Cyndi's List

**A Comprehensive List of
40,000 Genealogy Sites on the Internet**

Cyndi's List

A Comprehensive List of
40,000 Genealogy Sites on the Internet

Cyndi Howells

Published by Genealogical Publishing Co., Inc.
1001 N. Calvert St., Baltimore, MD 21202
Second printing 1999
Library of Congress Catalogue Card Number 97-78337
International Standard Book Number 0-8063-1556-3
Made in the United States of America

Cover artwork designed by Mark Brill

Contents

Acknowledgments

There are two special groups and two special individuals that have made the work on *Cyndi's List* and on this book possible. I want these people to know how much I appreciate their friendship, their support and their ongoing encouragement.

The members of the Tacoma-Pierce County Genealogical Society are responsible for creating in me the need to organize the resources I found online and to help make it a simpler task to find those resources. Understanding the group's desire to learn more about using the Internet as a successful genealogical research tool helped me to understand that the same desire existed worldwide. I am proud to be a member of such an enthusiastic, supportive and forward-thinking group of people.

Every visitor to *Cyndi's List* over the past three years has helped contribute to the usefulness of the web site in a multitude of ways. Each request, comment or criticism that I have received by e-mail has been an indicator of what people need or hope to find when they use the list for their online genealogical research. Thousands of e-mail messages have been filled with encouragement, friendship and wonderful success stories. I am eternally grateful to those who have taken time from their busy schedules to let me know how using *Cyndi's List* has affected their research.

In preparing *Cyndi's List* to be published in book form, I decided to undertake an incredible task in identifying as many "broken" or non-functioning links as possible, in order to make the book as accurate as possible. I couldn't have done this without the help of my online friend and fellow researcher, Jennifer Godwin. Jen's fantastic attention to detail and her personal knowledge of genealogical research and the Internet made this monumental task a relative breeze.

Most of all, I owe my thanks to my husband, Mark. He has encouraged me every step of the way and has made it possible for me to create, maintain and expand *Cyndi's List* so that it has become what it is today. It was Mark's idea to go online and it was with his urging that I created our personal web site for genealogy, along with *Cyndi's List*. In creating the site and through the process of continually updating and improving the site, Mark has been my proofreader, my test-surfer, my second set of critical eyes and my sounding board for ideas. I couldn't have done any of this without him.

Cyndi Howells
January 1999

Foreword

Of all people, I am the least surprised by the phenomenal success of *Cyndi's List of Genealogy Sites on the Internet*. The millions of visits per year which the site receives, the dozens and dozens of honors bestowed on *Cyndi's List,* her best selling book *Netting Your Ancestors,* and the media attention given to "a housewife from Puyallup" appear to me to be a natural outcome for all of Cyndi's hard work and dedication. The online results of *Cyndi's List* are merely the visible tip of the iceberg when compared to the large amount of behind-the-scenes work that Cyndi puts into her web site. Being one of the privileged few to watch Cyndi develop *Cyndi's List,* I'm not surprised by the results—it proves what dedication to a labor of love can accomplish.

When Cyndi first got on the Internet and began teaching herself web authoring more than three years ago, *Cyndi's List* immediately reflected the passion for her interests which Cyndi has shown in every one of her undertakings. Attention to detail, a constant drive to improve, and a fundamental desire to make order out of chaos are traits of character within Cyndi which shine in everything that she does. Cyndi's love of genealogy and family history is evident in *Cyndi's List.* Like an artist, Cyndi has studied the mosaic tiles which comprise genealogical information on the Internet, and has meticulously laid them out in a cohesive pattern for all to see and benefit from. Like a librarian, Cyndi has carefully created her massive index of genealogy web sites and cross-referenced them so that visitors to *Cyndi's List* can find what they're seeking regardless of how they approach their research. Like a teacher, Cyndi has patiently volunteered her time and efforts helping tens of thousands of family historians to better understand this wonderful tool called the Internet. Small wonder that *Cyndi's List of Genealogical Sites on the Internet* has become the premier index to genealogy and family history resources on the Internet.

While technology continues to change the way in which we access information, the much-predicted "paperless world" has failed to materialize. In fact, the advent of the personal computer has increased the use of paper as software tools have made the sharing of well-presented information increasingly easy to commit to paper. There is something comforting about the tactile feel of paper. Ink on paper has the mark of permanence unmatched by electronically-stimulated pixels on a glowing screen. So it is with this book—a printed version of Cyndi's tremendous web site. Now people can feel, touch, and read *Cyndi's List,* and it is available to them even when the power is turned off! This book is ideal for those with limited Internet time, because they can use it as a guide before spending their time searching online. It is also convenient for those who pay for their Internet connectivity by the minute. Institutions of the printed word (remember libraries?) will find this book invaluable as a reference to the brave new world of the Internet. Here, in print, is the organized, cross-referenced index to genealogy and family history sites on the Internet which is *Cyndi's List.* The special care which Cyndi brings to her web site is now available for you to hold in your hands in the form of this book. No doubt this volume will have a special place next to the personal computers of many Internet genealogists as they continue the never-ending search for their ancestors.

Mark Howells
January 1999

Introduction

The need for a printed version of *Cyndi's List* has become more and more apparent as time has passed. *Cyndi's List* has become a traditional online research tool for people worldwide. Many individuals have written to me asking for a printed version of the site in order to help them prepare in advance for the time spent doing their research online. Libraries and Family History Centers have also expressed a need for the *Cyndi's List* book. Having a printed version of the web site in their collections, sitting next to each Internet computer terminal, will aid their patrons in spending their limited time online in a productive manner. Anyone who has limited access to the Internet, whether through financial limitations or time limitations, will find this book useful in predetermining what resources will best fit their research efforts.

The History of *Cyndi's List*

My web site, *Cyndi's List of Genealogy Sites on the Internet,* located at http://www.CyndisList.com, was first published online on March 4, 1996. The list was made up of my own personal set of categorized bookmarks for genealogy and was a part of the personal web site created by my husband, Mark Howells, and me. The list of bookmarks began when I shared a printed page with my local genealogical society members at our monthly meeting. As I have often recounted, upon learning that I had a list of genealogy bookmarks to share, the members of the Tacoma-Pierce County Genealogical Society jumped on me like a pack of ravenous wolves. They wanted that list and it didn't stop there. That evening the editor of our quarterly, Nancy Peterson, asked me if I could expand on the idea and come up with five or six pages of genealogy web site addresses. I agreed and even offered to categorize the lot. Thus it began.

When I began work on *Mark and Cyndi's Family Tree,* I asked Mark if he thought I should include my list of bookmarks. Would anyone find them useful? He said, "Sure, why not?" Famous last words for a man who has now learned to wear a lot of wrinkled laundry and who now knows the people at the fast-food drive-up windows by name. *Cyndi's List* began with 1,025 links listed on one page. Today, *Cyndi's List* has more than 40,000 categorized and cross-referenced links in over 100 categories listed on more than 300 individual web pages. The site has more than 64,000 visitors each day, with a total of more than 7 million people having stepped through the front door of the site to date. Each month I add approximately 1,000 new links and I correct about 500 broken links. What originally began as a small hobby and an online contribution, has now become more than a full time job—a job I enjoy immensely.

How to Use *Cyndi's List*—The Book

The book is identical to the web site, with only a few exceptions. Each of the categories is found in alphabetical order. Within each category you will find a small category index. Each of these sub-categories contains links listed alphabetically by the title shown on the web site. The differences between the book version and the web site are as follows:

- The book does not include the Personal Home Pages category found on the site.

- On each U.S. state page in the book, the USGenWeb section has been trimmed down to include only the state-level addresses. Individual county resources can be found by visiting those web sites, or by visiting the *Cyndi's List* web site.
- Miscellaneous category pages or sections were removed from the book in order to conserve space. Check the web site for the most current and complete list of links.
- Every attempt has been made to ensure that the information in this book is as accurate as possible. All addresses in the book were verified for accuracy prior to going to print. However, web addresses are fluid and they can change daily. Visit the *Cyndi's List* web site for a current list of links. The web site is updated regularly, so the links found there would be more current than those found in the book.

Visiting a Site Found in the *Cyndi's List* Book

Once you locate an address in the book that you would like to visit, you have a choice of two methods to use to visit that site:

1. Manually type the address into the Location or Address box in your web browser.
2. Visit the appropriate category page on *Cyndi's List* and click on the link from there.

When an Address in the *Cyndi's List* Book Doesn't Work

If you find an address in this book that doesn't work, follow these steps to determine the correct address:

1. Carefully check the address you typed, looking for missing characters. Be sure to type all addresses exactly as they are given, taking care to include uppercase and lowercase letters as shown in this book.
2. Visit the appropriate category page on the *Cyndi's List* web site and look for the link listed there. The web site will always be more current than the book because it is updated on a regular basis.
3. If the link on the *Cyndi's List* web site is also not working, use the "Report a Broken Link" form on that category page to report the link to me. I will update it as quickly as possible.

How to Use *Cyndi's List*—The Web Site

I work on the site daily, adding new links, updating links, correcting broken links and removing outdated or non-functioning links. I receive more than 200 e-mail messages each day with requests from visitors to the site for specific resources to be added to the list. As the list has grown and taken on a life of its own, I have continually altered the way that I work on the site. Out of necessity, I have created several supporting, administrative web pages collectively falling under the heading of "About Using *Cyndi's List*." Following is a summary of the information found on each of these web pages. The information detailed there is designed to aid people in using the site productively, while also helping to make my job as easy as possible. Daily work on *Cyndi's List* is a full-time job, so I appreciate visitors who follow the guidelines and the requests specified on these pages.

Cyndi's List of Genealogy Sites on the Internet
http://www.CyndisList.com

This is the main index page for the site. It contains links to each page found within *Cyndi's List*. The top of the page has current update information, the date the site was last updated, and the number of links added, updated or removed. The next section on the page contains links to each of the supporting informational pages detailed below. Following that is the Category Index. There are links to each category page, listed alphabetically by the title of that page. Under the name for each category the visitor will find the date shown for the last update of that category page. Some of the category headings also contain a brief description.

"No-Frills" Category Index
http://www.CyndisList.com/nofrills.htm

This is an alphabetical list of the category pages found on *Cyndi's List*. This index doesn't contain update dates, descriptions or cross-referencing between categories; it is just a simple list of the category pages, shown alphabetically by title. For a more detailed version see the main index page at http://www.CyndisList.com

Make *Cyndi's List* Your Homepage!
http://www.CyndisList.com/yourhome.htm

Make *Cyndi's List* the first page you see when you start your web browser. The site is here for you to use as a jumping-off point in your daily online research. Think of *Cyndi's List* as a card catalog to the genealogy section in the massive research library that is the Internet.

The CyndisList Mailing List
http://www.CyndisList.com/maillist.htm

The CyndisList Mailing List is a free e-mail announcement list, created to keep users of the *Cyndi's List* web site (http://www.CyndisList.com) regularly updated regarding the activities on *Cyndi's List,* including any or all of the following:

1. Frequent updates to the site
2. Number of new links
3. Number of updated/corrected links
4. Number of deleted links
5. Names of categories that have been updated
6. Descriptions of new features or improvements to the site
7. Answers to frequently asked questions
8. Announcements and/or news regarding important online or offline resources
9. Details on what Cyndi is up to
10. Anything else that Cyndi wants to announce!

On each day that I make updates to *Cyndi's List*, a computer-generated report is sent to the mailing list with details on the number of links added, updated or deleted on the list. In addition, I send out a personally written note approximately once a week. This note includes information on my latest projects, work on the web site and other miscellaneous genealogical research information.

To subscribe, send an e-mail message to: CyndisList-request@rootsweb.com
In the body include only one word: subscribe

What's New on *Cyndi's List*
http://www.CyndisList.com/whatsnew.htm

This is an index to each of the monthly, temporary, uncategorized pages of new links on *Cyndi's List.* As new links are submitted to me via the "Submit a New Link" form on each category page, they will temporarily be added to a page of uncategorized links for that month. Once I place these links in their permanent home on various category pages on *Cyndi's List,* I will remove them from these temporary, uncategorized pages. New links are added to the individual category pages on *Cyndi's List* as I have time to visit, verify and examine each web site. You can identify new links and updated links on *Cyndi's List* by looking for a NEW or UPDATED graphic next to the links.

Submit a New Link to *Cyndi's List*

http://www.CyndisList.com/newlink.htm

Do you have a new web site for genealogy? Do you know of a web site that isn't yet linked on *Cyndi's List?* I intend to add categorized links for all genealogical resources that I find on the Internet. Currently I add approximately 1,000 new links every month and do my best to keep up with all requests that I receive. Send me any new web sites you know about and I'll try to add them to the list as soon as possible. Please don't send me repetitive requests for the same link. Once I receive the new link requests:

- I will visit each site to verify that the address is correct.
- I will use the title exactly as it is shown on the web site.
- I will determine the categories under which the links will be set up.
- I cannot guarantee how soon I will set up the link, but I'll do my best to get it done quickly.
- New links will be temporarily added to a set of pages titled "What's New on *Cyndi's List?*"

* Please note that this form is for links to web sites only. Please do not submit queries with e-mail addresses.

Create a Link to *Cyndi's List*

http://www.CyndisList.com/linkto.htm

If you have a web site of your own, use this page to set up a link to *Cyndi's List.* The page supplies the graphics and the HTML code you need to create the link.

FAQ (Frequently Asked Questions)—About Cyndi and *Cyndi's List*

http://www.CyndisList.com/faq.htm

I receive hundreds of e-mail messages each day, and many of them are filled with questions about me, my list, the time I spend working on the list, etc. I hope that this list of FAQs will solve some of the misconceptions and satisfy everyone's curiosity.

About Sending E-mail to Cyndi

http://www.CyndisList.com/e-mail.htm

Please read this page before sending me e-mail. Many of the questions you may have about the book or the web site are addressed on this page and also on the FAQ page.

Cyndi's Genealogy Home Page Construction Kit

http://www.CyndisList.com/construc.htm

Tips, hints, links and more to help you create your personal genealogy home page.

Internet Stuff You Need to Know

http://www.CyndisList.com/internet.htm

I created this page in order to point fellow genealogists to responsible, helpful resources online that will aid them in understanding some of the mysteries of the Internet. There are a lot of misconceptions, rumors, hoaxes and other bits of misinformation floating about. Hopefully, this page will help to dismiss some of the worries and clear up any confusion. This page includes links for the following topics:

- Computer Viruses
- Cookies
- Copyright Resources on the Web
- E-mail Chain-Letters, Folklore, Hoaxes, Misunderstandings & Scams
- Internet & Computer Terminology

- Netiquette
- Newbies
- Privacy Issues
- Software Features and Utilities
- Spam
- Y2K ~ Year 2000

Disclaimers

http://www.CyndisList.com/disclaim.htm

1. The content on *Cyndi's List* is subject to the owner's discretion. The owner is Cyndi Howells.
2. Links will be added to *Cyndi's List* at the owner's discretion.
3. There is no guarantee that all links will be included on *Cyndi's List*.
4. There is no guarantee that links will be added to *Cyndi's List* within a specific time frame.
5. All new resources submitted for inclusion on *Cyndi's List* will be reviewed by the owner prior to categorization.
   - Each URL will be verified for accuracy.
   - Each web site title will be reviewed for correct categorization and alphabetization.
   - Categorization of each link will be at the discretion of the owner.
6. The purpose of *Cyndi's List* is to provide a categorized and cross-referenced index to genealogical resources found online. The intent is for the site to be all-inclusive; however, the owner reserves the right to add and remove links at any time and at her discretion.
7. Links will be added and/or removed without any prior notification at the discretion of the owner.
8. The owner is not responsible for the content found on other web sites that are found linked on *Cyndi's List*.
9. Links to commercial enterprises found on *Cyndi's List* are included as a courtesy. Unless otherwise stated, the existence of these links on *Cyndi's List* does not imply endorsement of the services or products provided by those commercial enterprises.
10. The owner will not knowingly link to sites that derive from or participate in fraudulent or illegal behavior.
11. The owner is not responsible for problems that arise from sites found on the index that derive from or participate in fraudulent or illegal behavior.

ACADIAN, CAJUN & CREOLE
http://www.CyndisList.com/acadian.htm

- Acadia University—Vaughan Memorial Library
  http://www.acadiau.ca/vaughan/
  Wolfville, Nova Scotia, Canada

- Acadian Archives—UMFK
  http://www.umfk.maine.edu/infoserv/archives/welcome.htm

- Acadian-Cajun Genealogy & History
  http://www.acadian-cajun.com/

- ACADIAN-CAJUN Mailing List
  http://members.aol.com/gfsjohnf/gen_mail_country-
  can.html#ACADIAN-CAJUN

- Acadian-Cajun Mailing List
  http://members.aol.com/gfsjohnf/gen_mail_country-
  can.html#Acadian1

- Acadian Cultural Society Page de la Maison
  http://www.angelfire.com/ma/1755/index.html

- Acadian/French-Canadian SURNAME Researchers
  http://www.acadian.org/genealogy/resrch.html
  From the Acadian Genealogy Homepage.

- Acadian Genealogy Homepage
  http://www.acadian.org/

- Acadian Genealogy Links
  http://www.globalserve.net/~gcrose/acadianl.html

- Acadian GenWeb
  http://www.geocities.com/Heartland/Acres/2162/

- Acadian History and Genealogy
  http://ourworld.compuserve.com/homepages/lwjones/
  acadianh.htm
  *From Linda Jones' Genealogy—Acadian and French-Canadian
  Style web site.*

- The Acadian Odyssey—L'Odysée Acadienne
  http://www.schoolnet.ca/collections/acadian/intro/

- Les Acadiens aux îles Saint-Pierre et Miquelon
  http://www.cancom.net/~encyspm/acadie/EAcadien.html
  Islands off the coast of Canada, under the sovereignty of France.

- The Acadians of Nova Scotia
  http://www.grassroots.ns.ca/comgrp/acad.htm

- Avoyelleans: French Creoles
  http://www.geocities.com/BourbonStreet/1781/

- The "Cajun/Acadian" Chat Room
  http://www.acadian.org/genealogy/chat.html
  From the Acadian Genealogy Homepage.

- Cajun Clickers Genealogy SIG—Baton Rouge,
  Louisiana
  http://www.intersurf.com/~cars/

- Canadian Genealogy and History Links—Acadian
  http://www.islandnet.com/~jveinot/cghl/acadian.html

- Cape Breton Pictorial Cookbook—Acadian
  http://www.taisbean.com/CBcookbook/acadian.html

- Centre de recherches généalogiques du Québec
  http://www.cam.org/~cdrgduq/
  *Parchment certificates for sale with more than 4000 names from
  French-Canadian and Acadian origins.*

- The Early Acadian Period in Nova Scotia 1605–1755
  http://www.ednet.ns.ca/educ/museum/arch/acadia.htm
  From Archaeology in Nova Scotia.

- Encyclopedia of Cajun Culture
  http://www.cajunculture.com/

- Genealogy of Acadia
  http://www.cam.org/~beaur/gen/acadie-e.html
  From Denis Beauregard.

- The German-Acadian Coast Historical &
  Genealogical Society
  http://www.rootsweb.com/~lastjohn/geracadn.htm
  Destrehan, Louisiana

- The Gumbo Pages
  http://www.gumbopages.com/
  *Culture, history, etc. Previously titled Guide to Acadiana—
  Acadiana: Les Paroisses Acadiennes.*

- Les Acadiens—from Portage Technologies
  http://www.taisbean.com/portage/

- St. Augustine Historical Society—Creole Heritage
  Preservation
  http://www.cp-tel.net/creole/
  Isle Brevelle, Louisiana

- Société Des Acadiens Et Acadiennes Du
  Nouveau-Brunswick
  http://www.rbmulti.nb.ca/saanb/saanb.htm

- Society of Acadian Descendants
  http://www.acadian.org/genealogy/sad.html

- Université de Moncton—Centre d'études acadiennes
  http://www.umoncton.ca/etudeacadiennes/centre/cea.html
  New Brunswick, Canada

◆ Acadian Family Sites

- The Acadian JOHNSON Association / Association
  Des JOHNSON D'acadie
  http://www.geocities.com/BourbonStreet/5102/index.html

- The ARSENAULT / ARSENEAU / ARSENEAULT
  / ARCENEAUX Genealogy Web Site
  http://www.rbmulti.nb.ca/acadie/familles/arsenaul/arseno.htm

- Ben's Genealogical Research—Regarding
  Le BLANC's
  http://personal.nbnet.nb.ca/leblanc2/gen.html

- The CHAPMAN's Homepage
  http://www3.ns.sympatico.ca/chapy/
  *CHAPMAN, BOUDREAU, MacKENZIE, MORAN, LANDRY,
  MEALEY, SIMPSON, GOULD/DOIRON*

- Cyndie BROUSSARD's Genealogy Website
  http://www.intersurf.com/~cajunpcr/
  *BEARD, BLANCHARD, BROUSSARD, COOPER, DAVIS,
  DUHON, HENRY, INGRAM, LUCKY, MORELAND, NICKS,
  THIBODEAUX, TRAHAN, VANCE*

- Genealogy—Acadian and French-Canadian Style
  http://ourworld.compuserve.com/homepages/lwjones/
  homepage.htm
  *General resources and information for surnames: BABIN,
  BARD, BOUCHER, BOURDAGES, FOURNIER, GAGNON,
  PLOURDE, POIRIER, and VAILLANCOURT*

- HEBERT Family Genealogy
  http://www.acadian-cajun.com/hebert.htm

- Histoire et généalogie—THIBAUDEAU—
  THIBODEAU—History and Genealogy
  http://www.qouest.net/~jljmt/index.htm
  *Pierre THIBEAUDEAU, le pionnier Acadien. THIBODAUX,
  THIBEAUDEAU, THIBAUDEAUX, THIBODEAUX,
  TEBEDORE, TIBEDORE, THIBODEAULT, THIBAUDEAULT,
  THYBAUDEAU, THIBEDEAU, TIBIDO, THIBIDAUX,
  THIBAUDAU, THIBODOT, BODEAU, BODO, THIBADEAU,
  THEBADO, TIBBEDEAUX, TIBADO, TOLADO*

- Jim FRASER'S Genealogy Stuff
  http://www2.shore.net/~jaf/genpage.htm
  *FRASER (Guysborough Co, NS), WOMBLE (NC), FOUGERE,
  DYE (KY), ARNOLD, DOTY, and many early Acadians. Many
  names from the 1671 Port Royal census; Ile Madame.*

- The MELANSON / MELANCON / MALONSON /
  MALANSON Family Project
  http://www.geocities.com/Heartland/Meadows/7961/

- SAMSON Family Home Page
  http://www.familytreemaker.com/users/s/a/m/
  Charles-A-Samson
  *The Samson Family Homepage traces the descendants of the
  first Samson immigrants to New France (Quebec) in 1665. Also:
  BOUDROT, MARTEL, FOUGERE, LANDRY, FOREST, and
  MARCHAND.*

- The SAULNIER Genealogy HomePage
  http://www.geocities.com/Heartland/Acres/6946/
  *Descendants of Louis Saulnier and Louise Bastinaud dit
  Pelletier, who arrived in Acadia (now Nova Scotia) c.1685.*

- Steve FLEMING's Family
  http://www.erols.com/someday/Steve.html
  *Dedicated to Genealogy on the German-Acadian Coast of
  Louisiana.*

- WALKER—VAUGHN—Acadian Genealogy
  http://pw2.netcom.com/~daglo/gloria.html
  WALKER, VAUGHN, and MORASSE

ADOPTION

http://www.CyndisList.com/adoption.htm

Category Index:

- General Resource Sites
- Mailing Lists, Newsgroups & Chat
- Orphan Trains

- Professional Researchers, Volunteers & Other Research Services

---

◆ General Resource Sites

- Adoption.com
  http://www.adoption.com/index.shtml

- Adoption Information, Laws and Reforms
  http://www.webcom.com/kmc/
  From Kevin McCarty.

- Adoption Search
  http://www.adoptionsearch.com/
  The world's first adoption-focused search engine.

- Adoption Search and Reunion
  http://www.highfiber.com/~rema/index.html

- AdoptioNetwork
  http://www.adoption.org/

- An Adoptee's Right to Know
  http://www.plumsite.com/shea/

- Adoptee Searcher's Handbook ~ Canada
  http://www.login.net/inverc/search.htm

- Ancestor's Attic Discount Genealogy Books— Adoption Books
  http://members.tripod.com/~ancestorsattic/index.html#ADOPT

- Angry Grandma's Adoptees' Links
  http://199.79.239.12/~laswi/bookmark.htm

- Becky West's Adoption Page
  http://www.geocities.com/Heartland/Prairie/8066/adoption.htm

- Birthmoms Support List
  http://www.geocities.com/Heartland/6436/

- BirthQuest
  http://www.birthquest.org/
  Online searchable database for searching adoptees, birth parents, adoptive parents and siblings.

- The Canada-Wide National Registry & Family Finders
  http://www.adopting.org/ffcwnr.html
  Adoption resources & registry.

- Canadian Adoptees Registry and Classifieds
  http://www.bconnex.net/~rickm/

- Carrie's Adoptee & Genealogy Page
  http://www.mtjeff.com/~bodenst/page3.html

- Dawn's Birthmother/Adoption Resource Page
  http://members.tripod.com/~HevensDawn/adoption.html

- Forget Me Not Family Society
  http://www.portal.ca/~adoption/

- Irish Adoptees in Search of Roots & Wings
  http://members.aol.com/COD18460/IRISHADOPTEES.html

- Janyce's Root Diggin' Dept.—People Searching & Adoption
  http://www.janyce.com/gene/search.html

- Jenine—A Birthmother's Story
  http://www1.kingston.net/~recovery/jenine.html
  Links to resources for birthmothers.

- Looking for someone? Find them here!
  http://home.inreach.com/diak3/

- Luanne Pruesner's Internet Adoption Page
  http://users.aol.com/luannep/adoption.htm

- Mari's Place—Adoption Links
  http://www.netreach.net/~steed/

- Missing Birth Children—from Genealogical Journeys in Time
  http://pages.prodigy.com/Strawn/missingc.htm

- Missing Birth Parents—from Genealogical Journeys in Time
  http://pages.prodigy.com/Strawn/missingb.htm

- Missing Persons—from Genealogical Journeys in Time
  http://ourworld.compuserve.com/homepages/Strawn/missingp.htm

- Office for National Statistics—Adoption Certificates ~ U.K.
  http://www.ons.gov.uk/services/adoption.htm

- Oregon Adoptive Rights Association
  http://www.oara.org/

- ""Petition""—Opening of All Adoption Records
  http://home.att.net/~lewiskincaid/index.html.04.html

- Reunion Registry.com
  http://www.reunionregistry.com/

- Reunions Online Adoption Registry
  http://www.absnw.com/reunions/
- Searching in Ireland—Resources for Irish-Born Adoptees
  http://www.netreach.net/~steed/search.html
- Searching For People
  http://ddi.digital.net/~islander/
- The Seeker Magazine
  http://www.the-seeker.com/
- The Volunteer Search Network (VSN) Information Page
  http://www.vsn.org/
- World Wide Web Library of Adoptee Related Sites
  http://www.bastards.org/web.htm
- Yahoo!....Adoption
  http://www.yahoo.com/Society_and_Culture/Families/ Parenting/Adoption/
- Yellow Rose Reunions
  http://home.texoma.net/~wfbonner/
- Yourfamily.com—Long Lost Family Bulletin Board
  http://www.yourfamily.com/lost_family.shtml

◆ Mailing Lists, Newsgroups & Chat

- Adoptees Internet Mailing List
  http://www.webreflection.com/aiml/
- ADOPTEES Mailing List
  http://members.aol.com/johnf14246/ gen_mail_general.html#ADOPTEES
  For legal adoptees and "adoptee-lites" (people who were raised without one or both birth parents, but who were never legally adopted) to seek advice in conducting a search.
- The Adoptees Newsgroup Home Page— soc.adoption.adoptees
  http://www.geocities.com/Heartland/Acres/8126/
- ADOPT-FR Mailing List
  http://members.aol.com/johnf14246/ gen_mail_general.html#ADOPT-FR
- adopt-gene Mailing List
  http://members.aol.com/johnf14246/ gen_mail_general.html#adopt-gene
  For the discussion of problems related to adoption.
- ADOPTING Mailing List
  http://members.aol.com/johnf14246/ gen_mail_general.html#ADOPTING
  For anyone touched by adoption. This list offers search help, support, and tips on research related to adoption.
- ADOPTION Mailing List
  http://members.aol.com/johnf14246/ gen_mail_general.html#ADOPTION
  Discussions of anything and everything connected with adoption.

- FAMILIES-TOUCHED-BY-ADOPTION-L Mailing List
  http://members.aol.com/johnf14246/ gen_mail_general.html#FamAdop
  For anyone personally touched by adoption and wishing to trace/share their heritage, genealogists seeking biological/ adoptive family information to include an adoptee on their family tree, and for sharing guidelines for searching public records. Also see the associated web page at http://www.onelist.com/subscribe.cgi/FamAdopt
- IRISH-ADOPTEES-SEARCH Mailing List
  http://members.aol.com/gfsjohnf/gen_mail_country- unk.html#IRISH-ADOPTEES-SEARCH
- Usenet Newsgroup alt.adoption
  news:alt.adoption
  For adoptees, birthparents, adoptive parents.
- Usenet Newsgroup soc.adoption.adoptees
  news:soc.adoption.adoptees
  The Adoptees Newsgroup.
- Webchat Broadcasting System: Adult Adoptees Chat
  http://pages.wbs.net/webchat3.so?cmd=cmd_ doorway:Adult_Adoptees_Chat

◆ Orphan Trains

- Iowa Orphan Train Project
  http://www.maquoketa.k12.ia.us/orphan_train.html
- Orphan Train Adoptees
  http://www.system.missouri.edu/shs/orphan.html
- Orphan Train Genealogy
  http://www.ancestry.com/magazine/articles/orphan.htm
  By Marilyn Irvin Holt for Ancestry Magazine.
- Orphan Train Heritage Society of America, Inc.
  http://pda.republic.net/othsa/
- Orphan Train Resources
  http://www.maquoketa.k12.ia.us/ot%20resource.html
- Orphan Train Riders History
  http://www.hamilton.net/subscribers/hurd/index.html
- Orphan Trains
  http://www.outfitters.com/~melissa/ot/ot.html
- The Orphan Trains
  http://www.pbs.org/wgbh/pages/amex/orphan/index.html
  A PBS American Experience television show regarding this unusual immigrant experience.
- Orphan Trains of Kansas
  http://kuhttp.cc.ukans.edu/carrie/kancoll/articles/orphans/ index.html
  - A History of the Orphan Trains
    http://raven.cc.ukans.edu/carrie/kancoll/articles/orphans/ or_hist.htm
  - Index of Children Who Rode the Orphan Trains to Kansas
    http://raven.cc.ukans.edu/carrie/kancoll/articles/orphans/ or_child.htm

○ Kansas Orphan Train "Time-Line"
  http://raven.cc.ukans.edu/carrie/kancoll/articles/orphans/
  or_timel.htm

○ Orphan Train Bibliographies
  http://www.ukans.edu/carrie/kancoll/articles/orphans/
  or_bibli.htm

○ A Partial List of Institutions That Orphan Train
  Children Came From
  http://raven.cc.ukans.edu/carrie/kancoll/articles/orphans/
  or_homes.htm

○ A Partial List of Kansas Orphan Train Arrivals
  http://raven.cc.ukans.edu/carrie/kancoll/articles/orphans/
  or_arriv.htm

○ Riders on an Orphan Train to Kansas—1911
  http://raven.cc.ukans.edu/carrie/kancoll/articles/
  orphan_train_1911.html

● Orphan Trains of Nebraska
  http://www.rootsweb.com/~neadoptn/Orphan.htm

● The Orphan Trains: Placing Out in America
  http://st2.yahoo.com/ancestry/brtheortrain.html
  A book by Marilyn Irvin Holt, for sale from Ancestry.

● Orphan Trains to Missouri
  http://www.system.missouri.edu/upress/spring1997/
  patrick.htm
  Information about a book from the University of Missouri Press.

● They Rode the Orphan Trains
  http://www.rootsweb.com/~mogrundy/orphans.html

◆ Professional Researchers, Volunteers & Other Research Services

● Adoption Searches & Investigations
  http://www3.sympatico.ca/searches/
  London, Ontario, Canada

● AIS—Asset Information Services
  http://pages3.simplenet.com/ais.htm
  San Diego, California. Missing persons and adoption searches.

● AAG International Research—Professional
  Genealogists and Family Historians
  http://www.intl-research.com/
  Accredited genealogists & family historians specializing in family history research, development & publication. Accredited by the Family History Library in Salt Lake City, the world's largest genealogical library. Tax deductions for LDS research.

● Assets and Family Research Consultants
  E-mail: sharsam@adan.kingston.net
  Toronto, Ontario, Canada. Researcher with 15 years experience, specializing in adoption-related searches. Contact Sharon Chianelli at 1-613-352-1163 or by e-mail at: sharsam@adan.kingston.net

● genealogyPro—Adoption Researchers
  http://genealogyPro.com/directories/adoption.html

AFRICAN-AMERICAN
http://www.CyndisList.com/african.htm

Category Index:

- ◆ General Resource Sites
- ◆ History & Culture
- ◆ Libraries, Archives & Museums
- ◆ Mailing Lists, Newsgroups & Chat
- ◆ Military
- ◆ People & Families

- ◆ Professional Researchers, Volunteers & Other Research Services
- ◆ Publications, Software & Supplies
- ◆ Records: Census, Cemeteries, Land, Obituaries, Personal, Taxes and Vital
- ◆ Slavery
- ◆ Societies & Groups

◆ General Resource Sites

- ● African American Genealogy
  http://www.familytreemaker.com/issue12.html

- ● African-American Genealogy Ring
  http://www.geocities.com/Heartland/Prairie/6288/afamgenring.html

- ● African American History and Genealogy Resources
  http://www.ilinks.net/~mcmaster/
  Includes a partial list of Charleston's antebellum black Catholics.

- ● African-American How-To Guide From Family Tree Maker
  http://www.familytreemaker.com/00000360.html

- ● African American Lifelines
  http://ourworld.compuserve.com/homepages/Cliff_m/
  How-to for beginners

- ● African-American Sources
  http://www.comsource.net/~tnolcox/africanamerican.htm
  Indiana

- ● The African—Native Genealogy Homepage
  http://members.aol.com/angelaw859/index.html
  Celebrating the Estelusti—The Freedmen Oklahoma's Black Indians of the Cherokee, Chickasaw, Choctaw, Creek, and Seminole Nations.

- ● African Studies WWW (U. Penn)
  http://www.sas.upenn.edu/African_Studies/AS.html

- ● Afrigeneas—African American Roots
  http://www.msstate.edu/Archives/History/afrigen/index.html

- ● Afro American Registry
  E-mail: cristal@ripco.com
  E-mail address for the registry.

- ● ALGenWeb: Ethnic Groups: African-American Genealogy and History Sites
  http://members.aol.com/blountal/Afmain.html

- ● Black/African Related Resources
  http://www.sas.upenn.edu/African_Studies/Home_Page/mcgee.html

- ● Blacks in Alaska History Project, Inc.
  http://www.servcom.com/akblkhist/

- ● Christine's Genealogy Website
  http://www.ccharity.com/
  A wealth of African-American resources for genealogy as well as Christine's personal research: The RUSSELLs & COBBs of Jackson, Tennessee; the CHARITYs of Surry and Charles City County, Virginia; the ANDERSONs and PERKINS of Shuqualak, Mississippi; and the SIMMONS of Detroit, Michigan.

- ● Internet Resources for Students of Afro-American History
  http://www.libraries.rutgers.edu/rulib/socsci/hist/afrores.htm

◆ History & Culture

- ● African American History
  http://www.msstate.edu/Archives/History/USA/Afro-Amer/afro.html
  Links from the Historical Text Archive at Mississippi State University.

- ● African-American History Links
  http://www.plcmc.lib.nc.us/online/links/african.htm#history
  From the Public Library of Charlotte-Mecklenburg County, North Carolina.

- ● Boston African-American National Historic Site
  http://www.nps.gov/boaf/

- ● Lest We Forget
  http://www.coax.net/people/LWF/default.htm
  Documents with focus on the history and culture of African-Americans.

  - ○ Genealogy
    http://www.coax.net/people/lwf/genes.htm
    Index page from the LEST WE FORGET Web Site.

- ● The North Star: Tracing The Underground Railroad
  http://www.ugrr.org/

- A Selection of Underground Railroad Resources
  http://www.ugrr.org/web.htm
- To Know My Name—A Chronological History of African Americans in Santa Cruz County
  http://www.cruzio.com/~sclibs/history/know1.html
  California
- Underground Railroad—Taking the Train to Freedom
  http://www.nps.gov/undergroundrr/contents.htm
- The Universal Black Pages—History Links
  http://www.gatech.edu/bgsa/blackpages/history.html
- The Walk to Canada—Tracing the Underground Railroad
  http://www.npca.org/walk.html

◆ Libraries, Archives & Museums

- African-American Genealogy Sources in the Louisiana Division of the New Orleans Public Library
  http://home.gnofn.org/~nopl/guides/black.htm
- African American Perspectives: Pamphlets from the Daniel A.P. Murray Collection, 1818–1907
  http://lcweb2.loc.gov/ammem/aap/aaphome.html
- Afro-American Sources in Virginia—A Guide to Manuscripts
  http://www.upress.virginia.edu/plunkett/mfp.html
- Amistad Research Center
  http://www.arc.tulane.edu/
- Carnegie Library of Pittsburgh—Pennsylvania Department: African-American Genealogy
  http://www.clpgh.org/CLP/Pennsylvania/oak_penna32.html
- IPL Museum of African American History, Detroit, Michigan
  http://www.ipl.org/exhibit/maah/
- Kentucky's African-American Genealogical Sources at the Kentucky Department for Libraries and Archives
  http://www.kdla.state.ky.us/arch/blkhist.htm
- The Museum of Afro-American History Boston
  http://www.afroammuseum.org/
  Massachusetts
- The Museum of Slavery in the Atlantic
  http://squash.la.psu.edu/~plarson/smuseum/homepage.html
- Selections from The African-American Mosaic: A Library of Congress Exhibit
  http://lcweb.loc.gov/exhibits/african/intro.html

- Third Person, First Person: Slave Voices from the Special Collections Library
  http://scriptorium.lib.duke.edu/slavery/
  Broadside Collection, Special Collections Library, Duke University.

◆ Mailing Lists, Newsgroups & Chat

- Afrigeneas Mailing list
  http://members.aol.com/johnf14246/gen_mail_general.html#AFRIGENEAS
- AL-AfricaAmer Mailing List
  http://members.aol.com/gfsjohnf/gen_mail_states-al.html#AL-AfricaAmer
  For anyone with an interest in African American genealogy in Alabama.
- GEN-AFRICAN Mailing List
  http://members.aol.com/gfsjohnf/gen_mail_country-gen.html#GEN-AFRICAN
  Gatewayed with the soc.genealogy.african newsgroup for the discussion of African genealogy.
- SLAVEINFO Mailing List
  http://members.aol.com/gfsjohnf/gen_mail_states-gen.html#SLAVEINFO
  For the sharing of genealogical data about slaves in the United States including wills/deeds that show sales and transfer of ownership, vital records (e.g., birth, marriage, death), and information/queries on specific slaves that may be part of your ancestry.

◆ Military

- African-American Civil War Memorial
  http://www.itd.nps.gov/cwss/dcmem.html
- African American Warriors
  http://www.abest.com/~cklose/aawar.htm
- The Buffalo Soldiers on the Western Frontier
  http://www.imh.org/imh/buf/buftoc.html
  From the International Museum of the Horse.
- The Civil War
  http://www.coax.net/people/lwf/data.htm
  Several links and articles from "Lest We Forget."
- Fifty-fourth Massachusetts Infantry
  http://extlab1.entnem.ufl.edu/olustee/54th_MS_inf.html
- Guide to Tracing Your African American Civil War Ancestor
  http://www.coax.net/people/lwf/cwguide.htm
- History of African Americans in the Civil War
  http://www.itd.nps.gov/cel/africanh.html
- NPS African-American Civil War Sites
  http://www.itd.nps.gov/cel/aa-sites.html
- United States Colored Troops (USCT)
  http://www.itd.nps.gov/cwss/usct.html

- United States Colored Troops Resident in Baltimore at the Time of the 1890 Census
  http://www.mdarchives.state.md.us/msa/speccol/3096/html/00010001.html

- United States Colored Troops: The Civil War
  http://www.coax.net/people/lwf/usct.htm

◆ People & Families

- African American MABRYs
  http://www.execpc.com/~dcollins/african.html

- The African American OGBURNs and the House of OGBURNs
  http://www.oginet.com/Chronicles/hoogbrn.htm

- The Willie L. ROBINSON Family Home Page
  http://www.familytreemaker.com/users/r/o/b/Willie-L-Robinson/
  AMOS, ARNOLD, BAILEY, HARDY, HANEY, CROSSLEY, DILLON, STEWART, KEYS, PORTER, CROCKETT, SIMMONS, GREEN, RICHARD, GOFF, PEAVY, CRUMP, LARD, TATE, VARNADO, McNULTY, MARSHALL and YANKAWAY

◆ Professional Researchers, Volunteers & Other Research Services

- AAG International Research—Professional Genealogists and Family Historians
  http://www.intl-research.com/
  Accredited genealogists & family historians specializing in family history research, development & publication. Accredited by the Family History Library in Salt Lake City, the world's largest genealogical library. Tax deductions for LDS research.

- Board for Certification of Genealogists—Roster of Those Certified—Specializing in African American Genealogy
  http://www.genealogy.org/~bcg/rosts_@a.html

◆ Publications, Software & Supplies

- African-American Ancestors Among the Five Civilized Tribes
  http://www.coax.net/people/lwf/blkind.htm
  Description of book for sale.

- African American Genealogy: A Bibliography for Beginners
  http://www.kdla.state.ky.us/arch/biblforb.htm

- Ancestor's Attic Discount Genealogy Books— African American Genealogy Books
  http://members.tripod.com/~ancestorsattic/index.html#secAA

- Frontier Press Bookstore—African American History / Research
  http://www.doit.com/frontier/frontier.cgi?category=afr

- GenealogyBookShop.com—African American
  http://www.genealogybookshop.com/genealogybookshop/files/General,African_American/index.html
  The online store of Genealogical Publishing Co., Inc. & Clearfield Company.

- Heritage Books—African American
  http://www.heritagebooks.com/afr-am.htm

- A Student's Guide to African American Genealogy
  http://www.oryxpress.com/scripts/book.idc?acro=FTAFR
  A book for sale.

- Willow Bend Bookstore—African-American
  http://www.willowbend.net/black.htm

◆ Records: Census, Cemeteries, Land, Obituaries, Personal, Taxes and Vital (Born, Married, Died & Buried)

- African Americans listed in the 1850 & 1860 Madison County, Tennessee Free Census Schedule
  http://www.ccharity.com/tennessee/freetenn.htm

- African Burial Ground Archeological Project
  http://www.afrinet.net/~hallh/abg.html
  Manhattan

- Black Studies—A select catalog of National Archives microfilm
  http://www.nara.gov/publications/microfilm/blackstudies/blackstd.html

- Freedmen's Bureau Records
  http://www.freedmensbureau.com
  From Christine's Genealogy Website.

  ○ Freedman's Bureau, Marriages in Arkansas 1861–1869
    http://www.freedmensbureau.com/arkansas/arkansasmarriages.htm

  ○ Freedman's Bureau, Marriages in Jacksonville, Florida 1861–1869
    http://www.freedmensbureau.com/florida/florida.htm

  ○ Freedman's Bureau, Marriages in Mississippi 1863–1865
    http://www.freedmensbureau.com/mississippi/mississippimarriages.htm

  ○ Freedman's Bureau, Marriages in Tennesee 1865–1869
    http://www.freedmensbureau.com/tennessee/marriages/tennesseemarriages.htm

  ○ Freedman's Bureau, Marriages in Washington, D.C. 1861–1869, Part 1
    http://www.freedmensbureau.com/washingtondc/dcmarriages1.htm

- Freedman's Bureau, Marriages in Washington, D.C. 1861–1869, Part 2
  http://www.freedmensbureau.com/washingtondc/dcmarriages2.htm
- Freedmen's Bureau Register of Marriages in Gloucester, Virginia 1861–1869
  http://www.freedmensbureau.com/virginia/gloucester.htm
- Noxubee County, Mississippi Slave Schedule— 1860 Census
  http://www.ccharity.com/mississippi/1860noxumortpt1.htm
- Register of Free Blacks Augusta County, Virginia
  http://jefferson.village.virginia.edu/vshadow2/govdoc/fblack.html
- Register of Free Negroes and Mulattoes in The Corporation of Staunton
  http://jefferson.village.virginia.edu/vshadow2/govdoc/fblack2.html
- Slave Entries in Wills, Deeds, Etc.
  http://www.netcom.com/~jog1/slavedocs.html
  Kentucky, South Carolina, Tennessee, Virginia
- Slave Information from Various Loudoun Co., VA Documents, 13 Dec 1809 to 30 June 1861
  http://www.rootsweb.com/~valoudou/slaves.html

◆ Slavery

- American Slave Narratives: An Online Anthology
  http://xroads.virginia.edu/~HYPER/wpa/wpahome.html
- Amistad America, Inc.—Building the Freedom Schooner
  http://www.amistadamerica.org/
- Amistad—"Give Us Free"
  http://news.courant.com/special/amistad/
- Documenting the American South—North American Slave Narratives, Beginnings to 1920
  http://sunsite.unc.edu/docsouth/neh/neh.html
- Excerpts from Slave Narratives
  http://vi.uh.edu/pages/mintz/primary.htm
- Exploring Amistad: Race and the Boundaries of Freedom in Antebellum Maritime America
  http://amistad.mysticseaport.org/
- The North Star: Tracing The Underground Railroad
  http://www.ugrr.org/
- A Selection of Underground Railroad Resources
  http://www.ugrr.org/web.htm
- Slave Entries in Wills, Deeds, Etc.
  http://www.netcom.com/~jog1/slavedocs.html
  Kentucky, South Carolina, Tennessee, Virginia

- Slave Information from Various Loudoun Co., VA Documents, 13 Dec 1809 to 30 June 1861
  http://www.rootsweb.com/~valoudou/slaves.html
- Slaveowners and Slaves In and Around Dauphin County, Pennsylvania
  http://www.geocities.com/Athens/Parthenon/6329/index.html
- Slavery and Abolition—A Journal of Slave and Post-Slave Studies
  http://www.frankcass.com/jnls/sa.htm
- Slavery in Dauphin County, Pennsylvania
  http://www.geocities.com/Athens/Parthenon/6329/
- Testimony of the Canadian Fugitives
  http://history.cc.ukans.edu/carrie/docs/texts/canadian_slaves.html
- Third Person, First Person: Slave Voices from the Special Collections Library
  http://scriptorium.lib.duke.edu/slavery/
  Broadside Collection, Special Collections Library, Duke University.
- Underground Railroad—Taking the Train to Freedom
  http://www.nps.gov/undergroundrr/contents.htm
- The Walk to Canada—Tracing the Underground Railroad
  http://www.npca.org/walk.html
- Women and Slavery
  http://weber.u.washington.edu/~sunstar/ws200/slavery.htm
- Yahoo!...US History...Slavery
  http://www.yahoo.com/Arts/Humanities/History/U_S__History/Slavery/

◆ Societies & Groups

- African-American Genealogical Societies Around the U.S.A.
  http://www.everton.com/oe2-7/afamlist.htm
- African American Genealogical Society of Northern California
  http://www.aagsnc.org/
  Oakland, California. Preserve and promote the study of records of a genealogical and historical nature relating to African American ancestry.
- African-American Genealogy Group (AAGG)
  http://www.libertynet.org/~gencap/aagg.html
  Philadelphia, Pennsylvania
- Afro-American Historical and Genealogical Society
  http://www.erols.com/trirose/aahgs.htm

ASIA & THE PACIFIC
http://www.CyndisList.com/asia.htm

- Ancestor's Attic Discount Genealogy Books—
  Asian Genealogy Books
  http://members.tripod.com/~ancestorsattic/index.html#secAS

- Ancestors from the former Dutch East Indies
  http://ourworld.compuserve.com/homepages/paulvanV/eastindi.htm

- ANU—Asian Studies: Online Chinese Libraries
  http://online.anu.edu.au/Asia/Chi/ChiLib.html

- ARMENIA Mailing List
  http://members.aol.com/gfsjohnf/gen_mail_country-arm.html#ARMENIA

- Asia GenWeb
  http://www.rootsweb.com/~asiagw/
  - Japan—World GenWeb Project
    http://www.rootsweb.com/~jpnwgw/
  - Philippines Genealogy Web Project
    http://www.geocities.com/Heartland/Ranch/9121/

- Books We Own—Oceania
  http://www.rootsweb.com/~bwo/oceania.html

- British Ancestors in India
  http://www.ozemail.com.au/~clday/

- The British in Singapore and Malaya
  http://user.itl.net/~glen/BritishinSingapore%26Malaya.html

- Chinese Historical Society of Southern California
  http://www.chssc.org/

- Chinese Surnames
  http://www.geocities.com/Tokyo/3919/

- Chinese Surname Queries
  http://www.ziplink.net/~rey/ch/queries/

- ChouOnline 1997
  http://www.idis.com/ChouOnline/
  *Sponsored by The Chou Clansmen Association of America.
  Covers various clan names including: Chow, Chang, Lum,
  Ching, Goo, Woo, Ing, Sun, Chiang, Ho, Kee, Kwock, Lau, Loui,
  Mao, Wong, Yap, Lai, and Choy. Also: Dang, Young, Chock, and
  Tom.*

- Civilian Internees of the Japanese in Singapore
  during WWII
  http://user.itl.net/~glen/CivilianInternees.html
  as well as messages regarding that site
  http://user.itl.net/~glen/CivilianInternees2.html
  From Alex Glendinning's Asian Pages.

- Commonwealth War Graves Commission
  http://www.cwgc.org/
  *Details of 1.7 million members of UK and Commonwealth forces
  who died in the 1st and 2nd World Wars and other wars, and
  60,000 civilian casualties of WWII. Gives details of grave site,
  date of death, age, usually parents/widow's address.*

- The Cochin Churchbook
  http://www.telebyte.nl/~dessa/cochin.htm
  *Baptism & marriages from the Dutch Church in Cochin, India
  (1754–1804).*

- Dutch East-Indies Informationpoint
  http://home.wxs.nl/~vdbroeke/
  *A "guide" for everybody who is interested in Eurasian culture in
  the Netherlands.*

- English East India Company Ships
  http://www.ships.dircon.co.uk/eic/eic.htm
  *Shipping Losses in the Mercantile Service 1600–1834 (includes
  Shipwrecks, Captures & Missing Vessels).*

- Genealogical Gleanings—Royal & Noble Lineages
  of Tonga, Fiji, Hawaii, Burma and Cambodia
  http://www.uq.net.au/~zzhsoszy/index.html

- Genealogy in Non-Western Civilizations
  http://win-www.uia.ac.be/u/pavp/gengen.html#nwest
  India, China, Japan, the Arab World, the Jews.

- Hakka Chinese Homepage
  http://www.asiawind.com/hakka/

- Hindu Names
  http://www.rajiv.org/iu/hindunam.txt

- Historical Maps of Australia and the Pacific
  http://www.lib.utexas.edu:80/Libs/PCL/Map_collection/
  historical/history_austral_pacific.html
  *From The Perry-Castañeda Library Map Collection, The
  University of Texas at Austin.*

- The Imperial Family of Japan
  http://www.geocities.com/Tokyo/Temple/3953/
  *Biographies and information for the emperors and their families
  since 1850.*

- INDIA Mailing List
  http://members.aol.com/gfsjohnf/gen_mail_country-ind.html#INDIA1
  *For anyone who is interested in tracing their British and
  European Ancestors in British India.*

- India Office Records: Sources for Family History
  Research
  http://www.bl.uk/collections/oriental/records/iorfamhi.html
  *The British Library Oriental and India Office Collections
  (OIOC).*

- Indian Last Names
  http://www.nssl.uoknor.edu/~lakshman/names.html

- Jamal's Yellow Pages of Pakistan
  http://www.jamals.com/

- KOREA Mailing List
  http://members.aol.com/gfsjohnf/gen_mail_country-kor.html#KOREA

- Lareau Web Parlour
  http://www.wavefront.com/~pjlareau/
  - HMS Bounty Genealogies
    http://www.wavefront.com/~pjlareau/bounty6.html
  - Lareau Web Parlour Genealogy Site
    http://www.wavefront.com/~pjlareau/geneal1.html
  - Pitcairn Island Web Site
    http://www.wavefront.com/~pjlareau/pitc1.html
- Map of Palau
  http://www.lib.utexas.edu/Libs/PCL/Map_collection/
  islands_oceans_poles/Palau.jpg
  From the Perry-Castañeda Library at the Univ. of Texas at Austin.
- National Japanese American Historical Society
  http://www.nikkeiheritage.org/
- Pacific_Islands Mailing List
  http://members.aol.com/gfsjohnf/gen_mail_country-
  gen.html#Pacific_Islands
  For the discussion and collaboration on genealogy and family history of indigenous peoples from the Pacific. Also see the associated web page at http://www.genweb.net/~niueis/pacific.htm
- PANICKER Family History, Kerala, India
  http://web2.airmail.net/panicker/
  Based on The Panicker Kudumba Charithram Handbook.
- The POYNTZ Family in India
  http://www.hal-pc.org/~poyntz/india.html
  Selected Extracts from the India Presidencies of Bengal, Bombay and Madras Ecclesiastical Returns of Baptisms, Marriages and Burials 1713–1948.
- Soldiers Whom the World Have Forgotten
  http://www.geocities.com/Athens/Acropolis/9460/index.html
  Dedicated to the memory of soldiers & their families who died in and around Bangalore, India.

- Sosen of Sasebo—The Sasebo Chapter, NSDAR
  http://www.geocities.com/Heartland/Plains/1789/
  National Daughters of the American Revolution, Sasebo, Japan.
- SRILANKA Mailing List
  http://members.aol.com/gfsjohnf/gen_mail_country-
  sri.html#SRILANKA
- A Student's Guide to Chinese American Genealogy
  http://www.oryxpress.com/scripts/book.idc?acro=FTCHN
  A book for sale.
- THIEN Genealogy Home Page
  http://www.geocities.com/Tokyo/3998/index.html
  The genealogy of Francis THIEN Chung Kong, a Malaysian Chinese Hakka. DENG, TENG, TANG, THIEN, THEAN, THIAN.
- Yahoo!...China...History
  http://dir.yahoo.com/Regional/Countries/China/
  Arts_and_Humanities/History/
- Yahoo!...India...Genealogy
  http://dir.yahoo.com/Regional/Countries/India/
  Arts_and_Humanities/History/Genealogy/
- Yahoo!...Indonesia...History
  http://dir.yahoo.com/Regional/Countries/Indonesia/
  Arts_and_Humanities/History/
- Yahoo!...Japan...History
  http://dir.yahoo.com/Regional/Countries/Japan/
  Arts_and_Humanities/History/
- Yahoo!...Korea,South...History
  http://dir.yahoo.com/Regional/Countries/Korea__South/
  Arts_and_Humanities/History/

AUSTRALIA & NEW ZEALAND
http://www.CyndisList.com/austnz.htm

Category Index:
◆ General Resource Sites
◆ Government & Cities
◆ History & Culture
◆ How To
◆ Libraries, Archives & Museums
◆ Mailing Lists, Newsgroups & Chat
◆ Maps, Gazetteers & Geographical Information
◆ Military
◆ Newspapers

◆ People & Families
◆ Professional Researchers, Volunteers & Other Research Services
◆ Publications, Software & Supplies
◆ Queries, Message Boards & Surname Lists
◆ Records: Census, Cemeteries, Land, Obituaries, Personal, Taxes and Vital
◆ Ships: Convict Lists, Passenger Lists, Etc.
◆ Societies & Groups

◆ General Resource Sites

● AGWeb—The Australasian Genealogy Web
http://home.vicnet.net.au/~AGWeb/agweb.htm

● AustraliaGenWeb
http://www.rootsweb.com/~auswgw/

● Australia's Immigration and Family History Centre
http://www.rypac.com.au/~frasertravel/hervey/family/family.htm

● Australian Family History Compendium
http://www.cohsoft.com.au/afhc/

  ○ Genealogy Addresses for the Australian Capital Territory
  http://www.cohsoft.com.au/afhc/act.html

  ○ Genealogy Addresses for the State of New South Wales
  http://www.cohsoft.com.au/afhc/nsw.html

  ○ Genealogy Addresses for Northern Territory
  http://www.cohsoft.com.au/afhc/nt.html

  ○ Genealogy Addresses for the State of Queensland
  http://www.cohsoft.com.au/afhc/qld.html

  ○ Genealogy Addresses for the State of South Australia
  http://www.cohsoft.com.au/afhc/sa.html

  ○ Genealogy Addresses for the State of Tasmania
  http://www.cohsoft.com.au/afhc/tas.html

  ○ Genealogy Addresses for the State of Victoria
  http://www.cohsoft.com.au/afhc/vic.html

  ○ Genealogy Addresses for the State of Western Australia
  http://www.cohsoft.com.au/afhc/wa.html

● Australian Institute of Genealogical Studies Inc.
http://www.alphalink.com.au/~aigs/

● BROWNE Tasmanian Genealogy
http://www.vision.net.au/~jbrowne/
Convicts, family files, cemetery records, Tasmanian Webring, Tasmanian Forum.

● The Central Register of Indexing Projects in Australia
http://www.st.net.au/~judyweb/register.html

● David Scott's List of Australian (and NZ) Ged2html Sites
http://www1.tpgi.com.au/users/dscott/aust_gen.htm

● Family History Events—Australian Family History Compendium
http://www.cohsoft.com.au/afhc/announce.html

● Family History Research Centres List
http://home.vicnet.net.au/~provic/guides/guide18.htm
From the Public Record Office of Victoria.

● Genealogy Bulletin Board Systems for Australia
http://www.genealogy.org/~gbbs/gblaustr.html

● Genealogy Bulletin Board Systems for New Zealand
http://www.genealogy.org/~gbbs/gblnewze.html

● Genealogy in Australia
http://www.pcug.org.au/~mpahlow/welcome.html

● Genealogy New Zealand
http://www.voyager.co.nz/~ianclap/gennz.htm
From Ian Clapham.

● The Genealogy Resource Page & Cemetery Database of the Hunter Valley NSW Australia
http://bhss.inia.net.au/patmay/

- Genealogy from Gerringong
  http://www.ozemail.com.au/~johngrah/
  Information for Illawarra area of New South Wales, Australia, especially for the town of Gerringong and its surrounds. Also for the Westernport Settlement of 1826–28 in what is now the state of Victoria, Australia. Also the VIDLER surname.

- Gum Tree Genealogy Ring
  http://members.tripod.com/~Jules_in_oz/gumtree/

- Moggill Local History
  http://192.148.225.23/bruce/mogg.html
  ANSTEAD, BIRD, BOYLE, CURRIE, BAINBRIDGE, CAMPBELL, DOYLE, FINLAY, HALLETT, LATHER, MAKEPEACE, OWENS, SEXTON, SHIELD, SUGARS, TWINE and WESTCOTT Families.

- New Zealand White Pages
  http://www.whitepages.co.nz/

- Resources in Australia and New Zealand
  http://www.tc.umn.edu/~pmg/Australia.html

- South Australian Family History & Genealogy
  http://www.adelaide.net.au/~bazle/

- Southern Cross Genealogy
  http://www.southernx.com.au/
  Australia's national ISP for Genealogists and Historians.

- Tasmanian Genealogy Webring
  http://www.vision.net.au/~jbrowne/newpage1.htm

- Tasmanian Sources
  http://www.vision.net.au/~tmartin/moemartin/tasour.html

- Telecom New Zealand White Pages
  http://www.whitepages.co.nz/

- Telstra—Australian White & Yellow Pages
  http://www.telstra.com.au/

- White Pages Phone Directory for Australia
  http://www.whitepages.com.au/

- Yahoo!...Australia...Genealogy
  http://www.yahoo.com/Regional/Countries/Australia/Arts_and_Humanities/Humanities/History/Genealogy/

◆ Government & Cities

- Australian Commonwealth Government
  http://www.fed.gov.au/

- Parliament of New South Wales
  http://www.parliament.nsw.gov.au/

◆ History & Culture

- GOLD 150—Celebrating 150 Years of Australian Gold-Rush History
  http://www.ballarat.edu.au/krause/external/sovhill/gold150//sovhill.htm

- Milton Ulladulla History Site
  http://www.shoalhaven.net.au/~cathyd/

- Strahan, Sarah Island Convict Site, South West Tasmania
  http://www.ozemail.com.au/~kemoon/Strahan.html

◆ How To

- Australian Genealogy How To Guide
  http://www.familytreemaker.com/00000362.html

- Research Tips for Queensland
  http://www.st.net.au/~judyweb/tips-qld.html

◆ Libraries, Archives & Museums

- The Archives Authority of New South Wales
  http://www.records.nsw.gov.au/

- Archives Office of Tasmania
  http://www.tased.edu.au/archives/archives.htm
  - Guide to Reference Services
    http://www.tased.edu.au/archives/refguide.htm
  - Tasmanian Family Link
    http://www.eos.tased.edu.au/pioneers/
    A database made up of records of births, deaths, and marriages, as well as other events, that is designed to connect families with ancestors who lived in Tasmania in the 19th century.

- Australia—New Zealand—Family History Centers
  http://lds.org/en/2_How_Do_I_Begin/Where_is_Locations/13_Australia-New_Zealand.html

- Australia Family History Centers
  http://www.genhomepage.com/FHC/Australia.html
  A list of addresses, phone numbers and hours of operation from the Genealogy Home Page.

- Australian Capital Territory & National Institution Libraries
  http://sunsite.anu.edu.au/search/lib/

- Australian Libraries Gateway (ALG)
  http://www.nla.gov.au/libraries/

- Canterbury Public Library
  http://www.ccc.govt.nz/library/
  New Zealand

- Directory of Archives in Australia—Australian Society of Archivists
  http://www.asap.unimelb.edu.au/asa/directory/asa_dir.htm

- Geelong Historical Records Centre
  http://www.zades.com.au/geelong/ghrc.html

- Genealogy Library: Flinders University
  http://pcm.pcmedia.com.au/tags/docs/flinders.html

- The Library and Information Service of Western Australia—Genealogy (Family History)
  http://www.liswa.wa.gov.au/gencoll.html

- National Archives of Australia
  http://www.naa.gov.au/index.htm
  - Fact Sheets Subject Index
    http://www.naa.gov.au/research/factsheet/factshet.htm#gene
  - Finding Families—The Guide to the National Archives of Australia for Genealogists
    http://www.naa.gov.au/PUBLICAT/GUIDES/HTML/family.htm
    A book for sale.

- Services to Researchers
  http://www.naa.gov.au/research/index.htm
  - Getting Started
    http://www.naa.gov.au/research/start/start.htm
- National Archives of New Zealand / Te Whare Tohu Tuhituhinga O Aotearoa
  http://www.archives.dia.govt.nz/
- National Library of Australia
  http://www.nla.gov.au/
- National Library of New Zealand
  http://www.natlib.govt.nz/
- The New South Wales Parliamentary Archives
  http://www.parliament.nsw.gov.au/gi/archives/default.html
- North Shore Libraries
  http://pollux.dslak.co.nz:8001/nsl/nsl.htm
  New Zealand
- Northern Territory Library
  http://www.nt.gov.au/ntl/
- State Library of New South Wales
  http://www.slnsw.gov.au/
  - Family History Service
    http://www.slnsw.gov.au/grl/family/family.htm
  - Mitchell and Dixson Libraries—Australian Research Collections
    http://www.slnsw.gov.au/ml/mitchell.htm
- State Library of Queensland
  http://www.slq.qld.gov.au/
  - The Family History Unit
    http://www.slq.qld.gov.au/gen.htm
  - John Oxley Library
    http://www.slq.qld.gov.au/jo.htm
  - Maps Unit
    http://www.slq.qld.gov.au/maps.htm
- State Library of South Australia
  http://www.slsa.sa.gov.au/
  - Family History Source Sheets
    http://www.slsa.sa.gov.au/lib_guide/fh/fh.htm
- State Library of Tasmania Home Page
  http://www.tased.edu.au/library/
  - Heritage Collections
    http://www.tased.edu.au/library/heritage/
- State Library of Victoria
  http://www.slv.vic.gov.au/
  - Australiana Collections
    http://www.slv.vic.gov.au/slv/latrobe/
  - Genealogy and Family History Homepage
    http://www.slv.vic.gov.au/slv/genealogy/
  - Map Collection—An Introduction
    http://www.slv.vic.gov.au/slv/maps/
- Newspaper Collection
  http://www.slv.vic.gov.au/slv/newspapers/
- Sydney City Archives
  http://www.aa.gov.au/AA_WWW/OtherArch/SydneyCity/SydneyCity.html
- Ulverstone Local History Museum
  http://www.tassie.net.au/~cbroadfi/LocalHistoryMuseum.htm
  Tasmania
- The University of New England and Regional Archives
  http://www.une.edu.au/archives/
  Armidale
- The University of Queensland Library
  http://www.library.uq.edu.au/
- University of Sydney Archives
  http://www.usyd.edu.au/su/archives/

◆ Mailing Lists, Newsgroups & Chat

- Genealogy Resources on the Internet—Australia Mailing Lists
  http://members.aol.com/gfsjohnf/gen_mail_country-aus.html
  and New Zealand Mailing Lists
  http://members.aol.com/gfsjohnf/gen_mail_country-nez.html
  Each of the mailing list links below points to this site, wonderfully maintained by John Fuller.
- ARIA Mailing List
  http://members.aol.com/gfsjohnf/gen_mail_country-aus.html#ARIA-L
  For Australians and New Zealanders who are researching their Italian Heritage, Culture and Ancestry.
- AUS-NQ Mailing List
  http://members.aol.com/gfsjohnf/gen_mail_country-aus.html#AUS-NQ
  For anyone with genealogical or historical interests in North Queensland, Australia, north from the Tropic of Capricorn to Cape York and west to the Northern Territory border.
- AUS-NSW-Hunter-Valley Mailing List
  http://members.aol.com/gfsjohnf/gen_mail_country-aus.html#AUS-NSW-Hunter-Valley
  For anyone with a genealogical interest in Hunter Valley, New South Wales, Australia, which encompasses the cities of Newcastle, Maitland, Cessnock, and Singleton.
- AUS-NSW-SE Mailing List
  http://members.aol.com/gfsjohnf/gen_mail_country-aus.html#AUS-NSW-SE
  For anyone with a genealogical interest in New South Wales (NSW), Australia.
- AUS-QLD-SE-Germans Mailing List
  http://members.aol.com/gfsjohnf/gen_mail_country-aus.html#AUS-QLD-SE-Germans
  For anyone with a genealogical interest in the descendants of the Germans who migrated to South East Queensland, Australia.
- AUS-Tasmania Mailing List
  http://members.aol.com/gfsjohnf/gen_mail_country-aus.html#AUS-Tasmania

- AUSTRALIA Mailing List
  http://members.aol.com/gfsjohnf/gen_mail_country-aus.html#AUSTRALIA
  "The Conference of Australian History." For anyone with an interest in Australian History—not exclusively genealogy—including the history of events involving Australians or their ancestors elsewhere in the world. Also see the associated web page at http://www.antiquodes.com.au/~jsnelson/rootsweb.html

- Australian Genealogy Chat Sessions
  http://www.uq.net.au/~zzsbrown/irc.htm

- DPS-SYDNEY Mailing List
  http://members.aol.com/johnf14246/gen_mail_general.html#DPS-SYDNEY
  For the Sydney Dead Persons Society (DPS).

- EMIGRATION-SHIPS-REQUEST Mailing List
  http://members.aol.com/johnf14246/gen_mail_general.html#EMIGRATION-SHIPS
  A mailing list for anyone who wants to discuss the ships their ancestors arrived on or post passenger lists for any ships.

- FHANQ Mailing List
  http://members.aol.com/gfsjohnf/gen_mail_country-aus.html#FHANQ
  For the members of the Family History Association of North Queensland, Australia to discuss Association activities and to share genealogy information on the ancestors and descendants of North Queensland families.

- GENANZ Mailing list gatewayed with the soc.genealogy.australia+nz newsgroup
  http://members.aol.com/gfsjohnf/gen_mail_country-aus.html#GENANZ-L
  For the discussion of Australia and New Zealand genealogy. See also the GENANZ Home Page.
  http://www.rootsweb.com/~billingh/genanz-l.htm

◆ Maps, Gazetteers & Geographical Information

- AUSLIG On the Web—Australian Surveying & Land Information Group
  http://www.auslig.gov.au/

- Australia Towns Index
  http://www.atn.com.au/contents.htm

- Australian Gazetteer
  http://www.ke.com.au/cgi-bin/texhtml?form=AustGaz

- Australian Geographic Place Names (Gazetteer)
  http://www.erin.gov.au/database/gaze_ack.html

- Historical Maps of Australia and the Pacific
  http://www.lib.utexas.edu:80/Libs/PCL/Map_collection/historical/history_austral_pacific.html
  From the Perry-Castañeda Library Map Collection, The University of Texas at Austin.

- History of Australian Places Index
  http://www.zades.com.au/ozindex/ozindex.html

- LINZ—The New Zealand Geographic Place-Names Database
  http://www.linz.govt.nz/databases/geographic/geoname.html

- Map of New Zealand—Guide to Cities & Towns
  http://www.atonz.com/genealogy/nza2.gif

- National Library of Australia Map Collection
  http://www.nla.gov.au/1/gencoll/maps.html

◆ Military

- 460 Squadron RAAF
  http://www.st.net.au/~dunn/460sqdn.htm
  Australians serving in WWII

- Australian Genealogy Researching Armed Services Personnel
  http://www.pcug.org.au/~mjsparke/mj_page1.html

- Australian War Medals
  http://www.ozemail.com.au/~qphoto/index.html
  Provides background information on campaign & gallantry awards given to Australian forces. Includes some medal rolls listing individual recipients of medals. Also has a research resource page for researching Australian servicemen.

- "G" for George
  http://www.st.net.au/~dunn/g4george.htm
  The Avro Lancaster B1 on display in the Aeroplane Hall at the Australian War Memorial in Canberra, ACT, Australia.

- New Zealand Defence Forces, 1860–1883
  http://www.atonz.com/genealogy/nzdefence.html

- The Queensland Defence Force
  http://www.ozemail.com.au/~adjutant/moreton/qdf.html

◆ Newspapers

- Australian Newspapers
  http://www.slsa.sa.gov.au/lib_guide/subjects/news/austnews.htm
  A list from the State Library of South Australia.

- Newspaper Collection
  http://www.slv.vic.gov.au/slv/newspapers/
  At the State Library of Victoria.

◆ People & Families

- Allieliza's Genealogy Homepage
  http://www.geocities.com/Athens/Parthenon/2486/
  Surnames: BALL, BATMAN, BEST, BROOKS, CUBITT, DALY, DOBSON, GOODSON, HAINES, KIRCUP, LOCKING, MITCHELL, NELSON, OSBOURNE, SIMPSON, SMITH, STAGG, STANLEY, TETLEY, WEST. Areas: Lincolnshire, Yorkshire, Norfolk. Also, a one name study of the surname CUBITT. All areas, worldwide.

- Andrea JOHNSON's Genealogy Page
  http://www.geocities.com/Heartland/7031/
  SHORT, REDKNAP, DWYER, ADAMS, McARDLE, VON GEYER, DYSON, FOX

- Andrew KEMP's Genealogy Page
  http://opax.swin.edu.au/andrew/genealogy.html
  KEMP, VAN DER VEN, MURPHY, De JONG, WELSH, DETHRIDGE and MOREY

- Anni's Page
  http://www.bendigo.net.au/~oconnell/anni.htm
  BRADLEY, O'CONNELL, YOUNG, BARNSTABLE, WHEELER, McGAWLEY, O'CALLAGHAN & CARTWRIGHT

- The Ascott Martyrs
  http://www.geocities.com/Heartland/Plains/6081/
  An Historical Link to the PRATLY, PRATLEY and PRATTLEY Families of New Zealand.

- ATKINSON Family Epistle
  http://home.clear.net.nz/pages/joanne_atk/
  BAIRD, BROOKS, LOFTUS, MOORE, MOSS, PEASE, POUND, REEVE, TOMBS

- The Australian BLAIR Family
  http://www.pcug.org.au/~kenblair/

- Barry's Genealogical Site
  http://www.fox.net.au/~beetee/
  Melbourne, Australia. THRIPPLETON / THREAPLETON / THREAPLAND, AUSTIN, PEARSON, STANSFIELD, VERITY and WAITE.

- The BEER Family Tree
  http://www-users.dragon.net.au/bestoc/beerft.html
  ARMFIELD, BARKER, BEECHAM, BEER, KELLAWAY / KILLAWAY, ATTERSOLL, BERCHTEN, COLLARD, HOLT, GIBBONS (or GIBBINS), BROWN, THOMPSON and RUSSAM

- BREW Family Genealogy Page
  http://www.sigment.com/brew/
  Brew One Name Study Genealogy Site with searchable databases.

- Bruce FAIRHALL's Home Page
  http://www.ros.com.au/~bfairhall/index.htm

- Chris MITCHELL's Home Page
  http://www.i.net.au/wheels/homepage.htm

- Clan JOHNSTON/E Association of Australia
  http://www.felglow.com.au/webpgs/valdes/index.htm
  Society for all JOHNSTON, JOHNSTONE, and JOHNSTOUNE in Australia and New Zealand. Has genealogical officer and maintains a one-name database.

- Convicts, Characters & Cads—The Ancestors of Scott and Fiona Brown
  http://www.uq.net.au/~zzsbrown/family/
  Surnames including BROWN, SMITH, CALLOW, PHILLIPS, MORTON, MOUGHTIN. The site also includes an Australian Genealogy Bulletin Board.

- Daniel BLACKWELL: Tasmanian Genealogy and Convict History
  http://www.ozemail.com.au/~kemoon/Danielb.html
  Grandfather's Grandfather—The story of Daniel BLACKWELL and his descendants.

- David SCOTT's Home Page
  http://www1.tpgi.com.au/users/dscott/david.htm
  SCOTT, RANSOM, ALLEN, PRICE, JACKSON, FISCHER, MOYSES, POLKINGHORNE

- David Scott's List of Australian (and NZ) Genweb Sites
  http://www1.tpgi.com.au/users/dscott/aust_gen.htm

- Des LAWLOR's Family Tree in Australia
  http://www.hotkey.net.au/~annah/
  LAWLOR / LAWLER, GLOVER, HEIT, O'MAHONEY, FIELDER, WALTERS, McGREEVY, RELLER

- The DUBBELD Connection
  http://www.nor.com.au/users/jdubbeld/

- First Families 2001
  http://home.vicnet.net.au/~family/
  A database and collection of stories about the people of Australia, past and present.

- From a Distant FIELD—The Living Edition on the Internet
  http://acsys.anu.edu.au/FromADistantField/
  Descendants of the New South Wales (Australia) pioneers, EDWARD and ELIZABETH FIELD.

- Genealogy In Action—The Homepage of Gary PATTON
  http://www.dragnet.com.au/~pattogar/
  CAMPBELL, COLLINS, PATTON, GUERNSEY, HARRISON, REIJERSE (REYERSE), SHEARGOLD, SULLIVAN

- Genealogy in Australia
  http://www2.hunterlink.net.au/~ddrge/genealogy/contents.html
  Bobs Internet Guide to Genealogy in Australia. Terminology, Resources and Descendant lists for ELDRIDGE, GEARY, MEEHAN with more coming.

- Genealogy, REEVES, LAYTON, EMSLIE, STONYER
  http://www.es.co.nz/~treeves/geneal.htm

- Genealogy—SUGARS
  http://192.148.225.23/bruce/bruce.html
  SUGARS, BREED, ROBERTS, STINTON, THIESFIELD, PAGE, MERRITT

- Gold Diggers Mine Site
  http://www.thehub.com.au/~gatfield/welcome.html
  GATFIELD, AVIS

- Henrietta MAY's Genealogy Page
  http://mayhem.atnf.csiro.au/index.html
  BAYLY/BAYLEY, WATCHORN, WESTBROOK, CRISP, GAGGIN

- HEWLETT BEUZEVILLE ROUSSEL Family Home Page
  http://www.home.aone.net.au/mclark/

- History and Family Tree of John JEWELL
  http://www.dcscomp.com.au/jewell/family-history/
  His Ancestors in Cornwall and His Descendants in Australia 1567–1996.

- HUNTER Family Genealogy
  http://www.deakin.edu.au/~heather/hunter.htm
  HUNTER, BROWN, PENMAN, KENNEDY, CUNNINGHAM, TERRIS

- Ian DALWOOD Genealogy & Family History
  http://www.pcug.org.au/~idalwood/
  DALWOOD, TREVETT, MARSDEN, FENTON, COCKBURN

- Jenny's Favorite Family History Sites
  http://www.wn.com.au/jabol/
  CRIPPS, CAMPBELL, LYMBURNER/DELISSER, CADDY, MacKAY, MANSELL

- Jewish Genealogy in Australia
  http://www.zeta.org.au/~feraltek/genealogy/index.html

- Judy WEBSTER's Genealogy Info-Page
  http://www.st.net.au/~judyweb/index.html
  Several helpful articles online.

- Julie's Genealogy Page
  http://www.alpha.com.au/teamalpha/genealogy.html
  DALY, STEVENS, HARRISON, COLLIS, WILSON, HARLEY, MCDONALD, VOAKES, MATTHEWS, GRUBB, BOSMAN, WOUTERS, JACKSON, BULLEY, HODGSON, SUCKLING, WHITTINGHAM, HOLLIS, KNOLL. Julie's mother, Nancy STEVENS was born Beatrice Mary DALY and she is looking for her birthmother, Kathleen (Kate) DALY.

- KENDALL Families in New South Wales, Australia
  http://www.northnet.com.au/~kendalli/index.html
  Web pages for all KENDALL families who lived in New South Wales, Australia, from 1788 until 1888. Information has been extracted from the IGI, convicts records and the Blue Books of the colony 1788–1824. Much of the information is incomplete and requires additional work. Assistance greatly appreciated.

- KIMPTON & LEDWICH Family History
  http://www.crt.net.au/~stormy1/
  KIMPTON, LEDWICH, COPELY, DORAN, MORGAN, COYLE, BROADBENT, SMITH, STARR, FREEMAN and more.

- The LANGHAM Genealogy Page
  http://www.onthenet.com.au/~tonylang/Mainpage.html

- Lauren THOMSON's Genealogy Home Page
  http://www.starnet.com.au/lthomson/lauren.htm
  BULL, GIRT, SALISBURY, SETFORD, RICHARDSON, TURNER, WOODS, WRAY

- Leith Hutton's Genealogy Homepage
  http://www.geocities.com/Athens/Forum/3709/
  Leith Hutton's Genealogy Homepage is host to a number of useful resources, including: the Australasia Births, Deaths and Marriages Exchange, the New Zealand Genealogical Resource Bureau and GenSearch Ring. It is also host to my personal genealogical research, including a transcription of my great grandfather's journal.

- Leone FABRE—Genealogy, Family History and Victorian Links
  http://www.geocities.com/Heartland/8267/
  ROBERTS, NORMAN, PETERSON, WHITE, METCALF, FROST

- The LIPSCOMB Home Page
  http://www.geocities.com/Heartland/Plains/9053/
  LIPSCOMB, ADAMS, BARRON, WILLIS and STEWART

- LOITERTON Family Homepage
  http://www.hinet.net.au/~jblstat/loitsearch.html

- Lyn's Genealogy Pages
  http://users.hunterlink.net.au/~ddlc/
  CLARKE, POULTER, GLENN, McGLASHAN, HALLETT, LEONARD, NEWEY, CORBETT

- Maureen MARTIN's Genealogy Home Page
  http://www.vision.net.au/~tmartin/moemartin/
  Genealogy related to Tasmania.

- The MIDDLEMISS Family, 1769–1996, From Berwick-on-Tweed to New Zealand
  http://home.clear.net.nz/pages/middlemiss/
  Descendants of Andrew MIDDLEMIST, born 1769 in Berwick-On-Tweed.

- The MURRAY Clan Society of Queensland
  http://www.globec.com.au/~egan/
  For anyone bearing the surname of: MURRAY, MACMURRAY, MORAY, MURRIE, MORROW or the Clan's affiliated septs: BALNEAVES, DINSMORE, DUNSMORE, FLEMING, GERAGHTY, GINSMORE, HARRINGTON, MACMORROW, NEAVES, PIPER, PYPER, SMALL, SMAIL, SMEAL, SPAULDING, THOMAS or TOMAS.

- MURRAY, EGGLESTONE, JAMES, DODD Genealogy
  http://www.home.aone.net.au/murray/surnames.htm
  MLN Scotland to Australia 1766—Now.

- The MUTIMER Family Home Page
  http://www.lzs.com.au/~lmutimer

- The NAIBOR Genealogy Page
  http://www.ozemail.com.au/~naibor/
  ANDERSON, ATHERTON, BARNARD, CLARKE, FOWLER, HANCOCK, HUNTER, JENSEN, KERRISON, MAPLETOFT, PEDERSEN, STYLES

- Narryna Genealogy Page
  http://www.geocities.com/Heartland/Acres/2316/
  MUNNS, JENSEN, McMANUS, HAIG, LEWIS, NIELSSEN, SMITH and STREETS

- NEWMAN Family Genealogy
  http://www.ozemail.com.au/~nnewman/
  HANSBERRY

- NICKSON Family Tree
  http://www.fortunecity.com/millenium/abbeydale/38/index.html
  NICKSON, LEEL

- O'MALLEY Family in Australia—The Descendants of John MALAY
  http://www.users.bigpond.com/omalley/
  Malay, Maley, Malley, O'Malley family of Westbury Tasmania, Australia.

- Our Family Trees
  http://www.atonz.com/genealogy/
  DAVIS, KEMPT, MEAD/E, PATEMAN, RUFF, WALFORD, ZANDER

- Our Home Page On Genealogy
  http://www.iniaccess.net.au/~steves/
  BLAIR, IRWIN, SIMMONS and WADE

- The OzEmail Home Page of John SYMONDS
  http://www.ozemail.com.au/~jlsymo/
  SYMONDS, CAUST, LLOYD, WHITE, HILL, VERRAN

- The OzEmail Home Page of John WARD
  http://www.ozemail.com.au/~wardjc/
  WARD (Coventry), LORD (Rossendale), ARCHER, REDMAN, WILLAN, WITTON, GARNETT (Kendal, Kirby Lonsdale, Dent, Sedbergh), ANDERSON, HOTSON, LOCKIE (Langholm, Dumfs.), McGREGOR, ANDERSON (Perthshire, Stirlingshire).

- Pat's Genealogy Page
  http://msowww.anu.edu.au/~barling/gene.htm
  CASHIN, BARLING, KELLY, McSHANE

- Patricia DOWNES' Genealogy Pages
  http://www.pcug.org.au/~pdownes/
  MERRICK, CASHION

- PEPPER Genealogical Stuff
  http://www.alphalink.com.au/~peppy/index.htm
  HANCOCK, REED, HECKFORD, ROLASON, HEARNS

- Peter DUNN's Research Interests
  http://www.st.net.au/~dunn/research.htm
  ARUNDELL, DOUGHERTY, DUNN, GOULEVITCH, JENSON, MALONEY, MORAN, MORTENSEN, O'NEILL, WALDER

- Peter HODGE's Home Page
  http://www.pcug.org.au/~phodge/
  Information regarding the brig "Indian" from Falmouth in mid-1843 bound for Launceston, Tasmania; the "Emigrant" sailed from Plymouth on 9 August 1850 bound for Moreton Bay; and more on emigration, etc.

- Phil SMITH Genealogy Home Page
  http://www.ozemail.com.au/~kegs/
  ALLAN, CAVINATO, CHASELING, COOPER, CRISMOND, EVERINGHAM, JONES, NORRIS, QUARMAN, RHYMES, SMITH, SULLIVAN

- QUINANE Genealogy Home Page
  http://www.tip.net.au/~ivecm/hist.htm
  Home Page of the Quinane's from Tipperary, Ireland who emigrated to Australia between 1850 and 1880.

- Rob's Family Tree
  http://www.cs.auckland.ac.nz/~rob/FamilyTree/
  Ancestors of Robert Edwin BURROWES and Rachel Elizabeth ADAMS. 8,898 Individuals, 3,637 Families with indexes and search engine.

- Sally HAMMON's Home Page
  http://202.139.254.245/
  COULSELL, DALE, WHITE, FRAZER, FAWCKNER, VAN DAMME

- Sally's Research Center
  http://members.net-tech.com.au/shine/sally.htm
  LAMBDEN, MACKIE, LOVERIDGE, COLE, BOASE, Mc GACHEN, FISHER, AUSTIN, ALLEN, ROBINSON, BURROWS, GOOLD, BUCHANAN

- The SAW Family Genealogy and History
  http://web.access.net.au/jarks/home.html
  McCAULEY, SAW

- The SHEATHERS—Our Australian Heritage
  http://www.wts.com.au/~pwsheather/phil/australi.html

- Susie ZADA's Home Page
  http://www.zades.com.au/susiez/home.html
  FUSSEN, GIARDINA, SCHUBERT, NIALL, MURRAY, NAUGHTEN

- The SUTHERS Page
  http://student.curtin.edu.au/~psutherssp/suthers.html

- SWADLING's World
  http://www.hinet.net.au/~linswad/
  SWADLING, LANE, MUDIE, BARNETT, LOGUE, COLEMAN, TIERNEY, WILLIAMS, BRITTON, BATE, KJELSBERG, GREEN

- Ted McCLOSKEY's Home Page
  http://www.hinet.net.au/~tedmac/homepage.htm
  GEELAN from Co. Longford, Ireland, McCLOSKEY from Co. Derry and Co. Antrim, Ireland, VANNI from Vellano, Tuscany, Italy.

- The Unofficial Page of the Clan EGAN Association—Australian Branch
  http://www.globec.com.au/~egan/egan.htm
  Gaelic: MACAODHAGAIN, MacEGAN, EGAN, EAGAN, EAGEN, KEEGAN, HAGEN

- Vicki's Genealogy Page
  http://www.geocities.com/Heartland/Plains/3576/
  BARRETT, DING, DUNNING, FIELDER, NEILL, OLIVER, PLATTEN, RHODES, SLATER, SYKES

- VIDLER Family in Australia
  http://www.ozemail.com.au/~johngrah/vidler.html
  VIDLER, COPPER, KING, CURRAN, CHAPMAN, QUINCE

- Whakapapa Maori Genealogy
  http://ourworld.compuserve.com/homepages/rhimona/whakapap.htm

◆ Professional Researchers, Volunteers & Other Research Services

- A.A. Genealogy
  http://www.lisp.com.au/~coffey/index.htm
  Family Tree research in Australia and overseas.

- Adelaide proformat
  http://www.users.on.net/proformat/jaunay.html

- The Australasian Association of Genealogists and Record Agents
  http://home.vicnet.net.au/~aagra/

- Australia's Immigration and Family History Centre
  http://www.peg.apc.org/~frasertravel/hervey/family/research.htm
  Janet Reakes

- Cemetery Searches—Sydney, Australia
  http://homepages.tig.com.au/~tezz/netscape.htm
  This service will locate your ancestors' graves and take photos if required.

- Garrison Communications—Family History Research Services
  http://www.garrison.gil.com.au/
  Specialising in Queensland, Australia, with expertise in English, Scottish, Welsh and Irish records.

- Genealogy Helplist—Australia
  http://members.aol.com/dfbradshaw/au.html

- Genealogy Helplist—New Zealand
  http://posom.com/hl/nzl/index.shtml

- genealogyPro—Professional Genealogists for Australia
  http://genealogyPro.com/directories/Australia.html

- genealogyPro—Professional Genealogists for New Zealand
  http://genealogyPro.com/directories/NewZealand.html

- Gold Coast Family History Research Group Inc.
  http://www.qid.net.au/hacs/clients/history1.htm
  Southport, Queensland, Australia
- KENNEDY RESEARCH—Australian and International Family History Research
  http://www.marque.com.au/kenres/
  Professional researcher
- Marbract Services—NSW Birth, Death & Marriage Certificate Transcription Service
  http://www.marbract.com.au/
  NSW Births 1788–1905, NSW Marriages 1788–1918 & NSW Deaths 1788–1945, Australia.
- National Heritage Datapoint
  http://www.vicnet.net.au/vicnet/family/datapoint/dpoint.htm
- New Zealand Genealogy & History
  http://www.angelfire.com/ak/Register2/index.html
  Research by Heather Walden.
- New Zealand Research
  http://www.st.net.au/~ailsa/
  Ailsa Corlett, professional researcher.
- Professional Genealogical Research in Queensland
  http://www.st.net.au/~judyweb/prof.html
  Judy Webster
- Professional Genealogist in New Zealand for the UK and Ireland—Tony Fitzgerald
  http://genealogypro.com/tfitzgerald.html

◆ Publications, Software & Supplies

- Adelaide proformat Bookshop
  http://www.users.on.net/proformat/books.html
- Australian Family Tree Connections Magazine
  http://www.aftc.com.au/
- Books We Own—Australia
  http://www.rootsweb.com/~bwo/australia.html
- Books We Own—New Zealand
  http://www.rootsweb.com/~bwo/nz.html
- Evagean Genealogy Publishing
  http://webnz.com/evagean/
  New Zealand
- EZITREE Family History Program
  http://www.ram.net.au/users/ezitree/
  DOS program.
- Fast Books
  http://www.fastbooks.com.au/
  Perfect Bound Paperback Books, Glebe NSW, Australia.
- Genealogy Books & Accessories by Janet Reakes
  http://www.peg.apc.org/~frasertravel/hervey/family/books.htm
  From Australia's Immigration and Family History Centre.

- Genius Family Tree
  http://www.gensol.com.au/
  Windows—"The easy genealogy program."
- Gould Books—Family & Local History Specialist
  http://www.gould.com.au/
  Books, maps, charts, computing, microfiche, video & audio.
- Macbeth Genealogical Services
  http://www.macbeth.com.au/
  Books, fiche, maps, and CD-ROMs.
- My Family History
  http://www.ozemail.com.au/~pkortge/MFH.html
  For Windows WFW & Windows 95, from Australia.
- New Zealand Society of Genealogists— Hardcopy Publications
  http://homepages.ihug.co.nz/~nzsg/Publications/hardcopy_main.html
- New Zealand Society of Genealogists— Microfiche Publications
  http://homepages.ihug.co.nz/~nzsg/Publications/fiche_main.html
- RMIT Publishing Genealogy
  http://www.rmitpublishing.com.au/products/genealogy.html
  Australian databases on CD.
- Time Booksellers—Rare & Collectible Books
  http://www.anzaab.com.au/~timebook/index.html
- WinGen (Windows Genealogy)
  http://members.tripod.com/~WinGen95/
  Shareware from New Zealand.
- Yesteryear Links
  http://www.uq.net.au/yesteryearlinks/
  Queensland, Australia

◆ Queries, Message Boards & Surname Lists

- Australia Convicts Message Board
  http://www.InsideTheWeb.com/messageboard/mbs.cgi/mb80720
- Australian Family Tree Connections Missing Ancestors
  http://www.aftc.com.au/missanc.html
- Australian Family Tree Connections Surname Register
  http://www.aftc.com.au/surname.html
- Australian Genealogy Bulletin Board
  http://www.InsideTheWeb.com/messageboard/mbs.cgi/mb5856
- CANSW—Cornish Surname Interests & Family Queries
  http://www.ozemail.com.au/~jlsymo/cornsurn.htm
- Online Australasian Names Research Directory
  http://www.users.on.net/proformat/ausnames.html

◆ Records: Census, Cemeteries, Land, Obituaries, Personal, Taxes and Vital (Born, Married, Died & Buried)

- 1880–1920 Otago Daily Times Births Deaths Marriages, Anniversaries Index, Dunedin, New Zealand
  http://www.es.co.nz/~treeves/geneal.htm
  See the details near the end of this page.

- Anne's UK Certificates for Australians
  http://freespace.virgin.net/mark.wainwright6/uk_certificates/
  An Australian living in London who can obtain copies of English, Scottish & Welsh Birth, Marriage and Death Certificates in exchange for payment in Australian dollars.

- Australasia Births, Deaths and Marriages Exchange
  http://www.geocities.com/Athens/Forum/3709/exchange/
  The aim of the Australasia Births, Deaths and Marriages Exchange is to provide to genealogists a free resource, to share information about details contained on birth, death and marriage registrations registered in Australia, New Zealand and Papua New Guinea.

- Australian Registrars of Births, Deaths & Marriages
  http://www.users.on.net/proformat/regs.html

- Cemeteries in and around Gunning Shire, New South Wales
  http://www.pcug.org.au/~gchallin/cemeteries/top.htm

- Censuses in Australian Colonies
  http://www.users.on.net/proformat/census.html

- Civil Registration—Australian BDM Criteria
  http://www.users.on.net/proformat/bdm.html

- Commonwealth War Graves Commission
  http://www.cwgc.org/
  Details of 1.7 million members of UK and Commonwealth forces who died in the 1st and 2nd World Wars and other wars, and 60,000 civilian casualties of WWII. Gives details of grave site, date of death, age, usually parents/widow's address.

- Current Cost of Australian Certificates
  http://202.139.254.245/cert_aus.htm
  From Sally Hammon's home page.

- Deaths and Memoriams Extracted From the 'New Zealand Herald' 1993
  http://www.geocities.com/Heartland/6123/dth_names.html
  From New Zealand. Find a surname of interest then e-mail the owner of the page for details.

- District Registrars in South Australia
  http://www.users.on.net/proformat/dregs.html

- Index Projects at the Public Record Office, Victoria's Archives
  http://home.vicnet.net.au/~provic/index.htm

- Location of South Australian Records
  http://www.users.on.net/proformat/research.html
  Including some research guidelines.

- Lonely Graves in South Australia
  http://www.users.on.net/proformat/graves.html

- Marriage Witness Indexes for United Kingdom, Australia, and New Zealand
  http://www.genuki.org.uk/mwi/

- Moggill Cemetery
  http://192.148.225.23/bruce/cemetery.html
  A suburb of Brisbane, Queensland, Australia.

- New South Wales Family History Document Service
  http://www.ihr.com.au/
  A service which provides you with image files of historical documents used for researching people in New South Wales between 1850 and 1920.

- New South Wales Registry of Births, Deaths and Marriages
  http://www.agd.nsw.gov.au/bdm/

- New Zealand Births, Deaths & Marriages Office
  http://inform.dia.govt.nz/internal_affairs/businesses/doni_pro/bdm_pro/bdm.html
  and their research service
  http://inform.dia.govt.nz/internal_affairs/businesses/doni_pro/bdm_pro/research/researchindex.html

- Public Record Office—Victoria's Archives
  http://home.vicnet.net.au/~provic/welcome.htm

- South Australian Cemeteries
  http://www.users.on.net/proformat/cems.html

- Spencer Holy Trinity Cemetery
  http://www.terrigal.net.au/~history/spencer.htm
  Cemetery Index for sale.

◆ Ships: Convict Lists, Passenger Lists, Etc.

- AUSNZ Passenger Lists
  http://www.users.on.net/proformat/auspass.html

- Australia's First Fleet
  http://www.pcug.org.au/~pdownes/dps/1stflt.htm
  Convicts transported from England in 1788.

- Australia's Second Fleet
  http://www.pcug.org.au/~pdownes/dps/2ndflt.htm
  Convicts transported from England in 1790.

- Australia's Third Fleet
  http://www.pcug.org.au/~pdownes/dps/3rdflt.txt
  Convicts transported from England in 1791.

- Fifty Years in Queensland:—Living Pioneer Colonists
  http://192.148.225.23/bruce/qldpio.html
  A supplement article to "The Queenslander" Jubilee Issue:— 7 August 1909, which lists names, ages and year of arrival and the ship's name.

- Geelong Maritime Museum
  http://www.zades.com.au/geelong/maritime.html

- Index to Inward Overseas Passengers from Foreign Ports 1852–1859
  http://home.vicnet.net.au/~provic/185259/5259indx.htm
  From the PRO Victoria.

- Lincolnshire Archives Index of Convict Records 1787–1840
  http://www.demon.co.uk/lincs-archives/convicts.htm

- National Archives of Ireland: Transportation Records
  http://www.nationalarchives.ie/search01.html
  Convicts from Ireland to Australia, 1788 to 1868.

- "Parsee"—Passenger List—Moreton Bay—11 January 1853
  http://192.148.225.23/bruce/plink.html

- Passenger List of the Palestine
  http://www.benet.net.au/~brandis/gendata/palestine.html
  From Plymouth, England, 29 November 1852 to Perth, Western Australia, 28 April 1853.

- Passengers on the Emigrant Ship "Emigrant"
  http://www.swinhope.demon.co.uk/genuki/Transcriptions/Emigrant.html
  Sailed from Sunderland 10 September 1852; arrived Melbourne 3 January 1853.

- Passengers on the Emigrant Ship "Lizzie Webber"
  http://www.swinhope.demon.co.uk/genuki/Transcriptions/LizzieWebber.html
  Sailed from Sunderland 31 July 1852; arrived Melbourne 4 December 1852.

- Passengers on the Emigrant Ship "Lord Delaval"
  http://www.swinhope.demon.co.uk/genuki/Transcriptions/LordDelaval.html
  Sailed from Berwick-upon-Tweed on September 13th 1852 for London and on to Port St. Philip, Victoria, Australia.

- Passengers on the Emigrant Ship "Saldanha"
  http://www.swinhope.demon.co.uk/genuki/Transcriptions/Saldanha.html
  Sailed from Liverpool in the summer of 1856 for Victoria, Australia.

- Peter HODGE's Home Page
  http://www.pcug.org.au/~phodge/
  Information regarding the brig "Indian" from Falmouth in mid-1843 bound for Launceston, Tasmania; the "Emigrant" sailed from Plymouth on 9 August 1850 bound for Moreton Bay; and more on emigration, etc.

- Sailing Ship the INDIA Lost at Sea 1841
  http://www.home.gil.com.au/~bbiggar/india.htm
  Sailed from Greenock Scotland on 4 June 1841 bound for the Australian colony of Port Phillip.

- Ships to Western Australia 1829–1849
  http://www.benet.net.au/~brandis/gendata/1829_49.html

- Ships to Western Australia 1899
  http://www.benet.net.au/~brandis/gendata/1899ship.html

- Ships to Western Australia 1900
  http://www.benet.net.au/~brandis/gendata/1900ship.html

- Ships to Western Australia January and February 1901
  http://www.benet.net.au/~brandis/gendata/1901ship.html

- South Australian Passenger Lists 1836–1840
  http://www.users.on.net/proformat/ships36.html

- South Australian Passenger Lists 1841–1846
  http://www.users.on.net/proformat/ships41.html

- South Australian Passenger Lists 1847–1886
  http://www.users.on.net/proformat/ships47.html

- South Australian Transported Convicts
  http://www.users.on.net/proformat/convicts.html

- The Wellington Valley Convicts, 1823–31
  http://www.newcastle.edu.au/department/hi/roberts/convicts.htm
  A database of more than 1,000 convicts.

- Women and Female Children of the Royal Admiral 1792
  http://www.shoalhaven.net.au/~cathyd/raladies.html

◆ Societies & Groups

- Albury-Wodonga Dead Persons Society
  http://candela.dragnet.com.au/~pattogar/dps.htm
  Victoria, New South Wales

- Archer's Computer Interest Group List—Australia
  http://www.genealogy.org/~ngs/cigs/ngl3otau.html

- ARHS/nsw—Australian Railway Historical Society, New South Wales Division
  http://www.accsoft.com.au/~arhsnsw/

- AusSI Special Interest Groups
  http://www.zeta.org.au/~aussi/administration/sigs.htm

- Australian Institute of Genealogical Studies Inc.
  http://www.alphalink.com.au/~aigs/
  Blackburn, Victoria, Australia

- Australian Jewish Genealogical Society
  http://www.zeta.org.au/~feraltek/genealogy/ajgs/index.html

- Australian Local Family History Societies
  http://www.ihr.com.au./societies.html

- Australian Railway Historical Society (ARHS)—(Victorian Division Inc.)
  http://home.vicnet.net.au/~arhsvic/

- Australia Railway Historical Society—Queensland Division
  http://zerlargal.humbug.org.au/~arhsqld/

- Australian Society of Archivists
  http://www.aa.gov.au/AA_WWW/ProAssn/ASA/ASA.html

- Ballarat & District Genealogical Society
  http://www.ballaratgenealogy.org.au/
  Victoria, Australia

- Bellarine Historical Society Inc.
  http://www.zades.com.au/bellhs/bellhs.html
  Covering the Bellarine Peninsula in Victoria, Australia.

- Brisbane Dead Persons Society
  http://www.st.net.au/~dps/

- The City of Cessnock Historical Society
  http://users.hunterlink.net.au/~ddlc/cessnock.htm
- Clare Regional History Group
  http://www.ozemail.com.au/~jlsymo/clareone.htm
- Cornish Association of New South Wales
  http://www.ozemail.com.au/~jlsymo/cansw.htm
- Cornish Association of New South Wales
  http://www.zynet.co.uk/jlobb/cansw/canswref.htm
- Cornish Association of Victoria
  http://www.dcscomp.com.au/jewell/cav/index.htm
- Dead Persons Society
  http://pcm.pcmedia.com.au/tags/docs/dps.html
- Dead Persons Society (DPS) Canberra ACT
  Australia—Home Page
  http://www.pcug.org.au/~chowell/dpshome.htm
- Dead Persons Society, Melbourne, Victoria,
  Australia
  http://home.vicnet.net.au/~dpsoc/welcome.htm
- Dead Persons Society, Newcastle, NSW
  http://bhss.inia.net.au/patmay/dps/
- Dromana and District Historical Society Inc.
  http://home.vicnet.net.au/~dromana/
- Echuca / Moama Family History Group, Inc.
  http://avoca.vicnet.net.au/~emfhistory/
- First Fleet Fellowship
  http://home.vicnet.net.au/~firstff/
  *A historical society for people who have ancestors who arrived
  in Australia in 1788 aboard one of the ships of the First Fleet.*
- The Geelong Family History Group Inc. (GFHG)
  http://home.vicnet.net.au/~gfamhist/index.htm
- Geelong Historical Society
  http://www.zades.com.au/geelong/ghs.html
- Genealogical Society of Queensland Inc.
  http://www.st.net.au/~dunn/gsq.htm
- Genealogical Society of Victoria Inc.
  http://www.alphalink.com.au/~gsv/
- Geraldton Family History Society
  http://www.wn.com.au/gfhs/
  *Western Australian Society. Includes a listing of members
  surname interests.*
- Gerringong and District Historical Society
  http://www.ozemail.com.au/~johngrah/gdhs.html
- Gold Coast Dead Persons Society
  http://www.worldlink.com.au/dps/
- The Heraldry and Genealogy Society of
  Canberra Inc.
  http://www.netspeed.com.au/hagsoc/
- Lithgow and District Family History Society Inc.
  http://www.lisp.com.au/~ldfhs/
  New South Wales

- Mallacoota & District Historical Society
  http://home.vicnet.net.au/~coota/community/history.htm
- Melbourne PAF Users Group
  http://www.cohsoft.com.au/afhc/melbpaf.html
- Mildura & District Genealogical Society Inc.
  http://users.mildura.net.au/users/genealogy/
- The Military Historical Society of Australia
  http://www.pcug.org.au/~astaunto/mhsa.htm
- Milton Ulladulla History Groups
  http://www.shoalhaven.net.au/~cathyd/groups.html
- New Zealand Society of Genealogists, Inc.
  http://www.genealogy.org.nz/
- Perth Dead Person's Society
  http://carmen.murdoch.edu.au/community/dps/default.html
- Qld Association of Local and Family History
  Societies
  http://www.st.net.au/~judyweb/qalfhs.html
  Queensland
- Queensland Family History Society Inc.
  http://www.qfhs.org.au/
  *Large reference library with most major research resources
  (focusing on Australasia, British Isles, and Germany). Largest
  genealogical CD-ROM collection in Australia. Currently
  compiling 1.3 million Queensland Genealogical Master Index to
  sources. 1,400 members. New members always welcome.*
- Royal Historical Society of Victoria
  http://home.vicnet.net.au/~rhsvic/
- Society of Australian Genealogists
  http://www.ozemail.com.au/~socgenes/sag.html
- South Australian Genealogy & Heraldry Society Inc.
  http://saghs.mtx.net/
- The Sydney Dead Persons Society
  http://www.ozemail.com.au/~johngrah/dps.html
- The Townsville and District Dead Persons' Society
  http://www.ozemail.com.au/~dpsnq/
  North Queensland, Australia
- Victorian GUM (Genealogists Using
  Microcomputers) Inc.
  http://www.vicgum.asn.au/
- Wagga Wagga & District Family History Society
  (Inc)
  http://members.xoom.com/FHS/
  *Contains Members' Interest Register and general information
  about the situation and facilities of the society.*
- Western Australian Genealogical Society Inc.
  http://cleo.murdoch.edu.au/~wags/
- Woodend and District Heritage Society
  http://www.asap.unimelb.edu.au/asa/directory/data/399.htm
  Local & Family History Resource Centre, Woodend, Victoria.

AUSTRIA / ÖSTERREICH
http://www.CyndisList.com/austria.htm

Category Index:
- General Resource Sites
- Libraries, Archives & Museums
- Mailing Lists, Newsgroups & Chat
- Maps, Gazetteers & Geographical Information
- People & Families

- Professional Researchers, Volunteers & Other Research Services
- Publications, Software & Supplies
- Queries, Message Boards & Surname Lists

◆ General Resource Sites

- Austrian Genealogy—AustriaGenWeb
  http://www.rootsweb.com/~autwgw/
  Genealogical research in Austria. Information, links and posting of queries.

- Family History / Genealogy from the Unofficial Homepage for Austria of The Church of Jesus Christ of Latter-day Saints
  http://www.ettl.co.at/mormon/english/gen_gy.htm

- Genealogical Research in Austria
  http://www.genealogy.net/gene/reg/AUT/austria-en.html

- Genealogical Research in the Lands of the Former Austro-Hungarian Monarchy—Guide to Archives and Parish-Registers
  http://www.netway.at/ihff/

- Post & Telekom Austria—Elektronisches Telefonbuch
  http://www.etb.at/

◆ Libraries, Archives & Museums

- Archives in Austria
  http://www.bawue.de/~hanacek/info/aarchive.htm
  Addresses and descriptions in German.

- Family History Centers in Germany, Austria and Switzerland
  http://www.genealogy.net/gene/faqs/LDS.de

- Österreichische Nationalbibliothek / National Library of Austria
  http://www.onb.ac.at/

- Wiener Stadt-und Landesarchiv / Viennese City & National Archives
  http://www.magwien.gv.at/ma08/m08_leit.htm

◆ Mailing Lists, Newsgroups & Chat

- AUSTRIA Mailing List
  http://members.aol.com/gfsjohnf/gen_mail_country-aut.html#AUSTRIA

◆ Maps, Gazetteers & Geographical Information

- 1858 Map of Vienna
  http://www.lib.utexas.edu/Libs/PCL/Map_collection/historical/Vienna_1858.jpg

- Map of Austria
  http://www.lib.utexas.edu/Libs/PCL/Map_collection/europe/Austria.GIF
  From the Perry-Castañeda Library at the Univ. of Texas at Austin.

◆ People & Families

- Austria/Hungary Empire
  http://www.worldroots.com/brigitte/royal/royal10.htm
  Historic and genealogical information about royal and nobility family lines.

◆ Professional Researchers, Volunteers & Other Research Services

- Arno Schmitt, Journalist from San Diego, California
  E-mail: reporter@adnc.com
  He can help to find relatives, links or sources regarding ancestors by placing articles in German, Austrian and/or Swiss newspapers. For details, e-mail Arno at: reporter@adnc.com

- Family Tree Genealogical and Probate Research Bureau Ltd.
  http://www.hungary.net/familytree/
  Professional research service covering the area of what was formerly the Austro-Hungarian Empire, including: Hungary, Slovakia, Czech Republic, Austria, Italy, Transylvania, Croatia, Slovenia, former Yugoslavia (Banat), and the Ukraine (Sub-Carpathian).

- Institute for Historical Family Research / IHFF Genealogie Gesellschaft mbH
  http://www.netway.at/ihff/index.htm
  Professional Researcher specializing in: Austria, Czech & Slovak Republics, Hungary, Slovenian Republic, Croatia, Galicia, others. There are many articles and helpful research guides on this site.

◆ Publications, Software & Supplies

- Frontier Press Bookstore—Austria
  http://www.doit.com/frontier/frontier.cgi?category=aus

◆ Queries, Message Boards & Surname Lists

- Lineages' Free On-line Queries—Austria
  http://www.lineages.com/queries/BrowseByCountry.asp

BELGIUM / BELGIQUE / BELGIË
http://www.CyndisList.com/belgium.htm

Category Index:

- ◆ General Resource Sites
- ◆ Libraries, Archives & Museums
- ◆ Mailing Lists, Newsgroups & Chat
- ◆ Maps, Gazetteers & Geographical Information
- ◆ People & Families
- ◆ Professional Researchers, Volunteers & Other Research Services

- ◆ Publications, Software & Supplies
- ◆ Queries, Message Boards & Surname Lists
- ◆ Records: Census, Cemeteries, Land, Obituaries, Personal, Taxes and Vital
- ◆ Societies & Groups

◆ General Resource Sites

- Belgium—Immigrants in America
  http://www.ping.be/picavet/
  A complete guide for descendants of Belgian immigrants looking for their roots in Belgium.

- Benelux Research
  gopher://omega.ufsia.ac.be

- The Emigration from the Waasland to the United States and Canada 1830–1950
  http://www.geocities.com/Heartland/Plains/5666/Picavet.html
  or an alternate site
  http://www.concentric.net/~Mikerice/hl/more/gpicavet.shtml
  A project by Georges Picavet.

- Genealogie in Limburg
  http://home.wxs.nl/~eugdub/

- Genealogy Benelux Home Page
  http://www.ufsia.ac.be/genealogy/

- Genealogy in Belgium
  http://win-www.uia.ac.be/u/pavp/index.html

- Genealogy in Belgium
  http://www.cam.org/~beaur/gen/belgiq-e.html
  From Denis Beauregard. Mostly in French until English translation is complete.

- Infobel—Find Business & Residential Addresses in Belgium
  http://www.infobel.be/

- STORME's Genealogy Page
  http://www.ufsia.ac.be/~estorme/genealogy.html
  Many great Benelux resource links. STORME, van WAESBERGHE, de LAUSNAY, BLOCK, SCHEERDERS, van SCHOUBROEK, de SCHRYVER, BOSTEELS.

- "Wallonia"—Genealogy Database from French-speaking Belgium
  http://www.ufsia.ac.be/genealogy/wallonia/wallonia.htm
  Brussels and Wallonia

- Yahoo!...Belgium...Genealogy
  http://dir.yahoo.com/Regional/Countries/Belgium/Society_and_Culture/History/Genealogy/

◆ Libraries, Archives & Museums

- Archives of Mechelen, Belgium Sources for Genealogy
  http://www.tornado.be/~marc.alcide/archief/archiefe.htm

- Les Centres Généalogiques SDJ / LDS Family History Centers
  http://www2.et.byu.edu/~harmanc/paris/genealogie.html
  France, Belgique, Suisse, Canada

- Stadsarchief van Mechelen. Aanbod voor Genealogen / Archives of Mechelen. Main sources for genealogy
  http://www.tornado.be/~marc.alcide/archief/archief.html

◆ Mailing Lists, Newsgroups & Chat

- BELGIUM-ROOTS Mailing List
  http://members.aol.com/gfsjohnf/gen_mail_country-blg.html#BELGIUM-ROOTS
  For the descendants of Belgian emigrants/immigrants who are interested in researching their roots in Belgium.

- GENBNL-L Mailing List
  http://members.aol.com/gfsjohnf/gen_mail_country-blg.html#DUTCH
  For research in the Benelux region (Belgium, the Netherlands, and Luxembourg). Gatewayed with the soc.genealogy.benelux newsgroup.

◆ Maps, Gazetteers & Geographical Information

- Belgium Place Names
  http://www.ping.be/picavet/Waas_America_Research21.shtml

- Map of Belgium
  http://www.lib.utexas.edu/Libs/PCL/Map_collection/europe/
  BELGIUM.GIF
  From the Perry-Castañeda Library at the Univ. of Texas at Austin.

◆ People & Families

- BLONDIA and family
  http://members.aol.com/rblondia/genealogy/index.htm

- Familiearchief—Panis, Geusens, Houben, Lindmans
  en vele andere families
  http://www.falcon.be/familiearchief/

- Genealogiepagina van Luc SILLIS
  http://www.club.innet.be/~agfa0190/genealogie.htm

- Kwartierstaat van Nada Kimberley KLAPS
  http://ping4.ping.be/~ping2011/Klaps.html
  KLAPS, PHETSUWAN, HERMANS, NINSUWAN, GOOSSENS, VERNELEN, JAME, CRAEGHS, MARTENS, SMEYERS

- LOUWAGIE Genealogical Tree, From
  1190 Till Today
  http://www.stleocol-bru.be/sl/loage.htm
  From Belgium. Lauage, Lauwagie, Lawaese, Lawaisse, Louage, Louagé, Louagie, Louwaege, Louwage and Lowagie.

- Homepage of the Family Association
  VANDENBEMPT
  http://www.club.innet.be/~ind1991/
  Vandenbempt, Vanden Bempt, Van den Bempt, Vanderbemde(n), Vander Bemde(n), Van der Bemde(n), Vandenbempde(n), Vanden Bempde(n), van den Beempde, Van den Beemd, van den Beemd, van den Beemt, Vanebempt, Debempt.

- Index of Persons—Famille ADAMS et apparentees
  http://users.skynet.be/sky39882/geneal/persons.htm
  ADAMS, KLEPPER, VAN ACHTER, De KIMPE, VANDERHAEGEN

- Male Descendants of Gerardus VAN WIJCK
  http://www.ping.be/~ping2855/

- Marc VERMEIRSSEN's Homepage
  http://bewoner.dma.be/mvermeir/
  Vermeirssen, Vermeerssen, Vermeirsschen, Vermeirssch, Vermeerren.

- The ORBAN's
  http://www.geocities.com/CapeCanaveral/7473/orban.html
  Belgium, Hungary

- La Page Genealogique De Gilbert MINETTE
  http://users.skynet.be/sky40172/index.htm

- Pascal JANSSENs Genealogy Page
  http://pucky.uia.ac.be/~janssen/genealogy/
  HEBBINCKHUYS, CEULEMANS, SCHAUWERS

- VAN BEESEN: Ma Généalogie et autres liens
  http://club.ib.be/patrick.van.beesen/

- VAN THIENEN Genealogy
  http://www.ping.be/~pin02229/genealog.htm
  Van Thienen, Vanthienen, van Thienen, Van Thienen, Van Tienen, Vantienen, van Tienen, Van Tiene, von Thienen, Von Thienen, de Tenis, de Thenis. In Belgium, The Netherlands, Germany, France, Argentina, Canada, USA, New Zealand and Australia.

◆ Professional Researchers, Volunteers & Other Research Services

- Genealogy Helplist—Belgium
  http://posom.com/hl/bel/index.shtml

◆ Publications, Software & Supplies

- Books We Own—Belgium
  http://www.rootsweb.com/~bwo/belgium.html

- PRO-GEN Genealogie à la Carte
  http://home.wxs.nl/~progen/home.html
  Dutch genealogy program capable of outputs in Dutch, English, French, Frisian and German.

◆ Queries, Message Boards & Surname Lists

- Lineages' Free On-line Queries—Belgium
  http://www.lineages.com/queries/BrowseByCountry.asp

- Project Ahnentafels in Limburg / Project Limburgse
  Kwartierstaten
  http://ping4.ping.be/~ping2011/Ahnen.html

◆ Records: Census, Cemeteries, Land, Obituaries, Personal, Taxes and Vital (Born, Married, Died & Buried)

- Digital Resources Netherlands and Belgium
  http://home.wxs.nl/~hjdewit/links_en.html
  Digital resources available on the internet, bulletin board systems and on diskette/CD-ROM.

- Stadsarchief van Mechelen. Aanbod voor
  Genealogen
  http://www.mechelen.be/archief/archief.html
  Archives of Mechelen. Main sources for genealogy.

  - Criminaliteit te Mechelen van 1773 tot 1795
    http://www2.cipal.be/Mechelen/archief/Vonnissn.htm
    Criminal records between 1773 and 1795.

  - Mechelen: Register Van De Belastingen Op De
    Huizen Anno 1722: Sint Katelijneparochie
    http://www.mechelen.be/archief/katelijn.htm
    House Tax Registry anno 1722: Sint Katelijne.

○ Mechelse conscrits of (kandidaat-)soldaten voor het Franse leger (1798–1814)
http://www2.cipal.be/Mechelen/archief/ConscritIndex2.html
Conscrits for the French army (1798–1814).

◆ Societies & Groups

● Archer's Computer Interest Group List—Belgium
http://www.genealogy.org/~ngs/cigs/ngl3otbe.html

● Cercle de Généalogie et d'Héraldique de l'U.E. / E.U. Society for Genealogy and Heraldry
http://ourworld.compuserve.com/homepages/cghue_eusgh/cghue2.htm

● Club De Genealogie De Sambreville (Belgique)
http://www.multimania.com/bcollard/

● Fédération Généalogique et Héraldique de Belgique / Belgische Federatie voor Genealogie en Heraldiek
http://win-www.uia.ac.be/u/pavp/societies.html#bfgh

● Genealogical Society of Flemish Americans
http://members.xoom.com/GSFA
GSFA publishes a newsletter and helps people trace their Flemish and Belgian heritage.

● GENSESEM—Cercle de généalogie de Chimay
http://users.skynet.be/sky38740/

● PRO-GEN gebruikersgroep LIMBURG / PRO-GEN users' group LIMBURG
http://ping4.ping.be/~ping2011/

● Vlaamse Vereniging voor Familiekunde—V.V.F.— Flemish Society of Genealogists
http://win-www.uia.ac.be/u/pavp/societies.html#vvf

BIOGRAPHIES
http://www.CyndisList.com/biograph.htm

- American Life Histories: Manuscripts from the
  Federal Writers' Project, 1936–1940
  http://lcweb2.loc.gov/ammem/wpaintro/wpahome.html
  *"These life histories were written by the staff of the Folklore
  Project of the Federal Writers' Project for the U.S. Works
  Progress (later Work Projects) Administration (WPA) from
  1936–1940. The Library of Congress collection includes 2,900
  documents representing the work of over 300 writers from
  24 states."*

- Augustine GODWIN of Wyoming Township, Kent
  County, Michigan
  http://homepages.rootsweb.com/~godwin/family/
  augustine.html

- Autobiography of the Rev. William GILL
  http://www.genuki.org.uk/big/eng/Indexes/REVWGILL.txt
  A list of names indexed from the book.

- Biographical Dictionary
  http://www.s9.com/biography/
  Covers more than 19,000 notable men and women.

- Biographical Sketches Relating to Sussex County
  http://www.gate.net/~pascalfl/bioindex.html
  New Jersey

- Biographies and Histories from Around the World
  http://vader.castles.com/ftprints/web80000.html

- Biographies & Newspaper Articles
  http://www.genweb.net/~bowers/lane/pollyp.htm
  From the LANE Descendants Homepage.

- Biographies from the Memorial and
  Biographical Record
  http://www.rootsweb.com/~usgenweb/sd/biography/
  memor.htm
  South Dakota

- Biographies of Henry County Families
  http://www.geocities.com/Heartland/Plains/8977/biodex.htm
  Illinois

- Biography of Jeptha THORNTON
  http://www.rootsweb.com/~ordougla/jeptha.htm
  An Oregon pioneer.

- Biography of Joanna QUAID
  http://www.pclink.com/kg0ay/quaid.htm
  *She was born in Ireland and made the trek to the United States
  in 1836.*

- Beers Biographical Record Online—Washington
  County, Pennsylvania
  http://www.chartiers.com/beers-project/beers.html
  *Biographical Sketches of Prominent and Representative Citizens
  and of many of the Early Settled Families.*

- Boyhood Memories of Col. Ed NIX, U.S. Marshal of
  the Oklahoma Territory
  http://www.geocities.com/Heartland/Hills/5391/nix.html
  By Gene KUYKENDALL.

- California County Biographies and Histories
  http://www.compuology.com/cpl/cpl_bio.htm

- A Centennial Tribute: Creators of the Legacy
  http://www.commerce.digital.com/palo-alto/historical-assoc/
  centennial-bios/home.html
  Palo Alto, California

- Colonial Hall: Biographies of America's
  Founding Fathers
  http://www.webcom.com/bba/ch/

- Cowlitz County Biographies
  http://www.halcyon.com/jennyrt/wacowlitz/bios.html
  Washington

- Decatur County, Iowa Genealogy—Pioneer
  Biographies
  http://www.geocities.com/Heartland/Hills/7094/bios.htm

- Francis Marion GAY, Co. F 65th Reg.
  Georgia Infantry
  http://www.izzy.net/~michaelg/fm-gay.htm

- Frontier Press Bookstore—Biography
  http://www.frontierpress.com/frontier.cgi?category=biog

- Genealogical Investigation into Charles J. ARIS
  http://www.oz.net/~markhow/chasaris.htm
  *World War I veteran, 16th Queen's Own Lancers, a cavalry unit
  of the British Army.*

- Harrison County Iowa Biographies
  http://www.rootsweb.com/~iaharris/bio/genealog.htm

- Heritage Gateway—Pioneer Journals
  http://heritage.uen.org/cgi-bin/websql/pioneer.hts?type=1
  Members of the LDS church.

- Historical Events & People Worldwide
  http://www.CyndisList.com/historic.htm
  See this category on Cyndi's List for related links.

- Indiana Biography
  http://www.ipfw.edu/ipfwhist/indiana/biog.htm
  *From the Department of History, Indiana University-Purdue
  University Fort Wayne.*

- Isaac Spears SANDERLIN, Private, Co. I, 100th
  Ohio Volunteer Infantry in the Civil War
  http://www.oz.net/~cyndihow/isaac.htm
  Cyndi's 3rd great-grandfather.

- Journals of Early Members of the Church of Jesus Christ of Latter-day Saints
  http://www.math.byu.edu/~smithw/Lds/LDS/Early-Saints/
  Journals, diaries, biographies and autobiographies of some early Mormons and others who knew Joseph Smith, Jr.

- Kentuckiana Konnections—Biographies
  http://www.floyd-pavey.com/kentuckiana/kyiana/county/biolinks.html
  Kentucky & Indiana

- KYBIOGRAPHIES Mailing List
  http://members.aol.com/gfsjohnf/gen_mail_states-ky.html#KYBIOGRAPHIES
  A read-only mailing list (no queries or submissions) transmitting biographies on all the Kentucky people cited in the old histories (e.g., Perrins, Collins, church histories).

- Letters and Stories—A Pioneer's Story—By Joe PLETCHER, told August 5, 1905
  http://www.geocities.com/Heartland/Hills/5807/story.html

- Letters from an Iowa Soldier in the Civil War
  http://www.ucsc.edu./civil-war-letters/home.html
  Part of a collection written by Newton Robert SCOTT, Private, Company A, of the 36th Infantry, Iowa Volunteers to Hannah CONE, his friend and later his wife.

- Lewis County Biographies
  http://www.halcyon.com/jennyrt/bios/bios.html
  Washington

- The Life and Times of South Dakota Pioneers
  http://members.aol.com/drfransen/letters/home.htm

- Life of Polly HART LANE
  http://www.genweb.net/~bowers/lane/pollyp.htm
  Polly Pierce (Pierre) Hart LANE born in 1802 in Kentucky.

- The Life of "Racket" JOHNSON
  http://homepages.rootsweb.com/~godwin/family/racket.html
  As told by his grandson, George Thomas Johnson. About 1794–95 in Sussex.

- Linn County Biography Index
  http://www.rootsweb.com/~ialinn/bios/bio-index.htm
  Iowa

- Louisa County Genealogical Society Biographies
  http://www.rootsweb.com/~ialouisa/lbios.htm
  Iowa

- MA RYAN, Co B 14th Miss Vol Inf CSA
  http://www.izzy.net/~michaelg/ma-ryan.htm
  Experience of a Confederate Soldier in Camp and Prison in The Civil War 1861–1865.

- Mercer's Maids—Pioneer Brides of 1864
  http://members.tripod.com/~PeriM/Brides.html
  Washington

- Muscatine County Iowa—Pioneers Page
  http://www.geocities.com/Heartland/8613/people.html

- MyStory—The Complete Autobiography Writing System!
  http://www.mystorywriter.com/

- My Virtual Reference Desk—Biography / Who's Who
  http://www.refdesk.com/factbiog.html

- Notable Women Ancestors
  http://www.rootsweb.com/~nwa/

- Out Of Our Past (Stories and Histories of Our Ancestors)
  http://vader.castles.com/ftprints/web50000.html

- Photographs & Memories
  http://www.CyndisList.com/photos.htm
  See this category for related links. Learn how to preserve your own family's stories and put together biographical information regarding one of your own ancestors—or yourself.

- Robert MIDDLETON of Maryland 1651–1708
  http://home.earthlink.net/~middleton/robert.html

- Sabbath Keepers in History
  http://www.ozemail.com.au/~sdbbris/books/new/index2.htm
  From the Time of Christ to the 19th Century. Reprints from "Seventh Day Baptists in Europe and America" Volume 1 (pp 11–115), American Sabbath Tract Society, Plainfield, New Jersey, 1910.

- Samuel Campbell GOODAKER, 1844–c1920, by Charles Goodaker
  http://www.geocities.com/Heartland/Hills/5391/good7.html

- SD Biographies
  http://www.rootsweb.com/~usgenweb/sd/biography/bios.htm

- This One is on Me
  http://www.iwaynet.net/~lsci/Panhandle/Home.html
  By Dr. James Lee Fisher (1895–1987). The life-story of an old doctor who saw many changes in medicine, in industry, in social customs, and the world in general.

- Time Line for Charles Ransom DeLAP 1828–1945
  http://www.rootsweb.com/~orklamat/delap.html
  An Oregon pioneer.

- U.S. Biographies Project
  http://members.tripod.com/~debmurray/usbios/usbiog.html
  A project by Jeff Murphy. Adopt a state and put biographies online!

  - Arkansas Biographies Project
    http://www.rootsweb.com/~usgenweb/ar/biography/bios-ark1.htm

  - California County Biographies and Histories
    http://www.compuology.com/cpl/cpl_bio.htm

  - Indiana Biographies
    http://members.tripod.com/~debmurray/indybios/indiana1.htm

  - Iowa Biographies Project
    http://www.genhist.com/IABios/

  - Kentucky Biographies Project
    http://www.starbase21.com/kybiog/

○ KYBIOG-L—Kentucky Biographies Project
http://members.aol.com/gfsjohnf/gen_mail_states-ky.html#KYBIOG-L
Established to gather biographies of Kentucky citizens as well as those who have moved from Kentucky to other states and whose biographies in that state make reference to their Kentucky backgrounds.

○ Louisiana Biographies
http://www.geocities.com/BourbonStreet/6934/

○ Ohio Biographies Project
http://members.aol.com/webbergrp/ohbios/home.htm

○ USBIOG Mailing List
http://members.aol.com/gfsjohnf/gen_mail_states-gen.html#USBIOG
For people who are interested in helping coordinate a collection of biographies within their state as part of the US Biographies project.

○ Virginia Biographies Project
http://members.aol.com/webbergrp/vabios/home.htm

○ WA Biographies Project
http://www.halcyon.com/jennyrt/WABios/index.html

● La Vie De DUPLEIX
http://members.aol.com/MDruez/dupleix.htm
Francois Joseph Dupleix, governor of Pondicherry for Louis XV of France in India (mid 18th century).

● Webster County Biographies
http://www.rootsweb.com/~kywebste/biogs/biogs.htm
Kentucky

● Xerxes KNOX, Private, Co. G, 3rd Iowa Cavalry in the Civil War
http://www.oz.net/~cyndihow/xerxes.htm
Cyndi's 3rd great-grandfather and a prisoner at Camp Ford in Tyler, Texas.

● Yukon / Alaska Pioneer Biographies
http://yukonalaska.miningco.com/msub15.htm

BOOKS
http://www.CyndisList.com/books.htm

Category Index:

◆ General Sources

◆ Family History Publishers

◆ Locality & Topic Specific

◆ Mailing Lists, Newsgroups & Chat

◆ Used Books, Rare Books & Book Search Services

◆ General Sources

- A1Books
  http://www.a1books.com/
  Do a search on a keyword such as "genealogy."

- AGLL Genealogical Services
  http://www.agll.com/
  American Genealogical Lending Library.

- AGLL Genealogical Services Mailing List
  http://members.aol.com/johnf14246/
  gen_mail_software.html#AGLL
  For announcements of new genealogical products and sales promotions from AGLL.

- alt.bookstore
  http://www.altbookstore.com/

- Amazon.com Books
  http://www.amazon.com/
  Do a search on a keyword such as "genealogy."

- Ancestor Trails
  http://www.ancestor.com/at/

- Ancestors Attic—Discount Genealogy Bookshop
  http://members.tripod.com/~ancestorsattic/index.html

- Ancestry.com Online Store
  http://shop.ancestry.com/
  Books, Computers, Maps, Miscellaneous, Services.

- Appleton's Fine Used Bookseller and Genealogy
  http://www.appletons.com/genealogy/homepage.html
  Charlotte, North Carolina. Genealogy books, software, CD-ROMs, and more. Free genealogy catalog and e-mail list.

- Back Tracks Genealogy Books
  http://www.naxs.com/abingdon/backtrak/catalog.htm

- Barnette's Family Tree Book Company
  http://www.barnettesbooks.com/

- Blairs' Book Service
  http://www.glbco.com/
  With a searchable database.

- The Book Craftsman
  http://www.bookcraftsman.com/
  Restoration of books, custom binding.

- Book Stacks Unlimited, Inc.
  http://www.books.com/scripts/news.exe
  - Book Stacks Publishers' Place
    http://www.books.com/scripts/place.exe
  - Book Stacks Electronic Library
    http://www.books.com/scripts/lib.exe

- Books We Own List
  http://www.rootsweb.com/~bwo/index.html
  A list of resources owned by others who are willing to do lookups in them.

- Boyd Publishing Company Catalog
  http://www.hom.net/~gac/

- Broken Arrow Publishing
  http://clanhuston.com/
  Genealogical and historical publications.

- Ericson Books
  http://www.ericsonbooks.com/
  Nacogdoches, Texas

- Essex Books
  http://www.HERTGE.COM/essex/

- Family History Bookshop—The Institute of Heraldic and Genealogical Studies
  http://www.cs.ncl.ac.uk/genuki/IHGS/Catalogue.html

- Family Tree Bookshop
  http://www.bluecrab.org/famtree/
  Easton, Maryland

- Federation of Family History Societies Publications ~ U.K.
  http://www.ffhs.org.uk/pubs/index.htm

- Frontier Press Bookstore—Genealogical and Historical Books
  http://www.frontierpress.com/frontier.cgi

- GEN-BOOKS Mailing List
  http://members.aol.com/johnf14246/
  gen_mail_general.html#GEN-BOOKS
  For anyone with an interest in the buying or selling of new or used genealogy books and CDs made from these books.

- GenByte BookStore
  http://www.rootsweb.com/~pictou/genbyte.htm

- Genealogical Gleanings
  http://www.pcola.gulf.net/~llscott/tableofc.htm
  by Laura Lee Scott.

- Genealogical Journeys In Time—Books for Sale
  http://ourworld.compuserve.com/homepages/Strawn/
  booksfor.htm

- Genealogical Services & The Genealogy Store
  http://www.genservices.com/

- Genealogy Books & Accessories by Janet Reakes
  http://www.peg.apc.org/~frasertravel/hervey/family/books.htm
  From Australia's Immigration And Family History Centre.

- Genealogy Books By Jeannette Holland Austin
  http://www.genealogy-books.com/index.htm

- GenealogyBookShop.com
  http://www.genealogybookshop.com/genealogybookshop/
  index.html
  *The online store of Genealogical Publishing Co., Inc. &
  Clearfield Company.*

- Genealogy Unlimited—Home Page
  http://www.itsnet.com/~genun/

- GEN-MAT-REQUEST Mailing List
  http://members.aol.com/johnf14246/
  gen_mail_general.html#GEN-MAT
  *For anyone who has an interest in the buying or selling of new
  or used genealogical materials (e.g., books, newsletters, CDs,
  magazines).*

- GEN-MAT-15 Mailing List
  http://members.aol.com/johnf14246/
  gen_mail_general.html#GEN-MAT-15
  *For anyone who desires to post the availability of new or used
  genealogical materials (e.g., books, newsletters, CDs, magazines) or services for sale at a price of $15 or less.*

- GLOBAL Genealogical Supply
  http://www.globalgenealogy.com/

- Golden West Marketing
  http://www.greenheart.com/rdietz/
  *Surname exchange, limited free searches of database, book list,
  professional researchers.*

- The Handy Book for Genealogists
  http://www.everton.com/ads/hbook.htm
  From Everton Publishers.

- Hearthstone Bookshop
  http://www.hearthstonebooks.com/
  Alexandria, Virginia

- Heraldry Today
  http://www.heraldrytoday.co.uk/
  Books for heraldry and genealogy.

- Heritage Books Archives
  http://www.hb-archives.com
  *A research resource which includes a free index to books
  published on the WWW by Heritage Books and a free index to
  other books and CD-ROMs published by Heritage Books.*

- Heritage Books, Inc.
  http://www.heritagebooks.com/
  *Books and CD-ROMs with over 1,000 titles in print. Weekly
  drawings for free books and databases.*

- Higginson Book Company
  http://www.higginsonbooks.com/
  In Salem, Massachusetts. Specializing in genealogy and history.

- The Internet Bookshop
  http://www.bookshop.co.uk/
  Online bookshop in the U.K.

- Lineages, Inc.: Bookstore
  http://www.lineages.com/catalog/BooksTopical.asp

- Lost In Time
  http://www.lostintime.com/
  Books, CDs, software, maps, and accessories.

- Mark and Cyndi's Library
  http://www.oz.net/~markhow/library.htm
  *A list of the genealogy books in our collection, with authors,
  addresses, ISBN numbers and ordering information via
  Amazon.com*

- The Memorabilia Corner
  http://members.aol.com/TMCorner/index.html
  *Forms, flags, maps, software, CDs, tapes, microfilm &
  microfiche, books, periodicals, photographic conservation &
  archival materials.*

- Mountain Press
  http://www.mountainpress.com
  *Books for the southeastern section of the United States from
  Pennsylvania to Texas, with the emphasis on Tennessee and
  Virginia.*

- National Archives Book Store
  http://www.nara.gov/nara/bookstore/books.html

- National Historical Publishing Co.—Introduction
  http://smtp.tbox.com/natlhist/

- Online Pioneers Genealogy Bookstore
  http://www.eskimo.com/~mnarends/book/books.html

- Origins—A Genealogy Book Store
  http://www.angelfire.com/biz/origins1/
  Wisconsin

- Picton Press
  http://www.pictonpress.com/

- Provincial Press
  http://www.provincialpress.com/
  *Reference Books by Winston De Ville, Fellow, American Society
  of Genealogists.*

- SK Publications
  http://www.skpub.com/genie/
  Genealogy research consultants & census books for sale.

- S & N Genealogy Supplies
  http://ourworld.compuserve.com/homepages/
  Genealogy_Supplies/

- Storbeck's Genealogy Books Maps CD-ROM
  http://www.storbecks.com/
- Sunnydaze Genealogical Research Material & Antiques
  http://www.sunnydaze.com/
- Tattered Cover Book Store
  http://www.tatteredcover.com/
- Willow Bend Books
  http://www.willowbend.net/
- Windmill Publications, Inc.
  http://www.comsource.net/~windmill/
- Yahoo!...Genealogy...Publications
  http://dir.yahoo.com/Business_and_Economy/Companies/
  Information/Genealogy/Publications/
- Ye Olde Genealogie Shoppe
  http://www.yogs.com/

◆ Family History Publishers

- Curtis Media, Inc.
  http://members.aol.com/curmedia/curtish.htm
  Bedford, Texas. Publishers of genealogy and history books.
- Custom Computer Creation—Genealogy Book Publishing
  http://www.dlcwest.com/~mgwood/book.html
- Evagean Genealogy Publishing
  http://webnz.com/evagean/
  New Zealand
- Fast Books
  http://www.fastbooks.com.au/
  Perfect Bound Paperback Books, Glebe NSW, Australia.
- Genealogy Publishing Service
  http://www.intertekweb.com/gpsbook/
- The Gregath Publishing Company
  http://www.gregathcompany.com/
  Wyandotte, Oklahoma
- Heritage Books, Inc.
  http://www.heritagebooks.com/authinfo.htm
  Author information—So You Want to Publish a Book?
- Newberry Street Press
  http://www.nehgs.org/NewburySt/press-02.htm
  The special publications division of the New England Historic Genealogical Society.
- Yahoo!...Genealogy...Family History Publishers
  http://dir.yahoo.com/Business_and_Economy/Companies/
  Information/Genealogy/Family_History_Publishers/
- Storytellers
  http://www.storytellers.net/
  Publishers of books & CDs to preserve your family stories.

◆ Locality & Topic Specific

- Advance Genealogy Systems
  http://www.quantumlynx.com/advance/
  Software & books. Canada.
- American Genealogical Research at the DAR, Washington, D.C.
  http://www.dar.org/library/libpub.html
  A terrific book for sale from the DAR
- Ancient Pedigrees
  http://www.infowest.com/ancient/index.html
  A collection of published works called "The World Book of Generations."
- Antigonish Books of Genealogical and Historical Interest
  http://www.rootsweb.com/~pictou/biblio.htm
  Nova Scotia, Canada
- Arkansas Ancestors—Arkansas and Alabama Genealogy Resource Books
  http://www.genrecords.com/arkansasancestors/index.htm
- Arkansas Research—Desmond Walls Allen
  http://biz.ipa.net/arkresearch/
  Arkansas genealogy books for sale including: Death Records, 1850 Census Indexes, Land Patent Series, County Records, Ozark Folk Tales, Military Records, and more.
- Avotaynu, Inc. Home Page
  http://www.avotaynu.com/
  Products and information for Jewish genealogy.
- The Best Books on German Passenger Liners
  http://www.genealogy.net/brigitte/ships.htm
- Beyond Bartholomew—The Portland Area History
  http://www.seark.net/~history/
  Arkansas. A book for sale by the author. The book's table of contents and a family name list are online here also.
- Books Related to Irish Migration
  http://www2.ebtech.net/~kleonard/Irish.html
  A list by Karen Leonard.
- Bridges Genealogy Books and Services
  http://pw2.netcom.com/~huskyfan/genealogy.html
  Pictou County, Nova Scotia, North Carolina and Virginia
- Broad View Books
  http://broadviewbooks.com/
  Used Genealogy Books, Local History of Massachusetts, Connecticut, Rhode Island, Vermont and New England.
- Byron Sistler and Associates, Inc.
  http://www.mindspring.com/~sistler/
  Over 900 books covering records from Tennessee, Virginia, North Carolina, and Kentucky.
- Camp Pope Bookshop
  http://members.aol.com/ckenyoncpb/index.htm
  Specializing in out-of-print books on the American Civil War, Iowa & the Trans-Mississippi Theater.

- Cemetery Survey of the Eastern District of Douglas County, Missouri
  http://pages.prodigy.com/PTPM52A.LaineS/
  Book for sale.

- Chapman Record Cameos
  http://www.genuki.org.uk/big/Chapman.html
  U.K. A series of books by Colin R. Chapman, noted British genealogist.

- Cherokee Proud: A Guide for Tracing and Honoring Your Cherokee Ancestors
  http://www.powersource.com/gallery/tonymack/

- Curley—Koen Book Distributors
  http://pw2.netcom.com/~jcurley1/CKBooks.html
  Census indexes for Guysborough County, Nova Scotia, Canada.

- Family Line Publications
  http://pages.prodigy.com/Strawn/family.htm
  Books covering Delaware, Maryland, New Jersey, Pennsylvania, Virginia, and Washington, DC.

- A Genealogist's Guide to Discovering Your Italian Ancestors
  http://www.erols.com/lynnn/dyia/main.html
  A book for sale, with excerpts and its table of contents online.

- Genealogy for Armenians
  http://www.itsnet.com/home/gfa/
  This site has excerpts from a book for sale of the same title.

- Genealogy Titles from the Vermont Historical Society Book List
  http://www.state.vt.us/vhs/shop/genebks.htm

- Gibson Guides—Location Guides for Family and Local Historians
  http://www.genuki.org.uk/big/Gibson.html
  U.K. A set of guides to the whereabouts of records, available from the Federation of Family History Societies.

- Gorin Genealogical Publishing
  http://members.tripod.com/~GorinS/index.html
  and an alternate address
  http://members.aol.com/kygen/gorin.htm
  Publications cover mostly Kentucky, also has some for Logan County, Illinois and Fentress & Overton Counties, Tennessee.

- Gould Books—Family & Local History Specialist
  http://www.gould.com.au/
  Australia

- Guidon Books
  http://www.guidon.com/index.html
  Has an extensive collection of new and out of print books on the American Civil War and Western Americana.

- Hope Farm Press & Bookshop
  http://www.hopefarm.com/
  New York State Regional History, Folklore, Nature, Military, Native American and Genealogy—Covering Western New York, Adirondacks, Hudson Valley, Catskill Mts & Finger Lakes.

- Iberian Publishing Company's Online Catalog
  http://www.iberian.com/
  Specializing in reference works for genealogists and historians researching the Virginias and other Southeastern U.S. States circa. 1650–1850.

- Indiana Historical Society Publications
  https://www.dgltd.com/ihs1830/publications.html

- Interlink Bookshop & Genealogical Services
  http://www.pacificcoast.net/~ibgs/
  Victoria, B.C. Canada

- Iowa Counties—Iowa Internet Book Store
  http://iowa-counties.com/bookstore/

- J & W Enterprises
  http://www.dhc.net/~jw/
  One stop book source on the Internet, specializing in southern states source material.

- Jewish Roots in Poland—Pages from the Past and Archival Inventories
  http://www.rtrfoundation.org/
  A new book by Miriam Weiner.

- Kinseeker Publications
  http://www.angelfire.com/biz/Kinseeker/index.html
  Michigan and Wisconsin

- Kinship—"Genealogy Resources for Kith and Kin"
  http://www.kinshipny.com/
  Publishers of New York State Research Material.

- Lunenburg County / Nova Scotia Genealogy Book List
  http://www.rootsweb.com/~canns/lunenburg/booklist.htm

- Macbeth Genealogical Services
  http://www.macbeth.com.au/
  Books, fiche, maps, and CD-ROMs. Australia.

- Martin Genealogy Publications
  http://www.angelfire.com/biz/martingenpub/
  Alabama and Florida

- Mechling Associates, Inc. Western Pennsylvania Genealogy & History Books
  http://members.aol.com/armechling/mechweb.html

- Military Publications International Directory
  http://www.islandnet.com/~duke/idmp.htm
  Book for sale from Canada.

- Mines Road Books
  http://cmug.com/~minesroad/
  Fremont, California. Specialize in researching and publishing California history and genealogy.

- Monroe DAVIS' Family Book Shelf
  http://members.aol.com/monroegd/index.html
  DAVIS, VAUGHN, WATKINS

- National Historical Publishing Company
  http://www.tbox.com/natlhist/default.html
  Books regarding pension files and service records for the Revolutionary War, War of 1812, Mexican War and Civil War. Indexes to Old Wars and Indian Wars.

- The Naval & Military Press Web Page
  http://www.naval-military-press.co.uk/
  A large selection of military books, many with of interest to the genealogist.

- Netting Your Ancestors—Genealogical Research on the Internet
  http://www.CyndisList.com/netting.htm
  My book from Genealogical Publishing Co.

- New Zealand Society of Genealogists— Hardcopy Publications
  http://homepages.ihug.co.nz/~nzsg/Publications/hardcopy_main.html

- Nova Scotia Book Dealers—Used & Rare
  http://www.shelburne.nscc.ns.ca/nsgna/nbst.html

- Nova Scotia / New Brunswick Bookstores— Used & Rare
  http://www.rootsweb.com/~canns/lunenburg/bookstores.htm

- Old Times Not Forgotten: A History of Drew County
  http://www.seark.net/~rdea/
  Arkansas. A book for sale by the author. The book's table of contents and a family name list are online here also.

- OLochlainns Irish Families
  http://www.irishroots.com/
  The home page of the Irish Genealogical Foundation and OLochlainns Irish Family Journal.

- The Ontario Genealogical Society's Publications List
  http://www.ogs.on.ca/pubs.htm
  Books for sale from the OGS.

- Oregon-California Trails Association (OCTA) Bookstore
  http://calcite.rocky.edu/octa/bookstor.htm

- Ovilla, Texas History Book
  http://www.flash.net/~cmiracle/

- Park Genealogical Books
  http://www.parkbooks.com/
  Specialists in genealogy and local history for Minnesota, Wisconsin, North and South Dakota and the surrounding area.

- Ozark Books
  http://home.att.net/~rdfortner/
  Supplier of books about the Missouri and Arkansas Ozarks, including Branson.

- Pictou Books of Genealogical and Historical Interest
  http://www.rootsweb.com/~pictou/libpic1.htm
  Nova Scotia, Canada

- Pleasant Creek Online Bookstore
  http://members.aol.com/stevecunni/wv7thcav/books.html
  Civil War books.

- Prima's Official Companion to Family Tree Maker Version 5
  http://www.primapublishing.com/PageBuilder.asp?Page=76151677
  By Myra Vanderpool Gormley, C.G.

- Public Record Office Bookshop ~ U.K.
  http://www.pro.gov.uk/bookshop/default.htm

- Publications on Rowan County, North Carolina by Jo White Linn
  http://www.geocities.com/Heartland/Hills/5391/jowlinn.html

- Quintin Publications
  http://www.quintinpublications.com/
  Materials relating to Canada.

- Read Ireland Bookstore
  http://www.readireland.ie/

- Regi Magyarorszag "Old Hungary" Bookstore
  http://www.dholmes.com/rm-book.html
  Specializing in Hungarian & Slovak Genealogy.

- Rhode Island Families Association— Genealogical Publications and Research
  http://www.erols.com/rigr/
  Indexed articles from the Rhode Island Genealogical Register, as well as publications from a variety of records: probate, wills, vital, cemeteries, etc.

- The Rural Citizen Online Bookstore
  http://www.ruralcitizen.com/
  Specializes in Southern and Confederate history, culture and heritage.

- S.E.L. Enterprises
  http://www.mentornet.org/sel.htm
  Publications (books, magazines, periodicals & maps) for researching your English, Irish, Scots and Welsh ancestors.

- Selected Bibliography, Book List Channel Islands
  http://Fox.nstn.ca:80/~nstn1528/booklist.htm

- The Sleeper Co.: Genealogy Books on Washington Co., NY
  http://www.sleeperco.com/

- Society of Genealogists Bookshop Online ~ U.K.
  http://www.sog.org.uk/acatalog/welcome.html

- A Student's Guide to...
  http://www.oryxpress.com/subjidx.htm
  African American Genealogy, British American, German American, Chinese American, Irish American, Japanese American, Italian American, Jewish American, Native American, Mexican American, Polish American, Scandinavian American.

- Tacoma-Pierce County Genealogical Society— Publications for Sale
  http://www.rootsweb.com/~watpcgs/pubs.htm
  Washington

- TCI Genealogical Resources
  http://www.tcigenealogy.com/
  Books for research in the Caribbean, Cuba, Central & South America.

- TLC Genealogy Books
  http://www.tlc-gen.com/
  Specializing in Colonial VA, KY, MD, OH, PA, NC, etc.

- Victoria History of the Counties of England
  http://ihr.sas.ac.uk/vch/vchnew.asc.html

- West Virginia Book Company
  http://www.wvbookco.com/

- West Virginia Histories Homepage
  http://www.clearlight.com/~wvhh/
  A listing of history books that have been published relating to West Virginia.

- Westland Publications Genealogy—
  Find Immigrant Ancestors
  http://www.theriver.com/westlandpubn/
  Monographic publications of translated documents from Germany, Great Britain, France, Switzerland, and Central Europe.

- Yesteryear Links
  http://www.st.net.au/~grinly/
  Queensland, Australia

◆ Mailing Lists, Newsgroups & Chat

- AGLL Genealogical Services Mailing List
  http://members.aol.com/johnf14246/
  gen_mail_software.html#AGLL
  For announcements of new genealogical products and sales promotions from AGLL.

- Appleton's Mailing List
  http://members.aol.com/johnf14246/
  gen_mail_general.html#Appleton
  A read-only list with information on new genealogy software, CD-ROMs, books, and more from Appleton's Books and Genealogy.

- GEN-BOOKS Mailing List
  http://members.aol.com/johnf14246/
  gen_mail_general.html#GEN-BOOKS
  For anyone with an interest in the buying or selling of new or used genealogy books and CDs made from these books.

- GEN-MARKET Mailing List
  http://members.aol.com/johnf14246/
  gen_mail_general.html#GEN-MARKET
  Gatewayed with the soc.genealogy.marketplace newsgroup for commercial postings of unique interest to genealogists.

- GEN-MAT Mailing List
  http://members.aol.com/johnf14246/
  gen_mail_general.html#GEN-MAT
  This is a mailing list for anyone who has an interest in the buying or selling of new or used genealogical materials (e.g., books, newsletters, CDs, magazines).

- GEN-MAT-15 Mailing List
  http://members.aol.com/johnf14246/
  gen_mail_general.html#GEN-MAT-15
  For anyone who desires to post the availability of new or used genealogical materials (e.g., books, newsletters, CDs, magazines) or services for sale at a price of $15 or less.

- GEN-MAT-HX Mailing List
  http://members.aol.com/johnf14246/
  gen_mail_general.html#GEN-MAT-HX
  For anyone who has an interest in the buying or selling of new or used biographies and history books. Publishers of such books are welcome, as are resellers (businesses or individuals cleaning bookshelves).

- GenSwap Mailing List
  http://members.aol.com/johnf14246/
  gen_mail_general.html#GenSwap
  For exchanging research time and swaping records for records with others (e.g., researching in your area for someone else in exchange for like efforts on their part).

◆ Used Books, Rare Books & Book Search Services

- 84 Charing Cross, EH?—Good Used/Rare Books
  http://www.84cc.com/
  Michigan

- The Advanced Book Exchange
  http://www.abebooks.com/

- alt.bookstore Used Book Exchange
  http://www.altbookstore.com/usedexchange.html

- Ambra Books & Lesley Aitchison
  http://www.cornwall-online.co.uk/ambrabooks/
  Buying and selling antiquarian and secondhand books, manuscripts, documents, maps, plans, photographs, albums, and ephemera relating to Cornwall and the West Country—Devon, Dorset, Gloucestershire, Somerset & Wiltshire in the United Kingdom.

- The Avid Reader Used and Rare Books
  http://www.avidreader.com/
  Chapel Hill, North Carolina

- Barbara Green's Used Genealogy Books
  http://home.earthlink.net/~genbooks/

- Bibliofind
  http://www.bibliofind.com/
  Booksearch, antiquarian books, old books, used books, rare books.

- Book Look
  http://www.booklook.com/
  America's largest out-of-print book search service.

- A Bookman's Indiana/A Guide to the State's Used Bookshops & Bibliophilic Resources
  http://www2.inetdirect.net/~charta/Ind_bks.html

- **Books Out-of-Print**
  http://www.bowker.com/bop/home/index.html
  More than 900,000 out-of-print or out-of-stock-indefinitely titles from 1979 to the present.

- **Broad View Books**
  http://broadviewbooks.com/
  Used Genealogy Books, Local History of Massachusetts, Connecticut, Rhode Island, Vermont and New England.

- **FLI Antiques & Genealogy**
  http://www.wwd.net/user/tklaiber/index.htm
  Publications for Ohio and Kentucky.

- **Genealogical Journeys In Time—Used Reference Books for Sale**
  http://ourworld.compuserve.com/homepages/Strawn/booklist.htm

- **Genealogy Book Exchange**
  http://www.internetcs.com/bookexch/index.htm

- **Iguana Publishing Books and Maps— Genealogy & History**
  http://mav.net/genealogy/
  Old, new and used.

- **Interloc, Inc.**
  http://www.interloc.com/
  A large collection of out-of-print books.

- **Internet Used Book Store**
  http://www.rede.com/books/
  See their genealogy section.

- **Janet's Used Genealogy & History Books**
  http://home.earthlink.net/~janetm1/

- **The McGowan Book Company**
  http://www.mcgowanbooks.com/
  Specializing in locating, buying and selling rare books, Civil War memorabilia, photographs and documents. Also, materials for Americana, African-American history, Church history and Military history.

- **Madigan's Books—Buy & Sell Books of Genealogical Interest**
  http://www.advant.com/madigan/

- **MX BookFinder: Search for Out of Print and Used Books**
  http://www.mxbf.com/

- **Nova Scotia / New Brunswick Bookstores— Used & Rare**
  http://www.rootsweb.com/~canns/lunenburg/bookstores.htm

- **Old Books on the Strait**
  http://www.olypen.com/oldbooks/
  Antiquarian and used book business, also a book search service.

- **Powell's Books**
  http://www.powells.com/
  Portland, Oregon. Used, new and out of print books.

- **Rare Book Reprints**
  http://members.aol.com/rarebk
  Old, "lost," scarce, and rare Carter family books and genealogies.

- **Roots and Branches**
  http://members.aol.com/RebelSher1/index.html
  Used books, forms, maps and the Civil War info.

- **Roy Henderson—World-Wide Booksearch Service**
  http://ourworld.compuserve.com/homepages/RoyHenderson/

- **Shorey's Bookstore Inc.**
  http://www.serv.net/shorey/
  Seattle, Washington. Used & rare books, out-of-print book searches.

- **Stacey's Book Search Page**
  http://www.highfiber.com/~rmcclend/Index.html
  Genealogy and American/Local History and Miscellaneous Other Items.

- **Time Booksellers—Rare & Collectible Books**
  http://www.anzaab.com.au/~timebook/index.html
  Australia

- **Tuttle Antiquarian Books**
  http://www.rmharris.com/pub/rmharris/alldlrs/ne/05701tut.html
  Rutland, Vermont

- **UMI's Books on Demand Program**
  http://www.umi.com/hp/Support/BOD/
  A collection of more than 140,000 out-of-print books that can be xerographically reproduced on demand.

- **Yahoo!....Books: Antique, Rare and Used**
  http://dir.yahoo.com/Business_and_Economy/Companies/Books/Shopping_and_Services/Booksellers/Antique__Rare__and_Used/

- **Yahoo!....Books: Book Search Services**
  http://dir.yahoo.com/Business_and_Economy/Companies/Books/Shopping_and_Services/Book_Search_Services/

- **Ye Olde Genealogie Shoppe—Flea Market**
  http://www.yogs.com/fleamkt.htm

CALENDARS & DATES
http://www.CyndisList.com/calendar.htm

- 1790–1840 Census Birth Year Reference Chart
  http://www.genrecords.com/library/birthyear2.htm

- 1850–1920 Census Birth Year Reference Chart
  http://www.genrecords.com/library/birthyear.htm

- 10,000-Year Calendar
  http://CalendarHome.com/tyc/home.html
  Choose menu options and view a month or year calendar for any year 1 to 10000 A.D.

- American Plantations and Colonies—Genealogy—Calendar Confusion
  http://www.primenet.com/~langford/sidebars/calendar.htm

- Birthdate Calculator
  http://enws347.eas.asu.edu:8000/~buckner/bdform.html
  Calculates birthdate from date of death in year, month, day format.

- Calculating Birth Year Based on Census Information
  http://home.mem.net/~rac7253/gen/cenindx.htm

- Calculation of the Ecclesiastical Calendar
  http://cssa.stanford.edu/~marcos/ec-cal.html

- Calendar Form
  http://www.earth.com/calendar
  You type in a month and year—future or past—and it returns a calendar of that month.

- Calendar Conversions
  http://www.genealogy.org/~scottlee/calconvert.cgi
  Scott Lee's free on-line service for converting to/from dates in Gregorian, Julian, French republican and Jewish calendars.

- Calendar Stories
  http://win-www.uia.ac.be/u/pavp/calendars.html
  From the Genealogy in Belgium Home Page.

- Calendars and Their History
  http://astro.nmsu.edu/~lhuber/leaphist.html

- Calendar Zone
  http://www.calendarzone.com/

- The Date of Easter
  http://www.ely.anglican.org/cgi-bin/easter

- The Date of Easter from the Royal Greenwich Observatory
  http://www.ast.cam.ac.uk/RGO/leaflets/easter/easter.html

- Dates of Easter Sunday and Perpetual Calendar, 1550–2049 (for Great Britain and the Colonies)
  http://www.swinhope.demon.co.uk/genuki/easter/

- DAYS Calendar Program for Genealogists
  http://www.thygesen.suite.dk/

- Determining Date of Birth—"Formula 8870"
  http://www.rootsweb.com/~hcpd/formula.htm

- Easter Dating Method
  http://www.assa.org.au/edm.html

- English Calendar
  http://spider.albion.edu/fac/engl/calendar/
  Interactive calendar helps you calculate: Ecclesiastical Calendar, Old and New Style Dating, Day of the week, Regnal Years.

- InnoVision Technologies—Roman Numeral Conversion
  http://www.ivtech.com/roman/

- JavaScript Birthdate Calculator
  http://enws347.eas.asu.edu:8000/~buckner/bdjscr.html

- Leap Year, 1582–1752 (a query)
  http://www.crocker.com/~merrill/family/leapyear.html

- Old Style and New Style Dates—A Summary for Genealogists
  http://www.genuki.org.uk/big/dates.txt

- Old Style & New Style Dates for the Quaker Calendar
  http://www.everton.com/usa/GENEALOG/GENEALOG.QUAKERC1

- Quaker Dates
  http://www.illuminatrix.com/andria/quaker.html

- Roman Digits
  http://utopia.knoware.nl/users/eprebel/Numbers/RomanDigits/index.html

- Roman Numeral Conversion
  http://www.damtp.cam.ac.uk/user/bp10004/cgi_roman.html
  A site that will convert dates for you, following a strict set of rules for the dates.

- Roman Numeral Date Conversion Table
  http://www2.inetdirect.net/~charta/Roman_numerals.html

- Roman Numerals
  http://www.deadline.demon.co.uk/roman/front.htm
  A list of dates converted Arabic numerals to Roman numerals for the years 1450 to 2100.

- Roman Numerals
  http://www.morgan.net.au/roman.htm

- Roman Numerals (Numbers)
  http://www.lib.auburn.edu/serials/docs/training/manual/roman.html

- The ROOTS-L Library: Dates and Calendars
  http://www.rootsweb.com/roots-l/filelist.html
  - 3 Charts for Date to Day of the Week Conversions
    ftp://ftp.rootsweb.com/pub/roots-l/genealog/
    genealog.dateday
  - A Perpetual Calendar
    ftp://ftp.rootsweb.com/pub/roots-l/genealog/
    genealog.perpcal
  - Another Perpetual Calendar
    ftp://ftp.rootsweb.com/pub/roots-l/genealog/
    genealog.perpcal2
  - Old Style & New Style Dates For The
    Quaker Calendar
    ftp://ftp.rootsweb.com/pub/roots-l/genealog/
    genealog.quakerc1

CANADA—GENERAL CANADA SITES
http://www.CyndisList.com/gencan.htm

Category Index:

- ◆ Canada GenWeb Project
- ◆ General Resource Sites
- ◆ Government & Cities
- ◆ History & Culture
- ◆ Libraries, Archives & Museums
- ◆ Mailing Lists, Newsgroups & Chat
- ◆ Maps, Gazetteers & Geographical Information
- ◆ Military
- ◆ Newspapers

- ◆ People & Families
- ◆ Professional Researchers, Volunteers & Other Research Services
- ◆ Publications, Software & Supplies
- ◆ Records: Census, Cemeteries, Land, Obituaries, Personal, Taxes and Vital
- ◆ Religion & Churches
- ◆ Societies & Groups

◆ Canada GenWeb Project

- ● Canada Genealogy / Généalogie du Canada—GenWeb Project Home Page
  http://www.rootsweb.com/~canwgw/index.html
  - ○ Acadian GenWeb
    http://www.geocities.com/Heartland/Acres/2162/
  - ○ Alberta GenWeb
    http://www.geocities.com/Heartland/Hills/3508/albertagenweb.html
  - ○ British Columbia GenWeb Project
    http://www.rootsweb.com/~canbc/
  - ○ Manitoba GenWeb Project
    http://www.rootsweb.com/~canmb/index.htm
  - ○ New Brunswick / Nouveau-Brunswick GenWeb
    http://www.bitheads.ca/nbgenweb/index.htm
  - ○ Newfoundland & Labrador GenWeb Project
    http://www.huronweb.com/genweb/nf.htm
  - ○ Northwest Territories GenWeb Project
    http://www.rootsweb.com/~cannt/nwt.htm
  - ○ Nova Scotia GenWeb Project
    http://www.rootsweb.com/~canns/index.html
  - ○ Ontario GenWeb
    http://www.geneofun.on.ca/ongenweb/
  - ○ The Island Register—Prince Edward Island GenWeb Project
    http://www.isn.net/~dhunter/pegenweb.html
  - ○ Projet GenWeb du Québec
    http://www.rootsweb.com/~canqc/index.htm
  - ○ Saskatchewan GenWeb
    http://www.rootsweb.com/~cansk/Saskatchewan/
  - ○ Yukon GenWeb
    http://www.rootsweb.com/~canyk/

◆ General Resource Sites

- ● Atlantic Canadian Genealogy Links
  http://www3.ns.sympatico.ca/chapy/glinks.htm
- ● Bob's your Uncle, eh!
  http://indexes.mtrl.toronto.on.ca/genealogy/index.htf
  A search engine for genealogy in Canada.
- ● Canada 411 White Pages
  http://canada411.sympatico.ca/
- ● Canada Post Corporation / Société canadienne des postes
  http://www.canadapost.ca/
  Postal rates & codes, etc.
- ● The Canada-Wide National Registry & Family Finders
  http://www.adopting.org/ffcwnr.html
  Adoption resources & registry.
- ● Canadian Conference of Mennonite Brethren Churches
  http://www.cdnmbconf.ca/mb/mbdoc.htm
- ● Canadian Genealogy and History Links
  http://www.islandnet.com/~jveinot/cghl/cghl.html
  From OCFA and BCCFA.
- ● Canadian Genealogy Gopher Sites
  gopher://Alpha.CC.UToledo.edu/11GOPHER_ROOT%3a%5b000000.RESEARCH-RESOURCES.GENEALOGY.canadian-genealogy%5d
- ● Canadian Genealogy Made Easy!!
  http://www.geocities.com/Heartland/4051/

- Canadian Heraldry/L'Heraldique
  http://www.schoolnet.ca/collections/governor/heraldry/
  index.html

- Genealogy Bulletin Board Systems—
  Canadian Index
  http://www.genealogy.org/~gbbs/gbbscaix.html

- Genealogy Resources on the Internet:
  Canada/Canadian
  http://www-personal.umich.edu/~cgaunt/canada.html

- ROOTS-L Resources: Canada
  http://www.rootsweb.com/roots-l/canada.html

- Westminster—Canadian Postal Code
  Lookup Service
  http://www.westminster.ca/cdnlook.htm
  Also has U.S. Zip codes.

- Yahoo!...Canada...Genealogy
  http://www.yahoo.com/Regional/Countries/Canada/
  Arts_and_Humanities/Humanities/History/Genealogy/

◆ Government & Cities

- Yahoo! Canada....Cities
  http://www.yahoo.ca/Regional/Countries/Canada/Cities/

◆ History & Culture

- 1755—The French and Indian War Home Page
  http://web.syr.edu/~laroux/

- Canadian Confederation
  http://www.nlc-bnc.ca/confed/e-1867.htm

- Canadian Cowboy—History
  http://www.ccinet.ab.ca/bjj/history.htm

- Canadian Heritage Information Network
  http://www.chin.gc.ca/

- Canadian History—20th Century
  http://www.ualberta.ca/~slis/guides/canada/cansub.htm

- Canadian Institute for Historical Microreproductions
  http://www.nlc-bnc.ca/cihm/cihm.htm

- Canadian Journal of History—Annales canadiennes
  d'histoire
  http://www.usask.ca/history/cjh/

- Canadian Maritime Commerce & Canadian
  Maritime Heritage
  http://www.marmus.ca/

- Celebrating Women's Achievements: 21 Pioneers
  http://www.nlc-bnc.ca/digiproj/women/ewomen.htm

- CultureNet
  http://www.culturenet.ucalgary.ca/indexen.html

- Department of Canadian Heritage
  http://www.pch.gc.ca/english.htm

- Links to Canada's Past
  http://www.citenet.net/users/g.vanert/history.html
  From the Canada Pages: History.

- Significant Dates in Canadian Railway History
  http://infoweb.magi.com/~churcher/candate/candate.htm

- The Territorial Evolution of Canada
  http://www.nlc-bnc.ca/confed/maps.htm

◆ Libraries, Archives & Museums

- Canada Family History Centers
  http://www.lib.byu.edu/~uvrfhc/canada.html

- Canadian Archival Resources on the Internet
  http://www.usask.ca/archives/menu.html

- Canadian Archive Addresses
  gopher://Gopher.UToledo.edu:70/
  00GOPHER_ROOT%3A%5B000000.RESEARCH-
  RESOURCES.GENEALOGY.CANADIAN-
  GENEALOGY%5DCANADIAN-ARCHIVE-ADDRESSES.

- Canadian Genealogy and History Links—
  Archives—Libraries—Museums
  http://www.islandnet.com/~jveinot/cghl/archives.html

- Canadian Institute for Historical Microreproductions
  http://www.nlc-bnc.ca/cihm/cihm.htm
  *Established to preserve early printed materials (books, annuals,
  and periodicals) on microfilm for availability to libraries and
  archives.*

- Canadian Library Association
  http://www.cla.amlibs.ca/

- The Canadian Library Index
  http://www.lights.com/canlib/

- Les Centres Généalogiques SDJ / LDS Family
  History Centers
  http://www2.et.byu.edu/~harmanc/paris/genealogie.html
  France, Belgique, Suisse, Canada

- Family History Centres in Canada
  http://www.shelburne.nscc.ns.ca/nsgna/fhc/cdnfhc.htm

- The Genealogical Institute of the Maritimes
  http://www.cfn.cs.dal.ca/cfn/Recreation/GANS/gim.html

- Historical Documents from the National Library
  of Canada
  http://www.nlc-bnc.ca/confed/historic.htm

- HYTELNET Library Catalogs: Canada
  http://library.usask.ca/hytelnet/ca0/ca000.html
  *Before you use any of the Telnet links, make note of the user
  name, password and any other logon information.*

- List of Canadian Archives Addresses
  http://www.byu.edu/rel1/jsblab/genealog/programs/text/
  can-arch.txt

- Maritime History Archive at Memorial University
  of Newfoundland
  http://www.mun.ca/mha/

- The National Archives of Canada /
  Archives Nationales du Canada
  http://www.archives.ca/
  - Genealogy Research—National Archives
    http://www.archives.ca/www/Genealogy.html
- National Library of Canada / Bibliothèque nationale
  du Canada
  http://www.nlc-bnc.ca/
- Queen's University Libraries
  http://stauffer.queensu.ca/
  Kingston
  - Genealogy
    http://stauffer.queensu.ca/inforef/guides/genealogy.htm
  - Genealogy Resources in Government Documents
    http://stauffer.queensu.ca/webdoc/genealogy/
- Special Collections Spécialisées
  http://library.usask.ca/spcol/index.html
  *Directory of special collections of research value in
  Canadian libraries.*
- United Church of Canada Archives Network
  http://www.uccan.org/archives/home.htm
- webCATS: Library Catalogues on the World Wide
  Web—Canada
  http://library.usask.ca/hywebcat/countries/CA.html

◆ Mailing Lists, Newsgroups & Chat

- ACADIAN-CAJUN Mailing List
  http://members.aol.com/gfsjohnf/gen_mail_country-
  can.html#ACADIAN-CAJUN
  For anyone with Acadian-Cajun ancestry worldwide.
- Acadian-Cajun Mailing List
  http://members.aol.com/gfsjohnf/gen_mail_country-
  can.html#Acadian1
  *For anyone with a genealogical, historical, or general interest
  in the Acadian and Cajun people of Canada and Louisiana.*
- CANADIAN-ROOTS-L Mailing List
  http://members.aol.com/gfsjohnf/gen_mail_country-
  can.html#CANADIAN-ROOTS
- CAN-ORANGE Mailing List
  http://members.aol.com/gfsjohnf/gen_mail_country-
  can.html#CAN-ORANGE
  *For persons interested in the genealogy, culture, and history of
  persons who came to Canada as members of the Orange
  Association and their descendants and followers. Also see the
  associated web page at http://members.tripod.com/~firstlight_2/
  canorange.htm*
- GERMAN-CANADIAN Mailing List
  http://members.aol.com/gfsjohnf/gen_mail_country-
  can.html#GERMAN-CANADIAN
  *For the discussion of issues concerning the settlement of
  German speaking immigrants coming from anywhere to Canada.*
- Irish-Canadian Mailing List
  http://members.aol.com/gfsjohnf/gen_mail_country-
  ire.html#Irish-Canadian
  *For anyone interested in the genealogy, culture, and historical
  contribution of people who immigrated from Ireland to Canada.*

- loyalists-in-canada Mailing List
  http://members.aol.com/gfsjohnf/gen_mail_country-
  can.html#LOYALIST
  *For those with loyalist ancestors to help one another research
  their loyalist history and to post any facts on the subject that
  they desire. Loyalists are defined as those who left the United
  States for Canada after the American Revolution for a number
  of reasons.*
- METISGEN Mailing List
  http://members.aol.com/johnf14246/
  gen_mail_general.html#METISGEN
  *For the discussion and sharing of information regarding the
  Metis and their descendants. The Metis are North America's Fur
  Trading Children . . . the new nation of individuals born within
  North America from the first unions of natives and whites.*
- SCHAKEL-NL Mailing List
  http://members.aol.com/gfsjohnf/gen_mail_country-
  net.html#SCHAKEL-NL
  *For discussions of news events and issues of interest to Canadi-
  ans and Americans of Dutch origin; Dutch heritage, customs
  and traditions; immigrant experiences; questions about Dutch
  legislation, laws, regulations, history etc.; living the Dutch way
  (e.g., travel, food, drinks); and the ties that bind us. Queries
  from genealogists related to their Dutch ancestry are welcome.*
- SURNAMES-CANADA Mailing List
  http://members.aol.com/gfsjohnf/gen_mail_country-
  can.html#SURNAMES-CANADA
  *For surname queries related to Canada. Gatewayed with the
  soc.genealogy.surnames.canada newsgroup.*
- UPPER-CANADA Mailing List
  http://members.aol.com/gfsjohnf/gen_mail_country-
  can.html#UPPER-CANADA
  *For anyone with a genealogical interest in Upper Canada, the
  region split from the Province of Quebec after the American
  Revolution, including its history and settlement by Loyalists and
  British and German soldiers, up to and including the year 1841.*

◆ Maps, Gazetteers & Geographical Information

- Association of Canadian Map Libraries and Archives
  http://www.sscl.uwo.ca/assoc/acml/acmla.html
- Canada National Atlas Information Service
  http://www.nais.ccm.emr.ca/
- Canadian Geographical Names / Les noms
  géographiques du Canada
  http://GeoNames.NRCan.gc.ca/
  - Canadian Geographical Names—Publications
    http://GeoNames.NRCan.gc.ca/english/publications.html
    *List of available publications on geographical names
    including policy documents and manuals, gazetteers,
    glossaries, newsletters and brochures.*
  - Origins of Canada's Geographical Names
    http://GeoNames.NRCan.gc.ca/english/schoolnet/origin.html
  - Query by Geographical Name
    http://Geonames.NRCan.gc.ca/english/cgndb.html
  - Current Names Selected by Coordinates
    http://Geonames.NRCan.gc.ca/english/cgndb_coord.html
    *Search this database of over 500,000 geographical names by
    name, feature type, region and by province.*

- Excite Travel: Canada Maps
  http://www.city.net/countries/canada/maps/
- Historical Atlas of Canada Data Dissemination
  Project
  http://geog.utoronto.ca/hacddp/hacpage.html
- K.B. Slocum Books and Maps—Canada
  http://www.treasurenet.com/cgi-bin/treasure/kbslocum/scan/
  se=Louisiana/sf=mapstate

◆ Military

- The Black Watch (Royal Highland Regiment)
  of Canada
  http://www.odyssee.net/~kerra/bwhome.html
- Books of Remembrance
  http://www.schoolnet.ca/collections/books/
  *Contain the names of Canadians who fought in wars and died
  either during or after them.*
- Canadian Air Aces and Heroes—WWI,
  WWII and Korea
  http://www.accessweb.com/users/mconstab/
- Canadian Expeditionary Force (CEF)—
  Records Database
  http://www.archives.ca/db/cef/index.html
  *An index to the personnel files of over 600,000 soldiers that
  enlisted during the First World War.*
- Canadian Genealogy and History Links—Military
  http://www.islandnet.com/~jveinot/cghl/military.html
- The Canadian Great War Homepage
  http://www.rootsweb.com/~ww1can/
  Canada's Role in World War I, 1914–1918.
- Canadian Military Genealogical FAQ
  http://www.igs.net/~donpark/canmilfaq.htm
- Canadian POW/MIA Information Centre
  http://www.ipsystems.com/powmia/
- Canadian Vietnam Casualties
  http://www.ipsystems.com/powmia/names/names.html
- Canadian War Museum
  http://www.cmcc.muse.digital.ca/cwm/cwmeng/cwmeng.html
- Fatal Casualties in Canadian Contingents
  of the Boer War
  http://www.islandnet.com/~duke/boercas.htm
- The Lincoln and Welland Regiment
  http://www.iaw.on.ca:80/~awoolley/lincweld.html
  A reserve infantry battalion of the Canadian Forces.
- Military of Old Canada
  http://www.inforamp.net/~griffish/gene/mil/mil1.html
- Museum of the Regiments
  http://www.nucleus.com/~regiments/
- The Queen's York Rangers (1st American Regiment)
  http://www.inforamp.net/~ihooker/ranger.htm

- RCAF Personnel—Honours and Awards—
  1939–1949
  http://www.achq.dnd.ca/awards/index.htm
  *An index of 9,200 awards to approx. 8,300 RCAF personnel,
  announced between 1940 and 1949, for services during the
  Second World War.*
- RCMP History
  http://www.rcmp-grc.gc.ca/html/history.htm
- World War I Canadian Infantry & Cavalry Index
  http://www.bookkeeping.com/rings/genealogy/ww1.html
- World War I Journal of John SPRACKLIN
  http://www.scruznet.com/~sprack/journ1.html
  *1917, served with the Canadian Mounted Rifles Battalion in
  France.*

◆ Newspapers

- Newspapers at the National Library of Canada
  http://www.nlc-bnc.ca/services/enews.htm

◆ People & Families

- Canadian Adoptees Registry and Classifieds
  http://www.bconnex.net/~rickm/
- Canadian Genealogy and History Links—Personal
  http://www.islandnet.com/~jveinot/cghl/personal.html
- Genealogy—Acadian and French Canadian
  http://ourworld.compuserve.com/homepages/lwjones/
- Geographical Index to the Tribes of the United
  States and Canada
  http://hanksville.phast.umass.edu:8000/cultprop/contacts/
  tribal/US.html
- Internment of Ukrainians in Canada 1914–1920
  http://www.infoukes.com/history/internment/
- Irish-Canadian List
  http://www.bess.tcd.ie/roots/irishcan.htm
- Loyalists
  http://www.CyndisList.com/loyalist.htm
  See this category on Cyndi's List for related links.
- Paul Bunnell will search your Loyalist ancestors—
  Send e-mail to Paul for details
  E-mail: benjamin@capecod.net
- Prussian-Russian-Canadian Mennonite
  Genealogical Resources
  http://www.mmhs.org/mmhsgen.htm
- Testimony of the Canadian Fugitives
  http://history.cc.ukans.edu/carrie/docs/texts/
  canadian_slaves.html
- The Walk to Canada—Tracing the Underground
  Railroad
  http://www.npca.org/walk.html
- Women in Canadian History
  http://www.niagara.com/~merrwill/

- Young Immigrants to Canada
  http://www.dcs.uwaterloo.ca/~marj/genealogy/homeadd.html

◆ Professional Researchers, Volunteers & Other Research Services

- Board for Certification of Genealogists—Roster of Those Certified—Specializing in Canada
  http://www.genealogy.org/~bcg/rosts_@c.html
- Bowers Genealogy Services
  http://www.interlog.com/~kbowers/bgs2.htm
  England, Scotland, Canada
- Canadian Metis Genealogy
  http://genweb.net/~pbg/metis.htm
- The Genealogical Research Library, Toronto, Canada
  http://www.grl.com/
  Professional research services & publications.
- Genealogy Helplist—Canada
  http://www.geocities.com/Heartland/Hills/1285/hlCan.html
- genealogyPro—Professional Genealogists for Canada
  http://genealogyPro.com/directories/Canada.html
- inGeneas Canadian Genealogical Research Services
  http://www.ingeneas.com/
  Ottawa, Ontario, Canada
- The Official Iowa Counties Professional Genealogist and Researcher's Registry for Canada
  http://www.iowa-counties.com/gene/canada.htm
- Traces From Your Past
  http://www.cadvision.com/traces/
  Genealogical Publications, Services and Resources to assist the Family Historian researching in Canada and the United Kingdom.

◆ Publications, Software & Supplies

- Ancestor's Attic Discount Genealogy Books— Canadian Genealogy Books
  http://members.tripod.com/~ancestorsattic/index.html#secCA
- Books We Own—Canada
  http://www.rootsweb.com/~bwo/can_gr.html
- Family History News
  http://www.globalserve.net/~parrspub/
  Canadian genealogical publication.
- Frontier Press Bookstore—Canada
  http://www.frontierpress.com/frontier.cgi?category=can
- GenealogyBookShop.com—Canada
  http://www.genealogybookshop.com/genealogybookshop/files/The_World,Canada/index.html
  The online store of Genealogical Publishing Co., Inc. & Clearfield Company.

- Heritage Books—Canadian
  http://www.heritagebooks.com/indian.htm
- Global Genealogical Supply—Misc. Canadian Genealogy & Local History Books
  http://www.globalgenealogy.com/cdamisc.htm
- Willow Bend Bookstore—Canada and Canadians
  http://www.willowbend.net/cdn.htm

◆ Records: Census, Cemeteries, Land, Obituaries, Personal, Taxes and Vital (Born, Married, Died & Buried)

- 1901 Census of Canada—Film Numbers
  http://www.tbaytel.net/bmartin/census.htm
- Canadian Vital Statistics Addresses
  gopher://Gopher.UToledo.edu:70/
  00GOPHER_ROOT%3A%5B000000.RESEARCH-
  RESOURCES.GENEALOGY.CANADIAN-
  GENEALOGY%5DCANADIAN-VITAL-STATISTICS-ADDRESSES.
- Commonwealth War Graves Commission
  http://www.cwgc.org/
  Details of 1.7 million members of UK and Commonwealth forces who died in the 1st and 2nd World Wars and other wars, and 60,000 civilian casualties of WWII. Gives details of grave site, date of death, age, usually parents/widow's address.
- The National Registration File of 1940
  http://www.tbaytel.net/bmartin/natreg.htm
  Canada registered everyone at least 16 years old in 1940. These records can provide real help to the genealogist. Full information on these records and how to access them.

◆ Religion & Churches

- Christianity.Net Church Locator—Canada
  http://www.christianity.net/cgi/location.exe?Canada
- Church Online!—Canada by Province
  http://www.churchonline.com/canadap/canadap.html
- Churches dot Net—Global Church Web Pages— Canada
  http://www.churches.net/churches/full.htm#CAN

◆ Societies & Groups

- The American-Canadian Genealogical Society
  http://ourworld.compuserve.com:80/homepages/ACGS/homepage.htm
  Leaders in French-Canadian Genealogical Research.
- Archer's Computer Interest Group List—Canada
  http://www.genealogy.org/~ngs/cigs/ngl3otcd.html
- Canada's National History Society
  http://www.cyberspc.mb.ca/~otmw/cnhs/cnhs.html
- Canadian Federation of Genealogical and Family History Societies (CanFed)
  http://www.geocities.com/Athens/Troy/2274/index.html

- Canadian Friends Historical Association
  http://home.interhop.net/~aschrauwe/
- Canadian Genealogical Societies
  gopher://Gopher.UToledo.edu:70/
  00GOPHER_ROOT%3A%5B000000.RESEARCH-
  RESOURCES.GENEALOGY.CANADIAN-
  GENEALOGY%5DCANADIAN-GENEALOGICAL-GROUPS.
- Canadian Genealogy and History Links—
  Organizations and Societies
  http://www.islandnet.com/~jveinot/cghl/organization.html

- Canadian Peacekeeping Veterans Association
  http://www.islandnet.com/~duke/cpva.htm
- IOOF Lodge Website Directory—Canada
  http://norm28.hsc.usc.edu/IOOF/International/Canada.html
  Independent Order of Odd Fellows and Rebekahs.
- Mennonite Historical Society of Canada
  http://www.lib.uwaterloo.ca/MHSC/mhsc.html
- The United Empire Loyalists' Association of Canada
  http://www.npiec.on.ca/~uela/uela1.htm
  Toronto, Ontario, Canada

CANADA—ALBERTA
http://www.CyndisList.com/alberta.htm

Category Index:

- Events & Activities
- General Resource Sites
- Government & Cities
- Libraries, Archives & Museums
- Mailing Lists, Newsgroups & Chat
- Maps, Gazetteers & Geographical Information
- Military
- Newspapers

- People & Families
- Professional Researchers, Volunteers & Other Research Services
- Publications, Software & Supplies
- Records: Census, Cemeteries, Land, Obituaries, Personal, Taxes and Vital
- Religion & Churches
- Societies & Groups

◆ Events & Activities

- Alberta Family Histories Society—Gensoft
  http://www.calcna.ab.ca/afhs/gensoft.html

- Alberta Family Histories Society—Wild Rose Seminar
  http://www.calcna.ab.ca/afhs/seminar.html

◆ General Resource Sites

- Alberta GenWeb
  http://www.geocities.com/Heartland/Hills/3508/albertagenweb.html

- Canadian Genealogy and History Links—Alberta
  http://www.islandnet.com/~jveinot/cghl/alberta.html

- Genealogy Resources on the Internet: Alberta
  http://www-personal.umich.edu/~cgaunt/canada.html#Alberta

- Traces: Genealogy Alberta
  http://www.cadvision.com/traces/alta/alberta.html
  New site providing on-line indexes to a variety of material. Small look up fee applies in SOME instances. Main interest area is Calgary & southwestern Alberta.

◆ Government & Cities

- Government of Alberta
  http://www.gov.ab.ca/

- Yahoo! Canada....Alberta: Cities
  http://www.yahoo.ca/Regional/Countries/Canada/Provinces_and_Territories/Alberta/Cities/

◆ Libraries, Archives & Museums

- Alberta Provincial Government Libraries
  http://www.gov.ab.ca/library/aglchome.html

- Alberta Railway Museum
  http://www.discoveredmonton.com/RailwayMuseum/

- Calgary & Edmonton Railway Museum
  http://www.discoveredmonton.com/RailMuseum/

- Calgary Public Library
  http://www.public-library.calgary.ab.ca/

- City of Edmonton Archives
  http://www.gov.edmonton.ab.ca/parkrec/archives/
  In the Prince of Wales Armouries, Heritage Centre.

- Edmonton Public Library
  http://www.publib.edmonton.ab.ca/
  - Tracing Your Family Tree
    http://www.publib.edmonton.ab.ca/famtree.html

- Glenbow Archives
  http://www.glenbow.org/archives.htm

- Glenbow Library
  http://www.glenbow.org/library.htm

- HYTELNET—Library Catalogs: Canada: Alberta
  http://library.usask.ca/hytelnet/ca0/AB.html
  Before you use any of the Telnet links, make note of the user name, password and any other logon information.

- The Hudson's Bay Company Archives
  http://www.gov.mb.ca/chc/archives/hbca/index.html
  From the Provincial Archives of Manitoba, Canada.

- Lethbridge Family History Center
  http://www.leth.net/fhc/

- Okotoks Family History Center
  http://www.cadvision.com/johansss/oktitle.htm

- Provincial Archives of Alberta
  http://www.gov.ab.ca/~mcd/mhs/paa/paa.htm

- United Church of Canada Archives Network: Alberta and Northwest Conference Archives
  http://www.uccan.org/archives/alberta.htm
  A summary of their holdings and contact information.

- Whyte Museum of the Canadian Rockies
  http://www.whyte.org/
  Has an archives research library.

◆ Mailing Lists, Newsgroups & Chat

- ALBERTA Mailing List
  http://members.aol.com/gfsjohnf/gen_mail_country-can.html#ALBERTA

- alberta Mailing List
  http://members.aol.com/gfsjohnf/gen_mail_country-can.html#ALBERTA-CANADA

- CANADIAN ROOTS Mailing List
  http://members.aol.com/gfsjohnf/gen_mail_country-can.html#CANADIAN-ROOTS

- SURNAMES-CANADA Mailing List
  http://members.aol.com/gfsjohnf/gen_mail_country-can.html#SURNAMES-CANADA
  For surname queries related to Canada. Gatewayed with the soc.genealogy.surnames.canada newsgroup.

◆ Maps, Gazetteers & Geographical Information

- Canadian Geographical Names / Les noms géographiques du Canada
  http://GeoNames.NRCan.gc.ca/

  ○ Canadian Geographical Names—Publications
    http://GeoNames.NRCan.gc.ca/english/publications.html
    List of available publications on geographical names including policy documents and manuals, gazetteers, glossaries, newsletters and brochures.

  ○ Origins of Canada's Geographical Names
    http://GeoNames.NRCan.gc.ca/english/schoolnet/origin.html

  ○ Query by Geographical Name
    http://Geonames.NRCan.gc.ca/english/cgndb.html

  ○ Current Names Selected by Coordinates
    http://Geonames.NRCan.gc.ca/english/cgndb_coord.html
    Search this database of over 500,000 geographical names by name, feature type, region and by province.

- Excite Maps: Alberta
  http://city.net/maps/view/?mapurl=/countries/canada/alberta

◆ Military

- Alberta's War Memorials
  http://www.stemnet.nf.ca/monuments/ab.htm
  A project to preserve information about War Memorials throughout Canada on the World Wide Web. The descriptions of these individual cenotaphs often includes names and other information on the dead which can be of interest to the genealogist.

- The Regiment
  http://www.telusplanet.net/public/keco/regiment.html
  History of the South Alberta Light Horse.

- The South Alberta Regiment
  http://www.steelchariots.net/29armd.htm
  History of the South Alberta Regiment.

◆ Newspapers

- E&P Media Info Links—Newspaper Sites in Alberta
  http://www.mediainfo.com/emediajs/browse-results.htm?region=alberta&category=newspaper+++++++++

◆ People & Families

- Hutterite Genealogy Cross-Index
  http://feefhs.org/hut/indexhut.html

- Tribes and Bands of Alberta
  http://hanksville.phast.umass.edu:8000/cultprop/contacts/tribal/AB.html

◆ Professional Researchers, Volunteers & Other Research Services

- Gen-Find Research Associates
  http://www.gen-find.com/
  Specialists in Genealogy Research for Ontario & Western Canada, Scotland, Ireland. Also the rest of Canada and Forensic & Probate/Heir Research and 20th Century Research.

◆ Publications, Software & Supplies

- Global Genealogical Supply—Western Canada Genealogical & Local History Books
  http://www.globalgenealogy.com/cdawest.htm

◆ Records: Census, Cemeteries, Land, Obituaries, Personal, Taxes and Vital (Born, Married, Died & Buried)

- Alberta Genealogical Society Master Name Index
  http://www.compusmart.ab.ca/abgensoc/nameindex.html
  A database of about 400,000 names, including mostly cemetery records and tombstone inscriptions. They can search the database for a small fee.

- Births, Deaths and Marriages Reported in Calgary, Alberta Newspapers, 1883–1899
  http://www.calcna.ab.ca/afhs/news.html

- City of Edmonton's Department of Cemeteries
  E-mail: cemetery@wnet.gov.edmonton.ab.ca
  Send e-mail to: cemetery@wnet.gov.edmonton.ab.ca to find out about your ancestors buried in Edmonton, Alberta, Canada.

- Edmonton Parks and Recreation—Searching for a Family Member in Our Cemeteries
  http://www.gov.edmonton.ab.ca/parkrec/cemetery/search.htm
  Database of people interred more than 25 years ago (close to 60,000 people) that are in Edmonton Municipal Cemeteries.

- Hilda Baptist Cemetery, Hilda, Alberta, Canada
  http://pixel.cs.vt.edu/library/cemeteries/canada/link/hilda1.txt

- Index to the 1891 Dominion Census Lethbridge
  Sub-District, Alberta, Northwest Territories
  http://mypage.direct.ca/d/dobee/lethmain.html

◆ Religion & Churches

- Christianity.Net Church Locator—Alberta
  http://www.christianity.net/cgi/location.exe?Canada+Alberta

- Church Online!—Alberta
  http://www.churchonline.com/canadap/ab/ab.html

- Churches of the World—Alberta
  http://www.churchsurf.com/churches/Canada/Alberta
  From the ChurchSurf Christian Directory.

◆ Societies & Groups

- The Alberta Chapter, Germans from
  Russia Heritage Society
  http://www.grhs.com/alberta.html

- Alberta Family Histories Society
  http://www.calcna.ab.ca/afhs/

- Alberta Genealogical Society
  http://www.compusmart.ab.ca/abgensoc/
  - Brooks & District Branch of the Alberta
    Genealogical Society
    http://www.eidnet.org/local/bburrows/bbags/
  - Fort McMurray Branch of the Alberta
    Genealogical Society
    http://www.tnc.com/tncn/fmgs/ft_main.htm

  - Grande Prairie & District Branch Alberta
    Genealogical Society
    http://www.telusplanet.net/public/turnbl/ags/gpbranch.html
  - Lethbridge & District Branch of the Alberta
    Genealogical Society
    http://www.bulli.com/~owenr/agsleth/agsleth.htm

- American Historical Society of Germans from
  Russia—Calgary Canada Chapter
  http://www.ahsgr.org/calgary.html

- IOOF Lodge Website Directory—Alberta
  http://norm28.hsc.usc.edu/IOOF/International/Alberta.html
  Independent Order of Odd Fellows and Rebekahs.

- Mennonite Historical Society of Alberta
  http://members.home.net/rempel/mhsa/
  *The MHSA is a new society developed to support those who are
  interested in basic Mennonite history, those doing Mennonite
  genealogy/family history research, and those who are interested
  in the preservation and display of Mennonite historical documents and cultural artifacts.*

- La Societe Genealogique du Nord-Ouest
  http://genweb.net/~pbg/sgno.htm
  Edmonton

- Societe Historique et Genealogique de Smoky River
  http://www.telusplanet.net/public/genealfa/English.html
  *The "largest French-Canadian genealogical resource library in
  Western Canada" located in Donnelly, Alberta, Canada in the
  centre of the Smoky River area in the Peace River region of
  Northern Alberta.*

CANADA—BRITISH COLUMBIA
http://www.CyndisList.com/bc.htm

Category Index:
◆ General Resource Sites
◆ Government & Cities
◆ History & Culture
◆ Libraries, Archives & Museums
◆ Mailing Lists, Newsgroups & Chat
◆ Maps, Gazetteers & Geographical Information
◆ Newspapers
◆ People & Families

◆ Professional Researchers, Volunteers &
  Other Research Services
◆ Publications, Software & Supplies
◆ Records: Census, Cemeteries, Land, Obituaries,
  Personal, Taxes and Vital
◆ Religion & Churches
◆ Societies & Groups

◆ General Resource Sites
● British Columbia GenWeb Project
  http://www.rootsweb.com/~canbc/
● Canadian Genealogy and History Links—
  British Columbia
  http://www.islandnet.com/~jveinot/cghl/british-columbia.html
● Genealogy Bulletin Board Systems for
  British Columbia
  http://www.genealogy.org/~gbbs/gblbc.html
● Genealogy Resources on the Internet:
  British Columbia
  http://www-personal.umich.edu/~cgaunt/canada.html#BC

◆ Government & Cities
● City of Vancouver, B.C., Municipal Government
  http://www.city.vancouver.bc.ca/
● City of Victoria
  http://www.city.victoria.bc.ca/
● Government of British Columbia
  http://www.gov.bc.ca/
● Yahoo! Canada....British Columbia: Cities
  http://www.yahoo.ca/Regional/Countries/Canada/
  Provinces_and_Territories/British_Columbia/Cities/

◆ History & Culture
● The British Columbia History Internet/
  World-Wide Web Page
  http://www.victoria.tc.ca/bchistory.html
● British Columbia Museums Association
  http://www.islandnet.com/~bcma/museums/culture.html
● The Great Depression
  http://trinculo.educ.sfu.ca/pgm/depress/greatdepress.html
  Focusing on the city of Vancouver.

◆ Libraries, Archives & Museums
● Archives Association of British Columbia
  http://www.harbour.com/AABC/
● British Columbia Archival Resources
  http://www.harbour.com/AABC/bcarch.html
● British Columbia Archives & Records Service
  http://www.bcarchives.gov.bc.ca/index.htm
● British Columbia Museums Association
  http://www.islandnet.com/~bcma/museums/culture.html
  "Cultural Heritage in British Columbia."
● City of Richmond Archives
  http://www.city.richmond.bc.ca/archives/archives.html
● City of Vancouver Archives
  http://www.city.vancouver.bc.ca/ctyclerk/archives/
  index.html-ssi
● City of Victoria Archives and Records Division
  http://www.city.victoria.bc.ca/archives/index.htm
  ○ Genealogical Research
    http://www.city.victoria.bc.ca/archives/genogy.htm
● The Hudson's Bay Company Archives
  http://www.gov.mb.ca/chc/archives/hbca/index.html
  From the Provincial Archives of Manitoba, Canada.
● HYTELNET—Library Catalogs: Canada:
  British Columbia
  http://library.usask.ca/hytelnet/ca0/BC.html
  *Before you use any of the Telnet links, make note of the user
  name, password and any other logon information.*
● Nanaimo Community Archives
  http://bbs.sd68.nanaimo.bc.ca/nol/community/nca.htm
● Simon Fraser University Archives
  http://www.sfu.ca/archives/
● Surrey Public Library
  http://www.city.surrey.bc.ca/SPL/

- UBC Library Special Collections and University Archives
  http://www.library.ubc.ca/spcoll/
- United Church of Canada Archives Network: British Columbia Conference Archives
  http://www.uccan.org/archives/britishcolumbia.htm
  A summary of their holdings and contact information.
- Vancouver Public Library Central Branch— Special Collections
  http://www.vpl.vancouver.bc.ca/branches/LibrarySquare/spe/home.html

◆ Mailing Lists, Newsgroups & Chat

- british-columbia Mailing List
  http://members.aol.com/gfsjohnf/gen_mail_country-can.html#BRITISH-COLUMBIA-CANADA
- CANADIAN ROOTS Mailing List
  http://members.aol.com/gfsjohnf/gen_mail_country-can.html#CANADIAN-ROOTS
- SURNAMES-CANADA Mailing List
  http://members.aol.com/gfsjohnf/gen_mail_country-can.html#SURNAMES-CANADA
  For surname queries related to Canada. Gatewayed with the soc.genealogy.surnames.canada newsgroup.

◆ Maps, Gazetteers & Geographical Information

- BC Geographical Names Information System
  http://www.env.gov.bc.ca/~bcnames/
  Searchable database
- Canadian Geographical Names / Les noms géographiques du Canada
  http://GeoNames.NRCan.gc.ca/
  - Canadian Geographical Names—Publications
    http://GeoNames.NRCan.gc.ca/english/publications.html
    List of available publications on geographical names including policy documents and manuals, gazetteers, glossaries, newsletters and brochures.
  - Origins of Canada's Geographical Names
    http://GeoNames.NRCan.gc.ca/english/schoolnet/origin.html
  - Query by Geographical Name
    http://Geonames.NRCan.gc.ca/english/cgndb.html
  - Current Names Selected by Coordinates
    http://Geonames.NRCan.gc.ca/english/cgndb_coord.html
    Search this database of over 500,000 geographical names by name, feature type, region and by province.
- Cartographic Records
  http://142.36.5.25:80/cartogr/general/maps.html
- Excite Maps: British Columbia
  http://city.net/maps/view/?mapurl=/countries/canada/british_columbia

◆ Newspapers

- The First Newspapers on Canada's West Coast: 1858–1863
  http://members.tripod.com/~Hughdoherty/index.htm

◆ People & Families

- Doukhobor Home Page
  http://www.dlcwest.com/~r.androsoff/index.htm
  A group of Russian peasants that split from the Russian Orthodox Church. Large groups of Doukhobors emigrated to Canada and homesteaded in Saskatchewan and British Columbia.
- Tribes and Bands of British Columbia
  http://hanksville.phast.umass.edu:8000/cultprop/contacts/tribal/BC.html

◆ Professional Researchers, Volunteers & Other Research Services

- Gen-Find Research Associates
  http://www.gen-find.com/
  Specialists in Genealogy Research for Ontario & Western Canada, Scotland, Ireland. Also the rest of Canada and Forensic & Probate/Heir Research and 20th Century Research.

◆ Publications, Software & Supplies

- Global Genealogical Supply—Western Canada Genealogical & Local History Books
  http://www.globalgenealogy.com/cdawest.htm
- Interlink Bookshop & Genealogical Services
  http://www.pacificcoast.net/~ibgs/
  Victoria, B.C. Canada

◆ Records: Census, Cemeteries, Land, Obituaries, Personal, Taxes and Vital (Born, Married, Died & Buried)

- British Columbia Cemetery Finding Aid
  http://www.islandnet.com/bccfa/homepage.html
- British Columbia Vital Statistics Agency
  http://www.hlth.gov.bc.ca/vs/
  - British Columbia Vital Statistics Agency— New Adoption Act
    http://www.hlth.gov.bc.ca/vs/adoption/
  - British Columbia Birth Event
    http://www.hlth.gov.bc.ca/vs/births/
  - British Columbia Marriage Event
    http://www.hlth.gov.bc.ca/vs/marriage/
  - British Columbia Death Event
    http://www.hlth.gov.bc.ca/vs/death/

○ British Columbia Wills Registry
http://www.hlth.gov.bc.ca/vs/wills/

○ British Columbia Genealogy
http://www.hlth.gov.bc.ca/vs/genealogy/

● Nominal Census Homepage
http://royal.okanagan.bc.ca/census/index.html
Data for the southern interior of the Province of British Columbia, Canada.

○ Canada Census, 1881—Yale District
http://royal.okanagan.bc.ca/census/yale1881.html

○ Canada Census, 1891—Yale District
http://royal.okanagan.bc.ca/census/yale1891.html

○ The IRC Census, 1877
http://royal.okanagan.bc.ca/census/ind1877.html
Indian Reserve Commission

○ The OMI Census, 1877
http://royal.okanagan.bc.ca/census/omi1877.html
A nominal census of Native peoples taken by the Catholic missionary order, Oblates of Mary Immaculate (OMI).

● Parksville Qualicum Marriages, 1948–1994
http://macn.bc.ca/~d69hist/marriage.html
Mid-Vancouver Island, BC, Canada

● Vernon and District Family History Society—Cemetery Monument Inscriptions
http://www.junction.net/vernhist/V4.html
B.C., Canada

● Vital Events Indexes—BC Archives
http://www2.bcarchives.gov.bc.ca/textual/governmt/vstats/v_events.htm

○ Marriage Registration Index Search Gateway, 1872 to 1921
http://www2.bcarchives.gov.bc.ca/cgi-bin/www2vsm

○ Death Registration Index, 1872 to 1976
http://www2.bcarchives.gov.bc.ca/cgi-bin/www2vsd

◆ Religion & Churches

● Christianity.Net Church Locator—British Columbia
http://www.christianity.net/cgi/location.exe?Canada+British_Columbia

● Church Online!—British Columbia
http://www.churchonline.com/canadap/bc/bc.html

● Churches of the World—British Columbia
http://www.churchsurf.com/churches/Canada/British_Columbia/index.htm
From the ChurchSurf Christian Directory.

◆ Societies & Groups

● Abbotsford Genealogical Group
http://www3.bc.sympatico.ca/abbotsfordgengroup/AGG.HTML

● Brewery Creek Historical Society
http://www.interchg.ubc.ca/leslief/bchs/index.html
Vancouver

● The British Columbia Folklore Society
http://www.folklore.bc.ca/

● British Columbia Genealogical Society
http://www.npsnet.com/bcgs/

● British Columbia Historical Federation
http://www.selkirk.bc.ca/bchf/main1.htm

● British Columbia Military Heritage Society
http://www.clearcf.uvic.ca/bcmhs/

● Campbell River Genealogy Club
http://www.connected.bc.ca/~genealogy/

● District 69 Historical Society
http://www.macn.bc.ca/~d69hist/

● Germans From Russia Heritage Society, British Columbia Chapter
http://feefhs.org/grhs/grhs-bc.html

● Heritage Society of British Columbia
http://www.islandnet.com/~hsbc/

● Heritage Vancouver Society
http://home.istar.ca/~glenchan/hvsintro.shtml

● IOOF Lodge Website Directory—British Columbia
http://norm28.hsc.usc.edu/IOOF/International/BritishColumbia.html
Independent Order of Odd Fellows and Rebekahs.

● Kamloops Family History Society
http://www.ocis.net/kfhs/

● Kelowna & District Genealogical Society
http://www.wkpowerlink.com/~gjespers/kdgs.html

● Nanaimo Family History Society
http://www.island.net/~tghayes/

● Nanaimo Historical Society
http://www.sd68.nanaimo.bc.ca/nol/community/nhistsoc.htm

● The Old Cemeteries Society—Victoria Tombstone Tales of Ross Bay Cemetery
http://www.oldcem.bc.ca/

● The Slovak Heritage and Cultural Society of British Columbia
http://www.iarelative.com/slovakbc.htm

● South Cariboo Genealogy Group
http://www.web-trek.net/stern/cariboo.html

● South Okanagan Genealogical Society
http://www.vip.net/sogs/
Penticton, British Columbia

● The Vancouver Historical Society
http://www.vcn.bc.ca/vhs/

● Vernon and District Family History Society
http://www.junction.net/vernhist/

● Victoria Genealogical Society
http://www.islandnet.com/~vgs/homepage.html

CANADA—MANITOBA
http://www.CyndisList.com/manitoba.htm

Category Index:

- General Resource Sites
- Government & Cities
- Libraries, Archives & Museums
- Mailing Lists, Newsgroups & Chat
- Maps, Gazetteers & Geographical Information
- People & Families

- Professional Researchers, Volunteers & Other Research Services
- Publications, Software & Supplies
- Records: Census, Cemeteries, Land, Obituaries, Personal, Taxes and Vital
- Religion & Churches
- Societies & Groups

◆ General Resource Sites

- Canadian Genealogy and History Links—Manitoba
  http://www.islandnet.com/~jveinot/cghl/manitoba.html

- Doing Genealogy
  http://www.mbnet.mb.ca/~mhc/genealog.htm

- Genealogy Resources on the Internet: Manitoba
  http://www-personal.umich.edu/~cgaunt/
  canada.html#MANITOBA

- Manitoba GenWeb Project
  http://www.rootsweb.com/~canmb/index.htm

- Mennonite Heritage Centre
  http://www.mbnet.mb.ca/~mhc/
  Winnipeg

◆ Government & Cities

- Manitoba Government—Explore Manitoba
  http://www.gov.mb.ca/

- Yahoo! Canada....Manitoba: Cities
  http://www.yahoo.ca/Regional/Countries/Canada/
  Provinces_and_Territories/Manitoba/Cities/

◆ Libraries, Archives & Museums

- Brandon University Catalogue
  http://library.uwaterloo.ca/catalogues/cataloghelp/loginc/
  brandon.html

- The Hudson's Bay Company Archives
  http://www.gov.mb.ca/chc/archives/hbca/index.html
  From the Provincial Archives of Manitoba, Canada

- HYTELNET Library Catalogs: Canada: Manitoba
  http://library.usask.ca/hytelnet/ca0/MB.html
  Before you use any of the Telnet links, make note of the user name, password and any other logon information.

- Manitoba Legislative Library
  http://www.gov.mb.ca/leg-lib/
  Check out links to newspapers, family histories and research materials.

- Manitoba Public Library Services
  http://www.gov.mb.ca/chc/pls/

- Provincial Archives of Manitoba
  http://www.gov.mb.ca/chc/archives/index.html
  Includes location information, hours of operation, and an access guide listing current holdings.

- United Church of Canada Archives Network: Manitoba and Northwestern Ontario Conference Archives
  http://www.uccan.org/archives/manitoba.htm
  A summary of their holdings and contact information

- University of Manitoba Libraries Catalogue
  http://library.uwaterloo.ca/catalogues/cataloghelp/loginc/
  manitoba.html

- University of Winnipeg Catalogue
  http://library.uwaterloo.ca/catalogues/cataloghelp/loginc/
  winnipeg.html

- Winnipeg Public Library Catalogue
  http://library.uwaterloo.ca/catalogues/cataloghelp/loginc/
  winnipegP.html

◆ Mailing Lists, Newsgroups & Chat

- CANADIAN ROOTS Mailing List
  http://members.aol.com/gfsjohnf/gen_mail_country-
  can.html#CANADIAN-ROOTS

- manitoba Mailing List
  http://members.aol.com/gfsjohnf/gen_mail_country-
  can.html#MANITOBA-CANADA

- SURNAMES-CANADA Mailing List
  http://members.aol.com/gfsjohnf/gen_mail_country-can.html#SURNAMES-CANADA
  For surname queries related to Canada. Gatewayed with the soc.genealogy.surnames.canada newsgroup.

◆ Maps, Gazetteers & Geographical Information

- Canadian Geographical Names / Les noms géographiques du Canada
  http://GeoNames.NRCan.gc.ca/
  - Canadian Geographical Names—Publications
    http://GeoNames.NRCan.gc.ca/english/publications.html
    List of available publications on geographical names including policy documents and manuals, gazetteers, glossaries, newsletters and brochures.
  - Origins of Canada's Geographical Names
    http://GeoNames.NRCan.gc.ca/english/schoolnet/origin.html
  - Query by Geographical Name
    http://Geonames.NRCan.gc.ca/english/cgndb.html
    Current Names Selected by Coordinates
    http://Geonames.NRCan.gc.ca/english/cgndb_coord.html
    Search this database of over 500,000 geographical names by name, feature type, region and by province.
- Excite Maps: Manitoba
  http://city.net/maps/view/?mapurl=/countries/canada/manitoba

◆ People & Families

- An Introduction to Jewish Genealogy in Manitoba
  http://www.concentric.net/~Lkessler/genbegin.shtml
- The Jewish Genealogical Exploration Guide for Manitoba and Saskatchewan (J-GEMS)
  http://www.concentric.net/~Lkessler/jgems.shtml
- Tribes and Bands of Manitoba
  http://hanksville.phast.umass.edu:8000/cultprop/contacts/tribal/Man.html

◆ Professional Researchers, Volunteers & Other Research Services

- Gen-Find Research Associates
  http://www.gen-find.com/
  Specialists in Genealogy Research for Ontario & Western Canada, Scotland, Ireland. Also the rest of Canada and Forensic & Probate/Heir Research and 20th Century Research.

◆ Publications, Software & Supplies

- Global Genealogical Supply—Western Canada Genealogical & Local History Books
  http://www.globalgenealogy.com/cdawest.htm

◆ Records: Census, Cemeteries, Land, Obituaries, Personal, Taxes and Vital (Born, Married, Died & Buried)

- Consolidated Index of the Church Family Registers (Mennonite)
  http://www.mbnet.mb.ca/~mhc/allindxm.htm
  Bergthaler (Russia) 1843, Chortitzer (Manitoba) 1878, Chortitzer (Manitoba) 1887, Chortitzer (Manitoba) 1907

◆ Religion & Churches

- Christianity.Net Church Locator—Manitoba
  http://www.christianity.net/cgi/location.exe?Canada+Manitoba
- Church Online!—Manitoba
  http://www.churchonline.com/canadap/mb/mb.html
- Churches of the World—Manitoba
  http://www.churchsurf.com/churches/Canada/Manitoba/index.htm
  From the ChurchSurf Christian Directory.

◆ Societies & Groups

- East European Genealogical Society, Inc. (EEGS)
  http://feefhs.org/ca/frg-eegs.html
  Formerly known as the East European Branch of the Manitoba Genealogical Society, Canada.
- The Genealogical Institute of the Jewish Historical Society of Western Canada
  http://www.concentric.net/~lkessler/geninst.shtml
- IOOF Lodge Website Directory—Manitoba
  http://norm28.hsc.usc.edu/IOOF/International/Manitoba.html
  Independent Order of Odd Fellows and Rebekahs.
- Manitoba Genealogical Society
  http://www.mbnet.mb.ca/~mgs/
- Manitoba Mennonite Historical Society
  http://www.mmhs.org/
- La Société Historique de Saint-Boniface
  http://home.ican.net/~shsb/index.htm

CANADA—MILITARY
http://www.CyndisList.com/milcan.htm

Category Index:
- General Resource Sites
- Historical Military Conflicts, Events or Wars
- Libraries, Archives & Museums
- Mailing Lists, Newsgroups & Chat
- Medals, Awards & Tributes

- Publications, Software & Supplies
- Records: Military, Pension, Burial
- Regimental Rosters, Histories and Home Pages
- Societies & Groups

◆ General Resource Sites
- Canadian Air Aces and Heroes—WWI, WWII and Korea
  http://www.accessweb.com/users/mconstab/
- Canadian Genealogy and History Links—Military
  http://www.islandnet.com/~jveinot/cghl/military.html
- Canadian Military Genealogical FAQ
  http://www.ott.igs.net/~donpark/canmilfaq.htm
- The Canadian Military Heritage Project
  http://www.rootsweb.com/~canmil/index.html
- Canadian POW/MIA Information Centre
  http://www.ipsystems.com/powmia/
- RCMP History
  http://www.rcmp-grc.gc.ca/html/history.htm
- Veterans Affairs / Anciens Combattants Canada
  http://www.vac-acc.gc.ca/

◆ Historical Military Conflicts, Events or Wars

18th & 19th Century Conflicts
- 1755—The French and Indian War Home Page
  http://web.syr.edu/~laroux/
- The French and Indian War—Montcalm and Wolfe
  http://www.kiva.net/~gorham/wolfe.html
- The Hessians
  http://www.cgo.wave.ca/~hessian/
  The loyal German auxiliary soldiers, of King George III, who settled in Canada, after the American Revolution 1776–1783.
- Loyalists
  http://www.CyndisList.com/loyalist.htm
  See this category on Cyndi's List for related links.

The Boer War
- The Anglo Boer War Discussion Page
  http://www.icon.co.za/~dup42/talk.htm
  This mailing list is for the discussion of the Anglo Boer War and other military related topics pre-1900.
- Fatal Casualties In Canadian Contingents of the Boer War
  http://www.islandnet.com/~duke/boercas.htm
- FOB-LIST—Friends of the Boers—E-mail List
  http://www.webcom.com/perspekt/eng/mlist/fob.html
  The primary topic of this mailing list is the centenary commemoration of the 2nd Anglo Boer war (1899–1902).
- League of Researchers of South African Historical Battlefields
  http://www.icon.co.za/~dup42/Welcome.html
- The South African War Virtual Library
  http://www.uq.net.au/~zzrwotto/

World War I ~ The Great War
- Canadian Air Aces and Heroes—WWI, WWII and Korea
  http://www2.awinc.com/users/mconstab/
- Canadian Expeditionary Force (CEF)—Records Database
  http://www.archives.ca/db/cef/index.html
  An index to the personnel files of over 600,000 soldiers that enlisted during the First World War.
- The Canadian Great War Homepage
  http://www.rootsweb.com/~ww1can/
  Canada's Role in World War I, 1914–1918.
- Valour Remembered—Canada and the First World War
  http://www.vac-acc.gc.ca/historical/firstwar/vrww1.htm
- The World War I Document Archive
  http://www.lib.byu.edu/~rdh/wwi/
  Assembled by volunteers of the World War I Military History List (WWI-L).

- The Western Front Association—Remembering 1914–1918
  http://ourworld.compuserve.com/homepages/cf_baker/
- World War I Canadian Infantry & Cavalry Index
  http://www.bookkeeping.com/rings/genealogy/ww1.html
- World War I Journal of John SPRACKLIN
  http://www.scruznet.com/~sprack/journ1.html
  1917, served with the Canadian Mounted Rifles Battalion in France.
- World War I—Trenches on the Web
  http://www.worldwar1.com/

World War II

- Canadian Air Aces and Heroes— WWI, WWII and Korea
  http://www.accessweb.com/users/mconstab/
- World War II on the Web
  http://www.geocities.com/Athens/Oracle/2691/welcome.htm

The Korean War

- Canadian Air Aces and Heroes—WWI, WWII and Korea
  http://www2.awinc.com/users/mconstab/
- Korean War Project
  http://www.koreanwar.org/
- The Korean War Project Searchable Database
  http://www.netpath.com/~korea/cgi-bin/kccf_search.cgi
  Over 33,000 individuals listed as KIA/MIA.

Vietnam

- Canadian Vietnam Casualties
  http://www.ipsystems.com/powmia/names/names.html
- Military history: Vietnam War (1961–1975)
  http://www.cfcsc.dnd.ca/links/milhist/viet.html
- The Vietnam Veterans' Memorial Wall
  http://thewall-usa.com/
  With a searchable database.
- The Vietnam Veterans Memorial Wall—Index
  http://www.cpeq.com/~wall/

◆ Libraries, Archives & Museums

- Canadian War Museum
  http://www.cmcc.muse.digital.ca/cwm/cwmeng/cwmeng.html
- The Military History Collections of The New York Public Library
  http://www.nypl.org/research/chss/subguides/milhist/home.html
- Museum of the Regiments
  http://www.nucleus.com/~regiments/

◆ Mailing Lists, Newsgroups & Chat

- AMERICAN-REVOLUTION Mailing List
  http://members.aol.com/gfsjohnf/gen_mail_states-gen.html#AMERICAN-REVOLUTION
  For the discussion of events during the American Revolution and genealogical matters related to the American Revolution. The French-Indian Wars and the War of 1812 are also suitable topics for discussion.
- FOB-LIST—Friends Of the Boers—E-mail List
  http://www.webcom.com/perspekt/eng/mlist/fob.html
  The primary topic of this mailing list is the centenary commemoration of the 2nd Anglo Boer war (1899–1902).
- LOYALIST-IN-CANADA Mailing List
  http://members.aol.com/gfsjohnf/gen_mail_country-can.html#LOYALIST
  For those with loyalist ancestors to help one another research their loyalist history and to post any facts on the subject that they desire. Loyalists are defined as those who left the United States for Canada after the American Revolution for a number of reasons.
- soc.history.war.us-revolution Newsgroup
- soc.history.war.vietnam Newsgroup
- soc.history.war.world-war-ii Newsgroup
- WARof1812 Mailing List
  http://members.aol.com/johnf14246/gen_mail_general.html#WARof1812
- WW20-ROOTS-L Mailing List
  http://members.aol.com/johnf14246/gen_mail_general.html#WW20-ROOTS-L
  For the discussion of genealogy in all 20th century wars.

◆ Medals, Awards & Tributes

- The Vietnam Veterans' Memorial Wall
  http://thewall-usa.com/
  With a searchable database
- The Vietnam Veterans Memorial Wall—Index
  http://www.cpeq.com/~wall/

◆ Publications, Software & Supplies

- Books of Remembrance
  http://www.schoolnet.ca/collections/books/
  Contain the names of Canadians who fought in wars and died either during or after them.
- Boyd Publishing Company—Misc. Military
  http://www.hom.net/~gac/miscmil.htm
- Global Genealogy—Canadian Genealogy & History Books: The Loyalists
  http://www.globalgenealogy.com/loyalist.htm
- Hearthstone Bookshop—Military Records
  http://www.hearthstonebooks.com/Military_Records.html
- Heritage Books—Loyalists
  http://www.heritagebooks.com/loyal.htm

- Heritage Books—Revolutionary War
  http://www.heritagebooks.com/revwar.htm
- Heritage Books—War of 1812
  http://www.heritagebooks.com/war1812.htm
- Military Publications International Directory
  http://www.islandnet.com/~duke/idmp.htm
  Book for sale from Canada
- Willow Bend Bookstore—Military
  http://www.willowbend.net/military.htm
- Willow Bend Bookstore—War of 1812
  http://www.willowbend.net/1812.htm

◆ Records: Military, Pension, Burial

- Canadian Expeditionary Force (CEF)—
  Records Database
  http://www.archives.ca/db/cef/index.html
  An index to the personnel files of over 600,000 soldiers that enlisted during the First World War.
- Canadian Vietnam Casualties
  http://www.ipsystems.com/powmia/names.html
- Commonwealth War Graves Commission
  http://www.cwgc.org/
  Details of 1.7 million members of UK and Commonwealth forces who died in the 1st and 2nd World Wars and other wars, and 60,000 civilian casualties of WWII. Gives details of grave site, date of death, age, usually parents/widow's address.
- Fatal Casualties In Canadian Contingents of the Boer War
  http://www.islandnet.com/~duke/boercas.htm
- World War I Canadian Infantry & Cavalry Index
  http://www.bookkeeping.com/rings/genealogy/ww1.html

◆ Regimental Rosters, Histories and Home Pages

- 1st Battalion, The Royal New Brunswick Regiment (Carleton and York)
  http://www4.brunnet.net/242/rnbr.htm
- The Black Watch (Royal Highland Regiment) of Canada
  http://www.odyssee.net/~kerra/bwhome.html
- The Cameron Highlanders of Ottawa (CHofO)
  http://infobase.ic.gc.ca/chofo/cameron.htm

- The Canadian Air Force / la Force Aérienne Canadienne
  http://www.achq.dnd.ca/
- Captain Samuel Hayden's Company of the King's Rangers
  http://www.erols.com/candidus/kings.htm
- King's Rangers
  http://www.cam.org/~dmonk/
- The Lincoln and Welland Regiment
  http://www.iaw.on.ca:80/~awoolley/lincweld.html
  A reserve infantry battalion of the Canadian Forces.
- PPCLI—The Princess Patricias Canadian Light Infantry
  http://www.nucleus.com/~ppcli/main.html
- The Queen's York Rangers (1st American Regiment)
  http://www.connection.com/~qyrang/
  An armoured reconnaissance regiment of the Canadian Forces Militia.
- The Rifleman Online—The Queen's Own Rifles of Canada
  http://www.qor.com/
- The Royal Canadian Regiment
  http://www.rcr.clevernet.on.ca/
- The (Unofficial) Canadian Army Home Page
  http://www.cyberus.ca/~army/army/

◆ Societies & Groups

- 48th Highlanders of Canada, Old Comrades Association
  http://www.rose.com/~ronk/
- British Columbia Military Heritage Society
  http://www.clearcf.uvic.ca/bcmhs/
- Canadian Peacekeeping Veterans Association
  http://www.islandnet.com/~duke/cpva.htm
- General Society of the War of 1812
  http://LanClio.org/1812.htm
- The Western Front Association—Remembering 1914–1918
  http://ourworld.compuserve.com/homepages/cf_baker/

CANADA—NEW BRUNSWICK
http://www.CyndisList.com/newbruns.htm

Category Index:

- General Resource Sites
- Government & Cities
- History & Culture
- Libraries, Archives & Museums
- Mailing Lists, Newsgroups & Chat
- Maps, Gazetteers & Geographical Information
- Military
- Newspapers
- People & Families

- Professional Researchers, Volunteers & Other Research Services
- Publications, Software & Supplies
- Queries, Message Boards & Surname Lists
- Records: Census, Cemeteries, Land, Obituaries, Personal, Taxes and Vital
- Religion & Churches
- Societies & Groups

◆ General Resource Sites

- **Canadian Genealogy and History Links—New Brunswick**
  http://www.islandnet.com/~jveinot/cghl/new-brunswick.html

- **The Chignecto Project Web Archives & Workbench**
  http://www.chignecto.net/
  A historical and genealogical web site for Nova Scotia and New Brunswick.

- **Climbing Your Family Tree—Finding/Tracing/Researching Your Ancestors in New Brunswick, Canada**
  http://www.gov.nb.ca/supply/archives/climbing.htm

- **Free queries for New Brunswick, Canada**
  E-mail: devlin7@ibm.net
  Rooters searching in Westmorland, Albert, Kings, Kent and Northumberland counties of New Brunswick, Canada can post a free query to Missing Links, a weekly geneaolgy newspaper column written and managed by Sandra Devlin. Queries should be to a maximum of 30 words PLUS forwarding address. Don't forget your snail mail, fax or voice mail, as well as e-mail addresses. Send queries to: devlin7@ibm.net

- **Genealogy in Queens County, New Brunswick**
  http://home.earthlink.net/~jkthompson/genealogy/qc_gene.htm

- **Genealogy Resources on the Internet: New Brunswick**
  http://www-personal.umich.edu/~cgaunt/canada.html#NB

- **New Brunswick / Nouveau-Brunswick GenWeb**
  http://www.bitheads.ca/nbgenweb/index.htm

- **Université de Moncton—Centre d'études acadiennes**
  http://www.umoncton.ca/etudeacadiennes/centre/cea.html

◆ Government & Cities

- **Province of New Brunswick / Province du Nouveau-Brunswick**
  http://www.gov.nb.ca/

- **Yahoo! Canada....New Brunswick: Cities**
  http://www.yahoo.ca/Regional/Countries/Canada/Provinces_and_Territories/New_Brunswick/Cities/

◆ History & Culture

- **History of the Miramichi**
  http://www.mibc.nb.ca/HISTORY/Default.html

◆ Libraries, Archives & Museums

- **HYTELNET Library Catalogs: Canada: New Brunswick**
  http://library.usask.ca/hytelnet/ca0/NB.html
  Before you use any of the Telnet links, make note of the user name, password and any other logon information.

- **Planter Studies Centre**
  http://ace.acadiau.ca/history/PLSTCNTR.HTM

- **Provincial Archives of New Brunswick**
  http://www.gov.nb.ca/supply/archives/index.htm

  - **Climbing Your Family Tree**
    http://www.gov.nb.ca/supply/archives/climbing.htm

  - **County Guides for the Province of New Brunswick**
    http://www.gov.nb.ca/supply/archives/guides.htm
    The guides that were previously found linked from this page are now available for download as Word documents via this link.

- University of New Brunswick Libraries
  http://www.lib.unb.ca/
  - Archives and Special Collections
    http://degaulle.hil.unb.ca/library/archives/
  - Genealogical Resources, Harriet Irving Library
    http://www.lib.unb.ca/Help/Subject_guides/Genealogy.html
  - Loyalist Collection—Harriet Irving Library
    http://www.lib.unb.ca/Collections/Loyalist/
  - Reference Department
    http://www.lib.unb.ca/Research/Department/
- United Church of Canada Archives Network: Maritime Conference Archives
  http://www.uccan.org/archives/maritime.htm
  A summary of their holdings and contact information.

◆ Mailing Lists, Newsgroups & Chat

- CANADIAN ROOTS Mailing List
  http://members.aol.com/gfsjohnf/gen_mail_country-can.html#CANADIAN-ROOTS
- new-brunswick Mailing List
  http://members.aol.com/gfsjohnf/gen_mail_country-can.html#NEW-BRUNSWICK-CANADA
- NewBrunswick Mailing List
  http://members.aol.com/gfsjohnf/gen_mail_country-can.html#NewBrunswick
- SURNAMES-CANADA Mailing List
  http://members.aol.com/gfsjohnf/gen_mail_country-can.html#SURNAMES-CANADA
  For surname queries related to Canada. Gatewayed with the soc.genealogy.surnames.canada newsgroup.

◆ Maps, Gazetteers & Geographical Information

- Canadian Geographical Names / Les noms géographiques du Canada
  http://GeoNames.NRCan.gc.ca/
  - Canadian Geographical Names—Publications
    http://GeoNames.NRCan.gc.ca/english/publications.html
    List of available publications on geographical names including policy documents and manuals, gazetteers, glossaries, newsletters and brochures.
  - Origins of Canada's Geographical Names
    http://GeoNames.NRCan.gc.ca/english/schoolnet/origin.html
  - Query by Geographical Name
    http://Geonames.NRCan.gc.ca/english/cgndb.html
  - Current Names Selected by Coordinates
    http://Geonames.NRCan.gc.ca/english/cgndb_coord.html
    Search this database of over 500,000 geographical names by name, feature type, region and by province.
- Excite Maps: New Brunswick
  http://city.net/maps/view/?mapurl=/countries/canada/new_brunswick

◆ Military

- 1st Battalion, The Royal New Brunswick Regiment (Carleton and York)
  http://www4.brunnet.net/242/rnbr.htm
- The Aroostook War—Maine vs. New Brunswick, 1839
  http://www.stanford.edu/~jenkg/family/aroostook.html

◆ Newspapers

- Saint John Times Globe
  http://www.nbpub.nb.ca/TIMES/INDEX.HTM
  Contact information and history regarding this newspaper.
- Telegraph Journal Online
  http://www.nbpub.nb.ca/TELE/INDEX.HTM

◆ People & Families

- The McKINNEYs of Summer Hill And Their Neighbors
  http://personal.nbnet.nb.ca/davmc/frames.htm
  Dedicated to James Alexander McKinney and his wife, Mary Ann (Murphy) McKinney who immigrated from County Tyrone, Northern Ireland in 1825 and their neighbors, pioneers, who cleared the forest land and established the communities of Summer Hill, Dunns Corner and Headline.
- SWEET Family of New Brunswick, Canada
  http://personal.nbnet.nb.ca/bobsweet/home.htm
  BANNISTER, DALY, DOWNIE, DRIDEN, HARKAN, HOPPER, LACHYE, LEEMAN, McLAUGHLIN, McLEOD, POWER, WHITE, MELANSON
- Tribes and Bands of New Brunswick
  http://hanksville.phast.umass.edu:8000/cultprop/contacts/tribal/NB.html
- The VIENNEAU Genealogy
  http://www3.nbnet.nb.ca/davienn/Testpage2ang.htm
  VIENNEAU, CORMIER, THÉRIAULT, RICHARD, HUARD, LAGACÉ, COUTURE, PITRE

◆ Professional Researchers, Volunteers & Other Research Services

- LIFELINES Genealogical Research
  http://www.webspawner.com/users/DonDixonGRSC/
  Don Dixon, GRS(C), LIFELINES Genealogical Research/ Genealogical and family history research for New Brunswick and Nova Scotia, Canada.

◆ Publications, Software & Supplies

- Books We Own—New Brunswick
  http://www.rootsweb.com/~bwo/can_nb.html
- Global Genealogical Supply—Atlantic Provinces Genealogical & Local History Books
  http://www.globalgenealogy.com/cdaatlan.htm

- Nova Scotia / New Brunswick Bookstores—
Used & Rare
http://www.rootsweb.com/~canns/lunenburg/bookstores.htm

- W.K.R.P. (Washington/Charlotte Kounty Records
Preservation) Newsletter
E-mail: shwkrp@aol.com
*A quarterly newsletter concerning research being done in
Washington Co., Maine and Charlotte County, New Brunswick.
For details e-mail Sharon at: shwkrp@aol.com*

◆ Queries, Message Boards & Surname Lists

- Queries for New Brunswick
http://www.geocities.com/Heartland/4051/nbq.htm

◆ Records: Census, Cemeteries, Land, Obituaries, Personal, Taxes and Vital (Born, Married, Died & Buried)

- PANB/UNB Cadastral Database—Searching the
Grantbook Database
http://degaulle.hil.unb.ca/library/data/panb/panbweb.html
Records of land settlement in New Brunswick, 1765–1800.

◆ Religion & Churches

- Christianity.Net Church Locator—New Brunswick
http://www.christianity.net/cgi/
location.exe?Canada+New_Brunswick

- Church Online!—New Brunswick
http://www.churchonline.com/canadap/nb/nb.html

- Churches of the World—New Brunswick
http://www.churchsurf.com/churches/Canada/New_Brunswick
From the ChurchSurf Christian Directory.

◆ Societies & Groups

- Genealogical Society of New Brunswick,
Saint John Branch
http://www.sjfn.nb.ca/Community_Hall/g/gene1900.html

- IOOF Lodge Website Directory—Atlantic Provinces
http://norm28.hsc.usc.edu/IOOF/International/
AtlanticProvinces.html
Independent Order of Odd Fellows and Rebekahs.

- New Brunswick Genealogical Society
http://www.bitheads.com/nbgs/

- Société Des Acadiens Et Acadiennes Du
Nouveau-Brunswick
http://www.rbmulti.nb.ca/saanb/saanb.htm

CANADA—NEWFOUNDLAND & LABRADOR
http://www.CyndisList.com/newf-lab.htm

Category Index:
- General Resource Sites
- Government & Cities
- History & Culture
- Libraries, Archives & Museums
- Mailing Lists, Newsgroups & Chat
- Maps, Gazetteers & Geographical Information
- People & Families

- Professional Researchers, Volunteers & Other Research Services
- Records: Census, Cemeteries, Land, Obituaries, Personal, Taxes and Vital
- Religion & Churches
- Societies & Groups

◆ General Resource Sites
- Al Beagan's "Genealogy Notes" of Newfoundland
  http://www.capecod.net/~abeagan/nfld.htm
- Canadian Genealogy and History Links—Newfoundland
  http://www.islandnet.com/~jveinot/cghl/newfoundland.html
- Genealogy Resources on the Internet: Newfoundland and Labrador
  http://www-personal.umich.edu/~cgaunt/canada.html#NFL
- Newfoundland & Labrador GenWeb Project
  http://www.huronweb.com/genweb/nf.htm
- Newfoundland Genealogy Resources
  http://web.cs.mun.ca/~santhony/genea.html
- Newfoundland's South Coast Genealogy
  http://www.geocities.com/Pipeline/Halfpipe/7046/

◆ Government & Cities
- Government of Newfoundland & Labrador
  http://www.gov.nf.ca/
- Yahoo! Canada....Newfoundland: Cities
  http://www.yahoo.ca/Regional/Countries/Canada/Provinces_and_Territories/Newfoundland/Cities/

◆ History & Culture
- The Colony of Avalon ~ Ferryland
  http://www.mediatouch.com/avalon/
- Newfoundland, Its Origin, Its Rise and Fall, Also an Epitome of the Jersey Crisis in January 1886. An Episode of the History of Jersey
  http://Fox.nstn.ca:80/~nstn1528/sullivan.htm

- Religion, Society and Culture In Newfoundland and Labrador
  http://www.ucs.mun.ca/~hrollman/

◆ Libraries, Archives & Museums
- Association of Newfoundland and Labrador Archives
  http://www.infonet.st-johns.nf.ca/providers/anla/anlahome.html
- Government of Newfoundland and Labrador Provincial Archives Division
  http://www.gov.nf.ca/tcr/cultural/archives.htm
- HYTELNET Library Catalogs: Canada: Newfoundland
  http://library.usask.ca/hytelnet/ca0/NF.html
  Before you use any of the Telnet links, make note of the user name, password and any other logon information.
- Maritime History Archive at Memorial University of Newfoundland
  http://www.mun.ca/mha/
- United Church of Canada Archives Network: Newfoundland and Labrador Conference Archives
  http://www.uccan.org/archives/newfoundland.htm
  A summary of their holdings and contact information.

◆ Mailing Lists, Newsgroups & Chat
- atlantic-province Mailing List
  http://members.aol.com/gfsjohnf/gen_mail_country-can.html#ATLANTIC-PROVINCES-CANADA
  For the Atlantic Provinces of Canada—Nova Scotia, Newfoundland, Labrador, and Prince Edward Island.
- CANADIAN ROOTS Mailing List
  http://members.aol.com/gfsjohnf/gen_mail_country-can.html#CANADIAN-ROOTS

- Newfoundland and Labrador Genealogical Society Mailing List
  http://www3.nf.sympatico.ca/nlgs/nlgsml.htm
- NFLD-LAB Mailing List
  http://members.aol.com/gfsjohnf/gen_mail_country-can.html#NFLD-LAB
- NFLD-ROOTS Mailing List
  http://members.aol.com/gfsjohnf/gen_mail_country-can.html#NFLD-ROOTS
- NLGS-L Mailing List
  http://members.aol.com/gfsjohnf/gen_mail_country-can.html#NLGS-L
  Maintained by the Newfoundland and Labrador Genealogical Society (NLGS), for anyone with a genealogical interest in this Canadian province.
- SURNAMES-CANADA Mailing List
  http://members.aol.com/gfsjohnf/gen_mail_country-can.html#SURNAMES-CANADA
  For surname queries related to Canada. Gatewayed with the soc.genealogy.surnames.canada newsgroup.

◆ Maps, Gazetteers & Geographical Information

- Canadian Geographical Names / Les noms géographiques du Canada
  http://GeoNames.NRCan.gc.ca/
  - Canadian Geographical Names—Publications
    http://GeoNames.NRCan.gc.ca/english/publications.html
    List of available publications on geographical names including policy documents and manuals, gazetteers, glossaries, newsletters and brochures.
  - Origins of Canada's Geographical Names
    http://GeoNames.NRCan.gc.ca/english/schoolnet/origin.html
  - Query by Geographical Name
    http://Geonames.NRCan.gc.ca/english/cgndb.html
  - Current Names Selected by Coordinates
    http://Geonames.NRCan.gc.ca/english/cgndb_coord.html
    Search this database of over 500,000 geographical names by name, feature type, region and by province.
- Excite Maps: Newfoundland
  http://city.net/maps/view/?mapurl=/countries/canada/newfoundland

◆ People & Families

- Tribes and Bands of Newfoundland
  http://hanksville.phast.umass.edu:8000/cultprop/contacts/tribal/NF.html

◆ Professional Researchers, Volunteers & Other Research Services

- Gen-Find Research Associates
  http://www.gen-find.com/
  Specialists in Genealogy Research for Ontario & Western Canada, Scotland, Ireland. Also the rest of Canada and Forensic & Probate/Heir Research and 20th Century Research.

◆ Records: Census, Cemeteries, Land, Obituaries, Personal, Taxes and Vital (Born, Married, Died & Buried)

- David's Family History Stuff
  http://www.dms.auburn.edu/~pikedav/family_history/
  Including many census resources for Newfoundland.

◆ Religion & Churches

- Christianity.Net Church Locator—Newfoundland
  http://www.christianity.net/cgi/location.exe?Canada+Newfoundland
- Church Online!—Newfoundland and Labrador
  http://www.churchonline.com/canadap/nf/nf.html
- Churches of the World—Newfoundland
  http://www.churchsurf.com/churches/Canada/Newfoundland
  From the ChurchSurf Christian Directory.

◆ Societies & Groups

- IOOF Lodge Website Directory—Atlantic Provinces
  http://norm28.hsc.usc.edu/IOOF/International/AtlanticProvinces.html
  Independent Order of Odd Fellows and Rebekahs.
- Newfoundland and Labrador Genealogical Society Home Page
  http://www3.nf.sympatico.ca/nlgs/

CANADA—NORTHWEST TERRITORIES & THE YUKON
http://www.CyndisList.com/nw-yukon.htm

Category Index:
- General Resource Sites
- Government & Cities
- History & Culture
- Libraries, Archives & Museums
- Mailing Lists, Newsgroups & Chat
- Maps, Gazetteers & Geographical Information
- Newspapers
- People & Families

- Professional Researchers, Volunteers & Other Research Services
- Publications, Software & Supplies
- Records: Census, Cemeteries, Land, Obituaries, Personal, Taxes and Vital
- Religion & Churches
- Societies & Groups

◆ General Resource Sites
- Canadian Genealogy and History Links—Northwest Territories
  http://www.islandnet.com/~jveinot/cghl/northwest-territories.html
- Canadian Genealogy and History Links—Yukon
  http://www.islandnet.com/~jveinot/cghl/yukon.html
- Genealogy Resources on the Internet: Northwest Territories
  http://www-personal.umich.edu/~cgaunt/canada.html#NWT
- Genealogy Resources on the Internet: Yukon Territory
  http://www-personal.umich.edu/~cgaunt/canada.html#YT
- Northwest Territories GenWeb Project
  http://www.rootsweb.com/~cannt/nwt.htm
- Yukon & Alaska Genealogy Centre
  http://yukonalaska.com/pathfinder/gen/index.html
- Yukon GenWeb
  http://www.rootsweb.com/~canyk/
- Yukon White Pages
  http://whitepages.yknet.yk.ca/
  A listing of holders of Internet e-mail accounts in the Yukon.

◆ Government & Cities
- City of Yellowknife
  http://www.city.yellowknife.nt.ca/
- Government of the Northwest Territories
  http://www.ssimicro.com/~xpsognwt/Net/index.html

- Government of the Northwest Territories
  http://www.gov.nt.ca/
- Government of Yukon
  http://www.gov.yk.ca/
- Yahoo! Canada....Northwest Territories: Cities
  http://www.yahoo.ca/Regional/Countries/Canada/Provinces_and_Territories/Northwest_Territories/Cities/
- Yahoo! Canada....Yukon: Cities
  http://www.yahoo.ca/Regional/Countries/Canada/Provinces_and_Territories/Yukon/Cities/

◆ History & Culture
- Constantine and Brown: First Mounties in the Yukon
  http://www.rcmp-grc.gc.ca/html/qu-c-b.htm
  From the RCMP Historical Branch.
- Prince of Wales Northern Heritage Centre, Yellowknife, Northwest Territories, Canada
  http://pwnhc.learnnet.nt.ca/
- Yukon and Alaska History—The Mining Company
  http://yukonalaska.miningco.com/

◆ Libraries, Archives & Museums
- The Hudson's Bay Company Archives
  http://www.gov.mb.ca/chc/archives/hbca/index.html
  From the Provincial Archives of Manitoba, Canada.
- Northwest Territories Archives
  http://pwnhc.learnnet.nt.ca/programs/archive.htm
- NWT Archives Photographic Database
  http://pwnhc.learnnet.nt.ca/programs/search.htm
  250,000 photographs preserved at the NWT Archives, Yellowknife, Northwest Territories.

- United Church of Canada Archives Network: Alberta and Northwest Conference Archives
  http://www.uccan.org/archives/alberta.htm
  A summary of their holdings and contact information.

- Whitehorse Services: Museums
  http://www.yukonweb.com/community/whitehorse/services/museums.html

- Yellowknife Public Library
  http://www.ssimicro.com/~xlibrary/

- Yukon Archives
  http://yukoncollege.yk.ca/archives/yukarch.html

- Yukon Public Libraries
  http://www.yukoncollege.yk.ca/archives/yuklibrs.html

◆ Mailing Lists, Newsgroups & Chat

- CANADIAN ROOTS Mailing List
  http://members.aol.com/gfsjohnf/gen_mail_country-can.html#CANADIAN-ROOTS

- northern-canada Mailing List
  http://members.aol.com/gfsjohnf/gen_mail_country-can.html#NORTHERN-CANADA

- SURNAMES-CANADA Mailing List
  http://members.aol.com/gfsjohnf/gen_mail_country-can.html#SURNAMES-CANADA
  For surname queries related to Canada. Gatewayed with the soc.genealogy.surnames.canada newsgroup.

◆ Maps, Gazetteers & Geographical Information

- Canadian Geographical Names / Les noms géographiques du Canada
  http://GeoNames.NRCan.gc.ca/

  o Canadian Geographical Names—Publications
    http://GeoNames.NRCan.gc.ca/english/publications.html
    List of available publications on geographical names including policy documents and manuals, gazetteers, glossaries, newsletters and brochures.

  o Origins of Canada's Geographical Names
    http://GeoNames.NRCan.gc.ca/english/schoolnet/origin.html

  o Query by Geographical Name
    http://Geonames.NRCan.gc.ca/english/cgndb.html

  o Current Names Selected by Coordinates
    http://Geonames.NRCan.gc.ca/english/cgndb_coord.html
    Search this database of over 500,000 geographical names by name, feature type, region and by province.

- Excite Maps: Yukon Territory
  http://city.net/maps/view/?mapurl=/countries/canada/yukon_territory

◆ Newspapers

- Northern News Services Limited
  http://www.nnsl.com/
  Serving communities in Canada's Arctic Northwest Territories and Nunavut, Yellowknife.

- Nunatsiaq News
  http://www.nunanet.com/~nunat/

- Slave River Journal Interactive
  http://www.auroranet.nt.ca/srj/

- Whitehorse Star Daily
  http://www.whitehorsestar.com/

- Yukon News Online
  http://www.yukon-news.com/

◆ People & Families

- Tribes and Bands of Northwest Territories
  http://hanksville.phast.umass.edu:8000/cultprop/contacts/tribal/NWT.html

- Tribes and Bands of Yukon
  http://hanksville.phast.umass.edu:8000/cultprop/contacts/tribal/YK.html

- Yukon / Alaska Pioneer Biographies
  http://yukonalaska.miningco.com/msub15.htm

◆ Professional Researchers, Volunteers & Other Research Services

- Gen-Find Research Associates
  http://www.gen-find.com/
  Specialists in Genealogy Research for Ontario & Western Canada, Scotland, Ireland. Also the rest of Canada and Forensic & Probate/Heir Research and 20th Century Research.

- Yukon Historic Research
  http://www.yukonweb.com/business/yhr/

◆ Publications, Software & Supplies

- Global Genealogical Supply—Western Canada Genealogical & Local History Books
  http://www.globalgenealogy.com/cdawest.htm

◆ Records: Census, Cemeteries, Land, Obituaries, Personal, Taxes and Vital (Born, Married, Died & Buried)

- Family Chronicle—Alaska-Yukon Goldrush Participants
  http://www.interlog.com/~magazine/klond/klondike.htm

● Ghosts of the Klondike Gold Rush
http://Gold-Rush.org/
Check out the "Pan for Gold Database."

◆ Religion & Churches

● Christianity.Net Church Locator—Northwest
Territories
http://www.christianity.net/cgi/
location.exe?Canada+Northwest_Territories

● Churches of the World—Northwest Territories
http://www.churchsurf.com/churches/Canada/
Northwest_Territories
From the ChurchSurf Christian Directory.

● Churches of the World—Yukon Territory
http://www.churchsurf.com/churches/Canada/Yukon_Territory
From the ChurchSurf Christian Directory.

◆ Societies & Groups

● Dawson City Museum and Historical Society
http://users.yknet.yk.ca/dcpages/Museum.html
Has the largest historical collection in the Yukon Territory.

● The N.W.T. Genealogical Society
http://www.ssimicro.com/nonprofit/nwtgs/

CANADA—NOVA SCOTIA
http://www.CyndisList.com/novascot.htm

Category Index:

- General Resource Sites
- Government & Cities
- History & Culture
- Libraries, Archives & Museums
- Mailing Lists, Newsgroups & Chat
- Maps, Gazetteers & Geographical Information
- Newspapers
- People & Families

- Professional Researchers, Volunteers & Other Research Services
- Publications, Software & Supplies
- Records: Census, Cemeteries, Land, Obituaries, Personal, Taxes and Vital
- Religion & Churches
- Societies & Groups

◆ General Resource Sites

- Canadian Genealogy and History Links— Nova Scotia
  http://www.islandnet.com/~jveinot/cghl/nova-scotia.html
- Cape Breton Roots
  http://www.geocities.com/Heartland/Plains/1368/index.html
  Cape Breton Genealogical Resources from Ann Capstick.
- The Chignecto Project Web Archives & Workbench
  http://www.chignecto.net/
  A historical and genealogical web site for Nova Scotia and New Brunswick.
- Family Roots of Pictou and Antigonish Counties, Nova Scotia
  http://www.rootsweb.com/~pictou/index.htm
  ROBERTSON, OULTON, CUNNINGHAM, LOGAN, PUSHEE, WILLIAMS
- The Genealogical Institue of the Maritimes
  http://www.cfn.cs.dal.ca/cfn/Recreation/GANS/gim.html
- Genealogical Record of Colchester Co.
  http://www.shelburne.nscc.ns.ca/nsgna/miller/surnames.htm
- Genealogy Resources on the Internet: Nova Scotia
  http://www-personal.umich.edu/~cgaunt/canada.html#NS
- The Halifax Explosion
  http://www.halifaxinfo.com/B/B4.html
- The Nova Scotia Genealogy Resources Page
  http://www.ccn.cs.dal.ca/~ab443/genealog.html
- Nova Scotia GenWeb Project
  http://www.rootsweb.com/~canns/index.html

◆ Government & Cities

- Government of Nova Scotia Canada
  http://www.gov.ns.ca/index.htm

- Yahoo! Canada....Nova Scotia: Cities
  http://www.yahoo.ca/Regional/Countries/Canada/Provinces_and_Territories/Nova_Scotia/Cities/

◆ History & Culture

- The Black Cultural Centre for Nova Scotia
  http://home.istar.ca/~bccns/index.shtml
- Cape Breton Pictorial Cookbook
  http://www.taisbean.com/CBcookbook/home.html
- The Early Acadian Period in Nova Scotia 1605–1755
  http://www.ednet.ns.ca/educ/museum/arch/acadia.htm
  From Archaeology in Nova Scotia.
- Highland Village—A Living History Museum & Cultural Centre
  http://eagle.uccb.ns.ca/lona/menu.html
- History of Coal Mining in Nova Scotia— The Louis Frost Notes 1685 to 1962
  http://www.cbnet.ns.ca/cbnet/comucntr/coalhist/lfindex.html
- History of the Scots in New Scotland (Nova Scotia)
  http://www.cfn.cs.dal.ca/Humanities/FSCNS/Scots_NS/About_Clans/HtySctNS.html
- Nova Scotia's Electronic Attic
  http://www.alts.net/ns1625/index.html
  Specializing in on-line information about Nova Scotia.
- The Pier 21 Society
  http://www.pier21.ns.ca/
  On the Halifax waterfront, this is the site where over 1.5 million immigrants entered the country between 1928 and 1971.
- Titanic ~ The Unsinkable Ship and Halifax
  http://titanic.gov.ns.ca/
  A site from Halifax, Nova Scotia, Canada, including a list of those buried in cemeteries in Halifax.

◆ Libraries, Archives & Museums

- Acadia University—Vaughan Memorial Library
  http://www.acadiau.ca/vaughan/
  Wolfville

- Archaeology in Nova Scotia—Nova Scotia Museum
  http://www.ednet.ns.ca/educ/museum/arch/index.htm

- Beaton Institute Archives, Cape Breton, Nova Scotia
  http://eagle.uccb.ns.ca/beaton/beaton.html

- Colchester Historical Museum and Archives
  http://www.shelburne.nscc.ns.ca/nsgna/col/col_main.htm
  Truro

- The Council of Nova Scotia Archives (CNSA)
  http://fox.nstn.ca/~cnsa/index.html

- Dartmouth N.S. Family History Centre
  http://www.shelburne.nscc.ns.ca/nsgna/fhc/fhc.htm

- Dartmouth Regional Library
  http://www.ccn.cs.dal.ca/Libraries/DartLibrary/drl.html

- HYTELNET Library Catalogs: Canada: Nova Scotia
  http://library.usask.ca/hytelnet/ca0/NS.html
  Before you use any of the Telnet links, make note of the user name, password and any other logon information.

- Nova Scotia Library Homepages
  http://www.stmarys.ca/administration/library/apla/
  aplalib2.html

- Nova Scotia Provincial Library
  http://www.nshpl.library.ns.ca/

  - Nova Scotia Regional Libraries
    http://www.nshpl.library.ns.ca/regionals/

    - Annapolis Valley Regional Library
      http://www.nshpl.library.ns.ca/regionals/avr/

    - Cape Breton Regional Library
      http://www.nshpl.library.ns.ca/regionals/cbr/

    - Colchester-East Hants Regional Library
      http://www.nshpl.library.ns.ca/regionals/ceh/

    - Cumberland Regional Library
      http://www.nshpl.library.ns.ca/regionals/cur/

    - Eastern Counties Regional Library
      http://www.nshpl.library.ns.ca/regionals/ecr/

    - Halifax Regional Library
      http://www.ccn.cs.dal.ca/Libraries/HCRL/
      HalifaxLibraryHome.html

    - Pictou-Antigonish Regional Library
      http://www.nshpl.library.ns.ca/regionals/par/

    - South Shore Regional Library
      http://www.nshpl.library.ns.ca/regionals/ssr/
      Lunenburg and Queens counties.

    - Western Counties Regional Library
      http://www.nshpl.library.ns.ca/regionals/wcr/

  - Online Catalogue on NcompasS
    http://www.nshpl.library.ns.ca/services/techserv/
    about_NcompasS/opac.html
    Instructions for using Telnet to access this catalog.

- Planter Studies Centre
  http://ace.acadiau.ca/history/PLSTCNTR.HTM

- Queens County Museum
  http://www.geocities.com/Paris/2669/
  Home of the Thomas H. Raddall Research Centre.

- United Church of Canada Archives Network: Maritime Conference Archives
  http://www.uccan.org/archives/maritime.htm
  A summary of their holdings and contact information.

- Yarmouth County Museum and Archives
  http://ycn.library.ns.ca/museum/yarcomus.htm

◆ Mailing Lists, Newsgroups & Chat

- atlantic-province Mailing List
  http://members.aol.com/gfsjohnf/gen_mail_country-
  can.html#ATLANTIC-PROVINCES-CANADA
  For the Atlantic Provinces of Canada—Nova Scotia, Newfoundland, Labrador, and Prince Edward Island.

- CANADIAN ROOTS Mailing List
  http://members.aol.com/gfsjohnf/gen_mail_country-
  can.html#CANADIAN-ROOTS

- ILMADAME Mailing List
  http://members.aol.com/gfsjohnf/gen_mail_country-
  can.html#ILMADAME

- LUNEN-LINKS Mailing List
  http://members.aol.com/gfsjohnf/gen_mail_country-
  can.html#LUNEN-LINKS
  For Lunenberg County.

- NOVA-SCOTIA Mailing List
  http://members.aol.com/gfsjohnf/gen_mail_country-
  can.html#NOVA-SCOTIA
  and the accompanying FAQ page
  http://www.rootsweb.com/~canns/nsfaq.html

- NSROOTS Mailing List
  http://members.aol.com/gfsjohnf/gen_mail_country-
  can.html#NSROOTS
  A "moderated" mailing list, sponsored by the Nova Scotia Genealogy Network Association.

- Pictouroots Mailing List
  http://members.aol.com/gfsjohnf/gen_mail_country-
  can.html#Pictouroots
  Also see the associated web page at
  http://www.onelist.com/subscribe.cgi/pictouroots

- SURNAMES-CANADA Mailing List
  http://members.aol.com/gfsjohnf/gen_mail_country-
  can.html#SURNAMES-CANADA
  For surname queries related to Canada. Gatewayed with the soc.genealogy.surnames.canada newsgroup.

◆ Maps, Gazetteers & Geographical Information

- Canadian Geographical Names / Les noms géographiques du Canada
  http://GeoNames.NRCan.gc.ca/

○ Canadian Geographical Names—Publications
http://GeoNames.NRCan.gc.ca/english/publications.html
*List of available publications on geographical names
including policy documents and manuals, gazetteers,
glossaries, newsletters and brochures.*

○ Origins of Canada's Geographical Names
http://GeoNames.NRCan.gc.ca/english/schoolnet/origin.html

○ Query by Geographical Name
http://Geonames.NRCan.gc.ca/english/cgndb.html

○ Current Names Selected by Coordinates
http://Geonames.NRCan.gc.ca/english/cgndb_coord.html
*Search this database of over 500,000 geographical names by
name, feature type, region and by province.*

• Excite Maps: Nova Scotia
http://city.net/maps/view/?mapurl=/countries/canada/
nova_scotia

• Nova Scotia Highway Map
http://destination-ns.com/map/roadmap.htm

◆ Newspapers

• The Daily News Worldwide
http://www.hfxnews.southam.ca/
Halifax, Nova Scotia

• The Halifax Herald
http://www.herald.ns.ca/

• Nova Scotian Newspapers
http://www.shelburne.nscc.ns.ca/nsgna/nnewsp.html

◆ People & Families

• The Acadians of Nova Scotia
http://www.grassroots.ns.ca/comgrp/acad.htm

• BISSETT Family
http://www.giammo.com/Bissett/
*Descendants of Jacques BISSETT & Anne Catherine METTHEY,
who emigrated to Nova Scotia in 1752.*

• Christopher GORMAN's Genealogy Page
http://www.lookup.com/Homepages/70616/home.html
GORMAN, DALRYMPLE, HENNIGAR

• The DALRYMPLEs of Nova Scotia
http://home.mem.net/~dalrympl/

• The DUNN Family of Castle Bay and Dominion,
Cape Breton Island
http://www.geocities.com/~dunnfamily/

• Fishing?—It was "A WAY OF LIFE" and
Lost At Sea
http://www.geocities.com/Heartland/Prairie/7527/
*Dedicated to Atlantic Canada fishermen and mariners lost at
sea, their families and survivors. And to all those from other
countries who were lost at sea.*

• Four Nova Scotia Families
http://www.widomaker.com/~gwk/
*Information about descendants of four families who settled in
Nova Scotia in the mid 1700s—three Rice families who settled in
the Annapolis Valley in 1760 and the Graham family who
arrived at Halifax about 1749.*

• A Internet home for George Rose, and Atlantic
Canada Genealogy
http://www.chebucto.ns.ca/~ab936/Profile.html

• Jim FRASER'S Genealogy Related Info
http://www2.shore.net/~jaf/genpage.htm
*FRASER (Guysborough Co, NS), WOMBLE (NC), FOUGERE,
DYE (KY), ARNOLD, DOTY, and many early Acadians.*

• Karen FARMER's Kinfolk—Genealogy in Nova
Scotia, Ontario and Quebec
http://www.geocities.com/Heartland/Plains/7525/
*BEZANSON, CLEROUX, CROCKETT, FARMER, LANGILLE,
STEVENS & TATTRIE*

• Lloyd MAC DONALD Genealogy Page
http://members.tripod.com/~lemac2/index.html
*ROY, HENDERSON, MAC DONALD, URQUHART,
MAC LEOD*

• Randall's Genealogy Page
http://www.interlog.com/~prandall/intro.html
*Special focus on Bayfield, Antigonish County. ATWATER,
CUNNINGHAM, HULBERT, IRISH, KINNEY, NICHOLS,
RANDALL, STROPLE, WAMBACH, WILLIAMS, etc.*

• Scots in New Scotland (Nova Scotia)
http://www.ccn.cs.dal.ca/Heritage/FSCNS/ScotsHome.html

• Tom ROGERS Family History
http://www.geocities.com/Heartland/Prairie/8062/
genealogy.html
*BUSBY, COOK, GARRON, KNOWLES, LACEY, NICKERSON,
ROGERS, WILSON*

• Tribes and Bands of Nova Scotia
http://hanksville.phast.umass.edu:8000/cultprop/contacts/
tribal/NS.html

◆ Professional Researchers, Volunteers & Other Research Services

• Gen-Find Research Associates
http://www.gen-find.com/
*Specialists in Genealogy Research for Ontario & Western
Canada, Scotland, Ireland. Also the rest of Canada and Forensic
& Probate/Heir Research and 20th Century Research.*

• LIFELINES Genealogical Research
http://www.webspawner.com/users/DonDixonGRSC/
*Don Dixon, GRS(C), LIFELINES Genealogical Research/
Genealogical and family history research for New Brunswick
and Nova Scotia, Canada.*

• Roots Cape Breton Genealogy & Family
History Centre
http://eagle.uccb.ns.ca/lona/roots.html
A computer-assisted research service.

◆ Publications, Software & Supplies

• Antigonish Books of Genealogical and
Historical Interest
http://www.rootsweb.com/~pictou/biblio.htm

- Books We Own—Nova Scotia
  http://www.rootsweb.com/~bwo/can_ns.html
- Bridges Genealogy Books And Services
  http://pw2.netcom.com/~huskyfan/genealogy.html
  Pictou County, Nova Scotia Death Records.
- Curley—Koen Book Distributors
  http://pw2.netcom.com/~jcurley1/CKBooks.html
  Census indexes for Guysborough County.
- Global Genealogical Supply—Atlantic Provinces
  Genealogical & Local History Books
  http://www.globalgenealogy.com/cdaatlan.htm
- Louisa's World—A Genealogy in Context
  http://www3.ns.sympatico.ca/dmcclare/TITLE.HTM
  From the 1815 Diary of a Nova Scotia Farm Girl, Louisa Collins, of Colin Grove, Dartmouth.
- Lunenburg County / Nova Scotia Genealogy
  Book List
  http://www.rootsweb.com/~canns/lunenburg/booklist.htm
- Nova Scotia Book Dealers—Used & Rare
  http://www.shelburne.nscc.ns.ca/nsgna/nbst.html
- Nova Scotia / New Brunswick Bookstores—
  Used & Rare
  http://www.rootsweb.com/~canns/lunenburg/bookstores.htm
- Pictou Books of Genealogical and Historical Interest
  http://www.rootsweb.com/~pictou/libpic1.htm

◆ Queries, Message Boards & Surname Lists

- Nova Scotians searching surnames
  http://www.chebucto.ns.ca/~ab936/search.html

◆ Records: Census, Cemeteries, Land, Obituaries, Personal, Taxes and Vital (Born, Married, Died & Buried)

Cemeteries, Funeral Homes & Obituaries

- Abstracts from the Court of Probate Records for
  Annapolis County, Nova Scotia
  http://www.widomaker.com/~gwk/abstract.htm
  We are indebted to Wayne W. Walker for making a copy of his Abstracts from the Court of Probate Records for Annapolis County, Nova Scotia available to us on the Internet. The Abstracts are available for download as a ZIP (compressed) file. The text is in ASCII text format which can be read by all word processors.
- Beaton Cemetery, Millbrook, Pictou County
  http://www.rootsweb.com/~pictou/beaton.htm
- Black River Cemetery, Pictou County
  http://www.rootsweb.com/~pictou/blackriv.htm
- Blanchard Road Cemetery, Pictou County
  http://www.rootsweb.com/~pictou/blanch.htm

- Brookville Cemetery, Pictou County
  http://www.rootsweb.com/~pictou/brookvll.htm
- Burial Point Cemetery, Merigomish
  http://www.rootsweb.com/~pictou/bpoint.htm
- Cemeteries of Pictou County
  http://www.rootsweb.com/~pictou/oldest.htm
  Excerpted from "The Stone Book of Pictou County" by Donald Nicholson. The statistics are listed by cemetery, including the oldest birth year, oldest death year, oldest age at death.
- Chester New Baptist Cemetery, Lunenburg
  http://www.rootsweb.com/~canns/lunenburg/chnbaptist.html
- Chester Basin Old Baptist Cemetery, Lunenburg
  http://www.rootsweb.com/~canns/lunenburg/cbobaptist.html
- Death Notices of Some Early Pictou County Settlers
  http://www.rootsweb.com/~pictou/obits.htm
- East River St. Mary's Cemetery, Pictou County
  http://www.rootsweb.com/~pictou/eastriv.htm
- Eden Lake Cemetery, Pictou County
  http://www.rootsweb.com/~pictou/edenlake.htm
- Fox Brook Private Cemetery
  http://www.rootsweb.com/~pictou/foxpriv.htm
- Fraser Cemetery, Blanchard Road, Pictou County
  http://www.rootsweb.com/~pictou/fraserb.htm
- Glen Bard Cemetery, James River,
  Antigonish County
  http://www.rootsweb.com/~pictou/antiglb.htm
- Gunn Cemetery, Eden Lake, Pictou County
  http://www.rootsweb.com/~pictou/gunn.htm
- Guysborough County Cemetery Listings
  http://www.geocities.com/Heartland/Plains/7525/Cemetery/cemindex.htm
- Halifax County—Cemetery Listings
  http://www.geocities.com/Heartland/Meadows/3515/Cemetery.htm
- Hattie Cemetery, Avondale, Pictou County
  http://www.rootsweb.com/~pictou/hattie.htm
- Heatherton Cemetery, Old Section,
  Antigonish County
  http://www.rootsweb.com/~pictou/hethold.htm
- Hillside Cemetery, Trenton, Pictou County
  http://www.rootsweb.com/~pictou/hillside.htm
- Hodson Cemetery, Pictou County
  http://www.rootsweb.com/~pictou/hodson.htm
- Kenzieville Cemetery, Pictou County
  http://www.rootsweb.com/~pictou/kenzie.htm
- McKenzie Cemetery, Salt Springs, Pictou County
  http://www.rootsweb.com/~pictou/mckenzie.htm
- McLean Cemetery, Hopewell, Pictou County
  http://www.rootsweb.com/~pictou/mclhope.htm

- Meiklefield Cemetery, Meiklefield, Pictou County
  http://www.rootsweb.com/~pictou/mekfd.htm
- Murray Point Cemetery, Pictou County
  http://www.rootsweb.com/~pictou/murpt.htm
- Old Cemetery, Salt Springs, Pictou County
  http://www.rootsweb.com/~pictou/oldcem.htm
- Pictou Island Pioneer Cemetery
  http://www.rootsweb.com/~pictou/pioneer.htm
- Pictou Island Presbyterian Church Cemetery
  http://www.rootsweb.com/~pictou/prezz.htm
- Rocky Mountain Cemetery, Pictou County
  http://www.rootsweb.com/~pictou/rocky.htm
- Roman Catholic Cemetery, Merigomish
  http://www.rootsweb.com/~pictou/rcmeri.htm
- Saint Andrew's Cemetery, Old Section, Antigonish County
  http://www.rootsweb.com/~pictou/stanold.htm
- Salt Springs Cemetery, Pictou County
  http://www.rootsweb.com/~pictou/ssprings.htm
- Stewart's Cemetery, Antigonish County
  http://www.rootsweb.com/~pictou/stewart.htm
- Victoria County Cemetery Transcriptions
  http://members.tripod.com/~lemac2/index-16.html

Census Indexes & Census Records

- 1901 Census—Lunenburg County, Nova Scotia
  http://www.rootsweb.com/~canns/lunenburg/1901census.html
- Halifax Census (1752), A–E
  http://www.geocities.com/Heartland/Prairie/6261/hfxcensus1.htm

  F–K
  http://www.geocities.com/Heartland/Prairie/6261/hfxcensus2.htm

  L–Q
  http://www.geocities.com/Heartland/Prairie/6261/hfxcensus3.htm

  R–Z
  http://www.geocities.com/Heartland/Prairie/6261/hfxcensus4.htm
- Nova Scotia Census Data
  http://www.genealogy.org/~soccgs/census.html
- Nova Scotia Census on Microfilm
  http://www.shelburne.nscc.ns.ca/nsgna/ncensus.html

Land Records & Tax Rolls

- Registry of Deeds—Nova Scotia
  http://www.shelburne.nscc.ns.ca/nsgna/ndeed.html

Ships, Passenger Lists & Immigration

- Dove Passenger List—1801
  http://www.rootsweb.com/~pictou/dove1.htm
  Arriving in Pictou County, Nova Scotia, Canada.

- Hector Passenger List
  http://www.rootsweb.com/~pictou/hector1.htm
  Voyage to Pictou, Nova Scotia in 1773.
- Humphreys Passenger List—1806
  http://www.rootsweb.com/~pictou/hmphreys.htm
- Lunenburg County, NSGenWeb—Passenger Lists
  http://www.rootsweb.com/~canns/lunenburg/shiplists.html
  - Cornwallis Ships to Halifax—1749
    http://www.rootsweb.com/~canns/cornwallis.html
  - Passenger Lists for Ships Carrying the "Foreign Protestants" to Nova Scotia
    http://www.rootsweb.com/~canns/lunenburg/shiplist2.html
    59 Families 16 May 1752 "SPEEDWELL."
  - Passenger Lists for Ships Carrying the "Foreign Protestants" to Nova Scotia
    http://www.rootsweb.com/~canns/lunenburg/shiplist3.html
    59 Families 30 May 1752 "BETTY."
  - Passenger Lists for Ships Carrying the "Foreign Protestants" to Nova Scotia
    http://www.rootsweb.com/~canns/lunenburg/shiplist11.html
    73 Families 18 May 1751 "SPEEDWELL."
  - Passenger Lists for Ships Carrying the "Foreign Protestants" to Nova Scotia
    http://www.rootsweb.com/~canns/lunenburg/shiplist4.html
    85 Families 2 Jul 1751 "PEARL."
  - Passenger Lists for Ships Carrying the "Foreign Protestants" to Nova Scotia
    http://www.rootsweb.com/~canns/lunenburg/shiplist5.html
    85 Families 5 Jun 1752 "GALE."
  - Passenger Lists for Ships Carrying the "Foreign Protestants" to Nova Scotia
    http://www.rootsweb.com/~canns/lunenburg/shiplist6.html
    85 Families 6 Jun 1752 "PEARL."
  - Passenger Lists for Ships Carrying the "Foreign Protestants" to Nova Scotia
    http://www.rootsweb.com/~canns/lunenburg/shiplist9.html
    99 Families 29 Jun 1750 "ANN."
  - Passenger Lists for Ships Carrying the "Foreign Protestants" to Nova Scotia
    http://www.rootsweb.com/~canns/lunenburg/shiplist1.html
    100 Families of German Protestants 25 Jun 1751 "MURDOCH."
  - Passenger Lists for Ships Carrying the "Foreign Protestants" to Nova Scotia
    http://www.rootsweb.com/~canns/lunenburg/shiplist7.html
    119 Families 30 May 1752 "SALLY."
  - Passenger Lists for Ships Carrying the "Foreign Protestants" to Nova Scotia
    http://www.rootsweb.com/~canns/lunenburg/shiplist8.html
    Foreign Names of Those Arriving with Cornwallis, 1749 and Others of Interest Arriving in 1749.

o Passenger Lists for Ships Carrying the "Foreign Protestants" to Nova Scotia
   http://www.rootsweb.com/~canns/lunenburg/shiplist12.html
   Settlers Who Are Presumed to Have Arrived on the "ALDER-NEY" or the "NANCY" in August and September 1750.

● Nova Scotia Bound
  http://www.geocities.com/Heartland/Meadows/8429/index.html
  A partial list of ships bound for Nova Scotia between 1750 and 1862.

   o The Albion Ship List, Surnames A–L
      http://www.geocities.com/Heartland/Meadows/8429/albal.html

   o The Albion Ship List, Surnames M–Z
      http://www.geocities.com/Heartland/Meadows/8429/albmz.html
      Arrived in Halifax, Nova Scotia, Canada on May 6, 1774 from Hull, Yorkshire, England.

   o The British Queen Passenger List
      http://www.geocities.com/Heartland/Meadows/8429/britqn.html
      Sailed for Nova Scotia from Liverpool, England on April 1st, 1862.

   o The Duke of York Passenger List
      http://www.geocities.com/Heartland/Meadows/8429/dyork.html
      Arrived in Halifax, Nova Scotia from Liverpool, England on May 1, 1772.

   o Elisabeth and Ann Passenger List
      http://www.geocities.com/Heartland/Meadows/8429/elisann.html
      Sailed for Nova Scotia from Thurso, North Britain on November 8th, 1806.

   o The Frank Flint Passenger List
      http://www.geocities.com/Heartland/Meadows/8429/flint.html
      Sailed for Halifax, Nova Scotia from Liverpool, England on May 28th, 1862.

   o The Humphreys Passenger List
      http://www.geocities.com/Heartland/Meadows/8429/hmphry.html
      Sailed for Nova Scotia from Tobermory, North Britain on July 14th, 1806.

   o The Jenny Ship List
      http://www.geocities.com/Heartland/Meadows/8429/jenny.html
      To Halifax, Nova Scotia, Canada from Hull, Yorkshire, England in April of 1775.

   o The Providence Passenger List
      http://www.geocities.com/Heartland/Meadows/8429/prvdnc.html
      Arrived in Halifax on June 1, 1774 from Newcastle Northumberland.

   o The Rambler Passenger List
      http://www.geocities.com/Heartland/Meadows/8429/rambler.html
      Sailed for Nova Scotia from Thurso, North Britain on November 8th, 1806.

   o The Thomas and William or the Prince George Passenger List
      http://www.geocities.com/Heartland/Meadows/8429/tmwlad.html
      Arrived at Halifax from Scarborough, Yorkshire on May 14/16, 1774.

   o The Two Friends Ship List
      http://www.geocities.com/Heartland/Meadows/8429/2friends.html
      Arrived in Halifax, Nova Scotia on May 9, 1774 from Hull, Yorkshire.

● Nova Scotia Passenger Lists—The Speedwell and The Ann
  http://www.rootsweb.com/~ote/nsship.htm

● Oughton Passenger List—1804
  http://www.rootsweb.com/~pictou/oughton.htm

● The Sarah—1801
  http://www.rootsweb.com/~pictou/sarah1.htm
  To Pictou, Nova Scotia.

● Spencer Passenger List—1806
  http://www.rootsweb.com/~pictou/spencer.htm

Vital Records—Birth, Marriage & Death

● Baptisms in Pictou County by Rev. James MacGregor, D.D
  http://www.rootsweb.com/~pictou/bapt1.htm

● Births and Baptisms at Barney's River
  http://www.rootsweb.com/~pictou/birbp.htm
  Pictou County

● Candlish Church, Free Presbyterian, Barney's River, Pictou County, Nova Scotia Marriages—1812–1883
  http://www.rootsweb.com/~pictou/marchr.htm

● Fortress of Louisbourg Parish Records (1713–1758)
  http://www.schoolnet.ca:80/collections/louisbourg/genealogy/index.html

● Lunenburg, Nova Scotia Will Extracts
  http://www.geocities.com/Heartland/Meadows/5699/willtab.html

● Marriages in Pictou County by Rev. James McGregor
  http://www.rootsweb.com/~pictou/hitches.htm

● Nova Scotia Vital Statistics Division of Business and Consumer Services
  http://www.gov.ns.ca/bacs/vstat/

● Nova Scotia Vital Statistics Information from NSGNA
  http://www.shelburne.nscc.ns.ca/nsgna/nvitals.html

● Registrars of Probate Information from NSGNA
  http://www.shelburne.nscc.ns.ca/nsgna/npro.html

● Surnames of Barney's River, Nova Scotia
  http://www.rootsweb.com/~pictou/names.htm
  From Pictou County Death Records for the period of 1864–1877.

◆ Religion & Churches

- Anglican Parish Ministry
  http://www.ccn.cs.dal.ca/Religion/AnglicanChurchNS/parishes.html
  For Nova Scotia and Prince Edward Island.

- Christianity.Net Church Locator—Nova Scotia
  http://www.christianity.net/cgi/location.exe?Canada+Nova_Scotia

- Church Online!—Nova Scotia
  http://www.churchonline.com/canadap/ns/ns.html

- Churches of the World—Nova Scotia
  http://www.churchsurf.com/churches/Canada/Nova_Scotia
  From the ChurchSurf Christian Directory.

- United Church Congregations and Pastoral Charges in Halifax Presbytery
  http://www.cfn.cs.dal.ca/Religion/UCCPresbytery/_Charges.html

◆ Societies & Groups

- Cape Sable Historical Society
  http://www.bmhs.ednet.ns.ca/cshs.htm

- Genealogical Association of Nova Scotia
  http://www.ccn.cs.dal.ca/Recreation/GANS/gans_homepage.html

- Hantsport & Area Historical Society
  http://www.shelburne.nscc.ns.ca/nsgna/hpt/hport.htm

- IOOF Lodge Website Directory—Atlantic Provinces
  http://norm28.hsc.usc.edu/IOOF/International/AtlanticProvinces.html
  Independent Order of Odd Fellows and Rebekahs.

- The Kings Historical Society and Old Kings Courthouse Museum
  http://www.go.ednet.ns.ca/~ip96003/

- North Queens Heritage Society
  http://www.rootsweb.com/~canns/queens/qcnorth.html

- The Nova Scotia Genealogy Network Association
  http://www.shelburne.nscc.ns.ca/nsgna/
  Dozens of great resources here!

- Nova Scotia Highland Village Society
  http://eagle.uccb.ns.ca/Iona/history.html

- Pictou County Genealogy & Heritage Society and McCulloch House Museum
  http://www.geocities.com/Colosseum/7374/

- Queens County Historical Society
  http://www.rootsweb.com/~canns/queens/qchist.html

- The Royal Nova Scotia Historical Society
  http://www.shelburne.nscc.ns.ca/nsgna/rnshs/index.html
  Dartmouth

- Shelburne County Genealogical Society
  http://www.shelburne.nscc.ns.ca/nsgna/sg/sg_home.htm

- South Shore Genealogical Society
  http://www.lunco.com/genealogy/index.htm
  Lunenburg and Queens Counties

- West Hants Historical Society
  http://www.glinx.com/users/whhs/

CANADA—ONTARIO

http://www.CyndisList.com/ontario.htm

Category Index:

- General Resource Sites
- Government & Cities
- History & Culture
- Libraries, Archives & Museums
- Mailing Lists, Newsgroups & Chat
- Maps, Gazetteers & Geographical Information
- Military
- Newspapers
- People & Families

- Professional Researchers, Volunteers & Other Research Services
- Publications, Software & Supplies
- Queries, Message Boards & Surname Lists
- Records: Census, Cemeteries, Land, Obituaries, Personal, Taxes and Vital
- Religion & Churches
- Societies & Groups

◆ General Resource Sites

- Canadian Genealogy and History Links—Ontario
  http://www.islandnet.com/~jveinot/cghl/ontario.html

- Genealogy Bulletin Board Systems for Ontario
  http://www.genealogy.org/~gbbs/gblon.html

- Genealogy Research in Ontario
  http://www.xcelco.on.ca/~genealog/#Ontario

- Genealogy Resources on the Internet: Ontario
  http://www-personal.umich.edu/~cgaunt/
  canada.html#ONTARIO

- Glengarry County Ontario and Area
  http://members.tripod.com/~GLENGARRY/index.html

- Norfolk Genealogy
  http://alpha.nornet.on.ca/~jcardiff/

- Ontario Genealogy Resource Page
  http://wwnet.com/~treesrch/ontario.html

- Ontario GenWeb
  http://www.geneofun.on.ca/ongenweb/

- Société Franco-Ontarienne d'histoire et de Généalogie Réunion
  E-mail: jsauve@istar.ca
  Annuelle 6-7-8 juin 1997 Nes Liskeard, Ont. For details send e-mail to: jsauve@istar.ca

◆ Government & Cities

- Government of Ontario, Canada
  http://www.gov.on.ca/

- Yahoo! Canada....Ontario: Cities
  http://www.yahoo.ca/Regional/Countries/Canada/
  Provinces_and_Territories/Ontario/Cities/

◆ History & Culture

- Ontario: History
  http://www.gov.on.ca/MBS/english/its_ontario/ont-hist/
  index.html

- The Toronto History Page
  http://www.interlog.com/~pfalex/

◆ Libraries, Archives & Museums

- Archives Association of Ontario
  http://www.fis.utoronto.ca/groups/aao/

- Archives of Ontario
  http://www.gov.on.ca/MCZCR/archives/index.html

- At Port Bruce—Local History and Genealogy
  http://www.ptbruce.kanservu.ca/Genealogy/index.html

- Chatham Public Library
  http://www.wincom.net/CHATHAM/library.htm

- Conrad Grebel College Genealogical Resources
  http://www.lib.uwaterloo.ca/MHSC/gen.html
  Lists genealogical resources held in Conrad Grebel College and the Mennonite Archives of Ontario.

- Directory of Ontario Public Libraries / Répertoire des bibliothéques de l'Ontario, 1995–1996
  http://www.sols.on.ca/director/dpublib.html

- Doon Heritage Crossroads—Waterloo Regional Curatorial Centre
  http://www.oceta.on.ca/region.waterloo/doon/docs/
  dooncurat.html

- Family History Centres in Ontario
  http://www.gov.on.ca/MCZCR/archives/english/geneal/
  fmlyhist.htm

- HALINET Home Page—The Public Libraries of Halton
  http://www.hhpl.on.ca/
- Hamilton Public Library
  http://www.hpl.hamilton.on.ca/DEFAULT.HTM
  - Special Collections
    http://www.hpl.hamilton.on.ca/LOCAL/SPCOLL/Speccol.htm
    - Canadiana
      http://www.hpl.hamilton.on.ca/LOCAL/SPCOLL/CANA.HTM
    - Genealogy
      http://www.hpl.hamilton.on.ca/LOCAL/SPCOLL/GENEA.HTM
    - Local History
      http://www.hpl.hamilton.on.ca/LOCAL/SPCOLL/LOCAL.HTM
- HYTELNET Library Catalogs: Canada: Ontario
  http://library.usask.ca/hytelnet/ca0/ON.html
  Before you use any of the Telnet links, make note of the user name, password and any other logon information.
- Leamington Public Library / Bibliothèque publique de Leamington
  http://www.lccia.net/~lpl/
  - Local History Databases
    http://www.lccia.net/~lpl/english.htm
- London Public Library
  http://discover.lpl.london.on.ca/
- Marine Museum of the Great Lakes at Kingston
  http://www.marmus.ca/marmus/index.html
- Mississauga Library System
  http://www.city.mississauga.on.ca/library/default.htm
- The Niagara Historical Resource Centre
  http://vaxxine.com/fa/notlpl/nhrc.htm
- Queen's University Archives
  http://stauffer.queensu.ca/webarch/
  Kingston
- Queen's University Libraries
  http://stauffer.queensu.ca/
  Kingston
  - Genealogy
    http://stauffer.queensu.ca/inforef/guides/genealogy.htm
  - Genealogy Resources in Government Documents
    http://stauffer.queensu.ca/webdoc/genealogy/
- Region of Peel Archives
  http://www.region.peel.on.ca/heritage/archives.htm
- The St. Thomas Public Library
  http://www.elgin.net/stpl/public_library.html
- United Church of Canada Archives Network: Manitoba and Northwestern Ontario Conference Archives
  http://www.uccan.org/archives/manitoba.htm
  A summary of their holdings and contact information.

- United Church of Canada / Victoria University Archives
  http://vicu.utoronto.ca/archives/archives.htm
  Located in Ontario. The holdings in the archives include records for The Presbyterian Church in Canada; The Methodist Church (Canada); The Congregational Union of Canada; Local Union Churches; and the Evangelical United Brethren Church. There are also personal papers, biographical files and photographs.
- The University of Waterloo Electronic Library
  http://www.lib.uwaterloo.ca/
- The Uxbridge-Scott Museum
  http://www.uxbridge.com/museum/mhome.html
  Including Quaker heritage
- Wainfleet Township Public Library
  http://ont.net/wainfleet/library/wtpl.htm
  - Wainfleet Township Public Library Genealogy Page
    http://ont.net/wainfleet/library/genmain.htm

◆ Mailing Lists, Newsgroups & Chat

- CANADIAN ROOTS Mailing List
  http://members.aol.com/gfsjohnf/gen_mail_country-can.html#CANADIAN-ROOTS
- EONTGEN-L Mailing List
  http://members.aol.com/gfsjohnf/gen_mail_country-can.html#EONTGEN-L
  For discussions of history, geography and genealogy related to Eastern Ontario, Canada: Prince Edward; Hastings; Lennox & Addington; Frontenac; Leeds & Grenville; Lanark; Stormont, Glengarry & Dundas; Prescott & Russell; and Carleton Counties.
- loyalists-in-canada Mailing List
  http://members.aol.com/gfsjohnf/gen_mail_country-can.html#LOYALIST
  For those with loyalist ancestors to help one another research their loyalist history and to post any facts on the subject that they desire. Loyalists are defined as those who left the United States for Canada after the American Revolution for a number of reasons.
- NIAGARA-ONT Surname Mailing List
  http://members.aol.com/gfsjohnf/gen_mail_country-can.html#NIAGARA-ONT
  For anyone with a genealogical interest in the Niagara Region of Ontario, Canada.
- ONDURHAM Mailing List
  http://members.aol.com/gfsjohnf/gen_mail_country-can.html#ONDURHAM
  Durham County
- OntarioGenWeb Chat Forum
  http://www.rootsweb.com/~canon/chat.html
- ontario Mailing List
  http://members.aol.com/gfsjohnf/gen_mail_country-can.html#ONTARIO-CANADA
- ONTARIO Mailing List
  http://members.aol.com/gfsjohnf/gen_mail_country-can.html#ONTARIO

- SURNAMES-CANADA Mailing List
  http://members.aol.com/gfsjohnf/gen_mail_country-can.html#SURNAMES-CANADA
  For surname queries related to Canada. Gatewayed with the soc.genealogy.surnames.canada newsgroup.

- UOVGEN—The Upper Ottawa Valley Genealogy Mailing List
  http://members.aol.com/gfsjohnf/gen_mail_country-can.html#UOVGEN
  and the corresponding web page
  http://www.valleynet.on.ca/~aa127/uovgen/uovgen.html
  For Renfrew and Pontiac Counties of the Upper Ottawa Valley region of Ontario and Quebec.

◆ Maps, Gazetteers & Geographical Information

- Canadian Geographical Names / Les noms géographiques du Canada
  http://GeoNames.NRCan.gc.ca/
  - Canadian Geographical Names—Publications
    http://GeoNames.NRCan.gc.ca/english/publications.html
    List of available publications on geographical names including policy documents and manuals, gazetteers, glossaries, newsletters and brochures.
  - Origins of Canada's Geographical Names
    http://GeoNames.NRCan.gc.ca/english/schoolnet/origin.html
  - Query by Geographical Name
    http://Geonames.NRCan.gc.ca/english/cgndb.html
  - Current Names Selected by Coordinates
    http://Geonames.NRCan.gc.ca/english/cgndb_coord.html
    Search this database of over 500,000 geographical names by name, feature type, region and by province.

- Excite Maps: Ontario
  http://city.net/maps/view/?mapurl=/countries/canada/ontario

- Ontario Locator
  http://www.rootsweb.com/~canon/locator/

- Present Day Ontario
  http://www.rootsweb.com/~canon/locator/pdontmap.html

◆ Military

- The Cameron Highlanders of Ottawa (CHofO)
  http://infobase.ic.gc.ca/chofo/cameron.htm

- Roll of the 1st Regiment, Hastings County, Midland District, Upper Canada Militia
  http://www.iwaynet.net/~bobphillips/muster.htm

◆ Newspapers

- The Hamilton Spectator
  http://www.southam.com/hamiltonspectator/

- The Kingston Whig-Standard
  http://www.southam.com/kingstonwhigstandard/

- Kitchener Waterloo Record Online
  http://www.southam.com/kitchenerwaterloorecord/

- Ottawa Citizen Online
  http://www.ottawacitizen.com/

- The Windsor Star
  http://www.southam.com/windsorstar/

◆ People & Families

- Claude's Place on the Web
  http://www.geocities.com/~couimet/
  OUIMET, PROULX, LECLAIR, THEORET, CORTENBACH, SEEGERS, KNAAPEN and JOORDENS

- Le HOUYMET Internet—Home on the Internet of Les Descendants de Jean OUIMET, Inc.
  http://www.geocities.com/~couimet/lehouymet.html
  Ouimet, Houymet, Vilmet, Wemet, Wemett, Wuillemette, Wilmot and numerous other spelling variations.

- Karen FARMER's Kinfolk—Genealogy in Nova Scotia, Ontario and Quebec
  http://www.geocities.com/Heartland/Plains/7525/
  BEZANSON, CLEROUX, CROCKETT, FARMER, LANGILLE, STEVENS & TATTRIE

- Les's Canadian Genealogy Page
  http://members.home.net:80/lwhite1/
  ESCH, WHITE, CRANE

- The Metis Nation of Ontario
  http://www.metisnation.org/

- The NELSON and McRAE Genealogy Page
  http://www.geocities.com/Heartland/Plains/7683/
  CAMERON, LINDENTHOLER, McRAE, NALLEY, ROSTAD, ZUTTER

- PILGRIM's Landing
  http://www.cyberus.ca/~pmarchan/pilgrim.html

- The RODRIGUE Families
  http://www.er.uqam.ca/nobel/g17176/rodrigue/engindex.html
  Quebec and Ontario in Canada, Louisiana and New England in the U.S.

- Searching for My Leeds County Ancestors
  http://wp.com/wright/home1.html
  WRIGHT, CHISHLOM, BEST, LOCKWOOD, GARRETT, LANGDON, LASHLEY

- Tribes and Bands of Ontario
  http://hanksville.phast.umass.edu:8000/cultprop/contacts/tribal/ON.html

- Young Immigrants to Canada
  http://www.dcs.uwaterloo.ca/~marj/genealogy/homeadd.html

◆ Professional Researchers, Volunteers & Other Research Services

- Adoption Searches & Investigations
  http://www3.sympatico.ca/searches/
  London, Ontario

- Assets and Family Research Consultants
  E-mail: sharsam@adan.kingston.net
  Toronto, Ontario, Canada
  Researcher with 15 years experience, specializing in adoption-related searches. Contact Sharon Chianelli at 1-613-352-1163 or by e-mail at: sharsam@adan.kingston.net

- Bruce Murduck—Historical, Geographical and Genealogical Research Services
  http://www.ikweb.com/murduck/genealogy/rsrchndx.htm
  Researcher in Ontario, Canada.

- Diane's Michigan Genealogy Page
  http://members.aol.com/DJOslund/index.html
  Professional Genealogist serving Southeastern Michigan, Southwestern Ontario, Northwestern Ohio.

- Ed's Ancestral Research Services
  http://www.execulink.com/~patpamed/index.html
  Specializing in research for Ontario, Canada, but capable of global research.

- Forebears Research & Associates
  http://www3.sympatico.ca/bill.forebears/
  London, Ontario

- The Genealogical Research Library
  http://www.grl.com/
  Toronto, Ontario

- Gen-Find Research Associates
  http://www.gen-find.com/
  Specialists in Genealogy Research for Ontario & Western Canada, Scotland, Ireland, Forensic Genealogy & 20th Century Research.

- Glenn King—Genealogy
  E-mail: kingdav@limestone.kosone.com
  *For details send e-mail to Glenn at: e-mail kingdav@ limestone.kosone.com
  Research, Canadian and U.K. records.*

- inGeneas Canadian Genealogical Research Services
  http://www.ingeneas.com/
  Ottawa

- The Official Iowa Counties Professional Genealogist and Researcher's Registry for Ontario
  http://www.iowa-counties.com/gene/oc.htm

- Research Etc.—Genealogy—Serving Muskoka District and Simcoe County
  http://www.bracebridge.com/genealogy/research.html
  Nancy Monnell, Orillia, Ontario Canada.

◆ Publications, Software & Supplies

- Books We Own—Ontario
  http://www.rootsweb.com/~bwo/can_o.html

- Global Genealogical Supply—Ontario Genealogical & Local History Books
  http://www.globalgenealogy.com/cdaont.htm

- The Ontario Genealogical Society's Publications List
  http://www.ogs.on.ca/pubs.htm
  Books for sale from the OGS.

◆ Queries, Message Boards & Surname Lists

- Lanark County Genealogical Society Members' Queries
  http://www.globalgenealogy.com/LCGS/LCGSQURY.HTM

- Queries—OntarioGenWeb
  http://www.rootsweb.com/~canon/ontquery.html

- Surnames—OntarioGenWeb
  http://www.geocities.com/SoHo/Nook/5996/firstsurnamepage.html

- Waterloo Genealogy Co-operative
  http://members.aol.com/ernm/roots/waterloo.html
  Colleagues Researching Waterloo, Ontario, Canada.

◆ Records: Census, Cemeteries, Land, Obituaries, Personal, Taxes and Vital (Born, Married, Died & Buried)

- 1842 Malahide Township Elgin County, Ontario Census Index
  http://www.ptbruce.kanservu.ca/Genealogy/1842Census.html

- 1871 Ontario Census Index
  http://www.archives.ca/db/1871/1871_Census_Search.html

- Bill Martin's Genealogy Page
  http://www.tbaytel.net/bmartin/
  Has several articles for Ontario genealogical research, including lists of microfilm numbers for ordering from the archives or an FHC.
  - The Archives of Ontario Microfilm InterLoan Catalog
    http://www.tbaytel.net/bmartin/archives.htm
  - Birth, Marriage, Death Indexes for Ontario, Canada
    http://www.tbaytel.net/bmartin/bmd.htm
  - Birth, Marriage and Death Application Form Instructions
    http://www.tbaytel.net/bmartin/registry.htm
  - LDS Film Numbers for Ontario Birth Registrations
    http://www.tbaytel.net/bmartin/lds-b.htm
  - LDS Film Numbers for Ontario Death Registrations
    http://www.tbaytel.net/bmartin/lds-d.htm
  - LDS Film Numbers for Ontario Marriage Registrations
    http://www.tbaytel.net/bmartin/lds-m.htm

- Erin Township, Wellington Co., Ontario Records
  http://www.chelmsford.com/home/priestner/Wellington.htm

- Lambton County Cemetery Index
  http://www.sarnia.com/groups/ogs/logs1.html

- Land Records in Ontario
  http://wwnet.com/~treesrch/ontland.html
- OCFA—The Ontario Cemetery Finding Aid
  http://www.islandnet.com/ocfa/homepage.html
- Ontario 1871 Census
  http://stauffer.queensu.ca/docsunit/searchc71.html
  and a new searchable format as well
  http://130.15.161.15/1871.htm
- Ontario Vital Statistics Bulletin
  http://www.gov.on.ca/MCZCR/archives/english/geneal/
  vtlstats.htm
  *Researching Birth, Death and Marriage Records in Ontario
  from the Archives of Ontario.*

◆ Religion & Churches

- Christianity.Net Church Locator—Ontario
  http://www.christianity.net/cgi/location.exe?Canada+Ontario
- Church Online!—Ontario
  http://www.churchonline.com/canadap/on/on.html
- Churches in Elgin County
  http://www.eversweb.on.ca/Churches-Elgin/
- Churches of the World—Ontario
  http://www.churchsurf.com/churches/Canada/Ontario
  From the ChurchSurf Christian Directory.

◆ Societies & Groups

- The British Isles Family History Society of
  Greater Ottawa
  http://www.cyberus.ca/~bifhsgo/
- Bruce County Genealogical Society
  http://www.compunik.com/vmall/bcgs/index.htm
- East Durham Historical Society
  http://www.nhb.com/edhs.htm
  Port Hope
- IOOF Lodge Website Directory—Ontario
  http://norm28.hsc.usc.edu/IOOF/International/Ontario.html
  Independent Order of Odd Fellows and Rebekahs.
- Lanark County Genealogical Society
  http://www.globalgenealogy.com/LCGS/
- Leeds & Grenville Genealogical Society
  http://www.cybertap.com/genealogy/
- The London & Middlesex Historical Society
  http://www.fanshawec.on.ca/~Debra/intro1.htm
- Millbrook & Cavan Historical Society
  http://www.kawartha.net/~mchs/mchs.htm
- Norfolk Historical Society
  http://www.norfolklore.com/
  Simcoe
- Ontario Genealogical Society
  http://www.ogs.on.ca/

- Brant County Branch, Ontario Genealogical
  Society
  http://www.wchat.on.ca:80/public/dwinn/dwinn1/
  ogsbrant.htm
- Bruce and Grey Branch of the Ontario
  Genealogical Society
  http://www.bmts.com/~bgogs/
- Elgin County Branch, Ontario Genealogical
  Society
  http://home.ican.net/~bedmonds/ElginOGS/
- Halton-Peel Branch, Ontario Genealogical Society
  http://www.hhpl.on.ca/sigs/ogshp/ogshp.htm
- Hamilton Branch, Ontario Genealogical Society
  http://www.hwcn.org/link/HBOGS/
- Kent County Branch of the Ontario Genealogical
  Society
  http://www.angelfire.com/on/kentogs/
- Kingston Branch, Ontario Genealogical Society
  http://post.queensu.ca/~murduckb/kgbrogs.htm
- Lambton County Branch, Ontario Genealogical
  Society
  http://www.sarnia.com/groups/ogs/lambton_page.html
- London & Middlesex County Branch of the
  Ontario Genealogical Society
  http://www.mirror.org/groups/genealogy/index.html
- Nipissing District Branch, Ontario Genealogical
  Society
  http://www.onlink.net/~twc/nipogs.htm
- The Norfolk County Branch of the Ontario
  Genealogical Society
  http://www.oxford.net/~mihaley/ogsnb/main.htm
- Ottawa Branch, Ontario Genealogical Society
  http://www.cyberus.ca/~ogsottawa/ogsottawa.htm
- La page de la SFOHG
  http://alumni.laurentian.ca/www/physplant/sfohg/
  societe.htm
  *Home page of the "Société franco-ontarienne d'histoire et de
  généalogie."*
- Quinte Branch, Ontario Genealogical Society
  http://www.pec.on.ca/history/geneol.html
- Sault Ste. Marie & District of Algoma, Branch of
  Ontario Genealogical Society
  http://www.soonet.ca/sdbogs-genealogy/
- Simcoe County Branch, Ontario Genealogical
  Society
  http://www.genweb.net/~simcoe/
- Sudbury Branch, Ontario Genealogical Society
  http://www.sudbury.com/Family_Services/Family_
  History/OGS/
- Waterloo-Wellington Branch, Ontario
  Genealogical Society
  http://www.dcs.uwaterloo.ca/~marj/genealogy/ww.html

- St. Catharines Historical Society
  http://www.niagara.com/~dmdorey/hssc/hssc.html

- Société Franco-Ontarienne d'histoire et de généalogie (SFOGH)
  http://www.glen-net.ca/sfohg/

- The Stormont, Dundas and Glengarry Historical Society
  http://www.cnwl.igs.net/~slm/sd&ghs.htm
  Cornwall, Ontario, Canada

- Temiskaming Genealogy Group
  http://www.nt.net/~timetrav/

- Toronto Cornish Association (TCA)
  http://www.digiserve.com/msyoung/tca.htm
  For those living in Ontario who are interested in the County of Cornwall in the UK.

- The United Empire Loyalists' Association of Canada
  http://www.npiec.on.ca/~uela/uela1.htm
  Toronto, Ontario, Canada

- Upper Ottawa Valley Genealogical Group
  http://www.valleynet.on.ca/Culture/Genealogy/UOVGG/index.html

- Waterloo Historical Society
  http://www.dcs.uwaterloo.ca/~marj/history/whs.html

- Wellington County Historical Society
  http://www.dcs.uwaterloo.ca/~marj/history/wellington.html

CANADA—PRINCE EDWARD ISLAND
http://www.CyndisList.com/pei.htm

Category Index:
- General Resource Sites
- Government & Cities
- History & Culture
- Libraries, Archives & Museums
- Mailing Lists, Newsgroups & Chat
- Maps, Gazetteers & Geographical Information
- People & Families

- Professional Researchers, Volunteers & Other Research Services
- Publications, Software & Supplies
- Queries, Message Boards & Surname Lists
- Records: Census, Cemeteries, Land, Obituaries, Personal, Taxes and Vital
- Religion & Churches
- Societies & Groups

◆ General Resource Sites
- Canadian Genealogy and History Links—
  Prince Edward Island
  http://www.islandnet.com/~jveinot/cghl/prince-edward-island.html
- Genealogy Resources on the Internet:
  Prince Edward Island
  http://www-personal.umich.edu/~cgaunt/canada.html#PEI
- The Island Register
  http://www.isn.net/~dhunter/index.html
  Prince Edward Island's First Genealogy Home Page.
- Prince Edward Island GenWeb Project
  http://www.isn.net/~dhunter/pegenweb.html
- Robertson Library Research Guide for Genealogy
  http://www.upei.ca/~library/info/guides/geneal.html

◆ Government & Cities
- The Prince Edward Island Information Centre
  http://www.gov.pe.ca/
- Yahoo! Canada....Prince Edward Island: Cities
  http://www.yahoo.ca/Regional/Countries/Canada/Provinces_and_Territories/Prince_Edward_Island/Cities/

◆ History & Culture
- Heritage Highlights
  http://www.isn.net/~dhunter/heritage.html
- Pioneer Life on P.E.I.
  http://www.isn.net/~dhunter/life.html
- Prince Edward Island Information Centre
  http://www.gov.pe.ca/

◆ Libraries, Archives & Museums
- HYTELNET Library Catalogs: Canada:
  Prince Edward Island
  http://library.usask.ca/hytelnet/ca0/PEI.html
  Before you use any of the Telnet links, make note of the user name, password and any other logon information.
- Prince Edward Island Museum and
  Heritage Foundation
  http://www.metamedia.pe.ca/peimuseum/
  and a description from the Island Register site
  http://www.isn.net/~dhunter/peimhf.html
- Prince Edward Island Provincial Library Service
  http://www.library.pe.ca/
- Prince Edward Island Public Archives and
  Records Office
  http://www.gov.pe.ca/educ/archives/archives_index.html
- Robertson Library Homepage—University of
  Prince Edward Island
  http://www.upei.ca/~library/
- United Church of Canada Archives Network:
  Maritime Conference Archives
  http://www.uccan.org/archives/maritime.htm
  A summary of their holdings and contact information.

◆ Mailing Lists, Newsgroups & Chat
- atlantic-province Mailing List
  http://members.aol.com/gfsjohnf/gen_mail_country-can.html#ATLANTIC-PROVINCES-CANADA
  For the Atlantic Provinces of Canada—Nova Scotia, Newfoundland, Labrador, and Prince Edward Island.
- CANADIAN ROOTS Mailing List
  http://members.aol.com/gfsjohnf/gen_mail_country-can.html#CANADIAN-ROOTS

- PEI-ROOTS Mailing List
  http://members.aol.com/gfsjohnf/gen_mail_country-
  can.html#PEI-ROOTS

- SURNAMES-CANADA Mailing List
  http://members.aol.com/gfsjohnf/gen_mail_country-
  can.html#SURNAMES-CANADA
  *For surname queries related to Canada. Gatewayed with the
  soc.genealogy.surnames.canada newsgroup.*

◆ Maps, Gazetteers & Geographical Information

- Canadian Geographical Names / Les noms
  géographiques du Canada
  http://GeoNames.NRCan.gc.ca/

  ○ Canadian Geographical Names—Publications
    http://GeoNames.NRCan.gc.ca/english/publications.html
    *List of available publications on geographical names
    including policy documents and manuals, gazetteers,
    glossaries, newsletters and brochures.*

  ○ Origins of Canada's Geographical Names
    http://GeoNames.NRCan.gc.ca/english/schoolnet/origin.html

  ○ Query by Geographical Name
    http://Geonames.NRCan.gc.ca/english/cgndb.html

  ○ Current Names Selected by Coordinates
    http://Geonames.NRCan.gc.ca/english/cgndb_coord.html
    *Search this database of over 500,000 geographical names by
    name, feature type, region and by province.*

- Excite Maps: Prince Edward Island
  http://city.net/maps/view/?mapurl=/countries/canada/
  prince_edward_island

◆ People & Families

- The DYMENT Genealogy—Prince Edward Island
  http://www.sentex.net/~dyment/pei-gen/index.html
  *DYMENT, LADNER, ENMAN, NISBET, and FOLLAND. Also
  some MOORE and RAMSAY from P.E.I.*

- Marge Reid's Irish-Canadian Heritage
  http://homepages.rootsweb.com/~mvrgen/mvrgen/irish.html
  Databases, transcriptions, indexes and more.

- Prince Edward Island Surnames
  http://www.isn.net/~dhunter/gindex.html

- Tribes and Bands of Prince Edward Island
  http://hanksville.phast.umass.edu:8000/cultprop/contacts/
  tribal/PEI.html

◆ Professional Researchers, Volunteers & Other Research Services

- Gen-Find Research Associates
  http://www.gen-find.com/
  *Specialists in Genealogy Research for Ontario & Western
  Canada, Scotland, Ireland. Also the rest of Canada and Forensic
  & Probate/Heir Research and 20th Century Research.*

◆ Publications, Software & Supplies

- Books We Own—Prince Edward Island
  http://www.rootsweb.com/~bwo/can_pei.html

- Global Genealogical Supply—Atlantic Provinces
  Genealogical & Local History Books
  http://www.globalgenealogy.com/cdaatlan.htm

◆ Queries, Message Boards & Surname Lists

- Prince Edward Island Surname List
  http://www.geocities.com/Heartland/Acres/4835/index.html

◆ Records: Census, Cemeteries, Land, Obituaries, Personal, Taxes and Vital (Born, Married, Died & Buried)

- 1768 St. John's Island Heads of Household Census
  http://www.isn.net/~dhunter/1768.html

- Central United Cemetery—Dunstaffnage
  http://www.rootsweb.com/~pictou/cucdun.htm

- Covehead Tracadie Marriages 1887–1900
  http://homepages.rootsweb.com/~mvreid/pei/34mar.html
  For Covehead, Corran Ban, Tracadie in Queens County.

- Index to PEI Database Reports
  http://www.eskimo.com/~mvreid/peibidx.html
  *A wonderful collection of resources from Marge Reid, including
  probate records, surname indexes for marriage and burial
  records and much more.*

- Index to PEI Probate Records
  http://www.eskimo.com/~mvreid/peiprbt.html

- Index to the 1891 Census of Prince Edward Island
  http://homepages.rootsweb.com/~mvreid/pei/34mar.html

- Little Sands Cemetery
  http://www.rootsweb.com/~pictou/lilsands.htm

- Long Creek Baptist Church Cemetery
  http://www.rootsweb.com/~pictou/longcree.htm

- Lovely Nelly Passenger Lists, 1774 & 1775
  http://www.rootsweb.com/~pictou/lnell1.htm
  From Galloway, Scotland to Prince Edward Island.

- The Passenger List of the "Alexander," and the
  Glenaladale Settlers
  http://www.isn.net/~dhunter/alexandr.html
  *May 1772 from Greenock, Scotland to Prince Edward Island,
  Canada.*

- Passenger List of the "Jane"
  http://www.isn.net/~dhunter/jane.html
  From Drimindarach, Scotland, July 12, 1790.

- Passenger List of the "Lucy" 1790
  http://www.isn.net/~dhunter/lucy.html
  *In the company of the "Jane," from Scotland to Prince Edward
  Island, Canada.*

- PEI Burial Records—1892–1900
  http://homepages.rootsweb.com/~mvreid/pei/34burabs.html
  St. Eugene's (CoveHead), St. Michael's (Corran Ban), St. Bonaventure's (Tracadie)

- Prince Edward Island Cemeteries Page
  http://www.isn.net/~dhunter/cem.html
  Includes "Extract from the Death Registers," St. Patrick's Roman Catholic Church in Ft. Augustus, P.E.I.

- Wood Island Cemetery (established 1882)
  http://www.rootsweb.com/~pictou/wdi.htm

- Wood Islands Pioneer Cemetery 1807–1910
  http://www.rootsweb.com/~pictou/wdislan.htm

◆ Religion & Churches

- Christianity.Net Church Locator—
  Prince Edward Island
  http://www.christianity.net/cgi/
  location.exe?Canada+Prince_Edward_Island

- Church Online!—Prince Edward Island
  http://www.churchonline.com/canadap/pe/pe.html

- Churches of the World—Prince Edward Island
  http://www.churchsurf.com/churches/Canada/
  Prince_Edward_Island
  From the ChurchSurf Christian Directory.

◆ Societies & Groups

- IOOF Lodge Website Directory—Atlantic Provinces
  http://norm28.hsc.usc.edu/IOOF/International/
  AtlanticProvinces.html
  Independent Order of Odd Fellows and Rebekahs.

- The Prince Edward Island Genealogical Society
  http://www.isn.net/~dhunter/peigs.html

- The Prince Edward Island Museum and
  Heritage Foundation
  E-mail: peimuse@cycor.ca
  E-mail them at: peimuse@cycor.ca and they will accept general queries, as well as queries about books that are available on PEI genealogy and history.

CANADA—QUEBEC
http://www.CyndisList.com/quebec.htm

Category Index:

- General Resource Sites
- Government & Cities
- History & Culture
- Libraries, Archives & Museums
- Mailing Lists, Newsgroups & Chat
- Maps, Gazetteers & Geographical Information
- Military
- People & Families

- Professional Researchers, Volunteers & Other Research Services
- Publications, Software & Supplies
- Records: Census, Cemeteries, Land, Obituaries, Personal, Taxes and Vital
- Religion & Churches
- Societies & Groups

◆ General Resource Sites

- Canadian Genealogy and History Links—Quebec
  http://www.islandnet.com/~jveinot/cghl/quebec.html
- Denis Beauregard Genealogy Page
  http://www.cam.org/~beaur/gen/welcome.html
- Genealogy Bulletin Board Systems for Quebec
  http://www.genealogy.org/~gbbs/gblpq.html
- Genealogy of Quebec's Native People and francophone Metis
  http://www.cam.org/~beaur/gen/amerin-e.html
- Genealogy Resources on the Internet: Quebec
  http://www-personal.umich.edu/~cgaunt/canada.html#QUEBEC
- Pontiac County, Quebec Genealogical Resources
  http://www.valleynet.on.ca/~aa127/uovgen/pontiac.html
- Projet GenWeb du Québec
  http://www.rootsweb.com/~canqc/index.htm
- Quebec Genealogy Page
  http://www.cam.org/~beaur/gen/quebec-e.html

◆ Government & Cities

- Gouvernement du Québec / Government of Québec
  http://www.gouv.qc.ca/anglais/
- Yahoo! Canada....Quebec: Cities
  http://www.yahoo.ca/Regional/Countries/Canada/Provinces_and_Territories/Quebec/Cities/

◆ History & Culture

- Montreal Important Dates
  http://www.cam.org/~fishon1/date.html

- La Ville de Rivière-du-Loup
  http://icrdl.net/~mlagace/rdl.htm
  The City of Rivière-du-Loup
  http://icrdl.net/~mlagace/rdla.htm
  by Mireille LAGACÉ.

◆ Libraries, Archives & Museums

- Archives Nationales du Québec
  http://www.anq.gouv.qc.ca/
- Les Centres Généalogiques SDJ / LDS Family History Centers
  http://www.et.byu.edu/~harmanc/paris/genealogie.html
  France, Belgique, Suisse, Canada
- HYTELNET Library Catalogs: Canada: Quebec
  http://library.usask.ca/hytelnet/ca0/PQ.html
  Before you use any of the Telnet links, make note of the user name, password and any other logon information.
- United Church of Canada Archives Network: Montreal and Ottawa Conference Archives
  http://www.uccan.org/archives/montreal.htm
  A summary of their holdings and contact information.

◆ Mailing Lists, Newsgroups & Chat

- CANADIAN ROOTS Mailing List
  http://members.aol.com/gfsjohnf/gen_mail_country-can.html#CANADIAN-ROOTS
- GEN-FF Mailing List
  http://members.aol.com/gfsjohnf/gen_mail_country-fra.html#GEN-FF-L
  Discussion of Francophone genealogy. Gatewayed with fr.rec.genealogie. Mainly in French.

- GEN-FR Mailing List
  http://members.aol.com/gfsjohnf/gen_mail_country-fra.html#GEN-FR-L
  Discussion of Francophone genealogy. Gatewayed with soc.genealogy.french. Mainly in English.

- QC-ETANGLO Mailing List
  http://members.aol.com/gfsjohnf/gen_mail_country-can.html#QC-ETANGLO
  For anyone researching Anglo-Protestant roots within any of the 11 Quebec, Canada counties that make up the Eastern Townships (i.e., Arthabaska, Brome, Compton, Drummond, Megantic, Missisquoi, Richmond, Shefford, Sherbrooke, Stanstead, Wolfe).

- quebec Mailing List
  http://members.aol.com/gfsjohnf/gen_mail_country-can.html#QUEBEC-CANADA

- SURNAMES-CANADA Mailing List
  http://members.aol.com/gfsjohnf/gen_mail_country-can.html#SURNAMES-CANADA
  For surname queries related to Canada. Gatewayed with the soc.genealogy.surnames.canada newsgroup.

- UOVGEN—The Upper Ottawa Valley Genealogy Mailing List
  http://members.aol.com/gfsjohnf/gen_mail_country-can.html#UOVGEN
  and the corresponding web page
  http://www.valleynet.on.ca/~aa127/uovgen/uovgen.html
  For Renfrew and Pontiac Counties of the Upper Ottawa Valley region of Ontario and Quebec.

- UPPER-CANADA Mailing List
  http://members.aol.com/gfsjohnf/gen_mail_country-can.html#UPPER-CANADA
  For anyone with a genealogical interest in Upper Canada, the region split from the Province of Quebec after the American Revolution, including its history and settlement by Loyalists and British and German soldiers, up to and including the year 1841.

◆ Maps, Gazetteers & Geographical Information

- Canadian Geographical Names / Les noms géographiques du Canada
  http://GeoNames.NRCan.gc.ca/
  - Canadian Geographical Names—Publications
    http://GeoNames.NRCan.gc.ca/english/publications.html
    List of available publications on geographical names including policy documents and manuals, gazetteers, glossaries, newsletters and brochures.
  - Origins of Canada's Geographical Names
    http://GeoNames.NRCan.gc.ca/english/schoolnet/origin.html
  - Query by Geographical Name
    http://Geonames.NRCan.gc.ca/english/cgndb.html
  - Current Names Selected by Coordinates
    http://Geonames.NRCan.gc.ca/english/cgndb_coord.html
    Search this database of over 500,000 geographical names by name, feature type, region and by province.

- Excite Maps: Quebec
  http://city.net/maps/view/?mapurl=/countries/canada/quebec

◆ Military

- 1755—The French and Indian War Home Page
  http://web.syr.edu/~laroux/

◆ People & Families

- Aline's French-Canadian Ancestors
  http://members.tripod.com/~AlineB/index.html
  CHARTRAND, DESJARDINS, ROIREAU DIT LALIBERTY, LIBERTY

- Association des Familles MORISSETTE Inc.
  http://www.genealogie.org/famille/morissette/morissette.htm

- Bienvenue chez Mireille LAGACÉ
  http://icrdl.net/~mlagace/
  LAGACÉ, DICKNER, ROY, DUMONT

- Les Descendants des FRÉCHETTE, Inc.
  http://www.angelfire.com/ca/frechette/

- Descendents of Andre MORIN and Marguerite MOREAU
  http://www.newnorth.net/~kind/morin.html
  Settled in Quebec around 1665 and married in 1670.

- Donna's Genealogy Homepage
  http://members.aol.com/donnawalt/donnas.htm
  ANTAYA, BOULAY, BOEMIER, BERGERON, BOURDEAU, DROUILLARD, CLERMONT, DEMERS, MONTMINY, PELLITIER and many more.

- Don's Home Page of Genealogy of the DUBE's
  http://www.geocities.com/Heartland/Pointe/4910/castle.html
  ST-LAURENT, DEVINE, BRODEUR, DUBE, LANDRY, BONENFANT, BRETON, CHAMPION, LONDON, ARCENEAULT, LYONS and McEWIN (McKEONE)

- Généalogie TELLIER / LAFORTUNE
  http://www3.sympatico.ca/mlafortu/
  LETELLIER, TELLIER, LAFORTUNE

- Genealogy Home Page of Jacques L'HEUREUX
  http://www.concentric.net/~lheureux/genealogy.html
  L'HEUREUX, LEUREAU, BARIL, DUMONT, MUELLER, MERLE AND ST-ARNAULT, ST-ARNAUD

- Hebridean Scots of the Province of Quebec
  http://www.geocities.com/~hebridscots/
  BOHLMAN, BRUMBAUGH, CLAPPER, FELDHAHN, FELDHAN, FELDTON, FELTON, FRANT, FRIEND, WALDRON

- Le HOUYMET Internet—Home on the Internet of Les Descendants de Jean OUIMET, Inc.
  http://www.geocities.com/~couimet/lehouymet.html
  Ouimet, Houymet, Vilmet, Wemet, Wemett, Wuillemette, Wilmot and numerous other spelling variations.

- Hugi's Homepage
  http://www.connect.ab.ca/~hjobin/
  Researching French Quebec names. DESHETRES, DESHAIES, DESHAYES, PAGE, PROU, PROULX, JOBIN.

- Karen FARMER's Kinfolk—Genealogy in Nova Scotia, Ontario and Quebec
  http://www.geocities.com/Heartland/Plains/7525/
  BEZANSON, CLEROUX, CROCKETT, FARMER, LANGILLE, STEVENS & TATTRIE

- The LAROCQUE Family of America Home Page
  http://www.easynet.on.ca/~larocque/laroc1e.htm
  Descendants of Philibert Couillaud de La Roque de Roquebrune who came to Canada in 1665 with the regiment of Carignan, from France.

- La page de la famille PAYER
  http://ww.total.net/~jlpayer/
  BAYER, PAYER, PAYEUR

- The PICHE, PICHETTE and DUPRE Families
  http://www.abacom.com/~dgdupre/

- Régis CORBIN
  http://www.hawk.igs.net/~letanu/
  CORBIN and BELZILE (Gagnon dit)

- The RODRIGUE Families
  http://www.er.uqam.ca/nobel/g17176/rodrigue/engindex.html
  Quebec and Ontario in Canada, Louisiana and New England in the U.S.

- Les ROUSSEL en Amérique du Nord / ROUSSEL Families in North America
  http://www.cam.org/~mauricel

- Tribes and Bands of Quebec
  http://hanksville.phast.umass.edu:8000/cultprop/contacts/tribal/QU.html

◆ Professional Researchers, Volunteers & Other Research Services

- Eastern Townships of Quebec Genealogy
  http://www.virtuel.qc.ca/simmons/
  Marlene Simmons has indexed 490,000 church, census, newspaper, cemetery, some Vermont vital records, and other miscellaneous records.

- The Official Iowa Counties Professional Genealogist and Researcher's Registry for Quebec
  http://www.iowa-counties.com/gene/qc.htm

◆ Publications, Software & Supplies

- Books We Own—Quebec
  http://www.rootsweb.com/~bwo/can_q.html

- Centre de recherches généalogiques du Québec
  http://www.cam.org/~cdrgduq/
  Parchment certificates for sale with more than 4,000 names from French-Canadian and Acadian origins.

- Global Genealogical Supply—Quebec (Lower Canada) Genealogical & Local History Books
  http://www.globalgenealogy.com/cdaque.htm

◆ Records: Census, Cemeteries, Land, Obituaries, Personal, Taxes and Vital (Born, Married, Died & Buried)

- French Canadian Heads-of-Households in the Province of Quebec in 1871—Cities Beginning with A–C
  http://www.oz.net/~johnbang/genealogy/quebecac.txt
  D–L
  http://www.oz.net/~johnbang/genealogy/quebecdl.txt
  L–M
  http://www.oz.net/~johnbang/genealogy/quebeclm.txt

- Index to the 1744 Quebec City Census
  http://www.oz.net/~johnbang/genealogy/1744indx.txt

◆ Religion & Churches

- Christianity.Net Church Locator—Quebec
  http://www.christianity.net/cgi/location.exe?Canada+Quebec

- Church Online!—Quebec
  http://www.churchonline.com/canadap/pq/pq.html

- Churches of the World—Quebec
  http://www.churchsurf.com/churches/Canada/Quebec
  From the ChurchSurf Christian Directory.

◆ Societies & Groups

- Club De Généalogie De Longueuil
  http://www.total.net:8080/~clubcgl/index1.html

- Fédération des Familles-Souches Québécoises Inc.
  http://www.mediom.qc.ca/~ffsq/

- Fédération québécoise des sociétés de généalogie
  http://www.federationgenealogie.qc.ca/

- FRANCETRES: Genealogie du Quebec—Sociétés de généalogie/Genealogical Societies
  http://www.cam.org/~beaur/gen/qc-bib-f.html#societes

- IOOF Lodge Website Directory—Quebec
  http://norm28.hsc.usc.edu/IOOF/International/Quebec.html
  Independent Order of Odd Fellows and Rebekahs.

- Libertel: SGEQ—Répertoire des associations de familles
  http://www.libertel.org/site/sgeq/familles.htm

- Quebec Family History Society Home Page
  http://www.cam.org/~qfhs/index.html

- Société de généalogie de Québec
  http://www.genealogie.org/club/sgq/sgq.htm

- Société d'Histoire et de Généalogie de Rivière-du-Loup
  http://icrdl.net/~mlagace/shgrdla.htm

- Société d'Histoire et de Généalogie
  Maria-Chapdelaine
  http://www.destination.ca/~francois/shg/societe.html

- Société généalogique d'Argenteuil—
  Argenteuil County Genealogical Society
  http://www.hawk.igs.net/~letanu/sga.htm

- Société Généalogique Canadienne-Française
  http://www.sgcf.com/
  Montreal

- Société Généalogique De L'est Du Québec (SGEQ)
  http://www.genealogie.org/club/sgeq/sgeq.htm

CANADA—SASKATCHEWAN

http://www.CyndisList.com/sask.htm

Category Index:

- ◆ General Resource Sites
- ◆ Government & Cities
- ◆ Libraries, Archives & Museums
- ◆ Mailing Lists, Newsgroups & Chat
- ◆ Maps, Gazetteers & Geographical Information
- ◆ Newspapers
- ◆ People & Families

- ◆ Professional Researchers, Volunteers & Other Research Services
- ◆ Publications, Software & Supplies
- ◆ Queries, Message Boards & Surname Lists
- ◆ Records: Census, Cemeteries, Land, Obituaries, Personal, Taxes and Vital
- ◆ Religion & Churches
- ◆ Societies & Groups

◆ General Resource Sites

- ● Canadian Genealogy and History Links— Saskatchewan
  http://www.islandnet.com/~jveinot/cghl/saskatchewan.html

- ● Genealogy Resources on the Internet: Saskatchewan
  http://www-personal.umich.edu/~cgaunt/canada.html#SASK

- ● St. Joseph's Colony
  http://www.rootsweb.com/~skstjose/stjoseph.html

- ● Saskatchewan GenWeb
  http://www.rootsweb.com/~cansk/Saskatchewan/

- ● Saskatchewan Yellow Pages
  http://www.saskyellowpages.com/
  - ○ Residential Search
    http://www.saskyellowpages.com/search/main.cgi
  - ○ Business Search
    http://www2.saskyellowpages.com/

◆ Government & Cities

- ● City of Regina—Regina's Heritage Index
  http://www.cityregina.com/info/heritage/index.shtml

- ● Government of Saskatchewan
  http://www.gov.sk.ca/default.htm

- ● Yahoo! Canada....Saskatchewan: Cities
  http://www.yahoo.ca/Regional/Countries/Canada/Provinces_and_Territories/Saskatchewan/Cities/

◆ Libraries, Archives & Museums

- ● The Hudson's Bay Company Archives
  http://www.gov.mb.ca/chc/archives/hbca/index.html
  From the Provincial Archives of Manitoba, Canada.

- ● HYTELNET Library Catalogs: Canada: Saskatchewan
  http://library.usask.ca/hytelnet/ca0/SK.html
  Before you use any of the Telnet links, make note of the user name, password and any other logon information.

- ● United Church of Canada Archives Network: Saskatchewan Conference Archives
  http://www.uccan.org/archives/saskatchewan.htm
  A summary of their holdings and contact information.

- ● University of Saskatchewan—Department of History
  http://www.usask.ca/history/

◆ Mailing Lists, Newsgroups & Chat

- ● CANADIAN ROOTS Mailing List
  http://members.aol.com/gfsjohnf/gen_mail_country-can.html#CANADIAN-ROOTS

- ● CAN-SASKATCHEWAN Mailing List
  http://members.aol.com/gfsjohnf/gen_mail_country-can.html#CAN-SASKATCHEWAN

- ● saskatchewan Mailing List
  http://members.aol.com/gfsjohnf/gen_mail_country-can.html#SASKATCHEWAN-CANADA

- ● SURNAMES-CANADA Mailing List
  http://members.aol.com/gfsjohnf/gen_mail_country-can.html#SURNAMES-CANADA
  For surname queries related to Canada. Gatewayed with the soc.genealogy.surnames.canada newsgroup.

◆ Maps, Gazetteers & Geographical Information

- ● Canadian Geographical Names / Les noms géographiques du Canada
  http://GeoNames.NRCan.gc.ca/

○ Canadian Geographical Names—Publications
http://GeoNames.NRCan.gc.ca/english/publications.html
*List of available publications on geographical names
including policy documents and manuals, gazetteers,
glossaries, newsletters and brochures.*

○ Origins of Canada's Geographical Names
http://GeoNames.NRCan.gc.ca/english/schoolnet/origin.html

○ Query by Geographical Name
http://Geonames.NRCan.gc.ca/english/cgndb.html

○ Current Names Selected by Coordinates
http://Geonames.NRCan.gc.ca/english/cgndb_coord.html
*Search this database of over 500,000 geographical names by
name, feature type, region and by province.*

● Excite Maps: Saskatchewan
http://city.net/maps/view/?mapurl=/countries/canada/
saskatchewan

◆ Newspapers

● Leader-Post Online
http://www.leader-post.sk.ca/
Regina

● Prince Albert Daily Herald Online Edition
http://www.paherald.sk.ca/prin/Start.htm

● The StarPhoenix Online
http://www.saskstar.sk.ca/
Saskatoon

◆ People & Families

● Doukhobor Home Page
http://www.dlcwest.com/~r.androsoff/index.htm
*A group of Russian peasants that split from the Russian Ortho-
dox Church. Large groups of Doukhobors emigrated to Canada
and homesteaded in Saskatchewan and British Columbia.*

● Hutterite Genealogy HomePage and Cross-Index
http://feefhs.org/hut/indexhut.html

● The Jewish Genealogical Exploration Guide for
Manitoba and Saskatchewan (J-GEMS)
http://www.concentric.net/~Lkessler/jgems.shtml

● Tribes and Bands of Saskatchewan
http://hanksville.phast.umass.edu:8000/cultprop/contacts/
tribal/SK.html

◆ Professional Researchers, Volunteers & Other Research Services

● Gen-Find Research Associates
http://www.gen-find.com/
*Specialists in Genealogy Research for Ontario & Western
Canada, Scotland, Ireland. Also the rest of Canada and Forensic
& Probate/Heir Research and 20th Century Research.*

◆ Publications, Software & Supplies

● Books We Own—Saskatchewan
http://www.rootsweb.com/~bwo/can_sas.html

● Global Genealogical Supply—Western Canada
Genealogical & Local History Books
http://www.globalgenealogy.com/cdawest.htm

◆ Queries, Message Boards & Surname Lists

● Genealogical Queries from the Saskatchewan
Genealogical Society
http://www.saskgenealogy.com/queries/queries.htm

◆ Records: Census, Cemeteries, Land, Obituaries, Personal, Taxes and Vital (Born, Married, Died & Buried)

● City of Saskatoon: Woodlawn Cemetery
http://www.city.saskatoon.sk.ca/departments/public_works/
cemetery/default.htm

○ The Nutana Cemetery—Saskatoon's
Pioneer Cemetery
http://www.city.saskatoon.sk.ca/departments/public_works/
cemetery/nutana/nutana1.htm

● Prairie Epitaph—Catholic Cemetery in Salvador,
Saskatchewan
http://mars.ark.com/~rbell/html/history/epitaph.html
Many German Russian families.

● Saskatchewan Cemetery Index
http://www.saskgenealogy.com/cemetery/cemetery.htm

◆ Religion & Churches

● Christianity.Net Church Locator—Saskatchewan
http://www.christianity.net/cgi/
location.exe?Canada+Saskatchewan

● Church Online!—Saskatchewan
http://www.churchonline.com/canadap/sk/sk.html

● Churches of the World—Saskatchewan
http://www.churchsurf.com/churches/Canada/Saskatchewan
From the ChurchSurf Christian Directory.

◆ Societies & Groups

● IOOF Lodge Website Directory—Saskatchewan
http://norm28.hsc.usc.edu/IOOF/International/
Saskatchewan.html
Independent Order of Odd Fellows and Rebekahs.

● Saskatchewan Genealogical Society
http://www.saskgenealogy.com/

CEMETERIES & FUNERAL HOMES
http://www.CyndisList.com/cemetery.htm

Category Index:

- ◆ Cemeteries & Funeral Homes
- ◆ How To
- ◆ Mailing Lists, Newsgroups & Chat
- ◆ Publications, Software & Supplies
- ◆ Societies & Groups

◆ Cemeteries & Funeral Homes

- Abney Park Cemetery Trust
  http://www.abney-park.org.uk/
  London, England

- Addison Township Cemetery Index
  http://www.dcgs.org/addison/
  Du Page County, Illinois

- African Burial Ground Archeological Project
  http://www.afrinet.net/~hallh/abg.html
  Manhattan

- Alberta Genealogical Society Master Name Index
  http://www.compusmart.ab.ca/abgensoc/nameindex.html
  Canada. A database of about 400,000 names, including mostly cemetery records and tombstone inscriptions. They can search the database for a small fee.

- Allen County, Ohio Cemetery Page
  http://www.geocities.com/Heartland/Plains/5409/cem.html
  From The GIERHART Family Inn.

- Allendale / Bamberg / Barnwell County Cemeteries
  http://www.rootsweb.com/~scbarnwe/Cemeteries.htm
  South Carolina

- Anchorage Memorial Park Cemetery
  http://www.atu.com/community/points/pnt016.html
  Alaska

- The Apache Cemetery, at Apache, Cochise County, Arizona
  http://www.amug.org/~mzwhiz/cemetery.html

- Aquia Church Page
  http://www.illuminet.net/aquiachurch/cemetary.html
  Cemetery listing of Aquia Episcopal Church, Stafford, Virginia (Stafford County). Includes cemetery locations and map.

- Arlington National Cemetery
  http://www.arlingtoncemetery.com/

- Arlington National Cemetery
  http://www.mdw.army.mil/cemetery.htm
  General information and a map.

- Associated Catholic Cemeteries, Archdiocese of Seattle
  http://www.acc-seattle.com/
  Washington

- Autauga County, Alabama Cemetery Listings
  http://searches.rootsweb.com/cgi-bin/autauga/auta-cem.pl

- Beaton Cemetery, Millbrook, Pictou County
  http://www.rootsweb.com/~pictou/beaton.htm
  Nova Scotia, Canada

- Becker County, Minnesota, Cemeteries
  http://www.rootsweb.com/~mnbecker/cemeteries.htm
  List of cemeteries in Becker County, Minnesota with links to GNIS which gives location and online map.

- Black River Cemetery, Pictou County
  http://www.rootsweb.com/~pictou/blackriv.htm
  Nova Scotia, Canada

- Blanchard Road Cemetery, Pictou County
  http://www.rootsweb.com/~pictou/blanch.htm
  Nova Scotia, Canada

- Books for Sale: Douglas County, Missouri— Cemetery Survey of the Eastern District of Douglas County, Missouri
  http://members.aol.com/LaineBelle/HomePage.html

- Boren-Reagor Springs Cemetery
  http://www.geocities.com/Heartland/Prairie/1746/boren.html
  The Boren-Reagor Springs Cemetery page has biographical information on individuals buried in the cemetery with a completed listing of all who are buried there. Links included to Civil War History of those buried in the cemetery and of other Boren descendants. Also included in the history of the Lee-Peacock Feud. Texas.

- British Columbia Cemetery Finding Aid
  http://www.islandnet.com/bccfa/homepage.html
  Canada

- Brookville Cemetery, Pictou County
  http://www.rootsweb.com/~pictou/brookvll.htm
  Nova Scotia, Canada

- Brown Co. IL Bell-Perry Cemeteries
  http://www.geocities.com/Heartland/Valley/7991/
  b_p_cems.html
- Buck Creek Cemetery, Colquitt County, Georgia
  http://www.ij.net/phickey/buckck.htm
- Burial Point Cemetery, Merigomish
  http://www.rootsweb.com/~pictou/bpoint.htm
  Nova Scotia, Canada
- Burials of Easton, Plainfield, Mount Bethel,
  Forks and Dryland
  http://www.geocities.com/Heartland/6508/#Burials of
  Easton,Plainfield,Mount Bethel,Forks and Dryland,
  Pennsylvania
- Camden and Charlton County Cemetery Records
  Online
  http://www.gate.net/~tutcher/cemetery/ceme_index.html
  Georgia
- Camp Moore Confederate Cemetery and Museum
  http://home.gulfsouth.verio.net/~harper1/
- Carter County Missouri Cemeteries
  http://www.mindspring.com/~sapart/cartcmtr.html
  - Aldrich Valley Cemetery
    http://www.mindspring.com/~sapart/aldrchcm.html
  - Brame Cemetery
    http://www.mindspring.com/~sapart/brmecemt.html
  - Bristol Cemetery
    http://www.mindspring.com/~sapart/bristlcm.html
  - Eastwood Cemetery
    http://www.mindspring.com/~sapart/cemin.html
  - Midco Cemtery
    http://www.mindspring.com/~sapart/midcocmt.html
  - Seats Family Cemetery
    http://www.mindspring.com/~sapart/seatscmt.html
- Cascade County Montana Cemetery Index
  http://www.rootsweb.com/~mtcascad/cemetery/cemet.html
- Cayuga County, NYGenWeb Project Cemetery List
  http://www.rootsweb.com/~nycayuga/cemetery.htm
- Cemeteries
  http://www.totentanz.de/cemetery.htm
  Formerly titled World Wide Index of Cemeteries on the Net.
  - Cemeteries in Africa
    http://www.totentanz.de/africa.htm
  - Cemeteries in Asia
    http://www.totentanz.de/asia.htm
  - Cemeteries in Australia
    http://www.totentanz.de/australi.htm
  - Cemeteries in America
    http://www.totentanz.de/america.htm
  - Cemeteries in Europe
    http://www.totentanz.de/europe.htm

  - US Cemeteries
    http://www.totentanz.de/usa.htm
- Cemeteries
  http://www.geocities.com/Heartland/Acres/4348/
  cemeteries.html
  *Two abandoned cemeteries in Cabell County and Wayne County,
  West Virginia.*
- Cemeteries, Graveyards, Burying Grounds
  http://www.potifos.com/cemeteries.html
  Links to resources on cemetery history and preservation.
- Cemeteries in and around Gunning Shire,
  New South Wales
  http://www.pcug.org.au/~gchallin/cemeteries/top.htm
  Australia
- Cemeteries in Onondaga County, New York
  http://www.rootsweb.com/~nyononda/CEMETERY.HTM
- Cemeteries Listed on the U.S. Civil War Center
  web page
  http://www.cwc.lsu.edu/links/hist.htm#Cemeteries
- The Cemeteries of Chautauqua County, NY
  http://www.rootsweb.com/~nychauta/CEMETERY/
  TOWN_CEM.HTM
- Cemeteries of Martha's Vineyard
  http://www.vineyard.net/vineyard/history/cemetery/cemlist.htm
  *Massachusetts. Links to photographs, transcripts, and notes on
  gravestones at Company Place Cemetery, West Chop Cemetery,
  Christiantown, and other sites on Martha's Vineyard.*
- The Cemeteries of Minnesota
  http://www.gac.edu/~kengelha/cemeteries.html
  List of cemeteries in Minnesota, county by county.
- Cemeteries of Monroe Co., MI
  http://206.42.132.11/havekost/cemetery.htm
  Michigan
- Cemeteries of Orleans County, New York
  http://www.rootsweb.com/~nyorlean/cemetery.htm
- Cemeteries of Pictou County
  http://www.rootsweb.com/~pictou/oldest.htm
  *Excerpted from "The Stone Book of Pictou County" by Donald
  Nicholson. The statistics are listed by cemetery, including the
  oldest birth year, oldest death year, oldest age at death. Nova
  Scotia, Canada.*
- The Cemeteries of Rutherford County, NC
  http://rfci.net/wdfloyd/
- Cemeteries of Tallahatchie County Mississippi
  http://www.rootsweb.com/~mstallah/cemeteries/index.html
- Cemeteries Online!
  http://martin.simplenet.com/Cemeteries/
  *Database of cemeteries in south-eastern and south-central
  Pennsylvania.*
- Cemetery Index for Tioga and Bradford Counties in
  PA and Chemung County in NY
  http://www.rootsweb.com/~pabradfo/cemindex.htm

- Cemetery Inscriptions in Little Compton, Newport County, Rhode Island
  ftp://ftp.rootsweb.com/pub/usgenweb/ri/newport/cemetery/cemetery.txt
- Cemetery Interment Lists on the Internet
  http://www.interment.net/
- Cemetery Junction—The Internet Directory of Active and Retired Cemeteries
  http://www.daddezio.com/cemetery/index.html
- Cemetery Records of Hampton, New Hampshire
  http://www.hampton.lib.nh.us/hampton/graves/graves.htm
- Cemetery Searches, Sydney Australia
  http://homepages.tig.com.au/~tezz/netscape.htm
  This service will locate your ancestors' graves and take photos if required.
- Central United Cemetery—Dunstaffnage
  http://www.rootsweb.com/~pictou/cucdun.htm
  Prince Edward Island, Canada
- Chalmette National Cemetery
  http://www.cwc.lsu.edu/projects/dbases/chalmla.htm
  Louisiana
- Charleston Race Course Prison Dead, SC
  http://members.aol.com/edboots/charlestondead.html
  Union Civil War Prisoners of War originally buried at the Charleston Race Course Cemetery and later reinterred at the Beaufort National Cemetery.
- Chester Basin Old Baptist Cemetery
  http://www.rootsweb.com/~canns/lunenburg/cbobaptist.html
  Chester Basin, Lunenburg, Nova Scotia, Canada
- Chester Cemeteries Online
  http://www.rootsweb.com/~pacheste/chetgrav.htm
  Pennsylvania
- Chester New Baptist Cemetery
  http://www.rootsweb.com/~canns/lunenburg/chnbaptist.html
  Chester, Lunenburg, Nova Scotia, Canada
- Churches and Cemetery Records of Anson County, NC
  http://www.rootsweb.com/~ncanson/cemet.htm
- City of Edmonton's Department of Cemeteries
  E-mail: cemetery@wnet.gov.edmonton.ab.ca
  Send e-mail to: cemetery@wnet.gov.edmonton.ab.ca to find out about your ancestors buried in Edmonton, Alberta, Canada.
- City of Saskatoon: Woodlawn Cemetery
  http://www.city.saskatoon.sk.ca/departments/public_works/cemetery/default.htm
  - The Nutana Cemetery—Saskatoon's Pioneer Cemetery
    http://www.city.saskatoon.sk.ca/departments/public_works/cemetery/nutana/nutana1.htm
- City of the Silent
  http://www.best.com/~gazissax/city.html

- Clark County Cemeteries
  http://www.geocities.com/Heartland/Plains/5881/index.html
  Indiana
- Cloverdale Cemetery
  http://www.rootsweb.com/~nmhidalg/cloverdale.html
  Hidalgo County, New Mexico
- Confederate Burials in Mound City National Cemetery
  http://www.outfitters.com/illinois/history/civil/cwmoundcitycem.html
  Illinois
- Confederate Soldiers Rest, Elmwood Cemetery, Memphis, Tennessee
  http://www.people.memphis.edu/~jcothern/soldrest.htm
- Congregation Mikveh Israel Cemetery
  http://199.234.236.10/iha/_mikvehc.html
  Philadelphia, Pennsylvania
- Conneaut Valley Area Soldiers' Graves
  http://www.granniesworld.com/cvahs/cem/sold/index.html
  Pennsylvania
- The Connecticut Gravestone Network
  http://members.aol.com/ctgravenet/index.htm
- Corinth National Cemetery
  http://www2.tsixroads.com/Corinth_MLSANDY/cnc.html
  Mississippi
- Covington County, Alabama Cemeteries
  http://members.aol.com/genweblisa/covcem1.htm
- Covington County, Alabama Cemeteries
  http://members.aol.com/genweblisa/covcem2.htm
- Crawford Co., IN Cemetery Records
  http://www.floyd-pavey.com/kentuckiana/kyiana/county/crawford/ccemetery.html
  Indiana
- DC Cemeteries
  http://www.ihot.com/~christis/cemetery/cemetery.htm
- Decatur County, Tennessee Cemeteries
  http://funnelweb.utcc.utk.edu/~ddonahue/decatur/decatur.htm
- Delaware County Cemeteries
  http://www.rootsweb.com/~nydelawa/cem.html
  New York
- Delmarva Cemeteries
  http://www.shoreweb.com/cindy/cemetery.htm
  Maryland
- Dermott City Cemetery, Chicot County, Arkansas, "A–L"
  http://www.seark.net/~sabra/dercemty.txt
  "M–Z"
  http://www.seark.net/~sabra/dercem2.txt
- Downers Grove and Lisle Township Cemetery Index
  http://www.dcgs.org/downers/
  Du Page County, Illinois

- Dunstable, Massachusetts Burying Grounds
  http://members.tripod.com/DANRUTH/DunstableCem.html
  A list of the occupants of several cemeteries in Dunstable, Massachusetts. Primary family names include BLOOD, RIDEOUT, ROBBINS, SPAULDING and SWALLOW.

- Eakins Cemetery Records
  http://www.geocities.com/SoHo/Lofts/6448/EakinsCem.html
  Ponder, Denton County, Texas

- East River St. Mary's, Pictou County
  http://www.rootsweb.com/~pictou/eastriv.htm
  Nova Scotia, Canada

- Eden Lake Cemetery, Pictou County
  http://www.rootsweb.com/~pictou/edenlake.htm
  Nova Scotia, Canada

- Edmonton Parks and Recreation—Searching for a Family Member in Our Cemeteries
  http://www.gov.edmonton.ab.ca/parkrec/cemetery/search.htm
  Alberta, Canada. Database of people interred more than 25 years ago (close to 60,000 people) that are in Edmonton Municipal Cemeteries.

- Edmunds County, South Dakota, Cemetery Census—Interactive Search
  http://www.rootsweb.com/cgi-bin/sdedmunds/cemetery.pl

- The Electric Cemetery
  http://www.ionet.net/~cousin/

- Erie County, New York Cemeteries Past and Present
  http://members.tripod.com/~wnyroots/
  This site is updated weekly.

- Evergreen Cemetery, New Haven, Connecticut
  http://www.geocities.com/TheTropics/1127/evergren.html

- Farnam, Nebraska Cemetery
  http://www.4w.com/pages/hoppe/cemetery/

- Find A Grave: Noteworthy Gravesites
  http://www.findagrave.com/
  A listing of celebrity's gravesites.

- Forest Lawn Cemetery and Garden Mausoleums
  http://www.forest-lawn.com/
  Buffalo, New York

- Forks Church Yard—Lutheran Reformed
  http://www.geocities.com/Heartland/6508/FORKS.HTM

- Fox Brook Private Cemetery
  http://www.rootsweb.com/~pictou/foxpriv.htm
  Nova Scotia, Canada

- Fraser Cemetery, Blanchard Road, Pictou County
  http://www.rootsweb.com/~pictou/fraserb.htm
  Nova Scotia, Canada

- Fredericksburg Confederate Cemetery
  http://www.nps.gov/frsp/rebcem.htm
  Virginia

- Fredericksburg National Cemetery
  http://www.nps.gov/frsp/natcem.htm
  Virginia

- Friedensgemeinde Cemetery, Froid, Montana
  http://pixel.cs.vt.edu/library/cemeteries/montana/link/damm.txt

- Funeral Net
  http://www.funeralnet.com/
  Funeral home directory for the U.S.

- Funeral Homes on the Internet
  http://www.funeral.net/info/fnhinet.html

- Gallup Cemetery, Voluntown, Connecticut
  http://www.geocities.com/Vienna/1516/gallup1.html

- Genealogical Research at Oak Woods Cemetery
  http://homepages.rootsweb.com/~godwin/reference/oakwoods.html
  Chicago, Illinois

- The Genealogy Resource Page & Cemetery Database of the Hunter Valley NSW Australia
  http://bhss.inia.net.au/patmay/

- Glen Bard Cemetery, James River, Antigonish County
  http://www.rootsweb.com/~pictou/antiglb.htm
  Nova Scotia, Canada

- Graveyards of Chicago ~ Illinois
  http://www.graveyards.com/

- Grays Harbor County Washington Cemeteries
  http://www.geocities.com/Heartland/Hills/6201/cemeteries.html
  A list of cemeteries and their addresses, plus information on a book in the works from the Grays Harbor Genealogical Society.

- Greensboro Cemetery, Tomnolan, Mississippi
  ftp://ftp.rootsweb.com/pub/usgenweb/ms/webster/cemeteries/greensboro.txt

- Greenway Cemetery, Greenway, South Dakota
  http://pixel.cs.vt.edu/library/cemeteries/sodak/link/grnway.txt

- Greenwood Cemetery: History ~ Tallahassee, Florida
  http://www.state.fl.us/citytlh/public_works/grnwdhst.html

- Ground Work—Genealogy on the Internet—Cemeteries
  http://members.aol.com/ssmadonna/cemeteries.htm

- A Guide to Mount Hope Cemetery, Rochester, New York
  http://www.ci.rochester.ny.us/fun/mthope/mthope.htm

- Gunn Cemetery, Eden Lake, Pictou County
  http://www.rootsweb.com/~pictou/gunn.htm
  Nova Scotia, Canada

- Guysborough County Cemetery Listings ~ Nova Scotia, Canada
  http://www.geocities.com/Heartland/Plains/7525/Cemetery/cemindex.htm

- Halifax County—Cemetery Listings ~ Nova Scotia, Canada
  http://www.geocities.com/Heartland/Meadows/3515/Cemetery.htm

- Harper County Cemeteries ~ Kansas
  http://www.ohmygosh.com/genealogy/cemetery.htm
- Hattie Cemetery, Avondale, Pictou County ~ Nova Scotia, Canada
  http://www.rootsweb.com/~pictou/hattie.htm
- Hazleton Cemetery ~ Indiana
  http://www.comsource.net/~tnolcox/cemetery3.htm
- Heatherton Cemetery, Old Section, Antigonish County ~ Nova Scotia, Canada
  http://www.rootsweb.com/~pictou/hethold.htm
- Henderson County, Tennessee Cemeteries
  http://funnelweb.utcc.utk.edu/~ddonahue/henderson/hender.htm
- Herkimer/Montgomery Counties Cemetery Resources ~ New York
  http://www.rootsweb.com/~nyherkim/cemeteries.html
  Lists of cemeteries, private cemeteries, funeral homes and microfilm resources at the LDS Family History Centers.
- Hilda Baptist Cemetery, Hilda, Alberta, Canada
  http://pixel.cs.vt.edu/library/cemeteries/canada/link/hilda1.txt
- Hillside Cemetery, Trenton, Pictou County
  http://www.rootsweb.com/~pictou/hillside.htm
  Nova Scotia, Canada
- Historic Cemeteries in Berlin ~ Germany
  http://www.kulturbox.de/friedhof/index_e.htm
- Historic Cemeteries of Los Angeles ~ California
  http://www.usc.edu/isd/archives/la/cemeteries/
- Historic Congressional Cemetery ~ Washington, D.C.
  http://www.geocities.com/Heartland/Meadows/4633/index.html
- Historic Graveyards of The Berkshires ~ Massachusetts
  http://www.berkshireweb.com/plexus/graveyards/graveyards.html
- Historic Laurel Hill Cemetery ~ Philadelphia, Pennsylvania
  http://design.coda.drexel.edu/students/rmiller/assn2b.html
- Historical Notes—Calvary Cemetery ~ Seattle, Washington
  http://www.acc-seattle.com/cchistry.html
- History of the Seminole Indian Scout Cemetery ~ Brackettville, Texas
  http://www.coax.net/people/lwf/his_sisc.htm
- Hodson Cemetery, Pictou County ~ Nova Scotia, Canada
  http://www.rootsweb.com/~pictou/hodson.htm
- Holmes Funeral Co. Book—Saratoga Springs, New York
  http://freenet.buffalo.edu/~ae487/holmes.html
  Aug. 1854 to Dec. 1856.
- Hope Congregational Cemetery, Bethune, Colorado
  http://pixel.cs.vt.edu/library/cemeteries/colorado/link/bethune1.txt
- Howard Cemetery Armsby Road Sutton, Massachusetts
  http://www.geocities.com/Heartland/Valley/1410/sutton/armsby.html
- Huguenot Cemetery
  http://www.geocities.com/Heartland/Hills/8299/cemetery/hug_cem.htm
  St. John's County, Florida
- Immanuel Lutheran Church Cemetery, Bethune, Colorado
  http://pixel.cs.vt.edu/library/cemeteries/colorado/link/bethune2.txt
- Inactive Cemeteries of Lewis County as transcribed by Lowville Grange #71 in 1965
  http://www.rootsweb.com/~nylewis/inactive.htm
  New York
- Index of Graves at Liberty Hill Primitive Baptist Cemetery ~ Alabama
  http://www.geocities.com/Heartland/Meadows/9105/xlibhill.htm
- The Indiana Pioneer Cemeteries Restoration Project
  http://www.rootsweb.com/~inpcrp/
- Indian Graves and Cemeteries
  http://history.cc.ukans.edu/heritage/werner/indigrav.html
- Inhabitants of the Silent City— Warnock Cemetery ~ Indiana
  http://www.comsource.net/~tnolcox/cemetery2.htm
- International Jewish Cemetery Project
  http://www.jewishgen.org/cemetery/index.htm
- Internet Cemetery / Crematoria Directory
  http://www.funeral.net/info/ceminetdir.html
- Internet Funeral Service Directory
  http://www.funeral.net/info/fhinetdir.html
- Jackson County, Iowa Cemeteries
  http://www.rootsweb.com/~iajackso/Cemetery.html
- Jefferson County, Texas Cemeteries
  http://www.rootsweb.com/~txjeffer/burials/cemeteri.htm
- Jerauld County Cemetery Index
  http://pixel.cs.vt.edu/library/cemeteries/sodak/link/jerauld.txt
- JewishGen Hotline: Jewish Cemeteries in New York City
  http://www.jewishgen.org/mentprog/m_nycem.htm
- Kenzieville Cemetery, Pictou County ~ Nova Scotia, Canada
  http://www.rootsweb.com/~pictou/kenzie.htm

- Kinder McRill Memorial Cemetery ~
  Kinder, Louisiana
  http://fp1.centuryinter.net/KinderCemetery/

- Kootenai County Cemetery ~ Idaho
  http://www.ior.com/~jmakovec/genealogy/kc_cem.htm

- Lambton County Cemetery Index ~ Ontario, Canada
  http://www.sarnia.com/groups/ogs/logs1.html

- Lehigh County Cemetery Locations ~ Pennsylvania
  http://www.geocities.com/Heartland/6508/#Lehigh County

- Letcher County Cemetery Records ~ Kentucky
  http://webpages.metrolink.net/~bcaudill/kygenweb/
  cem_recs.htm

- Linwood Cemetery, Columbus, Georgia
  http://members.aol.com/CGAutry/linwood.html

- Little Sands Cemetery ~
  Prince Edward Island, Canada
  http://www.rootsweb.com/~pictou/lilsands.htm

- List of Soldiers in the Three Princeton Cemeteries
  (1889) ~ Indiana
  http://www.comsource.net/~tnolcox/cemetery1.htm

- Long Creek Baptist Church Cemetery
  http://www.rootsweb.com/~pictou/longcree.htm
  Prince Edward Island, Canada

- Lookups from the "Galveston, Indiana Cemetery
  Index, from the Platbooks and Files"
  E-mail: beheler@netusa1.net
  *For Cass, Howard or Miami Counties in Indiana. Send e-mail to
  Debra Beheler.*

- Lyona Cemetery List of Burials
  http://wwwp.exis.net/~bgugler/crecords.htm
  Dickinson County, Kansas

- McKenney Cemetery, Harrison County, Kentucky
  http://www.mindspring.com/~jogt/kygen/mckcem.htm

- McKenzie Cemetery, Salt Springs, Pictou County ~
  Nova Scotia, Canada
  http://www.rootsweb.com/~pictou/mckenzie.htm

- McLean Cemetery, Hopewell, Pictou County ~
  Nova Scotia, Canada
  http://www.rootsweb.com/~pictou/mclhope.htm

- Meiklefield Cemetery, Meiklefield, Pictou County ~
  Nova Scotia, Canada
  http://www.rootsweb.com/~pictou/mekfd.htm

- Memorial Links
  http://www.kiva.net/~markh/memorial.html

- Michigan Cemetery Page
  http://www.rootsweb.com/~migenweb/mi-cemetery.html

- The Middle Animas Cemetery
  http://www.rootsweb.com/~nmhidalg/manimas.html
  Animas, Hidalgo County, New Mexico

- Mills Cemetery, Garland, Texas
  http://www.geocities.com/TheTropics/1127/mills.html

- Moggill Cemetery
  http://192.148.225.23/bruce/cemetery.html
  A suburb of Brisbane, Queensland, Australia.

- Montgomery County Cemetery Project ~
  Pennsylvania
  http://members.aol.com/tmyers8644/mccem.html

- Monumental Inscriptions for Genealogists
  http://www.neep.demon.co.uk/mis/index.htm

- Morgan County Cemeteries Lookups—Missouri
  E-mail: wmwwms@laurie.net
  *Send e-mail to William & Dorothy Williams at
  wmwwms@laurie.net for lookups to be done in their personal
  catalog of Morgan County Cemeteries in Missouri. They have
  visited each of these gravesites and recorded all necessary
  details for each grave, including the parents of children and
  maiden name of wives if known. Their database has over 22,000
  burials in over 150 cemeteries. Records cover only Morgan
  County's present boundries for 1830 through 1996. Copies of
  these records can also be found in the State Archives, State
  Historical Library, and the Morgan County Library. Make sure
  to send a reasonable request and don't forget to thank William &
  Dorothy for their tremendous generosity!*

- Moss Cemetery, Marble, Cherokee County,
  North Carolina
  http://main.nc.us/OBCGS/mosscem.htm

- Mount Hope Cemetery ~ Bangor, Maine
  http://www.mthopebgr.com/

- Mt. Adams Cemetery, Glenwood, Klickitat
  County, Washington
  ftp://ftp.rootsweb.com/pub/usgenweb/wa/klickitat/cemetery/
  mtadams.txt

- Mt. View Research Cemetery Index Page
  County, Virginia
  http://www.geocities.com/Heartland/Valley/9793/
  cemeteryindex.htm

- Murray Point Cemetery, Pictou County ~
  Nova Scotia, Canada
  http://www.rootsweb.com/~pictou/murpt.htm

- National Cemetery System—Department
  of Veteran Affairs
  http://www.cem.va.gov/

- Nevada County, Arkansas Cemetery Records
  http://www.pcfa.org/depot_museum/cemetery/

- Niagara County, NY Cemeteries
  http://members.aol.com/Moecow/index2.html

- North East Florida & some South East George
  counties—Listing of over 300 Cemeteries
  E-mail: cmobley@magicnet.net
  *Send e-mail to Carl Mobley, with SPECIFIC given names &
  surnames and he will do a lookup for you.*

- Northampton County Cemetery Locations ~
  Pennsylvania
  http://www.geocities.com/Heartland/6508/#Cemeteries

- OCFA—The Ontario Cemetery Finding Aid
  http://www.islandnet.com/ocfa/homepage.html

- Old Blandford Church and Cemetery ~
  Petersburg, Virginia
  http://www.rootsweb.com/~vacpeter/cemetery/blandfd1.htm

- Old Burial Ground of Middle Fork of Raven
  Creek—Harrison County, Kentucky
  http://members.aol.com/kygenweb/raven.htm

- The Old Cemeteries Society—Victoria Tombstone
  Tales of Ross Bay Cemetery
  http://www.oldcem.bc.ca/
  British Columbia, Canada

- Old Cemetery, Salt Springs, Pictou County ~
  Nova Scotia, Canada
  http://www.rootsweb.com/~pictou/oldcem.htm

- Old City Cemetery: History ~ Tallahassee, Florida
  http://www.state.fl.us/citytlh/public_works/occhist.html

- Old Huntsville Magazine: Cemetery Records of
  Madison County Alabama
  http://oldhuntsville.com/oldhuntsville/p187.htm

- Old Huntsville Magazine—A Listing of Cemeteries
  in Madison County, Alabama
  http://oldhuntsville.com/oldhuntsville/p303.htm

- Old Kinne Cemetery, Voluntown, Connecticut
  http://www.geocities.com/Vienna/1516/kinne4.html

- Old Methodist Church Cemetery, Venus,
  Pennsylvania
  http://members.aol.com/jadolby/index.htm

- Old Patoka Cemetery ~ Indiana
  http://www.comsource.net/~tnolcox/cemetery4.htm

- Old Spanish Cemetery ~ St. John's County, Florida
  http://www.geocities.com/Heartland/Hills/8299/cemetery/
  spa_cem.htm

- Our Lady of Good Counsel Church Cemetery ~
  St. John's County, Florida
  http://www.geocities.com/Heartland/Hills/8299/cemetery/
  cons_cem.htm

- Paris Cemeteries ~ France
  http://www.parisnet.com/english/city/unusual/cimetieres.htm

- Pariscope: Cemeteries ~ France
  http://pariscope.fr/Pariscope/Visiter/Cimetieres/
  Welcome.E.html

- PEI Burial Records—1892–1900 ~ Canada
  http://www.eskimo.com/~mvreid/34burabs.html
  *St Eugene's (CoveHead), St Michael's (Corran Ban),
  St Bonaventure's (Tracadie)*

- Perry County Indiana Tombstone Inscriptions
  http://www.floyd-pavey.com/kentuckiana/kyiana/cemetery/
  perrytombstones.html

- Petersburg National Battlefield—Poplar Grove
  National Cemetery ~ Virginia
  http://www.nps.gov/pete/pe_pop.htm

- Pictou Island Pioneer Cemetery ~
  Nova Scotia, Canada
  http://www.rootsweb.com/~pictou/pioneer.htm

- Pictou Island Presbyterian Church Cemetery ~
  Nova Scotia, Canada
  http://www.rootsweb.com/~pictou/prezz.htm

- Pin Oak Cemetery, Milam County, Texas
  http://www.geocities.com/Heartland/Hills/7475/poc.html

- Pioneer Cemetery—Horseshoe Bend,
  Boise County, Idaho
  http://www.rootsquest.com/~idaho/boise/cemhsb.html

- Placerville Cemetery—Boise County, Idaho
  http://www.rootsquest.com/~idaho/boise/cemplacer.html

- Pleasant Grove Methodist Cemetery
  http://home.att.net/~dpdklong/PleasantGrove.html
  Chilton County, Alabama, 1848–1978.

- The Political Graveyard
  http://politicalgraveyard.com/index.html
  *"The Web Site That Tells Where the Dead Politicians are
  Buried."*

- Potter Field Cemetery, 1887–1957, Omaha,
  Douglas County, Nebraska
  http://www.geocities.com/Heartland/Plains/3730/stone5.html

- Prairie Epitaph—Catholic Cemetery in Salvador,
  Saskatchewan
  http://mars.ark.com/~rbell/html/history/epitaph.html
  Many German Russian families.

- Preserving Cemetery Data: The North Carolina
  Cemetery Survey and Protective Legislation
  http://www.arch.dcr.state.nc.us/cemetery.htm

- Prince Edward Island Cemeteries Page
  http://www.isn.net/~dhunter/cem.html
  *Includes "Extract from the Death Registers, St. Patrick's Roman
  Catholic Church in Ft. Augustus, P.E.I.*

- Quaker Burying Ground Morris, New York,
  Surnames A–M
  http://www.rootsweb.com/~nyotsego/morbga.htm

  Surnames N–Z
  http://www.rootsweb.com/~nyotsego/morbgb.htm

- Raven Creek Cemetery, Harrison County, Kentucky
  http://pw1.netcom.com/~jog1/ravencreek.html

- Rhode Island Cemeteries Database Home Page
  http://members.tripod.com/~debyns/cemetery.html

- Rock Island County Cemeteries ~ Illinois
  http://www.rootsweb.com/~ilrockis/cemetery/cemetery.htm

- Rocky Mountain Cemetery, Pictou County ~
  Nova Scotia, Canada
  http://www.rootsweb.com/~pictou/rocky.htm

- The Rodeo Cemetery
  http://www.rootsweb.com/~nmhidalg/rodeocem.html
  Rodeo, Hidalgo County, New Mexico

- Roman Catholic Cemetery, Merigomish ~
  Nova Scotia, Canada
  http://www.rootsweb.com/~pictou/rcmeri.htm

- Saint Andrew's Cemetery, Old Section,
  Antigonish County ~ Nova Scotia, Canada
  http://www.rootsweb.com/~pictou/stanold.htm

- St. Augustine National Cemetery
  http://www.geocities.com/Heartland/Hills/8299/cemetery/
  nat_cem.htm
  St. John's County, Florida

- St. John Memorial Gardens ~ Louisiana
  http://www.rootsweb.com/~lastjohn/stjcem1.htm

- Salt Springs Cemetery, Pictou County ~
  Nova Scotia, Canada
  http://www.rootsweb.com/~pictou/ssprings.htm

- San Francisco Cemeteries
  http://userwww.sfsu.edu/~jblcktt/SFCemeteries.html

- Saskatchewan Cemetery Index ~ Canada
  http://www.saskgenealogy.com/cemetery/cemetery.htm

- Shiloh Cemetery, Delta County, Texas
  http://www.geocities.com/Vienna/1516/shiloh.html

- Skinnersville Cemetery Amherst NY
  http://www.geocities.com/Heartland/Acres/4218/
  skinnersville.html

- South Australian Cemeteries
  http://www.users.on.net/proformat/cems.html

- Spencer Holy Trinity Cemetery
  http://www.terrigal.net.au/~history/spencer.htm
  Australia. Cemetery Index for sale.

- Stephens County Oklahoma Cemeteries
  http://www.geocities.com/Heartland/Ridge/1308/MAPS.html

- Stewart's Cemetery, Antigonish County ~
  Nova Scotia, Canada
  http://www.rootsweb.com/~pictou/stewart.htm

- Stony Cemetery ~ Denton County, Texas
  http://www.geocities.com/SoHo/Lofts/6448/StonyCem.html

- Strong or Crawford Cemetery ~ Indiana
  http://www.floyd-pavey.com/kentuckiana/kyiana/cemetery/
  strong.html

- Sussex County, NJ Cemetery Indexes ~ New Jersey
  http://www.gate.net/~pascalfl/cemidx.html

- Texas Roots—Limestone County Cemetery Surveys
  http://www.glade.net/~hcox/cemeteries/cemeteryintro.html

- Texas State Cemetery
  http://www.cemetery.state.tx.us/

- Toledo's Attic Woodlawn Cemetery
  Biographies ~ Ohio
  http://www.history.utoledo.edu/att/wood/woodindex.html

- Tombstone Records from Monroe Co., New York
  and a Few Church Records
  http://home.eznet.net/~halsey/cem.html

- Tombstone Transcription Project
  http://www.angelfire.com/va/dullesgirl/index.html
  *Ozora Baptist Church Cemetery, Grayson, Gwinnett
  County, GA.*

- T Point Cemetery, Clayhole, Kentucky
  http://www.seidata.com/~lhoffman/what.html

- Union Baptist Church Inscriptions
  http://www.geocities.com/Heartland/Meadows/3011/un.htm
  Lipscomb, Alabama

- University of Oxford, Ashmolean Museum, The
  Department of Antiquities Monumental Brasses
  http://antiqs-iii.ashmol.ox.ac.uk/ash/departments/
  antiquities/brass/
  England

- Upper Beard Cemetery ~ Indiana
  http://www.floyd-pavey.com/kentuckiana/kyiana/cemetery/
  upperbeard.html

- Upsala, Minnesota Cemetery Index
  http://upstel.net/~johns/CemIndex/CemIndex.html

- USCWC Cemetery Listings
  http://www.cwc.lsu.edu/cwc/projects/cemindex.htm
  From the U.S. Civil War Center.

- USGenWeb Tombstone Transcription Project
  http://www.rootsweb.com/~cemetery/

- USGS Mapping Information: GNIS Data Base
  Query Form
  http://www-nmd.usgs.gov/www/gnis/gnisform.html
  *Type in your County & State name and in the Feature box type
  in the word Cemetery.*

- The Utica Cemetery ~ Michigan
  http://www.concentric.net/~Ekkm/Utica.html

- Uttoxeter Road Cemetery, Derby, Derbyshire,
  England, UK
  http://www.derbycity.com/derby/tombs.html

- Vernon and District Family History Society—
  Cemetery Monument Inscriptions
  http://www.junction.net/vernhist/V4.html
  B.C., Canada

- Victoria County Cemetery Transcriptions ~
  Nova Scotia, Canada
  http://members.tripod.com/~lemac2/index-16.html

- Washington Cemetery Project
  http://www.rootsweb.com/~usgenweb/wa/wacem.htm
  From the US GenWeb Archives.
  - Eden Valley Cemetery
    ftp://ftp.rootsweb.com/pub/usgenweb/wa/wahkiakum/
    cemetery/edenvall.txt
    Also known as Buskala Family Cemetery.
  - Elma Catholic Cemetery
    ftp://ftp.rootsweb.com/pub/usgenweb/wa/graysharbor/
    cemetery/elmacath.txt
    Also known as St. Joseph's Cemetery.
  - Fern Hill Cemetery, Wahkiakum County
    ftp://ftp.rootsweb.com/pub/usgenweb/wa/wahkiakum/
    cemetery/fernhill.txt
  - Grays River Grange Cemetery,
    Wahkiakum County
    ftp://ftp.rootsweb.com/pub/usgenweb/wa/wahkiakum/
    cemetery/graysriv.txt
  - Greenwood Cemetery, Cathlamet,
    Wahkiakum County
    ftp://ftp.rootsweb.com/pub/usgenweb/wa/wahkiakum/
    cemetery/greenwd.txt
  - Johns River Cemetery, Markham, Washington
    ftp://ftp.rootsweb.com/pub/usgenweb/wa/graysharbor/
    cemetery/jriver.txt
  - Mt. Adams Cemetery, Glenwood, Klickitat
    County, Washington
    ftp://ftp.rootsweb.com/pub/usgenweb/wa/klickita/cemetery/
    mtadams.txt
  - Old Schafer Homestead Cemetery
    ftp://ftp.rootsweb.com/pub/usgenweb/wa/graysharbor/
    cemetery/schafer.txt
    *Also known as Schafer Valley Cemetery and Satsop Valley
    Cemetery. Some of the graves here were moved to Shafer
    Cemetery and to Fern Hill Cemetery.*
  - Pioneer Cemetery in Cathlamet,
    Wahkiakum County
    ftp://ftp.rootsweb.com/pub/usgenweb/wa/wahkiakum/
    cemetery/pioneer.txt
  - Rosburg Cemetery, Wahkiakum County
    ftp://ftp.rootsweb.com/pub/usgenweb/wa/wahkiakum/
    cemetery/rosburg.txt
  - Seal River Cemetery, Wahkiakum County
    ftp://ftp.rootsweb.com/pub/usgenweb/wa/wahkiakum/
    cemetery/sealriv.txt
- Washington County Cemetery Project ~ Indiana
  http://vax1.vigo.lib.in.us/~jmounts/cem.htm
- Waterford Rural Cemetery Records ~ New York
  http://www.rootsweb.com/~nysarato/cembeg.htm
- Werkheiser Cemetery-Forks Township
  http://www.geocities.com/Heartland/6508/#Werkheiser
  Cemetery

- Willoughby Cemetery, Great Valley, Cattaraugus
  County, New York
  ftp://ftp.rootsweb.com/pub/usgenweb/ny/cattaraugus/
  greatvalley/ceme0001.txt
- Wood Island Cemetery (established 1882)
  http://www.rootsweb.com/~pictou/wdi.htm
  Prince Edward Island, Canada
- Wood Islands Pioneer Cemetery 1807–1910
  http://www.rootsweb.com/~pictou/wdislan.htm
  Prince Edward Island, Canada
- World Wide Cemetery
  http://www.cemetery.org/
  *A place for Internet users to erect permanent monuments to
  the dead.*
- Yahoo!...Cemeteries
  http://dir.yahoo.com/Society_and_Culture/Death_and_Dying/
  End_of_Life_Issues/Funeral_Services/Cemeteries/
- Yahoo!...Funeral Homes
  http://dir.yahoo.com/Business_and_Economy/Companies/
  Funerals/Funeral_Homes/
- Yale Peabody Museum: Geographic Names
  Information System (GNIS)
  http://www.peabody.yale.edu/other/gnis/
  *Search the USGS Geographic Names Database. You can limit
  the search to a specific county in this state and search for any of
  the following features: airport arch area arroyo bar basin bay
  beach bench bend bridge **building** canal cape **cemetery** channel
  church cliff crater crossing dam falls flat forest gap geyser
  glacier gut harbor hospital island isthmus lake lava levee locale
  mine oilfield other park pillar plain ppl range rapids reserve
  reservoir ridge **school** sea slope spring stream summit swamp
  tower trail tunnel valley well woods.*
- York Township Cemetery Index
  http://www.dcgs.org/york/
  Du Page County, Illinois
- The Young-Sanders Center
  http://youngsanders.org/
  *For the study of the War Between the States in Louisiana.
  Contains searchable database of over 10,000 Confederate
  soldiers buried in Louisiana with cemetery locations.*

◆ How To

- All About Cemeteries and Funeral Homes
  http://www.familytreemaker.com/00000049.html
- CGN Cemetery Do's & Don'ts
  http://members.aol.com/ctgravenet/dosdonts.htm
  *Includes: Cleaning Basics, Graveyard Maintenance, Gravestone
  Rubbings, Reading Inscriptions, Should You Seal or Waterproof
  Gravestones?*
- Doing Your Cemetery Survey
  http://www.netusa1.net/~hartmont/cemsurvey.htm
- Finding a Burial Place in Cemeteries or
  Cemetery Records
  http://www.familytreemaker.com/00000480.html

- Finding a Death Date in Cemeteries or Cemetery Records
  http://www.familytreemaker.com/00000442.html
- Finding the Hidden Treasures in Tombstone Rubbings
  http://www.firstct.com/fv/t_examp.html
- Frontier Press Bookstore—Cemetery Research / Preservation
  http://www.frontierpress.com/frontier.cgi?category=ceme
- Graven Images
  http://www.rootsweb.com/~ote/grave.htm
  Describes the symbolism of motifs on gravestones—from The Olive Tree.
- How to do Tombstone Rubbings
  http://www.mindspring.com/~mooregen/tombstone.htm
- Locating Cemeteries and Cemetery Records
  http://www.familytreemaker.com/00000050.html
- Researching and Recording Civil War Veterans Burials in Michigan Cemeteries
  http://www.centuryinter.net/suvcw.mi/gr-recgv.html
- Standards for Transcribing Cemetery Headstones
  ftp://ftp.rootsweb.com/pub/roots-l/genealog/genealog.headston
- Tombstone Rubbings
  http://www.firstct.com/fv/t_stone.html

◆ Mailing Lists, Newsgroups & Chat

- ALEXTREE Mailing List
  http://members.aol.com/gfsjohnf/gen_mail_states-nc.html#ALEXTREE
  For anyone with an interest in the cemeteries of Western North Carolina. Areas of discussion will include page updates, local cemetery news and announcements, and preservation strategies.
- CEMETERY Mailing List
  http://members.aol.com/johnf14246/gen_mail_general.html#CEMETERY
  For people interested in the many aspects of family graves from caring for the grave of one ancestor to the restoration and preservation of the family cemetery.
- GRAVE-L Mailing List
  http://www.best.com/~gazissax/silence/mlist.html
  "Grave-L is a new mailing list explicitly for taphophiles—lovers of cemeteries and funerals. It will be of particular interest to historians, genealogists, funeral directors, cemetery workers, and others concerned with the preservation, folklore, and history of graveyards."

- INSCRIPTIONS-L Mailing List
  http://members.aol.com/johnf14246/gen_mail_general.html#INSCRIPTIONS
  For anyone who has an interest in genealogy and local history related to Monumental Inscriptions including gravestones, monuments, and war memorials.
- MI-ENGLAND Mailing List
  http://members.aol.com/gfsjohnf/gen_mail_country-unk.html#MI-ENGLAND
  For those interested in Monumental Inscriptions on gravestones, etc. in England.

◆ Publications, Software & Supplies

- Genealogical Cemetery Database
  http://www.dhc.net/~design/desig1-4.htm
  Software program from Design Software.
- Tomb With A View
  http://members.aol.com/TombView/twav.html
  A newsletter devoted to the appreciation, study and preservation of historic U.S. cemeteries. It includes articles, book reviews and an extensive listing of special events in or about cemeteries, such as tours, lectures and special celebrations.
- View•logy—Memorials That Tell A Story
  http://www.leif.com/
  An electronic display unit that installs into traditional grave markers, which includes a visual eulogy.

◆ Societies & Groups

- Association for Gravestone Studies Home Page
  http://www.berkshire.net/ags/
- Commission for the Preservation of Pioneer Jewish Cemeteries and Landmarks
  http://www.jfed.org/mcemcom.htm
  Northern California
- Commonwealth War Graves Commission
  http://www.cwgc.org/
  Details of 1.7 million members of UK and Commonwealth forces who died in the 1st and 2nd World Wars and other wars, and 60,000 civilian casualties of WWII. Gives details of grave site, date of death, age, usually parents/widow's address.
- Iowa Funeral Directors Association Members
  http://www.istatinc.com/ifda_members.html
- The Vermont Old Cemetery Association
  http://homepages.together.net/~btrutor/voca/vocahome.htm

CENSUS RELATED SITES WORLDWIDE

http://www.CyndisList.com/census2.htm

◆ Census Tools & Information

- Calculating Birth-Year Based on Census Information
  http://home.mem.net/~rac7253/gen/cenindx.htm

- The Census Enumerators' Books
  http://www.staffs.ac.uk/schools/humanities_and_soc_sciences/
  census/cebs.htm
  An introduction to the surviving source material for the censuses done in the United Kingdom in the 1800s. While geared to sociologists, this site is helpful to family historians for under-standing the source documents which they use in their research.

- Census Information from GENUKI
  http://www.genuki.org.uk/big/eng/census.html
  For England, Scotland & Wales.

- Censuses in Australian Colonies
  http://www.users.on.net/proformat/census.html
  Listing of census availability and locations of records.

- Family Census Research
  http://www.dhc.net/~design/fcr30.htm
  Software program for organizing census records.

- Finding an Address in the Transcription of the 1881 Census of England and Wales
  http://people.enternet.com.au/~tmj/c81-adrs.htm

- Getting into the Norwegian Census
  http://www.isv.uit.no/seksjon/rhd/nhdc/michael02.htm

- Researching with Census Records
  http://www.familytreemaker.com/issue13.html
  From Family Tree Maker Online.

- Soundex Conversion Program from Genealogy Online
  http://www.genealogy.org/soundex.shtml

- Soundex Conversion Program—Surname to Soundex Code
  http://searches.rootsweb.com/cgi-bin/Genea/soundex.sh

- The Soundex Machine
  http://www.nara.gov/genealogy/soundex/soundex.html
  A form to convert surnames to soundex codes; from the National Archives.

- Tom Nunamaker's Census Age Calculator
  http://toshop.com/censuscalc.cfm

- Using the Soundex System
  http://www.ancestry.com/home/George_Morgan/03-20-98.htm
  From "Along Those Lines . . ." by George G. Morgan.

◆ International Census Indexes & Records

- 1768 St. John's Island Heads of Household Census
  http://www.isn.net/~dhunter/1768.html
  Prince Edward Island, Canada

- 1842 Malahide Township Elgin County, Ontario Census Index
  http://www.ptbruce.kanservu.ca/Genealogy/1842Census.html

- 1871 Cornwall Census Query
  http://www.kindredkonnections.com/cgi-bin/crcensus?-1+0+English
  England. From Kindred Konnections.

- 1871 Ontario Census Index ~ Census
  http://www.archives.ca/db/1871/1871_Census_Search.html

- 1891 Census of East Hamlet, Ludlow, Shropshire ~ England
  ftp://ftp.rootsweb.com/pub/wggenweb/england/ludlow/
  easthamlet/shropshire/census/eastha91.txt

- 1901 Census—Lunenburg County, Nova Scotia
  http://www.geocities.com/Heartland/6625/1901census.html

- 1901 Census of Canada—Film Numbers
  http://www.tbaytel.net/bmartin/census.htm

- Censuses of Gloucestershire and Southern Warwickshire
  http://www.silk.net/personal/gordonb/cotswold.htm
  Over 300 census extracts (150,000 entries) for this area in England.

- Dale Street Bridewell, Liverpool—1871
  http://www.globalserve.net/~scouse/bridwell.htm

- General Don's Militia Survey of 1815
  http://www.societe-jersiaise.org/alexgle/Don.html
  Channel Islands

- Halifax Census (1752), A–E
  http://www.geocities.com/Heartland/Prairie/6261/
  hfxcensus1.htm

  F–K
  http://www.geocities.com/Heartland/Prairie/6261/
  hfxcensus2.htm

  L–Q
  http://www.geocities.com/Heartland/Prairie/6261/
  hfxcensus3.htm

  R–Z
  http://www.geocities.com/Heartland/Prairie/6261/
  hfxcensus4.htm

- Index to the 1744 Quebec City Census
  http://www.oz.net/~johnbang/genealogy/1744indx.txt
  Quebec, Canada

- Index to the 1891 Census of Prince Edward
  Island ~ Canada
  http://www.edu.pe.ca/paro/1891/index.asp

- Index to the 1891 Dominion Census Lethbridge
  Sub-District, Alberta, Northwest Territories
  http://mypage.direct.ca/d/dobee/lethmain.html

- Mecklenburg-Schwerin Census Records
  http://pages.prodigy.net/jhbowen/census.htm

- NFHS Internet Branch—The 1851 British Census
  Index on CD-ROM—Its availability & usage
  http://www.rootsweb.com/~nfhs/ib/1851cd.htm
  *Describes the contents and use of this census index for the
  English counties of Devon, Norfolk, and Warwickshire which
  includes over 1.5 million individuals. Ordering information for
  this low cost CD-ROM is provided for 5 different countries.*

- Nominal Census Homepage
  http://royal.okanagan.bc.ca/census/index.html
  *Data for the southern interior of the Province of British
  Columbia, Canada.*

  - Canada Census, 1881—Yale District
    http://royal.okanagan.bc.ca/census/yale1881.html

  - Canada Census, 1891—Yale District
    http://royal.okanagan.bc.ca/census/yale1891.html

  - The IRC Census, 1877
    http://royal.okanagan.bc.ca/census/ind1877.html
    Indian Reserve Commission

  - The OMI Census, 1877
    http://royal.okanagan.bc.ca/census/omi1877.html
    *A nominal census of Native peoples taken by the Catholic
    missionary order, Oblates of Mary Immaculate (OMI).*

- Norway—1801 Census
  http://www.uib.no/hi/1801page.html

- Nova Scotia Census Data
  http://www.genealogy.org/~soccgs/census.html

- Ontario 1871 Census
  http://stauffer.queensu.ca/docsunit/searchc71.html
  and a new searchable format as well
  http://130.15.161.15/1871.htm

- Ron Taylor's UK Census Finding Aids and Indexes
  http://rontay.digiweb.com/
  Mainly from the 1851 Census.

  - Born in France and Germany Census Indexes
    http://rontay.digiweb.com/france

  - Institutionalised Census Indexes
    http://rontay.digiweb.com/institute
    *Including Paupers, Inmates, Convicts, Prisoners and
    Prostitutes.*

  - Occupations Census Indexes
    http://rontay.digiweb.com/visit/occupy/

  - Scots and Irish Strays Census Indexes
    http://rontay.digiweb.com/scot

  - Strays by County Census Indexes
    http://rontay.digiweb.com/county

  - Visitors Census Indexes
    http://rontay.digiweb.com/visit/

- Unruh's South Russian Mennonite Census,
  1795–1814
  http://pixel.cs.vt.edu/library/census/link/bhu.txt

CHAT & INTERNET RELAY CHAT (IRC)
http://www.CyndisList.com/chat.htm

Category Index:

◆ Genealogy Chat & IRC Channels Listed by Networks / Server

◆ Genealogy Chat & IRC Home Pages
◆ General IRC Software & How To Guides

◆ Genealogy Chat & IRC Channels Listed by Networks / Server

● AfterNET
irc.afternet.org:6667

　○ #GenealogyForum
　　http://www.rare.on.ca/users/genealogyforum/index.htm

　○ #Genealogy-n-UK

　○ #Genealogy-Native
　　http://www.icomnet.com/~cheyanne/

● AnotherNet
irc.another.net:6667

　○ #genealogy

● DALnet
http://www.lookup.com/Homepages/89108/dalnetgy.html
irc.dal.net:7000

　○ #Canadian Gen

　○ #Fianna (Irish research)

　○ #genealogy-events

　○ #genealogy-help
　　http://www.geocities.com/Heartland/Ranch/4656/

　○ #Genealogy_IRC
　　http://genweb.net/~genirc/

　○ #Gen_Family_Tree

　○ #Gentrace

　○ Lunenburg County, Nova Scotia, Canada
　　#lunie-links

● EFnet
irc.chat.org:6667

　○ #FTMCC

　○ #genealogies

　○ #genealogy
　　http://www.voicenet.com/~bparker1/CHANNEL/index.htm

　○ #roots

● IIGS
http://www.iigs.org/irc/index.htm.en
irc.IIGS.org:6667 or 7000

　○ #Australia
　　http://www.uq.net.au/~zzsbrown/irc.htm

　○ #BNL
　　http://www.iigs.org/cgi/ircthemes/ircthemes#Belgium, Netherlands, Luxemburg

　○ #Canadian-Gen
　　http://www.iigs.org/cgi/ircthemes/ircthemes#Canadian Genealogy

　○ #genealogie.fr

　○ #Ger-Rus
　　http://www.geocities.com/Heartland/Acres/4123/irc.htm

　○ #IIGS-Meet

　○ #IIGS-UKgen
　　http://www.iigs.org/cgi/ircthemes/ircthemes#UK Genealogy

　○ #Ireland-gen

　○ #KY-Estill
　　http://www.iigs.org/cgi/ircthemes/ircthemes#Estill County, Kentucky Research

　○ #SE-KY
　　http://www.rootsweb.com/~seky/irc.html

　○ #USMil
　　http://www.geocities.com/Heartland/4119/us-mil.htm

● NewNet
irc.newnet.net:6667

　○ #family_history

　○ #genealogy
　　http://www.eskimo.com/~mevers/rogue.htm

　○ #genealogy101

● RootsWeb
irc.rootsweb.com:6667 or 7000

　○ #MSGenWeb
　　http://www.rootsweb.com/~msgenweb/chat.shtml

● SCS Net
irc.scscorp.net:6667

　○ #genealogy

　○ #Stephenson_Co_IL
　　http://www.rootsweb.com/~ilstephe/chat.html

　○ #Sturtevant
　　http://www.goodnet.com/~julweed/chat.html

- WebMaster
  irc.webmaster.com:6667

  o #TMG
    http://www.communique.net/~davidl/tmg-chat/tmg-chat.htm
    The Master Genealogist software program.

◆ Genealogy Chat & IRC Home Pages

- Ancestral Findings—Ancestral Chat
  http://web.mountain.net/~wfmoney/cd/chat.htm

- Australian Genealogy Chat Sessions
  http://www.uq.net.au/~zzsbrown/irc.htm

- The "Cajun/Acadian" Chat Room
  http://www.acadian.org/genealogy/chat.html
  From the Acadian Genealogy Homepage.

- Charlotte's Genealogy Conference Room
  http://www.cci-internet.com/~coats/genechat.htm

- The DALnet Genealogy Channels
  http://www.geocities.com/SiliconValley/1641/genechat.html

- Folks Online—FolksChat
  http://www.folksonline.com/folks/commun/folkschat/
  folkschat.htm#chatnow

- #Genealogy Forum
  http://www.rare.on.ca/users/genealogyforum/index.htm
  Genealogy Channel on Internet Relay Chat (IRC).

- #Genealogy-Help Chat Page on DALnet
  http://www.geocities.com/Heartland/Ranch/4656/

- Genealogy Online—Chat Room
  http://www.genealogy.org/~genchat/

- Genealogy_IRC = International Researcher's Club Page
  http://genweb.net/~genirc/

- Genealogy-Native-American
  http://www.icomnet.com/~cheyanne/
  #Genealogy-Native-American Channel on AfterNET.

- Genealogy-Net—Gene-Net "One on One"
  http://www.geocities.com/Heartland/Meadows/6820/
  genenet.htm

- GEN-IRC Mailing List
  http://members.aol.com/johnf14246/
  gen_mail_general.html#GEN-IRC

- GMW Chat Page
  http://www.citynet.net/mostwanted/prechat.htm
  From Genealogy's Most Wanted.

- Home Page for Genealogy on IRC
  http://www.genealogy.org/~jkatcmi/genealogy-irc/
  welcome.html

  o Channels and NetWorks
    http://www.genealogy.org/~jkatcmi/genealogy-irc/
    geneycha.htm
    A guide for beginners.

- o #genealogy IRC
    http://www.eskimo.com/~mevers/genealogy.html
    Channel Stats—Geney01's #genealogy SPY Page!

  o IRC info to deal with channel and Geney01
    http://www.genealogy.org/~jkatcmi/genealogy-irc/
    geneyirc.htm

  o Regarding the Use of IRC in Genealogy Research
    http://www.genealogy.org/~jkatcmi/genealogy-irc/
    geneyfaq.htm

- IIGS—International Internet Genealogical Society, I.R.C. Internet Relay Chat
  http://www.iigs.org/irc/index.htm.en

- IRC Channels Events Home Page
  http://www.geocities.com/Heartland/Meadows/6820/

- IRC Chat Line—#Ger-Rus
  http://www.geocities.com/Heartland/Acres/4123/irc.htm
  For researching Germans from Russia.

- Lee Chat at the Lee County Genealogy Society
  http://www.riversidemarketing.com/lcgs/chat.htm

- Lincoln Co. WV Genealogy Chat Room
  http://www.oklahoma.net/~davidm/lincoln/chat.htm

- McCALLISTER/McALLISTER/etc Chat Room
  http://www.oklahoma.net/~davidm/chat.htm

- Mississippi Genealogy IRC Chats
  http://www.rootsweb.com/~msgenweb/chat.shtml

- NewNet #Genealogy's Rogues Gallery
  http://www.eskimo.com/~mevers/rogue.htm

- North Carolina Genealogy QuickChat Web Chat
  http://www.lochfort.net/ajpweb/remote/chat/genchat.html

- Northeast Pennsylvania IRC Chat—#Luzerne_Co_Genealogy
  http://www.rootsweb.com/~paluzern/chat.htm

- OntarioGenWeb Chat Forum
  http://www.rootsweb.com/~canon/chat.html

- Stephenson County Chat ~ Illinois
  http://www.rootsweb.com/~ilstephe/chat.html

- Sturtevant Ancestors Chat
  http://www.goodnet.com/~julweed/chat.html

- The Unofficial EFnet #genealogy Channel Home Page
  http://www.voicenet.com/~bparker1/CHANNEL/index.htm

  o The EFnet Genealogy Channel Beginners' Guide to Online Genealogy
    http://www.voicenet.com/~bparker1/CHANNEL/beginner.htm

- Webchat Broadcasting System: Adult Adoptees Chat
  http://pages.wbs.net/webchat3.so?cmd=cmd_doorway:
  Adult_Adoptees_Chat

- Webchat Broadcasting System: Genealogy
  http://pages.wbs.net/webchat3.so?cmd=cmd_doorway:
  Genealogy

◆ General IRC Software & How To Guides

- The Comprehensive IRC Network List
  http://www.irchelp.org/irchelp/networks/

- Chat Etiquette: The Do's and Don'ts of On-Line Conversation
  http://acm.ewu.edu/homepage/wmundell/chatet.htm

- Chatter's Jargon Dictionary
  http://www.tiac.net/users/scg/jargpge.htm

- DALnet IRC—FAQ
  http://deckard.mc.duke.edu/irchelp/mirc/aol.html
  http://www.dal.net/howto/FAQ.default.html
  Directions for Setting up mIRC for AOL Customers.

- EFnet #IRChelp Help Archive
  http://www.irchelp.org/

- Getting the Most from mIRC
  http://www.rare.on.ca/users/genealogyforum/MIRCing.htm

- ichat
  http://www.ichat.com/
  Plug-in software for your browser.

- ICQ
  http://www.mirabilis.com/index.html

- I.I.G.S.—Instructions, FAQs and Links for IRC
  http://www.iigs.org/irc/irclinks.htm.en

- IRC Intro File for Newbies using Windows
  http://www.geocities.com/SiliconValley/Park/6000/ircintro.html

- The MacIRC Home Page
  http://www.macirc.com/
  Software for Macintosh.

- mIRC: Homepage of the IRC Chat Client mIRC
  http://www.geocities.com/SiliconValley/Park/6000/index.html
  Software for Windows.

- NewIRCusers.com
  http://www.newircusers.com/

- The Official Ircle Home Page
  http://www.ircle.houseit.com/
  Software for Macintosh.

- OrbitIRC
  http://www.dlcwest.com/~orbitirc/index.html
  Software for Windows 95.

- ParaChat—Wweb-based 100% Java chat software
  http://www.paralogic.com/

- The PIRCH Page
  http://www.bcpl.lib.md.us/~frappa/pirch.html
  IRC client software for the Windows 3.x, Windows 95 and Windows NT.

- A Quick Guide to Basic mIRC Commands
  http://www.voicenet.com/~bparker1/CHANNEL/mircguide.htm

- The Scripters Guild
  http://www.geocities.com/SiliconValley/Heights/1246/

- Shareware.com—IRC Downloads
  http://search.shareware.com/code/engine/Find?frame=none&logop=and&cfrom=quick&orfile=True&hits=25&search=IRC&category=All-Categories

- Straight Talk About IRC
  http://www.rare.on.ca/users/genealogyforum/TalkIRC.htm

- Stroud's IRC App Reviews
  http://cws.internet.com/32irc-reviews.html

- XiRCON
  http://www.xircon.com/
  IRC Client for Windows 95/NT.

- Yahoo!...Computers and Internet...Chat
  http://dir.yahoo.com/Computers_and_Internet/Internet/Chat/

CITING SOURCES
http://www.CyndisList.com/citing.htm

Category Index:
- ◆ Citations in Genealogy
- ◆ Citing Electronic Sources

- ◆ Forms

◆ Citations in Genealogy

- Carla's Tips for Sources
  http://www.familytreemaker.com/19_carla.html
  by Carla Ridenour

- A Cite For Sore Eyes—Quality Citations for Electronic Genealogy Sources
  http://www.oz.net/~markhow/writing/cite.htm
  By Mark Howells.

- Citing the Messages
  http://www.ancestry.com/home/bestofgc/citing.htm
  A sample article by Drew Smith from Genealogical Computing.

- Citing Your Sources
  http://www.genealogy.org/~bcg/skbld959.html
  From the Board for Certification of Genealogists—Skill Building—September 1995.

- EVIDENCE! Citation & Analysis For The Family Historian
  http://www.genealogical.com/evidence.htm
  A terrific new book by Elizabeth Shown Mills.

- How To Cite Sources
  http://www.familytreemaker.com/19_wylie.html
  by John Wylie.

- Producing Quality Research Notes
  http://www.genealogy.org/~bcg/skbld971.html
  From the Board for Certification of Genealogists—Skill Building—January 1997.

- Serious Citations
  http://www.ancestry.com/home/George_Morgan/02-27-98.htm
  From "Along Those Lines . . ." by George G. Morgan.

- Why Bother? The Value of Documentation in Family History Research
  http://www.familytreemaker.com/19_kory.html
  by Kory Meyerink, MLS, AG.

◆ Citing Electronic Sources

- APA-Style Citations of Electronic Sources
  http://www.cas.usf.edu/english/walker/apa.html

- Beyond the MLA Handbook: Documenting Electronic Sources on the Internet
  http://falcon.eku.edu/honors/beyond-mla/

- Bibliographic Formats for Citing Electronic Information
  http://www.uvm.edu/~ncrane/estyles/

- A Brief Citation Guide for Internet Sources in History and the Humanities
  http://h-net2.msu.edu/~africa/citation.html

- Citation Guides for Electronic Documents
  http://www.nlc-bnc.ca/ifla/I/training/citation/citing.htm
  A good list of links to citation resources.

- Citation Style for Internet Sources
  http://www.cl.cam.ac.uk/users/maw13/citation.html

- Citation Style Guides for Internet and Electronic Sources
  http://www.library.ualberta.ca/library_html/help/pathfinders/style/

- A Cite For Sore Eyes—Quality Citations for Electronic Genealogy Sources
  http://www.oz.net/~markhow/writing/cite.htm
  By Mark Howells

- Citing Electronic Information in History Papers
  http://www.people.memphis.edu/~mcrouse/elcite.html

- Citing Internet—APA Style
  http://www.nhmccd.cc.tx.us/contracts/lrc/kc/CitingElecSources-apa.html

- Citing the Messages
  http://www.ancestry.com/home/bestofgc/citing.htm
  A sample article by Drew Smith from Genealogical Computing.

- Citing Online Sources
  http://clever.net/quinion/words/citation.htm

- Citing Online Sources—MLA Style
  http://www.nhmccd.cc.tx.us/contracts/lrc/kc/mla-internet.html

- Columbia Online Style: MLA-Style Citations of Electronic Sources
  http://www.cas.usf.edu/english/walker/mla.html

- Documenting Sources
  http://www.familytreemaker.com/issue19.html
  From Family Tree Maker Online.

- Electronic Sources: APA Style of Citation
  http://www.uvm.edu/~xli/reference/apa.html

- Electronic Sources: MLA Style of Citation
  http://www.uvm.edu/~xli/reference/mla.html

- Electronic Style...the Final Frontier
  http://funnelweb.utcc.utk.edu/~hoemann/style.html

- Guide for Citing Electronic Information
  http://www.wilpaterson.edu/wpcpages/library/citing.htm
  From the Sarah Byrd Askew Library, William Patterson University of New Jersey.

- A Guide to Citing Internet Sources
  http://www.ups.edu/library/research/CITEURLS.htm
  Collins Memorial Library, University of Puget Sound.

- MLA Style
  http://www.mla.org/main_stl.htm

- MLA-Style Citations of Electronic Sources
  http://www.cas.usf.edu/english/walker/mla.html
  or this alternate site
  http://www.lib.berkeley.edu/TeachingLib/Guides/Internet/MLAStyleSheet.html

- World Wide Words—Citing Online Sources
  http://clever.net/quinion/words/citation.htm

◆ Forms

- Genealogy Research Log
  http://www.genrecords.com/forms/genealogyresearchlog.pdf
  Form to print and use from the Genealogy Records Service. Requires the Adobe Acrobat Reader Plugin in order to print the form: http://www.adobe.com/prodindex/acrobat/readstep.html

- Research Log
  http://www.lds.org/en/2_How_Do_I_Begin/Research_Log.html
  From the LDS church.

- Research Log
  http://www.pbs.org/kbyu/ancestors/teachersguide/tg-images/resrchlg.gif
  From the Ancestors television program, with an alternate form in .pdf format that requires the Adobe Acrobat Reader Plugin in order to print the form.
  http://www.pbs.org/kbyu/ancestors/teachersguide/pdf/reschlog.pdf

CORRESPONDENCE
Postage, Payments & Letter Writing
http://www.CyndisList.com/correspd.htm

Category Index:

◆ Forms & Form Letters
◆ General Resource Sites

◆ Postage & Payments
◆ Postal Services Worldwide

◆ Forms & Form Letters

● Ancestry.com—County Courthouses Record Request Form Letter
http://www.ancestry.com/download/countyform.htm

● Ancestry.com—Naturalization Record Request Form Letter
http://www.ancestry.com/download/naturalform.htm

● Family Tree Maker Online Genealogy How-To—Form Letters and Other Aids
http://www.familytreemaker.com/00000023.html

　○ Correspondence Table
http://www.familytreemaker.com/00000007.html

　○ Form Letters in English
http://www.familytreemaker.com/ltr_english.html

　○ Form Letters in French
http://www.familytreemaker.com/ltr_french.html

　○ Form Letters in German
http://www.familytreemaker.com/ltr_german.html

　○ Form Letters in Italian
http://www.familytreemaker.com/ltr_italian.html

　○ Form Letters in Spanish
http://www.familytreemaker.com/ltr_spanish.html

● Form Letters for German Genealogy
http://www.genealogy.net/gene/www/ghlp/muster.html

● Sample Letters in German to Obtain Genealogical Information
gopher://Gopher.UToledo.edu:70/00GOPHER_ROOT%
3A%5BRESEARCH-RESOURCES.GENEALOGY.GERMAN-
GENEALOGY%5DGERMAN-SAMPLE-LETTER.FOR-
INFORMATION-REQUESTS

● Supplies, Charts, Forms, Etc.
http://www.CyndisList.com/supplies.htm
See this category on Cyndi's List for related links.

● Universal Family Group Sheet
http://www.geocities.com/Heartland/Meadows/7970/vfgs.html
An online form which allows you to enter your data and e-mail it to another researcher.

◆ General Resource Sites

● Effective Correspondence: The Bad Manners of Just One Genealogist, Reflect on All of Us
http://www.ancestry.com/lessons/howto/letters.htm

● Essentials of a Genealogical Letter
http://www.rootscomputing.com/howto/checkl/checkl.htm
Scroll to the bottom of this web page to read the article.

● The Forms Needed to Order Records from the National Archives
http://www.ancestry.com/columns/george/05-15-98.htm
From "Along Those Lines . . ." by George G. Morgan.

● Genealogy Correspondence: The Writing Rite Done Right
http://www.ancestry.com/columns/george/09-11-98.htm
From "Along Those Lines . . ." by George G. Morgan.

● Lineages' First Steps—Write Successful Genealogy Queries
http://www.lineages.com/FirstSteps/WriteQueries.asp

● Researching From Abroad
http://www.genuki.org.uk/ab/
From the GENUKI web site.

● 6 Steps to Writing a Successful Genealogy Query
http://www.firstct.com/fv/query.html

● What is the proper format for addressing a "snail mail" letter to a foreign country?
http://www.oz.net/~markhow/genuki/NFK/norffaq.htm#address
From the Norfolk-L Genealogy Mailing List Frequently Asked Questions web pages.

◆ Postage & Payments

● Britain in the USA—British Currency and Postage Stamps
http://www.britain-info.org/bis/fsheets/5.stm

● Currency Calculator
http://www.x-rates.com/calculator.html

● Interactive Currency Table
http://www.xe.net/currency/table.htm

- International Reply Coupon Affair
  http://www.ancestry.com/columns/myra/Shaking_Family_Tree 08-20-98.htm
  By Myra Vanderpool Gormley, C.G.

- International Reply Coupons
  http://opera.iinet.net.au/~davwat/wfhs/irc.html
  A brief description from the Watkins Family History Society.

- Ruesch International, Inc.—
  Global Payments Services
  http://www.ruesch.com/
  Affordable payment options for sending money to other countries.

- The Universal Currency Converter
  http://www.xe.net/currency/classic/

- What is the best way to send payments to the United Kingdom from abroad?
  http://www.oz.net/~markhow/genuki/NFK/ norffaq.htm#Payments
  From the Norfolk-L Genealogy Mailing List Frequently Asked Questions web pages.

◆ Postal Services Worldwide

- Australia Post—Correct Addressing
  http://www.auspost.com.au/index.asp?link_id=2.241

- Canada Post—How to Format the Postal Code and the Address
  http://www.canadapost.ca/CPC2/addrm/pclookup/ pcinfo.html#how

- Postal Authorities
  http://www.execpc.com/~joeluft/postauth.html
  Listed by country.

- Royal Mail—Postal Services Guide ~ U.K.
  http://www.royalmail.com/guide/contents.htm

- United States Postal Service—Addressing and Packaging Your Mail
  http://www.usps.gov/csmrguid/addrpack.htm
  A portion of the "Consumer's Guide to Postal Services and Products."

DATABASES, SEARCH SITES, SURNAME LISTS
http://www.CyndisList.com/database.htm

Category Index:

- ◆ Commercial
- ◆ General
- ◆ Locality Specific
- ◆ Military
- ◆ People & Families

- ◆ Records: Census, Cemeteries, Land, Obituaries, Personal, Taxes and Vital
- ◆ ROOTS-L and RootsWeb
- ◆ Services
- ◆ Societies & Groups

◆ Commercial

- Ancestry Library Search
  http://www.ancestry.com/ancestry/search.asp
  Social Security Death Index (SSDI), PERSI, Ancestry World Tree and 10 Day Free Trial Databases.

- Everton Publishers
  http://www.everton.com/
  Databases include "Roots" Cellar, Family File, Pedigree Library and GEDSEARCH. Also databases for England, some census and death records.

- Family Tree Maker Online
  http://www.familytreemaker.com/
  Search the Family Finder Index online.

- Design Software
  http://www.dhc.net/~design/search.htm
  Misc. searches and other useful utilities.

- Golden West Marketing
  http://www.greenheart.com/rdietz/
  Surname exchange, limited free searches of database, book list, professional researchers.

- Kindred Konnections
  http://www.kindredkonnections.com/
  Online searching through a 70-million name genealogy archive. Socal Security Death Index (March 1997 release), Free Surname Research, Census Indexes, Pedigree linked GEDCOM Library, and hundreds of resource files.

- Legends and Legacies Family Tree Collection
  http://interchange.idc.uvic.ca:80/~legends/library/trees/famtree.html

- Next of Kin
  http://www.lineages.com/NextOfKin/default.asp
  From Lineages, Inc.

- Westland Publications Genealogy—Find Immigrant Ancestors
  http://www.theriver.com/westlandpubn/
  Search from Thousands of Surnames and Hundreds of Place Names in Germany, Great Britain, France, Switzerland, and Central Europe.

- World Family Tree Submitter List
  http://www.inlink.com/~nomi/wftlist/index.html

- Yahoo! Business and Economy:Companies: Information:Genealogy:Databases
  http://dir.yahoo.com/Business_and_Economy/Companies/Information/Genealogy/Databases/

◆ General

- BirthQuest
  http://www.access.digex.net/~vqi/top.html
  Online searchable database for searching adoptees, birth parents, adoptive parents and siblings.

- Common Threads
  http://www.gensource.com/common/
  A searchable database with e-mail addresses for submitters.

- Design Software—Genealogy Databases on the World Wide Web, A–M
  http://www.dhc.net/~design/datainda.htm
  N–Z
  http://www.dhc.net/~design/dataindx.htm

- FEEFHS Cross Index of 27 Surname databases
  http://feefhs.org/index/indexsur.html

- GEDDEX—GEDCOM Index from A.J. Morris
  http://www.genealogy.org/~ajmorris/geddex/geddex.htm

- GENDEX Database
  http://www.gendex.com/
  A searchable index of over 7.7 million names in 2,259 databases, each actively maintained and updated by the database owner.

- GeneaNet Genealogical Database Network
  http://www.geneanet.org/
  Database indexing surnames from before 1850 & corresponding contact information—online or offline.

- Genealogists Index to the World Wide Web
  http://members.aol.com/Genwebindx/index.htm

- GenMatch
  http://206.139.152.113/GenMatch/genmatch.htm
  Compares & finds matches on online databases.

- GenServ—Family History
  http://www.genserv.com/
  Over 9,370,000 names in 7,000+ GEDCOM databases.

- Growth of Linked Pedigree Databases
  http://www.bearhaven.com/family/growth.html
  A month-by-month list of the growth of some large genealogy databases.

- Indexes Unlimited
  http://www.eburg.com/~fowlerc/browse.html
  Book indexes online.

- my-ged.com—the best little gedcom server on the WWW
  http://www.my-ged.com/

- Online Genealogical Database Index
  http://www.gentree.com/
  From Tim Doyle.

- Personal Home Pages
  http://www.CyndisList.com/personal.htm
  See this category on Cyndi's List for related links.

- Queries & Message Boards
  http://www.CyndisList.com/queries.htm
  See this category on Cyndi's List for related links.

- Scott McGee's GenWeb Page
  http://www.genealogy.org/~smcgee/genweb/genweb.html

- Searchable Genealogy Links [Lauren Knoblauch]
  http://www.bc1.com/users/sgl/
  A large selection of world-wide searchable genealogy links. Sorted geographically and alphabetically.

- Surname Springboard
  http://www.geocities.com/~alacy/spring.htm
  Dedicated to internet researchers who have indexed their GEDCOM data & converted it to HTML pages.

- Surnames, Family Associations & Family Newsletters
  http://www.CyndisList.com/surnames.htm
  See this category on Cyndi's List for related links.

- The SurnameWeb
  http://www.surnameweb.org/
  The Surname Genealogy Web Project.

- What's Your Line?
  http://www.uvol.com/www1st/redeem/surnames.html
  List of surnames being researched from the WWW 1st Ward LDS site.

- World Wide Cemetery
  http://www.interlog.com/~cemetery/

- WWW genealogy databases
  http://www.genhomepage.com/genwww.html

- Yates Publishing—The Computerized Ancestor
  http://www.montana.com/yates/index.html

◆ Locality Specific

- Anglesey, Wales Surname List
  http://www.genuki.org.uk/big/wal/Surnames/agy.htm

- Angus Scotland Surnames List
  http://www.geocities.com/Athens/Parthenon/5020/Angus/

- Argyllshire, Scotland Surname List
  http://members.aol.com/sloinne/Argyll/Surnames.htm

- Australian Family Tree Connections Surname Register
  http://www.aftc.com.au/surname.html

- Ayrshire Surname Database ~ Scotland
  http://home.clara.net/iainkerr/genuki/AYR/SID/indexsid.htm

- Banffshire Surname List ~ Scotland
  http://www.rootsweb.com/~sctban/

- Bedfordshire Surnames List ~ England
  http://homepages.ihug.co.nz/~hughw/bedf.html

- Berkshire Surnames List
  http://www.geocities.com/Heartland/Ranch/5973/berksurname.htm

- Berwickshire Surnames List ~ Scotland
  http://www.geocities.com/Heartland/Valley/2039/

- Breconshire, Wales Surnames List
  http://www.genuki.org.uk/big/wal/Surnames/bre.htm

- Brule County, SD, History Index—Interactive Search
  http://www.rootsweb.com/cgi-bin/sdbrulehist/sdbrule.pl
  From the South Dakota Historical Collections, Vol. XXIII, pages 1–184 (1947).

- Buckinghamshire Surnames List ~ England
  http://www.csranet.com/~dcarlsen/genuki/BKM/bucksurname.html

- Caernarfonshire, Wales Surnames List
  http://www.genuki.org.uk/big/wal/Surnames/cae.htm

- Caithness Surnames Research List ~ Scotland
  http://www.frayston.demon.co.uk/genuki/cai/surnames.htm

- Cambridgeshire Surnames List ~ England
  http://www.personal.u-net.com/~gaer/cam/SurnamesList.html

- Cardiganshire, Wales Surnames List
  http://www.genuki.org.uk/big/wal/Surnames/cgn.htm

- Carmarthenshire, Wales Surnames List
  http://www.genuki.org.uk/big/wal/Surnames/cmn.htm

- Channel Islands Genealogy—Surname Interests List
  http://members.aol.com/johnf14246/ci/surnames.html

- Cheshire Surnames List ~ England
  http://www.users.zetnet.co.uk/blangston/surnames/

- Chinese Surnames
  http://www.geocities.com/Tokyo/3919/

- Clackmannanshire Surname List ~ Scotland
  http://www.dgnscrn.demon.co.uk/genuki/CLK/misc/surnames/

- Co. Tyrone, N. Ireland Fellow Genealogists
  http://pw2.netcom.com/~vanessa1/tyrone.html

- Cornwall, England—Surnames List ~ England
  http://www.cs.ncl.ac.uk/genuki/SurnamesList/Cornwall/

- County Antrim Surname Interest List ~ Ireland
  http://www.rootsweb.com/~irldub/antrim/antrimsr.htm

- County Down Surname List ~ Northern Ireland
  http://www.amitar.com.au/~deel/downlist.htm

- County Galway Surname List ~ Ireland
  http://www.labyrinth.net.au/~quibellg/galway.htm

- County Kerry Surname Interest List ~ Ireland
  http://www.bendigo.net.au/~oconnell/kerry.htm

- County Kilkenny Ireland Genealogy "Surnames
  of Kilkenny"
  http://www.rootsweb.com/~irlkik/ksurname.htm

- County Limerick, Ireland Surnames and Queries
  http://www.geocities.com/Athens/Parthenon/6108/limerick.htm

- The County Mayo Surname Interest List ~ Ireland
  http://www.cs.ncl.ac.uk/genuki/SurnamesList/MAY.html

- County of Stirlingshire Surname List
  http://www.jeack.com.au/~treaclbk/surnames/stirling.htm

- County Sligo, Ireland Surname List
  http://www.rootsweb.com/~irlsli/surnam.html

- County Sutherland, Scotland Surname List
  http://members.aol.com/sloinne/Sutherland/Surnames.htm

- County Westmeath Surname List ~ Ireland
  http://www.amitar.com.au/~deel/westlist.htm

- Cumbria Surnames List ~ England
  http://cumbria-surnames.worldward.com/index.mv

- Danish Emigration Archives
  http://users.cybercity.dk/~ccc13656/uk/home2.htm
  Searchable database for 1869 to 1904, working on records thru 1940.

- DDD Danish Demographic Database
  http://ddd.sa.dk/ddd2.htm
  Search a partial census database for 1787–1850 and the Danish emigrant database for 1868–1900.

- Denbighshire, Wales Surnames List
  http://www.genuki.org.uk/big/wal/Surnames/den.htm

- Derbyshire Surnames List ~ England
  http://homepage.ihug.co.nz/~hughw/dby.htm

- Devon, England—Surnames List
  http://www.gendex.com/users/branscombe/genuki/devindex.htm

- East and North Riding Surname Interest List ~
  England
  http://www.jodenoy.clara.net/erynry/erynry.htm

- East Lothian Surnames List ~ Scotland
  http://www.users.zetnet.co.uk/vdunstan/genuki/ELN/Surnames/

- East of London Surname Overview
  http://ourworld.compuserve.com/homepages/jordan/eolsur01.htm
  Includes the Boroughs of: Hackney, Tower Hamlets within Middlesex County, and Newham, Redbridge, Barking and Dagenham, and Havering within Essex County.

- Essex Surnames List ~ England
  http://www.sullom.demon.co.uk/essex/surnames.html

- FINNDEX—The Finnish Genealogical
  Research Index
  http://members.aol.com/finndex/finndex.htm

- Flintshire, Wales Surnames List
  http://www.genuki.org.uk/big/wal/Surnames/fln.htm

- Fylkesarkivet i Sogn og Fjordane—Databases
  http://www.sffarkiv.no/sffbasar/default.asp

- GENUKI Surname Lists
  http://www.cs.ncl.ac.uk/genuki/SurnamesList/
  Lists for each county in the United Kingdom and Ireland.

- German Ancestors
  http://www.haaga.com/germany/default.htm
  Post your German surnames on this alphabetical surname index.

- German-Bohemian Immigrant Surname Database
  http://www.rootsweb.com/~gbhs/database.html

- Ghosts of the Klondike Gold Rush
  http://www.gold-rush.org/
  Check out the "Pan for Gold Database."

- Glamorganshire, Wales Surnames List
  http://www.genuki.org.uk/big/wal/Surnames/gla.htm

- Gloucestershire Surnames List ~ England
  http://tolstoi.saccii.net.au/~dsteel/glsnames.htm

- Hampshire Surnames List ~ England
  http://dspace.dial.pipex.com/c.broomfield/ham.htm

- Herefordshire Surnames List ~ England
  http://freespace.virgin.net/isabel.easter/mem.html

- HERRICK Library's Listing of SURNAMES in
  Ottawa County Michigan
  http://www.macatawa.org/~brianter/herrick.htm

- The Hertfordshire Surnames List ~ England
  http://mwi.home.ml.org/hertford.html

- Huntingdonshire Surnames List ~ England
  http://www.genuki.org.uk/big/eng/HUN/Surnames.html

- Julie's Welsh Surnames List
  http://home.on.rogers.wave.ca/bozzy/index.html
  A page for posting Welsh surnames being researched online.

- Kent England Surname Interests
  http://www.centrenet.co.uk/~cna49/kfhs2.htm

- Kingdom of Fife Surnames List ~ Scotland
  http://www.genuki.org.uk/big/scot/Fife/fife.surnames.html

- Kinross-shire Surname List ~ Scotland
  http://www.dgnscrn.demon.co.uk/genuki/KRS/misc/surnames/index.html

- Lanarkshire Surnames List ~ Scotland
  http://www.fan.net.au/~scoop/lanark.htm

- Leicestershire Surnames List ~ England
  http://www.lodp.demon.co.uk/LEI.html

- Leitrim-Roscommon Surname Search ~ Ireland
  http://www.thecore.com/let_ros/surname_intro.html
- Lincolnshire Surnames ~ England
  http://www.excel.net/~nclark/sur1.htm
- The Liverpool (& area) Surnames List ~ England
  http://www.globalserve.net/~scouse/list.htm
- London Jews Database
  http://www.jewishgen.org/databases/londweb.htm
- Louisiana Land Records—Interactive Search
  http://searches.rootsweb.com/cgi-bin/laland/laland.pl
  Pre-1908 Homestead and Cash Entry Patents from the Bureau of Land Management's General Land Office (GLO) Automated Records Project.
- Mecklenburg-Vorpommern Query System
  http://pages.prodigy.net/jhbowen/c3.htm
- Merionethshire, Wales Surnames List
  http://www.genuki.org.uk/big/wal/Surnames/mer.htm
- The Midlothian, Scotland Surnames List
  http://pages.prodigy.net/richrob/midlothian/midlothian.htm
- Missouri Surname Researchers List
  http://www.geocities.com/Heartland/Plains/7113/surnames.htm
- Monmouthshire, Wales Surnames List
  http://www.genuki.org.uk/big/wal/Surnames/mon.htm
- Montgomeryshire, Wales Surnames List
  http://www.genuki.org.uk/big/wal/Surnames/mgy.htm
- Nairnshire Surnames List ~ Scotland
  http://www.geocities.com/~brooms/genuki/surnames/index.html
- Names of Mecklenburg-Schwerin Emigrants 1844–1915
  http://pages.prodigy.net/jhbowen/emig.htm
- Niedersachsen Germany Queries
  http://cgi.rootsweb.com/~genbbs/genbbs.cgi/Germany/Niedersachsen
- NORDGUIDE
  http://info.rbt.no/nordguide/nordguide.html
  A directory of databases in the Nordic Countries.
- Nordrhein-Westfalen (North Rhine Westphalia) Surnames ~ Germany
  http://www.rootsweb.com/~cotter/nr-wf/surnames.html
- Norfolk Surnames List ~ England
  http://freespace.virgin.net/isabel.easter/Norfolk/Surnames.htm
- North East Lancashire Surname List ~ England
  http://ourworld.compuserve.com/homepages/GAFOSTER/n-e-lanc.htm
- Northamptonshire Surnames List ~ England
  http://www.skynet.co.uk/genuki/big/eng/NTH/Surnames/
- Northumberland and Durham, England—Surnames List
  http://gendex.com/users/branscombe/genuki/nblindex.htm

- Northwest History Databases from the Tacoma Public Library
  http://www.tpl.lib.wa.us/nwr/nwdata.htm
- Nostro Albero
  http://www.geocities.com/SiliconValley/Park/3063/nostrow.htm
  With a searchable database of 5,300 Italian surnames.
- Nottinghamshire Surnames List ~ England
  http://homepages.ihug.co.nz/~hughw/notts.html
- Oklahoma Surnames
  http://www.rootsweb.com/~oknames/
- Online Australasian Names Research Directory
  http://www.users.on.net/proformat/ausnames.html
- On-line Dorset Names Research Directory
  http://www.users.on.net/proformat/dornames.html
- On-line Irish Names Research Directory
  http://www.users.on.net/proformat/irlnames.html
- On-line Search for Maiden Names of Women in South Holland
  http://www.itsnet.com/~pauld/ksh/
  Searchable database to be used in conjunction with the "Klappers of Zuid Holland" ("Indexes of South Holland"). Approx. 250,000 maiden names, from between 1695 and 1811.
- The Orkney Surnames List
  http://www.tiac.net/users/teschek/genuki/OKI/surnames.htm
- Oxfordshire Surname Interest List (OXSIL) ~ England
  http://www.rootsweb.com/~oxsil/
- Peeblesshire Surnames List ~ Scotland
  http://www.rootsweb.com/~sctpbs/PSL.htm
- Pembrokeshire, Wales Surnames List
  http://www.genuki.org.uk/big/wal/Surnames/pem.htm
- Pennsylvania Dutch (Queries Posted Immediately and Surnames Indexed Every Tuesday)
  http://cgi.rootsweb.com/~genbbs/genbbs.cgi/USA/Pa/Dutch
- Perthshire, Scotland Surnames List
  http://www.geocities.com/Heartland/Plains/3176/perthlist/index.html
- Portuguese Genealogist Master Database
  http://www.lusaweb.com/mstrlst.html-ssi
- Prince Edward Island Surname List
  http://www.geocities.com/Heartland/Acres/4835/index.html
- Radnorshire, Wales Surnames List
  http://www.genuki.org.uk/big/wal/Surnames/rad.htm
- Rafal T. Prinke—Surname List (English)
  http://hum.amu.edu.pl/~rafalp/GEN/wykaz-eng.html
- Rafal T. Prinke—Surname List / Lista Nazwisk (Polish)
  http://hum.amu.edu.pl/~rafalp/GEN/wykaz.html
- Renfrewshire Surnames List ~ Scotland
  http://www.skylinc.net/~lasmith/rfwnames/

- The Rutland Surnames List ~ England
  http://www.lodp.demon.co.uk/RUT.html
- Search the USGenWeb Archives Digital Library
  http://www.rootsweb.com/~usgenweb/ussearch.htm
- Selkirkshire Surnames List ~ Scotland
  http://www.users.zetnet.co.uk/vdunstan/genuki/SEL/Surnames/
- Shropshire Surname Interest List ~ England
  http://www.genuki.org.uk/big/eng/Surnames/sal.htm
- Siciliani in the World
  http://diemme.diemme.it/italiani/sicilia/
  E-mail addresses for people researching Sicilian surnames.
- Somerset & Dorset Surnames Index
  http://www.bakery.co.uk/sandd/
- Somerset Surnames Interest List ~ England
  http://www.genuki.org.uk/big/eng/Surnames/som.htm
- Staffordshire Surname Interest List ~ England
  http://www.genuki.org.uk/big/eng/Surnames/sts.htm
- Suffolk Surname List (& More!) ~ England
  http://www.visualcreations.com/pers/leeann/suffolk/
- Surname Index for Kentuckiana Genealogy ~ Kentucky & Indiana
  http://cgi.rootsweb.com/surhelp-bin/
  surindx.pl?site=kyiana&letter=a
- Surname List: Dumfriesshire, Kirkcudbrightshire & Wigtownshire ~Scotland
  http://www.users.globalnet.co.uk/~brownfam/dfsnames.html
- Surname Page for Schleswig-Holstein, Germany
  http://www.rootsweb.com/~deuscn/surnam.htm
- Surrey Surname Interest List ~ England
  http://www.genuki.org.uk/big/eng/Surnames/sry.htm
- Sussex Surnames List ~ England
  http://dspace.dial.pipex.com/c.broomfield/ssxname.htm
- The Texas Genealogy Register
  http://www.lsjunction.com/gen.htm
- Texas Surnames
  http://www.rootsweb.com/~txrusk/txsurnames.html
- Tipperary Surname Interest List ~ Ireland
  http://homepages.ihug.co.nz/~hughw/tip.html
- Tisbury History: On-Line Historical Archives ~ Massachusetts
  http://www.vineyard.net/vineyard/history/
- USGenWeb Archives
  http://www.rootsweb.com/~usgenweb/
- USGenWeb Archives Search Page
  http://searches.rootsweb.com/usgwarch.html
- Valdez Museum & Historical Archive—Rush Participants Database
  http://www.alaska.net/~vldzmuse/valdez.htm
  Alaska. Valdez Gold Rush 1898–1899, Names Database.

- The Warwickshire Surnames List ~ England
  http://homepages.ihug.co.nz/~hughw/warwick.html
- The Wellington Valley Convicts, 1823–31
  http://www.newcastle.edu.au/department/hi/roberts/
  convicts.htm
  A database of over 1,000 convicts.
- West Indies Surname Interests List
  http://ourworld.compuserve.com/homepages/vroyal/
- West Lothian Surname List ~ Scotland
  http://www.rootsweb.com/~sctwln/
- West Riding Yorkshire Surname Interests ~ England
  http://members.aol.com/wrylist/wry.htm
- Wexford Surname Interest List ~ Ireland
  http://homepages.ihug.co.nz/~hughw/wexford.html
- Wiltshire Surname Interests List ~ England
  http://www.genuki.org.uk/big/eng/WIL/interests/surnames.html
- Wisconsin Land Records—Interactive Search
  http://searches.rootsweb.com/cgi-bin/wisconsin/wisconsin.pl
  Pre-1908 Homestead and Cash Entry Patents from the BLM.
- Worcestershire Surname Interest List ~ England
  http://www.jump.net/~salter/WORSIL.html

◆ Military

- American Revolutionary War Soldiers & Their Descendants
  http://www.rootsweb.com/~ars/index.htm
  A surname list of soldiers, with e-mail addresses to contact the researchers.
- Canadian Expeditionary Force (CEF)— Records Database
  http://www.archives.ca/db/cef/index.html
  An index to the personnel files of over 600,000 soldiers that enlisted during the First World War.
- The Civil War Soldiers and Sailors System (CWSS)
  http://www.itd.nps.gov/cwss/
  Read a description of the project, then use the searchable database at:
  Civil War Soldiers and Sailors System Name Search.
  http://www.itd.nps.gov/cgi-bin/dualz.test
- Confederate Pension Rolls, Veterans and Widows
  http://image.vtls.com/collections/CW.html
  From the Library of Virginia Digital Collections.
- Database of Illinois' Civil War Veterans
  http://www.sos.state.il.us/depts/archives/datcivil.html
  From the Illinois State Archives, this is an index of over 250,000 men in 175 regiments as they are listed in 8 volumes of the Report of the Adjutant General of the State of Illinois, published in 1900–1901.
- Index To Militia Rolls—Olive Tree Genealogy
  http://www.rootsweb.com/~ote/indexmil.htm
  Rolls for New Jersey and New York.
- Kansas Enlistments (1861–1865)
  http://www.lineages.com/military/ks_enlistments.asp
  Searchable database index from Lineages, Inc.

- The Korean War Project
  http://www.koreanwar.org/

- Our Ancestors Who Served in the War of 1812
  http://www.rootsweb.com/~kyharris/1812vets.htm

- Pearl Harbor Casualties List
  http://www.mit.edu:8001/afs/athena/activity/a/afrotc/www/names

- Pearl Harbor Casualties (U.S.)
  http://www.lineages.com/military/PearlHarbor.asp
  Searchable database from Lineages, Inc.

- Pearl Harbor—Civilian and Military Personnel Casualties
  ftp://ftp.rootsweb.com/pub/usgenweb/hi/military/pearl.txt

- Recruitment of Illinois Regiments—Civil War, 1861–1865—County Search or see these databases to search by company:
  http://www.outfitters.com/illinois/history/civil/searchco.html

  o Recruitment of Illinois Artillery Regiments— Civil War, 1861–1865
    http://www.outfitters.com/illinois/history/civil/searchart.html

  o Recruitment of Illinois Cavalry Regiments— Civil War, 1861–1865
    http://www.outfitters.com/illinois/history/civil/searchcav.html

  o Recruitment of Illinois Infantry Regiments— Civil War, 1861–1865
    http://www.outfitters.com/illinois/history/civil/searchreg.html

- Search the Virginia Rosters
  http://jefferson.village.virginia.edu/vshadow/rostersearch.html

- VietNam Casualty Search Page
  http://www.no-quarter.org/
  Database compiled by Thomas Holloway.

- Vietnam Era POW/MIA Database
  http://lcweb2.loc.gov/pow/powhome.html
  At the Library of Congress.

- The VietNam Veterans' Memorial Wall
  http://thewall-usa.com/
  With a searchable database.

- The Wall on the Web
  http://www.vietvet.org/thewall/thewallm.html
  Over 58,000 names in this list.

- World War I Canadian Infantry & Cavalry Index
  http://www.bookkeeping.com/rings/genealogy/ww1.html

◆ People & Families

- HMS Bounty Genealogies
  http://wavefront.wavefront.com/~pjlareau/bounty6.html

- Huguenot Surnames Index—from Australian Family Tree Connections Magazine
  http://www.aftc.com.au/huguenot.html

- Index to: Religious Personnel in Russia 1853–1854
  http://www.memo.com/jgsr/database/deych.cgi

- The JewishGen Family Finder (JGFF)
  http://www.jewishgen.org/jgff/

- Master Index to President's Genealogical Data
  http://www.dcs.hull.ac.uk/public/genealogy/presidents/gedx.html

- OMII Genealogy Project & Kidron Heritage Center
  http://www.bright.net/~swisstea/index.html
  A Swiss Mennonite & German Amish genealogy project.

- Pennsylvania Dutch (Queries Posted Immediately and Surnames Indexed Every Tuesday)
  http://cgi.rootsweb.com/~genbbs/genbbs.cgi/USA/Pa/Dutch

- Surname Helper—Search for a Surname
  http://cgi.rootsweb.com/surhelp/srchall.html
  A searchable database of queries and surname registrations posted on various genealogy sites, including USGenWeb and WorldGenWeb.

◆ Records: Census, Cemeteries, Land, Obituaries, Personal, Taxes and Vital (Born, Married, Died & Buried)

- 1871 Ontario Census Index
  http://www.archives.ca/db/1871/1871_Census_Search.html

- 1872 Foreign-Born Voters of California
  http://feefhs.org/fbvca/fbvcagri.html

- Ancestry Home Town—Social Security Death Index (SSDI)
  http://www.ancestry.com/ssdi/advanced.htm

- Arkansas Land Records—Interactive Search
  http://searches.rootsweb.com/cgi-bin/arkland/arkland.pl

- Census Related Sites Worldwide
  http://www.CyndisList.com/census2.htm
  See this category on Cyndi's List for related links.

- Censuses of the Cotswolds and Southern Warwickshire
  http://www.silk.net/personal/gordonb/cotswold.htm
  Dozens of census extracts for this area in England.

- Database to an Index of Indiana Marriages Through 1850
  http://www.statelib.lib.in.us/www/indiana/genealogy/mirr.html
  Indiana State Library, Genealogy Division.

- Everton's On-Line Search—Social Security Death Index
  http://emh.everton.com/ssmdi.html

- Faculty Office Marriage Licence Index
  http://ourworld.compuserve.com/homepages/David_Squire/faculty.htm
  Index of marriage licences issued by the Master of Faculties of the Archbishop of Canterbury for the period 1714 to 1850, England.

- Genealogical Death Indexing System, Michigan
  http://www.mdch.state.mi.us/PHA/OSR/gendis/index.htm
  A database containing 81,540 Michigan death records from 1867–1874 and a portion of 1875 from the Division of Vital Records and Health Statistics.

- Genealogy Online's Event's Database
  http://events.genealogy.org/main.html
  Add to this database and/or search this database of events such as birth, marriage or death, by surname.

- Index of Marriages and Deaths in New York Weekly Museum, 1788–1817
  http://www.itsnet.com/~pauld/newyork/

- The Joiner Marriage Index
  http://homepages.enterprise.net/pjoiner/mindex/mindex.html
  A Marriage Database for County Durham, and the North Riding of Yorkshire in England.

- Kentucky Vital Records Index
  http://ukcc.uky.edu/~vitalrec/
  Marriage / Divorce / Death

- Lincoln County, Tennessee, Marriages—Interactive Search
  http://www.rootsweb.com/cgi-bin/tnlincoln/tnlincoln.pl

- Madison County, Iowa Marriages 1850–1880
  http://searches.rootsweb.com/cgi-bin/Genea/iowa

- Marriage History Search Form
  http://thor.ddp.state.me.us/archives/plsql/
  archdev.Marriage_Archive.search_form
  Index to Maine Marriages 1892–1966.

- Marriages from the Sherburn Hospital Registers (1695–1837)
  http://www.cs.ncl.ac.uk/genuki/Transcriptions/DUR/SHO.html
  Northumberland and Durham, England

- Marriages in Rankin County, Mississippi
  http://www.vanished.com/pages/free_lib/rankin_co.html

- Miami Valley Genealogical Index ~ Ohio
  http://www.pcdl.lib.oh.us/miami/miami.htm
  Surname index of census, tax, marriage & wills records for these counties: Butler, Champaign, Clark, Darke, Greene, Hamilton, Mercer, Miami, Montgomery, Preble, Shelby, Warren.

- Norway—1801 Census
  http://www.uib.no/hi/1801page.html

- Nova Scotia Census Data 1891 Antigonish County
  http://www.genealogy.org/~soccgs/census.html

- Obituary Daily Times
  http://www.best.com/~shuntsbe/obituary/

- Ohio Online Death Certificate Index, 1913–1927, and 1933–1937
  http://www.ohiohistory.org/dindex/search.cfm
  Searchable database from the Ohio Historical Society, Archives/Library.

- The Old 300 Genealogical Database
  http://www.tgn.net/~bchm/Genealogy/gene.html
  Texas. "The "Old 300" database actually includes a core listing of all settlers who had received land grants in Austin's Colony by the eve of the war for independence from Mexico."

- SAMPUBCO
  http://www.wasatch.com/~dsam/sampubco/index.htm
  Will Testators Indexes, Naturalization Records Indexes and Census Indexes online. You can order copies of the original source documents for a small fee.

- The San Francisco Call (Newspaper) Database 1875–1905
  http://feefhs.org/fdb2/sfcall0.html

- Scots Origins
  http://www.origins.net/GRO/
  An online pay-per-view database of searchable indexes of the GRO(S) index to births/baptisms and banns/marriages from the Old Parish Registers dating from 1553 to 1854, plus the indexes to births, deaths and marriages from 1855 to 1897. The 1881 census data is expected later this year and an index to the 1891 census records is coming soon.

- Seventh-day Adventist Periodical Index
  http://143.207.5.3:82/search/
  Has a searchable obituary index and more.

- Släktdatas registerarkiv/ Searchable parish registers ~ Sweden
  http://sd.datatorget.educ.goteborg.se/cdata/
  reginfo.php3?lang=english#english

- Tacoma Obituary Database ~ Washington
  http://www.tpl.lib.wa.us/nwr/obitscgi.htm

- U.S. Census
  http://www.CyndisList.com/census.htm
  See this category on Cyndi's List for related links.

- U.S. Census Bureau Name Search
  http://www.census.gov/ftp/pub/genealogy/www/
  namesearch.html
  This provides name frequency in America from the 1990 census.

- Vicar-General Marriage Licence Index
  http://ourworld.compuserve.com/homepages/David_Squire/
  vicgen1.htm
  Index of marriage licences issued by the office of the Vicar-General of the Archbishop of Canterbury for the period 1701 to 1850, England.

- Virginia Quit Rent Rolls, 1704
  http://www.lineages.com/vault/rents_1704_results.asp

- Vital Events Indexes—BC Archives
  http://www2.bcarchives.gov.bc.ca/textual/governmt/vstats/
  v_events.htm
  - Marriage Registration Index Search Gateway, 1872 to 1921
    http://www2.bcarchives.gov.bc.ca/cgi-bin/www2vsm
  - Death Registration Index, 1872 to 1976
    http://www2.bcarchives.gov.bc.ca/cgi-bin/www2vsd

- York County, South Carolina, Census Index—
  Interactive Search
  http://www.rootsweb.com/cgi-bin/scyork/scyork.pl
  1790 to 1850 heads of household.

◆ ROOTS-L and RootsWeb

- RootsWeb Surname List—Interactive Data Edit/
  Submission Form
  http://rsl.rootsweb.com/cgi-bin/rsledit.cgi

- RSL Search Program Alternate site
  http://gen.roc.wayne.edu/fsl.html

- Roots Location List Name Finder
  http://searches.rootsweb.com/cgi-bin/Genea/rll

- ROOTS-L Library
  http://www.rootsweb.com/roots-l/filelist.html
  Dozens of reference files full of hidden goodies.

- RootsWeb Genealogical Data Cooperative—
  Search Engines
  http://www.rootsweb.com/rootsweb/searches/
  *Several searchable databases on this site, with more coming
  online each day!*

- RootsWeb Surname List—Interactive Search
  http://rsl.rootsweb.com/cgi-bin/rslsql.cgi

- RootsWeb Surname List or RSL Readme File
  http://www.rootsweb.com/roots-l/family.readme.html

- Search the Archive of ROOTS-L Messages from
  1987 through present
  http://searches.rootsweb.com/roots-l.search.html

◆ Services

- Ancestral Findings
  http://web.mountain.net/~wfmoney/cd/
  Free CD searches—limited to 2 individuals per day.

- Free GEDCOM Matching Service (Georgia-Lina
  Historical Society)
  E-mail: gedsearch@aol.com
  Send GEDCOM or Tiny Tafel to e-mail address.

- Nova's Genealogy Page
  http://users.aol.com/novajohn/nova.htm
  *Nova will search her Social Security Death Index CD-ROM
  for you.*

◆ Societies & Groups

- Bedfordshire Family History Society—Member's
  Interests
  http://www.kbnet.co.uk/brianp/interests.html
  A list of surnames being researched by the members.

- The Genealogical Society of Broward County
  Surname List ~ Florida
  http://www.rootsweb.com/~flgsbc/surmenu.html

- Index of Names Being Researched by Arizona State
  Genealogical Society Members
  http://www.goodnet.com/~eb43571/nindex.html

- Livermore-Amador Genealogical Society
  Surname Index
  http://www.l-ags.org/surname.html
  With over 10,000 surname-locality entries.

- MLFHS Internet Group Members Interests
  http://www.onthenet.com.au/~tonylang/Mainpage.html
  *Surnames from members of the Manchester and Lancashire
  Family History Society in England.*

- National Genealogical Society—Projects Registry
  http://www.kindredkonnections.com/ngsproj/
  A database of genealogical and family history projects.

- Orangeburgh German-Swiss Genealogical Society
  Surnames List
  http://www.netside.com/~genealogy/surnames.shtml
  Immigrants and First Families in South Carolina.

- The Skaneateles Historical Society
  http://www.skaneateles.com/historical/
  *New York. They have vital statistics records online, including
  marriage records and death records. A database of over 15,000
  records compiled from the old newspaper records from 1831
  through 1899.*

- South Carolina Historical Society—Surname Guide
  http://www.historic.com/schs/gbrowse/browse.html

- South Dakota Genealogical Society Quarterly
  Index—Interactive Search
  http://www.rootsweb.com/cgi-bin/sdgsqart/sdgsqart.pl

- Tacoma-Pierce County Genealogical Society—
  Ancestor Exchange Index
  http://www.rootsweb.com/~watpcgs/ancexch.htm
  Washington

DIARIES & LETTERS
http://www.CyndisList.com/diaries.htm

- Civil War Diaries
  http://sparc5.augustana.edu/library/civil.html

- Civil War Diary of Bingham Findley JUNKIN, 100th Pennsylvania Volunteer Infantry ("Roundheads")
  http://www.iwaynet.net/~lsci/junkin/

- The Civil War Diary of E.B. ROOT
  http://www.netrom.com/~merklee/Diary.html

- Civil War: Iowa Volunteers
  http://www.alaska.net/~design/civilwar/
  Including excerpts from a Civil War diary and letters.

- The Diary of "Honest" John Martin
  http://www.burgoyne.com/pages/ballark/JohnMartin.html
  Portions of the diary of John Martin, who was sentenced to Van Diemen's land charged with treason for fighting for home rule in the 1800's. Accounts of his voyage, conversations with John Mitchel, etc.

- Diary of Mexican-American War: Elias F. HINEY
  http://www.genweb.net/~samcasey/elias.html
  Elias Hiney served in Company B, First Regiment of Pennsylvania Volunteers from December 15, 1846 through July 27, 1848 and kept a diary through his entire term of service.

- Diary of Raymond ALLEN
  http://www.rootsweb.com/~pabradfo/allendia.htm
  Diary of a cattle drive from Windham Twp, Bradford County, PA to Connecticut, 1864.

- Diary of Rev. Clay MacCauley
  http://jefferson.village.virginia.edu/vshadow2/personal/mccauley.html

- Documenting the American South: First Person Narratives of the American South
  http://metalab.unc.edu/docsouth/fpn/fpn.html
  From the University of North Carolina at Chapel Hill.

- Enchanted Mountains Genealogy Society— Diary of Joseph Beaman Oviatt
  http://www.geocities.com/Heartland/Park/3294/diary.html
  Winter of 1847–1848, Keating Township, McKean County, PA.

- Letter from Adeline Winn of Concord, Massachusetts
  http://www.rootsweb.com/~valoudou/1831conc.html
  Written to Mary Dulin (Jenners) Braden of Clinton Co., Indiana March 2, 1831.

- Letter from Mrs. Elizabeth Braden of Waterford, VA
  http://www.rootsweb.com/~valoudou/1830june.html
  To Burr & Mary Braden of Lafayette, IN 21 June 1830.

- Letters from an Iowa Soldier in the Civil War
  http://www.ucsc.edu./civil-war-letters/home.html
  Part of a collection written by Newton Robert SCOTT, Private, Company A, of the 36th Infantry, Iowa Volunteers to Hannah CONE, his friend and later his wife.

- Letters from Forgotten Ancestors
  http://www.tngenweb.usit.com/tnletters/
  A Tennessee Genealogy History Project.

- Letters of the Civil War
  http://www.geocities.com/Pentagon/7914/
  A compilation of letters from the soldiers, sailors, nurses, politicians, ministers and journalists from the newspapers of the cities and towns of Massachusetts, April 1861–December 1865.

- A Michigan Civil War Physician's Diary
  http://www.sos.state.mi.us/history/museum/techstuf/civilwar/diarybac.html
  Excerpts from Dr. Cyrus Bacon's diary.

- SCETI: Women's Studies
  http://www.library.upenn.edu/etext/diaries/
  From the University of Pennsylvania Library / Schoenberg Center for Electronic Text & Image.
  - Manuscript Diaries of Grace Gilchrist Frend, 1907–1941
    http://www.library.upenn.edu/etext/diaries/gilchrist/
  - Manuscript Diary of Elizabeth Cowperthwaite, 1857–1858
    http://www.library.upenn.edu/etext/diaries/cowper1857/
  - Manuscript Diary of Fanny Ruschenberger, 1858–1881
    http://www.library.upenn.edu/etext/diaries/fanny/
  - Manuscript Diary of Margaret A. Eadie, 1901–1909
    http://www.library.upenn.edu/etext/diaries/eadie/
  - Manuscript Diary of Margaret T. Spaulding, 1870
    http://www.library.upenn.edu/etext/diaries/spaulding1870/
  - Manuscript Diary of Susan Sherman, 1850–1851
    http://www.library.upenn.edu/etext/diaries/sherman1850/

- Women's Civil War Diaries and Papers—Locations
  http://homepages.rootsweb.com/~haas/cwdiaries.html

EASTERN EUROPE
http://www.CyndisList.com/easteuro.htm

Category Index:

- FEEFHS ~ Federation of East European Family History Societies
- General Resource Sites
- History & Culture
- Language
- Libraries, Archives & Museums
- Mailing Lists, Newsgroups & Chat
- Maps, Gazetteers & Geographical Information

- People & Families
- Professional Researchers, Volunteers & Other Research Services
- Publications, Software & Supplies
- Religion & Churches
- Societies & Groups
- World GenWeb

◆ FEEFHS ~ Federation of East European Family History Societies

- FEEFHS—Federation of East European Family History Societies
  http://feefhs.org/
  - Ethnic, Religious and National Index of HomePages and FEEFHS Resource Guide Listings of organizations associated with FEEFHS from 14 countries
    http://feefhs.org/ethnic.html
  - FEEFHS Ethnic, Religious and National Cross-Indexes:
    - Austro-Hungarian Empire
      http://feefhs.org/ah/indexah.html
    - Baltic Countries: Estonia, Latvia and Lithuania
      http://feefhs.org/baltic/indexblt.html
    - Banat
      http://feefhs.org/banat/indexban.html
    - Canadian
      http://feefhs.org/ca/indexcan.html
    - Carpatho-Rusyn, Rusin, Ruthenia
      http://feefhs.org/rusyn/indexcru.html
    - Croatia Genealogy
      http://feefhs.org/cro/indexcro.html
    - Czech Republic
      http://feefhs.org/indexcz.html
    - Galicia—(Galizien)
      http://feefhs.org/gal/indexgal.html
    - Germans from Russia Historical Collection
      http://feefhs.org/grhc/indexgrc.html
    - Germans from Russia Heritage Society
      http://feefhs.org/grhs/indexgrh.html

- Hutterite Genealogy
  http://feefhs.org/hut/indexhut.html
- Jewish Genealogy
  http://feefhs.org/indexjew.html
- Mennonite
  http://feefhs.org/men/indexmen.html
- Polish
  http://feefhs.org/pol/indexpol.html
- Slovak Republic
  http://feefhs.org/indexsk.html
- Slovenia Genealogy
  http://feefhs.org/slovenia/indexsi.html
- Swiss
  http://feefhs.org/ch/indexch.html
- FEEFHS Full Text Web Site Index Search Engine
  http://feefhs.org/feefhsei.html
- FEEFHS Location (Address) Index of FEEFHS Member Organizations and other East European Genealogy Organizations
  http://feefhs.org/location.html
- FEEFHS Significant Additions Index
  http://feefhs.org/webm/sigad96.html
- FEEFHS Web Site Master Index
  http://feefhs.org/masteri.html

◆ General Resource Sites

- AEGEE's former Yugoslavia Information
  http://www.tue.nl/aegee/hrwg/exyu/index.html
- Alex Glendinning's Hungarian Pages
  http://user.itl.net/~glen/Hungarianintro.html
- Austria / Österreich
  http://www.CyndisList.com/austria.htm
  See this category on Cyndi's List for related links.

- Carpatho-Rusyn Genealogy
  http://www.rusyn.com/

- Carpatho-Rusyn Knowledge Base
  http://www.carpatho-rusyn.org/

- The Carpatho-Rusyn Surname Project
  http://www.carpatho-rusyn.org/surnames.htm

- Czech Republic, Bohemia and Moravia
  Genealogical Research
  http://www.iarelative.com/czech/

- Dags' Latvian Genealogy Page
  http://feefhs.org/baltic/lv/frg-dag.html

- Eastern Slovakia, Slovak and Carpatho-Rusyn
  Genealogy Research
  http://www.iarelative.com/slovakia.htm

- European Focus
  http://www.eurofocus.com/
  Photographic portfolios of ancestral towns in Europe created for Genealogy enthusiasts in Germany, Italy, Poland, Scandinavia, Great Britain and more.

- Genealogical Research in the Lands of the Former
  Austro-Hungarian Monarchy—Guide to Archives
  and Parish-Registers
  http://www.netway.at/ihff/

- The Genealogist—Hungarian Genealogy
  http://www.xcelco.on.ca/~genealog/hungary.html

- Genealogy and Heraldry in Slovenia
  http://genealogy.ijp.si/

- Genealogy for Armenians
  http://www.itsnet.com/home/gfa/
  This site has excerpts from a book for sale of the same title.

- German Genealogy: Donauschwaben / Danube-
  Swabians
  http://www.genealogy.net/gene/reg/ESE/dschwaben.html

- German-Prussian Genealogy Links
  http://www.geocities.com/SiliconValley/Haven/1538/
  germanpg.html

- Germans from Russia
  http://www.CyndisList.com/germruss.htm
  See this category on Cyndi's List for related links.

- Germany / Deutschland
  http://www.CyndisList.com/germany.htm
  See this category on Cyndi's List for related links.

- Greek Telephone Directories
  http://www.hellasyellow.gr/

- Help in searching for ancestors from the Sudetenland
  http://www.genealogy.net/gene/reg/SUD/sudet_en.html
  German settlement area in Bohemia/Moravia/Austrian Silesia—>Czechoslovakia—> Czech Republik.

- Home Page of the Unofficial Dvinsk Genealogy SIG
  http://www.geocities.com/Heartland/Valley/4100/

- How to Do Croatian Genealogy
  http://www.durham.net/facts/crogen/

- Institute Country Index
  http://www.columbia.edu/cu/sipa/REGIONAL/ECE/country.html
  Links to online resources for several countries from the Institute on East Central Europe at Columbia University.

- The Italo-Albanian Heritage Pages
  http://members.aol.com/itaalb1/web/arberesh.htm

- Jewish Records Indexing—Poland
  http://www.jewishgen.org/reipp/

- Myron Gruenwald's Page—Germany, Prussia,
  Pomerania
  http://home.aol.com/myrondpl

- Patrick Janis' Czech Genealogy Page
  http://www.genealogy.org/~czech/index.html

- Poland / Polska
  http://www.CyndisList.com/poland.htm
  See this category on Cyndi's List for related links.

- The Pomeranian Page
  http://www.execpc.com/~kap/pommern1.html

- Prussian Genealogy Links
  http://www.geocities.com/SiliconValley/Haven/1538/
  prussia.html

- Prussian-Russian-Canadian Mennonite
  Genealogical Resources
  http://www.mmhs.org/mmhsgen.htm

- Slovak and Rusyn Roots; Getting Started
  http://feefhs.org/socslav/hudick1.html

- Switzerland
  http://www.CyndisList.com/swiss.htm
  See this category on Cyndi's List for related links.

- Telefonski imenik Slovenije—Slovenian
  Telephone Directory
  http://tis.telekom.si/

- Ukrainian Genealogy
  http://www.infoukes.com/genealogy/

- Western Europe
  http://www.CyndisList.com/westeuro.htm
  See this category on Cyndi's List for related links.

- Yahoo!...Armenia...Genealogy
  http://dir.yahoo.com/Regional/Countries/Armenia/
  Arts_and_Humanities/History/Genealogy/

- Yahoo!...Ukraine...Genealogy
  http://dir.yahoo.com/Regional/Countries/Ukraine/
  Arts_and_Humanities/History/Genealogy/

◆ History & Culture

- History of Europe, Slavic States
  http://www.worldroots.com/brigitte/royal/royal4.htm
  Historic and genealogical information about royal and nobility family lines.

- History of German Settlements in Southern Hungary
  http://feefhs.org/banat/bhistory.html
- The Russian Post-Emancipation Household Two Villages in the Moscow Area
  http://www.uib.no/hi/herdis/HerdisKolle.html
  By Herdis Kolle. A description of Russian peasant family life.

◆ Language

- The Cyrillic Alphabet
  http://www.friends-partners.org/oldfriends/language/russian-alphabet.html
  A written & audio guide to pronouncing the letters of the Russian alphabet.
- English-Czech Dictionary
  http://ww2.fce.vutbr.cz/bin/ecd
- English-Hungarian Dictionary
  http://www.sztaki.hu/services/engdict/index.jhtml
- FEEFHS Database of Professional Translators Specializing in East European Genealogy
  http://feefhs.org/frg/frg-pt.html
- Slovak Translation Services by Jana Cupková Holmes
  http://www.dholmes.com/janatran.html
- Terms, Phrases, Dictionaries & Glossaries
  http://www.CyndisList.com/terms.htm
  See this category on Cyndi's List for related links.

◆ Libraries, Archives & Museums

- Archives in Czech Republic
  http://www.genealogy.net/gene/reg/SUD/sudet_crarch_en.html
- HELKA—The Helsinki University Libraries OPAC
  http://renki.helsinki.fi/gabriel/en/countries/finland-opac-en.html
  Catalog of the Helsinki University Library system. It has a large collection of official publications of the former Russian Empire.
- Martynas Mazvydas National Library of Lithuania / Lietuvos Nacionaline Martyno Mazvydo Biblioteka
  http://lnb.lrs.lt/
- Mestska knihovna v Praze / Municipal Library of Prague
  http://www.mlp.cz/
- National and University Library, Ljubljana, Slovenija
  http://www.nuk.uni-lj.si/
- Public Libraries of Europe
  http://dspace.dial.pipex.com/town/square/ac940/eurolib.html
- Slovene Archives
  http://www.pokarh-mb.si/home.html

◆ Mailing Lists, Newsgroups & Chat

- Banat Genealogy Mailing List Home Page
  http://feefhs.org/banat/frgbanat.html
- BANAT Mailing List
  http://members.aol.com/gfsjohnf/gen_mail_country-hun.html#BANAT
  For those doing research in the Banat region of what was formerly Hungary.
- BDO Mailing List
  http://members.aol.com/gfsjohnf/gen_mail_country-rus.html#BDO
  The Beresan District Odessa (BDO) mailing list is for anyone with a genealogical interest in the Beresan Colonies which were made up of Germans who immigrated to Russia, beginning in the first decade of the 19th century, at the request of Alexander I, Tsar of Russia. The Colonies were located Northeast of the city of Odessa on the Black Sea.
- BERDICHEV Mailing List
  http://members.aol.com/gfsjohnf/gen_mail_country-rus.html#BERDICHEV
  For anyone with a genealogical interest in Berdichev, Ukraine, Russia with a focus on Jewish genealogy.
- Boslovlist Mailing List
  http://members.aol.com/gfsjohnf/gen_mail_country-ukr.html#Boslovlist
  A mailing list for anyone with a genealogical interest in the town of Boslov (Boguslav) in the Ukraine.
- BUKOVINA-GEN Mailing List
  http://members.aol.com/gfsjohnf/gen_mail_country-rom.html#BUKOVINA-GEN
  For those researching their genealogy and family history in Bukovina, a former crownland of the Austrian Empire (a.k.a. Bucovina, Bukowina, Bukovyna, or Buchenland), now divided between Romania and Ukraine.
- EURO-JEWISH Mailing List
  http://members.aol.com/johnf14246/gen_mail_general.html#EURO-JEWISH
  For anyone with a genealogical interest in the Migration, History, Culture, Heritage and Surname search of the Jewish people from Europe to the United States and their descendants in the United States.
- GEN-SLAVIC Mailing List
  http://members.aol.com/gfsjohnf/gen_mail_country-pol.html#GEN-SLAVIC
  Gatewayed with the soc.genealogy.slavic newsgroup.
- GERMAN-BOHEMIAN-L Mailing List
  http://members.aol.com/gfsjohnf/gen_mail_country-ger.html#GERMAN-BOHEMIAN-L
  About the culture, genealogy and heritage of the German-speaking people of Bohemia and Moravia, now the Czech Republic.
- Hellenes-Diaspora Mailing List
  http://members.aol.com/gfsjohnf/gen_mail_country-gre.html#Hellenes-Diaspora
  For anyone with an interest in Hellenes in the Diaspora. The list will address concerns regarding Hellenes finding long lost friends, family, or connections in Greece or elsewhere around the world and for research concerning their Hellenic family trees.

- HERBARZ Mailing List
  http://members.aol.com/gfsjohnf/gen_mail_country-
  lit.html#HERBARZ
  *For the discussion of Polish and Lithuanian heraldry, the history
  of the armorial clans, and the genealogy of noble families.*

- Hungarian American List (HAL)
  http://members.aol.com/gfsjohnf/gen_mail_country-
  hun.html#HUNGARIAN
  *A mailing list for those interested in expressing, sharing, and
  exchanging their views, ideas, and feelings about Hungary,
  Hungarians, Hungarian-Americans, and Hungarian culture and
  genealogy.*

- HUNGARY Mailing List
  http://members.aol.com/gfsjohnf/gen_mail_country-
  hun.html#HUNGARY1

- LITHUANIA Mailing List
  http://members.aol.com/gfsjohnf/gen_mail_country-
  lit.html#LITHUANIA

- med-gene Mailing List
  http://members.aol.com/gfsjohnf/gen_mail_country-
  gen.html#med-gene
  *For anyone with a genealogical interest in the Mediterranean
  area.*

- MORAVIA Mailing List
  http://members.aol.com/gfsjohnf/gen_mail_country-
  ger.html#MORAVIA
  *For anyone with a genealogical interest in Moravia, now part
  of the Czech Republic.*

- OW-PREUSSEN-L Mailing List
  http://members.aol.com/gfsjohnf/gen_mail_country-
  ger.html#OW-PREUSSEN-L
  *For those interested in sharing and exchanging information on
  genealogy and history which has a connection to the former
  East and West Prussia.*

- PolandBorderSurnames Mailing List
  http://members.aol.com/gfsjohnf/gen_mail_country-
  pol.html#PolandBorderSurnames
  *For anyone researching genealogy in the former historical
  borders of Poland including Estonia, Latvia, Lithuania, Belarus,
  Ukraine, Moldova, Slovakia, Czech Republic, Moravia, Hungary, Russia, the Balkans, and East Prussia.*

- POMMERN-L Mailing List
  http://members.aol.com/gfsjohnf/gen_mail_country-ger.
  html#POMMERN-L
  *Genealogy and history which has a connection to Pommerania,
  both the current Polish part and remaining German parts of the
  former Prussian province.*

- PreussenAmericans Mailing List
  http://members.aol.com/gfsjohnf/gen_mail_country-ger.
  html#PreussenAmericans
  *For anyone with a genealogical interest in Prussian immigrants
  to America.*

- PRUSSIA-ROOTS Mailing List
  http://members.aol.com/gfsjohnf/gen_mail_country-
  ger.html#PRUSSIA-ROOTS
  *For anyone with a genealogical interest in Brandenburg,
  Hannover (or Hanover), Ostpreussen (East Prussia), Pommern
  (Pomerania), Posen, Provinz Sachsen (Province of Saxony—
  northern Saxony), Schleswig-Holstein, Schlesien (Silesia),
  Westpreussen (West Prussia), Lubeck, Hamburg, and Bremen.*

- Radoshkovichlist Mailing List
  http://members.aol.com/gfsjohnf/gen_mail_country-lit.
  html#Radoshkovichlist
  *A mailing list for anyone with a genealogical interest in the town
  of Radoshkovich (a town on the road from Vilna to Minsk in
  Eastern Europe).*

- SLOVAK-L Mailing List
  http://members.aol.com/gfsjohnf/gen_mail_country-slo.
  html#SLOVAK-L

- SLOVAK-WORLD Mailing List
  http://members.aol.com/gfsjohnf/gen_mail_country-slo.
  html#SLOVAK-W

- SUGUSELTS Mailing List
  http://members.aol.com/gfsjohnf/gen_mail_country-est.
  html#SUGUSELTS
  An Estonian-language Genealogy list.

- Turkish_Jews Mailing List
  http://members.aol.com/gfsjohnf/gen_mail_country-ser.
  html#Turkish_Jews
  *For Shephardic Jewish genealogists with roots in the former
  Turkish Ottoman Empire including Turkey, Serbia, Greece, and
  Yugoslavia.*

- WorldGenWeb-Preussen Mailing List
  http://members.aol.com/gfsjohnf/gen_mail_country-
  ger.html#WorldGenWeb-Preussen

◆ Maps, Gazetteers & Geographical Information

- FEEFHS East European Map Room—Map Index
  http://feefhs.org/maps/indexmap.html

- Genealogy Unlimited—Home Page
  http://www.itsnet.com:80/home/genun/public_html/
  Maps, books & supplies for sale.

- From the Perry-Castañeda Library Map Collection at
  the Univ. of Texas at Austin:
  http://www.lib.utexas.edu/Libs/PCL/Map_collection/
  Map_collection.html
  - Maps of Europe
    http://www.lib.utexas.edu/Libs/PCL/Map_collection/
    europe.html
    - Map of Albania
      http://www.lib.utexas.edu/Libs/PCL/Map_collection/
      europe/Albania.GIF
    - Map of Bosnia Herzegovina
      http://www.lib.utexas.edu/Libs/PCL/Map_collection/
      europe/BosniaHerzegovina.jpg
    - Map of Bulgaria
      http://www.lib.utexas.edu/Libs/PCL/Map_collection/
      europe/Bulgaria.jpg
    - Map of Chechnya
      http://www.lib.utexas.edu/Libs/PCL/Map_collection/
      commonwealth/Chechnya.jpg
    - Map of Croatia
      http://www.lib.utexas.edu/Libs/PCL/Map_collection/
      europe/Croatia.jpg

- Map of Cyprus
  http://www.lib.utexas.edu/Libs/PCL/Map_collection/europe/Cyprus.GIF
- Map of Czech Republic
  http://www.lib.utexas.edu/Libs/PCL/Map_collection/europe/CzechRepublic.jpg
- Map of Estonia
  http://www.lib.utexas.edu/Libs/PCL/Map_collection/europe/Estonia.GIF
- Map of Ethnic Groups of Eastern Europe
  http://www.lib.utexas.edu/Libs/PCL/Map_collection/europe/EEurope_Ethnic_95.jpg
- Map of Greece
  http://www.lib.utexas.edu/Libs/PCL/Map_collection/europe/greece.jpg
- Map of Hungary
  http://www.lib.utexas.edu/Libs/PCL/Map_collection/europe/Hungary.jpg
- Map of Latvia
  http://www.lib.utexas.edu/Libs/PCL/Map_collection/europe/Latvia.GIF
- Map of Lithuania
  http://www.lib.utexas.edu/Libs/PCL/Map_collection/europe/Lithuania.GIF
- Map of Macedonia
  http://www.lib.utexas.edu/Libs/PCL/Map_collection/europe/MACEDONIA.GIF
- Map of Romania
  http://www.lib.utexas.edu/Libs/PCL/Map_collection/europe/Romania.GIF
- Map of Serbia
  http://www.lib.utexas.edu/Libs/PCL/Map_collection/europe/Serbia.GIF
- Map of Slovakia
  http://www.lib.utexas.edu/Libs/PCL/Map_collection/europe/Slovakia_map.jpg
- Map of Slovenia
  http://www.lib.utexas.edu/Libs/PCL/Map_collection/europe/Slovenia.jpg

- Map of Odessa
  http://members.aol.com/tgostin/graphics/odessa2.jpg
- Maps of Croatia and Bosnia-Herzegovina
  http://www.applicom.com/maps/
- Home Page of Hungarian Cartography
  http://lazarus.elte.hu/gb/hunkarta/kezdo.htm

◆ People & Families

- Dictionary of the Titled Nobility of Russia
  http://www.booksatoz.com/tims/genealogy/russian.htm
- The Family LOKUCIEWSKI
  http://www.btinternet.com/~hydro.lek/lokuhome.htm
  From 1560, in Eastern Poland now part of Belarus/Lithuania/Poland.

- Genealogija Rodbine BUTINA iz Kostela, Slovenija, Vasje Butina
  http://www.creativ.si/genealog/
  The BUTINA'S Family Genealogy from Kostel, Slovenia by Vasja Butina. BUTINA, BATINICA, GOLIK, KAJFEZ, MIHELCIC, REBOLJ, SUMI, ZDRAVIC, ZIDAR, ZUPANCIC.
- Generations...Foot Steps of My Life— The BUJAKI Family
  http://Home1.GTE.Net/grampi/generations.htm
  BUJAKI, BUJAK, KOZO, ZBOROWSKI, SLAVIK
- MIODOWNIK and NOWAK Homepage
  http://205.214.171.123/rdm/
- My Hungarian Ancestry: The Edelényi SZABÓ Family of Pápa, County Veszprem, Hungary
  http://user.itl.net/~glen/edelenyiszabo.html
- My Hungarian Ancestry: The SZEDMÁKY FAMILY
  http://user.itl.net/~glen/szedmakys.html
- Nenad VEKARIC Home Page
  http://www.geocities.com/Athens/Delphi/6320/
  Head of the Institute for Historical Sciences, Croatian Academy of Sciences and Arts, Dubrovnik-Croatia. Author of several books, including some for genealogy in Croatia. Croatian surnames: AGUZIN, BRBORA, KELEZ, KNEGO, MILOSLAVIC, PENDO, SKURIC, SVILOKOS, VIOLIC, VLAHUTIN.
- The ORBAN's
  http://www.geocities.com/CapeCanaveral/7473/orban.html
  Belgium, Hungary
- PENZAR Family Home Page
  http://www.geocities.com/Heartland/1302/
  Post your Croatian genealogy queries here.
- The PISZCZOR Pages
  http://www.iwaynet.net/~crashe/index.html
- PLUHOVOY, Ukranian Genealogy
  http://www.pluvoy.com/pluhovoy.html
  PLUHOVOY, KOSTENKO, MAXIMENKO, THOMASHENKO
- Russian Royal Links
  http://www.worldroots.com/brigitte/royal/royal2.htm
- Tilo GOMOLL Homepage
  http://home.t-online.de/home/tilo.gomoll/
  West Prussia, now Poland.

◆ Professional Researchers, Volunteers & Other Research Services

- Board for Certification of Genealogists—Roster of Those Certified—Specializing in Europe/USSR
  http://www.genealogy.org/~bcg/rosts_@e.html

- CZECH Info Center: Find A Czech Ancestor /
  Mate Pribuzne v Zamori?
  http://www.muselik.com/cac/
  14-day free trial, then you subscribe.

- Czechoslovak Genealogical Society Int'l—
  Professional Genealogical Researchers for Czech
  and Slovak Republics
  http://members.aol.com/cgsi/research.htm

- Family Tree Genealogical and Probate Research
  Bureau Ltd.
  http://www.familytree.hu/
  *Professional research service covering the area of what was
  formerly the Austro-Hungarian Empire, including: Hungary,
  Slovakia, Czech Republic, Austria, Italy, Transylvania, Croatia,
  Slovenia, former Yugoslavia (Banat), and the Ukraine
  (Sub-Carpathian).*

- FEEFHS Database of Professional Genealogists
  Specializing in East European Genealogy
  http://feefhs.org/frg/frg-pg.html

- Genealogy Helplist—Russia
  http://perso.club-internet.fr/montardi/berdnikov/Genealogy-
  Helplist-Russia/

- genealogyPro—Professional Genealogists for
  Central and Eastern Europe
  http://genealogyPro.com/directories/Europe.html

- genealogyPro—Professional Genealogists for
  Czech Republic
  http://genealogyPro.com/directories/CzechRepublic.html

- HungaroGens Genealogisches Büro / HungaroGens
  Genealogical Bureau
  http://www.genealogy.net/hungarogens/
  *Genealogical research in Hungary, Austria, Slovakia, Rumania,
  Slovenia, Jugoslavia.*

- IHFF Genealogie Gesellschaft mbH
  http://www.netway.at/ihff/
  *Professional Researcher specializing in: Austria, Czech &
  Slovak Republics, Hungary, Slovenian Republic, Croatia,
  Galicia, others.*

- P.A.T.H. Finders—Personal Ancestral Tours &
  History
  http://www.abilnet.com/pathfinders/
  *Specializing in Family History and Travel in the Czech and
  Slovak Republics.*

- Routes to Roots
  http://www.routestoroots.com/
  Tracing Jewish Roots in Poland, Ukraine, Moldova and Belarus.

◆ Publications, Software & Supplies

- Bohemian Genealogy Bibliography
  http://192.231.205.235/ISC102.HTM

- Books We Own—Czech Republic
  http://www.rootsweb.com/~bwo/czech.html

- Books We Own—The Republic of Slovakia
  http://www.rootsweb.com/~bwo/slovakia.html

- "DEPOPULATED PLINA" The Book by Ante Erak
  http://jagor.srce.hr/~merak/indexpli.htm
  Plina is an area in Croatia.

- Frontier Press Bookstore—Czechoslovakian
  Ancestry
  http://www.frontierpress.com/frontier.cgi?category=cze

- Frontier Press Bookstore—European Ancestry
  http://www.frontierpress.com/frontier.cgi?category=europe

- Frontier Press Bookstore—Hungarian Ancestry
  http://www.frontierpress.com/frontier.cgi?category=hung

- GenealogyBookShop.com—Hungary/Hungarian
  http://www.genealogybookshop.com/genealogybookshop/files/
  The_World,Hungary_Hungarian/index.html
  *The online store of Genealogical Publishing Co., Inc. &
  Clearfield Company.*

- GenealogyBookShop.com—Russia/Russian
  http://www.genealogybookshop.com/genealogybookshop/files/
  The_World,Russia_Russian/index.html
  *The online store of Genealogical Publishing Co., Inc. &
  Clearfield Company.*

- Genealogy Unlimited—Home Page
  http://www.itsnet.com:80/home/genun/public_html/
  Maps, books & supplies for sale.

- Marriages in Plauschwarren, East Prussia
  1778–1802
  http://www.mmhs.org/prussia/plauschm.htm

- Regi Magyarorszag "Old Hungary" Bookstore
  http://www.dholmes.com/rm-book.html
  Specializing in Hungarian & Slovak Genealogy.

- Wandering Volhynians
  http://pixel.cs.vt.edu/pub/sources/wv.txt
  *A Magazine for the Descendants of Germans From
  Volhynia and Poland.*

- Wandering Volhynians—
  German-Volhynian Newsletter
  http://feefhs.org/ca/frg-wv.html

◆ Religion & Churches

- German Baptists in Volhynia ~ Ukraine
  http://mypage.direct.ca/d/dobee/volhynia.html

- The Hungarian Reformed Church in Paris 1938
  http://user.itl.net/~glen/HungariansinParis.html
  A Parisi Magyar Reformatus Egyhaz Presbiteriuma.

- Index to: Religious Personnel in Russia 1853–1854
  http://www.memo.com/jgsr/database/deych.cgi

- Jewish
  http://www.CyndisList.com/jewish.htm
  See this category on Cyndi's List for related links.

- Jewish Roots in Romania—Radacini Evreiesti
  in Romania
  http://www.accordnet.com/jewish-dorohoi/

- Mennonite
  http://www.CyndisList.com/menno.htm
  See this category on Cyndi's List for related links.

◆ Societies & Groups

- **Bukovina Society of the Americas**
  http://members.aol.com/LJensen/bukovina.html

- **Carpatho-Rusyn Society Page**
  http://www.carpatho-rusyn.org/crs/
  Slovakia / Carpathian Mts.

- **Czech & Slovak American Genealogy Society of Illinois**
  http://members.aol.com/chrismik/csagsi/csagsi.htm

- **Czechoslovak Genealogical Society, International**
  http://members.aol.com/CGSI/index.html

- **Czech Heritage Society of Texas**
  http://www.genealogy.org/~czech/

- **FEEFHS—Federation of East European Family History Societies**
  http://feefhs.org/

- **FEEFHS Location (Address) Index of FEEFHS Member Organizations**
  http://feefhs.org/location.html
  And other East European Genealogy Organizations.

- **The German-Bohemian Heritage Society**
  http://www.rootsweb.com/~gbhs/

- **German-Bohemian Heritage Society, USA**
  http://www.genealogy.net/gene/reg/SUD/sudet_GBHS.html

- **Hungarian/American Friendship Society (HAFS)**
  http://www.dholmes.com/hafs.html
  Specializing in Hungarian & Slovak Genealogy.

- **Lithuanian American Genealogy Society (Lgs)**
  http://feefhs.org/baltic/lt/frg-lags.html

- **The Slovak Heritage and Cultural Society of British Columbia**
  http://www.iarelative.com/slovakbc.htm

- **Slovenian Genealogical Society / Slovensko Rodoslovno Dru[Tvo**
  http://genealogy.ijp.si/slovrd/rd.htm

- **Slovenian Genealogical Society**
  E-mail: janez.toplisek@fov.uni-mb.si

- **Slovenian Genealogy Society (International Headquarters)**
  http://feefhs.org/slovenia/frg-sgsi.html

- **Slovenian Genealogy Society, Ohio Chapter**
  http://feefhs.org/slovenia/frgsgsoh.html

- **Transylvania Saxon Genealogy and Heritage Society, Inc. ~ Ohio**
  http://feefhs.org/ah/hu/tsghs/frgtsghs.html

◆ World GenWeb

- **Hungary Genealogy—World GenWeb**
  http://www.rootsweb.com/~wghungar/

EVENTS & ACTIVITIES
http://www.CyndisList.com/events.htm

Category Index:
◆ Events Calendars

◆ Reunions

◆ Seminars & Classes

◆ Events Calendars

● Australian Family History Events
http://www.cohsoft.com.au/afhc/announce.html

● Calendar of Events in NY State
http://www.rootsweb.com/~nygenweb/gencal.htm

● Eastern Washington Genealogical Society, 1998/1999 Calendar
http://www.onlinepub.net/ewgs/calendar1.html

● Federation of Genealogical Societies Calendar of Events
http://www.fgs.org/~fgs/fgs-curr.htm

● Genealogical Events Across North America
http://familyhistory.flash.net/events.html
From The Family History Show in Texas.

● Genealogical Forum of Oregon, Inc. Special Events
http://www.gfo.org/special.htm

● Genealogy Upcoming Events, Classes, Opportunities—San Diego County Area
http://www.cgssd.org/events.html

● GENEVA—The GENUKI diary of GENealogical EVents and Activities ~ U.K.
http://users.ox.ac.uk/~malcolm/genuki/geneva/

● GenieSpeak—Genealogy Speakers Bureau
http://www.geniespeak.com
Created to promote and increase contacts between societies and speakers (at all levels), and to list upcoming events and workshop resources.

● German Genealogy: Genealogical Events
http://www.genealogy.net/gene/ghlp/events.html

● Germans from Russia Heritage Collection Upcoming Events
http://www.lib.ndsu.nodak.edu/gerrus/events.html

● Heritage Quest Events Center
http://www.heritagequest.com/cgi-bin/
page.exe?catalog=EventsCenter&file=Sort.htm&&@sort@comp.
EVcomp=EventPlace:a
A calendar of events, seminars and conferences held by societies and organizations. Sort the calendar by name, place or date.

● Heritage Quest Genealogy Road Show
http://www.heritagequest.com/genealogy/magazine/html/
hq_roadshow.html

● NARA Calendar of Events
http://www.nara.gov/nara/events/events.html
For the National Archives facilities in and around Washington, DC and nationwide.

● N.E.H.G.S. Calendar of Events—New England Historic Genealogical Society
http://www.nehgs.org/education/events.htm

● NGS Calendar
http://www.ngsgenealogy.org/news/content/calendar.html
National Genealogical Society

● OGS Sponsored Events
http://www.ogs.on.ca/ogsevent.htm
Ontario Genealogical Society

● Ohio Genealogical Society Calendar of Events
http://www.greenapple.com/~ksmith/events.html

● Pennsylvania Genealogical Events
http://www.libertynet.org/gencap/events.html

● SHHAR Calendar
http://members.aol.com/shhar/calendar.html
The Society of Hispanic Historical and Ancestral Research.

● Society of Genealogists: Lectures, Visits and Courses ~ U.K.
http://www.sog.org.uk/events/

● Tacoma-Pierce County Genealogical Society— Activity Calendar ~ Washington
http://www.rootsweb.com/~watpcgs/activity.htm

● Tacoma-Pierce County Genealogical Society— Monthly Meetings ~ Washington
http://www.rootsweb.com/~watpcgs/meetings.htm

● This Week in Genealogy
http://members.aol.com/genwebindx/twig.htm

● TNGenWeb Project's Calendar of Events for Tennessee
http://www.tngenweb.org/events.htm

● Upcoming Events—from Family Tree Maker Online
http://www.familytreemaker.com/othrevnt.html

- Virginia Genealogical Society Events
  http://www.vgs.org/events.htm
- Washington State Genealogical Society—
  Genealogical Events Calendar
  http://www.rootsweb.com/~wasgs/wsgscal.htm
- Wisconsin Calendar of Lineage Events
  http://www.execpc.com/~drg/drgllcal.html

◆ Reunions

- ALGenWeb Family Reunions ~ Alabama
  http://www.edge.net/~deke/algenweb/reunion.html
- BOND Family Reunion
  E-mail: receiver@visioncom.net
  Every Labor Day Sunday in Wiggins, Mississippi. E-mail A.M. Bond at receiver@visioncom.net for more details.
- ClassMates Online
  http://www.classmates.com/
  Helps high school alumni friends find each other
- CORNING Family Reunion
  http:/bold.coba.unr.edu/corning/reunion/1fam.html
  Corning Family Reunion, Yarmouth, Nova Scotia, Canada, July 22 to 25, 1999.
- Family Reunion Page for the Central Texas Area
  http://www.aisi.net/GenWeb/mclennanco/mainreun.htm
- Kentucky Family Reunions
  http://www.mindspring.com/~jbawden/reunion/index.html
- MUMMEY Family Reunion Website
  http://ecicnet.org/~uboat977/
  Mummey/Mummy family genealogy, with Hammond and Smith allied lines, information on annual Mummey reunion.
- Ohio Family Reunions
  http://www.rootsweb.com/~ohgenweb/reunion.htm
- Pat's Reunion Help and More!
  http://www.pacifier.com/~patbauer/
  Vancouver, Washington
- Posted Family Reunions
  http://www.genealogy-books.com/reunions.htm
- Reunion Hall
  http://www.nowandthen.com/reunion/index.html
- Seekers of the Lost International Reunion Registry
  http://www.seeklost.com/
- TANNAHILL Family Reunion
  http://home.att.net/~Tannahill/
  April 3, 1999, Fort Worth, Texas, USA.
- Thinking About a Reunion?
  http://www.familytreemaker.com/32_reunion.html
- What Should We Do at the Reunion?
  http://www.familytreemaker.com/34_reunion.html

◆ Seminars & Classes

- 1999 OGS Annual Conference
  http://www.greenapple.com/~ksmith/ogsconf.html
  April 23 & 24, 1999, Toledo Hilton/ Dana Conference Center, Ohio.
- 1999 Research Trip to Ireland
  http://www.ngsgenealogy.org/feature/content/feature2.html
  Sponsored by National Genealogical Society, 18–24 September 1999.
- Alberta Family Histories Society—
  Gensoft ~ Canada
  http://www.calcna.ab.ca/afhs/gensoft.html
- Alberta Family Histories Society—
  Wild Rose Seminar ~ Canada
  http://www.calcna.ab.ca/afhs/seminar.html
- Federation of Genealogical Societies—
  FGS Conferences
  http://www.fgs.org/~fgs/fgs-conf.htm
  Contact: fgs-office@fgs.org or 1-888-FGS-1500.
- Fifth New England Regional
  Genealogical Conference
  http://www.rootsweb.com/~maplymou/conf/confmain.htm
  October 22–15, 1998 in Portland, Maine.
- Genealogical Conferences & Workshops
  http://www.globalgenealogy.com/confmain.htm
  List from GLOBAL Genealogical Supply.
- The Genealogical Institute of Mid-America (GIMA)
  http://www.misslink.net/neill/gima.html
  The 6th annual Institute will be held 12–15 July 1999 in Springfield, IL (instructors include Lloyd Bockstruck, Sandra Luebking, and Michael Neill).
- GENTECH99
  http://www.gentech.org/~gentech/99home.htm
  January 22–23, 1999, Salt Lake City, Utah.
- GENTECH2000
  http://www.gentech.org/~gentech/2000home.htm
  San Diego, California, 27–29 January 2000.
- Institute of Genealogical Studies
  http://www.cyberramp.net/~igs/
  From the Dallas Genealogical Society.
- National Genealogical Society—1999 Conference
  in the States
  http://www.ngsgenealogy.org/feature/content/feature.html
  12–15 May 1999 in Richmond, Virginia.
- North Carolina Genealogical Society
  Workshops Schedule
  http://www.ncgenealogy.org/workshops/
- Portuguese Genealogy Workshop
  http://www.dholmes.com/workshop.html
  Sacramento LDS Family History Center, Carmichael, California.

- Québec Family History Society—
  Facilities and Activities
  http://www.cam.org/~qfhs/Facili.html
- Salt Lake Institute of Genealogy
  http://www.infouga.org/institut.htm

- Samford University Institute of Genealogy and
  Historical Research
  http://www.Samford.Edu/schools/ighr/ighr.html
  Alabama
- Utah Genealogical Association Annual Conference
  http://www.infouga.org/confrnce.htm

FAMILY BIBLES
http://www.CyndisList.com/bibles.htm

- Antiquarian Books & Bindery ~ Atlanta, Georgia
  http://205.206.160.250/home/kaolink/
  Specializing in Bible restoration. Also a selection of rare books for sale.

- Bible and Family Records Index
  http://www.cslnet.ctstateu.edu/bible.htm
  At the History and Genealogy Unit, Connecticut State Library.

- The Bible Archives (TBA)
  http://www.geocities.com/Heartland/Fields/2403/
  This is a collection of records transcribed from family Bibles, baptism booklets, death books, etc.

- Bible Records
  http://www.rootsweb.com/~sccalhou/bible1.htm
  From the Calhoun County, South Carolina USGenWeb site.

- Bible Records of Orange County, Indiana
  http://www.rootsweb.com/~inorange/prebible.htm

- Bible Records Online—Pittsylvania County, Virginia
  http://www.rootsweb.com/~vapittsy/bible.htm

- Bible Records—Taylor County, Georgia
  http://www.rootsweb.com/~gataylor/taybib.htm

- Bibles—Giles County ~ Tennessee
  http://www.rootsweb.com/~tngiles/bible/bible.htm

- Bibles with a Kentucky Connection
  http://www.nlt.net/kygenweb/bibles.html

- Bladen County, NC Bible Records Vol. 1
  http://www.geocities.com/Heartland/Plains/8415/bladen1.html

- Bladen County, NC Bible Records Vol. 2
  http://www.geocities.com/Heartland/Plains/8415/bladen2.html

- Bladen County, NC Bible Records Vol. 3
  http://www.geocities.com/Heartland/Plains/8415/bladen3.html

- Bladen County, NC Bible Records Vol. 4
  http://www.geocities.com/Heartland/Plains/8415/bladen4.html

- BLOUNT Family Bible
  http://www.genealogy.org/~ajmorris/misc/bible02.htm

- The Book Craftsman—Restoration of Family Bibles
  http://www.bookcraftsman.com/

- Computer Jeannie—Harrison TOTTY Bible
  http://www.jcrogers.com/totty.htm

- The CORNELL and GROOT Family from the GROOT Family Bible Record
  http://vader.castles.com/ftprints/web51110.html

- Craighead Co. Bible Records ~ Arkansas
  http://www.couchgenweb.com/craighead/bible.htm

- David and Abigail PATTON Bible
  http://www.geocities.com/Heartland/Hills/6538/Patton1.htm

- DAY Family Bible, 1835–1946
  http://www.geocities.com/Heartland/Meadows/1759/bible.html
  The family Bible of Spencer Eliphalet Day and Wealthy A. Nichols of Monroe Co., NY.

- DUNCAN Bible Record (Lee Co.) ~ Alabama
  ftp://ftp.rootsweb.com/pub/usgenweb/al/lee/bible/duncan.txt

- Excerpts from the BURGAN Family Bible
  http://www.geocities.com/Heartland/Acres/3183/bible.html

- Family_Bible Mailing List
  http://members.aol.com/johnf14246/
  gen_mail_general.html#Family_Bibles
  For the entry ONLY of information on any and all family bibles.

- Family Bible Records in Onondaga County, New York
  http://www.rootsweb.com/~nyononda/BIBLE.HTM

- Family Bible Records—Old Buncombe County Genealogical Society ~ North Carolina
  http://main.nc.us/OBCGS/Bible.htm

- Family Bibles
  http://users.erinet.com/31363/family.htm
  "Rescued" family Bibles for sale.

- Family Bibles
  http://www.rootsweb.com/~minewayg/fmbible.html
  LARABEE, TITUS, DICKINSON, WARREN, HUNTER, WANTZ, AMES, DARLING, FOOT, JOHNSON, STRATTON HESS, COLLINS, BURT, JUDD, KINSEY

- GARRETT Bible Records— James Madison Garrett, Sr.
  ftp://ftp.rootsweb.com/pub/usgenweb/al/lowndes/bible/garrett.txt

- ghotes of Virginia—Family Bible Pages
  http://www.esva.net/ghotes/fbrindex.htm

- HART and REYNOLDS Family Bible
  http://www.genealogy.org/~ajmorris/misc/bible01.htm

- Hopkins County Genealogical Society Bibles
  http://www.rootsweb.com/~usgenweb/ky/bibles/hcgs/toc.html

- Index to Online Bible Records
  http://www.genealogy-books.com/idxbible.htm

- Ira J. TUCKER Bible Record
  ftp://ftp.rootsweb.com/pub/usgenweb/al/pike/bible/tucker.txt

- Iroquois Co. Genealogical Society—Bible Records Collection ~ Illinois
  http://www.rootsweb.com/~ilicgs/bible/bibindex.htm

- Jeannie Rogers—Harrison TOTTY Bible Record
  http://www.jcrogers.com/totty.htm
- Joseph Henry PATTON Bible
  http://www.geocities.com/Heartland/Hills/6538/Patton2.htm
- Kentucky Bible Records Collection Project
  http://www.geocities.com/Heartland/7578/index.html
- KYNERD (also spelled KINARD later)
  Bible Record
  ftp://ftp.rootsweb.com/pub/usgenweb/al/perry/kynerd.txt
- Lafleur Archives
  http://www.lafleur.org/
  Provides birth, death and marriage records from authentic Bible records. There are scanned images of Bibles when possible.
- Lenawee Co. Mi Bible Records Forum
  http://cgi.rootsweb.com/~genbbs/genbbs.cgi/USA/Mi/LenaweeBibl
- Library of Virginia, Bible Records and
  Genealogical Notes
  http://www.vsla.edu/archives/biblerecs.html
- Morgan County, Indiana, Bible Records
  http://www.geocities.com/Heartland/Meadows/8056/inmorgan/biblerec.html
- NEGenWeb Ancestors' Lost & Found
  http://www.rootsweb.com/~neresour/ancestors/index.html
  Dedicated to reuniting families with the Nebraska memorabilia their ancestors left behind: photos, family Bibles, etc.
- Pennsylvania Family Bibles
  http://www.geocities.com/Heartland/3955/bibles.htm
- Philemon HAWKINS Bible
  http://www.lofthouse.com/warren/bibles/query001.htm#44
- Poovy's Bible Records
  http://www.geocities.com/SouthBeach/8189/BibleRecord.html
  Bible records of Mr. & Mrs. John J. MYERS (Whitmell, Pittsylvania County, Virginia).
- Questioning the Bible
  http://www.ancestry.com/columns/george/08-14-98.htm
  From "Along Those Lines . . ." by George Morgan.
- Revolutionary War Period Bible, Family &
  Marriage Records
  http://www.dhc.net/~revwar/
  Index to microfilm volumes of abstracts from pension files.
- Robert L. Taylor's Maine Family Bible Archives
  http://www.rootsweb.com/~meandrhs/taylor/bible/maine.html
- ROBERTSON Family Bible
  http://www.geocities.com/Heartland/Plains/4880/bible.html
  Belonging to James Wiley Robertson (1849–1925) and Millie Ann Jones Robertson (1850–1935).
- Sumner County, Tennessee Bible Records Project
  http://www.tngenweb.org/sumner/sumnbibl.htm

- VTLS Archives & Manuscripts—Bible Records
  http://image.vtls.com:80/bible/virtua.html
  From the Library of Virginia.
- Warren Co Bibles North Carolina Index to
  Surnames, Queries, and Researchers
  http://www.lofthouse.com/warren/bibles/qryindex.htm
- Wayne County Tennessee Bible Records
  http://www.netease.net/wayne/bible.htm
- WPA Reports for Culpeper Co., VA—Bibles
  http://www.rootsweb.com/~takelley/cbibles.htm

◆ Family Tree Maker Online—"How To" Guide

- Finding Birthplace with Bible Records
  http://www.familytreemaker.com/00000419.html
- Finding Marriage Places with Bible Records
  http://www.familytreemaker.com/00000506.html
- Finding Death Dates with Bible Records
  http://www.familytreemaker.com/00000434.html
- Finding a Place of Death with Bible Records
  http://www.familytreemaker.com/00000455.html
- Finding a Burial Place with Bible Records
  http://www.familytreemaker.com/00000472.html
- Finding the Minimum Information for
  Bible Records—Birth Date
  http://www.familytreemaker.com/00000403.html
- Finding the Minimum Information for
  Bible Records—Birthplace
  http://www.familytreemaker.com/00000420.html
- Finding the Minimum Information for
  Bible Records—Spouse's Name
  http://www.familytreemaker.com/00000561.html
- Finding the Minimum Information for
  Bible Records—Marriage Dates
  http://www.familytreemaker.com/00000490.html
- Finding the Minimum Information for
  Bible Records—Divorce or Subsequent Marriage
  http://www.familytreemaker.com/00000576.html
- Finding the Minimum Information for
  Bible Records—Death Date
  http://www.familytreemaker.com/00000435.html
- Finding the Minimum Information for
  Bible Records—Place of Death
  http://www.familytreemaker.com/00000456.html
- Finding the Minimum Information for
  Bible Records—Burial Place
  http://www.familytreemaker.com/00000473.html

FEMALE ANCESTORS
http://www.CyndisList.com/female.htm

Category Index:

◆ General Resource Sites

◆ Military

◆ Our Foremothers

◆ Societies & Groups

◆ Women's History Resources

◆ General Resource Sites

● Discovering Your Female Ancestors
http://www.ancestry.com/home/
Myra_Vanderpool_Gormley\Shaking_Family_Tree03-26-98.htm
*From Shaking Your Family Tree by Myra Vanderpool
Gormley, C.G.*

● Female Ancestry
http://www.ancestry.com/magazine/articles/female.htm
by Roseann R. Hogan, Ph.D.

● First Name Basis
http://www.hypervigilance.com/genlog/firstname.html
*To aid you in researching when all you know is the first name
of a person. Focuses on unusual first names and women's first
names when maiden names are unknown.*

● The First Woman Who...
http://main.nc.us/OBCGS/firstwomen.htm

● A Genealogist's Guide to Discovering Your Female
Ancestors: Special Strategies for Uncovering Hard-
To-Find Information About Your Female Lineage
http://www.oz.net/~markhow/library.htm#female
*A book for sale from Amazon.com, by Sharon Debartolo
Carmack.*

● A Guide to Materials on Women in The United
Methodist Church Archives
http://www.gcah.org/women.htm
*From The General Commission on Archives and History for
The United Methodist Church.*

● Notable Women Ancestors
http://www.rootsweb.com/~nwa/

● Remember the Ladies
http://pw1.netcom.com/~rilydia/chase/kate.html
and an alternate address
http://www.geocities.com/Heartland/4678/kate.html

● Schoolmarms on the Frontier
http://www.ancestry.com/columns/myra/
Shaking_Family_Tree06-04-98.htm
*From Shaking Your Family Tree by Myra Vanderpool
Gormley, C.G.*

◆ Military

● American Women in Uniform, Veterans Too!
http://userpages.aug.com/captbarb/

● CIVIL-WAR-WOMEN Mailing List
http://members.aol.com/gfsjohnf/gen_mail_states-
gen.html#CIVIL-WAR-WOMEN
*For those who are researching women that served or assisted in
the American Civil War.*

● Civil War Women—Primary Sources on the Internet
http://scriptorium.lib.duke.edu/women/cwdocs.html

● Women and the Civil War
http://odyssey.lib.duke.edu/women/civilwar.html
*Manuscript sources in the Special Collections Library at
Duke University.*

● Women in Military Service for America Memorial
Foundation, Inc.
http://www.wimsa.org/

● Women Soldiers of the Civil War
http://www.nara.gov/publications/prologue/women1.html

● Women's Civil War Diaries and Papers—Locations
http://homepages.rootsweb.com/~haas/cwdiaries.html

◆ Our Foremothers

● Anne MARBURY HUTCHINSON
http://www.rootsweb.com/~nwa/ah.html
*Born in 1591 in Alford, Lincolnshire, England, died 1643 in
East Chester, New York.*

● Biographies of Historical Women
http://www.inform.umd.edu:8080/EdRes/Topic/
WomensStudies/ReadingRoom/History/Biographies/

● Biography of Joanna QUAID
http://www.pclink.com/kg0ay/quaid.htm
*She was born in Ireland and made the trek to the United States
in 1836.*

● Distinguished Women of Past and Present
http://www.netsrq.com/~dbois/

● Early Illinois Women & Other Unsung Heroes
http://www.rsa.lib.il.us/~ilwomen/

- Elizabeth SIMPSON (HAIGH) BRADSHAW of the Martin Handcart Company
  http://www.geocities.com/Heartland/Pointe/7083/index.html
- The Hannah DUSTIN Story
  http://www.net1plus.com/users/locke/hannah.htm
- Life of Polly Hart LANE
  http://www.genweb.net/~bowers/lane/pollyp.htm
  Polly Pierce (Pierre) Hart LANE born in 1802 in Kentucky.
- Mercer's Maids—Pioneer Brides of 1864 ~ Washington
  http://members.tripod.com/~PeriM/Brides.html
- National First Ladies Library
  http://www.firstladies.org/
- Notable Women Ancestors
  http://www.rootsweb.com/~nwa/
- "The Petticoat Invasion": Women at the College of William and Mary 1918–1945
  http://www.swem.wm.edu/SPCOL/women/mainwom.html
- Pocahontas Descendants
  http://www.rootscomputing.com/howto/pocahn/pocahn.htm
  Descendants of Powhatan (Father of Pocahontas).
- 75 Suffragists
  http://www.inform.umd.edu/EdRes/Topic/WomensStudies/ReadingRoom/History/Vote/75-suffragists.html
- Women and Female children of the Royal Admiral 1792
  http://www.shoalhaven.net.au/~cathyd/raladies.html

◆ Societies & Groups

- Dames of the Loyal Legion of the United States of America
  http://www.usmo.com/~momollus/DOLLUS.HTM
- Daughters of Union Veterans of the Civil War
  http://suvcw.org/duv.htm
- National Society Colonial Dames XVII Century
  http://www.geocities.com/Heartland/Meadows/4399/cdxvii.html

- National Society of the Daughters of the American Revolution, General Samuel Hopkins Chapter
  http://www.rootsweb.com/~kyhender/Henderson/DAR/dar.htm
  Henderson County, Kentucky
- National Society of the Daughters of the American Revolution Home Page
  http://www.dar.org/index.html
- United Daughters of the Confederacy
  http://www.hqudc.org/

◆ Women's History Resources

- American Women's History: A Research Guide
  http://frank.mtsu.edu/~kmiddlet/history/women.html
- Guide to Women's History Materials in Manuscript Collections at the Indiana Historical Society
  http://www.dgltd.com/ihs1830/wombib.htm
- Living the Legacy: The Women's Rights Movement 1848–1998
  http://www.legacy98.org/
- National Museum of Women's History
  http://www.nmwh.org/
- The National Women's History Project
  http://www.nwhp.org/welcome.html
- Nevada Women's History Project
  http://www.unr.edu/unr/sb204/nwhp/
- Women and Slavery
  http://weber.u.washington.edu/~sunstar/ws200/slavery.htm
- Women in Canadian History
  http://www.niagara.com/~merrwill/
- Women in History
  http://www.clements.umich.edu/Gurls/Gurl.html
  A new guide to manuscripts of the Clements Library, University of Michigan, Ann Arbor, Michigan.
- Women's History Web Links
  http://www.socialstudies.com/womenlinks.html
- Yahoo!...Women's History
  http://dir.yahoo.com/Arts/Humanities/History/Women_s_History/

FINDING PEOPLE

Phone Numbers, E-Mail Addresses, Mailing Addresses, Places, Etc.
http://www.CyndisList.com/finding.htm

Category Index:

◆ City Directories

◆ E-Mail Addresses and Web Sites

◆ People Searching

◆ Snail Mail Addresses

◆ Telephone Directories

◆ City Directories

● Analyzing City Directories
http://www.genealogy.org/~bcg/skbld965.html
From the Board for Certification of Genealogists—Skill Building—May 1996.

● Chicago City Directories on Microfilm ~ Illinois
http://www.mcs.net/~jimjoyce/genealogy/ccdindex.html

● City Directories
http://www.ancestry.com/columns/george/03-06-98.htm
From "Along Those Lines . . ." by George Morgan.

● City Directories at the Library of Congress
http://www.kinquest.com/genealogy/citydir.html

● City Directories at the Tennessee State Library & Archives
http://www.state.tn.us/sos/statelib/pubsvs/cdirect.htm

● City Directories of the United States—Guide to the Microfilm Collection
http://scfn.thpl.lib.fl.us/thpl/main/spc/city_directories.htm
From the Special Collections Department of the Tampa-Hillsborough County Public Library System.

● City Directories: Windows on the Past
http://www.ancestry.com/columns/myra/
Shaking_Family_Tree03-19-98.htm
From Shaking Your Family Tree, by Myra Vanderpool Gormley, C.G.

● Glendale City Directories ~ California
http://www.library.ci.glendale.ca.us/city_dir.html

● Telephone and City Directories in the Library of Congress: A Finding Guide
gopher://marvel.loc.gov/00/research/reading.rooms/genealogy/
bibs.guides/telephon
By Barbara B. Walsh, Reference Specialist, November 1994.

● TSLAC City Directories Available in the State Archives
http://www.tsl.state.tx.us/lobby/citydirs.htm
Texas State Library and Archives Commission

◆ E-Mail Addresses and Web Sites

● 555-1212.com
http://www.555-1212.com/
Look up telephone numbers, e-mail addresses, web sites, and area code lookups also.

● Bigfoot
http://www.bigfoot.com/
Global e-mail directory

● Find mE-Mail
http://www.findmemail.com/

● Finding People on the Internet
http://alabanza.com/kabacoff/Inter-Links/phone.html

● Gibraltar E-Mail Directory
http://www.gibraltar.gi/localinfo/gibdirectory.html

● InfoSpace
http://www.infospace.com/

● Internet Address Finder
http://www.iaf.net/

● Personal Seek
http://www.personalseek.com/

● Search Engines
http://www.CyndisList.com/search.htm
See this category on Cyndi's List for related links. Find people, topics and resources on the Internet.

● Searching For People
http://ddi.digital.net/~islander/

● Semaphore's National Address Browser & Where Did They Go? Databases
http://www.semaphorecorp.com/default.html

● Sharkey's Search Engine Index: People and Businesses
http://www2.hawaii.edu/~sharkey/links/search/people/
people.htm

● Sunny's CyberConnexion...
http://www.geocities.com/TheTropics/3233/

- WorldPages
  http://www.worldpages.com/
  Your one-stop directory for telephone, e-mail and web site connections.

- WhoWhere? People Finder
  http://www.whowhere.lycos.com/
  Find e-mail addresses and people on the Internet.

- Yahoo! People Search
  http://people.yahoo.com/

- Yukon White Pages
  http://whitepages.yknet.yk.ca/
  A listing of holders of Internet e-mail accounts in the Yukon.

◆ People Searching

- Adoption
  http://www.CyndisList.com/adoption.htm
  See this category on Cyndi's List for related links.

- ClassMates Online
  http://www.classmates.com/
  Helps high school alumni friends find each other.

- CyberPages International—Lost and Missing Relatives
  http://www.cyberpages.com/lostprsn.htm

- Find People Fast
  http://www.fpf.com/

- Janyce's Root Diggin' Dept.—People Searching & Adoption
  http://www.janyce.com/gene/search.html

- Military—Buddies, Pals, Shipmates, Families, and Friends
  http://www.shipmates.com/

- Military Search Bulletin Board
  http://www.shadow.net/~tferrer/search.html

- New Zealand White Pages
  http://www.whitepages.co.nz/

- People Finder
  http://www.peoplesite.com/

- Professional Researchers, Volunteers & Other Research Services
  http://www.CyndisList.com/profess.htm
  See this category on Cyndi's List for related links.

- Reunion Hall
  http://www.nowandthen.com/reunion/index.html

- Searching For People
  http://ddi.digital.net/~islander/

- The Seeker Magazine
  http://www.the-seeker.com/

- Seekers of the Lost International Reunion Registry
  http://www.seeklost.com/

- Semaphore's National Address Browser & Where Did They Go? Databases
  http://www.semaphorecorp.com/default.html

- USTRACE
  http://www.ustrace.com/
  Missing persons, background checks, etc.

◆ Snail Mail Addresses

- 411 Locate
  http://www.411Locate.com/

- Big Book Directory
  http://www.bigbook.com/
  Business yellow pages

- Canada 411 White Pages
  http://canada411.sympatico.ca/

- Canada Post Corporation / Société canadienne des postes
  http://www.canadapost.ca/
  Postal rates & codes, etc.

- Les codes postaux des villes françaises / Postal Codes for Towns in France
  http://www.unice.fr/html/French/codePostal.html

- Database America People Finder
  http://www.databaseamerica.com/html/gpfind.htm

- Deutsche Post AG
  http://www.postag.de/
  Postal codes, etc.

- Finding People on the Internet
  http://alabanza.com/kabacoff/Inter-Links/phone.html

- Geographic Name Server
  gopher://riceinfo.rice.edu:1103/1geo
  Look up US place names by city or zip code.

- Infobel—Find Business & Residential Addresses in Belgium
  http://www.infobel.be/

- InfoSpace
  http://www.infospace.com/

- InterNIC White Pages Directory Services
  http://www.internic.net/tools/wp.html

- The Lycos People Finder
  http://www.lycos.com/pplfndr.html

- Maps, Gazetteers and Geographical Information
  http://www.CyndisList.com/maps.htm
  See this category on Cyndi's List for related links.

- National Address and ZIP+4 Browser
  http://www.semaphorecorp.com/

- POSTINFO: World-Address postal information service
  http://www.world-address.com/postinfo/

- RootsWeb Surname List Country Abbreviations
  http://www.rootsweb.com/roots-l/cabbrev1.html
  Listed by Country.

  o Abbreviations from the RootsWeb Surname List
    http://www.rootsweb.com/roots-l/cabbrev2.html
    Listed by Abbreviation.

- Searching For People
  http://ddi.digital.net/~islander/

- Semaphore's National Address Browser &
  Where Did They Go? Databases
  http://www.semaphorecorp.com/default.html

- Sharkey's Search Engine Index: People and
  Businesses
  http://www2.hawaii.edu/~sharkey/links/search/people/people.htm

- Sunny's CyberConnexion...
  http://www.geocities.com/TheTropics/3233/

- USPS Address and ZIP Code Information
  http://www.usps.gov/ncsc/

- Westminster—Canadian Postal Code
  Lookup Service
  http://www.westminster.ca/cdnlook.htm
  Also has U.S. Zip codes.

- Yahoo! People Search
  http://people.yahoo.com/

- Zip Codes and Phone Numbers
  http://www.microserve.com/~john/pages/numbers.html

◆ Telephone Directories

- 555-1212.com
  http://www.555-1212.com/
  Look up telephone numbers, e-mail addresses, web sites, and area code lookups also.

- AnyWho: Find People—Find E-mail—Toll-Free
  Directory Search
  http://www.tollfree.att.net/tf.html

- BigYellow: Your Yellow Pages on the Web
  http://www1.bigyellow.com/

- Canada 411 White Pages
  http://canada411.sympatico.ca/

- Database America People Finder
  http://www.databaseamerica.com/html/gpfind.htm

- Finding People on the Internet
  http://alabanza.com/kabacoff/Inter-Links/phone.html

- Greek Telephone Directories
  http://www.hellasyellow.gr/

- InfoSpace
  http://www.infospace.com/

- InterNIC White Pages Directory Services
  http://www.internic.net/tools/wp.html

- Jamal's Yellow Pages of Pakistan
  http://www.jamals.com/

- The Lycos People Finder
  http://www.lycos.com/pplfndr.html

- New Zealand White Pages
  http://www.whitepages.co.nz/

- On-Line Phone Directories of the World by
  Bob Coret
  http://www.coret.demon.nl/phone

- P & T Luxembourg OnLine!
  http://www.editus.lu/
  Online telephone directory.

- LES PAGES BLANCHES—les annuaires de France
  Telecom, Pages jaunes, Pages Blanches, Les
  marques, Les rues commercantes, Les pages pro,
  Adresses E-mail, Voila, assistance de cartographie
  http://www.pagesjaunes.fr/wbpm_pages_blanches.cgi?

- Post & Telekom Austria—
  Elektronisches Telefonbuch
  http://www.etb.at/

- Saskatchewan Yellow Pages
  http://www.saskyellowpages.com/
  Residential Search
  http://www2.saskyellowpages.com/
  Business Search
  http://www.saskyellowpages.com/search/main.cgi

- Searching For People
  http://ddi.digital.net/~islander/

- Semaphore's National Address Browser &
  Where Did They Go? Databases
  http://www.semaphorecorp.com/default.html

- Sharkey's Search Engine Index:
  People and Businesses
  http://www2.hawaii.edu/~sharkey/links/search/people/people.htm

- Spanish Yellow Pages—Páginas
  Amarillas Multimedia
  http://www.paginas-amarillas.es/

- Sunny's CyberConnexion...
  http://www.geocities.com/TheTropics/3233/

- Switchboard
  http://www.switchboard.com/
  If you don't have access to a phone CD try this site for addresses and phone numbers.

- Telecom New Zealand White Pages
  http://www.whitepages.co.nz/

- Telefonski imenik Slovenije—
  Slovenian Telephone Directory
  http://tis.telekom.si/

- Telephone and City Directories in the Library of Congress: A Finding Guide
  gopher://marvel.loc.gov/00/research/reading.rooms/genealogy/bibs.guides/telephon
  By Barbara B. Walsh, Reference Specialist, November 1994.

- Telephone Directories on the Web
  http://www.contractjobs.com/tel/

- Telstra—Australian White & Yellow Pages
  http://www.telstra.com.au/

- TIV Tele-Info Verlag, Online Auskunft Deutschland
  http://www.teleinfo.de/abfragen/bin/neuabfrage.pl
  Online telephone book for Germany.

- The Ultimate White Pages
  http://www.theultimates.com/white/

- White Pages Phone Directory for Australia
  http://www.whitepages.com.au/

- WorldPages
  http://www.worldpages.com/
  Your one-stop directory for telephone, e-mail and web site connections.

- Yahoo! People Search
  http://people.yahoo.com/

FRANCE

http://www.CyndisList.com/france.htm

- ALSACE-GENEALOGY Mailing List
  http://members.aol.com/gfsjohnf/gen_mail_country-fra.html#ALSACE-L
  and the corresponding web page
  http://members.aol.com/jaw5623/private/alsace/listes.html
  For anyone interested in Alsace, a border region of France and Germany.

- ALSACE-LORRAINE Mailing List
  http://members.aol.com/gfsjohnf/gen_mail_country-fra.html#ALSACE-LORRAINE

- The American-French Genealogical Society
  http://users.ids.net/~afgs/afgshome.html
  Rhode Island

- ANCESTRA—Logiciel de généalogie
  http://myweb.worldnet.fr/~franke/genealogie/ancestra.htm
  From France, for Windows 3.1 & 95.

- The Anglo-French Family History Society
  http://www.karolus.org/org/assoc/as-euro/as-affhs.htm
  Andover, Hampshire, Great Britain

- Archer's Computer Interest Group List—France
  http://www.genealogy.org/~ngs/cigs/ngl3otfr.html

- BASQUE Mailing List
  http://members.aol.com/gfsjohnf/gen_mail_country-fra.html#BASQUE
  A "moderated" mailing list, gatewayed with the soc.culture.basque "moderated" newsgroup, that provides Basques the world over with a virtual place to discuss social, political, cultural or any other issues related to Basques, or to request information and discuss matters related to the basque people and/or their culture. Genealogy queries are an acceptable topic for the list.

- BASQUE-L Mailing List
  http://members.aol.com/gfsjohnf/gen_mail_country-fra.html#BASQUE-L
  A forum for the dissemination and exchange of information on Basque culture. Genealogy-related issues are often discussed on the list though the main topics of discussion are socio-political current affairs, gastronomy, Basque music, poetry, anthropology (e.g., origin of Basques), etc.

- Bibliothèque Nationale de France /
  National Library of France
  http://www.bnf.fr/

- Bienvenue en Alsace! / Welcome to Alsace!
  http://members.aol.com/jaw5623/private/alsace/

- Books We Own—France
  http://www.rootsweb.com/~bwo/france.html

- Brother's Keeper Software
  http://ourworld.compuserve.com/homepages/Brothers_Keeper/
  Downloadable shareware program for Windows. The latest version contains English, French, Norwegian, Danish, Swedish, German, and Dutch.

- Calendar Conversions
  http://www.genealogy.org/~scottlee/calconvert.cgi
  Scott Lee's free on-line service for converting to/from dates in Gregorian, Julian, French republican and Jewish calendars.

- Centre Departemental D'histoire Des Familles
  http://www.telmat-net.fr/~cdhf/

- Centre Généalogique des Pyrénées-Atlantiques
  (Béarn et Pays Basque)
  http://www.world-address.com/cgpa/

- Les Centres Généalogiques SDJ /
  LDS Family History Centers
  http://www2.et.byu.edu/~harmanc/paris/genealogie.html
  France, Belgique, Suisse, Canada

- Le Cercle Généalogique du Sud-Aveyronm ~
  Millau, France
  http://www.geocities.com/Heartland/8308/

- Le Cercle Généalogique et Héraldique de
  L'Auvergne et du Velay
  http://pages.pratique.fr/~phegymeg/adlv/cghav.htm

- Les cercles généalogiques d'Alsace, de Lorraine et
  de Sarre / Genealogical societies in Alsace, in
  Lorraine and in Saar
  http://perso.club-internet.fr/rweinl/cercl_en.htm

- Les codes postaux des villes françaises /
  Postal Codes for Towns in France
  http://www.unice.fr/html/French/codePostal.html

- The Communities of Alsace A–Z
  http://members.aol.com/RobtBehra/AlsaceA-Z/GenInfo.htm

- Le Dictionnaire des communes
  http://www.es-conseil.fr/pramona/p1gen.htm#dico
  If you are searching for a place name in France, or Algeria, Philippe RAMONA will do a lookup for you in this book: "Dictionnaire des Communes de la France, de l'Algérie et des autres colonies Françaises" (Paris 1866).

- Encyclopédie de Saint-Pierre et Miquelon—
  La France en Amérique du Nord
  http://209.205.50.254/encyspmweb/
  France in North America

- Fédération Française de Généalogie
  http://members.aol.com/GHCaraibe/pub/pubffga.html

- FranceGenWeb
  http://francegenweb.org/
  Part of the WorldGenWeb project.

- FRANCÊTRES: Généalogie en France /
  Genealogy in France
  http://www.world-address.com/francetres/

- FRANCÊTRES: Généalogie en France / Genealogy in France—Centres généalogiques mormons / Genealogical LDS centers
  http://www.world-address.com/francetres/gefrldho.htm
- FRANCÊTRES: Genealogy in France
  http://www.cam.org/~beaur/gen/france-e.html
  By Denis Beauregard.
- From Alsace to Lorraine.....through Saarland— Robert WEINLAND's Home Page
  http://perso.club-internet.fr/rweinl/
  Many French resources listed here.
- GENEA64 Mailing List
  http://members.aol.com/gfsjohnf/gen_mail_country-fra.html#GENEA64
  For anyone with a genealogical interest in the French Regions of Bearn and Pays Basque.
- GENEAL / GENE2000—Généalogie en Europe / Genealogy in Europe
  http://www.gene2000.com/
- GenealogyBookShop.com—France/French
  http://www.genealogybookshop.com/genealogybookshop/files/The_World,France_French/index.html
  The online store of Genealogical Publishing Co., Inc. & Clearfield Company.
- Genealogy—France (professional researchers)
  http://www.wp.com/GEFRANCE/
- Genealogy in France
  http://www.cam.org/~beaur/gen/france-e.html
  From Denis Beauregard.
- GENEALOR: Généalogie en Lorraine (France) / Genealogy in Lorraine (France)
  http://www.world-address.com/genealor/
- GENEALOR Mailing List
  http://members.aol.com/gfsjohnf/gen_mail_country-fra.html#GENEALOR
  For anyone with a genealogical interest in the French region of Lorraine.
- Généatique pour windows / Geneatique for Windows
  http://www.cdip.com/
- GeneDraw Software
  http://home.nordnet.fr/~ppuech/pregd3.html
- GENENORD—Le Web Des Associations Généalogiques Des Provinces du Nord
  http://www.genenord.tm.fr/
- GEN-FF Mailing List
  http://members.aol.com/gfsjohnf/gen_mail_country-fra.html#GEN-FF-L
  Discussion of Francophone genealogy. Gatewayed with fr.rec.genealogie. Mainly in French.
- GEN-FR Mailing List
  http://members.aol.com/gfsjohnf/gen_mail_country-fra.html#GEN-FR-L
  Discussion of Francophone genealogy. Gatewayed with soc.genealogy.french. Mainly in English.

- Genus Genealogy Program
  http://www.mediabase.fi/suku/genupgb.htm
  Windows program available in six languages: Dutch, English, Finnish, French, German and Swedish.
- German Genealogy: Elsass / Alsace
  http://www.genealogy.net/gene/reg/ELS-LOT/alsace.html
- GRIOT Alternative—Généalogie et démographie informatique
  http://www.cybernaute.com/jgagnon/griot/index.htm
- HEREDIS PRO pour Windows
  http://www.es-conseil.fr/pramona/p1gen.htm#sommet
  Download a demo of this French genealogy software.
- History of Europe in Medieval Times, France
  http://www.worldroots.com/brigitte/royal/royal6.htm
  Historic and genealogical information about royal and nobility family lines.
- Huguenot Mailing List
  http://members.aol.com/johnf14246/gen_mail_general.html#Huguenot
- Images de la France d'Autrefois / Old French Picture Postcards
  http://france.mediasys.fr:8060/Pages/Sommaire.html
  Searchable by locality.
- JamoDat—Win-Family Software
  http://www.jamodat.dk/
  Available in Danish, Swedish, Norwegian, French, German and English.
- KAROLUS—from the Fédération Française de Généalogie
  http://www.karolus.org/
  An Internet database dedicated to genealogy, heraldic, archiving of related documentation. There are many helpful articles & lists on this site to help you with French genealogical research.
- Lineages' Free On-line Queries—France
  http://www.lineages.com/queries/BrowseByCountry.asp
- Map of France
  http://www.lib.utexas.edu/Libs/PCL/Map_collection/europe/France.GIF
  From the Perry-Castañeda Library at the Univ. of Texas at Austin.
- Nomade—Sciences humaines et sociales...Histoire: Généalogie
  http://www.nomade.fr/sciences_sociales/sciences_humaines/histoire/genealogie/
  French web directory with many links to personal home pages for genealogy.
- Les pages Zoom de France Telecom—annuaire du telephone / France Telecom Directories
  http://www.pageszoom.com/files/nojava/francais/commun/sommaire.html
- Paris Cemeteries
  http://www.parisnet.com/english/city/unusual/cimetieres.htm
- Pariscope: Cemeteries
  http://pariscope.fr/Pariscope/Visiter/Cimetieres/Welcome.E.html

- PRO-GEN Genealogie à la Carte
  http://home.pi.net/~progen/
  Dutch genealogy program capable of outputs in Dutch, English, French, Frisian and German.

- Union Des Cercles Genealogiques et Heraldiques de Normandie
  http://members.aol.com/ucghn/index.htm

- Union des Cercles Généalogiques Lorrains
  http://www.world-address.com/ucgl/

- Usenet Newsgroup fr.rec.genealogie
  In French, mostly. Gatewayed with Mailing List GEN-FF.

- Usenet Newsgroup soc.genealogy.french
  Gatewayed with Mailing List GEN-FR

- World-Address postal information service: France
  http://www.world-address.com/postinfo/postfrho.htm

- Yahoo!...France...Genealogy
  http://dir.yahoo.com/Regional/Countries/France/
  Arts_and_Humanities/History/Genealogy/

◆ French Family Sites

- Bernard et Claudette PARANQUE, Généalogie
  http://myweb.worldnet.net/~paranqu/genea/dragonet.html
  PARANQUE, RÉGIS, LABATUT, BONASSE, De PONTEVES, CHABERT, de ROUX, NÉGREL

- JEAN en 3 D (Druez, Desnos, Dupleix)
  http://members.aol.com/JDruez/index.htm
  (France):DRUEZ—DEMARE—FONTAINE—DRU—MATHIEU—GUYOT—HULBERT, (England): ARCHER

- LOEB Family Tree
  http://www.labri.u-bordeaux.fr/Equipe/CombAlg/membre/loeb/tree/index.html
  French and Jewish research

- MEYER-HEITZ-JOHO de l'Alsace et Lorraine
  http://www.autumnstar.com/Genealogy/Meyer/

- La page généalogique d'Yves GUIGNARD
  http://www.geneanet.net/

- Page personnelle de Dominique MAGNIER
  http://books.dreambook.com/dmagnier/livredor.html

- La page Web de CHEVIET's Family
  http://perso.club-internet.fr/cheviet/
  Ascendance d'Antoine et Mathilde CHEVIET

- Recherches généalogiques en France: le site de Paul-Marc HEUDRE
  http://members.aol.com/heudre/index.htm

- VIALLET et arbre généalogique / VIALLET and Tree
  http://www.mygale.org/07/viallet/

GERMANS FROM RUSSIA

http://www.CyndisList.com/germruss.htm

Category Index:

- General Resource Sites
- Mailing Lists, Newsgroups & Chat
- Maps, Gazetteers & Geographical Information
- People & Families
- Publications

- Records: Census, Cemeteries, Land, Obituaries, Personal, Taxes and Vital
- Societies & Groups
- Villages & Colonies

◆ General Resource Sites

- German-Russian Genealogy Links
  http://www.geocities.com/SiliconValley/Haven/1538/germ_rus.html

- Germans from Russia Heritage Collection
  http://www.lib.ndsu.nodak.edu/gerrus/index.html
  From North Dakota State University & Michael Miller.

- Germans from Russia Heritage Society—GRHS—Cross-Index
  http://feefhs.org/grhs/indexgrh.html

- Germans from Russia Historical Collection—GRHC—Cross Index—from FEEFHS
  http://feefhs.org/grhc/indexgrc.html

- German / Russian Roots
  http://www.geocities.com/Heartland/Acres/4123/ger-rus.htm

- Manisfesto of the Empress Catherine II, issued July 22, 1763
  http://members.aol.com/jktsn/manifest.htm

- ODESSA ... a German-Russian Genealogical Library
  http://pixel.cs.vt.edu/library/odessa.html

- St. Joseph's Colony
  http://www.rootsweb.com/~skstjose/stjoseph.html
  Saskatchewan, Canada

- Who Are the Germans from Russia?
  http://www.feefhs.org/frgcdcwt.html

◆ Mailing Lists, Newsgroups & Chat

- BDO Mailing List
  http://members.aol.com/gfsjohnf/gen_mail_country-rus.html#BDO
  The Beresan District Odessa (BDO) mailing list is for anyone with a genealogical interest in the Beresan Colonies which were made up of Germans who immigrated to Russia, beginning in the first decade of the 19th century, at the request of Alexander I, Tsar of Russia. The Colonies were located Northeast of the city of Odessa on the Black Sea.

- BESS-GR: Bessarabian Germans From Russia Electronic Discussion Group
  http://www.lib.ndsu.nodak.edu/gerrus/listbessgr.html

- GCRA Mailing List
  http://www.lib.ndsu.nodak.edu/gerrus/listgcra.html
  For those interested in Germans from Russia research and family research oriented specifically to the Glueckstal Colonies of Bergdorf, Glueckstal, Kassel, and Neudorf and their daughter colonies.

- GER-VOLGA Mailing List
  http://members.aol.com/gfsjohnf/gen_mail_country-rus.html#GER-VOLGA
  For those who are researching Germans from the Volga Valley area of Russia.

- GRDB Mailing List
  http://members.aol.com/gfsjohnf/gen_mail_country-rus.html#GRDB
  For the discussion of genealogy databases containing German-Russians and their descendants, being developed by the American Historical Society of Germans from Russian (AHSGR).

- GR-GENEALOGY Mailing List
  http://members.aol.com/gfsjohnf/gen_mail_country-rus.html#GR-GENEALOGY
  For discussions of Germans from Russia genealogy and family research.

- GR-HERITAGE Mailing List
  http://members.aol.com/gfsjohnf/gen_mail_country-rus.html#GR-HERITAGE
  For general discussions of Germans from Russia history, culture, and folklore.

- IRC Chat Line—#Ger-Rus
  http://www.geocities.com/Heartland/Acres/4123/irc.htm
  For researching Germans from Russia.

- Kutschurgan Mailing List
  http://members.aol.com/gfsjohnf/gen_mail_country-rus.html#Kutschurgan
  For anyone with a genealogical interest in the Kutschurgan Colonies which were made up of Germans who immigrated to Russia, beginning in the first decade of the 19th century, at the request of Alexander I, Tsar of Russia. The Colonies were located Northwest of the city of Odessa on the Black Sea.

- Master E-mail Listing for Germans From Russia
  http://pixel.cs.vt.edu/library/boxes/stahl/mastlist.html
- SURNAMES-GERMAN Mailing List
  http://members.aol.com/gfsjohnf/gen_mail_country-ger.html#SURNAMES-GERMAN
  For surname queries related to German speaking countries. Gatewayed with the soc.genealogy.surnames.german newsgroup.

◆ Maps, Gazetteers & Geographical Information

- Map of Odessa
  http://members.aol.com/tgostin/graphics/odessa2.jpg
- Old-Samara—Volga-German Colonies Map
  http://pixel.cs.vt.edu/library/boxes/stahl/kochmap.gif

◆ People & Families

- The ANTONS: German—Russian Heritage 1720–1995
  http://www.bconnex.net/~ganton/genealogy.html
- AVANT Genealogy Page
  http://www.avalon.net/~avant/Page.htm
  Village of Dreispitz, Volga, Russia and Village of Tarutino, Bessarabia, Russia. BOETTCHER, DICK, DOERING, HEID, HEINITZ, HERBEL, HULSCHER, KOSCH/KOTH?, KRAUSE, MANSKE, ROLOFF, UTTKE, WARNKE, WENDLAND
- Dennis and Patricia Evans' Family History
  http://www.cadvision.com/evansdg/INDEX-1.HTM
  EVANS, HARRAY, GRIFFITHS, REED, STEINERT, BORTH, STREGGER, SCHMIDT
- ELL Family Heritage Page
  http://mars.ark.com/~rbell/html/ellfam.htm
  ELL, FLECK, JUNG, WOLFE, SCHAAN/SCHAN, HEGEL/HAGEL, HIMMILSPACH
- Famous Germans from Russia
  http://www-personal.umich.edu/~steeles/gerrus/
- FEHR's Famous Family
  http://www3.bc.sympatico.ca/donfehr/fehr.htm
  The family of Benjamin Fehr and his wife, Elisabeth, in Manitoba and Saskatchewan, Canada.
- The GEYER Family: Germans from Russia
  http://www.angelfire.com/ny/earthstar/geyer.html
  Descendants of Frederick W. C. Geyer, born about 1808 and his wife Margaret, born about 1813.
- GUENTHER Genealogy—Passionate Possessions of Faith
  http://home1.gte.net/kanetani/guenther/index.htm
  A book for sale about The Jacob Guenther Family 1725–present, including GOERTZEN, DUERKSEN, PETERS, WARKENTIN, ADRIAN, LOEWEN, PETKAU, ISAAC, FADENRECHT, THIESSEN and others.

- Harold EHRMAN's Web Page
  http://www.jovanet.com/~hmehrman/
  EHRMANN, DOCKTER, HAUCK, KNOERTZER
- HOCHHALTER's WWW Page
  http://www.srv.net/~kata9b/eehpg.html
  HOCHHALTER, RUDOLPH, STOLZ, ZIMBELMANN
- HOHNSTEIN / HOHENSTEIN Surname Project
  http://members.xoom.com/tsterkel/surname_projects/hohnstei.htm
- Hutterite Genealogy Cross-Index
  http://feefhs.org/hut/indexhut.html
- John WALL's Family Tree
  http://www.oz.net/~compass/family/fam_tree.htm
  BAIRD, BURGESS / EASTERLING, CLARK / WHORTON or HORTON, GIESWEIN, JOHNSON, PEANECKER or PINNECKER or PENAGER or PINAGER, WALL. Gnadenfeld, Russia; Puschen, Germany.
- LANGMACHER Surname Project
  http://members.xoom.com/tsterkel/surname_projects/langmach.htm
- REMMICK Home Site
  http://members.aol.com/remmick1/Remmick.Home.Site.index.html/
  German-Russian heritage connected to Edenkoben, Palatinate migration to Worms/Odessa, S. Russia then Streeter, ND, USA. Remmick, Roemmich, Remick, Remich, Roemigius, Roemig.
- SCHUMAN SCHUMANN Surname Project
  http://members.xoom.com/tsterkel/surname_projects/schuman.htm
- STAERKEL, STOERKEL, STÄRKEL, STÖRKEL, STARKEL, STERKEL Surname Project
  http://members.xoom.com/tsterkel/surname_projects/sterkel.htm
- The Volga Germans—A Brief History
  http://www.lhm.org/LID/lidhist.htm

◆ Publications

- The Folks—Books Listing
  http://pixel.cs.vt.edu/pub/sources/booklist.txt
- The "German-Russian Books" list
  http://pixel.cs.vt.edu/pub/sources/grbooks.txt
- Wandering Volhynians
  http://pixel.cs.vt.edu/pub/sources/wv.txt
  A Magazine for the Descendants of Germans From Volhynia and Poland.
- Wandering Volhynians—German-Volhynian Newsletter
  http://feefhs.org/ca/frg-wv.html

◆ Records: Census, Cemeteries, Land, Obituaries, Personal, Taxes and Vital (Born, Married, Died & Buried)

- The Bessarabian Collection
  http://pixel.cs.vt.edu/library/bess/
  Includes the Bessarabian Index, the Christian Fiess Indices, The Koblenz Exodus Questionnaires/Forms Index and much more.

- Cemeteries
  http://pixel.cs.vt.edu/library/cemeteries/

- Census Records
  http://pixel.cs.vt.edu/library/census/
  - Barnes County, North Dakota 1900 Census of Germans from Russia
    http://pixel.cs.vt.edu/library/census/link/barnes00.txt
  - Barnes County, North Dakota 1910 Census of Germans from Russia
    http://pixel.cs.vt.edu/library/census/link/barnes10.txt
  - Barnes County, North Dakota 1920 Census of Germans from Russia
    http://pixel.cs.vt.edu/library/census/link/barnes20.txt
  - Campbell County, South Dakota 1910 Census of German Russians
    http://pixel.cs.vt.edu/library/census/link/camp10.txt
  - Charles Mix County, South Dakota 1910 Census of German Russians
    http://pixel.cs.vt.edu/library/census/link/cmix10.txt
  - Clark County, South Dakota 1910 Census of German Russians
    http://pixel.cs.vt.edu/library/census/link/clark10.txt
  - Grimes County, Texas 1900 Census, Germans from Russia
    http://pixel.cs.vt.edu/library/census/link/grimes00.txt
  - Grimes County, Texas 1910 Census, Germans from Russia
    http://pixel.cs.vt.edu/library/census/link/grimes10.txt
  - Grimes County, Texas 1920 Census, Germans from Russia
    http://pixel.cs.vt.edu/library/census/link/grimes20.txt
  - McPherson County, South Dakota 1900 Census of German Russians
    http://pixel.cs.vt.edu/library/census/link/mcpher00.txt
  - McPherson County, South Dakota 1910 Census of German Russians
    http://pixel.cs.vt.edu/library/census/link/mcpher10.txt
  - Unruh's South Russian Mennonite Census, 1795–1814
    http://pixel.cs.vt.edu/library/census/link/bhu.txt
  - Walworth County, South Dakota 1900 Census of German Russians
    http://pixel.cs.vt.edu/library/census/link/wal00.txt
  - Walworth County, South Dakota 1910 Census of German Russians
    http://pixel.cs.vt.edu/library/census/link/wal10.txt

- Friedensgemeinde Cemetery, Froid, Montana
  http://pixel.cs.vt.edu/library/cemeteries/montana/link/damm.txt

- The Gluecksthal Reformed Church, Odessa Township, McPherson Co., South Dakota
  http://pixel.cs.vt.edu/library/churches/link/glueck.txt
  Birth records, now in the possession of the Eureka Reformed Church.

- Greenway Cemetery, Greenway, South Dakota
  http://pixel.cs.vt.edu/library/cemeteries/sodak/link/grnway.txt

- Hilda Baptist Cemetery, Hilda, Alberta, Canada
  http://pixel.cs.vt.edu/library/cemeteries/canada/link/hilda1.txt

- Hope Congregational Cemetery, Bethune, Colorado
  http://pixel.cs.vt.edu/library/cemeteries/colorado/link/bethune1.txt

- Immanuel Lutheran Church Cemetery, Bethune, Colorado
  http://pixel.cs.vt.edu/library/cemeteries/colorado/link/bethune2.txt

- Jerauld County Cemetery Index
  http://pixel.cs.vt.edu/library/cemeteries/sodak/link/jerauld.txt

- Prairie Epitaph—Catholic Cemetery in Salvador, Saskatchewan
  http://mars.ark.com/~rbell/html/history/epitaph.html
  Many German Russian families.

- St. Petersburg Records Database for Glueckstal Colonies
  http://pixel.cs.vt.edu/library/boxes/ehrman/index.html

◆ Societies & Groups

- American Historical Society of Germans from Russia
  http://www.ahsgr.org/
  Lincoln, Nebraska
  - Arizona Sun Chapter
    http://www.ahsgr.org/azsun.html
  - Calgary Canada Chapter
    http://www.ahsgr.org/calgary.html
  - Central California Chapter
    http://www.ahsgr.org/cacentra.html
  - Central Oklahoma Chapter
    http://www.ahsgr.org/okcentra.html
  - Central Washington Chapter
    http://www.ahsgr.org/wacentra.html

- Denver Metro Chapter
  http://www.ahsgr.org/codenver.html
- Florida Suncoast Chapter
  http://www.ahsgr.org/flsuncst.html
- Golden Wheat Chapter
  http://www.ahsgr.org/ksgolden.html
- Greater Seattle Chapter
  http://www.ahsgr.org/waseattl.html
- Kansas Sunflower Chapter
  http://www.ahsgr.org/kssunflo.html
- Lincoln Nebraska Chapter
  http://www.ahsgr.org/nelincol.html
- Nation's Capital Area Chapter
  http://www.ahsgr.org/dcapitol.html
- North Star Chapter—Minnesota
  http://www.ahsgr.org/mnnostar.html
- Northeast Nebraska Chapter
  http://www.ahsgr.org/nenorthe.html
- Northeastern Kansas Chapter
  http://www.ahsgr.org/ksnorthe.html
- Northern Colorado Chapter
  http://www.ahsgr.org/conorthe.html
- Northern Illinois Chapter
  http://www.ahsgr.org/ilnorthe.html
- Olympic Peninsula Chapter—Washington
  http://www.ahsgr.org/waolypen.html
- Oregon Chapter
  http://www.ahsgr.org/orportla.html
- Southeastern Wisconsin Chapter
  http://www.ahsgr.org/wisouthe.html
- Southern California Chapter
  http://www.jovanet.com/~hmehrman/ahsgr/casocal.html
- Southwest Michigan Chapter
  http://www.ahsgr.org/misouthw.html
- Ventura Chapter
  http://www.jovanet.com/~hmehrman/ahsgr/cavent.html
- Washington Rainier Chapter of Tacoma
  http://www.ahsgr.org/warainer.html

- **Bukovina Society of the Americas**
  http://members.aol.com/LJensen/bukovina.html
- **German-Russian Genealogical Societies**
  http://pixel.cs.vt.edu/library/societies.html
- **Germans From Russia Heritage Society**
  http://www.grhs.com/
  Bismarck, North Dakota
  - Alberta Chapter
    http://www.grhs.com/alberta.html
  - British Columbia Chapter
    http://feefhs.org/grhs/grhs-bc.html

- Puget Sound Chapter
  http://www.grhs.com/pugetsnd.html
- **Glückstal Colonies Research Association (GCRA)**
  http://www.feefhs.org/FRGGCRA/gcra.html

◆ Villages & Colonies

- **AHSGR Village Research Coordinators**
  http://www.ahsgr.org/ahsgrvcs.html
  American Historical Society of Germans From Russia.
- **Alt-Danzig & Neu-Danzig, Russia**
  http://members.aol.com/fisherjoy/danzig.html
- **Dietel (Russian Name: Oleshna/Aleshniki)**
  ftp://ftp.netcom.com/pub/di/dietel/dietel.htm
- **Glückstal Surnames Found in the St. Petersburg Records Database**
  http://feefhs.org/FRGGCRA/gcra3.html
- **Gnadenfeld Molotschna, South Russia, 1835 through 1943**
  http://www.primenet.com/~rempel/gnadenfeld/gndntoc.htm
  Memories of Good Times and of Hard Times, Collected by J. C. Krause, Yarrow, British Columbia, 1954.
- **GRHS Village Coordinators**
  http://www.grhs.com/grhsvcs.html
  Germans From Russia Heritage Society.
- **Herzog, Russia Homepage**
  http://www.geocities.com/Heartland/Estates/5138/
- **History of the Glückstal Colonies**
  http://feefhs.org/FRGGCRA/gcra1.html
- **Home Page for Village of Novo Nikolaevka**
  http://www.best.com/~heli/genealogy/nn.html
- **The Hussenbach Villages of Russia**
  http://www.teleport.com/~stahl/hussenba.html
- **Kutschurgan Villages Web Site**
  http://www.kutschurgan.com/
  Catholic Villages of the Kutschurgan Colony just NW of Odessa.
- **Leichtling Home Page**
  http://www.geocities.com/Heartland/Flats/5505/
  Leichtling, Saratov, Volga, Russia
- **Lower Jeruslan River Colonies Research Project**
  http://members.home.net/jeruslanvillages/
- **Messer (aka ust Solicha) Village Database**
  http://members.xoom.com/tsterkel/village_projects/messer.htm
- **Norka (aka Weigand) Village Database**
  http://members.xoom.com/tsterkel/village_projects/norka.htm
- **Norka Village**
  http://www.jps.net/wulfie/norka.htm
- **Obermunjor, Russia Home Page**
  http://www.geocities.com/Heartland/Flats/2799/

- Paulskoye, Russia—A Volga German Village
  http://members.aol.com/TCWeeder/index.paulskoye.html
- RemMick's Borodino Bessarabia Home Site
  http://members.aol.com/RemMick/
  BorodinoBessarabia.index.html/
- St. Petersburg Records Database for Glueckstal Colonies
  http://pixel.cs.vt.edu/library/boxes/ehrman/index.html
- Saratov, Volga, Russia Villages
  http://www.avalon.net/~avant/villages.html
  - Village of Dobrinka
    http://www.avalon.net/~avant/dobrinka.html
  - Village of Kraft
    http://www.avalon.net/~avant/kraft.html
  - Village of Mueller
    http://www.avalon.net/~avant/mueller.html
  - Village of Schwab
    http://www.avalon.net/~avant/schwab.html
  - Village of Stephan
    http://www.avalon.net/~avant/stephan.html
  - Villages of Dreispitz and Shcherbakovka
    http://www.avalon.net/~avant/dreispitz.html
  - Villages of Galka and Holstein
    http://www.avalon.net/~avant/galka.html
- Stahl am Tarlyk (a.k.a. Stepnoje) Village Database
  http://members.xoom.com/tsterkel/village_projects/stahl_t.htm
- Surnames in Mueller
  http://www.avalon.net/~avant/mueller-surnames.html
- Village Compilations—Genealogies
  http://pixel.cs.vt.edu/library/villages/
- Village Coordinators, by Village or http:// pixel.cs.vt.edu/library/vc.html
  http://pixel.cs.vt.edu/library/village.html
  Village Coordinators, by Surname.

- Village Genealogy Research—Germans from Volga, Russia
  http://members.xoom.com/tsterkel/village_projects/
  villages.htm
  Dedicated to Family History Research for the Russia Volga Colonies: Stahl am Tarlyk, Norka and Messer.
- The Village History Project
  http://pixel.cs.vt.edu/library/history/
- Village of Balzer
  http://www.teleport.com/~herbf/balzer.htm
  Volga Russian Germans
- The Village of Brunnental, Russia
  http://pixel.cs.vt.edu/library/boxes/stahl/index.html
- Village of Frank, Russia
  http://www.colo.com/frank/
- The Village of Grimm, Russia
  http://www.angelfire.com/ca/GRIMM/index.html
- Village of Kolb, Russia
  http://pixel.cs.vt.edu/library/kolb.html
- Village of Kratzke, Russia / Zum Dorf von Kratzke, Russland
  http://www.thegrid.net/kratzke/
- Village of Schilling, Russia
  http://home.earthlink.net/~garymartens/schilling.html
- Village Records and Compilations
  http://pixel.cs.vt.edu/library/villages/
  From the Odessa German-Russian Genealogical Library.
- The Volga Deutsch Home Page for Fischer
  http://members.aol.com/RAToepfer/index.htm
- Walter, Russia or (Grechinaya Luka) which means...... Buckwheat Bend
  http://securitydoors.com/walter/
- Yagodnaya Polyana, Russia
  http://pta6000.pld.com:80/skmug1/

GERMANY / DEUTSCHLAND
http://www.CyndisList.com/germany.htm

Category Index:

- General Resource Sites
- How To
- Language, Handwriting & Script
- Libraries, Archives & Museums
- Locality Specific & Migration
- Mailing Lists, Newsgroups & Chat
- Maps, Gazetteers & Geographical Information
- People & Families

- Professional Researchers, Volunteers & Other Research Services
- Publications, Software & Supplies
- Queries, Message Boards & Surname Lists
- Records: Census, Cemeteries, Land, Obituaries, Personal, Taxes and Vital
- Societies & Groups
- WorldGenWeb—Germany Genealogy

◆ General Resource Sites

- Deutsche Post AG
  http://www.postag.de/
  Postal codes, etc.

- Genealogie Im Sudetenland / Böhmen
  http://www.pingweb.de/Kummer/

- German Genealogy Cross-Index—from FEEFHS
  http://feefhs.org/indexger.html

- German Genealogy: Genealogical Events
  http://www.genealogy.net/gene/ghlp/events.html

- German Genealogy Home Page
  http://www.genealogy.net/gene/index.html

  - German Genealogy Home Page
    http://w3g.med.uni-giessen.de/gene/
    Mirror site in Giessen, Germany.

  - German Genealogy Home Page
    http://www.genealogy.net/gene/
    Mirror site in Kerpen, Germany.

  - Index to States, Provinces, and Regions
    http://www.genealogy.net/gene/reg/rindex.htm

- German Genealogy Links
  http://www.geocities.com/SiliconValley/Haven/1538/german.html

- German Genealogy Sites and Organizations
  http://www.execpc.com/~kap/gene-de.html
  From Kent's Genealogy Trading Post.

- German Genealogy? Start Here!
  http://www.daddezio.com/germgen.html
  From D'ADDEZIO.com

- German Migration Resource Center
  http://www.germanmigration.com/
  Books for sale, a reunion calendar, information about the Hannover Chronicle, and a spot for posting queries about your immigrant German ancestors.

- German-Prussian Genealogy Links
  http://www.geocities.com/SiliconValley/Haven/1538/germanpg.html

- Germany Genealogy—World GenWeb
  http://www.rootsweb.com/~wggerman/

- Internet Sources of German Genealogy
  http://www.bawue.de/~hanacek/info/edatbase.htm

- Misc. German Genealogy Information
  http://www.worldroots.com/brigitte/b4_index.html
  and Germany Information
  http://www.worldroots.com/brigitte/germinfo.htm
  From Brigitte Gastel Lloyd.

- OMII Genealogy Project & Kidron Heritage Center
  http://www.wgbc.org/hindex.htm
  A Swiss Mennonite & German Amish genealogy project.

- Prussian Genealogy Links
  http://www.geocities.com/SiliconValley/Haven/1538/prussia.html

- The SGGS "German Card"
  http://feefhs.org/sggs/sggs-gc.html

- TIV Tele-Info Verlag, Online Auskunft Deutschland
  http://www.teleinfo.de/abfragen/bin/neuabfrage.pl
  Online telephone book for Germany.

- Yahoo!...Germany...Genealogy
  http://dir.yahoo.com/Regional/Countries/Germany/Arts_and_Humanities/History/Genealogy/

◆ How To

- Finding Where Your Ancestors Came From in Germany
  http://www.angelfire.com/biz/origins1/ancestors.html

- German Genealogical Research Before The Church Records Begin
http://www.kinquest.com/genealogy/researching.html
Tips and hints by Lisa Petersen.

- German Research at Libraries and Archives in Baden-Wuerttemberg
http://www.kinquest.com/genealogy/badwue.html
Tips and hints by Lisa Petersen.

- German Research in Stuttgart Libraries and Archives
http://www.kinquest.com/genealogy/stuttgart.html
Tips and hints by Lisa Petersen.

- Hints for researchers outside Germany
http://www.bawue.de/~hanacek/info/darchi99.htm#english

◆ Language, Handwriting & Script

- Deutsch <-> Englisches Wörterbuch
http://www.tu-chemnitz.de/urz/netz/forms/dict.html

- Form Letters for German Genealogy
http://www.genealogy.net/gene/www/ghlp/muster.html

- Genealogical Dictionaries—Old German Professions & Old German Medical Terms and Causes of Death
http://home.navisoft.com/scrolls/dictinry.htm

- German-English Letter Translation Specialists
http://www.win.bright.net/~deichsa/welcome.html

- German-English On-line Dictionary
http://dictionaries.travlang.com/GermanEnglish/

- German Genealogy: Translation Service
http://www.genealogy.net/gene/www/abt/translation.html

- German Illness Translations
http://pixel.cs.vt.edu/library/articles/link/illness.txt

- German Study Group / German Words
http://205.216.138.19/~websites/lynnd/vuword.html

- German Translation Service > Old Script
http://www.win.bright.net/~jakeschu/welcome.html

- German Translator—Genealogical, Literary, Technical, Civil, Business Documents
http://people.delphi.com/delaneyj/index.html

- A Glossary Of German Words Used in Official Documents
gopher://Gopher.UToledo.edu:70/
00GOPHER_ROOT%3A%5BRESEARCH-
RESOURCES.GENEALOGY.GERMAN-GENEALOGY%5DA-
GLOSSARY-OF-GERMAN-WORDS.USED-IN-OFFICIAL-
DOCUMENTS

- GMS Gesellschaft für multilinguale Systeme / German to English Online Dictionary
http://www.gmsmuc.de/english/

- Moravians—German Script Tutorial
http://www.mun.ca/rels/morav/script.html
With Moravian Archival examples.

  - German Script Alphabet
http://www.mun.ca/rels/morav/pics/tutor/mscript2.html

- Old German Handwritten Scripts
http://www2.genealogy.net/gene/misc/scripts.html

- Old German Professions and Occupations
http://www.worldroots.com/brigitte/occupat.htm

- Sample Letters in German to Obtain Genealogical Information
gopher://Gopher.UToledo.edu:70/
00GOPHER_ROOT%3A%5BRESEARCH-
RESOURCES.GENEALOGY.GERMAN-GENEALOGY%5DGERMAN-
SAMPLE-LETTER.FOR-INFORMATION-REQUESTS

- Walden Font
http://www.waldenfont.com/
Several different fonts for sale, including: The Gutenberg Press German Fraktur Fonts and German Script.

◆ Libraries, Archives & Museums

- Archives in Germany
http://www.bawue.de/~hanacek/info/earchive.htm

- Bavarian State Libraries and the Bavarian Library Network / Bayerischen Staatlichen Bibliotheken und dem Bibliotheksverbund Bayern
http://www.bib-bvb.de/

- Berlin Central and State Library / Zentral— und Landesbibliothek Berlin (ZLB)
http://www.kulturbox.de/berlin/zlb/

- Civil Archives Libraries and Museums of Saxony
http://rosella.apana.org.au/~jgk/civil.html

- Cologne Public Library / StadtBibliothek Köln
http://www.stbib-koeln.de/

- Die Deutsche Bibliothek
http://www.ddb.de/

- Family History Centers in Germany, Austria and Switzerland
http://www.genealogy.net/gene/faqs/LDS.de

- HBZ Hochschulbibliothekszentrum Des Landes Nordrhein-Westfalen
http://www.hbz-nrw.de/
HBZ—The online utility and service center for academic libraries in North Rhine-Westphalia.

- Württembergische Landesbibliothek Stuttgart / Wuerttemberg State Library
http://www.wlb-stuttgart.de/~www/wlbinfo-home.html
Regional library for Baden-Wuerttemberg, for the administrative districts of Stuttgart and Tuebingen.

◆ Locality Specific & Migration

- Bühlertal, Baden Home Page
http://www.geocities.com/Heartland/Prairie/3974/index.html

- The Communities of Alsace A–Z
  http://members.aol.com/RobtBehra/AlsaceA-Z/GenInfo.htm
- Eastern Europe
  http://www.CyndisList.com/easteuro.htm
  See this category on Cyndi's List for related links.
- Emigrants from Nattheim to USA /
  Nattheimer Auswanderer nach Amerika
  http://members.aol.com/fmaili/emigrat1.htm
- Emigrants from Oggenhausen to USA /
  Oggenhausener Auswanderer nach Amerika
  http://members.aol.com/fmaili/emigrat2.htm
- From Alsace to Lorraine... ... across Saar
  http://perso.club-internet.fr/rweinl/
  Many French resources listed here.
- Genealogical Research in Bavaria
  http://www.worldroots.com/misc/bg_misc/bavausw.html
- German-Bohemian Immigrant Surname Database
  http://www.rootsweb.com/~gbhs/database.html
- German Genealogy: Elsass / Alsace
  http://www.genealogy.net/gene/reg/ELS-LOT/alsace.html
- German Genealogy: Donauschwaben /
  Danube-Swabians
  http://www.genealogy.net/gene/reg/ESE/dschwaben.html
- Germans From Russia
  http://www.CyndisList.com/germruss.htm
  See this category on Cyndi's List for related links.
- The Great Palatine Migration
  http://www.zekes.com/~dspidell/palatine.html
- Help in searching for ancestors from the Sudetenland
  http://www.genealogy.net/gene/reg/SUD/sudet_en.html
  *German settlement area in Bohemia/Moravia/Austrian Silesia—
  >Czechoslovakia—> Czech Republik.*
- History of German Settlements in Southern Hungary
  http://feefhs.org/banat/bhistory.html
- Kraig Ruckel's Palatine & Pennsylvania Dutch
  Genealogy Home Page
  http://www.geocities.com/Heartland/3955/
- Myron Gruenwald's Page—Germany, Prussia,
  Pomerania
  http://home.aol.com/myrondpl
- Ostfriesian Genealogical Research by MJ Neill
  http://www.asc.csc.cc.il.us/~mneill/html/ostfriesland.html
  By Michael Neill.
- Ostfriesland
  http://www.summitsoftware.com/pwa/ostfriesen.htm
- Ostfriesland Ancestors
  http://www.alaska.net/~dsewell/
- Palatine History
  http://www.rootsweb.com/~ote/palatine.htm
  From The Olive Tree.

- Palatines to America Homepage
  http://www.genealogy.org/~palam/
- The Pomeranian Page
  http://www.execpc.com/~kap/pommern1.html
- Prussian-Russian-Canadian Mennonite
  Genealogical Resources
  http://www.mmhs.org/mmhsgen.htm
- Saxony Online
  http://rosella.apana.org.au/~jgk/saxon.html
  KEHRER and KETTNISS
- Vörstetten, Baden, Germany
  http://www.genealogy.org/~smoore/vorstetten.html
- Western Europe
  http://www.CyndisList.com/westeuro.htm
  See this category on Cyndi's List for related links.
- The Wind-Mill
  http://www.geocities.com/Heartland/6166/index.html
  *Devoted to exploring Frisian/Ostfriesen/North German heritage
  and history.*
- Wittgenstein History and Genealogy
  http://www.action-research.com/gene/wittpage.htm
  *The former counties of Wittgenstein-Berleburg and Wittgenstein-
  Wittgenstein in the south of the Sauerland.*

◆ Mailing Lists, Newsgroups & Chat

- Genealogy Resources on the Internet—Germany/
  Prussia Mailing Lists
  http://members.aol.com/gfsjohnf/gen_mail_country-ger.html
  *Each of the mailing list links below points to this site, wonder-
  fully maintained by John Fuller.*
- ALSACE-GENEALOGY Mailing List
  http://members.aol.com/gfsjohnf/gen_mail_country-
  ger.html#ALSACE-L
  and the corresponding web page
  http://members.aol.com/jaw5623/private/alsace/alsace.html
  *For anyone interested in Alsace, a border region of France and
  Germany.*
- ALSACE-LORRAINE Mailing List
  http://members.aol.com/gfsjohnf/gen_mail_country-
  ger.html#ALSACE-LORRAINE
- AUS-QLD-SE-Germans Mailing List
  http://members.aol.com/gfsjohnf/gen_mail_country-
  ger.html#AUS-QLD-SE-Germans
  *For anyone with a genealogical interest in the descendants of
  the Germans who migrated to South East Queensland, Australia.*
- BADEN-WURTTEMBERG Mailing List
  http://members.aol.com/gfsjohnf/gen_mail_country-
  ger.html#BADEN-WURTTEMBERG
  For Baden, Hohenzollern, and Wurttemberg.
- BAVARIA Mailing List
  http://members.aol.com/gfsjohnf/gen_mail_country-
  ger.html#GER-BAVARIA
  *For the kingdom, province and state of Bavaria including the
  city of Munich.*

- BUNDESLAND Mailing List
  http://members.aol.com/gfsjohnf/gen_mail_country-
  ger.html#BUNDESLAND
  *For those trying to find their German roots and interested in
  German history.*

- deu-gene Mailing List
  http://members.aol.com/gfsjohnf/gen_mail_country-
  ger.html#deu-gene

- FRANKEN-L Mailing List
  http://members.aol.com/gfsjohnf/gen_mail_country-
  ger.html#FRANKEN-L
  *For those interested in sharing and exchanging information on
  genealogy and history which has a connection to the area of the
  three sections of northern Bavaria called Oberfranken,
  Mittelfranken and Unterfranken.*

- fido.ger.genealogy Newsgroup

- GEN-DE Mailing List gatewayed with the
  news:soc.genealogy.german
  http://members.aol.com/gfsjohnf/gen_mail_country-
  ger.html#GEN-DE-L
  soc.genealogy.german newsgroup

- GERMAN-AMERICAN Mailing List
  http://members.aol.com/gfsjohnf/gen_mail_states-
  gen.html#GERMAN-AMERICAN
  *For genealogy related to German immigrants and their families
  AFTER their arrival in America.*

- GERMAN-BOHEMIAN-L Mailing List
  http://members.aol.com/gfsjohnf/gen_mail_country-
  ger.html#GERMAN-BOHEMIAN-L
  *About the culture, genealogy and heritage of the German-
  speaking people of Bohemia and Moravia, now the Czech
  Republic.*

- GERMANNA_COLONIES Mailing List
  http://members.aol.com/gfsjohnf/gen_mail_states-
  va.html#GERMAN_COLONIES
  *For descendants of the Germanna Colonies (i.e., the original
  German settlements in Virginia under Governor Spotswood;
  there were three colonies established, the first being in 1714).*

- GERMAN-KINGDOMS Mailing List
  http://members.aol.com/gfsjohnf/gen_mail_country-
  ger.html#GERMAN-KINGDOMS
  *For anyone with a genealogical interest in the Duchies of
  Thuringen (Thuringia) including Reuss altere Linie, Reuss
  jungere Linie, Saxe-Altenburg (Sachsen-Altenburg), Saxe-
  Coburg-Gotha (Sachsen-Koburg-Cotha), Saxe-Meiningen
  (Sachsen-Meiningen), Saxe-Weimar-Eisenach (Sachsen-Weimar-
  Eisenach), Schwarzburg-Rudolstadt, Schwarzburg-
  Sondershausen, Anhalt, and Schaumberg-Lippe; Braunschweig
  (Brunswick); Lippe (aka: Lippe-Detmold); Oldenburg; Waldeck;
  Mecklenburg-Schwerin; and Mecklenburg-Strelitz.*

- GERMAN-TEXAN Mailing List
  http://members.aol.com/gfsjohnf/gen_mail_states-
  tx.html#GERMAN-TEXAN
  *For anyone with a genealogical interest in German and Central
  European immigrants to Texas, especially Germans in the 19th
  century.*

- HANNOVER-L Mailing List
  http://members.aol.com/gfsjohnf/gen_mail_country-
  ger.html#HANNOVER-L
  *Genealogy and history which has a connection to the former
  Kingdom of Hannover.*

- HESSE Mailing List
  http://members.aol.com/gfsjohnf/gen_mail_country-
  ger.html#GER-HESSEN
  *For the kingdoms, principalities, provinces, and state of Hessen
  (Hesse-Darmstadt, Hesse-Starkenburg, Hesse-Nassau, Waldeck,
  Rheinhessen) including the city of Frankfurt-A/Main.*

- MECKLENBURG-L Mailing List
  http://members.aol.com/gfsjohnf/gen_mail_country-
  ger.html#MECKLENBURG-L
  *Genealogy and history which has a connection to the general
  area of Mecklenburg.*

- MORAVIA Mailing List
  http://members.aol.com/gfsjohnf/gen_mail_country-
  ger.html#MORAVIA
  *For anyone with a genealogical interest in Moravia, now part of
  the Czech Republic.*

- NIEDERSACHSEN Mailing List
  http://members.aol.com/gfsjohnf/gen_mail_country-
  ger.html#NIEDERSACHSEN

- OLDENBURG-L Mailing List
  http://members.aol.com/gfsjohnf/gen_mail_country-
  ger.html#OLDENBURG-L
  *For those interested in sharing and exchanging information on
  genealogy and history which has a connection to the former
  Grand Duchy of Oldenburg.*

- OSTFRIESEN Mailing List
  http://members.aol.com/gfsjohnf/gen_mail_country-
  ger.html#OSTFRIESEN
  *For anyone with a genealogical, cultural or historical interest
  in Ostfriesland (East Friesia), Germany. Also see the Ostfriesen
  E-Mail Discussion List Web Page at http://www.summitsoftware.
  com/pwa/ostfries2.htm*

- OW-PREUSSEN-L Mailing List
  http://members.aol.com/gfsjohnf/gen_mail_country-
  ger.html#OW-PREUSSEN-L
  *Genealogy and history which has a connection to the former
  East and West Prussia.*

- PFALZ Mailing List
  http://members.aol.com/gfsjohnf/gen_mail_country-
  ger.html#PFALZ
  *For anyone with a genealogical interest in the Palatine of
  Germany (area now divided between Saarland, Rheinland-Pfalz
  and Hessen, formerly Bavaria's Rhenish Pfalz).*

- PolandBorderSurnames Mailing List
  http://members.aol.com/gfsjohnf/gen_mail_country-
  ger.html#PolandBorderSurnames
  *A mailing list of surnames for anyone researching genealogy in
  the former historical borders of Poland including Estonia,
  Latvia, Lithuania, Belarus, Ukraine, Moldova, Slovakia, Czech
  Republic, Moravia, Hungary, Russia, the Balkans, and East
  Prussia.*

- POMMERN-L Mailing List
  http://members.aol.com/gfsjohnf/gen_mail_country-ger.html#POMMERN-L
  Genealogy and history which has a connection to Pommerania, both the current Polish part and remaining German parts of the former Prussian province.

- PreussenAmericans Mailing List
  http://members.aol.com/gfsjohnf/gen_mail_country-ger.html#PreussenAmericans
  For anyone with a genealogical interest in Prussian immigrants to America.

- PRUSSIA-ROOTS Mailing List
  http://members.aol.com/gfsjohnf/gen_mail_country-ger.html#PRUSSIA-ROOTS
  For anyone with a genealogical interest in Brandenburg, Hannover (or Hanover), Ostpreussen (East Prussia), Pommern (Pomerania), Posen, Provinz Sachsen (Province of Saxony—northern Saxony), Schleswig-Holstein, Schlesien (Silesia), Westpreussen (West Prussia), Lubeck, Hamburg, and Bremen.

- SACHSEN-ANHALT-L Mailing List
  http://members.aol.com/gfsjohnf/gen_mail_country-ger.html#SACHSEN-ANHALT-L
  Genealogy and history which has a connection to the present area of the state of Sachsen-Anhalt.

- SCHLESIEN-L Mailing List
  http://members.aol.com/gfsjohnf/gen_mail_country-pol.html#SCHLESIEN-L
  For those with a genealogical interest in the former Prussian province of Schlesien (Silesia), which is now mostly in Poland.

- SCHLESWIG-HOLSTEIN-ROOTS Mailing List
  http://members.aol.com/gfsjohnf/gen_mail_country-ger.html#SCHLESWIG-HOLSTEIN-ROOTS
  For anyone with a genealogical interest in the German province/state of Schleswig-Holstein.

- SURNAMES-GERMAN Mailing List
  http://members.aol.com/gfsjohnf/gen_mail_country-ger.html#SURNAMES-GERMAN
  For surname queries related to German speaking countries. Gatewayed with the soc.genealogy.surnames.german newsgroup.

- TRIER-ROOTS Mailing List
  http://members.aol.com/gfsjohnf/gen_mail_country-ger.html#GER-TRIER-ROOTS
  For anyone with a genealogical interest in Luxembourg, the Saarland, the Rheinland, Westfalen (Westphalia), and the Pfalz (used to be between Rheinland and Baden, belonged to Bavaria but is now part of Rheinpfalz).

- GEN-DE Mailing List
  http://members.aol.com/gfsjohnf/gen_mail_country-ger.html#GEN-DE-L
  Gatewayed with the soc.genealogy.german newsgroup

- WESTFALEN-L Mailing List
  http://members.aol.com/gfsjohnf/gen_mail_country-ger.html#WESTFALEN-L
  Genealogy and history which has a connection to the general area of Westphalia.

- WorldGenWeb-Preussen Mailing List
  http://members.aol.com/gfsjohnf/gen_mail_country-ger.html#WorldGenWeb-Preussen

◆ Maps, Gazetteers & Geographical Information

- Ancient Germania
  http://www.lib.utexas.edu/Libs/PCL/Map_collection/historical/Ancient_Germania.jpg

- The Carolingian Empire 768–911
  http://www.rootsweb.com/~wggerman/karemp.htm

- Deutschland um 1378 / Germany in 1378
  http://www8.informatik.uni-erlangen.de/html/wwp/deutschland1378.html

- Deutschland um 1547 / Germany in 1547
  http://www8.informatik.uni-erlangen.de/html/wwp/deutschland1547.html

- Deutschland um 1648 / Germany in 1648
  http://www8.informatik.uni-erlangen.de/html/wwp/deutschland1648.html

- Genealogy Unlimited—Home Page
  http://www.itsnet.com:80/home/genun/public_html/
  Maps, books & supplies for sale.

- GEOserv—a German town locator
  http://www2.genealogy.net/gene/www/abt/geoserv.html

- The German Confederation 1815–1871
  http://www.rootsweb.com/~wggerman/map1.htm

- Germany at the time of the Reformation, 1517
  http://www.rootsweb.com/~wggerman/gerref.htm

- Germany under Bismarck and the struggle for Unification, 1815–1871
  http://www.rootsweb.com/~wggerman/gerbis.htm

- Map of Baden
  http://members.aol.com/tgostin/graphics/baden.jpg

- Map of Germany
  http://www.lib.utexas.edu/Libs/PCL/Map_collection/europe/Germany.jpg
  From the Perry-Castañeda Library at the Univ. of Texas at Austin.

- Munich 1858
  http://www.lib.utexas.edu/Libs/PCL/Map_collection/historical/Munich_1858.jpg

- Nuremberg 1858
  http://www.lib.utexas.edu/Libs/PCL/Map_collection/historical/Nuremberg_1858.jpg

- The Weimar Republic 1918–1933
  http://www.rootsweb.com/~wggerman/weim.htm

◆ People & Families

- Andreas HANACEK's Genealogy Page
  http://www.bawue.de/~hanacek/egene/egenepag.htm

- BOCKELMANN Genealogy Homepage
  http://ourworld.compuserve.com/homepages/Bockelmann/
  BOCKELMANN, BOSTELMANN, KAISER OR KAYSER, MAACK, PUTENSEN. Nördliches Niedersachsen, Landkreis Harburg und Landkreis Lüneburg, Salzhausen und Umgebung / north of Lower Saxony, district Harburg and district Lüneburg.

- BRAND—BRANDT Genealogie und Familienforschung in der Gemeinde Reichartshausen
  http://home.t-online.de/home/Brand.Karl-Heinz/
  Baden Württemberg

- Genealogical Office LAMPING Family
  http://www.lamping.demon.nl/genea/
  Descendants of LAMPING, LAMPINK and LAMBING. German & Dutch roots.

- Genealogische Forschungen DIETZ-LENSSEN
  http://members.aol.com/pixcool/genindex.htm
  DIETZ and LENSSEN surnames; deals with GERMAN-TEXAN emigration.

- Genealogische Quellen im Internet
  http://ourworld.compuserve.com/homepages/KMedeke/genealog.htm
  MEDEKE, LEDERER, DIEKMANN, FRITZE and MOORMANN

- Genealogy of the EYMANN Family
  http://www.iig.uni-freiburg.de/~eymann/genealog.htm
  Germany, Switzerland and the U.S.

- German Ancestors up to the Middle Ages
  http://www.worldroots.com/ged/max/
  11,000 individuals, 3,400 surnames from all over Germany. Some lines reaching far into the Middle Ages and beyond. Main families: AMBURGER, BARTHOLOMÉ, BERTHEAU, BOEHTLINGK, BRÜCKNER, DISSELHOFF, FLIEDNER, GSCHNEIDINGER, JEITER, KRAUßE, KRÖNLEIN, MÜLLER, PALMER, SCHIELE, WAGNER.

- HANDWERK Family Research in Germany
  http://pw2.netcom.com/~richardz/handwe3.html
  Hantwerck; Handwercker; Handtwerck; Handwerk and Handwerg.

- Harm's Genealogie Seiten / Harms Genealogy Site
  http://home.dinx.de/rieper/
  RIEPER, WINDBICHLER

- Hermann's Genealogie—Seiten
  http://members.aol.com/Hermann001/welcome.htm
  Genealogy in Bokuwina, Germany and some parts of France.

- Klaus-Peter WESSEL's Genealogy Home Page
  http://home.t-online.de/home/klaus-peter.wessel/
  WESSEL, NOLTING, DOEHR/DOER/DOERE, KINDERVATER, BOEKEMEIER, KLEEMEIER, CZECH, KONIK. Town of VLOTHO, located in North-Rhine Westfalia, Germany.

- Links to Royal and Nobility Genealogy Data
  http://www.worldroots.com/brigitte/royal/royal.htm

- Maili's World
  http://members.aol.com/fmaili/persons.htm
  Frank MAILAENDER'S family from South Germany back to 1570. MAILANDER, MAIER, FAUL, ESSLINGER, SCHMIDT, WIEDENMANN, FREYTAG all from the area Heidenheim near Ulm, South Germany.

- Mennonites
  http://www.CyndisList.com/menno.htm
  See this category on Cyndi's List for related links.

- Michael M. ZIEFLE's Genealogical Home Page
  http://ourworld.compuserve.com/Homepages/M_Ziefle/

- REINHART Genealogy and Niedernberg, Germany
  http://ourworld.compuserve.com/homepages/niedernberg/niedernberg.html

- SCHWENKNet
  http://www.cyberhighway.net/~gordons/
  Dedicated primarily to those living descendants of Conrad Schwenk (1601–1686), weaver, of Laichingen, Baden-Wuerttemberg in So. Germany.

- Thomas SCHARNOWSKI Home Page
  http://home.t-online.de/home/thomas.scharnowski/
  Ancestors from Württemberg and East Prussia; also surname CZARNOWSKI.

- WW-Person
  http://www8.informatik.uni-erlangen.de/html/ww-person.html
  A database of persons of German nobility.

◆ Professional Researchers, Volunteers & Other Research Services

- Arno Schmitt, Journalist from San Diego, California
  E-mail: reporter@adnc.com
  He can help to find relatives, links or sources regarding ancestors by placing articles in German, Austrian and/or Swiss newspapers. For details, e-mail Arno at: reporter@adnc.com

- Genealogy Helplist—Germany
  http://posom.com/hl/deu/index.shtml

- genealogyPro—Professional Genealogists for Germany
  http://genealogyPro.com/directories/Germany.html

- IHFF Genealogie Gesellschaft mbH
  http://www.netway.at/ihff/index.htm
  Professional Researcher specializing in: Austria, Czech & Slovak Republics, Hungary, Slovenian Republic, Croatia, Galicia, others.

- Richard M. Pope, Certified Genealogist
  http://w3.nai.net/~absuax/
  Specializing in: Connecticut, Massachusetts, New York City, Germany.

- Schröeder & Fülling GbR, German Genealogy Research Firm
  http://ourworld.compuserve.com/homepages/German_Genealogy/homepage.htm

◆ Publications, Software & Supplies

- Books We Own—Germany
  http://www.rootsweb.com/~bwo/germany.html

- Brother's Keeper Software
  http://ourworld.compuserve.com/homepages/Brothers_Keeper/
  Downloadable shareware program for Windows. The latest version contains English, French, Norwegian, Danish, Swedish, German and Dutch.

- DYNAS-TREE
  http://www.xterna-net.de/GerdBauch/dynastree/gb/index.shtml
  Win95 or NT. German or English.

- Frontier Press Bookstore—Germany
  http://www.frontierpress.com/frontier.cgi?category=ger

- GenealogyBookShop.com—Germany/German
  http://www.genealogybookshop.com/genealogybookshop/files/
  The_World,Germany_German/index.html
  The online store of Genealogical Publishing Co., Inc. & Clearfield Company.

- Genealogy Unlimited—Home Page
  http://www.itsnet.com:80/home/genun/public_html/
  Maps, books & supplies for sale.

- Genus Genealogy Program
  http://www.mediabase.fi/suku/genupgb.htm
  Windows program available in six languages: Dutch, English, Finnish, French, German and Swedish.

- Heritage Books—German
  http://www.heritagebooks.com/german.htm

- JamoDat—Win-Family Software
  http://www.jamodat.dk/
  Available in Danish, Swedish, Norwegian, French, German and English.

- PRO-GEN Genealogie à la Carte
  http://home.pi.net/~progen/
  Dutch genealogy program capable of outputs in Dutch, English, French, Frisian and German.

- Stammbaum 4.0 in Stichworten
  http://www3.pair.com/hblanken/stb.htm
  Genealogy software for Windows.

- STAMMBAUM: The Journal of German-Jewish Genealogical Research
  http://www.jewishgen.org/stammbaum/

- Wandering Volhynians
  http://pixel.cs.vt.edu/pub/sources/wv.txt
  A Magazine for the Descendants of Germans From Volhynia and Poland.

- Willow Bend Bookstore—Germans and Germany
  http://www.willowbend.net/ger.htm

- The Wind-Mill: A Periodical of Frisian/Germanic Heritage
  http://members.aol.com/gowindmill/index.html

◆ Queries, Message Boards & Surname Lists

- German Ancestors
  http://www.haaga.com/germany/default.htm
  Post your German surnames on this alphabetical surname index.

- Mecklenburg-Vorpommern Query System
  http://pages.prodigy.net/jhbowen/c3.htm

- Niedersachsen Germany Queries
  http://cgi.rootsweb.com/~genbbs/genbbs.cgi/Germany/
  Niedersachsen

- Nordrhein-Westfalen (North Rhine Westphalia) Surnames
  http://www.rootsweb.com/~cotter/nr-wf/surnames.html

- Surname Page for Schleswig-Holstein, Germany
  http://www.rootsweb.com/~deuscn/surnam.htm

◆ Records: Census, Cemeteries, Land, Obituaries, Personal, Taxes and Vital (Born, Married, Died & Buried)

- Historic Cemeteries in Berlin
  http://www.kulturbox.de/friedhof/index_e.htm

- Index To Palatine Passenger Lists
  http://www.rootsweb.com/~ote/palalist.htm

- Marriages in Plauschwarren, East Prussia 1778–1802
  http://www.mmhs.org/prussia/plauschm.htm

- Mecklenburg-Schwerin Census Records
  http://pages.prodigy.net/jhbowen/census.htm

- Names of Mecklenburg-Schwerin Emigrants 1844–1915
  http://pages.prodigy.net/jhbowen/emig.htm

- Search Weil im Schoenbuch Marriages
  http://www.kinquest.com/genealogy/marriages.html
  Württemberg, Germany

◆ Societies & Groups

- Anglo-German Family History Society—AG-FHS
  http://feefhs.org/uk/frgagfhs.html
  United Kingdom

- Archer's Computer Interest Group List—Germany
  http://www.genealogy.org/~ngs/cigs/ngl3otge.html

- Emsland Heritage Society
  http://www.geocities.com/Heartland/4018/
  For ALL those interested in the genealogies and histories of the people and towns of the area of Germany-bordering Netherlands>upper north west>North sea> Ems Canal. Towns include: Papenburg, Sögel, Werlte, Hüven, Stavern, Lähn, Spelle and others.

- Genealogical Societies for Saxony—Regional and Local
  http://rosella.apana.org.au/~jgk/society.html

- German-Bohemian Heritage Society
  http://www.rootsweb.com/~gbhs/
  New Ulm, Minnesota

- German Society of Pennsylvania
  http://www.german-society.org/
  and a description from GENCAP
  http://www.libertynet.org/~gencap/germanpa.html

- Germanic Genealogy Society
  http://www.mtn.org/mgs/branches/german.html
  Saint Paul, Minnesota

- Sacramento German Genealogy Society, Inc. ~ California
  http://feefhs.org/sggs/frg-sggs.html

- Verein für Familien—und Wappenkunde in Württemberg und Baden e.V.
  http://www2.genealogy.net/gene/vereine/VFWKWB/index.html

◆ WorldGenWeb— Germany Genealogy

- Germany Genealogy
  http://www.rootsweb.com/~wggerman/
  - Baden-Württemberg GenWeb Page
    http://www.rootsweb.com/~deubadnw/
  - Bayern (Bavaria) Germany Genealogy
    http://www.rootsweb.com/~deubay
  - Berlin Surname Queries
    http://www.geocities.com/Heartland/Ranch/1927/
  - Brandenburg, Germany
    http://www.rootsweb.com/~deubrg/
  - Bremen GenWeb
    http://members.aol.com/highsky767/index.html

  - Hamburg Germany World GenWeb Page
    http://www.rootsweb.com/~deuham/index.htm
  - Hessen Germany Genealogy World GenWeb Page
    http://web.nstar.net/~dwat6911/
  - Mecklenburg Vorpommern, Germany
    http://pages.prodigy.net/jhbowen/
  - Niedersachsen (Lower Saxony) GenWeb
    http://www.geocities.com/~pfoad/
  - Nordrhein-Westfalen—North Rhine-Westphalia Genealogy
    http://www.rootsweb.com/~deunrhwf/
  - Prussia / Preussen
    http://www.rootsweb.com/~deupru/
  - Rheinland-Pfalz Germany
    http://members.tripod.com/~brandilyn/
  - Saarland
    http://www.rootsweb.com/~deusaa/
  - Sachsen-Anhalt
    http://www.geocities.com/Heartland/Meadows/3456/sachsenanhalt1.html
  - Saxony
    http://www.rootsweb.com/~wggerman/sachseng.htm
  - Schleswig-Holstein, Deutschland
    http://www.rootsweb.com/~deuscn/index.htm
  - Thüringen, Deutschland
    http://www.geocities.com/Heartland/Prairie/1843/home.html

HANDWRITING & SCRIPT

http://www.CyndisList.com/handwrit.htm

- Deciphering Old Handwriting
  http://www.firstct.com/fv/oldhand.html
- Examples of Letters of the 17th Century Found in Parish Registers
  http://www.rootsweb.com/~genepool/oldalpha.htm
- German Translation Service > Old Script
  http://www.win.bright.net/~jakeschu/welcome.html
- Moravians—German Script Tutorial
  http://www.mun.ca/rels/morav/script.html
  With Moravian Archival examples.
  - German Script Alphabet
    http://www.mun.ca/rels/morav/pics/tutor/mscript2.html
- Name and Word Spellings
  http://www.familytreemaker.com/00000015.html
  Includes a brief explanation of errors caused by handwriting.
- Old German Handwritten Scripts
  http://www2.genealogy.net/gene/misc/scripts.html
- Old Handwriting Samples
  http://www.rootsweb.com/~ote/writing.htm

- Reading Early American Handwriting
  http://www.genealogical.com/newrel.htm
  A new book by Kip Sperry.
- Searching Old Records—Reading Old Handwriting and Looking for Names
  http://members.aol.com/AdamCo9991/genealogytips9.html
- Society of Genealogists Bookshop: Handwriting ~ U.K.
  http://www.sog.org.uk/acatalog/A000_41.html
- Understanding Colonial Handwriting
  http://www.genealogybookshop.com/genealogybookshop/files/General,Guides_and_Manuals/5647.html
  From GenealogyBookShop.com, the online store of Genealogical Publishing Co., Inc. & Clearfield Company.
- Walden Font
  http://www.waldenfont.com/
  Several different fonts for sale, including: The Gutenberg Press German Fraktur Fonts and German Script.

HANDY ONLINE STARTING POINTS
http://www.CyndisList.com/handy.htm

Category Index:
- General Lists of Links
- Getting Started
- Locality & Ethnic Specific
- Volunteers, Lookups & Free Searches
- Web Rings for Genealogy

◆ General Lists of Links

- **AOL Members' Genealogy Related Web Pages**
  http://members.aol.com/AHowe1/genwebpgs.html

- **A Barrel of Links**
  http://cpcug.org/user/jlacombe/mark.html

- **Best Genealogy Links on the Web**
  http://pages.prodigy.net/middleton/topten.html
  From Pam Middleton's home page.

- **The Big Page of Genealogy Links**
  http://members.tripod.com/~bigpage/

- **Chat Genealogy Homepages**
  http://members.wbs.net/homepages/s/h/e/sherrya.html

- **The CyberTree Genealogy Database**
  http://home.sprynet.com/sprynet/lgk71/CybrTree.htm

- **Design Software**
  http://www.dhc.net/~design/sites.htm
  Genealogy and Other Sites of Interest around the World.

- **Everton's—On-Line—International Genealogical Resources**
  http://www.everton.com/resources/world-resource.html

- **Everton's—On-Line—US Genealogical Resources**
  http://www.everton.com/resources/usa-resource.html

- **Family Tree Maker Genealogy SiteFinder**
  http://www.familytreemaker.com/links/index.html

- **Family Tree Maker Online User Home Pages**
  http://www.familytreemaker.com/users/

- **Ford Genealogy Club Home Page**
  http://www.wwnet.net/~krugman1/fgc/

- **Genealogical Journeys In Time**
  http://ourworld.compuserve.com/homepages/Strawn/

- **Genealogical WWW pages**
  http://www.tic.com/gen.html

- **Genealogy Exchange & Surname Registry**
  http://www.genexchange.com
  The GenExchange is a comprehensive "raw" genealogy web site with over 160MB of searchable data.

- **Genealogy Forum on CompuServe®**
  http://ourworld.compuserve.com/homepages/roots/

- **Genealogy Home Page**
  http://www.genhomepage.com/full.html

- **Genealogy is My Hobby!**
  http://home.earthlink.net/~middleton/
  From Pam Middleton. Posting Of Surnames/Queries/Homepage Urls—Free!

- **Genealogy on the Internet**
  http://www.geocities.com/Heartland/6266/genealogy.htm
  From Alan Mann, A.G.

- **Genealogy Online**
  http://www.genealogy.org/

- **Genealogy Resources on the Internet**
  http://members.aol.com/johnf14246/internet.html
  From John Fuller and Chris Gaunt.

- **Genealogy's Most Wanted—Links To Other Sites**
  http://www.citynet.net/mostwanted/links.html

- **GenSearcher—The All-in-One Genealogy Search Page**
  http://www.geocities.com/Heartland/Acres/8310/gensearcher.html

- **GenWeb.Net**
  http://www.genweb.net
  A site for genealogy and history research. Free web space and over 10,000 mailing lists.

- **The Grannies' Genealogy Helper Menu**
  http://www.toolcity.net/~vadkins/gen/index.html
  Links to home pages; contacts for newspaper & newsletter queries; other genealogy services.

- **Ground Work—Genealogy on the Internet**
  http://members.aol.com/ssmadonna/index.htm

- **Helm's Genealogy Toolbox**
  http://genealogy.tbox.com/

- **Horus' H-GIG—Genealogy Links for Historians**
  http://www.ucr.edu/h-gig/hist-preservation/genea.html

- **Internet Genealogical Directory / Annuaire Généalogique Internet**
  http://www.chez.com/agi/intro.htm

- **Juliana's Links**
  http://www.ancestry.com/ancestry/testurllinks/search.asp
  A searchable list of genealogy links from Ancestry.com

- Nerd World: Genealogy
  http://www.nerdworld.com/nw192.html

- Nerd World: Personal Pages—Genealogy
  http://www.nerdworld.com/cgi-bin/
  subjects.cgi?usr=582&cat=1124

- Olive Tree Genealogy
  http://www.rootsweb.com/~ote/
  *Huguenots & Walloons, Ontario Loyalists, Mohawk, Mennonite,
  Palatines and Dutch Research.*

- Cook Memorial Public Library District—Genealogy
  Referral Page
  http://www.cooklib.org/genrefer.htm

- Parsons Genealogy Registry
  http://www.parsonstech.com/genealogy/registry.html

- Personal Views of Genealogy on the Internet
  http://www.everton.com/personal.html

- RAND Genealogy Club Home Page
  http://www.rand.org/personal/Genea/

- Reunion Users with Home Pages
  http://www.leisterpro.com/doc/Users.html

- RootsComputing
  http://www.rootscomputing.com/index.htm

- ROOTS-L Home Page
  http://www.rootsweb.com/roots-l/roots-l.html

- The RootsWeb Genealogical Data Cooperative
  http://www.rootsweb.com/

- Searchable Genealogy Links
  [Lauren KNOBLAUCH]
  http://www.bc1.com/users/sgl/

- Sharing Family History on the Internet
  http://www.geocities.com/~wallyg/internet.htm

- Sharkey's Links to Genealogical Links
  http://www2.hawaii.edu/~sharkey/links/genealog/genealog.htm

- Tripod—Interact—Genealogy Pod Publishers
  http://www.tripod.com/pod_central/pods/genealogy/publishers/

- Ultimate Family Tree: Family Web Pages
  http://www.uftree.com/UFT/Nav/familywebpagesview.html

- WebCrawler: Genealogy
  http://webcrawler.com/WCGuide/home_and_family/hobbies/
  genealogy/

- What's New With the Genealogy Home Page
  http://www.genhomepage.com/whats_new.html

- WhoWhere? Personal Home Pages—Home
  Pages:Personal Interests:Genealogy
  http://homepages.whowhere.com/Personal_Interests/
  Genealogy/

- YAHOO!—Arts:Humanities:History:Genealogy
  http://www.yahoo.com/Arts/Humanities/History/Genealogy/

- Yahoo!—Arts: Humanities: History: Genealogy:
  Beginners' Guides
  http://www.yahoo.com/Arts/Humanities/History/Genealogy/
  Beginners__Guides/

- Yahoo!—Arts: Humanities: History:
  Genealogy: Indices
  http://www.yahoo.com/Arts/Humanities/History/Genealogy/
  Indices/

- Yahoo!—Arts: Humanities: History:
  Genealogy: Lineages & Surnames
  http://www.yahoo.com/Arts/Humanities/History/Genealogy/
  Lineages_and_Surnames/

- Yahoo!—Arts: Humanities: History:
  Genealogy: Lookups
  http://www.yahoo.com/Arts/Humanities/History/Genealogy/
  Lookups/

- Yahoo!—Arts: Humanities: History:
  Genealogy: Organizations
  http://www.yahoo.com/Arts/Humanities/History/Genealogy/
  Organizations/

- Yahoo!—Arts: Humanities: History:
  Genealogy: Regional and Ethnic Resources
  http://www.yahoo.com/Arts/Humanities/History/Genealogy/
  Regional_and_Ethnic_Resources/

- Yahoo!—Arts: Humanities: History:
  Genealogy: Usenet
  http://www.yahoo.com/Arts/Humanities/History/Genealogy/
  Usenet/

- Yourfamily.com Family Home Pages
  http://yourfamily.com/family.cgi

- Yvon CYR's Genealogy Related WWW Hotlist
  http://www.acadian.org/genealogy/lk-sites.html

◆ Getting Started

- Ancestry Search
  http://www.ancestry.com/
  *Social Security Death Index (SSDI) and other searchable
  databases.*

- Family Tree Maker's Genealogy "How To" Guide
  http://www.familytreemaker.com/mainmenu.html

- GEN-NEWBIE-L Home Page
  http://www.rootsweb.com/~newbie/

- GEN-NEWBIE-L Mailing List
  http://members.aol.com/johnf14246/
  gen_mail_general.html#GEN-NEWBIE-L
  *A mailing list where people who are new to computers and
  genealogy may interact using a computer's e-mail program.*

- How To
  http://www.CyndisList.com/howto.htm
  *See this category on Cyndi's List for dozens of links to helpful
  sites and articles.*

- ROOTS-L Mailing List
  http://members.aol.com/johnf14246/
  gen_mail_general.html#ROOTS-L
  THE list to start with online! Broad-based genealogy topics and over 10,000 subscribers.

- RootsWeb Surname List Search Engine on Rootsweb
  http://rsl.rootsweb.com/cgi-bin/rslsql.cgi

◆ Locality & Ethnic Specific

- The Afrigeneas Homepage
  http://www.msstate.edu/Archives/History/afrigen/index.html
  For African ancestry.

- Belgium—Immigrants in America
  http://www.ping.be/picavet/
  A complete guide for descendants of Belgian immigrants looking for their roots in Belgium.

- Canadian Genealogy & History Links
  http://www.islandnet.com/~jveinot/cghl/cghl.html

- Federation of East European Family History Societies—FEEFHS
  http://feefhs.org/

- Genealogy Benelux Home Page
  http://www.ufsia.ac.be/genealogy/

- German Genealogy Home Page
  http://www.genealogy.net/gene/index.html

- Hispanic Genealogy Crossroads
  http://members.aol.com/mrosado007/crossroads.htm
  Categorized resources from the AOL Hispanic Genealogy Group.

- IRLGEN: Tracing Your Irish Ancestors
  http://www.bess.tcd.ie/roots_ie.htm

- The Italian Genealogy Home Page
  http://www.italgen.com/

- JewishGen: The Official Home of Jewish Genealogy
  http://www.jewishgen.org/

- Native American Genealogy
  http://members.aol.com/bbbenge/front.html

- ROOTS-L Resources: United States Resources
  http://www.rootsweb.com/roots-l/usa.html

- The UK & Ireland Genealogical Information Service (GENUKI)
  http://midas.ac.uk/genuki

- The USGenWeb Project
  http://www.usgenweb.org/

◆ Volunteers, Lookups & Free Searches

- Ancestral Findings
  http://web.mountain.net/~wfmoney/cd/
  Free CD searches—limited to 2 persons per day.

- Books We Own List
  http://www.rootsweb.com/~bwo/index.html
  A list of resources owned by others who are willing to do lookups in them.

- Free Genealogy Lookups
  http://www.pnx.com/unicorn/sites/lookups.htm
  From a variety of CDs and books listed on this page.

- Genealogists At VU Look-ups
  http://www.concentric.net/~Cande/lookups.shtml

- Genealogy Helplist
  http://posom.com/hl/
  List of volunteers willing to help others in specific areas.

- The Look-up Exchange
  http://www.geocities.com/Heartland/Plains/8555/lookup.html
  A county-by-county list of resources covering England, Scotland, Wales and the Isle of Man, made available by volunteers for free look-ups.

- Lookups from Genealogical CDs
  http://www.seidata.com/~lhoffman/cdlist.html
  People who own genealogy CDs and are willing to do lookups for others.

- Lookups from Privately Owned Publications
  http://www.seidata.com/~lhoffman/private.html
  People volunteering to do lookups in their own personal library.

- Los Angeles City Directory 1930
  E-mail: billcapp@ix.netcom.com
  E-mail Bill Cappello at billcapp@ix.netcom.com and he will do a reasonable number of specific lookups for you. Allow two weeks for a reply.

- Nova's Genealogy Page
  http://www.buffnet.net/~nova/
  Nova will search her Social Security Death Index CD-ROM for you.

- Resources With A Wide Array Of Genealogical Interest
  http://members.aol.com/djungclas/common/resource.htm

- Susan Bryant
  E-mail: sbry@dowco.com
  Has a Pro-CD Canadian Home Phone CD. E-mail Susan with specific details and she will do a quick lookup for you.

◆ Web Rings for Genealogy

A popular new service on the Internet! A web ring is made up of links to web sites with a common topic or theme. Follow the links around the ring and perhaps you'll come across the web page belonging to that long-lost cousin you've been searching for! For details visit the Web Ring Homepage, http://www.webring.org/

- African-American Genealogy Ring
  http://www.geocities.com/Heartland/Prairie/6288/
  afamgenring.html

- Civil War Virtual Archive Web Ring
  http://www.geocities.com/Athens/Forum/1867/cwring.html

- CWOL Webring (Civil War On-line)
  http://www.geocities.com/CapitolHill/8472/webring.html

- Genealogy Pages Web Ring
  http://www.geocities.com/Heartland/8907/gp/gpring.html
- The GenePool Ring
  http://netrover.com/~pilgrim/gpwr/gpwebring.htm
- GenRing Information Center
  http://www.geocities.com/Athens/3082/genring.html
  For amateur genealogists & members of the USGenWeb project to link their web sites together.
- GenSearch Web Ring
  http://www.geocities.com/Athens/Forum/3709/webring.html
- Gum Tree Genealogy Ring ~ Australia
  http://members.tripod.com/~Jules_in_oz/gumtree/
- Heartland Genealogical Society Web Ring
  http://www.geocities.com/Heartland/Ranch/2416/hgsring.html
- Jewish Roots Ring
  http://pw1.netcom.com/~barrison/jewgenwebring.html
- Kentuckiana Genealogy WebRing
  http://www.floyd-pavey.com/kentuckiana/kyiana/webring.html
  Kentucky & Indiana

- The Louisiana Genealogy Web Ring Home Page
  http://members.xoom.com/LaGenWebRing/WebRing.html
- Maggie's Ohio Web Ring
  http://www.infinet.com/~dzimmerm/Ring/ohring.html
- Our Heritage Around the World Web Ring
  http://www.ourancestry.com/webring1.html
- Reunion Users Web Ring
  http://www.geocities.com/Heartland/Plains/9053/reunion.html
  For users of the Reunion software program by Leisterpro.
- Ring of Scottish Clans Information Center
  http://www.sirius.com/~black/webring/index.htm
  Celebrating the culture, history, music and families of Scotland.
- Tasmanian Genealogy Webring
  http://www.vision.net.au/~jbrowne/newpage1.htm
- The Tennessee Genealogy & History Web Ring
  http://web.utk.edu/~kizzer/genehist/tghring/
- The Trees' of Families Web Ring Form
  http://www.geocities.com/Heartland/Hills/1749/webring.htm
- The UK Genealogy Webring
  http://www.kbnet.co.uk/brianp/webring.html

HERALDRY

http://www.CyndisList.com/heraldry.htm

- About Achievement of Arms (tm)
  http://members.aol.com/grammarman/grammarstuff/
  aboutachieve.html
  Software for designing shields, crests, etc.

- The Augustan Society, Inc.
  http://www.augustansociety.org
  *An International Genealogical, Historical, Heraldic and
  Chivalric Society.*

- Alve, Heráldica Española—Spanish Heraldry
  http://www.artenet-cb.es/alve.html

- The American College of Heraldry
  http://users.aol.com/ballywoodn/acheraldry.html

- An Anachronist's Encyclopaedia—Heraldry
  http://www.acc.umu.se/~lkj/uma/her.html

- Blasón Virtual, Heráldica en la Red
  http://www.ctv.es/blason/

- Blazon and Blazon95 Software
  http://www.platypus.clara.co.uk/blazon.htm

- Blazons! Software
  http://www.blazons.com/

- The British Heraldic Archive
  http://www.kwtelecom.com/heraldry/

- Caltrap's*Corner
  http://caltrap.bbsnet.com/

- Canadian Heraldry/L'Heraldique
  http://www.schoolnet.ca/collections/governor/heraldry/
  index.html

- Centro De Estudios Heraldicos
  http://www.net64.es/heraldica/

- The College of Arms
  http://www.kwtelecom.com/heraldry/collarms/index.html

- Crests and Coats of Arms
  http://britain.nyc.ny.us/bis/fsheets/3.HTM#crests
  A paragraph from Britain in the USA: Genealogical Research.

- English Heraldic Dictionary
  http://jagor.srce.hr/~zheimer/heraldry/h.htm

- Family Tree Genealogical and Probate Research
  Bureau Ltd.
  http://www.familytree.hu/
  *Professional research service covering the area of what was
  formerly the Austro—Hungarian Empire, including: Hungary,
  Slovakia, Czech Republic, Austria, Italy, Transylvania, Croatia,
  Slovenia, former Yugoslavia (Banat), and the Ukraine
  (Sub-Carpathian).*

- Genealogia e Heráldica Portuguesa—
  Portuguese Genealogy and Heraldry
  http://www.nca.pt/individual/babel/
  álvaro HOLSTEIN Home Page.

- Genealogy and Heraldry in Slovenia
  http://genealogy.ijp.si/

- GenealogyBookShop.com—Heraldry
  http://www.genealogybookshop.com/genealogybookshop/files/
  General,Heraldry/index.html
  *The online store of Genealogical Publishing Co., Inc. &
  Clearfield Company.*

- genealogyPro—Professional Researchers
  Specializing in Heraldry
  http://genealogyPro.com/directories/heraldry.html

- The Great Hall of the Clans
  http://www.tartans.com/hall.html

- Heraldic Arts Heraldry Page
  http://www.demon.co.uk/heritage/heraldry/

- Heraldic Primer: Table of Contents
  http://www.sca.org/heraldry/primer/

- Heráldica Española, Heraldry for Surnames
  of Spanish Origin
  http://www.ctv.es/artes/
  *(Heráldica y escudos de armas de apellidos españoles,
  genealogía, escudos de armas—Heraldry for surnames of
  Spanish origin, coats of arms, genealogy).*

- Heraldica—François Velde's Heraldry Site
  http://www.heraldica.org/intro.htm

- Heraldica Hispana
  http://www.alc.es/heraldica/heral_en.htm

- Heraldry and Vexillology
  http://www.du.edu/~tomills/flags.html

- Heraldry on the Internet
  http://digiserve.com/heraldry/

- Heraldry Page by M.N. Razumkin
  http://sunsite.cs.msu.su/heraldry/
  The Crown of Russian Empire—The Unofficial Home Page.

- The Heraldry Society
  http://www.kwtelecom.com/heraldry/hersoc/

- Heraldry Software
  http://digiserve.com/heraldry/hersoft.htm

- Heraldry Today
  http://www.heraldrytoday.co.uk/
  Books for heraldry and genealogy.

- HERBARZ Mailing List
  http://members.aol.com/gfsjohnf/gen_mail_country-lit.html#HERBARZ
  For the discussion of Polish and Lithuanian heraldry, the history of the armorial clans, and the genealogy of noble families.

- The Institute of Heraldic and Genealogical Studies ~ U.K.
  http://www.cs.ncl.ac.uk/genuki/IHGS/

- International Civic Arms
  http://www.bng.nl/ngw/indexgb.htm
  Over 9,500 arms of towns, states and countries.

- International Research—Association of Accredited Genealogists
  http://www.intl-research.com/heraldry.htm
  Accredited genealogists & family historians specializing in family history research, development & publication. Accredited by the Family History Library in Salt Lake City, the world's largest genealogical library. Tax deductions for LDS research.

- Italian Heraldry, Nobility and Genealogy
  http://www.italgen.com/heraldry.htm

  o How Professional Genealogists Determine Ancestral Nobility in Italy
    http://www.italgen.com/nobilit.htm

- Jeff Alvey Genealogy History Heraldry
  http://www.fred.net/jefalvey/jeffhera.html

- Jürgen Maus, Grabador De Escudos, Iniciales Y Emblemas * Lapidarios
  http://www.net64.es/jmaus/
  He is an engraver of coat of arms, initials and emblems in semi and precious stones.

- Kleine Einführung in die Wappenkunde / Introduction in Heraldry
  http://www.geocities.com/Colosseum/1959/wappen.html

- Kyl's Illustrative and Educational Guide to Heraldry and Blazoning in our Current Middle Ages
  http://www.geocities.com/Athens/Forum/4433/index.html

- Pimbley's Dictionary of Heraldry
  http://www.digiserve.com/heraldry/pimbley.htm

- The Points of Heraldry—The Basics of Heraldic Design and Terminology
  http://www2.okstate.edu/pages/Services/heraldry.html

- Reynolds Hunter Y Puebla Heráldica Y Blasones—Heraldries
  http://www.audinex.es/~hunter/

- Uasal—A Server for Irish Nobility, Heraldry and Genealogy
  http://www.finearts.sfasu.edu/uasal/welcome.html

- Usenet Newsgroup rec.heraldry

- Yahoo!....Genealogy:Heraldry & Name Histories
  http://dir.yahoo.com/Business_and_Economy/Companies/Information/Genealogy/Heraldry___Name_Histories/

HISPANIC, CENTRAL & SOUTH AMERICA, & THE WEST INDIES

Including Mexico, Latin America & the Caribbean
http://www.CyndisList.com/hispanic.htm

Category Index:

- ◆ General Resource Sites
- ◆ Libraries, Archives & Museums
- ◆ Mailing Lists, Newsgroups & Chat
- ◆ People & Families
- ◆ Professional Researchers, Volunteers & Other Research Services

- ◆ Publications, Software & Supplies
- ◆ Queries, Message Boards & Surname Lists
- ◆ Records: Census, Cemeteries, Land, Obituaries, Personal, Taxes and Vital
- ◆ Societies & Groups
- ◆ WorldGenWeb Project

◆ General Resource Sites

- AOL Hispanic Genealogy Group's Home Page
  http://users.aol.com/mrosado007/index.htm

- Barbados Genealogy
  http://www.mindspring.com/~jsruss/bdos/barbados.htm

- Barbados Information
  http://home.cwnet.com/dynasty/barbados.htm

- Bibliography for Researchers of Jamaican Genealogy and History
  http://www6.pair.com/silvera/jamgen/jgbibliography.html

- CLNET Genealogy Sources
  http://latino.sscnet.ucla.edu/Test/genealogy.ref.html
  List of Hispanic published resources.

- Cuban Genealogy How To Guide
  http://www.familytreemaker.com/00000365.html

- Dutch Antilles
  http://ourworld.compuserve.com/homepages/paulvanV/nedantil.htm

- Family History of Jamaica, West Indies
  http://users.pullman.com/mitchelm/jamaica.htm
  From Madeleine Mitchell. ARSCOTT, COVER, MURRAY, LEVY.

- Family Tree Maker's How-To Guide—Institute of Genealogy and History for Latin America
  http://www.familytreemaker.com/00000140.html

- genealogia.com
  http://www.genealogia.com
  A Comprehensive Hispanic Genealogy Research Web Site Covering all Hispanics Countries Including Spain and Brazil.

- Genealogical Research in South America
  http://www.saqnet.co.uk/users/hrhenly/latinam1.html
  With an emphasis on British settlement.

- Généalogie et Histoire de la Caraïbe
  http://members.aol.com/GHCaraibe/index.html

- Genealogy in Costa Rica
  http://www.nortronica.com/genealogy/

- German Genealogy: BRAZIL
  http://www.genealogy.net/gene/reg/WELT/brasil.html
  German migration to Brasil.

- Hispanic Genealogical Research Center of New Mexico
  http://www.hgrc-nm.org/

- Hispanic Genealogy Address Book by Country
  http://members.aol.com/mrosado007/crossroads.htm#HGAB

- Hispanic Genealogy Crossroads
  http://members.aol.com/mrosado007/crossroads.htm
  Categorized resources from the AOL Hispanic Genealogy Group.

- Hispanic Genealogy Page on Compuserve
  http://ourworld.compuserve.com/homepages/Alfred_Sosa/

- Hispanic Genealogy—The Institute of Genealogy and History for Latin America
  http://www.infowest.com/l/lplatt/

- Index to "Historia de Familias Cubanas, Vols. 1–9"—(Histories of Cuban Families)
  http://www.cubagenweb.org/jaruco.htm

- Jamaican Jewish Genealogy
  http://www6.pair.com/silvera/jamgen/index.html

- Mexican Genealogy How To Guide
  http://www.familytreemaker.com/00000379.html

- Spain, Portugal & The Basques / España, Portugal, y
  El Pais Vosco
  http://www.CyndisList.com/spain.htm
  See this category on Cyndi's List for related links.

- The Taino Genealogy Project
  http://www.hartford-hwp.com/taino/docs/proj-6.html

- The Taino Inter-Tribal Council
  http://www.hartford-hwp.com/taino/index.html

- The Tom & Dollie Genealogy Page
  http://spot.Colorado.EDU/~madridt/Home.html

- Tracing Hispanic/Mexican-American Roots
  gopher://latino.sscnet.ucla.edu/11/Researcher/
  Arts%20%26%20Humanities/Genealogy/

- United States Index
  See these category pages on Cyndi's List for related links.
  - Arizona
    http://www.CyndisList.com/az.htm
  - California
    http://www.CyndisList.com/ca.htm
  - New Mexico
    http://www.CyndisList.com/nm.htm
  - Texas
    http://www.CyndisList.com/tx.htm

- West Indian Genealogy Links
  http://ourworld.compuserve.com/homepages/vroyal/links.htm

- Where to Find Jamaican Genealogical Information
  http://www6.pair.com/silvera/jamgen/jgwhere.html

- Yahoo!...Hispanic...Genealogy
  http://dir.yahoo.com/Arts/Humanities/History/Genealogy/
  Regional_and_Ethnic_Resources/Hispanic/

- Yahoo!...Mexico...Genealogy
  http://dir.yahoo.com/Regional/Countries/Mexico/
  Arts_and_Humanities/History/Genealogy/

◆ Libraries, Archives & Museums

- Rio Grande Valley Library System—
  Special Collections Branch
  http://www.cabq.gov/rgvls/specol.html
  Albuquerque. Strong in the areas of New Mexico and Hispanic genealogy.

◆ Mailing Lists, Newsgroups & Chat

- BAHAMAS Mailing List
  http://members.aol.com/gfsjohnf/gen_mail_country-
  bah.html#BAHAMAS
  For anyone with a genealogical interest in the country of the Bahamas.

- BRAZIL Mailing List
  http://members.aol.com/gfsjohnf/gen_mail_country-
  bra.html#BRAZIL
  For anyone with genealogical interest in Brazil.

- Caribbean Historical & Genealogical Journal
  http://www.tcigenealogy.com/
  From TCI Genealogical Resources.

- CARIBBEAN Mailing List
  http://members.aol.com/gfsjohnf/gen_mail_country-
  gen.html#CARIBBEAN
  For anyone with a genealogical or historical interest in the West Indies and the Caribbean.

- CUBA Mailing List
  http://members.aol.com/gfsjohnf/gen_mail_country-
  cub.html#CUBA

- Genealogia Mailing List
  http://members.aol.com/gfsjohnf/gen_mail_country-
  bra.html#Genealogia
  For those interested in genealogy in Brazil. The list is dedicated to the search for information on the origins of families, registers in Brazil and abroad, histories of immigrants, meanings of surnames, etc.

- GEN-HISPANIC Mailing List
  http://members.aol.com/gfsjohnf/gen_mail_country-
  gen.html#GEN-HISPANIC
  For the discussion of Hispanic genealogy. Gatewayed with the soc.genealogy.hispanic newsgroup.

- MadeiraExiles Mailing List
  http://members.aol.com/gfsjohnf/gen_mail_country-
  wes.html#MadeiraExiles
  Devoted to the research of Dr. Robert Reid Kalley's Portuguese Presbyterian exiles from Madeira, Portugal who emigrated to Trinidad and then to Illinois (ca 1846–1854). Postings regarding research of related exiles who settled in Trinidad, Antigua, St. Kitts, Jamaica, Demerara, etc. are also welcome.

- MEXICO Mailing List
  http://members.aol.com/gfsjohnf/gen_mail_country-
  mex.html#MEXICO

- REPUBLICA-DOMINICANA Mailing List
  http://members.aol.com/gfsjohnf/gen_mail_country-
  dom.html#REPUBLICA-DOMINICANA

- Search Soc.genealogy.west-indies Posts
  http://searches.rootsweb.com/sgwest-indies.html

- SOUTH-AM-EMI Mailing List
  http://members.aol.com/johnf14246/gen_mail_geo-
  nonusa.html#SOUTH-AM-EMI
  A mailing list for the discussion and sharing of information regarding emigrants from the United Kingdom to South America during the eighteenth and nineteenth centuries.

- TX-MEX Mailing List
  http://members.aol.com/gfsjohnf/gen_mail_states-tx.html
  #TX-MEX
  For anyone with ancestors who immigrated to Texas from Mexico.

- Usenet Newsgroup soc.genealogy.hispanic

- Usenet Newsgroup soc.genealogy.west-indies

◆ People & Families

- David SILVERA's Home Page
  http://www6.pair.com/silvera/
  Primarily focused on the Spanish and Portuguese Jewish community in Jamaica, West Indies.

- De Windt's Family Home Page (1810–1996)
  http://users.aksi.net/~wilfredo/dewindt.html
  Curaçao and Dominican Republic

- Lucy's Page
  http://www.geocities.com/Heartland/Meadows/4296/family.html
  MÁLAGA y BERNEDO

- Michael ROSADO's Genealogy Home Page
  http://users.aol.com/mrosado007/personal/index.htm
  ROSADO PAGÁN, COLÓN CAPÓ, ROSADO DECLET, PAGÁN DECLET, COLÓN LEBRÓN, CAPÓ NAVARRO

- MORALES-LANGUASCO Genealogical Research Home Page
  http://www.viaccess.net/~paiewons/homepage.htm
  MORALES, LANGUASCO, ROBAINNE, ALVAREZ, CASTELLANOS, CHEVALIER, De WINDT, Del VALLE, ESCUDERO, LEROUX, PAIEWONSKY, PELEGRÍN, PERELLÓ, RODRÍGUEZ de ASTUDILLO, SENIOR, VICTORIA

- A Page For My Family
  http://members.tripod.com/~blueflower/index.htm

- La Página de Genealogía de José Rivera Nieves
  http://www.geocities.com/Heartland/Prairie/9311/

- Valerio F. LAUBE—Home Page Genealogia
  http://www.netuno.com.br/~vflaube/vfl_05.htm
  Brazil. LAUBE, ZOZ, WELTER, MARQUARDT

- Viola's Web Home
  http://members.aol.com/vrsadler/index.html
  CÁRDENAS, CASTAÑEDA, ELIZONDO, LAZCANO, MARTÍNEZ, RODRÍGUEZ, VILLA

◆ Professional Researchers, Volunteers & Other Research Services

- Board for Certification of Genealogists—Roster of Those Certified—Specializing in Mexico
  http://www.genealogy.org/~bcg/rosts_@m.html

- Genealogy Helplist—Brazil
  http://posom.com/hl/bra/index.shtml

- Manchego Consulting
  http://members.aol.com/manchegoc/homepage.html
  Hispanic genealogy research and book publishing.

◆ Publications, Software & Supplies

- Books We Own—Caribbean
  http://www.rootsweb.com/~bwo/caribbean.html

- Frontier Press Bookstore—Hispanic Research
  http://www.frontierpress.com/frontier.cgi?category=hisp

- GenealogyBookShop.com—Bahamas/Bahamian
  http://www.genealogybookshop.com/genealogybookshop/files/The_World,Bahamas_Bahamian/index.html

  Barbados
  http://www.genealogybookshop.com/genealogybookshop/files/The_World,Barbados/index.html

  Jamaica/Jamaican
  http://www.genealogybookshop.com/genealogybookshop/files/The_World,Jamaica_Jamaican/index.html

  Bermuda
  http://www.genealogybookshop.com/genealogybookshop/files/The_World,Bermuda/index.html

  Spain/Spanish/Hispanic
  http://www.genealogybookshop.com/genealogybookshop/files/The_World,Spain_Spanish_Hispanic/index.html
  The online store of Genealogical Publishing Co., Inc. & Clearfield Company.

- A Student's Guide to Mexican American Genealogy
  http://www.oryxpress.com/scripts/book.idc?acro=FTMEX
  A book for sale from Oryx Press.

◆ Queries, Message Boards & Surname Lists

- West Indies Surname Interests List
  http://ourworld.compuserve.com/homepages/vroyal/

◆ Records: Census, Cemeteries, Land, Obituaries, Personal, Taxes and Vital (Born, Married, Died & Buried)

- Texas General Land Office—Spanish and Mexican land titles in Texas
  http://www.glo.state.tx.us/central/arc/spanmex.html

◆ Societies & Groups

- Asociación de Genealogía Judía de Argentina
  http://www.marben.com.ar/toldot
  Página Oficial de la Asociacion de Genealogia Judia de Argentina. Jewish Genealogical Society of Argentina (Official Site).

- Genealogical Society of Hispanic America
  http://www.ancestry.com/SocietyHall/viewmember.asp?results=81
  GSHA is 11 years old with five chapters in Colorado & California. Members specialize in Hispanic research in the American Southwest & Mexico. Over 75% are descendants of the Spanish colonists of New Mexico.

- Hispanic Genealogical Society
  http://www.brokersys.com/~joguerra/jose.html
  Houston, Texas

- Hispanic Genealogical Society of New York
  http://www.webcom.com/hgsny/
- Instituto Dominicano De Genealogia, Inc.
  http://members.tripod.com/~vmpv/idg
- Jewish Genealogical Society of Argentina
  http://www.jewishgen.org/infofiles/ar-jgs.txt
- Jewish Genealogical Society of Brazil /
  Sociedade Genealógica Judaica do Brasil
  http://www.lookup.com/homepages/82259/sgjbing.htm
- The Puerto Rican / Hispanic Genealogical Society
  http://www.rootsweb.com/~prhgs/
- Sociedad Puertorriqueña de Genealogía
  http://www.usc.clu.edu/spg/
  San Juan, Puerto Rico
- The Society of Hispanic Historical and
  Ancestral Research (SHHAR)
  http://members.aol.com/shhar/index.html
- Spanish American Genealogical Association
  http://members.aol.com/sagacorpus/saga.htm
  Corpus Christi , Texas

◆ WorldGenWeb Project

- WorldGenWeb Project
  http://www.worldgenweb.org/
  - ○ CaribbeanGenWeb
    http://www.rootsweb.com/~caribgw/
    - BajanGenWeb
      http://www.rootsweb.com/~brbwgw/
      The CaribbeanGenWeb site for Barbados.
    - Bermuda Genealogy
      http://www.rootsweb.com/~bmuwgw/bermuda.htm
    - Cuban Genealogy Resources
      http://www.cubagenweb.org/
    - Dominican Republic Caribbean GenWeb
      http://www.rootsweb.com/~domwgw/mhhbcgw.htm
    - La Genealogía de Puerto Rico (The Genealogy
      of Puerto Rico)
      http://www.rootsweb.com/~prwgw/index.html

- Genealogie d'Haiti
  http://www.rootsweb.com/~htiwgw/
- Genealogy of the Bahamas Islands
  http://www.geocities.com/Heartland/Prairie/3226/
  Bahamas/index.html
- Genealogy of Jamaica
  http://www.rootsweb.com/~jamwgw/index.htm
- Genealogy of Netherland Antilles
  http://www.rootsweb.com/~caribgw/dutch.htm
- U.S. (Danish) Virgin Islands—St. Thomas,
  St. Croix, St. John
  http://www.rootsweb.com/~usvi/
- WorldGenWeb page for Grenada
  http://www.rootsweb.com/~grdwgw/
- WorldGenWeb page for Saint Vincent and
  the Grenadines
  http://www.rootsweb.com/~vctwgw/
  - ○ CentralAmGenWeb
    http://www.rootsweb.com/~centamgw/
    - Belize
      http://www.rootsweb.com/~blzwgw/
    - La Genealogía de El Salvador
      http://www.rootsweb.com/~slvwgw/
    - Honduras GenWeb
      http://www.rootsweb.com/~hndwgw/honduras.html
  - ○ MexicoGenWeb Project
    http://www.rootsweb.com/~mexwgw/
  - ○ SouthAmGenWeb
    http://www.rootsweb.com/~sthamgw/
    - Argentina WorldGenWeb
      http://www.rootsweb.com/~perwgw/Argentina
    - Brazil Genealogy / Genealogia no Brasil
      http://www.rootsweb.com/~brawgw/
    - Genealogía de Venezuela—
      Venezuelan Genealogy
      http://www.geocities.com/Heartland/Ranch/2443/
    - Peru—The WorldGenWeb Project
      http://www.rootsweb.com/~perwgw/

HISTORICAL EVENTS & PEOPLE WORLDWIDE
http://www.CyndisList.com/historic.htm

Category Index:

- Ellis Island, New York
- General History Resources
- Heading West
- The Mayflower

- People & Families
- Societies & Groups
- The Titanic
- War & The Military

◆ Ellis Island, New York

- The American Immigrant Wall of Honor
  http://www.wallofhonor.com/

- The Ellis Island Home Page
  http://www.ellisisland.org/

- Ellis Island (I-Channel)
  http://www.i-channel.com/features/ellis/

- New York, NY, Ellis Island—Immigration: 1900–1920
  http://cmp1.ucr.edu/exhibitions/immigration_id.html
  University of California, Riverside, Keystone-Mast Collection, California Museum of Photography. Photographs of immigrants, ships & Ellis Island.

◆ General History Resources

- Historical Documents
  gopher://ucsbuxa.ucsb.edu:3001/11/.stacks/.historical
  Text files of documents such as the Declaration of Independence, the Magna Carta, the Mayflower Compact and more.

- The Historical Text Archive (HTA)
  http://www.msstate.edu/Archives/History/
  Housed at Mississippi State University.

- History Buff's Home Page
  http://www.historybuff.com/index.html
  Created by the Newspaper Collectors Society of America.

- The History Net
  http://www.thehistorynet.com/home.htm
  Where History Lives on the Web.

- The History Place
  http://www.historyplace.com/index.html

- Horus' Web Links to History Resources
  http://www.ucr.edu/h-gig/horuslinks.html

- HyperHistory Online
  http://www.hyperhistory.com/online_n2/History_n2/a.html

- Index of Resources for Historians
  http://kuhttp.cc.ukans.edu/history/index.html

- Irish History on the Web
  http://wwwvms.utexas.edu/~jdana/irehist.html

- U.S.—History
  http://www.CyndisList.com/hist-us.htm
  See this category on Cyndi's List for related links.

- WWW Sites for Historians
  http://www.hist.unt.edu/09-www.htm

- Yahoo!...History
  http://dir.yahoo.com/Arts/Humanities/History/

◆ Heading West

- Explorers of the West
  http://upanet.uleth.ca/~Haig/

- The Hudson's Bay Company Archives
  http://www.gov.mb.ca/chc/archives/hbca/index.html
  From the Provincial Archives of Manitoba, Canada.

- Mountain Men and the Fur Trade
  http://www.xmission.com/~drudy/amm.html
  Sources of the History of the Fur Trade in the Rocky Mountain West.

- trails west Mailing List
  http://members.aol.com/gfsjohnf/gen_mail_states-gen.html#trails-west
  For those who want to research their family history and post facts on their move west in North America. The trails addressed by the list started at the very beginning of the settlement of North America and are not just the ones in western North America.

◆ The Mayflower

- The ALDEN House Museum
  http://www.alden.org/
  The home of John & Priscilla Alden in Duxbury, Massachusetts.

- The General Society of Mayflower Descendants
  http://www.mayflower.org/

- A Mayflower & New England Study
  http://www.mayflowerfamilies.com/

- Mayflower Database
  http://www.geocities.com/Heartland/Bluffs/4313/
- MAYFLOWER Mailing List
  http://members.aol.com/gfsjohnf/gen_mail_states-gen.html#MAYFLOWER
  A mailing list for the discussion and sharing of information regarding the descendants of the Mayflower passengers in any place and at any time.
- Mayflower Web Page
  http://members.aol.com/calebj/mayflower.html

◆ People & Families

- Association for the Preservation of Virginia Antiquities—Jamestown Rediscovery
  http://www.apva.org/
  - A Brief History of Jamestown
    http://www.apva.org/history/index.html
- Biographical Dictionary
  http://www.s9.com/biography/
  Covers more than 19,000 notable men and women.
- Descendants of * of the Ark NOAH
  http://www.parsonstech.com/genealogy/trees/dmalec/burkhamm.htm
- Descendants of Royalty, Historical Figures
  http://www.worldroots.com/brigitte/royal/royal11.htm
- Genealogy of Mankind from Adam to Japheth, Shem, and Ham
  http://www.geocities.com/Tokyo/4241/geneadm2.html
- HMS Bounty Genealogies
  http://www.wavefront.com/~pjlareau/bounty6.html
- The Irish Famine, 1845–1850
  http://avery.med.virginia.edu/~eas5e/Irish/Famine.html
- Lewis & Clark—The Journey of the Corps of Discovery
  http://www.pbs.org/lewisandclark/
  The companion web site for the PBS series by Ken Burns.
- List of Officers and Sailors in the First Voyage of Columbus in 1492
  http://www.rootsweb.com/~ote/colship.htm
  Nina, Pinta, Santa Maria
- Lusitania (1907–1915)
  http://www.liv.ac.uk/~archives/cunard/ships/lusitan.htm
  From the Cunard Archives web site.
- Magellan's Voyages from *The Discovery of America* by John Fiske published in 1892
  http://www.rootsweb.com/~ote/magship.htm
  The Victoria and the Trinidad.

- METISGEN Mailing List
  http://members.aol.com/johnf14246/gen_mail_general.html#METISGEN
  For the discussion and sharing of information regarding the Metis and their descendants. The Metis are North America's Fur Trading Children . . . the new nation of individuals born within North America from the first unions of natives and whites.
- Notable Women Ancestors
  http://www.rootsweb.com/~nwa/
- Palatine Emigrants by Kraig Ruckel
  http://www.geocities.com/Heartland/3955/palatine.htm
- Palatines to America Homepage
  http://www.genealogy.org:80/~palam/
- Pocahontas Descendants
  http://www.rootscomputing.com/howto/pocahn/pocahn.htm
  Descendants of Powhatan (Father of Pocahontas).
- The Political Graveyard
  http://politicalgraveyard.com/index.html
  "The Web Site That Tells Where the Dead Politicians are Buried."
- Researching the Genealogy of Almanzo and Laura Ingalls Wilder
  http://members.tripod.com/~PennyN/LIWgen.html
- Robert BURNS Family History
  http://fox.nstn.ca/~jburness/burns.html
  Family history of the Scottish poet Robert Burns including 130 descendants and over 800 other relatives.
- Roman Emperors—The Imperial Index
  http://www.salve.edu/~dimaiom/impindex.html
  An Online Encyclopedia of Roman Emperors.
- ROOTS-L Resources: Historical Groups
  http://www.rootsweb.com/roots-l/hist_groups.html
  Links to several articles and sites regarding various groups, such as the Lewis & Clark expedition and many more.
- A Roster of the Lewis & Clark Expedition
  http://www.rootsweb.com/~genepool/lewiclar.htm
- Royalty & Nobility
  http://www.CyndisList.com/royalty.htm
  See this category on Cyndi's List for related links.
- A Shakespeare Genealogy
  http://daphne.palomar.edu/shakespeare/timeline/genealogy.htm

◆ Societies & Groups

- The Historical Association ~ U.K.
  http://www.history.org.uk/
- The National Society Magna Charta Dames and Barons
  http://www.magnacharta.org/
- Railroad Historical Societies
  http://tucson.com/concor/histsoc.html

◆ The Titanic

- Encyclopedia Titanica
  http://www.rmplc.co.uk/eduweb/sites/phind/

- In Memoriam: RMS Titanic
  http://miso.wwa.com/~dsp//titanic/

- The Original Titanic Home Page
  http://www.home.gil.com.au/~dalgarry/

- RMS Titanic: Her Passengers and Crew
  http://www.rmplc.co.uk/eduweb/sites/phind/home.html

- Titanic and Other White Star Ships
  http://members.aol.com/MNichol/Titanic.index.html

- Titanic Passenger List
  http://vsla.edu/vnp/titanic/p2.htm

- Titanic ~ The Unsinkable Ship and Halifax
  http://titanic.gov.ns.ca/
  A site from Halifax, Nova Scotia, Canada, including a list of those buried in cemeteries in Halifax.

◆ War & The Military

- The Alamo
  http://numedia.tddc.net/sa/alamo/

- AMERICAN-REVOLUTION Mailing List
  http://members.aol.com/gfsjohnf/gen_mail_states-gen.html#AMERICAN-REVOLUTION
  For the discussion of events during the American Revolution and genealogical matters related to the American Revolution. The French-Indian Wars and the War of 1812 are also suitable topics for discussion.

- Canada—Military
  http://www.CyndisList.com/milcan.htm
  See this category on Cyndi's List for related links.

- Dad's War: Finding and Telling Your Father's World War II Story
  http://members.aol.com/dadswar/

- Descendants of Mexican War Veterans
  http://members.aol.com/dmwv/home.htm

- The French and Indian Raid on Deerfield, Massachusetts, 1704
  http://uts.cc.utexas.edu/~churchh/deerfild.html

- Korean War Project
  http://www.koreanwar.org/

- The Mexican-American War Memorial Homepage
  http://sunsite.unam.mx/revistas/1847/

- Michael D. Meals' Revolutionary War Links
  http://q.continuum.net/~histnact/revwar/revwar.html

- Military Resources Worldwide
  http://www.CyndisList.com/milres.htm
  See this category on Cyndi's List for related links.

- Pearl Harbor Casualties List
  http://www.mit.edu:8001/afs/athena/activity/a/afrotc/www/names

- Secrets of the Norman Invasion
  http://www.cablenet.net/pages/book/index.htm
  With plates of the Bayeux Tapestry.

- A Selection of Underground Railroad Resources
  http://www.ugrr.org/web.htm

- United States Holocaust Memorial Museum
  http://www.ushmm.org/

- U.S. Civil War ~ The War for Southern Independence
  http://www.CyndisList.com/cw.htm
  See this category on Cyndi's List for related links.

- U.S. Military
  http://www.CyndisList.com/military.htm
  See this category on Cyndi's List for related links.

- Vietnam Era POW/MIA Database
  http://lcweb2.loc.gov/pow/powhome.html
  At the Library of Congress.

- The Wars of Religion
  http://www.lepg.org/wars.htm

HIT A BRICK WALL?

http://www.CyndisList.com/hitbrick.htm

- **Books We Own**
  http://www.rootsweb.com/~bwo/index.html
  Sometimes it is best to set aside your research problem and put your thoughts elsewhere for a while. Whenever I've done this I can always come back to the problem with a fresh set of eyes. Try volunteering to help others for a while instead. The Books We Own site is a great way to begin!

- **Cyndi's Genealogy Home Page Construction Kit**
  http://www.CyndisList.com/construc.htm
  Create your own web page in order to put up a list of your surnames and your research questions, problems & mysteries!

- **Finding People**
  http://www.CyndisList.com/finding.htm
  Phone Numbers, E-Mail Addresses, Mailing Addresses, Places, Etc.

- **First Name Basis**
  http://www.hypervigilance.com/genlog/firstname.html
  To aid you in researching when all you know is the first name of a person. Focuses on unusual first names and women's first names when maiden names are unknown.

- **Genealogy's Most Wanted**
  http://www.citynet.net/mostwanted/
  One of the first sites online to help us get past this brick wall!.

- **GEN-UNSOLVED-MYSTERIES Mailing List**
  http://members.aol.com/johnf14246/
  gen_mail_general.html#GEN-UNSOLVED-MYSTERIES
  For people whose family genealogies include "unsolved mysteries." Postings should include only mysterious disappearances or appearances, unsolved murders, questionable incarcerations, and other mysterious or unsolved events in an ancestor's life. Postings should not include "brick walls" since these would be repetitive of the content of other lists.

- **How To**
  http://www.CyndisList.com/howto.htm
  Stop by the "How To" category on this site and read through multiple helpful articles on all sorts of research topics. Perhaps the answer is hidden in one of these online resources!

- **How-to get past the "Stone Wall Syndrome"**
  http://www.firstct.com/fv/stone.html
  A terrific article from Robert Ragan's Treasure Maps site.

- **Library of Congress**
  http://lcweb.loc.gov/homepage/lchp.html
  One visitor to my site suggested checking the Library of Congress to see if your ancestor had a biography or an autobiography written about him or her. Another visitor pointed out that you should specifically check with the genealogy section "which contains genealogies sent to the the LC, some of them merely typed, many not published."

- **Mailing Lists & Newsgroups**
  http://www.CyndisList.com/mailnews.htm
  Join a mailing list for your specific surname or your research locality. Communicate regularly with others who are researching the same names or in the same areas and share ideas, hints, tips and advice.

- **Professional Researchers, Volunteers & Other Research Services**
  http://www.CyndisList.com/profess.htm
  If all else fails you might consider hiring a professional researcher to do some of the work for you. I can't personally endorse any of the researchers on this page, so you must use your best judgement in obtaining their services. You might also try to "swap" volunteer services with others who need help in your areas of expertise or resources.

- **Queries & Message Boards**
  http://www.CyndisList.com/queries.htm
  Search through thousands of online queries by other researchers. Make up your own basic/generic query for each person you are working on and post it in as many spots as you can as you sift through other's queries. Stop by each of the USGenWeb pages for the counties you are researching in and look through their queries also.

- **Search Engines**
  http://www.CyndisList.com/search.htm
  Use any of the search engines on this page to do a search on a specific surname, place name or keyword that you are interested in. Read the help files and the FAQ for each search engine and learn how they each work. Try different combinations of words & phrases to maximize your search results.

- **Sources of Genealogical Information**
  http://www.rootsweb.com/~genepool/sources.htm
  "Have you reached a dead-end in your research? Have you looked in these records yet?!" A checklist of resources you shouldn't overlook in your research. From Joanne Rabun and the Gene Pool.

- **UFO-ROOTS Mailing List**
  http://members.aol.com/johnf14246/
  gen_mail_general.html#UFO-ROOTS
  For those whose ancestors arrived from outer space to make connections with others sharing this problem, discuss their ancestry, and provide advice on possible avenues for further research.

- **Web Rings**
  http://www.CyndisList.com/handy.htm
  See this section on the Handy Online Starting Points category page on Cyndi's List.
  Web rings are popping up on genealogy web sites all over the net. A "web ring" is a series of web sites connected to one another via a special link table set up for sites that fit a specific topic. There are several web rings for genealogy, covering everything from general genealogical web sites to the Civil War, Jewish genealogy and Reunion software users. When you see a web ring table on a site you can choose to follow the link to the next site on that ring, or you can skip ahead 5 links or you can choose a random link on the ring. Doesn't this sound like the type of thing you should do when you hit that brick wall in your research? It reminds me of randomly stopping your arm as you rewind a roll of microfilm and you spot your long-lost ancestor on the page in front of you!

- **When Your Family History Research Hits the Wall**
  http://www.parkbooks.com/Html/res_guid.html
  A research guide from Park Genealogical Books.

HOW TO
http://www.CyndisList.com/howto.htm

Category Index:

- Ancestors Television Series
- Education
- Electronic Genealogical Research
- Family Tree Maker Online
- General Genealogical Guides, Hints & Tips
- Getting Started

- LDS Family History Centers & The Family History Library
- Mailing Lists, Newsgroups & Chat
- Methods & Techniques
- Publications, Software & Supplies
- Specific Topics or Areas of Research
- Tools for Your Research

◆ Ancestors Television Series

- Ancestors Home Page
  http://www.pbs.org/kbyu/ancestors/
  - Ancestors Charts & Records
    http://www.pbs.org/kbyu/ancestors/teachersguide/charts-records.html
  - Ancestors Teacher's Guide
    http://www.pbs.org/kbyu/ancestors/teachersguide/
    From the television program on PBS, a teacher's guide for starting a family history project.
  - Ancestors Viewer's Guide To Getting Started
    http://www.pbs.org/kbyu/ancestors/viewersguide/

◆ Education

- Bellevue Community College Continuing Education Online Courses
  http://www.conted.bcc.ctc.edu/users/online/
  - Introduction to Genealogy Online
    http://www.conted.bcc.ctc.edu/users/marends/
    Instructor Marthe Arends
  - Weaving Your Memory Web: Preserving Family Stories for Future Generations
    http://www.conted.bcc.ctc.edu/users/bhofmann/
    Instructor William Hofmann
- BYU Genealogy and Family History Conference
  http://coned.byu.edu/cw/cwgen/
- BYU Independent Study—Family History Courses
  http://coned.byu.edu/is/
- The Elderhostel Home Page
  http://www.elderhostel.org/
- Family Tree Maker's Genealogy Site: Online Genealogy Classes
  http://www.familytreemaker.com/university.html
  From Karen Clifford, Genealogy Research Associates and Marthe Arends, Online Pioneers.

- Federation of Genealogical Societies— FGS Conferences
  http://www.fgs.org/~fgs/fgs-conf.htm
- The Genealogical Institute of Mid-America (GIMA)
  http://www.misslink.net/neill/gima.html
  The 6th annual Institute will be held 12–15 July 1999 in Springfield, IL (instructors include Lloyd Bockstruck, Sandra Luebking, and Michael Neill).
- Genealogy Classes offered through Madison Area Technical College ~ Wisconsin
  http://www.rootsweb.com/~widane/class.htm
- Genealogy Lectures, Seminars, and Workshops
  http://www.misslink.net/neill/lecture.html
  By Michael John Neill, M.S.
- Genealogy Lesson Plans
  http://members.aol.com/rechtman/genclass.html
- Genealogy—Part of the History/Social Studies Web Site for K–12 Teachers
  http://www.execpc.com/~dboals/geneo.html
- GENTECH, Inc.
  http://www.gentech.org/~gentech/
  A non-profit organization designed to educate genealogists in the use of technology for gathering, storing, sharing and evaluating their research.
- The Institute of Heraldic and Genealogical Studies
  http://www.cs.ncl.ac.uk/genuki/IHGS/
  In Northgate, Canterbury, Kent, England. Offers a correspondence course in genealogy.
- International Internet Genealogical Society University
  http://www.iigs.org/university/index.htm.en
- National Genealogical Society Home Study Course
  http://www.ngsgenealogy.org/education/content/basic/intro.html
  "American Genealogy: A Basic Course."

- National Institute on Genealogical Research
  http://natgeninst.genealogy.org/

- New England Historic Genealogical Society
  Education Department
  http://www.nehgs.org/Education/EDhome.htm

- Repeat Performance—Audio/Video
  Recording Services
  http://www.repeatperformance.com/
  *Tapes of classes and presentations at several genealogy
  conferences and seminars for the last 18 years.*

- Samford University Institute of Genealogy and
  Historical Research ~ Alabama
  http://www.samford.edu/schools/ighr/ighr.html

- Spectrum Virtual University:
  Global Village Classrooms
  http://www.vu.org/campus.html
  *Has two courses for genealogy: Introduction to Online Geneal-
  ogy; Writing Family and Personal History. Also learn about the
  associated mailing list at http://members.aol.com/johnf14246/
  gen_mail_general.html#Internet_Genealogy*

- UW Certificate Program in Genealogy and
  Family History
  http://www.edoutreach.washington.edu/extinfo/certprog/gfh/
  default.htm
  From the University of Washington in Seattle.

◆ Electronic Genealogical Research

- Cyndi's Genealogy Home Page Construction Kit
  http://www.CyndisList.com/construc.htm

- Developing a Family Homepage—
  from Yourfamily.com
  http://yourfamily.com/making_hp.shtml

- Handy Online Starting Points
  http://www.CyndisList.com/handy.htm
  See this category on Cyndi's List for related links.

- The Internet & Webbing Your Family History
  http://www.pe.net/~lucindaw/internet/internet.htm
  From the Harper County Genealogical Society.

- Netting Your Ancestors—Genealogical Research
  on the Internet
  http://www.CyndisList.com/netting.htm
  Cyndi's book from Genealogical Publishing Co.

- Online Research Techniques from Everton's:
  Part 1
  http://www.everton.com/oe2-5/ort1.htm
  Part 2
  http://www.everton.com/oe2-6/ort2.htm
  Part 3
  http://www.everton.com/oe2-7/ort3.htm
  Part 4
  http://www.everton.com/oe2-8/ort4.htm

- Practical Genealogy Research—Making the Internet
  Work for You
  http://www.zen.co.uk/home/page/joe.houghton/
  RESEARCH.HTM

- Software & Computers
  http://www.CyndisList.com/software.htm
  See this category on Cyndi's List for related links.

- Transforming Your GEDCOM Files Into Web Pages
  http://www.oz.net/~markhow/writing/gedcom.htm
  By Mark Howells.

◆ Family Tree Maker Online

- Family Tree Maker's Genealogy "How-To" Guide
  http://www.familytreemaker.com/mainmenu.html
  - Back Issues of Family Tree Maker Online
    http://www.familytreemaker.com/backissu.html
    - African American Genealogy
      http://www.familytreemaker.com/issue12.html
    - Aspects of Internet Genealogy
      http://www.familytreemaker.com/issue29.html
    - Caring for Your Family Photos
      http://www.familytreemaker.com/issue10.html
    - Celebrating Kinship Connections—and Mom!
      http://www.familytreemaker.com/issue16.html
    - Documenting Sources
      http://www.familytreemaker.com/issue19.html
    - Family Archive CD Spotlight
      http://www.familytreemaker.com/issue22.html
    - Family Associations
      http://www.familytreemaker.com/issue26.html
    - Family History Books
      http://www.familytreemaker.com/issue21.html
    - Family Reunions
      http://www.familytreemaker.com/issue1.html
    - Family Traditions
      http://www.familytreemaker.com/issue9.html
    - Finding and Using Previous Research
      http://www.familytreemaker.com/issue15.html
    - Finding Your New England Ancestors
      http://www.familytreemaker.com/issue25.html
    - Genealogical Journeys—Vacationing with
      Your Ancestors
      http://www.familytreemaker.com/issue17.html
    - Irish Research Resources
      http://www.familytreemaker.com/issue30.html
    - Learning About Your Immigrant Ancestors
      http://www.familytreemaker.com/issue8.html
    - Making Your Overseas Connection
      http://www.familytreemaker.com/issue31.html
    - The National Archives
      http://www.familytreemaker.com/issue3.html

- Oral Histories
  http://www.familytreemaker.com/issue2.html
- Organizing for the New Year
  http://www.familytreemaker.com/issue27.html
- Professional Research
  http://www.familytreemaker.com/issue20.html
- Researching Civil War Soldiers
  http://www.familytreemaker.com/issue7.html
- Researching Irish Roots
  http://www.familytreemaker.com/issue4.html
- Researching Revolutionary War Veterans
  http://www.familytreemaker.com/issue24.html
- Researching with Census Records
  http://www.familytreemaker.com/issue13.html
- Researching with Church Records
  http://www.familytreemaker.com/issue5.html
- Researching Your Family's Marriages
  http://www.familytreemaker.com/issue11.html
- Trees, Trees, Trees!
  http://www.familytreemaker.com/issue23.html
- What's in a Surname?
  http://www.familytreemaker.com/issue18.html
- Why Genealogy Conferences?
  http://www.familytreemaker.com/issue28.html
- World Family Tree Spotlight
  http://www.familytreemaker.com/issue14.html
- Your Family's Health History
  http://www.familytreemaker.com/issue6.html
- Family Tree Maker's Genealogy Site:
  Online Genealogy Classes
  http://www.familytreemaker.com/university.html
  From Karen Clifford, Genealogy Research Associates and Marthe Arends, Online Pioneers.

◆ General Genealogical Guides, Hints & Tips

- 20 Ways to Avoid Genealogical Grief
  http://www.rootsweb.com/roots-l/20ways.html
- Backward Footprints
  http://www.geocities.com/CapitolHill/1025/faq.html
- Checklist of Home Sources
  http://www.rootscomputing.com/howto/checkl/checkl.htm
- The Genealogist's Guide—from Heritage Associates
  http://www.granniesworld.com/heritage/guide.htm
- The GenTutor Approach to Climbing
  Your Family Tree
  http://members.aol.com/GenTutor/tutor.html
- Professional Researchers, Volunteers &
  Other Research Services
  http://www.CyndisList.com/profess.htm
  See this category on Cyndi's List for related links.

- Research Tips on Gathering Your
  Family Information
  http://ourworld.compuserve.com/homepages/Strawn/tips.htm
- Tracing Our Roots
  http://www.hhcn.com/family/kellow/index.html
  Column by Brenda Burns Kellow, featured in the Plano Star Courier, Plano, Texas.
- Tracing Our Roots
  http://www.harrisburg.com/root.html
  Column by Schuyler Brossman, featured in The Press And Journal Extra, Middletown, Pennsylvania.
- Treasure Maps: The "How-To" Genealogy Site
  http://www.firstct.com/fv/tmaps.html
- Tri-City Herald Genealogy Online
  http://www.tri-cityherald.com/genealogy/
  Dozens of helpful columns written by Terry Day and Donna Potter Phillips.
- Wanda's Genealogy Tips
  http://wlake.com/wandas/genepage.html
- What You Should Know Before Hiring A
  Professional Genealogist
  http://www.genservices.com/help_guides/HiringAPro.html

◆ Getting Started

- 26 Genealogy Tips
  http://www.A1WebDesign.com/rebick/26tips.htm
  From Robert Bickham Family Genealogy.
- Beginner's Guide to Family History Research
  http://biz.ipa.net/arkresearch/guide.html
  and an alternate site
  http://www.dhc.net/~jw/guide.html
  By Desmond Walls Allen and Carolyn Earle Billingsley.
- Beginning Family History, UK National Register of
  Archives—information leaflets ~ GENUKI
  http://www.genuki.org.uk/big/RCH/Beginning.html
- Beginning Steps At Home On the Internet
  http://www.nauvoo.com/family/chamblee/ncjohnston/begin.html
- Calgary Free-Net:Genealogy—Tracing Your
  Family Tree
  http://www.FreeNet.Calgary.ab.ca/science/genealogy/begingene.html
- A Crash Course In Genealogy
  http://www.grl.com/grl/start.shtml
  From the Genealogical Research Library.
- Everton Publishers—Getting Started
  http://www.everton.com/intro1.htm
- Family Tree Finders
  http://www.sodamail.com/site/ftf.shtml
  A Monday through Friday newsletter that provides interesting and useful information for tracing your family tree. It's geared to beginners and experienced family tree trackers of any age! Written by well known genealogist, Rhonda R. McClure.

- First Steps in Genealogy
  http://www.gcpl.lib.oh.us/services/gcr/gen_resources/1ststeps.htm
  From the Greene County Public Library, Ohio.

- Genealogy 101
  http://www.wizard.com/~bascs/101a.htm

- A Genealogy Primer
  http://www.sky.net/~mreed/primer.htm

- GEN-NEWBIE-L Home Page
  http://www.rootsweb.com/~newbie/

- GEN-NEWBIE-L Mailing List
  http://members.aol.com/johnf14246/gen_mail_general.html#GEN-NEWBIE-L
  A mailing list where people who are new to computers and genealogy may interact using a computer's e-mail program.

- Getting Started
  http://www.herald.co.uk/local_info/genuki/new_user.html

- Getting Started in Genealogy and Family History
  http://www.genuki.org.uk/gs/

- Getting Started With Genealogical Research
  http://httpsrv.ocs.drexel.edu/grad/sg94e3fd/WEDNESDA.HTM

- Helpful Hints for Successful Searching
  http://www.rootsweb.com/~irlwat/instruct.htm

- How Do I Begin?
  http://www.lds.org/en/2_How_Do_I_Begin/0-How_Do_I_Begin.html
  From the official LDS Church web site.

- How To......
  http://www.cohsoft.com.au/afhc/faq.html
  From the Australian Family History Compendium.

- How To Trace One's Ancestors
  http://www.genealogy.org/~ajmorris/misc/tracing.htm

- How To Trace Your Family Tree—Notes For Beginners
  http://members.aol.com/gfhsoc/beginner.htm
  From the Glamorgan Family History Society.

- Lost_Newbies Mailing List
  http://members.aol.com/johnf14246/gen_mail_general.html#Lost_Newbies
  For people who are new to genealogy and/or the use of the Internet in genealogical research.

- National Genealogical Society—NGS Beginner's Kit
  http://www.ngsgenealogy.org/education/content/beginkit.html

- National Genealogical Society—Suggestions for Beginners
  http://www.ngsgenealogy.org/getstart/content/suggest.html

- NEWGEN Mailing List
  http://members.aol.com/johnf14246/gen_mail_general.html#NEWGEN
  Created to assist those who are quite new to genealogy.

- Research Aids for the Family Historian
  http://www.rootsweb.com/~genepool/ogsaids.htm

- ROOTS-L Resources: Info and Tips for Beginning Genealogy
  http://www.rootsweb.com/roots-l/starting.html

- Suggestions for Beginners in Genealogy
  http://pcm.pcmedia.com.au/tags/docs/ngstips1.html

- Suggestions for Tracing Your Family Tree
  http://www.system.missouri.edu/shs/familytr.html
  From the State Historical Society of Missouri.

- Tips & Tricks for the Beginner—Genealogy 101
  http://www.kalglo.com/gentips.htm

- Tracing Your Family Tree
  http://freenet.calgary.ab.ca/afhs/bhbegin.html
  By Brian W. Hutchison for the Alberta Family Histories Society.

- Treasure Maps: The "How-To" Genealogy Site
  http://www.firstct.com/fv/tmaps.html

- Ultimate Family Tree: Get Started with Setting Out
  http://www.uftree.com/UFT/Nav/howtossetting.html

- Your Great Ancestral Hunt—A Beginner's Course for Discovering Your Family
  http://www.familytreemaker.com/101/lesson1/course1_01.html
  By Karen Clifford, A.G. from Family Tree Maker. Over 60 pages of step-by-step instructions and tips for first time family history hunters. Includes self-tests.

◆ LDS Family History Centers & The Family History Library

- Family Search: The Family History Library Catalog (FHLC)
  http://www.firstct.com/fv/fhlc.html

- FamilySearch FAQ: Answers to Your Questions About FamilySearch
  http://www.utw.com/~tornado/
  - The Ancestral File—Questions and Answers
    http://www.utw.com/~tornado/ancfile.html
  - The Family History Library Catalog
    http://www.utw.com/~tornado/fhlibcat.html
  - General Information About FamilySearch
    http://www.utw.com/~tornado/general.html

- The Genealogist—The Family History Library
  http://www.xcelco.on.ca/~genealog/famhilib.htm

- Guide To LDS Family History Library, Salt Lake City, Utah
  http://www.jewishgen.org/infofiles/lds-slc.txt
  A JewishGen InfoFile

- LDS & Family History Centers
  http://www.CyndisList.com/lds.htm
  See this category on Cyndi's List for related links.

- LDS Family History Centers—The Largest Collection In The World!
  http://www.firstct.com/fv/lds1.html
  A tutorial from the Treasure Maps site.

- LDS Family History Library, Salt Lake City, Utah
  http://www.everton.com/GENEALOG/GENEALOG.LDSFHLIB
  Description, maps, etc.

- ROOTS-L Resources: Family History Centers and Library
  http://www.rootsweb.com/roots-l/fhc.html

- Salt Lake City, Family History Library Information
  http://www.aros.net/~drwaff/slcfhl.htm

- Salt Lake City Here We Come!
  http://www.rootsweb.com/~genepool/slc.htm

- Welcome To The Family History Center™
  http://www.lds.org/en/2_Welcome_to_the_FHC/
  Welcome_to_the_FHC.html
  An online brochure from the official LDS Church web site.

- What Is a Family History Center™?
  http://www.lds.org/en/2_How_Do_I_Begin/3-What_is.html
  From the official LDS Church web site.

- What is the I.G.I.?—aka The International Genealogical Index
  http://www.livgenmi.com/fhcigi.htm
  A definition help page by Helen S. Ullmann, C.G.

◆ Mailing Lists, Newsgroups & Chat

- Family Tree Finders
  http://www.sodamail.com/site/ftf.shtml
  A Monday through Friday newsletter that provides interesting and useful information for tracing your family tree. It's geared to beginners and experienced family tree trackers of any age! Written by well known genealogist, Rhonda R. McClure.

- GEN-NEWBIE-L Mailing List
  http://members.aol.com/johnf14246/
  gen_mail_general.html#GEN-NEWBIE-L
  A mailing list where people who are new to computers and genealogy may interact using a computer's e-mail program.

- GENMTD-L Mailing List
  http://members.aol.com/johnf14246/
  gen_mail_general.html#GENMTD-L
  Gatewayed with the soc.genealogy.methods newsgroup for the discussion of genealogy research techniques and resources.

- GEN-ROOTERS Mailing List
  http://members.aol.com/johnf14246/
  gen_mail_general.html#GEN-ROOTERS
  For members of the Church of Jesus Christ of Latter-day Saints to share ideas and helpful hints on the "how-to's" of genealogy.

- GEN-SHARE Mailing List
  http://members.aol.com/johnf14246/
  gen_mail_general.html#GEN-SHARE
  For "seasoned" genealogy researchers to share sources and get help with tough problems. This list is not for the posting of queries addressing searches for specific ancestors and is not recommended for those new to genealogy.

- GENTEEN-L Mailing List
  http://members.aol.com/johnf14246/
  gen_mail_general.html#GENTEEN-L
  For teenagers and young adults who are interested in genealogical research or others who have suggestions or ideas for young genealogists.

- GenTips-L Mailing List
  http://members.aol.com/johnf14246/
  gen_mail_general.html#GenTips-L
  For anyone who has an interest in genealogy. This list hopes to provide tips about obtaining genealogy records and is useful for both beginning genealogists and experts.

- NEWGEN Mailing List
  http://members.aol.com/johnf14246/
  gen_mail_general.html#NEWGEN
  Created to assist those who are quite new to genealogy.

- RESEARCH-HOWTO Mailing List
  http://members.aol.com/johnf14246/
  gen_mail_general.html#RESEARCH-HOWTO
  For those who are just getting started in genealogy research and those who are not novices but need information on where to go when "dead ends" are encountered.

◆ Methods & Techniques

- Board for Certification of Genealogists— Skillbuilding, Index of Available Columns
  http://www.genealogy.org/~bcg/skbldidx.html

- Deciphering Old Handwriting
  http://www.firstct.com/fv/oldhand.html

- Documenting Sources
  http://www.familytreemaker.com/issue19.html
  From Family Tree Maker Online.

- Doing Your Cemetery Survey
  http://www.netusa1.net/~hartmont/cemsurvey.htm

- Elements of a Research Plan
  http://www.micronet.net/users/~searcy/researchplan.htm

- Frontier Press Bookstore—Methodology
  http://www.frontierpress.com/frontier.cgi?category=method

- Genealogy Goals
  http://www.1adventure.com/FutureWork/ConBusTr/
  genealog.htm
  By Dennis Piccirillo.

- GENMTD-L Mailing List
  http://members.aol.com/johnf14246/
  gen_mail_general.html#GENMTD-L
  Genealogy methods & non-net resources. Gatewayed with the soc.genealogy.methods newsgroup.

- How Do I Keep All This Stuff Straight?
  http://www.ancestry.com/columns/George/04-24-98.htm
  From "Along Those Lines . . ." by George Morgan.

- How-to get past the "Stone Wall Syndrome"
  http://www.firstct.com/fv/stone.html

- Lineages' First Steps—Write Successful Genealogy Queries
  http://www.lineages.com/FirstSteps/WriteQueries.asp

- Numbering Systems in Genealogy
  http://www.genealogy.org/~st-clair/numbers/

- Organization of Genealogical Materials
  http://www.rootsweb.com/~ote/organize.htm

- Organizing Your Family History
  http://www.micronet.net/users/~searcy/organizing.htm

- Organizing Your Research: Research Records
  http://www.parkbooks.com/Html/res_org.html
  A research guide from Park Genealogical Books.

- Principles of Web Searching
  http://www.mannlib.cornell.edu/workshops/WebSearching/
  index.html

- St. Clair County, Michigan Sample Queries
  http://www.rootsweb.com/~mistclai/sample-queries.html
  A humorous and instructive guide to how NOT to write a query. Provides excellent advice on how to compose an effective query. Applicable for all queries in any locality.

- Standards for Sound Genealogical Research
  http://www.ngsgenealogy.org/about/content/committees/
  gene_stan.html
  Recommended by the National Genealogical Society.

- Standards For Transcribing Cemetery Headstones
  ftp://ftp.rootsweb.com/pub/roots-l/genealog/
  genealog.headston

- Standards for Using Records Repositories and Libraries
  http://www.ngsgenealogy.org/about/content/committees/
  gene_stan.html
  Recommended by the National Genealogical Society.

◆ Publications, Software & Supplies

- *American Genealogical Research at the DAR, Washington, D.C.*
  http://www.dar.org/library/libpub.html

- Books We Own—Genealogy, General Reference
  http://www.rootsweb.com/~bwo/gen_ref.html

- Computer Genealogist—New Technology for Genealogy—PERiodical Source Index
  http://www.credible.com/genealg7.html
  An article from Computer Credible Magazine by Alan E. Mann.

- Frontier Press Bookstore—Beginning Genealogy
  http://www.frontierpress.com/frontier.cgi?category=begin

- GenealogyBookShop.com—Guides and Manuals
  http://www.genealogybookshop.com/genealogybookshop/files/
  General,Guides_and_Manuals/index.html
  The online store of Genealogical Publishing Co., Inc. & Clearfield Company.

- Global Genealogy—General Genealogy Topics & How-To Books
  http://www.globalgenealogy.com/howto.htm

- Heritage Books—Research Aids
  http://www.heritagebooks.com/resaids.htm

- Trade Genealogy Audio Tapes
  http://www.rootsweb.com/~widane/Trade.htm

- Unpuzzling Your Past: A Basic Guide to Genealogy
  http://www.amazon.com/exec/obidos/ISBN=1558703969/
  A book for beginning genealogy by Emily Anne Croom. Available from Amazon.com Books. I recommend this book to everyone who is just starting to trace their family tree.

- U.S. Research Outlines
  http://www.firstct.com/fv/usout.html

- Where to Write for Vital Records
  http://www.cdc.gov/nchswww/howto/w2w/w2welcom.htm

- Willow Bend Bookstore—How To Genealogy
  http://www.willowbend.net/howto.htm

- Willow Bend Bookstore—Research Aids
  http://www.willowbend.net/ra.htm

◆ Specific Topics or Areas of Research

Military

- How To Obtain A Revolutionary War Pension File
  http://www.teleport.com/~carolynk/howtofil.htm

- How to Obtain Military Pension Files from the Department of Veterans Affairs
  http://www.kinquest.com/genealogy/va.html

- How to Order Military & Pension Records for Union Civil War Veterans
  http://www.oz.net/~cyndihow/pensions.htm
  From the National Archives.

- War of 1812 Records: Where and How do I get them?
  http://www.rootsweb.com/~kyharris/1812how.htm

Records: Census, Cemeteries, Land, Obituaries, Personal, Taxes and Vital (Born, Married, Died & Buried)

- FAQ: Obtaining a Copy of a Social Security Number Application
  http://members.aol.com/reginamari/ancestry/ssnfaq.html
  The how and why of obtaining a copy of an SSN Application for genealogical purposes. Includes sample SSN applications.

- Finding a Marriage Date
  http://www.familytreemaker.com/11_mrgdt.html
  by Karen Clifford, A.G.

- How Newspapers Can Help You With Your Research
  http://www.everton.com/oe3-18/papers.htm
  From Everton's Genealogical Helper Online.

- How to Use Soundex for United States Census Records
  http://sparc.hpl.lib.tx.us/hpl/soundex.html

- Information on Land Records
  http://www.avana.net/~lhaasdav/landinfo.html

- Land Record Reference
  http://www.ultranet.com/~deeds/landref.htm
- Ordering Birth Registration Certificates from the United Kingdom
  http://www.oz.net/~markhow/ukbirths.htm
  Using the LDS Family History Center Resources.
- Retracing the Trails of Your Ancestors Using Deed Records
  http://www.ultranet.com/~deeds/deeds.htm
  By William Dollarhide, from the Genealogy Bulletin, Issue No. 25, Jan–Feb 1995.
- US Land & Property Research
  http://users.arn.net/~billco/uslpr.htm
  By Bill Utterback for the IIGS University.
- Using Census Records
  http://www.micronet.net/users/~searcy/records.htm
- Using the Census Soundex
  http://www.familyhistory.com/faqs/narasdex.htm
- Using the Soundex System
  http://www.ancestry.com/home/George_Morgan/03-20-98.htm
  From "Along Those Lines . . ." by George G. Morgan.

Ships, Passenger Lists & Immigration

- How To Find Your Immigrant Ancestor— Passenger and Immigration Lists Index
  http://www.rader.org/how_to.htm
- How to Get Your Ancestor's Papers from the Immigration and Naturalization Service
  http://www.italgen.com/immigrat.htm
- LDS Passenger Manifests—Jan Grippo's Guide to Using the Passenger Lists at Your Local Family History Center
  http://homepage.interaccess.com/~arduinif/ldsmanif.htm
- Passport Application Record Information From the National Archives
  http://homepages.rootsweb.com/~godwin/reference/passport.html
- Requesting Your Ancestor's Naturalization Records from the INS
  http://www.brigadoon.com/~jwilson/gen/maher/immigrate.html
  A guide by Dennis Piccirillo.

Specialty Records or Topics

- How to do Genealogical Research using FBI Files?
  http://members.aol.com/rechtman/fbi.html
- How to do Tombstone Rubbings
  http://www.mindspring.com/~mooregen/tombstone.htm
- Locating Published Genealogies
  http://www.familytreemaker.com/15_genes.html
  by Donna Przecha. From Family Tree Maker Online.

- Local Histories: Finding and Evaluating
  http://www.familytreemaker.com/15_local.html
  by Myra Vanderpool Gormley, C.G. From Family Tree Maker Online.
- Primer on Collecting Old & Historic Newspapers
  http://www.historybuff.com/primer.html
- The U.S. Railroad Retirement Board and Genealogical Information
  http://www.rrb.gov/geneal.html
- Using Federal Documents In Genealogical Research—U.S.
  http://www.history.rochester.edu/jssn/page1.htm
- Was Your Ancestor a Doctor?
  http://user.itl.net/~glen/doctors.html

Specific Localities & Ethnic Groups

- African American Lifelines
  http://ourworld.compuserve.com/homepages/Cliff_m/
  How-to for beginners.
- Ancestors from Norway—Getting Started
  http://www.geocities.com/Heartland/Plains/5100/na15.html
- Compiling a Family Tree—Getting started
  http://www.cw.globalweb.co.uk/buchan/records.htm
  From the Central Buchan Project. Provides information for beginning research with emphasis on the holdings of the local Buchan Registration Offices and repositories in Scotland.
- Finding Where Your Ancestors Came From in Germany
  http://www.angelfire.com/biz/origins1/ancestors.html
- German Genealogical Research Before The Church Records Begin
  http://www.kinquest.com/genealogy/researching.html
  Tips and hints by Lisa Petersen.
- German Research at Libraries and Archives in Baden-Wuerttemberg
  http://www.kinquest.com/genealogy/badwue.html
  Tips and hints by Lisa Petersen.
- German Research in Stuttgart Libraries and Archives
  http://www.kinquest.com/genealogy/stuttgart.html
  Tips and hints by Lisa Petersen.
- How To Guide for Native Americans
  http://members.aol.com/bbbenge/page12.html
- Have You Found a Swedish Ancestor?
  http://www.geocities.com/Heartland/Meadows/7095/swede.html
- Hvordan Finner Jeg Etterkommere Av De Som Utvandret Til USA? / How Do I Find Descendants of a Norwegian Immigrant to the USA?
  http://members.xoom.com/follesdal/na14.html
  In Norwegian; for Norwegians who are tracing descendants of a Norwegian immigrant to the USA.

- An Introduction to Jewish Genealogy in Manitoba
  http://www.concentric.net/~Lkessler/genbegin.shtml
- Native American Genealogy
  http://www.system.missouri.edu/shs/nativeam.html
  A guide from the State Historical Society of Missouri.
- Researching Ancestors from the United Kingdom
  http://www.oz.net/~markhow/uksearch.htm
  Using the LDS Family History Center Resources.
- The Search for the Parents of Franciska TRAUTVETTER—A Study in Downstate Illinois Resources
  http://www.misslink.net/neill/francis.html
  By Michael John Neill.
- Swedish Information Service—Internet Resources for Tracing Your Swedish Roots
  http://www.webcom.com/sis/geneal.html
- Tim's Tips on Pennsylvania German Research
  http://www.geocities.com/Heartland/Plains/3816/how2.html

◆ Tools for Your Research

- Calendars & Dating
  http://www.CyndisList.com/calendar.htm
- Family Relationship Chart to Download from David's Home Page
  http://www.agate.net/~davids/_genea/dl01.htm
- Finding People
  http://www.CyndisList.com/finding.htm
  Phone Numbers, E-Mail Addresses, Mailing Addresses, Places, Etc.
- Form Letters for German Genealogy
  http://www.genealogy.net/gene/www/ghlp/muster.html
- Genealogy Dictionary
  http://home.att.net/~dottsr/diction.html

- The Handy-Dandy Cousin Chart
  http://www2.ebtech.net/~kleonard/chart.html
- Libraries
  http://www.CyndisList.com/libes.htm
- Maps, Gazetteers and Geographical Information
  http://www.CyndisList.com/maps.htm
- Newspapers
  http://www.CyndisList.com/newspapr.htm
- Relationship Chart
  http://www.eng.uci.edu/students/mpontius/pontius/7-7.html
- Research It!—One stop reference desk
  http://iTools.com/research-it/research-it.html
- Search Engines
  http://www.CyndisList.com/search.htm
- Section and Acres Charts by Janyce
  http://www.janyce.com/misc/section.html
- Soundex Conversion Program from Genealogy Online
  http://www.genealogy.org/soundex.shtml
- Soundex Conversion Program—Surname to Soundex Code
  http://searches.rootsweb.com/cgi-bin/Genea/soundex.sh
- The Soundex Machine
  http://www.nara.gov/genealogy/soundex/soundex.html
  A form to convert surnames to soundex codes; from the National Archives.
- Supplies, Charts, Forms, Etc.
  http://www.CyndisList.com/supplies.htm
- Terms, Phrases, Dictionaries & Glossaries
  http://www.CyndisList.com/terms.htm

HUGUENOT

http://www.CyndisList.com/huguenot.htm

- Experiences of the French Huguenots in America
  http://pages.prodigy.com/VRHZ10A/ressegui.htm

- France
  http://www.CyndisList.com/france.htm
  See this category on Cyndi's List for related links

- The French Protestant Church of London
  http://ihr.sas.ac.uk/ihr/associnstits/huguenots.mnu.html

- Huguenot & Protestant Reformed Chronology
  http://www.kopower.com/~jimchstn/timeline.htm
  From the Pierre Chastain Family Association.

- Huguenot Cemetery
  http://www.geocities.com/Heartland/Hills/8299/cemetery/
  hug_cem.htm
  St. John's County, Florida

- The Huguenot Cross
  http://www.geocities.com/Heartland/Valley/8140/x-eng.htm

- Huguenot Historical Society
  http://members.aol.com/HuguenotHS/index.html
  New Paltz, New York

- Huguenot Historical Society
  http://home.earthlink.net/~rctwig/hhs1.htm
  New Paltz, New York

- Huguenot History
  http://history.cc.ukans.edu/heritage/cousin/huguenot.html

- Huguenot History
  http://www.home.aone.net.au/mclark/huguenot_history.htm

- Huguenot Mailing List
  http://members.aol.com/johnf14246/
  gen_mail_general.html#Huguenot

- Huguenot Refugees
  http://www.rootsweb.com/~ote/hugship.htm
  On the ship "Mary and Ann," August 12, 1700, Virginia, James City and on the ship "Peter and Anthony" from London to James River in Virginia, 20th of Sept. 1700.

- Huguenot Refugees in the Cape Colony of South Africa
  http://www.rootsweb.com/~ote/hugsa.htm

- Huguenot Resources—Olive Tree Genealogy
  http://www.rootsweb.com/~ote/hugres.htm

- Huguenot Society of South Africa
  http://www.geocities.com/Heartland/Valley/8140/

- The Huguenot Society of Texas of the National Huguenot Society
  http://www.startext.net/homes/huguenot/

- Huguenot Society of Wisconsin
  http://www.execpc.com/~drg/wihs.html

- Huguenot Source List—Olive Tree Genealogy
  http://www.rootsweb.com/~ote/hugsour.htm

- Huguenot Sources
  http://www.kopower.com/~jimchstn/hugsrcs2.htm
  From the Pierre Chastain Family Association.

- Huguenot Surnames Index—from Australian Family Tree Connections Magazine
  http://www.aftc.com.au/huguenot.html

- Huguenots
  http://www.geocities.com/SoHo/3809/Huguen.htm

- Huguenots to England
  http://www.rootsweb.com/~ote/hugeng.htm

- Olive Tree Genealogy—Huguenots & Walloons
  http://www.rootsweb.com/~ote/hw.htm

- Ottosen Online—Research of Danish Huguenot History
  http://home4.inet.tele.dk/mo2sn/huguenot.html

- Pierre CHASTAIN Family Association
  http://www.kopower.com/~jimchstn/

- The National Huguenot Society
  http://huguenot.netnation.com/
  The National Huguenot Society is an organization devoted to: 1. Coordinating activities of member societies, and promoting and supporting fulfillment of their common purposes which include: a. perpetuating the memory and promoting the principles and virtues of the Huguenots; b. commemorating the great events of Huguenot history; c. collecting and preserving historical data and relics illustrative of Huguenot life, manners, and customs; 2. To give expression to the Huguenot tenets of faith and liberty, and to promote their understanding for the good of the United States; 3. To encourage and foster the organization of new member Societies within states, territories of the United States, and the District of Columbia where none currently exist.

- Netherlands / Nederland
  http://www.CyndisList.com/nether.htm
  See this category on Cyndi's List for more links.

- South Africa / Suid-Afrika
  http://www.CyndisList.com/soafrica.htm
  See this category on Cyndi's List for more links.

- The Wars of Religion
  http://world.std.com/~cti/wars.htm

- Who were the Huguenots?
  http://www.geocities.com/Heartland/Valley/8140/hist-hug.htm

- Willow Bend Books—Huguenot Genealogy
  http://www.willowbend.net/hugu.htm

◆ Huguenot Family Sites

- BOESHORE (BESHORE) Family History
  http://www.enerspace.com/beshore.htm

- The DEYO Family in America
  http://www.deyo.org/deyo.htm

- The DuPREE Family Research Page
  http://members.aol.com/Borgite/dupre.html
  Decandants of Josias DuPre' and Mynota.

- DuVAL Family Association
  http://www.geocities.com/Heartland/Ridge/7508/
  Descendants of Daniel DuVal and his wife Philadelphia DuBois who were French Huguenots.

- The FUQUA Family Foundation
  http://www.concentric.net/~fuqua/
  Guillaume Fouquet, b. 1667, came to Virginia from France.

- Genealogy Resources: Steps in Time
  http://www.geocities.com/Heartland/Meadows/4399/
  VILLEPONTEAUX

- The GOURDIN / GOURDINE Family Home Page
  http://members.aol.com/gourdinr/index.htm
  A French-African-American Family from South Carolina.

- HEWLETT BEUZEVILLE ROUSSEL Family Home Page
  http://www.home.aone.net.au/mclark/

- Huguenot Ancestry
  http://www.uftree.com/UFT/WebPages/huguenot/default/index.htm
  BILLIOU, DU BOIS, LARZALERE, RAMBOUT

- The Huguenot Families UZIELE and CASIER
  http://www.rootsweb.com/~ote/casuz.htm

- The Huguenots
  http://www.freeyellow.com/members5/huguenot/
  Huguenots in Denmark. Descendants of Pierre DEVANTIER born 1637 in France.

- LaRUE & Allied Families
  http://web.nstar.net/~dwat6911/myheart.htm

- Life's Short; Plunge In.
  http://members.aol.com/Nlalabungu/index.html
  BURN, WILMOT, DUPREE, VENZKE

- MARTIN Family: the Huguenot Emigrant Generation
  http://www.vcu.edu/engweb/home/huguenot.html

- Pierre CHASTAIN Family Association
  http://www.kopower.com/~jimchstn/

- VALLEAU Family Association
  http://www.geocities.com/Heartland/Prairie/1181/

- VILJOEN Family Homepage
  http://www.geocities.com/Heartland/Acres/4040/index.html
  Villion, Campenaar

HUMOR & PROSE
http://www.CyndisList.com/humor.htm

- **Alien Spaceship Theory of Genealogy**
  http://www.gendex.com/users/clbates/lovitt/spaceship2.html

- **Are You a Genealogist?**
  ftp://ftp.rootsweb.com/pub/roots-l/genealog/genealog.gposter
  An ASCII art poster.

- **Are you a Genealogist?**
  http://www.geocities.com/Heartland/Plains/3634/
  Genealogist.htm

- **Carl Barks's Duck Family Tree**
  http://www.update.uu.se/~starback/disney-comics/chars/
  cb-tree.html
  Donald Duck's pedigree!

- **Carol's Genealogy Taglines**
  http://www.rootsweb.com/~genepool/taglines.htm

- **Chester County Chuckles**
  http://www.rootsweb.com/~pacheste/chester.htm
  *Located on the Chester County page of the Pennsylvania
  GenWeb project.*

- **Christmas Humor**
  http://www.wizard.com/~bascs/chhumor.htm

- **David's Genealogy Taglines**
  http://www.agate.net/~davids/_genea/taglines.htm

- **A "Dear Abby" Entry on Genealogy**
  http://comedy.clari.net/rhf/jokes/90q1/12.html

- **The Elusive Ancestor by Merrell Kenworthy**
  http://www.angelfire.com/fl/Sumter/elusive.html

- **Genealogical Taglines for Your Use**
  http://www.wizard.com/~bascs/taglines.htm

- **GenealogyBookShop.com—Humor**
  http://www.genealogybookshop.com/genealogybookshop/files/
  General,Humor/index.html
  *The online store of Genealogical Publishing Co., Inc. &
  Clearfield Company.*

- **Genealogy Epitaphs, Quotes, Poems**
  http://www.netins.net/showcase/kadinger/anthology.htm

- **Genealogy Humor**
  http://www.idcomm.com/personal/bbunce/humor.htm

- **Genealogy Humor**
  http://www.chrysalis.org/sanford/cgn/humor.htm

- **Genealogy Humor???**
  http://toadstool.2u.to/gabriele/humor.html

- **Genealogy Is...**
  http://main.nc.us/OBCGS/geneis.html

- **Genealogy Laughs Page**
  http://www.rootsweb.com/~txcass/laughs/laughs.htm

- **Genealogy Poem by Sandy Coleman**
  http://www.geocities.com/Athens/Forum/1996/POEM.HTM

- **Genealogy Poetry and Prose**
  http://www.seidata.com/~lhoffman/poems.html

- **Genealogy Songs & Movies**
  http://www.geocities.com/Heartland/Plains/7038/Songs.html

- **Geneverse—A Collection Of Original Verse By
  Genealogists Inspired By Genealogy**
  http://www.geocities.com/Athens/1491/

- **Geneitis: The Genealogist's Disease**
  http://www.GeoCities.com/Heartland/Plains/5137/geneitis.htm

- **GenHumor Mailing List**
  http://members.aol.com/johnf14246/
  gen_mail_general.html#GenHumor
  *For the exchange of genealogy amd family humor including
  poems and jokes.*

- **A Glow in the Forest**
  http://www.netins.net/showcase/pafways/glow.htm?
  A collection of taglines from Pafways in Iowa.

- **Grandma Climbed The Family Tree**
  http://www.ledet.com/genealogy/misc/grandmatree.html

- **Humor**
  http://ram.ramlink.net/~cbarker/humor.htm

- **Humorous Reading**
  http://www.wizard.com/~bascs/humor.htm
  Some computer humor as well as genealogical humor here.

- **"If . . ."—A Poem for Genealogists**
  http://www.geocities.com/Heartland/Plains/5137/ifgene.htm

- **The Inevitable Laws of Genealogy**
  http://www.micronet.net/users/~searcy/laws.htm

- **JEFFCO Genealogy Stories—Humorous**
  http://www.ticnet.com/jeffco/stories.html

- **Kentuckiana Genealogy—Humor**
  http://www.floyd-pavey.com/kentuckiana/kyiana/humor.html

- **Laws of Genealogy**
  ftp://ftp.rootsweb.com/pub/roots-l/genealog/
  genealog.genelaws

- **Limericks of the Month**
  http://www.chrysalis.org/sanford/cgn/limerick.htm

- **Mary Daily's Genealogy—Poem**
  http://www.geocities.com/Heartland/Meadows/1096/poem.html

- **One Liners**
  http://main.nc.us/OBCGS/oneliners.htm

- Our Ancestors Poem
  http://www.geocities.com/Heartland/Meadows/8965/ancestors.html

- The Outhouse—Genealogy Humor
  http://members.aol.com/RootsLady/lady/outhouse.htm

- Twas The Day Before Yesterday
  http://pw1.netcom.com/~eapii/genealogy/stuff.html#p3
  by Linnie Vanderford Poyneer.

- Ye Olde English Sayings
  http://www.rootsweb.com/~genepool/sayings.htm

- You Know You're An Addicted Genealogist. . .
  http://www.micronet.net/users/~searcy/addicted.htm

ITALY / ITALIA
http://www.CyndisList.com/italy.htm

Category Index:

- General Resource Sites
- History & Culture
- How To
- Mailing Lists, Newsgroups & Chat
- Maps, Gazetteers & Geographical Information
- People & Families

- Professional Researchers, Volunteers & Other Research Services
- Publications, Software & Supplies
- Queries, Message Boards & Surname Lists
- Societies & Groups

◆ General Resource Sites

- Arduini & Pizzo—An Italian Genealogy
  http://homepage.interaccess.com/~arduinif/
  Many resources for Italian genealogical research.

- Cimorelli Enterprises HomePage
  http://www.cimorelli.com/

- The Italian Genealogy Home Page
  http://www.italgen.com/

- Italian Genealogy? Start Here!
  http://www.daddezio.com/index.html
  The D'ADDEZIO surname, articles and other helpful tools for Italian research.

- The Italo-Albanian Heritage Pages
  http://members.aol.com/itaalb1/web/arberesh.htm

- Joe's Italian Genealogy Page
  http://www.phoenix.net/~joe/

- Lou ALFANO's GeoCities Web Site
  http://www.geocities.com/Athens/Acropolis/1709/index.html
  Dedicated to Italian Genealogy, History & Culture.

- Nostro Albero
  http://www.geocities.com/SiliconValley/Park/3063/nostrow.htm
  With a searchable database of 5,300 Italian surnames.

- PIE Homepage
  http://www.cimorelli.com/pie/piesani.htm

- Radici—The Italian Genealogy Webclub
  http://www.initaly.com/gene/
  Lets you build your own Online Family Bible, share the results of your research and network with other Italian descendants all over the world.

- Yahoo!...Italy...Genealogy
  http://dir.yahoo.com/Regional/Countries/Italy/
  Arts_and_Humanities/Humanities/History/Genealogy/

◆ History & Culture

- Torrione Castle—an unusual example of a Museum for History
  http://www.gvo.it/VdSF/torrione1.html
  From Italy. Be sure to check out their Vialardi di Sandigliano lineage library.

- The Trentino Site—Genealogy, Culture, History
  http://members.aol.com/sromano937/index.htm
  A Little About the Province of Trento, especially Val di Non.

◆ How To

- How to Research your Italian Ancestry?
  http://members.aol.com/geneaita/indexen.html

- Italian Genealogy How-To Guide
  http://www.familytreemaker.com/00000375.html

◆ Mailing Lists, Newsgroups & Chat

- Genealogy Resources on the Internet— Italy Mailing Lists
  http://members.aol.com/gfsjohnf/gen_mail_country-ita.html
  Each of the mailing list links below points to this site, wonderfully maintained by John Fuller.

- ARIA Mailing List
  http://members.aol.com/gfsjohnf/gen_mail_country-ita.html#ARIA-L
  For Australians and New Zealanders who are researching their Italian Heritage, Culture and Ancestry.

- CALITRI Mailing List
  http://members.aol.com/gfsjohnf/gen_mail_country-ita.html#CALITRI
  A mailing list for those who are interested in their Calitrani (people from Calitri, Italy) heritage. Towns of interest include Calitri, Andretta, Bisaccia, Pescopagano, Ruvo, Santangelo Lombardi, and other surrounding towns.

- COMUNES_OF_ITALY Mailing List
  http://members.aol.com/gfsjohnf/gen_mail_country-ita.html#COMUNES_OF_ITALY
  For those who are interested in Italian genealogy, culture and all things Italian.

- GEN-ITALIAN Mailing List
  http://members.aol.com/gfsjohnf/gen_mail_country-ita.html#GEN-ITALIAN
  Gatewayed with the soc.genealogy.italian newsgroup.

- ICC—The Il Circolo Calabrese Mailing List
  http://members.aol.com/gfsjohnf/gen_mail_country-ita.html#ICC
  For anyone with a genealogical interest in the Calabria region of Italy (the southernmost region of the Italian peninsula, the 'toe' of the boot).

- italy-gene Mailing List
  http://members.aol.com/gfsjohnf/gen_mail_country-ita.html#italy-gene

- PIE Mailing List
  http://members.aol.com/gfsjohnf/gen_mail_country-ita.html#PIE
  For Italian genealogical research.

- SARDINIA Mailing List
  http://members.aol.com/gfsjohnf/gen_mail_country-sar.html#SARDINIA

◆ Maps, Gazetteers & Geographical Information

- Map of Italy
  http://www.lib.utexas.edu/Libs/PCL/Map_collection/europe/Italy.jpg
  From the Perry-Castañeda Library at the Univ. of Texas at Austin.

- Map of San Marino
  http://www.lib.utexas.edu/Libs/PCL/Map_collection/europe/SanMarino.jpg
  From the Perry-Castañeda Library at the Univ. of Texas at Austin.

- Map of Vatican City
  http://www.lib.utexas.edu/Libs/PCL/Map_collection/europe/Vaticancity.jpg
  From the Perry-Castañeda Library at the Univ. of Texas at Austin.

◆ People & Families

- Angelo GRIFASI ~ Milan
  http://joshua.micronet.it/utenti/mgrifasi/home.html
  Sicily, Pics, Sicilian Cooking, Names curiosities, Palermo, Milano, Ravanusa.

- FISCHETTI / SORVILLO Family Genealogy
  http://members.aol.com/rich353/index.htm
  FISCHETTI, DIGIUSEPPE, BORGIA, SORVILLO, GRAZIANO, VISCARDO, COPPOLA, GRILLO, OLIVERI

- Giorgio ALESSANDRI's Home Page
  http://www.agora.stm.it/G.Alessandri/home.htm
  Including a case study on a recent genealogical research project and an article on church records over time.

- An Italian Family Homepage
  http://users.ox.ac.uk/~bras0599/
  FILIPPELLI, BARBUTO, BONACCI, SCALZO, LIA

- Joseph and Joyce ANELLO
  http://www.geocities.com/Heartland/Plains/6917/
  The ANELLO, PUSATERI, LETO and VENTURA families from Caccamo and Termini, Sicily.

- Our Calabrian Heritage
  http://members.aol.com/GLilli/index.html
  A study of the Village of Oriolo, Cosenza, in the Italian Region of Calabria, its History, People and Culture.

- Siciliani in the World
  http://diemme.diemme.it/italiani/sicilia/
  E-mail addresses for people researching Sicilian surnames.

- Spence Sacco BURTON's Homepage
  http://members.home.net/sfburton
  SACCO, SANTANGELO, INDELICATO, DILORENZO, (DI) SILVESTRO, TODARO, GAIMO, BURTON, SPENCE. Sicilian genealogy, culture etc. Italian language pages available.

- The Vasto Page—La Pagina Vastese
  http://www.geocities.com/Athens/Acropolis/1709/VastoPag.htm
  Comune of Vasto, Province of Chieti, Region of Abruzzo.

◆ Professional Researchers, Volunteers & Other Research Services

- Emilio—Escort of SICILY
  http://www.mediatel.it/public/emilio/
  Professional Italian researcher and tour guide.

- Family Tree Genealogical and Probate Research Bureau Ltd.
  http://www.hungary.net/familytree/
  Professional research service covering the area of what was formerly the Austro-Hungarian Empire, including: Hungary, Slovakia, Czech Republic, Austria, Italy, Transylvania, Croatia, Slovenia, former Yugoslavia (Banat), and the Ukraine (Sub-Carpathian).

- Genealogy Helplist—Italy
  http://posom.com/hl/ita/index.shtml

- genealogyPro—Professional Genealogists for Italy
  http://genealogyPro.com/directories/Italy.html

- New Jersey and Italian Genealogical Research Services
  http://www.italgen.com/sponsors/piccirillo/index.htm

- Sicilian Research
  http://www.inconnect.com/~gjnixon/ki00011.htm

◆ Publications, Software & Supplies

- Ancestor's Attic Discount Genealogy Books—
  Italian Genealogy Books
  http://members.tripod.com/~ancestorsattic/index.html#secIT

- Frontier Press Bookstore—Italy
  http://www.frontierpress.com/frontier.cgi?category=ital

- A Genealogist's Guide to Discovering Your
  Italian Ancestors
  http://www.erols.com/lynnn/dyia/main.html
  A book for sale, with excerpts and its table of contents online.

- GenealogyBookShop.com—Italy/Italian
  http://www.genealogybookshop.com/genealogybookshop/files/
  The_World,Italy_Italian/index.html
  *The online store of Genealogical Publishing Co., Inc. &
  Clearfield Company.*

◆ Queries, Message Boards & Surname Lists

- Lineages' Free On-line Queries—Italy
  http://www.lineages.com/queries/BrowseByCountry.asp

◆ Societies & Groups

- The Buffalo & Western New York Italian
  Genealogy Society
  http://freenet.buffalo.edu/~roots/bawnigs.htm

- Il Circolo Calabrese
  http://www.girimonti.com/icc/

- Il Circolo Filippo Mazzei—The Washington D.C.
  Metropolitan Area Italian Genealogical Society
  http://www.geocities.com/Athens/Acropolis/1709/Mazzei.htm

- Italian Genealogical Society of America
  http://users.loa.com/~del2jdcd/igsa.html
  Cranston, Rhode Island

- The Italian Genealogical Group
  http://www.italiangen.org/

JEWISH
http://www.CyndisList.com/jewish.htm

Category Index:

◆ General Resource Sites
◆ Libraries, Archives & Museums
◆ Locality Specific
◆ Mailing Lists, Newsgroups & Chat
◆ People & Families

◆ Professional Researchers, Volunteers &
   Other Research Services
◆ Publications, Software & Supplies
◆ Records: Census, Cemeteries, Land, Obituaries,
   Personal, Taxes and Vital
◆ Societies & Groups

◆ General Resource Sites

● Avotaynu, Inc. Home Page
  http://www.avotaynu.com/
  Products and information for Jewish genealogy.

● Calendar Conversions
  http://www.genealogy.org/~scottlee/calconvert.cgi
  Scott Lee's free on-line service for converting to/from dates in Gregorian, Julian, French republican and Jewish calendars.

● Cross-Index to HomePages of Jewish Genealogy— from FEEFHS
  http://feefhs.org/indexjew.html

● Jamaican Jewish Genealogy
  http://www6.pair.com/silvera/jamgen/index.html

● Jewish Family & Life: Jewish Genealogy on the Web
  http://www.jewishfamily.com/Features/996/genealogy.htm
  An article by Yaffa Klugerman.

● JewishGen Family Finder (JGFF)—ONLINE
  http://www.jewishgen.org/jgff/

● JewishGen FAQ—Frequently Asked Questions
  http://www.jewishgen.org/infofiles/faq.html

● JewishGen: The Official Home of Jewish Genealogy
  http://www.jewishgen.org/

● Jewish Records Indexing—Poland
  http://www.jewishgen.org/reipp/

● Jewish Roots Ring
  http://pw1.netcom.com/~barrison/jewgenwebring.html
  A web ring for Jewish genealogy sites.

● JGL: Jewish Genealogy Links
  http://jewish.genealogy.org
  A list of several hundred Jewish Genealogy Links, cross-indexed by subject.

● JGSR Jewish Genealogy Page
  http://jgsr.hq.net/jgsr/

● Sephardic Genealogy Sources
  http://www.orthohelp.com/geneal/sefardim.htm

◆ Libraries, Archives & Museums

● The Balch Institute for Ethnic Studies
  http://www.libertynet.org/~balch/
  Home of the Philadelphia Jewish Archives Center.

● Beth Hatefutsoth Museum of the Jewish People
  http://www.bh.org.il/
  The Nahum Goldmann Museum of the Jewish Diaspora.

  ○ Beth Hatefutsoth Family Names Database
    http://www.bh.org.il/Names/index.htm

  ○ The Douglas E. Goldman Jewish Genealogy Center
    http://www.bh.org.il/Geneology/index.htm

● United States Holocaust Memorial Museum
  http://www.ushmm.org/

◆ Locality Specific

● An Introduction to Jewish Genealogy in Manitoba
  http://www.concentric.net/~Lkessler/genbegin.shtml

● The Jewish Genealogical Exploration Guide for Manitoba and Saskatchewan (J-GEMS)
  http://www.concentric.net/~Lkessler/jgems.shtml

● Jewish Genealogy in Australia
  http://www.zeta.org.au/~feraltek/genealogy/index.html

● Jewish Genealogy in South Africa: Getting Started
  http://www.jewishgen.org/mentprog/m_rsa.htm

● Jewish Records Indexing—Poland
  http://www.jewishgen.org/JRI-PL/

● Jewish Roots in Romania—Radacini Evreiesti in Romania
  http://www.accordnet.com/jewish-dorohoi

- Researching Jewish Genealogies in South Africa—
Part A
http://www.jewishgen.org/infofiles/za-infoa.txt
- Researching Jewish Genealogies in South Africa—
Part B
http://www.jewishgen.org/infofiles/za-infob.txt

◆ Mailing Lists, Newsgroups & Chat

- BERDICHEV Mailing List
http://members.aol.com/gfsjohnf/gen_mail_country-rus.html#BERDICHEV
For anyone with a genealogical interest in Berdichev, Ukraine, Russia with a focus on Jewish genealogy.
- EURO-JEWISH Mailing List
http://members.aol.com/johnf14246/gen_mail_general.html#EURO-JEWISH
For anyone with a genealogical interest in the Migration, History, Culture, Heritage and Surname search of the Jewish people from Europe to the United States and their descendants in the United States.
- IsraelGenWeb Mailing List
http://members.aol.com/gfsjohnf/gen_mail_country-isr.html#IsraelGenWeb
- JEWISHGEN Mailing List
http://members.aol.com/johnf14246/gen_mail_general.html#JEWISHGEN
Gatewayed with the soc.genealogy.jewish newsgroup.
- Jewish Museum of Belgium
http://members.aol.com/johnf14246/gen_mail_general.html#JEWBEL
For anyone who is interested in Jewish genealogy; in Belgian or English.
- KULANU-L Mailing List
http://members.aol.com/johnf14246/gen_mail_general.html#KULANU-L
Kulanu ("all of us") is an organization of individuals of varied backgrounds and practices dedicated to finding lost and dispersed remnants of the Jewish people.
- Turkish_Jews Mailing List
http://members.aol.com/gfsjohnf/gen_mail_country-ser.html#Turkish_Jews
For Shephardic Jewish genealogists with roots in the former Turkish Ottoman Empire including Turkey, Serbia, Greece, and Yugoslavia.
- Usenet Newsgroup soc.genealogy.jewish

◆ People & Families

- GROSS-STEINBERG Family Tree
http://www.geocities.com/Heartland/6721/
Surnames from Austria, Lithuania, and Poland.
- LOEB Family Tree
http://www.labri.u-bordeaux.fr/Equipe/CombAlg/membre/loeb/tree/index.html
French and Jewish research.

◆ Professional Researchers, Volunteers & Other Research Services

- genealogyPro—Professional Researchers Specializing in Jewish Genealogy
http://genealogyPro.com/directories/Jewish.html
- Routes to Roots
http://www.routestoroots.com/
Tracing Jewish Roots in Poland, Ukraine, Moldova and Belarus.

◆ Publications, Software & Supplies

- Ancestor's Attic Discount Genealogy Books—Jewish Genealogy Books
http://members.tripod.com/~ancestorsattic/index.html#secJW
- Avotaynu, Inc. Home Page
http://www.avotaynu.com/
Products and information for Jewish genealogy.
- Frontier Press Bookstore—Jewish Research
http://www.frontierpress.com/frontier.cgi?category=jewish
- Heritage Books—Jewish
http://www.heritagebooks.com/jewish.htm
- ILANOT—Software for Jewish Genealogy
http://www.bh.org.il/Geneology/index.htm#ilanot
- Jewish Roots in Poland—Pages from the Past and Archival Inventories
http://www.rtrfoundation.org/
A new book by Miriam Weiner.
- STAMMBAUM: The Journal of German-Jewish Genealogical Research
http://www.jewishgen.org/stammbaum/
- Willow Bend Bookstore—Jewish Genealogy
http://www.willowbend.net/jewish.htm

◆ Records: Census, Cemeteries, Land, Obituaries, Personal, Taxes and Vital (Born, Married, Died & Buried)

- Commission for the Preservation of Pioneer Jewish Cemeteries and Landmarks
http://www.jfed.org/mcemcom.htm
Northern California
- Index to: Religious Personnel in Russia 1853–1854
http://www.memo.com/jgsr/database/deych.cgi
- International Jewish Cemetery Project
http://www.jewishgen.org/cemetery/index.htm
- JewishGen Hotline: Jewish Cemeteries in New York City
http://www.jewishgen.org/mentprog/m_nycem.htm

- London Jews Database
  http://www.jewishgen.org/databases/londweb.htm

◆ Societies & Groups

- American Jewish Historical Society
  http://www.ajhs.org/
  Waltham, Massachusetts

- Asociación de Genealogía Judía de Argentina
  http://www.marben.com.ar/toldot
  Página Oficial de la Asociacion de Genealogia Judia de Argentina. Jewish Genealogical Society of Argentina (Official Site).

- Association of Jewish Genealogical Societies (AJGS)
  http://www.jewishgen.org/ajgs/index.html

- Australian Jewish Genealogical Society
  http://www.zeta.org.au/~feraltek/genealogy/ajgs/index.html

- Dallas Jewish Historical Society ~ Texas
  http://www.dvjc.org/history/

- Dallas Virtual Jewish Community—Jewish Genealogy Home Page
  http://www.dvjc.org/history/genealogy.shtml

- GenDex = / Groups and Societies
  http://www.netins.net/showcase/pafways/groups.htm#GROUPS

- The Genealogical Institute of the Jewish Historical Society of Western Canada
  http://www.concentric.net/~lkessler/geninst.shtml
  Winnipeg, Manitoba, Canada

- The Israel Genealogical Society
  http://www.navitek.com/igs/

- Jewish Genealogical Society, Los Angeles (JGSLA)
  http://www.jewishgen.org/jgsla/

- Jewish Genealogical Society of Argentina
  http://www.jewishgen.org/infofiles/ar-jgs.txt

- Jewish Genealogical Society of Brazil / Sociedade Genealógica Judaica do Brasil
  http://www.lookup.com/homepages/82259/sgjbing.htm

- Jewish Genealogical Society of Great Britain
  http://www.ort.org/jgsgb/index.htm

- Jewish Genealogical Society of Greater Boston
  http://www.jewishgen.org/boston/jgsgb.html

- Jewish Genealogical Society of Philadelphia
  http://www.jewishgen.org/jgsp/

- Jewish Genealogical Society of Rochester ~ New York
  http://hq.net/jgsr/

- Jewish Genealogical Society of Sacramento ~ California
  http://www1.jewishgen.org/ajgs/jgs-sacramento/

- Jewish Genealogical Society of St. Louis
  http://www.stlcyberjew.com/jgs-stl/

- Jewish Genealogical Society of St. Louis, Computer SIG
  http://www.stlcyberjew.com/jgs-stl/SIGhome.htm

- The Jewish Genealogy Society of Greater Washington, D.C.
  http://www.jewishgen.org/jgsgw/

- Jewish Genealogical Society of Philadelphia
  http://www.jewishgen.org/jgsp/

- The Jewish Genealogy Society of Long Island ~ New York
  http://www.jewishgen.org/jgsli

- The Jewish Historical Society of Central Jersey
  http://www.jewishgen.org/jhscj/

- Jewish Historical Society of Maryland
  http://www.jhsm.org/

- Jewish Historical Society of South Carolina
  http://www.scsn.net/users/efolley/jhssc/jhssc_home.html

- Nederlandse Kring voor Joodse Genealogie / Netherlands Society for Jewish Genealogy
  http://www.nljewgen.org/

- San Francisco Bay Area Jewish Genealogical Society (SFBA JGS)
  http://www.jewishgen.org/sfbajgs/

KIDS & TEENS
http://www.CyndisList.com/kids.htm

- Ancestors Teacher's Guide
  http://www.pbs.org/kbyu/ancestors/teachersguide/
  From the television program on PBS, a teacher's guide for starting a family history project.

- AskERIC InfoGuide—Family History for Middle Schools
  http://ericir.syr.edu/plweb-cgi/fastweb?getdoc+infoguides+
  infoguides+730+0+wAAA+family%26history

- BRAE'S Genealogy for Kids
  http://members.aol.com/braehenry/kids.html

- Family: A Mini-Unit for Teaching Students More About Family
  http://teacherlink.ed.usu.edu/resources/ed_lesson_plans/
  socst/CKHOOSTE/%7F%7F%7FFAMILY2.HTM

- Frontier Press Bookstore—Children's Guides to Research
  http://www.frontierpress.com/frontier.cgi?category=children

- Genealogy: A Great Way To Teach Just About Any Subject
  http://ole.net/ole/1996/may/NetLesso/gene/gene.html

- Genealogy Books for Kids & Teaching
  http://member.aol.com/TMCorner/book_kid.htm

- Genealogy for Children
  http://home.iSTAR.ca/~ljbritt/

- Genealogy for Kids Room
  http://www.geocities.com/EnchantedForest/5283/genekids.htm

- Genealogy Instruction Beginners, Teenagers, and Kids
  http://home.earthlink.net/~howardorjeff/instruct.htm

- Genealogy Merit Badge
  http://usscouts.org/mb/mb056.html
  Criteria from the Boy Scouts of America.

- The Genealogy Merit Badge of the Boy Scouts of America
  http://www.oz.net/~markhow/BSA/meritbdg.htm

- Genealogy—Part of the History/Social Studies Web Site for K–12 Teachers
  http://www.execpc.com/~dboals/geneo.html

- Genealogy Unit Lesson
  http://www.geocities.com/Heartland/Plains/3729/LESSON.HTM

- Genealogy WebQuest
  http://www.ultranet.com/~olmckey/quest.htm

- GEN-NEWBIE-L Mailing List
  http://members.aol.com/johnf14246/
  gen_mail_general.html#GEN-NEWBIE-L
  A mailing list where people who are new to computers and genealogy may interact using a computer's e-mail program.

- GENTEEN-L Mailing List
  http://members.aol.com/johnf14246/
  gen_mail_general.html#GENTEEN-L
  For teenagers and young adults who are interested in genealogical research or others who have suggestions or ideas for young genealogists.

- KIDPROJ Family History Projects 1997
  http://www.kidlink.org/KIDPROJ/FamHistory/links.html

- MOMS_N_ME-ROOTS Mailing List
  http://members.aol.com/johnf14246/
  gen_mail_general.html#MOMS_N_ME-ROOTS
  To aid moms of all ages, but especially those with young children, in researching their family. Also welcome are any ideas for helping mothers teach their children about their heritage and the importance of family research.

- National Genealogical Society—Youth Resources Committee
  http://www.genealogy.org/~ngs/fhesshp.html

- Not Merely Ancestors: A Guide for Teaching Genealogy in the Schools
  http://www.genealogybookshop.com/genealogybookshop/files/
  General,Guides_and_Manuals/9119.html
  A book for sale from GenealogyBookShop.com

- Outline of Lesson Plans
  http://nisus.sfusd.k12.ca.us/schwww/sch634/
  Outlinelessons.html
  From the Spanish Family History Project, James Lick Middle School.

- Roots for Kids: A Genealogy Guide for Young People
  http://www.genealogybookshop.com/genealogybookshop/files/
  General,Guides_and_Manuals/422.html
  A book for sale from GenealogyBookShop.com

- Storbeck's Genealogy Books for Kids
  http://www.storbecks.com/kids.htm

- A Student's Guide to...
  http://www.oryxpress.com/subjidx.htm
  African American Genealogy, British American, German American, Chinese American, Irish American, Japanese American, Italian American, Jewish American, Native American, Mexican American, Polish American, Scandinavian American.

- Teaching History Through Genealogy
  http://members.aol.com/ranenb/index.htm
  Free online class for ages 8–14 and parent.

- USGenWeb Kidz Project
  http://www.rootsweb.com/~usgwkidz/

- WorldGenWeb For Kids
  http://www.rootsweb.com/~wgwkids/

LAND RECORDS, DEEDS, HOMESTEADS, ETC.

http://www.CyndisList.com/land.htm

- **Analyzing Deeds for Useful Clues**
  http://www.genealogy.org/~bcg/skbld951.html
  From the Board for Certification of Genealogists—Skill Building—January 1995.

- **Ancestry.com—Land Entry Files—NATF Form 84**
  http://www.ancestry.com/research/land84.htm

- **Arkansas Land Records—Interactive Search**
  http://searches.rootsweb.com/cgi-bin/arkland/arkland.pl

- **The Bureau of Land Management—Eastern States, General Land Office**
  http://www.glorecords.blm.gov/
  The Official Land Patent Records Site. This site has a searchable database of over two million pre-1908 Federal land title records, including scanned images of those records. The Eastern Public Land States covered in this database are: Alabama, Arkansas, Florida, Illinois, Indiana, Louisiana, Michigan, Minnesota, Mississippi, Missouri, Ohio, Wisconsin.

  ○ **Early Land Laws**
    http://www.glorecords.blm.gov/landlaws.htm

    • **Cash Entry Act**
      http://www.glorecords.blm.gov/cash.htm
      Sixteenth Congress. Sess. I. Ch. 51 1820.

    • **Homestead Act**
      http://www.glorecords.blm.gov/homestead.htm
      Thirty-Seventh Congress. Sess. II. Ch. 75. 1862.

    • **Military Survey and United Brethren Act**
      http://www.glorecords.blm.gov/military.htm
      Approved, June 1, 1796.

  ○ **The Electronic Reading Room**
    http://www.blm.gov/nhp/efoia/
    Bureau of Land Management Headquarters Office and Field Facilities.

  ○ **Land Descriptions**
    http://www.glorecords.blm.gov/land_desc.htm

- **The Bureau of Land Management—Idaho**
  http://www.id.blm.gov/

- **Computer Programs for Drawing Plat Maps**
  http://www.outfitters.com/genealogy/land/compmaps.html

- **Deed Data Pool**
  http://www.ultranet.com/~deeds/pool.htm
  Downloadable deed files for Kentucky, New York, Pennsylvania, Virginia & West Virginia.

- **Deeds, Homestead Records and Store Accounts in Georgia**
  http://www.rootsweb.com/~gagenweb/records/dhrsa.htm

- **Early Land Entries—Orange County, Indiana**
  http://www.rootsweb.com/~inorange/preland.htm

- **An Essay on Land Records, Their History and Use in Genealogy Research**
  http://homepages.rootsweb.com/~haas/

- **The Essex County Registry of Deeds**
  http://207.244.88.10/
  Salem, Massachussetts

- **Federal Land Records for Arkansas**
  http://www.rootsweb.com/~usgenweb/ar/fedland.htm

- **Federal Tract Books of Oklahoma Territory**
  http://www.sirinet.net/~lgarris/swogs/tract.html

- **Frederick Co., Maryland Descents—Court Records from 1794–1837**
  http://members.aol.com/DorindaMD/descents.html

- **Frontier Press Bookstore—Land in America**
  http://www.frontierpress.com/frontier.cgi?category=land

- **Genealogical Riches In The American State Papers**
  http://www.lineages.com/rooms/reading/statepapers.asp

- **Genealogical Riches In The American State Papers**
  http://home.rmci.net/dyingst/papers.HTM

- **GenealogyBookShop.com—Land Records**
  http://www.genealogybookshop.com/genealogybookshop/files/General,Land_Records/index.html
  The online store of Genealogical Publishing Co., Inc. & Clearfield Company.

- **General Land Office Records CD-ROMs For Sale**
  http://www.access.gpo.gov/su_docs/sale/sale334.html

- **Graphical Display of the Federal Township and Range System ~ U.S.**
  http://www.outfitters.com/genealogy/land/twprangemap.html
  Explains the division of townships and sections.

- **History & Use of Land Records**
  http://main.nc.us/OBCGS/searchland-rec.htm
  By Linda Haas Davenport.

- **HM Land Registry Home Page**
  http://www.open.gov.uk/landreg/home.htm
  United Kingdom

- **The Homestead Act of 1862**
  http://www.apics253.com/~deeds/homestead.htm
  By Richard Pence.

- **The Homestead Act May 20, 1862**
  http://www.pbs.org/weta/thewest/wpages/wpgs650/homestd.htm

- **Homesteaders Left Marks on Land and Paper**
  http://www.ancestry.com/columns/myra/Shaking_Family_Tree07-24-97.htm
  From Shaking Your Family Tree by Myra Vanderpool Gormley, C.G.

- Homesteading Records—Tracking Your Ancestors in South Dakota
  http://members.aol.com/gkrell/homestead/home.html

- Homestead papers copied by Faith Libelo
  E-mail: fsl.genie.research@erols.com
  She can visit the National Archives for you and copy the files. E-mail Faith at fsl.genie.research@erols.com for details.

- Illinois Public Domain Land Sales (19th Century)
  http://www.sos.state.il.us:80/depts/archives/data_lan.html

- An Introduction to the History of Tennessee's Confusing Land Laws
  http://web.utk.edu/~kizzer/genehist/research/landlaws.htm
  By Billie R. McNamara

- Indiana Land Records Search by CompuGen Systems
  http://members.aol.com/CGSystems/LRSearch.html

- INGALLS Homestead File
  http://www.nara.gov/nara/EXTRA/ingalls.html
  Scanned images of 24 original documents pertaining to the DeSmet, South Dakota homestead of the family of Laura Ingalls Wilder. A terrific example from the National Archives and Records Administration.

- Kansas Land Records
  http://pixel.cs.vt.edu/library/land/kansas/

- Land Office Patents and Grants Collection Index
  http://image.vtls.com/collections/LO.html
  Electronic Card Indexes, Digital Collections Home Page, The Library of Virginia.

- Land Office Records at the Indiana State Archives
  http://www.state.in.us/icpr/webfile/land/land_off.html
  - Fort Wayne, Indiana Land Office Database Search Page
    http://www.state.in.us/icpr/webfile/land/srch_fw.html
  - The Indianapolis Donation
    http://www.state.in.us/icpr/webfile/donation/donindex.html
  - Laporte/Winamac, Indiana Land Office Database Search Page
    http://www.state.in.us/icpr/webfile/land/search.html

- Land Ownership Maps in the Library of Congress
  http://www.kinquest.com/genealogy/lom.html
  A list by state, county and year, of the maps available in the collection held at the Library of Congress.

- Land Record Reference
  http://www.ultranet.com/~deeds/landref.htm

- Land Record Research Directory
  http://www.ultranet.com/~deeds/research.htm
  List of other researchers and the areas in which they are researching.

- Land Records—Becker County, Minnesota GenWeb
  http://www.rootsweb.com/~mnbecker/land.htm

- Land Records for Ireland
  http://www.bess.tcd.ie/irlgen/landrec.htm

- Land Records in Ontario
  http://wwnet.com/~treesrch/ontland.html

- Legal Land Descriptions in the USA
  http://www.outfitters.com/genealogy/land/land.html
  - Legal Land Descriptions in Federal Township and Range System
    http://www.outfitters.com/genealogy/land/twprange.html
  - Legal Land Descriptions in Indiscriminate Metes and Bounds
    http://www.outfitters.com/genealogy/land/metesbounds.html

- Louisiana Land Records—Interactive Search
  http://searches.rootsweb.com/cgi-bin/laland/laland.pl
  Pre-1908 Homestead and Cash Entry Patents from the Bureau of Land Management's General Land Office (GLO) Automated Records Project.

- Massachusetts Registries of Deeds
  http://www.browntech.com/ma_cnty.html
  Click on map to obtain address and homepage for Registry of Deeds for your county.

- Milestone Historic Documents— The Northwest Ordinance
  http://earlyamerica.com/earlyamerica/milestones/ordinance/index.html
  An Ordinance for the Government of the Territory of the United States, North-West of the River Ohio. As it appears in the Supplement to the First Volume of the Columbian Magazine, Philadelphia, 1787. Explains the Northwest Ordinance and its significance, with the full text and a scanned copy of the original document online.

- Morgan County Public Library—GenAssist— The Genealogy Assistant
  http://www.scican.net/~morglib/genasist/genasist.html
  - Morgan County Indiana Original Land Sales From U.S. Government—Sorted by Location
    http://www.scican.net/~morglib/genasist/landsal2.html
  - Morgan County Indiana Original Land Sales From U.S. Government—Sorted by Name
    http://www.scican.net/~morglib/genasist/landsal1.html

- National Land Survey of Finland
  http://www.nls.fi/index_e.html

- New York Indorsed Land Papers, 1643–1676
  http://www.tlc-gen.com/newyork.htm

- North Dakota Land Records
  http://pixel.cs.vt.edu/library/land/nodak/

- Northwest Ordinance of 1787
  http://www.statelib.lib.in.us/WWW/ihb/nword.html

- The Old 300 Genealogical Database
  http://www.tgn.net/~bchm/Genealogy/gene.html
  Texas. "The 'Old 300' database actually includes a core listing of all settlers who had received land grants in Austin's Colony by the eve of the war for independence from Mexico."

- Original Lot Holders, Buffalo, New York
  http://www.localnet.com/~andrle/erie/buffalo/lots.htm

- PANB/UNB Cadastral Database—
  Searching the Grantbook Database
  http://degaulle.hil.unb.ca/library/data/panb/panbweb.html
  Records of land settlement in New Brunswick, 1765–1800.

- Pennsylvania Original Land Records
  http://www.innernet.net/hively/
  Series for York County.

- Public Record Office—Finding Aids—
  A–Z Index of All Leaflets ~ U.K.
  http://www.pro.gov.uk/leaflets/riindex.htm

  o Common Lands (#95)
    http://www.pro.gov.uk/leaflets/RI095.HTM

  o Crown and Royalist Lands, 1642–1660:
    Confiscations, Sales and Restorations (#88)
    http://www.pro.gov.uk/leaflets/RI088.HTM

  o Land Grants In America and American
    Loyalists' Claims (#34)
    http://www.pro.gov.uk/leaflets/RI034.HTM

  o Sources for the History of Religious Houses and
    Their Lands, c.1000–1530 (#103)
    http://www.pro.gov.uk/leaflets/ri103.htm

  o Valuation Office Records Created Under
    The Finance (1909–1910) Act (#68)
    http://www.pro.gov.uk/leaflets/ri068.htm

- Registers of Scotland Executive Agency
  http://www.open.gov.uk/ros/roshome.htm
  Guide to Land, Sasine, Personal and Other Registers.

- Registry of Deeds—Nova Scotia
  http://www.shelburne.nscc.ns.ca/nsgna/ndeed.html

- Retracing the Trails of Your Ancestors Using
  Deed Records
  http://www.ultranet.com/~deeds/deeds.htm
  *By William Dollarhide, from the Genealogy Bulletin, Issue
  No. 25, Jan–Feb 1995.*

- San Francisco Title Abstract Index
  http://pages.prodigy.net/greentrucking/GenPage/sfindex.htm
  1850 to 1918

- SDGenWeb County Land Records
  http://members.aol.com/drfransen/land/home.htm

- South Dakota Land Records
  http://pixel.cs.vt.edu/library/land/sodak/

- Surveying Units and Terms
  http://members.aol.com/RootsLady/universal/survey1.htm

- Texas General Land Office—Archives and Records
  http://www.glo.state.tx.us/central/arc/index.html

- Texas General Land Office—Map Collection
  http://www.glo.state.tx.us/central/arc/mapscol.html

- Texas General Land Office—Spanish and Mexican
  land titles in Texas
  http://www.glo.state.tx.us/central/arc/spanmex.html

- US Land & Property Research
  http://users.arn.net/~billco/uslpr.htm
  By Bill Utterback for the IIGS University.

- US Public Land Survey Methods
  http://www.rootsweb.com/~mistclai/landsurv.htm

- U.S. Public Lands—Public Domain System
  http://www.apics253.com/~deeds/public.htm

- Where to Obtain Land Patents/Warrants
  http://www.avana.net/~lhaasdav/Patentlocations.html

- Wisconsin Land Records—Interactive Search
  http://searches.rootsweb.com/cgi-bin/wisconsin/wisconsin.pl
  Pre-1908 Homestead and Cash Entry Patents from the BLM.

LDS & FAMILY HISTORY CENTERS

The Church of Jesus Christ of Latter-day Saints
http://www.CyndisList.com/lds.htm

Category Index:

- ◆ Family History Centers ~ General Information
- ◆ Family History Centers ~ Locations
- ◆ The Family History Library & Salt Lake City
- ◆ History of the LDS Church
- ◆ Mailing Lists, Newsgroups & Chat

- ◆ Microfilm & Microfiche
- ◆ Miscellaneous LDS Church & Genealogy Resources
- ◆ Professional Researchers, Volunteers & Other Research Services
- ◆ Research Tools

◆ Family History Centers ~ General Information

- LDS Family History Centers
  http://www.jewishgen.org/infofiles/ldscntr.txt
  A JewishGen InfoFile

- LDS Family History Centers—
  The Largest Collection In The World!
  http://www.firstct.com/fv/lds1.html
  A tutorial from the Treasure Maps site.

- ROOTS-L Resources: Family History Centers and Library
  http://www.rootsweb.com/roots-l/fhc.html

- Welcome To The Family History Center™
  http://www.lds.org/en/2_Welcome_to_the_FHC/
  Welcome_to_the_FHC.html
  An online brochure from the official LDS Church web site.

- What Is a Family History Center™?
  http://www.lds.org/en/2_How_Do_I_Begin/3-What_is.html
  From the official LDS Church web site.

- Where Is the Nearest Family History Center™?
  http://www.lds.org/en/2_How_Do_I_Begin/4_Where_is.html
  A list of phone numbers by state & province from the official LDS Church web site.

◆ Family History Centers ~ Locations

- Atlanta Area Family History Centers in Georgia
  http://www.mindspring.com/~noahsark/lds-fhc.html

- Byrd Springs Family History Center
  http://members.aol.com/r3morgan/byrd.htm
  Huntsville, Alabama

- Les Centres Généalogiques SDJ / LDS Family History Centers
  http://www2.et.byu.edu/~harmanc/paris/genealogie.html
  France, Belgique, Suisse, Canada

- Cherry Hill Family History Center
  http://www.cyberenet.net/~gsteiner/njgenweb/chnjfhc.txt
  New Jersey

- Chesapeake, Virginia Family History Center
  http://sites.communitylink.org/cpl/famhistory.html

- Columbia Missouri Family History Center
  http://www.synapse.com/bocomogenweb/LDSFHC.HTM

- Concord/Walnut Creek California Family History Center
  http://feefhs.org/lds/fhc/frg-fhcc.html

- Dartmouth Nova Scotia Family History Centre
  http://www.shelburne.nscc.ns.ca/nsgna/fhc/fhc.htm

- Denver Family History Center
  http://pw1.netcom.com/~rossmi/denfhc.html
  Colorado

- Family History Center, Washington DC Temple
  http://www.access.digex.net/~giammot/FHC/

- Family History Centers
  http://www.genhomepage.com/FHC/fhc.html

- Family History Centres in Canada
  http://www.shelburne.nscc.ns.ca/nsgna/fhc/cdnfhc.htm

- Family History Centers in Germany, Austria and Switzerland
  http://www.genealogy.net/gene/faqs/LDS.de

- Family History Centers in North Alabama
  http://members.aol.com/terryann/other.htm

- Family History Centers of The Church of Jesus Christ of Latter-day Saints
  http://www.deseretbook.com/famhis/

- Family History Centres in Ontario
  http://www.gov.on.ca/MCZCR/archives/english/geneal/fmlyhist.htm

- Family History Centres in the UK
  http://www.dungeon.com/~deltatango/mormon.html
- FRANCÊTRES: Généalogie en France / Genealogy
  in France—Centres généalogiques mormons /
  Genealogical LDS centers
  http://www.world-address.com/francetres/gefrldho.htm
- Howell Family History Center ~ Michigan
  http://www.LivGenMI.com/howfhc.htm
- The Jersey Family History Centre of the
  L.D.S. Church
  http://user.itl.net/~glen/ldsci.html
  Channel Islands
- Lakewood Family History Center ~ Colorado
  http://pw1.netcom.com/~rossmi/lwfhc.html
- The LDS Family History Center in
  Huntsville, Alabama
  http://members.aol.com/terryann2/fhcinal.htm
- LDS Family History Centers
  http://www.genhomepage.com/FHC/
  *The Genealogy Home Page is collecting addresses & info
  regarding your local FHC.*
- LDS Family History Centers United States
  of America
  http://www.everton.com/fhcusa.html
- LDS Family History Centers United States
  of America
  http://www.dungeon.com/~deltatango/fhcusa.html
- LDS Family History Centres in the British Isles,
  including Ireland and Scotland
  http://www.genuki.org.uk/big/LDS/centres.txt
- Leesburg Family History Center ~ Florida
  http://www.angelfire.com/fl/Sumter/genealogy.html
- Lethbridge Family History Center
  http://www.leth.net/fhc/
  Alberta, Canada
- The Lexington Kentucky Family History Center
  http://www.uky.edu/StudentOrgs/LDSSA/FHCpage.html
- Los Angeles Family History Center
  http://www.rootsweb.com/~bifhsusa/fhcwhere.html
  From the British Isles Family History Society—U.S.A. web site.
- Madison Alabama Family History Center
  http://members.aol.com/terryann/madison.htm
- The Madison, WI Stake Family History Center ~
  Wisconsin
  http://www.cae.wisc.edu/~porterb/lds/fam_hist.html
- Okotoks Family History Center
  http://www.cadvision.com/johansss/oktitle.htm
  Alberta, Canada
- Orchard Park FHC, Erie County, New York
  http://www.localnet.com/~andrle/erie/orchard_park/opfhc.htm

- Other Central New Jersey Family History Centers
  http://members.aol.com/DSSaari/prifhc.htm#Other
- Pensacola, Florida Family History Center
  http://www.rootsweb.com/~flescamb/fhc.htm
- San Diego Family History Centers
  http://www.cgssd.org/centers.html
- Santa Clara Family History Center ~ California
  http://reality.sgi.com/csp/scfhc/
- The Unofficial Home Page of the Princeton
  Family History Center
  http://members.aol.com/dssaari/prifhc.htm
- Utah Valley Regional Family History Center
  http://www.lib.byu.edu/~uvrfhc/
  *On the fourth floor of the Harold B. Lee Library on the campus
  of Brigham Young University.*
- Williamsville FHC, Erie County, New York
  http://www.localnet.com/~andrle/erie/amherst/wmfhc.htm
- World Family History Centers (as of January 1995)
  http://www.lib.byu.edu/~uvrfhc/states.html

◆ The Family History Library & Salt Lake City

- The Church of Jesus Christ of Latter-day Saints
  and the Family History Library
  http://www.genhomepage.com/LDS.html
  From the Genealogy Home Page.
- Genealogical Society of Utah
  http://www.mormons.org/daily/family_history/
  genealogical_society_eom.htm
  Description from All About Mormons.
- Genealogical Society of Utah
  http://www.itd.nps.gov/cwss/gsu.html
  *Description from the National Park Service, Civil War Soldiers
  and Sailors System web site.*
- The Genealogist—The Family History Library
  http://www.xcelco.on.ca/~genealog/famhilib.htm
- Guide To LDS Family History Library,
  Salt Lake City, Utah
  http://www.jewishgen.org/infofiles/lds-slc.txt
  A JewishGen InfoFile.
- LDS Family History Library, Salt Lake City, Utah
  http://www.everton.com/genealog/genealog.ldsfhlib
  Description, maps, etc.
- News of the Family History Library in
  Salt Lake City
  http://members.aol.com/terryann2/lib_news.htm
- ROOTS-L Resources: Family History Centers
  and Library
  http://www.rootsweb.com/roots-l/fhc.html
- Salt Lake City, Family History Library Information
  http://www.aros.net/~drwaff/slcfhl.htm

- Salt Lake City Here We Come!
  http://www.rootsweb.com/~genepool/slc.htm
- Utah Valley PAF Users Group—The Salt Lake Family History Library
  http://www.genealogy.org/~uvpafug/fhlslc.html

◆ History of the LDS Church

- Handcart Companies
  http://eddy.media.utah.edu/medsol/UCME/h/HANDCART.html
- Heritage Gateway
  http://heritage.uen.org/cgi-bin/websql/index.hts
- Journals of Early Members of the Church of Jesus Christ of Latter-day Saints
  http://www.math.byu.edu/~smithw/Lds/LDS/Early-Saints/
  Journals, diaries, biographies and autobiographies of some early Mormons and others who knew Joseph Smith, Jr.
- Max Bertola's—The Mormon Pioneer Story
  http://www.uvol.com/pioneer/homepage.html
- Mormon History Resource Page
  http://www.indirect.com:80/www/crockett/history.html
  - Mormon Diaries/Journals and Biographies
    http://www.indirect.com:80/www/crockett/bios.html
  - Mormon History Resource Page—Pioneer Period
    http://www.indirect.com:80/www/crockett/pioneer.html
- The Mormon Pioneer Trail
  http://www.americanwest.com/trails/pages/mormtrl.htm
  From the American West Home Page.
- The Mormon Pioneer Trail
  http://www.omaha.org/trails/main.htm
  From the Douglas-Sarpy Counties Mormon Trails Association.
- The Mormon Trail
  http://www.esu3.k12.ne.us:80/districts/elkhorn/ms/curriculum/Mormon1.html
- MormonTrail.com—The Pioneer Experience
  http://www.mormontrail.com/
  The Official Web Site for Stories, Facts, and Ship Logs on the Mormon Trail Pioneers.
- Tracing Mormon Pioneers
  http://www.vii.com/~nelsonb/pioneer.htm
  - Mormon Emigrant Ships (1840–1868)
    http://www.vii.com/~nelsonb/pioneer.htm#ships
  - Scandinavian Saints
    http://www.vii.com/~nelsonb/scand.htm
    For researching members of the LDS church from the Scandinavian Mission in the time period of 1852–1868.
  - South African Emigration 1853–1865
    http://www.vii.com/~nelsonb/safrica.htm

◆ Mailing Lists, Newsgroups & Chat

- ELIJAH-L Mailing List
  http://members.aol.com/johnf14246/gen_mail_general.html#ELIJAH-L
  For believing members of the Church of Jesus Christ of Latter-day Saints to discuss their ideas and experiences relating with genealogy in the LDS Church.
- FHCNET Mailing List
  http://members.aol.com/johnf14246/gen_mail_general.html#FHCNET
  For directors and others closely associated with the operation of Latter-day Saint family history centers (FHCs). Topics for discussion include staff training, microfilm circulation, collection development, FamilySearch, equipment maintenance, and patron services.
- GEN-ROOTERS Mailing List
  http://members.aol.com/johnf14246/gen_mail_general.html#GEN-ROOTERS
  For members of the Church of Jesus Christ of Latter-day Saints to share ideas and helpful hints on the "how-to's" of genealogy.
- HANDCART Mailing List
  http://members.aol.com/gfsjohnf/gen_mail_states-ut.html#HANDCART
  For anyone who has an interest in the genealogy, journals, and stories of the Pioneers of the Church of Jesus Christ of Latter-day Saints who settled in the Salt Lake Valley from 1847 to 1860.
- LDS-Genealogy Mailing List FAQ and Subscription Info
  http://members.tripod.com/~Genealogy_Infocenter/ldsgen-list.html
- MORMON-INDEX Mailing List
  http://members.aol.com/johnf14246/gen_mail_general.html#MORMON-INDEX
  Provides a weekly newsletter containing queries about Mormon Internet Resources, responses to those queries, announcements of Mormon Internet Resources, and compilations of resources by subject.
- PAF Mailing List
  http://members.aol.com/johnf14246/gen_mail_software.html#PAF
  For discussions relating to the Personal Ancestral File program put out by the LDS.
- PAF-2.31-USERS Mailing List
  http://members.aol.com/johnf14246/gen_mail_software.html#PAF-2.31-USERS
- PAF-3-USERS Mailing List
  http://members.aol.com/johnf14246/gen_mail_software.html#PAF-3-USERS

◆ Microfilm & Microfiche

- California Death Index Information
  http://www.micronet.net/users/~searcy/indexinfo.htm
  A list of microfiche/film numbers by year and surname.

- Halifax County, Nova Scotia LDS/PANS
  Film Numbers
  http://www.geocities.com/Heartland/Prairie/6261/films.htm
- LDS Film Numbers for Ontario Birth Registrations
  http://www.geocities.com/Heartland/9332/lds-b.htm
- LDS Film Numbers for Ontario Death Registrations
  http://www.geocities.com/Heartland/9332/lds-d.htm
- LDS Film Numbers for Ontario Marriage
  Registrations
  http://www.geocities.com/Heartland/9332/lds-m.htm
- LDS Microfilm for Loudoun Co., VA
  http://www.rootsweb.com/~valoudou/film.html
- LDS Microfilms and Microfiche for
  Coshocton Co., Ohio
  http://www.pe.net/~sharyn/lds.html
- LDS Polish Jewish LDS Microfilms
  http://www.jewishgen.org/reipp/jri-lds.htm
  JewishGen
- Microfilm of Connecticut Records at LDS Family
  History Centers
  http://www.cslnet.ctstateu.edu/ldsmicro.htm
- Scottish Reference Information
  http://www.ktb.net/~dwills/13300-scottishreference.htm
  An extensive list of parish numbers and microfilm numbers to aid in doing Scottish research at an LDS Family History Center.

◆ Miscellaneous LDS Church & Genealogy Resources

- All About Mormons
  http://www.mormons.org/
  - Family History
    http://www.mormons.org/daily/family_history/index.htm
- Brigham Young University Libraries
  http://www.byu.edu/libraries/
  - Utah Valley Regional Family History Center
    http://www.lib.byu.edu/dept/uvrfhc/
    On the fourth floor of the Harold B. Lee Library on the campus of Brigham Young University.
- BYU-ISSL—Family History Research
  http://issl.cs.byu.edu/famHist/home.html
- Church of Jesus Christ of Latter-day Saints
  http://www.lds.org/
- Family History / Genealogy from the Unofficial
  Homepage for Austria of The Church of Jesus Christ
  of Latter-day Saints
  http://www.ettl.co.at/mormon/english/gen_gy.htm
- JSB Family History Lab
  http://reled.byu.edu/famhist/

- The Mormon Connection—The LDS Church and
  Genealogy
  http://www.leisterpro.com/doc/Articles/MormConn.html
- Redeem the Dead
  http://www.uvol.com/www1st/redeem/redeem.html
- Submitting Names for Temple Ordinances
  http://www.pcola.gulf.net/~llscott/templery.htm
- The WWW L.D.S. Visitors Center
  http://www.mich.com/~romulans/lds.html

◆ Professional Researchers, Volunteers & Other Research Services

People Specializing in Research or Resources at the Family History Library in Salt Lake City.

- AAG International Research—Professional
  Genealogists and Family Historians
  http://www.intl-research.com/
  Accredited genealogists & family historians specializing in family history research, development & publication. Accredited by the Family History Library in Salt Lake City, the world's largest genealogical library. Tax deductions for LDS research.
- Ancestors Lost and Found
  http://www.ancestorsfound.com/
  Salt Lake City, Utah
- Association of Professional Genealogists—
  Salt Lake Chapter
  http://www.gensource.com/APGSLC.html
- The Basque Genealogy Homepage
  Research Services
  http://www.primenet.com/~fybarra/Research.html
  Specializing in Basque records from the province of Vizcaya. These records are on microfilm at the Salt Lake Family History Library, but do not get circulated.
- Genealogy Ancestors Search
  http://www.wasatch.com/~lance/
  By Family Ties Research, Sandy, Utah.
- Genie Genealogy Research
  http://genealogy.hypermart.net
  Genie Genealogy provides professional genealogy research services to help you find your ancestors. Whether you're a novice or expert, discover your family tree now—quickly and affordably. Genie also offers web page design, picture scanning, report printing, data entry, and LDS-specific genealogy services.
- GSS—Genealogical Search Services
  http://www.itsnet.com/~gss/
  Research at the Family History Library in Salt Lake City, Utah.
- Heirlines Family History and Genealogy Research
  Services
  http://www.heirlines.com
- Heritage Consulting and Services

http://www.heritageconsulting.com/
Salt Lake City, Utah

- Kinsearch Genealogical Services
  http://home.utah-inter.net/kinsearch/index.html
  Provides genealogical research services at the Family History Library (FHL) in Salt Lake City.

- Natalie Cottrill Genealogical Research
  http://www.nataliesnet.com/
  United States research at the Salt Lake City, Utah Family History Library.

- The Official Iowa Counties Professional Genealogist and Researcher's Registry for LDS—Salt Lake City, Utah, USA
  http://www.iowa-counties.com/gene/lds.htm

- Quik-Search—A Document Retrieval Service for Genealogists and Historians
  http://www.inconnect.com/~gjnixon/
  Document retrieval from the Family History Library Collections in Salt Lake City, Utah.

- SAMPUBCO
  http://www.wasatch.com/~dsam/sampubco/index.htm
  Will Testators Indexes, Naturalization Records Indexes and Census Indexes online. You can order copies of the original source documents for a small fee. This service pertains only to entries found in the indexes on this web site.

◆ Research Tools

- Family History Library Catalog Description
  http://www.genuki.org.uk/big/LDS/catorg.txt

- Family History Library Catalog Topics
  http://www.genuki.org.uk/big/LDS/topics.txt
  Listed & cross-referenced for use in England, that allow for differences in American and English usage.

- Family Search: The Family History Library Catalog (FHLC)
  http://www.firstct.com/fv/fhlc.html

- FamilySearch FAQ: Answers to Your Questions About FamilySearch
  http://www.utw.com/~tornado/
  - The Ancestral File—Questions and Answers
    http://www.utw.com/~tornado/ancfile.html
  - The Family History Library Catalog
    http://www.utw.com/~tornado/fhlibcat.html
  - General Information About FamilySearch
    http://www.utw.com/~tornado/general.html

- FHL Publications List
  http://www.firstct.com/fv/lds4.html

- LDS Passenger Manifests—Jan Grippo's Guide to Using the Passenger Lists at Your Local Family History Center
  http://homepage.interaccess.com/~arduinif/tools/ldsmanif.htm

- U.S. Research Outlines
  http://www.firstct.com/fv/usout.html

- Welcome To The Family History Center™
  http://www.lds.org/en/2_Welcome_to_the_FHC/Welcome_to_the_FHC.html
  An online brochure from the official LDS Church web site.

- What Is a Family History Center™?
  http://www.lds.org/en/2_How_Do_I_Begin/3-What_is.html
  From the official LDS Church web site.

- What is the I.G.I.?—aka The International Genealogical Index
  http://www.livgenmi.com/fhcigi.htm
  A definition help page by Helen S. Ullmann, C.G.

- Where Is the Nearest Family History Center™?
  http://www.lds.org/en/2_How_Do_I_Begin/4_Where_is.html
  A list of phone numbers by state & province from the official LDS Church web site.

LIBRARIES, ARCHIVES & MUSEUMS
http://www.CyndisList.com/libes.htm

Category Index:

◆ General Library Resources

◆ Telnet

◆ General Library Resources

- ALA—Links to Library Web Resources
  http://www.ala.org/library/weblinks.html
- Australian Libraries Gateway (ALG)
  http://www.nla.gov.au/libraries/
- The Canadian Library Index
  http://www.lights.com/canlib/
- The Care and Feeding of Genealogical Librarians
  http://www.ancestry.com/home/George_Morgan/01-23-98.htm
  From "Along Those Lines . . ." by George G. Morgan.
- CURL—The Consortium of University Research Libraries
  http://www.curl.ac.uk/
  British Isles
- CyberTree Genealogy Database—Dewey Decimal System Other Helpful Codes
  http://home.sprynet.com/sprynet/lgk71/dew-othr.htm
- CyberTree Genealogy Database—Dewey Decimal System Regional Numbering
  http://home.sprynet.com/sprynet/lgk71/dew-regn.htm
- CyberTree Genealogy Database—Dewey Decimal System United States
  http://home.sprynet.com/sprynet/lgk71/dew-stat.htm
- Directory of Genealogy Libraries In the U.S.
  http://www.greenheart.com/rdietz/gen_libs.htm
- Directory of Virginia Libraries
  http://www.vsla.edu:80/directory/
- Find Libraries Online
  gopher://libgopher.cis.yale.edu:70/11/
- Gabriel—Gateway to Europe's National Libraries
  http://portico.bl.uk/gabriel/en/welcome.html
- HYTELNET on the World Wide Web
  http://library.usask.ca/hytelnet/
  An index of library catalogs online, with links to the telnet addresses and complete logon instructions. For Telnet, you must have Telnet software to access. Make note of logon and password when you begin. Read more about Telnet below.
- International Federation of Library Associations and Institutions
  http://www.nlc-bnc.ca/ifla/

- IPL—Internet Public Library
  http://www.ipl.org/
- Librarians Serving Genealogists: Genealogy Libraries on the WWW
  http://www.genealogy.org/~holdiman/LSG/libraries.html
- The Library of Congress—State Library Web Listing
  http://lcweb.loc.gov/global/library/statelib.html
- Library Resource List
  http://www.dpi.state.wi.us/www/lib_res.html
  From the State of Wisconsin, a list of over 500 Internet resources that will be of interest to the library community.
- LIBRIS—Nationellt Bibliotekssystem—Svenska Bibliotek I Samverkan / Union Catalogue of Swedish Libraries
  http://www.libris.kb.se/
- Libweb—Library Servers via WWW
  http://sunsite.berkeley.edu/Libweb/
- Map Libraries—WWW Links
  http://www-map.lib.umn.edu/map_libraries.html
- OCLC Online Computer Library Center Home Page
  http://www.oclc.org/oclc/menu/home1.htm
- Project EARL—Connecting Public Libraries to the Network ~ U.K.
  http://www.earl.org.uk/
- Public Libraries of Europe
  http://dspace.dial.pipex.com/town/square/ac940/eurolib.html
- Public Libraries with Internet Services
  http://www.halcyon.com/treasure/virtual/library.html
- Ready, 'Net, Go! Archival Internet Resources
  http://www.tulane.edu/~lmiller/ArchivesResources.html
- SJCPL's List of Public Libraries with WWW Services
  http://sjcpl.lib.in.us/homepage/PublicLibraries/PubLibSrvsGpherWWW.html
- SJCPL's List of Public Libraries with Telnet Services
  http://sjcpl.lib.in.us/homepage/PublicLibraries/PubLibSrvsTelnet.html

- Standards for Using Records Repositories
  and Libraries
  http://www.ngsgenealogy.org/about/content/committees/
  gene_stan.html
  Recommended by the National Genealogical Society.

- State Library Web Sites
  http://www.dpi.state.wi.us/www/statelib.html

- The UK Public Libraries Page
  http://dspace.dial.pipex.com/town/square/ac940/ukpublib.html

- United States Depository Libraries
  http://www.facsnet.org/report_tools/findem_fast/appendix.html
  *"A list of federal regional depository libraries, so-called super
  libraries."*

- U.S. Public Libraries with Websites
  http://www.capecod.net/epl/public.libraries.html

- webCATS: Library Catalogues on the
  World Wide Web
  http://library.usask.ca/hywebcat/

- Yahoo!...History...Archives
  http://dir.yahoo.com/Arts/Humanities/History/Archives/

- Yahoo!...Reference...Libraries
  http://dir.yahoo.com/Reference/Libraries/

  - Yahoo!...Reference...Academic Libraries
    http://dir.yahoo.com/Reference/Libraries/
    Academic_Libraries/

  - Yahoo!...Reference...Digital Libraries
    http://dir.yahoo.com/Reference/Libraries/Digital_Libraries/

  - Yahoo!...Reference...Public Libraries
    http://dir.yahoo.com/Reference/Libraries/Public_Libraries/

  - Yahoo!...Reference...School Libraries
    http://dir.yahoo.com/Reference/Libraries/School_Libraries/

  - Yahoo!...Reference...Special Collections
    http://dir.yahoo.com/Reference/Libraries/
    Special_Collections/

  - Yahoo!...Reference...U.S. State Libraries
    http://dir.yahoo.com/Reference/Libraries/
    U_S__State_Libraries/

- Yahoo!...Science...Maps...Libraries
  http://dir.yahoo.com/Science/Geography/Cartography/Maps/
  Libraries/

◆ Telnet

*Many libraries have their card catalogs available online via Telnet.
Telnet allows you to access a computer in another location via your
Internet connection, and interact with that computer as if you were
sitting right in front of it. For instance, using Telnet, you can search
Quest, the Seattle Public Library's catalog. In order to access a
catalog via Telnet, you will need to be sure that you have Telnet
access through your Internet Service Provider and you will also
need to have Telnet software installed on your computer. You can
download a shareware version of Telnet software from any of these
shareware sites:*

- NONAGS—Shareware & Freeware
  http://www.nonags.com/

- Stroud's Consummate Winsock Applications
  http://cws.internet.com/

- TUCOWS, The Worlds Best Collection of
  Internet Software
  http://www.tucows.com

*You can use the Telnet software on its own after dialing up your
Internet connection or you can configure your web browser to
launch your Telnet software program each time you click on a
Telnet link on a web site. You will find several Telnet links throughout the list of libraries on Cyndi's List. Once you've accessed a
Telnet site be sure to make a note of the logon and password in case
you are asked for it again during your Telnet session.*

- SJCPL's List of Public Libraries with Telnet Services
  http://sjcpl.lib.in.us/homepage/PublicLibraries/
  PubLibSrvsTelnet.html

- Telnet Tips
  http://library.usask.ca/hytelnet/telnet.html

LOYALISTS

http://www.CyndisList.com/loyalist.htm

- AMERICAN-REVOLUTION Mailing List
  http://members.aol.com/gfsjohnf/gen_mail_states-gen.html#AMERICAN-REVOLUTION
  For the discussion of events during the American Revolution and genealogical matters related to the American Revolution. The French-Indian Wars and the War of 1812 are also suitable topics for discussion.

- British Headquarters Papers, New York City 1774–1783 The Carleton Papers
  http://www2.magmacom.com/~ekipp/kingname.htm
  The King's Name Project.

- Butler's Rangers
  http://iaw.on.ca/~awoolley/brang/brang.html

- Frontier Press Bookstore—Loyalists
  http://www.frontierpress.com/frontier.cgi?category=loyal

- GenealogyBookShop.com—Loyalists
  http://www.genealogybookshop.com/genealogybookshop/files/General,Loyalists/index.html
  The online store of Genealogical Publishing Co., Inc. & Clearfield Company.

- Global Genealogy—Books—The Loyalists
  http://www.globalgenealogy.com/loyalist.htm

- Heritage Books, Inc.—Loyalist
  http://www.heritagebooks.com/loyal.htm

- The King's Men: Loyalist Units in New York and North America
  http://www.geocities.com/Athens/Delphi/4171/kingsmen.htm

- A Loyalist Bibliography
  http://www.magma.ca/~ekipp/loybib.htm

- Loyalist Books, Documents and Related Materials
  http://www.shelburne.nscc.ns.ca/nsgna/sg/sg_loy.htm

- Loyalist Collection—Harriet Irving Library
  http://www.lib.unb.ca/Collections/Loyalist/
  University of New Brunswick

- Loyalist Genealogy
  http://personal.nbnet.nb.ca/bmercer/index.html/Loyalist.htm

- loyalists-in-canada Mailing List
  http://members.aol.com/gfsjohnf/gen_mail_country-can.html#LOYALIST
  For those with loyalist ancestors to help one another research their loyalist history and to post any facts on the subject that they desire. Loyalists are defined as those who left the United States for Canada after the American Revolution for a number of reasons.

- Loyalist Units
  http://www.brigade.org/loy.html
  From the Brigade of the American Revolution Home Page at http://www.brigade.org/welcome.html

- The Loyalists
  http://www.rootsweb.com/~canwgw/ns/digby/perm/loyalist.htm
  From the Digby County, Nova Scotia GenWeb site.

- Loyalists of Digby, Nova Scotia
  http://www.rootsweb.com/~canwgw/ns/digby/perm/article1.htm
  and Black Loyalists of Digby, Nova Scotia
  http://www.rootsweb.com/~canwgw/ns/digby/perm/article2.htm

- Maine Loyalists
  http://www.rootsweb.com/~usgenweb/me/washington/loyalist.htm

- The Maryland Loyalist Battalion Home Page
  http://www.erols.com/grippo/

- Maryland Loyalists and the American Revolution
  http://www.erols.com/candidus/index.htm

- Muster Roll at Gulliver's Hole, St. Mary's Bay and Sissiboo
  http://www.rootsweb.com/~canwgw/ns/digby/perm/muster1.htm
  Digby, Nova Scotia, Canada

- New York State Library—Loyalist Records
  http://unix2.nysed.gov/genealogy/loyalist.htm

- The Olive Tree Genealogy Homepage—Index to Ontario Loyalists
  http://www.rootsweb.com/~ote/indexloy.htm

- Paul Bunnell will search your Loyalist ancestors— Send e-mail to Paul for details
  E-mail: benjamin@capecod.net

- The United Empire Loyalists' Association of Canada
  http://www.npiec.on.ca/~uela/uela1.htm
  Toronto, Ontario, Canada

◆ Loyalist People & Family Sites

- Ancestors of Julia and Tim RICE
  http://www.familytreemaker.com/users/r/i/c/Craig—Rice/index.html

- Edward KIPP: Family History, KIP/KIPP Genealogy, Loyalist Genealogy, Princeton, Ontario, Alumni Western, HTML Basics
  http://www2.magmacom.com/~ekipp/index.html

- William OSTERHOUT, United Empire Loyalist
  http://citd.scar.utoronto.ca/ANTC28/Osterhout.html

MAGAZINES, JOURNALS, COLUMNS, NEWSLETTERS & PAMPHLETS
http://www.CyndisList.com/magazine.htm

Category Index:

- ◆ Magazines, Journals & Columns ~ Online Editions
- ◆ Magazines, Journals & Columns ~ Snail Mail Delivery
- ◆ Newsletters & Pamphlets

◆ Magazines, Journals & Columns ~ Online Editions

- Ancestry.com Genealogy Columns
  http://www.ancestry.com/columns/index.htm
  - ○ "Along Those Lines . . ." by George G. Morgan
    http://www.ancestry.com/columns/george/index.htm
  - ○ DearMYRTLE'S Daily Genealogy Column by Myrtle!
    http://www.ancestry.com/columns/myrtle/index.htm
  - ○ Eastman's Online Genealogy Newsletter by Dick Eastman
    http://www.ancestry.com/columns/eastman/index.htm
  - ○ Shaking Your Family Tree by Myra Vanderpool Gormley
    http://www.ancestry.com/columns/myra/index.htm
- ComputerCredible Magazine: Index of Computer Genealogy Articles
  http://www.credible.com/geneallist.html
- Family Search by Sharon Burns
  http://connections.oklahoman.net/familysearch/home.html
  From the Oklahoman Online newspaper.
- The Family Tree Online
  http://www.teleport.com/~binder/famtree.shtml
- Genealogical Thoughts by Gary Boyd Roberts
  http://www.nehgs.org/GBR/GBRColumn.htm
  A weekly web site column from the NEHGS Senior Research Scholar.
- Jewish Family & Life: Jewish Genealogy on the Web
  http://www.jewishfamily.com/Features/996/genealogy.htm
  An article by Yaffa Klugerman.
- Journal of Online Genealogy
  http://www.onlinegenealogy.com/
  Promoting the Use of Computers and the Internet in Family History Research.

- Lineage Links—My Heritage Quest Column
  http://www.CyndisList.com/hqllinks.htm
  A list of links featured in Cindy's column for Heritage Quest Magazine, a bi-monthly publication.
- Southern Queries Genealogy Magazine
  http://www.mindspring.com/~freedom1/sq/sq.htm
- Southern Roots—Southern Style Online Magazine & Shoppe
  http://www.southern-style.com/genealog.htm
- A Time for Sharing—Native American SIG Newsletter
  http://members.aol.com/kathyehyde/news/index.htm
- Tracing Our Roots
  http://www.hhcn.com/family/kellow/index.html
  Column by Brenda Burns Kellow, featured in the Plano Star Courier, Plano, Texas.
- Tracing Our Roots
  http://www.harrisburg.com/root.html
  Column by Schuyler Brossman, featured in The Press And Journal Extra, Middletown, Pennsylvania.
- Tri-City Herald Genealogy Online
  http://www.tri-cityherald.com/genealogy/
  Dozens of helpful columns written by Terry Day and Donna Potter Phillips.
- The William and Mary Quarterly
  http://www.jstor.org/journals/00435597.html
  A searchable database from the JSTOR Journal Collection online. This covers three series dating from 1892 through 1991.

◆ Magazines, Journals & Columns ~ Snail Mail Delivery

- Alabama Heritage Magazine
  http://www.as.ua.edu/heritage/
- American Genealogy Magazine
  http://www4.viaweb.com/datatrace/
- Ancestry Magazine
  http://www2.viaweb.com/ancestry/anmag.html

- Australian Family Tree Connections Magazine
  http://www.aftc.com.au/

- Caribbean Historical & Genealogical Journal
  http://www.tcigenealogy.com/
  From TCI Genealogical Resources.

- The Computer Genealogist
  http://www.nehgs.org/publications/necg.htm
  A newsletter from the New England Historic Genealogical Society.

- Computers in Genealogy
  http://www.sog.org.uk/cig/
  A Quarterly Publication of the Society of Genealogists, U.K.

- Council of Genealogy Columnists
  http://www.rootsweb.com/~cgc/index.htm

- Everton's Genealogical Helper
  http://www.everton.com/
  Since 1947—the largest genealogical magazine in the world.

- Family Chronicle Magazine
  http://www.familychronicle.com/

- Family History News
  http://www.globalserve.net/~parrspub/
  Canadian genealogical publication.

- Family Puzzlers
  http://www.avana.net/~amymws/heritage.htm

- Family Tree Magazine
  http://www.family-tree.co.uk/
  England

- Genealogical Computing
  http://www2.viaweb.com/ancestry/gencom.html

- Genealogical Journal
  http://www.infouga.org/journal.htm
  From the Utah Genealogical Association.

- The Genealogists Magazine: Indexes
  http://www.sog.org.uk/genmag/
  The quarterly publication of the Society of Genealogists, UK.

- Genealogy and Tennessee—GENEALOGY FRIENDS:Partyline News
  http://users.aol.com/genny1/done.html
  FREE Queries, mail or e-mail.

- GEN-MAT-REQUEST Mailing List
  http://members.aol.com/johnf14246/
  gen_mail_general.html#GEN-MAT
  For anyone who has an interest in the buying or selling of new or used genealogical materials (e.g., books, newsletters, CDs, magazines).

- GEN-MAT–15 Mailing List
  http://members.aol.com/johnf14246/
  gen_mail_general.html#GEN-MAT–15
  For anyone who desires to post the availability of new or used genealogical materials (e.g., books, newsletters, CDs, magazines) or services for sale at a price of $15 or less.

- Heritage Quest Magazine
  http://www.heritagequest.com/

- Irish Roots Magazine HomePage
  http://www.iol.ie/~irishrts/

- Isle of Man Family History Society Journal
  http://www.ee.surrey.ac.uk/Contrib/manx/famhist/fhsjidx.htm
  Volume i 1979 to Volume xii 1990, articles scanned and online!

- Journals & Newsletters covering Genealogy in South Africa
  http://www.geocities.com/Heartland/8256/others.html

- Kentucky Explorer Magazine
  http://www.win.net/kyexmag/KEhome.html
  Kentucky's Most Unique History & Genealogy Publication.

- Local History Magazine
  http://www.local-history.co.uk/
  United Kingdom

- Mennonite Family History Magazine
  http://www.masthof.org/mfh.html

- Minnesota Genealogical Journal
  http://www.parkbooks.com/Html/mgjbroch.html

- Mobile Genealogical Society: The News Stand
  http://www.siteone.com/clubs/mgs/newstand.htm
  Links to genealogical columns that appear in newspapers and accept announcements and/or queries.

- The New England Historical and Genealogical Register
  http://www.nehgs.org/publications/register.htm
  Quarterly published by the New England Historic Genealogical Society.

- NGS Quarterly—A Journal for Today's Family Historian
  http://www.ngsgenealogy.org/about/content/publications/
  quarterly.html
  From the National Genealogical Society in the U.S.

- Northwest Ohio Quarterly
  http://www.history.utoledo.edu/NWOQ.HTML
  A joint publication of the History Department of the University of Toledo, the Maumee Valley Historical Society and the Toledo-Lucas County Public Library.

- Old Huntsville Magazine
  http://oldhuntsville.com/oldhuntsville/
  Alabama

- Reunions Magazine Homepage
  http://www.execpc.com/~reunions/
  Family reunions, class reunions etc.

- STAMMBAUM: The Journal of German-Jewish Genealogical Research
  http://www.jewishgen.org/stammbaum/index.html

- Tidewater Virginia Families
  http://www.erols.com/tvf/
  "A Magazine of History and Genealogy." An independent quarterly journal.

- Western Kentucky Journal
  http://pw1.netcom.com/~cpalmer/wkj/wkj.htm

- The Wind-Mill: A Periodical of Frisian/
  Germanic Heritage
  http://members.aol.com/gowindmill/index.html

- Yahoo!...Genealogy...Magazines
  http://dir.yahoo.com/Arts/Humanities/History/Genealogy/
  Magazines/

◆ Newsletters & Pamphlets

- family Backtracking—The Newsletter of the
  Puget Sound Genealogical Society
  http://www.rootsweb.com/~wapsgs/news.htm
  Washington

- Family Tree Finders
  http://www.sodamail.com/site/ftf.shtml
  *A Monday through Friday newsletter that provides interesting
  and useful information for tracing your family tree. It's geared to
  beginners and experienced family tree trackers of any age!
  Written by well known genealogist, Rhonda R. McClure.*

- FHL Publications List
  http://www.firstct.com/fv/lds4.html
  For the Family History Library, Salt Lake City, Utah.

- The Genealogist's Guides—
  from Heritage Associates
  http://www.granniesworld.com/heritage/guide.htm

- Genealogy Today Newsletter
  http://www.enoch.com/genealogy/newslet.htm

- GEN-EDITOR Mailing List
  http://members.aol.com/johnf14246/
  gen_mail_general.html#GEN-EDITOR
  *For editors/publishers of genealogical, surname and family
  newsletters to have a place to discuss and share ideas and tips.*

- Generations Newsletter
  http://www.rupert.net/~lkool/page13.html
  *A genealogy newsletter published 6 times per year (to be
  increased to 12 very soon), which contains articles of interest to
  anyone researching their family history in South Africa.*

- Georgia Research Helper
  http://www.genealogy-books.com/research.htm
  A Newsletter published quarterly.

- Greene Genes: A Genealogical Quarterly About
  Greene County, New York
  E-mail: greene-genes@msn.com
  *For details send e-mail to Patricia Morrow at
  greene-genes@msn.com*

- Jeans & Genes—The newsletter of the Rockdale
  County Genealogical Society
  http://www.mindspring.com/~bevr/html/newsletters.html

- Joe's Genealogy E-mail Newsletter
  http://www.zen.co.uk/home/page/joe.houghton/NEWSLTR.HTM

- Legends and Legacies Free Newsletter
  "Hot Chocolate"
  http://www.legends.ca/newslttr/newsmain.html
  Published twice annually in May and November.

- Manx Methodist Historical Society Newsletter
  http://www.ee.surrey.ac.uk/Contrib/manx/methdism/mhist/
  index.htm
  Index to Newsletters 1–24.

- Mic Barnette's Columns, Genealogy & History
  http://www.geocities.com/BourbonStreet/Delta/7552/
  From The Houston Chronicle.

- MISSING LINKS: A Weekly Newsletter for
  Genealogists
  http://www.rootsweb.com/~mlnews/
  *By Julia M. Case and Myra Vanderpool Gormley. Homepage of
  Missing Links, weekly genealogy E-Zine with a sample issue,
  plus its archives dating back to August 1996. Also see the
  archive of back-issues at ftp://ftp.rootsweb.com/pub/mlnews/ To
  subscribe, send a NEW e-mail message to MISSING-LINKS-L-
  request@rootsweb.com and in the body of the message enter
  only one word: subscribe.*

- NGS/CIG Digest
  http://www.ngsgenealogy.org/about/content/publications/
  cig_digest.html
  *From the Computer Interest Group, from the National Genea-
  logical Society in the U.S. This is bound within each issue of the
  NGS Newsletter.*

- NGS Newsletter
  http://www.ngsgenealogy.org/about/content/publications/
  newslet.html
  Bi-monthly, from the National Genealogical Society in the U.S.

- Online Pioneers Genealogy Page
  http://www.eskimo.com/~mnarends/

- O Progresso—The quarterly newsletter of the
  Portuguese Historical & Cultural Society (PHCS)
  http://www.dholmes.com/o-prog.html

- RootsWeb Review: Genealogical Data Cooperative
  Weekly News
  http://www.rootsweb.com/~review/
  *Homepage of RootsWeb Review, a weekly E-zine, pertaining to
  the news of RootsWeb Data Cooperative and of matters of
  interest to online genealogists worldwide. Also see the archive of
  back-issues at ftp://ftp.rootsweb.com/pub/review/
  To subscribe, send a NEW e-mail message to ROOTSWEB-
  REVIEW-L-request@rootsweb.com and in the body of the
  message enter only one word: subscribe.*

- Slovak Heritage Live
  http://www.iarelative.com/bc_live.htm
  *A quarterly publication of the Slovak Heritage and Cultural
  Society of British Columbia.*

- Surnames, Family Associations &
  Family Newsletters
  http://www.CyndisList.com/surnames.htm
  See this category on Cyndi's List for related links.

- Treasure Maps's FREE Monthly E-mail Newsletter
  http://www.firstct.com/fv/sub.html

- The Tri-County Researcher
  http://www.ovnet.com/~tcr/
  *A West Virginia Genealogical Publication covering Marshall,
  Tyler, & Wetzel Counties.*

- U.S. Research Outlines
  http://www.firstct.com/fv/usout.html

- Where to Write for Vital Records
  http://www.cdc.gov/nchswww/howto/w2w/w2welcom.htm

- Wandering Volhynians
  http://pixel.cs.vt.edu/pub/sources/wv.txt
  A Magazine for the Descendants of Germans From Volhynia and Poland.

- Wandering Volhynians—
  German-Volhynian Newsletter
  http://feefhs.org/ca/frg-wv.html

- W.K.R.P. (Washington/Charlotte Kounty
  Records Preservation) Newsletter
  E-mail: shwkrp@aol.com
  A quarterly newsletter concerning research being done in Washington Co., Maine and Charlotte County, New Brunswick. For details e-mail Sharon at: shwkrp@aol.com

MAILING LISTS & NEWSGROUPS

http://www.CyndisList.com/mailnews.htm

Category Index:

- Mailing Lists & Newsgroups Briefly Defined
- The Complete Resource for Mailing Lists & Newsgroups
- Buy, Sell or Trade
- Cemeteries & Obituaries
- The First Mailing Lists to Start With Online
- For Announcements Only
- General Mailing Lists
- Helpful Articles and Web Sites
- How-To & Research Methods

- Mailing List Archives
- Military
- Miscellaneous
- Newsletters (Read-only Mailing Lists)
- Queries & Surnames
- Religion & Churches
- Settling North America
- Software & Computers
- Specific Localities & Ethnic Groups
- Usenet Newsgroups and Others

◆ Mailing Lists & Newsgroups Briefly Defined

- Mailing Lists & Newsgroups are very similar to one another:
  - They are free to subscribe to and you participate in specific genealogical or historical discussions via e-mail.
  - To participate in a newsgroup you need to have news reader software, such as Free Agent (http://www.forteinc.com/forte/agent/index.html) or the news reader program that is already resident in many web browsers.
  - To participate in a mailing list you send e-mail commands to a computer software program (i.e., Listserv, Smartlist, etc.) in order to be automatically added to the list. You send e-mail messages to a different address in order to communicate with the other members of the mailing list.
  - My own personal preference is mailing lists because there are a larger number of genealogy mailing lists to choose from (more than 4,000) than there are genealogy newsgroups (a bit over 30). With mailing lists the messages come to me via e-mail, which means I have one less thing to remember to go and check on, as you would have to do regularly with newsgroups.

◆ The Complete Resource for Mailing Lists & Newsgroups

- Genealogy Resources On the Internet by John Fuller & Chris Gaunt
  http://members.aol.com/johnf14246/internet.html
  Start here for a complete listing of all the currently available mailing lists & newsgroups—including details for subscribing and descriptions of topics covered. You can also find categorized links in the list below to many of the mailing lists detailed on this site.
  - Genealogy Resources: Mailing Lists
    http://members.aol.com/johnf14246/gen_mail.html
    - General Mailing Lists
      http://members.aol.com/johnf14246/gen_mail_general.html
    - Software Mailing Lists
      http://members.aol.com/johnf14246/gen_mail_software.html
    - Non-USA Geographic Mailing Lists
      http://members.aol.com/johnf14246/gen_mail.html
      See the list, arranged by country, on the main index page.
    - United States Mailing Lists
      http://members.aol.com/johnf14246/gen_mail.html
      See the list, arranged by state, on the main index page
    - Surname Mailing Lists
      http://members.aol.com/johnf14246/gen_mail.html
      See the alphabetical table at the bottom of the main index page.
  - Genealogy Resources: Usenet Newsgroups
    http://members.aol.com/johnf14246/gen_use.html

◆ Buy, Sell or Trade

- AGLL Genealogical Services Mailing List
  http://members.aol.com/johnf14246/
  gen_mail_software.html#AGLL
  For announcements of new genealogical products and sales promotions from AGLL.

- Appleton's Mailing List
  http://members.aol.com/johnf14246/
  gen_mail_general.html#Appleton
  A read-only list with information on new genealogy software, CD-ROMs, books, and more from Appleton's Books and Genealogy.

- GEN-BOOKS Mailing List
  http://members.aol.com/johnf14246/
  gen_mail_general.html#GEN-BOOKS
  For anyone with an interest in the buying or selling of new or used genealogy books and CDs made from these books.

- GEN-MARKET Mailing List
  http://members.aol.com/johnf14246/
  gen_mail_general.html#GEN-MARKET
  For commercial postings of unique interest to genealogists. Gatewayed with the soc.genealogy.marketplace newsgroup.

- GEN-MAT Mailing List
  http://members.aol.com/johnf14246/
  gen_mail_general.html#GEN-MAT
  This is a mailing list for anyone who has an interest in the buying or selling of new or used genealogical materials (e.g., books, newsletters, CDs, magazines).

- GEN-MAT-15 Mailing List
  http://members.aol.com/johnf14246/
  gen_mail_general.html#GEN-MAT-15
  For anyone who desires to post the availability of new or used genealogical materials (e.g., books, newsletters, CDs, magazines) or services for sale at a price of $15 or less.

- GEN-MAT-HX Mailing List
  http://members.aol.com/johnf14246/
  gen_mail_general.html#GEN-MAT-HX
  For anyone who has an interest in the buying or selling of new or used biographies and history books. Publishers of such books are welcome, as are resellers (businesses or individuals cleaning bookshelves).

- GenSwap Mailing List
  http://members.aol.com/johnf14246/
  gen_mail_general.html#GenSwap
  For exchanging research time and swaping records for records with others (e.g., researching in your area for someone else in exchange for like efforts on their part).

◆ Cemeteries & Obituaries

- CEMETERY Mailing List
  http://members.aol.com/johnf14246/
  gen_mail_general.html#CEMETERY
  For people interested in the many aspects of family graves from caring for the grave of one ancestor to the restoration and preservation of the family cemetery.

- CLA-L: Cemetery Listing Association Mailing List
  http://members.aol.com/johnf14246/
  gen_mail_general.html#CLA-L
  The purpose of the CLA is to collect cemetery research by individual genealogists and make it available across the Internet.

- GEN-OBIT Mailing List
  http://members.aol.com/johnf14246/
  gen_mail_general.html#GEN-OBIT

- GRAVE-L Mailing List
  http://www.best.com/~gazissax/silence/mlist.html
  "Grave-L is a new mailing list explicitly for taphophiles—lovers of cemeteries and funerals. It will be of particular interest to historians, genealogists, funeral directors, cemetery workers, and others concerned with the preservation, folklore, and history of graveyards."

- INSCRIPTIONS-L Mailing List
  http://members.aol.com/johnf14246/
  gen_mail_general.html#INSCRIPTIONS
  For anyone who has an interest in genealogy and local history related to Monumental Inscriptions including gravestones, monuments, and war memorials.

◆ The First Mailing Lists to Start With Online

- GEN-NEWBIE-L Mailing List
  http://members.aol.com/johnf14246/
  gen_mail_general.html#GEN-NEWBIE-L
  A mailing list where people who are new to computers and genealogy may interact using a computer's e-mail program.

- GEN-NEWBIE-L Home Page
  http://www.rootsweb.com/~newbie/

- GENTEEN Mailing List
  http://members.aol.com/johnf14246/
  gen_mail_general.html#GENTEEN-L
  For teenagers and young adults who are interested in genealogical research or others who have suggestions or ideas for young genealogists.

- Lost_Newbies Mailing List
  http://members.aol.com/johnf14246/
  gen_mail_general.html#Lost_Newbies
  For people who are new to genealogy and/or the use of the Internet in genealogical research.

- NEWGEN Mailing List
  http://members.aol.com/johnf14246/
  gen_mail_general.html#NEWGEN
  Created to assist those who are quite new to genealogy.

- ROOTS-L Mailing List
  http://members.aol.com/johnf14246/
  gen_mail_general.html#ROOTS-L
  Broad-based genealogy topics—over 10,000 subscribers.

- WEB-NEWBIE Mailing List
  http://members.aol.com/johnf14246/
  gen_mail_general.html#WEB-NEWBIE
  For beginners who have questions on the Internet, Internet methods, genealogy on the Internet, and how to build a web page.

◆ For Announcements Only

- The CyndisList Mailing List
  http://www.CyndisList.com/maillist.htm
  An announcements-only list for information regarding daily updates to the Cyndi's List web site.

- NEW-GENLIST Mailing List
  http://members.aol.com/johnf14246/
  gen_mail_general.html#NEW-GENLIST
  For announcing new genealogy mailing lists.

- NEW-GEN-URL Mailing List
  http://members.aol.com/johnf14246/
  gen_mail_general.html#NEW-GEN-URL
  For announcing new or updated genealogy-related web sites.

- USIGS Mailing List
  http://members.aol.com/johnf14246/
  gen_mail_general.html#USIGS
  The Announcement mailing list for the United States Internet Genealogical Society.

◆ General Mailing Lists

- ALT-GENEALOGY Mailing List
  http://members.aol.com/johnf14246/
  gen_mail_general.html#ALT-GENEALOGY
  For general genealogical discussions. Gatewayed with the alt.genealogy newsgroup.

- GenChat Mailing List
  http://members.aol.com/johnf14246/
  gen_mail_general.html#GenChat
  For discussions of anything having to do with genealogy.

- GENEALOGY-L Mailing List
  http://members.aol.com/johnf14246/
  gen_mail_general.html#GENEALOGY-L

- gene-helpline Mailing List
  http://members.aol.com/johnf14246/
  gen_mail_general.html#gene-helpline

- Genexchange-L Mailing List
  http://members.aol.com/johnf14246/
  gen_mail_general.html#Genexchange-L

- GENMSC Mailing List
  http://members.aol.com/johnf14246/
  gen_mail_general.html#GENMSC-L
  For general genealogical discussions that don't fit within one of the other soc.genealogy. newsgroups. Gatewayed with the soc.genealogy.misc newsgroup.*

- GenTips-L Mailing List
  http://members.aol.com/johnf14246/
  gen_mail_general.html#GenTips-L
  For anyone who has an interest in genealogy. This list hopes to provide tips about obtaining genealogy records and is useful for both beginning genealogists and experts.

- H-Net Discussion Networks
  http://www.h-net.msu.edu/lists/
  Dozens of mailing lists for history and social studies.

- ROOTS-L Mailing List
  http://members.aol.com/johnf14246/
  gen_mail_general.html#ROOTS-L
  Broad-based genealogy topics—over 10,000 subscribers.

◆ Helpful Articles and Web Sites

- Ancestry.com—Mailing Lists: Tips For Posting An Effective Query
  http://www.ancestry.com/research/listservs.htm

- AOL NetFind | Newsgroup Etiquette
  http://www.aol.com/netfind/scoop/newsgroup_etiquette.html

- AOL NetFind | Newsgroup Scoop Glossary
  http://www.aol.com/netfind/scoop/newsgroup_glossary.html

- Basic newsgroup and mailing list "Netiquette"
  http://www.herald.co.uk/local_info/genuki/netiquette.html

- Birds of a Feather
  http://www.birdsofafeather.net/
  Mailing list service.

- DejaNews—An "Official" Usenet Primer
  http://www.dejanews.com/info/primer3.shtml

- DejaNews—The Source for Internet Newsgroups
  http://www.dejanews.com/
  Search the newsgroups for a specific topic or keyword and read the archived messages.

- DejaNews—What is Usenet?
  http://www.dejanews.com/help/dnusenet_1.html

- Digest Freeware—Dave Hein's Genealogy Page
  http://ourworld.compuserve.com/homepages/david_hein/geneal.htm
  Converts mail list digests into hypertext to view in a web browser.

- Interlinks—E-Mail Discussion Groups
  http://alabanza.com/kabacoff/Inter-Links/listserv.html

- Larry Stephens Genealogy Page—
  E-mail Lists I Own
  http://php.indiana.edu/~stephenl/ownlists.htm

- ListServe.com Internet Power Tool—Publicly Accessible Mailing Lists
  http://www.neosoft.com/internet/paml/

- LISTSERV Help—Larry Stephens Genealogy Page
  http://php.indiana.edu/~stephenl/listhelp.htm

- LISTSERV—The Mailing List Management Classic
  http://www.lsoft.com/listserv.stm
  Software program that runs many mailing lists.

- Liszt: Searchable Directory of e-Mail Discussion Groups
  http://www.liszt.com/

- Mailing Lists Are Fun!
  http://www.ancestry.com/columns/George/03-13-98.htm
  From "Along Those Lines . . ." by George Morgan.

- Maiser Help
  http://www.fagg.uni-lj.si/maiser.htm

- The Net: User Guidelines and Netiquette
  http://www.fau.edu/rinaldi/net/dis.html
  For Listservs/Mailing Lists/ Discussion Groups, by Arlene Rinaldi.

- Newsgroup Participation and Citizenship: Some Basic Information
  http://www.onlinegenealogy.com/aug96/newsgroups.html
  By Margaret Olson for the Journal of Online Genealogy.

- News Rover—Scans, downloads and decodes Usenet newsgroup messages
  http://www.NewsRover.com
  Usenet search agent that scans Usenet genealogy newsgroups and downloads messages that are of interest to your research.

- The Reporter's Guide to Mailing Lists
  http://www.daily.umn.edu/~broeker/guide.html

- RootsWeb User Mailing Lists
  http://www.rootsweb.com/~maillist/
  A categorized list of the mailing lists currently hosted on the RootsWeb servers.

- Search the List of Lists
  http://catalog.com/vivian/interest-group-search.html

- soc.genealogy Newsgroups and Associated Mailing Lists: A Short History
  http://www.onlinegenealogy.com/jul96/newsgroups1.html
  By Margaret Olson for the Journal of Online Genealogy.

- Vicki's Home Page—Genealogy Listservers, Newsgroups & Special Homepages
  http://www.eskimo.com/~chance/lists.html
  Great alphabetical list of Newsgroups and Mailing Lists with subscription details.

- Yahoo!.....Mailing Lists
  http://dir.yahoo.com/Computers_and_Internet/Internet/Mailing_Lists/

◆ How-To & Research Methods

- GENCLASS Mailing List
  http://members.aol.com/johnf14246/gen_mail_general.html#GENCLASS
  For the members of the free genealogy classes offered by Diana Hanson and the USGenWeb Project. Also see the associated web page at http://www.rootsweb.com/~genclass/

- GENMTD Mailing List
  http://members.aol.com/johnf14246/gen_mail_general.html#GENMTD-L
  For the discussion of genealogy research techniques and resources. Gatewayed with the soc.genealogy.methods newsgroup.

- GEN-ROOTERS Mailing List
  http://members.aol.com/johnf14246/gen_mail_general.html#GEN-ROOTERS
  For members of the Church of Jesus Christ of Latter-day Saints to share ideas and helpful hints on the "how-to's" of genealogy.

- GEN-SHARE Mailing List
  http://members.aol.com/johnf14246/gen_mail_general.html#GEN-SHARE
  For "seasoned" genealogy researchers to share sources and get help with tough problems. This list is not for the posting of queries addressing searches for specific ancestors and is not recommended for those new to genealogy.

- GENTEEN Mailing List
  http://members.aol.com/johnf14246/gen_mail_general.html#GENTEEN-L
  For teenagers and young adults who are interested in genealogical research or others who have suggestions or ideas for young genealogists.

- GenTips-L Mailing List
  http://members.aol.com/johnf14246/gen_mail_general.html#GenTips-L
  For anyone who has an interest in genealogy. This list hopes to provide tips about obtaining genealogy records and is useful for both beginning genealogists and experts.

- Internet_Genealogy Mailing List
  http://members.aol.com/johnf14246/gen_mail_general.html#Internet_Genealogy
  For students of Marthe Arends' Practical Internet Genealogy series of courses at Virtual University.

- NEWGEN Mailing List
  http://members.aol.com/johnf14246/gen_mail_general.html#NEWGEN
  Created to assist those who are quite new to genealogy.

- RESEARCH-HOWTO Mailing List
  http://members.aol.com/johnf14246/gen_mail_general.html#RESEARCH-HOWTO
  For those who are just getting started in genealogy research and those who are not novices but need information on where to go when "dead ends" are encountered.

◆ Mailing List Archives

- List archives at LISTSERV.INDIANA.EDU
  http://listserv.indiana.edu/archives/index.html
  Browse through the online archives for several genealogy mailing lists run by Larry Stephens.

- ROOTS-L Mailing List
  http://www.rootsweb.com/roots-l/roots-l.html
  At 10 years of age, this is the great-grandmother of all genealogy mailing lists!

  ○ ROOTS-L Archive—Log Files of Messages to the List
    ftp://ftp.rootsweb.com/pub/roots-l/archive/

  ○ ROOTS-L Archive—Messages from August 1996 through the present
    ftp://ftp.rootsweb.com/pub/roots-l/messages/

  ○ ROOTS-L Daily Index of Mailing List Messages
    http://www.rootsweb.com/roots-l/index/

  ○ ROOTS-L Message Archives
    http://searches.rootsweb.com/roots-l.search.html

  ○ ROOTS-L Recent Postings
    gopher://gort.canisius.edu/1m/.otherlib/.discussion/.lists/ROOTS-L

- Rootsweb List Archive Searches Using CNIDR's ISearch
  http://www.shelby.net/shelby/jr/robertsn/rwsearch.htm
  An unofficial set of recommendations on how to construct search queries on the Rootsweb archives that use the CNIDR search software—from John Robertson.

- Rootsweb Mailing List Archives
  http://lists.rootsweb.com/~archiver/
  In beta testing: Marc Nozell's threaded version in hierarchical order by date. Includes only mailing lists that asked to participate.

- RootsWeb Mailing Lists—Interactive Search
  http://searches.rootsweb.com/cgi-bin/listsearch.pl
  In beta testing: Karen Isaacson's searchable web form. Does not include all mailing lists yet.

- Search Features for a RootsWeb Mailing List
  http://www.rootsweb.com/rootsweb/members/archives.html
  Search messages for the last 2–4 weeks via e-mail command.

◆ Military

- AMERICAN-REVOLUTION Mailing List
  http://members.aol.com/gfsjohnf/gen_mail_states-gen.html#AMERICAN-REVOLUTION
  For the discussion of events during the American Revolution and genealogical matters related to the American Revolution. The French-Indian Wars and the War of 1812 are also suitable topics for discussion.

- AMREV-HESSIANS Mailing List
  http://members.aol.com/gfsjohnf/gen_mail_states-gen.html#AMREV-HESSIANS
  For anyone with a genealogical interest in the Hessian soldiers (German auxiliary troops employed by King George III of England) who remained in America after the American Revolution.

- The Anglo Boer War Discussion Page
  http://www.icon.co.za/~dup42/talk.htm
  This mailing list is for the discussion of the Anglo Boer War and other military related topics pre-1900.

- FOB-LIST—Friends of the Boers—E-mail List
  http://www.webcom.com/perspekt/eng/mlist/fob.html
  The primary topic of this mailing list is the centenary commemoration of the 2nd Anglo Boer war (1899–1902).

- U.S. Civil War
  http://www.CyndisList.com/cw.htm
  See this category on Cyndi's List for mailing list links.

- U.S. Military
  http://www.CyndisList.com/military.htm
  See this category on Cyndi's List for mailing list links.

- WARof1812 Mailing List
  http://members.aol.com/johnf14246/gen_mail_general.html#WARof1812

- WW20-ROOTS-L Mailing List
  http://members.aol.com/johnf14246/gen_mail_general.html#WW20-ROOTS-L
  For the discussion of genealogy in all 20th century wars.

◆ Miscellaneous

- ADOPTEES Mailing List
  http://members.aol.com/johnf14246/gen_mail_general.html#ADOPTEES
  For legal adoptees and "adoptee-lites" (people who were raised without one or both birth parents, but who were never legally adopted) to seek advice in conducting a search.

- ADOPT-FR Mailing List
  http://members.aol.com/johnf14246/gen_mail_general.html#ADOPT-FR

- adopt-gene Mailing List
  http://members.aol.com/johnf14246/gen_mail_general.html#adopt-gene
  For the discussion of problems related to adoption.

- ADOPTING Mailing List
  http://members.aol.com/johnf14246/gen_mail_general.html#ADOPTING
  For anyone touched by adoption. This list offers search help, support, and tips on research related to adoption.

- ADOPTION Mailing List
  http://members.aol.com/johnf14246/gen_mail_general.html#ADOPTION
  Discussions of anything and everything connected with adoption.

- BlackSheep Mailing List
  http://members.aol.com/johnf14246/gen_mail_general.html#BlackSheep
  For the International Black Sheep Society of Genealogists (IBSSG) which includes all those who have a dastardly, infamous individual of public knowledge and ill-repute somewhere in their family . . . preferably in their direct lines. This individual must have been publicly pilloried in disgrace for acts of a significantly anti-social nature. Also see the associated web page at http://homepages.rootsweb.com/~blksheep/

- emigration-ships Mailing List
  http://members.aol.com/johnf14246/gen_mail_general.html#EMIGRATION-SHIPS
  A mailing list for anyone who wants to discuss the ships their ancestors arrived on or post passenger lists for any ships.

- FAMILIES-TOUCHED-BY-ADOPTION-L Mailing List
  http://members.aol.com/johnf14246/gen_mail_general.html#FamAdop
  For anyone personally touched by adoption and wishing to trace/share their heritage, genealogists seeking biological/adoptive family information to include an adoptee on their family tree, and for sharing guidelines for searching public records. Also see the associated web page at http://members.aol.com/FamAdop/index.html

- Family_Bible Mailing List
  http://members.aol.com/johnf14246/gen_mail_general.html#Family_Bibles
  For the entry ONLY of information on any and all family bibles.

- FHCNET Mailing List
  http://members.aol.com/johnf14246/gen_mail_general.html#FHCNET
  For directors and others closely associated with the operation of Latter-Day Saint family history centers (FHCs). Topics for discussion include staff training, microfilm circulation, collection development, FamilySearch, equipment maintenance, and patron services.

- **FOLKLORE** Mailing List
  http://members.aol.com/johnf14246/
  gen_mail_general.html#FOLKLORE
  A mailing list for the exchange of folklore—folk medicine and recipes.

- **GENEALIB** Mailing List
  http://members.aol.com/johnf14246/
  gen_mail_general.html#GENEALIB
  For librarians who specialize in genealogy.

- **GEN-EDITOR** Mailing List
  http://members.aol.com/johnf14246/
  gen_mail_general.html#GEN-EDITOR
  For editors/publishers of genealogical, surname and family newsletters to have a place to discuss and share ideas and tips.

- **GenHumor** Mailing List
  http://members.aol.com/johnf14246/
  gen_mail_general.html#GenHumor
  For the exchange of genealogy amd family humor including poems and jokes.

- **GEN-IRC** Mailing List
  http://members.aol.com/johnf14246/
  gen_mail_general.html#GEN-IRC
  Internet Relay Chat

- **GEN-MEDIEVAL** Mailing List
  http://members.aol.com/johnf14246/
  gen_mail_general.html#GEN-MEDIEVAL
  For genealogy and family history discussion among people researching individuals living during medieval times. Gatewayed with thesoc.genealogy.medieval newsgroup.

- **GEN-ROYAL** Mailing List
  http://members.aol.com/johnf14246/
  gen_mail_general.html#GEN-ROYAL

- **GEN_SOCIETIES** Mailing List
  http://members.aol.com/johnf14246/
  gen_mail_general.html#GEN_SOCIETIES
  For persons involved with establishing a local genealogical society in order to share program ideas, discuss means of promoting growth within a group, discuss how to work with libraries, and other related topics.

- **GENTEEN** Mailing List
  http://members.aol.com/johnf14246/
  gen_mail_general.html#GENTEEN-L
  For teenagers and young adults who are interested in genealogical research or others who have suggestions or ideas for young genealogists.

- **GenToday** Mailing List
  http://members.aol.com/johnf14246/
  gen_mail_general.html#GenToday
  For the online newsletter, Genealogy Today, http://www.enoch.com/genealogy/newslet.htm, for the discussion and sharing of information among subscribers for genealogy in any place and at any time.

- **GEN-UNSOLVED-MYSTERIES** Mailing List
  http://members.aol.com/johnf14246/
  gen_mail_general.html#GEN-UNSOLVED-MYSTERIES
  For people whose family genealogies include "unsolved mysteries." Postings should include only mysterious disappearances or appearances, unsolved murders, questionable incarcerations, and other mysterious or unsolved events in an ancestor's life. Postings should not include "brick walls" since these would be repetitive of the content of other lists.

- **GLSHIPS** Mailing List
  http://members.aol.com/gfsjohnf/gen_mail_states-gen.html#GLSHIPS
  For anyone who is researching ancestors who participated in the shipping industry on the Great Lakes of the northeastern United States.

- **HOMESPUN** Mailing List
  http://members.aol.com/johnf14246/
  gen_mail_general.html#HOMESPUN
  For those who want to have a bit of fun reminiscing. Subscribers are welcome to share memories, traditions, poems, humor, stories, recipes, folklore and home remedies.

- **IIGS-UNIVERSITY** Mailing List
  http://members.aol.com/johnf14246/
  gen_mail_general.html#IIGS-UNIVERSITY
  For volunteers who are working on the International Internet Genealogical Society (IIGS) University project.

- **IIGS-UNIVERSITY-LIBRARY** Mailing List
  http://members.aol.com/johnf14246/
  gen_mail_general.html#IIGS-UNIVERSITY-LIBRARY
  For volunteers who are working on the International Internet Genealogical Society (IIGS) University Library project.

- **itinerantroots** Mailing List
  http://www.onelist.com/subscribe.cgi/itinerantroots
  For genealogy resources relating to itinerant professions: circus, theatre, music hall, vaudeville, fairs, showmen, portable theatres, etc.

- **Mariners** Mailing List
  http://members.aol.com/johnf14246/
  gen_mail_general.html#Mariners
  For anyone who is researching their seafaring ancestors.

- **METISGEN** Mailing List
  http://members.aol.com/johnf14246/
  gen_mail_general.html#METISGEN
  For the discussion and sharing of information regarding the Metis and their descendants. The Metis are North America's Fur Trading Children . . . the new nation of individuals born within North America from the first unions of natives and whites.

- **MOMS_N_ME-ROOTS** Mailing List
  http://members.aol.com/johnf14246/
  gen_mail_general.html#MOMS_N_ME-ROOTS
  To aid moms of all ages, but especially those with young children, in researching their family. Also welcome are any ideas for helping mothers teach their children about their heritage and the importance of family research.

- **NOTABLE-WOMEN-ANCESTORS** Mailing List
  http://members.aol.com/johnf14246/
  gen_mail_general.html#NOTABLE-WOMEN-ANCESTORS
  For the discussion of female ancestors (famous and not-so-famous) and methods of researching women in conjunction with the NWA web site (http://www.rootsweb.com/~nwa).

- **Photo Generations—Home of the PhotoGen Mailing List Page**
  http://www.webcom.com/cityg/photogen/index.html
  The Photography and Genealogy Mailing List.

- **ProResearchers** Mailing List
  http://members.aol.com/johnf14246/
  gen_mail_general.html#ProResearchers
  Just for Professional Researchers to discuss their industry.

- **SALEM-WITCH Mailing List**
http://members.aol.com/gfsjohnf/gen_mail_states-ma.html#SALEM-WITCH
A genealogy and history mailing list for descendants of the people involved in the Salem Witchcraft Trials of 1692—the accusers and the accused, the afflicted and the executed, as well as the magistrates, clergy, jurors, and anyone affected by the proceedings. Also see the associated web page at http://www.ogram.org/17thc/salem-witch-list.shtml

- **TheShipsList Mailing List**
http://members.aol.com/johnf14246/gen_mail_general.html#TheShipsList
For anyone interested in the ships our ancestors migrated on. Subjects include emigration/immigration, ports of entry, ports of departure, ship descriptions and history, passenger lists and other related information.

- **UFO-ROOTS Mailing List**
http://members.aol.com/johnf14246/gen_mail_general.html#UFO-ROOTS
For those whose ancestors arrived from outer space to make connections with others sharing this problem, discuss their ancestry, and provide advice on possible avenues for further research.

- **WORDS Mailing List**
http://members.aol.com/johnf14246/gen_mail_general.html#WORDS
A light-hearted discussion of English-English/American-English phrases and how they might have originated. Also see the associated web page at http://www.rootsweb.com/~genepool/amerispeak.htm

◆ Newsletters (Read-only Mailing Lists)

- **Ancestry Daily News**
http://www.ancestry.com/whatsnew.htm

- **The CyndisList Mailing List**
http://www.CyndisList.com/maillist.htm
An announcements-only list for information regarding daily updates to the Cyndi's List web site.

- **Eastman's Online Genealogy Newsletter**
Send a NEW e-mail message to: listserv@peach.ease.lsoft.com and in the body of the message enter only the following (replacing "Jane Doe" with your own first and last name): subscribe rootscomputing Jane Doe.

- **Family Tree Finders**
http://www.sodamail.com/site/ftf.shtml
A Monday through Friday newsletter that provides interesting and useful information for tracing your family tree. It's geared to beginners and experienced family tree trackers of any age! Written by well known genealogist, Rhonda R. McClure.

- **MISSING LINKS: A Weekly Newsletter for Genealogists**
http://www.rootsweb.com/~mlnews/
By Julia M. Case and Myra Vanderpool Gormley. Homepage of Missing Links, weekly genealogy E-Zine with a sample issue, plus its archives dating back to August 1996. Also see the archive of back-issues at ftp://ftp.rootsweb.com/pub/mlnews/ To subscribe, send a NEW e-mail message to MISSING-LINKS-L-request@rootsweb.com and in the body of the message enter only one word: subscribe.

- **RootsWeb Review: Genealogical Data Cooperative Weekly News**
http://www.rootsweb.com/~review/
Homepage of RootsWeb Review, a weekly E-zine, pertaining to the news of RootsWeb Data Cooperative and of matters of interest to online genealogists worldwide. Also see the archive of back-issues at ftp://ftp.rootsweb.com/pub/review/ To subscribe, send a NEW e-mail message to ROOTSWEB-REVIEW-L-request@rootsweb.com and in the body of the message enter only one word: subscribe.

- **The Treasure Maps Monthly E-mail Newsletter**
http://www.firstct.com/fv/sub.html

◆ Queries & Surnames

- **GOONS-L Mailing List**
http://members.aol.com/johnf14246/gen_mail_general.html#GOONS-L
For members of the Guild of One-Name Studies (GOONS) to promote discussion of matters concerned with One-Name Studies and the Guild.

- **QEXPRESS Mailing List**
http://members.aol.com/johnf14246/gen_mail_general.html#QEXPRESS
For people who are using the USGenWeb/WorldGenWeb Query Express system.

- **ROLL-CALL Mailing List**
http://members.aol.com/gfsjohnf/gen_mail_surnames-gen.html#ROLL-CALL
For the posting of "roll calls" (lists) of the surnames you are researching so that others can determine if there is a common interest.

- **RSL-UPDATE Mailing List**
http://members.aol.com/gfsjohnf/gen_mail_surnames-gen.html#RSL-UPDATE
The RootsWeb Surname List database monthly update of new surnames.

- **soc.genealogy.surnames.* / SURNAMES-* FAQ files**
http://www.rootsweb.com/~surnames/

- **Surname Mailing Lists—Genealogy Resources on the Internet**
http://members.aol.com/johnf14246/gen_mail.html
See the alphabetical listing at the bottom of the main index.

- **SURNAME-QUERY Mailing List**
http://members.aol.com/gfsjohnf/gen_mail_surnames-gen.html#SURNAME-QUERY
For users to send queries on specific surname searches.

- **SURNAMES Mailing List**
http://members.aol.com/gfsjohnf/gen_mail_surnames-gen.html#SURNAMES
Surname queries central database. Gatewayed with the soc.genealogy.surnames.global newsgroup.

- **SURNAMES-BRITAIN Mailing List**
http://members.aol.com/gfsjohnf/gen_mail_country-unk.html#SURNAMES-BRITAIN
For surname queries related to Great Britain. Gatewayed with the soc.genealogy.surnames.britain newsgroup.

- **SURNAMES-CANADA** Mailing List
  http://members.aol.com/gfsjohnf/gen_mail_surnames-gen.html#SURNAMES-CANADA
  For surname queries related to Canada. Gatewayed with the soc.genealogy.surnames.canada newsgroup.

- **SURNAMES-GERMAN** Mailing List
  http://members.aol.com/gfsjohnf/gen_mail_surnames-gen.html#SURNAMES-GERMAN
  For surname queries related to German speaking countries. Gatewayed with the soc.genealogy.surnames.german newsgroup.

- **SURNAMES-IRELAND** Mailing List
  http://members.aol.com/gfsjohnf/gen_mail_country-unk.html#SURNAMES-IRELAND
  For surname queries related to Ireland and Northern Ireland. Gatewayed with the soc.genealogy.surnames.ireland newsgroup.

- **SURNAMES-MISC** Mailing List
  http://members.aol.com/gfsjohnf/gen_mail_surnames-gen.html#SURNAMES-MISC
  For surname queries for regions not addressed elsewhere in the soc.genealogy.surnames.* hierarchy. Gatewayed with the soc.genealogy.surnames.misc newsgroup.

- **SURNAMES-USA** Mailing List
  http://members.aol.com/gfsjohnf/gen_mail_surnames-gen.html#SURNAMES-USA
  For surname queries related to the United States. Gatewayed with the soc.genealogy.surnames.usa newsgroup.

◆ Religion & Churches

- **BRETHREN** Mailing List
  http://members.aol.com/johnf14246/gen_mail_general.html#BRETHREN
  Includes such church groups as Tunkers/Dunkers, Church of the Brethren, and German Baptists.

- **ELIJAH-L** Mailing List
  http://members.aol.com/johnf14246/gen_mail_general.html#ELIJAH-L
  For believing members of the Church of Jesus Christ of Latter-day Saints to discuss their ideas and experiences relating with genealogy in the LDS Church.

- **GEN-ROOTERS** Mailing List
  http://members.aol.com/johnf14246/gen_mail_general.html#GEN-ROOTERS
  For members of the Church of Jesus Christ of Latter-day Saints to share ideas and helpful hints on the "how-to's" of genealogy.

- **HANDCART** Mailing List
  http://members.aol.com/gfsjohnf/gen_mail_states-ut.html#HANDCART
  For anyone who has an interest in the genealogy, journals, and stories of the Pioneers of the Church of Jesus Christ of Latter-day Saints who settled in the Salt Lake Valley from 1847 to 1860.

- **Huguenot** Mailing List
  http://members.aol.com/johnf14246/gen_mail_general.html#Huguenot

- **JEWISHGEN** Mailing List
  http://members.aol.com/johnf14246/gen_mail_general.html#JEWISHGEN
  The JewishGen Conference. Discussions of Jewish genealogy. JewishGen is gatewayed with the soc.genealogy.jewish newsgroup.

- **LDS-Genealogy** Mailing List FAQ and Subscription Info
  http://members.tripod.com/~Genealogy_Infocenter/ldsgen-list.html

- **MCF-ROOTS** Mailing List
  http://members.aol.com/gfsjohnf/gen_mail_states-gen.html#MCF-ROOTS
  A mailing list (Maryland Catholics on the Frontier) for the discussion of descendants of Maryland Catholics who migrated first to Kentucky and then to other parts of the frontier.

- **MENNO.REC.ROOTS** Mailing List
  http://members.aol.com/johnf14246/gen_mail_general.html#MENNO.REC.ROOTS
  A Mennonite genealogy and family research interest group.

- **MENNO-ROOTS** Mailing List
  http://members.aol.com/johnf14246/gen_mail_general.html#MENNO-ROOTS

- **MORAVIANCHURCH** Mailing List
  http://members.aol.com/johnf14246/gen_mail_general.html#MORAVIANCHURCH
  For the world-wide Moravian Church, the oldest Protestant denomination. This list is for an exchange of Moravian records, genealogies, references, and historical information; especially in Europe and Colonial America.

- **MORMON-INDEX** Mailing List
  http://members.aol.com/johnf14246/gen_mail_general.html#MORMON-INDEX
  Provides a weekly newsletter containing queries about Mormon Internet Resources, responses to those queries, announcements of Mormon Internet Resources, and compilations of resources by subject.

- **QUAKER-L** Mailing List
  http://members.aol.com/johnf14246/gen_mail_general.html#QUAKER-L

- **QUAKER-ROOTS** Discussion Group
  http://www.rootsweb.com/~quakers/quaker-r.htm

◆ Settling North America

- **CA-GOLDRUSH** Mailing List
  http://members.aol.com/gfsjohnf/gen_mail_states-ca.html#CA-GOLDRUSH
  For anyone who is interested in early California miners and settlers, especially in northern California, 1848–1880.

- **Colonial-America** Mailing List
  http://members.aol.com/gfsjohnf/gen_mail_states-gen.html#Colonial-America
  For discussing the history of our ancestors.

- **DUTCH-COLONIES** Mailing List
  http://members.aol.com/gfsjohnf/gen_mail_states-nj.html#DUTCH-COLONIES
  For New York and New Jersey Colonies, known as New Amsterdam.

- **emigration-ships** Mailing List
  http://members.aol.com/johnf14246/gen_mail_general.html#EMIGRATION-SHIPS
  A mailing list for anyone who wants to discuss the ships their ancestors arrived on or post passenger lists for any ships.

- GERMAN-AMERICAN Mailing List
  http://members.aol.com/gfsjohnf/gen_mail_states-gen.html#GERMAN-AMERICAN
  For anyone interested in genealogy related to German immigrants and their families AFTER their arrival in America.

- GERMANNA_COLONIES Mailing List
  http://members.aol.com/gfsjohnf/gen_mail_states-va.html#GERMAN_COLONIES
  For descendants of the Germanna Colonies (i.e., the original German settlements in Virginia under Governor Spotswood; there were three colonies established, the first being in 1714).

- GERMAN-TEXAN Mailing List
  http://members.aol.com/gfsjohnf/gen_mail_states-tx.html#GERMAN-TEXAN
  For anyone with a genealogical interest in German and Central European immigrants to Texas, especially Germans in the 19th century.

- Homesteaders Mailing List
  http://members.aol.com/gfsjohnf/gen_mail_states-gen.html#Homesteaders
  For researching the history of our homesteaders anscestors; to share information on how they lived, post stories from your family, and share genealogical information.

- IMMI-GRAND Mailing List
  http://members.aol.com/johnf14246/gen_mail_general.html#IMMI-GRAND
  For those attempting to do genealogical research whose grandparents (or parents) arrived in the USA after 1875.

- MAYFLOWER Mailing List
  http://members.aol.com/gfsjohnf/gen_mail_states-gen.html#MAYFLOWER
  A mailing list for the discussion and sharing of information regarding the descendants of the Mayflower passengers in any place and at any time.

- Overland-Trails Mailing List
  http://members.aol.com/gfsjohnf/gen_mail_states-gen.html#Overland-Trails
  Discussions concerning the history, preservation, and promotion of the Oregon, California, Sante Fe, and other historic trails in the Western USA.

- PENNA-DUTCH Mailing List
  http://members.aol.com/gfsjohnf/gen_mail_states-pa.html#PENNA-DUTCH
  For anyone who is researching their Pennsylvania Dutch ancestry or has other genealogical or historical interests in the Pennsylvania Dutch. Also see the associated web page at http://homepages.rootsweb.com/~padutch/lists.html

- SANTA-FE-TRAIL Mailing List
  http://members.aol.com/gfsjohnf/gen_mail_states-gen.html#SANTA-FE-TRAIL

- SCHAKEL-NL Mailing List
  http://members.aol.com/gfsjohnf/gen_mail_country-net.html#SCHAKEL-NL
  For discussions of news events and issues of interest to Canadians and Americans of Dutch origin; Dutch heritage, customs and traditions; immigrant experiences; questions about Dutch legislation, laws, regulations, history etc.; living the Dutch way (e.g., travel, food, drinks); and the ties that bind us. Queries from genealogists related to their Dutch ancestry are welcome.

- Scotch-Irish-L Mailing List
  http://members.aol.com/gfsjohnf/gen_mail_country-unk.html#Scotch-Irish-L
  For Scotch-Irish or Ulster Scots genealogy and culture. These people began a period of heavy emigration from Ulster in the early 1700's and played a large part in the American Revolution.

- TheShipsList Mailing List
  http://members.aol.com/johnf14246/gen_mail_general.html#TheShipsList
  For anyone interested in the ships our ancestors migrated on. Subjects include emigration/immigration, ports of entry, ports of departure, ship descriptions and history, passenger lists and other related information.

- SLAVEINFO Mailing List
  http://members.aol.com/gfsjohnf/gen_mail_states-gen.html#SLAVEINFO
  For the sharing of genealogical data about slaves in the United States including wills/deeds that show sales and transfer of ownership, vital records (e.g., birth, marriage, death), and information/queries on specific slaves that may be part of your ancestry.

- Southern-Trails Mailing List
  http://members.aol.com/gfsjohnf/gen_mail_states-gen.html#Southern-Trails
  For the discussion and sharing of information regarding migration routes in the Southern United States and the people who used them.

- trails west Mailing List
  http://members.aol.com/gfsjohnf/gen_mail_states-gen.html#trails-west
  For those who want to research their family history and post facts on their move west in North America. The trails addressed by the list started at the very beginning of the settlement of North America and are not just the ones in western North America.

◆ Software & Computers

- AGLL Genealogical Services Mailing List
  http://members.aol.com/johnf14246/gen_mail_software.html#AGLL
  For announcements of new genealogical products and sales promotions from AGLL.

- BBANNOUNCE-L Mailing List
  http://members.aol.com/johnf14246/gen_mail_software.html#BBANNOUNCE-L
  Maintained by the Banner Blue Division of Broderbund Software for product announcements (10–15 postings a year).

- BK5forum Mailing List
  http://members.aol.com/johnf14246/gen_mail_software.html#BK5forum
  For the discussion of the Brother's Keeper genealogy program. The list is for the Scandinavian countries so please note that the language for this list is Norwegian, Danish and Swedish.

- BK5-L Mailing List
  http://members.aol.com/johnf14246/gen_mail_software.html#BK-L
  A mailing list for the discussion of the Brother's Keeper genealogy program.

- **CFT-WIN Mailing List**
  http://members.aol.com/johnf14246/
  gen_mail_software.html#CFT-WIN
  Discussion and support for Cumberland Family Software products.

- **Clooz Mailing List**
  http://members.aol.com/johnf14246/
  gen_mail_software.html#Clooz
  For users of the Clooz genealogy utility software program.

- **FAMILIE_OG_SLEKT Mailing List**
  http://members.aol.com/johnf14246/
  gen_mail_software.html#FAMILIE_OG_SLEKT
  For discussions of the "Familie og Slekt" Norwegian genealogy software program.

- **FAMILY-ORIGIN-USERS Mailing List**
  http://members.aol.com/johnf14246/
  gen_mail_software.html#FAMILY-ORIGINS-USERS

- **FAMILYROOTS Mailing List**
  http://members.aol.com/johnf14246/
  gen_mail_software.html#FAMILYROOTS
  For DOS and Macintosh users of Quinsept's Family Roots genealogy software who were "orphaned" when Steve Vorenberg closed the Quinsept company in August 1997. Also see the associated web page at http://www.ogram.org/familyroots/familyroots-list.shtml

- **FT2TMG Mailing List**
  http://members.aol.com/johnf14246/
  gen_mail_software.html#FR2TMG
  For those who have questions and comments relating to importing (DOS) Family Roots (FR) data into The Master Genealogist (TMG) (Windows).

- **FTMTECH-L Mailing List**
  http://members.aol.com/johnf14246/
  gen_mail_software.html#FTMTECH-L
  Maintained by the Banner Blue Division of Broderbund Software for the discussion of technical issues regarding the Family Tree Maker genealogy program.

- **GEDCOM-L Mailing List**
  http://members.aol.com/johnf14246/
  gen_mail_software.html#GEDCOM-L
  A technical mailing list to discuss the GEDCOM specifications.

- **GENCMP Mailing list**
  http://members.aol.com/johnf14246/
  gen_mail_general.html#GENCMP-L
  For the discussion of genealogical computing and net resources. Gatewayed with the soc.genealogy.computing newsgroup.

- **LegacyNews Mailing List**
  http://members.aol.com/johnf14246/
  gen_mail_software.html#LegacyNews
  A read-only mailing list maintained by Millennia Corporation for announcements of interest to users of the Legacy Family Tree genealogy software program.

- **LegacyUserGroup Mailing List**
  http://members.aol.com/johnf14246/
  gen_mail_software.html#LegacyUserGroup
  For users of the Legacy Family Tree genealogy software program to share ideas with other Legacy users.

- **NEW-GENLIST Mailing List**
  http://members.aol.com/johnf14246/
  gen_mail_general.html#NEW-GENLIST
  For announcing new genealogy mailing lists.

- **NEW-GEN-URL Mailing List**
  http://members.aol.com/johnf14246/
  gen_mail_general.html#NEW-GEN-URL
  Information on genealogy-related web sites

- **NO-SLEKT-PROGRAMMER Mailing List**
  http://members.aol.com/gfsjohnf/gen_mail_country-nor.html#NO-SLEKT-PROG
  Norwegian genealogy conference for discussion of computer programs and other computer-related questions as they relate to genealogy. The conference is conducted in Norwegian. Gatewayed with the no.slekt.programmer newsgroup.

- **PAF Mailing List**
  http://members.aol.com/johnf14246/
  gen_mail_software.html#PAF
  For discussion and help regarding the use of all versions of the Personal Ancestral File genealogy program.

- **PAF-2.31-USERS Mailing List**
  http://members.aol.com/johnf14246/
  gen_mail_software.html#PAF-2.31-USERS

- **PAF-3-USERS Mailing List**
  http://members.aol.com/johnf14246/
  gen_mail_software.html#PAF-3-USERS

- **ReunionTalk Mailing List**
  http://members.aol.com/johnf14246/
  gen_mail_software.html#ReunionTalk
  For discussions of Reunion, the family tree software for Macintosh and Windows.

- **Sierra Generations Mailing List**
  http://www.sierra.com/sierrahome/familytree/community/discussion/

- **TMG-L Mailing List**
  http://members.aol.com/johnf14246/
  gen_mail_software.html#TMG-L
  For those interested in The Master Genealogist software program.

- **Y2K Mailing List**
  http://members.aol.com/johnf14246/
  gen_mail_general.html#Y2K
  For the discussion of Year 2000 issues as they relate to genealogy.

◆ Specific Localities & Ethnic Groups

- **ACADIAN-CAJUN Mailing List**
  http://members.aol.com/gfsjohnf/gen_mail_country-can.html#ACADIAN-CAJUN

- **Acadian-Cajun Mailing List**
  http://members.aol.com/gfsjohnf/gen_mail_country-can.html#Acadian1

- Afrigeneas Mailing list
  http://members.aol.com/johnf14246/
  gen_mail_general.html#AFRIGENEAS
  For African-American genealogy.

- ALSACE-GENEALOGY Mailing List
  http://members.aol.com/gfsjohnf/gen_mail_country-fra.html#ALSACE-L
  For anyone interested in Alsace, a border region of France and Germany. Also see the associated web page at http://members.aol.com/jaw5623/private/alsace/listes.html

- ALSACE-LORRAINE Mailing List
  http://members.aol.com/gfsjohnf/gen_mail_country-fra.html#ALSACE-LORRAINE

- ARIA Mailing List
  http://members.aol.com/gfsjohnf/gen_mail_country-ita.html#ARIA-L
  For Australians and New Zealanders who are researching their Italian Heritage, Culture and Ancestry.

- ARMENIA Mailing List
  http://members.aol.com/gfsjohnf/gen_mail_country-arm.html#ARMENIA

- Australia & New Zealand Mailing Lists
  http://www.CyndisList.com/austnz.htm
  See this category on Cyndi's List for mailing list links.

- AUSTRIA Mailing List
  http://members.aol.com/gfsjohnf/gen_mail_country-aut.html#AUSTRIA

- BAHAMAS Mailing List
  http://members.aol.com/gfsjohnf/gen_mail_country-bah.html#BAHAMAS
  For anyone with a genealogical interest in the country of the Bahamas.

- BANAT Mailing list
  http://members.aol.com/gfsjohnf/gen_mail_country-hun.html#BANAT
  For those doing research in the Banat region of what was formerly Hungary.

- BASQUE Mailing List
  http://members.aol.com/gfsjohnf/gen_mail_country-fra.html#BASQUE
  A "moderated" mailing list, gatewayed with the soc.culture.basque "moderated" newsgroup, that provides Basques the world over with a virtual place to discuss social, political, cultural or any other issues related to basques, or to request information and discuss matters related to the basque people and/or their culture. Genealogy queries are an acceptable topic for the list.

- BASQUE-L Mailing List
  http://members.aol.com/gfsjohnf/gen_mail_country-fra.html#BASQUE-L
  A forum for the dissemination and exchange of information on Basque culture. Genealogy-related issues are often discussed on the list though the main topics of discussion are socio-political current affairs, gastronomy, Basque music, poetry, anthropology (e.g., origin of Basques), etc.

- BDO Mailing List
  http://members.aol.com/gfsjohnf/gen_mail_country-rus.html#BDO
  The Beresan District Odessa (BDO) mailing list is for anyone with a genealogical interest in the Beresan Colonies which were made up of Germans who immigrated to Russia, beginning in the first decade of the 19th century, at the request of Alexander I, Tsar of Russia. The Colonies were located Northeast of the city of Odessa on the Black Sea.

- BELGIUM-ROOTS Mailing List
  http://members.aol.com/gfsjohnf/gen_mail_country-blg.html#BELGIUM-ROOTS
  For the descendants of Belgian emigrants/immigrants who are interested in researching their roots in Belgium.

- BERDICHEV Mailing List
  http://members.aol.com/gfsjohnf/gen_mail_country-rus.html#BERDICHEV
  For anyone with a genealogical interest in Berdichev, Ukraine, Russia with a focus on Jewish genealogy.

- Boslovlist Mailing List
  http://members.aol.com/gfsjohnf/gen_mail_country-ukr.html#Boslovlist
  A mailing list for anyone with a genealogical interest in the town of Boslov (Boguslav) in the Ukraine.

- BRAZIL Mailing List
  http://members.aol.com/gfsjohnf/gen_mail_country-bra.html#BRAZIL
  For anyone with genealogical interest in Brazil.

- BUKOVINA-GEN Mailing List
  http://members.aol.com/gfsjohnf/gen_mail_country-rom.html#BUKOVINA-GEN
  For those researching their genealogy and family history in Bukovina, a former crownland of the Austrian Empire (a.k.a. Bucovina, Bukowina, Bukovyna, or Buchenland), now divided between Romania and Ukraine.

- CALITRI Mailing List
  http://members.aol.com/gfsjohnf/gen_mail_country-ita.html#CALITRI
  A mailing list for those who are interested in their Calitrani (people from Calitri, Italy) heritage. Towns of interest include Calitri, Andretta, Bisaccia, Pescopagano, Ruvo, Santangelo Lombardi, and other surrounding towns.

- Canada Mailing Lists
  http://www.CyndisList.com/canada.htm
  See this category on Cyndi's List for mailing list links.

- CARIBBEAN Mailing List
  http://members.aol.com/gfsjohnf/gen_mail_country-gen.html#CARIBBEAN
  For anyone with a genealogical or historical interest in the West Indies and the Caribbean.

- CHANNEL-ISLANDS Mailing List
  http://members.aol.com/gfsjohnf/gen_mail_country-unk.html#CHANNEL-ISLANDS
  For anyone with a genealogical interest in the Channel Islands (Jersey and the Bailiwick of Guernsey) which lie off the Normandy coast of France.

- CUBA Mailing List
  http://members.aol.com/gfsjohnf/gen_mail_country-cub.html#CUBA

- COMUNES_OF_ITALY Mailing List
  http://members.aol.com/gfsjohnf/gen_mail_country-
  ita.html#COMUNES_OF_ITALY
  *For those who are interested in Italian genealogy, culture and
  all things Italian.*

- England Mailing Lists
  http://www.CyndisList.com/england.htm
  See this category on Cyndi's List for mailing list links.

- EURO-JEWISH Mailing List
  http://members.aol.com/johnf14246/
  gen_mail_general.html#EURO-JEWISH
  *For anyone with a genealogical interest in the Migration,
  History, Culture, Heritage and Surname search of the Jewish
  people from Europe to the United States and their descendants
  in the United States.*

- FINNGEN Mailing List
  http://members.aol.com/gfsjohnf/gen_mail_country-
  fin.html#FINNGEN
  For Finnish genealogy.

- GEN-AFRICAN Mailing List
  http://members.aol.com/gfsjohnf/gen_mail_country-
  gen.html#GEN-AFRICAN
  *For the discussion of African genealogy. Gatewayed with the
  soc.genealogy.african newsgroup.*

- GENBNL-L Mailing List
  http://members.aol.com/gfsjohnf/gen_mail_country-
  blg.html#DUTCH
  *For research in the Benelux region (Belgium, the Netherlands,
  and Luxembourg). Gatewayed with the soc.genealogy.benelux
  newsgroup.*

- GENEALOR Mailing List
  http://members.aol.com/gfsjohnf/gen_mail_country-
  fra.html#GENEALOR
  *For anyone with a genealogical interest in the French region of
  Lorraine.*

- GENEA64 Mailing List
  http://members.aol.com/gfsjohnf/gen_mail_country-
  fra.html#GENEA64
  *For anyone with a genealogical interest in the French Regions
  of Bearn and Pays Basque.*

- Genealogia Mailing List
  http://members.aol.com/gfsjohnf/gen_mail_country-
  bra.html#Genealogia
  *For those interested in genealogy in Brazil. The list is dedicated
  to the search for information on the origins of families, registers
  in Brazil and abroad, histories of immigrants, meanings of
  surnames, etc.*

- GENEALOR Mailing List
  http://members.aol.com/gfsjohnf/gen_mail_country-
  fra.html#GENEALOR
  *For anyone with a genealogical interest in the French region of
  Lorraine.*

- GEN-FF Mailing List
  http://members.aol.com/gfsjohnf/gen_mail_country-
  fra.html#GEN-FF-L
  Gatewayed with the news:fr.rec.genealogie

- fr.rec.genealogie newsgroup.
  *For the discussion of Francophone genealogy—the genealogy
  of French-speaking people (traffic probably mainly in French).*

- GEN-FR Mailing List
  http://members.aol.com/gfsjohnf/gen_mail_country-
  fra.html#GEN-FR-L
  *For the discussion of Francophone genealogy—the genealogy of
  French-speaking people. Gatewayed with the
  soc.genealogy.french newsgroup.*

- GEN-HISPANIC Mailing List
  http://members.aol.com/gfsjohnf/gen_mail_country-
  gen.html#GEN-HISPANIC
  *For the discussion of Hispanic genealogy. Gatewayed with the
  soc.genealogy.hispanic newsgroup.*

- GEN-ITALIAN Mailing List
  http://members.aol.com/gfsjohnf/gen_mail_country-
  ita.html#GEN-ITALIAN
  Gatewayed with the soc.genealogy.italian newsgroup.

- GEN-NORDIC Mailing List
  http://members.aol.com/gfsjohnf/gen_mail_country-
  den.html#GEN-NORDIC
  *For the discussion of genealogy in the Scandinavian countries,
  including: Denmark, Finland, Greenland, Iceland, Norway and
  Sweden. Gatewayed with the soc.genealogy.nordic newsgroup.*

- GENPOL Mailing List
  http://members.aol.com/gfsjohnf/gen_mail_country-
  pol.html#GENPOL
  For Polish genealogy.

- GEN-SLAVIC Mailing List
  http://members.aol.com/gfsjohnf/gen_mail_country-
  pol.html#GEN-SLAVIC
  Gatewayed with the soc.genealogy.slavic newsgroup.

- Germans from Russia Mailing Lists
  http://www.CyndisList.com/germruss.htm
  See this category on Cyndi's List for mailing list links.

- Germany Mailing Lists
  http://www.CyndisList.com/germany.htm
  See this category on Cyndi's List for mailing list links.

- Hellenes-Diaspora Mailing List
  http://members.aol.com/gfsjohnf/gen_mail_country-
  gre.html#Hellenes-Diaspora
  *For anyone with an interest in Hellenes in the Diaspora. The
  list will address concerns regarding Hellenes finding long lost
  friends, family, or connections in Greece or elsewhere around
  the world and for research concerning their Hellenic family
  trees.*

- HERBARZ Mailing List
  http://members.aol.com/gfsjohnf/gen_mail_country-
  lit.html#HERBARZ
  *For the discussion of Polish and Lithuanian heraldry, the history
  of the armorial clans, and the genealogy of noble families.*

- Huguenot Mailing List
  http://members.aol.com/johnf14246/
  gen_mail_general.html#Huguenot

- Hungarian American List (HAL)
  http://members.aol.com/gfsjohnf/gen_mail_country-
  hun.html#HUNGARIAN
  *A mailing list for those interested in expressing, sharing, and
  exchanging their views, ideas, and feelings about Hungary,
  Hungarians, Hungarian-Americans, and Hungarian culture and
  genealogy.*

- HUNGARY Mailing List
  http://members.aol.com/gfsjohnf/gen_mail_country-hun.html#HUNGARY1

- ICC—The Il Circolo Calabrese Mailing List
  http://members.aol.com/gfsjohnf/gen_mail_country-ita.html#ICC
  For anyone with a genealogical interest in the Calabria region of Italy (the southernmost region of the Italian peninsula, the 'toe' of the boot).

- ICELAND Mailing List
  http://members.aol.com/gfsjohnf/gen_mail_country-ice.html#ICELAND

- INDIA Mailing List
  http://members.aol.com/gfsjohnf/gen_mail_country-ind.html#INDIA1
  For anyone who is interested in tracing their British and European Ancestors in British India.

- INDIAN-ROOTS-L Mailing List
  http://members.aol.com/gfsjohnf/gen_mail_states-gen.html#INDIAN-ROOTS
  For Native Americans.

- Indian-Territory-Roots Mailing List
  http://members.aol.com/gfsjohnf/gen_mail_states-ok.html#Indian-Territory-Roots
  For anyone with a genealogical interest in Indian Territory—an area that in 1907 became the eastern and south/south-eastern part of Oklahoma.

- Ireland & Northern Ireland Mailing Lists
  http://www.CyndisList.com/ireland.htm
  See this category on Cyndi's List for mailing list links.

- ISLE-OF-MAN Mailing List
  http://members.aol.com/gfsjohnf/gen_mail_country-unk.html#ISLE-OF-MAN
  United Kingdom

- IsraelGenWeb Mailing List
  http://members.aol.com/gfsjohnf/gen_mail_country-isr.html#IsraelGenWeb

- italy-gene Mailing List
  http://members.aol.com/gfsjohnf/gen_mail_country-ita.html#italy-gene

- Jewish Museum of Belgium
  http://members.aol.com/johnf14246/gen_mail_general.html#JEWBEL
  For anyone who is interested in Jewish genealogy; in Belgian or English.

- KOREA Mailing List
  http://members.aol.com/gfsjohnf/gen_mail_country-kor.html#KOREA

- Kutschurgan Mailing List
  http://members.aol.com/gfsjohnf/gen_mail_country-rus.html#Kutschurgan
  For anyone with a genealogical interest in the Kutschurgan Colonies which were made up of Germans who immigrated to Russia, beginning in the first decade of the 19th century, at the request of Alexander I, Tsar of Russia. The Colonies were located Northwest of the city of Odessa on the Black Sea.

- LITHUANIA Mailing List
  http://members.aol.com/gfsjohnf/gen_mail_country-lit.html#LITHUANIA

- LOWER-DELMARVA-ROOTS Mailing List
  http://members.aol.com/gfsjohnf/gen_mail_states-md.html#LOWER-DELMARVA-ROOTS
  Sussex and Kent Counties in Delaware; Dorchester, Wicomico, Somerset, and Worcester in Maryland; Northampton and Accomack in Virginia.

- loyalists-in-canada Mailing List
  http://members.aol.com/gfsjohnf/gen_mail_country-can.html#LOYALIST
  For those with loyalist ancestors to help one another research their loyalist history and to post any facts on the subject that they desire. Loyalists are defined as those who left the United States for Canada after the American Revolution for a number of reasons.

- MadeiraExiles Mailing List
  http://members.aol.com/gfsjohnf/gen_mail_country-wes.html#MadeiraExiles
  Devoted to the research of Dr. Robert Reid Kalley's Portuguese Presbyterian exiles from Madeira, Portugal who emigrated to Trinidad and then to Illinois (ca 1846–1854). Postings regarding research of related exiles who settled in Trinidad, Antigua, St. Kitts, Jamaica, Demerara, etc. are also welcome.

- med-gene Mailing List
  http://members.aol.com/gfsjohnf/gen_mail_country-gen.html#med-gene
  For anyone with a genealogical interest in the Mediterranean area.

- Melungeon Mailing List
  http://members.aol.com/gfsjohnf/gen_mail_states-gen.html#MELUNGEO
  For people conducting Melungeon and/or Appalachian research including Native American, Portuguese, Turkish, Black Dutch, and other unverifiable mixed statements of ancestry or unexplained rumors, with ancestors in TN, KY, VA, NC, SC, GA, AL, WV, and possibly other places.

- MEXICO Mailing List
  http://members.aol.com/gfsjohnf/gen_mail_country-mex.html#MEXICO

- NORWAY Mailing List
  http://members.aol.com/gfsjohnf/gen_mail_country-nor.html#NORWAY

- NO-SLEKT Mailing List
  http://members.aol.com/gfsjohnf/gen_mail_country-nor.html#NO-SLEKT
  Gatewayed with the no.slekt newsgroup. Norwegian genealogy conference covering any topic in genealogy except computer programs for genealogical use and searches for lost relatives and ancestors. The conference is conducted in Norwegian.

- NO-SLEKT-ETTERLYSNING Mailing List
  http://members.aol.com/gfsjohnf/gen_mail_country-nor.html#NO-SLEKT-ETT
  Gatewayed with the no.slekt.etterlysning newsgroup. Norwegian genealogy conference for searching relatives and ancestors in Norway and eventual discussions of such searches if there are dubious links published. The conference is conducted in Norwegian.

- **NO-SLEKT-PROGRAMMER** Mailing List
http://members.aol.com/gfsjohnf/gen_mail_country-nor.html#NO-SLEKT-PROG
Gatewayed with the no.slekt.programmer newsgroup. Norwegian genealogy conference for discussion of computer programs and other computer-related questions as they relate to genealogy. The conference is conducted in Norwegian.

- **Pacific_Islands** Mailing List
http://members.aol.com/gfsjohnf/gen_mail_country-gen.html#Pacific_Islands
For the discussion and collaboration on genealogy and family history of indigenous peoples from the Pacific. Also see the associated web page at http://www.genweb.net/~niueis/pacific.htm

- **PIE** Mailing List
http://members.aol.com/gfsjohnf/gen_mail_country-ita.html#PIE
For Italian genealogical research. Also see the associated web page at http://www.cimorelli.com/pie/piehome.htm

- **PolandBorderSurnames** Mailing List
http://members.aol.com/gfsjohnf/gen_mail_country-pol.html#PolandBorderSurnames
For anyone researching genealogy in the former historical borders of Poland including Estonia, Latvia, Lithuania, Belarus, Ukraine, Moldova, Slovakia, Czech Republic, Moravia, Hungary, Russia, the Balkans, and East Prussia.

- **POLAND-ROOTS** Mailing List
http://members.aol.com/gfsjohnf/gen_mail_country-pol.html#POLAND-ROOTS

- **PolishLessons** Mailing List
http://members.aol.com/gfsjohnf/gen_mail_country-pol.html#PolishLessons
To assist Poland researchers in translating Polish documents and to further their research while visiting/researching in Poland.

- **POMMERN-L** Mailing List
http://members.aol.com/gfsjohnf/gen_mail_country-pol.html#POMMERN-L
For those interested in sharing and exchanging information on genealogy and history which has a connection to Pommerania, both the current Polish part and remaining German parts of the former Prussian province.

- **PORTUGAL** Mailing List
http://members.aol.com/gfsjohnf/gen_mail_country-por.html#PORTUGAL

- **Radoshkovichlist** Mailing List
http://members.aol.com/gfsjohnf/gen_mail_country-lit.html#Radoshkovichlist
A mailing list for anyone with a genealogical interest in the town of Radoshkovich (a town on the road from Vilna to Minsk in Eastern Europe).

- **REPUBLICA-DOMINICANA** Mailing List
http://members.aol.com/gfsjohnf/gen_mail_country-dom.html#REPUBLICA-DOMINICANA

- **SARDINIA** Mailing List
http://members.aol.com/gfsjohnf/gen_mail_country-sar.html#SARDINIA

- **SaudiArabia** Mailing List
http://members.aol.com/gfsjohnf/gen_mail_country-sau.html#SaudiArabia

- **SCHAKEL-NL** Mailing List
http://members.aol.com/gfsjohnf/gen_mail_country-net.html#SCHAKEL-NL
For discussions of news events and issues of interest to Canadians and Americans of Dutch origin; Dutch heritage, customs and traditions; immigrant experiences; questions about Dutch legislation, laws, regulations, history etc.; living the Dutch way (e.g., travel, food, drinks); and the ties that bind us. Queries from genealogists related to their Dutch ancestry are welcome.

- **SCHLESIEN-L** Mailing List
http://members.aol.com/gfsjohnf/gen_mail_country-pol.html#SCHLESIEN-L
For those with a genealogical interest in the former Prussian province of Schlesien (Silesia), which is now mostly in Poland.

- **Scotland** Mailing Lists
http://www.CyndisList.com/scotland.htm
See this category on Cyndi's List for mailing list links.

- **SLOVAK-L** Mailing List
http://members.aol.com/gfsjohnf/gen_mail_country-slo.html#SLOVAK-L

- **SLOVAK-WORLD** Mailing List
http://members.aol.com/gfsjohnf/gen_mail_country-slo.html#SLOVAK-W

- **SOUTH-AFRICA** Mailing List
http://members.aol.com/gfsjohnf/gen_mail_country-soa.html#SOUTH-AFRICA

- **SOUTH-AM-EMI** Mailing List
http://members.aol.com/gfsjohnf/gen_mail_country-unk.html#SOUTH-AM-EMI
A mailing list for the discussion and sharing of information regarding emigrants from the United Kingdom to South America during the eighteenth and nineteenth centuries.

- **SPAIN** Mailing List
http://members.aol.com/gfsjohnf/gen_mail_country-spa.html#SPAIN

- **SRILANKA** Mailing List
http://members.aol.com/gfsjohnf/gen_mail_country-sri.html#SRILANKA

- **SWEDEN** Mailing List
http://members.aol.com/gfsjohnf/gen_mail_country-swe.html#SWEDEN

- **SWEDES** Mailing List
http://members.aol.com/gfsjohnf/gen_mail_country-swe.html#SWEDES

- **SWITZERLAND** Mailing List
http://members.aol.com/gfsjohnf/gen_mail_country-swi.html#SWITZERLAND

- **TRIER-ROOTS** Mailing List
http://members.aol.com/gfsjohnf/gen_mail_country-lux.html#GER-TRIER-ROOTS
For anyone with a genealogical interest in Luxembourg, the Saarland, the Rheinland, Westfalen (Westphalia), and the Pfalz (used to be between Rheinland and Baden, belonged to Bavaria but is now part of Rheinpfalz).

- Turkish_Jews Mailing List
  http://members.aol.com/gfsjohnf/gen_mail_country-ser.html#Turkish_Jews
  For Shephardic Jewish genealogists with roots in the former Turkish Ottoman Empire including Turkey, Serbia, Greece, and Yugoslavia.

- Unionist-Culture Mailing List
  http://members.aol.com/gfsjohnf/gen_mail_country-unk.html#Unionist-Culture
  For anyone with a genealogical or cultural interest in the Unionist communities of Ireland (those areas that wish to remain part of the union with England).

- United Kingdom & Ireland Mailing Lists
  http://www.CyndisList.com/uksites.htm
  and General UK Sites
  http://www.CyndisList.com/genuk.htm
  See these categories on Cyndi's List for mailing list links.

- United States Mailing Lists
  http://www.CyndisList.com/usa.htm
  and General USA Sites
  http://www.CyndisList.com/genusa.htm
  See these categories on Cyndi's List for mailing list links.

- VALDRES Mailing List
  http://members.aol.com/gfsjohnf/gen_mail_country-nor.html#VALDRES
  For the discussion and sharing of information regarding the Valdres region of Norway and immigrants from that region.

- Wales Mailing Lists
  http://www.CyndisList.com/wales.htm
  See this category on Cyndi's List for mailing list links.

◆ Usenet Newsgroups and Others

"Gatewayed with" means that the mailing list mirrors the associated newsgroup. All postings seen on the newsgroup will also be seen on the mailing list and vice versa. "FAQ" stands for Frequently Asked Questions and generally is a "help file" for a specific topic.

- alt.adoption
  For adoptees, birthparents, adoptive parents.

- alt.genealogy
  For general discussion.
  - Gatewayed with the ALT-GENEALOGY Mailing List
    http://members.aol.com/johnf14246/gen_mail_general.html#ALT-GENEALOGY

- alt.obituaries

- alt.scottish.clans

- alt.war.civil.usa
  - Web page
    http://www.public.usit.net/mruddy/index.html

- dk.historie.genealogi
  Danish newsgroup.

- fido.ger.genealogy
  German newsgroup.

- fr.rec.genealogie
  In French, mostly.
  - Gatewayed with the GEN-FF Mailing List
    http://members.aol.com/gfsjohnf/gen_mail_country-fra.html#GEN-FF-L

- no.slekt
  Mostly in Norwegian.
  - Archived messages
    http://www.sn.no/disnorge/norge.htm
  - Gatewayed with the NO-SLEKT Mailing List.
    http://members.aol.com/gfsjohnf/gen_mail_country-nor.html#NO-SLEKT

- no.slekt.programmer
  Mostly in Norwegian.
  - Web site
    http://www.sn.no/disnorge/
  - Gatewayed with NO-SLEKT-PROGRAMMER Mailing List.
    http://members.aol.com/gfsjohnf/gen_mail_country-nor.html#NO-SLEKT-PROG

- rec.heraldry

- soc.adoption.adoptees
  - The Adoptees Newsgroup
    http://www.geocities.com/Heartland/Acres/8126/

- soc.genealogy.african
  - Archived messages
    http://searches.rootsweb.com/sgafrican.html
  - Gatewayed with the Afrigeneas Mailing list.
    http://members.aol.com/johnf14246/gen_mail_general.html#AFRIGENEAS

- soc.genealogy.australia+nz
  Australia & New Zealand.
  - Archived messages
    http://www.anatomy.su.oz.au/danny/usenet/
  - FAQ
    http://www.rootsweb.com/~billingh/genanz-l.htm
  - Home page
    http://www.rootsweb.com/~billingh/
  - Gatewayed with the GENANZ Mailing list.
    http://members.aol.com/gfsjohnf/gen_mail_country-aus.html#GENANZ-L

- soc.genealogy.benelux
  Belgium, Netherlands, Luxembourg
  - Archived messages
    http://www.ufsia.ac.be/genealogy/genealog.htm
  - Gatewayed with the GENBNL-L Mailing list
    http://members.aol.com/gfsjohnf/gen_mail_country-blg.html#DUTCH

- soc.genealogy.britain
  - Gatewayed with the GENBRIT Mailing list.
    http://members.aol.com/gfsjohnf/gen_mail_country-unk.html#GENBRIT

- **soc.genealogy.computing**
  Genealogical computing & net resources.
  - Gatewayed with the GENCMP Mailing list
    http://members.aol.com/johnf14246/
    gen_mail_general.html#GENCMP-L
- **soc.genealogy.french**
  Discussion of Francophone genealogy.
  - Gatewayed with GEN-FR Mailing List.
    http://members.aol.com/gfsjohnf/gen_mail_country-
    fra.html#GEN-FR-L
- **soc.genealogy.german**
  - Web site
    http://www.genealogy.net/
  - FAQ
    http://www.genealogy.net/gene/faqs/sgg.html
  - Gatewayed with the GEN-DE Mailing List
    http://members.aol.com/gfsjohnf/gen_mail_country-
    ger.html#GEN-DE-L
- **soc.genealogy.hispanic**
- **soc.genealogy.ireland**
  - Gatewayed with the GENIRE Mailing List.
    http://members.aol.com/gfsjohnf/gen_mail_country-
    unk.html#GENIRE
- **soc.genealogy.jewish**
  - FAQ
    http://www.jewishgen.org/faqinfo.html
  - Gatewayed with the JEWISHGEN Mailing List
    http://members.aol.com/johnf14246/
    gen_mail_general.html#JEWISHGEN
- **soc.genealogy.marketplace**
  - FAQ
    http://www.prairienet.org/~mjolson/market.html
  - GEN-MARKET Mailing List
    http://members.aol.com/johnf14246/
    gen_mail_general.html#GEN-MARKET
- **soc.genealogy.medieval**
  - FAQ
    http://www.rand.org/personal/Genea/faqmed.html
  - Gatewayed with the GEN-MEDIEVAL
    Mailing List
    http://members.aol.com/johnf14246/
    gen_mail_general.html#GEN-MEDIEVAL
- **soc.genealogy.methods**
  Genealogy methods & non-net resources.
  - Web site
    http://www.rootsweb.com/~aet/
  - Archived messages
    http://searches.rootsweb.com/sgmethods.html
  - Gatewayed with the GENMTD Mailing List
    http://members.aol.com/johnf14246/
    gen_mail_general.html#GENMTD-L

- **soc.genealogy.misc**
  General genealogical discussions.
  - FAQ
    http://www.herald.co.uk/local_info/genuki/socgmisc.html
  - Gatewayed with the GENMSC Mailing List
    http://members.aol.com/johnf14246/
    gen_mail_general.html#GENMSC-L
- **soc.genealogy.nordic**
  - Gatewayed with the GEN-NORDIC Mailing List.
    http://members.aol.com/gfsjohnf/gen_mail_country-
    nor.html#GEN-NORDIC
- **soc.genealogy.slavic**
  - Web site
    http://feefhs.org/socslav/frg-slav.html
  - Gatewayed with the GEN-SLAVIC Mailing List
    http://members.aol.com/gfsjohnf/gen_mail_country-
    pol.html#GEN-SLAVIC
- **soc.genealogy.surnames.global**
  - SURNAMES-* FAQ files
    http://www.rootsweb.com/~surnames/
  - Gatewayed with the SURNAMES Mailing List
    http://members.aol.com/gfsjohnf/gen_mail_surnames-
    gen.html#SURNAMES
- **soc.genealogy.surnames.britain**
  Surname queries related to Great Britain.
  - SURNAMES-* FAQ files
    http://www.rootsweb.com/~surnames/
  - Gatewayed with SURNAMES-BRITAIN
    Mailing List
    http://members.aol.com/gfsjohnf/gen_mail_country-
    unk.html#SURNAMES-BRITAIN
- **soc.genealogy.surnames.canada**
  Surname queries related to Canada.
  - SURNAMES-* FAQ files
    http://www.rootsweb.com/~surnames/
  - Gatewayed with SURNAMES-CANADA
    Mailing List
    http://members.aol.com/gfsjohnf/gen_mail_surnames-
    gen.html#SURNAMES-CANADA
- **soc.genealogy.surnames.german**
  Surname queries related to Germany.
  - SURNAMES-* FAQ files
    http://www.rootsweb.com/~surnames/
  - Gatewayed with SURNAMES-GERMAN
    Mailing List
    http://members.aol.com/gfsjohnf/gen_mail_surnames-
    gen.html#SURNAMES-GERMAN
- **soc.genealogy.surnames.ireland**
  Surname queries related to Ireland and Northern Ireland.
  - SURNAMES-* FAQ files
    http://www.rootsweb.com/~surnames/

- ○ Gatewayed with SURNAMES-IRELAND Mailing List
  http://members.aol.com/gfsjohnf/gen_mail_surnames-gen.html#SURNAMES-IRELAND
- soc.genealogy.surnames.misc
  - ○ SURNAMES-* FAQ files
    http://www.rootsweb.com/~surnames/
  - ○ Gatewayed with SURNAMES-MISC Mailing List
    http://members.aol.com/gfsjohnf/gen_mail_surnames-gen.html#SURNAMES-MISC
- soc.genealogy.surnames.usa
  - ○ SURNAMES-* FAQ files
    http://www.rootsweb.com/~surnames/
  - ○ Gatewayed with SURNAMES-USA Mailing List
    http://members.aol.com/gfsjohnf/gen_mail_surnames-gen.html#SURNAMES-USA

- soc.genealogy.west-indies
  - ○ Archived Messages
    http://searches.rootsweb.com/sgwest-indies.html
- soc.history.moderated
- soc.history.war.us-civil-war
- soc.history.war.us-revolution
- soc.history.war.vietnam
- soc.history.war.world-war-ii
- swnet.sci.genealogi
  Swedish newsgroup.

MAPS, GAZETTEERS & GEOGRAPHICAL INFORMATION
http://www.CyndisList.com/maps.htm

Category Index:

- City Directories
- General Resource Sites
- Historical Maps, Atlases & Gazetteers
- Interactive Online Map Creation
- Libraries, Archives & Museums

- Local Boundary Resources
- National Geographic Information
- Software
- Vendors

◆ City Directories

- **Analyzing City Directories**
  http://www.genealogy.org/~bcg/skbld965.html
  From the Board for Certification of Genealogists—Skill Building—May 1996.

- **Chicago City Directories on Microfilm**
  http://www.mcs.net/~jimjoyce/genealogy/ccdindex.html
  Illinois

- **City Directories at the Library of Congress**
  http://www.kinquest.com/genealogy/citydir.html

- **City Directories**
  http://www.ancestry.com/columns/george/03-06-98.htm
  From "Along Those Lines . . ." by George Morgan.

- **City Directories of the United States—Guide to the Microfilm Collection**
  http://scfn.thpl.lib.fl.us/thpl/main/spc/city_directories.htm
  From the Special Collections Department of the Tampa-Hillsborough County Public Library System.

- **City Directories: Windows on the Past**
  http://www.ancestry.com/columns/myra/
  Shaking_Family_Tree03-19-98.htm
  From Shaking Your Family Tree, by Myra Vanderpool Gormley, C.G.

- **Glendale City Directories**
  http://www.library.ci.glendale.ca.us/city_dir.html
  California

- **Telephone and City Directories in the Library of Congress: A Finding Guide**
  gopher://marvel.loc.gov/00/research/reading.rooms/genealogy/
  bibs.guides/telephon
  By Barbara B. Walsh, Reference Specialist, November 1994.

- **TSLAC City Directories Available in the State Archives**
  http://www.tsl.state.tx.us/lobby/citydirs.htm
  Texas State Library and Archives Commission.

◆ General Resource Sites

- **Ancestry Groups in the United States**
  http://www.lmic.state.mn.us/dnet/maplib/ancestry/
  usancest.htm
  Maps which show how many people in each county of the United States identify with certain ancestry groups.

- **Books We Own—Atlases and Gazetteers**
  http://www.rootsweb.com/~bwo/atlas.html

- **Cartography Resources**
  http://geog.gmu.edu/projects/maps/cartogrefs.html

- **CGRER Netsurfing: Maps and References**
  http://www.cgrer.uiowa.edu/servers/servers_references.html
  Huge compilation of links from the University of Iowa.

- **Geographic Information Systems—Resources on the Web**
  http://www-map.lib.umn.edu/gis.html
  List from the John R. Borchert Map Library, Univ. of Minnesota.

- **Getty Thesaurus of Geographic Names**
  http://www.ahip.getty.edu/tgn_browser/

- **John Robertson's Genealogy & Maps**
  http://www.geocities.com/Heartland/2297/
  Historical county lines; genealogy atlas "how-to" and more.

- **Map Related Web Sites**
  http://www.lib.utexas.edu/Libs/PCL/Map_collection/map_sites/
  map_sites.html

- **Maps Can Help You Trace Your Family Tree**
  http://info.er.usgs.gov/fact-sheets/genealogy/index.html

- **Oddens's Bookmarks—The Fascinating World of Maps and Mapping**
  http://kartoserver.geog.uu.nl/html/staff/oddens/oddens.htm

◆ Historical Maps, Atlases & Gazetteers

- 1872 County Map of Colorado, Dakota, Indian Nations, Kansas, Montana, Nebraska & Wyoming
  http://www.ismi.net/chnegw/1872title.htm

- 1895 World Atlas—U.S.
  http://www.LivGenMI.com/1895.htm

- American Memory Railroad Maps 1828–1900
  http://memory.loc.gov/ammem/gmdhtml/rrhtml/rrhome.html
  From the Geography and Map Division, Library of Congress.

- Andreas' Historical Atlas of Dakota ~ 1884
  http://www.rootsweb.com/~usgenweb/sd/andreas/1884

- Cartographic Images—Ancient, Medieval & Renaissance Maps
  http://www.iag.net/~jsiebold/carto.html

- Le Dictionnaire des communes
  http://www.es-conseil.fr/pramona/p1gen.htm#dico
  If you are searching for a place name in France, or Algeria, Philippe RAMONA will do a lookup for you in this book: "Dictionnaire des Communes de la France, de l'Algérie et des autres colonies Françaises" (Paris 1866).

- FEEFHS Map Room—Background and Map Index
  http://feefhs.org/maps/indexmap.html

- Greenwood's Map of London 1827
  http://www.bathspa.ac.uk/greenwood/home.html

- Historic Maps of the Netherlands
  http://grid.let.rug.nl/~welling/maps/maps.html

- Historical Atlas of Canada Data Dissemination Project
  http://geog.utoronto.ca/hacddp/hacpage.html

- Historical Map Web Sites
  http://www.lib.utexas.edu/Libs/PCL/Map_collection/map_sites/hist_sites.html
  A list by the Perry-Castañeda Library Map Collection, The University of Texas at Austin.

- Historical Maps
  http://www.lib.utexas.edu:80/Libs/PCL/Map_collection/historical/history_main.html
  From The Perry-Castañeda Library Map Collection, The University of Texas at Austin.

- Historical Maps
  http://www.rootsweb.com/~wggerman/maps.htm
  For Germany from WorldGenWeb.

- Map 1797—Plan of Great Yarmouth, Norfolk by William Faden
  http://www.gtyarmouth.co.uk/html/map_1797.htm
  England

- Maps of National Historic & Military Parks, Memorials, and Battlefields
  http://www.lib.utexas.edu/Libs/PCL/Map_collection/National_parks/historic_parks.html#military
  United States

- New York State Historical Maps
  http://www.sunysb.edu/libmap/nymaps.htm

- Old Maps of the Channel Islands
  http://user.itl.net/~glen/maps.html

- OSSHE Historical & Cultural Atlas Resource
  http://darkwing.uoregon.edu/~atlas/

- Panoramic Maps Collection
  http://lcweb2.loc.gov/ammem/pmhtml/panhome.html
  From the Geography and Map Division, Library of Congress.

- Pioneer Trails from U.S. Land Surveys
  http://history.cc.ukans.edu/heritage/werner/werner.html

- Sanborn Fire Insurance Maps
  http://www.lib.berkeley.edu/EART/snb-intr.html
  A description from the Earth Sciences and Map Library at the University of California at Berkeley.

- Texas General Land Office Archives— Map Collection
  http://www.glo.state.tx.us/central/arc/mapscol.html

- Texas Historic Sites Atlas
  http://atlas.thc.state.tx.us/

- U.S. Territorial Maps 1775–1920
  http://xroads.virginia.edu/~MAP/terr_hp.html

- Wisconsin County Maps, 1901
  http://www.kinquest.com/1901Atlas/1901atlas.html

◆ Interactive Online Map Creation

- MapBlast!
  http://www.mapblast.com/
  Create detailed street maps.

- MapQuest!
  http://www.mapquest.com/
  Interactive atlas for U.S. streets and more.

- Microsoft Expedia Maps
  http://www.expediamaps.com/

- Multi Media Mapping
  http://uk5.multimap.com/map/places.cgi
  An interactive atlas of Great Britain. Enter the name of a British city, town or village to get a clickable, zoomable, detailed map.

- U.S. Surname Distribution Maps
  http://www.hamrick.com/names/index.html

◆ Libraries, Archives & Museums

- Association of Canadian Map Libraries and Archives
  http://www.sscl.uwo.ca/assoc/acml/acmla.html

- The Bodleian Library Map Room
  http://www.rsl.ox.ac.uk/nnj/

- Harvard Map Collection
  http://icg.harvard.edu/~maps/

- Heritage Map Museum Home Page
  http://www.carto.com/
  Antique maps from 15th to 19th century.

- Map and Geographic Information Center
  http://magic.lib.uconn.edu/
  University of Connecticut, Homer Babbidge Library.

- The Map Collection at the University of Stony Brook, New York
  http://www.sunysb.edu/library/ldmaps.htm

- Map Libraries—List from the John R. Borchert Map Library, Univ. of Minnesota
  http://www-map.lib.umn.edu/map_libraries.html

- Perry-Castañeda Library Map Collection
  http://www.lib.utexas.edu/Libs/PCL/Map_collection/
  Map_collection.html
  The General Libraries, The University of Texas at Austin.

- Rare Map Collection at the Hargrett Library, University of Georgia
  http://www.libs.uga.edu/darchive/hargrett/maps/maps.html

- UVA Library Geographic Information Center
  http://viva.lib.virginia.edu/gic/
  ○ Digital Resources Catalog
     http://viva.lib.virginia.edu/gic/catalog/
  ○ Maps Collection
     http://viva.lib.virginia.edu/gic/services/services_maps.html
  ○ Virginia Digital Map Library
     http://viva.lib.virginia.edu/gic/maps/maps_va.html
  ○ Virginia Locator Service
     http://viva.lib.virginia.edu/gic/va_locator/locator.html

- Western Association of Map Libraries
  http://gort.ucsd.edu/mw/waml/waml.html

- Yahoo!...Science...Maps...Libraries
  http://dir.yahoo.com/Science/Geography/Cartography/Maps/
  Libraries/

◆ Local Boundary Resources

- Administrative Regions of the British Isles
  http://www.genuki.org.uk/big/Regions/
  From GENUKI.

- Boundaries of the United States and the Several States
  http://www.ac.wwu.edu/~stephan/48states.html
  with an animated GIF map of the Settlement of the United States
  http://www.rootsweb.com/~kygreenu/images/48states.gif

- Counties of England, Scotland and Wales Prior to the 1974 Boundary Changes
  http://www.genuki.org.uk/big/BRITAIN2.GIF

- County Map of Scotland
  http://www.users.zetnet.co.uk/vdunstan/genuki/maps/
  sct_cmap.html
  From the GENUKI web site for Scotland.

- Evolution of United States County Boundaries
  http://www.ac.wwu.edu/~stephan/Animation/us.html
  *and an animated GIF showing county boundaries for 1650,
  1700, 1750, and census years from 1790 onward*
  http://www.ac.wwu.edu/~stephan/Animation/us.gif

- Graphical Display of the Federal Township and Range System
  http://www.outfitters.com/genealogy/land/twprangemap.html
  U.S. Explains the division of townships and sections.

- Historical County Lines
  http://www.geocities.com/Heartland/2297/maps.htm

- Land Ownership Maps in the Library of Congress
  http://www.kinquest.com/genealogy/lom.html
  *A list by state, county and year, of the maps available in the
  collection held at the Library of Congress.*

- Leitrim-Roscommon Map Collection
  http://www.thecore.com/let_ros/LR_maps.html
  *Ireland. Maps that display the Parishes, Baronies and Poor Law
  Unions for these two counties.*

- List of United States Counties—Home Page
  http://www.genealogy.org/PAF/www/counties/

◆ National Geographic Information

- AUSLIG on the Web—Australian Surveying & Land Information Group
  http://www.auslig.gov.au/

- Australian Gazetteer
  http://www.ke.com.au/cgi-bin/texhtml?form=AustGaz
  Online demo version of a software program.

- Australian Geographic Place Names (Gazetteer)
  http://www.erin.gov.au/database/gaze_ack.html

- BC Geographical Names Information System
  http://www.env.gov.bc.ca/~bcnames/
  Canada. Searchable database.

- British Geological Survey Maps
  http://www.bgs.ac.uk/bgs/w3/isg/maps.html

- Canada National Atlas Information Service (NAIS)
  http://www-nais.ccm.emr.ca/

- Canadian Geographical Names / Les noms géographiques du Canada
  http://GeoNames.NRCan.gc.ca/
  ○ Canadian Geographical Names—Publications
     http://GeoNames.NRCan.gc.ca/english/publications.html
     *List of available publications on geographical names
     including policy documents and manuals, gazetteers,
     glossaries, newsletters and brochures.*
  ○ Origins of Canada's Geographical Names
     http://GeoNames.NRCan.gc.ca/english/schoolnet/origin.html
  ○ Query by Geographical Name
     http://Geonames.NRCan.gc.ca/english/cgndb.html
  ○ Current Names Selected by Coordinates
     http://Geonames.NRCan.gc.ca/english/cgndb_coord.html
     *Search this database of over 500,000 geographical names by
     name, feature type, region and by province.*

- Color Landform Atlas of the United States
  http://fermi.jhuapl.edu/states/states.html

- Country Maps from W3 Servers in Europe
  http://www.tue.nl/europe/

- The Data Wales Maps Page
  http://www.data-wales.co.uk/walesmap.htm
- Gazetteer for Scotland
  http://www.geo.ed.ac.uk/~scotgaz/gazhome.htm
  Under development at the Department of Geography at the University of Edinburgh.
- Geographic Names Database
  ftp://ftp.eecs.umich.edu/pub/eecs/geo/
  - Format of the Geographic Names Database
    ftp://ftp.eecs.umich.edu/pub/eecs/geo/README
- Geographic Name Server
  http://www.mit.edu:8001/geo
  Find location, county name and zip code.
- Geographic Name Server
  gopher://riceinfo.rice.edu:1103/1geo
  Look up US place names by city or zip code.
- Geographic Server by State
  gopher://george.peabody.yale.edu:71/1
- GEOserv—A German Town Locator
  http://www2.genealogy.net/gene/www/abt/geoserv.html
- Government Documents and Map Department
  http://govdoc.ucdavis.edu/
  U.S. At the University of California, Davis.
- History of Australian Places Index
  http://www.zades.com.au/ozindex/ozindex.html
- Home Page of Hungarian Cartography
  http://lazarus.elte.hu/gb/hunkarta/kezdo.htm
- Large Map of Wales
  ftp://sunsite.unc.edu/pub/academic/languages/welsh/wales.gif
- LINZ—The New Zealand Geographic Place-Names Database
  http://www.linz.govt.nz/databases/geographic/geoname.html
- Map of New Zealand—Guide to Cities & Towns
  http://www.atonz.com/genealogy/nza2.gif
- Maps of Croatia and Bosnia-Herzegovina
  http://www.applicom.com/maps/
- The Ordnance Survey—Gazetteer of Place Names
  http://www.campus.bt.com/CampusWorld/pub/OS/Gazetteer/index.html
  Searchable database for UK.
- Ordnance Survey Home Page
  http://www.ordsvy.gov.uk/
  National Mapping Agency of Great Britain.
- National Imagery and Mapping Agency—GEOnet Names Server
  http://164.214.2.59/gns/html/index.html
  United States NIMA GNPS Query Form for searching a database of foreign geographic feature names.
- National Library of Australia Map Collection
  http://www.nla.gov.au/1/gencoll/maps.html

- Natural Resources Canada
  http://www.NRCan.gc.ca/
- Tiger Mapping Service Home Page (US Census Bureau)
  http://tiger.census.gov/
- UK Sensitive Map to Universities
  http://scitsc.wlv.ac.uk/ukinfo/uk.map.html
- United States Board on Geographic Names
  http://mapping.usgs.gov/www/gnis/bgn.html
  A description from the USGS Mapping Information web site.
- U.S. Gazetteer—From the U.S. Census Bureau
  http://www.census.gov/cgi-bin/gazetteer
- USGS National Mapping Information
  http://mapping.usgs.gov/
  - USGS Mapping Information: Foreign Geographic Names Gazetteers
    http://mapping.usgs.gov/www/gnis/foreign.html
  - USGS Mapping Information: Geographic Names Information System
    http://mapping.usgs.gov/www/gnis/
  - USGS Mapping Information: GNIS Data Base Query Form
    http://mapping.usgs.gov/www/gnis/gnisform.html
  - USGS Mapping Information: The National Gazetteer
    http://164.214.2.59/gns/html/index.html
  - USGS National Mapping Division Reference Collection Library and Historical Map Archives
    http://mapping.usgs.gov/html/2library.html
  - USGS NSDI Clearinghouse—Geographic Names Information System (GNIS)
    http://nsdi.usgs.gov/nsdi/products/gnis.html
- Yale Peabody Museum: Geographic Names Information System (GNIS)
  http://www.peabody.yale.edu/other/gnis/
  *Search the USGS Geographic Names Database. You can limit the search to a specific county in this state and search for any of the following features: airport arch area arroyo bar basin bay beach bench bend bridge **building** canal cape **cemetery** channel **church** cliff crater crossing dam falls flat forest gap geyser glacier gut harbor hospital island isthmus lake lava levee locale mine oilfield other park pillar plain ppl range rapids reserve reservoir ridge **school** sea slope spring stream summit swamp tower trail tunnel valley well woods.*

◆ Software

- CensusCD+Maps
  http://www.censuscd.com/cdmaps/censuscd_maps.htm
- Computer Programs for Drawing Plat Maps
  http://www.outfitters.com/genealogy/land/compmaps.html
- Deed Mapper Software
  http://www.ultranet.com/~deeds/

- Gold Bug
  http://www.goldbug.com/
  Historical map reproductions & county mapping software.
- Stephen Archer's Genealogical Software Home Page
  http://ourworld.compuserve.com/homepages/steve_archer/
  GenMap UK, a Windows mapping program designed mainly for UK genealogical and historical mapping.

◆ Vendors

- Baldwin's Old Prints, Maps & Charts
  http://commercial.visi.net/baldwins/
- City and Town Plan Reproductions for Genealogy—From Generations Press
  http://members.aol.com/townplans/index.html
- The David Morgan Home Page
  http://www.davidmorgan.com/
  Has British Ordnance Survey maps for sale.
- Frontier Press Bookstore—Atlases
  http://www.frontierpress.com/frontier.cgi?category=atlas
- Frontier Press Bookstore—Maps
  (Finding and Making Use of Maps)
  http://www.frontierpress.com/frontier.cgi?category=map
- GenealogyBookShop.com—Atlases/Gazetteers/Place Names
  http://www.genealogybookshop.com/genealogybookshop/files/General,Atlases_Gazetteers_Place_Names/index.html
  The online store of Genealogical Publishing Co., Inc. & Clearfield Company.
- Genealogy Unlimited, Inc.
  http://www.itsnet.com:80/home/genun/public_html/
  Genealogical books, forms, and supplies; historical, topographic, and modern European maps; and archival supplies.
- Generations Press Maps—City & Town Plans for Genealogy
  http://members.aol.com/townplans/
- Gleason's Old Maps Etc.
  http://members.aol.com/oldmapsetc/index.html
  Photocopies of Old Maps, Old Prints, and Old Articles of Interest to Genealogists and Historians Pertaining to Indiana, Illinois, Ohio, New Jersey, Pennsylvania, and more to come.
- Global Genealogy—Historical & Contemporary Maps & Atlases
  http://www.globalgenealogy.com/mapsmain.htm
- The Henry H. Schryver Collection
  http://www.bigwave.ca/~avanhald/
  A collection of historical maps and books on the geography of North America.

- International Map Trade Association (IMTA)
  http://www.maptrade.org/
- K.B. Slocum Books and Maps
  http://www.treasurenet.com/kbslocum/welcome.html
  A huge selection of old U.S. state and city maps.
- Kickapoo Maps
  http://www.kickapoo.com/
- Macbeth Genealogical Services
  http://www.macbeth.com.au/
  Books, fiche, maps, and CD-ROMs. Australia.
- The Memorabilia Corner
  http://members.aol.com/TMCorner/index.html
  Forms, flags, maps, software, CDs, tapes, microfilm & microfiche, books, periodicals, photographic conservation & archival materials.
- Old Maps of New England & New York—Villages, Towns & Cities & Other Items of Historical Interest
  http://members.aol.com/oldmapsne/index.html
- Pacific Shore Maps
  http://www.electriciti.com/psmaps/index.html
  Antique maps and charts from around the world.
- Patton Maps—Alfred B. Patton, Inc.
  http://www.pattonmaps.com/
- Reproductions of Old Town Maps in New England
  http://www.biddeford.com/~lkane/
- Roots and Branches
  http://members.aol.com/RebelSher1/index.html
  Used books, forms, maps and the Civil War info.
- Scharlau Prints and Maps
  http://www.scharlau.co.uk/
  Etchings, antiquarian engravings, maps and prints of Scotland.
- S.E.L. Enterprises
  http://www.mentornet.org/sel.htm
  Publications (books, magazines, periodicals & maps) for researching your English, Irish, Scots and Welsh ancestors.
- Storbeck's Genealogy Books Maps CD-ROM
  http://www.storbecks.com/
- Travel Genie—Detailed Maps for Genealogy
  http://www.netins.net/showcase/travelgenie
- The Willow Bend Books Mapstore
  http://www.willowbend.net/maps.htm
- Ye Olde Genealogie Shoppe—Forms, Charts, Maps & Goodies
  http://www.yogs.com/

MARRIAGES
http://www.CyndisList.com/marriage.htm

Category Index:

- ◆ How To
- ◆ Locality Specific

- ◆ Professional Researchers, Volunteers &
  Other Research Services

◆ How To

- England and Wales Birth, Marriage, and
  Death Certificate Information
  http://shoppersmart.com/otown/registrations/

- Finding a Marriage Date
  http://www.familytreemaker.com/11_mrgdt.html
  By Karen Clifford, A.G.

- Finding Marriage Places with Bible Records
  http://www.familytreemaker.com/00000506.html

- Finding the Minimum Information for
  Bible Records—Marriage Dates
  http://www.familytreemaker.com/00000490.html

- Finding the Minimum Information for
  Bible Records—Divorce or Subsequent Marriage
  http://www.familytreemaker.com/00000576.html

- Researching Your Family's Marriages
  http://www.familytreemaker.com/issue11.html

- Terms of Confusement: Dowry and Dower
  http://www.ancestry.com/columns/myra/
  Shaking_Family_Tree10-02-97.htm
  *From Shaking Your Family Tree by Myra Vanderpool
  Gormley, C.G.*

◆ Locality Specific

- 1880–1920 Otago Daily Times Births Deaths
  Marriages, Anniversaries Index, Dunedin,
  New Zealand
  http://www.es.co.nz/~treeves/geneal.htm
  See the details near the end of this page.

- Al POTTS' Marion County, Ohio Page
  http://idt.net/~allenp19/
  *Marion County, Ohio Marriages Volume I 1824–1835 and
  Volume II 1835–1839; Meeker Union Cemetery Records, Meeker
  Ohio pictures and more.*

- Alblasserwaard Genealogie Page
  http://www.geocities.com/Paris/4744/ALBWRDGENPAGE.HTM
  Several marriage indexes here for the early 1800's.

- Andover, Maine Marriages 1805 to 1863
  http://members.aol.com/andoverme/marriage.html

- Australasia Births, Deaths and Marriages Exchange
  http://www.geocities.com/Athens/Forum/3709/exchange/
  *The aim of the Australasia Births, Deaths and Marriages
  Exchange is to provide to genealogists a free resource, to share
  information about details contained on birth, death and
  marriage registrations registered in Australia, New Zealand and
  Papua New Guinea.*

- Australian Registrars of Births Deaths & Marriages
  http://www.users.on.net/proformat/regs.html

- Baker County Marriages, 1877–1930
  http://www.magicnet.net/~cmobley/mgs.html
  Florida

- Barrington Courier-Review Indexes
  http://www.bal.alibrary.com/bcr.html
  Illinois. Births, deaths and marriages from 1890 to 1996.

- Birth, Marriage, Death Indexes for Ontario, Canada
  http://www.geocities.com/Heartland/9332/bmd.htm

- Births, Deaths and Marriages Reported in Calgary,
  Alberta Newspapers, 1883–1899
  http://www.calcna.ab.ca/afhs/news.html
  Canada

- British Columbia Marriage Event
  http://www.hlth.gov.bc.ca/vs/marriage/

- Buncombe County, NC Marriage Records
  http://main.nc.us/OBCGS/wedindx.htm

- Caldwell County, Texas Marriages, 1848–1886
  ftp://ftp.rootsweb.com/pub/usgenweb/tx/caldwell/marriage/
  1848.txt

- Candlish Church, Free Presbyterian, Barney's River,
  Pictou County, Nova Scotia Marriages—1812–1883
  http://www.rootsweb.com/~pictou/marchr.htm

- Carter County, Missouri Marriages—1860 thru 1881
  http://www.mindspring.com/~sapart/mar1860.html

- Carter County Missouri Marriages—
  Book "A" 1881–1890
  http://www.mindspring.com/~sapart/cc188190.html

- Carter County Missouri Marriage Book "B"
  1890–1898
  http://www.mindspring.com/~sapart/crtmrgb.html

- Castine Marriages 1892–1960
  http://www.kalama.com/~mariner/casmarry.htm
  Maine

- Christian County Marriages 1799–1820
  http://www.aplusdata.com/kyseeker/christmarriages.cfm
  Kentucky

- Clark County, Nevada Government and Services
  http://www.co.clark.nv.us/
  - Marriage Inquiry System
    http://www.co.clark.nv.us/recorder/mar_disc.htm
    A searchable index of marriages from 1984 through the present.

- Clinton County, Indiana Marriages
  http://www.rootsweb.com/~inclinto/marriages.html

- The Cochin Churchbook
  http://www.telebyte.nl/~dessa/cochin.htm
  Baptism & marriages from the Dutch Church in Cochin, India (1754–1804).

- Colorado Marriages and Divorces Search
  http://www.quickinfo.net/madi/comadi.html
  Marriages (from 1975 to 1997) and divorces (from 1975 to July 1998).

- Covehead Tracadie Marriages 1887–1900
  http://www.eskimo.com/~mvreid/34mar.html
  For Covehead, Corran Ban, Tracadie in Queens County, Prince Edward Island, Canada.

- Crawford County Marriages 1877–1887
  http://www.rootsweb.com/~arcrawfo/marriage.htm
  Arkansas

- Database to an Index of Indiana Marriages Through 1850
  http://www.statelib.lib.in.us/www/indiana/genealogy/mirr.html
  Indiana State Library, Genealogy Division.

- Desoto Co. Marriages, June 28, 1887 thru March 24, 1892
  http://www.rootsweb.com/~fldesoto/marriages.htm
  Florida

- Early Alpena County Marriages 1871
  http://www.rootsweb.com/~mialpena/early.htm
  Michigan

- Early Marriages By Albertus C. Van Raalte
  http://www.macatawa.org/~devries/Earlym.htm
  From Southern Ottawa County, Michigan, and Northern Allegan County, Michigan.

- Early Marriages of Newaygo County
  http://www.rootsweb.com/~minewaygo/marriag.html
  Michigan

- Early Marriages and Deaths of Village Residents
  http://www.iserv.net/~bryant/grmarr.txt
  Grand Rapids, Michigan

- Early Marriages of Wood County
  http://home.sprynet.com/sprynet/bweiford/woodcoma.htm
  West Virginia

- Erin Township, Wellington Co., Ontario Records
  http://www.chelmsford.com/home/priestner/Wellington.htm
  Canada. Various marriage records from 1831 through 1908.

- Faculty Office Marriage Licence Index
  http://ourworld.compuserve.com/homepages/David_Squire/faculty.htm
  Index of marriage licences issued by the Master of Faculties of the Archbishop of Canterbury for the period 1714 to 1850.

- Freedman's Bureau, Marriages in Arkansas 1861–1869
  http://www.freedmensbureau.com/arkansas/arkansasmarriages.htm

- Freedman's Bureau, Marriages in Jacksonville, Florida 1861–1869
  http://www.freedmensbureau.com/florida/florida.htm

- Freedman's Bureau, Marriages in Mississippi 1863–1865
  http://www.freedmensbureau.com/mississippi/mississippimarriages.htm

- Freedman's Bureau, Marriages in Tennesee 1865–1869
  http://www.freedmensbureau.com/tennessee/marriages/tennesseemarriages.htm

- Freedman's Bureau, Marriages in Washington, D.C. 1861–1869, Part 1
  http://www.freedmensbureau.com/washingtondc/dcmarriages1.htm
  Part 2
  http://www.freedmensbureau.com/washingtondc/dcmarriages2.htm

- Freedmen's Bureau Register of Marriages in Gloucester, Virginia 1861–1869
  http://www.freedmensbureau.com/virginia/gloucester.htm

- Every Name Index to Town Marriage Records in Tisbury, MA 1850–1875
  http://www.vineyard.net/vineyard/history/tmindex.htm
  - Index to Marriages in Tisbury by Bride's Name 1844–1940
    http://www.vineyard.net/vineyard/history/bridesi.htm
    Index to marriages in Tisbury, Mass. by bride's name, for the period 1844–1940. Prepared by the staff of the Tisbury Town Clerk's office.
  - Index to Marriages in Tisbury by Groom's Name 1844–1940
    http://www.vineyard.net/vineyard/history/groomsi.htm
    Index to marriages in Tisbury, Mass. by groom's name, for the period 1844–1940. Prepared by the staff of the Tisbury Town Clerk's office.

- Henderson County Marriages 1806–1860
  http://www.aplusdata.com/kyseeker/hendmarriages.cfm
  Kentucky

- Hillsborough County, Florida Marriage Records—
Index
http://www.lib.usf.edu/spccoll/guide/m/ml/guide.html
*Records online from 4 Jan 1878 to 11 May 1884, including a
photo of the original document.*

- Hillsborough County Marriage Records
http://www.lib.usf.edu/spccoll/marriage.html
*List of the special collections at University of South Florida
Tampa Campus Library.*

- Hood County Texas Genealogical Society
Index of Records
http://www.genealogy.org/~granbury/index.htm
Including Birth, Marriage, Tax, & many other online records.

- Index of Marriages and Deaths in New York Weekly
Museum, 1788–1817
http://www.itsnet.com/~pauld/newyork/

- Index to Death & Marriage Notices in the Vineyard
Gazette 1884–1939 A–K
http://www.vineyard.net/vineyard/history/vgind1.htm

- Index to Death & Marriage Notices in the Vineyard
Gazette 1884–1939 L–Z
http://www.vineyard.net/vineyard/history/vgind2.htm

- Index to Marriage Notices in the Vineyard Gazette,
1850–1863
http://www.vineyard.net/vineyard/history/gazmar63.htm
*Index to marriage notices in the Vineyard Gazette by bride and
groom—mainly covers marriages on Martha's Vineyard and
Dukes County, Mass. Covers years 1850–1863. Includes names,
residences, date and place of marriage, and newspaper issue.*

- Index to PEI Database Reports
http://homepages.rootsweb.com/~mvreid/pei/peidbidx.html
*A wonderful collection of resources from Marge Reid, including
probate records, surname indexes for marriage and burial
records and much more.*

- Ionia County, Michigan—Early Marriage Records—
Indexed by Groom
http://www.rootsweb.com/~miionia/more.txt

- Jean's Maine Genealogy Page
http://www.mnopltd.com/jean/
*Index of deaths and marriages as published in the Ellsworth
Herald its successor, the Ellsworth American October 24, 1851
through December 29, 1865.*

- Jo Daviess Co., IL Marriage Records
http://members.tripod.com/~Chemingway/Mrg.html
Volume B: 1855–1865, Volume E, 1870–1885.

- The Joiner Marriage Index
http://homepages.enterprise.net/pjoiner/mindex/mindex.html
*A Marriage Database for County Durham, and the North
Riding of Yorkshire.*

- Kentucky Residents Married in
Shawneetown, Illinois
http://www.rootsweb.com/~kyhender/Henderson/ill.htm

- Kentucky Vital Records Index
http://ukcc.uky.edu/~vitalrec/
Marriage / Divorce / Death

- Lafleur Archives
http://www.lafleur.org/
*Provides birth, death and marriage records from authentic Bible
records. There are scanned images of Bibles when possible.*

- LDS Film Numbers for Ontario Marriage
Registrations
http://www.geocities.com/Heartland/9332/lds-m.htm

- Leon County Marriage Records Search Form
http://www.clerk.leon.fl.us/marriage/marriage_index.html
Florida

- Lenawee County Michigan Newspaper 'Michigan
Expositor' Notices of Marriages and Deaths in 1850
http://members.aol.com/Lenaweemi/extractions1850.html

- Lincoln County, Oklahoma Early Marriages
http://www.skypoint.com/~jkm/oklincoln/marriage.html

- Lincoln County, Tennessee, Marriages—
Interactive Search
http://www.rootsweb.com/cgi-bin/tnlincoln/tnlincoln.pl

- Llanelli Marriages 1833–1837 St. Elli Parish
Church, South Wales, UK
ftp://ftp.rootsweb.com/pub/wggenweb/southwales/vitals/
llanelli.txt
*Also Llanelli Marriages 1864–1867. Taken from Llanelli
Guardian Births, Deaths & Marriages.*

- A Little Bit of Ireland
http://home.att.net/~labaths/
*From Cathy Joynt Labath, contains many transcribed records:
birth, marriage, cemeteries, deeds, directories, etc.*

- Louisiana Weddings
http://www.angelfire.com/tx/1850censusrecords/
laweddings.html

- Madison County, Iowa Marriages 1850–1880
http://searches.rootsweb.com/cgi-bin/Genea/iowa

- Marriage History Search Form
http://thor.ddp.state.me.us/archives/plsql/
archdev.Marriage_Archive.search_form
Index to Maine Marriages 1892–1966.

- Marriage Records of Knott County, Kentucky
http://www.rootsweb.com/~kyknott/marriages.html

- Marriages in Tisbury, 1850–1853
http://www.vineyard.net/vineyard/history/tmar1b.htm
*Transcript of the town marriage register for the town of Tisbury,
Mass., covering the years 1850–1853.*

- Marriages in Tisbury, 1853–1875
http://www.vineyard.net/vineyard/history/tmar2.htm
*Transcript of town marriage register for the town of Tisbury,
Mass. for the years 1853–1875.*

- Marriage Witness Indexes for United Kingdom, Australia, and New Zealand
  http://www.genuki.org.uk/mwi/

- Marriages and Deaths, A–D
  http://www.geocities.com/Heartland/Plains/3558/admarrig.htm
  Pennsylvania. 1810–1818. Many from Luzerne, Bradford, & Susquehanna Counties.

- Marriages and Deaths, E–G
  http://www.geocities.com/Heartland/Plains/3558/egmarrig.htm
  Pennsylvania. 1810–1818. Many from Luzerne, Bradford, & Susquehanna Counties.

- Marriages from the Sherburn Hospital Registers (1695–1837)
  http://www.cs.ncl.ac.uk/genuki/Transcriptions/DUR/SHO.html
  Northumberland and Durham, England

- Marriages from the Texas Telegraph, 1841–50
  http://www.geocities.com/Vienna/1516/houmart.html
  Houston, Texas

- Marriages in Kalkaska County, Michigan 1871–1875
  http://members.aol.com/kingsley/kas-mar.html

- Marriages in Parishes in Castlebar-Westport Area
  http://people.delphi.com/patdeese/MARR.HTML
  Ireland

- Marriages in Pictou County by Rev. James McGregor
  http://www.rootsweb.com/~pictou/hitches.htm
  Nova Scotia, Canada

- Marriages in Plauschwarren, East Prussia 1778–1802
  http://www.mmhs.org/prussia/plauschm.htm

- Marriages in Rankin County, Mississippi
  http://www.vanished.com/pages/free_lib/rankin_co.html

- Marriages of Norfolk County, Virginia, 1851–1865
  This book, compiled and published by Elizabeth B. Hanbury, lists the 1300+ marriages and all pertinent information for each given in the county marriage register for that period. Arranged alphabetically by grooms' last names; brides' names are indexed. For details send e-mail to Elizabeth at:ehanbury@pilot.infi.net

- Miami Valley Genealogical Index
  http://www.pcdl.lib.oh.us/miami/miami.htm
  Surname index of census, tax, marriage & wills records for these counties: Butler, Champaign, Clark, Darke, Greene, Hamilton, Mercer, Miami, Montgomery, Preble, Shelby, Warren.

- Michiana Genealogical Index—MGI
  http://www.qtm.net/~ftmiami/remarc/
  A surname source database for birth, death, marriage, license, divorce and cemetery records. Representing over 500,000 records from southwestern Michigan and northern Indiana.

- Middlesex England Parish Records
  http://www.enol.com/~infobase/gen/parish/
  Database of records between 1563 and 1895, listed alphabetically by groom's last name.

- Mt. View Research Page County, Virginia Marriages 1831–1864
  http://www.rootsweb.com/~vapage/marriages.htm

- Mt. View Research Page County, Virginia Marriages 1831–1864 Bride Index
  http://www.rootsweb.com/~vapage/marriagesbride.htm

- Mt. View Research Shenandoah County, Virginia Marriages 1850–1859
  http://www.rootsweb.com/~vapage/shenandoahmarrac.htm

- New South Wales Registry of Births, Deaths and Marriages
  http://www.agd.nsw.gov.au/bdm/

- New Zealand Births, Deaths & Marriages Office
  http://inform.dia.govt.nz/internal_affairs/businesses/doni_pro/bdm_pro/bdm.html
  and their research service
  http://inform.dia.govt.nz/internal_affairs/businesses/doni_pro/bdm_pro/research/researchindex.html

- ONS Services—Certificates of Births, Marriages and Deaths
  http://www.ons.gov.uk/services/cert.htm
  England and Wales

- Ontario Vital Statistics Bulletin
  http://www.gov.on.ca/MCZCR/archives/english/geneal/vtlstats.htm
  Researching Birth, Death and Marriage Records in Ontario from the Archives of Ontario.

- Parksville Qualicum Marriages, 1948–1994
  http://macn.bc.ca/~d69hist/marriage.html
  Mid-Vancouver Island, BC, Canada

- Pinellas Genealogy Society, Inc.
  http://www.geocities.com/Heartland/Plains/8283/
  Includes a database of 1970–1974 Pinellas County Marriages and Engagements.

- Pipestone County Museum Marriage Records
  http://www.pipestone.mn.us/Museum/MALEMAR.HTM
  Minnesota

- The POYNTZ Family in India
  http://www.hal-pc.org/~poyntz/india.html
  Selected Extracts from the India Presidencies of Bengal, Bombay and Madras Ecclesiastical Returns of Baptisms, Marriages and Burials 1713–1948.

- Quaker Marriages
  http://www.rootsweb.com/~quakers/quakmarr.htm

- Record of Marriages and Deaths 1826–1836
  http://www.geocities.com/Heartland/Plains/3558/voliv.htm
  Pennsylvania. Found in "Proceedings and Collections of the Wyoming Historical & Geological Society," Vol. IV.

- Records of the Reformed Dutch Church in New York—Marriages, 1639–1699
  http://www.rootsweb.com/~ote/rdcmarr.htm

- Registrar of Births, Deaths and Marriages, Dundee
  http://www.dundeecity.gov.uk/dcchtml/sservices/rbdm.html
  Scotland

- Revolutionary War Period Bible, Family & Marriage Records
  http://www.dhc.net/~revwar/
  Index to microfilm volumes of abstracts from pension files.

- Reynolds County Marriage Records 1870–1891
  http://www.mindspring.com/~sapart/reymag.html

- Ripley County Missouri Marriage Records {1833–1860}
  http://members.tripod.com/~tmsnyder/Ripley.htm_

- San Francisco County Ancestors' Marriage Notices
  http://www.sfo.com/~timandpamwolf/sfmar.htm
  California

- Search Idaho Marriage Record Index
  http://abish.ricks.edu/fhc/gbsearch.asp
  Search engine for marriages in Arizona, Idaho, Nevada, Oregon, Utah 1850–1951.

- Search Weil im Schoenbuch Marriages
  http://www.kinquest.com/genealogy/marriages.html
  Württemberg, Germany

- The Skaneateles Historical Society
  http://www.skaneateles.com/historical/
  New York. They have vital statistics records online, including marriage records and death records. A database of over 15,000 records compiled from the old newspaper records from 1831 through 1899.

- Some South Georgia Marriage Records
  http://www.ij.net/phickey/marriage.htm

- The St. Catherine's Marriage Index
  http://www.cs.ncl.ac.uk/genuki/StCathsTranscriptions/

- Sussex County Marriages
  http://www.gate.net/~pascalfl/marrndx.html
  New Jersey

- Tattnall County, Georgia Marriage Records 1805–1845
  http://www.teesee.com/marriage/tattnall/marriage1.htm

- Town Marriage Records in Tisbury, 1850–1875: An Index of Recorded Names
  http://www.vineyard.net/vineyard/history/tmindex.htm

- Trigg County Marriages 1820–1900
  http://www.aplusdata.com/kyseeker/triggmarriages.cfm
  Kentucky

- Tulare County Marriages—1852 to June, 1893
  http://www.compuology.com/cagenweb/tckcm.htm
  California

- Tulare County Marriages—July 1, 1893 to Dec. 31, 1909
  http://www.compuology.com/cagenweb/tcm.htm
  California

- UK Marriage Related Information
  http://members.aol.com/aisling13/ixukwit.htm

- Vicar-General Marriage Licence Index
  http://ourworld.compuserve.com/homepages/David_Squire/vicgen1.htm
  Index of marriage licences issued by the office of the Vicar-General of the Archbishop of Canterbury for the period 1701 to 1850, England.

- Vital Events Indexes—BC Archives
  http://www2.bcarchives.gov.bc.ca/textual/governmt/vstats/v_events.htm

  ○ Marriage Registration Index Search Gateway, 1872 to 1921
    http://www2.bcarchives.gov.bc.ca/cgi-bin/www2vsm

- Vital Records Extracted From "The Life, Travels, and Ministry of Milton M. Everly"
  http://www.aloha.net/~jan/milton.txt
  September 1901–September 1903. Extractions of records for marriages, some baptisms, and funerals.

- Walpole History Vital Records to 1850
  http://www.walpole.ma.us/hhisdocvitalrecords.htm
  Massachusetts

◆ Professional Researchers, Volunteers & Other Research Services

- Anne's UK Certificates for Australians
  http://freespace.virgin.net/mark.wainwright6/uk_certificates/
  An Australian living in London who can obtain copies of English, Scottish & Welsh Birth, Marriage and Death Certificates in exchange for payment in Australian dollars.

- Marbract Services—NSW Birth, Death & Marriage Certificate Transcription Service
  http://www.marbract.com.au/
  Australia. NSW Births 1788–1905, NSW Deaths and Marriages 1788–1918.

MEDICAL, MEDICINE, GENETICS
http://www.CyndisList.com/medical.htm

Category Index:

- Civil War Medicine & Hospitals
- Diseases & Medical Terms
- Doctors
- General Resource Sites
- Genetics & Family Health
- History

◆ Civil War Medicine & Hospitals

- Civil War and 19th Century Medical Terminology
  http://members.aol.com/jweaver300/grayson/medterm.htm

- Civil War Medicine
  http://www.powerweb.net/bbock/war/

- Civil War Medicine Vocabulary
  http://www.cee.indiana.edu/gopher/
  Turner_Adventure_Learning/Gettysburg_Archive/
  Other_Resources/Medicine_Vocabulary.txt

- Medical Services, Civil War
  http://carlisle-www.army.mil/usamhi/RefBibs/medical/
  civwar.htm
  A working bibliography of MHI sources.

- Medical Staff Press
  http://www.iserv.net/~civilmed/

- National Museum of Civil War Medicine
  http://www.civilwarmed.org/

- Resources in Civil War Medicine
  http://www.collphyphil.org/FIND_AID/histcvwr.htm
  At The Library of the College of Physicians of Philadelphia.

- Virginia's Confederate Military Hospitals
  http://members.aol.com/jweaver300/grayson/hospital.htm

◆ Diseases & Medical Terms

- Archaic Medical Expressions for Genealogists, A–K
  http://www.gpiag-asthma.org/drpsmith/amt1.htm

- Archaic Medical Expressions for Genealogists, L–Z
  http://www.gpiag-asthma.org/drpsmith/amt2.htm

- Colonial Diseases & Cures
  http://www.genweb.net/~samcasey/disease.html

- Genealogical Dictionaries—Old German Professions
  & Old German Medical Terms and Causes of Death
  http://home.navisoft.com/scrolls/dictinry.htm

- German Illness Translations
  http://pixel.cs.vt.edu/library/articles/link/illness.txt

- Glossary of Diseases
  http://www.rootsweb.com/~ote/disease.htm

- Kentuckiana Genealogy—Disease Chart
  http://www.floyd-pavey.com/kentuckiana/kyiana/kyiana/
  disease.html

- Modern Names or Definitions of Illnesses
  of Our Ancestors, A–K
  http://www.genrecords.com/library/disease.htm

- Modern Names or Definitions of Illnesses
  of Our Ancestors, L–Z
  http://www.genrecords.com/library/diseases2.htm
  From the Genealogy Record Service Library.

- Old Disease Names & Their Modern Definitions
  http://www.netusa1.net/~hartmont/medicalterms.htm

- Old Medical Terminology
  http://members.aol.com/AdamCo9991/medicalterminolgy.html

- Outdated Medical Terminology
  http://www.familytreemaker.com/00000014.html

- The People's Plague Online: Tuberculosis Resources
  http://www0.pbs.org/ppol/resource.html

- SFS Outdated Medical Terms
  http://www.demon.co.uk/sfs/diseases.htm

◆ Doctors

- Deceased American Physicians' Records
  http://www.ngsgenealogy.org/library/content/ama_info.html
  *A research service available from the National Genealogical
  Society.*

- Medical Profession Last Names A–L
  http://rontay.digiweb.com/visit/occupy/physa.htm

- Medical Profession Last Names M–Z
  http://rontay.digiweb.com/visit/occupy/physm.htm
  *From the Occupations Census Indexes, Ron Taylor's UK Census
  Finding Aids and Indexes.*

- Tennessee Confederate Physicians: An Introduction
  http://www.state.tn.us/sos/statelib/pubsvs/docintro.htm
  *From the Tennessee State Library and Archives—Historical and
  Genealogical Information.*

- Was Your Ancestor a Doctor?
  http://user.itl.net/~glen/doctors.html

◆ General Resource Sites

- FOLKLORE Mailing List
  http://members.aol.com/johnf14246/
  gen_mail_general.html#FOLKLORE
  A mailing list for the exchange of folklore—folk medicine and recipes.

- Frontier Press Bookstore—Genetics and Genealogy
  http://www.frontierpress.com/frontier.cgi?category=genetics

- Frontier Press Bookstore—Medical History
  http://www.frontierpress.com/frontier.cgi?category=medical

- U.S. National Library of Medicine (NLM)—History of Medicine Division
  http://www.nlm.nih.gov/hmd/hmd.html

  - Does HMD have sources for genealogical research?
    http://www.nlm.nih.gov/hmd/faq-hmd.html#genealogy

◆ Genetics & Family Health

- American Journal of Medical Genetics
  http://www.interscience.wiley.com/jpages/0148-7299/

- Compiling your family medical history—
  How important is it?
  http://www.mayohealth.org/mayo/9612/htm/family.htm

- Genealogy and Genetics
  http://www.geocities.com/Heartland/Pointe/1439/
  Genealogy with a special reason: Stanley Diamond's Beta-Thalassemia genetic trait research project.

- Genetic Disorders, Databases, and Genealogy
  http://habitant.org/genetics.htm

- Know Your Family's Cancer History
  http://www.childfund.org/history.htm

- Lifelinks International
  http://www.lifelinks.mb.ca/
  A family medical history and personal record keeping program.

- National Genealogical Society—
  Family Health History
  http://www.ngsgenealogy.org/about/content/committees/
  famhealth.html

- Your Family's Health History
  http://www.familytreemaker.com/issue6.html

- Your Medical Heritage
  http://www.pbs.org/kbyu/ancestors/viewersguide/episode-eight.html
  From the Ancestors television program on PBS.

◆ History

- Epidemics
  http://main.nc.us/OBCGS/epidemics.htm

- Epidemics and Military Battles
  http://www.ento.vt.edu/IHS/militaryEpidemics.html

- Epidemics in U.S.—1657–1918
  http://members.aol.com/AdamCo9991/epidemics.html

- From Quackery to Bacteriology: The Emergence of Modern Medicine in 19th Century America
  http://www.cl.utoledo.edu/canaday/quackery/quack-index.html

- Health and Hygiene in the Nineteenth Century
  http://www.stg.brown.edu/projects/hypertext/landow/victorian/
  health/health10.html

- History of the Health Sciences World Wide Web Links
  http://www2.mc.duke.edu/misc/MLA/HHSS/histlink.htm

- National Library of Medicine: Exhibitions in the History of Medicine
  http://www.nlm.nih.gov/exhibition/exhibition.html

- Resources for Medical History Papers
  http://www.usuhs.mil/meh/histres.html

- Some Historically Significant Epidemics
  http://www.botany.duke.edu/microbe/chrono.htm

- The USGenWeb Project—Information for Researchers—Epidemics
  http://www.usgenweb.org/researchers/epidemics.html

MEDIEVAL

http://www.CyndisList.com/medieval.htm

- Cartographic Images—Ancient, Medieval & Renaissance Maps
  http://www.iag.net/~jsiebold/carto.html

- Dominion & Domination of the Gentle Sex: The Lives of Medieval Women
  http://library.advanced.org/12834/

- Frequently Asked Questions (FAQs) for soc.genealogy.medieval
  http://www.rand.org/personal/Genea/faqmed.html

- Frontier Press Bookstore—Medieval/ Renaissance Studies
  http://www.frontierpress.com/frontier.cgi?category=medieval

- GEN-MEDIEVAL Mailing List
  http://members.aol.com/johnf14246/ gen_mail_general.html#GEN-MEDIEVAL

- History of Europe in Medieval Times, Anglo-Saxons
  http://www.worldroots.com/brigitte/royal/royal7.htm
  Historic and genealogical information about royal and nobility family lines.

- Images of Medieval Art And Architecture— Maps of Great Britain
  http://www1.pitt.edu/~medart/menuengl/mainmaps.html

- Internet Medieval Sourcebook
  http://www.fordham.edu/halsall/sbook.html

- Medieval England 1066–1399—Bibliography
  http://www.history.bangor.ac.uk/H3H03/h3h03bib.htm
  From a course at the School of History and Welsh History / Adran Hanes a Hanes Cymru, University of Wales, Bangor.

- Medieval Genealogy—From Everton's
  http://www.everton.com/oe1–15/gen-med.htm

- Medieval Studies
  http://www.georgetown.edu/labyrinth/Virtual_Library/ Medieval_Studies.html

- NetSERF—The Internet Connection for Medieval Resources
  http://netserf.cua.edu/

- The Shaping of the Medieval World— Medieval Web Links
  http://www.fordham.edu/halsall/med/medweb.html

- Torrione Castle—an unusual example of a Museum for History
  http://www.gvo.it/VdSF/torrione1.html
  From Italy. Be sure to check out their Vialardi di Sandigliano lineage library.

- Usenet Newsgroup soc.genealogy.medieval
  Gatewayed with the GEN-MEDIEVAL Mailing List.

MENNONITE

http://www.CyndisList.com/menno.htm

- The Amish, the Mennonites, and the Plain People of the Pennsylvania Dutch Country
  http://www.800padutch.com/amish.html

- A Bibliography of Anabaptist—Mennonite Works at the Mennonite Historical Library, Canadian Mennonite Bible College
  http://www.mbnet.mb.ca/~mhc/biblio.htm

- The California Mennonite Historical Society
  http://www.fresno.edu/cmhs/home.htm

- Canadian Conference of Mennonite Brethren Churches
  http://www.cdnmbconf.ca/mb/mbdoc.htm

- The Center for Mennonite Brethren Studies
  http://www.fresno.edu/cmbs/home.htm
  Fresno, California

- Centre for Mennonite Brethren Studies
  http://www.cdnmbconf.ca/mb/cmbs.htm
  Winnipeg, Manitoba

- Consolidated Index of the Church Family Registers (Mennonite)
  http://www.mbnet.mb.ca/~mhc/allindxm.htm
  Bergthaler (Russia) 1843, Chortitzer (Manitoba) 1878, Chortitzer (Manitoba) 1887, Chortitzer (Manitoba) 1907.

- Early Russian Mennonite History—Part One
  http://members.aol.com/jktsn/mennohis.htm

- The Thiessen Family and The Mennonite Diaspora—Part Two
  http://members.aol.com/jktsn/mennodia.htm

- Lancaster Mennonite Historical Society
  http://lanclio.org/lmhs.htm
  Pennsylvania

- Manitoba Mennonite Historical Society
  http://www.mmhs.org/
  Canada

- Masthof Press
  http://www.masthof.org/
  Genealogical and historical books, including many for Mennonite, Amish and Brethren research.

- MennoLink Mennonite Information Center
  http://www.prairienet.org/community/religion/mennonite/menno.html

- Mennonite Brethren Herald
  http://www.cdnmbconf.ca/mb/mbherald.htm
  Be sure to see their online editions & current obituaries section.

- Mennonite Connections on the WWW
  http://www-personal.umich.edu/~bpl/menno.html

- Mennonite Cross-Index—from FEEFHS
  http://feefhs.org/men/indexmen.html

- Mennonite Family History Magazine
  http://www.masthof.org/mfh.html

- Mennonite Heritage Centre
  http://www.mbnet.mb.ca/~mhc/
  Winnipeg, Manitoba, Canada

- Mennonite Historian Magazine
  http://www.mbnet.mb.ca/~mhc/menhist.htm

- The Mennonite Historians of Eastern Pennsylvania
  http://www.mhep.org/

- Mennonite Historical Society of Alberta
  http://members.home.net/rempel/mhsa/
  The MHSA is a new society developed to support those who are interested in basic Mennonite history, those doing Mennonite genealogy/family history research, and those who are interested in the preservation and display of Mennonite historical documents and cultural artifacts.

- Mennonite Library and Archives
  http://www.bethelks.edu/services/mla/
  Bethel College North Newton, Kansas

- Mennonite Research Corner
  http://www.ristenbatt.com/genealogy/mennonit.htm

- Mennonites in Canada
  http://www.mhsc.ca/
  The web site for the Mennonite Historical Society of Canada.

- MENNO.REC.ROOTS Mailing List
  http://members.aol.com/johnf14246/gen_mail_general.html#MENNO.REC.ROOTS
  A Mennonite genealogy and family research interest group.

- MENNO-ROOTS Mailing List
  http://members.aol.com/johnf14246/gen_mail_general.html#MENNO-ROOTS

- Olive Tree Genealogy
  http://www.rootsweb.com/~ote/
  Huguenots & Walloons, Ontario Loyalists, Mohawk, Mennonite, Palatines and Dutch Research.

- OMII Genealogy Project & Kidron Heritage Center
  http://www.wgbc.org/hindex.htm
  A Swiss Mennonite & German Amish genealogy project.

- Prussian-Russian-Canadian Mennonite Genealogical Resources
  http://www.mmhs.org/mmhsgen.htm

- Unruh's South Russian Mennonite Census, 1795–1814
  http://pixel.cs.vt.edu/library/census/link/bhu.txt

- WENGER Home Page
  http://www.wengersundial.com/wengerfamily/
  A database of over 78,000 names of individuals, mostly descended from 18th century Mennonites, River Brethren (Brethren in Christ) and German Baptist Brethren who settled in Lancaster, Lebanon and Franklin Counties of Pennsylvania, in Ontario, Canada and in Washington Co., Maryland and Botetourt Co., Virginia.

MICROFILM & MICROFICHE

http://www.CyndisList.com/micro.htm

Category Index:

◆ Film/Fiche Numbers
◆ National Archives

◆ Vendors

◆ Film/Fiche Numbers

● 1901 Census of Canada—Film Numbers
http://www.tbaytel.net/bmartin/census.htm

● California Death Index Information
http://www.micronet.net/users/~searcy/indexinfo.htm
A list of microfiche/film numbers by year and surname.

● Halifax County, Nova Scotia LDS/PANS
Film Numbers
http://www.geocities.com/Heartland/Prairie/6261/films.htm

● LDS Film Numbers for Ontario Birth Registrations
http://www.geocities.com/Heartland/9332/lds-b.htm

● LDS Film Numbers for Ontario Death Registrations
http://www.geocities.com/Heartland/9332/lds-d.htm

● LDS Film Numbers for Ontario
Marriage Registrations
http://www.geocities.com/Heartland/9332/lds-m.htm

● LDS Microfilm for Loudoun Co., VA
http://www.rootsweb.com/~valoudou/film.html

● LDS Microfilms and Microfiche for
Coshocton Co., Ohio
http://www.pe.net/~sharyn/lds.html

● LDS Polish Jewish Microfilm Lists
http://www.jewishgen.org/reipp/jri-lds.htm
JewishGen

● Microfilm of Connecticut Records at LDS Family
History Centers
http://www.cslnet.ctstateu.edu/ldsmicro.htm

● Scottish Reference Information
http://www.ktb.net/~dwills/13300-scottishreference.htm
*An extensive list of parish numbers and microfilm numbers to
aid in doing Scottish research at an LDS Family History Center.*

◆ National Archives

● National Archives and Records Administration
http://www.nara.gov/
United States

  ○ The Federal Population Censuses—
  Catalogs of NARA Microfilm
  http://www.nara.gov/publications/microfilm/census/
  census.html

  • 1790–1890 Federal Population Censuses—
  Catalog of NARA Microfilm
  http://www.nara.gov/publications/microfilm/census/1790–
  1890/17901890.html

  • 1900 Federal Population Census—
  Catalog of NARA Microfilm
  http://www.nara.gov/publications/microfilm/census/1900/
  1900.html

  • 1910 Federal Population Censuses—
  Catalog of NARA Microfilm
  http://www.nara.gov/publications/microfilm/census/1910/
  1910.html

  • 1920 Federal Population Census—
  Catalog of NARA Microfilm
  http://www.nara.gov/publications/microfilm/census/1920/
  1920.html

  ○ How to Use NARA's Census Microfilm Catalogs
  http://www.nara.gov/genealogy/microcen.html

  ○ National Archives Microfilm Catalogs Online

  • American Indians—A Select Catalog of NARA
  Microfilm Publications
  http://www.nara.gov/publications/microfilm/amerindians/
  indians.html

  • Black Studies—A Select Catalog of NARA
  Microfilm Publications
  http://www.nara.gov/publications/microfilm/blackstudies/
  blackstd.html

- Federal Court Records—A Select Catalog of NARA Microfilm Publications
  http://www.nara.gov/publications/microfilm/courts/fedcourt.html
- Genealogical and Biographical Research—A Select Catalog of NARA Microfilm Publications
  http://www.nara.gov/publications/microfilm/biographical/genbio.html
- Immigrant and Passenger Arrivals—A Select Catalog of NARA Microfilm Publications
  http://www.nara.gov/publications/microfilm/immigrant/immpass.html
- Microfilm of Connecticut Records at LDS Family History Centers
  http://www.cslnet.ctstateu.edu/ldsmicro.htm
- Microfilm Resources for Research—A Comprehensive Catalog
  http://www.nara.gov/publications/microfilm/comprehensive/compcat.html
- Military Service Records—A Select Catalog of NARA Microfilm Publications
  http://www.nara.gov/publications/microfilm/military/service.html
- National Archives Microfilm Collection in Seattle
  http://www.rootsweb.com/~watpcgs/narafilm.htm
  A list of 549 microfilm publications available at the Pacific Alaska Region branch of NARA.
- National Archives Microfilm Rental Program
  http://www.nara.gov/publications/microfilm/micrent.html

◆ Vendors

- AncestorSpy—CDs and Microfiche
  http://www.ancestorspy.com
- Avotaynu Microfiche
  http://www.avotaynu.com/microf.html
  Products and information for Jewish genealogy.
- Durham and Northumberland Family History Microfiche
  http://www.jwillans.freeserve.co.uk/default.html
  England
- Heritage Quest's Resources on Microfilm and Fiche
  http://www.heritagequest.com/genealogy/microfilm/
- The Memorabilia Corner
  http://members.aol.com/TMCorner/index.html
  Forms, flags, maps, software, CDs, tapes, microfilm & microfiche, books, periodicals, photographic conservation & archival materials.
- New Zealand Society of Genealogists— Microfiche Publications
  http://homepages.ihug.co.nz/~nzsg/Publications/fiche_main.html
- Yesteryear Links
  http://www.st.net.au/~grinly/
  Queensland, Australia

MILITARY RESOURCES WORLDWIDE
http://www.CyndisList.com/milres.htm

Category Index:

- General Resource Sites
- Libraries, Archives & Museums
- Mailing Lists, Newsgroups & Chat
- Professional Researchers, Volunteers & Other Research Services

- Publications, Software & Supplies
- Records: Military, Pension, Burial
- Societies & Groups

◆ General Resource Sites

- **43rd Wessex Association**
  http://www.digiserve.com/msyoung/43rd.htm
  England

- **460 Squadron RAAF**
  http://www.st.net.au/~dunn/460sqdn.htm
  Australians serving in WWII.

- **Australian Genealogy Researching Armed Services Personnel**
  http://www.pcug.org.au/~mjsparke/mj_page1.html

- **Australian War Medals**
  http://www.ozemail.com.au/~qphoto/index.html
  Provides background information on campaign & gallantry awards given to Australian forces. Includes some medal rolls listing individual recipients of medals. Also has a research resource page for researching Australian servicemen.

- **The British Army**
  http://www.army.mod.uk

- **The British Empire & Commonwealth Land Forces**
  http://www.du.edu/~tomills/military/empire.htm

- **British infantry regiment name changes (1881)**
  http://www.tdrake.demon.co.uk/infantry.htm

- **The Buffalo Soldiers on the Western Frontier**
  http://www.imh.org/imh/buf/buftoc.html
  From the International Museum of the Horse.

- **The Buff's (The Royal East Kent Regiment)**
  http://www.digiserve.com/peter/buffs/
  England

- **Canada—Military**
  http://www.CyndisList.com/milcan.htm
  See this category on Cyndi's List for related links.

- **Duke of Cornwall's Light Infantry**
  http://www.digiserve.com/msyoung/dcli.htm
  England. 32nd & 46th Regiments of Foot.

- **"G" for George**
  http://www.st.net.au/~dunn/g4george.htm
  The Avro Lancaster B1 on display in the Aeroplane Hall at the Australian War Memorial in Canberra, ACT, Australia.

- **Genealogical Investigation into Charles J. ARIS**
  http://www.oz.net/~markhow/chasaris.htm
  World War 1 veteran, 16th Queen's Own Lancers, a cavalry unit of the British Army.

- **The Great War—HELLFIRE CORNER**
  http://www.fylde.demon.co.uk/welcome.htm
  Tom Morgan's Great War Web Pages.

- **A Group Photograph—Before, Now, and In-Between (A History Project)**
  http://www.mister-t.demon.co.uk/
  A genealogical project that came about from a group photograph of the officers of the 8th Royal Berkshire Regiment taken at their training camp on Salisbury Plain in July 1915.

- **The Mexican-American War Memorial Homepage**
  http://sunsite.unam.mx/revistas/1847/

- **Military History**
  http://www.cfcsc.dnd.ca/links/milhist/index.html
  From the War, Peace and Security Guide, Canadian Forces College.

- **The Military History Page**
  http://www.du.edu/~tomills/military/index.html
  - ○ Land Forces of Britain, the Empire and Commonwealth
    http://www.du.edu/~tomills/military/empire.htm

- **Military Search Bulletin Board**
  http://www.shadow.net/~tferrer/search.html

- **New Zealand Defence Forces, 1860–1883**
  http://www.atonz.com/genealogy/nzdefence.html

- **The Queensland Defence Force**
  http://www.ozemail.com.au/~adjutant/moreton/qdf.html

- **Rongstad's Worldwide Military Links**
  http://members.aol.com/rhrongstad/private/milinksr.htm

- The Royal Navy Ship—HMS Opal
  http://pages.prodigy.com/SC/familyhx/familyhx3.html
- The Scots At War Project
  http://www-saw.arts.ed.ac.uk/saw.html
  A tribute to the men and women who served their country in the 20th century. Includes information on genealogy for Scottish soldiers.
    - Genealogical Help Service—Ancestor Hunting
      http://www-saw.arts.ed.ac.uk/misc/genealogy/ancestor.html
    - Genealogical Help Service—The Armed and Civilian Services
      http://www-saw.arts.ed.ac.uk/misc/genealogy/military.html
    - Military Service Museums for Scotland
      http://www-saw.arts.ed.ac.uk/misc/genealogy/museums.html
- Scottish Military Historical Society—Index of Military Sites To Visit
  http://www.virtual-pc.com/journal/other.htm
- Soldiers Whom the World Have Forgotten
  http://www.geocities.com/Athens/Acropolis/9460/index.html
  Dedicated to the memory of soldiers & their families who died in and around Bangalore, India.
- U.S.—Civil War ~ The War for Southern Independence
  http://www.CyndisList.com/cw.htm
  See this category on Cyndi's List for related links.
- U.S.—Military
  http://www.CyndisList.com/military.htm
  See this category on Cyndi's List for related links.
- War Chart
  http://www.genrecords.com/library/war.htm
  From the Genealogy Record Service.
- World War I—Trenches on the Web
  http://www.worldwar1.com/
- World War II on the Web
  http://www.geocities.com/Athens/Oracle/2691/welcome.htm

◆ Libraries, Archives & Museums

- Genealogie: Sudetenland, Böhmen/Bohemia, Mähren/Moravia—Militärarchive und militärische Personalunterlagen / Military Archives and Records
  http://w3g.med.uni-giessen.de/gene/reg/SUD/sudet_miarch.html
- Military Archives in Germany
  http://www.bawue.de/~hanacek/info/earchive.htm#CC
- The National Army Museum
  http://www.failte.com/nam/index.htm
  London, England
- The South African War Virtual Library
  http://www.uq.net.au/~zzrwotto/

- The World War I Document Archive
  http://www.lib.byu.edu/~rdh/wwi/
  Assembled by volunteers of the World War I Military History List (WWI-L).

◆ Mailing Lists, Newsgroups & Chat

- AMERICAN-REVOLUTION Mailing List
  http://members.aol.com/gfsjohnf/gen_mail_states-gen.html#AMERICAN-REVOLUTION
  For the discussion of events during the American Revolution and genealogical matters related to the American Revolution. The French-Indian Wars and the War of 1812 are also suitable topics for discussion.
- The Anglo Boer War Discussion Page
  http://www.icon.co.za/~dup42/talk.htm
  This mailing list is for the discussion of the Anglo Boer War and other military related topics pre-1900.
- FOB-LIST—Friends Of the Boers—E-mail List
  http://www.webcom.com/perspekt/eng/mlist/fob.html
  The primary topic of this mailing list is the centenary commemoration of the 2nd Anglo Boer War (1899–1902).
- WW20-ROOTS-L Mailing List
  http://members.aol.com/johnf14246/gen_mail_general.html#WW20-ROOTS-L
  For the discussion of genealogy in all 20th century wars.

◆ Professional Researchers, Volunteers & Other Research Services

- Bob's Public Records Office Searches—Kew, London, England
  http://www.users.dircon.co.uk/~searcher/
  Including these records: Military, Royal Navy, Merchant Navy, Convict, Railway, West Indies, Passenger Lists, History Projects.

◆ Publications, Software & Supplies

- The Naval & Military Press Web Page
  http://www.naval-military-press.co.uk/
  A large selection of military books, many of interest to the genealogist.
- The Order of the Virtuti Militari and its Cavaliers 1792–1992
  http://www.wwdir.com/order/
  This book has 26,506 names of persons and military organizations. It is presented in English and Polish.
- Polish Military History Books
  http://www.wwdir.com/polishbk.html
  Polish Orders, Medals, Badges, and Insignia. Military and Civilian Decorations, 1705 to 1985.

◆ Records: Military, Pension, Burial

- British Military Records
  http://www.genuki.org.uk/big/BritMilRecs.html

- Commonwealth War Graves Commission
  http://www.cwgc.org/
  Details of 1.7 million members of UK and Commonwealth forces who died in the 1st and 2nd World Wars and other wars, and 60,000 civilian casualties of WWII. Gives details of grave site, date of death, age, usually parents/widow's address.

- The Trafalgar Roll
  http://www.genuki.org.uk/big/eng/Trafalgar/
  A list of 1640 officers and men who fought at the Battle of Trafalgar.

◆ Societies & Groups

- Crimean War Research Society
  http://homepages.ihug.co.nz/~phil/crimean.htm
  U.K.

- DISPATCH—Scottish Military Historical Society
  http://subnet.virtual-pc.com/~mc546367/journal.htm

- League of Researchers of South African Historical Battlefields
  http://www.icon.co.za/~dup42/Welcome.html

- The Military Historical Society of Australia
  http://www.pcug.org.au/~astaunto/mhsa.htm

- The South African Military History Society / Die Suid-Afrikaanse Krygshistoriese Vereeniging
  http://rapidttp.com/milhist/

- The Western Front Association—Remembering 1914–1918
  http://ourworld.compuserve.com/homepages/cf_baker/

NATIVE AMERICAN
http://www.CyndisList.com/native.htm

Category Index:

- General Resource Sites
- History & Culture
- Libraries, Archives & Museums
- Mailing Lists, Newsgroups & Chat
- People & Families
- Professional Researchers, Volunteers & Other Research Services

- Publications, Software & Supplies
- Records: Census, Cemeteries, Land, Obituaries, Personal, Taxes and Vital
- Societies & Groups
- Specific Tribal or Nation Resources
- USGenWeb Project ~ Native Americans

◆ General Resource Sites

- The African—Native Genealogy Homepage
  http://members.aol.com/angelaw859/index.html
  Celebrating the Estelusti ~ The Freedmen Oklahoma's Black Indians of the Cherokee, Chickasaw, Choctaw, Creek, and Seminole Nations.

- AISES Gopher Site
  gopher://bioc02.uthscsa.edu/11/AISESnet%20Gopher

- American Indian Studies
  http://www.csulb.edu/~aisstudy/

- American Indian Tribal Directory
  http://www.indians.org./tribes/

- Genealogy of Quebec's Native People and Francophone Metis
  http://www.cam.org/~beaur/gen/amerin-e.html

- How To Guide for Native Americans
  http://members.aol.com/bbbenge/page12.html
  By Paul R. Sarrett, Jr.

- Links to Aboriginal Resources
  http://www.bloorstreet.com/300block/aborl.htm

- Native American Genealogy
  http://members.aol.com/bbbenge/front.html

- Native American Genealogy
  http://www.system.missouri.edu/shs/nativeam.html
  A guide from the State Historical Society of Missouri.

- Native American Genealogy in Alabama
  http://www.asc.edu/archives/referenc/notat.html#Native
  From the Alabama Dept. of Archives and History.

- Native American Gopher Entry at Berkeley
  gopher://garnet.berkeley.edu:1250/11/.race/.native

- Native American Home Page
  http://home1.gte.net/cicsd/index.htm
  Terri Moore's page with Arkansas, Oklahoma and Native American information.

- Native American Research in Michigan
  http://members.aol.com/roundsky/introduction.html
  Using the Ottawa, Chippewa and Potawatomi tribes as examples.

- Native American Research in Wisconsin
  http://members.aol.com/RoundSky/Wis-intro.html

- Native American Research Page
  http://maple.lemoyne.edu/~bucko/indian.html

- Native American Sites
  http://www.pitt.edu/~lmitten/indians.html

- National Archives Resources— Native American "Rolls"
  http://members.aol.com/bbbenge/page13.html
  By Paul R. Sarrett, Jr.

- Native American Resources
  http://members.aol.com/bbbenge/page14.html
  By Paul R. Sarrett, Jr.

- NativeWeb
  http://www.nativeweb.org/

- OTA's Native American Resource Page
  http://bilbo.isu.edu/ota/nativea.html

- Tribes, States and Government Agency
  http://members.aol.com/bbbenge/newlinks.html

- Unique Peoples
  http://www.CyndisList.com/peoples.htm
  See this category on Cyndi's List for related links.

◆ History & Culture

- Native American History and Culture
  http://www.etsu-tn.edu/cas/history/natam.htm

◆ Libraries, Archives & Museums

- California Indian Library Collections
  http://www.mip.berkeley.edu/cilc/brochure/brochure.html

- Native American Research from the Library
  of Michigan
  http://www.libofmich.lib.mi.us/genealogy/nativeamerican.html

- Tennessee State Library and Archives
  http://www.state.tn.us/sos/statelib/pubsvs/cherokee.htm
  *Historical and Genealogical Information—Suggestions for
  Native American Research (Cherokee).*

◆ Mailing Lists, Newsgroups & Chat

- CHEROKEE Mailing List
  http://members.aol.com/gfsjohnf/gen_mail_states-
  gen.html#CHEROKEE

- CherokeeGene Mailing List
  http://members.aol.com/gfsjohnf/gen_mail_states-
  gen.html#CherokeeGene

- CREEK-SOUTHEAST Mailing List
  http://members.aol.com/gfsjohnf/gen_mail_states-
  gen.html#CREEK-SOUTHEAST
  *For anyone interested in the genealogy and history of the Creek
  Indians of the Southeastern United States, and those living
  among the Creeks.*

- Genealogy-Native
  http://nctc.com/~cheyanne/index.htm
  #Genealogy-Native Channel on AfterNET.

- INDIAN-ROOTS-L Mailing List
  http://members.aol.com/gfsjohnf/gen_mail_states-
  gen.html#INDIAN-ROOTS

- Indian-Territory-Roots Mailing List
  http://members.aol.com/gfsjohnf/gen_mail_states-
  ok.html#Indian-Territory-Roots
  *For anyone with a genealogical interest in Indian Territory—an
  area that in 1907 became the eastern and south/south-eastern
  part of Oklahoma.*

- ITCREEKN Mailing List
  http://members.aol.com/gfsjohnf/gen_mail_states-
  ok.html#ITCREEKN
  *For anyone with a genealogical interest in the Creek Nation,
  Indian Territory.*

- MELUNGEO Mailing List
  http://members.aol.com/gfsjohnf/gen_mail_states-
  gen.html#MELUNGEO
  *For people conducting Melungeon and/or Appalachian research
  including Native American, Portuguese, Turkish, Black Dutch,
  and other unverifiable mixed statements of ancestry or unexplained rumors, with ancestors in TN, KY, VA, NC, SC, GA, AL,
  WV, and possibly other places.*

- NA-FORUM-L Mailing List
  http://members.aol.com/gfsjohnf/gen_mail_states-
  gen.html#NA-FORUM
  *For anyone with an interest in North American Indian history
  and/or their Indian family history.*

- natam-gene Mailing List
  http://members.aol.com/gfsjohnf/gen_mail_states-
  gen.html#natam-gene
  For anyone with a genealogical interest in Native Americans.

- NISHNAWBE Mailing List
  http://members.aol.com/gfsjohnf/gen_mail_states-
  wi.html#NISHNAWBE
  *For anyone researching Native Americans in Michigan and
  Wisconsin, and the fur traders connected with them.*

◆ People & Families

- Descendants of Moytoy
  http://www.familytreemaker.com/users/h/i/c/James-R-Hicks/
  GENE5-0001.html
  Supreme Chief of the Cherokee 1730–1760.

- Descendants of Nancy WARD
  http://www.nancyward.com/

- MOYTOY—Descendants of Moytoy
  http://www.rootsquest.com/~coatsfar/wardnancd.html
  Supreme Chief of the Cherokee 1730–1760.

- Pocahontas Descendants
  http://www.rootscomputing.com/howto/pocahn/pocahn.htm
  Descendants of Powhatan (Father of Pocahontas).

◆ Professional Researchers, Volunteers & Other Research Services

- AAG International Research—Professional
  Genealogists and Family Historians
  http://www.intl-research.com/
  *Accredited genealogists & family historians specializing in
  family history research, development & publication. Accredited
  by the Family History Library in Salt Lake City, the world's
  largest genealogical library. Tax deductions for LDS research.*

- Board for Certification of Genealogists—
  Roster of Those Certified—Specializing in
  Native American Genealogy
  http://www.genealogy.org/~bcg/rosts_@n.html

- Past Tracker
  http://www.harborside.com/home/r/rice/index.html
  *Coos Bay, Oregon. Native American and New England specialty
  searches.*

◆ Publications, Software & Supplies

- African-American Ancestors Among the Five
  Civilized Tribes
  http://www.coax.net/people/lwf/blkind.htm
  Description of book for sale.

- Ancestor's Attic Discount Genealogy Books—
  Native American Genealogy Books
  http://members.tripod.com/~ancestorsattic/index.html#secNA

- Cherokee Proud: A Guide for Tracing and Honoring Your Cherokee Ancestors
  http://www.powersource.com/gallery/tonymack/

- Frontier Press—Native American Research
  http://www.frontierpress.com/frontier.cgi?category=ind

- GenealogyBookShop.com—Native American/Indian
  http://www.genealogybookshop.com/genealogybookshop/files/
  General,Native_American_Indian/index.html
  The online store of Genealogical Publishing Co., Inc. & Clearfield Company.

- Heritage Books—Indian
  http://www.heritagebooks.com/indian.htm

- Indian Blood
  http://indianbl.digigo.com/

- The Memorabilia Corner
  http://members.aol.com/TMCorner/index.html
  Located in Oklahoma with many Native American resources. Forms, flags, maps, software, CDs, tapes, microfilm & micro-fiche, books, periodicals, photographic conservation & archival materials.

- Michigan's Native Americans—A Selective Bibliography
  http://www.libofmich.lib.mi.us/genealogy/minatamerbib.html

- A Student's Guide to Native American Genealogy
  http://www.oryxpress.com/scripts/book.idc?acro=FTNA

- A Time for Sharing—Native American SIG Newsletter
  http://members.aol.com/kathyehyde/news/index.htm

◆ Records: Census, Cemeteries, Land, Obituaries, Personal, Taxes and Vital (Born, Married, Died & Buried)

- 1851 Census of Cherokee's East of the Misssissippi—The Siler Rolls
  http://members.aol.com/lredtail/siler.html

- American Indians—A select catalog of National Archives microfilm
  http://www.nara.gov/publications/microfilm/amerindians/
  indians.html

- Indian Captives of Early American Pioneers
  http://www.rootsweb.com/~indian/index.htm

- Indian Graves and Cemeteries
  http://history.cc.ukans.edu/heritage/werner/indigrav.html

- Intruders and Non-Citizens in the Creek Nation 1875–1895
  http://www.rootsweb.com/~itcreek/records2.htm

- Nominal Census Homepage
  http://royal.okanagan.bc.ca/census/index.html
  Data for the southern interior of the Province of British Columbia, Canada.

- Canada Census, 1881—Yale District
  http://royal.okanagan.bc.ca/census/yale1881.html

- Canada Census, 1891—Yale District
  http://royal.okanagan.bc.ca/census/yale1891.html

- The IRC Census, 1877
  http://royal.okanagan.bc.ca/census/ind1877.html
  Indian Reserve Commission

- The OMI Census, 1877
  http://royal.okanagan.bc.ca/census/omi1877.html
  A nominal census of Native peoples taken by the Catholic missionary order, Oblates of Mary Immaculate (OMI).

- Selected Index of Intruders and Non-Citizens in the Creek Nation (1876–1897)
  http://www.rootsweb.com/~itcreek/records1.htm

◆ Societies & Groups

- The Cherokee National Historical Society
  http://www.Powersource.com/heritage/

- Lenni Lenape Historical Society and Museum of Indian Culture
  http://www.lenape.org/
  Allentown, Pennsylvania

◆ Specific Tribal or Nation Resources

- The Ani-Stohini/Unami Nation
  http://www.ani-stohini-unami.com/
  An Algonquian language group speaking Native American tribe located in the rural Appalachian Mountain Counties of Washington, Smyth, Grayson, Wythe, Carroll, Patrick, and Floyd in the Commonwealth of Virginia and in Surry County, North Carolina.

- The Blackfeet
  http://blackfeet.3rivers.net/history.htm

- Cherokee Research
  - 1851 Census of Cherokee's east of the Misssissippi—The Siler Rolls
    http://members.aol.com/lredtail/siler.html
  - Bibliography for Cherokee History (in Appalachia)
    http://pluto.clinch.edu/appalachia/melungeon/cherokee.htm
  - Cherokee Cousins—Cherokee Genealogy, Language Culture
    http://www.powersource.com/powersource/cousins/
    default.html
    Research service
  - Cherokee Genealogy
    http://www.phoenix.net/~martikw/geneal.html
  - Cherokee Genealogy—A Selected Resource List on the Cherokee Indians
    http://www.kirch.net/melodie.html

- ○ The Cherokee Genealogy Page
  http://www.geocities.com/Hollywood/Academy/6713/CherokeeGenealogy/
- ○ Cherokee Legion—"Georgia State Guards"
  http://www.scsn.net/users/sage/cl_index.htm
- ○ Cherokee Messenger
  http://www.powersource.com/powersource/cherokee/default.html
- ○ The Cherokee Page
  http://members.aol.com/bbbenge/page10.html
- ○ A Guide to Cherokee Confederate Military Units, 1861–1865
  http://www.scv.org/cherokee.htm
- ○ A Guide To Discovering Your Cherokee Ancestors
  http://www.public.usit.net/jerercox/guide.html
- ○ History of the Cherokee— White Indian's Homepage
  http://pages.tca.net/martikw/
- ○ NC Cherokee Reservation Genealogy
  http://www.intertekweb.com/gpsbook/cherokee/index.html
- ○ The Official Homepage of the Cherokee Indian Reservation
  http://www.cherokee-nc.com/
- ○ So Your Grandmother Was a Cherokee Princess?
  http://www.powersource.com/powersource/cherokee/gene.html
- ○ The Trail of Tears Lawrence County Arkansas
  http://147.97.31.30/lawrence/trail1.htm
- ○ Yansudi's Cherokee Heritage Page
  http://www.public.usit.net/jerercox/index.html
- Cheyenne Genealogy Research
  http://www.mcn.net/~hmscook/roots/cheyenne.html
- The Chickasaw and Their Cessions
  http://www.tngenweb.usit.com/tnfirst/chickasaw/
  Tennessee
- Chickasaw Historical Research Page
  http://www.flash.net/~kma/
- The Choctaw Nation
  http://members.aol.com/bbbenge/page5.html
- Confederated Tribes of the Chehalis
  http://coopext.cahe.wsu.edu/~chehalis/
  Washington
- First Nations Histories
  http://www.dickshovel.com/Compacts.html
- FLGenWeb Project—Native American Information and Links
  http://www.rootsweb.com/~flgenweb/tribes.htm
  Florida
- A Guide to the Great Sioux Nation
  http://www.state.sd.us/state/executive/tourism/sioux/sioux.htm

- Indian People of the Edisto River
  http://www.pride-net.com/native_indians/edisto.html
- Lakota Page—The Great Sioux Nation
  http://members.aol.com/bbbenge/page6.html
- Lakota Wowapi Oti Kin—Lakota Information Home Page
  http://maple.lemoyne.edu/~bucko/lakota.html
- The Mohawk Nation of Akwesasne
  http://www.peacetree.com/akwesasne/home.htm
- The Naragansetts
  http://members.aol.com/bbbenge/page21.htm
- Native Genealogy
  http://www.edwards1.com/rose/genealogy/native-gen/native-gen.htm
  For the People of the three fires, the Ojibwa, Ottawa and Potawatomi.
- Ojibwe Language and Culture, by Nancy Vogt
  http://hanksville.phast.umass.edu/misc/ojibwe/index.html
- Oneida Indian Nation of NY
  http://one-web.org/oneida/
- The Osage
  http://members.aol.com/bbbenge/page16.html
- The Plains and Emigrant Tribes of Kansas
  http://history.cc.ukans.edu/heritage/old_west/indian.html
- Pueblo Cultural Center
  http://hanksville.phast.umass.edu/defs/independent/PCC/PCC.html
- Seminole Nation of Oklahoma—Historic Preservation Office
  http://www.cowboy.net/native/seminole/historic.html
- The Seminole Tribe of Florida
  http://www.seminoletribe.com/
- Suquamish Tribe
  http://www.suquamish.nsn.us/
  Washington
- The Taino Genealogy Project
  http://www.hartford-hwp.com/taino/docs/proj-6.html
- The Taino Inter-Tribal Council
  http://www.hartford-hwp.com/taino/index.html
- Terri Moore's Native American Home Page
  http://home1.gte.net/cicsd/index.htm
  Arkansas, Oklahoma and Native American Information.
- Viki's Little Corner of the Web
  http://www.novia.net/~vikia/
  ROARK, COLBERT, LOVE, KEMP, FRAZIER, McKINNEY & Chickasaw Native American History and Genealogy.
  - ○ Chickasaw Families Database
    http://www.novia.net/~vikia/KerryArmstrong.html
    Over 18,000 names.

- Wampanoag History
  http://www.dickshovel.com/wampa.html
  Massachusetts

◆ USGenWeb Project ~ Native Americans

- Idaho Indian Reservations—USGenWeb Project
  http://www.wsu.edu:8080/~mbsimon/idahoindians/index.html
  - Coeur d'Alene Reservation
    http://www.wsu.edu:8080/~mbsimon/idahoindians/index.html#coeur
  - Duck Valley Reservation
    http://www.wsu.edu:8080/~mbsimon/idahoindians/index.html#duck
  - Fort Hall Reservation
    http://www.wsu.edu:8080/~mbsimon/idahoindians/index.html#forthall
    Home to the Shoshone and Bannock Tribes.
  - Nez Perce Reservation
    http://www.wsu.edu:8080/~mbsimon/idahoindians/index.html#nezperce
- NC Cherokee Reservation Genealogy
  http://www.intertekweb.com/gpsbook/cherokee/index.html
  - Sources & References
    http://www.intertekweb.com/gpsbook/cherokee/sources.htm
    Includes Cherokee Rolls: East of the Mississippi and West of the Mississippi.
- Twin Territories—Oklahoma/Indian Territory Project
  http://www.rootsweb.com/~itgenweb/index.htm
  - Cherokee Nation
    http://www.rootsweb.com/~itcherok/
  - Chickasaw Nation
    http://www.rootsweb.com/~itchicka/
  - Choctaw Nation
    http://www.rootsweb.com/~itchocta

  - Creek Nation
    http://www.rootsweb.com/~itcreek/index.htm
  - Seminole Nation
    http://www.rootsweb.com/~itsemino/seminoleit.htm
  - Cherokee Outlet
    http://www.harvestcomm.net/personal/bjsbytes/outlet.htm
  - Cheyenne & Arapaho
    http://www.geocities.com/Heartland/Hills/1263/itcheyarapindx.html
  - Kiowa, Comanche & Apache
    http://www.geocities.com/Heartland/Hills/1263/itcomancindx.html
  - No Man's Land
    http://www.rootsweb.com/~okbeaver/NoMansLand/nomansld.htm
  - Osage Nation
    http://www.rootsweb.com/~itosage/
  - Pottawatomie
    http://tri.net/~kheidel/nativeamer/index.html
  - Quapaw Agency Lands
    http://www.rootsweb.com/~itquapaw/index.htm
  - Sovereign Nation of the Kaw
    http://www.rootsweb.com/~itkaw/KanzaNation.html
  - Unassigned Lands
    http://www.geocities.com/Heartland/Park/9448/
- South Dakota Native American Genealogy
  http://www.geocities.com/Heartland/Plains/8430/
- Washington Indian Reservation Orders
  http://www.rootsweb.com/~usgenweb/wa/indians/resorder.htm
- Washington Indian Treaties
  http://www.rootsweb.com/~usgenweb/wa/indians/treaties.htm
- Washington Tribes
  http://www.travel-in-wa.com/DISTINCTLY/tribes.html
  List of addresses for tribes in the state.

NETHERLANDS / NEDERLAND

http://www.CyndisList.com/nether.htm

Category Index:

- General Resource Sites
- Libraries, Archives & Museums
- Locality Specific & Migration
- Mailing Lists, Newsgroups & Chat
- Maps, Gazetteers & Geographical Information
- People & Families

- Professional Researchers, Volunteers & Other Research Services
- Publications, Software & Supplies
- Records: Census, Cemeteries, Land, Obituaries, Personal, Taxes and Vital
- Societies & Groups

◆ General Resource Sites

- Ancestors from the former Dutch East Indies
  http://ourworld.compuserve.com/homepages/paulvanV/eastindi.htm
- Arie Jan Stasse's Home Page
  http://www.geocities.com/Paris/4744/
- Benelux Research
  gopher://omega.ufsia.ac.be
- Dutch Antilles
  http://ourworld.compuserve.com/homepages/paulvanV/nedantil.htm
- Dutch East-Indies Informationpoint
  http://home.wxs.nl/~vdbroeke/
  A "guide" for everybody who is interested in Eurasian culture in the Netherlands.
- Dutch Research Corner
  http://www.ristenbatt.com/genealogy/dutch_rc.htm
- Genealogica Brabantica—Noord-Brabant
  http://www.xs4all.nl/~defonte/brabant.htm
- Genealogische Links—Genealogy Links in The Netherlands / Wortels naar het Verleden
  http://members.tripod.com/~westland/index.htm
- Genealogy Benelux Home Page
  http://www.ufsia.ac.be/genealogy/
- Genealogy Bulletin Board Systems for the Netherlands
  http://www.genealogy.org/~gbbs/gblnethe.html
- Het Centraal Bureau voor Genealogie / The Central Bureau for Genealogy
  http://www.cbg.nl/
- Holland Page
  http://ourworld.compuserve.com/homepages/paulvanv/

- International Civic Arms
  http://www.bng.nl/ngw/indexgb.htm
  Over 9,500 arms of towns, states and countries.
- Links naar databestanden met gegevens uit primaire bronnen
  http://home.wxs.nl/~hjdewit/links.html
- STORME's Genealogy Page
  http://www.ufsia.ac.be/~estorme/genealogy.html
  Many great Benelux resource links. STORME, van WAESBERGHE, de LAUSNAY, BLOCK, SCHEERDERS, van SCHOUBROEK, de SCHRYVER, BOSTEELS.
- Web-wijzer Genealogie
  http://www.multiweb.nl/~don_arnoldus/glinks_nl.htm
  Web-wijzer Genealogie (Dutch). A linking system to websites which will be of interest to genealogic researchers.
- Yahoo!...Netherlands...Genealogy
  http://dir.yahoo.com/Regional/Countries/Netherlands/Arts_and_Humanities/History/Genealogy/
- Yvette's Dutch Genealogy Homepage
  http://www.twente.nl/~genealogy/

◆ Libraries, Archives & Museums

- Archiefdiensten In Nederland
  http://www.ufsia.ac.be/genealogy/pages/geninfo/archi_nl.txt
- The Dutch Archives
  http://ourworld.compuserve.com/homepages/paulvanv/dutcharc.htm
  Detailed information in English about the various archives in the Netherlands with links describing their collections & how to use them.
- Gemeentebibliotheek Utrecht / Municipal Public Library Utrecht (Netherlands)
  http://www.gbu.nl/
- Koninklijke Bibliotheek / The National Library of the Netherlands
  http://www.konbib.nl/

- Municipal Archives of Zwolle
  http://www.obd.nl/instel/gemarchzw/gemareng.htm
- NBD—Nederlandse Bibliotheek Dienst /
  Netherlands Library Service
  http://www.nbd.nl/www/owa/page
- Netherlands Historical Data Archive
  http://oasis.leidenuniv.nl/nhda/nhda-welcome-uk.html
- Stadsbibliotheek Maastricht / City Library of
  Maastricht
  http://www.sbm.nl/
- Stadsbibliotheek Vlaardingen / City Library of
  Vlaardingen
  http://www.dsv.nl/DSV/kijken-en-kopen/lezen/bibliotheek/
  bibindex.htm
- State Archives in the province of Overijssel
  http://obd-server.obd.nl/www-data/instel/arch/rkarchen.htm
- Stichting Vrienden West Zeeuws-Vlaamse Archieven
  http://www.cyber.nl/zeeuw_archief/welcome.html
  Archive site in Dutch.

◆ Locality Specific & Migration

- Hoeksche Waard—Martine's Historical Homepage
  http://stad.dsl.nl/~martine/zoehwe.htm
- Limburg Genealogy
  http://home.pi.net/~eugdub/homeeng.htm
- Ostfriesian Research: American Sources and
  Suggestions by Micheal Neill
  http://csc.techcenter.org/~mneill/ostfries.html
- Project Ahnentafels in Limburg / Project
  Limburgse Kwartierstaten
  http://ping4.ping.be/~ping2011/Ahnen.html

◆ Mailing Lists, Newsgroups & Chat

- GENBNL-L Mailing List
  http://members.aol.com/gfsjohnf/gen_mail_country-
  blg.html#DUTCH
  *For research in the Benelux region (Belgium, the Netherlands,
  and Luxembourg). Gatewayed with the soc.genealogy.benelux
  newsgroup.*
- SCHAKEL-NL Mailing List
  http://members.aol.com/gfsjohnf/gen_mail_country-
  net.html#SCHAKEL-NL
  *For discussions of news events and issues of interest to Canadi-
  ans and Americans of Dutch origin; Dutch heritage, customs
  and traditions; immigrant experiences; questions about Dutch
  legislation, laws, regulations, history etc.; living the Dutch way
  (e.g., travel, food, drinks); and the ties that bind us. Queries
  from genealogists related to their Dutch ancestry are welcome.*

◆ Maps, Gazetteers & Geographical Information

- Historic Maps of the Netherlands
  http://grid.let.rug.nl/~welling/maps/maps.html
- Map of Amsterdam
  http://members.aol.com/tgostin/graphics/amstrdam.jpg
- Map of The Netherlands
  http://www.lib.utexas.edu/Libs/PCL/Map_collection/europe/
  Netherlands.jpg
  *From the Perry-Castañeda Library at the Univ. of Texas at
  Austin.*

◆ People & Families

- Adrian and Jenny VANDERHOEVEN's Dutch
  Genealogy Page—Families Are Forever
  http://users.deseretonline.com/adrian/index.html
- Andrys STIENSTRA's Home Page
  http://web.inter.nl.net/hcc/Andrys.Stienstra/
  *STIENSTRA surname and info on the Hazadata software
  program.*
- Arie Jan STASSE's Home Page
  http://www.geocities.com/Paris/4744/
- Aartje's Dutch Ancestry Page
  http://www.northrim.net/Aartje/
  *VAN OS, VROEGH, KEIJ, BROUWER, PLANKEN, KRUIJS,
  LABEE, SOUWER, VAN BRUGGEN, VAN BRAKEL, DEN
  HARTOG, VAN DER FLIER, HOL, DE KIEFTE, VAN STENIS*
- AUGUSTEIJN Genealogy / Stamboom
  AUGUSTEIJN
  http://web.inter.NL.net/hcc/Eric.Aug/
- Bas en Fredie
  http://www.telebyte.nl/~dessa/english1.htm
  TUIJL, van
- BATTJES, DEBOER, SCHAAF & VERVER
  Families
  http://members.aol.com/ververhp/htmlmain.htm
- BUWALDA Family Tree
  http://www.noord.bart.nl/~abuwalda
  *Andre A. Buwalda's page from the Netherlands, for his Frisian
  surname and allied family lines.*
- The DIJKGRAAF Family Genealogy Page
  http://www.geocities.com/~dijkgraaf/
  *De WIT(T), DIJKGRAAF/DYKGRAAF, MEUWIS /
  MEEUWIS(SEN), SMOUTER*
- Dutch Family Genealogies—BANGMA, KAT,
  SCHUURMAN and VRIEND
  http://home.earthlink.net/~jkthompson/genealogy/NL_gene.htm
- Genealogical Office LAMPING Family
  http://www.lamping.demon.nl/genea/
  *Descendants of LAMPING, LAMPINK and LAMBING. German
  & Dutch roots.*

- Genealogie
  http://homepage.cistron.nl/~dagospel/genealogie/
  bookmark.nl.htm
  HENDERSON, Van RIEDE, HENDRIKSON, MACOR, van RIJ, van den HAM

- Genealogie GUEQUIERRE
  http://www.worldaccess.nl/~driessen/eduard/geguinl.htm
  France—> Netherlands—> Wis. USA

- Genealogie Homepage Van Henk DE PAUW & Ans Van DER GUN
  http://callisto.worldonline.nl/~hadepauw/

- Genealogie homepage van Piet en Willeke MOLEMA-SMITSHOEK
  http://www.medewerker.hro.nl/w_t_molema/
  Zoetermeer. MOLEMA, SMITSHOEK, BALJE and GELLING

- Genealogie van de familie HANSWIJK
  http://www.mediaport.org/~johnh/genealog/welkom.htm
  HANSWIJK, VAN HANSWIJK, HANSWIJCK

- Genealogie SJOLLEMA Index
  http://www.rendo.dekooi.nl/~sjollema/genealogie.htm

- Genealogische Homepage van Herman de WIT
  http://home.wxs.nl/~hjdewit/home_en.html
  ABBRING, DACHVERLIES, De JONGE, KLERCK, MODDER, De ROTH, SCHOOFS, De SMIT, WEIJERS, De WIT

- De Genealogische Pagina van Hans HOMAN FREE
  http://web.inter.NL.net/hcc/Hanshoman.Free/
  HOMAN, FREE, OORTMAN, KUIPER, VAN VLIET, DILLING, IN DRENTHE, GRONINGEN and ZUIDHOLLAND

- Genealogy Homepage by Guus van den NESTE
  http://people.zeelandnet.nl/jetsen/
  Surnames: van den Neste, Vanden Neste, Vandenneste, De Jong, De Reus.

- Genealogy Homepage of Bart van Gurp
  http://web.inter.NL.net/hcc/B.van.Gurp/geneng.htm
  van GURP, NUIJTEN, WILLEMSEN, SCHNEIJDERBERG

- Genealogy Homepage of Peter van MARKUS
  http://users.bart.nl/~pvmarkus/
  Descendants of Pieter Louissen van Markus, married 1718 Catharina van Wijck.

- Genealogy of the family van DORT
  http://www.geocities.com/Paris/6547/index.htm
  Netherlands, Sri Lanka, Malaysia, Belgium, U.S., Canada, Australia.

- Genealogy of the PESCHIER family
  http://www.students.cs.ruu.nl/people/jpeschie/genealog.htm

- Genealogy of the Royal Family of The Netherlands
  http://www.xs4all.nl/~kvenjb/gennl.htm

- Genealogy REINDERS / Kwartierstaat REINDERS
  http://www.tref.nl/bunnik/bn/genealog.htm
  REINDERS, De VRIES, VERSCHLEUSS, NIEKAMP, STOKDIJK, ONDERSTAL, VERSCHLEUSZ, SIKKINK, DOETS

- Gil ANEMA's Genealogy Page
  http://ourworld.compuserve.com/homepages/GLA/
  Genbody.htm
  ANEMA, BROUWER, DELEEUW, DROS/DROST, GORDIJN, GRAAF, GROENEVELD, GROOT, HARKEMA, JELLESMA, KOOGER, LEMKE, OTTEN, POSTHUMUS, SALM, STARK, SLOT, TIMMER, VANPROOYEN / VANPROOIJEN, VLAMING / VLAMINGH / FLAMING

- HjV's Dutch Descendant & Ancestors Page
  http://www.nfra.nl/~hjv/genealogy/dap_nl.html
  A list of links to web sites for Dutch family lines.

- De HOEGE Woeninck
  http://www.xs4all.nl/~bv25/hgwng1.html
  Hoogewoning, Hoogewooning, Hoogewoonink

- Homepage Folkert van der MOLEN
  http://home.pi.net/~folmolen/

- Homepage Genealogy RO(O)S(Z)E(N)BOOM
  http://leden.tref.nl/pjdepenn/default.htm
  Rooseboom, Roosenboom, Roseboom, Rosenboom, Roozenboom, Roozeboom, Rozeboom, Rozenboom—Worldwide

- Home Page of Bob CORET
  http://www.coret.demon.nl/
  CORET and BRIZEE

- Homepage of Henk F.M. BARKHOF
  http://home.pi.net/~hbarkhof/
  BARKHOF, FRANZEN, AMBAUM, REMLINGER, LOEFF

- The HomePage of Jos de KLOE
  http://www.geocities.com/Paris/1634/homepage/index.htm
  WESTERLAKEN, de KLOE, du CLOU(X), NAAIJEN

- Homepage van de familie ARNOLDUS
  http://www.multiweb.nl/~don_arnoldus/g_idx_nl.htm
  ARNOLDUS, GUYT/GUIJT/GUIT, WITTE, van RIJSWIJK and MARTIN

- Homepage Van De Familie SJOLLEMA
  http://www.noord.bart.nl/~tipama/

- De Homepage van Gerard KELDERMAN
  http://www.worldaccess.nl/~kelderg/gerard.htm

- Homepage Van Ton & Ria
  http://www.xs4all.nl/~tonput/
  Van der PUTTE, BERGMAN (BORGMAN), OOMS (MET ALLE VARIANTEN), VISSERS, JOOSTEN, LOKERMAN

- Huguenot
  http://www.CyndisList.com/huguenot.htm
  See this category on Cyndi's List for related links.

- Index of Persons—Harry WEDEMEIJER
  http://utopia.knoware.nl/users/hwede/genealogy/
  VAN LEEUWEN, and WEDEMEIJER

- Kwartieren van HELVOORT, SEUREN, CRAANE en VERHOEVEN
  http://www.flnet.nl/~0vhelvoort02/genealog/

- Kwartierstaat REINDERS
  http://www.tref.nl/bunnik/bn/genealog.htm
  REINDERS, De VRIES, VERSCHLEUSS, STOKDIJK, ONDERSTAL, SIKKINK, DOETS, VAN VELDEN, RUSSON

- LAMBRECHTSEN Online
  http://utopia.knoware.nl/users/evim/index.html
  Joos Lambrechtsen, born November 9th 1597 in Petegem near Deinze in East-Flanders.

- LETHER / LEETHER Family Genealogical Society
  http://www.presstige.nl/Genealogy/

- Marcel NIJSKENS New Home Page
  http://www.yi.com/home/NijskensMarcel/
  NIJSKENS, NIESKENS, NISKENS, HEIJNEN, REIJGERSBERG, van de VELDE, ARENDONK

- Martine's Historische Homepage—Academisch Historisch Museum Leiden
  http://www.leidenuniv.nl/bvdu/ahm/zoe.htm
  ZOETEMAN, SOETEMAN

- OFFRINGA Familytree with more than 3,000 Offringa's
  http://home.pi.net/~offringa/index.htm
  From Dick Offringa in Emmeloord, Netherlands.

- RIPER Genealogy Site
  http://home.wxs.nl/~riper/
  RIEPER, RIPER, VAN RIPER, De WIT, WESSELS, Van WAETERSCHOODT

- Ronald BALHAN's Genealogy Page
  http://almere.flnet.nl/~0balhan01/roots/nroots.htm

- The ROTHUIZEN / RODENHOUSE Family Web Site
  http://www.sigma.net/etymes/
  Eleven generations (with about 500 names) of the family of Anton and Wilhelmina Rothuizen (who changed the family name to Rodenhouse in 1919), originally from Osterbeek, Gelderland, Netherlands. The site makes a case for the theory that all those named "Rothuizen" or "Rotshuizen" might be related.

- Ruben WOUDSMA's Genealogic Page
  http://www.geocities.com/Athens/8018/FAMTREE.HTM
  WOUDSMA, SPAANDER, HIDDEMA, VOLGER, DAMSMA, HUIZINGA

- Rude's Genealogy
  http://www.xs4all.nl/~rude/ruud/genea.html
  RAATS, VAN AARDEN, VAN DEN KIEBOOM, VAN VELDHOOVEN, ROYEN, VERLINDEN, VERHIEST, HENNEVANGER, ZONNEVELD, OBER, VAN KAMPEN, LUCASSEN, ZIMMERMANN

- SIFA: Stichting Indisch Familie Archief
  http://www.xs4all.nl/~polleke/
  A private collection of family documentation from the Dutch-East Indies period.

- SMIT's Page
  http://www.worldaccess.nl/~ksmit/
  SMIT, v. OOSTOM (OSTRUM)

- Stamboom van de Familie KREIKE
  http://huizen.dds.nl/~bkreike/

- SWINX Zoeklijst Nederlandse Familienamen
  http://www.multiweb.nl/~don_arnoldus/swinx/index.html
  Netherlands. SWINX = Surname Website INdeX

- VAN HEES Family History
  http://www.foxberry.net/rvanhees/home.html-ssi
  VAN HEES, KROEZE, DIRKSE, VANDENBOSCH, BURGE

- The WIERENGA Family Site
  http://www.macatawa.org/~donweers/
  ALLART, DeKORNE, WIERENGA

- Yntze van der HONING Home Page
  http://home.wxs.nl/~yntze/
  JONGEDIJK (YOUNGEDYKE), BOEK, SCHRAM, EVERTS, VAN DER HONING and other surnames.

◆ Professional Researchers, Volunteers & Other Research Services

- Genealogy Helplist—Netherlands
  http://www.cybercomm.net/~freddie/helplist/nethlnd.htm

- Holland Family History
  http://home.wxs.nl/~hfh/engels.htm

- Holland Page Helpdesk
  http://ourworld.compuserve.com/homepages/paulvanv/helpdesk.htm

◆ Publications, Software & Supplies

- Books We Own—Netherlands
  http://www.rootsweb.com/~bwo/nether.html

- Brother's Keeper Software
  http://ourworld.compuserve.com/homepages/Brothers_Keeper/
  Downloadable shareware program for Windows. The latest version contains English, French, Norwegian, Danish, Swedish, German, and Dutch.

- Frontier Press Bookstore—Dutch
  http://www.frontierpress.com/frontier.cgi?category=dutch

- GenealogyBookShop.com—Netherlands/Dutch
  http://www.genealogybookshop.com/genealogybookshop/files/The_World,Netherlands_Dutch/index.html
  The online store of Genealogical Publishing Co., Inc. & Clearfield Company.

- GensData voor Windows
  http://web.inter.nl.net/hcc/F.Berkhof/proefblz.htm
  Dutch genealogy program for Windows 3.1 or Windows 95.

- Genus Genealogy Program
  http://www.mediabase.fi/suku/genupgb.htm
  Windows program available in six languages: Dutch, English, Finnish, French, German and Swedish.

- Haza-Data Website
  http://www.hazadata.com
  Dutch genealogy software program. Also versions in English, German, Swedish, Norwegian, Polish.

- Heritage Books—Dutch
  http://www.heritagebooks.com/dutch.htm

- PRO-GEN Genealogie à la Carte
  http://home.wxs.nl/~progen/home.html
  Dutch genealogy program capable of outputs in Dutch, English, French, Frisian and German.

◆ Records: Census, Cemeteries, Land, Obituaries, Personal, Taxes and Vital (Born, Married, Died & Buried)

- Alblasserwaard Genealogie Page
  http://www.geocities.com/Paris/4744/ALBWRDGENPAGE.HTM
  Several marriage indexes here for the early 1800's.

- The Cochin Churchbook
  http://www.telebyte.nl/~dessa/cochin.htm
  Baptism & marriages from the Dutch Church in Cochin, India (1754–1804).

- Digital Resources Netherlands and Belgium
  http://home.wxs.nl/~hjdewit/links_en.html
  Digital resources available on the internet, bulletin board systems and on diskette/CD-ROM.

- On-line Search for Maiden Names of Women in South Holland
  http://www.itsnet.com/~pauld/ksh/
  Searchable database to be used in conjunction with the "Klappers of Zuid Holland" ("Indexes of South Holland"). Approx. 250,000 maiden names, from between 1695 and 1811.

◆ Societies & Groups

- Afdeling Computergenealogie Van De Nederlandse Genealogische Vereniging—Gens Data
  http://www.gensdata.demon.nl/

- Archer's Computer Interest Group List— Netherlands
  http://www.genealogy.org/~ngs/cigs/ngl3otnt.html

- Genealogische Vereniging Prometheus / Genealogical Society Prometheus
  http://duttcbs.tn.tudelft.nl/genealogie/hg1.html
  Delft, Netherlands

- Nederlandse Genealogische Vereniging
  http://www.ngv.nl/

- Nederlandse Kring voor Joodse Genealogie / Netherlands Society for Jewish Genealogy
  http://www.nljewgen.org/

NEWSPAPERS
http://www.CyndisList.com/newspapr.htm

◆ General Resources   ◆ Alphabetical listing

◆ General Resources

- ABC Newspaper Hotlink Directory
  http://www.accessabc.com/hotlinks/newspapr.html

- AJR NewsLink Newspaper Index
  http://www.newslink.org/news.html
  American Journalism Review

- Cybermart News Online
  http://www.cybermart.net/Newspapers/US_News/index.html
  Index of over 2,500 newspapers and magazines.

- Ecola Newstand: Newspapers
  http://www.ecola.com/news/press/
  Worldwide

- Editor & Publisher Interactive Online
  Newspaper Database
  http://www.mediainfo.com/ephome/npaper/nphtm/online.htm

- Frontier Press Bookstore—Newspapers
  http://www.frontierpress.com/frontier.cgi?category=news

- Historic Newspaper Archives
  http://www.historicnewspaper.com/
  Actual historic newspapers to give as gifts. Dating from 1880's to present.

- History Buff's Home Page
  http://www.historybuff.com
  Produced by The Newspaper Collectors Society of America.
  - Primer on Collecting Old & Historic Newspapers
    http://www.historybuff.com/primer.html

- How Newspapers Can Help You With Your Research
  http://www.everton.com/oe3-18/papers.htm
  From Everton's Genealogical Helper Online.

- Library of Congress Newspaper and Current
  Periodical Reading Room
  http://lcweb.loc.gov/rr/news/ncp.html

- Newspapers
  http://lcweb.loc.gov/rr/news/lcnewsp.html
  Periodicals
  http://lcweb.loc.gov/rr/news/lcper.html
  - 17th & 18th Century Foreign Newspapers
    http://lcweb.loc.gov/rr/news/17th/178th.html
  - Full-Text Journals Available in the Newspaper and
    Current Periodical Reading Room
    http://lcweb.loc.gov/rr/news/full.html
  - How to Find a Newspaper in this Reading Room
    gopher://marvel.loc.gov:70/00/research/reading.rooms/
    newspaper/bibs.guides/newspap.bib

  - Internet Resources Outside the Library
    of Congress
    http://lcweb.loc.gov/rr/news/othint.html
  - Lists of Newspaper & Periodical Resources
    on the Internet
    http://lcweb.loc.gov/rr/news/lists.html
  - Online Newspaper Indexes Available in the
    Newspaper and Current Periodical Reading Room
    http://lcweb.loc.gov/rr/news/npindex2.html

- MEDIA-Link: Newspapers
  http://www.dds.nl/~kidon/papers.html
  Listings for Europe, USA, Americas, Asia, Africa and Oceania.

- MediaSite Newspapers—International Newspapers
  http://www.potter.net/mediasite/international.html

- MediaSite Newspapers—U.S. and
  Canadian Newspapers
  http://www.potter.net/mediasite/newspaper.html

- My Virtual Newspaper
  http://www.refdesk.com/paper.html
  List of great newspaper links by country & by state.

- Newspaper Association of America—Hotlinks
  http://www.naa.org/hotlinks/index.html

- Newspapers on the Net
  http://www.give.com/papers.html

- New York State Newspaper Project—
  For Newspaper Collectors
  http://unix2.nysed.gov/nysnp/buysell.htm
  A list of dealers of collectible newspapers.

- Using Newspapers for Genealogical Research
  http://www.system.missouri.edu/shs/newspap.html
  From the State Historical Society of Missouri.

- Yahoo!...News and Media...Newspapers
  http://dir.yahoo.com/News_and_Media/Newspapers/

◆ "A"

- Aftenposten Interaktiv
  http://www.aftenposten.no/
  Oslo, Norway

- An Phoblacht / Republican News
  http://www.irlnet.com/aprn/index.html
  Belfast & Dublin

- The Anchorage Daily News
  http://www.adn.com/
  Alaska

- The Ann Arbor News—Michigan Live
  http://aa.mlive.com/

- Arizona Central: Arizona Republic Archives
  http://www.azcentral.com/archive/

- The Arizona Daily Star
  http://www.azstarnet.com/public/pubstar/dstar.cgi

- The Arizona Newspaper Project
  http://www.lib.az.us/research/c-news.htm

- The Atlanta Journal-Constitution
  http://www.accessatlanta.com/ajc/
  Georgia

- Austin 360: News: Austin American-Statesman
  http://www.Austin360.com/news/
  Texas

- Australian Newspapers
  http://www.slsa.sa.gov.au/lib_guide/subjects/news/
  austnews.htm
  A list from the State Library of South Australia.

◆ "B"

- Bangor Daily News Interactive
  http://www.bangornews.com/
  Maine

- The Berkshire Eagle
  http://www.newschoice.com/newspapers/newengland/eagle/
  Massachusetts

- The Bismarck Tribune
  http://www.ndonline.com/
  North Dakota

- Boulder News
  http://www.bouldernews.com/
  Colorado

- The Brainerd Daily Dispatch Online
  http://www.brainerddispatch.com/
  Minnesota

◆ "C"

- Carson Appeal Newspaper Index, 1865–66,
  1879–80, 1881, 1885–86
  http://www.clan.lib.nv.us/docs/NSLA/ARCHIVES/appeal/
  appeal1.htm

- Chicago Newspaper Network
  http://www.chicago-news.com/
  Illinois. "Your guide to 70 newspapers serving the city and suburbs."

- The Chicago Sun-Times Online
  http://www.suntimes.com/index/

- The Connaught Telegraph, Co Mayo, West of Ireland
  http://www.mayo-ireland.ie/Connaught.htm

- Connecticut Newspaper Project
  http://www.cslnet.ctstateu.edu/cnp.htm

◆ "D"

- The Daily Journal
  http://www.daily-journal.com/
  Kankakee, Ilinois

- The Daily ME
  http://www.thedailyme.com/
  Maine

- The Daily News Online
  http://www.tdn.com/
  Longview-Kelso, Washington

- The Daily News Worldwide
  http://www.hfxnews.southam.ca/
  Halifax, Nova Scotia, Canada

- The Dallas Morning News
  http://www.dallasnews.com/
  Texas

- Decatur Daily Democrat
  http://www.decaturnet.com/paper/
  Indiana

- The Denver Post Online
  http://www.denverpost.com/

- The Detroit Free Press—The Freep
  http://www.freep.com/index.htm
  Michigan

- The Detroit News
  http://www.detnews.com/
  Michigan

- Duluth News-Tribune
  http://www.duluthnews.com/
  Minnesota

◆ "E"

- Eastern Counties Network
  http://www.ecn.co.uk/index.htm
  England. East Anglian Daily Times, Eastern Daily Press, Evening News, Evening Star.

- Echo Press Online
  http://www.echopress.com/
  Alexandria, Minnesota

- ESCN Database Reports
  http://ourworld.compuserve.com/homepages/
  escn_database_reports/
  Quick Reference Indexes to the Early South Carolina Newspapers.

- Excerpts From Old Newspapers
  http://www.ida.net/users/dhanco/news.htm

◆ "F"

- The First Newspapers on Canada's West Coast: 1858–1863
  http://members.tripod.com/~Hughdoherty/index.htm

- The Florida Times-Union Online, Jacksonville, Florida
  http://www.times-union.com/

◆ "G"

- Galway Advertiser
  http://ireland.iol.ie/resource/ga/
  Ireland

- The Gate
  http://www.sfgate.com/
  From the San Francisco Chronicle & the San Francisco Examiner.

- Gebbie Press—Daily Newspapers on the Web
  http://www.gebbieinc.com/dailyint.htm

- Greensboro News & Record Online
  http://www.greensboro.com/nronline/index.htm
  North Carolina

◆ "H"

- The Halifax Herald
  http://www.herald.ns.ca/
  Nova Scotia, Canada

- The Hamilton Spectator
  http://www.southam.com/hamiltonspectator/
  Ontario, Canada

- The Heritage Newspapers
  http://www.heritagenews.com/
  Michigan

- Historical Text Archive— Old Gazettes & Newspapers
  http://www.msstate.edu:80/Archives/History/USA/gazette.html

- HomeTown Online
  http://www.htnews.com/
  Newspapers for Howell, Michigan.

- Honolulu Star-Bulletin
  http://www.starbulletin.com/
  Hawaii

- Houston Chronicle Interactive
  http://www.chron.com/
  Texas

◆ "I"

- In-Forum
  http://www.in-forum.com/
  Fargo, North Dakota

- The Independent
  http://www.indenews.com/
  Serving the Hudson Berkshire Corridor, New York.

- Indiana Newspaper Search by CompuGen Systems
  http://members.aol.com/CGSystems/NXSearch.html

- The Irish News
  http://www.irishnews.com/
  Belfast

- The Irish People—The Voice of Irish Republicanism in America
  http://larkspirit.com/IrishPeople/

- The Irish Times on the Web
  http://www.irish-times.com/
  Dublin

- The Irish Voice Online
  http://www.irishvoice.com/
  New York

- The Issaquah Press
  http://www.blueworld.com/iol/isspress/
  Washington. Includes Historic Articles.

◆ "J"

- The Joplin Globe
  http://www.joplinglobe.com/
  Missouri

◆ "K"

- The Kingston Whig-Standard
  http://www.southam.com/kingstonwhigstandard/
  Ontario, Canada

- Kitchener Waterloo Record Online
  http://www.southam.com/kitchenerwaterloorecord/
  Ontario, Canada

- The Knoxville Gazette
  http://www.ultranet.com/~smack/news.htm
  Transcribed historical articles related to genealogy, from November 5, 1791 thru January 14, 1792. More transcriptions to come in this ongoing project from Tennessee.

◆ "L"

- The Landmark Newspaper
  http://www.thelandmark.com/
  Serving the Wachusett Region: Holden, Paxton, Princeton, Rutland, Sterling, Massachusetts.

- Leader-Post Online
  http://www.leader-post.sk.ca/
  Regina, Saskatchewan, Canada

- The Limerick Post Newspaper
  http://ireland.iol.ie/~lpost/
  Ireland

- The London Gazette
  http://www.history.rochester.edu/London_Gazette/
  Selected online editions for 1674, 1675, 1676, 1678 and 1692 from Electronic Historical Publications.

- Los Angeles Times
  http://www.latimes.com/

- Lubbock Online
  http://www.lubbockonline.com/
  Texas

◆ "M"

- The Minnesota Daily Online
  http://www.daily.umn.edu/
  Minneapolis-St. Paul

- Missoulian Online
  http://www.missoulian.com/
  Montana

- The Monroe Evening News
  http://www.MONROENEWS.COM/index.html
  Michigan

- Montague County Shopper Online
  http://www.morgan.net/shopper/
  Texas

- Mountain Democrat Online
  http://www.mtdemocrat.com/
  California's Oldest Newspaper, Placerville, California.

◆ "N"

- N.C. Newspaper Project
  http://statelibrary.dcr.state.nc.us/tss/newspape.htm
  North Carolina

- Nevada Newspaper Indexes
  http://www.clan.lib.nv.us/docs/NSLA/ARCHIVES/newsind.htm
  Nevada State Library and Archives and Records.

- New England Old Newspaper Index Project of Maine
  http://www.geocities.com/Heartland/Hills/1460/

- New Jersey Daily Newspapers
  http://www.naa.org/hotlinks/nj.html
  From NAA, Newspaper Association of America.

- New York State Newspaper Project
  http://www.nysl.nysed.gov/nysnp/

- The New York Times on the Web
  http://www.nytimes.com/

- Newspaper and Current Periodical Room—
  Library of Congress
  http://lcweb.loc.gov/global/ncp/ncp.html

- Newspaper Clippings—Kansas City Public Library
  http://www.kcpl.lib.mo.us/sc/clips/newsclips.htm
  Missouri. In the Special Collections Department. Some are online.

- Newspaper Collection
  http://www.slv.vic.gov.au/slv/newspapers/
  At the State Library of Victoria, Australia.

- Newspaper Titles Online
  http://lcweb.loc.gov/global/ncp/oltitles.html
  From the Library of Congress Internet Resource Page.

- Newspapers at the National Library of Canada
  http://www.nlc-bnc.ca/services/enews.htm

- North East Newspapers
  http://www.aberdeenshire.gov.uk/ne_news.htm
  Held by the North East of Scotland Library Service.

- Northern News Services Limited
  http://www.nnsl.com/
  Yellowknife, NW Territories, Canada. Serving communities in Canada's Arctic Northwest Territories and Nunavut.

- Northscape News: The Grand Forks Herald Online
  http://www.northscape.com/

- Nova Scotian Newspapers
  http://www.shelburne.nscc.ns.ca/nsgna/nnewsp.html

- Nunatsiaq News
  http://www.nunanet.com/~nunat/
  NW Territories, Canada

◆ "O"

- Observer-Reporter Online
  http://www.observer-reporter.com/
  Washington, Pennsylvania

- Oklahoma Newspaper Project
  http://www.keytech.com:80/~frizzell/
  A project to preserve newspapers on microfilm.

- The Oklahoman Online
  http://www.oklahoman.com/

- Ottawa Citizen Online
  http://www.ottawacitizen.com/
  Ontario, Canada

◆ "P"

- Pilot Online—The Virginian-Pilot
  http://www.pilotonline.com/
  Hampton Roads

- Pioneer Planet
  http://www.pioneerplanet.com/
  St. Paul, Minnesota

- Portland Press Herald Online
  http://www.portland.com/
  Maine

- Prince Albert Daily Herald Online Edition
  http://www.paherald.sk.ca/prin/Start.htm
  Saskatchewan, Canada

- The Providence Journal-Bulletin
  http://www.providencejournal.com/main.htm
  Rhode Island

◆ "R"

- Recorder Online
  http://www.recordernews.com/
  Amsterdam, New York

- The Register-Herald, Preble County, Ohio
  http://www.registerherald.com/

- The Richmond Times-Dispatch
  http://www.gateway-va.com/pages/tdmain.htm
  Virginia

- The Roanoke Times Online
  http://www.roanoke.com/
  Virginia

- Rockford Register Star
  http://www.rrstar.com/
  Illinois

◆ "S"

- Sacramento Bee
  http://www.sacbee.com/
  California

- Saint John Times Globe
  http://www.nbpub.nb.ca/TIMES/INDEX.HTM
  Saint John, New Brunswick, Canada. Contact information and history regarding this newspaper.

- The Salt Lake Tribune
  http://www.sltrib.com/
  Utah

- San Francisco Bay Guardian
  http://www.sfbayguardian.com/

- The Seattle Times
  http://www.seattletimes.com/
  Washington

- The Shelbyville News Online
  http://www.shelbynews.com/
  Indiana

- Sioux City Journal Online
  http://www.siouxcityjournal.com/
  Iowa

- Slave River Journal Interactive
  http://www.auroranet.nt.ca/srj/
  NW Territories, Canada

- Southwest Virginia Enterprise
  http://www.wythenews.com/
  Wytheville, Virginia

- SPAN—Serials, Periodicals, and Newspapers
  http://span.mlc.lib.mi.us:9000/
  A database of over 201,000 journals, magazines and newspapers found in Michigan's libraries.

- The Star—Kansas City
  http://www.kcstar.com/
  Missouri

- Star Tribune Online
  http://www.startribune.com/
  Minneapolis-St. Paul, Minnesota

- StarLine On Line: The Morning Star
  http://starnews.wilmington.net/
  Wilmington, North Carolina

- StarNet—The Arizona Daily Star
  http://www.azstarnet.com/

- The StarPhoenix Online
  http://www.saskstar.sk.ca/
  Saskatoon, Saskatchewan, Canada

- Stephen A. Goldman Historical Newspapers
  http://www.historybuff.com/mall/goldman/index.html

- Svenska Dagbladet—Nyheter
  http://www.svd.se/svd/ettan/dagens/index.html
  Sweden

◆ "T"

- The Tampa Tribune on the Web
  http://www.tampatrib.com/
  Florida

- Telegraph Journal Online
  http://www.nbpub.nb.ca/TELE/INDEX.HTM
  New Brunswick, Canada

- Timothy Hughes Rare & Early Newspapers
  http://www.rarenewspapers.com/

- Trib-Net—The News Tribune
  http://www.tribnet.com/
  Tacoma, Washington

- Tri-City Herald Online
  http://www.tri-cityherald.com/
  Kennewick, Pasco and Richland, Washington

◆ "U"

- The United States Newspaper Program Participants
  http://www.neh.fed.us/html/usnp.html

- US Newspaper Archives on the Web
  http://sunsite.unc.edu/slanews/internet/archives.html

- UW Suzzallo Library Microform and Newspaper Collections
  http://www.lib.washington.edu/libinfo/libunits/suzzallo/mcnews/
  University of Washington in Seattle

◆ "V"

- Valley of the Shadow Newspapers
  http://jefferson.village.Virginia.EDU/vshadow2/newspapers.html
  From the Civil War project at the University of Virginia.

- The Virginia Newspaper Project
  http://vsla.edu/vnp/home.html

◆ "W"

- Washington Newspaper Publishers Association
  http://www.wnpa.com/editor/

- The Washington Post
  http://www.washingtonpost.com/

- The Washington Times National Weekly Edition
  http://www.washtimes-weekly.com/

- The Wenatchee World
  http://www.wenworld.com/
  Washington

- West Central Tribune
  http://www.wctrib.com/
  Willmar, Minnesota

- Westchester County Newspaper Collections
  http://pages.prodigy.com/HFBK19A/wcgsrs10.htm
  New York

- Western Oklahoma Newspaper Research
  http://members.tripod.com/~smcb/research.html

- Western People
  http://www.mayo-ireland.ie/WPeople.htm
  Mayo, Ireland

- Whitehorse Star Daily
  http://www.whitehorsestar.com/
  Yukon, Canada

- Wichita Online—A Service of the Wichita Eagle
  http://www.wichitaeagle.com/

- The Windsor Star
  http://www.southam.com/windsorstar/
  Ontario, Canada

- The Wire—News from AP
  http://wire.ap.org/WireWelcome/

◆ "Y"

- Yukon News Online
  http://www.yukon-news.com/

OBITUARIES

http://www.CyndisList.com/obits.htm

- Arrangements.com
  http://www.arrangements.com/
  For posting obituaries and funeral details.

- The Berkshire Eagle—Obituaries
  http://www.newschoice.com/webnews/index/nebeobt3i.asp
  Massachusetts

- BPL's Obituary Database
  http://www.bpl.org/WWW/Obits.html
  Massachusetts. This is a Telnet database from the Boston Public Library.

- Butler County, OH Older Obituaries
  http://www.rootsweb.com/~ohbutler/obit.html

- Campbell County, South Dakota, Obitbook—
  Interactive Search
  http://www.rootsweb.com/cgi-bin/sdcampbell/obitbook.pl

- Cemeteries—Wakulla County, FL
  http://mailer.fsu.edu/~rthompso/cemetery.html

- Cleveland News Index—Search on the word
  "Obituaries"
  http://www-catalog.cpl.org/CLENIX
  Database from 1976 to present.

- Cumberlink Obituaries
  http://www.cumberlink.com/obits/archive.html
  From the Sentinel, Carlisle, Pennsylvania.

- Death Notices
  http://www.funeral.net/info/notices.html
  Online forum to post your notices. Maintained by Armstrong Funeral Home and Funeral.Net

- Death Notices from Saratoga Whig Newspaper,
  1840–1842
  http://freenet.buffalo.edu/~ae487/awhig.html
  New York

- Death Notices of Some Early Pictou County Settlers
  http://www.rootsweb.com/~pictou/obits.htm
  Nova Scotia, Canada

- Deaths and Funerals—Chattanooga Free Press
  http://www.chatfreepress.com/obituary/
  Tennessee

- Deaths and Memoriams Extracted from the
  'New Zealand Herald' 1993
  http://www.geocities.com/Heartland/6123/dth_names.html
  From New Zealand. Find a surname of interest then e-mail the owner of the page for details.

- Deaths from Kerwin's 1888 Saratoga Springs
  City Directory
  http://freenet.buffalo.edu/~ae487/1888.html
  New York

- Detroit Free Press—Death Notices
  http://www.freep.com/death_notices/index.htm
  Michigan

- Detroit Free Press—Obituaries
  http://www.freep.com/index/obituaries.htm
  Michigan

- The Detroit News—Obituaries & Death Notices
  http://www.detnews.com/
  Scroll through the index on this page and click on the link to Obituaries.

- Fargo Forum Obituary Index
  http://www.lib.ndsu.nodak.edu/ndirs/bio&genealogy/
  forumobits.html
  Eastern North Dakota or Northwestern Minnesota. 40,000 names for obituaries posted from 1985 through 1995 and approx. 2,000 obituaries from earlier years.

- The Florida Times-Union Online Obituaries
  http://www.times-union.com/tu-online/obituaries/
  Jacksonville, Florida

- Fort Worth Star-Telegram Local Death Notices—
  Texas
  http://www.startext.com/today/news/local/fw/
  Scroll to the bottom of this page and click on the link for "Local Death Notices."

- Funeral Notices—The Arizona Daily Star
  http://www.azstarnet.com/public/electrifieds/0002.htm

- GEN-OBIT Mailing List
  http://members.aol.com/johnf14246/
  gen_mail_general.html#GEN-OBIT

- Gospel Advocate Obituary Index
  http://www.ag.uiuc.edu/~mcmillan/Restlit/Database/gaobit.html
  Compiled by members of the Lehman Avenue church of Christ in Bowling Green, Kentucky.

- Greensboro News & Record Online Obituaries Index
  http://www.greensboro.com/nronline/Index/miobits.htm
  Under construction as of February 1, 1997.

- Hopkins County Obituaries—Kentucky
  http://www.rootsweb.com/~kygenweb/hopkins/obits/index.html

- Index to Obituaries Taken From The Southern
  Democrat, Blount County, Alabama 1915–1940
  http://members.aol.com/blountal/Obit.html

- Internet Obituary Network
  http://www.obits.com/

- Joplin Area Deaths—The Joplin Globe
  http://www.joplinglobe.com/4state/deaths.html
  Missouri

- Kansas City Star Obituaries
  http://www.kcstar.com/cgi-bin/class?template=clq-obit.htm&category=0&database=daily

- KnoxNews.com—News—Obituaries
  http://www.knoxnews.com/news/obituaries/
  Tennessee. Knoxville News-Sentinel Online.

- Lexington Herald-Leader On-Line Obituaries
  http://www.kentuckyconnect.com/heraldleader/obituaries/
  Kentucky

- Mennonite Brethren Herald
  http://www.cdnmbconf.ca/mb/mbherald.htm
  Be sure to see their online editions & current obituaries section.

- Michigan Live: Obituaries
  http://www.mlive.com/obits/

- Minnesota Obituaries—September 1995 to present
  http://www.pconline.com/~mnobits/index.htm

- Monroe Evening News Obituaries
  http://www.MONROENEWS.COM/newshtml/Obits.htm
  Michigan

- Montague County Shopper Online—Obituaries
  http://ww2.morgan.net/Shopper/obits.htm
  Texas

- The New Orleans Times Picayune Obituary Listings Index
  http://www.challenger.net/local/users/lindas/times1.htm

- North Central Iowa Newspaper Obituaries
  http://www.netins.net/showcase/pafways/obitone.htm

- Obituaries from News-Star, Monroe, LA
  http://www.bayou.com/~suelynn/obits.html

- Obituaries from the Houston Morning Star, Texas—
  1839
  http://www.geocities.com/Vienna/1516/houobi.html
  1840
  http://www.geocities.com/Vienna/1516/houobi40.html
  1841
  http://www.geocities.com/Vienna/1516/houobi41.html
  1842
  http://www.geocities.com/Vienna/1516/houobi42.html
  1843
  http://www.geocities.com/Vienna/1516/houobi43.html
  1844
  http://www.geocities.com/Vienna/1516/houobi44.html

- Obituaries—Gibson County, Indiana
  http://www.comsource.net/~tnolcox/obituaries.htm

- Obituaries, The Citizens' Voice Newspaper, Wilkes-Barre, PA
  http://citizensvoice.com/obituaries.html

- Obituary Abstracts of Coshocton Co. OH
  http://www.pe.net/~sharyn/obits.html

- Obituary Daily Times
  http://www.rootsweb.com/~obituary/

- The Obituary Page
  http://catless.ncl.ac.uk/Obituary/

- Observer-Reporter Obituary Archive
  http://www.chartiers.com/worobits/index.html
  Pennsylvania. Obituaries for Washington and Greene counties from August 1997 through present.

- OKbits—1883–1997 Obits & Tidbits
  http://www.rootsweb.com/~okbits/index.htm

- Old Obituaries In Stephens County Oklahoma
  http://www.geocities.com/Heartland/Ridge/1308/OBITS.html

- Philadelphia Daily News: Deaths
  http://www.phillynews.com/programs/go-pdn/deaths/
  Pennsylvania

- Philadelphia Inquirer: Obituaries
  http://www.phillynews.com/programs/go-inq/obituaries/
  Pennsylvania

- Preble County Obituary Index
  http://206.103.255.36/getobit.htm
  Ohio. More than 10,500 obituaries reported in the Register-Herald for 1980–1995.

- Providence Journal Obituaries
  http://www.projo.com/report/pjb/indexes/ob.htm
  Rhode Island

- Roanoke Times Online Obituaries
  http://www.roanoke.com/classifieds/obits.html
  Virginia

- Rock Island County Obituaries
  http://www.rootsweb.com/~ilrockis/bio_obit/obits.htm
  Illinois

- The Salt Lake Tribune—Utah Section
  http://www.sltrib.com/
  Go to the Utah section and find the links for Utah Births and Utah Deaths.

- San Francisco County Genealogy—Ancestors' Obituaries and Death Notices
  http://www.sfo.com/~timandpamwolf/sfranobi.htm
  California

- Search Obituaries found in Dayton Newspaper 1985–97
  http://www.dayton.lib.oh.us/htbin/obit

- Sellers' Western Kentucky Obituaries
  http://cgi.rootsweb.com/~genbbs/genbbs.cgi/USA/Ky/SellersObits

- Seventh-day Adventist Periodical Index
  http://143.207.5.3:82/search/
  Has a searchable obituary index.

- Sioux City Journal Online—Daily Obituaries
  http://www.siouxcityjournal.com/editorial/obit.html
  Iowa

- SouthEast Texas Obituaries
  http://members.aol.com/RootsLady/universal/obituari.htm

- Southwest Virginia Enterprise—Obituaries
  http://www.wythenews.com/obit.htm
  Obituaries from the latest edition of this newspaper in Wythe County, Virginia.
  Also see their archives for past editions from previous dates which also include obituaries
  http://www.wythenews.com/archive.htm

- Tacoma Obituary Database
  http://www.tpl.lib.wa.us/nwr/obitscgi.htm
  Washington state

- Tampa Tribune Obituary Index
  http://tampatrib.com/news/obitindx.htm
  Florida

- Telegram & Gazette Online—Obituaries
  http://www.telegram.com/news/obits/
  Worcester, Massachusetts

- Times-Dispatch Obituaries—Richmond, Virginia
  http://www.gateway-va.com/pages/tdstory/obtindex.htm

- The Times Record Obituary Page
  http://www.timesrecord.com/obituaries
  Brunswick, Maine

- Umatilla County, Oregon—USGenWeb Archives
  http://www.rootsweb.com/~usgenweb/or/umfiles.htm
  Includes Abstracts of obituaries from Hermiston newspapers.

- Usenet Newsgroup
  alt.obituaries

- Webster County Kentucky Obituaries
  http://www.rootsweb.com/~kywebste/obits/obits.htm

- Yahoo!...Obituaries
  http://dir.yahoo.com/Society_and_Culture/Death_and_Dying/End_of_Life_Issues/Obituaries/

OCCUPATIONS
http://www.CyndisList.com/occupatn.htm

- American Vaudeville Museum
  http://vaudeville.org/page12.html
  Has a place to post questions about vaudeville performers.

- Brickmakers Index
  http://www.genuki.org.uk/big/eng/bwi.html
  Index of brickfield workers and owners gathered from census, local histories and directories in England, mainly from southeast England.

- CA-GOLDRUSH Mailing List
  http://members.aol.com/gfsjohnf/gen_mail_states-ca.html
  #CA-GOLDRUSH
  For anyone who is interested in early California miners and settlers, especially in northern California, 1848–1880.

- The Circus, Theatre & Music Hall Families Page
  http://www.users.globalnet.co.uk/~paulln/circus.htm

- COALMINERS Mailing List
  http://members.aol.com/gfsjohnf/gen_mail_country-unk.html#COALMINERS
  For anyone whose ancestors were coalminers in the United Kingdom or the United States.

- The Coal Mines of West Virginia
  http://www.rootsweb.com/~wvgenweb/coal/index.htm

- Colonial Occupations
  http://www.rootsweb.com/~rigenweb/ocupaton.html

- Colonial Occupations
  http://www.rootsweb.com/~genepool/jobs.htm

- Colonial Occupations
  http://www.netusa1.net/~hartmont/index.htm#Occupations

- Colonial Occupations
  http://www.genweb.net/~samcasey/occupation.html

- Deceased American Physicians' Records
  http://www.ngsgenealogy.org/library/content/ama_info.html
  A research service available from the National Genealogical Society.

- The Divers Index
  http://www.thehds.dircon.co.uk/divers/divers.htm
  An Index of Historical Divers and Their Work.

- Index to "Paupers in Workhouses 1861" (10% sample)
  http://www.genuki.org.uk/big/eng/Paupers/
  This lists adult paupers in workhouses in England and Wales.

- Down to the Sea in Ships
  http://www.star.net/misuraca/down2c.htm
  A list of men fishing out of Gloucester, Massachusetts who were lost at sea.

- Fishing?—It was "A WAY OF LIFE"
  http://www.geocities.com/Heartland/Prairie/7527/
  Devoted to and dedicated to the fishermen, mariners, their families and survivors in Nova Scotia. Has memorials, lists of lost fisherman, photographs, newspaper and book extracts, and much more.

- Ghosts of the Klondike Gold Rush
  http://www.gold-rush.org/
  Check out the "Pan for Gold Database."

- GOLD 150—Celebrating 150 Years of Australian Gold-Rush History
  http://www.ballarat.edu.au/krause/external/sovhill/gold150//sovhill.htm

- Gold Prospectors of Colorado
  http://www.GPOC.idsite.com/

- The Historical Diving Society
  http://www.thehds.dircon.co.uk/
  U.K.

- Is That a Postmaster in Your Family Tree?
  http://www.ancestry.com/columns/george/02-06-98.htm
  From "Along Those Lines . . ." by George G. Morgan.

- itinerantroots Mailing List
  http://www.onelist.com/subscribe.cgi/itinerantroots
  For genealogy resources relating to itinerant professions; circus, theatre, music hall, vaudeville, fairs, showmen, portable theatres, etc.

- Kentuckiana Genealogy—Occupation Chart
  http://www.floyd-pavey.com/kentuckiana/kyiana/kyiana/occupations.html

- Lacinskie nazwy zawodow = Latin Names of Occupations
  http://hum.amu.edu.pl/~rafalp/GEN/zawody.htm
  Latin to Polish translations.

- Law Enforcement Memorial Links
  http://www.policememorial.com/memoriallinks.htm
  Links to many sites regarding law enforcement officials who died in the line of duty. Some have historic lists of names.

- A List of Occupations
  http://cpcug.org/user/jlacombe/terms.html

- Mariners Mailing List
  http://members.aol.com/johnf14246/gen_mail_general.html#Mariners
  For anyone who is researching their seafaring ancestors.

- METISGEN Mailing List
  http://members.aol.com/johnf14246/
  gen_mail_general.html#METISGEN
  *For the discussion and sharing of information regarding the
  Metis and their descendants. The Metis are North America's Fur
  Trading Children . . . the new nation of individuals born within
  North America from the first unions of natives and whites.*

- Mining History Association
  http://members.aol.com/MiningHA/index.htm

- Mining History Network
  http://info.ex.ac.uk/~RBurt/MinHistNet/welcome.html

- Mountain Men and the Fur Trade
  http://www.xmission.com/~drudy/amm.html
  *Sources of the History of the Fur Trade in the Rocky
  Mountain West.*

- Obsolete Occupations
  http://www.rootsweb.com/~ote/occs.htm
  *Some Medieval and Obsolete English Trade and Professional
  Terms Used From 1086–1400. From The Olive Tree.*

- Occupations Census Indexes
  http://rontay.digiweb.com/visit/occupy/
  From Ron Taylor's UK Census Finding Aids and Indexes.

- Occupations and their Descriptions
  http://www.onthenet.com.au/~tonylang/occupa.htm
  From the Langham Genealogy Page.

- Old German Professions and Occupations
  http://www.worldroots.com/brigitte/occupat.htm

- Old Time Jobs
  http://www.seidata.com/~lhoffman/jobdesc.html

- Our Firemen—A History of the New York
  Fire Departments
  http://members.aol.com/dcbreton2/FDNY/FDNY_Notes.html
  Includes an every-name index.

- Post Office Records
  http://www.nara.gov/genealogy/postal.html
  From the National Archives and Records Administration.

- Transcript of the Entry of "Professions and Trades"
  for Grinton in Baine's Directory of 1823
  http://www.genuki.org.uk/big/eng/YKS/NRY/Grinton/
  Grinton23.html
  England

- Public Record Office—Finding Aids—
  A–Z Index of All Leaflets
  http://www.pro.gov.uk/leaflets/riindex.htm
  U.K.

  ○ Apprenticeship Records as Sources for
    Genealogy (#44)
    http://www.pro.gov.uk/leaflets/ri044.htm

  ○ Civilian Nurses and Nursing Services (#113)
    http://www.pro.gov.uk/leaflets/ri113.htm

  ○ Coal Mining Records In The Public Record
    Office (#82)
    http://www.pro.gov.uk/leaflets/RI082.Htm

  ○ Dockyard Employees: Documents (#15)
    http://www.pro.gov.uk/leaflets/ri015.htm

  ○ Metropolitan Police Records of Service (#53)
    http://www.pro.gov.uk/leaflets/ri053.htm

  ○ Records of Attorneys and Solicitors in The Public
    Record Office (#112)
    http://www.pro.gov.uk/leaflets/ri112.htm

  ○ Records of the Ministry of Labour (#130)
    http://www.pro.gov.uk/leaflets/ri130.htm

  ○ Records of the Registrar General of Shipping and
    Seamen (#5)
    http://www.pro.gov.uk/leaflets/ri005.htm

  ○ Records of the Royal Irish Constabulary (#11)
    http://www.pro.gov.uk/leaflets/ri011.htm

- Railroads
  http://www.CyndisList.com/railroad.htm
  See this category on Cyndi's List for related links.

- RiverRats Mailing List
  http://members.aol.com/gfsjohnf/gen_mail_states-
  gen.html#RiverRats
  *For discussions of the Mississippi River "people" living on,
  working on, and involved in life on the "river." Any family living
  in any county bordering the Mississippi River, or living "on" the
  river, is welcome.*

- Schoolmarms on the Frontier
  http://www.ancestry.com/columns/myra/
  Shaking_Family_Tree06-04-98.htm
  *From Shaking Your Family Tree by Myra Vanderpool Gormley,
  C.G.*

- The Society of Brushmakers' Descendants
  http://www.thenet.co.uk/~socy-brush-desc/index.html
  Essex, England

- Society of Genealogists Bookshop—Trades,
  Professions and Offenders
  http://www.sog.org.uk/bookshop/Q25.html

- The Steam Engine Makers Database
  http://www.geog.qmw.ac.uk/lifeline/sem_db/
  sem_db_home.html

- Tennessee Confederate Physicians: An Introduction
  http://www.state.tn.us/sos/statelib/pubsvs/docintro.htm
  *From the Tennessee State Library and Archives—Historical and
  Genealogical Information.*

- Valdez Gold Rush Centennial
  http://www.alaska.net/~vldzmuse/goldrush1.htm

  ○ Valdez Museum & Historical Archive—
    Rush Participants Database
    http://www.alaska.net/~vldzmuse/valdez.htm
    Valdez Gold Rush 1898–1899, Names Database.

- Was Your Ancestor a Doctor?
  http://user.itl.net/~glen/doctors.html

ODDS & ENDS

Interesting & Unusual Genealogy Sites That Don't Fit In Other Categories.
http://www.CyndisList.com/odds.htm

Category Index:

- Genealogy Web Site Awards
- Lost & Found
- Money

- Names
- Stories, Tall Tales & Legends
- This & That

◆ Genealogy Web Site Awards

- 1998 Genealogical Inspirational Award
  http://home.earthlink.net/~howardorjeff/award3.htm

- ATAWAYTAGO Monthly Awards
  http://www.ohmygosh.com/genealogy/ATAWAYTAGO.htm

- Back to the Roots Genealogical Homepage
  Award of Excellence
  http://members.aol.com/kfwendt/award/myawards.html

- Baden-Württemberg Genealogical Award
  http://www.rootsweb.com/~deubadnw/award.html

- BaiCon Award
  http://www.geocities.com/Heartland/4714/award.html

- Charlotte's Webpage Genealogy
  Award of Excellence
  http://members.tripod.com/~rcjack/winaward.html

- Cherished Memories & CS Designs Site Award
  http://www.geocities.com/Heartland/Valley/2248/
  siteawrd2.html
  *Excellence in Homepage Design Award, Genealogy Sharing
  Award, Genealogy Award of Excellence.*

- Cool Site of the Month for Genealogists
  http://www.cogensoc.org/cgs/cgs-cool.htm
  From the Colorado Genealogical Society.

- DeWanna's Home on the Web—Family Tree Award
  http://www.geocities.com/Heartland/Hills/4693/impaward.html

- Diggin' Up My Roots Award
  http://www.geocities.com/Heartland/Prairie/6288/
  digaward.html

- Dona's Web Awards Nomination Booth
  http://members.aol.com/sshield2/awardspg.html
  The Cain Connections Ancestral Award.

- Family Chronicle—Top Ten Genealogy
  Websites Nominees
  http://www.familychronicle.com/webpicks.htm

- Family Genealogical Leaf Award
  http://www.sowega.net/~ramses/getaward.html

- Gail's Genealogy Wonderland
  http://members.aol.com/gailn8058/nominees.htm

- Gathering Leaves Award
  http://www.geocities.com/Heartland/Estates/7131/
  gathering_leaves.html

- Genealogical Excellence Award
  http://www.kiva.net/~markh/award.html

- Genealogical Journeys in Time
  http://pages.prodigy.com/Strawn/topsite.htm

- The Genealogy & History International Award Site
  http://www.ringnett.no/home/bjornstad/awards/index.html

- Genealogy Corner Genealogy Homepage Award
  http://www.geocities.com/Heartland/1657/genealogy.html

- Genealogy Home Page Award of Excellence
  http://www.geocities.com/Heartland/Plains/7906/award.html

- Genealogy is My Hobby—Excellence in Genealogy
  Home Page Award
  http://home.earthlink.net/~middleton/nom.html

- Genealogy is My Hobby—Genealogy Hot Pick
  of the Month
  http://home.earthlink.net/~middleton/gbhot.html

- Genealogy Web Page Excellence Awards
  http://www.geocities.com/Heartland/Meadows/5219/

- Genealogy's Most Wanted Featured Site
  of the Month
  http://www.citynet.net/mostwanted/featured.html

- The Genie Bug Award for Genealogy Excellence
  http://www.geocities.com/Heartland/Valley/8506/award.html

- The Gierhart Family Inn's Genealogy's Helping
  Hand Award
  http://www.geocities.com/Heartland/Plains/5409/awards.html

- Gracie's Family Tree—Winner's Circle
  http://www.geocities.com/Heartland/Ranch/1322/winners.html

- Honoring Our Ancestors Award
  http://www.mtjeff.com/~bodenst/Award_page.htm

- Our Ancestry Excellence in Genealogy Award
  http://www.ourancestry.com/nominate.html
- A Passage in Time Genealogical Homepage Award of Excellence
  http://www.geocities.com/Heartland/1146/winaward.html
- Relatively Speaking
  http://www.geocities.com/Heartland/Meadows/1147/winaward..html
- Robert Bickham Family Genealogy Monthly Site Award
  http://www.a1webdesign.com/rebick/site.html
- Rose's Genealogy Place Website Award For Excellence
  http://www.edwards1.com/rose/genealogy/award-details.htm
- Sam's Spectacular Genealogy Homepage Award
  http://www.genweb.net/~samcasey/specaward.html
- Sharon Herrington's Awards Page
  http://www.geocities.com/Heartland/Hills/8563/awards.htm
- The Siggy Award
  http://www.usigs.org/registry/registry.htm
  USIGS "Access Free Records Online for Genealogy."
- Suffolk List's Award
  http://www.visualcreations.com/pers/leeann/suffolk/awards.html
- The Wilder Place Genealogy Exellence Award
  http://www.newwave.net/~lmwilder/gen_award_app.htm
- Wood World Award of Excellence
  http://www.dlcwest.com/~mgwood/award.html

◆ Lost & Found

- Ancestral Photos
  http://pw1.netcom.com/~cityslic/photos.htm
  Pictures found at auctions and in antique stores.
- "Fallen Leaves" Lost Leaves Photos
  http://www.agcig.org/leaves.htm
- Family Papers
  http://www.teleport.com/~jimren/
  A service that helps family historians locate and own original documents pertaining to their ancestors.
- f.i.r.s.t.—Family Items Registry and Search Technology
  http://www.first-usa.com/
  A searchable database of antiques and collectibles of interest to genealogists.
- Ford and Nagle
  http://users.erinet.com/31363/fordand.htm
  Historians, Genealogists, and Collectors of Antique Family Photos, Family Bibles, and Family Documents.
  - Antique Family Photos—A–G
    http://users.erinet.com/31363/photos.htm
    H–Q
    http://users.erinet.com/31363/photos2.htm

  - R–Z
    http://users.erinet.com/31363/photo3.htm
  - Family Bibles
    http://users.erinet.com/31363/family.htm
  - Family Documents
    http://users.erinet.com/31363/docs1.htm
- Granny's Lost & Found
  http://www.geocities.com/~grannys_attic/lostfoun.html
  Lost: out of print books and films. Found: old photos, journals, documents, and letters.
- Missing Photographs
  http://www.missingphotos.com
  A company dedicated to reuniting people interested in their genealogy with previously unknown or lost family photographs.
- NEGenWeb Ancestors' Lost & Found
  http://www.rootsweb.com/~neresour/ancestors/index.html
  Dedicated to reuniting families with the Nebraska memorabilia their ancestors left behind: photos, family Bibles, etc.
- PhotoFind Searchable Database
  http://www.everton.com/photofind/phfind.html
- Your Family Heirlooms
  http://www.yourantiques.com/home.html
- Your Past Connections, Inc.
  http://www.pastconnect.com/
  Helps you find original items from your family's past. Items such as: cards, letters, certificates, books, etc.

◆ Money

- The Currency and Measurements History Lexicon of Norway
  http://www.ringnett.no/home/bjornstad/measure/Index.html
- Current Value of Old Money
  http://www.ex.ac.uk/~RDavies/arian/current/howmuch.html
- The History of U.S. Paper Money
  http://very.simplenet.com/currency/rhist.htm
- History of Money from Ancient Times to the Present Day by Glyn Davies
  http://www.ex.ac.uk/~RDavies/arian/llyfr.html
- Money in North American History
  http://www.ex.ac.uk/~RDavies/arian/northamerica.html
  From Wampum to Electronic Funds Transfer.
- Money of the Republic of Texas
  http://www.lsjunction.com/facts/tx_money.htm
  Financing the public debt and implementing a stable currency system were among the many challenges facing the government of the Republic of Texas.

◆ Names

- By Any Other Name...
  http://www.w-link.net/~maegwin/menagerie/name.htm
  Discover the meaning of your name.
- Family Naming Traditions
  http://www.rootsweb.com/~genepool/naming.htm

- First Name Basis
  http://www.hypervigilance.com/genlog/firstname.html
  To aid you in researching when all you know is the first name of a person. Focuses on unusual first names and women's first names when maiden names are unknown.

- Given Name Index
  http://www.geocities.com/Heartland/Hills/1739/givennames.html

- A Listing of Some 18th and 19th Century American Nicknames
  http://www.cslnet.ctstateu.edu/nickname.htm

- Nicknames and Naming Traditions
  http://www.tngenweb.usit.com/franklin/frannick.htm

- Our Ancestor's Nicknames
  http://www.uftree.com/UFT/HowTos/SettingOut/nickname1.html

- Quirky Surnames
  http://members.xoom.com/present/

- The USGenWeb Project—Info for Researchers—Names
  http://www.usgenweb.org/researchers/names.html

◆ Stories, Tall Tales & Legends

- Biographies
  http://www.CyndisList.com/biograph.htm
  See this category on Cyndi's List for related links.

- Excerpts From Old Newspapers
  http://www.ida.net/users/dhanco/news.htm

- MythNET Genealogical Charts
  http://www.infotoronto.com/mythnet/chart.html
  Genealogy of the characters in Greek mythology.

- Oral History & Interviews
  http://www.CyndisList.com/oral.htm
  See this category on Cyndi's List for related links.

- Serendipity.....Genealogical Discoveries with a Little Help from Above
  http://www.rootsweb.com/~genepool/serendipity/index.html
  Submit your personal story & read amazing stories from other genealogists!

- Ye Olde Wive's Tales
  http://www.ida.net/users/dhanco/tales.htm

◆ This & That

- AmeriSpeak: Expressions of Our Ancestors
  http://www.rootsweb.com/~genepool/amerispeak.htm
  A place to record those phrases that have been passed down through the generations in your family.

- The Circus, Theatre & Music Hall Families Page
  http://www.users.globalnet.co.uk/~paulln/circus.htm

- Cyndi's Genealogy Home Page Construction Kit
  http://www.CyndisList.com/construc.htm

- "Dear Friend Robert Merry": Letters from Nineteenth-Century American Children
  http://members.tripod.com/~merrycoz/MUSEUM/MERYCOZ.HTM
  From a collection of letters written by subscribers to Robert Merry's Museum, including an index of information gathered on many of the children who wrote the letters.

- The Family History Show
  http://familyhistory.flash.net/
  A radio talk show on the Texas State Network with Michael Matthews.

- The Family Letter
  http://www.FamilyLetter.com/
  A circular "letter" that allows your family all around the world to stay in touch online. You must subcribe to this new Everton's service in order to use it.

- A Genealogical Tool Kit
  http://www.cslnet.ctstateu.edu/toolkit.htm
  A complete list of the items you need to take with you when you visit cemeteries, archives, libraries, and town halls.

- The Genealogy Merit Badge of the Boy Scouts of America
  http://www.oz.net/~markhow/BSA/meritbdg.htm
  This is where it all started for my husband, Mark!

- Gifts from Our Forefathers—From the Gene Pool
  http://www.rootsweb.com/~genepool/gifts.htm

- Halbert's Under Cease and Desist Order
  http://www.genealogy.org/~ngs/halberts.html

- International Black Sheep Society of Genealogists (IBSSG)
  http://homepages.rootsweb.com/~blksheep/
  For those who have a dastardly, infamous individual of public knowledge and ill-repute in their family . . . within 1 degree of consanguinity of their direct lines. This individual must have been pilloried in disgrace for acts of a significantly anti-social nature. Also learn about the associated mailing list at http://members.aol.com/johnf14246 gen_mail_general.html#BlackSheep

- Notable Women Ancestors
  http://www.rootsweb.com/~nwa/

- A Study of Genealogists & Family Historians
  http://watarts.uwaterloo.ca/~rdlamber/genstudy.htm

- Ye Olde English Sayings
  http://www.rootsweb.com/~genepool/sayings.htm

ORAL HISTORY & INTERVIEWS
http://www.CyndisList.com/oral.htm

- The Art of the Oral Historian
  http://www.library.ucsb.edu/speccoll/oralhlec.html

- Association of Personal Historians
  http://www.personalhistorians.org/

- Baylor University Institute for Oral History:
  Oral History Workshop on the Web
  http://www.baylor.edu/~Oral_History/Workshop_welcome.html

- Capturing the Past: How to Prepare & Conduct and
  Oral History Interview
  http://www.kbyu.org/capturingpast/

- CIMS Oral History Page
  http://coombs.anu.edu.au/~cims/oralhist.html
  *An extensive list of links to oral history repositories from the
  Centre for Immigration and Multicultural Studies, Australian
  National University.*

- Clio Whispers About Oral History
  http://home.earthlink.net/~raulb/Clio-2.html

- DearMYRTLE's Genealogy for Beginners—
  Interviewing Relatives
  http://www.ancestry.com/lessons/beginners/lesson21.htm

- Doing Oral History
  http://www.gcah.org/oral.html
  *From The General Commission on Archives and History—
  The United Methodist Church, Archival Leaflet Series.*

- Ellis Island Oral History Project
  http://www.i-channel.com/features/ellis/oralhist.html

- Family Tree Maker's Genealogy Site: Back Issue:
  Oral Histories
  http://www.familytreemaker.com/issue2.html

- Family Tree Maker's Genealogy Site: Suggested
  Topics and Questions for Oral Histories
  http://www.familytreemaker.com/00000030.html

- Grandpa Wouldn't Talk Until I Put on the
  Oral History "Spurs"
  http://www.jangle.com/articles/grandpa.htm

- Guidelines for Doing Oral History
  http://www.cms.ccsd.k12.co.us/SONY/Orbeta1/orlguide.htm
  From the American Memory, Library of Congress web site.

- The History Channel Projects—Oral History:
  Telling the Story of the Past
  http://www.historychannel.com/hometownhistory/
  oralhistory.html

- How to Tape Instant Oral Biographies
  http://www.oz.net/~markhow/library.htm#tape
  by Bill Zimmerman, a book for sale from Amazon.com

- Interview Absolutely Everyone!
  http://www.ancestry.com/columns/george/04-03-98.htm
  From "Along Those Lines . . ." by George Morgan.

- Journal Jar Ideas
  http://www.omnicron.com/~fluzby/sister-share/journal.htm

- Legal Issues for Oral Histories
  http://primarysources.msu.edu/curricula/intro/upsthree/howto/
  legal.html

- One-Minute Guide to Oral Histories
  http://library.berkeley.edu/BANC/ROHO/1minute.html
  From the University of California, Berkeley.

- Oral Histories
  http://www.everton.com/GENEALOG/GENEALOG.ORALHIST
  by Patricia Jocius, from the Everton Publishers web site.

- Oral History and Folklore of the Miami Valley, Ohio
  http://www.muohio.edu/~oralhxcwis/index.htmlx
  From the Miami Valley Cultural Heritage Project.

- Oral History Association
  http://www.baylor.edu/~OHA/
  Includes an extensive list of links to oral history repositories.

- Oral History Internet Resources
  http://scnc.leslie.k12.mi.us/~charnle2/ohlinks.html

- Oral History Interview, Questions and Topics
  http://www1.jewishgen.org/infofiles/quest.txt

- Oral History Interviews, Why, How, Help with
  Oral Family History
  http://www.marple.com/whyoral.html

- The Oral History Program, University of
  Alaska Fairbanks
  http://www.uaf.edu/library/oralhist/home.html

- Oral History Questions
  http://www.ping.be/picavet/
  Waas_America_Research03.shtml#OralHistoryQuestions
  From the Belgium Immigrants in America web site.

- Oral History Questions—The Gene Pool
  http://www.rootsweb.com/~genepool/oralhist.htm

- An Oral History Primer
  http://bob.ucsc.edu/library/reg-hist/ohprimer.html

- Oral History Society
  http://www.essex.ac.uk/sociology/oralhis.htm

- Oral History Support Materials
  http://www.mov.vic.gov.au/Hidden_Histories/
  classroom_materials/oral.html
  *From the Museum Victoria and the Department of Education in
  Australia.*

- Oral History Techniques and Procedures
  http://www.army.mil/cmh-pg/books/oral.htm
  By Stephen E. Everett for the Center of Military History.

- PIE Interview Guide—Family Folklore Interviewing Guide and Questionnaire
  http://www.cimorelli.com/pie/library/intrview.htm

- PIE—The Art of Interviewing Relatives and Getting Answers to Your Questions
  http://www.cimorelli.com/pie/library/intr_art.htm

- Preserving Community / Cuentos del Varrio
  http://web.nmsu.edu/~publhist/ohindex.html
  An Oral History Instruction Manual.

- Preserving Family Stories
  http://www.ancestry.com/columns/myra/
  Shaking_Family_Tree02-19-98.htm
  From Shaking Your Family Tree by Myra Vanderpool Gormley, C.G.

- Southern Oral History Program—How To
  http://www.unc.edu/depts/sohp/info.html

- The Third Degree: Tips for a Successful Interview
  http://www.ancestry.com/magazine/articles/interview.htm
  From Ancestry Magazine, Jan/Feb 1998, Volume 16, Number 1 by George Thurston.

- Tips for Interviewers
  http://library.berkeley.edu/BANC/ROHO/rohotips.html
  From the University of California, Berkeley.

- Tools for Oral History
  http://www.fortlewis.edu/acad-aff/swcenter/tools.htm#Tools for Oral History:
  From the Fort Lewis College Center of Southwest Studies in Colorado.

- University of Kentucky Oral History Program
  http://www.uky.edu/Libraries/Special/oral_history/

- USU Oral History Program—How to Collect Oral Histories
  http://www.usu.edu/~oralhist/oh_howto.html
  From Utah State University.

- Virginia Folklife Program Oral History Workshop: A Basic Guide to the Concepts, Techniques and Strategies of Oral History Research
  http://minerva.acc.virginia.edu/vfh/vfp/oh2.html

- Yourfamily.com—Videos, Albums, and Taped Oral Histories
  http://yourfamily.com/histories.shtml

PHOTOGRAPHS & MEMORIES

Preserving Your Family's Heirlooms, Treasures & Genealogical Research.
http://www.CyndisList.com/photos.htm

Category Index:

- ◆ Lost & Found
- ◆ Novelties
- ◆ Photo Archives, Collections and Libraries
- ◆ Photo Restoration & Care
- ◆ Photos—Miscellaneous

- ◆ Preservation & Conservation
- ◆ Scanners & Electronic Preservation
- ◆ Telling Your Story
- ◆ Vendors

◆ Lost & Found

- **Ancestral Photos**
  http://pw1.netcom.com/~cityslic/photos.htm
  Pictures found at auctions and in antique stores.

- **AncesTree**
  http://www.ancestree.com/
  "The Family Tree with Photographs."

- **"Fallen Leaves" Lost Leaves Photos**
  http://www.agcig.org/leaves.htm

- **Ford and Nagle**
  http://users.erinet.com/31363/fordand.htm
  Historians, Genealogists, and Collectors of Antique Family Photos, Family Bibles, and Family Documents.

  - ○ **Antique Family Photos—A–G**
    http://users.erinet.com/31363/photos.htm
    H–Q
    http://users.erinet.com/31363/photos2.htm
    R–Z
    http://users.erinet.com/31363/photo3.htm
  - ○ **Family Bibles**
    http://users.erinet.com/31363/family.htm
  - ○ **Family Documents**
    http://users.erinet.com/31363/docs1.htm

- **Family Papers**
  http://www.teleport.com/~jimren/
  A service that helps family historians locate and own original documents pertaining to their ancestors.

- **Granny's Lost & Found**
  http://www.geocities.com/~grannys_attic/lostfoun.html
  Lost: out of print books and films. Found: old photos, journals, documents, and letters.

- **Lenore Frost's Dating Family Photos Homepage**
  http://www.alphalink.com.au/~lfrost/Homepage/
  A book to help date old photographs, and a project to reunite photos and families, mostly Australian, some British.

- **Missing Photographs**
  http://www.missingphotos.com
  A company dedicated to reuniting people interested in their genealogy with previously unknown or lost family photographs.

- **NEGenWeb Ancestors' Lost & Found**
  http://www.rootsweb.com/~neresour/ancestors/index.html
  Dedicated to reuniting families with the Nebraska memorabilia their ancestors left behind: photos, family Bibles, etc.

- **PhotoFind Searchable Database**
  http://www.everton.com/photofind/phfind.html

◆ Novelties

- **Dirilyte Family Tree Plaques & Gifts**
  http://www.dirilyte.com/famtree.htm

- **Friar Bob Tuck's Home Page**
  http://www.isn.net/friartuck/#Ancestor Portraits
  An artist who paints portraits of your ancestors based on their photographs.

- **Memorial Video Tributes**
  http://www.mlvp.com/memory7.htm
  Our Video Production Company produces Video Memorializations or Memorial Tributes on Video for the clients of Funeral Homes and individuals. We use the family photos, slides, film, video, and other memorabilia. We transfer these items to video and produce a video tape with music, that the family will value forever.

- **Metallic Reflections**
  http://www.extremezone.com/~metallic/
  Family tree genealogy ornaments.

- **Photographic Family Trees by DooleyNoted Enterprises**
  http://members.aol.com/Timdooley/index.html
  Your favorite family photos scanned, enhanced and put into your family tree ancestor chart. T-shirts, wallhangings, pillows make great gifts for family reunions, birthdays and anniversaries!

- **Photo Saver—Personal Screensaver**
  http://www.photosaver.com/
  Turn your favorite photos into a personal screensaver.

- Reunion T-Shirts
  http://www.bowplus.com/t-shirts/
  Personalized family t-shirts.

◆ Photo Archives, Collections and Libraries

- The 19th Century Exchange
  http://www.webcom.com/cityg/exchange/index.html
  Nineteenth-Century Exchange promotes the exchange of information about 19th and early 20th century photography between genealogists, collectors, photography historians or anyone with an interest in antique photographs and their makers.

- Chicago Imagebase
  http://www.uic.edu/depts/ahaa/imagebase/
  Find a wealth of information at this site from before the Great Fire of 1871 to the present including the Fire Insurance Maps of Chicago, Robinson Atlases of Downtown Chicago (ca. 1886), Sanborn Atlas Maps, Rand McNally's Bird's-Eye Views and Guide to Chicago (ca. 1893), Historical View Books, and much more! Browse the imagebase collection by artist/architect, building and era. Find information on Using Historical Maps and Dating Buildings by Stylistic Analysis. View contemporary aerial views (ca. 1986) and photographs 1970–1990's of Chicago.

- City Gallery
  http://www.webcom.com/cityg/
  Including a Directory of Photography Historians and a Photography mailing list.

- Civil War Family Photographs
  http://members.tripod.com/~cwphotos/

- The Daguerreotype: The Daguerreian Society Homepage
  http://www.austinc.edu/dag

- Daguerreotypes 1842–1862
  http://lcweb2.loc.gov/ammem/daghtml/daghome.html
  From the Library of Congress, American Memory collection.

- Introduction to Imaging: Issues in Constructing an Image Database
  http://www.gii.getty.edu/intro_imaging/Tbl.html

- Lost Memory—Libraries and Archives Destroyed in the Twentieth Century
  http://www.unesco.org/webworld/mdm/administ/en/detruit.html

- National Monuments Record at the RCHME
  http://www.rchme.gov.uk/nmr.html
  UK national archive of old photographs, plans, aerial photographs.

- Photo Adventures—Museum of History and Industry
  http://www.historymuse-nw.org/photo%20adventures/photo_ad.htm
  A collection of historical photographs from the Pacific Northwest and Alaska.

- Repositories of Primary Sources
  http://www.uidaho.edu/special-collections/Other.Repositories.html
  A listing of over 3000 websites describing holdings of manuscripts, archives, rare books, historical photographs, and other primary sources for the research scholar.

- Touring Turn-of-the-Century America: Photographs from the Detroit Publishing Company, 1880–1920
  http://lcweb2.loc.gov/detroit/dethome.html
  From American Memory, Library of Congress.

◆ Photo Restoration & Care

- A-1 Digiflux Photo Restoration
  http://www.htcomp.net/tfunk/photorestoration.html
  Digital Photo Restoration for torn, scratched, water damaged, faded, abused photos. Colorize your old B&W pictures! Personalized service.

- Ab Initio Books & Vintage Image Services
  http://www.abinitiobooks.com
  Ab Initio Books is a publisher of quality family histories. We also restore old images for publication or as a photographic print.

- Care and Preservation of Photographs
  http://www.gcah.org/care.html
  From The General Commission on Archives and History—The United Methodist Church.

- Care of Photographs
  http://pucky.uia.ac.be/~janssen/genealogy/photos1.html
  By Northeast Document Conservation Center.

- Caring for Your Family Photos
  http://www.familytreemaker.com/issue10.html
  From Family Tree Maker Online.

- Castle Photographic—Photo Restoration
  http://home.earthlink.net/~castlefoto/restore.htm

- Classy Image
  http://www.classyimage.com/
  Restoration and alteration of old & new photographs; photography; web page design & graphics design.

- Computer Imaging & Genealogy
  http://www.terraworld.net/users/r/rbrook/
  Scanning and photograph restoration services.

- DIGI-RE-DU Photo Restoration
  http://www.cco.net/~digiredu/

- Gardner Graphics Photo Restoration
  http://www.halcyon.com/dianne/index.htm

- Guidelines For Preserving Your Photographic Heritage
  http://www.geocities.com/Heartland/6662/photopre.htm

- Horn Graphics
  http://www.horngraphics.com/
  Tacoma, Washington. Photograph restoration and digital imaging.

- Human Touch Restorations
  http://www.localaccess.com/DAVEH/

- Just Black & White's Tips for Preserving Your
  Photographs and Documents
  http://www.maine.com/photos/tip.htm

- Nilsson Imaging—Photo Restoration
  http://www.nilsson.olm.net/PhotoRes/index.htm
  *Restore your photographs to their original splendor. Don't let
  the adverse effects of time rob you of your precious memories.*

- Northern States Conservation Center:
  Care by Type—Photographs
  http://www.collectioncare.org/cci/ccicph.html

- PhotoGraphics Copy & Restoration Service
  http://fixpix.com
  *Restoration of damaged and faded photos and documents.
  Photos and documents to CD and Powerpoint slides.*

- Photo Restoration
  http://members.tripod.com/~PhotoDoc/photodoc.html
  *Mike the Photo Doc restores old, faded, torn, fire or water
  damaged photos. Visit my site to view a before and after photo
  and to get contact information.*

- Photo Restoration by The Photo Medic
  http://www.photo-medic.com
  *Photo-Medic repairs and restores old and damaged photos. If an
  old photo has faded or darkened over the decades, Photo-Medic
  can enhance the image to better see the people long since gone.*

- Photos Restored by SCL—Shawnee Color Lab
  http://www.shawneecolorlab.com
  *"Photos Torn, Scratched, or Faded? We can restore them for
  you . . . SATISFACTION GUARANTEED!"*

- Re-Image
  http://www.re-image.com/
  Photographic restoration.

- Roots 'n Shoots
  http://www.wwonline.com/~pbatek/
  Photo restoration.

- Williams Computer Services—
  Photo and Document Restoration
  http://www.prairienet.org/photo/

◆ Photos—Miscellaneous

- 19th Century Photography for Genealogists
  http://www.genealogy.org/~ajmorris/photo/photo.htm
  by A.J. Morris.

  ○ Dating 19th Century Card Mounted Portraits
    http://www.genealogy.org/~ajmorris/photo/dates.htm

  ○ History of Photography—A Thumbnail Sketch
    http://www.genealogy.org/~ajmorris/photo/history.htm

  ○ Photography and Genealogy
    http://www.genealogy.org/~ajmorris/photo/pg.htm

  ○ Types of Photographs
    http://www.genealogy.org/~ajmorris/photo/types.htm

- Photo Generations—Home of the PhotoGen
  Mailing List Page
  http://www.webcom.com/cityg/photogen/index.html
  The Photography and Genealogy Mailing List.

- Photography as a Tool in Genealogy
  http://www.teleport.com/~fgriffin/photos.txt
  An article w/definitions & descriptions of types of photographs.

◆ Preservation & Conservation

- AIC Caring for Your Treasures
  http://sul-server-2.stanford.edu/aic/treasure/
  *From the American Institute for Conservation of Historic &
  Artistic Works.*

- Archival Products Newsletter
  http://www.archival.com/newsletter.html

  ○ Helpful Tips For Preserving Your Precious
    Documents And Memorabilia
    http://www.archival.com/NA13.html
    *Tips on Creating an Archival Scrapbook or Photo Album by
    Nancy Kraft for the Iowa Conservation and Preservation
    Consortium.*

  ○ Technical Tips—Care of Books, Documents
    and Photographs
    http://www.archival.com/NA16.html

- Caring for Your Artifacts: Preservation Fact Sheets
  http://www.hfmgv.org/histories/cis/pfs.html

- CoOL—Conservation OnLine—Resources for
  Conservation Professionals
  http://palimpsest.stanford.edu/

- Document and Photo Preservation FAQ
  http://www.seidata.com/~lhoffman/faq.html

- How To Save Your Stuff From a Disaster
  http://home.earthlink.net/~artdoc/
  *A book by Fine Art Conservator Scott M. Haskins with complete
  instructions on how to protect and save your family history,
  heirlooms and collectables.*

- The Library of Congress—Preservation
  http://lcweb.loc.gov/preserv/

  ○ Collections Care and Conservation
    http://lcweb.loc.gov/preserv/pubscare.html

  ○ Handouts from the 2nd Annual Preservation
    Awareness Workshop
    http://lcweb.loc.gov/preserv/aware2.html

  ○ Library of Congress Frequently Asked Questions:
    Preservation
    http://lcweb.loc.gov/preserv/presfaq.html

- Memory of the World: A Guide to Standards,
  Recommended Practices and Reference Literature
  Related to the Preservation of Documents of All
  Kinds
  http://www.unesco.org/webworld/mdm/administ/en/guide/
  guidetoc.htm

- National Archives and Records Administration: Preservation
  http://www.nara.gov/nara/preserva/

- NCPTT: National Center for Preservation Technology and Training
  http://www.ncptt.nps.gov/pir/
  A searchable database of Internet resources for heritage conservation, historic preservation and archaeology.

- Northeast Document Conservation Center
  http://www.nedcc.org/

  ○ Northeast Document Conservation Center— NEDCC Technical Leaflets
    http://www.nedcc.org/leaf.htm

- Northern States Conservation Center: Collection Care
  http://www.collectioncare.org/cci/cci.html

  ○ Northern States Conservation Center: Care by Type
    http://www.collectioncare.org/cci/ccic.html

    • Archives
      http://www.collectioncare.org/cci/ccica.html

    • Books
      http://www.collectioncare.org/cci/ccicboo.html

    • Electronic Data
      http://www.collectioncare.org/cci/ccice.html

    • Newspapers
      http://www.collectioncare.org/cci/ccicne.html

    • Paper
      http://www.collectioncare.org/cci/ccicpa.html

    • Photographs
      http://www.collectioncare.org/cci/ccicph.html

    • Sound Recordings
      http://www.collectioncare.org/cci/ccicso.html

    • Textiles
      http://www.collectioncare.org/cci/ccict.html

- Preserving Personal Papers and Photographs: General Guidelines
  http://www.lib.az.us/archives/preserve.htm
  From the Arizona State Archives.

- Preserving Photographs for Photographers and Family Historians
  http://members.aol.com/ARKivist/photos.htm
  Learn to build a lasting family photo heritage through a low cost, information packed, four week e-mail format class.

- Public Record Office—Preservation
  http://www.pro.gov.uk/preservation/default.htm

  ○ An Introduction to 19th and Early 20th Century Photographic Processes
    http://www.pro.gov.uk/preservation/photos.htm

  ○ An Introduction to English Paper
    http://www.pro.gov.uk/preservation/paper.htm

  ○ An Introduction to Parchment
    http://www.pro.gov.uk/preservation/parchment.htm

- A Simple Book Repair Manual
  http://www.dartmouth.edu/~preserve/tofc.html

- Tips for the Care of Water-Damaged Family Heirlooms and Other Valuables
  http://palimpsest.stanford.edu/aic/disaster/tentip.html

◆ Scanners & Electronic Preservation

- The Complete Guide to Scanning
  http://www.ulead.com/new/scanner.htm

- CompuDimension
  http://www.ao.net/~compudimension/
  Scanning services.

- Computer Imaging & Genealogy
  http://www.terraworld.net/users/r/rbrook/
  Scanning and photograph restoration services.

- Dennis Transfer to CD-ROM
  http://members.tripod.com/~crosley1/
  Specializing in transferring old 35mm film and VCR tapes to CD-ROMs.

- Digital Treasures
  http://www.digitaltreasures.com/
  Memories CDs and home film to video transfers.

- Family History Video
  http://www.familyhistoryvideo.com/
  A service which uses old photographs, slides, and home movies to produce video documentary of your family.

- Family Tree Video
  http://www.i-netmall.com/shops/familytreevideo/

- A Few Scanning Tips: Scanner Basics 101
  http://www.scantips.com/

- Genealogical Image Scanning
  http://netnow.micron.net/~wnetzlof/scansvc/scan10.htm
  Photographs, documents, maps. Scanning, enhancement, restoration.

- Gleason Genealogical Research and Digital Imaging
  http://www.tiac.net/users/gleason/

- Horn Graphics
  http://www.horngraphics.com/
  Tacoma, Washington. Photograph restoration and digital imaging.

- Memorial Video Tributes
  http://www.mlvp.com/memory7.htm
  Our Video Production Company produces Video Memorializations or Memorial Tributes on Video for the clients of Funeral Homes and individuals. We use family photos, slides, film, video, and other memorabilia. We transfer these items to video and produce a video tape with music, that the family will value forever.

- Northern States Conservation Center:
  Care by Type—Electronic Data
  http://www.collectioncare.org/cci/ccice.html

- PixScan
  http://pixscan.itool.com
  PixScan will scan photos, slides and 35mm negatives for a very modest fee.

- Plum Video Productions
  http://www.plumvideo.com/
  All sorts of video products, film transfers, slides, photos, etc. Including a Family History Video Album.

- The Scanning FAQ
  http://www.infomedia.net/scan/

- Video Photo Albums
  http://pw1.netcom.com/~mgjhson/index.html

- Virtual Archives Home
  http://www.virtualarchives.com
  Virtual Archives specializes in the digital storage of documents and images. Our Digital Archive service is perfect for preserving family histories in document and photograph form.

◆ Telling Your Story

- Biographies
  http://www.CyndisList.com/biograph.htm
  See this category on Cyndi's List for related links.

- Books
  http://www.CyndisList.com/books.htm
  See this category on Cyndi's List for related links.

- The Center for Life Stories Preservation
  http://members.aol.com/storycntr/index.html
  Family Stories—Military Memoirs—Reunions—Genealogy—Anniversaries.

- Family History Books
  http://www.familytreemaker.com/issue21.html
  From Family Tree Maker Online.

- Family History Questionnaire
  http://www.genrecords.com/library/question.htm
  From the Genealogy Record Service Library.

- Family History Writing & Preparing Your Family History For Publication
  http://www.ozemail.com.au/~nkyle/

- Hawk House Chronicles of Genealogy
  http://www.hsv.tis.net/~skbs/FamilyHY/HHC.html
  Immortalize your ancestors' lives in story form.

- How To Write and Publish Your Family Book
  http://www.intertekweb.com/gpsbook/howto.html
  Book for sale from Genealogy Publishing Service.

- Kindred Keepsakes
  http://www.rootsweb.com/~genepool/keepsakes.htm
  Genealogy charts; tips & hints for publishing your own family keepsakes.

- Oral History & Interviews
  http://www.CyndisList.com/oral.htm
  See this category on Cyndi's List for related links.

- Publish Your Own Family Keepsakes
  http://www.rootsweb.com/~genepool/keepsakes.htm

- Turning Memories Into Memoirs
  http://www.turningmemories.com/

- Weaving Your Memory Web: Preserving Family Stories for Future Generations
  http://www.conted.bcc.ctc.edu/users/bhofmann/
  Online course from Bellevue Community College, Instructor William Hofmann.

- Yourfamily.com
  http://yourfamily.com/
  Create your own family homepage, taped oral history & heirloom photo-album.

◆ Vendors

- AAG International Research—Professional Genealogists and Family Historians
  http://www.intl-research.com/
  Accredited genealogists & family historians specializing in family history research, development & publication. Accredited by the Family History Library in Salt Lake City, the world's largest genealogical library. Tax deductions for LDS research.

- Antiquarian Books & Bindery
  http://205.206.160.250/home/kaolink/
  Atlanta, Georgia. Specializing in Bible restoration. Also a selection of rare books for sale.

- The Book Craftsman
  http://www.bookcraftsman.com/
  Restoration of Books, Custom binding.

- Creative Memories
  http://www.creative-memories.com/

- Custom Family Trees & Charts by Olsongraphics
  http://www.olsonetc.com/

- European Focus
  http://www.eurofocus.com/
  Photographic portfolios of ancestral towns in Europe created for Genealogy enthusiasts in Germany, Italy, Poland, Scandinavia, Great Britain and more.

- Family Base Computer Archiving & Scrapbooking Software
  http://www.luminae.com/familyb.htm

- Family History Network
  http://www.familyhistorynetwork.com
  We help families create scrapbooks of photos, souvenirs, and stories. We consult by phone and e-mail, and provide scanning, custom design, and production services.

- Family Photo Album for Windows
  http://www.cf-software.com/fpa.htm

- Family Trees, Family History and Genealogy
  http://dspace.dial.pipex.com/georgethomson/CALLGEN.HTM
  Charts by a professional calligrapher.

- Frontier Press Bookstore—
  Photography and Genealogy
  http://www.frontierpress.com/frontier.cgi?category=photo

- Frontier Press Bookstore—Preservation
  http://www.frontierpress.com/frontier.cgi?category=preserv
- GeneagraphX Wall Charts
  http://ipxnet.com/home/perry/
  Photo preservation, CD-ROMs, etc.
- Genealogy Unlimited, Inc.—Archival Supplies
  http://www.itsnet.com/~genun/archival.html
- geneamedia
  http://homepage.tinet.ie/~geneamedia/
  Photography and film services for genealogists with Irish roots.
- The Memorabilia Corner
  http://members.aol.com/TMCorner/index.html
  Forms, flags, maps, software, CDs, tapes, microfilm & microfiche, books, periodicals, photographic conservation & archival materials.
- Native Soil
  http://www.nativesoil.com/
  Point to point marketing of historical documents with special emphasis on property deeds.
- Olsongraphics Custom Genealogy Family Trees
  http://www.olsonetc.com/
- Petersen Reproductions
  http://www.datacruz.com/~bapetersen/pr1888.htm
  Reproductions of antique prints and family tree charts.
- PhotoBritain—Photos of Your Ancestors Past
  http://www.photobritain.ndirect.co.uk/
  A service to provide photographs of your British ancestor's past life. You provide the details of your ancestors' place of work, workplace or church and PhotoBritain can provide you with a photographic record to treasure.
- Photo Services for Genealogists
  http://www.avana.net/~donflinn/index.htm

- Plum Video Productions
  http://www.plumvideo.com/
  All sorts of video products, film transfers, slides, photos, etc. Including a Family History Video Album.
- The Scrapbooking Idea Network
  http://www.scrapbooking.com/
  Archival Storage and Career Information Sponsored by Jennia K. Hart, PJC.
- Seattle FilmWorks
  http://www.filmworks.com/
  Digital image processing—download your pictures from the Internet!
- Storytellers
  http://www.storytellers.net/
  Publishers of books & CDs to preserve your family stories.
- Supplies, Charts, Forms, Etc.
  http://www.CyndisList.com/supplies.htm
  See this category on Cyndi's List for related links.
- Suppliers—Sources of Conservation Supplies
  http://palimpsest.stanford.edu/bytopic/suppliers/
- Virtual Archives Home
  http://www.virtualarchives.com
  Virtual Archives specializes in the digital storage of documents and images. Our Digital Archive service is perfect for preserving family histories in document and photograph form.
- Ye Olde Genealogy Charts, Ltd.
  http://www.webcom.com/charts/
- Yourfamily.com
  http://yourfamily.com/
  Create your own family homepage, taped oral history & heirloom photo-album.

POLAND / POLSKA
http://www.CyndisList.com/poland.htm

Category Index:

- General Resource Sites
- History & Culture
- Libraries, Archives & Museums
- Mailing Lists, Newsgroups & Chat
- Maps, Gazetteers & Geographical Information
- People & Families

- Professional Researchers, Volunteers & Other Research Services
- Publications, Software & Supplies
- Queries, Message Boards & Surname Lists
- Records: Census, Cemeteries, Land, Obituaries, Personal, Taxes and Vital
- Societies & Groups

◆ General Resource Sites

- Bibliography of Polish Genealogy and Heraldry
  http://hum.amu.edu.pl/~rafalp/GEN/bibl-eng.html

- Federation of East European Family History Societies—FEEFHS
  http://feefhs.org/

- Galicia—(Galizien) Cross-Index
  http://feefhs.org/gal/indexgal.html
  FEEFHS

- Genealogical Research In The Lands of the Former Austro-Hungarian Monarchy—Guide to Archives and Parish-Registers
  http://www.netway.at/ihff/

- Genealogy and Poland—A Guide
  http://members.aol.com/genpoland/genpolen.htm

- German-Prussian Genealogy Links
  http://www.geocities.com/SiliconValley/Haven/1538/germanpg.html

- Jewish Records Indexing—Poland
  http://www.jewishgen.org/JRI-PL/

- Lacinskie nazwy zawodow = Latin names of occupations
  http://hum.amu.edu.pl/~rafalp/GEN/zawody.htm
  Latin to Polish translations.

- Myron Gruenwald's Page—Germany, Prussia, Pomerania
  http://home.aol.com/myrondpl

- The Order of the Virtuti Militari and its Cavaliers 1792–1992
  http://www.wwdir.com/order/
  This book has 26,506 names of persons and military organizations. It is presented in English and Polish.

- PolandGenWeb
  http://www.rootsweb.com/~polwgw/polandgen.html
  Part of the WorldGenWeb project.

- The Polish Genealogy Home Page
  http://hum.amu.edu.pl/~rafalp/GEN/plgenhp.htm

- Polish Genealogy Links
  http://www.geocities.com/SiliconValley/Haven/1538/Polishpg.html

- Polish Listings Cross Index—from FEEFHS
  http://feefhs.org/pol/indexpol.html

- The Pomeranian Page
  http://www.execpc.com/~kap/pommern1.html

- Prussian Genealogy Links
  http://www.geocities.com/SiliconValley/Haven/1538/prussia.html

- Tracing Your Roots In Poland— by Leonard Markowitz
  http://www.jewishgen.org/infofiles/pl-trav.txt

- Yahoo!...Poland...Genealogy
  http://dir.yahoo.com/Regional/Countries/Poland/Arts_and_Humanities/History/Genealogy/

◆ History & Culture

- History of Europe, Slavic States
  http://www.worldroots.com/brigitte/royal/royal4.htm
  Historic and genealogical information about royal and nobility family lines.

◆ Libraries, Archives & Museums

- Archiwum Archidiecezjalne w Poznaniu / Archdiocesan Archive in Poznan
  http://www.wsdsc.poznan.pl/arch/

- Public Libraries of Europe
  http://dspace.dial.pipex.com/town/square/ac940/eurolib.html
- Archiwa Panstwowe / State Archives
  http://ciuw.warman.net.pl/alf/archiwa/index.eng.html

◆ Mailing Lists, Newsgroups & Chat

- Genealogy Resources on the Internet—
  Poland Mailing Lists
  http://members.aol.com/gfsjohnf/gen_mail_country-pol.html
  Each of the mailing list links below points to this site, wonderfully maintained by John Fuller.
- GENPOL Mailing List
  http://members.aol.com/gfsjohnf/gen_mail_country-pol.html#GENPOL
- GEN-SLAVIC Mailing List
  http://members.aol.com/gfsjohnf/gen_mail_country-pol.html#GEN-SLAVIC
  Gatewayed with the soc.genealogy.slavic newsgroup.
- HERBARZ Mailing List
  http://members.aol.com/gfsjohnf/gen_mail_country-pol.html#HERBARZ
  For the discussion of Polish and Lithuanian heraldry, the history of the armorial clans, and the genealogy of noble families.
- PolandBorderSurnames Mailing List
  http://members.aol.com/gfsjohnf/gen_mail_country-pol.html#PolandBorderSurnames
  For anyone researching genealogy in the former historical borders of Poland including Estonia, Latvia, Lithuania, Belarus, Ukraine, Moldova, Slovakia, Czech Republic, Moravia, Hungary, Russia, the Balkans, and East Prussia.
- POLAND-ROOTS Mailing List
  http://members.aol.com/gfsjohnf/gen_mail_country-pol.html#POLAND-ROOTS
- PolishLessons Mailing List
  http://members.aol.com/gfsjohnf/gen_mail_country-pol.html#PolishLessons
  To assist Poland researchers in translating Polish documents and to further their research while visiting/researching in Poland.
- POMMERN-L Mailing List
  http://members.aol.com/gfsjohnf/gen_mail_country-pol.html#POMMERN-L
  For those interested in sharing and exchanging information on genealogy and history which has a connection to Pommerania, both the current Polish part and remaining German parts of the former Prussian province.
- PRUSSIA-ROOTS Mailing List
  http://members.aol.com/gfsjohnf/gen_mail_country-ger.html#PRUSSIA-ROOTS
  For anyone with a genealogical interest in Brandenburg, Hannover (or Hanover), Ostpreussen (East Prussia), Pommern (Pomerania), Posen, Provinz Sachsen (Province of Saxony—northern Saxony), Schleswig-Holstein, Schlesien (Silesia), Westpreussen (West Prussia), Lubeck, Hamburg, and Bremen.

- SCHLESIEN-L Mailing List
  http://members.aol.com/gfsjohnf/gen_mail_country-pol.html#SCHLESIEN-L
  For those with a genealogical interest in the former Prussian province of Schlesien (Silesia), which is now mostly in Poland.

◆ Maps, Gazetteers & Geographical Information

- FEEFHS East European Map Room—Map Index
  http://feefhs.org/maps/indexmap.html
- Genealogy Unlimited—Home Page
  http://www.itsnet.com:80/home/genun/public_html/
  Maps, books & supplies for sale.
- Map of Ethnic Groups of Eastern Europe
  http://www.lib.utexas.edu/Libs/PCL/Map_collection/europe/EEurope_Ethnic_95.jpg
  From the Perry-Castañeda Library at the Univ. of Texas at Austin.
- Map of Poland
  http://www.lib.utexas.edu/Libs/PCL/Map_collection/europe/Poland.jpg
  From the Perry-Castañeda Library at the Univ. of Texas at Austin.

◆ People & Families

- The Family LOKUCIEWSKI
  http://www.btinternet.com/~hydro.lek/lokuhome.htm
  From 1560, in Eastern Poland now part of Belarus/Lithuania/Poland.
- MIODOWNIK and NOWAK Homepage
  http://205.214.171.123/rdm/
- Rafal T. Prinke Home Page
  http://hum.amu.edu.pl/~rafalp/

◆ Professional Researchers, Volunteers & Other Research Services

- IHFF Genealogie Gesellschaft mbH
  http://www.netway.at/ihff/index.htm
  Professional Researcher specializing in: Austria, Czech & Slovak Republics, Hungary, Slovenian Republic, Croatia, Galicia, others.
- Routes to Roots
  http://www.routestoroots.com/
  Tracing Jewish Roots in Poland, Ukraine, Moldova and Belarus.

◆ Publications, Software & Supplies

- Ancestor's Attic Discount Genealogy Books—
  Polish Genealogy Books
  http://members.tripod.com/~ancestorsattic/index.html#secPO

- Frontier Press Bookstore—European Ancestry
  http://www.frontierpress.com/frontier.cgi?category=europe

- Frontier Press Bookstore—Polish Ancestry
  http://www.frontierpress.com/frontier.cgi?category=polish

- GenealogyBookShop.com—Poland/Polish
  http://www.genealogybookshop.com/genealogybookshop/files/
  The_World,Poland_Polish/index.html
  *The online store of Genealogical Publishing Co., Inc. &
  Clearfield Company.*

- Genealogy Unlimited—Home Page
  http://www.itsnet.com:80/home/genun/public_html/
  Maps, books & supplies for sale.

- Jewish Roots in Poland—Pages from the Past
  and Archival Inventories
  http://www.rtrfoundation.org/
  A new book by Miriam Weiner.

- Polish Military History Books
  http://www.wwdir.com/polishbk.html
  *Polish Orders, Medals, Badges, and Insignia. Military and
  Civilian Decorations, 1705 to 1985.*

- A Student's Guide to Polish American Genealogy
  http://www.oryxpress.com/scripts/book.idc?acro=FTPOL

- Wandering Volhynians
  http://pixel.cs.vt.edu/pub/sources/wv.txt
  *A Magazine for the Descendants of Germans From Volhynia
  and Poland.*

◆ Queries, Message Boards & Surname Lists

- The Carpatho-Rusyn Surname Project
  http://www.carpatho-rusyn.org/surnames.htm

- Lineages' Free On-line Queries—Poland
  http://www.lineages.com/queries/BrowseByCountry.asp

- Rafal T. Prinke—Surname List (English)
  http://hum.amu.edu.pl/~rafalp/GEN/wykaz-eng.html

- Rafal T. Prinke—Surname List / Lista Nazwisk
  (Polish)
  http://hum.amu.edu.pl/~rafalp/GEN/wykaz.html

- Silesian / Schlesien Research List—SILRL
  http://feefhs.org/de/sil/silrl/silrl.html

◆ Records: Census, Cemeteries, Land, Obituaries, Personal, Taxes and Vital (Born, Married, Died & Buried)

- LDS Polish Jewish LDS Microfilms
  http://www.jewishgen.org/reipp/jri-lds.htm
  JewishGen

- Marriages in Plauschwarren, East Prussia
  1778–1802
  http://www.mmhs.org/prussia/plauschm.htm

◆ Societies & Groups

- Federation of East European Family History
  Societies—FEEFHS
  http://feefhs.org/

- Polish Genealogical Society of America
  http://www.pgsa.org/
  Chicago, Illinois

- Polish Genealogical Society of California—PGSCA
  http://feefhs.org/pol/pgsca/frgpgsca.html

- Polish Genealogical Society of Connecticut and the
  Northeast
  http://members.aol.com/pgsne2/

- Polish Genealogical Society of Massachusetts
  http://feefhs.org/pol/frgpgsma.html

- Polish Genealogical Society of Minnesota
  http://www.mtn.org/mgs/branches/polish.html

- Polish Genealogical Society of New York State
  http://www.pgsnys.org/

PRIMARY SOURCES
http://www.CyndisList.com/primary.htm

Category Index:

◆ How To Locate or Order Copies of Offline Primary Sources

◆ Online Primary Sources

◆ How To Locate or Order Copies of Offline Primary Sources

● How to Obtain a Revolutionary War Pension File
http://www.teleport.com/~dongky/pension.htm

● How to Obtain Military Pension Files from the Department of Veterans Affairs
http://www.kinquest.com/genealogy/va.html

● National Personnel Records Center
http://www.nara.gov/nara/frc/nprc.html

● Requesting Your Ancestor's Naturalization Records from the INS
http://www.brigadoon.com/~jwilson/gen/maher/immigrate.html
A guide by Dennis Piccirillo.

● Scots Origins
http://www.origins.net/GRO/
An online pay-per-view database of searchable indexes of the GRO(S) index to births/baptisms and banns/marriages from the Old Parish Registers dating from 1553 to 1854, plus the indexes to births, deaths and marriages from 1855 to 1897. The 1881 census data is expected later this year and an index to the 1891 census records is coming soon.

● U.S. Civil War Pension & Military Records

   ○ Arkansas History Commission—Request Form For Photocopies of Arkansas Confederate Pensions
   http://www.state.ar.us/ahc/form4.txt

   ○ Arkansas History Commission—Request Form For Photocopies of Arkansas Military Service Records
   http://www.state.ar.us/ahc/form3.txt

   ○ Civil War Records
   http://www.nara.gov/genealogy/civilwar.html
   An article from the National Archives.

   ○ Civil War Records—An Introduction and Invitation
   http://www.nara.gov/publications/prologue/musick.html
   An article by Michael P. Musick from the National Archives web site.

   ○ Civil War Veterans: Copies of military & pension records
   E-mail: inquire@arch2.nara.gov
   Send e-mail to order form NATF 80, Veteran's Records (before WWI only). You will need to give them your postal mailing address.

   ○ Confederate Ancestor Research Guide
   http://www.scv.org/scvgen02.htm

   ○ Confederate Military Records at the Archives
   http://www.scdah.sc.edu/confedrc.htm
   South Carolina

   ○ Confederate Military Records—Civil War Military Records in the U.S. National Archives
   http://www2.msstate.edu/~gam3/cw/resources/bib-comp.html
   A how-to guide by Howard Beckman.

   ○ Confederate Pension Records
   http://www.nara.gov/genealogy/confed.html
   An article from the National Archives.

   ○ Confederate Pension Rolls, Veterans and Widows
   http://image.vtls.com/collections/CW.html
   From the Library of Virginia Digital Collections.

   ○ Florida Confederate Pension Application Files
   http://www.dos.state.fl.us/dlis/barm/PensionIntroduction.htm
   Search this online index then follow the instructions for ordering a copy of the pension file.

   ○ Georgia Confederate Pension Applications—State of Georgia Department of Archives & History
   http://docuweb.gsu.edu/scripts/ColBrows.dll?CollectionContent&915703266-3&MainCollection\\Open+Collections+-\\Georgia+Civil+War+Pension+Records
   "The purpose of this community service project is to digitize the microfilm associated with the pension applications of Georgia's Confederate soldiers and their widows."

   ○ How to Order Military & Pension Records for Union Civil War Veterans from the National Archives
   http://www.oz.net/~cyndihow/pensions.htm
   by Cyndi Howells.

   ○ How to Request Michigan Civil War Ancestor's Military Records from the National Archives
   http://www.centuryinter.net/suvcw.mi/gr-recwv.html

○ Index to Confederate Pension Applications
http://www.tsl.state.tx.us/lobby/cpi/introcpi.htm
Texas

○ United States Civil War Service and
Pension Records
http://www.history.rochester.edu/jssn/page5.htm
Scanned image examples.

○ Virtual Victoria: Confederate Pension
Applicant Index
http://www.viptx.net/victoria/history/pensions/index.html
An index to all of the applicants from Victoria County, Texas.

● Vital Records Information—State Index
http://vitalrec.com/index.html

● Where to Write for Vital Records
http://www.cdc.gov/nchswww/howto/w2w/w2welcom.htm
Download site.

◆ Online Primary Sources

● The Bureau of Land Management—Eastern States,
General Land Office
http://www.glorecords.blm.gov/
*The Official Land Patent Records Site. This site has a
searchable database of over two million pre-1908 Federal land
title records, including scanned images of those records. The
Eastern Public Land States covered in this database are:
Alabama, Arkansas, Florida, Illinois, Indiana, Louisiana,
Michigan, Minnesota, Mississippi, Missouri, Ohio, Wisconsin.*

● Canadian Expeditionary Force (CEF)—
Records Database
http://www.archives.ca/db/cef/index.html
*An index to the personnel files of over 600,000 soldiers that
enlisted during the First World War. Copies of over 50,000
pages of Attestation papers have been scanned and are available
online here.*

● Hillsborough County, Florida Marriage
Records—Index
http://www.lib.usf.edu/spccoll/guide/m/ml/guide.html
*Records online from 4 Jan 1878 to 11 May 1884, including a
scanned photo of the original document.*

● INGALLS Homestead File
http://www.nara.gov/nara/EXTRA/ingalls.html
*Scanned images of 24 original documents pertaining to the
DeSmet, South Dakota homestead of the family of Laura Ingalls
Wilder. A terrific example from the National Archives and
Records Administration.*

● Lafleur Archives
http://www.lafleur.org/
*Provides birth, death and marriage records from authentic Bible
records. There are scanned images of Bibles when possible.*

● The Library of Virginia
http://www.vsla.edu/index.html

○ The Library of Virginia—Archival and
Information Services
http://www.vsla.edu/archives/index.html

○ The Library of Virginia Digital Collections
http://198.17.62.51/

    ■ LVA Electronically Available Card Indexes
http://198.17.62.51/collections/

○ The Library of Virginia Genealogy Home Page
http://www.vsla.edu/archives/genie.html

○ The Library of Virginia—Online Catalogs and
Image Databases
http://www.vsla.edu/lva/col.html

○ Research Guides and Finding Aids at the
Library of Virginia
http://www.vsla.edu/research.html

● NARA Archival Information Locator
http://www.nara.gov/nara/EXTRA/nail2.html
*A pilot database of selected holdings with digital copies of
selected textual documents, photographs, maps, and sound
recordings.*

● United States Civil War Service and
Pension Records
http://www.history.rochester.edu/jssn/page5.htm
Scanned image examples.

PRISONS, PRISONERS & OUTLAWS
http://www.CyndisList.com/prisons.htm

Category Index:

- Convicts to Australia
- General Resource Sites
- Historic Prisons & Penitentiaries
- Notorious Characters

- Pirates, Privateers & Buccaneers
- U.S. Civil War Prisons & Prisoners
- The Wild West

❖ Convicts to Australia

- Australia Convicts Message Board
  http://www.insidetheweb.com/messageboard/mbs.cgi/
  mb80720

- Australia's First Fleet
  http://www.pcug.org.au/~pdownes/dps/1stflt.htm
  Convicts transported from England in 1788.

- Australia's Second Fleet
  http://www.pcug.org.au/~pdownes/dps/2ndflt.htm
  Convicts transported from England in 1790.

- Australia's Third Fleet
  http://www.pcug.org.au/~pdownes/dps/3rdflt.txt
  Convicts transported from England in 1791.

- Convicts, Characters & Cads—The Ancestors
  of Scott and Fiona Brown
  http://www.uq.net.au/~zzsbrown/family/
  *Surnames including BROWN, SMITH, CALLOW, PHILLIPS,
  MORTON, MOUGHTIN. The site also includes an Australian
  Genealogy Bulletin Board.*

- Daniel BLACKWELL: Tasmanian Genealogy and
  Convict History
  http://www.ozemail.com.au/~kemoon/Danielb.html
  *Grandfather's Grandfather—The story of Daniel BLACKWELL
  and his Descendants.*

- Lincolnshire Archives Index of Convict Records
  1787–1840
  http://www.demon.co.uk/lincs-archives/convicts.htm

- National Archives of Ireland: Transportation Records
  http://www.nationalarchives.ie/search01.html
  Convicts from Ireland to Australia, 1788 to 1868.

- South Australian Transported Convicts
  http://www.users.on.net/proformat/convicts.html

- Strahan, Sarah Island Convict Site,
  South West Tasmania
  http://www.ozemail.com.au/~kemoon/Strahan.html

- The Wellington Valley Convicts, 1823–31
  http://www.newcastle.edu.au/department/hi/roberts/
  convicts.htm
  A database of over 1,000 convicts.

◆ General Resource Sites

- An Abstract of the Civil Law and Statute Law Now
  in Force, in Relation to Pyracy (1726)
  http://www2.prestel.co.uk/orton/family/pyracy.html

- Civilian Internees of the Japanese in Singapore
  during WWII
  http://user.itl.net/~glen/CivilianInternees.html
  Also messages regarding that site.
  http://user.itl.net/~glen/CivilianInternees2.html
  From Alex Glendinning's Asian Pages.

- Executions in England from 1606
  http://www.fred.net/jefalvey/execute.html

- The Family History System—Executions in
  England from 1606
  http://www.fhsystem.demon.co.uk/fhsytem5.htm

- genealogyPro—Criminal—Arrest Researchers
  http://genealogyPro.com/directories/criminal-arrest.html

- GEN-UNSOLVED-MYSTERIES Mailing List
  http://members.aol.com/johnf14246/
  gen_mail_general.html#GEN-UNSOLVED-MYSTERIES
  *For people whose family genealogies include "unsolved
  mysteries." Postings should include only mysterious disappearances or appearances, unsolved murders, questionable incarcerations, and other mysterious or unsolved events in an
  ancestor's life. Postings should not include "brick walls" since
  these would be repetitive of the content of other lists.*

- International Black Sheep Society of Genealogists
  (IBSSG)
  http://homepages.rootsweb.com/~blksheep/
  *For those who have a dastardly, infamous individual of public
  knowledge and ill-repute in their family . . . within 1 degree of
  consanginuity of their direct lines. This individual must have
  been pilloried in disgrace for acts of a significantly anti-social
  nature.*

- Internment of Ukrainians in Canada 1914–1920
  http://www.infoukes.com/history/internment/

- OKLAHOMBRES Online!
  http://www.qns.com/~dcordry/hombres.html
  *Dedicated to the careful, correct research and preservation of
  lawman and outlaw history.*

- Transported Felons Hang on Family Trees
  http://www.ancestry.com/columns/myra/
  Shaking_Family_Tree12-18-97.htm
  *From Shaking Your Family Tree by Myra Vanderpool Gormley,
  C.G.*

◆ Historic Prisons & Penitentiaries

- Anamosa State Penitentiary
  http://www.geocities.com/Heartland/2201/index.html
  Iowa

- Beveren-Waas, Prisons 1857
  http://pucky.uia.ac.be/~janssen/genealogy/bev-gev.html
  Belgium

- Colorado State Archives Penitentiary and
  Reformatory Records
  http://www.state.co.us/gov_dir/gss/archives/prison.html

- Dale Street Bridewell, Liverpool—1871
  http://www.globalserve.net/~scouse/bridwell.htm

- Eastern State Penitentiary
  http://www.libertynet.org/e-state/
  Pennsylvania

- History of the Maine State Prison
  http://www.midcoast.com/~tomshell/prison.html

- Inmates of the Ohio State Penitentiary
  http://www.genealogy.org/~smoore/marion/badguys.htm
  *For every inmate of the Ohio State Penitentiary (Columbus)
  with a Marion County connection, admissions for the years
  1834–1875.*

- Newgate—Newgate Prison
  http://www.fred.net/jefalvey/newgate.html
  *England. A list of inmates, victims and those associated with
  the prison.*

- Old Idaho Penitentiary
  http://www.idoc.state.id.us/IRTI/site/3xoold.html

- Old Newgate Prison
  http://www.viewzone.com/oldnewgate.html
  East Granby, Connecticut

◆ Notorious Characters

- Evolution of an Outlaw Band: The Making of the
  Barker-Karpis Gang—Part 1
  http://www.qns.com/~dcordry/Barker1.html
  Part 2
  http://www.qns.com/~dcordry/Barker2.html

- Famous Cases—FBI
  http://www.fbi.gov/famcases/famcases.htm

- The John Dillinger File
  http://www.geocities.com/~jdillinger/

- Notorious Ancestors
  http://www.geocities.com/Heartland/Acres/8310/notorious.html

- Yahoo!...Outlaws
  http://dir.yahoo.com/Society_and_Culture/Crime/Outlaws/

◆ Pirates, Privateers & Buccaneers

- Anne Bonny's Home Page
  http://www.geocities.com/CollegePark/4704/annebonny.html
  "The most notorious female pirate that ever lived."

- Beej's Pirate Image Archive
  http://www.ecst.csuchico.edu/~beej/pirates/

- Blackbeard the Pirate
  http://www.blackbeardthepirate.com/blackbeard1.htm

- Grace O'Malley
  http://members.aol.com/GFSSam/notable/grace.html

- Hawkins Scurvy Crew
  http://www.geocities.com/Heartland/Pointe/8616/pirates.html
  *Dedicated to pirates, their lifestyle, their music, and the history
  they created.*

- Piracy
  http://huizen.nhkanaal.nl/~wastrel/

- Pirate Roster
  http://www.geocities.com/Athens/Aegean/3111/
  pirate_roster.html

- Pirates Homepage
  http://www.powerup.com.au~glen/pirate.htm

- Pirates of the Caribbean
  http://icarus.cc.uic.edu/~jdrege1/toby/pirates/pirates.html

- Pirates, Privateers, Buccaneers
  http://www.columbia.edu/~tg66/piratepage.htm

- Wild Women and Salty Dogs
  http://www.discovery.com/DCO/doc/1012/world/history/
  2pirates/2pirates.html
  *"Pirates were thieves and looters and hard drinkers. They loved
  wild women. Sometimes they were wild women."*

- Yahoo!...Pirates
  http://dir.yahoo.com/Arts/Humanities/History/
  Maritime_History/Pirates/

◆ U.S. Civil War Prisons & Prisoners

- 36th Iowa Infantry POW's at Camp Ford, Tyler, TX
  http://www.rootsweb.com/~iaappano/pow.htm

- Alton in the Civil War—Alton Prison
  http://www.altonweb.com/history/civilwar/confed/index.html
  Illinois

- ANDERSONVILLE Mailing List
  http://members.aol.com/gfsjohnf/gen_mail_states-
  gen.html#ANDERSONVILLE
  *For the descendants and interested historians of Andersonville,
  the Civil War's most notorious prison camp, to swap knowledge
  and research the lives of Union prisoners before, during, and
  after their time in Andersonville.*

- Andersonville National Historic Site
  http://www.nps.gov/ande/
  from the National Park Service.

- Camp Douglas, Illinois
  http://www.outfitters.com/illinois/history/civil/
  campdouglas.html
  Prison camp and training camp.

- Confederate Soldier—Rock Island Illinois
  http://www.insolwwb.net/~egerdes/rockisld.htm
  Confederate POW's Listed in Arkansas Units Who Died in Rock Island, IL Prison Camp.

- CW-POW Mailing List
  http://members.aol.com/gfsjohnf/gen_mail_states-gen.html#CW-POW
  For the discussion and sharing of information regarding the Civil War prisoner of war camps and prisoners of war, both Union and Confederate.

- Friends of the Florence Stockade
  http://members.aol.com/qmsgtboots/florence.html
  Florence, South Carolina

- Kansas Prisoners of War at Camp Ford, Texas 1863–1865
  http://history.cc.ukans.edu/heritage/research/campford.html

- MA Ryan, Co B 14th Miss Vol Inf CSA
  http://www.izzy.net/~michaelg/ma-ryan.htm
  Experience of a Confederate Soldier in Camp and Prison in The Civil War 1861–1865.

- Ohio Prisoner of War Camp Sources
  http://www.infinet.com/~lstevens/a/prison.html

- Union Civil War Prison at Elmira, NY
  http://www2.netdoor.com/~52rcourt/elmiran.htm

- Union Civil War Prison at Point Lookout, Maryland
  http://www2.netdoor.com/~52rcourt/lookoutn.htm

- Xerxes Knox, Private, Co. G, 3rd Iowa Cavalry in the Civil War
  http://www.oz.net/~cyndihow/xerxes.htm
  Cyndi's 3rd great-grandfather and a prisoner at Camp Ford in Tyler, Texas.

◆ The Wild West

- Billy the Kid Outlaw Gang
  http://www.nmia.com/~btkog/index.html

- Kansas Gunfighters
  http://history.cc.ukans.edu/heritage/research/gunfighters.html

- Marshals, Lawmen, Rangers: Historical Characters on the Family Tree
  http://www.ancestry.com/columns/myra/
  Shaking_Family_Tree11-20-97.htm
  From Shaking Your Family Tree by Myra Vanderpool Gormley, C.G.

- Outlaws and Lawmen of the Old West
  http://www.sky.net/~fogel/oldwest.htm

- Scribe's Tribute to Billy the Kid
  http://www.geocities.com/SouthBeach/Marina/2057/
  Billy_the_Kid.html

- Scribe's Tribute to Jesse James
  http://www.geocities.com/SouthBeach/Marina/2057/
  Jesse_James.html

- Western Outlaw-Lawman History Association
  http://www.flash.net/~pggreen/

- The Wild West—Outlaws
  http://www.calweb.com/~rbbusman/outlaws/outlaws.html

- Wild West Personalities Produce Bang-Up Pedigree
  http://www.uftree.com/UFT/FamousFamilyTrees/Earp/
  index.html
  By Myra Vanderpool Gormley, CG.

- The Wild Wild West
  http://www.gunslinger.com/west.html

PROFESSIONAL RESEARCHERS, VOLUNTEERS & OTHER RESEARCH SERVICES
http://www.CyndisList.com/profess.htm

Category Index:
- General Resources
- Speakers & Authors
- Alphabetical listing

◆ General Resources

- Are You Ready to Become a Professional?
  http://www.apgen.org/~apg/ready.html
  From the Association of Professional Genealogists web site.

- Association of Professional Genealogists
  http://www.apgen.org/
  Denver, Colorado
  - APG Mailing List
    http://members.aol.com/johnf14246/
    gen_mail_general.html#APG
  - The National Capital Area Chapter of the Association of Professional Genealogists
    http://www.apgen.org/ncac/
    Washington, DC

- Board for Certification of Genealogists
  http://www.genealogy.org/~bcg/
  Washington, D.C.
  - Board for Certification of Genealogists—Roster of Those Certified—State/Country Index
    http://www.genealogy.org/~bcg/rost_ix.html

- Certification of Genealogists—Why Should a Professional Genealogist be Certified and What is Involved in that Process?
  http://www.rootscomputing.com/howto/certify/certify.htm
  By Gale Williams Bamman.

- CGC Mailing List
  http://members.aol.com/johnf14246/
  gen_mail_general.html#CGC
  For the members of Council of Genealogy Columnists (CGC) in order to keep in touch and plan and discuss various CGC events and functions.

- Council of Genealogy Columnists
  http://www.rootsweb.com/~cgc/index.htm

- Determining When You Need a Professional Genealogist
  http://www.familytreemaker.com/20_myra.html
  By Myra Vanderpool Gormley, CG for Family Tree Maker Online.

- Hiring a Professional Genealogist
  http://www.jewishgen.org/infofiles/profgen.txt
  A JewishGen InfoFile.

- How to Become a Professional Genealogist
  http://www.familytreemaker.com/20_hnkly.html
  By Kathleen Hinckley, CGRS for Family Tree Maker Online.

- On the Trail of a Credentialled Genealogist
  http://www.familytreemaker.com/20_trail.html
  Finding the Ancestry of Etna Briggs, by Karen Clifford, AG.

- ProResearchers Mailing List
  http://members.aol.com/johnf14246/
  gen_mail_general.html#ProResearchers
  Just for Professional Researchers to discuss their industry.

- So You're Going to Hire a Professional Genealogist
  http://www.apgen.org/hire.htm

- What You Should Know Before Hiring a Professional Genealogist
  http://www.genservices.com/help_guides/HiringAPro.html

◆ Speakers & Authors

- Ancestor Detective Speakers Bureau
  http://www.ancestordetective.com/bureau.htm
  The speakers bureau for professional genealogical speakers and program planners. Web brochures highlight speakers' qualifications and experience.

- AzGAB Speakers
  http://www.azgab.org/speakers/speakers.html
  Arizona

- Cyndi's Speaking Schedule & Calendar
  http://www.CyndisList.com/speaking.htm

- FEEFHS Database of Professional Authors and Lecturers
  http://feefhs.org/frg/frg-a&l.html
  Specializing in Central and East European Genealogy.

- GenieSpeak—Genealogy Speakers Bureau
  http://www.geniespeak.com
  Created to promote and increase contacts between societies and speakers (at all levels), and to list upcoming events and workshop resources.

- Genealogical Speaker's Guild
  http://www.genspeakguild.org/
- Georgia Genealogical Society Speakers Directory
  http://www.america.net/~ggs/speakers.htm
- Heritage Quest Genealogy Road Show
  http://www.heritagequest.com/genealogy/roadshow/
- Kip Sperry, Brigham Young University
  http://reled.byu.edu/chist/sperryk/sperryk.htm
  Author of Reading Early American Handwriting and Genealogical Research in Ohio.
- Michael Neill's Genealogy Lecturing
  http://www.misslink.net/neill/lecture.html
- Repeat Performance—Audio/Video Recording Services
  http://www.repeatperformance.com/
  Tapes of classes and presentations at several genealogy conferences and seminars for the last 18 years.
- Shaking Family Trees by Myra Vanderpool Gormley, CG
  http://homepages.rootsweb.com/~gormleym/speak.htm

◆ "A"

- A+ Genealogy Research Service
  http://www.genealogy-research.com/
- A.A. Genealogy
  http://www.lisp.com.au/~coffey/index.htm
  Family Tree research in Australia and overseas.
- A Net Information Services—Genealogical Research—Finland and Scandinavia
  http://event.jyu.fi/ajantieto/
- AAG International Research—Professional Genealogists and Family Historians
  http://www.intl-research.com/
  Accredited genealogists & family historians specializing in family history research, development & publication. Accredited by the Family History Library in Salt Lake City, the world's largest genealogical library. Tax deductions for LDS research.
- Adelaide proformat
  http://www.users.on.net/proformat/jaunay.html
  Australia
- AID Kinresearch—Släktservice Hemsida / AID Kinresearch Swedish Genealogy
  http://hem1.passagen.se/aidkin/
- AIS—Asset Information Services
  http://pages3.simplenet.com/ais.htm
  San Diego, California. Missing persons and adoption searches.
- AL, GA, TN Genealogy Researcher
  http://members.aol.com/CindyJ4/algatn.htm

- American Records Research Services
  http://www.records.org
  A research service providing assistance to obtain important genealogical information from National Archives Records, LDS Database Searches, San Francisco Bay Area Research, California Vital Records, Sutro Library Research and computer searches.
- Amy Johnson Crow, CG
  http://www.amyjohnsoncrow.com
  Genealogical research in Ohio and Ohioans in the Civil War.
- Ancestor Detective Speakers Bureau
  http://www.ancestordetective.com/bureau.htm
  The speakers bureau for professional genealogical speakers and program planners. Web brochures highlight speakers' qualifications and experience.
- Ancestor Research Service
  http://home.att.net/~rva/Genealogy/index.htm
  Kathleen Van Ausdal, specializing in United States, British Isles, Denmark, Germany.
- Ancestors in the Attic
  http://ladyecloud.hypermart.net/Ancestors.htm
  Oregon
- Ancestors Lost and Found
  http://www.ancestorsfound.com/
  Salt Lake City, Utah
- Ancestral Investigations
  http://www.ancestralinvestigation.com/
  "Offers a variety of research services at a reasonable rate, including internet research, US Archive research, CD and book searches, and organization of family information."
- Ancestral Findings
  http://web.mountain.net/~wfmoney/cd/
  Free CD searches—limited to 2 persons per day.
- Ancestral Research in Ulster
  http://www.a-research.demon.co.uk/
  Genealogy research service specialising in the nine counties of Ulster, Northern Ireland.
- Ancestral Roots
  E-mail: AncestralRoots@annescales.freeserve.co.uk
  Genealogical Research in SE Wales: Glamorgan and Monmouthshire/Gwent. For details please send e-mail to: Anne Scales MSc BA, AncestralRoots@annescales.freeserve.co.uk
- Ancient History
  http://www.spessart.com/users/ggraham/anchist1.htm
  Yamhill County, Oregon
- Ann McRoden Mensch, Professional Genealogist
  http://home.att.net/~mensch-family/Resume.htm
  Researching at the Allen County Public Library.
- Arno Schmitt, Journalist from San Diego, California
  E-mail: reporter@adnc.com
  He can help to find relatives, links or sources regarding ancestors by placing articles in German, Austrian and/or Swiss newspapers. For details, e-mail Arno at: reporter@adnc.com

- AskQuailind@—Document Delivery Service for Genealogists and Family Historians
  http://www.AskQuailind.com/
  San Mateo, California

- Assets and Family Research Consultants
  E-mail: sharsam@adan.kingston.net
  Toronto, Ontario, Canada. Researcher with 15 years experience, specializing in adoption-related searches. Contact Sharon Chianelli at 1-613-352-1163 or by e-mail at: sharsam@adan.kingston.net

- Association of Professional Genealogists
  http://www.apgen.org/~apg/
  Denver, Colorado

- The Australasian Association of Genealogists and Record Agents
  http://home.vicnet.net.au/~aagra/

- Australia's Immigration and Family History Centre
  http://www.peg.apc.org/~frasertravel/hervey/family/research.htm
  Janet Reakes

◆ "B"

- Back To Roots—Family History Service
  http://www.wwide.co.uk/backtoroots/
  From the United Kingdom.

- Back Tracks Genealogy Service
  http://www.naxs.com/abingdon/backtrak/default.htm
  Abingdon, Virginia

- Barbara Jean Mathews, CG
  http://www.gis.net/~bmathews/
  Professional Genealogical Research In Connecticut and Eastern Massachusetts.

- The Basque Genealogy Homepage Research Services
  http://www.primenet.com/~fybarra/Research.html
  Specializing in Basque records from the province of Vizcaya. These records are on microfilm at the Salt Lake Family History Library, but do not get circulated.

- Bill Madon—New York State Genealogy Research Services
  http://www.treesearch.com/treesearch.html

- Birmingham Public Libraries Genealogical Research
  http://lirn.viscount.org.uk/earl/members/birmingham/gene.htm
  England

- Board for Certification of Genealogists
  http://www.genealogy.org/~bcg/
  Washington, D.C.

- Bob's Public Records Office Searches—Kew, London, England
  http://www.users.dircon.co.uk/~searcher/
  Including these records: Military, Royal Navy, Merchant Navy, Convict, Railway, West Indies, Passenger Lists, History Projects.

- Books We Own List
  http://www.rootsweb.com/~bwo/index.html
  A list of resources owned by others who are willing to do lookups in them.

- Bowers Genealogy Services
  http://www.interlog.com/~kbowers/bgs2.htm
  England, Scotland, Canada

- Brian Walker—Family History Research in all London Record Offices
  http://ourworld.compuserve.com/homepages/brianwalker1/
  Specializes in London area record repositories including the Family Records Centre, the Public Record Office, Somerset House, Guildhall Library, Society of Genealogists Library, and others.

- British Ancestral Research
  http://www.brit-a-r.demon.co.uk/

- Bruce Murduck—Historical, Geographical and Genealogical Research Services
  http://www.ikweb.com/murduck/genealogy/rsrchndx.htm
  Researcher in Ontario, Canada.

◆ "C"

- Canadian Metis Genealogy
  http://genweb.net/~pbg/metis.htm

- The Cavalier Research Group
  http://www.cavaliergroup.org/
  Central Virginia

- Celtic Origins
  http://www.genealogy.ie/
  Dublin, Ireland

- Cemetery Searches, Sydney Australia
  http://homepages.tig.com.au/~tezz/netscape.htm
  This service will locate your ancestors' graves and take photos if required.

- The Census Giver
  http://www.censusgiver.com/
  A no-frills, quick turn-around search and retrieval of US Federal Census records from the National Archives.

- Center For Genealogical Research / Cabinet d'Etudes Généalogiques
  http://genrsch.com/
  U.S. & Switzerland

- Centre Departemental D'histoire Des Familles
  http://www.telmat-net.fr/~cdhf/
  France

- Charles Herbert Crookston—Family History Research
  E-mail: charleshc@sfo.com
  Specializing pre-1906 San Francisco Earthquake and Fire Research and Northern California research. Send e-mail to: charleshc@sfo.com

- Cherokee Cousins—Cherokee Genealogy, Language, Culture
  http://www.powersource.com/powersource/cousins/default.html

- Chicago Genealogy and Family History Research Services
  http://members.aol.com/ChiSearch
  Professional research done in Chicago and Cook Co., Ilinois. Special research projects for Italian Family History and Medical Genealogy.

- Civil War Pensions, Revolutionary War Records and Homestead Papers Copied by Faith Libelo
  E-mail: fsl.genie.research@erols.com
  She can visit the National Archives for you and copy the files. E-mail Faith at fsl.genie.research@erols.com for details.

- Commissioning a Genealogical Search
  http://www.bess.tcd.ie/irlgen/commiss.htm
  Ireland

- CompuGen Systems Home Page.
  http://members.aol.com/CGSystems/index.html
  Newspaper and land records index searches for Indiana.

- Connie Lenzen—Certified Genealogical Research Specialist
  http://www.orednet.org/~clenzen/
  Research in Oregon and southwest Washington.

- Council of Genealogy Columnists
  http://www.rootsweb.com/~cgc/index.htm

- Czechoslovak Genealogical Society Int'l— Professional Genealogical Researchers for Czech and Slovak Republics
  http://members.aol.com/cgsi/research.htm

◆ **"D"**

- D & A Lambert Genealogical and Historical Research Service
  http://www.channel1.com/~davidl/
  New England and Civil War research.

- Davis Genealogy Page and Genealogical Research Services
  http://home.sprynet.com/sprynet/ecdavis/davisgen.htm
  Specializing in research for Greene and Christian Counties, Missouri.

- DelMarVa Roots
  http://www.intercom.net/user/bobroots/tindex.html
  Genealogical record searches for the State of Delaware.

- Detroit Search
  http://pages.prodigy.net/kdall/yourpage.html
  Michigan

- Diane E. Greene
  E-mail: 102007.1244@compuserve.com
  United States Research—Salt Lake City Family Library (Salt Lake City, UT) and Daughters of the American Revolution Library (Washington, D.C.) Family research, lineage applications prepared. Free brochure. For details e-mail Diane at 102007.1244@compuserve.com

- Diane's Michigan Genealogy Page
  http://members.aol.com/DJOslund/index.html
  Professional Genealogist serving Southeastern Michigan, Southwestern Ontario, Northwestern Ohio.

- Dickenson Research & Photo-Video Evidence
  http://PersonalWebs.myriad.net/jdickenson/
  Huntsville, Texas. Specializing in Locating Missing Heirs in Estate Cases and General Genealogical Research.

- Doherty Enterprises Professional Genealogical Research
  http://www.magpage.com/~tdoherty/tpdserve.html
  Delaware

- Donna's Genealogy Services
  http://www.globaldialog.com/~kilroyd/genserv.htm
  Watertown, Wisconsin

◆ **"E"**

- Eastern Townships of Quebec Genealogy
  http://www.virtuel.qc.ca/simmons/
  Marlene Simmons has indexed 490,000 church, census, newspaper, cemetery, some Vermont vital records, and other miscellaneous records.

- Ed's Ancestral Research Services
  http://www.execulink.com/~patpamed/index.html
  Specializing in research for Ontario, Canada, but capable of global research.

- Emilio—Escort of SICILY
  http://www.mediatel.it/public/emilio/
  Professional Italian researcher and tour guide.

- Eneclann: Irish Genealogical Research Services
  http://www.eneclann.tcd.ie/genealogy.htm

◆ **"F"**

- Family Detective
  http://www.familydetective.com
  Family Detective finds people such as lost family and friends, former classmates, military buddies, unknown or missing heirs, adoptees, and cousins. Kathleen W. Hinckley combines her skills as a professional genealogist and private investigator, utilizing the Internet, public records, and genealogical sources to locate living persons.

- Family History Land
  http://www.familyhistoryland.com/
  Tucson, Arizona

- Family History Research
  http://www.mharper36.demon.co.uk/
  U.K. sources, particularly in London.

- Family Line Research from TPCGS
  http://www.rootsweb.com/~watpcgs/famline.htm
  For the Tacoma-Pierce County, Washington area.

- Family Tree Genealogical and Probate Research
  Bureau Ltd.
  http://www.familytree.hu/
  Professional research service covering the area of what was formerly the Austro—Hungarian Empire, including: Hungary, Slovakia, Czech Republic, Austria, Italy, Transylvania, Croatia, Slovenia, former Yugoslavia (Banat), and the Ukraine (Sub-Carpathian).

- Family Tree Research in the Outer Hebrides
  of Scotland
  http://www.hebrides.com/busi/coleis/
  A professional research service based in Taobh Tuath (Norton).

- Famylies Genealogical Research
  http://www.famylies.com/

- Fawn Associates
  http://www.wizvax.net/fawn/
  Estate Genealogy, Heir Identification, Unclaimed Funds Recovery.

- FEEFHS Database of Professional Genealogists
  Specializing in East European Genealogy
  http://feefhs.org/frg/frg-pg.html

- Forebears Research & Associates
  http://www3.sympatico.ca/bill.forebears/
  London, Ontario, Canada

- 4SIGHT RESEARCH—The Research Specialists,
  Surrey, England
  http://www.netlink.co.uk/users/beavis/

- Free GEDCOM Matching Service (Georgia-Lina
  Historical Society)
  E-mail: gedsearch@aol.com
  Send GEDCOM or Tiny Tafel by e-mail.

- Free Genealogy Lookups
  http://www.pnx.com/unicorn/sites/lookups.htm
  From a variety of CDs and books listed on this page.

◆ **"G"**

- Gail Graham, Independent Genealogist & Research
  Specialist
  http://www.spessart.com/users/ggraham/gailg.htm
  Specializing in Yamhill County, Oregon; and Oregon in General.

- Garrison Communications—Family History
  Research Services
  http://www.garrison.gil.com.au/
  Specialising in Queensland, Australia, with expertise in English, Scottish, Welsh and Irish records.

- Genealogical and Historical Research
  http://lonestar.simplenet.com/genealogy/researchservices.html

- Genealogical Journeys in Time Biographies
  http://pages.prodigy.com/Strawn/bio.htm
  An index of individual biographies and a service that will photocopy the biographies for you from the books in their local library.

- Genealogical Journeys In Time (Research Services)
  http://ourworld.compuserve.com/homepages/Strawn/referenc.htm

- Genealogical Research in Scotland
  http://website.lineone.net/~gary.young/
  Gary Young, Dunbartonshire, Scotland.

- The Genealogical Research Library
  http://www.grl.com/
  Toronto, Ontario, Canada

- Genealogical Services & The Genealogy Store
  http://www.genservices.com/

- Genealogist and Record Agent Ireland
  http://indigo.ie/~records/

- Genealogists at VU Look-ups
  http://www.concentric.net/~Cande/lookups.shtml

- Genealogy Ancestors Search
  http://www.wasatch.com/~lance/
  By Family Ties Research, Sandy, Utah.

- Genealogy—France
  http://www.wp.com/GEFRANCE/

- Genealogy Helplist
  http://posom.com/hl/
  List of volunteers willing to help others in specific areas.

- Genealogy NOW!
  http://208.129.36.5:80/genealogy/
  Educational Materials, Family/Name Searches, Picture and Text Scanning Services.

- genealogyPro—Directory of Professional
  Genealogists
  http://genealogyPro.com/
  An advertising and marketing directory for professional genealogists, adoption researchers, historians and translators.

- Genealogy Record Service
  http://www.genrecords.com/

- Genealogy Research by Diane Tofte Kropp
  http://lonestar.simplenet.com/genres.html
  Pearland, Texas

- Genealogy Research—Family Tree Studies
  (New England)
  http://www.webcs.com/genealogy/
  Massachusetts

- Genealogy Research Services
  http://home.pacbell.net/cageni/
  California

- Genealogy Search
  http://www.genealogysearch.com/

- Genealogy Services, Malta
  http://www.waldonet.net.mt/~sultan/gene.htm

- Gen-Find Research Associates
  http://www.gen-find.com/
  Specialists in Genealogy Research for Ontario & Western Canada, Scotland, Ireland, Forensic Genealogy & 20th Century Research.

- Genie Genealogy Research
  http://genealogy.hypermart.net
  Genie Genealogy provides professional genealogy research services to help you find your ancestors. Whether you're a novice or expert, discover your family tree now—quickly and affordably. Genie also offers web page design, picture scanning, report printing, data entry, and LDS-specific genealogy services.

- GenSwap Mailing List
  http://members.aol.com/johnf14246/
  gen_mail_general.html#GenSwap
  For exchanging research time and swapping records for records with others (e.g., researching in your area for someone else in exchange for like efforts on their part).

- Georgia Genealogy Research Services
  http://LeeGenealogy.ofamerica.com/garesh.htm

- Gleason Genealogical Research and Digital Imaging
  http://www.tiac.net/users/gleason/

- Glenn King—Genealogy Ontario, Canada
  E-mail: kingdav@limestone.kosone.com
  Research, Canadian and U.K. records. For details send e-mail to Glenn at: e-mail kingdav@limestone.kosone.com

- GMW Helpers
  http://www.citynet.net/mostwanted/ra/assist.htm
  A list of research volunteers from Genealogy's Most Wanted.

- Gold Coast Family History Research Group Inc.
  http://www.qid.net.au/hacs/clients/history1.htm
  Southport, Queensland, Australia

- Golden West Marketing
  http://www.greenheart.com/rdietz/
  Surname exchange, limited free searches of database, book list, professional researchers.

- GSS—Genealogical Search Services
  http://www.itsnet.com/~gss/
  Research at the Family History Library in Salt Lake City, Utah.

◆ "H"

- Hands Across Time—Professional Ancestral Research Service
  http://www.4free.com/hands/

- Heirlines Family History and Genealogy Research Services
  http://www.heirlines.com
  Salt Lake City, Utah

- Henry's Genealogy Services
  http://home.earthlink.net/~hgrs/
  Augusta, Georgia. "Genealogy research of all kinds at reasonable rates."

- Heritage Associates
  http://www.granniesworld.com/heritage/
  New England Research, specializing in pre-1850 north coast Massachusetts.

- Heritage Consulting and Services
  http://www.heritageconsulting.com/
  Salt Lake City, Utah

- Hidden Heritage—United Kingdom Genealogy Research
  http://www.gloster.demon.co.uk/
  Specializing around Gloucestershire, England. Including Herefordshire, Worcestershire, Avon and Somerset.

- Higgins Family History and Other Services
  http://www.concentric.net/~Higginsj/
  Family history typing & publishing, document scanning for documentation, research Dallas/Fort Worth available resources including government archives.

- Holland Family History
  http://home.wxs.nl/~hfh/engels.htm
  Netherlands

- Holland Page Helpdesk
  http://ourworld.compuserve.com/homepages/paulvanv/
  helpdesk.htm

- Holly Heinsohn Texas Genealogy
  http://www.hrkropp.com/wizzf.html

- HungaroGens Genealogisches Büro / HungaroGens Genealogical Bureau
  http://www.genealogy.net/hungarogens/
  Genealogical research in Hungary, Austria, Slovakia, Rumania, Slovenia, Jugoslavia.

◆ "I"

- IHFF Genealogie Gesellschaft mbH
  http://www.netway.at/ihff/
  Professional Researcher specializing in: Austria, Czech & Slovak Republics, Hungary, Slovenian Republic, Croatia, Galicia, others.

- Independent Researchers at the PRO
  http://www.open.gov.uk/pro/independ.htm
  United Kingdom. This site provides instructions on how you can receive the UK Public Record Office's official listing of independent researchers by e-mail. Listings of specialists in various record categories held by the PRO are available.

- inGeneas Canadian Genealogical Research Services
  http://www.ingeneas.com/
  Ottawa, Ontario, Canada

- International Genealogical Search
  http://www.heirsearch.com/

- Irish Family History Foundation
  http://www.mayo-ireland.ie/roots.htm
- Irish Professional Genealogists
  http://www.iol.ie/~irishrts/Professionals.html
- IRLGEN—Commissioning a Genealogical Search
  http://www.bess.tcd.ie/irlgen/commiss.htm
- Isle of Man—Manx Family History Search
  http://www.oz.net/~ccaine/djd/
  Donna Douglass can help you with your research.
- Italian Genealogical and Heraldic Institute
  http://www.italgen.com/sponsors/ighi/index.htm

◆ **"J"**

- James F. Justin Family Tree Research Services
  http://members.aol.com/jkjustin/gensrch.html
  Genealogy Research Service for New Jersey marriage records, birth records, death certificates, census returns, wills, court records and deeds also Philadelphia National Archives.
- JET Genealogical Research
  http://members.tripod.com/~Janet_E_Tabares/index.html
  Houston, Texas

◆ **"K"**

- KBA Research. Ancestral Research Services in the U.K
  http://members.aol.com/kbaresch
  Locate your ancestors, by using KBA Research, a professional, reliable and cost-effective service.
- KENNEDY RESEARCH—Australian and International Family History Research
  http://www.marque.com.au/kenres/
- Kindred Konnections
  http://www.kindredkonnections.com/
  Family History Research Center.
- KinHelp
  http://www.web-ecosse.com/genes/genes2.htm
  A Scottish oriented genealogical service by Gordon Johnson.
- Kinsearch Genealogical Services
  http://home.utah-inter.net/kinsearch/index.html
  Provides genealogical research services at the Family History Library (FHL) in Salt Lake City.

◆ **"L"**

- Land Record Research Directory
  http://www.ultranet.com/~deeds/research.htm
  Shows you other researchers who are doing LAND RECORD work in various parts of the country.

- Lassen & Lassen: Certified Genealogical Records Specialists
  E-mail: slassen@infoave.net
  Work in Ashe, Wilkes, Watauga, and Alleghany Cos., NC and in Grayson Co., VA. Additional nearby counties by special arrangement. Specialties are research, reportage, and on-site photography. For details e-mail slassen@infoave.net
- Legends & Legacies Writing Services
  http://www.legends.ca
- Library Stacks—An Historical Research and Reference Service
  http://members.aol.com/libstacks/libstacks.html
  Centered in the Boston area, Library Stacks is a professional service which provides research and reference assistance to antique dealers, attorneys, authors, booksellers, curators, family historians, genealogists, graduate students and historians whose genealogical and historical interests lie within the New England states.
- LIFELINES Genealogical Research
  http://www.webspawner.com/users/DonDixonGRSC/
  Don Dixon, GRS(C), LIFELINES Genealogical Research/ Genealogical and family history research for New Brunswick and Nova Scotia, Canada.
- Lineages, Inc.: Services
  http://www.lineages.com/catalog/services.asp
- Lists of Independent Researchers
  http://www.pro.gov.uk/readers/independent.htm
  How to Retrieve a List of Independent Researchers by E-mail from the PRO.
- Lonestar Genealogy
  http://lonestar.simplenet.com/genealogy.html
  Jeannette Prouse is a professional researcher living in Texas who does research services for the entire United States.
- The Look-up Exchange
  http://www.geocities.com/Heartland/Plains/8555/lookup.html
  A county-by-county list of resources covering England, Scotland, Wales and the Isle of Man, made available by volunteers for free look-ups.
- Lookups from Genealogical CDs
  http://www.seidata.com/~lhoffman/cdlist.html
  People who own genealogy CDs and are willing to do lookups for others.
- Lookups from Privately Owned Publications
  http://www.seidata.com/~lhoffman/private.html
  People volunteering to do lookups in their own personal library.
- Los Angeles City Directory 1930
  E-mail Bill Cappello at billcapp@ix.netcom.com and he will do a reasonable number of specific lookups for you. Allow two weeks for a reply.

◆ **"M"**

- Manchego Consulting
  http://members.aol.com/manchegoc/homepage.html
  Hispanic genealogy research and book publishing.

- Marbract Services—NSW Birth, Death & Marriage Certificate Transcription Service
  http://www.marbract.com.au/
  Australia. NSW Births 1788–1905, NSW Marriages 1788–1918 & NSW Deaths 1788–1945.

- Mentro Cymru—Tracing Your Welsh Heritage with Origin Quest
  http://dialspace.dial.pipex.com/pamb.mentro-cymru/

- Michigan Genealogist for Michigan—Karen Olszeski
  http://genealogypro.com/kolszeski.html

- Minnesota GenSearch
  http://members.aol.com/mngensrch/mngensrch.htm

- Molander's Genealogy Service
  http://www.algonet.se/~family/
  For Sweden and Norway.

◆ "N"

- Natalie Cottrill Genealogical Research
  http://www.nataliesnet.com/
  United States research at the Salt Lake City, Utah Family History Library.

- The National Archives of Ireland: Genealogical and Historical Researchers
  http://www.nationalarchives.ie/gen_researchers.html
  Postal addresses of professional researchers in Ireland.

- The National Capital Area Chapter of the Association of Professional Genealogists
  http://www.apgen.org/ncac/
  Washington, DC

- National Heritage Datapoint
  http://www.vicnet.net.au/vicnet/family/datapoint/dpoint.htm
  Australia

- New Jersey and Italian Genealogical Research Services
  http://www.italgen.com/sponsors/piccirillo/index.htm

- New Jersey Genealogical Research Service
  http://www.njgrs.com/

- New Zealand Genealogy & History
  http://www.angelfire.com/ak/Register2/index.html
  Research by Heather Walden.

- New Zealand Research
  http://www.st.net.au/~ailsa/
  Ailsa Corlett, professional researcher.

- Nicholas J. Davey, Researcher for Glamorgan and Monmouthshire, Wales
  E-mail: ndavey@baynet.co.uk
  E-mail Nicholas Davey for details at: ndavey@baynet.co.uk

- Nova's Genealogy Page
  http://www.buffnet.net/~nova/
  Nova will search her Social Security Death Index CD-ROM for you.

◆ "O"

- The Official Iowa Counties Genealogy— Professional Genealogical Researchers
  http://www.iowa-counties.com/gene/
  This site has a page where you can post complaints and opinions regarding professional researchers that you feel haven't treated you right.

- Oklahoma and Arkansas Research by Monroe Davis
  http://www.geocities.com/Eureka/Park/5315/research.htm

- Oz-Tech—Find Out Who is Researching Your British Isles Families...
  http://www.brigadoon.com/~oztech/

◆ "P"

- The PA1776 Researchers List
  http://www.pa1776.com/PAGENE/rsr01.htm
  For help with Pennsylvania genealogical research.

- Palatine & Pennsylvania-Dutch Genealogy Personally Owned Genealogy Resources
  http://www.geocities.com/Heartland/3955/resources.htm

- Past Tracker
  http://www.harborside.com/home/r/rice/index.html
  Coos Bay, Oregon. Native American and New England specialty searches.

- P.A.T.H. Finders—Personal Ancestral Tours & History
  http://www.abilnet.com/pathfinders/
  Specializing in Family History and Travel in the Czech and Slovak Republics.

- Paul Bunnell will search your Loyalist ancestors— Send e-mail to Paul for details
  E-mail: benjamin@capecod.net

- Per Search
  http://users.aol.com/vcassoc/

- Philadelphia Family Finder
  http://hometown.aol.com/ladybrvhrt/private/index.html
  Pennsylvania

- Portuguese Genealogy by Doug da Rocha Holmes
  http://www.dholmes.com/rocha1.html
  Professional researcher specializing in Azorean genealogy and Portuguese translation.

- Professional Family History Services
  http://pages.prodigy.net/john_flora/pfhs.htm
  California

- Professional Genealogical Research in Queensland
  http://www.st.net.au/~judyweb/prof.html
  Australia. Judy Webster.

- Professional Genealogist for Georgia—Shannon Wilson
  http://genealogypro.com/swilson.html

- Professional Genealogist for Western Kentucky—
  Bill Utterback
  http://genealogypro.com/b-utterback.html
  Bill Utterback, CGRS—Research in the Jackson Purchase Counties of Western Kentucky.

- Professional Genealogist in New Zealand for the UK
  and Ireland—Tony Fitzgerald
  http://genealogypro.com/tfitzgerald.html

- Professional Genealogists Familiar With Connecticut
  State Library Collections
  http://www.cslnet.ctstateu.edu/list.htm

- Professional Genealogists' Network
  http://ww2.esn.net/~ancestral/pgn/
  North Carolina

- ProResearchers Mailing List
  http://members.aol.com/johnf14246/
  gen_mail_general.html#ProResearchers
  Just for Professional Researchers to discuss their industry.

- Public Record Office Searches by Roger E. Nixon
  http://ourworld.compuserve.com/homepages/rogerenixon/
  All military, naval, seamen, naturalisations, migrants, police, convicts, FO, HO, CO searched. Wide range of subjects. Check my list first.

- Public Record Searches
  http://www.users.dircon.co.uk/~searcher/index.htm
  U.K. R.W. O'Hara in Kew, Richmond.

◆ "Q"

- Quik-Search—A Document Retrieval Service for
  Genealogists and Historians
  http://www.inconnect.com/~gjnixon/
  Document retrieval from the Family History Library Collections in Salt Lake City, Utah.

◆ "R"

- Research Etc.—Genealogy—Serving Muskoka
  District and Simcoe County
  http://www.bracebridge.com/genealogy/research.html
  Nancy Monnell, Orillia, Ontario Canada.

- The Research Resource
  http://www.toolcity.net/~vadkins/gen/resndx.html

- Research Undertaken at the Leicestershire
  Record Office
  http://ourworld.compuserve.com/homepages/bwmconsultants/
  Research.htm
  England

- Resources with a Wide Array of
  Genealogical Interest
  http://members.aol.com/djungclas/common/resource.htm
  Lists a variety of volunteer services.

- Rhode Island Families Association—
  Genealogical Publications and Research
  http://www.erols.com/rigr/
  Research for Rhode Island, New England, Probate, and DAR including membership.

- Rhonda R. McClure Genealogical Services
  http://www.thegenealogist.com/

- Richard M. Pope, Certified Genealogist
  http://w3.nai.net/~absuax/
  Specializing in Connecticut, Massachusetts, New York City, Germany.

- Robert M. Wilbanks IV, Genealogist & Historian
  http://www.getnet.com/~rmwiv/

- Rootbound Genealogy's Research Services
  http://www.angelfire.com/il/Rootbound/research.html

- Roots & Branches Genealogy—Becki Hagood
  E-mail: Roots4Gen@aol.com
  North Carolina statewide professional researcher. For details send e-mail to Becky at: Roots4Gen@aol.com

- Roots Cape Breton Genealogy & Family
  History Centre
  http://eagle.uccb.ns.ca/lona/roots.html
  A computer-assisted research service, Nova Scotia, Canada.

- Routes to Roots
  http://www.routestoroots.com/
  Tracing Jewish Roots in Poland, Ukraine, Moldova and Belarus.

- Rural New York State Family Research
  http://www.newyorkstateresearch.com/
  Genealogical Services for Central, Western, and Northern New York.

◆ "S"

- SAMPUBCO
  http://www.wasatch.com/~dsam/sampubco/index.htm
  Will Testators Indexes, Naturalization Records Indexes and Census Indexes online. You can order copies of the original source documents for a small fee.

- Schröeder & Fülling GbR, German Genealogy
  Research Firm
  http://ourworld.compuserve.com/homepages/
  German_Genealogy/homepage.htm

- Scotfinder Home Page
  http://ourworld.compuserve.com/homepages/scotfinder/

- Scots Ancestry Research Society
  http://www.royalmile.com/scotsancestry/

- Scottish Ancestry Research (Graham Maxwell)
  http://members.aol.com/grmaxwell/ancestry/index.htm

- Scottish Family Research
  http://www.linnet.co.uk/linnet/tour/67015.htm

- Scottish Family Search
  http://www.demon.co.uk/sfs/sfshome.htm

- Scottish Roots—Ancestral Research Services
  http://www.scottish-roots.co.uk/
- The Service Area
  http://www.toolcity.net/~vadkins/gen/svc.html
  From The Grannies' Genealogy Helper Menu.
- Sicilian Research
  http://www.inconnect.com/~gjnixon/ki00011.htm
  Italy
- SK Publications
  http://www.skpub.com/genie/
  Genealogy research consultants & census books for sale.
- So Many Branches
  http://www.angelfire.com/biz/SoManyBranches/
  Western New York, Northern Pennsylvania, Michigan and Northern Ohio Genealogical Research.
- Southern California Chapter Association of Professional Genealogists
  http://www.compuology.com/sccapg/
- Studio Galloway—Genealogy, Heraldry, Paintings, Illustrations
  http://www.firmnet.ch/galloway/index_e.html
  Switzerland
- Surnames.com
  http://www.surnames.com/default.htm
- Susan Bryant
  E-mail: sbry@dowco.com
  Has a Pro-CD Canadian Home Phone CD. E-mail Susan with specific details and she will do a quick lookup for you.

◆ "T"

- TCI—Threshold Concepts, Inc. Genealogy Research Services Group
  http://www.xmission.com/~tconcept/
  Professional Research Services, Photo/Document Services, Family History Publication Services.
- Ted Gostin, Professional Genealogist
  http://members.aol.com/tgostin/index.html
  Specializing in Jewish genealogy and Southern California resources.
- Thistle Roots Research
  http://www.geocities.com/Heartland/Plains/3735/
  George Cormack's Scottish genealogical resource based in Edinburgh.
- Time Machine: Ancestral Research
  E-mail: LaLynn@aol.com
  Alabama. Laura Flanagan, member of the Limestone County Historical Society, SPGS, NGS with 7 years experience, working toward certification. For details send e-mail to Laura at: LaLynn@aol.com
- Traces From Your Past
  http://www.cadvision.com/traces/
  Genealogical Publications, Services and Resources to assist the Family Historian researching in Canada and the United Kingdom.

- Tree Climber Genealogy Research
  http://www.ida.net/users/elaine/services.htm
  Elaine Johnson in Idaho.

◆ "V"

- Vamp Volunteers Help in Southeast Georgia
  E-mail: vamp@gnatnet.net
  Send her an e-mail with details.
- The Vanished Mall—History, Genealogy and Family History Mall
  http://www.vanished.com/
  Newspaper and city directory research service as well as other resources.
- Virginia Family Research
  http://www.mindspring.com/~jkward/Index.html
  Virginia genealogy, Virginia Confederate records, Revolutionary records.
- The Virginia Genealogy Store—Research Services
  http://www.wp.com/genealogy/page9.html

◆ "W"

- What You Should Know Before Hiring a Professional Genealogist
  http://www.genservices.com/help_guides/HiringAPro.html
- Will Search Ireland Co. Ltd
  http://indigo.ie/~willsrch/
- Willow Bend Research Services
  http://www.willowbend.net/service.htm
  Research in the Northern Virginia and the Washington, D.C. area, including military records from the National Archives.
- WiSearch
  http://www.msn.fullfeed.com/~wisearch/
  Professional research into your Wisconsin roots, specializing in the 1820–1920 time period. Census, vital records, land records, naturalization and much more. Offering on-site photography too!
- Worcestershire Family History Research
  http://www.users.globalnet.co.uk/~bill04/
  England
- World Family Tree Submitter List
  http://www.inlink.com/~nomi/wftlist/index.html
  Contact info for submitters to Broderbunds WFT CDs.

◆ "Y"

- Yahoo!...Genealogy...Researchers
  http://dir.yahoo.com/Business_and_Economy/Companies/Information/Genealogy/Researchers/
- Yorkshire Genealogical Research Specialist
  http://ourworld.compuserve.com/homepages/jksdelver/
  England
- Yukon Historic Research
  http://www.yukonweb.com/business/yhr/
  Canada

QUAKER
http://www.CyndisList.com/quaker.htm

- Canadian Friends Historical Association
  http://home.interhop.net/~aschrauwe/

- Finding Your Quaker Roots
  http://www.rootsweb.com/~quakers/quakfind.htm

- Frontier Press Bookstore—Quaker Ancestry
  http://www.frontierpress.com/frontier.cgi?category=quaker

- GenDex = / Groups and Societies
  http://www.netins.net/showcase/pafways/groups.htm#GROUPS

- Glossary of Quaker Terms
  http://www.rootsweb.com/~quakers/quakdefs.htm

- Guilford College Friends Historical Collection
  http://www.guilford.edu/LibraryArt/fhc.htm
  Greensboro, North Carolina

- Hearthstone Books—Quaker
  http://www.hearthstonebooks.com/Quakers.html

- Heritage Books—Quaker
  http://www.heritagebooks.com/quaker.htm

- Meeting Organization of the Society of Friends (Quakers)
  http://www.rootsweb.com/~quakers/quakmtg2.htm

- Old Style & New Style Dates for the Quaker Calendar
  http://www.everton.com/usa/GENEALOG/GENEALOG.QUAKERC1

- Picton Press—Quaker
  http://www.midcoast.com/~picton/public_html.BASK/catalog/religion.htm#quaker

- Quaker Abbreviations
  http://www.everton.com/GENEALOG/GENEALOG.QUAKER

- Quaker Burying Ground Morris, New York, Surnames A–M
  http://www.rootsweb.com/~nyotsego/morbga.htm
  Surnames N–Z
  http://www.rootsweb.com/~nyotsego/morbgb.htm

- Quaker Corner
  http://www.rootsweb.com/~quakers/index.htm

- Quaker Customs & Beliefs
  http://www.rootsweb.com/~quakers/quakinfo.htm

- Quaker Dates
  http://www.illuminatrix.com/andria/quaker.html

- Quaker Families On Line
  http://www.aracnet.com/~pslamb/findquak.htm

- QUAKER-L Mailing List
  http://members.aol.com/johnf14246/gen_mail_general.html#QUAKER-L

- Quaker Marriages
  http://www.rootsweb.com/~quakers/quakmarr.htm

- Quaker Monthly Meetings
  http://www.rootsweb.com/~quakers/quakmtg.htm
  Searchable database.

- Quaker Queries
  http://www.localaccess.com/rubym/QuakerQu.htm
  Submit your queries for free to this publication. Search the online index to one of the recent issues.

- Quaker Queries & Archives
  http://www.rootsweb.com/~quakers/queries.htm

- QUAKER-ROOTS Discussion Group
  http://www.rootsweb.com/~quakers/quaker-r.htm

- Quaker Silhouettes
  http://www.rootsweb.com/~quakers/quaksilo.htm

- The Quaker Wall
  http://home.att.net/~G.G.Hughes/quakwal.html
  List the Quaker names you are researching.

- The Quaker Yeoman Online
  http://www.aracnet.com/~pslamb/quaker.htm

- Quakers [Society of Friends] in Illinois
  http://www.outfitters.com/illinois/history/family/quakers/quakers1.html

- Rahway & Plainfield Monthly Meeting
  http://members.tripod.com/~PlainfieldFriends/
  Includes Register of Births—1705–1890, Register of Deaths—1705–1892, Plainfield Burial Ground.

- The Religious Society of Friends
  http://www.quaker.org/

- Religious Society of Friends—by Kirby Urner
  http://www.teleport.com/~pdx4d/quakes.html

- Research Resources for Quaker Genealogy
  http://www.rootsweb.com/~quakers/resource.htm

- Tripod is an online library program shared by three colleges in Pennsylvania with Quaker resources and collections:
  - ○ Quaker Collection—Haverford College Special Collections
    http://www.haverford.edu/library/sc/qcoll.html
  - ○ Friends Historical Library at Swarthmore College
    http://www.swarthmore.edu/Library/friends/
  - ○ Bryn Mawr
    http://tripod.brynmawr.edu/
  - ○ Read a Guide to Searching Tripod
    http://www.brynmawr.edu/Library/Docs/tripod_guide.html
    Then connect to the telnet://tripod.brynmawr.edu Tripod program directly using your telnet software and access capabilities. Must have Telnet software to access. Make note of logon and password when you begin. Read more about Telnet above.

- Where Did Hinshaw Put Those Quaker Records?
  http://www.rootsweb.com/~quakers/hinshaw.htm
- Willow Bend Bookstore—Quaker Genealogy
  http://www.willowbend.net/quaker.htm

QUERIES & MESSAGE BOARDS
http://www.CyndisList.com/queries.htm

Category Index:

- ◆ General Queries
- ◆ How To

- ◆ Locality Specific

◆ General Queries

- C. More Bones' Query Page—
  From the Skeleton Closet
  http://members.aol.com/cmorebones/queries.htm

- Family Workings
  http://www.familyworkings.com/

- Folks Online: Folks Family Message Tree
  http://www.folksonline.com/bbs3/

- GenConnect at RootsWeb
  http://cgi.rootsweb.com/~genbbs/
  A system for USGenWeb & WorldGenWeb queries, biographies and obituaries.

  - ○ Family Associations
    http://cgi.rootsweb.com/~genbbs/indx/FamAssoc.html

  - ○ Global Surname Search
    http://cgi.rootsweb.com/~genbbs/genbbs.cgi?search

    - • Search Help
      http://cgi.rootsweb.com/~genbbs/helpsrch.html

  - ○ Special Collections
    http://cgi.rootsweb.com/~genbbs/indx/Special.html

  - ○ USA Visitor Center
    http://cgi.rootsweb.com/~genbbs/usaindex.html

  - ○ Visitor Center Hints and Tips
    http://cgi.rootsweb.com/~genbbs/HINTS/index.html

  - ○ World Visitor Center
    http://cgi.rootsweb.com/~genbbs/qindex.html

- Genealogical Journeys in Time Queries Page
  http://ourworld.compuserve.com/homepages/Strawn/allqueri.htm

- Genealogical Journeys in Time Researchers Surname Page
  http://ourworld.compuserve.com/homepages/Strawn/allsurna.htm

- Genealogy Connection
  http://www.olywa.net/twohousewives/geneol.htm

- Genealogy Exchange and Surname Registry
  http://www.genexchange.com/index.cfm

- Genealogy Friends—Genealogy Queries
  http://members.xoom.com/rebelj/gf/index.html

- Genealogical Services—Genealogy Discussions
  http://www.genservices.com/cgi-bin/jerry/bbs/bbs_forum.cgi?forum=discussion

- Genealogy's Most Wanted
  http://www.citynet.net/mostwanted/

- GRD—The Genealogical Research Directory
  http://www.ozemail.com.au/~grdxxx/
  The world's largest listing of surname queries published annually in book form, now on CD-ROM.

- Helm's Genealogy Toolbox—Query Central
  http://genealogy.tbox.com/query/index.html

- IIGS—International Internet Genealogical Society Queries
  http://www.iigs.org/queries/

- Irene's Genealogy Post Forum
  http://www.thecore.com/~hand/genealogy/post/

- Lineages' Free On-line Queries
  http://www.lineages.com/queries/default.asp

- "Lutheran Roots" Genealogy Exchange Message Board
  http://www.aal.org/lutheran_roots/

- NGS News & Events: Queries
  http://www.ngsgenealogy.org/news/content/queries.html
  From the National Genealogical Society in the U.S.

- Parsons Genealogy Registry
  http://www.parsonstech.com/genealogy/registry.html

- Quaker Queries
  http://www.localaccess.com/rubym/QuakerQu.htm
  Submit your queries for free to this publication. Search the online index to one of the recent issues.

- The Query Corner
  http://www.toolcity.net/~vadkins/gen/querymen.html
  Contact these writers to place a query in their newspaper columns or newsletters.

- SURNAME-QUERY Mailing List
  http://members.aol.com/gfsjohnf/gen_mail_surnames-gen.html#SURNAME-QUERY
  For users to send queries on specific surname searches.

- The Tropical Forum—Genealogy Research
  http://www.naples-fl.com/webforum/genealogy/index.html
  From Karen's Root Cellar.

◆ How To

- Internet Genealogy Lesson 2: Creating
  Effective Queries
  http://www.familytreemaker.com/201/lesson2/course2_01.html
  From an online course by Marthe Arends.

- Lineages' First Steps—Write Successful
  Genealogy Queries
  http://www.lineages.com/FirstSteps/WriteQueries.asp

- St. Clair County Michigan Sample Queries
  http://www.rootsweb.com/~mistclai/sample-queries.html
  A humorous and instructive guide to how NOT to write a query.
  Provides excellent advice on how to compose an effective query.
  Applicable for all queries in any locality.

- 6 Steps to Writing a Successful Genealogy Query
  http://www.firstct.com/fv/query.html

◆ Locality Specific

- Alabama Queries
  http://www.geocities.com/Heartland/Meadows/9105/
  queries.htm

- Australian Family Tree Connections Missing
  Ancestors
  http://www.aftc.com.au/missanc.html

- Australian Genealogy Bulletin Board
  http://www.InsideTheWeb.com/messageboard/mbs.cgi/mb5856

- Bedfordshire Family History Society—
  Members' Interests
  http://www.kbnet.co.uk/brianp/interests.html
  A list of surnames being researched by the members.

- Chinese Surname Queries
  http://www.ziplink.net/~rey/ch/queries/

- Dallas County, Texas QueryBase
  http://www.geocities.com/TheTropics/1926/dallasquery.html
  Postings thru present date.

- Free Queries for New Brunswick, Canada
  E-mail: devlin7@ibm.net
  Rooters searching in Westmorland, Albert, Kings, Kent and
  Northumberland counties of New Brunswick, Canada can post a
  free query to Missing Links, a weekly genealogy newspaper
  column written and managed by Sandra Devlin. Queries should
  be to a maximum of 30 words PLUS forwarding address. Don't
  forget your snail mail, fax or voice mail, as well as e-mail
  addresses. Send queries to: devlin7@ibm.net

- Genealogical Queries from the Saskatchewan
  Genealogical Society
  http://www.saskgenealogy.com/queries/queries.htm

- GENUKI Query Searchable Form
  http://www.genuki.org.uk/query.html

- Gibson County Queries
  http://www.comsource.net/~tnolcox/queries.htm
  Indiana

- Irish Family History Foundation—Bulletin Boards
  http://mail.mayo-ireland.ie/WebX?14@^1320@.ee6b2a8
  Organized with folders for each county.

- The Italian Genealogy Web Forum
  http://www.italgen.com/wwwboard/wwwboard.shtml

- JEFFCO—New York Genealogical Posts
  http://www.ticnet.com/jeffco/nyposts/nyposts.html

- Kentuckiana Genealogy—Index to Surnames,
  Queries, and Researchers
  http://www.floyd-pavey.com/kentuckiana/qryindex.htm
  Kentucky & Indiana

- Lanark County Genealogical Society
  Members' Queries
  http://www.globalgenealogy.com/LCGS/LCGSQURY.HTM
  Ontario, Canada

- Litchfield County, Connecticut QueryBase
  http://www.geocities.com/TheTropics/1926/litchquery.html
  Postings thru present date.

- Lonestar Genealogy—Texas Surnames
  http://lonestar.simplenet.com/genealogy/txqueries.html

- Manx Genealogy Bulletin Board
  http://www.isle-of-man.com/interests/genealogy/bulletin/

- New Haven County, Connecticut QueryBase
  http://www.geocities.com/TheTropics/1926/nhquery.html
  Postings thru present date.

- New York State Queries
  http://www.cet.com/~weidnerc/newyork.html

- Palatine & Pennsylvania-Dutch Queries
  http://www.rootsweb.com/~panames/queries.html

- Queries for Monroe Co., NY
  http://home.eznet.net/~halsey/monroe/query.htm

- Queries for New Brunswick
  http://www.geocities.com/Heartland/4051/nbq.htm
  Canada

- Queries on The Coshocton Page—Ohio
  http://www.cu.soltec.com/~photo/coshocton.html

- Scanian Genealogy Homepage Efterlysningar
  1997 / Queries 1997
  http://cgi.algonet.se/htbin/
  cgiwrap?user=anderzb&script=query.cgi

- Scanian Genealogy Homepage Efterlysningar
  1996 / Queries 1996
  http://www.algonet.se/~anderzb/genea/queframe.htm
  Queries from the Swedish province of Scania.

- Stark County Ohio Genealogical Researchers—
Query Page
http://www.webcom.com/schori/querys.html

- Tacoma-Pierce County Genealogical Society
Queries Index
http://www.rootsweb.com/~watpcgs/queries.htm
Washington. Queries from 1994 to present.

- Virginia Genealogical Society Queries
http://www.vgs.org/queries.htm

RAILROADS
http://www.CyndisList.com/railroad.htm

Category Index:

- General Resource Sites
- Libraries, Archives & Museums
- More Railway Links Lists

- Official Railroad Web Sites
- Orphan Trains
- Societies & Groups

◆ General Resource Sites

- American Memory Railroad Maps 1828–1900
  http://memory.loc.gov/ammem/gmdhtml/rrhtml/rrhome.html
  From the Geography and Map Division, Library of Congress.

- The Chicago Tunnel Company Railroad
  http://members.aol.com/POKeefe571/tunnel1.html
  Learn all about a 60 mile underground railroad that operated with 146 locomotives and 3000 freight cars 40 feet below the streets of downtown Chicago.

- The Duluth, South Shore, and Atlantic Railway Home Page
  http://habitant.org/dssa/

- Existing Railroad Stations in New York State
  http://www.spectra.net/~woolever/depot/index2.html

- Frontier Press Bookstore—Railroad History
  http://www.frontierpress.com/frontier.cgi?category=railroad

- Idaho Historical Railroads
  http://members.aol.com/idahorail/ihr_main.htm

- Massachusetts Bay Railroad Enthusiasts
  http://www.massbayrre.org
  Mass Bay RRE is is a non-profit organization that promotes the enjoyment of Railroads.

- Minnesota by Rail
  http://www.parkbooks.com/Html/res_rail.html
  Research Notes from Park Genealogical Books.

- The Ontario Genealogical Society's Publications List
  http://www.ogs.on.ca/pubs.htm
  See their book titled "Canadian Railway Records: A Guide for Genealogists."

- Public Record Office, Records Information— Records Relating To Railways
  ftp://sable.ox.ac.uk/pub/users/malcolm/genealogy/pro/ri032.txt
  United Kingdom

- Railroad Research Resources
  http://hera.csus.edu/students/team/rsrch.html
  Written for railroad history hobbyists, but has good information for the genealogist as well.

- Railroads in Kansas
  http://history.cc.ukans.edu/heritage/research/rr/railroads.html

- Records of Railways
  http://www.pro.gov.uk/leaflets/ri032.htm
  U.K. Public Record Office, Records Information Leaflet No. 32.

- Riding the Rails Up Paper Mountain: Researching Railroad Records in the National Archives
  http://www.nara.gov/publications/prologue/railrd1.html
  By David A. Pfeiffer for Prologue, the quarterly of the National Archives and Records Administration.

- Society of Genealogists Bookshop— Trades, Professions And Offenders
  http://www.sog.org.uk/bookshop/Q25.html
  See Railwaymen section. This is for UK railwaymen only.

- United States Railroad Retirement Board
  http://www.rrb.gov/index.html

  - The U.S. Railroad Retirement Board and Genealogical Information
    http://www.rrb.gov/geneal.html

  - U.S. Railroad Retirement Board—Railroad Industry & Railroad Union Home Pages
    http://www.rrb.gov/rrlinks.html

◆ Libraries, Archives & Museums

- Age of Steam Railroad Museum—Dallas Texas
  http://www.startext.net/homes/railroad
  An overview and virtual tour of our Railroad Museum which is located at historic Fair Park in Dallas, Texas.

- Alberta Railway Museum
  http://www.discoveredmonton.com/RailwayMuseum/
  Canada

- The B&O Railroad Museum
  http://www.borail.org/
  Baltimore, Maryland

- BC Rail Ltd. Historical Archives
  http://www.bcrail.com/bcr/archives.htm
  Formerly the Pacific Great Eastern Railway, British Columbia, Canada.

- Calgary & Edmonton Railway Museum
  http://www.discoveredmonton.com/RailMuseum/
  Alberta, Canada

- California State Railroad Museum Library
  http://www.csrmf.org/library
  Holds records for: Atchison, Topeka & Santa Fe Railway, Western Pacific Railroad, Central Pacific, Southern Pacific Railroads.

- Erie Lackawanna Railroad Inventory
  http://www.uakron.edu/archival/ErieLack/erie1.htm
  University of Akron Archival Services.

- Guide to Railroad Archives at the Thomas J. Dodd Research Center
  http://www.lib.uconn.edu/DoddCenter/ASC/raillist.htm
  University of Connecticut.

- Guide to the New York, New Haven and Hartford Railroad Archives
  http://www.lib.uconn.edu/DoddCenter/ASC/nhtrains.htm
  University of Connecticut, Thomas J. Dodd Research Center.

- Indiana Historical Society—Manuscripts Available at the IHS Library
  http://www2.ihs1830.org/ihs1830/man1.htm
  Look under "L" for information about the Lake Erie & Western Railroad Records.

- Manuscript Sources for Railroad History Research at the Special Collections Department of the University Libraries at Virginia Tech
  http://scholar2.lib.vt.edu/spec/railroad/rrintro.htm

- The National Railway Museum, York
  http://www.nmsi.ac.uk/nrm/
  England

- North American Railroad Museums
  http://www.uprr.com/uprr/ffh/history/narr-mus.htm
  A list of addresses and phone numbers from the Union Pacific Railroad web site.

- Railroad Museums
  http://www.rrhistorical.com/nmra/museums.html
  A list of links. Some of these museums have archives available.

- State Archives of Michigan—Circular No. 13, Railroad Records
  gopher://gopher.sos.state.mi.us:70/00/history/archives/c13

- University of Nevada, Reno—Railroad Manuscript Collections
  http://www.library.unr.edu/~specoll/railroad.html

- University of Tennessee, Knoxville, Hoskins Library: Herbert E. Copeland Railroadiana Collection
  http://toltec.lib.utk.edu/~spec_coll/manuscripts/a0847

- University of Tennessee, Knoxville, Hoskins Library: Knoxville Railway and Light Company
  http://toltec.lib.utk.edu/~spec_coll/manuscripts/a1502

- University of Tennessee, Knoxville, Hoskins Library: Railroad Records Collection
  http://toltec.lib.utk.edu/~spec_coll/manuscripts/a1108

- University of Tennessee, Knoxville, Hoskins Library: Smoky Mountain Railroad Collection
  http://toltec.lib.utk.edu/~spec_coll/manuscripts/a0424

- University of Tennessee, Knoxville, Hoskins Library: Tennessee Central Railroad Company Collection
  http://toltec.lib.utk.edu/~spec_coll/manuscripts/a1702

- Wyoming State Archives
  http://commerce.state.wy.us/cr/Archives/
  Has records for the Union Pacific railroad.

- Yahoo!...Trains and Railroads....Museums
  http://dir.yahoo.com/Business_and_Economy/Transportation/Trains_and_Railroads/Museums/

◆ More Railway Links Lists

- The Information Train Station
  http://railroads.dm.net/linkmain.html

- Interesting Railroad Related Resources
  http://locomotive.raildreams.com/links.html

- Just Railroads
  http://www.bytehead.com/~cpawlus/copy_of_sssmre/a.htm

- Links for Railfans to Explore
  http://web1.tusco.net/rail/railfan.html

- Railpace Interlocking
  http://www.railpace.com/interlocking/

- Railroad Information Online
  http://krypton.mankato.msus.edu/~schumann/www/rr/railfan.html

- RailServe—Historical Societies & Preservation
  http://www.railserve.com/Historical/

- Side Tracked
  http://www.railroad.net/side_track/

◆ Official Railroad Web Sites

- BC Rail, Inc.
  http://www.bcrail.com/bcr/index.htm
  British Columbia, Canada

- Canadian National Railway Company / Canadien National
  http://www.cn.ca/

- Canadian Pacific Railway
  http://www.cprailway.com/

- The Union Pacific Railroad
  http://www.uprr.com/
  - The Union Pacific Collection at the Western Heritage Museum
    http://www.uprr.com/uprr/ffh/history/museum.htm
    Omaha, Nebraska

- Union Pacific Railroad History
  http://www.uprr.com/uprr/ffh/history/
- White Pass & Yukon Route
  http://www.whitepassrailroad.com/
- Yahoo!...Trains and Railroads
  http://dir.yahoo.com/Business_and_Economy/Transportation/
  Trains_and_Railroads/

◆ Orphan Trains

- Iowa Orphan Train Project
  http://www.maquoketa.k12.ia.us/orphan_train.html
- Orphan Train Adoptees
  http://www.system.missouri.edu/shs/orphan.html
- Orphan Train Genealogy
  http://www.ancestry.com/magazine/articles/orphan.htm
  By Marilyn Irvin Holt for Ancestry Magazine.
- Orphan Train Heritage Society of America, Inc.
  http://pda.republic.net/othsa/
- Orphan Train Resources
  http://www.maquoketa.k12.ia.us/ot%20resource.html
- Orphan Train Riders History
  http://www.hamilton.net/subscribers/hurd/index.html
- Orphan Trains
  http://www.outfitters.com/~melissa/ot/ot.html
- The Orphan Trains
  http://www.pbs.org/wgbh/pages/amex/orphan/index.html
  *A PBS American Experience television show regarding this
  unusual immigrant experience.*
- Orphan Trains of Kansas
  http://kuhttp.cc.ukans.edu/carrie/kancoll/articles/orphans/
  index.html
  - A History of the Orphan Trains
    http://raven.cc.ukans.edu/carrie/kancoll/articles/orphans/
    or_hist.htm
  - Index of Children Who Rode the Orphan Trains to
    Kansas
    http://raven.cc.ukans.edu/carrie/kancoll/articles/orphans/
    or_child.htm
  - Kansas Orphan Train "Time-Line"
    http://raven.cc.ukans.edu/carrie/kancoll/articles/orphans/
    or_timel.htm
  - Orphan Train Bibliographies
    http://www.ukans.edu/carrie/kancoll/articles/orphans/
    or_bibli.htm
  - A Partial List of Institutions That Orphan Train
    Children Came From
    http://raven.cc.ukans.edu/carrie/kancoll/articles/orphans/
    or_homes.htm
  - A Partial List of Kansas Orphan Train Arrivals
    http://raven.cc.ukans.edu/carrie/kancoll/articles/orphans/
    or_arriv.htm

- Riders on an Orphan Train to Kansas—1911
  http://raven.cc.ukans.edu/carrie/kancoll/articles/
  orphan_train_1911.html
- Orphan Trains of Nebraska
  http://www.rootsweb.com/~neadoptn/Orphan.htm
- The Orphan Trains: Placing Out in America
  http://st2.yahoo.com/ancestry/brtheortrain.html
  A book by Marilyn Irvin Holt, for sale from Ancestry.
- Orphan Trains to Missouri
  http://www.system.missouri.edu/upress/spring1997/
  patrick.htm
  Information about a book from the University of Missouri Press.
- They Rode the Orphan Trains
  http://www.rootsweb.com/~mogrundy/orphans.html

◆ Societies & Groups

- ARHS/nsw—Australian Railway Historical Society,
  New South Wales Division
  http://www.accsoft.com.au/~arhsnsw/
- Australian Railway Historical Society (ARHS)—
  (Victorian Division Inc.)
  http://home.vicnet.net.au/~arhsvic/
- Australia Railway Historical Society—
  Queensland Division
  http://zerlargal.humbug.org.au/~arhsqld/
- The Bridge Line Historical Society
  http://www.fileshop.com/personal/jashaw/rhs/blhs.html
  *Albany, New York. Historical Society of the Delaware & Hudson
  Railroad.*
- Burlington Route Historical Society (BRHS)
  http://www.getnet.com/~dickg/nmra/sigs/BRHS/CBQ.html
- The Chesapeake & Ohio Historical Society
  http://cohs.marshall.edu/
- The Chicago & Eastern Illinois Railroad Historical
  Society
  http://www2.justnet.com/cei/
- Chicago & North Western Historical Society
  http://www.cnwhs.org/
  Illinois
- Collis P. Huntington Railroad Historical Society
  http://www.serve.com/cphrrhs/
  West Virginia
- Fort Wayne Railroad Historical Society
  http://www.steamloco765.org/
  Indiana
- Grand Trunk Western Historical Society
  http://www.rrhistorical.com/gtwhs/index.html
  Michigan

- The Great Northern Railway Historical Society
  http://www.getnet.com/~dickg/nmra/sigs/GNHS/GN.html

- Historical Model Railway Society
  http://www.hmrs.org.uk/
  U.K.

- The Louisville & Nashville Railroad Historical Society
  http://www.rrhistorical.com/lnhs/index.html
  Kentucky

- The Maryland and Pennsylvania Railroad Preservation and Historical Society
  http://www.arrowweb.com/Ma&Pa/
  Spring Grove, Pennsylvania

- Milwaukee Road Historical Association
  http://www.mrha.com/
  Antioch, Illinois. Chicago, Milwaukee, St. Paul, and Pacific Railroad. This link is for Uncle Reggie!

- National Railway Historical Society
  http://www.rrhistorical.com/nrhs/
  Philadelphia, Pennsylvania

- National Railway Historical Society, UK Chapter
  http://www.siam.co.uk/siam/nrhsuk.shtml

- New Jersey Midland Railroad Historical Society
  http://ourworld.compuserve.com/homepages/njmidland/

- New York, Susquehanna & Western Technical & Historical Society, Inc.
  http://www.americaninternet.com/nyswths/index.htm

- The Northern Pacific Railway Historical Association
  http://pw2.netcom.com/~whstlpnk/np.html

- Ontario & Western Railway Historical Society
  http://shell.idt.net/~nyowrhs/
  New York

- Oregon Electric Railway Historical Society
  http://www.reed.edu/~reyn/oerhs.html

- Pacific Coast Chapter—Railway & Locomotive Historical Society
  http://www.mp1.com/
  Folsom, California

- The Pacific Northwest Chapter of the National Railway Historical Society
  http://www.easystreet.com/pnwc/
  Portland, Oregon

- Railroad Historical Societies
  http://tucson.com/concor/histsoc.html

- Railroad Historical & Preservation Societies: N America
  http://www.rrhistorical.com/nmra/histsoc.html

- International
  http://www.rrhistorical.com/nmra/whistsoc.html
  An excellent list of historical links from the National Model Railroad Association.

- Railway Ancestors Family History Society
  http://www.railwayancestors.demon.co.uk/
  U.K.

- San Bernardino Railroad Historical Society
  http://www.rrhistorical.com/sbrhs/
  California

- Santa Clara River Valley Railroad Historical Society Inc.
  http://www.fishnet.net/~johngart/
  California

- Santa Fe Railway Historical & Modeling Society
  http://www.atsfrr.com/Society/

- Seattle, Portland & Spokane (SP&S) Railway Historical Society
  http://www.teleport.com/~amacha/spsrhs.htm
  Vancouver, Washington

- Shore Line Historical Society
  http://www.getnet.com/~dickg/nmra/sigs/ShoreLine/ShoreLine.html
  Chicago, Illinois. For anyone with an interest in the Chicago North Shore and Milwaukee, the Chicago South Shore and South Bend, and/or the Chicago Aurora and Elgin railroads, including: Chicago Rapid Transit, Chicago Surface Lines, Chicago and West Towns Railways, Evanston Railway, Hammond Whiting and East Chicago Railway, and The Milwaukee Electric Railway and Light Company.

- Soo Line Historical and Technical Society
  http://www.rrhistorical.com/sooline/index.html
  Wisconsin

- Union Pacific Historical Society
  http://www.uphs.org/
  Cheyenne, Wyoming

- Wabash Railroad Historical Society
  http://users.aol.com/wabashrr/wabash.html

- The Washington State Railroads Historical Society
  http://home1.gte.net/jimbowe/WSRHS1.htm
  Pasco, Washington

- Yahoo!...Trains and Railroads....Historical Societies
  http://dir.yahoo.com/Business_and_Economy/Transportation/Trains_and_Railroads/Museums/Historical_Societies/

RECIPES, COOKBOOKS & FAMILY TRADITIONS

http://www.CyndisList.com/recipes.htm

- Cape Breton Pictorial Cookbook
  http://www.taisbean.com/CBcookbook/home.html
  Nova Scotia
- Favorite Family Recipes—From the Gene Pool
  http://www.rootsweb.com/~genepool/recipes.htm
- FOLKLORE Mailing List
  http://members.aol.com/johnf14246/
  gen_mail_general.html#FOLKLORE
  A mailing list for the exchange of folklore—folk medicine and recipes.
- Grandma's Kitchen—Recipes That
  Span Generations
  http://www.geocities.com/Heartland/Valley/9094/recipes.html
- HOMESPUN Mailing List
  http://members.aol.com/johnf14246/
  gen_mail_general.html#HOMESPUN
  For those who want to have a bit of fun reminiscing. Subscribers are welcome to share memories, traditions, poems, humor, stories, recipes, folklore and home remedies.
- More Bits 'N Pieces—Recipes, Cures and More
  http://www.ida.net/users/dhanco/misc.htm
- Old & Treasured Recipes
  http://www.firstct.com/fv/famrecip.html
  From the Treasure Maps site.
- Recipes & Foodways—Germans from Russia
  Heritage Collection
  http://www.lib.ndsu.nodak.edu/gerrus/recipes.html
- Slovak Heritage Live—Christmas Food and Drink
  http://www.iarelative.com/xmas/bc_food.htm

RELIGION & CHURCHES
http://www.CyndisList.com/religion.htm

Category Index:

◆ Directories
◆ General Resource Sites
◆ Libraries, Archives & Museums
◆ Locality Specific
◆ Mailing Lists, Newsgroups & Chat

◆ Publications, Software & Supplies
◆ Records: Census, Cemeteries, Land, Obituaries, Personal, Taxes and Vital
◆ Societies & Groups

◆ Directories

● Church of Scotland Churches
http://www.churchnet.org.uk/churchnet/ukdirect/scotland.htm

● National Directory of Congregations of the Presbyterian Church (U.S.A.)
http://www.pff.net/pc-list.html

● NetChurch Church Directory—United States
http://www.netchurch.com/churchlist_active_US.asp

◆ General Resource Sites

● Anabaptists
http://www.anabaptists.org/

● Ask The Amish!
http://www.800padutch.com/askamish.html

● Church of the Brethren
http://www.brethren.org/

● Doukhobor Home Page
http://www.dlcwest.com/~r.androsoff/index.htm
A group of Russian peasants that split from the Russian Orthodox Church. Large groups of Doukhobors emigrated to Canada and homesteaded in Saskatchewan and British Columbia.

● Greek Orthodox Archdiocese of America
http://www.goarch.org/

● The Hall of Church History
http://www.gty.org/~phil/hall.htm
An interesting site with definitions, descriptions and links to a variety of resources for each religious group it highlights.

  ○ The Anabaptists
  http://www.gty.org/~phil/anabapt.htm
  ○ The Arminians
  http://www.gty.org/~phil/arminian.htm
  ○ The Catholics
  http://www.gty.org/~phil/catholic.htm
  ○ The Puritans
  http://www.gty.org/~phil/puritans.htm

  ○ The Reformers
  http://www.gty.org/~phil/rformers.htm
  ○ The Baptists
  http://www.gty.org/~phil/baptist.htm
  ○ The Eastern Orthodox
  http://www.gty.org/~phil/orthodox.htm
  ○ The Medieval Churchmen
  http://www.gty.org/~phil/medieval.htm

● History of the Early American Presbyterian Church
http://sdsspc1.physics.lsa.umich.edu/amckay/presintr.htm

● Huguenot
http://www.CyndisList.com/huguenot.htm
See this category on Cyndi's List for related links.

● Hutterite Genealogy Cross-Index
http://feefhs.org/hut/indexhut.html

● Hutterite Genealogy HomePage
http://feefhs.org/hut/frg-hut.html

● Hutterite Society
http://www.press.jhu.edu/press/books/titles/s97/s97hohu.htm
A book by John A. Hostetler, for sale from the Johns Hopkins University Press.

● Jewish
http://www.CyndisList.com/jewish.htm
See this category on Cyndi's List for related links.

● LDS
http://www.CyndisList.com/lds.htm
See this category on Cyndi's List for related links.

● The "Lutheran Roots" Genealogy Exchange
http://www.aal.org/LutheransOnline/Gene_Ex/

● Mennonite
http://www.CyndisList.com/menno.htm
See this category on Cyndi's List for related links.

● The Moravian Church
http://home.ptd.net/~boddie/moravians.html

● The Moravian Church Home Page
http://www.moravian.org/

- Olive Tree Genealogy
  http://www.rootsweb.com/~ote/
  Huguenots & Walloons, Ontario Loyalists, Mohawk, Mennonite, Palatines and Dutch Research.

- OMII Genealogy Project & Kidron Heritage Center
  A Swiss Mennonite & German Amish genealogy project.

- Orthodox Church in America
  http://www.oca.org/

- Quaker
  http://www.CyndisList.com/quaker.htm
  See this category on Cyndi's List for related links.

- The Roman Catholic Archdiocese of Philadelphia
  http://www.archdiocese-phl.org/

- Seventh-day Adventist Church
  http://www.adventist.org/

- Shaker Manuscripts On-Line—Prophecies, Revelations and World Outreach from the Early Shaker
  http://www.passtheword.org/SHAKER-MANUSCRIPTS/

- United Methodist History
  http://gbgm-umc.org/UMhistory/

- The Wars of Religion
  http://www.lepg.org/wars.htm

- Yahoo!...Religious...Genealogy
  http://dir.yahoo.com/Arts/Humanities/History/Genealogy/Regional_and_Ethnic_Resources/Scandinavia/

◆ Libraries, Archives & Museums

- Archives—Evangelical Lutheran Church in America (ELCA)
  http://www.elca.org/os/archives/intro.html

- Archiwum Archidiecezjalne w Poznaniu / Archdiocesan Archive in Poznan
  http://www.wsdsc.poznan.pl/arch/
  Poland

- Catholic Archives of Texas
  http://www.onr.com/user/cat/

- Covenant Archives and Historical Library
  http://www.northpark.edu/library/Archives/Covenant_Archives/index.html
  Located at North Park College and Theological Seminary, Chicago, Illinois.

- General Commission on Archives and History; The United Methodist Church
  http://www.gcah.org/
  - Archival Holdings
    http://www.gcah.org/arch_hol.htm
  - Directory for Local and Regional United Methodist Archives
    http://www.gcah.org/Conference/umcdirectory.htm

  - Ministerial Genealogical Research Information
    http://www.gcah.org/minister.htm
  - Museum Exhibit
    http://www.gcah.org/museum.htm
  - Researching Your United Methodist Ancestors: A Brief Guide
    http://www.gcah.org/Searching.htm

- The Historical Foundation of the Cumberland Presbyterian Church and the Cumberland Presbyterian Church in America
  http://www.cumberland.org/hfcpc/
  Memphis, Tennessee

- Methodist Archives and Research Centre
  http://rylibweb.man.ac.uk/data1/dg/text/method.html
  at the John Rylands University Library in Manchester, UK. See the link for Researching your Family History on this site.

- Missouri United Methodist Archives
  http://cmc2.cmc.edu/arc.html
  At the Smiley Library, Central Methodist College, Fayette, Missouri.

- Shaker Museum at South Union, Kentucky—Links to Other Shaker Information
  http://www.logantele.com/~shakmus/othersites.htm

- United Church of Canada Archives Network
  http://www.uccan.org/archives/home.htm

- United Church of Canada / Victoria University Archives
  http://vicu.utoronto.ca/archives/archives.htm
  Located in Ontario, the holdings in the archives include records for the Presbyterian Church in Canada; the Methodist Church (Canada); the Congregational Union of Canada; Local Union Churches; and the Evangelical United Brethren Church. There are also personal papers, biographical files and photographs.

◆ Locality Specific

- The Amish, The Mennonites, and The Plain People of the Pennsylvania Dutch Country
  http://www.800padutch.com/amish.html

- Anglican Parish Ministry
  http://www.ccn.cs.dal.ca/Religion/AnglicanChurchNS/parishes.html
  For Nova Scotia and Prince Edward Island, Canada.

- Catholic Churches of Maine
  http://www.mint.net/~frenchcx/mecath1.htm

- The Charter of the Second Reformed Protestant Dutch Church of Warren, New York
  http://www.rootsweb.com/~nyherkim/wchurch.html

- The Church of England
  http://www.church-of-england.org/

- The Church of Scotland
  http://www.cofs.org.uk/

- Churches in Elgin County
  http://www.eversweb.on.ca/Churches-Elgin/
  Ontario, Canada

- Cumberland Presbyterian Links
  http://members.aol.com/srobin7056/cplinks.html

- The Free Church of Scotland
  http://www.freechurch.org/

- Genline—Svenska Kyrkböcker Online / Swedish Church Records On-line
  http://www.genline.se/

- German Baptists in Volhynia
  http://mypage.direct.ca/d/dobee/volhynia.html
  Ukraine

- The Historical Foundation of the Cumberland Presbyterian Church and the Cumberland Presbyterian Church in America
  http://www.cumberland.org/hfcpc/
  Memphis, Tennessee

- A Historical Sketch of the Brethren in Christ Church
  http://www.easynet.on.ca/~johnb/tunkers/
  "Known as Tunkers in Canada," by George Cober, Gormley, Ontario.

- Holy Trinity Church, Boston, Massachusetts
  http://www.eskimo.com/~mvreid/htc.html
  This site by Marge Reid has a multitude of resources for the church including the 1895 HTC Parish Directory and an HTC researchers directory, as well as many others.

- The Hungarian Reformed Church in Paris 1938
  http://user.itl.net/~glen/HungariansinParis.html
  A Parisi Magyar Reformatus Egyhaz Presbiteriuma.

- Moravian Settlers in North Carolina
  http://www.erols.com/fmoran/morav.html
  From the Jarvis Family Home Page.

- Presbytery of Orkney, Church of Scotland
  http://members.aol.com/OrkneyPrsb/index.htm

- The Presbytery of the Yukon
  http://www.alaska.net/~dao/YukonPresbytery/
  PRESBYTERY_MAIN.html
  Eagle, Alaska

- Suffolk Church Pictures
  http://www.geocities.com/Heartland/Acres/1231/
  England

- Sumner County Churches
  http://www.tngenweb.usit.com/sumner/sumnchur.htm
  Tennessee

- United Church Congregations and Pastoral Charges in Halifax Presbytery
  http://www.cfn.cs.dal.ca/Religion/UCCPresbytery/
  _Charges.html
  Nova Scotia, Canada

◆ Mailing Lists, Newsgroups & Chat

- BRETHREN Mailing List
  http://members.aol.com/johnf14246/
  gen_mail_general.html#BRETHREN
  Includes such church groups as Tunkers/Dunkers, Church of the Brethren, and German Baptists. Also see the associated web page at http://homepages.rootsweb.com/~padutch/lists.html

- ELIJAH-L Mailing List
  http://members.aol.com/johnf14246/
  gen_mail_general.html#ELIJAH-L
  For believing members of the Church of Jesus Christ of Latter-day Saints to discuss their ideas and experiences relating with genealogy in the LDS Church.

- GEN-ROOTERS Mailing List
  http://members.aol.com/johnf14246/
  gen_mail_general.html#GEN-ROOTERS
  For members of the Church of Jesus Christ of Latter-day Saints to share ideas and helpful hints on the "how-to's" of genealogy.

- HANDCART Mailing List
  http://members.aol.com/johnf14246/gen_mail_geo-usa.html#HANDCART
  For anyone who has an interest in the genealogy, journals, and stories of the Pioneers of the Church of Jesus Christ of Latter-day Saints who settled in the Salt Lake Valley from 1847 to 1860.

- JEWISHGEN Mailing List
  http://members.aol.com/johnf14246/
  gen_mail_general.html#JEWISHGEN
  The JewishGen Conference. Discussions of Jewish genealogy. JewishGen is gatewayed with the soc.genealogy.jewish newsgroup.

- MCF-ROOTS Mailing List
  http://members.aol.com/gfsjohnf/gen_mail_states-gen.html#MCF-ROOTS
  A mailing list (Maryland Catholics on the Frontier) for the discussion of descendants of Maryland Catholics who migrated first to Kentucky and then to other parts of the frontier.

- MENNO.REC.ROOTS Mailing List
  http://members.aol.com/johnf14246/
  gen_mail_general.html#MENNO.REC.ROOTS
  A Mennonite genealogy and family research interest group.

- MENNO-ROOTS Mailing List
  http://members.aol.com/johnf14246/
  gen_mail_general.html#MENNO-ROOTS

- MORAVIANCHURCH Mailing List
  http://members.aol.com/johnf14246/
  gen_mail_general.html#MORAVIANCHURCH
  For the world-wide Moravian Church, the oldest Protestant denomination. This list is for an exchange of Moravian records, genealogies, references, and historical information; especially in Europe and Colonial America.

- MORMON-INDEX Mailing List
  http://members.aol.com/johnf14246/
  gen_mail_general.html#MORMON-INDEX
  Provides a weekly newsletter containing queries about Mormon Internet Resources, responses to those queries, announcements of Mormon Internet Resources, and compilations of resources by subject.

- QUAKER-L Mailing List
  http://members.aol.com/johnf14246/
  gen_mail_general.html#QUAKER-L
- QUAKER-ROOTS Discussion Group
  http://www.rootsweb.com/~quakers/quaker-r.htm

◆ Publications, Software & Supplies

- Books We Own—US—Religious Groups
  http://www.rootsweb.com/~bwo/us_religious.html
- GenealogyBookShop.com—Religions
  http://www.genealogybookshop.com/genealogybookshop/files/
  General,Religions/index.html
  *The online store of Genealogical Publishing Co., Inc. &
  Clearfield Company.*
- Heritage Books—Seventh Day Baptists
  http://www.heritagebooks.com/baptist.htm
- Manx Methodist Historical Society Newsletter
  http://www.ee.surrey.ac.uk/Contrib/manx/methdism/mhist/
  index.htm
  Index to Newsletters 1–23.
- Picton Press—Religion
  http://www.midcoast.com/~picton/public_html.BASK/catalog/
  religion.htm
- Sabbath Keepers in History
  http://www.ozemail.com.au/~sdbbris/books/new/index2.htm
  *From the Time of Christ to the 19th Century. Reprints from
  "Seventh Day Baptists in Europe and America" Volume 1
  (pp 11–115), American Sabbath Tract Society, Plainfield, New
  Jersey. 1910.*

◆ Records: Census, Cemeteries, Land, Obituaries, Personal, Taxes and Vital (Born, Married, Died & Buried)

- Church Records in Onondaga County
  http://www.rootsweb.com/~nyononda/CHURCH/CHURCH.HTM
  New York
- Church Records for Ireland
  http://www.bess.tcd.ie/irlgen/church.htm
- The Cochin Churchbook
  http://www.telebyte.nl/~dessa/cochin.htm
  *Baptism & marriages from the Dutch Church in Cochin, India
  (1754–1804).*

- Early Members of the First Baptist Church, Holyoke, Massachusetts 1803–1828
  http://www.rootsweb.com/~mahampde/baptist.htm
- Lehigh County Historical Society Church Records Collection
  http://www.geocities.com/Heartland/3955/lehchurches.htm
  Pennsylvania
- Name Index to Barton W. Stone's Christian Messenger
  http://www.mun.ca/rels/restmov/texts/resources/index/
  index.html
  *Names and dates from as early as 1827; transcribed by Ruth E.
  Browning.*
- Records of Egypt Reformed Church Lehigh County, Pennsylvania 1734–1834
  http://www.geocities.com/Heartland/3955/lehegypt.htm
  From Pennsylvania Archives, Sixth Series, Volume 6.
- Records of the Cayuga and Fosterville United Methodist Churches Cayuga County, New York
  http://www.rootsweb.com/~nycayuga/caymeth.htm
- Researching with Church Records
  http://www.familytreemaker.com/issue5.html
  From Family Tree Maker Online.
- Seventh-day Adventist Periodical Index
  http://143.207.5.3:82/search/
  Has a searchable obituary index and more.

◆ Societies & Groups

- Catholic Family History Society of London, England
  http://feefhs.org/uk/frg-cfhs.html
- Fellowship of Brethren Genealogists
  http://www.cob-net.org/fobg/
- The Presbyterian Historical Society
  http://www.libertynet.org/~gencap/presbyhs.html
  Philadelphia, Pennsylvania
- Shaker Heritage Society
  http://www.crisny.org/not-for-profit/shakerwv/
  Albany, New York
- Texas Catholic Historical Society
  http://www.history.swt.edu/Catholic_Southwest.htm
- United States Catholic Historical Society
  http://www.catholic.org/uschs/

ROOTS-L & ROOTSWEB
http://www.CyndisList.com/rootsl.htm

Category Index:
- ◆ ROOTS-L Mailing List
- ◆ ROOTS-L Library, Archives and Files
- ◆ Roots Databases
- ◆ RootsWeb

◆ ROOTS-L Mailing List

- ROOTS-L is the original genealogy mailing list, founded in 1988. It currently has more than 10,000 subscribers and is sponsored and maintained by RootsWeb
  http://www.rootsweb.com/
  - ○ To subscribe to the ROOTS-L mailing list send an e-mail message to:
    ROOTS-L-request@rootsweb.com
    In the body of the message type only this one word: subscribe
    Be sure not to use a signature file with this message.
    Save a copy of the welcome message that you receive for future reference.
- ROOTS-L Home Page
  http://www.rootsweb.com/roots-l/roots-l.html
- ROOTS-L Resources: Info and Tips for Using ROOTS-L
  http://www.rootsweb.com/roots-l/rootshelp.html
- Welcome: Getting Started with ROOTS-L
  ftp://ftp.rootsweb.com/pub/roots-l/roots-l.welcome
  - ○ Welcome 1: ROOTS-L: How it Works #1
    ftp://ftp.rootsweb.com/pub/roots-l/roots-l.welcome1
  - ○ Welcome 2: ROOTS-L: How it Works #2
    ftp://ftp.rootsweb.com/pub/roots-l/roots-l.welcome2
  - ○ Welcome 3: ROOTS-L Frequently Asked Questions (FAQ)
    ftp://ftp.rootsweb.com/pub/roots-l/roots-l.welcome3
- ROOTS-L Archive—Log Files of Messages to the List
  ftp://ftp.rootsweb.com/pub/roots-l/archive/
- ROOTS-L Archive—Messages from August 1996 through the Present
  ftp://ftp.rootsweb.com/pub/roots-l/messages/
- ROOTS-L Daily Index of Mailing List Messages
  http://www.rootsweb.com/roots-l/index/
- ROOTS-L Message Archives
  http://searches.rootsweb.com/roots-l.search.html

- ROOTS-L Recent Postings
  gopher://gort.canisius.edu/1m/.otherlib/.discussion/.lists/ROOTS-L

◆ ROOTS-L Library, Archives and Files

- ROOTS-L Archives
  ftp://ftp.rootsweb.com/pub/roots-l/
- ROOTS-L File Catalog
  ftp://ftp.rootsweb.com/pub/roots-l/roots-l.catalog
- ROOTS-L Helpfile
  ftp://ftp.rootsweb.com/pub/roots-l/roots-l.helpfile
- ROOTS-L Index of FAQ Files
  ftp://ftp.rootsweb.com/pub/roots-l/faq/faq.index
- ROOTS-L: Internet Resources for Genealogy
  http://www.rootsweb.com/roots-l/intergen.html
- ROOTS-L Library
  http://www.rootsweb.com/roots-l/filelist.html
  An amazing collection of articles and links for you to explore.

◆ Roots Databases

- Roots Location List Name Finder
  http://searches.rootsweb.com/cgi-bin/Genea/rll
  - ○ Roots Location List—Entries for North America
    ftp://ftp.rootsweb.com/pub/roots-l/family/family.locnamer
  - ○ Roots Location List—Entries for the Rest of the World
    ftp://ftp.rootsweb.com/pub/roots-l/family/family.locworld
  - ○ Roots Location List—Addresses of Submitters
    ftp://ftp.rootsweb.com/pub/roots-l/family/family.locaddr
- RootsWeb Surname List—Interactive Search
  http://rsl.rootsweb.com/cgi-bin/rslsql.cgi
  An easily searchable database maintained by volunteer Karen Isaacson. The RSL contains more than 600,000 surnames, submitted by nearly 75,000 genealogists.

- RSL Search Program—Alternate
  http://gen.roc.wayne.edu/fsl.html
  - ○ Overview of the RootsWeb Surname List (RSL)
    http://www.rootsweb.com/roots-l/family.readme.html
  - ○ RootsWeb Surname List—Interactive Data Edit/ Submission Form
    http://rsl.rootsweb.com/cgi-bin/rsledit.cgi
    - • RootsWeb Surname List Country Abbreviations
      http://www.rootsweb.com/roots-l/cabbrev1.html
      Listed by Country.
    - • Abbreviations from the RootsWeb Surname List
      http://www.rootsweb.com/roots-l/cabbrev2.html
      Listed by Abbreviation.
  - ○ RootsWeb Surname List: Index to Files
    http://www.rootsweb.com/roots-l/rsl-index.html
  - ○ RSL-UPDATE Mailing List
    http://members.aol.com/gfsjohnf/gen_mail_surnames-gen.html#RSL-UPDATE
    The RootsWeb Surname List database monthly update of new surnames.

◆ RootsWeb

- RootsWeb is home to thousands of genealogy mailing lists (http://www.rootsweb.com/~maillist), many genealogical society web sites (http://www.rootsweb.com/~websites/gensoc.htm), USGenWeb county and state web sites (http://www.rootsweb.com/~usgenweb/) several searchable databases (http://www.rootsweb.com/rootsweb/ searches/), many USGenWeb archive files (http://www.rootsweb.com/~websites/usgenweb.htm), and dozens of other users' web sites and genealogical resources. This volunteer effort has been created, maintained and largely financed by Dr. Brian Leverich and Karen Isaacson. The online genealogical community owes them much appreciation for their wonderful generosity and for the hundreds of hours they spend to make our online research time an easy, enjoyable and productive pastime! If you enjoy participating in genealogy mailing lists, please consider becoming a RootsWeb Sponsor (http://www.rootsweb.com/rootsweb/how-to-subscribe.html).

- RootsWeb Genealogical Data Cooperative
  http://www.rootsweb.com/
  - ○ How to Subscribe to RootsWeb
    http://www.rootsweb.com/rootsweb/how-to-subscribe.html
    - • Member Services
      http://www.rootsweb.com/rootsweb/members/
  - ○ More About RootsWeb
    http://www.rootsweb.com/rootsweb/more-about-rootsweb/

- RootsWeb Guest Pages
  http://www.rootsweb.com/~websites/

- RootsWeb Search Engines
  http://www.rootsweb.com/rootsweb/searches/

- User Mailing Lists Hosted by RootsWeb
  http://www.rootsweb.com/~maillist

ROYALTY & NOBILITY
http://www.CyndisList.com/royalty.htm

- 1066 List of Knights: List of Those Accompanying William the Conqueror on His Invasion of England in 1066
  http://www.rootsweb.com/~ote/knight.htm

- Ancestors of King Edward III of England and Philippa of Hainault
  http://uts.cc.utexas.edu/~churchh/edw3chrt.html

- The British Monarchy—The Official Web Site
  http://www.royal.gov.uk/

- The Courtly Lives of Royals, Peerage, Saints, and Their Genealogy
  http://members.aol.com/MJKnecht/index.html

- Dictionary of the Titled Nobility of Russia
  http://www.booksatoz.com/tims/genealogy/russian.htm

- European Royal and Nobility Genealogical Databases
  http://www.worldroots.com/brigitte/royal/royal00.htm
  From Brigitte Ingeborg Gastel. Historic and genealogical information about royal and nobility family lines.

  o History, Royal and Nobility Genealogy Data
    http://www.worldroots.com/brigitte/b9_index.html

    - The Ancient Holy Roman Empire
      http://www.worldroots.com/brigitte/royal/royal3.htm

    - Austria/Hungary Empire
      http://www.worldroots.com/brigitte/royal/royal10.htm

    - Descendants of Royalty, Historical Figures
      http://www.worldroots.com/brigitte/royal/royal11.htm

    - History of England in Medieval Times
      http://www.worldroots.com/brigitte/royal/royal8.htm

    - History of England in Medieval Times, Biographies and portraits of the English Royals
      http://www.worldroots.com/brigitte/royal/royal13.htm

    - History of England in Medieval Times, Irish and Scotish Royalty
      http://www.worldroots.com/brigitte/royal/royal14.htm

    - History of Europe in Medieval Times, Anglo-Saxons
      http://www.worldroots.com/brigitte/royal/royal7.htm

    - History of Europe in Medieval Times, France
      http://www.worldroots.com/brigitte/royal/royal6.htm

    - History of Europe in Medieval Times, Scandinavia
      http://www.worldroots.com/brigitte/royal/royal1.htm

- History of Europe, Slavic States
  http://www.worldroots.com/brigitte/royal/royal4.htm

- History of Europe, the Mediterranean
  http://www.worldroots.com/brigitte/royal/royal5.htm

- Links to Royal and Nobility Genealogy Data
  http://www.worldroots.com/brigitte/royal/royal.htm

- Monaco
  http://www.worldroots.com/brigitte/royal/royal12.htm

- My Family Research Pages on Descendants of Royal Historical Figures
  http://www.worldroots.com/brigitte/royal/royal17.htm

- Private Nobility/Royal Links
  http://www.worldroots.com/brigitte/royal/royal9.htm

- Royal Genealogical Data Research Books used by Brian C. Tompsett
  http://www.worldroots.com/brigitte/roybooks.htm

- Russian Royal Links
  http://www.worldroots.com/brigitte/royal/royal2.htm

- Family Tree Genealogical and Probate Research Bureau Ltd.
  http://www.familytree.hu/
  Professional research service covering the area of what was formerly the Austro-Hungarian Empire, including: Hungary, Slovakia, Czech Republic, Austria, Italy, Transylvania, Croatia, Slovenia, former Yugoslavia (Banat), and the Ukraine (Sub-Carpathian).

- Genealogical Gleanings—Royal & Noble Lineages of Tonga, Fiji, Hawaii, Burma and Cambodia
  http://www.uq.net.au/~zzhsoszy/index.html

- GenealogyBookShop.com—Royal and Noble
  http://www.genealogybookshop.com/genealogybookshop/files/General,Royal_and_Noble/index.html
  The online store of Genealogical Publishing Co., Inc. & Clearfield Company.

- Genealogy of Mankind from Adam to Japheth, Shem, and Ham
  http://www.geocities.com/Tokyo/4241/geneadm2.html

- Genealogy of the Royal Family of The Netherlands
  http://www.xs4all.nl/~kvenjb/gennl.htm

- GEN-ROYAL Mailing List
  http://members.aol.com/johnf14246/gen_mail_general.html#GEN-ROYAL

- The Imperial Family of Japan
  http://www.geocities.com/Tokyo/Temple/3953/
  Biographies and information for the emperors and their families since 1850.

- Joan's Royal Favourites & Links Page
  http://www.xs4all.nl/~kvenjb/favour.htm

- Kings & Queens of Europe
  http://www.camelotintl.com/royal/europe.html

- Kungl. Hovstaterna / The Royal Court in Sweden
  http://www.royalcourt.se/

- LFM van de Pas Genealogics
  http://www.iinet.net.au/~leovdpas/genealogics.html
  Over 300,000 entries in this database contain Royalty, Landed Gentry and all other levels of society.

- The Lineage of the Royal Princes of England
  http://www.geocities.com/CapitolHill/4793/

- Manorial Society of Great Britain
  http://www.msgb.co.uk/msgb/index.html

- Mark Humphrys' Family History Page
  http://www.ed.ac.uk/~humphrys/FamTree/

  - Royal Descents of Famous People
    http://www.ed.ac.uk/~humphrys/FamTree/Royal/famous.descents.html

- Monarchs of England
  http://www.britannia.com/history/monarchs/mondex.html

- The Noblemen of Bohun
  http://www.rand.org/personal/Genea/bohon.html

- Roman Emperors—The Imperial Index
  http://www.salve.edu/~dimaiom/impindex.html
  An Online Encyclopedia of Roman Emperors.

- Royal and Noble Genealogical Data on the Web
  http://www.dcs.hull.ac.uk/public/genealogy/GEDCOM.html

  - Directory of Royal Genealogical Data
    http://www.dcs.hull.ac.uk/public/genealogy/royal/
    and an alternate site
    http://www.tardis.ed.ac.uk/~bct/public/genealogy/royal/

    - Master Index to Royal Genealogical Data—Ordered by Lastname
      http://www.dcs.hull.ac.uk/public/genealogy/royal/gedx.html

- Royal Genealogies—Menu
  http://ftp.cac.psu.edu/~saw/royal/royalgen.html

- The Royal History Homepage
  http://www.ringnett.no/home/bjornstad/royals/

  - The Monarchs & Regents of Denmark for Near 1100 Years
    http://www.ringnett.no/home/bjornstad/royals/Denmark.html

  - The Monarchs & Regents of England & Great Britain for Near 1200 Years
    http://www.ringnett.no/home/bjornstad/royals/England.html

  - The Monarchs & Regents of Norway for Near 1150 Years
    http://www.ringnett.no/home/bjornstad/royals/Norway.html

  - The Monarchs & Regents of Scotland for Near 600 Years
    http://www.ringnett.no/home/bjornstad/royals/Scotland.html

  - The Monarchs & Regents of Sweden for Near 1000 Years
    http://www.ringnett.no/home/bjornstad/royals/Sweden.html

- The Royalty in History Site
  http://www.xs4all.nl/~kvenjb/kings.htm

- Some Family History of Charles, Prince of Wales
  http://www.uftree.com/UFT/FamousFamilyTrees/royal/FG/HTML/CHARLES/index.htm

- Uasal—A Server for Irish Nobility, Heraldry and Genealogy
  http://www.finearts.sfasu.edu/uasal/welcome.html

- WW-Person
  http://www8.informatik.uni-erlangen.de/html/ww-person.html
  A data base of the higher nobility in Europe.

SCANDINAVIA & THE NORDIC COUNTRIES INDEX

- ◆ General Scandinavia & Nordic Sites
- ◆ Denmark / Danmark
- ◆ Finland / Suomi
- ◆ Iceland / Ísland
- ◆ Norway / Norge
- ◆ Sweden / Sverige

GENERAL SCANDINAVIA & NORDIC SITES
http://www.CyndisList.com/genscan.htm

Category Index:

- General Resource Sites
- History & Culture
- Libraries, Archives & Museums
- Mailing Lists, Newsgroups & Chat

- People & Families
- Professional Researchers, Volunteers & Other Research Services
- Publications, Software & Supplies

◆ General Resource Sites

- Electronic Resources for the Scandinavian Scholar
  http://www.montana.edu/sass/resource.htm
  From the Society for the Advancement of Scandinavian Study.

- Greenlandic Resources
  http://www.montana.edu/sass/greenlnd.htm
  From the Society for the Advancement of Scandinavian Study.

- NORDGUIDE
  http://info.rbt.no/nordguide/nordguide.html
  A directory of databases in the Nordic Countries.

- Nordic Notes on the Net
  http://nordicnotes.com/

- Yahoo!...Scandinavia...Genealogy
  http://dir.yahoo.com/Arts/Humanities/History/Genealogy/
  Regional_and_Ethnic_Resources/Scandinavia/

◆ History & Culture

- History of Europe in Medieval Times, Scandinavia
  http://www.worldroots.com/brigitte/royal/royal1.htm
  Historic and genealogical information about royal and nobility family lines.

◆ Libraries, Archives & Museums

- The Faroese National Archives
  http://www.sleipnir.fo/natarc.htm

◆ Mailing Lists, Newsgroups & Chat

- GEN-NORDIC Mailing List
  http://members.aol.com/gfsjohnf/gen_mail_country-
  den.html#GEN-NORDIC
  For the discussion of genealogy in the Scandinavian countries, including: Denmark, Finland, Greenland, Iceland, Norway and Sweden. Gatewayed with the soc.genealogy.nordic newsgroup.

◆ People & Families

- Sami Resources
  http://www.montana.edu/sass/sami.htm
  From the Society for the Advancement of Scandinavian Study.

- Scandinavian Saints
  http://www.vii.com/~nelsonb/scand.htm
  From the Tracing Mormon Pioneers web site. For researching members of the LDS church from the Scandinavian Mission in the time period of 1852–1868.

◆ Professional Researchers, Volunteers & Other Research Services

- A Net Information Services—Genealogical Research—Finland and Scandinavia
  http://event.jyu.fi/ajantieto/
  Professional researchers.

◆ Publications, Software & Supplies

- Frontier Press Bookstore—Scandinavian Ancestry
  http://www.frontierpress.com/frontier.cgi?category=sca
  Books for sale.

- JamoDat—Win-Family Software
  http://www.jamodat.dk/
  Available in Danish, Swedish, Norwegian, French, German and English.

DENMARK / DANMARK
http://www.CyndisList.com/denmark.htm

Category Index:

- General Resource Sites
- Government & Cities
- History & Culture
- Language & Names
- Libraries, Archives & Museums
- Mailing Lists, Newsgroups & Chat
- Maps, Gazetteers & Geographical Information
- Newspapers

- People & Families
- Professional Researchers, Volunteers & Other Research Services
- Publications, Software & Supplies
- Records: Census, Cemeteries, Land, Obituaries, Personal, Taxes and Vital
- Religion & Churches
- Societies & Groups

◆ General Resource Sites

- The Danish Genealogical Research Guide / Hvem Forsker Hvad
  http://www.hvemforskerhvad.dk/

- Danish Resources
  http://www.montana.edu/sass/denmark.htm
  From the Society for the Advancement of Scandinavian Study.

- Danmark Genealogy Resources
  http://members.tripod.com/~Youda/denmark.htm

- Faroese Resources
  http://www.montana.edu/sass/faroe.htm
  From the Society for the Advancement of Scandinavian Study.

- Greenlandic Resources
  http://www.montana.edu/sass/greenlnd.htm
  From the Society for the Advancement of Scandinavian Study.

- NORDGUIDE
  http://info.rbt.no/nordguide/nordguide.html
  A directory of databases in the Nordic Countries.

- Nordic Notes on the Net
  http://nordicnotes.com/
  ○ Denmark Genealogy
    http://nordicnotes.com/html/denmark.html

◆ Government & Cities

- City.Net Directory—Denmark
  http://www.city.net/countries/denmark/

- City.Net Directory—Faroe Islands
  http://www.city.net/countries/faroe_islands/

- Yahoo!...Denmark...Cities and Towns
  http://dir.yahoo.com/Regional/Countries/Denmark/Cities_and_Towns/

- Yahoo!...Denmark...Counties
  http://dir.yahoo.com/Regional/Countries/Denmark/Counties/

◆ History & Culture

- History of Europe in Medieval Times, Scandinavia
  http://www.worldroots.com/brigitte/royal/royal1.htm
  Historic and genealogical information about royal and nobility family lines.

◆ Language & Names

- Danish-English Genealogy Dictionary
  http://ourworld.compuserve.com/homepages/NormanMadsen/danish.htm

- Origins of Danish Names
  http://www.ida.net/users/dhanco/dnames.htm

- Show the ANDERSENs
  http://www.bear.dk/
  Danish-English Dictionary of often used genealogy words; a short guide of Danish names and their tradition; links. MORS, AARHUS, FYN, JORDAN.

◆ Libraries, Archives & Museums

- Århus Kommunes Biblioteker / The Public Libraries of Aarhus
  http://www.aakb.bib.dk/

- The Danish Archives
  http://ourworld.compuserve.com/homepages/paulvanv/danishar.htm
  A description and informational site.

- Danish Emigration Archive At Aalborg
  http://feefhs.org/dk/frg-deaa.html
  FEEFHS Resource Guide Listing.

- Danish Emigration Archives
  http://users.cybercity.dk/~ccc13656/uk/home2.htm
  Searchable database for 1869 to 1904, working on records thru 1940.

- Danish Immigrant Archive at Dana College
  http://www.dana.edu/~pformo/archive.htm
  Blair, Nebraska

- Danish State Archives—Statens Arkiver
  http://www.sa.dk/

- HYTELNET—Library Catalogs: Denmark
  http://library.usask.ca/hytelnet/dk0/dk000.html
  Before you use any of the Telnet links, make note of the user name, password and any other logon information.

- Roskilde Bibliotek / Roskilde Library
  http://www.roskildebib.dk/

- The Royal Library, Copenhagen
  http://www.kb.bib.dk/

- webCATS: Library Catalogues on the World Wide Web—Denmark
  http://library.usask.ca/hywebcat/countries/DK.html

◆ Mailing Lists, Newsgroups & Chat

- dk.historie.genealogi Newsgroup
  news:dk.historie.genealogi

- GEN-NORDIC Mailing List
  http://members.aol.com/gfsjohnf/gen_mail_country-den.html#GEN-NORDIC
  For the discussion of genealogy in the Scandinavian countries, including: Denmark, Finland, Greenland, Iceland, Norway and Sweden. Gatewayed with the soc.genealogy.nordic newsgroup.

◆ Maps, Gazetteers & Geographical Information

- Map of Denmark
  http://www.lib.utexas.edu/Libs/PCL/Map_collection/europe/Denmark.jpg
  From the Perry-Castañeda Library at the Univ. of Texas at Austin.

◆ Newspapers

- AJR NewsLink—Denmark Newspapers
  http://www.newslink.org/euden.html

- AJR NewsLink—Faroe Islands Newspapers
  http://www.newslink.org/eufar.html

- E&P Media Info Links—Newspaper Sites in Denmark
  http://www.mediainfo.com/emediajs/browse-results.htm?region=denmark&category=newspaper+++++++++

- The Ultimate Collection of News Links: Denmark
  http://www.pppp.net/links/news/Denmark.html

- Yahoo!...Newspapers...Denmark
  http://dir.yahoo.com/News_and_Media/Newspapers/Browse_By_Region/Countries/Denmark/

◆ People & Families

- Bjorn's Genealogy
  http://home4.inet.tele.dk/skin_rup/
  SKINNERUP

- Henriette IDESTRUPs hjemmeside om slægtsforskning
  http://users.cybercity.dk/~bkb2098/INDEX.HTML
  From Thisted County, Hjoerring County, Aalborg City and Soroe County, Denmark.

- The Monarchs & Regents of Denmark for Near 1100 Years
  http://www.ringnett.no/home/bjornstad/royals/Denmark.html

- Scandinavian Saints
  http://www.vii.com/~nelsonb/scand.htm
  From the Tracing Mormon Pioneers web site. For researching members of the LDS church from the Scandinavian Mission in the time period of 1852–1868.

◆ Professional Researchers, Volunteers & Other Research Services

- Genealogy Helplist—Denmark
  http://www.image.dk/~alexandr/helplist.html

- genealogyPro—Directory of Genealogists for Denmark
  http://genealogyPro.com/directories/Denmark.html

◆ Publications, Software & Supplies

- Books We Own—Denmark
  http://www.rootsweb.com/~bwo/denmark.html

- Brother's Keeper Software
  http://ourworld.compuserve.com/homepages/Brothers_Keeper/
  Downloadable shareware program for Windows. The latest version contains English, French, Norwegian, Danish, Swedish, German, and Dutch.

- Frontier Press Bookstore—Scandinavian Ancestry
  http://www.frontierpress.com/frontier.cgi?category=sca

- Hvem Forsker Hvad / Danish Genealogical Research Guide
  http://www.hvemforskerhvad.dk
  In English & Danish, a guide to Danish research published annually.

- JamoDat—Win-Family Software
  http://www.jamodat.dk/
  Available in Danish, Swedish, Norwegian, French, German and English.

◆ Records: Census, Cemeteries, Land, Obituaries, Personal, Taxes and Vital (Born, Married, Died & Buried)

- DDD Danish Demographic Database
  http://ddd.sa.dk/ddd2.htm
  Search a partial census database for 1787–1850 and the Danish emigrant database for 1868–1900.

◆ Religion & Churches

- Christianity.Net Church Locator—Denmark
  http://www.christianity.net/cgi/location.exe?Denmark

- Churches of the World—Denmark
  http://www.churchsurf.com/churches/world/Denmark/
  From the ChurchSurf Christian Directory.

◆ Societies & Groups

- Archer's Computer Interest Group List—Denmark
  http://www.genealogy.org/~ngs/cigs/ngl3otdk.html

- Danish-American Genealogical Group
  http://www.mtn.org/mgs/branches/danish.html

- Dansk Slægtsgårdsforening / Danish Society for Family Farms
  http://www.gbar.dtu.dk/~c957051/slaegtsgaard/

- DIS-Danmark—Databehandling i Slægtsforskning
  http://users.cybercity.dk/~dko6959/

- Roskildeegnens Selskab for Genealogi og Personalhistorie / Genealogy Society in Roskilde, Denmark
  http://www.webpoint.dk/jvo/rsgp/

- Ry Slægtshistoriske Forening / Ry Genealogical Society
  http://home3.inet.tele.dk/kaagaard/

FINLAND / SUOMI
http://www.CyndisList.com/finland.htm

Category Index:

◆ General Resource Sites
◆ Government & Cities
◆ History & Culture
◆ Libraries, Archives & Museums
◆ Mailing Lists, Newsgroups & Chat
◆ Maps, Gazetteers & Geographical Information
◆ Newspapers
◆ People & Families

◆ Professional Researchers, Volunteers & Other Research Services
◆ Publications, Software & Supplies
◆ Queries, Message Boards & Surname Lists
◆ Records: Census, Cemeteries, Land, Obituaries, Personal, Taxes and Vital
◆ Religion & Churches
◆ Societies & Groups

◆ General Resource Sites

● English-Finnish Dictionary
http://www.mofile.fi/-db.htm

● Family History Finland—World GenWeb
http://www.open.org/rumcd/genweb/finn.html

● Finnish Resources
http://www.montana.edu/sass/finland.htm
From the Society for the Advancement of Scandinavian Study.

● Genealogy & Family History—David S. Saari, Ph.D.
http://members.aol.com/dssaari/index.htm

  ○ Beginner's Guide to Finnish Family History Research
  http://members.aol.com/dssaari/guide.htm

● NORDGUIDE
http://info.rbt.no/nordguide/nordguide.html
A directory of databases in the Nordic Countries.

● Nordic Notes on the Net
http://nordicnotes.com/

  ○ Finland Genealogy
  http://nordicnotes.com/html/finland.html

● Sukututkimus Suomessa—Finnish Genealogy
http://home.kolumbus.fi/~sepa/suomessa.html
In Finnish.

● Sukututkimusta Suomessa / Genealogical Research in Finland
http://www.genealogia.org/

◆ Government & Cities

● City.Net Directory—Finland
http://www.city.net/countries/finland/

● Yahoo!...Finland...Cities and Towns
http://dir.yahoo.com/Regional/Countries/Finland/Cities_and_Towns/

◆ History & Culture

● History of Europe in Medieval Times, Scandinavia
http://www.worldroots.com/brigitte/royal/royal1.htm
Historic and genealogical information about royal and nobility family lines.

◆ Libraries, Archives & Museums

● Äänekosken kaupunginkirjasto—Aanekoski City Library
http://www.aanekoski.fi/kirjasto/

● Fredrika Biblioteken
http://www.kustnet.fi/~fredrika/

● HELKA—The Helsinki University Libraries OPAC
http://renki.helsinki.fi/gabriel/en/countries/finland-opac-en.html
Catalog of the Helsinki University Library system. It has a large collection of official publications of the former Russian Empire.

● Helsinki City Library / Helsingin Kaupunginkirjasto
http://www.lib.hel.fi/

● HYTELNET—Library Catalogs: Finland
http://library.usask.ca/hytelnet/fi0/fi000.html
Before you use any of the Telnet links, make note of the user name, password and any other logon information.

● MUISTI Tietokanta / Databas / Data Base
http://linnea.helsinki.fi/~muisti/MUISTI.html
The joint database of digitized national material of libraries, archives, and museums.

● National Repository Library
http://www.varasto.uku.fi/

- webCATS: Library Catalogues on the World Wide Web—Finland
  http://library.usask.ca/hywebcat/countries/Fl.html

◆ Mailing Lists, Newsgroups & Chat

- FINNGEN Mailing List
  http://members.aol.com/gfsjohnf/gen_mail_country-fin.html#FINNGEN

- GEN-NORDIC Mailing List
  http://members.aol.com/gfsjohnf/gen_mail_country-den.html#GEN-NORDIC
  For the discussion of genealogy in the Scandinavian countries, including: Denmark, Finland, Greenland, Iceland, Norway and Sweden. Gatewayed with the soc.genealogy.nordic newsgroup.

◆ Maps, Gazetteers & Geographical Information

- Map of Finland
  http://www.lib.utexas.edu/Libs/PCL/Map_collection/europe/Finland.jpg
  From the Perry-Castañeda Library at the Univ. of Texas at Austin.

◆ Newspapers

- AJR NewsLink—Finland Newspapers
  http://www.newslink.org/eufin.html

- E&P Media Info Links—Newspaper Sites in Finland
  http://www.mediainfo.com/emediajs/browse-results.htm?region=finland&category=newspaper+++++++++

- The Ultimate Collection of News Links: Finland
  http://www.pppp.net/links/news/Finland.html

◆ People & Families

- MÄNTTÄRI Family Association Ltd.
  http://www.kolumbus.fi/manttari/home-pag/main.htm

- Sami Resources
  http://www.montana.edu/sass/sami.htm
  From the Society for the Advancement of Scandinavian Study.

◆ Professional Researchers, Volunteers & Other Research Services

- A Net Information Services—Genealogical Research—Finland and Scandinavia
  http://event.jyu.fi/ajantieto/
  Professional researchers.

- Genealogy Helplist—Finland
  http://jocke.twistercom.fi/suku.html

- genealogyPro—Professional Genealogists for Finland
  http://genealogyPro.com/directories/Finland.html

◆ Publications, Software & Supplies

- Books We Own—Finland
  http://www.rootsweb.com/~bwo/finland.html

- Frontier Press Bookstore—Scandinavian Ancestry
  http://www.frontierpress.com/frontier.cgi?category=sca

- JamoDat—Win-Family Software
  http://www.jamodat.dk/
  Available in Danish, Swedish, Norwegian, French, German and English.

◆ Queries, Message Boards & Surname Lists

- FINNDEX—The Finnish Genealogical Research Index
  http://members.aol.com/finndex/finndex.htm

◆ Records: Census, Cemeteries, Land, Obituaries, Personal, Taxes and Vital (Born, Married, Died & Buried)

- National Land Survey of Finland
  http://www.nls.fi/index_e.html

◆ Religion & Churches

- Churches dot Net—Global Church Web Pages—Finland
  http://www.churches.net/churches/internat.htm#finland

- Churches of the World—Finland
  http://www.churchsurf.com/churches/world/Finland/
  From the ChurchSurf Christian Directory.

◆ Societies & Groups

- Archer's Computer Interest Group List—Finland
  http://www.genealogy.org/~ngs/cigs/ngl3otfi.html

- Cokato Finnish-American Historical Society
  http://cokato.mn.us/org/fahs.html
  Cokato, Minnesota

- Finnish American Heritage Society of CT
  http://www.rt.com/fahs-ct/
  Connecticut

- Finnish-American Historical Society of the West
  http://www.teleport.com/~finamhsw/
  Portland, Oregon

- Genealogical Society of Finland
  http://www.genealogia.org/ssse.htm

- Sukututkimusyhdistyksiä—Släktforskarföreningar—Genealogical Societies
  http://www.genealogia.org/stutkyh/index.htm

- Swedish Finn Historical Society
  http://home1.gte.net/SFHS/index.htm
  Seattle, Washington

ICELAND / ÍSLAND
http://www.CyndisList.com/iceland.htm

Category Index:

- General Resource Sites
- Government & Cities
- History & Culture
- Libraries, Archives & Museums
- Mailing Lists, Newsgroups & Chat
- Maps, Gazetteers & Geographical Information
- Newspapers

- Professional Researchers, Volunteers & Other Research Services
- Publications, Software & Supplies
- Records: Census, Cemeteries, Land, Obituaries, Personal, Taxes and Vital
- Societies & Groups

◆ General Resource Sites

- Icelandic GenWeb
  http://nyherji.is/~halfdan/aett/aettvef.htm

- Icelandic Last Names
  http://www.cs.umd.edu/~bthj/bthj/nofn.html

- Icelandic Names
  http://www.itn.is/~gunnsi/family.htm

- Icelandic Resources
  http://www.montana.edu/sass/iceland.htm
  From the Society for the Advancement of Scandinavian Study.

- NORDGUIDE
  http://info.rbt.no/nordguide/nordguide.html
  A directory of databases in the Nordic Countries.

- Nordic Notes on the Net
  http://nordicnotes.com/
  - Iceland Genealogy
    http://nordicnotes.com/html/iceland.html

- Yahoo!...Iceland...Genealogy
  http://dir.yahoo.com/Regional/Countries/Iceland/Arts_and_Humanities/History/Genealogy/

◆ Government & Cities

- City.Net Directory—Iceland
  http://www.city.net/countries/iceland/

- Yahoo!...Iceland...Cities and Towns
  http://dir.yahoo.com/Regional/Countries/Iceland/Cities_and_Towns/

◆ History & Culture

- A Bit about Icelandic Culture
  http://www.eyeoniceland.com/culture.html

- The Emigration from Iceland to America
  http://nyherji.is/~halfdan/westward/vestur.htm

- History of Europe in Medieval Times, Scandinavia
  http://www.worldroots.com/brigitte/royal/royal1.htm
  Historic and genealogical information about royal and nobility family lines.

- History of Iceland
  http://www.arctic.is/islandia/history/

◆ Libraries, Archives & Museums

- HYTELNET—Library Catalogs: Iceland
  http://library.usask.ca/hytelnet/is0/is000.html
  Before you use any of the Telnet links, make note of the user name, password and any other logon information.

- Landsbókasafn Íslands—Háskólabókasafn / National and University Library of Iceland
  http://www.bok.hi.is/

◆ Mailing Lists, Newsgroups & Chat

- ICELAND Mailing List
  http://members.aol.com/gfsjohnf/gen_mail_country-ice.html#ICELAND

- GEN-NORDIC Mailing List
  http://members.aol.com/gfsjohnf/gen_mail_country-den.html#GEN-NORDIC
  For the discussion of genealogy in the Scandinavian countries, including: Denmark, Finland, Greenland, Iceland, Norway and Sweden. Gatewayed with the soc.genealogy.nordic newsgroup.

◆ Maps, Gazetteers & Geographical Information

- Lonely Planet—Iceland Map
  http://www.lonelyplanet.com/dest/eur/graphics/map-ice.htm

- Map of Iceland
  http://www.lib.utexas.edu/Libs/PCL/Map_collection/europe/Iceland.GIF
  From the Perry-Castañeda Library at the Univ. of Texas at Austin.

◆ Newspapers

- AJR NewsLink—Iceland Newspapers
  http://www.newslink.org/euice.html

- E&P Media Info Links—Newspaper Sites in Iceland
  http://www.mediainfo.com/emediajs/browse-results.htm?region=iceland&category=newspaper+++++++++

- The Ultimate Collection of News Links: Iceland
  http://www.pppp.net/links/news/Iceland.html

◆ Professional Researchers, Volunteers & Other Research Services

- Genealogy Helplist—Iceland
  http://posom.com/hl/isl/index.shtml

◆ Publications, Software & Supplies

- Frontier Press Bookstore—Scandinavian Ancestry
  http://www.frontierpress.com/frontier.cgi?category=sca

- JamoDat—Win-Family Software
  http://www.jamodat.dk/
  Available in Danish, Swedish, Norwegian, French, German and English.

◆ Records: Census, Cemeteries, Land, Obituaries, Personal, Taxes and Vital (Born, Married, Died & Buried)

- The National Registry
  http://www.statice.is/depart/natreg.htm
  A register of all those who have been domiciled in Iceland since 1952.

- Registration: To all people of Icelandic origin living in the United States and Canada
  http://www.iceland.org/regist.htm

◆ Societies & Groups

- Icelandic Genealogical Society
  http://nyherji.is/~halfdan/aett/aettengl.htm

NORWAY / NORGE
http://www.CyndisList.com/norway.htm

Category Index:

- General Resource Sites
- Government & Cities
- History & Culture
- How To
- Language & Names
- Libraries, Archives & Museums
- Mailing Lists, Newsgroups & Chat
- Maps, Gazetteers & Geographical Information
- Newspapers

- People & Families
- Professional Researchers, Volunteers & Other Research Services
- Publications, Software & Supplies
- Records: Census, Cemeteries, Land, Obituaries, Personal, Taxes and Vital
- Religion & Churches
- Societies & Groups

◆ General Resource Sites

- Ancestors from Norway
  http://members.xoom.com/follesdal/
  Research guide for Norwegian-American genealogy.

- Arne Moen's Home Page from Norway
  http://home.sol.no/~amoen/genealogi.html
  In Norwegian with many links to Scandinavian genealogy sites.

- Bamble Genealogiske Side / Bamble Genealogical Page
  http://home.sol.no/~sorter/
  Including probate records from Bamble & Langesund.

- Kragerø Genealogical Page. By Per Stian Bjørnø Kjendal
  http://home.sol.no/~kjendal/engelsk.html
  Many Norwegian resources, especially for the Kragerø area, including maps, records sources and an index of those who emigrated during 1843–1899.

- Medieval Scandinavia
  http://www.ringnett.no/home/bjornstad/
  Previously the The Bjørnstad History and Genealogy Web Site of Norway. Information for Hemsedal, Hallingdal, Ringerike and Hole of Buskerud County and Lom/Vågå in Gudbrandsdal of Oppland County.

- NORDGUIDE
  http://info.rbt.no/nordguide/nordguide.html
  A directory of databases in the Nordic Countries.

- Nordic Notes on the Net
  http://nordicnotes.com/
  ○ Norwegian Genealogy
    http://nordicnotes.com/html/norway.html

- Norway Genealogy—World GenWeb
  http://www.rootsweb.com/~wgnorway/

- Norway Roots—Norske Røtter og Slektsgransking
  http://www.geocities.com/Heartland/3856/

- Norwegian Resources
  http://www.montana.edu/sass/norway.htm
  From the Society for the Advancement of Scandinavian Study.

- Skien Genealogiske Side / Skien Genealogical Page
  http://login.eunet.no/~jchriste/
  Including tax lists & parish registers.

◆ Government & Cities

- City.Net Directory—Norway
  http://www.city.net/countries/norway/

- Luster Kommune
  http://fjordinfo.vestdata.no/offentleg/kommunar/lusterkomm/luster.htm

- Yahoo!...Norway...Cities and Towns
  http://dir.yahoo.com/Regional/Countries/Norway/Cities_and_Towns/

- Yahoo!...Norway...Counties
  http://dir.yahoo.com/Regional/Countries/Norway/Counties/

◆ History & Culture

- The Currency and Measurements History Lexicon of Norway
  http://www.ringnett.no/home/bjornstad/measure/Index.html

- History of Europe in Medieval Times, Scandinavia
  http://www.worldroots.com/brigitte/royal/royal1.htm
  Historic and genealogical information about royal and nobility family lines.

- The History of Norway—from ODIN
  http://odin.dep.no/html/nofovalt/depter/ud/nornytt/uda-286.html

- Medieval Scandinavia
  http://www.ringnett.no/home/bjornstad/
  Previously the The Bjørnstad History and Genealogy Web Site of Norway. Information for Hemsedal, Hallingdal, Ringerike and Hole of Buskerud County and Lom/Vågå in Gudbrandsdal of Oppland County.

- The Viking History Homepage
  http://www.ringnett.no/home/bjornstad/vikings/index.html

◆ How To

- Ancestors from Norway
  http://members.xoom.com/follesdal/
  Research guide for Norwegian-American genealogy.

  o Ancestors from Norway—Getting Started
    http://members.xoom.com/follesdal/na15.html

  o Hvordan Finner Jeg Etterkommere Av De Som Utvandret Til USA? / How Do I Find Descendants of a Norwegian Immigrant to the USA?
    http://members.xoom.com/follesdal/na14.html
    In Norwegian; for Norwegians who are tracing descendants of a Norwegian immigrant to the USA.

- How To Trace Your Ancestors in Norway
  http://www.norway.org/ancestor.htm

- How to Trace Your Ancestors in Norway— From ODIN
  http://odin.dep.no/html/nofovalt/depter/ud/publ/96/ancestors/prep.html

- Norwegian Genealogy How To Guide
  http://www.familytreemaker.com/00000378.html

◆ Language & Names

- Norwegian Naming Practices
  http://www.uib.no/hi/nameprac.htm

◆ Libraries, Archives & Museums

- Fylkesarkivet i Sogn og Fjordane— Utvandring—Emigration
  http://www.sffarkiv.no/sffutv.htm
  Norway

- HYTELNET—Library Catalogs: Norway
  http://library.usask.ca/hytelnet/no0/no000.html
  Before you use any of the Telnet links, make note of the user name, password and any other logon information.

- The Norwegian Emigration Center
  http://www.utvandrersenteret.no/index.htm
  Stavanger

- The Norwegian Emigrant Museum
  http://www.hamarnett.no/emigrantmuseum/

- Registreringssentral for Historiske Data (RHD) / Norwegian Historical Data Centre (NHDC)
  http://www.isv.uit.no/seksjon/rhd/

- Universitetsbiblioteket i Oslo—UBO / University of Oslo Library (UBO)
  http://www.ub.uio.no/
  Norway

- Vesterheim Genealogical Center and Naeseth Library
  http://www.salamander.com/~vesterheim/madison.html
  Madison, Wisconsin

- webCATS: Library Catalogues on the World Wide Web—Norway
  http://library.usask.ca/hywebcat/countries/NO.html

◆ Mailing Lists, Newsgroups & Chat

- GEN-NORDIC Mailing List
  http://members.aol.com/gfsjohnf/gen_mail_country-den.html#GEN-NORDIC
  For the discussion of genealogy in the Scandinavian countries, including: Denmark, Finland, Greenland, Iceland, Norway and Sweden. Gatewayed with the soc.genealogy.nordic newsgroup.

- NORWAY Mailing List
  http://members.aol.com/gfsjohnf/gen_mail_country-nor.html#NORWAY

- NO-SLEKT Mailing List
  http://members.aol.com/gfsjohnf/gen_mail_country-nor.html#NO-SLEKT
  Gatewayed with the news:no.slekt

- no.slekt newsgroup
  Norwegian genealogy conference covering any topic in genealogy except computer programs for genealogical use and searches for lost relatives and ancestors. The conference is conducted in Norwegian.

- NO-SLEKT-ETTERLYSNING Mailing List
  http://members.aol.com/gfsjohnf/gen_mail_country-nor.html#NO-SLEKT-ETT
  Gatewayed with the news:no.slekt.etterlysning

- no.slekt.etterlysning newsgroup
  Norwegian genealogy conference for searching relatives and ancestors in Norway and eventual discussions of such searches if there are dubious links published. The conference is conducted in Norwegian.

- NO-SLEKT-PROGRAMMER Mailing List
  http://members.aol.com/gfsjohnf/gen_mail_country-nor.html#NO-SLEKT-PROG
  Gatewayed with the news:no.slekt.programmer

- no.slekt.programmer newsgroup
  Norwegian genealogy conference for discussion of computer programs and other computer-related questions as they relate to genealogy. The conference is conducted in Norwegian.

- VALDRES Mailing List
  http://members.aol.com/gfsjohnf/gen_mail_country-nor.html#VALDRES
  For the discussion and sharing of information regarding the Valdres region of Norway and immigrants from that region.

◆ Maps, Gazetteers & Geographical Information

- Map of Norway
  http://www.lib.utexas.edu/Libs/PCL/Map_collection/europe/
  Norway.GIF
  From the Perry-Castañeda Library at the Univ. of Texas at Austin.

◆ Newspapers

- Aftenposten Interaktiv
  http://www.aftenposten.no/
  Oslo, Norway

- AJR NewsLink—Norway Newspapers
  http://www.newslink.org/eunor.html

- E&P Media Info Links—Newspaper Sites in Norway
  http://www.mediainfo.com/emediajs/browse-
  results.htm?region=norway&category=newspaper+++++++++

- The Ultimate Collection of News Links: Norway
  http://www.pppp.net/links/news/Norway.html

- Yahoo!...Newspapers...Norway
  http://dir.yahoo.com/News_and_Media/Newspapers/Regional/
  Countries/Norway/

◆ People & Families

- Arne MOEN's Home Page from Norway
  http://home.sol.no/~amoen/genealogi.html
  In Norwegian with many links to Scandinavian genealogy sites.

- Homepage of Hilde WAASETH & Per Ivar NICOLAISEN
  http://w1.2741.telia.com/~u274100021/
  From Norway. KJELVIK and MYRLAND in Minnesota, USA, RØSET, NICOLAISEN / NIKOLAISEN, KOEHL / KØHL, REITAN, LERHAGEN, GULSTAD, ESAIASSEN.

- Hr. Åkre's Family History—Åkre Slekthistorie og Slektregister
  http://www.primenet.com/~akre/family.html
  AKRE (ÅKRE), VANVIK, HAMMER, ENEBERG, MONTGOMERY

- Jangaarden / The JANGAARD Home Page
  http://w1.2701.telia.com/~u270100245/
  For descendants of Jangaarden and people related to anybody from Jangaarden. GISKE, GISKEGJERDE, SKJONG, VALDERHAUG, SÆTER, NORDSTRAND, URKEDAL, NØRVE, FARSTAD, HUSØY.

- OJ's Homepage—Otto JORGENSEN
  http://home.sol.no/~ojorgens/

- The Royal History Homepage
  http://www.ringnett.no/home/bjornstad/royals/

  - The Monarchs & Regents of Norway for Near 1150 Years
    http://www.ringnett.no/home/bjornstad/royals/Norway.html

- Sami Resources
  http://www.montana.edu/sass/sami.htm
  From the Society for the Advancement of Scandinavian Study.

- Stein Norem WISTED's Genealogy pages
  http://www.sorco.no/~snw/sokn-eng.htm
  Includes pages on Sokndal parish in Rogaland, Norway.

- Svein ULVUND Home Page
  http://login.eunet.no/~ulvund/
  SUNDVE, SKJERVHEIM, ULVUND, LID

- Sverre Geir LUDWIGSEN's Home Page
  http://home.sol.no/~sgl/index.htm
  FOSS, LEIN, WAAGØ, SANDØY, LUDWIGSEN, CASPERÆTTEN, FRENGEN. Norway, Sweden, Denmark, Germany, USA, Canada back to year 1490.

◆ Professional Researchers, Volunteers & Other Research Services

- Genealogy Helplist—Norway
  http://posom.com/hl/nor/index.shtml

- genealogyPro—Professional Genealogists for Norway
  http://genealogyPro.com/directories/Norway.html

- Molander's Genealogy Service
  http://www.algonet.se/~family/
  Professional researchers for Sweden and Norway.

◆ Publications, Software & Supplies

- Books We Own—Norway
  http://www.rootsweb.com/~bwo/norway.html

- Brother's Keeper Software
  http://ourworld.compuserve.com/homepages/Brothers_Keeper/
  Downloadable shareware program for Windows. The latest version contains English, French, Norwegian, Danish, Swedish, German, and Dutch.

- FAMILIE_OG_SLEKT Mailing List
  http://members.aol.com/johnf14246/
  gen_mail_software.html#FAMILIE_OG_SLEKT
  For discussions of the "Familie og Slekt" Norwegian genealogy software program.

- Frontier Press Bookstore—Scandinavian Ancestry
  http://www.frontierpress.com/frontier.cgi?category=sca

- Heritage Books—Norwegian
  http://www.heritagebooks.com/norweg.htm

- JamoDat—Win-Family Software
  http://www.jamodat.dk/
  Available in Danish, Swedish, Norwegian, French, German and English.

◆ Records: Census, Cemeteries, Land, Obituaries, Personal, Taxes and Vital (Born, Married, Died & Buried)

- Fylkesarkivet i Sogn og Fjordane—Databases
  http://www.sffarkiv.no/sffbasar/default.asp

- Getting into the Norwegian Census
  http://www.isv.uit.no/seksjon/rhd/nhdc/michael02.htm

- Gjerpen—Slekt
  http://home.sol.no/~gstrom/
  Including census & churchbook resources.

- Norway—1801 Census
  http://www.uib.no/hi/1801page.html

- Porsgrunn Genealogiske Side / Porsgrunn Genealogical Page
  http://home.sol.no/~holmjohn/
  Including church books & probate records for Brevik, land records for Eidanger.

- Teleslekt
  http://teleslekt.nbr.no/
  A database project; census.

◆ Religion & Churches

- Christianity.Net Church Locator—Norway
  http://www.christianity.net/cgi/location.exe?Norway

- The Church and Parish Homepage
  http://www.ringnett.no/home/bjornstad/church/Index.html

- Churches dot Net—Global Church Web Pages—Norway
  http://www.churches.net/churches/internat.htm#nor

- Churches of the World—Norway
  http://www.churchsurf.com/churches/world/Norway/
  From the ChurchSurf Christian Directory.

◆ Societies & Groups

- Archer's Computer Interest Group List—Norway
  http://www.genealogy.org/~ngs/cigs/ngl3otno.html

- Dis Nord-Trøndelag
  http://w1.2741.telia.com/~u274100021/dis/
  Computer group in Steinkjer, Norway.

- DIS-Norges hjemmeside in Norwegian
  http://www.sn.no/disnorge/

- Grenland Genealogy Society
  http://home.sol.no/~kjendal/grenland.html
  Part of Telemark in Norway.

- Lee Internet Club
  http://www.listservice.net/lee/lee1e.htm
  The Home Page for you who have Norwegian ancestors, particularly from Vik in Sogn.

- The Norwegian-American Bygdelagenes Fellesraad
  http://www.lexiaintl.org/sylte/bygdelag.html

- Norwegian-American Historical Association
  http://www.stolaf.edu/stolaf/other/naha/naha.html

- Norwegian Emigrant Museum Genealogical Society
  http://www.hamarnett.no/emigrantmuseum/gensocie.htm
  Norway

- Norwegian Genealogy Computer Interest Group
  http://www.uio.no/~achristo/genealog.html

- Sognefjordlaget in America
  http://home.c2i.net/bolstad/sfjlag.htm

- Sons of Norway Home Page
  http://www.sofn.com/

- Sons of Norway, Innherad Lodge
  http://www.amilar.com/SON/Am_idx.html
  Levanger, Norway

- Sons of Norway, NordTex Lodge 1-594, Dallas, Texas
  http://web2.airmail.net/gus/nordtex.htm

- Telelaget of America—A Norwegian-American bygdelag
  http://www.geocities.com/Heartland/Hills/1545/
  Bloomington, Minnesota

SWEDEN / SVERIGE
http://www.CyndisList.com/sweden.htm

Category Index:

- General Resource Sites
- Government & Cities
- History & Culture
- How To
- Language & Names
- Libraries, Archives & Museums
- Mailing Lists, Newsgroups & Chat
- Maps, Gazetteers & Geographical Information
- Newspapers

- People & Families
- Professional Researchers, Volunteers & Other Research Services
- Publications, Software & Supplies
- Queries, Message Boards & Surname Lists
- Records: Census, Cemeteries, Land, Obituaries, Personal, Taxes and Vital
- Religion & Churches
- Societies & Groups

◆ General Resource Sites

- Anders Berg's Homepage
  http://www.algonet.se/~anderzb/
  With Swedish resources.

- DataDux Släktforskning Genealogy
  http://www.datadux.se/
  In Swedish & English.

- European Emigration—A Review of Swedish Emigration to America
  http://www.americanwest.com/swedemigr/pages/emigra.htm

- Genealogi—Ulf Berggren
  http://www.nada.kth.se/~ulfb/genealogi.html

- Genealogy in Sweden / Släktforskning i Sverige
  http://sd.datatorget.educ.goteborg.se/
  In Swedish.

- NORDGUIDE
  http://info.rbt.no/nordguide/nordguide.html
  A directory of databases in the Nordic Countries.

- Nordic Notes on the Net
  http://nordicnotes.com/
  - Sweden Genealogy
    http://nordicnotes.com/html/sweden.html

- Skånsk Släktforskning
  http://www.algonet.se/~anderzb/genea/skane.htm
  Swedish genealogy resources. In Swedish & some English.

- Släktforskning i Sverige / Genealogy in Sweden
  http://www.lysator.liu.se/~pober/slfo.html
  In Swedish.

- Svenska Släktforskarlänkar
  http://www.itv.se/~a1089/genealogy/gen-sv.htm

- Sweden Genealogy—World GenWeb
  http://www.rootsweb.com/~wgsweden/

- Swedish Genealogy
  http://www.abc.se/~m6921/geneal.html
  In Swedish only.

- Swedish Genealogy How To Guide
  http://www.familytreemaker.com/00000386.html

- Swedish Information Service—Internet Resources for Tracing Your Swedish Roots
  http://www.webcom.com/sis/geneal.html

- Swedish Resources
  http://www.montana.edu/sass/sweden.htm
  From the Society for the Advancement of Scandinavian Study.

- Tabergs Bergslag
  http://www.algonet.se/~p-ryden/tab.html
  Månsarp, Barnarp and Sandseryd, together called the mining district of Taberg—Tabergs Bergslag, in Smaland of Sweden.

◆ Government & Cities

- City.Net Directory—Sweden
  http://www.city.net/countries/sweden/

- Yahoo!...Sweden...Cities and Towns
  http://dir.yahoo.com/Regional/Countries/Sweden/Cities_and_Towns/

- Yahoo!...Sweden...Counties
  http://dir.yahoo.com/Regional/Countries/Sweden/Counties/

◆ History & Culture

- History of Europe in Medieval Times, Scandinavia
  http://www.worldroots.com/brigitte/royal/royal1.htm
  Historic and genealogical information about royal and nobility family lines.

◆ How To

- Have You Found a Swedish Ancestor?
  http://www.geocities.com/Heartland/Meadows/7095/
  swede.html

◆ Language & Names

- Lexin Svensk-Engelskt Lexikon / Lexin Swedish-English Dictionary
  http://sd.datatorget.educ.goteborg.se/cdata/sv-eng.html?lang=english#english

- Så Stavar du Namnen—Släktforskarförbundets Namnlista / How to Spell First Names—The Swedish Genealogical Association's Names List
  http://www.genealogi.se/namnnorm.htm
  Explanations by Håkan Skogsjö.

◆ Libraries, Archives & Museums

- American Swedish Historical Museum
  http://www.libertynet.org/~ashm/
  Philadelphia, Pennsylvania

- HYTELNET—Library Catalogs: Sweden
  http://library.usask.ca/hytelnet/se0/se000.html
  Before you use any of the Telnet links, make note of the user name, password and any other logon information.

- Kungl. Biblioteket, Sveriges Nationalbibliotek / The Royal Library, National Library of Sweden
  http://www.kb.se/

- LIBRIS—Nationellt Bibliotekssystem—Svenska Bibliotek I Samverkan / Union Catalogue of Swedish Libraries
  http://www.libris.kb.se/

- Malmö Stadsbibliotek / Malmö City Library
  http://www.msb.malmo.se/

- Mölndals Stadsbibliotek / Mölndal Public Library
  http://www.molndal.se/bibl/uk.htm

- North Park University's Library, Archives and Instructional Media
  http://www.northpark.edu/library/
  Chicago, Illinois

  ○ Archival Research Collections at North Park College
    http://www.northpark.edu/library/Archives/
    Including information for the Swedish-American Archives of Greater Chicago, the Covenant Archives and Historical Library, and the Archives of the Society for the Advancement of Scandinavian Study.

- Swenson Swedish Immigration Research Center
  http://www.augustana.edu/administration/swenson/
  Illinois

- webCATS: Library Catalogues on the World Wide Web—Sweden
  http://library.usask.ca/hywebcat/countries/SE.html

◆ Mailing Lists, Newsgroups & Chat

- GEN-NORDIC Mailing List
  http://members.aol.com/gfsjohnf/gen_mail_country-den.html#GEN-NORDIC
  For the discussion of genealogy in the Scandinavian countries, including: Denmark, Finland, Greenland, Iceland, Norway and Sweden. Gatewayed with the soc.genealogy.nordic newsgroup.

- SWEDEN Mailing List
  http://members.aol.com/gfsjohnf/gen_mail_country-swe.html#SWEDEN

- SWEDES Mailing List
  http://members.aol.com/gfsjohnf/gen_mail_country-swe.html#SWEDES

- swnet.sci.genealogi Newsgroup

◆ Maps, Gazetteers & Geographical Information

- Map of Sweden
  http://www.lib.utexas.edu/Libs/PCL/Map_collection/europe/
  Sweden.jpg
  From the Perry-Castañeda Library at the Univ. of Texas at Austin.

◆ Newspapers

- AJR NewsLink—Sweden Newspapers
  http://www.newslink.org/euswed.html

- E&P Media Info Links—Newspaper Sites in Sweden
  http://www.mediainfo.com/emediajs/browse-results.htm?region=sweden&category=newspaper+++++++++

- Svenska Dagbladet—Nyheter
  http://www.svd.se/svd/ettan/dagens/index.html

- The Ultimate Collection of News Links: Sweden
  http://www.pppp.net/links/news/Sweden.html

- Yahoo!...Newspapers...Sweden
  http://dir.yahoo.com/News_and_Media/Newspapers/Regional/
  Countries/Sweden/

◆ People & Families

- Håkan Asmundsson's Websida
  http://home1.swipnet.se/~w-14440/
  *JÖNSSON, SAMUELSSON, ANDERSSON, LARSSON.
  Information for Swedish provinces of: ÖSTERGÖTLAND,
  SMÅLAND, SKÅNE.*

- Kurt MAXE Släktforskning
  http://hem.passagen.se/kurremax/maxe.htm
  MAXE, KARLSSON, CARLSDOTTER, PERSSON

- The Monarchs & Regents of Sweden for
  Near 1000 Years
  http://www.ringnett.no/home/bjornstad/royals/Sweden.html
- Rolf BROBECK—Genealogy
  http://home1.swipnet.se/~w-11647/rolf/rolfbe.htm
- Sami Resources
  http://www.montana.edu/sass/sami.htm
  From the Society for the Advancement of Scandinavian Study.
- STENFELT Family Genealogy
  http://www.ndepot.com/stenfelt/
  *Traces primarily the STENFELT lineage including the varia-
  tions STONEFELT, STONEFIELD and STENFELDT, from
  Georg STENFELT to the known current living descendants. Also
  partial royal (Sweden) lineages of Vasa and Stråle.*
- Sven-Arne ADOLFSSON's Home Page
  http://www.yi.com/home/AdolfssonSven-arne/
  *JOHANSSON from Bouslaen and other names from Blekinge,
  Skane Sweden.*

◆ Professional Researchers, Volunteers & Other Research Services

- AID Kinresearch—Släktservice Hemsida / AID
  Kinresearch Swedish Genealogy
  http://hem1.passagen.se/aidkin/
- Genealogy Helplist—Sweden
  http://posom.com/hl/swe/index.shtml
- genealogyPro—Professional Genealogists for
  Sweden
  http://genealogyPro.com/directories/Sweden.html
- Molander's Genealogy Service
  http://www.algonet.se/~family/
  Professional researchers for Sweden and Norway.

◆ Publications, Software & Supplies

- Brother's Keeper Software in Swedish
  http://ourworld.compuserve.com/homepages/Brothers_Keeper/
  or in English
  http://www.torget.se/users/b/bertun/bk.html
  *Downloadable shareware program for Windows. The latest
  version contains English, French, Norwegian, Danish, Swedish,
  German, and Dutch.*
- Frontier Press Bookstore—Scandinavian Ancestry
  http://www.frontierpress.com/frontier.cgi?category=sca
- GenealogyBookShop.com—Sweden/Swedish
  http://www.genealogybookshop.com/genealogybookshop/files/
  The_World,Sweden_Swedish/index.html
  *The online store of Genealogical Publishing Co., Inc. &
  Clearfield Company.*

- Genus Genealogy Program
  http://www.mediabase.fi/suku/genupgb.htm
  *Windows program available in six languages: Dutch, English,
  Finnish, French, German and Swedish.*
- JamoDat—Win-Family Software
  http://www.jamodat.dk/
  *Available in Danish, Swedish, Norwegian, French, German and
  English.*
- Nättidningen RÖTTER—för dig som släktforskar
  http://www.genealogi.se/index.htm
  *An e-zine from the Swedish Federation of Genealogical
  Societies.*

◆ Queries, Message Boards & Surname Lists

- Scanian Genealogy Homepage Efterlysningar 1997 /
  Queries 1997
  http://cgi.algonet.se/htbin/
  cgiwrap?user=anderzb&script=query.cgi
- Scanian Genealogy Homepage Efterlysningar 1996 /
  Queries 1996
  http://www.algonet.se/~anderzb/genea/queframe.htm
  Queries from the Swedish province of Scania.

◆ Records: Census, Cemeteries, Land, Obituaries, Personal, Taxes and Vital (Born, Married, Died & Buried)

- Släktdatas Registerarkiv / Searchable
  Parish Registers
  http://sd.datatorget.educ.goteborg.se/cdata/
  reginfo.php3?lang=english#english

◆ Religion & Churches

- Christianity.Net Church Locator—Sweden
  http://www.christianity.net/cgi/location.exe?Sweden
- Churches dot Net—Global Church Web Pages—
  Sweden
  http://www.churches.net/churches/internat.htm#swe
- Churches of the World—Sweden
  http://www.churchsurf.com/churches/world/Sweden/
  From the ChurchSurf Christian Directory.
- Genline—Svenska Kyrkböcker Online / Swedish
  Church Records On-line
  http://www.genline.se/
- Släktdatas Registerarkiv / Searchable
  Parish Registers
  http://sd.datatorget.educ.goteborg.se/cdata/
  reginfo.php3?lang=english#english

◆ Societies & Groups

- Archer's Computer Interest Group List—Sweden
  http://www.genealogy.org/~ngs/cigs/ngl3otsw.html

- Computer Genealogy Society of Sweden /
  Föreningen för datorhjälp i släktforskningen
  http://www.dis.se/

- Föreningar i riksförbundet Länk—och adresslista /
  Member Societies of The Federation of Swedish
  Genealogical Societies
  http://www.genealogi.se/links3.htm
  Local and regional genealogical societies in Sweden.

- Sveriges Släktforskarförbund / The Swedish
  Federation of Genealogical Societies
  http://www.genealogi.se/forbund.htm

- The Swedish Colonial Society
  http://www.libertynet.org/~gencap/scs.html
  Philadelphia, Pennsylvania

- Swedish Finn Historical Society
  http://home1.gte.net/SFHS/index.htm
  Seattle, Washington

- Swedish Genealogy Group
  http://www.mtn.org/mgs/branches/swedish.html
  Minnesota

SHIPS, PASSENGER LISTS & IMMIGRATION
http://www.CyndisList.com/ships.htm

Category Index:

◆ Famous & Historical Ships

- Amistad America, Inc.—Building the Freedom Schooner
  http://www.amistadamerica.org/

- Amistad—"Give Us Free"
  http://news.courant.com/special/amistad/

- Amistad Links
  http://www.amistad.org/

- Exploring Amistad: Race and the Boundaries of Freedom in Antebellum Maritime America
  http://amistad.mysticseaport.org/

- Encyclopedia Titanica
  http://www.rmplc.co.uk/eduweb/sites/phind/

- The General Society of Mayflower Descendants
  http://www.mayflower.org/

- HMS Bounty Genealogies
  http://wavefront.wavefront.com/~pjlareau/bounty6.html

- In Memoriam: RMS Titanic
  http://miso.wwa.com/~dsp//titanic/

- List of Officers and Sailors in the First Voyage of Columbus in 1492
  http://www.rootsweb.com/~ote/colship.htm
  Nina, Pinta, Santa Maria

- Lusitania (1907–1915)
  http://www.liv.ac.uk/~archives/cunard/ships/lusitan.htm

- Magellan's Voyages from *The Discovery of America*
  http://www.rootsweb.com/~ote/magship.htm
  By John Fiske published in 1892. The Victoria and the Trinidad.

- Mayflower Database
  http://www.geocities.com/Heartland/Bluffs/4313/

- Mayflower Passenger List
  http://members.aol.com/calebj/passenger.html

- Mayflower Passengers
  http://www.ida.net/users/dhanco/mayflr.htm

- A Mayflower Study
  http://www.maddoxinteractive.com/mayflower/

- The Original Titanic Home Page
  http://www.home.gil.com.au/~dalgarry/

- RMS Lusitania
  http://vif16.icair.iac.org.nz/lusitan.htm

- RMS Titanic: Her Passengers and Crew
  http://www.rmplc.co.uk/eduweb/sites/phind/home.html

- The Sultana: Death on the Dark River (1865)
  http://www.rootsweb.com/~genepool/sultana.htm

- Titanic and Other White Star Ships
  http://members.aol.com/MNichol/Titanic.index.html

- Titanic Passenger List
  http://vsla.edu/vnp/titanic/p2.htm

- Titanic
  http://titanic.gov.ns.ca/
  The Unsinkable Ship and Halifax. A site from Halifax, Nova Scotia, Canada, including a list of those buried in cemeteries in Halifax.

- Welcome to the Mayflower Web Page
  http://members.aol.com/calebj/mayflower.html

◆ General Resource Sites

- Ancestry.com—Ship Passenger Arrival Records—Form 81
  http://www.ancestry.com/research/ships.htm

- The Divers Index
  http://www.thehds.dircon.co.uk/divers/divers.htm
  An Index of Historical Divers and Their Work.

- Downward Bound—Great Lakes Shipping Genealogy Index
  http://www.rootsweb.com/~migls/

- Early Types of Sailing Ships
  http://www.rootsweb.com/~ote/defship.htm

- Emigration / Ship Lists and Resources
  http://www.geocities.com/Heartland/5978/Emigration.html
  From Addie's Genealogy Home Page.

- Genealogy Resources on the Internet: Passenger Lists; Ships; Ship Museums
  http://www-personal.umich.edu/~cgaunt/pass.html

- German and American Sources for German Emigration to America
  http://www.genealogy.net/gene/www/emig/emigrati.htm

- German Genealogy: Emigration from Germany to America
  http://www.genealogy.net/gene/www/emig/emigr.html

- Links: Ships
  http://pc-78-120.udac.se:8001/www/nautica/Pointers/Ships.html
  From the Maritime History Virtual Archives.

- Locating Ship Passenger Lists
  http://www.familytreemaker.com/8_mgpal.html
  by Myra Vanderpool Gormley, C.G.

- Maritime History
  http://www.st-and.ac.uk/~www_sa/personal/md4/
  Information on captured vessels, which appear in the records of the High Court of Admiralty in the U.K.

- Mark Rosenstein's Sailing Page
  http://www.apparent-wind.com/sailing-page.html

- Ocean Liner Passenger Lists Catalog
  http://www.oceanliner.com/passlist.htm
  From New Steamship Consultants.

- Passenger Lists General Info from the JewishGen FAQ
  http://www.jewishgen.org/faqinfo.html#Passenger

- Passenger Lists and Immigration-Related Materials
  http://www.hpl.lib.tx.us/clayton/px001.html
  A Guide from the Clayton Library in Houston, Texas.

- Public Record Office—Finding Aids—A–Z Index of All Leaflets
  http://www.pro.gov.uk/leaflets/riindex.htm
  U.K.

  - Emigrants: Documents in the Public Record Office (#71)
    http://www.pro.gov.uk/leaflets/ri071.htm

  - Immigrants: Documents in the Public Record Office (#70)
    http://www.pro.gov.uk/leaflets/ri070.htm

  - Passport Records (#69)
    http://www.pro.gov.uk/leaflets/ri069.htm

  - Records of HM Coastguard (#8)
    http://www.pro.gov.uk/leaflets/ri008.htm

  - Records of the Registrar General of Shipping and Seamen (#5)
    http://www.pro.gov.uk/leaflets/ri005.htm

  - Records Relating to RMS Titanic (#81)
    http://www.pro.gov.uk/leaflets/ri081.htm

  - Records Relating to Shipwrecks (#65)
    http://www.pro.gov.uk/leaflets/ri065.htm

- Shipping Terminology
  http://www.isn.net/~dhunter/terms.html
  With a Prince Edward Island Slant.

◆ Immigration & Naturalization

- 17th Century Immigrants To New York Registry
  http://www.rootsweb.com/~ote/dnybook.htm

- Ancestry.com—Naturalization Record Request Form Letter
  http://www.ancestry.com/download/naturalform.htm

- Angel Island—The Pacific Gateway
  http://www.i-channel.com/angelisland/
  Angel Island Immigration Station, San Francisco Bay, 1910 to 1940.

- The American Immigrant Wall of Honor
  http://www.wallofhonor.com/

- The Ellis Island Home Page
  http://www.ellisisland.org/

- Ellis Island (I-Channel)
  http://www.i-channel.com/features/ellis/

- Finding Immigration Records—U.S.
  http://www.history.rochester.edu/jssn/page2.htm
  Including a scanned image example

- Historical Events & People Worldwide
  http://www.CyndisList.com/historic.htm
  See this category on Cyndi's List for related links to Ellis Island, "Heading West" and the Mayflower.

- How to Get Your Ancestor's Papers from the Immigration and Naturalization Service
  http://www.italgen.com/immigrat.htm

- Immigrant and Passenger Arrivals
  http://www.nara.gov/publications/microfilm/immigrant/immpass.html
  A select catalog of National Archives microfilm.

- Immigration History Research Center (IHRC) at the University of Minnesota
  http://www.umn.edu/ihrc/
  An international resource on American immigration and ethnic history.

- Irish Emigrants
  http://genealogy.org/~ajmorris/ireland/ireemg1.htm

- Learning About Your Immigrant Ancestors
  http://www.familytreemaker.com/issue8.html

- McLean County, IL, Immigration Records
  http://www.mclean.gov/cc/imgrecs/imgrecs.html

- Naturalization Records
  http://www.nara.gov/genealogy/natural.html
  From the U.S. National Archives and Records Administration.

- Naturalization Records—U.S.
  http://www.history.rochester.edu/jssn/page3.htm
  Including a scanned image example.

- Naturalizations: Researching Philadelphia Records
  http://www.phila.gov/phils/Docs/Inventor/natz.htm
- New York, NY, Ellis Island—Immigration: 1900–1920
  http://cmp1.ucr.edu/exhibitions/immigration_id.html
  University of California, Riverside, Keystone-Mast Collection, California Museum of Photography. Photographs of immigrants, ships & Ellis Island.
- North Dakota Naturalization Records Index
  http://www.lib.ndsu.nodak.edu/database/naturalrec.html
- Q & A: Naturalization 1749
  http://www.worldroots.com/misc/bg_misc/qa6.html
- U.S. Immigration and Naturalization Service (INS)
  http://www.ins.usdoj.gov/index.html
  - INS Forms Available for Download
    http://www.ins.usdoj.gov/forms/index.html
    Download forms such as G-639, Freedom of Information / Privacy Act.

◆ Libraries, Archives & Museums

- The Balch Institute for Ethnic Studies
  http://www.libertynet.org/~balch/
  Includes a research library with materials on immigration studies.
- Cunard Archives at Liverpool University
  http://www.liv.ac.uk/~archives/cunard/chome.htm
  - Cunard Archives: Information on Passengers and Emigrants
    http://www.liv.ac.uk/~archives/cunard/pass.htm
  - Cunard Archives: Ships Index
    http://www.liv.ac.uk/~archives/cunard/ships/ndx.htm
  - Cunard Archives: Ships' Log Books
    http://www.liv.ac.uk/~archives/cunard/logs.htm
- Fylkesarkivet i Sogn og Fjordane—Utvandring— Emigration
  http://www.sffarkiv.no/sffutv.htm
  Norway
- Geelong Maritime Museum
  http://www.zades.com.au/geelong/maritime.html
  Australia
- Hampton Roads Naval Museum
  http://naval-station.norfolk.va.us/navy.html
  Norfolk, Virginia
- The Mariners' Museum—Newport News, Virginia
  http://www.mariner.org/
  Archives, manuscripts, manifests & research services available.
- Maritime History Archive at Memorial University of Newfoundland
  http://www.mun.ca/mha/
- The Maritime History Virtual Archives
  http://pc-78-120.udac.se:8001/WWW/Nautica/Nautica.html

- Marine Museum of the Great Lakes at Kingston
  http://www.marmus.ca/marmus/index.html
  Ontario, Canada
- National Archives of Ireland: Transportation Records
  http://www.nationalarchives.ie/search01.html
  Convicts from Ireland to Australia, 1788 to 1868.
- Naval Historical Center
  http://www.history.navy.mil/
  U.S. Navy History, Department of the Navy.
- Passenger Lists—Hamburg 1850–1934—Film List for the LDS FHC
  http://www.genealogy.net/gene/www/emig/ham_pass.html
- Smith's Master Index of North American Maritime Museum Internet Resources
  http://www.bobhudson.com/Smiths/index.html
- Wisconsin Maritime Museum
  http://dataplusnet.com/maritime/maritime.html

◆ Mailing Lists, Newsgroups & Chat

- emigration-ships Mailing List
  http://members.aol.com/johnf14246/gen_mail_general.html#EMIGRATION-SHIPS
  A mailing list for anyone who wants to discuss the ships their ancestors arrived on or post passenger lists for any ships.
- GLSHIPS Mailing List
  http://members.aol.com/gfsjohnf/gen_mail_states-gen.html#GLSHIPS
  For anyone who is researching ancestors who participated in the shipping industry on the Great Lakes of the northeastern United States.
- IMMI-GRAND Mailing List
  http://members.aol.com/johnf14246/gen_mail_general.html#IMMI-GRAND
  For those attempting to do genealogical research whose grandparents (or parents) arrived in the USA after 1875.
- Mariners Mailing List
  http://members.aol.com/johnf14246/gen_mail_general.html#Mariners
  For anyone who is researching their seafaring ancestors.
- MAYFLOWER Mailing List
  http://members.aol.com/gfsjohnf/gen_mail_states-gen.html#MAYFLOWER
  A mailing list for the discussion and sharing of information regarding the descendants of the Mayflower passengers in any place and at any time.
- TheShipsList Mailing List
  http://members.aol.com/johnf14246/gen_mail_general.html#TheShipsList
  For anyone interested in the ships our ancestors migrated on. Subjects include emigration/immigration, ports of entry, ports of departure, ship descriptions and history, passenger lists and other related information.
- SULTANA Mailing List
  http://members.aol.com/gfsjohnf/gen_mail_states-gen.html#SULTANA
  For anyone who is researching the 2,000+ soldiers aboard the ill-fated steamship Sultana which exploded in 1865.

◆ Publications, Microfilm & Microfiche

- The Best Books on German Passenger Liners
  http://www.worldroots.com/brigitte/ships.htm

- GenealogyBookShop.com—Immigration/Passenger Lists/Naturalizations
  http://www.genealogybookshop.com/genealogybookshop/files/General,Immigration_Passenger_Lists_Naturalizations/index.html
  The online store of Genealogical Publishing Co., Inc. & Clearfield Company.

- Germans to America: Lists of Passengers Arriving at U.S. Ports
  http://www.genealogy.net/gene/www/emig/GermansToAmerica.html
  A description of the books by Ira A. Glazier and P. William Filby, along with a breakdown of the volume numbers and which years are covered in each volume.

- Hamburg Passenger Lists, 1850–1934
  http://www.genealogy.net/gene/www/emig/ham_pass.html
  List of microfilm numbers for the LDS Family History Library.

- How to Find Your Immigrant Ancestor—Passenger and Immigration Lists Index
  http://www.rader.org/how_to.htm
  Tips on using these volumes by Filby.

- Immigrant and Passenger Arrivals
  http://www.nara.gov/publications/microfilm/immigrant/immpass.html
  A select catalog of National Archives microfilm.

- LDS Passenger Manifests—Jan Grippo's Guide to Using the Passenger Lists at Your Local Family History Center
  http://homepage.interaccess.com/~arduinif/tools/ldsmanif.htm

◆ Ship, Passenger & Crew Lists

General Lists of Links

- American Plantations and Colonies—Ship Index
  http://www.primenet.com/~langford/ships/shiplist.htm

- CIMO—Cimorelli Immigration Manifests Online
  http://www.cimorelli.com/vbclient/shipmenu.htm
  An online collection of databases comprised of the Morton Allan Directory, M1066 Microfilm series from NARA, various newspaper articles, Internet sources, and personal contribution.

- Emigration / Ship Lists and Resources
  http://www.geocities.com/Heartland/5978/Emigration.html
  From Addie's Genealogy Home Page.

- Genealogy Resources on the Internet: Passenger Lists; Ships; Ship Museums
  http://www-personal.umich.edu/~cgaunt/pass.html

- Ground Work—Passenger Lists
  http://members.aol.com/ssmadonna/ships.htm

- Immigrant Ship Information
  http://www.fortunecity.com/littleitaly/amalfi/13/ships.htm
  An alphabetical list of ships, with details on each ship as submitted to various Internet mailing lists.

- The Olive Tree Genealogy—Index to Passenger Lists
  http://www.rootsweb.com/~ote/indexshp.htm
  - Index to Miscellaneous Ships' Passenger Lists
    http://www.rootsweb.com/~ote/miscship.htm
  - Index to New Netherland Ships' Passenger Lists
    http://www.rootsweb.com/~ote/nyship.htm
  - Index to Nova Scotia Passenger Lists
    http://www.rootsweb.com/~ote/nsship.htm
  - Index to Palatine Passenger Lists
    http://www.rootsweb.com/~ote/palalist.htm
  - Irish Ship Lists
    http://www.rootsweb.com/~ote/iriship.htm
  - Miscellaneous Ships' Passenger Lists
    http://www.rootsweb.com/~ote/neship.htm
  - Passenger Lists from England and Scotland to North Carolina
    http://www.rootsweb.com/~ote/caroship.htm
  - Ships' Passenger Lists Index by Year
    http://www.rootsweb.com/~ote/shipindx.htm

- On the Trail of Our Ancestors—Index to Ships' Passenger Lists
  http://www.ristenbatt.com/genealogy/shipind1.htm
  by Donna Speer Ristenbatt.

- The Ship Information Database / La Base de données d'information sur les navires
  http://www.chin.gc.ca/ship
  From the Canadian Heritage Information Network.

- Ships Passenger Lists
  http://home.erols.com/fmoran/ships.html

- Una's Genealogy Stuff
  http://idt.net/~unatg/
  Has transcriptions of several passenger lists from Liverpool to NYC.

Shipwrecks

- English East India Company Ships
  http://www.ships.dircon.co.uk/eic/eic.htm
  Shipping Losses in the Mercantile Service 1600–1834 (includes Shipwrecks, Captures & Missing Vessels).

- Lost Boats
  http://www.subnet.com/MEMORIAL/lostboat.htm
  A list of US submarines, the crew and the passengers that were lost since 1915.

- Passenger List: Angel Gabriel
  http://members.aol.com/dcurtin1/gene/gabriel.htm
  Wrecked off Pemaquid Pt., Maine on Aug. 15, 1635.

- Research Sources and Technique with Special Emphasis on the Great Lakes Region
  http://www.xnet.com/~acpinc/research.html

- Sandusky Shipwrecks
  http://pilot.msu.edu/user/hancockp/index.htm

Specific Ships, Localities or Topics

- 1749 Phoenix Passenger List
  http://www.execpc.com/~trarbach/Patience/1749Phoenix.html

- 1768 Ship Arrivals, Charleston, SC
  ftp://ftp.rootsweb.com/pub/usgenweb/sc/ships/1768ship.txt

- AHSGR Ship and Immigration Records
  http://pixel.cs.vt.edu/library/ships/
  American Historical Society of Germans from Russia.

- American Plantations and Colonies—Ships to America Index
  http://www.primenet.com/~langford/ships/shiplist.htm

- AUSNZ Passenger Lists
  http://www.users.on.net/proformat/auspass.html

- Australia's First Fleet
  http://www.pcug.org.au/~pdownes/dps/1stflt.htm
  Convicts transported from England in 1788.

- Australia's Second Fleet
  http://www.pcug.org.au/~pdownes/dps/2ndflt.htm
  Convicts transported from England in 1790.

- Australia's Third Fleet
  http://www.pcug.org.au/~pdownes/dps/3rdflt.txt
  Convicts transported from England in 1791.

- Bark "Charlotte Harrison"—July 1850 Passenger List
  http://www.execpc.com/~haroldr/hrsnlist.htm

- British Barque "Tay"—August 1840 Passenger List
  http://www.execpc.com/~haroldr/taylist.htm

- The Canary Islanders' Migration to Louisiana 1778–1783
  http://www.rootsweb.com/~lastbern/passenger.htm
  Aboard: SS Sacremento, San Ignacio de Loyola, La Victoria, Sanuan Nepomuceno, La Santa Faz, El Sagrada Corazon de Jeses, Fragata Llamada Margarita, SS Trinidad.

- Chester County Ships' Lists
  http://199.72.15.191/Sites/Gen/Chet2/scripts/ListShips.asp
  Located on the Chester County page of the Pennsylvania GenWeb project.

- Chignecto—Web Archives—Ships— Passengers-by-Ship
  http://www.chignecto.net/cwa/ships.nsf?OpenDatabase
  Nova Scotia, New Brunswick

- Dove Passenger List—1801
  http://www.rootsweb.com/~pictou/dove1.htm
  Arriving in Pictou County, Nova Scotia, Canada.

- Down to the Sea in Ships
  http://www.star.net/misuraca/down2c.htm
  A list of men fishing out of Gloucester, Massachusetts who were lost at sea.

- Emigrant Ships, Newspaper Clippings on the Lammershagen & Other
  http://home.sol.no/holum/emigrantship.htm

- The Emigrants from the Waasland (Flanders, Belgium) to the United States and Canada 1830–1950
  http://www.ping.be/picavet/
  - Transatlantic Passenger Ships 1830–1859
    http://www.ping.be/picavet/Waas_America_Travel01.shtml
  - Transatlantic Passenger Ships 1860–1899
    http://www.ping.be/picavet/Waas_America_Travel02.shtml
  - Transatlantic Passenger Ships 1900–1913
    http://www.ping.be/picavet/Waas_America_Travel03.shtml
  - Transatlantic Passenger Ships 1919–1921
    http://www.ping.be/picavet/Waas_America_Travel04.shtml
  - Transatlantic Passenger Ships 1921–1950
    http://www.ping.be/picavet/Waas_America_Travel05.shtml

- Fifty Years in Queensland:— Living Pioneer Colonists
  http://192.148.225.23/bruce/qldpio.html
  A supplement article to "The Queenslander" Jubilee Issue:— 7 August 1909, which lists names, ages and year of arrival and the ship's name.

- Fishing?—It was "A WAY OF LIFE" and Lost At Sea
  http://www.geocities.com/Heartland/Prairie/7527/
  Dedicated to Atlantic Canada fishermen and mariners lost at sea, their families and survivors. And to all those from other countries who were lost at sea.

- "Franklin"—From Liverpool to New York, June 22, 1827
  ftp://ftp.rootsweb.com/pub/usgenweb/ny/passengerlists/ship0002.txt

- The Germanic—Partial List of Passengers from Ireland to NY in June, 1903
  http://genealogy.org/~ajmorris/ireland/ireemg3.htm

- "Gildart" Passenger List
  ftp://ftp.rootsweb.com/pub/usgenweb/md/ships/gildart.txt
  Scottish rebels from Liverpool 5 May 1747 to Port North, Potomack, Maryland: 5 August 1747.

- Grand River West and the Queen of Greenock
  http://www.isn.net/~dhunter/stpatricks.html

- Hamburg Passenger Lists, 1850–1934
  http://www.genealogy.net/gene/www/emig/ham_pass.html
  An index of the microfilm numbers for the 486 reels at the Family History Library in Salt Lake City. The original lists are held at Hamburg State Archive/Staatsarchiv, Bestand Auswandereramt.

- Hector Passenger List
  http://www.rootsweb.com/~pictou/hector1.htm
  Voyage to Pictou, Nova Scotia in 1773.

- Huguenot Refugees
  http://www.rootsweb.com/~ote/hugship.htm
  On the ship Mary and Ann, August 12, 1700, Virginia, James City and from London to James River in Virginia, 20th of Sept.

- Humphreys Passenger List—1806
  http://www.rootsweb.com/~pictou/hmphreys.htm

- Immigrant Ships Carrying Some of the First Colonists to the West Michigan Area
  http://www.macatawa.org/~devries/Shipindex.htm

- Index to Inward Overseas Passengers from Foreign Ports 1852–1859
  http://home.vicnet.net.au/~provic/185259/5259indx.htm
  From the PRO Victoria, Australia.

- Irish Passenger Lists
  http://freespace.virgin.net/alan.tupman/sites/irish.htm

- Irish Passenger Lists
  http://members.tripod.com/~Data_Mate/irish/Irish.htm

- "Isabellabath"
  http://www.macatawa.org/~devries/isabath.html
  From the Netherlands to New York on December 19, 1846.

- The Island Register Shipping Stories, Info, and Folklore
  http://www.isn.net/~dhunter/ships.html
  Prince Edward Island, Canada

- "Johnson" Passenger List
  ftp://ftp.rootsweb.com/pub/usgenweb/md/ships/johnson.txt
  Prisoners, shipped on 5 May 1747 Port Oxford, Maryland 17 July 1747.

- Liners of the Golden Age
  http://www.powerscourt.com/liners/index.htm

- List of Ships Conveying Emigrants to Virginia Before 1625–6
  http://www.rootsweb.com/~ote/vaship.htm
  From the Olive Tree.

- List of Ships to Philadelphia
  http://www.genealogy.org/~palam/ships.htm

- List or Manifest of Alien Passengers for the United States Immigration Officer at Port of Arrival—San Francisco, California—September 4th, 1930
  http://members.aol.com/jktsn/shiplst2.htm

- Lovely Nelly Passenger Lists, 1774 & 1775
  http://www.rootsweb.com/~pictou/lnell1.htm
  From Galloway, Scotland to Prince Edward Island.

- Lunenburg County, NSGenWeb—Passenger Lists
  http://www.rootsweb.com/~canns/lunenburg/shiplists.html

  ○ Cornwallis Ships to Halifax—1749
    http://www.rootsweb.com/~canns/cornwallis.html

○ Passenger Lists for Ships Carrying the "Foreign Protestants" to Nova Scotia
  http://www.rootsweb.com/~canns/lunenburg/shiplist2.html
  59 Families 16 May 1752 "SPEEDWELL."

○ Passenger Lists for Ships Carrying the "Foreign Protestants" to Nova Scotia
  http://www.rootsweb.com/~canns/lunenburg/shiplist3.html
  59 Families 30 May 1752 "BETTY."

○ Passenger Lists for Ships Carrying the "Foreign Protestants" to Nova Scotia
  http://www.rootsweb.com/~canns/lunenburg/shiplist11.html
  73 Families 18 May 1751 "SPEEDWELL."

○ Passenger Lists for Ships Carrying the "Foreign Protestants" to Nova Scotia
  http://www.rootsweb.com/~canns/lunenburg/shiplist4.html
  85 Families 2 Jul 1751 "PEARL."

○ Passenger Lists for Ships Carrying the "Foreign Protestants" to Nova Scotia
  http://www.rootsweb.com/~canns/lunenburg/shiplist5.html
  85 Families 5 Jun 1752 "GALE."

○ Passenger Lists for Ships Carrying the "Foreign Protestants" to Nova Scotia
  http://www.rootsweb.com/~canns/lunenburg/shiplist6.html
  85 Families 6 Jun 1752 "PEARL."

○ Passenger Lists for Ships Carrying the "Foreign Protestants" to Nova Scotia
  http://www.rootsweb.com/~canns/lunenburg/shiplist9.html
  99 Families 29 Jun 1750 "ANN."

○ Passenger Lists for Ships Carrying the "Foreign Protestants" to Nova Scotia
  http://www.rootsweb.com/~canns/lunenburg/shiplist1.html
  100 Families of German Protestants 25 Jun 1751 "MURDOCH."

○ Passenger Lists for Ships Carrying the "Foreign Protestants" to Nova Scotia
  http://www.rootsweb.com/~canns/lunenburg/shiplist7.html
  119 Families 30 May 1752 "SALLY."

○ Passenger Lists for Ships Carrying the "Foreign Protestants" to Nova Scotia
  http://www.rootsweb.com/~canns/lunenburg/shiplist8.html
  Foreign Names of Those Arriving with Cornwallis, 1749 and Others Of Interest Arriving in 1749.

○ Passenger Lists for Ships Carrying the "Foreign Protestants" to Nova Scotia
  http://www.rootsweb.com/~canns/lunenburg/shiplist12.html
  Settlers Who Are Presumed to Have Arrived on the "ALDERNEY" or the "NANCY" in August and September 1750.

- LusaWeb Portuguese Immigrant Ship Lists
  http://www.lusaweb.com/shiplist.cfm

- Marine Museum of the Great Lakes at Kingston—Mills Ship List
  http://130.15.161.15/mills.htm
  Canada and the Great Lakes.

- Marine Museum of the Great Lakes at Kingston—Wallace Ship List
  http://130.15.161.15/wallace.htm
  Canada and the Great Lakes.

- Molly Passenger List—October 16, 1741
  http://www.placercoe.k12.ca.us/kgissy/molly.htm
  Rotterdam, Holland—Deal, England—Philadelphia, PA.

- Montcalm Passenger List
  http://mypage.direct.ca/d/dobee/pilgrim.html
  From Montreal on July 16, 1936 to Antwerp and London. This was one of several steamships that sailed from Canada to Europe in the summer of 1936, carrying Great War veterans and their families to ceremonies regarding the war.

- Mormon Emigrant Ships (1840–1868)
  http://www.vii.com/~nelsonb/pioneer.htm#ships

- Nova Scotia Bound
  http://www.geocities.com/Heartland/Meadows/8429/index.html
  A partial list of ships bound for Nova Scotia between 1750 and 1862.

  o The Albion Ship List, Surnames A–L
    http://www.geocities.com/Heartland/Meadows/8429/albal.html
    Arrived in Halifax, Nova Scotia, Canada on May 6, 1774 from Hull, Yorkshire, England.

  o The Albion Ship List, Surnames M–Z
    http://www.geocities.com/Heartland/Meadows/8429/albmz.html
    Arrived in Halifax, Nova Scotia, Canada on May 6, 1774 from Hull, Yorkshire, England.

  o The British Queen Passenger List
    http://www.geocities.com/Heartland/Meadows/8429/britqn.html
    Sailed for Nova Scotia from Liverpool, England on April 1st, 1862.

  o The Duke of York Passenger List
    http://www.geocities.com/Heartland/Meadows/8429/dyork.html
    Arrived in Halifax, Nova Scotia from Liverpool, England on May 1, 1772.

  o Elisabeth and Ann Passenger List
    http://www.geocities.com/Heartland/Meadows/8429/elisann.html
    Sailed for Nova Scotia from Thurso, North Britain on November 8th, 1806.

  o The Frank Flint Passenger List
    http://www.geocities.com/Heartland/Meadows/8429/flint.html
    Sailed for Halifax, Nova Scotia from Liverpool, England on May 28th, 1862.

  o The Humphreys Passenger List
    http://www.geocities.com/Heartland/Meadows/8429/hmphry.html
    Sailed for Nova Scotia from Tobermory, North Britain on July 14th, 1806.

  o The Jenny Ship List
    http://www.geocities.com/Heartland/Meadows/8429/jenny.html
    To Halifax, Nova Scotia, Canada from Hull, Yorkshire, England in April of 1775.

  o The Providence Passenger List
    http://www.geocities.com/Heartland/Meadows/8429/prvdnc.html
    Arrived in Halifax on June 1, 1774 from Newcastle Northumberland.

  o The Rambler Passenger List
    http://www.geocities.com/Heartland/Meadows/8429/rambler.html
    Sailed for Nova Scotia from Thurso, North Britain on November 8th, 1806.

  o The Thomas and William or the Prince George Passenger List
    http://www.geocities.com/Heartland/Meadows/8429/tmwlad.html
    Arrived at Halifax from Scarborough, Yorkshire on May 14/16, 1774.

  o The Two Friends Ship List
    http://www.geocities.com/Heartland/Meadows/8429/2friends.html
    Arrived in Halifax, Nova Scotia on May 9, 1774 from Hull, Yorkshire.

- Nova Scotia Passenger Lists—The Speedwell and the Ann
  http://www.rootsweb.com/~ote/nsship.htm

- Oughton Passenger List—1804
  http://www.rootsweb.com/~pictou/oughton.htm

- "Parsee"—Passenger List—Moreton Bay—11 January 1853
  http://192.148.225.23/bruce/plink.html

- Passenger and Emigrant Lists
  http://www.bess.tcd.ie/roots/PROTOTYP/emg_plst.htm

- Passenger List: Angel Gabriel
  http://members.aol.com/dcurtin1/gene/gabriel.htm
  Wrecked off Pemaquid Pt., Maine on Aug. 15, 1635.

- Passenger List: Lyon 1632
  http://members.aol.com/dcurtin1/gene/lyon.htm

- Passenger List of Ship Ben Nevis
  http://home.sprynet.com/sprynet/harrisfarm/bennevis.htm
  Ship Register Wendish Colonists of Texas, 1854, from Liverpool, England to Queenstown, Ireland to Galveston, Texas.

- The Passenger List of the "Alexander," and the Glenaladale Settlers
  http://www.isn.net/~dhunter/alexandr.html
  1772–1997, Prince Edward Island, Canada.

- Passenger List of the Brig "Fanny"
  http://www.isn.net/~dhunter/fanny.html
  From Charlottetown to California Nov 12 1849.

- Passenger list of the "British Queen," 1790
  http://www.isn.net/~dhunter/british_queen.html

- Passenger List of the "Clarendon"—1808 from Oban, N. Britain
  http://www.isn.net/~dhunter/clarendon.html

- Passenger List of the "Elizabeth and Ann"—1806 from Thurso, N. Britain
  http://www.isn.net/~dhunter/liz_ann.html

- Passenger List of the "Falmouth"—1770 from Greenock
  http://www.isn.net/~dhunter/falmouth.html

- Passenger List of the "Jane"
  http://www.isn.net/~dhunter/jane.html
  From Drimindarach, Scotland to Prince Edward Island, 12 July 1790.

- Passenger List of the "Lively"—1775 from Britain
  http://www.isn.net/~dhunter/lively.html

- Passenger List of the "Lucy"
  http://www.isn.net/~dhunter/lucy.html
  Sailed in the company of the "Jane," from Drimindarach, Scotland to Prince Edward Island, 12 July 1790.

- Passenger List of the Pakeha
  http://www.isn.net/~dhunter/pakeha.html
  From Prince Edward Island to New Zealand, December 23, 1863.

- Passenger List of the Palestine
  http://www.benet.net.au/~brandis/gendata/palestine.html
  From Plymouth, England, 29 November 1852 to Perth, Western Australia, 28 April 1853.

- Passenger List of the "Rambler"—1806 from Tobermory, N. Britain
  http://www.isn.net/~dhunter/rambler.html

- Passenger List of the Schooner Jeannette
  http://home.hiwaay.net/~guillory/genealogy/personal/jeannette.html

- Passenger List, Ship Anne, 1623
  http://members.aol.com/calebj/anne.html

- Passenger List, Ship Fortune, 1621
  http://members.aol.com/calebj/fortune.html

- Passenger List: Planter 1635
  http://members.aol.com/dcurtin1/gene/planter.htm

- Passenger Lists from Ireland—1803
  http://www.ida.net/users/dhanco/passlst.htm

- Passenger Lists from Ireland #2—1803
  http://www.ida.net/users/dhanco/passlst2.htm

- Passenger Lists of 1855 Migration
  http://www.geocities.com/Heartland/Prairie/3974/plists.html
  From Bühlertal, Baden, Germany.

- Passenger Ship Records—PA Archives
  http://www.rootsweb.com/~usgenweb/pa/1pa/ship.htm

- Passenger Ships' Lists, Pennsylvania
  http://www.ristenbatt.com/genealogy/shipind.htm
  Between 1728 and 1772.

- Passengerlist Lammershagen
  http://home.sol.no/holum/passengerlist.htm

- Passengers Aboard the Ship Bowditch (of Boston)
  http://genealogy.org/~ajmorris/ireland/ireemg2.htm
  From Liverpool, arrived at New York May 27, 1839.

- Passengers of the "Henry and Francis," 1685
  ftp://ftp.rootsweb.com/pub/usgenweb/nj/ships/1685nj.txt

- "Passengers of the Prince Edward"
  http://www.isn.net/~dhunter/pedward.html
  To New Zealand from Charlottetown Harbour, 1859.

- Passengers on the Emigrant Ship "Emigrant"
  http://www.swinhope.demon.co.uk/genuki/Transcriptions/Emigrant.html
  Sailed from Sunderland 10 September 1852; arrived Melbourne 3 January 1853.

- Passengers on the Emigrant Ship "Guy Mannering"
  http://www.swinhope.demon.co.uk/genuki/Transcriptions/GuyMannering.html
  Sailed from Liverpool on May 22nd 1849; arrived New York, June 28th.

- Passengers on the Emigrant Ship "Lizzie Webber"
  http://www.swinhope.demon.co.uk/genuki/Transcriptions/LizzieWebber.html
  Sailed from Sunderland 31 July 1852; arrived Melbourne 4 December 1852.

- Passengers on the Emigrant Ship "Lord Delaval"
  http://www.swinhope.demon.co.uk/genuki/Transcriptions/LordDelaval.html
  Sailed from Berwick upon Tweed on September 13th 1852 for London and on to Port St Philip, Victoria, Australia.

- Passengers on the Emigrant Ship "Saldanha"
  http://www.swinhope.demon.co.uk/genuki/Transcriptions/Saldanha.html
  Sailed from Liverpool in the summer of 1856 for Victoria, Australia.

- The Patience 1751
  http://www.execpc.com/~trarbach/Patience/patience_home.html

- Peter Hodge's Home Page
  http://www.pcug.org.au/~phodge/
  Information regarding the brig "Indian" from Falmouth in mid-1843 bound for Launceston, Tasmania; the "Emigrant" sailed from Plymouth on 9 August 1850 bound for Moreton Bay; and more on emigration, etc.

- Portuguese Passenger Ship Master List
  http://www.dholmes.com/ships.html

- Prince of Wales—June 28 1813 from Stromness, Orkney, Scotland
  http://members.tripod.com/~tmsnyder/PW_LIST.htm

- "Queen of the Colonies" Web Site
  http://www.garrison.gil.com.au/queen.html

- Reconstructed Passenger List of the German Ship Lammershagen
  http://home.sol.no/holum/germanship.htm

- Sailing Ship the INDIA Lost at Sea 1841
  http://www.home.gil.com.au/~bbiggar/india.htm
  Sailed from Greenock Scotland on 4 June 1841 bound for the Australian colony of Port Phillip.

- Saint Andrew Galley
  http://www.enter.net/~stenlake/list.html
  September 26, 1737, Palatinates from Rotterdam and Cowes.

- St. George Partial Passenger List, Liverpool to NY 1847
  ftp://ftp.rootsweb.com/pub/usgenweb/ny/passengerlists/ship0003.txt

- Samuel—The English Immigrant Ship
  http://members.aol.com/groffh/samuel.htm
  It brought many immigrants from the Palatinate, Germany, and Switzerland to Philadelphia.

- The Sarah—1801
  http://www.rootsweb.com/~pictou/sarah1.htm
  To Pictou, Nova Scotia.

- Sarah Hyde Passenger List, 1854 from Antwerp to New York
  http://www.seidata.com/~lhoffman/hyde.html

- Ship Bowditch Passenger List
  http://www.rootsweb.com/~ote/iriship1.htm
  From The Olive Tree.

- The Ship Defence, 1635
  http://www.citynet.net/personal/gunn/defence.html

- Ship Diligent—Passenger List and General Info
  http://www.geocities.com/Heartland/Ranch/4750/LassShip.html

- Ship Edinburgh Passenger Lists
  http://www.execpc.com/~haroldr/edbrglst.htm
  From Campbeltown, Scotland to Cape Fear, North Carolina in 1770 and to Island of St. Johns (Prince Edward Island) in 1771.

- Ship *Griffin* Passenger List 1749
  http://www.worldroots.com/misc/bg_misc/ship02.html

- The Ship Marianne
  http://members.aol.com/lhchristen/marianne.htm
  Voyage from Bremen to Baltimore, Departing August 11, 1843, and Arriving September 25, 1843.

- Ship Mortonhouse
  ftp://ftp.rootsweb.com/pub/usgenweb/pa/1pa/ships/1729mrtn.txt
  Sailed from Rotterdam to Philadelphia August 17, 1729.

- Palatine Immigrant Ship Patience Home Page
  http://www.execpc.com/~trarbach/Patience/patience_home.html

- Ship WILMINGTON Passenger List
  http://www.execpc.com/~haroldr/wlmtnlst.htm
  From Belfast to New York, 9 July 1803.

- Ships & Captains...1874 Publication
  http://www.seidata.com/~lhoffman/ships.html
  A list of ships and their masters, and emigrants, transcribed from a book edited by John Camden Hotten and published by Chatto and Windus, London 1874.

- Ships of our Ancestors
  http://www.worldroots.com/misc/bg_misc/ship01.html

- Ships to Western Australia 1829–1849
  http://www.benet.net.au/~brandis/gendata/1829_49.html

- Ships to Western Australia 1899
  http://www.benet.net.au/~brandis/gendata/1899ship.html

- Ships to Western Australia 1900
  http://www.benet.net.au/~brandis/gendata/1900ship.html

- Ships to Western Australia January and February 1901
  http://www.benet.net.au/~brandis/gendata/1901ship.html

- South Australian Passenger Lists 1836–1840
  http://www.users.on.net/proformat/ships36.html

- South Australian Passenger Lists 1841–1846
  http://www.users.on.net/proformat/ships41.html

- South Australian Passenger Lists 1847–1886
  http://www.users.on.net/proformat/ships47.html

- Spencer Passenger List—1806
  http://www.rootsweb.com/~pictou/spencer.htm

- SS Lucania Partial Passenger List, Ire to NY 1898
  ftp://ftp.rootsweb.com/pub/usgenweb/ny/passengerlists/ship0001.txt

- S.S. Yukon—Ship Passenger List
  http://www.rootsweb.com/~akgenweb/yukon.htm

- Steam Ship Seneca, Hobocken, NJ, 1879
  http://members.tripod.com/~tmsnyder/SS.htm

- Two Lists of Intending Passengers to the New World, 1770 and 1771
  http://www.execpc.com/~haroldr/edbrglst.htm
  Ship "Edinburgh" voyage from Campbeltown, Scotland to Cape Fear, North Carolina in 1770 and to Island of St. Johns (Prince Edward Island) in 1771.

- The Winthrop Fleet of 1630
  http://members.aol.com/dcurtin1/gene/winthrop.htm

- Women and Female Children of the Royal Admiral 1792
  http://www.shoalhaven.net.au/~cathyd/raladies.html

◆ Societies & Groups

- Association for Great Lakes Maritime History
  http://little.nhlink.net/wgm/glmh/glmh.html

- The Great Lakes Shipwreck Historical Society
  http://www.lssu.edu/shipwreck/
  Michigan

- The Historical Diving Society
  http://www.thehds.dircon.co.uk/
  U.K.

- Marine Historical Society of Detroit
  http://www.oakland.edu/~ncschult/mhsd/

- Puget Sound Maritime Historical Society
  http://www.psmaritime.org/
  Seattle, Washington

- The Saginaw River Marine Historical Society
  http://www.concentric.net/~Djmaus/srmhs.htm

- Titanic Historical Society
  http://www.titanic1.org/

- Wisconsin Marine Historical Society
  http://www.wisconsinwebdesign.com/wmhs/homeport.htm

SOCIETIES & GROUPS—GENERAL
http://www.CyndisList.com/society.htm

Category Index:

- ◆ Ethnic Organizations
- ◆ Fraternal Organizations
- ◆ General Resource Sites
- ◆ Lineage Societies
- ◆ Military Societies

- ◆ National Societies
- ◆ Religious Organizations

- ◆ *See also the complete alphabetical listing of societies on the* Cyndi's List *web site at http://www.CyndisList.com/society.htm*

◆ Ethnic Organizations

- ● Ancient Order of Hibernians in America—National Web Page
  http://www.aoh.com

- ● Association of Jewish Genealogical Societies (AJGS)
  http://www.jewishgen.org/ajgs/index.html

- ● National Japanese American Historical Society
  http://www.nikkeiheritage.org

- ● Polish Genealogical Society of America
  http://www.pgsa.org

- ● Society of Acadian Descendants
  http://www.acadian.org/genealogy/sad.html

- ● The Society of Hispanic Historical and Ancestral Research (SHHAR)
  http://members.aol.com/shhar/index.html

- ● Sons of Norway Home Page
  http://www.sofn.com

◆ Fraternal Organizations

- ● BPO Elks Online
  http://www.elks.org

- ● the e-m@son website
  http://www.freemasonry.org
  A Masonic starting point for the Freemason, e-mason & non-Mason.

- ● Independent Order of Odd Fellows and Rebekahs
  http://norm28.hsc.usc.edu/IOOF.shtml

  - ○ Family History Research
    http://norm28.hsc.usc.edu/IOOF/FamilyResearch.html
    Instructions and details from I.O.O.F.

- ● Knights of Columbus
  http://www.kofc-supreme-council.org

- ● Lions International
  http://www.lions.org

- ● Masonic Resources on the Internet
  http://www.flash.net/~mason/links.html

- ● The Order of Knights of Pythias
  http://www.pythias.org
  An international, non-sectarian fraternal order, founded in 1864.

- ● The Shrine and Shriners Hospital
  http://shrinershq.org

◆ General Resource Sites

- ● American Association for State and Local History
  http://www.Nashville.Net/~aaslh/

- ● Association for Gravestone Studies Home Page
  http://www.berkshire.net/ags/

- ● The Association of One-Name Studies
  http://www.mediasoft.net/ScottC/aons.htm

- ● GEN-EDITOR Mailing List
  http://members.aol.com/johnf14246/gen_mail_general.html#GEN-EDITOR
  For editors/publishers of genealogical, surname and family newsletters to have a place to discuss and share ideas and tips.

- ● GEN_SOCIETIES Mailing List
  http://members.aol.com/johnf14246/gen_mail_general.html#GEN_SOCIETIES
  For persons involved with establishing a local genealogical society in order to share program ideas, discuss means of promoting growth within a group, discuss how to work with libraries, and other related topics.

- ● Guild of One-Name Studies
  http://www.one-name.org
  United Kingdom

- ● Railroad Historical Societies
  http://tucson.com/concor/histsoc.html

◆ Lineage Societies

- ● Board for Certification of Genealogists—Roster of Those Certified—Specializing in Lineage Societies
  http://www.genealogy.org/~bcg/rosts_@l.html

- Daughters of Union Veterans of the Civil War
  http://suvcw.org/duv.htm

- First Families of Tennessee
  http://www.korrnet.org/eths/firstfam.htm
  A Heritage Program of the East Tennessee Historical Society.

- First Fleet Fellowship
  http://home.vicnet.net.au/~firstff/
  A historical society for people who have ancestors who arrived in Australia in 1788 aboard one of the ships of the First Fleet.

- GenealogyBookShop.com—Lineage Records/ Hereditary Societies
  http://www.genealogybookshop.com/genealogybookshop/files/General,Lineage_Records_Hereditary_Societies/index.html
  The online store of Genealogical Publishing Co., Inc. & Clearfield Company.

- The General Society of Mayflower Descendants
  http://www.mayflower.org

- Holland Society of New York
  http://members.aol.com/hollsoc/
  Descendants in the direct male line from those who lived in the colonies under Dutch rule in America before or during 1675.

- Jamestowne Society
  http://www.jamestowne.org
  For descendants of the Virginia settlers in the first permanent English settlement in America.

- The National Society Magna Charta Dames and Barons
  http://www.magnacharta.org

- National Society of the Daughters of the American Revolution Home Page
  http://www.dar.org

- National Society Sons and Daughters of the Pilgrims
  http://www.nssdp.org
  The NSSDP is a national lineage society whose members have proven lineal descent from any immigrant to the American Colonies prior to 1700.

- National Society of the Sons of the American Revolution
  http://www.sar.org
  Louisville, Kentucky

- Order of Descendants of Ancient Planters
  http://tyner.simplenet.com/PLANTERS.HTM
  People who arrived in Virginia before 1616, remained for a period of three years, paid their passage, and survived the massacre of 1622.

- The Order of the Founders and Patriots of America
  http://www.mindspring.com/~wxman2/gp/

- Society of California Pioneers
  http://www.wenet.net/~pioneers/

- Sons of Confederate Veterans Home Page
  http://www.scv.org
  - Sons of Confederate Veterans Genealogy Network
    http://www.scv.org/scvgen00.htm

- Confederate Ancestor Research Guide
  http://www.scv.org/scvgen02.htm

- Sons of Union Veterans of the Civil War
  http://suvcw.org

- United Daughters of the Confederacy
  http://www.hqudc.org

- The United Empire Loyalists' Association of Canada
  http://www.npiec.on.ca/~uela/uela1.htm
  Toronto, Ontario, Canada

◆ Military Societies

- The American Legion National Headquarters
  http://www.legion.org

- Army Alumni Organizations
  http://www.army.mil/vetinfo/vetloc.htm

- The Army Home Page Organizations Index
  http://www.army.mil/ORG/ALL.HTM
  Alphabetical index of a numerous variety of organizations within the Army or related to the Army.

- The Aztec Club of 1847
  http://www.concentric.net/~walika/aztec.htm
  Military society of the Mexican War.

- Canadian Peacekeeping Veterans Association
  http://www.islandnet.com/~duke/cpva.htm

- Confederate Memorial Association
  http://www.confederate.org

- Crimean War Research Society ~ U.K.
  http://homepages.ihug.co.nz/~phil/crimean.htm

- Dames of the Loyal Legion of the United States of America
  http://www.usmo.com/~momollus/DOLLUS.HTM

- Daughters of Union Veterans of the Civil War
  http://suvcw.org/duv.htm

- DISPATCH—Scottish Military Historical Society
  http://subnet.virtual-pc.com/~mc546367/journal.htm

- General Society of Colonial Wars
  http://www.ubalt.edu/www/gscw/

- General Society of the War of 1812
  http://LanClio.org/1812.htm

- Grand Army of the Republic (GAR)
  http://pages.prodigy.com/CGBD86A/garhp.htm

- League of Researchers of South African Historical Battlefields
  http://www.icon.co.za/~dup42/Welcome.html

- Legion Ville—First Training Camp of the United States Army, 1792
  http://tristate.pgh.net/~bsilver/legion.htm
  The Legion Ville Historical Society, Inc., The Anthony Wayne Historical Society, Inc. Includes transcriptions of West Point Orderly Books, 1792–1796.

- The Military Historical Society of Australia
  http://www.pcug.org.au/~astaunto/mhsa.htm
- Military Order of the Loyal Legion of the United States
  http://suvcw.org/mollus.htm
- National Civil War Association
  http://reenact.org/ncwa/
- National Society Colonial Dames XVII Century
  http://www.geocities.com/Heartland/Meadows/4399/cdxvii.html
- National Society of the Daughters of the American Revolution Home Page
  http://www.dar.org
- National Society of the Sons of the American Revolution
  http://www.sar.org
  Louisville, Kentucky
- Order of Indian Wars of the United States
  http://members.tripod.com/~Historic_Trust/indian.htm
- Sons of Confederate Veterans Home Page
  http://www.scv.org
  - Sons of Confederate Veterans Genealogy Network
    http://www.scv.org/scvgen00.htm
    - Confederate Ancestor Research Guide
      http://www.scv.org/scvgen02.htm
- Sons of Union Veterans of the Civil War
  http://suvcw.org
- United Daughters of the Confederacy
  http://www.hqudc.org
- Veterans of Foreign Wars
  http://www.vfw.org
- The Western Front Association—Remembering 1914–1918
  http://ourworld.compuserve.com/homepages/cf_baker/
- Women in Military Service for America Memorial Foundation, Inc.
  http://www.wimsa.org

◆ National Societies

- The American Historical Association
  http://chnm.gmu.edu/aha/index.html
- Association of Professional Genealogists
  http://www.apgen.org/~apg/
  Denver, Colorado
- Canada's National History Society
  http://www.cyberspc.mb.ca/~otmw/cnhs/cnhs.html
- Dead Persons Society
  http://pcm.pcmedia.com.au/tags/docs/dps.html
  Australia

- The Federation of Family History Societies ~ U.K.
  http://www.ffhs.org.uk/
- Federation of Genealogical Societies ~ U.S.
  http://www.fgs.org
- The Institute of Heraldic and Genealogical Studies ~ U.K.
  http://www.cs.ncl.ac.uk/genuki/IHGS/
- National Genealogical Society
  http://www.ngsgenealogy.org
  Arlington, Virginia
- National Railway Historical Society
  http://www.rrhistorical.com/nrhs/
- National Trust for Historic Preservation ~ U.S.
  http://www.nthp.org
- Nederlandse Genealogische Vereniging
  http://www.ngv.nl/
- Society of Australian Genealogists
  http://www.ozemail.com.au/~socgenes/sag.html
- Society of Genealogists, UK
  http://www.sog.org.uk/
- Sveriges Släktforskarförbund / The Swedish Federation of Genealogical Societies
  http://www.genealogi.se/forbund.htm

◆ Religious Organizations

- Association of Jewish Genealogical Societies (AJGS)
  http://www.jewishgen.org/ajgs/index.html
- Catholic Family History Society of London, England
  http://feefhs.org/uk/frg-cfhs.html
- Fellowship of Brethren Genealogists
  http://www.cob-net.org/fobg/
- Knights of Columbus
  http://www.kofc-supreme-council.org
- The National Huguenot Society
  http://huguenot.netnation.com
  The National Huguenot Society is an organization devoted to: 1. Coordinating activities of member societies, and promoting and supporting fulfillment of their common purposes which include: a. perpetuating the memory and promoting the principles and virtues of the Huguenots; b. commemorating the great events of Huguenot history; c. collecting and preserving historical data and relics illustrative of Huguenot life, manners, and customs; 2. To give expression to the Huguenot tenets of faith and liberty, and to promote their understanding for the good of the United States; 3. To encourage and foster the organization of new member Societies within states, territories of the United States, and the District of Columbia where none currently exist.
- The Presbyterian Historical Society
  http://www.libertynet.org/gencap/presbyhs.html
  Philadelphia, Pennsylvania
- The United States Catholic Historical Society
  http://www.catholic.org/uschs/

SOFTWARE & COMPUTERS

http://www.CyndisList.com/software.htm

Category Index:

- CD-ROMs: Books, Databases & Indexes
- Genealogy Software Programs
- Genealogy Software Programs That Generate HTML & Web Pages
- Helpful Internet Software Programs
- Mailing Lists, Newsgroups & Chat

- Miscellaneous Download and Reference Sites
- Miscellaneous Software
- Publications, Magazines & Newsletters
- Societies & Groups
- Tools & Utilities
- Vendors

◆ CD-ROMs: Books, Databases & Indexes

- **American Heritage Imaging, Inc.**
  http://www.a-h-i-inc.com/

- **Ancestral Findings**
  http://web.mountain.net/~wfmoney/cd/
  Free CD searches—limited to 2 persons per day.

- **Ancestry Reference Library on CD-ROM**
  http://www.familyhistory.com/products/ancestry.htm
  For Windows or Mac

- **Appleton's Fine Used Bookseller and Genealogy— Genealogy CD-ROMs and Diskettes**
  http://www.appletons.com/genealogy/genemcdr.html
  Hundreds of genealogy CD-ROMs (including Family Tree Maker) and genealogy software programs for sale. Free demos available to download.

- **Automated Research, Inc.—Genealogists Serving Genealogists CDs**
  http://www.aricds.com/

- **CensusCD**
  http://www.censuscd.com/cd/censuscd.htm

- **CensusCD+Maps**
  http://www.censuscd.com/cdmaps/censuscd_maps.htm

- **Census View—Actual Census on CD-ROM**
  http://www.galstar.com/~censusvu/

- **Cornish Roots!**
  http://www.cornwall-net.co.uk/multimed/roots.htm
  A CD-ROM being produced in Cornwall, England.

- **Family Archive CD Spotlight**
  http://www.familytreemaker.com/issue22.html

- **Family Archive Viewer, Version 4.0**
  http://www.familytreemaker.com/abtffiv.html
  Software from Broderbund which allows you to read their CD-ROM products.

- **Family Forest**
  http://www.FamilyForest.com/
  CD-ROM indexes.

- **Family Tree Maker's Family Archive CDs**
  http://www.familytreemaker.com/facds.html

- **Free Genealogy Lookups**
  http://www.pnx.com/unicorn/sites/lookups.htm
  From a variety of CDs and books listed on this page.

- **Frontier Press Bookstore**
  http://www.frontierpress.com/frontier.cgi

- **Genealogical CD-ROM Reference List**
  http://www.kersur.net/~ccooper/states/gencdrom.htm

- **GenealogyBookShop.com—CD-ROM Publications**
  http://www.genealogybookshop.com/genealogybookshop/files/General,CD-ROM_Publications/index.html
  The online store of Genealogical Publishing Co., Inc. & Clearfield Company.

- **GenRef, Inc.—Family History CDs**
  http://www.genref.com/

- **Global Data CD Publishers: Genealogy Page**
  http://www.tcd.net/~globalcd/genealogy.html

- **Global Heritage Center**
  http://www.ledet.com/genealogy/ghc.html
  CD-ROMs and software.

- **GRD—The Genealogical Research Directory**
  http://www.ozemail.com.au/~grdxxx/
  The world's largest listing of surname queries published annually in bookform, now on CD-ROM.

- **Guild Press of Indiana—Civil War CD-ROMs**
  http://www.guildpress.com/cdroms.htm#civilwar

- **Heritage Books, Inc.**
  http://www.heritagebooks.com/
  CD-ROMs available.

- **Lookups from Genealogical CDs**
  http://www.seidata.com/~lhoffman/cdlist.html
  People who own genealogy CDs and are willing to do lookups for others.

- Lost in Time
  http://www.lostintime.com/
  Books, CDs, software, maps, and accessories.

- Macbeth Genealogical Services
  http://www.macbeth.com.au/
  Books, fiche, maps, and CD-ROMs. Australia.

- The Memorabilia Corner
  http://members.aol.com/TMCorner/index.html
  Forms, flags, maps, software, CDs, tapes, microfilm & microfiche, books, periodicals, photographic conservation & archival materials.

- Quintin Publications
  http://www.quintinpublications.com/
  Materials relating to Canada.

- RMIT Publishing Genealogy
  http://www.rmitpublishing.com.au/products/genealogy.html
  Australian databases on CD.

- S&N Genealogy Supplies
  http://www.genealogy.demon.co.uk/

- Storbeck's Genealogy Books Maps CD-ROM
  http://www.storbecks.com/

- World Family Tree Submitter Information Service
  http://www.familytreemaker.com/cgi-bin/subinfo.cgi
  Use the information from your WFT CD to look up the submitter information in this database.

- World Family Tree Submitter List
  http://www.inlink.com/~nomi/wftlist/index.html
  Names, addresses and e-mail addresses for various submitters to the WFT CD-ROMs.

◆ Genealogy Software Programs

- Ancestors and Descendants®
  http://www.AIA-AnD.com/
  For IBM-compatible PCs, regardless of operating system.

- ANCESTRA—Logiciel de généalogie
  http://myweb.worldnet.fr/~franke/genealogie/ancestra.htm
  From France, for Windows 3.1 & 95.

- Ancestral Quest
  http://www.ancquest.com/
  For Windows, downloadable demos available.

- Behold—The Genealogist's Companion and Research Tool
  http://www.concentric.net/~Lkessler/behold.shtml
  Shareware for Windows 95 and 3.1.

- Brother's Keeper Software
  http://ourworld.compuserve.com/homepages/Brothers_Keeper/
  Downloadable shareware program for Windows. The latest version contains English, French, Norwegian, Danish, Swedish, German, and Dutch.

- Computer Programs for Drawing Plat Maps
  http://www.outfitters.com/genealogy/land/compmaps.html

- Cumberland Family Software
  http://www.cf-software.com/
  Shareware program for Windows.

- Drake Software Genealogy Programs and Information
  http://www.tdrake.demon.co.uk/genindex.htm
  BIRDIE (British Isles Regional Display of IGI Extracts) for Windows, Buckinghamshire Posse Comitatus (1798), British Date Calculator and more.

- DYNAS-TREE
  http://www.xterna-net.de/GerdBauch/dynastree/gb/index.shtml
  Win95 or NT. German or English.

- EZITREE Family History Program
  http://www.ram.net.au/users/ezitree/
  DOS program from Australia.

- Family Base—Your Computer Scrapbook
  http://www.familybase.com/
  Create a multimedia scrapbook from your photos and videos. For Windows 3.1x or higher and for Macintosh.

- Family Census Research
  http://www.dhc.net/~design/fcr30.htm
  Software program for organizing census records. Runs under DOS or Windows.

- Family History Composer for the Macintosh
  http://home.att.net/~paulrswan/cygsoft/
  A genealogical utility which creates a family history document in a new, elegantly designed format focused on your direct ancestors.

- Family Matters® Genealogy Software—From MatterWare
  http://members.aol.com/matterware/index.html
  Shareware for Windows.

- Family Origins® for Windows and Windows 95
  http://ourworld.compuserve.com/homepages/formalsoft/

- Family Reunion 5.0 for Windows
  http://www.accessintl.com/famware/

- Family Scrapbook Genealogy Software by Chris Long
  http://users.southeast.net/~vesd/
  or an alternate site
  http://www.pcug.org.au/~chowell/fsbf.htm
  For DOS.

- Family Tracker by Rex Myer
  http://www.surfutah.com/web/famtrak/famtrak.html
  For Windows 3.1 or higher.

- Family Treasures from Family Technologies
  http://www.famtech.com/histprod.htm
  For Windows 3.1 or higher. Additional databases available that work with this program.

- Family Tree Journal
  http://www.cherrytreesoftware.com/

- Family Tree Maker—Latest Versions
  http://www.familytreemaker.com/ftmvers.html
  For Windows and Macintosh.

- Gene Macintosh Genealogy Software
  http://www.ics.uci.edu/~eppstein/gene/

- Genealogical Cemetery Database
  http://www.dhc.net/~design/desig1-4.htm
  Design Software, Texas. Software program for organizing cemetery records. Runs under DOS or Windows.

- The Genealogical Companion v2.2a
  http://www.geocities.com/SiliconValley/2399/tgc.htm
  A freeware Windows program which compliments the Family Origins® standard set of reports.

- Genealogy Software Guide
  http://www.eskimo.com/~mnarends/gsg.html
  A wonderful new book by Marthe Arends.

- Généatique pour windows / Geneatique for Windows
  http://www.cdip.com/
  French software.

- GeneDraw
  http://home.nordnet.fr/~ppuech/pregd3.html
  France

- Genelines—Companion Software for Genealogy
  http://www.progenysoftware.com/genelines.html
  *A charting companion for Family Tree Maker 4.x * and PAF 3.0.*

- Generations—from Sierra
  http://www.sierra.com/sierrahome/familytree/
  Previously Reunion for Windows.

- Geni—A Genealogical Browser for the Psion 3a and 3c
  http://www-theory.dcs.st-andrews.ac.uk/~mnd/export/geni/

- Genius Family Tree
  http://www.gensol.com.au/
  Windows. "The easy genealogy program."

- GensData voor Windows
  http://web.inter.nl.net/hcc/F.Berkhof/proefblz.htm
  Dutch genealogy program for Windows 3.1 or Windows 95.

- GIM Home Page—Genealogical Information Manager
  http://www.mindspring.com/~dblaine/gimhome.html
  Shareware for DOS

- Grenham's Irish Recordfinder
  http://indigo.ie/~rfinder/
  A software system designed to help you determine relevant resources for your specific Irish genealogical research.

- GRIOT Alternative—French Language Genealogy Software
  http://www.planete.qc.ca/pages/griot/index.html

- Haza-Data Website
  http://www.hazadata.com
  Dutch genealogy software program. Also versions in English, German, Swedish, Norwegian, Polish.

- Helm's Genealogy Toolbox—Genealogy Yellow Pages—Software
  http://genealogy.tbox.com/yelpgs/software/software.htm

- HEREDIS PRO pour Windows
  http://www.es-conseil.fr/pramona/p1gen.htm#sommet
  Download a demo of this French genealogy software.

- Heritage Genealogy Software
  http://www.eskimo.com/~grandine/heritage.html
  Ver. 3.01 for Mac.

- ILANOT—Software for Jewish Genealogy
  http://www.bh.org.il/Geneology/index.htm#ilanot

- JamoDat—Win-Family Software
  http://www.jamodat.dk/
  Available in Danish, Swedish, Norwegian, French, German and English.

- Kin Ware Family History Software for Windows 95 and NT
  http://www.commercial.com/kinware/
  Family Explorer.

- Legacy 2.0 Family Tree
  http://www.legacyfamilytree.com/
  Windows.

- LifeLines—Genealogy Software for UNIX
  http://www.genealogy.org/~ttw/lines/lines.html
  Alternate site
  http://www1.shore.net/~ttw/lines/lines.html

- Macintosh Genealogy Programs
  http://www.cyberenet.net/~gsteiner/macgsfaq/macprog.html

- Macintosh Genealogy Software FAQ
  http://www.cyberenet.net/~gsteiner/macgsfaq/

- The Master Genealogist
  http://www.WhollyGenes.com/
  For Windows or DOS.

- My Family History
  http://www.ozemail.com.au/~pkortge/MFH.html
  For Windows WFW & Windows 95, from Australia.

- Parents 4.6 Genealogy Software for Windows
  http://ourworld.compuserve.com/homepages/NickleWare/

- Parsons Technology Creative Studio
  http://www.parsonstech.com/genealogy/index.html
  Windows software: Family Origins, Family Atlas & Family Images Software.

- Pedigree Family History System
  http://ourworld.compuserve.com/homepages/pedigreesoftware/
  For MSDOS and also runs under Windows. A full Windows 3.1 and Win95 version is expected in Spring 1999.

- Prima's Official Companion to Family Tree Maker Version 5
  http://www.primapublishing.com/PageBuilder.asp?Page=76151677
  By Myra Vanderpool Gormley, C.G.

- PRO-GEN Genealogie à la Carte
  http://home.wxs.nl/~progen/home.html
  Dutch genealogy program capable of outputs in Dutch, English, French, Frisian and German.

- Quinsept's Family Roots "Orphans"
  http://www.ogram.org/familyroots/index.shtml
  Information page for users of the Family Roots program by Quinsept, a company which closed in August 1997.

- Relations 2.3
  http://www.edm.shaw.wave.ca/~msd/relations2.html
  A Genealogy shareware program for Newton devices.

- Reunion Home Page
  http://www.leisterpro.com/
  Software for Macintosh.

- SpanSoft Genealogy Software
  http://ourworld.compuserve.com/homepages/SpanSoft/
  "Kith and Kin"—shareware for Windows 3.1 and "TreeDraw"
  for Windows.

- Stammbaum 4.0 in Stichworten
  http://www3.pair.com/hblanken/stb.htm
  From Germany, for Windows.

- Stephen Archer's Genealogical Software Home Page
  http://ourworld.compuserve.com/homepages/steve_archer/
  IGIREAD, a file conversion utility (DOS) for the IGI on
  CD-ROM and GenMap UK, a Windows mapping program
  designed mainly for UK genealogical and historical mapping.

- Ultimate Family Tree
  http://www.uftree.com/
  From Palladium Interactive.

- WinGen (Windows Genealogy)
  http://members.tripod.com/~WinGen95/
  Shareware from New Zealand.

◆ Genealogy Software Programs That Generate HTML & Web Pages

New versions of many popular genealogy software programs now include the ability to generate HTML web pages from your genealogy database file. Several companies which make genealogy software also offer you server space for a basic home page on the Internet as part of your software purchase.

- Ancestral Quest
  http://www.ancquest.com/
  For Windows, downloadable demos available.

- Family Origins
  http://www.parsonstech.com/software/famorig.html

- Family Tree Maker
  http://www.familytreemaker.com/

- Kinship Archivist
  http://www.kinshiparchivist.com/
  Shareware program that will create web pages.

- The Master Genealogist
  http://www.WhollyGenes.com/

- Reunion 5 for Macintosh
  http://www.leisterpro.com/

- Ultimate Family Tree
  http://www.uftree.com/
  From Palladium Interactive.

◆ Helpful Internet Software Programs

- Digest Freeware—Dave Hein's Genealogy Page
  http://ourworld.compuserve.com/homepages/david_hein/
  geneal.htm
  Converts mail list digests into hypertext to view in a web
  browser.

- Free HTML Pedigree Chart & Family Group
  Sheet—from Elaine Johnson
  http://www.ida.net/users/elaine/pedigre2.HTM

- GED2HTML: A GEDCOM to HTML Translator
  http://www.gendex.com/ged2html/
  Use this software to put your GEDCOM on your web page.

- GED2WWW
  http://www.netcom.com/~lhoward/ged2www.html
  Free software to convert GEDCOM files to HTML web pages.
  Emphasis on producing a minimal amount of HTML.

- GEDCOM to HTML service on RootsWeb.com
  http://www.rootsweb.com/~nozell/gedcom-service.html
  A demo by Marc Nozell.

- Gedpage
  http://www.frontiernet.net/~rjacob/gedpage.htm
  A program that will convert your GEDCOM file to web pages
  using a family group sheet format.

- GenBrowser 1.0
  http://www.pratt.lib.md.us/~bharding/rippleeffect/
  GenBrowser.html
  HTML2GED for downloading GEDCOM information from the
  Internet. Automated searching of genealogy indexes and web
  search engines.

- Hank Zimmerman's [Unofficial] Eudora Site
  http://www.ka.net/eudora/
  Many links to Eudora e-mail program resources.

- HTMLGenie
  http://www.geneaware.com/
  A GEDCOM to HTML conversion program that permits the user
  to output their genealogical data in one of 4 formats.

- Indexed GEDCOM Method for Genweb Authoring
  http://www.rootsweb.com/~gumby/igm.html

- JavaGED
  http://www.kersur.net/~ccooper/JavaGEDHome.html
  A Java applet shareware program designed to display your
  GEDCOM file using the interactive capabilities of the Java
  programming language.

- Kinship Archivist v1.3
  http://www.frugal.com/~evjendan/ancestry.html

- PafWeb 1.0—Family Histories and Genealogies
  Over the Internet
  http://rmeservy.byu.edu/

- Sparrowhawk
  http://www.tjp.washington.edu/bdm/genealogy/
  sparrowhawk.html
  A GEDCOM-to-HTML conversion program for the Macintosh.

- Transforming Your GEDCOM Files Into Web Pages
  http://www.oz.net/~markhow/writing/gedcom.htm
  By Mark Howells.
- uFTi 1.5 for Windows 95 and NT
  http://www.ufti.demon.co.uk/homepage.htm
  For creating HTML web pages.
- webGED: Progenitor
  http://www.access.digex.net/~giammot/webged/
  Produces a complete set of files for a self-contained, searchable WWW site from a GEDCOM file, using Java.
- Webified Genealogy—WebGen
  http://www.surfutah.com/web/webgene/index.html
  GEDCOM viewer.

◆ Mailing Lists, Newsgroups & Chat

- AGLL Genealogical Services Mailing List
  http://members.aol.com/johnf14246/
  gen_mail_software.html#AGLL
  For announcements of new genealogical products and sales promotions from AGLL.
- BBANNOUNCE-L Mailing List
  http://members.aol.com/johnf14246/
  gen_mail_software.html#BBANNOUNCE-L
  Maintained by the Banner Blue Division of Broderbund Software for product announcements (10–15 postings a year).
- BK5forum Mailing List
  http://members.aol.com/johnf14246/
  gen_mail_software.html#BK5forum
  For the discussion of the Brother's Keeper genealogy program. The list is for the Scandinavian countries so please note that the language for this list is Norwegian, Danish and Swedish.
- BK5-L Mailing List
  http://members.aol.com/johnf14246/
  gen_mail_software.html#BK-L
  A mailing list for the discussion of the Brother's Keeper genealogy program.
- CFT-WIN Mailing List
  http://members.aol.com/johnf14246/
  gen_mail_software.html#CFT-WIN
  Discussion and support for Cumberland Family Software products.
- Clooz Mailing List
  http://members.aol.com/johnf14246/
  gen_mail_software.html#Clooz
  For users of the Clooz genealogy utility software program.
- FAMILIE_OG_SLEKT Mailing List
  http://members.aol.com/johnf14246/
  gen_mail_software.html#FAMILIE_OG_SLEKT
  For discussions of the "Familie og Slekt" Norwegian genealogy software program.
- FAMILY-ORIGIN-USERS Mailing List
  http://members.aol.com/johnf14246/
  gen_mail_software.html#FAMILY-ORIGINS-USERS

- FAMILYROOTS Mailing List
  http://members.aol.com/johnf14246/
  gen_mail_software.html#FAMILYROOTS
  For DOS and Macintosh users of Quinsept's Family Roots genealogy software who were "orphaned" when Steve Vorenberg closed the Quinsept company in August 1997. Also see the Quinsept's Family Roots "Orphans" Web Page at http://www.ogram.org/familyroots/familyroots-list.shtml
- FT2TMG Mailing List
  http://members.aol.com/johnf14246/
  gen_mail_software.html#FR2TMG
  For those who have questions and comments relating to importing (DOS) Family Roots (FR) data into The Master Genealogist (TMG) (Windows).
- FTMTECH-L Mailing List
  http://members.aol.com/johnf14246/
  gen_mail_software.html#FTMTECH-L
  Maintained by the Banner Blue Division of Broderbund Software for the discussion of technical issues regarding the Family Tree Maker genealogy program.
- GEDCOM-L Mailing List
  http://members.aol.com/johnf14246/
  gen_mail_software.html#GEDCOM-L
  A technical mailing list to discuss the GEDCOM specifications.
- GENCMP Mailing List
  http://members.aol.com/johnf14246/
  gen_mail_general.html#GENCMP-L
  Gatewayed with the soc.genealogy.computing newsgroup for the discussion of genealogical computing and net resources.
- GEN-MAT-REQUEST Mailing List
  http://members.aol.com/johnf14246/
  gen_mail_general.html#GEN-MAT
  For anyone who has an interest in the buying or selling of new or used genealogical materials (e.g., books, newsletters, CDs, magazines).
- GEN-MAT-15-REQUEST Mailing List
  http://members.aol.com/johnf14246/
  gen_mail_general.html#GEN-MAT-15
  For anyone who desires to post the availability of new or used genealogical materials (e.g., books, newsletters, CDs, magazines) or services for sale at a price of $15 or less.
- LegacyNews Mailing List
  http://members.aol.com/johnf14246/
  gen_mail_software.html#LegacyNews
  A read-only mailing list maintained by Millennia Corporation for announcements of interest to users of the Legacy Family Tree genealogy software program.
- LegacyUserGroup Mailing List
  http://members.aol.com/johnf14246/
  gen_mail_software.html#LegacyUserGroup
  For users of the Legacy Family Tree genealogy software program to share ideas with other Legacy users.
- LINES-L Mailing List
  http://members.aol.com/johnf14246/
  gen_mail_software.html#LINES-L
  For LifeLines Genealogical Database and Report Generator.

- PAF Mailing List
  http://members.aol.com/johnf14246/
  gen_mail_software.html#PAF
  For discussion and help regarding the use of all versions of the Personal Ancestral File genealogy program.

- PAF-2.31-USERS Mailing List
  http://members.aol.com/johnf14246/
  gen_mail_software.html#PAF-2.31-USERS

- PAF-3-USERS Mailing List
  http://members.aol.com/johnf14246/
  gen_mail_software.html#PAF-3-USERS

- ReunionTalk Mailing List
  http://www.leisterpro.com/doc/listform.html

- Sierra Generations Mailing List
  http://www.sierra.com/sierrahome/familytree/community/
  discussion/

- #TMG IRC Chat
  http://www.communique.net/~davidl/tmg-chat/tmg-chat.htm
  For the Master Genealogist software program.

- TMG-L Mailing List
  http://members.aol.com/johnf14246/
  gen_mail_software.html#TMG-L
  For those interested in The Master Genealogist software program.

- Usenet Newsgroup soc.genealogy.computing
  Genealogical computing & net resources. Gatewayed with the GENCMP-L mailing list.

- Y2K Mailing List
  http://members.aol.com/johnf14246/
  gen_mail_general.html#Y2K
  For the discussion of Year 2000 issues as they relate to genealogy.

◆ Miscellaneous Download and Reference Sites

- Computing For Genealogists—Catalogue Page
  http://www.zen.co.uk/home/page/joe.houghton/CATLOG1.HTM

- Everton's Genealogical Software on the Internet
  http://www.everton.com/d1.htm

- Genealogy and Computers Kindergarten
  http://www.rootsweb.com/~GENHOME/gccg1.htm

- Genealogy Software—Freeware/Shareware
  http://www.geocities.com/Heartland/Plains/3959/Generev.htm
  List from Chuck Roberts.

- Genealogy Software from Peter Dunn
  http://www.star.brisnet.org.au:80/~dunn/
  Ships on disk & genealogy references on disk.

- Genealogy Software Springboard
  http://www.toltbbs.com/~kbasile/software.html
  Pros and cons of various programs.

- Louis Kessler's Genealogical Program Links
  http://www.concentric.net/~Lkessler/gplinks.shtml

- Macintosh Genealogy Software FAQ
  http://www.cyberenet.net/~gsteiner/macgsfaq/

- PAF Review—Home Page
  http://www.genealogy.org/~paf/

- Your Roots are Showing
  http://macworld.zdnet.com/pages/june.95/Column.899.html
  Mac genealogy software review.

◆ Miscellaneous Software

- About Achievement of Arms™
  http://members.aol.com/grammarman/grammarstuff/
  aboutachieve.html
  Software for designing shields, crests, etc.

- Blazon and Blazon95 Software
  http://www.platypus.clara.co.uk/blazon.htm

- Blazons! Software
  http://www.blazons.com/

- Family Base Computer Archiving & Scrapbooking Software
  http://www.luminae.com/familyb.htm

- Family Photo Album for Windows
  http://www.cf-software.com/fpa.htm

- Genealogy Clip Art
  http://www.wf.net/~jyates/genart.html

- Genealogy Clip Art Catalog
  http://www.wwwebit.com/bayberry/geneclip/geneclip.html-ssi

- Heraldry Software
  http://digiserve.com/heraldry/hersoft.htm

- MyStory—The Complete Autobiography Writing System!
  http://www.mystorywriter.com/

- Walden Font
  http://www.waldenfont.com/
  Several different fonts for sale, including: The Gutenberg Press German Fraktur Fonts, The Civil War Press, Old State House, German Script, US Presidents.

◆ Publications, Magazines & Newsletters

- The Computer Genealogist
  E-mail: nehgs@nehgs.org
  A newsletter from the New England Historic Genealogical Society. For a free sample send e-mail to: nehgs@nehgs.org

- ComputerCredible Magazine: Index of Computer Genealogy Articles
  http://www.credible.com/geneallist.html

- Computers in Genealogy
  http://www.sog.org.uk/cig/
  A quarterly publication of the Society of Genealogists, U.K.

- The Digital Digest
  http://jb.com/~carla/
  Dedicated to the use of computers in the study of genealogy and family history.

- Eastman's Online Genealogy Newsletter
  http://www.ancestry.com/home/eastarch.htm

- GenealogyBookShop.com—Computers
  http://www.genealogybookshop.com/genealogybookshop/files/General,Computers/index.html
  The online store of Genealogical Publishing Co., Inc. & Clearfield Company.

- Journal of Online Genealogy
  http://www.onlinegenealogy.com/
  Promoting the use of computers and the internet in family history research.

- Genealogical Computing
  http://www2.viaweb.com/ancestry/gencom.html

- Online Pioneers Genealogy Page
  http://www.eskimo.com/~mnarends/

◆ Societies & Groups

- Afdeling Computergenealogie Van De Nederlandse Genealogische Vereniging—Gens Data
  http://www.gensdata.demon.nl/
  Netherlands

- Amateur Computer Group of New Jersey— Genealogy Special Interest Group
  http://www.castle.net/~kb4cyc/gensig.html

- Archer's Computer Interest Group List—In the United States, Canada, and Abroad
  http://www.genealogy.org/~ngs/cigs/welcome.html

- Arizona Genealogy Computer Interest Group
  http://www.agcig.org/

- Birmingham PAF Users Group
  http://www.unistarcomputers.com/paf/
  Alabama

- Blue Mountain PAF Users Group
  http://www.eoni.com/~paf/
  Eastern Oregon & Southeast Washington.

- Central Florida Computer Society
  http://www.cfcs.org/

- Central Texas PC Users Group, Austin— Genealogy SIG
  http://www.ctpcug.com./sigs.htm#gen

- Central Valley PAF Users Group
  http://www.geocities.com/TimesSquare/7957/index.htm
  Fresno, California

- Computer Genealogy Society of Long Island
  http://members.macconnect.com/users/v/vitev/genesocli/
  New York

- The Computer Genealogy Society of San Diego (CGSSD)
  http://cgssd.genweb.org/cgssd/
  California

- Computer Genealogy Society of Sweden / Föreningen för datorhjälp i släktforskningen
  http://www.dis.se/

- DIS-Danmark—Databehandling i Slægtsforskning
  http://users.cybercity.dk/~dko6959/

- Dis Nord-Trøndelag
  http://w1.2741.telia.com/~u274100021/dis/
  Computer group in Steinkjer, Norway.

- Elkhart PC Users Group Genealogy SIG
  http://www.skyenet.net/~stevens/gensig1.htm
  Indiana

- GCSGA—Genealogical Computer Society of GA
  http://members.xoom.com/gcsga/
  Atlanta, Georgia

- GENCAP: Genealogical Computing Association of Pennsylvania
  http://www.libertynet.org/~gencap/

- GenCom PC Users Group of Shreveport, Louisiana
  http://www.softdisk.com/comp/gencom/

- Genealogical Computer Society of Georgia
  http://www.mindspring.com/~noahsark/gcsga.html

- Genealogical Society of South Africa— Computer Interest Group
  http://www.geocities.com/Athens/7783/

- GenSIG—Personal Computer Club of Charlotte, NC, Inc
  http://www.chem.uncc.edu/pccc/gensig/

- GENTECH Information
  http://www.gentech.org/~gentech/
  "GENTECH, Inc. is an independent, non-profit organization chartered in the state of Texas to educate genealogists in the use of technology for gathering, storing, sharing and evaluating their research."

- HAL-PC Genealogy SIG Home Page
  http://www.hal-pc.org/~jeans/gene.shtml
  Houston, Texas

- Melbourne PAF Users Group
  http://www.cohsoft.com.au/afhc/melbpaf.html
  Australia

- Milwaukee PAF Users Group Home Page
  http://www.execpc.com/~bheck/mpafug.html

- Mother Lode PAF User Group
  http://www.nccn.net/leisure/crafthby/genealog.htm
  Nevada City, California

- North East Ohio-Computer Aided Genealogy—NEO-CAG
  http://members.harborcom.net/~kliotj/neocag/

- Norwegian Genealogy Computer Interest Group
  http://www.uio.no/~achristo/genealog.html

- PAF-WAYS, A Genealogy/Computer Users Group
  http://www.netins.net/showcase/pafways/
  North-Central Iowa

- Pike's Peak Computer Genealogists
  http://members.aol.com/cliffpoint/ppcg/index.html
  Colorado

- PRO-GEN gebruikersgroep LIMBURG / PRO-GEN users' group LIMBURG
  http://ping4.ping.be/~ping2011/
  Belgium

- Roots Users Group of Arlington, Virginia
  http://www.genealogy.org/~rug/

- Silicon Valley PAF Users Group Home Page
  http://www.genealogy.org/~svpafug/

- Southern Oregon PAF Users Group (SO-PAF-UG)
  http://www.webtrail.com/sopafug/index.html

- TMG Users Groups
  http://www.WhollyGenes.com/html/ugroups.htm
  The Master Genealogist.

- Utah Valley PAF Users Group—Home Page
  http://www.genealogy.org/~uvpafug/

- Victorian GUM (Genealogists Using Microcomputers) Inc.
  http://www.vicgum.asn.au/
  Australia

◆ Tools & Utilities

- Brian Harney's WebPages, Software Corner
  http://members.aol.com/bdharney2/bh16.htm
  2 GEDCOM programs including R3GED2FT which aids in transferring Roots III data to Family Tree Maker for Windows.

- Clooz
  http://www.ancestordetective.com/clooz.htm
  A database for systematically storing all of the clues to your ancestry that you have been collecting. Requires Microsoft Windows 95.

- DAYS Calendar Program for Genealogists
  http://www.thygesen.suite.dk/

- Deed Mapper Software
  http://www.ultranet.com/~deeds/
  For IBM PC compatibles running DOS 3.3 or higher.

- FixSex 1.0
  http://www.pratt.lib.md.us/~bharding/rippleeffect/FixSex.html
  A utility to help you fix the sex codes in a GEDCOM file.

- GEDClean Home Page
  http://www.raynorshyn.com/gedclean/
  A utility used to "clean" info about living individuals out of a GEDCOM file in order to maintain privacy.

- The GEDCOM Standard Release 5.5
  http://www.tiac.net/users/pmcbride/gedcom/55gctoc.htm

- GEDCOM Utilities
  http://www.rootsweb.com/~gumby/ged.html
  Includes: addnote, gedcaps, gedliving.

- GEDCOM Viewer
  http://www.northnet.com.au/~generic/gedcom/

- Ged-Commander for Windows95
  http://www.btinternet.com/~genealogy/gedcmdr.htm
  A utility which allows you to manually edit or merge GEDCOM files.

- GEDPrivy
  http://members.aol.com/gedprivy/index.html
  A program to create privacy for data in genealogy files (GEDCOMs).

- GEN-BOOK Home Page
  http://www.foothill.net/~genbook/
  GENerate a GENealogy BOOK from PAF to WordPerfect or MSWord.

- Genie Helper Soundex Code Conversion Software for PC
  http://jnb.home.mindspring.com/soundex.html

- IXM, Software for Creating "Back of the Book Indexes"
  http://members.aol.com/bdharney2/bh6.htm

- KINWRITE Plus
  http://www2.dtc.net/~ldbond/
  Converts a PAF file into a book.

- MacPAF Report Utility
  http://members.aol.com/nexialist/index.html

- PAF*Mate Genealogy Program
  http://www.dhc.net/~design/pafmate1.htm
  Available from Design Software.

- Progeny Software—Companion Software for Quality Charts and Reports
  http://www.progenysoftware.com/
  *Download demos of PAF*Mate and GED*Mate.*

- Res Privata
  http://www.ozemail.com.au/~naibor/rpriv.html
  An easy to use application for filtering private data from genealogy database (GEDCOM or GED) files. It can filter birth, death, marriage, adoption, notes, source and other details.

- Soundex Code Generator—Macintosh
  http://www2.vivid.net/~brisance/

◆ Vendors

- Advance Genealogy Systems
  http://www.quantumlynx.com/advance/
  Software & books.

- Ancestor Trails
  http://www.ancestor.com/at/

- Ancestor's Attic Discount Genealogy Books—
  Software & Computer Genealogy Books
  http://members.tripod.com/~ancestorsattic/index.html#COMP

- Ancestry Superstore
  http://www.ancestry.com/home/mall.htm
  Books, Computers, Maps, Miscellaneous, Services.

- Appleton's Fine Used Bookseller and Genealogy
  http://www.appletons.com/genealogy/homepage.html
  *Charlotte, North Carolina. Genealogy books, software,
  CD-ROMs, and more. Free genealogy catalog and e-mail list.*

- Dangar Associates Home Page
  http://www.genealogy.org/users/Dangar/welcome.html

- Design Software
  http://www.dhc.net/~design/
  Specialized genealogy software & other genealogy links.

- Genealogical Services & The Genealogy Store
  http://www.genservices.com/

- GLOBAL Genealogical Supply
  http://www.globalgenealogy.com/

- Global Heritage Center
  http://www.ledet.com/genealogy/ghc.html
  CD-ROMs and software.

- Gould Books—Family & Local History Specialist
  http://www.gould.com.au/Computer.htm
  *Computer software catalogue from Australia. Also books, maps,
  charts, microfiche, video & audio.*

- Hearthstone Bookshop
  http://www.hearthstonebooks.com/
  Alexandria, Virginia

- Joe's Genealogy—Genealogy Software Links
  http://www.zen.co.uk/home/page/joe.houghton/
  SOFTWARE.HTM

- Lineages, Inc.: Software
  http://www.lineages.com/catalog/SoftwareDisplay.asp

- Lofthouse Publishing—Genealogy Software
  http://www.Lofthouse.com/

- Lost In Time
  http://www.lostintime.com/
  Books, CDs, software, maps, and accessories.

- The Memorabilia Corner
  http://members.aol.com/TMCorner/index.html
  *Forms, flags, maps, software, CDs, tapes, microfilm & micro-
  fiche, books, periodicals, photographic conservation & archival
  materials.*

- Pandect Services
  http://ourworld.compuserve.com/homepages/pandect/
  *Family history software and services from Leicestershire,
  England.*

- Platte Valley Books, Gifts and Genealogical Supplies
  http://www.hht.com/bus/secure/platte~1.html

- Roots & Branches
  http://www.inconnect.com/~bdi/roots_branches/
  roots&branches.html

- S & N Genealogy Supplies
  http://ourworld.compuserve.com/homepages/
  Genealogy_Supplies/
  and their mirror site
  http://www.genealogy.demon.co.uk/

- Tanner Computer Services—Genealogy Services
  http://www.xroads.com/~tcs/genealogy/genealogy.html
  *Their Genealogy Software Registry has lists of vendors with
  addresses, phone numbers, prices, etc. They also have computer-
  related genealogy books.*

- TWR Computing
  http://www.dungeon.com/~clapstile/
  *Computers and software for family historians and
  genealogists.*

- Yahoo!...Genealogy...Software
  http://dir.yahoo.com/Business_and_Economy/Companies/
  Information/Genealogy/Software/

SOUTH AFRICA / SUID-AFRIKA
http://www.CyndisList.com/soafrica.htm

Category Index:
- General Resource Sites
- Libraries, Archives & Museums
- Mailing Lists, Newsgroups & Chat
- Military
- People & Families
- Professional Researchers, Volunteers & Other Research Services

- Publications, Software & Supplies
- Queries, Message Boards & Surname Lists
- Records: Census, Cemeteries, Land, Obituaries, Personal, Taxes and Vital
- Societies & Groups

◆ General Resource Sites

- **Advice on How to Conduct South African Research**
  E-mail: mercon@global.co.za
  Send e-mail to Mr. Conrad Mercer at mercon@global.co.za and he will share his knowledge of family history research in South Africa. However he DOES NOT provide research services. See also the link below to his web site: South African Genealogy.

- **Genealogical Institute of South Africa**
  http://www.sun.ac.za/gisa/index.html

- **Genealogy Bulletin Board Systems for South Africa**
  http://www.genealogy.org/~gbbs/gblsouth.html

- **LEHMKUHL Family Home Page**
  http://www.rupert.net/~lkool/

- **South African Genealogy**
  http://home.global.co.za/~mercon/index.htm
  From Conrod Mercer, past president of the Genealogical Society of South Africa.

◆ Libraries, Archives & Museums

- **Albany Museum Ancestry Research—Genealogy**
  http://www.ru.ac.za/departments/am/geneal.html

- **The South African War Virtual Library**
  http://www.uq.edu.au/~zzrwotto/

◆ Mailing Lists, Newsgroups & Chat

- **The Anglo Boer War Discussion Page**
  http://www.icon.co.za/~dup42/talk.htm
  This mailing list is for the discussion of the Anglo Boer War and other military related topics pre-1900.

- **FOB-LIST—Friends of the Boers—E-mail List**
  http://www.webcom.com/perspekt/eng/mlist/fob.html
  The primary topic of this mailing list is the centenary commemoration of the 2nd Anglo Boer War (1899–1902).

- **SOUTH-AFRICA Mailing List**
  http://members.aol.com/gfsjohnf/gen_mail_country-soa.html#SOUTH-AFRICA

◆ Military

- **The Anglo Boer War Discussion Page**
  http://www.icon.co.za/~dup42/talk.htm
  This mailing list is for the discussion of the Anglo Boer War and other military related topics pre-1900.

- **The Boer War—South Africa, 1899–1902**
  http://www.geocities.com/Athens/Acropolis/8141/boerwar.html

- **Commonwealth War Graves Commission**
  http://www.cwgc.org/
  Details of 1.7 million members of UK and Commonwealth forces who died in the 1st and 2nd World Wars and other wars, and 60,000 civilian casualties of WWII. Gives details of grave site, date of death, age, usually parents/widow's address.

- **Fatal Casualties In Canadian Contingents of the Boer War**
  http://www.islandnet.com/~duke/boercas.htm

- **FOB-LIST—Friends of the Boers—E-mail List**
  http://www.webcom.com/perspekt/eng/mlist/fob.html
  The primary topic of this mailing list is the centenary commemoration of the 2nd Anglo Boer War (1899–1902).

- **League of Researchers of South African Historical Battlefields**
  http://www.icon.co.za/~dup42/Welcome.html

- **The South African War Virtual Library**
  http://www.uq.net.au/~zzrwotto/

◆ People & Families

- **Huguenot Refugees in the Cape Colony of South Africa**
  http://www.rootsweb.com/~ote/hugsa.htm

- **Jewish Genealogy in South Africa: Getting Started**
  http://www.jewishgen.org/mentprog/m_rsa.htm

- **LEHMKUHL Family Home Page**
  http://www.rupert.net/~lkool/

- **The MERCER Family**
  http://www.geocities.com/Heartland/Acres/6302/
  A chronicle of the antecedents of a South African Mercer.

- The POTGIETER Genealogy Pages
  http://www.geocities.com/Heartland/Park/7152/
  If you are interested to trace your Potgieter family roots in South Africa, then this is the place for you to start. This site hosts genealogy information, a mailing list, a discussion forum, biographies and history.
- Researching Jewish Genealogies in South Africa—Part A
  http://www.jewishgen.org/infofiles/za-infoa.txt
- Researching Jewish Genealogies in South Africa—Part B
  http://www.jewishgen.org/infofiles/za-infob.txt
- VILJOEN Family Homepage
  http://www.geocities.com/Heartland/Acres/4040/index.html
  Villion, Campenaar
- Whit's End: WHITLOCK / WHITFIELD Genealogy
  http://home.pix.za/dw/dw000002/index.htm
  The genealogy of the Whitlock and Whitfield families in England and South Africa over a period of about 800 years and 26 generations.

◆ Professional Researchers, Volunteers & Other Research Services

- Genealogy Helplist—South Africa
  http://posom.com/hl/zaf/index.shtml

◆ Publications, Software & Supplies

- Generations Newsletter
  http://www.rupert.net/~lkool/page13.html
  A genealogy newsletter published 6 times per year (to be increased to 12 very soon), which contains articles of interest to anyone researching their family history in South Africa.
- Journals & Newsletters Covering Genealogy in South Africa
  http://www.geocities.com/Heartland/8256/others.html

◆ Queries, Message Boards & Surname Lists

- South African Surname Search
  http://www.rupert.net/~lkool/page11.html

◆ Records: Census, Cemeteries, Land, Obituaries, Personal, Taxes and Vital (Born, Married, Died & Buried)

- Commonwealth War Graves Commission
  http://www.cwgc.org/
  Details of 1.7 million members of UK and Commonwealth forces who died in the 1st and 2nd World Wars and other wars, and 60,000 civilian casualties of WWII. Gives details of grave site, date of death, age, usually parents/widow's address.

- Fatal Casualties in Canadian Contingents of the Boer War
  http://www.islandnet.com/~duke/boercas.htm

◆ Societies & Groups

- Archer's Computer Interest Group List—Union of South Africa
  http://www.genealogy.org/~ngs/cigs/ngl3otsa.html
- The Genealogical Researchgroup Port Elizabeth
  http://www.cs.upe.ac.za/staff/csagdk/GNGPE/
- The Genealogical Society of South Africa
  http://genweb.net/~mercon/
  - Durban and Coastal Branch
    http://genweb.net/~mercon/DurbanC.htm
  - East Cape Branch
    http://genweb.net/~mercon/ECape.htm
  - East Gauteng Branch
    http://genweb.net/~mercon/EGauteng.html
  - Free State Branch
    http://genweb.net/~mercon/OFS.htm
  - Natal Midlands Branch
    http://genweb.net/~mercon/NatalM.htm
  - Northern Transvaal Branch
    http://genweb.net/~mercon/NTvl.htm
  - Southern Transvaal Branch
    http://genweb.net/~mercon/STvl.htm
    Saxonwold
  - Western Cape Branch
    http://genweb.net/~mercon/WCape.htm
- Genealogical Society of South Africa—Computer Interest Group
  http://www.geocities.com/Athens/7783/
- Huguenot Society of South Africa
  http://www.geocities.com/Heartland/Valley/8140/
- League of Researchers of South African Historical Battlefields
  http://www.icon.co.za/~dup42/Welcome.html
- The South African Military History Society / Die Suid-Afrikaanse Krygshistoriese Vereeniging
  http://rapidttp.com/milhist/
- The South East Witwatersrand Family History Society
  http://www.geocities.com/Heartland/8256/
  Gauteng, Republic of South Africa.
- UPEGIS
  http://www.cs.upe.ac.za/staff/csagdk/GisRes/UPEGIS/
  The University of Port Elizabeth Genealogical Information System.

SPAIN, PORTUGAL & THE BASQUE COUNTRY / ESPAÑA, PORTUGAL Y EL PAÍS VASCO

http://www.CyndisList.com/spain.htm

Category Index:

- ◆ General Resource Sites
- ◆ History & Culture
- ◆ Libraries, Archives & Museums
- ◆ Mailing Lists, Newsgroups & Chat
- ◆ Maps, Gazetteers & Geographical Information
- ◆ People & Families

- ◆ Professional Researchers, Volunteers & Other Research Services
- ◆ Publications, Software & Supplies
- ◆ Queries, Message Boards & Surname Lists
- ◆ Records: Census, Cemeteries, Land, Obituaries, Personal, Taxes and Vital
- ◆ Societies & Groups

◆ General Resource Sites

- Azore Islands—WorldGenWeb Project
  http://www.pacifier.com/~kcardoz/azoresindex.html
  Learn about the Azores with maps that show each island and the villages and churches there. Post a query here.

- Azores: Source of Immigration to the Americas
  http://www.lusaweb.com/azhist.htm

- Basque Genealogy Homepage
  http://www.primenet.com/~fybarra/
  From Susan Yvarra. YBARRA, ARESTI, AYO, URIGUEN, ARISTEGUI, MENDICOTE, MIRAGAYA and SESUMAGA.

- Blasón Virtual, Heráldica en la Red
  http://www.ctv.es/blason/

- Buber's Basque Page
  http://weber.u.washington.edu/~buber/Basque/Diaspora/
  *Euskaldunen Diaspora Eta Genealogia * The Basque Diaspora and Genealogy * La Diaspora Y Genealogia Vascas * La Disaspora Et Genealogie Basque.*

- Buber's Basque Page: Genealogical Tips
  http://weber.u.washington.edu/~buber/Basque/Diaspora/search.html
  Tips for doing genealogical research, tailored for researchers of the Basque Country.

- Centre Généalogique des Pyrénées-Atlantiques (Béarn et Pays Basque)
  http://www.world-address.com/cgpa/

- Centro De Estudios Heraldicos
  http://www.net64.es/heraldica/

- Fernando CANDIDO's Portuguese Genealogy Home Page
  http://www.freenet.edmonton.ab.ca/~fcandido/

- Genealogical Resources for Researching in the Azores, Portugal
  http://www.LusaWeb.com/resource.htm

- Heraldica Hispana
  http://www.alc.es/heraldica/heral_en.htm

- Hispanic, Central & South America, & the West Indies
  http://www.CyndisList.com/hispanic.htm
  Including Mexico, Latin America & the Caribbean. See this category on Cyndi's List for related links.

- Hispanic Genealogy Address Book—Portugal
  http://users.aol.com/mrosado007/portugal.htm

- LusaWeb—Portuguese Genealogy Resources
  http://www.lusaweb.com/html/genea.cfm

- Madeira: Sharing and Searching
  http://www.geocities.com/Heartland/Plains/9462/

- Portuguese Genealogist Master Database
  http://www.lusaweb.com/mstrlst.cfm

- Portuguese Genealogy Information Page from Doug da Rocha Holmes
  http://www.dholmes.com/rocha2.html

- Portuguese Genealogy Lexique
  http://www.freenet.edmonton.ab.ca/~fcandido/lexique.html
  Portuguese-English translations of genealogy terms.

- Portuguese Genealogy Workshop
  http://www.dholmes.com/workshop.html

- Portuguese Resources on the Web
  http://www.maui.net/~makule/port.html

- Research Guide Genealogical Resources, Madeira, Portugal
  http://www.geocities.com/Heartland/Hills/1065/GUIDE.HTML

- Reynolds Hunter y Puebla Heráldica y Blasones—Heraldries
  http://www.audinex.es/~hunter/

- Spain Genealogy Address Book
  http://user.aol.com/mrosado007/spain.htm
- Spanish Yellow Pages—Páginas Amarillas Multimedia
  http://www.paginas-amarillas.es/
- Western Europe
  http://www.CyndisList.com/westeuro.htm
  See this category on Cyndi's List for related links.

◆ History & Culture

- LusaWeb: Portuguese-American Communities on the World Wide Web
  http://www.LusaWeb.com/
- Portuguese/Azorean History Articles
  http://www.lusaweb.com/history.htm

◆ Libraries, Archives & Museums

- Arquivo da Universidade de Coimbra
  http://www.ci.uc.pt/auc/
  Portugal
- Arquivo Distrital de Beja (Portugal)
  http://www.cidadevirtual.pt/arq-dist-beja/
- Biblioteca Nacional / Portuguese National Library
  http://www.biblioteca-nacional.pt/
  Portugal
- Biblioteca Nacional de España / National Library of Spain
  http://www.bne.es/
- Biblioteca Pública e Arquivo de Angra do Heroísmo
  http://www.gzcah.pt//arede/entid/bpaah.htm
  Portugal
- Instituto Da Biblioteca Nacional E Do Livro—IBL
  http://www.ibl.pt/
  Portugal

◆ Mailing Lists, Newsgroups & Chat

- BASQUE Mailing List
  http://members.aol.com/gfsjohnf/gen_mail_country-fra.html#BASQUE
  A "moderated" mailing list, gatewayed with the soc.culture.basque "moderated" newsgroup, that provides Basques the world over with a virtual place to discuss social, political, cultural or any other issues related to Basques, or to request information and discuss matters related to the Basque people and/or their culture. Genealogy queries are an acceptable topic for the list.
- BASQUE-L Mailing List
  http://members.aol.com/gfsjohnf/gen_mail_country-fra.html#BASQUE-L
  A forum for the dissemination and exchange of information on Basque culture. Genealogy-related issues are often discussed on the list though the main topics of discussion are socio-political current affairs, gastronomy, Basque music, poetry, anthropology (e.g., origin of Basques), etc.

- MadeiraExiles Mailing List
  http://members.aol.com/gfsjohnf/gen_mail_states-il.html#MadeiraExiles
  Devoted to the research of Dr. Robert Reid Kalley's Portuguese Presbyterian exiles from Madeira, Portugal who emigrated to Trinidad and then to Illinois (ca 1846–1854).
- PORTUGAL Mailing List
  http://members.aol.com/gfsjohnf/gen_mail_country-por.html#PORTUGAL
- SPAIN Mailing List
  http://members.aol.com/gfsjohnf/gen_mail_country-spa.html#SPAIN

◆ Maps, Gazetteers & Geographical Information

- Map of Portugal
  http://www.lib.utexas.edu/Libs/PCL/Map_collection/europe/Portugal.jpg
  From the Perry-Castañeda Library at the Univ. of Texas at Austin.
- Map of Spain
  http://www.lib.utexas.edu/Libs/PCL/Map_collection/europe/Spain.jpg
  From the Perry-Castañeda Library at the Univ. of Texas at Austin
- Topographic Maps of the Azores Islands
  http://www.dholmes.com/az-maps.html
  Maps for sale for each of the islands.

◆ People & Families

- ABARCA. Genealogía y Heráldica del apellido
  http://www.ctv.es/USERS/abarca/
  de Aragón (España)
- El apellido ALFARO / The Surname ALFARO
  http://members.tripod.com/~Antonioalfaro/
  Spain, Portugal, Italy, Chile, Argentina, Brazil, Peru, Ecuador, Costa Rica, Panama, Puerto Rico, Mexico, the United States.
- Basque Genealogy Homepage
  http://www.primenet.com/~fybarra/
  From Susan Yvarra. YBARRA, ARESTI, AYO, URIGUEN, ARISTEGUI, MENDICOTE, MIRAGAYA and SESUMAGA.
- The COBRA Family Genealogy Home Page
  http://www.geocities.com/Athens/Acropolis/3515/
  History and genealogy of the Cobra Family in Portugal and its modern branches in Canada, Brazil, and the U.S.A.
- The (Do) ESPIRITO SANTO Family Club / Clube Das Famílias "Do ESPÍRITO SANTO"
  http://members.tripod.com/~EspiritoSanto/
- A Família Lima Verde
  http://www.geocities.com/Heartland/2177/lv.htm
  In Portuguese.
- Genealogía de Imanol M. Pagola SALAZAR
  http://www.geocities.com/Heartland/Hills/7393/

- Genealogia e Heráldica Portuguesa—Portuguese Genealogy and Heraldry
  http://www.nca.pt/individual/babel/
  álvaro HOLSTEIN Home Page.

- Genealogia Imanol M. Pagola SALAZAR
  http://www.geocities.com/Heartland/7399/

- The MEDEIROS Web—Heraldry and Genealogy
  http://www.maui.net/~makule/medgene.html

- Nelson SILVA Genealogy—Genealogia
  http://aramis.inescn.pt/~nsilva/gen/
  With categorized links for Genealogy in Portugal—Genealogia em Portugal.

- Papagaia's Journey of Discovery
  http://www.geocities.com/Heartland/Hills/1065/

- Portuguese Family Histories Home Page
  http://www.dholmes.com/fam-hist.html

- Portuguese Genealogy Home Pages
  http://www.geocities.com/CapitolHill/6506/Genealogy.html

◆ Professional Researchers, Volunteers & Other Research Services

- The Basque Genealogy Homepage Research Services
  http://www.primenet.com/~fybarra/Research.html
  Specializing in Basque records from the province of Vizcaya. These records are on microfilm at the Salt Lake Family History Library, but do not get circulated.

- genealogyPro—Professional Genealogists for Spain and Basque Country
  http://genealogyPro.com/directories/Spain.html

- Portuguese Genealogy by Doug da Rocha Holmes
  http://www.dholmes.com/rocha1.html
  Professional researcher specializing in Azorean genealogy and Portuguese translation.

◆ Publications, Software & Supplies

- The Forgotten Portuguese: The Melungeons and Other Groups—The Portuguese Making of America
  http://www.clinch.edu/appalachia/melungeon/mira.htm
  A book for sale, by Manuel Mira.

- GenealogyBookShop.com—Spain/Spanish/Hispanic
  http://www.genealogybookshop.com/genealogybookshop/files/
  The_World,Spain_Spanish_Hispanic/index.html
  The online store of Genealogical Publishing Co., Inc. & Clearfield Company.

- O Progresso—The Quarterly Newsletter of the Portuguese Historical & Cultural Society (PHCS)
  http://www.dholmes.com/o-prog.html

- Portuguese Gift Shop
  http://www.dholmes.com/portgift.html
  Books, documents, maps, and more.

- Portuguese Pioneers of the Sacramento Valley
  http://www.dholmes.com/new-book.html
  A new book project.

◆ Queries, Message Boards & Surname Lists

- Basque Surname Research
  http://weber.u.washington.edu/~buber/Basque/Surname/
  surlist.html

- Lineages' Free On-line Queries—Portugal & Spain
  http://www.lineages.com/queries/BrowseByCountry.asp

- Portuguese Genealogist Master List
  http://www.dholmes.com/master-l.html
  - Angola
    http://www.dholmes.com/angola.html
  - Azores / Açores
    http://www.dholmes.com/azores.html
    - Corvo
      http://www.dholmes.com/corvo.html
    - Faial
      http://www.dholmes.com/faial.html
    - Flores
      http://www.dholmes.com/flores.html
    - Graciosa
      http://www.dholmes.com/graciosa.html
    - Pico
      http://www.dholmes.com/pico.html
    - Santa Maria
      http://www.dholmes.com/smaria.html
    - São Jorge
      http://www.dholmes.com/sajorge.html
    - São Miguel
      http://www.dholmes.com/smiguel.html
    - Terceira
      http://www.dholmes.com/terceira.html
  - Brasil
    http://www.dholmes.com/brasil.html
  - Cabo Verde (Cape Verde)
    http://www.dholmes.com/caboverd.html
  - Madeira
    http://www.dholmes.com/madeira.html
  - Mainland Portugal
    http://www.dholmes.com/portugal.html
  - Porto Santo
    http://www.dholmes.com/psanto.html

◆ Records: Census, Cemeteries, Land, Obituaries, Personal, Taxes and Vital (Born, Married, Died & Buried)

- LusaWeb Portuguese Immigrant Ship Lists
  http://www.lusaweb.com/shiplist.cfm

- Portuguese Passenger Ship Master List
  http://www.dholmes.com/ships.html

- Portuguese Voters of 1872 in California
  http://www.dholmes.com/voters.html

◆ Societies & Groups

- Hawaii Portuguese Genealogical Society
  http://www.lusaweb.com/pgsh.htm

- Portuguese Historical & Cultural Society (PHCS)
  http://www.dholmes.com/calendar.html
  Sacramento, California

SUPPLIES, CHARTS, FORMS, ETC.
http://www.CyndisList.com/supplies.htm

Category Index:
- ◆ General Resource Sites
- ◆ Mailing Lists, Newsgroups & Chat
- ◆ Online Charts & Forms to Print
- ◆ Vendors

◆ General Resource Sites

- • Charts, Forms and Logs
  http://www.geocities.com/Heartland/Valley/2248/explain.html
  An explanation of terms, types of forms, etc.

- • The Forms Needed to Order Records from the National Archives
  http://www.ancestry.com/columns/george/05-15-98.htm
  From "Along Those Lines . . ." by George G. Morgan.

- • National Genealogical Society—
  NGS Beginner's Kit
  http://www.ngsgenealogy.org/education/content/beginkit.html

- • National Genealogical Society—Genealogical Forms and Research Aids
  http://www.ngsgenealogy.org/education/content/gen_forms.html

- • The SGGS "German Card"
  http://feefhs.org/sggs/sggs-gc.html

- • Universal Family Group Sheet
  http://www.geocities.com/Heartland/Meadows/7970/vfgs.html
  An online form which allows you to enter your data and e-mail it to another researcher.

◆ Mailing Lists, Newsgroups & Chat

- • GEN-MARKET Mailing List
  http://members.aol.com/johnf14246/gen_mail_general.html#GEN-MARKET
  Gatewayed with the soc.genealogy.marketplace newsgroup for commercial postings of unique interest to genealogists.

- • GEN-MAT-REQUEST Mailing List
  http://members.aol.com/johnf14246/gen_mail_general.html#GEN-MAT
  This is a mailing list for anyone who has an interest in the buying or selling of new or used genealogical materials (e.g., books, newsletters, CDs, magazines).

- • GEN-MAT-15-REQUEST Mailing List
  http://members.aol.com/johnf14246/gen_mail_general.html#GEN-MAT-15
  For anyone who desires to post the availability of new or used genealogical materials (e.g., books, newsletters, CDs, magazines) or services for sale at a price of $15 or less.

◆ Online Charts & Forms to Print

- • Abstract Printable Forms for Census Records ~ U.S.
  http://www.familytreemaker.com/00000061.html
  - ○ 1790
    http://www.familytreemaker.com/00000062.html
  - ○ 1800
    http://www.familytreemaker.com/00000063.html
  - ○ 1810
    http://www.familytreemaker.com/00000064.html
  - ○ 1820–1
    http://www.familytreemaker.com/00000065.html
  - ○ 1820–2
    http://www.familytreemaker.com/00000066.html
  - ○ 1830–1
    http://www.familytreemaker.com/00000067.html
  - ○ 1830–2
    http://www.familytreemaker.com/00000068.html
  - ○ 1840–1
    http://www.familytreemaker.com/00000069.html
  - ○ 1840–2
    http://www.familytreemaker.com/00000070.html
  - ○ 1850
    http://www.familytreemaker.com/00000071.html
  - ○ 1860
    http://www.familytreemaker.com/00000072.html
  - ○ 1870–1
    http://www.familytreemaker.com/00000073.html
  - ○ 1870–2
    http://www.familytreemaker.com/00000074.html
  - ○ 1880–1
    http://www.familytreemaker.com/00000075.html
  - ○ 1880–2
    http://www.familytreemaker.com/00000076.html
  - ○ 1890–1
    http://www.familytreemaker.com/00000077.html
  - ○ 1890–2
    http://www.familytreemaker.com/00000078.html
  - ○ 1900–1
    http://www.familytreemaker.com/00000079.html

- 1900–2
  http://www.familytreemaker.com/00000080.html
- 1910–1
  http://www.familytreemaker.com/00000081.html
- 1910–2
  http://www.familytreemaker.com/00000082.html
- 1910–3
  http://www.familytreemaker.com/00000083.html
- 1920–1
  http://www.familytreemaker.com/00000084.html
- 1920–2
  http://www.familytreemaker.com/00000085.html
- 1920–3
  http://www.familytreemaker.com/00000086.html

- **AHSGR Genealogical Forms**
  http://www.ahsgr.org/ahsgrfrm.html
  Forms for members of the American Historical Society of Germans From Russia.

- **Ancestors Charts and Records**
  http://www.pbs.org/kbyu/ancestors/teachersguide/charts-records.html
  From the television program on PBS. Includes a Pedigree Chart, Family Group Record, 2nd Page Family Group Record, Timeline Page, Research Log, Family and Home Information Sources Checklist, and Child's Pedigree Chart.

- **Checklist of Home Sources**
  http://www.rootscomputing.com/howto/checkl/checkl.htm

- **Everton's Free Forms**
  http://www.everton.com/charts/freeform.html
  Pedigree Chart and Family Group Sheet.

- **Genealogy Chart**
  http://www.gcpl.lib.oh.us/services/gcr/gen_resources/gtree.htm

- **Genealogy Charts!**
  http://www.genealogy-mall.com/freechar.htm
  - Family Group Record: Page 1
    http://www.genealogy-mall.com/fgr.htm
  - Family Group Record: Page 2
    http://www.genealogy-mall.com/fgr2.htm
  - Pedigree Chart
    http://www.genealogy-mall.com/pedchart.htm
  - 1790 Census Abstract Form
    http://www.genealogy-mall.com/1790cens.htm
  - 1800 Census Abstract Form
    http://www.genealogy-mall.com/1800cens.htm
  - Soundex Card
    http://www.genealogy-mall.com/sndxcard.htm

- **Greene County Room Genealogy Resources Genealogy Tree**
  http://www.gcpl.lib.oh.us/services/gcr/gen_resources/gtree.htm

- **GRS—Genealogy Records Service—Free Genealogy Charts & Forms**
  http://www.genrecords.com/forms.htm
  Includes Four Generation Ancestor Chart, Research Log, Four Generation Chart w/Tree, Blank Soundex Cards, Four Generation Vertical Chart, Vertical Family Group Sheet, Cousin Finder Chart, Cemetery Abstract Chart, Marriage Abstract Chart, Abstract for Soundex Research, Census History Form for Individuals. Requires the free Adobe Acrobat Reader Plugin.
  http://www.adobe.com/prodindex/acrobat/readstep.html

- **Lineages' First Steps—Get Organized**
  http://www.lineages.com/FirstSteps/Basic.asp
  Download a free toolkit of genealogical forms.

- **Pedigree Chart—From the LDS Church**
  http://www.lds.org/en/2_How_Do_I_Begin/Pedigree_Chart.html

- **Research Log**
  http://www.lds.org/en/2_How_Do_I_Begin/Research_Log.html
  From the LDS church.

- **ROOTS-L Resources: Printable Forms**
  http://www.rootsweb.com/roots-l/forms.html
  Postscript forms to print.

- **Rory's Genealogy Pages—Family Record Sheet**
  http://www.erols.com/emcrcc/Family_Record.htm

- **Rory's Genealogy Pages—Four Generation Pedigree Chart**
  http://www.erols.com/emcrcc/pedigree.htm

- **Rory's Genealogy Pages—Research Log**
  http://www.erols.com/emcrcc/Res_Log.htm

- **Rory's Genealogy Pages—Resources Checklist**
  http://www.erols.com/emcrcc/Resources_Checklist.htm

- **U.S. Census Summary Chart**
  http://www2.primecomm.net/trees/chart.htm

◆ Vendors

- **Appleton's Fine Used Bookseller and Genealogy**
  http://www.appletons.com/genealogy/homepage.html

- **Barnette's Family Tree Book Company— Genealogy Charts**
  http://www.barnettesbooks.com/charts.htm

  Genealogy Forms
  http://www.barnettesbooks.com/forms.htm

- **Custom Family Trees & Charts by Olsongraphics**
  http://www.olsonetc.com/

- **Dacrid's Genealogy Prints**
  http://www.dacrid.com/playit/genealgy.htm

- **Design Software—Genealogy Charts & Forms**
  http://www.dhc.net/~design/desig1-5.htm

- **Genealogical Services & The Genealogy Store**
  http://www.genservices.com/

- **Genealogy Unlimited—Home Page**
  http://www.itsnet.com/~genun/

- GLOBAL Genealogical Supply
  http://www.globalgenealogy.com/

- Grant Misbach's Genealogy & Family History Charts
  http://www.misbach.org/charts/index.html

- GRL Genealogy Supplies
  http://www.grl.com/grl/supplies.shtml
  Charts, albums and software from the Genealogical Research Library.

- Hearthstone Bookshop
  http://www.hearthstonebooks.com/
  Alexandria, Virginia

- Keeping Memories Alive—Scrapbook Supplies
  http://www.scrapbooks.com/

- The Memorabilia Corner
  http://members.aol.com/TMCorner/index.html
  Forms, flags, maps, software, CDs, tapes, microfilm & microfiche, books, periodicals, conservation & archival materials.

- Olsongraphics Custom Genealogy Family Trees
  http://www.olsonetc.com/

- Petersen Reproductions
  http://www.datacruz.com/~bapetersen/pr1888.htm
  Reproductions of antique prints and family tree charts.

- Quintin Publications
  http://www.quintinpublications.com/
  Materials relating to Canada.

- Roots and Branches
  http://members.aol.com/RebelSher1/index.html
  Used books, forms, maps and the Civil War info.

- ROOTSTAMPS
  http://www.whitemtns.com/~roots/
  Rubber stamp collection for genealogists.

- Sunnydaze Genealogical Research Material & Antiques
  http://www.sunnydaze.com/

- Suppliers—Sources of Conservation Supplies
  http://palimpsest.stanford.edu/bytopic/suppliers/

- Ye Olde Genealogie Shoppe—Forms, Charts, Maps & Goodies
  http://www.yogs.com/

- Ye Olde Genealogy Charts, Ltd.
  http://www.webcom.com/charts/

SURNAMES, FAMILY ASSOCIATIONS & FAMILY NEWSLETTERS

Sites or resources dedicated to SPECIFIC, individual family surnames. Listed alphabetically by SURNAME.
http://www.CyndisList.com/surnames.htm

Category Index:

- General Surname Sites
- Mailing Lists, Newsgroups & Chat
- Publications, Software & Supplies
- Alphabetical Listing by Surname

◆ General Surname Sites

- **Acadian/French-Canadian SURNAME Researchers**
  http://www.acadian.org/genealogy/resrch.html
  From the Acadian Genealogy Homepage.

- **Acadian Genealogy Homepage—List of Surnames on the Acadian CD**
  http://www.acadian.org/genealogy/surnames.html

- **Advice from the Experts: Running a Family Association**
  http://www.familytreemaker.com/26_runfm.html

- **The Association of One-Name Studies**
  http://www.willowbend.net/aons.htm

- **Brasenhill Genealogy Page**
  http://www.brasenhill.com/research/
  For the surname researcher—a site with links to home pages and an index of surnames and soundex codes as well.

- **Broken Arrow Publishing * Genealogy * Surname Origins**
  http://clanhuston.com/name/name.htm

- **Chinese Surnames**
  http://www.geocities.com/Tokyo/3919/

- **Common Threads**
  http://www.gensource.com/common/
  A searchable database with e-mail addresses for submitters.

- **Connect with Surnames**
  http://www.geocities.com/Heartland/Bluffs/7708/

- **Database, Search Sites, Surname Lists**
  http://www.CyndisList.com/database.htm
  See this category on Cyndi's List for related links.

- **Design Software—Genealogy Databases on the World Wide Web, A–M**
  http://www.dhc.net/~design/datainda.htm
  N–Z
  http://www.dhc.net/~design/dataindx.htm

- **Family Associations 101**
  http://www.familytreemaker.com/26_famas.html

- **Family Chronicle—Surname Origin List**
  http://www.familychronicle.com/surname.htm

- **Family History Research Register**
  http://symbcon.co.uk/fhistory/
  Register your surnames here and search the list for entries by others.

- **Fédération des Familles-Souches Québécoises Inc.**
  http://www.mediom.qc.ca/~ffsq/

- **FEEFHS Cross Index of 27 Surname Databases**
  http://feefhs.org/index/indexsur.html

- **GenConnect at RootsWeb—Family Associations**
  http://cgi.rootsweb.com/~genbbs/indx/FamAssoc.html

- **GENDEX Database**
  http://www.gendex.com
  A searchable index of over 1 million names.

- **Genealogy Exchange and Surname Registry**
  http://www.genexchange.com/index.cfm

- **GENUKI Surname Lists**
  http://www.cs.ncl.ac.uk/genuki/SurnamesList/
  Lists for each county in the United Kingdom and Ireland.

- **Global Genealogy—Family Histories & Genealogies**
  http://www.globalgenealogy.com/famhist.htm

- **Guild of One-Name Studies**
  http://www.one-name.org
  United Kingdom

- **Janyce's Surname to Researcher Directory**
  http://www.janyce.com/gene/names/surname.html

- **Kinseeker Publications Surname Newsletters**
  http://www.angelfire.com/biz/Kinseeker/newsletters.html

- **Legends and Legacies Family Tree Collection**
  http://www.legends.ca/library/trees/famtree.html

- **The Origins of Family Names**
  http://www.rootscomputing.com/howto/names/names.htm

- **Personal Home Pages**
  http://www.CyndisList.com/personal.htm
  See this category on Cyndi's List for related links.

- Queries & Message Boards
  http://www.CyndisList.com/queries.htm
  See this category on Cyndi's List for related links.

- Quirky Surnames
  http://members.xoom.com/present/

- The Relevance of Surnames in Genealogy
  http://www.sog.org.uk/leaflets/surnames.html
  Society of Genealogists Information Leaflet No. 7, from the U.K.

- RootsWeb Surname List
  http://www.rootsweb.com/rootsweb/searches/rslsearch.html

- RootsWeb Surname List Search Engine
  on Rootsweb
  http://rsl.rootsweb.com/cgi-bin/rslsql.cgi

- Stone Soup for Genealogists (Publishing a
  One-family Periodical)
  http://www.familytreemaker.com/26_wylie1.html

- The Story of Your Name
  http://www.lookup.com/homepages/69888/home.html

- Surname List and Their Researchers
  http://www.lookup.com/Homepages/55085/bulls.html/
  geo3.html/geo3.html#here
  List with e-mail addresses for people to contact.

- Surname Springboard
  http://www.geocities.com/~alacy/spring.htm
  *Dedicated to internet researchers who have indexed their
  GEDCOM data & converted it to HTML pages.*

- The SurnameWeb
  http://www.surnameweb.org
  The Surname Genealogy Web Project.

- Top 50 Surnames in the United States
  http://www.genrecords.com/library/usnames.htm

- SWINX Zoeklijst Nederlandse Familienamen
  http://www.multiweb.nl/~don_arnoldus/swinx/index.html
  Netherlands. SWINX = Surname Website INdeX.

- U.S. Surname Distribution Maps
  http://www.hamrick.com/names/index.html
  - Local Names in Each State
    http://www.hamrick.com/names/localnam.txt
  - Top 100 Names in the State of....
    http://www.hamrick.com/names/top100.txt

- USGenWeb Lineage Researcher Pages
  http://www.rootsweb.com/~lineage/

- Webified Genealogy
  http://www.surfutah.com/web/webgene/
  Search by surname and soundex code.

- What's in a Surname?
  http://www.familytreemaker.com/issue18.html

◆ Mailing Lists, Newsgroups & Chat

- Genealogy Resources on the Internet—
  "General" Surname Mailing Lists
  http://members.aol.com/gfsjohnf/gen_mail_surnames-gen.html

- GEN-EDITOR Mailing List
  http://members.aol.com/johnf14246/
  gen_mail_general.html#GEN-EDITOR
  *For editors/publishers of genealogical, surname and family
  newsletters to have a place to discuss and share ideas and tips.*

- GOONS-L Mailing List
  http://members.aol.com/johnf14246/
  gen_mail_general.html#GOONS-L
  *For members of the Guild of One-Name Studies (GOONS) to
  promote discussion of matters concerned with One-Name
  Studies and the Guild.*

- ROLL-CALL Mailing List
  http://members.aol.com/gfsjohnf/gen_mail_surnames-
  gen.html#ROLL-CALL
  *For the posting of "roll calls" (lists) of the surnames you are
  researching so that others can determine if there is a common
  interest.*

- RSL-UPDATE Mailing List
  http://members.aol.com/gfsjohnf/gen_mail_surnames-
  gen.html#RSL-UPDATE
  *The RootsWeb Surname List database monthly update of
  new surnames.*

- soc.genealogy.surnames.* / SURNAMES-*
  FAQ files
  http://www.rootsweb.com/~surnames/

- Surname Mailing Lists—Genealogy Resources on
  the Internet
  http://members.aol.com/johnf14246/gen_mail.html
  See the alphabetical listing at the bottom of the main index.

- SURNAME-QUERY Mailing List
  http://members.aol.com/gfsjohnf/gen_mail_surnames-
  gen.html#SURNAME-QUERY
  For users to send queries on specific surname searches.

- SURNAMES Mailing List
  http://members.aol.com/gfsjohnf/gen_mail_surnames-
  gen.html#SURNAMES
  *Surname queries central database. Gatewayed with the
  soc.genealogy.surnames.global newsgroup.*

- SURNAMES-BRITAIN Mailing List
  http://members.aol.com/gfsjohnf/gen_mail_surnames-
  gen.html#SURNAMES-BRITAIN
  *For surname queries related to Great Britain. Gatewayed with
  the soc.genealogy.surnames.britain newsgroup.*

- SURNAMES-CANADA Mailing List
  http://members.aol.com/gfsjohnf/gen_mail_surnames-
  gen.html#SURNAMES-CANADA
  *For surname queries related to Canada. Gatewayed with the
  soc.genealogy.surnames.canada newsgroup.*

- SURNAMES-GERMAN Mailing List
  http://members.aol.com/gfsjohnf/gen_mail_surnames-gen.html#SURNAMES-GERMAN
  For surname queries related to German speaking countries. Gatewayed with the soc.genealogy.surnames.german newsgroup.

- SURNAMES-IRELAND Mailing List
  http://members.aol.com/gfsjohnf/gen_mail_surnames-gen.html#SURNAMES-IRELAND
  For surname queries related to Ireland and Northern Ireland. Gatewayed with the soc.genealogy.surnames.ireland newsgroup.

- SURNAMES-MISC Mailing List
  http://members.aol.com/gfsjohnf/gen_mail_surnames-gen.html#SURNAMES-MISC
  For surname queries for regions not addressed elsewhere in the soc.genealogy.surnames. hierarchy. Gatewayed with the soc.genealogy.surnames.misc newsgroup.*

- SURNAMES-USA Mailing List
  http://members.aol.com/gfsjohnf/gen_mail_surnames-gen.html#SURNAMES-USA
  For surname queries related to the United States. Gatewayed with the soc.genealogy.surnames.usa newsgroup.

◆ Publications, Software & Supplies

- Ancestor Publishers Microfiche—Family Histories
  http://www.firstct.com/fv/surnames.html

- Books We Own—Family History by Surname
  http://www.rootsweb.com/~bwo/surindex.html

- Boyd Publishing Company—Family Histories
  http://www.hom.net/~gac/family.htm

- GenealogyBookShop.com—Family Histories
  http://www.genealogybookshop.com/genealogybookshop/files/General,Family_Histories/index.html
  The online store of Genealogical Publishing Co., Inc. & Clearfield Company.

- GenealogyBookShop.com—Surnames and Personal Names
  http://www.genealogybookshop.com/genealogybookshop/files/General,Surnames_and_Personal_Names/index.html
  The online store of Genealogical Publishing Co., Inc. & Clearfield Company.

- Heritage Books—Genealogies
  http://www.heritagebooks.com/geneal.htm

- Willow Bend Bookstore—Families
  http://www.willowbend.net/fg.htm

- Willow Bend Bookstore—Genealogies
  http://www.willowbend.net/genfam.htm

- Willow Bend Bookstore—Surnames
  http://www.willowbend.net/surname.htm

- Yahoo!...Genealogy:Publications:Individual Family
  http://dir.yahoo.com/Business_and_Economy/Companies/Information/Genealogy/Publications/Individual_Family_Histories/

◆ Surnames Beginning with "A"

- Family Tree Maker Online User Home Pages—A
  http://www.familytreemaker.com/users/a/index.html

- Genealogy's Most Wanted—Surnames Beginning with "A"
  http://www.citynet.net/mostwanted/a.htm

- H-GIG Surname Registry—Surnames Beginning A
  http://www.ucr.edu/h-gig/surdata/surname1.html

- Higginson Book Company—Surnames Beginning with A
  http://www.higginsonbooks.com/a.htm

- inGeneas Table of Common Surname Variations and Surname Misspellings—A–B
  http://www.ingeneas.com/A2B.html

- Surname Springboard Index—A
  http://www.geocities.com/~alacy/spring_i.htm

- SurnameWeb Surname Registry—A Index
  http://www.surnameweb.org/registry/a.htm

- Genealogy Resources on the Internet—"A" Surname Mailing Lists
  http://members.aol.com/gfsjohnf/gen_mail_surnames-a.html
  This site is wonderfully maintained by John Fuller. It includes mailing list information for the following surnames and their variant spellings:
  ABERCROMBIE (includes Abbercrombie, Abbercrumby), ABERNATHY (includes Abernethy), ABSTON, ACKER, ACKERMAN (includes Ackermann, Aukerman, Ackeman, Akerman, Acerman), ACUFF (includes Ecoff, Eickhoff, Ayscough, Eckhoff, Achuff, Acoff), ADAIR, ADAMS (includes McAdams, Addams, Adamson), AdcockFamily, ADKINS (includes Adkinson, Atkins, Atkinson), AGAN, AGEE, AGNEW, AILSTOCK (includes Aylstock, Alestock), AKERS (includes Ackers, Acree, Akerman, McAkers, Eckers), AKINS, ALBEE (includes Albe, Allbee, Alby, Albie, Aulby), ALBERT (includes Aulbert, Alburt, Alberts), ALBRECHT (includes Aubrecht, Ahubrecht, Ahlbrecht, Albright), ALCORN (includes Alcon, Allcorn), ALDEN (includes Aldin), ALDERSON (includes Aldersen, Aldersan), ALDRICH (includes Aldridge), ALEXANDER (includes McAlexander, Elaxander, Alexein), ALFORD (includes Alfred, Allford, Halford, Hallford, Holford, Olford, Ollford), ALGEO (includes Ajo, Aldgeo, Aldioye, Aldjeo, Aldjo, Aldjoe, Aldjoy, Algar, Algee, Algeo, Alger, Algie, Algoe, Algo, Algow, Aljeo, Aljho, Aljo, Aljoy, Allgeo, Allgoe, Alljo, Aljoe, Alljoy, Auldje, Auldjo, Auldjoy, Awldioy, Ciojo, Hallio, Ouldjo), ALLEE-ROOTS (includes D'Ailly, Alyee, Alyie, Alyea, Allie), allen_gen, ALLEN-NEW-ENGLAND/NY/NJ/PA, ALLERTON, ALLISON (includes Alison, Ellison, Elison), ALMOND (includes Almon, Alman, Almand), ALTMAN (includes Aultman, Altmann), ALVERSON (includes Alvison, Alberson, Olverson), AMBURGEY, AMONETT (includes Amonette, Ammonet, Ammonette, Amonet), ANDERSON, ANDREWS (includes Anderson, Andrus, Anders, Andres, Andrew, Andrewsen, Anderssen, Andress, McAndrews), ANNABLE/ANABLE (includes Anible), ANSLEY (includes Annesley, Ainsley, Ainslie, Aynsley, Ausley, Antley, Angley, Endsley, Ensley), ANSPACH (includes Anspaugh, Aunspach), APPLE, APPLEGATE, ARLEDGE (includes Aldridge, Allred), ARMSTRONG (includes Armstrang, Fortenbra, Fortebraccio), ARNOLD, ARRENDELL (includes Arendell, Arendall, Arandal, Arundle), ARTHUR (includes Arther, Arter), ARWOOD (includes Arrowood, Earwood, Garrowood, Harrowood,

Yearwood), ASHBY, ASHER-L, ASHLEY, ASHWILL, ASHWORTH, ATHEY (includes Athy, Athon, Athan, Athen, Athons, Athens, Athans), ATKEY, ATKINSON (includes Adkinson, Atkisson, Adkisson), ATTAKULLAKULLA, ATWELL, ATWOOD (includes Attwood, Atewood, Attewood, Atwod, Atte Wode), AUGER (includes Augur, Augir, Audger, Aunger, Agar, Odger, Angier, Augier, Anger, Elger, Alger), AUSTIN, AUTRY (includes Autrey, Autery, Awtry, Awtrey, Awtray, d'Autry, D'Autry, Dautry, Outry, Otray, Aughtry, Auttry, Autri, Alterius), AVERY, AYLOR (includes Alor, Ehler, Ahler, Ohler, McEller).

- **ABERCROMBIE Family Association**
  http://www.america.net/~ka4wujga/

- **Descendants of George ABERNETHY De Barrie**
  http://www.parsonstech.com/genealogy/trees/babernat/Abernath.htm

- **Centralized ABNEY Archives**
  http://www.geocities.com/Heartland/Park/2300/

- **1997 ACKERMAN Reunion Home Page**
  http://pw1.netcom.com/~oasissys/ackerman.html
  Saturday, June 28th, Tres Pinos, California.

- **ACKLEY Family Genealogy**
  http://www.geocities.com/heartland/prairie/4437
  Descendants of Nicholas Ackley, Zebulon Ackley and Scoby Ackley.

- **ACKLEY Family Historical Society**
  http://www.isoa.net/~lackley/

- **ACUFF Archives Homepage**
  http://www.public.usit.net/mcnamara/archives.htm
  ACUFF, ECOFF, EEKHOFF, and their spelling variants.

- **Hot on the Trail: ADAIR**
  http://homepages.rootsweb.com/~jclaytn/adair.html
  Adair Surname (GA>LA>MS>TX).

- **ADAMS' Family Home Page**
  http://205.213.168.3/adams.html
  Adams-McKain Family Newsletter.

- **ADKINS Family Information**
  http://fly.hiwaay.net/~jjadkins/genealogy/adkinsinfo.html

- **ALABASTER One Name Study**
  http://ourworld.compuserve.com/homepages/Laraine_Hake/

- **The ALBERT Family Tree**
  http://www.humboldt1.com/~cealbert/index.html
  Representing the Alberts and related families who settled Butler County, Pennsylvania.

- **ALDEN House Museum and ALDEN Kindred of America**
  http://www.alden.org
  Descendants of John Alden and Priscilla Mullins, passengers on the Mayflower.

- **David's Place—ALDERSON Genealogy**
  http://www.slip.net/~dgf/

- **The ALDINGER Family Homepage**
  http://www.aldinger.com/family/

- **The National ALDRICH Family Association**
  http://www.geocities.com/SouthBeach/Marina/2343/

- **ALDRIDGE / ARLEDGE Family Homepage**
  http://www.tx3.com/~arledge/
  For Aldridge, Aldrich, Arledge, Aldred, Allred.

- **El Apellido ALFARO / The Surname ALFARO**
  http://members.tripod.com/~Antonioalfaro/
  Spain, Portugal, Italy, Chile, Argentina, Brazil, Peru, Ecuador, Costa Rica, Panama, Puerto Rico, Mexico, the United States.

- **ALFORD American Family Association**
  http://www.alford.com/alford/aafa/homepage.html

- **ALGEO Family Newsletter**
  E-mail: kepler@oro.net
  For details e-mail Marianne Keplet at kepler@oro.net

- **The ALLEN Family Project**
  http://www.vineyard.net/vineyard/history/allen/allenhp.htm
  Fifteen generations of the descendants of George Allen of Sandwich 1637.

- **ALLEN Town—The ALLEN Family of Gilmer County, Georgia**
  http://www.geocities.com/Heartland/Hills/3513/

- **ALLISON Genealogy**
  http://pages.prodigy.com/Allison/

- **The Gathering of the ALLISON Clan**
  http://www.allison-clan.com

- **The ALLRED Family Organization, Inc.**
  http://www.bayside.net/users/afo/index.htm

- **The ALLRED Family Roster**
  http://www.scvnet.net/~allred/
  Every Name Index of over 118,000 Allred family members and 10,400 unique surnames.

- **ALLYN Family History**
  http://www2.whidbey.net/ballyn
  Descendants of Thomas and Matthew Allyn, two brothers who immigrated to Barnstable, Massachusetts in 1637.

- **ALTON-ALLTON-AULTON Association**
  http://members.aol.com/altonnews/aaaafn.htm

- **Jeff ALVEY Genealogy History**
  http://www.fred.net/jefalvey/jeffmain.html
  Jeff's index of Alveys from 1500 to present.

- **Everett ANDERSON Memorial Collection of Colonial Virginia ANDERSON Families**
  http://homepages.rootsweb.com/~anderson/virginia.html

- **The ANDREWS Family Collection**
  http://members.aol.com/gandr22/andrews.htm
  100 & growing distinct families of: Andrews, Anderson, Anders, Andrus, Andros.

- **The Descendants of Francis ANDRUS**
  http://www5.pair.com/vtandrew/andrews/andrews.htm

- **APGAR Family Association, Inc.**
  http://www.apgarfamily.com
  Descendants of Johannes Peter Apgar who settled in Hunterdon Co., NJ in the mid-18th century.

- **APPLEGATE Genealogy Home Page**
  http://www2.vcn.com/~applegatej/

- ARMSTRONG Genealogy and History Center
  http://www.gendex.com/~guest/martin/enigma/index.htm
- ARNOLD Ancestry Home Page—ARNOLD
  Ancestry Newsletter
  http://members.aol.com/kinseeker6/arnold.html
- The ARSENAULT / ARSENEAU / ARSENEAULT
  / ARCENEAUX Genealogy Web Site
  http://personal.nbnet.nb.ca/djsavard/Arseno/arseno.htm
- The ARTHUR Family Register
  http://ourworld.compuserve.com/homepages/David_Ramsdale/
  homepage.htm
  *From the parochs of Abercorn, Bathgate, Borrowstouness,
  Carriden, Dalmeny, Ecclesmachen, Kirkliston, Linlithgow,
  Livingston, South Queensferry, Torphichen and Whitburn in the
  county of West Lothian, Scotland.*
- The ASBILL Family
  http://arapaho.nsuok.edu/~asbill/asbillpg.htm
  *Some more common variant spellings of the name: Asbill,
  Asbell, Azbel(l), Asbyll and Azbill.*
- The ASBURY Family Home Page
  http://millennium.fortunecity.com/doddington/483/
  *Descendants of Henry Asbury, abt 1650–1707, from England to
  Westmoreland County, Virginia.*
- ASCOLANI Family Home Page
  http://www.geocities.com/Heartland/2999/ascolani.htm
- AUGER Surname Family Center
  http://my.voyager.net/hamp/auger/
  Augur, Aunger, Audger, Augier, Augar, Anger.
- The AUSTILL / AUSTELL Family Genealogy Page
  http://members.aol.com/elzyaust/index.htm
- AUSTIN Families Association of America (AFAOA)
  http://www.rahul.net/afaoa/index.html
- AUTRY Genealogy Page
  http://homepages.rootsweb.com/~autry/
  *Autry, Autrey, Autery, Awtry, Awtrey, Awtray, d'Autry, D'Autry,
  Dautry, Outry, Otray, Aughtry, Auttry, Autri, Alterius.*
- AUVENSHINE Family Tree
  http://www.flash.net/~genie/
- AXSOM Association of America
  http://users.southeast.net/~leaxsom/
- AXTELL Family Organization
  http://www.sover.net/~daxtell/axtell/
  Axtell, Axtel, Axtelle

◆ Surnames Beginning with "B"

- Family Tree Maker Online User Home Pages—B
  http://www.familytreemaker.com/users/b/index.html
- Genealogy's Most Wanted—Surnames Beginning
  with "B"
  http://www.citynet.net/mostwanted/b.htm
- H-GIG Surname Registry—Surnames Beginning B
  http://www.ucr.edu/h-gig/surdata/surname2.html

- Higginson Book Company—Surnames Beginning
  with B
  http://www.higginsonbooks.com/b.htm
- inGeneas Table of Common Surname Variations and
  Surname Misspellings—A–B
  http://www.ingeneas.com/A2B.html
- Surname Springboard Index—B
  http://www.geocities.com/~alacy/spring_b.htm
- SurnameWeb Surname Registry—B Index
  http://www.surnameweb.org/registry/b.htm
- Genealogy Resources on the Internet—"B" Surname
  Mailing Lists
  http://members.aol.com/gfsjohnf/gen_mail_surnames-b.html
  *This site is wonderfully maintained by John Fuller. It includes
  mailing list information for the following surnames and their
  variant spellings:*
  *B530 (Bennett/Bennet and allied families), BABB, BABCOCK,
  BACHMAN (includes Bachmann, Backman), BACKER-
  BAKER_Jacobus, BADGLEY, Baerfamily, BAGGARLY (includes
  Beggarly, Beggerly), BAGLEY (includes Bagby, Bagsby, Bigsby,
  Baxley, McBagly), BAGWELL, BAILEY (includes Bailee, Baley,
  Boehle), BAIRD (includes Beard), BAKER (includes Baxter,
  Becker, Baxley, Backster, Packer), BAKER_BOLIN (includes
  Bolen, Bowlin, Bolling, Bowling), BAKER-GENEALOGY,
  BAKER-ROOTS, BALDINGER, BALDWIN, BALES (includes
  Bailes, Beals, Bayles), BALL, BALL, EDWARD (Edward Ball
  and other Newark, NJ founding families), BALLARD, BALLEAU
  (includes Balleaux, Ballew), BALLEW (includes Blue, Beleu,
  Balew), Balliet-L, BALLINGER (includes Ballenger, Ballanger,
  Bollinger, Bellinger), BANKS (includes Bancks), BANKSTON
  (includes Bankson, Bankstone, Bengtsson), BARBEE, BARBER,
  BARDEN (includes Bardin, Bardon), BARGELT, BARGER
  (includes Bargar, Barrier, Berger), BARIL, BARKER, BARLOW,
  BARNES (includes Barnet, Barns, Barney, Bjairnes, Bournes,
  Byrnes, Parnes, Barnett, Burnes), BARNETT, BARNHART
  (includes Barnhardt), BARRETT (includes Barrott, Barrette,
  Barritt), BARRINGER (includes Baringer, Berringer), BARTH
  (includes Barthel), BARTLETT, BARTLETT-ROOTS, BARTON
  (includes Barten, Bartin, Bartinn, Borton, Barden, Burton,
  Banton, Baston, Bastin), BARWIS (includes Barwyse, Berwis),
  BASFORD (includes Bassford), BASHAM (includes Bassham),
  BASS, BASTIN (includes Bastyn, Baston, Basten, Bastjn,
  Beisstin, Bashteen, Bastian), BATEMAN (includes Batemon,
  Batman), BATES, BATTERTON-L, Battlist, BAUCOM (includes
  Baucum, Bawcom, Baughcom, Balcombe, Balcom, Balkcom,
  Van Baucom), BAUGHEN (includes Baughan, Baugham,
  Baughn, Bauffin, Baffin, Boffin, Boughan, Boughn, Bohon,
  Bangham, Banghan), BAXLEY, BAYNE-ROOTS (includes Bane,
  Baine, Bain, Bean, Beane), BEACH (includes Beech), BEALL
  (includes Bell, Beal, Bealle), BEAN (includes Been, Beene,
  MacBean), BEAR (includes Bar, Bare, Bair, Bahr, Behr),
  BEARD, BEARDEN (includes Beardon), BEASLEY (includes
  Beaszly, Beesley), BEAUDRY (includes Baudry), BEAUVAIS
  (includes Bauvais, Bova, St. Gemme, St. Gem, St. James,
  Vanesse dit Beauvais, Coderre, dit Beauvais, Beauvet, Bauvet),
  BECHTEL (includes Bechdol, Bachtel, Bechtold, Bechthold,
  Beachtel, Bachtell, Bechtell, Buchtel, Beghtol, Bechtolt, Bechtol,
  Baechtold, Bechdolt, Becktal, Bechtal, Bechtle, Bectal, Beghtel,
  Beghtol, Beightol, Bachtold, Backtell, Bechtl, Becktel, Becthel,
  Bucktel, Buechtel), BECK, BECKHAM (includes Beckum,
  Bekum), BECRAFT, BEDFORD-SURNAME, BEEDE (includes
  Bede, Beedee, Beedy), BEELER (includes Bealer, Biller, Buhler,
  Beiler, Byler, other related B460 spellings), BEERS, BEESON,
  BEHYMER (includes Becklehimer, Picklesimer), BEIERS
  (includes Byers, Boyer, Byar), BELCHER, BELDEN (includes
  Belding, Baildon), BELL, BELLAH, BEMIS (includes Bemiss),
  BENDER (includes Binder), BENGE (includes Bange, Bench,
  Bengay, Bengey, Benjay, Benjey, Binch, Bing, Binge, Bunch,*

Byng, Bynge), BENN, BENSLEY (includes Benslay, Bensle), BENSON (includes Bensen, Bentsen, Bensingh, Bennison), BENTLEY (includes Bently), BENTON, BERG, BERGER (includes Burger), BERNHARD (includes Bernhart, Burnhard, Burnhart, Barnhart, Bernard, Burham), BERRY (includes Barry, Barrie), BERRYHILL, BEST, BEVILL (includes Beville), BEZANSON (includes Bescanson), BEZY, BFHA-L (Barney), BIAS (includes Byas, Byus, Byars), BIBBINS (includes Bevan(s), Bevin(s), Bivin(s), Blevin(s)), BIBLE-FAMILY, BICKFORD-TALK (includes Beckford), BIDDLE, BIDDY, BIGALK-S (includes Bigalke, Begalke, Begalka), BIGGER (includes Biggers, Biggor(s), Biggar(s), Bieger(s)), BIGGS, BILBREY (includes Billberry), BILLINGS (includes Billing), BILYEU (includes Billiou, Balew, Ballou, Belieu, Belew, Boileau), BING (includes Byng), BIRD (includes Byrd, Burd), BIRKHOLZ (includes Berkholz, Burkholz, Birkholtz), BISE (includes Bice), BISH (includes Bisch), BISHOP-L (includes Bishopp, Bischoff), BISSETT, BLACK, BLACKBURN, BLACKLOCK, BLACKSTOCK, BLACKWELL, BLADES, BLAGDON (includes Blagden, Blackden), Blagg-genealogy, BLAIR (includes Blare, van Blaricom, van Blare), BLAKE, BLAKELY (includes Blackly, Blakeney), BLALOCK (includes Blaylock), BLANCHARD (includes Blancher, Blanchar), BLANKENSHIP, BLANSHAN (includes Blanchan), BLATTENBERGER (includes Blottenberger, Blattenberg, Plattenberger, Plattenburg), BLEVINS (includes Blevin, Blivins), BLOCHER (includes Blocker, Blokker, Plocher, Ploucher), BLOUNT (includes Blunt, Blund, Blound), BLOWERS (includes Bloor, Bloors, Blowes, Blower), BLOYD-GROUP (includes Bloid, Bloyed, Bloyth), BLUNDELL, BLYTHE (includes Blyth, Blithe), BOARD-ROOTS, BOATRIGHT (includes Boatwright), BOAZ, Bobrofffamily, BODEWIN, BODKIN (includes Botkin), BOGGESS (includes Bagguss, Baugus, Boggas, Bogiss, Bougus), BOGGS, BOHANNON (includes Bohanon, Bohannan, Bohana, Buchanan, Buchannan, Bucannan), BOHN (includes Bahn), BOLAM (includes Bolan, Bolum, Bollum), BOLCH (includes Balch, Balich, Boalich, Bohlich, Bohlig, Bolch, Boleck, Boley, Bolich, Bolick, Boliek, Bolig, Boligh, Bolih, Bolish, Bollich, Bollick, Bollig, Bolligh, Bolock, Bolsch), BOLEY (includes Bowley, Bolley), BOLIN, BOLISON, BOLLINGER (includes Bolinger, Bullinger, Ballinger), BOLSTER (includes Balster, Boldster, Bowlster, Bollster, Boldsteerman), BOND (includes Bonds, Bonde, Bondes, Bone, Bondi), BONE (includes Boane, Boon), BONHAM (includes Benham, Bonnum, Bonnem), BONNER (includes Banner, Boner, Benner), BONNETTE (includes Bonet, Bonnet, Bonnett, Bont, Bonte, Bontea, Bonadeau, Bonnedau), BONSALL (includes Bonsal, Bonsale, Bonsell), BOOKOUT, BOOMHOUR (includes Baumhouer, Boomhower, Bumhower), BOONE (includes Boon, Bohun), BOOTH, BOREMAN (includes Boarman), BOREN (includes Bowen), BOSSUOT (includes Bossuet), BOSWELL (includes Boswill, Baswell), BOTTOM (includes Bottoms, BOTTORFF (includes Batdorf, Putoff), BOTWINICKlist, BOUDREAU (includes Budrot, Boudreaux, Boudreault), BOULWARE (includes Bowler, Boler, Bouler), BOVEE (includes Bovie, Bovy, Beaufils, Bovier, Bouvier), BOWDEN (includes Baudon, Baudouin, Boden, Boudoin, Bowdoin, Bowdin, Bowdon, Bowdown), BOWEN (includes Bowin), BOWER (includes Bowers, Bauer, Bauers), BOWIE, BOWLES, BOWLING (includes Bowlin, Bolen, Bolin, Bolling, Boling), BOWSER (includes Bausser), BOYCE (includes Boice, Boise, Boys), BOYD, BOYD (includes Boid, Boide, Boit, Boyde, O'Boyd, McBoyd), BOYLE (includes Boil, Boile, Bole), BOYNTON (includes Boyington), BOZEMAN (includes Bozman, Bosman), BP2000-L (Beatty and variations), BRADBURY-L (includes Bradberry), BRADEN, BRADFORD (includes Brafford, Bradforthe), BRADLEY (includes Bradlee, Bradely, Bradleigh, Bratley, Badley), BRADSHAW (includes Bratshaw), BRADY (includes Braddy, Bradi, Bradie), BRAGG (includes Brag), BRAINERD (includes Brainard), BRANCH, BRAND, BRANDON, BRANHAM (includes Bramham, Branam, Branum, Branin, Branen, Brannon, any surname starting with, "Bran"), BRANIFF (includes Breniff), BRANSON (includes Bransen,

Bransan), BRASWELL-L, BRATCHER (includes Brashear, Brassiear, Brasher, Brazier, Brasier, Bradshaw, Bratshaw), BRATTON, BRAUN, BRAY (includes Brady, Pray, Brie, Brill(y), McBrey), BRAYfamily, BREEDLOVE (includes Breadlove, Bradlove), BREESE (includes Brees), BREITHAUPT, BREMNER, BRESHEARS (includes Breashears, Brashears, Brasher, Brashier, Brazier, Broshers, Bratcher, Brucher, Bezer, Brasseur, Bradshawe, Bashaw, Basham), BREWER, BRICE (includes Bryce, Bruce), BRICK, BRICKER (includes Brunker), BRIDGES (includes Bridger), BRIDGEWATER, BRIDGMAN (includes Bridgeman), BRIGGS (includes Brygge, Brigge, Bryggs), BRIGHT (includes Brecht, Bryte), BRINKLEY (includes Binkley, Brinkly), BRINSON (includes Brunson, Brimson), BRISBIN, BRITTINGHAM, BRIXEY (includes Bricksey), BROADAWAY (includes Broadway), BROADFOOT (includes Bradford, Bredfort, Proudfoot), BROADHURST (includes Broaddus), BROADWATER (includes Broadwaters), BROBST (includes Probst), BROCK, BROCKETT, BROCKWAY, BRODBECK (includes Broatbeck, Brobeck, Broderick), BROGAN, BROOKE, BROOKS (includes Brookes), BROOME (includes Broom), BROOMHALL (includes Broomall, Broomell), BROTZMAN (includes Brutzman, Prutzman, Prottsman), BROUGHTON, BROWDER, BROWN, BROWNING, BROWNLEE (includes Brownlie), BROWN-LEONARD, BROYLES (includes Breyhel, Bruel, Bruhel, Breuel, Brile, Briles, Broil, Broils, Broiles, Broyhill), BRUBAKER (includes Brubacher, Brubacker, Brewbaker), BRUCE (includes Brus, Bruse, Brusse, de Brus, de Bruse, de Brusse), BRUCE, GEORGE (descendants of Scot immigrant George Bruce (c1635–1692 Massachusetts), BRUMFIELD (includes Broomfield, Bromfield), BRUMMETTE, BRUNDAGE, BRUNNER (includes Bruner), BRUTON, BRYANT, BUCHANAN, BUCHHEIT-ROOTS (includes Buckheit, Buheit, Buchite, Buckite, Buhite, Buchhardt), BUCHMAN (includes Buchmann, Buckman, Buckmann), BUCKLAND (includes Bucklen, Bucklin), BUCKLEW, BUCKLEY, BULL, BULLOCK (includes Bulloch, Bollock, Bullick, Boughloch), BUMP (includes Bumpas, Bumpass, Bumpers, Bumps, Bumpus), BUNCH, BUNDY, BUNGARD, BUNKER, BURBIDGE (includes Burbage, Burbridge, Burridge), BURBURY (includes Burbery, Burberry, Burbeary), BURCH (includes Birch, Burtch), BURDETTE (includes Burdett, Burdete, Burdet), BURDICK, BURFORD (includes Burfoot, Burfort, Burfotte), BURGE, BURGESS (includes Burges, Burgis, Burgiss), BURGETT (includes Burget, Burgette, Burgert), BURK (includes Burks, Burke, Burkes, Berk, Berks, Birk, Birks), BURKE, BURKE, BURLEY (includes Burleigh, Berley), BURLINGAME (includes Burlingham, Burlingam, Burlinham), BURNETT (includes Burnet), BURNS, Burton_Genealogy, BURT-SOUTHERN-USA, BUSBY (includes Busbee, Buzbee, Buzby, Busbin, Busbie), BUSH, BUSHFIELD, BUSHNELL, BUSS, BUSSELL (includes Busselle, Bustle, Busell, Beisell, Buzzell, Buswell), BUTCHER (includes Bücher), BUTLER, BUTT (includes Butts, Butte, Butz), BYBEE (includes Biby, Bibbey, Byby), BYERS.

- **BACHMAN / BAUGHMAN Genealogy**
  http://members.aol.com/ewbaugh/index.htm
  Descendants of Ulrich Bachmann (1610) of Lauperswil, Signau District, Canton Berne, Switzerland.

- **BAILEY/BAYLEY, BAILY, Etc.**
  http://www.angelfire.com/mo/BaileyInfo
  Information on all BAILEYs, all spellings and all areas, descendant charts, births, marriages, deaths, books, periodicals.

- **BAILEY/BAYLEY, etc. Family Research & Home of the Bailey Database**
  http://www.geocities.com/Heartland/Ridge/9537/index.htm
  Database for all Bailey/Bayley, etc. anywhere/anyplace.

- **BAILEY Periodicals and Publications**
  http://www.rootsweb.com/~sueskay/misc/bailey.htm

- Catherine BAILLON Royal Connection Research Association
  http://habitant.org/baillon/

- BAKER Surname
  http://homepages.rootsweb.com/~jclaytn/baker.html
  Baker surname: (MA>NC>KT>TX).

- BALDRIDGE Family Historical Society
  http://home1.gte.net/bfhs/bald.htm

- The BALL Room: Descendants of Edward Ball (1640–1724) of NJ
  http://www.rootsweb.com/~genepool/edballnj.htm

- Descendants of Edward BALL of New Jersey—GEDCOM Repository Site
  http://www.altlaw.com/edball/

- BANKS / BANKES Families (U.S.)
  http://members.aol.com/rayhbanks/title.html

- BARBER Family History
  http://www.wco.com/~barber/family/
  Descendants of Samuel Barber, born around 1785 in Maryland.

- The BARD Family Web Page
  http://www.localnet.com/~cbard/Bard_Gen_Page/Bard_Cool_Gen_index.html

- BARGER Family History Society
  http://members.tripod.com/~suzid/index.html

- BARKER Mailing List Home Page
  http://www.rootsweb.com/~scwhite/barker/index.html

- Irene's Family Web Page—BARNARD & BUTTLE
  http://www.geocities.com/Athens/6896/

- The BARNEY Family Historical Association
  http://www.barneyfamily.org

- BARNEY Family History Association
  http://www.rootsweb.com/~daisy/1bfha.htm

- BARNHOUSE Branches—A Surname Resource Center
  http://www.nataliesnet.com/barnhouse
  Surname genealogy research for all U.S. Barnhouse branches.

- The History & Genealogy of John S. BARNS
  http://www.geocities.com/Heartland/3958/

- BARR Family Tree Trackers
  http://hometown.aol.com/MGBARR/INDEX.HTML

- BARROW Family Association of America
  http://www.geocities.com/Heartland/Flats/9562/
  The purpose of the Barrow Family Association is to encourage the collection and publication of genealogical records of those Barrow men and women who were early colonists in Virginia and North Carolina and their descendants. However, all Barrow descendants are invited to link to this site with the hope that this will encourage additional research and cross-referencing.

- BARTLETT Genealogy Foundation
  http://www.bartlettgenealogy.com

- BASTIN Family Website
  http://www.geocities.com/Heartland/Prairie/9714/
  Descendants of Thomas & Hannah Bastin (1745–1834) of Caswell Co., North Carolina.

- BATCHELDER / BATCHELLER Family Origins
  http://www.mindspring.com/~jogt/surnames/batcheld.htm
  Excerpts from: Batchelder, Batcheller Genealogy, by F. C. Pierce, 1898.

- The BATES Family of Old Virginia
  E-mail: WittBates@aol.com
  A family association in Centreville, Virginia. For details send e-mail to WittBates@aol.com

- The BATHURST Home Page
  http://www.geocities.com/Heartland/Acres/5783/

- The BEACH Family Journal
  http://members.aol.com/eugeneb/home.htm
  Home page of the Beach Family Journal; a genealogical newsletter devoted to Beach/Beech family history. For descendants of Richard, John and Thomas BEACH, of New Haven, Connecticut, together with all other BEACH or BEECH families in America.

- Descendants of Richard, John and Thomas BEACH of Connecticut
  http://www5.pair.com/vtandrew/beach/beach.htm

- The BEALL HomePage
  http://www.geocities.com/Athens/5568/beallstuff.html

- BEARD / BAIRD Genealogy
  http://www.outfitters.com/~chelle/

- BEATTY Project 2000
  http://www.digroots.com/Beatty.htm
  Beaty / Beatty Families.

- Charlene Beaty Bailey's BEATY-SNOWDON Genealogy Page
  http://www.digroots.com/beatsnow.htm
  Descendants of John Jesse BEATY (b. 1821) and Mary Frances SNOWDON (b. 1823).

- Famille BEAUSOLEIL Association Inc. / BROUSSARD Family Reunion
  http://www.vrml.k12.la.us/vermilion/famille/

- The BEAVINGTON Papers—502 Years of BEAVINGTON Genealogy
  http://www.silk.net/personal/gordonb/
  England, 1495–1997. BEVENTON, BEVINGTON.

- The Home Page Dedicated to BEDINGFIELD Family Research
  http://members.aol.com/TPaplanus/tpaplanus.html

- Mary's Place—Your BEEBE Connection
  http://www.bright.net/~bbe/

- BEEKS Lineage
  http://homestead.com/beeksbeaksbeakes/beekslineage.html
  At least 7 different lines of Beeks with various spelling of Beeks, Beaks, Beakes.

- Rick BEGEMAN's Home Page
  http://www.best.com/~rickb794/be02000.html

- The Irish Heritage of the Surname BEGLEY
  http://www.cris.com/~Maguire/IndexBegley.shtml

- BEHYMER Genealogy Group
  http://www.geocities.com/Heartland/Hills/3927/
  And all variant spellings.

- BELKNAP Family History Page
  http://home.earthlink.net/~cwtram/belknap.html

- The BELKNAP / BELNAP Homepage
  http://www.belknap.net/011596a.htm

- Clan BELL—BELL Family Association of the United States
  http://members.aol.com/rbell45369/clanbell.htm

- BENGE Research Network
  http://www.users.mis.net/~chesnut/pages/benge.htm
  Bange, Bench, Bengay, Bengey, Benjay, Benjey, Binch, Bing, Binge, Bunch, Byng, Bynge.

- BENNINGTON Family Homepage (and BENINGTON and BINNINGTON)
  http://www.dcfinc.com/genealogy/benningt.html
  Index to "Bennington Bulletin" newsletter. Early history of the surname. Author has database with over 10,000 connected names and sources.

- The BENOY Page
  http://www.benoy.com/family/index.htm

- BENSON Families Newsletter
  E-mail: alanbenson@delphi.com
  Quarterly newsletter for Benson and other related surnames (Bensen, Bentsen, Bensingh, Bennison, Bjornson, etc.). E-mail Alan Benson for details at: alanbenson@delphi.com

- BENNETT—B530 Mail List
  http://primusweb.com/genealogy/B530/
  Benet, Bennet, Bennett . . . Families.

- BERRY Family Genealogy—Descendants of John BERRY born 1749 in Lancashire, England
  http://ourworld.compuserve.com/homepages/JOHNBERRY/homepage.htm

- BERRY Resource Center
  http://www.flash.net/~skaspar/resberry.htm

- BETHEL / BETHELL Genealogy
  http://pages.prodigy.com/DDHW32A/
  A book for sale titled, The Early Bethells and Their Descendants 1635–1994.

- BETHUNE
  http://members.aol.com/PBeth26/bethune.html
  This site includes e-mail addresses for 12 different researchers of the Bethune surname. We believe that all Bethunes have a common ancestry and our goal is to find our common bond.

- BETTERTON Families of the World Web Site
  http://www.geocities.com/Heartland/Prairie/2570/betterto.htm

- BEVERLY Family Newsletter
  http://ourworld.compuserve.com/homepages/rbeverly/bfamnews.htm

- BEVERLY Query Page
  http://ourworld.compuserve.com/homepages/rbeverly/bevquery.htm

- BEVIER / ELTING Family Association
  http://home.earthlink.net/~rctwig/bevier.htm

- BEVIER—ELTING Family Association
  http://members.aol.com/Edie143/elt7_web.html
  Including a page with information and a photograph of the Bevier-Elting House on Huguenot Street in New Paltz, New York.

- BEVIS & COFFEE Descendants
  http://www.digroots.com/bevicoff.htm
  Descendants of John A. Bevis and John M. Coffey.

- BIBBINS Genealogy Website
  http://www.rootsweb.com/~tlmorris/bibbins/index.html
  Bibben(s), Bibbon(s), Bevin(s), Bevan(s), soundex code B152.

- The Family BIBLE or the http://www.rootsweb.com/~bible/
  http://www.geocities.com/Heartland/2252/
  The Bible Family.

- BICKHAM Family Home Page
  http://www.bickham.org

- On Beacon Hill
  http://www.bicknell.net
  The complete reference for BICKNELL & BECKNELL family, over 6,000 entries, coats of arms, origins, message forum— much more!

- BIDEWELL One Name Study
  http://www.familytreemaker.com/users/b/i/d/William-H-Bidewell/

- BIFFLE Researchers Newsletter
  E-mail: j-rose@tc.umn.edu
  Send e-mail to Janet Roseen at j-rose@tc.umn.edu for details.

- The BIGELOW Society
  http://www.slic.com/bigelow/bigsoc1.htm

- BIRKHOLZ Family History Search
  http://www.geocities.com/Athens/8020/birkholz.html
  Birkholz, Berkholz, Burkholz, etc.

- BIRNEY Genealogical Pages
  http://www3.sympatico.ca/ken.birney
  For Birneys world-wide. Trying to find common ancestry.

- BISSETT Family
  http://www.giammo.com/Bissett/
  Descendants of Jacques Bisett & Anne Catherine Metthey, who emigrated to Nova Scotia in 1752.

- BISSETT Family Home Page
  http://www.barney.org/bissett.html
  Bissett, Bisset, Basok, Beceit, Besack, Besat, Besate, Besek, Beset, Bessat, Bis, Biscet, Biset, Biseth, Bisey, Bissait, Bissaite, Bissart, Bissat, Bissate, Bissed, Bisseth, Bissit, Bissott, Bizat, Bize, Bizet, Bizett, Bizitt, Bizzet, Bizzett, Buset, Buseit, Bysat, Byset, Byseth, Byssate and Byssot

- BITTING Family History
  http://ourworld.compuserve.com/homepages/bitting/
  Bitting Family in America. Descendants of Henrich and Ann Catherina Bitting who immigrated to Pennsylvania in 1723.

- BLACKBURN Family Association, Inc.
  http://www.blackburn-tree.org
  The descendants of John BLACKBURN Sr. b. 17__ Ireland & Mary COURTNEY b. 1701 Ireland (1st wife) & Rachel MORTON b. 1694 Ireland (2nd wife).

- BLACKWELL Genealogy Study Group Notebook
  http://oasys.drc.com/~blackwell/

- The BLACKWELL Researchers Newsletter
  http://www.angelfire.com/mo/howdy2u/blawell.html

- The BLACKWELLs of Mississippi
  http://e2.empirenet.com/~jayken/blackwell/

- The Australian BLAIR Family
  http://www.pcug.org.au/~kenblair/

- BLAIRs of the World
  http://home.sprynet.com/sprynet/srblair/

- BLAIR Society for Genealogical Research
  http://blairsociety.org

- Guide to BLAIR Genealogy
  http://members.home.net/jcblair/blair.htm
  A complete source for all your Blair genealogy needs.

- The Thomas BLAIR Family
  http://www.familytreemaker.com/users/t/i/l/Susan-G-Tillman/
  Of Pennsylvania and Maryland

- The BLAKE Files
  http://www.geocities.com/Heartland/Acres/9900/
  Genealogy of the Blake Families of Ohio & New England with roots in Somerset, England. Descendants of William Blake who sailed from Plymouth, England on March 20, 1630 aboard the "Mary and John" and arrived in Nastasket, Massachusetts on May 30, 1630.

- BLAKESLEE Log Cabin
  http://www.ashtabula.net/blakeslee/
  Descendants of Samuel Blakeslee, pioneer Sala Blakeslee's genealogy, life and history are documented. His original log cabin is now listed in the National Register of Historic Places.

- A BLALOCK Genealogy Page
  http://www.clark.net/pub/jcblal/geneal.html
  Blalock, Blaylock, Blacklock

- BLANKENSHIP
  http://members.aol.com/AunteeChel/blankenship.html
  A website devoted to the lineage of Ralph Blankenship (1662–1714) of Henrico Co., VA presented in family group sheet format with links to history, graphics, sources, other Blankenship researchers, plus more. Contributions welcomed!

- BLEACH Genealogy
  http://www.awwwsome.com/dab/genealogy/
  Family of Jacob Joseph Bleach.

- Jim Boulden's BLEECKER Genealogy Home Page
  http://ourworld.compuserve.com:80/homepages/JBoulden/

- BLEECKER Genealogy Homepage
  http://ourworld.compuserve.com/homepages/JBoulden/
  Descendants of Jan Jansen Bleecker (1641–1732) the progenitor of the name in America.

- BLENCOWE Families Association
  http://www.geocities.com/Heartland/5088/
  Blenco, Blencoe, Blencow, Blencowe, Blenko, Blinco, Blincoe, Blincow, Blinchko, Blinko

- BLODGETT Ancestors in England & America
  http://www.rootsweb.com/~genepool/blodgett2.htm
  Descendants of Thomas BLOWGATE (abt 1490–1560).

- BLONDIA and family
  http://members.aol.com/rblondia/genealogy/index.htm
  A Belgian family.

- BLOOR Family Web Site
  http://www.bloor.demon.co.uk/

- The National BLUE Family Association
  http://www.glasscity.net/users/sbitter/BlueF1.htm

- Nils BLYTH—Home Page
  http://www.ActOnline.com.au/~nblyth/index.shtml
  BLYTH or BLYTHE families from the Scotish borders and the north of England.

- BOHNSACK Bonds Newsletter
  E-mail: dhoffgr@sensible-net.com or ajbohnsack@aol.com
  An exchange of Bohnsack surnames. Will also include other variations of BOHNSACK: BOHN, BOHNENEN, etc. For details e-mail Donna Hoff-Grambau at dhoffgr@sensible-net.com or Alice J. Bohnsack at ajbohnsack@aol.com

- BOLCH Genealogy
  http://www.geocities.com/Heartland/Plains/2953/
  Descendants of Johan Adam Bolch and his wife Anna Christina, who landed in Philadelphia on 24 September 1753 on the ship Neptune from Rotterdam. Balch, Balich, Boalich, Bohlich, Bohlig, Bolch, Boleck, Boley, Bolich, Bolick, Boliek, Bolig, Boligh, Bolih, Bolish, Bollich, Bollick, Bollig, Bolligh, Bolock, Bolsch.

- The BOLLING Family Association
  http://www.crosslink.net/~bolling/

- BOND Family Reunion
  E-mail: receiver@visioncom.net
  Every Labor Day Sunday in Wiggins, Mississippi. E-mail A.M. Bond at receiver@visioncom.net for more details.

- BONJOUR Family Genealogy
  http://www.geocities.com/Heartland/2700/index.html

- Descendants of Frank BOOKER
  http://www.geocities.com/Heartland/Acres/5731/booker.html
  Born 1521 in Challinsford, Essex, England.

- The BOOKOUT Web
  http://www.rootsweb.com/~daisy/bookout.htm
  BOOKOUT family, including BOECKHOUT, BOUCHOUT, BUCKHOUT, BOOKHOUT or any other related spelling.

- Ancestors and Descendants of the BOONE Family
  http://personal.bhm.bellsouth.net/bhm/s/h/sharrah/boone.html
  Including information on the famous Daniel BOONE.

- The BOONE Family
  http://www.rootsweb.com/~kygenweb/boone.html

- BOOTH Family History
  http://members.tripod.com/~kbush/index.htm
  Descendants of William BOOTH, Sr. born 3 Oct 1786 in Virginia.

- The BOßECKER Family History Web Site
  http://www.mindspring.com/~sbosecker/
  Bosecker/Boseker

- The World-Wide BOULDIN Page
  http://www.bouldin.org
  Bouldin, Boulden

- The BOULDING BOULDEN BOLLYNG Family of East Kent
  http://www.geocities.com/Heartland/Estates/4205/

- The BOURCIER / BOURSIER Genealogy Page
  http://www.magma.ca/~rbour/
  A list of about 400 marriages in the Bourcier family, 1673–1980. This is a French-Canadian family.

- L'Association des BOUTIN d'Amérique Inc.
  http://www.lookup.com/homepages/85950/boutin.html

- BOWEN Depository
  http://homepages.rootsweb.com/~kenbowen/
  A site for the genealogy study of all Bowen lines.

- BOWER Family Homestead
  http://www.geocities.com/Heartland/Park/4501
  A clearinghouse for researchers of the Bower[s] or Bauer[s] surname.

- The BOYD Family Pages
  http://www.swgroup.com/Boyd/

- BOYNTON Genealogy
  http://www.pluvoy.com/boynton.html

- BRADBURN Family Genealogy
  http://www.vvm.com/~bradburn

- BRADER Genealogy
  http://www.freeyellow.com/members2/terrymc98/brader.html
  Looking for information about James and Sarah E. (Dodson) Brader. James died on October 29, 1906 in Nanticoke, PA. His wife, Sarah Dodson was born on December 26, 1858.

- The BRADLEE Genealogical Society Homepage
  http://www.bradlee.org

- The Olive Tree Genealogy: The Norwegian BRADT Family
  http://www.rootsweb.com/~ote/albradt.htm
  Albert Andriessen De NOORMAN aka BRADT and his first wife, Annetie Barents (Van) ROTTMERS, was one of the earliest settlers in New Netherland. He sailed, accompanied by his wife, Annetje Barents of "Rolmers," and two children, on October 8, 1636, on the "Rensselaerswyck," which arrived at New Amsterdam March 4, 1637.

- BRADY Family
  http://www.wf.net/~billk/Brady.html
  Descendants of William Wallace BRADY and Harriett Rebecca BRYAN.

- BRADY Family Heritage Association
  http://members.aol.com/rbrady6925/brady_heritage.htm
  Hugh BRADY and wife Hannah and their seven sons, their wives and children. Announcing the discovery of the 254-year old two story homestead. Also a proposed reincarnation of a BRADY Family Heritage Association and newsletter.

- BRAINERD / BRAINARD Genealogy
  http://www.geocities.com/Heartland/Park/7294/
  One line of Brainerds from 1641–1935. Descendants of Daniel Brainerd who arrived in Hartford, Connecticut in or about the year 1649. Brainerd, Spencer, Arnold, Bushnell, Austin, Cone, Bailey, Clark, Wheeler, Morse.

- BRAKE Family History
  http://www.eg.bucknell.edu/~hyde/brake/
  The purpose of this web site is to encourage research and exchange of genealogical information on—as well as preserve—the family history of the Virginia/West Virginia BRAKE families descending from Johan Jacob and Mary Margaret BRAKE of Germany.

- The BRAMBLETT / BRAMLETT Information Center
  http://www.bramblett.com
  A site dedicated to collecting and disseminating information on descendants (and ancestors!) of the original American Bramlett—William Bramlett, Sr. who was in VA by no later than 1715. Surnames Bramblett, Bramlett, Bramlitt, and all variations.

- BRAMMER Branches Newsletter
  E-mail: brammer@erols.com
  A quarterly newsletter for descendants of BRAMMER pioneers of colonial Virginia. For details e-mail Charles Brammer at brammer@erols.com

- BRAMMER Family and Its Branches
  http://hometown.aol.com/ohioroots
  For BRAMMER descendants of Colonial Virginia. Contains over 200 searchable family group sheets, that are indexed, linked and cross linked, to make your search easier.

- The BRANIFF Resource Centre
  http://members.tripod.com/braniffcentre/index.htm
  An index of resources both on-line and off-line regarding the surname Braniff and similar surnames. BRYNOFF, BRUNOFF, BROWNAFF, BROUNNOFF, BRANIF, BRANNIFF, BRENIFF.

- BRANSCOMBE Home Page
  http://www.geocities.com/Athens/2155/home.html
  Branscombes, Branscomes, Branscombs, Branscums & Brownscombes.

- BRANSOM / BRANSON Information Center
  http://members.aol.com/ImaBR/page2/index.htm
  A site for ALL known data for the BRANSOM / BRANSON surname, including, births, burials, census, deaths, land records, wills, etc.

- BRANSON Surname Mailing List
  http://www.sonic.net/~yvonne/branson.html
  Includes Bransen, Bransan.

- BRASWELL Family Page
  http://www.pbmo.net/suburb/braswell/

- BRATTON Worldwide Clan
  http://grampa.GenDex.COM/~guest/69751/BrattonHomePage/

- BREADMORE One-Name Study
  http://www.tylehurst.demon.co.uk/breadmore/
- Descendants of Jakob BRENN
  http://www.parsonstech.com/genealogy/trees/sbrenn12/
  jbrenn.htm
  *Born before 1685 and married to Maria HOEFFLIN before
  1701.*
- BREW Family Genealogy Page
  http://www.sigment.com/brew/
  *Brew One Name Study Genealogy Site with searchable
  databases.*
- The BRICKHOUSE Family Association
  http://home.sprynet.com/sprynet/bricks/
- BRILEY and Allied Families
  http://www.pipeline.com/~margomc/
- The BRINGIER Family Home Page and BRINGIER
  Tomb Association
  http://www.connecti.com/~bringie/
- The BROCKLEHURST Revival Society
  http://www.fbrocko.demon.co.uk/brs.html
- BRONSON, BROWNSON, BRUNSON
  http://www.geocities.com/Heartland/Ridge/2509/
  brownson.html
- BROOMHALL Genealogy
  http://www.springhillfarm.com/broomhall
  *BROOMHALL, including BROOMALL and BROOMELL. While
  most of our research has been in Pennsylvania USA, we have
  some in OH and other states. This family is found in the UK,
  USA, Canada, Australia and New Zealand.*
- Descendants of Peter BROWNE (of ancient
  Windsor, Connecticut)
  http://members.aol.com/ptrbrwn
  *Born ca. 1632 at Plymouth (Duxbury), Massachusetts, died
  9 March 1691/92 in Windsor, Hartford County, Connecticut.*
- BROWN Family Genealogical Society
  http://www.brownfamily.org
- BROYLES/BRILES Family History
  http://homepages.rootsweb.com/~george/index.shtml
  *Produced and maintained for the tens of thousands of descen-
  dants of the immigrant Johannes BREYHEL (or John BROYLES,
  Johannes BREUEL and other variations of the name). Broyles,
  Briles, Bryles, Brile, Briel, Broil, Broiles, Bryoll, Breÿhel, Brül,
  Breuel, Brohl, Bruel, Breiel, Brouel, Bruile, Broyhill.*
- The Clan BUCHANAN
  http://www.tartans.com/clans/Buchanan/buchanan.html
- BUCK Genealogy Website
  http://www.rootsweb.com/~tlmorris/buck/index.html
- The BUCKNER Page
  http://enws347.eas.asu.edu/~buckner/buckner.html
- BUELL Family Research Project
  http://www.geocities.com/Heartland/Pointe/3237/FAMILY.HTM
- BUMP Family Association
  http://medgen.iupui.edu/~rebecca/bump.html
  Bump, Bumpas, Bumpass, Bumps, Bumpus, etc.

- BUNKER Family Association
  http://www.BunkerFamilyAssn.org/index.html
- BUNN Family Page
  http://www.geocities.com/Heartland/Hills/6858/
- BURBURY Family History Web Page
  http://www.vision.net.au/~dburbury/burbury.htm
- BURDICKs on the Web!
  http://ra.nilenet.com/~hburdick/botw.html
  *The Descendants of Robert BURDICK of Rhode Island, arriving
  from England in 1651.*
- BURKS Genealogy Study Group
  http://members.tripod.com/~bjcasey/index.html
  *Dedicated to the Burks/Burk families of Virginia, especially
  information on early Burk, Burks, of Goochland, Albemarle,
  Amherst and surrounding counties.*
- BURNESS One-Name Study
  http://fox.nstn.ca/~jburness/burness.html
  *Study of the surname Burness which originated in
  Kincardineshire Scotland.*
- BURRELL / BURRILL Family Association
  E-mail: Barbara_L_Burrill@compuserve.com
  *A quarterly newsletter for research on the names Burrell,
  Burrill, Burwell. E-mail Barbara Burrill for details at:
  Barbara_L_Burrill@compuserve.com*
- BURT Family Genealogy
  http://www.rootsweb.com/~burtsou/
  *The genealogy of the Burt family of the southeastern
  United States.*
- BUSBEE / BUSBY Family Homepage
  http://home.cdsnet.net/~nashoba/index.htm
- BUS'D'KER Family Genealogy
  http://www.mnsinc.com/royb/directry.htm
  *Includes Busdiecker, Busdieker, Busdeker, Bushdiecker,
  Bussdieker, Buszdieker, Busdicker, Busdecker, Busdeicker.*
- BUSH Family Genealogy
  http://www.geocities.com/Heartland/Plains/9130/
  *Descendants of Philip Bush and Mary Bryan, circa 1732,
  Orange County, Virginia.*
- BUSHFIELD Family History
  http://www.angelfire.com/in/bushfield/index.html
- BUSTARD Genealogy Home Page
  http://www.infc.ulst.ac.uk/~dave/Bustard/
- Genealogija Rodbine BUTINA iz Kostela, Slovenija,
  Vasje Butina
  http://www.creativ.si/genealog/
  *The BUTINA'S Family Genealogy from Kostel, Slovenia by
  Vasja Butina. BUTINA, BATINICA, GOLIK, KAJFEZ,
  MIHELCIC, REBOLJ, SUMI, ZDRAVIC, ZIDAR, ZUPANCIC.*
- BUTLERs in Jackson County, Tennessee
  http://www2.aros.net/~cbutler//index.htm
  *Early Butlers in Jackson County, TN and their descendants.
  BUTLER, MONTGOMERY, KINDALL, KIRKPATRICK,
  TINSELY, DAVIS, USSERY, PLUMLEE, SERGENT.*
- The BUTLER Society
  http://www.butler-soc.org

- BUTTON Genealogy Page
  http://members.harborcom.net/~cpr/Button.html

- HOELSCHER-BUXKEMPER Family Heritage Association
  http://www.hostville.com/hoelscher/

◆ Surnames Beginning with "C"

- Family Tree Maker Online User Home Pages—C
  http://www.familytreemaker.com/users/c/index.html

- Genealogy's Most Wanted—Surnames Beginning with "C"
  http://www.citynet.net/mostwanted/c.htm

- H-GIG Surname Registry—Surnames Beginning C
  http://www.ucr.edu/h-gig/surdata/surname3.html

- Higginson Book Company—Surnames Beginning with C
  http://www.Higginsonbooks.com/c.htm

- inGeneas Table of Common Surname Variations and Surname Misspellings—C
  http://www.ingeneas.com/C.html

- Surname Springboard Index—C
  http://www.geocities.com/~alacy/spring_c.htm

- SurnameWeb Surname Registry—C Index
  http://www.surnameweb.org/registry/c.htm

- Genealogy Resources on the Internet—"C" Surname Mailing Lists
  http://members.aol.com/gfsjohnf/gen_mail_surnames-c.html
  This site is wonderfully maintained by John Fuller. It includes mailing list information for the following surnames and their variant spellings:
  CABANIS (includes Chabanis, Cabaniss, Cabiness), CAGLE (includes Kegel), CAHILL, CAIN (includes Kane, Cane), CALDWELL (includes Caldeuuelle, Callwell, Cauldwell, Cawldwell, Coldwell, Colewell, Coldwold), CALES (includes Cale, Cail, Cayle, Caile, Kail), CALKIN (includes Calkins, Caulkin, Caulkins, Corkin), CALL (includes Calle, Caule), CALLAHAN (includes Callaghan, O'Callaghan), CALLAWAY (includes Calaway, Caloway, Calloway), CALLICOTT, CALVERT, CAMERON, CAMP, CAMPBELL-L, CANBY, CANNON (includes Canon), CANTER, CANTRELL, CAPLES (includes Cables, Kapels, Chapels), CAPPS, CAPSTACK (includes Capstick), CARDWELL, CARLILE (includes Carlisle), CARLSON (includes Carlsson, Karlson, Karlsson, Klassen), CARMACK, CARMAN (includes Carmon, Karmann), CARMAN-ROOTS, CARPENTER (includes Zimmerman), CARR (includes Kerr, Karr, Corr, Car, Kar), CARRICK (includes Kerrick), CARRINGTON (includes Carington, Karrington), CARROLL (includes Karel, Carrell, O'Carroll), CarruthFam (includes Carrouth, Caruth, Coruth, Cruth), CARSON (includes Carlson, Kerr, Carr, Karson, McCawson), CARTER (includes McCarter), CARTMILL (includes Cartmell, Cartmille, Cartmel), CARTY (includes McCarty, Carthy, McCarthy, Cardie, McCardie), CARVER, ROBERT, CARWILE (includes Calwell, Cardwell, Carswell, Carwell, Carlile, Carlisle, Carlyle, Cargile, Cargill, Carvile, Carvill, Corwyle, Corwell, Corwile, Corlyle), CARY (includes Carey), CASE-FAMILY (includes Cass), CASEY (includes Cayce, Kasey, O'Casey, MacKasey, Kayce, O'Cathasaigh, Catharsay, Causey, Cacey, Kissee, Casy, Cosey), CASH (includes Cach, Kash), Cash, CASHMORE (includes Cashmoore, Cashmores), CASSIDY (includes O'Cassidy,

  Cassiday, Cassady), CASSIE, CASSIL (includes Cassils, Casselberry, Cassel, Cassell, Cassells, Casselman, Cassels, Castell, Castle, Castleberry, Castleman, Castles, Casel, Casil, Casell, Casill), CASTEEL (includes Casteal, Castile), CASTOR (includes Kuster, Koster, Custer, Kusterd, Kuester, Kester, Custard, Kustard, Kistard, Kister, Gerster, Caster, Castor, Kastor, Koester, Kiester, Keister), CASWELL (includes Casswell, Carswell, Caswill, Keswell), CATE (includes Cates, Kate, Kates), CATO (includes Cater), CAUBLE (includes Coppel, Copel, Copple, Cobble, Cobel, Cobble, Kabble, Kabel, Kople, Kobble), CAUGHEY (includes McCaughey, Coughey, Cahey, Haughey, Eachaidh, Eochaidh, Coffee, Coffey, Cowfy, Keogh, Hoy, Kehoe, MacKeogh, O'Hoey, MacEochaidh), CAUSBY (includes Causbie, Cosby, Cozby), CAUSER, CAVIN (includes Cavins, Caven, Cavan), CAVITT (includes Cavett, Cavit, Cavet, Kivett, Kivet), CECIL (includes Cissell, Sessell, Sesil), CESSNA (includes Cessne, Cissne, Cisney, Cisna), CHAMBERS, CHAMBLEE (includes Chamlee, Chambley, Shamblee, Shambly, Shamly), CHANDLER, CHANEY (includes Cheney, Cheyney, Chesney), CHAPMAN (includes Chipman, Cheapman, Chapelman, Kapmann, Shapman, Shepman), CHAPPELL (includes Cappello, Kappel, Schappel), CHARITY, CHASE (includes Chace, Chazy), CHASTAIN (includes Castine, Chastaine, Chasteen, Chasten, Chastine, Chesteen, Shasteen, Shastid, Shastine), CHAUDOIN (includes Chaudowen, Chaddoan, Chaddoen, Chad-Owens, Chaudron, Shadowen, Shadowens, Shadowin, Shadowins, Shadoan, Shadoin, Shadden, Shaddin, Shad-Owens, Shadowing), CHEATHAM, CHEEK, CHEEVER (includes Chivers), CHENAULT (includes Chennault), CHESNEY (includes Chesnee, Chesnai, Chezney, Chesnau, Chesnet, McChesney), CHESNUT (includes Chastain, Chesnai, Chesnau, Chesnet, Chesney, Chesnutt, Chestnut, Chestnutt, McChesney), CHEW (includes Chewe), CHEYNE, CHICHESTER (includes Chidester), CHICKERING, CHILDERS (includes Childress, Childes, Childe, Child, Childs, Chilton, Chilters, Children), CHILTON (includes Shelton, Chelton), CHISKE (includes Chisk), CHITWOOD-L, CHOATE (includes Choat, Choats, Shoat, Shoate), CHRANE, CHRISTIAN, CHRISTMAS (includes Christmus), CHUMBLEY (includes Chumbly, Chumley, Chumly, Chumney, Crumbley), CLACK, CLAFLIN-L (includes MackClothlan, MacLachlan, MacLachlan, MakClachlane, MakLauchlane, M'Clachlene, MakClauchlane, McLauchlane, M'Lauchlane, M'Clauchlane, M'Lauchan, McClauchlan, McLauchlane, M'Clachlane, M'Claichlane, MacLaughlin), CLANTON, CLARKE (includes Clark, Clerke), CLARY (includes Cleary, Clare, Clara, O'Clary, O'Cleary, McClary, McCleary), CLAY (includes Klee, Kleh, Cleh, Clehy), CLAYPOOL (includes Claypoole, Cleypole, Claypole), CLAYTON, CLAYWORTH, CLEAVELAND (includes Cleveland, Clyveland, Clive-land, Cliveland, Caluvium (Roman), Cleve, Cleiveland), CLEMENT-Benjamin, CLEMENTS (includes Klementz, Clemence, Clement, Clemons, Claymore), CLEMMER (includes Klemmer, Klymer), CLENDINEN (includes Clendennin, Clendenin, Clendenning, Cledenan, Clendenon, Clendennon, Clendennan, Glendinning, Clindinning), CLEVENGER (includes Cleavenger, Clevinger, Clavenger), CLICK (includes Cleek, Gluck), CLIFTON (includes Clifftion, Clefton, Clipton, Cliftin), CLIMAS (includes Clemas, Clymas), CLINE (includes Clyne, Klein), CLONINGER (includes Cloniger, Glaninger, Kloninger), CLOSSON (includes Clason, Clauson), CLOUD, CLOUDMAN, CLOUGH (includes Cluff, Clow), CLOYES (includes Cloyse, Clayes, Cloice, Cloys), CLUTTERBUCK (includes Clotterbuck, Clutterbook), COATES-L (includes Coats, Coate), COBB (includes Cobbe, Caub), COCHRAN (includes Cockerell, Cockrell, McCorcoran, Cockerham), COCKEREL, COCKRELL (includes Cockerel, Cockrill, Cockerell, Cockrel, Cockerill, Cockriel), COE (includes Coo, Coes, Coey, Koe), COFFEY (includes Coffee, Coffin), COFFIELD (includes Cofield, Caufield, Coffel, Coffelt, Kauffeld), COFFIN, COFFMAN (includes Kaufman, Kaufmann, Kauffmann), COKER, COLBURN (includes Coalborne, Coalburn, Cobern, Cobourn, Cobron, Cobrun, Cobun, Coburn, Cockborn, Cockburn, Coebourne, Colbern, Colborn, Colborne, Colbourn, Colbourne, Colburn, Colburne, Coleborn, Coleburn,

Colbron, Colbrun, Coulborn, Coulborne, Coulbourn, Coulbourne, Coulburn), COLBY (includes Colbie, Colbey, Coleby), COLD, COLE (includes Coal, Kohl), COLEGROVE (includes Colgrove), COLEMAN, COLEY, COLLETT (includes Collet, Collitt), COLLIER, COLLING (includes Collin, Collins, Collings, Colinge, Collinet), COLLINS, COLQUHOUN (includes Cahoon, Calhoun), COLVILLE (includes Carville, Colvil), COLVIN (includes Calvin, Colven), COMBS (includes Com, Comb, Combe, Combes, Combs, Come, Coom, Coomb, Coombe, Coombes, Coombs, Coumbes, Kom, Kome, Komes), COMPTON, COMSTOCK, CONATY (includes Connachtaighs, Connerty), CONES, CONGLETON, CONKLIN-L, CONLON (includes O'Conlon, O'Conlan, Conlan, O'Conlin, Conlin, O'Conlen, Conlen), CONN (includes Con), CONNELLY (includes Conley, Connally, Connolly), CONNOLLY (includes Conly, Conely, Colepely, Conley), CONOVER (includes Coavenhoven, Coenhoven, Cofenhofen, Coneover, Connoven, Connower, Connoyer, Conoven, Conver, Couen Houen, Couenhouen, Coughvenhoven, Counoven, Counover, Couvenhoven, Couwehowen, Couwenhove, Couwenhoven, Couwenhowen, Couwenoven, Coven, Hoven, Covenhove, Covenhoven, Covenhover, Cowerhoven, Cownnover, Cownouer, Cownover, Cownovr, Coyenhoven, Crownover, Koienhoven, Koienoven, Konover, Korenoven, Kouenhoven, Kouveoven, Kouwenhove, Kouwenhoven, Kouwenove, Kouwenoven, Kovenhoven, Kowenhoven, Kownoven, Koyenhoven, Van Couwenhoven, Van Couwenhoven, Van Covenhoven, Van, Cowenhoven, Van Kouwenhoven), CONROY, CONVERSE (includes Conyerse), COOK (includes Cooke, Kuch, Koch), COOKSEY, COOLEY-L, COOMBER (includes Comber, Cumber), COON (includes Coons, Koon(s), Kuhn(s), Maccoone, McCune), COOPER (includes Kooper, Koeper, Kupfer, Kuyper, Coopers, Cooperman, Coper, Coober, Coopey, Copper), COPELAND (includes Coplen, Coplan, Copelan, Coupland), COPPOCK (includes Koppic, Kopec, Coppick, Cuppack, Coppage, McCobic), CORBETT (includes Corbet, Corbitt, Corbit), CORBIN (includes Corbett), CORLEY (includes Cawley, Cauley), CORN (includes Corns, Cornn, Corne, Cornes, Cornns), CORNELIUS (includes Corneliusen, Kornelius, Corder, Cornelli), CORNELL (includes Cornwell, Cornwall, Cornewell), CORNETT (includes Cornet, Canute), CORRELL (includes Currell, Corell), CORRIGAN (includes O'Corrigain, O'Corrigan, O'Carrigan, O'Corrican, O'Kerrigan, Carrigan, Corrican, Kerrigan), CORSON (includes Colson, Courson, DeCoursey, Courssen, Coarson, Corzine, Carsten; a branch is, Vroom), COSHOW (includes Cashew, Cusho, Kershaw), COSSEY, COTNER (includes Gortner, Goertner, Curtner, Carther, Cortner, Kartner), COTTINGHAM, COTTLE, COTTON, COTTRELL (includes Cottrill, Cotterell, Cotteral), COUCH (includes Crouch, Kouch), COUILLARD (includes Couillard, Coulliard, Couliard, Coulard, Coullard, Couilyard, Coulyard, Coolyard, Colyard), COULING (includes Cowling), COULOMBE (includes Coulome, Colombe, Colomb), COUNTRYMAN (includes Gunterman, Gunderman, Gonterman, Kunderman, Kunterman, Cunderman, Contreman, Counterman, Gautherman), COUNTS (includes Countz, Koontz), COURTNEY, COUTON (includes Couston, Couthon, Coutton, Coaston, Cowstonne), COUTS (includes Kutz, Kouts, Coots, Cootts, Coutts, Koutz), COVENTRY (includes Covingtry), COVERT (includes Coevert, Coovert, Coever), COVEY, COWAN (includes Cowen, Cown, McCowan), COWART, COWEN (includes Cowing), COWING, COWLEY (includes Cooley), COX-L, COY (includes Coye), COZART (includes Cossart, Cozad, Cassart, Kosart, Kozad), CRABBE (includes Crabb, Craib), CRABTREE, CRAFT (includes Kraft), CRAIG, CRAIN (includes Crane, Craine), CRAM, CRANDALL (includes Crandell, Crandle, Crandol), CRANFORD, CRAVEN, CRAWFORD (includes Craford, Crafford, Crowfoot), CREAGER (includes Krieger, Kruger, Cregar, Creger, Crugar, Creggar, Krueger), CREE (includes Cre, Crie, Crea, Crey), CREECH (includes Creach, Screech, Screach, Cruch), CREED (includes Creede, Creedon), CREEL (includes Creal), CRENSHAW (includes Crinshaw, Cranshaw, Crashaw), CREVLIN, CREWS (includes Cruise, Cruse, Crewse), CRILLEY (includes Crilly), CRINER (includes Creiner, Greiner, Kreiner, Kriner, Crider), CRIPPEN (includes Crippin, Grippen), CRIPPEN-NEWS (includes Crippin, Grippen, Grippin), CRISP (includes Chrisp, Crispe), CROCKER, CROCKETT, CROESEN (includes Cruise, Cruser, Crusen, Cruzen, Kroesen, Krewson, Krusen, Kruser), CRONK (includes Craunk, Kronk, Kraunk, Cronkhite, Krank), CRONWOVEN, CROOK (includes Crooks), CROSS, CROSTHWAITE (includes Crosthwait, Crosswaite, Crosswait, Crosswhite), CROUSE (includes Krouse, Krause), CROW, CROWDER, CRUMLEY (includes Crumly), CRUMPTON, CRUNKLETON, CRUSER (includes Kruser, Crusa, Croesen), CRYAN (includes O'cryan, O'crean, Crean, Crehan, O'cregan, O'croidheain), CULBERT (includes Cuthbert, Culpert), CULBERTSON, CULLOP (includes Kohlhop, Culop), CULP/KOLB, CULPEPPER (includes Culpeper, Colepeper), Cumbeefamily, CUNDIFF (includes Condiff, Conduff), CUNNINGHAM (includes Cunnyngham, Konningham, Koenigam, Cummings), CUPP (includes Kopp, Kop, Cop, Cope, Cup, Cap), CURCIE, CURNUTT/CURNUTTE (includes Carnutt, Cornutt, Kurnutt), CURNUTTE, CURRENCE (includes Currance, Currens, Currans), CURRY, CURTIS (includes Curtiss), CUSHMAN, CUTHRELL (includes Cuthriell, Cutrell), CUTLIP (includes Cutlipp, Cutliff, Cutliffe, Cudlip, Cudlipp, Cutlett, all C341 Soundex names), CUTRIGHT (includes Cartright).

- CADDLE & Varients Genealogy Homepage
  http://ourworld.compuserve.com/homepages/Terry_caddle/homepage.htm
  Caddle, Caddel, Caddell, Cadell, Cadel, Cadle

- CAHILL Cooperative Ancestors—Over 300 Families on File
  http://pages.prodigy.com/IA/cahillancestors/cahillancestors.html
  CAHILL / COHILL / CAHALL, etc. Also a newsletter available.

- CAIN Connections Genealogy Site
  http://members.aol.com/dkainc/index.html

- CALLAHANs WWW Home Page Introduction
  http://www.interactive.net/~mailman/
  Callahan, Callaghan, O'Callaghan

- CALLAWAY Family Association
  http://www.lgc.peachnet.edu/callaway/cfa1.htm

- CALMES Notes Newsletter
  E-mail: genecox@bluebon.net
  "Calmes Notes," a newsletter, is published four times each year, for descendants of Marquis de la Calmes, the Huguenot, who came to America in the late 1600s. The descendants are organized in the Genealogical Society of Versailles, named in honor of his grandson, Marquis Calmes, IV, who served as a captain in the Revolutionary War and later as a brigadier general with Kentucky troops in the War of 1812. General Calmes founded and laid out the town of Versailles, Kentucky, which he named in honor of his friend and associate, General Lafayette. The general and his wife, the former Priscilla Heale, are buried in a mausoleum in what is now a horse farm pastured about midway between Versailles and Lexington. The society named in his honor maintains the mausoleum. "Calmes Notes" covers information of interest about the early Calmes' families and their descendants. For details, send e-mail to Eugene Cox at genecox@bluebon.net

- Descendants of Lord Baltimore CALVERT
  http://www.familytreemaker.com/users/s/p/e/Vicki-K-Spencer/

- CAMP Family
  http://www.new-jerusalem.com/genealogy/barbara/camp.htm

- The CAMPBELL Database
  http://www.csihq.com/campbell/
  With Campbell marriage records and census records.

- CANNON Family Home Page
  http://www.rootsweb.com/~auntjean/cannon/index.htm
  Cannon / Kennon

- CANUPnet Genealogy
  http://www.hal-pc.org/~canupnet/geno.html
  *Canup, Cannup, Canupp, Cannupp, Cunnup, Canups, Cannups, Canupps, Caneup, Cunnop, Canop, Kanup, Kannup, Kanupp, Kanups, also some *Knup, and Knupp**

- CAPLES Surname Mailing List
  http://rampages.onramp.net/~lcompton/caples/index.html
  Includes Cables, Kapels, Chapels.

- CAPLICE Family Records
  http://www.st.net.au/~dunn/caplice.htm

- The CAPSHAW Family History
  http://www.magicnet.net/~jerryc/

- The CAR(E)Y Family Research Page
  http://home.earthlink.net/~howardorjeff/cary/

- CARLTON(Clafee) & MASON Descendants
  http://www.digroots.com/carlmaso.htm
  William Branch Carlton (or Clafee) b. 1856 m. Ethel Mason.

- CARMAN Family History
  http://home.att.net/~rcarman/

- CARMICHAEL Descendants of Comrie, Perthshire, Scotland
  http://members.aol.com/tch6535/carmichael/carmichael.htm
  For the descendants of the CARMICHAEL families originating from Comrie, Perthshire, Scotland. Includes CARMICHAEL, COMRIE, DRUMMOND, MORRISON, ROBERTSON, STEVEN, HEDDRICK, McLAREN, McGREGOR, ANDERSON.

- CAROTHERS Genealogy
  http://users.deltanet.com/users/dcaroth/public_html/carothers.html

- The CARRIKER Family Homepage
  http://pages.prodigy.com/CARRIKER/

- CARROLL Home Page—CARROLL Cables Newsletter
  http://members.aol.com/kinseeker6/carroll.html

- CARSTARPHEN Family Homepage
  http://www.edwards1.com/rose/genealogy/carstar/carstar.html
  And many variant spellings.

- CARTWRIGHT Research Center
  http://www.fortunecity.com/millenium/sherwood/163/index.html
  A one name study center for the Cartwright surname, any place, any time including any variation of spelling: Cartright, Cutright, and others.

- CASE Genealogy
  http://www.maggiesworld.com/case.htm
  Descendants of Ephriam Alpha CASE, born around Albany, New York in 1823.

- The CASEY Family Association
  http://home.swbell.net/cfa/

- The CASTOR Association of America
  http://members.tripod.com/~EbneterG/index-9.html
  Caster, Custer, Kester and other variants

- The CASWELL Homepage
  http://www.moonrakers.com/caswell/
  Carswell, Casswell, Caswill, Caswall, Karswell, Coswell, Cassill, etc.

- The CATO Homepage
  http://www.webkeeper.com/cato/c.html
  CATO & CATOE, many CATER, CATOR, CAYTOR, CAYTER, CAYTO, CATE, KAYTO, CATON and numerous other spellings.

- CHADY homepage
  http://www.cs.stedwards.edu/~chady/

- CHAMBERLAIN Chain
  http://www.cet.com/~weidnerc/

- The World CHAMBERLAIN Genealogical Society
  http://www.livingonline.com/~welmar/wcs.html

- The Association of CHARRON and DUCHARME, Inc
  E-mail: dmiale@exis.net
  For details e-mail Dick Miale at dmiale@exis.net or in French e-mail Pierre Ducharme at: duchap00libertel.montreal.qc.ca

- Pierre CHASTAIN Family Association
  http://www.kopower.com/~jimchstn/

- CHEESBROUGH One Name Study Home Page
  http://www.users.globalnet.co.uk/~gdl/cheesbro.htm

- CHENOWETH Family
  http://www.accessone.com/~jegge/chenweth.htm
  Descendants of John CHENOWETH & Mary CALVERT.

- CHESNUT / CHESTNUT Research Network
  http://www.users.mis.net/~chesnut/pages/chessurn.htm
  Chastain, Chesnai, Chesnau, Chesnet, Chesney, Chesnutt, Chestnut, Chestnutt, McChesney

- La page Web de CHEVIET's Family
  http://perso.club-internet.fr/cheviet/
  France. Ascendance d'Antoine et Mathilde CHEVIET.

- CHEYNE Home Page
  http://www.rootsweb.com/~cheyne/

- CHICKEN Family Histories
  http://ourworld.compuserve.com/homepages/Chicken_Matthews/

- The CHOQUET-CHOQUETTE Genealogy
  http://www.cam.org/~jchoque/english.html

- The CHRISTLIEB-CHRISLIP-CRISLIP Family Association
  http://pages.prodigy.net/jeffchristlieb/ccc.html

- CHURCH Family Chronicles
  http://members.aol.com/kinseeker6/church.html

- CISCO / SISCO Genealogy Data
  http://www-epi.soph.uab.edu/cisco/htm/
  Descendants of Moses SISCO, b. 28 Sep 1799 in Newark, New Jersey.

- A CLAGGETT Family History
  http://www.tedsite.mcmail.com
  Kent, England

- CLARDY Family Genealogy
  http://www.huscarl.com/clardy/index.htm
  A clearinghouse for information on the Clardy family and their associations.

- CLARK Family Home Page
  http://www.teleplex.net/gclark/index.html
  Dedicated to the descendants of John B. Clark of Rowan/Davie County, NC, and to all the Clark Family Researchers that choose to contribute, download, or add to our database.

- CLARK Genealogical Society
  http://www3.sympatico.ca/clark/begin.htm

- The Descendants of James CLARK of Vermont
  http://members.aol.com/MShermanL/clark.html
  Born 1601 probably in England, died probably in Vermont.

- CLAYTON Surname
  http://homepages.rootsweb.com/~jclaytn/clayton.html
  Clayton Surname: (DE>GA>AL>TX).

- CLAYWORTHs Online
  http://www.vaxxine.com/genrace/clayworth/

- CLEVELAND Family Chronicles
  http://www.angelfire.com/il/ClevelandFamilyChron/index.html

- The CLIFTON Family Home Page
  http://www.rootsweb.com/~clifton/clifton/

- The Decendants of John CLINE
  http://members.tripod.com/~jlschneider/index.htm

- CLOUGH-L Home Page
  http://genweb.net/~clough/
  Descendants of John Clough (1613–1691).

- The CLOUTIER—CLUTCHEY Family—
  A Genealogical History
  http://www.naples.net/~clutchey/
  Zacharie CLOUTIER, to Canada in 1634.

- CLUGSTON Family History & Genealogy
  http://www.cstone.net/~clugston/

- COATES-L Surname Mailing List
  http://www.aa.net/~jdcoates/list/coates-l.htm
  Includes Coats, Coate.

- COATNEY Surname List Home Page
  http://COATNEY.listbot.com
  A list for the discussion of the COATNEY Surname—any place, any time.

- The COBBETT Study Group
  http://members.aol.com/cobbettsg/

- COBERNUS, KOBERNUS, KOBERNUSS, KOBERNUSZ Family Home Page
  http://members.aol.com/gkobernus/index.html

- The COBRA Family Genealogy Home Page
  http://www.geocities.com/Athens/Acropolis/3515/
  History and genealogy of the Cobra Family in Portugal and its modern branches in Canada, Brazil, and the U.S.A.

- COCKRELL Collections
  http://www.futureone.com/~burgess/cockweb.html
  All Cockrell, Cockrill, Cockerill families in America.

- COFFEY Cousins' Clearinghouse
  http://www.geocities.com/Heartland/Plains/6233/coffeycousins.html

- The COHEN / COWEN/ COWAN Family History Page
  http://home.texoma.net/~mmcmullen/co/cohen.htm

- The FONDREN and COLE Families
  http://members.aol.com/jogt/fondren.htm
  Of North Carolina and South Carolina.

- COLEMAN Surname Mailing List
  http://rampages.onramp.net/~lcompton/coleman/index.html

- The COLERIDGE Family Genealogy
  http://www.geocities.com/Athens/4017/
  Including the poet, Samuel Taylor Coleridge.

- The COLLING System BBS
  http://www.pi.se/collings-system/

- COLLINS Bulletin Board
  http://pages.prodigy.com/YWMZ46A/CBB.htm

- COLLINS Mess or Mess of COLLINS
  http://pages.prodigy.com/YWMZ46A/collinsm.htm

- The COLVIN Family History Page
  http://www.rootsweb.com/~mcolvin/colvinfh/

- COLYER Genealogy
  http://www.mychoice.net/colyer55/
  Colier, Collier, Collyer, Colyar, Colyear, Colyer.

- The COMBS &c. RootsWeb Research Project
  http://www.rootsweb.com/~combs/index.html
  Includes Comb, Combe, Combes, Come, Comes, Coomb, Coombe, Coombes, Coome, Coomes.

- L'Association des COMEAU D'Amérique
  http://home.istar.ca/~acomeau/aca/bonjour.htm

- COMPTON Home Site
  http://www.geocities.com/Heartland/Acres/4730/compton/compton.html

- CONDER Family
  http://www.duke.edu/web/chlamy/conder.html
  Descendants of Lewis Conder and Elizabeth Muller or Miller.

- CONKLIN-L Surname Mailing List
  http://www.rootsweb.com/~nozell/CONKLIN-L/

- CONNOLLY Genealogy Forum
  http://www.connollyweb.com/geneology/
- CONOVER Family Genealogy
  http://www.conovergenealogy.com
  Descendants of Wolpert Gerretse Van Kouwenhoven.
- COOPER Home Page—COOPER Collections Newsletter
  http://members.aol.com/kinseeker6/cooper.html
- COPELAND Cuzzins Newsletter
  E-mail: CarlCindy2@aol.com
  For details send e-mail to Lucinda (Cindy) Olsen, editor and publisher, at CarlCindy2@aol.com
- SStapor's COPELAND Home Page
  http://members.aol.com/SStapor/Copeland.html
  The descendants of Joel Copeland 1734–1814 of Overton Co., TN. He was the g-g-grandson of John Copeland (b 1616) the immigrant.
- CORFMAN Family Web Site
  http://www.corfman.com
  Also KORFFMANN.
- CORMIER Family
  E-mail: moxie40@vivanet.com
  Send e-mail to Robin Finley at moxie40@vivanet.com
- CORNELL Family Genealogy
  http://www.netusa1.net/~kb9lwn/gene.html
  Cornell/Cornwell/Cornwall Families of Central Ontario, Canada and Central New York.
- CORNING Connections
  http://mrmac-jr.scs.unr.edu/corning/corning.html
- CORNING Family Reunion
  http:/bold.coba.unr.edu/corning/reunion/1fam.html
  Corning Family Reunion, Yarmouth, Nova Scotia, Canada, July 22 to 25, 1999.
- COUCH Genealogy
  http://www.couchgenweb.com
- The COULTER / COALTER Family—Genealogy
  http://www.internet-partners.com/mcdonald/index.htm
- COUNTRYMAN Surname Mailing List
  http://www.nmmi.cc.nm.us/~nancy/countryman
  Includes Gunterman, Gunderman, Gonterman, Kunderman, Kunterman, Cunderman, Contreman, Counterman, Gautherman.
- COURTNEY Chronicle On-Line Family Magazine
  http://www.geocities.com/RainForest/3608/
- A COURTNEY's Descendants Family History
  http://www2.netdoor.com/~52rcourt/histn.htm
  John Ellis Courtney, abt. 1821–1864.
- COUSINS/COZENS/COUZENS Family Genealogy
  http://web2.airmail.net/lwi941/
  From Virginia since 1694.
- COUTANT / COTANT Genealogy
  http://members.aol.com/scotant/index.htm
  History from 1142 to 1997.

- COVEY Family Research Page
  http://www.geocities.com/Heartland/Plains/7614/COVEY.HTM
- COVINGTON
  http://members.aol.com/covingtonw/home.htm
  Descendants of Terrel Covington, born in Richmond County, NC.
- COWAN Clan United
  http://www.sure.net/~rcowan/index.html
- COWAN Clues Genealogy Newsletter
  http://www.angelfire.com/ar/cowanclues/index.html
- The COWAN List
  http://members.tripod.com/~TMock/cowan.htm
  Cowan, Cowen
- COWHERD Genealogy
  http://www.geocities.com/Heartland/Prairie/4917/
  Descendants of James COWARD, immigrant who came to Virginia from England in 1688.
- COX Family Genealogy
  http://www.jax-inter.net/users/bjcox/
  Benjamin J COX (1773–1846) et al. Links to more COX family resources, etc.
- The CRABBE Family Page
  http://www.geocities.com/Heartland/Ranch/7299/
  World-Wide One-Name Study of CRABBE families.
- CRAGG the name
  http://www.ozemail.com.au/~woolwash/cragg/engcragg1.htm
  CRAGG—Cumberland County, England
  http://www.ozemail.com.au/~woolwash/cragg/engcragg2.htm
  CRAGG—Keswick, Cumberland County, England
  http://www.ozemail.com.au/~woolwash/cragg/engcragg3.htm
  CRAGG—Workington, Cumberland County, England
  http://www.ozemail.com.au/~woolwash/cragg/engcragg4.htm
- CRAIG Genealogy
  http://www.qni.com/~geo/craig.htm
  Descendants of Samuel Craig, born 1760 in York County, Pennsylvania.
- CRAIGMYLE Genealogy
  http://members.aol.com/Rdkfour/craigmyle.html
- CRAMP(E) One Name Association
  http://www.geocities.com/Heartland/Flats/7866/
- Some CRANDALL, CRAIN, COWAN, & CLARY Genealogy
  http://www.geocities.com/MotorCity/1949/
- CRANDALL Family Association
  http://pages.prodigy.com/NY/cranfamassoc/index.html
- CRANE Family Message Board
  http://www.koke.com/crane/
- CRANKSHAW Family History
  http://www.angelfire.com/ga/Crankshaw/

- CRAWCOUR Connections—The CRAWCOUR Family One Name Study
  http://www.geocities.com/Heartland/8256/crawcour.html

- Dick CRAWLEY Genealogy
  http://www.accucomm.net/~owc/
  Member of C.C.I.E. (CRAWLEY Cousins Information Exchange).

- The CREE Family History Society
  http://www.leicester.co.uk/cree/

- The CRESAP Society
  http://www.rootsweb.com/~cresap/

- The CREUTZBERG Home
  http://www.creutzberg.com

- The CRIBBS Family History & Genealogy Homepage
  http://www.geocities.com/Heartland/Bluffs/7748/cribbs.htm

- CRIE Surname
  http://homepages.rootsweb.com/~jclaytn/crie.html
  Crie Surname: (Scotland>ME>MO>TX).

- CRIPPEN-CRIPPIN Family Journal
  http://www.intrepid.net/~fanfare/crippen.html

- CRISPELL Family Association
  http://home.earthlink.net/~rctwig/crispell.htm

- The CRIST Family on the Net
  http://users.aol.com/stephenmce/crist/index.htm

- The CRITESER Crossroad
  http://ourworld.compuserve.com/homepages/waltcr/waltcr.htm

- CROOM Genealogy Web Site
  http://members.aol.com/crooiii/croopage.htm
  Descendants of Daniel Croom, bc 1683 VA; also Cooper, Herring, Henry, Howard, Malpass, Moore, familes of eastern North Carolina.

- The CROSSMAN Society
  http://www.geocities.com/Heartland/Meadows/1246/index.html

- CROSSNOE Genealogy
  http://www.apex.net/users/crossnoe
  Resource Center and information for the surname CROSSNOE, CROSSNO, CROSNOE, CROSNO, CROSSNORE, and CROSSNOW.

- CROUSE Crossroads
  http://members.tripod.com/~jdk3/index.html
  Descendants of Mathias Crouse born ca. 1750.

- The CROWTHER Family Tree Project
  http://members.aol.com/crowtrees/index.html
  From England and South Carolina.

- CROY Family Homepage
  http://www.croy.org

- The CRUMBAUGH/CRUMBACH Family of Maryland, Kentucky and Illinois
  http://www.mindspring.com/~jogt/kygen/crumba2.htm

- CRUMPTON—Genealogy
  http://www.Thomson.net/land/crumpgen.htm
  Descendants of Luke CRUMPTON, b. abt. 1765.

- CUJAK / ZIELKE / SILKE / ZUELKE Genealogy
  http://pages.prodigy.net/dave_lossos/cujak.htm

- CULPEPPER Connections!
  http://gen.culpepper.com
  The Culpepper Family History Site. An extensive genealogical database of over 4,000 Colepepers, Culpepers and Culpeppers. Also includes an archival section, historical documents, place names, researchers, and more.

- Isaac CUMMINGS Family Association
  http://www.mtjeff.com/~bodenst/ICFA/index.htm

- CUNNINGHAM Descendants
  http://www.ovis.net/~billcham/cunningm/
  Descendants of Alexander Cunningham, born in Scotland about 1498.

- CURSITERs of Orkney—Orkney Genealogy Website
  http://www.cursiter.com

- Genealogical Research Center for the CYRENNE or SYRENNE families in Canada
  http://www3.sympatico.ca/gpfern/EHOME.HTM

◆ Surnames Beginning with "D"

- Family Tree Maker Online User Home Pages—D
  http://www.familytreemaker.com/users/d/index.html

- Genealogy's Most Wanted—Surnames Beginning with "D"
  http://www.citynet.net/mostwanted/d.htm

- H-GIG Surname Registry—Surnames Beginning D
  http://www.ucr.edu/h-gig/surdata/surname4.html

- Higginson Book Company—Surnames Beginning with D
  http://www.higginsonbooks.com/d.htm

- inGeneas Table of Common Surname Variations and Surname Misspellings—D–E
  http://www.ingeneas.com/D2E.html

- Surname Springboard Index—D
  http://www.geocities.com/~alacy/spring_d.htm

- SurnameWeb Surname Registry—D Index
  http://www.surnameweb.org/registry/d.htm

- Genealogy Resources on the Internet— "D" Surname Mailing Lists
  http://members.aol.com/gfsjohnf/gen_mail_surnames-d.html
  This site is wonderfully maintained by John Fuller. It includes mailing list information for the following surnames and their variant spellings:
  DABNEY (includes de Aubigne, de Aubigny, Daubinge), DAGGETT (includes Dagget, Dagett, Doggett, Dogett), DAHLEM (includes Dahlen, Dalem, Dallem), DALBY-S (includes Dalbey, Dolby, Dolbey, Dolbie, Dalbie), DALTON

(includes Daulton, Dolton, Dolten), DALY (includes O'Daly, Daley, Daily), DAMPIER (includes Dampear, Dampierre, Damphear, Damphere), DANFORTH (includes Danforthe, Danford, Danforde, Daneford, Darnford, Darneforde, Dampford, Dampforde, Dernford, Dernforth, Derneforthe), DANIEL, DANN (includes Dan), DANNAR (includes Danner), DARBY (includes Derby, Darbyshire), DARLAND (includes Darlandt, Dorland, Dorlandt, Durland, Durlandt), DARLING, DARNELL, DAVAR-DEVER (includes Daver, Davers, Davor, Devar, Devers), DAVENPORT, DAVIDOW, DAVIDSON (includes Davison), DAVIS (includes Davies, Dave, Daves, Davey, Daveys, Davison, Davisson), DAVIS1, DAWSON, DAY (includes Dey), DAY, DEAL (includes Deel, Diehl, Dial), DEAN, DEARBORN (includes Dearborne), DEARDORFF (includes Diedorff), DEBELL (includes Dobell), DEBOLT (includes DeBolt, Debolt, Diebold, Dieboldt), DECAMP (includes D'Camp, Van Camp, Van Campen), DECK (includes Dech, Dick, Dach, Dack, Dych), DECKER, DECOSTE (includes Coste), DeCUIR (includes Decuir, Decuire, Decuyre, deCuir), DEETER (includes Teeter, Deeder, Dieter), DEFORD, DEFRANCE, DeGARMO, DEGENHARDT (includes Degenhard, Degenhart, Dagenhart, Degenhart, Degener), DEGRAFFENREID, DeHAAS (includes Haas, Hass, Haff), DeHart, DEHAVEN (includes Den Hoffen, Ten Hauven, Inhoff), DELAHUNTY (includes Delahanty, Delehanty, Delahunt), DELAMARRE (includes Delamar, Delamer), DELASHMUTT (includes Delahsmut, de la Chamotte), DELAUDER (includes Delatter, Delatrre, Delawter, Delater, De Lattre, Delator), DELLINGER (includes Dillinger), DeLOACH (includes DeLoache, DeLoatch, DeLoch, D'Loatche), DELZELL (includes Dalziel, Dalyell, Dalzell), DEMASTUS (includes Demasters, Demastis, Demastes), DEMUTH (includes Damuth, Demuth, DeMuth), DENBY, DENDY (includes Dandy, Dandie, Denday), DENNEY (includes Denny), DENNIS, DENNISON (includes Tennison, Dannygston, Donohosen, Danielston), DENT, DENTMAIL, DENTON (includes Dent), DEPUY (includes DePui, DePue, Depue, DuPue, Dupue, DePuis, Depuis, DePew, Depew, Dupee, DePoe, Dupree, DePu, Duppery), DERR (includes Duerr, Durr, Dir, Doerr), DeSPAIN, DEVASIER (includes DeVasher, Devasure, Devazier, Devazur), DEVAUGHN, DEVORE, DEW (includes Dewe, Dews, Dewes, Due, Dhu, Deu, Deugh), DEWEESE (includes Dewees, Dewese, Dewease, Duese, Duest), DEWHURST (includes Dewhirst, du Hurst, d'Hurst), DEWITT, DEWOLF (includes Dewolff, Dolph, Deaolph, D'Olf), DICKERSON (includes Dickson), DILLARD (includes Dilliard, Dillards, Dilyard), DILLON (includes Dillion, Dillen, Dillin, Dellow, Delon, Delone, Dillian, Dillieon, Dillow, Dillyan, Dillyon, Dilon, Dilow, Dulon), DINGLER (includes Dengler, Dingle), DINGMAN, DINKIN (includes Dinkins), DISHONG (includes Deshong, Deshon, Dischong), DISMUKES (includes Dysmokes, Demeux, Demaux, Demeausse, Disquemue, Dixmund, Disimieu), DITTMAN, DIXON (includes Dixson, Dickson), DOAK, DOAN (includes Doane), DOBBIE-L (includes Dobie), DOBBS (includes Daubs, Dabbs), DOCKSTADER (includes Docksteader, Doxtoder, Doxteader), DODD, DODGE (includes Doidge, Dogge), DODSON (includes Dotson), DOHERTY, DOLLEY (includes Dolly, Doly), DONAGHY (includes Doneghy, MacDonagh, O'Donaghy, McDonough), DONALDSON (includes Donalson, Donelson), DOOLEY (includes Dooly, Dula, Dooling, Dowling, Duley), DORAN, DORLAND, DORNER (includes Doerner), DORSET-FAMILY (includes Dorsett, Doorset), DORSEY, DOTSON, DOUGHERTY (includes Daughardy, Daugherty, Daughetee, Daughetry, Daughhetee, Daughhettee, Daughtery, Daughtrey, Daughtry, Doughertey, Doughrety, Doughterty), DOUGLAS (includes Douglass), DOVE, DOVER, DOW, DOWDA (includes Dowdy), DOWER, DOWNEY, DOWNING, DOXSIE (includes Doxie, Doxey, Doxsee, Doxy, Dox, Docksey, Doxee), DOYLE, DOZIER, DRAKE (includes Dratz, Drak, Drakes), DRAPER, DREESE-ROOTS (includes Dries, Dreis, Drease, Tries, Treis, Trease, Treece, Treese), DREISBACH-L, DRENNON (includes Drennan, Drennen), DRINKARD, DRUMM (includes Trumm, Tromm), DRYER (includes Dreyer, Drier, VanDryer), DUANE (includes Devine), DUBOIS (includes

Du Bois), DUBOSE, DUGGER-LIST (includes Duger, Duggar, Dugar), DUKE (includes Dukes), DUMAS, DUMONT, DUNBAR, DUNCAN (includes Dinkins, Dockin, Dunkan, Dunkin, Denkens), DUNCAN-ROOTS (includes Dunkin, Dancun, Dockan, Dankan, Durkin, Denkens), DUNGAN, DUNHAM-DONHAM, DUNLAP, Dunlap, DUNLEVY (includes Dunleavy), DUNN, DUNNING, DUNSMOOR (includes Dunsmore, Dinsmoor, Dinsmore, Densmore), DUNTON (includes Dunten, Dutton), DURANT, DURBIN, DURHAM (includes Durham, Duran, Duren, Daram), DURKAN (includes Durkin, MacDurkin, MacDurkan, MacDurcan, MacDurkain, MacCurkan, Durcan, Gurkin, Gurken, Zurkin), DURMAN (includes Durmon, Dorman), DUSENBERRY (includes Dusenbury), DUTCHER (includes Ducher, Duyster, De Duyster, De Duytser, De Duytscher), DUTTON, DUVALL (includes DeVall, DeVeault, DeVolld, Deuel, Devault, Devol, Dewell, Divell, Divil, Divoll, Dowell, DuVal, DuVall, Duvol, Duwault, Duel, Formy-Duvall), DWINELL (includes Dunnel, Donnel), DWYER (includes O'Dwyer, Dwire, Dwyre, Dwyar, Dwier), DYER, DYESS (includes Dyes, Dice, Dias, Diaz, Diez, Dyas), DYSART (includes Dysert, Diesert, Disart), DYSON.

- **Descendants of Valentin DAHLEM**
  http://www.netropolis.net/jpounds/dahlem/dahlem.htm
  Gathered from a family tree created in Germany by Direktor Hermann Dahlem. Appended with descendants of Freidrich Wilhelm Dahlem.

- **DAHLSTEDT Family Roots**
  http://sony.inergy.com/DahlstedtRoots/
  Descendants of Nils DAHLSTEDT, born in 1749, died in Mönsterås, May 20,1817.

- **The DALRYMPLEs of Nova Scotia and Stair**
  http://home.mem.net/~dalrympl/
  Descendants of James Dalrymple (b.1761) of Nova Scotia and descendants of James Dalrymple, First Viscount of Stair.

- **DALTON Genealogical Society**
  http://members.aol.com/DaltonGene/index.html

- **The Descendants of Crohan DALY in America**
  http://www.crocker.com/~pford/
  Their emigration from Ireland to America in 1863.

- **The Olive Tree Genealogy: The DAMEN Family of New York**
  http://www.rootsweb.com/~ote/damen.htm
  Descendants of Jan Cornelise Damen, from Bunnik, a village on the Ryn in Utrecht, and his wife Fytie/Sophia Martens. Jan and Sophia were in Long Island by 1650.

- **The DAMERON-DAMRON Family Association**
  http://pw1.netcom.com/~choppy/ddfa.html

- **D'ARCHE Family History**
  http://www.wenet.net/~ddarche/page4.html

- **Coteau de France—DASPIT de Saint-Amand**
  http://www.concentric.net/~Jpdaspit/history1.htm
  "The name derives from the part of Louisiana where Pierre Daspit de Saint Amand's land grant was located."

- **DaVAR Individuals**
  http://www.macatawa.org/~brianter/davar.htm

- **A Genealogy of the DAVIDSON / DAVISON Family**
  http://user.maas.net/~coffee/wdd.htm
  Devoted to the Davidson/Davison Family of Amelia and Prince Edward Counties, VA., Anson County, NC., Maury County, TN. and Polk, Dallas and Newton Counties, MO.

- Diggin' for DAVISes Newsletter
  http://www.greenheart.com/rdietz/diggin1.htm
  Available on the GoldenWest Marketing page.

- The DAVIS Family History: The Immigrants and Colonists (1500–1847)
  http://www.davisfamily.org

- DAVIS Genealogy—Descendants—1800, WAR, ENG
  http://www.itmagic.demon.co.uk/genealogy/davis.htm
  Descendants of William DAVIS & Sarah.

- DAWSON Family History Project
  http://ntfp.globalserve.net/dawson/

- The World of DAYs
  http://www.day-family.freeserve.co.uk/
  Worldwide One Name Study for the surname DAY and it's variants DAYE, DEY and DEYE.

- DeBORD (Debord DeBord DeBoard) Surname
  E-mail: Rdebord@aol.com
  Raleigh P. DeBORD has a wealth of information dating back to 1703. For details e-mail him at: Rdebord@aol.com

- DEEDS World
  http://www.iowa-counties.com/genealogy/

- The DeFRANCE Family Home Page
  http://www.helenet.com/~larry/fam_home.html

- DENG Clan Genealogy
  http://www.geocities.com/Tokyo/3998/deng.htm

- DENT Family Research Center
  http://www.rootsweb.com/~auntjean/dent/

- Descendants of Toussaint Hunault Dit DESCHAMPS
  http://www.familytreemaker.com/users/l/a/c/Frances-J-Lachance/index.html
  Over 18,000 descendants of Toussaint Hunault dit Deschamps and Marie Lorguieul. They apparently met aboard ship, arrived in Canada in 1653, and married a year later.

- The DESMOND Family History Page
  http://ourworld.compuserve.com/homepages/Rebel_Earl/

- DeVORE/DEVORE/deVORE/DEVOOR/DuFOUR Genealogy Page
  http://www.geocities.com/Heartland/3946/

- DEWEES—DEWEESE Family Home Page
  http://home.earthlink.net/~tdewees/
  DEWEES—DEWEESE—DEWESE—DEWEASE

- DeWITT Family Lines of North America
  http://pages.prodigy.com/DeWitt/

- DEYO Family Association
  http://home.earthlink.net/~rctwig/deyo.htm

- The DEYO Family in America
  http://www.deyo.org/deyo.htm

- What The DICKENS?
  http://ladyecloud.hypermart.net/Dickens.htm
  Dicken(s) and Dickin(s)

- DIGBY
  E-mail: adigger@ghplus.infi.net
  List of 1,200 marriages into the Digby line, 1200–1900 in England. E-mail Joe at adigger@ghplus.infi.net for details.

- The William DIGGS Family
  http://www.aracnet.com/~pslamb/diggs.htm
  Descendants of William Degge and Judith Haley, Louisa Co., Virginia & Anson Co., North Carolina.

- Descendants of Henry and Elinor DILLON
  http://www.parsonstech.com/genealogy/trees/ddillon/dillon.htm
  From Franklin Co., Virginia., Monroe Co., Virginia and Raleigh Co., West Virginia.

- DIMMOCK Roots and Offshoots
  http://www.fpworkshop.com/genealogy/
  Descendants of Thomas Dimmock of Barnstable, Massachusetts. Includes: Demick, Demmick, Dimick, Dimmack, Dimmick, Dimmock, Dimmuck, Dimock, Dimuck, Dymoke.

- DINGMAN Genealogy Info Site
  http://www.geocities.com/Heartland/Plains/4858/
  For descendants of Adam DINGMAN (to North America in about 1650) and other DINGMAN researchers.

- DISTLER Family Genealogy
  http://www.iquest.net/~ddistler/distler/
  Distler, Diestler, Dishler and other variant spellings.

- DITTUS Family Home Page
  http://members.aol.com/psdb/dittus/index.htm
  A Gathering Place for all Dittus Family Lines.

- TheDIXONs.Net—The Web Site for the Dixons of the World
  http://thedixons.net
  If you are a Dixon yourself, or are pursuing genealogy of the Dixon surname, we have e-mail addresses and web space for you!

- The DOANE Family Association, Inc.
  http://www.doane.edu/dfa/dfa2.htm

- DOCKERY Family Association, Inc.
  http://www.tib.com/dfai/
  The Hanging Dog Community six miles due north of Murphy, NC, the ancestral home of most early settlers with the surnames identified on this page.

- The DODGE Family Association
  http://www.dodgefamily.org

- DOGGETTs and Other Cousins
  http://doggettfam.org/index.htm
  Devoted to the study of the family history of the Rev. Benjamin Doggett of Lancaster County, Virginia.

- DONLON Family History, Ireland
  http://www.hylit.com/info/Genealogy/Donlon.html
  A genealogy of the Donlon family, recently of Westmeath, Ireland, and originally of Galway. The Galway genealogy starts as far back as 1400.

- The DONLEY Family—Genealogy
  http://www.internet-partners.com/donley/index.htm

- The DONNAN Home Page
  http://www.clis.com/donnan/
  Donnan, Donan, Donnon

- DONSHEA DUNSHEA DUNSHEE
  Genealogy Page
  http://www.angelfire.com/ny/earthstar/index.html
  Scots-Irish ancestors.

- Genealogy of the Family van DORT
  http://www.geocities.com/Paris/6547/index.htm
  Netherlands, Sri Lanka, Malaysia, Belgium, U.S., Canada, Australia.

- DOSS Family Association & Newsletter
  E-mail: yyex00a@prodigy.com
  For details e-mail Libbie Griffin at yyex00a@prodigy.com

- Genealogy for DOTTERER / DUDDERAR /
  DUDDRA / DUTRO / DUDDERA / DOTTER /
  DUTTERER / DUTROW / DUTTEROW /
  DUTTER
  http://www.angelfire.com/az/rdutter/

- The DOWBIGGIN Family History Society
  http://www.netmagic.net/~taz/dfhs.html

- DRAKE Family Genealogy WorldWide
  http://www.users.bigpond.com/lrandrew/drake/drakepage.htm

- DRESSER Family Genealogy Page
  http://plainfield.bypass.com/~jdresser/index.html

- DREWRY Family History in America
  http://www.anniebees.com/Drewry/Drewry.htm
  The Ancestors and Descendants of Harry Moss Drewry 1886–1970.

- Looking for DREW's? Look no further!
  http://members.stratos.net/mikeandcindy/drew.htm

- DRIVER Family Historical Society
  http://tdcweb.com/tdfhs/

- DRUMM News
  http://hometown.aol.com/drummnews/DrummNews.html
  A web site and newsletter for anyone researching the Drum and/ or Drumm surname.

- DuBOIS Family Association
  http://home.earthlink.net/~rctwig/dubois.htm

- The Association of CHARRON and
  DUCHARME, Inc.
  E-mail: dmiale@exis.net
  For details e-mail Dick Miale at dmiale@exis.net or in French e-mail Pierre Ducharme at: duchap00libertel.montreal.qc.ca

- DUDLEY Homepage and Database
  http://www.geocities.com/Heartland/Hills/8388/

- The DUFFIELD Family
  http://access.mountain.net/~braxton/duffield.html
  Dufield/Duffields

- DUFFUS—Sept of Clan Sutherland—
  1000 Years of History
  http://www.duffus.com
  Genealogy and history of Duffus for last 1000 years.

- DUKESHIRE Lines
  http://www.mdc.net/~wmduke/
  A family association, publications and a database including the surnames DUKESHIRE, RAWDING, BEELER, FEINDELL, RINGER, FREEMAN.

- The DULONG Family
  http://habitant.org/dulong/

- Genealogy of the DUMM Family of Fairfield
  County, Ohio
  http://www.clark.net/pub/jcblal/dumm/dumm.html
  Descendants of Casper Dumm (1720–1802) and of Jacob Dumm (1792–1864).

- DUNAVANT Genealogy
  http://members.aol.com/CrysDH/index.html

- DUNCAN Surname Association
  http://www.tyrell.net/~wad/dsa/dsa.htm

- DUNGAN and Related Families
  http://www.mindspring.com/~jogt/surnames/dungan.htm
  Descendants of Thomas Dungan, son of William Dungan, a perfumer, from London, England, born about 1606.

- History of the DUNHAM-DONHAM Family
  in America
  http://www.geocities.com/Heartland/5275/dunham.htm
  Descendants of Deacon John DUNHAM, born about 1589, died 2 March 1668/69 in Plymouth, Massachusetts.

- The DUNN Family of Castle Bay and Dominion,
  Cape Breton Island
  http://www.geocities.com/~dunnfamily/
  Nova Scotia, Canada

- William DUNN from Little Bray, Devon, England
  http://www.st.net.au/~dunn/wdunn.htm

- The DUNTON Family Home Site
  http://www.web-ster.com/~miked/
  Dunton, Dunten, Dutton

- The DuPREE Family Research Page
  http://members.aol.com/Borgite/dupre.html
  Descendants of Josias DuPre' and Mynota.

- The DUPRE Page—La Famille DUPRÉ
  http://members.aol.com/Nlalabungu/dupree.html

- The DUQUET(TE) Family Forest
  http://www.berkshire.net/~ferris/ged2www/duquet.htm
  French-Canadian DUQUET(TE)s, DUCAT(TE)s, DUKET(TE)s.

- The Thomas DURFEE Family Tree
  http://members.aol.com/MShermanL/durfee.html
  Descendants of Thomas Durfee, born 1643 in England, died July 1712 in Portsmouth, Rhode Island.

- The DURHAM Family Home Page
  http://www.familytreemaker.com/users/s/t/o/Terri-L-Stone/
  Descendants of Robert DURHAM, born 1811 and Elizabeth Riggs, born 1825.

- The Society of Genealogy of DURKEE
  http://www2.andrews.edu/~calkins/durkeefa.html

- The DUSTIN/DUSTON Family Association
  http://www.net1plus.com/users/locke/dustin1.htm
- DUTCHER Family
  http://www.genealogy.org/~smoore/dutchers/
- DuVAL Family Association
  http://www.geocities.com/Heartland/Ridge/7508/
  Descendants of Daniel DuVal and his wife Philadelphia DuBois who were French Huguenots.
- DWYER Family Home Page
  http://www.rootsweb.com/~takelley/dwyer/dwyer.htm
- The New England DYER Connection
  http://www.geocities.com/Heartland/Plains/4663/
  Genealogies of five different DYER families in New England from the 17th century. Also a reference to "Genealogies of the Families of Braintree, Ma" by Sprague.
- DYESS Family
  http://www.geocities.com/Heartland/5438/

◆ Surnames Beginning with "E"

- Family Tree Maker Online User Home Pages—E
  http://www.familytreemaker.com/users/e/index.html
- Genealogy's Most Wanted—Surnames Beginning With "E"
  http://www.citynet.net/mostwanted/e.htm
- H-GIG Surname Registry—Surnames beginning E
  http://www.ucr.edu/h-gig/surdata/surname5.html
- Higginson Book Company—Surnames Beginning With E
  http://www.higginsonbooks.com/e.htm
- inGeneas Table of Common Surname Variations and Surname Misspellings—D–E
  http://www.ingeneas.com/D2E.html
- Surname Springboard Index—E
  http://www.geocities.com/~alacy/spring_e.htm
- SurnameWeb Surname Registry—E Index
  http://www.surnameweb.org/registry/e.htm
- Genealogy Resources on the Internet—"E" Surname Mailing Lists
  http://members.aol.com/gfsjohnf/gen_mail_surnames-e.html
  This site is wonderfully maintained by John Fuller. It includes mailing list information for the following surnames and their variant spellings:
  ELGINS_ONLINE, ELKINS (includes Alkins, Alkens, Elkens, Elkons, Elkuns, Alkons, Alkuns), ELL (includes Elle, Ehle, Elles, Ells), ELLEDGE (includes Elige, Ellage), ELLER (includes Ellers, Oehler), ELLINGHAM, ELLIOTT, ELLIS, ELMORE (includes Elmo, Almore, Ulmo, Olmeer, Elmer, McElmo, StElmo), ELROD, EMERSON, EMERY (includes Emry, Emory, Embry), EMERY (includes Embry), EMMES (includes Emms, Emes, Ems), EMMONS, ENGBERG, ENDICOTT (includes Endecott), ENGLAND, ENGLE (includes Engel, Engler), ENGLISH-FAMILY (includes Ingliss), ENNIS, ENO (includes Enos, Enno, Henno, Hennot), ENYART (includes Enyard, Enyeart, Inyart), EPLER, EPPERSON (includes Apperson), EPPESgenealogy, ERICKSON (includes Ericcson, Ericsson,

Ericson, Erikson), ERSKINE, ERWIN, ESTELLE (includes Estell, Estill, Estil, Estle, Estal, Estile), ESTEP (includes Eastep, Esstep, Esttep, Estepp), ESTES (includes Estis, Estive, Estep, Eastus), ETCHESON (includes Etchison, Etchenson), ETHERIDGE (includes Ethridge, Etheredge), EUBANKS, EVANS, EVELAND (includes Iffland, Ifflandt, Iffelandt), EVERINGHAM (includes Everham, Evernham, Evringham), EWING (includes Ewen, Ewin, MacEwen, MacEwin).

- EARTHY Family Genealogy
  http://www.earthy.co.uk/Genealogy
- EASTMAN Genealogy and History
  http://www.netcom.com/~seven007/index.html
  Descendants of Roger EASTMAN, born 1610, immigrated to America about 1638 on the ship "Confidence" to the Massachusetts Bay Colony.
- Descendants of the EAST WOOD
  E-mail: AllysonMT@aol.com
  For details send e-mail to Allyson Tilton at AllysonMT@aol.com. Allyson Monroe Tilton, 148 Belglen Lane, Los Gatos, CA 95032.
- EDDLEMAN Database Home Page
  http://www.netusa1.net/~eddleman/eddleman.htm
- The EDDLEMAN Genealogy Library
  http://www.disknet.com/indiana_biolab/eg.htm
  "The Largest International Online Collection of Authentic Edelmann—Eddleman Genealogy Data."
- EDENFIELD Genealogical Society
  http://www.hom.net/~egs/
  A searchable database of over 20,000. Edenfield descendants, as well as background information on the Edenfield surname and place-name, a village in Lancashire, England.
- The EDSON Genealogical Association
  http://members.aol.com/EdsonEGA/EdsonEga.html
- The Unofficial Page of the Clan EGAN Association—Australian Branch
  http://www.globec.com.au/~egan/egan.htm
  Gaelic: MACAODHAGAIN. MacEGAN, EGAN, EAGAN, EAGEN, KEEGAN, HAGEN.
- World Wide EGGLESTON Family Roots Home Page
  http://hometown.aol.com/MREgleston/index.html
- The ELAM Family Research Page
  http://www.geocities.com/Heartland/Prairie/6831/
- ELAM Genealogy
  http://www.webpak.net/~kyblue/elam.htm
- ELDER Family Newsletter
  http://www.intrepid.net/~fanfare/EFN.html
- ELGIN Net
  http://www.elgins.com
- ELKINS Surname
  E-mail: oldbooks@olypen.com
  E-mail Steve Elkins at oldbooks@olypen.com for more details on his research.
- ELL Family Heritage Page
  http://mars.ark.com/~rbell/html/ellfam.htm

- The Dabner Wansley ELLIOTT Family Home Page
  http://www.familytreemaker.com/users/e/l/l/John-C-Elliott/
  index.html
  Lumpkin Co., Hall Co, Dawson Co., and Forsyth Co., Georgia.

- ELSEY Family Association & the ELSEY
  Echoes Newsletter
  E-mail: Ellzeyj@msn.com
  *Elsey, Ellzey, Elzey, Ellzea, Elsea, Ellsea, Elzie, Elsy. For details
  send e-mail to Joan Ellzey at: Ellzeyj@msn.com*

- BEVIER / ELTING Family Association
  http://home.earthlink.net/~rctwig/bevier.htm

- BEVIER—ELTING Family Association
  http://members.aol.com/Edie143/elt7_web.html
  *Including a page with information and a photograph of the
  Bevier-Elting House on Huguenot Street in New Paltz, New
  York.*

- ELWOOD Echoes
  http://ladyecloud.hypermart.net/Elwood.htm
  Elwood, Ellwood

- EMMERICH EMERICH EMERICK EMRICK
  EMRICH
  http://genweb.net/~dlemrick/

- The EMPSON Family Page
  http://www.ezwebpages.com/Empson/

- EMRY / EMERY Family Genealogy
  http://www.jps.net/memry/emrygen.html

- ENGELBACH Home Page
  http://soli.inav.net/~jme240
  *ENGELBACH, ENGLEBACH, ENGLEBACK. This site is
  devoted to the world-wide surname of ENGELBACH and
  the families, past and present. A world-wide ENGELBACH
  Gathering Place.*

- Descendants of John Marcus ENGELHORN II
  http://www.wenet.net/~jschremp/eng1782.html
  Born December 11, 1782, died October 25, 1869.

- ENGLE News Letter
  *Includes any spelling of the name Engel, Ingall, Engall, etc. For
  details send e-mal to Lisa Herdahl at: THZQ38A@prodigy.com*

- The ENRIGHT Family Home Page
  http://www.familytreemaker.com/users/w/e/b/
  Bruce-J-Webster-Jr/

- ERSKINE Surname Mailing List
  http://www.spirallight.com/erskine/

- The (Do) ESPIRITO SANTO Family Club /
  Clube Das Famílias "Do ESPÍRITO SANTO"
  http://members.tripod.com/~EspiritoSanto/

- The ESSIG / ESSICK Family
  http://www.inetica.com/~irwayne/genealogy/ESS_hist.htm
  *Descendants of Rudolph Essig and sons, Georg Abraham and
  Hans Michael. Arrived in Philadelphia from Wurtenburg,
  Germany, on the "Princes Agusta" on September 16, 1736.*

- ESTESLinks
  http://www.panama.gulf.net/~estes/el/el.htm

- ESTLE Family Bulletin
  E-mail: flakey@eurekanet.com
  *A newsletter for various Estle families & spellings which could
  include Estell, Estile, Estille, Estelle, Estal, Estoal, Estle, Estel,
  Estele, Estil, Estill just to name a few. For details send e-mail to
  Arleen Estle at: flakey@eurekanet.com*

- EUSTACE Family History Homepage
  http://dspace.dial.pipex.com/town/square/ga40/index.htm

- EVANS Ancestors
  http://skyport.com/spirit/evansl/evhtml.htm
  GEDCOM files collected from the Evans Surname Mailing List.

- The EVANS Genealogy Harbour
  http://members.aol.com/levans3352/public/index.html
  Descendants of John William Evans.

- EVERSOLE / EBERSOHL Research Network
  http://www.users.mis.net/~chesnut/pages/eversole.htm
  *Includes Abersold, Abersole, Aebersold, Aebersole, Ebersold,
  Ebersole, Eibersold, Eibersolt, Eversold, Eversole, Eversoll.*

- EWING Home Page—EWING Exchange
  Newsletter
  http://members.aol.com/Kinseeker6/ewing.html

- EYRE Home Page
  http://mail.standard.net.au/~daneyre/

- Genealogy of the EYMANN Family
  http://www.iig.uni-freiburg.de/~eymann/genealog.htm
  Germany, Switzerland and the U.S.

◆ Surnames Beginning with "F"

- Family Tree Maker Online User Home Pages—F
  http://www.familytreemaker.com/users/f/index.html

- Genealogy's Most Wanted—Surnames Beginning
  with "F"
  http://www.citynet.net/mostwanted/f.htm

- H-GIG Surname Registry—Surnames Beginning F
  http://www.ucr.edu/h-gig/surdata/surname6.html

- Higginson Book Company—Surnames Beginning
  with F
  http://www.higginsonbooks.com/f.htm

- inGeneas Table of Common Surname Variations and
  Surname Misspellings—F–G
  http://www.ingeneas.com/F2G.html

- Surname Springboard Index—F
  http://www.geocities.com/~alacy/spring_f.htm

- SurnameWeb Surname Registry—F Index
  http://www.surnameweb.org/registry/f.htm

- Genealogy Resources on the Internet—"F" Surname Mailing Lists
  http://members.aol.com/gfsjohnf/gen_mail_surnames-f.html
  This site is wonderfully maintained by John Fuller. It includes mailing list information for the following surnames and their variant spellings:
  FACKRELL, FAILE (includes Fail, Fails), FAIN (includes Fayne, Fane, Fann, Fine, Few), FAIRCHILD, FAIRFAX, FAMBRO (includes Fambrough), FANTOM (includes Fantham, Fanton), FARLEY (includes Farler), FARMER, FARNI (includes Farney, Forney), FARNSWORTH (includes Fanef, Faneuf, Farneth, Farnworth, Phaneuf, Farneworth, Farnom, Farnot, Fearneworth, Fearnoth, Fernworth), FARR (includes Pharr, Far), FARRELL, FARRIS (includes Faris, Faries, Pharris, Phares, Pharis), FARTHING, FAUBION (includes Fabion, Fawbian, Fabian), FAULKNER (includes Falconar, Falconer, Falkner, Falkner, Faulconer, Faulknor, Folkner, Forkner, Fortner), FAUST (includes Foust), FAWCETT (includes Faucett, Faucette), FEAGIN (includes Feagan, Fagin, Fagan), FEATHERS (includes Feather, Fetter, Fetters, Fether, Vetter), FEGLEY (includes Fagley, Figley, Voegeli), FELTHAM, FELTON (includes Felten), FEREBEE, FERGUS, FERGUSON (includes Fergesen, Fergerson, Furgusun, Fergersen), FERNALD (includes Furnald), FERREE (includes Fehree, Ferry, Fery, Fairy, Forry, Furry, Firry, Soundex F600), FIELDS (includes Field), FIES (includes Fees, Fiess, Fiese, Feis, Feise, Feese), FIGGERS (includes Figures, Figers, Figuars, Figge, Fegins, Fegans, Fegens, Feagans, Feagins, Feugers, Figgerst), FIKE (includes Fyke, Fykes), FILLMORE (includes Phillmore, Fillmour, Fillimore), FILSON, FINCH (includes Fink, Feench, Funk, Wench, Venigs, Fenwick, McFince), FINE (includes Fein, Fyn, Vine, Fines), FINKBEINER (includes Finkenbiner, Finkenbender), FINNERTY (includes Finerty, Finarty, Finnarty, Fenerty, Fennerty, Fenarty, Fenaughty), FISHER (includes Fischer), FISKE (includes Fisk), FITZ-RANDOLPH-S (includes Fitz Ralph, Fitz Ranulf), FIVEASH (includes Fiveashe, Fivash, Fireash, Viveash), FIVEASH-FAMILY-ASSOCIATION (includes Fiveashe, Fivash, Fireash, Viveash), FLAGG (includes Flegg), FLANAGAN, FLANNERY, FLANNIGAN, FLATT, FLAX (includes Flacks, Flaks), FLEAGLE (includes Flagle, Fliegel, Fluegel), FLEMING, FLESHER (includes Flescher, Fleisher, Fleischer), FLESHMAN, FLETCHER, FLICK, FLINCHUM (includes Flincham, Flinchem, Finchem, Finchum, Fincham), FLINN (includes Flin, Fline, Flyn, Fling), FLINT (includes Flynt, Flinte, Flintt), FLIPPO, FLOHR (includes Floor, Flor), FLORA (includes Flory, Fleury, Florin, Flori, Floray, Flury, Florea, Florey), FLOWERS, FLYNN (includes Flinn, O'Flynn, Flin), FOALE, FODEN, FOLAND (includes Folland, Folant, Wohland, Yoland, Volland), FOLSOM (includes Fulsom, Folsum, Folsome, Folson, Foulsham, Folsham), FOOTE (includes Foot), FORCE (includes Forse, Fors, Vorce, La Force, De La Force), FORD, FORDYCE (includes Fordice, Fordise), FOREHAND, FOREY (includes Forry, Forrey, Foray), FORSYTHE (includes Forsyth, Forsithe), FORTIER, FORTNER, FORTUNE (includes LaFortune), FORWOOD, FOSTER (includes Forster), FOUNTAINE (includes de la Fountaine, Fountain, Fontain), FOUTCH (includes Fouch, Fouche), FOWLER (includes Fouller), FOX (includes Fuchs), FRAMPTON, FRANCOEUR, FRANKLIN, FRANTZ (includes Frantzin), FREE, FREELAND, FREELS, FREEMAN, FREILING (includes Freyling, Fruhling, Fruyling, Veryling, Freeling), FRENCH, FRETWELL, FRIEDMAN (includes Friedmann, Freeman, Freedman), FRIEND, FROMKE-genealogy, FROST, FRUGE (includes Ferger, Fruget, Fruger), FRY (includes Frei, Frye, Frey), FRYAR (includes Fryer, Friar, Frier), FUCICH, FULCHER, FULFORD, FULLER, FULLER, Ezekiel, FULMER (includes Fullmer, Folmer, Follmer, Vollmer), FULTON, FULTONVA, FUTRILL (includes Futrille, Futral, Futrell, Fewtral), FYFE-list (includes Fyff, Fife, Phyfe, Fyffe).

- My Neck of the Woods
  http://www.ounceofprevention.ca/history.htm
  FAIR, FLEMING

- FANCHER Family Genealogy
  http://members.tripod.com/~KandyF/index.html

- FANNING Family Newsletter
  http://members.aol.com/bsmith1311/fanning.htm
  Online version of the Fanning Family Newsletter, a family history and family genealogy newsletter for the descendants of Bill and Ellie Fanning of Fayetteville, Tennessee.

- FARNSWORTH and PHANEUF
  http://www.microtec.net/~aphane/english.htm

- Cherry Stone Creek—Official Home of the FARTHING Family in America
  http://www.geocities.com/Heartland/Plains/9515/

- FAUGHNAN Genealogy Home Page
  http://members.aol.com/faughnan1/Faughnan/faugh.htm

- FAULCONER Family
  http://www.mindspring.com/~jogt/surnames/faulcon.htm
  Virginia and Kentucky.

- FAULKNER Researchers Page
  http://www.geocities.com/Heartland/Prairie/3597/
  Falconar, Falconer, Falkiner, Falkner, Faulknor, Forkner, Fortner.

- The FEATHERSTONE Society
  http://www.geocities.com/~pfeatherstone/

- FEHR's Famous Family
  http://www3.bc.sympatico.ca/donfehr/fehr.htm
  The family of Benjamin Fehr and his wife, Elisabeth, in Manitoba and Saskatchewan, Canada.

- The FIG Tree News—FENTON International Genealogy
  http://weatherhead.cwru.edu/homes/figtree/

- FERGUSON Home Page—FERGUSON Files Newsletter
  http://members.aol.com/Kinseeker6/ferguson.html

- The Descendants of Jeffery FERRIS of England
  http://members.aol.com/MShermanL/ferris.html
  Born 1610 in England; died May 31, 1666 in Greenwich, Connecticut.

- The FEULING Family Genealogy
  http://www.star.net/People/~mga60/feulhome.htm

- From a Distant FIELD—The Living Edition on the Internet
  http://acsys.anu.edu.au/FromADistantField/
  Descendants of the New South Wales (Australia) pioneers, EDWARD and ELIZABETH FIELD.

- The FIFIELD One-Name Study
  http://top.monad.net/~pfwells/

- FIGHT/FIGHTMASTER Family
  http://members.aol.com/jogt/fightfam.htm

- FINLEY Family History
  http://opac.sonoma.edu/finley

- FITZSIMMONS Family Web Page
  http://www.geocities.com/Heartland/Valley/1410/fitzsimmons/
  index.html
  Fitzsimmons, Fitsimmons, Fitzimmons

- FLELLO—A One Name Study
  http://home.clara.net/flello/pag014.htm

- From FLENNIKEN to FLANNIGAN
  http://www.geocities.com/Heartland/Valley/2967/

- FLESHMAN/FLEISCHMANN Family History &
  Databases
  http://homepages.rootsweb.com/~george/flesh.html

- FLETCHER Family Research Bulletin
  http://www.cswnet.com/~fletcher/

- FLETCHER Family Tree
  http://www.oise.utoronto.ca/~dfletcher/Fletcher.html
  *Descendants of William Fletcher (1721–1769) and Janet
  Littlejohn.*

- FLEUETTE Family Association
  http://www.kersur.net/~fleuette/
  Fluet, Fluette and Fleuette

- FLOORE Family History
  http://www.geocities.com/Heartland/Meadows/5110
  *Searching for the ancestors and descendants of Samuel
  FLOORE who settled around Louisville, Kentucky between 1795
  and 1800.*

- FLOURNOY Genealogy Website
  http://home1.gte.net/jtflourn/flournoy/index.htm

- Stephen FLUHARTY Descendants
  http://www.ovis.net/~billcham/sfluh/
  *Descendants of Stephen Fluharty, born 1746 and died 1825 in
  West Virginia.*

- FLYNN Clan of America
  http://pages.prodigy.com/GPGJ41A/flynn.htm

- The FOGARTY Page
  http://www.albedo.net/~fogarty/genealogy.htm

- FOLSOM Family Association of America
  http://www.shadow.net/~miamibig/folsom/

- The FONDREN and COLE Families
  http://members.aol.com/jogt/fondren.htm
  Of North Carolina and South Carolina.

- FONNESBECK / Deerstream
  http://www.fortunecity.com/millenium/castleton/262/
  Excellent Interests Fonnesbeck Genealogy Page.

- FOORD One Name Study
  *Including FOORD, FOORDE, FORDE but not FORD unless the
  variant has a direct link. Database includes both submitted
  family trees and historical information. Contributors and
  queries very welcome. Not online, only via E-mail:
  lfoord@saturn.execulink.com*

- The FORBES Families of North Carolina
  http://www.geocities.com/Heartland/Pointe/2430/index.html

- The William FORD Society
  http://users.erinet.com/31363/fordfam.htm
  *Descendants of William Ford who was born in 1722 in Charles
  County, Maryland and died in 1821 in what is now Taylor
  County, West Virginia.*

- FORNEY Families in America
  http://www.netins.net/showcase/rittel/forney/database/
  forney.html
  Farni, Forneick, Fornick, Fornich, Forny, & Furney

- FORREST Family Home Page
  http://members.aol.com/harley1369/forrest.html
  *Forrest-Forrester-Forist-Forest-Forraster, and other variant
  spellings.*

- The FORTIN Genealogy Page
  http://www.gaudreau.org/arthur/genealogy/fortin.sht

- The FORTINEUX Family Home Page
  http://www.public.usit.net/davegoff/fortineux.htm
  *The Fortineux family lived in the Palatinate in the 17th century
  and descendants include persons living in North America today
  with the surnames Fortney, Fortna, Furtney, and Fordney.*

- FOSBROOKE Surname, England
  *E-mail Richard Jones at richardj@converting.co.uk and he will
  check his extensive database.*

- The FOUNTAIN Family Outline
  http://www.mosquitonet.com/~luht/FOUNT.HTM

- The FOUST/FAUST Family
  http://members.aol.com/jogt/foustfam.htm
  Of North Carolina and Tennessee.

- FOUST / FAUST Genealogy Resource Page
  http://w2.parkland.cc.il.us/~jfoust/Foust/f_foust.htm

- Descendants of John and Jane FRANCIS
  http://www.geocities.com/Heartland/Plains/4268/
  Including the FRANCIS/FRANCE Family Newsletter.

- The FRANCISCO Researcher
  E-mail Rick at rdsmyrna@aol.com for details on this newsletter.

- "The House of FRANCISCUS"
  *Book with over 7,200 descendants of Christophel Franciscus.
  E-mail Jan Johnson at jj@amug.org for lookups in this book—
  Francisco or Franciscus.*

- Genealogy & Heraldry of the FRANCOM Family
  http://users.aol.com/mefrancom/genealogy/index.html

- Les Descendants des FRÉCHETTE, Inc.
  http://www.angelfire.com/ca/frechette/

- The FREDERICK Genealogy Home Page
  http://www.greatnorthern.net/~terryf/Frederick.html
  *Descendants of John Frederick, born 12 Sept. 1787 and
  Mary Ann Easterday.*

- Descendants of John FREEMAN, Sr. of Bladen Co.,
  NC b c 1775
  http://members.aol.com/markfreemn/freemanj.html

- FREER Family Genealogy Research
  http://home.cc.umanitoba.ca/~sfreer/

- Solomon FREER Family Association
  For details send e-mail to John H. Freer at
  jfrog@hop-uky.campus.mci.net

- FREER / LOW Family Association
  http://home.earthlink.net/~rctwig/freer.htm

- FREEZE & FRIES Family History
  http://www.geocities.com/Heartland/1134/
  From New Jersey in the early 1700s to everywhere in the
  present time.

- Heinrich FREY Family Association
  http://members.aol.com/deancestor/HFFA.htm

- The FRIEL Seanachie
  http://www.azstarnet.com/~opus/laura/friel.htm
  Dedicated to preserving the Friel family legacy in Ireland, the
  UK, and the Americas.

- FRIEND Family Association of America
  http://pages.prodigy.com/MChipman/

- FRISTOE Genealogy
  http://www.mindspring.com/~fristoe/
  Fristo, Fristow, Fristowe, Frestow, Friston, etc.

- FULBRIGHT Family Association
  http://www.concentric.net/~Mcclaran/fulbright.htm
  VOLLBRECHT—FULBRIGHT

- Edward FULLER (Mayflower Passenger)
  Genealogy
  http://pages.prodigy.net/dave_lossos/cooper.htm

- The FULTZ Family Genealogy
  http://www.geocities.com/Heartland/1415/fultz.html
  Fultz, Fults, Fulce, Fulks, etc. In honor of the descendants of
  Obadiah Fults/z or see also the following site.

- Descendants of Obadiah FULKS-FULTZ
  1765–1845—Home Page
  http://www.familytreemaker.com/users/f/u/l/Patrick-M-Fultz/
  index.html

- The FUQUA Family Foundation
  http://www.concentric.net/~fuqua/

- FURR Family Web Page
  http://members.aol.com/bfurr1/index.html
  With over 5,000 descendants of Heinrich Furrer (Furr), mostly
  from North Carolina and Mississippi.

- The FURR Surname
  http://www.geocities.com/Heartland/Estates/5554
  This page contains the results of my many years of research of
  the descendants of Heinrich Furrer of Cabarrus County, North
  Carolina, including the Mississippi Furrs. Additions or correc-
  tions are welcomed. I have also collected some information on
  other Furr families, particularly the Virginia Furrs. I believe,
  but cannot prove, that there is a connection between the North
  Carolina and Virginia Furrs. I and other Furr researchers are
  also continuing our quest for the ancestors of Heinrich Furrer.
  There are two likey candidates, but so far no definitive, primary-
  source material to "prove" which one is correct.

- FUTCH Family Roots
  http://www.geocities.com/~glenn_futch/
  Descendants of Jacob Futch, from Germany to North Carolina
  in 1709.

◆ Surnames Beginning with "G"

- Family Tree Maker Online User Home Pages—G
  http://www.familytreemaker.com/users/g/index.html

- Genealogy's Most Wanted—Surnames Beginning
  with "G"
  http://www.citynet.net/mostwanted/g.htm

- H-GIG Surname Registry—Surnames Beginning G
  http://www.ucr.edu/h-gig/surdata/surname7.html

- Higginson Book Company—Surnames Beginning
  with G
  http://www.higginsonbooks.com/g.htm

- inGeneas Table of Common Surname Variations and
  Surname Misspellings—F–G
  http://www.ingeneas.com/F2G.html

- Surname Springboard Index—G
  http://www.geocities.com/~alacy/spring_g.htm

- SurnameWeb Surname Registry—G Index
  http://www.surnameweb.org/registry/g.htm

- Genealogy Resources on the Internet—"G" Surname
  Mailing Lists
  http://members.aol.com/gfsjohnf/gen_mail_surnames-g.html
  This site is wonderfully maintained by John Fuller. It includes
  mailing list information for the following surnames and their
  variant spellings:
  GABBARD (includes Gabbert, Gebert, Gebhard, Gebhardt),
  GADDIS, GADDY (includes Gaddie, Gady, Gadde), GAINES,
  GALBRAITH (includes Galbreath, Gilbreath, Gilreath, Gilbreth,
  Kilbreath, Kulbeth, Colbreath), GALLAGHER (includes
  Gallacher, Gallaugher, Golliher), GALLIVAN (includes Galvin,
  Gallavan), GALLOWAY, GAMAGE, GAMEL (includes Gammel,
  Gammell, Gamell, Gamill, Gammil, Gammill, Gamble, Gambol,
  Gambel, Gambell, Gambelle, Gambill, Gambil, Gambrell,
  Gambrill), GANNON (includes Ganon, Gann, Gammon,
  Gamon), GANT (includes Gantt, Gaunt, Gauntt, Gent, Ghent),
  GARBER (includes Gerber, Garver, Carver), GARDNER,
  GARLAND, GARNER, GARNETT (includes Garnet),
  GAROUTTE (includes Garrott, Garrot, Garott, Gariot, Garrett,
  Garriott, Gerratt, Gariott, Garriot), GARRETT (includes
  Garratt, Garret, Garot), GARRISON (includes Garretson),
  GARST (includes Gerst, Gharst), GARVIN (includes Garven,
  Garvan, Garvey, McGarvin, O'Garvin, O'Garvey), Gastwirth,
  GATES, GATEWOOD, GAY (includes Gayre, Guy), GEARHART
  (includes Gerhardt, Gerhart, Gearheart, Gierhart, Gerald,
  Gerard, Gerault), GEER (includes Gere, Gear, Gehr), GEIGER
  (includes Kiger, Kyger, Keiger, Gyger, Giger, Gieger), GENIK
  (includes Genyk, Gennick), GENSMER (includes Genzmer,
  Gensemer), GENTRY, GEORGE, GERALD (includes Gerrald,
  Garrell, Garrall), GERARD (includes Gerrard, Garrard),
  GERBIG, GERDAU, GERE, GERHARDSTEIN (includes
  Gerhartzstein, Geroldstein, Gerolstein, Gerholstein,
  Girardstein), GESELL (includes Gazelle, Gezell), GETHINGS,
  GEYER (includes Geier, Gyer, Gayer, Guyer, Geer, Geere, Gear,
  Gier, Gehr, Coyer), GIBBONS (includes Gibbins, Gibens), Gibbs
  (includes Gibb, Gibbes, Gibbses, Gybbys), GIBSON-L,
  GIDDINGS (includes Giddins, Giddens, Gideon), GIFFORD
  (includes Gafford), GILL, GILLAM (includes Gillim, Gillem,
  Gilham, Gilliam, Gillham, Gillum), GILLESPIE (includes
  Gillaspy), GILLEY, GILLIHAN (includes Gillahan, Gillehan,
  G(a,e,i)ll(a,e,i)h(a,e,i)(m,n)), GILMAN (includes Gillman),
  GILMORE (includes Gilmour, Gilmoore, Gilmer), GILREATH,
  GIRDLER, GIST (includes Guest, Guess, Giss, Gass, Gess),
  GIVIDON (includes Jividen), GLANTON, GLASGOW, GLASS

(includes Glas, Glasse), GLATTFELDER (includes Glotfelty, Glatfelder, Gladfelter, Clodfelter, Glotfelter, Clotfelter), GLENN (includes Glen, Glynn), GLIDDEN, GLINES, GLOVER, GOAD, GOBER (includes Gobee, Gobe), GODDARD (includes Godard), GODFREY, GODOWN (includes Godon, Godoun, Goedowne, Godowne, Goodown, Godowns), GODSHALK (includes Godschall, Godschalk, Godshall, Godtschalk, Gotschall, Gottschalk, Gottshall, Gottshalk), GODWIN (includes Godwyn, Godwynne, Godwine, Godwinne, Godin, Gadwin), GOFF, GOHR (includes Gohre, Gohrke, Gohring, Gohrs, Gohres, Gohrban), GOLDBERG, GOLDEN, GOLDMAN (includes Goldmann), GONSALUS, GOODENOW (includes Goodenowe, Goodenough, Goodno, Goodnow, Goodinowe, Goodyknow, Goodynow, Goodenough, Goodnough), GOODGAME, GOODLETT, GOODMAN, GOODRICH, GOODSON, GOODWIN, GORDON, GORDY (includes Gorden, Gordie, Gordey, Gorday, Gawdy), GORE (includes Goar, Goare, Goore, Gohr), GORIN-family, GORRELL (includes Gorel, Goril, Gorrill, Garrell, Garil, Garel), GOSSETT, GOTCHER (includes the allied family of Boren), GOTTFRIED, GOUCHER-S, GOULD (includes Gold), GOWDY (includes Goudy), GOWEN (includes Gowan, Goyne, Goins), GRACE, GRAF (includes Graff, Graph), GRAHAM, GRALEY (includes Grayley, Graille), GRAMMAR (includes Grammar, Grahmar), GRANGER (includes Grainger), GRANSTRAND (includes Grandstrand), GRANT, GRANTHAM (includes Granttham, Granthum), GRASBY, GRATTIDGE (includes Gratwick, Gratwich, Greatorex), GRAVES (includes Graff), GRAVES-FAM-ASSOC (includes Greaves), GRAVITT (includes Gravit, Gravat, Gravatt, Gravatte, Gravet, Gravett, Gravette), GRAY (includes Grey), GRAYBEAL (includes Graybill, Grable), GRAYSON, GREATHOUSE (includes Groethausen, Grothouss, Grothausen, Grothauss, Grothausze, Grosshaus, Grothaus, Gratehouse, Greatehouse, Grotehouse, Graytower, Greethouse, Grotehose, Gratchouse), GREEN (includes Greene), GREENE (includes Green), GREENHALGH, GREENSLIT (includes Greenslet), GREENSTREET (includes Greenstret, Greenstrait), GREENWOOD, GREER (includes Grier), GREGG (includes Mac Gregor, Greig), GREGORY, GREGORY-L (includes Grigory, Gregery, Gregary, Gregor), GRENFELL, GRIERSON (includes Greirson, Greerson, Greirson, Grier, Griere, Greer, Greere, Greir, Greire, Grear, Greear, McGreer, McGrier, O'Greer), GRIFF (includes Griffith, Griffiths, Griffeth, Griffeths, Griffin, Griffins), GRIFFIN, GRIGGS (includes Grigg), Griggs, GRIMM (includes Grim), GRIMSLEY (includes Grimslee, Grimsly), GRISSO (includes Gresso), GRISSOM (includes Grisham, Grishem, Grissam, Grissum, Grisum), GRISWOLD, GRIZZLE (includes Grizzel, Grizzell), GROGAN (includes Croghan), GROOM (includes Grooms), GROTE (includes Groot, Groat, DeGroote, DeGroat, DeGrote), GROVER, GRUBBS, GRUBER-L, GRUNEWALD (includes Greenawalt, Greenwald, Gruenewald), GUARDIAN (includes Gard, Garde, Guard), GUESMAN (includes Guseman), GUICE, GUIDRY (includes Guidrey, Guedry, Gaidry, Guildry, Gaitry), GUILLORY-L, GUNTER, GUSHLOW, GUSTIN (includes Gustine), GUTHRIE (includes Guthree, Guttrie, Lahiff), GWIN (includes Gwinn, Guin, Gwynn).

- Rev. John F. GAGNIER
  http://home.eznet.net/~jgagnier/
  GAGNIER, GAGNE

- The GAINES Place
  http://www.geocities.com/Heartland/Plains/7221/

- GAIR Genealogy—Descendants—1800,MDX,ENG
  http://www.itmagic.demon.co.uk/genealogy/gair.htm
  Descendants of William GAIR (1836-?) and Hannah JOHNSON.

- All GAITHER's in America
  http://home.inreach.com/calcoca/family.htm

- The Clan GALBRAITH
  http://www.tartans.com/clans/Galbraith/galbraith.html
  CALBREATH, COLBREATH, CULBREATH, GALBREATH, GILBREATH, GILREATH, KILBREATH, KULBETH and other variant spellings.

- GALLINGER Mail Group Archives
  http://www.inforamp.net/~griffish/gene/gall/gall1.html
  Dedicated to tracing the family of Michael Gallinger and his wife Agatha Ady (Alyda).

- GANDY Gathering Genealogy
  http://www.geocities.com/Heartland/Pointe/1462/

- GANTTREES Newsletter
  E-mail Ben GANTT at bengantt@hal-pc.org for subscription details. Covers the GANT(T), GENT, GAUN(T) families in the U.S.

- GARRISON Surname Mailing List
  http://www.sonic.net/~yvonne/garrison.html
  Includes Garretson.

- The GAUDREAU Genealogy Page
  http://www.gaudreau.org/arthur/genealogy/gaudreau.sht
  Gaudreau, Gaudreault, Gautras, Gautreau, Geaudreau, Godereau, Godrault, Godreau, Godreault, Gotereau, Gotreau, Gottrau, Gottreau, and Goudreau.

- GAUER Family Home Page
  http://users.uniserve.com/~morbeus
  The Gauer surname is very unusual. Gauer folks are related in some way. This is a collection of everything I have been able to find about people with the Gauer surname. Gauers started in Germany but can now be found all over the world. If you have a Gauer anywhere in your family history this is the place to look.

- GAUNT / GAUNTT / GANT / GANTT Families Page
  http://www-personal.umich.edu/~cgaunt/Gaunt/gaunt.html

- GEEnealogy—Genealogy of the GEE Family
  http://www2.arkansas.net/~mgee/genealo.html

- Descendants of Reuben and Ann (Handley) GEORGE
  http://www.rootsweb.com/~moandrew/george/reub-1.html
  Married in 1797, Greenbrier Co., WV; lived in Monroe Co., WV; moved to Butler Co., OH about 1810.

- GERAGHTY World Genealogy
  For details on this group, send e-mail to williamm@4dcomm.com

- GERHARDSTEIN
  http://www.3-cities.com/~larry/gerhardstein/gerhardstein.html

- GEROW / GIRAUD Family Association
  http://home.earthlink.net/~rctwig/gerow.htm

- GERRANS Kin FHS
  http://www.geocities.com/Athens/4725/

- GERSTENBERGER Genealogy Home Page—The GERSTENBERGER Immigrants and Their Descendants in America
  http://members.aol.com/gerstdf/index.htm
  A Compendium of Vital Statistics by Duane Francis Gerstenberger, M.D., MPH, and Ruthelma Millie Vedder Gerstenberger.

- The GEYER Family: Germans from Russia
  http://www.angelfire.com/ny/earthstar/geyer.html
  Descendants of Frederick W. C. Geyer, born about 1808 and his wife Margaret, born about 1813.

- The GIBSON Family from New York State's Hudson River Valley
  http://members.aol.com/GibbJ/index.html

- The GIBSON Family Tree
  http://www.geocities.com/Heartland/Meadows/6579/
  Descendants of William Gibson, born ca. 1700.

- GIBSON Home Page—Gathering GIBSONs Newsletter
  http://members.aol.com/Kinseeker6/gibson.html

- GIDEON's Trumpet—The GIDEON Genealogy Home Page
  http://members.tripod.com/~rootbound/index.html

- The GIRDLER Family
  http://www.girdler.com

- Searching GIVNEY Names
  http://www.geocities.com/Heartland/Estates/4121/

- GLADNEY Home Page
  http://members.aol.com/retteacher/gladney.html
  In South Carolina, descendants of Richard GLADNEY, b. ca. 1670 Res. Kinbally, Skerry Parish, Antrim, IRELAND.

- The Origins of the GLENDINNINGs
  http://user.itl.net/~glen/glendinningorigins.html

- GLENISTER Family History and Worldwide One Name Study
  http://www.glenister.demon.co.uk/

- GOCHENOUR Genealogy
  http://web2.airmail.net/wagoch/gene.htm
  From the editor of the "The Trail Seekers" newsletter for Gochenour/Coughenour/Gochnauer.

- GODBOUT Genealogy
  http://members.xoom.com/godbout/genealog.htm

- The GODDARD Association's Homepage
  http://www.eese.qut.edu.au/~mgoddard/gae_gaa1.htm

- GODWIN Surname Mailing List
  http://homepages.rootsweb.com/~godwin/surname/
  Includes Godwyn, Godwynne, Godwine, Godwinne.

- Most Wanted GODWINs
  http://homepages.rootsweb.com/~godwin/surname/mostwanted.html

- The GOFF/GOUGH Family Page
  http://www.inmind.com/people/dcooper/

- GOLDER / GOULDER / GOLDEN Family Genealogy Listings
  http://www.facstaff.bucknell.edu/goldcoop/geneal.html
  Descendants of William Golder, born 1613 in Ireland, died 1680, Long Island, NY.

- The All GOLDFARB Site
  http://www.mrbig.com/goldhome2.html

- GOODENOW E-Mailer Home Page
  http://users.ilnk.com/ejcornell/Goodenow.htm

- The GOODMAN Family
  http://www.bcpl.lib.md.us/~dmg/goodman.html
  With a clearinghouse for all people researching GOODMAN.

- GOODSON Genealogy
  http://www.tntech.edu/~beg/goodson/index.html

- The Descendants of Arne Henriksen GOPLEN
  http://www.familytreemaker.com/users/g/o/p/Lawrence-M-Goplen/

- GORDON Genealogy
  http://www.geocities.com/Heartland/5917/GORDON2.HTM

- The GORE Family Connection
  http://www.yucca.net/jglocke/

- GOSSETT/GOSSET Genealogy
  http://www.surfsouth.com/~fgossett/

- GOTCHER Family Home Page
  http://www.wsu.edu:8080/~giles/gotcher/gotcher.htm
  Variations: Goacher / Goatcher / Gochar / Gochar / Gocher / Gotcher / Goucher.

- GOTTSEGEN Family Home Page
  http://www.ccil.org/~jcg/home.html

- Jan GOULEVITCH, DFC
  http://www.st.net.au/~dunn/goolie.htm
  Born 21 Feb 1919 in Blagoveshschensk in Siberia, died 24 Dec 1994 in Townsville, Australia.

- GOURDIN-GOURDINE Family Association
  http://www.blackcamisards.com/gourdin/index.html
  A French-African-American Family from South Carolina.

- GOWEN Research Foundation
  http://www.llano.net/gowen/
  Gowen, Gowen, Gowan, Gowans, Gowing, Goin, Going, Goins, Goings, Gooing, Goan, Goan, Goen, Goens, Gowin, Gowins, Goyne, Goynes, Guyne, Guynes.

- The GRAHAM Family Page
  http://www.spessart.com/users/ggraham/graham1.htm

- GRAHAM Home Page—GRAHAM Group Newsletter
  http://members.aol.com/Kinseeker6/graham.html

- The Edward GRANTHAM Family
  http://www.familytreemaker.com/users/g/r/a/Christopher-P-Grantham/index.html
  Descendants of Edward Grantham, born 1643 and died September 1704 in Grantham's Reeds, Surry Co., VA.

- The GRANTHAM Gazette
  A quarterly newsletter devoted to the Grantham surname. For details send e-mail to Ron Johnson and Lori Grantham at: rjohnson@graham.main.nc.us

- The GRAVES Family Association
  http://www.gravesfa.org

- GRAVITT Surname Mailing List
  http://www.geocities.com/Heartland/Plains/4235/Gravform.htm
  Includes Gravit, Gravat, Gravatt, Gravatte, Gravet, Gravett, Gravette.

- The GREEN(E) Family Genealogy Page
  http://al7fl.abts.net/green-page/green.htm
- The Samuel Thomas GREENE Genealogical Page
  http://www.cgocable.net/~ccarbin/greene.html
  The first deaf teacher of deaf students in the Canadian province of Ontario, October 1870.
- GREENWOOD Genealogies, 1154–1914
  http://www.rootsweb.com/~genepool/grnwdind.htm
- GREGG Family Documents and History
  http://pw1.netcom.com/~jog1/greggndex.html
  GREGG / GRIGGS / GREGGS
- GRIBBLE One Name Site
  http://www.users.bigpond.com/jgribble/
- GRICE Family Home Page
  http://ourworld.compuserve.com/homepages/ra_grice/grice.htm
- GRIFF* Mail Group Archives
  http://www.inforamp.net/~griffish/gene/griff/griff1.html
  For surnames beginning with GRIFF; i.e., GRIFFITH, GRIFFITHS, GRIFFETH, GRIFFETHS, GRIFFIN, GRIFFINS, etc.
- GRIGGS Mailing List
  http://www.onelist.com/subscribe.cgi/griggs
  Devoted to researching the Griggs family, especially the descendants/ancestors of Michael and/or Jeremiah Michael Griggs of early Virginia.
- "Saints & Sinners" Genealogical Newsletter—GRIGGS Researchers
  http://members.aol.com/scribblerg/saints.htm
  Gregg, Griggle, Grigges, Grigs, Gregs.
- National GRIGSBY Family Society
  http://www.grigsby.org
- The Official GRIM—GRIMM Family Home Page
  http://fvl.k12.mi.us/~grimm/index.html
- GRINNELL Family Association
  http://www.gate.net/~grinnell/
- GRISSOM Surname Mailing List
  http://www.geocities.com/~fannincounty/grissom-grists.html
  Includes Grisham, Grishem, Grissam, Grissum, Grisum.
- The GRISWOLD Family Association
  http://www.griswoldfamily.org
- Canadian GROBE Home Page
  http://www.ionline.net/~grobee/1.htm
  Descendants of Johann GROBE and Sophia KULOW.
- GRONINGER Family Record Newsletter
  E-mail Jon Kroninger at jonk59@interaccess.com for details. Name variations are: GRONINGER, GRENINGER, CRONINGER, CHRONINGER, KRONINGER.
- GROOMS
  http://www.rio.com/~shoch/grooms.html
  Descendants of Abraham GROOMS, born 1740 in Gunpowder Falls, Maryland and Margaret SATTERFIELD.

- The GROOMS Family Page
  http://www.angelfire.com/mo/groomsfamilypage/index.html
- The GROTON Family Trees
  http://cpplus.com/grotonresearch
  The Groton Family Trees, researching all branches of the Groton, Grotton, Graton, Groten, Grotten and Gratten families in North America. Research dates back to Thomas Groton circa 1650, in Massachusetts and William Groton circa 1650, in Virginia. Inquiries are welcolme.
- GRÜNINGER Families of the World
  http://www.dnc.net/users/squirrel/gruninger/gruninger.htm
  Dedicated to establishing the link between Johannes Reinhart Grüninger and the Grüninger families around the world. Grueninger, Grininger, Grüniger, Grieninger, Grienninger, Geininger, Groninger, Groininger, Gürninger and other variant spellings.
- GRUWELL Gatherings Site Index
  http://members.aol.com/rngruwell/
- The GUARNIERI Home Web Page
  http://www.Guarnieri.com
- GUENTHER Genealogy—Passionate Possessions of Faith
  http://home1.gte.net/kanetani/guenther/index.htm
  A book for sale about The Jacob Guenther Family 1725–present, including GOERTZEN, DUERKSEN, PETERS, WARKENTIN, ADRIAN, LOEWEN, PETKAU, ISAAC, FADENRECHT, THIESSEN and others.
- The GUILLIATT Family Home Page
  http://www.crabtree.demon.co.uk/
- Clan GUNN Society of North America
  http://www.nsynch.com/~clangunn
- GUTH / GOOD Researchers
  http://www.erie.net/~sjones/ggresearchers.html
- The GYLLENHAAL Family Tree Project
  http://www.voicenet.com/~egyllenh/Html/treepage.html

◆ Surnames Beginning with "H"

- Family Tree Maker Online User Home Pages—H
  http://www.familytreemaker.com/users/h/index.html
- Genealogy's Most Wanted—Surnames Beginning with "H"
  http://www.citynet.net/mostwanted/h.htm
- H-GIG Surname Registry—Surnames Beginning H
  http://www.ucr.edu/h-gig/surdata/surname8.html
- Higginson Book Company—Surnames Beginning with H
  http://www.higginsonbooks.com/h.htm
- inGeneas Table of Common Surname Variations and Surname Misspellings—H–J
  http://www.ingeneas.com/H2J.html
- Surname Springboard Index—H
  http://www.geocities.com/~alacy/spring_h.htm

- SurnameWeb Surname Registry—H Index
  http://www.surnameweb.org/registry/h.htm
- Genealogy Resources on the Internet—"H" Surname
  Mailing Lists
  http://members.aol.com/gfsjohnf/gen_mail_surnames-h.html
  This site is wonderfully maintained by John Fuller. It includes mailing list information for the following surnames and their variant spellings:
  HACKETT (includes Hacket), HACKWORTH (includes Hackworthe, Hack), HAFFEY (includes Haffy), HAGAMAN (includes Hageman, Hagerman, Hegeman), HAGAN, HAGER, HAGERTY (includes Haggerty, Hegarty, Heagerty, Heaggarty, O'Heagarty, O'Hagerty, O'Haggerty), HAGOOD (includes Haygood, Haigwood, Heygood), HAIRE (includes Hair, O'Hair, O'Haegher), HAKE, HALDEMAN-L, HALE (includes Haile, Heale), HALEY (includes Hailey, Haly), HALFACRE (includes Halfaker, Huffaker), HALL, HALLFORD (includes Halford), HALLMAN (includes Heilman, Heilmann), HALLMARK, HALSEY_LIST, HALTERMAN (includes Halderman, Haltiman), HAMAKER (includes Hamacher, Haymaker), HAMBY, HAMILTON, HAMLIN (includes Hamblin), HAMMACK (includes Hammock, Hamack), HAMMAN (includes Hammon, Hammond, Hammen, Hammin), HAMMETT, HAMMONTREE, HAMNER (includes Hanmer), HAMRICK (includes Hambrick, Hemric), HANCE, HANCOCK (includes Handcock), HANCOCK_Capt_John, HAND (includes Hann), HANDLEY (includes Handly, Hanley, Hanly), HANEY (includes Hany, Heany, Heaney, Heny), HANKINS, HANKS (includes Hank, Hanke, Hankey, Hancks, Hanckes, Henks, Henke, Henkins), HANLON (includes O'Hanlon), HANNA (includes Hannah, Hannay), HANRATTY (includes Hanretty), HARDESTY (includes Hardisty, Hardiesty, Hardestie, Hardister, Hardester), HARDIN (includes Harden, Harding), HARDMAN (includes Hardeman, Hardiman, Hardyman), HARDWICK, HARDY (includes Hardee, Hardie), HARGETT (includes Hargratt, Hargate), HARGIS (includes Hargas, Harges, Hargiss, Hargus), HARGREAVES (includes Hargreave, Hargrave, Hargraves, Hargrove, Hargroves), HARKEY (includes antecedent surnames Herch, Herche, Herche Der Junge), HARLESS-L (includes Harles, Harlos, Herlass), HARLOW (includes Harlowe, Harlough), HARMAN (includes Harmon), HARNED (includes Harnett, Horned), HARPER (includes Arp, Arpe, Harp, Harpe), HARRADEN (includes Harreden), HARRAH (includes Harrow, O'Harrow, Harra), HARRELL (includes Harrill, Haral, Harral, Harold, Harrold), HARRGENE (Harrington, Herrington, Harington), HARRIS-HUNTERS, HARRISON (includes Harison, Harrisson, Harreston, Herrison), HARRIS-VA, HART (includes Hartt, Heart), HARTLEB-FAMILY, HARTLEY, HARTMAN (includes Hartmann), HARTSELL (includes Hartzell, Hartsel, Hartzel), HARTSHORN (includes Hartshorne, Hartson), HARTSOOK (includes Herzog, Hartsock, Heartsock, Hartog, Hartough, Hartsough), HARVEY (includes Harvie), HARVIN, HARWOOD (includes Harrod, Harewood, Horwood), HASSELL, HATCH (includes Hacche, Hach), HATCHER, HATFIELD, HATHAWAY (includes Haddaway, Hataway), HATHCOCK, HAUGHN (includes Hahn), HÄUSER, HAVINS (includes Havens), HAWK (includes Hawkes, Hawks, Hauk), HAWKINS (includes Hawkyns, Hawking), HAYDEN (includes Heydon, Haydon, Hadden, Haden, Hyden), HAYES (includes Hays, Hayse, Haze), HAYHURST, HAYNES (includes Hanes, Haines), HAZELRIGG (includes Heselridge), HEACKER (includes Hecker, Hacker, Hüecker), HEAD (includes Headlee, Headley, Headly), HEADEN, HEALEY (includes Healy), HEARNE (includes Hearn, Hern, Herrin, Herron, Heron), HEATH (includes Heathcock, Heathcote, Heather, Heatherington), HECKMAN (includes Heckaman, Hickman), HECTOR (includes Hecter, Hecktor, Heckter, Hektor, Hekter), HEDDEN (includes Headen, Heden, Heddan, Heddin, Heddins, Hadden, Haddon, Heady, Heddy), HEDGES (includes Hedge), HEDRICK (includes Headrick), HEFFRON (includes Heffernan), HEFLIN (includes Hefflin, Heflen, Heffernon), HEINRICH, HELM (includes Helms, Hellums, Elam, Ellams,

Hallam, Kellums, Nelms, Halm, Helmig, Helmoldus, Chelm, Cellums, Shelem, Shalem, Gelm, Hellmann, Helmstedter, Helmreich, Hjelm, Helmont, Helmbold, Swethelm, Helmsley, McHelm, Helmers, Elmo, Helmes, Holmes), HELMAN (includes Hellman, Hellmann, Heilman, Heylman), HELMICK, HEMING (includes Hemming), HEMOND (includes Hemon, Hemont, Haimond, Emond, Emon, Emont, Aymond, Aymong, Aymon, Aumont, Aumond), HENDERSON, HENDERSON (Clan Henderson), HENDERSON-CANADA, HENDRICKS, HENDRICKSON, HENDRICKS (includes Hendrix, Hendrickson), HENDRY, HENES, HENKEL, HENLY (includes Henley, Hendly, Hendley), HENNING (includes Hening), HENNION (includes Henion, Henyon, Henyan), HENRY (includes Henri, Henery, McHenry), HENSLEY, HEPLER (includes Heppler, Hoppler), HERBERT (includes Abear, Abert, Abair), HERD (includes Heard, Hird, Hurd), HERMAN (includes Hermann, Herrman, Herrmann), HERRING (includes Herrin, Herron), HERSUM (includes Hersom, Hershum, Horsam, Horsom, Horsum), HESLER (includes Hessler, Heslar, Hesslar, Hosler, Hossler), HESTER, HETTINGER, HETZEL (includes Hezel, Heltzel), HEWITT-COLEMAN, HIATT (includes Hyatt, Hiett, Hyett), HIBBS, HICKAM (includes Hickem, Hickham, Hickhem), HICKEY (includes Hicke, Hicki, Hickie, Hicky), HICKMAN, HICKS, HIGBIE (includes Higbee, Higby), HIGGINBOTHAM (includes Higgingbottom, Hickingbottom, Hickenbottom, Hickingbotham), HIGGINS (includes Higgie, O'Higgins, Higgens, O'Higgeen, O'Huigin), HIGHTOWER, HILES (includes Hyles), HILL (includes Hills, Hille), HILLIER (includes Hillierd, Hilliar, Hilliard, Hillyer), HILTON (includes Hylton), HIMES, HINES, HINKSON (includes Hinkston), HINSHAW (includes Henshaw, Henshall), HIPP (includes Hepp, Hip, Hipps, Hepps), HITCHCOCK, HITE, HITT, HOBAN (includes Hoben, Hobin, Hooban, Howbane, Huban, Hubane), HOBBS, HOCH, HOCKADAY (includes Hockday, Hoccaday, Hochaday, Hoccadie, Hockerdy), HODGES (includes Hodge, Hedge), HOEY (includes Hoy, Haughey), HOFBAUER (includes Hoffbauer), HOFF (includes Huff, Hough), HOFFMAN (includes Hofman, Hoffmann, Hofmann, Huffman, Hufman), HOFFPAUIR (includes Hoffpauer, Huffpower), HOGAN, HOGGETT (includes Hoggatt), HOISINGTON (includes Hossington, Hosington, Hassington, Hissington, Hossenton, Hyselton, Hesselton), HOKE, HOLBERT (includes Halbert, Hulbert), HOLBERT (includes Halbert, Haubert, Hurlburt, Howbert), HOLBROOK, HOLDER (includes Holdour, Holdor), HOLLAND, HOLLANDS (includes Holland, Holand, Oland), HOLLER (includes Hollar, Haller), HOLLETT, HOLLEY, HOLLIDAY (includes Halliday, Halladay, Holladay, Halladie), HOLLINGER (includes Hullinger), HOLLINGSWORTH, HOLLISTER, HOLLOWAY, HOLLOWELL (includes Hallowell, Holliwell, Halliwell, Hollewell, Hallewell), HOLMAN (includes Hollman, Hallman), HOLMES (includes Hohmes, Holemes, Holms, Hom, Home, Homes, Hooms), HOLSAPPLE (includes Holsopple, Holtzapfel), HOLSTROM, HOLT (includes Holte), HOLTON, HOMME, HOMMEL (includes Hommell, Homel, Hummel, Humel, Humble), HONEA (includes Honey, Honay), HONEYCUTT (includes Honneycutt, Honeycut, Honeycut, Huneycutt, Hunneycut, Huneycut, Hunneycut, Honicutt, Honnicutt, Honicut, Honnicut, Hunicutt, Hunnicutt, Hunicut, Hunnicut), HOOKER, HOOKS (includes Hook), HOOPER, HOOTER, HOOVER, HOPE (includes Hoppe), HOPKINS, HOPPER (includes Hooper, Hoppe, Hoppen), HORN, HORNBECK (includes Hornback), HORNER, HORNSBY (includes Hornby), HORTON (includes Horten, Orton), HORTON-family, HOSEY (includes Hossey, Hosea, Hozey, Hosse, Hose), Hotchkiss, HOUCHENS (includes Houchins, Houchen, Houchin), HOUGHTON (includes Haughton), HOUSDEN (includes Housdon, Howsden, Howsdon, Howson), HOUSE, HOUSTON (includes Huston), HOWARD-family (includes Hayward, Howarth), HOWDER (includes Houder, Houter, Hauder, Hauter), HOWE (includes How), HOWELL, HOWERY (includes Hauri, Haury, Hourie, Howrey, Howrie, Howry), HOWLAND, HOYT (includes Haight), HOYT-HAIGHT, HUBAND (includes Hubolt), HUBBARD (includes Hobart, Hubert, Hibbard, Hubbel, Halbert, O'Hubbard), HUBER,

HUDDLESTON (includes Hudelson), HUDNALL, HUDSON, HUFF-HUFFINES-HOFFHEINTZ, HUFFMAN (includes Hufman, Hofman, Hoffman), HUGGINS (includes Hudgins), HUGHES (includes McHugh, McCue, Huge, Hough, Hews, Hughs, Hughey), HULL, HULSE-FAMILY (includes Hulce, Huls, Hults, Hultz, Holsaert, Hulsart, Hulseheart), HUMAN (includes Humann, Hueman, Hughman, Hewman), HUMFLEET (includes Umfleet), HUMPHREYS (includes Humphries, Humphrey, Umphrey), HUNGERFORD, HUNSAKER, HUNSUCKER (includes Hunsicker, Hunsinger, Honsooker, Huntsucker, Hunsecker, Huntsicker), HUNT, HUNTER, HUNTOON (includes Hunton, Hanton, Henton, Hinton, Honton, Hynton), HURLESS, HURLEY, HURREN, HURST, HURSTER, HURTfamily, HURTFIELD, HURT-HURTT, HUSKEY (includes Husky), HUSON, HUSSEY (includes Huse, Husse, Hussy), HUSTED (includes Huested, Hustead), HUTCHINSON (includes Hudgins, Houghton, Hodgeson, Huggins, Hutcheson), HUTCHISON (includes Hutchinson, Hutcheson, Hutcherson, Hutchins), HUTTO, HYDE.

- HAEFNER Family Tree Outline
  http://www.sky.net/~shaefner/famtree.htm
  Descendants of William and Frank ?? HAEFNER.

- The Descendants of Hans Jacob HAGEY
  http://alpha.nornet.on.ca/~hlhagey/
  Largely a genealogical history of Daniel HAGEY and his wife Elizabeth BERGEY who emigrated to Canada in 1822.

- Johannes HAHN Family History
  http://users.twave.net/lhsetzer/hahn.html
  Descendants of Johannes Hahn, born 1712 in Frechenfeld, Germany, died 1793 in Lincoln, Catawba, NC.

- HALE Genealogy
  http://www.qni.com/~geo/jhale.htm
  Descendants of John Hale, Revolutionary War soldier, born 1753.

- HALEY Surname Discussion List
  http://www.geocities.com/Heartland/Ranch/1764/maillist.html

- The HALLs and HENNINGs of Ireland
  http://members.aol.com/Rdkone/HallMain.html
  Descendants of Samuel Hall and Robert Henning.

- HALTERMAN Hollow
  http://www.scioto.org/Halterman/index.html
  Halterman, Halderman, Haltiman, Haldeman.

- Will of Stephen HAMM
  http://members.aol.com/jogt/hammwl.htm

- HAMILTON Historical Newsletter
  E-mail Ann Kirkpatrick Hull at IMAKSICKAR@aol.com for details.

- HAMILTON National Genealogical Society, Inc.
  http://www.qni.com/~hamgen/index.html
  A non-profit organization devoted to assembling and preserving genealogical and historical materials pertaining to the Hamilton (ALL spellings: Hamelton, Hamleton, Hambleton, Hambelton) and Allied families. Membership is open to all persons interested in genealogical research and preservation of records. We publish a Monthly Newsletter "The Connector."

- HAMLEY, HAMBLY & HAMLYN Family History Society
  http://freespace.virgin.net/ham.famis/

- HAMLIN-List Genealogy
  http://www.forbin.com/users/gwinslow/hamlin/
  mirror site
  http://www.geocities.com/Heartland/Hills/2496/Hamlin/
  Site contains GEDCOM files from multiple HAMLIN, HAMLYN, HAMLEN, HAMBLIN, HAMBLYN, HAMBLEN researchers. Also has links to other HAMLIN, HAMLYN, HAMLEN, HAMBLIN, HAMBLYN, HAMBLEN researchers and query page on our "lost" HAMLIN, HAMLYN, HAMLEN, HAMBLIN, HAMBLYN, HAMBLEN ancestors.

- The North American HAMMILL Family Forum
  http://www.webcom.com/hammill/
  Hammill, Hammil, Hamill, Hamil, Hammel, Hammell, Hamel, Hamell.

- HAMMOND Genealogy
  http://www.arq.net/~ljacobs/hamm1.htm
  Descendants of William Hammond who died in Swansea, MA in 1675.

- HAMMONS Genealogy Page
  http://genweb.net/Hammons
  A data base for all spellings of Hammonds including Ammons.

- The HANCOCK Family History Page
  http://www.geocities.com/Heartland/Meadows/9255/index.html

- The HANDLEY Genealogy Index Page
  http://members.aol.com/Sftrail/handley/

- HANDWERK Family Research in Germany
  http://pw2.netcom.com/~richardz/handwe3.html
  Hantwerck, Handwercker, Handtwerck, Handwerk and Handwerg.

- The HANNA Surname Resource Center
  http://members.theglobe.com/slhanna/hanna.html
  The site is for the study of the Hanna, Hannah, Hannay, Hanner surnames and variations. Its purpose is to link to relevant sites, to collect information and to present this information on the web so that it can be freely accessed.

- The HARDICK Page
  http://www.hardick.org
  Hardick, Hardiek, Hardieck, Haardiek, Haardick & Haardieck.

- The HARDIN Family Compendium
  http://www.flex.net/~hardin/

- HARDWICK Hunters
  http://www.s-hornbeck.com/hardhunt.htm
  A clearing house for HARDWICK Hunters, queries.

- HARDWICK Hunting Newsletter
  http://www.s-hornbeck.com/hardwick.htm

- HARGETT Database Home Page
  http://www.netusa1.net/~eddleman/hargett.htm

- The HARLAN Family in America
  http://www.harlanfamily.org

- HARMER Family Association
  http://www.angelfire.com/wa/harmer1/index.html

- HARMON Genealogical Society
  http://www.geocities.com/Heartland/Valley/4236/

- HARMON Heritage
  http://www.ida.net/users/cherylb/
  Descendants of Nehemiah HARMON (1728–1806).

- The HARNEDs of North America
  http://homepages.rootsweb.com/~harned/
  Site for the Harned family of North America, descendants of Edward Harnett, at Salem by 1637, including Harnet, Harnett, Horned.

- HARNEY Home Page
  http://www.xmission.com/~harney2/

- HARRINGTON Genealogy Association
  http://www.genealogy.org/~bryce/harrgene.html

- Southern HARRINGTON Genealogy WebSite
  http://www.cinti.net:2000/~johnh/

- The HARRISON Genealogy Repository
  http://moon.ouhsc.edu/rbonner/harintro.htm

- My HARRISON Line
  http://harrison.simplenet.com
  Descendants of Richard HARRISON, born about 1663, Leeds, Yorkshire, England.

- HARRIS Surname Webring
  http://www.geocities.com/Heartland/Flats/4239/harris.html
  Harris Surname Webring links genealogy pages that have research on the surname Harris.

- The HARROD Family Page
  http://www.hypervigilance.com/genlog/harrod.html
  Descendants of James (abt. 1668) and Maria (Kent) Harrod, from Bedfordshire, England in about 1720–1722.

- HART Family Association
  http://www.opcweb.com/hart/hfa.htm
  Including Hart, Heart, O'Hart, Harte, and Hartt.

- HARTMAN Genealogy
  http://www.java-connect.com/hartman/
  Descendants of John HARTMAN and Margaret SCHADEL. The HARTMAN families on these pages originated in the 1890's in Southside, Pittsburgh, PA.

- HARTWELLs of America
  http://www.hartwell.org

- The HARVEY Genealogist / The HARVEY Resource
  http://www.geocities.com/Heartland/6575/
  A surname association that includes Harvy, Harvie, Hervey, Hervy and Hervie.

- HASBROUCK Family Association
  http://home.earthlink.net/~rctwig/hasbrouc.htm

- The HATCLIFFE Family
  http://www.bendigo.net.au/~lisid/
  *Ide Haddeclive * de Hatclyf * Attlyf * Hatteclyf * Hatlyff * Hatley * Hatclyffe * Hatlefe * Hatlif * Hatchcliffe * Hatliff * Hatcliff.*

- HATFIELD Genealogy Homepage
  http://members.aol.com/HatwellE/genealogy.html

- HATT Family Research Page
  http://www.geocities.com/Heartland/Plains/7614/hatt.htm
  Including Hate, Haight, Height, Hat, Hott, Hite, Hedyt, Hoyt, Heit, Hitt, etc.

- HAVEKOST Genealogy
  http://www.tdi.net/havekost/

- HAWES HAWS Roots in Kentucky Genealogy and Beyond
  http://members.aol.com/JimHawes/Hawes.html
  This page is dedicated to persons researching one of the oldest names in American history, "HAWES—HAWS."

- HAYDEN Family History
  http://www.pastracks.com/hayden/

- HAYDEN Family History
  http://www.hayden.org
  Heydon, Haydon, Haden, Hadden, Hyden, Headen, Haddon and others. Sponsored by some of The Descendants of Joseph Thompson Hayden.

- HEABERLIN Family Genealogy
  http://www.pulpgen.com/gen/heaberlin/
  Descendants of Andrew Heaberlin, a weaver, who emigrated from Germany to Maryland around the time of the American Revolution.

- HEATHFamily.org—The Official HEATH Family Website
  http://www.heathfamily.org

- HEBERT Family Genealogy
  http://www.acadian-cajun.com/hebert.htm

- The HEBERT Genealogy Page
  http://www.gaudreau.org/arthur/genealogy/hebert.sht

- HEDGES Family History Website
  http://ourworld.compuserve.com/homepages/PHedges/

- HEDRICK Surname Mailing List
  http://members.aol.com/TreeCrazyD/hedric_l.html
  Includes Headrick.

- The HEIMBACH Genealogy HomePage
  http://www.nimbus.org/f.genealogy/HeimbachGenlgyPage.html

- HEINRICH Family History
  http://www.geocities.com/~gdheinrich/
  The Heinrich Family and many German Moravian, Moravian, German Bohemian, Bohemian, German Russian, German, & Czech Families.

- HELM/HELMS Family Research Page
  http://genealogy.tbox.com/research/helm.html

- The Status of the Search for the NC HELMS Brothers Parents (1690–1750)
  http://idt.net/~jfultz19/helms-1.htm
  by Ira L. Helms, Jr.

- Family Pedigree of the HELSBY Family
  http://www.geocities.com/Hollywood/1880/Famtree.html
  A Norman–French Pedigree by Thomas Helsby, Esq., of Lincoln's Inn.

- HEMINGWAY / HEMENWAY Genealogy
  http://www.hemingway.net
- HENDERSHOT Family Genealogy
  http://www.mindspring.com/~noahsark/family.html
- The HENDERSON Genealogy Page
  http://www.concentric.net/~rayii/henderson.shtml
- HENDRIX / HENDRICKS Family Archives
  http://www.geocities.com/Athens/9640/index.html
- HENLEY Family Genealogy
  http://www.vii.com/~jensenet/henley/
  Henley/Henly/Hensley/Hensly/Hendly/Hendley. Origins in Virginia branched out to North and South Carolinas then the normal migration route of Alabama, Mississippi, etc.
- HENRY and Related Families of Harrison County, Kentucky
  http://www.mindspring.com/~jogt/surnames/henry2.htm
- The HENRY Herald
  http://ladyecloud.hypermart.net/Henry.htm
  Henri(e), Henery, Henry.
- Genealogy of the HERSHEY's
  http://www.raccoon.com/~hershey/
- HIBLER & HIBBLER Family History
  http://www.geocities.com/Heartland/Hills/3280/index.html
  From New Jersey in the early 1700s to everywhere in the present time.
- HICKEY Heritage Newsletter
  A Hickey Family Research Newsletter, for all Hickey, Hicky, Hickie, Hikky families. For details send e-mail to Diane Heap, Editor at kstander@pol.net or Carol B. Wahl, Contributing Editor at wahlwrks@fishnet.net
- HICKS Genealogy Homepage
  http://www.annie.co.jp/~dhicks/
- The HICKS / HIX Database Home Page
  http://www.familytreemaker.com/users/h/i/c/Joan-M-Hicks/
  Devoted to descendants of the surname Hicks or Hix with lines originating in New England and New York in colonial times.
- HICKS / HIX Home Page
  http://members.aol.com/kvhicks/index.htm
  With a HICKS newsletter.
- The HIDDEN One-Name Study
  http://www.btinternet.com/~nick.hidden/index.htm
- HIESTAND Family Genealogy
  http://www.rootsweb.com/~takelley/hiestand/hiestand.htm
  Heistand, Heiston, Histand, Heastand, Hasting, etc.
- The HIGHTOWER Files
  http://web2.airmail.net/phi868/hightowr.htm
  For the Hightower families in America, circa 1650 to the present.
- HIGHTOWER News
  http://hightower.indstate.edu/HightowerNews/default.html
- HILDRETH Family Association
  http://www.Hildreth.net

- HILL Families of America
  http://edge.edge.net/~gbhill/
- HILL Family History Page
  http://home.texoma.net/~mmcmullen/hi/hill.htm
- A HILLARD (HILLIARD) Genealogy
  http://members.aol.com/vichillard/hillard/hillard.htm
  Descendants of William Hillard who came to America in the spring of 1635.
- Descendants of Johann Jacob HILTZ (HULS)
  http://www.parsonstech.com/genealogy/trees/chiltz/Hiltz.htm
- HINMAN Family Association & Newsletter
  Has a database of nearly 28,000 names and nearly 10,000 marriages. For details send e-mail to Munson Hinman at topbari@pacbell.net
- The HINSHAW Family Association
  http://www.blueneptune.com/~hinshaw/
- HIRKO Family Genealogy Project
  http://members.aol.com/buffhirko/index1.html
- HISE Family Association
  http://www.clark.net/pub/mjloyd/hise.html
  Many variations: HEISS, HICE, HEISE, HAIS, HEYSS, HIES.
- HIXON HIXSON HICKSON Genealogy Page— A One Name Study
  http://ourworld.compuserve.com/homepages/Tyn_Rhos/
- HLAVATY Family Page
  http://www.cjnetworks.com/~wrs/hlav.htm
  Descendants of Frans Hlavaty and Barbara Riener.
- HOCKADAY Home Page
  http://www.panam.edu/dept/csl/hockaday/Hockaday.html
- HOCKENSMITH / HOCKERSMITH Family Association Homepage
  http://america.net/~timhock/
  Hawkersmith, Hockensmith, Hockersmith, Hackenschmidt.
- HODGES Family Association
  http://bluepost.tcimet.net/hodges/
- De HOEGE Woeninck
  http://www.xs4all.nl/~bv25/hgwng1.html
  Netherlands. Hoogewoning, Hoogewooning, Hoogewoonink.
- HOELSCHER-BUXKEMPER Family Heritage Association
  http://www.hostville.com/hoelscher/
- HOEY Family News
  http://members.aol.com/arthurh583/index.html
  Researching HOEY, HOY, and HAUGHEY surnames.
- HOFF / HUFF Family
  http://www.sensible-net.com/dhoffgr/hoff.wbg/
  Descendants of Johann Jacob Hoff/Huff/Hough of Bradford County, Pennsylvania.
- HOHNSTEIN / HOHENSTEIN Surname Project
  http://members.xoom.com/tsterkel/surname_projects/hohnstei.htm

- HOLCOMB and ROBERSON/ROBINSON
  http://members.aol.com/jogt/holcomms.htm

- HOLLAND Family History and Tree
  http://home.hiwaay.net/~dfaust/holland/holintro.htm
  Approximately 1,800 descendants of Jimmie and Jerutha White Holland who settled in North Carolina in the 1700's.

- HOLLENBECK and HALLENBECK Genealogy
  http://members.aol.com/Rdkone/hollenbeck.html

- The Holler—Net, HOLLER—HOLLAR—HALLER
  http://www.insolwwb.net/~rholler/net.htm

- HOLLINGSWORTH—A Genealogy in Progress
  http://homepages.rootsweb.com/~jayken/hollingsworth/hollindx.htm

- HOLLINGSWORTH Heritage
  http://home1.gte.net/edarrah/hollings.htm
  Hollingsworth family history, descendants of Valentine Hollingsworth, Sr.

- HOLLOWAY Genealogy Home Page
  http://www2.connectnet.com/users/markch/

- HOLT Genealogy and Family History Site
  http://www.holt.org

- HONEYMAN-Hunters
  http://www.islandnet.com/~gopher/honeyman.htm

- HONEYWELL Family Association
  http://members.aol.com/parkshoney/hfa.html

- HOOKER Families
  http://members.aol.com/bigtruffel/hooker.html
  A web site in support of the HOOKER family mail list includes reports of families being researched by list members.

- HOPKINS Clearing House
  http://members.tripod.com/~ahopkins/index.htm

- HORGAN Genealogy—Descendants—1830, MDX, ENG
  http://www.itmagic.demon.co.uk/genealogy/horgan.htm
  Descendants of David HORGAN (1839–1891) and Sarah LONG.

- HORINE Family History
  http://www.iwaynet.net/~lsci/horine/
  Descendants of Johann Tobias Horine (1725–1773).

- HORN Family Genealogy
  http://www.qni.com/~geo/horn.htm
  Descendants of David Llewellyn Horn.

- HORNBECK Hunters
  http://www.s-hornbeck.com/hunter.htm
  A clearing house for HORNBECK Hunters, queries.

- Warnaar HORNBECK (The Book) and Descendants of Warnaar HORNBECK Born c1645
  http://www.s-hornbeck.com/hornbeck.htm

- HOUSTON / HUSTON Association
  http://clanhuston.com/huston.htm
  News, History, and Queries for Descendants of Scotland & Ulster, affiliated with Clan McDonald.

- HOVEY Family Connections
  http://www.geocities.com/Heartland/Pointe/3480/index.html
  For all HOVEYs, especially descendants of Daniel Hovey of Ipswich, Massachusetts.

- HOWARD Family Electronic Newsletter
  http://ourworld.compuserve.com/homepages/Ramonyca_Howard/howardfa.htm

- The HOWARD Family Home Page
  http://home.att.net/~DHoward2/home.htm
  This site list date of birth, marriage, and death for members of the James Howard Family of Montgomery County, Virginia.

- The HOWARD Historian
  http://www.pcez.com/~howardh/

- HOWARD Surname
  http://homepages.rootsweb.com/~jclaytn/howard.html
  Howard surname: (GA>AL>TX).

- HOWE Surname Mailing List
  http://www.zekes.com/~dwells/howe.html
  Includes How.

- The HOWELL Connection
  http://members.tripod.com/~Sporn/index.html

- HOWERTON Heritage
  http://members.tripod.com/~JFHowerton/index.html

- The Descendants of William HUBBARD
  http://www5.pair.com/vtandrew/hubbard/hubbard.htm

- HUDNALL Family Association
  http://www.hudnall-family.com

- HUDSON Family Association
  http://members.tripod.com/HameLia/hfa.html

- HUDSONs of Amelia
  http://members.tripod.com/~HameLia/
  Descendants of Richard Hudson III, born about 1660, in Henrico County, Virginia.

- HUFF / HOUGH / HOFF Newsletter
  For details, e-mail Max Huff, Editor at mhuff@sccsi.com

- HUGHES Genealogy
  http://pages.prodigy.net/dave_lossos/hughes.htm

- HULME Family Newsletter
  http://www.avana.net/~amymws/hfn.htm

- HULSHIZER Heritage
  http://www.geocities.com/Heartland/Meadows/9332/
  Hulshizer, Hulsizer, Holshouser, Holtshouser.

- HUNGERFORD Great Hall
  http://www.escape.ca/~nthomas/hall.htm

- HUNSUCKER Family Genealogy
  http://www.geocities.com/Heartland/Ranch/8679/
  Hunsucker, Hunsicker, Huntzicker, Huntzinger, Hunsinger, Honaker, Hunsaker and all name variations.

- The HUNT Line Online
  http://www.genweb.net/~hunt/index.html

- HUNTList Website
  http://members.aol.com/huntlist/index.html

- HUNTINGTON Family Association
  http://www.huntington.tierranet.com

- HURLBUT—HURLBURT Genealogy
  http://www.idsonline.com/userweb/hurlburt/
  The descendants of Thomas Hurlbut who came to America about the year 1630.

- Wills of John and Mary HUTCHERSON— Harrison Co., KY
  http://members.aol.com/jogt/hutch.htm
  Formerly of Spotsylvania Co., Virginia.

- HUXTABLE Family Research
  http://www.st.net.au/~dunn/huxtable.htm
  Huxtable, Hokestaple, Hosestaple, Hucstapull, Hukestabull, Hucstapyll. Huxtable = "a spur of land with a post."

- HYLAND Family, Cork/Tipperary, Ireland
  http://www.hylit.com/info/Genealogy/Hyland.html
  A genealogy of the Hyland family of North Cork, Ireland. Other variants of the Hyland name: O'Faolain, Whelan, Phelan.

◆ Surnames Beginning with "I"

- Family Tree Maker Online User Home Pages—I
  http://www.familytreemaker.com/users/i/index.html

- Genealogy's Most Wanted—Surnames Beginning with "I"
  http://www.citynet.net/mostwanted/i.htm

- H-GIG Surname Registry—Surnames Beginning I
  http://www.ucr.edu/h-gig/surdata/surname9.html

- Higginson Book Company—Surnames Beginning with I
  http://www.higginsonbooks.com/i.htm

- inGeneas Table of Common Surname Variations and Surname Misspellings—H–J
  http://www.ingeneas.com/H2J.html

- Surname Springboard Index—I
  http://www.geocities.com/~alacy/spring_i.htm

- SurnameWeb Surname Registry—I Index
  http://www.surnameweb.org/registry/i.htm

- Genealogy Resources on the Internet—"I" Surname Mailing Lists
  http://members.aol.com/gfsjohnf/gen_mail_surnames-ij.html
  This site is wonderfully maintained by John Fuller. It includes mailing list information for the following surnames and their variant spellings:
  ICENOGLE (includes Eisennagel), INGALLS (includes Engolls, Ingolls, Ingals), INGERSOLL (includes Ingerson, Ingersole, Ingersol), INGRAM (includes Ingraham, Ingrahame, Ingrams), INMAN (includes Innman, Inmann, Hinman), IRELAN (includes Ireland), IRVIN (includes Irvine, Irving), ISAACS (includes Isacks, Isaacks), ISBELL (includes Isbel, Isabell), ISENBERG (includes Eisenberg), ISLEY (includes Iseley, Iseli, Sele, Icely), ITTERMANN (includes Itterman), IVIE (includes Ivey, Ivy), IZATT (includes Isatt, Iset, Izet).

- ICENOGLE Genealogy
  http://www.cswnet.com/~bbarnes/Icenogle.htm
  A web site for Eisennagel, Icenogle, Isnogle, etc. genealogy.

- deYgolvyndenne—a.k.a The Most Mispelled Name In History
  http://users.uniserve.com/~wiggulde/iggs.htm
  Today: IGGULDEN, IGGLESDEN, IGGLEDEN and EGGLEDEN.

- Descendants of William IMUS
  http://www.parsonstech.com/genealogy/trees/rdwyer/imus%20fam.htm
  Lineage of the Imus family in America.

- INGERSOLL Family Genealogy Research
  http://www.ingersoll.net

- The INMAN Compendium
  http://www.surnameweb.org/centers/i/inman/index.htm
  Inman, Inmon

- INMAN Genealogical Database
  http://www.rootsweb.com/~gumby/genweb/Inman/Inman.html
  A database that contains 1,001 names.

- Descendants of Andrew and Anna IRION
  http://members.aol.com/sherryew/Irion/Fam00072.html
  Ancestry and descendants of Andrew J. and Anna K. (ZELLER) IRION of Brittheim, Wurtemburg, Germany. Surnames include: WAGNER, WURM, OTTO, SCHMIDT.

- The ISELI Family Web Site
  http://iseli.simplenet.com
  ESELI, ESELY, ESLEY, ISALY, ISELI, ISELY, ISLEY, & ISLIE in America. ISEL, IZEL, YSELLE, YSELI, & YSSEL in South Africa.

◆ Surnames Beginning with "J"

- Family Tree Maker Online User Home Pages—J
  http://www.familytreemaker.com/users/j/index.html

- Genealogy's Most Wanted—Surnames Beginning with "J"
  http://www.citynet.net/mostwanted/j.htm

- H-GIG Surname Registry—Surnames Beginning J
  http://www.ucr.edu/h-gig/surdata/surname10.html

- Higginson Book Company—Surnames Beginning with J
  http://www.higginsonbooks.com/j.htm

- inGeneas Table of Common Surname Variations and Surname Misspellings—H–J
  http://www.ingeneas.com/H2J.html

- Surname Springboard Index—J
  http://www.geocities.com/~alacy/spring_j.htm

- SurnameWeb Surname Registry—J Index
  http://www.surnameweb.org/registry/j.htm

- Genealogy Resources on the Internet—"J" Surname Mailing Lists
  http://members.aol.com/gfsjohnf/gen_mail_surnames-ij.html
  This site is wonderfully maintained by John Fuller. It includes mailing list information for the following surnames and their variant spellings:
  JACKSON, JACO, JACOBS, JAGGARD (includes Jagger, Jagard), JAMES (includes Jamison, Jimeson, Jameson, Jamieson, Hymeson, Jomes, Jame, Jamie, Chameson, Hameson,

Iameson, Gunn, Games, Chames, Jacobs, Gemison), JAMESON (includes Jamieson, Jamison, Jamerson, Jemmison, Jemmerson, Jimerson), JANES (includes Jaynes), JARRELL-L (includes Garrell, Jerrell, Jarriel), JARRETT (includes Jerrett, Jarret, Jaret), JARVIS, JASTER, JAY, JEFFERS (includes Jeffres, Jefferis, Jeffords), JEFFERSON, JEFFREY (includes Jeffery), JENKINS, JENNINGS, JEPHSON (includes Jepson), JERNIGAN (includes Journagen, Jarnigan, Churnigan, Kernican, Gernikan), JERRETT, JESSEE (includes Jesse, Jessie, Jessy), JETTON (includes Jeton, Gitton), JEWELL (includes Jule, Juell), JEWETT, JOBE (includes Job, Jobes), JOHN (includes Johns), JOHNSON (includes Johnston, Jonson, Jonsen, Johanson), JOHNSON (descendants of Thomas H. Johnson (c/a 1759–1835), founder of Johnson County, Tennessee), JOINER (includes Joyner), JONES, JOPLIN (includes Jopling), JORDAN (includes Jardon, Jerden, Jerdon, Jorden, Jordon, Jourdan, Jourden, Jourdon, Jourdain), JOSLIN, JOYCE, JUDSON, JUHL (includes Juul, Jul, Jewell), JUNGCK (includes Jungk, Jung, Youngck, Yungck, Young), JURY, JUSTICE (includes Justis, Justus, Justiss, Gustafsson).

- **JACKSON Brigade Association, Inc.**
  http://www.eg.bucknell.edu/~hyde/jackson/
  Genealogical Association for Descendants of John JACKSON (1715–1801). The purpose of the Jackson Brigade Association, Inc. is to research, preserve and exchange genealogical information about the family in the United States who are descendants of John and Elizabeth (Cummins) Jackson; and to strengthen family ties.

- **The JAMES Family Web Site— JAMES Surname Web**
  http://www.rootsweb.com/~daisy/jameskin.htm

- **Descendants of Jonas and Stina JANSSON**
  http://www.ndepot.com/jansson/
  Jonas born May 6, 1820 in Syltebacka, Brålanda Sweden and Stina born November 23, 1823 in adjacent Kjelleberg, Brålanda Sweden. They emigrated to the US (ultimately Nicollet County, MN) in 1865.

- **JARMAN Genealogy & Family History**
  http://www.inct.net/~german/
  JARMAN, JARMON, GERMAN, GEARMAN, JERMAN families of North Carolina, Tennessee or the lower South.

- **The JAYCOCK Family Tree**
  http://members.home.net/mpjaycock/tree.html
  Research for the name Jaycock in Canada and the UK. Also Jeacock.

- **The JELBERT Society**
  http://www.boswarva.demon.co.uk/jelbsoc.html

- **JENKS Genealogy Center**
  http://members.aol.com/JenksNews/index.html
  Jenks, Jenkes, Jenckes, Jenques, Gynkes, Jinks, Janks, Jankes.

- **Anders JENSEN from Aalborg, Denmark**
  http://www.st.net.au/~dunn/jensen.htm

- **JERNIGAN Family Home Page**
  http://members.aol.com/jernigan01/homepg1.htm
  Some of the spellings include Jarnagan, Jarnegan, Jannikin, Janagen, Jernagan, Jonikan, Johnikin, Jonikin, Journagan, Jernegan, Jermegan, Jonerkin, Jernican, Jurnigan, Gernigan, Jerningham, Jarningham, and so on.

- **History and Family Tree of John JEWELL**
  http://www.dcscomp.com.au/jewell/family-history/
  His Ancestors in Cornwall and his Descendants in Australia 1567–1996.

- **JICKLING Connection**
  http://members.aol.com/famhistbuf/jickling.htm
  Jickling and variant spellings, any time and any place. Family newsletter (by e-mail or snail) and family directory.

- **The Acadian JOHNSON Association / Association Des JOHNSON D'acadie**
  http://www.geocities.com/BourbonStreet/5102/index.html

- **The A.D. JOHNSON Family Association**
  http://users.penn.com/~rbt/index.html

- **Descendants of William JOHNSON Sr.**
  http://www.netins.net/showcase/vbciowa/genie/Johnson/Johnson.htm
  Born Dec. 17, 1789 in Dauphin Co., PA. Died Sept. 23, 1845 in Van Buren Co., IA.

- **The JOHNSON Page**
  http://www.geocities.com/Heartland/Plains/7614/johnson.htm
  A resource of the Johnson Mailing List. Johnson, Johnston, Johansen, Johanson, Johansson, Johnsen, Jonsen, Jonson, Johnstone, Johnstoune, Jansen, Jansson, Janssen, Jenson, Jeansonne, Jodneston.

- **Descendants of Eli JOHNSTON**
  http://www.nextek.net/djohnson/swartz.htm
  The Johnston Genealogy in Ohio beginning with Eli Johnston who died in 1841 in Butler County, Ohio. The Johnston surname was changed to Johnson in the mid 1850s. Surnames: JOHNSTON, JOHNSON, TERRY, MERCER, HANBY.

- **JOHNSTON Clan History & Scottish Links**
  http://members.aol.com/ntgen/taylor/jnstnhistory.html

- **Clan JOHNSTON/E Association of Australia**
  http://www.felglow.com.au/webpgs/valdes/index.htm
  Society for all, JOHNSTON, JOHNSTONE, and JOHNSTOUNE in Australia and New Zealand. Has genealogical officer and maintains a one-name database.

- **The Clan JOHNSTONE Heritage Page**
  http://home.eznet.net/~jeff/clan.html

- **JOINER / JOYNER One Name Study**
  http://homepages.enterprise.net/pjoiner/joiner/joiner.html

- **JOPLIN Surname Mailing List**
  http://www.geocities.com/~fannincounty/joplin-jingles.html
  Includes Jopling.

- **JUDD Family Home Page**
  http://www.rootsweb.com/~takelley/judd/judd.htm

- **The JUDKINS Family Association**
  http://users.aol.com/judkinsfa/judkins.htm

- **The JUDSON Connection**
  http://www.geocities.com/TheTropics/1926/judson.html

- **JUETT / JOUETT / JEWETT Family**
  http://www.mindspring.com/~jogt/surnames/juett.htm

- **JUNOD Généalogie—Lignières—Neuchâtel—Suisse**
  http://www.junod.ch/
  Genealogy and history of the JUNOD from Neuchâtel, Switzerland since the 15th century, including emigration to the USA.

◆ Surnames Beginning with "K"

- Family Tree Maker Online User Home Pages—K
  http://www.familytreemaker.com/users/k/index.html

- Genealogy's Most Wanted—Surnames Beginning with "K"
  http://www.citynet.net/mostwanted/k.htm

- H-GIG Surname Registry—Surnames Beginning K
  http://www.ucr.edu/h-gig/surdata/surname11.html

- Higginson Book Company—Surnames Beginning with K
  http://www.higginsonbooks.com/k.htm

- inGeneas Table of Common Surname Variations and Surname Misspellings—K–L
  http://www.ingeneas.com/K2L.html

- Surname Springboard Index—K
  http://www.geocities.com/~alacy/spring_k.htm

- SurnameWeb Surname Registry—K Index
  http://www.surnameweb.org/registry/k.htm

- Genealogy Resources on the Internet—"K" Surname Mailing Lists
  http://members.aol.com/gfsjohnf/gen_mail_surnames-k.html
  This site is wonderfully maintained by John Fuller. It includes mailing list information for the following surnames and their variant spellings:
  KALER (includes Kalor, Kaylor, Kayler), KANGASfamily, KARBOWSKI (includes Karbowsky, Karboski, Karbosky, Carboski), KARDA, KARP (includes Carp, Karpinski, Karpelenko), KASTNER (includes Castner, Cassner, Kassner, Cosner, Cossner, Costner), KEALY, KEARNS, KEATING (includes Keaton, Keeting), KEECH (includes Keach, Ketch), KEENER (includes Canor, Keehner, Keinar, Keiner, Kienar, Kiener, Kuehner, Kyhner, Kyner), KEETER (includes Keiter), KEFFER (includes Kieffer), KEGLEY, KEIM (includes Kime, Kimes, Koyme, Kymes, Kaim, Keym, Kiehm, Kimery), KEISTER, KEITH, KEITHLEY (includes Keithly, Keathley, Keathly), KELCH (includes Keltch, Koelsch), KELLAM (includes Killam, Kilham, Kellum), KELLETT (includes Kellet, Kellitt), KELLEY (includes Kelly, O'Kelly), KELLOGG, KELSEY (includes Kelso, Kelsy, Kelly, Kelley), KEMMERER (includes Kammerer, Cammerer), KEMP, Kempers (includes Camper), KENDALL (includes Kindel, Kindell, Kindal, Kindall, Kindle), KENDERDINE (includes Kinderdine), KENNAMER (includes Kennemer, Kenimer, Kennemur), KENNEDY, KENNELLY (includes Kenealy, Kennealy), KENT (includes Kente, Cant, Cante, Kind, Kindt, Kint, Keent), KENTON, KENYON (includes Kinyon, Kenion, Kinion, Kennon), KEOUGH (includes Keogh, Kehoe), KERBOW (includes Kirbo, Kirbow, Kerbo, Kerbow, Curbo, Curbow, Cerbeaux, Carbaugh), KERN (includes Kerns, Kearn, Kearns, Karn, Karns), KERR (includes Ker, Carr), KERSEY (includes Keirsey, Kiersey), KESSLER (includes Kesler, Kepler), KIDD, KIFFER (includes Kifer), KIKER-LIST (includes Keicher, Kiger, Kyker, Cyger, Soundex K260), KILBY (includes Kilbey, Killbee), KILDAY, KILE (includes Keil), KILGORE, KILLIAN (includes Kilian, Killion), KILLINGSWORTH, KILROY, KIMBALL (includes Kimbell, Kimbrell, Kimble, Kemble, Kembold), KIMBERLIN (includes Kummerling, Kimberling), KIMMEL (includes Komel, Kummel), KINCAID (includes Kincade, Kincaide, Kinkade, Kinkaid, Kinkead, Kinket), KINCHEN, KING (includes Koenig), KINGSLEY (includes Kinsley, Kingseley), KINNEY (includes Keene, Keeney, Kenny, Kenney, Kinne, Kinnie, McKinney, Kinnear), KINNICK (includes Kennick), KINSMAN, KINTER, KINZER (includes Kintzer, Kinser, Kenser, Kincer, Kuntzer,

Ginter), KIPP (includes Kip, Kyp, de Kype, DeKype), KIRBY-KERBY, KIRKHAM, KIRKLAND, KIRKMAN (includes Kirchman), KIRKPATRICK (includes Kilpatrick), KIRTLEY (includes Kertly, Kertley, Kirtlett, Kirtly), KIRTON (includes Kerton, Kirkton, de Kirketon, Kirktoune, Kierton), KIRWIN (includes Kirwan, Kerwin, Curwin), KITCH (includes Kitsch, Kitszch, Kech, Kich), KLAGES, KLEINHENN, KLINCKE (includes Klimcke, Klinke, Klinkey, Clinky), KLINGENSMITH, KLUSMEYER (includes Klusmire, Klusmeijer), KNAPP (includes Knap, Knopp), KNAUER, KNIGHT-TIMES (includes Knight, Night, Knecht, Kniht), KNISLEY (includes Kneisley, Kniesley, Nisley, Nicley, Nissley), KNOTTS (includes Knott, Nott, Notts, Nutt), KNOWLTON, KOBEL (includes Coble), KOBERSTEIN (includes Coverstone), KOEHLER (includes Kohler, Köhler, Keller, Kahler, Culler, Kuehler, Kohlar, Koller, Von K"hler, Koellar, Caler, K"hler, Kähler, Callar, Kellar, Caller, Kellar, Calor, Kroehler, Caylor, Kailer, Kaler, Collar, Kalor, Kayler, Kaylor, Kohl, Kohle), KOENIG (includes Konig), KOOGLER (includes Kugler, Coogler), KOPP (includes Kob), KORNEGAY (includes Cornegay, Carnagee), KRAMER (includes Cramer, Krammer, Crammer, Kraemer, Craemer, Creamer, Kreamer, Kremer), KRAUS, KRIJGSMAN (includes Krijgsma, Krygsman), KRUEGER (includes Kruger, Krieger), KRUTSINGER (includes Cutsinger, Curtsinger, Krutzinger, Katsinger), KUEHL-L (includes Kühl), KUNEY, KUNKEL (includes Conkle, Gunkel, Kunkle, Kunckel, Gunckel, Konkel, Konkle, Kunkler, Kunkelmann, Kinkel, Conkel), KUYKENDALL (includes Van Kuykendaal, Kikendall, Kirkendall, Coykendall, Cuykendall), KYLE, KYLER.

- The KARBOWSKI(Y) Family Home Page
  http://www.rootsweb.com/~clifton/karbowsk/

- Clan K/CAVANAUGH
  http://incolor.inetnebr.com/aris3301/clan.htm
  and many variant spellings

- The KEAREY Clans
  http://www.ctv.es/USERS/kearey/

- KEATHLEY / KEITHLEY Genealogy
  http://webusers.anet-dfw.com/~skeath/
  Keathley, Keithley, Kethley or any other variant.

- The KEEFE Homepage
  http://www.keefe.org

- Highland Rim KEEN and Kin Family Newsletter
  KEEN, KEENE, KEAN, KEANE. The owner maintains a 75,000 name database, with the main areas of interest being in Virginia, North Carolina, Tennessee, Kentucky, Illinois, Indiana, Missouri and Arkansas. For details e-mail Edward Keen at ejkeen@juno.com

- KEENEY Genealogy
  http://www.keeney.net

- KEESLING Genealogy
  http://www.geocities.com/Heartland/Plains/3299/kegen.htm
  Kißling / Kisling / Kissling / Keesling

- The KEITH Genealogy Book Project
  http://pages.prodigy.com/KeithName/

- KEITHLEY Surname Mailing List
  http://www.rootsweb.com/~karen/keithley/
  Includes Keithly, Keathley, Keathly.

- KeithName
  http://pages.prodigy.com/KeithName
  KEITH, KEETH, KEATH, KIETH, KEYTH, etc., including genealogies in North America, the family's general history and clan notables in Scotland.

- KELLEY Heritage Quest
  http://members.aol.com/famlyfndr/kelley.htm
  KELLEY / KELLY Research Homepage.

- KELLEY / KELLY Family History
  http://www.geocities.com/Heartland/Estates/7201/
  Descendants of Moses Kelley/Kelly born 1754 in Maryland and served in the Revolutionary War.

- The Origins of the KELLOGG Family
  http://www.winternet.com/~rlkelog/KelloggHistory/History.html

- KELLY-CLAN of County Armagh, Northern Ireland
  http://www.kelly-clan.com
  A KELLY-CLAN web site to help all Kelly's / Kelley's of the world research their family line.

- KELTON Family HomePage
  http://rampages.onramp.net/~ekelton/index.html

- KEMP Family Association
  http://www.geocities.com/TheTropics/1926/

- KEMP Family Chronicles
  http://www.angelfire.com/in/genman/index.html
  Descendants of Nathaniel L. (Nathan) Kemp born ca. 1774 in North Carolina.

- KENDALL Families in New South Wales, Australia
  http://www.northnet.com.au/~kendalli/index.html
  Web pages for all KENDALL families who lived in New South Wales, Australia, from 1788 until 1888. Information has been extracted from the IGI, convicts records and the Blue Books of the colony 1788–1824. Much of the information is incomplete and requires additional work. Assistance greatly appreciated.

- KENNERLY Family Research
  http://home.earthlink.net/~kkenerly/kennerly.htm
  KENNERLY, KENERLY, KENNERLEY, KENERLEY and related Families.

- KENT Family Genealogy
  http://www.athens.net/~ethelind/genealogy/kent/kent.html
  Descendants of Thomas (1749–1835) and Ann(e) (Ralston) Kent of Ireland and Pennsylvania.

- The KENTON Kin Association
  http://www.rootsweb.com/~daisy/kenton.htm

- The KERCHEVAL Genealogy Homepage
  http://kercheval.simplenet.com
  Descendants of Samuel KERCHEVAL, Jr., born ca. 1720, of Virginia.

- KERCHNER Genealogy Home Page
  http://www.kalglo.com/kerchner.htm

- The KERN Genealogy Homepage
  http://www.enter.net/~stenlake/kern.html

- The Clan KERR Society
  http://www.tartans.com/clans/Kerr/society/society.html

- KERSEY Family Research Links
  http://www.halcyon.com/millerm/html/links.htm

- The KERSEY Page
  http://www.artwells.com/kersey/
  For the descendants of James KERSEY (1867–1960) and Sarah Jane LEIGH Kersey (1873–1936).

- Genealogy of the KETTLE Family
  http://www.altern8.demon.co.uk/anna/kettle/

- KIDD Konnections
  http://www.geocities.com/Heartland/Meadows/9710/

- KIDWELL Genealogy
  For details send e-mail to Marilyn Kidwell at 75467.64@compuserve.com

- KIGER Kounter Newsletter
  For the surnames KIGER, KYGER, KIKER, and GEIGER. E-mail Joan Young for details at JYoung6180@AOL.COM

- KILBOURNE Genealogy Home Page
  http://www.paonline.com/csanders/Kilborn/RR_TOC.htm
  Descendants of Richard Kylborn. Particularly the Michigan and Pennsylvania branches.

- Pages for List for Genealogy of KILIANs, KILLIANs, KILLIONs, ...
  http://www.genealogy.org/~green/Killian.html

- The KILLION / KILLIAN Genealogy Page
  http://www.mcs.net/~shs/killion.html
  Focusing on Irish descent.

- KIMBALL Genealogy Online
  http://www.kimbell.org
  KIMBALL, KIMBELL, KIMBRELL, KIMBRIEL, KIMBLE, and KEMBLE.

- The KIMMEL Family Record
  http://home1.gte.net/kimmel/genealogy.htm
  For Kimmel, Kimmell, Kimel, Kimmal, Kummel, Keehmle surname variations.

- The KINCAID Researcher
  http://www.alphalink.com.au/~kincaidr/
  For Kincaid, Kincade, Kinkade, Kinkead, Kinket, etc.

- KINNEY Family Genealogy Page
  http://www.greggkinney.com/

- KINNEY Genealogy Odds and Ends
  http://www.geocities.com/Heartland/Meadows/5699/kinney.html

- The KINNICK Project
  http://cadvantage.com/~vision2a/kinnick.html

- The Association of the Descendants of John and Tabitha KIRK
  http://www.cleverlink.com/kirk/

- The House of KIRKPATRICK International Association
  http://members.tripod.com/~PPPat/index.html

- KIRKPATRICK Genealogy Web Page
  http://www.geocities.com/heartland/6540/
  And related families of Kilpatrick and Gilpatrick.

- KIRKPATRICK Historical Newsletter
  E-mail Ann Kirkpatrick Hull at IMAKSICKAR@aol.com for details.

- KIRK Society Web Page
  http://www.digiserve.co.uk/kirk/kirksoc.htm
  Including variant spellings: Kirk, Kirke, Kyrke, Kircke, Kyrcke, Cirk, Cirke, Cyrke, Kircke...

- KIRTON On The Web
  http://homepages.enterprise.net/kirton/

- Michael & Mary KISER of Virginia
  http://www.geocities.com/Heartland/Hills/6359/kiser/kiser.html
  They and their ten children came to the Shenandoah Valley of Virginia in about 1783.

- Will of Peter KIVETT
  http://members.aol.com/jogt/kivettwl.htm

- KLEINECKE Family
  http://www.wf.net/~billk/Kleinecke.html
  Descendants of Charles Fritz KLEINECKE and Mary Henrietta HOENIS.

- Genealogy for KLEINS—KLINES—CLINES
  http://www.genealogy.org/~yoderj/

- KLÖPFER, KLOEPFER, and KLEOPFER Genealogy
  http://members.aol.com/Rdkone/Kleopfer.html

- KNEE One-Name Study
  http://homepages.nildram.co.uk/~kneearch/HomeHTM.html
  Including some instances of Nee, Kne, Kney, Ney.

- KNICKERBOCKER Family Home Page
  http://www.knic.com

- KNOWLTON Genealogy Home Page
  http://www.benetech.com/knowlton/
  A collaborative effort of the members of the mailing list.

- COBERNUS, KOBERNUS, KOBERNUSS, KOBERNUSZ Family Home Page
  http://members.aol.com/gkobernus/index.html

- The KOLODNY Family World Page
  http://www.geocities.com/~kolodny/

- KONVALINKA Home Page
  http://ourworld.compuserve.com/homepages/jkonvalinka/

- Home (Page) of the KRÄHENBÜHL Family
  http://www.vianet.net.au/~kraybill/kraybill.htm
  Kraehenbuehl, Krähenbühl, Kreienbuhl, Kraybill, Krabill, Krebill, Krebiel, Krehbiel, Graybill, Grabill, Crabill and others.

- KRAMER Genealogy Page
  http://www.sentex.net/~kramer/genealogy/
  Krämer—Kramer—Krammer—Kraemer—Kremer—Kremmer—CrÄmer—Cramer—Crammer—Craemer—Cremer—Cremmer.

- Genealogical Data and Genealogy of the KRAUTWURST Family
  http://home.eznet.net/~larryn/
  Descendants of Martin Krautwurst of Groß-Breitenbach in Thuringia, Germany, 1515.

- The KUCHARIK Connection
  http://pages.prodigy.com/kucharik/

- KUEHL / KÜHL Connections
  http://www.rootsweb.com/~wiwood/MAK-roots/Kuehl/s-kuehl.htm

- KUHN Kuzns
  http://ladyecloud.hypermart.net/Kuhn.htm
  Coon, Cune, Koon, Kuehn, Kunz, Koonse, Koontz, Kuntz and other variations.

- The KUHRING Family's Homepage
  http://ourworld.compuserve.com/homepages/annette_c_jost/
  KURING, KUHRICK, CHURING

- The KUNKEL-KUNKLE-CONKLE-GUNKEL "Spindle" Family Genealogy Newsletter
  http://www.flash.net/~conkle/INDEX.HTM

- KUNZE Family Home Page
  http://www.ghgcorp.com/smutchler/genek.html
  The KUNZE family is of New York City, and Brooklyn areas.

- The KUYKENDALL Genealogy Page
  http://w3.gorge.net/forest/
  Coykendall, Kirkendall, Keykendall, Kikendall, Cuykendall, Kuykindolph, Kirkendol, Curkendall, Kuyrkendall, Kuykendal.

◆ Surnames Beginning with "L"

- Family Tree Maker Online User Home Pages—L
  http://www.familytreemaker.com/users/l/index.html

- Genealogy's Most Wanted—Surnames Beginning with "L"
  http://www.citynet.net/mostwanted/l.htm

- H-GIG Surname Registry—Surnames Beginning L
  http://www.ucr.edu/h-gig/surdata/surname12.html

- Higginson Book Company—Surnames Beginning with L
  http://www.higginsonbooks.com/l.htm

- inGeneas Table of Common Surname Variations and Surname Misspellings—K–L
  http://www.ingeneas.com/K2L.html

- Surname Springboard Index—L
  http://www.geocities.com/~alacy/spring_l.htm

- SurnameWeb Surname Registry—L Index
  http://www.surnameweb.org/registry/l.htm

- Genealogy Resources on the Internet—"L" Surname Mailing Lists
  http://members.aol.com/gfsjohnf/gen_mail_surnames-l.html
  This site is wonderfully maintained by John Fuller. It includes mailing list information for the following surnames and their variant spellings:
  LABERGE, LABOYTEAUX (includes LaBerteaux, Laboyteau, Labertew, LeBoiteaux, Le Boyteulx, Boiteau, Boiteaux, Petue), LACY (includes Lacey, De Lacy), LADD, LAFFERTY (includes Laferty, Laverty), LAFFOON-L, LAFONTAINE (includes Lariou dit Lafontaine), LAIB (includes Laible, Laibach), LAIRD (includes Lard, Leard), LALONDE (includes De Lalonde, D'aoust), LAMB, LAMBERT (includes Lambeth), LAMBERTON, Lambgenealogy, LAMPKIN (includes Lamkin), LANCASTERGen, LANDON (includes Landen, Langden,

Langdon), LANE, LANGEN, LANGFORD, LANGHORN (includes Langhorne), LANGILLE (includes Langel, Langile, Languilles), LANGLEY (includes Langly), LANGSTON (includes Langstone, Lankston), LANIER, LANNING (includes Laning), LANPHEAR (includes Lanphere, Lamphear, Lamphere), LANSDOWNE (includes Lansdown), LANSING, LANTRIP (includes Lanthrip, Lanthrop, Landtroop), LAPRADE, LARIMER (includes Larmore, Lorimer, Larimore, Larmer), LARRABEE (includes Laribee, Larabee, Laraby, Larobouy), LARUE, LARZELERE (includes Larzalere, Larzeilier), LASH (includes Lesh, Lasch), LASSITER (includes all Soundex Code L236 such as Laciter, Lasater, Lasseter, Lasster, Lester, Leister, Laycestre, Lyster, Luster), LATHAM (includes Lathem, Lathim, Lathom, Lathum, Laytham, Leatham, Leathem, Leathim, Leathom, Leathum, Letham, Leytham, Lapham), LATHROP (includes Lothrop, Lothropp), LATIMER (includes Lattimer, Latimore, Latimar), LATOURETTE (includes La Tourette, LaTourette, Laturett), LATTA (includes Latty, Latto, Lattea), LAUDERDALE, LAUGHLIN (includes O'Laughlin, MacLaughlin, Loughlin), Laughlin-L, LAUGHTON (includes Lawton), LAVALLEY (includes Lavalle, Lavallee, La Valley), LAWHORN (includes Lawhorne, Lowhorn, Lawhern, Lawhon, Laugherne, Lahon, Lahorn), LAWRENCE, LAWS (includes Law, Lawes), LAWSHAE, LAWSON, LAY, LAYZELL (includes Lazell, Lazsell, Layzsell, Laszelle, Laselle, Lascelles), LEACH (includes Leech, Leitch), LEATHERMAN (includes Lederman), LEDBETTER (includes Leedbetter, Leadbetter), LEDFORD (includes Lydford, Leadford), LEDLOW (includes Ledlowe, Ledloe, Ledlo, Leadlow, Letlow, Letloe, Letlo, Ludlow, Ludloe, Ludlo), LEE (includes Lea, O'Leahy, Leigh, Levy, Leay, Schlee, Ley), LEEMING, LEENET, LEEPER (includes Lieper, Leiper, Leaper), LEE-ROOTS, LEETE (includes Leet), LEGG (includes Legge), LEGGETT (includes Legat, Legate, Legatt, Legett, LeGett, LeGette, Legget, Leggette, Leggit, Leggitt, Liggett), LEHMAN (includes Lehmann, Layman, Lahman, Lemons, Lemmons, Lemon, Lemmon), LEHMANN_of_Alsace (includes Lehman, Layman, Laymon, Leeman), LEHNHERR, LEIMEISTER, LEMASTERS (includes Lemaster, Lamaster, Lamasters, Lemaitre), LEMLEY, LENT, LENTZ (includes Lence, Lance, Lantz), LENTZ-genealogy, LEONARD (includes Lowenart, Loweryd, Learned, Lernert, Lenhardt), LESAGE (includes LeSage, Le'Sage, Lesage', LaSage, Lasage, La'Sage, Lasage'), LESLIE (includes Lesley, Lessley), LETSON (includes Litson, Ledson, Lidson), LEUZE, LEVERICH (includes Leveridge), LEVESQUE, LEVINESS (includes LaViness, LaVigne, LeVines, Levines, Levine, LeVigne), LEWALLEN (includes Lewellen, Lieuallen, Llewellyn, Luallen), LEWIN, LEWIS, LHEUREUX (includes Lereau, L'Hereault, L'Herault, L'Heros, Lurix, Happy), LIENHARD, LIGHT, LIGON, LILLY (includes Lily, Lilie, Lylie), LIMOGESgenealogy (includes Lamarge, Lamudge, Lamugh, Lemoge, Lemoges, Lemogne), LINCOLN, LIND, LINDLEY, LINDSAY (includes Lindsey, Linsey), LINES-FAMILY (includes Line, Lyne, Lynes), LINTHICUM, LINTNER (includes Lindner, Lindtner), LIPPERTS, LIPSCOMB, LITCHFIELD (includes Lechfeild, Lechfeld, Lechfield, Leechfield, Lichfeild, Lichfield, Litchfeald, Litchfeeld, Litchfeild, Litchfelde, Litchfild), LITTLE (includes Littell, Littel, Litel, Lytel, Lytell, Lyttelle, Littelle, Lyttle, Lyttle), LITTLEFIELD-ROOTS, LITTLEFORD, LITTLEPAGE, LITTLETON, LITTRELL (includes Litteral, Literal, Luttrell), LIVERMORE, LIVINGSTON (includes Livingstone, Levingston), LOCKE (includes Lock), LOCKER (includes Locher), LOCKHART, LOCKWOOD (includes De Lockwood), LODEN, LOFTIN, LOGAN, LOGUE, LOKRIG (Lokrig Family Association members; includes Laughridge, Loachridge, Lochridge, Lockridge, Lorthridge, Lothridge, Lotridge, Lottridge, Loughridge, Loughrige), LOKRIG (general list; includes Laughridge, Loachridge, Lochridge, Lockridge, Lorthridge, Lothridge, Lotridge, Lottridge, Loughridge, Loughrige), LONG, LONGCORE (includes Longcor, Longcoure, Langhaar), LONGSTREET (includes Langestraet, Langstraat), LONGWELL (includes Longwill, Langwell, Langwall), LONSDALE, LOOKINGBILL (includes Luckenbell, Lukenbell, Luckenbill, Lookabell, Luckenbaugh), LOOMIS (includes Lummys,

Lummuys, Lummyus, Lomax), LOONEY (includes Luna, Lunney, Leeney, O'Looney), LOOPER, LORANCE (includes Lowrance), LORD, LORDS, LOTT (includes Lot, Lotte, Lote), LOVE, LOVEALL (includes Lovell, Lovall, Loval, Lovel), LOVEJOY, LOVELACE (includes Loveless, Lovlis, Lovlys, Lovlace), LOVETTE (includes Lovett, Lovet), LOVICK (includes Lovicke), LOVING (includes Lovin), LOWDEN (includes Loudoun, Louden, Lowdoun), LOWDER (includes Louder, Loudder, Lauder, Loder), LOWE (includes Low, Lo, Lough), LOWRY (includes Lowery, Lowrey), LOYD-LLOYD, LUCAS, LUCKY (includes Luckey, McLuckey, McLucky), LUCY (includes Luce, Lucey, Lossee), LUDDINGTON (includes Ludington), LUFBORROW, LUFSEY (includes Leavcy, Leivsay, Leivsey, Leofsiege, Leofsy, Levacy, Levesee, Levisee, Levsay, Lievsay, Lifsay, Lifsey, Lipsey, Litsey, Livasy, Livcey, Livecy, Livesa, Livesaly, Livesay, Livese, Liveseay, Liveseley, Livesey, Livesie, Livesley, Lively, Livesy, Livessay, Livesy, Livezay, Livezey, Livey, Liveze, Livezely, Livezey, Livezley, Livezly, Livezy, Lovcey, Lovci, Lovecey, Lovesay, Lovesee, Lovesey, Lovesy, Lufcy, Luffsey, Lufsey, Lyffsey), LUMBLEY (includes Lumley, Lumbey, Lumly, Lumby), LUMLEY, LUND (includes Lunn, Lunde), LUNDY, LUNSFORD (includes Lunceford, Lonsford, Lansford, Luntsford), LUSH (includes Lushe), LUSK (includes Loosk), LUTHER (includes Luter, Louther), LUTZINGER (includes Ledsinger, Litsinger, Schlessinger, Letsinger), LYKE (includes Leick, Like, Leich), LYKINS, LYNCH (includes Linch), LYNN-ROOTS, LYONS (includes Lyon), LYONS, JOHN, LYTTON (includes Litton, Litten, Letton).

- **LABADIE** Family Reunion
  http://members.aol.com/redwing386/labadie.html
  May 4th, 1997, Kalamazoo, Michigan.

- Les familles **LABROSSE** et Raymond
  http://www3.sympatico.ca/rlabrosse/

- Elton & Bonnie **LACEY**'s Family Homepage
  http://homepages.rootsweb.com/~elacey/

- The **LACOMBE** Page
  http://cpcug.org/user/jlacombe/index.html

- **LADD** Digging Ground & Kentucky **LADD**'s
  http://www.geocities.com/Heartland/Meadows/5807/

- La**FEVRE** Family Association
  http://home.earthlink.net/~rctwig/lafever.htm

- **LAIDMAN** One Name Study
  http://www.mharper36.demon.co.uk/laidmen.htm

- **LAIRD** Family, Carrick-on-Shannon, Leitrim, Ireland
  http://www.hylit.com/info/Genealogy/Laird.html
  A genealogy of the Laird family of Killukin, Roscommon (near Carrick-on-Shannon, Co. Leitrim, Ireland), starting around 1730.

- The **LAMBERT** Family Archive and Home Pages
  http://www.motor-software.co.uk/home/

- The **LAMBERTUS** Family Homepage
  http://netrover.com/~brilamb
  Genealogy of the Lambertus family, who came to Canada in 1835, from the southern regions of Germany.

- **LAMBRECHTSEN** Online
  http://utopia.knoware.nl/users/evim/index.html
  Netherlands. Joos Lambrechtsen, born November 9, 1597 in Petegem near Deinze in East-Flanders.

- Clan LAMONT Society of North America
  http://www.jps.net/ogdenj/lamont/lamont.htm
  Information on the Scottish clan Lamont, its septs, and its modern clan societies in the U.S., Canada, Australia, and Scotland.

- LAMPERT Home Page
  http://www.lamperts.com
  Descendants of Jacob R. Lampert, immigrated from Flasch, Switzerland in the 1800's.

- Genealogical Office LAMPING Family
  http://www.lamping.demon.nl/genea/
  Descendants of LAMPING, LAMPINK and LAMBING. German & Dutch roots.

- LAMPSON WITMUS Family Organization
  http://ww2.sd.cybernex.net/~pawalker/lampwit.html
  For descendants of William LAMPSON, born 1761 in Boston, Mass. and Wilhelm WITTMUETZ born 1799 in Ruegen Island, Germany.

- LANE Descendants
  http://www.genweb.net/~bowers/lane/index.shtml

- Descendants of # 1 Pieter LANGEDIJK
  http://www.parsonstech.com/genealogy/trees/jlangedi/LANGEDIJ.htm

- LANGILLE Family Homepage
  http://www.geocities.com/Heartland/Plains/7525/langille.htm
  Descendants of Daniel Langille & Annie France Brandt born in 1687 & 1689 in Montbeliard.

- LANGMACHER Surname Project
  http://members.xoom.com/tsterkel/surname_projects/langmach.htm

- LANIGAN Family History, Waterford, Cork, Ireland
  http://www.hylit.com/info/Genealogy/Lanigan.html
  A genealogy of the Lanigan family of Waterford and then of Cork, Ireland.

- LANTY Genealogy and Literature
  http://members.tripod.com/~lanty/index.html
  Research into the Lanty name in genealogy, literature, geography, and race horse names.

- Laporte dit St-Georges Family Association
  E-mail Baxter D. LaPorte for more information at: baxter@total.net

- LAQUE Genealogy Home Page
  http://www.familytreemaker.com/users/r/o/b/Linda-G-Robin/index.html

- LARBALESTIER Family Home Page
  http://www.angelfire.com/fl/larbalestier/index.html
  Channel Islands.

- LAREAU Family Online
  http://www.wavefront.com/~pjlareau/lareaufo.html

- The LAROCQUE Family of America Home Page
  http://www.easynet.on.ca/~larocque/laroc1e.htm
  Descendants of Philibert Couillaud de La Roque de Roquebrune who came to Canada in 1665 with the regiment of Carignan, from France.

- LASATER Lineages Newsletter
  For details send e-mail to Lucinda (Cindy) Olsen, editor and publisher, at CarlCindy2@aol.com

- The LATTA Genealogy Newsletter
  http://www.latta.org

- The LATTIN Notebook
  http://pages.prodigy.com/military/lattin.htm

- LAUBACH Family Association
  http://darkstar.icdc.com/~gordonl/

- LAUDENSLAGER Genealogy Home Page
  http://www.kalglo.com/laudslgr.htm

- The LAWRENCE One-Name Study
  http://home.sprynet.com/sprynet/lawren05/

- LAWSON One Name Study Home Page
  http://www.users.globalnet.co.uk/~gdl/lawson.htm

- John LAZELL / LASSELL of Hingham, Massachusetts abt. 1619–1700
  http://www.geocities.com/Heartland/Ranch/4750/

- LAKE and LEAKE Family Home Page
  http://www.dcfinc.com/genealogy/lakeleak.html
  Index to "Lake/Leake Newsletter." Projects in progress: Lake/Leake/Leek database. 1850 census extraction.

- The National Association of LEAVITT Families, Inc.
  http://pw2.netcom.com/~bayouboy/Entrance.html

- The 'Le COCQ' family of Alderney— Channel Islands
  http://www.guernsey.net/~genealogy/LeCocq/RR_TOC.htm

- Association des Familles LEDUC
  http://www.geocities.com/Heartland/5063/index.html

- LEE Genealogy—of English Descent
  http://www.geocities.com/Heartland/7748/

- Ye Olde LEE Genealogy
  http://LeeGenealogy.ofamerica.com

- La Généalogie des LEFEBVRE dit BOULANGER
  http://terminal1.mtl.net/~rboulan/

- La Généalogie de Sylvain LEFEBVRE et la Descendance de Pierre LEFEBVRE
  http://www.genieaudio.com/lefebvre/

- LEFTWICH Historical Association
  For details send e-mail to Patricia HUTSON at: sadie@gate.net

- The LEHNHERR Genealogy
  http://www.lehnherr.com/genealogy/

- LE NEUF Family Research Project
  http://habitant.org/leneuf/

- LESSARD Genealogy Home Page
  http://pages.prodigy.com/CUGF40A/
  Descendants of Louis (Paul) LESSARD Family from Chambois in lower Normandy, France.

- LETHER / LEETHER Family Genealogical Society
  http://www.presstige.nl/Genealogy/
  Netherlands

- 10 Generations of/de LÉVESQUE—Descendants of Robert LÉVESQUE
  http://www.geocities.com/Eureka/Plaza/4458/index2.html

- LEWIS Family Genealogical Resource
  http://www.lewisgenealogy.com
  Any Lewis research, particularly for descendants of John Lewis, Pioneer b. 1678 d. 1762.

- The LEWIS Family Newsletter
  http://pages.prodigy.com/jimlewis/

- LEWIS Lineages
  http://www.onlinepub.net/lewis.html

- The Descendants of Simon L'HÉRAULT dit L'HEUREUX
  http://www.concentric.net/~lheureux/genealogy/simon_lereau.html
  Simon L'HERAULT emigrated to Quebec in 1652 and is the ancestor of the L'HEUREUX, LEREAU, LEUREAU and LEVREAU families.

- LINDER Family Association
  E-mail: rumples949@aol.com
  For details, send e-mail to Bonnie Dailey at rumples949@aol.com

- LINDER Family Page
  http://www.serve.com/jitter/linder.htm
  Henry Pertle Linder (1830–1908).

- Clan LINDSAY Association, USA, Inc.
  http://www.odu.edu/~src/Lindsay/

- LINDSAY Family Newsletter
  For details e-mail Barbee Reid at BMReid92@aol.com

- Descendants of Col. John LINDSEY
  http://www.netins.net/showcase/vbciowa/genie/Lindsay/Lindsay.htm
  Born in 1725, died in 1785 or 1787 in South Carolina.

- LISTON—Worldwide One-Name Study
  http://liston.ourfamily.com

- George LITTLE Family Association
  http://www.execpc.com/~budtamms/glfa.htm
  A tailor on Unicorn Street (near London Bridge), came to America in 1640 and was one of the first settlers in Newbury, Massachusetts.

- The LITTLEFIELD Family Research Page
  http://www.eden.com/~gregandi/lfd.html
  The descendants of Edmund Littlefield of Wells, Maine.

- The LITTLEFIELD Genealogy Pages
  http://www.nis.za/homepgs/alittle/lfield.htm
  The descendants of Francis Littlefield and his son James Littlefield of Titchfield, Hampshire, UK.

- LIVINGSTON Family History
  http://www.geocities.com/Heartland/Estates/7131/
  Descendants of Henry Reed E. Livingston, born October 10, 1818 in Somerset County, Pennsylvania.

- LIVINGSTON Lines Newsletter
  http://ro.com/~ewhitten/

- The Family of Simon LOBDELL
  http://www.frii.com/~dougl/Genea/index.htm

- LOCKE Family Association
  http://www.tiac.net/users/dhayes/

- LOCKE Genealogy
  http://www.net1plus.com/users/locke/
  William Locke of Woburn, MA, 1628–1720.

- The LOGAN Letter
  http://pages.prodigy.com/TheLOGANLETTER/
  A newsletter based on Andrew LOGAN and his descendants.

- LOITERTON Family Homepage
  http://www.hinet.net.au/~jblstat/loitsearch.html

- The LOKRIG Family Association
  http://www.geocities.com/Heartland/Hills/8593/
  Genealogy research and exchange for all spellings of surnames sounding like Lokrig (Lockridge, Lochridge, Laughridge, Loughridge, Loughrige, Laughrige, Loachridge, Lorthridge, Lothridge, Lottridge, Lotridge, and any other variant).

- The Family LOKUCIEWSKI
  http://www.btinternet.com/~hydro.lek/lokuhome.htm
  From 1560, in Eastern Poland now part of Belarus/Lithuania/Poland.

- Descendants of Henry LONGCRIER, Sr.
  http://www.geocities.com/Heartland/Ranch/7402/

- David Uhrey's LONGFELLOW Connection
  http://www.geocities.com/heartland/ridge/6281
  Descendants of William Longfellow born 1679.

- LONGWELL, LONGWILL, LANGWELL, LANGRALL and Related Families
  http://www.familytreemaker.com/users/l/o/n/Laurie-M-Longwell/index.html

- Family Group Record of William Spencer LORDS
  http://www.lordsfamily.org/research/wslords/index.html
  Born 13 October 1820 at Alton, Penobscot, Maine.

- LOSOS Genealogy
  http://pages.prodigy.net/dave_lossos/losos.htm

- LOUWAGIE Genealogical Tree, From 1190 Till Today
  http://www.stleocol-bru.be/sl/loage.htm
  From Belgium. Lauage, Lauwagie, Lawaese, Lawaisse, Louage, Louagé, Louagie, Louwaege, Louwage and Lowagie.

- LOVELAND Family History
  http://www.tmcl.demon.co.uk/loveland/index.htm

- The LOVETT-LOVITT Genealogy Page
  http://www.gendex.com/users/clbates/lovitt/
  LOVETT/LOVITT (all areas, all lines), JAMES, RICHARDSON, McDONALD, McDANIEL. Includes census and other records for the Lovett surname.

- FREER / LOW Family Association
  http://home.earthlink.net/~rctwig/freer.htm

- LOWARY Home Page
  http://www.synapse.com/lowary/
  Dedicated to the Lowary, Lowery, Lowrey, Lowry, Loughry names and any other spelling variations.

- Keeping A LOWE Profile
  http://www.geocities.com/Heartland/Plains/2684/
  A genealogy newsletter for the LOWE surname including these variant spellings: Lowe, Low, Lough, Loe, Louw & Lau.

- LOWELL Genealogy
  http://www.interpath.net/~plowell/lowell.html
  Descendants of William LOWLE of Yardley in County Worcester, England. Born 1288, County Worcester, England.

- LOWMAN Family Genealogy
  http://www.feist.com/~slvwng/lowman.html
  Harvey County, Kansas.

- The LUCKY Tree
  http://www.rootsweb.com/~daisy/lucky.htm
  Descendants of William LUCKY and Nancy Ann PREWITT.

- LUCRAFT One-Name Study
  http://www.lucraft.demon.co.uk/
  Variants: LUCKRAFT, LUCCRAFT, LUCKARIFT, LOWCROFTE, LOCRAFT.

- Stéphane LUCE's Homepage
  http://www.multi-medias.ca/luce/
  The immigration of Phillippe LUCE from Jersey to Canada (1861).

- House of LUMSDEN Association
  http://wkweb4.cableinet.co.uk/donmanson/hofla.html

- LUNNY News Home Page
  http://homepage.dave-world.net/~lunny/

- Good Ol' Mountain News
  http://members.aol.com/bonessgt/GOMN.htm
  Dedicated to The LUNSFORD (and variants) All-Time, World-Wide Family Tree. LUNSFORD, LUNCFORD, LUNDSFORD and LUNCEFORD.

- LUTHER Surname Mailing List
  http://www.geocities.com/~fannincounty/luther-lines.html
  Includes Luter, Louther.

- LYNCH Genealogy
  http://www.qni.com/~geo/lynch.htm
  Descendants of Joshua W. Lynch, born 1790 in Maryland.

- LYNCH Home Page—LYNCH Family Association
  http://members.aol.com/lynchlinch/lynchlinch.html

- LYNN/LINN Lineage Quarterly
  http://www.geocities.com/Heartland/9723/

- LYNNs of Prince William Co., Virginia
  http://members.aol.com/lynnpwco/index.htm
  LYNN surname in Prince William Co., Virginia.

- John LYONS Genealogy
  http://www.aznet.net/~davidl/geneal/files/lyons001.htm
  John Lyons, born circa 1750; died circa 1834, St. Landry Parish, LA.

- The LYON(S) Families Association of America
  http://www.neca.com/~bclyon/lyon(s).htm

- WDC GenWeb—LYTTON Study Group
  http://www.primenet.com/~dlytton/wdc/lytton.html
  Lytton, Litton, Letton, Letten, Leyton, Litten, etc.

◆ Surnames Beginning with "M"

- Family Tree Maker Online User Home Pages—M
  http://www.familytreemaker.com/users/m/index.html

- Genealogy's Most Wanted—Surnames Beginning with "M"
  http://www.citynet.net/mostwanted/m.htm

- Genealogy's Most Wanted—Surnames Beginning with "Mc"
  http://www.citynet.net/mostwanted/mc.htm

- H-GIG Surname Registry—Surnames Beginning M
  http://www.ucr.edu/h-gig/surdata/surname13.html

- Higginson Book Company—Surnames Beginning with M
  http://www.higginsonbooks.com/m.htm

- inGeneas Table of Common Surname Variations and Surname Misspellings—M
  http://www.ingeneas.com/M.html

- Surname Springboard Index—M
  http://www.geocities.com/~alacy/spring_m.htm

- SurnameWeb Surname Registry—M Index
  http://www.surnameweb.org/registry/m.htm

- Genealogy Resources on the Internet—"M" Surname Mailing Lists
  http://members.aol.com/gfsjohnf/gen_mail_surnames-m.html
  This site is wonderfully maintained by John Fuller. It includes mailing list information for the following surnames and their variant spellings:
  MABE (includes Maib, Mayaab), MABRY (includes Mayberry, Marbury, Mabrie), MACARTHUR, MACFARLAND, MACKENZIE (includes MacKenzie, McKenzie, McKinzie, McKensie), MACKEY, MacQueen (includes McQueen), MACRAE (includes Ra, Rae, Rea optionally prefixed [Mac,Mc,M ,M'][C,K,G] or postfixed [i]th,w,y), MADDEN, MADDOCK-L (includes Maddix, Maddock, Maddocks, Maddox, Maddux, Mattix, Mattock, Mattocks, Mattox, Muddock, Muddox. Muttock, Muttox), MADDUXCousins (includes Maddox, Maddeaux, Maddocks, Mattocks, Madog), MADERAS (includes Madaris, Medearis, Medaris, McDarris), MADILL (includes Mac Dougall), MAGGARD (includes Maegert, Magot, Maggot, Maggott, Mackert), MAGILL (includes McGill), MAHON, MAJORS (includes Major, Magers), MALEY (includes Malley, Maly, Mayley, Mealey, Mealy, Mailey), MALIK, MALISH (includes Mehlish, Mehlisch, Malisch), MALONE (includes Maloney, Mahoney, Mallory, O'Malley, Molone), MALOWNEY (includes Maloney, Mullowney, Moloney, Mallowney, Malowny, Malowany), MANCILL, MANIS (includes Manes, Mannis, Manous, Manious, Mannis, Minus, Maines, Manas, Menis, Mannix, Manice, Mannice, Maniss, Manus, Magnus, McNamee, McName, Mennis, Maners, Manners), MANLEY (includes Manly, Mannley, any other M540 soundex variations), MANN (includes Man, Munn, Monn, Mahon, any other M500 soundex surname), MANN, MANNING, MAPLES, MARCHANT, MARJORIBANKS (includes Marchbank, Marchbanks, Marshbanks, Banks), MARKER (includes Maercker, Merker), MARKHAM (includes Marcum, Marcom, Markram, Markam), MARLATT/MALOTT/MELLOTT (includes Marlett, Merlette,

Melott, Melot), Marleyfamily, MARLOW (includes Marlowe), MARONEY (includes Moroney, Mulrooney, Murrowney, Marooney, Maroni, Murroney, O'Moroney), MARQUESS (includes Marquis, Marques), MARSEE (includes Marsie, Marsey, Marcie, Massa, Massey, Massy, Marcee, Marcey), MARSHALL, MARSTELLER (includes Mostoller, Marstiller, Masteller, Mosteller, Marstella), MARSTON (includes Marsden, Marsten, Marson), MARTELL, MARTENEY (includes Marteny, Marteeney, Marteeny, Martini, Mastery), MARTIN (includes Martyne, Maryte, Martyn, Martye, Martel, Morton, Martinez), Martin_family, MARVILL, MASHBURN, MASON, MASSEY (includes Massy), MASTERS (includes Master, Meschter, Meister, Maaster, Maestre), MASTERSON, MASTIN (includes Masten, Maston), MATHER, MATHESON (includes Mathieson, Mathison, Matheison, Mathewson), MATHIS (includes Mathes, Mathias, Matis, Mathys, Matthias), MATLOCK (includes Medlock, Meadloak, Midlott, Modluck), MATNEY (includes Mattingley, Matinglee, Matenle, Matinlee, Matinglee, Matingley, Matenler, Matteny, Mateney), MATTHEWS (includes Mathissen, Mathes, Matherson, Mathias, Marthaws), MATTINGLY (includes Mattenlee, Matteey, Matley, Matney from 1792–1817), MATTIX (includes Mattox, Maddox, Maddock), MATZ (includes Motts, Motz), MAULDIN (includes Mauldon, Maldin, Malden, Moldin, Molding, Maulding, Maulden, Mulden, Modlin, Madlin), MAUPIN, MAURER (includes Maurers, Mauer, Mower, Mowers), MAXEY, MAXWELL, MAY (includes Maye, Mays, Mayes, Mayhew, Mayhue, Mayberry, Mayflower), MAYFIELD (includes Mayfeldt), MAYNARD (includes Mainard, Mainord, Manard), MAYRAND (includes Merand, Merrand), McALINDEN (includes McLinden, Maclinden), McALLISTER (includes MacAlester, McAlister, Allister, Alester), McBRIDE, McCALL, McCALLUM (includes Malcolm, McCallum, McCollum, Collum), McCANDLESS/McCANDLISH (includes McCanles, McCanless, McCandliss, McCandlass, Chandless, Candish, M'Caunles, McCanlies, Quinlish, Quinlisk, O'Quinlish, Quinless), McCANN, McCARLEY, McCARTT (includes McCart, McKart), McCARTY (includes McArty, McCarthy), McClain (includes McCain, McCane), McCLANAHAN (includes McClenahan, McClenaghan), McCLENNEN (includes McLennan, McClennan), McCLINTOCK (includes McClintoch, McLintock, McClintick, McClintic, McLintick), McCLUNG (includes McClun, McClurg), McCLURE (includes McLure, McClurg, Clary, McCleary, McClaran, MacLarry), McCLURG, McCLUSKEY, McCOLLUM (includes McCallum, MacCollum, McCollom), McCOMBS (includes McComb, Macomb, McCoombs, Macoombs, McCombe, McCombes, Macomber, McComber, McCombie, McComas, Coombs), McCONLOUGH, McCORD (includes Corder, McCardell, Cardin, McGarr, McKord), McCORMICK (includes McCormack), McCOY (includes McKoy, McCoig, McKay), McCRACKEN (includes McCrackin), McCRAW (includes McGraw), McCUBBINS (includes MacCubbin, MacCubein, MakCubyn, MakCumbyn), McCULLEY (includes McCully), McCullough, McCUNE, McCURDY (includes Macurdy, McKirdy, MacKirdy, MacCurdy), McCUTCHEON, McDONALD, McDOW, McDowell (includes MacDowell, McDowel), mcelroy, McELWEE (includes McElway, McIlwee, McIlway), McENTEE (includes McAtee, McIntee, MacAtee, MacIntee, MacEntee, MacEtye), McEVER (includes McEvers, McEaver, McEavers, McIver, McIvers, McKeever, McKeevers, McCever, McCevers, McKeaver, McKeavers), McEWEN (includes MacEwen, McEwan, McEwin), McFADDIN (includes McFadden), McFAUL (includes McFall), McGEE (includes Mc Gee, MacGee, Mac Gee), McGEHEE (includes McGhee, Magee, Megee, Megehee), Mcgillivary, McGIMPSEY (includes McJimsey, McJimpsey, McGimsey), McGinnisGen, McGLAUGHON (includes McGlaun, McGlaughn), McGOVNEY (includes McGivney), McGOWAN (includes Magowan, MacGowan, McGowen, McGown, McGoune, O'Gowan, Smith, Smythe, McCown, McCowan), McGRAW, McGregor-L (includes MacGregor), McGREW, McGUIGAN, McGUIRE (includes Maguire, MacGuire, McQuire, MacQuire), McHONE (includes Mahone), McHUGH (includes McCue, MacHugh, MacCue, McKew,

McQue), McILVAINE (includes McIlvaine(e), McElvain(e), McElwain(e), McIlwain(e), Macelvaine, Mcelvany, Malven, Malvern, Malvin, McIlvane), McKAY, McKEAN, MCKEEL, McKEON (includes McKeown, McKeone), McKEY (includes McKay, McKee, McKie), McKINLEY, McKNELLY, McKNIGHT (includes MacKnight, McKnitt, McKnit), McKOWN (includes McKeown, McGowan), McLAUGHLIN, McLENDON-McCLENDON, McLEOD, McMAHON (includes McMahan, McMahen, McMachen, Mahon, Mahan), McMAINS (includes McMain, MacMain, McManis), McMASTER (includes McMasters, MacMaster, MacMasters), McMILLEN (includes MacMillen, M(a)cMillan, M(a)cMillon, M(a)cMullan, M(a)cMullon, M(a)cMullen, M(a)cMillian, M(a)cMellon), McMINN, McNABB (includes McKnab), McNEAL, McNeese, McNEILLY (includes McNeely, McNeily, McNeilley, McNeeley), McNEW (includes McKnew, MacNew, MacKnew), McNUTT, McPHAIL (includes McPhall, McFail, McFail), McQUEEN, McSPADDEN, McSWAIN-L, McTAGGART-s, McTURK (includes MacTurk), McWHORTER (includes McWhirter, McWherter, MacWhorter), McWILLIAMS (includes Micwilliams, Macwilliams, Mickwilliams, Mackwilliams), MEACHAM (includes Meecham, Meechum, Mecham, Mitchum, Mitcham), MEAD (includes Meade, Meady, Mede), MEADOR (includes Meadors), MEADOWS, MEDLEY, MEEHAN (includes Mehan, Meighan, Meighen), MEGER, MELLOTT, MELROSE (includes Mellrose, Milrose, Millrose, Malross), MELTON, Menapace, MENDENHALL, MERCER (includes Mercier, Messer), MEREDITH (includes Meredydd, Morgetiud, Merrilth), MERIWETHER (includes Merriweather, Merriwether, Meriweather), MERRILL (includes Merrell, Merils), MERRY, MESSENGER, METCALF, METHVIN (includes Methven), MICHAEL (includes Mikel, Michaels), MICHELS (includes Michaels), MIDDLEBROOKS, MIDDLETON, MIESS (includes Mease, Meece, Mehs, Musse), MIGHILL (includes McGill, MacGill), MIKELL, MILAM (includes Mileham, Milem, Mylem), MILAM-UK, MILLAN (includes Million, Millon, Milan), MILLER (includes Milner, Milnik, Muller, Hagermiller, Reimiller, Muiller, Mueller), Miller-name-jewish, MILLIGAN, MILLS, MILLS_William, MIMS (includes Mymmes, Mymms, Mimms, Minns), MINESINGER (includes Meinsinger, Meinzinger), MINIER (includes Manier, Minegar, Mynhier, Minear, Minniear, Minnir, Mineer, Menear, Mynheer, Menier), MINOR (includes Miner, Meinhert, Maynor, Minar, Minnear, Minherr), MINTON (includes Mintor, Mintern, Minthorn, Mintin, Minten, Mineton), MITCHELL (includes Michell, Mischel), MITCHELL, MITER (includes Mitter, Mitre), MOBLEY, MOCK-GEN-L (includes Mauk, Mauck, Mack, Macht, Mauch, Maught), MODLIN (includes Maudlin, Maudlen), MOE (includes Mow, LeMoe, Lemoux), MOFFITT (includes Moffett), MOLDT (includes Molt), MOLLETT (includes Mullett, Mollette), MOLSBERRY (includes Malsbury), MOLYNEUX (includes Mullinax, Mulnix, Mullenneaux, Molineux, Moliner, Molynes), MONCRIEF, MONEY (includes Monnett, Mooney), MONROE, MONTGOMERY (includes Montgolfier, Montague, McGomry), MOODY (includes Mooty), MOON (includes Moone, Mohun), MOONEY (includes Mainey, Meeny, Moony, O'Mooney), MOORE-L, MOORE-POLING, MOORE-research, MOORHEAD (includes Muirhead, Moorehead, Morehead, Morhead), MOREAU (includes Merau, Maureau, Maure, Moro, Moreaux, Moreault), MOREFIELD (includes Moorefield, Mofield), MOREHOUSE (includes Morhouse, Moorhouse), MORELOCK, MORFORD, MORGAN (includes Morgain, Ap Morgan, Rhys Morgan, Rose Morgan), MORLEY, MORNINGSTAR, MORRIS, MORRISON, MORRISSEY, MORROW, MORROW-KY, MORSE, MOSES (includes Moser, Moshe, Mosley, Moss, Mosher, Moseley), MOSEY, MOSHER (includes Mosier), MOUDY, MOUNT (includes Mounts), MOUSER, MOWERY (includes Mowry), MOYE (includes Moy), MUDD (includes Mud, Modh), MUGG, MULLEE (includes Malley, Molloy, Mulloy, Maillee, O'Mailaooha), MULLINS (includes Mullen, Mullens, Mullin, Mullinnex, Mullineaux), MULLIS, MUMFORD (includes Munford, Monfort, Momphard), MUNDAY, MUNN, MURDUCK-L (includes Murdock, Murdoch, Murdocke,

Murducke, Mardock, Merdock, Moorduck, Midduck),
MURNANE (includes Marnane), MURPHY (includes
Murphrey), MURPHY-ROOTS (includes O'Muracha, O'Murphy,
Murchoe, Morphy, MacMurrough, MacMurrough Kavanagh,
MacMurrow, Morrowson, Murrough, Morrough, Morrogh,
Murrow, Morrow, MacMurchy, Murchison), MURRAY (includes
Moray, Murrey, Murry, Murrie, Merry, Murrihy, MacMurry,
MacMorry, MacMorray, MacMurray, McMurray, MacMorrow,
Morrow, Currie, Curry, MacKilmurray, Kilmurry, Kilmary,
Kilmore, Gilmore), MUSE (includes Mewes, Mews, Muis),
MYATT (includes Miot, Miatt), MYERS (includes Myer, Meyers,
Meyer, Meier).

- McANINCH Family History Newsletter
  E-mail Frank McANINCH at FrankMac@worldnet.att.net for
  subscription & database details. For the surnames McAninch /
  McIninch /McNinch and variations.

- The Descendants of Patrick and Jane Greene
  McCAHAN
  http://www.adeptweb.com/mccahan/
  Patrick born March 14, 1766, about twenty miles north of
  Dublin, Ireland.

- West Virginia McCALLISTER Genealogy
  http://www.oklahoma.net/~davidm/
  Specializes in (but is not limited to) West Virginia McCallister
  genealogy lines. McCallister is generic for the various spellings
  such as McAlister, McAllister, McCalister, McCollister,
  McCallester, McCallaster, McCalaster, McAllaster, etc.

- The McCARLEY Genealogy Station
  http://members.aol.com/PipL7x3/index.html

- McCHRYSTAL, McCRYSTAL, McCRISTALL
  Surnames and All Variants
  E-mail John Hollis at John.Hollis@london-research.gov.uk and
  he will search his database for you.

- McCLANAHAN Time Online
  http://www.geocities.com/Heartland/Prairie/3895/

- McCLENDONs and McLENDONs—Genealogy:
  McCLENDONs and McLENDONs on the Internet
  http://www.users.mis.net/~patmc/mcclendo.html

- McCLOSKEY International Family
  http://www.hinet.net.au/~tedmac/macnet.htm

- The McCORD Family Association On-line
  http://mccord.home.mindspring.com

- McCULLAR Genealogy Page
  http://pages.prodigy.com/jmccullar/mccullar.htm
  Includes McCULLAR, McCULLARS, McCULLER,
  McCULLERS, McCULLOUGH.

- The Unofficial McCULLOUGH Family
  Genealogy Page
  http://members.aol.com/mcjill/index.html

- The McCUTCHAN Family Tree
  http://www.mccutchan.org

- McDANIEL Family of Maryland and Kentucky
  http://members.aol.com/jogt/mcdaniel.htm

- The McDONALD Family—Genealogy
  http://www.internet-partners.com/mcdonald/index.htm

- McGEE Surname Researchers
  http://www.geocities.com/Heartland/Prairie/3570/
  McGee, MacGee, Magee, McGhee, McGhie, McGahey,
  McGhee, MaGeeHee, McGeehan, McGahan and others.

- Clan McGINNIS Home Page
  http://users.why.net/wejr/Publish/
  Descendants of William Erasmus McGINNIS and Cora Pauline
  ENGLISH, 1865–1942.

- McGINNIS Genealogy
  http://ddi.digital.net/~hmcginni/McGinnis.html

- McGINNIS Genealogy Home Page
  http://members.tripod.com/~cheysmom/index.html
  Dedicated to descendants of William McGinnis and his wife
  Mary Micheltree and other McGinnis'.

- McGUIRT Genealogy Homepage
  http://cust.iamerica.net/aircom/mcguirt.html

- Clan McINTOSH
  http://www.mcintoshweb.com/clanmcintosh/main.asp

- McKINNEY Genealogy
  http://www.mckinneys.org

- McKINNEY / McKENNEY Family Miscellaneous
  Documents and Data
  http://www.mindspring.com/~jogt/surnames/mckendoc.htm

- Descendants of John McMAHAN, Jr.
  http://www.halcyon.com/jmashmun/mcmahan/index.html
  Born 23 May 1741 in County Cavan, Ireland.

- McMONEGAL of Westchester County and the
  Bronx, New York
  http://members.aol.com/popmick/mcmon.htm
  Descendants of John McMONEGAL, then Dominick
  McMONEGAL of Ireland.

- McNEESE / McNEES / McNIECE Family
  Genealogical Research
  http://www.mcneese.com

- McNELIS Genealogy Home Page
  http://www.personal.psu.edu/faculty/j/w/jwd6/mcnelis.htm
  McNellis, McNealus, McNeilis, McNeelis, McNail, McNaylis,
  McNealie, Mcneilly, McNealis, McNeil, McNeilis, McNelis,
  McNelus, McNolos.

- The Descendants of Paul McPHERSON 1734–1828
  of The King's 17th Foot Regiment
  http://www.geocities.com/Heartland/Prairie/8367/

- McQUEEN Surname Page
  http://home.earthlink.net/~mpdavis/gen/mcqueen.htm
  Including: McQuin, MacQuin, McQuinn, MacQuinn, McQuean,
  MacQuean and Queen.

- McSWAN Home Page
  http://www.durham.igs.net/~lmcswan
  Origins and lineage of the McSwan and MacSwans of Australia,
  Canada, England, Scotland and the United States.

- The Name McTURK or MacTURK
  http://home.clara.net/iainkerr/McTurk.htm

- McWH*RTER Genealogy
  http://pages.prodigy.com/mcwgen/
  *McWHORTER, McWHIRTER, McWHERTER, McWORTER,
  MEWHORTER, McQUIRTER, McQUARTER, MAWHORTER,
  MEWHIRTER, MEWHERTER, McQUERTER, McWHARTER,
  MAWHIRTER, etc.*

- MABRY Page
  http://www.execpc.com/~dcollins/mabry.html
  *For names: MABERY, MABERRY, MABRAY, MABREY, MABRY,
  MAYBERRY.*

- Genealogy: MABRY Relatives Plus Some Other
  Sources
  http://www.genealogy.org/~soccgs/census.html

- The MacARTHUR Family Tree Project
  http://www.web.netactive.co.za/~donmac/

- Clan MacCALLUM / MALCOLM Society
  http://www.sni.net/~dougm/ClanMacCallum/

- MacDERMOT Clan Association Homepage
  http://aoife.indigo.ie/~mcdermot/

- THORBURN-MACFIE Family Society
  http://home1.swipnet.se/~w-10723/thormac1.htm
  *Descendants of William Thorburn and his wife Jessy (née
  Macfie) who in July 1823 removed to Sweden from Leith in
  Scotland.*

- Unofficial M(a)cINTYRE Genealogy Homepage
  http://www.rpi.edu/~makowj/mcintyre.genie.html

- Clan MacKAY
  http://www.geocities.com/Heartland/Park/8030

- The MACK / MOCK Connection
  http://personal.mia.bellsouth.net/mia/t/m/tmock/connect.htm

- Clan MacKENZIE Society in the Americas
  E-mail: gwmckenz@freenet.mb.ca

- MacKNEW / McNEW
  http://www.geocities.com/Heartland/Ranch/1984/
  *Descendants of Jeremiah MacKNEW I who emigrated in 1668 to
  Charles County, MD.*

- Clan MacLACHLAN
  http://www.shirenet.com/MacLachlan

- The Descendants of James MacLACHLAN
  http://www5.pair.com/vtandrew/mcglauf/mcglauf.htm

- MADDOCK-L Surname Mailing List
  http://www.ikweb.com/murduck/genealogy/maddock-l/
  intro.htm
  *Includes Maddix, Maddock, Maddocks, Maddox, Maddux,
  Mattix, Mattock, Mattocks, Mattox, Muddock, Muddox. Muttock,
  Muttox.*

- The MADDOX Family
  http://www.tfs.net/~gbyron/kin/maddox.html
  *History to 500 a.d., 6000 names with photos and history of
  Maddox, Madoc, Maddux, Mattox, Maddock.*

- MADDUXCousins
  http://users.cwnet.com/maverik/
  *Descendants of Alexander Maddox, born 1613, arrived in
  Virginia 1635, died 1660. Variant spellings: Madawg, Madog,
  Maddeaux, Maddocks, Maddox, Maddux, Mattix, Mattocks,
  Mattox.*

- David MADER Family History
  http://www.jmts.com/mader/
  History of the David Mader Family in America.

- MAGNY Family Association
  http://home.earthlink.net/~rctwig/magny.htm

- MAGUIRE Clan
  http://users.uniserve.com/~makyta/welcome.html

- Our Irish Heritage of the Surname MAGUIRE
  http://www.cris.com/~Maguire/IndexIrish2.shtml

- MAHER (MEAGHER / MAHAR) Surname
  http://homepages.rootsweb.com/~maher/
  *Information for those researching the Maher, Meagher, Mahar
  (and variants) surname.*

- The MAINE Family Tree
  http://www.stlawu.edu/amai:http/gen1.htm
  *Descendants of Ezekiel MAINE, born 1641, York, Maine, died
  June 1714 in Stonington, Connecticut and Mary HATCH born
  03 Oct 1652 in Stonington.*

- MALEY Family Web Site
  http://www.maley.org

- MALOWNEY
  http://www.irishgenealogy.com/MALOWNEY.htm
  *Malonek, Maloney, Malowany, Malowny, Malowney, Mallowney,
  Moloney, Mullowney.*

- The Mandeville Newsletter
  *A quarterly newsletter devoted to the Mandeville family lines, all
  branches, any spelling variations (Mandeville, Manvil,
  Mandevil, D'Mandewijl, Manderville, Mandeviel, De
  Mandeville, Manterville, etc.). For details send e-mail to Sharon
  West at Shhhharon@aol.com*

- The MANGUM Family
  http://fly.hiwaay.net/~lparham/
  Mangham, Mangrum, Mangram, Mangun, Mangam, etc.

- The MANSKER Chronicles
  http://home.earthlink.net/~dmansker/
  *Descendants of Ludwig Mäintzger, from Germany to Philadel-
  phia in September of 1749. Mansker, Minsker, Mintsker, Mansco,
  Mesker, Meinzer, and all of the other variations on the family
  name.*

- MÄNTTÄRI Family Association Ltd.
  http://www.kolumbus.fi/manttari/home-pag/main.htm
  Finland

- Peter van MARKUS Homepage
  http://www.bART.nl/~pvmarkus/
  *From the Netherlands. Descendants of Pieter Louissen van
  Markus, married 1718 Catharina van Wijck.*

- MARR Family
  http://www.wf.net/~billk/Marr.html
  *Descendants of Martha Maria TAYLOR and Nathaniel Hancock
  MARR.*

- The MARSDEN Page
  http://ourworld.compuserve.com/homepages/johnmarsden/mars-1.htm

- Henry MARTIN of Cumberland County, VA (d. 1752)
  http://bladerunner.dartmouth.edu/~emily/H.Martin.html

- The MARTIN's
  http://www.angelfire.com/tx/lineage/index.html
  Documented history of William Martin VA>NC>SC>TN>MS.

- The MASTERS Family Association
  http://www.geocities.com/Heartland/Prairie/4153/

- Dan MATNEY and Allied Families
  http://www.angelfire.com/or/matney/

- The MAULE Family History Home Page
  http://www.maule.u-net.com/home~1.htm
  Maule, Mawl, Mall.

- MAULE Genealogy Homepage
  http://www.vcilp.org/~maule/maulehpg.htm

- MAUPIN Family
  http://www.geocities.com/Heartland/Bluffs/6987/
  Descendants of Gabriel Maupin and His Wife Marie Hersent of Gargeau, France; Amsterdam, Netherlands and Williamsburg, Virginia & Their Son Daniel Maupin and His Wife Margaret Via of Albemarle County, Virginia.

- MAYHEAD Family
  http://www.alan-rosie.demon.co.uk/
  Mayhead and variants, one name study—Mayhead, Mayhood, Madhead.

- MAYNARD Project
  http://www.wizard.net/~aldonna/maynard.htm
  Descendants of John Maynard of Sudbury, Massachusetts.

- M(E)AT(T)YE(A)R One Name Study
  http://home.clara.net/dchilds/mtyr-ons.html
  MATCHER, MATEAR/EER, MATHIAR, MATIER, MATTEAR, MATTIA, MATYE(A)R, MEA(T)CHER, MEATCHIER, MEATYE(A)R, ME(S/T)TAYER or Le METAYER, METIAR/ER/ OR, MET(T)YE(A)R.

- The MEDEIROS Home Page
  http://www.maui.net/~makule/medhome.html

- MEDERNACH
  http://gallery.uunet.lu/M.Brouwer/index.html
  The village Medernach or the name Medernach from Luxembourg.

- MEDLEY Surname Mailing List
  http://www.jas.net/~sueowens/meddir.htm

- The MELANSON / MELANCON / MALONSON / MALANSON Family Project.
  http://www.geocities.com/Heartland/Meadows/7961/

- MELLOR One Name Study
  http://ourworld.compuserve.com/homepages/mike_mellor_coventry/

- MENDENHALL Family Association
  http://www.mendenhall.org

- The MERIWETHER Society, Inc.
  http://members.aol.com/tmsimc/index.html
  Established by descendants of Nicholas Meriwether I (1631–1678).

- The MERRILL Newsletter
  http://www.netcom.com/~lilhall/merrill.html

- MERRILLs of Franklin County, MA
  http://www.bearhaven.com/merrills.htm

- Number of MERRILLs in the United States, 1850–1990
  http://www.bearhaven.com/family/merrill/p1850–1990.html

- Miles MERWIN Association
  http://www.merwin.org

- Genealogy of the MESERVE Family
  http://www.ultranet.com/~fmeserve/

- Messerville
  http://www.hci.net/~windsong/
  For the Messer surname, including the descendants of Captain "Robert" Messer.

- MESSINGER Family History: Immigrants in 1732 to Pennsylvania
  http://www.wyoming.com/~Carol/Messinger.shl
  Includes 8 generations of the descendants of Johannes and Elisabeth Messinger in PA, OH, IL and OR.

- The METCALFE Society
  http://www.metcalfe.org.uk/
  Home Page of the METCALFE Society devoted to researching the name Metcalfe and all its variants, including Medcalf, Metcoff and the like. Society was founded in the UK in 1980 and has more than 450 active members worldwide.

- Association des Familles MICHAUD, Inc.
  http://www.genealogie.org/famille/michaud/
  This site describes Michaud Families' Association, explain their Coat of Arms, gives highlights of ancestor Pierre Micheau's life in New France.

- The MIDDLEMISS Family, 1769–1996, From Berwick-on-Tweed to New Zealand
  http://home.clear.net.nz/pages/middlemiss/
  Descendants of Andrew MIDDLEMIST, born 1769 in Berwick On Tweed.

- MIDDLETON Home Page
  http://members.aol.com/donmid1/families/middletn.htm
  Descendants of James Middleton born 1750 died 1798 in Broadcreek Hundred, Sussex County, Delaware.

- MIDDLETON Queries
  http://home.earthlink.net/~middleton/query.html

- The Other MIDDLETON Home Page
  http://members.aol.com/srwings/middleton/middleton.htm
  Descendants & ancestors of John Andrew MIDDLETON born about 1833 in Virginia.

- The MIDGLEY Page
  http://home.earthlink.net/~petegm/index.html

- The MILAM Family History
  http://www.getnet.com/~rmwiv/milam.html

- MILLER Genealogy
  http://www.qni.com/~geo/miller.htm
  For the descendants of Reason Miller, born January 7, 1817.

- MILLESON Genealogy Home Page
  http://ourworld.compuserve.com/homepages/milleson/

- MILLS Ancestry
  http://www.geocities.com/Heartland/8496/
  Descendants, ancestors and allied families of the Mills of colonial New York and New England, as well as throughout the US and Canada to the present time.

- MILLS Musings
  http://ladyecloud.hypermart.net/Mills.htm

- The MITCHELL Family Association HomePage
  http://www.netcom.com/~lilhall/mitchellfamasn.html

- The MIXON / MIXSON Family Web Site
  http://www.lakelanier.com/mixons/index.htm

- MOBLEY Surname Home Page
  http://www.genealogy.org/~mobley/

- The MOCK Family Historian
  http://www.cybergate.com/~rmoore/mock.html

- MOCK-GEN-L Surname Mailing List
  http://home.ease.lsoft.com/archives/mock-gen-l.html
  Includes Mauk, Mauck, Mack, Macht, Mauch, Maught.

- MOFFITT Surname Mailing List
  http://www.sonic.net/~yvonne/moffitt.html
  Includes Moffett.

- The MOHLER Family Tree
  http://pw2.netcom.com/~mohlerl/lances.htm
  History of the Mohler family in the U.S., starting with Lancaster County, Pennsylvania.

- The Gathering of the MOHRs
  http://www.whitesite.com/mohr/
  Mohr, Moore, Maurer & Mowrer Genealogy.

- The Clan MONTGOMERY Society International
  http://www.geocities.com/Heartland/Acres/6070/index.htm

- The MONTGOMERY Family Home Page
  http://www3.sk.sympatico.ca/monta/

- MOORE-L Web Page
  http://www.rootsweb.com/~nozell/MOORE-L/

- MOORE News—A Weekly E-mail Newsletter
  Send e-mail to Joyce Browning at Jbrown7169@aol.com for details.

- MOORE-POLING Web Page
  http://www.zoomnet.net/~sllewis/moore/index.html
  Descendants of Daniel Moore, born abt 1760 and Deborah Poling, born 1774 in Virginia.

- MORAAL Family History
  http://come.to/moraal
  Tales and family trees from the Moraal family.

- Descendants of Andre MORIN and Marguerite MOREAU
  http://www.newnorth.net/~kind/morin.html
  Settled in Quebec around 1665 and married in 1670.

- Association des Familles MORISSETTE Inc.
  http://www.genealogie.org/famille/morissette/morissette.htm
  Quebec

- MORRIS Family Association
  http://genweb.net/~morris/

- MORRIS Genealogy Web Site
  http://www.geocities.com/Heartland/Hills/1914/genealogy.htm
  COFFEY, CONLEY, GREEN, HERRING, MILLER, PENNELL, PHILLIPS, TEACHEY, YATES

- MORRIS Home Page—MORRIS Members Newsletter
  http://members.aol.com/Kinseeker6/morris.html

- The MORSE Society
  http://morssweb.com/morse/index.htm
  American and Canadian Descendants of Samuel Morse, Anthony Morse, William Morse, Joseph Morse, John Moss.

- The MORT Family Homepage
  http://www.execpc.com/~drg/mort.html
  Genealogy & Research on all American Mort Families.

- MORTIBOYS Family History
  http://www.mortiboy.freeserve.co.uk/fh.htm
  Mortiboys, Mortiboy, Morteboy

- MOWER Family History Association
  http://www.xmission.com/~mower/

- The MUCHMORE Families
  http://www.poncacitynews.com/muchmoreorg/muchmore.htm
  MUCHMORE, MUCHEMORE, MUTCHMORE, MUTCHMOR, MICHELMORE, GARARD, BRUEN, LUM, KITCHEL plus "muchmore." A Genealogy of the Descendants of John & Hannah Muchmore John & Anne Muchemore and All Allied Families.

- The MULBERRY Family Of Idaho
  http://www.netcom.com/~jog1/mulberry/ofidaho.html

- The MULBERRY Family Of Kentucky
  http://www.netcom.com/~jog1/mulberry/jacob.html

- The MUMMA-MOOMAW Family Page
  http://www.mumma.org/mumma.html
  Mewmaw, Moomau, Moomaw, Muma, Mumau, Mumaugh, Mumaw, Mumma, Mummah, Mummau and Mummaw.

- MUMMEY Family Reunion Website
  http://ecicnet.org/~uboat977/
  Mummey/Mummy family genealogy, with Hammond and Smith allied lines, information on annual Mummey reunion.

- Thomas MUNSON Foundation
  http://www.thomas-munson.org

- MURDUCK-L Surname Mailing List
  http://www.ikweb.com/murduck/genealogy/murduck-l/intro.htm
  Includes Murdock, Murdoch, Murdocke, Murducke, Mardock, Merdock, Moorduck, Midduck.

- **MURNANEs of Tipperary, Cork and Limerick**
  http://www.murnane.org

- **MURPHY Home Page—MURPHY Mates Newsletter**
  http://members.aol.com/Kinseeker6/murphy.html

- **The MURRAY Clan Society of Queensland**
  http://www.globec.com.au/~egan/
  For anyone bearing the surname of: MURRAY, MACMURRAY, MORAY, MURRIE, MORROW or the Clan's affiliated septs: BALNEAVES, DINSMORE, DUNSMORE, FLEMING, GERAGHTY, GINSMORE, HARRINGTON, MACMORROW, NEAVES, PIPER, PYPER, SMALL, SMAIL, SMEAL, SPAULDING, THOMAS or TOMAS.

- **MURRAY Family Web**
  http://www.murrayfamily.org
  Descendants of Patrick Murray who married circa 1795 and resided on the Townland of Curragh, Clondulane, Fermoy, Co. Cork, Ireland.

- **MUSETTI Surname Resource Center**
  http://www.geocities.com/Heartland/Valley/2702/musetti.htm
  A place for MUSETTI's around the world to gather and share genealogical information. Site includes: Family Crest, Origin of Surname, Addresses, Passenger Arrivals, Military Records, Social Security Records, etc.

- **MUTCHLER Family Home Page**
  http://www.ghgcorp.com/smutchler/genem.html
  From Wörth, Alsace Lorriane area of France and Germany around the early 1600s.

- **The MUTIMER Family Home Page**
  http://www.lzs.com.au/~lmutimer
  Australia

◆ Surnames Beginning with "N"

- **Family Tree Maker Online User Home Pages—N**
  http://www.familytreemaker.com/users/n/index.html

- **Genealogy's Most Wanted—Surnames Beginning with "N"**
  http://www.citynet.net/mostwanted/n.htm

- **H-GIG Surname Registry—Surnames Beginning N**
  http://www.ucr.edu/h-gig/surdata/surname14.html

- **Higginson Book Company—Surnames Beginning with N**
  http://www.higginsonbooks.com/n.htm

- **inGeneas Table of Common Surname Variations and Surname Misspellings—N–Q**
  http://www.ingeneas.com/N2Q.html

- **Surname Springboard Index—N**
  http://www.geocities.com/~alacy/spring_n.htm

- **SurnameWeb Surname Registry—N Index**
  http://www.surnameweb.org/registry/n.htm

- **Genealogy Resources on the Internet—"N" Surname Mailing Lists**
  http://members.aol.com/gfsjohnf/gen_mail_surnames-no.html
  This site is wonderfully maintained by John Fuller. It includes mailing list information for the following surnames and their variant spellings:
  NAGLE (includes Nagel, Naugle), NANCE, NAPIER (includes Napeir, Nepair, Nepeir, Neper, Napare, Naper, Naipper), NASH, NEAL, NEELEY (includes Neely, Nealy, Neley, Neelly, Nely), NEEP (includes Knipe, Heap, Sneap), NEGRYCH (includes Negrich), NEHS, NEIBAUR (includes Neubauer), NEIGHBOURS (includes Nabors), NEIKIRK (includes Nikirk, Newkirk, Neukirch, Neukrich, Nykirk, any Soundex N262), NEILL, NELLIS-L (includes Nelles), NELSON, NERNES (includes Nerness, Nernaes), NESBITT (includes Nesbit), NESMITH, NETTROUR, NEVEU (includes Nephew, Nevue, Nauvau, Naview), NEVILLE (includes Nevill, Nevills, Neavill, Neaveill, Nevel, Nevell, Nevels, Nevils, Neufville; North, America), NEVILLE-Origins (includes Nevill, Nevills, Neavill, Neaveill, Nevel, Nevell, Nevels, Nevils, Neufville; other, than North America), NEVISON (includes Nevinson, Navison, Neverson), NEVITT (includes Knevitt), NEW (includes Neu), NEWBERRY (includes Newbery, Newbury), NEWCOMB (includes Newcombe, Newcomber), NEWFIELD (includes Newfelt, Neufieldt), NEWMAN (includes Newsome, Newmon, Newmen, Newsame, Newsam, Newsom), NEWSOM (includes Newsome, Nusom), NEWTON, NEYLAND (includes Neeland, Neylans, Kneeland), NICHOLS (includes Nickels, Nickles, Nuckolls, Nicol), NICHOLSON, Nicholsonfam, NIMS, NISWONGER, NIX (includes Nicks), NOBLE (includes Nobel), NOBLIN, NOE, NOEL, NOLF (includes Nulph, Nolff, Nulf), NORFLEET (includes Northfleete), NORMAN, NORRIS (includes Noreys, Norreys, Norrice, Norriss), NORTH (includes Northend, Northern), NORTHCUTT (includes Northcut, Northcott, Northcot), NORTHWAY (includes Northaway), NORTON (includes Naughton), NORWOOD (includes Northwoode), NOTHNAGLE (includes Nothnagel), NOWLIN (includes Nolan, Nolen, Knowlan, Knowland, Nowland, Noland, Nowlan, Nowlen, O'Nawlin), NUCKOLLS, NUNNELLEY (includes Nunely, Nunley), NUTTER.

- **The NAFZGER Genealogy Home Page**
  http://sailfish.exis.net/~tjnoff/
  NAFZGER / NOFFSINGER

- **The NALE Family Page**
  http://www.nidlink.com/~rsnale/

- **NANCE Family History Web Page**
  http://cust.iamerica.net/tnance/history.htm

- **NAUGHTON Genealogy Page**
  http://miso.wwa.com/~naughton/genealogy.html

- **The Descendants of George NAYLOR of Bradford England**
  http://www5.pair.com/vtandrew/naylor/joenaylr.htm

- **The Official NEELEY'S Web Site— The NEELEY'S From Whence They Came**
  http://www.genweb.net/~neeley
  The NEELEY'S [all spelling varations] Neely/Neelly/Nealy/ Neley, etc. of Europe?, Pennsylvania, Indiana, North Carolina, Tennessee, Oklahoma, California. Descendants of William NEELEY & Eleanor?

- **Family History—Genealogy of the NEEP / KNAPP Family**
  http://www.neep.demon.co.uk/fhist/neep-knapp.htm

- NEFF Genealogy
  http://ourworld.compuserve.com/homepages/neff_genealogy/
  For the Exchange of NAEF, NAF, NAFF, NAVE, NEAVE, NEEF, NEFF, etc.

- NESBITT / NISBET Society (UK Branch)
  http://www.angelfire.com/ne/nesbitt/index.html

- The NESBITT / NISBET Society (US Branch)
  http://www.ibydeit.com

- NEVILLE Heritage Society
  http://www.prairienet.org/neville/homepage.html

- NEWBERRY Surname Mailing List
  http://www.geocities.com/Heartland/Estates/8415/
  Includes Newbery, Newbury.

- Hugo le NEWCOMEN
  http://www.ziplink.net/~joelinda/hugo.htm
  Lord of the Manor of Saltfleetby in Lincolnshire, England.

- Augusta NEWMAN
  http://csc.techcenter.org/~mneill/augusta.html

- NICKERSON Family Association
  http://www.capecod.net/nfaoncape
  NICKERSON the founder of Chatham MA on Cape Cod and descendants throughout North America especially those Planters and Loyalists that went to NS and NB Canada.

- NISWONGER's Nest
  http://members.xoom.com/Niswonger/

- Of NOBLE Lineage
  http://ourworld.compuserve.com/homepages/noble/

- NORDMEYER Homepage
  http://www.nordmeyer.com
  Nordmeyer Family homepage for 4+ generations (and growing!). Descendants of Heinrict (F. G.) Nordmeyer (1821–1882).

- The NORWOOD Family Page
  http://www.geocities.com/Heartland/Estates/4805/index.html
  The Massachusetts and Maine Lines, Descendants of Francis Norwood.

- NUCKOLLS Kindred Worldwide
  http://www.nuckolls.org

- NUETZELs on the Web
  http://www.nuetzel.com/family/

- The NUTTER Family Bulletin Board
  http://members.aol.com/NutterWV/index.htm
  Descendants of Christopher NUTTER, born abt 1638–1642 and Mary DORMAN.

- The NYE Family Home Page
  http://www.crosslink.net/~bobnye/nyehome.htm

◆ Surnames Beginning with "O"

- Family Tree Maker Online User Home Pages—O
  http://www.familytreemaker.com/users/o/index.html

- Genealogy's Most Wanted—Surnames Beginning with "O"
  http://www.citynet.net/mostwanted/o.htm

- H-GIG Surname Registry—Surnames Beginning O
  http://www.ucr.edu/h-gig/surdata/surname15.html

- Higginson Book Company—Surnames Beginning with O
  http://www.higginsonbooks.com/o.htm

- inGeneas Table of Common Surname Variations and Surname Misspellings—N-Q
  http://www.ingeneas.com/N2Q.html

- Surname Springboard Index—O
  http://www.geocities.com/~alacy/spring_o.htm

- SurnameWeb Surname Registry—O Index
  http://www.surnameweb.org/registry/o.htm

- Genealogy Resources on the Internet—"O" Surname Mailing Lists
  http://members.aol.com/gfsjohnf/gen_mail_surnames-no.html
  This site is wonderfully maintained by John Fuller. It includes mailing list information for the following surnames and their variant spellings:
  OAKLEY, OBRIEN (includes Byrom, Bynum, Byran, Biron, Brian), OCONNELL, OCONNOR (includes O'Conner, Connor, Conner, O'Conor), ODELL (includes Odel, Odle, O'Dell, O'Del), ODELL (includes O'Dell), ODEN, ODENBAUGH (includes Odenbach, Offenbach, Adenbach, Adenbaugh, Von Adenbach), ODONNELL (includes Odonell, O'Donnel), ODOR (includes Oder), OESTERREICH, OGLESBY, OKENNEDY (includes Canady, Kenedy, Kennedy), OLDS (includes Old, Auld, Aulds), OLEARY (includes Leary, O'leary), OLIPHANT, OLIVE, OLIVER, OLLIS, OLMSTED (includes Almstead, Umstedt), OLSEN (includes Olson), OMeara (includes O'mara, Mara, Meara), ONEALL (includes O'Neill, O'Neal, O'Neil, Neal, Neale), OOTEN (includes Euten, Ooton), OPDYCK (includes Updike, Op den Dyck, Opdycke), ORBAN (includes Orbin, Orbant, Orbaneja, Orbanic), OREAR (includes O'Rear, ORear, Orrear, Orea), ORR, OSBORN (includes Osborne, Ozburn, Ozbirn, Osbourne), OSBORNE, OSGOOD, OSTENDARP, OSTRANDER (includes Oostrander, Hostrander, Van Ostrander, Van Nostrunt, Vanostran, Ostervanter, Ostrancer, Ostronden, Ostrandt, Osslander, Osatrander, Noortstrande), OSTROM (includes Ostrum, Oosteroom), OVERALL (includes Overhall), OVERBAUGH (includes Oberbach), OVERSTREET, OVERTON, OWEN (includes Owens, Oen, Owing), OXLEY.

- O'BRIEN Genealogy (Bandon, Cork, Ireland)
  http://www.hylit.com/info/Genealogy/OBrien.html
  A genealogy of the O'Brien family of West Cork.

- O'CONNOR—Ireland to Iowa
  http://www.aplusdata.com/genexchange/ajabby/OConnor/index.html

- O'DEA Online
  http://homepage.tinet.ie/~odeaclan/
  Home Page of the Dysert O'Dea Clan Association (Clan Ua Déaghaid) for those with surnames O'Dea, O'Day, Dee, or Day. Includes a short clan history, application for Clan Association membership, a genealogical exchange, and details on the Fourth International O'Dea Clan Gathering in July 1999.

- ODELLs: Lost & Found
  http://members.tripod.com/~mygenerations/odellslostandfound.html
  Odell, O'Dell, Odle

- O'DOCHARTAIGH County Donegal—The Great Clann O'DOCHARTAIGH
  http://pages.prodigy.net/bkbaker1/index.html
  Daugherty, Dougherty, Doherty, Dohetee, Docharty, and other variants of O'Dochartaigh.

- Offringa Familytree with more than 3,000 Offringas
  http://home.pi.net/~offringa/index.htm
  From Dick Offringa in Emmeloord, Netherlands.

- OGBOURNE Chronicles
  http://www.oginet.com/Chronicles/
  Historical & Genealogical Information relating to the names of OGBOURNE, OGBORNE, OGBORN, OGBURN.

- The African American OGBURNs And The House of OGBURNs
  http://www.oginet.com/Chronicles/hoogbrn.htm

- O'KEEFFE Home Page
  http://www.usinternet.com/users/jokeefe/home.htm

- OLDHAM Genealogical Database
  http://www.rootsweb.com/~gumby/genweb/Oldham/Oldham.html
  A database that contains 16,578 names.

- OLIVER Surname Mailing List
  http://www.sonic.net/~yvonne/oliver.html

- The Boston OLLIS Family Home Page
  http://www.familytreemaker.com/users/o/l/l/Prentis-L-Ollis/index.html
  For descendants of Boston Ollis, born abt. 1743 in Wales, died March 9, 1835, buried in Morgan County, TN.

- The O'MAHONY Society
  http://cat.spindata.com/mahony/

- O'MALLEY family in Australia—The Descendants of John MALAY
  http://www.users.bigpond.com/omalley/
  Malay, Maley, Malley, O'Malley family of Westbury Tasmania, Australia.

- O'MARY Genealogy Homepage
  http://www.syspac.com/~somary/gene.html

- O'NEILL Clan Homepage
  http://www.seregin.com.au/oneill/

- The Descendants of William OPENSHAW
  http://www5.pair.com/vtandrew/openshaw/openshaw.htm

- OPP Genealogy
  http://pages.prodigy.net/dave_lossos/opp.htm

- ORAVECZ Families Web Site
  http://www.oravecz.org
  General site for all Oravecz families. Currently includes descendants of George Oravecz, Sr. and Miller and Partsch ancestors of Miriam Jane Partsch Oravecz. Hosting: Oravecz, Oravec, Oravetz, Oravets, Oravez, Oravis, and Orawetz.

- The ORBAN's
  http://www.geocities.com/CapeCanaveral/7473/orban.html
  Belgium, Hungary

- O'ROURKE Family Genealogy Home Page
  http://www.geocities.com/Heartland/Plains/3552/orourke.htm
  Dedicated to the research and discussion of genealogy on the O'Rourke, Rourke, O'Rorke, Roark, O'Roarke family lines.

- ORTON Family History Society
  http://www2.prestel.co.uk/orton/fhs/index.html

- OSBORNE Origins
  http://home.att.net/~osborne_origins/

- O'SHIELDS / O'SHEILDS Family History
  http://home.texoma.net/~mmcmullen/o/oshield.htm

- The OSTRANDER Family Association (OFA)
  http://home.earthlink.net/~ostrander/index.html
  Ostranders in America Since 1660.

- OSTRANDER KELLEY Family Page
  http://www.familytreemaker.com/users/k/e/l/terence—kelley/index.html
  Descendants of Pieter Ostrander who married Rebecca Traphagen in 1679 in New Amsterdam.

- Dr. Bodo OTTO Association
  http://www.geocities.com/Heartland/Prairie/8833/

- Le HOUYMET Internet—Home on the Internet of Les Descendants de Jean OUIMET, Inc.
  http://www.geocities.com/~couimet/lehouymet.html
  Ouimet, Houymet, Vilmet, Wemet, Wemett, Wuillemette, Wilmot and numerous other spelling variations.

- The OULTON Project
  http://www.cct.infi.net/~funbooks/html/index/oulton.htm
  An attempt to trace the Oultons back to the Irish-Norse Vikings who settled in Cheshire England. Also includes most all Oulton genealogy in America.

- OUTTEN Family History
  http://members.aol.com/outtengene/Outten.htm
  Descendants of John Outten of Somerset County, Maryland.

- OWSLEY Family Historical Society
  http://home.dwave.net/~skeeter/owsley.html

- OXFORDs of America
  http://www.geocities.com/Heartland/Acres/3974/

◆ Surnames Beginning with "P"

- Family Tree Maker Online User Home Pages—P
  http://www.familytreemaker.com/users/p/index.html

- Genealogy's Most Wanted—Surnames Beginning with "P"
  http://www.citynet.net/mostwanted/p.htm

- H-GIG Surname Registry—Surnames Beginning P
  http://www.ucr.edu/h-gig/surdata/surname16.html

- Higginson Book Company—Surnames Beginning with P
  http://www.higginsonbooks.com/p.htm

- inGeneas Table of Common Surname Variations and Surname Misspellings—N–Q
  http://www.ingeneas.com/N2Q.html

- Surname Springboard Index—P
  http://www.geocities.com/~alacy/spring_p.htm

- SurnameWeb Surname Registry—P Index
  http://www.surnameweb.org/registry/p.htm

- Genealogy Resources on the Internet—"P" Surname Mailing Lists
  http://members.aol.com/gfsjohnf/gen_mail_surnames-p.html
  This site is wonderfully maintained by John Fuller. It includes mailing list information for the following surnames and their variant spellings:
  PACK, PADDOCK (includes Paddack, Paddick, Padduck, Padock, Padack, Padick, Paduck), PAGE, PALMER, PANKRATZ, PANNEBECKER (includes Pennybacker, Pennybaker, Pennebaker, Pfannebakker, Pennypacker, Pannebaker, Panebaker, Panebecker, Pannabecker, Pannebecker), PARDUE (includes Perdue), PARHAM (includes Paaram), PARISH (includes Parrish, Paris, Parys, Pary), PARKER-ROOTS, PARKHURST, PARKS (includes Park), PARR (includes Paar), PARRACK (includes Parrick, Parrock, Parack, Parick, Parock), PARRENT (includes Parent), PARRIOTT (includes Parriot, Pariot, Parrot), PARSONS, PARTEE (includes Pardee), PASCHAL, PASCOE, PASS (includes Pas, Passe, Pace), PATE (includes Pait, Payte, Pates), PATENAUDE (includes Patnode, Patnoe, Paternostre, Patno), PATRICK (includes Patrik, Patric, Patricks), PATTON (includes Patten, Payton), PATTERSON (includes Peterson, Patrickson, Paterson, Batterson), PATZKOWSKI (includes Pasckowski, Paszkowski, Patzkowsky, Paczkoswki, Pacskowski), PAUGH, PAUL-ROOTS (includes Paull, Paule), PAVY, PAXTON, PAYANT (includes Payan), PAYNE (includes Paine, Payn), PEABODY, PEACOCK, PEALE (includes Peal), PEARSALL (includes Parshall, Peirsol), PEAVLER (includes Peveler, Peevler, Peavley, Peevley, Pevley), PECK, PEDDICORD (includes Peddycoard, Petticoat, Peddycort), PEDEN (includes Paden, Peeden), PEDIGO (includes Peregoy, Perrigo, Perigo, Petigo, Petticoat), PEDLEY (includes Pedly), PEEBLES, PEEK (includes Peak, Peake), PEELE (includes Peelle, Peel, Peal), PEER (includes LaPeer, Peers), PEERY-L, PEFFLEY (includes Peffly, Peffle, Pefley, Pefly), PENIX (includes Pennock, Penick, Pinnex, Pinex, Phenix), PENLAND (includes Penlan, Penlin, Pendland, Pendlum), PENLEY, PENN, PENNEY_family, PENNINGTON (includes Peninton, Penitone, Pennton, Piniton, Penistone, Peddington, Penninton), PENNOYER (includes Penoyer, Pennoire), PENNY (includes Penney), PEPPER, PERCIVAL, PERILLOUX (includes Perioux, Periou, Perrilloux, Perriloux, Perrillioux), PERKINS, PERLEY (includes Pearley, Pearly, Perly, Parly, Parley, Pearlee), PERRY (includes Parrie), PERRYMAN (includes Periman, Perriman), PETERMAN, PETERS (includes Peter, Peterson), PETERSON, PETERSON, PETREY (includes Petry, Pettry, Petrie, Pettrie, Petre, Pettre, Petree, Pettrey), PETTENGILL (includes Pettingell, Pettingill, Pettengall, Pettengale), PETTIGREW (includes Peticru, Petticrew, Bettigrew), PETTIT-L, PETTUS (includes Pettis), PETTY, PEYTON, PFISTER (includes Pfisterer), PFOUTS (includes Pfautz, Pfoutz, Fouts, Foutz), PHELAN (includes Phalen, Phalon, Pheland, Felan), PHELPS, PHENIX (includes Fenix, Feeneys, Phoenix, Penninck, Fenwick, Pfennigs, Fenex), PHIFER (includes Fifer, Fiffer, Phiffer, Pfeiffer, Pfeifer), PHILBRICK (includes Philbricke, Philbreck, Philbrook, Fillbrick, Felbrigg, Fylbrigg), PHILLIPPI (includes Soundex P410), PHILLIPS (includes Philips, Philipps), PHIPPS (includes Phips, Fipps), PICKERING, PIERCE (includes Piers, Peirs, Perse, Peirce, Peirse, Peers, Pairs), PIERSON (includes Pearson, Peirson), PIGOTT (includes Piggott, Pygott, Pigate), PIKE, PILGRIM (includes Pillgrim, Pilgram, Pilgrem, Pilgrum), PIMENTEL, PINE, PINSON (includes Penson), PIPPIN (includes Pippen, Pepin, Papin, Pappin), PIRZ, PITSENBARGER (includes Pitzenberger), PITTMAN (includes Pitman), PIXLER-BIXLER, PLACE (includes Plaise, Pleas, de la Place), Platt, PLETSCH (includes Pletch), PLOWMAN (includes Ploughman), PLUMMER (includes Plumer), PLUNKETT, POARCH (includes Porch), POE, POINDEXTER, POLING (includes Poland, Polen), POLK (includes Pogue, Pollack, Pollock), POLLEY-L (includes Polly), POLSTON (includes Poulson, Polson, Poston), PONDER (includes Pounder, Pounders, Pinder, Pender, Pynder), POOLE (includes Pool, Pettypool, Pettypoole, Van Pool, Van Poole), POPE, POPWELL (includes Poppleweil, Popplewell), PORTER, PORTERFIELD (includes Potterfield, Porteous, Borderfield, Porter), PORTWINE (includes Potvin), PORTWOOD, POSEY, POST, POTTEIGER, POTTS (includes Philpott, MacKillop, Pott, Pot, Potter, Botts, Bott, Bot), POUNCEY, POWELL, POWERS (includes Power, Bowers, Poors, Poore, Bauers), POYTHRESS, PRATHER (includes Prater, Prayter, Praytor, Prator), PREADMORE (includes Predmore, Pridemore, Pridmore, Prigmore), PRESTON, PRICE (includes Pryce), PRICHARD (includes Pritchard), PRIDGEN, PRIEST, PRINCE (includes Printz, Prinns), PROCTOR (includes Procter, Prochtor, Prochter), PROFFITT (includes Proffit, Profitt, Profit, Prophet), PROWSE (includes Prouz, Prose, Prouse, Prouze), PRUITT (includes Prewitt, Prewet, Pruit, Prout, Pratt), PRYOR (includes Prior, Prier, Pryer, Pryar), PUCKETT, PUGH, PURDY (includes Purdey, Purdee, Purdon, Purdie), PURSLEY (includes Presley, Purcell, Pursell, Purselley), PURVIANCE (includes Perviance, Pervines, Purvines, Purveance), PUSHEE (includes Pushie, Poucie), PYLE (includes Pyles, Pile, Piles, Pihl), PYRON (includes Peron, Peronne, Perron, Piran, Pirent, Pierent, Pryon, Pyrain, Pyram, Pyrant, Pyrom, Pyront, Pyrum, Pyrun).

- PAAR Genealogy Research Project
  http://www.fp.nxs.net/jpaar/genealogy/paar/paar.htm

- The PACE Network
  http://users.aol.com/pacenetwrk/pace.htm

- PAGEOT-PAGEAU-PAJOT Genealogy Home Page
  http://www.novagate.com/~rpaggeot/

- Those Prolific PAINs
  http://members.tripod.com/~ProlificPains/index.html
  Payn, Payne, Pane, Paine and Pain.

- Walter PALMER Society
  http://www.walterpalmer.com
  For descendants of Walter Palmer who arrived in Salem, Massachusetts in June 1629.

- The PAMPLIN Family & Connections Home Page
  http://userwww.service.emory.edu/~wpampli/pamplin.html

- The PARK/E/S Family Research Page
  http://home.earthlink.net/~howardorjeff/park/

- The PARKE Society, Inc.
  http://ourworld.compuserve.com/homepages/Tad_Parks/
  Clearinghouse for research on all Park/e/s immigrants from the British Isles.

- PARLE / PEARL Family Association
  http://www.geocities.com/Athens/Acropolis/4933/parle.html
  A gathering point for information concerning the surname Parle and all possible variations including Pearl.

- PARSONS Family Association
  The Parsons Family of the South Branch of the Potomac and Cheat River VA/WV. For details send e-mail to Katherine Ray at KATHYR@prodigy.net

- GenPARTEE
  http://www.geocities.com/Heartland/Plains/4143/genpartee.html
  A web site for the Partee Surname Discussion Group.

- The PARTEE Pages
  http://pages.prodigy.com/Goodtrader/partee.htm
  For the PARTEE surname in North Carolina and Georgia.

- The PARTRIDGE Family Nest
  http://members.aol.com/pedrix/index.htm

- The PATE-PAIT Historical Society
  http://www.mindspring.com/~caryonline/pphs/

- Descendants of James PATERSON
  http://homepages.ihug.co.nz/~Sallanp/paterson.htm

- PATTERSON Home Page—PATTERSON People Newsletter
  http://members.aol.com/Kinseeker6/patterson.html

- The PATTON Exchange
  http://members.aol.com/M55442/index.html

- Cissie P's PAYNE Genealogy Page
  http://members.aol.com/CissieP/index.html
  PAYNE / PAINE / PAIN

- The Joseph PAYNE Family of Virginia, Tennessee and Mississippi
  http://members.aol.com/jogt/payne.htm

- The PAYNEs of Virginia
  http://www.icon.net/~sdcaller/payne.htm
  Descendants of John Payne, born ca 1615 in England.

- PEABODY Family Home Pages
  http://www.pbdy.com
  Velton Peabody's compilation of ALL Peabodys in the U.S.

- PEACOCK Family Association of the South
  http://www.peacockfamily.org

- The PEELE Family Association
  http://www.txdirect.net/~hpeele/
  Peelle, Peele, Peel and Peal. Horace PEELE's Genealogy, Etc.—The First PEELLE Family in America.

- PEERY Family History Home Page
  http://www.cc.utah.edu/~pdp7277/

- PEGRAM Family Album
  http://www.patch.net
  Descendants of Daniel Pegram (c1720–1776) of Williamsburg, VA and Warren County, NC.

- PELLAND Family Genealogy
  http://www.cyberbeach.net/~jrpellan/pellan2.htm
  PELLAND, PELLAN, PELLANT, PENLAN

- Association des Familles PELLETIER
  http://www.quebectel.com/pelletier/

- PELLETIER Genealogy
  http://www.genealogy.org/~gapellet/

- PENDERGRAFT and PENDERGRASS Family Web Page
  http://www.ticnet.com/lpenderg/pendergr.htm
  Descendants of James Pendergrass (Prendergast), who was born about 1640 in Ireland and came to Virginia in about 1668.

- PENNEBAKER History
  http://www.communique.net/~pepbaker/pennebkr.htm
  Pannebakker, Pannebecker, Pfannebecker

- PENNINGTON Research Association Homepage
  http://penningtonresearch.org
  The Pennington Research Association (PRA) was founded for the sole purpose of the collection, preservation, maintenance, and dissemination of materials relating to the genealogical structure of the Pennington Family. We strive to be the most comprehensive source of accurate genealogical information, material and events concerning the Pennington Family. We will strive to utilize Internet technology as an informative and educational tool for our members and all other genealogy researchers.

- The PENNY / PENNEY Home Page
  http://www.inch.com/~penney/gene/

- The Northwest Twig of the PEPPAN / PEPIN Family Tree
  http://www.escargot.com/lisap
  The descendants of Louis Seymour Peppan and his wife, Emma Sarah Peppan nee Houston.

- Association Des Familles PERRON D'Amérique
  http://www.oricom.ca/pperron/

- PESCE Family Web Page
  http://www.geocities.com/Heartland/Valley/1410/pesce_index.html

- PETERMAN Surname Web Site
  http://members.aol.com/rootshuntr/dir/peterlist.html

- The PETTIGROVE Genealogy Page
  http://www.personal.psu.edu/faculty/j/w/jwd6/pettigro.htm

- The PEYTON Society of Virginia Mailing List
  For persons who may be descended from a Peyton living in Virginia before 1800. For details send e-mail to Harold Davey at: hdavey@moon.jic.com

- Home Pages of Richard PFOUTS
  http://home.earthlink.net/~pfoutsr/
  Pfautz, Pfoutz, Fouts, Foutz

- PHEBUS Genealogy Index
  http://www.phebus.com
  Phoebus, Pheobus, Phebues, Febus, etc.

- PHELPS Connections
  http://www.phelps-connections.org

- PHIFER Surname Research
  http://rampages.onramp.net/~lcompton/phifer/index.html

- The PHILIPP/PHILLIPS Family from Alsace to Ohio
  http://www.geocities.com/Heartland/Acres/4585
  Read about the Phillips family from Fairfield County, Ohio and their Philipp ancestors from Friesen, Alsace, France. Related names include Buechler, Kilburger, Krile, Messbarger, Piper, Rauch, Saum, Steck and Winter.

- PHILLIPS Family 1593–1997
  http://members.aol.com/PSulzer/Phillips.html
  This line originated in County Norfolk, UK before 1593 with Christopher Phillips.

- The Association of the PICHE Families
  http://www.abacom.com/~dgdupre/#The association of the Piche families

- PICKLES Genealogy Home Page
  http://www.paonline.com/csanders/Pickles/RR_TOC.htm
  Descendants of John PICKLES and Hannah WHITNEY, principally of England and Michigan.

- PICOT Home Page • Page Web PICOT
  http://Fox.nstn.ca:80/~nstn1528/index.html

- The Descendants of Richard PIERCE
  http://www5.pair.com/vtandrew/pierce/pierce.htm

- PIERCE Surname Mailing List
  http://members.aol.com/rootshuntr/dir/PHist.html
  Includes Piers, Peirs, Perse, Peirce, Peirse, Peers, Pairs.

- PILCHER Family Roots
  http://www.geocities.com/Heartland/Hills/7046/

- PILGRIM's Landing
  http://www.cyberus.ca/~pmarchan/pilgrim.html

- PIPKIN Family Association
  http://www.u.arizona.edu/~freitas/pipkin.html

- The PITSENBARGER Family of America
  http://www.calweb.com/~wally/darke/w-pits1.htm

- PIXLEY Family Online
  http://www.wavefront.com/~pjlareau/pixleyfo.html

- Ancêtre de tous les PLAMONDON en Amérique du nord
  http://www.qbc.clic.net/~mrplam/plamgenf.html

- The PLATT Page
  http://users.aol.com/CPlatt1/platt.html

- The POHL Page
  http://members.aol.com/kenpohl/index.htm
  Descendants of Christian F. Pohl.

- POINDEXTER Descendants Association
  http://www.geocities.com/~poingdestre/
  American descendants of the Poingdestre Family, Isle of Jersey, Channel Islands. George Poingdestre, arrived in the Colony of Virginia in 1657.

- POLLARD Family of VA and KY
  http://members.aol.com/jogt/pollard.htm

- Welcome to the World of POLLEY!
  http://pages.prodigy.com/CJTP10A/polley.htm
  Descendants of David POLLEY.

- Descendants of Henry Washington POPLIN
  http://www.scsn.net/users/summit/poplin.html

- The POPWELL Family
  http://home.att.net/~dpdklong/Popwell.htm
  The Popwell family, descended from Ruben Poppleweil, first arriving in Alabama in 1828. With links to a four-generation family tree and other related families.

- The Olive Tree Genealogy: The New Jersey POST Family
  http://www.rootsweb.com/~ote/post.htm
  Descendants of Adriaen Crijnen POST & Clara (Claartje) MOOCKERS. Adriaen and Clara settled on Staten Island in 1655. By 1665 he was living in Bergen New Jersey and is the ancestor of most NJ POSTs.

- The POTGIETER Genealogy Pages
  http://www.geocities.com/Heartland/Park/7152/
  If you are interested to trace your Potgieter family roots in South Africa, then this is the place for you to start. This site hosts genealogy information, a mailing list, a discussion forum, biographies and history.

- The POTTEN Pages
  http://www.vaugrat.demon.co.uk/

- POTTER Profiles
  http://www.screensaves.com/potter.htm

- The POYNTZ Family in India
  http://www.hal-pc.org/~poyntz/india.html
  Selected Extracts from the India Presidencies of Bengal, Bombay and Madras Ecclesiastical Returns of Baptisms, Marriages and Burials 1713–1948.

- Dennis PRANGNELL's Home Page
  http://www.pragndr.demon.co.uk/index.htm
  Prangell, Pragnell

- PRATER.org
  http://www.prater.org

- PRATHER Family History Mailing List
  http://www.angelfire.com/in/prather/index.html

- The Ascott Martyrs
  http://www.geocities.com/Heartland/Plains/6081/
  An Historical Link to the PRATLY, PRATLEY and PRATTLEY Families of New Zealand.

- The Descendants of Thomas PRATT
  http://members.aol.com/MShermanL/pratt.html
  Born Abt 1615 London, England, died 1705–1706 Watertown, Massachusetts.

- PrenticeNet
  http://www.prenticenet.com
  Prentiss, Prentis, Prentys, and other variations.

- PRESTON Genealogy
  http://cust2.iamerica.net/fpreston/prestong.htm
  Mostly on Prestons of Southwest Virginia but also some in New England, England and Ireland.

- PRIDGEN Family Genealogy—PRIDGEN Pages of the Past
  http://www.geocities.com/Heartland/Meadows/6297
  Site for Pridgen Family trees, Bibles, military info and address for Pridgen Family mailing list on the Internet. This is for the Pridgen Family anywhere, anytime.

- PRIEST Family Research
  http://members.aol.com/famlyfndr/priest1.htm

- PRIME Time 1275–1997—The PRIME Family History Centre
  http://www.taunton.demon.co.uk/
  A national and global one name study of the name PRIME.

- Provenzano.org
  http://www.provenzano.org
  A website entirely devoted to helping users tracing geneolgy concerning the Provenzano surname.

- The PYATT Family Home Page
  http://www3.sympatico.ca/dg.pyatt/
  Descendants of James Pyatt—to Canada in the 1860's.

◆ Surnames Beginning with "Q"

- Family Tree Maker Online User Home Pages—Q
  http://www.familytreemaker.com/users/q/index.html

- Genealogy's Most Wanted—Surnames Beginning with "Q"
  http://www.citynet.net/mostwanted/q.htm

- H-GIG Surname Registry—Surnames Beginning Q
  http://www.ucr.edu/h-gig/surdata/surname17.html

- Higginson Book Company—Surnames Beginning with Q
  http://www.higginsonbooks.com/q.htm

- inGeneas Table of Common Surname Variations and Surname Misspellings—N–Q
  http://www.ingeneas.com/N2Q.html

- Surname Springboard Index—Q
  http://www.geocities.com/~alacy/spring_q.htm

- SurnameWeb Surname Registry—Q Index
  http://www.surnameweb.org/registry/q.htm

- Genealogy Resources on the Internet— "Q" Surname Mailing Lists
  http://members.aol.com/gfsjohnf/gen_mail_surnames-qr.html
  This site is wonderfully maintained by John Fuller. It includes mailing list information for the following surnames and their variant spellings:
  QUALLS-QUARLES, QUARTERMAN (includes Quartermaine), QUEBEDEAUX (includes Quebedeau, Quevedo), QUEEN, QUESENBERRY, QUICK, QUIGGLE, QUILLIAN (includes Quilliam, Quillan, Quillen, Quillin, MacQuillian, McQuillen, McQuillin, McQuillan), QUINN (includes O'Quinn), QUIRAM (includes Quirandt, Quirant, Quirin, Quiring, Queram, Kwiram, Kweram, Kwirandt, Kwirant, Chwiram).

- QUAID Families Clearing House
  http://www.pclink.com/kg0ay/quaidclr.htm

- QUAITE Family Association—Clan Farquharson
  http://clanhuston.com/quaite.htm

- QUARTERMAN Family History Project
  http://www.quarterman.org

- QUINANE Genealogy Home Page
  http://www.tip.net.au/~ivecm/hist.htm
  Home Page of the Quinane's from Tipperary, Ireland who emigrated to Australia between 1850 and 1880.

- QUINN Quarterly Newsletter
  http://www.users.uswest.net/~ottino/newslett.htm

- QUISENBERRY Chat
  http://forums.delphi.com/preview/main.asp?sigdir=Quisenberry
  Quisenberry, Quesenberry, Quiesenberry, Cushingberry.

◆ Surnames Beginning with "R"

- Family Tree Maker Online User Home Pages—R
  http://www.familytreemaker.com/users/r/index.html

- Genealogy's Most Wanted—Surnames Beginning with "R"
  http://www.citynet.net/mostwanted/r.htm

- H-GIG Surname Registry—Surnames Beginning R
  http://www.ucr.edu/h-gig/surdata/surname18.html

- Higginson Book Company—Surnames Beginning with R
  http://www.higginsonbooks.com/r.htm

- inGeneas Table of Common Surname Variations and Surname Misspellings—R–S
  http://www.ingeneas.com/R2S.html

- Surname Springboard Index—R
  http://www.geocities.com/~alacy/spring_r.htm

- SurnameWeb Surname Registry—R Index
  http://www.surnameweb.org/registry/r.htm

- Genealogy Resources on the Internet—"R" Surname Mailing Lists
  http://members.aol.com/gfsjohnf/gen_mail_surnames-qr.html
  This site is wonderfully maintained by John Fuller. It includes mailing list information for the following surnames and their variant spellings:
  R100 (includes Reiff, Reif, Rieff, Reif, Rife, Riffe, Riffey), R360 (includes Reader, Raeder, Roder, Roeder, Rotter), RABB (includes Rab, Raab), RABURN (includes Rayburn, Raborn, Rayborn, Raiburn, Raiborn, Raybourne), RACKHAM, RADER (includes Raider), RADFORD, RADLEY (includes Radly), RAGAN-ROOTS (includes Reagan, Regan), RAGSDALE (includes Bragsdale, Ridgedale, Ragsdall, Regisdale, Racksdale), RAINS/RAINES (includes Ranes, Reynes, Raynes), RAMEY (includes Remy, Rhamy, Ramie), RAMONAT, RAMSEY (includes Ramsay, Ramseur), RANDOLPH, RANEY (includes Riney), RANGER, RAPE (includes Reap, Reph), RASBERRY (includes Raspberry), RASEY (includes Racey, Raisee, Raisey, Raisy, Rasy, Razee, Razey, Razy, Reasey), RASURE (includes Razor, Rasor), RATLIFF (includes Ratcliff, Ratliffe, Radcliff, Rattle), RAY (includes Wray), RAYNESlist (includes Raines), READ (includes Reade, Reed, Reid), RECKINGER, RECTOR (includes Richter, Recter, Rektor), REDDICK (includes Riddick, Redick, Redrick, Rhedick), REDDING, REDUS (includes Readus, Reedis, Redish), REDWINE (includes Reitweil, Riedweyl, Redwile, Riethweil, Reedwile), REEB-ROOTS, REEDER, REESE (includes Rees), REEVES (includes Reaves, Rieves, Reeve), REGISTER (includes Regester), REIFSNYDER (includes Raifsnider, Reiffschneider), REISER (includes Reisser, Rieser), REISINGER (includes Risinger), REMBERT (includes Rambert), REMICK, REMINGTON (includes Remmington), REMPEL (includes Remple), RENICK (includes Rennick, Rennix), RENNER (includes Runner), RENNIE (includes Raynie), REYNIERSEN (includes Reynerson, Rynearson, Rinearson, Rhynearson, Rynerson), REYNOLDS, RHEA (includes Rea, Wray, Rae, Ray), RHODES (includes Rodes, Rhoades), RHONE (includes Rohn, Rahn), RHYMES (includes Rimes, Rhimes, Rymes), RHYNO (includes Rhino, Rino, Reneau,

Ryno), RIACH (includes Riabhach, Reoch, Raich, Rioch, Reiach), RICE, RICH (includes Ritch, Ryche, Riche), RICHARDS, RICHARDSON-L (includes Richards), RICHBOURG (includes Richebourg, Richburg, Richbourgh), RICHMOND, RICHTER (includes Reighter, Richster), RICKABAUGH (includes Rickaback, Rickenbaugh. Rickabough), RICKER (includes Ricard, Riccar, Recore), RICKETSON, RICKEYRoots, RIDDLE (includes Riddles, Riddell, Ridle, Reidle, Ritle, Ruddle, Rydale, Rydel), RIDENOUR, RIDER (includes Ryder), RIDGWAY (includes Ridgwaie, Ridgeway, Rugewaye, Rudgwy, Rydeware, Rydgeway, Wrydgway), RIEDINGER, RIEGEL (includes Reagle, Riggle), RIGGS, RIGSBY, RIKER (includes Ryker, Rycke, Rycken), RILEY, RIPPETOE (includes Rippeto, Rippeteau), RITCHEY (includes Richey, Richy, Ritchie), RITTENHOUSE (includes Rettinghousen, Rittinghuysen), RITTER (includes Writter), RIVERS, ROACHE_ROCHE (includes Roach, Roch), ROACH/ ROCHE, ROARK (includes Ruark, Rork, O'Rork, Rourick, Rowark), ROBERTS, ROBERTS, REUBEN, ROBERTSON, ROBEY (includes Roby), ROBINETT (includes Robinet, Robinette, Robnet), ROBINS, ROBINSON (includes Robertson, Robison, Robeson, Roberson, Robbins, Robins), ROBLEE (includes Robblee, Rublee, Robleyer, Rublier, Robley), ROCKETT, RODDIN, RODMAN (includes Redmond, Rodham, Redman, Broadman, (H)Rothmann, Roadman, Hrodman, Rathman, Rutman, Redmon, Rothman, Rideman, Brodman), ROEMHILDT (includes Rhoemhildt, Roemhild), ROGASCH (includes Rogash, Roggosch), ROGERS (includes Rodgers), ROHRBOUGH (includes Rohrbaugh, Rohrbach, Rohrabaugh, Rohrabacher, Rorapaugh), ROHRER (includes Rhorer, Rorer, Rorrer, Roher), ROHWER (includes Roher, Rohr, Rower, Rorer, Rohwedder), ROLAND (includes Rowland, Rawlings, Rawlin, Rollens, Rollings, Rollins, Rolin), ROLFE, ROLL (includes Raal, Rall, Ral, Rol, Rool, Rools, Mengalrol and the patronym Mangles), ROMANS, ROMINE (includes Romeyn, Romain, Romaine, Romines, Romeyns, Romains, Romaines, Remine), ROOK (includes Rooke, Rooks), ROPER, ROSE (includes Roosa, Rosa, Rutsen, Ruzen), ROSENBERGER (includes Rosenberg), ROSEVEAR, ROSS, ROSSITER (includes Rossitter, Rosseter), ROTH (includes Rothe, Wroth), ROUNSEVELL, ROUSE (includes Roush, Rausch), ROUTH (includes Ruth), ROWE (includes Row), ROWLETT (includes Rawlett, Rowlette, Roulet), ROWLEY-FAMILY, ROWND (includes Round, Rownds, Rounds), ROY (includes Roye), ROYAL-Surname (includes Royall), ROYCE (includes Royse, Roys, Rice), ROYER, ROYSTON (includes Roystone), RUCKEL (includes Rockel, Ruckle, Ruttle), RUCKER (includes Rücker), RUDACILLE (includes Rudisill, Rudisilla, Rudaciller), RUDD (includes Rud), RUDDELL (includes Ruddel, Rudel, Ruddle, Rudle), RUDE, RUE (includes LaRue, Rew), RUFFIN, RUMMEL_Rooters (includes Rumel, Rummell, Romel, Rommel), RUNNELS, RUNYON (includes Runyan, Runion), RUSH, RUSH (includes Rushe), RUSSELL, RUSSELL-UK, RUST (includes Russ), RUTHERFORD, RUTLEDGE (includes Rutlidge, Rutlege, Rutlige, Rutlage), RYAN, RYAN_Clan_Assoc_US (includes Rian, Mulryans, Mhaolrians), RYE, RYMES.

- **RADER Genealogy Home Page**
  http://www.rader.org
  Rader, Reader, Raeder, Roder, Roeder, Rotter.

- **Descendants of James RAMPLEY**
  http://csc.techcenter.org/~mneill/jamesramp.html

- **RAMSDALE Family Register**
  http://ourworld.compuserve.com/homepages/David_Ramsdale/homepage.htm
  Ramsdall, Ramsdell, Ramsdill and Ramsdaille.

- **RAMSDELL Genealogical Archive**
  http://www5.pair.com/vtandrew/ramsdell/archive.htm
  Ramsdell, Ramsdale, Ramsden, Ramsdall, Ramsdill, Ramsdal and Ramsdel.

- **RAMSEY Researchers**
  http://www.geocities.com/Heartland/Plains/1717/ram.htm

- **The RANGER Family History Home Page**
  http://www.familytreemaker.com/users/r/a/n/R-D-Ranger/index.html
  Descendants of Amos Ranger, born April 1766.

- **RANSOM Family Genealogy**
  http://www.peak.org/~mransom/ransom.html
  RANSOM / RANSOME and RANSON / RANSONE resources.

- **RARICK Families**
  http://www.infinet.com/~wkfisher/Rarick.html
  RARICK, RAIRIGH family history. Descendants of George Rairigh (Rarick), Sr. born 22 Aug. 1793 in Cowanshannock Twp., Armstrong County, Pennsylvania.

- **The RATCLIFF Family Tree**
  http://www.geocities.com/CollegePark/Campus/1719/tree.html
  Ratcliff, Ratliff, Radcliff.

- **The RATHBONE Register**
  http://www.stanford.edu/~dorcas/Rathbone.html
  The largest one-name study of the surname RATHBONE and its variations, including—RATHBORN(E), RATHBOURN(E), RATHBURN(E), RABON(E) RATHBOND, RATHBAN(D) etc.

- **REBBECK One Name Study, Newsletter**
  For details send e-mail to Judy Rebbeck Watten at RayjudyW@aol.com

- **REED Family Home Page**
  http://users.ilnk.com/creed/reed1.htm
  Descendants of Jacob Reed, 1729–1820, Leesburg, Virginia.

- **Paul REEVES Home Page**
  http://members.aol.com/rreeves204/reeves.html

- **The REEVES Registry**
  http://www.vantek.net/reevesregistry.com
  REAVE, REAVES, REAVIS, REEVE, REEVES, REIVE, REIVES, REVE, REVES, RIEVE, RIEVES, RIVE, RIVES, RYVE, RYVES

- **A Gathering of REIDYs**
  http://www.mindspring.com/~jreidy/reidy.htm

- **REINHART Genealogy and Niedernberg, Germany**
  http://ourworld.compuserve.com/homepages/niedernberg/niedernberg.html

- **REMMICK Home Site**
  http://members.aol.com/remmick1/Remmick.Home.Site.index.html/
  German-Russian heritage connected to Edenkoben, Palatinate migration to Worms/Odessa, S. Russia then Streeter, ND, USA. Remmick, Roemmich, Remick, Remich, Roemigius, Roemig.

- **The RENDALL Network**
  http://rendall.net

- **RENNERs of Frederick Co., Maryland**
  http://www.innova.net/~goob/genealogy.html
  Descendants of Abraham Renner & Elizabeth Overholtz.

- **REPLOGLE-REPROGLE Genealogy: The Family History of a Surname**
  http://www.geocities.com/Heartland/Pointe/7517
  Concerned with all descendants of the immigrants to America with the surname Replogle or Reprogle (or Reblogel in the German), both male and female.

- The RETTIG Genealogy Home Page
  http://members.aol.com/JWR184/rettig.html

- REYNOLDS Home Page—REYNOLDS
  Records Newsletter
  http://members.aol.com/Kinseeker6/reynolds.html

- RHYMES Family Genealogy
  http://wymple.gs.net/~longstrt/rhymes.html
  Descendants of John Rhyne, born 1745 in North Carolina.

- Le Groupe RHYNO
  http://www.geocities.com/Heartland/2194/rhyno.html
  Other possible spellings are Reynaud, Renaud, Reneau, Reno,
  Ryno, Rino, Rhino and more.

- Deacon Edmund RICE (1638) Association
  http://web2.airmail.net/drrice/

- The RICE Family: "End-of-the-Century Publishing
  Project"
  http://heaven.gofast.net/~rosemary/

- Samuel Whitney RICHARDS—His Wives, Children
  and Descendants
  http://www.n1.net/~mcward/swr.htm
  Born 9 August 1824 in Richmond, Berkshire, Massachusetts.

- Descendants of Robert RICHARDSON
  (c1637–1682)
  http://www.intercom.net/local/richardson/
  Owned a 2000 acre plantation, land grant dated November 9,
  1666, in Somerset County, later Worcester County Maryland.

- RICHBOURG Surname
  http://homepages.rootsweb.com/~jclaytn/richbourg.html
  Richbourg Surname: France>SC>AL>MS>TX.

- RICHFORD One-Name Study
  http://ourworld.compuserve.com/homepages/
  Kevin_H_Jennings/

- RICHTER Family History Page
  http://home.texoma.net/~mmcmullen/r/richter.htm

- RICKEY Family Association
  For details send e-mail to Stanton M. Rickey at
  rickeyroot@aol.com

- The Descendants of Jonas RICKS and Other RICKS
  Families in America
  http://www.geocities.com/Heartland/Plains/1948/index.html
  Mainly for Jonas Ricks, who was in Rowan County, North
  Carolina, in 1768, died in Guilford County 1821.

- RICKLEFS Family Center
  http://home.earthlink.net/~ricklefsr/
  RICKLEFS, RICKLEF, RICKLES, RICKEL, RICKELS,
  RICKLEFSEN plus other derivations.

- RIDER Family Chronicles
  http://www.geocities.com/Heartland/Hills/5650/

- RIDGWAY—RIDGEWAY Surname Study
  http://207.49.108.197/tango/pjohnson/

- RIFFE—R100 Mailing List
  http://www.cdc.net/~primus/genealogy/R100/R100.htm
  Reiff, Reif, Rief, Riffe, Rife . . . Families.

- RIGG—RIGGS Home Page
  http://www.geocities.com/Heartland/Hills/4192/Rigindx.html

- RILEY Genealogy Home Page
  http://www.paonline.com/csanders/Riley/RR_TOC.htm
  Descendants of Barnabas O'REILLY and Anna Marie FERREE
  of south central Pennsylvania.

- The RING Family Tree Homepage
  http://www.angelfire.com/md/ringtree/index.html
  Descendatns of Dennis Ring, emigrated from Cork, Ireland to
  New York via Liverpool in 1839.

- ROACH * ROACHE * ROCHE Genealogy
  Research
  http://www.geocities.com/Heartland/Acres/5725/

- The ROAN Irish Surname Page
  http://www.geocities.com/Athens/Delphi/4658/Roan.01.html
  Roan, Rohan, Roughan, Rowan.

- ROARK Surname Research "Texas Clan"
  Home Page
  http://www.phaenom.com.roark
  Roark in Texas—One-Name research for all surnames Roark,
  Roarke, Rourk, Rourke, O'Roark, O'Roarke, O'Rourk, &
  O'Rourke in Texas since the Repulic was settled.

- HOLCOMB and ROBERSON/ROBINSON
  http://members.aol.com/jogt/holcomms.htm

- Chuck ROBERTS Genealogy Page
  http://www.geocities.com/Heartland/Plains/3959/
  Index of over 1,300+ ROBERTS.

- ROBERTSON Families of the World
  http://www.shelby.net/shelby/jr/robertsn/

- ROBICHAUD Genealogy Exchange
  http://www.webgate.net/~earlr/
  Robichaud, Robichaux, Robicheau, Robicheaux, Robich.
  29,000+ names.

- Descendants of Goddard ROCKENFELLER
  http://www.netins.net/showcase/vbciowa/genie/Rockefellow/
  rock.htm
  Born in 1590 in Fahr, Germany.

- The RODRIGUE Families
  http://www.er.uqam.ca/nobel/g17176/rodrigue/engindex.html
  Quebec and Ontario in Canada, Louisiana and New England in
  the U.S.

- ROGERS Hunters Home Page
  http://users.ilnk.com/ejcornell/Rogers.htm

- ROMINE Family Group Genealogy
  http://www.geocities.com/Heartland/Plains/8574/
  Includes Romeyn, Romain, Romaine, Romines, Romeyns,
  Romains, Romaines, Remine, etc.

- Homepage Genealogy RO(O)S(Z)E(N)BOOM
  http://leden.tref.nl/pjdepenn/default.htm
  Rooseboom, Roosenboom, Roseboom, Rosenboom,
  Roozenboom, Roozeboom, Rozeboom, Rozenboom—Worldwide.

- ROSE Family Association Nationwide
  http://ourworld.compuserve.com/homepages/ChristineR/
  Rose surname throughout the U.S.

- ROSSON Genealogy Page
  http://www.geocities.com/Heartland/Valley/5785/
- ROTHENHÖFER (ROTHENHOEFER) Lineages
  http://www.azstarnet.com/~bkcntry/rotnhofr/index.htm
  Rothenhöfer Lineages explores this surname and its derivational forms. The site is principally directed at identifying the pre-1750 lineages throughout modern southwest Germany.
- The ROTHUIZEN / RODENHOUSE
  Family Web Site
  http://www.sigma.net/etymes/
  Eleven generations (with about 500 names) of the family of Anton and Wilhelmina Rothuizen (who changed the family name to Rodenhouse in 1919), originally from Osterbeek, Gelderland, Netherlands. The site makes a case for the theory that all those named "Rothuizen" or "Rotshuizen" might be related.
- ROUSE Family Genealogy
  http://www.geocities.com/Heartland/Hills/2342/rindex.html
- ROUNSEFELL One-Name Study
  http://members.xoom.com/4Grant/
- Les ROUSSEL en Amérique du Nord /
  ROUSSEL Families in North America
  http://www.cam.org/~mauricel
- John McKAY's Web Site—Descendants of
  Willis ROUTT
  http://www.aa.net/~jfmckay/
- ROYER Family in America
  http://www.cet.com/~royerr/
- The ROYER Family in Canada
  http://www.intplsrv.net/jroyer/gen/genhome.htm
- Descendants of Isaac RUCKER of
  Amerhert County, Virginia
  http://csc.techcenter.org/~mneill/ruckerisaac.html
- Wills of Peter RUCKER & John RUCKER
  http://members.aol.com/jogt/ruckerwl.htm
- The RÜCKER FAMILY SOCIETY
  http://www.mindspring.com/~jogt/surnames/ruckerfs.htm
- RUDISILL Family Association Page
  http://www.geocities.com/Heartland/Estates/6698/
- The RUE Family in the U.S.A.
  http://www.catskill.net/rue/family/rue/
- RUGGLES Family
  http://gator1.brazosport.cc.tx.us/~truggles/rug.htm
- The RUSSELL Family—Genealogy
  http://www.internet-partners.com/russell/index.htm
- The RUTLEDGE Family Association
  http://www.rootsweb.com/~rutledge/

◆ Surnames Beginning with "S"

- Family Tree Maker Online User Home Pages—S
  http://www.familytreemaker.com/users/s/index.html
- Genealogy's Most Wanted—Surnames Beginning
  with "S"
  http://www.citynet.net/mostwanted/s.htm
- H-GIG Surname Registry—Surnames Beginning S
  http://www.ucr.edu/h-gig/surdata/surname19.html
- Higginson Book Company—Surnames Beginning
  with S
  http://www.higginsonbooks.com/s.htm
- inGeneas Table of Common Surname Variations and
  Surname Misspellings—R–S
  http://www.ingeneas.com/R2S.html
- Surname Springboard Index—S
  http://www.geocities.com/~alacy/spring_s.htm
- SurnameWeb Surname Registry—S Index
  http://www.surnameweb.org/registry/s.htm
- Genealogy Resources on the Internet—
  "S" Surname Mailing Lists
  http://members.aol.com/gfsjohnf/gen_mail_surnames-s.html
  This site is wonderfully maintained by John Fuller. It includes mailing list information for the following surnames and their variant spellings:
  S425 (includes all soundex S425), SAATHOFF, SACKETT (includes Sacket, Seckett, Secket, Sachet, Sacet, Sackette, Sackitt, Sackat, Sackatt, Sackutt), SADLER, SAFFELL (includes Saffle, Saffel, Saffels), SAFLEY (includes Saftley, Safly, Saphley, Sapley, Saufley, Sofley, Softly), SAGER (includes Seger), SAHLSTRÖM (includes Salstrom, Sahlström), SAILOR, SAINT (includes Sant), SALISBURY (includes Sailsberry, Sailsbery, Salesbury, Salisburie, Salsberry, Salsbery, Salsburie, Salsburry, Salsbury, Salsibury, Salusbury, Saulisbury, Saulsberry, Saulsbery, Saulsbury), SALLEE (includes Sallé, Salle', Salle, Salee, Sally, Salley, Saley, Saly, Sallée, Sallie, Sailey, Salla, Sallings), SALLS (includes Sarles, Searles, Serls), SALO, SALYER, SAMPLES (includes Sample, Semple, Sempel), SAMPLES (includes Sample, Semple), SANDERS (includes Sander, Saunders, Sounder, Souder), SANDIDGE (includes Sandage, Sandige, Sandridge, Sandredge, Sandwich), SANDS, SANDUSKY, SANFORD (includes Sandford, Samford), SANT, SAPP, SARGENT (includes Sargeant, Sergent), SARTIN (includes Sartain, Sertain, Certain, Certing, Sarton), SASSER-L, SATTERFIELD, SAUER (includes Sauers, Sower, Sowers), SAUVAGEAU, SAVAGE, SAVILLE (includes Savil, Savill, Sayvell, Civil), SAWYER, SAXTON, SAYRES (includes Sayers, Sayer, Sears), SCARBOROUGH (includes Scarboro, Scarbrough, Scarborrow, Scarbro), SCHAGEL (includes Scadgel, Scegel, Schadgel), SCHAUB (includes Schawb, Schaup, Schauble, Schaible, Scheuble, Schüblin, Schaab, Shobe, Schoup), SCHAUER (includes Shauer, Shower), SCHELL (includes Shell, Shull, Shaul, Shoul, Schelle), SCHILLING, SCHISSLER (includes Schiesler, Schisler, Schoessler, Schuessler, Shisler, Schizler), SCHLEMMER (includes Schlemer, Schlimmer, Slimmer), SCHLOTTE (includes von Schlotte), SCHMIDT (includes Schmitt, Schmite, Schmide, Schmid), SCHMIDTKE, SCHMOYER (includes Schmeyer, Smoyer), SCHNEBELE (includes Snavely, Snively), SCHNORF, SCHOENEBERGER (includes Sheneberger, Shenberger, Shoneberger, Shaneberger), SCHOLL (includes Sholl, Shull), SCHREIBER (includes Schriever, Shriver, Schreibman, Schreber), SCHROEDER (includes Schroder, Schrader), SCHULTE-L, SCHULTZ (includes Shultz, Schulz, Schulze, Shults), SCHWENK, SCISM (includes Scissom, Scisson, Sissom, Sisson, Scizm, Chisholm, Chism, Cissom, Cism, Cisme, Cissum, Cisson), SCOBEE, SCOGIN (includes Scoggin, Scoggins, Scroggin, Scroggins, Scogen, Scoggen), SCOL (includes Sutfin, Sutphen, Sutphin, Zutphen), SCOTT, SCOTT, CLAN, SCOTTFam, Scottish-

WHITSON (Whitson with a Scottish heritage), SCOVILLE (includes Scovill, Schovel, Scovell), SEAL (includes Seals, Seale, Seales), SEAMAN, SEARS, SEAY, SECOR (includes Sicard, Seacord, Secord), SEDGWICK-L (includes Sedwick), SEE (includes Sie, Sea, Zea, Zie, Zeh, Cie), SEELY (includes Sealy, Selly, Seligh, Salee, Sallee, Saley, Salley), SELBY (includes Selbey), SELF (includes Selph, Selfe), SELLERS (includes Cellers, Sollars, Zellers), SELLON (includes Sellen), SELLS (includes Cells, Cell), SETTLE, SEVCIK, SEVIER (includes Severe, Xavier), SEWELL (includes Seawell, Sowell, Showell), SEXTON (includes Saxton, Saxon, Sesten, Saxe), SEYMOUR, SHACKELFORD (includes Shackford, Shackleford, Shakford), SHACKLETT (includes Shacklette, Shacklet, Jacquelot), SHADE, SHAFFER (includes Shafer, Shaeffer, Schaeffer, Schaefer, Schaffer, Schafer), SHANER (includes Schaner, Schoener, Shiner, Shoner, O'Shaner, Shane, O'Shane), SHANK, SHANNON (includes Shannahan), SHARP, SHATTO (includes Chateau, Schatteau, Schaddeau, Shaddeau, Shatow, Shedo, Scheddo, Schedo, Shattoe, Shado, Shadow, Shadel, Shadell, Shadle, Shaddle, Shaddo, Schatto, Schaddo, Shatts, Shotta, Shattow, Shattoo, Shato), SHAW, SHAWHAN (includes Shawn, Shahan, Shehane, Sheehane, Shehawn, Shehawne, Shehauon, Shehorn, Shahorn, Sheehaan, Sheahorn, Shehan, Shaughen, Sheohan, Shaan, Shehen), SHEELY (includes Sheeley, Shealy, Schiel, Schiele, Schiehl, Schiell), SHEETS (includes Sheetz, Scheets, Scheetz), SHELDON, SHELDRICK (includes Shildrick, Sheldrack, Sheldrake, Shildrake), SHELTON, SHEPHERD-SHEPPARD, SHERBONDY (includes Sherbundy, Shobundy, Shorbundy, Shorbondy), SHERBURNE, SHERMAN (includes Shearman), SHERRILL, SHERROD, SHERWOOD, SHIELDS (includes Shiels, Shield, Shiel, O'Shields, O'Shield), SHIELDS_Daniel, SHIFLETT, SHIPPEE (includes Shippy, Scheppe, Shippey), SHIRER, SHIRLEY (includes Sheale, Shurley), SHIVER, SHOCKEY (includes Schacke), SHOE-MAKER (includes Shumaker, Schumacher), SHOFNER, SHOLAR (includes Sholer, Sholars, Scholer, Scholar), SHOOK, SHORB (includes Schorb, Schorben, Sherb, Sherbs, Shorp, Shurp), SHORES, SHORT, SHORTRIDGE, SHOTWELL (includes Shadwell, Shotwill, Shotto), SHOUN (includes Shown, Shawn), SHOWERS, SHREWSBURY (includes Shrewsberry), SHRIVER, SHRUM (includes Schramm), SHUFF (includes Schoff, Schoffe, Schuff), SHUFFETT (includes Shuffet, Shoffit, Shuffit, Shuffitt), SHUMAN (includes Schuman, Schumann, Scheman, Sewman, Sheman, Shewman, Shoeman, Shueman, Suman), SHUMWAY (includes Shamway, Chamois), SIDDON, SIDES (includes Sites, Zeits), SIMCOCK (includes Simcox, Symcock), SIMONDS (includes Simons, Symonds, Symons, Simon, Symons, Simmonds, Simmons), SIMPSON (includes Simson), SIMS, SINCLAIR, SINDELAR, SINGLETON, SINKS, SIRES (includes Siers, Syers, Sias, Cyrus), SISCO (includes Francisco, Cisco), SISLER, SKAGGS (includes Scaggs, Skeggs, Sceggs), SKELTON, SKENE (includes Skeen, Skeens, Skeans), SKIFF, SKILES (includes Skyles), SKIPWORTH (includes Skipper, Skipwith), SLAGLE (includes Slagel), SLATON (includes Slaten, Slatton), SLAUTER (includes Slaughter), SLAVEN-SLAVEY (includes Slavin, Slavens, Slavy), SLEDGE (includes Slech, Sligo, Sluggo, Schleicher, Slaker), SLOAN-SLONE, SLOAT (includes Sloet, Slote, Slot, Slott, Slute, Sluet, Slaught, Van der Sloot, Sloet), SLONAKER (includes Sloneker, Sloniker, Slonneger, Schlunneger, Schluneger, Schloneker), SLUDER, SLY (includes Slye, Sligh), SMALL, SMALLEY, SMALLWOOD, SMART (includes Smartt), SMITH, SMITH, GEORGE STERLING, SMITH, NIMROD, SMITHSON, SMOTHERMAN (includes Smitherman), SMOTHERS, SNEAD, SNELSON (includes Snelston, Senellestone, Senelestune), SNODDY, SNOW (includes Snaw, Show, Schnee, Snowman), SNOWDON (includes Snowden), SNYDER (includes Snider, Schneider), SOLOMON, SOMERVILLE (includes Sommerville, Sumervell, Summerville), SORENSON, SORRELL (includes Sorrells, Sorrelle, Sorrel, Sorell, Sorel), SORTORE (includes Sortor, Sorter), SOUCY (includes Souci, Soucie, Soucis, Soucisse, Sucese), SOULE (includes Sowle, Sole), SOUTHON (includes Southen, Sowton, Souton), SOWDER (includes Souder,

Sowders, Souders), SPALDING (includes Spaulding), SPANN, SPEARMAN, SPEARS (includes Spear, Speer, Speers, Speir, Speirs), SPECK, SPEESE (includes Spees, Spies, Speece), SPEIDEL (includes Spidell, Spidle, Spydel, soundex code S134), SPELL, SPENCE (includes Spens), SPENCER (includes Spenser, Spincer, Spinser), SPICER, SPIKER (includes Speicher, Spyker, Spicker), SPILMAN (includes Spillman, Spelman, Spellman, Spielman, Espielman), SPINA, SPINKS, SPINNEY, SPIVEY (includes Spiva), SPOFFORD, SPONBERG (includes Sponeburgh, Sponburg), SPORES (includes Spore, Spoor, Spoors, Spur, Spurr, Spahr, Spohr, Sparr, Spoar), SPRADLIN, SPRINGER, SPRINGMAN (includes Springmann), SPROUSE (includes Sprouce), SPRUILL (includes Sprueil, Sprule, Sprewel, Spruell, Sproul), SPRY (includes Sprey, Spray, Sprie, Spree, Sprye), SQUIRE, STAATS (includes Statts, Stadts, States, Stats, Staat, Staet), STACKHOUSE, STAFFORD, STAGG (includes Stage, Stag, Staggs, Steg, Stegg, Stegge, Stegges, Du Stage), STAGNER (includes Stagnor, Stegner, Steigner), STALLINGS (includes Stalings, Stallons, Stalins, Stallins, Stalions, Stallions, Stillings, Stilings), STAMPER, STANFORD, STANGER (includes Stenger), STANLEY (includes Standley, Standly, Stanly), STANTON, STAPLES (includes Steeples, Staple), STAPLETON (includes Stapelton, Stableton, Stebleton, Stapylton, Stepleton, Steveldon, Stapulton, Stapilton, Stapledon, Staplton, Stebelton, Steppleton, Stapledown), STAPP (includes Stepp, Stapf), STARK (includes Starke, Starks), STARLING (includes Starlin, Starlyn, Starlyng, Starlynge), ST-ARNAUD (includes St. Arnou, St. Arnould, St. Arnoud, St. Arnaux, St. Arnault), STARNER-FAMILY, STARR (includes Star), STARRITT (includes Sterrett, Stirrat, Stirret, Stirrit. Starrat, Stirrat), STATEN (includes Staton), STAUFFACHER, STEARNS (includes Starnes, Stearne, Sterne, Sterns, Stearnes), STEBBINS (includes Stebbings), STEELE (includes Steel, Stahl, McSteely, Sterling, Stoele), STEELE (includes Steel, Stahl), STEGALL_N_STRATTON, STEICHEN (includes Stechen), STEINKE, STEPHENS-L (includes Stevens, Stephenson), STERNsurname, STEVENSON, STEWART (includes Stuart, Steuart, Steward), STICE, STICKNEY, STIDHAM (includes Stiddem, Steadman, Stedman), STILLWELL (includes Stilwell), STINNETT (includes Stennett, Stinet, Stinit), STITES, STITT, STJOHN, STLOUIS, STOCKER (includes Stucker, Stooker), STOCKSLAGER (includes Stocksleger), STOCKTON, STOKES, STOKES, STOLZ-REQUEST (includes Stoltz, Stultz, Stults), STONE, STONER, STONE-Spencer, ST. ONGE (includes Saintonge), STOOPS, STORCKE (includes Stork, Storckman, Storch, Storke, Storckwitz, Storc, Storck), STORM (includes Storms, Sturm), STORY (includes Storie, Storey, Stori), STOUT, STOVER, STOWE (includes Stow), STOWELL (includes Stowel, Stoel, Stawell), STOWERS, STRADTMAN (includes Strattman, Stradmann, Strathman), STRAIGHT (includes Strait, Streit), STRAIN (includes Soundex S365), STRASSER (includes Strawser, Strauser, Strausser, Strazer, Strauzer), STRAUSS, STREET, STREETER (includes Streater), STRICKLAND (includes Stricklin), STRICKLER (includes Stickler), STROCK (includes Strack), STROHSCHNEIDER, STRONG (includes Stronge, Strongman, Straughan, Straughn, Strang, Strange, Strangeman, Strachan, Strawn), STROUD (includes McStroud, Straub, Staub, Strauss, Stroupe, Strode), STUDDARD (includes Studard, Stoddard), STULTZ, STUMP (includes Stomp), STURGEON, SUDBURY (includes Sudberry, Sedberry, Sutberry), SUDDARTH (includes Sudderth, Suddoth, Sudduth, Suddith, Suddata, Suddreth), SUGGS (includes Sugg), SULLIVAN (includes Sullavan, Sullivant, Sullavant, O'Sullivan, O'Sullavan, O'Sullivant, McSullivan, McSullavan, McSullivant), SUMMERS, SUMNER (includes Somner, Summoner, Somnier, Sumners), SUMPTER (includes Sumter), SURBER (includes Sorber, Serber, Sarver, Server, Surbaugh), SURGENER (includes Surginer, Surginor, Sojourner), SUTTON, SWAIN (includes Swaine, Swayne, Swaim, Swaime, Swayme, Swem), SWANBOROUGH (includes Swansborough), SWAYZE (includes Swezey, Swayzie, Sweazy, Swasey, Sweezey), SWEET (includes Sweat, Sweatt, Sweatte), SWENSON, SWEPSON (includes Sweptson, Swepston, Swepstone, Swepton, Sweepson,

Sweepston, Sweepstone, Sweepton, Sivepson), SWIFT, SWINDLE, SWINFORD, SWINGLE, SWISHER-SWEITZER-var, SWOPE (includes Schwab, Swoope), SWORDS (includes Soards, Sowards, Sword), SYLVESTER.

- **SACKETT Surname Mailing List**
  http://www.nmmi.cc.nm.us/~nancy/sackett
  Includes Sacet, Seckett, Secket, Sachet, Sacet, Sackette, Sackitt, Sackat, Sackatt, Sackutt, Sackville, Saccavilla.

- **SAMSON Family Home Page**
  http://www.familytreemaker.com/users/s/a/m/Charles-A-Samson
  The Samson Family Homepage traces the descendants of the first Samson immigrants to New France (Quebec) in 1665.

- **SANDERS & SAUNDERS**
  http://www.geocities.com/Heartland/Plains/7614/sanders.htm
  A site for SANDERS and SAUNDERS Family History.

- **SANDERS Genealogy Home Page**
  http://www.paonline.com/csanders/Sanders/RR_TOC.htm
  Fom the south central Pennsylvania area.

- **The SANKEY One Name Study**
  http://www.sankey.demon.co.uk/genindex.html

- **SAPP Family History, Genealogy**
  http://members.aol.com/Sapps/SFH.html

- **The SASSO Meeting Place**
  http://members.aol.com/combit3/index.html
  A simple webpage for anyone researching the surname of Sasso especially, but not limited to those with roots in New York.

- **The SAULNIER Genealogy HomePage**
  http://www.geocities.com/Heartland/Acres/6946/
  Descendants of Louis Saulnier and Louise Bastinaud dit Pelletier, who arrived in Acadia (now Nova Scotia) c.1685.

- **The SAVAGE Family**
  http://home.att.net/~dpdklong/Savage.htm
  The SAVAGE family of central Alabama, with stories of their origin and an unusual Civil War story.

- **SCAMP—The Genealogy of a Gypsy Family**
  http://ourworld.compuserve.com/homepages/rogerbaker/

- **SCHAEFFER Genealogy**
  http://www.geocities.com/Heartland/Prairie/5275
  Schaeffer surname list, Schaeffer Photographs, Pennsylvania Deutsch, early settlers of Ohio and Illinois.

- **The SCHAKES of La Charette 1855–1996**
  http://www.rootsweb.com/~mowarren/schake/intro.html
  From Humfeld, Lippe (Germany) of the Teutoburger Forest to Charette Township, Warren County, Missouri.

- **SCHLAUDECKERS of the World**
  http://pages.prodigy.com/OH/schlaudecker/

- **SCHNELLER Genealogy**
  http://pages.prodigy.net/dave_lossos/schnel.htm

- **SCHOENEBERGER Surname Web Site**
  http://members.aol.com/rootshuntr/dir/Sch.html
  Includes Sheneberger, Shenberger, Shoneberger, Shaneberger.

- **SCHOONMAKER Family Association**
  http://home.earthlink.net/~rctwig/schoon.htm

- **The SCHRYVER Page**
  http://www.schryver.org
  Schryver, Schryver, Schriber, Schriver, de Schryver, De Schryver.

- **SCHULER Family Genealogy**
  http://ourworld.compuserve.com/homepages/RSchuler/schulerf.htm
  Descendants of Gabriel Schuler of Skippack, Montgomery County, Pennsylvania (c.1672–1779).

- **SCHUMAN SCHUMANN Surname Project**
  http://members.xoom.com/tsterkel/surname_projects/schuman.htm

- **SCHWEISSGÜT Historical Society**
  http://www.sns-access.com/~lamackey/swise.html
  Schwainsgute, Schweisgut, Schweisgood, Schweisgute, Schweisguth, Schweissgut, Schweissguth, Schweiszguth, Swaisgood, Sweisgood, Swicegood, Sweisguth, Swysgood, Weisgut.

- **SCHWEITZER, SWISHER, SWITZER Website**
  http://members.aol.com/TNash74528/Index.html

- **SCHWENKNet**
  http://www.cyberhighway.net/~gordons/
  Dedicated primarily to those living descendants of Conrad Schwenk (1601–1686), weaver, of Laichingen, Baden-Wuerttemberg in So. Germany.

- **SCOTT Family Lines**
  http://www.flash.net/~mscott/
  Descendatns of Uchtredius Filius SCOTT through Milton SCOTT.

- **The SEALE Family**
  http://www.dallas.net/~seale/

- **Descendants of Capt. John SEAMAN, Hempstead, Long Island, NY**
  http://www.familytreemaker.com/users/r/u/b/James-David-Rubins-CA/index.html

- **SEARLES Genealogy—Descendants of Joseph SEARLES and Elizabeth CARTER**
  http://home.sprynet.com/sprynet/mholland02/searles1.htm

- **SEARLES in Westchester County, New York**
  http://members.aol.com/jl3bluhm/sarles.htm
  SARLES, SARLLS, SARLS, SERLS, SIRLS, and SURLES

- **SEARS Family Association**
  http://www.genealogy.org/~lrsears

- **SEELYE Genealogy**
  http://pages.prodigy.net/seelyedan/seelye.htm
  SEELYE, SEELEY, SEELYE

- **SELF Family Newsletter**
  http://members.tripod.com/~SelfFamilyNewsletter/index.html
  A family publication started in 1982 for the surnames—Self, Selfe, Selph, abd other variants.

- **SELF PORTRAITS: The Self Family NetLetter**
  http://www.inland.net/~tim/

- **SELLERS Family Genealogy**
  http://www.netins.net/showcase/sellerfamily/
  SELLERS, SOLLARS, CELLARS, ZELLERS

- The SENSEBACH Family Research Assocation Home Page
  http://www.geocities.com/Heartland/Meadows/4596/
  Sensabaugh, Sensebaugh, Sensibaugh, Sencabaugh, Sencebaugh, Sencibaugh, Sensiboy, Sinsabaugh, Sinsapaugh, Sincebaugh, Cencebaugh, Sencenbaugh, Sensenbaugh, Sensanbaugh, Sincerbeaux, Cincebeaux, Cincebox, Sinsebox, Sincerbox, Sencerbox, Sencaboy.

- SERNÉ Genealogie
  http://www.tip.nl/users/m.c.serne
  Genealogy of the family Serné, Sernee, Serne. About 4000 names. This family lives in Holland, Canada, USA and Australia (and more).

- SEWELL Family History ~1760–1997~
  http://www.edm.net/~Pjsewell/
  Descendants of English Abraham SEWELL and Mary CARPENTER.

- SEXTON Genealogy Research Page
  http://www.genealogy.org/~sexton/
  SEXTON, SEXTEN, SAXON, SAXTON, SAXE

- The SHANKLAND One-Name Group
  http://ourworld.compuserve.com/homepages/shankland/

- SHANNON Genealogy & History
  http://www.geocities.com/Heartland/Hills/5600/

- SHANNON Searchers Newletter
  For details send e-mail to Joyce Shannon Bridges at JSBRIDG@aol.com

- SHEA Genealogy Links
  http://www.geocities.com/Heartland/Valley/1410/
  shea_index.html
  Shea, Shay

- The SHEALTIEL Family Worldwide
  http://www.shealtiel.org
  Saltiel, Shaltiel, Shaaltiel, Sealtiël, Chaltiel, Chartiel and Schaltiel.

- Descendants of John SHEARIN
  http://www.parsonstech.com/genealogy/trees/gshearin/
  SHEARIN.htm
  Born about 1626 in England. Includes Shearin, Shearon, Sherron and many more.

- The SHEATHERS—Our Australian Heritage
  http://www.wts.com.au/~pwsheather/phil/australi.html

- The SHELBY Exchange
  http://www.familytreemaker.com/users/t/r/o/Judith-A-Trolinger/
  Home page and quarterly newsletter.

- SHELDON Family Association
  http://members.aol.com/sheldons1/index.htm

- My SHELTON Family
  http://www.mindspring.com/~jogt/surnames/sheltfam.htm
  One Branch from Virginia.

- My SHERMAN Family Page
  http://members.aol.com/MALUTZ/tips.html

- The SHERMANs of Yaxley Home Page
  http://members.aol.com/macpinhead/sherman.html
  The group is name for Tom Sherman (1422–1493) of Yaxley, Suffolk, England, one of the earliest proven ancestors.

- SHERMANs of Yaxley
  http://www.geocities.com/Heartland/Ranch/3064/sherman.htm
  This site contains wills transcribed from "Some of the Descendants of Philip Sherman, First Secretary of Rhode Island" by Roy V. Sherman.

- The SHERRILL/SHERRELL Family Assn.
  http://www.abraxis.com/tuckahoe/shersher/shersher.html

- SHIFFER Genealogy Page
  http://home.att.net/~jsgehrig/index.html
  Home page for the name SHIFFER. Lists the descendants of Edward Shiffer, born 1828 in Pennsylvania.

- SHIFLETT Family Genealogy
  http://www.geocities.com/Heartland/Hills/4575/
  Shiflet, Shifflett, Shiplet, Shiplett, Shifflet.

- SHIPPEE, SHIPPEY, SHIPPY Genealogy
  http://www.geocities.com/Heartland/Plains/4799/shippee.html

- The SHIRLEY Association
  http://www.shirleyassociation.com

- The SHIVERS Family Newsletter
  E-mail Glydie Nelson for details at: glydie@alaska.net

- SHOCKLEY Descendants
  http://www.escape.com/~patpnyc/shockley.htm

- SHOEMAKE Family History Page
  http://www.tlxnet.net/~bradjudy/

- SHUCK Family Home Page
  http://homepage.interaccess.com/~nealu/shuck.htm
  Information exchange for researchers of the Shuck surname including the spelling variants Shook, Shock, Shoc, Shoch, Schuck, Schook, Schock, Schoc, Schoch, Schuh, Shue and Schug.

- SHUGART Family Tree and Genealogy
  http://www.familytreemaker.com/users/s/h/u/Eric—Shugart/
  index.html
  Descendants of John Shugart, born 1725 in Pennsylvania.

- SHULLEY Genealogy Home Page
  http://www.paonline.com/csanders/Shulley/RR_TOC.htm
  Descendants of Frederick Shulley of south central Pennsylvania.

- SHULL Family Genealogy
  http://www.geocities.com/Heartland/Ranch/8593/
  Shull genealogy from Jonathan Shull and Abraham Shull.

- The SHUMWAY Root Cellar
  http://www.shumway.org

- The SIDNEY Internet Directory
  http://www.i-way.co.uk/~sid/sidney.html
  The World Wide Web site of all things Sidney. Includes the surname Sydney.

- The SIMARD Genealogy Page
  http://www.gaudreau.org/arthur/genealogy/simard.sht

- The SIMS et al. GEDCOM Project
  http://www.world.std.com/~lsimms/simms2.html
  A centralized collection of over 2,000 Sims surnames and variant spellings: Sims, Simms, Syms, Symms, Symes, Symmes, Sim, Simm, Sime, Simmes, Syme, Symme, Sym, Symm, Sems, Semms, Semes, Semmes, Symns, Symmns et al.

- SINEX Family Newsletter
  Send e-mail to Antoinette Waughtel Sorensen at waughtel@oz.net for details.

- Genealogie van de familie SJOLLEMA
  http://www.noord.bart.nl/~tipama/genealogie.htm
  Netherlands

- SKILES—SKYLES Website
  http://members.techheadnet.com/skifri/index.htm

- SKINNER Family Association
  http://www.geocities.com/Paris/1051/SkinnerFamAssc.htm

- SKIPWORTH Family Homepage
  http://members.aol.com/bartology/bartology/
  SkipworthHome.html

- Revealing Family Ancestry—
  SLAGG Family History
  http://www.hal-pc.org/~jsb/page36.html

- SLÄKTEN STÅLNACKE—STÅLNACKEN suku
  The Family Stålnacke
  http://angelfire.com/ri/stolnacke/index.html
  Sweden, Finland and Norway.

- Descendants of Thomas SLEDD
  http://csc.techcenter.org/~mneill/thomassledd.html

- The SLEE One Name Study
  http://www.homeusers.prestel.co.uk/naylor/slee.htm

- SLUDERs Online—A SLUDER Family Association
  http://members.aol.com/tomsluder/sluder.htm

- SMALTZ Genealogy—Part 1
  http://pages.prodigy.com/MD/xnra99a/xnra99a3.html
  With links to Part 2 and other surnames.

- SMART Memorial Preservation Society
  http://www.geocities.com/Heartland/Meadows/7602/
  Descendants of Reverend James SMART, born October 13, 1714 in Prince George Co., Virginia and his wife Elizabeth LEDBETTER.

- Joseph SMITH
  http://www.aracnet.com/~pslamb/joseph.htm
  Of Anson County, North Carolina.

- SMITH Families of England and New England Newsletter
  For details send e-mail to Lucinda (Cindy) Olsen, editor and publisher, at CarlCindy2@aol.com

- SMITH Genealogy
  http://members.aol.com/ImaBR/index.html
  Descendants of Freeman R. SMITH, b. 25 Oct. 1814 in North Carolina.

- Some Descendants of James SMITH of Weymouth, Massachusetts
  http://www.prenticenet.com/home/vandy/smith.htm

- The SMITHSON Association
  http://members.aol.com/Rickishay/shp.html/
  The Smithson Family Exchange Newsletter, mailing list, photo archive and more.

- The SMITTER Family Tree
  http://users.netonecom.net/~pwn/smitter/index.html
  Descendants of Wobbes SMITTER, born in the 1700's, died in 1823.

- SMOOT Ancestry
  http://www.familytreemaker.com/users/s/m/o/Steve-L-Smoot/
  Devoted to the descendants of William SMUTE, born 1596.

- SMUIN Genealogy pages
  http://www.smuin.demon.co.uk/pages/geneo1.htm
  SMUIN, SMEWING, SMEWIN, etc.

- Descendants of Freeman SNELGROVE
  http://www.parsonstech.com/genealogy/trees/psnellgr/
  charlie.htm

- The SNELSON DataBase & Index
  http://www.ozemail.com.au/~jsnelson/snelson.html

- SNIPES Family History, Person County, North Carolina
  http://www.geocities.com/Heartland/Estates/3882/Snipes.html
  Descendants of Richard SNAPE, born in Oxford Co., England.

- SNIPES Family of America Home Page
  http://www.familytreemaker.com/users/s/n/i/Robert-T-Snipes/

- SNYDER Surnames Search
  http://www.angelfire.com/fl/SNYDER/index.html

- The SOLE Society
  http://village.vossnet.co.uk/t/timsoles/sole.htm
  Sole, Saul, Sewell, Solley and their variants.

- SORRELL Genealogy
  http://www.webpak.net/~kyblue/sorrell/index.htm

- The SORTORE Family
  http://www.mcn.net/~hmscook/jsortore/sortore.html
  Also SORTOR and SORTER.

- SOUTHER Family Association
  http://www.geocities.com/Heartland/Estates/9785/
  SoutherHomePage.html
  Foremost genealogical site on the web for the surname Souther. Descendants of Joseph Souther of Boston, MA including Hingham, Cohasset & Quincy, MA. Surnames: Sprague, Stowell, Gill, Hersey, Pineo, Hersey, Tower, Lincoln.

- SOUTHON One-Name Study
  http://home.clara.net/iainkerr/southon.htm
  Sotheran, Sothern, Sotheron, Southan, Southin, Southen, Southon, Southerin, Southern, Sowtan, Sowten, Sowton, Sudran, Sudrenn, Sudron, Sutherin, Suthern, Sutherns, Suthren, Suthryn.

- SOUTH Surname Home Page
  http://users.aol.com/cmsouth/

- The SOUTHWORTH Home Page
  http://members.aol.com/sforg/index.html

- SOWDER / SOUDER Collections
  http://www.geocities.com/~jdanielson/sowder.htm

- The SOWDER Genealogical & Historical Society
  http://www.familytreemaker.com/users/s/o/w/DALE-E-
  SOWDER/

- The SPELTZ Web
  http://www.speltz.com
- SPENCER Historical and Genealogical Society, Inc.
  http://advicom.net/~lcrowe/shgs.htm
- The SPIKER / SPEICHER / SPYKER Family National Registry
  http://users.intercomm.com/spike/
- The International SPRACKLEN Home Page
  http://www.phaenom.com/spracklen
  Spracklen, Spracklin, Sprackling, Sprackland, Spradlin, Spradling, Sparklin etc. in England, Canada, South Africa and the US.
- SPRAGUE Database
  http://www.mhtc.net/~rewcsdb/sprague.htm
  Compiled by Richard E. (Dick) Weber, over 81,000 individuals.
- SPROUSE Family Page
  http://pages.prodigy.net/jeffone/
- Descendants of Dr. Godfrey SPRUILL
  http://www.rootsweb.com/~takelley/spruill/godfrey.htm
  Born about 1650 in Scotland and died about 1719 in North Carolina.
- The SPURLOCK Family Association
  http://www.geocities.com/Heartland/Hills/4411/
- The STACY Journal
  http://www.otn.net/stacy/
  A comprehensive study of the Stacy families from England and in America. Descendants of Thomas Stacy of Saffron Walden, England.
- STAERKEL, STOERKEL, STÄRKEL, STÖRKEL, STARKEL, STERKEL Surname Project
  http://members.xoom.com/tsterkel/surname_projects/sterkel.htm
- The STAMPER Family
  http://home.att.net/~BoKay1/index.html
- STANDERFER, etc. Research Site
  http://www.carolyar.com
  Standerfer, Standifer, Standefer, Standiford, Standforth, Sanderford, Sandefur, Sandefer, Standford, Sanford, etc.
- Descendants of Thomas STARR
  http://www.parsonstech.com/genealogy/trees/rrooy1/starr.htm
  Born about 1540 in New Romney, Kent, England.
- The STEAD / STEED One-Name Study
  http://www.canterbury.ac.uk/depts/acad/science/staff/shelagh.htm
- The W.T. STEAD Page
  http://www.iinet.net.au/~sharpen/stead.htm
  Dedicated to William Thomas Stead (1849–1912).
- STEELE Quarterly News
  For details send e-mail to Tammy Steele at: Tlsteeled@aol.com
- The STELLJES Genealogy Project
  http://www.geocities.com/ResearchTriangle/1794/Stelljes.html
  STELJES, STELLJIS

- STENFELT Family Genealogy
  http://www.ndepot.com/stenfelt/
  Traces primarily the STENFELT lineage including the variations STONEFELT, STONEFIELD and STENFELDT, from Georg STENFELT to the known current living descendants. Also partial royal (Sweden) lineages of Vasa and Stråle.
- The STENLAKE Genealogy Homepage
  http://www.enter.net/~stenlake/stenlake.html
- The STEPIEN's
  http://www.geocities.com/Heartland/Prairie/8473/stepien.html
- Clan STERLING-STIRLING Online
  http://home1.gte.net/mcej/index.htm
- STERRY Worldwide
  http://www.zip.com.au/~rsterry/gen/
- STEVENSON Family History from the Eastern Shore of Maryland, Worcester Co, MD to Woodford Co, KY to Putnam Co, IN by Margaretta Stevenson 1968.
  ftp://ftp.rootsweb.com/pub/STEVBOOK.EXE
  This is an executable file that you can download via FTP by clicking on the link above. It is an 877KB file, including a viewer and a scanned copy of this book. This book lists STEVENSON's in Worcester Co, Maryland from about 1700–1790, Woodford Co, KY 1790–1824, and then Indiana from early 1800's. Other surnames mentioned are CROPPER, COX, LITTLETON, WHITTINGTON, FASSITT, CAMPBELL, NELSON. If you have any questions, contact George Stevenson by e-mail at: george@psychoed.com
- John STEVENSON of Boston, 1637
  http://users.aol.com/jhstevenso/surnames.htm
  and his descendants.
- STEVICK Family Tree Index
  http://bhs.broo.k12.wv.us/homepage/alumni/dstevick/tree/index.htm
- STEWART Clan Newsletter
  http://members.aol.com/jlcooke/scn.htm
  For Stewart, Steward, and Stuart.
- STILES Family of America & Affiliated Familes, Inc.
  http://www.psci.net/~rstiles/
- STITT Surname Mailing List
  http://www.ctaz.com/~shadgraf/stitt-l.htm
- STIVER Family Home Page
  http://members.aol.com/flstiver/stiver.html
  Descendants of Dietrich STÖVER and wife Magdalena EBERWEIN of Frankenberg, Germany. STÖVER, STOEVER, STAVER, STIVER.
- The STOCKDILL Family History Society
  http://ourworld.compuserve.com/homepages/roystock/
- The STOCKMAN Family Newsletter
  http://www.zianet.com/stockman_allen/
  History and genealogy of the STOCKMAN/STUCKMAN family in the United States.

- STOUT Family History Page
  http://home.earthlink.net/~cwtram/stout.html

- My STOVALL Family
  http://members.aol.com/ImaBR/STOVALL.htm
  Descendants of George STOVALL, born ca. 1555, probably in Surrey, England.

- STOVALL Family Association
  http://www.bhm.tis.net/~stovall/sfa/index.html

- STOVER / STOBER Genealogy Page
  http://www.geocities.com/Heartland/Hills/8220/
  Ancestors and Descendants of Johan Valentin Stober/Stover (1692–1741) with emphasis on the Stover families of Centre County, PA.

- Trekking STOVER Cousins Webpage
  http://www.geocities.com/Heartland/Meadows/1043/
  Descendants of Jacob Stover and Sarah Boone. Jacob Stover came to America from Switzerland in 1710.

- Genealogical Journeys in Time—STRAWN Surname & others
  http://ourworld.compuserve.com/homepages/Strawn/

- STREEPERS in America
  http://www.n1.net/~mcward/sia.htm
  Descendants of Wilhelm/Willem STREYPERS and Mary/Mercken WILLEMSEN LUCKEN.

- STREVEL Genealogy Website
  http://members.aol.com/bstr2/index.htm
  Dedicated to Johannes Striebel and his descendants.

- SFAA Homepage—STRONG Family Association of America
  http://www.geocities.com/Heartland/Prairie/4715/

- STRONG Genealogy Network
  http://www.geocities.com/Heartland/Meadows/5744/
  Strong, Stronge, Strang, Strange, L'Estrange, etc.

- The STRONG Quest
  http://ro.com/~rts2/
  Research on the surname Strong(e), anywhere, anytime, including any phonetic, graphic, or etymologic equivalents, such as Strang(e) and Straughan, Strawn, etc. Home Page on the WWW of the Strong Mail List.

- STRONG Roots Database
  http://fly.hiwaay.net/~jgilbert/main/srd-toc.htm

- SULLIVAN! SULLIVAN! SULLIVAN!
  http://www-leland.stanford.edu/~meehan/sullivan/sull.html

- SULOUFF or SULOFF, We're One Family
  http://www.geocities.com/Heartland/Ranch/8094/
  Descendants of Johannes ZULAUF, arrived from Germany at Staten Island on 15 August 1776.

- SURGENER Genealogy Research Sources
  http://home.rmci.net/adamewa
  Research records collection for the Surgener name and its many variations: Surginer, Surginor, Sojourner, etc.

- Milo SUTTON Home Page
  http://www.geocities.com/Heartland/5248/
  Links to many Sutton resources including a newsletter and mailing list.

- The SUTTON Searchers Newletter Genealogy Homepage
  http://sutton.org

- Seining SWAIMs
  http://www.geocities.com/Heartland/Ridge/9157/
  Descendants of William A. Swaim, North Carolina.

- The SWATEK / SVATEK Genealogy Page
  http://www.swatek.com/genealogy.htm
  Descendants of Frank A. Swatek/Svatek and Josephine Richter.

- SWINDLEY Family History Page
  http://www.swindley.demon.co.uk/famhist/swindleys.html

- SWINSCOE Home Page
  http://www.users.bigpond.com/waugh/frames.htm
  SWINSCOE, SWINSCOW, SWAINSCOE

- Jacob Rivers SWISHER Descendants
  http://members.delphi.com/floa/index.html

- Genealogical Research Center for the CYRENNE or SYRENNE Families in Canada
  http://www3.sympatico.ca/gpfern/EHOME.HTM

◆ Surnames Beginning with "T"

- Family Tree Maker Online User Home Pages—T
  http://www.familytreemaker.com/users/t/index.html

- Genealogy's Most Wanted—Surnames Beginning with "T"
  http://www.citynet.net/mostwanted/t.htm

- H-GIG Surname Registry—Surnames Beginning T
  http://www.ucr.edu/h-gig/surdata/surname20.html

- Higginson Book Company—Surnames Beginning with T
  http://www.higginsonbooks.com/t.htm

- inGeneas Table of Common Surname Variations and Surname Misspellings—T–Z
  http://www.ingeneas.com/T2Z.html

- Surname Springboard Index—T
  http://www.geocities.com/~alacy/spring_t.htm

- SurnameWeb Surname Registry—T Index
  http://www.surnameweb.org/registry/t.htm

- Genealogy Resources on the Internet—"T" Surname Mailing Lists
  http://members.aol.com/gfsjohnf/gen_mail_surnames-t.html
  This site is wonderfully maintained by John Fuller. It includes mailing list information for the following surnames and their variant spellings:
  TABAR (includes Taber, Tabor), TACKETT (includes Tackitt), TAFT, TAGGART (includes McTaggart, MacTaggart), TALIAFERRO (includes Talifero, Toliver, Talafero), TALLENT, TALLEY (includes Tally), TALLMAN (includes Tallmon, Tollman, Talman, Taleman), TANDY, TANNER, TANQUARY (includes Tanquery, Toncray, Tonkery, Toncre, Tonkery, Tonkray, Tonchre), TAPPTICO (includes Tapp), TAPSCOTT (includes Tapscot, Tabscott), TARDIF-TARDY (includes Tardiff, Tardieu), TARKINGTON (includes Tarkenton), TARRANT, Tarshis, TART (includes Tarte, Tartt), TARVIN, TARWATER (includes

Theurwachter, Torwater, Tawater), TATE (includes Tait, Tatum), TATMAN (includes Tateman, Totman), TATUM (includes Tatem, Tatom, Tatam), TAULBEE (includes Talbee, Tolby, Talby), TAYLOR, Taylorans, TEACHOUT (includes Tietsort, Titsworth), TEAGUE (includes Tegge), TEASLEY (includes Teasler), TEBBETTS (includes Tibbetts), TEEL-TEAL, TEER, TEMPLE (includes Temples), TENNANT, TENNEY (includes Tinney), TEPPER (includes Topper, Toeppfer), TERPENING (includes Teerpenning, Terpenning, Tarpanning, Tarpeny, Terbening), TERRIL, TESLER (includes Tessler, Teszler, Teslyar, Tsesler, Tchesler, Dessler), TETER, TEVAULT (includes Devolt), TEWKSBURY, THAMES (includes Timms, Tims), THATCHER (includes Thacher), THAXTON (includes Thackston), THOMAS (includes Tomas, Thomason), THOMASON (includes Thomasson, Thompson, Thomas), THOMPSON (includes Thomson, Tompson), THOR (includes Tor), THORESON (includes Toreson), THORN (includes Thorne), THORNBURG (includes Thornberg, Thornburgh), THORNHILL, THORNTON, THRASHER (includes Thresher), THREET (includes Threat, Threatte, Thweat, Thweatte, Thwreat), THRIFT, THROWER (includes Trower), THRUSH, THURLOW (includes Thurloe, Thallow, Tallow, Thorlow, Thirlow, Thorley), THURSTON, TIBBS (includes Tebbs), TIDD-genealogy, TIDWELL (includes Tidywell, Tadwell), TIFFIN, TIGNOR (includes Tigner, Tickner), TILLER, TIMBRELL (includes Timbrel), TIMM, TIMMONS, TINCHER, TING, TINGLEY, TINGSTROM, TINKER (includes Tincher), TIPTON, TITUS-Dutch, TOCA, TODD, TOLAND (includes Tolland, Tolan, Tolen), TOLER (includes Tolar, Tollar, Toller), TOLLETT, TOMAN, TOMBLIN, TOMLINSON (includes Tomalinson, Tomlin, Tomilson, Timlinson), TOMPKINS, TOOMBS (includes Toms, Tombs), TOSELEY (includes Tosley), TOTEN (includes Tatan, Tatin, Taton, Tattan, Tattin, Tatton, Tatum, Tootan, Tooten, Totin, Toton, Tottan, Tottin, Totton, Tutan, Tuten, Tutin, Tuttan, Tutten, Tutton, and any other T350 Soundex-based, surname), TOTTEN, TOTTY (includes Tottie, Tottey, Tottye, Toddy, Toddie, Toty, Tolly, Tollie Tutte, Tutty), TOURTELLOTTE (includes Tourtillott, Tortlot, Tourtellott), TOWERS, TOWNE, TOWNER, TOWNSEND, TRABUE (includes Trabuc), TRANT, TRAYLOR (includes Traylo, Trailer, Trayler, Trailor), TREADWELL (Treadwell/Tredwell database maintenance), TREADWELL (Treadwell/Tredwell queries and discussions), TREAT, TREMBLE (includes Trembly, Trembley), TRENT, TRETTER, TRICE-L, TRIMBLE, TRIMMER, TRIPP, TRITTON (includes Tritten, Tryton), TRORBAUGH (includes Trorbach), TROTTER (includes Trot, Tretter), TROTTIER, TROWBRIDGE, TROWER, TROXEL (includes Troxell, Trachsel), TRUAX (includes Truex, Trueax, Truaxe, Du Trieux), TRUE (includes Trew), TRUELOVE, TRUITT-L (includes Truett), TRYON (includes Tryan, Trion, Trial, Tryall), TUBBS, TUCKER (includes Tuck, Tucks), TULLOS, TUNISON, TURBERVILLE (includes Turbeville, Troublefield, Turbervyle), TURK (includes Turck), TURNBULL, TURNER (includes Turney, Doerner, Durner, Tarner, Terner, Tourneau, Tirner, Torner, Tearner), TURVEY (includes Turvy), TUTCHER, TUTTLE, TWEEDY1, TWIDWELL, TWOMEY (includes Tome, Toomay, Toomee, Toomey, Tumee, Tumey, Tuomy, Twoomy, O'Tuama), TYER, TYLER (includes Tighler, Tiler, Tiller, Tylor), TYO (includes Taillon), TYSON.

- The TACKETT Family Association
  http://www.jps.net/jtackitt/index.html

- The TAFT Family Association Home Page
  http://members.aol.com/sbroker12/taft/index.html

- TALIAFERRO
  http://www.gensouth.com/taliaferro/

- TALIAFERRO Times
  http://www.spingola.com/ds/TaliaferroTimes/TT.htm
  This site contains 50 back issues of the Taliaferro Times, a now defunct e-mail newsletter of interest to persons researching the surname Taliaferro. Lots of great information.

- Genealogy of the TANKERSLEY Family in the United States
  http://members.aol.com/gkobernus/tankindx.html
  Descended from an old English family of that name in Tankersley Parish, Yorkshire, England.

- TANNAHILL Family Reunion
  http://home.att.net/~Tannahill/
  April 3, 1999, Fort Worth, Texas USA.

- The TARPEY Home Page
  http://sun1.bham.ac.uk/C.M.Tarpey/tarpeys/

- TARVIN Family Association
  http://tarvin.genweb.org

- TATE Family History Page
  http://home.texoma.net/~mmcmullen/ta/tate.htm

- The TATUM Archives
  http://www.rootsquest.com/~ranlewis/
  A collection of information, links and researchers of the Tatum family of the United States.

- TAYLOR Family History
  http://www.scruz.net/~jt/Grace/HISTORY.htm
  Genealogy of William TAYLOR & Elizabeth WELLS of Lincolnshire England, then immigrated to Cincinnati; descendants in Iowa, Kansas, Indiana & Colorado.

- Descendants of Henry TEACHOUT (1781–1852) of Chittenden Co, Vermont
  http://www.teachout.org/gen/index.html

- The TEAL Family History Homepage
  http://www.dteal.dircon.co.uk/
  TEAL family history in Yorkshire, UK. Decendants of Thomas Teal 1705–1771 of the Parish of Fewston in the Washburn Valley.

- TEGEN / TEGAN Genealogy
  http://www.inetworld.net/~tegen/Genealogy/genealogy.html

- TENNENT Genealogy Tree
  http://www.wolfe.net/~dtennent/Tennents.html

- TERRY Family
  http://www.wf.net/~billk/Terry.html
  Descendants of James Doss TERRY and Katharina FERBER.

- The TERWILLIGER Family Association
  http://home.earthlink.net/~rctwig/

- TEWKSBURY Tracings—A Surname Resource Center
  http://www.nataliesnet.com/tewksbury
  Tewksbury family in the U.S. Genealogy site, queries, source records, links, researchers list, descendancies, etc.

- Famille THERRIEN
  http://www.genealogie.org/famille/therrien/
  Home page for the Therrien Family Association also known as "Le Ralliement des familles Jean et Pierre Therrien."

- Histoire et généalogie—THIBAUDEAU—THIBODEAU—History and Genealogy
  http://www.qouest.net/~jljmt/index.htm
  Pierre THIBEAUDEAU, le pionnier Acadien. THIBODAUX, THIBEAUDEAU, THIBAUDEAUX, THIBODEAUX, TEBEDORE, TIBEDORE, THIBODEAULT, THIBAUDEAULT, THYBAUDEAU, THIBEDEAU, TIBIDO, THIBIDAUX, THIBAUDAU, THIBODOT, BODEAU, BODO, THIBADEAU, THEBADO, TIBBEDEAUX, TIBADO, TOLADO

- THOMAS Family Archives
  http://www.geocities.com/Heartland/Hills/2603/
  Descendants of Job Thomas b. c 1736 Virginia.

- THOMAS Family Tree
  http://homepage.dave-world.net/~davidt/Thomas.html
  Descendants of Michael Thomas, born 1759 Fayette Co, Pennsylvania, died 1840 Ross Co, Ohio and Elizabeth Bennett.

- THOMAS Genealogy
  http://www.ghgcorp.com/tbraithw/genthoma.html

- Andrew THOMPSON of Wythe and Bland Counties, Virginia and Descendants
  http://www.neticus.com/~cgaisfor/Family/Cragun/index.htm

- THOMPSON Family Genealogy Page
  http://www.indy.net/~barneyt/thompson.htm
  The Thompson Family of Prince Edward County, Virginia Butler and Trigg Counties, Kentucky and the Florida Parishes of Louisiana: The Descendants of Thomas Thompson, 1740–1810.

- THOMPSON One Name Study
  http://www.geocities.com/Athens/2249/

- THORBURN-MACFIE Family Society
  http://home1.swipnet.se/~w-10723/thormac1.htm
  Descendants of William Thorburn and his wife Jessy (née Macfie) who in July 1823 removed to Sweden from Leith in Scotland.

- THORNDELL Descendants, 1599–1999
  http://members.aol.com/davethornl/thorndell/index.htm
  Descendants of Edward Thorndell and Ann Scollock married 14 Jan 1599 in Gloucestershire, England.

- THRASHER Genealogy
  http://www.eskimo.com/~greg/thrasher.html
  A mailing list, queries, cemetery information and more.

- THURMAN's Quest
  http://www.megabits.net/~lthurman/
  THURMAN and related Surname on-line repository with 6 major databases and over 25,000 on-line names.

- The TILLOTSON Project
  http://www.tillotson.net
  TILLOTSON, TILSTON, TILLERSON, TILSON, TILLITSON, TILLETSON, TILLISON, TILESTONE, TILESTON, TILLSON, TILLESTON

- TIMPERLEY Family History and Genealogy
  http://ourworld.compuserve.com/homepages/mtimperley/
  Alternate Spellings: Temperley, Temperly, Timberley, Timberly, de Timperley, Timperly.

- TINNEY Surname
  http://www.geocities.com/Heartland/Ranch/5409/

- Descendants of John TINSLEY
  http://csc.techcenter.org/~mneill/tinsjohn.html

- The TIPTON Family Association Of America
  http://pages.prodigy.net/seelyedan/tipton.htm

- The TITTERTON Family Web Site
  http://www.titterton.mcmail.com
  TITTERTON families live all around the world and not just in the UK. The web site looks at the origin of the surname and the various families using the name.

- Decendants of Silius TITUS
  http://www.familytreemaker.com/users/p/e/t/Richard-L-Pettitt/

- The TOADVINE Family
  http://www.intercom.net/user/toadvine/index.html
  Nicholas TOADVINE from Guernsey Island to Maryland in approx. 1675.

- TODD Family Message Board
  http://www.rootsweb.com/~genepool/toddboard.htm

- The TOLLINGTON Home Page
  http://www.hotstar.net/~moose/index.htm

- TONEY Genealogy Exchange
  http://www.toneyweb.com/exchange/

- TOWSE Tree Family HomePage
  http://members.tripod.com/~DCohig/index.html
  Towse surname worldwide.

- The TRACEWELL Family Genealogy Site
  http://www.bonk.com/tracewell/

- TRAMMELL Family History Page
  http://home.earthlink.net/~cwtram/trammell.html

- TRAMMELL Surname Webring
  http://www.geocities.com/Heartland/Flats/4239/trammell.html

- R.W. TRASK Family Home Page
  http://www.geocities.com/Heartland/8860/
  With a listing of other TRASK researchers.

- TRASK Genealogy Web Site
  http://www.i-way.co.uk/~lawrie/family/index.htm

- The TRAUTVETTERs of Hancock County, Illinois
  http://asc.csc.cc.il.us/~mneill/trautv/trautv.htm
  Originating in and around Bad Salzungen, Thuringen, Germany.

- TREASE Family Home Page
  http://www.geocities.com/Heartland/Pointe/1420
  Surname information on TREASE, TREECE, TREACE, TRIECE.

- TRETHEWY Page
  http://www.angelfire.com/mi/cornwall/tre.index.html
  Variants: TRETHEWY, TRETHEWEY, TRETHEWIE and TRETHEWAY, originating in Cornwall.

- TREVATHAN & TREVETHAN—A Family from Cornwall
  http://www.geocities.com/BourbonStreet/7769/

- TRUDE Family Genealogy
  http://www.intplsrv.net/tltrude/
  Trude or DeTrude in America and Canada.

- The TRUMBLE-TRUMBULL Family History and Genealogy
  http://www.trumble-trumbull.com
  Everything about the Trumble/Trumbull families in America.

- TRUSLER / TRUSLOW Surname Home Page
  http://home.earthlink.net/~artcheryl/

- The TUCKER Kingdom Web Ring
  http://earth.vol.com/~ecochran/ring.html

- World TUDDENHAM Family Tree
  http://www.users.globalnet.co.uk/~jerryt/

- TUPMAN Family Data
  http://freespace.virgin.net/alan.tupman/sites/down1.htm

- TURNBULL History
  http://www.falls.igs.net/~corey/turnbull.htm

- The James TURNER Family of Amherst Co., VA, Sumner Co., TN and Marshall Co., MS
  http://members.aol.com/jogt/turnerja.htm

- TURNER Archive & Historical Records Collection
  http://members.aol.com/tahrc/
  Descendants of Jesse Porter Turner & Malinda Francis Barnhart Turner, Boone County, Missouri.

- TURNER Family Genealogy
  http://members.aol.com/PSulzer/Turner.html
  Descendants of John TURNER and his son Fielding, born 1706 Northumberland Co., Virginia.

- TWEEDIE or TWEEDY Genealogy and Family History
  http://www.apgate.com/fam_his/index.html
  Information regarding this family's origins in the Scottish Border Country.

- TWITCHELL Links
  http://golden.adams.net/~etwitch/
  Descendants of Benjamin TWITCHELL who immigrated from Buckinghamshire, England in about 1630. Includes these spellings: TWICHEL, TWICHELL, TWITCHEL.

- TYLCOAT TYLECOTE TALCOTT Genealogy
  http://ourworld.compuserve.com/homepages/dave_tylcoat/

- The TYREE Name
  http://users.aol.com/rtyree/a/TyreeName.html
  TYRIE, TIRI, TYREE, etc. in Scotland.

◆ Surnames Beginning with "U"

- Family Tree Maker Online User Home Pages—U
  http://www.familytreemaker.com/users/u/index.html

- Genealogy's Most Wanted—Surnames Beginning with "U"
  http://www.citynet.net/mostwanted/u.htm

- H-GIG Surname Registry—Surnames Beginning U
  http://www.ucr.edu/h-gig/surdata/surname21.html

- Higginson Book Company—Surnames Beginning with U
  http://www.higginsonbooks.com/u.htm

- inGeneas Table of Common Surname Variations and Surname Misspellings—T–Z
  http://www.ingeneas.com/T2Z.html

- Surname Springboard Index—U
  http://www.geocities.com/~alacy/spring_u.htm

- SurnameWeb Surname Registry—U Index
  http://www.surnameweb.org/registry/u.htm

- Genealogy Resources on the Internet—"U" Surname Mailing Lists
  http://members.aol.com/gfsjohnf/gen_mail_surnames-uv.html
  This site is wonderfully maintained by John Fuller. It includes mailing list information for the following surnames and their variant spellings:
  UHL (includes Uhle), ULLMAN (includes all U455 soundex names such as Uhlman, Ullmann), UNANGST, UNDERWOOD, UPSHAW (includes Upshur, Upsher, Upcher, Upshire, ApShaw), UPTON, URAN (includes Urin, Urann), URBAN, UTLEY (includes Uttley).

- The UFKES Genealogy Home Page
  http://asc.csc.cc.il.us/~mneill/ufkes/main.html
  Descendants of Hinrich Jansen UFKES (1797–1873) and his wife Trientje Eilts POST (1803–1878) of the Holtrop and Wiesens area of Ostfriesland, Germany.

- ULLMER Genealogy Page
  http://www.du.edu/~cullmer/gene.html
  Decendents of Joseph Ullmer 1853–1910.

- The UNGERLEIDER Family Foundation
  http://members.aol.com/jackunger/family/index.html

- The URRY Family—URRY An Isle of Wight Family
  http://www.marcireau.fr/urry/urry.htm
  URRAY, URY, URIE, URRIE, URI, URRI, UREY, HURRY, ORRY, ORRI, HORREY

- USSERY / USERY / USRY / URSERY / ESSARY and Associated Families
  http://www.netunlimited.net/~ccasey/

◆ Surnames Beginning with "V"

- Family Tree Maker Online User Home Pages—V
  http://www.familytreemaker.com/users/v/index.html

- Genealogy's Most Wanted—Surnames Beginning with "V"
  http://www.citynet.net/mostwanted/v.htm

- H-GIG Surname Registry—Surnames Beginning V
  http://www.ucr.edu/h-gig/surdata/surname22.html

- Higginson Book Company—Surnames Beginning with V
  http://www.higginsonbooks.com/v.htm

- inGeneas Table of Common Surname Variations and Surname Misspellings—T–Z
  http://www.ingeneas.com/T2Z.html

- Surname Springboard Index—V
  http://www.geocities.com/~alacy/spring_v.htm

- SurnameWeb Surname Registry—V Index
  http://www.surnameweb.org/registry/v.htm

- Genealogy Resources on the Internet—"V" Surname
  Mailing Lists
  http://members.aol.com/gfsjohnf/gen_mail_surnames-uv.html
  *This site is wonderfully maintained by John Fuller. It includes
  mailing list information for the following surnames and their
  variant spellings:*
  *VALKENBURG (includes Valkenburgh, Valckenburg,
  Valckenburgh, Van Valkenburg, Van, Valckenburgh, Falkenburg,
  Falckenburgh), VanARSDALE (includes VanArsdalen), Van_
  BIBBER (includes Van Bebber, Van Beber, Vanbibber, Vanbebber,
  Bebber), VANCE (includes Vanss, Vans, Vaux, Wauss, Waus,
  Vass, Vauss, Vaus), VANCLEAVE (includes Van Cleef, Van
  Cleve), VANDERGRIFT (includes Vandegrift, Vandagriff,
  Vandigriff, Vandegriff, Vandergriffe), VANDERPOOL (includes
  Van De Poel), VANDOVER (includes Vandaver, Vandever,
  Vandiver, Vandivier, Vandiviere), VanDUSEN (includes
  Vandusen, Van Deusen, Van Deursen, Van Duzee, Van Duzer,
  Van Duzen), VanGUNDY, VanHOOK (includes VanHoeck,
  VanHoek), VANHORNE (includes Van Horn, Van Hoorn),
  VANKEUREN (includes Van Curen), VanKIRK,
  VANLANDINGHAM (includes Vallandingham), VANNORMAN
  (includes VanAernam, VanArlem, VanArnam, VanArnem,
  VanArnhem, VanArnon, VanOrman), VANORDEN (includes Van
  Naarden), VANOVER, VANSCOY (includes Van Scoy, Van Sky,
  Van Scoyoc, Van Schaick, Vernooy), VARNADO (includes
  Varnedo, Varnydo, Varnadoe, Varnedeau), VARNER (includes
  Verner, Werner, Warner, Ferner, Vernor, Venable), VAUGHAN
  (includes Vaughn), VEAL (includes Veale), VERNON, VEST,
  VESTAL (includes Vastal, Vestall, Vestol, Vastel), VIA (includes
  Viah, Viar, Vier, Viet), VICKER (includes Wicker, Vickery,
  Vickers, Weicher, Weigert, Wica, Whicker), VIEAU (includes
  Viau, Vieaux, Vieu, Vieo), VINES (includes Vine), VINING
  (includes Vinen, Venning), VINSON, VOGT (includes Voght),
  VONFREYMANN, VOSS (includes Vass, Vause, Vosse, Vase),
  VOTAW (includes Votau, Vatau, Voteau, Votan, Vatan, Vatow,
  Votow, Vataw, Votaugh, Vataugh, Vatough, Voutow, Voutaw,
  Vawten, Vater, Votar, Votare), VROOMAN.*

- VALLEAU Family Association
  http://www.geocities.com/Heartland/Prairie/1181/

- Surnames Beginning with VAN, VANDER &
  VANDEN Newsletter
  *For details send e-mail to Lucinda (Cindy) Olsen, editor and
  publisher, at CarlCindy2@aol.com*

- VAN AKEN and VAN AUKEN Genealogy
  http://wworks.com/~macbeth/

- VanAUKEN Family History & Genealogy
  http://pages.prodigy.com/VT/vanauken/
  *VanAuken / VanAken / VanNocker. Dutch family who settled in
  America as early as 1652.*

- VANCE Family Association
  http://ourworld.compuserve.com/homepages/VFA/

- Homepage of the Family Association
  VANDENBEMPT
  http://www.club.innet.be/~ind1991/
  *Vandenbempt, Vanden Bempt, Van den Bempt, Vanderbemde(n),
  Vander Bemde(n), Van der Bemde(n), Vandenbempde(n), Vanden
  Bempde(n), van den Beempde, Van den Beemd, van den Beemd,
  van den Beemt, Vanebempt, Debempt.*

- The VANDENBOSCH Family in America
  http://www.macatawa.org/~dobo/
  Descendants of Tamme VANDENBOSCH 1798–1874.

- VANDERGRIFT Family of America
  http://members.tripod.com/vandergrift/index.htm

- The Ancestors & Families of David Chris
  HANKINS—The Descendants of Hendrick
  VANDOLAH
  http://www.vitrex.net/~foffer/index.html

- The National VAN HOOK Genealogical Homepage
  http://home.att.net/~vanhook/

- VAN HORN Family Genealogy Online
  http://members.localnet.com/~zeus/Van%20Horn/
  Van%20Horn.htm
  *13 generations of the VAN HORN family of Burt (Charlotville),
  New York.*

- The VAN NORMAN Family Association
  http://www.multiboard.com/~spettit/vnfam.html

- The Olive Tree Genealogy: The VAN SLYKE
  Family
  http://www.rootsweb.com/~ote/vslyke.htm
  *The descendants of Cornelise Antonissen VAN SLYKE, 1604–
  1676 and his Mohawk Wife Ots-Toch. Cornelis settled in
  Rensellaerswyck in 1634. Cornelis and his nephew Willem
  Pieterse VAN SLYKE aka NEEF, were the ancestors of the VAN
  SLYKE families in New York.*

- VAN TASSEL Family History Homepage
  http://members.aol.com/RickVT/index.html
  One-name study of the Van Tassel family.

- VAN THIENEN Genealogy
  http://www.ping.be/~pin02229/genealog.htm
  *Van Thienen, Vanthienen, van Thienen, Van Thienen, Van Tienen,
  Vantienen, van Tienen, Van Tiene, von Thienen, Von Thienen, de
  Tenis, de Thenis. In Belgium, The Netherlands, Germany,
  France, Argentina, Canada, USA, New Zealand and Australia.*

- National Association of the VAN
  VALKENBURG Family
  http://haven.ios.com/~wordup/navvf/navvf.html
  *Descendants of Lambert VAN VALCKENBURG of the Nether-
  lands and Annetie JACOBS of Schleswig, Holstein, married in
  Amsterdam in 1642, came to North America and became
  colonists in New Amsterdam in 1644.*

- The VAN VOORHEES Association
  http://www.vanvoorhees.org
  *Includes Van Voorhees, Van Voorhies, Van Vorhies, Van Voris,
  Van Vorous, Van Voorhis, Van Vource, Van Voorus, Van Vorys,
  and Van Vories.*

- The VAN ZANDT Society
  http://www.user1.netcarrier.com/~muriel/VanZandtSociety/
  *International society for research of Van Zandt, and other
  spellings, including Van Sant, Vanzant, Vinzant, Van Zant, van de
  Sandt, and others.*

- VARNUM Genealogy
  http://www.geocities.com/Heartland/Plains/7945/

- Marc VERMEIRSSEN's Homepage
  http://bewoner.dma.be/mvermeir/
  Vermeirssen, Vermeerssen, Vermeirsschen, Vermeirssch, Vermeerren.

- VIAU / VIEAU / VIEUX
  http://www.geocities.com/Heartland/Acres/1636/
  Descendants of Michel Viau of France, b. 1655.

- The VIENNEAU Genealogy
  http://www3.nbnet.nb.ca/davienn/Testpage2ang.htm
  and a French version
  http://www3.nbnet.nb.ca/davienn/Testpage2.htm
  Descendants of Michel Vienneau and Thérèse Baude, including these surnames: Vienneau, Huard, Cormier, Richard, Thériault, Lagacé, Pitre, Couture. All from Atlantic region in Canada.

- VINING Genealogy Exchange
  http://www.geocities.com/Heartland/Plains/3863/

- The VOELL Family Website
  http://www.voell.com
  Interactive news, calanders, and picture archives.

- VOSSELLER Home Page
  http://members.tripod.com/~jvhc/
  Vosseller, Fusler, Vosler, Vossler, Vusler.

◆ Surnames Beginning with "W"

- Family Tree Maker Online User Home Pages—W
  http://www.familytreemaker.com/users/w/index.html

- Genealogy's Most Wanted—Surnames Beginning with "W"
  http://www.citynet.net/mostwanted/w.htm

- H-GIG Surname Registry—Surnames Beginning W
  http://www.ucr.edu/h-gig/surdata/surname23.html

- Higginson Book Company—Surnames Beginning with W
  http://www.higginsonbooks.com/w.htm

- inGeneas Table of Common Surname Variations and Surname Misspellings—T–Z
  http://www.ingeneas.com/T2Z.html

- Surname Springboard Index—W
  http://www.geocities.com/~alacy/spring_w.htm

- SurnameWeb Surname Registry—W Index
  http://www.surnameweb.org/registry/w.htm

- Genealogy Resources on the Internet—"W" Surname Mailing Lists
  http://members.aol.com/gfsjohnf/gen_mail_surnames-w.html
  This site is wonderfully maintained by John Fuller. It includes mailing list information for the following surnames and their variant spellings:
  WADDELL, WADE (includes Wayde, Waid, Wayd, Waddel), WAFFORD (includes Warford, Wofford, Walford), WAGNON, WAGONER (includes Wagoner, Waggoner), WALDEN (includes Waldan, Waldin, Waldon, Waldun), WALKER, WALTON, WARFIELD, WALKER, JOHN (ancestors and descendants of John Walker of Wigton, Scotland (1677–1734)), WALL (includes Walls), WALLACE (includes Wallis, Wallas), WALLER (includes De Waller), WALLING, WALSH, WALTERS, WAMSLEY, WARD

(includes Warde), WARD-KYDAVIESS, WARD-LIST, WARE (includes Wear, Wair, Warr), WARNER, WARNOX (includes Warnock), WARREN, WARRICK, WASHBURN, WATERS (includes Watters, Watrous), WATKINS, WATSON, WATTS, WAUGH, WAY, WAYNE (includes Wain, O'Wayne, McWayne, Weign, Weyne, Wynne), WEATHERLY (includes Wetherly, Wetherleigh, Withersby), WEAVER (includes Wever, Weber), WEBB, WEBER (includes Webber), WEBSTER, WEDDINGTON (includes Waddington), WEDDLE, WEDERELL, WEDGWOOD (includes Wedgewood), WEEKLEY (includes Weekly, Weakley, Weakly), WEEMS (includes Wemyss, Weams, Weemes), WEISHAUPT, WELBAUM (includes Wellbaum), WELCH, WELLS, WELLSFamilyAssociation (announcements of new items added to Wells Family Research Association, website), WELLS, JAMES, WELLS, ZACHARIAH, WELSH, WELTY (includes Weldy, Welday, Velty, Felty), WENT (includes Wendt), WENTWORTH, WERTZ (includes Werts, Wurtz), WESLEY, WESNER (includes Weisner, Westner, Wessner, Wisener), WESSLING (includes Wesling, Wesseling), WEST, WESTBROOK (includes Westbroke, Westbrok), WESTON, WETZELL (includes Wetzel), WHALEY (includes Whalley, Whally, Whalen), WHATLEY (includes Watley, Whately, Wheatley, Wheatly, Whitley, Whitely), WHEAT, WHEATLEY (includes Wheatly), WHEELER, WHELESS, WHILLANS (includes Wealands, Wealans, Wealens, Wealleans, Weallens, Wheelans, Wheeleans, Whelans, Whelens, Whellens, Whillace, Whillance, Whillas, Wholans, Willance, Willands), WHIPPLE, WHISNANT (includes Wissenandt, Visanand, Whisenhunt, Whisenant, Whisonant), WHITAKER (includes Whittaker, Whitacre), WHITE (includes Whyte, Whiet), WHITEHEAD, WHITE-L, WHITESIDE (includes Whitesides), WHITFORD, WHITMER (includes Whitmore, Witmer, Witmore, Vitmer, Widmer), WHITNEY, WHITSETT, WHITSON, WHITTEN, WHITWELL, WIBLE (includes Weible, Wibel), WICK (includes Wicks, Week, Weeks), WIDENER (includes Weidner, Widner), WIER (includes Weir, Wehr), WIGDERSON, WIGGINS (includes Wiggens, Wiggs), WIGGS (Wigglesworth surname; includes Wiglesworth, Wigelsworth), WIGHT (includes Whight, Wycht), WILAND (includes Wilant, Weyland, Weylant, Wyland, Wyand, Weyand, Wiant, Wiand), WILBANKS (includes Willbanks, Woolbanks), WILCOX (includes Willcox, Willcoxson), WILDE (includes Wild, Wilder, Wyld, Wylde, Wilds), WILEY (includes Wylie, Wylly), WILHITE (includes Wilhoit, Wilheit, Willert, Wilert), WILKES (includes Wilks, Welkes, Walkes, Wolkes, Volkes, Wellkes, McWilk), WILKIN (includes Wilkins), WILKINSON (includes McQuilkin, McQuilken, McQuilkan), WILLETT, WILLIAMS (includes McWilliams, Willis, Wilkinson, Williamson, O'Williams), WILLIAMS, WILLIS, WILLOUGHBY (includes Wilobe, Willabe, Willowbe), WILLS, WILLSTROP (includes Wilstrop, Wylestrope, Wilstrope, Vilstrup, Wilstrup), WILMOT (includes Wilmarth, Willmuth, Wilmottsen, Willmouth, Walmarth, Wilmoth), WILMOTH (includes Wilmot, Wilmoarth, Wilmuth, Wilmouth, Wilmount, Wilmath), WILSFORD (includes Willeford, Wilford, Willesford, Williford), WILSON (includes Willson), WILSON, WILSON, WINCHELL (includes Wincall), WINDHAM (includes Wyndham, Windom, Windam), WINDSOR (includes Winsor), WINEGARDNER (includes Winegartner, Weingartner, Winegarden, Winegarten, Weingarden, Weingarten, Winegardener, Winegart, Weingart, Wingart, Wingert), WINELAND (includes Weinland), WING (includes Winge, Wyng, Wynge), WINGET-WINGATE (includes Wyngate, Wingett), WINGFIELD (includes Winfield), WINGO, WINKELER (includes Winkler, Winckler), WINKLE (includes Winkel but not Van Winkle), WINN (includes Wynne, Wynn, Winne), WINN (Winn Family and Kinship Association), WINNINGHAM (includes Winingham, Willingham, Winham, Wingham), WINSLOW, WINTER, WINTON (includes Wynton), WIRE_family, WISE (includes Wees, Weese, Weis, Weise, Weiss, Weisse, Weisz, Wice, Wiece, Wiese, Wiess, Wyse, Wyss), WISELY, WISEMAN, WISTAR, WITCHER, WITHERSPOON (includes Weatherspoon, Wotherspoon), WITT, WOLFE (includes Wolf, Wolff, Woolf, Wulf, Wulff, Rolfe, Rolph), WOLFGANG-cuzns, WOLFSKILL (includes Wolfskhel, Wolfkill), WOLTZ/WALTZ (includes Wolz, Walz, Waltzer, Waltser), WOLVERTON (includes

Woolverton, Wolberton, Wolferton, Wulferton, Wolferstan, Wulferstan, Wolvington, Wolverstone), WOODALL, WOODARD *(includes Woodward),* WOODCOCK, WOODHOUSE *(includes Wodehouse, Woodhousem, Woodhouser),* WOODRUFF *(includes Woodroof, Woodrough, Woodruffe),* WOODS *(includes Wood),* WOODSON, WOODWORTH, WOOLFORD, WOOLLEY, WOOLWINE *(includes Wohlwein),* WOOLWORTH, WOOSLEY *(includes Wooseley, Ousley, Owsley),* WOOTEN *(includes Wooton, Wootton),* WORKMAN *(includes Wortman),* WORLEY *(includes Warley, Werly, deWerly, Wherley, Whorley, Wirley, Wyrley),* WORSHAM, WORTHINGTON, WORWAG *(includes Wörwag, Woerwag, Werenwag),* WRATHALL *(includes Wrathall-Bull in Australia),* WRAY *(includes Ray),* WRENN *(includes Wren),* WRIGHT, WYATT *(includes Wiatt, Wiat, Wyatte, Wyat),* WYCKOFF.

- **Descendants of Thomas Young WADDELL**
  http://www.parsonstech.com/genealogy/trees/jwaddel1/wadle.htm
  and a companion site
  http://www.telcomplus.net/jwaddell/
  Of Polk County, Missouri.

- **WADE Families Page**
  http://ds.dial.pipex.com/richard.rwsd/

- **Lucy Ann WALBERT Genealogy & Lineage**
  http://www.kalglo.com/walbert.htm

- **WALLER Family**
  http://home.sprynet.com/sprynet/GWaller/

- **WALSH Family Genealogy Home Page**
  http://pw2.netcom.com/~walshdw/index.html

- **WALSH Surname Mailing List**
  http://pw2.netcom.com/~walshdw/maillist.html

- **The WALTERHOUSE Family Page**
  http://home.comm.net/~walterhouse/

- **The WALTER(S) and Allied Families Genealogy Page**
  http://www.familytreemaker.com/users/w/a/l/John-A-Walters/index.html
  Descendants of Thomas Walter(s), died 6 Jul 1724 in Charlestown, MA, and Hannah Gray.

- **WAMSLEY~WEB Newsletter**
  For details send e-mail to Wanda Wamsley Balducci at: Wamsleyweb@aol.com

- **Descendants of Nancy WARD**
  http://www.nancyward.com

- **WARNER and BURLINGAME Descendants**
  http://www.digroots.com/burlwarn.htm
  Descendants of Eliza Warner and Jeremiah Burlingame.

- **WARNER—Who, When & Where Home Page**
  http://members.aol.com/kinseeker6/warner.html

- **Richard WARREN (Mayflower Passenger) Genealogy**
  http://pages.prodigy.net/dave_lossos/warren.htm

- **WASDIN / WASDEN Family Home Page**
  http://www.why.net/home/waz/

- **WASHBURN Family History Page**
  http://home.earthlink.net/~cwashburn/history.html
  John Washburn Jr. (1621–1686) and His Descendants.

- **The National Society of the WASHINGTON Family Descendants**
  http://members.tripod.com/~NSWFD/
  Members are descendants of any of the ancestors of George Washington who lived in Colonial America between 1607 and 1732.

- **WATERS / WATTERS (and Sometimes WALTERS) Genealogy**
  http://www.cwo.com/~genetti/

- **Worldwide WATERS Research Site**
  http://www.fortunecity.com/millenium/lilac/38/index.html

- **WATKINS Family History Society**
  http://www.iinet.net.au/~davwat/wfhs/

- **A WEAVER's Source Book: Uphome with Jonas and Emma**
  http://www.sitematrix.com/uphome
  Information about a recent 304-page publication of stories and genealogy for the Weaver family. The book spans the 500 years since the Radical Reformation, tracing fifteen generations of one family in the Swiss-Anabaptist Waber-Weber-Weaver lineage.

- **WEAVER Surname Mailing List**
  http://www.geocities.com/~fannincounty/weaver-webs.html
  Includes Wever, Weber.

- **WEBB One Name Register**
  http://www.btinternet.com/~wonr
  GOONS registered society for WEBB surname and variants.

- **The WEBB Site**
  http://www.geocities.com/Heartland/Valley/2009
  Homepage of the The Webb One Name Register (GOONS Member).

- **World Wide WEBNER Home Page**
  http://www.systime.com/~micah/family/wwwebner.html

- **The WEDGWOOD Family Worldwide**
  http://www.geocities.com/Heartland/3203/

- **WEEDMAN Family Genealogy**
  http://ourworld.compuserve.com/homepages/HNWEEDMAN/

- **WEEKS Family Genealogy**
  http://www2.southwind.net/~rwweeks/weeksg.html
  Descendants of George Weeks, born abt 1603, Devonshire, England and Jane Clapp, born abt 1604, Salcombe Regis, Devonshire, England.

- **WEEKS Family Registry**
  http://www.geocities.com/~weekseekers/
  A registry of the descendants of Benjamin and Mary Chase Weeks of Falmouth, Massachusetts and Carteret County, North Carolina.

- **WEEMS Family History**
  http://www.genealogy.org/~weems/

- **WEGG Genealogy and One Name Study**
  http://www.wegg.mcmail.com

- Descendants of James WELL(E)S
  http://www.parsonstech.com/genealogy/trees/HJack/Wells.htm
  10 Generations of Wells from 1600 in Virginia through Delaware, Maryland, Pennsylvania to New York in 1995.

- The WELLS Family Research Association
  http://www.rootsweb.com/~wellsfam/wfrahome.html

- WELLS Surname Mailing List
  http://www.zekes.com/~dwells/list.html

- WELTY Family Genealogy
  http://users.aol.com/ocicat/welty.html

- WENGER Home Page
  http://www.wengersundial.com/wengerfamily/
  A database of over 78,000 names of individuals, mostly descended from 18th century Mennonites, River Brethren (Brethren in Christ) and German Baptist Brethren who settled in Lancaster, Lebanon and Franklin Counties of Pennsylvania, in Ontario, Canada and in Washington Co., Maryland and Botetourt Co., Virginia.

- The WENTZEL(L) Genealogy Society
  http://www.qcis.ns.ca/wentzell/

- WEST Genealogy Page and WEST Surname Search
  http://members.tripod.com/~westgenealogy
  A page about the West family, history of the surname, a page to research fellow Wests, and links to West surname mailing lists and more!

- The Descendants of John and Sarah WESTON in America
  http://members.aol.com/microfud/private/weston.html

- The WEYMOUTH Home Page
  http://www.tiac.net/users/weymouth/

- WHALEY6: Roots—Branches, Twigs, & Leaves
  http://members.aol.com/Whaley6/index.htm
  Dedicated to the descendants of Elijah McAnally & Alexander WHALEY.

- WHATLING Family History—A One Name Study
  http://www.visualcreations.com/pers/leeann/whatling/index.html

- Descendants of Rev. Thomas WHEAT (1789–1860)
  http://www.familytreemaker.com/users/w/h/e/John-M-Wheat/

- WHEAT Front Page
  http://www.geocities.com/Heartland/7785/

- Francis WHEAT Genealogy
  http://www.geocities.com/Heartland/7785/FrancisWheat2.htm
  Born February 21, 1737/38 in St. John Piscataway, Prince George's, Maryland.

- The WHINNERY Research Network
  http://members.aol.com/janfwatson/
  WHINERY, WHINNERY, WHINREY

- The WHIPPLE Web Site
  http://www.whipple.org

- WHISNANT Surname Center
  http://homepages.rootsweb.com/~whisnant/
  Whisnant, Whisenant, Whisenand, Whisonant, Whisante, Whisenhunt, Visinand.

- Alfred WHITE Family Organization
  http://www.geocities.com/Athens/Forum/6215/awfo.htm
  For records pertaining to the ancestors and descendants of pioneers Alfred Talmon WHITE (1778–1853/54) and his wife, Mary PERRY (1785–1866/68).
  http://www.netpathway.com/~bennie/white/index.html

- WHITE Genealogy—Descendants—1800, SOM
  http://www.itmagic.demon.co.uk/genealogy/white.htm
  Descendants of William Thomas WHITE and Elizabeth FERRIS.

- Whit's End: WHITLOCK / WHITFIELD Genealogy
  http://home.pix.za/dw/dw000002/index.htm
  The genealogy of the Whitlock and Whitfield families in England and South Africa over a period of about 800 years and 26 generations.

- WHITNEY Family Genealogy
  http://www.erols.com/rlward1/whitney/index.html
  Resources for all WHITNEY families, including vital, census, probate, and military records, genealogies, queries, a bibliography, famous people, and much more!

- WHITNEY Genealogical Database
  http://www.rootsweb.com/~gumby/genweb/Whitney/Whitney.html
  A database that contains 6,654 people, 6,652 names.

- WHITON Genealogy and Family History
  http://www.concentric.net/~whitmark/index.shtml
  WHITEN, WHITING, WHITTEN, and WITON

- The WHITSONs of the World Home Page
  http://www.tusc.net/~tcla/geneal/whitson/

- WHITTED Family Homepage
  http://www.geocities.com/Heartland/Meadows/5097/
  Descendants of the Anderson and Mariah Whitted family, originally of Hillsboro Township (now Hillsborough), North Carolina.

- The WHITTLETON Family WEB Site
  http://www.whittleton.com

- The WHITWORTH Family Genealogy Home Page
  http://www.familytreemaker.com/users/w/h/i/Gwen-W-Whitworth-Jr/
  Information for the WHITWORTH Family Association. Descendants of William H. WHITWORTH, born February 22, 1841 in Franklin County, Missouri, and died October 21, 1913 in Missouri.

- WIBE—A Family from Norway
  http://www.accessone.com/~jegge/wibe.htm

- WIDDOWS One-Name Study
  http://www.lamerton.demon.co.uk/wid-onst.htm

- WIGLEY Surname Webring
  http://www.geocities.com/Heartland/Flats/4239/webring.html

- WILBANKS-WILLBANKS Family History
  http://www.getnet.com/~rmwiv/wilbanks.html

- Mark's Genealogy Page—WILCOX, WILLCOX, WILCOCKSE
  http://members.tripod.com/~MARK_DAMON_SMITH/INDEX.HTM

- WILCOX Genealogy Area
  http://www.magnate.demon.co.uk/genealogy/gene.htm
  Wilcox in England.

- WILHOIT/WILHITE Family History
  http://homepages.rootsweb.com/~george/wilhoit.html

- WILKINSON Connection Newsletter
  For all Wilkinson, Wilkerson, Wilkenson, Wilkins, Wilkens, etc. researchers. $15.00/year, quarterly. Submit queries or info by snail mail or by E-mail: Peggy Rockwell Gleich, Editor, PO Box 8003, Janesville WI 53547-8003, pgleich@aol.com

- WILKINSONS on the Web
  http://www.wilkinsons.com/Wilkinsons.html

- WILLARD Family Association Home Page
  http://www.discover.net/~rwillard/wfa.html

- Your WILLIAMS Home Page
  http://www.soltec.net/~photo/
  This site is for ALL Williams descendants. Searchable database by NAME or STATE. Over 6,500 submissions, submit your own!

- WILSFORD Family
  http://www.mindspring.com/~jogt/surnames/wilsford.htm

- WILSON's Network
  http://members.tripod.com/~Wilson_Network/index.htm

- WIMBERLY Family Genealogy
  http://members.accessus.net/~twimberly/index.htm

- WINCH Genealogical Database
  http://www.rootsweb.com/~gumby/genweb/Winch/Winch.html
  A database that contains 18,307 names.

- The WINDEMUTH Family Organization
  http://www.kern.com/maykoski/wintermute.htm

- The WINDEMUTH Family Organization
  http://www.intaccess.com/wintermute/
  Descendants of Johan Christoph WINDEMUTH and Mary Marguerite KLEPPLINGER. WINDEMUTH, WINTAMUTE, WINTEMUTE, WINTERMOTE, WINTERMUTE, WINTERMUTH.

- The WINEMILLER Family Inn
  http://www.winemiller.org

- WINGFIELD Family Society
  http://www.wingfield.org

- The WINGO Family Page
  http://www.spessart.com/users/ggraham/wingo.htm

- Genealogy Homepage for WINN~WYNN~WYNNE & Assciated Families
  http://members.aol.com/lunetta595/main.html
  Descendants of Dr. Thomas Wynne, born 1627 in Wales.

- Wandering WINTER(S)
  http://www.geocities.com/Heartland/Hills/8929/

- The WINTHROP Society
  http://members.aol.com/WinthropSQ/society.htm
  For those with proven descent from one or more passengers of the Winthrop fleet, or of others who settled in the Massachusetts Bay Colony before December 31, 1632.

- Descendants of Johannes Conrad WIRZ and Anna GOETSCHY
  http://pages.prodigy.net/reed_wurts/cpwurts/surnames.html
  Descendants of Johannes Conrad Wirz and Anna Goetschy, compiled mostly from a book by Charles Pemberton Wurts published in 1889, with additions by Reed M. W. Wurts.

- The WISEMAN Family Association
  http://members.tripod.com/~dwiseman/index.html

- LAMPSON WITMUS Family Organization
  http://ww2.sd.cybernex.net/~pawalker/lampwit.html
  For descendants of William LAMPSON, born 1761 in Boston, Mass. and Wilhelm WITTMUETZ born 1799 in Ruegen Island, Germany.

- WITHERSPOON Family Research Home Page
  http://members.tripod.com/~witherspoon/

- WITTENBERG Family Association
  http://members.aol.com/wittnberg/index.htm
  Also WHITTENBURG, WHITTENBERG, WITTENBERG, WITTENBURG.

- WITT / WHITT / WHIT Newsletters
  http://www.halcyondays.com/famnames/witt/wittnews.htm

- The WLADYKA Genealogy Forum
  http://cbt.bungi.com/surnamewladyka/

- WOLDIN-SITZ Family History
  http://www.catskill.net/rue/family/woldin/

- WOLF Home Page—Wandering WOLFs Newsletter
  http://members.aol.com/Kinseeker6/wolf.html

- WOLFENSBERGER Family Association
  http://www.icon.net/~wolfberg/
  Also: Wolfersberger, Wolfersparger, Wolfensparger, Wolfenbarger, Wolfenberger, Wolfinbarger, Sparger and Spargur.

- WOLVERTON / WOOLVERTON Family Heritage Society
  http://www.ualr.edu/~mamiller1/

- The WOMACK Genealogy Network (WGN)
  http://members.aol.com/womacknet/home.html

- The Descendants of Peter Atte WOOD of England and Henry WOOD of Plymouth Massachusetts
  http://www5.pair.com/vtandrew/wood/wood.htm

- WOOD Family
  http://members.aol.com/HatwellE/WoodFamilyHistory.html
  Jacob Wood Descendant's Family History.

- WOOD World—WOOD Family Genealogy
  http://www.dlcwest.com/~mgwood/

- WOODHAM Family Association
  http://www.geocities.com/~rewoodham/woodham.html

- WOODRUFF Genealogy
  http://www.geocities.com/Heartland/Acres/3792/
  For all WOODRUFF's Anytime, Anywhere.

- My Neck of the WOODS
  http://www.ounceofprevention.ca/history.htm
  Researching the WOODS family from the Isle of Wight. Also surnames Fair, Fleming, and Smart.

- WOODWARDs WeSearch Newsletter
  http://www.studiosr.com/woodward/
  Provides access to the subject index to the quarterly publication (beginning October 1992) of the WOODWARDs WeSearch Newsletter embracing all Woodwards (including spelling variations) throughout the United States. Access is also provided for an application form and links to URL for subscribers home pages.

- Wo*l*m Genealogy
  http://www.geocities.com/Heartland/Plains/2316/
  Genealogy of WOOLAM, WOOLEM, WOOLUM, ULM, ULLUM, WOLLAM, WOOLLAM, WOOLLUM Families.

- WORTHINGTON
  http://members.aol.com/hdw3/worthington.html
  A website devoted to the lineage of Capt. John Worthington (1650–1701) of Anne Arundel Co., Md presented in family group sheet format with links to Ancestors, Sources, other Worthington researchers, plus much more! Contributions welcomed.

- The WORTMAN Family Tree
  http://ourworld.compuserve.com/homepages/Warren_Wortman/
  Descendants of Milton Lad Wortman.

- The WRIGHT Areas
  http://pw1.netcom.com/~jjordan2/ritearea.html

- WRIGHT Researchers
  http://www.athens.net/~ethelind/genealogy/wright/wright.html

- The WRIGHT Tidbits
  http://www.geocities.com/Heartland/5917/Tidbits.htm

- World WYKES Web
  http://www.enduser.co.uk/wykes/

- WYMAN Family
  http://www.wyman.org

- WYNN Family and Kinsman Association, Est. 1971
  http://www.ausaweb.com/drwynn
  WYNNE including variant spellings: Wynne Winne Wynn Winn Gwynne Gwynn Gwyn Win Winnie Gwynn Gwyn Gwyne.

◆ Surnames Beginning with "X"

- Family Tree Maker Online User Home Pages—X
  http://www.familytreemaker.com/users/x/index.html

- Genealogy's Most Wanted—Surnames Beginning with "X"
  http://www.citynet.net/mostwanted/x.htm

- H-GIG Surname Registry—Surnames Beginning X–Z
  http://www.ucr.edu/h-gig/surdata/surname24.html

- Higginson Book Company—Surnames Beginning with X
  http://www.higginsonbooks.com/x.htm

- inGeneas Table of Common Surname Variations and Surname Misspellings—T–Z
  http://www.ingeneas.com/T2Z.html

- Surname Springboard Index—X
  http://www.geocities.com/~alacy/spring_x.htm

- SurnameWeb Surname Registry—X Index
  http://www.surnameweb.org/registry/x.htm

◆ Surnames Beginning with "Y"

- Family Tree Maker Online User Home Pages—Y
  http://www.familytreemaker.com/users/y/index.html

- Genealogy's Most Wanted—Surnames Beginning with "Y"
  http://www.citynet.net/mostwanted/y.htm

- H-GIG Surname Registry—Surnames Beginning X–Z
  http://www.ucr.edu/h-gig/surdata/surname24.html

- Higginson Book Company—Surnames Beginning with Y
  http://www.higginsonbooks.com/y.htm

- inGeneas Table of Common Surname Variations and Surname Misspellings—T–Z
  http://www.ingeneas.com/T2Z.html

- Surname Springboard Index—Y
  http://www.geocities.com/~alacy/spring_y.htm

- SurnameWeb Surname Registry—Y Index
  http://www.surnameweb.org/registry/y.htm

- Genealogy Resources on the Internet—"Y" Surname Mailing Lists
  http://members.aol.com/gfsjohnf/gen_mail_surnames-xyz.html
  This site is wonderfully maintained by John Fuller. It includes mailing list information for the following surnames and their variant spellings:
  YANCEY (includes Yancy), YATES (includes Yeats, Yeates), YAWN (includes Yaun, Yon, Yonn), YEAZEL (includes Yazel, Yeasle, Yeazle, Yazell), YELTON, YINGLING (includes Yungling, Juengling, England, Yinglin), YOCUM (includes Yoakum, Yokum, Yocom, Jochem, Joachim), YODER (includes Joder, Jotter, Yeater, Yetter, Yoders, Yoter, Yother, Yotter, Youter, Youther, Yuter, Yutter), YORK, YORSTON, YOST (includes Jost), YOUNG, YOUNGBLOOD (includes Jungblut, Jungbluth, Jongblud), YOUNKER (includes Yonker, Yunker), YOUNKIN-NEWS (includes Youngkin, Youngken, Yonkin, Junghen).

- YANCEY Cousins United
  http://members.aol.com/YANCEY7/index.htm
  Yancy, Yance, Yonce, Yoncy, Yaney, Yanney, Nanny, Nanney

- The YARBERRY Family Tree
  http://www.vabch.com/kyarberr/yarberry.html
  Yarberry / Yarbrough / Yarborough family and closely associated families.

- My YEARY Line
  http://user.icx.net/~booboo/paternal.html
  Descendants of Henry YEARY, Sr., born 1730 in Virginia and Elizabeth CROXSTALL, born 1729 in Maryland.

- Official Home Page of the YELVERTON / YELVINGTON / ELVINGTON Families of America
  http://www.execpc.com/~kvcw/

- YODER Family Information Archives Online
  http://www.yodernewsletter.org
- YOUNKIN Family News Bulletin
  http://www.intrepid.net/genealogy/junghen/

◆ Surnames Beginning with "Z"

- Family Tree Maker Online User Home Pages—Z
  http://www.familytreemaker.com/users/z/index.html
- Genealogy's Most Wanted—Surnames Beginning with "Z"
  http://www.citynet.net/mostwanted/z.htm
- H-GIG Surname Registry—Surnames Beginning X–Z
  http://www.ucr.edu/h-gig/surdata/surname24.html
- Higginson Book Company—Surnames Beginning with Z
  http://www.higginsonbooks.com/z.htm
- inGeneas Table of Common Surname Variations and Surname Misspellings—T–Z
  http://www.ingeneas.com/T2Z.html
- Surname Springboard Index—Z
  http://www.geocities.com/~alacy/spring_z.htm
- SurnameWeb Surname Registry—Z Index
  http://www.surnameweb.org/registry/z.htm

- Genealogy Resources on the Internet— "Z" Surname Mailing Lists
  http://members.aol.com/gfsjohnf/gen_mail_surnames-xyz.html
  This site is wonderfully maintained by John Fuller. It includes mailing list information for the following surnames and their variant spellings:
  ZAHM, ZELL (includes Zeller, von Zell), ZICKEFOOSE (includes Zicafoose, Zickafoose), ZIEGLER (includes Zeigler, Zaigler), ZIELINSKI, ZIMBLE (includes Zimbal, Zimball, Zimbul), ZIMMERMAN, ZINK, ZIRKLE (includes Zircle, Zerkle, Zerkel, Circle, Sircle), Ziv, ZUG (includes Zook, Zuck, Zaug), ZUTZ.
- ZAMMIT Connection
  http://pw1.netcom.com/~azammit/ZAMMIT.html
- ZEMAITIS Homepage
  http://www.webmart.net/~zemaitis/zemaitis.htm
  Origin of Zemaitis surname and Lithuanian heritage.
- ZETTERBERG's Genealogy Page
  http://members.aol.com/lynnzr/life1/index.htm
  Searching for information in Sweden on a Carl Albin F. Zetterberg born between 1840–1850.
- Michael M. ZIEFLE—The Family ZIEFLE
  http://ourworld.compuserve.com/Homepages/M_Ziefle/ziefle_e.htm
- ZIELINSKI Family Journal
  http://www.infi.net/~ajabby/joframe.html

SWITZERLAND / SUISSE / SCHWEIZ
http://www.CyndisList.com/swiss.htm

- Archives de l'Etat de Neuchâtel / Neuchâtel State Archives
  http://www.etatne.ch/adm/dipac/archives/accueil.htm
- Arno Schmitt, Journalist from San Diego, California
  E-mail: reporter@adnc.com
  He can help to find relatives, links or sources regarding ancestors by placing articles in German, Austrian and/or Swiss newspapers. For details, e-mail Arno at: reporter@adnc.com
- Books We Own—Switzerland
  http://www.rootsweb.com/~bwo/switz.html
- Center For Genealogical Research / Cabinet d'Etudes Généalogiques
  http://genrsch.com/
- Les Centres Généalogiques SDJ / LDS Family History Centers
  http://www2.et.byu.edu/~harmanc/paris/genealogie.html
  France, Belgique, Suisse, Canada.
- Doug SCHOREY's Pages within SwissGen
  http://www.eye.ch/swissgen/schori/swiss.htm
- Family History Centers in Germany, Austria and Switzerland
  http://www.genealogy.net/gene/faqs/LDS.de
- FEEFHS Ethnic, Religious and National Cross-Indexes: Swiss Cross-Index
  http://feefhs.org/ch/indexch.html
- Frontier Press Bookstore—Switzerland
  http://www.frontierpress.com/frontier.cgi?category=swiss
- Genealogical Dictionaries—Old German Professions & Old German Medical Terms and Causes of Death
  http://home.navisoft.com/scrolls/dictinry.htm
- GenealogyBookShop.com—Switzerland/Swiss
  http://www.genealogybookshop.com/genealogybookshop/files/The_World,Switzerland_Swiss/index.html
  The online store of Genealogical Publishing Co., Inc. & Clearfield Company.
- Genealogy Helplist—Switzerland
  http://posom.com/hl/che/index.shtml
- Genealogy in French-Speaking Switzerland
  http://www.unige.ch/biblio/ses/jla/gen/swiss-e.html
- Information about Switzerland
  http://www.ethz.ch/swiss/Switzerland_Info.html
- Map of Switzerland
  http://www.lib.utexas.edu/Libs/PCL/Map_collection/europe/Switzerland.jpg
  From the Perry-Castañeda Library at the Univ. of Texas at Austin.
- Neuchâtel Genealogy Society / Société Neuchâteloise de Généalogie
  http://www.junod.ch/SNG/SNG_index.html
  Short queries or professional help on families that came from Neuchâtel county.

- OMII Genealogy Project & Kidron Heritage Center
  http://www.bright.net/~swisstea/index.html
  A Swiss Mennonite & German Amish genealogy project.
- Schweizerische Landesbibliothek / Swiss National Library
  http://www.snl.ch/
- Staatsarchiv Des Kantons Luzern
  http://www.staluzern.ch/
- Studio Galloway—Genealogy, Heraldry, Paintings, Illustrations
  http://www.firmnet.ch/galloway/index_e.html
  Professional researcher.
- The Swiss Connection (Swiss Newsletter)
  http://www.feefhs.org/ch/tsc/frg-tsc.html
- Swiss Genealogy
  http://www.mindspring.com/~philipp/che.html
- Swiss Genealogy on the Internet
  http://www.eye.ch/swissgen/
- Swiss Genealogy on the Internet—Mirror Site
  http://www.genealogy.net/gene/reg/CH/
- Swiss Genealogy on the Internet—Mirror Site
  http://w3g.med.uni-giessen.de/gene/reg/CH/
- Swiss State Archives—Addresses
  http://www.etatne.ch/adm/auto/archives/arcch_en.htm
- SWITZERLAND Mailing List
  http://members.aol.com/gfsjohnf/gen_mail_country-swi.html#SWITZERLAND
- Yahoo!...Switzerland...Genealogy
  http://dir.yahoo.com/Regional/Countries/Switzerland/Arts_and_Humanities/History/Genealogy/

◆ Swiss Family Sites

- ANDRIST Home Page
  http://ourworld.compuserve.com/homepages/andrist/
  Information on Andrist history, legends, genealogy, heraldry, the sites in Switzerland where the name comes from.
- BACHMAN / BAUGHMAN Genealogy
  http://members.aol.com/ewbaugh/index.htm
  Descendants of Ulrich Bachmann (1610) of Lauperswil, Signau District, Canton Berne, Switzerland.
- JUNOD Généalogie—Lignières—Neuchâtel—Suisse
  http://www.junod.ch/
  Genealogy and history of the JUNOD from Neuchâtel, Switzerland since the 15th century, including emigration to the USA.

TAXES
http://www.CyndisList.com/taxes.htm

Category Index:
◆ General Resource Sites

◆ Tax Lists

◆ General Resource Sites

- Finding Minimum Information for Tax Records
  http://www.familytreemaker.com/00000671.html

- Finding Residences with Tax Records
  http://www.familytreemaker.com/00000670.html

- Public Record Office—Finding Aids—A–Z Index of All Leaflets
  http://www.pro.gov.uk/leaflets/riindex.htm
  U.K.

  ○ Customs and Excise Records as Sources for Biography and Family History (#106)
    http://www.pro.gov.uk/leaflets/RI106.HTM

  ○ Tax Records as a Source for Local and Family History c. 1198 To 1698 (#56)
    http://www.pro.gov.uk/leaflets/ri056.htm

  ○ Tithe Records in the Public Record Office (#41)
    http://www.pro.gov.uk/leaflets/ri041.htm

◆ Tax Lists

- 1759 Rowan County Tax List
  http://www.erols.com/fmoran/1759.html
  North Carolina

- 1780 Montgomery County Tax List
  http://www.rootsweb.com/~ncmontgo/m1780tax.html
  North Carolina

- 1786 Taxables located in Captain Krous' District, Surry County (Present-Day Forsyth)
  http://www.erols.com/fmoran/1786.html
  North Carolina

- 1786 Taxables located in Captain Atkins' District, Surry County
  http://www.erols.com/fmoran/1786a.html
  North Carolina. Located in southern region of present-day Surry, along the Yadkin River.

- 1815 Taxables—Cumberland County, NC
  http://www.rootsweb.com/~nccumber/1815taxables.htm

- Assessment of Taxes on Real Estate, Monroe County, Alabama 1854
  http://members.aol.com/GenWebLisa/monrotax.htm

- The Assessors Roll of Crown Point—1818
  http://www.bestweb.net/~csmfox/cp1818.htm
  Essex County, New York

- The Assessor's Roll of Crown Point—1835
  http://www.bestweb.net/~csmfox/crownp.htm
  Essex County, New York

- Dauphin County Tax Lists
  http://maley.net/dauphin/tax_lists.htm
  Pennsylvania

- Greene County, Tennessee 1783 Tax List
  http://www.tngenweb.org/greene/tax001.htm

- Greene County, TN, Early Tax Lists
  http://www.tngenweb.org/greene/earlytax.htm

- Henderson County Tax Roll 1799
  http://members.aol.com/patander73/h1799tax.html
  Kentucky

- Houston, Texas Tax List, September, 1839
  http://www.geocities.com/Vienna/1516/taxlist.html
  From the Houston Morning Star Newspaper.

- Kanawha County Tax Lists
  http://www.rootsweb.com/~wvkanawh/Tax/index.html
  West Virginia

- List of Montgomery County Tax Payers in 1779
  http://www.rootsweb.com/~ncmontgo/m1779tax.html
  North Carolina

- A List of Taxable Persons & Estates for the Year 1777 in Brandywine Hundred, New Castle County, DE
  ftp://ftp.rootsweb.com/pub/usgenweb/de/new_castle/tax/brtx1777.txt

- Louisa County Tax List
  http://www.rootsweb.com/~ialouisa/taxes.htm
  Iowa

- New Kent Co. Land Tax—1782
  http://www.geocities.com/Heartland/4945/nktax1782.html
  Virginia

- Stamford Grand Lists
  http://www.cslnet.ctstateu.edu/stamford/granlist.htm
  Taxation in Stamford, CT from 1641 to the Code of 1821.

- Sumner County Tax Records and Other Lists
  http://www.tngenweb.org/sumner/sumnlist.htm
  Tennessee

- Sussex County Taxlists
  http://www.gate.net/~pascalfl/taxindx.html
  New Jersey

- Tax List Perquimans County NC 1702
  (Taxables, Tithables)
  http://gort.ucsd.edu/hc/perq1702.html

- Tax List Perquimans County NC 1754
  (Taxables, Tithables)
  http://gort.ucsd.edu/hc/perq1754.html

- Tax Lists: 1734 Philadelphia County Taxables:
  Berks County Portion
  ftp://ftp.rootsweb.com/pub/usgenweb/pa/berks/taxlist/
  tax1734.txt
  Pennsylvania

- Tax Lists: 1753 Assessment List—Heidelberg
  Township, Lancaster County
  ftp://ftp.rootsweb.com/pub/usgenweb/pa/berks/taxlist/
  1753heid.txt
  Pennsylvania

- Texas County Tax Rolls
  http://isadore.tsl.state.tx.us/g/genealogy/.files/tax
  Information on how to order these records on microfilm.

TERMS, PHRASES, DICTIONARIES & GLOSSARIES
http://www.CyndisList.com/terms.htm

Category Index:

- Abbreviations
- Diseases & Medical Terms
- Foreign Language Dictionaries & Translation Sites
- Genealogy Dictionaries & Glossaries
- Land

- Miscellaneous
- Occupations
- Other Online Dictionaries, Glossaries, Etc.
- Relationships & Cousin Charts

◆ Abbreviations

- Abbreviations
  http://home.sprynet.com/sprynet/lgk71/2abbrevi.htm

- Abbreviations and Terms Used in Soundex Cards
  http://www.geocities.com/Heartland/plains/7193/satusc.htm

- Abbreviations Found in Genealogy
  http://www.rootsweb.com/~rigenweb/abbrev.html

- Abbreviations Used in Genealogy
  http://www.uq.net.au/~zzmgrinl/abbrev.html

- Alphabet Soup: Understanding the Genealogical Community
  http://www.familytreemaker.com/33_kathy.html

- Census and Soundex Relationship Abbreviations
  http://www.genrecords.com/library/abbreviations.htm
  From the Genealogy Record Service Library.

- Genealogical Abbreviations
  http://www.pcola.gulf.net/~llscott/abbrevia.htm

- The Genealogists' Handbook—Common (and Not So Common) Abbreviations
  http://www.floyd-pavey.com/kentuckiana/kyiana/kyiana/
  abbreviations.html
  From Kentuckiana Genealogy.

- Genealogy Abbreviation List
  http://www.niagara.com/~hanam/abbreviations/
  abbreviations.txt

- Genealogy Abbreviations
  http://www.genweb.net/~samcasey/abbr.html

- ROOTS-L Resources: Abbreviations Used in Genealogy
  http://www.rootsweb.com/roots-l/abbrevs.html

◆ Diseases & Medical Terms

- Archaic Medical Expressions for Genealogists, A–K
  http://www.gpiag-asthma.org/drpsmith/amt1.htm

- Archaic Medical Expressions for Genealogists, L–Z
  http://www.gpiag-asthma.org/drpsmith/amt2.htm

- Colonial Diseases & Cures
  http://www.genweb.net/~samcasey/disease.html

- Genealogical Dictionaries—Old German Professions & Old German Medical Terms and Causes of Death
  http://home.navisoft.com/scrolls/dictinry.htm

- German Illness Translations
  http://pixel.cs.vt.edu/library/articles/link/illness.txt

- Glossary of Diseases
  http://www.rootsweb.com/~ote/disease.htm

- Kentuckiana Genealogy—Disease Chart
  http://www.floyd-pavey.com/kentuckiana/kyiana/kyiana/
  disease.html

- Modern Names or Definitions of Illnesses of Our Ancestors, A–K
  http://www.genrecords.com/library/disease.htm

- Modern Names or Definitions of Illnesses of Our Ancestors, L–Z
  http://www.genrecords.com/library/diseases2.htm
  From the Genealogy Record Service Library.

- Old Disease Names & Their Modern Definitions
  http://www.netusa1.net/~hartmont/medicalterms.htm

- Outdated Medical Terminology
  http://www.familytreemaker.com/00000014.html

- SFS Outdated Medical Terms
  http://www.demon.co.uk/sfs/diseases.htm

◆ Foreign Language Dictionaries & Translation Sites

- AltaVista Translation Service
  http://babelfish.altavista.digital.com/cgi-bin/translate?
  Input a URL for a web site or a block of plain text and this site will translate for you to/from the following languages: English, French, German, Italian, Portuguese, and Spanish.

- The Cyrillic Alphabet
  http://www.friends-partners.org/oldfriends/language/russian-alphabet.html
  A written & audio guide to pronouncing the letters of the Russian alphabet.

- Deutsch <-> Englisches Wörterbuch
  http://www.tu-chemnitz.de/urz/netz/forms/dict.html

- Dictionaries and Other Useful Sources
  http://nucleus.hut.fi/~peura/dictionaries.html

- English-Czech Dictionary
  http://ww2.fce.vutbr.cz/bin/ecd

- English-Finnish Dictionary
  http://www.mofile.fi/-db.htm

- English-Hungarian Dictionary
  http://www.sztaki.hu/services/engdict/index.jhtml

- Foreign Language Dictionaries
  http://www.travlang.com/languages/

- Foreign Language Translators and Dictionaries
  http://www.educ.kent.edu/CoE/Resources/ref/dict/foreign/index.html

- Genealogy Exchange & Surname Registry—Translation Volunteers
  http://www.genexchange.com/tSearch.CFM

- German-English Letter Translation Specialists
  http://www.win.bright.net/~deichsa/welcome.html

- German-English On-line Dictionary
  http://www.travlang.com/GermanEnglish/

- German Genealogy: Translation Service
  http://www.genealogy.net/gene/www/abt/translation.html

- German Script Translation Chart
  http://www.geocities.com/Heartland/Hills/5971/script.htm

- German Translator—Genealogical, Literary, Technical, Civil, Business Documents
  http://people.delphi.com/delaneyj/index.html

- GLOBALINK
  http://www.globalink.com/
  Free Translation Service.

- GMS Gesellschaft für multilinguale Systeme / German to English Online Dictionary
  http://www.gmsmuc.de/english/

- Languages and translation
  http://www.iol.ie/~mazzoldi/lang/
  A collection of useful links and resources for translators.

- Latin Primer
  http://www.vii.com/~nelsonb/latin.htm

- Lexin Svensk-Engelskt Lexikon / Lexin Swedish-English Dictionary
  http://www.nada.kth.se/skolverket/sve-eng.html

- The Linguist List: Dictionaries, Etc.
  http://www.emich.edu/~linguist/dictionaries.html

- Online Language Dictionaries and Translators
  http://rivendel.com:80/~ric/resources/dictionary.html

- Portuguese Genealogy Lexique
  http://www.freenet.edmonton.ab.ca/~fcandido/lexique.html
  Portuguese-English translations of genealogy terms.

- Research It!
  http://www.iTools.com/research-it/research-it.html
  Has a foreign language universal translator.

- Slovak Translation Services by Jana Cupková Holmes
  http://www.dholmes.com/janatran.html

- Svensk-engelskt släkt-lexikon / Swedish-English Genealogy Dictionary
  http://sd.datatorget.educ.goteborg.se/cdata/sv-eng.html?lang=english#english

- SYSTRAN Online Translation
  http://www.systranet.com/english/trans.html

- Tolken97 v3.2
  http://www.algonet.se/~hagsten/
  Shareware program from Sweden—language-translator, texteditor, dictionary, etc.

- The Translator's Home Companion—On-line Dictionaries and Glossaries
  http://www.rahul.net/lai/glossaries.html

- travlang's Translating Dictionaries
  http://dictionaries.travlang.com/
  Including: English, German, Dutch, French, Spanish, Danish, Portuguese, Afrikaans, Esperanto.

- A Web of On-Line Dictionaries
  http://www.facstaff.bucknell.edu/rbeard/diction.html
  A huge index of a variety of available dictionaries, including foreign translation sites.

◆ Genealogy Dictionaries & Glossaries

- Charlotte's Web Genealogical Dictionary
  http://www.charweb.org/gen/gendict.html

- Charts for Reference in Genealogy Research
  http://members.tripod.com/~Silvie/charts.html
  Glossary Chart, Occupation Chart, War Chart, Disease Chart.

- Danish-English Genealogy Dictionary
  http://ourworld.compuserve.com/homepages/NormanMadsen/danish.htm

- Family Finders Glossary of Genealogy Terms
  http://www.iosphere.net/~jholwell/fam-find/glossary.html

- Genealogy Definitions
  http://home.earthlink.net/~howardorjeff/i8.htm

- Genealogy Dictionary
  http://home.att.net/~dottsr/diction.html

- Genealogy Dictionary from Dick Eastman
  http://w3g.med.uni-giessen.de/CGB/genetxt/buzzwo.rds

- Genealogy Dictionary from Family Tree Maker
  http://www.familytreemaker.com/00000736.html

- Genealogy Terms
  http://www.genweb.net/~samcasey/terms.html

- German Study Group / German Words
  http://205.216.138.19/~websites/lynnd/vuword.html

- Glossary of Genealogical Terms
  http://www.rootsweb.com/~canwgw/ns/digby/perm/
  glossary.htm

- Glossary of Unusual Words Found in Wills etc.
  http://ourworld.compuserve.com/homepages/dave_tylcoat/
  gloss.htm

- Index of Genealogical Related Terms
  http://www.trailerpark.com/tango/pjohnson/term_index.html
  (the ones that might trip you up)

- Parsons Genealogy Definition—Genealogy Glossary
  http://www.parsonstech.com/genealogy/def.html

- A Partial List of Latin Genealogy Terms and Their
  English Equivalents
  http://homepage.interaccess.com/~arduinif/tools/latin.htm

- ROOTS-L Resources: Genealogical Terms and
  Definitions
  http://www.rootsweb.com/roots-l/definitions.html

- Ultimate Family Tree—Glossary of Genealogical
  Terms and Abbreviations
  http://www.uftree.com/UFT/Nav/glossary.html

- The USGenWeb Project Information for
  Researchers—Genealogy Vocabulary
  http://www.usgenweb.org/researchers/vocab.html

◆ Land

- Section and Acres Charts by Janyce
  http://www.janyce.com/misc/section.html

- Surveying Units and Terms
  http://members.aol.com/RootsLady/universal/survey1.htm

◆ Miscellaneous

- AmeriSpeak: Expressions of Our Ancestors
  http://www.rootsweb.com/~genepool/amerispeak.htm

- Civil War Soldier Vocabulary
  http://www.cee.indiana.edu/gopher/
  Turner_Adventure_Learning/Gettysburg_Archive/
  Other_Resources/Soldier_Vocabulary.txt

- Definition of Early Immigrants
  http://www.rootsweb.com/~ote/def.htm

- A Glossary of German Words Used in
  Official Documents
  gopher://Gopher.UToledo.edu:70/00GOPHER_
  ROOT%3A%5BRESEARCH-RESOURCES.GENEALOGY.
  GERMAN-GENEALOGY%5DA-GLOSSARY-OF-GERMAN-
  WORDS.USED-IN-OFFICIAL-DOCUMENTS

- Glossary of Unusual Words Found in Wills etc.
  http://ourworld.compuserve.com/homepages/dave_tylcoat/
  glossary.htm

- Graven Images
  http://www.rootsweb.com/~ote/grave.htm
  *Describes the symbolism of motifs on gravestones—from
  The Olive Tree.*

- Nicknames List
  http://www.tngenweb.usit.com/franklin/frannick.htm

- Our Ancestors' Nicknames
  http://www.uftree.com/UFT/HowTos/SettingOut/nickname1.html

- Shipping Terminology
  http://www.isn.net/~dhunter/terms.html
  With a Prince Edward Island Slant.

- Society of Genealogists Bookshop: Glossaries,
  Handwriting & Latin
  http://www.sog.org.uk/bookshop/Q8.html
  U.K.

- Terms of Confusement: Dowry and Dower
  http://www.ancestry.com/columns/myra/
  Shaking_Family_Tree10-02-97.htm
  *From Shaking Your Family Tree by Myra Vanderpool Gormley,
  C.G.*

- WORDS Mailing List
  http://members.aol.com/johnf14246/gen_mail_general.
  html#WORDS
  *A lighthearted discussion of English-English/American-English
  phrases and how they might have originated. Also see the
  associated web page at http://www.rootsweb.com/~genepool/
  amerispeak.htm*

- Ye Olde English Sayings
  http://www.rootsweb.com/~genepool/sayings.htm

◆ Occupations

- Colonial Occupations
  http://www.rootsweb.com/~rigenweb/ocupaton.html

- Colonial Occupations
  http://www.rootsweb.com/~genepool/jobs.htm

- Colonial Occupations
  http://www.netusa1.net/~hartmont/index.htm#Occupations

- Colonial Occupations
  http://www.genweb.net/~samcasey/occupation.html

- Genealogical Dictionaries—Old German Professions
  & Old German Medical Terms and Causes of Death
  http://home.navisoft.com/scrolls/dictinry.htm

- Kentuckiana Genealogy—Occupation Chart
  http://www.floyd-pavey.com/kentuckiana/kyiana/kyiana/
  occupations.html

- A List of Occupations
  http://cpcug.org/user/jlacombe/terms.html

- Obsolete Occupations
  http://www.rootsweb.com/~ote/occs.htm
  *Some Medieval And Obsolete English Trade And Professional
  Terms Used From 1086–1400. From The Olive Tree.*

- Occupations and Their Descriptions
  http://www.onthenet.com.au/~tonylang/occupa.htm
  From the Langham Genealogy Page.

- Old German Professions and Occupations
  http://www.worldroots.com/brigitte/occupat.htm

- Old Time Jobs
  http://www.seidata.com/~lhoffman/jobdesc.html

◆ Other Online Dictionaries, Glossaries, Etc.

- Hypertext Webster's Interface—from Various
  Webster's Dictionary Services on the Internet
  http://c.gp.cs.cmu.edu:5103/prog/webster

- A Web of On-Line Dictionaries
  http://www.facstaff.bucknell.edu/rbeard/diction.html
  *A huge index of a variety of available dictionaries, including
  foreign translation sites.*

- Online Dictionaries, Glossaries and Encylopedias
  http://www-ocean.tamu.edu/~baum/hyperref.html

- On-line Reference Works
  http://www.cs.cmu.edu/references.html
  Dictionaries, Internet resources, maps, and much more!

◆ Relationships & Cousin Charts

- A Chart for Figuring Relationships
  http://www.rootscomputing.com/howto/cousin/cousin.htm

- A Chart for Figuring Relationships
  http://www.rootsweb.com/~genepool/cousins.htm

- A Chart of Consanguinity
  http://www.geocities.com/BourbonStreet/1769/consangu.html

- Cousin Calculator
  http://www.prenticenet.com/roots/tools/cusncalc/cusncalc.htm

- Cousin-Finder
  http://www.ionet.net/~cousin/dale23.html

- Cousins & Cousinhood—It's all Strictly Relative
  http://homepage.interaccess.com/~arduinif/tools/cousins.htm

- "Cousins" & "Removed" explained by Janyce
  http://www.janyce.com/gene/cousins.html

- Cousins Explained
  http://www.obliquity.com/family/misc/cousin.html

- Everton's—On-Line—Relationship Chart
  http://www.everton.com/relation/relation.htm

- Family Derivative—Cousins, How Far Removed
  http://www.cswnet.com/~mgoad/cousins.htm

- Family Relationships Chart
  http://www.tic.net/~lewis/cousin.html

- The Gene Pool: A Chart for Figuring Relationships
  http://www.rootsweb.com/~genepool/cousins.htm

- GRL Relationship Chart
  http://www.grl.com/grl/relationship.shtml

- GRS-Our Library-Cousin Chart
  http://www.genrecords.com/library/cousin.htm

- The Handy-Dandy Cousin Chart
  http://www2.ebtech.net/~kleonard/chart.html

- The Nature of Kinship—Glossary Menu
  http://www.palomar.edu/more/beh_sci/kinship/kin_74.htm
  An Introduction to Descent Systems and Family Organization.

- Relationship Chart
  http://www.eng.uci.edu/students/mpontius/pontius/7-7.html

- Relationship Chart
  http://www.agate.net/~davids/_genea/dl01.htm
  Download from David's Home Page.

- Relationship Chart—How are We Related?
  http://www.jewishgen.org/infofiles/related.txt
  A JewishGen InfoFile.

- Table of Consanguinity
  http://www.heirsearch.com/cons.html
  Showing degrees of relationship by blood.

- What Is a First Cousin, Twice Removed?
  http://www.familytreemaker.com/16_cousn.html
  From Family Tree Maker Online.

TRAVEL & RESEARCH
http://www.CyndisList.com/travel.htm

Category Index:

- ◆ General Resource Sites
- ◆ Elderhostels for Genealogical Research Trips
- ◆ Planning a Research Trip to the Family History Library in Salt Lake City, Utah?
- ◆ Planning a Research Trip to Washington, DC?

◆ General Resource Sites

- 1999 Research Trip to Ireland
  http://www.ngsgenealogy.org/feature/content/feature2.html
  Sponsored by National Genealogical Society, 18–24 September 1999.

- Czech Republic & Slovakia Genealogical/ Cultural Tours
  http://members.aol.com/jzel/tourfly.htm

- European Focus
  http://www.eurofocus.com/html/privatetours.html
  Personalized, private tours to your ancestral town.

- Genealogical Journeys—Vacationing with Your Ancestors
  http://www.familytreemaker.com/issue17.html
  From Family Tree Maker's Back Issues.

  - ○ Before Your Trip: Doing Your Homework
    http://www.familytreemaker.com/17_before.html

  - ○ A Genealogist's Post-Vacation Checklist
    http://www.familytreemaker.com/17_after.html

  - ○ Packing for a Genealogical Journey
    http://www.familytreemaker.com/17_pack.html

- A Genealogical Tool Kit
  http://www.cslnet.ctstateu.edu/toolkit.htm
  A complete list of the items you need to take with you when you visit cemeteries, archives, libraries, and town halls.

- The JewishGen TraveLink Database
  http://www.jewishgen.org/interactive/tr_main.html

- Kiwanis International Convention—Unlock Your Family Heritage..
  http://www.kiwanis.com/librycon.htm

- Libraries—Cyndi's List
  http://www.CyndisList.com/libes.htm
  Planning a research trip? Look through online library catalogs to determine what resources you will be able to access while visiting each city or town.

- Planning A Genealogical Vacation
  http://www.ancestry.com/columns/george/06-19-98.htm
  From "Along Those Lines . . ." by George G. Morgan.

- Routes to Roots
  http://www.routestoroots.com/
  Tracing Jewish Roots in Poland, Ukraine, Moldova and Belarus.

- RV-n-Genealogists
  http://www.everton.com/rvgen/index.html
  From Evertons'—dedicated to genealogy and the RV lifestyle.

- Specialty Travel Index: Genealogy
  http://www.spectrav.com/genealogy.html

- Travel Genie
  http://www.netins.net/showcase/travelgenie/
  Detailed Maps for Travel and Genealogy Since 1985.

◆ Elderhostels for Genealogical Research Trips

- BYU Elderhostel Home Page—Conferences and Workshops
  http://coned.byu.edu/cw/cwelderh/

- Canada Elderhostel—Elderhostel Programs
  http://www.compu-clone.ns.ca/~jdaisley/elder.htm

- Elderhostel Canada
  http://www.csi.nb.ca/nbtour/htm/customer/eldrhstl.htm

- The Elderhostel Home Page
  http://www.elderhostel.org

  - ○ Elderhostel—Search the U.S. & Canada Catalogs
    http://www.elderhostel.org/catalog/select.html

- New Hampshire Society of Genealogists Elderhostel Description
  http://www.tiac.net/users/nhsog/prelderh.htm

- Ricks College Elderhostel Programs
  http://www.ricks.edu/Ricks/ContEd/elderh.htm
  Idaho

- VCOA—Richmond Elderhostel Programs
  http://views.vcu.edu/vcoa/eldhosr.htm
  Virginia

◆ Planning a Research Trip to the Family History Library in Salt Lake City, Utah?

- The Church of Jesus Christ of Latter-day Saints and the Family History Library
  http://www.genhomepage.com/LDS.html
  From the Genealogy Home Page.

- Excite Travel: Salt Lake City, Utah
  http://www.city.net/countries/united_states/utah/salt_lake_city/

- Guide To LDS Family History Library, Salt Lake City, Utah
  http://www.jewishgen.org/infofiles/lds-slc.txt
  A JewishGen InfoFile.

- Hotels and Travel in Utah
  http://www.hotelstravel.com/usut.html

- LDS & Family History Centers
  http://www.CyndisList.com/lds.htm
  See this category on Cyndi's List for related links.

- LDS Family History Library, Salt Lake City, Utah
  http://www.everton.com/genealog/genealog.ldsfhlib
  Description, maps, etc.

- Max Bertola's Mormon Temple Square Visitor Center
  http://www.uvol.com/www1st/tsquare/

- News of the Family History Library in Salt Lake City
  http://members.aol.com/terryann2/lib_news.htm

- Salt Lake City, Family History Library Information
  http://www.aros.net/~drwaff/slcfhl.htm

- Salt Lake City Here We Come!
  http://www.rootsweb.com/~genepool/slc.htm

- Salt Lake Family History Library
  http://www.genealogy.org/~uvpafug/fhlslc.html
  From the Utah Valley PAF Users Group.

- Visit Salt Lake
  http://www.saltlake.org/
  From the Salt Lake Convention & Visitors Bureau.

- Yahoo!...Salt Lake City...Travel
  http://travel.yahoo.com/Destinations/North_America/Countries/United_States/States/Utah//Cities/Salt_Lake_City/

◆ Planning a Research Trip to Washington, DC?

- The Center—A Guide to Genealogical Research in the National Capital Area
  http://www.genealogybookshop.com/genealogybookshop/files/The_United_States,District_of_Columbia/5175.html
  A great book by Christina K. Schaefer. We found this very useful in planning our last trip to DC.

- Excite Travel: Washington, District of Columbia
  http://www.city.net/countries/united_states/district_of_columbia/washington/

- Hearthstone Bookshop
  http://www.hearthstonebooks.com/
  Alexandria, Virginia

- Hotels and Travel in Washington DC
  http://www.hotelstravel.com/usdc.html

- Library of Congress
  http://www.CyndisList.com/libofcon.htm
  See this category on Cyndi's List for related links.

- National Archives
  http://www.CyndisList.com/na.htm
  See this category on Cyndi's List for related links.

- National Archives and Records Administration
  http://www.nara.gov/
  - NARA Calendar of Events
    http://www.nara.gov/nara/events/events.html
    For the National Archives facilities in and around Washington, DC and nationwide.
  - National Archives: Washington, DC Area Facilities
    http://www.nara.gov/nara/dc/dcarea.html

- National Genealogical Society—Library Services
  http://www.genealogy.org/~ngs/library.html
  Arlington, Virginia

- National Society of the Daughters of the American Revolution Home Page
  http://www.dar.org/index.html
  - American Genealogical Research at the DAR, Washington, D.C.
    http://www.dar.org/library/libpub.html
    A terrific book for sale from the DAR.
  - DAR Museum
    http://www.dar.org/museum/index.html
  - Genealogical Research Library
    http://www.dar.org/library/library.html

- NUCMC Listing of Archives and Manuscript Repositories in the District of Columbia
  http://lcweb.loc.gov/coll/nucmc/dcsites.html
  Links to information about resources other than those held in the Library of Congress.

- Tips for Genealogical Researchers in the District of Columbia
  http://members.aol.com/dcgenweb/dctips.html

- U.S.—District of Columbia—DC
  http://www.CyndisList.com/dc.htm
  See this category on Cyndi's List for related links.

- Yahoo!...Washington, D.C....Travel
  http://travel.yahoo.com/Destinations/North_America/Countries/United_States/States/District_of_Columbia/metros/DC/

UNIQUE PEOPLES & CULTURES
http://www.CyndisList.com/peoples.htm

Category Index:

◆ Gypsy, Romani, Romany & Travellers

◆ Melungeons

◆ Miscellaneous

◆ Gypsy, Romani, Romany & Travellers

- Association of Gypsies/Romani International, Inc.
  http://www.gypsies.net/

- Gypsies and Travellers
  http://www.herts.ac.uk/UHPress/Gypsies.html
  Books published by the University of Hertfordshire Press.

- Gypsy Collections at the University of Liverpool
  http://sca.lib.liv.ac.uk/collections/gypsy/intro.htm

  ○ Gypsy Collections—Families
    http://sca.lib.liv.ac.uk/collections/gypsy/families.htm

  ○ Irish Travellers Today
    http://sca.lib.liv.ac.uk/collections/gypsy/travell.htm

  ○ Journal of the Gypsy Lore Society
    http://sca.lib.liv.ac.uk/collections/gypsy/journal.htm

- Gypsys Across America
  http://www.gypsys.com/

- The International Romani Union
  http://www.rroma.com/tiru.htm

- itinerantroots Mailing List
  http://www.onelist.com/subscribe.cgi/itinerantroots
  For genealogy resources relating to itinerant professions; circus, theatre, music hall, vaudeville, fairs, showmen, portable theatres, etc.

- The Patrin Web Journal—Romani (Gypsy) Culture and History
  http://www.geocities.com/Paris/5121/patrin.htm

- The Romani Archives
  http://www.rroma.com/archives/archives.htm

- SCAMP—The Genealogy of a Gypsy Family
  http://ourworld.compuserve.com/homepages/rogerbaker/

- SOCAS—Gypsies and Travellers: Resources on the World Wide Web
  http://www.cf.ac.uk/uwcc/socas/links/gypsies.html

◆ Melungeons

- First Union: The Melungeons Revisited
  http://www6.roanoke.infi.net/~leisure/brc/melung/melung.html
  An article from Blue Ridge Country Magazine.

- The Louisiana Redbones
  http://dogwoodpress.myriad.net/dcm/redbone.html

- Melungeon Mailing List
  http://members.aol.com/gfsjohnf/gen_mail_states-gen.html#MELUNGEO
  For people conducting Melungeon and/or Appalachian research including Native American, Portuguese, Turkish, Black Dutch, and other unverifiable mixed statements of ancestry or unexplained rumors, with ancestors in TN, KY, VA, NC, SC, GA, AL, WV, and possibly other places.

- Melungeon Ancestry Research Page—The Melungeon Outpost
  http://www.bright.net/~kat/melung.htm
  A Place For Connection, Sharing and Research.

- A Melungeon HomePage
  http://www.melungeons.org./index.html

  ○ *Appalachian Clan Mines Web Sites for Ancestral Clues*
    http://www.melungeons.org./dw1_wsj.htm
    by Fred R. Bleakley for the Wall Street Journal.

  ○ *The Forgotten Portuguese: The Melungeons And Other Groups—The Portuguese Making of America*
    http://www.melungeons.org./mira.htm
    A book for sale, by Manuel Mira.

  ○ *THE MELUNGEONS: The Pioneers of the Interior Southeastern United States*
    http://www.melungeons.org./gallegos.htm
    A book for sale, by Eloy Gallegos.

  ○ *The National Melungeon Registry*
    http://www.melungeons.org./mel_nmr.htm

  ○ *Under One Sky—The Melungeon Information Exchange*
    http://www.melungeons.org./mel_uos.htm

- Melungeons and Other Mestee Groups
  http://www.hypertext.com/blackirish/melungeons.html
- Melungeons: Read More About It
  http://www.bright.net/~kat/readmor.htm
  Bibliography of suggested reading.
- Possible Melungeon Surnames
  http://www.bright.net/~kat/melnam.htm
- Southeastern Kentucky Melungeon Information Exchange
  http://www.bright.net/~kat/skmie.htm

◆ Miscellaneous

- The African-Native Genealogy Homepage
  http://members.aol.com/angelaw859/index.html
  Celebrating the Estelusti~The Freedmen Oklahoma's Black Indians of the Cherokee, Chickasaw, Choctaw, Creek, and Seminole Nations.
- Doukhobor Home Page
  http://www.dlcwest.com/~r.androsoff/index.htm
  A group of Russian peasants that split from the Russian Ortho-dox Church. Large groups of Doukhobors emigrated to Canada and homesteaded in Saskatchewan and British Columbia.

- International Black Sheep Society of Genealogists (IBSSG)
  http://homepages.rootsweb.com/~blksheep/
  For those who have a dastardly, infamous individual of public knowledge and ill-repute in their family . . . within 1 degree of consanginuity of their direct lines. This individual must have been pilloried in disgrace for acts of a significantly anti-social nature.
- METISGEN Mailing List
  http://members.aol.com/johnf14246/gen_mail_general.html#METISGEN
  For the discussion and sharing of information regarding the Metis and their descendants. The Metis are North America's Fur Trading Children . . . the new nation of individuals born within North America from the first unions of natives and whites.
- The Metis Nation of Ontario
  http://www.metisnation.org/
- Notorious Ancestors
  http://www.geocities.com/Heartland/Acres/8310/notorious.html
- Sami Resources
  http://www.montana.edu/sass/sami.htm
- Texas Wendish Heritage Society
  http://home.sprynet.com/sprynet/harrisfarm/wendish.htm

UNITED KINGDOM & IRELAND INDEX

U.K. & IRELAND—GENERAL UK SITES
http://www.CyndisList.com/genuk.htm

Category Index:

- ◆ Colonies & Possessions
- ◆ General Resource Sites
- ◆ History & Culture
- ◆ How To
- ◆ Libraries, Archives & Museums
- ◆ Mailing Lists, Newsgroups & Chat
- ◆ Maps, Gazetteers & Geographical Information
- ◆ Military
- ◆ Newspapers

- ◆ People & Families
- ◆ Professional Researchers, Volunteers & Other Research Services
- ◆ Publications, Software & Supplies
- ◆ Queries, Message Boards & Surname Lists
- ◆ Records: Census, Cemeteries, Land, Obituaries, Personal, Taxes and Vital
- ◆ Societies & Groups

◆ Colonies & Possessions

- ● Australia & New Zealand
  http://www.CyndisList.com/austnz.htm
  See this category on Cyndi's List for related links.

- ● Canada
  http://www.CyndisList.com/canada.htm
  See this category on Cyndi's List for related links.

- ● British Ancestors in India
  http://www.ozemail.com.au/~clday/

- ● The British in Singapore and Malaya
  http://user.itl.net/~glen/BritishinSingapore%26Malaya.html

- ● Commonwealth War Graves Commission
  http://www.cwgc.org/
  Details of 1.7 million members of UK and Commonwealth forces who died in the 1st and 2nd World Wars and other wars, and 60,000 civilian casualties of WWII. Gives details of grave site, date of death, age, usually parents/widow's address.

- ● English East India Company Ships
  http://www.ships.dircon.co.uk/eic/eic.htm
  Shipping Losses in the Mercantile Service 1600–1834 (includes Shipwrecks, Captures & Missing Vessels).

- ● Falkland Island Genealogy
  http://members.tripod.com/~FalklandIslands/Genealogy.html

- ● Hispanic, Central & South America, & the West Indies
  http://www.CyndisList.com/hispanic.htm
  Including Mexico, Latin America & the Caribbean. See this category on Cyndi's List for related links.

- ● India Office Records: Sources for Family History Research
  http://www.bl.uk/collections/oriental/records/iorfamhi.html
  The British Library Oriental and India Office Collections (OIOC).

- ● Maltese Genealogy Corner.
  http://www.fred.net/malta/roots.html

- ● Soldiers Whom the World have Forgotten
  http://www.geocities.com/Athens/Acropolis/9460/index.html
  Dedicated to the memory of soldiers & their families who died in and around Bangalore, India.

- ● South Africa
  http://www.CyndisList.com/soafrica.htm
  See this category on Cyndi's List for related links.

- ● United States
  http://www.CyndisList.com/usa.htm
  See this category on Cyndi's List for related links.

◆ General Resource Sites

- ● Genealogy Bulletin Board Systems for the United Kingdom
  http://www.genealogy.org/~gbbs/gblunite.html

- ● GENEVA—The GENUKI diary of GENealogical EVents and Activities
  http://users.ox.ac.uk/~malcolm/genuki/geneva/

- ● ROOTS-L Resources: United Kingdom and Ireland
  http://www.rootsweb.com/roots-l/uki.html

- ● The UK Genealogy Webring
  http://www.kbnet.co.uk/brianp/webring.html

- ● The UK & Ireland Genealogical Information Service (GENUKI)
  http://www.genuki.org.uk
  - ○ UK+Ireland Genealogy Index
    http://www.genuki.org.uk/mindex.html

○ The UK and Ireland
  http://www.genuki.org.uk/big/

  • Channel Islands
    http://user.itl.net/~glen/genukici.html

  • England
    http://www.genuki.org.uk/big/eng/

  • Ireland
    http://hiwaay.net/~white/genuki/irl.html

  • Isle of Man
    http://www.genuki.org.uk/big/lom.html

  • Scotland
    http://www-theory.dcs.st-and.ac.uk/~mnd/genuki/scot.html

  • Wales
    http://www.genuki.org.uk/big/wal/

- UK Surname Frequency, 1851–1996
  http://www.tdrake.demon.co.uk/surname.htm
  The top 88 surnames in 1996 compared to the 1851 UK census.

- Yahoo!...United Kingdom...Genealogy
  http://dir.yahoo.com/Regional/Countries/United_Kingdom/Arts_and_Humanities/Humanities/History/Genealogy/

◆ History & Culture

- American and British History Resources on the Internet
  http://www.libraries.rutgers.edu/rulib/socsci/hist/amhist.html

- Gaelic & Gaelic Culture
  http://sunsite.unc.edu/gaelic/

- History of England in Medieval Times
  http://www.worldroots.com/brigitte/royal/royal8.htm
  Historic and genealogical information about royal and nobility family lines.

- Secrets of the Norman Invasion
  http://www.cablenet.net/pages/book/index.htm
  With plates of the Bayeux Tapestry.

- Victorian History Overview
  http://www.stg.brown.edu/projects/hypertext/landow/victorian/history/histov.html

◆ How To

- Beginning Family History, UK National Register of Archives—Information Leaflets ~ GENUKI
  http://www.genuki.org.uk/big/RCH/Beginning.html

- How to Trace Your Family Tree—Notes for Beginners
  http://members.aol.com/gfhsoc/beginner.htm
  From the Glamorgan Family History Society.

- Researching Ancestors from the United Kingdom Using the LDS Family History Center Resources
  http://www.oz.net/~markhow/uksearch.htm

- Researching from Abroad ~ GENUKI
  http://www.genuki.org.uk/ab/

- Emery Paper, Version 3—A–Z of British Genealogical Research ~ GENUKI
  http://www.genuki.org.uk/big/EmeryPaper.html

◆ Libraries, Archives & Museums

- The British Heraldic Archive
  http://www.kwtelecom.com/heraldry/

- British Isles Family History Centers
  http://www.lib.byu.edu/~uvrfhc/england.html

- The British Library
  http://www.bl.uk/index.html

- Cunard Archives at Liverpool University
  http://www.liv.ac.uk/~archives/cunard/chome.htm

- CURL—The Consortium of University Research Libraries
  http://www.curl.ac.uk/

- Family History Centres in the UK
  http://www.dungeon.com/~deltatango/mormon.html

- Guildhall Library Manuscripts Collection
  http://ihr.sas.ac.uk/ihr/ghmnu.html

- The Hudson's Bay Company Archives
  http://www.gov.mb.ca/chc/archives/hbca/index.html
  From the Provincial Archives of Manitoba, Canada.

- HYTELNET—Library Catalogs: United Kingdom
  http://library.usask.ca/hytelnet/uk0/uk000.html
  Before you use any of the Telnet links, make note of the user name, password and any other logon information.

- LDS Family History Centres in the British Isles, Including Ireland and Scotland
  http://www.genuki.org.uk/big/LDS/centres.txt

- Methodist Archives and Research Centre
  http://rylibweb.man.ac.uk/data1/dg/text/method.html
  At the John Rylands University Library in Manchester, UK. See the link for Researching your Family History on this site.

- The National Army Museum ~ London
  http://www.failte.com/nam/index.htm

- The Post Office Archives and Record Services
  http://www.cs.ncl.ac.uk/genuki/PostOffice/

- Project EARL—Connecting Public Libraries to the Network
  http://www.earl.org.uk/

- Royal Commission on Historical Manuscripts
  http://www.hmc.gov.uk/
  Information on manuscript collections relating to British history.

- UK Archival Repositories on the Internet
  http://www.archivesinfo.net/uksites.html

- The UK Public Libraries Page
  http://dspace.dial.pipex.com/town/square/ac940/ukpublib.html

- University of Essex—The Data Archive
  http://dawww.essex.ac.uk/
- webCATS: Library Catalogues on the World Wide
  Web—United Kingdom
  http://library.usask.ca/hywebcat/countries/UK.html

◆ Mailing Lists, Newsgroups & Chat

- BORDER Mailing List
  http://members.aol.com/gfsjohnf/gen_mail_country-unk.
  html#BORDER
  *For anyone interested in genealogy, history, or culture related to
  the counties which surround the border of Scotland and
  England.*
- COALMINERS Mailing List
  http://members.aol.com/gfsjohnf/gen_mail_country-unk.
  html#COALMINERS
  *For anyone whose ancestors were coalminers in the United
  Kingdom or the United States.*
- Falklands Mailing List
  http://members.aol.com/gfsjohnf/gen_mail_country-unk.
  html#Falklands
  For anyone with a genealogical interest in the Falkland Islands.
- GENBRIT Mailing List
  http://members.aol.com/gfsjohnf/gen_mail_country-unk.
  html#GENBRIT
  *For the discussion of genealogy in Great Britain and the islands.
  Gatewayed with the soc.genealogy.britain newsgroup.*
- GENIRE Mailing List—Ireland
  http://members.aol.com/gfsjohnf/gen_mail_country-unk.
  html#GENIRE
  Gatewayed with the soc.genealogy.ireland newsgroup.
- INDIA Mailing List
  http://members.aol.com/gfsjohnf/gen_mail_country-ind.
  html#INDIA1
  *For anyone who is interested in tracing their British and
  European Ancestors in British India.*
- SOG-NEWS Mailing List
  http://members.aol.com/gfsjohnf/gen_mail_country-unk.
  html#SOG-NEWS
  *A read-only mailing list for anyone interested in the activities of
  the Society of Genealogists (of Great Britain), in particular non-
  members of the Society. This list will be used by the Society to
  publicise Society events, courses, special library acquisitions,
  etc. or for comments on genealogical issues.*
- SOG-UK Mailing List
  http://members.aol.com/gfsjohnf/gen_mail_country-unk.
  html#SOG-UK
  *For the members of the Society of Genealogists (of Great
  Britain) for topics related to genealogy, the Society resources, or
  Society issues.*
- SOUTH-AM-EMI Mailing List
  http://members.aol.com/gfsjohnf/gen_mail_country-unk.
  html#SOUTH-AM-EMI
  *A mailing list for the discussion and sharing of information
  regarding emigrants from the United Kingdom to South America
  during the eighteenth and nineteenth centuries.*

- SURNAMES-BRITAIN Mailing List
  http://members.aol.com/gfsjohnf/gen_mail_country-unk.
  html#SURNAMES-BRITAIN
  *For surname queries related to Great Britain. Gatewayed with
  the soc.genealogy.surnames.britain newsgroup.*
- SURNAMES-IRELAND Mailing List
  http://members.aol.com/gfsjohnf/gen_mail_country-unk.
  html#SURNAMES-IRELAND
  *Gatewayed with the soc.genealogy.surnames.ireland newsgroup
  For surname queries related to Ireland and Northern Ireland.*
- Unionist-Culture Mailing List
  http://members.aol.com/gfsjohnf/gen_mail_country-unk.
  html#Unionist-Culture
  *For anyone with a genealogical or cultural interest in the
  Unionist communities of Ireland (those areas that wish to remain
  part of the union with England).*

◆ Maps, Gazetteers & Geographical Information

- Administrative Regions of the British Isles ~
  GENUKI
  http://www.genuki.org.uk/big/Regions/
- The Bodleian Library Map Room
  http://www.rsl.ox.ac.uk/nnj/
- British Geological Survey Maps
  http://www.bgs.ac.uk/bgs/w3/isg/maps.html
- Chapman Country & County Codes (Pre 1974)
  http://www.netcentral.co.uk/~wjh/ccodes.html
- Counties of England, Scotland and Wales Prior to
  the 1974 Boundary Changes
  http://www.genuki.org.uk/big/BRITAIN2.GIF
- The David Morgan Home Page
  http://www.davidmorgan.com/
  Has British Ordnance Survey maps for sale.
- Geographical search—UK or elsewhere
  http://www.nkw.ac.uk/bgs/w3/isg/ukornot.html
- Multi Media Mapping
  http://uk5.multimap.com/map/places.cgi
  *An interactive atlas of Great Britain. Enter the name of a British
  city, town or village to get a clickable, zoomable, detailed map.*
- The Ordnance Survey—Gazetteer of Place Names
  http://www.campus.bt.com/CampusWorld/pub/OS/Gazetteer/
  index.html
  Searchable database for UK.
- Ordnance Survey Home Page
  http://www.ordsvy.gov.uk/
  National Mapping Agency of Great Britain.
- UK Sensitive Map to Universities
  http://scitsc.wlv.ac.uk/ukinfo/uk.map.html

◆ Military

- The British Army
  http://www.army.mod.uk

- The British Empire & Commonwealth Land Forces
  http://www.du.edu/~tomills/military/empire.htm
- British Infantry Regiment Name Changes (1881)
  http://www.tdrake.demon.co.uk/infantry.htm
- British Military Records
  http://www.genuki.org.uk/big/BritMilRecs.html
- The Buff's (The Royal East Kent Regiment)
  http://www.digiserve.com/peter/buffs/
- Commonwealth War Graves Commission
  http://www.cwgc.org/
  Details of 1.7 million members of UK and Commonwealth forces who died in the 1st and 2nd World Wars and other wars, and 60,000 civilian casualties of WWII. Gives details of grave site, date of death, age, usually parents/widow's address.
- Dispatch Military Journal
  http://subnet.virtual-pc.com/~mc546367/journal.htm
  Journal for Scottish Military History and Regiments, Scottish Military Historical Society.
- The National Army Museum
  http://www.failte.com/nam/index.htm
  London, England
- The Scots at War Project
  http://www-saw.arts.ed.ac.uk/saw.html
  A tribute to the men and women who served their country in the 20th century. Includes information on genealogy for Scottish soldiers.
  - Genealogical Help Service—Ancestor Hunting
    http://www-saw.arts.ed.ac.uk/misc/genealogy/ancestor.html
  - Genealogical Help Service—The Armed and Civilian Services
    http://www-saw.arts.ed.ac.uk/misc/genealogy/military.html
  - Military Service Museums for Scotland
    http://www-saw.arts.ed.ac.uk/misc/genealogy/museums.html
- Scottish Military Historical Society—Index of Military Sites to Visit
  http://www.virtual-pc.com/journal/other.htm
- The Trafalgar Roll
  http://www.genuki.org.uk/big/eng/Trafalgar/
  A list of 1640 officers and men who fought at the Battle of Trafalgar.

◆ Newspapers

- AJR NewsLink: United Kingdom Newspapers
  http://www.newslink.org/euuk.html
- Cybermart News Online: United Kingdom Newspapers
  http://www.cybermart.net/Newspapers/Countries/United_Kingdom/index.html
- Ecola Newstand: United Kingdom Newspapers
  http://www.ecola.com/news/press/eu/uk/

- The Ultimate Collection of News Links: United Kingdom
  http://www.pppp.net/links/news/UK.html
- Yahoo!...Newspapers...United Kingdom
  http://dir.yahoo.com/News_and_Media/Newspapers/Regional/Countries/United_Kingdom/

◆ People & Families

- British Ancestors in India
  http://www.ozemail.com.au/~clday/
- The British Monarchy—The Official Web Site
  http://www.royal.gov.uk/
- The French Protestant Church of London
  http://ihr.sas.ac.uk/ihr/associnstits/huguenots.mnu.html
- Huguenots to England
  http://www.rootsweb.com/~ote/hugeng.htm
- The Monarchs & Regents of England & Great Britain for Near 1200 Years
  http://www.ringnett.no/home/bjornstad/royals/England.html
- Soldiers Whom the World have Forgotten
  http://www.geocities.com/Athens/Acropolis/9460/index.html
  Dedicated to the memory of soldiers & their families who died in and around Bangalore, India.

◆ Professional Researchers, Volunteers & Other Research Services

- 4SIGHT RESEARCH—The Research Specialists, Surrey, England
  http://www.netlink.co.uk/users/beavis/
- Back to Roots—Family History Service
  http://www.wwide.co.uk/backtoroots/
- Board for Certification of Genealogists—Roster of Those Certified—Specializing in British Isles
  http://www.genealogy.org/~bcg/rosts_@b.html
- Bob's Public Records Office Searches—Kew, London, England
  http://www.users.dircon.co.uk/~searcher/
  Including these records: Military, Royal Navy, Merchant Navy, Convict, Railway, West Indies, Passenger Lists, History Projects.
- Bowers Genealogy Services
  http://www.interlog.com/~kbowers/bgs2.htm
  England, Scotland, Canada
- Brian Walker—Family History Research in All London Record Offices
  http://ourworld.compuserve.com/homepages/brianwalker1/
  Specializes in London area record repositories including the Family Records Centre, the Public Record Office, Somerset House, Guildhall Library, Society of Genealogists Library, and others.

- British Ancestral Research
  http://www.brit-a-r.demon.co.uk/

- Genealogy Helplist—United Kingdom
  http://www.cybercomm.net/~freddie/helplist/uk.htm

- Lists of Independent Researchers
  http://www.pro.gov.uk/readers/independent.htm
  How to Retrieve a List of Independent Researchers by E-mail from the PRO.

- The Look-up Exchange
  http://www.geocities.com/Heartland/Plains/8555/lookup.html
  A county-by-county list of resources covering England, Scotland, Wales and the Isle of Man, made available by volunteers for free look-ups.

- Professional Genealogist ... Tony Fitzgerald
  http://www.iosphere.net/~jholwell/fam-find/nz/9706106.html
  British research from New Zealand.

- Public Record Searches ~ U.K.
  http://www.users.dircon.co.uk/~searcher/index.htm
  R.W. O'Hara in Kew, Richmond.

- Traces From Your Past
  http://www.cadvision.com/traces/
  Genealogical Publications, Services and Resources to assist the Family Historian researching in Canada and the United Kingdom.

◆ Publications, Software & Supplies

- Ancestor's Attic Discount Genealogy Books— British Genealogy Books
  http://members.tripod.com/~ancestorsattic/index.html#secBR

- Britain in the USA: Family Tracing Fact Sheets
  http://148.100.56.24/bis/fsheets/leaffam.htm

- The British Isles Parish Locator Programs
  http://www.users.globalnet.co.uk/~gdl/parfind.htm

- Cambridge University Press
  http://www.cup.cam.ac.uk/

- Chapman Record Cameos
  http://www.genuki.org.uk/big/Chapman.html
  A series of books by Colin R. Chapman, noted British genealogist.

- Drake Software Genealogy Programs and Information
  http://www.tdrake.demon.co.uk/genindex.htm
  BIRDIE (British Isles Regional Display of Igi Extracts) for Windows, Buckinghamshire Posse Comitatus (1798), British Date Calculator and more.

- Family History Bookshop—The Institute of Heraldic and Genealogical Studies
  http://www.cs.ncl.ac.uk/genuki/IHGS/Catalogue.html

- Family History Library Catalog Description
  http://www.genuki.org.uk/big/LDS/catorg.txt

- Family History Library Catalog Topics
  http://www.genuki.org.uk/big/LDS/topics.txt
  Listed & cross-referenced for use in England, that allow for differences in American and English usage.

- Family Tree Magazine
  http://www.family-tree.co.uk/

- Federation of Family History Societies Publications
  http://www.ffhs.org.uk/pubs/index.htm

- Frontier Press Bookstore—British (General)
  http://www.frontierpress.com/frontier.cgi?category=brit

- GenealogyBookShop.com—Great Britain/British
  http://www.genealogybookshop.com/genealogybookshop/files/The_World,Great_Britain_British/index.html
  The online store of Genealogical Publishing Co., Inc. & Clearfield Company.

- Geni—A Genealogical Browser for the Psion 3a and 3c
  http://www-theory.dcs.st-andrews.ac.uk/~mnd/export/geni/

- Gibson Guides—Location Guides for Family and Local Historians
  http://www.genuki.org.uk/big/Gibson.html
  A set of guides to the whereabouts of records, available from the Federation of Family History Societies.

- Local History Magazine
  http://www.local-history.co.uk/

- The Naval & Military Press Web Page
  http://www.naval-military-press.co.uk/
  A large selection of military books, many with of interest to the genealogist.

- Pandect Services
  http://ourworld.compuserve.com/homepages/pandect/
  Family history software and services from Leicestershire, England.

- Public Record Office Bookshop
  http://www.pro.gov.uk/bookshop/default.htm

- S.E.L. Enterprises
  http://www.mentornet.org/sel.htm
  Publications (books, magazines, periodicals & maps) for researching your English, Irish, Scots and Welsh ancestors.

- Society of Genealogists Bookshop Online
  http://www.sog.org.uk/acatalog/welcome.html

- Stephen Archer's Genealogical Software Home Page
  http://ourworld.compuserve.com/homepages/steve_archer/
  IGIREAD, a file conversion utility (DOS) for the IGI on CD-ROM and GenMap UK, a Windows mapping program designed mainly for UK genealogical and historical mapping.

- UK Online Newspapers
  http://www-mice.cs.ucl.ac.uk/misc/uk/newspaper.html

◆ Queries, Message Boards & Surname Lists

- GENUKI Surname Lists
  http://www.cs.ncl.ac.uk/genuki/SurnamesList/
  Lists for each county in the United Kingdom and Ireland.

- Lineages' Free On-line Queries—England, Ireland, Scotland & Wales
  http://www.lineages.com/queries/BrowseByCountry.asp

◆ Records: Census, Cemeteries, Land, Obituaries, Personal, Taxes and Vital (Born, Married, Died & Buried)

- Anne's UK Certificates for Australians
  http://freespace.virgin.net/mark.wainwright6/uk_certificates/
  An Australian living in London who can obtain copies of English, Scottish & Welsh Birth, Marriage and Death Certificates in exchange for payment in Australian dollars.

- Births Deaths & Marriages Exchange
  http://web.ukonline.co.uk/graham.pitt/bdm/

- British Military Records
  http://www.genuki.org.uk/big/BritMilRecs.html

- The Census Enumerators' Books
  http://www.staffs.ac.uk/schools/humanities_and_soc_sciences/census/cebs.htm
  An introduction to the surviving source material for the censuses done in the United Kingdom in the 1800s. While geared to sociologists, this site is helpful to family historians for understanding the source documents which they use in their research.

- Civil Registration ~ GENUKI
  http://www.genuki.org.uk/big/eng/civreg/

- Commonwealth War Graves Commission
  http://www.cwgc.org/
  Details of 1.7 million members of UK and Commonwealth forces who died in the 1st and 2nd World Wars and other wars, and 60,000 civilian casualties of WWII. Gives details of grave site, date of death, age, usually parents/widow's address.

- India Office Records: Sources for Family History Research
  http://portico.bl.uk/oioc/records/iorfamhi.html
  The British Library Oriental and India Office Collections (OIOC).

- HM Land Registry Home Page ~ United Kingdom
  http://www.open.gov.uk/landreg/home.htm

- Marriage Witness Indexes for United Kingdom, Australia, and New Zealand
  http://www.genuki.org.uk/mwi/

- Office for National Statistics, Registration Division—Adoptions
  http://www.emap.com/ons/public/reg.shtml

- ONS Publication Index—Birth, Death or Marriage Certificates for England and Wales
  http://www.emap.com/ons/public/certificate.shtml

- Ordering Birth Registration Certificates from the United Kingdom Using the LDS Family History Center Resources
  http://www.oz.net/~markhow/ukbirths.htm

- Parish Register Copies in the Library of the Society of Genealogists
  http://www.sog.org.uk/prc/

- The Public Record Office Home Page
  http://www.pro.gov.uk/
  - About the Family Records Centre
    http://www.pro.gov.uk/about/frc/
  - Information For Genealogists
    http://www.pro.gov.uk/readers/genealogists/default.htm
    - Public Record Office—Family Fact Sheets
      http://www.pro.gov.uk/readers/genealogists/familyfacts.htm
  - Public Record Office—Finding Aids—A–Z Index of All Leaflets
    http://www.pro.gov.uk/leaflets/riindex.htm
    - Admiralty Records as Sources for Biography and Genealogy (#2)
      http://www.pro.gov.uk/leaflets/ri002.htm
    - Air Records as Sources for Biography and Family History (#13)
      http://www.pro.gov.uk/leaflets/ri013.htm
    - Births, Marriages and Deaths (#39)
      http://www.pro.gov.uk/leaflets/ri039.htm
    - British Army Records as Sources for Biography and Genealogy (#59)
      http://www.pro.gov.uk/leaflets/ri059.htm
    - Family History in England and Wales (#14)
      http://www.pro.gov.uk/leaflets/ri014.htm
    - Genealogy Before the Parish Registers (#28)
      http://www.pro.gov.uk/leaflets/ri028.htm
    - Public Records Outside the Public Record Office (#124)
      http://www.pro.gov.uk/leaflets/ri124.htm

- Public Record Office Leaflets ~ GENUKI
  http://users.ox.ac.uk/~malcolm/genuki/big/pro/leaflets.htm

- Ron Taylor's UK Census Finding Aids and Indexes
  http://rontay.digiweb.com/
  Mainly from the 1851 Census.
  - Born in France and Germany Census Indexes
    http://rontay.digiweb.com/france/
  - Institutionalised Census Indexes
    http://rontay.digiweb.com/institute
    Including Paupers, Inmates, Convicts, Prisoners and Prostitutes.
  - Occupations Census Indexes
    http://rontay.digiweb.com/visit/occupy/
  - Scots and Irish Strays Census Indexes
    http://rontay.digiweb.com/scot/
  - Strays by County Census Indexes
    http://rontay.digiweb.com/county
  - Visitors Census Indexes
    http://rontay.digiweb.com/visit/

◆ Societies & Groups

- Anglo-German Family History Society—AG-FHS
  http://feefhs.org/uk/frgagfhs.html

- British Isles Family History Society—U.S.A.
  http://www.rootsweb.com/~bifhsusa/
  Los Angeles, California

- Crimean War Research Society
  http://homepages.ihug.co.nz/~phil/crimean.htm

- The Federation of Family History Societies
  http://www.ffhs.org.uk/

- Friends of the PRO
  http://www.pro.gov.uk/friends/default.htm
  This voluntary organization helps index and acquire materials at the Public Records Office.

- Guild of One-Name Studies
  http://www.one-name.org/

- The Historical Association
  http://www.history.org.uk/

- The Historical Diving Society
  http://www.thehds.dircon.co.uk/

- The Institute of Heraldic and Genealogical Studies
  http://www.cs.ncl.ac.uk/genuki/IHGS/

- Jewish Genealogical Society of Great Britain
  http://www.ort.org/jgsgb/index.htm

- Manorial Society of Great Britain
  http://www.msgb.co.uk/msgb/index.html

- National Railway Historical Society, UK Chapter
  http://www.siam.co.uk/siam/nrhsuk.shtml

- Railway Ancestors Family History Society
  http://www.railwayancestors.demon.co.uk/

- Society of Genealogists
  http://www.sog.org.uk/

CHANNEL ISLANDS
http://www.CyndisList.com/channel.htm

Category Index:

- General Resource Sites
- History & Culture
- Libraries, Archives & Museums
- Mailing Lists, Newsgroups & Chat
- Maps, Gazetteers & Geographical Information

- People & Families
- Queries, Message Boards & Surname Lists
- Records: Census, Cemeteries, Land, Obituaries, Personal, Taxes and Vital
- Societies & Groups

◆ General Resource Sites

- Al BEAGAN's "Genealogy Notes"—The Island of Jersey
  http://www.capecod.net/~abeagan/jersey.htm
- Alex GLENDINNING's Channel Islands Pages
  http://user.itl.net/~glen/CIintro.html
  - The Alderney Index
    http://user.itl.net/~glen/alderneyhistoryindex.html
  - Channel Islands Family History: Reading the Records: A Tutorial
    http://user.itl.net/~glen/CItutorial.html
  - Research in the Channel Islands: Alderney Ancestry
    http://user.itl.net/~glen/alderney.html
  - Research in the Channel Islands—FAQs (Frequently Asked Questions)
    http://user.itl.net/~glen/CIResearch.html
  - Research in the Channel Islands FAQs (Frequently Asked Questions)—Links Page
    http://user.itl.net/~glen/CIResearch2.html
  - Research in the Channel Islands: Sark Ancestry
    http://user.itl.net/~glen/sark.html
- Alex GLENDINNING's Société Jersiaise Page
  http://www.societe-jersiaise.org/alexgle/index.html
- The Bailiwick of Guernsey—Genealogy Interest Site
  http://www.guernsey.net/~genealogy/
- Channel Islands Genealogy
  http://members.aol.com/johnf14246/ci.html
  From John Fuller.
  - Volunteers/Lookups
    http://members.aol.com/johnf14246/ci/volunteers.html
- A Chronology of Jersey
  http://Fox.nstn.ca:80/~nstn1528/chro_en.htm
- Guernsey Family History Page
  http://www.guernsey.net/~abott/famhist.html

- International Internet Genealogical Society—Channel Islands—CHI Pages: Jersey, Guernsey, Alderney & Sark
  http://user.itl.net/~glen/IIGSci.html
- Selected Bibliography, Book List Channel Islands
  http://Fox.nstn.ca:80/~nstn1528/booklist.htm
- The UK & Ireland Genealogical Information Service (GENUKI)
  http://www.genuki.org.uk/
  - Channel Islands Genealogy—from GENUKI
    http://user.itl.net/~glen/genukici.html
    - Guernsey Genealogy
      http://user.itl.net/~glen/guernsey.html
    - Jersey Genealogy
      http://user.itl.net/~glen/jersey.html

◆ History & Culture

- Alderney: Evacuation and Occupation 1940–45
  http://user.itl.net/~glen/aldocc.html
- Guernsey Datestones
  http://user.itl.net/~glen/stonegsy.html
- Historical Descriptions of the Channel Islands
  http://user.itl.net/~glen/description.html
  From Grose's "The Antiquities of England and Wales," published 1777.
- The Jersey Datestones Project
  http://www.societe-jersiaise.org/alexgle/stonejsy.html
- Les pages Jèrriaises
  http://www.societe-jersiaise.org/geraint/jerriais.html
  About the native language—Jersey Norman-French.
- Newfoundland, Its Origin, Its Rise and Fall, Also an Epitome of the Jersey Crisis in January 1886. An Episode of the History of Jersey
  http://Fox.nstn.ca:80/~nstn1528/sullivan.htm

- Social Life in Jersey in the Early Seventeenth Century
  http://Fox.nstn.ca:80/~nstn1528/social.htm

◆ Libraries, Archives & Museums

- The Jersey Family History Centre of the L.D.S. Church
  http://user.itl.net/~glen/ldsci.html

- The Priaulx Library
  http://user.itl.net/~glen/priaulx.html
  St Peter Port, Guernsey

- Société Jersiaise Library Collection
  http://user.itl.net/~glen/societe.html

◆ Mailing Lists, Newsgroups & Chat

- CHANNEL-ISLANDS Mailing List
  http://members.aol.com/gfsjohnf/gen_mail_country-unk.
  html#CHANNEL-ISLANDS
  For anyone with a genealogical interest in the Channel Islands (Jersey and the Bailiwick of Guernsey) which lie off the Normandy coast of France.

- GENBRIT Mailing List
  http://members.aol.com/gfsjohnf/gen_mail_country-unk.
  html#GENBRIT
  For the discussion of genealogy in Great Britain and the islands. Gatewayed with the soc.genealogy.britain newsgroup.

- SURNAMES-BRITAIN Mailing List
  http://members.aol.com/gfsjohnf/gen_mail_country-unk.
  html#SURNAMES-BRITAIN
  For surname queries related to Great Britain. Gatewayed with the soc.genealogy.surnames.britain newsgroup.

◆ Maps, Gazetteers & Geographical Information

- Administrative Regions of the British Isles ~ GENUKI
  http://www.genuki.org.uk/big/Regions/

  ○ Crown Dependencies
    http://www.genuki.org.uk/big/Regions/Crown.html

- Map of Jersey Parishes
  http://user.itl.net/image/maps/jsyall.gif

- Old Maps of the Channel Islands
  http://user.itl.net/~glen/maps.html

◆ People & Families

- Clive and Cathy LeMESURIER Family Home Page
  http://www.familytreemaker.com/users/l/e/m/Clive-
  P-Lemesurier/index.html
  Raulin LeMesurier from 1274 in Guernsey and Martino LeMesurier, 1299 in St. Pierre du Bois, Guernsey.

- FALLA Family Home Page
  http://www.familytreemaker.com/users/f/a/l/John-M-Falla/
  index.html

- du Feu Family Home Page
  http://www.geocities.com/Heartland/Meadows/3551/index.html
  Has over 900 people from 1590 to the present day.

- Genealogy of the MESERVE Family
  http://www.ultranet.com/~fmeserve/

- G-wear George
  http://members.wbs.net/homepages/g/w/e/gweargeorge.html
  SMITH, HODGES, TIBBLES, PICKET(T), BARNINGHAM

- Jersey and My Family History
  http://ourworld.compuserve.com:80/homepages/JBrannan/
  jersey.htm
  By James BRANNAN. RENOUF, CAMPBELL, BLAMPIED, DU PRE, HUE, DORET, PIQUET.

- John FULLER's Home Page
  http://members.aol.com/johnf14246/index.html

- LARBALESTIER Family Home Page
  http://www.angelfire.com/fl/larbalestier/index.html

- The 'Le COCQ' family of Alderney—Channel Islands
  http://www.guernsey.net/~genealogy/LeCocq/RR_TOC.htm

- The Le GROS Families of Jersey
  http://user.itl.net/~hsm/history/legros.htm
  CONEFREY, REMON, DENIZE, JEANDRON, LE MAISTRE, HERAULT, DE STE CROIX

- Home Page for Geoff WRIGHT
  http://www.societe-jersiaise.org/members/geoffw/index.html
  Channel Islands Mailing List and more.

- LUCE Genealogy: Jersey: Channels Islands
  http://www.webspawner.com/users/victor/

- The Origins of the GLENDINNINGs
  http://user.itl.net/~glen/glendinningorigins.html

- PICOT Home Page • Page Web PICOT
  http://Fox.nstn.ca:80/~nstn1528/index.html

- POINDEXTER Descendants Association
  http://www.geocities.com/~poingdestre/
  American descendants of the Poingdestre Family, Isle of Jersey, Channel Islands. George Poingdestre, arrived in the Colony of Virginia in 1657.

- Stéphane LUCE's Web Site / Le site Web de Stéphane LUCE
  http://pages.infinit.net/mercure/
  The immigration of Phillippe LUCE to Canada (1861).

- Stephen Foote's Genealogy Home Page
  http://ourworld.compuserve.com/homepages/stephen_foote/
  In Guernsey—FOOTE, OZANNE, PRIAULX, MARQUAND, FALLA, BISSON.

- The TOADVINE Family
  http://www.intercom.net/user/toadvine/index.html
  Nicholas TOADVINE from Guernsey Island to Maryland in approx. 1675.

◆ Queries, Message Boards & Surname Lists

- Channel Islands Genealogy—Surname Interests List
  http://members.aol.com/johnf14246/ci/surnames.html

- Geoff Wright's Channel Islands Queries Pages
  http://www.societe-jersiaise.org/members/geoffw/ci-web-q.html

◆ Records: Census, Cemeteries, Land, Obituaries, Personal, Taxes and Vital (Born, Married, Died & Buried)

- General Don's Militia Survey of 1815
  http://www.societe-jersiaise.org/alexgle/Don.html

- Index of Marriages of Jersey Surname in Québec, Canada
  http://pages.infinit.net/mercure/

- Jersey Archives Service
  http://www.jersey.gov.uk/heritage/archives/jasweb.html

- Livres des Perchages of the Fiefs in Guernsey
  http://user.itl.net/~glen/livresdesperchages.html

- The Public Record Office Home Page
  http://www.pro.gov.uk/

- ○ About the Family Records Centre
  http://www.pro.gov.uk/about/frc/

- ○ Information for Genealogists
  http://www.pro.gov.uk/readers/genealogists/default.htm

  - • Public Record Office—Family Fact Sheets
    http://www.pro.gov.uk/readers/genealogists/familyfacts.htm

- States of Guernsey Island Archives Service
  http://user.itl.net/~glen/archgsy.html

◆ Societies & Groups

- Channel Islands Family History Society
  http://user.itl.net/~glen/AbouttheChannelIslandsFHS.html

- The Family History Section of La Société Guernesiaise
  http://user.itl.net/~glen/fhssocguer.html

- Gaspésian Channel Islands' Society ~ Canada
  http://www.geocities.com/Athens/Forum/5443/h_g/channel.htm

- The Jersey Merchant Seamen's Benefit Society
  http://www.societe-jersiaise.org/alexgle/JMSBS.html

- Société Jersiaise ~ Channel Islands
  http://www.societe-jersiaise.org/

  - ○ Guide to the Library and Photographic Archive
    http://www.societe-jersiaise.org/pages/library.html

ENGLAND
http://www.CyndisList.com/england.htm

Category Index:

- General Resource Sites
- GENUKI Resources by County
- Government & Cities
- History & Culture
- How To
- Libraries, Archives & Museums
- Mailing Lists, Newsgroups & Chat
- Maps, Gazetteers & Geographical Information
- Military
- Newspapers

- People & Families
- Professional Researchers, Volunteers & Other Research Services
- Publications, Software & Supplies
- Queries, Message Boards & Surname Lists
- Records: Census, Cemeteries, Land, Obituaries, Personal, Taxes and Vital
- Religion & Churches
- Societies & Groups

◆ General Resource Sites

- Berkshire Family History Page
  http://www.moonrakers.com/berkshire/

- Bert's English Genealogy Page
  http://www.vii.com/~nelsonb/brit4.htm
  Includes History of the Church of England, a Latin primer, and an overview of English research methods.

- The Black Country Pages
  http://www.geocities.com/Heartland/Prairie/6697/
  An area in the English Midlands, to the north and west of Birmingham. Covers towns such as Stourbridge, Lye, Dudley, Wolverhampton, Wednesbury, Walsall, West Bromwich, Brierley Hill, Halesowen and others.

- Cheshire Parishes Index
  http://www.users.zetnet.co.uk/blangston/genuki/chspars/

- Cornish Pages
  http://www.zynet.co.uk/jlobb/

- Cornwall Online—The Cornish Internet Magazine
  http://www.cornwall-online.co.uk/
  - Cornish History
    http://www.cornwall-online.co.uk/history/history1.htm
  - Cornwall Online's Genealogy Pages
    http://www.cornwall-online.co.uk/genealogy.htm

- Durham and Northumberland Family History Microfiche
  http://www.jwillans.freeserve.co.uk/default.html

- East Anglian Village Research
  http://www.btinternet.com/~p.w.w/
  Essex, Suffolk, Cambridgeshire and Norfolk.

- Genealogy in Darwen & Blackburn Lancashire, England
  http://ourworld.compuserve.com/homepages/GAFOSTER/

- Genealogy in Somerset
  http://www.compulink.co.uk/~somrec/yosomfam.htm

- GK Genealogy
  http://www.users.dircon.co.uk/~stogyman/gk1/indexgk1.html
  England Genealogical Research.

- Lincolnshire Genealogical Research
  http://www.excel.net/~nclark/

- Lincolnshire Genealogy Forum
  http://www.cotcom.net/genealgy.htm

- Moonrakers.com
  http://www.moonrakers.com/netindex.htm
  The Best Source For Your Family History In Wiltshire, England.

- The PARSONAGE Pages
  http://www.geocities.com/Heartland/Plains/8555/
  With links to Worcestershire and Birmingham resources.

- Peter's Genealogy and East Kent Page
  http://www.digiserve.com/peter/

- Pigot's Commercial Directory of Derbyshire 1835
  http://www.genuki.org.uk/big/eng/Derbys/Transcriptions/Pigot/about.html

- Somerset & Dorset Pages
  http://www.ozemail.com.au/~jlsymo/somerdor.htm

- Surrey History Service
  http://www.surreycc.gov.uk:80/libraries-leisure/shs/

- The UK & Ireland Genealogical Information Service (GENUKI)
  http://www.genuki.org.uk/

- West Riding Research
  http://ourworld.compuserve.com/homepages/StevieBruce/
  *Genealogical research within the old county division of the
  'West Riding of Yorkshire,' England.*

- Yahoo!...England...Genealogy
  http://dir.yahoo.com/Regional/Countries/United_Kingdom/
  England/Arts_and_Humanities/History/Genealogy/

◆ GENUKI Resources by County

- The UK & Ireland Genealogical Information Service
  (GENUKI)
  http://www.genuki.org.uk/

  o English Genealogy Index
    http://www.genuki.org.uk/big/eng/

    - Bedfordshire Genealogy
      http://www.blunham.demon.co.uk/genuki/BDF/

    - Berkshire Genealogy
      http://www.genuki.org.uk/big/eng/BRK/

    - Buckinghamshire Genealogy
      http://met.open.ac.uk/genuki/big/eng/BKM/

    - Cambridgeshire Genealogy
      http://www.genuki.org.uk/big/eng/CAM/

    - Cheshire Genealogy
      http://www.users.zetnet.co.uk/blangston/genuki/chs.htm

    - Cornwall Genealogy
      http://www.cfhs.demon.co.uk/

    - Cumberland Genealogy
      http://www.genuki.org.uk/big/eng/CUL/

    - Derbyshire Genealogy
      http://www.homeusers.prestel.co.uk/renfrew/genuki/DBY/

    - Devon Genealogy
      http://www.cs.ncl.ac.uk/genuki/DEV/

    - Dorset Genealogy
      http://www.genuki.org.uk/big/eng/DOR/

    - Durham Genealogy
      http://homepages.enterprise.net/pjoiner/genuki/DUR/

    - Essex Genealogy
      http://privatewww.essex.ac.uk/~esfh/genuki/

    - Gloucestershire Genealogy
      http://www.genuki.org.uk/big/eng/GLS/

    - Hampshire Genealogy
      http://www.genuki.org.uk/big/eng/HAM/

    - Herefordshire Genealogy
      http://www.genuki.org.uk/big/eng/HEF/

    - Hertfordshire Genealogy
      http://homepages.enterprise.net/pjoiner/genuki/HRT/

    - Huntingdonshire Genealogy
      http://www.genuki.org.uk/big/eng/HUN/

    - Kent Genealogy
      http://users.ox.ac.uk/~malcolm/genuki/big/eng/KEN/

- Lancashire Genealogy
  http://www.genuki.org.uk/big/eng/LAN/

- Leicestershire Genealogy
  http://www.genuki.org.uk/big/eng/LEI/

- Lincolnshire Genealogy
  http://www.genuki.org.uk/big/eng/LIN/

- London Genealogy
  http://www.gold.ac.uk/genuki/LND/

- Middlesex Genealogy
  http://www.gold.ac.uk/genuki/MDX/

- Norfolk Genealogy
  http://www.uea.ac.uk/~s090/genuki/NFK/

- Northamptonshire Genealogy
  http://www.skynet.co.uk/genuki/big/eng/NTH/

- Northumberland Genealogy
  http://www.swinhope.demon.co.uk/genuki/NBL/

- Nottinghamshire Genealogy
  http://www.homeusers.prestel.co.uk/renfrew/genuki/NTT/

- Oxfordshire Genealogy
  http://users.ox.ac.uk/~malcolm/genuki/big/eng/OXF/

- Rutland (or Rutlandshire) Genealogy
  http://www.skynet.co.uk/genuki/big/eng/RUT/

- Shropshire Genealogy
  http://www.essex.ac.uk/AMS/genuki/SAL/

- Somerset Genealogy
  http://www.genuki.org.uk/big/eng/SOM/

- Staffordshire Genealogy
  http://www.genuki.org.uk/big/eng/STS/

- Suffolk Genealogy
  http://www.genuki.org.uk/big/eng/SFK/

- Surrey Genealogy
  http://www.gold.ac.uk/genuki/SRY/

- Sussex Genealogy
  http://www.gold.ac.uk/genuki/SSX/

- Warwickshire Genealogy
  http://www.genuki.org.uk/big/eng/WAR/

- Westmorland Genealogy
  http://www.awitc.demon.co.uk/genuki/WES/

- Wiltshire Genealogy
  http://www.genuki.org.uk/big/eng/WIL/

- Worcestershire Genealogy
  http://www.genuki.org.uk/big/eng/WOR/

- Yorkshire Genealogy
  http://www.blunham.demon.co.uk/genuki/YKS/

◆ Government & Cities

- Leeds Library & Information Services—
  Local History Photographic Collection
  http://www.leeds.gov.uk/library/loc_hist/archive.html

- Spon End Coventry—A Local History
  http://www.geocities.com/CollegePark/3384/

- Wakefield History—A Descriptive History of The Wakefield Battles; and a Short Account of This Ancient and Important Town
  http://www.genuki.org.uk/big/eng/YKS/wake/

- Yorkshire Information Centre, Yorkshire, Northern England
  http://www.yorkshirenet.co.uk/

- Yorkshire Past and Present
  http://www.genuki.org.uk/big/eng/YKS/ypp/
  Scanned version of a book by the same name.

◆ History & Culture

- English Heritage
  http://www.english-heritage.org.uk/

- Tudor England
  http://tudor.simplenet.com/

- Yahoo!...England...History
  http://dir.yahoo.com/Regional/Countries/United_Kingdom/
  England/Arts_and_Humanities/History/

◆ How To

- English Research by Barbara Meyers
  http://www.vii.com/~nelsonb/engre.htm

- Ordering Birth Registration Certificates from England & Wales
  http://www.oz.net/~markhow/ukbirths.htm
  Using the LDS Family History Center Resources.

- Researching Ancestors from the United Kingdom
  http://www.oz.net/~markhow/uksearch.htm
  Using the LDS Family History Center Resources.

- Researching from Abroad—from GENUKI
  http://www.genuki.org.uk/ab/

◆ Libraries, Archives & Museums

- Birmingham Central Library—Genealogical Research
  http://assist.cs.bham.ac.uk/html/council/library/genealogy/

- Birmingham Public Libraries Genealogical Research
  http://lirn.viscount.org.uk/earl/members/birmingham/gene.htm

- Bodleian Library, University of Oxford
  http://www.bodley.ox.ac.uk/

- Cambridge University Library
  http://www.lib.cam.ac.uk/

- Corporation of London Libraries
  http://www.earl.org.uk/partners/corp_of_london/index.html

- Gateshead Central Library—Local Studies Department
  http://www.swinhope.demon.co.uk/genuki/DUR/GatesheadLib/

- Greater Manchester Archives: A Guide to Local Repositories
  http://www.gmcro.u-net.com/purple1.htm

- Guildhall Library Manuscripts Collection ~ London
  http://ihr.sas.ac.uk/ihr/ghmnu.html

- John Rylands University Library of Manchester
  http://rylibweb.man.ac.uk/index.html

- LARGO: Libraries and Archives Research Guide Online ~ London
  http://pitcairn.lib.uci.edu/largo/largo/largo.html

- Leeds City Council—Local and Family History Library
  http://www.leeds.gov.uk/library/services/locnfam.html/

- Leeds University Library
  http://www.leeds.ac.uk/library/library.html
  Yorkshire, England

- Liverpool Central Library
  http://www.liverpool.gov.uk/public/council_info/direct-info/
  leisure/libraries/central.htm

- Museum of London
  http://www.museum-london.org.uk/

- The National Railway Museum, York
  http://www.nmsi.ac.uk/nrm/

- Newcastle Local Studies Library
  http://www.swinhope.demon.co.uk/genuki/NBL/NCLLib/

- University of Liverpool Library
  http://cwis.liv.ac.uk/Library/libhomep.html

- University of London Library
  http://www.ull.ac.uk/ull/

- University of Southampton Library Archive and Manuscript Collections
  http://www.soton.ac.uk/~papers1/collections/index.html

- The University of York, Borthwick Institute of Historical Research
  http://www.york.ac.uk/inst/bihr/
  - Summary of Holdings
    http://www.york.ac.uk/inst/bihr/holdings.htm
  - Searching Service
    http://www.york.ac.uk/inst/bihr/service.htm

- University of York Library—LibWeb Library and Information Services on the Web
  http://www.york.ac.uk/services/library/welcome.htm

◆ Mailing Lists, Newsgroups & Chat

- BEDFORD Mailing List
  http://members.aol.com/gfsjohnf/gen_mail_country-unk.
  html#BEDFORD
  Bedfordshire, Buckinghamshire and Hertfordshire.

- BERKSHIRE Mailing List
  http://members.aol.com/gfsjohnf/gen_mail_country-unk.
  html#BERKSHIRE

- BORDER Mailing List
  http://members.aol.com/gfsjohnf/gen_mail_country-unk.
  html#BORDER
  For anyone interested in genealogy, history, or culture related to the counties which surround the border of Scotland and England.

- Bristol_and_Somerset Mailing List
  http://members.aol.com/gfsjohnf/gen_mail_country-unk.
  html#Bristol_and_Somerset

- BUCKS Mailing List ~ Buckinghamshire
  http://members.aol.com/gfsjohnf/gen_mail_country-unk.
  html#BUCKS

- CHESHIRE Mailing List
  http://members.aol.com/gfsjohnf/gen_mail_country-unk.
  html#CHESHIRE

- CLAYWORTH Mailing List
  http://members.aol.com/gfsjohnf/gen_mail_country-unk.
  html#CLAYWORTH
  For the discussion and sharing of information regarding the Clayworth surname in any place and at any time and also for the village of Clayworth, Nottinghamshire, England.

- CORNISH-L Mailing List
  http://members.aol.com/gfsjohnf/gen_mail_country-unk.
  html#CORNISH-L
  For anyone interested in immigrants from the county of Cornwall, England to the United States.

- CUMBERLAND Mailing List
  http://members.aol.com/gfsjohnf/gen_mail_country-unk.
  html#CUMBERLAND

- DERBYSGEN Mailing List ~ Derbyshire
  http://members.aol.com/gfsjohnf/gen_mail_country-unk.
  html#DERBYSGEN

- DEVON Mailing List
  http://members.aol.com/gfsjohnf/gen_mail_country-unk.
  html#DEVON

- DORSET Mailing List
  http://members.aol.com/gfsjohnf/gen_mail_country-unk.
  html#DORSET

- DUR-NBL Mailing List
  http://members.aol.com/gfsjohnf/gen_mail_country-unk.
  html#DUR-NBL
  For anyone with a pure genealogical interest in the counties of Durham and Northumberland in the Northeast part of England.

- england-gene Mailing List
  http://members.aol.com/gfsjohnf/gen_mail_country-unk.
  html#england-gene

- ENGLISH-FENS Mailing List
  http://members.aol.com/gfsjohnf/gen_mail_country-unk.
  html#ENGLISH-FENS
  For anyone with a genealogical interest in the counties of Cambridgeshire and Huntingdonshire.

- ENG-WESTMORLAND Mailing List
  http://members.aol.com/gfsjohnf/gen_mail_country-unk.
  html#ENG-WESTMORLAND

- ESSEX-UK Mailing List
  http://members.aol.com/gfsjohnf/gen_mail_country-unk.
  html#ESSEX-UK

- GENBRIT Mailing List
  http://members.aol.com/gfsjohnf/gen_mail_country-unk.
  html#GENBRIT
  For the discussion of genealogy in Great Britain and the islands. Gatewayed with the soc.genealogy.britain newsgroup.

- GLOUCESTER Mailing List
  http://members.aol.com/gfsjohnf/gen_mail_country-unk.
  html#GLOUCESTER

- HAMPSHIRE Mailing List
  http://members.aol.com/gfsjohnf/gen_mail_country-unk.
  html#HAMPSHIRE

- Isle-of-Thanet Mailing List ~ Kent
  http://members.aol.com/gfsjohnf/gen_mail_country-unk.
  html#Isle-of-Thanet

- ISLE-OF-WIGHT Mailing List
  http://members.aol.com/gfsjohnf/gen_mail_country-unk.
  html#ISLE-OF-WIGHT

- KENT-ENG Mailing List
  http://members.aol.com/gfsjohnf/gen_mail_country-unk.
  html#KENT-ENG

- kentgene Mailing List
  http://members.aol.com/gfsjohnf/gen_mail_country-unk.
  html#kentgene

- LANCSGEN Mailing List ~ Lancashire
  http://members.aol.com/gfsjohnf/gen_mail_country-unk.
  html#LANCSGEN

- LEICESTERSHIRE-PLUS Mailing List
  http://members.aol.com/gfsjohnf/gen_mail_country-unk.
  html#LEICESTERSHIRE-PLUS
  Counties of Leicestershire and Rutland.

- Lincs-Genealogy Mailing List—Lincolnshire, England
  http://members.aol.com/gfsjohnf/gen_mail_country-unk.
  html#Lincs-Genealogy

- LONDON Mailing List
  http://members.aol.com/gfsjohnf/gen_mail_country-unk.
  html#LONDON

- Middlesex_County_UK Mailing List
  http://members.aol.com/gfsjohnf/gen_mail_country-unk.
  html#Middlesex_County_UK

- MIDMARCH Mailing List
  http://members.aol.com/gfsjohnf/gen_mail_country-unk.
  html#MIDMARCH
  For anyone with a genealogical or historical interest in the counties of Breconshire, Herefordshire, Monmouthshire, Shropshire, Staffordshire and Worcestershire.

- MI-ENGLAND Mailing List
  http://members.aol.com/gfsjohnf/gen_mail_country-unk.
  html#MI-ENGLAND
  For those interested in Monumental Inscriptions on gravestones, etc. in England.

- Moonrakers Mailing List
  http://members.aol.com/gfsjohnf/gen_mail_country-unk.
  html#Moonrakers
  *For anyone with a genealogical or historical interest in the
  county of Wiltshire, England.*

- NORFOLK Mailing List
  http://www.oz.net/~markhow/genuki/NFK/norfmail.htm

- NORTHANTS Mailing List ~ Northampton
  http://members.aol.com/gfsjohnf/gen_mail_country-unk.
  html#NORTHANTS

- NORTHUMBRIA Mailing List ~ Northumberland
  and Durham
  http://members.aol.com/gfsjohnf/gen_mail_country-unk.
  html#NORTHUMBRIA

- NOTTSGEN Mailing List ~ Nottingham
  http://members.aol.com/gfsjohnf/gen_mail_country-unk.
  html#NOTTSGEN

- OXFORDSHIRE Mailing List
  http://members.aol.com/gfsjohnf/gen_mail_country-unk.
  html#OXFORDSHIRE

- STAFFORDSHIRE Mailing List
  http://members.aol.com/gfsjohnf/gen_mail_country-unk.
  html#STAFFORDSHIRE

- SUFFOLK Mailing List
  http://members.aol.com/gfsjohnf/gen_mail_country-unk.
  html#SUFFOLK

- SURNAMES-BRITAIN Mailing List
  http://members.aol.com/gfsjohnf/gen_mail_country-unk.
  html#SURNAMES-BRITAIN
  *For surname queries related to Great Britain. Gatewayed with
  the soc.genealogy.surnames.britain newsgroup.*

- SUSSEX-PLUS Mailing List
  http://members.aol.com/gfsjohnf/gen_mail_country-unk.
  html#SUSSEX-PLUS
  *For anyone with a genealogical or historical interest in the
  county of Sussex, England and the adjacent counties of Surrey,
  Kent and Hampshire. Also see the associated web page at http://
  homepages.enterprise.net/crghenly/sussex-plus.html*

- WARWICK Mailing List ~ Warwickshire
  http://members.aol.com/gfsjohnf/gen_mail_country-unk.
  html#WARWICK

- WESSEX-PLUS Mailing List
  http://members.aol.com/gfsjohnf/gen_mail_country-unk.
  html#WESSEX-PLUS
  *For anyone who has an interest in genealogy or general and
  local history related to and incorporating the counties of
  Berkshire, Bristol, Devon, Dorset, Gloucestershire, Isle of
  Wight, Hampshire, Oxfordshire, Somerset, and Wiltshire,
  England.*

- WEST-RIDING Mailing List
  http://members.aol.com/gfsjohnf/gen_mail_country-unk.
  html#WEST-RIDING
  *For anyone with a genealogical interest in West Riding,
  Yorkshire, England prior to 1974.*

- WILTSHIRE-EMI Mailing List
  http://members.aol.com/gfsjohnf/gen_mail_country-unk.
  html#WILTSHIRE-EMI
  *Regarding emigrants from Wiltshire County, England to
  anywhere in the world in any timeframe.*

- YORKSGEN Mailing List
  http://members.aol.com/gfsjohnf/gen_mail_country-unk.
  html#YORKSGEN
  Yorkshire

◆ Maps, Gazetteers & Geographical Information

- Administrative Regions of the British Isles
  http://www.genuki.org.uk/big/Regions/
  From GENUKI

  ○ Administrative Areas of England
    http://www.genuki.org.uk/big/Regions/England.html

- Counties of England, Scotland and Wales Prior
  to the 1974 Boundary Changes
  http://www.genuki.org.uk/big/BRITAIN2.GIF

- Great Yarmouth Central
  http://www.gtyarmouth.co.uk/Pictures/Maps/
  Gt_Yarmouth_Central_Map.JPG

- Great Yarmouth North
  http://www.gtyarmouth.co.uk/Pictures/Maps/
  Gt_Yarmouth_North_Map.JPG

- Great Yarmouth South
  http://www.gtyarmouth.co.uk/Pictures/Maps/
  Gt_Yarmouth_South_Map.JPG

- Greenwood's Map of London 1827
  http://www.bathspa.ac.uk/greenwood/home.html

- Leeds City Council—City Centre Maps
  http://www.leeds.gov.uk/tourinfo/locate/citymaps/centre/
  city_map.html

- Map 1797—Plan of Great Yarmouth, Norfolk by
  William Faden
  http://www.gtyarmouth.co.uk/html/map_1797.htm

- Map of Kent
  http://www.digiserve.com/peter/kent.htm

- Map of Winchester
  http://members.aol.com/tgostin/graphics/winchstr.jpg

- Multi Media Mapping
  http://uk5.multimap.com/map/places.cgi
  *An interactive atlas of Great Britain. Enter the name of a British
  city, town or village to get a clickable, zoomable, detailed map.*

- Ordnance Survey—Gazetteer of Place Names
  http://www.campus.bt.com/CampusWorld/pub/OS/Gazetteer/
  index.html

- Victoria History of the Counties of England
  http://ihr.sas.ac.uk/vch/vchnew.asc.html

◆ Military

- 43rd Wessex Association
  http://www.digiserve.com/msyoung/43rd.htm

- The Buff's (The Royal East Kent Regiment)
  http://www.digiserve.com/peter/buffs/

- Duke of Cornwall's Light Infantry
  http://www.digiserve.com/msyoung/dcli.htm
  32nd & 46th Regiments of Foot

- A Group Photograph—Before, Now, and In-Between
  (A History Project)
  http://www.mister-t.demon.co.uk/
  *A genealogical project that came about from a group photo-
  graph of the officers of the 8th Royal Berkshire Regiment taken
  at their training camp on Salisbury Plain in July 1915.*

- The Trafalgar Roll
  http://www.genuki.org.uk/big/eng/Trafalgar/
  *A list of 1640 officers and men who fought at the Battle of
  Trafalgar.*

◆ Newspapers

- Eastern Counties Network
  http://www.ecn.co.uk/index.htm
  *East Anglian Daily Times, Eastern Daily Press, Evening News,
  Evening Star.*

- E&P Media Info Links—Newspaper Sites in
  England
  http://www.mediainfo.com/emediajs/browse-results.
  htm?region=england&category=newspaper+++++++++

- The London Gazette
  http://www.history.rochester.edu/London_Gazette/
  *Selected online editions for 1674, 1675, 1676, 1678 and 1692
  from Electronic Historical Publications.*

◆ People & Families

- Alan's Genealogy & Cheshire, England Page
  http://members.tripod.com/~AlanCheshire/index.html

- The Ascott Martyrs
  http://www.geocities.com/Heartland/Plains/6081/
  *An Historical Link to the PRATLY, PRATLEY and PRATTLEY
  Families of New Zealand.*

- Autobiography of the Rev. William GILL
  http://www.genuki.org.uk/big/eng/Indexes/REVWGILL.txt
  A list of names indexed from the book.

- Genealogical Investigation into Charles J. ARIS
  http://www.oz.net/~markhow/chasaris.htm
  *World War 1 veteran, 16th Queen's Own Lancers, a cavalry unit
  of the British Army.*

- A Genealogist's Devon Connection
  http://www.geocities.com/Athens/Acropolis/3033/

- The Lineage of the Royal Princes of England
  http://www.geocities.com/CapitolHill/4793/

- London Jews Database
  http://www.jewishgen.org/databases/londweb.htm

- The Monarchs & Regents of England &
  Great Britain for Near 1200 Years
  http://www.ringnett.no/home/bjornstad/royals/England.html

◆ Professional Researchers, Volunteers & Other Research Services

- Brian Walker—Family History Research in all
  London Record Offices
  http://ourworld.compuserve.com/homepages/brianwalker1/
  *My husband, Mark, has used this professional researcher in the
  UK with excellent results. He specializes in London area record
  repositories including the Family Records Centre, the Public
  Record Office, Somerset House, Guildhall Library, Society of
  Genealogists Library, and others. His rates are reasonable and
  he accepts personal checks in foreign currencies.*

- England Look-up Exchange
  http://www.geocities.com/Heartland/Plains/8555/england.html

- Family History Research
  http://www.mharper36.demon.co.uk/
  U.K. sources, particularly in London.

- GenealogyPro—Professional Genealogists for
  England and Wales
  http://genealogyPro.com/directories/England-Wales.html

- Hidden Heritage—United Kingdom Genealogy
  Research
  http://www.gloster.demon.co.uk/
  *Specializing around Gloucestershire, England. Including
  Herefordshire, Worcestershire, Avon and Somerset.*

- KBA Research. Ancestral Research Services
  in the U.K
  http://members.aol.com/kbaresch
  *Locate your ancestors, by using KBA Research, a professional,
  reliable and cost-effective service.*

- The Official Iowa Counties Professional Genealogist
  and Researcher's Registry for England
  http://www.iowa-counties.com/gene/england.htm

- Public Record Office Searches by Roger E. Nixon
  http://ourworld.compuserve.com/homepages/rogerenixon/
  *All military, naval, seamen, naturalisations, migrants, police,
  convicts, FO, HO, CO searched. Wide range of subjects. Check
  my list first.*

- Research Undertaken at the Leicestershire
  Record Office
  http://ourworld.compuserve.com/homepages/bwmconsultants/
  Research.htm

- Seaham Super Index
  http://dspace.dial.pipex.com/town/street/kch66/
  *For county Durham. This database can be searched for a small
  fee to the author. It contains census returns, trade directories
  and more.*

- Worcestershire Family History Research
  http://www.users.globalnet.co.uk/~bill04/

- Yorkshire Genealogical Research Specialist
  http://ourworld.compuserve.com/homepages/jksdelver/

◆ Publications, Software & Supplies

- Ambra Books & Lesley Aitchison
  http://www.cornwall-online.co.uk/ambrabooks/
  Buying and selling antiquarian and secondhand books, manuscripts, documents, maps, plans, photographs, albums, and ephemera relating to Cornwall and the West Country—Devon, Dorset, Gloucestershire, Somerset & Wiltshire.

- Books We Own—England
  http://www.rootsweb.com/~bwo/england.html

- Cornish Roots!
  http://www.cornwall-net.co.uk/multimed/roots.htm
  A new CD-ROM being produced in Cornwall in 1997.

- Family Tree Magazine
  http://www.family-tree.co.uk/

- Frontier Press Bookstore—English Research
  http://www.frontierpress.com/frontier.cgi?category=eng

- GenealogyBookShop.com—England/English
  http://www.genealogybookshop.com/genealogybookshop/files/The_World,England_English/index.html
  The online store of Genealogical Publishing Co., Inc. & Clearfield Company.

- Hearthstone Bookshop—England
  http://www.hearthstonebooks.com/England.html

- Heritage Books—English
  http://www.heritagebooks.com/english.htm

- S.E.L. Enterprises
  http://www.mentornet.org/sel.htm
  Publications (books, magazines, periodicals & maps) for researching your English, Irish, Scots and Welsh ancestors.

- Victoria History of the Counties of England
  http://ihr.sas.ac.uk/vch/vchnew.asc.html

- Willow Bend Bookstore—England
  http://www.willowbend.net/eng.htm

◆ Queries, Message Boards & Surname Lists

- MLFHS Internet Group Members Interests
  http://www.onthenet.com.au/~tonylang/Mainpage.html
  Surnames from members of the Manchester and Lancashire Family History Society in England.

- North East Lancashire Surname List
  http://ourworld.compuserve.com/homepages/GAFOSTER/n-e-lanc.htm

- Somerset and Dorset Surnames and Queries
  http://www.ozemail.com.au/~jlsymo/sdnames.htm

- Somerset & Dorset Surnames Index
  http://www.bakery.co.uk/sandd/

- The UK & Ireland Genealogical Information Service (GENUKI)
  http://www.genuki.org.uk/
  - Surname Lists Index from GENUKI
    http://www.cs.ncl.ac.uk/genuki/SurnamesList/
    - Bedfordshire Surnames List
      http://homepages.ihug.co.nz/~hughw/bedf.html
    - Berkshire Surnames List
      http://www.geocities.com/Heartland/Ranch/5973/berksurname.htm
    - Buckinghamshire Surnames List
      http://www.csranet.com/~dcarlsen/genuki/BKM/bucksurname.html
    - Cambridgeshire Surnames List
      http://www.personal.u-net.com/~gaer/cam/SurnamesList.html
    - Cheshire Surnames List
      http://www.users.zetnet.co.uk/blangston/surnames/
    - Cornwall, England—Surnames List
      http://www.cs.ncl.ac.uk/genuki/SurnamesList/Cornwall/
    - Cumbria Surnames List
      http://cumbria-surnames.worldward.com/index.mv
    - Derbyshire Surnames List
      http://homepage.ihug.co.nz/~hughw/dby.htm
    - Devon, England—Surnames List
      http://www.gendex.com/users/branscombe/genuki/devindex.htm
    - East and North Riding Surname Interest List
      http://www.jodenoy.clara.net/erynry/erynry.htm
    - East of London Surname Overview
      http://ourworld.compuserve.com/homepages/jordan/eolsur01.htm
      Includes the Boroughs of: Hackney, Tower Hamlets within Middlesex County, and Newham, Redbridge, Barking and Dagenham, and Havering within Essex County.
    - Essex Surnames List
      http://www.sullom.demon.co.uk/essex/surnames.html
    - Gloucestershire Surnames List
      http://tolstoi.saccii.net.au/~dsteel/glsnames.htm
    - Hampshire Surnames List
      http://dspace.dial.pipex.com/c.broomfield/ham.htm
    - Herefordshire Surnames List
      http://freespace.virgin.net/isabel.easter/mem.html
    - The Hertfordshire Surnames List
      http://homepages.ihug.co.nz/~hughw/hertford.html
    - Huntingdonshire Surnames List
      http://www.genuki.org.uk/big/eng/HUN/Surnames.html
    - Kent England Surname Interests
      http://www.centrenet.co.uk/~cna49/kfhs2.htm
    - Leicestershire Surnames List
      http://www.lodp.demon.co.uk/LEI.html
    - Lincolnshire Surnames
      http://www.excel.net/~nclark/sur1.htm

- The Liverpool (& area) Surnames List
  http://www.globalserve.net/~scouse/list.htm
- Norfolk Surnames List
  http://freespace.virgin.net/isabel.easter/Norfolk/Surnames.htm
- Northamptonshire Surnames List
  http://www.skynet.co.uk/genuki/big/eng/NTH/Surnames/
- Northumberland and Durham, England—Surnames List
  http://gendex.com/users/branscombe/genuki/nblindex.htm
- Nottinghamshire Surnames List
  http://homepages.ihug.co.nz/~hughw/notts.html
- On-line Dorset Names Research Directory
  http://www.users.on.net/proformat/dornames.html
- Oxfordshire Surname Interest List (OXSIL)
  http://www.rootsweb.com/~oxsil/
- The Rutland Surnames List
  http://www.lodp.demon.co.uk/RUT.html
- Shropshire Surname Interest List
  http://www.genuki.org.uk/big/eng/Surnames/sal.htm
- Somerset Surnames Interest List
  http://www.genuki.org.uk/big/eng/Surnames/som.htm
- Staffordshire Surname Interest List
  http://www.genuki.org.uk/big/eng/Surnames/sts.htm
- Suffolk Surname List (& More!)
  http://www.visualcreations.com/pers/leeann/suffolk/
- Surrey Surname Interest List
  http://www.genuki.org.uk/big/eng/Surnames/sry.htm
- Sussex Surnames List
  http://dspace.dial.pipex.com/c.broomfield/ssxname.htm
- The Warwickshire Surnames List
  http://homepages.ihug.co.nz/~hughw/warwick.html
- West Riding Yorkshire Surname Interests
  http://members.aol.com/wrylist/wry.htm
- Wiltshire Surname Interests List
  http://www.genuki.org.uk/big/eng/WIL/interests/surnames.html
- Worcestershire Surname Interest List
  http://www.jump.net/~salter/WORSIL.html

◆ Records: Census, Cemeteries, Land, Obituaries, Personal, Taxes and Vital (Born, Married, Died & Buried)

- 1871 Cornwall Census Query
  http://www.kindredkonnections.com/cgi-bin/crcensus?-1+0+English
- 1891 Census of East Hamlet, Ludlow, Shropshire
  ftp://ftp.rootsweb.com/pub/wggenweb/england/ludlow/easthamlet/shropshire/census/eastha91.txt

- Abney Park Cemetery Trust ~ London
  http://www.abney-park.org.uk/
- Anne's UK Certificates for Australians
  http://freespace.virgin.net/mark.wainwright6/uk_certificates/
  An Australian living in London who can obtain copies of English, Scottish & Welsh Birth, Marriage and Death Certificates in exchange for payment in Australian dollars.
- Bob Holloway's Genealogy Page for Source Information
  http://members.aol.com/aisling13/index.htm
  Terrific index to zipped or compressed data files and other online resources.
  - Cemetery Name Lists & Monumental Inscriptions
    http://members.aol.com/aisling13/ixmis.htm
  - Dale Street Bridewell, Liverpool—1871
    http://www.globalserve.net/~scouse/bridwell.htm
  - Miscellaneous or Personally Held Source Material
    http://members.aol.com/aisling13/ixmisc.htm
  - Parish Register Details
    http://members.aol.com/aisling13/ixparish.htm
  - UK Census Material
    http://members.aol.com/aisling13/ixukcen.htm
  - UK Marriage Related Information
    http://members.aol.com/aisling13/ixukwit.htm
- Brickmakers Index
  http://www.genuki.org.uk/big/eng/bwi.html
  Index of brickfield workers and owners gathered from census, local histories and directories in England, mainly from southeast England.
- Census Information from GENUKI
  http://www.genuki.org.uk/big/eng/census.html
  For England, Scotland & Wales.
- Censuses of Gloucestershire and Southern Warwickshire
  http://www.silk.net/personal/gordonb/cotswold.htm
  Over 300 census extracts (150,000 entries) for this area in England.
- Civil Registration in England and Wales ~ GENUKI
  http://www.genuki.org.uk/big/eng/civreg/
- England and Wales Birth, Marriage, and Death Certificate Information
  http://shoppersmart.com/otown/registrations/
- England Genealogy—Lesson Eight—Tax and Fee Records
  http://www.ideaschool.org/courses/general/gen201_8.htm
- English and Welsh Register Offices
  http://www.genuki.org.uk/big/eng/RegOffice/
- Executions in England from 1606
  http://www.fred.net/jefalvey/execute.html
- Faculty Office Marriage Licence Index
  http://ourworld.compuserve.com/homepages/David_Squire/faculty.htm
  Index of marriage licences issued by the Master of Faculties of the Archbishop of Canterbury for the period 1714 to 1850.

- The Family History System—Executions in England from 1606
  http://www.fhsystem.demon.co.uk/fhsytem5.htm

- Finding an Address in the Transcription of the 1881 Census of England and Wales
  http://people.enternet.com.au/~tmj/c81-adrs.htm

- Genealogy—David ROLES
  http://www.ualberta.ca/~droles/gen/gen.html
  Includes articles with information on using various English records, as well as blank forms to print for use in your research.

  o Census Records
    http://www.ualberta.ca/~droles/gen/cen.html

  o England Parish Registers
    http://www.ualberta.ca/~droles/gen/par.html

  o English Military records
    http://www.ualberta.ca/~droles/gen/mil.html

- George BELL's Indexes
  http://www.swinhope.demon.co.uk/genuki/NBL/Bell.html
  A large collection of indexes to a variety of records—some available online, but most available on microfiche for sale.

- The Greater Manchester County Record Office
  http://www.personal.u-net.com/~gmcro/home.htm

- Hackney Archives Department
  http://www.hackney.gov.uk/archive/first1.htm
  From the London Borough of Hackney.

- Halifax Parish Church Registers
  http://www.blunham.demon.co.uk/genuki/YKS/WRY/Halifax/halifax.txt
  1542, 1543, 1545

- Index to "Paupers in Workhouses 1861" (10% Sample)
  http://www.genuki.org.uk/big/eng/Paupers/
  This lists adult paupers in workhouses in England and Wales.

- The Joiner Marriage Index
  http://homepages.enterprise.net/pjoiner/mindex/mindex.html
  A Marriage Database for County Durham, and the North Riding of Yorkshire.

- Lancashire Record Office
  http://www.lancashire.com/lcc/edu/ro/index.htm

- Lincolnshire Archives
  http://www.lincs-archives.com/
  A Service Provided by Lincolnshire County Council, England.

- Marriages from the Sherburn Hospital Registers (1695–1837)
  http://www.cs.ncl.ac.uk/genuki/Transcriptions/DUR/SHO.html
  Northumberland and Durham, England.

- Middlesex England Parish Records
  http://www.enol.com/~infobase/gen/parish/
  Database of records between 1563 and 1895, listed alphabetically by groom's last name.

- Newgate—Newgate Prison ~ England
  http://www.fred.net/jefalvey/newgate.html
  A list of inmates, victims and those associated with the prison.

- NFHS Internet Branch—The 1851 British Census Index on CD-ROM—Its Availbility & Usage
  http://www.rootsweb.com/~nfhs/ib/1851cd.htm
  Describes the contents and use of this census index for the English counties of Devon, Norfolk, and Warwickshire which includes over 1.5 million individuals. Ordering information for this low cost CD-ROM is provided for 5 different countries.

- Norfolk Record Office (NRO)
  http://www.norfolk.gov.uk/council/departments/nro/nroindex.htm

- Northumberland Record Office
  http://www.swinhope.demon.co.uk/genuki/NBL/NorthumberlandRO/
  Northumberland County Council Amenities Division.

- ONS Services—Certificates of Births, Marriages and Deaths
  http://www.ons.gov.uk/services/cert.htm
  England and Wales.

- Ordering Birth Registration Certificates from England & Wales
  http://www.oz.net/~markhow/ukbirths.htm
  Using the LDS Family History Center Resources.

- Parish Register Copies in the Library of the Society of Genealogists
  http://www.sog.org.uk/prc/

- Paul DURRANT's Genealogy Home Page
  http://www.durrant.demon.co.uk/genealogy/
  Has a downloadable transcript of the 1881 Census for Cromer, Norfolk.

- The Public Record Office Home Page
  http://www.pro.gov.uk/

  o About the Family Records Centre
    http://www.pro.gov.uk/about/frc/

  o Information For Genealogists
    http://www.pro.gov.uk/readers/genealogists/default.htm

    - Public Record Office—Family Fact Sheets
      http://www.pro.gov.uk/readers/genealogists/familyfacts.htm

- Register Offices in Staffordshire
  http://www.staffordshire.gov.uk/locgov/county/register.htm

- Ron Taylor's UK Census Finding Aids and Indexes
  http://rontay.digiweb.com/

  o Strays by County Census Indexes
    http://207.176.42.192/county/

    - Bedfordshire Strays
      http://207.176.42.192/county/bdf.htm

    - Buckingham Strays
      http://207.176.42.192/county/bkm.htm

    - Essex Strays—Surnames A–E
      http://207.176.42.192/county/essa.htm

      Essex Strays—Surnames F–K
      http://207.176.42.192/county/essf.htm

Essex Strays—Surnames L–O
http://207.176.42.192/county/ESSL.htm

Essex Strays—Surnames P–S
http://207.176.42.192/county/essp.htm

Essex Strays—Surnames T–Z
http://207.176.42.192/county/esst.htm

- Kent Strays—Surnames A–E
http://207.176.42.192/county/kenta.htm

Kent Strays—Surnames F–K
http://207.176.42.192/county/kenf.htm

Kent Strays—Surnames P–S
http://207.176.42.192/county/kenl.htm

Kent Strays—Surnames L–O
http://207.176.42.192/county/kenp.htm

Kent Strays—Surnames T–Z
http://207.176.42.192/county/kent.htm

- Lancashire Strays—Surnames A–E
http://207.176.42.192/county/lana.htm

Lancashire Strays—Surnames F–K
http://207.176.42.192/county/lanf.htm

Lancashire Strays—Surnames P–S
http://207.176.42.192/county/lanl.htm

Lancashire Strays—Surnames L–O
http://207.176.42.192/county/lanp.htm

Lancashire Strays—Surnames T–Z
http://207.176.42.192/county/lant.htm

- Middlesex Strays—Surnames A–E
http://207.176.42.192/county/mdxa.htm

Middlesex Strays—Surnames F–K
http://207.176.42.192/county/mdxf.htm

Middlesex Strays—Surnames P–S
http://207.176.42.192/county/mdxl.htm

Middlesex Strays—Surnames L–O
http://207.176.42.192/county/mdxp.htm

Middlesex Strays—Surnames T–Z
http://207.176.42.192/county/mdxt.htm

- Surrey Strays—Surnames A–E
http://207.176.42.192/county/srya.htm

Surrey Strays—Surnames F–K
http://207.176.42.192/county/sryf.htm

Surrey Strays—Surnames P–S
http://207.176.42.192/county/sryl.htm

Surrey Strays—Surnames L–O
http://207.176.42.192/county/srys.htm

Surrey Strays—Surnames T–Z
http://207.176.42.192/county/sryt.htm

- The St. Catherine's Marriage Index
http://www.cs.ncl.ac.uk/genuki/StCathsTranscriptions/

- Surrey History Service
http://www.surreycc.gov.uk:80/libraries-leisure/shs/

- Tyne & Wear Archives Service
http://ris.niaa.org.uk/archives/index.html
Family History Resources, Newcastle upon Tyne.

- University of Oxford, Ashmolean Museum, The Department of Antiquities Monumental Brasses
http://antiqs-iii.ashmol.ox.ac.uk/ash/departments/antiquities/brass/

- Uttoxeter Road Cemetery, Derby, Derbyshire, England, UK
http://www.derbycity.com/derby/tombs.html

- Vicar-General Marriage Licence Index
http://ourworld.compuserve.com/homepages/David_Squire/vicgen1.htm
Index of marriage licences issued by the office of the Vicar-General of the Archbishop of Canterbury for the period 1701 to 1850, England.

- West Sussex Records Office
http://www.westsussex.gov.uk/cs/ro/rohome.htm

- West Yorkshire Archive Service
http://www.archives.wyjs.org.uk/index.htm

  o Sources for the Family Historian
  http://www.archives.wyjs.org.uk/fhinfo.htm

- Wiltshire Index Service
http://www.cadvision.com/traces/wis.html
Fee-based service. Burials, Beneficiaries & 1871 Census Surname Indexes, Wiltshire, England.

◆ Religion & Churches

- Brief History of the Church of England
http://www.vii.com/~nelsonb/chist.htm

- Church of England
http://www.church-of-england.org/

- Norfolk Churches Directory
http://www.uea.ac.uk/~e340/ncd/ncd.htm

◆ Societies & Groups

- The Anglo-French Family History Society
http://www.karolus.org/org/assoc/as-euro/as-affhs.htm
Andover, Hampshire, Great Britain

- Archer's Computer Interest Group List—England
http://www.genealogy.org/~ngs/cigs/ngl3oten.html

- Barnsley Family History Society
http://ourworld.compuserve.com/homepages/Ian_Townend/bfhs01.htm

- Bedfordshire Family History Society
http://www.bfhs.org.uk/

- Berkshire Family History Society
http://www.vellum.demon.co.uk/genuki/BRK/berksfhs/

- Bewcastle Heritage Society
http://ourworld.compuserve.com/homepages/noble/bewsoc.htm
Cumbria County, England

- The Birmingham and Midland Society for Genealogy and Heraldry
  http://www.bmsgh.org/

- Bradford Family History Society
  http://www.genuki.org.uk/big/eng/YKS/bfhs/

- Bristol & Avon Family History Society
  http://www.cix.co.uk/~kgroves/ba/index.html

- Buckinghamshire Family History Society
  http://www.clues.demon.co.uk/bucksfhs/

- Buckinghamshire Genealogical Society
  http://met.open.ac.uk/group/kaq/bgs.htm

- California Cornish Cousins
  http://www.calflytech.com/ccc/

- Cambridge University Heraldic & Genealogical Society
  http://www.cam.ac.uk/CambUniv/Societies/cuhags/

- Cambridgeshire Family History Society
  http://www.cf.ac.uk/uwcc/comp/drayton/genuki/CAM/camfhs/

- Catholic Family History Society of London, England
  http://feefhs.org/uk/frg-cfhs.html

- Cleveland Family History Society
  http://homepages.enterprise.net/pjoiner/cfhs/cfhs.html

- Cornwall Family History Society
  http://www.cfhs.demon.co.uk/Society/

- Cornwall Family History Society—Electronic Members List
  http://lochnet.co.uk/talijen/cfhs/cfhs.html

- The Coventry and Warwickshire Network— Coventry Family History Society
  http://www.coventry.org.uk/heritage/familyhistory/index.html

- Cumbria FHS
  http://www.genuki.org.uk/big/eng/CUL/cumbFHS/

- The Derbyshire Ancestral Research Group
  http://www.yacc.demon.co.uk/genuki/DBY/darg.htm

- Derbyshire Family History Society
  http://web.ukonline.co.uk/Members/gj.hadfield/dbyfhs.htm

- The Devon Family History Society
  http://www.devonfhs.org.uk
  The offical site for information about meetings, publications, indexes and our own building, Tree House.

- The East of London Family History Society
  http://ourworld.compuserve.com/homepages/jordan/eolfhs.htm

- East Surrey Family History Society
  http://www.gold.ac.uk/genuki/SRY/esfhs/

- East Yorkshire Family History Society
  http://www.btinternet.com/~banyan.ed/

- Epsom Family History Group ~ Surrey
  http://ourworld.compuserve.com/homepages/G_Walker/efhs.htm

- Essex Society for Family History
  http://www.genuki.org.uk/big/eng/ESS/efhs/

- The Family History Society of Cheshire
  http://www.users.zetnet.co.uk/blangston/fhsc/

- The Federation of Family History Societies
  http://www.ffhs.org.uk/

- Felixstowe Family History Society
  http://www.genuki.org.uk/big/eng/SFK/ffhs/
  Suffolk County, England

- Folkestone & District Family History Society
  http://www.jmcrid.demon.co.uk/fdfhs/
  Southeast Kent, England

- Furness Family History Society
  http://members.aol.com/FurnessFHS/fpw0.htm
  Cumbria County, England

- Gloucestershire Family History Society (GFHS)
  http://www.compulink.co.uk/~rd/GENUKI/gfhs.htm

- The Hampshire Genealogical Society
  http://www.hantsgensoc.demon.co.uk/

- Herefordshire Family History Society
  http://freespace.virgin.net/bruce.donaldson/

- Hillingdon Family History Society
  http://www.gold.ac.uk/genuki/MDX/Hillingdon_FHS.txt
  London, England

- Huddersfield & District Family History Society
  http://www.hdfhs.demon.co.uk/
  West Riding, Yorkshire, England

- Huntingdonshire Family History Society
  http://www.genuki.org.uk/big/eng/HUN/HFHS/
  Cambridgeshire, England

- The Isle of Axholme Family History Society
  http://www.linktop.demon.co.uk/axholme/
  Lincolnshire

- Isle of Wight Family History Society
  http://www.dina.clara.net/iowfhs/

- Kent Family History Society
  http://www.centrenet.co.uk/~cna49/kfhs.htm

- Lancashire Family History and Heraldry Society
  http://www.lfhhs.mcmail.com/

- Lancashire Parish Register Society
  http://www.genuki.org.uk/big/eng/LAN/lprs/

- Leicestershire & Rutland Family History Society
  http://www.geocities.com/Heartland/Pointe/3446/

- Lincolnshire Family History Society
  http://www.genuki.org.uk/big/eng/LIN/lfhs/

- Liverpool & South West Lancashire Family History Society
  http://www.compulink.co.uk/~lexsys/lexsysge.htm

- London & North Middlesex Family History Society
  http://www.lnmfhs.dircon.co.uk/
  A helpful parish map on this site provides a geographic description of the Soceity's area of coverage along with their neighboring socieites in this very important research area covered by multiple socieites.

- Manchester & Lancashire FHS
  http://www.mlfhs.demon.co.uk/

- Mid Norfolk Family History Society
  http://www.uea.ac.uk/~s300/genuki/NFK/organisations/midnfhs/

- Norfolk Family History Society
  http://www.uea.ac.uk/~s300/genuki/NFK/organisations/nfhs/

  o The Internet Branch of the Norfolk Family History Society
    http://www.rootsweb.com/~nfhs/ib/index.htm

- North Cheshire Family History Society
  http://www.genuki.org.uk/big/eng/CHS/NorthChesFHS/

- Northamptonshire Family History Society
  http://ourworld.compuserve.com/homepages/NORTHAMPTONSHIRE_FHS/

- Northumberland & Durham Family History Society
  http://www.geocities.com/Athens/6549/

- North West Kent Family History Society
  http://users.ox.ac.uk/~malcolm/NWKFHS/

- Nottinghamshire Family History Society
  http://www.netcomuk.co.uk/~jeffop/index.html

- Nuneaton & North Warwickshire Family History Society
  http://members.aol.com/NNWFHS/

- Oxfordshire Family History Society
  http://users.ox.ac.uk/~malcolm/genuki/big/eng/OXF/OFHS/

- The Record Society of Lancashire and Cheshire
  http://www.personal.u-net.com/~gmcro/leaflet.htm

- Ripon Historical Society and the Ripon, Harrogate & District Family History Group
  http://www.users.globalnet.co.uk/~gdl/rh1.htm

- Sheffield and District Family History Society
  http://mtx.net.au/~exy/sheffield_fhs.html

- Shropshire Family History Society
  http://www.essex.ac.uk/AMS/genuki/SAL/shrop_12.html

- The Society of Brushmakers' Descendants ~ Essex
  http://www.thenet.co.uk/~socy-brush-desc/index.html

- Society of Indexers Genealogical Group
  http://ourworld.compuserve.com/homepages/David_Squire/sigg.htm

- Somerset & Dorset Family History Society
  http://ourworld.compuserve.com/homepages/Alan_J_Brown/

- Spon End Local History Society ~ Coventry
  http://www.geocities.com/CollegePark/3384/

- Suffolk Family History Society
  http://www.genuki.org.uk/big/eng/SFK/sfhs/sfhs.htm

- Sussex Family History Group
  http://www.sfhg.org.uk/

- Toronto Cornish Association (TCA)
  http://www.digiserve.com/msyoung/tca.htm
  For those living in Ontario who are interested in the County of Cornwall in the UK.

- Tunbridge Wells Family History Society
  http://www.kcckal.demon.co.uk/twfhsmain.htm

- Warwickshire Family History Society
  http://freespace.virgin.net/diane.lindsay/wfhs.htm

- West Middlesex Family History Society
  http://home.clara.net/dchilds/wmfhs/

- West Surrey Family History Society
  http://www.surreyweb.org.uk/wsfhs/

- Wharfedale Family History Group
  http://www.users.globalnet.co.uk/~gdl/wfhg1.htm
  Area north-west of Leeds along the Wharfedale Valley, England.

- Wiltshire Family History Society
  http://www.genuki.org.uk/big/eng/WIL/WFHS/

- The Yorkshire Archaeological Society— Family History Section
  http://www.users.globalnet.co.uk/~gdl/yasfhs.htm
  Leeds, England

IRELAND & NORTHERN IRELAND
http://www.CyndisList.com/ireland.htm

Category Index:

- General Resource Sites
- GENUKI Resources by County
- History & Culture
- How To
- Irish Family History Foundation ~ County Heritage Centres
- Libraries, Archives & Museums
- Mailing Lists, Newsgroups & Chat
- Maps, Gazetteers & Geographical Information
- Newspapers

- People & Families
- Professional Researchers, Volunteers & Other Research Services
- Publications, Software & Supplies
- Queries, Message Boards & Surname Lists
- Records: Census, Cemeteries, Land, Obituaries, Personal, Taxes and Vital
- Societies & Groups
- WorldGenWeb Project

◆ General Resource Sites

- The A to Z of Irish Genealogy Web Sites
  http://www.irish-insight.com/a2z-genealogy/

- The Ballykilcline World Wide-Web Site
  http://www.ballykilcline.com/

- Co.Antrim's Main Web Page
  http://www.genealogy.org/~liam/
  Including The Antrim Surname Interest List.

- Fianna Hideaway & Guide to Irish Genealogy
  http://www.rootsweb.com/~fianna/

- The Fianna: Irish Ancestry & History Research
  http://www.geocities.com/Heartland/Meadows/4404/

- Heraldry in Ireland
  http://www.finearts.sfasu.edu/uasal/heraldry.html

- Ireland: The Internet Collection
  http://itdsrv1.ul.ie/Information/Ireland.html

- Irish Adoptees in Search of Roots & Wings
  http://members.aol.com/COD18460/IRISHADOPTEES.html

- Irish Ancestors
  http://www.ireland.com/ancestor/
  A comprehensive guide to Irish research. From John Grenham and the Irish Times on the Web.

  o Browse
    http://www.ireland.com/ancestor/browse/index.htm
    A general overview of some of the records relevant to Irish family history research.

    - Addresses
      http://www.ireland.com/ancestor/browse/address/index.htm

- Counties
  http://www.ireland.com/ancestor/browse/counties/index.htm
  Including the provinces of:

    Connaught
    http://www.ireland.com/ancestor/browse/counties/connaught/index.htm

    Leinster
    http://www.ireland.com/ancestor/browse/counties/leinster/index.htm

    Munster
    http://www.ireland.com/ancestor/browse/counties/munster/index.htm

    Ulster
    http://www.ireland.com/ancestor/browse/counties/ulster/index.htm

- Emigration
  http://www.ireland.com/ancestor/browse/emigration/index.htm

- How To
  http://www.ireland.com/ancestor/browse/guide/index.htm

- Records
  http://www.ireland.com/ancestor/browse/records/index.htm

  o Gen.ie Research Service
    http://www.ireland.com/ancestor/database/index.htm

  o Magazine
    http://www.ireland.com/ancestor/magazine/index.htm
    Monthly articles.

  o Placenames Database
    http://www.ireland.com/ancestor/placename/index.cfm

- ○ Surname Search
  http://www.ireland.com/ancestor/surname/surnameentry.cfm
- Irish Chronicles Project
  http://www.genealogy.org/~ajmorris/ireland/icp/icp.htm
- Irish Family History Foundation—Bulletin Boards
  http://mail.mayo-ireland.ie/WebX?14@^1320@.ee6b2a8
  Organized with folders for each county.
- Irish Genealogy: The Celtic Connection
  http://www.geocities.com/Heartland/Prairie/8088/ire.html
- Irish Genealogy from A.J. Morris
  http://www.genealogy.org/~ajmorris/ireland/ireland.htm
  Surnames, Biographies, Publications, Emigrants, EIREphile, Counties & Internet Links.
- Irish Genealogy Links
  http://www.geocities.com/SiliconValley/Haven/1538/irish.html
- Irish Genealogy on the Web
  http://www.rootsweb.com/~irish/
  Presented by the Irish Genealogical Society, Int'l (IGSI).
- Irish History, Surnames and Timeline
  http://www.ida.net/users/dhanco/names.htm
- Leitrim-Roscommon Genealogy homepage
  http://www.thecore.com/let_ros/
- A Little Bit of Ireland
  http://home.att.net/~labaths/
  From Cathy Joynt Labath, contains many transcribed records: birth, marriage, cemeteries, deeds, directories, etc.
- Looking for Irish in All the Right Places
  http://celtic.stanford.edu/pub/post/Dec/Genealogy
- Northern Irish References—Ulster Province Family History
  http://members.aol.com/Manus/ulsterref.html
- Uasal—A Server for Irish Nobility, Heraldry and Genealogy
  http://www.finearts.sfasu.edu/uasal/welcome.html
- Ulster Origins Genealogy Site
  http://picard.holodeck.org/ulster/index.html
- Yahoo!...Ireland...Genealogy
  http://dir.yahoo.com/Regional/Countries/Ireland/Arts_and_Humanities/Humanities/History/Genealogy/

◆ GENUKI Resources by County

- The UK & Ireland Genealogical Information Service (GENUKI)
  http://www.genuki.org.uk/
  - ○ Ireland Genealogy Index
    http://hiwaay.net/~white/genuki/irl.html
    - Antrim
      http://www.cs.ncl.ac.uk/genuki/irl/Antrim/
    - Armagh
      http://www.cs.ncl.ac.uk/genuki/irl/Armagh/

- Carlow
  http://www.cs.ncl.ac.uk/genuki/irl/Carlow/
- Cavan
  http://www.cs.ncl.ac.uk/genuki/irl/Cavan/
- Clare
  http://www.cs.ncl.ac.uk/genuki/irl/Clare/
- Cork
  http://www.cs.ncl.ac.uk/genuki/irl/Cork/
- Derry (Londonderry)
  http://www.cs.ncl.ac.uk/genuki/irl/Derry/
- Donegal
  http://www.cs.ncl.ac.uk/genuki/irl/Donegal/
- Down
  http://www.cs.ncl.ac.uk/genuki/irl/Down/
- Dublin
  http://www.cs.ncl.ac.uk/genuki/irl/Dublin/
- Fermanagh
  http://www.cs.ncl.ac.uk/genuki/irl/Fermanagh/
- Galway
  http://www.cs.ncl.ac.uk/genuki/irl/Galway/
- Kerry
  http://www.cs.ncl.ac.uk/genuki/irl/Kerry/
- Kildare
  http://www.cs.ncl.ac.uk/genuki/irl/Kildare/
- Kilkenny
  http://www.cs.ncl.ac.uk/genuki/irl/Kilkenny/
- Laois (Queen's County)
  http://www.cs.ncl.ac.uk/genuki/irl/Laois/
- Leitrim
  http://www.cs.ncl.ac.uk/genuki/irl/Leitrim/
- Limerick
  http://www.cs.ncl.ac.uk/genuki/irl/Limerick/
- Longford
  http://www.cs.ncl.ac.uk/genuki/irl/Longford/
- Louth
  http://www.cs.ncl.ac.uk/genuki/irl/Louth/
- Mayo
  http://www.cs.ncl.ac.uk/genuki/irl/Mayo/
- Meath
  http://www.cs.ncl.ac.uk/genuki/irl/Meath/
- Monaghan
  http://www.cs.ncl.ac.uk/genuki/irl/Monaghan/
- Offaly (King's County)
  http://www.cs.ncl.ac.uk/genuki/irl/Offaly/
- Roscommon
  http://www.cs.ncl.ac.uk/genuki/irl/Roscommon/
- Sligo
  http://www.cs.ncl.ac.uk/genuki/irl/Sligo/
- Tipperary
  http://www.cs.ncl.ac.uk/genuki/irl/Tipperary/
- Tyrone
  http://www.cs.ncl.ac.uk/genuki/irl/Tyrone/

- Waterford
  http://www.cs.ncl.ac.uk/genuki/irl/Waterford/
- Westmeath
  http://www.cs.ncl.ac.uk/genuki/irl/Westmeath/
- Wexford
  http://www.cs.ncl.ac.uk/genuki/irl/Wexford/
- Wicklow
  http://www.cs.ncl.ac.uk/genuki/irl/Wicklow/

◆ History & Culture

- Facts About Ireland
  http://www.irlgov.ie/iveagh/foreignaffairs/facts/fai/HOME.HTML
- The Irish Famine, 1845–1850
  http://avery.med.virginia.edu/~eas5e/Irish/Famine.html
- Irish History on the Web
  http://wwwvms.utexas.edu/~jdana/irehist.html
- Views of the Famine
  http://vassun.vassar.edu/~sttaylor/FAMINE/

◆ How To

- Aid to Genealogical Research in Clogheen
  & District
  http://www.amireland.com/clogheen/clogpage/roots.html
- Finding Your Ancestors in Ireland
  http://www.familytreemaker.com/4_pocket.html
- Researching Irish Roots
  http://www.familytreemaker.com/issue4.html
- Scotch-Irish Research
  http://www.familytreemaker.com/00000384.html
- Tracing Your Roots
  http://users.homenet.ie/~aduffy/fingal.html

◆ Irish Family History Foundation ~ County Heritage Centres

Each county now has a local heritage centre and many of these centres also offer a search service for a small fee. "The Irish Family History Foundation is the co-ordinating body for a network of government approved genealogical research centres in the Republic of Ireland (Eire) and in Northern Ireland which have computerised tens of millions of Irish ancestral records of different types."

- Irish Family History Foundation
  http://www.mayo-ireland.ie/Roots.htm
  - Bru Boru Heritage Centre (South Tipperary)
    http://www.mayo-ireland.ie/Geneal/STipp.htm
  - Carlow Research Centre
    http://www.mayo-ireland.ie/Geneal/Carlow.htm

- Cavan Research Centre
  http://www.mayo-ireland.ie/Geneal/Cavan.htm
- Clare Heritage and Genealogical Centre
  http://www.mayo-ireland.ie/Geneal/Clare.htm
- County Armagh Genealogy-Armagh Ancestry
  http://www.mayo-ireland.ie/Geneal/Armagh.htm
- County Cork-Mallow Heritage Centre
  http://www.mayo-ireland.ie/Geneal/Cork.htm
- County Derry or Londonderry Genealogy Centre
  http://www.mayo-ireland.ie/Geneal/Derry.htm
- County Roscommon Heritage and Genealogy Society
  http://www.mayo-ireland.ie/Geneal/Roscmmn.htm
- County Sligo Heritage and Genealogy Centre
  http://www.mayo-ireland.ie/Geneal/Sligo.htm
- Donegal Ancestry in County Donegal
  http://www.mayo-ireland.ie/Geneal/Donegal.htm
- Dun Laoghaire Rathdown Heritage Society
  http://www.mayo-ireland.ie/Geneal/DunLghre.htm
- Dun na Si Heritage Centre-Westmeath
  http://www.mayo-ireland.ie/Geneal/Wstmeath.htm
- East Galway Family History Society
  http://www.mayo-ireland.ie/Geneal/EtGalway.htm
- Fingal Heritage Group, County Dublin
  http://www.mayo-ireland.ie/Geneal/Fingal.htm
- Heritage World (Fermanagh and Tyrone)
  http://www.mayo-ireland.ie/Geneal/FnghTyrn.htm
- Kildare Heritage and Genealogy Company
  http://www.mayo-ireland.ie/Geneal/Kildare.htm
- Kilkenney Ancestry
  http://www.mayo-ireland.ie/Geneal/Kilknny.htm
- Killarney Genealogical Centre
  http://www.mayo-ireland.ie/Geneal/Kerry.htm
- Laois & Offaly Family History Research Centre
  http://www.mayo-ireland.ie/Geneal/LaoisOff.htm
- Leitrim Genealogy Centre
  http://www.mayo-ireland.ie/Geneal/Leitrim.htm
- Limerick Regional Archives
  http://www.mayo-ireland.ie/Geneal/Limerick.htm
- Longford Research Centre
  http://www.mayo-ireland.ie/Geneal/Longford.htm
- Meath Heritage Centre
  http://www.mayo-ireland.ie/Geneal/Meath.htm
- Meath-Louth Family Research Centre
  http://www.mayo-ireland.ie/Geneal/Louth.htm
- Monaghan Research Centre
  http://www.mayo-ireland.ie/Geneal/Monaghan.htm
- North Mayo Family Research Centre
  http://www.mayo-ireland.ie/Geneal/NrthMayo.htm
- South Mayo Family Research Centre
  http://www.mayo-ireland.ie/Geneal/SouMayo.htm

- ○ Tipperary North Family Research Centre
  http://www.mayo-ireland.ie/Geneal/NTipp.htm
- ○ Ulster Historical Foundation
  http://www.mayo-ireland.ie/Geneal/AntmDown.htm
  For Counties Antrim & Down.
- ○ Waterford Research Centre
  http://www.mayo-ireland.ie/Geneal/Waterfrd.htm
- ○ Wexford Genealogy Centre
  http://www.mayo-ireland.ie/Geneal/Wexford.htm
- ○ West Galway Family History Society
  http://www.mayo-ireland.ie/Geneal/WtGalway.htm
- ○ Wicklow Research Centre
  http://www.mayo-ireland.ie/Geneal/Wicklow.htm

◆ Libraries, Archives & Museums

- Dublin City Public Libraries
  http://www.iol.ie/resource/dublincitylibrary/
- HYTELNET—Library Catalogs: Ireland
  http://library.usask.ca/hytelnet/ie0/ie000.html
  Before you use any of the Telnet links, make note of the user name, password and any other logon information.
- Irish Ancestors—Heritage Centres
  http://www.ireland.com/ancestor/browse/address/heritage.html
- National Archives of Ireland
  http://www.nationalarchives.ie/index.html
- National Library of Ireland
  http://www.heanet.ie/natlib/
  - ○ Family History Research at the National Library
    http://www.heanet.ie/natlib/family_research.html
  - ○ National Library of Ireland Collections
    http://www.heanet.ie/natlib/collections/
    - • Manuscripts
      http://www.heanet.ie/natlib/collections/manuscripts.html
    - • Newspapers and Periodicals
      http://www.heanet.ie/natlib/collections/newsper.html
- webCATS: Library Catalogues on the World Wide Web—Ireland
  http://library.usask.ca/hywebcat/countries/IE.html

◆ Mailing Lists, Newsgroups & Chat

- Antrim Mailing List
  http://members.aol.com/gfsjohnf/gen_mail_country-ire.html#Antrim
- Beara Mailing List
  http://members.aol.com/gfsjohnf/gen_mail_country-ire.html#Beara
  Berehaven Peninsula, counties of Cork and Kerry.
- CIVIL-WAR-IRISH Mailing List
  http://members.aol.com/gfsjohnf/gen_mail_country-ire.html#CIVIL-WAR-IRISH
  For those with a genealogical interest in the Irish participants in the American Civil War and their descendants.

- CoTipperary Mailing List
  http://members.aol.com/gfsjohnf/gen_mail_country-ire.html#CoTipperary
- CoTyroneIreland Mailing List
  http://members.aol.com/gfsjohnf/gen_mail_country-ire.html#CoTyroneIreland
- CountyCork Mailing List
  http://members.aol.com/gfsjohnf/gen_mail_country-ire.html#CountyCork
- DONEGALEIRE Mailing List
  http://members.aol.com/gfsjohnf/gen_mail_country-ire.html#DONEGALEIRE
- FERMANAGH Mailing List
  http://members.aol.com/gfsjohnf/gen_mail_country-ire.html#FERMANAGH
- FIANNA Mailing List
  http://members.aol.com/gfsjohnf/gen_mail_country-ire.html#FIANNA
  For those who are researching Irish ancestry and history to discuss ways of improving their skills in searching for their Irish ancestors.
- GENBRIT Mailing List
  http://members.aol.com/gfsjohnf/gen_mail_country-unk.html#GENBRIT
  For the discussion of genealogy in Great Britain and the islands. Gatewayed with the soc.genealogy.britain newsgroup.
- GENIRE Mailing List
  http://members.aol.com/gfsjohnf/gen_mail_country-ire.html#GENIRE
  Gatewayed with the soc.genealogy.ireland newsgroup.
- greenisle-gene Mailing List
  http://members.aol.com/gfsjohnf/gen_mail_country-ire.html#greenisle-gene
- IRELAND Mailing List
  http://members.aol.com/gfsjohnf/gen_mail_country-ire.html#IRELAND
  For anyone with a genealogical or historical interest in the island of Ireland.
- IrelandGenWeb Mailing List
  http://members.aol.com/gfsjohnf/gen_mail_country-ire.html#IrelandGenWeb
- IRISH-ADOPTEES-SEARCH Mailing List
  http://members.aol.com/gfsjohnf/gen_mail_country-ire.html#IRISH-ADOPTEES-SEARCH
- Irish-Canadian Mailing List
  http://members.aol.com/gfsjohnf/gen_mail_country-ire.html#Irish-Canadian
  For anyone interested in the genealogy, culture, and historical contribution of people who immigrated from Ireland to Canada.
- IRL-ANTRIM Mailing List
  http://members.aol.com/gfsjohnf/gen_mail_country-ire.html#IRL-ANTRIM

- IRL-BALLYKILCLINE Mailing List
  http://members.aol.com/gfsjohnf/gen_mail_country-ire.
  html#IRL-BALLYKILCLINE
  For the Ballykilcline Society; an association of people bearing a surname, or having descended from an ancestor with a surname, of the tenant farmers from Ballykilcline, Kilglass Parish, County Roscommon, Ireland.

- IRL-KERRY Mailing List
  http://members.aol.com/gfsjohnf/gen_mail_country-ire.
  html#IRL-KERRY

- KILKENNY Mailing List
  http://members.aol.com/gfsjohnf/gen_mail_country-ire.
  html#KILKENNY
  Also see the associated web page at http://www.rootsweb.com/ ~irlkik/maillist.htm

- LETTERMULLEN-GALWAY Mailing List
  http://members.aol.com/gfsjohnf/gen_mail_country-ire.
  html#LETTERMULLEN-GALWAY

- MAYO Mailing List
  http://members.aol.com/gfsjohnf/gen_mail_country-ire.
  html#MAYO

- NIR-DOWN Mailing List
  http://members.aol.com/gfsjohnf/gen_mail_country-ire.
  html#NIR-DOWN

- N-Ireland Mailing List
  http://members.aol.com/gfsjohnf/gen_mail_country-ire.
  html#N-Ireland

- NorthernIrelandGenWeb Mailing List
  http://members.aol.com/gfsjohnf/gen_mail_country-ire.
  html#NorthernIrelandGenWeb

- ROSCOMMON Mailing List
  http://members.aol.com/gfsjohnf/gen_mail_country-ire.
  html#ROSCOMMON

- Scotch-Irish-L Mailing List
  http://members.aol.com/gfsjohnf/gen_mail_country-ire.
  html#Scotch-Irish-L
  For Scotch-Irish or Ulster Scots genealogy and culture. These people began a period of heavy emigration from Ulster in the early 1700's and played a large part in the American Revolution.

- SHAMROCK Mailing List
  http://members.aol.com/gfsjohnf/gen_mail_country-ire.
  html#SHAMROCK
  For those trying to find their Celtic/Irish roots and for Irish historic research.

- SURNAMES-BRITAIN Mailing List
  http://members.aol.com/gfsjohnf/gen_mail_country-unk.
  html#SURNAMES-BRITAIN
  For surname queries related to Great Britain. Gatewayed with the soc.genealogy.surnames.britain newsgroup.

- SURNAMES-IRELAND Mailing List
  http://members.aol.com/gfsjohnf/gen_mail_country-ire.
  html#SURNAMES-IRELAND
  For surname queries related to Ireland and Northern Ireland. Gatewayed with the soc.genealogy.surnames.ireland newsgroup.

- Unionist-Culture Mailing List
  http://members.aol.com/gfsjohnf/gen_mail_country-ire.
  html#Unionist-Culture
  For anyone with a genealogical or cultural interest in the Unionist communities of Ireland (those areas that wish to remain part of the union with England).

- WATERFORD Mailing List
  http://members.aol.com/gfsjohnf/gen_mail_country-ire.
  html#WATERFORD

- WEXFORD Mailing List
  http://members.aol.com/gfsjohnf/gen_mail_country-ire.
  html#WEXFORD

◆ Maps, Gazetteers & Geographical Information

- Administrative Regions of the British Isles
  http://www.genuki.org.uk/big/Regions/
  From GENUKI.

  ○ Administrative Areas of Northern Ireland
     http://www.genuki.org.uk/big/Regions/NIreland.html

  ○ Administrative Areas of the Republic of Ireland
     http://www.genuki.org.uk/big/Regions/Ireland.html

- Chapman Codes for Ireland
  http://www.genuki.org.uk/big/IrelandCodes.GIF

- Irish Ancestors—Placenames: Irish Administrative Divisions
  http://www.ireland.com/ancestor/Placename/admin.htm

- Leitrim-Roscommon Map Collection
  http://www.thecore.com/let_ros/LR_maps.html
  Maps that display the Parishes, Baronies and Poor Law Unions for these two counties.

- Map of Ireland
  http://www.lib.utexas.edu/Libs/PCL/Map_collection/europe/
  Ireland.jpg
  From the Perry-Castañeda Library at the Univ. of Texas at Austin.

- Ordnance Survey—Gazetteer of Place Names
  http://www.campus.bt.com/CampusWorld/pub/OS/Gazetteer/
  index.html

◆ Newspapers

- AJR NewsLink: Irish Newspapers
  http://www.newslink.org/euire.html

- An Phoblacht / Republican News
  http://www.irlnet.com/aprn/index.html
  Belfast & Dublin.

- The Connaught Telegraph, Co Mayo, West of Ireland
  http://www.mayo-ireland.ie/Connaught.htm

- Cybermart News Online: Ireland Newspapers
  http://www.cybermart.net/Newspapers/Countries/Ireland/
  index.html

- E&P Media Info Links—Newspaper Sites in Ireland
  http://www.mediainfo.com/emediajs/browse-results.
  htm?region=ireland&category=newspaper+++++++++
- Ecola Newstand: Ireland Newspapers
  http://www.ecola.com/news/press/eu/ie/
- Galway Advertiser
  http://ireland.iol.ie/resource/ga/
- The Irish News ~ Belfast
  http://www.irishnews.com/
- The Irish People—The Voice of Irish Republicanism
  in America
  http://larkspirit.com/IrishPeople/
- The Irish Times on the Web ~ Dublin
  http://www.irish-times.com/
- The Irish Voice Online ~ New York
  http://www.irishvoice.com/
- The Limerick Post Newspaper
  http://ireland.iol.ie/~lpost/
- The Ultimate Collection of News Links: Ireland
  http://www.pppp.net/links/news/Ireland.html
- Western People ~ Mayo
  http://www.mayo-ireland.ie/WPeople.htm
- Yahoo!...Newspapers...Ireland
  http://dir.yahoo.com/News_and_Media/Newspapers/Regional/
  Countries/Ireland/

◆ People & Families

- Co. Tyrone, N. Ireland Fellow Genealogists
  http://pw2.netcom.com/~vanessa1/tyrone.html
- Irish Clans Then and Now
  http://pages.prodigy.com/GPGJ41A/clans.htm
- The Irish in 19th-Century Portsmouth, New
  Hampshire
  http://www.geocities.com/CollegePark/9887/ports.html
- The Myth of the Black Irish
  http://www.hypertext.com/blackirish/
- O'Kelly High Kings of Ireland
  http://www.iol.ie/~okelly/okelly.htm
  CD-ROM for sale.
- Searching in Ireland—Resources for Irish-Born
  Adoptees
  http://www.netreach.net/~steed/search.html

◆ Professional Researchers, Volunteers & Other Research Services

- Ancestral Research in Ulster
  http://www.a-research.demon.co.uk/
  Genealogy research service specialising in the nine counties of Ulster, Northern Ireland.

- Board for Certification of Genealogists—Roster of
  Those Certified—Specializing in British Isles
  http://www.genealogy.org/~bcg/rosts_@b.html
- Celtic Origins ~ Dublin
  http://www.genealogy.ie/
- Eneclann: Irish Genealogical Research Services
  http://www.eneclann.tcd.ie/genealogy.htm
- Genealogist and Record Agent Ireland
  http://indigo.ie/~records/
- Genealogy Helplist—Ireland
  http://www.geocities.com/Athens/Delphi/4715/genealog/
  helpireland.html
- genealogyPro—Professional Genealogists
  for Ireland
  http://genealogyPro.com/directories/Ireland.html
- Gen-Find Research Associates
  http://www.gen-find.com/
  Specialists in Genealogy Research for Ontario & Western Canada, Scotland, Ireland, Forensic Genealogy & 20th Century Research.
- Irish Professional Genealogists
  http://www.iol.ie/~irishrts/Professionals.html
- The National Archives of Ireland: Genealogical
  and Historical Researchers
  http://www.nationalarchives.ie/gen_researchers.html
  Postal addresses of professional researchers in Ireland.
- Will Search Ireland Co. Ltd
  http://indigo.ie/~willsrch/

◆ Publications, Software & Supplies

- Ancestor's Attic Discount Genealogy Books—
  Irish Genealogy Books
  http://members.tripod.com/~ancestorsattic/index.html#secIR
- Books We Own—Ireland
  http://www.rootsweb.com/~bwo/ireland.html
- Books Related to Irish Migration
  http://www2.ebtech.net/~kleonard/Irish.html
- Frontier Press Bookstore—Irish Research
  http://www.frontierpress.com/frontier.cgi?category=ire
- GenealogyBookShop.com—Ireland/Irish
  http://www.genealogybookshop.com/genealogybookshop/files/
  The_World,Ireland_Irish/index.html
  The online store of Genealogical Publishing Co., Inc. & Clearfield Company.
- Grenham's Irish Recordfinder
  http://indigo.ie/~rfinder/
  A software system designed to help you determine relevant resources for your Irish genealogical research.
- Hearthstone Bookshop—Ireland
  http://www.hearthstonebooks.com/Ireland.html

- Irish Roots Magazine HomePage
  http://www.iol.ie/~irishrts/

- OLochlainns Irish Families
  http://www.irishroots.com/
  The home page of the Irish Genealogical Foundation and OLochlainns Irish Family Journal.

- Read Ireland Bookstore
  http://www.readireland.ie/

- S.E.L. Enterprises
  http://www.mentornet.org/sel.htm
  Publications (books, magazines, periodicals & maps) for researching your English, Irish, Scots and Welsh ancestors.

- Tracing Your Irish Ancestors
  http://www.ireland.com/ancestor/credit/grenham.htm
  By John Grenham.

◆ Queries, Message Boards & Surname Lists

- GenConnect Ireland Visitor Center
  http://cgi.rootsweb.com/~genbbs/index/Ireland.html

- Local Names Ireland
  http://names.local.ie/

- The UK & Ireland Genealogical Information Service (GENUKI)
  http://www.genuki.org.uk/
  - GENUKI Surname Lists
    http://www.cs.ncl.ac.uk/genuki/SurnamesList/
    - Co. Tyrone, N. Ireland Fellow Genealogists
      http://pw2.netcom.com/~vanessa1/tyrone.html
    - County Antrim Surname Interest List
      http://www.rootsweb.com/~irldub/antrim/antrimsr.htm
    - County Down Surname List
      http://www.amitar.com.au/~deel/downlist.htm
    - County Galway Surname List
      http://www.labyrinth.net.au/~quibellg/galway.htm
    - County Kerry Surname Interest List
      http://www.bendigo.net.au/~oconnell/kerry.htm
    - County Kilkenny Ireland Genealogy "Surnames of Kilkenny"
      http://www.rootsweb.com/~irlkik/ksurname.htm
    - County Limerick, Ireland Surnames and Queries
      http://www.geocities.com/Athens/Parthenon/6108/limerick.htm
    - The County Mayo Surname Interest List
      http://www.cs.ncl.ac.uk/genuki/SurnamesList/MAY.html
    - County Sligo, Ireland Surname List
      http://www.rootsweb.com/~irlsli/surnam.html
    - County Westmeath Surname List
      http://www.amitar.com.au/~deel/westlist.htm

- Leitrim-Roscommon Surname Search
  http://www.thecore.com/let_ros/surname_intro.html

- On-line Irish Names Research Directory
  http://www.users.on.net/proformat/irlnames.html

- Tipperary Surname Interest List
  http://homepages.ihug.co.nz/~hughw/tip.html

- Wexford Surname Interest List
  http://homepages.ihug.co.nz/~hughw/wexford.html

◆ Records: Census, Cemeteries, Land, Obituaries, Personal, Taxes and Vital (Born, Married, Died & Buried)

- Irish Ancestors—The Records
  http://www.ireland.com/ancestor/browse/records/index.htm
  - Census Records
    http://www.ireland.com/ancestor/browse/records/census/index.htm
  - Church Records
    http://www.ireland.com/ancestor/browse/records/church/index.htm
  - Land Records
    http://www.ireland.com/ancestor/browse/records/land/index.htm
  - State Registration of Births, Marriages & Deaths
    http://www.ireland.com/ancestor/browse/records/state/index.htm
  - Wills
    http://www.ireland.com/ancestor/browse/records/wills/index.htm

- Irish Emigrants List
  http://www.genealogy.org/~ajmorris/ireland/ireemg.htm

- Marriages in Parishes in Castlebar-Westport Area
  http://people.delphi.com/patdeese/MARR.HTML

- National Archives of Ireland
  http://www.nationalarchives.ie/index.html

- National Archives of Ireland: Transportation Records
  http://www.nationalarchives.ie/search01.html
  Convicts from Ireland to Australia, 1788 to 1868.

- Passenger Lists from Ireland—1803
  http://www.ida.net/users/dhanco/passlst.htm

- Passenger Lists from Ireland #2—1803
  http://www.ida.net/users/dhanco/passlst2.htm

- Public Record Office of Northern Ireland
  http://proni.nics.gov.uk/

- Una's Genealogy Stuff
  http://idt.net/~unatg/
  Has transcriptions of births, baptisms, marriages, several passenger lists from Liverpool to NYC, etc.

◆ Societies & Groups

- The American Irish Historical Society
  http://www.aihs.org/
  New York

- Ancient Order of Hibernians in America
  http://www.aoh.com

- Ancient Order of Hibernians in Ohio
  http://www.intcom.net/~tomt/aoh/ohio/aohohio.html

- County Roscommon Family History Society
  http://www.iol.ie/bizpark/c/crfhs/

- County Tipperary Historical Society
  http://www.iol.ie/~tipplibs/Welcome.htm

- Irish American Archives Society
  http://www.intcom.net/~tomt/aoh/ohio/iaas.html
  Cleveland, Ohio

- The Irish-American Club
  http://www.en.com/irishclub/
  East Side—Cleveland, Ohio

- Irish Ancestors—Heritage Centres
  http://www.ireland.com/ancestor/browse/address/heritage.html

- The Irish Ancestral Research Association (TIARA)
  http://world.std.com/~ahern/TIARA.html
  Sudbury, Massachusetts

- Irish Family History Foundation
  http://www.mayo-ireland.ie/roots.htm

- Irish Family History Society
  http://www.mayo-ireland.ie/Geneal/IFHisSoc.htm

- Irish Genealogical Society, International ~ Ireland
  http://www.rootsweb.com/~irish/index.html

- Irish Genealogical Society of Wisconsin
  http://www.execpc.com/~igsw/

- Local Family History Societies in Ireland
  http://www.iol.ie/~irishrts/Societies.html

- North of Ireland Family History Society
  http://www.mni.co.uk/nifhs/

- Offaly Historical and Archaeological Society
  http://ireland.iol.ie/~ohas
  The family history research centre for the Irish counties of Laois and Offaly.

- Ulster Historical Foundation
  http://www.uhf.org.uk/

- Ulster-Scots Heritage Council
  http://ourworld.compuserve.com/homepages/w_bradley/

◆ WorldGenWeb Project

- IrelandGenWeb Project
  http://www.rootsweb.com/~irlwgw/

  - Antrim
    http://mtnia.com/mmhill/Antrim.htm

- Armagh
  http://www.geocities.com/Heartland/Plains/9095/armagh.html

- Carlow
  http://cgi.rootsweb.com/~genbbs/genbbs.cgi/Ireland/Carlow

- Cavan
  http://members.tripod.com/~Al_Beagan/tcavan.htm

- Clare
  http://members.aol.com/Anj6787/ctyclare.html

- Cork
  http://www.rootsweb.com/~irlcor/

- Donegal
  http://www.inetall.net/rjo/donegal/

- Down
  http://www.carebear.demon.co.uk/down.html

- Dublin
  http://homepages.rootsweb.com/~cheps/Dublin/index.htm

- Fermanagh
  http://cgi.rootsweb.com/~genbbs/genbbs.cgi/Ireland/Fermanagh

- Galway
  http://www.geocities.com/Heartland/Plains/9095/Galway.html

- Kerry
  http://cgi.rootsweb.com/~genbbs/genbbs.cgi/Ireland/Kerry

- Kildare
  http://cgi.rootsweb.com/~genbbs/genbbs.cgi/Ireland/Kildare

- Kilkenny
  http://www.rootsweb.com/~irlkik/

- Laois (Queens County)
  http://cgi.rootsweb.com/~genbbs/genbbs.cgi/Ireland/Laios

- Leitrim
  http://www.rootsweb.com/~irllet/index.htm

- Limerick
  http://www.geocities.com/Athens/Parthenon/6108/limerick.htm

- Londonderry / Derry
  http://homepages.rootsweb.com/~cheps/Derry/index.htm

- Longford
  http://personal.nbnet.nb.ca/tmoffatt/Longford_queries.html

- Louth
  http://www.worldgenweb.org/ireland/louth/louth.htm

- Mayo
  http://www.geocities.com/Heartland/Acres/4031/mayo.html

- Meath
  http://cgi.rootsweb.com/~genbbs/genbbs.cgi/Ireland/Meath

- Monaghan
  http://www.exis.net/ahd/monaghan/

- Offaly (Kings County)
  http://cgi.rootsweb.com/~genbbs/genbbs.cgi/Ireland/Offaly

- Roscommon
  http://www.rootsweb.com/~irlrosco

- Sligo
  http://www.rootsweb.com/~irlsli/index.html
- Tipperary
  http://www.cyberbeach.net/~mkelly/iregenweb.htm
- Tyrone
  http://www.teesee.com/CoTyrone/tyrone.html
- Waterford
  http://www.rootsweb.com/~irlwat/waterford.htm

- Westmeath
  http://cgi.rootsweb.com/~genbbs/genbbs.cgi/Ireland/Westmeath
- Wexford
  http://www.rootsweb.com/~irlwex/wex.htm
- Wicklow
  http://cgi.rootsweb.com/~genbbs/genbbs.cgi/Ireland/Wicklow

ISLE OF MAN
http://www.CyndisList.com/isleman.htm

Category Index:

- General Resource Sites
- Mailing Lists, Newsgroups & Chat
- Maps, Gazetteers & Geographical Information
- Professional Researchers, Volunteers & Other Research Services

- Queries, Message Boards & Surname Lists
- Records: Census, Cemeteries, Land, Obituaries, Personal, Taxes and Vital
- Societies & Groups

◆ General Resource Sites

- Manx Genealogy Bulletin Board
  http://www.isle-of-man.com/interests/genealogy/bulletin/

- A Manx Notebook
  http://www.ee.surrey.ac.uk/Contrib/manx/index.html
  An Electronic Compendium of Matters Past and Present Connected with the Isle of Man.

- Parishes of the Isle of Man and their Churches
  http://www.ee.surrey.ac.uk/Contrib/manx/parishes/index.htm

- The UK & Ireland Genealogical Information Service (GENUKI)
  http://www.genuki.org.uk/
  - Isle of Man Genealogy—From GENUKI
    http://www.genuki.org.uk/big/lom.html

- Welcome to the Isle of Man
  http://www.isle-of-man.com/
  Many resources—be sure to see their genealogy page link.

◆ Mailing Lists, Newsgroups & Chat

- GENBRIT Mailing List
  http://members.aol.com/gfsjohnf/gen_mail_country-unk.html#GENBRIT
  For the discussion of genealogy in Great Britain and the islands. Gatewayed with the soc.genealogy.britain newsgroup.

- Manx Mailing List
  http://members.aol.com/gfsjohnf/gen_mail_country-unk.html#Manx

- SURNAMES-BRITAIN Mailing List
  http://members.aol.com/gfsjohnf/gen_mail_country-unk.html#SURNAMES-BRITAIN
  For surname queries related to Great Britain. Gatewayed with the soc.genealogy.surnames.britain newsgroup.

◆ Maps, Gazetteers & Geographical Information

- Administrative Regions of the British Isles
  http://www.genuki.org.uk/big/Regions/
  From GENUKI.
  - Crown Dependencies
    http://www.genuki.org.uk/big/Regions/Crown.html

◆ Professional Researchers, Volunteers & Other Research Services

- Isle of Man Look-up Exchange
  http://www.isle-of-man.com/interests/genealogy/look-up.htm

- Isle of Man—Manx Family History Search
  http://www.oz.net/~ccaine/djd/
  Donna Douglass can help you with your research.

◆ Queries, Message Boards & Surname Lists

- Database of Researchers—Isle of Man Genealogy
  http://www.isle-of-man.com/interests/genealogy/database.htm

◆ Records: Census, Cemeteries, Land, Obituaries, Personal, Taxes and Vital (Born, Married, Died & Buried)

- The Public Record Office Home Page
  http://www.pro.gov.uk/
  - About the Family Records Centre
    http://www.pro.gov.uk/about/frc/

○ Information for Genealogists
http://www.pro.gov.uk/readers/genealogists/default.htm

    • Public Record Office—Family Fact Sheets
http://www.pro.gov.uk/readers/genealogists/
familyfacts.htm

◆ Societies & Groups

• Isle of Man Family History Society
http://www.isle-of-man.com/interests/genealogy/fhs/

• Isle of Man Family History Society Journal
http://www.ee.surrey.ac.uk/Contrib/manx/famhist/fhsjidx.htm
Volume i 1979 to Volume xii 1990, articles scanned and online!

• Manx Methodist Historical Society Newsletter
http://www.ee.surrey.ac.uk/Contrib/manx/methdism/mhist/
index.htm
Index to Newsletters 1–24.

• North American Manx Association
http://www.isle-of-man.com/interests/genealogy/nama/
index.htm

SCOTLAND
http://www.CyndisList.com/scotland.htm

Category Index:

- General Resource Sites
- GENUKI Resources by County
- Government & Cities
- History & Culture
- How To
- Libraries, Archives & Museums
- Mailing Lists, Newsgroups & Chat
- Maps, Gazetteers & Geographical Information
- Military
- Newspapers

- People & Families
- Professional Researchers, Volunteers & Other Research Services
- Publications, Software & Supplies
- Queries, Message Boards & Surname Lists
- Records: Census, Cemeteries, Land, Obituaries, Personal, Taxes and Vital
- Religion & Churches
- Societies & Groups

◆ General Resource Sites

- The 100 Most Common Surnames in Scotland—1995
  http://www.open.gov.uk/gros/surnames.htm
- Clans & Tartans
  http://www.sgiandhu.com/clans/online/index.html
- CURSITERs of Orkney—Orkney Genealogy Website
  http://www.cursiter.com/
- Family Tree Research in the Outer Hebrides of Scotland
  http://www.hebrides.com/busi/coleis/
- The Gathering of the Clans
  http://www.tartans.com/
  Site devoted to all things Scottish.
- The Internet Guide to Scotland
  http://ourworld.compuserve.com/homepages/RJWinters/scotland.htm
- Researching From Abroad—from GENUKI
  http://www.genuki.org.uk/ab/
- Ring of Scottish Clans Information Center
  http://www.sirius.com/~black/webring/index.htm
  A web ring site. Celebrating the culture, history, music and families of Scotland.
- Scotland WorldGenWeb Project
  http://www.rootsweb.com/~sctwgw/
- The Scottish Page
  http://homepages.rootsweb.com/~scottish/
  Devoted to the research of Scottish ancestry, especially that of Dumfries-Galloway.

- The UK & Ireland Genealogical Information Service (GENUKI)
  http://www.genuki.org.uk/
- Yahoo!...Scotland...Genealogy
  http://dir.yahoo.com/Regional/Countries/United_Kingdom/Scotland/Arts_and_Humanities/History/Genealogy/

◆ GENUKI Resources by County

- The UK & Ireland Genealogical Information Service (GENUKI)
  http://www.genuki.org.uk/
  ○ Scottish Genealogy Index
    http://www-theory.dcs.st-and.ac.uk/~mnd/genuki/scot.html
    - Aberdeenshire Genealogy
      http://www.urie.demon.co.uk/genuki/ABD/aberdeen.htm
    - Angus Genealogy
      http://www.dundee.ac.uk/~anicoll/genuki/ANS/
    - Argyll Genealogy
      http://www.roe.ac.uk/genuki/argyll/index.html
    - Ayrshire Genealogy
      http://home.clara.net/iainkerr/genuki/AYR/
    - Banffshire Genealogy
      http://www-theory.dcs.st-and.ac.uk/~mnd/counties/banff.html
    - Berwickshire Genealogy
      http://www.users.zetnet.co.uk/vdunstan/genuki/BWK/
    - Bute Genealogy
      http://www-theory.dcs.st-and.ac.uk/~mnd/counties/bute.html
    - Caithness Genealogy
      http://www.frayston.demon.co.uk/genuki/cai/

- Clackmannanshire Genealogy
  http://www.dgnscrn.demon.co.uk/genuki/CLK/
- Dumbartonshire Genealogy
  http://www.skylinc.net/~lasmith/genuki/DNB/
- Dumfriesshire Genealogy
  http://www.burgoyne.com/pages/djaggi/genuki/county/
  dumfries.htm
- East Lothian
  http://freespace.virgin.net/david.howie/genuki/ELN/
  index.html
- Fife Genealogy
  http://www.sol.co.uk/w/w.owen/genuki/FIF/index.htm
- Inverness-shire Genealogy
  http://www.roe.ac.uk/genuki/inv/index.html
  This includes part of Lewis, North & South Uist and Skye.
- Kincardineshire Genealogy
  http://www.btinternet.com/~mmorton/genuki/KCD/
- Kinross-shire Genealogy
  http://www.dgnscrn.demon.co.uk/genuki/KRS/
- Kirkcudbrightshire Genealogy
  http://www.burgoyne.com/pages/djaggi/genuki/
  kirkcudb.htm
- Lanarkshire Genealogy
  http://www.users.zetnet.co.uk/rdixon/genuki/LKS/
  index.htm
- Midlothian (Edinburghshire) Genealogy
  http://www.btinternet.com/~mmgene/genuki/mln/
  mlothian.htm
- Moray Genealogy
  http://www-theory.dcs.st-and.ac.uk/~mnd/genuki/
  counties/moray.html
- Nairnshire Genealogy
  http://www.geocities.com/~brooms/genuki/
- Orkney Genealogy
  http://www.tiac.net/users/teschek/genuki/OKI/
- Peeblesshire Genealogy
  http://www.users.zetnet.co.uk/vdunstan/genuki/PEE/
- Perthshire Genealogy
  http://www.dundee.ac.uk/~gbuttars/genuki/PER/PER.htm
- Renfrewshire Genealogy
  http://www.skylinc.net/~lasmith/genuki/RFW
- Ross & Cromarty
  http://www.roe.ac.uk/genuki/roc/index.html
  This includes part of the island of Lewis.
- Roxburghshire Genealogy
  http://www.users.zetnet.co.uk/vdunstan/genuki/ROX/
- Selkirkshire Genealogy
  http://www.users.zetnet.co.uk/vdunstan/genuki/SEL/
- Shetland Genealogy
  http://www-theory.dcs.st-and.ac.uk/~mnd/genuki/
  counties/shetland.html
- Stirlingshire Genealogy
  http://www-theory.dcs.st-and.ac.uk/~mnd/genuki/
  counties/stirling.html

- Sutherland Genealogy
  http://www-theory.dcs.st-and.ac.uk/~mnd/genuki/
  counties/sutherland.html
- West Lothian (Linlithgowshire) Genealogy
  http://www-theory.dcs.st-and.ac.uk/~mnd/genuki/WLN/
- Wigtownshire Genealogy
  http://www.burgoyne.com/pages/djaggi/genuki/county1/
  wigtown.htm

◆ Government & Cities

- City of Edinburgh Council
  http://www.edinburgh.gov.uk/
- Glasgow City Council
  http://www.glasgow.gov.uk/
- The Scottish Office
  http://www.scotland.gov.uk/

◆ History & Culture

- Notable Dates in Scottish History
  http://www.geo.ed.ac.uk/home/scotland/histdates.html
- Stones of Scotland
  http://www.stonepages.com/utenti/dmeozzi/Scotland/
  Scotland.html
- Tartan Day
  http://www.tartanday.com/
- Tartans of Scotland
  http://www.tartans.scotland.net/
- Yahoo!...Scotland...History
  http://dir.yahoo.com/Regional/Countries/United_Kingdom/
  Scotland/Arts_and_Humanities/History/

◆ How To

- Compiling a Family Tree—Getting Started
  http://www.cw.globalweb.co.uk/buchan/records.htm
  *From the Central Buchan Project. Provides information for
  beginning research with emphasis on the holdings of the local
  Buchan Registration Offices and repositories.*
- Introduction to Scottish Family History
  http://www-theory.dcs.st-and.ac.uk/~mnd/genuki/intro.html
- Scotch-Irish Research
  http://www.familytreemaker.com/00000384.html
  From Family Tree Maker Online.
- Tracing your Scottish Ancestry
  http://www.geo.ed.ac.uk/home/Scotland/genealogy.html

◆ Libraries, Archives & Museums

- Angus Archives
  http://www.angus.gov.uk/history/history.htm
  *Records for the seven burghs of Arbroath, Brechin, Carnoustie,
  Forfar, Kirriemuir, Montrose and Monifieth.*

- Archives & Libraries in Scotland
  http://www-theory.dcs.st-and.ac.uk/~mnd/genuki/archives.html

- Edinburgh University Library—Library and Information Resources
  http://www.lib.ed.ac.uk/

- Genealogy & Family History in the North East of Scotland
  http://www.aberdeenshire.gov.uk/famhist.htm
  From the North East of Scotland Library Service.

- Glasgow University Archives and Business Records Centre
  http://www.archives.gla.ac.uk/
  Preserves academic, business, and health records for the west of Scotland.

  o Business Archives Council of Scotland
    http://www.archives.gla.ac.uk/bacs/default.html
    For the preservation of Scottish business records at Glasgow University.

  o Greater Glasgow Health Board (GGHB) Archive
    http://www.archives.gla.ac.uk/gghb/default.html
    Archives of the hospitals in the Glasgow area held by Glasgow University.

  o Scottish Brewing Archive (SBA)
    http://www.archives.gla.ac.uk/sba/default.html
    Repository for business records from the brewing industry past and present at Glasgow University.

  o University Archives
    http://www.archives.gla.ac.uk/arcbrc/default.html

- National Library of Scotland
  http://www.nls.uk/

- South Ayrshire Libraries—Scottish & Local History Library
  http://www.south-ayrshire.gov.uk/Library/scot_local/Localhistory2.htm

  o Genealogical Collection
    http://www.south-ayrshire.gov.uk/Library/scot_local/genealogy.htm

- St. Andrews University Library
  http://www-library.st-and.ac.uk/

- University of Dundee Department of Archives and Manuscripts
  http://www.dundee.ac.uk/Archives/

◆ Mailing Lists, Newsgroups & Chat

- ABERDEEN Mailing List
  http://members.aol.com/gfsjohnf/gen_mail_country-unk.html#ABERDEEN

- ANGUS Mailing List
  http://members.aol.com/gfsjohnf/gen_mail_country-unk.html#ANGUS

- AYRSHIRE Mailing List
  http://members.aol.com/gfsjohnf/gen_mail_country-unk.html#AYRSHIRE

- BORDER Mailing List
  http://members.aol.com/gfsjohnf/gen_mail_country-unk.html#BORDER
  For anyone interested in genealogy, history, or culture related to the counties which surround the border of Scotland and England.

- ButeshireGenWeb Mailing List
  http://members.aol.com/gfsjohnf/gen_mail_country-unk.html#ButeshireGenWeb

- CAPE-FEAR-SCOTS Mailing List
  http://members.aol.com/gfsjohnf/gen_mail_country-unk.html#CAPE-FEAR-SCOTS
  For anyone researching Scottish immigrants to the Cape Fear region of North Carolina prior to 1850.

- DUMFRIES-GALLOWAY Mailing List
  http://members.aol.com/gfsjohnf/gen_mail_country-unk.html#DUMFRIES-GALLOWAY
  For anyone with a genealogical interest in the counties of Dumfries, Wigtown, and Kirkcudbright, Scotland, United Kingdom.

- GENBRIT Mailing List
  http://members.aol.com/gfsjohnf/gen_mail_country-unk.html#GENBRIT
  For the discussion of genealogy in Great Britain and the islands. Gatewayed with the soc.genealogy.britain newsgroup.

- LANARK Mailing List
  http://members.aol.com/gfsjohnf/gen_mail_country-unk.html#LANARK
  Lanarkshire

- MIDLOTHIAN Mailing List
  http://members.aol.com/gfsjohnf/gen_mail_country-unk.html#MIDLOTHIAN
  For anyone with a genealogical interest in the counties of East Lothian, Midlothian and West Lothian, Scotland, Great Britain.

- MORAY Mailing List
  http://members.aol.com/gfsjohnf/gen_mail_country-unk.html#MORAY
  For anyone with a genealogical interest in the counties of Morayshire, Banffshire and Nairnshire, Scotland, United Kingdom.

- ORKNEY Mailing List
  http://members.aol.com/gfsjohnf/gen_mail_country-unk.html#ORKNEY

- PERTHSHIRE Mailing List
  http://members.aol.com/gfsjohnf/gen_mail_country-unk.html#PERTHSHIRE
  For anyone with a genealogical or historical interest in the county of Perthshire, Scotland, Great Britain.

- ROSSGEN Mailing List
  http://members.aol.com/gfsjohnf/gen_mail_country-unk.html#ROSSGEN
  For anyone with a genealogical or historical interest in the county of Ross and Cromarty, Scotland, Great Britain.

- Scotch-Irish-L Mailing List
  http://members.aol.com/gfsjohnf/gen_mail_country-unk.html#Scotch-Irish-L
  For Scotch-Irish or Ulster Scots genealogy and culture. These people began a period of heavy emigration from Ulster in the early 1700's and played a large part in the American Revolution.

- SCOTLAND-GENWEB Mailing List
  http://members.aol.com/gfsjohnf/gen_mail_country-unk.
  html#SCOTLAND-GENWEB

- SCT-FIFE Mailing List
  http://members.aol.com/gfsjohnf/gen_mail_country-unk.
  html#SCT-FIFE

- SCT-INVERNESS Mailing List
  http://members.aol.com/gfsjohnf/gen_mail_country-unk.
  html#SCT-INVERNESS

- SCT-ISLAY Mailing List
  http://members.aol.com/gfsjohnf/gen_mail_country-unk.
  html#SCT-ISLAY

- SCT-ISLEOFMULL Mailing List
  http://members.aol.com/gfsjohnf/gen_mail_country-unk.
  html#SCT-ISLEOFMULL

- SCT-KINCARDINE Mailing List
  http://members.aol.com/gfsjohnf/gen_mail_country-unk.
  html#SCT-KINCARDINE

- SCT-KIRKCUDBRIGHTSHIRE Mailing List
  http://members.aol.com/gfsjohnf/gen_mail_country-unk.
  html#SCT-KIRKCUDBRIGHTSHIRE

- SCT-STIRLINGSHIRE Mailing List
  http://members.aol.com/gfsjohnf/gen_mail_country-unk.
  html#SCT-STIRLINGSHIRE

- SURNAMES-BRITAIN Mailing List
  http://members.aol.com/gfsjohnf/gen_mail_country-unk.
  html#SURNAMES-BRITAIN
  *For surname queries related to Great Britain. Gatewayed with
  the soc.genealogy.surnames.britain newsgroup.*

- Usenet Newsgroup
  alt.scottish.clans

◆ Maps, Gazetteers & Geographical Information

- Administrative Regions of the British Isles
  http://www.genuki.org.uk/big/Regions/
  From GENUKI

  ○ Administrative Areas of Scotland
    http://www.genuki.org.uk/big/Regions/Scotland.html

- Counties of England, Scotland and Wales Prior to
  the 1974 Boundary Changes
  http://www.genuki.org.uk/big/BRITAIN2.GIF

- County Map of Scotland
  http://www.users.zetnet.co.uk/vdunstan/genuki/maps/
  sct_cmap.html
  From the GENUKI web site for Scotland.

- The Derivation of Edinburgh's Street Names
  http://www.ebs.hw.ac.uk/STREETS/welcome.html

- Edinburgh City Centre Map
  http://www.efr.hw.ac.uk/EDC/maps/city-centre-map.html

- Edinburgh Suburbs Map
  http://www.efr.hw.ac.uk/EDC/maps/suburbs-map.html

- Gazetteer for Scotland
  http://www.geo.ed.ac.uk/scotgaz/
  *Under development at the Department of Geography at the
  University of Edinburgh.*

- Map of the Clans of Scotland
  ftp://ftp.csn.net/McCallum/maps/map.jpg

- Local Government in Scotland—Council Maps
  http://www.scotland.gov.uk/library/documents3/fs12-11.htm
  From the Scottish Office.

- Multi Media Mapping
  http://uk5.multimap.com/map/places.cgi
  *An interactive atlas of Great Britain. Enter the name of a British
  city, town or village to get a clickable, zoomable, detailed map.*

- Ordnance Survey—Gazetteer of Place Names
  http://www.campus.bt.com/CampusWorld/pub/OS/Gazetteer/
  index.html

- Scharlau Prints and Maps
  http://www.scharlau.co.uk/
  Etchings, antiquarian engravings, maps and prints of Scotland.

◆ Military

- Dispatch Military Journal
  http://subnet.virtual-pc.com/~mc546367/journal.htm
  *Journal for Scottish Military History and Regiments, Scottish
  Military Historical Society.*

- The Scots at War Project
  http://www-saw.arts.ed.ac.uk/saw.html
  *A tribute to the men and women who served their country in the
  20th century. Includes information on genealogy for Scottish
  soldiers.*

  ○ Genealogical Help Service—Ancestor Hunting
    http://www-saw.arts.ed.ac.uk/misc/genealogy/ancestor.html

  ○ Genealogical Help Service—The Armed and
    Civilian Services
    http://www-saw.arts.ed.ac.uk/misc/genealogy/military.html

  ○ Military Service Museums for Scotland
    http://www-saw.arts.ed.ac.uk/misc/genealogy/
    museums.html

- Scottish Military Historical Society—Index of
  Military Sites to Visit
  http://www.virtual-pc.com/journal/other.htm

◆ Newspapers

- E&P Media Info Links—Newspaper Sites
  in Scotland
  http://www.mediainfo.com/emediajs/browse-results.
  htm?region=scotland&category=newspaper+++++++++

- North East Newspapers
  http://www.aberdeenshire.gov.uk/ne_news.htm
  Held by the North East of Scotland Library Service.

◆ People & Families

- The Monarchs & Regents of Scotland for Near 600 Years
  http://www.ringnett.no/home/bjornstad/royals/Scotland.html

- Robert BURNS Family History
  http://fox.nstn.ca/~jburness/burns.html
  Family history of the Scottish poet Robert Burns including 130 descendants and over 800 other relatives.

◆ Professional Researchers, Volunteers & Other Research Services

- Family Tree Research in the Outer Hebrides of Scotland
  http://www.hebrides.com/busi/coleis/
  A professional research service based in Taobh Tuath (Norton).

- Genealogical Research in Scotland
  http://website.lineone.net/~gary.young/
  Gary Young, Dunbartonshire, Scotland.

- genealogyPro—Professional Genealogists for Scotland
  http://genealogyPro.com/directories/Scotland.html

- Gen-Find Research Associates
  http://www.gen-find.com/
  Specialists in Genealogy Research for Ontario & Western Canada, Scotland, Ireland, Forensic Genealogy & 20th Century Research.

- KinHelp
  http://www.web-ecosse.com/genes/genes2.htm
  A Scottish oriented genealogical service by Gordon Johnson.

- Scotfinder Home Page
  http://ourworld.compuserve.com/homepages/scotfinder/

- Scotland Look-up Exchange
  http://www.geocities.com/Heartland/Acres/6317/sct.htm

- Scots Ancestry Research Society
  http://www.royalmile.com/scotsancestry/

- Scottish Ancestry Research (Graham Maxwell)
  http://members.aol.com/grmaxwell/ancestry/index.htm

- Scottish Family Research
  http://www.linnet.co.uk/linnet/tour/67015.htm

- Scottish Family Search
  http://www.demon.co.uk/sfs/sfshome.htm

- Scottish Roots—Ancestral Research Services
  http://www.scottish-roots.co.uk/

- Thistle Roots Research
  http://www.geocities.com/Heartland/Plains/3735/
  George Cormack's Scottish genealogical resource based in Edinburgh.

◆ Publications, Software & Supplies

- Ancestor's Attic Discount Genealogy Books—Scottish Genealogy Books
  http://members.tripod.com/~ancestorsattic/index.html#secSC

- Books We Own—Scotland
  http://www.rootsweb.com/~bwo/scotland.html

- David Dobson M. Phil., (St Andrews)
  http://www.users.zetnet.co.uk/dobson.genealogy/
  Over 40 publications for Scottish research.

- Frances McDonnell Publications
  http://www.users.zetnet.co.uk/dobson.genealogy/frances.html

- Frontier Press Bookstore—Scottish Research
  http://www.frontierpress.com/frontier.cgi?category=scot

- GenealogyBookShop.com—Scotland/Scottish
  http://www.genealogybookshop.com/genealogybookshop/files/The_World,Scotland_Scottish/index.html
  The online store of Genealogical Publishing Co., Inc. & Clearfield Company.

- Hearthstone Bookshop—Scotland
  http://www.hearthstonebooks.com/Scotland.html

- Heritage Books—Scotland
  http://www.heritagebooks.com/scottish.htm

- Scottish Bibliography—From GENUKI
  http://www-theory.dcs.st-and.ac.uk/~mnd/genuki/biblio.html

- The Scottish Genealogy Society Sales and Publications
  http://www.taynet.co.uk/users/scotgensoc/sales.htm

- S.E.L. Enterprises
  http://www.mentornet.org/sel.htm
  Publications (books, magazines, periodicals & maps) for researching your English, Irish, Scots and Welsh ancestors.

- South Ayrshire Council—Publications for Sale
  http://www.south-ayrshire.gov.uk/Library/scot_local/Publics.htm

- Willow Bend Bookstore—Scotland and Scots-Irish
  http://www.willowbend.net/sco.htm

- Willow Bend Bookstore—Scots/Scots-Irish
  http://www.willowbend.net/scots.htm

◆ Queries, Message Boards & Surname Lists

- The UK & Ireland Genealogical Information Service (GENUKI)
  http://www.genuki.org.uk/
  ○ Surname Lists Index from GENUKI
    http://www.cs.ncl.ac.uk/genuki/SurnamesList/
    • Angus Scotland Surnames List
      http://www.geocities.com/Athens/Parthenon/5020/Angus/
    • Argyllshire, Scotland Surname List
      http://members.aol.com/sloinne/Argyll/Surnames.htm

- Ayrshire Surname Database
  http://home.clara.net/iainkerr/genuki/AYR/SID/
  indexsid.htm
- Banffshire Surname List
  http://www.rootsweb.com/~sctban/
- Berwickshire Surnames List
  http://www.geocities.com/Heartland/Valley/2039/
- Caithness Surnames Research List
  http://www.frayston.demon.co.uk/genuki/cai/
  surnames.htm
- Clackmannanshire Surname List
  http://www.dgnscrn.demon.co.uk/genuki/CLK/misc/
  surnames/
- County of Stirlingshire Surname List
  http://www.jeack.com.au/~treaclbk/surnames/stirling.htm
- County Sutherland, Scotland Surname List
  http://members.aol.com/sloinne/Sutherland/Surnames.htm
- East Lothian Surnames List
  http://www.users.zetnet.co.uk/vdunstan/genuki/ELN/
  Surnames/
- Kingdom of Fife Surnames List
  http://www.genuki.org.uk/big/scot/Fife/fife.surnames.html
- Kinross-shire Surname List
  http://www.dgnscrn.demon.co.uk/genuki/KRS/misc/
  surnames/index.html
- Lanarkshire Surnames List
  http://www.fan.net.au/~scoop/lanark.htm
- The Midlothian, Scotland Surnames List
  http://pages.prodigy.net/richrob/midlothian/
  midlothian.htm
- Nairnshire Surnames List
  http://www.geocities.com/~brooms/genuki/surnames/
  index.html
- The Orkney Surnames List
  http://www.tiac.net/users/teschek/genuki/OKI/
  surnames.htm
- Peeblesshire Surnames List
  http://www.rootsweb.com/~sctpbs/PSL.htm
- Perthshire, Scotland Surnames List
  http://www.geocities.com/Heartland/Plains/3176/perthlist/
  index.html
- Renfrewshire Surnames List
  http://www.skylinc.net/~lasmith/rfwnames/
- Selkirkshire Surnames List
  http://www.users.zetnet.co.uk/vdunstan/genuki/SEL/
  Surnames/
- Surname List: Dumfriesshire, Kirkcudbrightshire
  & Wigtownshire
  http://www.users.globalnet.co.uk/~brownfam/
  dfsnames.html
- West Lothian Surname List
  http://www.rootsweb.com/~sctwln/

◆ Records: Census, Cemeteries, Land, Obituaries, Personal, Taxes and Vital (Born, Married, Died & Buried)

- Anne's UK Certificates for Australians
  http://freespace.virgin.net/mark.wainwright6/uk_certificates/
  An Australian living in London who can obtain copies of English, Scottish & Welsh Birth, Marriage and Death Certificates in exchange for payment in Australian dollars.
- Ayrshire Archives
  http://www.south-ayrshire.gov.uk/Archives/Default.htm
  Hold the records of the former Ayr County Council and its predecessor organizations.
- Census Information from GENUKI
  http://www.genuki.org.uk/big/eng/census.html
  For England, Scotland & Wales.
- Dundee City Archive and Record Centre
  http://www.dundeecity.gov.uk/dcchtml/sservices/archives.html
- First Glasgow Directory 1787
  http://www.geocities.com/Heartland/Hills/2100/glasgowdir.htm
- General Register Office for Scotland Home Page
  http://www.open.gov.uk/gros/groshome.htm
  - GRO(S)—Frequently Asked Questions
    http://www.open.gov.uk/gros/faq.htm
  - Leaflet S1—List of Main Records in the Care of the Registrar General
    http://www.open.gov.uk/gros/leaflet1.htm
  - Leaflet S2—Searching by Our Staff for a Particular Event ('Particular Search')
    http://www.open.gov.uk/gros/leaflet2.htm
  - Leaflet S3—Guidance for General Search Customers in New Register House
    http://www.open.gov.uk/gros/leaflet3.htm
  - Leaflet S4—Group Evening Visits to New Register House
    http://www.open.gov.uk/gros/leaflet4.htm
  - Leaflet S5—Advertisements for Genealogical Services
    http://www.open.gov.uk/gros/leaflet5.htm
- Glasgow City Archives
  http://users.colloquium.co.uk/~glw_archives/src001.htm
  Holds the records of the Glasgow (City) Corporation, private, business, shipbuilding records and more.
- The Public Record Office Home Page
  http://www.pro.gov.uk/
  The Public Records Office holds a few records for Scotland. These include: service records for Scots serving in the British army after 1707 in Scottish regiments and non-Scottish regiments; some Scottish militia records; records regarding the Risings of 1715 and 1745; and some Scottish emigration records.

○ PRO Leaflet No. 4—Sources for the History of the Jacobite Rising of 1715 and 1745
ftp://sable.ox.ac.uk/pub/users/malcolm/genealogy/pro/ri004.txt
From the Public Record Office.

- Registrar of Births, Deaths and Marriages, Dundee
http://www.dundeecity.gov.uk/dcchtml/sservices/rbdm.html

- Registers of Scotland Executive Agency
http://www.open.gov.uk/ros/roshome.htm
Guide to Land, Sasine, Personal and Other Registers.

- Ron Taylor's UK Census Finding Aids and Indexes
http://rontay.digiweb.com/

  ○ Strays by County Census Indexes
  http://207.176.42.192/county/

    • Aberdeen Strays
    http://207.176.42.192/county/abd.htm

    • Angus Strays
    http://207.176.42.192/county/ans.htm

    • Argyll Strays
    http://207.176.42.192/county/arl.htm

    • Ayrshire Strays
    http://207.176.42.192/county/ayr.htm

    • Banff Strays
    http://207.176.42.192/county/ban.htm

    • Berwick Strays
    http://207.176.42.192/county/bew.htm

- Scots Origins
http://www.origins.net/GRO/
An online pay-per-view database of searchable indexes of the GRO(S) index to births/baptisms and banns/marriages from the Old Parish Registers dating from 1553 to 1854, plus the indexes to births, deaths and marriages from 1855 to 1897. The 1881 census data is expected later this year and an index to the 1891 census records is coming soon.

- Scottish Record Office
http://www-theory.dcs.st-and.ac.uk/~mnd/genuki/intro.html#SRO
The Scottish Record Office in Edinburgh is the home of the national archives of Scotland. Records of particular interest to family historians include: wills and testaments, non-conformist church records, Kirk Session records of the Established Church of Scotland, many legal and court records, land and estate records, and maps and plans.

  ○ A Guide to Family History by the Scottish Record Office
  http://www-saw.arts.ed.ac.uk/misc/genealogy/guide.html
  From the Scots at War Project.

○ Scottish Reference Information
http://www.ktb.net/~dwills/scotref/13300-scottishreference.htm
An extensive list of parish numbers and microfilm numbers to aid in doing Scottish research at an LDS Family History Center.

◆ Religion & Churches

- The Church of Scotland
http://www.cofs.org.uk/

- The Free Church of Scotland
http://www.freechurch.org/

- Presbytery of Orkney, Church of Scotland
http://members.aol.com/OrkneyPrsb/index.htm

- UK Churches—Church of Scotland
http://www.churchnet.org.uk/ukchurches/scotland/

◆ Societies & Groups

- Aberdeen & North East Scotland Family History Society
http://www.rsc.co.uk/anesfhs/

- Borders Family History Society
http://www.users.zetnet.co.uk/vdunstan/genuki/misc/bordersFHS.html
Covers the Scottish border counties of Roxburghshire, Berwickshire, Selkirkshire and Peeblesshire.

- Clan LAMONT Society of North America
http://www.jps.net/ogdenj/lamont/lamont.htm

- DISPATCH—Scottish Military Historical Society
http://subnet.virtual-pc.com/~mc546367/journal.htm

- Dumfries & Galloway Family History Society
http://www.users.globalnet.co.uk/~brownfam/dgfhs.html

- Fife Family History Society
http://wkweb4.cableinet.co.uk/donmanson/ffhs.html

- Glasgow & West of Scotland Family History Society
http://users.colloquium.co.uk/~alistair/gwsfhs/

- Scottish Genealogy Society
http://www.taynet.co.uk/users/scotgensoc/

- The Scottish Tartans Society
http://www.tartans.electricscotland.com/

- Tay Valley Family History Society
http://www.sol.co.uk/t/tayvalleyfhs/
Includes the former counties of Angus, Perthshire, Fife and Kinross in Scotland.

WALES / CYMRU
http://www.CyndisList.com/wales.htm

Category Index:

- ◆ General Resource Sites
- ◆ GENUKI Resources by County
- ◆ Government & Cities
- ◆ History & Culture
- ◆ Libraries, Archives & Museums
- ◆ Mailing Lists, Newsgroups & Chat
- ◆ Maps, Gazetteers & Geographical Information

- ◆ Professional Researchers, Volunteers & Other Research Services
- ◆ Publications, Software & Supplies
- ◆ Queries, Message Boards & Surname Lists
- ◆ Records: Census, Cemeteries, Land, Obituaries, Personal, Taxes and Vital
- ◆ Societies & Groups

◆ General Resource Sites

- ● North Wales Internet Genealogy Pages
  http://www.nwi.co.uk/famhist/fhinfo.htm
- ● Researching Ancestors from the United Kingdom
  http://www.oz.net/~markhow/uksearch.htm
  Using the LDS Family History Center Resources.
- ● South & West Wales Genealogical Index
  http://members.aol.com/swalesidx/
- ● The UK & Ireland Genealogical Information Service (GENUKI)
  http://www.genuki.org.uk/
  - ○ Digging Up Your Roots in Wales
    http://www.genuki.org.uk/big/wal/wales.html
    By Daniel L. Parry.
  - ○ Researching from Abroad
    http://www.genuki.org.uk/ab/
  - ○ Using the IGI for Wales and Monmouthshire
    http://www.genuki.org.uk/big/wal/WalesIGI.html
- ● Yahoo!...Wales...Genealogy
  http://dir.yahoo.com/Regional/Countries/United_Kingdom/Wales/Arts_and_Humanities/History/Genealogy/

◆ GENUKI Resources by County

- ● The UK & Ireland Genealogical Information Service (GENUKI)
  http://www.genuki.org.uk/
  - ○ Welsh Genealogy Index
    http://www.genuki.org.uk/big/wal/index.html
    - • Anglesey Genealogy
      http://www.genuki.org.uk/big/wal/AGY/
    - • Breconshire (Brecknockshire) Genealogy
      http://www.rapidagent.co.uk/genuki/BRE/
    - • Caernarvonshire Genealogy
      http://www.genuki.org.uk/big/wal/CAE/

- • Cardiganshire Genealogy
  http://www.semlyn.demon.co.uk/genuki/CGN/
- • Carmarthenshire Genealogy
  http://www.semlyn.demon.co.uk/genuki/CMN/
- • Denbighshire Genealogy
  http://www.genuki.org.uk/big/wal/DEN/
- • Flintshire Genealogy
  http://www.genuki.org.uk/big/wal/FLN/
- • Glamorgan Genealogy
  http://www.genuki.org.uk/big/wal/GLA/
- • Merionethshire Genealogy
  http://www.genuki.org.uk/big/wal/MER/
- • Monmouthshire Genealogy
  http://www.genuki.org.uk/big/wal/MON/
- • Montgomeryshire Genealogy
  http://www.rapidagent.co.uk/genuki/MGY/
- • Pembrokeshire Genealogy
  http://www.semlyn.demon.co.uk/genuki/PEM/
- • Radnorshire Genealogy
  http://www.rapidagent.co.uk/genuki/RAD/

◆ Government & Cities

- ● The Welsh Office / Y Swyddfa Gymreig
  http://www.welsh-ofce.gov.uk/

◆ History & Culture

- ● Wales—Other Sites of Interest
  http://www.madog.org/hotlist.html
- ● Welsh Language Course
  http://www.cs.brown.edu/fun/welsh/Welsh.html
- ● Yahoo!...Wales...History
  http://dir.yahoo.com/Regional/Countries/United_Kingdom/Wales/Arts_and_Humanities/History/

◆ Libraries, Archives & Museums

- A Guide to Genealogical Sources at the National Library of Wales
  http://www.genuki.org.uk/big/wal/NLW.html
  From the GENUKI Project.

- Llyfrgell Genedlaethol Cymru / National Library of Wales
  http://www.llgc.org.uk/
  ○ Department of Manuscripts and Records
    http://www.llgc.org.uk/lc/lcs0001.htm
    • A Guide to Genealogical Sources at National Library of Wales
      http://www.llgc.org.uk/lc/gg01.htm

◆ Mailing Lists, Newsgroups & Chat

- BlaenauGwent Mailing List
  http://members.aol.com/gfsjohnf/gen_mail_country-unk.
  html#BlaenauGwent
  For anyone with a genealogical interest in the areas of Nantyglo, Blaina, Brynmawr, Tredegar, Abertillery, and Llanhilleth in the county of Monmouthshire (Gwent), Great Britain.

- CARMARTHENSHIRE Mailing List
  http://members.aol.com/gfsjohnf/gen_mail_country-unk.
  html#CARMARTHENSHIRE

- CLWYD Mailing List
  http://members.aol.com/gfsjohnf/gen_mail_country-unk.
  html#CLWYD
  Sponsored by the Clwyd Family History Society for anyone with a genealogical or historical interest in north-east Wales, United Kingdom—in effect, the pre-1974 counties of Flintshire, Denbighshire and northern Meirioneth.

- COALMINERS Mailing List
  http://members.aol.com/gfsjohnf/gen_mail_country-unk.
  html#COALMINERS
  For anyone whose ancestors were coalminers in the United Kingdom or the United States.

- DYFED Mailing List
  http://members.aol.com/gfsjohnf/gen_mail_country-unk.
  html#DYFED
  For anyone with a genealogical interest in the Wales, United Kingdom counties of Cardiganshire, Carmartheshire, and Pembrokeshire.

- GENBRIT Mailing List
  http://members.aol.com/gfsjohnf/gen_mail_country-unk.
  html#GENBRIT
  For the discussion of genealogy in Great Britain and the islands. Gatewayed with the soc.genealogy.britain newsgroup.

- GLAMORGAN Mailing List
  http://members.aol.com/gfsjohnf/gen_mail_country-unk.
  html#GLAMORGAN

- POWYS Mailing List
  http://members.aol.com/gfsjohnf/gen_mail_country-unk.
  html#POWYS
  For anyone with a genealogical interest in the Wales, United Kingdom counties of Breconshire, Radnor, Montgomeryshire, Flint, Denbigh, Caernarfon, Anglesey, and Merionthshire.

- SURNAMES-BRITAIN Mailing List
  http://members.aol.com/gfsjohnf/gen_mail_country-unk.
  html#SURNAMES-BRITAIN
  For surname queries related to Great Britain. Gatewayed with the soc.genealogy.surnames.britain newsgroup.

- Wales-CC Mailing List
  http://members.aol.com/gfsjohnf/gen_mail_country-unk.
  html#Wales-CC
  For use by the WorldGenWeb County Coordinators for Wales, United Kingdom, to discuss the creation of single sources for genealogy databases dealing with their areas and the development of related County web pages.

- WELSH-L Mailing List
  http://members.aol.com/gfsjohnf/gen_mail_country-unk.
  html#WELSH-L
  For discussion of questions of the Welsh language, Welsh culture, history and politics, and to offer a forum for speakers and learners of the Welsh language.

◆ Maps, Gazetteers & Geographical Information

- Administrative Regions of the British Isles ~ From GENUKI
  http://www.genuki.org.uk/big/Regions/
  ○ Administrative Areas of Wales
    http://www.genuki.org.uk/big/Regions/Wales.html

- A Clickable Map of Cardiff
  http://www.cm.cf.ac.uk/lsmaps/cardiff.html

- Counties of England, Scotland and Wales Prior to the 1974 Boundary Changes
  http://www.genuki.org.uk/big/BRITAIN2.GIF

- The Data Wales Maps Page
  http://www.data-wales.co.uk/walesmap.htm

- Large Map of Wales
  ftp://sunsite.unc.edu/pub/academic/languages/welsh/wales.gif

- Multi Media Mapping
  http://uk5.multimap.com/map/places.cgi
  An interactive atlas of Great Britain. Enter the name of a British city, town or village to get a clickable, zoomable, detailed map.

- Ordnance Survey—Gazetteer of Place Names
  http://www.campus.bt.com/CampusWorld/pub/OS/Gazetteer/
  index.html

◆ Professional Researchers, Volunteers & Other Research Services

- Ancestral Roots
  E-mail: AncestralRoots@annescales.freeserve.co.uk
  Genealogical Research in SE Wales: Glamorgan and Monmouthshire/Gwent. For details please send e-mail to: Anne Scales MSc BA, AncestralRoots@annescales.freeserve.co.uk

- GenealogyPro—Professional Genealogists for England and Wales
  http://genealogyPro.com/directories/England-Wales.html

- Mentro Cymru—Tracing Your Welsh Heritage with Origin Quest
  http://dialspace.dial.pipex.com/pamb.mentro-cymru/
- Nicholas J. Davey, Researcher for Glamorgan and Monmouthshire
  E-mail: ndavey@baynet.co.uk
  E-mail Nicholas Davey for details at: ndavey@baynet.co.uk
- Wales Look-up Exchange
  http://freespace.virgin.net/m.harbach/wales/lookupw.html

◆ Publications, Software & Supplies

- Books We Own—Wales
  http://www.rootsweb.com/~bwo/wales.html
- Frontier Press Bookstore—Welsh Research
  http://www.frontierpress.com/frontier.cgi?category=welsh
- GenealogyBookShop.com—Wales/Welsh
  http://www.genealogybookshop.com/genealogybookshop/files/The_World,Wales_Welsh/index.html
  The online store of Genealogical Publishing Co., Inc. & Clearfield Company.
- Hearthstone Books—Wales
  http://www.hearthstonebooks.com/Wales.html
- Heritage Books—Welsh
  http://www.heritagebooks.com/welsh.htm
- S.E.L. Enterprises
  http://www.mentornet.org/sel.htm
  Publications (books, magazines, periodicals & maps) for researching your English, Irish, Scots and Welsh ancestors.
- Willow Bend Bookstore—Wales and Welshmen
  http://www.willowbend.net/wales.htm

◆ Queries, Message Boards & Surname Lists

- Julie's Welsh Surnames List
  http://home.on.rogers.wave.ca/bozzy/index.html
  A page for posting Welsh surnames being researched online.
- The UK & Ireland Genealogical Information Service (GENUKI)
  http://www.genuki.org.uk/
  - GENUKI Surname Lists
    http://www.cs.ncl.ac.uk/genuki/SurnamesList/
    - Anglesey, Wales
      http://www.genuki.org.uk/big/wal/Surnames/agy.htm
    - Breconshire, Wales
      http://www.genuki.org.uk/big/wal/Surnames/bre.htm
    - Caernarfonshire, Wales
      http://www.genuki.org.uk/big/wal/Surnames/cae.htm
    - Cardiganshire, Wales
      http://www.genuki.org.uk/big/wal/Surnames/cgn.htm

- Carmarthenshire, Wales
  http://www.genuki.org.uk/big/wal/Surnames/cmn.htm
- Denbighshire, Wales
  http://www.genuki.org.uk/big/wal/Surnames/den.htm
- Flintshire, Wales
  http://www.genuki.org.uk/big/wal/Surnames/fln.htm
- Glamorgan, Wales
  http://www.genuki.org.uk/big/wal/Surnames/gla.htm
- Merionethshire, Wales
  http://www.genuki.org.uk/big/wal/Surnames/mer.htm
- Monmouthshire, Wales
  http://www.genuki.org.uk/big/wal/Surnames/mon.htm
- Montgomeryshire, Wales
  http://www.genuki.org.uk/big/wal/Surnames/mgy.htm
- Pembrokeshire, Wales
  http://www.genuki.org.uk/big/wal/Surnames/pem.htm
- Radnorshire, Wales
  http://www.genuki.org.uk/big/wal/Surnames/rad.htm

◆ Records: Census, Cemeteries, Land, Obituaries, Personal, Taxes and Vital (Born, Married, Died & Buried)

- Anne's UK Certificates for Australians
  http://freespace.virgin.net/mark.wainwright6/uk_certificates/
  An Australian living in London who can obtain copies of English, Scottish & Welsh Birth, Marriage and Death Certificates in exchange for payment in Australian dollars.
- Cardiff Records Home Page
  http://easyweb.easynet.co.uk/~psewell/cr/cr.html
- Census Information from GENUKI
  http://www.genuki.org.uk/big/eng/census.html
  For England, Scotland & Wales.
- Civil Registration in England and Wales
  http://www.genuki.org.uk/big/eng/civreg/
  GENUKI
- Cyngor Archifau Cymru / Archives Council Wales
  http://www.llgc.org.uk/cac/
  - Sefydliadau Archifol Cymru / Archive Repositories in Wales
    http://www.llgc.org.uk/cac/cac0023.htm
    - Anglesey County Record Office
      http://www.llgc.org.uk/cac/cac0036.htm
    - Caernarfon Record Office
      http://www.llgc.org.uk/cac/cac0053.htm
    - Carmarthenshire Archives Service
      http://www.llgc.org.uk/cac/cac0028.htm
    - Ceredigion Archives
      http://www.llgc.org.uk/cac/cac0009.htm

- Conwy Archives Service
  http://www.llgc.org.uk/cac/cac0035.htm
- Denbighshire Record Office
  http://www.llgc.org.uk/cac/cac0011.htm
- Flintshire Record Office
  http://www.llgc.org.uk/cac/cac0032.htm
- Glamorgan Record Office
  http://www.llgc.org.uk/cac/cac0026.htm
- Gwent Record Office
  http://www.llgc.org.uk/cac/cac0004.htm
- Merioneth Record Office
  http://www.llgc.org.uk/cac/cac0030.htm
- Pembrokeshire Record Office
  http://www.llgc.org.uk/cac/cac0002.htm
- West Glamorgan Archive Service
  http://www.llgc.org.uk/cac/cac0019.htm
- Wrexham Archives Service
  http://www.llgc.org.uk/cac/cac0038.htm

- England and Wales Birth, Marriage, and Death Certificate Information
  http://shoppersmart.com/otown/registrations/
- English and Welsh Register Offices
  http://www.genuki.org.uk/big/eng/RegOffice/
- Finding an Address in the Transcription of the 1881 Census of England and Wales
  http://people.enternet.com.au/~tmj/c81-adrs.htm
- Index to "Paupers in Workhouses 1861" (10% sample)
  http://www.genuki.org.uk/big/eng/Paupers/
  This lists adult paupers in workhouses in England and Wales
- Llanelli Marriages 1833–1837 St Elli Parish Church, South Wales, UK
  ftp://ftp.rootsweb.com/pub/wggenweb/southwales/vitals/llanelli.txt
  Also Llanelli Marriages 1864–1867 Taken from Llanelli Guardian Births, Deaths & Marriages.
- ONS Services—Certificates of Births, Marriages and Deaths
  http://www.ons.gov.uk/services/cert.htm
  England and Wales.
- Ordering Birth Registration Certificates from the England & Wales
  http://www.oz.net/~markhow/ukbirths.htm
  Using the LDS Family History Center Resources.
- Powys County Archives Office
  http://www.powys.gov.uk/pcc/archives/default.HTM
  - Powys Archives—Guide to Holdings: Brecknockshire Records
    http://www.powys.gov.uk/pcc/archives/info/Brec/BREC1.HTM

  - Powys Archives—Guide to Holdings: Montgomeryshire Records
    http://www.powys.gov.uk/pcc/archives/info/Mont/MONT1.HTM
  - Powys Archives—Guide to Holdings: Radnorshire Records
    http://www.powys.gov.uk/pcc/archives/info/Rad/RADN1.HTM
- The Public Record Office Home Page
  http://www.pro.gov.uk/
  - About the Family Records Centre
    http://www.pro.gov.uk/about/frc/
  - Information For Genealogists
    http://www.pro.gov.uk/readers/genealogists/default.htm
    - Public Record Office—Family Fact Sheets
      http://www.pro.gov.uk/readers/genealogists/familyfacts.htm
- Ron Taylor's UK Census Finding Aids and Indexes
  http://rontay.digiweb.com/
  - Strays by County Census Indexes
    http://207.176.42.192/county/
    - Anglesey Strays
      http://207.176.42.192/county/agy.htm

◆ Societies & Groups

- Cardiganshire Family History Society / Cymdeithas Hanes Teuluoedd Ceredigion
  http://www.celtic.co.uk/~heaton/cgnfhs/
- Carmarthenshire Family History Society
  http://members.aol.com/cmnfhs1/
- Clwyd Family History Society
  http://www.genuki.org.uk/big/wal/FLN/ClwydFHS/
- Dyfed Family History Society
  http://www.westwales.co.uk/dfhs/dfhs.htm
- Glamorgan Family History Society
  http://members.aol.com/gfhsoc/index.htm
- Gwynedd Family History Society
  http://www.nol.co.uk/~gwyfhs/
- Montgomeryshire Genealogical Society / Cymdeithas Achyddol Maldwyn
  http://www.netcollect.co.uk/coins/Genealogy/
- Powys Family History Society
  http://ourworld.compuserve.com/homepages/michaelmacsorley/powys1.htm
- Roath Local History Society
  http://www.cf.ac.uk//ccin/main/socecon/roath/church/lochist.html
  Cardiff, Wales, U.K.

UNITED STATES INDEX

- ◆ U.S. – General U.S. Sites
- ◆ U.S. – Library of Congress
- ◆ U.S. – National Archives
- ◆ U.S. – Social Security
- ◆ U.S. – Territories & Possessions
- ◆ U.S. – Census
- ◆ U.S. – Civil War ~ War for Southern Independence
- ◆ U.S. – History
- ◆ U.S. – Military
- ◆ Alphabetical listing by state

GENERAL U.S. SITES
http://www.CyndisList.com/genusa.htm

Category Index:

- General Resource Sites
- Government & Cities
- History & Culture
- Libraries, Archives & Museums
- Mailing Lists, Newsgroups & Chat
- Maps, Gazetteers & Geographical Information
- Military
- Newspapers
- People & Families

- Professional Researchers, Volunteers & Other Research Services
- Publications, Software & Supplies
- Queries, Message Boards & Surname Lists
- Records: Census, Cemeteries, Land, Obituaries, Personal, Taxes and Vital
- Religion & Churches
- Societies & Groups

◆ General Resource Sites

- Genealogy in the United States from Everton's
  http://www.everton.com/usa.html

- Genealogy Resources on the Internet: United States
  http://www-personal.umich.edu/~cgaunt/united_states.html

- ROOTS-L Resources: United States Resources
  http://www.rootsweb.com/roots-l/usa.html
  Comprehensive list of research links, including many to history-related sites.

- Territories & Possessions
  http://www.CyndisList.com/territor.htm
  See this category on Cyndi's List for related links.

- USGenWeb Project
  http://www.usgenweb.org/
  - USGenWeb Archives—Table of Contents
    http://www.rootsweb.com/~usgenweb/
  - USGenWeb Census Project
    http://www.usgenweb.org/census/
  - USGenWeb Tombstone Transcription Project
    http://www.rootsweb.com/~cemetery/

- U.S. States Research Outlines
  http://www.everton.com/usa/us-gen.txt
  From the Family History Library, Salt Lake City, Utah.

- Yahoo!...United States...Genealogy
  http://dir.yahoo.com/Arts/Humanities/History/Genealogy/Regional_and_Ethnic_Resources/United_States/

◆ Government & Cities

- City.Net United States
  http://www.city.net/countries/united_states/
  A site meant for travel which contains links & resources for all sorts of U.S. geographic information.

- The International Chamber of Commerce & City-State-Province Directory
  http://Chamber-of-Commerce.com/

- State Search—Sponsored by NASIRE
  http://www.nasire.org/ss/index.html
  "Designed to serve as a topical clearinghouse to state government information on the Internet."
  - State Homepages
    http://www.nasire.org/ss/STstates.html

- USA CityLink Project
  http://banzai.neosoft.com/citylink/

◆ History & Culture

- U.S. History
  http://www.CyndisList.com/hist-us.htm
  See this category on Cyndi's List for related links.

◆ Libraries, Archives & Museums

- Directory of Genealogy Libraries in the U.S.
  http://www.greenheart.com/rdietz/gen_libs.htm

- Family History Centers
  http://www.genhomepage.com/FHC/
  Listing from the Genealogy Home Page, with a state by state index.

- Family History Centers in the USA
  http://www.everton.com/fhcusa.html
  From Everton's Genealogical Helper.

- Family History Centers of: The Church of Jesus Christ of Latter-day Saints
  http://www.deseretbook.com/famhis/
  State by state index.

- HYTELNET—Library Catalogs: United States
  http://library.usask.ca/hytelnet/usa/usall.html
  Before you use any of the Telnet links, make note of the user name, password and any other logon information.

- Japanese American National Museum
  http://www.artcom.com/museums/nv/gl/90012-39.htm
  Has a collection of microfiche records covering the Japanese American internment camps of WWII (1942–1945).

- LDS Family History Centers United States of America
  http://www.dungeon.com/~deltatango/fhcusa.html

- Library of Congress
  http://www.CyndisList.com/libofcon.htm
  See this category on Cyndi's List for related links.

- National Archives
  http://www.CyndisList.com/na.htm
  See this category on Cyndi's List for related links.

- NUCMC Listing of Archives and Manuscript Repositories in the United States
  http://lcweb.loc.gov/coll/nucmc/ussites.html
  Links to information about resources other than those held in the Library of Congress.

- U.S. Public Libraries with Websites
  http://www.capecod.net/epl/public.libraries.html

- webCATS: Library Catalogues on the World Wide Web—United States
  http://library.usask.ca/hywebcat/countries/US.html

◆ Mailing Lists, Newsgroups & Chat

Each of the mailing list links below points to this site, wonderfully maintained by John Fuller. Visit his site for county-specific mailing lists as well.

- See these pages on Cyndi's List for related mailing list topics:
  - U.S. Civil War
    http://www.CyndisList.com/cw.htm
  - U.S. Military
    http://www.CyndisList.com/military.htm

- COALMINERS Mailing List
  http://members.aol.com/gfsjohnf/gen_mail_country-unk.
  html#COALMINERS
  For anyone whose ancestors were coalminers in the United Kingdom or the United States.

- Colonial-America Mailing List
  http://members.aol.com/gfsjohnf/gen_mail_states-gen.
  html#Colonial-America
  For discussing the history of our ancestors.

- EURO-JEWISH Mailing List
  http://members.aol.com/johnf14246/gen_mail_general.
  html#EURO-JEWISH
  For anyone with a genealogical interest in the Migration, History, Culture, Heritage and Surname search of the Jewish people from Europe to the United States and their descendants in the United States.

- GERMAN-AMERICAN Mailing List
  http://members.aol.com/gfsjohnf/gen_mail_states-gen.
  html#GERMAN-AMERICAN
  For genealogy related to German immigrants and their families AFTER their arrival in America.

- GLSHIPS Mailing List
  http://members.aol.com/gfsjohnf/gen_mail_states-gen.
  html#GLSHIPS
  For anyone who is researching ancestors who participated in the shipping industry on the Great Lakes of the northeastern United States.

- Homesteaders Mailing List
  http://members.aol.com/gfsjohnf/gen_mail_states-gen.
  html#Homesteaders
  For researching the history of our homesteader ancestors; to share information on how they lived, post stories from your family, and share genealogical information.

- LOYALIST-IN-CANADA Mailing List
  http://members.aol.com/johnf14246/gen_mail_geo-nonusa.
  html#LOYALIST
  For those with loyalist ancestors to help one another research their loyalist history and to post any facts on the subject that they desire. Loyalists are defined as those who left the United States for Canada after the American Revolution for a number of reasons.

- Melungeon Mailing List
  http://members.aol.com/gfsjohnf/gen_mail_states-gen.
  html#MELUNGEO
  For people conducting Melungeon and/or Appalachian research including Native American, Portuguese, Turkish, Black Dutch, and other unverifiable mixed statements of ancestry or unexplained rumors, with ancestors in TN, KY, VA, NC, SC, GA, AL, WV, and possibly other places.

- METISGEN Mailing List
  http://members.aol.com/johnf14246/gen_mail_general.
  html#METISGEN
  For the discussion and sharing of information regarding the Metis and their descendants. The Metis are North America's Fur Trading Children . . . the new nation of individuals born within North America from the first unions of natives and whites.

- newengland-gene Mailing List
  http://members.aol.com/gfsjohnf/gen_mail_states-gen.
  html#newengland-gene

- Overland-Trails Mailing List
  http://members.aol.com/gfsjohnf/gen_mail_states-gen.
  html#Overland-Trails
  Discussions concerning the history, preservation, and promotion of the Oregon, California, Sante Fe, and other historic trails in the Western USA.

- PreussenAmericans Mailing List
  http://members.aol.com/gfsjohnf/gen_mail_country-ger.
  html#PreussenAmericans
  For anyone with a genealogical interest in Prussian immigrants to America.

- RiverRats Mailing List
  http://members.aol.com/gfsjohnf/gen_mail_states-gen.
  html#RiverRats
  For discussions of the Mississippi River "people" living on, working on, and involved in life on the "river." Any family living in any county bordering the Mississippi River, or living "on" the river, is welcome.

- SANTA-FE-TRAIL Mailing List
  http://members.aol.com/gfsjohnf/gen_mail_states-gen.
  html#SANTA-FE-TRAIL

- SCHAKEL-NL Mailing List
  http://members.aol.com/johnf14246/gen_mail_geo-nonusa.
  html#SCHAKEL-NL
  For discussions of news events and issues of interest to Canadians and Americans of Dutch origin; Dutch heritage, customs and traditions; immigrant experiences; questions about Dutch legislation, laws, regulations, history etc.; living the Dutch way (e.g., travel, food, drinks); and the ties that bind us. Queries from genealogists related to their Dutch ancestry are welcome.

- Scotch-Irish-L Mailing List
  http://members.aol.com/johnf14246/gen_mail_geo-nonusa.
  html#Scotch-Irish-L
  For Scotch-Irish or Ulster Scots genealogy and culture. These people began a period of heavy emigration from Ulster in the early 1700's and played a large part in the American Revolution.

- SLAVEINFO Mailing List
  http://members.aol.com/gfsjohnf/gen_mail_states-gen.
  html#SLAVEINFO
  For the sharing of genealogical data about slaves in the United States including wills/deeds that show sales and transfer of ownership, vital records (e.g., birth, marriage, death), and information/queries on specific slaves that may be part of your ancestry.

- Southern-Trails Mailing List
  http://members.aol.com/gfsjohnf/gen_mail_states-gen.
  html#Southern-Trails
  For the discussion and sharing of information regarding migration routes in the Southern United States and the people who used them.

- SURNAMES-USA Mailing List
  http://members.aol.com/gfsjohnf/gen_mail_surnames-gen.
  html#SURNAMES-USA
  For surname queries related to the United States. Gatewayed with the soc.genealogy.surnames.usa newsgroup.

- trails west Mailing List
  http://members.aol.com/gfsjohnf/gen_mail_states-gen.
  html#trails-west
  For those who want to research their family history and post facts on their move west in North America. The trails addressed by the list started at the very beginning of the settlement of North America and are not just the ones in western North America.

- USBIOG Mailing List
  http://members.aol.com/gfsjohnf/gen_mail_states-
  gen.html#USBIOG
  For people who are interested in helping coordinate a collection of biographies within their state as part of the US Biographies project.

◆ Maps, Gazetteers & Geographical Information

- Ancestry Groups in the United States—Maps
  http://www.lmic.state.mn.us/dnet/maplib/ancestry/
  usancest.htm

- Boundaries of the United States and the Several States
  http://www.wwu.edu/~stephan/48states.html
  with an animated GIF map of the settlement of the United States.
  http://www.rootsweb.com/~kygreenu/images/48states.gif

- Color Landform Atlas of the United States
  http://fermi.jhuapl.edu/states/states.html

- Evolution of United States County Boundaries
  http://www.wwu.edu/~stephan/Animation/us.html
  and an animated GIF showing county boundaries for 1650, 1700, 1750, and census years from 1790 onward.
  http://www.wwu.edu/~stephan/Animation/us.gif

- Geographic Names Database
  ftp://ftp.eecs.umich.edu/pub/eecs/geo/
  - Format of the Geographic Names Database
    ftp://ftp.eecs.umich.edu/pub/eecs/geo/README

- Geographic NameServer
  http://www.mit.edu:8001/geo
  Enter a city or place name and receive the county & state name as well as other geographic information.

- Historical County Lines
  http://www.geocities.com/Heartland/2297/maps.htm

- Historical Maps of the United States
  http://www.lib.utexas.edu:80/Libs/PCL/Map_collection/
  histus.html

- International Research—Migration Charts
  http://www.intl-research.com/migration.htm
  - Eastern United States Migration
    http://www.intl-research.com/images/eastbig.gif
  - Northern United States Migration
    http://www.intl-research.com/images/eastbig.gif
  - Western United States Migration
    http://www.intl-research.com/images/west.gif

- List of United States Counties—Home Page
  http://www.genealogy.org/PAF/www/counties/

- Tiger Mapping Service Home Page
  http://tiger.census.gov/

- U.S. County Outline Maps
  http://www.lib.utexas.edu/Libs/PCL/Map_collection/
  county_outline.html

- U.S. Gazetteer—From the U.S. Census Bureau
  http://www.census.gov/cgi-bin/gazetteer

- USGS Mapping Information: GNIS Data Base Query Form
  http://mapping.usgs.gov/www/gnis/gnisform.html

- U.S. Surname Distribution Maps
  http://www.hamrick.com/names/index.html

- U.S. Territorial Maps 1775–1920
  http://xroads.virginia.edu/~MAP/terr_hp.html

- WWW Thematic Mapping System
  http://www.census.gov/themapit/www/
  Create, view and print maps with specific themes from U.S. census data.

- Yale Peabody Museum: Geographic Names Information System (GNIS)
  http://www.peabody.yale.edu/other/gnis/
  Search the USGS Geographic Names Database. You can limit the search to a specific county in this state and search for any of the following features: airport arch area arroyo bar basin bay beach bench bridge **building** *canal cape* **cemetery** *channel* **church** *cliff crater crossing dam falls flat forest gap geyser glacier gut harbor hospital island isthmus lake lava levee locale mine oilfield other park pillar plain ppl range rapids reserve reservoir ridge* **school** *sea slope spring stream summit swamp tower trail tunnel valley well woods.*

- Yahoo! Maps
  http://www.proximus.com/yahoo/
  Enter a street address for a U.S. city or state and the map is displayed for you.

◆ Military

- Law Enforcement Memorial Links
  http://www.policememorial.com/memoriallinks.htm
  Links to many sites regarding law enforcement officials who died in the line of duty. Some have historic lists of names.

- U.S. Civil War ~ War for Southern Independence
  http://www.CyndisList.com/cw.htm
  See this category on Cyndi's List for related links.

- U.S. Military
  http://www.CyndisList.com/military.htm
  See this category on Cyndi's List for related links.

◆ Newspapers

- AJR NewsLink: National Newspapers
  http://www.newslink.org/dayn.html

- Cybermart News Online
  http://www.cybermart.net/Newspapers/US_News/

- E&P Media Info Links—Newspaper Sites in United States
  http://www.mediainfo.com/emediajs/media-types.htm?
  location=us++++++++++++++++++++++++++++++++++++++&
  category=newspaper+++++++++

- Gebbie Press—Daily Newspapers on the Web
  http://www.gebbieinc.com/dailyint.htm

- Ecola Newstand: United States Newspapers
  http://www.ecola.com/news/press/na/us/

- NAA Hotlinks: Alphabetical Listing of U.S. Daily Newspapers
  http://www.naa.org/hotlinks/all.html

- N-Net—United States Newspaper List
  http://www.n-net.com/

- The Ultimate Collection of News Links: Canada & USA—Nationwide & Online Only
  http://www.pppp.net/links/news/NA.html

- The United States Newspaper Program Participants
  http://www.neh.fed.us/html/usnp.html

- US Newspaper Archives on the Web
  http://sunsite.unc.edu/slanews/internet/archives.html

- Yahoo!...Newspapers...U.S. States
  http://dir.yahoo.com/News_and_Media/Newspapers/
  Browse_By_Region/U_S__States/

◆ People & Families

- Geographical Index to the Tribes of the United States and Canada
  http://hanksville.phast.umass.edu:8000/cultprop/contacts/
  tribal/US.html

- Just The Facts
  http://www.mindspring.com/~czar1/pres/
  Facts about U.S. Presidents, First Ladies and Vice Presidents.

- Loyalists
  http://www.CyndisList.com/loyalist.htm
  See this category on Cyndi's List for related links.

- Maryland Catholics on the Frontier
  http://www.pastracks.com/mcf/
  For descendants of Maryland Catholics who migrated westward. They first went to Kentucky and from there to other parts of the Frontier.

- The Melungeon Ancestry Research and Information Page
  http://www.bright.net/~kat/melung.htm

◆ Professional Researchers, Volunteers & Other Research Services

- AAG International Research—Professional Genealogists and Family Historians
  http://www.intl-research.com/
  Accredited genealogists & family historians specializing in family history research, development & publication. Accredited by the Family History Library in Salt Lake City, the world's largest genealogical library. Tax deductions for LDS research.

- Association of Professional Genealogists
  http://www.apgen.org/~apg/
  Denver, Colorado

- genealogyPro—Professional Genealogists for the United States
  http://genealogyPro.com/directories/USA.html

- The Official Iowa Counties Professional Genealogist and Researcher's Registry for United States
  http://www.iowa-counties.com/gene/us.htm

- Professional Genealogical Researchers—All Locations—World Wide
  http://www.iowa-counties.com/gene/professional.htm
  Includes a state by state index. From the Official Iowa Counties web site.

◆ Publications, Software & Supplies

- Ancestor Publishers Microfiche—United States
  http://www.firstct.com/fv/us.html

- Ancestor's Attic Discount Genealogy Books—United States Books
  http://members.tripod.com/~ancestorsattic/index.html#US

- Appleton's Fine Used Bookseller and Genealogy—US/State Genealogy Books
  http://www.appletons.com/genealogy/geneusbk.html

- Books We Own—United States Historical Events, General, and Multiple States
  http://www.rootsweb.com/~bwo/us_hist.html

- Books We Own—New England
  http://www.rootsweb.com/~bwo/new_england.html

- Books We Own—Southern U.S.
  http://www.rootsweb.com/~bwo/south.html

- Books We Own—Western U.S.
  http://www.rootsweb.com/~bwo/west.html

- GenealogyBookShop.com—The United States
  The online store of Genealogical Publishing Co., Inc. & Clearfield Company.
  http://www.genealogybookshop.com/genealogybookshop/files/The_United_States.html
  - Mid-Atlantic
    http://www.genealogybookshop.com/genealogybookshop/files/The_United_States,Mid-Atlantic/index.html
  - Midwest
    http://www.genealogybookshop.com/genealogybookshop/files/The_United_States,Midwest/index.html
  - New England
    http://www.genealogybookshop.com/genealogybookshop/files/The_United_States,New_England/index.html
  - South
    http://www.genealogybookshop.com/genealogybookshop/files/The_United_States,South/index.html
  - Vital Records
    http://www.genealogybookshop.com/genealogybookshop/files/General,Vital_Records/index.html

- Genealogy USA—Pentref Press
  http://www.genealogyusa.com/home.html
  Several quarterlies; specializing in colonial American genealogy, all eastern seaboard families, Quebec to Florida, 1600s to 1700s.

- Heritage Books—United States
  http://www.heritagebooks.com/us.htm

◆ Queries, Message Boards & Surname Lists

- Indian Captives of Early American Pioneers
  http://www.rootsweb.com/~indian/index.htm

◆ Records: Census, Cemeteries, Land, Obituaries, Personal, Taxes and Vital (Born, Married, Died & Buried)

- Arlington National Cemetery
  http://www.arlingtoncemetery.com/

- The Bureau of Land Management
  http://www.blm.gov/

- National Personnel Records Center
  http://www.nara.gov/nara/frc/nprc.html

- Requesting Your Ancestor's Naturalization Records from the INS
  http://www.brigadoon.com/~jwilson/gen/maher/immigrate.html
  A guide by Dennis Piccirillo.

- Social Security
  http://www.CyndisList.com/socsec.htm
  See this category on Cyndi's List for related links.

- Soundex Conversion Program from Genealogy Online
  http://www.genealogy.org/soundex.shtml

- Soundex Conversion Program—Surname to Soundex Code
  http://searches.rootsweb.com/cgi-bin/Genea/soundex.sh

- U.S. Census
  http://www.CyndisList.com/census.htm
  See this category on Cyndi's List for related links.

- USGenWeb Archive Census Project
  http://www.usgenweb.org/census/states/

- Using Federal Documents in Genealogical Research—U.S.
  http://www.history.rochester.edu/jssn/page1.htm

- Vital Records Information—United States
  http://vitalrec.com/index.html

- Where to Write for Vital Records Download Site
  http://www.cdc.gov/nchswww/howto/w2w/w2welcom.htm

◆ Religion & Churches

- Christianity.Net Church Locator—United States
  http://www.christianity.net/cgi/location.exe?United_States

- Church Online!—United States
  http://www.churchonline.com/usas/usas.html

- Church Profiles—United States
  http://www.church-profiles.com/states.html

- Churches dot Net—Global Church Web Pages—United States
  http://www.churches.net/churches/full.htm

- Churches of the World—United States
  http://www.churchsurf.com/churches/index.htm
  From the ChurchSurf Christian Directory.

- NetChurch Church Directory—United States
  http://www.netchurch.com/churchlist_active_US.asp
- The United States Catholic Historical Society
  http://www.catholic.org/uschs/

◆ Societies & Groups

- American Antiquarian Society
  gopher://mark.mwa.org/
  Founded in 1812 in Worcester, Massachusetts.
- The American Historical Association
  http://chnm.gmu.edu/aha/index.html
- America's First Families Society
  http://www.linkline.com/personal/xymox/
- Archer's Computer Interest Group List—
  U.S. National
  http://www.genealogy.org/~ngs/cigs/ngl1usus.html
- Dames of the Loyal Legion of the United States
  of America
  http://www.usmo.com/~momollus/DOLLUS.HTM
- Federation of Genealogical Societies
  http://www.fgs.org/
- Genealogical and Historical Societies in the USA
  http://www.outfitters.com/genealogy/gensoc/usgensoc.html

- National Genealogical Society
  http://www.ngsgenealogy.org/
  Arlington, Virginia
- National Japanese American Historical Society
  http://www.nikkeiheritage.org/index.html
- National Maritime Historical Society
  http://www.marineart.com/nmhs/index.shtml
- National Railway Historical Society
  http://www.rrhistorical.com/nrhs/
- National Society Colonial Dames XVII Century
  http://www.geocities.com/Heartland/Meadows/4399/cdxvii.html
- National Society of the Daughters of the American
  Revolution Home Page
  http://www.dar.org/index.html
- National Society Sons and Daughters of the Pilgrims
  http://www.nssdp.org
  *The NSSDP is a national lineage society whose members have
  proven lineal descent from any immigrant to the American
  Colonies prior to 1700.*
- United States Capitol Historical Society
  http://www.uschs.org/
- The United States Catholic Historical Society
  http://www.catholic.org/uschs/

U.S.—LIBRARY OF CONGRESS
http://www.CyndisList.com/libofcon.htm

- **Library of Congress Home Page**
  http://lcweb.loc.gov/
  - American Life Histories: Manuscripts from the Federal Writers' Project, 1936–1940
    http://lcweb2.loc.gov/ammem/wpaintro/wpahome.html
    "These life histories were written by the staff of the Folklore Project of the Federal Writers' Project for the U.S. Works Progress (later Work Projects) Administration (WPA) from 1936–1940. The Library of Congress collection includes 2,900 documents representing the work of over 300 writers from 24 states."
  - American Memory—Historical Collections for the National Digital Library
    http://rs6.loc.gov/amhome.html
  - City Directories at the Library of Congress
    http://www.kinquest.com/genealogy/citydir.html
  - Land Ownership Maps in the Library of Congress
    http://www.kinquest.com/genealogy/lom.html
    A list by state, county and year, of the maps available in the collection held at the Library of Congress.
  - Library of Congress: American Special Collections
    http://lcweb.loc.gov/spcoll/spclhome.html
  - Library of Congress Cataloging Directorate
    http://lcweb.loc.gov/catdir/catdir.html
  - Library of Congress Newspaper and Current Periodical Reading Room
    http://lcweb.loc.gov/rr/news/ncp.html
    Newspapers
    http://lcweb.loc.gov/rr/news/lcnewsp.html
    Periodicals
    http://lcweb.loc.gov/rr/news/lcper.html
    - 17th & 18th Century Foreign Newspapers
      http://lcweb.loc.gov/rr/news/17th/178th.html
    - Full-Text Journals Available in the Newspaper and Current Periodical Reading Room
      http://lcweb.loc.gov/rr/news/full.html
    - How To Find A Newspaper In This Reading Room
      gopher://marvel.loc.gov:70/00/research/reading.rooms/newspaper/bibs.guides/newspap.bib
    - Internet Resources Outside the Library of Congress
      http://lcweb.loc.gov/rr/news/othint.html
    - Lists of Newspaper & Periodical Resources on the Internet
      http://lcweb.loc.gov/rr/news/lists.html
    - Online Newspaper Indexes Available in the Newspaper and Current Periodical Reading Room
      http://lcweb.loc.gov/rr/news/npindex2.html
  - Library of Congress Online Catalog
    http://lcweb.loc.gov/homepage/online.html
    Search via Telnet or via the Web gateway with keywords.
  - Library of Congress WWW/Z39.50 Gateway
    http://lcweb.loc.gov/z3950/gateway.html
    Search Library of Congress Catalog and search other catalogs including colleges, universities and libraries.
  - National Union Catalog of Manuscript Collections (NUCMC)
    http://lcweb.loc.gov/coll/nucmc/nucmc.html
    A free-of-charge cooperative cataloging program operated by the Library of Congress.
    - NUCMC Cataloging
      http://lcweb.loc.gov/coll/nucmc/nucmccat.html
    - NUCMC Online Cataloging RLIN AMC File Search Form
      http://lcweb.loc.gov/z3950/rlinamc.html
      Via the Library of Congress gateway
  - Other Library of Congress Resources Menu
    http://lcweb.loc.gov/coll/nucmc/lc.html
    Including Library of Congress reading rooms with archival and manuscript material:
    - African and Middle Eastern Division
      gopher://marvel.loc.gov/11/research/reading.rooms/african
    - American Folklife Center
      http://lcweb.loc.gov/folklife
    - Asian Division
      gopher://marvel.loc.gov/11/research/reading.rooms/asian
    - European Division
      gopher://marvel.loc.gov/11/research/reading.rooms/european
    - Geography and Map Division
      gopher://marvel.loc.gov/11/research/reading.rooms/geography
    - Hispanic Division
      gopher://marvel.loc.gov/11/research/reading.rooms/hispanic
    - Local History and Genealogy Reading Room
      http://lcweb.loc.gov/rr/genealogy/
    - Manuscript Division
      gopher://marvel.loc.gov/11/research/reading.rooms/manuscripts
    - Prints and Photographs Division
      gopher://marvel.loc.gov/11/research/reading.rooms/prints
    - Rare Book and Special Collections Division
      gopher://marvel.loc.gov/11/research/reading.rooms/rare.books
  - The U. S. Newspaper Program Participants
    http://www.neh.fed.us/html/usnp.html
    A cooperative national effort to locate, catalog, preserve on microfilm, and make available to researchers newspapers published in the United States from the eighteenth century to the present. Funding provided by the National Endowment for the Humanities. Technical assistance furnished by the Library of Congress.

U.S.—NATIONAL ARCHIVES
http://www.CyndisList.com/na.htm

Category Index:

- ◆ General Resource Sites
- ◆ How To Articles & Guides
- ◆ Military
- ◆ Online Microfilm Catalogs from NARA

- ◆ Professional Researchers, Volunteers & Other Research Services
- ◆ Publications, Software & Supplies
- ◆ The United States Federal Census

◆ General Resource Sites

- National Archives and Records Administration (NARA)
  http://www.nara.gov/
  - Genealogical Research at the National Archives
    http://www.nara.gov/genealogy/
  - NAIL Home Page—NARA Archival Information Locator
    http://www.nara.gov/nara/nail.html
    A Pilot Database of Selected Holdings.
    - Genealogical Data in NAIL
      http://www.nara.gov/nara/nail/nailgen.html
  - NARA Calendar of Events
    http://www.nara.gov/nara/events/events.html
    For the National Archives facilities in and around Washington, DC and nationwide.
  - NATF Forms 80 & 81 Request
    E-mail: inquire@arch2.nara.gov
    Send e-mail to order NATF 80 Form for copies of military & pension records (before WWI only) & Form 81 Passenger Lists. You will need to give them your postal mailing address.
  - National Personnel Records Center, St. Louis, MO
    http://www.nara.gov/regional/stlouis.html
  - Naturalization Records
    http://www.nara.gov/genealogy/natural.html
  - Regional Archives—Addresses, Hours & General Information
    http://www.nara.gov/regional/nrmenu.html
    - NARA's Regional Archives General Information
      http://www.nara.gov/regional/nrmenu.html
    - Regional Archives Quicklist
      http://www.nara.gov/regional/quicklst.html
    - National Archives—Northeast Region (Boston)
      http://www.nara.gov/regional/boston.html
    - National Archives—Region (Pittsfield)
      http://www.nara.gov/regional/pittsfie.html
    - National Archives—Northeast Region (New York)
      http://www.nara.gov/regional/newyork.html

- • National Archives—Mid Atlantic Region (Philadelphia)
  http://www.nara.gov/regional/philacc.html
- • National Archives—Southeast Region (Atlanta)
  http://www.nara.gov/regional/atlanta.html
- • National Archives—Great Lakes Region (Chicago)
  http://www.nara.gov/regional/chicago.html
- • National Archives—Central Plains Region (Kansas City)
  http://www.nara.gov/regional/kansas.html
- • National Archives—Southwest Region (Fort Worth)
  http://www.nara.gov/regional/ftworth.html
- • National Archives—Rocky Mountain Region (Denver)
  http://www.nara.gov/regional/denver.html
- • National Archives—Pacific Region (Laguna Niguel)
  http://www.nara.gov/regional/laguna.html
- • National Archives—Pacific Region (San Bruno)
  http://www.nara.gov/regional/sanfranc.html
- • National Archives—Pacific Alaska Region (Seattle)
  http://www.nara.gov/regional/seattle.html
- • National Archives—Pacific Alaska Region (Anchorage)
  http://www.nara.gov/regional/anchorag.html

◆ How To Articles & Guides

- How To Order Military & Pension Records for Union Civil War Veterans from the National Archives
  http://www.oz.net/~cyndihow/pensions.htm
  By Cyndi Howells.
- The National Archives
  http://www.familytreemaker.com/issue3.html

- ○ Finding Your Way Through the National Archives
  http://www.familytreemaker.com/3_nara.html
- ○ The National Archives and Regional Centers—From FTM's How To Guide
  http://www.familytreemaker.com/00000091.html
- ○ Tales from the Genealogical Trenches
  http://www.familytreemaker.com/3_story.html
  "A Family Tree Maker customer tells you what he's found in the National Archives."
- Passport Application Record Information from the National Archives
  http://homepages.rootsweb.com/~godwin/reference/passport.html
- Riding the Rails Up Paper Mountain: Researching Railroad Records in the National Archives
  http://www.nara.gov/publications/prologue/railrd1.html
  By David A. Pfeiffer for Prologue, the quarterly of the National Archives and Records Administration.

◆ Military

- Civil War Records—An Introduction and Invitation
  http://www.nara.gov/publications/prologue/musick.html
  An article by Michael P. Musick from the National Archives web site.
- How To Order Military & Pension Records for Union Civil War Veterans from the National Archives
  http://www.oz.net/~cyndihow/pensions.htm
  By Cyndi Howells.
- Military Service Records—A Select Catalog of NARA Microfilm Publications
  http://www.nara.gov/publications/microfilm/military/service.html
- State-level Lists of Casualties—Korea and Vietnam
  http://www.nara.gov/nara/electronic/korvnsta.html
  From the NARA Center for Electronic Records.
  - ○ Korean Conflict State-Level Casualty Lists, Sorted by Home of Record
    http://www.nara.gov/nara/electronic/kcashr.html
    Sorted Alphabetically by Last Name of Casualty.
    http://www.nara.gov/nara/electronic/kcasal.html
  - ○ Vietnam Conflict State-Level Casualty Lists, Sorted by Home of Record
    http://www.nara.gov/nara/electronic/vcashr.html
    Sorted Alphabetically by Last Name of Casualty.
    http://www.nara.gov/nara/electronic/vcasal.html

◆ Online Microfilm Catalogs from NARA

- American Indians—A Select Catalog of NARA Microfilm Publications
  http://www.nara.gov/publications/microfilm/amerindians/indians.html

- Black Studies—A Select Catalog of NARA Microfilm Publications
  http://www.nara.gov/publications/microfilm/blackstudies/blackstd.html
- Federal Court Records—A Select Catalog of NARA Microfilm Publications
  http://www.nara.gov/publications/microfilm/courts/fedcourt.html
- Genealogical and Biographical Research—A Select Catalog of NARA Microfilm Publications
  http://www.nara.gov/publications/microfilm/biographical/genbio.html
- Immigrant and Passenger Arrivals—A Select Catalog of NARA Microfilm Publications
  http://www.nara.gov/publications/microfilm/immigrant/immpass.html
- Microfilm Resources for Research—A Comprehensive Catalog
  http://www.nara.gov/publications/microfilm/comprehensive/compcat.html
- Military Service Records—A Select Catalog of NARA Microfilm Publications
  http://www.nara.gov/publications/microfilm/military/service.html
- National Archives Microfilm Collection in Seattle
  http://www.rootsweb.com/~watpcgs/narafilm.htm
  A list of 549 microfilm publications available at the Pacific Alaska Region branch of NARA.

◆ Professional Researchers, Volunteers & Other Research Services

- Civil War pension, Revolutionary records and Homestead papers copied by Faith Libelo
  E-mail: fsl.genie.research@erols.com
  She can visit the National Archives for you and copy the files. E-mail Faith at fsl.genie.research@erols.com for details.

◆ Publications, Software & Supplies

- National Archives Book Store
  http://www.nara.gov/nara/bookstore/books.html
- National Archives Microfilm Catalogs Online
  http://gopher.nara.gov:70/1/genealog/holdings/catalogs
- Prologue—Quarterly of the National Archives and Records Administration
  http://www.nara.gov/publications/prologue/prologue.html
- Willow Bend Bookstore—National Archives
  http://www.willowbend.net/nara.htm

◆ The United States Federal Census

- Clues in Census Records, 1850–1920
  http://www.nara.gov/genealogy/cenclues.html

- The Federal Population Censuses—Catalogs of
  NARA Microfilm
  http://www.nara.gov/publications/microfilm/census/
  census.html

  o 1790–1890 Federal Population Censuses—
    Catalog of NARA Microfilm
    http://www.nara.gov/publications/microfilm/census/1790–
    1890/17901890.html

  o 1900 Federal Population Census—Catalog of
    NARA Microfilm
    http://www.nara.gov/publications/microfilm/census/1900/
    1900.html

  o 1910 Federal Population Censuses—Catalog of
    NARA Microfilm
    http://www.nara.gov/publications/microfilm/census/1910/
    1910.html

  o 1920 Federal Population Census—Catalog of
    NARA Microfilm
    http://www.nara.gov/publications/microfilm/census/1920/
    1920.html

- How to Use NARA's Census Microfilm Catalogs
  http://www.nara.gov/genealogy/microcen.html

- The Soundex Machine
  http://www.nara.gov/genealogy/soundex/soundex.html

- U.S. Census
  http://www.CyndisList.com/census.htm
  See this category on Cyndi's List for related links.

U.S.—SOCIAL SECURITY

http://www.CyndisList.com/socsec.htm

- Everton's On-Line Search—Social Security Death Index
  http://emh.everton.com/ssmdi.html

- Family Tree Maker Online
  http://www.familytreemaker.com/ffitop.html
  Search the Family Finder Index online. Find out if people can be located on the Social Security Death Index—SSDI.

- FAQ: Obtaining a Copy of a Social Security Number Application
  http://members.aol.com/reginamari/ancestry/ssnfaq.html
  The how and why of obtaining a copy of an SSN Application for genealogical purposes. Includes sample SSN applications.

- Lost Persons Letter Forwarding by the SSA
  ftp://ftp.rootsweb.com/pub/roots-l/genealog/genealog.lostper

- Nova's Genealogy Page
  http://www.buffnet.net/~nova/
  Nova will search her Social Security Death Index CD-ROM for you.

- Social Security Adminstration & Genealogy FAQ
  http://members.aol.com/rechtman/ssafaq.html

- Social Security Administration Home Page
  http://www.ssa.gov/

- Social Security Administration History Page
  http://www.ssa.gov/history/history.html

- Social Security Death Benefits Records
  http://scfn.thpl.lib.fl.us/thpl/main/spc/
  social_security_death_records.htm
  From the Special Collections Department of the Tampa-Hillsborough County Public Library System.

- Social Security Death Index—SSDI
  http://www.mtjeff.com/~bodenst/ssdi.html
  An informational page on how to use the information you get from searching the SSDI database.

- Social Security Death Index (SSDI) at Ancestry.com
  http://www.ancestry.com/ssdi/advanced.htm

  - Ancestry Library Social Security Death Index (SSDI)
    http://www.ancestry.com/ssdi/q01hlp.htm
    A helpful page with a description of the data and searching tips.

- Social Security Death Master File: A Much Misunderstood Index
  http://www.ancestry.com/ssdi/article.htm
  An article by Jake Gehring.

- Social Security Death Master File: Common Misconceptions
  http://www.ancestry.com/ssdi/miscon.htm

- Social Security Number FAQ
  http://www.cpsr.org/cpsr/privacy/ssn/ssn.faq.html

- Structure of Social Security Numbers
  http://www.cpsr.org/cpsr/privacy/ssn/ssn.structure.html

- Utilizing Social Security Death Index
  http://www.ancestry.com/columns/myra/
  Shaking_Family_Tree06-25-98.htm
  From Shaking Your Family Tree, by Myra Vanderpool Gormley, C.G.

U.S.—TERRITORIES AND POSSESSIONS
http://www.CyndisList.com/territor.htm

- American Samoa Vital Records Information
  http://vitalrec.com/as.html

- Canal Zone Vital Records Information
  http://vitalrec.com/cz.html

- Find-A-Grave by Location: Puerto Rico
  http://www.findagrave.com/grave/lpr.html
  Graves of noteworthy people.

- La Genealogía de Puerto Rico (The Genealogy of Puerto Rico)
  http://www.rootsweb.com/~prwgw/index.html
  The WorldGenWeb Project.

- Genealogy Exchange & Surname Registry—PRGenExchange
  http://www.genexchange.com/pr/index.cfm
  Puerto Rico

- Genealogy Helplist—Northern Mariana Islands
  http://www.concentric.net/~Mikerice/hl/usa/mp.shtml

- Guam Vital Records Information
  http://vitalrec.com/gu.html

- National Archives—Northeast Region (New York)
  http://www.nara.gov/regional/newyork.html

- National Archives—Northeast Region
  http://www.familytreemaker.com/00000099.html
  Records for New Jersey, New York, Puerto Rico, and the Virgin Islands.

- National Archives—Pacific Region (San Bruno)
  http://www.nara.gov/regional/sanfranc.html

- National Archives—Pacific Sierra Region
  http://www.familytreemaker.com/00000101.html
  Records for Northern California, Hawaii, Nevada (except Clark County), the Pacific Trust Territories, and American Samoa.

- Northern Mariana Islands Vital Records Information
  http://vitalrec.com/mp.html

- The Puerto Rican / Hispanic Genealogical Society
  http://www.rootsweb.com/~prhgs/

- PUERTORICO Mailing List
  http://members.aol.com/gfsjohnf/gen_mail_states-pr.html#PUERTORICO

- Puerto Rico Vital Records Information
  http://vitalrec.com/pr.html

- U.S. Virgin Islands—St. Thomas, St. Croix, St. John
  http://www.rootsweb.com/~usvi/
  The WorldGenWeb Project.

- The Vietnam Veterans Memorial—Guam
  http://grunt.space.swri.edu/statewall/guam/gm.htm

- The Vietnam Veterans Memorial—Puerto Rico
  http://grunt.space.swri.edu/statewall/prico/pr.htm

- The Vietnam Veterans Memorial—Virgin Islands
  http://grunt.space.swri.edu/statewall/vislands/vi.htm

- Virgin Islands Vital Records Information
  http://vitalrec.com/vi.html
  Saint Croix, Saint Thomas, Saint Thomas/John

U.S.—CENSUS
http://www.CyndisList.com/census.htm

Category Index:

◆ Census Tools & Information

◆ Soundex

◆ U.S. Census Indexes & Records

◆ Census Tools & Information

● 1790–1840 Census Birth Year Reference Chart
http://www.genrecords.com/library/birthyear2.htm

● 1850–1920 Census Birth Year Reference Chart
http://www.genrecords.com/library/birthyear.htm
From the Genealogy Record Service Library.

● Abstract Printable Forms for Census Records
http://www.familytreemaker.com/00000061.html

○ 1790
http://www.familytreemaker.com/00000062.html

○ 1800
http://www.familytreemaker.com/00000063.html

○ 1810
http://www.familytreemaker.com/00000064.html

○ 1820–1
http://www.familytreemaker.com/00000065.html

○ 1820–2
http://www.familytreemaker.com/00000066.html

○ 1830–1
http://www.familytreemaker.com/00000067.html

○ 1830–2
http://www.familytreemaker.com/00000068.html

○ 1840–1
http://www.familytreemaker.com/00000069.html

○ 1840–2
http://www.familytreemaker.com/00000070.html

○ 1850
http://www.familytreemaker.com/00000071.html

○ 1860
http://www.familytreemaker.com/00000072.html

○ 1870–1
http://www.familytreemaker.com/00000073.html

○ 1870–2
http://www.familytreemaker.com/00000074.html

○ 1880–1
http://www.familytreemaker.com/00000075.html

○ 1880–2
http://www.familytreemaker.com/00000076.html

○ 1890–1
http://www.familytreemaker.com/00000077.html

○ 1890–2
http://www.familytreemaker.com/00000078.html

○ 1900–1
http://www.familytreemaker.com/00000079.html

○ 1900–2
http://www.familytreemaker.com/00000080.html

○ 1910–1
http://www.familytreemaker.com/00000081.html

○ 1910–2
http://www.familytreemaker.com/00000082.html

○ 1910–3
http://www.familytreemaker.com/00000083.html

○ 1920–1
http://www.familytreemaker.com/00000084.html

○ 1920–2
http://www.familytreemaker.com/00000085.html

○ 1920–3
http://www.familytreemaker.com/00000086.html

● American Heritage Imaging, Inc.
http://www.a-h-i-inc.com/

● Ancestry.com—Census Records—Form 82
http://www.ancestry.com/research/census.htm

● Ancestry.com—Information in U.S. Federal Censuses 1790–1920
http://www.ancestry.com/research/census_questions.htm

● Ancestry.com—Tips On Using Census Records Effectively
http://www.ancestry.com/research/census_tips.htm

● Calculating Birth Year Based on Census Information
http://home.mem.net/~rac7253/gen/cenindx.htm

● Census and Soundex Relationship Abbreviations
http://www.genrecords.com/library/abbreviations.htm
From the Genealogy Record Service Library.

● Census Bureau Home Page
http://www.census.gov/

- ○ Census Bureau Genealogy Page
  http://www.census.gov/genealogy/www/
- CensusCD
  http://www.censuscd.com/cd/censuscd.htm
- CensusCD+Maps
  http://www.censuscd.com/cdmaps/censuscd_maps.htm
- CENSUS-CHAT Mailing List
  http://members.aol.com/johnf14246/gen_mail_general.
  html#CENSUS-CHAT
  Sponsored by the Census Project, for anyone who wants to discuss the Census, provide tips for locating Census information, and request Census lookups.
- The Census Giver
  http://www.censusgiver.com/
  A no-frills, quick turn-around search and retrieval of US Federal Census records from the National Archives.
- Census Online—Census Sites on the Web
  http://www.census-online.com/
- Census Related Sites Worldwide
  http://www.CyndisList.com/census2.htm
  See this category on Cyndi's List for related links.
- Census Schedules—U.S. Federal
  ftp://ftp.rootsweb.com/pub/roots-l/genealog/
  genealog.uscensus
  A listing of the items of information that can be found on each census between 1790 and 1900.
- Census View—Actual Census On CD-ROM
  http://www.galstar.com/~censusvu/
- Clues in Census Records, 1850–1920
  http://www.nara.gov/genealogy/cenclues.html
  From the National Archives web site.
- Come to Your Census
  http://home.sprynet.com/sprynet/lgk71/2census.htm
  Describes what is detailed on each of the U.S. Federal Censuses.
- Family Census Research
  http://www.dhc.net/~design/fcr30.htm
  Software program for organizing census records.
- Federal Census Records ~ A Brief Guide
  http://www.history.rochester.edu/jssn/page4.htm
- Finding Treasures in the U.S. Federal Census
  http://www.firstct.com/fv/uscensus.html
- "First in the Path of the Firemen"—The Fate of the 1890 Population Census
  http://www.nara.gov/publications/prologue/1890cen1.html
  Blake, Kellee. 1996. Prologue, National Archives and Records Administration. 28:1.
- Frontier Press Bookstore—Census Research Guides
  http://www.frontierpress.com/frontier.cgi?category=census
- GenealogyBookShop.com—Census
  http://www.genealogybookshop.com/genealogybookshop/files/
  General,Census/index.html
  The online store of Genealogical Publishing Co., Inc. & Clearfield Company.

- Genealogy Charts!
  http://www.genealogy-mall.com/freechar.htm
  - ○ 1790 Census Abstract Form
    http://www.genealogy-mall.com/1790cens.htm
  - ○ 1800 Census Abstract Form
    http://www.genealogy-mall.com/1800cens.htm
  - ○ Soundex Card
    http://www.genealogy-mall.com/sndxcard.htm
- Guide to the 1790–1890 Federal Population Censuses: Catalog of National Archives Microfilm
  http://www.genealogy.org/census/contents.shtml
- Historical Demographic, Economic, and Social Data for the United States, 1790–1860
  http://icg.harvard.edu/census/
- Kinsearch Genealogical Services—1790–1920 U.S. Federal Census Indexes
  http://home.utah-inter.net/kinsearch/CensIndxTable.html
  A chart of state-wide census indexes available at the Family History Library.
- Kinsearch Genealogical Services—1910 Census Finding Aids
  http://home.utah-inter.net/kinsearch/1910FindingAids.html
- National Archives
  http://www.CyndisList.com/na.htm
  See this category on Cyndi's List for related links.
  - ○ The Federal Population Censuses—Catalogs of NARA Microfilm
    http://www.nara.gov/publications/microfilm/census/
    census.html
    - 1790–1890 Federal Population Censuses—Catalog of NARA Microfilm
      http://www.nara.gov/publications/microfilm/census/1790–
      1890/17901890.html
    - 1900 Federal Population Census—Catalog of NARA Microfilm
      http://www.nara.gov/publications/microfilm/census/1900/
      1900.html
    - 1910 Federal Population Censuses—Catalog of NARA Microfilm
      http://www.nara.gov/publications/microfilm/census/1910/
      1910.html
    - 1920 Federal Population Census—Catalog of NARA Microfilm
      http://www.nara.gov/publications/microfilm/census/1920/
      1920.html
- Researching with Census Records
  http://www.familytreemaker.com/issue13.html
- Secrets of the Census
  http://www.familytreemaker.com/13_secrt.html
- S-K Publications: Census Books for Sale
  http://www.skpub.com/genie/census.html
  1800–1850 Census Books.

- Tiger Mapping Service Home Page
  http://tiger.census.gov/
  U.S. Census Bureau

- Tom Nunamaker's Census Age Calculator
  http://toshop.com/censuscalc.cfm

- U.S. Census Bureau—1990 Census Name Files
  http://www.census.gov/genealogy/names/
  This provides name frequency in America from the 1990 census.

- U.S. Census Summary Chart
  http://www2.primecomm.net/trees/chart.htm

- USGenWeb Census Project
  http://www.usgenweb.org/census/

- Using Census Records
  http://www.micronet.net/users/~searcy/records.htm

- What Kind of Information is in the Census Records?
  http://www.genrecords.com/library/lib1.htm
  From the Genealogy Record Service Library.

- What's on Each Census Record?
  http://www.genrecords.com/library/what.htm
  From the Genealogy Record Service Library.

◆ Soundex

- 1880 Soundex Card
  http://www.genrecords.com/library/1880soundex.htm
  From the Genealogy Record Service Library.

- 1900 Soundex Card
  http://www.genrecords.com/library/1900Soundex.htm
  From the Genealogy Record Service Library.

- 1910 Miracode Soundex
  http://www.genrecords.com/library/miracode.htm
  From the Genealogy Record Service Library.

- Abbreviations and Terms Used in Soundex Cards
  http://www.geocities.com/Heartland/plains/7193/satusc.htm

- Census and Soundex Relationship Abbreviations
  http://www.genrecords.com/library/abbreviations.htm
  From the Genealogy Record Service Library.

- Genie Helper Soundex Code Conversion Software for PC
  http://jnb.home.mindspring.com/soundex.html

- How to Use Soundex for United States Census Records
  http://www.hpl.lib.tx.us/clayton/soundex.html

- Kinsearch Genealogical Services—Description of the Soundex Indexing System
  http://home.utah-inter.net/kinsearch/Soundex.html

- Soundex Card
  http://www.genealogy-mall.com/sndxcard.htm

- Soundex Code Generator—Macintosh
  http://www2.vivid.net/~brisance/

- Soundex Coding
  http://www.jewishgen.org/infofiles/soundex.txt
  A JewishGen InfoFile which includes two parts: I. Russell (NARA)—II. Daitch-Mokotoff (D-M).

- Soundex Conversion Program from Genealogy Online
  http://www.genealogy.org/soundex.shtml

- Soundex Conversion Program—Surname to Soundex Code
  http://searches.rootsweb.com/cgi-bin/Genea/soundex.sh

- Soundexing and Genealogy
  http://www.avotaynu.com/soundex.html
  By Gary Mokotoff.

- The Soundex Machine
  http://www.nara.gov/genealogy/soundex/soundex.html
  A form to convert surnames to soundex codes; from the National Archives.

- Soundex Rules
  http://www.genealogy-mall.com/sndxrule.htm

- Surname to Soundex Converter
  http://www.geocities.com/Heartland/Hills/3916/soundex.html

- Using the Soundex System
  http://www.ancestry.com/home/George_Morgan/03-20-98.htm
  From "Along Those Lines . . ." by George G. Morgan.

◆ U.S. Census Indexes & Records

- 1785 Halifax County, Virginia Heads of Families
  http://www.genealogy.org/~ajmorris/misc/va1785hf.htm

- 1790 Census Database—Saratoga County, New York
  http://www.rootsweb.com/~nysarato/1790_int.htm

- 1790 Stokes County, North Carolina Census
  http://www.users.mis.net/~chesnut/pages/nstokes.htm

- 1790 Surry County, North Carolina Census
  http://www.users.mis.net/~chesnut/pages/nsurry.htm

- 1800 Census Anson County, North Carolina
  http://www.aracnet.com/~pslamb/census.htm

- The 1800 Horry County, South Carolina Census
  http://ourworld.compuserve.com/homepages/jotajota/horry1.htm

- 1809 Census of Madison County, Alabama
  http://hiwaay.net/~white/TVGS/1809mad.txt

- 1810 Census Culpeper County, Virginia
  http://www.rootsweb.com/~takelley/culp1810/culp1810.htm

- 1810 Harrison Co., Indiana Census for Harrison and Exeter Townships
  http://www.floyd-pavey.com/kentuckiana/kyiana/census/1810harrisonc.html

- 1820 Federal Census Orange County, Indiana
  http://twobees.com/1820/

- 1820 Floyd Co, KY Census Index
  http://www.bright.net/~kat/floydcen.htm

- 1820 United States Census Robertson County, Tennessee
  http://home.earthlink.net/~howardorjeff/1820.htm

- 1830 Census Record—Oldham County ~ Kentucky
  http://www.rootsweb.com/~usgenweb/ky/oldham/census/
  1830.html

- 1830 Crawford County Census Index ~ Pennsylvania
  http://www.granniesworld.com/cvahs/1830/index.html

- 1830 Federal Census for Sussex County, NJ Township Index
  http://www.gate.net/~pascalfl/1830twpx.html

- 1830 Greene County, Tennessee Census Index
  http://www.geocities.com/Heartland/Hills/8214/indextn.html

- 1830 Sumner County, TN Census Index
  http://www.tngenweb.usit.com/sumner/sumncndx.htm

- 1830 United States Census St. Bernard Parish, Louisiana
  http://www.rootsweb.com/~lastbern/stbern1830.htm

- 1840 Census—Linn County, Iowa
  http://www.rootsweb.com/~ialinn/census/1840.htm

- 1840 Lawrence County, Ky Census Index
  http://www.bright.net/~kat/lawrenc.htm

- 1840 Lowndes County, Georgia Federal Census Index
  http://www.ij.net/phickey/1840cens.htm

- 1840 Oldham County, Ky Census
  http://www.rootsweb.com/~usgenweb/ky/oldham/census/
  1840.html

- 1850 Census Beaver Township, Crawford County, Pennsylvania
  http://www.granniesworld.com/cvahs/bcen/

- 1850 Census Conneautville, Crawford County, Pennsylvania
  http://www.granniesworld.com/cvahs/census/index.html

- 1850 Census, Greene Co., Tennessee
  http://www.census-online.com/transcript/tn/greene/index.html

- 1850 Census Henderson County, Kentucky
  http://www.rootsweb.com/~kyhender/Henderson/hendky.txt

- 1850 Census, Jackson County, Tennessee
  http://www2.aros.net/~cbutler//census/jack50x.htm

- 1850 Census, Mercer County, Kentucky
  http://w3.one.net/~durp/50cenidx.htm

- 1850 Census, Robertson County, Texas
  http://www.geocities.com/Heartland/Plains/3451/1850.htm

- 1850 Census, Shenandoah Co., VA
  http://www.rootsweb.com/~vashenan/census.html

- 1850 Census Summerhill Township, Crawford County, Pennsylvania
  http://www.granniesworld.com/cvahs/scen/

- 1850 Census, Victoria County, Texas
  http://www.viptx.net/victoria/history/1850/

- 1850 Cocke Co., Tennessee Census
  http://www.liberty.com/home/hannibal/cocke.html

- 1850 Crawford Co., IN Census
  http://www.floyd-pavey.com/kentuckiana/kyiana/census/
  1850ccensus.html
  An ongoing project that currently only contains Jennings Township.

- 1850 Federal Census—Clinch County, Georgia
  http://www.rootsweb.com/~gaechols/echclcen.html

- 1850 Federal Census for Lewis County, Oregon Territory
  ftp://ftp.rootsweb.com/pub/usgenweb/wa/lewis/census/50lc.txt
  Included what is now Lewis, Thurston, and Pierce counties, Washington.

- 1850 Federal Census of Wayne County, Virginia
  http://www.rootsweb.com/~wvwayne/wayne50.htm

- 1850 Federal Census Orange County, Indiana
  http://www.geocities.com/~labooski/census/

- 1850 Federal Census Orleans County, NY
  http://www.rootsweb.com/~nyorlean/1850Cen.htm

- 1850 Florida Census: St. John's County
  http://www.geocities.com/Heartland/Hills/8299/1850cens.htm

- 1850 Lowndes County, Georgia Federal Census Index
  http://www.ij.net/phickey/1850cens.htm

- 1851 Census of Cherokee's East of the Misssissippi—The Siler Rolls
  http://members.aol.com/lredtail/siler.html

- 1858 Chehalis County Territorial Census
  ftp://ftp.rootsweb.com/pub/usgenweb/wa/graysharbor/census/
  58ccterr.txt
  Now Gray's Harbor County, Washington.

- 1860 Census Northumberland County, Virginia
  http://www.mosquitonet.com/~luht/CENSUS.HTM

- 1860 Federal Census of Tyrrell County, North Carolina
  http://www.rootsweb.com/~takelley/tyrr1860/tyrr1860.htm

- 1860 Henderson County Census ~ Kentucky
  ftp://ftp.rootsweb.com/pub/usgenweb/ky/henderson/census/
  cens1860.txt

- 1860 Thurston County Territorial Census ~ Washington
  ftp://ftp.rootsweb.com/pub/usgenweb/wa/thurston/census/
  60tcterr.txt

- 1860 Webster County Census ~ Kentucky
  http://www.rootsweb.com/~kywebste/census/1860/sl-001.htm
- 1865 Census of East Parish Tisbury, Mass.
  http://www.vineyard.net/vineyard/history/cen65t.htm
- 1865 New York State Census Orleans County
  http://www.rootsweb.com/~nyorlean/1865Cen.htm
- 1870 Census Lawrence Co., Kentucky
  http://ourworld.compuserve.com/homepages/GlenGallagher/law1870.htm
- 1870 Census Lawrence Co., Kentucky—Census Index
  http://ourworld.compuserve.com/homepages/GlenGallagher/L70index.htm
- 1870 Dimmit County, Texas Census
  http://www.rootsweb.com/~txdimmit/DC1870.htm
- 1870 Greenup County, Kentucky Census Data
  http://www.zoomnet.net/~blogan/1870grco.html
- 1870 U.S. Census for Penn Township (Castleton Post Office), Stark County, Illinois
  http://members.aol.com/ZCyberCat/private/castleton.html
- 1870 U.S. Census for Penn Township (Wyoming Post Office), Stark County, Illinois
  http://members.aol.com/ZCyberCat/private/census1.html
- 1880 Karnes County Census (Polish areas) ~ Texas
  http://paris.chem.yale.edu/~zondlo/karnes1880.html
- 1880 U.S. Census for Penn Township (aka Wyoming), Stark County, Illinois
  http://members.aol.com/ZCyberCat/private/1880census.html
- 1885 Anthony, Kansas Census
  http://www.ohmygosh.com/genealogy/records/1885Anthonycensus.htm
- 1885 Dakota Territory Census Database
  http://www.lib.ndsu.nodak.edu/database/1885census.html
- 1900 Dimmit County Census Index ~ Texas
  http://www.rootsweb.com/~txdimmit/DC1900.htm
- 1910 Benton County Census ~ Washington
  http://www.owt.com/ebchs/census.htm
- 1910 Dimmit County Census Index ~ Texas
  http://www.rootsweb.com/~txdimmit/dc1910.htm
- 1910 Federal Census—Fox Island Precinct, Pierce County, Washington
  ftp://ftp.rootsweb.com/pub/usgenweb/wa/pierce/census/10pcfoxi.txt
- 1920 Census of Saxtons River, Windham County, Vermont
  http://www.rootsweb.com/rootsweb/searches/vtsaxriv/
- African Americans Listed in the 1850 & 1860 Madison County, Tennessee Free Census Schedule
  http://www.ccharity.com/tennessee/freetenn.htm
- Autauga County, Alabama 1830 Census
  http://searches.rootsweb.com/cgi-bin/autauga/auta-1830.pl
- Autauga County, Alabama 1840 Census
  http://searches.rootsweb.com/cgi-bin/autauga/auta-1840.pl
- Barnes County, North Dakota 1900 Census of Germans from Russia
  http://pixel.cs.vt.edu/library/census/link/barnes00.txt
- Barnes County, North Dakota 1910 Census of Germans from Russia
  http://pixel.cs.vt.edu/library/census/link/barnes10.txt
- Barnes County, North Dakota 1920 Census of Germans from Russia
  http://pixel.cs.vt.edu/library/census/link/barnes20.txt
- Blount County, Alabama 1830 Census
  http://members.aol.com/WGenTwo/1830.htm
- Buckley, Pierce County, Washington 1890 Census
  ftp://ftp.rootsweb.com/pub/usgenweb/wa/pierce/census/90bucktn.txt
- Campbell County, South Dakota 1910 Census of German Russians
  http://pixel.cs.vt.edu/library/census/link/camp10.txt
- Censuses of Trigg County ~ Kentucky
  http://www.usroots.com/kyseeker/public_html/kentucky/trigg/Trigg/Census/censuses.html
- Census of Madison County (Alabama) Mississippi Territory Taken January 1809
  http://oldhuntsville.com/oldhuntsville/p591.htm
- Charles Mix County, South Dakota 1910 Census of German Russians
  http://pixel.cs.vt.edu:70/0/GRG/Census/cmix10.txt
- Clarke County, Mississippi 1840–1860 Census Surname Index
  http://www.netpathway.com/~bennie/cenindx2.html
- Clark County, South Dakota 1910 Census of German Russians
  http://pixel.cs.vt.edu:70/0/GRG/Census/clark10.txt
- Correlations: Warren County, Tennessee 1850 Census Database Project
  http://members.aol.com/APTurner/wctnhome.htm
  "The goal is to correlate the 1850 census records for Warren County, Tennessee with other types of records which show family connections: marriage, probate, court, land, Bible, Ancestral File, personal GEDCOM files, magazine articles, Internet newsgroup messages, and so forth."
- Crawford Co., IN 1820 Census
  http://www.floyd-pavey.com/kentuckiana/kyiana/census/1820cra.html
- Dakota Territory 1860 Census—Interactive Search
  http://www.rootsweb.com/cgi-bin/sdcensus/sd1860cen.pl

- Darke County, Ohio Census Indexes, Section Maps, History of Towns and Townships, and More
  http://php.ucs.indiana.edu/~jetorres/twps.html

- Douglas Co., Washington Territory, 1885 Territorial Census
  ftp://ftp.rootsweb.com/pub/usgenweb/wa/douglas/census/85dcterr.txt

- The Federal Census of 1850 for Effingham County, Illinois
  http://www.primenet.com/~powerss/census.html

- Fragments of the 1890 Census for Texas
  http://lonestar.simplenet.com/genealogy/genweb/1890tx.html

- Grimes County, Texas 1900 Census, Germans from Russia
  http://pixel.cs.vt.edu/library/census/link/grimes00.txt

- Grimes County, Texas 1910 Census, Germans from Russia
  http://pixel.cs.vt.edu/library/census/link/grimes10.txt

- Grimes County, Texas 1920 Census, Germans from Russia
  http://pixel.cs.vt.edu/library/census/link/grimes20.txt

- Hampden County, Massachusetts Granville 1790 Census
  http://www.rootsweb.com/~mahampde/census.htm

- Historical Census Records for Ontario County ~ New York
  http://raims.com/censusmenu.html

- Index of 1910 Federal Census, Pierce County, Wilkeson, Washington
  ftp://ftp.rootsweb.com/pub/usgenweb/wa/pierce/census/10pcwkin.txt

- Index of All Surnames Enumerated in the Benton Co., IA 1850 Federal Census
  http://www.rootsweb.com/~iabenton/1850.htm
  This page includes an offer for a lookup to be done in the 1850 Benton County Census.

- Index to 1910 Federal Census for Berlin Township, Marathon County, Wisconsin
  http://www.goodnet.com/~eb43571/berlin.htm

- Jones County, Iowa 1852 State Census
  http://www.rootsweb.com/~iajones/census/1852/52census.htm

- Jones County, Iowa 1854 Census
  http://www.rootsweb.com/~iajones/census/1854/54census.htm

- Jones County, Iowa—1856 Census
  http://www.rootsweb.com/~iajones/census/1856/56census.htm

- Kansas Censuses 1855–1875
  http://history.cc.ukans.edu/heritage/kshs/library/18551875.htm
  A guide to the records on microfilm.

- Kershaw County, South Carolina 1800 Federal Census
  http://homepages.rootsweb.com/~marykozy/census/kers1800.txt

- Lake County, Colorado 1870 US Census Index, A–J
  ftp://ftp.rootsweb.com/pub/usgenweb/co/lake/census/1870cenA_J.txt
  K–Z
  ftp://ftp.rootsweb.com/pub/usgenweb/co/lake/census/1870cenK_Z.txt

- Lehigh County, Pennsylvania Tax & Census Records
  http://www.geocities.com/Heartland/3955/lehtax.htm

- McPherson County, South Dakota 1900 Census of German Russians
  http://pixel.cs.vt.edu/library/census/link/mcpher00.txt

- McPherson County, South Dakota 1910 Census of German Russians
  http://pixel.cs.vt.edu/library/census/link/mcpher10.txt

- Madison Co., MS 1850 Federal Census
  http://www.rootsweb.com/~msmadiso/1850census/

- Massachusetts, Bristol County 1790 Census
  http://www.marketrends.net/mthome/census/1790census.html
  1800
  http://www.marketrends.net/mthome/census/1800census.html
  1810
  http://www.marketrends.net/mthome/census/1810census.html
  1850
  http://www.marketrends.net/mthome/census/1850census.html
  1860
  http://www.marketrends.net/mthome/census/1860census.html

- Morgan County Public Library—GenAssist— The Genealogy Assistant
  http://www.scican.net/~morglib/genasist/genasist.html

  o Morgan County, Indiana 1850 Federal Census Mortality Schedule
    http://www.scican.net/~morglib/genasist/mort1850.html

  o Morgan County, Indiana 1870 Federal Census Index of Households
    http://www.scican.net/~morglib/genasist/cens1870.html

  o Morgan County, Indiana 1880 Federal Census Index of Households
    http://www.scican.net/~morglib/genasist/cens1880.html

  o Morgan County, Indiana 1890 Enrollment of Soldiers
    http://www.scican.net/~morglib/genasist/enrl1890.html

  o Morgan County, Indiana 1910 Federal Census Index of Households
    http://www.scican.net/~morglib/genasist/cens1910.html

- Mt. View Research 1860 Federal Census Page Co., Va.
  http://www.geocities.com/Heartland/Valley/9793/census1860a.htm

- Mt. View Research 1870 Federal Census Page Co., Va.
  http://www.geocities.com/Heartland/Valley/9793/census1870a.htm

- New York State Census
  http://home.eznet.net/~halsey/NY/ny-census.htm

- Noxubee County, Mississippi Slave Schedule— 1860 Census
  http://www.ccharity.com/mississippi/1860noxumortpt1.htm

- Partial 1680 Pennsylvania Census—Along the Delaware River
  http://www.geocities.com/Heartland/3955/1680census.htm

- Russell County, Virginia 1860 Census
  http://rhobard.com/census/index.shtml

- San Francisco 1842 Census ~ California
  http://www.geocities.com/Heartland/Valley/2171/hc842.htm

- School Census of Students, Arline, Washington, 1911
  ftp://ftp.rootsweb.com/pub/usgenweb/wa/pierce/school/11arline.txt

- Search the 1860 Augusta County Census ~ Virginia
  http://jefferson.village.virginia.edu/vshadow2/govdoc/au.census1860.html

- Search the 1860 Franklin County Census ~ Pennsylvania
  http://jefferson.village.virginia.edu/vshadow2/govdoc/fr.census1860.html

- Surname Index to the Census of the Slovak People Living in Mahoning County, Ohio
  http://www.iarelative.com/22census/index.html

- Territorial and State Census Schedules in Washington
  ftp://ftp.rootsweb.com/pub/usgenweb/wa/census/waterr.txt

- Transcript of the Grant County, Kentucky 1860 Census
  http://home.att.net/~l.k.osborne/grnt1860/

- Walworth County, South Dakota 1900 Census of German Russians
  http://pixel.cs.vt.edu/library/census/link/wal00.txt

- Walworth County, South Dakota 1910 Census of German Russians
  http://pixel.cs.vt.edu/library/census/link/wal10.txt

- Wicomico County, Maryland Barren Creek District #1 1870 Census
  http://www.shoreweb.com/cindy/census/barren.htm

- Wicomico County, Maryland Quantico District 1870 Census
  http://www.shoreweb.com/cindy/census/quantico.htm

- Wicomico County, Maryland Sharptown District #10 1870 Census
  http://www.shoreweb.com/cindy/census/sharptown.htm

- Wicomico County, Maryland Tyaskin District #14 1870 Census
  http://www.shoreweb.com/cindy/census/tyaskin.htm

- York County, South Carolina, Census Index— Interactive Search
  http://www.rootsweb.com/cgi-bin/scyork/scyork.pl
  1790 to 1850 heads of household.

U.S.—CIVIL WAR / WAR FOR SOUTHERN INDEPENDENCE
http://www.CyndisList.com/cw.htm

Category Index:

- African-Americans in the War
- Battles, Battlefields & Cemeteries
- Forts, Barracks & Posts
- General Resource Sites
- General Resource Sites ~ By State or Locality
- Hospitals & Medicine
- Libraries, Archives & Museums
- Mailing Lists, Newsgroups & Chat
- The Navies
- Pension & Military Records

- People & Families
- Prisons & Prisoners
- Professional Researchers, Volunteers & Other Research Services
- Publications, Photographs & Supplies
- Reconstruction
- Regimental Rosters & Histories ~ The Confederacy
- Regimental Rosters & Histories ~ The Union
- Societies & Groups

◆ African-Americans in the War

- African-American Civil War Memorial
  http://www.itd.nps.gov/cwss/dcmem.html
- African American Warriors
  http://www.abest.com/~cklose/aawar.htm
- African Americans in the Civil War: Shamrock Hill Books
  http://members.aol.com/historybks/blk.htm
- Guide to Tracing Your African American Civil War Ancestor
  http://www.coax.net/people/LWF/cwguide.htm
- History of African Americans in the Civil War
  http://www.itd.nps.gov/cel/africanh.html
- NPS African-American Civil War Sites
  http://www.itd.nps.gov/cel/aa-sites.html
- United States Colored Troops (USCT)
  http://www.itd.nps.gov/cwss/usct.html
- United States Colored Troops Resident in Baltimore at the Time of the 1890 Census
  http://www.mdarchives.state.md.us/msa/speccol/3096/html/00010001.html
- United States Colored Troops: The Civil War
  http://www.coax.net/people/lwf/usct.htm

◆ Battles, Battlefields & Cemeteries

- Battle of Olustee ~ Florida
  http://extlab1.entnem.ufl.edu/olustee/index.html

- The Battle of Shiloh
  http://www.ot.centuryinter.net/nacent/bs/shiloh.htm
- Camp Moore Confederate Cemetery and Museum
  http://home.gulfsouth.verio.net/~harper1/
- Chalmette National Cemetery ~ Louisiana
  http://www.cwc.lsu.edu/projects/dbases/chalmla.htm
- Charleston Race Course Prison Dead, SC
  http://members.aol.com/edboots/charlestondead.html
  Union Civil War Prisoners of War originally buried at the Charleston Race Course Cemetery and later reinterred at the Beaufort National Cemetery.
- Chronological List of Civil War Battles
  http://users.aol.com/dlharvey/engage.htm
- Civil War Battle Summaries by State
  http://www2.cr.nps.gov/abpp/battles/bystate.htm
- Confederate Soldiers Rest, Elmwood Cemetery, Memphis, Tennessee
  http://www.people.memphis.edu/~jcothern/soldrest.htm
- Fort Henry, Tennessee
  http://users.aol.com/greenup1/page1.html
  Regarding CSA Soldier's Graves marked near Fort Henry.
- Fredericksburg Confederate Cemetery ~ Virginia
  http://www.nps.gov/frsp/rebcem.htm
- Fredericksburg National Cemetery ~ Virginia
  http://www.nps.gov/frsp/natcem.htm
- Gettysburg National Military Park ~ Pennsylvania
  http://www.nps.gov/gett/
- Perryville Battlefield ~ Kentucky
  http://www.farmnatldan.com/perry.htm

- Petersburg National Battlefield—Poplar Grove National Cemetery ~ Virginia
  http://www.nps.gov/pete/pe_pop.htm
- Researching and Recording Civil War Veterans Burials in Michigan Cemeteries
  http://www.centuryinter.net/suvcw.mi/gr-recgv.html
- USCWC Cemetery Listings
  http://www.cwc.lsu.edu/cwc/projects/cemindex.htm
  From the U.S. Civil War Center.

◆ Forts, Barracks & Posts

- Buffalo's 19th Century Army Barracks and the Towpath to Weedsport
  http://army.barracks.buffalonet.org/
- Fort deRussy
  http://www.geocities.com/BourbonStreet/5600/
  Marksville, Louisiana

◆ General Resource Sites

- ACWRoots Genealogy
  http://www.rootsweb.com/~acwroots/index.html
- American Civil War
  http://home.ptd.net/~nikki/civilwar.htm
  From the home page of Nikki Roth-Skiles, highlighting several regiments in which her ancestors served.
- The American Civil War
  http://homepages.dsu.edu/jankej/civilwar/civilwar.htm
  From Dakota State University.
- The American Civil War, 1861–1865
  http://www.access.digex.net/~bdboyle/cw.html
- American Civil War Home Page
  http://sunsite.utk.edu/civil-war/
- A Brief Introduction to Genealogy and the American Civil War
  http://www.outfitters.com/illinois/history/civil/cwgeneal.html
- The Civil War Archive
  http://www.civilwararchive.com/
- Civil War Related Sites in the National Park Service
  http://www.itd.nps.gov/cel/sites.html
- Civil War Resources
  http://www.usafa.af.mil/dfeng/cwarres.htm
- Civil War Resources from A.J. Morris
  http://www.genealogy.org/~ajmorris/cw/cw.htm
  Biographies, Units, Letters, Publications & Internet Links.
- Civil War Resources on the Internet: Abolitionism to Reconstruction (1830's–1890's)
  http://www.libraries.rutgers.edu/rulib/socsci/hist/civwar-2.html
- Civil War Soldier Vocabulary
  http://www.cee.indiana.edu/gopher/
  Turner_Adventure_Learning/Gettysburg_Archive/
  Other_Resources/Soldier_Vocabulary.txt

- The Civil War Soldiers and Sailors System (CWSS)
  http://www.itd.nps.gov/cwss/
  Read a description of the project, then use the searachable database at: Civil War Soldiers and Sailors System Name Search, http://www.itd.nps.gov/cgi-bin/dualz.test
- Civil War Virtual Archive Web Ring
  http://www.geocities.com/Athens/Forum/1867/cwring.html
  The Civil War Virtual Archive Web Ring links web sites containing primary reference material for those engaged in researching the American Civil War.
- Civil War WWW Information Archive
  http://www.access.digex.net/~bdboyle/cw.html
- The Confederate Network
  http://members.tripod.com/~jrw/
- CWOL Webring (Civil War On-line)
  http://www.geocities.com/CapitolHill/8472/webring.html
- Cycles of US History—Civil War Cycle (1792–1859)
  http://www.seanet.com/Users/pamur/civi.html
- Electric Cemetery
  http://www.ionet.net/~cousin/
  Many Civil War links.
- Finding a Civil War Ancestor
  http://www.ristenbatt.com/genealogy/civilwar.htm
- Genealogy and the American Civil War
  http://www.outfitters.com/illinois/history/civil/cwgeneal.html
- Index of Civil War Information Available on the Internet
  http://www.cwc.lsu.edu/civlink.htm
- Lineages, Inc.—Confederate States
  http://www.lineages.com/military/mil_csa.asp
- Lineages, Inc.—Military Research Room
  http://www.lineages.com/military/mil_cw.asp
  Civil War, 1861–1865.
- Military History: United States Civil War (1861–1865)
  http://www.cfcsc.dnd.ca/links/milhist/usciv.html
- Military Records for Genealogy—The Civil War Era
  http://www.usgenweb.com/military/civ.htm
- Researching Civil War Soldiers
  http://www.familytreemaker.com/issue7.html
- Tenny's Civil War Page
  http://www.mebbs.com/tenny/civilwar.htm
- U.S. Civil War Center
  http://www.cwc.lsu.edu/
- U.S. Civil War Center—Civil War Links Index
  http://www.cwc.lsu.edu/cwc/cvlink.htm
- War for Southern Independence Links
  http://members.tripod.com/~jrw2/index2.htm

◆ General Resource Sites ~ By State or Locality

- 1893 Nebraska Census of Civil War Veterans
  http://www.rootsweb.com/~neholt/1893/index.html

- Alton in the Civil War ~ Illinois
  http://www.altonweb.com/history/civilwar/index.html

- Bleeding Kansas Home Page
  http://members.aol.com/marcalford/pp235.htm
  The SHULERs and the War on the Border.

- The Blue and Gray Trail—The Civil War in North Georgia and Chattanooga
  http://ngeorgia.com/travel/bgtrail.html

- The Civil War in Arkansas
  http://www.civilwarbuff.org/

- The Civil War in Florida
  http://mailer.fsu.edu/~rthompso/csa-page.html
  Includes Wakulla, Franklin, Jefferson, and Leon counties. Includes muster rolls for units from the state.

- Civil War in West Virginia
  http://www.rootsweb.com/~hcpd/civilwar.htm

- The Civil War Page
  http://www.wwd.net/user/historical/Cwindex.html
  From The Lawrence Register web site (Lawrence County, Ohio).

- Civil War Records of Bucks and Northampton Counties
  http://www.geocities.com/heartland/6508/DURHAM6.HTM

- The Colorado Volunteers During the Civil War (1861–1865)
  http://www.state.co.us/gov_dir/gss/archives/civwar/civilwar.html

  - Colorado Civil War Casualties Index
    http://www.state.co.us/gov_dir/gss/archives/ciwardea.html

- Corinth, Mississippi—Civil War History
  http://www2.tsixroads.com/Corinth_MLSANDY/corciv.html

- Dakota Territory During the Civil War
  http://www.rootsweb.com/~usgenweb/sd/military/cw.htm
  Includes a roster of all known 1st Dakota Cavalry personnel.

- Finding Your Civil War Ancestor in Wisconsin
  http://www.execpc.com/~kap/wisc-cw.html

- Illinois in the Civil War
  http://www.outfitters.com/illinois/history/civil/civil.html

- Index of the Civil War in Missouri Links and Resources Available on the Internet
  http://www.usmo.com/~momollus/MOCWLINK.HTM

- Indiana in the Civil War
  http://www.thnet.com/~liggetkw/incw/cw.htm

- Kansas in the Civil War
  http://skyways.lib.ks.us/kansas/genweb/civilwar/index.html

- Kentucky Military Links
  http://www.rootsweb.com/~kymil/index.html

- Maine in the Civil War
  http://www.rootsweb.com/~mecivilw/mecivilw.htm

- Michigan in the Civil War
  http://users.aol.com/dlharvey/cwmireg.htm

- Mississippi Civil War Information
  http://www2.msstate.edu/~gam3/cw/index.html

- Missouri in the Civil War
  http://www.tri.net/~kheidel/mowar/

- New York State and the Civil War
  http://www.snymor.edu/pages/library/local_history/sites/

- North Carolina Civil War Home Page
  http://members.aol.com/jweaver303/nc/nccwhp.htm
  Collection of biographical and historical information pertaining to North Carolina and North Carolinians in the American Civil War.

- Ohio in the Civil War
  http://www.infinet.com/~lstevens/a/civil.html

- Old Times, Not Forgotten
  http://www.seark.net/~sabra/index.html
  Featuring links for Arkansas resources.

- Pennsylvania in the Civil War
  http://www.libertynet.org/gencap/pacw.html

- Roster of Ohio Soldiers 1861–1866
  http://members.aol.com/WmMartin1/ohio/

- Russell County, Virginia Civil War Website
  http://rhobard.com/russell/civilwar.html

- Tennessee Confederate Soldiers' Home Applications
  http://www.state.tn.us/sos/statelib/pubsvs/csh_intr.htm

- Texas Adjutant General Service Records 1836–1935
  http://www.tsl.state.tx.us/lobby/servrecs.htm

- TNGenWeb Civil War Resource Page
  http://www.tngenweb.org/cwsource.htm

- USGenWeb Civil War Veterans—Missouri Veterans
  http://www.tri.net/~kheidel/mowar/veterans.html

- Vermont in the Civil War
  http://www.geocities.com/Pentagon/1861/vt-cw.htm

- Valley of the Shadow: Living the Civil War in Pennsylvania and Virginia
  gopher://jefferson.village.virginia.edu:80/hGET%20/vshadow/vshadow.html

- Virginia Civil War Home Page
  http://members.aol.com/jweaver300/grayson/vacwhp.htm

- West Virginia in the Civil War
  http://www.wvcivilwar.com/

- Wisconsin Veterans Museum
  http://badger.state.wi.us/agencies/dva/museum/wvmmain.html

- The Young-Sanders Center
  http://youngsanders.org/
  For the study of the War Between the States in Louisiana. Contains searchable database of over 10,000 Confederate soldiers buried in Louisiana with cemetery locations.

◆ Hospitals & Medicine

- Civil War and 19th Century Medical Terminology
  http://members.aol.com/jweaver300/grayson/medterm.htm

- Civil War Medicine
  http://www.powerweb.net/bbock/war/

- Civil War Medicine Vocabulary
  http://www.cee.indiana.edu/gopher/
  Turner_Adventure_Learning/Gettysburg_Archive/
  Other_Resources/Medicine_Vocabulary.txt

- Hale's 31st Alabama / 49th Alabama, Port Hudson,
  LA Hospital Ledger
  http://fly.hiwaay.net/~jemcgee/hospital.htm

- Medical Services, Civil War
  http://carlisle-www.army.mil/usamhi/RefBibs/medical/
  civwar.htm
  A working bibliography of MHI sources.

- Medical Staff Press
  http://www.iserv.net/~civilmed/

- National Museum of Civil War Medicine
  http://www.civilwarmed.org/

- Resources in Civil War Medicine
  http://www.collphyphil.org/FIND_AID/histcvwr.htm
  At The Library of the College of Physicians of Philadelphia.

- Virginia's Confederate Military Hospitals
  http://members.aol.com/jweaver300/grayson/hospital.htm

◆ Libraries, Archives & Museums

- Grand Army of the Republic Civil War Museum
  and Library ~ Pennsylvania
  http://www.libertynet.org/~gencap/gar.html

- A Guide to the Civil War Materials of the Earl Gregg
  Swem Library at the College of William and Mary
  http://www.swem.wm.edu/SPCOL/CivilWar/webcw2.html

- USGenWeb Archives: West Virginia: Civil War Files
  http://www.rootsweb.com/usgenweb/wv/civilwar/

- Virginia Military Institute Archives
  http://www.vmi.edu/~archtml/index.html

◆ Mailing Lists, Newsgroups & Chat

- ACWBLUE Mailing List
  http://members.aol.com/gfsjohnf/gen_mail_states-gen.
  html#ACWBLUE
  *For those who are trying to find genealogical information from
  the Northern States during the period of and around the
  American Civil War.*

- ACWGREY Mailing List
  http://members.aol.com/gfsjohnf/gen_mail_states-gen.
  html#ACWGREY
  *For those who are trying to find genealogical information
  from the Southern States during the period of and around the
  American Civil War.*

- ANDERSONVILLE Mailing List
  http://members.aol.com/gfsjohnf/gen_mail_states-gen.
  html#ANDERSONVILLE
  *For the descendants and interested historians of Andersonville,
  the Civil War's most notorious prison camp, to swap knowledge
  and research the lives of Union prisoners before, during, and
  after their time in Andersonville.*

- CIVIL-WAR-IRISH Mailing List
  http://members.aol.com/gfsjohnf/gen_mail_states-gen.
  html#CIVIL-WAR-IRISH
  *For those with a genealogical interest in the Irish participants in
  the American Civil War and their descendants.*

- CIVIL-WAR Mailing List
  http://members.aol.com/gfsjohnf/gen_mail_states-gen.
  html#CIVIL-WAR
  Also see the associated web page at
  http://www.public.usit.net/mruddy/index.html

- CIVIL-WAR-WOMEN Mailing List
  http://members.aol.com/gfsjohnf/gen_mail_states-gen.
  html#CIVIL-WAR-WOMEN
  *For those with who are researching women that served or
  assisted in the American Civil War.*

- CSA-History Mailing List
  http://members.aol.com/gfsjohnf/gen_mail_states-gen.
  html#CSA-History
  *Confederate States of America Early History and Culture,
  genealogy, Migration Trails, War of Secession, Monuments,
  Cemeteries, Prisons, C.S.A. Regiments, Reconstruction, and
  other pertinent topics.*

- CW-POW Mailing List
  http://members.aol.com/gfsjohnf/gen_mail_states-gen.
  html#CW-POW
  *For the discussion and sharing of information regarding the
  Civil War prisoner of war camps and prisoners of war, both
  Union and Confederate.*

- H-CIVWAR Home Page
  http://h-net2.msu.edu/~civwar/
  *The H-Net discussion list dealing with the culture and history of
  the Civil War.*

- HONEYHILL Mailing List
  http://members.aol.com/gfsjohnf/gen_mail_states-gen.
  html#HONEYHILL
  *For anyone with a genealogical or historical interest in the
  Civil War battle of Honey Hill.*

- IL-CIVIL-WAR Mailing List
  http://members.aol.com/gfsjohnf/gen_mail_states-il.
  html#IL-CIVIL-WAR
  For Civil War researchers in Illinois.

- SULTANA Mailing List
  http://members.aol.com/gfsjohnf/gen_mail_states-gen.
  html#SULTANA
  *For anyone who is researching the 2,000+ soldiers aboard the
  ill-fated steamship Sultana which exploded in 1865.*

- Usenet Newsgroup
  alt.war.civil.usa

- Usenet Newsgroup
  soc.history.war.us-civil-war

- VAWBTSVETS Mailing List
  http://members.aol.com/gfsjohnf/gen_mail_states-va.
  html#VAWBTSVETS
  For anyone with a genealogical interest in the Virginia veterans of the War Between the States.

- WVWBTSVETS Mailing List
  http://members.aol.com/gfsjohnf/gen_mail_states-wv.
  html#WVWBTSVETS
  For anyone researching Civil War Verterans, both Confederate and Union, in West Virginia.

◆ The Navies

- The Civil War Ironclads Page
  http://members.aol.com/MaxDemon88/ironclad.html

- Confederate Naval Museum in Columbus, Georgia
  http://www.columbusga.com/ccvb/ccvb-cnm.html

- Confederate Navy Collections Index
  http://image.vtls.com/collections/CN.html
  From the Library of Virginia Digital Collections.

- CSS Virginia Home Page
  http://members.aol.com/vacsn/index.htm

- The Sultana: Death on the Dark River (1865)
  http://www.rootsweb.com/~genepool/sultana.htm

- SULTANA Mailing List
  http://members.aol.com/gfsjohnf/gen_mail_states-
  gen.html#SULTANA
  For anyone who is researching the 2,000+ soldiers aboard the ill-fated steamship Sultana which exploded in 1865.

- The U.S. Navy in the Civil War: Western Theatre
  http://www.webnation.com/~spectrum/usn-cw/index.phtml
  The "Brownwater Fleet."

- U.S.S. Harvest Moon
  http://members.aol.com/waltesmith/hmhome.htm
  Civil War Flagship of the South Atlantic Blockading Squadron 1864–1865.

◆ Pension & Military Records

- Arkansas History Commission—Request Form for Photocopies of Arkansas Confederate Pensions
  http://www.state.ar.us/ahc/form4.txt

- Arkansas History Commission—Request Form for Photocopies of Arkansas Military Service Records
  http://www.state.ar.us/ahc/form3.txt

- Civil War Records
  http://www.nara.gov/genealogy/civilwar.html
  An article from the National Archives.

- Civil War Records—An Introduction and Invitation
  http://www.nara.gov/publications/prologue/musick.html
  An article by Michael P. Musick from the National Archives web site.

- Civil War Veterans: Copies of Military & Pension Records
  E-mail: inquire@arch2.nara.gov
  Send e-mail to order form NATF 80, Veteran's Records (before WWI only). You will need to give them your postal mailing address.

- Confederate Ancestor Research Guide
  http://www.scv.org/scvgen02.htm

- Confederate Military Records at the Archives ~ South Carolina
  http://www.state.sc.us/scdah/confedrc.htm

- Confederate Military Records—Civil War Military Records in the U.S. National Archives
  http://www2.msstate.edu/~gam3/cw/resources/bib-comp.html
  A how-to guide by Howard Beckman.

- Confederate Pension Records
  http://www.nara.gov/genealogy/confed.html
  An article from the National Archives.

- Confederate Pension Rolls, Veterans and Widows
  http://image.vtls.com/collections/CW.html
  From the Library of Virginia Digital Collections.

- Florida Confederate Pension Application Files
  http://www.dos.state.fl.us/dlis/barm/PensionIntroduction.htm
  Search this online index then follow the instructions for ordering a copy of the pension file.

- Georgia Confederate Pension Applications—State of Georgia Department of Archives & History
  http://docuweb.gsu.edu/scripts/ColBrows.dll?
  CollectionContent&915703266-3&MainCollection\\
  Open+Collections+-\\Georgia+Civil+War+Pension+Records
  "The purpose of this community service project is to digitize the microfilm associated with the pension applications of Georgia's Confederate soldiers and their widows."

- How to Order Military & Pension Records for Union Civil War Veterans from the National Archives
  http://www.oz.net/~cyndihow/pensions.htm
  By Cyndi Howells.

- How to Request Michigan Civil War Ancestor's Military Records from the National Archives
  http://www.centuryinter.net/suvcw.mi/gr-recwv.html

- Index to Confederate Pension Applications ~ Texas
  http://www.tsl.state.tx.us/lobby/cpi/introcpi.htm

- The Library of Virginia Digital Collections
  http://198.17.62.51/
  - Confederate Navy
    http://198.17.62.51/collections/CN.html
  - Confederate Pension Rolls, Veterans and Widows
    http://198.17.62.51/collections/CW.html
  - Confederate Rosters
    http://198.17.62.51/collections/CF.html
  - Confederate Rosters—Supplement
    http://198.17.62.51/collections/CS.html

○ Confederate Units and Localities
http://198.17.62.51/collections/CU.html

● United States Civil War Service and Pension Records
http://www.history.rochester.edu/jssn/page5.htm
Scanned image examples.

● Virtual Victoria: Confederate Pension Applicant Index
http://www.viptx.net/victoria/history/pensions/index.html
An index to all of the applicants from Victoria County, Texas.

◆ People & Families

● Civil War Diary of Bingham Findley JUNKIN, 100th Pennsylvania Volunteer Infantry ("Roundheads")
http://www.iwaynet.net/~lsci/junkin/

● The Civil War Diary of E.B. ROOT
http://www.netrom.com/~merklee/Diary.html

● Civil War Medal of Honor Recipients, A–L
http://imabbs.army.mil/cmh-pg/mohciv.htm

M–Z
http://imabbs.army.mil/cmh-pg/mohciv2.htm

● Civil War Women—Primary Sources on the Internet
http://scriptorium.lib.duke.edu/women/cwdocs.html

● Francis Marion Gay, Co. F 65th Reg. Georgia Infantry
http://www.izzy.net/~michaelg/fm-gay.htm

● Genealogy of the Davis Family
http://www.ruf.rice.edu/~pjdavis/gene.htm
Jefferson Davis, President of C.S.A.

● Isaac Spears Sanderlin, Private, Co. I, 100th Ohio Volunteer Infantry in the Civil War
http://www.oz.net/~cyndihow/isaac.htm
Cyndi's 3rd great-grandfather.

● Letters from an Iowa Soldier in the Civil War
http://www.ucsc.edu./civil-war-letters/home.html
Part of a collection written by Newton Robert SCOTT, Private, Company A, of the 36th Infantry, Iowa Volunteers to Hannah CONE, his friend and later his wife.

● Letters of the Civil War
http://www.geocities.com/Pentagon/7914/
A compilation of letters from the soldiers, sailors, nurses, politicians, ministers and journalists from the newspapers of the cities and towns of Massachusetts, April 1861–December 1865.

● MA Ryan, Co B 14th Miss Vol Inf CSA
http://www.izzy.net/~michaelg/ma-ryan.htm
Experience of a Confederate Soldier in Camp and Prison in The Civil War 1861–1865.

● The Other Civil War Veterans in Cyndi's Family
http://www.oz.net/~cyndihow/civilwar.htm
Cartwright, Ingle, Sanderlin and Walterhouse.

● Tennessee Confederate Physicians: An Introduction
http://www.state.tn.us/sos/statelib/pubsvs/docintro.htm
From the Tennessee State Library and Archives—Historical and Genealogical Information.

● Women and the Civil War
http://odyssey.lib.duke.edu/women/civilwar.html
Manuscript sources in the Special Collections Library at Duke University.

● Women Soldiers of the Civil War
http://www.nara.gov/publications/prologue/women1.html

● Women's Civil War Diaries and Papers—Locations
http://homepages.rootsweb.com/~haas/cwdiaries.html

● Xerxes Knox, Private, Co. G, 3rd Iowa Cavalry in the Civil War
http://www.oz.net/~cyndihow/xerxes.htm
Cyndi's 3rd great-grandfather and a prisoner at Camp Ford in Tyler, Texas.

◆ Prisons & Prisoners

● 36th Iowa Infantry POWs at Camp Ford, Tyler, Tx
http://www.rootsweb.com/~iaappano/pow.htm

● Alton in the Civil War—Alton Prison ~ Illinois
http://www.altonweb.com/history/civilwar/confed/index.html

● Andersonville National Historic Site
http://www.nps.gov/ande/
From the National Park Service.

● Camp Douglas, Illinois
http://www.outfitters.com/illinois/history/civil/campdouglas.html
Prison camp and training camp.

● Charleston Race Course Prison Dead, SC
http://members.aol.com/edboots/charlestondead.html
Union Civil War Prisoners of War originally buried at the Charleston Race Course Cemetery and later reinterred at the Beaufort National Cemetery.

● Confederate Soldier—Rock Island Illinois
http://www.insolwwb.net/~egerdes/rockisld.htm
Confederate POW's Listed in Arkansas Units Who Died in Rock Island, IL Prison Camp.

● Friends of the Florence Stockade
http://members.aol.com/qmsgtboots/florence.html
Florence, South Carolina

● Kansas Prisoners of War at Camp Ford, Texas 1863–1865
http://history.cc.ukans.edu/heritage/research/campford.html

● MA Ryan, Co B 14th Miss Vol Inf CSA
http://www.izzy.net/~michaelg/ma-ryan.htm
Experience of a Confederate Soldier in Camp and Prison in The Civil War 1861–1865.

● Ohio Prisoner of War Camp Sources
http://www.infinet.com/~lstevens/a/prison.html

- Union Civil War Prison at Elmira, NY
  http://www2.netdoor.com/~52rcourt/elmiran.htm
- Union Civil War Prison at Point Lookout, Maryland
  http://www2.netdoor.com/~52rcourt/lookoutn.htm
- Xerxes Knox, Private, Co. G, 3rd Iowa Cavalry
  in the Civil War
  http://www.oz.net/~cyndihow/xerxes.htm
  *Cyndi's 3rd great-grandfather and a prisoner at Camp Ford in
  Tyler, Texas.*

◆ Professional Researchers, Volunteers & Other Research Services

- Civil War Pension Files Copied by Faith Libelo
  E-mail: fsl.genie.research@erols.com
  *She can visit the National Archives for you and copy the files. E-
  mail Faith at fsl.genie.research@erols.com for details.*
- D & A Lambert Genealogical and Historical
  Research Service
  http://www.channel1.com/~davidl/
  New England and Civil War research.
- Virginia Family Research
  http://www.mindspring.com/~jkward/Index.html
  *Virginia genealogy, Virginia Confederate records, Revolutionary
  records.*

◆ Publications, Photographs & Supplies

- America's Civil War Magazine
  http://www.thehistorynet.com/AmericasCivilWar/
- Boyd Publishing Company—Civil War
  http://www.hom.net/~gac/civilwar.htm
- Camp Pope Bookshop
  http://members.aol.com/ckenyoncpb/index.htm
  *Specializing in out-of-print books on the American Civil War,
  Iowa & the Trans-Mississippi Theater State.*
- Civil War Diaries
  http://www.augustana.edu/library/civil.html
- Civil War Family Photographs
  http://members.tripod.com/~cwphotos/
- The Civil War Music Store
  http://bizweb.lightspeed.net/~cwms/
  Authentic music of the Civil War.
- Civil War Photograph Collection
  http://lcweb.loc.gov/spcoll/048.html
  Library of Congress.
- Civil War Times Magazine
  http://www.thehistorynet.com/CivilWarTimes/
- Frontier Press Bookstore—Civil War
  http://www.frontierpress.com/frontier.cgi?category=civwar

- GenealogyBookShop.com—Civil War
  http://www.genealogybookshop.com/genealogybookshop/files/
  General,Civil_War/index.html
  *The online store of Genealogical Publishing Co., Inc. &
  Clearfield Company.*
- Guidon Books
  http://www.guidon.com/index.html
  *Has an extensive collection of new and out of print books on the
  American Civil War and Western Americana.*
- Guild Press of Indiana—Civil War Books, part 1
  http://www.guildpress.com/civil_war_books.htm

  and part 2
  http://www.guildpress.com/civil_war_books2.htm
- Guild Press of Indiana—Civil War CD-ROMs
  http://www.guildpress.com/cdroms.htm#civilwar
- James River Publications Civil War Homepage
  http://www.erols.com/jreb/civilwar.htm
- The McGowan Book Company
  http://www.mcgowanbooks.com/
  *Specializing in locating, buying and selling rare books, Civil
  War memorabilia, photographs and documents. Also, materials
  for Americana, African-American history, Church History and
  Military history.*
- MHI Photograph Database—Catalog of CW Photos
  http://www.city-gallery.com/resource/pa/Reviews/Collections/
  Military_History_Institute_Photographs.html
- Miles of History—Online Auction
  http://collectorsnet.com/miles/
- North South Trader's Civil War Magazine
  http://www.nstcivilwar.com/
- The Official Records of the Union and
  Confederate Armies
  http://www.soldiersearch.com/aorintro.htm
  128 volumes, including index. Also available on CD-ROM.
- Ohio Civil War Genealogy Journal
  http://www.ogs.org/civil.htm
  A quarterly publication from The Ohio Genealogical Society.
- The OR—The Official Record of the Union and
  Confederate Armies in the War of the Rebellion
  http://www.public.usit.net/mruddy/or.htm
  *A description, as well as a synopsis of the contents in each
  volume.*
  http://www.public.usit.net/mruddy/synopses.htm
- The Rural Citizen Online Bookstore
  http://www.ruralcitizen.com/
  *Specializes in Southern and Confederate history, culture and
  heritage.*
- Selected Civil War Photographs—American
  Memory Collection, Library of Congress
  http://lcweb2.loc.gov/ammem/cwphome.html
- SoldierSearch.com—Civil War Research and
  Genealogy Materials
  http://www.soldiersearch.com/
  *Featuring products from Broadfoot Publishing, including
  several CD-ROMs.*

- Valley of the Shadow Newspapers
  http://jefferson.village.Virginia.EDU/vshadow2/
  newspapers.html
  From the Civil War project at the University of Virginia.

- Valor in Gray—Recipients of the Confederate Medal of Honor
  http://www.mindspring.com/~valor-in-gray/
  A new book from Gregg S. Clemmer.

- West Virginia Book Company
  http://www.wvbookco.com/

- Willow Bend Bookstore—Civil War
  http://www.willowbend.net/cw.htm

◆ Reconstruction

- Aftermath of the Civil War—Reconstruction Era 1865–77
  http://www.libarts.sfasu.edu/history/133_Unit4D.html

- The American South During Reconstruction
  http://www.cyberverse.com/~burkean/
  american_south_during_reconstruc.htm

- A Bitter Peace—The Reconstruction of Georgia
  http://ngeorgia.com/history/recon.shtml

- Chapter 13: Reconstruction & the New South
  http://www.cwo.com/~guru/ushch13.html

- The Compromise of 1877
  http://www.npcts.edu/acad/history/WebChron/USA/
  1877Comp.html

- Explain the Rise of the Black Ghetto During the Period 1880–1920
  http://www.foobar.co.uk/~allat51/chris/desk/ghetto.html

- The Legacy of the Civil War
  http://getafix.isgtec.com/glenweb/legacy.html

- Reconstruction 1865–1877
  http://www.marshall.edu/history/mccarthy/hst331/lecture/
  reconst.i

- Reconstruction by Frederick Douglass
  http://etext.lib.virginia.edu/cgibin/browse-
  mixed?id=DouReco&tag=public&images=images/
  modeng&data=/lv1/Archive/eng-parsed

- The Reconstruction of the South After the Civil War
  http://gps.lhric.org/middle/ems/rcpeters.htm

◆ Regimental Rosters & Histories ~ The Confederacy

- 1st Confederate Division
  http://fly.hiwaay.net/~dsmart/1stdiv.html

- 1st. Infantry Regiment, Alabama, C.S.A.
  http://home.sprynet.com/sprynet/harrisfarm/ahar02.htm

- 1st Maryland Battery, C.S.A.
  http://www.concentric.net/~Danaher/MD1stAty/

- 3rd Arkansas Infantry Regiment
  http://www.wcnet.org/~bminton/

- 4th Alabama Infantry
  http://www.geocities.com/BourbonStreet/Delta/7265/

- 6th Missouri Infantry, Company A, 4th Battalion
  http://www.sunflower.org/~6thmo/6thmo.htm

- 6th Texas Cavalry Battalion—Gould's Texas Battalion
  http://www.io.com/~dwhite/gould.html
  A history of the battalion and a muster roll for Company E.

- 6th Texas Infantry—A Civil War Historical and Genealogical Resource Page
  http://lonestar.texas.net/~thompson/

- 7th Texas Infantry
  http://www.why.net/home/sdavis/7thTexas/index.htm

- 8th Tennessee Cavalry, C.S.A.
  http://www.jagunet.com/~mbar/8tncav.htm

- 8th Virginia Cavalry—Wayne County, West Virginia
  http://ourworld.compuserve.com/homepages/GlenGallagher/
  8thva.htm

- 11th Mississippi Infantry
  http://www.why.net/home/sdavis/11thMiss/index.htm

- 16th Virginia Cavalry—Wayne County, West Virginia
  http://ourworld.compuserve.com/homepages/GlenGallagher/
  16thva.htm

- 19th Alabama Infantry Regiment, Army of Tennessee, C.S.A.
  http://www.19thalabama.org/

- The 19th Georgia Regimental History
  http://www.fred.net/stevent/19GA/19ga.html

- 19th Louisiana
  http://www.access.digex.net/~bdboyle/19LA.txt

- 20th (Russell's) Tennessee Cavalry, C.S.A.
  http://home.olemiss.edu/~cmprice/cav.html

- 25th TN Inf. CSA
  http://userzweb.lightspeed.net/~richardm/zolly.htm

- 26th Mississippi Infantry, C.S.A.
  http://members.aol.com/shardwik/cw/26thms.html

- 29th Alabama Infantry Regiment, C.S.A.
  http://www.geocities.com/Heartland/Estates/3071/index.html

- 30th Arkansas Infantry CSA, Co. A & L
  http://www.cswnet.com/~bbarnes/30th_Ark_inf_Clay.htm

- 30th Regiment of Virginia Infantry, Regimental History
  http://www.access.digex.net/~bdboyle/30thva.html

- 32nd Infantry Regiment of Alabama Volunteers, Company "D"
  http://www.netpathway.com/~bennie/compdal.html

- The 35th Texas Cavalry
  http://www.io.com/~dwhite/35thTX.html
  A brief history of the 35th Texas Cavalry and extracts from the pension application of Mrs. John Hale.

- 36th Alabama Infantry—Company G
  http://www.edge.net/~deke/algenweb/36th_AL.htm

- 42nd Alabama Infantry
  http://www.alaska.net/~bearpaw/Alabama42.htm

- 44th Tennessee Infantry Regiment, C.S.A.
  http://www.geocities.com/BourbonStreet/4455/

- 47th Tennessee Infantry Regiment, C.S.A.
  http://www.geocities.com/Pentagon/4740/

- 48th Alabama Infantry
  http://fly.hiwaay.net/~jrgeorge/48histry.html

- 49th Alabama (CSA) During the Civil War
  http://fly.hiwaay.net/~jemcgee/
  Initially known as "Hale's 31st Alabama."

- 50th Regiment Georgia Volunteer Infantry Army of Northern Virginia, C.S.A.
  http://www.ij.net/phickey/50.htm
  Colquitt County, Georgia, Colquitt Marksmen or Colquitt Volunteers.

- 51st Virginia Infantry
  http://www.clark.net/pub/mjloyd/home.html
  on Mary Jo Loyd's Home Page.

- 55th Alabama
  http://www.access.digex.net/~bdboyle/55al.txt

- Alabama Civil War Regimental Histories
  http://www.tarleton.edu/~kjones/alregts.html

- Alabama Infantry Regiments
  http://www.erols.com/jreb/alabama.html
  Books for sale, as well as links to regimental sites.

- Battalion History of First Maryland Cavalry Battalion, C.S.A.
  http://www.cybcon.com/~warren/MD1_hist.html

- Blount County, Alabama Companies and Soldiers in the Armies of the C.S.A.
  http://members.aol.com/egun/CSA.html

- Cherokee Legion—"Georgia State Guards"
  http://www.scsn.net/users/sage/cl_index.htm

- Civil War Units File—CSA National and States A–M
  http://sunsite.utk.edu/civil-war/unit4.html
  E-mail contacts.

- Civil War Units File—CSA States N–V
  http://sunsite.utk.edu/civil-war/unit5.html
  E-mail contacts.

- Co H 30th Arkansas Infantry Regiment, C.S.A.
  http://www.insolwwb.net/~egerdes/civilwar/30ark.htm

- Co I 30th Arkansas Infantry Regiment, C.S.A.
  http://www.insolwwb.net/~egerdes/civilwar/coiark.htm

- Colquitt's Brigade
  http://extlab1.entnem.ufl.edu/olustee/colquitt.html
  Sixth Georgia Infantry.

- Co. B, 11th Battalion Georgia Volunteer Artillery Americus, GA.
  http://www.ij.net/phickey/ga11.htm
  Known as "Cutts Battalion," Sumter Flying Artillery.

- Co. F, 65th Regiment Georgia Volunteer Infantry Army of Tennessee, C.S.A.
  http://www.izzy.net/~michaelg/fm-gay.htm

- Company A, Fifth Regiment Mississippi Cavalry
  http://www.gower.net/bclayton/coa5reg.html

- Company G, 8th Georgia Regiment, C.S.A.
  http://www.mindspring.com/~jtfleming/CoG_1.htm
  History of Company G, 8th Georgia Regiment, C.S.A. ("The Pulaski Volunteers"), by David Green Fleming," originally published in the summer of 1879.

- Company Muster Roll Enterprise Tigers Company D 37th
  http://www.netpathway.com/~buckley/tiger.html

- Confederate Regimental History Links
  http://www.tarleton.edu/~kjones/confeds.html

- Confederate Rosters
  http://image.vtls.com/collections/CF.html
  From the Library of Virginia Digital Collections.

- Confederate Rosters—Supplement
  http://image.vtls.com/collections/CS.html
  From the Library of Virginia Digital Collections.

- Confederate Soldiers from Shelby County, Alabama and Surrounding Counties
  http://www.mindspring.com/~spbarber429/shelbycsa.htm

- Confederate Soldiers from the Shenandoah Valley
  http://home.tampabay.rr.com/shenandoah/civilwar.html

- Confederate Units and Localities
  http://image.vtls.com/collections/CU.html
  From the Library of Virginia Digital Collections.

- Cpt. John L. KUYKENDALL of Greene County, Arkansas
  http://www.grnco.net/~michael/civwar.htm

- CSA 9th Florida Infantry
  http://members.aol.com/Kwiley/index.html

- "E" Company, 4th Missouri Infantry, C.S.A.
  http://www.mo-net.com/~mwilliams/reenactor.html

- Eighth Regiment—Infantry Company G, Tolson Guard of Jasper County Mississippi
  http://www.netpathway.com/~buckley/tolson.html

- Fifth Mississippi Regiment, C.S.A.
  http://www.izzy.net/~michaelg/5ms-1.htm

- The Fifth Missouri Infantry—CSA
  http://www.cedarcroft.com/cw/5mo.html

- Fifteenth Alabama Infantry Regiment
  http://www.mindspring.com/~edeagle/15AVC/
  Campsite for information on the Original Regiment & for Reenactment 15th Alabama Infantry, Company A.

- Fifteenth Mississippi Infantry Regiment CSA
  http://web2.airmail.net/phi868/wigfall.html

- First Georgia Regulars
  http://extlab1.entnem.ufl.edu/olustee/1st_GA_regulars.html

- First Kentucky Brigade, C.S.A.—The Orphan Brigade
  http://www.rootsweb.com/~orphanhm/

- Forty-Eighth Alabama Infantry
  http://members.aol.com/egun/48th.html

- Georgia 15th Infantry Regiment
  http://members.aol.com/lissiet/15thcamp.htm

- Georgia 49th Infantry Regiment
  http://members.aol.com/lissiet/49thcamp.htm

- A Guide to Cherokee Confederate Military Units, 1861–1865
  http://www.scv.org/cherokee.htm

- H Co. 19th Alabama
  http://www.dnaco.net/~csmartin/hco_19th.html

- Harrison's Brigade
  http://extlab1.entnem.ufl.edu/olustee/harrison.html

- History of Law's Alabama Brigade, 1862–1865
  http://www.tarleton.edu/~kjones/lawsbrig.html
  Including information & muster rolls for: 4th Alabama Regiment, 15th Alabama Regiment, 44th Alabama Regiment, 47th Alabama Regiment and 48th Alabama Regiment.

- History of the 3rd Georgia Volunteer Infantry
  http://www.forttejon.org/ga3/ga3history.html

- History of the 18th Alabama Infantry Regiment—CSA
  http://www.mindspring.com/~spbarber429/18ala.htm

- History of the 19th (Dawson's) Arkansas Infantry Regiment
  http://rampages.onramp.net/~jtcreate/19hist.htm

- History of the 33rd Alabama Infantry
  http://members.aol.com/wwhitby/33rd.html

- History of the 47th Alabama Volunteer Infantry Regiment
  http://www.geocities.com/heartland/ridge/9202
  This is a Confederate Army Regimental History of the 47th Alabama Infantry. It now includes unit rosters, (alphabetical order for ease of searching), and will eventually contain other genealogical information related to individuals which were listed on the rosters such as age at enlistment, occupation at enlistment, etc., and burial places of the members of the unit. I will also be including and soliciting for information from decendants of the unit to include on this page. The page will include about 1000 names of the soldiers of the 47th but will be unique in that it will eventually chronicle battles, casualties, campsite locations, etc.

- Index to the 32nd Arkansas Infantry M-317 Compiled Service Records
  http://www.insolwwb.net/~egerdes/32index.htm

- Muster Roll Captain R. R. Sissell's Company, Hopkins County, Texas
  http://www.geocities.com/Vienna/1516/muster.html

- Muster Roll of Company B, 51st Regiment Georgia Volunteer Infantry
  http://www.ij.net/phickey/51.htm

- Nineteenth Georgia Infantry
  http://extlab1.entnem.ufl.edu/olustee/19th_GA_inf.html

- Newton's 8th Arkansas Cavalry CSA
  http://members.aol.com/newtons8th/index.html

- Official Historic Web Site of the 10th Texas Infantry
  http://members.aol.com/SMckay1234/

- Parsons' Texas Cavalry Brigade
  http://www.why.net/home/sdavis/Parsons/index.htm
  Regimental rosters for the 12th, 19th, 21st, 30th and Morgan's Regiment Texas Cavalry.

- Roster of Company I, 28th Texas Cavalry (Dismounted)
  http://www.io.com/~dwhite/col28.html

- Roster of Confederate Soldiers in Colquitt County, Georgia
  http://www.ij.net/phickey/colconfed.htm

- Search the Virginia Rosters
  http://jefferson.village.virginia.edu/vshadow/rostersearch.html

- Shaver's 7th Regiment and Other Companies with Lawrence County and Surrounding Area Soldiers
  http://www.insolwwb.net/~egerdes/civilwar/
  Arkansas

- Sixth Georgia Infantry
  http://extlab1.entnem.ufl.edu/olustee/6th_GA_inf.html

- Sixty-Fourth Georgia Infantry Regiment
  http://extlab1.entnem.ufl.edu/olustee/64th_GA_inf.html

- Swann's Battalion Virginia Cavalry
  http://members.aol.com/jweaver302/CW/swann.htm

- Third Florida Infantry, Company B—St. Augustine Blues (CSA)
  http://www.geocities.com/Heartland/Hills/8299/military/3fl_inf.htm

- Thirty-Second Georgia Infantry
  http://extlab1.entnem.ufl.edu/olustee/32nd_GA_inf.html

- Thurmond's Virginia Partisan Rangers
  http://members.aol.com/jweaver302/CW/thurmond.htm

- Trans-Mississippi Rifles (TMR)
  http://members.aol.com/rlhtmr/index.html

- Twenty-Eighth Battalion, Georgia Siege Artillery
  http://extlab1.entnem.ufl.edu/olustee/28th_GA_art.html

- Twenty-Eighth Georgia Infantry
  http://extlab1.entnem.ufl.edu/olustee/28th_GA_inf.html

- Twenty-Seventh Georgia Infantry
  http://extlab1.entnem.ufl.edu/olustee/27th_GA_inf.html

- Twenty-Third Georgia Infantry
  http://extlab1.entnem.ufl.edu/olustee/23rd_GA_inf.html

- Virtual Victoria: Confederate Soldiers
  http://www.viptx.net/victoria/history/soldiers.html
  Rosters of soldiers from Victoria County, Texas.

◆ Regimental Rosters & Histories ~ The Union

- 1st Kansas Volunteer Infantry
  http://www.access.digex.net/~bdboyle/1stks.txt

- 1st Regiment Michigan Sharpshooters
  http://users.aol.com/dlharvey/sharps.htm

- 4th Ohio Volunteer Cavalry
  http://www.geocities.com/Heartland/Plains/7614/4th_ohio.htm

- The 5th New York Volunteer Infantry—"Duryee's Zouaves"
  http://www.zouave.org/

- 5th Regiment New Hampshire Volunteers
  http://www.mv.com/ipusers/n33db/fifth.html

- 6th Kentucky Volunteer Infantry Regiment
  http://www.rootsweb.com/~jadmire/kyhenry/6thky.htm

- 6th Regiment, Ohio Volunteer Infantry
  http://www.access.digex.net/~bdboyle/6thohio.txt

- 7th Illinois Cavalry
  http://www.outfitters.com/illinois/history/civil/cwc7-agr1.html

- The 7th West Virginia Infantry Homepage
  http://members.aol.com/dwmellott/7wv.htm
  "The voice of the Bloody Seventh"

- 8th Iowa Cavalry from Appanoose County, Iowa
  http://www.ionet.net/~cousin/dale3.html

- The 8th Missouri Volunteer Infantry, US
  http://www.apci.net/~prozac/

- 9th Illinois Cavalry
  http://www.outfitters.com/illinois/history/civil/cwc9.html

- 9th Massachusetts Battery
  http://www.geocities.com/pentagon/8279
  Civil War Site for historical and reenacting 9th Massachusetts Battery. Lists where each was from, occupation, muster in and out dates, date of death, injuries. etc.

- 10th Iowa Volunteer Infantry
  http://www.geocities.com/Heartland/Plains/7614/10thiowa.htm

- 10th Kansas Volunteer Infantry
  http://www.telepath.com/erics/10kansas1.html

- 10th Mass. Volunteer Infantry Regiment
  http://members.aol.com/mass10th/index.html

- 11th Massachusetts Infantry—"Boston Volunteers"
  http://members.aol.com/rdmorss/11home.htm

- 12th Indiana Volunteer Infantry Regiment
  http://www.access.digex.net/~bdboyle/12in.txt

- 12th Kansas Volunteer Infantry, Company K
  http://www.geocities.com/MotorCity/1949/cok12ks.htm

- 12th Kentucky Infantry Regiment (US)
  http://www.edm.net/~Pjsewell/12th.htm

- 12th New York Cavalry
  http://snycorva.cortland.edu/~woosterk/12cav.html

- 13th Corp Organization as Part of the Army of the Tennessee
  http://www.intersource.com/~bjohnson/corp.html

- 14th Kentucky Infantry
  http://ram.ramlink.net/~cbarker/14kyinf.htm

- 15th Massachusetts Volunteer Infantry
  http://www.augsburg.baynet.de/~ba021308/

- 15th New Jersey Volunteer Infantry
  http://www.erols.com/jbeegle/15thform.html

- 16th Massachusetts Volunteer Infantry
  http://members.aol.com/inf16mavol/16thmass.html
  Dedicated to my great-great-grandfather, Isaac F. Kennaston, this site lists the rosters of the 16th Mass., and links to known descendants and other Civil War sites.

- 16th Ohio Volunteer Infantry Home Page
  http://www.mkwe.com/home.htm

- 17th Illinois Infantry
  http://www.outfitters.com/illinois/history/civil/cw17.html

- 18th Massachusetts Volunteer Infantry
  http://www.geocities.com/Pentagon/8509/

- 19th Indiana Volunteer Infantry—Company A
  http://members.iquest.net/~virx/19th.html

- 20th Maine Volunteer Infantry Company G
  http://midas.org/npo/cwar/acwa/20mevcog.html

- 20th Regiment of Massachusetts Volunteer Infantry—"The Harvard Regiment"
  http://www.med.Virginia.EDU/~mmd5f/

- 22nd Massachusetts Volunteer Infantry
  http://www.geocities.com/Pentagon/3622/
  A Civil War Rifle Unit, reenactment group.

- 27th Indiana Volunteer Infantry
  http://www.fortunecity.com/victorian/browning/186/27thindiana.html

- 27th Regiment, Massachusetts Volunteer Infantry
  http://members.aol.com/mass27th/

- 28th Maine, Battle Report
  http://www.access.digex.net/~bdboyle/28thme.txt

- 28th Massachusetts Volunteer Infantry
  http://209.61.8.248/

- 28th Regiment, Wisconsin Volunteer Infantry
  http://www.execpc.com/~kap/wisc28.html

- 36th Iowa Infantry
  http://www.rootsweb.com/~iaappano/36ia.htm

- 36th Ohio Volunteer Infantry, Union Civil War Regiment 1861–1865
  http://www.angelfire.com/oh/36OVI/
  Site dedicated to preserving the history of the 36th Ohio Volunteer Infantry, a Civil War unit formed in Washington County, Ohio. Searching for descendants of the men of the 36th. Gathering material for a regimental history to be written by a military historian.

- 39th Regiment of New York Infantry— "Garibaldi Guard"
  http://hebron.ee.gannon.edu/~frezza/39NYSV/RegHist.html

- 42nd Indiana Volunteer Infantry—Army of the Cumberland, U.S.A.
  http://www.19thalabama.org/42ndind.html

- The 44th Regt. Massachusetts Volunteer Militia— The Second New England Guards Regiment
  http://members.aol.com/dcurtin1/44th_reg.htm

- 48th Ohio Veteran Volunteer Infantry
  http://www.ben2.ucla.edu/~worth/history48ovvi.html

- 49th Indiana Volunteer Infantry, 'Company F'— Reenactment Unit
  http://www.intersource.com/~bjohnson/49th.html

- 49th Ohio Volunteer Infantry
  http://www.infinet.com/~lstevens/49oh.html

- 53rd Kentucky Mounted Infantry
  http://www.geocities.com/Heartland/5170/53rdkent.htm

- 53rd Massachusetts Volunteer Infantry
  http://www.intac.com/~blenderm/53rd_Mass_f/53rd_Mass.html

- 54th. Mass. Volunteer Infantry, Co. I
  http://www.awod.com/gallery/probono/cwchas/54ma.html

- 55th Illinois Infantry
  http://www.outfitters.com/illinois/history/civil/cw55.html

- 56th Regiment Massachusetts Volunteers
  http://www.tiac.net/users/dhayes/56th/

- 59th Illinois Infantry
  http://www.outfitters.com/illinois/history/civil/cw59.html

- 61st PA Volunteers, Regimental History
  http://www.access.digex.net/~bdboyle/61st.txt

- The 72nd New York Volunteer Infantry
  http://home.inreach.com/mavgw/72nd.htm

- 74th Illinois Infantry
  http://www.outfitters.com/illinois/history/civil/cw74.html

- 75th Illinois Infantry
  http://www.outfitters.com/illinois/history/civil/cw75.html

- 76th Ohio Volunteer Infantry
  http://www.infinet.com/~lstevens/civwar/

- 101st Pennsylvania Volunteer Infantry
  http://members.aol.com/qmsgtboots/101pa.html

- 103d Regiment Pennsylvania Volunteer Infantry
  http://users.aol.com/evanslaug/103rd.html

- 104th Pa. Volunteer Infantry
  http://www.voicenet.com/~104pa/

- 112th New York Infantry—The Chautauqua Regiment
  http://home.earthlink.net/~cwashburn/112th_ny.html

- 114th Pennsylvania Volunteer Infantry, Co. A— "Collis' Zouaves"
  http://www.concentric.net/~sthutch/114th.html

- 115th NY Volunteer Infantry
  http://www.rootsweb.com/~nyherkim/general115.html

- 125th Pennsylvania Regiment—Memorial
  http://members.aol.com/PA125thReg/home.htm
  Roster of all companies of the 125th Pennsylvania Regiment Volunteers in the Civil War.

- The 126th Ohio Volunteer Infantry: Letters, Accounts, Oral Histories
  http://www.iwaynet.net/~lsci/

- 187th Regiment Pennsylvania Volunteer Infantry
  http://Bip.concept.se/user/187pvi/

- Alabama Regiments in the Armies of the United States
  http://members.aol.com/egun/Union.html

- Civil War: Iowa Volunteers
  http://www.alaska.net/~design/civilwar/
  Including excerpts from a Civil War diary and letters.

- Civil War New York 21st Volunteers
  http://www.surfer-net.com/lbeilein/civil.htm

- The Civil War Pages—78th Pennsylvania Volunteer Infantry
  http://members.tripod.com/~ProlificPains/cwpages.htm

- Civil War Record for Black Hawk County, Iowa
  http://www.iowa-counties.com/blackhawk/civilwar/index.shtml
  Including: First Cavalry, Ninth Infantry, Twelfth Infantry, and Thirty-First Infantry.

- Civil War Rolls for Washington County, Pennsylvania
  http://www.chartiers.com/crumrine/civil-index.html

- Civil War Soldiers from Jefferson County, Pennsylvania
  http://www.geocities.com/Heartland/Plains/8021/civil1.htm

- Civil War Units File—USA National and States A–I
  http://sunsite.utk.edu/civil-war/unit1.html
  E-mail contacts.

- Civil War Units File—USA States K–N
  http://sunsite.utk.edu/civil-war/unit2.html
  E-mail contacts.

- Civil War Units File—USA States O–W
  http://sunsite.utk.edu/civil-war/unit3.html
  E-mail contacts.

- Company D, Tenth WV Volunteers (116 men)
  http://members.tripod.com/~drmalec/cod10.htm

- Company I, 111th NYS Volunteer Infantry
  Regiment 1862
  http://www.ultranet.com/~smack/111th.html

- Database of Illinois' Civil War Veterans
  http://www.sos.state.il.us/depts/archives/datcivil.html
  *From the Illinois State Archives, this is an index of over 250,000
  men in 175 regiments as they are listed in 8 volumes of the
  Report of the Adjutant General of the State of Illinois, published
  in 1900–1901.*

- The Eighty-Fourth Pennsylvania Volunteer
  http://mason.gmu.edu/~rgainer/
  Infantry Homepage.

- Fifty-Fourth Massachusetts Infantry
  http://extlab1.entnem.ufl.edu/olustee/54th_MS_inf.html

- Forty-Fourth Regiment Massachusetts Volunteer
  Militia (Infantry)
  http://members.aol.com/dcurtin1/44th_reg.htm

- Fourteenth Brooklyn New York State Militia,
  "Red Legged Devils"
  http://www.mncs.k12.mn.us/~14nysm/

- Fourteenth Regiment, Kansas Volunteer Calvary
  http://www.ukans.edu/~hisite/franklin/military/
  KS14thRegCav.htm

- The Fourth Arkansas Union Infantry
  http://www.insolwwb.net/~egerdes/4thunion.htm

- History of 48th Illinois Infantry
  http://www.outfitters.com/illinois/history/civil/cw48-hist.html

- History of Ninety-Ninth Infantry
  http://www.outfitters.com/illinois/history/civil/cw99-agr.html

- History of the Seventy-Sixth Illinois Volunteer
  Infantry Regiment
  http://www.outfitters.com/illinois/history/civil/cw76-hist.html

- Illinois in the Civil War
  http://www.rootsweb.com/~ilcivilw/
  A USGenWeb and ILGenWeb project to put rosters online.

- Index—Company I, Second Pennsylvania Cavalry
  http://www.granniesworld.com/cvahs/CompanyI/

- Index to Kansas Volunteer Regiment Enlistments,
  1861–1865
  http://www.ukans.edu/heritage/kshs/archives/agorpt.htm

- Lawrence County in the Civil War ~ Ohio
  http://www.geocities.com/Heartland/5060/lawcocw.htm

- Massachusetts Third Infantry
  http://www.geocities.com/Heartland/Valley/1410/
  ma3_index.html

- Massachusetts Volunteer Cavalry 1st Regiment
  http://members.aol.com/Shortyhack/1stmass.html

- Michigan Regimental Rosters
  http://users.aol.com/dharvey125/rosters.htm

- Muster Roll—West Virginia 15th Vol. Infantry
  http://sunsite.utk.edu/civil-war/wvamuster.html

- New York 2nd Regiment Veteran Cavalry—
  "Empire Light Cavalry"
  http://www.geocities.com/Heartland/2101/2dvetcav.html

- New York Volunteers 188th Regiment Co. A
  http://home.swbell.net/jcanders/index.html

- Ninth Regiment Infantry Indiana Volunteers
  Company E
  http://www.csinet.net/lt1Mike/

- Ninety-Ninth Infantry Regiment of Illinois
  Volunteers, Muster Roll of Company "D"
  http://www.outfitters.com/illinois/history/civil/cw99dndx.html

- NY 16th Regiment Infantry Page
  http://www.geocities.com/Heartland/2101/16index.html

- Ohio Volunteer Infantry 4th Regiment
  http://members.aol.com/Shortyhack/Ohio4.html

- Ohio Volunteer Infantry 51st Regiment
  http://members.aol.com/Shortyhack/ohio51.html

- Ohio Volunteer Infantry 66th Regiment
  http://members.aol.com/Shortyhack/66ohio.html

- Ohio Volunteer Infantry 142nd Regiment
  http://members.aol.com/Shortyhack/142ohio.html

- Pennsylvania Volunteers of the Civil War, 81st
  Regiment Company D
  http://www.geocities.com/Heartland/Hills/3916/cwpa81d.html

- Pennsylvania Volunteers of the Civil War,
  Emergency and State Militia Troops of 1863, 53rd
  Regiment Company I
  http://www.geocities.com/Heartland/Hills/3916/cwpa53i.html

- Pennsylvania Volunteers of the Civil War, Ninety-
  Sixth Regiment, Company F
  http://www.geocities.com/Heartland/Hills/3916/cwpa96f.html

- Pennsylvania Volunteers of the Civil War, Sixteenth
  Regiment, Company D
  http://www.geocities.com/Heartland/Hills/3916/cwpa16d.html

- Pennsylvania Volunteers of the Civil War, Sixteenth
  Regiment, Company I
  http://www.geocities.com/Heartland/Hills/3916/cwpa16i.html

- Recruitment of Illinois Regiments—Civil War,
  1861–1865—County Search
  http://www.outfitters.com/illinois/history/civil/searchco.html

- Recruitment of Illinois Artillery Regiments—Civil War, 1861–1865
  http://www.outfitters.com/illinois/history/civil/searchart.html
  - Recruitment of Illinois Cavalry Regiments—Civil War, 1861–1865
  http://www.outfitters.com/illinois/history/civil/searchcav.html
  - Recruitment of Illinois Infantry Regiments—Civil War, 1861–1865
  http://www.outfitters.com/illinois/history/civil/searchreg.html
- Regimental History 148th Pennsylvania Volunteers
  http://www.gettysburg.edu/~sdreese/148.html
- Roster Members of 187th Regiment, Pennsylvania Volunteer Infantry
  http://www.clark.net/pub/monte/files/187rost.txt
  Still Living 35 years from the date of discharge, 3 August 1865.
- Roster of Men Joining the U.S. Army from Pitcher, Chenango County, New York in the Years 1861–1865
  http://www.frontiernet.net/~elburro/roster01.htm
- Roster of 24th Iowa Infantry
  http://www.rootsweb.com/~ialinn/civil_war/24th/24_indx.htm
  Formed in Linn County, Iowa.
- Roster of the 101st Pennsylvania Volunteer Infantry
  http://members.aol.com/qmsgtboots/101roster.html
- Roster of the 2nd Massachusetts Volunteer Heavy Artillery, Companies G & H and Field & Staff Officers
  http://members.aol.com/CWPPDS/2ma.html
- Second Kansas Volunteer Cavalry
  http://home.earthlink.net/~balocca/cavalry.html
- The Seventeenth New York Volunteer Infantry, Company B
  http://members.tripod.com/~bwhelply/17NYVI.html
- Seventh Illinois Mounted Infantry, Enlisted Men of Company "H"
  http://members.tripod.com/~rjsnyder/Seventh.htm
- Seventh New Hampshire Infantry
  http://extlab1.entnem.ufl.edu/olustee/7th_NH_inf.html
- The Seventh West Virginia Cavalry
  http://members.aol.com/stevecunni/wv7thcav/index.html
  Formerly the Eighth [West] Virginia Infantry and the Eighth West Virginia Mounted Infantry U.S. Civil War, Union Army, 1861–1865.
- Sixth Ohio Volunteer Infantry
  http://www.intcom.net/~tomt/6ovihome.htm
- Stephen Williamson's Ancestor Page with Information on the 14th WV Volunteer Infantry
  http://pw2.netcom.com/~steve443/williamson.html

- Table of Contents for the 15th Iowa Infantry
  http://www.geocities.com/Heartland/Plains/3730/table.htm
- Third West Virginia Infantry
  http://www.rootsweb.com/~hcpd/3rdinf/3rdinf.htm
  aka Sixth West Virginia Vets Volunteer Cavalry.
- Union Army Regimental History Index
  http://www.tarleton.edu/~kjones/unions.html
- War History and Record One Hundred and Twenty-Ninth Illinois Infantry
  http://www.mtco.com/~martisiq/129_il.htm
  Company D—Winchester, Illinois.

◆ Societies & Groups

- American Civil War Association
  http://acwa.org/
  A California Reenactment Organization.
- Ann Arbor Civil War Roundtable ~ Michigan
  http://www.izzy.net/~michaelg/aacwrt.htm
- Civil War Plymouth Pilgrims Descendants Society
  http://members.aol.com/CWPPDS/homepage.html
  For the descendants of the Union Soldiers and Sailors engaged and captured at the Battle of Plymouth, NC, April 17–20th, 1864 who became known as the "Plymouth Pilgrims."
- The Civil War Round Table of Dallas
  http://members.tripod.com/~DallasCWRT
- Civil War Roundtable of Southern West Virginia
  http://members.tripod.com/~cwrswv/index.html
- Confederate Memorial Association
  http://www.confederate.org/
- Dames of the Loyal Legion of the United States of America
  http://www.usmo.com/~momollus/DOLLUS.HTM
- Daughters of Union Veterans of the Civil War
  http://suvcw.org/duv.htm
- Department of Michigan Sons of Union Veterans of the Civil War
  http://www.centuryinter.net/suvcw.mi/index.html
- Friends of the Florence Stockade
  http://members.aol.com/qmsgtboots/florence.html
  Florence, South Carolina
- General Robert C. Newton Camp #197, Sons of Confederate Veterans
  http://www.aristotle.net/~tomezell/scv197.htm
  Little Rock, Arkansas
- The Governor Henry H. Crapo Camp No. 145—Sons of Union Veterans of the Civil War
  http://gfn1.genesee.freenet.org/suvmi145/
  Michigan
- Grand Army of the Republic (GAR)
  http://pages.prodigy.com/CGBD86A/garhp.htm

- The Grand Army of the Republic In Michigan
  http://www.centuryinter.net/suvcw.mi/garmi.html
- Military Order of the Loyal Legion of the United States
  http://suvcw.org/mollus.htm
- The Missouri Division, Sons of Confederate Veterans
  http://www.missouri-scv.org/
- National Civil War Association
  http://www.ncwa.org/
- Order of Confederate Rose, Belle Boyd Chapter, Shreveport, Louisiana
  http://www.angelfire.com/la/BelleBoydOCR/index.html
- Sons of Confederate Veterans—Colonel Robert G. Shaver Camp #1655, Jonesboro, Arkansas
  http://members.tripod.com/~arkansas/

- Sons of Confederate Veterans Home Page
  http://www.scv.org/
  - Sons of Confederate Veterans Genealogy Network
    http://www.scv.org/scvgen00.htm
    - Confederate Ancestor Research Guide
      http://www.scv.org/scvgen02.htm
- Sons of Union Veterans of the Civil War
  http://suvcw.org/
- United Daughters of the Confederacy
  http://www.hqudc.org/
- Wayne Van Zandt Chapter, Military Order of the Stars and Bars
  http://www.aristotle.net/~tomezell/mosb.htm
  Little Rock, Arkansas

U.S.—HISTORY
http://www.CyndisList.com/hist-us.htm

Category Index:

- Ellis Island, New York
- General History Resources
- Heading West
- Historic Sites, Monuments & National Treasures
- Libraries & Archives
- The Mayflower

- People & Families
- Presidents & Politicians
- Societies & Groups
- War & the Military
- The Wild West

◆ Ellis Island, New York

- The American Immigrant Wall of Honor
  http://www.wallofhonor.com/

- The Ellis Island Home Page
  http://www.ellisisland.org/

- Ellis Island—Through America's Gateway
  http://www.i-channel.com/features/ellis/

- New York, NY, Ellis Island—Immigration:
  1900–1920
  http://cmp1.ucr.edu/exhibitions/immigration_id.html
  *University of California, Riverside, Keystone-Mast Collection,
  California Museum of Photography. Photographs of immigrants,
  ships & Ellis Island.*

- Statue of Liberty National Monument and
  Ellis Island
  http://www.nps.gov/stli/

◆ General History Resources

- The Age of Imperialism
  http://www.smplanet.com/imperialism/toc.html

- American and British History Resources on
  the Internet
  http://www.libraries.rutgers.edu/rulib/socsci/hist/amhist.html

- American History Resources Web Sites Index
  http://www.historybuff.com/resources/index.html

- Colonial-America Mailing List
  http://members.aol.com/gfsjohnf/gen_mail_states-
  gen.html#Colonial-America
  For discussing the history of our ancestors.

- Historical Events & People Worldwide
  http://www.CyndisList.com/historic.htm
  See this category on Cyndi's List for related links.

- History Buff's Home Page
  http://www.historybuff.com/index.html
  Created by the Newspaper Collectors Society of America.

- The History Net
  http://www.thehistorynet.com/home.htm
  Where History Lives on the Web.

- History of the United States
  http://www.msstate.edu:80/Archives/History/USA/usa.html

- HyperHistory Online
  http://www.hyperhistory.com/online_n2/History_n2/a.html

- Index of Resources for Historians
  http://kuhttp.cc.ukans.edu/history/index.html

- Making of America
  http://www.umdl.umich.edu/moa/index.html
  *Scanned images in this collection which contains approximately
  1,600 books and 50,000 journal articles with 19th century
  imprints.*

- The National Park Service—Links to the Past ~ U.S.
  http://www.cr.nps.gov/

- The Time Page—An Examination of Cycles in
  U.S. History
  http://www.seanet.com/Users/pamur/time.html

- WebChron: The Web Chronology Project—
  The United States of America
  http://www.npcts.edu/acad/history/WebChron/USA/USA.html

- Web Resources in Early American History
  http://www.clements.umich.edu/Links/Linkhist.html

- WWW Sites for Historians
  http://www.hist.unt.edu/09-www.htm

- Yahoo!...History
  http://dir.yahoo.com/Arts/Humanities/History/

- Yahoo!...History: US History
  http://dir.yahoo.com/Arts/Humanities/History/U_S__History/

◆ Heading West

- The American West—Development & History
  http://www.americanwest.com/

- The American West—Frontier Trails Brief History
  http://www.americanwest.com/trails/
- CA-GOLDRUSH Mailing List
  http://members.aol.com/gfsjohnf/gen_mail_states-ca.
  html#CA-GOLDRUSH
  *For anyone who is interested in early California miners and
  settlers, especially in northern California, 1848–1880.*
- Central Nevada Emigrant Trail Association
  (CNETA)
  http://ourworld.compuserve.com/homepages/trailofthe49ers/
- DONNER Party
  http://www.tahoenet.com/tdhs/tpdonner.html
- The DONNER Party
  http://members.aol.com/danmrosen/donner/index.htm
- Early American Trails and Roads
  http://members.aol.com/RoadTrails/roadtrai.html
- The End of the Oregon Trail Interpretive Center
  http://www.teleport.com/~eotic/index.html
- The Frontier in American Culture
  http://www.lib.washington.edu/exhibits/FRONTIER/index.html
  From the The University of Washington Libraries.
- Ghosts of the Klondike Gold Rush
  http://www.gold-rush.org/
  Check out the "Pan for Gold Database."
- Homesteaders Mailing List
  http://members.aol.com/gfsjohnf/gen_mail_states-
  gen.html#Homesteaders
  *For researching the history of our homesteader anscestors;
  to share information on how they lived, post stories from your
  family, and share genealogical information.*
- The Hudson's Bay Company Archives
  http://www.gov.mb.ca/chc/archives/hbca/index.html
  From the Provincial Archives of Manitoba, Canada.
- In Search of the Oregon Trail
  http://www.pbs.org/opb/oregontrail/index.html
  From a PBS series of the same name.
- International Research—Migration Charts
  http://www.intl-research.com/migration.htm
  - Eastern United States Migration
    http://www.intl-research.com/images/eastbig.gif
  - Northern United States Migration
    http://www.intl-research.com/images/eastbig.gif
  - Western United States Migration
    http://www.intl-research.com/images/west.gif
- Milestone Historic Documents—The Northwest
  Ordinance
  http://earlyamerica.com/earlyamerica/milestones/ordinance/
  index.html
  *An Ordinance for the Government of the Territory of the United
  States, North-West of the River Ohio. As it appears in the
  Supplement to the First Volume of the Columbian Magazine,
  Philadelphia, 1787. Explains the Northwest Ordinance and its
  significance, full text online and scanned copy of original
  document.*

- The Mormon Pioneer Trail
  http://www.americanwest.com/trails/pages/mormtrl.htm
  From the American West Home Page.
- The Mormon Pioneer Trail
  http://www.omaha.org/trails/main.htm
  From the Douglas-Sarpy Counties Mormon Trails Association.
- The Mormon Trail
  http://www.esu3.k12.ne.us:80/districts/elkhorn/ms/curriculum/
  Mormon1.html
- MormonTrail.com—The Pioneer Experience
  http://www.mormontrail.com/
  *The Official Web Site for Stories, Facts, and Ship Logs on the
  Mormon Trail Pioneers.*
- Mountain Men and the Fur Trade
  http://www.xmission.com/~drudy/amm.html
  *Sources of the History of the Fur Trade in the Rocky
  Mountain West.*
- New Light on the Donner Party
  http://www.metrogourmet.com/crossroads/KJhome.htm
- Northwest Ordinance of 1787
  http://www.statelib.lib.in.us/WWW/ihb/nword.html
- The Oregon-California Trails Association (OCTA)
  http://calcite.rocky.edu/octa/octahome.htm
- Oregon Pioneers—The Wagon Train of 1843
  http://www.peak.org/~mransom/pioneers.html
- Oregon Trail Pioneers—The Oregon Territory
  http://www.teleport.com/~sflora/ortrail.htm
- OREGON TRAIL: The Trail West
  http://www.ukans.edu/kansas/seneca/oregon/
- The Orphan Trains
  http://www.pbs.org/wgbh/pages/amex/orphan/index.html
  *A PBS American Experience television show regarding this
  unusual immigrant experience.*
- Orphan Trains of Kansas
  http://kuhttp.cc.ukans.edu/carrie/kancoll/articles/orphans/
- The Overland Trail
  http://www.over-land.com/
  - Links to Personalities of the West
    http://www.over-land.com/westpers.html
  - Links to The Oregon Trail
    http://www.over-land.com/trore.html
  - Links to Trails West
    http://www.over-land.com/trwest.html
  - Links to Western History
    http://www.over-land.com/westhist.html
- Overland-Trails Mailing List
  http://members.aol.com/gfsjohnf/gen_mail_states-
  gen.html#Overland-Trails
  *Discussions concerning the history, preservation, and promotion
  of the Oregon, California, Sante Fe, and other historic trails in
  the Western USA.*
- Pioneer Trails from U.S. Land Surveys
  http://history.cc.ukans.edu/heritage/werner/werner.html

- Pony Express Home Station
  http://www.ccnet.com/~xptom
- SANTA-FE-TRAIL Mailing List
  http://members.aol.com/gfsjohnf/gen_mail_states-gen.html#SANTA-FE-TRAIL
  For sharing ideas, adventures, questions, and answers regarding the Santa Fe Trail.
- Southern-Trails Mailing List
  http://members.aol.com/gfsjohnf/gen_mail_states-gen.html#Southern-Trails
  For the discussion and sharing of information regarding migration routes in the Southern United States and the people who used them.
- trails-west Mailing List
  http://members.aol.com/gfsjohnf/gen_mail_states-gen.html#trails-west
  For those who want to research their family history and post facts on their move west in North America.
- Valdez Gold Rush Centennial
  http://www.alaska.net/~vldzmuse/goldrush1.htm
  - Valdez Museum & Historical Archive—Rush Participants Database
    http://www.alaska.net/~vldzmuse/valdez.htm
    Valdez Gold Rush 1898–1899, Names Database.

◆ Historic Sites, Monuments & National Treasures

- Historic Congressional Cemetery
  http://www.geocities.com/Heartland/Meadows/4633/index.html
  Washington, D.C.
- Historic Valley Forge
  http://www.libertynet.org/iha/valleyforge/
- History of the Erie Canal
  http://www.history.rochester.edu/canal/
- Liberty Hall Historic Site
  http://www.libertyhall.org/
- Monticello, Home of Thomas Jefferson
  http://www.monticello.org/
- Mount Vernon
  http://www.mountvernon.org/
  The home of our first president, George Washington.
- National Historic Landmarks Program
  http://www.cr.nps.gov/history/nhl/nhlpgm.html
- The National Park Service
  http://www.nps.gov
- National Register of Historic Places
  http://www.cr.nps.gov/nr/nrhome.html
- Red Hill—The Patrick Henry National Memorial
  http://www.redhill.org/
  The last home and burial place of Patrick HENRY. Tells all about his life, the home, buildings [7] and the Patrick HENRY Foundation.

- Statue of Liberty National Monument and Ellis Island
  http://www.nps.gov/stli/

◆ Libraries & Archives

- American Memory—Historical Collections for the National Digital Library
  http://lcweb2.loc.gov/ammem/ammemhome.html
  From the Library of Congress.
- Archiving Early America—Historic Documents from 18th Century America
  http://earlyamerica.com/
- Historical Documents
  gopher://ucsbuxa.ucsb.edu:3001/11/.stacks/.historical
  Text files of documents such as the Declaration of Independence, the Magna Carta, the Mayflower Compact and more.
- The Historical Text Archive (HTA)
  http://www.msstate.edu/Archives/History/
  Housed at Mississippi State University.
- Lest We Forget
  http://www.coax.net/people/lwf/
  Documents with focus on the history and culture of African-Americans.
- Life History Manuscripts From the Folklore Project, WPA Federal Writer's Project 1936
  http://lcweb2.loc.gov/ammem/wpaintro/wpahome.html
- Presidential Libraries
  http://www.nara.gov/nara/president/address.html
- Yahoo!...Presidential Libraries
  http://dir.yahoo.com/Arts/Humanities/History/U_S__History/Archives/Presidential_Libraries/

◆ The Mayflower

- The ALDEN House Museum
  http://www.alden.org/
  The home of John & Priscilla Alden in Duxbury, Massachusetts.
- The General Society of Mayflower Descendants
  http://www.mayflower.org/
- A Mayflower & New England Study
  http://www.mayflowerfamilies.com/
- Mayflower Database
  http://www.geocities.com/Heartland/Bluffs/4313/
- MAYFLOWER Mailing List
  http://members.aol.com/gfsjohnf/gen_mail_states-gen.html#MAYFLOWER
  A mailing list for the discussion and sharing of information regarding the descendants of the Mayflower passengers in any place and at any time.
- Mayflower Web Page
  http://members.aol.com/calebj/mayflower.html

◆ People & Families

- 17th c. Colonial New England, with Special Emphasis on the Salem Witchcraft Trials of 1692
  http://www.ogram.org/17thc/index.shtml

- African-American
  http://www.CyndisList.com/african.htm
  See this category on Cyndi's List for related links.

- African American Pioneers
  http://www.localnet.com/~adonis2/pioall.htm

- Ancestry of Lizzie BORDEN
  http://www.uftree.com/UFT/FamousFamilyTrees/Borden/index.htm

- BOONE Ancestors and Descendants
  http://booneinfo.com/
  Including information on the famous Daniel BOONE.

- The BOONE Family
  http://www.rootsweb.com/~kygenweb/boone.html

- The BOONE-LINCOLN Genealogical Connection
  http://www.everton.com/usa/GENEALOG/GENEALOG.BOONLINC

- DONNER Party
  http://www.tahoenet.com/tdhs/tpdonner.html

- The DONNER Party
  http://members.aol.com/danmrosen/donner/index.htm

- GERMAN-AMERICAN Mailing List
  http://members.aol.com/gfsjohnf/gen_mail_states-gen.html#GERMAN-AMERICAN
  For anyone interested in genealogy related to German immigrants and their families AFTER their arrival in America.

- Lewis & Clark—The Journey of the Corps of Discovery
  http://www.pbs.org/lewisandclark/
  The companion web site for the PBS series by Ken Burns

- METISGEN Mailing List
  http://members.aol.com/johnf14246/gen_mail_general.html#METISGEN
  For the discussion and sharing of information regarding the Metis and their descendants. The Metis are North America's Fur Trading Children . . . the new nation of individuals born within North America from the first unions of natives and whites.

- Native American
  http://www.CyndisList.com/native.htm
  See this category on Cyndi's List for related links.

- Notable Women Ancestors
  http://www.rootsweb.com/~nwa/

- Palatine Emigrants by Kraig Ruckel
  http://www.geocities.com/Heartland/3955/palatine.htm

- Palatines to America Homepage
  http://www.genealogy.org:80/~palam/

- Pocahontas Descendants
  http://www.rootscomputing.com/howto/pocahn/pocahn.htm
  Descendants of Powhatan (Father of Pocahontas).

- Researching the Genealogy of Almanzo and Laura INGALLS WILDER
  http://members.tripod.com/~PennyN/LIWgen.html

- RiverRats Mailing List
  http://members.aol.com/gfsjohnf/gen_mail_states-gen.html#RiverRats
  For discussions of the Mississippi River "people" living on, working on, and involved in life on the "river." Any family living in any county bordering the Mississippi River, or living "on" the river, is welcome.

- ROOTS-L Resources: Historical Groups
  http://www.rootsweb.com/roots-l/hist_groups.html
  Links to several articles and sites regarding various groups, such as the Lewis & Clark expedition and many more.

- A Roster of the Lewis & Clark Expedition
  http://www.rootsweb.com/~genepool/lewiclar.htm

- SALEM-WITCH Mailing List
  http://members.aol.com/gfsjohnf/gen_mail_states-ma.html#SALEM-WITCH
  A genealogy and history mailing list for descendants of the people involved in the Salem Witchcraft Trials of 1692—the accusers and the accused, the afflicted and the executed, as well as the magistrates, clergy, jurors, and anyone affected by the proceedings.

- Salem Witch Trials Chronology
  http://www.star.net/salem/memorial/default.htm

- Unique Peoples & Cultures
  http://www.CyndisList.com/peoples.htm
  See this category on Cyndi's List for related links.

- Yahoo!...History: Exploration: Cook, James (1728–1779)
  http://dir.yahoo.com/Arts/Humanities/History/Exploration/Cook__James__1728_1779_/
  Dozens of links about this famous explorer.

◆ Presidents & Politicians

- Ancestry of John Quincy ADAMS
  http://www.uftree.com/UFT/FamousFamilyTrees/Adams/index.htm

- Ancestry of Thomas JEFFERSON
  http://www.uftree.com/UFT/FamousFamilyTrees/Jefferson/index.htm

- Colonial Hall: Biographies of America's Founding Fathers
  http://www.webcom.com/bba/ch/

- Dead Presidents
  http://starship.skyport.net/crew/manus/Presidents/index.html

- Genealogy of the DAVIS Family
  http://www.ruf.rice.edu/~pjdavis/gene.htm
  Jefferson Davis, President of C.S.A.

- Governor John WEBSTER of Hartford, Connecticut and Hadley, Massachusetts
  http://www.rootsweb.com/~genepool/websjohn.htm

- History Buff's Presidential Library
  http://www.historybuff.com/presidents/index.html

- Just the Facts
  http://www.mindspring.com/~czar1/pres/
  Facts about U.S. Presidents, First Ladies and Vice Presidents.

- Master Index to Presidents' Genealogical Data
  http://www.dcs.hull.ac.uk/public/genealogy/presidents/gedx.html

- National First Ladies Library
  http://www.firstladies.org/

- The National Society of the WASHINGTON Family Descendants
  http://members.tripod.com/~NSWFD/
  Members are descendants of any of the ancestors of George Washington who lived in Colonial America between 1607 and 1732.

- The Political Graveyard
  http://politicalgraveyard.com/
  "The Web Site That Tells Where the Dead Politicians are Buried."

- Presidential Ancestral Charts
  http://www.megabits.net/~lthurman/prsdnt/prsdnt.html
  For Washington, Adams, Jefferson, Pierce, Lincoln, Harrison, Bush.

- Presidential Genealogies on the Web
  http://homepages.rootsweb.com/~godwin/reference/prez.html
  A comprehensive list of links.

◆ Societies & Groups

- National Railway Historical Society
  http://www.rrhistorical.com/nrhs/

- National Trust for Historic Preservation
  http://www.nthp.org/

- The Order of the Founders and Patriots of America
  http://www.mindspring.com/~wxman2/gp/

- Railroad Historical Societies
  http://tucson.com/concor/histsoc.html

- Supreme Court Historical Society
  http://www.supremecourthistory.org/

◆ War & The Military

- The Alamo
  http://numedia.tddc.net/sa/alamo/

- AMERICAN-REVOLUTION Mailing List
  http://members.aol.com/gfsjohnf/gen_mail_states-gen.html#AMERICAN-REVOLUTION

- The Aroostook War—Maine vs. New Brunswick, 1839
  http://www.stanford.edu/~jenkg/family/aroostook.html

- Custer Battlefield Historical & Museum Association
  http://www.intuitive.com/custer/

- The French and Indian Raid on Deerfield, Massachusetts, 1704
  http://uts.cc.utexas.edu/~churchh/deerfield.html

- Historic Valley Forge
  http://www.libertynet.org/iha/valleyforge/

- Military Resources Worldwide
  http://www.CyndisList.com/milres.htm
  See this category on Cyndi's List for related links.

- Pearl Harbor Casualties List
  http://www.mit.edu:8001/afs/athena/activity/a/afrotc/www/names

- A Selection of Underground Railroad Resources
  http://www.ugrr.org/web.html

- U.S. Civil War ~ The War for Southern Independence
  http://www.CyndisList.com/cw.htm
  See this category on Cyndi's List for related links.

- U.S. Military
  http://www.CyndisList.com/military.htm
  See this category on Cyndi's List for related links.

◆ The Wild West

- Billy the Kid Outlaw Gang
  http://www.nmia.com/~btkog/index.html

- History Buff's Reference Library—Old West History Articles
  http://www.historybuff.com/library/refwest.html

- Jim Janke's Old West Page
  http://homepages.dsu.edu/jankej/oldwest/oldwest.htm

- Kansas Gunfighters
  http://history.cc.ukans.edu/heritage/research/gunfighters.html

- OKLAHOMBRES Online!
  http://www.qns.com/~dcordry/hombres.html
  Dedicated to the careful, correct research and preservation of lawman and outlaw history.

- The Old West Living History Foundation
  http://www.gunfighter.com/owlhf/

- Outlaws and Lawmen of the Old West
  http://www.sky.net/~fogel/oldwest.htm

- Scribe's Tribute to Billy the Kid
  http://www.geocities.com/SouthBeach/Marina/2057/Billy_the_Kid.html

- Scribe's Tribute to Jesse James
  http://www.geocities.com/SouthBeach/Marina/2057/Jesse_James.html

- Western Outlaw-Lawman History Association
  http://www.flash.net/~pggreen/

- The Wild West
  http://www.calweb.com/~rbbusman/index.html

- Wild West Personalities Produce Bang-Up Pedigree
  http://www.uftree.com/UFT/FamousFamilyTrees/Earp/index.html
  By Myra Vanderpool Gormley, CG.

- The Wild Wild West
  http://www.gunslinger.com/west.html

U.S.—MILITARY

http://www.CyndisList.com/military.htm

Category Index:

- ◆ General Resource Sites
- ◆ Historical Military Conflicts, Events or Wars
- ◆ Libraries, Archives & Museums
- ◆ Mailing Lists, Newsgroups & Chat
- ◆ Maps, Gazetteers & Geographical Information
- ◆ Medals, Awards & Tributes

- ◆ Military History Resources
- ◆ Professional Researchers, Volunteers & Other Research Services
- ◆ Publications, Software & Supplies
- ◆ Records: Military, Pension, Burial
- ◆ Societies & Groups

◆ General Resource Sites

- ● African American Warriors
  http://www.abest.com/~cklose/aawar.htm

- ● Canada—Military
  http://www.CyndisList.com/milcan.htm
  See this category on Cyndi's List for related links.

- ● Law Enforcement Memorial Links
  http://www.policememorial.com/memoriallinks.htm
  Links to many sites regarding law enforcement officials who died in the line of duty. Some have historic lists of names.

- ● Lineages, Inc.—Military Research Room
  http://www.lineages.com/military/default.asp

  - ○ American Revolution, 1775–1783
    http://www.lineages.com/military/mil_rw.asp

  - ○ Civil War, 1861–1865
    http://www.lineages.com/military/mil_cw.asp

  - ○ Korean War, 1950–1953
    http://www.lineages.com/military/mil_kor.asp

  - ○ Old Northwest and Old Southwest Indian Wars, 1783–1796
    http://www.lineages.com/military/mil_old.asp

  - ○ Patriot's War, 1837–1838
    http://www.lineages.com/military/mil_pat.asp

  - ○ Persian Gulf War, 1990–1991
    http://www.lineages.com/military/mil_gulf.asp

  - ○ Philippine Insurrection, 1899–1902
    http://www.lineages.com/military/mil_phil.asp

  - ○ Spanish-American War, 1898
    http://www.lineages.com/military/mil_span.asp

  - ○ Texan War of Independence, 1836
    http://www.lineages.com/military/mil_tx.asp

  - ○ Vietnam War, 1961–1973
    http://www.lineages.com/military/mil_vn.asp

  - ○ War of 1812
    http://www.lineages.com/military/mil_1812.asp

  - ○ War with the Barbary Pirates, 1801–1805
    http://www.lineages.com/military/mil_pir.asp

  - ○ World War I, 1914–1918 (U.S., 1917–1918)
    http://www.lineages.com/military/mil_ww1.asp

  - ○ World War II, 1939–1945 (U.S., 1941–1945)
    http://www.lineages.com/military/mil_ww2.asp

- ● The Military Network
  http://www.military-network.com/

- ● Military Resources Worldwide
  http://www.CyndisList.com/milres.htm
  See this category on Cyndi's List for related links.

- ● Online Military Resources
  http://www.cooklib.org/Focus/4military.htm
  A list from the Cook Memorial Public Library District in Libertyville, Illinois.

- ● U.S. Army Home Page
  http://www.army.mil/

- ● U.S.—Civil War ~ The War for Southern Independence
  http://www.CyndisList.com/cw.htm
  See this category on Cyndi's List for related links.

- ● USIGS Military Collection
  http://www.usigs.org/library/military/

- ● War Chart
  http://www.genrecords.com/library/war.htm
  From the Genealogy Record Service.

◆ Historical Military Conflicts, Events or Wars

The American Revolutionary War

- ● The American Revolutionary War Home Page
  http://www.ccs.neu.edu/home/bcortez/revwar/RevWeb.html

- American Revolutionary War Soldiers &
  Their Descendants
  http://www.rootsweb.com/~ars/index.htm
  A surname list of soldiers, with e-mail addresses to contact the researchers.

- The Brigade of the American Revolution Home Page
  http://www.brigade.org/welcome.html

- Culpeper Minute Battalion
  http://www.meridiantc.com/nwta/index.html
  Virginia

- Drums Along the Mohawk
  http://www.geocities.com/Athens/Delphi/4171/
  The story of the American Revolution on the New York Frontier.

- Loyalists
  http://www.CyndisList.com/loyalist.htm
  See this category on Cyndi's List for related links.

- Maryland Loyalists and the American Revolution
  http://www.erols.com/candidus/index.htm

- Michael Meals Presents: www.revwar.com
  http://www.revwar.com/

- Military History: American Revolution (1775–1783)
  http://www.cfcsc.dnd.ca/links/milhist/usrev.html

- Revolutionary Soldiers of Chautauqua County
  http://www.rootsweb.com/~nychauta/MILITARY/REVSOL.HTM
  New York

- Revolutionary War Muster Rolls Northampton
  County, Pennsylvania
  http://www.geocities.com/Heartland/3955/rev.htm
  Names extracted from the Pennsylvania Archives, 2nd Series, Volume XIV.

- Revolutionary War Period Bible, Family &
  Marriage Records
  http://www.dhc.net/~revwar/
  Index to microfilm volumes of abstracts from pension files.

- Revolutionary War Soldiers Living in the State of
  Ohio in 1818–1819
  http://php.ucs.indiana.edu/~jetorres/ohiorev.html

- Sons of the American Revolution
  http://www.sar.org
  National Society, Louisville, Kentucky.

- USIGS Military Collection—The Revolutionary
  War Era
  http://www.usigs.org/library/military/links/rev.htm

The War of 1812

- General Society of the War of 1812
  http://LanClio.org/1812.htm

- Military History: War of 1812 (1812–1814)
  http://www.cfcsc.dnd.ca/links/milhist/1812.html

- USIGS Military Collection—The War of 1812 Era
  http://www.usigs.org/library/military/links/1812.htm

- War of 1812 Records: Where and How Do I
  Get Them?
  http://www.rootsweb.com/~kyharris/1812how.htm

- The War of 1812—Why, What and Who?
  http://www.rootsweb.com/~kyharris/1812war.htm

The Mexican-American War

- Descendants of Mexican War Veterans
  http://members.aol.com/dmwv/home.htm

- The Mexican-American War Memorial Homepage
  http://sunsite.unam.mx/revistas/1847/

- USIGS Military Collection—The Mexican-
  American War Era
  http://www.usigs.org/library/military/links/mex-am.htm

Civil War / War for Southern Independence

- Civil War / War for Southern Independence
  http://www.CyndisList.com/cw.htm
  See this category on Cyndi's List for related links.

The Spanish-American War

- The Spanish-American War—Remember the Maine
  http://www.smplanet.com/imperialism/remember.html

- Spanish-American War Centennial Website
  http://www.powerscourt.com/war/

- Spanish-American War Medal of Honor Recipients
  http://www.army.mil/cmh-pg/mohspan.htm

- Spanish-American War Page
  http://www.ecsis.net/~jrwilobe/

- A Splendid Little War
  http://www.smplanet.com/imperialism/splendid.html

- Texas Volunteers, Spanish-American War Military
  Rolls, 1898–1901
  http://isadore.tsl.state.tx.us/.dir/mil.dir/.files/mrw.txt

- USIGS Military Collection—The Spanish-American
  War Era
  http://www.usigs.org/library/military/links/span.htm

World War I—The Great War

- Military History: World War I (1914–1918)
  http://www.cfcsc.dnd.ca/links/milhist/wwi.html

- USIGS Military Collection—World War I Era
  http://www.usigs.org/library/military/links/wwi.htm

World War II

- Dad's War: Finding and Telling Your Father's
  World War II Story
  http://members.aol.com/dadswar/

- Military History: World War II (1939–1945)
  http://www.cfcsc.dnd.ca/links/milhist/wwii.html
- Pearl Harbor Casualties List
  http://www.mit.edu:8001/afs/athena/activity/a/afrotc/www/names
- Pearl Harbor Casualties (U.S.)
  http://www.lineages.com/military/PearlHarbor.asp
  Searchable database from Lineages, Inc.
- Pearl Harbor—Civilian and Military Personnel Casualties
  ftp://ftp.rootsweb.com/pub/usgenweb/hi/military/pearl.txt
- USIGS Military Collection—World War II Era
  http://www.usigs.org/library/military/links/wwii.htm
- WNY Genealogy—World War II Honor Roll
  http://members.tripod.com/~NSampson/ww2wny.html
  New York
- World War II on the Web
  http://www.geocities.com/Athens/Oracle/2691/welcome.htm
- WW II: Americans Who Liberated Belgium
  http://www.ping.be/picavet/Belgium_USA_WW2_01.shtml

The Korean War

- Korean Conflict State-Level Casualty Lists, Sorted by Home of Record
  http://www.nara.gov/nara/electronic/kcashr.html
  Sorted Alphabetically by Last Name of Casualty
  http://www.nara.gov/nara/electronic/kcasal.html
  From the National Archives and Records Administration, Center for Electronic Records.
- Korean War Project
  http://www.koreanwar.org
- Military History: Korean War (1950–1953)
  http://www.cfcsc.dnd.ca/links/milhist/korea.html
- State-level Casualty Lists from the Korean Conflict (1951–57)
  http://www.nara.gov/nara/electronic/kcas.html
  From the National Archives and Records Administration.
- USIGS Military Collection—The Korean War Era
  http://www.usigs.org/library/military/links/korea.htm
- WNY Korean War
  http://www.freeyellow.com/members2/samdecker/KoreanWar.html
  A list of men and women from the Western NY area who gave their lives during the Korean War (1950–1953).

Vietnam

- Military History: Vietnam War (1961–1975)
  http://www.cfcsc.dnd.ca/links/milhist/viet.html
- USIGS Military Collection—The Vietnam War Era
  http://www.usigs.org/library/military/links/vietnam.htm
- Vietnam Conflict State-Level Casualty Lists, Sorted by Home of Record
  http://www.nara.gov/nara/electronic/vcashr.html

Sorted Alphabetically by Last Name of Casualty
http://www.nara.gov/nara/electronic/vcasal.html
From the National Archives and Records Administration, Center for Electronic Records.

- Vietnam Era POW/MIA Database
  http://lcweb2.loc.gov/pow/powhome.html
  Library of Congress.
- The Vietnam Veterans' Memorial Wall
  http://thewall-usa.com/
  With a searchable database.
- The Wall on the Web
  http://www.vietvet.org/thewall/thewallm.html
  Over 58,000 names in this list.

◆ Libraries, Archives & Museums

- The Military History Collections of The New York Public Library
  http://www.nypl.org/research/chss/subguides/milhist/home.html
- United States Air Force Museum
  http://www.wpafb.af.mil/museum/
- The U.S. Army Military History Institute
  http://carlisle-www.army.mil/usamhi/
  and a description from GENCAP
  http://www.libertynet.org/~gencap/usarmymhi.html
- Wisconsin Veterans Museum
  http://badger.state.wi.us/agencies/dva/museum/wvmmain.html

◆ Mailing Lists, Newsgroups & Chat

- Mailing lists for the U.S. Civil War can be found at
  http://www.CyndisList.com/cw.htm
- Genealogy Resources on the Internet—General USA Mailing Lists
  http://members.aol.com/gfsjohnf/gen_mail_states-gen.html
  Each of the mailing list links below points to this site, wonderfully maintained by John Fuller.
- 1776 Mailing List
  http://members.aol.com/gfsjohnf/gen_mail_states-gen.html#1776
  For genealogical and historical research surrounding 1776 and the American Revolution.
- AMERICAN-REVOLUTION Mailing List
  http://members.aol.com/gfsjohnf/gen_mail_states-gen.html#AMERICAN-REVOLUTION
  For the discussion of events during the American Revolution and genealogical matters related to the American Revolution. The French-Indian Wars and the War of 1812 are also suitable topics for discussion.
- AMREV-HESSIANS Mailing List
  http://members.aol.com/gfsjohnf/gen_mail_states-gen.html#AMREV-HESSIANS
  For anyone with a genealogical interest in the Hessian soldiers (German auxiliary troops employed by King George III of England) who remained in America after the American Revolution.

- LOYALIST-IN-CANADA Mailing List
  http://members.aol.com/gfsjohnf/gen_mail_country-can.html#LOYALIST
  For those with loyalist ancestors to help one another research their loyalist history and to post any facts on the subject that they desire. Loyalists are defined as those who left the United States for Canada after the American Revolution for a number of reasons.

- soc.history.war.us-revolution Newsgroup

- soc.history.war.vietnam Newsgroup

- soc.history.war.world-war-ii Newsgroup

- WARof1812 Mailing List
  http://members.aol.com/johnf14246/gen_mail_general.html#WARof1812

- WW20-ROOTS-L Mailing List
  http://members.aol.com/johnf14246/gen_mail_general.html#WW20-ROOTS-L
  For the discussion of genealogy in all 20th century wars.

◆ Maps, Gazetteers & Geographical Information

- Maps of National Historic & Military Parks, Memorials, and Battlefields
  http://www.lib.utexas.edu/Libs/PCL/Map_collection/National_parks/historic_parks.html#military

◆ Medals, Awards & Tributes

- Blindauer's Tribute to All Purple Heart Recipients
  http://www.excel.net/~sebring/index.htm

- Medal of Honor Citations, Full-text Listings
  http://imabbs.army.mil/cmh-pg/moh1.htm
  From the U.S. Army Center of Military History.

- United States Marine Corps—Medal of Honor Recipients
  http://www.usmc.mil/moh/

- United States Military Medals
  http://users.aol.com/gman755/medals/medals2.html

- The Vietnam Veterans' Memorial Wall
  http://thewall-usa.com/
  With a searchable database.

- The Vietnam Veterans Memorial Wall—Index
  http://www.cpeq.com/~wall/

◆ Military History Resources

- First Visit by a US Naval Vessel to Hawaii, 1826—"The Battle of Honolulu"
  ftp://ftp.rootsweb.com/pub/usgenweb/hi/history/dolphin.txt

- Legion Ville—First Training Camp of the United States Army, 1792
  http://tristate.pgh.net/~bsilver/legion.htm
  The Legion Ville Historical Society, Inc., The Anthony Wayne Historical Society, Inc. Includes transcriptions of West Point Orderly Books, 1792–1796.

- Naval Historical Center
  http://www.history.navy.mil/

- Pacific Northwest Military History and Reenacting Web Site
  http://www.hevanet.com/1860colt/pnwmain.html

- U.S. Air Force Historical Research Agency
  http://www.au.af.mil/au/afhra/

- U.S. Army Center of Military History
  http://www.army.mil/cmh-pg/

◆ Professional Researchers, Volunteers & Other Research Services

- Revolutionary War Records Copied by Faith Libelo
  E-mail: fsl.genie.research@erols.com
  She can visit the National Archives for you and copy the files. E-mail Faith at fsl.genie.research@erols.com for details.

- Virginia Family Research
  http://www.mindspring.com/~jkward/Index.html
  Virginia genealogy, Virginia Confederate records, Revolutionary records.

◆ Publications, Software & Supplies

- Ancestor's Attic Discount Genealogy Books—United States—Military Books
  http://members.tripod.com/~ancestorsattic/index.html#USMIL

- Boyd Publishing Company—Misc. Military
  http://www.hom.net/~gac/miscmil.htm

- GenealogyBookShop.com—Frontier Wars
  http://www.genealogybookshop.com/genealogybookshop/files/General,Frontier_Wars/index.html

  Military
  http://www.genealogybookshop.com/genealogybookshop/files/General,Military/index.html

  Pension Records
  http://www.genealogybookshop.com/genealogybookshop/files/General,Pension_Records/index.html

  Revolutionary War
  http://www.genealogybookshop.com/genealogybookshop/files/General,Revolutionary_War/index.html

  War of 1812
  http://www.genealogybookshop.com/genealogybookshop/files/General,War_of_1812/index.html
  The online store of Genealogical Publishing Co., Inc. & Clearfield Company.

- Hearthstone Bookshop—Military Records
  http://www.hearthstonebooks.com/Military_Records.html

- Heritage Books—Loyalists
  http://www.heritagebooks.com/loyal.htm

- Heritage Books—Revolutionary War
  http://www.heritagebooks.com/revwar.htm

- Heritage Books—War of 1812
  http://www.heritagebooks.com/war1812.htm

- National Historical Publishing Company
  http://www.tbox.com/natlhist/default.html
  Books regarding pension files and service records for the Revolutionary War, War of 1812, Mexican War and Civil War. Indexes to Old Wars and Indian Wars.

- Willow Bend Bookstore—Military
  http://www.willowbend.net/military.htm

- Willow Bend Bookstore—War of 1812
  http://www.willowbend.net/1812.htm

◆ Records: Military, Pension, Burial

- Ancestry.com—Military Records—Pre World War I (Form 80)
  http://www.ancestry.com/research/military80.htm

- Ancestry.com—Military Records—World War I and After (Form 180)
  http://www.ancestry.com/research/military180.htm

- Arlington National Cemetery
  http://www.mdw.army.mil/cemetery.htm
  General information and a map.

- FAQ Regarding Military Records Requests
  http://members.aol.com/rechtman/faq-army.html

- How to Obtain a Revolutionary War Pension File
  http://www.teleport.com/~carolynk/howtofil.htm

- How To Obtain Military Pension Files from the Department of Veterans Affairs
  http://www.kinquest.com/genealogy/va.html

- How to Order Military & Pension Records for Union Civil War Veterans from the National Archives
  http://www.oz.net/~cyndihow/pensions.htm
  By Cyndi Howells.

- Index to Militia Rolls—Olive Tree Genealogy
  http://www.rootsweb.com/~ote/indexmil.htm
  Rolls for New Jersey and New York.

- Introduction to the Connecticut Military Census of 1917
  http://www.cslnet.ctstateu.edu/milcens.htm

- Legion Ville—First Training Camp of the United States Army, 1792
  http://tristate.pgh.net/~bsilver/legion.htm
  The Legion Ville Historical Society, Inc., The Anthony Wayne Historical Society, Inc. Includes transcriptions of West Point Orderly Books, 1792–1796.

- Lost Boats
  http://www.subnet.com/MEMORIAL/lostboat.htm
  A list of US submarines, the crew and the passengers that were lost since 1915.

- Master Index of (U.S.) Army Records
  http://www.army.mil/cmh-pg/records.htm

- Medal of Honor Citations, Full-Text Listings
  http://imabbs.army.mil/cmh-pg/moh1.htm
  From the U.S. Army Center of Military History.

- Military Records—From Family Tree Maker Online
  http://www.familytreemaker.com/00000801.html

- Military Service Records—A Select Catalog of National Archives Microfilm
  http://www.nara.gov/publications/microfilm/military/service.html

- National Cemetery System—Department of Veteran Affairs
  http://www.va.gov/cemetery/index.htm

- National Personnel Records Center, St. Louis, MO
  http://www.nara.gov/regional/stlouis.html

- Pearl Harbor Casualties List
  http://www.mit.edu:8001/afs/athena/activity/a/afrotc/www/names

- Pearl Harbor Casualties (U.S.)
  http://www.lineages.com/military/PearlHarbor.asp
  Searchable database from Lineages, Inc.

- Pearl Harbor—Civilian and Military Personnel Casualties
  ftp://ftp.rootsweb.com/pub/usgenweb/hi/military/pearl.txt

- Researching Through Military Records
  http://www.familytreemaker.com/00000106.html

- Revolutionary War Period Bible, Family & Marriage Records
  http://www.dhc.net/~revwar/
  Index to microfilm volumes of abstracts from pension files.

- Tennessee World War I Veterans
  http://www.state.tn.us/sos/statelib/pubsvs/ww1intro.htm
  A database for select counties in Tennessee. From the Tennessee State Library and Archives.

- USIGS Military Collection Links
  http://www.usigs.org/library/military/links/index.htm

- War of 1812 Pay Rolls and Muster Rolls Collection Index
  http://image.vtls.com/collections/WA.html

◆ Societies & Groups

- Army Alumni Organizations
  http://www.army.mil/vetinfo/vetloc.htm

- The Aztec Club of 1847
  http://www.concentric.net/~walika/aztec.htm
  Military society of the Mexican War.

- General Society of the War of 1812
  http://LanClio.org/1812.htm

- "Knights of the Air" 114th Aviation Company Association
  http://www.familyville.com/data/lusmyp/knight461/

- Legion Ville—First Training Camp of the United States Army, 1792
  http://tristate.pgh.net/~bsilver/legion.htm
  The Legion Ville Historical Society, Inc., The Anthony Wayne Historical Society, Inc. Includes transcriptions of West Point Orderly Books, 1792–1796.

- National Society of the Daughters of the American Revolution Home Page
  http://www.dar.org/index.html

- Order of Indian Wars of the United States
  http://members.tripod.com/~Historic_Trust/indian.htm

- Sons of the American Revolution
  http://www.sar.org
  National Society, Louisville, Kentucky.

- Sons of the Revolution in the State of California
  http://www.walika.com/sr.htm

- Sons of the Revolution in the State of Illinois
  http://www.execpc.com/~drg/sril.html

- Sons of the Revolution in the State of Michigan
  http://www.execpc.com/~sril/srmi.html

- Veterans of Foreign Wars
  http://www.vfw.org

- The Western Front Association—Remembering 1914–1918
  http://ourworld.compuserve.com/homepages/cf_baker/

- Women in Military Service for America Memorial Foundation, Inc.
  http://www.wimsa.org

U.S.—ALABAMA—AL
http://www.CyndisList.com/al.htm

Category Index:

- General Resource Sites
- Government & Cities
- History & Culture
- Libraries, Archives & Museums
- Mailing Lists, Newsgroups & Chat
- Maps, Gazetteers & Geographical Information
- Military
- Newspapers
- People & Families

- Professional Researchers, Volunteers & Other Research Services
- Publications, Software & Supplies
- Queries, Message Boards & Surname Lists
- Records: Census, Cemeteries, Land, Obituaries, Personal, Taxes and Vital
- Religion & Churches
- Societies & Groups
- USGenWeb Project

◆ General Resource Sites

- **Alabama Family Reunions**
  http://www.edge.net/~deke/algenweb/reunion.html

- **Amelia's Alabama Genealogy**
  http://www.bham.mindspring.com/~awillcut/home.html

- **Autauga County, Alabama Genealogical Information**
  http://www.tntech.edu/~beg/autauga/index.html

- **Blount County, Alabama Genealogy**
  http://members.aol.com/egun/Blhome.html

- **Everton's Sources of Genealogical Information in Alabama**
  http://www.everton.com/usa/al.htm

- **Family Tree Maker's Genealogy "How To" Guide—Alabama**
  http://www.familytreemaker.com/00000175.html

- **Genealogy Bulletin Board Systems for Alabama**
  http://www.genealogy.org/~gbbs/gblal.html

- **Genealogy Exchange & Surname Registry—ALGenExchange**
  http://www.genexchange.com/al/index.cfm

- **Genealogy Resources on the Internet: Alabama**
  http://www-personal.umich.edu/~cgaunt/alabama.html

- **HUDSON Genealogy and History in Limestone County, Alabama**
  http://fly.hiwaay.net/~kenth/

- **LDS Research Outline for Alabama**
  http://www.everton.com/usa/al-0801B.txt

- **Lineages' Genealogy Site: Alabama**
  http://www.lineages.com/rooms/usa/state.asp?StateCode=AL

- **Related Alabama Links**
  http://www.asc.edu/archives/related.html
  From the Alabama Department of Archives & History.

- **ROOTS-L United States Resources: Alabama**
  http://www.rootsweb.com/roots-l/USA/al.html
  Comprehensive list of research links, including many to history-related sites.

- **Tracking Your Roots**
  http://members.aol.com/GenWebLisa/
  Many resources for Conecuh, Covington & Marengo Counties & a lot more!

◆ Government & Cities

- **50states.com—Alabama State Information Resource**
  http://www.50states.com/alabama.htm
  A list of general information for each state, including a list of colleges, state symbols, links to maps, newspapers, and other miscellaneous state information.

- **Alabama Cities Index—Alabama Information Sources**
  http://www.cptr.ua.edu/alacity.htm

- **AlaWeb—Alabama State Government**
  http://www.state.al.us/govern.html

- **Excite Travel by City.Net—Alabama**
  http://www.city.net/countries/united_states/alabama/
  Includes links to web pages for government, cities, schools, libraries, newspapers and maps.

- **Mobile History and Culture**
  http://www.mobile.org/hc/hc-home.phtml

- Official City Web Sites for the State of Alabama
  http://OfficialCitySites.org/alabama.htm

- Yahoo! Get Local...Alabama Cities
  http://dir.yahoo.com/Regional/U_S__States/Alabama/Cities/
  Maps, yellow pages, white pages, newspapers and other local information.

- Yahoo! Get Local...Alabama Counties and Regions
  http://dir.yahoo.com/Regional/U_S__States/Alabama/
  Counties_and_Regions/
  Maps, yellow pages, white pages, newspapers and other local information.

◆ History & Culture

- Alabama History On-Line
  http://www.asc.edu/archives/aho.html

- Historic Postcards of Alabama
  http://www.slis.ua.edu/projects/PCARDS/pcard.htm

- Internet Resources for Special Collections and Alabama History
  http://www.lib.auburn.edu/special/docs/netindex.html
  From Auburn University Libraries.

- Ray's Alabama History
  http://www.mindspring.com/~rjones/

- Yahoo!...History...Alabama
  http://dir.yahoo.com/Arts/Humanities/History/
  Browse_By_Region/U_S__States/Alabama/

◆ Libraries, Archives & Museums

- Alabama Dept. of Archives & History Homepage
  http://www.asc.edu/archives/agis.html

  o Church Records
    http://www.asc.edu/archives/referenc/church.html

  o Family History and Genealogy
    http://www.asc.edu/archives/referenc/family.html

  o Military Records
    http://www.asc.edu/archives/referenc/military.html

  o Newspapers on Microfilm
    http://www.asc.edu/archives/newsp/newsp.html

- Alabama Family History Centers
  http://www.genhomepage.com/FHC/Alabama.html
  A list of addresses, phone numbers and hours of operation from the Genealogy Home Page.

- Alabama Public Library Service
  http://www.apls.state.al.us/

- Anniston-Calhoun County Public Library
  http://pages.prodigy.net/tracks/ANNLIB.HTM

- Auburn University Libraries—Aubie Plus
  http://www.lib.auburn.edu/index.html

  o Archives and Manuscripts Department
    http://www.lib.auburn.edu/archive/

  o Special Collections Department
    http://www.lib.auburn.edu/special/

- Birmingham Public Library
  http://www.bham.lib.al.us/

  o Tutwiler Collection of Southern History and Literature—Genealogical Research
    http://www.bham.lib.al.us/departments/Southern/Gene.htm

- Byrd Springs Family History Center
  http://members.aol.com/r3morgan/byrd.htm
  Huntsville, Alabama

- Family History Centers—Alabama
  http://www.deseretbook.com/famhis/al.html

- Family History Centers—Alabama
  http://www.lib.byu.edu/~uvrfhc/centers/alabama.html

- Family History Centers in North Alabama
  http://members.aol.com/terryann/other.htm

- HYTELNET—Library Catalogs: USA: Alabama
  http://library.usask.ca/hytelnet/usa/AL.html
  Before you use any of the Telnet links, make note of the user name, password and any other logon information.

- The LDS Family History Center in Huntsville, Alabama
  http://members.aol.com/terryann2/fhcinal.htm

- Madison Alabama Family History Center
  http://members.aol.com/terryann/madison.htm

- Mobile Public Library
  http://www2.acan.net/~mplhp/index.html

  o Local History and Genealogy
    http://www2.acan.net/~mplhp/lhg.htm

- NUCMC Listing of Archives and Manuscript Repositories in Alabama
  http://lcweb.loc.gov/coll/nucmc/alsites.html
  Links to information about resources other than those held in the Library of Congress.

- Repositories of Primary Sources: Alabama
  http://www.uidaho.edu/special-collections/east1.html#usal
  A list of links to online resources from the Univ. of Idaho Library, Special Collections and Archives.

- University of South Alabama Archives
  http://www.usouthal.edu/archives/archome.htm

- webCATS: Library Catalogues on the World Wide Web—Alabama
  http://library.usask.ca/hywebcat/states/AL.html

◆ Mailing Lists, Newsgroups & Chat

- Genealogy Resources on the Internet—Alabama Mailing Lists
  http://members.aol.com/gfsjohnf/gen_mail_states-al.html
  Each of the mailing list links below points to this site, wonderfully maintained by John Fuller. Visit this site for county-specific mailing lists as well.

- ALABAMA Mailing List
  http://members.aol.com/gfsjohnf/gen_mail_states-al.html#ALABAMA

- AL-AfricaAmer Mailing List
  http://members.aol.com/gfsjohnf/gen_mail_states-al.html#AL-AfricaAmer
  For anyone with an interest in African American genealogy in Alabama.

- AL-Rooters Mailing List
  http://members.aol.com/gfsjohnf/gen_mail_states-al.html#AL-Rooters

- COVINGTON Mailing List
  http://members.aol.com/gfsjohnf/gen_mail_states-al.html#COVINGTON
  For Covington County research.

- DEEP-SOUTH-ROOTS-L Mailing List
  http://members.aol.com/gfsjohnf/gen_mail_states-al.html#DEEP-SOUTH-ROOTS
  Alabama, Florida, Georgia & Mississippi

- GADADE Mailing List
  http://members.aol.com/gfsjohnf/gen_mail_states-al.html#GADADE
  For anyone with a genealogical interest in the Dade County, Georgia area. Researchers for Walker County, Georgia; Marion County, Tennessee; and Dekalb and Jackson Counties, Alabama are invited to join as well.

- Melungeon Mailing List
  http://members.aol.com/gfsjohnf/gen_mail_states-gen.html#MELUNGEO
  For people conducting Melungeon and/or Appalachian research including Native American, Portuguese, Turkish, Black Dutch, and other unverifiable mixed statements of ancestry or unexplained rumors, with ancestors in TN, KY, VA, NC, SC, GA, AL, WV, and possibly other places.

- RAN-CLAY Mailing List
  http://members.aol.com/gfsjohnf/gen_mail_states-al.html#RAN-CLAY
  For anyone who has an interest in genealogy related to the east-central Alabama counties of Autauga, Bullock, Calhoun, Chambers, Cherokee, Chilton, Clay, Cleburne, Coosa, Elmore, Etowah, Lee, Macon, Montgomery, Randolph, Russell, St.Clair, Shelby, Talladega and Tallapoosa, and the Georgia border counties, all of which was once Indian territory and subject to boundary changes. See also the East Central Alabama Researchers web site for more details: http://www.shelby.net/shelby/jr/ecar/

◆ Maps, Gazetteers & Geographical Information

- 1895 U.S. Atlas—Alabama
  http://www.LivGenMI.com/1895al.htm

- Alabama Clickable Image Map
  http://www.eng.auburn.edu/alabama/map.html

- Alabama Counties
  http://www.asc.edu/archives/counties.html

- American Memory Panoramic Maps 1847–1929—Alabama
  http://lcweb2.loc.gov/cgi-bin/query/S?ammem/gmd:@filreq(@field(STATE+alabama)+@field(COLLID+pmmap))
  From the Geography and Map Division, Library of Congress.

- American Memory Railroad Maps 1828–1900—Alabama
  http://memory.loc.gov/cgi-bin/query/S?ammem/gmd:@filreq(@field(STATE+alabama)+@field(COLLID+rrmap))
  From the Geography and Map Division, Library of Congress.

- Color Landform Atlas: Alabama
  http://fermi.jhuapl.edu/states/al_0.html
  Including a map of counties and a map for 1895.

- Excite Maps: Alabama Maps
  http://www.city.net/maps/view/?mapurl=/countries/united_states/alabama
  Zoom in on these maps all the way to the street level.

- HPI County InfoSystem—Counties in Alabama
  http://www.com/hpi/alcty/index.html

- K.B. Slocum Books and Maps—Alabama
  http://www.treasurenet.com/cgi-bin/treasure/kbslocum/scan/se=Alabama/sf=mapstate

- List of Alabama Counties
  http://www.genealogy.org/~st-clair/counties/state_al.html

- Map of Alabama Counties
  http://govinfo.kerr.orst.edu/gif/states/al.gif
  From the Government Information Sharing Project, Information Services, Oregon State University.

- Map of Alabama Counties
  http://www.lib.utexas.edu/Libs/PCL/Map_collection/states/Alabama.gif
  From the Perry-Castañeda Library at the Univ. of Texas at Austin.

- U.S. Census Bureau—Alabama Profiles
  http://www.census.gov/datamap/www/01.html

- Yale Peabody Museum: GNIS—Alabama
  http://www.peabody.yale.edu/other/gnis/AL.html
  Search the USGS Geographic Names Database. You can limit the search to a specific county in this state and search for any of the following features: airport arch area arroyo bar basin bay beach bench bend bridge **building** *canal cape* **cemetery** *channel* **church** *cliff crater crossing dam falls flat forest gap geyser glacier gut harbor hospital island isthmus lake lava levee locale mine oilfield other park pillar plain ppl range rapids reserve reservoir ridge* **school** *sea slope spring stream summit swamp tower trail tunnel valley well woods.*

◆ Military

- 1st Infantry Regiment, Alabama, C.S.A.
  http://home.sprynet.com/sprynet/harrisfarm/ahar02.htm

- 4th Alabama Infantry
  http://www.geocities.com/BourbonStreet/Delta/7265/

- 19th Alabama Infantry Regiment, Army of Tennessee, C.S.A.
  http://www.19thalabama.org/

- 29th Alabama Infantry Regiment, C.S.A.
  http://www.geocities.com/Heartland/Estates/3071/index.html

- 32nd Infantry Regiment of Alabama Volunteers, Company "D"
  http://www.netpathway.com/~bennie/compdal.html

- 36th Alabama Infantry—Company G
  http://www.edge.net/~deke/algenweb/36th_AL.htm

- 42nd Alabama Infantry
  http://www.alaska.net/~bearpaw/Alabama42.htm

- 48th Alabama Infantry
  http://fly.hiwaay.net/~jrgeorge/48histry.html

- 49th Alabama (CSA) During the Civil War
  http://fly.hiwaay.net/~jemcgee/
  Initially known as "Hale's 31st Alabama."

- 55th Alabama
  http://www.access.digex.net/~bdboyle/55al.txt

- Alabama Civil War Regimental Histories
  http://www.tarleton.edu/~kjones/alregts.html

- Alabama Infantry Regiments
  http://www.erols.com/jreb/alabama.html
  Books for sale, as well as links to regimental sites.

- Alabama Regiments in the Armies of the United States
  http://members.aol.com/egun/Union.html

- Blount County, Alabama Companies and Soldiers in the Armies of the C.S.A.
  http://members.aol.com/egun/CSA.html

- The Civil War Archive—Union Regiments—Alabama
  http://www.civilwararchive.com/unional.htm

- Civil War Battle Summaries by State—Alabama
  http://www2.cr.nps.gov/abpp/battles/bystate.htm#al

- Confederate Soldiers from Shelby County, Alabama and Surrounding Counties
  http://www.mindspring.com/~spbarber429/shelbycsa.htm

- Fifteenth Alabama Infantry Regiment
  http://www.mindspring.com/~edeagle/15AVC/
  Campsite for information on the Original Regiment & for Reenactment 15th Alabama Infantry, Company A.

- Forty-Eighth Alabama Infantry
  http://members.aol.com/egun/48th.html

- H Co. 19th Alabama
  http://www.dnaco.net/~csmartin/hco_19th.html

- Hale's 31st Alabama / 49th Alabama, Port Hudson, LA Hospital Ledger
  http://fly.hiwaay.net/~jemcgee/hospital.htm

- History of Law's Alabama Brigade, 1862–1865
  http://www.tarleton.edu/~kjones/lawsbrig.html
  Including information & muster rolls for: 4th Alabama Regiment, 15th Alabama Regiment, 44th Alabama Regiment, 47th Alabama Regiment and 48th Alabama Regiment.

- History of the 18th Alabama Infantry Regiment, C.S.A.
  http://www.mindspring.com/~spbarber429/18ala.htm

- History of the 47th Alabama Volunteer Infantry Regiment
  http://www.geocities.com/heartland/ridge/9202
  This is a Confederate Army Regimental History of the 47th Alabama Infantry. It now includes unit rosters, (alphabetical order for ease of searching), and will eventually contain other genealogical information related to individuals which were listed on the rosters such as age at enlistment, occupation at enlistment, etc., and burial places of the members of the unit. I will also be including and soliciting for information from decendants of the unit to include on this page. The page will include about 1000 names of the soldiers of the 47th but will be unique in that it will eventually chronicle battles, casualties, campsite locations, etc.

- History of the 33rd Alabama Infantry
  http://members.aol.com/wwhitby/33rd.html

- Korean Conflict State-Level Casualty Lists—Alabama
  http://www.nara.gov/nara/electronic/alhrlist.html
  From the National Archives and Records Administration, Center for Electronic Records.

- Old Huntsville Magazine—War of 1812 Soldiers from North Alabama
  http://oldhuntsville.com/oldhuntsville/p581.htm

- Vietnam Conflict State-Level Casualty Lists—Alabama
  http://www.nara.gov/nara/electronic/alhrviet.html
  From the National Archives and Records Administration, Center for Electronic Records.

- The Vietnam Veterans Memorial—Alabama
  http://grunt.space.swri.edu/statewall/alab/al.htm

◆ Newspapers

- AJR NewsLink—Alabama Newspapers
  http://www.newslink.org/alnews.html

- E&P Media Info Links—Newspaper Sites in Alabama
  http://www.mediainfo.com/emedia/browse-results.htm?region=alabama&category=newspapers++++++++

- Ecola Newstand: Alabama
  http://www.ecola.com/news/press/na/us/al/

- NAA Hotlinks to Newspapers Online—Alabama
  http://www.naa.org/hotlinks/searchResult.asp?param=AL-Alabama&City=1

- N-Net—Alabama Newspapers
  http://www.n-net.com/al.htm

- The Ultimate Collection of News Links: USA—Alabama
  http://www.pppp.net/links/news/USA-AL.html

- Yahoo!...Newspapers...Alabama
  http://www.yahoo.com/News_and_Media/Newspapers/Browse_By_Region/U_S__States/Alabama/

◆ People & Families

- ALGenWeb: Ethnic Resources
  http://www.edge.net/~deke/algenweb/ethnic.html

- ALGenWeb: Ethnic Groups: African-American
  Genealogy and History Sites
  http://members.aol.com/blountal/Afmain.html

- Native American Genealogy in Alabama
  http://www.asc.edu/archives/referenc/notat.html#Native
  Records not at the Alabama Dept. of Archives and History.

- Old Huntsville Magazine—Officials of
  Madison County 1810–1970
  http://oldhuntsville.com/oldhuntsville/p306.htm

- Tribes and Villages of Alabama
  http://hanksville.phast.umass.edu:8000/cultprop/contacts/
  tribal/AL.html

- WPA Life Histories from Alabama
  http://lcweb2.loc.gov/ammem/wpaintro/alcat.html
  *Manuscripts from the Federal Writer's Project, 1936–1940,
  Library of Congress.*

◆ Professional Researchers, Volunteers & Other Research Services

- AL, GA, TN Genealogy Researcher
  http://members.aol.com/CindyJ4/algatn.htm

- Board for Certification of Genealogists—Roster of
  Those Certified—Specializing in Alabama
  http://www.genealogy.org/~bcg/rosts_al.html

- Genealogy Helplist—Alabama
  http://posom.com/hl/usa/al.shtml

- The Official Iowa Counties Professional Genealogist
  and Researcher's Registry for Alabama
  http://www.iowa-counties.com/gene/al.htm

- Time Machine: Ancestral Research
  E-mail: LaLynn@aol.com
  *Laura Flanagan, member of the Limestone County Historical
  Society, SPGS, NGS with 7 years experience, working toward
  certification. For details send e-mail to Laura at:
  LaLynn@aol.com*

◆ Publications, Software & Supplies

- Alabama Heritage Magazine
  http://www.as.ua.edu/heritage/

- AncestorSpy—CDs and Microfiche for Alabama
  http://www.ancestorspy.com/alabama.htm

- The Annie Calhoun Book Shop
  http://pages.prodigy.net/tracks/ACBS.HTM
  Part of the Anniston-Calhoun County Public Library.

- Arkansas Ancestors—Arkansas and Alabama
  Genealogy Resource Books
  http://www.genrecords.com/arkansasancestors/index.htm

- Barbara Green's Used Genealogy Books—Alabama
  http://home.earthlink.net/~genbooks/lochist.html#AL

- Barnette's Family Tree Books—Alabama
  http://www.barnettesbooks.com/alabama.htm

- Books We Own—Alabama
  http://www.rootsweb.com/~bwo/alabama.html

- Boyd Publishing Company—Alabama
  http://www.hom.net/~gac/alabama.htm

- Frontier Press Bookstore—Alabama
  http://www.frontierpress.com/frontier.cgi?category=al

- Genealogical CD-ROM Reference List—Alabama
  http://www.kersur.net/~ccooper/states/al_cdrom.htm

- GenealogyBookShop.com—Alabama
  http://www.genealogybookshop.com/genealogybookshop/files/
  The_United_States,Alabama/index.html
  *The online store of Genealogical Publishing Co., Inc. &
  Clearfield Company.*

- Hearthstone Bookshop—Alabama
  http://www.hearthstonebooks.com/cgi-bin/webc.cgi/st_main.
  html?catid=72&sid=2PH5t29sm

- Heritage Books—Alabama
  http://www.heritagebooks.com/al.htm

- Heritage Quest—Microfilm Records for the
  State of Alabama
  http://www.heritagequest.com/genealogy/microfilm/alabama/

- J & W Enterprises
  http://www.dhc.net/~jw/
  *One stop book source on the Internet, specializing in southern
  states source material.*

- Lost in Time Books—Alabama
  http://www.lostintime.com/catalog/books/bookst/bo01000.htm

- Martin Genealogy Publications
  http://www.angelfire.com/biz/martingenpub/
  Alabama and Florida.

- The Memorabilia Corner Books—Alabama
  http://members.aol.com/TMCorner/book_ala.htm

- The Memorabilia Corner Census View CDs—
  Alabama
  http://members.aol.com/TMCorner/cen_al.htm

- Old Huntsville Magazine
  http://oldhuntsville.com/oldhuntsville/

- S-K Publications—Alabama 1830–1850
  Census Books
  http://www.skpub.com/genie/census/al/

- Southern Queries Genealogy Magazine
  http://www.mindspring.com/~freedom1/sq/sq.htm

- The University of Alabama Press
  http://www.uapress.ua.edu/

- Willow Bend Bookstore—Alabama
  http://www.willowbend.net/al.htm

◆ Queries, Message Boards & Surname Lists

- Alabama Queries
  http://www.geocities.com/Heartland/Meadows/9105/queries.htm

- GenConnect Alabama Visitor Center
  http://cgi.rootsweb.com/~genbbs/indx/Al.html
  A system for posting queries, Bibles, biographies, deeds, obituaries, pensions, wills.

◆ Records: Census, Cemeteries, Land, Obituaries, Personal, Taxes and Vital (Born, Married, Died & Buried)

- The 1790–1890 Federal Population Censuses: Catalog of National Archives Microfilm
  http://www.genealogy.org/census/contents.shtml

  - Census Schedules and Microfilm Roll Numbers for Alabama:

    1830
    http://www.genealogy.org/census/1830_schedules/Alabama.html

    1840
    http://www.genealogy.org/census/1840_schedules/Alabama.html

    1850
    http://www.genealogy.org/census/1850_schedules/Alabama.html

    1860
    http://www.genealogy.org/census/1860_schedules/Alabama.html

    1870
    http://www.genealogy.org/census/1870_schedules/Alabama.html

    1880
    http://www.genealogy.org/census/1880_schedules/Alabama.html

    1880 Soundex
    http://www.genealogy.org/census/1880.sdx_schedules/T734.html

- 1809 Census of Madison County Alabama
  http://hiwaay.net/~white/TVGS/1809mad.txt

- Alabama Vital Records Information
  http://vitalrec.com/al.html

- Assessment of Taxes on Real Estate, Monroe County, Alabama 1854
  http://members.aol.com/GenWebLisa/monrotax.htm

- Autauga County, Alabama 1830 Census
  http://searches.rootsweb.com/cgi-bin/autauga/auta-1830.pl

- Autauga County, Alabama 1840 Census
  http://searches.rootsweb.com/cgi-bin/autauga/auta-1840.pl

- Autauga County, Alabama Cemetery Listings
  http://searches.rootsweb.com/cgi-bin/autauga/auta-cem.pl

- Autauga County, Alabama Super Index
  http://searches.rootsweb.com/cgi-bin/autauga/auta-super.pl
  Search a consolidated index of Autauga County resources.

- Blount County, Alabama 1830 Census
  http://members.aol.com/WGenTwo/1830.htm

- The Bureau of Land Management—Eastern States, General Land Office
  http://www.glorecords.blm.gov/
  The Official Land Patent Records Site. This site has a searchable database of over two million pre-1908 Federal land title records, including scanned images of those records. The Eastern Public Land States covered in this database are: Alabama, Arkansas, Florida, Illinois, Indiana, Louisiana, Michigan, Minnesota, Mississippi, Missouri, Ohio, Wisconsin.

- Cemeteries of the United States—Alabama Cemeteries—County Index
  http://www.gac.edu/~kengelha/uscemeteries/alabama.html

- Census of Madison County (Alabama) Mississippi Territory Taken January 1809
  http://oldhuntsville.com/oldhuntsville/p591.htm

- Census Online—Links to Census Sites on the Web—Alabama
  http://www.census-online.com/links/AL_data.html

- County Courthouse Addresses
  http://www.familytreemaker.com/00000230.html

- Index to Covington County, Alabama Deaths A–F
  http://members.aol.com/GenWebLisa/covdeath.htm
  G–M
  http://members.aol.com/GenWebLisa/covde2.htm

- Covington County, Alabama Cemeteries
  http://members.aol.com/genweblisa/covcem1.htm

- Covington County, Alabama Cemeteries
  http://members.aol.com/genweblisa/covcem2.htm

- Find-A-Grave by Location: Alabama
  http://www.findagrave.com/grave/lal.html
  Graves of noteworthy people.

- Ground Work Genealogy on the Internet: Alabama
  http://members.aol.com/ssmadonna/al.htm

- Index of Graves at Liberty Hill Primitive Baptist Cemetery
  http://www.geocities.com/Heartland/Meadows/9105/xlibhill.htm

- Index to Obituaries Taken from the Southern Democrat, Blount County, Alabama 1915–1940
  http://members.aol.com/blountal/Obit.html

- Interment.net: Alabama Cemeteries
  http://www.interment.net/us/al/index.htm
  A list of links to other sites.

- Marengo Co., AL Estate Records Index Vol I:
  1846–1858
  http://members.aol.com/genweblisa/marengo.htm
- National Archives—Southeast Region (Atlanta)
  http://www.nara.gov/regional/atlanta.html
- National Archives—Southeast Region from
  Family Tree Maker
  http://www.familytreemaker.com/00000104.html
  *Records for Alabama, Florida, Georgia, Kentucky, Mississippi,
  North Carolina, South Carolina, and Tennessee.*
- Old Huntsville Magazine: Cemetery Records of
  Madison County, Alabama
  http://oldhuntsville.com/oldhuntsville/p187.htm
- Old Huntsville Magazine—A Listing of Cemeteries
  in Madison, County, Alabama
  http://oldhuntsville.com/oldhuntsville/p303.htm
- Old Huntsville Magazine—Purchasers of Huntsville
  Town Lots from Original Owners
  http://oldhuntsville.com/oldhuntsville/p588.htm
- Pleasant Grove Methodist Cemetery
  http://home.att.net/~dpdklong/PleasantGrove.html
  Chilton County, Alabama, 1848–1978.
- The Political Graveyard—Cemeteries in Alabama
  http://politicalgraveyard.com/geo/AL/kmindex.html
- Preplanning Network—Funeral Home and
  Cemetery Directory—Alabama
  http://www.preplannet.com/alfhcem.htm
- Register of Births—Conecuh County, AL:
  1881–1883
  http://members.aol.com/GenWebLisa/conecuh.htm
- Union Baptist Church Inscriptions
  http://www.geocities.com/Heartland/Meadows/3011/un.htm
  Lipscomb, Alabama
- USGenWeb Census Project Alabama
  http://www.usgenweb.org/census/states/alabama/alabama.htm
- USGenWeb Tombstone Transcription Project—
  Alabama
  http://www.rootsweb.com/~cemetery/alabama.html
- VitalChek Network—Alabama
  http://www.vitalchek.com/stateselect.asp?state=AL
- Where to Write for Vital Records—Alabama
  http://www.cdc.gov/nchswww/howto/w2w/alabama.htm
  From the National Center for Health Statistics (NCHS).

◆ Religion & Churches

- Christianity.Net Church Locator—Alabama
  http://www.christianity.net/cgi/location.exe?
  United_States+Alabama
- Churches dot Net—Global Church Web Pages—
  Alabama
  http://www.churches.net/churches/alabama.html
- Church Online!—Alabama
  http://www.churchonline.com/usas/al/al.html
- Church Profiles—Alabama
  http://www.church-profiles.com/al/al.html
- Churches of the World—Alabama
  http://www.churchsurf.com/churches/Alabama/index.htm
  From the ChurchSurf Christian Directory.

◆ Societies & Groups

- AlaBenton Genealogical Society
  http://pages.prodigy.net/tracks/ABENINQ.HTM
  Anniston, Alabama
- Archer's Computer Interest Group List—Alabama
  http://www.genealogy.org/~ngs/cigs/ngl1usal.html
- Birmingham PAF Users Group
  http://www.unistarcomputers.com/paf/
- Grand Lodge F & A M of Alabama
  http://www.alagl.org/
- IOOF Lodge Website Directory—Alabama
  http://norm28.hsc.usc.edu/IOOF/USA/Alabama/Alabama.html
  Independent Order of Odd Fellows and Rebekahs.
- Mobile Genealogical Society
  http://www.siteone.com/clubs/mgs/index.html
- Tennessee Valley Genealogical Society
  http://hiwaay.net/~white/TVGS/tvgs.html

◆ USGenWeb Project

- Alabama Genealogy—USGenWeb Project
  State Page
  http://www.usgenweb.org/al
- Alabama—USGenWeb Archives Table of Contents
  http://www.rootsweb.com/~usgenweb/al/alfiles.htm
- Alabama—USGenWeb FTP Archives
  ftp://ftp.rootsweb.com/pub/usgenweb/al/
- Alabama—Queries
  http://www.edge.net/~deke/algenweb/query.html

U.S.—ALASKA—AK
http://www.CyndisList.com/ak.htm

Category Index:

◆ General Resource Sites
◆ Government & Cities
◆ History & Culture
◆ Libraries, Archives & Museums
◆ Mailing Lists, Newsgroups & Chat
◆ Maps, Gazetteers & Geographical Information
◆ Military
◆ Newspapers
◆ People & Families

◆ Professional Researchers, Volunteers & Other Research Services
◆ Publications, Software & Supplies
◆ Queries, Message Boards & Surname Lists
◆ Records: Census, Cemeteries, Land, Obituaries, Personal, Taxes and Vital
◆ Religion & Churches
◆ Societies & Groups
◆ USGenWeb Project

◆ General Resource Sites

● Everton's Sources of Genealogical Information in Alaska
http://www.everton.com/usa/ak.htm

● Family Tree Maker's Genealogy "How To" Guide— Alaska
http://www.familytreemaker.com/00000176.html

● Genealogical Resources in Anchorage, Alaska
http://www.micronet.net/users/~searcy/AKRes.htm

● Genealogy Exchange & Surname Registry— AKGenExchange
http://www.genexchange.com/ak/index.cfm

● Genealogy Resources on the Internet: Alaska
http://www-personal.umich.edu/~cgaunt/alaska.html

● LDS Research Outline for Alaska
http://www.everton.com/usa/ak-0802B.txt

● Lineages' Genealogy Site: Alaska
http://www.lineages.com/rooms/usa/state.asp?StateCode=AK

● ROOTS-L United States Resources: Alaska
http://www.rootsweb.com/roots-l/USA/ak.html
Comprehensive list of research links, including many to history-related sites.

◆ Government & Cities

● 50states.com—Alaska State Information Resource
http://www.50states.com/alaska.htm
A list of general information for each state, including a list of colleges, state symbols, links to maps, newspapers, and other miscellaneous state information.

● Excite Travel by City.Net—Alaska
http://www.city.net/countries/united_states/alaska/
Includes links to web pages for government, cities, schools, libraries, newspapers and maps.

● Official City Web Sites for the State of Alaska
http://OfficialCitySites.org/alaska.htm

● State of Alaska Home Page
http://www.state.ak.us/

● Yahoo! Get Local...Alaska Boroughs and Regions
http://dir.yahoo.com/Regional/U_S__States/Alaska/ Boroughs_and_Regions/
Maps, yellow pages, white pages, newspapers and other local information.

● Yahoo! Get Local...Alaska Cities
http://dir.yahoo.com/Regional/U_S__States/Alaska/Cities/
Maps, yellow pages, white pages, newspapers and other local information.

◆ History & Culture

● Alaska Historical Commission—Office of History and Archaeology
http://www.dnr.state.ak.us/parks/oha_web/ahc.htm

● Valdez Gold Rush Centennial
http://www.alaska.net/~vldzmuse/goldrush1.htm

  ○ Valdez Museum & Historical Archive—Rush Participants Database
  http://www.alaska.net/~vldzmuse/valdez.htm
  Valdez Gold Rush 1898–1899, Names Database.

● Yahoo!...History...Alaska
http://dir.yahoo.com/Arts/Humanities/History/ Browse_By_Region/U_S__States/Alaska/

◆ Libraries, Archives & Museums

- Alaska Family History Centers
  http://www.genhomepage.com/FHC/Alaska.html
  A list of addresses, phone numbers and hours of operation from the Genealogy Home Page.

- Alaska Department of Education—Division of Libraries, Archives and Museums
  http://www.educ.state.ak.us/lam/
  - Alaska Archives and Records Management
    http://www.educ.state.ak.us/lam/archives/home.html
  - Alaska State Library
    http://www.educ.state.ak.us/lam/library.html
  - Alaska State Museum
    http://www.educ.state.ak.us/lam/museum/asmhome.html
  - Statewide Library Electronic Doorway Home Page
    http://sled.alaska.edu/index.html
    - State Library Catalog (SLED) Telnet
      telnet://sled.alaska.edu:23
      Must have Telnet software to access. Make note of logon and password when you begin. Read more about Telnet on the "Libraries, Archives & Museums—General" category page on Cyndi's List.
      http://www.CyndisList.com/lib-gen.htm#Telnet

- Anchorage Municipal Libraries
  http://www.ci.anchorage.ak.us/Services/Departments/Culture/Library/index.html
  - Collections & Resources
    http://www.ci.anchorage.ak.us/Services/Departments/Culture/Library/collect.html

- Family History Centers—Alaska
  http://www.deseretbook.com/famhis/ak.html

- Family History Centers—Alaska
  http://www.lib.byu.edu/~uvrfhc/centers/alaska.html

- HYTELNET—Library Catalogs: USA: Alaska
  http://library.usask.ca/hytelnet/usa/AK.html
  Before you use any of the Telnet links, make note of the user name, password and any other logon information.

- NUCMC Listing of Archives and Manuscript Repositories in Alaska
  http://lcweb.loc.gov/coll/nucmc/aksites.html
  Links to information about resources other than those held in the Library of Congress.

- Repositories of Primary Sources: Alaska
  http://www.uidaho.edu/special-collections/west.html#usak
  A list of links to online resources from the Univ. of Idaho Library, Special Collections and Archives.

- University of Alaska Telnet
  telnet://gnosis.alaska.edu:23
  Must have Telnet software to access. Make note of logon and password when you begin. Read more about Telnet on the "Libraries, Archives & Museums—General" category page on Cyndi's List.
  http://www.CyndisList.com/lib-gen.htm#Telnet

- Valdez Museum and Historical Archive
  http://www.alaska.net/~vldzmuse/

- webCATS: Library Catalogues on the World Wide Web—Alaska
  http://library.usask.ca/hywebcat/states/AK.html

◆ Mailing Lists, Newsgroups & Chat

- Genealogy Resources on the Internet—Alaska Mailing Lists
  http://members.aol.com/gfsjohnf/gen_mail_states-ak.html
  Each of the mailing list links below points to this site, wonderfully maintained by John Fuller. Visit this site for county-specific mailing lists as well.

- AK-Rooters Mailing List
  http://members.aol.com/gfsjohnf/gen_mail_states-ak.html#AK-Rooters

- WESTERN-ROOTS-L Mailing list
  http://members.aol.com/gfsjohnf/gen_mail_states-ak.html#WESTERN-ROOTS-L
  Washington, Oregon, Alaska, Idaho, Montana, Wyoming, California, Nevada, Hawaii, Colorado, Utah, Arizona, and New Mexico.

◆ Maps, Gazetteers & Geographical Information

- 1895 U.S. Atlas—Alaska
  http://www.LivGenMI.com/ak1895mp.htm

- American Memory Railroad Maps 1828–1900—Alaska
  http://memory.loc.gov/cgi-bin/query/S?ammem/gmd:@filreq(@field(STATE+alaska)+@field(COLLID+rrmap))
  From the Geography and Map Division, Library of Congress.

- Color Landform Atlas: Alaska
  http://fermi.jhuapl.edu/states/ak_0.html
  Including a map of counties and a map for 1895.

- Excite Maps: Alaska Maps
  http://www.city.net/maps/view/?mapurl=/countries/united_states/alaska
  Zoom in on these maps all the way to the street level.

- HPI County InfoSystem—Counties in Alaska
  http://www.com/hpi/akcty/index.html

- K.B. Slocum Books and Maps—Alaska
  http://www.treasurenet.com/cgi-bin/treasure/kbslocum/scan/se=Alaska/sf=mapstate

- List of Alaska Boroughs and Regions
  http://www.genealogy.org/~st-clair/counties/state_ak.html

- Map of Alaska Boroughs and Regions, Map #1
  http://govinfo.kerr.orst.edu/gif/states/ak.gif

  Map #2
  http://govinfo.kerr.orst.edu/gif/states/ak1.gif

Map #3
http://govinfo.kerr.orst.edu/gif/states/ak2.gif

Map #4
http://govinfo.kerr.orst.edu/gif/states/ak3.gif
From the Government Information Sharing Project, Information Services, Oregon State University.

- Map of Alaska Boroughs and Regions
  http://www.lib.utexas.edu/Libs/PCL/Map_collection/states/Alaska.gif
  From the Perry-Castañeda Library at the Univ. of Texas at Austin.

- U.S. Census Bureau—Alaska Profiles
  http://www.census.gov/datamap/www/02.html

- Yale Peabody Museum: GNIS—Alaska
  http://www.peabody.yale.edu/other/gnis/AK.html
  *Search the USGS Geographic Names Database. You can limit the search to a specific county in this state and search for any of the following features: airport arch area arroyo bar basin bay beach bench bend bridge **building** canal cape **cemetery** channel **church** cliff crater crossing dam falls flat forest gap geyser glacier gut harbor hospital island isthmus lake lava levee locale mine oilfield other park pillar plain ppl range rapids reserve reservoir ridge **school** slope spring stream summit swamp tower trail tunnel valley well woods.*

◆ Military

- Korean Conflict State-Level Casualty Lists—Alaska
  http://www.nara.gov/nara/electronic/akhrlist.html
  From the National Archives and Records Administration, Center for Electronic Records.

- Vietnam Conflict State-Level Casualty Lists—Alaska
  http://www.nara.gov/nara/electronic/akhrviet.html
  From the National Archives and Records Administration, Center for Electronic Records.

- The Vietnam Veterans Memorial—Alaska
  http://grunt.space.swri.edu/statewall/alaska/ak.htm

◆ Newspapers

- AJR NewsLink—Alaska Newspapers
  http://www.newslink.org/asnews.html

- The Alaska Newspaper Project
  http://www.educ.state.ak.us/lam/library/hist/newspaper.html

- The Anchorage Daily News
  http://www.adn.com/

- E&P Media Info Links—Newspaper Sites in Alaska
  http://www.mediainfo.com/emedia/browse-results.htm?region=alaska&category=newspaper+++++++++

- Ecola Newstand: Alaska
  http://www.ecola.com/news/press/na/us/ak/

- NAA Hotlinks to Newspapers Online—Alaska
  http://www.naa.org/hotlinks/searchResult.asp?param=AK-Alaska&City=1

- N-Net—Alaska Newspapers
  http://www.n-net.com/ak.htm

- The Ultimate Collection of News Links: USA—Alaska
  http://www.pppp.net/links/news/USA-AK.html

- Yahoo!...Newspapers...Alaska
  http://www.yahoo.com/News_and_Media/Newspapers/Browse_By_Region/U_S__States/Alaska/

◆ People & Families

- Affiliated Tribes of Northwest Indians
  http://www.atni.org/~tribes/
  For Alaska, California, Idaho, Montana, Oregon, Washington.

- Agrafena's Children: the Old Families of Ninilchik, Alaska
  http://www.mcn.net/~wleman/agrafena/agrafena.htm

- Albert Aris: Genealogical Gold From The Internet
  http://www.oz.net/~markhow/arisgold.htm
  Mark Howells' great-grandfather who worked at a gold mine in Alaska.

- Blacks in Alaska History Project, Inc.
  http://www.servcom.com/akblkhist/

- Ghosts of the Klondike Gold Rush
  http://www.gold-rush.org/
  Check out the "Pan for Gold Database."

- Ninilchik Families
  http://www.geocities.com/Heartland/Hills/4416/families.htm
  Includes AGRAFENA, COOPER, CRAWFORD, KELLY, KVASNIKOFF, MATSON, OSKOLKOFF.

- Tribes and Villages of Alaska
  http://hanksville.phast.umass.edu:8000/cultprop/contacts/tribal/AK.html

- Valdez Museum & Historical Archive—Rush Participants Database
  http://www.alaska.net/~vldzmuse/valdez.htm
  Valdez Gold Rush 1898–1899, Names Database.

- Yukon / Alaska Pioneer Biographies
  http://yukonalaska.miningco.com/msub15.htm

◆ Professional Researchers, Volunteers & Other Research Services

- Board for Certification of Genealogists—Roster of Those Certified—Specializing in Alaska
  http://www.genealogy.org/~bcg/rosts_ak.html

- Genealogy Helplist—Alaska
  http://www.cybercomm.net/~freddie/helplist/ak.htm

- The Official Iowa Counties Professional Genealogist and Researcher's Registry for Alaska
  http://www.iowa-counties.com/gene/ak.htm

◆ Publications, Software & Supplies

- Barbara Green's Used Genealogy Books—Alaska
  http://home.earthlink.net/~genbooks/lochist.html#AK

- Barnette's Family Tree Books—Alaska
  http://www.barnettesbooks.com/alaska.htm

- Frontier Press Bookstore—Alaska
  http://www.frontierpress.com/frontier.cgi?category=ak

- Genealogical CD-ROM Reference List—Alaska
  http://www.kersur.net/~ccooper/states/ak_cdrom.htm

- Heritage Books—Alaska
  http://www.heritagebooks.com/ak.htm

- Heritage Quest—Microfilm Records for the State of Alaska
  http://www.heritagequest.com/genealogy/microfilm/alaska/

- Lost in Time Books—Alaska
  http://www.lostintime.com/catalog/books/bookst/bo02000.htm

- Willow Bend Bookstore—Alaska
  http://www.willowbend.net/ak.htm

◆ Queries, Message Boards & Surname Lists

- GenConnect Alaska Visitor Center
  http://cgi.rootsweb.com/~genbbs/indx/Ak.html
  A system for posting queries, Bibles, biographies, deeds, obituaries, pensions, wills.

◆ Records: Census, Cemeteries, Land, Obituaries, Personal, Taxes and Vital (Born, Married, Died & Buried)

- Alaska Vital Records Information
  http://vitalrec.com/ak.html

- Anchorage Memorial Park Cemetery
  http://www.atu.com/community/points/pnt016.html

- BLM—Alaska's Electronic Reading Room
  http://www-a.blm.gov/nhp/efoia/ak/
  United States Bureau of Land Management.

- County Courthouse Addresses
  http://www.familytreemaker.com/00000231.html

- Find-A-Grave by Location: Alaska
  http://www.findagrave.com/grave/lak.html
  Graves of noteworthy people.

- National Archives—Pacific Alaska Region (Anchorage)
  http://www.nara.gov/regional/anchorag.html

- National Archives—Alaska Region from Family Tree Maker. Records for Alaska
  http://www.familytreemaker.com/00000094.html

- The Political Graveyard—Cemeteries in Alaska
  http://politicalgraveyard.com/geo/AK/kmindex.html

- S.S. Yukon—Ship Passenger List
  http://www.rootsweb.com/~akgenweb/yukon.htm

- USGenWeb Census Project Alaska
  http://www.usgenweb.org/census/states/alaska.htm

- USGenWeb Tombstone Transcription Project—Alaska
  http://www.rootsweb.com/~cemetery/alaska.html

- VitalChek Network—Alaska
  http://www.vitalchek.com/stateselect.asp?state=AK

- Where to Write for Vital Records—Alaska
  http://www.cdc.gov/nchswww/howto/w2w/alaska.htm
  From the National Center for Health Statistics (NCHS).

◆ Religion & Churches

- Christianity.Net Church Locator—Alaska
  http://www.christianity.net/cgi/location.exe?United_States+Alaska

- Church Online!—Alaska
  http://www.churchonline.com/usas/ak/ak.html

- Church Profiles—Alaska
  http://www.church-profiles.com/ak/ak.html

- Churches of the World—Alaska
  http://www.churchsurf.com/churches/Alaska/index.htm
  From the ChurchSurf Christian Directory.

- The Presbytery of the Yukon
  http://www.alaska.net/~dao/YukonPresbytery/PRESBYTERY_MAIN.html
  Eagle, Alaska

◆ Societies & Groups

- Alaska Historical Society
  http://www.polarnet.com/users/fgs/research/clubs/AKHistorical.htm

- Archer's Computer Interest Group List—Alaska
  http://www.genealogy.org/~ngs/cigs/ngl1usak.html

- Eagle Historical Society
  http://www.polarnet.com/users/fgs/research/clubs/EagleHistory.htm

- Fairbanks Genealogical Society
  http://www.polarnet.com/users/fgs/

- IOOF Lodge Website Directory—Alaska
  http://norm28.hsc.usc.edu/IOOF/USA/Alaska/Alaska.html
  Independent Order of Odd Fellows and Rebekahs.

- Masonry in Alaska
  http://www.alaska-mason.org/

◆ USGenWeb Project

- Alaska Genealogy—USGenWeb Project State Page
  http://www.usgenweb.org/ak

- Alaska—Queries
  http://www.rootsweb.com/~akgenweb/queries.htm

- Alaska—USGenWeb Archives Table of Contents
  http://www.rootsweb.com/~usgenweb/ak/akfiles.htm

- Alaska—USGenWeb FTP Archives
  ftp://ftp.rootsweb.com/pub/usgenweb/ak/

U.S.—ARIZONA—AZ
http://www.CyndisList.com/az.htm

Category Index:

- General Resource Sites
- Government & Cities
- History & Culture
- Libraries, Archives & Museums
- Mailing Lists, Newsgroups & Chat
- Maps, Gazetteers & Geographical Information
- Military
- Newspapers
- People & Families

- Professional Researchers, Volunteers & Other Research Services
- Publications, Software & Supplies
- Queries, Message Boards & Surname Lists
- Records: Census, Cemeteries, Land, Obituaries, Personal, Taxes and Vital
- Religion & Churches
- Societies & Groups
- USGenWeb Project

◆ General Resource Sites

- Everton's Sources of Genealogical Information in Arizona
  http://www.everton.com/usa/az.htm

- Family Tree Maker's Genealogy "How To" Guide— Arizona
  http://www.familytreemaker.com/00000177.html

- Genealogy Bulletin Board Systems for Arizona
  http://www.genealogy.org/~gbbs/gblaz.html

- Genealogy Exchange & Surname Registry— AZGenExchange
  http://www.genexchange.com/az/index.cfm

- Genealogy Resources on the Internet: Arizona
  http://www-personal.umich.edu/~cgaunt/arizona.html

- LDS Research Outline for Arizona
  http://www.everton.com/usa/az-0803B.txt

- Lineages' Genealogy Site: Arizona
  http://www.lineages.com/rooms/usa/state.asp?StateCode=AZ

- ROOTS-L United States Resources: Arizona
  http://www.rootsweb.com/roots-l/USA/az.html
  Comprehensive list of research links, including many to history-related sites.

◆ Government & Cities

- 50states.com—Arizona State Information Resource
  http://www.50states.com/arizona.htm
  A list of general information for each state, including a list of colleges, state symbols, links to maps, newspapers, and other miscellaneous state information.

- Excite Travel by City.Net—Arizona
  http://www.city.net/countries/united_states/arizona/
  Includes links to web pages for government, cities, schools, libraries, newspapers and maps.

- Official City Web Sites for the State of Arizona
  http://OfficialCitySites.org/Arizona.htm

- State of Arizona World Wide Web
  http://www.state.az.us/

- Yahoo! Get Local...Arizona Cities
  http://dir.yahoo.com/Regional/U_S__States/Arizona/Cities/
  Maps, yellow pages, white pages, newspapers and other local information.

- Yahoo! Get Local...Arizona Counties and Regions
  http://dir.yahoo.com/Regional/U_S__States/Arizona/Counties_and_Regions/
  Maps, yellow pages, white pages, newspapers and other local information.

◆ History & Culture

- Ghost Towns of Arizona
  http://www.ghosttowns.com/states/az/az.html

- Yahoo!...History...Arizona
  http://dir.yahoo.com/Arts/Humanities/History/Browse_By_Region/U_S__States/Arizona/

◆ Libraries, Archives & Museums

- Arizona Department of Libraries, Archives and Public Records
  http://www.lib.az.us/
  - ○ Archives Division
    http://www.lib.az.us/archives/

- Resources for Local History Research
  http://www.lib.az.us/archives/local.htm
  - Library Extension Division
    http://www.lib.az.us/extension/index.html
  - Records Management Division
    http://www.lib.az.us/records/index.html
- Arizona Family History Centers
  http://www.genhomepage.com/FHC/Arizona.html
  A list of addresses, phone numbers and hours of operation from the Genealogy Home Page.
- Arizona State University Libraries
  http://www.asu.edu/lib/
  - Arizona Collection
    http://www.asu.edu/lib/archives/arizona.htm
  - Arizona Historical Foundation
    http://www.asu.edu/lib/ahf/
  - Arizona State University's Special Collections
    http://www.asu.edu/lib/speccoll/
  - Department of Archives & Manuscripts
    http://www.asu.edu/lib/archives/dampage.htm
- Family History Centers—Arizona
  http://www.deseretbook.com/famhis/az.html
- Family History Centers—Arizona
  http://www.lib.byu.edu/~uvrfhc/centers/arizona.html
- HYTELNET—Library Catalogs: USA: Arizona
  http://library.usask.ca/hytelnet/usa/AZ.html
  Before you use any of the Telnet links, make note of the user name, password and any other logon information.
- NUCMC Listing of Archives and Manuscript Repositories in Arizona
  http://lcweb.loc.gov/coll/nucmc/azsites.html
  Links to information about resources other than those held in the Library of Congress.
- Repositories of Primary Sources: Arizona
  http://www.uidaho.edu/special-collections/west.html#usaz
  A list of links to online resources from the Univ. of Idaho Library, Special Collections and Archives.
- The Tucson-Pima Library
  http://www.azstarnet.com/packages/072-3864.htm
- webCATS: Library Catalogues on the World Wide Web—Arizona
  http://library.usask.ca/hywebcat/states/AZ.html

◆ Mailing Lists, Newsgroups & Chat

- Genealogy Resources on the Internet—Arizona Mailing Lists
  http://members.aol.com/gfsjohnf/gen_mail_states-az.html
  Each of the mailing list links below points to this site, wonderfully maintained by John Fuller. Visit this site for county-specific mailing lists as well.

- PARADISE-PROJECT Mailing List
  http://members.aol.com/gfsjohnf/gen_mail_states-az.html#PARADISE-PROJECT
  For the discussion and sharing of information regarding the Paradise Valley Genealogy Project in Maricopa County, Arizona. The purpose of this project is to assist patrons of the LDS Paradise Valley Stake in the use of their stake Family History Center, both for personal Family History Work and participation in Family Temple Work.
- WESTERN-ROOTS-L Mailing list
  http://members.aol.com/gfsjohnf/gen_mail_states-az.html#WESTERN-ROOTS-L
  Washington, Oregon, Alaska, Idaho, Montana, Wyoming, California, Nevada, Hawaii, Colorado, Utah, Arizona, and New Mexico.

◆ Maps, Gazetteers & Geographical Information

- 1895 U.S. Atlas—Arizona
  http://www.LivGenMI.com/1895az.htm
- American Memory Panoramic Maps 1847–1929—Arizona
  http://lcweb2.loc.gov/cgi-bin/query/S?ammem/gmd:@filreq(@field(STATE+arizona)+@field(COLLID+pmmap))
  From the Geography and Map Division, Library of Congress.
- American Memory Railroad Maps 1828–1900—Arizona
  http://memory.loc.gov/cgi-bin/query/S?ammem/gmd:@filreq(@field(STATE+arizona)+@field(COLLID+rrmap))
  From the Geography and Map Division, Library of Congress.
- Color Landform Atlas: Arizona
  http://fermi.jhuapl.edu/states/az_0.html
  Including a map of counties and a map for 1895.
- Excite Maps: Arizona Maps
  http://www.city.net/maps/view/?mapurl=/countries/united_states/arizona
  Zoom in on these maps all the way to the street level.
- HPI County InfoSystem—Counties in Arizona
  http://www.com/hpi/azcty/index.html
- K.B. Slocum Books and Maps—Arizona
  http://www.treasurenet.com/cgi-bin/treasure/kbslocum/scan/se=Arizona/sf=mapstate
- List of Arizona Counties
  http://www.genealogy.org/~st-clair/counties/state_az.html
- Map of Arizona Counties
  http://govinfo.kerr.orst.edu/gif/states/az.gif
  From the Government Information Sharing Project, Information Services, Oregon State University.
- Map of Arizona Counties
  http://www.lib.utexas.edu/Libs/PCL/Map_collection/states/Arizona.gif
  From the Perry-Castañeda Library at the Univ. of Texas at Austin.
- U.S. Census Bureau—Arizona Profiles
  http://www.census.gov/datamap/www/04.html

- Yale Peabody Museum: GNIS—Arizona
  http://www.peabody.yale.edu/other/gnis/AZ.html
  Search the USGS Geographic Names Database. You can limit the search to a specific county in this state and search for any of the following features: airport arch area arroyo bar basin bay beach bench bend bridge **building** *canal cape* **cemetery** *channel* **church** *cliff crater crossing dam falls flat forest gap geyser glacier gut harbor hospital island isthmus lake lava levee locale mine oilfield other park pillar plain ppl range rapids reserve reservoir ridge* **school** *sea slope spring stream summit swamp tower trail tunnel valley well woods.*

◆ Military

- Korean Conflict State-Level Casualty Lists—Arizona
  http://www.nara.gov/nara/electronic/azhrlist.html
  From the National Archives and Records Administration, Center for Electronic Records.

- Vietnam Conflict State-Level Casualty Lists—Arizona
  http://www.nara.gov/nara/electronic/azhrviet.html
  From the National Archives and Records Administration, Center for Electronic Records.

- The Vietnam Veterans Memorial—Arizona
  http://grunt.space.swri.edu/statewall/ariz/az.htm

◆ Newspapers

- AJR NewsLink—Arizona Newspapers
  http://www.newslink.org/aznews.html

- Arizona Central: Arizona Republic Archives
  http://www.azcentral.com/archive/

- The Arizona Daily Star
  http://www.azstarnet.com/public/pubstar/dstar.cgi

- The Arizona Newspaper Project
  http://www.lib.az.us/research/c-news.htm

- E&P Media Info Links—Newspaper Sites in Arizona
  http://www.mediainfo.com/emedia/browse-results.htm?region=arizona&category=newspaper+++++++++

- Ecola Newstand: Arizona
  http://www.ecola.com/news/press/na/us/az/

- NAA Hotlinks to Newspapers Online—Arizona
  http://www.naa.org/hotlinks/searchResult.asp?param=AZ-Arizona&City=1

- N-Net—Arizona Newspapers
  http://www.n-net.com/az.htm

- StarNet—The Arizona Daily Star
  http://www.azstarnet.com/

- The Ultimate Collection of News Links: USA—Arizona
  http://www.pppp.net/links/news/USA-AZ.html

- Yahoo!...Newspapers...Arizona
  http://www.yahoo.com/News_and_Media/Newspapers/Browse_By_Region/U_S__States/Arizona/

◆ People & Families

- Tribes and Villages of Arizona
  http://hanksville.phast.umass.edu:8000/cultprop/contacts/tribal/AZ.html

◆ Professional Researchers, Volunteers & Other Research Services

- Board for Certification of Genealogists—Roster of Those Certified—Specializing in Arizona
  http://www.genealogy.org/~bcg/rosts_az.html

- Family History Land
  http://www.familyhistoryland.com/
  Tucson, Arizona

- Genealogy Helplist—Arizona
  http://www.cybercomm.net/~freddie/helplist/az.htm

- The Official Iowa Counties Professional Genealogist and Researcher's Registry for Arizona
  http://www.iowa-counties.com/gene/az.htm

◆ Publications, Software & Supplies

- Barbara Green's Used Genealogy Books—Arizona
  http://home.earthlink.net/~genbooks/lochist.html#AZ

- Frontier Press Bookstore—Arizona
  http://www.frontierpress.com/frontier.cgi?category=az

- Genealogical CD-ROM Reference List—Arizona
  http://www.kersur.net/~ccooper/states/az_cdrom.htm

- Heritage Quest—Microfilm Records for the State of Arizona
  http://www.heritagequest.com/genealogy/microfilm/arizona/

- The Memorabilia Corner—Books: Arizona
  http://members.aol.com/TMCorner/book_arz.htm

◆ Queries, Message Boards & Surname Lists

- GenConnect Arizona Visitor Center
  http://cgi.rootsweb.com/~genbbs/indx/Az.html
  A system for posting queries, Bibles, biographies, deeds, obituaries, pensions, wills.

◆ Records: Census, Cemeteries, Land, Obituaries, Personal, Taxes and Vital (Born, Married, Died & Buried)

- The 1790–1890 Federal Population Censuses: Catalog of National Archives Microfilm
  http://www.genealogy.org/census/contents.shtml

- Census Schedules and Microfilm Roll Numbers for Arizona:

  1870
  http://www.genealogy.org/census/1870_schedules/Arizona.html

  1880
  http://www.genealogy.org/census/1880_schedules/Arizona.html

  1880 Soundex
  http://www.genealogy.org/census/1880.sdx_schedules/T735.html

- The Apache Cemetery, at Apache, Cochise County, Arizona
  http://www.amug.org/~mzwhiz/cemetery.html

- Arizona Resources—Vital Records
  http://aztec.asu.edu:80/genealogy/resource.html

- Arizona Vital Records Information
  http://vitalrec.com/az.html

- Arizona WPA Interview Records
  http://www.getnet.com/~jeannie/wpaintro.html

- BLM—Arizona Electronic Reading Room
  http://www.blm.gov/nhp/efoia/az/
  United States Bureau of Land Management.

- Cemeteries of the United States—Arizona Cemeteries—County Index
  http://www.gac.edu/~kengelha/uscemeteries/arizona.html

- County Courthouse Addresses
  http://www.familytreemaker.com/00000232.html

- Find-A-Grave by Location: Arizona
  http://www.findagrave.com/grave/laz.html
  Graves of noteworthy people.

- Funeral Notices—The Arizona Daily Star
  http://www.azstarnet.com/public/electrifieds/0002.htm

- Interment.net: Arizona Cemeteries
  http://www.interment.net/us/az/index.htm
  A list of links to other sites.

- National Archives—Pacific Region (Laguna Niguel)
  http://www.nara.gov/regional/laguna.html

- National Archives—Pacific Southwest Region
  http://www.familytreemaker.com/00000102.html
  Records for Arizona, Southern California, and Clark County, Nevada.

- The Political Graveyard—Cemeteries in Arizona
  http://politicalgraveyard.com/geo/AZ/kmindex.html

- Preplanning Network—Funeral Home and Cemetery Directory—Arizona
  http://www.preplannet.com/arizfhcem.htm

- Ricks College—Family History Center Genesis Project
  http://abish.ricks.edu/fhc/gbsearch.asp
  Search engine for marriages in Arizona, Idaho, Nevada, Oregon, Utah 1850–1951.

- USGenWeb Census Project Arizona
  http://www.usgenweb.org/census/states/arizona.htm

- USGenWeb Tombstone Transcription Project—Arizona
  http://www.rootsweb.com/~cemetery/arizona.html

- VitalChek Network—Arizona
  http://www.vitalchek.com/stateselect.asp?state=AZ

- Where to Write for Vital Records—Arizona
  http://www.cdc.gov/nchswww/howto/w2w/arizona.htm
  From the National Center for Health Statistics (NCHS).

◆ Religion & Churches

- Christianity.Net Church Locator—Arizona
  http://www.christianity.net/cgi/location.exe?United_States+Arizona

- Church Online!—Arizona
  http://www.churchonline.com/usas/az/az.html

- Church Profiles—Arizona
  http://www.church-profiles.com/az/az.html

- Churches dot Net—Global Church Web Pages—Arizona
  http://www.churches.net/churches/arizona.html

- Churches of the World—Arizona
  http://www.churchsurf.com/churches/Arizona/index.htm
  From the ChurchSurf Christian Directory.

◆ Societies & Groups

- American Historical Society of Germans from Russia—Arizona Sun Chapter
  http://www.ahsgr.org/azsun.html

- Archer's Computer Interest Group List—Arizona
  http://www.genealogy.org/~ngs/cigs/ngl1usaz.html

- Arizona Genealogical & Historical Societies
  http://www.azgab.org/orgs.htm

- Arizona Genealogy Computer Interest Group
  http://www.agcig.org/

- Arizona Genealogy Societies
  http://aztec.asu.edu:80/genealogy/society.html

- Arizona Historical Society, Central Arizona Division
  http://www.tempe.gov/ahs/

- Arizona Historical Society, Northern Arizona Division
  http://www.azstarnet.com/~azhist/nadgeneral.htm

- Arizona Historical Society, Rio Colorado Division
  http://www.tempe.gov/ahs/yuma.htm

- Arizona Historical Society, Southern Arizona Division
  http://www.azstarnet.com/~azhist/

- Arizona Society Daughters of the American Revolution
  http://www.smallbiznetwork.com/asdar/asdar.htm
- Arizona State Genealogical Society
  http://www.rootsweb.com/~asgs/
- AzGAB—Arizona Genealogy Advisory Board
  http://www.azgab.org/
- Family History Society of Arizona
  http://www.fhsa.org/
- The Family History Society of Arizona—Arizona Genealogical Societies
  http://www.fhsa.org/society.html
- IOOF Lodge Website Directory—Arizona
  http://norm28.hsc.usc.edu/IOOF/USA/Arizona/Arizona.html
  Independent Order of Odd Fellows and Rebekahs.

- Northern Arizona Genealogical Society
  http://www.geocities.com/Heartland/3955/NAGS.htm
- Oracle Historical Society
  http://www.ferberts.com/ohs/

◆ USGenWeb Project

- Arizona Genealogy—USGenWeb Project State Page
  http://www.usgenweb.org/az
- Arizona—USGenWeb Archives Table of Contents
  http://www.rootsweb.com/~usgenweb/az/azfiles.htm
- Arizona—USGenWeb FTP Archives
  ftp://ftp.rootsweb.com/pub/usgenweb/az/

U.S.—ARKANSAS—AR
http://www.CyndisList.com/ar.htm

Category Index:

- General Resource Sites
- Government & Cities
- History & Culture
- Libraries, Archives & Museums
- Mailing Lists, Newsgroups & Chat
- Maps, Gazetteers & Geographical Information
- Military
- Newspapers
- People & Families

- Professional Researchers, Volunteers & Other Research Services
- Publications, Software & Supplies
- Queries, Message Boards & Surname Lists
- Records: Census, Cemeteries, Land, Obituaries, Personal, Taxes and Vital
- Religion & Churches
- Societies & Groups
- USGenWeb Project

◆ General Resource Sites

- Everton's Sources of Genealogical Information in Arkansas
  http://www.everton.com/usa/ar.htm
- Family Tree Maker's Genealogy "How To" Guide—Arkansas
  http://www.familytreemaker.com/00000178.html
- Genealogy Bulletin Board Systems for Arkansas
  http://www.genealogy.org/~gbbs/gblar.html
- Genealogy Exchange & Surname Registry—ARGenExchange
  http://www.genexchange.com/ar/index.cfm
- Genealogy Resources on the Internet: Arkansas
  http://www-personal.umich.edu/~cgaunt/arkansas.html
- LDS Research Outline for Arkansas
  http://www.everton.com/usa/ar-0804B.txt
- Lineages' Genealogy Site: Arkansas
  http://www.lineages.com/rooms/usa/state.asp?StateCode=AR
- ROOTS-L United States Resources: Arkansas
  http://www.rootsweb.com/roots-l/USA/ar.html
  Comprehensive list of research links, including many to history-related sites.

◆ Government & Cities

- 50states.com—Arkansas State Information Resource
  http://www.50states.com/arkansas.htm
  A list of general information for each state, including a list of colleges, state symbols, links to maps, newspapers, and other miscellaneous state information.

- Arkansas Home Page
  http://www.state.ar.us/
  State of Arkansas
- Excite Travel by City.Net—Arkansas
  http://www.city.net/countries/united_states/arkansas/
  Includes links to web pages for government, cities, schools, libraries, newspapers and maps.
- Official City Web Sites for the State of Arkansas
  http://OfficialCitySites.org/arkansas.htm
- Yahoo! Get Local...Arkansas Cities
  http://dir.yahoo.com/Regional/U_S__States/Arkansas/Cities/
  Maps, yellow pages, white pages, newspapers and other local information.
- Yahoo! Get Local...Arkansas Counties and Regions
  http://dir.yahoo.com/Regional/U_S__States/Arkansas/Counties_and_Regions/
  Maps, yellow pages, white pages, newspapers and other local information.

◆ History & Culture

- The Turnbo Manuscripts
  http://198.209.8.166/turnbo/about.html
  By Silas Claiborne Turnbo, 1844–1925. "A collection of approximately eight hundred short tales, stories and vignettes that reflect life along the White River Valley in northwest Arkansas and southwest Missouri during the latter half of the 19th century."
- Yahoo!...History...Arkansas
  http://dir.yahoo.com/Arts/Humanities/History/Browse_By_Region/U_S__States/Arkansas/

◆ Libraries, Archives & Museums

- Arkansas Family History Centers
  http://www.genhomepage.com/FHC/Arkansas.html
  A list of addresses, phone numbers and hours of operation from the Genealogy Home Page.

- The Arkansas History Commission and State Archives
  http://www.state.ar.us/ahc/index.htm

- Arkansas State Library
  http://www.asl.lib.ar.us/

- Family History Centers—Arkansas
  http://www.deseretbook.com/famhis/ar.html

- Family History Centers—Arkansas
  http://www.lib.byu.edu/~uvrfhc/centers/arkansas.html

- Fort Smith Public Library
  http://www.fspl.lib.ar.us/
  - Genealogy Department
    http://www.fspl.lib.ar.us/genmain.html
  - Reference Department
    http://www.fspl.lib.ar.us/refmain.html

- HYTELNET—Library Catalogs: USA: Arkansas
  http://library.usask.ca/hytelnet/usa/AR.html
  Before you use any of the Telnet links, make note of the user name, password and any other logon information.

- Nevada County Depot Museum
  http://wolfden.swsc.k12.ar.us/depot_museum/

- NUCMC Listing of Archives and Manuscript Repositories in Arkansas
  http://lcweb.loc.gov/coll/nucmc/arsites.html
  Links to information about resources other than those held in the Library of Congress.

- Repositories of Primary Sources: Arkansas
  http://www.uidaho.edu/special-collections/east1.html#usar
  A list of links to online resources from the Univ. of Idaho Library, Special Collections and Archives.

- University of Arkansas Libraries
  http://www.uark.edu/campus-resources/libinfo/
  - Special Collections Division
    http://www.uark.edu/libinfo/speccoll/
    - Short Guide: Biographical and Family History Research
      http://www.uark.edu/libinfo/speccoll/shortguides/genealogy.html

- webCATS: Library Catalogues on the World Wide Web—Arkansas
  http://library.usask.ca/hywebcat/states/AR.html

◆ Mailing Lists, Newsgroups & Chat

- Genealogy Resources on the Internet—Arkansas Mailing Lists
  http://members.aol.com/gfsjohnf/gen_mail_states-ar.html
  Each of the mailing list links below points to this site, wonderfully maintained by John Fuller. Visit this site for county specific mailing lists as well.

- AGS Mailing List
  http://members.aol.com/gfsjohnf/gen_mail_states-ar.html#AGS
  Sponsored by The Arkansas Genealogical Society (AGS), for anyone interested in the activities of the Society or genealogical research in Arkansas.

- ARKANSAS-ROOTS-L Mailing List
  http://members.aol.com/gfsjohnf/gen_mail_states-ar.html#ARKANSAS-ROOTS-L

- AR-Rooters Mailing List
  http://members.aol.com/gfsjohnf/gen_mail_states-ar.html#AR-Rooters

◆ Maps, Gazetteers & Geographical Information

- 1895 U.S. Atlas—Arkansas
  http://www.LivGenMI.com/1895ar.htm

- American Memory Panoramic Maps 1847–1929—Arkansas
  http://lcweb2.loc.gov/cgi-bin/query/S?ammem/gmd:@filreq(@field(STATE+arkansas)+@field(COLLID+pmmap))
  From the Geography and Map Division, Library of Congress.

- American Memory Railroad Maps 1828–1900—Arkansas
  http://memory.loc.gov/cgi-bin/query/S?ammem/gmd:@filreq(@field(STATE+arkansas)+@field(COLLID+rrmap))
  From the Geography and Map Division, Library of Congress.

- Color Landform Atlas: Arkansas
  http://fermi.jhuapl.edu/states/ar_0.html
  Including a map of counties and a map for 1895.

- Excite Maps: Arkansas Maps
  http://www.city.net/maps/view/?mapurl=/countries/united_states/arkansas
  Zoom in on these maps all the way to the street level.

- HPI County InfoSystem—Counties in Arkansas
  http://www.com/hpi/arcty/index.html

- K.B. Slocum Books and Maps—Arkansas
  http://www.treasurenet.com/cgi-bin/treasure/kbslocum/scan/se=Arkansas/sf=mapstate

- List of Arkansas Counties
  http://www.genealogy.org/~st-clair/counties/state_ar.html

- Map of Arkansas Counties
  http://govinfo.kerr.orst.edu/gif/states/ar.gif
  From the Government Information Sharing Project, Information Services, Oregon State University.

- Map of Arkansas Counties
  http://www.lib.utexas.edu/Libs/PCL/Map_collection/states/Arkansas.gif
  From the Perry-Castañeda Library at the Univ. of Texas at Austin.

- U.S. Census Bureau—Arkansas Profiles
  http://www.census.gov/datamap/www/05.html

- Yale Peabody Museum: GNIS—Arkansas
  http://www.peabody.yale.edu/other/gnis/AR.html
  *Search the USGS Geographic Names Database. You can limit
  the search to a specific county in this state and search for any of
  the following features: airport arch area arroyo bar basin bay
  beach bench bend bridge* **building** *canal cape* **cemetery** *channel*
  church *cliff crater crossing dam falls flat forest gap geyser
  glacier gut harbor hospital island isthmus lake lava levee locale
  mine oilfield other park pillar plain ppl range rapids reserve
  reservoir ridge* **school** *sea slope spring stream summit swamp
  tower trail tunnel valley well woods.*

◆ Military

- 3rd Arkansas Infantry Regiment
  http://www.wcnet.org/~bminton/

- 30th Arkansas Infantry CSA, Co. A & L
  http://www.cswnet.com/~bbarnes/30th_Ark_inf_Clay.htm

- Arkansas History Commission—Request Form for
  Photocopies of Arkansas Confederate Pensions
  http://www.state.ar.us/ahc/form4.txt

- Arkansas History Commission—Request Form for
  Photocopies of Arkansas Military Service Records
  http://www.state.ar.us/ahc/form3.txt

- The Civil War Archive—Union Regiments—
  Arkansas
  http://www.civilwararchive.com/unionar.htm

- Civil War Battle Summaries by State—Arkansas
  http://www2.cr.nps.gov/abpp/battles/bystate.htm#ar

- The Civil War in Arkansas
  http://www.civilwarbuff.org/

- Cpt John L. KUYKENDALL of Greene County,
  Arkansas
  http://www.grnco.net/~michael/civwar.htm

- Co H 30th Arkansas Infantry Regiment, C.S.A.
  http://www.insolwwb.net/~egerdes/civilwar/30ark.htm

- Co I 30th Arkansas Infantry Regiment, C.S.A.
  http://www.insolwwb.net/~egerdes/civilwar/coiark.htm

- Confederate Soldier—Rock Island Illinois
  http://www.insolwwb.net/~egerdes/rockisld.htm
  *Confederate POW's Listed in Arkansas Units Who Died in Rock
  Island, IL Prison Camp.*

- The Fourth Arkansas Union Infantry
  http://www.insolwwb.net/~egerdes/4thunion.htm

- History of the 19th (Dawson's) Arkansas Infantry
  Regiment
  http://rampages.onramp.net/~jtcreate/19hist.htm

- Index to the 32nd Arkansas Infantry M-317
  Compiled Service Records
  http://www.insolwwb.net/~egerdes/32index.htm

- Korean Conflict State-Level Casualty Lists—
  Arkansas
  http://www.nara.gov/nara/electronic/arhrlist.html
  *From the National Archives and Records Administration, Center
  for Electronic Records.*

- Newton's 8th Arkansas Cavalry CSA
  http://members.aol.com/newtons8th/index.html

- Shaver's 7th Regiment and Other Companies with
  Lawrence County and Surrounding Area Soldiers
  http://www.insolwwb.net/~egerdes/civilwar/

- Vietnam Conflict State-Level Casualty Lists—
  Arkansas
  http://www.nara.gov/nara/electronic/arhrviet.html
  *From the National Archives and Records Administration, Center
  for Electronic Records.*

- The Vietnam Veterans Memorial—Arkansas
  http://grunt.space.swri.edu/statewall/arkansas/ar.htm

◆ Newspapers

- AJR NewsLink—Arkansas Newspapers
  http://www.newslink.org/aknews.html

- E&P Media Info Links—Newspaper Sites in
  Arkansas
  http://www.mediainfo.com/emedia/browse-results.
  htm?region=arkansas&category=newspaper+++++++++

- Ecola Newstand: Arkansas
  http://www.ecola.com/news/press/na/us/ar/

- NAA Hotlinks to Newspapers Online—Arkansas
  http://www.naa.org/hotlinks/searchResult.asp?param=
  AR-Arkansas&City=1

- N-Net—Arkansas Newspapers
  http://www.n-net.com/ar.htm

- The Ultimate Collection of News Links: USA—
  Arkansas
  http://www.pppp.net/links/news/USA-AR.html

- Yahoo!...Newspapers...Arkansas
  http://www.yahoo.com/News_and_Media/Newspapers/
  Browse_By_Region/U_S__States/Arkansas/

◆ The Original Arkansas Genealogy

- The Original Arkansas Genealogy—from Bill Couch
  http://www.couchgenweb.com/arkansas/

- Arkansas Connections Page
  http://www.rootsweb.com/~usgenweb/ar/connections/
  connect.htm
  For links to sites with surnames having Arkansas 'connections.'

- Arkansas Unknown County Queries
  http://rampages.onramp.net/~colleag/arkansas/unknown.htm

◆ People & Families

- The Trail of Tears Lawrence County Arkansas
  http://147.97.31.30/lawrence/trail1.htm

- Trail of Tears
  http://www.cswnet.com/~bbarnes/Trail_of_Tears.htm
  Conway County, Faulkner County and Pope County, Arkansas.

- Tribes and Villages of Arkansas
  http://hanksville.phast.umass.edu:8000/cultprop/contacts/tribal/AR.html

◆ Professional Researchers, Volunteers & Other Research Services

- Board for Certification of Genealogists—Roster of Those Certified—Specializing in Arkansas
  http://www.genealogy.org/~bcg/rosts_ar.html

- Genealogy Helplist—Arkansas
  http://posom.com/hl/usa/ar.shtml

- The Official Iowa Counties Professional Genealogist and Researcher's Registry for Arkansas
  http://www.iowa-counties.com/gene/ar.htm

- Oklahoma and Arkansas Research by Monroe Davis
  http://www.geocities.com/Eureka/Park/5315/research.htm

◆ Publications, Software & Supplies

- AncestorSpy—CDs and Microfiche for Arkansas
  http://www.ancestorspy.com/ar.htm

- Arkansas Ancestors—Arkansas and Alabama Genealogy Resource Books
  http://www.genrecords.com/arkansasancestors/index.htm

- Arkansas Research
  http://biz.ipa.net/arkresearch/
  Desmond Walls Allen. Arkansas genealogy books for sale including: Death Records, 1850 Census Indexes, Land Patent Series, County Records, Ozark Folk Tales, Military Records, and more.

- Barbara Green's Used Genealogy Books—Arkansas
  http://home.earthlink.net/~genbooks/lochist.html#AR

- Barnette's Family Tree Books—Arkansas
  http://www.barnettesbooks.com/arkansas.htm

- Beyond Bartholomew—The Portland Area History
  http://www.seark.net/~history/
  Arkansas. A book for sale by the author. The book's table of contents and a family name list are online here also.

- Books We Own—Arkansas
  http://www.rootsweb.com/~bwo/arkansas.html

- Boyd Publishing Company—Arkansas
  http://www.hom.net/~gac/arcasas.htm

- Frontier Press Bookstore—Arkansas
  http://www.frontierpress.com/frontier.cgi?category=ar

- Genealogical CD-ROM Reference List—Arkansas
  http://www.kersur.net/~ccooper/states/ar_cdrom.htm

- GenealogyBookShop.com—Arkansas
  http://www.genealogybookshop.com/genealogybookshop/files/The_United_States,Arkansas/index.html
  The online store of Genealogical Publishing Co., Inc. & Clearfield Company.

- Hearthstone Bookshop—Arkansas
  http://www.hearthstonebooks.com/cgi-bin/webc.cgi/st_main.html?catid=73&sid=2PH5t29sm

- Heritage Books—Arkansas
  http://www.heritagebooks.com/ar.htm

- Heritage Quest—Microfilm Records for the State of Arkansas
  http://www.heritagequest.com/genealogy/microfilm/arkansas/

- J & W Enterprises
  http://www.dhc.net/~jw/
  One stop book source on the Internet, specializing in southern states source material.

- Lost in Time Books—Arkansas
  http://www.lostintime.com/catalog/books/bookst/bo03000.htm

- The Memorabilia Corner Books—Arkansas
  http://members.aol.com/TMCorner/book_ark.htm

- The Memorabilia Corner Census View CDs—Arkansas
  http://members.aol.com/TMCorner/cen_ark.htm

- Old Times Not Forgotten: A History of Drew County
  http://www.seark.net/~rdea/
  A book for sale by the author. The book's table of contents and a family name list are online here also.

- Ozark Books
  http://home.att.net/~rdfortner/
  Supplier of books about the Missouri and Arkansas Ozarks, including Branson.

- S-K Publications—Arkansas 1830–1850 Census Books
  http://www.skpub.com/genie/census/ar/

- Southern Queries Genealogy Magazine
  http://www.mindspring.com/~freedom1/sq/sq.htm

- Willow Bend Bookstore—Arkansas
  http://www.willowbend.net/ar.htm

◆ Queries, Message Boards & Surname Lists

- GenConnect Arkansas Visitor Center
  http://cgi.rootsweb.com/~genbbs/indx/Ar.html
  A system for posting queries, Bibles, biographies, deeds, obituaries, pensions, wills.

◆ Records: Census, Cemeteries, Land, Obituaries, Personal, Taxes and Vital (Born, Married, Died & Buried)

- The 1790–1890 Federal Population Censuses: Catalog of National Archives Microfilm
  http://www.genealogy.org/census/contents.shtml

  o Census Schedules and Microfilm Roll Numbers for Arkansas:

    1830
    http://www.genealogy.org/census/1830_schedules/Arkansas.html

    1840
    http://www.genealogy.org/census/1840_schedules/Arkansas.html

    1850
    http://www.genealogy.org/census/1850_schedules/Arkansas.html

    1860
    http://www.genealogy.org/census/1860_schedules/Arkansas.html

    1870
    http://www.genealogy.org/census/1870_schedules/Arkansas.html

    1880
    http://www.genealogy.org/census/1880_schedules/Arkansas.html

    1880 Soundex
    http://www.genealogy.org/census/1880.sdx_schedules/T736.html

- Arkansas Land Records—Interactive Search
  http://searches.rootsweb.com/cgi-bin/arkland/arkland.pl

- Arkansas Vital Records Information
  http://vitalrec.com/ar.html

- The Bureau of Land Management—Eastern States, General Land Office
  http://www.glorecords.blm.gov/
  The Official Land Patent Records Site. This site has a search-able database of over two million pre-1908 Federal land title records, including scanned images of those records. The Eastern Public Land States covered in this database are: Alabama, Arkansas, Florida, Illinois, Indiana, Louisiana, Michigan, Minnesota, Mississippi, Missouri, Ohio, Wisconsin.

- Cemeteries of the United States—Arkansas Cemeteries—County Index
  http://www.gac.edu/~kengelha/uscemeteries/arkansas.html

- Census Online—Links to Census Sites on the Web—Arkansas
  http://www.census-online.com/links/AR_data.html

- County Courthouse Addresses
  http://www.familytreemaker.com/00000233.html

- Crawford County Marriages 1877–1887
  http://www.rootsweb.com/~arcrawfo/marriage.htm

- Dermott City Cemetery, Chicot County, Arkansas, "A–L"
  http://www.seark.net/~sabra/dercemty.txt
  "M–Z"
  http://www.seark.net/~sabra/dercem2.txt

- Federal Land Records for Arkansas
  http://www.rootsweb.com/~usgenweb/ar/fedland.htm

- Find-A-Grave by Location: Arkansas
  http://www.findagrave.com/grave/lar.html
  Graves of noteworthy people

- Freedman's Bureau, Marriages in Arkansas, 1861–1869
  http://ccharity.com/freedmens/arkansasmarriages.htm

- Interment.net: Arkansas Cemeteries
  http://www.interment.net/us/ar/index.htm
  A list of links to other sites.

- National Archives—Southwest Region (Fort Worth)
  http://www.nara.gov/regional/ftworth.html

- National Archives—Southwest Region
  http://www.familytreemaker.com/00000105.html
  Records for Arkansas, Louisiana, Oklahoma, Texas, and a portion of New Mexico.

- Nevada County Arkansas Cemetery Records
  http://www.pcfa.org/depot_museum/cemetery/

- The Political Graveyard—Cemeteries in Arkansas
  http://politicalgraveyard.com/geo/AR/kmindex.html

- Preplanning Network—Funeral Home and Cemetery Directory—Arkansas
  http://www.preplannet.com/arkfhcem.htm

- USGenWeb Census Project Arkansas
  http://www.usgenweb.org/census/states/arkansas.htm

- USGenWeb Tombstone Transcription Project—Arkansas
  http://www.rootsweb.com/~cemetery/arkansas.html

- VitalChek Network—Arkansas
  http://www.vitalchek.com/stateselect.asp?state=AR

- Where to Write for Vital Records—Arkansas
  http://www.cdc.gov/nchswww/howto/w2w/arkansas.htm
  From the National Center for Health Statistics (NCHS).

◆ Religion & Churches

- Christianity.Net Church Locator—Arkansas
  http://www.christianity.net/cgi/location.exe?United_States+Arkansas

- Church Online!—Arkansas
  http://www.churchonline.com/usas/ar/ar.html

- Church Profiles—Arkansas
  http://www.church-profiles.com/ar/ar.html

- Churches dot Net—Global Church Web Pages—Arkansas
  http://www.churches.net/churches/arkansas.html

- Churches of the World—Arkansas
  http://www.churchsurf.com/churches/Arkansas/index.htm
  From the ChurchSurf Christian Directory.

◆ Societies & Groups

- Archer's Computer Interest Group List—Arkansas
  http://www.genealogy.org/~ngs/cigs/ngl1usar.html

- Arkansas Genealogical Society
  http://www.rootsweb.com/~args/

- Arkansas State Society National Society, Daughters of the American Revolution
  http://www.mtncom.com/noarweb/dar/

- Ark-La-Tex Genealogical Association
  http://www.softdisk.com/comp/aga/

- Baxter County, Arkansas, Historical and Genealogical Society
  http://www.geocities.com/Athens/2101/bchgs.html

- Benton County Cemetery Preservation Group
  http://www.nwa.quik.com/bccpg/

- Carroll County Arkansas Historical & Genealogical Society Home Page
  http://www.geocities.com/Heartland/Plains/4594/cchs.html

- Genealogy Society of Craighead County Arkansas
  http://www.insolwwb.net/~nlmatthews/newsletter.htm

- General Robert C. Newton Camp #197, Sons of Confederate Veterans
  http://www.aristotle.net/~tomezell/scv197.htm
  Little Rock, Arkansas

- Greene County Historical & Genealogical Society
  http://www.grnco.net/~michael/gchgs.htm

- IOOF Lodge Website Directory—Arkansas
  http://norm28.hsc.usc.edu/IOOF/USA/Arkansas/Arkansas.html
  Independent Order of Odd Fellows and Rebekahs.

- Madison County Genealogical & Historical Society
  http://members.aol.com/ptice/mcghsinf.htm

- Marion Chapter of the Daughters of the American Revolution Records
  http://cavern.uark.edu/libinfo/speccoll/darmarionaid.html

- The Most Worshipful Grand Lodge Free and Accepted Masons of Arkansas
  http://www.cei.net/~khat/

- Sons of Confederate Veterans—Colonel Robert G. Shaver Camp #1655, Jonesboro, Arkansas
  http://members.tripod.com/~arkansas/

- Washington County Historical Society
  http://biz.ipa.net/wchs/

- Wayne Van Zandt Chapter, Military Order of the Stars and Bars
  http://www.aristotle.net/~tomezell/mosb.htm
  Little Rock, Arkansas

◆ USGenWeb Project

- Arkansas Genealogy—USGenWeb Project State Page
  http://www.usgenweb.org/ar

- Arkansas—USGenWeb Archives Table of Contents
  http://www.rootsweb.com/~usgenweb/ar/arfiles.htm

- Arkansas—USGenWeb FTP Archives
  ftp://ftp.rootsweb.com/pub/usgenweb/ar/

- Arkansas—Queries
  http://www.rootsweb.com/~argenweb/queries.htm

- Arkansas Biographies Project
  http://www.rootsweb.com/~usgenweb/ar/biography/bios-ark1.htm

U.S.—CALIFORNIA—CA
http://www.CyndisList.com/ca.htm

Category Index:

- General Resource Sites
- Government & Cities
- History & Culture
- Libraries, Archives & Museums
- Mailing Lists, Newsgroups & Chat
- Maps, Gazetteers & Geographical Information
- Military
- Newspapers
- People & Families

- Professional Researchers, Volunteers & Other Research Services
- Publications, Software & Supplies
- Queries, Message Boards & Surname Lists
- Records: Census, Cemeteries, Land, Obituaries, Personal, Taxes and Vital
- Religion & Churches
- Societies & Groups
- USGenWeb Project

◆ General Resource Sites

- Everton's Sources of Genealogical Information in California
http://www.everton.com/usa/ca.htm
- Family History Research Sources for San Francisco City and County
http://feefhs.org/fhc-dave.html
- Family Tree Maker's Genealogy "How To" Guide—California
http://www.familytreemaker.com/00000179.html
- Genealogy Bulletin Board Systems for California
http://www.genealogy.org/~gbbs/gblca.html
- Genealogy Exchange & Surname Registry—CAGenExchange
http://www.genexchange.com/ca/index.cfm
- Genealogy Resources on the Internet: California
http://www-personal.umich.edu/~cgaunt/calif.html
- Genealogy Upcoming Events, Classes, Opportunities—San Diego County Area
http://www.cgssd.org/events.html
- LDS Research Outline for California
http://www.everton.com/usa/ca-0805B.txt
- Lineages' Genealogy Site: California
http://www.lineages.com/rooms/usa/state.asp?StateCode=CA
- NORCAL Genealogy Index
http://homepages.rootsweb.com/~yvonne/NORCAL%20index/
A State-Wide Index to Genealogical Information in California.
- ROOTS-L United States Resources: California
http://www.rootsweb.com/roots-l/USA/ca.html
Comprehensive list of research links, including many to history-related sites.

◆ Government & Cities

- 50states.com—California State Information Resource
http://www.50states.com/californ.htm
A list of general information for each state, including a list of colleges, state symbols, links to maps, newspapers, and other miscellaneous state information.
- California State Home Page
http://www.ca.gov/
- Excite Travel by City.Net—California
http://www.city.net/countries/united_states/california/
- I Love L.A.
http://www-leland.stanford.edu/~jenkg/angeles/la.html
Dedicated to the history, culture and landmarks of Los Angeles.
- Official City Web Sites for the State of California
http://OfficialCitySites.org/california.htm
- San Francisco History
http://www.geocities.com/Heartland/Valley/2171/sfcem.htm
- Yahoo! Get Local...California Cities
http://dir.yahoo.com/Regional/U_S__States/California/Cities/
Maps, yellow pages, white pages, newspapers and other local information.
- Yahoo! Get Local...California Counties and Regions
http://dir.yahoo.com/Regional/U_S__States/California/Counties_and_Regions/
Maps, yellow pages, white pages, newspapers and other local information.

◆ History & Culture

- California History
http://www.geocities.com/Athens/Forum/1464/

- California State Historical Landmarks
  http://www.donaldlaird.com/landmarks/
- Ghost Towns of California
  http://www.ghosttowns.com/states/ca/ca.html
- History, Culture, Economy & Natural Resources of California
  http://library.ca.gov/california/cahhisto.html
- History Resources for California
  http://www.jspub.com/~jsp/hisresrc.html
- I Love L.A.
  http://www-leland.stanford.edu/~jenkg/angeles/la.html
  Dedicated to the history, culture and landmarks of Los Angeles.
- Junipero Serra and the California Missions
  http://home.earthlink.net/~foghorn1/
- Los Angeles: Past, Present & Future
  http://www.usc.edu/Library/Ref/LA/
- San Bernardino History
  http://www.fp.csnsys.com/pioneer/
  Information on the San Bernardino Sesquicentennial Celebration Events and a place to register San Bernardino Colony descendants.
- San Francisco
  http://www.geocities.com/Heartland/Valley/2171/
  1842 census, 1850 directory, 1857 assessor's list, newspapers and other historical information.
- San Francisco History
  http://www.geocities.com/Heartland/Valley/2171/sfcem.htm
- Yahoo!...History...California
  http://dir.yahoo.com/Arts/Humanities/History/
  Browse_By_Region/U_S__States/California/

◆ Libraries, Archives & Museums

- Alameda County Library
  http://www.aclibrary.org/
  ○ The Pleasanton Genealogy Library
    http://www.aclibrary.org/system/genlib.html
- California Family History Centers
  http://www.genhomepage.com/FHC/California.html
  A list of addresses, phone numbers and hours of operation from the Genealogy Home Page.
- California Secretary of State—California State Archives
  http://www.ss.ca.gov/archives/archives.htm
  ○ Collections in the Archives
    http://www.ss.ca.gov/archives/archives_e.htm
    • Family History Resources
      http://www.ss.ca.gov/archives/level3_genie.htm
- California State Library
  http://www.library.ca.gov/
  ○ Selected Guide to Sources for Genealogy in the California History Section
    http://www.library.ca.gov/html/genealogy.html

- California State Railroad Museum Library
  http://www.csrmf.org/library
  Holds records for: Atchison, Topeka & Santa Fe Railway, Western Pacific Railroad, Central Pacific, Southern Pacific Railroads.
- Concord/Walnut Creek California Family History Center
  http://feefhs.org/lds/fhc/frg-fhcc.html
- Family History Centers—California
  http://www.deseretbook.com/famhis/ca.html
- Family History Centers—California
  http://www.lib.byu.edu/~uvrfhc/centers/california.html
- Glendale Public Library
  http://library.ci.glendale.ca.us/
- HYTELNET—Library Catalogs: USA: California
  http://library.usask.ca/hytelnet/usa/CA.html
  Before you use any of the Telnet links, make note of the user name, password and any other logon information.
- I Love L.A.—Historic and Cultural Museums, Missions and Adobes
  http://www-leland.stanford.edu/~jenkg/angeles/missions.html
- Libraries with Genealogy Holdings in the San Diego Area
  http://www.cgssd.org/libraries.html
- Los Angeles Family History Center
  http://www.rootsweb.com/~bifhsusa/fhcwhere.html
  From the British Isles Family History Society—U.S.A. web site.
- Los Angeles Public Library
  http://www.lapl.org/
  ○ History and Genealogy Department
    http://www.lapl.org/central/hihp.html
    One of the largest genealogy collections west of the Mississsppi.
  ○ Photo Database & Virtual Gallery
    http://catalog.lapl.org:1080/a_photo.html
    Over 2.5 million prints in a variety of collections dating back to 1880.
- NUCMC Listing of Archives and Manuscript Repositories in California
  http://lcweb.loc.gov/coll/nucmc/casites.html
  Links to information about resources other than those held in the Library of Congress.
- Other Libraries and Organizations in Southern California
  http://www.usc.edu/Library/Ref/Ethnic/socalorgan.html
- Repositories of Primary Sources: California
  http://www.uidaho.edu/special-collections/west.html#usca
  A list of links to online resources from the Univ. of Idaho Library, Special Collections and Archives.
- Research Libraries in Los Angeles
  http://www.usc.edu/isd/archives/la/libraries/
- Riverside City and County Public Library
  http://www.co.riverside.ca.us/community/rccpl/

- Ruben Salazar Library, Sonoma State University
  http://libweb.sonoma.edu/
  Rohnert Park, California
  - Special Collections / University Archives
    http://libweb.sonoma.edu/special/
    - Finley McFarling Genealogy Collection
      http://libweb.sonoma.edu/special/finley.html
- San Diego Family History Centers
  http://www.cgssd.org/centers.html
- San Diego Public Library
  http://www.sannet.gov/public-library/index.html
- San Francisco Public Library—General Collections Homepage: Genealogy Page
  http://sfpl.lib.ca.us/gencoll/gencolgn.htm
- San Jose Public Library: Genealogy
  http://www.sjpl.lib.ca.us/adult/genea.htm
- Santa Clara Family History Center
  http://reality.sgi.com/csp/scfhc/
- Southern California Genealogical Society Library
  http://www.cwire.com/scgs/library.html
  Burbank, California
- Stanford University Libraries & Information Resources
  http://www-sul.stanford.edu/
- The Sutro Library—A Branch of the California State Library
  http://nick.sfpl.lib.ca.us/gencoll/gencolsu.htm
  San Francisco
- Torrance Public Library
  http://www.ci.torrance.ca.us/city/dept/library/torrlib.htm
  - Genealogy Resources at Civic Center Library
    http://www.ci.torrance.ca.us/city/dept/library/GENEALOG.HTM
- USC University Libraries
  http://www.usc.edu/Library/index.html
- webCATS: Library Catalogues on the World Wide Web—California
  http://library.usask.ca/hywebcat/states/CA.html

◆ Mailing Lists, Newsgroups & Chat

- Genealogy Resources on the Internet—California Mailing Lists
  http://members.aol.com/gfsjohnf/gen_mail_states-ca.html
  Each of the mailing list links below points to this site, wonderfully maintained by John Fuller. Visit this site for county-specific mailing lists as well.
- CA-GOLDRUSH Mailing List
  http://members.aol.com/gfsjohnf/gen_mail_states-ca.html#CA-GOLDRUSH
  For anyone who is interested in early California miners and settlers, especially in northern California, 1848–1880.

- CA-Rooters Mailing List
  http://members.aol.com/gfsjohnf/gen_mail_states-ca.html#CA-Rooters
- CAROOTS Mailing List
  http://members.aol.com/gfsjohnf/gen_mail_states-ca.html#CAROOTS
- NORCAL-L Mailing List
  http://members.aol.com/gfsjohnf/gen_mail_states-ca.html#NORCAL
  For the discussion and sharing of information regarding the genealogy and history of NORthern CALifornia.
- SOCAL Mailing List
  http://members.aol.com/gfsjohnf/gen_mail_states-ca.html#SOCAL
  For the discussion and sharing of information regarding the genealogy and history of SOuthern CALifornia.
- WESTERN-ROOTS-L Mailing list
  http://members.aol.com/gfsjohnf/gen_mail_states-ca.html#WESTERN-ROOTS-L
  Washington, Oregon, Alaska, Idaho, Montana, Wyoming, California, Nevada, Hawaii, Colorado, Utah, Arizona, and New Mexico.

◆ Maps, Gazetteers & Geographical Information

- 1895 U.S. Atlas—California
  http://www.LivGenMI.com/1895ca.htm
- American Memory Panoramic Maps 1847–1929—California
  http://lcweb2.loc.gov/cgi-bin/query/S?ammem/gmd:@filreq(@field(STATE+california)+@field(COLLID+pmmap))
  From the Geography and Map Division, Library of Congress.
- American Memory Railroad Maps 1828–1900—California
  http://memory.loc.gov/cgi-bin/query/S?ammem/gmd:@filreq(@field(STATE+california)+@field(COLLID+rrmap))
  From the Geography and Map Division, Library of Congress.
- Color Landform Atlas: California
  http://fermi.jhuapl.edu/states/ca_0.html
  Including a map of counties and a map for 1895.
- Excite Maps: California Maps
  http://www.city.net/maps/view/?mapurl=/countries/united_states/california
  Zoom in on these maps all the way to the street level.
- HPI County InfoSystem—Counties in California
  http://www.com/hpi/cacty/index.html
- K.B. Slocum Books and Maps—California
  http://www.treasurenet.com/cgi-bin/treasure/kbslocum/scan/se=California/sf=mapstate
- List of California Counties
  http://www.genealogy.org/~st-clair/counties/state_ca.html
- Map of California Counties, Map #1
  http://govinfo.kerr.orst.edu/gif/states/ca.gif

Map #2
http://govinfo.kerr.orst.edu/gif/states/ca1.gif

Map #3
http://govinfo.kerr.orst.edu/gif/states/ca2.gif

Map #4
http://govinfo.kerr.orst.edu/gif/states/caorig.gif
From the Government Information Sharing Project, Information Services, Oregon State University.

- Map of California Counties
http://www.lib.utexas.edu/Libs/PCL/Map_collection/states/
California.gif
From the Perry-Castañeda Library at the Univ. of Texas at Austin.

- U.S. Census Bureau—California Profiles
http://www.census.gov/datamap/www/06.html

- Yale Peabody Museum: GNIS—California
http://www.peabody.yale.edu/other/gnis/CA.html
*Search the USGS Geographic Names Database. You can limit the search to a specific county in this state and search for any of the following features: airport arch area arroyo bar basin bay beach bench bend bridge **building** canal cape **cemetery** channel **church** cliff crater crossing dam falls flat forest gap geyser glacier gut harbor hospital island isthmus lake lava levee locale mine oilfield other park pillar plain ppl range rapids reserve reservoir ridge **school** sea slope spring stream summit swamp tower trail tunnel valley well woods.*

◆ Military

- The Civil War Archive—Union Regiments—California
http://www.civilwararchive.com/unionca.htm

- Korean Conflict State-Level Casualty Lists—California
http://www.nara.gov/nara/electronic/cahrlist.html
From the National Archives and Records Administration, Center for Electronic Records.

- Vietnam Conflict State-Level Casualty Lists—California
http://www.nara.gov/nara/electronic/cahrviet.html
From the National Archives and Records Administration, Center for Electronic Records.

- The Vietnam Veterans Memorial—California
http://grunt.space.swri.edu/statewall/calif/ca.htm

◆ Newspapers

- AJR NewsLink—California Newspapers
http://www.newslink.org/canews.html

- The California Newspaper Project
http://cbsr26.ucr.edu/cnp/index.html

- E&P Media Info Links—Newspaper Sites in California
http://www.mediainfo.com/emedia/browse-results.
htm?region=california&category=newspaper+++++++++

- Ecola Newstand: California
http://www.ecola.com/news/press/na/us/ca/

- The Gate
http://www.sfgate.com/
From the San Francisco Chronicle & the San Francisco Examiner.

- Los Angeles Times
http://www.latimes.com/

- Mountain Democrat Online
http://www.mtdemocrat.com/
California's Oldest Newspaper, Placerville, California.

- NAA Hotlinks to Newspapers Online—California
http://www.naa.org/hotlinks/searchResult.asp?param=
CA-California&City=1

- N-Net—California Newspapers
http://www.n-net.com/ca.htm

- Sacramento Bee
http://www.sacbee.com/

- San Francisco Bay Guardian
http://www.sfbayguardian.com/

- The Ultimate Collection of News Links:
USA—California
http://www.pppp.net/links/news/USA-CA.html

- Yahoo!...Newspapers...California
http://www.yahoo.com/News_and_Media/Newspapers/
Browse_By_Region/U_S__States/California/

◆ People & Families

- Affiliated Tribes of Northwest Indians
http://www.atni.org/~tribes/
For Alaska, California, Idaho, Montana, Oregon, Washington.

- California Cornish Cousins
http://www.kingsnet.com/users/rroberts/ccc/CCCmain.html

- A Centennial Tribute: Creators of the Legacy
http://www.commerce.digital.com/palo-alto/historical-assoc/
centennial-bios/home.html
Palo Alto, California

- Family Names of Early Portuguese Immigrants in California
http://www.LusaWeb.com/genames.htm

- To Know My Name—A Chronological History of African-Americans in Santa Cruz County
http://www.cruzio.com/~sclibs/history/know1.html

- Tribes and Rancherias of California
http://hanksville.phast.umass.edu:8000/cultprop/contacts/
tribal/CA.html

◆ Professional Researchers, Volunteers & Other Research Services

- AIS—Asset Information Services
http://pages3.simplenet.com/ais.htm
San Diego, California. Missing persons and adoption searches.

- American Records Research Services
  http://www.records.org
  A research service providing assistance to obtain important genealogical information from National Archives Records, LDS Database Searches, San Francisco Bay Area Research, California Vital Records, Sutro Library Research and computer searches.

- AskQuailind@—Document Delivery Service for Genealogists and Family Historians
  http://www.AskQuailind.com/
  San Mateo, California

- Board for Certification of Genealogists—Roster of Those Certified—Specializing in California
  http://www.genealogy.org/~bcg/rosts_ca.html

- California Genealogy Index
  http://cmug.com/~minesroad/genealogy.html
  From Mines Road Books. Search the index online and order research to be done on the surname you find in the index.

- Charles Herbert Crookston—Family History Research
  E-mail: charleshc@sfo.com
  Specializing pre 1906 San Francisco Earthquake and Fire Research and Northern California research. Send e-mail to: charleshc@sfo.com

- Genealogy Helplist—California
  http://www.geocities.com/Heartland/Ranch/6995/

- Genealogy Research Services
  http://home.pacbell.net/cageni/

- The Official Iowa Counties Professional Genealogist and Researcher's Registry for California
  http://www.iowa-counties.com/gene/ca.htm

- Professional Family History Services
  http://pages.prodigy.net/john_flora/pfhs.htm

◆ Publications, Software & Supplies

- AncestorSpy—CDs and Microfiche for California
  http://www.ancestorspy.com/calif.htm

- Barbara Green's Used Genealogy Books—California
  http://home.earthlink.net/~genbooks/lochist.html#CA

- Barnette's Family Tree Books—California
  http://www.barnettesbooks.com/california.htm

- Books We Own—California
  http://www.rootsweb.com/~bwo/california.html

- Boyd Publishing Company—California
  http://www.hom.net/~gac/califor.htm

- Frontier Press Bookstore—California
  http://www.frontierpress.com/frontier.cgi?category=ca

- GenealogyBookShop.com—California
  http://www.genealogybookshop.com/genealogybookshop/files/The_United_States,California/index.html
  The online store of Genealogical Publishing Co., Inc. & Clearfield Company.

- Heritage Books—California
  http://www.heritagebooks.com/ca.htm

- Heritage Quest—Microfilm Records for the State of California
  http://www.heritagequest.com/genealogy/microfilm/california/

- Los Angeles City Directory 1930
  E-mail: billcapp@ix.netcom.com
  E-mail Bill Cappello at billcapp@ix.netcom.com and he will do a reasonable number of specific lookups for you. Allow two weeks for a reply.

- Lost in Time Books—California
  http://www.lostintime.com/catalog/books/bookst/bo04000.htm

- The Memorabilia Corner—Books: California
  http://members.aol.com/TMCorner/book_cal.htm

- Mines Road Books ~ Fremont
  http://cmug.com/~minesroad/
  Specialize in researching and publishing California history and genealogy.

- Portuguese Pioneers of the Sacramento Valley
  http://www.dholmes.com/new-book.html
  A new book project.

- Willow Bend Bookstore—California
  http://www.willowbend.net/ca.htm

◆ Queries, Message Boards & Surname Lists

- GenConnect California Visitor Center
  http://cgi.rootsweb.com/~genbbs/indx/Ca.html
  A system for posting queries, Bibles, biographies, deeds, obituaries, pensions, wills.

- Livermore-Amador Genealogical Society Surname Index
  http://www.l-ags.org/surname.html
  With over 10,000 surname-locality entries.

◆ Records: Census, Cemeteries, Land, Obituaries, Personal, Taxes and Vital (Born, Married, Died & Buried)

- The 1790–1890 Federal Population Censuses: Catalog of National Archives Microfilm
  http://www.genealogy.org/census/contents.shtml
  - Census Schedules and Microfilm Roll Numbers for California:
    1850
    http://www.genealogy.org/census/1850_schedules/California.html
    1860
    http://www.genealogy.org/census/1860_schedules/California.html

1870
http://www.genealogy.org/census/1870_schedules/
California.html

1880
http://www.genealogy.org/census/1880_schedules/
California.html

1880 Soundex
http://www.genealogy.org/census/1880.sdx_schedules/
T737.html

- 1872 Foreign-Born Voters of California
  http://feefhs.org/fbvca/fbvcagri.html

- BLM—California Electronic Reading Room
  http://www.blm.gov/nhp/efoia/ca/
  United States Bureau of Land Management.

- California Death Index Information
  http://www.micronet.net/users/~searcy/indexinfo.htm
  A list of microfiche/film numbers by year and surname.

- California Vital Records Information
  http://vitalrec.com/ca.html

- Cemeteries of the United States—California
  Cemeteries—County Index
  http://www.gac.edu/~kengelha/uscemeteries/california.html

- Census Online—Links to Census Sites on the Web—
  California
  http://www.census-online.com/links/CA_data.html

- County Courthouse Addresses
  http://www.familytreemaker.com/00000234.html

- Downey Cemetery
  http://www.downeyca.org/histor5.htm#Downey Cemetery

- Find-A-Grave by Location: California
  http://www.findagrave.com/grave/lca.html
  Graves of noteworthy people.

- Historic Cemeteries of Los Angeles
  http://www.usc.edu/isd/archives/la/cemeteries/

- Interment.net: California Cemeteries
  http://www.interment.net/us/ca/index.htm
  A list of links to other sites.

- National Archives—Pacific Region (San Bruno)
  http://www.nara.gov/regional/sanfranc.html

- National Archives—Pacific Sierra Region
  http://www.familytreemaker.com/00000101.html
  *Records for Northern California, Hawaii, Nevada (except Clark
  County), the Pacific Trust Territories, and American Samoa.*

- National Archives—Pacific Region (Laguna Niguel)
  http://www.nara.gov/regional/laguna.html

- National Archives—Pacific Southwest Region
  http://www.familytreemaker.com/00000102.html
  *Records for Arizona, Southern California, and Clark County,
  Nevada.*

- The Political Graveyard—Cemeteries in California
  http://politicalgraveyard.com/geo/CA/kmindex.html

- Portuguese Voters of 1872 in California
  http://www.dholmes.com/voters.html

- Preplanning Network—Funeral Home and
  Cemetery Directory—California
  http://www.preplannet.com/califfh.htm

- The San Francisco Call (Newspaper) Database
  1875–1905
  http://feefhs.org/fdb2/sfcall0.html

- San Francisco Cemeteries
  http://userwww.sfsu.edu/~jblcktt/SFCemeteries.html

- San Francisco County Ancestors' Marriage Notices
  http://www.sfo.com/~timandpamwolf/sfmar.htm

- San Francisco County Genealogy—Ancestors'
  Obituaries and Death Notices
  http://www.sfo.com/~timandpamwolf/sfranobi.htm

- San Francisco 1842 Census
  http://www.geocities.com/Heartland/Valley/2171/hc842.htm

- San Francisco History—Cemeteries
  http://www.geocities.com/Heartland/Valley/2171/hcmaaa.htm

- San Francisco Title Abstract Index
  http://pages.prodigy.net/greentrucking/GenPage/sfindex.htm
  1850 to 1918.

- Tulare County Marriages—1852 to June 1893
  http://www.compuology.com/cagenweb/tckcm.htm

- Tulare County Marriages—July 1, 1893 to
  Dec. 31, 1909
  http://www.compuology.com/cagenweb/tcm.htm

- USGenWeb Census Project California
  http://www.usgenweb.org/census/states/californ.htm

- USGenWeb Tombstone Transcription Project—
  California
  http://www.rootsweb.com/~cemetery/californ.html

- VitalChek Network—California
  http://www.vitalchek.com/stateselect.asp?state=CA

- Where to Write for Vital Records—California
  http://www.cdc.gov/nchswww/howto/w2w/californ.htm
  From the National Center for Health Statistics (NCHS).

◆ Religion & Churches

- Christianity.Net Church Locator—California
  http://www.christianity.net/cgi/
  location.exe?United_States+California

- Church Online!—California
  http://www.churchonline.com/usas/ca/ca.html

- Church Profiles—California
  http://www.church-profiles.com/ca/ca.html

- Churches dot Net—Global Church Web Pages—
  California
  http://www.churches.net/churches/californ.html

Churches of the World—California
http://www.churchsurf.com/churches/California/index.htm
From the ChurchSurf Christian Directory.

◆ Societies & Groups

- African American Genealogical Society of Northern California
  http://www.aagsnc.org/
  Oakland, California. Preserve and promote the study of records of a genealogical and historical nature relating to African American ancestry.

- American Civil War Association
  http://acwa.org/
  A California Reenactment Organization.

- American Historical Society of Germans from Russia—Central California Chapter
  http://www.ahsgr.org/cacentra.html

- American Historical Society of Germans from Russia—Southern California Chapter
  http://www.jovanet.com/~hmehrman/ahsgr/casocal.html

- American Historical Society of Germans from Russia—Ventura Chapter
  http://www.jovanet.com/~hmehrman/ahsgr/cavent.html

- Archer's Computer Interest Group List—California
  http://www.genealogy.org/~ngs/cigs/ngl1usca.html

- British Isles Family History Society—U.S.A. ~ Los Angeles
  http://www.rootsweb.com/~bifhsusa/

- California Cornish Cousins
  http://www.calflytech.com/ccc/

- California Genealogical Societies: Publications, Libraries and Research
  http://www.compuology.com/cagenweb/ca-socty.htm

- California Genealogical Society
  http://members.aol.com/calgensoc/home.htm
  San Francisco, California

- The California Historical Society
  http://www.calhist.org/

- The California Mennonite Historical Society
  http://www.fresno.edu/cmhs/home.htm

- California State Society of the National Society Daughters of the American Revolution
  http://members.home.net/swelch/cssdar/

- Central Valley PAF Users Group ~ Fresno, California
  http://www.geocities.com/TimesSquare/7957/index.htm

- Chinese Historical Society of Southern California
  http://www.chssc.org/

- Commission for the Preservation of Pioneer Jewish Cemeteries and Landmarks
  http://www.jfed.org/mcemcom.htm
  Northern California

- The Computer Genealogy Society of San Diego (CGSSD)
  http://www.cgssd.org/

- Contra Costa County Historical Society
  http://www.ecis.com/~oakhrst/history.html

- Fresno City and County Historical Society
  http://www.fcoe.k12.ca.us/home/histscty.html

- Fresno County Genealogical Society
  http://nc.sjvls.lib.ca.us:80/fresno/fgs/

- Genealogical and Historical Council of the Sacramento Valley
  http://feefhs.org/ghcsv/frgghcsv.html

- Genealogical Society of Hispanic America
  http://www.ancestry.com/SocietyHall/viewmember.asp?results=81
  GSHA is 11 years old with five chapters in Colorado & California. Members specialize in Hispanic research in the American Southwest & Mexico. Over 75% are descendants of the Spanish colonists of New Mexico.

- The Genealogical Society of the Morongo Basin
  http://www.yuccavalley.com/genealogy/
  In Yucca Valley, CA. Has downloadable surname registry.

- Grand Lodge of California Free and Accepted Masons
  http://www.freemason.org/

- Grass Roots Genealogical Group
  http://www.nccn.net/leisure/crafthby/genealog.htm
  Grass Valley, California

- Hi-Desert Genealogical Society
  http://www.vvo.com/comm/hdgs.htm

- High Sierra History Forum
  http://tahoenet.com/tdhs/index.html
  California / Nevada

- Independent Order of Odd Fellows and Rebekahs—Grand Lodge of California
  http://128.125.109.137/CA_IOOF.shtml

- Jewish Genealogical Society of Sacramento
  http://www1.jewishgen.org/ajgs/jgs-sacramento/

- Jewish Genealogical Society, Los Angeles (JGSLA)
  http://www.jewishgen.org/jgsla/

- JPL Genealogy Club
  http://www.jplerc.org/genealog/
  Employees of the Jet Propulsion Laboratory in California.

- Livermore-Amador Genealogical Society
  http://www.l-ags.org/

- Military Order of the Loyal Legion of the United States—California Commandery
http://www.walika.com/mollus.htm

- Mission Oaks Genealogy Club
http://www.2xtreme.net/mogc/index.html
Carmichael, California

- Mother Lode PAF User Group
http://www.nccn.net/leisure/crafthby/genealog.htm
Nevada City, California

- Nevada County Genealogical Society
http://www.nccn.net/leisure/crafthby/genealog.htm
Cedar Ridge, California

- Nevada County Historical Society
http://www.nccn.net/orgsclbs/history/histsoc/welcome.htm
Nevada City, California

- North San Diego County Genealogical Society
http://www.compuology.com/nsdcgs/

- Orange County California Genealogical Society (OCCGS)
http://occgs.com/

- Paradise Genealogical Society, Inc.
http://www.jps.net/pargenso/
Paradise, Butte County, California

- Pacific Coast Chapter—Railway & Locomotive Historical Society
http://www.mp1.com/
Folsom, California

- Palo Alto Historical Association
http://www.commerce.digital.com/palo-alto/historical-assoc/home.html

- Placer County Genealogical Society
http://www.webcom.com/~gunruh/pcgs.html
Auburn, California

- Polish Genealogical Society of California—PGSCA
http://feefhs.org/pol/pgsca/frgpgsca.html

- Portuguese Historical & Cultural Society (PHCS)
http://www.dholmes.com/calendar.html
Sacramento, California

- Questing Heirs Genealogical Society, Inc.
http://www.compuology.com/questing/
Long Beach

- Railroad Historical and Technical Societies of California/Nevada
http://www.io.com/~fano2472/ggrm/histsoc.html

- Sacramento German Genealogy Society, Inc.
http://feefhs.org/sggs/frg-sggs.html

- San Bernardino Railroad Historical Society
http://www.rrhistorical.com/sbrhs/

- San Diego Genealogical Society
http://www.genealogy.org/~sdgs/

- San Diego Historical Society
http://edweb.sdsu.edu/SDHS/

- San Francisco Bay Area Jewish Genealogical Society (SFBA JGS)
http://www.jewishgen.org/sfbajgs/

- San Mateo County Genealogical Society
http://www.genealogy.org/~smcgs/

- Santa Barbara County Genealogical Society
http://www.compuology.com/sbarbara/

- Santa Clara River Valley Railroad Historical Society Inc.
http://www.fishnet.net/~johngart/

- Santa Clarita Valley Historical Society
http://felix.scvnet.com/~highlites/scvhs/index.html

- Shasta Historical Society
http://www.shasta-co.k12.ca.us/www/rmah/SHS.html

- Silicon Valley PAF Users Group Home Page
http://www.genealogy.org/~svpafug/

- Sloughhouse Area Genealogy Society
http://www.rootsweb.com/~casags/
Sacramento, California

- SOCCGS Genealogy Home Page
http://genealogy.emcee.com/~soccgs/
South Orange County California Genealogical Society.

- Society of California Pioneers
http://www.wenet.net/~pioneers/

- Sonoma County Genealogical Society
http://www.scgs.org/

- Sons of the Revolution in the State of California
http://www.walika.com/sr.htm

- South Bay Cities Genealogical Society
http://www.rootsweb.com/~casbcgs/
Torrance, California

- Southern California Chapter Association of Professional Genealogists
http://www.compuology.com/sccapg/

- Southern California Genealogical Society
http://www.cwire.com/scgs/
Burbank, California

- Southern California Genealogical Society— French Canadian Interest Group
http://home.earthlink.net/~djmill/
Burbank, California

- Truckee-Donner Historical Society
http://www.tahoenet.com/tdhs/tpnewslt.html

- Whittier Area Genealogical Society
http://www.compuology.com/wags/

◆ USGenWeb Project

- California Genealogy—USGenWeb Project State Page
http://www.usgenweb.org/ca

- California County Biographies and Histories
http://www.compuology.com/cpl/cpl_bio.htm

- California—USGenWeb Archives Table of Contents
http://www.rootsweb.com/~usgenweb/ca/cafiles.htm

- California—USGenWeb FTP Archives
ftp://ftp.rootsweb.com/pub/usgenweb/ca/

U.S.—COLORADO—CO

http://www.CyndisList.com/co.htm

Category Index:

- General Resource Sites
- Government & Cities
- History & Culture
- Libraries, Archives & Museums
- Mailing Lists, Newsgroups & Chat
- Maps, Gazetteers & Geographical Information
- Military
- Newspapers
- People & Families

- Professional Researchers, Volunteers & Other Research Services
- Publications, Software & Supplies
- Queries, Message Boards & Surname Lists
- Records: Census, Cemeteries, Land, Obituaries, Personal, Taxes and Vital
- Religion & Churches
- Societies & Groups
- USGenWeb Project

◆ General Resource Sites

- Everton's Sources of Genealogical Information in Colorado
  http://www.everton.com/usa/co.htm

- Family Tree Maker's Genealogy "How To" Guide—Colorado
  http://www.familytreemaker.com/00000180.html

- Genealogy Bulletin Board Systems for Colorado
  http://www.genealogy.org/~gbbs/gblco.html

- Genealogy Exchange & Surname Registry—COGenExchange
  http://www.genexchange.com/co/index.cfm

- Genealogy Resources on the Internet
  http://www-personal.umich.edu/~cgaunt/colorado.html

- LDS Research Outline for Colorado
  http://www.everton.com/usa/co-0806B.txt

- Lineages' Genealogy Site: Colorado
  http://www.lineages.com/rooms/usa/state.asp?StateCode=CO

- ROOTS-L United States Resources: Colorado
  http://www.rootsweb.com/roots-l/USA/co.html
  Comprehensive list of research links, including many to history-related sites.

◆ Government & Cities

- 50states.com—Colorado State Information Resource
  http://www.50states.com/colorado.htm
  A list of general information for each state, including a list of colleges, state symbols, links to maps, newspapers, and other miscellaneous state information.

- Excite Travel by City.Net—Colorado
  http://www.city.net/countries/united_states/colorado/

- Official City Web Sites for the State of Colorado
  http://OfficialCitySites.org/colorado.htm

- State of Colorado Home Page
  http://www.state.co.us/

- Yahoo! Get Local...Colorado Cities
  http://dir.yahoo.com/Regional/U_S__States/Colorado/Cities/
  Maps, yellow pages, white pages, newspapers and other local information.

- Yahoo! Get Local...Colorado Counties and Regions
  http://dir.yahoo.com/Regional/U_S__States/Colorado/Counties_and_Regions/
  Maps, yellow pages, white pages, newspapers and other local information.

◆ History & Culture

- Colorado Lore, Legend and Fact
  http://www.ionet.net/~jellenc/hcg_fac.html

- Ghost Towns of Colorado
  http://www.ghosttowns.com/states/co/co.html

- Mountain Men and the Fur Trade
  http://www.xmission.com/~drudy/amm.html
  Sources of the History of the Fur Trade in the Rocky Mountain West.

- Yahoo!...History...Colorado
  http://dir.yahoo.com/Arts/Humanities/History/Browse_By_Region/U_S__States/Colorado/

◆ Libraries, Archives & Museums

- **Cedaredge Public Library**
  http://www.dci-press.com/deltacounty/libraries/cedaredge/index.html

- **Colorado Family History Centers**
  http://www.genhomepage.com/FHC/Colorado.html
  A list of addresses, phone numbers and hours of operation from the Genealogy Home Page.

- **Colorado State Archives**
  http://www.state.co.us/gov_dir/gss/archives/index.html
  - ○ **Colorado State Archives Genealogy Resources**
    http://www.state.co.us/gov_dir/gss/archives/geneal.html

- **Colorado State Library Services**
  http://www.cde.state.co.us/sllibsrv.htm

- **Denver Family History Center**
  http://pw1.netcom.com/~rossmi/denfhc.html

- **Denver Public Library**
  http://www.denver.lib.co.us/index.html

- **Family History Centers—Colorado**
  http://www.deseretbook.com/famhis/co.html

- **Family History Centers—Colorado**
  http://www.lib.byu.edu/~uvrfhc/centers/colorado.html

- **HYTELNET—Library Catalogs: USA: Colorado**
  http://library.usask.ca/hytelnet/usa/CO.html
  Before you use any of the Telnet links, make note of the user name, password and any other logon information.

- **Lakewood Family History Center**
  http://pw1.netcom.com/~rossmi/lwfhc.html

- **NUCMC Listing of Archives and Manuscript Repositories in Colorado**
  http://lcweb.loc.gov/coll/nucmc/cosites.html
  Links to information about resources other than those held in the Library of Congress.

- **Repositories of Primary Sources: Colorado**
  http://www.uidaho.edu/special-collections/west.html#usco
  A list of links to online resources from the Univ. of Idaho Library, Special Collections and Archives.

- **webCATS: Library Catalogues on the World Wide Web—Colorado**
  http://library.usask.ca/hywebcat/states/CO.html

◆ Mailing Lists, Newsgroups & Chat

- **Genealogy Resources on the Internet—Colorado Mailing Lists**
  http://members.aol.com/gfsjohnf/gen_mail_states-co.html
  Each of the mailing list links below points to this site, wonderfully maintained by John Fuller. Visit this site for county-specific mailing lists as well.

- **COCHAT Mailing List**
  http://members.aol.com/gfsjohnf/gen_mail_states-co.html#COCHAT
  for anyone interested in chatting about the State of Colorado. Topics cover the spectrum of Colorado interests, and genealogy is therefore an acceptable topic for the list.

- **WESTERN-ROOTS-L Mailing list**
  http://members.aol.com/gfsjohnf/gen_mail_states-co.html#WESTERN-ROOTS-L
  Washington, Oregon, Alaska, Idaho, Montana, Wyoming, California, Nevada, Hawaii, Colorado, Utah, Arizona, and New Mexico.

◆ Maps, Gazetteers & Geographical Information

- **1872 County Map of Colorado**
  http://www.ismi.net/chnegw/1872colorado.htm

- **1895 U.S. Atlas—Colorado**
  http://www.LivGenMI.com/1895co.htm

- **American Memory Panoramic Maps 1847–1929—Colorado**
  http://lcweb2.loc.gov/cgi-bin/query/S?ammem/gmd:@filreq(@field(STATE+colorado)+@field(COLLID+pmmap))
  From the Geography and Map Division, Library of Congress.

- **American Memory Railroad Maps 1828–1900—Colorado**
  http://memory.loc.gov/cgi-bin/query/S?ammem/gmd:@filreq(@field(STATE+colorado)+@field(COLLID+rrmap))
  From the Geography and Map Division, Library of Congress.

- **Color Landform Atlas: Colorado**
  http://fermi.jhuapl.edu/states/co_0.html
  Including a map of counties and a map for 1895.

- **Excite Maps: Colorado Maps**
  http://www.city.net/maps/view/?mapurl=/countries/united_states/colorado
  Zoom in on these maps all the way to the street level.

- **HPI County InfoSystem—Counties in Colorado**
  http://www.com/hpi/cocty/index.html

- **K.B. Slocum Books and Maps—Colorado**
  http://www.treasurenet.com/cgi-bin/treasure/kbslocum/scan/se=Colorado/sf=mapstate

- **List of Colorado Counties**
  http://www.genealogy.org/~st-clair/counties/state_co.html

- **Map of Colorado Counties**
  http://govinfo.kerr.orst.edu/gif/states/co.gif
  From the Government Information Sharing Project, Information Services, Oregon State University.

- **Map of Colorado Counties**
  http://www.lib.utexas.edu/Libs/PCL/Map_collection/states/Colorado.gif
  From the Perry-Castañeda Library at the Univ. of Texas at Austin.

- U.S. Census Bureau—Colorado Profiles
  http://www.census.gov/datamap/www/08.html

- Yale Peabody Museum: GNIS—Colorado
  http://www.peabody.yale.edu/other/gnis/CO.html
  *Search the USGS Geographic Names Database. You can limit the search to a specific county in this state and search for any of the following features: airport arch area arroyo bar basin bay beach bench bend bridge **building** canal cape **cemetery** channel **church** cliff crater crossing dam falls flat forest gap geyser glacier gut harbor hospital island isthmus lake lava levee locale mine oilfield other park pillar plain ppl range rapids reserve reservoir ridge **school** sea slope spring stream summit swamp tower trail tunnel valley well woods.*

◆ Military

- The Civil War Archive—Union Regiments—Colorado
  http://www.civilwararchive.com/unionco.htm

- Civil War Battle Summaries by State—Colorado
  http://www2.cr.nps.gov/abpp/battles/bystate.htm#co

- The Colorado Volunteers During the Civil War (1861–1865)
  http://www.state.co.us/gov_dir/gss/archives/civwar/civilwar.html
  - Colorado Civil War Casualties Index
    http://www.state.co.us/gov_dir/gss/archives/ciwardea.html

- Colorado Volunteers in the Spanish American War (1898)
  http://www.state.co.us/gov_dir/gss/archives/spamwar.html

- Korean Conflict State-Level Casualty Lists—Colorado
  http://www.nara.gov/nara/electronic/cohrlist.html
  From the National Archives and Records Administration, Center for Electronic Records.

- Vietnam Conflict State-Level Casualty Lists—Colorado
  http://www.nara.gov/nara/electronic/cohrviet.html
  From the National Archives and Records Administration, Center for Electronic Records.

- The Vietnam Veterans Memorial—Colorado
  http://grunt.space.swri.edu/statewall/colo/co.htm

◆ Newspapers

- AJR NewsLink—Colorado Newspapers
  http://www.newslink.org/conews.html

- Boulder News
  http://www.bouldernews.com/

- The Denver Post Online
  http://www.denverpost.com/

- E&P Media Info Links—Newspaper Sites in Colorado
  http://www.mediainfo.com/emedia/browse-results.htm?region=colorado&category=newspaper+++++++++

- Ecola Newstand: Colorado
  http://www.ecola.com/news/press/na/us/co/

- NAA Hotlinks to Newspapers Online—Colorado
  http://www.naa.org/hotlinks/searchResult.asp?param=CO-Colorado&City=1

- N-Net—Colorado Newspapers
  http://www.n-net.com/co.htm

- The Ultimate Collection of News Links: USA—Colorado
  http://www.pppp.net/links/news/USA-CO.html

- Yahoo!...Newspapers...Colorado
  http://www.yahoo.com/News_and_Media/Newspapers/Browse_By_Region/U_S__States/Colorado/

◆ People & Families

- Gold Prospectors of Colorado
  http://www.GPOC.idsite.com/

- Tribes and Villages of Colorado
  http://hanksville.phast.umass.edu:8000/cultprop/contacts/tribal/CO.html

◆ Professional Researchers, Volunteers & Other Research Services

- Board for Certification of Genealogists—Roster of Those Certified—Specializing in Colorado
  http://www.genealogy.org/~bcg/rosts_co.html

- Family Detective
  http://www.familydetective.com
  Family Detective—Researches regularly at Colorado State Archives, Colorado Historical Society, Denver Public Library and courthouses in Adams, Arapahoe, Boulder, Denver, and Jefferson counties. Will search the Denver Probate Indexes 1865–1983 for FREE.

- Genealogy Helplist—Colorado
  http://members.aol.com/DFBradshaw/co.html

- The Official Iowa Counties Professional Genealogist and Researcher's Registry for Colorado
  http://www.iowa-counties.com/gene/co.htm

◆ Publications, Software & Supplies

- AncestorSpy—CDs and Microfiche for Colorado
  http://www.ancestorspy.com/colorado.htm

- Barbara Green's Used Genealogy Books—Colorado
  http://home.earthlink.net/~genbooks/lochist.html#CO

- Books We Own—Colorado
  http://www.rootsweb.com/~bwo/colorado.html

- Boyd Publishing Company—Colorado
  http://www.hom.net/~gac/colorod.htm

- Frontier Press Bookstore—Colorado
  http://www.frontierpress.com/frontier.cgi?category=co
- Heritage Quest—Microfilm Records for the State of Colorado
  http://www.heritagequest.com/genealogy/microfilm/colorado/
- The Memorabilia Corner—Books: Colorado
  http://members.aol.com/TMCorner/book_col.htm

◆ Queries, Message Boards & Surname Lists

- GenConnect Colorado Visitor Center
  http://cgi.rootsweb.com/~genbbs/indx/Co.html
  A system for posting queries, Bibles, biographies, deeds, obituaries, pensions, wills.

◆ Records: Census, Cemeteries, Land, Obituaries, Personal, Taxes and Vital (Born, Married, Died & Buried)

- The 1790–1890 Federal Population Censuses: Catalog of National Archives Microfilm
  http://www.genealogy.org/census/contents.shtml
  - Census Schedules and Microfilm Roll Numbers for Colorado:
    1870
    http://www.genealogy.org/census/1870_schedules/Colorado.html
    1880
    http://www.genealogy.org/census/1880_schedules/Colorado.html
    1880 Soundex
    http://www.genealogy.org/census/1880.sdx_schedules/T738.html
- BLM—Colorado Electronic Reading Room
  http://www.blm.gov/nhp/efoia/co/
  United States Bureau of Land Management.
- CDPHE—Health Statistics and Vital Records Division
  http://www.state.co.us/gov_dir/cdphe_dir/hs/hshom.html
- Cemeteries of the United States—Colorado Cemeteries—County Index
  http://www.gac.edu/~kengelha/uscemeteries/colorado.html
- Census Online—Links to Census Sites on the Web—Colorado
  http://www.census-online.com/links/CO_data.html
- Colorado Department of Public Health and Environment—Vital Records
  http://www.state.co.us/gov_dir/cdphe_dir/hs/cshom.html
  Available years for birth, death, marriage, and divorce records: Births—1910–present, Deaths—1900–present, Marriages—1900–1939, 1975–present, Divorces—1900–1939, 1968–present.

- Colorado Marriages and Divorces Search
  http://www.quickinfo.net/madi/comadi.html
  Marriages (from 1975 to 1997) and divorces (from 1975 to July 1998).
- Colorado Vital Records Information
  http://vitalrec.com/co.html
- County Courthouse Addresses
  http://www.familytreemaker.com/00000235.html
- Find-A-Grave by Location: Colorado
  http://www.findagrave.com/grave/lco.html
  Graves of noteworthy people.
- Hope Congregational Cemetery, Bethune, Colorado
  http://pixel.cs.vt.edu/library/cemeteries/colorado/link/bethune1.txt
- Immanuel Lutheran Church Cemetery, Bethune, Colorado
  http://pixel.cs.vt.edu/library/cemeteries/colorado/link/bethune2.txt
- Interment.net: Colorado Cemeteries
  http://www.interment.net/us/co/index.htm
  A list of links to other sites.
- Lake County, Colorado 1870 US Census Index, A–J
  ftp://ftp.rootsweb.com/pub/usgenweb/co/lake/census/1870cenA_J.txt
- Lake County, Colorado 1870 US Census Index, K–Z
  ftp://ftp.rootsweb.com/pub/usgenweb/co/lake/census/1870cenK_Z.txt
- Mesa County Colorado Health Department—Vital Statistics
  http://www.rmwest.com/mchd/vs.htm
- National Archives—Rocky Mountain Region (Denver)
  http://www.nara.gov/regional/denver.html
- National Archives—Rocky Mountain Region
  http://www.familytreemaker.com/00000103.html
  Records for Colorado, Montana, North Dakota, South Dakota, Utah, Wyoming, and a portion of New Mexico.
- The Political Graveyard—Cemeteries in Colorado
  http://politicalgraveyard.com/geo/CO/kmindex.html
- Preplanning Network—Funeral Home and Cemetery Directory—Colorado
  http://www.preplannet.com/coloradofhcem.htm
- Pupils of the Colorado School for the Deaf and the Blind, 1874–1883
  http://www.henge.com/~holsclaw/deafblind/csdbproj.htm
  List of earliest students at the Institute/School, transcripts of early annual reports, sample research data.
- USGenWeb Census Project Colorado
  http://www.usgenweb.org/census/states/colorado.htm
- USGenWeb Tombstone Transcription Project—Colorado
  http://www.rootsweb.com/~cemetery/colorado.html

- VitalChek Network—Colorado
  http://www.vitalchek.com/stateselect.asp?state=CO

- Vital Records Extracted From "The Life, Travels, and Ministry of Milton M. Everly"
  http://www.aloha.net/~jan/milton.txt
  September 1901–September 1903. Extractions of records for marriages, some baptisms, and funerals.

- Where to Write for Vital Records—Colorado
  http://www.cdc.gov/nchswww/howto/w2w/colorado.htm
  From the National Center for Health Statistics (NCHS).

◆ Religion & Churches

- Christianity.Net Church Locator—Colorado
  http://www.christianity.net/cgi/location.exe?United_States+Colorado

- Church Online!—Colorado
  http://www.churchonline.com/usas/co/co.html

- Church Profiles—Colorado
  http://www.church-profiles.com/co/co.html

- Churches dot Net—Global Church Web Pages—Colorado
  http://www.churches.net/churches/colorado.html

- Churches of the World—Colorado
  http://www.churchsurf.com/churches/Colorado/index.htm
  From the ChurchSurf Christian Directory.

◆ Societies & Groups

- American Historical Society of Germans from Russia—Denver Metro Chapter
  http://www.ahsgr.org/codenver.html

- American Historical Society of Germans from Russia—Northern Colorado Chapter
  http://www.ahsgr.org/conorthe.html

- American Legion—Department of Colorado
  http://www.pcisys.net/~coloradolegion/

- Archer's Computer Interest Group List—Colorado
  http://www.genealogy.org/~ngs/cigs/ngl1usco.html

- Aspen Historical Society
  http://www.aspen.com/aspenonline/directory/mac/sponsors/artscouncil/sponsors/histsoc/index.histsoc.html

- Colorado Genealogical Society
  http://www.cogensoc.org/cgs/cgs-home.htm

- Colorado Historical Society
  http://www.aclin.org/other/historic/chs/

- Colorado State Society Daughters of the American Revolution
  http://members.aol.com/darcolo/

- Genealogical Society of Hispanic America
  http://www.ancestry.com/SocietyHall/viewmember.asp?results=81
  GSHA is 11 years old with five chapters in Colorado & California. Members specialize in Hispanic research in the American Southwest & Mexico. Over 75% are descendants of the Spanish colonists of New Mexico.

- The Grand Lodge of Colorado, A.F. & A.M.
  http://www.coloradomasons.org/

- IOOF Lodge Website Directory—Colorado
  http://norm28.hsc.usc.edu/IOOF/USA/Colorado/Colorado.html
  Independent Order of Odd Fellows and Rebekahs.

- Larimer County Genealogical Society
  http://jymis.com/~lcgs/lcgs.shtml
  Fort Collins, Colorado

- Old Colorado City Historical Society
  http://history.oldcolo.com/

- Pike's Peak Computer Genealogists
  http://members.aol.com/cliffpoint/ppcg/index.html

- Southeastern Colorado Genealogy Society, Inc.
  http://members.aol.com/annray5543/private/Local.html

- Victor Historic Preservation Commission
  http://www.victorhistory.org/

- Weld County Genealogical Society
  http://www.rootsweb.com/~cowcgs/index.htm
  Genealogy Society located in Greeley, Weld, Colorado. Serving Northeastern Colorado Area. Publications on County information available.

◆ USGenWeb Project

- Colorado Genealogy—USGenWeb Project State Page
  http://www.usgenweb.org/co

- Colorado—USGenWeb Archives Table of Contents
  http://www.rootsweb.com/~usgenweb/co/cofiles.htm

- Colorado—USGenWeb FTP Archives
  ftp://ftp.rootsweb.com/pub/usgenweb/co/

U.S.—CONNECTICUT—CT
http://www.CyndisList.com/ct.htm

Category Index:

- General Resource Sites
- Government & Cities
- History & Culture
- Libraries, Archives & Museums
- Locality Specific
- Mailing Lists, Newsgroups & Chat
- Maps, Gazetteers & Geographical Information
- Military
- Newspapers
- People & Families

- Professional Researchers, Volunteers & Other Research Services
- Publications, Software & Supplies
- Queries, Message Boards & Surname Lists
- Records: Census, Cemeteries, Land, Obituaries, Personal, Taxes and Vital
- Religion & Churches
- Societies & Groups
- USGenWeb Project

◆ General Resource Sites

- Everton's Sources of Genealogical Information in Connecticut
  http://www.everton.com/usa/ct.htm

- Family Tree Maker's Genealogy "How To" Guide—Connecticut
  http://www.familytreemaker.com/00000181.html

- Genealogy Bulletin Board Systems for Connecticut
  http://www.genealogy.org/~gbbs/gblct.html

- Genealogy Exchange & Surname Registry—CTGenExchange
  http://www.genexchange.com/ct/index.cfm

- Genealogy Resources on the Internet: Connecticut
  http://www-personal.umich.edu/~cgaunt/conn.html

- LDS Research Outline for Connecticut
  http://www.everton.com/usa/ct-0807B.txt

- Lineages' Genealogy Site: Connecticut
  http://www.lineages.com/rooms/usa/state.asp?StateCode=CT

- New England Connections
  http://www.geocities.com/Heartland/5274/nec.htm

- ROOTS-L United States Resources: Connecticut
  http://www.rootsweb.com/roots-l/USA/ct.html
  Comprehensive list of research links, including many to history-related sites.

◆ Government & Cities

- 50states.com—Connecticut State Information Resource
  http://www.50states.com/connecti.htm
  A list of general information for each state, including a list of colleges, state symbols, links to maps, newspapers, and other miscellaneous state information.

- Connecticut Government Information Page
  http://www.state.ct.us/

- Connecticut.com
  http://www.connecticut.com/

- Essex, Connecticut
  http://www.EssexCT.com/index.htm

- Excite Travel by City.Net—Connecticut
  http://www.city.net/countries/united_states/connecticut/

- Middletown, Connecticut
  http://www.middletownct.com/index.htm

- Norwich, Connecticut Now!
  http://www.norwich.org/

- Official City Web Sites for the State of Connecticut
  http://OfficialCitySites.org/connecticut.htm

- Old Saybrook, Connecticut
  http://www.OldSaybrook.com/index.htm

- Southington, Connecticut
  http://www.southington.com/index.htm

- Westbrook, Connecticut
  http://www.westbrookct.com/

- Yahoo! Get Local...Connecticut Cities
  http://dir.yahoo.com/Regional/U_S__States/Connecticut/Cities/
  Maps, yellow pages, white pages, newspapers and other local information.

- Yahoo! Get Local...Connecticut Counties and Regions or
  http://dir.yahoo.com/Regional/U_S__States/Connecticut/
  Counties_and_Regions/
  Maps, yellow pages, white pages, newspapers and other local information.

◆ History & Culture

- Old Newgate Prison
  http://www.viewzone.com/oldnewgate.html
  East Granby, Connecticut

- Yahoo!...History...Connecticut
  http://dir.yahoo.com/Arts/Humanities/History/
  Browse_By_Region/U_S__States/Connecticut/

◆ Libraries, Archives & Museums

- Archives in New England on the Internet
  http://www.lib.umb.edu/newengarch/nearch.html

- Connecticut Family History Centers
  http://www.genhomepage.com/FHC/Connecticut.html
  A list of addresses, phone numbers and hours of operation from the Genealogy Home Page.

- Connecticut State Archives
  http://www.cslnet.ctstateu.edu/archives.htm

- Connecticut Libraries
  http://spirit.lib.uconn.edu/ConnState/Libraries/CTLibraries.html

- Connecticut State Library
  http://www.cslnet.ctstateu.edu/
  - History and Genealogy Unit
    http://www.cslnet.ctstateu.edu/handg.htm

- Family History Centers—Connecticut
  http://www.deseretbook.com/famhis/ct.html

- Family History Centers—Connecticut
  http://www.lib.byu.edu/~uvrfhc/centers/connecticut.html

- Godfrey Memorial Library
  http://www.godfrey.org/
  Middletown, Connecticut

- Guide to Railroad Archives at the Thomas J. Dodd Research Center
  http://www.lib.uconn.edu/DoddCenter/ASC/raillist.htm
  University of Connecticut.

- Guide to the New York, New Haven and Hartford Railroad Archives
  http://www.lib.uconn.edu/DoddCenter/ASC/nhtrains.htm
  University of Connecticut, Thomas J. Dodd Research Center

- HYTELNET—Library Catalogs: USA: Connecticut
  http://library.usask.ca/hytelnet/usa/CT.html
  Before you use any of the Telnet links, make note of the user name, password and any other logon information.

- NUCMC Listing of Archives and Manuscript Repositories in Connecticut
  http://lcweb.loc.gov/coll/nucmc/ctsites.html
  Links to information about resources other than those held in the Library of Congress.

- Repositories of Primary Sources: Connecticut
  http://www.uidaho.edu/special-collections/east1.html#usct
  A list of links to online resources from the Univ. of Idaho Library, Special Collections and Archives.

- webCATS: Library Catalogues on the World Wide Web—Connecticut
  http://library.usask.ca/hywebcat/states/CT.html

◆ Locality Specific

- Also see the USGenWeb section for links to county-specific resources.

- Old Saybrook Genealogy Research Guide
  http://nw3.nai.net/~sanner/

◆ Mailing Lists, Newsgroups & Chat

- Genealogy Resources on the Internet—Connecticut Mailing Lists
  http://members.aol.com/gfsjohnf/gen_mail_states-ct.html
  Each of the mailing list links below points to this site, wonderfully maintained by John Fuller. Visit this site for county-specific mailing lists as well.

- Connecticut Mailing List
  http://members.aol.com/gfsjohnf/gen_mail_states-ct.
  html#Connecticut

- CT-MANSFIELD Mailing List—Town of Mansfield
  http://members.aol.com/gfsjohnf/gen_mail_states-ct.html#CT-MANSFIELD

- CT-TOLLANDCO Mailing List—Tolland County
  http://members.aol.com/gfsjohnf/gen_mail_states-ct.html#CT-TOLLANDCO

- CT-Waterbury Mailing List—Town of Waterbury
  http://members.aol.com/gfsjohnf/gen_mail_states-ct.html#CT-Waterbury

- CT-WINDHAMCO Mailing List—Windham County
  http://members.aol.com/gfsjohnf/gen_mail_states-ct.html#CT-WINDHAMCO

- GenConnecticut Mailing List
  http://members.aol.com/gfsjohnf/gen_mail_states-ct.
  html#GenConnecticut

- NORTHEAST-ROOTS-L Mailing List
  http://members.aol.com/gfsjohnf/gen_mail_states-ct.
  html#NORTHEAST-ROOTS
  Connecticut, Maine, Massachusetts, New Hampshire, Rhode Island & Vermont.

◆ Maps, Gazetteers & Geographical Information

- 1895 U.S. Atlas—Connecticut
  http://www.LivGenMI.com/1895ct.htm

- 1,933 Placenames from the 1884 Issue of Geer's Hartford City Directory
  ftp://ftp.rootsweb.com/pub/usgenweb/ct/ctstate/geography/gaz1884a.txt

- American Memory Panoramic Maps 1847–1929—Connecticut
  http://lcweb2.loc.gov/cgi-bin/query/S?ammem/gmd:@filreq(@field(STATE+connecticut)+@field(COLLID+pmmap))
  From the Geography and Map Division, Library of Congress.

- American Memory Railroad Maps 1828–1900—Connecticut
  http://memory.loc.gov/cgi-bin/query/S?ammem/gmd:@filreq(@field(STATE+connecticut)+@field(COLLID+rrmap))
  From the Geography and Map Division, Library of Congress.

- Color Landform Atlas: Connecticut
  http://fermi.jhuapl.edu/states/ct_0.html
  Including a map of counties and a map for 1895.

- Connecticut Cities—What City is in Which County?
  http://www.vineyard.net/vineyard/history/allen/CT_ctys.htm

- Excite Maps: Connecticut Maps
  http://www.city.net/maps/view/?mapurl=/countries/united_states/connecticut
  Zoom in on these maps all the way to the street level.

- HPI County InfoSystem—Counties in Connecticut
  http://www.com/hpi/ctcty/index.html

- K.B. Slocum Books and Maps—Connecticut
  http://www.treasurenet.com/cgi-bin/treasure/kbslocum/scan/se=Connecticut/sf=mapstate

- List of Connecticut Counties
  http://www.genealogy.org/~st-clair/counties/state_ct.html

- Map and Geographic Information Center
  http://magic.lib.uconn.edu/
  University of Connecticut, Homer Babbidge Library.

- Map of Connecticut Counties
  http://govinfo.kerr.orst.edu/gif/states/ct.gif
  From the Government Information Sharing Project, Information Services, Oregon State University.

- Map of Connecticut Counties
  http://www.lib.utexas.edu/Libs/PCL/Map_collection/states/Connecticut.gif
  From the Perry-Castañeda Library at the Univ. of Texas at Austin.

- Old Maps of New England (Maine, New Hampshire, Vermont, Connecticut, Rhode Island, Massachusetts) and New York
  http://members.aol.com/oldmapsne/index.html

- Reproductions of Old Town Maps in New England
  http://www.biddeford.com/~lkane/

- U.S. Census Bureau—Connecticut Profiles
  http://www.census.gov/datamap/www/09.html

- Yale Peabody Museum: GNIS—Connecticut
  http://www.peabody.yale.edu/other/gnis/CT.html
  *Search the USGS Geographic Names Database. You can limit the search to a specific county in this state and search for any of the following features: airport arch area arroyo bar basin bay beach bench bend bridge **building** canal cape **cemetery** channel **church** cliff crater crossing dam falls flat forest gap geyser glacier gut harbor hospital island isthmus lake lava levee locale mine oilfield other park pillar plain ppl range rapids reserve reservoir ridge **school** sea slope spring stream summit swamp tower trail tunnel valley well woods.*

◆ Military

- The Civil War Archive—Union Regiments—Connecticut
  http://www.civilwararchive.com/unionct.htm

- Introduction to the Connecticut Military Census of 1917
  http://www.cslnet.ctstateu.edu/milcens.htm

- Korean Conflict State-Level Casualty Lists—Connecticut
  http://www.nara.gov/nara/electronic/cthrlist.html
  From the National Archives and Records Administration, Center for Electronic Records.

- Vietnam Conflict State-Level Casualty Lists—Connecticut
  http://www.nara.gov/nara/electronic/cthrviet.html
  From the National Archives and Records Administration, Center for Electronic Records.

- The Vietnam Veterans Memorial—Connecticut
  http://grunt.space.swri.edu/statewall/conn/ct.htm

◆ Newspapers

- AJR NewsLink—Connecticut Newspapers
  http://www.newslink.org/cnnews.html

- Connecticut Newspaper Project
  http://www.cslnet.ctstateu.edu/cnp.htm

- E&P Media Info Links—Newspaper Sites in Connecticut
  http://www.mediainfo.com/emedia/browse-results.htm?region=connecticut&category=newspaper+++++++++

- Ecola Newstand: Connecticut
  http://www.ecola.com/news/press/na/us/ct/

- NAA Hotlinks to Newspapers Online—Connecticut
  http://www.naa.org/hotlinks/searchResult.asp?param=CT-Connecticut&City=1

- N-Net—Connecticut Newspapers
  http://www.n-net.com/ct.htm

- The Ultimate Collection of News Links: USA—Connecticut
  http://www.pppp.net/links/news/USA-CN.html

- Yahoo!...Newspapers...Connecticut
  http://www.yahoo.com/News_and_Media/Newspapers/
  Browse_By_Region/U_S__States/Connecticut/

◆ People & Families

- Directory of Underground Railroad Operators—
  Connecticut
  http://www.ugrr.org//names/map-ct.htm

- Governor John WEBSTER of Hartford, Connecticut
  and Hadley, Massachusetts
  http://www.rootsweb.com/~genepool/websjohn.htm

- Theodore Webster's Homepage—Home Page for
  Gov. John WEBSTER of Connecticut
  http://www1.cedar-rapids.net/theodore/

- Tribes and Villages of Connecticut
  http://hanksville.phast.umass.edu:8000/cultprop/contacts/
  tribal/CT.html

- WPA Life Histories from Connecticut
  http://lcweb2.loc.gov/ammem/wpaintro/ctcat.html
  *Manuscripts from the Federal Writer's Project, 1936–1940,
  Library of Congress.*

◆ Professional Researchers, Volunteers & Other Research Services

- Board for Certification of Genealogists—Roster of
  Those Certified—Specializing in Connecticut
  http://www.genealogy.org/~bcg/rosts_ct.html

- Genealogy Helplist—Connecticut
  http://www.cyberbeach.net/~mkelly/helplistUSA/ct.htm

- Heritage Associates
  http://www.granniesworld.com/heritage/
  *New England Research, specializing in pre-1850 north coast
  Massachusetts.*

- Library Stacks—An Historical Research and
  Reference Service
  http://members.aol.com/libstacks/libstacks.html
  *Centered in the Boston area, Library Stacks is a professional
  service which provides research and reference assistance to
  antique dealers, attorneys, authors, booksellers, curators, family
  historians, genealogists, graduate students and historians whose
  genealogical and historical interests lie within the New England
  states.*

- The Official Iowa Counties Professional Genealogist
  and Researcher's Registry for Connecticut
  http://www.iowa-counties.com/gene/ct.htm

- Professional Genealogists Familiar with Connecticut
  State Library Collections
  http://www.cslnet.ctstateu.edu/list.htm

- Richard M. Pope, Certified Genealogist
  http://w3.nai.net/~absuax/
  *Specializing in: Connecticut, Massachusetts, New York City,
  Germany.*

◆ Publications, Software & Supplies

- AncestorSpy—CDs and Microfiche for Connecticut
  http://www.ancestorspy.com/ctcat.htm

- Barbara Green's Used Genealogy Books—
  Connecticut
  http://home.earthlink.net/~genbooks/lochist.html#CT

- Barnette's Family Tree Books—Connecticut
  http://www.barnettesbooks.com/connecticut.htm

- Books We Own—Connecticut
  http://www.rootsweb.com/~bwo/connecticut.html

- Boyd Publishing Company—New England
  http://www.hom.net/~gac/newengla.htm

- Broad View Books
  http://broadviewbooks.com/
  *Used Genealogy Books, Local History of Massachusetts,
  Connecticut, Rhode Island, Vermont and New England.*

- Essex Books—New England
  http://www.HERTGE.COM/essex/neweng.htm

- Frontier Press Bookstore—Connecticut
  http://www.frontierpress.com/frontier.cgi?category=ct

- GenealogyBookShop.com—Connecticut
  http://www.genealogybookshop.com/genealogybookshop/files/
  The_United_States,Connecticut/index.html
  *The online store of Genealogical Publishing Co., Inc. &
  Clearfield Company.*

- Hearthstone Bookshop—Connecticut
  http://www.hearthstonebooks.com/cgi-bin/webc.cgi/
  st_main.html?catid=74&sid=2PH5t29sm

- Heritage Books—Connecticut
  http://www.heritagebooks.com/ct.htm

- Heritage Quest—Microfilm Records for the
  State of Connecticut
  http://www.heritagequest.com/genealogy/microfilm/
  connecticut/

- Lost in Time Books—Connecticut
  http://www.lostintime.com/catalog/books/bookst/bo05000.htm

- The Memorabilia Corner—Books: Connecticut
  http://members.aol.com/TMCorner/book_con.htm

- Picton Press—Connecticut
  http://www.midcoast.com/~picton/catalog/connecti.htm

- Willow Bend Bookstore—Connecticut
  http://www.willowbend.net/ct.htm

◆ Queries, Message Boards & Surname Lists

- GenConnect Connecticut Visitor Center
  http://cgi.rootsweb.com/~genbbs/indx/Ct.html
  *A system for posting queries, Bibles, biographies, deeds,
  obituaries, pensions, wills.*

- Litchfield County Queries
  http://www.geocities.com/TheTropics/1926/litchfield.html#4

- New England Connections Query Archive
  http://www.geocities.com/Heartland/5274/nequery.htm

- New Haven County Queries
  http://www.geocities.com/TheTropics/1926/newhaven.html#4

◆ Records: Census, Cemeteries, Land, Obituaries, Personal, Taxes and Vital (Born, Married, Died & Buried)

- The 1790–1890 Federal Population Censuses: Catalog of National Archives Microfilm
  http://www.genealogy.org/census/contents.shtml

  - Census Schedules and Microfilm Roll Numbers for Connecticut:

    1790
    http://www.genealogy.org/census/1790.html

    1800
    http://www.genealogy.org/census/1800_schedules/Connecticut.html

    1810
    http://www.genealogy.org/census/1810_schedules/Connecticut.html

    1820
    http://www.genealogy.org/census/1820_schedules/Connecticut.html

    1830
    http://www.genealogy.org/census/1830_schedules/Connecticut.html

    1840
    http://www.genealogy.org/census/1840_schedules/Connecticut.html

    1850
    http://www.genealogy.org/census/1850_schedules/Connecticut.html

    1860
    http://www.genealogy.org/census/1860_schedules/Connecticut.html

    1870
    http://www.genealogy.org/census/1870_schedules/Connecticut.html

    1880
    http://www.genealogy.org/census/1880_schedules/Connecticut.html

    1880 Soundex
    http://www.genealogy.org/census/1880.sdx_schedules/T739.html

- Cemeteries of the United States—Connecticut Cemeteries—County Index
  http://www.gac.edu/~kengelha/uscemeteries/connecticut.html

- Census Online—Links to Census Sites on the Web—Connecticut
  http://www.census-online.com/links/CT_data.html

- The Connecticut Gravestone Network
  http://members.aol.com/ctgravenet/index.htm

- Connecticut Vital Records Information
  http://vitalrec.com/ct.html

- County Courthouse Addresses
  http://www.familytreemaker.com/00000236.html

- Evergreen Cemetery, New Haven, Connecticut
  http://www.geocities.com/TheTropics/1127/evergren.html

- Find-A-Grave by Location: Connecticut
  http://www.findagrave.com/grave/lct.html
  Graves of noteworthy people.

- Gallup Cemetery, Voluntown, Connecticut
  http://www.geocities.com/Vienna/1516/gallup1.html

- Interment.net: Connecticut Cemeteries
  http://www.interment.net/us/ct/index.htm
  A list of links to other sites.

- Introduction to Colonial and State Census Records at the Connecticut State Library
  http://www.cslnet.ctstateu.edu/colcens.htm

- National Archives—Northeast Region (Boston)
  http://www.nara.gov/regional/boston.html

- National Archives—New England Region
  http://www.familytreemaker.com/00000098.html
  Records for Connecticut, Maine, Massachusetts, New Hampshire, Rhode Island, and Vermont.

- Old Kinne Cemetery, Voluntown, Connecticut
  http://www.geocities.com/Vienna/1516/kinne4.html

- The Political Graveyard—Cemeteries in Connecticut
  http://politicalgraveyard.com/geo/CT/kmindex.html

- Preplanning Network—Funeral Home and Cemetery Directory—Connecticut
  http://www.preplannet.com/confhcem.htm

- Stamford Grand Lists
  http://www.cslnet.ctstateu.edu/stamford/granlist.htm
  Taxation in Stamford, CT from 1641 to the Code of 1821.

- USGenWeb Census Project Connecticut
  http://www.usgenweb.org/census/states/connecti/connecti.htm

- USGenWeb Tombstone Transcription Project—Connecticut
  http://www.rootsweb.com/~cemetery/connecti.html

- VitalChek Network—Connecticut
  http://www.vitalchek.com/stateselect.asp?state=CT

- Where to Write for Vital Records—Connecticut
  http://www.cdc.gov/nchswww/howto/w2w/connect.htm
  From the National Center for Health Statistics (NCHS).

◆ Religion & Churches

- Christianity.Net Church Locator—Connecticut
  http://www.christianity.net/cgi/location.exe?
  United_States+Connecticut

- Church Online!—Connecticut
  http://www.churchonline.com/usas/ct/ct.html

- Church Profiles—Connecticut
  http://www.church-profiles.com/ct/ct.html

- Churches dot Net—Global Church Web Pages—
  Connecticut
  http://www.churches.net/churches/connecti.html

- Churches of the World—Connecticut
  http://www.churchsurf.com/churches/Connecticut/index.htm
  From the ChurchSurf Christian Directory.

◆ Societies & Groups

- Archer's Computer Interest Group List—
  Connecticut
  http://www.genealogy.org/~ngs/cigs/ngl1usct.html

- Brookfield Historical Society
  http://www.danbury.org/org/brookhc/index.htm

- Connecticut Historical Society
  http://www.hartnet.org/~chs/

- Connecticut Society of Genealogists, Inc.
  http://www.knic.com/csg/

- The Connecticut Society of the Sons of the
  American Revolution
  http://www.ctssar.org/

- Connecticut State Society of the National Society
  Daughters of the American Revolution
  http://members.aol.com/ctdar/dar.htm

- Finnish American Heritage Society of CT
  http://www.rt.com/fahs-ct/

- French Canadian Genealogical Society of
  Connecticut
  http://ourworld.compuserve.com/homepages/RLCarpenter/
  frenchca.htm

- The Gaylordsville Historical Society
  http://www.eci.com/Gaylordsville/

- Griswold Historical Society
  http://www.griswoldct.com/history/index.htm

- IOOF Lodge Website Directory—Connecticut
  http://norm28.hsc.usc.edu/IOOF/USA/Connecticut/
  Connecticut.html
  Independent Order of Odd Fellows and Rebekahs.

- The Killingly Historical Society
  http://www.commnet.edu/QVCTC/brian/KHS/kilz1.html

- Manchester Historical Society
  http://www.ci.manchester.ct.us./cheney/historic.htm

- Middlesex Genealogical Society
  http://darien.lib.ct.us/mgs/default.htm
  Darien, Connecticut

- Milford Historical Society
  http://www.geocities.com/SiliconValley/Park/3831/

- New England Historic Genealogical Society
  http://www.nehgs.org/

- New Fairfield Historical Society
  http://www.geocities.com/Athens/Forum/8992/

- The Old Saybrook Historical Society
  http://oldsaybrook.com/History/society.htm

- Polish Genealogical Society of Connecticut and
  the Northeast
  http://members.aol.com/pgsne2/

- Salmon Brook Historical Society
  http://www.harborside.com/home/p/p2241/sbhs.html
  Granby, Connecticut

- Saybrook Colony Founders Association
  http://www.rootsweb.com/~ctscfa/

- Stamford Historical Society
  http://www.cslnet.ctstateu.edu/stamford/index.htm

- Trumbull Historical Society
  http://trumbull.ct.us/history/

◆ USGenWeb Project

- Connecticut Genealogy—USGenWeb Project
  State Page
  http://www.usgenweb.org/ct

- Connecticut—USGenWeb Archives Table of
  Contents
  http://www.rootsweb.com/~usgenweb/ct/ctfiles.htm

- Connecticut—USGenWeb FTP Archives
  ftp://ftp.rootsweb.com/pub/usgenweb/ct/

- CTGEN Mailing List
  http://members.aol.com/gfsjohnf/gen_mail_states-ct.
  html#CTGEN
  *A part of the USGenWeb Project. For discussing the creation of
  a single source for all Connecticut genealogy databases.*

U.S.—DELAWARE—DE
http://www.CyndisList.com/de.htm

Category Index:

- General Resource Sites
- Government & Cities
- History & Culture
- Libraries, Archives & Museums
- Mailing Lists, Newsgroups & Chat
- Maps, Gazetteers & Geographical Information
- Military
- Newspapers
- People & Families

- Professional Researchers, Volunteers & Other Research Services
- Publications, Software & Supplies
- Queries, Message Boards & Surname Lists
- Records: Census, Cemeteries, Land, Obituaries, Personal, Taxes and Vital
- Religion & Churches
- Societies & Groups
- USGenWeb Project

◆ General Resource Sites

- Delaware Genealogical Information And Repositories
  http://delgensoc.org/delrep.html

- Everton's Sources of Genealogical Information in Delaware
  http://www.everton.com/usa/de.htm

- Family Tree Maker's Genealogy "How To" Guide—Delaware
  http://www.familytreemaker.com/00000182.html

- Genealogy Exchange & Surname Registry—DEGenExchange
  http://www.genexchange.com/de/index.cfm

- Genealogy Resources on the Internet: Delaware
  http://www-personal.umich.edu/~cgaunt/delaware.html

- Golden Lyon II Genealogical Research
  http://www.erols.com/rariggin/lyon.html
  Resource for studying related families of the Lower Eastern Shore—Allied Families of the Delmarva Peninsula.

- LDS Research Outline for Delaware
  http://www.everton.com/usa/de-0808B.txt

- Lineages' Genealogy Site: Delaware
  http://www.lineages.com/rooms/usa/state.asp?StateCode=DE

- ROOTS-L United States Resources: Delaware
  http://www.rootsweb.com/roots-l/USA/de.html
  Comprehensive list of research links, including many to history-related sites.

◆ Government & Cities

- 50states.com—Delaware State Information Resource
  http://www.50states.com/delaware.htm
  A list of general information for each state, including a list of colleges, state symbols, links to maps, newspapers, and other miscellaneous state information.

- Excite Travel by City.Net—Delaware
  http://www.city.net/countries/united_states/delaware/

- Official City Web Sites for the State of Delaware
  http://OfficialCitySites.org/delaware.htm

- State of Delaware
  http://www.state.de.us/

- Yahoo! Get Local...Delaware Cities
  http://dir.yahoo.com/Regional/U_S__States/Delaware/Cities/
  Maps, yellow pages, white pages, newspapers and other local information.

- Yahoo! Get Local...Delaware Counties and Regions
  http://dir.yahoo.com/Regional/U_S__States/Delaware/Counties_and_Regions/
  Maps, yellow pages, white pages, newspapers and other local information.

◆ History & Culture

- Yahoo!...History...Delaware
  http://dir.yahoo.com/Arts/Humanities/History/Browse_By_Region/U_S__States/Delaware/

◆ Libraries, Archives & Museums

- Delaware Family History Centers
  http://www.genhomepage.com/FHC/Delaware.html
  A list of addresses, phone numbers and hours of operation from the Genealogy Home Page.

- Delaware Public Archives
  http://del-aware.lib.de.us/archives/

- DelAWARE—The Digital Library of the First State
  http://www.lib.de.us

- Delaware's Public Library WWW Page
  http://kentnet.dtcc.edu/

- Family History Centers—Delaware
  http://www.deseretbook.com/famhis/de.html

- Family History Centers—Delaware
  http://www.lib.byu.edu/~uvrfhc/centers/delaware.html

- HYTELNET—Library Catalogs: USA: Delaware
  http://library.usask.ca/hytelnet/usa/DE.html
  Before you use any of the Telnet links, make note of the user name, password and any other logon information.

- NUCMC Listing of Archives and Manuscript Repositories in Delaware
  http://lcweb.loc.gov/coll/nucmc/desites.html
  Links to information about resources other than those held in the Library of Congress.

- Repositories of Primary Sources: Delaware
  http://www.uidaho.edu/special-collections/east1.html#usde
  A list of links to online resources from the Univ. of Idaho Library, Special Collections and Archives.

- webCATS: Library Catalogues on the World Wide Web—Delaware
  http://library.usask.ca/hywebcat/states/DE.html

◆ Mailing Lists, Newsgroups & Chat

- Genealogy Resources on the Internet—Delaware Mailing Lists
  http://members.aol.com/gfsjohnf/gen_mail_states-de.html
  Each of the mailing list links below points to this site, wonderfully maintained by John Fuller. Visit this site for county-specific mailing lists as well.

- DE-OLDSWEDES Mailing List
  http://members.aol.com/gfsjohnf/gen_mail_states-de.html#DE-OLDSWEDES
  For anyone interested in the genealogy of families associated with the Old Swedes (Holy Trinity) Church in Wilmington, Delaware.

- LOWER-DELMARVA-ROOTS Mailing List
  http://members.aol.com/gfsjohnf/gen_mail_states-de.html#LOWER-DELMARVA-ROOTS
  Sussex and Kent Counties in Delaware; Dorchester, Wicomico, Somerset, and Worcester in Maryland; Northampton and Accomack in Virginia.

- MID-ATLANTIC-ROOTS-L Mailing List
  http://members.aol.com/gfsjohnf/gen_mail_states-de.html#MID-ATLANTIC-ROOTS-L
  New Jersey, Maryland, Delaware, and the District of Columbia.

◆ Maps, Gazetteers & Geographical Information

- 1790 Delaware Census Map
  http://www.historyu.com/Village/SurvHouse/1790pages/90delaware.html

- 1895 U.S. Atlas—Delaware
  http://www.LivGenMI.com/1895de.htm

- American Memory Panoramic Maps 1847–1929—Delaware
  http://lcweb2.loc.gov/cgi-bin/query/S?ammem/gmd:@filreq(@field(STATE+delaware)+@field(COLLID+pmmap))
  From the Geography and Map Division, Library of Congress.

- American Memory Railroad Maps 1828–1900—Delaware
  http://memory.loc.gov/cgi-bin/query/S?ammem/gmd:@filreq(@field(STATE+delaware)+@field(COLLID+rrmap))
  From the Geography and Map Division, Library of Congress.

- Color Landform Atlas: Delaware
  http://fermi.jhuapl.edu/states/de_0.html
  Including a map of counties and a map for 1895.

- Excite Maps: Delaware Maps
  http://www.city.net/maps/view/?mapurl=/countries/united_states/delaware
  Zoom in on these maps all the way to the street level.

- HPI County InfoSystem—Counties in Delaware
  http://www.com/hpi/decty/index.html

- K.B. Slocum Books and Maps—Delaware
  http://www.treasurenet.com/cgi-bin/treasure/kbslocum/scan/se=Delaware/sf=mapstate

- List of Delaware Counties
  http://www.genealogy.org/~st-clair/counties/state_de.html

- Map of Delaware Counties
  http://govinfo.kerr.orst.edu/gif/states/de.gif
  From the Government Information Sharing Project, Information Services, Oregon State University.

- Map of Delaware Counties
  http://www.lib.utexas.edu/Libs/PCL/Map_collection/states/Delaware.gif
  From the Perry-Castañeda Library at the Univ. of Texas at Austin.

- U.S. Census Bureau—Delaware Profiles
  http://www.census.gov/datamap/www/10.html

- Yale Peabody Museum: GNIS—Delaware
  http://www.peabody.yale.edu/other/gnis/DE.html
  *Search the USGS Geographic Names Database. You can limit the search to a specific county in this state and search for any of the following features: airport arch area arroyo bar basin bay beach bench bend bridge **building** canal cape **cemetery** channel **church** cliff crater crossing dam falls flat forest gap geyser glacier gut harbor hospital island isthmus lake lava levee locale mine oilfield other park pillar plain ppl range rapids reserve reservoir ridge **school** sea slope spring stream summit swamp tower trail tunnel valley well woods.*

◆ Military

- The Civil War Archive—Union Regiments—Delaware
  http://www.civilwararchive.com/unionde.htm
- Korean Conflict State-Level Casualty Lists—Delaware
  http://www.nara.gov/nara/electronic/dehrlist.html
  From the National Archives and Records Administration, Center for Electronic Records.
- Vietnam Conflict State-Level Casualty Lists—Delaware
  http://www.nara.gov/nara/electronic/dehrviet.html
  From the National Archives and Records Administration, Center for Electronic Records.
- The Vietnam Veterans Memorial—Delaware
  http://grunt.space.swri.edu/statewall/del/de.htm

◆ Newspapers

- AJR NewsLink—Delaware Newspapers
  http://www.newslink.org/denews.html
- E&P Media Info Links—Newspaper Sites in Delaware
  http://www.mediainfo.com/emedia/browse-results.htm?region=delaware&category=newspaper+++++++++
- NAA Hotlinks to Newspapers Online—Delaware
  http://www.naa.org/hotlinks/searchResult.asp?param=DE-Delaware&City=1
- N-Net—Delaware Newspapers
  http://www.n-net.com/de.htm
- The Ultimate Collection of News Links: USA—Delaware
  http://www.pppp.net/links/news/USA-DE.html
- Yahoo!...Newspapers...Delaware
  http://www.yahoo.com/News_and_Media/Newspapers/Browse_By_Region/U_S__States/Delaware/

◆ People & Families

- Directory of Underground Railroad Operators—Delaware
  http://www.ugrr.org//names/map-de.htm
- Tribes and Villages of Delaware
  http://hanksville.phast.umass.edu:8000/cultprop/contacts/tribal/DE.html

◆ Professional Researchers, Volunteers & Other Research Services

- Board for Certification of Genealogists—Roster of Those Certified—Specializing in Delaware
  http://www.genealogy.org/~bcg/rosts_de.html
- DelMarVa Roots
  http://www.intercom.net/user/bobroots/tindex.html
  Genealogical record searches for the State of Delaware.
- Doherty Enterprises Professional Genealogical Research
  http://www.magpage.com/~tdoherty/tpdserve.html
- Genealogy Helplist—Delaware
  http://www.cyberbeach.net/~mkelly/helplistUSA/de.htm
- The Official Iowa Counties Professional Genealogist and Researcher's Registry for Delaware
  http://www.iowa-counties.com/gene/de.htm

◆ Publications, Software & Supplies

- AncestorSpy—CDs and Microfiche for Delaware
  http://www.ancestorspy.com/de.htm
- Barbara Green's Used Genealogy Books—Delaware
  http://home.earthlink.net/~genbooks/lochist.html#DE
- Barnette's Family Tree Books—Delaware
  http://www.barnettesbooks.com/delaware.htm
- Books We Own—Delaware
  http://www.rootsweb.com/~bwo/delaware.html
- Delaware Genealogical Research Guide
  http://delgensoc.org/dgsguide.html
- Family Line Publications
  http://pages.prodigy.com/Strawn/family.htm
  Books covering Delaware, Maryland, New Jersey, Pennsylvania, Virginia, and Washington DC.
- Frontier Press Bookstore—Delaware
  http://www.frontierpress.com/frontier.cgi?category=de
- GenealogyBookShop.com—Delaware
  http://www.genealogybookshop.com/genealogybookshop/files/The_United_States,Delaware/index.html
  The online store of Genealogical Publishing Co., Inc. & Clearfield Company.
- Hearthstone Bookshop—Delaware
  http://www.hearthstonebooks.com/cgi-bin/webc.cgi/st_main.html?catid=75&sid=2PH5t29sm
- Heritage Books—Delaware
  http://www.heritagebooks.com/de.htm
- Heritage Quest—Microfilm Records for the State of Delaware
  http://www.heritagequest.com/genealogy/microfilm/delaware/
- Lost in Time Books—Delaware
  http://www.lostintime.com/catalog/books/bookst/bo06000.htm
- The Memorabilia Corner—Books: Delaware
  http://members.aol.com/TMCorner/book_del.htm
- Picton Press—Delaware
  http://www.midcoast.com/~picton/public_html.BASK/catalog/state_dl.htm
- Southern Queries Genealogy Magazine
  http://www.mindspring.com/~freedom1/sq/sq.htm

- Willow Bend Bookstore—Delaware
  http://www.willowbend.net/de.htm

◆ Queries, Message Boards & Surname Lists

- GenConnect Delaware Visitor Center
  http://cgi.rootsweb.com/~genbbs/indx/De.html
  A system for posting queries, Bibles, biographies, deeds, obituaries, pensions, wills.

◆ Records: Census, Cemeteries, Land, Obituaries, Personal, Taxes and Vital (Born, Married, Died & Buried)

- The 1790–1890 Federal Population Censuses: Catalog of National Archives Microfilm
  http://www.genealogy.org/census/contents.shtml
  - Census Schedules and Microfilm Roll Numbers for Delaware:

    1800
    http://www.genealogy.org/census/1800_schedules/Delaware.html

    1810
    http://www.genealogy.org/census/1810_schedules/Delaware.html

    1820
    http://www.genealogy.org/census/1820_schedules/Delaware.html

    1830
    http://www.genealogy.org/census/1830_schedules/Delaware.html

    1840
    http://www.genealogy.org/census/1840_schedules/Delaware.html

    1850
    http://www.genealogy.org/census/1850_schedules/Delaware.html

    1860
    http://www.genealogy.org/census/1860_schedules/Delaware.html

    1870
    http://www.genealogy.org/census/1870_schedules/Delaware.html

    1880
    http://www.genealogy.org/census/1880_schedules/Delaware.html

    1880 Soundex
    http://www.genealogy.org/census/1880.sdx_schedules/T741.html

- Cemeteries of the United States—Delaware Cemeteries—County Index
  http://www.gac.edu/~kengelha/uscemeteries/delaware.html

- County Courthouse Addresses
  http://www.familytreemaker.com/00000182.html

- Delaware Vital Records Information
  http://vitalrec.com/de.html

- Directory of Historical Records in Delaware
  http://www.magpage.com/~tdoherty/dehisrec.html

- Find-A-Grave by Location: Delaware
  http://www.findagrave.com/grave/lde.html
  Graves of noteworthy people.

- Interment.net: Delaware Cemeteries
  http://www.interment.net/us/de/index.htm
  A list of links to other sites.

- A List of Taxable Persons & Estates for the Year 1777 in Brandywine Hundred, New Castle County, DE
  ftp://ftp.rootsweb.com/pub/usgenweb/de/new_castle/tax/brtx1777.txt

- National Archives—Mid Atlantic Region (Philadelphia) or
  http://www.nara.gov/regional/philacc.html

- National Archives—Mid-Atlantic Region
  http://www.familytreemaker.com/00000097.html
  Records for Delaware, Maryland, Pennsylvania, Virginia, and West Virginia.

- The Political Graveyard—Cemeteries in Delaware
  http://politicalgraveyard.com/geo/DE/kmindex.html

- Preplanning Network—Funeral Home and Cemetery Directory—Delaware
  http://www.preplannet.com/delawarefhcem.htm

- USGenWeb Census Project Delaware
  http://www.usgenweb.org/census/states/delaware.htm

- USGenWeb Tombstone Transcription Project—Delaware
  http://www.rootsweb.com/~cemetery/delaware.html

- VitalChek Network—Delaware
  http://www.vitalchek.com/stateselect.asp?state=DE

- Where to Write for Vital Records—Delaware
  http://www.cdc.gov/nchswww/howto/w2w/delaware.htm
  From the National Center for Health Statistics (NCHS).

◆ Religion & Churches

- Christianity.Net Church Locator—Delaware
  http://www.christianity.net/cgi/location.exe?United_States+Delaware

- Church Online!—Delaware
  http://www.churchonline.com/usas/de/de.html

- Church Profiles—Delaware
  http://www.church-profiles.com/de/de.html

- Churches dot Net—Global Church Web Pages—Delaware
  http://www.churches.net/churches/delaware.html

- Churches of the World—Delaware
  http://www.churchsurf.com/churches/Delaware/index.htm
  From the ChurchSurf Christian Directory.

◆ Societies & Groups

- Archer's Computer Interest Group List—Delaware
  http://www.genealogy.org/~ngs/cigs/ngl1usde.html

- Delaware Genealogical Society
  http://delgensoc.org/

- Downstate Genealogists
  http://members.aol.com/josefowski/index.html
  Focusing on the genealogy of Kent and Sussex Counties, Delaware.

- Historical Society of Delaware
  http://www.hsd.org/

- IOOF Lodge Website Directory—Delaware
  http://norm28.hsc.usc.edu/IOOF/USA/Delaware/Delaware.html
  Independent Order of Odd Fellows and Rebekahs.

- Lower Delmarva Genealogical Society
  http://bay.intercom.net/ldgs/index.html
  Delaware, Maryland and Virginia.

- Mike St. Clair's List of Societies & CIGS—Delaware
  http://www.genealogy.org/~gwsc/gwscusde.htm

◆ USGenWeb Project

- Delaware Genealogy—USGenWeb Project State Page
  http://www.usgenweb.org/de

- Delaware—USGenWeb Archives Table of Contents
  http://www.rootsweb.com/~usgenweb/de/defiles.htm

- Delaware—USGenWeb FTP Archives
  ftp://ftp.rootsweb.com/pub/usgenweb/de/

U.S.—DISTRICT OF COLUMBIA—DC
http://www.CyndisList.com/dc.htm

Category Index:
- ◆ General Resource Sites
- ◆ History & Culture
- ◆ Libraries, Archives & Museums
- ◆ Mailing Lists, Newsgroups & Chat
- ◆ Maps, Gazetteers & Geographical Information
- ◆ Military
- ◆ Newspapers
- ◆ Professional Researchers, Volunteers & Other Research Services

- ◆ Publications, Software & Supplies
- ◆ Queries, Message Boards & Surname Lists
- ◆ Records: Census, Cemeteries, Land, Obituaries, Personal, Taxes and Vital
- ◆ Religion & Churches
- ◆ Societies & Groups
- ◆ USGenWeb Project

◆ General Resource Sites

- 50states.com—District of Columbia Information Resource
  http://www.50states.com/dc.htm
  A list of general information for each state, including a list of colleges, state symbols, links to maps, newspapers, and other miscellaneous state information.

- Excite Travel by City.Net—District of Columbia
  http://www.city.net/countries/united_states/district_of_columbia/

- Everton's Sources of Genealogical Information in the District of Columbia
  http://www.everton.com/usa/dc.htm

- Family Tree Maker's Genealogy "How To" Guide—District of Columbia
  http://www.familytreemaker.com/00000223.html

- LDS Research Outline for District of Columbia
  http://www.everton.com/usa/dc-0809B.txt

- Lineages' Genealogy Site: District of Columbia Research Room
  http://www.lineages.com/rooms/usa/state.asp?StateCode=DC

- NARA Calendar of Events
  http://www.nara.gov/nara/events/events.html
  For the National Archives facilities in and around Washington, DC and nationwide.

- Official City Web Sites for the District of Columbia
  http://OfficialCitySites.org/washington-DC.htm

- Planning a Research Trip to Washington, DC?
  http://www.CyndisList.com/travel.htm#DC
  See the Travel & Research category on Cyndi's List for related links.

- ROOTS-L United States Resources: District of Columbia
  http://www.rootsweb.com/roots-l/USA/dc.html
  Comprehensive list of research links, including many to history-related sites.

◆ History & Culture

- Yahoo!...History...Washington, D.C.
  http://dir.yahoo.com/Arts/Humanities/History/Browse_By_Region/U_S__States/Washington__D_C_/

◆ Libraries, Archives & Museums

- Family History Center, Washington DC Temple
  http://www.access.digex.net/~giammot/FHC/

- HYTELNET—Library Catalogs: USA: District of Columbia
  http://library.usask.ca/hytelnet/usa/DC.html
  Before you use any of the Telnet links, make note of the user name, password and any other logon information.

- Library of Congress
  http://www.CyndisList.com/libofcon.htm
  See this category on Cyndi's List for related links.

- The National Archives
  http://www.CyndisList.com/na.htm
  See this category on Cyndi's List for related links.

- National Society of the Daughters of the American Revolution—Genealogical Research Library
  http://www.dar.org/library/library.html

- NUCMC Listing of Archives and Manuscript Repositories in the District of Columbia
  http://lcweb.loc.gov/coll/nucmc/dcsites.html
  Links to information about resources other than those held in the Library of Congress.

- Repositories of Primary Sources: District of Columbia
  http://www.uidaho.edu/special-collections/east1.html#usdc
  A list of links to online resources from the Univ. of Idaho Library, Special Collections and Archives.

- Research Library of Washington History
  http://www.wam.umd.edu/~pbowen/library.htm
  The collections of The Historical Society of Washington, D.C.

- webCATS: Library Catalogues on the World Wide Web—District of Columbia
  http://library.usask.ca/hywebcat/states/DC.html

◆ Mailing Lists, Newsgroups & Chat

- Genealogy Resources on the Internet—District of Columbia Mailing Lists
  http://members.aol.com/gfsjohnf/gen_mail_states-dc.html
  Each of the mailing list links below points to this site, wonderfully maintained by John Fuller. Visit this site for county-specific mailing lists as well.

- MID-ATLANTIC-ROOTS-L Mailing List
  http://members.aol.com/gfsjohnf/gen_mail_states-dc.html#MID-ATLANTIC-ROOTS-L
  New Jersey, Maryland, Delaware, and the District of Columbia.

- WashingtonDC Mailing List
  http://members.aol.com/gfsjohnf/gen_mail_states-dc.html#WashingtonDC

◆ Maps, Gazetteers & Geographical Information

- 1895 U.S. Atlas—District of Columbia
  http://www.livgenmi.com/1895doc

- American Memory Panoramic Maps 1847–1929—District of Columbia
  http://lcweb2.loc.gov/cgi-bin/query/S?ammem/gmd:
  @filreq(@field(STATE+@band(+district+of+columbia))+
  @field(COLLID+pmmap))
  From the Geography and Map Division, Library of Congress.

- American Memory Railroad Maps 1828–1900—District of Columbia
  http://memory.loc.gov/cgi-bin/query/S?ammem/gmd:
  @filreq(@field(STATE+@band(+district+of+columbia))+
  @field(COLLID+rrmap))
  From the Geography and Map Division, Library of Congress.

- Excite Maps: District of Columbia Maps
  http://www.city.net/maps/view/?mapurl=/countries/
  united_states/district_of_columbia
  Zoom in on these maps all the way to the street level.

- U.S. Census Bureau—District of Columbia Profiles
  http://www.census.gov/datamap/www/11.html

- Yahoo! Get Local...Washington, D.C.
  http://dir.yahoo.com/Regional/U_S__States/
  Washington__D_C_/
  Maps, yellow pages, white pages, newspapers and other local information.

- Yale Peabody Museum: GNIS—District of Columbia
  http://www.peabody.yale.edu/other/gnis/DC.html
  Search the USGS Geographic Names Database. You can limit the search to a specific county in this state and search for any of the following features: airport arch area arroyo bar basin bay beach bench bend bridge **building** *canal cape* **cemetery** *channel* **church** *cliff crater crossing dam falls flat forest gap geyser glacier gut harbor hospital island isthmus lake lava levee locale mine oilfield other park pillar plain ppl range rapids reserve reservoir ridge* **school** *sea slope spring stream summit swamp tower trail tunnel valley well woods.*

◆ Military

- The Civil War Archive—Union Regiments—District of Columbia
  http://www.civilwararchive.com/uniondc.htm

- Civil War Battle Summaries by State—District of Columbia
  http://www2.cr.nps.gov/abpp/battles/bystate.htm#dc

- Korean Conflict State-Level Casualty Lists—District of Columbia
  http://www.nara.gov/nara/electronic/dchrlist.html
  From the National Archives and Records Administration, Center for Electronic Records.

- Vietnam Conflict State-Level Casualty Lists—District of Columbia
  http://www.nara.gov/nara/electronic/dchrviet.html
  From the National Archives and Records Administration, Center for Electronic Records.

- The Vietnam Veterans Memorial—District of Columbia
  http://grunt.space.swri.edu/statewall/washdc/dc.htm

◆ Newspapers

- AJR NewsLink—District of Columbia Newspapers
  http://www.newslink.org/dcnews.html

- E&P Media Info Links—Newspaper Sites in District of Columbia
  http://www.mediainfo.com/emedia/browse-results.htm?region=
  districtofcolumbia&category=newspaper+++++++++

- Ecola Newstand: District of Columbia
  http://www.ecola.com/news/press/na/us/dc/

- NAA Hotlinks to Newspapers Online—District of Columbia
  http://www.naa.org/hotlinks/searchResult.asp?param=
  DC-District+of+Columbia&City=1

- N-Net—District of Columbia Newspapers
  http://www.n-net.com/dc.htm

- The Ultimate Collection of News Links: USA—District of Columbia
  http://www.pppp.net/links/news/USA-DC.html

- The Washington Post
  http://www.washingtonpost.com/

- The Washington Times National Weekly Edition
  http://www.washtimes-weekly.com/

- Yahoo!...Newspapers...District of Columbia
  http://dir.yahoo.com/News_and_Media/Newspapers/
  Browse_By_Region/U_S_States/Washington_D_C_/

◆ Professional Researchers, Volunteers & Other Research Services

- Board for Certification of Genealogists—Roster of Those Certified—Specializing in District of Columbia
  http://www.genealogy.org/~bcg/rosts_dc.html
- The Cavalier Research Group
  http://www.cavaliergroup.org/
- Genealogy Helplist—Washington DC
  http://posom.com/hl/usa/dc.shtml
- The Official Iowa Counties Professional Genealogist and Researcher's Registry for District of Columbia
  http://www.iowa-counties.com/gene/dc.htm

◆ Publications, Software & Supplies

- American Genealogical Research at the DAR, Washington, D.C.
  http://www.dar.org/library/libpub.html
- Barbara Green's Used Genealogy Books— Washington, D.C.
  http://home.earthlink.net/~genbooks/lochist.html#DC
- Family Line Publications
  http://pages.prodigy.com/Strawn/family.htm
  Books covering Delaware, Maryland, New Jersey, Pennsylvania, Virginia, and Washington DC.
- Frontier Press Bookstore—District of Columbia
  http://www.frontierpress.com/frontier.cgi?category=dc
- GenealogyBookShop.com—District of Columbia
  http://www.genealogybookshop.com/genealogybookshop/files/
  The_United_States,District_of_Columbia/index.html
  The online store of Genealogical Publishing Co., Inc. & Clearfield Company.
- Hearthstone Bookshop—District of Columbia
  http://www.hearthstonebooks.com/cgi-bin/webc.cgi/
  st_main.html?catid=76&sid=2PH5t29sm
- Heritage Books—District of Columbia
  http://www.heritagebooks.com/dc.htm
- Heritage Quest—Microfilm Records for the District of Columbia
  http://www.heritagequest.com/genealogy/microfilm/
  district_of_columbia/
- Lost in Time Books—District of Columbia
  http://www.lostintime.com/catalog/books/bookst/bo07000.htm
- The Memorabilia Corner—Books: District of Columbia
  http://members.aol.com/TMCorner/book_dc.htm

- Southern Queries Genealogy Magazine
  http://www.mindspring.com/~freedom1/sq/sq.htm
- Willow Bend Bookstore—District of Columbia
  http://www.willowbend.net/dc.htm

◆ Queries, Message Boards & Surname Lists

- GenConnect District of Columbia Visitor Center
  http://cgi.rootsweb.com/~genbbs/indx/DC.html
  A system for posting queries, Bibles, biographies, deeds, obituaries, pensions, wills.

◆ Records: Census, Cemeteries, Land, Obituaries, Personal, Taxes and Vital (Born, Married, Died & Buried)

- The 1790–1890 Federal Population Censuses: Catalog of National Archives Microfilm
  http://www.genealogy.org/census/contents.shtml
  o Census Schedules and Microfilm Roll Numbers for District of Columbia:
    1800
    http://www.genealogy.org/census/1800_schedules/
    District.of.Columbia.html
    1820
    http://www.genealogy.org/census/1820_schedules/
    District.of.Columbia.html
    1830
    http://www.genealogy.org/census/1830_schedules/
    District.of.Columbia.html
    1840
    http://www.genealogy.org/census/1840_schedules/
    District.of.Columbia.html
    1850
    http://www.genealogy.org/census/1850_schedules/
    District.of.Columbia.html
    1860
    http://www.genealogy.org/census/1860_schedules/
    District.of.Columbia.html
    1870
    http://www.genealogy.org/census/1870_schedules/
    District.of.Columbia.html
    1880
    http://www.genealogy.org/census/1880_schedules/
    District.of.Columbia.html
    1880 Soundex
    http://www.genealogy.org/census/1880.sdx_schedules/
    T742.html
- Cemeteries of the United States—District of Columbia Cemeteries—County Index
  http://www.gac.edu/~kengelha/uscemeteries/dc.html

- Census Online—Links to Census Sites on the Web—Washington D.C.
  http://www.census-online.com/links/DC_data.html
- County Courthouse Addresses
  http://www.familytreemaker.com/00000277.html
- DC Cemeteries
  http://www.ihot.com/~christis/cemetery/cemetery.htm
- DC State Center for Health Statistics
  http://www.ci.washington.dc.us/HEALTH/schs.htm
  The Vital Records Division has birth and death certificates.
- District of Columbia Vital Records Information
  http://vitalrec.com/dc.html
- Find-A-Grave by Location: District of Columbia
  http://www.findagrave.com/grave/ldc.html
  Graves of noteworthy people.
- Freedman's Bureau, Marriages in Washington, D.C. 1861–1869, Part 1
  http://ccharity.com/freedmens/dcmarriages1.htm
  Part 2
  http://ccharity.com/freedmens/dcmarriages2.htm
- Historic Congressional Cemetery
  http://www.geocities.com/Heartland/Meadows/4633/index.html
- National Archives, Washington, DC Area Sites
  http://www.nara.gov/nara/dc/dcarea.html
- National Archives—Washington, D.C.
  http://www.familytreemaker.com/00000093.html
- The Political Graveyard—Cemeteries in District of Columbia
  http://politicalgraveyard.com/geo/DC/kmindex.html
- USGenWeb Census Project District of Columbia
  http://www.usgenweb.org/census/states/district.htm
- USGenWeb Tombstone Transcription Project—District of Columbia
  http://www.rootsweb.com/~cemetery/district.html
- VitalChek Network—District of Columbia
  http://www.vitalchek.com/stateselect.asp?state=DC
- Where to Write for Vital Records—District of Columbia
  http://www.cdc.gov/nchswww/howto/w2w/dc.htm
  From the National Center for Health Statistics (NCHS).

◆ Religion & Churches

- Christianity.Net Church Locator—District of Columbia
  http://www.christianity.net/cgi/location.exe?United_States+District_of_Columbia
- Church Online!—District of Columbia
  http://www.churchonline.com/usas/dc/dc.html

- Church Profiles—District of Columbia
  http://www.church-profiles.com/dc/dc.html
- Churches of the World—District of Columbia
  http://www.churchsurf.com/churches/Washington_DC/
  From the ChurchSurf Christian Directory.

◆ Societies & Groups

- American Historical Society of Germans from Russia—Nation's Capital Area Chapter
  http://www.ahsgr.org/dcapitol.html
- Archer's Computer Interest Group List—District of Columbia
  http://www.genealogy.org/~ngs/cigs/ngl1usdc.html
- Historical Society of Washington, D.C.
  http://www.wam.umd.edu/~pbowen/welcome.htm
- Il Circolo Filippo Mazzei—The Washington DC Metropolitan Area Italian Genealogical Society
  http://www.geocities.com/Athens/Acropolis/1709/Mazzei.htm
- IOOF Lodge Website Directory—District of Columbia
  http://norm28.hsc.usc.edu/IOOF/USA/DC/DC.html
  Independent Order of Odd Fellows and Rebekahs.
- The Jewish Genealogy Society of Greater Washington, D.C.
  http://www.jewishgen.org/jgsgw/
- Mike St. Clair's List of Societies & CIGS—District of Columbia
  http://www.genealogy.org/~gwsc/gwscusdc.htm
- The National Capital Area Chapter of the Association of Professional Genealogists
  http://www.apgen.org/ncac/
- National Society of the Daughters of the American Revolution Home Page
  http://www.dar.org/index.html
- United States Capitol Historical Society
  http://www.uschs.org/
- Women in Military Service for America Memorial Foundation, Inc.
  http://www.wimsa.org/

◆ USGenWeb Project

- District of Columbia Genealogy—USGenWeb Project
  http://www.usgenweb.org/dc
- District of Columbia—USGenWeb Archives Table of Contents
  http://www.rootsweb.com/~usgenweb/dc/dcfiles.htm
- District of Columbia—USGenWeb FTP Archives
  ftp://ftp.rootsweb.com/pub/usgenweb/dc/

U.S.—FLORIDA—FL
http://www.CyndisList.com/fl.htm

Category Index:

- General Resource Sites
- Government & Cities
- History & Culture
- Libraries, Archives & Museums
- Mailing Lists, Newsgroups & Chat
- Maps, Gazetteers & Geographical Information
- Military
- Newspapers
- People & Families

- Professional Researchers, Volunteers & Other Research Services
- Publications, Software & Supplies
- Queries, Message Boards & Surname Lists
- Records: Census, Cemeteries, Land, Obituaries, Personal, Taxes and Vital
- Religion & Churches
- Societies & Groups
- USGenWeb Project

◆ General Resource Sites

- Escambia County, Florida Genealogy Research
  http://www.geocities.com/Heartland/Acres/5731/
  Family charts, obits, wills pertaining to Escambia Co, FL.

- Everton's Sources of Genealogical Information in Florida
  http://www.everton.com/usa/fl.htm

- Family Tree Maker's Genealogy "How To" Guide— Florida
  http://www.familytreemaker.com/00000183.html

- Genealogical Research in the Pensacola Area
  http://www.pcola.gulf.net/~gdeagan/wfgs.htm

- Genealogy Bulletin Board Systems for Florida
  http://www.genealogy.org/~gbbs/gblfl.html

- Genealogy Exchange & Surname Registry— FLGenExchange
  http://www.genexchange.com/fl/index.cfm

- Genealogy Resources on the Internet: Florida
  http://www-personal.umich.edu/~cgaunt/florida.html

- LDS Research Outline for Florida
  http://www.everton.com/usa/fl-0810B.txt

- Lineages' Genealogy Site: Florida
  http://www.lineages.com/rooms/usa/state.asp?StateCode=FL

- ROOTS-L United States Resources: Florida
  http://www.rootsweb.com/roots-l/USA/fl.html
  Comprehensive list of research links, including many to history-related sites.

◆ Government & Cities

- 50states.com—Florida State Information Resource
  http://www.50states.com/florida.htm
  A list of general information for each state, including a list of colleges, state symbols, links to maps, newspapers, and other miscellaneous state information.

- Excite Travel by City.Net—Florida
  http://www.city.net/countries/united_states/florida/

- Official City Web Sites for the State of Florida
  http://OfficialCitySites.org/florida.htm

- State of Florida and US Government
  http://www.firn.edu/flgov.html

- Yahoo! Get Local...Florida Cities
  http://dir.yahoo.com/Regional/U_S__States/Florida/Cities/
  Maps, yellow pages, white pages, newspapers and other local information.

- Yahoo! Get Local...Florida Counties and Regions
  http://dir.yahoo.com/Regional/U_S__States/Florida/
  Counties_and_Regions/
  Maps, yellow pages, white pages, newspapers and other local information.

◆ History & Culture

- Yahoo!...History...Florida
  http://dir.yahoo.com/Arts/Humanities/History/
  Browse_By_Region/U_S__States/Florida/

◆ Libraries, Archives & Museums

- Family History Centers—Florida
  http://www.deseretbook.com/famhis/fl.html

- Family History Centers—Florida
  http://www.lib.byu.edu/~uvrfhc/centers/florida.html
- Florida Department of State—Library and
  Information Services
  http://www.dos.state.fl.us/dlis/index.html
  - The Bureau of Archives and Records Management
    http://www.dos.state.fl.us/dlis/barm/archives.html
    - Florida Records Storage Center
      http://www.dos.state.fl.us/dlis/barm/fsrc.html
    - Florida State Archives
      http://www.dos.state.fl.us/dlis/barm/fsa.html
  - State Library of Florida Resources
    http://stafla.dlis.state.fl.us/
    - Search the State Library Catalog
      http://stafla.dlis.state.fl.us/MARION
- Florida Family History Centers
  http://www.genhomepage.com/FHC/Florida.html
  *A list of addresses, phone numbers and hours of operation from
  the Genealogy Home Page.*
- HYTELNET—Library Catalogs: USA: Florida
  http://library.usask.ca/hytelnet/usa/FL.html
  *Before you use any of the Telnet links, make note of the user
  name, password and any other logon information.*
- Lakes Regional Library Resources
  http://mh101.infi.net/~crazy1/lakelibr.htm
- Leesburg Family History Center
  http://www.angelfire.com/fl/Sumter/genealogy.html
- NUCMC Listing of Archives and Manuscript
  Repositories in Florida
  http://lcweb.loc.gov/coll/nucmc/flsites.html
  *Links to information about resources other than those held in the
  Library of Congress.*
- Pensacola, Florida Family History Center
  http://www.rootsweb.com/~flescamb/fhc.htm
- Repositories of Primary Sources: Florida
  http://www.uidaho.edu/special-collections/east1.html#usfl
  *A list of links to online resources from the Univ. of Idaho
  Library, Special Collections and Archives.*
- University of South Florida Tampa Campus Library
  http://www.lib.usf.edu/index.html
  - Special Collections Department
    http://www.lib.usf.edu/spccoll/
    - Genealogy Collection
      http://www.lib.usf.edu/spccoll/genea.html
- webCATS: Library Catalogues on the World Wide
  Web—Florida
  http://library.usask.ca/hywebcat/states/FL.html

◆ Mailing Lists, Newsgroups & Chat

- Genealogy Resources on the Internet—Florida
  Mailing Lists
  http://members.aol.com/gfsjohnf/gen_mail_states-fl.html
  *Each of the mailing list links below points to this site, wonder-
  fully maintained by John Fuller. Visit this site for county-specific
  mailing lists as well.*
- DEEP-SOUTH-ROOTS-L Mailing List
  http://members.aol.com/gfsjohnf/gen_mail_states-fl.
  html#DEEP-SOUTH-ROOTS
  Alabama, Florida, Georgia & Mississippi.
- FLORIDA Mailing List
  http://members.aol.com/gfsjohnf/gen_mail_states-fl.
  html#FLORIDA

◆ Maps, Gazetteers & Geographical Information

- 1895 U.S. Atlas—Florida
  http://www.LivGenMI.com/1895fl.htm
- American Memory Panoramic Maps 1847–1929—
  Florida
  http://lcweb2.loc.gov/cgi-bin/query/S?ammem/gmd:
  @filreq(@field(STATE+florida)+@field(COLLID+pmmap))
  From the Geography and Map Division, Library of Congress.
- American Memory Railroad Maps 1828–1900—
  Florida
  http://memory.loc.gov/cgi-bin/query/S?ammem/gmd:
  @filreq(@field(STATE+florida)+@field(COLLID+rrmap))
  From the Geography and Map Division, Library of Congress.
- Color Landform Atlas: Florida
  http://fermi.jhuapl.edu/states/fl_0.html
  Including a map of counties and a map for 1895.
- Excite Maps: Florida Maps
  http://www.city.net/maps/view/?mapurl=/countries/
  united_states/florida
  Zoom in on these maps all the way to the street level.
- HPI County InfoSystem—Counties in Florida
  http://www.com/hpi/flcty/index.html
- Interactive Florida County Atlas
  http://cartlab-www.freac.fsu.edu/interactivecountyatlas/
  atlas.html
- K.B. Slocum Books and Maps—Florida
  http://www.treasurenet.com/cgi-bin/treasure/kbslocum/scan/
  se=Florida/sf=mapstate
- List of Florida Counties
  http://www.genealogy.org/~st-clair/counties/state_fl.html
- Map of Florida Counties
  http://govinfo.kerr.orst.edu/gif/states/fl.gif
  *From the Government Information Sharing Project, Information
  Services, Oregon State University.*

- Map of Florida Counties
  http://www.lib.utexas.edu/Libs/PCL/Map_collection/states/
  Florida.gif
  *From the Perry-Castañeda Library at the Univ. of Texas at
  Austin.*

- U.S. Census Bureau—Florida Profiles
  http://www.census.gov/datamap/www/12.html

- Yale Peabody Museum: GNIS—Florida
  http://www.peabody.yale.edu/other/gnis/FL.html
  *Search the USGS Geographic Names Database. You can limit
  the search to a specific county in this state and search for any of
  the following features: airport arch area arroyo bar basin bay
  beach bench bend bridge **building** canal cape **cemetery** channel
  church cliff crater crossing dam falls flat forest gap geyser
  glacier gut harbor hospital island isthmus lake lava levee locale
  mine oilfield other park pillar plain ppl range rapids reserve
  reservoir ridge **school** sea slope spring stream summit swamp
  tower trail tunnel valley well woods.*

◆ Military

- Battle of Olustee
  http://extlab1.entnem.ufl.edu/olustee/index.html

- The Civil War Archive—Union Regiments—Florida
  http://www.civilwararchive.com/unionfl.htm

- Civil War Battle Summaries by State—Florida
  http://www2.cr.nps.gov/abpp/battles/bystate.htm#fl

- The Civil War in Florida
  http://mailer.fsu.edu/~rthompso/csa-page.html
  *Includes Wakulla, Franklin, Jefferson, and Leon counties.
  Includes muster rolls for units from the state.*

- CSA 9th Florida Infantry
  http://members.aol.com/Kwiley/index.html

- Florida Confederate Pension Application Files
  http://www.dos.state.fl.us/dlis/barm/PensionIntroduction.htm
  *Search this online index then follow the instructions for ordering
  a copy of the pension file.*

- Florida Medal of Honor Recipients
  http://www.geocities.com/Heartland/Hills/8299/military/
  moh.htm

- Korean Conflict State-Level Casualty Lists—Florida
  http://www.nara.gov/nara/electronic/flhrlist.html
  *From the National Archives and Records Administration,
  Center for Electronic Records.*

- Third Florida Infantry, Company B—St. Augustine
  Blues (CSA)
  http://www.geocities.com/Heartland/Hills/8299/military/
  3fl_inf.htm

- Vietnam Conflict State-Level Casualty Lists—
  Florida
  http://www.nara.gov/nara/electronic/flhrviet.html
  *From the National Archives and Records Administration,
  Center for Electronic Records.*

- The Vietnam Veterans Memorial—Florida
  http://grunt.space.swri.edu/statewall/florida/fl.htm

◆ Newspapers

- AJR NewsLink—Florida Newspapers
  http://www.newslink.org/flnews.html

- E&P Media Info Links—Newspaper Sites in Florida
  http://www.mediainfo.com/emedia/browse-results.
  htm?region=florida&category=newspaper+++++++++

- Ecola Newstand: Florida
  http://www.ecola.com/news/press/na/us/fl/

- NAA Hotlinks to Newspapers Online—Florida
  http://www.naa.org/hotlinks/searchResult.asp?param=
  FL-Florida&City=1

- The Florida Newspaper Project
  http://www.uflib.ufl.edu/flnews/

- The Florida Times-Union Online, Jacksonville,
  Florida
  http://www.times-union.com/

- N-Net—Florida Newspapers
  http://www.n-net.com/fl.htm

- The Tampa Tribune on the Web
  http://www.tampatrib.com/

- The Ultimate Collection of News Links:
  USA—Florida
  http://www.pppp.net/links/news/USA-FL.html

- Yahoo!...Newspapers...Florida
  http://dir.yahoo.com/News_and_Media/Newspapers/
  Browse_By_Region/U_S__States/Florida/

◆ People & Families

- FLGenWeb Project—Native American Information
  and Links
  http://www.rootsweb.com/~flgenweb/tribes.htm

- The Seminole Tribe of Florida
  http://www.gate.net/~semtribe/

- Tribes and Villages of Florida
  http://hanksville.phast.umass.edu:8000/cultprop/contacts/
  tribal/FL.html

- WPA Life Histories from Florida
  http://lcweb2.loc.gov/ammem/wpaintro/flcat.html
  *Manuscripts from the Federal Writer's Project, 1936–1940,
  Library of Congress.*

◆ Professional Researchers, Volunteers & Other Research Services

- Board for Certification of Genealogists—Roster of
  Those Certified—Specializing in Florida
  http://www.genealogy.org/~bcg/rosts_fl.html

- Genealogy Helplist—Florida
  http://www.reesestudio.net/genealogy/fl.htm

- The Official Iowa Counties Professional Genealogist and Researcher's Registry for Florida
  http://www.iowa-counties.com/gene/fl.htm

◆ Publications, Software & Supplies

- Barbara Green's Used Genealogy Books—Florida
  http://home.earthlink.net/~genbooks/lochist.html#FL

- Barnette's Family Tree Books—Florida
  http://www.barnettesbooks.com/florida.htm

- Books We Own—Florida
  http://www.rootsweb.com/~bwo/florida.html

- Boyd Publishing Company—Florida
  http://www.hom.net/~gac/florida.htm

- Frontier Press Bookstore—Florida
  http://www.frontierpress.com/frontier.cgi?category=fl

- GenealogyBookShop.com—Florida
  http://www.genealogybookshop.com/genealogybookshop/files/The_United_States,Florida/index.html
  The online store of Genealogical Publishing Co., Inc. & Clearfield Company.

- Heritage Quest—Microfilm Records for the State of Florida
  http://www.heritagequest.com/genealogy/microfilm/florida/

- Martin Genealogy Publications
  http://www.angelfire.com/biz/martingenpub/
  Alabama and Florida.

- Southern Queries Genealogy Magazine
  http://www.mindspring.com/~freedom1/sq/sq.htm

◆ Queries, Message Boards & Surname Lists

- GenConnect Florida Visitor Center
  http://cgi.rootsweb.com/~genbbs/indx/Fl.html
  A system for posting queries, Bibles, biographies, deeds, obituaries, pensions, wills.

- The Genealogical Society of Broward County Surname List
  http://www.rootsweb.com/~flgsbc/surmenu.html

◆ Records: Census, Cemeteries, Land, Obituaries, Personal, Taxes and Vital (Born, Married, Died & Buried)

- The 1790–1890 Federal Population Censuses: Catalog of National Archives Microfilm
  http://www.genealogy.org/census/contents.shtml
  - Census Schedules and Microfilm Roll Numbers for Florida:

1830
http://www.genealogy.org/census/1830_schedules/Florida.html

1840
http://www.genealogy.org/census/1840_schedules/Florida.html

1850
http://www.genealogy.org/census/1850_schedules/Florida.html

1860
http://www.genealogy.org/census/1860_schedules/Florida.html

1870
http://www.genealogy.org/census/1870_schedules/Florida.html

1880
http://www.genealogy.org/census/1880_schedules/Florida.html

1880 Soundex
http://www.genealogy.org/census/1880.sdx_schedules/T743.html

- 1850 Florida Census: St. John's County
  http://www.geocities.com/Heartland/Hills/8299/1850cens.htm

- Baker County Marriages, 1877–1930
  http://www.magicnet.net/~cmobley/mgs.html

- The Bureau of Land Management—Eastern States, General Land Office
  http://www.glorecords.blm.gov/
  The Official Land Patent Records Site. This site has a searchable database of over two million pre-1908 Federal land title records, including scanned images of those records. The Eastern Public Land States covered in this database are: Alabama, Arkansas, Florida, Illinois, Indiana, Louisiana, Michigan, Minnesota, Mississippi, Missouri, Ohio, Wisconsin.

- Cemeteries of the United States—Florida Cemeteries—County Index
  http://www.gac.edu/~kengelha/uscemeteries/florida.html

- Cemeteries—Wakulla County, FL
  http://mailer.fsu.edu/~rthompso/cemetery.html

- Census Online—Links to Census Sites on the Web—Florida
  http://www.census-online.com/links/FL_data.html

- County Courthouse Addresses
  http://www.familytreemaker.com/00000238.html

- Desoto Co Marriages, June 28, 1887 thru March 24, 1892
  http://www.rootsweb.com/~fldesoto/marriages.htm

- Find-A-Grave by Location: Florida
  http://www.findagrave.com/grave/lfl.html
  Graves of noteworthy people.

- Florida Census Records—Further Information
  http://www.lib.usf.edu/spccoll/guide/for/f11for.html
  From University of South Florida Tampa Campus Library.

- Florida Confederate Pension Application Files
  http://www.dos.state.fl.us/dlis/barm/PensionIntroduction.htm
  Search this online index then follow the instructions for ordering a copy of the pension file.

- The Florida Times-Union Online Obituaries
  http://www.times-union.com/tu-online/obituaries/
  Jacksonville, Florida

- Florida Vital Records Information
  http://vitalrec.com/fl.html

- Freedman's Bureau, Marriages in Jacksonville, Florida 1861–1869
  http://ccharity.com/freedmens/florida.htm

- Greenwood Cemetery: History ~ Tallahassee
  http://www.state.fl.us/citytlh/public_works/grnwdhst.html

- Hillsborough County, Florida Marriage Records—Index
  http://www.lib.usf.edu/spccoll/guide/m/ml/guide.html
  Records online from 4 Jan 1878 to 11 May 1884, including a photo of the original document.

- Hillsborough County Marriage Records
  http://www.lib.usf.edu/spccoll/marriage.html
  List of the special collections at University of South Florida Tampa Campus Library.

- Huguenot Cemetery
  http://www.geocities.com/Heartland/Hills/8299/cemetery/hug_cem.htm
  St. John's County

- Interment.net: Florida Cemeteries
  http://www.interment.net/us/fl/index.htm
  A list of links to other sites.

- Leon County Marriage Records Search Form
  http://www.clerk.leon.fl.us/marriage/marriage_index.html

- National Archives—Southeast Region (Atlanta)
  http://www.nara.gov/regional/atlanta.html

- National Archives—Southeast Region from Family Tree Maker
  http://www.familytreemaker.com/00000104.html
  Records for Alabama, Florida, Georgia, Kentucky, Mississippi, North Carolina, South Carolina, and Tennessee.

- North East Florida & Some South East George Counties—Listing of Over 300 Cemeteries.
  E-mail: cmobley@magicnet.net
  Florida counties include: Baker, Bradford, Columbia, Hamilton, Levy, Nassau, Union, (a few in Clay). Send e-mail to Carl Mobley, with SPECIFIC given names & surnames and he will do a lookup for you.

- Old City Cemetery: History ~ Tallahassee
  http://www.state.fl.us/citytlh/public_works/occhist.html

- Old Spanish Cemetery
  http://www.geocities.com/Heartland/Hills/8299/cemetery/spa_cem.htm
  St. John's County

- Our Lady of Good Counsel Church Cemetery
  http://www.geocities.com/Heartland/Hills/8299/cemetery/cons_cem.htm
  St. John's County

- The Political Graveyard—Cemeteries in Florida
  http://politicalgraveyard.com/geo/FL/kmindex.html

- Preplanning Network—Funeral Home and Cemetery Directory—Florida
  http://www.preplannet.com/florfh.htm

- St. Augustine National Cemetery
  http://www.geocities.com/Heartland/Hills/8299/cemetery/nat_cem.htm
  St. John's County

- Tampa Tribune Obituary Index
  http://tampatrib.com/news/obitindx.htm

- USGenWeb Census Project Florida
  http://www.usgenweb.org/census/states/florida.htm

- USGenWeb Tombstone Transcription Project—Florida
  http://www.rootsweb.com/~cemetery/florida.html

- VitalChek Network—Florida
  http://www.vitalchek.com/stateselect.asp?state=FL

- Where to Write for Vital Records—Florida
  http://www.cdc.gov/nchswww/howto/w2w/florida.htm
  From the National Center for Health Statistics (NCHS).

◆ Religion & Churches

- Christianity.Net Church Locator—Florida
  http://www.christianity.net/cgi/location.exe?United_States+Florida

- Church Online!—Florida
  http://www.churchonline.com/usas/fl/fl.html

- Church Profiles—Florida
  http://www.church-profiles.com/fl/fl.html

- Churches dot Net—Global Church Web Pages—Florida
  http://www.churches.net/churches/florida.html

- Churches of the World—Florida
  http://www.churchsurf.com/churches/Florida/index.htm
  From the ChurchSurf Christian Directory.

◆ Societies & Groups

- American Historical Society of Germans from Russia—Florida Suncoast Chapter
  http://www.ahsgr.org/flsuncst.html

- American Legion—State of Florida Department
  http://www.floridalegion.org/

- Archer's Computer Interest Group List—Florida
  http://www.genealogy.org/~ngs/cigs/ngl1usfl.html

- Bay County Genealogical Society
  http://www.rootsweb.com/~flbay/genealogical.htm
  Panama City, Florida

- Central Florida Computer Society
  http://www.cfcs.org/

- Central Florida Genealogical Society ~ Orlando
  http://www.geocities.com/Heartland/Ranch/4580/

- Citrus County Genealogical Society ~ Inverness
  http://mh101.infi.net/~crazy1/ccgs.htm

- East Central Florida Genealogical Society Co-op
  http://www.rootsweb.com/~flecfgsc/

- Florida Historical Society
  http://www.florida-historical-soc.org/

- Florida Society Sons of the American Revolution
  http://www.flssar.org/

- Florida State Genealogical Society
  http://www.rootsweb.com/~flsgs/

- Florida State Society Daughters of the American
  Revolution
  http://www.tnn.net/~nerowolf/fssdar.html

- The Genealogical Society of Broward County
  http://www.rootsweb.com/~flgsbc/

- The Huxford Genealogical Society, Inc.
  http://www.planttel.net/~hux/
  Homerville, Georgia. "Covering the Wiregrass Area of South Georgia and North Florida and Eastern U. S."

- Indian River Genealogical Society, Inc.
  http://www.rootsweb.com/~flindigs/
  Vero Beach, Florida

- IOOF Lodge Website Directory—Florida
  http://norm28.hsc.usc.edu/IOOF/USA/Florida/Florida.html
  Independent Order of Odd Fellows and Rebekahs.

- Jacksonville Genealogical Society
  http://users.southeast.net/~jgs/

- Lee County Genealogy Society
  http://www.riversidemarketing.com/lcgs/index.htm

- The Panama Canal Society of Florida, Inc.
  http://w3.one.net/~matthewa/societylink.html

- Pinellas Genealogy Society, Inc.
  http://www.geocities.com/Heartland/Plains/8283/
  Includes a database of 1970–1974 Pinellas County Marriages and Engagements.

- The Sons & Daughters of the Province and Republic
  of West Florida 1763–1810
  http://cust2.iamerica.net/mmoore/sonsdau.htm

- West Florida Genealogical Society
  http://www.rootsweb.com/~flescamb/wfgs.htm

◆ USGenWeb Project

- Florida Genealogy—USGenWeb Project State Page
  http://www.usgenweb.org/fl

- Florida—USGenWeb Archives Table of Contents
  http://www.rootsweb.com/~usgenweb/fl/flfiles.htm

- Florida—USGenWeb FTP Archives
  ftp://ftp.rootsweb.com/pub/usgenweb/fl/

U.S.—GEORGIA—GA
http://www.CyndisList.com/ga.htm

Category Index:

- General Resource Sites
- Government & Cities
- History & Culture
- Libraries, Archives & Museums
- Mailing Lists, Newsgroups & Chat
- Maps, Gazetteers & Geographical Information
- Military
- Newspapers
- People & Families

- Professional Researchers, Volunteers & Other Research Services
- Publications, Software & Supplies
- Queries, Message Boards & Surname Lists
- Records: Census, Cemeteries, Land, Obituaries, Personal, Taxes and Vital
- Religion & Churches
- Societies & Groups
- USGenWeb Project

◆ General Resource Sites

- Everton's Sources of Genealogical Information in Georgia
  http://www.everton.com/usa/ga.htm

- Family Tree Maker's Genealogy "How To" Guide— Georgia
  http://www.familytreemaker.com/00000184.html

- Genealogy Bulletin Board Systems for Georgia
  http://www.genealogy.org/~gbbs/gblga.html

- Genealogy Exchange & Surname Registry— GAGenExchange
  http://www.genexchange.com/ga/index.cfm

- Genealogy Resources on the Internet: Georgia
  http://www-personal.umich.edu/~cgaunt/georgia.html

- Georgia Genealogical Information
  http://www.mindspring.com/~bevr/index.html

- LDS Research Outline for Georgia
  http://www.everton.com/usa/ga-0811b.txt

- Lineages' Genealogy Site: Georgia
  http://www.lineages.com/rooms/usa/state.asp?StateCode=GA

- Paul Hickey's Genealogy Corner
  http://www.ij.net/phickey/
  Covers research in the South Georgia area, with many specific resources for Colquitt County, including cemetery records.

- ROOTS-L United States Resources: Georgia
  http://www.rootsweb.com/roots-l/USA/ga.html
  Comprehensive list of research links, including many to history-related sites.

- Spencer LAIRD's Homepage
  http://www.free.cts.com/crash/s/spencerl/index.html
  Georgia Surnames and Georgia Counties.

◆ Government & Cities

- 50states.com—Georgia State Information Resource
  http://www.50states.com/georgia.htm
  A list of general information for each state, including a list of colleges, state symbols, links to maps, newspapers, and other miscellaneous state information.

- Excite Travel by City.Net—Georgia
  http://www.city.net/countries/united_states/georgia/

- Georgia Online Network—GO
  http://www.state.ga.us/

- North Georgia
  http://ngeorgia.com/

- Official City Web Sites for the State of Georgia
  http://OfficialCitySites.org/georgia.htm

- Yahoo! Get Local...Georgia Cities
  http://dir.yahoo.com/Regional/U_S__States/Georgia/Cities/
  Maps, yellow pages, white pages, newspapers and other local information.

- Yahoo! Get Local...Georgia Counties and Regions
  http://dir.yahoo.com/Regional/U_S__States/Georgia/Counties_and_Regions/
  Maps, yellow pages, white pages, newspapers and other local information.

◆ History & Culture

- A Bitter Peace—The Reconstruction of Georgia
  http://ngeorgia.com/history/recon.shtml

- North Georgia History
  http://ngeorgia.com/history/

- Yahoo!...History...Georgia
  http://dir.yahoo.com/Arts/Humanities/History/Browse_By_Region/U_S__States/Georgia/

◆ Libraries, Archives & Museums

- Atlanta Area Family History Centers
  http://www.mindspring.com/~noahsark/lds-fhc.html

- Cherokee Regional Library, LaFayette, Georgia
  http://www.walker.public.lib.ga.us/

  - The Doris Coulter Hetzler Memorial Georgia
    History & Genealogy Room
    http://www.walker.public.lib.ga.us/ghr/

- Cobb County Public Library, Georgia Room
  http://www.mindspring.com/~bevr/html/cobb.html
  Marietta, Georgia

- Family History Centers—Georgia
  http://www.deseretbook.com/famhis/ga.html

- Family History Centers—Georgia
  http://www.lib.byu.edu/~uvrfhc/centers/georgia.html

- Georgia Department of Archives and History
  http://www.sos.state.ga.us/archives

- Georgia Family History Centers
  http://www.genhomepage.com/FHC/Georgia.html
  A list of addresses, phone numbers and hours of operation from the Genealogy Home Page.

- Georgia Office of Public Library Services
  http://www.gpls.public.lib.ga.us/

- Historical Organizations and Resources in Georgia
  http://www.sos.state.ga.us/archives/GHRAB/Directory/hr1.htm

- HYTELNET—Library Catalogs: USA: Georgia
  http://library.usask.ca/hytelnet/usa/GA.html
  Before you use any of the Telnet links, make note of the user name, password and any other logon information.

- Ladson Genealogical Library
  http://www.mindspring.com/~bevr/html/ladson.html
  Vidalia, Georgia

- NUCMC Listing of Archives and Manuscript
  Repositories in Georgia
  http://lcweb.loc.gov/coll/nucmc/gasites.html
  Links to information about resources other than those held in the Library of Congress.

- Other Georgia Libraries
  http://www.mindspring.com/~bevr/html/other_libraries.html

- Repositories of Primary Sources: Georgia
  http://www.uidaho.edu/special-collections/east1.html#usga
  A list of links to online resources from the Univ. of Idaho Library, Special Collections and Archives.

- University of Georgia Library
  http://www.mindspring.com/~bevr/html/uga.html
  Athens, Georgia

- Washington Memorial Library Genealogical
  and Historical Room
  http://www.mindspring.com/~bevr/html/washington.html
  Macon, Georgia

- webCATS: Library Catalogues on the World Wide
  Web—Georgia
  http://library.usask.ca/hywebcat/states/GA.html

◆ Mailing Lists, Newsgroups & Chat

- Genealogy Resources on the Internet—Georgia
  Mailing Lists
  http://members.aol.com/gfsjohnf/gen_mail_states-ga.html
  Each of the mailing list links below points to this site, wonderfully maintained by John Fuller. Visit this site for county-specific mailing lists as well.

- Appalachianfamily Mailing List
  http://members.aol.com/gfsjohnf/gen_mail_states-va.
  html#Appalachianfamily
  Appalachian Mountain Families including families from Georgia, North Carolina, South Carolina, Tennessee, Kentucky, Virginia, and West Virginia.

- CAMDEN Mailing List
  http://members.aol.com/gfsjohnf/gen_mail_states-ga.
  html#CAMDEN
  A mailing list for anyone with a genealogical or historical interest in Camden and Charlton Counties, Georgia (also includes Cumberland Island).

- DEEP-SOUTH-ROOTS-L Mailing List
  http://members.aol.com/gfsjohnf/gen_mail_states-ga.
  html#DEEP-SOUTH-ROOTS
  Alabama, Florida, Georgia & Mississippi.

- GA-Rooters Mailing List
  http://members.aol.com/gfsjohnf/gen_mail_states-ga.
  html#GA-Rooters

- GEORGIA Mailing List
  http://members.aol.com/gfsjohnf/gen_mail_states-ga.
  html#GEORGIA

- Melungeon Mailing List
  http://members.aol.com/gfsjohnf/gen_mail_states-gen.
  html#MELUNGEO
  For people conducting Melungeon and/or Appalachian research including Native American, Portuguese, Turkish, Black Dutch, and other unverifiable mixed statements of ancestry or unexplained rumors, with ancestors in TN, KY, VA, NC, SC, GA, AL, WV, and possibly other places.

- RAN-CLAY Mailing List
  http://members.aol.com/gfsjohnf/gen_mail_states-ga.
  html#RAN-CLAY
  For anyone who has an interest in genealogy related to the east-central Alabama counties of Autauga, Bullock, Calhoun, Chambers, Cherokee, Chilton, Clay, Cleburne, Coosa, Elmore, Etowah, Lee, Macon, Montgomery, Randolph, Russell, St.Clair, Shelby, Talladega and Tallapoosa, and the Georgia border counties, all of which was once Indian territory and subject to boundary changes.

◆ Maps, Gazetteers & Geographical Information

- 1895 U.S. Atlas—Georgia
  http://www.LivGenMI.com/1895ga.htm

- American Memory Panoramic Maps 1847–1929—Georgia
  http://lcweb2.loc.gov/cgi-bin/query/S?ammem/gmd:
  @filreq(@field(STATE+georgia)+@field(COLLID+pmmap))
  From the Geography and Map Division, Library of Congress.

- American Memory Railroad Maps 1828–1900—Georgia
  http://memory.loc.gov/cgi-bin/query/S?ammem/gmd:
  @filreq(@field(STATE+georgia)+@field(COLLID+rrmap))
  From the Geography and Map Division, Library of Congress.

- Color Landform Atlas: Georgia
  http://fermi.jhuapl.edu/states/ga_0.html
  Including a map of counties and a map for 1895.

- Excite Maps: Georgia Maps
  http://www.city.net/maps/view/?mapurl=/countries/
  united_states/georgia
  Zoom in on these maps all the way to the street level.

- Colquitt County Ga. Map
  http://www.ij.net/phickey/colquitt.htm
  Including church locations.

- Georgia County Boundries 1850
  http://www.ij.net/phickey/1850map.htm

- Georgia County Boundries 1860
  http://www.ij.net/phickey/1860map.htm

- Georgia County Boundries 1870
  http://www.ij.net/phickey/1870map.htm

- Georgia County Boundries 1880–1900
  http://www.ij.net/phickey/1880map.htm

- Georgia County Boundries 1910
  http://www.ij.net/phickey/1910map.htm

- HPI County InfoSystem—Counties in Georgia
  http://www.com/hpi/gacty/index.html

- K.B. Slocum Books and Maps—Georgia
  http://www.treasurenet.com/cgi-bin/treasure/kbslocum/scan/
  se=Georgia/sf=mapstate

- List of Georgia Counties
  http://www.genealogy.org/~st-clair/counties/state_ga.html

- Map of Georgia Counties, Map #1
  http://govinfo.kerr.orst.edu/gif/states/ga.gif

  Map of Region 1
  http://govinfo.kerr.orst.edu/gif/states/ga1.gif

  Map of Region 2
  http://govinfo.kerr.orst.edu/gif/states/ga2.gif
  From the Government Information Sharing Project, Information Services, Oregon State University.

- Map of Georgia Counties
  http://www.lib.utexas.edu/Libs/PCL/Map_collection/states/
  Georgia.gif
  From the Perry-Castañeda Library at the Univ. of Texas at Austin.

- Rare Map Collection at the Hargrett Library, University of Georgia
  http://www.libs.uga.edu/darchive/hargrett/maps/maps.html

- U.S. Census Bureau—Georgia Profiles
  http://www.census.gov/datamap/www/13.html

- Yale Peabody Museum: GNIS—Georgia
  http://www.peabody.yale.edu/other/gnis/GA.html
  *Search the USGS Geographic Names Database. You can limit the search to a specific county in this state and search for any of the following features: airport arch area arroyo bar basin bay beach bench bend bridge **building** canal cape **cemetery** channel **church** cliff crater crossing dam falls flat forest gap geyser glacier gut harbor hospital island isthmus lake lava levee locale mine oilfield other park pillar plain ppl range rapids reserve reservoir ridge **school** sea slope spring stream summit swamp tower trail tunnel valley well woods.*

◆ Military

- The 19th Georgia Regimental History
  http://www.fred.net/stevent/19GA/19ga.html

- 50th Regiment Georgia Volunteer Infantry Army of Northern Virginia, C.S.A.
  http://www.ij.net/phickey/50.htm
  Colquitt County, Georgia, Colquitt Marksmen or Colquitt Volunteers.

- The Blue and Gray Trail—The Civil War in North Georgia and Chattanooga
  http://ngeorgia.com/travel/bgtrail.html

- The Civil War Archive—Union Regiments—Georgia
  http://www.civilwararchive.com/unionga.htm

- Civil War Battle Summaries by State—Georgia
  http://www2.cr.nps.gov/abpp/battles/bystate.htm#ga

- Co. B, 11th Battalion Georgia Volunteer Artillery Americus, GA.
  http://www.ij.net/phickey/ga11.htm
  Known as "Cutts Battalion," Sumter Flying Artillery.

- Colquitt's Brigade
  http://extlab1.entnem.ufl.edu/olustee/colquitt.html
  Sixth Georgia Infantry.

- Company G, 8th Georgia Regiment, C.S.A.
  http://www.mindspring.com/~jtfleming/CoG_1.htm
  History of Company G, 8th Georgia Regiment, C.S.A. ("The Pulaski Volunteers"), by David Green Fleming," originally published in the summer of 1879.

- Francis Marion Gay, Co. F 65th Reg. Georgia Infantry
  http://www.izzy.net/~michaelg/fm-gay.htm
  Including the Muster Roll for Co. F, 65th Regiment Georgia Volunteer Infantry Army of Tennessee, C.S.A.

- First Georgia Regulars
  http://extlab1.entnem.ufl.edu/olustee/1st_GA_regulars.html

- Georgia Confederate Pension Applications—State of Georgia Department of Archives & History
http://docuweb.gsu.edu/scripts/ColBrows.dll?
CollectionContent&915703266-3&MainCollection\\Open+
Collections+-\\Georgia+Civil+War+Pension+Records
"The purpose of this community service project is to digitize the microfilm associated with the pension applications of Georgia's Confederate soldiers and their widows."

- Georgia 15th Infantry Regiment
http://members.aol.com/lissiet/15thcamp.htm

- Georgia 49th Infantry Regiment
http://members.aol.com/lissiet/49thcamp.htm

- Georgia Military Records
http://www.rootsweb.com/~gagenweb/records/military.htm

- Harrison's Brigade
http://extlab1.entnem.ufl.edu/olustee/harrison.html

- History of the 3rd Georgia Volunteer Infantry
http://www.forttejon.org/ga3/ga3history.html

- Korean Conflict State-Level Casualty Lists—Georgia
http://www.nara.gov/nara/electronic/gahrlist.html
From the National Archives and Records Administration, Center for Electronic Records.

- Muster Roll of Company B, 51st Regiment Georgia Volunteer Infantry
http://www.ij.net/phickey/51.htm

- Nineteenth Georgia Infantry
http://extlab1.entnem.ufl.edu/olustee/19th_GA_inf.html

- Roster of Confederate Soldiers In Colquitt County, Georgia
http://www.ij.net/phickey/colconfed.htm

- Sixth Georgia Infantry
http://extlab1.entnem.ufl.edu/olustee/6th_GA_inf.html

- Sixty-fourth Georgia Infantry Regiment
http://extlab1.entnem.ufl.edu/olustee/64th_GA_inf.html

- Thirty-second Georgia Infantry
http://extlab1.entnem.ufl.edu/olustee/32nd_GA_inf.html

- Twenty-eighth Battalion, Georgia Siege Artillery
http://extlab1.entnem.ufl.edu/olustee/28th_GA_art.html

- Twenty-eighth Georgia Infantry
http://extlab1.entnem.ufl.edu/olustee/28th_GA_inf.html

- Twenty-seventh Georgia Infantry
http://extlab1.entnem.ufl.edu/olustee/27th_GA_inf.html

- Twenty-third Georgia Infantry
http://extlab1.entnem.ufl.edu/olustee/23rd_GA_inf.html

- Vietnam Conflict State-Level Casualty Lists—Georgia
http://www.nara.gov/nara/electronic/gahrviet.html
From the National Archives and Records Administration, Center for Electronic Records.

- The Vietnam Veterans Memorial—Georgia
http://grunt.space.swri.edu/statewall/georgia/ga.htm

◆ Newspapers

- AJR NewsLink—Georgia Newspapers
http://www.newslink.org/ganews.html

- The Atlanta Journal-Constitution
http://www.accessatlanta.com/ajc/

- E&P Media Info Links—Newspaper Sites in Georgia
http://www.mediainfo.com/emedia/browse-results.
htm?region=georgia&category=newspaper+++++++++

- Ecola Newstand: Georgia
http://www.ecola.com/news/press/na/us/ga/

- The Georgia Newspaper Project
http://www.libs.uga.edu/darchive/aboutgnp.html

- NAA Hotlinks to Newspapers Online—Georgia
http://www.naa.org/hotlinks/searchResult.asp?param=
GA-Georgia&City=1

- N-Net—Georgia Newspapers
http://www.n-net.com/ga.htm

- The Ultimate Collection of News Links: USA—Georgia
http://www.pppp.net/links/news/USA-GA.html

- Yahoo!...Newspapers...Georgia
http://dir.yahoo.com/News_and_Media/Newspapers/
Browse_By_Region/U_S__States/Georgia/

◆ People & Families

- Tribes and Villages of Georgia
http://hanksville.phast.umass.edu:8000/cultprop/contacts/
tribal/GA.html

- WPA Life Histories from Georgia
http://lcweb2.loc.gov/ammem/wpaintro/gacat.html
Manuscripts from the Federal Writer's Project, 1936–1940, Library of Congress.

◆ Professional Researchers, Volunteers & Other Research Services

- AL, GA, TN Genealogy Researcher
http://members.aol.com/CindyJ4/algatn.htm

- Board for Certification of Genealogists—Roster of Those Certified—Specializing in Georgia
http://www.genealogy.org/~bcg/rosts_ga.html

- Free GEDCOM Matching Service (Georgia-Lina Historical Society)
E-mail: gedsearch@aol.com
Send GEDCOM or Tiny Tafel by e-mail.

- Genealogy Helplist—Georgia
  http://www.geocities.com/Heartland/Plains/9829/Ga.html
- Georgia Genealogy Research Services
  http://LeeGenealogy.ofamerica.com/garesh.htm
- Henry's Genealogy Services
  http://home.earthlink.net/~hgrs/
  Augusta, Georgia. "Genealogy research of all kinds at reasonable rates."
- The Official Iowa Counties Professional Genealogist and Researcher's Registry for Georgia
  http://www.iowa-counties.com/gene/ga.htm
- Professional Genealogist for Georgia— Shannon Wilson
  http://genealogypro.com/swilson.html

◆ Publications, Software & Supplies

- AncestorSpy—CDs and Microfiche for Georgia
  http://www.ancestorspy.com/ga.htm
- Barbara Green's Used Genealogy Books—Georgia
  http://home.earthlink.net/~genbooks/lochist.html#GA
- Barnette's Family Tree Books—Georgia
  http://www.barnettesbooks.com/georgia.htm
- Books We Own—Georgia
  http://www.rootsweb.com/~bwo/georgia.html
- Boyd Publishing Company—Georgia
  http://www.hom.net/~gac/georgia.htm
- Frontier Press Bookstore—Georgia
  http://www.frontierpress.com/frontier.cgi?category=ga
- GenealogyBookShop.com—Georgia
  http://www.genealogybookshop.com/genealogybookshop/files/The_United_States,Georgia/index.html
  The online store of Genealogical Publishing Co., Inc. & Clearfield Company.
- Genealogy—Warren County, Georgia
  http://www.Thomson.net/land/wcgagen.htm
  Two books for sale: Cemeteries & Genealogy Warren County, Georgia and Immediate Vicinity 1792–1987 and Warren County, Georgia 1793–1900 Genealogy II.
- Georgia Research Helper
  http://www.genealogy-books.com/research.htm
  A Newsletter published quarterly.
- Hearthstone Bookshop—Georgia
  http://www.hearthstonebooks.com/cgi-bin/webc.cgi/st_main.html?catid=77&sid=2PH5t29sm
- Heritage Books—Georgia
  http://www.heritagebooks.com/ga.htm
- Heritage Quest—Microfilm Records for the State of Georgia
  http://www.heritagequest.com/genealogy/microfilm/georgia/

- J & W Enterprises
  http://www.dhc.net/~jw/
  One stop book source on the Internet, specializing in southern states source material.
- Lost in Time Books—Georgia
  http://www.lostintime.com/catalog/books/bookst/bo08000.htm
- The Memorabilia Corner Books—Georgia
  http://members.aol.com/TMCorner/book_ga.htm
- The Memorabilia Corner Census View CDs— Georgia
  http://members.aol.com/TMCorner/cen_ga.htm
- Picton Press—Georgia
  http://www.midcoast.com/~picton/public_html.BASK/catalog/state_ga.htm
- S-K Publications—Georgia 1820–1850 Census Books
  http://www.skpub.com/genie/census/ga/
- Southern Queries Genealogy Magazine
  http://www.mindspring.com/~freedom1/sq/sq.htm
- Willow Bend Bookstore—Georgia
  http://www.willowbend.net/ga.htm

◆ Queries, Message Boards & Surname Lists

- GenConnect Georgia Visitor Center
  http://cgi.rootsweb.com/~genbbs/indx/Ga.html
  A system for posting queries, Bibles, biographies, deeds, obituaries, pensions, wills.

◆ Records: Census, Cemeteries, Land, Obituaries, Personal, Taxes and Vital (Born, Married, Died & Buried)

- The 1790–1890 Federal Population Censuses: Catalog of National Archives Microfilm
  http://www.genealogy.org/census/contents.shtml
  - Census Schedules and Microfilm Roll Numbers for Georgia:
    1820
    http://www.genealogy.org/census/1820_schedules/Georgia.html
    1830
    http://www.genealogy.org/census/1830_schedules/Georgia.html
    1840
    http://www.genealogy.org/census/1840_schedules/Georgia.html
    1850
    http://www.genealogy.org/census/1850_schedules/Georgia.html

1860
http://www.genealogy.org/census/1860_schedules/
Georgia.html

1870
http://www.genealogy.org/census/1870_schedules/
Georgia.html

1880
http://www.genealogy.org/census/1880_schedules/
Georgia.html

1880 Soundex
http://www.genealogy.org/census/1880.sdx_schedules/
T744.html

- 1840 Lowndes County Georgia Federal Census Index
  http://www.ij.net/phickey/1840cens.htm

- 1850 Lowndes County Georgia Federal Census Index
  http://www.ij.net/phickey/1850cens.htm

- 1850 Federal Census—Clinch County, Georgia
  http://www.rootsweb.com/~gaechols/echclcen.html

- Buck Creek Cemetery, Colquitt County, Georgia
  http://www.ij.net/phickey/buckck.htm

- Camden and Charlton County Cemetery Records Online
  http://www.gate.net/~tutcher/cemetery/ceme_index.html

- Cemeteries of the United States—Georgia Cemeteries—County Index
  http://www.gac.edu/~kengelha/uscemeteries/georgia.html

- Census Online—Links to Census Sites on the Web—Georgia
  http://www.census-online.com/links/GA_data.html

- County Courthouse Addresses
  http://www.familytreemaker.com/00000239.html

- Deeds, Homestead Records and Store Accounts in Georgia
  http://www.rootsweb.com/~gagenweb/records/dhrsa.htm

- Find-A-Grave by Location: Georgia
  http://www.findagrave.com/grave/lga.html
  Graves of noteworthy people.

- Freedmen's Bureau Records—Georgia
  http://www.freedmensbureau.com/georgia/index.htm

- Georgia Confederate Pension Applications—State of Georgia Department of Archives & History
  http://docuweb.gsu.edu/scripts/
  ColBrows.dll?CollectionContent&915703266-
  3&MainCollection\\Open+Collections+-
  \\Georgia+Civil+War+Pension+Records
  "The purpose of this community service project is to digitize the microfilm associated with the pension applications of Georgia's Confederate soldiers and their widows."

- Georgia Vital Records Information
  http://vitalrec.com/ga.html

- Ground Work Genealogy on the Internet: Georgia
  http://members.aol.com/ssmadonna/ga.htm

- Interment.net: Georgia Cemeteries
  http://www.interment.net/us/ga/index.htm
  A list of links to other sites.

- Linwood Cemetery, Columbus, Georgia
  http://members.aol.com/CGAutry/linwood.html

- National Archives—Southeast Region (Atlanta)
  http://www.nara.gov/regional/atlanta.html

- National Archives—Southeast Region from Family Tree Maker
  http://www.familytreemaker.com/00000104.html
  Records for Alabama, Florida, Georgia, Kentucky, Mississippi, North Carolina, South Carolina, and Tennessee.

- North East Florida & Some South East George Counties—Listing of Over 300 Cemeteries.
  E-mail: cmobley@magicnet.net
  Georgia counties include: Charlton, Brantley & Pierce and (one in Echols Co). Send e-mail to Carl Mobley, with SPECIFIC given names & surnames and he will do a lookup for you.

- Some South Georgia Marriage Records
  http://www.ij.net/phickey/marriage.htm

- The Political Graveyard—Cemeteries in Georgia
  http://politicalgraveyard.com/geo/GA/kmindex.html

- Preplanning Network—Funeral Home and Cemetery Directory—Georgia
  http://www.preplannet.com/georgiafhcem.htm

- Tattnall County, Georgia Marriage Records 1805–1845
  http://www.teesee.com/marriage/tattnall/marriage1.htm

- Tombstone Transcription Project
  http://www.angelfire.com/va/dullesgirl/index.html
  Ozora Baptist Church Cemetery, Grayson, Gwinnett County, GA.

- USGenWeb Census Project Georgia
  http://www.usgenweb.org/census/states/georgia/georgia.htm

- USGenWeb Tombstone Transcription Project—Georgia
  http://www.rootsweb.com/~cemetery/georgia.html

- VitalChek Network—Georgia
  http://www.vitalchek.com/stateselect.asp?state=GA

- Where to Write for Vital Records—Georgia
  http://www.cdc.gov/nchswww/howto/w2w/georgia.htm
  From the National Center for Health Statistics (NCHS).

◆ Religion & Churches

- Christianity.Net Church Locator—Georgia
  http://www.christianity.net/cgi/location.exe?
  United_States+Georgia

- Church Online!—Georgia
  http://www.churchonline.com/usas/ga/ga.html

- Church Profiles—Georgia
  http://www.church-profiles.com/ga/ga.html

- Churches dot Net—Global Church Web Pages—
  Georgia
  http://www.churches.net/churches/georgia.html

- Churches of the World—Georgia
  http://www.churchsurf.com/churches/Georgia/index.htm
  From the ChurchSurf Christian Directory.

◆ Societies & Groups

- Archer's Computer Interest Group List—Georgia
  http://www.genealogy.org/~ngs/cigs/ngl1usga.html

- Augusta Genealogical Society
  http://interoz.com/ags/

- Burke County Genealogical Society
  http://members.aol.com/J2525/gen.htm
  Waynesboro, Georgia

- GCSGA—Genealogical Computer Society of GA
  http://members.xoom.com/gcsga/
  Atlanta, Georgia

- Genealogical Computer Society of Georgia
  http://www.mindspring.com/~noahsark/gcsga.html

- Georgia Genealogical Society
  http://www.america.net/~ggs/index.html

- The Georgia Historical Society
  http://www.savannah-online.com/ghs/

- The Georgia Salzburger Society
  http://www.msstate.edu/Archives/History/salzb/

- Georgia State Society Daughters of the American
  Revolution
  http://www.geocities.com/Heartland/Ridge/4935/

- The Grand Lodge of Free and Accepted Masons for
  the State of Georgia
  http://www.glofga.org/

- Historical Organizations and Resources in Georgia
  http://www.sos.state.ga.us/archives/GHRAB/Directory/hr1.htm

- The Huxford Genealogical Society, Inc.
  http://www.planttel.net/~hux/
  *Homerville, Georgia. "Covering the Wiregrass Area of South
  Georgia and North Florida and Eastern U. S."*

- IOOF Lodge Website Directory—Georgia
  http://norm28.hsc.usc.edu/IOOF/USA/Georgia/Georgia.html
  Independent Order of Odd Fellows and Rebekahs.

- Marble Valley Historical Society
  http://www.ngeorgia.com/mvhs.html

- Northwest Georgia Historical & Genealogical
  Society
  http://www.rootsweb.com/~ganwhags/
  *In Rome, Georgia. Covering these counties: Bartow/Cass,
  Carroll, Catoosa, Cherokee, Cobb, Dade, Dawson, Douglas,
  Fannin, Floyd, Forsyth, Gilmer, Gordon, Hall, Habersham,
  Haralson, Lumpkin, Murray, Paulding, Pickens, Polk, Rabun,
  Towns, Union, Walker, White, Whitfield.*

- Roswell Historical Society
  http://www.ethom.com/roswell/histmone.htm

- Savannah River Valley Genealogical Society ~
  Hartwell
  http://www.srvgs.org/

- Southwest Georgia Genealogical Society
  http://www.geocities.com/Heartland/Meadows/7746/swggs/
  *Albany, Georgia. For these counties: Baker, Ben Hill, Calhoun,
  Clay, Colquitt, Crisp, Decatur, Dooly, Dougherty, Early, Grady,
  Irwin, Lee, Marion, Miller, Mitchell, Quitman, Randolph, Schley,
  Seminole, Stewart, Sumter, Terrell, Thomas, Tift, Turner, Webster,
  Wilcox, Worth.*

- Taylor County Genealogical Societies
  http://www.rootsweb.com/~gataylor/taygen.htm

- Union County Historical Society
  http://www.ngeorgia.com/uchs.html

◆ USGenWeb Project

- Georgia Genealogy—USGenWeb Project State Page
  http://www.usgenweb.org/ga

- Georgia—USGenWeb Archives Table of Contents
  http://www.rootsweb.com/~usgenweb/ga/gafiles.htm

- Georgia—USGenWeb FTP Archives
  ftp://ftp.rootsweb.com/pub/usgenweb/ga/

U.S.—HAWAII—HI
http://www.CyndisList.com/hi.htm

Category Index:

- General Resource Sites
- Government & Cities
- History & Culture
- Libraries, Archives & Museums
- Mailing Lists, Newsgroups & Chat
- Maps, Gazetteers & Geographical Information
- Military
- Newspapers
- People & Families

- Professional Researchers, Volunteers & Other Research Services
- Publications, Software & Supplies
- Queries, Message Boards & Surname Lists
- Records: Census, Cemeteries, Land, Obituaries, Personal, Taxes and Vital
- Religion & Churches
- Societies & Groups
- USGenWeb Project

◆ General Resource Sites

- Everton's Sources of Genealogical Information in Hawaii
  http://www.everton.com/usa/hi.htm
- Family Tree Maker's Genealogy "How To" Guide—Hawaii
  http://www.familytreemaker.com/00000185.html
- Genealogical Research
  http://www.hawaii.gov/health/vr_gene.htm
- Genealogical Resources In Hawaii
  http://www.hpcug.org/resource.htm
- Genealogy Exchange & Surname Registry—HIGenExchange
  http://www.genexchange.com/hi/index.cfm
- Genealogy Resources on the Internet: Hawaii
  http://www-personal.umich.edu/~cgaunt/hawaii.html
- LDS Research Outline for Hawaii
  http://www.everton.com/usa/hi-0812B.txt
- Lineages' Genealogy Site: Hawaii
  http://www.lineages.com/rooms/usa/state.asp?StateCode=HI
- ROOTS-L United States Resources: Hawaii
  http://www.rootsweb.com/roots-l/USA/hi.html
  Comprehensive list of research links, including many to history-related sites.

◆ Government & Cities

- 50states.com—Hawaii State Information Resource
  http://www.50states.com/hawaii.htm
  A list of general information for each state, including a list of colleges, state symbols, links to maps, newspapers, and other miscellaneous state information.

- Excite Travel by City.Net—Hawaii
  http://www.city.net/countries/united_states/hawaii/
- Hawaii State Government
  http://www.hawaii.gov/
- Hawaii's WWW Home Page
  http://www.hawaii.net/cgi-bin/hhp?
- Official City Web Sites for the State of Hawaii
  http://OfficialCitySites.org/hawaii.htm
- Yahoo! Get Local...Hawaii Cities
  http://dir.yahoo.com/Regional/U_S__States/Hawaii/Cities/
  Maps, yellow pages, white pages, newspapers and other local information.
- Yahoo! Get Local...Hawaii Counties and Regions
  http://dir.yahoo.com/Regional/U_S__States/Hawaii/Counties_and_Regions/
  Maps, yellow pages, white pages, newspapers and other local information.

◆ History & Culture

- Yahoo!...History: Exploration: Cook, James (1728–1779)
  http://dir.yahoo.com/Arts/Humanities/History/Exploration/Cook__James__1728_1779_/
  Dozens of links about this famous explorer.
- Yahoo!...History...Hawaii
  http://dir.yahoo.com/Arts/Humanities/History/Browse_By_Region/U_S__States/Hawaii/

◆ Libraries, Archives & Museums

- Family History Centers—Hawaii
  http://www.deseretbook.com/famhis/hi.html

- Family History Centers—Hawaii
  http://www.lib.byu.edu/~uvrfhc/centers/hawaii.html
- Hawaii State Archives
  http://www.state.hi.us/dags/archives/
- Hawaii State Public Library System
  http://www.hcc.hawaii.edu/hspls/
  Guide to Resources and Services.
- HYTELNET—Library Catalogs: USA: Hawaii
  http://library.usask.ca/hytelnet/usa/HI.html
  Before you use any of the Telnet links, make note of the user name, password and any other logon information.
- NUCMC Listing of Archives and Manuscript Repositories in Hawaii
  http://lcweb.loc.gov/coll/nucmc/hisites.html
  Links to information about resources other than those held in the Library of Congress.
- Repositories of Primary Sources: Hawaii
  http://www.uidaho.edu/special-collections/west.html#ushi
  A list of links to online resources from the Univ. of Idaho Library, Special Collections and Archives.
- University of Hawai'i at Manoa Library
  http://www2.hawaii.edu/lib/
  - Special Collections
    http://www2.hawaii.edu/~speccoll/
    - Hawaii War Records Depository
      http://www2.hawaii.edu/~speccoll/hwrd/
    - University of Hawaii Archives
      http://www2.hawaii.edu/~speccoll/arch/
- webCATS: Library Catalogues on the World Wide Web—Hawaii
  http://library.usask.ca/hywebcat/states/HI.html

◆ Mailing Lists, Newsgroups & Chat

- Genealogy Resources on the Internet—Hawaii Mailing Lists
  http://members.aol.com/gfsjohnf/gen_mail_states-hi.html
  Each of the mailing list links below points to this site, wonderfully maintained by John Fuller.
- HAWAII Mailing List
  http://members.aol.com/gfsjohnf/gen_mail_states-hi.html#HAWAII
- WESTERN-ROOTS-L Mailing list
  http://members.aol.com/gfsjohnf/gen_mail_states-hi.html#WESTERN-ROOTS-L
  Washington, Oregon, Alaska, Idaho, Montana, Wyoming, California, Nevada, Hawaii, Colorado, Utah, Arizona, and New Mexico.

◆ Maps, Gazetteers & Geographical Information

- American Memory Railroad Maps 1828–1900—Hawaii
  http://memory.loc.gov/cgi-bin/query/S?ammem/gmd:@filreq(@field(STATE+hawaii)+@field(COLLID+rrmap))
  From the Geography and Map Division, Library of Congress.
- Color Landform Atlas: Hawaii
  http://fermi.jhuapl.edu/states/hi_0.html
  Including a map of counties and a map for 1895.
- Excite Maps: Hawaii Maps
  http://www.city.net/maps/view/?mapurl=/countries/united_states/hawaii
  Zoom in on these maps all the way to the street level.
- HPI County InfoSystem—Counties in Hawaii
  http://www.com/hpi/hicty/index.html
- K.B. Slocum Books and Maps—Hawaii
  http://www.treasurenet.com/cgi-bin/treasure/kbslocum/scan/se=Hawaii/sf=mapstate
- List of Hawaii Counties
  http://www.genealogy.org/~st-clair/counties/state_ha.html
- Map of Hawaii Counties
  http://govinfo.kerr.orst.edu/gif/states/hi.gif
  From the Government Information Sharing Project, Information Services, Oregon State University.
- Map of Hawaii Counties
  http://www.lib.utexas.edu/Libs/PCL/Map_collection/states/Hawaii.gif
  From the Perry-Castañeda Library at the Univ. of Texas at Austin.
- U.S. Census Bureau—Hawaii Profiles
  http://www.census.gov/datamap/www/15.html
- Yale Peabody Museum: GNIS—Hawaii
  http://www.peabody.yale.edu/other/gnis/HI.html
  Search the USGS Geographic Names Database. You can limit the search to a specific county in this state and search for any of the following features: airport arch area arroyo bar basin bay beach bench bend bridge **building** *canal cape* **cemetery** *channel* **church** *cliff crater crossing dam falls flat forest gap geyser glacier gut harbor hospital island isthmus lake lava levee locale mine oilfield other park pillar plain ppl range rapids reserve reservoir ridge* **school** *sea slope spring stream summit swamp tower trail tunnel valley well woods.*

◆ Military

- First Visit by a US Naval Vessel to Hawaii, 1826—"The Battle of Honolulu"
  ftp://ftp.rootsweb.com/pub/usgenweb/hi/history/dolphin.txt
- Korean Conflict State-Level Casualty Lists—Hawaii
  http://www.nara.gov/nara/electronic/hihrlist.html
  From the National Archives and Records Administration, Center for Electronic Records.

- Pearl Harbor Casualties List
  http://www.mit.edu:8001/afs/athena/activity/a/afrotc/www/names
- Pearl Harbor Casualties (U.S.)
  http://www.lineages.com/military/PearlHarbor.asp
  Searchable database from Lineages, Inc.
- Pearl Harbor—Civilian and Military Personnel Casualties
  ftp://ftp.rootsweb.com/pub/usgenweb/hi/military/pearl.txt
- Vietnam Conflict State-Level Casualty Lists—Hawaii
  http://www.nara.gov/nara/electronic/hihrviet.html
  From the National Archives and Records Administration, Center for Electronic Records.
- The Vietnam Veterans Memorial—Hawaii
  http://grunt.space.swri.edu/statewall/hawaii/hi.htm

◆ Newspapers

- AJR NewsLink—Hawaii Newspapers
  http://www.newslink.org/hanews.html
- E&P Media Info Links—Newspaper Sites in Hawaii
  http://www.mediainfo.com/emedia/browse-results.htm?region=hawaii&category=newspaper+++++++++
- Ecola Newstand: Hawaii
  http://www.ecola.com/news/press/na/us/hi/
- NAA Hotlinks to Newspapers Online—Hawaii
  http://www.naa.org/hotlinks/searchResult.asp?param=HI-Hawaii&City=1
- Honolulu Star-Bulletin
  http://www.starbulletin.com/
- N-Net—Hawaii Newspapers
  http://www.n-net.com/hi.htm
- The Ultimate Collection of News Links: USA—Hawaii
  http://www.pppp.net/links/news/USA-HI.html
- Yahoo!...Newspapers...Hawaii
  http://dir.yahoo.com/News_and_Media/Newspapers/Browse_By_Region/U_S__States/Hawaii/

◆ People & Families

- Kua'ali'i Genealogy
  http://hawaii-shopping.com./~sammonet/genealogy.html
- People of Hawaii
  http://hanksville.phast.umass.edu:8000/cultprop/contacts/tribal/HI.html
- Portuguese Immigration to Hawaii, 1878–1913
  ftp://ftp.rootsweb.com/pub/usgenweb/hi/shiplists/portug.txt

◆ Professional Researchers, Volunteers & Other Research Services

- Board for Certification of Genealogists—Roster of Those Certified—Specializing in Hawaii
  http://www.genealogy.org/~bcg/rosts_hi.html
- Genealogy Helplist—Hawaii
  http://www.cybercomm.net/~freddie/helplist/hi.htm
- The Official Iowa Counties Professional Genealogist and Researcher's Registry for Hawaii
  http://www.iowa-counties.com/gene/hi.htm

◆ Publications, Software & Supplies

- Barbara Green's Used Genealogy Books—Hawaii
  http://home.earthlink.net/~genbooks/lochist.html#HI
- Books We Own—Hawaii
  http://www.rootsweb.com/~bwo/hawaii.html
- Frontier Press Bookstore—Hawaii
  http://www.frontierpress.com/frontier.cgi?category=hi
- Heritage Quest—Microfilm Records for the State of Hawaii
  http://www.heritagequest.com/genealogy/microfilm/hawaii/

◆ Queries, Message Boards & Surname Lists

- GenConnect Hawaii Visitor Center
  http://cgi.rootsweb.com/~genbbs/indx/Hi.html
  A system for posting queries, Bibles, biographies, deeds, obituaries, pensions, wills.

◆ Records: Census, Cemeteries, Land, Obituaries, Personal, Taxes and Vital (Born, Married, Died & Buried)

- Cemeteries of the United States—Hawaii Cemeteries—County Index
  http://www.gac.edu/~kengelha/uscemeteries/hawaii.html
- County Courthouse Addresses
  http://www.familytreemaker.com/00000240.html
- Find-A-Grave by Location: Hawaii
  http://www.findagrave.com/grave/lhi.html
  Graves of noteworthy people.
- Hawaii Vital Records Information
  http://vitalrec.com/hi.html
- How to Get State of Hawaii Vital Records Information
  http://www.state.hi.us/health/vr_howto.htm

- National Archives—Pacific Region (San Bruno)
  http://www.nara.gov/regional/sanfranc.html
- National Archives—Pacific Sierra Region
  http://www.familytreemaker.com/00000101.html
  Records for Northern California, Hawaii, Nevada (except Clark County), the Pacific Trust Territories, and American Samoa.
- The Political Graveyard—Cemeteries in Hawaii
  http://politicalgraveyard.com/geo/HI/kmindex.html
- USGenWeb Census Project Hawaii
  http://www.usgenweb.org/census/states/hawaii.htm
- USGenWeb Tombstone Transcription Project—Hawaii
  http://www.rootsweb.com/~cemetery/hawaii.html
- VitalChek Network—Hawaii
  http://www.vitalchek.com/stateselect.asp?state=HI
- Where to Write for Vital Records—Hawaii
  http://www.cdc.gov/nchswww/howto/w2w/hawaii.htm
  From the National Center for Health Statistics (NCHS).

◆ Religion & Churches

- Christianity.Net Church Locator—Hawaii
  http://www.christianity.net/cgi/location.exe?United_States+Hawaii
- Church Online!—Hawaii
  http://www.churchonline.com/usas/hi/hi.html
- Church Profiles—Hawaii
  http://www.church-profiles.com/hi/hi.html
- Churches of the World—Hawaii
  http://www.churchsurf.com/churches/Hawaii/index.htm
  From the ChurchSurf Christian Directory.

◆ Societies & Groups

- Archer's Computer Interest Group List—Hawaii
  http://www.genealogy.org/~ngs/cigs/ngl1ushi.html
- The Grand Lodge of Free and Accepted Masons of the State of Hawaii
  http://www.pixi.com/~masonsgl/
- Hawaii Portuguese Genealogical Society
  http://www.lusaweb.com/pgsh.htm
- The Hawaiian Historical Society
  http://www.hawaiianhistory.org/
- IOOF Lodge Website Directory—Hawaii
  http://norm28.hsc.usc.edu/IOOF/USA/Hawaii/Hawaii.html
  Independent Order of Odd Fellows and Rebekahs.
- Kona Historical Society
  http://lehua.ilhawaii.net/~khs/
- Maui Historical Society
  http://mauigateway.com/~lmctrigg/
- National Society Daughters of the American Revolution Hawai'i Chapter
  http://www.hpcug.org/hi-dar.html
- Sandwich Islands Genealogical Society
  http://www.hpcug.org/sandils.htm

◆ USGenWeb Project

- Hawaii Genealogy—USGenWeb Project State Page
  http://www.usgenweb.org/hi
- Hawaii—USGenWeb Archives Table of Contents
  http://www.rootsweb.com/~usgenweb/hi/hifiles.htm
- Hawaii—USGenWeb FTP Archives
  ftp://ftp.rootsweb.com/pub/usgenweb/hi/

U.S.—IDAHO—ID
http://www.CyndisList.com/id.htm

Category Index:

- General Resource Sites
- Government & Cities
- History & Culture
- Libraries, Archives & Museums
- Mailing Lists, Newsgroups & Chat
- Maps, Gazetteers & Geographical Information
- Military
- Newspapers
- People & Families

- Professional Researchers, Volunteers & Other Research Services
- Publications, Software & Supplies
- Queries, Message Boards & Surname Lists
- Records: Census, Cemeteries, Land, Obituaries, Personal, Taxes and Vital
- Religion & Churches
- Societies & Groups
- USGenWeb Project

◆ General Resource Sites

- Donovan's Genealogy Idaho
  http://home.rmci.net/dyingst/index.htm
- Everton's Sources of Genealogical Information in Idaho
  http://www.everton.com/usa/id.htm
- Family Tree Maker's Genealogy "How To" Guide—Idaho
  http://www.familytreemaker.com/00000186.html
- Genealogy Exchange & Surname Registry—IDGenExchange
  http://www.genexchange.com/id/index.cfm
- Genealogy Resources on the Internet: Idaho
  http://www-personal.umich.edu/~cgaunt/idaho.html
- LDS Research Outline for Idaho
  http://www.everton.com/usa/id-0813B.txt
- Lineages' Genealogy Site: Idaho
  http://www.lineages.com/rooms/usa/state.asp?StateCode=ID
- ROOTS-L United States Resources: Idaho
  http://www.rootsweb.com/roots-l/USA/id.html
  Comprehensive list of research links, including many to history-related sites.

◆ Government & Cities

- 50states.com—Idaho State Information Resource
  http://www.50states.com/idaho.htm
  A list of general information for each state, including a list of colleges, state symbols, links to maps, newspapers, and other miscellaneous state information.
- Excite Travel by City.Net—Idaho
  http://www.city.net/countries/united_states/idaho/

- Official City Web Sites for the State of Idaho
  http://OfficialCitySites.org/idaho.htm
- State of Idaho Home Page
  http://www.state.id.us/
- Yahoo! Get Local...Idaho Cities
  http://dir.yahoo.com/Regional/U_S__States/Idaho/Cities/
  Maps, yellow pages, white pages, newspapers and other local information.
- Yahoo! Get Local...Idaho Counties and Regions
  http://dir.yahoo.com/Regional/U_S__States/Idaho/Counties_and_Regions/
  Maps, yellow pages, white pages, newspapers and other local information.

◆ History & Culture

- Ghost Towns of Idaho
  http://www.ghosttowns.com/states/id/id.html
- A Hundred Years of the History of Idaho
  http://www.rootsweb.com/~idlemhi/history.htm
- Idaho Historical Railroads
  http://members.aol.com/idahorail/ihr_main.htm
- Idaho State Historical Society—Historic Sites
  http://www2.state.id.us/ishs/Sites.html
- Mountain Men and the Fur Trade
  http://www.xmission.com/~drudy/amm.html
  Sources of the History of the Fur Trade in the Rocky Mountain West.
- Weston Memories
  http://www.vii.com/~nelsonb/weston.htm
- Yahoo!...History...Idaho
  http://dir.yahoo.com/Arts/Humanities/History/Browse_By_Region/U_S__States/Idaho/

◆ Libraries, Archives & Museums

- Family History Centers—Idaho
  http://www.deseretbook.com/famhis/id.html

- Family History Centers—Idaho
  http://www.lib.byu.edu/~uvrfhc/centers/idaho.html

- HYTELNET—Library Catalogs: USA: Idaho
  http://library.usask.ca/hytelnet/usa/ID.html
  Before you use any of the Telnet links, make note of the user name, password and any other logon information.

- Idaho Family History Centers
  http://www.genhomepage.com/FHC/Idaho.html
  A list of addresses, phone numbers and hours of operation from the Genealogy Home Page.

- Idaho State Library
  http://www.lili.org/isl/hp.htm

- NUCMC Listing of Archives and Manuscript Repositories in Idaho
  http://lcweb.loc.gov/coll/nucmc/idsites.html
  Links to information about resources other than those held in the Library of Congress.

- Repositories of Primary Sources: Idaho
  http://www.uidaho.edu/special-collections/west.html#usid
  A list of links to online resources from the Univ. of Idaho Library, Special Collections and Archives.

- Special Collections and Archives at the University of Idaho Library
  http://www.lib.uidaho.edu/special-collections/

- webCATS: Library Catalogues on the World Wide Web—Idaho
  http://library.usask.ca/hywebcat/states/ID.html

◆ Mailing Lists, Newsgroups & Chat

- Genealogy Resources on the Internet—Idaho Mailing Lists
  http://members.aol.com/gfsjohnf/gen_mail_states-id.html
  Each of the mailing list links below point to this site, wonderfully maintained by John Fuller. Visit this site for county-specific mailing lists as well.

- WESTERN-ROOTS-L Mailing list
  http://members.aol.com/gfsjohnf/gen_mail_states-id.html#WESTERN-ROOTS-L
  Washington, Oregon, Alaska, Idaho, Montana, Wyoming, California, Nevada, Hawaii, Colorado, Utah, Arizona, and New Mexico.

◆ Maps, Gazetteers & Geographical Information

- 1895 U.S. Atlas—Idaho
  http://www.LivGenMI.com/1895id.htm

- American Memory Panoramic Maps 1847–1929—Idaho
  http://lcweb2.loc.gov/cgi-bin/query/S?ammem/gmd:@filreq(@field(STATE+idaho)+@field(COLLID+pmmap))
  From the Geography and Map Division, Library of Congress.

- American Memory Railroad Maps 1828–1900—Idaho
  http://memory.loc.gov/cgi-bin/query/S?ammem/gmd:@filreq(@field(STATE+idaho)+@field(COLLID+rrmap))
  From the Geography and Map Division, Library of Congress.

- Color Landform Atlas: Illinois
  http://fermi.jhuapl.edu/states/id_0.html
  Including a map of counties and a map for 1895.

- Excite Maps: Idaho Maps
  http://www.city.net/maps/view/?mapurl=/countries/united_states/idaho
  Zoom in on these maps all the way to the street level.

- HPI County InfoSystem—Counties in Idaho
  http://www.com/hpi/idcty/index.html

- K.B. Slocum Books and Maps—Idaho
  http://www.treasurenet.com/cgi-bin/treasure/kbslocum/scan/se=Idaho/sf=mapstate

- List of Idaho Counties
  http://www.genealogy.org/~st-clair/counties/state_id.html

- Map of Idaho Counties
  http://govinfo.kerr.orst.edu/gif/states/id.gif
  From the Government Information Sharing Project, Information Services, Oregon State University.

- Map of Idaho Counties
  http://www.lib.utexas.edu/Libs/PCL/Map_collection/states/Idaho.gif
  From the Perry-Castañeda Library at the Univ. of Texas at Austin.

- U.S. Census Bureau—Idaho Profiles
  http://www.census.gov/datamap/www/16.html

- Yale Peabody Museum: GNIS—Idaho
  http://www.peabody.yale.edu/other/gnis/ID.html
  Search the USGS Geographic Names Database. You can limit the search to a specific county in this state and search for any of the following features: airport arch area arroyo bar basin bay beach bench bend bridge **building** *canal cape* **cemetery** *channel* **church** *cliff crater crossing dam falls flat forest gap geyser glacier gut harbor hospital island isthmus lake lava levee locale mine oilfield other park pillar plain ppl range rapids reserve reservoir ridge* **school** *sea slope spring stream summit swamp tower trail tunnel valley well woods.*

◆ Military

- Civil War Battle Summaries by State—Idaho
  http://www2.cr.nps.gov/abpp/battles/bystate.htm#id

- Korean Conflict State-Level Casualty Lists—Idaho
  http://www.nara.gov/nara/electronic/idhrlist.html
  From the National Archives and Records Administration, Center for Electronic Records.

- Pacific Northwest Military History and Reenacting Web Site
  http://www.hevanet.com/1860colt/pnwmain.html

- Vietnam Conflict State-Level Casualty Lists—Idaho
  http://www.nara.gov/nara/electronic/idhrviet.html
  From the National Archives and Records Administration, Center for Electronic Records.

- The Vietnam Veterans Memorial—Idaho
  http://grunt.space.swri.edu/statewall/idaho/id.htm

◆ Newspapers

- AJR NewsLink—Idaho Newspapers
  http://www.newslink.org/idnews.html

- E&P Media Info Links—Newspaper Sites in Idaho
  http://www.mediainfo.com/emedia/browse-results.
  htm?region=idaho&category=newspaper+++++++++

- Ecola Newstand: Idaho
  http://www.ecola.com/news/press/na/us/id/

- NAA Hotlinks to Newspapers Online—Idaho
  http://www.naa.org/hotlinks/searchResult.asp?param=
  ID-Idaho&City=1

- N-Net—Idaho Newspapers
  http://www.n-net.com/id.htm

- The Ultimate Collection of News Links:
  USA—Idaho
  http://www.pppp.net/links/news/USA-ID.html

- Yahoo!...Newspapers...Idaho
  http://dir.yahoo.com/News_and_Media/Newspapers/
  Browse_By_Region/U_S__States/Idaho/

◆ People & Families

- Affiliated Tribes of Northwest Indians
  http://www.atni.org/~tribes/
  For Alaska, California, Idaho, Montana, Oregon, Washington.

- Tribes and Villages of Idaho
  http://hanksville.phast.umass.edu:8000/cultprop/contacts/
  tribal/ID.html

◆ Professional Researchers, Volunteers & Other Research Services

- Board for Certification of Genealogists—Roster of
  Those Certified—Specializing in Idaho
  http://www.genealogy.org/~bcg/rosts_id.html

- Genealogy Helplist—Idaho
  http://members.aol.com/DFBradshaw/id.html

- The Official Iowa Counties Professional Genealogist
  and Researcher's Registry for Idaho
  http://www.iowa-counties.com/gene/id.htm

◆ Publications, Software & Supplies

- Barbara Green's Used Genealogy Books—Idaho
  http://home.earthlink.net/~genbooks/lochist.html#ID

- Frontier Press Bookstore—Idaho
  http://www.frontierpress.com/frontier.cgi?category=id

- Heritage Quest—Microfilm Records for the State
  of Idaho
  http://www.heritagequest.com/genealogy/microfilm/idaho/

- The Memorabilia Corner—Books: Idaho
  http://members.aol.com/TMCorner/book_ida.htm

◆ Queries, Message Boards & Surname Lists

- GenConnect Idaho Visitor Center
  http://cgi.rootsweb.com/~genbbs/indx/Id.html
  *A system for posting queries, Bibles, biographies, deeds,
  obituaries, pensions, wills.*

◆ Records: Census, Cemeteries, Land, Obituaries, Personal, Taxes and Vital (Born, Married, Died & Buried)

- The 1790–1890 Federal Population Censuses:
  Catalog of National Archives Microfilm
  http://www.genealogy.org/census/contents.shtml
  - Census Schedules and Microfilm Roll Numbers
    for Idaho:
    1870
    http://www.genealogy.org/census/1870_schedules/
    Idaho.html
    1880
    http://www.genealogy.org/census/1880_schedules/
    Idaho.html
    1880 Soundex
    http://www.genealogy.org/census/1880.sdx_schedules/
    T745.html

- BLM—Idaho Electronic Reading Room
  http://www.blm.gov/nhp/efoia/id/
  United States Bureau of Land Management.

- The Bureau of Land Management—Idaho
  http://www.id.blm.gov/

- Cemeteries of the United States—Idaho
  Cemeteries—County Index
  http://www.gac.edu/~kengelha/uscemeteries/idaho.html

- Census Online—Links to Census Sites on
  the Web—Idaho
  http://www.census-online.com/links/ID_data.html

- County Courthouse Addresses
  http://www.familytreemaker.com/00000241.html

- Find-A-Grave by Location: Idaho
  http://www.findagrave.com/grave/lid.html
  Graves of noteworthy people.

- Genealogical Records in Idaho
  http://www.lib.uidaho.edu/special-collections/genealgl.htm
  From the University of Idaho Library, Special Collections Dept.

- Idaho Vital Records Information
  http://vitalrec.com/id.html

- Interment.net: Idaho Cemeteries
  http://www.interment.net/us/id/index.htm
  A list of links to other sites.

- Kootenai County Cemetery
  http://www.ior.com/~jmakovec/genealogy/kc_cem.htm

- Livestock Brands in Idaho
  http://www.lineages.com/rooms/reading/brands.asp

- National Archives—Pacific Alaska Region (Seattle)
  http://www.nara.gov/regional/seattle.html

- National Archives—Pacific Northwest Region
  http://www.familytreemaker.com/00000100.html
  Records for Idaho, Oregon and Washington.

- Pioneer Cemetery—Horseshoe Bend, Boise County, Idaho
  http://www.rootsquest.com/~idaho/boise/cemhsb.html

- Placerville Cemetery—Boise County, Idaho
  http://www.rootsquest.com/~idaho/boise/cemplacer.html

- The Political Graveyard—Cemeteries in Idaho
  http://politicalgraveyard.com/geo/ID/kmindex.html

- Preplanning Network—Funeral Home and Cemetery Directory—Idaho
  http://www.preplannet.com/idahofhcem.htm

- SAMPUBCO
  http://www.wasatch.com/~dsam/sampubco/index.htm
  Will Testators Indexes, Naturalization Records Indexes and Census Indexes online. You can order copies of the original source documents for a small fee.

- Search Idaho Marriage Record Index
  http://abish.ricks.edu/fhc/gbsearch.asp
  Search engine for marriages in Arizona, Idaho, Nevada, Oregon, Utah 1850–1951.

- USGenWeb Census Project Idaho
  http://www.usgenweb.org/census/states/idaho.htm

- USGenWeb Tombstone Transcription Project—Idaho
  http://www.rootsweb.com/~cemetery/idaho.html

- VitalChek Network—Idaho
  http://www.vitalchek.com/stateselect.asp?state=ID

- Where to Write for Vital Records—Idaho
  http://www.cdc.gov/nchswww/howto/w2w/idaho.htm
  From the National Center for Health Statistics (NCHS).

◆ Religion & Churches

- Christianity.Net Church Locator—Idaho
  http://www.christianity.net/cgi/location.exe?United_States+Idaho

- Church Online!—Idaho
  http://www.churchonline.com/usas/id/id.html

- Church Profiles—Idaho
  http://www.church-profiles.com/id/id.html

- Churches dot Net—Global Church Web Pages—Idaho
  http://www.churches.net/churches/idaho.html

- Churches of the World—Idaho
  http://www.churchsurf.com/churches/Idaho/index.htm
  From the ChurchSurf Christian Directory.

◆ Societies & Groups

- Archer's Computer Interest Group List—Idaho
  http://www.genealogy.org/~ngs/cigs/ngl1usid.html

- Idaho State Historical Society
  http://www2.state.id.us/ishs/index.html
  - Genealogy
    http://www2.state.id.us/ishs/Gen.html

- IOOF Lodge Website Directory—Idaho
  http://norm28.hsc.usc.edu/IOOF/USA/Idaho/Idaho.html
  Independent Order of Odd Fellows and Rebekahs.

- Latah County Historical Society
  http://www.moscow.com/Resources/latahhistory/

◆ USGenWeb Project

- Idaho Genealogy—USGenWeb Project State Page
  http://www.usgenweb.org/id

- Idaho Indian Reservations
  http://www.wsu.edu:8080/~mbsimon/idahoindians/index.html

- Idaho—USGenWeb Archives Table of Contents
  http://www.rootsweb.com/~usgenweb/id/idfiles.htm

- Idaho—USGenWeb FTP Archives
  ftp://ftp.rootsweb.com/pub/usgenweb/id/

- North Idaho Query Page
  http://www.rootsweb.com/~idgenweb/n_idaho.htm

- South Central Idaho Query Page
  http://www.rootsweb.com/~idgenweb/sc_idaho.htm

- Southeast Idaho Query Page
  http://www.rootsweb.com/~idgenweb/se_idaho.htm

U.S.—ILLINOIS—IL
http://www.CyndisList.com/il.htm

Category Index:

- General Resource Sites
- Government & Cities
- History & Culture
- Libraries, Archives & Museums
- Mailing Lists, Newsgroups & Chat
- Maps, Gazetteers & Geographical Information
- Military
- Newspapers
- People & Families

- Professional Researchers, Volunteers & Other Research Services
- Publications, Software & Supplies
- Queries, Message Boards & Surname Lists
- Records: Census, Cemeteries, Land, Obituaries, Personal, Taxes and Vital
- Religion & Churches
- Societies & Groups
- USGenWeb Project

◆ General Resource Sites

- Everton's Sources of Genealogical Information in Illinois
  http://www.everton.com/usa/il.htm

- Family Tree Maker's Genealogy "How To" Guide— Illinois
  http://www.familytreemaker.com/00000187.html

- The Genealogical Institute of Mid-America (GIMA)
  http://www.misslink.net/neill/gima.html

- Genealogy and Family History Research in Illinois
  http://www.outfitters.com/illinois/history/family/

- Genealogy & History in Fulton County, Illinois
  http://www.outfitters.com/illinois/history/family/fulton/fulton.html

- Genealogy Calendar of Upcoming Events—Illinois
  http://genealogy.org/~gcal/gcl1usil.html

- Genealogy Exchange & Surname Registry— ILGenExchange
  http://www.genexchange.com/il/index.cfm

- Genealogy Resources on the Internet: Illinois
  http://www-personal.umich.edu/~cgaunt/illinois.html

- LDS Research Outline for Illinois
  http://www.everton.com/usa/il-0814B.txt

- Lineages' Genealogy Site: Illinois
  http://www.lineages.com/rooms/usa/state.asp?StateCode=IL

- ROOTS-L United States Resources: Illinois
  http://www.rootsweb.com/roots-l/USA/il.html
  Comprehensive list of research links, including many to history-related sites.

◆ Government & Cities

- 50states.com—Illinois State Information Resource
  http://www.50states.com/illinois.htm
  A list of general information for each state, including a list of colleges, state symbols, links to maps, newspapers, and other miscellaneous state information.

- Excite Travel by City.Net—Illinois
  http://www.city.net/countries/united_states/illinois/

- Marrowbone History
  http://www.rootsweb.com/~ilmoult2/marrhist.html
  An index of names from "This WAS Marrowbone (1829–1889)."

- Official City Web Sites for the State of Illinois
  http://OfficialCitySites.org/Illinois.htm

- State of Illinois
  http://www.state.il.us/

- Yahoo! Get Local...Illinois Cities
  http://dir.yahoo.com/Regional/U_S__States/Illinois/Cities/
  Maps, yellow pages, white pages, newspapers and other local information.

- Yahoo! Get Local...Illinois Counties and Regions
  http://dir.yahoo.com/Regional/U_S__States/Illinois/Counties_and_Regions/
  Maps, yellow pages, white pages, newspapers and other local information.

◆ History & Culture

- Chicago Imagebase
  http://www.uic.edu/depts/ahaa/imagebase/
  Find a wealth of information at this site from before the Great Fire of 1871 to the present including the Fire Insurance Maps of Chicago, Robinson Atlases of Downtown Chicago (ca. 1886), Sanborn Atlas Maps, Rand McNally's Bird's-Eye Views and Guide to Chicago (ca. 1893), Historical View Books, and much more! Browse the imagebase collection by artist/architect, building and era. Find information on Using Historical Maps and Dating Buildings by Stylistic Analysis. View contemporary aerial views (ca. 1986) and photographs 1970–1990's of Chicago.

- The Chicago Tunnel Company Railroad
  http://members.aol.com/POKeefe571/tunnel1.html
  Learn all about a 60 mile underground railroad that operated with 146 locomotives and 3000 freight cars 40 feet below the streets of downtown Chicago.

- Illinois History Pages
  http://www.outfitters.com/illinois/history/

- The Illinois History Resource Page
  http://alexia.lis.uiuc.edu/~sorensen/hist.html

- Jon's Southern Illinois History Page
  http://www.midamer.net/users/jonm/index.htm

- Yahoo!...History...Illinois
  http://dir.yahoo.com/Arts/Humanities/History/
  Browse_By_Region/U_S__States/Illinois/

◆ Libraries, Archives & Museums

- Algonquin Area Public Library
  http://www.nslsilus.org/alkhome

- Augustana College Library
  http://www.augustana.edu/library/
  - Augustana College Special Collections
    http://www.augustana.edu/library/special/index.htm
    Including photographs, Civil War diaries, some biographies and more.

- Chicago Historical Society Library
  http://www.chicagohs.org/Collections/LIBRARY.html
  - Genealogical Research
    http://www.chicagohs.org/Collections/GENEALOGICAL.html

- Chicago Public Library
  http://www.chipublib.org/
  - CPL Social Sciences Genealogy
    http://www.chipublib.org/008subject/010ssh/genealogy.html

- Cook Memorial Public Library District
  http://www.cooklib.org/
  Libertyville

- Family History Centers—Illinois
  http://www.deseretbook.com/famhis/il.html

- Family History Centers—Illinois
  http://www.lib.byu.edu/~uvrfhc/centers/illinois.html

- HYTELNET—Library Catalogs: USA: Illinois
  http://library.usask.ca/hytelnet/usa/IL.html
  Before you use any of the Telnet links, make note of the user name, password and any other logon information.

- ILLINET Library Directory
  http://www.library.sos.state.il.us/lib_dir/lib_dir.html

- Illinois Family History Centers
  http://www.genhomepage.com/FHC/Illinois.html
  A list of addresses, phone numbers and hours of operation from the Genealogy Home Page.

- Illinois State Archives
  http://www.sos.state.il.us/depts/archives/arc_home.html

- Illinois State Library
  http://www.sos.state.il.us/depts/library/isl_home.html

- The Newberry Library
  http://www.newberry.org/
  Chicago, Illinois

- North Park University's Library, Archives and Instructional Media
  http://www.northpark.edu/library/
  Chicago
  - Archival Research Collections at North Park College
    http://www.northpark.edu/library/Archives/
    Including information for the Swedish-American Archives of Greater Chicago, the Covenant Archives and Historical Library, and the Archives of the Society for the Advancement of Scandinavian Study.

- North Suburban Library System (NSLS)
  http://www.nslsilus.org/~referenc/

- NUCMC Listing of Archives and Manuscript Repositories in Illinois
  http://lcweb.loc.gov/coll/nucmc/ilsites.html
  Links to information about resources other than those held in the Library of Congress.

- Repositories of Primary Sources: Illinois
  http://www.uidaho.edu/special-collections/east1.html#usil
  A list of links to online resources from the Univ. of Idaho Library, Special Collections and Archives.

- Schaumburg Township District Library
  http://www.stdl.org/

- Swenson Swedish Immigration Research Center
  http://www.augustana.edu/administration/swenson/

- Warren County Library
  http://www.maplecity.com/~wcpl/
  Monmouth, Illinois

- webCATS: Library Catalogues on the World Wide Web—Illinois
  http://library.usask.ca/hywebcat/states/IL.html

◆ Mailing Lists, Newsgroups & Chat

- Genealogy Resources on the Internet—Illinois Mailing Lists
  http://members.aol.com/gfsjohnf/gen_mail_states-il.html
  Each of the mailing list links below points to this site, wonderfully maintained by John Fuller. Visit this site for county-specific mailing lists as well.

- COOK-CO-IL Mailing List
  http://members.aol.com/gfsjohnf/gen_mail_states-il.html#COOK-CO-IL

- IL-CIVIL-WAR Mailing List
  http://members.aol.com/gfsjohnf/gen_mail_states-il.html#IL-CIVIL-WAR
  For Civil War researchers in Illinois.

- ILLINOIS-ROOTS-L Mailing List
  http://members.aol.com/gfsjohnf/gen_mail_states-il.html#ILLINOIS-ROOTS

- ILROOTS Mailing List
  http://members.aol.com/gfsjohnf/gen_mail_states-il.html#ILROOTS

- MadeiraExiles Mailing List
  http://members.aol.com/gfsjohnf/gen_mail_states-il.html#MadeiraExiles
  Devoted to the research of Dr. Robert Reid Kalley's Portuguese Presbyterian exiles from Madeira, Portugal who emigrated to Trinidad and then to Illinois (ca. 1846–1854).

- SOIL Mailing List
  http://members.aol.com/gfsjohnf/gen_mail_states-il.html#SOIL
  For anyone with a genealogical interest in Southern Illinois, from an east-west line running through St. Louis.

◆ Maps, Gazetteers & Geographical Information

- 1895 U.S. Atlas—Illinois
  http://www.LivGenMI.com/1895il.htm

- American Memory Panoramic Maps 1847–1929—Illinois
  http://lcweb2.loc.gov/cgi-bin/query/S?ammem/gmd:@filreq(@field(STATE+illinois)+@field(COLLID+pmmap))
  From the Geography and Map Division, Library of Congress.

- American Memory Railroad Maps 1828–1900—Illinois
  http://memory.loc.gov/cgi-bin/query/S?ammem/gmd:@filreq(@field(STATE+illinois)+@field(COLLID+rrmap))
  From the Geography and Map Division, Library of Congress.

- Color Landform Atlas: Illinois
  http://fermi.jhuapl.edu/states/il_0.html
  Including a map of counties and a map for 1895.

- Excite Maps: Illinois Maps
  http://www.city.net/maps/view/?mapurl=/countries/united_states/illinois
  Zoom in on these maps all the way to the street level.

- Find Illinois County for Specified City
  http://www.outfitters.com/illinois/searchcity.html

- Gleason's Old Maps, Etc.
  http://members.aol.com/oldmapsetc/illinois.html
  Photocopies of Old Maps, Prints and Articles of Historical and Genealogical Interest from Illinois.

- HPI County InfoSystem—Counties in Illinois
  http://www.com/hpi/ilcty/index.html

- K.B. Slocum Books and Maps—Illinois
  http://www.treasurenet.com/cgi-bin/treasure/kbslocum/scan/se=Illinois/sf=mapstate

- List of Iliinois Counties
  http://www.genealogy.org/~st-clair/counties/state_il.html

- Map of Illinois Counties
  http://govinfo.kerr.orst.edu/gif/states/il.gif
  From the Government Information Sharing Project, Information Services, Oregon State University.

- Map of Illinois Counties
  http://www.lib.utexas.edu/Libs/PCL/Map_collection/states/Illinois.gif
  From the Perry-Castañeda Library at the Univ. of Texas at Austin.

- U.S. Census Bureau—Illinois Profiles
  http://www.census.gov/datamap/www/17.html

- Yale Peabody Museum: GNIS—Illinois
  http://www.peabody.yale.edu/other/gnis/IL.html
  *Search the USGS Geographic Names Database. You can limit the search to a specific county in this state and search for any of the following features: airport arch area arroyo bar basin bay beach bench bend bridge **building** canal cape **cemetery** channel **church** cliff crater crossing dam falls flat forest gap geyser glacier gut harbor hospital island isthmus lake lava levee locale mine oilfield other park pillar plain ppl range rapids reserve reservoir ridge **school** sea slope spring stream summit swamp tower trail tunnel valley well woods.*

◆ Military

- 7th Illinois Cavalry
  http://www.outfitters.com/illinois/history/civil/cwc7-agr1.html

- 9th Illinois Cavalry
  http://www.outfitters.com/illinois/history/civil/cwc9.html

- 17th Illinois Infantry
  http://www.outfitters.com/illinois/history/civil/cw17.html

- 55th Illinois Infantry
  http://www.outfitters.com/illinois/history/civil/cw55.html

- 59th Illinois Infantry
  http://www.outfitters.com/illinois/history/civil/cw59.html

- 74th Illinois Infantry
  http://www.outfitters.com/illinois/history/civil/cw74.html

- 75th Illinois Infantry
  http://www.outfitters.com/illinois/history/civil/cw75.html

- Alton in the Civil War
  http://www.altonweb.com/history/civilwar/index.html

- Camp Douglas, Illinois
  http://www.outfitters.com/illinois/history/civil/campdouglas.html
  Prison camp and training camp.

- The Civil War Archive—Union Regiments—Illinois
  http://www.civilwararchive.com/unionil.htm
- Confederate Burials in Mound City National Cemetery
  http://www.outfitters.com/illinois/history/civil/
  cwmoundcitycem.html
- Database of Illinois' Civil War Veterans
  http://www.sos.state.il.us/depts/archives/datcivil.html
  From the Illinois State Archives, this is an index of over 250,000 men in 175 regiments as they are listed in 8 volumes of the Report of the Adjutant General of the State of Illinois, published in 1900–1901.
- History of 48th Illinois Infantry
  http://www.outfitters.com/illinois/history/civil/cw48-hist.html
- History of Ninety-Ninth Infantry
  http://www.outfitters.com/illinois/history/civil/cw99-agr.html
- History of the Seventy-Sixth Illinois Volunteer Infantry Regiment
  http://www.outfitters.com/illinois/history/civil/cw76-hist.html
- Illinois in the Civil War
  http://www.outfitters.com/illinois/history/civil/civil.html
- Illinois in the Civil War
  http://www.rootsweb.com/~ilcivilw/
  A USGenWeb and ILGenWeb project to put rosters online.
- Korean Conflict State-Level Casualty Lists—Illinois
  http://www.nara.gov/nara/electronic/ilhrlist.html
  From the National Archives and Records Administration, Center for Electronic Records.
- Ninety-Ninth Infantry Regiment of Illinois Volunteers, Muster Roll of Company "D"
  http://www.outfitters.com/illinois/history/civil/cw99dndx.html
- Recruitment of Illinois Regiments—Civil War, 1861–1865—County Search
  http://www.outfitters.com/illinois/history/civil/searchco.html
  - Recruitment of Illinois Artillery Regiments— Civil War, 1861–1865
    http://www.outfitters.com/illinois/history/civil/
    searchart.html
  - Recruitment of Illinois Cavalry Regiments— Civil War, 1861–1865
    http://www.outfitters.com/illinois/history/civil/
    searchcav.html
  - Recruitment of Illinois Infantry Regiments— Civil War, 1861–1865
    http://www.outfitters.com/illinois/history/civil/
    searchreg.html
- Seventh Illinois Mounted Infantry, Enlisted Men of Company "H"
  http://members.tripod.com/~rjsnyder/Seventh.htm

- Vietnam Conflict State-Level Casualty Lists— Illinois
  http://www.nara.gov/nara/electronic/ilhrviet.html
  From the National Archives and Records Administration, Center for Electronic Records.
- The Vietnam Veterans Memorial—Illinois
  http://grunt.space.swri.edu/statewall/illinois/il.htm
- War History and Record One Hundred and Twenty-Ninth Illinois Infantry
  http://www.mtco.com/~martisiq/129_il.htm
  Company D—Winchester, Illinois.

◆ Newspapers

- AJR News Link—Illinois Newspapers
  http://www.newslink.org/ilnews.html
- Chicago Newspaper Network
  http://www.chicago-news.com/
  "Your guide to 70 newspapers serving the city and suburbs."
- The Chicago Sun-Times Online
  http://www.suntimes.com/index/
- The Daily Journal
  http://www.daily-journal.com/
  Kankakee, Ilinois
- E&P Media Info Links—Newspaper Sites in Illinois
  http://www.mediainfo.com/emedia/browse-results.
  htm?region=illinois&category=newspaper+++++++++
- Ecola Newstand: Illinois
  http://www.ecola.com/news/press/na/us/il/
- NAA Hotlinks to Newspapers Online—Illinois
  http://www.naa.org/hotlinks/searchResult.asp?param=
  IL-Illinois&City=1
- N-Net—Illinois Newspapers
  http://www.n-net.com/il.htm
- Rockford Register Star
  http://www.rrstar.com/
- The Ultimate Collection of News Links: USA—Illinois
  http://www.pppp.net/links/news/USA-IL.html
- Yahoo!...Newspapers...Illinois
  http://dir.yahoo.com/News_and_Media/Newspapers/
  Browse_By_Region/U_S__States/Illinois/

◆ People & Families

- Directory of Underground Railroad Operators— Illinois
  http://www.ugrr.org//names/map-il.htm
- Early Illinois Women & Other Unsung Heroes
  http://www.rsa.lib.il.us/~ilwomen/

- The Search for the Parents of Franciska
  TRAUTVETTER—A Study in Downstate
  Illinois Resources
  http://www.misslink.net/neill/francis.html
  By Michael John Neill.

- Tribes and Villages of Illinois
  http://hanksville.phast.umass.edu:8000/cultprop/contacts/
  tribal/IL.html

- WPA Life Histories from Illinois
  http://lcweb2.loc.gov/ammem/wpaintro/ilcat.html
  *Manuscripts from the Federal Writer's Project, 1936–1940,
  Library of Congress.*

◆ Professional Researchers, Volunteers & Other Research Services

- Board for Certification of Genealogists—Roster of
  Those Certified—Specializing in Illinois
  http://www.genealogy.org/~bcg/rosts_il.html

- Chicago Genealogy and Family History
  Research Services
  http://members.aol.com/ChiSearch
  *Professional research done in Chicago and Cook Co., Illinois.
  Special research projects for Italian Family History and Medical
  Genealogy.*

- Genealogy Helplist—Illinois
  http://www.calarts.edu/~karynw/helplist/il.html

- The Official Iowa Counties Professional Genealogist
  and Researcher's Registry for Illinois
  http://www.iowa-counties.com/gene/il.htm

◆ Publications, Software & Supplies

- AncestorSpy—CDs and Microfiche for Illinois
  http://www.ancestorspy.com/il.htm

- Barbara Green's Used Genealogy Books—Illinois
  http://home.earthlink.net/~genbooks/lochist.html#IL

- Barnette's Family Tree Books—Illinois
  http://www.barnettesbooks.com/illinois.htm

- Books We Own—Illinois
  http://www.rootsweb.com/~bwo/illinois.html

- Boyd Publishing Company—Illinois
  http://www.hom.net/~gac/illinos.htm

- Frontier Press Bookstore—Illinois
  http://www.frontierpress.com/frontier.cgi?category=il

- GenealogyBookShop.com—Illinois
  http://www.genealogybookshop.com/genealogybookshop/files/
  The_United_States,Illinois/index.html
  *The online store of Genealogical Publishing Co., Inc. &
  Clearfield Company.*

- Gorin Genealogical Publishing
  http://members.tripod.com/~GorinS/index.html
  and an alternate address
  http://members.aol.com/kygen/gorin.htm
  *Publications cover mostly Kentucky, also has some for Logan
  County, Illinois and Fentress & Overton Counties, Tennessee.*

- Hearthstone Bookshop—Illinois
  http://www.hearthstonebooks.com/cgi-bin/webc.cgi/st_main.
  html?catid=78&sid=2PH5t29sm

- Heritage Books—Illinois
  http://www.heritagebooks.com/il.htm

- Heritage Quest—Microfilm Records for the State
  of Illinois
  http://www.heritagequest.com/genealogy/microfilm/illinois/

- Lost in Time Books—Illinois
  http://www.lostintime.com/catalog/books/bookst/bo09000.htm

- S-K Publications—Illinois 1820–1850 Census
  Books
  http://www.skpub.com/genie/census/il/

- Willow Bend Bookstore—Illinois
  http://www.willowbend.net/il.htm

- Ye Olde Genealogie Shoppe—Illinois
  http://www.yogs.com/maincat.htm#ILLINOIS

◆ Queries, Message Boards & Surname Lists

- Early Appearing Surnames from St. Clair County,
  Illinois
  http://www.frontiernet.net/~jimbridg/surname.htm

- GenConnect Ilinois Visitor Center
  http://cgi.rootsweb.com/~genbbs/indx/il.html
  *A system for posting queries, Bibles, biographies, deeds,
  obituaries, pensions, wills.*

◆ Records: Census, Cemeteries, Land, Obituaries, Personal, Taxes and Vital (Born, Married, Died & Buried)

- The 1790–1890 Federal Population Censuses:
  Catalog of National Archives Microfilm
  http://www.genealogy.org/census/contents.shtml
  - Census Schedules and Microfilm Roll Numbers
    for Illinois:
    1820
    http://www.genealogy.org/census/1820_schedules/
    Illinois.html
    1830
    http://www.genealogy.org/census/1830_schedules/
    Illinois.html

1840
http://www.genealogy.org/census/1840_schedules/
Illinois.html

1850
http://www.genealogy.org/census/1850_schedules/
Illinois.html

1860
http://www.genealogy.org/census/1860_schedules/
Illinois.html

1870
http://www.genealogy.org/census/1870_schedules/
Illinois.html

1880
http://www.genealogy.org/census/1880_schedules/
Illinois.html

1880 Soundex
http://www.genealogy.org/census/1880.sdx_schedules/
T746.html

- 1870 U.S. Census for Penn Township (Castleton Post Office), Stark County, Illinois
  http://members.aol.com/ZCyberCat/private/castleton.html

- 1870 U.S. Census for Penn Township (Wyoming Post Office), Stark County, Illinois
  http://members.aol.com/ZCyberCat/private/census1.html

- 1880 U.S. Census for Penn Township (aka Wyoming), Stark County, Illinois
  http://members.aol.com/ZCyberCat/private/1880census.html

- Addison Township Cemetery Index
  http://www.dcgs.org/addison/
  DuPage County, Illinois

- Barrington Courier-Review Indexes
  http://www.bal.alibrary.com/bcr.html
  Births, deaths and marriages from 1890 to 1996.

- Brown Co. IL Bell-Perry Cemeteries
  http://www.geocities.com/Heartland/Valley/7991/
  b_p_cems.html

- The Bureau of Land Management—Eastern States, General Land Office
  http://www.glorecords.blm.gov/
  The Official Land Patent Records Site. This site has a searchable database of over two million pre-1908 Federal land title records, including scanned images of those records. The Eastern Public Land States covered in this database are: Alabama, Arkansas, Florida, Illinois, Indiana, Louisiana, Michigan, Minnesota, Mississippi, Missouri, Ohio, Wisconsin.

- Cemeteries of the United States—Illinois Cemeteries—County Index
  http://www.gac.edu/~kengelha/uscemeteries/illinois.html

- Census Online—Links to Census Sites on the Web—Illinois
  http://www.census-online.com/links/IL_data.html

- Confederate Burials in Mound City National Cemetery
  http://www.outfitters.com/illinois/history/civil/
  cwmoundcitycem.html

- County Courthouse Addresses
  http://www.familytreemaker.com/00000242.html

- Downers Grove and Lisle Township Cemetery Index
  http://www.dcgs.org/downers/
  DuPage County, Illinois

- The Federal Census of 1850 for Effingham County, Illinois
  http://www.primenet.com/~powerss/census.html

- Find-A-Grave by Location: Illinois
  http://www.findagrave.com/grave/lil.html
  Graves of noteworthy people.

- Genealogical Research at Oak Woods Cemetery ~ Chicago
  http://homepages.rootsweb.com/~godwin/reference/
  oakwoods.html

- Graveyards of Chicago
  http://www.graveyards.com/

- Ground Work Genealogy on the Internet: Illinois
  http://members.aol.com/ssmadonna/il.htm

- Illinois Vital Records Information
  http://vitalrec.com/il.html

- Illinois Public Domain Land Sales (19th Century)
  http://www.sos.state.il.us:80/depts/archives/data_lan.html

- Interment.net: Illinois Cemeteries
  http://www.interment.net/us/il/index.htm
  A list of links to other sites.

- Jo Daviess Co., IL Marriage Records
  http://members.tripod.com/~Chemingway/Mrg.html
  Volume B: 1855–1865, Volume E, 1870–1885.

- McLean County, IL, Immigration Records
  http://www.mclean.gov/cc/imgrecs/imgrecs.html

- National Archives—Great Lakes Region (Chicago)
  http://www.nara.gov/regional/chicago.html

- National Archives—Great Lakes Region
  http://www.familytreemaker.com/00000096.html
  Records from Illinois, Indiana, Michigan, Minnesota, Ohio, and Wisconsin.

- The Political Graveyard—Cemeteries in Illinois
  http://politicalgraveyard.com/geo/IL/kmindex.html

- Preplanning Network—Funeral Home and Cemetery Directory—Illinois
  http://www.preplannet.com/ilfhcem.htm

- Rock Island County Cemeteries
  http://www.rootsweb.com/~ilrockis/cemetery/cemetery.htm

- Rock Island County Obituaries
  http://www.rootsweb.com/~ilrockis/bio_obit/obits.htm
- USGenWeb Census Project Illinois
  http://www.usgenweb.org/census/states/illinois.htm
- USGenWeb Tombstone Transcription Project—
  Illinois
  http://www.rootsweb.com/~cemetery/illinois.html
- VitalChek Network—Illinois
  http://www.vitalchek.com/stateselect.asp?state=IL
- Where to Write for Vital Records—Illinois
  http://www.cdc.gov/nchswww/howto/w2w/illinois.htm
  From the National Center for Health Statistics (NCHS).
- York Township Cemetery Index
  http://www.dcgs.org/york/
  DuPage County, Illinois

◆ Religion & Churches

- Christianity.Net Church Locator—Illinois
  http://www.christianity.net/cgi/location.exe?
  United_States+Illinois
- Church Online!—Illinois
  http://www.churchonline.com/usas/il/il.html
- Church Profiles—Illinois
  http://www.church-profiles.com/il/il.html
- Churches dot Net—Global Church Web Pages—
  Illinois
  http://www.churches.net/churches/illinois.html
- Churches of the World—Illinois
  http://www.churchsurf.com/churches/Illinois/index.htm
  From the ChurchSurf Christian Directory.
- Quakers [Society of Friends] in Illinois
  http://www.outfitters.com/illinois/history/family/quakers/
  quakers1.html

◆ Societies & Groups

- American Historical Society of Germans from
  Russia—Northern Illinois Chapter
  http://www.ahsgr.org/ilnorthe.html
- The American Legion of Illinois
  http://www.illegion.org/
- Archer's Computer Interest Group List—Illinois
  http://www.genealogy.org/~ngs/cigs/ngl1usil.html
- Blackhawk Genealogical Society
  http://www.rootsweb.com/~ilrockis/bhgs.htm
  Rock Island, Illinois
- Bureau County Genealogical Society
  http://www.anet-chi.com/~jeffb/bureau/bcgs.htm
  Princeton, Illinois

- Champaign County Genealogical Society
  http://www.tbox.com/ccgs/
- The Chicago & Eastern Illinois Railroad
  Historical Society
  http://www2.justnet.com/cei/
- Chicago & North Western Historical Society
  http://www.cnwhs.org/
- Chicago Historical Society
  http://www.chicagohs.org/
  ○ Collections
     http://www.chicagohs.org/Collections/CollectionsIntro.html
     · Genealogical Research
       http://www.chicagohs.org/Collections/
       GENEALOGICAL.html
- Czech & Slovak American Genealogy Society
  of Illinois
  http://members.aol.com/chrismik/csagsi/csagsi.htm
- Descendants of the Bishop Hill Colonists,
  Henry County, Illinois, USA
  http://www.outfitters.com/illinois/henry/
  bishop_hill_genealogy.html
- DuPage County (IL) Genealogical Society
  http://www.dcgs.org
- Elgin Genealogical Society
  http://nsn.nslsilus.org/elghome/egs/index.html
  Elgin, Illinois
- Evanston Historical Society
  http://www.adena.com/ehs/
  Evanston, Illinois
- Fox Valley Genealogical Society, Naperville, IL
  http://members.aol.com/fvgs1/index.html
- The Galva Historical Society
  http://www.galva.com/historic/index.htm
- Genealogical and Historical Societies in Illinois
  http://www.outfitters.com/genealogy/gensoc/gensoc.html#fam
- Genealogical & Historical Societies of Illinois
  http://www.rootsweb.com/~ilgenweb/society.htm
- Genealogy Society of Southern Illinois (GSSI)
  http://jal.cc.il.us/gssi.html
- Great River Genealogical Society
  http://www.outfitters.com/~grgs/
  Quincy, Adams County, Illinois
- Greene County Historical Society
  http://www.rootsweb.com/~ilgreene/gcgs.htm
- Henry County Genealogical Society
  http://www.geocities.com/Heartland/Hills/9101/
  Kewanee, Illinois
- Illinois Daughters of the American Revolution
  http://www.ezl.com/~hootowl/

- Illinois State Genealogical Society
  http://smtp.tbox.com/isgs/
- Illinois State Historical Society
  http://www.prairienet.org/ishs/
- IOOF Lodge Website Directory—Illinois
  http://norm28.hsc.usc.edu/IOOF/USA/Illinois/Illinois.html
  Independent Order of Odd Fellows and Rebekahs.
- Iroquois County Genealogical Society
  http://www.rootsweb.com/~ilicgs/index.htm
- Jersey County Genealogical Society
  http://www.rootsweb.com/~iljersey/jerco.htm
- Kane County Genealogical Society
  http://users.ilnk.com/ejcornell/Kane_co.htm
- Kankakee Valley Genealogical Society
  http://www.keynet.net/~lee/k3gensoc.html
- LaSalle County Genealogy Guild
  http://www.genealogy.org/~dpc/
- Lee County Genealogical Society
  http://www.rootsweb.com/~illee/lcgs.htm
  Dixon, Illinois
- Lee County Historical Society
  http://www.lchs.cin.net/
  Dixon, Illinois
- McLean County Historical Society
  http://oldwww.dave-world.net/community/mchs/
- McDonough County Genealogical Society
  http://www.macomb.com/mcgs/
- McHenry County Illinois Genealogical Society
  http://nsn.nslsilus.org/clkhome/mcigs/
- Macoupin County Genealogical Society
  http://www.rootsweb.com/~ilmacoup/m_gensoc.htm
- Madison County Genealogical Society
  http://ns.plantnet.com/~mcgs/
  Edwardsville, Illinois
- Marissa Historical And Genealogical Society
  http://library.wustl.edu/~spec/archives/aslaa/directory/marissa.html
  Marissa, Illinois
- Marshall County Historical Society
  http://www.rootsweb.com/~ilmarsha/mphs.htm
- Milwaukee Road Historical Association
  http://www.mrha.com/
  Antioch, Illinois. Chicago, Milwaukee, St. Paul, and Pacific Railroad.
- Montgomery County Genealogical Society
  http://www.rootsweb.com/~ilgreene/montgomery/gensoc.htm
- Northbrook Historical Society
  http://nsn.nslsilus.org/nbkhome/nbhsoc/

- Peoria County Genealogical Society
  http://www.rootsweb.com/~ilpeoria/pcgs.htm
- Perry County Historical Society
  http://www.fnbpville.com/perrycounty.html
- Polish Genealogical Society of America
  http://www.pgsa.org/
  Chicago, Illinois
- St. Clair County Genealogical Society
  http://www.compu-type.net/rengen/stclair/stchome.htm
- Sangamon County Genealogical Society
  http://www.rootsweb.com/~ilsangam/scgs.htm
- Shore Line Historical Society
  http://www.getnet.com/~dickg/nmra/sigs/ShoreLine/ShoreLine.html
  Chicago, Illinois. For anyone with an interest in the Chicago North Shore and Milwaukee, the Chicago South Shore and South Bend, and/or the Chicago Aurora and Elgin railroads, including: Chicago Rapid Transit, Chicago Surface Lines, Chicago and West Towns Railways, Evanston Railway, Hammond Whiting and East Chicago Railway, and The Milwaukee Electric Railway and Light Company.
- Sons of the Revolution in the State of Illinois
  http://www.execpc.com/~drg/sril.html
- South Suburban Genealogical and Historical Society
  http://www.rootsweb.com/~ssghs/ssghs.htm
  South Holland, Illinois. Covers: Bloom, Bremen, Calumet, Lemont, Orland, Palos, Rich, Thornton, and Worth in the southern part of Cook County; the Roseland and Pullman neighborhoods of the city of Chicago; Crete, Frankfort, Green Garden, Homer, Manhattan, Monee, New Lenox, Peotone, Washington, Will, and Wilton in the northern part of Will County.
- Tri-State Genealogical Society
  http://www.evansville.net/~tsgs/tsgs.html
  Indiana, Illinois and Kentucky
- Warren County Illinois Genealogical Society
  http://www.maplecity.com/~wcpl/genhome.html
  Monmouth
- White County Historical Society
  http://scribers.midwest.net/cbconly/wchs.htm

◆ USGenWeb Project

- Illinois Genealogy—USGenWeb Project State Page
  http://www.usgenweb.org/il
- Illinois—USGenWeb Archives Table of Contents
  http://www.rootsweb.com/~usgenweb/il/ilfiles.htm
- Illinois—USGenWeb FTP Archives
  ftp://ftp.rootsweb.com/pub/usgenweb/il/
- IL-Traces Mailing List
  http://members.aol.com/gfsjohnf/gen_mail_states-il.html#IL-Traces
  A tool of the ILGenWeb Archives. Items posted on this list will be placed in the archives files online.

U.S.—INDIANA—IN
http://www.CyndisList.com/in.htm

Category Index:

- General Resource Sites
- Government & Cities
- History & Culture
- Libraries, Archives & Museums
- Locality Specific
- Mailing Lists, Newsgroups & Chat
- Maps, Gazetteers & Geographical Information
- Military
- Newspapers
- People & Families

- Professional Researchers, Volunteers & Other Research Services
- Publications, Software & Supplies
- Queries, Message Boards & Surname Lists
- Records: Census, Cemeteries, Land, Obituaries, Personal, Taxes and Vital
- Religion & Churches
- Societies & Groups
- USGenWeb Project

◆ General Resource Sites

- Everton's Sources of Genealogical Information in Indiana
  http://www.everton.com/usa/in.htm

- Family Tree Maker's Genealogy "How To" Guide— Indiana
  http://www.familytreemaker.com/00000188.html

- Genealogy Bulletin Board Systesms for Indiana
  http://www.genealogy.org/~gbbs/gblin.html

- Genealogy Exchange & Surname Registry— INGenExchange
  http://www.genexchange.com/in/index.cfm

- Genealogy Resources on the Internet: Indiana
  http://www-personal.umich.edu/~cgaunt/indiana.html

- Hoosier Lines—Home Page for Ruth Montgomery
  http://www.netusa1.net/~hartmont/

- Indiana Biographies
  http://members.tripod.com/~debmurray/indybios/indiana1.htm

- Kentuckiana Genealogy WebRing
  http://www.floyd-pavey.com/kentuckiana/kyiana/webring.html
  Kentucky & Indiana

- LDS Research Outline for Indiana
  http://www.everton.com/usa/in-0815B.txt

- Lineages' Genealogy Site: Indiana
  http://www.lineages.com/rooms/usa/state.asp?StateCode=IN

- Links to Indiana Sites and World Wide Web Information
  http://www2.indianahistory.org/ihs1830/links.htm

- ROOTS-L United States Resources: Indiana
  http://www.rootsweb.com/roots-l/USA/in.html
  Comprehensive list of research links, including many to history-related sites.

◆ Government & Cities

- 50states.com—Indiana State Information Resource
  http://www.50states.com/indiana.htm
  A list of general information for each state, including a list of colleges, state symbols, links to maps, newspapers, and other miscellaneous state information.

- Access Indiana Information Network
  http://www.state.in.us/

- Bedford On-Line
  http://www.bedfordonline.com/bed.html

- Evansville Online
  http://www.evansville.net/

- Excite Travel by City.Net—Indiana
  http://www.city.net/countries/united_states/indiana/

- The Governors of Indiana
  http://www2.indianahistory.org/ihs1830/ingov.htm

- HoosierNet
  http://www.bloomington.in.us/
  Community Information and Internetworking for Monroe County, Indiana.

- Official City Web Sites for the State of Indiana
  http://OfficialCitySites.org/Indiana.htm

- Wayne County Government
  http://www.infocom.com/wayneco/

- Yahoo! Get Local...Indiana Cities
  http://dir.yahoo.com/Regional/U_S__States/Indiana/Cities/
  Maps, yellow pages, white pages, newspapers and other local information.

- Yahoo! Get Local...Indiana Counties and Regions
  http://dir.yahoo.com/Regional/U_S__States/Indiana/
  Counties_and_Regions/
  Maps, yellow pages, white pages, newspapers and other local information.

◆ History & Culture

- Fort Wayne History
  http://www.ipfw.edu/ipfwhist/fortwayn.htm

- Hoosier Heritage
  http://www2.indianahistory.org/ihs1830/heritage.htm

- Indiana Biography
  http://www.ipfw.edu/ipfwhist/indiana/biog.htm

- Indiana History
  http://www.ipfw.edu/ipfwhist/indihist.htm

- Yahoo!...History...Indiana
  http://dir.yahoo.com/Arts/Humanities/History/
  Browse_By_Region/U_S__States/Indiana/

◆ Libraries, Archives & Museums

- Allen County Public Library ~ Fort Wayne
  http://www.acpl.lib.in.us/
  - Historical Genealogy Collection
    http://www.acpl.lib.in.us/genealogy/genealogy.html
  - PERSI—Periodical Source Index
    http://www.acpl.lib.in.us/genealogy/persi.html
    - Periodical Source Index (PERSI) Order Form
      http://www.acpl.lib.in.us/database/graphics/
      order_form.html

- Evansville-Vanderburgh County Public Libraries
  http://www.evcpl.lib.in.us/

- Family History Centers—Indiana
  http://www.deseretbook.com/famhis/in.html

- Family History Centers—Indiana
  http://www.lib.byu.edu/~uvrfhc/centers/indiana.html

- Frankfort Community Public Library
  http://www.accs.net/fcpl/
  - Frankfort Library Genealogy Department
    http://www.accs.net/fcpl/gen.htm

- HYTELNET—Library Catalogs: USA: Indiana
  http://library.usask.ca/hytelnet/usa/IN.html
  Before you use any of the Telnet links, make note of the user name, password and any other logon information.

- Indiana Archival and Historical Repositories
  http://cawley.archives.nd.edu/sia/guide/reposito.htm

- Indiana Family History Centers
  http://www.genhomepage.com/FHC/Indiana.html
  A list of addresses, phone numbers and hours of operation from the Genealogy Home Page.

- Indiana State Archives
  http://www.ai.org/icpr/webfile/archives/homepage.html

- Indiana State Library, Indianapolis, Indiana
  http://www.statelib.lib.in.us
  - Indiana State Library Genealogy Section
    http://www.statelib.lib.in.us/www/indiana/genealogy/
    genmenu.html

- Indiana University Bloomington Libraries
  http://www.indiana.edu/~libweb/

- The Kokomo-Howard County Public Library
  http://www.kokomo.lib.in.us/
  - Genealogy and Local History Department
    http://www.kokomo.lib.in.us/genealogy/

- Lewis Historical Library—Vincennes University
  http://www.vinu.edu/lewis.htm

- Monroe County Public Library
  http://www.monroe.lib.in.us/
  - Collections
    http://www.monroe.lib.in.us/general_info/collections.html
    - MCPL Indiana Room—Genealogy Collections
      http://www.monroe.lib.in.us/indiana_room/genealogy.html
    - MCPL Indiana Room—Indiana and Local Collections
      http://www.monroe.lib.in.us/indiana_room/
      statelocal_collections.html

- Notre Dame Archives
  http://www.nd.edu/~archives/

- NUCMC Listing of Archives and Manuscript Repositories in Indiana
  http://lcweb.loc.gov/coll/nucmc/insites.html
  Links to information about resources other than those held in the Library of Congress.

- Repositories of Primary Sources: Indiana
  http://www.uidaho.edu/special-collections/east1.html#usin
  A list of links to online resources from the Univ. of Idaho Library, Special Collections and Archives.

- St. Joseph County Public Library
  http://www.sjcpl.lib.in.us/
  - SJCPL Local History & Genealogy Home Page
    http://www.sjcpl.lib.in.us/homepage/LocalHist/
    LocalHistory.html
    - SJCPL Genealogy Services
      http://sjcpl.lib.in.us/homepage/LocalHist/Genealogy.html
    - SJCPL Local History Services
      http://sjcpl.lib.in.us/homepage/LocalHist/LocalHist.html

- webCATS: Library Catalogues on the World Wide Web—Indiana
  http://library.usask.ca/hywebcat/states/IN.html

- Willard Library
  http://www.willard.lib.in.us/
  Evansville, Indiana

◆ Locality Specific

- Also see the USGenWeb section for links to county-specific resources.

- Kentuckiana Genealogy
  http://www.floyd-pavey.com/kentuckiana/
  Covering Indiana counties of: Clark, Crawford, Dubois, Floyd, Harrison, Perry, Scott and Washington; and Kentucky counties of Breckinridge, Jefferson, Hardin and Meade.

- NOLCOX Neighborhood
  http://www.comsource.net/~tnolcox/
  Terry's Page—Your Best Genealogical Connection To Gibson County, Indiana.

- Some Indiana Genealogy Homepage
  http://ourworld.compuserve.com/homepages/njmyers/
  Dearborn, Elkhart, Kosciusko, Marshall and St. Joseph Counties.

- Warrick County, Indiana History and Genealogy
  http://home.att.net/~SWilkin676/
  Genealogy and History data extracted from early Southern Indiana newspapers.

◆ Mailing Lists, Newsgroups & Chat

- Genealogy Resources on the Internet—Indiana Mailing Lists
  http://members.aol.com/gfsjohnf/gen_mail_states-in.html
  Each of the mailing list links below points to this site, wonderfully maintained by John Fuller. Visit this site for county-specific mailing lists as well.

- INDIANA_BIO Mailing List
  http://members.aol.com/gfsjohnf/gen_mail_states-in.html#INDIANA_BIO
  For the discussion of the Indiana Biographies Project which gathers biographies of Indiana citizens.

- INPCRP Mailing List
  http://members.aol.com/gfsjohnf/gen_mail_states-in.html#INPCRP
  For anyone interested in the Indiana Pioneer Cemeteries Restoration Project.
  http://www.rootsweb.com/~inpcrp/

- INROOTS-L Mailing List
  http://members.aol.com/gfsjohnf/gen_mail_states-in.html#INROOTS

- KENTUCKIANA Mailing List
  http://members.aol.com/gfsjohnf/gen_mail_states-ky.html#KENTUCKIANA
  For anyone with a genealogical, historical, or cultural interest in the Indiana counties of Clark, Crawford, Dubois, Floyd, Harrison, Orange, Perry, Scott and Washington, and the Kentucky counties of Breckinridge, Hardin, Jefferson and Meade.

- RANDOLPH COUNTY, INDIANA Mailing List
  http://members.aol.com/gfsjohnf/gen_mail_states-in.html#RAN-CTY

- WAYNE IN Mailing List—Wayne County, Indiana
  http://members.aol.com/gfsjohnf/gen_mail_states-in.html#WAYNE-IN

◆ Maps, Gazetteers & Geographical Information

- 1895 U.S. Atlas—Indiana
  http://www.LivGenMI.com/1895in.htm

- American Memory Panoramic Maps 1847–1929—Indiana
  http://lcweb2.loc.gov/cgi-bin/query/S?ammem/gmd:@filreq(@field(STATE+indiana)+@field(COLLID+pmmap))
  From the Geography and Map Division, Library of Congress.

- American Memory Railroad Maps 1828–1900—Indiana
  http://memory.loc.gov/cgi-bin/query/S?ammem/gmd:@filreq(@field(STATE+indiana)+@field(COLLID+rrmap))
  From the Geography and Map Division, Library of Congress.

- Color Landform Atlas: Indiana
  http://fermi.jhuapl.edu/states/in_0.html
  Including a map of counties and a map for 1895.

- Excite Maps: Indiana Maps
  http://www.city.net/maps/view/?mapurl=/countries/united_states/indiana
  Zoom in on these maps all the way to the street level.

- Gleason's Old Maps, Etc.
  http://members.aol.com/oldmapsetc/indiana.html
  Photocopies of Old Maps, Prints and Articles of Historical and Genealogical Interest from Indiana.

- HPI County InfoSystem—Counties in Indiana
  http://www.com/hpi/incty/index.html

- K.B. Slocum Books and Maps—Indiana
  http://www.treasurenet.com/cgi-bin/treasure/kbslocum/scan/se=Indiana/sf=mapstate

- List of Indiana Counties
  http://www.genealogy.org/~st-clair/counties/state_in.html

- Map of Indiana Counties
  http://govinfo.kerr.orst.edu/gif/states/in.gif
  From the Government Information Sharing Project, Information Services, Oregon State University.

- Map of Indiana Counties
  http://www.lib.utexas.edu/Libs/PCL/Map_collection/states/Indiana.gif
  From the Perry-Castañeda Library at the Univ. of Texas at Austin.

- U.S. Census Bureau—Indiana Profiles
  http://www.census.gov/datamap/www/18.html

- Yale Peabody Museum: GNIS—Indiana
  http://www.peabody.yale.edu/other/gnis/IN.html
  Search the USGS Geographic Names Database. You can limit the search to a specific county in this state and search for any of the following features: airport arch area arroyo bar basin bay beach bench bend bridge **building** *canal cape* **cemetery** *channel* **church** *cliff crater crossing dam falls flat forest gap geyser glacier gut harbor hospital island isthmus lake lava levee locale mine oilfield other park pillar plain ppl range rapids reserve reservoir ridge* **school** *sea slope spring stream summit swamp tower trail tunnel valley well woods.*

◆ Military

- 12th Indiana Volunteer Infantry Regiment
  http://www.access.digex.net/~bdboyle/12in.txt

- 19th Indiana Volunteer Infantry—Company A
  http://members.iquest.net/~virx/19th.html

- 27th Indiana Volunteer Infantry
  http://www.fortunecity.com/victorian/browning/186/
  27thindiana.html

- 42nd Indiana Volunteer Infantry—Army of the
  Cumberland, U.S.A.
  http://www.19thalabama.org/42ndind.html

- 49th Indiana Volunteer Infantry, 'Company F'—
  Reenactment Unit
  http://www.intersource.com/~bjohnson/49th.html

- The Civil War Archive—Union Regiments—Indiana
  http://www.civilwararchive.com/unionin.htm

- Civil War Battle Summaries by State—Indiana
  http://www2.cr.nps.gov/abpp/battles/bystate.htm#in

- Indiana in the Civil War
  http://www.thnet.com/~liggetkw/incw/cw.htm

- Korean Conflict State-Level Casualty Lists—Indiana
  http://www.nara.gov/nara/electronic/inhrlist.html
  *From the National Archives and Records Administration, Center
  for Electronic Records.*

- Ninth Regiment Infantry Indiana Volunteers
  Company E
  http://www.csinet.net/lt1Mike/

- State Archives Civil War Resources
  http://www.ai.org/icpr/webfile/civilwar/resource.html

- Vietnam Conflict State-Level Casualty Lists—
  Indiana
  http://www.nara.gov/nara/electronic/inhrviet.html
  *From the National Archives and Records Administration, Center
  for Electronic Records.*

- The Vietnam Veterans Memorial—Indiana
  http://grunt.space.swri.edu/statewall/indiana/in.htm

◆ Newspapers

- AJR NewsLink—Indiana Newspapers
  http://www.newslink.org/innews.html

- Decatur Daily Democrat
  http://www.decaturnet.com/paper/

- E&P Media Info Links—Newspaper Sites in Indiana
  http://www.mediainfo.com/emedia/browse-results.
  htm?region=indiana&category=newspaper+++++++++

- Ecola Newstand: Indiana
  http://www.ecola.com/news/press/na/us/in/

- NAA Hotlinks to Newspapers Online—Indiana
  http://www.naa.org/hotlinks/searchResult.asp?param=
  IN-Indiana&City=1

- The News-Sentinel, Fort Wayne, Indiana
  http://www.fortwayne.com/ns/

- N-Net—Indiana Newspapers
  http://www.n-net.com/in.htm

- The Shelbyville News Online
  http://www.shelbynews.com/

- The Ultimate Collection of News Links:
  USA—Indiana
  http://www.pppp.net/links/news/USA-IN.html

- Yahoo!...Newspapers...Indiana
  http://dir.yahoo.com/News_and_Media/Newspapers/
  Browse_By_Region/U_S__States/Indiana/

◆ People & Families

- African-American Sources
  http://www.comsource.net/~tnolcox/africanamerican.htm

- Directory of Underground Railroad Operators—
  Indiana
  http://www.ugrr.org//names/map-in.htm

- Kentuckiana Konnections—Biographies
  http://www.floyd-pavey.com/kentuckiana/kyiana/county/
  biolinks.html

- Ohio River Valley Families
  http://orvf.com/
  By Allen David Distler.

- Tribes and Villages of Indiana
  http://hanksville.phast.umass.edu:8000/cultprop/contacts/
  tribal/IN.html

- WPA Life Histories from Indiana
  http://lcweb2.loc.gov/ammem/wpaintro/incat.html
  *Manuscripts from the Federal Writer's Project, 1936–1940,
  Library of Congress.*

◆ Professional Researchers, Volunteers & Other Research Services

- Ann McRoden Mensch, Professional Genealogist
  http://home.att.net/~mensch-family/Resume.htm
  Researching at the Allen County Public Library.

- Board for Certification of Genealogists—Roster of
  Those Certified—Specializing in Indiana
  http://www.genealogy.org/~bcg/rosts_in.html

- Genealogy Helplist—Indiana
  http://www.rootsweb.com/~innoble/in.html

- Indiana Land Records Search by CompuGen
  Systems
  http://members.aol.com/CGSystems/LRSearch.html

- Indiana Newspaper Search by CompuGen Systems
  http://members.aol.com/CGSystems/NXSearch.html

- The Official Iowa Counties Professional Genealogist and Researcher's Registry for Indiana
  http://www.iowa-counties.com/gene/in.htm

◆ Publications, Software & Supplies

- AncestorSpy—CDs and Microfiche for Indiana
  http://www.ancestorspy.com/in.htm

- Barbara Green's Used Genealogy Books—Indiana
  http://home.earthlink.net/~genbooks/lochist.html#IN

- Barnette's Family Tree Books—Indiana
  http://www.barnettesbooks.com/indiana.htm

- A Bookman's Indiana | A Guide to the State's Used Bookshops & Bibliophilic Resources
  http://www2.inetdirect.net/~charta/Ind_bks.html

- Books We Own—Indiana
  http://www.rootsweb.com/~bwo/indiana.html

- Boyd Publishing Company—Indiana
  http://www.hom.net/~gac/indiana.htm

- Frontier Press Bookstore—Indiana
  http://www.frontierpress.com/frontier.cgi?category=in

- GenealogyBookShop.com—Indiana
  http://www.genealogybookshop.com/genealogybookshop/files/The_United_States,Indiana/index.html
  The online store of Genealogical Publishing Co., Inc. & Clearfield Company.

- Genealogy / Local History Publications By Stuart Harter
  http://members.aol.com/SAHarter/SAHPub.html

- Hearthstone Bookshop—Indiana
  http://www.hearthstonebooks.com/cgi-bin/webc.cgi/st_main.html?catid=79&sid=2PH5t29sm

- Heritage Books—Indiana
  http://www.heritagebooks.com/in.htm

- Heritage Quest—Microfilm Records for the State of Indiana
  http://www.heritagequest.com/genealogy/microfilm/indiana/

- The Hoosier Genealogist
  http://www2.indianahistory.org/ihs1830/thg.htm
  A quarterly publication devoted to information on Hoosier family history from the Indiana Historical Society.

- Indiana Historical Society Publications
  https://www.dgltd.com/ihs1830/publications.html

- Lost in Time Books—Indiana
  http://www.lostintime.com/catalog/books/bookst/bo10000.htm

- The Memorabilia Corner Books—Indiana
  http://members.aol.com/TMCorner/book_ind.htm

- The Memorabilia Corner Census View CDs—Indiana
  http://members.aol.com/TMCorner/cen_ind.htm

- S-K Publications—Indiana 1820–1850 Census Books
  http://www.skpub.com/genie/census/in/

- Willow Bend Bookstore—Indiana
  http://www.willowbend.net/in.htm

- Ye Olde Genealogie Shoppe—Indiana
  http://www.yogs.com/maincat.htm#INDIANA

◆ Queries, Message Boards & Surname Lists

- GenConnect Indiana Visitor Center
  http://cgi.rootsweb.com/~genbbs/indx/In.html
  A system for posting queries, Bibles, biographies, deeds, obituaries, pensions, wills.

- Gibson County Queries
  http://www.comsource.net/~tnolcox/queries.htm

- Indiana Surnames, Queries, Obituaries, Biographies and Genealogies On-Line
  http://vax1.vigo.lib.in.us/~jmounts/sqob.htm

- Kentuckiana Genealogy—Index to Surnames, Queries, and Researchers
  http://www.floyd-pavey.com/kentuckiana/qryindex.htm
  Kentucky & Indiana

- Surname Index for Kentuckiana Genealogy
  http://cgi.rootsweb.com/surhelp-bin/surindx.pl?site=kyiana&letter=a

◆ Records: Census, Cemeteries, Land, Obituaries, Personal, Taxes and Vital (Born, Married, Died & Buried)

- The 1790–1890 Federal Population Censuses: Catalog of National Archives Microfilm
  http://www.genealogy.org/census/contents.shtml
  - Census Schedules and Microfilm Roll Numbers for Indiana:
    1820
    http://www.genealogy.org/census/1820_schedules/Indiana.html
    1830
    http://www.genealogy.org/census/1830_schedules/Indiana.html
    1840
    http://www.genealogy.org/census/1840_schedules/Indiana.html
    1850
    http://www.genealogy.org/census/1850_schedules/Indiana.html
    1860
    http://www.genealogy.org/census/1860_schedules/Indiana.html

1870
http://www.genealogy.org/census/1870_schedules/
Indiana.html

1880
http://www.genealogy.org/census/1880_schedules/
Indiana.html

1880 Soundex
http://www.genealogy.org/census/1880.sdx_schedules/
T747.html

- 1810 Harrison Co., Indiana Census for Harrison and Exeter Townships
http://www.floyd-pavey.com/kentuckiana/kyiana/census/
1810harrisonc.html

- 1820 Federal Census Orange County, Indiana
http://twobees.com/1820/

- 1850 Crawford Co., IN Census
http://www.floyd-pavey.com/kentuckiana/kyiana/census/
1850ccensus.html
An ongoing project that currently only contains Jennings Township.

- 1850 Federal Census Orange County, Indiana
http://www.geocities.com/~labooski/census/

- Bible Records of Orange County, Indiana
http://www.rootsweb.com/~inorange/prebible.htm

- The Bureau of Land Management—Eastern States, General Land Office
http://www.glorecords.blm.gov/
The Official Land Patent Records Site. This site has a searchable database of over two million pre-1908 Federal land title records, including scanned images of those records. The Eastern Public Land States covered in this database are: Alabama, Arkansas, Florida, Illinois, Indiana, Louisiana, Michigan, Minnesota, Mississippi, Missouri, Ohio, Wisconsin.

- Cemeteries of the United States—Indiana Cemeteries—County Index
http://www.gac.edu/~kengelha/uscemeteries/indiana.html

- Census of the Indiana Territory for 1807
E-mail: jmounts@holli.com
E-mail Jerry Mounts at jmounts@holli.com with specific details and he will do a lookup for you. The counties at that time were: Dearborn, Clark, Knox and Randolph in Illinois.

- Census Online—Links to Census Sites on the Web—Indiana
http://www.census-online.com/links/IN_data.html

- Central State Hospital—Indiana Hospital for the Insane
http://www.ai.org/icpr/webfile/csh_aiin/chs.html
Will have a Commitment Records Database online in the future for 1848–1920.

- Clark County Cemeteries
http://www.geocities.com/Heartland/Plains/5881/index.html

- Clinton County, Indiana Marriages
http://www.rootsweb.com/~inclinto/marriages.html

- County Courthouse Addresses
http://www.familytreemaker.com/00000243.html

- Crawford Co., IN 1820 Census
http://www.floyd-pavey.com/kentuckiana/kyiana/census/
1820cra.html

- Crawford Co., IN Cemetery Records
http://www.floyd-pavey.com/kentuckiana/kyiana/county/
crawford/ccemetery.html

- Database to an Index of Indiana Marriages Through 1850
http://www.statelib.lib.in.us/www/indiana/genealogy/mirr.html
Indiana State Library, Genealogy Division.

- Early Land Entries—Orange County, Indiana
http://www.rootsweb.com/~inorange/preland.htm

- Find-A-Grave by Location: Indiana
http://www.findagrave.com/grave/lin.html
Graves of noteworthy people.

- Ground Work Genealogy on the Internet: Indiana
http://members.aol.com/ssmadonna/in.htm

- Hazleton Cemetery
http://www.comsource.net/~tnolcox/cemetery3.htm

- The Indiana Pioneer Cemeteries Restoration Project
http://www.rootsweb.com/~inpcrp/

- Indiana Vital Records Information
http://vitalrec.com/in.html

- Inhabitants of the Silent City—Warnock Cemetery
http://www.comsource.net/~tnolcox/cemetery2.htm

- Interment.net: Indiana Cemeteries
http://www.interment.net/us/in/index.htm
A list of links to other sites.

- Kosciusko County, Indiana—Index to the Early Wills 1844–1920
http://www.rootsweb.com/~inkosciu/willsndx.htm

- Land Office Records at the Indiana State Archives
http://www.state.in.us/icpr/webfile/land/land_off.html
  - Fort Wayne, Indiana Land Office Database Search Page
  http://www.state.in.us/icpr/webfile/land/srch_fw.html
  - The Indianapolis Donation
  http://www.state.in.us/icpr/webfile/donation/donindex.html
  - Laporte/Winamac, Indiana Land Office Database Search Page
  http://www.state.in.us/icpr/webfile/land/search.html

- List of Soldiers in the Three Princeton Cemeteries (1889)
http://www.comsource.net/~tnolcox/cemetery1.htm

- Lookups from the "Galveston, Indiana Cemetery Index, from the Platbooks and Files"
E-mail: beheler@netusa1.net
For Cass, Howard or Miami Counties in Indiana. Send e-mail to Debra Beheler at beheler@netusa1.net

- Michiana Genealogical Index—MGI
  http://www.qtm.net/~ftmiami/remarc/
  A surname source database for birth, death, marriage, license, divorce and cemetery records. Representing over 500,000 records from southwestern Michigan and northern Indiana.

- Morgan County, Indiana, Bible Records
  http://www.geocities.com/Heartland/Meadows/8056/inmorgan/biblerec.html

- Morgan County Public Library—GenAssist—The Genealogy Assistant
  http://www.scican.net/~morglib/genasist/genasist.html

  - Morgan County, Indiana 1850 Federal Census Mortality Schedule
    http://www.scican.net/~morglib/genasist/mort1850.html

  - Morgan County, Indiana 1870 Federal Census Index of Households
    http://www.scican.net/~morglib/genasist/cens1870.html

  - Morgan County, Indiana 1880 Federal Census Index of Households
    http://www.scican.net/~morglib/genasist/cens1880.html

  - Morgan County, Indiana 1890 Enrollment of Soldiers
    http://www.scican.net/~morglib/genasist/enrl1890.html

  - Morgan County, Indiana 1910 Federal Census Index of Households
    http://www.scican.net/~morglib/genasist/cens1910.html

  - Morgan County, Indiana Original Land Sales From U.S. Government—Sorted by Location
    http://www.scican.net/~morglib/genasist/landsal2.html

  - Morgan County, Indiana Original Land Sales From U.S. Government—Sorted by Name
    http://www.scican.net/~morglib/genasist/landsal1.html

- National Archives—Great Lakes Region (Chicago)
  http://www.nara.gov/regional/chicago.html

- National Archives—Great Lakes Region
  http://www.familytreemaker.com/00000096.html
  Records from Illinois, Indiana, Michigan, Minnesota, Ohio, and Wisconsin.

- Obituaries—Gibson County, Indiana
  http://www.comsource.net/~tnolcox/obituaries.htm

- Old Patoka Cemetery
  http://www.comsource.net/~tnolcox/cemetery4.htm

- Perry County, Indiana Tombstone Inscriptions
  http://www.floyd-pavey.com/kentuckiana/kyiana/cemetery/perrytombstones.html

- The Political Graveyard—Cemeteries in Indiana
  http://politicalgraveyard.com/geo/IN/kmindex.html

- Preplanning Network—Funeral Home and Cemetery Directory—Indiana
  http://www.preplannet.com/indfhcem.htm

- Strong or Crawford Cemetery
  http://www.floyd-pavey.com/kentuckiana/kyiana/cemetery/strong.html

- Upper Beard Cemetery
  http://www.floyd-pavey.com/kentuckiana/kyiana/cemetery/upperbeard.html

- USGenWeb Census Project Indiana
  http://www.usgenweb.org/census/states/indiana.htm

- USGenWeb Tombstone Transcription Project—Indiana
  http://www.rootsweb.com/~cemetery/indiana.html

- VitalChek Network—Indiana
  http://www.vitalchek.com/stateselect.asp?state=IN

- Washington County Cemetery Project
  http://vax1.vigo.lib.in.us/~jmounts/cem.htm

- Where to Write for Vital Records—Indiana
  http://www.cdc.gov/nchswww/howto/w2w/indiana.htm
  From the National Center for Health Statistics (NCHS).

◆ Religion & Churches

- Christianity.Net Church Locator—Indiana
  http://www.christianity.net/cgi/location.exe?United_States+Indiana

- Church Online!—Indiana
  http://www.churchonline.com/usas/in/in.html

- Church Profiles—Indiana
  http://www.church-profiles.com/in/in.html

- Churches dot Net—Global Church Web Pages—Indiana
  http://www.churches.net/churches/indiana.html

- Churches of the World—Indiana
  http://www.churchsurf.com/churches/Indiana/index.htm
  From the ChurchSurf Christian Directory.

- Indiana Catholic Page
  http://www.ipfw.edu/ipfwhist/indicath.htm

◆ Societies & Groups

- Allen County—Fort Wayne Historical Society
  http://www.ft-wayne.in.us/fort/FW_History/

- Allen County Genealogical Society of Indiana
  http://www.ipfw.edu/ipfwhist/historgs/acgsi.htm

- Archer's Computer Interest Group List—Indiana
  http://www.genealogy.org/~ngs/cigs/ngl1usin.html

- Besancon Historical Society
  http://www.ipfw.edu/ipfwhist/historgs/besanco.htm

- Elkhart PC Users Group Genealogy SIG
  http://www.skyenet.net/~stevens/gensig1.htm

- Fort Wayne Railroad Historical Society
  http://www.steamloco765.org/

- Genealogical Society of Whitley County
  http://home.whitleynet.org/genealogy/
- Genealogy Organizations in Indiana
  http://www2.ihs1830.org/ihs1830/genedir.htm
- Howard County Indiana Genealogical Society
  http://www.rootsweb.com/~inhoward/gensoc.html
- Indiana Daughters of the American Revolution
  http://www.ipfw.edu/ipfwhist/historgs/indar.htm
- Indiana Genealogical Society
  http://www.IndGenSoc.org/
- Indiana Historical Society
  http://www.indianahistory.org/
- Indiana Masons Online
  http://www.indianamasons.org/
- IOOF Lodge Website Directory—Indiana
  http://norm28.hsc.usc.edu/IOOF/USA/Indiana/Indiana.html
  Independent Order of Odd Fellows and Rebekahs.
- La Porte County Historical Society
  http://www.lapcohistsoc.org/
- Marion County-Indianapolis Historical Society
  http://members.iquest.net/~reboomer/mcihs.htm
- Mary Penrose Wayne Chapter, Daughters of the American Revolution
  http://www.ipfw.edu/ipfwhist/historgs/dar.htm
  Fort Wayne, Indiana
- Miami County Genealogical Society
  http://www.netusa1.net/~beheler/gensoc.html
- Monroe County Historical Society
  http://www.bluemarble.net/~julian/monroe.html
- Morgan County History and Genealogy Association
  http://www.rootsweb.com/~inmchaga/mchagai.html
- Orange County Genealogical Society
  http://www.rootsweb.com/~inorange/gensoc.htm
- Owen County Historical & Genealogical Society
  http://www.owen.in.us/owenhist/owen.htm
- Ripley County Historical Society
  http://www.seidata.com/~rchslib/
- South Bend Area Genealogical Society
  http://www.rootsweb.com/~insbags/index.htm
- Southern Indiana Genealogical Society
  http://www.ka.net/spcarpenter/SIGserve.htm
  New Albany, Indiana
- Starke County Genealogical Society of Indiana
  http://php.indiana.edu/~jmatsey/gen.htm
- Tri-State Genealogical Society
  http://www.evansville.net/~tsgs/tsgs.html
  Indiana, Illinois and Kentucky
- Vigo County Historical Society
  http://web.indstate.edu/community/vchs/
- Whitley County Historical Society
  http://home.whitleynet.org/historical/

◆ USGenWeb Project

- Indiana Genealogy—USGenWeb Project State Page
  http://www.usgenweb.org/in
- Indiana—USGenWeb Archives Table of Contents
  http://www.rootsweb.com/~usgenweb/in/infiles.htm
- Indiana—USGenWeb FTP Archives
  ftp://ftp.rootsweb.com/pub/usgenweb/in/

U.S.—IOWA—IA
http://www.CyndisList.com/ia.htm

Category Index:

- General Resource Sites
- Government & Cities
- History & Culture
- Libraries, Archives & Museums
- Mailing Lists, Newsgroups & Chat
- Maps, Gazetteers & Geographical Information
- Military
- Newspapers
- People & Families

- Professional Researchers, Volunteers & Other Research Services
- Publications, Software & Supplies
- Queries, Message Boards & Surname Lists
- Records: Census, Cemeteries, Land, Obituaries, Personal, Taxes and Vital
- Religion & Churches
- Societies & Groups
- USGenWeb Project

◆ General Resource Sites

- Dott's Genealogy Home Page ~ Iowa and Ohio
  http://home.att.net/~dottsr/
- Everton's Sources of Genealogical Information in Iowa
  http://www.everton.com/usa/ia.htm
- Family Tree Maker's Genealogy "How To" Guide—Iowa
  http://www.familytreemaker.com/00000189.html
- Genealogy Bulletin Board Systems for Iowa
  http://www.genealogy.org/~gbbs/gblia.html
- Genealogy Exchange & Surname Registry—IAGenExchange
  http://www.genexchange.com/ia/index.cfm
- Genealogy Resources on the Internet: Iowa
  http://www-personal.umich.edu/~cgaunt/iowa.html
- Iowa Genealogical Society—The Sesquicentennial, Pioneer and Century Certificates
  http://www.digiserve.com/igs/pioneer.htm
- Iowa Genealogy
  http://www.netins.net/showcase/iagenealogy/index.htm
- LDS Research Outline for Iowa
  http://www.everton.com/usa/ia-0816B.txt
- Lineages' Genealogy Site: Iowa
  http://www.lineages.com/rooms/usa/state.asp?StateCode=IA
- A North Iowa Genealogy Connection
  http://www.netins.net/showcase/pafways/

- The Official Iowa Counties Genealogy Page & Registry
  http://www.iowa-counties.com/gene/
  This site has an Iowa Genealogy Discussion Group for questions and answers; the Iowa Internet Book Store; and a directory of professional researchers worldwide, as well as a forum for posting complaints about professional researchers.
- ROOTS-L United States Resources: Iowa
  http://www.rootsweb.com/roots-l/USA/ia.html
  Comprehensive list of research links, including many to history-related sites.

◆ Government & Cities

- 50states.com—Iowa State Information Resource
  http://www.50states.com/iowa.htm
  A list of general information for each state, including a list of colleges, state symbols, links to maps, newspapers, and other miscellaneous state information.
- Excite Travel by City.Net—Iowa
  http://www.city.net/countries/united_states/iowa/
- Official City Web Sites for the State of Iowa
  http://OfficialCitySites.org/Iowa.htm
- State of Iowa Home Page
  http://www.state.ia.us/
- The Villages of Van Buren
  http://www.netins.net/showcase/villages/
- Yahoo! Get Local...Iowa Cities
  http://dir.yahoo.com/Regional/U_S__States/Iowa/Cities/
  Maps, yellow pages, white pages, newspapers and other local information.
- Yahoo! Get Local...Iowa Counties and Regions
  http://dir.yahoo.com/Regional/U_S__States/Iowa/Counties_and_Regions/
  Maps, yellow pages, white pages, newspapers and other local information.

◆ History & Culture

- Yahoo!...History...Iowa
  http://dir.yahoo.com/Arts/Humanities/History/
  Browse_By_Region/U_S__States/Iowa/

◆ Libraries, Archives & Museums

- Burlington Public Library
  http://www.burlington.lib.ia.us/

- Cedar Rapids Public Library Genealogical Holdings
  http://www.rootsweb.com/~ialinn/cr_lib.htm

- Family History Centers—Iowa
  http://www.deseretbook.com/famhis/ia.html

- Family History Centers—Iowa
  http://www.lib.byu.edu/~uvrfhc/centers/iowa.html

- HYTELNET—Library Catalogs: USA: Iowa
  http://library.usask.ca/hytelnet/usa/IA.html
  *Before you use any of the Telnet links, make note of the user
  name, password and any other logon information.*

- Iowa Family History Centers
  http://www.genhomepage.com/FHC/Iowa.html
  *A list of addresses, phone numbers and hours of operation from
  the Genealogy Home Page.*

- Iowa Libraries on the Web
  http://www.silo.lib.ia.us/web-dir.html
  A list from the State Library of Iowa.

- Kellogg, Iowa Historical Museum
  http://www.rootsweb.com/~iajasper/museum.htm

- NUCMC Listing of Archives and Manuscript
  Repositories in Iowa
  http://lcweb.loc.gov/coll/nucmc/iasites.html
  *Links to information about resources other than those held in the
  Library of Congress.*

- Repositories of Primary Sources: Iowa
  http://www.uidaho.edu/special-collections/east1.html#usia
  *A list of links to online resources from the Univ. of Idaho
  Library, Special Collections and Archives.*

- State Library of Iowa
  http://www.silo.lib.ia.us/

- webCATS: Library Catalogues on the World Wide
  Web—Iowa
  http://library.usask.ca/hywebcat/states/IA.html

◆ Mailing Lists, Newsgroups & Chat

- Genealogy Resources on the Internet—Illinois
  Mailing Lists
  http://members.aol.com/gfsjohnf/gen_mail_states-ia.html
  *Each of the mailing list links below points to this site, wonder-
  fully maintained by John Fuller. Visit this site for county-specific
  mailing lists as well.*

- IA-NEB-ROOTS Mailing List—Illinois & Nebraska
  http://members.aol.com/gfsjohnf/gen_mail_states-ia.
  html#IA-NEB-ROOTS-L

- IA-Rooters Mailing List
  http://members.aol.com/gfsjohnf/gen_mail_states-ia.
  html#IA-Rooters

◆ Maps, Gazetteers & Geographical Information

- 1882 Iowa State Gazetteer and Business Directory
  http://www.rootsweb.com/~usgenweb/ia/1882gaz.htm

- 1895 U.S. Atlas—Iowa
  http://www.LivGenMI.com/1895ia.htm

- American Memory Panoramic Maps 1847–1929—
  Iowa
  http://lcweb2.loc.gov/cgi-bin/query/S?ammem/gmd:
  @filreq(@field(STATE+iowa)+@field(COLLID+pmmap))
  From the Geography and Map Division, Library of Congress.

- American Memory Railroad Maps 1828–1900—
  Iowa
  http://memory.loc.gov/cgi-bin/query/S?ammem/gmd:
  @filreq(@field(STATE+iowa)+@field(COLLID+rrmap))
  From the Geography and Map Division, Library of Congress.

- Color Landform Atlas: Iowa
  http://fermi.jhuapl.edu/states/ia_0.html
  Including a map of counties and a map for 1895.

- Excite Maps: Iowa Maps
  http://www.city.net/maps/view/?mapurl=/countries/
  united_states/iowa
  Zoom in on these maps all the way to the street level.

- HPI County InfoSystem—Counties in Iowa
  http://www.com/hpi/iacty/index.html

- K.B. Slocum Books and Maps—Iowa
  http://www.treasurenet.com/cgi-bin/treasure/kbslocum/scan/
  se=Iowa/sf=mapstate

- List of Iowa Counties
  http://www.genealogy.org/~st-clair/counties/state_ia.html

- Map of Iowa Counties
  http://govinfo.kerr.orst.edu/gif/states/ia.gif
  *From the Government Information Sharing Project, Information
  Services, Oregon State University.*

- Map of Iowa Counties
  http://www.lib.utexas.edu/Libs/PCL/Map_collection/states/
  Iowa.gif
  *From the Perry-Castañeda Library at the Univ. of Texas at
  Austin.*

- Origin and Naming of Iowa Counties
  http://www.sos.state.ia.us/register/r7/r7origin.htm

- U.S. Census Bureau—Iowa Profiles
  http://www.census.gov/datamap/www/19.html

- Yale Peabody Museum: GNIS—Iowa
  http://www.peabody.yale.edu/other/gnis/IA.html
  *Search the USGS Geographic Names Database. You can limit the search to a specific county in this state and search for any of the following features: airport arch area arroyo bar basin bay beach bench bend bridge **building** canal cape **cemetery** channel **church** cliff crater crossing dam falls flat forest gap geyser glacier gut harbor hospital island isthmus lake lava levee locale mine oilfield other park pillar plain ppl range rapids reserve reservoir ridge **school** sea slope spring stream summit swamp tower trail tunnel valley well woods.*

◆ Military

- 8th Iowa Cavalry from Appanoose County, Iowa
  http://www.ionet.net/~cousin/dale3.html

- 10th Iowa Volunteer Infantry
  http://www.geocities.com/Heartland/Plains/7614/10thiowa.htm

- 36th Iowa Infantry
  http://www.rootsweb.com/~iaappano/36ia.htm

- 36th Iowa Infantry POWs At Camp Ford, Tyler, TX
  http://www.rootsweb.com/~iaappano/pow.htm

- The Civil War Archive—Union Regiments—Iowa
  http://www.civilwararchive.com/unionia.htm

- Civil War: Iowa Volunteers
  http://www.alaska.net/~design/civilwar/
  Including excerpts from a Civil War diary and letters.

- Civil War Record for Black Hawk County, Iowa
  http://www.iowa-counties.com/blackhawk/civilwar/index.shtml
  Including: First Cavalry, Ninth Infantry, Twelfth Infantry, and Thirty-First Infantry.

- Korean Conflict State-Level Casualty Lists—Iowa
  http://www.nara.gov/nara/electronic/iahrlist.html
  From the National Archives and Records Administration, Center for Electronic Records.

- Letters from an Iowa Soldier in the Civil War
  http://www.ucsc.edu./civil-war-letters/home.html
  Part of a collection written by Newton Robert SCOTT, Private, Company A, of the 36th Infantry, Iowa Volunteers to Hannah CONE, his friend and later his wife.

- Roster of 24th Iowa Infantry
  http://www.rootsweb.com/~ialinn/civil_war/24th/24_indx.htm
  Formed in Linn County, Iowa.

- Table of Contents for the 15th Iowa Infantry
  http://www.geocities.com/Heartland/Plains/3730/table.htm

- Vietnam Conflict State-Level Casualty Lists—Iowa
  http://www.nara.gov/nara/electronic/iahrviet.html
  From the National Archives and Records Administration, Center for Electronic Records.

- The Vietnam Veterans Memorial—Iowa
  http://grunt.space.swri.edu/statewall/iowa/ia.htm

- Xerxes Knox, Private, Company G, 3rd Iowa Cavalry in the Civil War
  http://www.oz.net/~cyndihow/xerxes.htm
  Cyndi's 3rd-great-grandfather & a successful escapee from Camp Ford, Tyler, Texas.

◆ Newspapers

- AJR NewsLink—Iowa Newspapers
  http://www.newslink.org/ianews.html

- E&P Media Info Links—Newspaper Sites in Iowa
  http://www.mediainfo.com/emedia/browse-results.htm?region=iowa&category=newspaper+++++++++

- Ecola Newstand: Iowa
  http://www.ecola.com/news/press/na/us/ia/

- NAA Hotlinks to Newspapers Online—Iowa
  http://www.naa.org/hotlinks/searchResult.asp?param=IA-Iowa&City=1

- N-Net—Iowa Newspapers
  http://www.n-net.com/ia.htm

- Sioux City Journal Online
  http://www.siouxcityjournal.com/

- The Ultimate Collection of News Links: USA—Iowa
  http://www.pppp.net/links/news/USA-IA.html

- Yahoo!...Newspapers...Iowa
  http://dir.yahoo.com/News_and_Media/Newspapers/Browse_By_Region/U_S__States/Iowa/

◆ People & Families

- Directory of Underground Railroad Operators—Iowa
  http://www.ugrr.org//names/map-ia.htm

- Linn County Biography Index
  http://www.rootsweb.com/~ialinn/bios/bio-index.htm

- Louisa County Genealogical Society Biographies
  http://www.rootsweb.com/~ialouisa/lbios.htm

- Tribes and Villages of Iowa
  http://hanksville.phast.umass.edu:8000/cultprop/contacts/tribal/IA.html

◆ Professional Researchers, Volunteers & Other Research Services

- Board for Certification of Genealogists—Roster of Those Certified—Specializing in Iowa
  http://www.genealogy.org/~bcg/rosts_ia.html

- Genealogy Helplist—Iowa
  http://www.geocities.com/Heartland/Acres/3525/helplist.html

- The Official Iowa Counties Professional Genealogist and Researcher's Registry for Iowa
  http://www.iowa-counties.com/gene/ia.htm

◆ Publications, Software & Supplies

- AncestorSpy—CDs and Microfiche for Iowa
  http://www.ancestorspy.com/ia.htm

- Barbara Green's Used Genealogy Books—Iowa
  http://home.earthlink.net/~genbooks/lochist.html#IA

- Barnette's Family Tree Books—Iowa
  http://www.barnettesbooks.com/iowa.htm

- Books We Own—Iowa
  http://www.rootsweb.com/~bwo/iowa.html

- Boyd Publishing Company—Iowa
  http://www.hom.net/~gac/iowa.htm

- Camp Pope Bookshop
  http://members.aol.com/ckenyoncpb/index.htm
  Specializing in out-of-print books on the American Civil War, Iowa & the Trans-Mississippi Theater.

- Frontier Press Bookstore—Iowa
  http://www.frontierpress.com/frontier.cgi?category=ia

- Heritage Quest—Microfilm Records for the State of Iowa
  http://www.heritagequest.com/genealogy/microfilm/iowa/

- Iowa Counties—Iowa Internet Book Store
  http://iowa-counties.com/bookstore/

- The Memorabilia Corner—Books: Iowa
  http://members.aol.com/TMCorner/book_iow.htm

- S-K Publications—Iowa 1850 Census Books
  http://www.skpub.com/genie/census/ia/

◆ Queries, Message Boards & Surname Lists

- GenConnect Iowa Visitor Center
  http://cgi.rootsweb.com/~genbbs/indx/la.html
  A system for posting queries, Bibles, biographies, deeds, obituaries, pensions, wills.

- Jones County, Iowa History and Genealogy Record 1996
  http://www.ia.net/~kccdiana/surnames.htm
  This is an index to a set of books for sale regarding Jones County, Iowa Surnames and Genealogy.

◆ Records: Census, Cemeteries, Land, Obituaries, Personal, Taxes and Vital (Born, Married, Died & Buried)

- The 1790–1890 Federal Population Censuses: Catalog of National Archives Microfilm
  http://www.genealogy.org/census/contents.shtml

- ○ Census Schedules and Microfilm Roll Numbers for Iowa:
  1840
  http://www.genealogy.org/census/1840_schedules/Iowa.html
  1850
  http://www.genealogy.org/census/1850_schedules/Iowa.html
  1860
  http://www.genealogy.org/census/1860_schedules/Iowa.html
  1870
  http://www.genealogy.org/census/1870_schedules/Iowa.html
  1880
  http://www.genealogy.org/census/1880_schedules/Iowa.html
  1880 Soundex
  http://www.genealogy.org/census/1880.sdx_schedules/T748.html

- 1840 Census—Linn County, Iowa
  http://www.rootsweb.com/~ialinn/census/1840.htm

- Cemeteries of the United States—Iowa Cemeteries—County Index
  http://www.gac.edu/~kengelha/uscemeteries/iowa.html

- Census Online—Links to Census Sites on the Web—Iowa
  http://www.census-online.com/links/IA_data.html

- County Courthouse Addresses
  http://www.familytreemaker.com/00000244.html

- Find-A-Grave by Location: Iowa
  http://www.findagrave.com/grave/lia.html
  Graves of noteworthy people.

- Index of All Surnames Enumerated in the Benton Co., IA 1850 Federal Census
  http://www.rootsweb.com/~iabenton/1850.htm
  This page includes an offer for a lookup to be done in the 1850 Benton County Census.

- Interment.net: Iowa Cemeteries
  http://www.interment.net/us/ia/index.htm
  A list of links to other sites.

- Iowa Funeral Directors Association Members
  http://www.istatinc.com/ifda_members.html

- Iowa Vital Records Information
  http://vitalrec.com/ia.html

- Jackson County, IA Cemeteries
  http://www.rootsweb.com/~iajackso/Cemetery.html

- Jones County, Iowa 1852 State Census
  http://www.rootsweb.com/~iajones/census/1852/52census.htm

- Jones County, Iowa 1854 Census
  http://www.rootsweb.com/~iajones/census/1854/54census.htm

- Jones County, Iowa 1856 Census
  http://www.rootsweb.com/~iajones/census/1856/56census.htm

- Louisa County Tax List
  http://www.rootsweb.com/~ialouisa/taxes.htm

- Madison County, Iowa Marriages 1850–1880
  http://searches.rootsweb.com/cgi-bin/Genea/iowa
- National Archives—Central Plains Region
  (Kansas City)
  http://www.nara.gov/regional/kansas.html
- National Archives—Central Plains Region from
  Family Tree Maker
  http://www.familytreemaker.com/00000095.html
  Records for Iowa, Kansas, Missouri, and Nebraska.
- North Central Iowa Newspaper Obituaries
  http://www.netins.net/showcase/pafways/obitone.htm
- The Political Graveyard—Cemeteries in Iowa
  http://politicalgraveyard.com/geo/IA/kmindex.html
- Preplanning Network—Funeral Home and
  Cemetery Directory—Iowa
  http://www.preplannet.com/iowafhcem.htm
- SAMPUBCO
  http://www.wasatch.com/~dsam/sampubco/index.htm
  *Will Testators Indexes, Naturalization Records Indexes and
  Census Indexes online. You can order copies of the original
  source documents for a small fee.*
- Sioux City Journal Online—Daily Obituaries
  http://www.siouxcityjournal.com/editorial/obit.html
- USGenWeb Census Project Iowa
  http://www.usgenweb.org/census/states/iowa/iowa.htm
- USGenWeb Tombstone Transcription Project—Iowa
  http://www.rootsweb.com/~cemetery/iowa.html
- VitalChek Network—Iowa
  http://www.vitalchek.com/stateselect.asp?state=IA
- Where to Write for Vital Records—Iowa
  http://www.cdc.gov/nchswww/howto/w2w/iowa.htm
  From the National Center for Health Statistics (NCHS).

◆ Religion & Churches

- Christianity.Net Church Locator—Iowa
  http://www.christianity.net/cgi/
  location.exe?United_States+Iowa
- Church Online!—Iowa
  http://www.churchonline.com/usas/ia/ia.html
- Church Profiles—Iowa
  http://www.church-profiles.com/ia/ia.html
- Churches dot Net—Global Church Web Pages—
  Iowa
  http://www.churches.net/churches/iowa.html
- Churches of the World—Iowa
  http://www.churchsurf.com/churches/Iowa/index.htm
  From the ChurchSurf Christian Directory.

◆ Societies & Groups

- Archer's Computer Interest Group List—Iowa
  http://www.genealogy.org/~ngs/cigs/ngl1usia.html
- Audubon County Genealogical Society
  http://www.netins.net/showcase/exiracc/acgs/
- Benton County Genealogical Society
  http://www.rootsweb.com/~iabenton/bcgs.htm
- Bremer County Iowa Genealogical Society
  http://www.rootsweb.com/~iabremer/gensoc.html
- Des Moines County Genealogical Society, Inc.
  http://www.geocities.com/Heartland/Valley/9825/
- Dubuque County Key City Genealogical Society
  http://users.mwci.net/~vschlarm/dckcgs/fromes.html
- Franklin County Genealogical Society
  http://www.willowtree.com/~yankeez/fcgs/page1.htm
  Hampton, Iowa
- The Grand Lodge of Iowa, A.F. & A.M.
  http://www.gl-ia.org/
- Harrison County Genealogical Society
  http://www.rootsweb.com/~iaharris/hcgs.htm
- The Historical Society of Pottawattamie
  County Iowa
  http://www.geocities.com/Heartland/Plains/5660/
- IOOF Lodge Website Directory—Iowa
  http://norm28.hsc.usc.edu/IOOF/USA/Iowa/Iowa.html
  Independent Order of Odd Fellows and Rebekahs.
- Iowa City Genealogical Society
  http://www.rootsweb.com/~iajohnso/icgensoc.htm
  Johnson County, Iowa
- Iowa Genealogical Society
  http://www.digiserve.com/igs/igs.htm
- Iowa Lakes Genealogy Society
  http://www.pionet.net/~nwiowa/spencer/clubs/ilgs.htm
  Spencer
- Iowa State Society of Daughters of the American
  Revolution
  http://www.geocities.com/Wellesley/7998/
- The Jasper County Genealogical Society
  http://www.rootsweb.com/~iajasper/jcgs/jcgs.htm
- Jones County Genealogical Society
  http://www.rootsweb.com/~iajones/research/research.htm#jcgs
- Kellogg, Iowa Historical Museum
  http://www.rootsweb.com/~iajasper/museum.htm
- Linn County Genealogical Society
  http://www.rootsweb.com/~ialinn/gen_soc.htm
- Linn County Historical Society
  http://www.rootsweb.com/~ialinn/hist_soc.htm
- Nishnabotna Genealogical Society of Shelby County
  http://www.rootsweb.com/~iashelby/scgs.htm
- Northeast Iowa Genealogical Society
  http://www.iowa-counties.com/blackhawk/gene.htm
  Black Hawk County, Iowa

- PAF-WAYS, A Genealogy/Computer Users Group
  http://www.netins.net/showcase/pafways/
  North Central Iowa
- Palo Alto County Genealogical Society
  http://www.rootsweb.com/~iapaloal/pageone.htm
- State Historical Society of Iowa
  http://www.state.ia.us/government/idca/shsi/
- Van Buren County Genealogical Society
  http://www.netins.net/showcase/vbciowa/vbcgs/vbcgs.htm
- Wapello County Genealogical Society
  http://www.rootsweb.com/~iawapegs/

◆ USGenWeb Project

- Iowa Genealogy—USGenWeb Project State Page
  http://www.usgenweb.org/ia
- IAGEN Mailing List
  http://members.aol.com/gfsjohnf/gen_mail_states-ia.
  html#IAGEN-L
  A mailing list (part of the USGenWeb Project) to provide communication among the IAGenWeb county coordinators and volunteers. The forum is open to individuals considering working within or having a valid interest in the IAGenWeb Project.
- Iowa Queries
  http://www.rootsweb.com/~iagenweb/queries/topquery.htm
- Iowa—USGenWeb Archives Table of Contents
  http://www.rootsweb.com/~usgenweb/ia/iafiles.htm
- Iowa—USGenWeb FTP Archives
  ftp://ftp.rootsweb.com/pub/usgenweb/ia/

U.S.—KANSAS—KS
http://www.CyndisList.com/ks.htm

Category Index:

- General Resource Sites
- Government & Cities
- History & Culture
- Libraries, Archives & Museums
- Locality Specific
- Mailing Lists, Newsgroups & Chat
- Maps, Gazetteers & Geographical Information
- Military
- Newspapers
- People & Families

- Professional Researchers, Volunteers & Other Research Services
- Publications, Software & Supplies
- Queries, Message Boards & Surname Lists
- Records: Census, Cemeteries, Land, Obituaries, Personal, Taxes and Vital
- Religion & Churches
- Societies & Groups
- USGenWeb Project

◆ General Resource Sites

- Dick Taylor's GHOSTCHASER
  http://www.ukans.edu/carrie/kancoll/chaser/
  Links to Kansas resources.

- Everton's Sources of Genealogical Information in Kansas
  http://www.everton.com/usa/ks.htm

- Family Tree Maker's Genealogy "How To" Guide—Kansas
  http://www.familytreemaker.com/00000190.html

- Genealogy Bulletin Board Systems in Kansas
  http://www.genealogy.org/~gbbs/gblks.html

- Genealogy Exchange & Surname Registry—KSGenExchange
  http://www.genexchange.com/ks/index.cfm

- Genealogy Resources on the Internet: Kansas
  http://www-personal.umich.edu/~cgaunt/kansas.html

- The Kansas Collection
  http://www.ukans.edu/carrie/kancoll/

- Kansas Heritage Center for Family and Local History
  http://history.cc.ukans.edu/heritage/

- Kansas Heritage's Interactive Genealogy
  http://falcon.cc.ukans.edu/~nsween/inter-gen.html

- LDS Research Outline for Kansas
  http://www.everton.com/usa/ks-0817B.txt

- Linda Wilson's Genealogy Page
  http://www.sunflower.org/~lmwilson/genpage.htm
  Information for Kansas vital and census records.

- Lineages' Genealogy Site: Kansas
  http://www.lineages.com/rooms/usa/state.asp?StateCode=KS

- Railroads in Kansas
  http://history.cc.ukans.edu/heritage/research/rr/railroads.html

- ROOTS-L United States Resources: Kansas
  http://www.rootsweb.com/roots-l/USA/ks.html
  Comprehensive list of research links, including many to history-related sites.

◆ Government & Cities

- 50states.com—Kansas State Information Resource
  http://www.50states.com/kansas.htm
  A list of general information for each state, including a list of colleges, state symbols, links to maps, newspapers, and other miscellaneous state information.

- Excite Travel by City.Net—Kansas
  http://www.city.net/countries/united_states/kansas/

- Official City Web Sites for the State of Kansas
  http://OfficialCitySites.org/Kansas.htm

- State of Kansas
  http://www.ink.org/

- Yahoo! Get Local...Kansas Cities
  http://dir.yahoo.com/Regional/U_S__States/Kansas/Cities/
  Maps, yellow pages, white pages, newspapers and other local information.

- Yahoo! Get Local...Kansas Counties and Regions
  http://dir.yahoo.com/Regional/U_S__States/Kansas/Counties_and_Regions/
  Maps, yellow pages, white pages, newspapers and other local information.

◆ History & Culture

- Old West Kansas
  http://history.cc.ukans.edu/heritage/old_west/old_west.html

- Yahoo!...History...Kansas
  http://dir.yahoo.com/Arts/Humanities/History/
  Browse_By_Region/U_S__States/Kansas/

◆ Libraries, Archives & Museums

- Family History Centers—Kansas
  http://www.deseretbook.com/famhis/ks.html

- Family History Centers—Kansas
  http://www.lib.byu.edu/~uvrfhc/centers/kansas.html

- HYTELNET—Library Catalogs: USA: Kansas
  http://library.usask.ca/hytelnet/usa/KS.html
  Before you use any of the Telnet links, make note of the user name, password and any other logon information.

- Kansas Family History Centers
  http://www.genhomepage.com/FHC/Kansas.html
  A list of addresses, phone numbers and hours of operation from the Genealogy Home Page.

- Kansas State Historical Society State Archives
  http://history.cc.ukans.edu/heritage/kshs/archives/
  archives.htm

- Kansas State Library
  http://skyways.lib.ks.us/KSL/

- Mennonite Library and Archives
  http://www.bethelks.edu/services/mla/
  Bethel College North Newton, Kansas.

- Midwest Historical and Genealogical Library
  http://skyways.lib.ks.us/genweb/mhgs/mhgs_library.htm
  Over 15,000 volumes and issues of books, magazines, manuscripts and collections in Wichita.

- NUCMC Listing of Archives and Manuscript Repositories in Kansas
  http://lcweb.loc.gov/coll/nucmc/kssites.html
  Links to information about resources other than those held in the Library of Congress.

- Repositories of Primary Sources: Kansas
  http://www.uidaho.edu/special-collections/west.html#usks
  A list of links to online resources from the Univ. of Idaho Library, Special Collections and Archives.

- W. A. Rankin Memorial Library, Wilson County, Kansas
  http://www.telepath.com/sysjer/rankin.htm

- webCATS: Library Catalogues on the World Wide Web—Kansas
  http://library.usask.ca/hywebcat/states/KS.html

◆ Locality Specific

- Also see the USGenWeb section for links to county-specific resources.

- Barber County, Kansas
  http://history.cc.ukans.edu/kansas/medicine/barberco.html

- Harper County, Kansas Home Page for Genealogy
  http://www.ohmygosh.com/genealogy/welcome.htm
  Local events & information, Harper County Cemetery records— Nine currently on-line, 1885 Harper County Census, Anthony Public Library's Genealogical Book Titles, Microfilm Titles, Microfilm Newspaper Titles and Harper County Genealogist's surnames & e-mail.

◆ Mailing Lists, Newsgroups & Chat

- Genealogy Resources on the Internet— Kansas Mailing Lists
  http://members.aol.com/gfsjohnf/gen_mail_states-ks.html
  Each of the mailing list links below points to this site, wonderfully maintained by John Fuller. Visit this site for county-specific mailing lists as well.

- KansasCity Mailing List
  http://members.aol.com/gfsjohnf/gen_mail_states-ks.
  html#KansasCity
  For anyone with a genealogical or historical interest in the greater Kansas City area (Kansas/Missouri).

- KANSAS-L Mailing List
  http://members.aol.com/gfsjohnf/gen_mail_states-ks.
  html#KANSAS-L
  Announcements and activities of the Kansas State Historical Society, a clearing house for announcements by other organizations, and a public forum for the discussion of Kansas heritage, both past and present.

- KANSASROOTS Mailing List
  http://members.aol.com/gfsjohnf/gen_mail_states-ks.
  html#KANSASROOTS

- KC-NGS Mailing List
  http://members.aol.com/gfsjohnf/gen_mail_states-ks.
  html#KC-NGS
  For anyone interested in the Northland Genealogy Society of Greater Kansas City.

- KC-NGS-NEWS Mailing List
  http://members.aol.com/gfsjohnf/gen_mail_states-ks.
  html#KC-NGS-NEWS
  For the members of the Northland Genealogical Society of Greater Kansas City.

- KS-KIN-L Mailing List
  http://members.aol.com/gfsjohnf/gen_mail_states-ks.
  html#KS-KIN-L

◆ Maps, Gazetteers & Geographical Information

- 1872 County Map of Kansas
  http://www.ismi.net/chnegw/1872kansas.htm

- 1895 U.S. Atlas—Kansas
  http://www.LivGenMI.com/1895ks.htm

- American Memory Panoramic Maps 1847–1929— Kansas
  http://lcweb2.loc.gov/cgi-bin/query/S?ammem/
  gmd:@filreq(@field(STATE+kansas)+@field(COLLID+pmmap))
  From the Geography and Map Division, Library of Congress.

- American Memory Railroad Maps 1828–1900—
  Kansas
  http://memory.loc.gov/cgi-bin/query/S?ammem/
  gmd:@filreq(@field(STATE+kansas)+@field(COLLID+rrmap))
  From the Geography and Map Division, Library of Congress.

- Color Landform Atlas: Kansas
  http://fermi.jhuapl.edu/states/ks_0.html
  Including a map of counties and a map for 1895.

- Excite Maps: Kansas Maps
  http://www.city.net/maps/view/?mapurl=/countries/
  united_states/kansas
  Zoom in on these maps all the way to the street level.

- HPI County InfoSystem—Counties in Kansas
  http://www.com/hpi/kscty/index.html

- K.B. Slocum Books and Maps—Kansas
  http://www.treasurenet.com/cgi-bin/treasure/kbslocum/scan/
  se=Kansas/sf=mapstate

- List of Kansas Counties
  http://www.genealogy.org/~st-clair/counties/state_ks.html

- Map of Kansas Counties
  http://govinfo.kerr.orst.edu/gif/states/ks.gif
  *From the Government Information Sharing Project, Information
  Services, Oregon State University.*

- Map of Kansas Counties
  http://www.lib.utexas.edu/Libs/PCL/Map_collection/states/
  Kansas.gif
  *From the Perry-Castañeda Library at the Univ. of Texas at
  Austin.*

- Old Kansas Area Maps
  http://history.cc.ukans.edu/carrie/kancoll/graphics/maps/
  maps.htm

- U.S. Census Bureau—Kansas Profiles
  http://www.census.gov/datamap/www/20.html

- Yale Peabody Museum: GNIS—Kansas
  http://www.peabody.yale.edu/other/gnis/KS.html
  *Search the USGS Geographic Names Database. You can limit
  the search to a specific county in this state and search for any of
  the following features: airport arch area arroyo bar basin bay
  beach bench bend bridge **building** canal cape **cemetery** channel
  church cliff crater crossing dam falls flat forest gap geyser
  glacier gut harbor hospital island isthmus lake lava levee locale
  mine oilfield other park pillar plain ppl range rapids reserve
  reservoir ridge **school** sea slope spring stream summit swamp
  tower trail tunnel valley well woods.*

◆ Military

- 1st Kansas Volunteer Infantry
  http://www.access.digex.net/~bdboyle/1stks.txt

- 10th Kansas Volunteer Infantry
  http://www.telepath.com/erics/10kansas1.html

- 12th Kansas Volunteer Infantry, Company K
  http://www.geocities.com/MotorCity/1949/cok12ks.htm

- Bleeding Kansas Home Page
  http://members.aol.com/marcalford/pp235.htm
  The SHULERs and the War on the Border.

- The Civil War Archive—Union Regiments—Kansas
  http://www.civilwararchive.com/unionks.htm

- Civil War Battle Summaries by State—Kansas
  http://www2.cr.nps.gov/abpp/battles/bystate.htm#ks

- Fourteenth Regiment, Kansas Volunteer Cavalry
  http://www.ukans.edu/~hisite/franklin/military/
  KS14thRegCav.htm

- Index to Kansas Volunteer Regiment Enlistments,
  1861–1865
  http://www.ukans.edu/heritage/kshs/archives/agorpt.htm

- Kansas Enlistments (1861–1865)
  http://www.lineages.com/military/ks_enlistments.asp
  Searchable database index from Lineages, Inc.

- Kansas in the Civil War
  http://skyways.lib.ks.us/kansas/genweb/civilwar/index.html

- Kansas Prisoners of War at Camp Ford, Texas
  1863–1865
  http://history.cc.ukans.edu/heritage/research/campford.html

- Korean Conflict State-Level Casualty Lists—Kansas
  http://www.nara.gov/nara/electronic/kshrlist.html
  *From the National Archives and Records Administration,
  Center for Electronic Records.*

- Second Kansas Volunteer Cavalry
  http://home.earthlink.net/~balocca/cavalry.html

- Soldiers in Kansas—Kansas State Historical Society
  State Archives
  http://history.cc.ukans.edu/heritage/kshs/resource/
  soldiers.htm

- Vietnam Conflict State-Level Casualty Lists—
  Kansas
  http://www.nara.gov/nara/electronic/kshrviet.html
  *From the National Archives and Records Administration,
  Center for Electronic Records.*

- The Vietnam Veterans Memorial—Kansas
  http://grunt.space.swri.edu/statewall/kansas/ks.htm

◆ Newspapers

- AJR NewsLink—Kansas Newspapers
  http://www.newslink.org/ksnews.html

- E&P Media Info Links—Newspaper Sites in Kansas
  http://www.mediainfo.com/emedia/browse-results.
  htm?region=kansas&category=newspaper+++++++++

- Ecola Newstand: Kansas
  http://www.ecola.com/news/press/na/us/ks/

- Guide to Newspapers on Microfilm
  http://history.cc.ukans.edu/heritage/kshs/library/news.htm

- NAA Hotlinks to Newspapers Online—Kansas
  http://www.naa.org/hotlinks/searchResult.asp?param=
  KS-Kansas&City=1

- N-Net—Kansas Newspapers
  http://www.n-net.com/ks.htm

- The Ultimate Collection of News Links:
  USA—Kansas
  http://www.pppp.net/links/news/USA-KS.html
- Wichita Online—A Service of the Wichita Eagle
  http://www.wichitaeagle.com/
- Yahoo!...Newspapers...Kansas
  http://dir.yahoo.com/News_and_Media/Newspapers/
  Browse_By_Region/U_S__States/Kansas/

◆ People & Families

- Directory of Underground Railroad Operators—
  Kansas
  http://www.ugrr.org//names/map-ks.htm
- Kansas Family History
  http://www.cc.ukans.edu/heritage/families/families_main.html
  Family group sheets & stores, listed by surname.
- Orphan Trains of Kansas
  http://kuhttp.cc.ukans.edu/carrie/kancoll/articles/orphans/
- The Plains and Emigrant Tribes of Kansas
  http://history.cc.ukans.edu/heritage/old_west/indian.html
- Tribes and Villages of Kansas
  http://hanksville.phast.umass.edu:8000/cultprop/contacts/
  tribal/KS.html

◆ Professional Researchers, Volunteers & Other Research Services

- Board for Certification of Genealogists—Roster of
  Those Certified—Specializing in Kansas
  http://www.genealogy.org/~bcg/rosts_ks.html
- Genealogy Helplist—Kansas
  http://posom.com/hl/usa/ks.shtml
- The Official Iowa Counties Professional Genealogist
  and Researcher's Registry for Kansas
  http://www.iowa-counties.com/gene/ks.htm

◆ Publications, Software & Supplies

- AncestorSpy—CDs and Microfiche for Kansas
  http://www.ancestorspy.com/ks.htm
- Barbara Green's Used Genealogy Books—Kansas
  http://home.earthlink.net/~genbooks/lochist.html#KS
- Barnette's Family Tree Books—Kansas
  http://www.barnettesbooks.com/kansas.htm
- Books of the Kansas Collection
  http://www.ukans.edu/carrie/kancoll/books/
- Books We Own—Kansas
  http://www.rootsweb.com/~bwo/kansas.html
- Boyd Publishing Company—Kansas
  http://www.hom.net/~gac/kansas.htm

- Frontier Press Bookstore—Kansas
  http://www.frontierpress.com/frontier.cgi?category=ks
- GenealogyBookShop.com—Kansas
  http://www.genealogybookshop.com/genealogybookshop/files/
  The_United_States,Kansas/index.html
  *The online store of Genealogical Publishing Co., Inc. &
  Clearfield Company.*
- Hearthstone Bookshop—Kansas
  http://www.hearthstonebooks.com/cgi-bin/webc.cgi/st_main.
  html?catid=80&sid=2PH5t29sm
- Heritage Books—Kansas
  http://www.heritagebooks.com/ks.htm
- Heritage Quest—Microfilm Records for the
  State of Kansas
  http://www.heritagequest.com/genealogy/microfilm/kansas/
- Lost in Time Books—Kansas
  http://www.lostintime.com/catalog/books/bookst/bo11000.htm
- The Memorabilia Corner—Books: Kansas
  http://members.aol.com/TMCorner/book_kan.htm
- Willow Bend Bookstore—Kansas
  http://www.willowbend.net/ks.htm

◆ Queries, Message Boards & Surname Lists

- GenConnect Kansas Visitor Center
  http://cgi.rootsweb.com/~genbbs/indx/Ks.html
  *A system for posting queries, Bibles, biographies, deeds,
  obituaries, pensions, wills.*
- Harper County Genealogical Society Queries
  http://www.pe.net/~lucindaw/kansas/genealog/hgs-qry.htm
- The Kansas Surname List
  http://raven.cc.ukans.edu/heritage/research/inter-gen/ks-
  gen1.html
- WGS Query Page—The Wichita Genealogical
  Society, Wichita, Kansas
  http://history.cc.ukans.edu/kansas/wgs/viewq.html

◆ Records: Census, Cemeteries, Land, Obituaries, Personal, Taxes and Vital (Born, Married, Died & Buried)

- The 1790–1890 Federal Population Censuses:
  Catalog of National Archives Microfilm
  http://www.genealogy.org/census/contents.shtml
  - Census Schedules and Microfilm Roll Numbers
    for Kansas:
    1860
    http://www.genealogy.org/census/1860_schedules/
    Kansas.html

1870
http://www.genealogy.org/census/1870_schedules/Kansas.html

1880
http://www.genealogy.org/census/1880_schedules/Kansas.html

1880 Soundex
http://www.genealogy.org/census/1880.sdx_schedules/T749.html

- 1885 Anthony, Kansas Census
http://www.ohmygosh.com/genealogy/records/1885Anthonycensus.htm

- Cemeteries of the United States—Kansas Cemeteries—County Index
http://www.gac.edu/~kengelha/uscemeteries/kansas.html

- Census Online—Links to Census Sites on the Web—Kansas
http://www.census-online.com/links/KS_data.html

- County Courthouse Addresses
http://www.familytreemaker.com/00000245.html

- Find-A-Grave by Location: Kansas
http://www.findagrave.com/grave/lks.html
Graves of noteworthy people.

- Harper County Cemeteries
http://www.ohmygosh.com/genealogy/cemetery.htm

- Interment.net: Kansas Cemeteries
http://www.interment.net/us/ks/index.htm
A list of links to other sites.

- Kansas City Star Obituaries
http://www.kcstar.com/cgi-bin/class?template=clq-obit.htm&category=0&database=daily

- Kansas Censuses 1855–1875
http://history.cc.ukans.edu/heritage/kshs/library/18551875.htm
A guide to the records on microfilm.

- Kansas Land Records
http://pixel.cs.vt.edu/library/land/kansas/

- Kansas Vital Records Information
http://vitalrec.com/ks.html

- Lyona Cemetery List of Burials
http://wwwp.exis.net/~bgugler/crecords.htm
Dickinson County, Kansas

- National Archives—Central Plains Region (Kansas City)
http://www.nara.gov/regional/kansas.html

- National Archives—Central Plains Region from Family Tree Maker
http://www.familytreemaker.com/00000095.html
Records for Iowa, Kansas, Missouri, and Nebraska.

- The Political Graveyard—Cemeteries in Kansas
http://politicalgraveyard.com/geo/KS/kmindex.html

- Preplanning Network—Funeral Home and Cemetery Directory—Kansas
http://www.preplannet.com/kansasfhcem.htm

- SAMPUBCO
http://www.wasatch.com/~dsam/sampubco/index.htm
Will Testators Indexes, Naturalization Records Indexes and Census Indexes online. You can order copies of the original source documents for a small fee..

- USGenWeb Census Project Kansas
http://www.usgenweb.org/census/states/kansas.htm

- USGenWeb Tombstone Transcription Project—Kansas
http://www.rootsweb.com/~cemetery/kansas.html

- VitalChek Network—Kansas
http://www.vitalchek.com/stateselect.asp?state=KS

- Where to Write for Vital Records—Kansas
http://www.cdc.gov/nchswww/howto/w2w/kansas.htm
From the National Center for Health Statistics (NCHS).

◆ Religion & Churches

- Christianity.Net Church Locator—Kansas
http://www.christianity.net/cgi/location.exe?United_States+Kansas

- Church Online!—Kansas
http://www.churchonline.com/usas/ks/ks.html

- Church Profiles—Kansas
http://www.church-profiles.com/ks/ks.html

- Churches dot Net—Global Church Web Pages—Kansas
http://www.churches.net/churches/kansas.html

- Churches of the World—Kansas
http://www.churchsurf.com/churches/Kansas/index.htm
From the ChurchSurf Christian Directory.

◆ Societies & Groups

- American Historical Society of Germans from Russia—Golden Wheat Chapter
http://www.ahsgr.org/ksgolden.html

- American Historical Society of Germans from Russia—Kansas Sunflower Chapter
http://www.ahsgr.org/kssunflo.html

- American Historical Society of Germans from Russia—Northeastern Kansas Chapter
http://www.ahsgr.org/ksnorthe.html

- The American Legion—Pearce-Keller Post 17
http://www.flinthills.com/~post17/index.html
Manhattan, Kansas

- Archer's Computer Interest Group List—Kansas
http://www.genealogy.org/~ngs/cigs/ngl1usks.html

- Branches & Twigs Genealogical Society
http://skyways.lib.ks.us/kansas/genweb/kingman/
branches.html
Kingman, Kansas

- Cherokee County Kansas Genealogical-Historical
Society, Inc.
http://skyways.lib.ks.us/kansas/genweb/cherokee/society/
cckghs.html

- Dickinson County Historical Society's
Heritage Center
http://history.cc.ukans.edu/heritage/abilene/herctr.html

- Franklin County Kansas Genealogical Society
http://www.ukans.edu/~hisite/franklin/fcgs/

- Harper County Genealogical Society
http://www.pe.net/~lucindaw/kansas/genealog/hgs.htm

- IOOF Lodge Website Directory—Kansas
http://norm28.hsc.usc.edu/IOOF/USA/Kansas/Kansas.html
Independent Order of Odd Fellows and Rebekahs.

- Johnson County Genealogical Society and
Library, Inc.
http://history.cc.ukans.edu/heritage/society/jcgs/
jcgs_main.html

- Kansas Council of Genealogical Societies
http://skyways.lib.ks.us/kansas/genweb/kcgs/index.html

- Kansas Genealogical Society
http://www.dodgecity.net/kgs/
Dodge City, Kansas

- Kansas State Historical Society
http://history.cc.ukans.edu/heritage/kshs/kshs1.html

- Labette County Genealogical Society, Inc.
http://skyways.lib.ks.us/genweb/society/parsons/
Parsons, Kansas

- Leavenworth County Historical Society
http://history.cc.ukans.edu/kansas/lchs/lchs.html

- Lyon County Historical Society and Museum
http://www.emporia.edu/S/www/slim/resource/lchs/
LyonCo.htm

- Midwest Historical and Genealogical Society
http://skyways.lib.ks.us/kansas/genweb/mhgs/index.html
Wichita, Kansas

- Nemaha County Genealogical Society
http://ukanaix.cc.ukans.edu/kansas/seneca/gensoc/
gensoc.html

- Nemaha County Historical Society
http://ukanaix.cc.ukans.edu/kansas/seneca/histsoc/
nemcohis.html

- Overland Park Historical Society
http://kcsun4.kcstar.com/schools/
OverlandParkHistoricalSociety/

- Reno County Genealogical Society
http://www.hplsck.org/gen.htm
Hutchinson, Kansas

- Riley County Genealogical Society & Library
http://www.flinthills.com/~rcgs/
Manhattan, Kansas

- Smoky Valley Genealogical Society
http://skyways.lib.ks.us/kansas/genweb/ottawa/smoky.html
Salina, Kansas

- Topeka Genealogical Society
http://www.cjnetworks.com/~gaulding/tgs.htm

- Wichita Genealogical Society
http://kuhttp.cc.ukans.edu/kansas/wgs/wgs.html

- Wyandotte County Historical Society and Museum
http://history.cc.ukans.edu/kansas/wchs/mainpage.html

◆ USGenWeb Project

- Kansas Genealogy—USGenWeb Project State Page
http://www.usgenweb.org/ks

- Kansas—USGenWeb Archives Table of Contents
http://www.rootsweb.com/~usgenweb/ks/ksfiles.htm

- Kansas—USGenWeb FTP Archives
ftp://ftp.rootsweb.com/pub/usgenweb/ks/

U.S.—KENTUCKY—KY
http://www.CyndisList.com/ky.htm

Category Index:

- General Resource Sites
- Government & Cities
- History & Culture
- Libraries, Archives & Museums
- Locality Specific
- Mailing Lists, Newsgroups & Chat
- Maps, Gazetteers & Geographical Information
- Military
- Newspapers
- People & Families

- Professional Researchers, Volunteers & Other Research Services
- Publications, Software & Supplies
- Queries, Message Boards & Surname Lists
- Records: Census, Cemeteries, Land, Obituaries, Personal, Taxes and Vital
- Religion & Churches
- Societies & Groups
- USGenWeb Project

◆ General Resource Sites

- Everton's Sources of Genealogical Information in Kentucky
  http://www.everton.com/usa/ky.htm
- Family Tree Maker's Genealogy "How To" Guide—Kentucky
  http://www.familytreemaker.com/00000191.html
- Genealogy Bulletin Board Systems for Kentucky
  http://www.genealogy.org/~gbbs/gblky.html
- Genealogy Exchange & Surname Registry—KYGenExchange
  http://www.genexchange.com/ky/index.cfm
- Genealogy Resources on the Internet: Kentucky
  http://www-personal.umich.edu/~cgaunt/kentucky.html
- Kentuckiana Genealogy WebRing
  http://www.floyd-pavey.com/kentuckiana/kyiana/webring.html
  Kentucky & Indiana
- LDS Research Outline for Kentucky
  http://www.everton.com/usa/ky-0818B.txt
- Lineages' Genealogy Site: Kentucky
  http://www.lineages.com/rooms/usa/state.asp?StateCode=KY
- ROOTS-L United States Resources: Kentucky
  http://www.rootsweb.com/roots-l/USA/ky.html
  Comprehensive list of research links, including many to history-related sites.

◆ Government & Cities

- 50states.com—Kentucky State Information Resource
  http://www.50states.com/kentucky.htm
  A list of general information for each state, including a list of colleges, state symbols, links to maps, newspapers, and other miscellaneous state information.
- Commonwealth of Kentucky Web Server
  http://www.state.ky.us/
- Excite Travel by City.Net—Kentucky
  http://www.city.net/countries/united_states/kentucky/
- Official City Web Sites for the State of Kentucky
  http://OfficialCitySites.org/Kentucky.htm
- Yahoo! Get Local...Kentucky Cities
  http://dir.yahoo.com/Regional/U_S__States/Kentucky/Cities/
  Maps, yellow pages, white pages, newspapers and other local information.
- Yahoo! GLet Local...Kentucky Counties and Regions
  http://dir.yahoo.com/Regional/U_S__States/Kentucky/Counties_and_Regions/
  Maps, yellow pages, white pages, newspapers and other local information.

◆ History & Culture

- The Appalachian Center at the University of Kentucky, Lexington
  http://www.uky.edu/RGS/AppalCenter/
- Liberty Hall Historic Site
  http://www.libertyhall.org/

- Logan's Fort
  http://www.logansfort.org./

- Yahoo!...History...Kentucky
  http://dir.yahoo.com/Arts/Humanities/History/
  Browse_By_Region/U_S__States/Kentucky/

◆ Libraries, Archives & Museums

- Family History Centers—Kentucky
  http://www.deseretbook.com/famhis/ky.html

- Family History Centers—Kentucky
  http://www.lib.byu.edu/~uvrfhc/centers/kentucky.html

- HYTELNET—Library Catalogs: USA: Kentucky
  http://library.usask.ca/hytelnet/usa/KY.html
  Before you use any of the Telnet links, make note of the user name, password and any other logon information.

- Kentucky Department for Libraries and Archives
  http://www.kdla.state.ky.us/
  - Genealogical Reference Correspondence Policy
    http://www.kdla.state.ky.us/arch/corpolic.htm
  - Kentucky's African-American Genealogical Sources at the Kentucky Department for Libraries and Archives
    http://www.kdla.state.ky.us/arch/blkhist.htm

- Kentucky Family History Centers
  http://www.genhomepage.com/FHC/Kentucky.html
  A list of addresses, phone numbers and hours of operation from the Genealogy Home Page.

- The Lexington Kentucky Family History Center
  http://www.uky.edu/StudentOrgs/LDSSA/FHCpage.html

- Lexington Public Library
  http://www.lpl.lib.ky.us/
  - The Reference Department
    http://www.lpl.lib.ky.us/reference/index.html
    - The Kentucky Room
      http://www.lpl.lib.ky.us/reference/kyroom.html
      - Resources for Genealogists
        http://www.lpl.lib.ky.us/reference/resource.html

- NUCMC Listing of Archives and Manuscript Repositories in Kentucky
  http://lcweb.loc.gov/coll/nucmc/kysites.html
  Links to information about resources other than those held in the Library of Congress.

- Repositories of Primary Sources: Kentucky
  http://www.uidaho.edu/special-collections/east1.html#usky
  A list of links to online resources from the Univ. of Idaho Library, Special Collections and Archives.

- webCATS: Library Catalogues on the World Wide Web—Kentucky
  http://library.usask.ca/hywebcat/states/KY.html

◆ Locality Specific

- Also see the USGenWeb section for links to county-specific resources.

- Eastern Kentucky Genealogy and History Connections
  http://www.bright.net/~kat/index.htm

- Kentuckiana Genealogy
  http://www.floyd-pavey.com/kentuckiana/
  Covering Indiana counties of: Clark, Crawford, Dubois, Floyd, Harrison, Perry, Scott and Washington; and Kentucky counties of Breckinridge, Jefferson, Hardin and Meade.

- Lawrence Co., KY Connections and Collections
  http://ourworld.compuserve.com/homepages/GlenGallagher/lawky.htm

◆ Mailing Lists, Newsgroups & Chat

- Genealogy Resources on the Internet—Kentucky Mailing Lists
  http://members.aol.com/gfsjohnf/gen_mail_states-ky.html
  Each of the mailing list links below points to this site, wonderfully maintained by John Fuller. Visit this site for county-specific mailing lists as well.

- Appalachianfamily Mailing List
  http://members.aol.com/gfsjohnf/gen_mail_states-va.html#Appalachianfamily
  Appalachian Mountain Families including families from Georgia, North Carolina, South Carolina, Tennessee, Kentucky, Virginia, and West Virginia.

- CAMPBELL-KY Mailing List
  http://members.aol.com/gfsjohnf/gen_mail_states-ky.html#CAMPBELL-KY
  For Campbell County, Kentucky and its spinoff counties of Kenton, Boone, Pendleton, Grant and Bracken Counties.

- COALMINERS Mailing List
  http://members.aol.com/gfsjohnf/gen_mail_country-unk.html#COALMINERS
  For anyone whose ancestors were coalminers in the United Kingdom or the United States.

- CUMBERLAND-RIVER Mailing List
  http://members.aol.com/gfsjohnf/gen_mail_states-ky.html#CUMBERLANDRR
  For anyone with a genealogical or historical interest in the Cumberland River region of Southeast Kentucky, including Whitley, Wayne, Pulaski, Knox, and McCreary counties.

- HOPKINS-CTY Mailing List—Hopkins County
  http://members.aol.com/gfsjohnf/gen_mail_states-ky.html#HOPKINS-CTY

- JACKSON-CLAY-OVERTON-CO-TN Mailing List
  http://members.aol.com/gfsjohnf/gen_mail_states-tn.html#JACKSON/CLAY
  Jackson, Clay and/or Overton Counties, as well as Smith County, Tennessee which was the parent county and bordering Monroe County, Kentucky.

- **KENTUCKIANA** Mailing List
  http://members.aol.com/gfsjohnf/gen_mail_states-ky.
  html#KENTUCKIANA
  For anyone with a genealogical, historical, or cultural interest in the Indiana counties of Clark, Crawford, Dubois, Floyd, Harrison, Orange, Perry, Scott and Washington, and the Kentucky counties of Breckinridge, Hardin, Jefferson and Meade.

- **KYBIOG-L—Kentucky Biographies Project**
  http://members.aol.com/gfsjohnf/gen_mail_states-ky.
  html#KYBIOG-L
  Established to gather biographies of Kentucky citizens as well as those who have moved from Kentucky to other states and whose biographies in that state make reference to their Kentucky backgrounds.

- **KYBIOGRAPHIES** Mailing List
  http://members.aol.com/gfsjohnf/gen_mail_states-ky.
  html#KYBIOGRAPHIES
  A read-only mailing list (no queries or submissions) transmitting biographies on all the Kentucky people cited in the old histories (e.g., Perrins, Collins, church histories).

- **KYJacksonPurchase** Mailing List
  http://members.aol.com/gfsjohnf/gen_mail_states-ky.
  html#KYJacksonPurchase
  For those whose family roots and research trace to the Jackson Purchase area of Western Kentucky, covering the counties of Calloway, Marshall, Graves, Fulton, Hickman, Ballard, Carlisle and McCracken.

- **KYRESEARCH** Mailing List
  http://members.aol.com/gfsjohnf/gen_mail_states-ky.
  html#KYRESEARCH
  A mailing list where the list owner will be sharing researching techniques for Kentucky with some being applicable to other locations.

- **KYROOTS** Mailing List
  http://members.aol.com/gfsjohnf/gen_mail_states-ky.
  html#KYROOTS

- **KYWBTSVETS** Mailing List
  http://members.aol.com/gfsjohnf/gen_mail_states-ky.
  html#KYWBTSVETS
  For anyone with a genealogical interest in Kentucky veterans of the War Between the States, both Confederate and Union.

- **LBL** Mailing List
  http://members.aol.com/gfsjohnf/gen_mail_states-ky.html#LBL
  For anyone with a genealogical interest in the Land Between the Lakes region of Kentucky covering Lyon, Caldwell, and Trigg Counties.

- **MCF-ROOTS**
  http://members.aol.com/gfsjohnf/gen_mail_states-gen.
  html#MCF-ROOTS
  A mailing list (Maryland Catholics on the Frontier) for the discussion of descendants of Maryland Catholics who migrated first to Kentucky and then to other parts of the frontier.

- **Melungeon** Mailing List
  http://members.aol.com/gfsjohnf/gen_mail_states-gen.
  html#MELUNGEO
  For people conducting Melungeon and/or Appalachian research including Native American, Portuguese, Turkish, Black Dutch, and other unverifiable mixed statements of ancestry or unexplained rumors, with ancestors in TN, KY, VA, NC, SC, GA, AL, WV, and possibly other places.

- **RUDDLESFORT** Mailing List
  http://members.aol.com/gfsjohnf/gen_mail_states-ky.
  html#RUDDLESFORT
  For interested historians, genealogists, and descendants of the survivors of the destruction of Ruddle's and Martin's Forts in pre-Bourbon County, Kentucky (Virginia) during the Revolutionary War.

- **SOUTH-CENTRAL-KENTUCKY** Mailing List
  http://members.aol.com/gfsjohnf/gen_mail_states-ky.
  html#SOUTH-CENTRAL-KY
  Counties of: Adair, Allen, Barren, Cumberland, Edmonson, Green, Hart, Metcalfe, Monroe, Russell, Taylor, and Warren.

- **WEST-CENTRAL-KY** Mailing List
  http://members.aol.com/gfsjohnf/gen_mail_states-ky.
  html#WEST-CENTRAL-KY
  For anyone with a genealogical interest in West-Central Kentucky, including the counties of Breckinridge, Butler, Daviess, Edmonson, Grayson, Hancock, Hardin, Hart, LaRue, McLean, Meade, and Ohio, which were all derived in large part from Old Hardin County as it was created in 1792.

- **WESTKENTUCKY** Mailing List
  http://members.aol.com/gfsjohnf/gen_mail_states-ky.
  html#WESTKENTUCKY
  Counties of Ballard, Caldwell, Calloway, Carlisle, Christian, Crittenden, Fulton, Graves, Henderson, Hickman, Hopkins, Livingston, Lyon, McCracken, Marshall, Trigg, Union, and Webster.

◆ Maps, Gazetteers & Geographical Information

- 1895 U.S. Atlas—Kentucky
  http://www.LivGenMI.com/1895ky.htm

- American Memory Panoramic Maps 1847–1929—Kentucky
  http://lcweb2.loc.gov/cgi-bin/query/S?ammem/gmd:
  @filreq(@field(STATE+kentucky)+@field(COLLID+pmmap))
  From the Geography and Map Division, Library of Congress.

- American Memory Railroad Maps 1828–1900—Kentucky
  http://memory.loc.gov/cgi-bin/query/S?ammem/gmd:
  @filreq(@field(STATE+kentucky)+@field(COLLID+rrmap))
  From the Geography and Map Division, Library of Congress.

- Color Landform Atlas: Kentucky
  http://fermi.jhuapl.edu/states/ky_0.html
  Including a map of counties and a map for 1895.

- An Electronic Guide to Kentucky Place Names
  http://www.uky.edu/KentuckyPlaceNames/

- Excite Maps: Kentucky Maps
  http://www.city.net/maps/view/?mapurl=/countries/
  united_states/kentucky
  Zoom in on these maps all the way to the street level.

- Historical Maps of Kentucky and Her Counties
  http://www.abraxis.com/beegee/Genealogy/Kentucky/Maps/
  kymaps.htm
  From December 31, 1776, to November 1, 1780, this area was called Kentucky County, Virginia.

- HPI County InfoSystem—Counties in Kentucky
  http://www.com/hpi/kycty/index.html
- K.B. Slocum Books and Maps—Kentucky
  http://www.treasurenet.com/cgi-bin/treasure/kbslocum/scan/
  se=Kentucky/sf=mapstate
- Kentucky Atlas & Gazetteer
  http://www.uky.edu/KentuckyAtlas/kentucky-gazetteer.html
- List of Kentucky Counties
  http://www.genealogy.org/~st-clair/counties/state_ky.html
- Map of Kentucky Counties, Map #1
  http://govinfo.kerr.orst.edu/gif/states/ky.gif

  Map #2
  http://govinfo.kerr.orst.edu/gif/states/ky1.gif

  Map #3
  http://govinfo.kerr.orst.edu/gif/states/ky2.gif

  Map #4
  http://govinfo.kerr.orst.edu/gif/states/kyorig.gif
  From the Government Information Sharing Project, Information Services, Oregon State University.
- Map of Kentucky Counties
  http://www.lib.utexas.edu/Libs/PCL/Map_collection/states/
  Kentucky.gif
  From the Perry-Castañeda Library at the Univ. of Texas at Austin.
- U.S. Census Bureau—Kentucky Profiles
  http://www.census.gov/datamap/www/21.html
- Yale Peabody Museum: GNIS—Kentucky
  http://www.peabody.yale.edu/other/gnis/KY.html
  *Search the USGS Geographic Names Database. You can limit the search to a specific county in this state and search for any of the following features: airport arch area arroyo bar basin bay beach bench bend bridge **building** canal cape **cemetery** channel **church** cliff crater crossing dam falls flat forest gap geyser glacier gut harbor hospital island isthmus lake lava levee locale mine oilfield other park pillar plain ppl range rapids reserve reservoir ridge **school** sea slope spring stream summit swamp tower trail tunnel valley well woods.*

◆ Military

- 6th Kentucky Volunteer Infantry Regiment
  http://www.rootsweb.com/~jadmire/kyhenry/6thky.htm
- 12th Kentucky Infantry Regiment (US)
  http://www.edm.net/~Pjsewell/12th.htm
- 14th Kentucky Infantry
  http://ram.ramlink.net/~cbarker/14kyinf.htm
- 53rd Kentucky Mounted Infantry
  http://www.geocities.com/Heartland/5170/53rdkent.htm
- The Civil War Archive—Union Regiments—Kentucky
  http://www.civilwararchive.com/unionky.htm
- Civil War Battle Summaries by State—Kentucky
  http://www2.cr.nps.gov/abpp/battles/bystate.htm#ky

- First Kentucky Brigade, C.S.A.—The Orphan Brigade
  http://www.rootsweb.com/~orphanhm/
- Kentucky Military Links
  http://www.rootsweb.com/~kymil/index.html
- Korean Conflict State-Level Casualty Lists—Kentucky
  http://www.nara.gov/nara/electronic/kyhrlist.html
  From the National Archives and Records Administration, Center for Electronic Records.
- Vietnam Conflict State-Level Casualty Lists—Kentucky
  http://www.nara.gov/nara/electronic/kyhrviet.html
  From the National Archives and Records Administration, Center for Electronic Records.
- The Vietnam Veterans Memorial—Kentucky
  http://grunt.space.swri.edu/statewall/kentucky/ky.htm

◆ Newspapers

- AJR NewsLink—Kentucky Newspapers
  http://www.newslink.org/kynews.html
- E&P Media Info Links—Newspaper Sites in Kentucky
  http://www.mediainfo.com/emedia/browse-results.
  htm?region=kentucky&category=newspaper+++++++++
- Ecola Newstand: Kentucky
  http://www.ecola.com/news/press/na/us/ky/
- NAA Hotlinks to Newspapers Online—Kentucky
  http://www.naa.org/hotlinks/searchResult.asp?param=
  KY-Kentucky&City=1
- N-Net—Kentucky Newspapers
  http://www.n-net.com/ky.htm
- The Ultimate Collection of News Links: USA—Kentucky
  http://www.pppp.net/links/news/USA-KY.html
- Yahoo!...Newspapers...Kentucky
  http://dir.yahoo.com/News_and_Media/Newspapers/
  Browse_By_Region/U_S__States/Kentucky/

◆ People & Families

- Brian Harney's Home Page, emphasis on Genealogy
  http://members.aol.com/bdharney2/index.htm
- Directory of Underground Railroad Operators—Kentucky
  http://www.ugrr.org/names/map-ky.htm
- Kentuckiana Konnections—Biographies
  http://www.floyd-pavey.com/kentuckiana/kyiana/county/
  biolinks.html
- Maryland Catholics on the Frontier
  http://www.pastracks.com/mcf/
  For descendants of Maryland Catholics who migrated westward. They first went to Kentucky and from there to other parts of the Frontier.

- The Melungeon Ancestry Research and Information Page
  http://www.bright.net/~kat/melung.htm
- Ohio River Valley Families
  http://orvf.com/
  By Allen David Distler.
- Southeastern Kentucky Melungeon Information Exchange
  http://www.bright.net/~kat/skmie.htm
  Also Tennessee, North Carolina and Virginia.
- Tribes and Villages of Kentucky
  http://hanksville.phast.umass.edu:8000/cultprop/contacts/tribal/KY.html
- Webster County Biographies
  http://www.rootsweb.com/~kywebste/biogs/biogs.htm

◆ Professional Researchers, Volunteers & Other Research Services

- Board for Certification of Genealogists—Roster of Those Certified—Specializing in Kentucky
  http://www.genealogy.org/~bcg/rosts_ky.html
- Genealogy Helplist—Kentucky
  http://posom.com/hl/usa/ky.shtml
- The Official Iowa Counties Professional Genealogist and Researcher's Registry for Kentucky
  http://www.iowa-counties.com/gene/ky.htm
- Professional Genealogist for Western Kentucky—Bill Utterback
  http://genealogypro.com/b-utterback.html
  Bill Utterback, CGRS—Research in the Jackson Purchase Counties of Western Kentucky.

◆ Publications, Software & Supplies

- AncestorSpy—CDs and Microfiche for Kentucky
  http://www.ancestorspy.com/ky.htm
- Barbara Green's Used Genealogy Books—Kentucky
  http://home.earthlink.net/~genbooks/lochist.html#KY
- Barnette's Family Tree Books—Kentucky
  http://www.barnettesbooks.com/kentucky.htm
- Books We Own—Kentucky
  http://www.rootsweb.com/~bwo/kentucky.html
- Boyd Publishing Company—Kentucky
  http://www.hom.net/~gac/kentuck.htm
- Byron Sistler and Associates, Inc.
  http://www.mindspring.com/~sistler/
  Over 900 books covering records from Tennessee, Virginia, North Carolina, and Kentucky.
- Frontier Press Bookstore—Kentucky
  http://www.frontierpress.com/frontier.cgi?category=ky

- FLI Antiques & Genealogy
  http://www.wwd.net/user/tklaiber/index.htm
  Publications for Ohio and Kentucky.
- GenealogyBookShop.com—Kentucky
  http://www.genealogybookshop.com/genealogybookshop/files/The_United_States,Kentucky/index.html
  The online store of Genealogical Publishing Co., Inc. & Clearfield Company.
- Gorin Genealogical Publishing
  http://members.tripod.com/~GorinS/index.html
  and an alternate address
  http://members.aol.com/kygen/gorin.htm
  Publications cover mostly Kentucky, also has some for Logan County, Illinois and Fentress & Overton Counties, Tennessee.
- Hearthstone Bookshop—Kentucky
  http://www.hearthstonebooks.com/cgi-bin/webc.cgi/st_main.html?catid=81&sid=2PH5t29sm
- Heritage Books—Kentucky
  http://www.heritagebooks.com/ky.htm
- Heritage Quest—Microfilm Records for the State of Kentucky
  http://www.heritagequest.com/genealogy/microfilm/kentucky/
- J & W Enterprises
  http://www.dhc.net/~jw/
  One stop book source on the Internet, specializing in southern states source material.
- Kentucky Biographies Project
  http://www.starbase21.com/kybiog/
- Kentucky Explorer Magazine
  http://www.win.net/kyexmag/KEhome.html
  Kentucky's Most Unique History & Genealogy Publication.
- Lost in Time Books—Kentucky
  http://www.lostintime.com/catalog/books/bookst/bo12000.htm
- The Memorabilia Corner Books—Kentucky
  http://members.aol.com/TMCorner/book_ken.htm
- The Memorabilia Corner Census View CDs—Kentucky
  http://members.aol.com/TMCorner/cen_ken.htm
- Owsley County Books
  E-mail: rlsmith@iac.net
  E-mail Robert Smith at rlsmith@iac.net and he can send you a list of books that he has for sale.
- S-K Publications—Kentucky 1810–1850 Census Books
  http://www.skpub.com/genie/census/ky/
- Southern Queries Genealogy Magazine
  http://www.mindspring.com/~freedom1/sq/sq.htm
- TLC Genealogy Books
  http://www.tlc-gen.com/
  Specializing in Colonial VA, KY, MD, OH, PA, NC, etc.
- Western Kentucky Journal
  http://pw1.netcom.com/~cpalmer/wkj/wkj.htm

- Willow Bend Bookstore—Kentucky
  http://www.willowbend.net/ky.htm
- Ye Olde Genealogie Shoppe—Kentucky
  http://www.yogs.com/kentucky.htm

◆ Queries, Message Boards & Surname Lists

- GenConnect Kentucky Visitor Center
  http://cgi.rootsweb.com/~genbbs/indx/Ky.html
  A system for posting queries, Bibles, biographies, deeds, obituaries, pensions, wills.
- Kentuckiana Genealogy—Index to Surnames, Queries, and Researchers
  http://www.floyd-pavey.com/kentuckiana/qryindex.htm
  Kentucky & Indiana.
- Surname Index for Kentuckiana Genealogy
  http://cgi.rootsweb.com/surhelp-bin/surindx.pl?site=kyiana&letter=a
- Surnames of Kentucky
  http://www.usgennet.org/~baicon/soky.html
  Includes message boards for: KY's Most Wanted Ancestors, KY's Unsolved Mysteries, Kentucky Queries, Kentucky's Missing.

◆ Records: Census, Cemeteries, Land, Obituaries, Personal, Taxes and Vital (Born, Married, Died & Buried)

- The 1790–1890 Federal Population Censuses: Catalog of National Archives Microfilm
  http://www.genealogy.org/census/contents.shtml
  - Census Schedules and Microfilm Roll Numbers for Kentucky:
    1810
    http://www.genealogy.org/census/1810_schedules/Kentucky.html
    1820
    http://www.genealogy.org/census/1820_schedules/Kentucky.html
    1830
    http://www.genealogy.org/census/1830_schedules/Kentucky.html
    1840
    http://www.genealogy.org/census/1840_schedules/Kentucky.html
    1850
    http://www.genealogy.org/census/1850_schedules/Kentucky.html
    1860
    http://www.genealogy.org/census/1860_schedules/Kentucky.html
    1870
    http://www.genealogy.org/census/1870_schedules/Kentucky.html
    1880
    http://www.genealogy.org/census/1880_schedules/Kentucky.html
    1880 Soundex
    http://www.genealogy.org/census/1880.sdx_schedules/T750.html
    1890 Special Schedules
    http://www.genealogy.org/census/1890-special_schedules/Kentucky.html
- 1820 Floyd Co., KY Census Index
  http://www.bright.net/~kat/floydcen.htm
- 1830 Census Record—Oldham County
  http://www.rootsweb.com/~usgenweb/ky/oldham/census/1830.html
- 1840 Lawrence County, KY Census Index
  http://www.bright.net/~kat/lawrenc.htm
- 1840 Oldham County, KY Census
  http://www.rootsweb.com/~usgenweb/ky/oldham/census/1840.html
- 1850 Census Henderson County, Kentucky
  http://www.rootsweb.com/~kyhender/Henderson/hendky.txt
- 1850 Census, Mercer County, Kentucky
  http://w3.one.net/~durp/50cenidx.htm
- 1860 Henderson County Census
  ftp://ftp.rootsweb.com/pub/usgenweb/ky/henderson/census/cens1860.txt
- 1860 Webster County Census
  http://www.rootsweb.com/~kywebste/census/1860/sl-001.htm
- 1870 Census Lawrence Co., Kentucky
  http://ourworld.compuserve.com/homepages/GlenGallagher/law1870.htm
- 1870 Census Lawrence Co., Kentucky—Census Index
  http://ourworld.compuserve.com/homepages/GlenGallagher/L70index.htm
- 1870 Greenup County, Kentucky Census Data
  http://www.zoomnet.net/~blogan/1870grco.html
- Bibles with a Kentucky Connection
  http://www.nlt.net/kygenweb/bibles.html
- Cemeteries of the United States—Kentucky Cemeteries—County Index
  http://www.gac.edu/~kengelha/uscemeteries/kentucky.html
- Censuses of Trigg County
  http://www.usroots.com/kyseeker/public_html/kentucky/trigg/Trigg/Census/censuses.html
- Census Online—Links to Census Sites on the Web—Kentucky
  http://www.census-online.com/links/KY_data.html
- Christian County Marriages 1799–1820
  http://www.aplusdata.com/kyseeker/christmarriages.cfm

- County Courthouse Addresses
  http://www.familytreemaker.com/00000246.html

- Deed Data Pool
  http://www.ultranet.com/~deeds/pool.htm
  Downloadable deed files for Kentucky, New York, Pennsylvania, Virginia & West Virginia.

- Edmonson County, Kentucky, Tax List for the Year 1825
  http://www.tlc-gen.com/edmonson.htm

- Find-A-Grave by Location: Kentucky
  http://www.findagrave.com/grave/lky.html
  Graves of noteworthy people.

- Gospel Advocate Obituary Index
  http://www.ag.uiuc.edu/~mcmillan/Restlit/Database/gaobit.html
  Compiled by members of the Lehman Avenue Church of Christ in Bowling Green, Kentucky.

- Ground Work Genealogy on the Internet: Kentucky
  http://members.aol.com/ssmadonna/ky.htm

- Henderson County Marriages 1806–1860
  http://www.aplusdata.com/kyseeker/hendmarriages.cfm

- Henderson County Tax Roll 1799
  http://members.aol.com/patander73/h1799tax.html

- Hopkins County Obituaries—Kentucky
  http://www.rootsweb.com/~kygenweb/hopkins/obits/index.html

- How to Get KY Death Certificates, 1911 to 1946 for $3.00 (plus postage)
  http://kyssar.hypermart.net/kyvital.htm
  Jessie Hagan will copy death certificates from this time period for $3 and a SASE. See this web site for details.

- Interment.net: Kentucky Cemeteries
  http://www.interment.net/us/ky/index.htm
  A list of links to other sites.

- Kentucky Bible Records Collection Project
  http://www.geocities.com/Heartland/7578/index.html

- Kentucky Death Certificate Photocopies
  E-mail: chesterward@mindspring.com
  Send e-mail to Chester Ward at chesterward@mindspring.comt for photocopies at $1.50 each, which includes postage. These are photocopies from the microfilm.

- Kentucky Death Certificates
  http://www.rootsweb.com/~kygenweb/ky-dcert.html
  Photocopies for the years 1911 thru 1945. Proceeds to help support online genealogical research through projects affiliated with USGenWeb.

- Kentucky Residents Married in Shawneetown, Illinois
  http://www.rootsweb.com/~kyhender/Henderson/ill.htm

- Kentucky State Death Certificate Index for 1911–1995
  E-mail: rlsmith@iac.net
  This is the same information as is contained on the next site below. Contact that site first and if you have problems contacting the site below you can then request a lookup from Robert Smith. Send e-mail to rlsmith@iac.net and be sure to include specific details.

- Kentucky Vital Records Index
  http://ukcc.uky.edu/~vitalrec/
  Marriage / Divorce / Death

- Kentucky Vital Records Information
  http://vitalrec.com/ky.html

- Letcher County Cemetery Records
  http://webpages.metrolink.net/~bcaudill/kygenweb/cem_recs.htm

- Lexington Herald-Leader On-Line Obituaries
  http://www.kentuckyconnect.com/heraldleader/obituaries/

- McKenney Cemetery, Harrison County, Kentucky
  http://www.mindspring.com/~jogt/kygen/mckcem.htm

- Marriage Records of Knott County, Kentucky
  http://www.rootsweb.com/~kyknott/marriages.html

- National Archives—Southeast Region (Atlanta)
  http://www.nara.gov/regional/atlanta.html

- National Archives—Southeast Region from Family Tree Maker
  http://www.familytreemaker.com/00000104.html
  Records for Alabama, Florida, Georgia, Kentucky, Mississippi, North Carolina, South Carolina, and Tennessee.

- Old Burial Ground of Middle Fork of Raven Creek—Harrison County, Kentucky
  http://members.aol.com/kygenweb/raven.htm

- Owsley County Help Needed?
  E-mail: rlsmith@iac.net
  Send e-mail to Robert Smith at rlsmith@iac.net and he will search his considerable personal resources for you.

- The Political Graveyard—Cemeteries in Kentucky
  http://politicalgraveyard.com/geo/KY/kmindex.html

- Preplanning Network—Funeral Home and Cemetery Directory—Kentucky
  http://www.preplannet.com/kentfhcem.htm

- Raven Creek Cemetery, Harrison County, Kentucky
  http://pw1.netcom.com/~jog1/ravencreek.html

- Sellers' Western Kentucky Obituaries
  http://cgi.rootsweb.com/~genbbs/genbbs.cgi/USA/Ky/SellersObits

- Slave Entries in Wills, Deeds, Etc.
  http://www.netcom.com/~jog1/slavedocs.html
  Kentucky, South Carolina, Tennessee, Virginia

- T Point Cemetery, Clayhole, Kentucky
  http://www.seidata.com/~lhoffman/what.html

- Transcript of the Grant County, Kentucky 1860 Census
  http://home.att.net/~l.k.osborne/grnt1860/

- Trigg County Marriages 1820–1900
  http://www.aplusdata.com/kyseeker/triggmarriages.cfm

- USGenWeb Census Project Kentucky
  http://www.usgenweb.org/census/states/kentucky.htm

- USGenWeb Tombstone Transcription Project—
  Kentucky
  http://www.rootsweb.com/~cemetery/kentucky.html
- VitalChek Network—Kentucky
  http://www.vitalchek.com/stateselect.asp?state=KY
- Webster County, Kentucky Obituaries
  http://www.rootsweb.com/~kywebste/obits/obits.htm
- Where to Write for Vital Records—Kentucky
  http://www.cdc.gov/nchswww/howto/w2w/kentuck.htm
  From the National Center for Health Statistics (NCHS).

◆ Religion & Churches

- Christianity.Net Church Locator—Kentucky
  http://www.christianity.net/cgi/
  location.exe?United_States+Kentucky
- Church Online!—Kentucky
  http://www.churchonline.com/usas/ky/ky.html
- Church Profiles—Kentucky
  http://www.church-profiles.com/ky/ky.html
- Churches dot Net—Global Church Web Pages—
  Kentucky
  http://www.churches.net/churches/kentucky.html
- Churches of the World—Kentucky
  http://www.churchsurf.com/churches/Kentucky/index.htm
  From the ChurchSurf Christian Directory.

◆ Societies & Groups

- Ancestral Trails Historical Society
  http://www.rootsweb.com/~kyaths/
- Archer's Computer Interest Group List—Kentucky
  http://www.genealogy.org/~ngs/cigs/ngl1usky.html
- Eastern Kentucky Genealogical Society
  http://www.wwd.net/user/sjackson/ekgs/ekgs.htm
  Ashland, Kentucky.
- The Filson Club Historical Society
  http://www.filsonclub.org/
- Harrodsburg Historical Society
  http://w3.one.net/~durp/hhs.htm
- Hart County Historical Society
  http://www.ovnet.com/userpages/feenerty/history.html
- Henderson County Historical &
  Genealogical Society
  http://www.rootsweb.com/~kyhender/Henderson/HCHGS/
  HCHGSpg.htm

- Hopkins County Genealogical Society
  http://www.nlt.net/hopkins/hcgs/index.html
- IOOF Lodge Website Directory—Kentucky
  http://norm28.hsc.usc.edu/IOOF/USA/Kentucky/Kentucky.html
  Independent Order of Odd Fellows and Rebekahs.
- Kentucky Genealogical Society
  http://members.aol.com/bdharney2/bh3.htm
- Kentucky Historical Society
  http://www.state.ky.us/agencies/khs/index.html
- The Kentucky Society, NSDAR
  http://www.mindspring.com/~jogt/dar_ky.htm
- Louisville & Nashville Railroad Historical Society
  http://www.rrhistorical.com/lnhs/index.html
- National Society of the Daughters of the American
  Revolution, General Samuel Hopkins Chapter
  http://www.rootsweb.com/~kyhender/Henderson/DAR/dar.htm
- Southern Kentucky Genealogical Society
  http://members.aol.com/kygen/skgs/index.htm
- Tri-State Genealogical Society
  http://www.evansville.net/~tsgs/tsgs.html
  Indiana, Illinois and Kentucky.
- Union County Historical Society Museum
  and Genealogy
  http://www.rootsweb.com/~kyunion/society.htm
  Morganfield, Kentucky
- Webster County Historical & Genealogical Society
  http://www.rootsweb.com/~kywebste/wch_gs.htm

◆ USGenWeb Project

- Kentucky Genealogy—USGenWeb Project
  State Page
  http://www.usgenweb.org/ky
- Kentucky—USGenWeb Archives Table of Contents
  http://www.rootsweb.com/~usgenweb/ky/kyfiles.html
- Kentucky—USGenWeb FTP Archives
  ftp://ftp.rootsweb.com/pub/usgenweb/ky/
- Kentucky Family Reunions
  http://www.mindspring.com/~jbawden/reunion/index.html
- KY-FOOTSTEPS Mailing List
  http://members.aol.com/gfsjohnf/gen_mail_states-ky.
  html#KY-FOOTSTEPS
  *For posting original genealogical source material for Kentucky
  where either more than one Kentucky county or a state other
  than Kentucky is mentioned. Also see the associated web page at
  http://www.rootsweb.com/~kygenweb/lists/kyfootsteps.html*

U.S.—LOUISIANA—LA
http://www.CyndisList.com/la.htm

Category Index:

- General Resource Sites
- Government & Cities
- History & Culture
- Libraries, Archives & Museums
- Mailing Lists, Newsgroups & Chat
- Maps, Gazetteers & Geographical Information
- Military
- Newspapers
- People & Families

- Professional Researchers, Volunteers & Other Research Services
- Publications, Software & Supplies
- Queries, Message Boards & Surname Lists
- Records: Census, Cemeteries, Land, Obituaries, Personal, Taxes and Vital
- Religion & Churches
- Societies & Groups
- USGenWeb Project

◆ General Resource Sites

- Everton's Sources of Genealogical Information in Louisiana
  http://www.everton.com/usa/la.htm
- Family Tree Maker's Genealogy "How To" Guide—Louisiana
  http://www.familytreemaker.com/00000192.html
- Genealogy Bulletin Board Systems for Louisiana
  http://www.genealogy.org/~gbbs/gblla.html
- Genealogy Exchange & Surname Registry—LAGenExchange
  http://www.genexchange.com/la/index.cfm
- Genealogy in Louisiana
  http://www.cam.org/~beaur/gen/louisi-e.html
  From Denis Beauregard.
- Genealogy Resources on the Internet: Louisiana
  http://www-personal.umich.edu/~cgaunt/la.html
- LDS Research Outline for Louisiana
  http://www.everton.com/usa/la-0819B.txt
- Lineages' Genealogy Site: Louisiana
  http://www.lineages.com/rooms/usa/state.asp?StateCode=LA
- The Louisiana Genealogy Web Ring Home Page
  http://members.xoom.com/LaGenWebRing/WebRing.html
- ROOTS-L United States Resources: Louisiana
  http://www.rootsweb.com/roots-l/USA/la.html
  Comprehensive list of research links, including many to history-related sites.

◆ Government & Cities

- 50states.com—Louisiana State Information Resource
  http://www.50states.com/louisian.htm
  A list of general information for each state, including a list of colleges, state symbols, links to maps, newspapers, and other miscellaneous state information.
- Excite Travel by City.Net—Louisiana
  http://www.city.net/countries/united_states/louisiana/
- Info Louisiana State of Louisiana
  http://www.state.la.us/
- Official City Web Sites for the State of Louisiana
  http://OfficialCitySites.org/Louisiana.htm
- Yahoo! Get Local...Louisiana Cities
  http://dir.yahoo.com/Regional/U_S__States/Louisiana/Parishes_and_Regions/
  Maps, yellow pages, white pages, newspapers and other local information.
- Yahoo! Get Local...Louisiana Parishes and Regions
  http://dir.yahoo.com/Regional/U_S__States/Louisiana/Cities/
  Maps, yellow pages, white pages, newspapers and other local information.

◆ History & Culture

- Foundation for Historical Louisiana
  http://www.fhl.org/indexa.html
- Yahoo!...History...Louisiana
  http://dir.yahoo.com/Arts/Humanities/History/Browse_By_Region/U_S__States/Louisiana/

◆ Libraries, Archives & Museums

- African-American Genealogy Sources in the Louisiana Division of the New Orleans Public Library
  http://home.gnofn.org/~nopl/guides/black.htm

- Family History Centers—Louisiana
  http://www.deseretbook.com/famhis/la.html

- Family History Centers—Louisiana
  http://www.lib.byu.edu/~uvrfhc/centers/louisana.html

- HYTELNET—Library Catalogs: USA: Louisiana
  http://library.usask.ca/hytelnet/usa/LA.html
  Before you use any of the Telnet links, make note of the user name, password and any other logon information.

- Louisiana Family History Centers
  http://www.genhomepage.com/FHC/Louisiana.html
  A list of addresses, phone numbers and hours of operation from the Genealogy Home Page.

- Louisiana State Archives
  http://www.sec.state.la.us/arch-1.htm

- New Orleans Public Library
  http://home.gnofn.org/~nopl/
  - ○ City Archives and Louisiana Division Special Collections
    http://home.gnofn.org/~nopl/spec/speclist.htm
    - ■ African-American Genealogical Materials
      http://home.gnofn.org/~nopl/guides/black.htm
    - ■ Genealogical Materials in the New Orleans Public Library's Louisiana Division and City Archives
      http://home.gnofn.org/~nopl/guides/genguide/ggcover.htm

- NUCMC Listing of Archives and Manuscript Repositories in Louisiana
  http://lcweb.loc.gov/coll/nucmc/lasites.html
  Links to information about resources other than those held in the Library of Congress.

- Repositories of Primary Sources: Louisiana
  http://www.uidaho.edu/special-collections/east1.html#usla
  A list of links to online resources from the Univ. of Idaho Library, Special Collections and Archives.

- Shreve Memorial Library Microform and Microfilm Holdings
  http://www.shreve.net/~japrime/lagenweb/shreve.htm

- State Library of Louisiana
  http://smt.state.lib.la.us/
  - ○ Searching for Your Louisiana Ancestors... and All That Jazz
    http://www.state.lib.la.us/Dept/LaSect/searchin.htm

- webCATS: Library Catalogues on the World Wide Web—Louisiana
  http://library.usask.ca/hywebcat/states/LA.html

◆ Mailing Lists, Newsgroups & Chat

- Genealogy Resources on the Internet—Louisiana Mailing Lists
  http://members.aol.com/gfsjohnf/gen_mail_states-la.html
  Each of the mailing list links below points to this site, wonderfully maintained by John Fuller. Visit this site for county-specific mailing lists as well.

- ACADIAN-CAJUN Mailing List
  http://members.aol.com/gfsjohnf/gen_mail_states-la.html#ACADIAN-CAJUN
  For anyone with Acadian-Cajun ancestry worldwide.

- Acadian-Cajun Mailing List
  http://members.aol.com/gfsjohnf/gen_mail_states-la.html#Acadian1
  For anyone with a genealogical, historical, or general interest in the Acadian and Cajun people of Canada and Louisiana.

- LOUISIANA-ROOTS-L Mailing List
  http://members.aol.com/gfsjohnf/gen_mail_states-la.html#LA-CAJUN-ROOTS-L

◆ Maps, Gazetteers & Geographical Information

- 1895 U.S. Atlas—Louisiana
  http://www.LivGenMI.com/1895la.htm

- American Memory Panoramic Maps 1847–1929—Louisiana
  http://lcweb2.loc.gov/cgi-bin/query/S?ammem/gmd:@filreq(@field(STATE+louisiana)+@field(COLLID+pmmap))
  From the Geography and Map Division, Library of Congress.

- American Memory Railroad Maps 1828–1900—Louisiana
  http://memory.loc.gov/cgi-bin/query/S?ammem/gmd:@filreq(@field(STATE+louisiana)+@field(COLLID+rrmap))
  From the Geography and Map Division, Library of Congress.

- Color Landform Atlas: Louisiana
  http://fermi.jhuapl.edu/states/la_0.html
  Including a map of counties and a map for 1895.

- Excite Maps: Louisiana Maps
  http://www.city.net/maps/view/?mapurl=/countries/united_states/louisiana
  Zoom in on these maps all the way to the street level.

- HPI County InfoSystem—Counties in Louisiana
  http://www.com/hpi/lacty/index.html

- K.B. Slocum Books and Maps—Louisiana
  http://www.treasurenet.com/cgi-bin/treasure/kbslocum/scan/se=Louisiana/sf=mapstate

- List of Louisiana Parishes
  http://www.genealogy.org/~st-clair/counties/state_la.html

- Map of Louisiana Parishes
  http://govinfo.kerr.orst.edu/gif/states/la.gif
  From the Government Information Sharing Project, Information Services, Oregon State University.

- Map of Louisiana Parishes
  http://www.lib.utexas.edu/Libs/PCL/Map_collection/states/
  Louisiana.gif
  From the Perry-Castañeda Library at the Univ. of Texas at Austin.

- U.S. Census Bureau—Louisiana Profiles
  http://www.census.gov/datamap/www/22.html

- Yale Peabody Museum: GNIS—Louisiana
  http://www.peabody.yale.edu/other/gnis/LA.html
  *Search the USGS Geographic Names Database. You can limit the search to a specific county in this state and search for any of the following features: airport arch area arroyo bar basin bay beach bench bend bridge **building** canal cape **cemetery** channel **church** cliff crater crossing dam falls flat forest gap geyser glacier gut harbor hospital island isthmus lake lava levee locale mine oilfield other park pillar plain ppl range rapids reserve reservoir ridge **school** sea slope spring stream summit swamp tower trail tunnel valley well woods.*

◆ Military

- 19th Louisiana
  http://www.access.digex.net/~bdboyle/19LA.txt

- The Civil War Archive—Union Regiments— Louisiana
  http://www.civilwararchive.com/unionla.htm

- Civil War Battle Summaries by State—Louisiana
  http://www2.cr.nps.gov/abpp/battles/bystate.htm#la

- Fort deRussy
  http://www.geocities.com/BourbonStreet/5600/
  Marksville, Louisiana

- Korean Conflict State-Level Casualty Lists— Louisiana
  http://www.nara.gov/nara/electronic/lahrlist.html
  From the National Archives and Records Administration, Center for Electronic Records.

- Vietnam Conflict State-Level Casualty Lists— Louisiana
  http://www.nara.gov/nara/electronic/lahrviet.html
  From the National Archives and Records Administration, Center for Electronic Records.

- The Vietnam Veterans Memorial—Louisiana
  http://grunt.space.swri.edu/statewall/louis/la.htm

- The Young-Sanders Center
  http://youngsanders.org/
  For the study of the War Between the States in Louisiana. Contains searchable database of over 10,000 Confederate soldiers buried in Louisiana with cemetery locations.

◆ Newspapers

- AJR NewsLink—Louisiana Newspapers
  http://www.newslink.org/lanews.html

- E&P Media Info Links—Newspaper Sites in Louisiana
  http://www.mediainfo.com/emedia/browse-results.
  htm?region=louisiana&category=newspaper+++++++++

- Ecola Newstand: Louisiana
  http://www.ecola.com/news/press/na/us/la/

- Louisiana Newspaper Project
  http://www.lib.lsu.edu/special/lnp.html

- NAA Hotlinks to Newspapers Online—Louisiana
  http://www.naa.org/hotlinks/searchResult.asp?param=
  LA-Louisiana&City=1

- N-Net—Louisiana Newspapers
  http://www.n-net.com/la.htm

- The Ultimate Collection of News Links: USA—Louisiana
  http://www.pppp.net/links/news/USA-LA.html

- Yahoo!....Newspapers....Louisiana
  http://dir.yahoo.com/News_and_Media/Newspapers/
  Browse_By_Region/U_S__States/Louisiana/

◆ People & Families

- Acadian, Cajun & Creole
  http://www.CyndisList.com/acadian.htm
  See this category on Cyndi's List for related links.

- Avoyelleans: French Creoles
  http://www.geocities.com/BourbonStreet/1781/

- Tribes and Villages of Louisiana
  http://hanksville.phast.umass.edu:8000/cultprop/contacts/
  tribal/LA.html

- WPA Life Histories from Louisiana
  http://lcweb2.loc.gov/ammem/wpaintro/lacat.html
  Manuscripts from the Federal Writer's Project, 1936–1940, Library of Congress.

◆ Professional Researchers, Volunteers & Other Research Services

- Board for Certification of Genealogists—Roster of Those Certified—Specializing in Louisiana
  http://www.genealogy.org/~bcg/rosts_la.html

- Genealogy Helplist—Louisiana
  http://posom.com/hl/usa/la.shtml

- The Official Iowa Counties Professional Genealogist and Researcher's Registry for Louisiana
  http://www.iowa-counties.com/gene/la.htm

◆ Publications, Software & Supplies

- AncestorSpy—CDs and Microfiche for Louisiana
  http://www.ancestorspy.com/la.htm

- Barbara Green's Used Genealogy Books—Louisiana
  http://home.earthlink.net/~genbooks/lochist.html#LA

- Barnette's Family Tree Books—Louisiana
  http://www.barnettesbooks.com/louisiana.htm

- Books We Own—Louisiana
  http://www.rootsweb.com/~bwo/louisiana.html
- Boyd Publishing Company—Louisiana
  http://www.hom.net/~gac/louis.htm
- Frontier Press Bookstore—Louisiana
  http://www.frontierpress.com/frontier.cgi?category=la
- GenealogyBookShop.com—Louisiana
  http://www.genealogybookshop.com/genealogybookshop/files/
  The_United_States,Louisiana/index.html
  *The online store of Genealogical Publishing Co., Inc. &
  Clearfield Company.*
- Hearthstone Bookshop—Louisiana
  http://www.hearthstonebooks.com/cgi-bin/webc.cgi/st_main.
  html?catid=82&sid=2PH5t29sm
- Heritage Quest—Microfilm Records for the
  State of Louisiana
  http://www.heritagequest.com/genealogy/microfilm/louisiana/
- J & W Enterprises
  http://www.dhc.net/~jw/
  *One stop book source on the Internet, specializing in southern
  states source material.*
- The Memorabilia Corner—Books: Louisiana
  http://members.aol.com/TMCorner/book_la.htm
- Southern Queries Genealogy Magazine
  http://www.mindspring.com/~freedom1/sq/sq.htm

◆ Queries, Message Boards & Surname Lists

- GenConnect Louisiana Visitor Center
  http://cgi.rootsweb.com/~genbbs/indx/La.html
  *A system for posting queries, Bibles, biographies, deeds,
  obituaries, pensions, wills.*

◆ Records: Census, Cemeteries, Land, Obituaries, Personal, Taxes and Vital (Born, Married, Died & Buried)

- The 1790–1890 Federal Population Censuses:
  Catalog of National Archives Microfilm
  http://www.genealogy.org/census/contents.shtml
  - Census Schedules and Microfilm Roll Numbers
    for Louisiana:
    1810
    http://www.genealogy.org/census/1810_schedules/
    Louisiana.html
    1820
    http://www.genealogy.org/census/1820_schedules/
    Louisiana.html
    1830
    http://www.genealogy.org/census/1830_schedules/
    Louisiana.html
    1840
    http://www.genealogy.org/census/1840_schedules/
    Louisiana.html
    1850
    http://www.genealogy.org/census/1850_schedules/
    Louisiana.html
    1860
    http://www.genealogy.org/census/1860_schedules/
    Louisiana.html
    1870
    http://www.genealogy.org/census/1870_schedules/
    Louisiana.html
    1880
    http://www.genealogy.org/census/1880_schedules/
    Louisiana.html
    1880 Soundex
    http://www.genealogy.org/census/1880.sdx_schedules/
    T751.html
    1890 Special Schedules
    http://www.genealogy.org/census/1890-special_schedules/
    Louisiana.html
- 1830 United States Census St. Bernard Parish,
  Louisiana
  http://www.rootsweb.com/~lastbern/stbern1830.htm
- The Bureau of Land Management—Eastern States,
  General Land Office
  http://www.glorecords.blm.gov/
  *The Official Land Patent Records Site. This site has a search-
  able database of over two million pre-1908 Federal land title
  records, including scanned images of those records. The Eastern
  Public Land States covered in this database are: Alabama,
  Arkansas, Florida, Illinois, Indiana, Louisiana, Michigan,
  Minnesota, Mississippi, Missouri, Ohio, Wisconsin.*
- The Canary Islander's Migration to Louisiana
  1778–1783
  http://www.rootsweb.com/~lastbern/passenger.htm
  *Aboard: SS Sacremento, San Ignacio de Loyola, La Victoria,
  Sanuan Nepomuceno, La Santa Faz, El Sagrada Corazon de
  Jeses, Fragata Llamada Margarita, SS Trinidad.*
- Cemeteries of the United States—Louisiana
  Cemeteries—County Index
  http://www.gac.edu/~kengelha/uscemeteries/louisiana.html
- Census Online—Links to Census Sites on the Web—
  Louisiana
  http://www.census-online.com/links/LA_data.html
- Chalmette National Cemetery
  http://www.cwc.lsu.edu/projects/dbases/chalmla.htm
- County Courthouse Addresses
  http://www.familytreemaker.com/00000247.html
- Find-A-Grave by Location: Louisiana
  http://www.findagrave.com/grave/lla.html
  Graves of noteworthy people.
- Interment.net: Louisiana Cemeteries
  http://www.interment.net/us/la/index.htm
  A list of links to other sites.

- Kinder McRill Memorial Cemetery
  http://fp1.centuryinter.net/KinderCemetery/
  Kinder, Louisiana

- Louisiana Land Records—Interactive Search
  http://searches.rootsweb.com/cgi-bin/laland/laland.pl
  Pre-1908 Homestead and Cash Entry Patents from the Bureau of Land Management's General Land Office (GLO) Automated Records Project.

- Louisiana Vital Records Information
  http://vitalrec.com/la.html

- Louisiana Weddings
  http://www.angelfire.com/tx/1850censusrecords/laweddings.html

- National Archives—Southwest Region (Fort Worth)
  http://www.nara.gov/regional/ftworth.html

- National Archives—Southwest Region
  http://www.familytreemaker.com/00000105.html
  Records for Arkansas, Louisiana, Oklahoma, Texas, and a portion of New Mexico.

- The New Orleans Times Picayune Obituary Listings Index
  http://www.challenger.net/local/users/lindas/times1.htm

- Obituaries from News-Star, Monroe, LA
  http://www.bayou.com/~suelynn/obits.html

- The Political Graveyard—Cemeteries in Louisiana
  http://politicalgraveyard.com/geo/LA/kmindex.html

- Preplanning Network—Funeral Home and Cemetery Directory—Louisiana
  http://www.preplannet.com/louisfhcem.htm

- St. John Memorial Gardens
  http://www.rootsweb.com/~lastjohn/stjcem1.htm

- USGenWeb Census Project Louisiana
  http://www.usgenweb.org/census/states/louisian/louisian.htm

- USGenWeb Tombstone Transcription Project—Louisiana
  http://www.rootsweb.com/~cemetery/louisian.html

- VitalChek Network—Louisiana
  http://www.vitalchek.com/stateselect.asp?state=LA

- Where to Write for Vital Records—Louisiana
  http://www.cdc.gov/nchswww/howto/w2w/louisia.htm
  From the National Center for Health Statistics (NCHS).

◆ Religion & Churches

- Christianity.Net Church Locator—Louisiana
  http://www.christianity.net/cgi/location.exe?United_States+Louisiana

- Church Online!—Louisiana
  http://www.churchonline.com/usas/la/la.html

- Church Profiles—Louisiana
  http://www.church-profiles.com/la/la.html

- Churches dot Net—Global Church Web Pages—Louisiana
  http://www.churches.net/churches/louisian.html

- Churches of the World—Louisiana
  http://www.churchsurf.com/churches/Louisiana/index.htm
  From the ChurchSurf Christian Directory.

◆ Societies & Groups

- Archer's Computer Interest Group List—Louisiana
  http://www.genealogy.org/~ngs/cigs/ngl1usla.html

- Ark-La-Tex Genealogical Association
  http://www.softdisk.com/comp/aga/

- Cajun Clickers Genealogy SIG—Baton Rouge, Louisiana
  http://www.intersurf.com/~cars/

- GenCom PC Users Group of Shreveport, Louisiana
  http://www.softdisk.com/comp/gencom/

- The German-Acadian Coast Historical & Genealogical Society
  http://www.rootsweb.com/~lastjohn/geracadn.htm
  Destrehan, Louisiana

- The Grand Lodge of the State of Louisiana, Free and Accepted Masons
  http://www.la-mason.com/gl.htm

- IOOF Lodge Website Directory—Louisiana
  http://norm28.hsc.usc.edu/IOOF/USA/Louisiana/Louisiana.html
  Independent Order of Odd Fellows and Rebekahs.

- Jefferson Genealogical Society
  http://www.gnofn.org/~jgs/

- Louisiana Genealogical & Historical Society
  http://cust2.iamerica.net/mmoore/lghs.htm
  Baton Rouge, Louisiana

- Louisiana Historical Society
  http://www.acadiacom.net/lahistsoc/

- The Natchitoches Genealogical & Historical Association Library
  http://www.rootsweb.com/~lanatchi/ngl.htm

- Order of Confederate Rose, Belle Boyd Chapter, Shreveport, Louisiana
  http://www.angelfire.com/la/BelleBoydOCR/index.html

- Pointe de L'eglise Historical and Genealogical Society
  http://pages.prodigy.com/FFWP26E/pointe.html
  Acadia Parish, Louisiana

- St. Augustine Historical Society—Creole Heritage Preservation
  http://www.cp-tel.net/creole/
  Isle Brevelle, Louisiana

- St. Bernard Genealogical Society
  http://www.rootsweb.com/~lastbern/stbgs.htm

- The Southwest Louisiana Genealogical Society, Inc.
  http://cust2.iamerica.net/mmoore/swlgs.htm
  Lake Charles, Louisiana

- Terrebonne Genealogical Society
  http://www.rootsweb.com/~laterreb/tgs.htm

- The Vermilion Genealogical Society
  http://cust2.iamerica.net/mmoore/VGS.htm
  Anacoco, Lousiana

- West Bank Genealogy Society
  http://www.rootsweb.com/~lajeffer/wbgs.html
  Harvey, Louisiana

- Winn Parish Genealogical & Historical Association
  http://www.rootsweb.com/~lawinn/wpgha.html
  Winnfield, Lousiana

◆ USGenWeb Project

- Louisiana Genealogy—USGenWeb Project State Page
  http://www.usgenweb.org/la

- LADATA Mailing List
  http://members.aol.com/gfsjohnf/gen_mail_states-la.html#LADATA
  For the posting of Louisiana genealogical source materials for eventual inclusion into the Louisiana GenWeb archives.

- Louisiana—USGenWeb Archives Table of Contents
  http://www.rootsweb.com/~usgenweb/la/lafiles.htm

- Louisiana—USGenWeb FTP Archives
  ftp://ftp.rootsweb.com/pub/usgenweb/la/

U.S.—MAINE—ME
http://www.CyndisList.com/me.htm

Category Index:

- General Resource Sites
- Government & Cities
- History & Culture
- Libraries, Archives & Museums
- Mailing Lists, Newsgroups & Chat
- Maps, Gazetteers & Geographical Information
- Military
- Newspapers
- People & Families

- Professional Researchers, Volunteers & Other Research Services
- Publications, Software & Supplies
- Queries, Message Boards & Surname Lists
- Records: Census, Cemeteries, Land, Obituaries, Personal, Taxes and Vital
- Religion & Churches
- Societies & Groups
- USGenWeb Project

◆ General Resource Sites

- Everton's Sources of Genealogical Information in Maine
  http://www.everton.com/usa/me.htm
- Family Tree Maker's Genealogy "How To" Guide—Maine
  http://www.familytreemaker.com/00000193.html
- Genealogy Exchange & Surname Registry—MEGenExchange
  http://www.genexchange.com/me/index.cfm
- Genealogy Resources on the Internet: Maine
  http://www-personal.umich.edu/~cgaunt/maine.html
- LDS Research Outline for Maine
  http://www.everton.com/usa/me-0820b.txt
- Lineages' Genealogy Site: Maine
  http://www.lineages.com/rooms/usa/state.asp?StateCode=ME
- New England Connections
  http://www.geocities.com/Heartland/5274/nec.htm
- ROOTS-L United States Resources: Maine
  http://www.rootsweb.com/roots-l/USA/me.html
  Comprehensive list of research links, including many to history-related sites.

◆ Government & Cities

- 50states.com—Maine State Information Resource
  http://www.50states.com/maine.htm
  A list of general information for each state, including a list of colleges, state symbols, links to maps, newspapers, and other miscellaneous state information.
- Excite Travel by City.Net—Maine
  http://www.city.net/countries/united_states/maine/

- Maine State Government WWW Page
  http://www.state.me.us/
- Official City Web Sites for the State of Maine
  http://OfficialCitySites.org/Maine.htm
- Town of Dexter, Maine
  http://www.dextermaine.org/
- Town of Garland, Maine
  http://www.thedailyme.com/garland/garland.html
- Yahoo! Get Local...Maine Cities
  http://dir.yahoo.com/Regional/U_S__States/Maine/Cities/
  Maps, yellow pages, white pages, newspapers and other local information.
- Yahoo! Get Local...Maine Counties and Regions
  http://dir.yahoo.com/Regional/U_S__States/Maine/Counties_and_Regions/
  Maps, yellow pages, white pages, newspapers and other local information.

◆ History & Culture

- The Center for Maine History
  http://www.mainehistory.com/
- History of the Maine State Prison
  http://www.midcoast.com/~tomshell/prison.html
- Maine History Firsts
  http://www.state.me.us/legis/general/history/hist2.htm
  From the Maine Legislature.
- Waterboro Public Library—History of Maine
  http://www.waterboro.lib.me.us/histme.htm
- Yahoo!...History...Maine
  http://dir.yahoo.com/Arts/Humanities/History/Browse_By_Region/U_S__States/Maine/

◆ Libraries, Archives & Museums

- Archives in New England on the Internet
  http://www.lib.umb.edu/newengarch/nearch.html

- Auburn Public Library
  http://www.auburn.lib.me.us/
  - Local History & Genealogy
    http://www.auburn.lib.me.us/genealogy.html

- Bangor Public Library
  http://www.bpl.lib.me.us/

- The Center for Maine History
  http://www.mainehistory.com/
  From the Maine Historical Society.
  - The Center for Maine History: Genealogy
    http://www.mainehistory.com/genealogy.html

- Curtis Memorial Library
  http://www.curtislibrary.com/
  - Curtis Memorial Library Genealogy
    http://www.curtislibrary.com/genealogy/

- Ellsworth Public Library
  http://www.ellsworth.lib.me.us/

- Family History Centers—Maine
  http://www.deseretbook.com/famhis/me.html

- Family History Centers—Maine
  http://www.lib.byu.edu/~uvrfhc/centers/maine.html

- HYTELNET—Library Catalogs: USA: Maine
  http://library.usask.ca/hytelnet/usa/ME.html
  Before you use any of the Telnet links, make note of the user name, password and any other logon information.

- Maine Family History Centers
  http://www.genhomepage.com/FHC/Maine.html
  A list of addresses, phone numbers and hours of operation from the Genealogy Home Page.

- Maine Libraries on the World Wide Web
  http://www.state.me.us/msl/melibson.htm

- Maine State Archives Web
  http://www.state.me.us/sos/arc/general/admin/mawww001.htm
  - Genealogical Research in the Maine State Archives
    http://www.state.me.us/sos/arc/archives/genealog/genie.htm

- Maine State Library
  http://www.state.me.us/msl/
  - Maine Libraries Online
    http://www.state.me.us/msl/mlo.htm

- NUCMC Listing of Archives and Manuscript Repositories in Maine
  http://lcweb.loc.gov/coll/nucmc/mesites.html
  Links to information about resources other than those held in the Library of Congress.

- Repositories of Primary Sources: Maine
  http://www.uidaho.edu/special-collections/east1.html#usme
  A list of links to online resources from the Univ. of Idaho Library, Special Collections and Archives.

- webCATS: Library Catalogues on the World Wide Web—Maine
  http://library.usask.ca/hywebcat/states/ME.html

◆ Mailing Lists, Newsgroups & Chat

- Genealogy Resources on the Internet—Maine Mailing Lists
  http://members.aol.com/gfsjohnf/gen_mail_states-me.html
  Each of the mailing list links below points to this site, wonderfully maintained by John Fuller. Visit this site for county-specific mailing lists as well.

- Maine Mailing List
  http://members.aol.com/gfsjohnf/gen_mail_states-me.html#maine

- MAME Mailing List
  http://members.aol.com/gfsjohnf/gen_mail_states-ma.html#MAME
  For anyone with a genealogical interest in the states of Massachusetts and Maine; both when they were "one" and after they were divided.

- NORTHEAST-ROOTS-L Mailing List
  http://members.aol.com/gfsjohnf/gen_mail_states-me.html#NORTHEAST-ROOTS
  Connecticut, Maine, Massachusetts, New Hampshire, Rhode Island & Vermont.

◆ Maps, Gazetteers & Geographical Information

- 1895 U.S. Atlas—Maine
  http://www.LivGenMI.com/1895me.htm

- American Memory Panoramic Maps 1847–1929—Maine
  http://lcweb2.loc.gov/cgi-bin/query/S?ammem/gmd:@filreq(@field(STATE+maine)+@field(COLLID+pmmap))
  From the Geography and Map Division, Library of Congress.

- American Memory Railroad Maps 1828–1900—Maine
  http://memory.loc.gov/cgi-bin/query/S?ammem/gmd:@filreq(@field(STATE+maine)+@field(COLLID+rrmap))
  From the Geography and Map Division, Library of Congress.

- Color Landform Atlas: Maine
  http://fermi.jhuapl.edu/states/me_0.html
  Including a map of counties and a map for 1895.

- Excite Maps: Maine Maps
  http://www.city.net/maps/view/?mapurl=/countries/united_states/maine
  Zoom in on these maps all the way to the street level.

- HPI County InfoSystem—Counties in Maine
  http://www.com/hpi/mecty/index.html

- K.B. Slocum Books and Maps—Maine
  http://www.treasurenet.com/cgi-bin/treasure/kbslocum/scan/se=Maine/sf=mapstate

- List of Maine Counties
  http://www.genealogy.org/~st-clair/counties/state_me.html

- Map of Maine Counties
  http://govinfo.kerr.orst.edu/gif/states/me.gif
  From the Government Information Sharing Project, Information Services, Oregon State University.

- Map of Maine Counties
  http://www.lib.utexas.edu/Libs/PCL/Map_collection/states/Maine.gif
  From the Perry-Castañeda Library at the Univ. of Texas at Austin.

- Old Maps of New England (Maine, New Hampshire, Vermont, Connecticut, Rhode Island, Massachusetts) and New York
  http://members.aol.com/oldmapsne/index.html

- Reproductions of Old Town Maps in New England
  http://www.biddeford.com/~lkane/

- U.S. Census Bureau—Maine Profiles
  http://www.census.gov/datamap/www/23.html

- Yale Peabody Museum: GNIS—Maine
  http://www.peabody.yale.edu/other/gnis/ME.html
  *Search the USGS Geographic Names Database. You can limit the search to a specific county in this state and search for any of the following features: airport arch area arroyo bar basin bay beach bench bend bridge **building** canal cape **cemetery** channel **church** cliff crater crossing dam falls flat forest gap geyser glacier gut harbor hospital island isthmus lake lava levee locale mine oilfield other park pillar plain ppl range rapids reserve reservoir ridge **school** sea slope spring stream summit swamp tower trail tunnel valley well woods.*

◆ Military

- 20th Maine Volunteer Infantry Company G
  http://midas.org/npo/cwar/acwa/20mevcog.html

- 28th Maine, Battle Report
  http://www.access.digex.net/~bdboyle/28thme.txt

- The Aroostook War—Maine vs. New Brunswick, 1839
  http://www.stanford.edu/~jenkg/family/aroostook.html

- The Civil War Archive—Union Regiments—Maine
  http://www.civilwararchive.com/unionme.htm

- Korean Conflict State-Level Casualty Lists—Maine
  http://www.nara.gov/nara/electronic/mehrlist.html
  From the National Archives and Records Administration, Center for Electronic Records.

- Maine in the Civil War
  http://www.rootsweb.com/~mecivilw/mecivilw.htm

- Military Records and Related Sources at the Maine State Archives
  http://www.state.me.us/sos/arc/archives/military/military.htm

- Vietnam Conflict State-Level Casualty Lists—Maine
  http://www.nara.gov/nara/electronic/mehrviet.html
  From the National Archives and Records Administration, Center for Electronic Records.

- The Vietnam Veterans Memorial—Maine
  http://grunt.space.swri.edu/statewall/maine/me.htm

◆ Newspapers

- AJR NewsLink—Maine Newspapers
  http://www.newslink.org/menews.html

- Bangor Daily News Interactive
  http://www.bangornews.com/

- The Daily ME
  http://www.thedailyme.com/

- E&P Media Info Links—Newspaper Sites in Maine
  http://www.mediainfo.com/emedia/browse-results.htm?region=maine&category=newspaper+++++++++

- Ecola Newstand: Maine
  http://www.ecola.com/news/press/na/us/me/

- NAA Hotlinks to Newspapers Online—Maine
  http://www.naa.org/hotlinks/searchResult.asp?param=ME-Maine&City=1

- New England Old Newspaper Index Project of Maine®
  http://www.geocities.com/Heartland/Hills/1460/

- N-Net—Maine Newspapers
  http://www.n-net.com/me.htm

- Portland Press Herald Online
  http://www.portland.com/

- The Ultimate Collection of News Links: USA—Maine
  http://www.pppp.net/links/news/USA-ME.html

- Yahoo!...Newspapers...Maine
  http://dir.yahoo.com/News_and_Media/Newspapers/Browse_By_Region/U_S__States/Maine/

◆ People & Families

- Directory of Underground Railroad Operators—Maine
  http://www.ugrr.org/names/map-me.htm

- Colonial Massachusetts and Maine Genealogies
  http://www.qni.com/~anderson/
  Information about approximately 5000 individuals who are descendants of the following surnames: Anderson, Blake, Brackett, Bradbury, Carver, Conant, Chute, Darling, Farrington, Hamblen/Hamblin/Hamlin, Haskell, Knight, Mansfield Mather, Noyes, Plumer/Plummer, Proctor, Sanford, Sawyer, Sewall, Shackford, Snow, Thurston, Waite, Watts, Woodward.

- Tribes and Villages of Maine
  http://hanksville.phast.umass.edu:8000/cultprop/contacts/tribal/ME.html

- WPA Life Histories from Maine
  http://lcweb2.loc.gov/ammem/wpaintro/mecat.html
  Manuscripts from the Federal Writer's Project, 1936–1940, Library of Congress.

◆ Professional Researchers, Volunteers & Other Research Services

- Board for Certification of Genealogists—Roster of Those Certified—Specializing in Maine
  http://www.genealogy.org/~bcg/rosts_me.html

- Genealogy Helplist—Maine
  http://www.calarts.edu/~karynw/helplist/me.html

- The Official Iowa Counties Professional Genealogist and Researcher's Registry for Maine
  http://www.iowa-counties.com/gene/me.htm

◆ Publications, Software & Supplies

- AncestorSpy—CDs and Microfiche for Maine
  http://www.ancestorspy.com/me.htm

- Barbara Green's Used Genealogy Books—Maine
  http://home.earthlink.net/~genbooks/lochist.html#ME

- Books We Own—Maine
  http://www.rootsweb.com/~bwo/maine.html

- Boyd Publishing Company—Maine
  http://www.hom.net/~gac/maine.htm

- Essex Books—New England
  http://www.HERTGE.COM/essex/neweng.htm

- Frontier Press Bookstore—Maine
  http://www.frontierpress.com/frontier.cgi?category=me

- GenealogyBookShop.com—Maine
  http://www.genealogybookshop.com/genealogybookshop/files/
  The_United_States,Maine/index.html
  The online store of Genealogical Publishing Co., Inc. & Clearfield Company.

- Genealogy USA—Pentref Press
  http://www.genealogyusa.com/home.html
  Several quarterlies, including "Forebears" for Maine families; specializing in colonial American genealogy, all eastern seaboard families, Quebec to Florida, 1600s to 1700s.

- Hearthstone Bookshop—Maine
  http://www.hearthstonebooks.com/cgi-bin/webc.cgi/st_main.
  html?catid=83&sid=2PH5t29sm

- Heritage Books—Maine
  http://www.heritagebooks.com/me.htm

- Heritage Quest—Microfilm Records for the State of Maine
  http://www.heritagequest.com/genealogy/microfilm/maine/

- Lost in Time Books—Maine
  http://www.lostintime.com/catalog/books/bookst/bo13000.htm

- The Memorabilia Corner—Books: Maine
  http://members.aol.com/TMCorner/book_ma.htm

- Picton Press—Maine
  http://www.midcoast.com/~picton/public_html.BASK/catalog/
  state_me.htm

- Willow Bend Bookstore—Maine
  http://www.willowbend.net/me.htm

- W.K.R.P. (Washington/Charlotte Kounty Records Preservation) Newsletter
  E-mail: shwkrp@aol.com
  A quarterly newsletter concerning research being done in Washington Co., Maine and Charlotte County, New Brunswick. For details e-mail Sharon at: shwkrp@aol.com

◆ Queries, Message Boards & Surname Lists

- GenConnect Maine Visitor Center
  http://cgi.rootsweb.com/~genbbs/indx/Me.html
  A system for posting queries, Bibles, biographies, deeds, obituaries, pensions, wills.

- New England Connections Query Archive
  http://www.geocities.com/Heartland/5274/nequery.htm

◆ Records: Census, Cemeteries, Land, Obituaries, Personal, Taxes and Vital (Born, Married, Died & Buried)

- The 1790–1890 Federal Population Censuses: Catalog of National Archives Microfilm
  http://www.genealogy.org/census/contents.shtml
  - Census Schedules and Microfilm Roll Numbers for Maine:
    1790
    http://www.genealogy.org/census/1790.html
    1800
    http://www.genealogy.org/census/1800_schedules/
    Maine.html
    1810
    http://www.genealogy.org/census/1810_schedules/
    Maine.html
    1820
    http://www.genealogy.org/census/1820_schedules/
    Maine.html
    1830
    http://www.genealogy.org/census/1830_schedules/
    Maine.html
    1840
    http://www.genealogy.org/census/1840_schedules/
    Maine.html
    1850
    http://www.genealogy.org/census/1850_schedules/
    Maine.html
    1860
    http://www.genealogy.org/census/1860_schedules/
    Maine.html
    1870
    http://www.genealogy.org/census/1870_schedules/
    Maine.html

1880
http://www.genealogy.org/census/1880_schedules/
Maine.html

1880 Soundex
http://www.genealogy.org/census/1880.sdx_schedules/
T752.html

1890 Special Schedules
http://www.genealogy.org/census/1890-special_schedules/
Maine.html

- Andover, Maine Marriages 1805 to 1863
  http://members.aol.com/andoverme/marriage.html

- Births in Standish
  ftp://ftp.rootsweb.com/pub/usgenweb/me/cumberland/
  standish/birth.txt
  *Compiled from Annual Town Reports for 1897–1902 and
  1904–1944.*

- Births, Intentions and Marriages 1775–1818 of
  Monmouth, Kennebec County, Maine
  ftp://ftp.rootsweb.com/pub/usgenweb/me/kennebec/
  monmouth/vitals/vr1.txt

- Castine Marriages 1892–1960
  http://www.kalama.com/~mariner/casmarry.htm

- Cemeteries of the United States—Maine
  Cemeteries—County Index
  http://www.gac.edu/~kengelha/uscemeteries/maine.html

- Census Online—Links to Census Sites on the Web—
  Maine
  http://www.census-online.com/links/ME_data.html

- County Courthouse Addresses
  http://www.familytreemaker.com/00000248.html

- Find-A-Grave by Location: Maine
  http://www.findagrave.com/grave/lme.html
  Graves of noteworthy people.

- Interment.net: Maine Cemeteries
  http://www.interment.net/us/me/index.htm
  A list of links to other sites.

- Jean's Maine Genealogy Page
  http://www.mnopltd.com/jean/
  *Index of deaths and marriages as published in the Ellsworth
  Herald its successor, the Ellsworth American October 24, 1851
  through December 29, 1865.*

- Judicial Records at the Maine State Archives
  http://www.state.me.us/sos/arc/archives/judicial/judicial.htm

- Maine Vital Records Information
  http://vitalrec.com/me.html

- Marriage History Search Form
  http://thor.ddp.state.me.us/archives/plsql/
  archdev.Marriage_Archive.search_form
  Index to Maine Marriages 1892–1966.

- Mount Hope Cemetery
  http://www.mthopebgr.com/
  Bangor, Maine

- National Archives—Northeast Region (Boston)
  http://www.nara.gov/regional/boston.html

- National Archives—New England Region
  http://www.familytreemaker.com/00000098.html
  *Records for Connecticut, Maine, Massachusetts, New
  Hampshire, Rhode Island, and Vermont.*

- The Political Graveyard—Cemeteries in Maine
  http://politicalgraveyard.com/geo/ME/kmindex.html

- Preplanning Network—Funeral Home and
  Cemetery Directory—Maine
  http://www.preplannet.com/mainefhcem.htm

- Robert L. Taylor's Maine Family Bible Archives
  http://www.rootsweb.com/~meandrhs/taylor/bible/maine.html

- The Times Record Obituary Page
  http://www.timesrecord.com/obituaries
  Brunswick, Maine

- USGenWeb Census Project Maine
  http://www.usgenweb.org/census/states/maine/maine.htm

- USGenWeb Tombstone Transcription Project—
  Maine
  http://www.rootsweb.com/~cemetery/maine.html

- VitalChek Network—Maine
  http://www.vitalchek.com/stateselect.asp?state=ME

- Vital Records of Wales, Maine
  ftp://ftp.rootsweb.com/pub/usgenweb/me/kennebec/wales/cem/
  cemvr.txt

- Where to Write for Vital Records—Maine
  http://www.cdc.gov/nchswww/howto/w2w/maine.htm
  From the National Center for Health Statistics (NCHS).

◆ Religion & Churches

- Catholic Churches of Maine
  http://www.mint.net/~frenchcx/mecath1.htm

- Christianity.Net Church Locator—Maine
  http://www.christianity.net/cgi/location.exe?
  United_States+Maine

- Church Online!—Maine
  http://www.churchonline.com/usas/me/me.html

- Church Profiles—Maine
  http://www.church-profiles.com/me/me.html

- Churches dot Net—Global Church Web Pages—
  Maine
  http://www.churches.net/churches/maine.html

- Churches of the World—Maine
  http://www.churchsurf.com/churches/Maine/index.htm
  From the ChurchSurf Christian Directory.

◆ Societies & Groups

- Androscoggin Historical Society
  http://www.rootsweb.com/~meandrhs/

- Archer's Computer Interest Group List—Maine
  http://www.genealogy.org/~ngs/cigs/ngl1usme.html
- Bethel Historical Society
  http://orion.bdc.bethel.me.us/~history/index.html
  Information about the Society, upcoming events, and selected articles from "The Courier," the society's quarterly publication.
- The Center for Maine History
  http://www.mainehistory.com/
  Houses the Maine Historical Society Research Library, the Maine History Gallery, and the historic Wadsworth-Longfellow House.
- Fryeburg Historical Society
  For details, send e-mail to museum@landmarknet.net
- Grand Lodge of Maine Ancient, Free and Accepted Masons
  http://www.nlbbs.com/~masonry/
- IOOF Lodge Website Directory—Maine
  http://norm28.hsc.usc.edu/IOOF/USA/Maine/Maine.html
  Independent Order of Odd Fellows and Rebekahs.
- Kennebunkport Historical Society
  http://www.kporthistory.org/
- Maine Genealogical Society
  http://www.rootsweb.com/~megs/MaineGS.htm
  Farmington

- Maine Old Cemetery Association
  http://www.rootsweb.com/~memoca/moca.htm
- New England Historic Genealogical Society
  http://www.nehgs.org/
- The Oakland (ME) Area Historical Society
  http://www.mint.net/~mdenis/oahs/Oakland.html
- Pejepscot Historical Society
  http://www.curtislibrary.com/pejepscot.htm

◆ USGenWeb Project

- Maine Genealogy—USGenWeb Project State Page
  http://www.usgenweb.org/me
- LMNC-Gen Mailing List
  http://members.aol.com/gfsjohnf/gen_mail_states-me.html#LMNC-Gen
  For discussing the creation of a single source for all Louisiana, Maine, and North Carolina genealogy databases.
- Maine—USGenWeb Archives Table of Contents
  http://www.rootsweb.com/~usgenweb/me/mefiles.htm
- Maine—USGenWeb FTP Archives
  ftp://ftp.rootsweb.com/pub/usgenweb/me/

U.S.—MARYLAND—MD
http://www.CyndisList.com/md.htm

Category Index:

- General Resource Sites
- Government & Cities
- History & Culture
- Libraries, Archives & Museums
- Mailing Lists, Newsgroups & Chat
- Maps, Gazetteers & Geographical Information
- Military
- Newspapers
- People & Families

- Professional Researchers, Volunteers & Other Research Services
- Publications, Software & Supplies
- Queries, Message Boards & Surname Lists
- Records: Census, Cemeteries, Land, Obituaries, Personal, Taxes and Vital
- Religion & Churches
- Societies & Groups
- USGenWeb Project

◆ General Resource Sites

- Everton's Sources of Genealogical Information in Maryland
  http://www.everton.com/usa/md.htm

- Family Tree Maker's Genealogy "How To" Guide—Maryland
  http://www.familytreemaker.com/00000194.html

- Genealogy Bulletin Board Systems for Maryland
  http://www.genealogy.org/~gbbs/gblmd.html

- Genealogy Exchange & Surname Registry—MDGenExchange
  http://www.genexchange.com/md/index.cfm

- Genealogy Resources on the Internet: Maryland
  http://www-personal.umich.edu/~cgaunt/maryland.html

- Golden Lyon II Genealogical Research
  http://www.erols.com/rariggin/lyon.html
  Resource for studying related families of the Lower Eastern Shore—Allied Families of the Delmarva Peninsula.

- Handley's Eastern Shore Maryland Genealogy Project
  http://bay.intercom.net/handley/

- LDS Research Outline for Maryland
  http://www.everton.com/usa/md-0821b.txt

- Lineages' Genealogy Site: Maryland
  http://www.lineages.com/rooms/usa/state.asp?StateCode=MD

- Maryland Eastern Shore Genealogy
  http://www.flash.net/~jhammell/

- Old Frederick County, Maryland
  http://members.aol.com/DorWinda/index.html

- ROOTS-L United States Resources: Maryland
  http://www.rootsweb.com/roots-l/USA/md.html
  Comprehensive list of research links, including many to history-related sites.

◆ Government & Cities

- 50states.com—Maryland State Information Resource
  http://www.50states.com/maryland.htm
  A list of general information for each state, including a list of colleges, state symbols, links to maps, newspapers, and other miscellaneous state information.

- Excite Travel by City.Net—Maryland
  http://www.city.net/countries/united_states/maryland/

- Maryland Electronic Capital
  http://www.mec.state.md.us/mec/

- Official City Web Sites for the State of Maryland
  http://OfficialCitySites.org/Maryland.htm

- Sailor's—Maryland's Public Information Network
  http://www.mec.state.md.us/

- Yahoo! Get Local...Maryland Cities
  http://dir.yahoo.com/Regional/U_S__States/Maryland/Cities/
  Maps, yellow pages, white pages, newspapers and other local information.

- Yahoo! Get Local...Maryland Counties and Regions
  http://dir.yahoo.com/Regional/U_S__States/Maryland/Counties_and_Regions/
  Maps, yellow pages, white pages, newspapers and other local information.

◆ History & Culture

- Yahoo!...History...Maryland
  http://dir.yahoo.com/Arts/Humanities/History/Browse_By_Region/U_S__States/Maryland/

◆ Libraries, Archives & Museums

- Baltimore County Public Library
  http://www.bcpl.lib.md.us/
  - ○ BCPL History and Genealogy InfoCenter
    http://www.bcpl.lib.md.us/centers/history/history.html

- The B&O Railroad Museum
  http://www.borail.org/
  Baltimore, Maryland

- Family History Center, Washington, DC Temple
  http://www.access.digex.net/~giammot/FHC/

- Family History Centers—Maryland
  http://www.deseretbook.com/famhis/md.html

- Family History Centers—Maryland
  http://www.lib.byu.edu/~uvrfhc/centers/maryland.html

- HYTELNET—Library Catalogs: USA: Maryland
  http://library.usask.ca/hytelnet/usa/MD.html
  Before you use any of the Telnet links, make note of the user name, password and any other logon information.

- Maryland Family History Centers
  http://www.genhomepage.com/FHC/Maryland.html
  A list of addresses, phone numbers and hours of operation from the Genealogy Home Page.

- Maryland State Archives
  http://www.mdarchives.state.md.us/

- NUCMC Listing of Archives and Manuscript Repositories in Maryland
  http://lcweb.loc.gov/coll/nucmc/mdsites.html
  Links to information about resources other than those held in the Library of Congress.

- Repositories of Primary Sources: Maryland
  http://www.uidaho.edu/special-collections/east1.html#usmd
  A list of links to online resources from the Univ. of Idaho Library, Special Collections and Archives.

- Sailor: Maryland Libraries
  http://www.sailor.lib.md.us/mdlibs/mdlibs.html
  Public libraries and university libraries.

- webCATS: Library Catalogues on the World Wide Web—Maryland
  http://library.usask.ca/hywebcat/states/MD.html

- Web Site MARYLAND—Libraries in Maryland
  http://www.pwl.com/maryland/library.html

◆ Mailing Lists, Newsgroups & Chat

- Genealogy Resources on the Internet—Maryland Mailing Lists
  http://members.aol.com/gfsjohnf/gen_mail_states-md.html
  Each of the mailing list links below points to this site, wonderfully maintained by John Fuller. Visit this site for county-specific mailing lists as well.

- BALTGEN-L Mailing List
  http://members.aol.com/gfsjohnf/gen_mail_states-md.html#BALTGEN-L
  Baltimore, Anne Arundel, Howard, Harford, and Carroll Counties.

- Baltocity Mailing List
  http://members.aol.com/gfsjohnf/gen_mail_states-md.html#Baltocity
  Baltimore City

- LOWER-DELMARVA-ROOTS Mailing List
  http://members.aol.com/gfsjohnf/gen_mail_states-md.html#LOWER-DELMARVA-ROOTS
  Sussex and Kent Counties in Delaware; Dorchester, Wicomico, Somerset, and Worcester in Maryland; Northampton and Accomack in Virginia.

- MCF-ROOTS
  http://members.aol.com/gfsjohnf/gen_mail_states-gen.html#MCF-ROOTS
  A mailing list (Maryland Catholics on the Frontier) for the discussion of descendants of Maryland Catholics who migrated first to Kentucky and then to other parts of the frontier.

- MID-ATLANTIC-ROOTS-L Mailing List
  http://members.aol.com/gfsjohnf/gen_mail_states-md.html#MID-ATLANTIC-ROOTS-L
  New Jersey, Maryland, Delaware, and the District of Columbia.

- QueenAnnes Mailing List
  http://members.aol.com/gfsjohnf/gen_mail_states-md.html#QueenAnnes
  For anyone with genealogical interest in the upper eastern shore counties of Maryland (i.e., Queen Anne's, Kent, Caroline).

- SOMGEN-L Mailing List
  http://members.aol.com/gfsjohnf/gen_mail_states-wv.html#SOMGEN-L
  For anyone with a genealogical interest in the Pennsylvania counties of Somerset, Bedford, Cambria and Fayette; the Maryland counties of Garrett and Allegany; and the border counties in West Virginia.

◆ Maps, Gazetteers & Geographical Information

- 1895 U.S. Atlas—Maryland
  http://www.LivGenMI.com/1895md.htm

- American Memory Panoramic Maps 1847–1929—Maryland
  http://lcweb2.loc.gov/cgi-bin/query/S?ammem/gmd:@filreq(@field(STATE+maryland)+@field(COLLID+pmmap))
  From the Geography and Map Division, Library of Congress.

- American Memory Railroad Maps 1828–1900—Maryland
  http://memory.loc.gov/cgi-bin/query/S?ammem/gmd:@filreq(@field(STATE+maryland)+@field(COLLID+rrmap))
  From the Geography and Map Division, Library of Congress.

- Color Landform Atlas: Maryland
  http://fermi.jhuapl.edu/states/md_0.html
  Including a map of counties and a map for 1895.

- Excite Maps: Maryland Maps
  http://www.city.net/maps/view/?mapurl=/countries/
  united_states/maryland
  Zoom in on these maps all the way to the street level.

- HPI County InfoSystem—Counties in Maryland
  http://www.com/hpi/mdcty/index.html

- K.B. Slocum Books and Maps—Maryland
  http://www.treasurenet.com/cgi-bin/treasure/kbslocum/scan/
  se=Maryland/sf=mapstate

- List of Maryland Counties
  http://www.genealogy.org/~st-clair/counties/state_md.html

- Map of Maryland Counties
  http://govinfo.kerr.orst.edu/gif/states/md.gif
  *From the Government Information Sharing Project, Information
  Services, Oregon State University.*

- Map of Maryland Counties
  http://www.lib.utexas.edu/Libs/PCL/Map_collection/states/
  Maryland.gif
  *From the Perry-Castañeda Library at the Univ. of Texas at
  Austin.*

- U.S. Census Bureau—Maryland Profiles
  http://www.census.gov/datamap/www/24.html

- Yale Peabody Museum: GNIS—Maryland
  http://www.peabody.yale.edu/other/gnis/MD.html
  *Search the USGS Geographic Names Database. You can limit
  the search to a specific county in this state and search for any of
  the following features: airport arch area arroyo bar basin bay
  beach bench bend bridge **building** canal cape **cemetery** channel
  church cliff crater crossing dam falls flat forest gap geyser
  glacier gut harbor hospital island isthmus lake lava levee locale
  mine oilfield other park pillar plain ppl range rapids reserve
  reservoir ridge **school** sea slope spring stream summit swamp
  tower trail tunnel valley well woods.*

◆ Military

- 1st Maryland Battery, C.S.A.
  http://www.concentric.net/~Danaher/MD1stAty/

- Battalion History of First Maryland Cavalry
  Battalion, C.S.A.
  http://www.cybcon.com/~warren/MD1_hist.html

- The Civil War Archive—Union Regiments—
  Maryland
  http://www.civilwararchive.com/unionmd.htm

- Civil War Battle Summaries by State—Maryland
  http://www2.cr.nps.gov/abpp/battles/bystate.htm#md

- Korean Conflict State-Level Casualty Lists—
  Maryland
  http://www.nara.gov/nara/electronic/mdhrlist.html
  *From the National Archives and Records Administration,
  Center for Electronic Records.*

- The Maryland Loyalist Battalion Home Page
  http://www.erols.com/grippo/

- Maryland Loyalists and the American Revolution
  http://www.erols.com/candidus/index.htm

- Vietnam Conflict State-Level Casualty Lists—
  Maryland
  http://www.nara.gov/nara/electronic/mdhrviet.html
  *From the National Archives and Records Administration,
  Center for Electronic Records.*

- The Vietnam Veterans Memorial—Maryland
  http://grunt.space.swri.edu/statewall/maryland/md.htm

◆ Newspapers

- AJR NewsLink—Maryland Newspapers
  http://www.newslink.org/mdnews.html

- E&P Media Info Links—Newspaper Sites
  in Maryland
  http://www.mediainfo.com/emedia/browse-results.
  htm?region=maryland&category=newspaper+++++++++

- Ecola Newstand: Maryland
  http://www.ecola.com/news/press/na/us/md/

- Maryland Newspaper Project
  http://www.mdarchives.state.md.us/msa/speccol/html/
  0003.html

- NAA Hotlinks to Newspapers Online—Maryland
  http://www.naa.org/hotlinks/searchResult.asp?param=
  MD-Maryland&City=1

- N-Net—Maryland Newspapers
  http://www.n-net.com/md.htm

- The Ultimate Collection of News Links:
  USA—Maryland
  http://www.pppp.net/links/news/USA-MD.html

- Yahoo!...Newspapers...Maryland
  http://dir.yahoo.com/News_and_Media/Newspapers/
  Browse_By_Region/U_S__States/Maryland/

◆ People & Families

- Directory of Underground Railroad Operators—
  Maryland
  http://www.ugrr.org//names/map-md.htm

- Maryland Catholics on the Frontier
  http://www.pastracks.com/mcf/
  *For descendants of Maryland Catholics who migrated westward.
  They first went to Kentucky and from there to other parts of the
  Frontier.*

- Maryland Loyalists and the American Revolution
  http://www.erols.com/candidus/index.htm

- Tribes and Villages of Maryland
  http://hanksville.phast.umass.edu:8000/cultprop/contacts/
  tribal/MD.html

◆ Professional Researchers, Volunteers & Other Research Services

- Board for Certification of Genealogists—Roster of Those Certified—Specializing in Maryland
  http://www.genealogy.org/~bcg/rosts_md.html

- Genealogy Helplist—Maryland
  http://posom.com/hl/usa/md.shtml

- The Official Iowa Counties Professional Genealogist and Researcher's Registry for Maryland
  http://www.iowa-counties.com/gene/md.htm

◆ Publications, Software & Supplies

- AncestorSpy—CDs and Microfiche for Maryland
  http://www.ancestorspy.com/md.htm

- Barbara Green's Used Genealogy Books—Maryland
  http://home.earthlink.net/~genbooks/lochist.html#MD

- Barnette's Family Tree Books—Maryland
  http://www.barnettesbooks.com/maryland.htm

- Books We Own—Maryland
  http://www.rootsweb.com/~bwo/maryland.html

- Family Line Publications
  http://pages.prodigy.com/Strawn/family.htm
  Books covering Delaware, Maryland, New Jersey, Pennsylvania, Virginia, and Washington, DC.

- The Family Tree Bookshop
  http://www.bluecrab.org/famtree/

- Frontier Press Bookstore—Maryland
  http://www.frontierpress.com/frontier.cgi?category=md

- GenealogyBookShop.com—Maryland
  http://www.genealogybookshop.com/genealogybookshop/files/The_United_States,Maryland/index.html
  The online store of Genealogical Publishing Co., Inc. & Clearfield Company.

- Hearthstone Bookshop—Maryland
  http://www.hearthstonebooks.com/cgi-bin/webc.cgi/st_main.html?catid=84&sid=2PH5t29sm

- Heritage Books—Maryland
  http://www.heritagebooks.com/md.htm

- Heritage Quest—Microfilm Records for the State of Maryland
  http://www.heritagequest.com/genealogy/microfilm/maryland/

- Lost in Time Books—Maryland
  http://www.lostintime.com/catalog/books/bookst/bo14000.htm

- Maryland Genealogy Research Books
  http://www.pastracks.com/states/maryland/marybooks.html
  A list of recommended books.

- The Memorabilia Corner—Books: Maryland
  http://members.aol.com/TMCorner/book_mar.htm

- Picton Press—Maryland
  http://www.midcoast.com/~picton/public_html.BASK/catalog/state_ml.htm

- S-K Publications—Maryland 1800–1850 Census Books
  http://www.skpub.com/genie/census/md/

- Southern Queries Genealogy Magazine
  http://www.mindspring.com/~freedom1/sq/sq.htm

- Ye Olde Genealogie Shoppe Books—Maryland
  http://www.yogs.com/maryland.htm

◆ Queries, Message Boards & Surname Lists

- Baltimore City, Maryland's Most Wanted
  http://www.InsideTheWeb.com/messageboard/mbs.cgi/mb106387

- GenConnect Maryland Visitor Center
  http://cgi.rootsweb.com/~genbbs/indx/Md.html
  A system for posting queries, Bibles, biographies, deeds, obituaries, pensions, wills.

◆ Records: Census, Cemeteries, Land, Obituaries, Personal, Taxes and Vital (Born, Married, Died & Buried)

- The 1790–1890 Federal Population Censuses: Catalog of National Archives Microfilm
  http://www.genealogy.org/census/contents.shtml
  - Census Schedules and Microfilm Roll Numbers for Maryland:
    1790
    http://www.genealogy.org/census/1790.html
    1800
    http://www.genealogy.org/census/1800_schedules/Maryland.html
    1810
    http://www.genealogy.org/census/1810_schedules/Maryland.html
    1820
    http://www.genealogy.org/census/1820_schedules/Maryland.html
    1830
    http://www.genealogy.org/census/1830_schedules/Maryland.html
    1840
    http://www.genealogy.org/census/1840_schedules/Maryland.html

1850
http://www.genealogy.org/census/1850_schedules/
Maryland.html

1860
http://www.genealogy.org/census/1860_schedules/
Maryland.html

1870
http://www.genealogy.org/census/1870_schedules/
Maryland.html

1880
http://www.genealogy.org/census/1880_schedules/
Maryland.html

1880 Soundex
http://www.genealogy.org/census/1880.sdx_schedules/
T753.html

1890 Special Schedules
http://www.genealogy.org/census/1890-special_schedules/
Maryland.html

- Baltimore & Anne Arundel County Last Will and Testaments
http://www.rootsweb.com/~mdbaltim/wills/xxwills.htm

- Cemeteries of the United States—Maryland Cemeteries—County Index
http://www.gac.edu/~kengelha/uscemeteries/maryland.html

- Census Online—Links to Census Sites on the Web—Maryland
http://www.census-online.com/links/MD_data.html

- County Courthouse Addresses
http://www.familytreemaker.com/00000249.html

- Delmarva Cemeteries
http://www.shoreweb.com/cindy/cemetery.htm

- Find-A-Grave by Location: Maryland
http://www.findagrave.com/grave/lmd.html
Graves of noteworthy people.

- Frederick Co., Maryland Descents—Court Records from 1794–1837
http://members.aol.com/DorindaMD/descents.html

- Interment.net: Maryland Cemeteries
http://www.interment.net/us/md/index.htm
A list of links to other sites.

- Maryland Vital Records Information
http://vitalrec.com/md.html

- National Archives—Mid Atlantic Region (Philadelphia)
http://www.nara.gov/regional/philacc.html

- National Archives—Mid-Atlantic Region
http://www.familytreemaker.com/00000097.html
Records for Delaware, Maryland, Pennsylvania, Virginia, and West Virginia.

- The Political Graveyard—Cemeteries in Maryland
http://politicalgraveyard.com/geo/MD/kmindex.html

- Preplanning Network—Funeral Home and Cemetery Directory—Maryland
http://www.preplannet.com/maryfhcem.htm

- United States Colored Troops Resident in Baltimore at the Time of the 1890 Census
http://www.mdarchives.state.md.us/msa/speccol/3096/html/00010001.html

- USGenWeb Census Project Maryland
http://www.usgenweb.org/census/states/maryland.htm

- USGenWeb Tombstone Transcription Project—Maryland
http://www.rootsweb.com/~cemetery/maryland.html

- VitalChek Network—Maryland
http://www.vitalchek.com/stateselect.asp?state=MD

- Where to Write for Vital Records—Maryland
http://www.cdc.gov/nchswww/howto/w2w/maryland.htm
From the National Center for Health Statistics (NCHS).

- Wicomico County, Maryland Barren Creek District #1 1870 Census
http://www.shoreweb.com/cindy/census/barren.htm

- Wicomico County, Maryland Quantico District 1870 Census
http://www.shoreweb.com/cindy/census/quantico.htm

- Wicomico County, Maryland Sharptown District #10 1870 Census
http://www.shoreweb.com/cindy/census/sharptown.htm

- Wicomico County, Maryland Tyaskin District #14 1870 Census
http://www.shoreweb.com/cindy/census/tyaskin.htm

◆ Religion & Churches

- Christianity.Net Church Locator—Maryland
http://www.christianity.net/cgi/location.exe?United_States+Maryland

- Church Online!—Maryland
http://www.churchonline.com/usas/md/md.html

- Church Profiles—Maryland
http://www.church-profiles.com/md/md.html

- Churches dot Net—Global Church Web Pages—Maryland
http://www.churches.net/churches/maryland.html

- Churches of the World—Maryland
http://www.churchsurf.com/churches/Maryland/index.htm
From the ChurchSurf Christian Directory.

- Maryland Catholics on the Frontier
http://www.pastracks.com/mcf/

◆ Societies & Groups

- **Allegheny Regional Family History Society**
  http://www.swcp.com/~dhickman/arfhs.html
  Area covers counties in northeast West Virginia, southwest Pennsylvania, western Maryland and northwest Virginia.

- **Anne Arundel Chapter—DAR**
  http://hometown.aol.com/ELLANWT/
  DAR_Ann_Arundel_CH_MD.htm

- **Archer's Computer Interest Group List—Maryland**
  http://www.genealogy.org/~ngs/cigs/ngl1usmd.html

- **Baltimore County Genealogical Society**
  http://www.serve.com/bcgs/bcgs.html

- **Carroll County Genealogical Society**
  http://www.carr.lib.md.us/ccgs/ccgs.html
  Westminster, Maryland

- **Daughters of American Colonists**
  http://members.aol.com/ELLANWT/DACPage.html
  The Ark and the Dove Chapter, Annapolis, Maryland.

- **Harford County Genealogical Society**
  http://www.rtis.com/reg/md/org/hcgs/

- **Historical Society of Carroll County**
  http://www.carr.org/hscc/

- **Historical Society of Cecil County**
  http://cchistory.org/

- **Howard County Genealogical Society, Inc.**
  http://users.aol.com/castlewrks/hcgs/index.html

- **IOOF Lodge Website Directory—Maryland**
  http://norm28.hsc.usc.edu/IOOF/USA/Maryland/Maryland.html
  Independent Order of Odd Fellows and Rebekahs.

- **Jewish Historical Society of Maryland**
  http://www.jhsm.org/

- **Lower Delmarva Genealogical Society**
  http://bay.intercom.net/ldgs/index.html
  Delaware, Maryland and Virginia.

- **Maryland Genealogical Society**
  http://www.rootsweb.com/~mdsgs/

- **Maryland Historical Society**
  http://www.mdhs.org/

- **Maryland State Society Daughters of the American Revolution**
  http://hometown.aol.com/ELLANWT/
  Maryland_State_Society_DAR.htm

- **St. Mary's County Genealogical Society**
  http://www.pastracks.com/smcgs/
  Leonardtown, Maryland

◆ USGenWeb Project

- **Maryland Genealogy—USGenWeb Project State Page**
  http://www.usgenweb.org/md

- **Maryland—USGenWeb Archives Table of Contents**
  http://www.rootsweb.com/~usgenweb/md/mdfiles.htm

- **Maryland—USGenWeb FTP Archives**
  ftp://ftp.rootsweb.com/pub/usgenweb/md/

- **MDGEN-L Mailing List**
  http://members.aol.com/gfsjohnf/gen_mail_states-md.html#MDGEN-L
  A part of the USGenWeb Project. For discussing the creation of a single source for all Maryland genealogy databases.

U.S.—MASSACHUSETTS—MA
http://www.CyndisList.com/ma.htm

Category Index:

- General Resource Sites
- Government & Cities
- History & Culture
- Libraries, Archives & Museums
- Mailing Lists, Newsgroups & Chat
- Maps, Gazetteers & Geographical Information
- Military
- Newspapers
- People & Families

- Professional Researchers, Volunteers & Other Research Services
- Publications, Software & Supplies
- Queries, Message Boards & Surname Lists
- Records: Census, Cemeteries, Land, Obituaries, Personal, Taxes and Vital
- Religion & Churches
- Societies & Groups
- USGenWeb Project

◆ General Resource Sites

- Everton's Sources of Genealogical Information in Massachusetts
  http://www.everton.com/usa/ma.htm
- Family Tree Maker's Genealogy "How To" Guide—Massachusetts
  http://www.familytreemaker.com/00000195.html
- Fifth New England Regional Genealogical Conference
  http://www.rootsweb.com/~maplymou/conf/confmain.htm
- Genealogical References
  http://idt.net/~ppl1/gencmb.html
  List of addresses and links for Massachusetts from the Plymouth Public Library.
- Genealogy Bulletin Board Systems for Massachusetts
  http://www.genealogy.org/~gbbs/gblma.html
- Genealogy Exchange & Surname Registry—MAGenExchange
  http://www.genexchange.com/ma/index.cfm
- Genealogy Resources on the Internet: Massachusetts
  http://www-personal.umich.edu/~cgaunt/mass.html
- LDS Research Outline for Massachusetts
  http://www.everton.com/usa/ma-0822b.txt
- Lineages' Genealogy Site: Massachusetts
  http://www.lineages.com/rooms/usa/state.asp?StateCode=MA
- New England Connections
  http://www.geocities.com/Heartland/5274/nec.htm
- ROOTS-L United States Resources: Massachusetts
  http://www.rootsweb.com/roots-l/USA/ma.html
  Comprehensive list of research links, including many to history-related sites.

◆ Government & Cities

- 50states.com—Massachusetts State Information Resource
  http://www.50states.com/massachu.htm
  A list of general information for each state, including a list of colleges, state symbols, links to maps, newspapers, and other miscellaneous state information.
- Charlemont, Massachusetts
  http://www.mohawktrail.com/charlemo.html
- Commonwealth of Massachusetts—MAGNet
  http://www.state.ma.us/
- Concord, Massachusetts
  http://www.concordma.com/
- Duxbury Online—Duxbury, Massachusetts
  http://www.duxburymass.com/welcome.html
- Early Brimfield—Hampden Co., MA
  http://www.rootsweb.com/~mahampde/brim.htm
- Excite Travel by City.Net—Massachusetts
  http://www.city.net/countries/united_states/massachusetts/
- Framingham History
  http://www.ixl.net/~stapleton/Framingham.html
- Franklin County Chamber of Commerce
  http://www.co.franklin.ma.us/
  Includes a map of the county with information for each of the cities.
- Gloucester, Massachusetts
  http://www.cape-ann.com/gloucester.html
- Historic Holyoke
  http://www.zapix.com/holyoke/
- History of Waltham
  http://www.waltham-community.org/history.html

- Lexington Community Web-Directory
  http://link.ci.lexington.ma.us/

- Needham, Massachusetts
  http://www.needhamonline.com/home.html

- New Bedford, Massachusetts
  http://www.newbedford.com/newbedford.html

- Official City Web Sites for the State
  of Massachusetts
  http://OfficialCitySites.org/Massachusetts.htm

- Old Sturbridge Village
  http://www.osv.org/

- Salem, Massachusetts
  http://www.salemweb.com/

- Shelburne Falls, Massachusetts
  http://www.mohawktrail.com/shelfall.html

- Yahoo! Get Local...Massachusetts Cities
  http://dir.yahoo.com/Regional/U_S__States/Massachusetts/
  Cities/
  *Maps, yellow pages, white pages, newspapers and other local
  information.*

- Yahoo! Get Local...Massachusetts Counties
  and Regions
  http://dir.yahoo.com/Regional/U_S__States/Massachusetts/
  Counties_and_Regions/
  *Maps, yellow pages, white pages, newspapers and other local
  information.*

◆ History & Culture

- 17th c. Colonial New England, with Special
  Emphasis on the Salem Witchcraft Trials of 1692
  http://www.ogram.org/17thc/index.shtml

- Boston African-American National Historic Site
  http://www.nps.gov/boaf/

- Boston History
  http://www.vboston.com/boshistory/index.htm

- The French and Indian Raid on Deerfield,
  Massachusetts, 1704
  http://uts.cc.utexas.edu/~churchh/deerfild.html

- History of the Blackstone River Valley
  http://www.blackstonevalley.com/history/

- The Massachusetts Enquirer
  http://www.maddoxinteractive.com/enquirer/

- Massachusetts Historical Sites & Societies
  http://www.masshome.com/hist.html

- Massachusetts Local History
  http://home.att.net/~mensch-family/MA_History.htm
  *Research Massachusetts local history by county, category & era
  via extensive collection of history and genealogy links, to learn
  about our ancestors and the history they lived.*

- Plymouth: Its' History and People
  http://wwx.media3.net/plymouth/history/index.htm

- Salem Witch Trials Chronology
  http://www.star.net/salem/memorial/default.htm

- Shays' Rebellion
  http://shaysnet.com/dshays.html
  A rebellion of farmers in Massachusetts.

- A Walking Tour of Plimoth Plantation
  http://www.lib.uconn.edu/ArchNet/Topical/Historic/Plimoth/
  Plimoth.html

- Yahoo!...History...Massachusetts
  http://dir.yahoo.com/Arts/Humanities/History/
  Browse_By_Region/U_S__States/Massachusetts/

◆ Libraries, Archives & Museums

- Archives in New England on the Internet
  http://www.lib.umb.edu/newengarch/nearch.html

- Boston Public Library
  http://www.boston.com/partners/bpl/bplhome.htm

- Family History Centers—Massachusetts
  http://www.deseretbook.com/famhis/ma.html

- Family History Centers—Massachusetts
  http://www.lib.byu.edu/~uvrfhc/centers/massachusetts.html

- Family History Resources at the Massachusetts
  Archives
  http://www.magnet.state.ma.us/sec/arc/arcfam/famidx.htm

- HYTELNET—Library Catalogs: USA:
  Massachusetts
  http://library.usask.ca/hytelnet/usa/MA.html
  *Before you use any of the Telnet links, make note of the user
  name, password and any other logon information.*

- Lawrence Public Library
  http://www.tiac.net/users/lfpl/index.shtml

- Massachusetts Archives Division
  http://www.state.ma.us/sec/arc/
  - Archival Records
    http://www.state.ma.us/sec/arc/arcarc/hol.htm
  - Researching Your Family's History at the
    Massachusetts Archives
    http://www.state.ma.us/sec/arc/arcfam/famidx.htm
  - Sources for Ethnic History/Genealogy
    http://www.state.ma.us/sec/arc/arcarc/hol3.htm

- Massachusetts Family History Centers
  http://www.genhomepage.com/FHC/Massachusetts.html
  *A list of addresses, phone numbers and hours of operation from
  the Genealogy Home Page.*

- The Massachusetts Library and Information Network
  http://www.mlin.lib.ma.us/
  - Massachusetts Libraries by Type
    http://www.mlin.lib.ma.us/cat_type.htm
  - Massachusetts Online Library Catalogs
    http://www.mlin.lib.ma.us/catalog.htm

- The Museum of Afro-American History Boston
  http://www.afroammuseum.org/

- NUCMC Listing of Archives and Manuscript Repositories in Massachusetts
  http://lcweb.loc.gov/coll/nucmc/masites.html
  Links to information about resources other than those held in the Library of Congress.

- Old Colony Library Network
  http://www.ocln.org/

- Plymouth Public Library
  http://idt.net/~ppl1/

  ○ Using the Plymouth Collection
    http://idt.net/~ppl1/plymouth_col.html

- Repositories of Primary Sources: Massachusetts
  http://www.uidaho.edu/special-collections/east1.html#usma
  A list of links to online resources from the Univ. of Idaho Library, Special Collections and Archives.

- State Library of Massachusetts
  http://www.state.ma.us/lib/

  ○ Special Collections of the State Library of Massachusetts
    http://www.state.ma.us/lib/sc/sc.htm

- Tisbury History: On-Line Historical Archives
  http://www.vineyard.net/vineyard/history/

- Vineyard Haven Public Library
  http://www.vineyard.net/org/vhpl/

- webCATS: Library Catalogues on the World Wide Web—Massachusetts
  http://library.usask.ca/hywebcat/states/MA.html

- Worcester Public Library
  http://www.worcpublib.org/

  ○ History and Genealogy
    http://www.worcpublib.org/internetresources/history.html

◆ Mailing Lists, Newsgroups & Chat

- Genealogy Resources on the Internet—Massachusetts Mailing Lists
  http://members.aol.com/gfsjohnf/gen_mail_states-ma.html
  Each of the mailing list links below points to this site, wonderfully maintained by John Fuller. Visit this site for county-specific mailing lists as well.

- BOSTON Mailing List—City of Boston
  http://members.aol.com/gfsjohnf/gen_mail_states-ma.html#BOSTON-L

- ESSEX-ROOTS Mailing List
  http://members.aol.com/gfsjohnf/gen_mail_states-ma.html#ESSEX-ROOTS
  For the discussion and sharing of information regarding the original settlers of Essex County, Massachusetts; their forebears from England; and their descendants throughout North America.

- GenMassachusetts Mailing List
  http://members.aol.com/gfsjohnf/gen_mail_states-ma.html#GenMassachusetts

- HTC-BOSTON Mailing List
  http://members.aol.com/gfsjohnf/gen_mail_states-ma.html#HTC-BOSTON
  For anyone researching their German roots in Boston, Massachusetts.

- MAME Mailing List
  http://members.aol.com/gfsjohnf/gen_mail_states-ma.html#MAME
  For anyone with a genealogical interest in the states of Massachusetts and Maine; both when they were "one" and after they were divided.

- Massachusetts Mailing List
  http://members.aol.com/gfsjohnf/gen_mail_states-ma.html#massachusetts

- NORTHEAST-ROOTS-L Mailing List
  http://members.aol.com/gfsjohnf/gen_mail_states-ma.html#NORTHEAST-ROOTS
  Connecticut, Maine, Massachusetts, New Hampshire, Rhode Island & Vermont.

- SALEM-WITCH Mailing List
  http://members.aol.com/gfsjohnf/gen_mail_states-ma.html#SALEM-WITCH
  A genealogy and history mailing list for descendants of the people involved in the Salem Witchcraft Trials of 1692—the accusers and the accused, the afflicted and the executed, as well as the magistrates, clergy, jurors, and anyone affected by the proceedings. Also see the associated web page at http://www.ogram.org/17thc/salem-witch-list.shtml

◆ Maps, Gazetteers & Geographical Information

- 1895 U.S. Atlas—Massachusetts
  http://www.LivGenMI.com/1895ma.htm

- American Memory Panoramic Maps 1847–1929—Massachusetts
  http://lcweb2.loc.gov/cgi-bin/query/S?ammem/gmd:@filreq(@field(STATE+massachusetts)+@field(COLLID+pmmap))
  From the Geography and Map Division, Library of Congress.

- American Memory Railroad Maps 1828–1900—Massachusetts
  http://memory.loc.gov/cgi-bin/query/S?ammem/gmd:@filreq(@field(STATE+massachusetts)+@field(COLLID+rrmap))
  From the Geography and Map Division, Library of Congress.

- AncestorSpy Massachusetts Gazetteer
  http://www.AncestorSpy.com/magaze.htm

- Color Landform Atlas: Massachusetts
  http://fermi.jhuapl.edu/states/ma_0.html
  Including a map of counties and a map for 1895.

- Excite Maps: Massachusetts Maps
  http://www.city.net/maps/view/?mapurl=/countries/united_states/massachusetts
  Zoom in on these maps all the way to the street level.

- HPI County InfoSystem—Counties in Massachusetts
  http://www.com/hpi/macty/index.html

- Index to Mass Towns
  http://www.texhoma.net/~lrsears/matowns.html

- K.B. Slocum Books and Maps—Massachusetts
  http://www.treasurenet.com/cgi-bin/treasure/kbslocum/scan/
  se=Massachusetts/sf=mapstate

- List of Massachusetts Counties
  http://www.genealogy.org/~st-clair/counties/state_ma.html

- Map of Massachusetts Counties
  http://govinfo.kerr.orst.edu/gif/states/ma.gif
  *From the Government Information Sharing Project, Information
  Services, Oregon State University.*

- Map of Massachusetts Counties
  http://www.lib.utexas.edu/Libs/PCL/Map_collection/states/
  Massachusetts.gif
  *From the Perry-Castañeda Library at the Univ. of Texas at
  Austin.*

- MassPike Offers Free Maps
  http://www.state.ma.us/masspike/freemap.htm

- Old Maps of New England (Maine, New Hampshire,
  Vermont, Connecticut, Rhode Island, Massachusetts)
  and New York
  http://members.aol.com/oldmapsne/index.html

- Reproductions of Old Town Maps in New England
  http://www.biddeford.com/~lkane/

- U.S. Census Bureau—Massachusetts Profiles
  http://www.census.gov/datamap/www/25.html

- Yale Peabody Museum: GNIS—Massachusetts
  http://www.peabody.yale.edu/other/gnis/MA.html
  *Search the USGS Geographic Names Database. You can limit
  the search to a specific county in this state and search for any of
  the following features: airport arch area arroyo bar basin bay
  beach bench bend bridge* **building** *canal cape* **cemetery** *channel*
  church *cliff crater crossing dam falls flat forest gap geyser
  glacier gut harbor hospital island isthmus lake lava levee locale
  mine oilfield other park pillar plain ppl range rapids reserve
  reservoir ridge* **school** *sea slope spring stream summit swamp
  tower trail tunnel valley well woods.*

◆ Military

- 9th Massachusetts Battery
  http://www.geocities.com/pentagon/8279
  *Civil War Site for historical and reenacting 9th Massachusetts
  Battery. Lists where each was from, occupation, muster in and
  out dates, date of death, injuries. etc.*

- 10th Mass. Volunteer Infantry Regiment
  http://members.aol.com/mass10th/index.html

- 11th Massachusetts Infantry—"Boston Volunteers"
  http://members.aol.com/rdmorss/11home.htm

- 15th Massachusetts Volunteer Infantry
  http://www.augsburg.baynet.de/~ba021308/

- 16th Massachusetts Volunteer Infantry
  http://members.aol.com/inf16mavol/16thmass.html
  *Dedicated to my great-great-grandfather, Isaac F. Kennaston,
  this site lists the rosters of the 16th Mass., and links to known
  descendants and other Civil War sites.*

- 18th Massachusetts Volunteer Infantry
  http://www.geocities.com/Pentagon/8509/

- 20th Regiment of Massachusetts Volunteer
  Infantry—"The Harvard Regiment"
  http://www.med.Virginia.EDU/~mmd5f/

- 22nd Massachusetts Volunteer Infantry
  http://www.geocities.com/Pentagon/3622/
  A Civil War Rifle Unit, reenactment group.

- 27th Regiment, Massachusetts Volunteer Infantry
  http://members.aol.com/mass27th/

- 28th Massachusetts Volunteer Infantry
  http://209.61.8.248/

- The 44th Regt. Massachusetts Volunteer Militia—
  the Second New England Guards Regiment
  http://members.aol.com/dcurtin1/44th_reg.htm

- 53rd Massachusetts Volunteer Infantry
  http://www.intac.com/~blenderm/53rd_Mass_f/
  53rd_Mass.html

- 54th. Mass. Volunteer Infantry, Co. I
  http://www.awod.com/gallery/probono/cwchas/54ma.html

- 56th Regiment Massachusetts Volunteers
  http://www.tiac.net/users/dhayes/56th/

- The Civil War Archive—Union Regiments—
  Massachusetts
  http://www.civilwararchive.com/unionma.htm

- Col. Bailey's 2nd Massachusetts Regiment
  http://www.ccs.neu.edu/home/bcortez/revwar/usa/ctl/02ma/
  02ma.html

- Fifty-Fourth Massachusetts Infantry
  http://extlab1.entnem.ufl.edu/olustee/54th_MS_inf.html

- Forty-Fourth Regiment Massachusetts Volunteer
  Militia (Infantry)
  http://members.aol.com/dcurtin1/44th_reg.htm

- Korean Conflict State-Level Casualty Lists—
  Massachusetts
  http://www.nara.gov/nara/electronic/mahrlist.html
  *From the National Archives and Records Administration,
  Center for Electronic Records.*

- Massachusetts Third Infantry
  http://www.geocities.com/Heartland/Valley/1410/
  ma3_index.html

- Massachusetts Volunteer Cavalry 1st Regiment
  http://members.aol.com/Shortyhack/1stmass.html

- Roster of the 2nd Massachusetts Volunteer
  Heavy Artillery, Companies G & H and Field &
  Staff Officers
  http://members.aol.com/CWPPDS/2ma.html

- Vietnam Conflict State-Level Casualty Lists—
  Massachusetts
  http://www.nara.gov/nara/electronic/mahrviet.html
  *From the National Archives and Records Administration,
  Center for Electronic Records.*

- The Vietnam Veterans Memorial—Massachusetts
  http://grunt.space.swri.edu/statewall/mass/ma.htm

◆ Newspapers

- AJR NewsLink—Massachusetts Newspapers
  http://www.newslink.org/manews.html

- The Berkshire Eagle
  http://www.newschoice.com/newspapers/newengland/eagle/

- E&P Media Info Links—Newspaper Sites in
  Massachusetts
  http://www.mediainfo.com/emedia/browse-results.
  htm?region=massachusetts&category=newspaper+++++++++

- Ecola Newstand: Massachusetts
  http://www.ecola.com/news/press/na/us/ma/

- The Landmark Newspaper
  http://www.thelandmark.com/
  *Serving the Wachusett Region: Holden, Paxton, Princeton,
  Rutland, Sterling, Massachusetts.*

- NAA Hotlinks to Newspapers Online—
  Massachusetts
  http://www.naa.org/hotlinks/searchResult.asp?param=
  MA-Massachusetts&City=1

- N-Net—Massachusetts Newspapers
  http://www.n-net.com/ma.htm

- The Ultimate Collection of News Links: USA—
  Massachusetts
  http://www.pppp.net/links/news/USA-MA.html

- Yahoo!...Newspapers...Massachusetts
  http://dir.yahoo.com/News_and_Media/Newspapers/
  Browse_By_Region/U_S__States/Massachusetts/

◆ People & Families

- The ALDEN House Museum
  http://www.alden.org/
  The home of John & Priscilla Alden in Duxbury, Massachusetts.

- Colonial Massachusetts and Maine Genealogies
  http://www.qni.com/~anderson/
  *Information about approximately 5,000 individuals who are
  descendants of the following surnames: Anderson, Blake,
  Brackett, Bradbury, Carver, Conant, Chute, Darling,
  Farrington, Hamblen/Hamblin/Hamlin, Haskell, Knight,
  Mansfield Mather, Noyes, Plumer/Plummer, Proctor, Sanford,
  Sawyer, Sewall, Shackford, Snow, Thurston, Waite, Watts,
  Woodward.*

- Directory of Underground Railroad Operators—
  Massachusetts
  http://www.ugrr.org//names/map-ma.htm

- Down to the Sea in Ships
  http://www.star.net/misuraca/down2c.htm
  A list of men fishing out of Gloucester who were lost at sea.

- Governor John WEBSTER of Hartford, Connecticut
  and Hadley, Massachusetts
  http://www.rootsweb.com/~genepool/websjohn.htm

- The Mayflower:
  - The General Society of Mayflower Descendants
    http://www.mayflower.org/
  - A Mayflower & New England Study
    http://www.mayflowerfamilies.com/
  - Mayflower Database
    http://www.geocities.com/Heartland/Bluffs/4313/
  - MAYFLOWER Mailing List
    http://members.aol.com/gfsjohnf/gen_mail_states-gen.
    html#MAYFLOWER
    *A mailing list for the discussion and sharing of information
    regarding the descendants of the Mayflower passengers in
    any place and at any time.*
  - Mayflower Web Page
    http://members.aol.com/calebj/mayflower.html

- The New England DYER Connection
  http://www.geocities.com/Heartland/Plains/4663/
  *Genealogies of five different DYER families in New England
  from the 17th century. Also a reference to "Genealogies of the
  Families of Braintree, Ma" by Sprague.*

- Tribes and Communities of Massachusetts
  http://hanksville.phast.umass.edu:8000/cultprop/contacts/
  tribal/MA.html

- WPA Life Histories from Massachusetts
  http://lcweb2.loc.gov/ammem/wpaintro/macat.html
  *Manuscripts from the Federal Writer's Project, 1936–1940,
  Library of Congress.*

◆ Professional Researchers, Volunteers & Other Research Services

- Barbara Jean Mathews, CG
  http://www.gis.net/~bmathews/
  *Professional genealogical research in Connecticut and
  eastern Massachusetts.*

- Board for Certification of Genealogists—Roster of
  Those Certified—Specializing in Massachusetts
  http://www.genealogy.org/~bcg/rosts_ma.html

- D & A Lambert Genealogical and Historical
  Research Services
  http://www.channel1.com/~davidl
  *Offering professional genealogical and historical research for
  Massachusetts genealogy since 1987.*

- Genealogy Helplist—Massachusetts
  http://www.calarts.edu/~karynw/helplist/ma.html

- Genealogy Research—Family Tree Studies
  (New England)
  http://www.webcs.com/genealogy/

- Heritage Associates
  http://www.granniesworld.com/heritage/
  *New England Research, specializing in pre-1850 north coast
  Massachusetts.*

- Library Stacks—An Historical Research and Reference Service
  http://members.aol.com/libstacks/libstacks.html
  Centered in the Boston area, Library Stacks is a professional service which provides research and reference assistance to antique dealers, attorneys, authors, booksellers, curators, family historians, genealogists, graduate students and historians whose genealogical and historical interests lie within the New England states.

- NEHGS Enquiries Service
  http://www.nehgs.org/EnquiryServ/enquire.htm
  From the New England Historic Genealogical Society.

- The Official Iowa Counties Professional Genealogist and Researcher's Registry for Massachusetts
  http://www.iowa-counties.com/gene/ma.htm

- Richard M. Pope, Certified Genealogist
  http://w3.nai.net/~absuax/
  Specializing in:Connecticut, Massachusetts, New York City, Germany.

◆ Publications, Software & Supplies

- AncestorSpy—CDs and Microfiche for Massachusetts
  http://www.ancestorspy.com/macat.htm

- Barbara Green's Used Genealogy Books— Massachusetts
  http://home.earthlink.net/~genbooks/lochist.html#MA

- Barnette's Family Tree Books—Massachusetts
  http://www.barnettesbooks.com/massachu.htm

- Books We Own—Massachusetts
  http://www.rootsweb.com/~bwo/mass.html

- Boyd Publishing Company—Massachusetts
  http://www.hom.net/~gac/massach.htm

- Broad View Books
  http://broadviewbooks.com/
  Used Genealogy Books, Local History of Massachusetts, Connecticut, Rhode Island, Vermont and New England.

- Essex Books—New England
  http://www.HERTGE.COM/essex/neweng.htm

- Frontier Press Bookstore—Massachusetts
  http://www.frontierpress.com/frontier.cgi?category=ma

- GenealogyBookShop.com—Massachusetts
  http://www.genealogybookshop.com/genealogybookshop/files/The_United_States,Massachusetts/index.html
  The online store of Genealogical Publishing Co., Inc. & Clearfield Company.

- Hearthstone Bookshop—Massachusetts
  http://www.hearthstonebooks.com/cgi-bin/webc.cgi/st_main.html?catid=85&sid=2PH5t29sm

- Heritage Books—Massachusetts, Part 1
  http://www.heritagebooks.com/ma1.htm

- Heritage Books—Massachusetts, Part 2
  http://www.heritagebooks.com/ma2.htm

- Heritage Quest—Microfilm Records for the State of Massachusetts
  http://www.heritagequest.com/genealogy/microfilm/massachusetts/

- Higginson Book Company
  http://www.higginsonbooks.com/
  In Salem, Massachusetts. Specializing in genealogy and history.

- Lost in Time Books—Massachusetts
  http://www.lostintime.com/catalog/books/bookst/bo15000.htm

- The Memorabilia Corner—Books: Massachusetts
  http://members.aol.com/TMCorner/book_mas.htm

- Mt. Massaemet Shadows
  http://merrill.wwh.net/massaemet/massaemet.html
  Index of Mt. Massaemet Shadows. Quarterly newsletter of Shelburne Historical Society, Shelburne, Franklin County, Massachusetts. Since 1975. 1985–1998 presently indexed. Back issues or selected pages available for a fee.

- Picton Press—Massachusetts
  http://www.midcoast.com/~picton/public_html.BASK/catalog/state_ma.htm

- Willow Bend Bookstore—Massachusetts
  http://www.willowbend.net/ma.htm

◆ Queries, Message Boards & Surname Lists

- GenConnect Massachusetts Visitor Center
  http://cgi.rootsweb.com/~genbbs/indx/Ma.html
  A system for posting queries, Bibles, biographies, deeds, obituaries, pensions, wills.

- New England Connections Query Archive
  http://www.geocities.com/Heartland/5274/nequery.htm

◆ Records: Census, Cemeteries, Land, Obituaries, Personal, Taxes and Vital (Born, Married, Died & Buried)

- The 1790–1890 Federal Population Censuses: Catalog of National Archives Microfilm
  http://www.genealogy.org/census/contents.shtml
  - Census Schedules and Microfilm Roll Numbers for Massachusetts:
    1790
    http://www.genealogy.org/census/1790.html
    1800
    http://www.genealogy.org/census/1800_schedules/Massachusetts.html
    1810
    http://www.genealogy.org/census/1810_schedules/Massachusetts.html
    1820
    http://www.genealogy.org/census/1820_schedules/Massachusetts.html

1830
http://www.genealogy.org/census/1830_schedules/
Massachusetts.html

1840
http://www.genealogy.org/census/1840_schedules/
Massachusetts.html

1850
http://www.genealogy.org/census/1850_schedules/
Massachusetts.html

1860
http://www.genealogy.org/census/1860_schedules/
Massachusetts.html

1870
http://www.genealogy.org/census/1870_schedules/
Massachusetts.html

1880
http://www.genealogy.org/census/1880_schedules/
Massachusetts.html

1880 Soundex
http://www.genealogy.org/census/1880.sdx_schedules/
T754.html

1890 Special Schedules
http://www.genealogy.org/census/1890-special_schedules/
Massachusetts.html

- The Berkshire Eagle—Obituaries
  http://www.newschoice.com/webnews/index/nebeobt3i.asp

- BPL's Obituary Database
  http://www.bpl.org/WWW/Obits.html
  This is a Telnet database from the Boston Public Library.

- Cemeteries of Martha's Vineyard
  http://www.vineyard.net/vineyard/history/cemetery/cemlist.htm
  *Links to photographs, transcripts, and notes on gravestones at
  Company Place Cemetery, West Chop Cemetery, Christiantown,
  and other sites on Martha's Vineyard.*

- Cemeteries of the United States—Massachusetts
  Cemeteries—County Index
  http://www.gac.edu/~kengelha/uscemeteries/
  massachusetts.html

- Census Online—Links to Census Sites on the Web—
  Massachusetts
  http://www.census-online.com/links/MA_data.html

- County Courthouse Addresses
  http://www.familytreemaker.com/00000250.html

- Dunstable, Massachusetts Burying Grounds
  http://members.tripod.com/DANRUTH/DunstableCem.html
  *A list of the occupants of several cemeteries in Dunstable,
  Massachusetts. Primary family names include BLOOD,
  RIDEOUT, ROBBINS, SPAULDING and SWALLOW.*

- The Essex County Registry of Deeds ~ Salem
  http://207.244.88.10/

- Find-A-Grave by Location: Massachusetts
  http://www.findagrave.com/grave/lma.html
  Graves of noteworthy people.

- Hampden County, Massachusetts Granville
  1790 Census
  http://www.rootsweb.com/~mahampde/census.htm

- Historic Graveyards of the Berkshires
  http://www.berkshireweb.com/plexus/graveyards/
  graveyards.html

- Historical Records of Tisbury, Massachusetts
  http://www.vineyard.net/vineyard/history/index.html

  o 1790 Federal Census of Tisbury, Dukes Co., Mass.
    http://www.vineyard.net/vineyard/history/cen1790i.htm

  o 1800 Federal Census of Tisbury, Dukes Co., Mass.
    http://www.vineyard.net/vineyard/history/cen1800i.htm

  o The 1850 Census of Tisbury, MA
    http://www.vineyard.net/vineyard/history/tiscen50.htm

  o The 1850 Census of Chilmark, MA
    http://www.vineyard.net/vineyard/history/chilcen50.htm

  o The 1850 Census of Edgartown, MA
    http://www.vineyard.net/vineyard/history/edgcen50.htm

  o 1862 Draft List: Tisbury Men Aged 18–45
    http://www.vineyard.net/vineyard/history/draftpag.htm

  o 1865 Census of East Parish Tisbury, Mass.
    http://www.vineyard.net/vineyard/history/cen65t.htm

  o 1897 Vineyard Haven and Tisbury Resident
    Directory
    http://www.vineyard.net/vineyard/history/td1897.htm

  o Deaths in Tisbury 1850–1875
    http://www.vineyard.net/vineyard/history/deathpag.htm

  o Every Name Index to Town Marriage Records in
    Tisbury, MA 1850–1875
    http://www.vineyard.net/vineyard/history/tmindex.htm

    • Index to Marriages in Tisbury by Bride's Name
      1844–1940
      http://www.vineyard.net/vineyard/history/bridesi.htm
      *Index to marriages in Tisbury, Mass. by bride's name, for
      the period 1844–1940. Prepared by the staff of the Tisbury
      Town Clerk's office.*

    • Index to Marriages in Tisbury by Groom's Name
      1844–1940
      http://www.vineyard.net/vineyard/history/groomsi.htm
      *Index to marriages in Tisbury, Mass. by groom's name, for
      the period 1844–1940. Prepared by the staff of the Tisbury
      Town Clerk's office.*

  o Index of Death Notices in the Vineyard Gazette
    1850–1875
    http://www.vineyard.net/vineyard/history/gazdeath.htm

  o Index to Death & Marriage Notices in the
    Vineyard Gazette 1884–1939 A–K
    http://www.vineyard.net/vineyard/history/vgind1.htm

  o Index to Death & Marriage Notices in the
    Vineyard Gazette 1884–1939 L–Z
    http://www.vineyard.net/vineyard/history/vgind2.htm

o Index to Marriage Notices in the Vineyard Gazette, 1850–1863
http://www.vineyard.net/vineyard/history/gazmar63.htm
Index to marriage notices in the Vineyard Gazette by bride and groom—mainly covers marriages on Martha's Vineyard and Dukes County, Mass. Covers years 1850–1863. Includes names, residences, date and place of marriage, and newspaper issue.

o Index to the 1850 Census of Dukes County, MA
http://www.vineyard.net/vineyard/history/cz50ind.htm

o Index to the 1860 Federal Census of Tisbury, MA
http://www.vineyard.net/vineyard/history/cen60.htm

o Index to the 1870 Federal Census of Tisbury, MA
http://www.vineyard.net/vineyard/history/cen70.htm

o Marriages in Tisbury, 1850–1853
http://www.vineyard.net/vineyard/history/tmar1b.htm
Transcript of the town marriage register for the town of Tisbury, Mass., covering the years 1850–1853.

o Marriages in Tisbury, 1853–1875
http://www.vineyard.net/vineyard/history/tmar2.htm
Transcript of town marriage register for the town of Tisbury, Mass. for the years 1853–1875. An every-name index to marriages in Tisbury for 1850–1875 is also available at http://www.vineyard.net/vineyard/history/tmindex.htm

o Name Extract of the 1910 Federal Census of Tisbury, MA
http://www.vineyard.net/vineyard/history/cen10.htm

o Surname Index to the 1910 Federal Census of Tisbury, MA
http://www.vineyard.net/vineyard/history/cen10ndx.htm

o Tisbury Deaths to the Year 1850: Adams to Linton
http://www.vineyard.net/vineyard/history/tvr.htm

Part Two: Look—Yale
http://www.vineyard.net/vineyard/history/tvrd2.htm
Transcribed from pp. 195–219 of "Vital Records of Tisbury Massachusetts to the Year 1850" published by the New England Historic Genealogy Society at the charge of the Eddy Town Record Fund. Boston, Mass., 1910. Part two, Look through Yale (pp. 219–244) is also available at http://www.vineyard.net/vineyard/history/tvrd2.htm

o Town Marriage Records in Tisbury, 1850–1875: An Index of Recorded Names
http://www.vineyard.net/vineyard/history/tmindex.htm

● Howard Cemetery Armsby Road Sutton, Massachusetts
http://www.geocities.com/Heartland/Valley/1410/sutton/armsby.html

● Interment.net: Massachusetts Cemeteries
http://www.interment.net/us/ma/index.htm
A list of links to other sites.

● Massachusetts, Bristol County 1790 Census
http://www.marketrends.net/mthome/census/1790census.html

● Massachusetts, Bristol County 1800 Census
http://www.marketrends.net/mthome/census/1800census.html

● Massachusetts, Bristol County 1810 Census
http://www.marketrends.net/mthome/census/1810census.html

● Massachusetts, Bristol County 1850 Census
http://www.marketrends.net/mthome/census/1850census.html

● Massachusetts, Bristol County 1860 Census
http://www.marketrends.net/mthome/census/1860census.html

● The Massachusetts Court System
http://www.state.ma.us/courts/courts.htm

● Massachusetts Registries of Deeds
http://www.browntech.com/ma_cnty.html
Click on map to obtain address and homepage for Registry of Deeds for your county.

● Massachusetts Vital Records Information
http://vitalrec.com/ma.html

● National Archives—Northeast Region (Boston)
http://www.nara.gov/regional/boston.html

● National Archives—New England Region
http://www.familytreemaker.com/00000098.html
Records for Connecticut, Maine, Massachusetts, New Hampshire, Rhode Island, and Vermont.

● National Archives—Northeast Region (Pittsfield)
http://www.nara.gov/regional/pittsfie.html

● National Archives—Pittsfield Region
http://www.familytreemaker.com/pittsfld.html

● The Political Graveyard—Cemeteries in Massachusetts
http://politicalgraveyard.com/geo/MA/kmindex.html

● Preplanning Network—Funeral Home and Cemetery Directory—Massachusetts
http://www.preplannet.com/massfhcem.htm

● Selected Surname—Index to Boston Births—1849–1869
http://www.eskimo.com/~mvreid/boshatch.html

● Telegram & Gazette Online—Obituaries ~ Worcester
http://www.telegram.com/news/obits/

● USGenWeb Census Project Massachusetts
http://www.usgenweb.org/census/states/massachu/massachu.htm

● USGenWeb Tombstone Transcription Project—Massachusetts
http://www.rootsweb.com/~cemetery/massachu.html

● VitalChek Network—Massachusetts
http://www.vitalchek.com/stateselect.asp?state=MA

● Walpole History Vital Records to 1850
http://www.walpole.ma.us/hhisdocvitalrecords.htm

● Where to Write for Vital Records—Massachusetts
http://www.cdc.gov/nchswww/howto/w2w/massach.htm
From the National Center for Health Statistics (NCHS).

◆ Religion & Churches

- Christianity.Net Church Locator—Massachusetts
  http://www.christianity.net/cgi/location.exe?
  United_States+Massachusetts
- Church Online!—Massachusetts
  http://www.churchonline.com/usas/ma/ma.html
- Church Profiles—Massachusetts
  http://www.church-profiles.com/ma/ma.html
- Churches dot Net—Global Church Web Pages—
  Massachusetts
  http://www.churches.net/churches/massachu.html
- Churches of the World—Massachusetts
  http://www.churchsurf.com/churches/Massachusetts/index.htm
  From the ChurchSurf Christian Directory.
- Early Members of the First Baptist Church, Holyoke,
  MA 1803–1828
  http://www.rootsweb.com/~mahampde/baptist.htm
- Holy Trinity Church, Boston, Massachusetts
  http://www.eskimo.com/~mvreid/htc.html
  *This site by Marge Reid has a multitude of resources for the
  church including the 1895 HTC Parish Directory and an HTC
  researchers directory, as well as many others.*

◆ Societies & Groups

- American Antiquarian Society
  gopher://mark.mwa.org/
  Founded in 1812 in Worcester, Massachusetts.
- American Jewish Historical Society
  http://www.ajhs.org/
  Waltham, Massachusetts
- Archer's Computer Interest Group List—
  Massachusetts
  http://www.genealogy.org/~ngs/cigs/ngl1usma.html
- The Arlington Historical Society
  http://www.arlhs.org
  *This website lists genealogical resources for the research of
  Menotomy/West Cambridge/Arlington, Massachusetts families.
  The society owns and operates the Smith Museum on Arlington
  history and the 1740s Jason Russell house.*
- Beverly Historical Society
  http://members.tripod.com/~BeverlyHS/
- Boston.com Historical Houses
  http://www.boston.com/goingout/activities/
  museumshouses.shtml
  Includes historical societies and museums as well.
- The Braintree Historical Society
  http://www.key-biz.com/ssn/Braintree/hist_soc.html
- Boylston Historical Society
  http://www.geocities.com/Heartland/Prairie/7688/
- The Cambridge Historical Society
  http://www.pastconnect.com/cambridge/

- Canton Historical Society
  http://www.canton.org/
- Cape Cod Genealogical Society
  http://members.xoom.com/ccgsWEB/
- Dedham Historical Society
  http://www.dedham.com/dhs/
- Essex Society of Genealogists
  http://www.esog.org/
- The Falmouth Historical Society
  http://www.fuzzylu.com/history/home.htm
- Historical Societies of Berkshire County
  http://www.berkshireweb.com/plexus/history/historic.html
- IOOF Lodge Website Directory—Massachusetts
  http://norm28.hsc.usc.edu/IOOF/USA/Massachusetts/
  Massachusetts.html
  Independent Order of Odd Fellows and Rebekahs.
- Ipswich Historical Society
  http://www.tiac.net/users/ncg/ihs.html
- The Irish Ancestral Research Association (TIARA)
  http://world.std.com/~ahern/TIARA.html
  Sudbury, Massachusetts
- Jamaica Plain Historical Society
  http://www.igc.org/jphs/
- Jewish Genealogical Society of Greater Boston
  http://www.jewishgen.org/boston/jgsgb.html
- Lincoln Historical Society
  http://www.tiac.net/users/morganti/historic.htm
- Massachusetts Daughters of the American
  Revolution
  http://members.aol.com/massdar/Massachusetts_DAR/
  mdar.htm
- Massachusetts Historical Sites & Societies
  http://www.masshome.com/hist.html
- Massachusetts Historical Society ~ Boston
  http://masshist.org/
- Massachusetts Studies Project—Local History—
  List of Societies & Groups
  http://k12s.phast.umass.edu/~masag/indexma.html
- The Most Worshipful Grand Lodge of Ancient Free
  and Accepted Masons of the Commonwealth of
  Massachusetts
  http://www.glmasons-mass.org/
- Natick Historical Society & Museum
  http://www.ixl.net/~natick/
- New England Historic Genealogical Society
  http://www.nehgs.org/
- Polish Genealogical Society of Massachusetts
  http://feefhs.org/pol/frgpgsma.html

- Rutland Historical Society, Inc.
  http://members.aol.com/bdleh/rutland/rhs.html
- Shrewsbury Historical Society
  http://www.geocities.com/CapeCanaveral/2771/
  ShrewsburyHistoricalSociety.html
- The Stoughton Historical Society
  http://www.channel1.com/~davidl/stoug.htm
- Topsfield Historical Society
  http://www.tiac.net/users/topshist/
- Winchester Historical Society
  http://www.tiac.net/users/mvz/winchest/histsoc.html
- The WINTHROP Society
  http://members.aol.com/WinthropSQ/society.htm
  *For those with proven descent from one or more passengers of
  the Winthrop fleet, or of others who settled in the Massachusetts
  Bay Colony before December 31, 1632*

◆ USGenWeb Project

- Massachusetts Genealogy—USGenWeb Project
  State Page
  http://www.usgenweb.org/ma
- Massachusetts—USGenWeb Archives Table of
  Contents
  http://www.rootsweb.com/~usgenweb/ma/mafiles.htm
- Massachusetts—USGenWeb FTP Archives
  ftp://ftp.rootsweb.com/pub/usgenweb/ma/

U.S.—MICHIGAN—MI
http://www.CyndisList.com/mi.htm

Category Index:

- General Resource Sites
- Government & Cities
- History & Culture
- Libraries, Archives & Museums
- Mailing Lists, Newsgroups & Chat
- Maps, Gazetteers & Geographical Information
- Military
- Newspapers
- People & Families

- Professional Researchers, Volunteers & Other Research Services
- Publications, Software & Supplies
- Queries, Message Boards & Surname Lists
- Records: Census, Cemeteries, Land, Obituaries, Personal, Taxes and Vital
- Religion & Churches
- Societies & Groups
- USGenWeb Project

◆ General Resource Sites

- **1994 Michigan County Clerks Genealogy Directory**
  http://www.sos.state.mi.us/history/archive/archgene.html

- **Everton's Sources of Genealogical Information in Michigan**
  http://www.everton.com/usa/mi.htm

- **Family Tree Maker's Genealogy "How To" Guide—Michigan**
  http://www.familytreemaker.com/00000196.html

- **Genealogy Bulletin Board Systems for Michigan**
  http://www.genealogy.org/~gbbs/gblmi.html

- **Genealogy Exchange & Surname Registry—MIGenExchange**
  http://www.genexchange.com/mi/index.cfm

- **Genealogy Resources on the Internet: Michigan**
  http://www-personal.umich.edu/~cgaunt/mich.html

- **LDS Research Outline for Michigan**
  http://www.everton.com/usa/mi-0823b.txt

- **Lineages' Genealogy Site: Michigan**
  http://www.lineages.com/rooms/usa/state.asp?StateCode=MI

- **Michigan Historical Center**
  http://www.sos.state.mi.us/history/history.html

- **ROOTS-L United States Resources: Michigan**
  http://www.rootsweb.com/roots-l/USA/mi.html
  Comprehensive list of research links, including many to history-related sites.

◆ Government & Cities

- **50states.com—Michigan State Information Resource**
  http://www.50states.com/michigan.htm
  A list of general information for each state, including a list of colleges, state symbols, links to maps, newspapers, and other miscellaneous state information.

- **Excite Travel by City.Net—Michigan**
  http://www.city.net/countries/united_states/michigan/

- **Michigan Historical Center (Michigan Department of State)**
  http://www.sos.state.mi.us/history/history.html

- **Michigan Local Government**
  http://mel.lib.mi.us/government/GOV-local-mi.html
  Links to Official Home Pages of Michigan County Governments and more.

- **Michigan State Government**
  http://www.migov.state.mi.us/

- **Official City Web Sites for the State of Michigan**
  http://OfficialCitySites.org/Michigan.htm

- **Yahoo! Get Local...Michigan Cities**
  http://dir.yahoo.com/Regional/U_S__States/Michigan/Cities/
  Maps, yellow pages, white pages, newspapers and other local information.

- **Yahoo! Get Local...Michigan Counties and Regions**
  http://dir.yahoo.com/Regional/U_S__States/Michigan/Counties_and_Regions/
  Maps, yellow pages, white pages, newspapers and other local information.

◆ History & Culture

- Michigan Through the Years—A Brief History of the Great Lake State
  http://www.sos.state.mi.us/history/michinfo/briefhis/briefhis.html

- Yahoo!...History...Michigan
  http://dir.yahoo.com/Arts/Humanities/History/Browse_By_Region/U_S__States/Michigan/

◆ Libraries, Archives & Museums

- The Bentley Historical Library at the Univ. of Michigan—Genealogy Resources
  http://www.umich.edu/~bhl/bhl/refhome/ugenie.htm

- Berrien County Libraries
  http://www.qtm.net/~genealogy/berrien/librarie.htm

- Detroit Public Library
  http://www.detroit.lib.mi.us/
  - Detroit Public Library—Special Collections
    http://www.detroit.lib.mi.us/special_collections.htm

- Family History Centers—Michigan
  http://www.deseretbook.com/famhis/mi.html

- Family History Centers—Michigan
  http://www.lib.byu.edu/~uvrfhc/centers/michigan.html

- Grand Rapids Public Library
  http://www.grapids.lib.mi.us/index.html
  - Local History Department
    http://www.grapids.lib.mi.us/localhis.htm
    - Family History Research Suggestions from the GRPL Local History Department
      http://www.grapids.lib.mi.us/famhist.htm

- Herrick District Library
  http://www.macatawa.org/~herrick/
  Holland, Michigan

- Howell Family History Center
  http://www.LivGenMI.com/howfhc.htm

- HYTELNET—Library Catalogs: USA: Michigan
  http://library.usask.ca/hytelnet/usa/MI.html
  Before you use any of the Telnet links, make note of the user name, password and any other logon information.

- The Library of Michigan
  http://www.libofmich.lib.mi.us/
  In the Michigan Library and Historical Center, Lansing, Michigan.
  - Library of Michigan Collections
    http://www.libofmich.lib.mi.us/collections/collections.html
    - Abrams Foundation Historical Collection: Genealogy and Local History
      http://www.libofmich.lib.mi.us/genealogy/genealogy.html

- Marguerite deAngeli Library Genealogy Collection
  http://www.lapeer.lib.mi.us/Library/Genealogy/Index.html
  Lapeer County

- Michigan Family History Centers
  http://www.genhomepage.com/FHC/Michigan.html
  A list of addresses, phone numbers and hours of operation from the Genealogy Home Page.

- Michigan Historical Center
  http://www.sos.state.mi.us/history/history.html
  Lansing, Michigan

- Michigan Library Association—Home Pages of Michigan Libraries
  http://www.mla.lib.mi.us/pages.html

- Mount Clemens Public Library
  http://www.macomb.lib.mi.us/mountclemens/
  - Genealogy Collection and Services
    http://www.macomb.lib.mi.us/mountclemens/genealog.htm
  - Mount Clemens Local History
    http://www.macomb.lib.mi.us/mountclemens/local.htm

- NUCMC Listing of Archives and Manuscript Repositories in Michigan
  http://lcweb.loc.gov/coll/nucmc/misites.html
  Links to information about resources other than those held in the Library of Congress.

- Public Libraries of Saginaw
  http://www.saginaw.lib.mi.us/index.htm
  - Eddy Historical and Genealogical Collection
    http://www.saginaw.lib.mi.us/services.htm#Eddy Historical and Genealogical Collection

- Repositories of Primary Sources: Michigan
  http://www.uidaho.edu/special-collections/east1.html#usmi
  A list of links to online resources from the Univ. of Idaho Library, Special Collections and Archives.

- State Archives of Michigan
  http://www.sos.state.mi.us/history/archive/archive.html
  - State Archives of Michigan—Circular No. 13, Railroad Records
    gopher://gopher.sos.state.mi.us:70/00/history/archives/c13

- Van Buren District Library
  http://cwic1.jackson.lib.mi.us/van/vanburen.htm
  Decatur, Michigan

- webCATS: Library Catalogues on the World Wide Web—Michigan
  http://library.usask.ca/hywebcat/states/MI.html

◆ Mailing Lists, Newsgroups & Chat

- Genealogy Resources on the Internet—Michigan Mailing Lists
  http://members.aol.com/gfsjohnf/gen_mail_states-mi.html
  Each of the mailing list links below points to this site, wonderfully maintained by John Fuller. Visit this site for county-specific mailing lists as well.

- MI-GENEALOGY Mailing List
  http://members.aol.com/gfsjohnf/gen_mail_states-mi.html#MI-GENEALOGY-L

- MI-WI-ROOTS-L Mailing List
http://members.aol.com/gfsjohnf/gen_mail_states-mi.
html#MI/WI-ROOTS
Michigan & Wisconsin

- NISHNAWBE Mailing List
http://members.aol.com/gfsjohnf/gen_mail_states-wi.
html#NISHNAWBE
For anyone researching Native Americans in Michigan and Wisconsin, and the fur traders connected with them.

- SouthwestMichigan Mailing List
http://members.aol.com/gfsjohnf/gen_mail_states-mi.
html#SouthwestMichigan
For genealogists researching ancestry in Southwest Michigan including, but not limited to, the counties of Berrien, Cass, Van Buren, Kalamazoo, and St. Joseph.

◆ Maps, Gazetteers & Geographical Information

- 1895 U.S. Atlas—Michigan
http://www.LivGenMI.com/1895mi.htm

- American Memory Panoramic Maps 1847–1929—Michigan
http://lcweb2.loc.gov/cgi-bin/query/S?ammem/gmd:
@filreq(@field(STATE+michigan)+@field(COLLID+pmmap))
From the Geography and Map Division, Library of Congress.

- American Memory Railroad Maps 1828–1900—Michigan
http://memory.loc.gov/cgi-bin/query/S?ammem/gmd:
@filreq(@field(STATE+michigan)+@field(COLLID+rrmap))
From the Geography and Map Division, Library of Congress.

- Color Landform Atlas: Michigan
http://fermi.jhuapl.edu/states/mi_0.html
Including a map of counties and a map for 1895.

- Excite Maps: Michigan Maps
http://www.city.net/maps/view/?mapurl=/countries/
united_states/michigan
Zoom in on these maps all the way to the street level.

- HPI County InfoSystem—Counties in Michigan
http://www.com/hpi/micty/index.html

- K.B. Slocum Books and Maps—Michigan
http://www.treasurenet.com/cgi-bin/treasure/kbslocum/scan/
se=Michigan/sf=mapstate

- List of Michigan Counties
http://www.genealogy.org/~st-clair/counties/state_mi.html

- Map of Michigan Counties, Map #1
http://govinfo.kerr.orst.edu/gif/states/mi1.gif

  Map #2
http://govinfo.kerr.orst.edu/gif/states/mi2.gif
From the Government Information Sharing Project, Information Services, Oregon State University.

- Map of Michigan Counties
http://www.lib.utexas.edu/Libs/PCL/Map_collection/states/
Michigan.gif
From the Perry-Castañeda Library at the Univ. of Texas at Austin.

- U.S. Census Bureau—Michigan Profiles
http://www.census.gov/datamap/www/26.html

- Yale Peabody Museum: GNIS—Michigan
http://www.peabody.yale.edu/other/gnis/MI.html
*Search the USGS Geographic Names Database. You can limit the search to a specific county in this state and search for any of the following features: airport arch area arroyo bar basin bay beach bench bend bridge **building** canal cape **cemetery** channel **church** cliff crater crossing dam falls flat forest gap geyser glacier gut harbor hospital island isthmus lake lava levee locale mine oilfield other park pillar plain ppl range rapids reserve reservoir ridge **school** sea slope spring stream summit swamp tower trail tunnel valley well woods.*

◆ Military

- 1st Regiment Michigan Sharpshooters
http://users.aol.com/dlharvey/sharps.htm

- The Civil War Archive—Union Regiments—Michigan
http://www.civilwararchive.com/unionmi.htm

- How to Request Michigan Civil War Ancestor's Military Records from the National Archives
http://www.centuryinter.net/suvcw.mi/gr-recwv.html

- Korean Conflict State-Level Casualty Lists—Michigan
http://www.nara.gov/nara/electronic/mihrlist.html
From the National Archives and Records Administration, Center for Electronic Records.

- Michigan in the Civil War
http://users.aol.com/dlharvey/cwmireg.htm

- Michigan Regimental Rosters
http://users.aol.com/dharvey125/rosters.htm

- Researching and Recording Civil War Veterans Burials in Michigan Cemeteries
http://www.centuryinter.net/suvcw.mi/gr-recgv.html

- Vietnam Conflict State-Level Casualty Lists—Michigan
http://www.nara.gov/nara/electronic/mihrviet.html
From the National Archives and Records Administration, Center for Electronic Records.

- The Vietnam Veterans Memorial—Michigan
http://grunt.space.swri.edu/statewall/mich/mi.htm

◆ Newspapers

- AJR NewsLink—Michigan Newspapers
http://www.newslink.org/minews.html

- The Ann Arbor News—Michigan Live
http://aa.mlive.com/

- The Detroit Free Press—The Freep
http://www.freep.com/index.htm

- The Detroit News
http://www.detnews.com/

- E&P Media Info Links—Newspaper Sites in Michigan
  http://www.mediainfo.com/emedia/browse-results.
  htm?region=michigan&category=newspaper+++++++++
- Ecola Newstand: Michigan
  http://www.ecola.com/news/press/na/us/mi/
- The Heritage Newspapers
  http://www.heritagenews.com/
- HomeTown Online
  http://www.htnews.com/
  Newspapers for Howell, Michigan.
- Michigan Newspaper Project
  http://www.libofmich.lib.mi.us/services/usnewsproj.html
- The Monroe Evening News
  http://www.MONROENEWS.COM/index.html
  Michigan
- NAA Hotlinks to Newspapers Online—Michigan
  http://www.naa.org/hotlinks/searchResult.asp?param=
  MI-Michigan&City=1
- N-Net—Michigan Newspapers
  http://www.n-net.com/mi.htm
- SPAN—Serials, Periodicals, and Newspapers
  http://span.mlc.lib.mi.us:9000/
  A database of over 201,000 journals, magazines and newspapers found in Michigan's libraries.
- The Ultimate Collection of News Links: USA—Michigan
  http://www.pppp.net/links/news/USA-MI.html
- Yahoo!...Newspapers...Michigan
  http://dir.yahoo.com/News_and_Media/Newspapers/
  Browse_By_Region/U_S__States/Michigan/

◆ People & Families

- Augustine GODWIN of Wyoming Township, Kent County, Michigan
  http://www-leland.stanford.edu/~jenkg/family/augustine.html
- Directory of Underground Railroad Operators— Michigan
  http://www.ugrr.org//names/map-mi.htm
- Michigan's Native Americans—A Selective Bibliography
  http://www.libofmich.lib.mi.us/genealogy/minatamerbib.html
- Native American Research in Michigan
  http://members.aol.com/roundsky/introduction.html
  Using the Ottawa, Chippewa and Potawatomi tribes as examples.
- Tribes and Villages of Michigan
  http://hanksville.phast.umass.edu:8000/cultprop/contacts/
  tribal/MI.html

◆ Professional Researchers, Volunteers & Other Research Services

- Board for Certification of Genealogists—Roster of Those Certified—Specializing in Michigan
  http://www.genealogy.org/~bcg/rosts_mi.html
- Detroit Search
  http://pages.prodigy.net/kdall/yourpage.html
- Diane's Michigan Genealogy Page
  http://members.aol.com/DJOslund/index.html
  Professional Genealogist serving Southeastern Michigan, Southwestern Ontario, Northwestern Ohio.
- Genealogy Helplist—Michigan
  http://www.omeganet.es/~boet/hl/mi.htm
- Michigan Genealogist for Michigan— Karen Olszeski
  http://genealogypro.com/kolszeski.html
- The Official Iowa Counties Professional Genealogist and Researcher's Registry for Michigan
  http://www.iowa-counties.com/gene/mi.htm
- So Many Branches
  http://www.angelfire.com/biz/SoManyBranches/
  Western New York, Northern Pennsylvania, Michigan and Northern Ohio Genealogical Research.

◆ Publications, Software & Supplies

- 84 Charing Cross, EH?—Good Used/Rare Books
  http://www.84cc.com/
- AncestorSpy—CDs and Microfiche for Michigan
  http://www.ancestorspy.com/mi.htm
- Barbara Green's Used Genealogy Books—Michigan
  http://home.earthlink.net/~genbooks/lochist.html#MI
- Books We Own—Michigan
  http://www.rootsweb.com/~bwo/michigan.html
- Boyd Publishing Company—Michigan
  http://www.hom.net/~gac/michiga.htm
- Frontier Press Bookstore—Michigan
  http://www.frontierpress.com/frontier.cgi?category=mi
- GenealogyBookShop.com—Michigan
  http://www.genealogybookshop.com/genealogybookshop/files/
  The_United_States,Michigan/index.html
  The online store of Genealogical Publishing Co., Inc. & Clearfield Company.
- Hearthstone Bookshop—Michigan
  http://www.hearthstonebooks.com/cgi-bin/webc.cgi/
  st_main.html?catid=86&sid=2PH5t29sm
- Heritage Quest—Microfilm Records for the State of Michigan
  http://www.heritagequest.com/genealogy/microfilm/michigan/

- Kinseeker Publications
  http://www.angelfire.com/biz/Kinseeker/index.html
- Lost in Time Books—Michigan
  http://www.lostintime.com/catalog/books/bookst/bo16000.htm
- The Memorabilia Corner—Books: Michigan
  http://members.aol.com/TMCorner/book_mi.htm
- S-K Publications—Michigan 1850 Census Books
  http://www.skpub.com/genie/census/mi/

◆ Queries, Message Boards & Surname Lists

- Detroit Genealogy Co-operative
  http://members.aol.com/ernm/roots/detroit.html
  Colleagues Researching Detroit, Michigan, USA.
- GenConnect Michigan Visitor Center
  http://cgi.rootsweb.com/~genbbs/indx/Mi.html
  A system for posting queries, Bibles, biographies, deeds, obituaries, pensions, wills.
- HERRICK Library's Listing of SURNAMES in Ottawa County Michigan
  http://www.macatawa.org/~brianter/herrick.htm

◆ Records: Census, Cemeteries, Land, Obituaries, Personal, Taxes and Vital (Born, Married, Died & Buried)

- The 1790–1890 Federal Population Censuses: Catalog of National Archives Microfilm
  http://www.genealogy.org/census/contents.shtml
  - Census Schedules and Microfilm Roll Numbers for Michigan:
    1820
    http://www.genealogy.org/census/1820_schedules/Michigan.html
    1830
    http://www.genealogy.org/census/1830_schedules/Michigan.html
    1840
    http://www.genealogy.org/census/1840_schedules/Michigan.html
    1850
    http://www.genealogy.org/census/1850_schedules/Michigan.html
    1860
    http://www.genealogy.org/census/1860_schedules/Michigan.html
    1870
    http://www.genealogy.org/census/1870_schedules/Michigan.html
    1880
    http://www.genealogy.org/census/1880_schedules/Michigan.html
    1880 Soundex
    http://www.genealogy.org/census/1880.sdx_schedules/T755.html
    1890 Special Schedules
    http://www.genealogy.org/census/1890-special_schedules/Michigan.html

- The Bureau of Land Management—Eastern States, General Land Office
  http://www.glorecords.blm.gov/
  The Official Land Patent Records Site. This site has a searchable database of over two million pre-1908 Federal land title records, including scanned images of those records. The Eastern Public Land States covered in this database are: Alabama, Arkansas, Florida, Illinois, Indiana, Louisiana, Michigan, Minnesota, Mississippi, Missouri, Ohio, Wisconsin.
- Cemeteries of Monroe Co., MI
  http://206.42.132.11/havekost/cemetery.htm
- Census Online—Links to Census Sites on the Web—Michigan
  http://www.census-online.com/links/MI_data.html
- County Courthouse Addresses
  http://www.familytreemaker.com/00000251.html
- Detroit Free Press—Death Notices
  http://www.freep.com/death_notices/index.htm
- Detroit Free Press—Obituaries
  http://www.freep.com/index/obituaries.htm
- The Detroit News—Obituaries & Death Notices
  http://www.detnews.com/
  Scroll through the index on this page and click on the link to Obituaries.
- Downward Bound Great Lakes Shipping Genealogy Index
  http://www.rootsweb.com/~migls/index.html
- Early Alpena County Marriages 1871
  http://www.rootsweb.com/~mialpena/early.htm
- Early Marriages by Albertus C. Van Raalte
  http://www.macatawa.org/~devries/Earlym.htm
  From Southern Ottawa County Michigan, and Northern Allegan County Michigan.
- Early Marriages of Newaygo County
  http://www.rootsweb.com/~minewayg/marriag.html
  Michigan
- Early Marriages and Deaths of Village Residents
  http://www.iserv.net/~bryant/grmarr.txt
  Grand Rapids, Michigan
- Find-A-Grave by Location: Michigan
  http://www.findagrave.com/grave/lmi.html
  Graves of noteworthy people.

- Genealogical Death Indexing System, Michigan
  http://www.mdch.state.mi.us/PHA/OSR/gendis/index.htm
  The current system contains information on 148,000 Michigan death records from 1867–1880 and portions of 1881 and 1882. Records for 1875 to 1882 have been newly added to the system during the week of September 14, 1998.

- Interment.net: Michigan Cemeteries
  http://www.interment.net/us/mi/index.htm
  A list of links to other sites.

- Ionia County, Michigan—Early Marriage Records—Indexed by Groom
  http://www.rootsweb.com/~miionia/more.txt

- Lenawee Co. MI Bible Records Forum
  http://cgi.rootsweb.com/~genbbs/genbbs.cgi/USA/Mi/LenaweeBibl

- Lenawee County Michigan Newspaper 'Michigan Expositor' Notices of Marriages and Deaths in 1850
  http://members.aol.com/Lenaweemi/extractions1850.html

- Marriages in Kalkaska County, Michigan 1871–1875
  http://members.aol.com/kingsley/kas-mar.html

- Michiana Genealogical Index—MGI
  http://www.qtm.net/~ftmiami/remarc/
  A surname source database for birth, death, marriage, license, divorce and cemetery records. Representing over 500,000 records from southwestern Michigan and northern Indiana.

- Michigan Cemetery Page
  http://www.rootsweb.com/~migenweb/mi-cemetery.html

- Michigan Live: Obituaries
  http://www.mlive.com/obits/

- Michigan Vital Records Information
  http://vitalrec.com/mi.html

- Monroe Evening News Obituaries
  http://www.MONROENEWS.COM/newshtml/Obits.htm

- National Archives—Great Lakes Region (Chicago)
  http://www.nara.gov/regional/chicago.html

- National Archives—Great Lakes Region
  http://www.familytreemaker.com/00000096.html
  Records from Illinois, Indiana, Michigan, Minnesota, Ohio, and Wisconsin.

- The Political Graveyard—Cemeteries in Michigan
  http://politicalgraveyard.com/geo/MI/kmindex.html

- Preplanning Network—Funeral Home and Cemetery Directory—Michigan
  http://www.preplannet.com/michfhcem.htm

- USGenWeb Census Project Michigan
  http://www.usgenweb.org/census/states/michigan/michigan.htm

- USGenWeb Tombstone Transcription Project—Michigan
  http://www.rootsweb.com/~cemetery/michigan.html

- The Utica Cemetery
  http://www.concentric.net/~Ekkm/Utica.html

- VitalChek Network—Michigan
  http://www.vitalchek.com/stateselect.asp?state=MI

- Where to Write for Vital Records—Michigan
  http://www.cdc.gov/nchswww/howto/w2w/michigan.htm
  From the National Center for Health Statistics (NCHS).

◆ Religion & Churches

- Christianity.Net Church Locator—Michigan
  http://www.christianity.net/cgi/location.exe?United_States+Michigan

- Church Online!—Michigan
  http://www.churchonline.com/usas/mi/mi.html

- Church Profiles—Michigan
  http://www.church-profiles.com/mi/mi.html

- Churches dot Net—Global Church Web Pages—Michigan
  http://www.churches.net/churches/michigan.html

- Churches of the World—Michigan
  http://www.churchsurf.com/churches/Michigan/index.htm
  From the ChurchSurf Christian Directory.

◆ Societies & Groups

- American Historical Society of Germans from Russia—Southwest Michigan Chapter
  http://www.ahsgr.org/misouthw.html

- Ann Arbor Civil War Roundtable
  http://www.izzy.net/~michaelg/aacwrt.htm

- Archer's Computer Interest Group List—Michigan
  http://www.genealogy.org/~ngs/cigs/ngl1usmi.html

- Berrien County Genealogical Society
  http://www.qtm.net/bcgensoc/

- Calhoun County Genealogical Society
  http://www.rootsweb.com/~micalhou/ccgs.htm
  Marshall, Michigan

- Charlevoix County Genealogical Society
  http://www.rootsweb.com/~micharle/cx-03.htm
  Boyne City, Michigan

- Daughters of the American Revolution of Michigan
  http://www.geocities.com/Heartland/Meadows/6543/

- Delta County Genealogical Society
  http://members.aol.com/DeltaMI4/home.html
  Escanaba, Michigan

- Department of Michigan Sons of Union Veterans of the Civil War
  http://www.centuryinter.net/suvcw.mi/index.html

- The Detroit Society for Genealogical Research, Inc
  http://www.dsgr.org/

- The Downriver Genealogical Society
  http://www.rootsweb.com/~midrgs/drgs.htm
  Wayne County

- Eaton County Genealogical Society
  http://www.sojourn.com/~mmgs/ecgs.html
  Charlotte

- Farmington Genealogical Society
  http://metronet.lib.mi.us/FCL/genealsoc.html

- Flint Genealogical Society
  http://www.rootsweb.com/~mifgs/

- The Ford Genealogy Club
  http://www.wwnet.net~krugman1/fgc/
  Dearborn, Michigan

- Fort Miami Heritage Society
  http://www.qtm.net/~ftmiami/

- French Canadian Heritage Society of Michigan
  http://habitant.org/fchsm/

- Genealogical, Historical, Social/Cultural, Hereditary, Ethnic & Reenactment Organizations as Well as Some Special Libraries, Museums & Archives in Michigan
  http://www.sojourn.com/~mmgs/societys.html

- Genealogical Society of Monroe County, Michigan
  http://www.tdi.net/havekost/gsmc.htm

- The Genealogists of the Clinton County Historical Society
  http://www.sojourn.com/~mmgs/gofcchs.html
  St. Johns

- The Governor Henry H. Crapo Camp No. 145— Sons of Union Veterans of the Civil War
  http://gfn1.genesee.freenet.org/suvmi145/

- The Grand Army of the Republic in Michigan
  http://www.centuryinter.net/suvcw.mi/garmi.html

- The Grand Lodge of Michigan Free and Accepted Masons
  http://gl-mi.org/

- Grand Traverse Area Genealogical Society
  http://members.aol.com/vwilson577/gtags.html
  Traverse City, Michigan

- Grand Trunk Western Historical Society
  http://www.rrhistorical.com/gtwhs/index.html

- Harrison Area Genealogy Society
  http://www.rootsweb.com/~miclare/harrison.htm

- The Houghton County Historical Museum
  http://habitant.org/houghton/

- Ingham County Genealogical Society
  http://userdata.acd.net/mmgs/icgs.html
  Mason

- Ionia County Genealogical Society
  http://www.rootsweb.com/~miionia/icgshome.htm

- IOOF Lodge Website Directory—Michigan
  http://norm28.hsc.usc.edu/IOOF/USA/Michigan/Michigan.html
  Independent Order of Odd Fellows and Rebekahs.

- Kalamazoo Valley Genealogical Society
  http://www.rootsweb.com/~mikvgs/

- Little Traverse Historical Society
  http://www.freeway.net/community/civic/historymuseum/
  Petoskey, Michigan

- Livingston County Genealogical Society
  http://www.LivGenMI.com/lcgslogo.htm
  Howell, Michigan

- The Marine Historical Society of Detroit
  http://www.oakland.edu/~ncschult/mhsd/

- Michigan American Legion
  http://www.michiganlegion.org/

- Michigan Genealogical Council
  http://www.geocities.com/Heartland/Meadows/2192/index.html

- Mid-Michigan Genealogical Society (MMGS)
  http://www.sojourn.com/~mmgs/

- Military Order of the Loyal Legion of the United States—Michigan Commandery
  http://pages.prodigy.net/pcinc/mollus.html

- Oakland County Pioneer and Historical Society
  http://www.med.umich.edu/HCHS/Files/Repositories/REPOS-MICH/Oakland/Oakland.html
  Pontiac, Michigan

- The Saginaw River Marine Historical Society
  http://www.concentric.net/~Djmaus/srmhs.htm

- Sons of the Revolution in the State of Michigan
  http://www.execpc.com/~sril/srmi.html

- Van Buren Regional Genealogical Society
  http://cwic1.jackson.lib.mi.us/van/vbrgs.htm
  Decatur, Michigan. For the counties of Allegan, Berrien, Cass, Kalamazoo and Van Buren.

- Western Michigan Genealogical Society
  http://www.iserv.net/~wmgs/

◆ USGenWeb Project

- Michigan Genealogy—USGenWeb Project State Page
  http://www.usgenweb.org/mi

- Michigan—USGenWeb Archives Table of Contents
  http://www.rootsweb.com/~usgenweb/mi/mifiles.htm

- Michigan—USGenWeb FTP Archives
  ftp://ftp.rootsweb.com/pub/usgenweb/mi/

U.S.—MINNESOTA—MN
http://www.CyndisList.com/mn.htm

Category Index:

- General Resource Sites
- Government & Cities
- History & Culture
- Libraries, Archives & Museums
- Mailing Lists, Newsgroups & Chat
- Maps, Gazetteers & Geographical Information
- Military
- Newspapers
- People & Families

- Professional Researchers, Volunteers & Other Research Services
- Publications, Software & Supplies
- Queries, Message Boards & Surname Lists
- Records: Census, Cemeteries, Land, Obituaries, Personal, Taxes and Vital
- Religion & Churches
- Societies & Groups
- USGenWeb Project

◆ General Resource Sites

- Everton's Sources of Genealogical Information in Minnesota
  http://www.everton.com/usa/mn.htm

- Family Tree Maker's Genealogy "How To" Guide—Minnesota
  http://www.familytreemaker.com/00000197.html

- Genealogy Bulletin Board Systems for Minnesota
  http://www.genealogy.org/~gbbs/gblmn.html

- Genealogy Exchange & Surname Registry—MNGenExchange
  http://www.genexchange.com/mn/index.cfm

- Genealogy Resources on the Internet: Minnesota
  http://www-personal.umich.edu/~cgaunt/minn.html

- Immigration History Research Center—Univ. of Minnesota
  http://www.umn.edu/ihrc/

- LDS Research Outline for Minnesota
  http://www.everton.com/usa/mn-0824b.txt

- Lineages' Genealogy Site: Minnesota
  http://www.lineages.com/rooms/usa/state.asp?StateCode=MN

- Minnesota Genealogy Research Notes
  http://www.parkbooks.com/Html/research.html
  A series of articles from Park Genealogical Books.

- ROOTS-L United States Resources: Minnesota
  http://www.rootsweb.com/roots-l/USA/mn.html
  Comprehensive list of research links, including many to history-related sites.

◆ Government & Cities

- 50states.com—Minnesota State Information Resource
  http://www.50states.com/minnesot.htm
  A list of general information for each state, including a list of colleges, state symbols, links to maps, newspapers, and other miscellaneous state information.

- Excite Travel by City.Net—Minnesota
  http://www.city.net/countries/united_states/minnesota/

- Minnesota Government Information and Services—Northstar
  http://www.state.mn.us/

- Official City Web Sites for the State of Minnesota
  http://OfficialCitySites.org/Minnesota.htm

- Yahoo! Get Local...Minnesota Cities
  http://dir.yahoo.com/Regional/U_S__States/Minnesota/Cities/
  Maps, yellow pages, white pages, newspapers and other local information.

- Yahoo! Get Local...Minnesota Counties and Regions
  http://dir.yahoo.com/Regional/U_S__States/Minnesota/Counties_and_Regions/
  Maps, yellow pages, white pages, newspapers and other local information.

◆ History & Culture

- Historical Encyclopedia of St. Paul, MN
  http://www.wavefront.com/~pjlareau/pep1.html

- Minnesota State Historic Preservation Office
  http://www.mnhs.org/prepast/mnshpo/mnshpo.html

- MN Historical Society: Historic Sites
  http://www.mnhs.org/sites/sites.html

- Yahoo!...History...Minnesota
  http://dir.yahoo.com/Arts/Humanities/History/
  Browse_By_Region/U_S__States/Minnesota/

◆ Libraries, Archives & Museums

- Family History Centers—Minnesota
  http://www.deseretbook.com/famhis/mn.html

- Family History Centers—Minnesota
  http://www.lib.byu.edu/~uvrfhc/centers/minnesota.html

- HYTELNET—Library Catalogs: USA: Minnesota
  http://library.usask.ca/hytelnet/usa/MN.html
  *Before you use any of the Telnet links, make note of the user
  name, password and any other logon information.*

- MHS Collections: State Archives
  http://www.mnhs.org/ebranch/mhs/research/c18.htm

- Minnesota Family History Centers
  http://www.genhomepage.com/FHC/Minnesota.html
  *A list of addresses, phone numbers and hours of operation from
  the Genealogy Home Page.*

- Minnesota Historical Society
  http://www.mnhs.org/index.html
  - The History Center
    http://www.mnhs.org/histctr/histctr.html
  - Using the Minnesota Historical Society's
    Collections for Research
    http://www.mnhs.org/index.html

- Minnesota Library Systems and Catalogs
  http://www.state.mn.us/libraries/index.html

- NUCMC Listing of Archives and Manuscript
  Repositories in Minnesota
  http://lcweb.loc.gov/coll/nucmc/mnsites.html
  *Links to information about resources other than those held in the
  Library of Congress.*

- Repositories of Primary Sources: Minnesota
  http://www.uidaho.edu/special-collections/east1.html#usmn
  *A list of links to online resources from the Univ. of Idaho
  Library, Special Collections and Archives.*

- Twin Cities Free-Net: Libraries
  http://freenet.msp.mn.us/library/

- Twin Cities Free-Net: Twin Cities Academic
  Libraries (Online Catalog)
  http://freenet.msp.mn.us/library/tcacad.html#uofm

- University of Minnesota Libraries
  http://www.lib.umn.edu/
  - Genealogy Resources Available at the
    University of Minnesota Libraries
    http://www.lib.umn.edu/reference/genealogy.html

- webCATS: Library Catalogues on the World Wide
  Web—Minnesota
  http://library.usask.ca/hywebcat/states/MN.html

◆ Mailing Lists, Newsgroups & Chat

- Genealogy Resources on the Internet—Minnesota
  Mailing Lists
  http://members.aol.com/gfsjohnf/gen_mail_states-mn.html
  *Each of the mailing list links below points to this site, wonder-
  fully maintained by John Fuller. Visit this site for county-specific
  mailing lists as well.*

- Minnesota Mailing List
  http://members.aol.com/gfsjohnf/gen_mail_states-mn.
  html#Minnesota

- NDSDMN-L Mailing List
  http://members.aol.com/gfsjohnf/gen_mail_states-mn.
  html#NDSDMN-L
  North Dakota, South Dakota and Minnesota.

◆ Maps, Gazetteers & Geographical Information

- 1895 U.S. Atlas—Minnesota
  http://www.LivGenMI.com/1895mn.htm

- American Memory Panoramic Maps 1847–1929—
  Minnesota
  http://lcweb2.loc.gov/cgi-bin/query/S?ammem/gmd:
  @filreq(@field(STATE+minnesota)+@field(COLLID+pmmap))
  From the Geography and Map Division, Library of Congress.

- American Memory Railroad Maps 1828–1900—
  Minnesota
  http://memory.loc.gov/cgi-bin/query/S?ammem/gmd:
  @filreq(@field(STATE+minnesota)+@field(COLLID+rrmap))
  From the Geography and Map Division, Library of Congress.

- Ancestry Groups in Minnesota—Maps
  http://www.lmic.state.mn.us/dnet/maplib/ancestry/
  mnancest.htm

- Color Landform Atlas: Minnesota
  http://fermi.jhuapl.edu/states/mn_0.html
  Including a map of counties and a map for 1895.

- Excite Maps: Minnesota Maps
  http://www.city.net/maps/view/?mapurl=/countries/
  united_states/minnesota
  Zoom in on these maps all the way to the street level.

- HPI County InfoSystem—Counties in Minnesota
  http://www.com/hpi/mncty/index.html

- K.B. Slocum Books and Maps—Minnesota
  http://www.treasurenet.com/cgi-bin/treasure/kbslocum/scan/
  se=Minnesota/sf=mapstate

- List of Minnesota Counties
  http://www.genealogy.org/~st-clair/counties/state_mn.html

- Map of Minnesota Counties
  http://govinfo.kerr.orst.edu/gif/states/mn.gif
  From the Government Information Sharing Project, Information Services, Oregon State University.

- Map of Minnesota Counties
  http://www.lib.utexas.edu/Libs/PCL/Map_collection/states/Minnesota.gif
  From the Perry-Castañeda Library at the Univ. of Texas at Austin.

- Minnesota Territorial Map 1849–1851
  http://www.rootsweb.com/~mngenweb/mnterr.htm

- U.S. Census Bureau—Minnesota Profiles
  http://www.census.gov/datamap/www/27.html

- Yale Peabody Museum: GNIS—Minnesota
  http://www.peabody.yale.edu/other/gnis/MN.html
  *Search the USGS Geographic Names Database. You can limit the search to a specific county in this state and search for any of the following features: airport arch area arroyo bar basin bay beach bench bend bridge **building** canal cape **cemetery** channel **church** cliff crater crossing dam falls flat forest gap geyser glacier gut harbor hospital island isthmus lake lava levee locale mine oilfield other park pillar plain ppl range rapids reserve reservoir ridge **school** sea slope spring stream summit swamp tower trail tunnel valley well woods.*

◆ Military

- The Civil War Archive—Union Regiments—Minnesota
  http://www.civilwararchive.com/unionmn.htm

- Civil War Battle Summaries by State—Minnesota
  http://www2.cr.nps.gov/abpp/battles/bystate.htm#mn

- Korean Conflict State-Level Casualty Lists—Minnesota
  http://www.nara.gov/nara/electronic/mnhrlist.html
  From the National Archives and Records Administration, Center for Electronic Records.

- Vietnam Conflict State-Level Casualty Lists—Minnesota
  http://www.nara.gov/nara/electronic/mnhrviet.html
  From the National Archives and Records Administration, Center for Electronic Records.

- The Vietnam Veterans Memorial—Minnesota
  http://grunt.space.swri.edu/statewall/minn/mn.htm

◆ Newspapers

- AJR NewsLink—Minnesota Newspapers
  http://www.newslink.org/mnnews.html

- E&P Media Info Links—Newspaper Sites in Minnesota
  http://www.mediainfo.com/emedia/browse-results.htm?region=minnesota&category=newspaper+++++++++

- Echo Press Online
  http://www.echopress.com/
  Alexandria, Minnesota

- The Brainerd Daily Dispatch Online
  http://www.brainerddispatch.com/

- Duluth News-Tribune
  http://www.duluthnews.com/

- Ecola Newstand: Minnesota
  http://www.ecola.com/news/press/na/us/mn/

- The Minnesota Daily Online
  http://www.daily.umn.edu/
  Minneapolist-St. Paul

- NAA Hotlinks to Newspapers Online—Minnesota
  http://www.naa.org/hotlinks/searchResult.asp?param=MN-Minnesota&City=1

- N-Net—Minnesota Newspapers
  http://www.n-net.com/mn.htm

- Pioneer Planet
  http://www.pioneerplanet.com/
  St. Paul, Minnesota

- Star Tribune Online
  http://www.startribune.com/
  Minneapolis-St. Paul, Minnesota

- The Ultimate Collection of News Links: USA—Minnesota
  http://www.pppp.net/links/news/USA-MN.html

- West Central Tribune
  http://www.wctrib.com/
  Willmar, Minnesota

- Yahoo!...Newspapers...Minnesota
  http://dir.yahoo.com/News_and_Media/Newspapers/Browse_By_Region/U_S__States/Minnesota/

◆ People & Families

- Tribes and Villages of Minnesota
  http://hanksville.phast.umass.edu:8000/cultprop/contacts/tribal/MN.html

◆ Professional Researchers, Volunteers & Other Research Services

- Board for Certification of Genealogists—Roster of Those Certified—Specializing in Minnesota
  http://www.genealogy.org/~bcg/rosts_mn.html

- Genealogy Helplist—Minnesota
  http://www.geocities.com/Heartland/Lane/5256/mn.htm

- Minnesota GenSearch
  http://members.aol.com/mngensrch/mngensrch.htm

- The Official Iowa Counties Professional Genealogist and Researcher's Registry for Minnesota
  http://www.iowa-counties.com/gene/mn.htm

◆ Publications, Software & Supplies

- AncestorSpy—CDs and Microfiche for Minnesota
  http://www.ancestorspy.com/mn.htm

- Barbara Green's Used Genealogy Books—
  Minnesota
  http://home.earthlink.net/~genbooks/lochist.html#MN

- Books We Own—Minnesota
  http://www.rootsweb.com/~bwo/minn.html

- Boyd Publishing Company—Minnesota
  http://www.hom.net/~gac/minniso.htm

- Frontier Press Bookstore—Minnesota
  http://www.frontierpress.com/frontier.cgi?category=mn

- Hearthstone Bookshop—Minnesota
  http://www.hearthstonebooks.com/cgi-bin/webc.cgi/
  st_main.html?catid=87&sid=2PH5t29sm

- Heritage Quest—Microfilm Records for the
  State of Minnesota
  http://www.heritagequest.com/genealogy/microfilm/minnesota/

- The Memorabilia Corner—Books: Minnesota
  http://members.aol.com/TMCorner/book_min.htm

- Minnesota Genealogical Journal
  http://www.parkbooks.com/Html/mgjbroch.html

- Park Genealogical Books
  http://www.parkbooks.com/
  *Specialists in genealogy and local history for Minnesota,
  Wisconsin, North and South Dakota and the surrounding area.*

◆ Queries, Message Boards & Surname Lists

- GenConnect Minnesota Visitor Center
  http://cgi.rootsweb.com/~genbbs/indx/Mn.html
  *A system for posting queries, Bibles, biographies, deeds,
  obituaries, pensions, wills.*

◆ Records: Census, Cemeteries, Land, Obituaries, Personal, Taxes and Vital (Born, Married, Died & Buried)

- The 1790–1890 Federal Population Censuses:
  Catalog of National Archives Microfilm
  http://www.genealogy.org/census/contents.shtml

  o Census Schedules and Microfilm Roll Numbers
    for Minnesota:
    1850
    http://www.genealogy.org/census/1850_schedules/
    Minnesota.html
    1860
    http://www.genealogy.org/census/1860_schedules/
    Minnesota.html
    1870
    http://www.genealogy.org/census/1870_schedules/
    Minnesota.html
    1880
    http://www.genealogy.org/census/1880_schedules/
    Minnesota.html
    1880 Soundex
    http://www.genealogy.org/census/1880.sdx_schedules/
    T756.html
    1890 Special Schedules
    http://www.genealogy.org/census/1890-special_schedules/
    Minnesota.html

- Becker County, Minnesota, Cemeteries
  http://www.rootsweb.com/~mnbecker/cemeteries.htm
  *List of cemeteries in Becker County, Minnesota with links to
  GNIS which gives location and online map.*

- The Bureau of Land Management—Eastern States,
  General Land Office
  http://www.glorecords.blm.gov/
  *The Official Land Patent Records Site. This site has a search-
  able database of over two million pre-1908 Federal land title
  records, including scanned images of those records. The Eastern
  Public Land States covered in this database are: Alabama,
  Arkansas, Florida, Illinois, Indiana, Louisiana, Michigan,
  Minnesota, Mississippi, Missouri, Ohio, Wisconsin.*

- The Cemeteries of Minnesota
  http://www.gac.edu/~kengelha/cemeteries.html
  List of cemeteries in Minnesota, county by county..

- County Courthouse Addresses
  http://www.familytreemaker.com/00000252.html

- Fargo Forum Obituary Index
  http://www.lib.ndsu.nodak.edu/ndirs/bio&genealogy/
  forumobits.html
  *Eastern North Dakota or Northwestern Minnesota. 40,000
  names for obituaries posted from 1985 through 1995 and
  approx. 2,000 obituaries from earlier years.*

- Find-A-Grave by Location: Minnesota
  http://www.findagrave.com/grave/lmn.html
  Graves of noteworthy people.

- Interment.net: Minnesota Cemeteries
  http://www.interment.net/us/mn/index.htm
  A list of links to other sites.

- Land Records—Becker County, Minnesota GenWeb
  http://www.rootsweb.com/~mnbecker/land.htm

- Minnesota Obituaries—September 1995 to present
  http://www.pconline.com/~mnobits/index.htm

- Minnesota Vital Records Information
  http://vitalrec.com/mn.html

- Minnesota Vital Statistics Page
  http://www.genealogy.org/~shardick/vital.html

- National Archives—Great Lakes Region (Chicago)
  http://www.nara.gov/regional/chicago.html

- National Archives—Great Lakes Region
  http://www.familytreemaker.com/00000096.html
  Records from Illinois, Indiana, Michigan, Minnesota, Ohio, and Wisconsin.

- Pipestone County Museum Marriage Records
  http://www.pipestone.mn.us/Museum/MALEMAR.HTM

- The Political Graveyard—Cemeteries in Minnesota
  http://politicalgraveyard.com/geo/MN/kmindex.html

- Preplanning Network—Funeral Home and Cemetery Directory—Minnesota
  http://www.preplannet.com/minnfhcem.htm

- Upsala, Minnesota Cemetery Index
  http://upstel.net/~johns/CemIndex/CemIndex.html

- USGenWeb Census Project Minnesota
  http://www.usgenweb.org/census/states/minnesot.htm

- USGenWeb Tombstone Transcription Project—Minnesota
  http://www.rootsweb.com/~cemetery/minne.html

- VitalChek Network—Minnesota
  http://www.vitalchek.com/stateselect.asp?state=MN

- Where to Write for Vital Records—Minnesota
  http://www.cdc.gov/nchswww/howto/w2w/minnesot.htm
  From the National Center for Health Statistics (NCHS).

◆ Religion & Churches

- Christianity.Net Church Locator—Minnesota
  http://www.christianity.net/cgi/location.exe?
  United_States+Minnesota

- Church Online!—Minnesota
  http://www.churchonline.com/usas/mn/mn.html

- Church Profiles—Minnesota
  http://www.church-profiles.com/mn/mn.html

- Churches dot Net—Global Church Web Pages—Minnesota
  http://www.churches.net/churches/minnesot.html

- Churches of the World—Minnesota
  http://www.churchsurf.com/churches/Minnesota/index.htm
  From the ChurchSurf Christian Directory.

◆ Societies & Groups

- American Historical Society of Germans from Russia—North Star Chapter—Minnesota
  http://www.ahsgr.org/mnnostar.html

- Archer's Computer Interest Group List—Minnesota
  http://www.genealogy.org/~ngs/cigs/ngl1usmn.html

- Becker County Historical Society
  http://www.angelfire.com/mn/bchs39/

- Blue Earth County Historical Society
  http://www.ic.mankato.mn.us/reg9/bechs/bechs1.html

- Clearwater County Historical Society
  http://www.rrv.net/bagleyweb/histcult.htm
  Bagley, Minnesota

- Cokato Finnish-American Historical Society
  http://cokato.mn.us/org/fahs.html
  Cokato, Minnesota

- Danish-American Genealogical Group
  http://www.mtn.org/mgs/branches/danish.html

- Douglas County Genealogical Society
  http://www.mtn.org/mgs/branches/douglas.html

- Douglas County Historical Society
  http://www.rea-alp.com/~historic/
  Alexandria, Minnesota

- English Genealogical Society
  http://www.mtn.org/mgs/branches/english.html

- German-Bohemian Heritage Society
  http://www.rootsweb.com/~gbhs/
  New Ulm, Minnesota

- Germanic Genealogy Society
  http://www.mtn.org/mgs/branches/german.html
  Saint Paul, Minnesota

- The Goodhue Area Historical Society
  http://www.ci.goodhue.mn.us/gahs/

- Goodhue County Historical Society
  http://www.goodhistory.org
  Red Wing, Minnesota

- The Grand Lodge of Minnesota Ancient Free and Accepted Masons
  http://mn-mason.org/

- Hubbard County Genealogical Society
  http://www.rootsweb.com/~mnhgs/hubco.htm
  Contains cenus, obits, history, vital stats.

- IOOF Lodge Website Directory—Minnesota
  http://norm28.hsc.usc.edu/IOOF/USA/Minnesota/Minnesota.html
  Independent Order of Odd Fellows and Rebekahs.

- Heart-O-Lakes Genealogical Society
  http://www.angelfire.com/mn/HOLGS/index.html
  Detroit Lakes, Minnesota

- Irish Genealogical Society, International
  http://www.rootsweb.com/~irish/

- Le Sueur County Historical Society
  http://www.lchs.mus.mn.us/

- Minnesota Genealogical Society
  http://www.mtn.org/mgs/

- Minnesota Historical Society
  http://www.mnhs.org/index.html

- Minnkota Genealogical Society
  http://www.rootsweb.com/~minnkota/
  Grand Forks, North Dakota & East Grand Forks, Minnesota.

- Olmsted County Genealogical Society & Historical Society Home Page
  http://www.millcomm.com/~gzimmer/ochs.html

- Olmsted County Historical Society
  http://www.millcomm.com/~ochs/

- Otter Tail County Historical Society
  http://www.prtel.com/ffalls/events/museum.htm

- Pipestone County Historical Society
  http://www.pipestone.mn.us/museum/HOMEPA~1.HTM

- Polish Genealogical Society of Minnesota
  http://www.mtn.org/mgs/branches/polish.html

- Renville County Genealogical Society
  http://ci.renville.mn.us/rcgs/

- Scott County Historical Society
  http://www.co.scott.mn.us/historic.htm

- Sherburne County Historical Society
  http://www.rootsweb.com/~mnschs/index.htm

- Swedish Genealogy Group
  http://www.mtn.org/mgs/branches/swedish.html

- Telelaget of America—A Norwegian-American bygdelag
  http://www.geocities.com/Heartland/Hills/1545/
  Bloomington, Minnesota

- Waseca County Historical Society
  http://www.platec.net/wchs/index.html

- Washington County Historical Society
  http://members.aol.com/washcogen/wchs.html

- Winona County Historical Society
  http://www.winonanet.com/orgs/wchs/

- Yankee Genealogical Society
  http://www.mtn.org/mgs/branches/yankee.html

◆ USGenWeb Project

- Minnesota Genealogy—USGenWeb Project State Page
  http://www.usgenweb.org/mn

- Minnesota—USGenWeb Archives Table of Contents
  http://www.rootsweb.com/~usgenweb/mn/mnfiles.htm

- Minnesota—USGenWeb FTP Archives
  ftp://ftp.rootsweb.com/pub/usgenweb/mn/

U.S.—MISSISSIPPI—MS
http://www.CyndisList.com/ms.htm

Category Index:

- General Resource Sites
- Government & Cities
- History & Culture
- Libraries, Archives & Museums
- Mailing Lists, Newsgroups & Chat
- Maps, Gazetteers & Geographical Information
- Military
- Newspapers
- People & Families

- Professional Researchers, Volunteers & Other Research Services
- Publications, Software & Supplies
- Queries, Message Boards & Surname Lists
- Records: Census, Cemeteries, Land, Obituaries, Personal, Taxes and Vital
- Religion & Churches
- Societies & Groups
- USGenWeb Project

◆ General Resource Sites

- Everton's Sources of Genealogical Information in Mississippi
  http://www.everton.com/usa/ms.htm

- Family Tree Maker's Genealogy "How To" Guide—Mississippi
  http://www.familytreemaker.com/00000198.html

- Genealogy Exchange & Surname Registry—MSGenExchange
  http://www.genexchange.com/ms/index.cfm

- Genealogy Resources on the Internet: Mississippi
  http://www-personal.umich.edu/~cgaunt/miss.html

- LDS Research Outline for Mississippi
  http://www.everton.com/usa/ms-0825b.txt

- Lineages' Genealogy Site: Mississippi
  http://www.lineages.com/rooms/usa/state.asp?StateCode=MS

- Mississippi Family Reunions
  http://www.rootsweb.com/~msgenweb/reunions.shtml

- ROOTS-L United States Resources: Mississippi
  http://www.rootsweb.com/roots-l/USA/ms.html
  Comprehensive list of research links, including many to history-related sites.

◆ Government & Cities

- 50states.com—Mississippi State Information Resource
  http://www.50states.com/mississi.htm
  A list of general information for each state, including a list of colleges, state symbols, links to maps, newspapers, and other miscellaneous state information.

- Excite Travel by City.Net—Mississippi
  http://www.city.net/countries/united_states/mississippi/

- Official City Web Sites for the State of Mississippi
  http://OfficialCitySites.org/Mississippi.htm

- State of Mississippi—Official Web Site
  http://www.state.ms.us/

- Yahoo! Get Local...Mississippi Cities
  http://dir.yahoo.com/Regional/U_S__States/Mississippi/Cities/
  Maps, yellow pages, white pages, newspapers and other local information.

- Yahoo! Get Local...Mississippi Counties and Regions
  http://dir.yahoo.com/Regional/U_S__States/Mississippi/Counties_and_Regions/
  Maps, yellow pages, white pages, newspapers and other local information.

◆ History & Culture

- Yahoo!...History...Mississippi
  http://dir.yahoo.com/Arts/Humanities/History/Browse_By_Region/U_S__States/Mississippi/

◆ Libraries, Archives & Museums

- Family History Centers—Mississippi
  http://www.deseretbook.com/famhis/ms.html

- Family History Centers—Mississippi
  http://www.lib.byu.edu/~uvrfhc/centers/mississippi.html

- HYTELNET—Library Catalogs: USA: Mississippi
  http://library.usask.ca/hytelnet/usa/MS.html
  Before you use any of the Telnet links, make note of the user name, password and any other logon information.

- Mississippi Department of Archives and History
  http://www.mdah.state.ms.us/index.html
  - Archives and Library Division
    http://www.mdah.state.ms.us/arlibtxt.html
  - Museum Division
    http://www.mdah.state.ms.us/musetxt.html
- Mississippi Family History Centers
  http://www.genhomepage.com/FHC/Mississippi.html
  A list of addresses, phone numbers and hours of operation from the Genealogy Home Page.
- Mississippi Library Commission
  http://www.mlc.lib.ms.us/
- NUCMC Listing of Archives and Manuscript Repositories in Mississippi
  http://lcweb.loc.gov/coll/nucmc/mssites.html
  Links to information about resources other than those held in the Library of Congress.
- Repositories of Primary Sources: Mississippi
  http://www.uidaho.edu/special-collections/east1.html#usms
  A list of links to online resources from the Univ. of Idaho Library, Special Collections and Archives.
- University of Mississippi Libraries
  http://www.olemiss.edu/depts/general_library/
  - Department of Archives and Special Collections
    http://www.olemiss.edu/depts/general_library/files/archhome.htm
- webCATS: Library Catalogues on the World Wide Web—Mississippi
  http://library.usask.ca/hywebcat/states/MS.html

◆ Mailing Lists, Newsgroups & Chat

- Genealogy Resources on the Internet—Mississippi Mailing Lists
  http://members.aol.com/gfsjohnf/gen_mail_states-ms.html
  Each of the mailing list links below points to this site, wonderfully maintained by John Fuller. Visit this site for county-specific mailing lists as well.
- DEEP-SOUTH-ROOTS-L Mailing List
  http://members.aol.com/gfsjohnf/gen_mail_states-ms.html#DEEP-SOUTH-ROOTS
  Alabama, Florida, Georgia & Mississippi.
- Mississippi Genealogy IRC Chats
  http://www.rootsweb.com/~msgenweb/chat.shtml
- MISSISSIPPI Mailing List
  http://members.aol.com/gfsjohnf/gen_mail_states-ms.html#MISSISSIPPI
- MSNWTERR Mailing List
  http://members.aol.com/gfsjohnf/gen_mail_states-ms.html#MSNWTERR
  For anyone with a genealogical interest in the Northwest portion of the Mississippi Territory. This area includes the current Mississippi counties of Calhoun, Coahoma, DeSoto, Lafayette, Marshall, Panola, Quitman, Tate, and Tunica.

- MSSWTERR Mailing List
  http://members.aol.com/gfsjohnf/gen_mail_states-ms.html#MSSWTERR
  For anyone with a genealogical interest in the Southwest Mississippi Territory prior to 1818.

◆ Maps, Gazetteers & Geographical Information

- 1895 U.S. Atlas—Mississippi
  http://www.LivGenMI.com/1895ms.htm
- American Memory Railroad Maps 1828–1900—Mississippi
  http://memory.loc.gov/cgi-bin/query/S?ammem/gmd:@filreq(@field(STATE+mississippi)+@field(COLLID+rrmap))
  From the Geography and Map Division, Library of Congress.
- Color Landform Atlas: Mississippi
  http://fermi.jhuapl.edu/states/ms_0.html
  Including a map of counties and a map for 1895.
- Excite Maps: Mississippi Maps
  http://www.city.net/maps/view/?mapurl=/countries/united_states/mississippi
  Zoom in on these maps all the way to the street level.
- HPI County InfoSystem—Counties in Mississippi
  http://www.com/hpi/mscty/index.html
- K.B. Slocum Books and Maps—Mississippi
  http://www.treasurenet.com/cgi-bin/treasure/kbslocum/scan/se=Mississippi/sf=mapstate
- List of Mississippi Counties
  http://www.genealogy.org/~st-clair/counties/state_ms.html
- Map of Mississippi Counties
  http://govinfo.kerr.orst.edu/gif/states/ms.gif
  From the Government Information Sharing Project, Information Services, Oregon State University.
- Map of Mississippi Counties
  http://www.lib.utexas.edu/Libs/PCL/Map_collection/states/Mississippi.gif
  From the Perry-Castañeda Library at the Univ. of Texas at Austin.
- Mississippi City/Town List
  http://www.rootsweb.com/~msctlist/ct-a.htm
- U.S. Census Bureau—Mississippi Profiles
  http://www.census.gov/datamap/www/28.html
- Yale Peabody Museum: GNIS—Mississippi
  http://www.peabody.yale.edu/other/gnis/MS.html
  *Search the USGS Geographic Names Database. You can limit the search to a specific county in this state and search for any of the following features: airport arch area arroyo bar basin bay beach bench bend bridge **building** canal cape **cemetery** channel **church** cliff crater crossing dam falls flat forest gap geyser glacier gut harbor hospital island isthmus lake lava levee locale mine oilfield other park pillar plain ppl range rapids reserve reservoir ridge **school** sea slope spring stream summit swamp tower trail tunnel valley well woods.*

◆ Military

- 11th Mississippi Infantry
  http://www.why.net/home/sdavis/11thMiss/index.htm

- 26th Mississippi Infantry, C.S.A.
  http://members.aol.com/shardwik/cw/26thms.html

- The Civil War Archive—Union Regiments—Mississippi
  http://www.civilwararchive.com/unionms.htm

- Civil War Battle Summaries by State—Mississippi
  http://www2.cr.nps.gov/abpp/battles/bystate.htm#ms

- Company A, Fifth Regiment Mississippi Cavalry
  http://www.gower.net/bclayton/coa5reg.html

- Company Muster Roll Enterprise Tigers Company D 37th
  http://www.netpathway.com/~buckley/tiger.html

- Corinth—Civil War History
  http://www2.tsixroads.com/Corinth_MLSANDY/corciv.html

- Eighth Regiment—Infantry Company G, Tolson Guard of Jasper County Mississippi
  http://www.netpathway.com/~buckley/tolson.html

- Fifth Mississippi Regiment, C.S.A.
  http://www.izzy.net/~michaelg/5ms-1.htm

- Fifteenth Mississippi Infantry Regiment CSA
  http://web2.airmail.net/phi868/wigfall.html

- Korean Conflict State-Level Casualty Lists—Mississippi
  http://www.nara.gov/nara/electronic/mshrlist.html
  From the National Archives and Records Administration, Center for Electronic Records.

- MA Ryan, Co B 14th Miss Vol Inf CSA
  http://www.izzy.net/~michaelg/ma-ryan.htm
  Experience of a Confederate Soldier in Camp and Prison in The Civil War 1861–1865.

- Mississippi Civil War Information
  http://www2.msstate.edu/~gam3/cw/index.html

- Vietnam Conflict State-Level Casualty Lists—Mississippi
  http://www.nara.gov/nara/electronic/mshrviet.html
  From the National Archives and Records Administration, Center for Electronic Records.

- The Vietnam Veterans Memorial—Mississippi
  http://grunt.space.swri.edu/statewall/miss/ms.htm

◆ Newspapers

- AJR NewsLink—Mississippi Newspapers
  http://www.newslink.org/msnews.html

- E&P Media Info Links—Newspaper Sites in Mississippi
  http://www.mediainfo.com/emedia/browse-results.htm?region=mississippi&category=newspaper+++++++++

- Ecola Newstand: Mississippi
  http://www.ecola.com/news/press/na/us/ms/

- NAA Hotlinks to Newspapers Online—Mississippi
  http://www.naa.org/hotlinks/searchResult.asp?param=MS-Mississippi&City=1

- N-Net—Mississippi Newspapers
  http://www.n-net.com/ms.htm

- The Ultimate Collection of News Links: USA—Mississippi
  http://www.pppp.net/links/news/USA-MS.html

- Yahoo!...Newspapers...Mississippi
  http://dir.yahoo.com/News_and_Media/Newspapers/Browse_By_Region/U_S__States/Mississippi/

◆ People & Families

- Tribes and Villages of Mississippi
  http://hanksville.phast.umass.edu:8000/cultprop/contacts/tribal/MS.html

◆ Professional Researchers, Volunteers & Other Research Services

- Board for Certification of Genealogists—Roster of Those Certified—Specializing in Mississippi
  http://www.genealogy.org/~bcg/rosts_ms.html

- Genealogy Helplist—Mississippi
  http://www2.netdoor.com/~armstsho/linda/ms.htm

- The Official Iowa Counties Professional Genealogist and Researcher's Registry for Mississippi
  http://www.iowa-counties.com/gene/ms.htm

◆ Publications, Software & Supplies

- Barbara Green's Used Genealogy Books—Mississippi
  http://home.earthlink.net/~genbooks/lochist.html#MS

- Barnette's Family Tree Books—Mississippi
  http://www.barnettesbooks.com/mississi.htm

- Books We Own—Mississippi
  http://www.rootsweb.com/~bwo/miss.html

- Boyd Publishing Company—Mississippi
  http://www.hom.net/~gac/mississ.htm

- Frontier Press Bookstore—Mississippi
  http://www.frontierpress.com/frontier.cgi?category=ms

- GenealogyBookShop.com—Mississippi
  http://www.genealogybookshop.com/genealogybookshop/files/The_United_States,Mississippi/index.html
  The online store of Genealogical Publishing Co., Inc. & Clearfield Company.

- Hearthstone Bookshop—Mississippi
  http://www.hearthstonebooks.com/cgi-bin/webc.cgi/
  st_main.html?catid=88&sid=2PH5t29sm
- Heritage Books—Mississippi
  http://www.heritagebooks.com/ms.htm
- Heritage Quest—Microfilm Records for the
  State of Mississippi
  http://www.heritagequest.com/genealogy/microfilm/
  mississippi/
- J & W Enterprises
  http://www.dhc.net/~jw/
  One stop book source on the Internet, specializing in southern states source material.
- Lost in Time Books—Mississippi
  http://www.lostintime.com/catalog/books/bookst/bo17000.htm
- The Memorabilia Corner—Books: Mississippi
  http://members.aol.com/TMCorner/book_mis.htm
- S-K Publications—Mississippi 1820–1850
  Census Books
  http://www.skpub.com/genie/census/ms/
- Southern Queries Genealogy Magazine
  http://www.mindspring.com/~freedom1/sq/sq.htm
- Willow Bend Bookstore—Mississippi
  http://www.willowbend.net/ms.htm

◆ Queries, Message Boards & Surname Lists

- GenConnect Mississippi Visitor Center
  http://cgi.rootsweb.com/~genbbs/indx/Ms.html
  A system for posting queries, Bibles, biographies, deeds, obituaries, pensions, wills.

◆ Records: Census, Cemeteries, Land, Obituaries, Personal, Taxes and Vital (Born, Married, Died & Buried)

- The 1790–1890 Federal Population Censuses:
  Catalog of National Archives Microfilm
  http://www.genealogy.org/census/contents.shtml
  - Census Schedules and Microfilm Roll Numbers
    for Mississippi:
    1820
    http://www.genealogy.org/census/1820_schedules/
    Mississippi.html
    1830
    http://www.genealogy.org/census/1830_schedules/
    Mississippi.html
    1840
    http://www.genealogy.org/census/1840_schedules/
    Mississippi.html
    1850
    http://www.genealogy.org/census/1850_schedules/
    Mississippi.html
    1860
    http://www.genealogy.org/census/1860_schedules/
    Mississippi.html
    1870
    http://www.genealogy.org/census/1870_schedules/
    Mississippi.html
    1880
    http://www.genealogy.org/census/1880_schedules/
    Mississippi.html
    1880 soundex
    http://www.genealogy.org/census/1880.sdx_schedules/
    T757.html
    1890 Special Schedules
    http://www.genealogy.org/census/1890-special_schedules/
    Mississippi.html
- The Bureau of Land Management—Eastern States,
  General Land Office
  http://www.glorecords.blm.gov/
  The Official Land Patent Records Site. This site has a searchable database of over two million pre-1908 Federal land title records, including scanned images of those records. The Eastern Public Land States covered in this database are: Alabama, Arkansas, Florida, Illinois, Indiana, Louisiana, Michigan, Minnesota, Mississippi, Missouri, Ohio, Wisconsin.
- Cemeteries of Tallahatchie County Mississippi
  http://www.rootsweb.com/~mstallah/talcocem.html
- Cemeteries of the United States—Mississippi
  Cemeteries—County Index
  http://www.gac.edu/~kengelha/uscemeteries/mississippi.html
- Census Online—Links to Census Sites on the Web—
  Mississippi
  http://www.census-online.com/links/MS_data.html
- Clarke County, MS 1840–1860 Census
  Surname Index
  http://www.netpathway.com/~bennie/cenindx2.html
- Corinth National Cemetery
  http://www2.tsixroads.com/Corinth_MLSANDY/cnc.html
- County Courthouse Addresses
  http://www.familytreemaker.com/00000253.html
- Find-A-Grave by Location: Mississippi
  http://www.findagrave.com/grave/lms.html
  Graves of noteworthy people.
- Freedmen's Bureau, Marriages in Mississippi
  1863–1865
  http://www.freedmensbureau.com/mississippi/
  mississippimarriages.htm
- Freedmen's Bureau Records—Mississippi
  http://www.freedmensbureau.com/mississippi/
- Greensboro Cemetery, Tomnolan, Mississippi
  ftp://ftp.rootsweb.com/pub/usgenweb/ms/webster/cemeteries/
  greensboro.txt

- Interment.net: Mississippi Cemeteries
  http://www.interment.net/us/ms/index.htm
  A list of links to other sites.
- Madison Co., MS 1850 Federal Census
  http://www.rootsweb.com/~msmadiso/1850census/
- Marriages in Rankin County, Mississippi
  http://www.vanished.com/pages/free_lib/rankin_co.html
- Mississippi Vital Records Information
  http://vitalrec.com/ms.html
- National Archives—Southeast Region (Atlanta)
  http://www.nara.gov/regional/atlanta.html
- National Archives—Southeast Region from Family Tree Maker
  http://www.familytreemaker.com/00000104.html
  Records for Alabama, Florida, Georgia, Kentucky, Mississippi, North Carolina, South Carolina, and Tennessee.
- Noxubee County, Mississippi Slave Schedule— 1860 Census
  http://www.ccharity.com/mississippi/1860noxumortpt1.htm
- The Political Graveyard—Cemeteries in Mississippi
  http://politicalgraveyard.com/geo/MS/kmindex.html
- USGenWeb Census Project Mississippi
  http://www.usgenweb.org/census/states/mississi/mississi.htm
- USGenWeb Tombstone Transcription Project— Mississippi
  http://www.rootsweb.com/~cemetery/missi.html
- VitalChek Network—Mississippi
  http://www.vitalchek.com/stateselect.asp?state=MS
- Where to Write for Vital Records—Mississippi
  http://www.cdc.gov/nchswww/howto/w2w/mississi.htm
  From the National Center for Health Statistics (NCHS).

◆ Religion & Churches

- Christianity.Net Church Locator—Mississippi
  http://www.christianity.net/cgi/
  location.exe?United_States+Mississippi
- Church Online!—Mississippi
  http://www.churchonline.com/usas/ms/ms.html
- Church Profiles—Mississippi
  http://www.church-profiles.com/ms/ms.html
- Churches dot Net—Global Church Web Pages— Mississippi
  http://www.churches.net/churches/mississi.html
- Churches of the World—Mississippi
  http://www.churchsurf.com/churches/Mississippi/index.htm
  From the ChurchSurf Christian Directory.

◆ Societies & Groups

- Alcorn County Genealogical Society
  http://www.rootsweb.com/~msacgs/index.html
- Archer's Computer Interest Group List—Mississippi
  http://www.genealogy.org/~ngs/cigs/ngl1usms.html
- Calhoun County Historical and Genealogical Society, Inc.
  http://usr.metamall.com/~rdiamond/
  Pittsboro, Mississippi
- Chickasaw County Historical & Genealogical Society
  http://www.rootsweb.com/~mschchgs/
- Dancing Rabbit Genealogical Society
  http://www2.netdoor.com/~drgs/
  Leake County, Mississippi
- Genealogical Society of Desoto County
  http://www.rootsweb.com/~msdesoto/gsdcm.htm
- Hancock County Historical Society
  http://www2.datasync.com/history/
- IOOF Lodge Website Directory—Mississippi
  http://norm28.hsc.usc.edu/IOOF/USA/Mississippi/
  Mississippi.html
  Independent Order of Odd Fellows and Rebekahs.
- Itawamba Historical Society
  http://www.network-one.com/~ithissoc/
- Judith Robinson Chapter Daughters of the American Revolution
  http://www.telapex.com/~dar/jrc.htm
  McComb, Mississippi
- Mississippi Genealogy—Genealogical and Historical Societies in Mississippi
  http://www.rootsweb.com/~msgenweb/gensocieties.shtml
- Mississippi State Society Daughters of the American Revolution
  http://www.telapex.com/~dar/mssdar.htm
- Neshoba County Genealogy Group
  http://www.geocities.com/SoHo/Lofts/5075/index.html
- Noxubee County Historical Society
  http://www.rootsweb.com/~longstrt/society.html
  Macon, Mississippi
- Pearl River Historical Society
  http://www.gulfcoastplus.com/histsoc/pearlriv.htm
- Scott County Genealogical Society
  http://usr.metamall.com/~glsmith/scgs/
  Forest, Scott County, Mississippi
- Sunflower County Historical Society
  http://www.rootsweb.com/~mssunflo/histsoc.htm
- Tippah County Historical Society
  http://ww2.dixie-net.com/tch/
- Tishomingo County Historical & Genealogical Society
  http://www.geocities.com/Heartland/Acres/1038/

- Vicksburg Genealogical Society
  http://www.rootsweb.com/~msvgs/index.htm

◆ USGenWeb Project

- Mississippi Genealogy—USGenWeb Project
  State Page
  http://www.usgenweb.org/ms

- Mississippi—USGenWeb Archives Table of
  Contents
  http://www.rootsweb.com/~usgenweb/ms/msfiles.htm

- Mississippi—USGenWeb FTP Archives
  ftp://ftp.rootsweb.com/pub/usgenweb/ms/

U.S.—MISSOURI—MO
http://www.CyndisList.com/mo.htm

Category Index:

- General Resource Sites
- Government & Cities
- History & Culture
- Libraries, Archives & Museums
- Mailing Lists, Newsgroups & Chat
- Maps, Gazetteers & Geographical Information
- Military
- Newspapers
- People & Families

- Professional Researchers, Volunteers & Other Research Services
- Publications, Software & Supplies
- Queries, Message Boards & Surname Lists
- Records: Census, Cemeteries, Land, Obituaries, Personal, Taxes and Vital
- Religion & Churches
- Societies & Groups
- USGenWeb Project

◆ General Resource Sites

- Anne Hood's Missouri Page
  http://home.sprynet.com/sprynet/Hood/missouri.htm

- Central Missouri Genealogical Forum
  http://www.coin.missouri.edu/community/genealogy/cent-mo/index.html

- Everton's Sources of Genealogical Information in Missouri
  http://www.everton.com/usa/mo.htm

- Family Tree Maker's Genealogy "How To" Guide—Missouri
  http://www.familytreemaker.com/00000199.html

- Genealogy Bulletin Board Systems for Missouri
  http://www.genealogy.org/~gbbs/gblmo.html

- Genealogy Exchange & Surname Registry—MOGenExchange
  http://www.genexchange.com/mo/index.cfm

- Genealogy in St. Louis
  http://pages.prodigy.net/dave_lossos/stl/gen.htm

- Genealogy Resources on the Internet: Missouri
  http://www-personal.umich.edu/~cgaunt/mo.html

- LDS Research Outline for Missouri
  http://www.everton.com/usa/mo-0826b.txt

- Linda Wilson's Genealogy Page
  http://www.sunflower.org/~lmwilson/genpage.htm
  Information for Kansas vital and census records.

- Lineages' Genealogy Site: Missouri
  http://www.lineages.com/rooms/usa/state.asp?StateCode=MO

- Missouri: Crossroads for Tracking Ancestors
  http://www.ancestry.com/columns/myra/Shaking_Family_Tree01-08-98.htm
  From Shaking Your Family Tree by Myra Vanderpool Gormley, C.G.

- Missouri Genealogy Webring
  http://members.tripod.com/~ripple4u/webring.htm

- Osage County, Missouri Genealogy Resources
  http://www.mindspring.com/~mgentges/

- ROOTS-L United States Resources: Missouri
  http://www.rootsweb.com/roots-l/USA/mo.html
  Comprehensive list of research links, including many to history-related sites.

- St. Louis, Mo.; Missouri; Phelps County, Mo.; Family and
  http://www.rollanet.org/~bdoerr/gene.htm

- St. Louis, MO Resources Valuable for Family History
  http://www.rollanet.org/~bdoerr/stlouis.htm
  Home page for Bob DOERR, with many great resources for St. Louis.

◆ Government & Cities

- 50states.com—Missouri State Information Resource
  http://www.50states.com/missouri.htm
  A list of general information for each state, including a list of colleges, state symbols, links to maps, newspapers, and other miscellaneous state information.

- Excite Travel by City.Net—Missouri
  http://www.city.net/countries/united_states/missouri/

- Missouri State Government Web
  http://www.state.mo.us/

- Official City Web Sites for the State of Missouri
  http://OfficialCitySites.org/Missouri.htm
- Yahoo! Get Local...Missouri Cities
  http://dir.yahoo.com/Regional/U_S__States/Missouri/Cities/
  Maps, yellow pages, white pages, newspapers and other local information.
- Yahoo! Get Local...Missouri Counties and Regions
  http://dir.yahoo.com/Regional/U_S__States/Missouri/
  Counties_and_Regions/
  Maps, yellow pages, white pages, newspapers and other local information.

◆ History & Culture

- 'Gone But Not Forgotten'—Missouri Pioneers
  http://www.rootsweb.com/~mopionee/
- History of Missouri
  http://ourworld.compuserve.com/homepages/mikenewman/hist-mo.htm
- The Turnbo Manuscripts
  http://198.209.8.166/turnbo/about.html
  By Silas Claiborne Turnbo, 1844–1925. "A collection of approximately eight hundred short tales, stories and vignettes that reflect life along the White River Valley in northwest Arkansas and southwest Missouri during the latter half of the 19th century."
- Yahoo!...History...Missouri
  http://dir.yahoo.com/Arts/Humanities/History/
  Browse_By_Region/U_S__States/Missouri/

◆ Libraries, Archives & Museums

- Adair County Public Library
  http://www.nemostate.edu/kirksville/library.html
  Kirksville, Missouri
- Christian County Library
  http://www.mlnc.com/~ccl/
  Ozark, Missouri
- Columbia Missouri Family History Center
  http://www.synapse.com/bocomogenweb/LDSFHC.HTM
- Dunklin County Library
  http://dunklin-co.lib.mo.us/index.html
- Family History Centers—Missouri
  http://www.deseretbook.com/famhis/mo.html
- Family History Centers—Missouri
  http://www.lib.byu.edu/~uvrfhc/centers/missouri.html
- Harry S. Truman Presidential Library & Museum
  http://sunsite.unc.edu/lia/president/truman.html
  Independence, Missouri
- HYTELNET—Library Catalogs: USA: Missouri
  http://library.usask.ca/hytelnet/usa/MO.html
  Before you use any of the Telnet links, make note of the user name, password and any other logon information.

- Kansas City Public Library
  http://www.kcpl.lib.mo.us/
  ○ The Special Collections Department of the Kansas City Public Library
    http://www.kcpl.lib.mo.us/sc/default.htm
    Local history, postcards, photographs, newspaper clippings, Ramos Collection, genealogy, biographies, maps, historic children's literature collection.
    • Genealogy
      http://www.kcpl.lib.mo.us/sc/gene/genealogy.htm
- Livingston County Library
  http://www.greenhills.net/~lclibr/index.html
  Chillicothe
- Mid-Continent Public Library, Independence, Missouri
  http://www.mcpl.lib.mo.us/
  ○ Genealogy & Local History Department
    http://www.mcpl.lib.mo.us/ge/
- Missouri Family History Centers
  http://www.genhomepage.com/FHC/Missouri.html
  A list of addresses, phone numbers and hours of operation from the Genealogy Home Page.
- Missouri State Archives
  http://mosl.sos.state.mo.us/rec-man/arch.html
- Missouri State Library
  http://mosl.sos.state.mo.us/lib-ser/libser.html
- Missouri United Methodist Archives
  http://cmc2.cmc.edu/arc.html
  At the Smiley Library, Central Methodist College, Fayette, Missouri.
- NUCMC Listing of Archives and Manuscript Repositories in Missouri
  http://lcweb.loc.gov/coll/nucmc/mosites.html
  Links to information about resources other than those held in the Library of Congress.
- Repositories of Primary Sources: Missouri
  http://www.uidaho.edu/special-collections/east1.html#usmo
  A list of links to online resources from the Univ. of Idaho Library, Special Collections and Archives.
- Springfield-Greene County Library
  http://www.orion.org/library/sgcl/
  Missouri
  ○ Genealogy
    http://www.orion.org/library/sgcl/genea/genea.htm
- St. Charles City-County Library District
  http://www.win.org/library/scccld.htm
  ○ The Bizelli-Fleming Local History Collection
    http://www.win.org/library/services/lhgen/cinmenu.htm
    Local History—Genealogy Home Page.
- St. Louis Public Library
  http://www.slpl.lib.mo.us/

- The University of Missouri—Western Historical Manuscript Collection—Columbia
  http://www.system.missouri.edu/whmc/
  - WHMC-Columbia / Collections
    http://www.system.missouri.edu/whmc/subject.htm
    - Ethnic Groups
      http://www.system.missouri.edu/whmc/ethnic.htm
    - Family and Personal Papers
      http://www.system.missouri.edu/whmc/family.htm
    - Genealogy
      http://www.system.missouri.edu/whmc/genea.htm
    - Local History
      http://www.system.missouri.edu/whmc/local.htm
    - Military
      http://www.system.missouri.edu/whmc/military.htm
    - Pioneer and Frontier Life
      http://www.system.missouri.edu/whmc/pioneer.htm
    - Social and Fraternal Organizations
      http://www.system.missouri.edu/whmc/socfrat.htm

- The University of Missouri—Western Historical Manuscript Collection—Kansas City
  http://www.umkc.edu/whmckc/index.htm
  - WHMC-KC Collections: Ethnic Communities
    http://www.umkc.edu/whmckc/Collections/ETHNIC.htm
  - WHMC-KC Collections: Military
    http://www.umkc.edu/WHMCKC/Collections/military.htm
  - WHMC-KC Collections: Populations
    http://www.umkc.edu/whmckc/Collections/populations.htm
    Includes Genealogy (family histories or records created for genealogists); Immigration/migrations/emigration; Community histories.

- The University of Missouri—Western Historical Manuscript Collection—Rolla
  http://www.umr.edu/~whmcinfo/index.html
  - WHMC-Rolla—Broad Subject Categories
    http://www.umr.edu/~whmcinfo/topics/
    - WHMC-Rolla—Family & Personal Papers
      http://www.umr.edu/~whmcinfo/topics/Family/
    - WHMC-Rolla—Genealogy
      http://www.umr.edu/~whmcinfo/topics/Gen/
    - WHMC-Rolla—Local History
      http://www.umr.edu/~whmcinfo/topics/Local/
    - WHMC-Rolla—Social & Fraternal Organizations
      http://www.umr.edu/~whmcinfo/topics/Soc/

- The University of Missouri—Western Historical Manuscript Collection—St. Louis
  http://www.umsl.edu/~whmc/
  - WHMC Collection Guides
    http://www.umsl.edu/~whmc/areas.html
    - Genealogy and Family History Collections
      http://www.umsl.edu/~whmc/whmfamg/index.html
    - Immigrant Collections
      http://www.umsl.edu/~whmc/whmimmg/index.html
    - Military History Collections
      http://www.umsl.edu/~whmc/whmmili/index.html

- webCATS: Library Catalogues on the World Wide Web—Missouri
  http://library.usask.ca/hywebcat/states/MO.html

◆ Mailing Lists, Newsgroups & Chat

- Genealogy Resources on the Internet—Missouri Mailing Lists
  http://members.aol.com/gfsjohnf/gen_mail_states-mo.html
  Each of the mailing list links below points to this site, wonderfully maintained by John Fuller. Visit this site for county-specific mailing lists as well.

- Audraincomo Mailing List
  http://members.aol.com/gfsjohnf/gen_mail_states-mo.html#Audraincomo
  Audrain County

- Camdencomo Mailing List
  http://members.aol.com/gfsjohnf/gen_mail_states-mo.html#Camdencomo
  Camden County

- KansasCity Mailing List
  http://members.aol.com/gfsjohnf/gen_mail_states-ks.html#KansasCity
  For anyone with a genealogical or historical interest in the greater Kansas City area (Kansas/Missouri).

- KC-NGS Mailing List
  http://members.aol.com/gfsjohnf/gen_mail_states-ks.html#KC-NGS
  For anyone interested in the Northland Genealogy Society of Greater Kansas City.

- KC-NGS-NEWS Mailing List
  http://members.aol.com/gfsjohnf/gen_mail_states-ks.html#KC-NGS-NEWS
  For the members of the Northland Genealogical Society of Greater Kansas City.

- Missouri-L Mailing List
  http://members.aol.com/gfsjohnf/gen_mail_states-mo.html#Missouri-L

- MISSOURI-ROOTS-L Mailing List
  http://members.aol.com/gfsjohnf/gen_mail_states-mo.html#MISSOURI-ROOTS

- StLouis-MO Mailing List
  http://members.aol.com/gfsjohnf/gen_mail_states-mo.html#StLouis-MO
  For anyone with a genealogical interest in the city of St. Louis, Missouri.

◆ Maps, Gazetteers & Geographical Information

- 1895 U.S. Atlas—Missouri
  http://www.LivGenMI.com/1895mo.htm

- American Memory Panoramic Maps 1847–1929—Missouri
  http://lcweb2.loc.gov/cgi-bin/query/S?ammem/gmd:
  @filreq(@field(STATE+missouri)+@field(COLLID+pmmap))
  From the Geography and Map Division, Library of Congress.

- American Memory Railroad Maps 1828–1900—Missouri
  http://memory.loc.gov/cgi-bin/query/S?ammem/gmd:
  @filreq(@field(STATE+missouri)+@field(COLLID+rrmap))
  From the Geography and Map Division, Library of Congress.

- Color Landform Atlas: Missouri
  http://fermi.jhuapl.edu/states/mo_0.html
  Including a map of counties and a map for 1895.

- Excite Maps: Missouri Maps
  http://www.city.net/maps/view/?mapurl=/countries/
  united_states/missouri
  Zoom in on these maps all the way to the street level.

- HPI County InfoSystem—Counties in Missouri
  http://www.com/hpi/mocty/index.html

- K.B. Slocum Books and Maps—Missouri
  http://www.treasurenet.com/cgi-bin/treasure/kbslocum/scan/
  se=Missouri/sf=mapstate

- List of Missouri Counties
  http://www.genealogy.org/~st-clair/counties/state_mo.html

- Map of Missouri Counties
  http://govinfo.kerr.orst.edu/gif/states/mo.gif
  From the Government Information Sharing Project, Information Services, Oregon State University.

- Map of Missouri Counties
  http://www.lib.utexas.edu/Libs/PCL/Map_collection/states/
  Missouri.gif
  From the Perry-Castañeda Library at the Univ. of Texas at Austin.

- Missouri Historical Maps
  http://www.rootsweb.com/~mogenweb/momaps.htm

- U.S. Census Bureau—Missouri Profiles
  http://www.census.gov/datamap/www/29.html

- Yale Peabody Museum: GNIS—Missouri
  http://www.peabody.yale.edu/other/gnis/MO.html
  *Search the USGS Geographic Names Database. You can limit the search to a specific county in this state and search for any of the following features: airport arch area arroyo bar basin bay beach bench bend bridge **building** canal cape **cemetery** channel **church** cliff crater crossing dam falls flat forest gap geyser glacier gut harbor hospital island isthmus lake lava levee locale mine oilfield other park pillar plain ppl range rapids reserve reservoir ridge **school** sea slope spring stream summit swamp tower trail tunnel valley well woods.*

◆ Military

- 6th Missouri Infantry, Company A, 4th Battalion
  http://www.sunflower.org/~6thmo/6thmo.htm

- The 8th Missouri Volunteer Infantry, US
  http://www.apci.net/~prozac/

- The Civil War Archive—Union Regiments—Missouri
  http://www.civilwararchive.com/unionmo.htm

- Civil War Battle Summaries by State—Missouri
  http://www2.cr.nps.gov/abpp/battles/bystate.htm#mo

- "E" Company, 4th Missouri Infantry, C.S.A.
  http://www.mo-net.com/~mwilliams/reenactor.html

- The Fifth Missouri Infantry—CSA
  http://www.cedarcroft.com/cw/5mo.html

- Index of the Civil War in Missouri Links and Resources Available on the Internet
  http://www.usmo.com/~momollus/MOCWLINK.HTM

- Korean Conflict State-Level Casualty Lists—Missouri
  http://www.nara.gov/nara/electronic/mohrlist.html
  From the National Archives and Records Administration, Center for Electronic Records.

- The Missouri Division, Sons of Confederate Veterans
  http://www.missouri-scv.org/

- Missouri in the Civil War
  http://www.tri.net/~kheidel/mowar/

- Sources for Military Records
  http://www.system.missouri.edu/shs/military.html

- USGenWeb Civil War Veterans—Missouri Veterans
  http://www.tri.net/~kheidel/mowar/veterans.html

- Vietnam Conflict State-Level Casualty Lists—Missouri
  http://www.nara.gov/nara/electronic/mohrviet.html
  From the National Archives and Records Administration, Center for Electronic Records.

- The Vietnam Veterans Memorial—Missouri
  http://grunt.space.swri.edu/statewall/missouri/mo.htm

◆ Newspapers

- AJR NewsLink—Missouri Newspapers
  http://www.newslink.org/monews.html

- E&P Media Info Links—Newspaper Sites in Missouri
  http://www.mediainfo.com/emedia/browse-results.
  htm?region=missouri&category=newspaper++++++++++

- Ecola Newstand: Missouri
  http://www.ecola.com/news/press/na/us/mo/

- The Joplin Globe
  http://www.joplinglobe.com/

- NAA Hotlinks to Newspapers Online—Missouri
  http://www.naa.org/hotlinks/searchResult.asp?param=
  MO-Missouri&City=1

- Newspaper Clippings—Kansas City Public Library
  http://www.kcpl.lib.mo.us/sc/clips/newsclips.htm
  In the Special Collections Department. Some are online.

- N-Net—Missouri Newspapers
  http://www.n-net.com/mo.htm

- The Star—Kansas City
  http://www.kcstar.com/

- The Ultimate Collection of News Links:
  USA—Missouri
  http://www.pppp.net/links/news/USA-MO.html

- Using Newspapers for Genealogical Research
  http://www.system.missouri.edu/shs/newspap.html
  From the State Historical Society of Missouri.

- Yahoo!...Newspapers...Missouri
  http://dir.yahoo.com/News_and_Media/Newspapers/
  Browse_By_Region/U_S__States/Missouri/

◆ People & Families

- Tribes and Villages of Missouri
  http://hanksville.phast.umass.edu:8000/cultprop/contacts/
  tribal/MO.html

- WPA Life Histories from Missouri
  http://lcweb2.loc.gov/ammem/wpaintro/mocat.html
  *Manuscripts from the Federal Writer's Project, 1936–1940,
  Library of Congress.*

◆ Professional Researchers, Volunteers & Other Research Services

- Board for Certification of Genealogists—Roster of
  Those Certified—Specializing in Missouri
  http://www.genealogy.org/~bcg/rosts_mo.html

- Davis Genealogy Page and Genealogical Research
  Services
  http://home.sprynet.com/sprynet/ecdavis/davisgen.htm
  *Specializing in research for Greene and Christian Counties,
  Missouri.*

- Genealogy Helplist—Missouri
  http://www.geocities.com/Heartland/Acres/4917/helplist.html

- The Official Iowa Counties Professional Genealogist
  and Researcher's Registry for Missouri
  http://www.iowa-counties.com/gene/mo.htm

◆ Publications, Software & Supplies

- AncestorSpy—CDs and Microfiche for Missouri
  http://www.ancestorspy.com/mo.htm

- Barbara Green's Used Genealogy Books—Missouri
  http://home.earthlink.net/~genbooks/lochist.html#MO

- Barnette's Family Tree Books—Missouri
  http://www.barnettesbooks.com/missouri.htm

- Books for Sale: Douglas County, Missouri
  http://members.aol.com/LaineBelle/HomePage.html
  *Cemetery Survey of the Eastern District of Douglas County,
  Missouri; Death Notices Abstracted from The Douglas County
  Herald, 1887–1910.*

- Books We Own—Missouri
  http://www.rootsweb.com/~bwo/missouri.html

- Boyd Publishing Company—Missouri
  http://www.hom.net/~gac/missouri.htm

- Frontier Press Bookstore—Missouri
  http://www.frontierpress.com/frontier.cgi?category=mo

- GenealogyBookShop.com—Missouri
  http://www.genealogybookshop.com/genealogybookshop/files/
  The_United_States,Missouri/index.html
  *The online store of Genealogical Publishing Co., Inc. &
  Clearfield Company.*

- Hearthstone Bookshop—Missouri
  http://www.hearthstonebooks.com/cgi-bin/webc.cgi/st_main.
  html?catid=89&sid=2PH5t29sm

- Heritage Books—Missouri
  http://www.heritagebooks.com/mo.htm

- Heritage Quest—Microfilm Records for the
  State of Missouri
  http://www.heritagequest.com/genealogy/microfilm/missouri/

- J & W Enterprises
  http://www.dhc.net/~jw/
  *One stop book source on the Internet, specializing in southern
  states source material.*

- Lost in Time Books—Missouri
  http://www.lostintime.com/catalog/books/bookst/bo18000.htm

- The Memorabilia Corner Books—Missouri
  http://members.aol.com/TMCorner/book_mo.htm

- The Memorabilia Corner Census View CDs—
  Missouri
  http://members.aol.com/TMCorner/cen_mo.htm

- Ozark Books
  http://home.att.net/~rdfortner/
  *Supplier of books about the Missouri and Arkansas Ozarks,
  including Branson.*

- S-K Publications—Missouri 1850 Census Books
  http://www.skpub.com/genie/census/mo/

- Southern Queries Genealogy Magazine
  http://www.mindspring.com/~freedom1/sq/sq.htm

- University of Missouri Press
  http://www.system.missouri.edu/upress/

- Willow Bend Bookstore—Missouri
  http://www.willowbend.net/mo.htm

◆ Queries, Message Boards & Surname Lists

- GenConnect Missouri Visitor Center
  http://cgi.rootsweb.com/~genbbs/indx/Mo.html
  *A system for posting queries, Bibles, biographies, deeds,
  obituaries, pensions, wills.*

- 'Gone But Not Forgotten'—Missouri Pioneers
  http://www.rootsweb.com/~mopionee/

- Missouri Surname Researchers List
  http://www.geocities.com/Heartland/Plains/7113/surnames.htm

◆ Records: Census, Cemeteries, Land, Obituaries, Personal, Taxes and Vital (Born, Married, Died & Buried)

- The 1790–1890 Federal Population Censuses: Catalog of National Archives Microfilm
  http://www.genealogy.org/census/contents.shtml
  - Census Schedules and Microfilm Roll Numbers for Missouri:

    1830
    http://www.genealogy.org/census/1830_schedules/Missouri.html

    1840
    http://www.genealogy.org/census/1840_schedules/Missouri.html

    1850
    http://www.genealogy.org/census/1850_schedules/Missouri.html

    1860
    http://www.genealogy.org/census/1860_schedules/Missouri.html

    1870
    http://www.genealogy.org/census/1870_schedules/Missouri.html

    1880
    http://www.genealogy.org/census/1880_schedules/Missouri.html

    1880 soundex
    http://www.genealogy.org/census/1880.sdx_schedules/T758.html

    1890 Special Schedules
    http://www.genealogy.org/census/1890-special_schedules/Missouri.html

- 1850 Census Lookups for Clinton County, MO.
  Send e-mail to Bob Cummings
  E-mail: gallion@gulf.net

- 1850 Census Lookups for Daviess County, MO.
  Send e-mail to Bob Cummings
  E-mail: gallion@gulf.net

- The Bureau of Land Management—Eastern States, General Land Office
  http://www.glorecords.blm.gov/
  The Official Land Patent Records Site. This site has a searchable database of over two million pre-1908 Federal land title records, including scanned images of those records. The Eastern Public Land States covered in this database are: Alabama, Arkansas, Florida, Illinois, Indiana, Louisiana, Michigan, Minnesota, Mississippi, Missouri, Ohio, Wisconsin.

- Carter County Missouri Cemeteries
  http://www.mindspring.com/~sapart/cartcmtr.html

  - Aldrich Valley Cemetery
    http://www.mindspring.com/~sapart/aldrchcm.html
  - Brame Cemetery
    http://www.mindspring.com/~sapart/brmecemt.html
  - Bristol Cemetery
    http://www.mindspring.com/~sapart/bristlcm.html
  - Eastwood Cemetery
    http://www.mindspring.com/~sapart/cemin.html
  - Midco Cemtery
    http://www.mindspring.com/~sapart/midcocmt.html
  - Seats Family Cemetery
    http://www.mindspring.com/~sapart/seatscmt.html

- Carter County, Missouri Marriages—1860 thru 1881
  http://www.mindspring.com/~sapart/mar1860.html

- Carter County Missouri Marriages, Book "A" 1881–1890
  http://www.mindspring.com/~sapart/cc188190.html

- Carter County Missouri Marriage, Book "B" 1890–1898
  http://www.mindspring.com/~sapart/crtmrgb.html

- Cemeteries of the United States—Missouri Cemeteries—County Index
  http://www.gac.edu/~kengelha/uscemeteries/missouri.html

- Census Online—Links to Census Sites on the Web—Missouri
  http://www.census-online.com/links/MO_data.html

- Christian County, Missouri Transcribed Records
  http://home.sprynet.com/sprynet/jenwbber/ccmo.htm

- County Courthouse Addresses
  http://www.familytreemaker.com/00000254.html

- Find-A-Grave by Location: Missouri
  http://www.findagrave.com/grave/lmo.html
  Graves of noteworthy people.

- Information About Census Records
  http://www.system.missouri.edu/shs/census.html
  From the State Historical Society of Missouri.

- Interment.net: Missouri Cemeteries
  http://www.interment.net/us/mo/index.htm
  A list of links to other sites.

- Joplin Area Deaths—The Joplin Globe
  http://www.joplinglobe.com/4state/deaths.html

- Kansas City Star Obituaries
  http://www.kcstar.com/cgi-bin/class?template=clq-obit.htm&category=0&database=daily

- Missouri Forms & Maps
  http://www.cchat.com/cupido/records.htm
  Downloadable forms for ordering vital records.

- Missouri Vital Records Information
  http://vitalrec.com/mo.html

- Morgan County Cemeteries Lookups—Missouri
  Send e-mail to William & Dorothy Williams at wmwwms@ laurie.net for lookups to be done in their personal catalog of Morgan County Cemeteries in Missouri. They have visited each of these gravesites and recorded all necessary details for each grave, including the parents of children and maiden name of wives if known. Their database has over 22,000 burials in over 150 cemeteries. Records cover only Morgan County's present boundries for 1830 through 1996. Copies of these records can also be found in the State Archives, State Historical Library, and the Morgan County Library. Make sure to send a reasonable request and don't forget to thank William & Dorothy for their tremendous generosity!

- National Archives—Central Plains Region (Kansas City)
  http://www.nara.gov/regional/kansas.html

- National Archives—Central Plains Region from Family Tree Maker
  http://www.familytreemaker.com/00000095.html
  Records for Iowa, Kansas, Missouri, and Nebraska.

- The Political Graveyard—Cemeteries in Missouri
  http://politicalgraveyard.com/geo/MO/kmindex.html

- Preplanning Network—Funeral Home and Cemetery Directory—Missouri
  http://www.preplannet.com/missourifhcem.htm

- Reynolds County Marriage Records 1870–1891
  http://www.mindspring.com/~sapart/reymag.html

- Ripley County Missouri Marriage Records {1833–1860}
  http://members.tripod.com/~tmsnyder/Ripley.htm_

- USGenWeb Census Project Missouri
  http://www.usgenweb.org/census/states/missouri/ missouri.htm

- USGenWeb Tombstone Transcription Project— Missouri
  http://www.rootsweb.com/~cemetery/missouri.html

- VitalChek Network—Missouri
  http://www.vitalchek.com/stateselect.asp?state=MO

- Vital Records for Missourians
  http://www.system.missouri.edu/shs/vital.html

- Where to Write for Vital Records—Missouri
  http://www.cdc.gov/nchswww/howto/w2w/missouri.htm
  From the National Center for Health Statistics (NCHS).

◆ Religion & Churches

- Christianity.Net Church Locator—Missouri
  http://www.christianity.net/cgi/ location.exe?United_States+Missouri

- Church Online!—Missouri
  http://www.churchonline.com/usas/mo/mo.html

- Church Profiles—Missouri
  http://www.church-profiles.com/mo/mo.html

- Churches dot Net—Global Church Web Pages— Missouri
  http://www.churches.net/churches/missouri.html

- Churches of the World—Missouri
  http://www.churchsurf.com/churches/Missouri/index.htm
  From the ChurchSurf Christian Directory.

◆ Societies & Groups

- The American Legion—Department of Missouri, Inc.
  http://www2.computerland.net/al/

- Archer's Computer Interest Group List—Missouri
  http://www.genealogy.org/~ngs/cigs/ngl1usmo.html

- Barry County Genealogical & Historical Society
  http://www.rootsweb.com/~mobarry/society.html

- Boone-Duden Historical Society
  http://norn.org/pub/other-orgs/bdhissoc/
  Regarding the Boone Settlement in St. Charles County, southern Warren County, and Lincoln County, Missouri.

- Cape Girardeau County Genealogical Society
  http://www.rosecity.net/genealog.html

- Carroll County Genealogical Association
  http://www.carolnet.com/ccga/
  Carrollton, Missouri

- Carroll County Historical Society
  http://www.carolnet.com/cchs/
  Carrollton, Missouri

- Central Missouri Genealogical Forum
  http://www.coin.missouri.edu/community/genealogy/cent-mo/ index.html

- Crawford County Historical Society
  http://www.avalon.net/~jmartin/Crawford/cchs.html
  Cuba, Missouri

- Fenton Historical Society
  http://www.crl.com/~keymastr/fenton/histsoc.html

- Greene County Historical Society
  http://www.rootsweb.com/~gcmohs/

- Grundy County Genealogical Society
  http://www.rootsweb.com/~mogrundy/gcgen.html

- IOOF Lodge Website Directory—Missouri
  http://norm28.hsc.usc.edu/IOOF/USA/Missouri/Missouri.html
  Independent Order of Odd Fellows and Rebekahs.

- Jefferson County Genealogical Society
  http://www.rootsweb.com/~mojcgs/jcgsinde.htm

- Jewish Genealogical Society of St. Louis
  http://www.stlcyberjew.com/jgs-stl/

- Jewish Genealogical Society of St. Louis, Computer SIG
  http://www.stlcyberjew.com/jgs-stl/SIGhome.htm

- Johnson County Historical Society
  http://www.digitalhistory.com/schools/
  JohnsonCountyHistoricalSociety/home.htm
  Warrensburg, Missouri

- Livingston County Genealogical Society
  http://www.greenhills.net/~fwoods/pages/lcgs.htm
  Chillicothe, Missouri

- Military Order of the Loyal Legion of the
  United States—Missouri Commandery
  http://www.usmo.com/~momollus/INDEX.HTM

- Mine Au Breton Historical Society
  http://www.rootsweb.com/~mowashin/mabhs.html

- The Missouri Division, Sons of Confederate
  Veterans
  http://www.missouri-scv.org/

- Missouri State Genealogical Association
  ("MoSGA")
  http://www.umr.edu/~mstauter/mosga/

- Missouri State Society Daughters of the
  American Revolution
  http://www.geocities.com/Heartland/Pointe/4136/

- Northwest Missouri Genealogical Society
  http://www.ccp.com/~stjoed/nwmgs.htm
  St. Joseph, Missouri

- Other Genealogical Societies in Missouri
  http://www.coin.missouri.edu/community/genealogy/cent-mo/
  other-mo-socs.html

- Ozarks Genealogical Society
  http://www.rootsweb.com/~ozarksgs/

- Phelps County Genealogical Society
  http://www.umr.edu/~whmcinfo/pcgs/

- Phelps County Historical Society
  http://www.umr.edu/~whmcinfo/pchs/

- St. Louis Genealogical Society
  http://www.rootsweb.com/~mostlogs/STINDEX.HTM

- State Historical Society of Missouri
  http://www.system.missouri.edu/shs/

  - SHS Guides To Genealogy Research
    http://www.system.missouri.edu/shs/guides.html

◆ USGenWeb Project

- Missouri Genealogy—Genealogy—USGenWeb
  Project State Page
  http://www.usgenweb.org/mo

- Missouri—USGenWeb Archives Table of Contents
  http://www.rootsweb.com/~usgenweb/mo/mofiles.htm

- Missouri—USGenWeb FTP Archives
  ftp://ftp.rootsweb.com/pub/usgenweb/mo/

- Missouri Queries
  http://www.rootsweb.com/~mogenweb/moqindex.htm

- MOGenWebTeen Page
  http://www.rootsweb.com/~mogenweb/moteen.htm

U.S.—MONTANA—MT
http://www.CyndisList.com/mt.htm

Category Index:

- General Resource Sites
- Government & Cities
- History & Culture
- Libraries, Archives & Museums
- Mailing Lists, Newsgroups & Chat
- Maps, Gazetteers & Geographical Information
- Military
- Newspapers
- People & Families

- Professional Researchers, Volunteers & Other Research Services
- Publications, Software & Supplies
- Queries, Message Boards & Surname Lists
- Records: Census, Cemeteries, Land, Obituaries, Personal, Taxes and Vital
- Religion & Churches
- Societies & Groups
- USGenWeb Project

◆ General Resource Sites

- Everton's Sources of Genealogical Information in Montana
  http://www.everton.com/usa/mt.htm

- Family Tree Maker's Genealogy "How To" Guide—Montana
  http://www.familytreemaker.com/00000200.html

- Genealogy Exchange & Surname Registry—MTGenExchange
  http://www.genexchange.com/mt/index.cfm

- Genealogy Resources on the Internet: Montana
  http://www-personal.umich.edu/~cgaunt/montana.html

- LDS Research Outline for Montana
  http://www.everton.com/usa/mt-0827b.txt

- Lineages' Genealogy Site: Montana
  http://www.lineages.com/rooms/usa/state.asp?StateCode=MT

- ROOTS-L United States Resources: Montana
  http://www.rootsweb.com/roots-l/USA/mt.html
  Extensive listing of articles & links for this state.

◆ Government & Cities

- 50states.com—Montana State Information Resource
  http://www.50states.com/montana.htm
  A list of general information for each state, including a list of colleges, state symbols, links to maps, newspapers, and other miscellaneous state information.

- Excite Travel by City.Net—Montana
  http://www.city.net/countries/united_states/montana/

- Montana Online: Homepage for the State of Montana
  http://www.mt.gov/

- Official City Web Sites for the State of Montana
  http://OfficialCitySites.org/montana.htm

- Yahoo! Get Local...Montana Cities
  http://dir.yahoo.com/Regional/U_S__States/Montana/Cities/
  Maps, yellow pages, white pages, newspapers and other local information.

- Yahoo! Get Local...Montana Counties and Regions
  http://dir.yahoo.com/Regional/U_S__States/Montana/Counties_and_Regions/
  Maps, yellow pages, white pages, newspapers and other local information.

◆ History & Culture

- Ghost Towns of Montana
  http://www.ghosttowns.com/states/mt/mt.html

- Mountain Men and the Fur Trade
  http://www.xmission.com/~drudy/amm.html
  Sources of the History of the Fur Trade in the Rocky Mountain West.

- Yahoo!...History...Montana
  http://dir.yahoo.com/Arts/Humanities/History/Browse_By_Region/U_S__States/Montana/

◆ Libraries, Archives & Museums

- Family History Centers—Montana
  http://www.deseretbook.com/famhis/mt.html

- Family History Centers—Montana
  http://www.lib.byu.edu/~uvrfhc/centers/montana.html

- HYTELNET—Library Catalogs: USA: Montana
  http://library.usask.ca/hytelnet/usa/MT.html
  Before you use any of the Telnet links, make note of the user name, password and any other logon information.

- Montana Family History Centers
  http://www.genhomepage.com/FHC/Montana.html
  A list of addresses, phone numbers and hours of operation from the Genealogy Home Page.

- Montana State Library
  http://msl.mt.gov/

- MSU-Bozeman Libraries
  http://www.lib.montana.edu/
  - Merrill G. Burlingame Special Collections
    http://www.lib.montana.edu/collect/spcoll/

- NUCMC Listing of Archives and Manuscript Repositories in Montana
  http://lcweb.loc.gov/coll/nucmc/mtsites.html
  Links to information about resources other than those held in the Library of Congress.

- Repositories of Primary Sources: Montana
  http://www.uidaho.edu/special-collections/west.html#usmt
  A list of links to online resources from the Univ. of Idaho Library, Special Collections and Archives.

- Yale Peabody Museum: GNIS—Montana
  http://www.peabody.yale.edu/other/gnis/MT.html
  *Search the USGS Geographic Names Database. You can limit the search to a specific county in this state and search for any of the following features: airport arch area arroyo bar basin bay beach bench bend bridge **building** canal cape **cemetery** channel **church** cliff crater crossing dam falls flat forest gap geyser glacier gut harbor hospital island isthmus lake lava levee locale mine oilfield other park pillar plain ppl range rapids reserve reservoir ridge **school** sea slope spring stream summit swamp tower trail tunnel valley well woods.*

◆ Mailing Lists, Newsgroups & Chat

- Genealogy Resources on the Internet—Montana Mailing Lists
  http://members.aol.com/gfsjohnf/gen_mail_states-mt.html
  Each of the mailing list links below points to this site, wonderfully maintained by John Fuller. Visit this site for county-specific mailing lists as well.

- COALMINERS Mailing List
  http://members.aol.com/gfsjohnf/gen_mail_country-unk.html#COALMINERS
  For anyone whose ancestors were coalminers in the United Kingdom or the United States.

- MONTANA Mailing List
  http://members.aol.com/gfsjohnf/gen_mail_states-mt.html#MONTANA

- WESTERN-ROOTS-L Mailing list
  http://members.aol.com/gfsjohnf/gen_mail_states-mt.html#WESTERN-ROOTS-L
  Washington, Oregon, Alaska, Idaho, Montana, Wyoming, California, Nevada, Hawaii, Colorado, Utah, Arizona, and New Mexico.

◆ Maps, Gazetteers & Geographical Information

- 1872 County Map of Montana
  http://www.ismi.net/chnegw/1872montana.htm

- 1895 U.S. Atlas—Montana
  http://www.LivGenMI.com/1895mt.htm

- American Memory Panoramic Maps 1847–1929—Montana
  http://lcweb2.loc.gov/cgi-bin/query/S?ammem/gmd:@filreq(@field(STATE+montana)+@field(COLLID+pmmap))
  From the Geography and Map Division, Library of Congress.

- American Memory Railroad Maps 1828–1900—Montana
  http://memory.loc.gov/cgi-bin/query/S?ammem/gmd:@filreq(@field(STATE+montana)+@field(COLLID+rrmap))
  From the Geography and Map Division, Library of Congress.

- Color Landform Atlas: Montana
  http://fermi.jhuapl.edu/states/mt_0.html
  Including a map of counties and a map for 1895.

- Excite Maps: Montana Maps
  http://www.city.net/maps/view/?mapurl=/countries/united_states/montana
  Zoom in on these maps all the way to the street level.

- HPI County InfoSystem—Counties in Montana
  http://www.com/hpi/mtcty/index.html

- K.B. Slocum Books and Maps—Montana
  http://www.treasurenet.com/cgi-bin/treasure/kbslocum/scan/se=Montana/sf=mapstate

- List of Montana Counties
  http://www.genealogy.org/~st-clair/counties/state_mt.html

- Map of Montana Counties
  http://govinfo.kerr.orst.edu/gif/states/mt.gif
  From the Government Information Sharing Project, Information Services, Oregon State University.

- Map of Montana Counties
  http://www.lib.utexas.edu/Libs/PCL/Map_collection/states/Montana.gif
  From the Perry-Castañeda Library at the Univ. of Texas at Austin.

- U.S. Census Bureau—Montana Profiles
  http://www.census.gov/datamap/www/30.html

◆ Military

- Korean Conflict State-Level Casualty Lists—Montana
  http://www.nara.gov/nara/electronic/mthrlist.html
  From the National Archives and Records Administration, Center for Electronic Records.

- Montana in the Military
  http://www.imt.net/~corkykn/military.html

- Vietnam Conflict State-Level Casualty Lists—Montana
  http://www.nara.gov/nara/electronic/mthrviet.html
  From the National Archives and Records Administration, Center for Electronic Records.

- The Vietnam Veterans Memorial—Montana
  http://grunt.space.swri.edu/statewall/montana/mt.htm

◆ Newspapers

- AJR NewsLink—Montana Newspapers
  http://www.newslink.org/mtnews.html

- E&P Media Info Links—Newspaper Sites in Montana
  http://www.mediainfo.com/emedia/browse-results.htm?region=montana&category=newspaper+++++++++

- Ecola Newstand: Montana
  http://www.ecola.com/news/press/na/us/mt/

- Missoulian Online
  http://www.missoulian.com/

- NAA Hotlinks to Newspapers Online—Montana
  http://www.naa.org/hotlinks/searchResult.asp?param=MT-Montana&City=1

- N-Net—Montana Newspapers
  http://www.n-net.com/mt.htm

- The Ultimate Collection of News Links: USA—Montana
  http://www.pppp.net/links/news/USA-MT.html

- Yahoo!...Newspapers...Montana
  http://dir.yahoo.com/News_and_Media/Newspapers/Browse_By_Region/U_S__States/Montana/

◆ People & Families

- Affiliated Tribes of Northwest Indians
  http://www.atni.org/~tribes/
  For Alaska, California, Idaho, Montana, Oregon, Washington.

- Tribes and Villages of Montana
  http://hanksville.phast.umass.edu:8000/cultprop/contacts/tribal/MT.html

- WPA Life Histories from Montana
  http://lcweb2.loc.gov/ammem/wpaintro/mtcat.html
  Manuscripts from the Federal Writer's Project, 1936–1940, Library of Congress.

◆ Professional Researchers, Volunteers & Other Research Services

- Board for Certification of Genealogists—Roster of Those Certified—Specializing in Montana
  http://www.genealogy.org/~bcg/rosts_mt.html

- Genealogy Helplist—Montana
  http://members.aol.com/DFBradshaw/mt.html

- The Official Iowa Counties Professional Genealogist and Researcher's Registry for Montana
  http://www.iowa-counties.com/gene/mt.htm

◆ Publications, Software & Supplies

- Barbara Green's Used Genealogy Books—Montana
  http://home.earthlink.net/~genbooks/lochist.html#MT

- Boyd Publishing Company—Montana
  http://www.hom.net/~gac/montana.htm

- Frontier Press Bookstore—Montana
  http://www.frontierpress.com/frontier.cgi?category=mt

- Heritage Quest—Microfilm Records for the State of Montana
  http://www.heritagequest.com/genealogy/microfilm/montana/

- Guide to Montana Reference Books & Media
  http://www.imt.net/~corkykn/book.html

◆ Queries, Message Boards & Surname Lists

- GenConnect Montana Visitor Center
  http://cgi.rootsweb.com/~genbbs/indx/Mt.html
  A system for posting queries, Bibles, biographies, deeds, obituaries, pensions, wills.

◆ Records: Census, Cemeteries, Land, Obituaries, Personal, Taxes and Vital (Born, Married, Died & Buried)

- The 1790–1890 Federal Population Censuses: Catalog of National Archives Microfilm
  http://www.genealogy.org/census/contents.shtml
  - Census Schedules and Microfilm Roll Numbers for Montana:
    1870
    http://www.genealogy.org/census/1870_schedules/Montana.html
    1880
    http://www.genealogy.org/census/1880_schedules/Montana.html
    1880 soundex
    http://www.genealogy.org/census/1880.sdx_schedules/T759.html
    1890 Special Schedules
    http://www.genealogy.org/census/1890-special_schedules/Montana.html

- BLM—Montana Electronic Reading Room
  http://www.blm.gov/nhp/efoia/mt/
  United States Bureau of Land Management.

- Cascade County Montana Cemetery Index
  http://www.initco.net/~ingelsp/cemetery/cemet.html

- Cemeteries of the United States—Montana Cemeteries—County Index
  http://www.gac.edu/~kengelha/uscemeteries/montana.html

- County Courthouse Addresses
  http://www.familytreemaker.com/00000255.html

- County Courthouse Records in Montana
  http://www.imt.net/~corkykn/county.html

- Find-A-Grave by Location: Montana
  http://www.findagrave.com/grave/lmt.html
  Graves of noteworthy people.

- Friedensgemeinde Cemetery, Froid, Montana
  http://pixel.cs.vt.edu/library/cemeteries/montana/link/damm.txt

- Interment.net: Montana Cemeteries
  http://www.interment.net/us/mt/index.htm
  A list of links to other sites.

- Montana State Vital Records
  http://www.imt.net/~corkykn/vital.html

- Montana Vital Records Information
  http://vitalrec.com/mt.html

- National Archives—Rocky Mountain Region (Denver)
  http://www.nara.gov/regional/denver.html

- National Archives—Rocky Mountain Region
  http://www.familytreemaker.com/00000103.html
  Records for Colorado, Montana, North Dakota, South Dakota, Utah, Wyoming, and a portion of New Mexico.

- The Political Graveyard—Cemeteries in Montana
  http://politicalgraveyard.com/geo/MT/kmindex.html

- USGenWeb Census Project Montana
  http://www.usgenweb.org/census/states/montana/montana.htm

- USGenWeb Tombstone Transcription Project—Montana
  http://www.rootsweb.com/~cemetery/montana.html

- VitalChek Network—Montana
  http://www.vitalchek.com/stateselect.asp?state=MT

- Where to Write for Vital Records—Montana
  http://www.cdc.gov/nchswww/howto/w2w/montana.htm
  From the National Center for Health Statistics (NCHS).

◆ Religion & Churches

- Christianity.Net Church Locator—Montana
  http://www.christianity.net/cgi/location.exe?United_States+Montana

- Church Online!—Montana
  http://www.churchonline.com/usas/mt/mt.html

- Church Profiles—Montana
  http://www.church-profiles.com/mt/mt.html

- Churches dot Net—Global Church Web Pages—Montana
  http://www.churches.net/churches/montana.html

- Churches of the World—Montana
  http://www.churchsurf.com/churches/Montana/index.htm
  From the ChurchSurf Christian Directory.

◆ Societies & Groups

- Archer's Computer Interest Group List—Montana
  http://www.genealogy.org/~ngs/cigs/ngl1usmt.html

- IOOF Lodge Website Directory—Montana
  http://norm28.hsc.usc.edu/IOOF/USA/Montana/Montana.html
  Independent Order of Odd Fellows and Rebekahs.

- The Miles City Genealogical Society
  http://www.geocities.com/Heartland/Fields/6175/
  Carter, Custer, Dawson, Fallon, Garfield, McCone, Prairie, Powder River, Richland, Rosebud, & Wibaux counties.

- Montana Historical Society
  http://www.his.mt.gov/

- Montana State Genealogical Society
  http://www.rootsweb.com/~mtmsgs/

- Tri-State Genealogical Society
  http://scream.iw.net/~shepherd/
  South Dakota, Wyoming, and Montana.

- Western Montana Genealogical Society
  http://www.rootsweb.com/~mtwmgs/

◆ USGenWeb Project

- Montana Genealogy—USGenWeb Project State Page
  http://www.usgenweb.org/mt

- Montana—USGenWeb Archives Table of Contents
  http://www.rootsweb.com/~usgenweb/mt/mtfiles.htm

- Montana—USGenWeb FTP Archives
  ftp://ftp.rootsweb.com/pub/usgenweb/mt

U.S.—NEBRASKA—NE
http://www.CyndisList.com/ne.htm

Category Index:

- General Resource Sites
- Government & Cities
- History & Culture
- Libraries, Archives & Museums
- Mailing Lists, Newsgroups & Chat
- Maps, Gazetteers & Geographical Information
- Military
- Newspapers
- People & Families

- Professional Researchers, Volunteers & Other Research Services
- Publications, Software & Supplies
- Queries, Message Boards & Surname Lists
- Records: Census, Cemeteries, Land, Obituaries, Personal, Taxes and Vital
- Religion & Churches
- Societies & Groups
- USGenWeb Project

◆ General Resource Sites

- Everton's Sources of Genealogical Information in Nebraska
  http://www.everton.com/usa/ne.htm

- Family Tree Maker's Genealogy "How To" Guide—Nebraska
  http://www.familytreemaker.com/00000201.html

- Genealogy Exchange & Surname Registry—NEGenExchange
  http://www.genexchange.com/ne/index.cfm

- Genealogy Resources on the Internet: Nebraska
  http://www-personal.umich.edu/~cgaunt/nebraska.html

- LDS Research Outline for Nebraska
  http://www.everton.com/usa/ne-0828b.txt

- Lineages' Genealogy Site: Nebraska
  http://www.lineages.com/rooms/usa/state.asp?StateCode=NE

- Patti's Home Page
  http://www.4w.com/pages/psimpson/

- ROOTS-L United States Resources: Nebraska
  http://www.rootsweb.com/roots-l/USA/ne.html
  Comprehensive list of research links, including many to history-related sites.

◆ Government & Cities

- 50states.com—Nebraska State Information Resource
  http://www.50states.com/nebraska.htm
  A list of general information for each state, including a list of colleges, state symbols, links to maps, newspapers, and other miscellaneous state information.

- Excite Travel by City.Net—Nebraska
  http://www.city.net/countries/united_states/nebraska/

- Nebraska State Government
  http://www.state.ne.us/

- Official City Web Sites for the State of Nebraska
  http://OfficialCitySites.org/Nebraska.htm

- Yahoo! Get Local...Nebraska Cities
  http://dir.yahoo.com/Regional/U_S__States/Nebraska/Cities/
  Maps, yellow pages, white pages, newspapers and other local information.

- Yahoo! Get Local...Nebraska Counties and Regions
  http://dir.yahoo.com/Regional/U_S__States/Nebraska/Counties_and_Regions/
  Maps, yellow pages, white pages, newspapers and other local information.

◆ History & Culture

- South Omaha, Douglas County, Nebraska 1886–1915 History
  http://www.geocities.com/Heartland/Plains/3730/so.html

- Yahoo!...History...Nebraska
  http://dir.yahoo.com/Arts/Humanities/History/Browse_By_Region/U_S__States/Nebraska/

◆ Libraries, Archives & Museums

- Danish Immigrant Archive at Dana College
  http://www.dana.edu/~pformo/archive.htm
  Blair, Nebraska

- Family History Centers—Nebraska
  http://www.deseretbook.com/famhis/ne.html

- Family History Centers—Nebraska
  http://www.lib.byu.edu/~uvrfhc/centers/nebraska.html
- HYTELNET—Library Catalogs: USA: Nebraska
  http://library.usask.ca/hytelnet/usa/NE.html
  Before you use any of the Telnet links, make note of the user name, password and any other logon information.
- Lincoln City Libraries
  http://www.lcl.lib.ne.us/
  For Lincoln and Lancaster County, Nebraska.
- Nebraska Family History Centers
  http://www.genhomepage.com/FHC/Nebraska.html
  A list of addresses, phone numbers and hours of operation from the Genealogy Home Page.
- Nebraska Library Commission
  http://www.nlc.state.ne.us/
- NUCMC Listing of Archives and Manuscript Repositories in Nebraska
  http://lcweb.loc.gov/coll/nucmc/nesites.html
  Links to information about resources other than those held in the Library of Congress.
- Repositories of Primary Sources: Nebraska
  http://www.uidaho.edu/special-collections/west.html#usne
  A list of links to online resources from the Univ. of Idaho Library, Special Collections and Archives.
- University of Nebraska-Lincoln, Libraries and Collections
  http://www.unl.edu/libr/libs/libscols.html
- webCATS: Library Catalogues on the World Wide Web—Nebraska
  http://library.usask.ca/hywebcat/states/NE.html

◆ Mailing Lists, Newsgroups & Chat

- Genealogy Resources on the Internet—Nebraska Mailing Lists
  http://members.aol.com/gfsjohnf/gen_mail_states-ne.html
  Each of the mailing list links below points to this site, wonderfully maintained by John Fuller. Visit this site for county-specific mailing lists as well.
- IA-NEB-ROOTS-L Mailing List—Iowa & Nebraska
  http://members.aol.com/gfsjohnf/gen_mail_states-ne.html#IA-NEB-ROOTS-L
- NEBRHeritage Mailing List
  http://members.aol.com/gfsjohnf/gen_mail_states-ne.html#NEBRASKA_HERITAGE
  For discussions on Nebraska history and life.
- NEBRRoots Mailing List
  http://members.aol.com/gfsjohnf/gen_mail_states-ne.html#NEBRROOTS

◆ Maps, Gazetteers & Geographical Information

- 1872 County Map of Nebraska
  http://www.ismi.net/chnegw/1872nebraska.htm

- 1895 U.S. Atlas—Nebraska
  http://www.LivGenMI.com/1895ne.htm
- American Memory Panoramic Maps 1847–1929—Nebraska
  http://lcweb2.loc.gov/cgi-bin/query/S?ammem/gmd:@filreq(@field(STATE+nebraska)+@field(COLLID+pmmap))
  From the Geography and Map Division, Library of Congress.
- American Memory Railroad Maps 1828–1900—Nebraska
  http://memory.loc.gov/cgi-bin/query/S?ammem/gmd:@filreq(@field(STATE+nebraska)+@field(COLLID+rrmap))
  From the Geography and Map Division, Library of Congress.
- Color Landform Atlas: Nebraska
  http://fermi.jhuapl.edu/states/ne_0.html
  Including a map of counties and a map for 1895.
- Excite Maps: Nebraska Maps
  http://www.city.net/maps/view/?mapurl=/countries/united_states/nebraska
  Zoom in on these maps all the way to the street level.
- HPI County InfoSystem—Counties in Nebraska
  http://www.com/hpi/necty/index.html
- K.B. Slocum Books and Maps—Nebraska
  http://www.treasurenet.com/cgi-bin/treasure/kbslocum/scan/se=Nebraska/sf=mapstate
- List of Nebraska Counties
  http://www.genealogy.org/~st-clair/counties/state_ne.html
- Map of Nebraska Counties
  http://govinfo.kerr.orst.edu/gif/states/ne.gif
  From the Government Information Sharing Project, Information Services, Oregon State University.
- Map of Nebraska Counties
  http://www.lib.utexas.edu/Libs/PCL/Map_collection/states/Nebraska.gif
  From the Perry-Castañeda Library at the Univ. of Texas at Austin.
- U.S. Census Bureau—Nebraska Profiles
  http://www.census.gov/datamap/www/31.html
- Yale Peabody Museum: GNIS—Nebraska
  http://www.peabody.yale.edu/other/gnis/NE.html
  *Search the USGS Geographic Names Database. You can limit the search to a specific county in this state and search for any of the following features: airport arch area arroyo bar basin bay beach bench bend bridge **building** canal cape **cemetery** channel **church** cliff crater crossing dam falls flat forest gap geyser glacier gut harbor hospital island isthmus lake lava levee locale mine oilfield other park pillar plain ppl range rapids reserve reservoir ridge **school** sea slope spring stream summit swamp tower trail tunnel valley well woods.*

◆ Military

- 1893 Nebraska Census of Civil War Veterans
  http://www.rootsweb.com/~neholt/1893/index.html
- The Civil War Archive—Union Regiments—Nebraska
  http://www.civilwararchive.com/unionne.htm

- Korean Conflict State-Level Casualty Lists—Nebraska
  http://www.nara.gov/nara/electronic/nehrlist.html
  From the National Archives and Records Administration, Center for Electronic Records.
- Vietnam Conflict State-Level Casualty Lists—Nebraska
  http://www.nara.gov/nara/electronic/nehrviet.html
  From the National Archives and Records Administration, Center for Electronic Records.
- The Vietnam Veterans Memorial—Nebraska
  http://grunt.space.swri.edu/statewall/nebraska/ne.htm

◆ Newspapers

- AJR NewsLink—Nebraska Newspapers
  http://www.newslink.org/nbnews.html
- E&P Media Info Links—Newspaper Sites in Nebraska
  http://www.mediainfo.com/emedia/browse-results.htm?region=nebraska&category=newspaper+++++++++
- Ecola Newstand: Nebraska
  http://www.ecola.com/news/press/na/us/ne/
- NAA Hotlinks to Newspapers Online—Nebraska
  http://www.naa.org/hotlinks/searchResult.asp?param=NE-Nebraska&City=1
- The Nebraska Newspaper Project
  http://www.unl.edu/nebnews/nnphome.html
- N-Net—Nebraska Newspapers
  http://www.n-net.com/ne.htm
- The Ultimate Collection of News Links: USA—Nebraska
  http://www.pppp.net/links/news/USA-NE.html
- Yahoo!...Newspapers...Nebraska
  http://dir.yahoo.com/News_and_Media/Newspapers/Browse_By_Region/U_S__States/Nebraska/

◆ People & Families

- Tribes and Villages of Nebraska
  http://hanksville.phast.umass.edu:8000/cultprop/contacts/tribal/NE.html
- WPA Life Histories from Nebraska
  http://lcweb2.loc.gov/ammem/wpaintro/necat.html
  Manuscripts from the Federal Writer's Project, 1936–1940, Library of Congress.

◆ Professional Researchers, Volunteers & Other Research Services

- Board for Certification of Genealogists—Roster of Those Certified—Specializing in Nebraska
  http://www.genealogy.org/~bcg/rosts_ne.html

- Genealogy Helplist—Nebraska
  http://posom.com/hl/usa/ne.shtml
- The Official Iowa Counties Professional Genealogist and Researcher's Registry for Nebraska
  http://www.iowa-counties.com/gene/ne.htm

◆ Publications, Software & Supplies

- AncestorSpy—CDs and Microfiche for Nebraska
  http://www.ancestorspy.com/ne.htm
- Barbara Green's Used Genealogy Books—Nebraska
  http://home.earthlink.net/~genbooks/lochist.html#NE
- Books We Own—Nebraska
  http://www.rootsweb.com/~bwo/nebraska.html
- Boyd Publishing Company—Nebraska
  http://www.hom.net/~gac/nebrask.htm
- Frontier Press Bookstore—Nebraska
  http://www.frontierpress.com/frontier.cgi?category=ne
- Heritage Quest—Microfilm Records for the State of Nebraska
  http://www.heritagequest.com/genealogy/microfilm/nebraska/
- The Memorabilia Corner—Books: Nebraska
  http://members.aol.com/TMCorner/book_neb.htm

◆ Queries, Message Boards & Surname Lists

- GenConnect Nebraska Visitor Center
  http://cgi.rootsweb.com/~genbbs/indx/Ne.html
  A system for posting queries, Bibles, biographies, deeds, obituaries, pensions, wills.

◆ Records: Census, Cemeteries, Land, Obituaries, Personal, Taxes and Vital (Born, Married, Died & Buried)

- The 1790–1890 Federal Population Censuses: Catalog of National Archives Microfilm
  http://www.genealogy.org/census/contents.shtml
  - Census Schedules and Microfilm Roll Numbers for Nebraska:
    1860
    http://www.genealogy.org/census/1860_schedules/Nebraska.html
    1870
    http://www.genealogy.org/census/1870_schedules/Nebraska.html
    1880
    http://www.genealogy.org/census/1880_schedules/Nebraska.html

1880 soundex
http://www.genealogy.org/census/1880.sdx_schedules/T760.html

1890 Special Schedules
http://www.genealogy.org/census/1890-special_schedules/Nebraska.html

- Census Online—Links to Census Sites on the Web—Nebraska
http://www.census-online.com/links/NE_data.html

- County Courthouse Addresses
http://www.familytreemaker.com/00000256.html

- Farnam, Nebraska Cemetery
http://www.4w.com/pages/hoppe/cemetery/

- Find-A-Grave by Location: Nebraska
http://www.findagrave.com/grave/lne.html
Graves of noteworthy people.

- Interment.net: Nebraska Cemeteries
http://www.interment.net/us/ne/index.htm
A list of links to other sites.

- National Archives—Central Plains Region (Kansas City)
http://www.nara.gov/regional/kansas.html

- National Archives—Central Plains Region from Family Tree Maker
http://www.familytreemaker.com/00000095.html
Records for Iowa, Kansas, Missouri, and Nebraska.

- Nebraska Vital Records Information
http://vitalrec.com/ne.html

- The Political Graveyard—Cemeteries in Nebraska
http://politicalgraveyard.com/geo/NE/kmindex.html

- Potter Field Cemetery, 1887–1957, Omaha, Douglas County, Nebraska
http://www.geocities.com/Heartland/Plains/3730/stone5.html

- Preplanning Network—Funeral Home and Cemetery Directory—Nebraska
http://www.preplannet.com/nebfhcem.htm

- USGenWeb Census Project Nebraska
http://www.usgenweb.org/census/states/nebraska/nebraska.htm

- USGenWeb Tombstone Transcription Project—Nebraska
http://www.rootsweb.com/~cemetery/nebraska/

- VitalChek Network—Nebraska
http://www.vitalchek.com/stateselect.asp?state=NE

- Where to Write for Vital Records—Nebraska
http://www.cdc.gov/nchswww/howto/w2w/nebraska.htm
From the National Center for Health Statistics (NCHS).

◆ Religion & Churches

- Christianity.Net Church Locator—Nebraska
http://www.christianity.net/cgi/location.exe?United_States+Nebraska

- Church Online!—Nebraska
http://www.churchonline.com/usas/ne/ne.html

- Church Profiles—Nebraska
http://www.church-profiles.com/ne/ne.html

- Churches dot Net—Global Church Web Pages—Nebraska
http://www.churches.net/churches/nebraska.html

- Churches of the World—Nebraska
http://www.churchsurf.com/churches/Nebraska/index.htm
From the ChurchSurf Christian Directory.

◆ Societies & Groups

- Adams County Genealogical Society
http://www.tcgcs.com/~achs/acgs.html

- Adams County Historical Society
http://www.hastingsnet.com/community/achs/

- American Historical Society of Germans from Russia—Lincoln Nebraska Chapter
http://www.ahsgr.org/nelincol.html

- American Historical Society of Germans from Russia—Northeast Nebraska Chapter
http://www.ahsgr.org/nenorthe.html

- Archer's Computer Interest Group List—Nebraska
http://www.genealogy.org/~ngs/cigs/ngl1usne.html

- Boone-Nance Genealogical Society
http://www.rootsweb.com/~nenance/bngensoc.html

- Custer County Historical Society
http://www.rootsweb.com/~necuster/
Broken Bow, Nebraska

- Eastern Nebraska Genealogical Society
http://www.connectfremont.org/CLUB/ENGS.HTM

- Historical Society of Douglas County
http://www.radiks.net/~hsdc-lac/

- Holdrege Area Genealogical Society
http://www.4w.com/pages/psimpson/phelpsgen.html
Holdrege, Phelps County, Nebraska

- IOOF Lodge Website Directory—Nebraska
http://norm28.hsc.usc.edu/IOOF/USA/Nebraska/Nebraska.html
Independent Order of Odd Fellows and Rebekahs.

- Naponee Historical Society, Nebraska
http://www.4w.com/pages/psimpson/naponeehist.html

- Nebraska State Genealogical Society
http://www.rootsweb.com/~negenweb/societies/stgnsoc.html

- Nebraska State Historical Society
  http://www.nebraskahistory.org/
- Southeast Nebraska Genealogical Society
  http://www.rootsweb.com/~negage/sengs.htm
  Beatrice, Nebraska

◆ USGenWeb Project

- Nebraska Genealogy—USGenWeb Project
  State Page
  http://www.usgenweb.org/ne
- Nebraska—USGenWeb Archives Table of Contents
  http://www.rootsweb.com/~usgenweb/ne/nefiles.htm
- Nebraska—USGenWeb FTP Archives
  ftp://ftp.rootsweb.com/pub/usgenweb/ne

U.S.—NEVADA—NV
http://www.CyndisList.com/nv.htm

Category Index:

- General Resource Sites
- Government & Cities
- History & Culture
- Libraries, Archives & Museums
- Mailing Lists, Newsgroups & Chat
- Maps, Gazetteers & Geographical Information
- Military
- Newspapers
- People & Families

- Professional Researchers, Volunteers & Other Research Services
- Publications, Software & Supplies
- Queries, Message Boards & Surname Lists
- Records: Census, Cemeteries, Land, Obituaries, Personal, Taxes and Vital
- Religion & Churches
- Societies & Groups
- USGenWeb Project

◆ General Resource Sites

- Everton's Sources of Genealogical Information in Nevada
  http://www.everton.com/usa/nv.htm

- Family Tree Maker's Genealogy "How To" Guide—Nevada
  http://www.familytreemaker.com/00000202.html

- Genealogy Bulletin Board Systems for Nevada
  http://www.genealogy.org/~gbbs/gblnv.html

- Genealogy Exchange & Surname Registry—NVGenExchange
  http://www.genexchange.com/nv/index.cfm

- Genealogy Resources on the Internet: Nevada
  http://www-personal.umich.edu/~cgaunt/nevada.html

- LDS Research Outline for Nevada
  http://www.everton.com/usa/nv-0829b.txt

- Lineages' Genealogy Site: Nevada
  http://www.lineages.com/rooms/usa/state.asp?StateCode=NV

- ROOTS-L United States Resources: Nevada
  http://www.rootsweb.com/roots-l/USA/nv.html
  Comprehensive list of research links, including many to history-related sites.

◆ Government & Cities

- 50states.com—Nevada State Information Resource
  http://www.50states.com/nevada.htm
  A list of general information for each state, including a list of colleges, state symbols, links to maps, newspapers, and other miscellaneous state information.

- Excite Travel by City.Net—Nevada
  http://www.city.net/countries/united_states/nevada/

- Official City Web Sites for the State of Nevada
  http://OfficialCitySites.org/Nevada.htm

- State of Nevada
  http://www.state.nv.us/

- Yahoo! Get Local...Nevada Cities
  http://dir.yahoo.com/Regional/U_S__States/Nevada/Cities/
  Maps, yellow pages, white pages, newspapers and other local information.

- Yahoo! Get Local...Nevada Counties and Regions
  http://dir.yahoo.com/Regional/U_S__States/Nevada/Counties_and_Regions/
  Maps, yellow pages, white pages, newspapers and other local information.

◆ History & Culture

- Central Nevada Emigrant Trail Association (CNETA)
  http://ourworld.compuserve.com/homepages/trailofthe49ers/

- Ghost Towns of Nevada
  http://www.ghosttowns.com/states/nv/nv.html

- Yahoo!...History...Nevada
  http://dir.yahoo.com/Arts/Humanities/History/Browse_By_Region/U_S__States/Nevada/

◆ Libraries, Archives & Museums

- Boulder City Library
  http://www.accessnv.com/bclibrary/

- Douglas County Library
  http://douglas.lib.nv.us/
  Minden, Nevada

- Family History Centers—Nevada
  http://www.deseretbook.com/famhis/nv.html

- Family History Centers—Nevada
  http://www.lib.byu.edu/~uvrfhc/centers/nevada.html

- HYTELNET—Library Catalogs: USA: Nevada
  http://library.usask.ca/hytelnet/usa/NV.html
  Before you use any of the Telnet links, make note of the user name, password and any other logon information.

- Las Vegas-Clark County Library District
  http://www.lvccld.lib.nv.us/

- Nevada Family History Centers
  http://www.genhomepage.com/FHC/Nevada.html
  A list of addresses, phone numbers and hours of operation from the Genealogy Home Page.

- Nevada State Library and Archives
  http://www.clan.lib.nv.us/docs/NSLA/nsla.htm
  - Nevada Library Catalogs & Electronic Resources
    http://www.clan.lib.nv.us/docs/NSLA/SERVICES/ref-cats.htm
  - Nevada State Archives and Records Management
    http://www.clan.lib.nv.us/docs/NSLA/ARCHIVES/arc-rec.htm
  - Nevada State Archives and Records Management—Genealogical Resources
    http://www.clan.lib.nv.us/docs/NSLA/ARCHIVES/geneal.htm
  - Nevada State Library and Archives Reference Services
    http://www.clan.lib.nv.us/docs/NSLA/SERVICES/refserv.htm

- NUCMC Listing of Archives and Manuscript Repositories in Nevada
  http://lcweb.loc.gov/coll/nucmc/nvsites.html
  Links to information about resources other than those held in the Library of Congress.

- Repositories of Primary Sources: Nevada
  http://www.uidaho.edu/special-collections/west.html#usnv
  A list of links to online resources from the Univ. of Idaho Library, Special Collections and Archives.

- University of Nevada, Reno Libraries
  http://www.library.unr.edu/
  - Special Collections Department
    http://www.library.unr.edu/~specoll/
  - University Archives
    http://www.library.unr.edu/~univarch/

- Washoe County Library Internet Branch
  http://www.washoe.lib.nv.us/
  Serving northern Nevada.

- webCATS: Library Catalogues on the World Wide Web—Nevada
  http://library.usask.ca/hywebcat/states/NV.html

◆ Mailing Lists, Newsgroups & Chat

- Genealogy Resources on the Internet—Nevada Mailing Lists
  http://members.aol.com/gfsjohnf/gen_mail_states-nv.html
  Each of the mailing list links below points to this site, wonderfully maintained by John Fuller. Visit this site for county-specific mailing lists as well.

- WESTERN-ROOTS-L Mailing list
  http://members.aol.com/gfsjohnf/gen_mail_states-nv.html#WESTERN-ROOTS-L
  Washington, Oregon, Alaska, Idaho, Montana, Wyoming, California, Nevada, Hawaii, Colorado, Utah, Arizona, and New Mexico.

◆ Maps, Gazetteers & Geographical Information

- 1895 U.S. Atlas—Nevada
  http://www.LivGenMI.com/1895nv.htm

- American Memory Panoramic Maps 1847–1929—Nevada
  http://lcweb2.loc.gov/cgi-bin/query/S?ammem/gmd:@filreq(@field(STATE+nevada)+@field(COLLID+pmmap))
  From the Geography and Map Division, Library of Congress.

- American Memory Railroad Maps 1828–1900—Nevada
  http://memory.loc.gov/cgi-bin/query/S?ammem/gmd:@filreq(@field(STATE+nevada)+@field(COLLID+rrmap))
  From the Geography and Map Division, Library of Congress.

- Color Landform Atlas: Nevada
  http://fermi.jhuapl.edu/states/nv_0.html
  Including a map of counties and a map for 1895.

- Excite Maps: Nevada Maps
  http://www.city.net/maps/view/?mapurl=/countries/united_states/nevada
  Zoom in on these maps all the way to the street level.

- HPI County InfoSystem—Counties in Nevada
  http://www.com/hpi/nvcty/index.html

- K.B. Slocum Books and Maps—Nevada
  http://www.treasurenet.com/cgi-bin/treasure/kbslocum/scan/se=Nevada/sf=mapstate

- List of Nevada Counties
  http://www.genealogy.org/~st-clair/counties/state_nv.html

- Map of Nevada Counties
  http://govinfo.kerr.orst.edu/gif/states/nv.gif
  From the Government Information Sharing Project, Information Services, Oregon State University.

- Map of Nevada Counties
  http://www.lib.utexas.edu/Libs/PCL/Map_collection/states/Nevada.gif
  From the Perry-Castañeda Library at the Univ. of Texas at Austin.

- U.S. Census Bureau—Nevada Profiles
  http://www.census.gov/datamap/www/32.html

- Yale Peabody Museum: GNIS—Nevada
  http://www.peabody.yale.edu/other/gnis/NV.html
  *Search the USGS Geographic Names Database. You can limit the search to a specific county in this state and search for any of the following features: airport arch area arroyo bar basin bay beach bench bend bridge **building** canal cape **cemetery** channel **church** cliff crater crossing dam falls flat forest gap geyser glacier gut harbor hospital island isthmus lake lava levee locale mine oilfield other park pillar plain ppl range rapids reserve reservoir ridge **school** sea slope spring stream summit swamp tower trail tunnel valley well woods.*

◆ Military

- The Civil War Archive—Union Regiments—Nevada
  http://www.civilwararchive.com/unionnv.htm
- Korean Conflict State-Level Casualty Lists— Nevada
  http://www.nara.gov/nara/electronic/nvhrlist.html
  From the National Archives and Records Administration, Center for Electronic Records.
- Vietnam Conflict State-Level Casualty Lists— Nevada
  http://www.nara.gov/nara/electronic/nvhrviet.html
  From the National Archives and Records Administration, Center for Electronic Records.
- The Vietnam Veterans Memorial—Nevada
  http://grunt.space.swri.edu/statewall/nevada/nv.htm

◆ Newspapers

- AJR NewsLink—Nevada Newspapers
  http://www.newslink.org/nvnews.html
- E&P Media Info Links—Newspaper Sites in Nevada
  http://www.mediainfo.com/emedia/browse-results.
  htm?region=nevada&category=newspaper+++++++++
- Ecola Newstand: Nevada
  http://www.ecola.com/news/press/na/us/nv/
- NAA Hotlinks to Newspapers Online—Nevada
  http://www.naa.org/hotlinks/searchResult.asp?param=
  NV-Nevada&City=1
- N-Net—Nevada Newspapers
  http://www.n-net.com/nv.htm
- The Ultimate Collection of News Links: USA—Nevada
  http://www.pppp.net/links/news/USA-NV.html
- Yahoo!...Newspapers...Nevada
  http://dir.yahoo.com/News_and_Media/Newspapers/
  Browse_By_Region/U_S__States/Nevada/

◆ People & Families

- Nevada Women's History Project
  http://www.unr.edu/unr/sb204/nwhp/
- Tribes and Villages of Nevada
  http://hanksville.phast.umass.edu:8000/cultprop/contacts/
  tribal/NV.html

◆ Professional Researchers, Volunteers & Other Research Services

- Board for Certification of Genealogists—Roster of Those Certified—Specializing in Nevada
  http://www.genealogy.org/~bcg/rosts_nv.html
- Genealogy Helplist—Nevada
  http://members.aol.com/DFBradshaw/nv.html
- The Official Iowa Counties Professional Genealogist and Researcher's Registry for Nevada
  http://www.iowa-counties.com/gene/nv.htm

◆ Publications, Software & Supplies

- Barbara Green's Used Genealogy Books—Nevada
  http://home.earthlink.net/~genbooks/lochist.html#NV
- Frontier Press Bookstore—Nevada
  http://www.frontierpress.com/frontier.cgi?category=nv
- GenealogyBookShop.com—Nevada
  http://www.genealogybookshop.com/genealogybookshop/files/
  The_United_States,Nevada/index.html
  The online store of Genealogical Publishing Co., Inc. & Clearfield Company.
- Heritage Quest—Microfilm Records for the State of Nevada
  http://www.heritagequest.com/genealogy/microfilm/nevada/
- The Memorabilia Corner—Books: Nevada
  http://members.aol.com/TMCorner/book_nev.htm

◆ Queries, Message Boards & Surname Lists

- GenConnect Nevada Visitor Center
  http://cgi.rootsweb.com/~genbbs/indx/Nv.html
  A system for posting queries, Bibles, biographies, deeds, obituaries, pensions, wills.

◆ Records: Census, Cemeteries, Land, Obituaries, Personal, Taxes and Vital (Born, Married, Died & Buried)

- The 1790–1890 Federal Population Censuses: Catalog of National Archives Microfilm
  http://www.genealogy.org/census/contents.shtml
  - Census Schedules and Microfilm Roll Numbers for Nevada:
    1860
    http://www.genealogy.org/census/1860_schedules/
    Nevada.html
    1870
    http://www.genealogy.org/census/1870_schedules/
    Nevada.html
    1880
    http://www.genealogy.org/census/1880_schedules/
    Nevada.html
    1880 soundex
    http://www.genealogy.org/census/1880.sdx_schedules/
    T761.html

1890 Special Schedules
http://www.genealogy.org/census/1890-special_schedules/
Nevada.html

- Birth and Death Records in Nevada
http://www.clan.lib.nv.us/docs/NSLA/ARCHIVES/birth.htm
*Includes addresses for the county recorders/auditors. From the
Nevada State Library and Archives.*

- BLM—Nevada's Electronic Reading Room
http://www.blm.gov/nhp/efoia/nv/
United States Bureau of Land Management.

- Carson Appeal Newspaper Index, 1865–66,
1879–80, 1881, 1885–86
http://www.clan.lib.nv.us/docs/NSLA/ARCHIVES/appeal/
appeal1.htm

- Clark County, Nevada Government and Services
http://www.co.clark.nv.us/
  - Marriage Inquiry System
  http://www.co.clark.nv.us/recorder/mar_disc.htm
  *A searchable index of marriages from 1984 through the
  present.*

- County Courthouse Addresses
http://www.familytreemaker.com/00000257.html

- Find-A-Grave by Location: Nevada
http://www.findagrave.com/grave/lnv.html
Graves of noteworthy people.

- National Archives—Pacific Region (San Bruno)
http://www.nara.gov/regional/sanfranc.html

- National Archives—Pacific Sierra Region
http://www.familytreemaker.com/00000101.html
*Records for Northern California, Hawaii, Nevada (except Clark
County), the Pacific Trust Territories, and American Samoa.*

- National Archives—Pacific Region (Laguna Niguel)
http://www.nara.gov/regional/laguna.html

- National Archives—Pacific Southwest Region
http://www.familytreemaker.com/00000102.html
*Records for Arizona, Southern California, and Clark County,
Nevada.*

- Nevada Newspaper Indexes
http://www.clan.lib.nv.us/docs/NSLA/ARCHIVES/newsind.htm
Nevada State Library and Archives and Records.

- Nevada Vital Records Information
http://vitalrec.com/nv.html

- The Political Graveyard—Cemeteries in Nevada
http://politicalgraveyard.com/geo/NV/kmindex.html

- Preplanning Network—Funeral Home and
Cemetery Directory—Nevada
http://www.preplannet.com/nevfhcem.htm

- Ricks College—Family History Center Genesis
Project
http://abish.ricks.edu/fhc/gbsearch.asp
*Search engine for marriages in Arizona, Idaho, Nevada,
Oregon, Utah 1850–1951.*

- USGenWeb Census Project Nevada
http://www.usgenweb.org/census/states/nevada.htm

- USGenWeb Tombstone Transcription Project—
Nevada
http://www.rootsweb.com/~cemetery/nevada.html

- VitalChek Network—Nevada
http://www.vitalchek.com/stateselect.asp?state=NV

- Where to Write for Vital Records—Nevada
http://www.cdc.gov/nchswww/howto/w2w/nevada.htm
From the National Center for Health Statistics (NCHS).

◆ Religion & Churches

- Christianity.Net Church Locator—Nevada
http://www.christianity.net/cgi/location.exe?
United_States+Nevada

- Church Online!—Nevada
http://www.churchonline.com/usas/nv/nv.html

- Church Profiles—Nevada
http://www.church-profiles.com/nv/nv.html

- Churches dot Net—Global Church Web Pages—
Nevada
http://www.churches.net/churches/nevada.html

- Churches of the World—Nevada
http://www.churchsurf.com/churches/Nevada/index.htm
From the ChurchSurf Christian Directory.

◆ Societies & Groups

- Archer's Computer Interest Group List—Nevada
http://www.genealogy.org/~ngs/cigs/ngl1usnv.html

- Banat Genealogy Society
http://feefhs.org/frgbanat.html

- High Sierra History Forum
http://www.tahoenet.com/tdhs/index.html
California / Nevada

- IOOF Lodge Website Directory—Nevada
http://norm28.hsc.usc.edu/IOOF/USA/Nevada/Nevada.html
Independent Order of Odd Fellows and Rebekahs.

- Nevada Historical Society
http://www.clan.lib.nv.us/docs/MUSEUMS/HIST/his-soc.htm

- Nevada State Society Daughters of the
American Revolution
http://members.aol.com/nvdar/state/state.htm

- Truckee-Donner Historical Society
http://www.tahoenet.com/tdhs/tpnewslt.html

- White Pine Historical and Archaeological Society
http://www.webpanda.com/white_pine_county/
historical_society/index.html
Ely, White Pine County, Nevada

◆ USGenWeb Project

- Nevada Genealogy—USGenWeb Project State Page
  http://www.usgenweb.org/nv

- Nevada—USGenWeb Archives Table of Contents
  http://www.rootsweb.com/~usgenweb/nv/nvfiles.htm

- Nevada—USGenWeb FTP Archives
  ftp://ftp.rootsweb.com/pub/usgenweb/nv/

- Nevada Query Page
  http://www.rootsweb.com/~nvgenweb/nvquery.htm

U.S.—NEW HAMPSHIRE—NH

http://www.CyndisList.com/nh.htm

Category Index:

- General Resource Sites
- Government & Cities
- History & Culture
- Libraries, Archives & Museums
- Mailing Lists, Newsgroups & Chat
- Maps, Gazetteers & Geographical Information
- Military
- Newspapers
- People & Families

- Professional Researchers, Volunteers & Other Research Services
- Publications, Software & Supplies
- Queries, Message Boards & Surname Lists
- Records: Census, Cemeteries, Land, Obituaries, Personal, Taxes and Vital
- Religion & Churches
- Societies & Groups
- USGenWeb Project

◆ General Resource Sites

- Everton's Sources of Genealogical Information in New Hampshire
  http://www.everton.com/usa/nh.htm

- Family Tree Maker's Genealogy "How To" Guide—New Hampshire
  http://www.familytreemaker.com/00000203.html

- Genealogy Bulletin Board Systems for New Hampshire
  http://www.genealogy.org/~gbbs/gblnh.html

- Genealogy Exchange & Surname Registry—NHGenExchange
  http://www.genexchange.com/nh/index.cfm

- Genealogy Resources on the Internet: New Hampshire
  http://www-personal.umich.edu/~cgaunt/newhamp.html

- LDS Research Outline for New Hampshire
  http://www.everton.com/usa/nh-0830b.txt

- Lineages' Genealogy Site: New Hampshire
  http://www.lineages.com/rooms/usa/state.asp?StateCode=NH

- New England Connections
  http://www.geocities.com/Heartland/5274/nec.htm

- ROOTS-L United States Resources: New Hampshire
  http://www.rootsweb.com/roots-l/USA/nh.html
  Comprehensive list of research links, including many to history-related sites.

◆ Government & Cities

- 50states.com—New Hampshire State Information Resource
  http://www.50states.com/newhamps.htm
  A list of general information for each state, including a list of colleges, state symbols, links to maps, newspapers, and other miscellaneous state information.

- Excite Travel by City.Net—New Hampshire
  http://www.city.net/countries/united_states/new_hampshire/

- Official City Web Sites for the State of New Hampshire
  http://OfficialCitySites.org/New-Hampshire.htm

- WEBSTER: The New Hampshire State Government Online Information Center
  http://www.state.nh.us/

- Yahoo! Get Local...New Hampshire Cities
  http://dir.yahoo.com/Regional/U_S__States/New_Hampshire/Cities/
  Maps, yellow pages, white pages, newspapers and other local information.

- Yahoo! Get Local...New Hampshire Counties and Regions
  http://dir.yahoo.com/Regional/U_S__States/New_Hampshire/Counties_and_Regions/
  Maps, yellow pages, white pages, newspapers and other local information.

◆ History & Culture

- New Hampshire's Historical Legacy
  http://www.nh.com/legacy/index.shtml

- Yahoo!...History...New Hampshire
  http://dir.yahoo.com/Arts/Humanities/History/
  Browse_By_Region/U_S__States/New_Hampshire/

◆ Libraries, Archives & Museums

- Archives in New England on the Internet
  http://www.lib.umb.edu/newengarch/nearch.html

- Family History Centers—New Hampshire
  http://www.deseretbook.com/famhis/nh.html

- Family History Centers—New Hampshire
  http://www.lib.byu.edu/~uvrfhc/centers/newhampshire.html

- HYTELNET—Library Catalogs: USA:
  New Hampshire
  http://library.usask.ca/hytelnet/usa/NH.html
  Before you use any of the Telnet links, make note of the user name, password and any other logon information.

- Lane Memorial Library, Hampton, NH
  http://www.hampton.lib.nh.us/
  - Hampton, N.H. History and Genealogy
    http://www.hampton.lib.nh.us/hampton/history.htm

- New Hampshire Division of Records Management and Archives
  http://www.state.nh.us/state/archives.htm

- New Hampshire Family History Centers
  http://www.genhomepage.com/FHC/New_Hampshire.html
  A list of addresses, phone numbers and hours of operation from the Genealogy Home Page.

- New Hampshire State Library
  http://www.state.nh.us/nhsl/index.html
  - Genealogy Section
    http://www.state.nh.us/nhsl/history/index.html

- NUCMC Listing of Archives and Manuscript Repositories in New Hampshire
  http://lcweb.loc.gov/coll/nucmc/nhsites.html
  Links to information about resources other than those held in the Library of Congress.

- Princeton University Library
  http://libweb.princeton.edu:2003/
  - History Resources
    http://www.princeton.edu/~pressman/history.htm
  - Microforms of Interest to Historical Research
    http://infoshare1.Princeton.EDU:2003/online/guide/history_microforms/

- Repositories of Primary Sources: New Hampshire
  http://www.uidaho.edu/special-collections/east2.html#usnh
  A list of links to online resources from the Univ. of Idaho Library, Special Collections and Archives.

- University of New Hampshire Libraries
  http://www.library.unh.edu/
  - Milne Special Collections and Archives
    http://wwwsc.library.unh.edu/specoll/

- webCATS: Library Catalogues on the World Wide Web—New Hampshire
  http://library.usask.ca/hywebcat/states/NH.html

◆ Mailing Lists, Newsgroups & Chat

- Genealogy Resources on the Internet—New Hampshire Mailing Lists
  http://members.aol.com/gfsjohnf/gen_mail_states-nh.html
  Each of the mailing list links below points to this site, wonderfully maintained by John Fuller. Visit this site for county-specific mailing lists as well.

- New-Hampshire Mailing List
  http://members.aol.com/gfsjohnf/gen_mail_states-nh.html#New-Hampshire

- NORTHEAST-ROOTS-L Mailing List
  http://members.aol.com/gfsjohnf/gen_mail_states-nh.html#NORTHEAST-ROOTS
  Connecticut, Maine, Massachusetts, New Hampshire, Rhode Island & Vermont.

◆ Maps, Gazetteers & Geographical Information

- 1895 U.S. Atlas—New Hampshire
  http://www.LivGenMI.com/1895nh.htm

- American Memory Panoramic Maps 1847–1929—New Hampshire
  http://lcweb2.loc.gov/cgi-bin/query/S?ammem/gmd:@filreq(@field(STATE+@band(+new+hampshire))+@field(COLLID+pmmap))
  From the Geography and Map Division, Library of Congress.

- American Memory Railroad Maps 1828–1900—New Hampshire
  http://memory.loc.gov/cgi-bin/query/S?ammem/gmd:@filreq(@field(STATE+@band(+new+hampshire))+@field(COLLID+rrmap))
  From the Geography and Map Division, Library of Congress.

- Color Landform Atlas: New Hampshire
  http://fermi.jhuapl.edu/states/nh_0.html
  Including a map of counties and a map for 1895.

- Excite Maps: New Hampshire Maps
  http://www.city.net/maps/view/?mapurl=/countries/united_states/new_hampshire
  Zoom in on these maps all the way to the street level.

- HPI County InfoSystem—Counties in New Hampshire
  http://www.com/hpi/nhcty/index.html

- K.B. Slocum Books and Maps—New Hampshire
  http://www.treasurenet.com/cgi-bin/treasure/kbslocum/scan/se=New.20Hampshire/sf=mapstate

- List of New Hampshire Counties
  http://www.genealogy.org/~st-clair/counties/state_nh.html

- Map of New Hampshire Counties
  http://govinfo.kerr.orst.edu/gif/states/nh.gif
  From the Government Information Sharing Project, Information Services, Oregon State University.

- Map of New Hampshire Counties
  http://www.lib.utexas.edu/Libs/PCL/Map_collection/states/New_Hampshire.gif
  From the Perry-Castañeda Library at the Univ. of Texas at Austin.

- Old Maps of New England (Maine, New Hampshire, Vermont, Connecticut, Rhode Island, Massachusetts) and New York
  http://members.aol.com/oldmapsne/index.html

- Reproductions of Old Town Maps in New England
  http://www.biddeford.com/~lkane/

- U.S. Census Bureau—New Hampshire Profiles
  http://www.census.gov/datamap/www/33.html

- Yale Peabody Museum: GNIS—New Hampshire
  http://www.peabody.yale.edu/other/gnis/NH.html
  *Search the USGS Geographic Names Database. You can limit the search to a specific county in this state and search for any of the following features: airport arch area arroyo bar basin bay beach bench bend bridge **building** canal cape **cemetery** channel **church** cliff crater crossing dam falls flat forest gap geyser glacier gut harbor hospital island isthmus lake lava levee locale mine oilfield other park pillar plain ppl range rapids reserve reservoir ridge **school** sea slope spring stream summit swamp tower trail tunnel valley well woods.*

◆ Military

- 2nd NH Light Company Home Page
  http://www.ccs.neu.edu/home/bcortez/revwar/usa/ctl/02lnh/02lnh.html

- 5th Regiment New Hampshire Volunteers
  http://www.mv.com/ipusers/n33db/fifth.html

- The Civil War Archive—Union Regiments—New Hampshire
  http://www.civilwararchive.com/unionnh.htm

- Korean Conflict State-Level Casualty Lists—New Hampshire
  http://www.nara.gov/nara/electronic/nhhrlist.html
  From the National Archives and Records Administration, Center for Electronic Records.

- Seventh New Hampshire Infantry
  http://extlab1.entnem.ufl.edu/olustee/7th_NH_inf.html

- Vietnam Conflict State-Level Casualty Lists—New Hampshire
  http://www.nara.gov/nara/electronic/nhhrviet.html
  From the National Archives and Records Administration, Center for Electronic Records.

- The Vietnam Veterans Memorial—New Hampshire
  http://grunt.space.swri.edu/statewall/nhamp/nh.htm

◆ Newspapers

- AJR NewsLink—New Hampshire Newspapers
  http://www.newslink.org/nhnews.html

- E&P Media Info Links—Newspaper Sites in New Hampshire
  http://www.mediainfo.com/emedia/browse-results.htm?region=newhampshire&category=newspaper+++++++++

- Ecola Newsstand: New Hampshire
  http://www.ecola.com/news/press/na/us/nh/

- NAA Hotlinks to Newspapers Online—New Hampshire
  http://www.naa.org/hotlinks/searchResult.asp?param=NH-New+Hampshire&City=1

- N-Net—New Hampshire Newspapers
  http://www.n-net.com/nh.htm

- The Ultimate Collection of News Links: USA—New Hampshire
  http://www.pppp.net/links/news/USA-NH.html

- Yahoo!...Newspapers...New Hampshire
  http://dir.yahoo.com/News_and_Media/Newspapers/Browse_By_Region/U_S__States/New_Hampshire/

◆ People & Families

- Directory of Underground Railroad Operators—New Hampshire
  http://www.ugrr.org//names/map-nh.htm

- The Irish in 19th-century Portsmouth, New Hampshire
  http://www.geocities.com/CollegePark/9887/ports.html

- Tribes and Villages of New Hampshire
  http://hanksville.phast.umass.edu:8000/cultprop/contacts/tribal/NH.html

- WPA Life Histories from New Hampshire
  http://lcweb2.loc.gov/ammem/wpaintro/nhcat.html
  Manuscripts from the Federal Writer's Project, 1936–1940, Library of Congress.

◆ Professional Researchers, Volunteers & Other Research Services

- Board for Certification of Genealogists—Roster of Those Certified—Specializing in New Hampshire
  http://www.genealogy.org/~bcg/rosts_nh.html

- Genealogy Helplist—New Hampshire
  http://www.calarts.edu/~karynw/helplist/nh.html

- Library Stacks—An Historical Research and
Reference Service
http://members.aol.com/libstacks/libstacks.html
*Centered in the Boston area, Library Stacks is a professional
service which provides research and reference assistance to
antique dealers, attorneys, authors, booksellers, curators, family
historians, genealogists, graduate students and historians whose
genealogical and historical interests lie within the New England
states.*

- The Official Iowa Counties Professional Genealogist
and Researcher's Registry for New Hampshire
http://www.iowa-counties.com/gene/nh.htm

◆ Publications, Software & Supplies

- AncestorSpy—CDs and Microfiche for
New Hampshire
http://www.ancestorspy.com/nh.htm

- Barbara Green's Used Genealogy Books—
New Hampshire
http://home.earthlink.net/~genbooks/lochist.html#NH

- Barnette's Family Tree Books—New Hampshire
http://www.barnettesbooks.com/new-hamp.htm

- Books We Own—New Hampshire
http://www.rootsweb.com/~bwo/nhamp.html

- Boyd Publishing Company—New England
http://www.hom.net/~gac/newengla.htm

- Essex Books—New England
http://www.HERTGE.COM/essex/neweng.htm

- Frontier Press Bookstore—New Hampshire
http://www.frontierpress.com/frontier.cgi?category=nh

- GenealogyBookShop.com—New Hampshire
http://www.genealogybookshop.com/genealogybookshop/files/
The_United_States,New_Hampshire/index.html
*The online store of Genealogical Publishing Co., Inc. &
Clearfield Company.*

- Hearthstone Bookshop—New Hampshire
http://www.hearthstonebooks.com/cgi-bin/webc.cgi/st_main.
html?catid=90&sid=2PH5t29sm

- Heritage Books—New Hampshire
http://www.heritagebooks.com/nh.htm

- Heritage Quest—Microfilm Records for the
State of New Hampshire
http://www.heritagequest.com/genealogy/microfilm/
new_hampshire/

- Lost in Time Books—New Hampshire
http://www.lostintime.com/catalog/books/bookst/bo20000.htm

- The Memorabilia Corner—Books: New Hampshire
http://members.aol.com/TMCorner/book_nh.htm

- Picton Press—New Hampshire
http://www.midcoast.com/~picton/public_html.BASK/catalog/
state_nh.htm

- Willow Bend Bookstore—New Hampshire
http://www.willowbend.net/nh.htm

◆ Queries, Message Boards & Surname Lists

- GenConnect New Hampshire Visitor Center
http://cgi.rootsweb.com/~genbbs/indx/NH.html
*A system for posting queries, Bibles, biographies, deeds,
obituaries, pensions, wills.*

- New England Connections Query Archive
http://www.geocities.com/Heartland/5274/nequery.htm

◆ Records: Census, Cemeteries, Land, Obituaries, Personal, Taxes and Vital (Born, Married, Died & Buried)

- The 1790–1890 Federal Population Censuses:
Catalog of National Archives Microfilm
http://www.genealogy.org/census/contents.shtml
  - Census Schedules and Microfilm Roll Numbers
for New Hampshire:
    1790
    http://www.genealogy.org/census/1790.html
    1800
    http://www.genealogy.org/census/1800_schedules/
New.Hampshire.html
    1810
    http://www.genealogy.org/census/1810_schedules/
New.Hampshire.html
    1820
    http://www.genealogy.org/census/1820_schedules/
New.Hampshire.html
    1830
    http://www.genealogy.org/census/1830_schedules/
New.Hampshire.html
    1840
    http://www.genealogy.org/census/1840_schedules/
New.Hampshire.html
    1850
    http://www.genealogy.org/census/1850_schedules/
New.Hampshire.html
    1860
    http://www.genealogy.org/census/1860_schedules/
New.Hampshire.html
    1870
    http://www.genealogy.org/census/1870_schedules/
New.Hampshire.html
    1880
    http://www.genealogy.org/census/1880_schedules/
New.Hampshire.html

1880 Soundex
http://www.genealogy.org/census/1880.sdx_schedules/
T762.html

1890 Special Schedules
http://www.genealogy.org/census/1890-special_schedules/
New.Hampshire.html

● Cemeteries of the United States—New Hampshire
Cemeteries—County Index
http://www.gac.edu/~kengelha/uscemeteries/
newhampshire.html

● Cemetery Records of Hampton, New Hampshire
http://www.hampton.lib.nh.us/hampton/graves/graves.htm

● Census Online—Links to Census Sites on the Web—
New Hampshire
http://www.census-online.com/links/NH_data.html

● County Courthouse Addresses
http://www.familytreemaker.com/00000258.html

● Find-A-Grave by Location: New Hampshire
http://www.findagrave.com/grave/lnh.html
Graves of noteworthy people.

● Interment.net: New Hampshire Cemeteries
http://www.interment.net/us/nh/index.htm
A list of links to other sites.

● National Archives-Northeast Region (Boston)
http://www.nara.gov/regional/boston.html

● National Archives—New England Region
http://www.familytreemaker.com/00000098.html
*Records for Connecticut, Maine, Massachusetts, New
Hampshire, Rhode Island, and Vermont.*

● New Hampshire Vital Records Information
http://vitalrec.com/nh.html

● The Political Graveyard—Cemeteries in
New Hampshire
http://politicalgraveyard.com/geo/NH/kmindex.html

● Preplanning Network—Funeral Home and
Cemetery Directory—New Hampshire
http://www.preplannet.com/newhamp.htm

● USGenWeb Census Project New Hampshire
http://www.usgenweb.org/census/states/newhamps.htm

● USGenWeb Tombstone Transcription Project—
New Hampshire
http://www.rootsweb.com/~cemetery/newhamp.html

● VitalChek Network—New Hampshire
http://www.vitalchek.com/stateselect.asp?state=NH

● Where to Write for Vital Records—New Hampshire
http://www.cdc.gov/nchswww/howto/w2w/newhamp.htm
From the National Center for Health Statistics (NCHS).

◆ Religion & Churches

● Christianity.Net Church Locator—New Hampshire
http://www.christianity.net/cgi/
location.exe?United_States+New_Hampshire

● Church Online!—New Hampshire
http://www.churchonline.com/usas/nh/nh.html

● Church Profiles—New Hampshire
http://www.church-profiles.com/nh/nh.html

● Churches dot Net—Global Church Web Pages—
New Hampshire
http://www.churches.net/churches/nhampshi.html

● Churches of the World—New Hampshire
http://www.churchsurf.com/churches/New_Hampshire/
index.htm
From the ChurchSurf Christian Directory.

◆ Societies & Groups

● The American-Canadian Genealogical Society
http://ourworld.compuserve.com:80/homepages/ACGS/
homepage.htm
Leaders in French-Canadian Genealogical Research.

● Hampton Historical Society
http://www.nh.ultranet.com/~hhs/HHSHome.htm

● IOOF Lodge Website Directory—New Hampshire
http://norm28.hsc.usc.edu/IOOF/USA/New_Hampshire/
New_Hampshire.html
Independent Order of Odd Fellows and Rebekahs.

● New England Historic Genealogical Society
http://www.nehgs.org/

● New Hampshire Historical Society
http://www.nhhistory.org/

● New Hampshire Society of Genealogists
http://www.tiac.net/users/nhsog/

◆ USGenWeb Project

● New Hampshire Genealogy—USGenWeb Project
State Page
http://www.usgenweb.org/nh

● New Hampshire—USGenWeb Archives Table of
Contents
http://www.rootsweb.com/~usgenweb/nh/nhfiles.htm

● New Hampshire—USGenWeb FTP Archives
ftp://ftp.rootsweb.com/pub/usgenweb/nh

U.S.—NEW JERSEY—NJ

http://www.CyndisList.com/nj.htm

Category Index:

- General Resource Sites
- Government & Cities
- History & Culture
- Libraries, Archives & Museums
- Mailing Lists, Newsgroups & Chat
- Maps, Gazetteers & Geographical Information
- Military
- Newspapers
- People & Families

- Professional Researchers, Volunteers & Other Research Services
- Publications, Software & Supplies
- Queries, Message Boards & Surname Lists
- Records: Census, Cemeteries, Land, Obituaries, Personal, Taxes and Vital
- Religion & Churches
- Societies & Groups
- USGenWeb Project

◆ General Resource Sites

- The Big GEDCOM Related Areas—New Jersey Online Resources
  http://www.altlaw.com/edball/biged4.htm
  From the Descendants of Edward BALL of New Jersey— GEDCOM Repository Site.

- Everton's Sources of Genealogical Information in New Jersey
  http://www.everton.com/usa/nj.htm

- Family Tree Maker's Genealogy "How To" Guide— New Jersey
  http://www.familytreemaker.com/00000204.html

- Genealogy Exchange & Surname Registry— NJGenExchange
  http://www.genexchange.com/nj/index.cfm

- Genealogy Resources on the Internet: New Jersey
  http://www-personal.umich.edu/~cgaunt/nj.html

- Horseneck Founders of New Jersey
  http://www.rootsweb.com/~genepool/nj.htm

- Lineages' Genealogy Site: New Jersey
  http://www.lineages.com/rooms/usa/state.asp?StateCode=NJ

- Pat Wardell's Home Page
  http://maple.nis.net/~wardell/
  Including resources for Bergen County, NJ—History & Genealogy.

- ROOTS-L United States Resources: New Jersey
  http://www.rootsweb.com/roots-l/USA/nj.html
  Comprehensive list of research links, including many to history-related sites.

◆ Government & Cities

- 50states.com—New Jersey State Information Resource
  http://www.50states.com/newjerse.htm
  A list of general information for each state, including a list of colleges, state symbols, links to maps, newspapers, and other miscellaneous state information.

- Excite Travel by City.Net—New Jersey
  http://www.city.net/countries/united_states/new_jersey/

- Official City Web Sites for the State of New Jersey
  http://OfficialCitySites.org/New-Jersey.htm

- State of New Jersey
  http://www.state.nj.us/

- Virtual Newark, New Jersey
  http://www.castle.net/~glenng/newark/newark.htm
  Cemeteries, churches, newspapers, street names, throughout the history of Newark.

- Yahoo! Get Local...New Jersey Cities
  http://dir.yahoo.com/Regional/U_S__States/New_Jersey/Cities/
  Maps, yellow pages, white pages, newspapers and other local information.

- Yahoo! Get Local...New Jersey Counties and Regions
  http://dir.yahoo.com/Regional/U_S__States/New_Jersey/Counties_and_Regions/
  Maps, yellow pages, white pages, newspapers and other local information.

◆ History & Culture

- New Jersey History
  http://scils.rutgers.edu/~macan/nj.history.html
  An Electronic Gateway to Online Information Related to the History of New Jersey.

- Yahoo!...History...New Jersey
  http://dir.yahoo.com/Arts/Humanities/History/
  Browse_By_Region/U_S__States/New_Jersey/

◆ Libraries, Archives & Museums

- Atlantic City Free Public Library
  http://library.atlantic.city.lib.nj.us/

- Atlantic County Library System
  http://commlink.atlantic.county.lib.nj.us/aclshome.htm

- Bergenfield Free Public Library
  http://gramercy.ios.com/~beldlib/

- Bernards Township Library
  http://www.bernards.org/library/
  Basking Ridge, New Jersey

- Cherry Hill Family History Center
  http://www.cyberenet.net/~gsteiner/njgenweb/chnjfhc.txt

- Division of Archives and Records Management
  http://www.state.nj.us/state/darm/darm.html

- Family History Centers—New Jersey
  http://www.deseretbook.com/famhis/nj.html

- Family History Centers—New Jersey
  http://www.lib.byu.edu/~uvrfhc/centers/newjersey.html

- HYTELNET—Library Catalogs: USA: New Jersey
  http://library.usask.ca/hytelnet/usa/NJ.html
  *Before you use any of the Telnet links, make note of the user
  name, password and any other logon information.*

- The Joint Free Public Library of Morristown
  and Morris Township—Local History and
  Genealogy Department
  http://www.makcom.com/jfpl/gene.htm

- Monmouth County Historical Association Library
  & Archives
  http://www.cjrlc.org/~mchalib/
  - Genealogical Collections
    http://www.cjrlc.org/~mchalib/genealogy.html

- New Jersey Family History Centers
  http://www.genhomepage.com/FHC/New_Jersey.html
  *A list of addresses, phone numbers and hours of operation from
  the Genealogy Home Page.*

- New Jersey League of Historical Societies—
  Central Region, Libraries and Archives
  http://scils.rutgers.edu/~macan/njc5.html

- New Jersey League of Historical Societies—
  North Region, Libraries and Archives
  http://scils.rutgers.edu/~macan/njn5.html

- New Jersey State Library
  http://www.state.nj.us/statelibrary/
  - Genealogy and Local History Office
    http://www.state.nj.us/statelibrary/libgene.htm

- Newark Public Library
  http://www.npl.org/
  - Special Collections Division
    http://www.npl.org/Pages/Collections/
    specialcollections1.html

- NJ History—New Jersey Libraries
  http://scils.rutgers.edu/~macan/library.html

- NUCMC Listing of Archives and Manuscript
  Repositories in New Jersey
  http://lcweb.loc.gov/coll/nucmc/njsites.html
  *Links to information about resources other than those held in the
  Library of Congress.*

- Other Central New Jersey Family History Centers
  http://members.aol.com/DSSaari/prifhc.htm#Other

- Repositories of Primary Sources: New Jersey
  http://www.uidaho.edu/special-collections/east2.html#usnj
  *A list of links to online resources from the Univ. of Idaho
  Library, Special Collections and Archives.*

- Seton Hall University Libraries
  http://www.shu.edu/library/
  - Special Collections Center
    http://www.shu.edu/library/speccoll.htm

- Sussex County Libraries, Historical Societies,
  Museums, Historical Sites and Other Points of
  Interest
  http://www.rootsweb.com/~njsussex/library.htm

- The Unofficial Home Page of the Princeton
  Family History Center
  http://members.aol.com/dssaari/prifhc.htm

- webCATS: Library Catalogues on the World Wide
  Web—New Jersey
  http://library.usask.ca/hywebcat/states/NJ.html

◆ Mailing Lists, Newsgroups & Chat

- Genealogy Resources on the Internet—New Jersey
  Mailing Lists
  http://members.aol.com/gfsjohnf/gen_mail_states-nj.html
  *Each of the mailing list links below points to this site, wonder-
  fully maintained by John Fuller. Visit this site for county-specific
  mailing lists as well.*

- DUTCH-COLONIES Mailing List
  http://members.aol.com/gfsjohnf/gen_mail_states-nj.
  html#DUTCH-COLONIES
  *For the discussion of the New York and New Jersey Colonies,
  known as New Amsterdam.*

- MID-ATLANTIC-ROOTS-L Mailing List
  http://members.aol.com/gfsjohnf/gen_mail_states-nj.
  html#MID-ATLANTIC-ROOTS-L
  New Jersey, Maryland, Delaware, and the District of Columbia.

- NJ Mailing List
  http://members.aol.com/gfsjohnf/gen_mail_states-nj.html#NJ

◆ Maps, Gazetteers & Geographical Information

- 1895 U.S. Atlas—New Jersey
  http://www.LivGenMI.com/1895nj.htm

- American Memory Panoramic Maps 1847–1929—New Jersey
  http://lcweb2.loc.gov/cgi-bin/query/S?ammem/gmd:
  @filreq(@field(STATE+@band(new+jersey))+
  @field(COLLID+pmmap))
  From the Geography and Map Division, Library of Congress.

- American Memory Railroad Maps 1828–1900—New Jersey
  http://memory.loc.gov/cgi-bin/query/S?ammem/gmd:
  @filreq(@field(STATE+@band(new+jersey))+
  @field(COLLID+rrmap))
  From the Geography and Map Division, Library of Congress.

- Color Landform Atlas: New Jersey
  http://fermi.jhuapl.edu/states/nj_0.html
  Including a map of counties and a map for 1895.

- Excite Maps: New Jersey Maps
  http://www.city.net/maps/view/?mapurl=/countries/
  united_states/new_jersey
  Zoom in on these maps all the way to the street level.

- Gleason's Old Maps, Etc.
  http://members.aol.com/oldmapsetc/nj.html
  Photocopies of Old Maps, Prints and Articles of Historical and Genealogical Interest from New Jersey.

- HPI County InfoSystem—Counties in New Jersey
  http://www.com/hpi/njcty/index.html

- informus—City and County Cross Reference
  http://www.informus.com/njxref.html

- K.B. Slocum Books and Maps—New Jersey
  http://www.treasurenet.com/cgi-bin/treasure/kbslocum/scan/
  se=New.20Jersey/sf=mapstate

- List of New Jersey Counties
  http://www.genealogy.org/~st-clair/counties/state_nj.html

- Map of New Jersey Counties
  http://govinfo.kerr.orst.edu/gif/states/nj.gif
  From the Government Information Sharing Project, Information Services, Oregon State University.

- Map of New Jersey Counties
  http://www.lib.utexas.edu/Libs/PCL/Map_collection/states/
  New_Jersey.gif
  From the Perry-Castañeda Library at the Univ. of Texas at Austin.

- U.S. Census Bureau—New Jersey Profiles
  http://www.census.gov/datamap/www/34.html

- Yale Peabody Museum: GNIS—New Jersey
  http://www.peabody.yale.edu/other/gnis/NJ.html
  Search the USGS Geographic Names Database. You can limit the search to a specific county in this state and search for any of the following features: airport arch area arroyo bar basin bay beach bench bend bridge **building** *canal cape* **cemetery** *channel* **church** *cliff crater crossing dam falls flat forest gap geyser glacier gut harbor hospital island isthmus lake lava levee locale mine oilfield other park pillar plain ppl range rapids reserve reservoir ridge* **school** *sea slope spring stream summit swamp tower trail tunnel valley well woods.*

◆ Military

- 15th New Jersey Volunteer Infantry
  http://www.erols.com/jbeegle/15thform.html

- The Civil War Archive—Union Regiments—New Jersey
  http://www.civilwararchive.com/unionnj.htm

- Index to Militia Rolls—Olive Tree Genealogy
  http://www.rootsweb.com/~ote/indexmil.htm
  Rolls for New Jersey and New York.

- Korean Conflict State-Level Casualty Lists—New Jersey
  http://www.nara.gov/nara/electronic/njhrlist.html
  From the National Archives and Records Administration, Center for Electronic Records.

- Vietnam Conflict State-Level Casualty Lists—New Jersey
  http://www.nara.gov/nara/electronic/njhrviet.html
  From the National Archives and Records Administration, Center for Electronic Records.

- The Vietnam Veterans Memorial—New Jersey
  http://grunt.space.swri.edu/statewall/njersey/nj.htm

◆ Newspapers

- AJR NewsLink—New Jersey Newspapers
  http://www.newslink.org/njnews.html

- E&P Media Info Links—Newspaper Sites in New Jersey
  http://www.mediainfo.com/emedia/browse-results.
  htm?region=newjersey&category=newspaper+++++++++

- Ecola Newstand: New Jersey
  http://www.ecola.com/news/press/na/us/nj/

- NAA Hotlinks to Newspapers Online—New Jersey
  http://www.naa.org/hotlinks/searchResult.asp?param=
  NJ-New+Jersey&City=1

- N-Net—New Jersey Newspapers
  http://www.n-net.com/nj.htm

- The Ultimate Collection of News Links: USA—New Jersey
  http://www.pppp.net/links/news/USA-NJ.html

- Yahoo!...Newspapers...New Jersey
  http://dir.yahoo.com/News_and_Media/Newspapers/
  Browse_By_Region/U_S__States/New_Jersey/

◆ People & Families

- Directory of Underground Railroad Operators—
  New Jersey
  http://www.ugrr.org//names/map-nj.htm

- Tribes and Villages of New Jersey
  http://hanksville.phast.umass.edu:8000/cultprop/contacts/
  tribal/NJ.html

◆ Professional Researchers, Volunteers & Other Research Services

- Board for Certification of Genealogists—Roster of
  Those Certified—Specializing in New Jersey
  http://www.genealogy.org/~bcg/rosts_nj.html

- Genealogy Helplist—New Jersey
  http://www.cybercomm.net/~freddie/helplist/nj.htm

- James F. Justin Family Tree Research Services
  http://members.aol.com/jkjustin/gensrch.html
  *Geneology Research Service for New Jersey marriage records,
  birth records, death certificates, census returns, wills, court
  records and deeds also Philadelphia National Archives.*

- New Jersey and Italian Genealogical Research
  Services
  http://www.italgen.com/sponsors/piccirillo/index.htm

- New Jersey Genealogical Research Service
  http://www.njgrs.com/

- The Official Iowa Counties Professional Genealogist
  and Researcher's Registry for New Jersey
  http://www.iowa-counties.com/gene/nj.htm

◆ Publications, Software & Supplies

- AncestorSpy—CDs and Microfiche for New Jersey
  http://www.ancestorspy.com/nj.htm

- Barbara Green's Used Genealogy Books—
  New Jersey
  http://home.earthlink.net/~genbooks/lochist.html#NJ

- Barnette's Family Tree Books—New Jersey
  http://www.barnettesbooks.com/new-jers.htm

- Books We Own—New Jersey
  http://www.rootsweb.com/~bwo/nj.html

- Boyd Publishing Company—New Jersey
  http://www.hom.net/~gac/newjersy.htm

- Family Line Publications
  http://pages.prodigy.com/Strawn/family.htm
  *Books covering Delaware, Maryland, New Jersey, Pennsylvania,
  Virginia, and Washington DC.*

- Frontier Press Bookstore—New Jersey
  http://www.frontierpress.com/frontier.cgi?category=nj

- GenealogyBookShop.com—New Jersey
  http://www.genealogybookshop.com/genealogybookshop/files/
  The_United_States,New_Jersey/index.html
  *The online store of Genealogical Publishing Co., Inc. &
  Clearfield Company.*

- Hearthstone Bookshop—New Jersey
  http://www.hearthstonebooks.com/cgi-bin/webc.cgi/
  st_main.html?catid=91&sid=2PH5t29sm

- Heritage Books—New Jersey
  http://www.heritagebooks.com/nj.htm

- Heritage Quest—Microfilm Records for the
  State of New Jersey
  http://www.heritagequest.com/genealogy/microfilm/
  new_jersey/

- Lost in Time Books—New Jersey
  http://www.lostintime.com/catalog/books/bookst/bo21000.htm

- The Memorabilia Corner—Books: New Jersey
  http://members.aol.com/TMCorner/book_nj.htm

- Reminiscences of Montclair, New Jersey
  http://www.rootsweb.com/~genepool/montcl.htm
  *Written by Montclair, New Jersey Resident Philip Doremus
  in 1908.*

- Willow Bend Bookstore—New Jersey
  http://www.willowbend.net/nj.htm

◆ Queries, Message Boards & Surname Lists

- GenConnect New Jersey Visitor Center
  http://cgi.rootsweb.com/~genbbs/indx/NJ.html
  *A system for posting queries, Bibles, biographies, deeds,
  obituaries, pensions, wills.*

◆ Records: Census, Cemeteries, Land, Obituaries, Personal, Taxes and Vital (Born, Married, Died & Buried)

- The 1790–1890 Federal Population Censuses:
  Catalog of National Archives Microfilm
  http://www.genealogy.org/census/contents.shtml

  ○ Census Schedules and Microfilm Roll Numbers
    for New Jersey:
    1830
    http://www.genealogy.org/census/1830_schedules/
    New.Jersey.html
    1840
    http://www.genealogy.org/census/1840_schedules/
    New.Jersey.html
    1850
    http://www.genealogy.org/census/1850_schedules/
    New.Jersey.html

1860
http://www.genealogy.org/census/1860_schedules/
New.Jersey.html

1870
http://www.genealogy.org/census/1870_schedules/
New.Jersey.html

1880
http://www.genealogy.org/census/1880_schedules/
New.Jersey.html

1880 soundex
http://www.genealogy.org/census/1880.sdx_schedules/
T763.html

1890 Special Schedules
http://www.genealogy.org/census/1890-special_schedules/
New.Jersey.html

- 1830 Federal Census for Sussex County, NJ Township Index
http://www.gate.net/~pascalfl/1830twpx.html

- Cemeteries of the United States—New Jersey Cemeteries—County Index
http://www.gac.edu/~kengelha/uscemeteries/new_jersey.html

- Census Online—Links to Census Sites on the Web—New Jersey
http://www.census-online.com/links/NJ_data.html

- County Courthouse Addresses
http://www.familytreemaker.com/00000204.html

- Find-A-Grave by Location: New Jersey
http://www.findagrave.com/grave/lnj.html
Graves of noteworthy people.

- Interment.net: New Jersey Cemeteries
http://www.interment.net/us/nj/index.htm
A list of links to other sites.

- Nancy Pascal's Genealogy Page
http://www.gate.net/~pascalfl/
Researching Sussex Co., NJ and the surrounding area.

  o Sussex County Marriages
  http://www.gate.net/~pascalfl/marrndx.html

  o Sussex County, NJ Cemetery Indexes
  http://www.gate.net/~pascalfl/cemidx.html

  o Sussex County Taxlists
  http://www.gate.net/~pascalfl/taxindx.html

  o Sussex County Will Abstracts Index
  http://www.gate.net/~pascalfl/wlabsdex.html

- National Archives—Northeast Region (New York)
http://www.nara.gov/regional/newyork.html

- National Archives—Northeast Region
http://www.familytreemaker.com/00000099.html
Records for New Jersey, New York, Puerto Rico, and the Virgin Islands.

- New Jersey Vital Records Information
http://vitalrec.com/nj.html

- The Political Graveyard—Cemeteries in New Jersey
http://politicalgraveyard.com/geo/NJ/kmindex.html

- Preplanning Network—Funeral Home and Cemetery Directory—New Jersey
http://www.preplannet.com/njfhcem.htm

- USGenWeb Census Project New Jersey
http://www.usgenweb.org/census/states/newjerse.htm

- USGenWeb Tombstone Transcription Project—New Jersey
http://www.rootsweb.com/~cemetery/newjer.html

- VitalChek Network—New Jersey
http://www.vitalchek.com/stateselect.asp?state=NJ

- Where to Write for Vital Records—New Jersey
http://www.cdc.gov/nchswww/howto/w2w/newjers.htm
From the National Center for Health Statistics (NCHS).

◆ Religion & Churches

- Christianity.Net Church Locator—New Jersey
http://www.christianity.net/cgi/
location.exe?United_States+New_Jersey

- Church Online!—New Jersey
http://www.churchonline.com/usas/nj/nj.html

- Church Profiles—New Jersey
http://www.church-profiles.com/nj/nj.html

- Churches dot Net—Global Church Web Pages—New Jersey
http://www.churches.net/churches/njersey.html

- Churches of the World—New Jersey
http://www.churchsurf.com/churches/New_Jersey/index.htm
From the ChurchSurf Christian Directory.

◆ Societies & Groups

- Amateur Computer Group of New Jersey—Genealogy Special Interest Group
http://www.castle.net/~kb4cyc/gensig.html

- Burlington County Historical Society
http://bc.emanon.net/cgi-bin/burl/county_historical_society

- Camden County Historical Society
http://www.cyberenet.net/~gsteiner/cchs/

- Cape May County Historical and Genealogical Society
http://www.cyberenet.net/~gsteiner/njgenweb/capemay/cmhgs.html

- City of Burlington Historical Society
http://bc.emanon.net/cgi-bin/burl/city_historical_society

- Cranford Historical Society
http://www.bobdevlin.com/crhissoc.html

- Cumberland County Historical Society
http://www.rootsweb.com/~njcumber/cumbernj.html

- Genealogical & Historical Organizations in New Jersey
  http://www.cyberenet.net/~gsteiner/njgenweb/njgenorg.html
- Genealogical Society of the Westfields
  http://www.bobdevlin.com/wsgenlo.html
  Westfield, New Jersey
- Gloucester County Historical Society
  http://www.rootsweb.com/~njglouce/gchs/
- Grand Lodge of New Jersey Free and Accepted Masons
  http://members.aol.com/glofnj/index.htm
- Historical Society of Princeton
  http://princetonol.com/groups/histsoc/
- IOOF Lodge Website Directory—New Jersey
  http://norm28.hsc.usc.edu/IOOF/USA/New_Jersey/New_Jersey.html
  Independent Order of Odd Fellows and Rebekahs.
- The Jewish Historical Society of Central Jersey
  http://www.jewishgen.org/jhscj/
- League of Historical Societies of New Jersey
  http://scils.rutgers.edu/~macan/leaguelist.html
- Metuchen-Edison Historical Society
  http://www.jhalpin.com/metuchen/met-ed.htm
- Monmouth County Genealogy Society
  http://nj5.injersey.com/~kjshelly/mcgs.html
- Monmouth County Historical Association
  http://www.monmouth.com/~mcha/index.html
- Moorestown Historical Society
  http://www.moorestown.com/community/history/
- New Jersey League of Historical Societies—Central Region, Historical Societies and Associations
  http://scils.rutgers.edu/~macan/njc1.html
- New Jersey League of Historical Societies—Northern Region, Historical Societies and Associations
  http://scils.rutgers.edu/~macan/njn1.html

- New Jersey League of Historical Societies—Southern Region, Historical Societies and Associations
  http://scils.rutgers.edu/~macan/njs1.html
- New Jersey Midland Railroad Historical Society
  http://ourworld.compuserve.com/homepages/njmidland/
- New York, Susquehanna & Western Technical & Historical Society, Inc.
  http://www.americaninternet.com/nyswths/index.htm
- Plainsboro Historical Society
  http://www.plainsboro.com/historical/
- Rahway Historical Society
  http://www.drover.org/
- Salem County Historical Society
  http://www.salemcounty.com/historicalsociety/
- Sussex County Libraries, Historical Societies, Museums, Historical Sites and Other Points of Interest
  http://www.rootsweb.com/~njsussex/library.htm
- The Unofficial Home Page of the Central Jersey Genealogy Club
  http://members.aol.com/dssaari/cjgc.htm

◆ USGenWeb Project

- New Jersey Genealogy—USGenWeb Project State Page
  http://www.usgenweb.org/nj
- New Jersey—USGenWeb Archives Table of Contents
  http://www.rootsweb.com/~usgenweb/nj/njfiles.htm
- New Jersey—USGenWeb FTP Archives
  ftp://ftp.rootsweb.com/pub/usgenweb/nj/

U.S.—NEW MEXICO—NM
http://www.CyndisList.com/nm.htm

Category Index:

- General Resource Sites
- Government & Cities
- History & Culture
- Libraries, Archives & Museums
- Mailing Lists, Newsgroups & Chat
- Maps, Gazetteers & Geographical Information
- Military
- Newspapers
- People & Families

- Professional Researchers, Volunteers & Other Research Services
- Publications, Software & Supplies
- Queries, Message Boards & Surname Lists
- Records: Census, Cemeteries, Land, Obituaries, Personal, Taxes and Vital
- Religion & Churches
- Societies & Groups
- USGenWeb Project

◆ General Resource Sites

- Everton's Sources of Genealogical Information in New Mexico
  http://www.everton.com/usa/nm.htm
- Family Tree Maker's Genealogy "How To" Guide—New Mexico
  http://www.familytreemaker.com/00000205.html
- Genealogy Bulletin Boards for New Mexico
  http://www.genealogy.org/~gbbs/gblnm.html
- Genealogy Exchange & Surname Registry—NMGenExchange
  http://www.genexchange.com/nm/index.cfm
- Genealogy Resources on the Internet: New Mexico
  http://www-personal.umich.edu/~cgaunt/newmex.html
- Hispanic Genealogical Research Center of New Mexico
  http://www.hgrc-nm.org/
- LDS Research Outline for New Mexico
  http://www.everton.com/usa/nm-0832b.txt
- Lineages' Genealogy Site: New Mexico
  http://www.lineages.com/rooms/usa/state.asp?StateCode=NM
- ROOTS-L United States Resources: New Mexico
  http://www.rootsweb.com/roots-l/USA/nm.html
  Comprehensive list of research links, including many to history-related sites.

◆ Government & Cities

- 50states.com—New Mexico State Information Resource
  http://www.50states.com/newmexic.htm
  A list of general information for each state, including a list of colleges, state symbols, links to maps, newspapers, and other miscellaneous state information.
- Excite Travel by City.Net—New Mexico
  http://www.city.net/countries/united_states/new_mexico/
- Official City Web Sites for the State of New Mexico
  http://OfficialCitySites.org/New-Mexico.htm
- State of New Mexico Government Information
  http://www.state.nm.us/
- Yahoo! Get Local...New Mexico Cities
  http://dir.yahoo.com/Regional/U_S__States/New_Mexico/Cities/
  Maps, yellow pages, white pages, newspapers and other local information.
- Yahoo! Get Local...New Mexico Counties and Regions
  http://dir.yahoo.com/Regional/U_S__States/New_Mexico/Counties_and_Regions/
  Maps, yellow pages, white pages, newspapers and other local information.

◆ History & Culture

- Ghost Towns of New Mexico
  http://www.ghosttowns.com/states/nm/nm.html
- Mountain Men and the Fur Trade
  http://www.xmission.com/~drudy/amm.html
  Sources of the History of the Fur Trade in the Rocky Mountain West.

- Yahoo!...History...New Mexico
  http://dir.yahoo.com/Arts/Humanities/History/
  Browse_By_Region/U_S__States/New_Mexico/

◆ Libraries, Archives & Museums

- Family History Centers—New Mexico
  http://www.deseretbook.com/famhis/nm.html

- Family History Centers—New Mexico
  http://www.lib.byu.edu/~uvrfhc/centers/newmexico.html

- HYTELNET—Library Catalogs: USA: New Mexico
  http://library.usask.ca/hytelnet/usa/NM.html
  Before you use any of the Telnet links, make note of the user name, password and any other logon information.

- New Mexico Commission of Public Records
  http://www.state.nm.us/cpr/
  o Archives and Historical Services Division
    http://www.state.nm.us/cpr/ahsd_top.htm

- New Mexico Family History Centers
  http://www.genhomepage.com/FHC/New_Mexico.html
  A list of addresses, phone numbers and hours of operation from the Genealogy Home Page.

- New Mexico State Library
  http://www.stlib.state.nm.us/
  o Southwest Room
    http://www.stlib.state.nm.us/sw.rm-info/swrpage.html

- NUCMC Listing of Archives and Manuscript Repositories in New Mexico
  http://lcweb.loc.gov/coll/nucmc/nmsites.html
  Links to information about resources other than those held in the Library of Congress.

- Repositories of Primary Sources: New Mexico
  http://www.uidaho.edu/special-collections/west.html#usnm
  A list of links to online resources from the Univ. of Idaho Library, Special Collections and Archives.

- Rio Grande Valley Library System—Special Collections Branch
  http://www.cabq.gov/rgvls/specol.html
  Albuquerque. Strong in the areas of New Mexico and Hispanic genealogy.

- webCATS: Library Catalogues on the World Wide Web—New Mexico
  http://library.usask.ca/hywebcat/states/NM.html

◆ Mailing Lists, Newsgroups & Chat

- Genealogy Resources on the Internet—New Mexico Mailing Lists
  http://members.aol.com/gfsjohnf/gen_mail_states-nm.html
  Each of the mailing list links below points to this site, wonderfully maintained by John Fuller. Visit this site for county-specific mailing lists as well.

- WESTERN-ROOTS-L Mailing list
  http://members.aol.com/gfsjohnf/gen_mail_states-nm.html#WESTERN-ROOTS-L
  Washington, Oregon, Alaska, Idaho, Montana, Wyoming, California, Nevada, Hawaii, Colorado, Utah, Arizona, and New Mexico.

◆ Maps, Gazetteers & Geographical Information

- 1895 U.S. Atlas—New Mexico
  http://www.LivGenMI.com/1895nm.htm

- American Memory Panoramic Maps 1847–1929—New Mexico
  http://lcweb2.loc.gov/cgi-bin/query/S?ammem/gmd:@filreq(@field(STATE+@band(+new+mexico))+@field(COLLID+pmmap))
  From the Geography and Map Division, Library of Congress.

- American Memory Railroad Maps 1828–1900—New Mexico
  http://memory.loc.gov/cgi-bin/query/S?ammem/gmd:@filreq(@field(STATE+@band(+new+mexico))+@field(COLLID+rrmap))
  From the Geography and Map Division, Library of Congress.

- Color Landform Atlas: New Mexico
  http://fermi.jhuapl.edu/states/nm_0.html
  Including a map of counties and a map for 1895.

- Excite Maps: New Mexico Maps
  http://www.city.net/maps/view/?mapurl=/countries/united_states/new_mexico
  Zoom in on these maps all the way to the street level.

- HPI County InfoSystem—Counties in New Mexico
  http://www.com/hpi/nmcty/index.html

- K.B. Slocum Books and Maps—New Mexico
  http://www.treasurenet.com/cgi-bin/treasure/kbslocum/scan/se=New.20Mexico/sf=mapstate

- List of New Mexico Counties
  http://www.genealogy.org/~st-clair/counties/state_nm.html

- Map of New Mexico Counties
  http://govinfo.kerr.orst.edu/gif/states/nm.gif
  From the Government Information Sharing Project, Information Services, Oregon State University.

- Map of New Mexico Counties
  http://www.lib.utexas.edu/Libs/PCL/Map_collection/states/New_Mexico.gif
  From the Perry-Castañeda Library at the Univ. of Texas at Austin.

- U.S. Census Bureau—New Mexico Profiles
  http://www.census.gov/datamap/www/35.html

- Yale Peabody Museum: GNIS—New Mexico
  http://www.peabody.yale.edu/other/gnis/NM.html
  *Search the USGS Geographic Names Database. You can limit the search to a specific county in this state and search for any of the following features: airport arch area arroyo bar basin bay beach bench bend bridge **building** canal cape **cemetery** channel **church** cliff crater crossing dam falls flat forest gap geyser glacier gut harbor hospital island isthmus lake lava levee locale mine oilfield other park pillar plain ppl range rapids reserve reservoir ridge **school** sea slope spring stream summit swamp tower trail tunnel valley well woods.*

◆ Military

- The Civil War Archive—Union Regiments—
  New Mexico
  http://www.civilwararchive.com/unionnm.htm

- Civil War Battle Summaries by State—New Mexico
  http://www2.cr.nps.gov/abpp/battles/bystate.htm#nm

- Korean Conflict State-Level Casualty Lists—
  New Mexico
  http://www.nara.gov/nara/electronic/nmhrlist.html
  *From the National Archives and Records Administration,
  Center for Electronic Records.*

- Vietnam Conflict State-Level Casualty Lists—
  New Mexico
  http://www.nara.gov/nara/electronic/nmhrviet.html
  *From the National Archives and Records Administration,
  Center for Electronic Records.*

- The Vietnam Veterans Memorial—New Mexico
  http://grunt.space.swri.edu/statewall/nmex/nm.htm

◆ Newspapers

- AJR NewsLink—New Mexico Newspapers
  http://www.newslink.org/nmnews.html

- E&P Media Info Links—Newspaper Sites in
  New Mexico
  http://www.mediainfo.com/emedia/browse-results.
  htm?region=newmexico&category=newspaper+++++++++

- Ecola Newstand: New Mexico
  http://www.ecola.com/news/press/na/us/nm/

- NAA Hotlinks to Newspapers Online—New Mexico
  http://www.naa.org/hotlinks/searchResult.asp?param=NM-
  New+Mexico&City=1

- N-Net—New Mexico Newspapers
  http://www.n-net.com/nm.htm

- The Ultimate Collection of News Links: USA—
  New Mexico
  http://www.pppp.net/links/news/USA-NM.html

- Yahoo!...Newspapers...New Mexico
  http://dir.yahoo.com/News_and_Media/Newspapers/
  Browse_By_Region/U_S__States/New_Mexico/

◆ People & Families

- Tribes and Villages of New Mexico
  http://hanksville.phast.umass.edu:8000/cultprop/contacts/
  tribal/NM.html

- WPA Life Histories from New Mexico
  http://lcweb2.loc.gov/ammem/wpaintro/nmcat.html
  *Manuscripts from the Federal Writer's Project, 1936–1940,
  Library of Congress.*

◆ Professional Researchers, Volunteers & Other Research Services

- Board for Certification of Genealogists—Roster of
  Those Certified—Specializing in New Mexico
  http://www.genealogy.org/~bcg/rosts_nm.html

- Genealogy Helplist—New Mexico
  http://posom.com/hl/usa/nm.shtml

- The Official Iowa Counties Professional Genealogist
  and Researcher's Registry for New Mexico
  http://www.iowa-counties.com/gene/nm.htm

◆ Publications, Software & Supplies

- Barbara Green's Used Genealogy Books—New
  Mexico
  http://home.earthlink.net/~genbooks/lochist.html#NM

- Frontier Press Bookstore—New Mexico
  http://www.frontierpress.com/frontier.cgi?category=nm

- Heritage Quest—Microfilm Records for the State of
  New Mexico
  http://www.heritagequest.com/genealogy/microfilm/
  new_mexico/

- The Memorabilia Corner—Books: New Mexico
  http://members.aol.com/TMCorner/book_nm.htm

- The New Mexico Chronicles
  http://www.ccvp.com/swhist/chronicl.html

◆ Queries, Message Boards & Surname Lists

- GenConnect New Mexico Visitor Center
  http://cgi.rootsweb.com/~genbbs/indx/NM.html
  *A system for posting queries, Bibles, biographies, deeds,
  obituaries, pensions, wills.*

◆ Records: Census, Cemeteries, Land, Obituaries, Personal, Taxes and Vital (Born, Married, Died & Buried)

- The 1790–1890 Federal Population Censuses:
  Catalog of National Archives Microfilm
  http://www.genealogy.org/census/contents.shtml
  ○ Census Schedules and Microfilm Roll Numbers
    for New Mexico:
    1850
    http://www.genealogy.org/census/1850_schedules/
    New.Mexico.html
    1860
    http://www.genealogy.org/census/1860_schedules/
    New.Mexico.html

1870
http://www.genealogy.org/census/1870_schedules/
New.Mexico.html

1880
http://www.genealogy.org/census/1880_schedules/
New.Mexico.html

1880 soundex
http://www.genealogy.org/census/1880.sdx_schedules/
T764.html

1890 Special Schedules
http://www.genealogy.org/census/1890-special_schedules/
New.Mexico.html

- BLM—New Mexico's Electronic Reading Room
  http://www.blm.gov/nhp/efoia/nm/
  United States Bureau of Land Management.

- Cloverdale Cemetery
  http://www.rootsweb.com/~nmhidalg/cloverdale.html
  Hidalgo County, New Mexico

- County Courthouse Addresses
  http://www.familytreemaker.com/00000260.html

- Find-A-Grave by Location: New Mexico
  http://www.findagrave.com/grave/lnm.html
  Graves of noteworthy people.

- Interment.net: New Mexico Cemeteries
  http://www.interment.net/us/nm/index.htm
  A list of links to other sites.

- The Middle Animas Cemetery
  http://www.rootsweb.com/~nmhidalg/manimas.html
  Animas, Hidalgo County, New Mexico

- National Archives—Rocky Mountain Region
  (Denver)
  http://www.nara.gov/regional/denver.html

- National Archives—Rocky Mountain Region
  http://www.familytreemaker.com/00000103.html
  Records for Colorado, Montana, North Dakota, South Dakota, Utah, Wyoming, and a portion of New Mexico.

- National Archives—Southwest Region (Fort Worth)
  http://www.nara.gov/regional/ftworth.html

- National Archives—Southwest Region
  http://www.familytreemaker.com/00000105.html
  Records for Arkansas, Louisiana, Oklahoma, Texas, and a portion of New Mexico.

- New Mexico Vital Records Information
  http://vitalrec.com/nm.html

- The Political Graveyard—Cemeteries in New Mexico
  http://politicalgraveyard.com/geo/NM/kmindex.html

- Preplanning Network—Funeral Home and Cemetery Directory—New Mexico
  http://www.preplannet.com/usafh.htm#New Mexico

- The Rodeo Cemetery
  http://www.rootsweb.com/~nmhidalg/rodeocem.html
  Rodeo, Hidalgo County, New Mexico

- USGenWeb Census Project New Mexico
  http://www.usgenweb.org/census/states/newmexic.htm

- USGenWeb Tombstone Transcription Project—New Mexico
  http://www.rootsweb.com/~cemetery/newmex.html

- VitalChek Network—New Mexico
  http://www.vitalchek.com/stateselect.asp?state=NM

- Where to Write for Vital Records—New Mexico
  http://www.cdc.gov/nchswww/howto/w2w/newmexic.htm
  From the National Center for Health Statistics (NCHS).

◆ Religion & Churches

- Christianity.Net Church Locator—New Mexico
  http://www.christianity.net/cgi/location.exe?
  United_States+New_Mexico

- Church Online!—New Mexico
  http://www.churchonline.com/usas/nm/nm.html

- Church Profiles—New Mexico
  http://www.church-profiles.com/nm/nm.html

- Churches dot Net—Global Church Web Pages—New Mexico
  http://www.churches.net/churches/nmexico.html

- Churches of the World—New Mexico
  http://www.churchsurf.com/churches/New_Mexico/index.htm
  From the ChurchSurf Christian Directory.

◆ Societies & Groups

- Grand Lodge of New Mexico Ancient Free & Accepted Masons
  http://204.134.124.1:80/leon/gl.htm

- IOOF Lodge Website Directory—New Mexico
  http://norm28.hsc.usc.edu/IOOF/USA/New_Mexico/
  New_Mexico.html
  Independent Order of Odd Fellows and Rebekahs.

- New Mexico Genealogical Society
  http://www.nmgs.org/
  Albuquerque

- Southern New Mexico Genealogical Society
  http://www.zianet.com/wheelerwc/GenSSNM/
  Lists of local cemeteries by county.

◆ USGenWeb Project

- New Mexico Genealogy—USGenWeb Project State Page
  http://www.usgenweb.org/nm

- New Mexico—USGenWeb Archives Table of Contents
  http://www.rootsweb.com/~usgenweb/nm/nmfiles.htm

- New Mexico—USGenWeb FTP Archives
  ftp://ftp.rootsweb.com/pub/usgenweb/nm/

U.S.—NEW YORK—NY
http://www.CyndisList.com/ny.htm

Category Index:

- General Resource Sites
- Government & Cities
- History & Culture
- Libraries, Archives & Museums
- Locality Specific
- Mailing Lists, Newsgroups & Chat
- Maps, Gazetteers & Geographical Information
- Military
- Newspapers
- People & Families

- Professional Researchers, Volunteers & Other Research Services
- Publications, Software & Supplies
- Queries, Message Boards & Surname Lists
- Records: Census, Cemeteries, Land, Obituaries, Personal, Taxes and Vital
- Religion & Churches
- Societies & Groups
- USGenWeb Project

◆ General Resource Sites

- Calendar of Events in NY State
  http://www.rootsweb.com/~nygenweb/gencal.htm
- Chris Andrle's New York State Genealogy Internet Resources
  http://www.localnet.com/~andrle/nysres.htm
- Everton's Sources of Genealogical Information in New York
  http://www.everton.com/usa/ny.htm
- Family Tree Maker's Genealogy "How To" Guide—New York
  http://www.familytreemaker.com/00000206.html
- Genealogy Bulletin Board Systems for New York
  http://www.genealogy.org/~gbbs/gblny.html
- Genealogy Exchange & Surname Registry—NYGenExchange
  http://www.genexchange.com/ny/index.cfm
- Genealogy Resources on the Internet: New York
  http://www-personal.umich.edu/~cgaunt/newyork.html
- Lineages' Genealogy Site: New York
  http://www.lineages.com/rooms/usa/state.asp?StateCode=NY
- New York State Governors
  http://www.rootsweb.com/~nygenweb/governors.htm
- ROOTS-L United States Resources: New York
  http://www.rootsweb.com/roots-l/USA/ny.html
  Extensive listing of articles & links for this state.

◆ Government & Cities

- 50states.com—New York State Information Resource
  http://www.50states.com/newyork.htm
  A list of general information for each state, including a list of colleges, state symbols, links to maps, newspapers, and other miscellaneous state information.
- Capital Region Communities
  http://www.crisny.org/communities/capreg.commun.html
  Including County, City, Town and Village level information for Albany, Rensselaer, Saratoga and Schenectady counties.
- Excite Travel by City.Net—New York
  http://www.city.net/countries/united_states/new_york/
- Government in New York State
  http://www.crisny.org/government/gov.ny.html
- New York State Government Information Locator Service
  http://www.nysl.nysed.gov/ils/
- New York State Governors
  http://www.rootsweb.com/~nygenweb/governors.htm
- Official City Web Sites for the State of New York
  http://OfficialCitySites.org/New-York.htm
- Yahoo! Get Local...New York Cities
  http://dir.yahoo.com/Regional/U_S__States/New_York/Cities/
  Maps, yellow pages, white pages, newspapers and other local information.
- Yahoo! Get Local...New York Counties and Regions
  http://dir.yahoo.com/Regional/U_S__States/New_York/Counties_and_Regions/
  Maps, yellow pages, white pages, newspapers and other local information.

◆ History & Culture

- The American Immigrant Wall of Honor
  http://www.wallofhonor.com/
  Ellis Island

- The Ellis Island Home Page
  http://www.ellisisland.org/

- Ellis Island—Through America's Gateway
  http://www.i-channel.com/features/ellis/

- History of the Erie Canal
  http://www.history.rochester.edu/canal/

- New Netherland Project
  http://www.nnp.org/
  A project to complete the transcription, translation, and publication of all Dutch documents in New York repositories relating to the seventeenth-century colony of New Netherland.

- New York, NY, Ellis Island—Immigration: 1900–1920
  http://cmp1.ucr.edu/exhibitions/immigration_id.html
  University of California, Riverside, Keystone-Mast Collection, California Museum of Photography. Photographs of immigrants, ships & Ellis Island.

- Old Fort Niagara
  http://www.oldfortniagara.org/
  Youngstown, NY

- Our Firemen, A History of the New York Fire Departments
  http://members.aol.com/dcbreton2/FDNY/FDNY_Notes.html
  Includes an every-name index.

- Yahoo!...History...New York
  http://dir.yahoo.com/Arts/Humanities/History/
  Browse_By_Region/U_S__States/New_York/

◆ Libraries, Archives & Museums

- Albany County Hall of Records Homepage
  http://www.albanycounty.com/achor/

- Columbia County History: On-Line Historical Archives
  http://apocalypse.berkshire.net/OnlineArchives/columbia/

- Family History Centers—New York
  http://www.deseretbook.com/famhis/ny.html

- Family History Centers—New York
  http://www.lib.byu.edu/~uvrfhc/centers/newyork.html

- HYTELNET—Library Catalogs: USA: New York
  http://library.usask.ca/hytelnet/usa/NY.html
  Before you use any of the Telnet links, make note of the user name, password and any other logon information.

- Library Resources in the Capital District
  http://www.crisny.org/libraries/lib.capreg.html

- The Military History Collections of the New York Public Library
  http://www.nypl.org/research/chss/subguides/milhist/home.html

- New York Family History Centers
  http://www.genhomepage.com/FHC/New_York.html
  A list of addresses, phone numbers and hours of operation from the Genealogy Home Page.

- New York Public Library
  http://www.nypl.org/
  - CATNYP: The Research Libraries' Catalogs
    http://catnyp.nypl.org/
  - New York Public Library—Center for the Humanities
    http://www.nypl.org/research/chss/chss.html
    - NYPL Center for the Humanities—Genealogical Research at the New York Public Library
      http://www.nypl.org/research/chss/lhg/research.html
    - NYPL Center for the Humanities— Map Division
      http://www.nypl.org/research/chss/map/map.html
    - NYPL Center for the Humanities— Research Guides
      http://www.nypl.org/research/chss/grd/resguides/rglist.html
    - NYPL Center for the Humanities—U.S. History, Local History & Genealogy Division
      http://www.nypl.org/research/chss/lhg/genea.html

- New York State Archives and Records Administration Home Page
  http://www.sara.nysed.gov/
  - Genealogical Sources in the New York State Archives
    http://www.sara.nysed.gov/holding/fact/genea-fa.htm
    New York State Archives Information Leaflet #1.
  - Guide to Records in the New York State Archives
    http://www.sara.nysed.gov/pubs/guideabs.htm
  - State Archives On-Line Catalog
    http://www.sara.nysed.gov/holding/opac.htm

- New York State Library Home Page
  http://www.nysl.nysed.gov/
  - Collections and Research Services
    http://www.nysl.nysed.gov/collser.htm
  - New York State Library: Genealogy
    http://www.nysl.nysed.gov/gengen.htm
  - New York State Newspaper Project
    http://www.nysl.nysed.gov/nysnp/

- NUCMC Listing of Archives and Manuscript Repositories in New York
  http://lcweb.loc.gov/coll/nucmc/nysites.html
  Links to information about resources other than those held in the Library of Congress.

- The Ontario County Records and Archives Center
  http://raims.com/home.html

- Orchard Park FHC, Erie County, New York
  http://www.localnet.com/~andrle/erie/orchard_park/opfhc.htm
- Penfield Library—State University of New York at Oswego
  http://www.oswego.edu/library/
  - Special (Historical) Collections
    http://www.oswego.edu/library/speccoll.html
- Repositories of Primary Sources: New York
  http://www.uidaho.edu/special-collections/east2.html#usny
  A list of links to online resources from the Univ. of Idaho Library, Special Collections and Archives.
- Schenectady County Public Library
  http://www.scpl.org/
- webCATS: Library Catalogues on the World Wide Web—New York
  http://library.usask.ca/hywebcat/states/NY.html
- Westchester County Archives
  http://www.westchesterclerk.com/arcintro.html
- Williamsville FHC, Erie County, New York
  http://www.localnet.com/~andrle/erie/amherst/wmfhc.htm

◆ Locality Specific

- Also see the USGenWeb section for links to county-specific resources.
- Buffalo—History & Genealogy
  http://members.aol.com/Frombufalo/index.html
- Chenango County, New York, Genealogical Resources...
  http://ourworld.compuserve.com/homepages/Bob_the_Squid/chenango.htm
- JEFFCO Upstate New York Genealogical Research and the HOLDEN Surname
  http://www.ticnet.com/jeffco/
- My Bronx Home Page
  http://www.dc.net/steven/bronx/
- Oswego Genealogy
  http://www.oswego.com/roots.html
- Roots: The Buffalo, New York Genealogy Forum
  http://freenet.buffalo.edu/~roots
  A good starting point for genealogical research in the Buffalo & Western NY area, with a comprehensive collection of links for Buffalo.
- Tom Lynch's Northeastern NY Genealogy Home Page
  http://freenet.buffalo.edu/~ae487/
- Tri-County Genealogy Sites of Joyce M. Tice
  http://www.rootsweb.com/~srgp/jmtindex.htm
  Bradford and Tioga Counties in Pennsylvania and Chemung County in New York.

- Westchester County Genealogical Resources
  http://pages.prodigy.com/HFBK19A/wcgsrs01.htm
  From the Westchester County Genealogical Society.
- WNY Genealogy
  http://www.angelfire.com/ny/WNYSampson/wnygenealogy.html

◆ Mailing Lists, Newsgroups & Chat

- Genealogy Resources on the Internet—New York Mailing Lists
  http://members.aol.com/gfsjohnf/gen_mail_states-ny.html
  Each of the mailing list links below points to this site, wonderfully maintained by John Fuller. Visit this site for county-specific mailing lists as well.
- BronxRoots Mailing List
  http://happytogether.com/bronx/
- DUTCH-COLONIES Mailing List
  http://members.aol.com/gfsjohnf/gen_mail_states-ny.html#DUTCH-COLONIES
  For the discussion of the New York and New Jersey Colonies, known as New Amsterdam.
- Dutchess-co-ny Mailing List
  http://members.aol.com/gfsjohnf/gen_mail_states-ny.html#Dutchess-co-ny
- GEN-NYS-L Mailing List
  http://members.aol.com/gfsjohnf/gen_mail_states-ny.html#GEN-NYS-L
- GEN-NYS-L Mailing List Web Page
  http://www.rootsweb.com/~nozell/GEN-NYS-L/
  Including archives of past correspondence.
- JeffHistGen Mailing List
  http://members.aol.com/gfsjohnf/gen_mail_states-ny.html#JeffHistGen
  For anyone with a genealogical or historical interest in Jefferson County, New York and the surrounding areas.
- LI-Rooters Mailing List
  http://members.aol.com/gfsjohnf/gen_mail_states-ny.html#LI-Rooters
  For anyone who has an interest in the four counties making up Long Island, New York; Kings (Brooklyn), Queens, Nassau, and Suffolk Counties.
- NewYork-ROOTS-L Mailing List
  http://members.aol.com/gfsjohnf/gen_mail_states-ny.html#NewYork-ROOTS
- NYFingerLakes Mailing List
  http://members.aol.com/gfsjohnf/gen_mail_states-ny.html#NYFingerLakes
  For anyone with a genealogical interest in the Finger Lakes counties of Cayuga, Livingston, Ontario, Schuyler, Seneca, Tompkins, Wayne and Yates in the state of New York.
- NYHIST-L
  http://members.aol.com/gfsjohnf/gen_mail_states-ny.html#NYHIST-L
  An edited discussion list provided by the New York State Archives and Records Administration as a forum for announcements, discussion, and research inquiries and referrals focused exclusively on New York State history including political, social, military, legal, and religious history.

- NY-Military Mailing List
  http://members.aol.com/gfsjohnf/gen_mail_states-ny.
  html#NY-Military
  For anyone who is researching New York ancestors who served in the military in any place and at any time.

- NYRichmond-Rooters Mailing List
  http://members.aol.com/gfsjohnf/gen_mail_states-ny.
  html#NYRichmond-Rooters
  For anyone with a historic or genealogical interest in Richmond County, New York (includes Staten Island).

- SULLCOUNTY Mailing List—Sullivan County
  http://members.aol.com/gfsjohnf/gen_mail_states-ny.
  html#SULLCOUNTY

◆ Maps, Gazetteers & Geographical Information

- 1895 U.S. Atlas—New York
  http://www.LivGenMI.com/1895ny.htm

- American Memory Panoramic Maps 1847–1929—New York
  http://lcweb2.loc.gov/cgi-bin/query/S?ammem/gmd:
  @filreq(@field(STATE+@band(new+york))+@field(COLLID+pmmap))
  From the Geography and Map Division, Library of Congress.

- American Memory Railroad Maps 1828–1900—New York
  http://memory.loc.gov/cgi-bin/query/S?ammem/gmd:
  @filreq(@field(STATE+@band(new+york))+@field(COLLID+rrmap))
  From the Geography and Map Division, Library of Congress.

- Color Landform Atlas: New York
  http://fermi.jhuapl.edu/states/ny_0.html
  Including a map of counties and a map for 1895.

- Excite Maps: New York Maps
  http://www.city.net/maps/view/?mapurl=/countries/
  united_states/new_york
  Zoom in on these maps all the way to the street level.

- HPI County InfoSystem—Counties in New York
  http://www.com/hpi/nycty/index.html

- K.B. Slocum Books and Maps—New York
  http://www.treasurenet.com/cgi-bin/treasure/kbslocum/scan/
  se=New.20York/sf=mapstate

- List of New York Counties
  http://www.genealogy.org/~st-clair/counties/state_ny.html

- Map of New York Counties
  http://govinfo.kerr.orst.edu/gif/states/ny.gif
  From the Government Information Sharing Project, Information Services, Oregon State University.

- Map of New York Counties
  http://www.lib.utexas.edu/Libs/PCL/Map_collection/states/
  New_York.gif
  From the Perry-Castañeda Library at the Univ. of Texas at Austin.

- New York State Historical Maps
  http://www.sunysb.edu/libmap/nymaps.htm

- Old Maps of New England (Maine, New Hampshire, Vermont, Connecticut, Rhode Island, Massachusetts) and New York
  http://members.aol.com/oldmapsne/index.html

- U.S. Census Bureau—New York Profiles
  http://www.census.gov/datamap/www/36.html

- Yale Peabody Museum: GNIS—New York
  http://www.peabody.yale.edu/other/gnis/NY.html
  Search the USGS Geographic Names Database. You can limit the search to a specific county in this state and search for any of the following features: airport arch area arroyo bar basin bay beach bench bend bridge **building** *canal cape* **cemetery** *channel* **church** *cliff crater crossing dam falls flat forest gap geyser glacier gut harbor hospital island isthmus lake lava levee locale mine oilfield other park pillar plain ppl range rapids reserve reservoir ridge* **school** *sea slope spring stream summit swamp tower trail tunnel valley well woods.*

◆ Military

- The 5th New York Volunteer Infantry—"Duryee's Zouaves"
  http://www.zouave.org/

- 12th New York Cavalry
  http://snycorva.cortland.edu/~woosterk/12cav.html

- 39th Regiment of New York Infantry—"Garibaldi Guard"
  http://hebron.ee.gannon.edu/~frezza/39NYSV/RegHist.html

- The 72nd New York Volunteer Infantry
  http://home.inreach.com/mavgw/72nd.htm

- 112th New York Infantry—The Chautauqua Regiment
  http://home.earthlink.net/~cwashburn/112th_ny.html

- 115th NY Volunteer Infantry
  http://www.rootsweb.com/~nyherkim/general115.html

- Buffalo's 19th Century Army Barracks and the Towpath to Weedsport
  http://army.barracks.buffalonet.org/

- The Civil War Archive—Union Regiments—New York
  http://www.civilwararchive.com/unionny.htm

- Civil War Medal of Honor Recipients from New York
  http://www.rootsweb.com/~nygenweb/civwarmoh.htm

- Civil War New York 21st Volunteers
  http://www.surfer-net.com/lbeilein/civil.htm

- Company I, 111th NYS Volunteer Infantry Regiment 1862
  http://www.ultranet.com/~smack/111th.html

- Fourteenth Brooklyn New York State Militia, "Red Legged Devils"
  http://www.mncs.k12.mn.us/~14nysm/

- Index To Militia Rolls—Olive Tree Genealogy
  http://www.rootsweb.com/~ote/indexmil.htm
  Rolls for New Jersey and New York.
- Korean Conflict State-Level Casualty Lists—New York
  http://www.nara.gov/nara/electronic/nyhrlist.html
  From the National Archives and Records Administration, Center for Electronic Records.
- New York 2nd Regiment Veteran Cavalry—"Empire Light Cavalry"
  http://www.geocities.com/Heartland/2101/2dvetcav.html
- New York State and the Civil War
  http://www.snymor.edu/pages/library/local_history/sites/
- New York Volunteers 188th Regiment Co. A
  http://home.swbell.net/jcanders/index.html
- NY 16th Regiment Infantry Page
  http://www.geocities.com/Heartland/2101/16index.html
- Revolutionary Soldiers of Chautauqua County
  http://www.rootsweb.com/~nychauta/MILITARY/REVSOL.HTM
- Roster of Men joining the U.S. Army from Pitcher, Chenango County, New York in the Years 1861–1865
  http://www.frontiernet.net/~elburro/roster01.htm
- The Seventeenth New York Volunteer Infantry, Company B
  http://members.tripod.com/~bwhelply/17NYVI.html
- Vietnam Conflict State-Level Casualty Lists—New York
  http://www.nara.gov/nara/electronic/nyhrviet.html
  From the National Archives and Records Administration, Center for Electronic Records.
- The Vietnam Veterans Memorial—New York
  http://grunt.space.swri.edu/statewall/nyork/ny.htm
- WNY Genealogy—World War II Honor Roll
  http://members.tripod.com/~NSampson/ww2wny.html
- WNY Korean War
  http://www.freeyellow.com/members2/samdecker/KoreanWar.html
  A list of men and women from the Western NY area who gave their lives during the Korean War (1950–1953).
- WW I Honor Roll—Amherst, NY
  http://www.geocities.com/Heartland/Acres/4218/honor_roll.html

◆ Newspapers

- AJR NewsLink—New York Newspapers
  http://www.newslink.org/nynews.html
- E&P Media Info Links—Newspaper Sites in New York
  http://www.mediainfo.com/emedia/browse-results.htm?region=newyork&category=newspaper+++++++++

- Ecola Newstand: New York
  http://www.ecola.com/news/press/na/us/ny/
- The Independent
  http://www.indenews.com/
  Serving the Hudson Berkshire Corridor, New York.
- NAA Hotlinks to Newspapers Online—New York
  http://www.naa.org/hotlinks/searchResult.asp?param=NY-New+York&City=1
- New York State Newspaper Project
  http://www.nysl.nysed.gov/nysnp/
- The New York Times on the Web
  http://www.nytimes.com/
- Newsday.com—Long Island and Queens, NY
  http://www.newsday.com/
- N-Net—New York Newspapers
  http://www.n-net.com/ny.htm
- Recorder Online
  http://www.recordernews.com/
  Amsterdam, New York
- The Ultimate Collection of News Links: USA—New York
  http://www.pppp.net/links/news/USA-NY.html
- Westchester County Newspaper Collections
  http://pages.prodigy.com/HFBK19A/wcgsrs10.htm
- Yahoo!...Newspapers...New York
  http://dir.yahoo.com/News_and_Media/Newspapers/Browse_By_Region/U_S__States/New_York/

◆ People & Families

- Directory of Underground Railroad Operators—New York
  http://www.ugrr.org//names/map-ny.htm
- Tribes and Villages of New York
  http://hanksville.phast.umass.edu:8000/cultprop/contacts/tribal/NY.html
- WPA Life Histories from New York
  http://lcweb2.loc.gov/ammem/wpaintro/nycat.html
  Manuscripts from the Federal Writer's Project, 1936–1940, Library of Congress.

◆ Professional Researchers, Volunteers & Other Research Services

- Bill Madon—New York State Genealogy Research Services
  http://www.treesearch.com/treesearch.html
- Board for Certification of Genealogists—Roster of Those Certified—Specializing in New York
  http://www.genealogy.org/~bcg/rosts_ny.html

- Genealogy Helplist—New York
  http://www.cybercomm.net/~freddie/helplist/ny.htm
- The Official Iowa Counties Professional Genealogist and Researcher's Registry for New York
  http://www.iowa-counties.com/gene/ny.htm
- Richard M. Pope, Certified Genealogist
  http://w3.nai.net/~absuax/
  Specializing in: Connecticut, Massachusetts, New York City, Germany.
- Rural New York State Family Research
  http://www.newyorkstateresearch.com/
  Genealogical Services for Central, Western, and Northern New York.
- So Many Branches
  http://www.angelfire.com/biz/SoManyBranches/
  Western New York, Northern Pennsylvania, Michigan and Northern Ohio Genealogical Research.

◆ Publications, Software & Supplies

- AncestorSpy—CDs and Microfiche for New York
  http://www.ancestorspy.com/nycat.htm
- Barbara Green's Used Genealogy Books—New York
  http://home.earthlink.net/~genbooks/lochist.html#NY
- Barnette's Family Tree Books—New York
  http://www.barnettesbooks.com/new-york.htm
- Books We Own—New York
  http://www.rootsweb.com/~bwo/new_york.html
- Boyd Publishing Company—New York
  http://www.hom.net/~gac/newyork.htm
- Frontier Press Bookstore—New York
  http://www.frontierpress.com/frontier.cgi?category=ny
- GenealogyBookShop.com—New York
  http://www.genealogybookshop.com/genealogybookshop/files/The_United_States,New_York/index.html
  The online store of Genealogical Publishing Co., Inc. & Clearfield Company.
- Greene Genes: A Genealogical Quarterly About Greene County, New York
  For details send e-mail to Patricia Morrow at greene-genes@msn.com
- Hearthstone Bookshop—New York
  http://www.hearthstonebooks.com/cgi-bin/webc.cgi/st_main.html?catid=92&sid=2PH5t29sm
- Heritage Books—New York
  http://www.heritagebooks.com/ny.htm
- Heritage Quest—Microfilm Records for the State of New York
  http://www.heritagequest.com/genealogy/microfilm/new_york/
- Hope Farm Press & Bookshop
  http://www.hopefarm.com/
  New York State Regional History, Folklore, Nature, Military, Native American and Genealogy—Covering Western New York, Adirondacks, Hudson Valley, Catskill Mts & Finger Lakes.

- Kinship—"Genealogy Resources for Kith and Kin"
  http://www.kinshipny.com/
  Publishers of New York State Research Material.
- Lost in Time Books—New York
  http://www.lostintime.com/catalog/books/bookst/bo22000.htm
- The Memorabilia Corner—Books: New York
  http://members.aol.com/TMCorner/book_ny.htm
- Picton Press—New York
  http://www.midcoast.com/~picton/public_html.BASK/catalog/state_ny.htm
- S-K Publications—New York 1850 Census Books
  http://www.skpub.com/genie/census/ny/
- The Sleeper Co.: Genealogy Books on Washington Co., NY
  http://www.sleeperco.com/
- Willow Bend Bookstore—New York
  http://www.willowbend.net/ny.htm

◆ Queries, Message Boards & Surname Lists

- 17th Century Immigrants to New York Registry
  http://www.rootsweb.com/~ote/dnybook.htm
- GenConnect New York Visitor Center
  http://cgi.rootsweb.com/~genbbs/indx/NY.html
  A system for posting queries, Bibles, biographies, deeds, obituaries, pensions, wills.
- JEFFCO—New York Genealogical Posts
  http://www.ticnet.com/jeffco/nyposts/nyposts.html
- New York State Queries
  http://www.cet.com/~weidnerc/newyork.html
- Queries for Monroe Co., NY
  http://home.eznet.net/~halsey/monroe/query.htm

◆ Records: Census, Cemeteries, Land, Obituaries, Personal, Taxes and Vital (Born, Married, Died & Buried)

- The 1790–1890 Federal Population Censuses: Catalog of National Archives Microfilm
  http://www.genealogy.org/census/contents.shtml
  - Census Schedules and Microfilm Roll Numbers for New York:
    1790
    http://www.genealogy.org/census/1790.html
    1800
    http://www.genealogy.org/census/1800_schedules/New.York.html
    1810
    http://www.genealogy.org/census/1810_schedules/New.York.html

1820
http://www.genealogy.org/census/1820_schedules/
New.York.html

1830
http://www.genealogy.org/census/1830_schedules/
New.York.html

1840
http://www.genealogy.org/census/1840_schedules/
New.York.html

1850
http://www.genealogy.org/census/1850_schedules/
New.York.html

1860
http://www.genealogy.org/census/1860_schedules/
New.York.html

1870
http://www.genealogy.org/census/1870_schedules/
New.York.html

1880
http://www.genealogy.org/census/1880_schedules/
New.York.html

1880 soundex
http://www.genealogy.org/census/1880.sdx_schedules/
T765.html

1890 Special Schedules
http://www.genealogy.org/census/1890-special_schedules/
New.York.html

- 1790 Census Database—Saratoga County, New York
  http://www.rootsweb.com/~nysarato/1790_int.htm

- 1850 Federal Census Orleans County, NY
  http://www.rootsweb.com/~nyorlean/1850Cen.htm

- 1865 New York State Census Orleans County
  http://www.rootsweb.com/~nyorlean/1865Cen.htm

- The Assessors Roll of Crown Point—1818
  http://www.bestweb.net/~csmfox/cp1818.htm
  Essex County, New York

- The Assessor's Roll of Crown Point—1835
  http://www.bestweb.net/~csmfox/crownp.htm
  Essex County, New York

- Cayuga County, NYGenWeb Project Cemetery List
  http://www.rootsweb.com/~nycayuga/cemetery.htm

- Cemeteries in Onondaga County
  http://www.rootsweb.com/~nyononda/CEMETERY.HTM

- The Cemeteries of Chautauqua County, NY
  http://www.rootsweb.com/~nychauta/CEMETERY/
  TOWN_CEM.HTM

- Cemeteries of Orleans County, New York
  http://www.rootsweb.com/~nyorlean/cemetery.htm

- Cemeteries of the United States—New York
  Cemeteries—County Index
  http://www.gac.edu/~kengelha/uscemeteries/new_york.html

- Cemetery Index for Tioga and Bradford Counties in
  PA and Chemung County in NY
  http://www.rootsweb.com/~pabradfo/cemindex.htm

- Census Online—Links to Census Sites on the Web—
  New York
  http://www.census-online.com/links/NY_data.html

- Church Records in Onondaga County
  http://www.rootsweb.com/~nyononda/CHURCH/CHURCH.HTM

- County Courthouse Addresses
  http://www.familytreemaker.com/00000261.html

- Court House Records in Onondaga County
  http://www.rootsweb.com/~nyononda/COURT/COURT.HTM

- Death Notices from Saratoga Whig Newspaper,
  1840–1842
  http://freenet.buffalo.edu/~ae487/awhig.html

- Deaths from Kerwin's 1888 Saratoga Springs City
  Directory
  http://freenet.buffalo.edu/~ae487/1888.html

- Deaths from the Western N.Y. Masonic Relief
  Association (1875–1893)
  http://home.eznet.net/~halsey/monroe/relief.htm

- Deed Data Pool
  http://www.ultranet.com/~deeds/pool.htm
  Downloadable deed files for Kentucky, New York, Pennsylvania,
  Virginia & West Virginia.

- Delaware County Cemeteries
  http://www.rootsweb.com/~nydelawa/cem.html

- The Department of Health Division of Vital Records,
  New York City
  http://www.tnp.com/nycgenweb/vital.htm

- Erie County, New York Cemeteries Past and Present
  http://members.tripod.com/~wnyroots/
  This site is updated weekly.

- Find-A-Grave by Location: New York
  http://www.findagrave.com/grave/lny.html
  Graves of noteworthy people.

- Forest Lawn Cemetery and Garden Mausoleums
  http://www.forest-lawn.com/
  Buffalo, New York

- Genealogical Sources in the New York State
  Archives
  http://unix6.nysed.gov/holding/fact/genea-fa.htm

- Ground Work Genealogy on the Internet: New York
  http://members.aol.com/ssmadonna/ny.htm

- A Guide To Mount Hope Cemetery, Rochester,
  New York
  http://www.ci.rochester.ny.us/fun/mthope/mthope.htm

- Herkimer/Montgomery Counties Cemetery
  Resources
  http://www.rootsweb.com/~nyherkim/cemeteries.html
  *Lists of cemeteries, private cemeteries, funeral homes and
  microfilm resources at the LDS Family History Centers.*

- Historical Census Records for Ontario County
  http://raims.com/censusmenu.html

- Holmes Funeral Co. Book—Saratoga Springs,
  New York
  http://freenet.buffalo.edu/~ae487/holmes.html
  Aug. 1854 to Dec. 1856.

- Inactive Cemeteries of Lewis County as Transcribed
  by Lowville Grange #71 in 1965
  http://www.rootsweb.com/~nylewis/inactive.htm

- Index of Marriages and Deaths in New York Weekly
  Museum, 1788–1817
  http://www.itsnet.com/~pauld/newyork/

- Interment.net: New York Cemeteries
  http://www.interment.net/us/ny/index.htm
  A list of links to other sites.

- JewishGen Hotline: Jewish Cemeteries in
  New York City
  http://www.jewishgen.org/mentprog/m_nycem.htm

- Military Service Records in the New York State
  Archives
  http://unix6.nysed.gov/holding/fact/mil.htm

- National Archives—Northeast Region (New York)
  http://www.nara.gov/regional/newyork.html

- National Archives—Northeast Region
  http://www.familytreemaker.com/00000099.html
  *Records for New Jersey, New York, Puerto Rico, and the
  Virgin Islands.*

- New York City Department of Records and
  Information Services, Municipal Archives
  http://www.tnp.com/nycgenweb/municipal.htm

- New York Indorsed Land Papers, 1643–1676
  http://www.tlc-gen.com/newyork.htm

- New York State Census
  http://home.eznet.net/~halsey/NY/ny-census.htm

- New York Vital Records Information
  http://vitalrec.com/ny.html

- Niagara County, NY Cemeteries
  http://members.aol.com/Moecow/index2.html

- Original Lot Holders, Buffalo, New York
  http://www.localnet.com/~andrle/erie/buffalo/lots.htm

- Passengers on the Emigrant Ship "Guy Mannering"
  http://www.swinhope.demon.co.uk/genuki/Transcriptions/
  GuyMannering.html
  *Sailed from Liverpool on May 22, 1849; arrived New York,
  June 28th.*

- The Political Graveyard—Cemeteries in New York
  http://politicalgraveyard.com/geo/NY/kmindex.html

- Preplanning Network—Funeral Home and
  Cemetery Directory—New York
  http://www.preplannet.com/nyfhcem.htm

- Records of the Reformed Dutch Church in
  New York—Marriages, 1639–1699
  http://www.rootsweb.com/~ote/rdcmarr.htm

- SAMPUBCO
  http://www.wasatch.com/~dsam/sampubco/index.htm
  *Will Testators Indexes, Naturalization Records Indexes and
  Census Indexes online. You can order copies of the original
  source documents for a small fee.*

- Skinnersville Cemetery Amherst, NY
  http://www.geocities.com/Heartland/Acres/4218/
  skinnersville.html

- Tombstone Records from Monroe Co., New York
  and a Few Church Records
  http://home.eznet.net/~halsey/cem.html

- USGenWeb Census Project New York
  http://www.usgenweb.org/census/states/newyork/newyork.htm

- USGenWeb Tombstone Transcription Project—
  New York
  http://www.rootsweb.com/~cemetery/newyork.html

- VitalChek Network—New York
  http://www.vitalchek.com/stateselect.asp?state=NY

- Vital Records Information—New York State
  Department of Health
  http://www.health.state.ny.us/nysdoh/consumer/vr.htm

- Waterford Rural Cemetery Records
  http://www.rootsweb.com/~nysarato/cembeg.htm

- Willoughby Cemetery, Great Valley, Cattaraugus
  County, New York
  ftp://ftp.rootsweb.com/pub/usgenweb/ny/cattaraugus/
  greatvalley/ceme0001.txt

- Where to Write for Vital Records—New York
  http://www.cdc.gov/nchswww/howto/w2w/newyork.htm
  From the National Center for Health Statistics (NCHS).

◆ Religion & Churches

- The Charter of the Second Reformed Protestant
  Dutch Church of Warren, New York
  http://www.rootsweb.com/~nyherkim/wchurch.html

- Christianity.Net Church Locator—New York
  http://www.christianity.net/cgi/location.exe?
  United_States+New_York

- Church Online!—New York
  http://www.churchonline.com/usas/ny/ny.html

- Church Profiles—New York
  http://www.church-profiles.com/ny/ny.html

- Churches dot Net—Global Church Web Pages—New York
  http://www.churches.net/churches/nyork.html
- Churches of the World—New York
  http://www.churchsurf.com/churches/New_York/index.htm
  From the ChurchSurf Christian Directory.
- Records of the Cayuga and Fosterville United Methodist Churches Cayuga County, New York
  http://www.rootsweb.com/~nycayuga/caymeth.htm

◆ Societies & Groups

- The American Irish Historical Society
  http://www.aihs.org/
- The Bridge Line Historical Society
  http://www.fileshop.com/personal/jashaw/rhs/blhs.html
  Albany
- Historical Society of the Delaware & Hudson Railroad
- Buffalo and Erie County Historical Society
  http://intotem.buffnet.net/bechs/
- Buffalo & Western New York Italian Genealogy Society
  http://freenet.buffalo.edu/~roots/bawnigs.htm
- Capital District Genealogical Society
  http://home.eznet.net/~halsey/NY/capital.htm
- Chautauqua County Genealogical Society
  http://www.rootsweb.com/~nychauta/Ccgs.htm
- Computer Genealogy Society of Long Island
  http://members.macconnect.com/users/v/vitev/genesocli/
- Delaware County Historical Association
  http://www.rootsweb.com/~nydelaha/
- Genealogical Societies in New York State
  http://home.eznet.net/~halsey/NY/gen-soc.htm
- Genealogical Society of Rockland County
  http://www.rootsweb.com/~nyrockla/GSRC/
- The German Genealogy Group
  http://www.geocities.com/Athens/Forum/2833/
  Plainview, New York
- Grand Lodge of New York—Masons
  http://www.nymasons.org/
- Hispanic Genealogical Society of New York
  http://www.webcom.com/hgsny/
- Holland Society of New York
  http://members.aol.com/hollsoc/
  Descendants in the direct male line from those who lived in the colonies under Dutch rule in America before or during 1675.
- Huguenot Historical Society
  http://members.aol.com/HuguenotHS/index.html
  New Paltz, New York

- Huguenot Historical Society
  http://home.earthlink.net/~rctwig/hhs1.htm
  New Paltz, New York
- Huntington Historical Society
  http://www.huntingtonli.org/hunthistorical/
- IOOF Lodge Website Directory—New York
  http://norm28.hsc.usc.edu/IOOF/USA/New_York/New_York.html
  Independent Order of Odd Fellows and Rebekahs.
- JEFFCO NY State Genealogical Societies Names and Addresses
  http://www.ticnet.com/jeffco/nysoc.html
- Jefferson County Genealogical Society
  http://www.rootsweb.com/~nyjeffer/jeffsoc.htm
- Jewish Genealogical Society of Rochester
  http://hq.net/jgsr/
- The Jewish Genealogy Society of Long Island
  http://www.jewishgen.org/jgsli
- Matinecock Lodge No. 806 F.&A.M.
  http://www.matinecock.org/
  Masonic Lodge, Oyster Bay, Long Island, New York.
- New York Genealogical & Biographical Society
  http://www.nygbs.org/
- New York State Organization National Society Daughters of the American Revolution
  http://www.borg.com/~emilies/nydar/
- Northeastern New York Genealogical Society
  http://freenet.buffalo.edu/~ae487/nnygs.html
- The On-Line Olean, Allegany, Portville and Hinsdale, NY Genealogical Society
  http://www.geocities.com/Heartland/Park/3294/oags.html
- Ontario & Western Railway Historical Society
  http://shell.idt.net/~nyowrhs/
- The Oyster Bay Historical Society
  http://members.aol.com/OBHistory/index.html
- Polish Genealogical Society of New York State
  http://www.pgsnys.org/
- Rensselaer County Historical Society
  http://www.crisny.org/not-for-profit/rchs/
- Rochester Genealogical Society
  http://home.eznet.net/~halsey/rgs.html
- Shaker Heritage Society
  http://www.crisny.org/not-for-profit/shakerwv/
  Albany, New York
- The Skaneateles Historical Society
  http://www.skaneateles.com/historical/
  They have vital statistics records online, including marriage records and death records. A database of over 15,000 records compiled from the old newspaper records from 1831 through 1899.

- Southern Tier Genealogical Society
  http://www.spectra.net/~ann/stgs.htm
  Vestal, New York

- The Three Village Historical Society
  http://members.aol.com/TVHS1/

- Tonawanda-Kenmore Historical Society
  http://freenet.buffalo.edu/~tot/htm/o_hsoc.htm

- Town of Newfane Historical Society
  http://www.localnet.com/~zeus/
  Niagara County, New York

- Westchester County Genealogical Society
  http://pages.prodigy.com/HFBK19A/wcgs.htm

- Western New York Genealogical Society Inc.
  http://www.pce.net/outram/wny.htm

◆ USGenWeb Project

- New York Genealogy—USGenWeb Project
  State Page
  http://www.usgenweb.org/ny

- New York—USGenWeb Archives Table of Contents
  http://www.rootsweb.com/~usgenweb/ny/nyfiles.htm

- New York—USGenWeb FTP Archives
  ftp://ftp.rootsweb.com/pub/usgenweb/ny/

U.S.—NORTH CAROLINA—NC
http://www.CyndisList.com/nc.htm

Category Index:

- General Resource Sites
- Government & Cities
- History & Culture
- Libraries, Archives & Museums
- Mailing Lists, Newsgroups & Chat
- Maps, Gazetteers & Geographical Information
- Military
- Newspapers
- People & Families

- Professional Researchers, Volunteers & Other Research Services
- Publications, Software & Supplies
- Queries, Message Boards & Surname Lists
- Records: Census, Cemeteries, Land, Obituaries, Personal, Taxes and Vital
- Religion & Churches
- Societies & Groups
- USGenWeb Project

◆ General Resource Sites

- Charlotte's Web Genealogy Page
  http://www.charweb.org/gen/
- Everton's Sources of Genealogical Information in North Carolina
  http://www.everton.com/usa/nc.htm
- Family Tree Maker's Genealogy "How To" Guide—North Carolina
  http://www.familytreemaker.com/00000208.html
- Genealogy Bulletin Board Systems for North Carolina
  http://www.genealogy.org/~gbbs/gblnc.html
- Genealogy Exchange & Surname Registry—NCGenExchange
  http://www.genexchange.com/nc/index.cfm
- Genealogy Resources on the Internet: North Carolina
  http://www-personal.umich.edu/~cgaunt/ncarolina.html
- LDS Research Outline for North Carolina
  http://www.everton.com/usa/nc-0834b.txt
- Lineages' Genealogy Site: North Carolina
  http://www.lineages.com/rooms/usa/state.asp?StateCode=NC
- North Carolina Encyclopedia
  http://hal.dcr.state.nc.us/nc/cover.htm
- North Carolina Genealogy QuickChat Web Chat
  http://www.lochfort.net/ajpweb/remote/chat/genchat.html
- Pitt County Compendium
  http://www.lib.ecu.edu/NCCollPCC/PCCweb/PCChome.html

- Pitt County Family Researchers
  http://www.geocities.com/Athens/Troy/1908/
- Preserving Cemetery Data: The North Carolina Cemetery Survey and Protective Legislation
  http://www.arch.dcr.state.nc.us/cemetery.htm
- ROOTS-L United States Resources: North Carolina
  http://www.rootsweb.com/roots-l/USA/nc.html
  Comprehensive list of research links, including many to history-related sites.
- Triangle Roots—A Genealogy Resource for Durham, Orange, and Wake Counties
  http://www.ils.unc.edu/familyhistory/roots.htm

◆ Government & Cities

- 50states.com—North Carolina State Information Resource
  http://www.50states.com/ncarolin.htm
  A list of general information for each state, including a list of colleges, state symbols, links to maps, newspapers, and other miscellaneous state information.
- Excite Travel by City.Net—North Carolina
  http://www.city.net/countries/united_states/north_carolina/
- Official City Web Sites for the State of North Carolina
  http://OfficialCitySites.org/North-Carolina.htm
- State of North Carolina—Public Information
  http://www.sips.state.nc.us/
- Yahoo! Get Local...North Carolina Cities
  http://dir.yahoo.com/Regional/U_S__States/North_Carolina/Cities/
  Maps, yellow pages, white pages, newspapers and other local information.

- Yahoo! Get Local...North Carolina Counties and Regions
  http://dir.yahoo.com/Regional/U_S__States/North_Carolina/Counties_and_Regions/
  Maps, yellow pages, white pages, newspapers and other local information.

◆ History & Culture

- The Early Vernacular of the North Carolina Mountains
  http://www.nando.net/smokies/smoke4.html
  With a partial glossary of early mountain vernacular.

- Yahoo!...History...North Carolina
  http://dir.yahoo.com/Arts/Humanities/History/Browse_By_Region/U_S__States/North_Carolina/

◆ Libraries, Archives & Museums

- Appalachian State University Libraries
  http://www.library.appstate.edu/home/

- Central North Carolina Regional Library
  http://ils.unc.edu/nclibs/centralnc/home.htm
  Serving Alamance and Chatham Counties.

- Cumberland County Public Library
  http://www.cumberland.lib.nc.us/

- Durham County Library
  http://ils.unc.edu/nclibs/durham/dclhome.htm

- Family History Centers—North Carolina
  http://www.deseretbook.com/famhis/nc.html

- Family History Centers—North Carolina
  http://www.lib.byu.edu/~uvrfhc/centers/northcarolina.html

- Greensboro Public Library
  http://www.greensboro.com/library/

- Guilford College Friends Historical Collection
  http://www.guilford.edu/LibraryArt/fhc.htm
  Greensboro, North Carolina

- HYTELNET—Library Catalogs: USA: North Carolina
  http://library.usask.ca/hytelnet/usa/NC.html
  Before you use any of the Telnet links, make note of the user name, password and any other logon information.

- New Hanover County Public Library
  http://www.co.new-hanover.nc.us/lib/libmain.htm

- North Carolina Division of Archives and History— Archives & Records Home Page
  http://www.ah.dcr.state.nc.us/sections/archives/
  - ○ Archival Services Branch
    http://www.ah.dcr.state.nc.us/sections/archives/arch/default.htm

- North Carolina State Archives—Genealogical Research
  http://www.ah.dcr.state.nc.us/sections/archives/arch/gen-res.htm

- North Carolina State Archives—Historical Research
  http://www.ah.dcr.state.nc.us/sections/archives/arch/hist-res.htm

  - ○ Records Services Branch
    http://www.ah.dcr.state.nc.us/sections/archives/rec/default.htm

- North Carolina Family History Centers
  http://www.genhomepage.com/FHC/North_Carolina.html
  A list of addresses, phone numbers and hours of operation from the Genealogy Home Page.

- North Carolina Public Libraries on the Web
  http://statelibrary.dcr.state.nc.us/library/publib.htm

- NUCMC Listing of Archives and Manuscript Repositories in North Carolina
  http://lcweb.loc.gov/coll/nucmc/ncsites.html
  Links to information about resources other than those held in the Library of Congress.

- Repositories of Primary Sources: North Carolina
  http://www.uidaho.edu/special-collections/east2.html#usnc
  A list of links to online resources from the Univ. of Idaho Library, Special Collections and Archives.

- The Robinson-Spangler Carolina Room
  http://www.plcmc.lib.nc.us/branch/main/carolina/default.htm
  At the Public Library of Charlotte-Mecklenburg County.

- Rockingham County Public Library
  http://www.rcpl.org/lib1.html

- Rowan Public Library's Edith M. Clark History Room
  http://www.lib.co.rowan.nc.us/hr/home.htm
  Salisbury, Rowan County, North Carolina.

- The Special Collections Library at Duke University
  http://scriptorium.lib.duke.edu/
  Durham, North Carolina

- State Library of North Carolina
  http://statelibrary.dcr.state.nc.us/ncslhome.htm

  - ○ Genealogical Research in North Carolina
    http://statelibrary.dcr.state.nc.us/iss/gr/genealog.htm

- UNC–Chapel Hill Libraries
  http://www.lib.unc.edu/

  - ○ Documenting the American South
    http://sunsite.unc.edu/docsouth/index.html

  - ○ History Collections
    http://www.lib.unc.edu/cdd/crs/hum/history/index.html

  - ○ Special Collections and Formats
    http://www.lib.unc.edu/cdd/crs/special/index.html

- webCATS: Library Catalogues on the World Wide Web—North Carolina
  http://library.usask.ca/hywebcat/states/NC.html

◆ Mailing Lists, Newsgroups & Chat

- Genealogy Resources on the Internet—North Carolina Mailing Lists
  http://members.aol.com/gfsjohnf/gen_mail_states-nc.html
  Each of the mailing list links below points to this site, wonderfully maintained by John Fuller. Visit this site for county-specific mailing lists as well.

- ALEXTREE Mailing List
  http://members.aol.com/gfsjohnf/gen_mail_states-nc.html#ALEXTREE
  For anyone with an interest in the cemeteries of Western North Carolina. Areas of discussion will include page updates, local cemetery news and announcements, and preservation strategies.

- Appalachianfamily Mailing List
  http://members.aol.com/gfsjohnf/gen_mail_states-va.html#Appalachianfamily
  Appalachian Mountain Families including families from Georgia, North Carolina, South Carolina, Tennessee, Kentucky, Virginia, and West Virginia.

- BrickChurchNC Mailing List
  http://members.aol.com/gfsjohnf/gen_mail_states-nc.html#BrickChurchNC
  For anyone with a genealogical or historical interest in the founders and members of The Brick Church that was founded 250 years ago in what is now Guilford County, North Carolina.

- CAPE-FEAR-SCOTS Mailing List
  http://members.aol.com/gfsjohnf/gen_mail_states-nc.html#CAPE-FEAR-SCOTS
  For anyone researching Scottish immigrants to the Cape Fear region of North Carolina prior to 1850.

- CATAWBA-WEST Mailing List
  http://members.aol.com/gfsjohnf/gen_mail_states-nc.html#CATAWBA-WEST
  For anyone with a genealogical interest in the region composed of the following North Carolina counties: Catawba, Lincoln, Gaston, Cleveland, Burke, and the NC area of the former Tryon county.

- Melungeon Mailing List
  http://members.aol.com/gfsjohnf/gen_mail_states-gen.html#MELUNGEO
  For people conducting Melungeon and/or Appalachian research including Native American, Portuguese, Turkish, Black Dutch, and other unverifiable mixed statements of ancestry or unexplained rumors, with ancestors in TN, KY, VA, NC, SC, GA, AL, WV, and possibly other places.

- NCORANGE Mailing List
  http://members.aol.com/gfsjohnf/gen_mail_states-nc.html#NCORANGE
  For anyone with a genealogical or historical interest in the area that became Orange County, North Carolina in 1752. This area not only includes the present Orange County but all or part of the following counties: Alamance, Caswell, Chatham, Durham, Guilford, Person, Randolph, Rockingham and Wake.

- NCROOTS Mailing List
  http://members.aol.com/gfsjohnf/gen_mail_states-nc.html#NCROOTS

- NCSCGENSWAP Mailing List
  http://members.aol.com/gfsjohnf/gen_mail_states-nc.html#NCSCGENSWAP
  For anyone wishing to swap research time in North and South Carolina.

- NCSCOTS-L Mailing List
  http://members.aol.com/gfsjohnf/gen_mail_states-nc.html#NCSCOTS-L
  For anyone who is studying the genealogy of Scottish immigrants to North Carolina.

- NC-SC-ROOTS-L Mailing List
  http://members.aol.com/gfsjohnf/gen_mail_states-nc.html#NC/SC-ROOTS
  North Carolina and South Carolina

- North Carolina Genealogy QuickChat Web Chat
  http://www.lochfort.net/ajpweb/remote/chat/genchat.html

- ROWANROOTS-L Mailing List
  http://members.aol.com/gfsjohnf/gen_mail_states-nc.html#ROWANROOTS-L
  For anyone with a genealogical or historical interest in the part of North Carolina known as "Old Rowan."

  ○ About RowanROOTS-L
    http://www.aa.net/~jdcoates/rowan/rowanroots-l.htm

◆ Maps, Gazetteers & Geographical Information

- 1895 U.S. Atlas—North Carolina
  http://www.LivGenMI.com/1895nc.htm

- American Memory Panoramic Maps 1847–1929—North Carolina
  http://lcweb2.loc.gov/cgi-bin/query/S?ammem/gmd:@filreq(@field(STATE+@band(north+carolina))+@field(COLLID+pmmap))
  From the Geography and Map Division, Library of Congress.

- American Memory Railroad Maps 1828–1900—North Carolina
  http://memory.loc.gov/cgi-bin/query/S?ammem/gmd:@filreq(@field(STATE+@band(north+carolina))+@field(COLLID+rrmap))
  From the Geography and Map Division, Library of Congress.

- Color Landform Atlas: North Carolina
  http://fermi.jhuapl.edu/states/nc_0.html
  Including a map of counties and a map for 1895.

- Excite Maps: North Carolina Maps
  http://www.city.net/maps/view/?mapurl=/countries/united_states/north_carolina
  Zoom in on these maps all the way to the street level.

- HPI County InfoSystem—Counties in North Carolina
  http://www.com/hpi/nccty/index.html

- K.B. Slocum Books and Maps—North Carolina
  http://www.treasurenet.com/cgi-bin/treasure/kbslocum/scan/
  se=North.20Carolina/sf=mapstate
- List of North Carolina Counties
  http://www.genealogy.org/~st-clair/counties/state_nc.html
- Map of North Carolina Counties
  http://govinfo.kerr.orst.edu/gif/states/nc.gif
  From the Government Information Sharing Project, Information Services, Oregon State University.
- Map of North Carolina Counties
  http://www.lib.utexas.edu/Libs/PCL/Map_collection/states/
  North_Carolina.gif
  From the Perry-Castañeda Library at the Univ. of Texas at Austin.
- U.S. Census Bureau—North Carolina Profiles
  http://www.census.gov/datamap/www/37.html
- Yale Peabody Museum: GNIS—North Carolina
  http://www.peabody.yale.edu/other/gnis/NC.html
  *Search the USGS Geographic Names Database. You can limit the search to a specific county in this state and search for any of the following features: airport arch area arroyo bar basin bay beach bench bend bridge **building** canal cape **cemetery** channel **church** cliff crater crossing dam falls flat forest gap geyser glacier gut harbor hospital island isthmus lake lava levee locale mine oilfield other park pillar plain ppl range rapids reserve reservoir ridge **school** sea slope spring stream summit swamp tower trail tunnel valley well woods.*

◆ Military

- The Civil War Archive—Union Regiments— North Carolina
  http://www.civilwararchive.com/unionnc.htm
- Civil War Battle Summaries by State— North Carolina
  http://www2.cr.nps.gov/abpp/battles/bystate.htm#nc
- Korean Conflict State-Level Casualty Lists— North Carolina
  http://www.nara.gov/nara/electronic/nchrlist.html
  From the National Archives and Records Administration, Center for Electronic Records.
- North Carolina Civil War Home Page
  http://members.aol.com/jweaver303/nc/nccwhp.htm
  Collection of biographical and historical information pertaining to North Carolina and North Carolinans in the American Civil War.
- North Carolina in the Revolutionary War
  http://www.rootsweb.com/~ncrevwar/ncrevwar.htm
- Vietnam Conflict State-Level Casualty Lists— North Carolina
  http://www.nara.gov/nara/electronic/nchrviet.html
  From the National Archives and Records Administration, Center for Electronic Records.
- The Vietnam Veterans Memorial—North Carolina
  http://grunt.space.swri.edu/statewall/ncarol/nc.htm

◆ Newspapers

- AJR NewsLink—North Carolina Newspapers
  http://www.newslink.org/ncnews.html
- E&P Media Info Links—Newspaper Sites in North Carolina
  http://www.mediainfo.com/emedia/browse-results.
  htm?region=northcarolina&category=newspaper+++++++++
- Ecola Newstand: North Carolina
  http://www.ecola.com/news/press/na/us/nc/
- Greensboro News & Record Online
  http://www.greensboro.com/nronline/index.htm
- NAA Hotlinks to Newspapers Online— North Carolina
  http://www.naa.org/hotlinks/searchResult.asp?param=
  NC-North+Carolina&City=1
- N.C. Newspaper Project
  http://statelibrary.dcr.state.nc.us/tss/newspape.htm
- N-Net—North Carolina Newspapers
  http://www.n-net.com/nc.htm
- StarLine On Line: The Morning Star
  http://starnews.wilmington.net/
  Wilmington, North Carolina
- The Ultimate Collection of News Links: USA—North Carolina
  http://www.pppp.net/links/news/USA-NC.html
- Yahoo!...Newspapers...North Carolina
  http://dir.yahoo.com/News_and_Media/Newspapers/
  Browse_By_Region/U_S__States/North_Carolina/

◆ People & Families

- Directory of Underground Railroad Operators— North Carolina
  http://www.ugrr.org//names/map-nc.htm
- Moravian Settlers in North Carolina
  http://www.erols.com/fmoran/morav.html
  From the Jarvis Family Home Page.
- Southeastern Kentucky Melungeon Information Exchange
  http://www.bright.net/~kat/skmie.htm
  Also Tennessee, North Carolina and Virginia.
- Tribes and Villages of North Carolina
  http://hanksville.phast.umass.edu:8000/cultprop/contacts/
  tribal/NC.html
- WPA Life Histories from North Carolina
  http://lcweb2.loc.gov/ammem/wpaintro/nccat.html
  Manuscripts from the Federal Writer's Project, 1936–1940, Library of Congress.

◆ Professional Researchers, Volunteers & Other Research Services

- Board for Certification of Genealogists—Roster of Those Certified—Specializing in North Carolina
  http://www.genealogy.org/~bcg/rosts_nc.html

- Genealogy Helplist—North Carolina
  http://posom.com/hl/usa/nc.shtml

- Lassen & Lassen: Certified Genealogical Records Specialists
  Work in Ashe, Wilkes, Watauga, and Alleghany Cos., NC and in Grayson Co., VA. Additional nearby counties by special arrangement. Specialties are research, reportage, and on-site photography. For details e-mail slassen@infoave.net

- The Official Iowa Counties Professional Genealogist and Researcher's Registry for North Carolina
  http://www.iowa-counties.com/gene/nc.htm

- Professional Genealogists' Network
  http://ww2.esn.net/~ancestral/pgn/

- Roots & Branches Genealogy—Becki Hagood
  North Carolina statewide professional researcher. For details send e-mail to Becky at: Roots4Gen@aol.com

◆ Publications, Software & Supplies

- AncestorSpy—CDs and Microfiche for North Carolina
  http://www.ancestorspy.com/nc.htm

- Appleton's Fine Used Bookseller and Genealogy
  http://www.appletons.com/genealogy/homepage.html
  Charlotte, North Carolina. Genealogy books, software, CD-ROMs, and more. Free genealogy catalog and e-mail list.

- Barbara Green's Used Genealogy Books— North Carolina
  http://home.earthlink.net/~genbooks/lochist.html#NC

- Barnette's Family Tree Books—North Carolina
  http://www.barnettesbooks.com/north-ca.htm

- Books We Own—North Carolina
  http://www.rootsweb.com/~bwo/ncar.html

- Boyd Publishing Company—North Carolina
  http://www.hom.net/~gac/northcar.htm

- Byron Sistler and Associates, Inc.
  http://www.mindspring.com/~sistler/
  Over 900 books covering records from Tennessee, Virginia, North Carolina, and Kentucky.

- Frontier Press Bookstore—North Carolina
  http://www.frontierpress.com/frontier.cgi?category=nc

- GenealogyBookShop.com—North Carolina
  http://www.genealogybookshop.com/genealogybookshop/files/The_United_States,North_Carolina/index.html
  The online store of Genealogical Publishing Co., Inc. & Clearfield Company.

- Hearthstone Bookshop—North Carolina
  http://www.hearthstonebooks.com/cgi-bin/webc.cgi/st_main.html?catid=93&sid=2PH5t29sm

- Heritage Books—North Carolina
  http://www.heritagebooks.com/nc.htm

- Heritage Quest—Microfilm Records for the State of North Carolina
  http://www.heritagequest.com/genealogy/microfilm/north_carolina/

- Iberian Publishing Company's Online Catalog
  http://www.iberian.com/
  Specializing in reference works for genealogists and historians researching the Virginias and other Southeastern U.S. States circa. 1650–1850.

- J & W Enterprises
  http://www.dhc.net/~jw/
  One stop book source on the Internet, specializing in southern states source material.

- Lost in Time Books—North Carolina
  http://www.lostintime.com/catalog/books/bookst/bo23000.htm

- The Memorabilia Corner Books—North Carolina
  http://members.aol.com/TMCorner/book_nc.htm

- The Memorabilia Corner Census View CDs— North Carolina
  http://members.aol.com/TMCorner/cen_nc.htm

- Publications on Rowan County, North Carolina by Jo White Linn
  http://www.geocities.com/Heartland/Hills/5391/jowlinn.html

- S-K Publications—North Carolina 1800–1850 Census Books
  http://www.skpub.com/genie/census/nc/

- Southern Queries Genealogy Magazine
  http://www.mindspring.com/~freedom1/sq/sq.htm

- TLC Genealogy Books
  http://www.tlc-gen.com/
  Specializing in Colonial VA, KY, MD, OH, PA, NC, etc.

- Willow Bend Bookstore—North Carolina
  http://www.willowbend.net/nc.htm

- Ye Olde Genealogie Shoppe Books—North Carolina
  http://www.yogs.com/maincat.htm#NORTH CAROLINA

◆ Queries, Message Boards & Surname Lists

- GenConnect North Carolina Visitor Center
  http://cgi.rootsweb.com/~genbbs/indx/NC.html
  A system for posting queries, Bibles, biographies, deeds, obituaries, pensions, wills.

◆ Records: Census, Cemeteries, Land, Obituaries, Personal, Taxes and Vital (Born, Married, Died & Buried)

- 1759 Rowan County Tax List
  http://www.erols.com/fmoran/1759.html

- 1780 Montgomery County Tax List
  http://www.rootsweb.com/~ncmontgo/m1780tax.html

- 1786 Taxables Located in Captain Krous' District, Surry County (Present-Day Forsyth)
  http://www.erols.com/fmoran/1786.html

- 1786 Taxables Located in Captain Atkins' District, Surry County
  http://www.erols.com/fmoran/1786a.html
  Located in southern region of present-day Surry, along the Yadkin River.

- The 1790–1890 Federal Population Censuses: Catalog of National Archives Microfilm
  http://www.genealogy.org/census/contents.shtml

  ○ Census Schedules and Microfilm Roll Numbers for North Carolina:

    1790
    http://www.genealogy.org/census/1790.html

    1800
    http://www.genealogy.org/census/1800_schedules/North.Carolina.html

    1810
    http://www.genealogy.org/census/1810_schedules/North.Carolina.html

    1820
    http://www.genealogy.org/census/1820_schedules/North.Carolina.html

    1830
    http://www.genealogy.org/census/1830_schedules/North.Carolina.html

    1840
    http://www.genealogy.org/census/1840_schedules/North.Carolina.html

    1850
    http://www.genealogy.org/census/1850_schedules/North.Carolina.html

    1860
    http://www.genealogy.org/census/1860_schedules/North.Carolina.html

    1870
    http://www.genealogy.org/census/1870_schedules/North.Carolina.html

    1880
    http://www.genealogy.org/census/1880_schedules/North.Carolina.html

    1880 soundex
    http://www.genealogy.org/census/1880.sdx_schedules/T766.html

    1890 Special Schedules
    http://www.genealogy.org/census/1890-special_schedules/North.Carolina.html

- 1790 Stokes County, North Carolina Census
  http://www.users.mis.net/~chesnut/pages/nstokes.htm

- 1790 Surry County, North Carolina Census
  http://www.users.mis.net/~chesnut/pages/nsurry.htm

- 1800 Census Anson County, North Carolina
  http://www.aracnet.com/~pslamb/census.htm

- 1815 Taxables—Cumberland County, NC
  http://www.rootsweb.com/~nccumber/1815taxables.htm

- 1860 Federal Census of Tyrrell County, North Carolina
  http://www.rootsweb.com/~takelley/tyrr1860/tyrr1860.htm

- Alamance County 1850 Mortality Schedule
  http://www.netpath.net/~lwatson/alms1850.htm

- Alamance County 1860 Mortality Schedule
  http://www.netpath.net/~lwatson/alms1860.htm

- Alamance County 1870 Mortality Schedule
  http://www.netpath.net/~lwatson/alms1870.htm

- Buncombe County, NC Marriage Records
  http://main.nc.us/OBCGS/wedindx.htm

- The Cemeteries of Rutherford County, NC
  http://rfci.net/wdfloyd/

- Cemeteries of the United States—North Carolina Cemeteries—County Index
  http://www.gac.edu/~kengelha/uscemeteries/north_carolina.html

- Census Online—Links to Census Sites on the Web—North Carolina
  http://www.census-online.com/links/NC_data.html

- Churches and Cemetery Records of Anson County, NC
  http://www.rootsweb.com/~ncanson/cemet.htm

- County Courthouse Addresses
  http://www.familytreemaker.com/00000262.html

- Find-A-Grave by Location: North Carolina
  http://www.findagrave.com/grave/lnc.html
  Graves of noteworthy people.

- Greensboro News & Record Online Obituaries Index
  http://www.greensboro.com/nronline/Index/miobits.htm
  Under construction as of February 1, 1997.

- Ground Work Genealogy on the Internet: North Carolina
  http://members.aol.com/ssmadonna/nc.htm

- Interment.net: North Carolina Cemeteries
http://www.interment.net/us/nc/index.htm
A list of links to other sites.

- List of Montgomery County Tax Payers in 1779
http://www.rootsweb.com/~ncmontgo/m1779tax.html

- Moss Cemetery, Marble, Cherokee County, North Carolina
http://main.nc.us/OBCGS/mosscem.htm

- National Archives—Southeast Region (Atlanta)
http://www.nara.gov/regional/atlanta.html

- National Archives—Southeast Region from Family Tree Maker
http://www.familytreemaker.com/00000104.html
Records for North Carolina, Florida, Georgia, Kentucky, Mississippi, North Carolina, South Carolina, and Tennessee.

- North Carolina Vital Records Information
http://vitalrec.com/nc.html

- Passenger Lists from England and Scotland to North Carolina
http://www.rootsweb.com/~ote/caroship.htm
From the Olive Tree.

- The Political Graveyard—Cemeteries in North Carolina
http://politicalgraveyard.com/geo/NC/kmindex.html

- Preplanning Network—Funeral Home and Cemetery Directory—North Carolina
http://www.preplannet.com/ncfhcem.htm

- Tax List Perquimans County, NC 1702 (Taxables, Tithables)
http://gort.ucsd.edu/hc/perq1702.html

- Tax List Perquimans County, NC 1754 (Taxables, Tithables)
http://gort.ucsd.edu/hc/perq1754.html

- USGenWeb Census Project North Carolina
http://www.usgenweb.org/census/states/northcar/northcar.htm

- USGenWeb Tombstone Transcription Project—North Carolina
http://www.rootsweb.com/~cemetery/n-car.html

- VitalChek Network—North Carolina
http://www.vitalchek.com/stateselect.asp?state=NC

- Warren Co., Bibles North Carolina Index to Surnames, Queries, and Researchers
http://www.lofthouse.com/warren/bibles/qryindex.htm

- Where to Write for Vital Records—North Carolina
http://www.cdc.gov/nchswww/howto/w2w/ncarolin.htm
From the National Center for Health Statistics (NCHS).

◆ Religion & Churches

- Christianity.Net Church Locator—North Carolina
http://www.christianity.net/cgi/location.exe?United_States+North_Carolina

- Church Online!—North Carolina
http://www.churchonline.com/usas/nc/nc.html

- Church Profiles—North Carolina
http://www.church-profiles.com/nc/nc.html

- Churches dot Net—Global Church Web Pages—North Carolina
http://www.churches.net/churches/ncarolin.html

- Churches of the World—North Carolina
http://www.churchsurf.com/churches/North_Carolina/index.htm
From the ChurchSurf Christian Directory.

◆ Societies & Groups

- Archer's Computer Interest Group List—North Carolina
http://www.genealogy.org/~ngs/cigs/ngl1usnc.html

- Balsam Roots—Haywood County Genealogical Society, Inc. of North Carolina
http://www.brinet.com/~hcgs/

- Catawba County Genealogical Society
http://www.co.catawba.nc.us/otheragency/ccgs/ccgsmain.htm

- Catawba County Historical Association
http://www.co.catawba.nc.us/otheragency/cchs/histassn.htm

- Cherokee County Historical Museum, Inc.
http://www.tib.com/cchm/

- Durham-Orange Genealogical Society of North Carolina
http://rtpnet.org/~dogs/index.html

- The Forsyth County Genealogical Society
http://www.erols.com/fmoran/gensoc/gensoc.html

- Genealogical Society of Rockingham & Stokes Counties, North Carolina Genealogy
http://ns.netmcr.com/~lonabec/gsrs.html

- Genealogical Society of Rowan County
http://www.lib.co.rowan.nc.us/hr/ges.htm

- GenSIG—Personal Computer Club of Charlotte, NC, Inc
http://www.chem.uncc.edu/pccc/gensig/

- Hyde County Historical and Genealogical Society
http://www.albemarle-nc.com/hyde/org/genelgy.htm

- IOOF Lodge Website Directory—North Carolina
http://norm28.hsc.usc.edu/IOOF/USA/North_Carolina/North_Carolina.html
Independent Order of Odd Fellows and Rebekahs.

- Jackson County Genealogical Society
  http://www.main.nc.us/jcgs/
- North Carolina Genealogical Society
  http://www.ncgenealogy.org/
- Old Buncombe County Genealogical Society
  http://main.nc.us/OBCGS/
- Old New Hanover Genealogical Society
  http://www.co.new-hanover.nc.us/lib/oldnew.htm
- Scotland County Genealogical Society
  http://www.txdirect.net/~hpeele/sctlnd5.htm
- Wake County Genealogical Society of
  North Carolina
  http://www.rtpnet.org/~wcgs/index.html

◆ USGenWeb Project

- North Carolina Genealogy—USGenWeb Project
  State Page
  http://www.usgenweb.org/nc
- North Carolina—USGenWeb Archives Table of
  Contents
  http://www.rootsweb.com/~usgenweb/nc/ncfiles.htm
- North Carolina—USGenWeb FTP Archives
  ftp://ftp.rootsweb.com/pub/usgenweb/nc/

U.S.—NORTH DAKOTA—ND
http://www.CyndisList.com/nd.htm

Category Index:

- General Resource Sites
- Government & Cities
- History & Culture
- Libraries, Archives & Museums
- Mailing Lists, Newsgroups & Chat
- Maps, Gazetteers & Geographical Information
- Military
- Newspapers
- People & Families

- Professional Researchers, Volunteers & Other Research Services
- Publications, Software & Supplies
- Queries, Message Boards & Surname Lists
- Records: Census, Cemeteries, Land, Obituaries, Personal, Taxes and Vital
- Religion & Churches
- Societies & Groups
- USGenWeb Project

◆ General Resource Sites

- Everton's Sources of Genealogical Information in North Dakota
  http://www.everton.com/usa/nd.htm
- Family Tree Maker's Genealogy "How To" Guide— North Dakota
  http://www.familytreemaker.com/00000209.html
- Genealogy Exchange & Surname Registry— NDGenExchange
  http://www.genexchange.com/nd/index.cfm
- Genealogy Resources on the Internet: North Dakota
  http://www-personal.umich.edu/~cgaunt/northdakota.html
- LDS Research Outline for North Dakota
  http://www.everton.com/usa/nd-0835b.txt
- Lineages' Genealogy Site: North Dakota
  http://www.lineages.com/rooms/usa/state.asp?StateCode=ND
- ROOTS-L United States Resources: North Dakota
  http://www.rootsweb.com/roots-l/USA/nd.html
  Comprehensive list of research links, including many to history-related sites.

◆ Government & Cities

- 50states.com—North Dakota State Information Resource
  http://www.50states.com/ndakota.htm
  A list of general information for each state, including a list of colleges, state symbols, links to maps, newspapers, and other miscellaneous state information.
- Excite Travel by City.Net—North Dakota
  http://www.city.net/countries/united_states/north_dakota/

- North Dakota State Government
  http://www.state.nd.us/
- Official City Web Sites for the State of North Dakota
  http://OfficialCitySites.org/North-Dakota.htm
- Yahoo! Get Local...North Dakota Cities
  http://dir.yahoo.com/Regional/U_S__States/North_Dakota/Cities/
  Maps, yellow pages, white pages, newspapers and other local information.
- Yahoo! Get Local...North Dakota Counties and Regions
  http://dir.yahoo.com/Regional/U_S__States/North_Dakota/Counties_and_Regions/
  Maps, yellow pages, white pages, newspapers and other local information.

◆ History & Culture

- Yahoo!...History...North Dakota
  http://dir.yahoo.com/Arts/Humanities/History/Browse_By_Region/U_S__States/North_Dakota/

◆ Libraries, Archives & Museums

- Chester Fritz Library, University of North Dakota
  http://www.und.nodak.edu/dept/library/index.html
  - Elwyn B. Robinson Department of Special Collections
    http://www.und.nodak.edu/dept/library/Collections/spk.html
    - Family History/Genealogy Room
      http://www.und.nodak.edu/dept/library/Collections/famhist.html

- Fred G. Aandahl Collection of Books on the Great Plains
  http://www.und.nodak.edu/dept/library/Collections/aand.html
- The North Dakota Book Collection
  http://www.und.nodak.edu/dept/library/Collections/ndbook.html
- North Dakota State Documents
  http://www.und.nodak.edu/dept/library/Collections/ndgtdocs.html
- Orin G. Libby Manuscript Collection
  http://www.und.nodak.edu/dept/library/Collections/oglman.html
- University Archives Collection
  http://www.und.nodak.edu/dept/library/Collections/uniarc.html

- Family History Centers—North Dakota
  http://www.deseretbook.com/famhis/nd.html
- Family History Centers—North Dakota
  http://www.lib.byu.edu/~uvrfhc/centers/northdakota.html
- North Dakota Family History Centers
  http://www.genhomepage.com/FHC/North_Dakota.html
  A list of addresses, phone numbers and hours of operation from the Genealogy Home Page.
- North Dakota State Library
  http://ndsl.lib.state.nd.us/
- North Dakota State University Libraries
  http://www.lib.ndsu.nodak.edu/
  ○ Germans from Russia Heritage Collection
    http://www.lib.ndsu.nodak.edu/gerrus/
  ○ Institute for Regional Studies
    http://www.lib.ndsu.nodak.edu/ndirs/
    - Biography & Genealogy
      http://www.lib.ndsu.nodak.edu/ndirs/bio&genealogy/index.html
    - Collections
      http://www.lib.ndsu.nodak.edu/ndirs/collections/index.html
  ○ University Archives
    http://www.lib.ndsu.nodak.edu/archives/
- NUCMC Listing of Archives and Manuscript Repositories in North Dakota
  http://lcweb.loc.gov/coll/nucmc/ndsites.html
  Links to information about resources other than those held in the Library of Congress.
- Red River Valley Heritage Resource Center
  http://www.atpfargo.com/hjem/
- Repositories of Primary Sources: North Dakota
  http://www.uidaho.edu/special-collections/west.html#usnd
  A list of links to online resources from the Univ. of Idaho Library, Special Collections and Archives.
- State Archives and Historical Research Library
  http://www.state.nd.us/hist/sal.htm

◆ Mailing Lists, Newsgroups & Chat

- Genealogy Resources on the Internet—North Dakota Mailing Lists
  http://members.aol.com/gfsjohnf/gen_mail_states-nd.html
  Each of the mailing list links below points to this site, wonderfully maintained by John Fuller. Visit this site for county-specific mailing lists as well.
- NDSDMN-L Mailing List
  http://members.aol.com/gfsjohnf/gen_mail_states-nd.html#NDSDMN-L
  North Dakota, South Dakota and Minnesota.

◆ Maps, Gazetteers & Geographical Information

- 1872 County Map of Dakota
  http://www.ismi.net/chnegw/1872dakota.htm
- 1895 U.S. Atlas—North Dakota
  http://www.LivGenMI.com/1895nd.htm
- American Memory Panoramic Maps 1847–1929—North Dakota
  http://lcweb2.loc.gov/cgi-bin/query/S?ammem/gmd:@filreq(@field(STATE+@band(north+dakota+))+@field(COLLID+pmmap))
  From the Geography and Map Division, Library of Congress.
- American Memory Railroad Maps 1828–1900—North Dakota
  http://memory.loc.gov/cgi-bin/query/S?ammem/gmd:@filreq(@field(STATE+@band(north+dakota+))+@field(COLLID+rrmap))
  From the Geography and Map Division, Library of Congress.
- Color Landform Atlas: North Dakota
  http://fermi.jhuapl.edu/states/nd_0.html
  Including a map of counties and a map for 1895.
- Excite Maps: North Dakota Maps
  http://www.city.net/maps/view/?mapurl=/countries/united_states/north_dakota
  Zoom in on these maps all the way to the street level.
- HPI County InfoSystem—Counties in North Dakota
  http://www.com/hpi/ndcty/index.html
- K.B. Slocum Books and Maps—North Dakota
  http://www.treasurenet.com/cgi-bin/treasure/kbslocum/scan/se=North.20Dakota/sf=mapstate
- List of North Dakota Counties
  http://www.genealogy.org/~st-clair/counties/state_nd.html
- Map of North Dakota Counties
  http://govinfo.kerr.orst.edu/gif/states/nd.gif
  From the Government Information Sharing Project, Information Services, Oregon State University.
- Map of North Dakota Counties
  http://www.lib.utexas.edu/Libs/PCL/Map_collection/states/North_Dakota.gif
  From the Perry-Castañeda Library at the Univ. of Texas at Austin.

- U.S. Census Bureau—North Dakota Profiles
  http://www.census.gov/datamap/www/38.html
- Yale Peabody Museum: GNIS—North Dakota
  http://www.peabody.yale.edu/other/gnis/ND.html
  *Search the USGS Geographic Names Database. You can limit the search to a specific county in this state and search for any of the following features: airport arch area arroyo bar basin bay beach bench bend bridge **building** canal cape **cemetery** channel **church** cliff crater crossing dam falls flat forest gap geyser glacier gut harbor hospital island isthmus lake lava levee locale mine oilfield other park pillar plain ppl range rapids reserve reservoir ridge **school** sea slope spring stream summit swamp tower trail tunnel valley well woods.*

◆ Military

- Civil War Battle Summaries by State—North Dakota
  http://www2.cr.nps.gov/abpp/battles/bystate.htm#nd
- Dakota Territory During the Civil War
  http://www.rootsweb.com/~usgenweb/sd/military/cw.htm
  Includes a roster of all known 1st Dakota Cavalry personnel.
- Korean Conflict State-Level Casualty Lists—North Dakota
  http://www.nara.gov/nara/electronic/ndhrlist.html
  From the National Archives and Records Administration, Center for Electronic Records.
- Vietnam Conflict State-Level Casualty Lists—North Dakota
  http://www.nara.gov/nara/electronic/ndhrviet.html
  From the National Archives and Records Administration, Center for Electronic Records.
- The Vietnam Veterans Memorial—North Dakota
  http://grunt.space.swri.edu/statewall/ndakota/nd.htm

◆ Newspapers

- AJR NewsLink—North Dakota Newspapers
  http://www.newslink.org/ndnews.html
- The Bismarck Tribune
  http://www.ndonline.com/
- E&P Media Info Links—Newspaper Sites in North Dakota
  http://www.mediainfo.com/emedia/browse-results.htm?region=northdakota&category=newspaper+++++++++
- Ecola Newstand: North Dakota
  http://www.ecola.com/news/press/na/us/nd/
- In-Forum
  http://www.in-forum.com/
  Fargo, North Dakota
- NAA Hotlinks to Newspapers Online—North Dakota
  http://www.naa.org/hotlinks/searchResult.asp?param=ND-North+Dakota&City=1
- N-Net—North DakotaNewspapers
  http://www.n-net.com/nd.htm

- Northscape News: The Grand Forks Herald Online
  http://www.northscape.com/
- The Ultimate Collection of News Links: USA—North Dakota
  http://www.pppp.net/links/news/USA-ND.html
- Yahoo!...Newspapers...North Dakota
  http://dir.yahoo.com/News_and_Media/Newspapers/Browse_By_Region/U_S__States/North_Dakota/

◆ People & Families

- Germans From Russia
  http://www.CyndisList.com/germruss.htm
  See this category on Cyndi's List for related links.
- Hutterite Genealogy HomePage and Cross-Index
  http://feefhs.org/hut/indexhut.html
- Tribes and Villages of North Dakota
  http://hanksville.phast.umass.edu:8000/cultprop/contacts/tribal/ND.html

◆ Professional Researchers, Volunteers & Other Research Services

- Board for Certification of Genealogists—Roster of Those Certified—Specializing in North Dakota
  http://www.genealogy.org/~bcg/rosts_nd.html
- Genealogy Helplist—North Dakota
  http://posom.com/hl/usa/nd.shtml
- The Official Iowa Counties Professional Genealogist and Researcher's Registry for North Dakota
  http://www.iowa-counties.com/gene/nd.htm

◆ Publications, Software & Supplies

- Barbara Green's Used Genealogy Books—North Dakota
  http://home.earthlink.net/~genbooks/lochist.html#ND
- Books We Own—North Dakota
  http://www.rootsweb.com/~bwo/ndakota.html
- Frontier Press Bookstore—North Dakota
  http://www.frontierpress.com/frontier.cgi?category=nd
- Heritage Quest—Microfilm Records for the State of North Dakota
  http://www.heritagequest.com/genealogy/microfilm/north_dakota/
- Park Genealogical Books
  http://www.parkbooks.com/
  Specialists in genealogy and local history for Minnesota, Wisconsin, North and South Dakota and the surrounding area.

◆ Queries, Message Boards & Surname Lists

- GenConnect North Dakota Visitor Center
  http://cgi.rootsweb.com/~genbbs/indx/ND.html
  A system for posting queries, Bibles, biographies, deeds, obituaries, pensions, wills.

◆ Records: Census, Cemeteries, Land, Obituaries, Personal, Taxes and Vital (Born, Married, Died & Buried)

- The 1790–1890 Federal Population Censuses: Catalog of National Archives Microfilm
  http://www.genealogy.org/census/contents.shtml
  - Census Schedules and Microfilm Roll Numbers for North Dakota:
    1860
    http://www.genealogy.org/census/1860_schedules/Dakota.html
    1870
    http://www.genealogy.org/census/1870_schedules/Dakota.html
    1880
    http://www.genealogy.org/census/1880_schedules/Dakota.html
    1880 soundex
    http://www.genealogy.org/census/1880.sdx_schedules/T740.html
    1890 Special Schedules
    http://www.genealogy.org/census/1890-special_schedules/North.Dakota.html

- 1885 Dakota Territory Census Database
  http://www.lib.ndsu.nodak.edu/database/1885census.html

- Barnes County, North Dakota 1900 Census of Germans from Russia
  http://pixel.cs.vt.edu/library/census/link/barnes00.txt

- Barnes County, North Dakota 1910 Census of Germans from Russia
  http://pixel.cs.vt.edu/library/census/link/barnes10.txt

- Barnes County, North Dakota 1920 Census of Germans from Russia
  http://pixel.cs.vt.edu/library/census/link/barnes20.txt

- Cemeteries of the United States—North Dakota Cemeteries—County Index
  http://www.gac.edu/~kengelha/uscemeteries/northdakota.html

- Census Online—Links to Census Sites on the Web—North Dakota
  http://www.census-online.com/links/ND_data.html

- County Courthouse Addresses
  http://www.familytreemaker.com/00000263.html

- Fargo Forum Obituary Index
  http://www.lib.ndsu.nodak.edu/ndirs/bio&genealogy/forumobits.html
  Eastern North Dakota or Northwestern Minnesota. 40,000 names for obituaries posted from 1985 through 1995 and approx. 2,000 obituaries from earlier years.

- Find-A-Grave by Location: North Dakota
  http://www.findagrave.com/grave/lnd.html
  Graves of noteworthy people.

- Interment.net: North Dakota Cemeteries
  http://www.interment.net/us/nd/index.htm
  A list of links to other sites.

- National Archives—Rocky Mountain Region (Denver)
  http://www.nara.gov/regional/denver.html

- National Archives—Rocky Mountain Region
  http://www.familytreemaker.com/00000103.html
  Records for Colorado, Montana, North Dakota, South Dakota, Utah, Wyoming, and a portion of New Mexico.

- North Dakota Land Records
  http://pixel.cs.vt.edu/library/land/nodak/

- North Dakota Naturalization Records Index
  http://www.lib.ndsu.nodak.edu/database/naturalrec.html

- North Dakota Vital Records Information
  http://vitalrec.com/nd.html

- The Political Graveyard—Cemeteries in North Dakota
  http://politicalgraveyard.com/geo/ND/kmindex.html

- USGenWeb Census Project North Dakota
  http://www.usgenweb.org/census/states/northdak.htm

- USGenWeb Tombstone Transcription Project—North Dakota
  http://www.rootsweb.com/~cemetery/ndakota.html

- VitalChek Network—North Dakota
  http://www.vitalchek.com/stateselect.asp?state=ND

- Where to Write for Vital Records—North Dakota
  http://www.cdc.gov/nchswww/howto/w2w/ndakota.htm
  From the National Center for Health Statistics (NCHS).

◆ Religion & Churches

- Christianity.Net Church Locator—North Dakota
  http://www.christianity.net/cgi/location.exe?United_States+North_Dakota

- Church Profiles—North Dakota
  http://www.church-profiles.com/nd/nd.html

- Churches dot Net—Global Church Web Pages—North Dakota
  http://www.churches.net/churches/ndakota.html

- Churches of the World—North Dakota
  http://www.churchsurf.com/churches/North_Dakota/index.htm
  From the ChurchSurf Christian Directory.

◆ Societies & Groups

- The American Legion—Department of North Dakota
  http://www.fm-net.com/ndlegion/

- Bismarck—Mandan Historical & Genealogical Society
  http://soli.inav.net/~dsenne/bmhgs_html/bmhgs.html

- Clay County Historical Society
  http://www.atpfargo.com/hjem/cchs/index.html

- Germans From Russia Heritage Society
  http://www.grhs.com
  Headquarters in Bismarck, North Dakota.

- IOOF Lodge Website Directory—North Dakota
  http://norm28.hsc.usc.edu/IOOF/USA/North_Dakota/North_Dakota.html
  Independent Order of Odd Fellows and Rebekahs.

- James River Genealogy Club
  http://www.rootsweb.com/~ndjrgc/index.htm
  Carrington

- Minnkota Genealogical Society
  http://www.rootsweb.com/~minnkota/
  Grand Forks, North Dakota & East Grand Forks, Minnesota

- Mouse River Loop Genealogical Society
  http://www.geocities.com/Athens/Forum/2079/mrlgs.html
  Bottineau, Burke, McHenry, Mountrail, Renville and Ward counties in North Dakota.

- Red River Valley Genealogical Society
  http://rrnet.com/~rrvgs/

- State Historical Society of North Dakota
  http://www.state.nd.us/hist/

◆ USGenWeb Project

- North Dakota Genealogy—USGenWeb Project State Page
  http://www.usgenweb.org/nd

- NDGENWEB Mailing List
  http://members.aol.com/gfsjohnf/gen_mail_states-nd.html#NDGENWEB
  For discussing the creation of a single source for all North Dakota genealogy databases.

- North Dakota—USGenWeb Archives Table of Contents
  http://www.rootsweb.com/~usgenweb/nd/ndfiles.htm

- North Dakota—USGenWeb FTP Archives
  ftp://ftp.rootsweb.com/pub/usgenweb/nd/

U.S.—OHIO—OH
http://www.CyndisList.com/oh.htm

Category Index:

- General Resource Sites
- Government & Cities
- History & Culture
- Libraries, Archives & Museums
- Locality Specific
- Mailing Lists, Newsgroups & Chat
- Maps, Gazetteers & Geographical Information
- Military
- Newspapers
- People & Families

- Professional Researchers, Volunteers & Other Research Services
- Publications, Software & Supplies
- Queries, Message Boards & Surname Lists
- Records: Census, Cemeteries, Land, Obituaries, Personal, Taxes and Vital
- Religion & Churches
- Societies & Groups
- USGenWeb Project

◆ General Resource Sites

- Dott's Genealogy Home Page
  http://home.att.net/~dottsr/
  Iowa and Ohio.

- Everton's Sources of Genealogical Information in Ohio
  http://www.everton.com/usa/oh.htm

- Family Tree Maker's Genealogy "How To" Guide—Ohio
  http://www.familytreemaker.com/00000210.html

- Genealogy Bulletin Board Systems for Ohio
  http://www.genealogy.org/~gbbs/gbloh.html

- Genealogy Exchange & Surname Registry—OHGenExchange
  http://www.genexchange.com/oh/index.cfm

- Genealogy Resources on the Internet: Ohio
  http://www-personal.umich.edu/~cgaunt/ohio.html

- The Lawrence Register—Southern Ohio's Genealogical and Historical Website
  http://www.wwd.net/user/historical/index.htm

- LDS Research Outline for Ohio
  http://www.everton.com/usa/oh-0836b.txt

- Lineages' Genealogy Site: Ohio
  http://www.lineages.com/rooms/usa/state.asp?StateCode=OH

- Maggie's Ohio Web Ring
  http://www.infinet.com/~dzimmerm/Ring/ohring.html

- ROOTS-L United States Resources: Ohio
  http://www.rootsweb.com/roots-l/USA/oh.html
  Comprehensive list of research links, including many to history-related sites.

◆ Government & Cities

- 50states.com—Ohio State Information Resource
  http://www.50states.com/ohio.htm
  A list of general information for each state, including a list of colleges, state symbols, links to maps, newspapers, and other miscellaneous state information.

- Excite Travel by City.Net—Ohio
  http://www.city.net/countries/united_states/ohio/

- Official City Web Sites for the State of Ohio
  http://OfficialCitySites.org/Ohio.htm

- Ohio and its Government
  http://winslo.ohio.gov/stgvtop.html

- State of Ohio Government Front Page
  http://www.ohio.gov/

- Toledo's Attic Virtual Museum
  http://www.history.utoledo.edu/attic

- Venedocia, Ohio Home Page
  http://www.geocities.com/Heartland/Hills/2761/

- Yahoo! Get Local...Ohio Cities
  http://dir.yahoo.com/Regional/U_S__States/Ohio/Cities/
  Maps, yellow pages, white pages, newspapers and other local information.

- Yahoo! Get Local...Ohio Counties and Regions
  http://dir.yahoo.com/Regional/U_S__States/Ohio/Counties_and_Regions/
  Maps, yellow pages, white pages, newspapers and other local information.

◆ History & Culture

- History of the Western Reserve
  http://www.infinet.com/~dzimmerm/western.html
- Yahoo!...History...Ohio
  http://dir.yahoo.com/Arts/Humanities/History/
  Browse_By_Region/U_S__States/Ohio/

◆ Libraries, Archives & Museums

- Bowling Green State University—Libraries & Learning Resources
  http://www.bgsu.edu/colleges/library/
  - Special Collections & Services
    http://www.bgsu.edu/colleges/library/special.html
    - Center for Archival Collections
      http://www.bgsu.edu/colleges/library/cac/cac.html
    - Historical Collections of the Great Lakes
      http://www.bgsu.edu/colleges/library/hcgl/hcgl.html
- Cincinnati Libraries
  http://cinci.com/info/libs.html
- Dayton & Montgomery County Public Library
  http://www.dayton.lib.oh.us/
  - Local History Collections
    http://www.dayton.lib.oh.us/adult/local-history.html
    - Genealogy Resources
      http://www.dayton.lib.oh.us/genealogy/index.html
    - Montgomery County Historical Society Collection
      http://www.dayton.lib.oh.us/archives/newcom2.htm
    - Shakers Collection
      http://www.dayton.lib.oh.us/archives/shakers.htm
- Family History Centers—Ohio
  http://www.deseretbook.com/famhis/oh.html
- Family History Centers—Ohio
  http://www.lib.byu.edu/~uvrfhc/centers/ohio.html
- Greene County Public Library
  http://www.gcpl.lib.oh.us/
  - Greene County Room, Local History and Genealogy
    http://www.gcpl.lib.oh.us/services/gcr/gcr.htm
- HYTELNET—Library Catalogs: USA: Ohio
  http://library.usask.ca/hytelnet/usa/OH.html
  Before you use any of the Telnet links, make note of the user name, password and any other logon information.
- Kent State University—Libraries & Media Services
  http://www.library.kent.edu/
  - Special Collections & Archives
    http://www.library.kent.edu/speccoll/
    - Regional Historical Collections
      http://www.library.kent.edu/speccoll/reghist/index.html

- NUCMC Listing of Archives and Manuscript Repositories in Ohio
  http://lcweb.loc.gov/coll/nucmc/ohsites.html
  Links to information about resources other than those held in the Library of Congress.
- Ohio Family History Centers
  http://www.genhomepage.com/FHC/Ohio.html
  A list of addresses, phone numbers and hours of operation from the Genealogy Home Page.
- Ohio Libraries and Genealogical Societies
  http://home.att.net/~dottsr/ohio.html
- Ohio Public Library Information Network (OPLIN)
  http://www.oplin.lib.oh.us/
- Ohio State University Libraries
  http://www.lib.ohio-state.edu/
- Ohio University Libraries
  http://www.library.ohiou.edu/index.htm
  - Ohio University Archives & Special Collections
    http://www.library.ohiou.edu/libinfo/depts/archives/archives.htm
  - Ohio University Library and Athens Area Genealogical Resources
    http://www.library.ohiou.edu/libinfo/depts/microforms/geneal.htm
- Preble County District Library
  http://www.pcdl.lib.oh.us/
  - The Preble County Room (Genealogy Department)
    http://www.pcdl.lib.oh.us/pcroom.htm
- Repositories of Primary Sources: Ohio
  http://www.uidaho.edu/special-collections/east2.html#usoh
  A list of links to online resources from the Univ. of Idaho Library, Special Collections and Archives.
- Toledo-Lucas County Public Library
  http://www.library.toledo.oh.us/
  - Local History
    http://www.library.toledo.oh.us/history/history1.htm
- The University of Akron Archival Services
  http://www.uakron.edu/archival/home1.htm
- webCATS: Library Catalogues on the World Wide Web—Ohio
  http://library.usask.ca/hywebcat/states/OH.html
- Western Reserve Historical Society Library
  http://www.wrhs.org/sites/library.htm
  Cleveland
- WINSLO—World Wide Web Info Network—State Library of Ohio
  http://winslo.ohio.gov/
  - State Library of Ohio Genealogy Department General Information
    http://winslo.ohio.gov/gendept.html

- Wright State University Libraries
  http://www.libraries.wright.edu/
  - History
    http://www.libraries.wright.edu/libnet/subj/his/
  - Paul Laurence Dunbar Library
    http://www.libraries.wright.edu/staff/dunbar/
    - Special Collections and Archives
      http://www.libraries.wright.edu/staff/dunbar/arch/schome.htm

◆ Locality Specific

- Also see the USGenWeb section for links to county-specific resources.
- Al POTTS' Marion County, Ohio Page
  http://idt.net/~allenp19/
  Marion County, Ohio Marriages Volume I 1824–1835 and Volume II 1835–1839; Meeker Union Cemetery Records, Meeker Ohio pictures and more.
- Allen County, Ohio Genealogy Homepage
  http://alpha.wcoil.com/~markg/allenco/main.html
- Clermont County, Ohio: Genealogy Resources
  http://members.tripod.com/~Jaibird/clermont.htm
- Darke County Genealogy Fair
  http://www.calweb.com/~wally/darke/fair1.htm
- Darke County, Ohio Genealogical Researchers Home Page
  http://php.ucs.indiana.edu/~jetorres/dco.html
- The Lawrence Register—Genealogical and Historical Website for Lawrence County, Ohio
  http://www.wwd.net/user/historical/
- Lower Scioto Valley
  http://www.scioto.org/LSV/index.html
  Ross, Pike, Scioto, Lawrence and Jackson Counties in Southern Ohio.
- Miami County, Ohio Genealogical Researchers Homepage
  http://www.tdn-net.com/genealogy/
- Miami Valley Genealogy On-line
  http://www.calweb.com/~wally/miami/miami1.htm
  Miami Valley, Ohio counties included in Region 7 of the Local Government Records project: Auglaize, Champaign, Clark, Darke, Greene, Logan, Mercer, Miami, Montgomery, Preble, Shelby.
- Scioto County Ohio Genealogy Hotspot
  http://www.scioto.org/Scioto/
- Scioto Trails: Paths From A Different Time And Place
  http://www.geocities.com/Heartland/5885/
- Sharyn's Genealogy Home Page
  http://www.pe.net/~sharyn/
  Info for Coshocton and surrounding counties.

◆ Mailing Lists, Newsgroups & Chat

- Genealogy Resources on the Internet—Ohio Mailing Lists
  http://members.aol.com/gfsjohnf/gen_mail_states-oh.html
  Each of the mailing list links below points to this site, wonderfully maintained by John Fuller. Visit this site for county-specific mailing lists as well.
- Coshoctonco Mailing List
  http://members.aol.com/gfsjohnf/gen_mail_states-oh.html#Coshoctonco
  Coshocton County, Ohio
- Darke County, Ohio
  http://members.aol.com/gfsjohnf/gen_mail_states-oh.html#DARKE
- Maggie_Ohio Mailing List
  http://members.aol.com/gfsjohnf/gen_mail_states-oh.html#Maggie_Ohio
  For discussing genealogy research and free simple genealogy lookups in the state of Ohio.
- MONTGOMERY_CO_OH Mailing List
  http://members.aol.com/gfsjohnf/gen_mail_states-oh.html#MONTGOMERY_CO_OH
- OHIO-ROOTS-L Mailing List
  http://members.aol.com/gfsjohnf/gen_mail_states-oh.html#OHIO-ROOTS
- OHIO-VALLEY Mailing List
  http://members.aol.com/gfsjohnf/gen_mail_states-oh.html#OHIO-VALLEY
  For anyone with a genealogical or historical interest in the Ohio Valley including the states of Ohio, West Virginia, and Pennsylvania.
- OHROOTS Mailing List
  http://members.aol.com/gfsjohnf/gen_mail_states-oh.html#OHROOTS
- PREBLE_CO_OH Mailing List
  http://members.aol.com/gfsjohnf/gen_mail_states-oh.html#PREBLE_CO_OH
- SCIOTO-VALLEY-OH Mailing List
  http://members.aol.com/gfsjohnf/gen_mail_states-oh.html#SCIOTO-VALLEY-OH
  Lower Scioto Valley including Ross, Pike, Scioto, Lawrence and Jackson counties.

◆ Maps, Gazetteers & Geographical Information

- 1895 U.S. Atlas—Ohio
  http://www.LivGenMI.com/1895oh.htm
- American Memory Panoramic Maps 1847–1929—Ohio
  http://lcweb2.loc.gov/cgi-bin/query/S?ammem/gmd:@filreq(@field(STATE+ohio)+@field(COLLID+pmmap))
  From the Geography and Map Division, Library of Congress.

- American Memory Railroad Maps 1828–1900—
  Ohio
  http://memory.loc.gov/cgi-bin/query/S?ammem/gmd:
  @filreq(@field(STATE+ohio)+@field(COLLID+rrmap))
  From the Geography and Map Division, Library of Congress.

- Color Landform Atlas: Ohio
  http://fermi.jhuapl.edu/states/oh_0.html
  Including a map of counties and a map for 1895.

- Darke County, Ohio Census Indexes, Section Maps,
  History of Towns and Townships, and More
  http://php.ucs.indiana.edu/~jetorres/twps.html

- Excite Maps: Ohio Maps
  http://www.city.net/maps/view/?mapurl=/countries/
  united_states/ohio
  Zoom in on these maps all the way to the street level.

- Gleason's Old Maps Etc.
  http://members.aol.com/oldmapsetc/ohio.html
  *Photocopies of Old Maps, Prints and Articles of Historical and
  Genealogical Interest from Ohio.*

- HPI County InfoSystem—Counties in Ohio
  http://www.com/hpi/ohcty/index.html

- K.B. Slocum Books and Maps—Ohio
  http://www.treasurenet.com/cgi-bin/treasure/kbslocum/scan/
  se=Ohio/sf=mapstate

- List of Ohio Counties
  http://www.genealogy.org/~st-clair/counties/state_oh.html

- Map of Ohio Counties
  http://govinfo.kerr.orst.edu/gif/states/oh.gif
  *From the Government Information Sharing Project, Information
  Services, Oregon State University.*

- Map of Ohio Counties
  http://www.lib.utexas.edu/Libs/PCL/Map_collection/states/
  Ohio.gif
  *From the Perry-Castañeda Library at the Univ. of Texas at
  Austin.*

- Ohio Counties Map
  http://www.genealogy.org/~baf/maps/ohio_map.html

- Ohio Migration Trails
  http://www.infinet.com/~dzimmerm/Gwen/migration.htm

- Ohio Place Names—Cities, Towns, & Townships
  Locations of Ohio, including Defunct Locations
  http://www.rootsweb.com/~ohdefunc/
  *Includes an 1851 listing of post offices that have names differing
  from the name of a town or locality.*

- U.S. Census Bureau—Ohio Profiles
  http://www.census.gov/datamap/www/39.html

- Yale Peabody Museum: GNIS—Ohio
  http://www.peabody.yale.edu/other/gnis/OH.html
  *Search the USGS Geographic Names Database. You can limit
  the search to a specific county in this state and search for any of
  the following features: airport arch area arroyo bar basin bay
  beach bench bend bridge **building** canal cape **cemetery** channel
  church cliff crater crossing dam falls flat forest gap geyser
  glacier gut harbor hospital island isthmus lake lava levee locale
  mine oilfield other park pillar plain ppl range rapids reserve
  reservoir ridge **school** sea slope spring stream summit swamp
  tower trail tunnel valley well woods.*

◆ Military

- 4th Ohio Volunteer Cavalry
  http://www.geocities.com/Heartland/Plains/7614/4th_ohio.htm

- 6th Regiment, Ohio Volunteer Infantry
  http://www.access.digex.net/~bdboyle/6thohio.txt

- 16th Ohio Volunteer Infantry Home Page
  http://www.mkwe.com/home.htm

- 36th Ohio Volunteer Infantry, Union Civil War
  Regiment 1861–1865
  http://www.angelfire.com/oh/36OVI/
  *Site dedicated to preserving the history of the 36th Ohio
  Volunteer Infantry, a Civil War unit formed in Washington
  County, Ohio. Searching for descendants of the men of the
  36th. Gathering material for a regimental history to be written
  by a military historian.*

- 48th Ohio Veteran Volunteer Infantry
  http://www.ben2.ucla.edu/~worth/history48ovvi.html

- 49th Ohio Volunteer Infantry
  http://www.infinet.com/~lstevens/49oh.html

- 76th Ohio Volunteer Infantry
  http://www.infinet.com/~lstevens/civwar/

- The 126th Ohio Volunteer Infantry: Letters,
  Accounts, Oral Histories
  http://www.iwaynet.net/~lsci/

- The Civil War Archive—Union Regiments—Ohio
  http://www.civilwararchive.com/unionoh.htm

- Civil War Battle Summaries by State—Ohio
  http://www2.cr.nps.gov/abpp/battles/bystate.htm#oh

- The Civil War Page
  http://www.wwd.net/user/historical/Cwindex.html
  From The Lawrence Register web site (Lawrence County, Ohio).

- Isaac Spears Sanderlin, Private, Company I, 100th
  Ohio Volunteer Infantry in the Civil War
  http://www.oz.net/~cyndihow/isaac.htm
  Cyndi's 3rd-great-grandfather.

- Korean Conflict State-Level Casualty Lists—Ohio
  http://www.nara.gov/nara/electronic/ohhrlist.html
  *From the National Archives and Records Administration, Center
  for Electronic Records.*

- Ohio Civil War Infantry
  http://www.infinet.com/~lstevens/a/infantry.html

- Ohio Civil War Genealogy Journal
  http://www.ogs.org/civil.htm
  A quarterly publication from The Ohio Genealogical Society.

- Ohio in the Civil War
  http://www.infinet.com/~lstevens/a/civil.html

- Ohio Volunteer Infantry 4th Regiment
  http://members.aol.com/Shortyhack/Ohio4.html

- Ohio Volunteer Infantry 51st Regiment
  http://members.aol.com/Shortyhack/ohio51.html

- Ohio Volunteer Infantry 66th Regiment
  http://members.aol.com/Shortyhack/66ohio.html

- Ohio Volunteer Infantry 142nd Regiment
  http://members.aol.com/Shortyhack/142ohio.html

- Revolutionary War Soldiers Living in the State of Ohio in 1818–1819
  http://php.ucs.indiana.edu/~jetorres/ohiorev.html

- Roster of Ohio Soldiers 1861–1866
  http://members.aol.com/WmMartin1/ohio/

- Sixth Ohio Volunteer Infantry
  http://www.intcom.net/~tomt/6ovihome.htm

- Vietnam Conflict State-Level Casualty Lists—Ohio
  http://www.nara.gov/nara/electronic/ohhrviet.html
  From the National Archives and Records Administration, Center for Electronic Records.

- The Vietnam Veterans Memorial—Ohio
  http://grunt.space.swri.edu/statewall/ohio/oh.htm

◆ Newspapers

- AJR NewsLink—Ohio Newspapers
  http://www.newslink.org/ohnews.html

- E&P Media Info Links—Newspaper Sites in Ohio
  http://www.mediainfo.com/emedia/browse-results.htm?region=ohio&category=newspaper+++++++++

- Ecola Newstand: Ohio
  http://www.ecola.com/news/press/na/us/oh/

- NAA Hotlinks to Newspapers Online—Ohio
  http://www.naa.org/hotlinks/searchResult.asp?param=OH-Ohio&City=1

- N-Net—Ohio Newspapers
  http://www.n-net.com/oh.htm

- The Register-Herald, Preble County, Ohio
  http://www.registerherald.com/

- The Ultimate Collection of News Links: USA—Ohio
  http://www.pppp.net/links/news/USA-OH.html

- Yahoo!...Newspapers...Ohio
  http://dir.yahoo.com/News_and_Media/Newspapers/Browse_By_Region/U_S__States/Ohio/

◆ People & Families

- Directory of Underground Railroad Operators— Ohio
  http://www.ugrr.org//names/map-oh.htm

- Murphy's Public House
  http://www.alltel.net/~dmurphy595
  Dedicated to the Irish and German families of Ohio.

- Ohio River Valley Families
  http://orvf.com/
  By Allen David Distler.

- Tribes and Villages of Ohio
  http://hanksville.phast.umass.edu:8000/cultprop/contacts/tribal/OH.html

◆ Professional Researchers, Volunteers & Other Research Services

- Amy Johnson Crow, CG
  http://www.amyjohnsoncrow.com
  Genealogical research in Ohio and Ohioans in the Civil War.

- Board for Certification of Genealogists—Roster of Those Certified—Specializing in Ohio
  http://www.genealogy.org/~bcg/rosts_oh.html

- Diane's Michigan Genealogy Page
  http://members.aol.com/DJOslund/index.html
  Professional Genealogist serving Southeastern Michigan, Southwestern Ontario, Northwestern Ohio.

- Genealogy Helplist—Ohio
  http://posom.com/hl/usa/oh.shtml

- The Official Iowa Counties Professional Genealogist and Researcher's Registry for Ohio
  http://www.iowa-counties.com/gene/oh.htm

- So Many Branches
  http://www.angelfire.com/biz/SoManyBranches/
  Western New York, Northern Pennsylvania, Michigan and Northern Ohio Genealogical Research.

◆ Publications, Software & Supplies

- AncestorSpy—CDs and Microfiche for Ohio
  http://www.ancestorspy.com/oh.htm

- Barbara Green's Used Genealogy Books—Ohio
  http://home.earthlink.net/~genbooks/lochist.html#OH

- Barnette's Family Tree Books—Ohio
  http://www.barnettesbooks.com/ohio.htm

- Books We Own—Ohio
  http://www.rootsweb.com/~bwo/ohio.html

- Boyd Publishing Company—Ohio
  http://www.hom.net/~gac/ohio.htm

- Frontier Press Bookstore—Ohio
  http://www.frontierpress.com/frontier.cgi?category=oh

- FLI Antiques & Genealogy
  http://www.wwd.net/user/tklaiber/index.htm
  Publications for Ohio and Kentucky.

- GenealogyBookShop.com—Ohio
  http://www.genealogybookshop.com/genealogybookshop/files/The_United_States,Ohio/index.html
  The online store of Genealogical Publishing Co., Inc. & Clearfield Company.

- The Grannies' Book Emporium
  http://www.granniesworld.com/books/
  Books for Ohio and Pennsylvania.

- Hearthstone Bookshop—Ohio
  http://www.hearthstonebooks.com/cgi-bin/webc.cgi/
  st_main.html?catid=94&sid=2PH5t29sm
- Heritage Books—Ohio
  http://www.heritagebooks.com/oh.htm
- Heritage Quest—Microfilm Records for the
  State of Ohio
  http://www.heritagequest.com/genealogy/microfilm/ohio/
- LDS Microfilms and Microfiche for Coshocton Co.,
  Ohio
  http://www.pe.net/~sharyn/lds.html
- Lost in Time Books—Ohio
  http://www.lostintime.com/catalog/books/bookst/bo24000.htm
- The Memorabilia Corner—Books: Ohio
  http://members.aol.com/TMCorner/book_oh.htm
- Northwest Ohio Quarterly
  http://www.history.utoledo.edu/NWOQ.HTML
  *A joint publication of the History Department of the University
  of Toledo, the Maumee Valley Historical Society and the Toledo-
  Lucas County Public Library.*
- Ohio Civil War Genealogy Journal
  http://www.greenapple.com/~ksmith/civil.html
  A quarterly publication from The Ohio Genealogical Society.
- S-K Publications—Ohio 1850 Census Books
  http://www.skpub.com/genie/census/oh/
- TLC Genealogy Books
  http://www.tlc-gen.com/
  Specializing in Colonial VA, KY, MD, OH, PA, NC, etc.
- Willow Bend Bookstore—Ohio
  http://www.willowbend.net/oh.htm
- Ye Olde Genealogie Shoppe Books—Ohio
  http://www.yogs.com/maincat.htm#OHIO

◆ Queries, Message Boards & Surname Lists

- GenConnect Ohio Visitor Center
  http://cgi.rootsweb.com/~genbbs/indx/Oh.html
  *A system for posting queries, Bibles, biographies, deeds,
  obituaries, pensions, wills.*
- Queries on the Coshocton Page—Ohio
  http://www.cu.soltec.com/~photo/coshocton.html

◆ Records: Census, Cemeteries, Land, Obituaries, Personal, Taxes and Vital (Born, Married, Died & Buried)

- The 1790–1890 Federal Population Censuses:
  Catalog of National Archives Microfilm
  http://www.genealogy.org/census/contents.shtml

- ○ Census Schedules and Microfilm Roll Numbers
  for Ohio:
  1820
  http://www.genealogy.org/census/1820_schedules/Ohio.html
  1830
  http://www.genealogy.org/census/1830_schedules/Ohio.html
  1840
  http://www.genealogy.org/census/1840_schedules/Ohio.html
  1850
  http://www.genealogy.org/census/1850_schedules/Ohio.html
  1860
  http://www.genealogy.org/census/1860_schedules/Ohio.html
  1870
  http://www.genealogy.org/census/1870_schedules/Ohio.html
  1880
  http://www.genealogy.org/census/1880_schedules/Ohio.html
  1880 soundex
  http://www.genealogy.org/census/1880.sdx_schedules/
  T767.html
  1890 Special Schedules
  http://www.genealogy.org/census/1890-special_schedules/
  Ohio.html
- Allen County, Ohio Cemetery Page
  http://www.geocities.com/Heartland/Plains/5409/cem.html
  From The GIERHART Family Inn.
- The Bureau of Land Management—Eastern States,
  General Land Office
  http://www.glorecords.blm.gov/
  *The Official Land Patent Records Site. This site has a search-
  able database of over two million pre-1908 Federal land title
  records, including scanned images of those records. The Eastern
  Public Land States covered in this database are: Alabama,
  Arkansas, Florida, Illinois, Indiana, Louisiana, Michigan,
  Minnesota, Mississippi, Missouri, Ohio, Wisconsin.*
- Butler County, OH Older Obituaries
  http://www.rootsweb.com/~ohbutler/obit.html
- Cemeteries of the United States—Ohio
  Cemeteries—County Index
  http://www.gac.edu/~kengelha/uscemeteries/ohio.html
- Census Online—Links to Census Sites on the Web—
  Ohio
  http://www.census-online.com/links/OH_data.html
- Cleveland News Index—Search on the word
  "Obituaries"
  http://www-catalog.cpl.org/CLENIX
  Database from 1976 to present.
- County Courthouse Addresses
  http://www.familytreemaker.com/00000264.html
- Darke County, Ohio Census Indexes, Section Maps,
  History of Towns and Townships, and More
  http://php.ucs.indiana.edu/~jetorres/twps.html

- Find-A-Grave by Location: Ohio
  http://www.findagrave.com/grave/loh.html
  Graves of noteworthy people.

- Interment.net: Ohio Cemeteries
  http://www.interment.net/us/oh/index.htm
  A list of links to other sites.

- Miami Valley Genealogical Index
  http://www.pcdl.lib.oh.us/miami/miami.htm
  Surname index of census, tax, marriage & wills records for these counties: Butler, Champaign, Clark, Darke, Greene, Hamilton, Mercer, Miami, Montgomery, Preble, Shelby, Warren.

- National Archives—Great Lakes Region (Chicago)
  http://www.nara.gov/regional/chicago.html

- National Archives—Great Lakes Region
  http://www.familytreemaker.com/00000096.html
  Records from Illinois, Indiana, Michigan, Minnesota, Ohio, and Wisconsin.

- Obituary Abstracts of Coshocton Co., OH
  http://www.pe.net/~sharyn/obits.html

- Ohio Online Death Certificate Index, 1913–1927, and 1933–1937
  http://www.ohiohistory.org/dindex/search.cfm
  Searchable database from the Ohio Historical Society, Archives/Library.

- Ohio Vital Records Information
  http://vitalrec.com/oh.html

- The Political Graveyard—Cemeteries in Ohio
  http://politicalgraveyard.com/geo/OH/kmindex.html

- Preble County Obituary Index
  http://206.103.255.36/getobit.htm
  More than 10,500 obituaries reported in the Register-Herald for 1980–1995.

- Preplanning Network—Funeral Home and Cemetery Directory—Ohio
  http://www.preplannet.com/ohiofh.htm

- SAMPUBCO
  http://www.wasatch.com/~dsam/sampubco/index.htm
  Will Testators Indexes, Naturalization Records Indexes and Census Indexes online. You can order copies of the original source documents for a small fee.

- Search Obituaries Found in Dayton Newspaper 1985–97
  http://www.dayton.lib.oh.us/htbin/obit

- Surname Index to the Census of the Slovak People Living in Mahoning County, Ohio
  http://www.iarelative.com/22census/index.html

- Toledo's Attic Woodlawn Cemetery Biographies
  http://www.history.utoledo.edu/att/wood/woodindex.html

- USGenWeb Census Project Ohio
  http://www.usgenweb.org/census/states/ohio/ohio.htm

- USGenWeb Tombstone Transcription Project—Ohio
  http://www.rootsweb.com/~cemetery/ohio.html

- VitalChek Network—Ohio
  http://www.vitalchek.com/stateselect.asp?state=OH

- Vital Records Extracted From "The Life, Travels, and Ministry of Milton M. Everly"
  http://www.aloha.net/~jan/milton.txt
  November 1897–April 1901. Extractions of records for marriages, some baptisms, and funerals.

- Where to Write for Vital Records—Ohio
  http://www.cdc.gov/nchswww/howto/w2w/ohio.htm
  From the National Center for Health Statistics (NCHS).

◆ Religion & Churches

- Christianity.Net Church Locator—Ohio
  http://www.christianity.net/cgi/location.exe?United_States+Ohio

- Church Online!—Ohio
  http://www.churchonline.com/usas/oh/oh.html

- Church Profiles—Ohio
  http://www.church-profiles.com/oh/oh.html

- Churches dot Net—Global Church Web Pages—Ohio
  http://www.churches.net/churches/ohio.html

- Churches of the World—Ohio
  http://www.churchsurf.com/churches/Ohio/index.htm
  From the ChurchSurf Christian Directory.

◆ Societies & Groups

- Ancient Order of Hibernians in Ohio
  http://www.intcom.net/~tomt/aoh/ohio/aohohio.html

- Archer's Computer Interest Group List—Ohio
  http://www.genealogy.org/~ngs/cigs/ngl1usoh.html

- Athens County Historical Society and Museum
  http://www.seorf.ohiou.edu/~xx023/

- Bellville Historical Society
  http://www.angelfire.com/oh/bellville/

- Berea Historical Society
  http://members.aol.com/bereahist/

- Botkins Historical Society
  http://members.aol.com/BotkinsHS/history/bhshome.html

- Centerville-Washington Township Historical Society
  http://www.mvcc.net/Centerville/histsoc/

- Cheviot Historical Society
  http://www.cheviot.org/historical.htm

- Cincinnati Historical Society Library
  http://www.cincymuseum.org/library.htm

- Darke County Ohio Genealogical Society
  http://php.indiana.edu/~jetorres/gensoc.html

- Genealogical Society Montgomery County, Ohio
  http://members.aol.com/ogsmont/

- The Grand Lodge of F. & A.M. of Ohio
  http://www.freemason.com./

- IOOF Lodge Website Directory—Ohio
  http://norm28.hsc.usc.edu/IOOF/USA/Ohio/Ohio.html
  Independent Order of Odd Fellows and Rebekahs.

- Irish American Archives Society
  http://www.intcom.net/~tomt/aoh/ohio/iaas.html
  Cleveland, Ohio

- Lake Erie Islands Historical Society
  http://www.leihs.org/

- Lakewood Historical Society
  http://www.lkwdpl.org/histsoc/

- Lawrence County Genealogy Society
  http://www.wwd.net/user/historical/gensoc.htm

- Military Order of the Loyal Legion of the
  United States—Ohio Commandery
  http://suvcw.org/oh/mollus/mollus_oh.htm

- New Albany Plain Township Historical Society
  http://members.tripod.com/~blulego/napths.htm

- Noble County Historical Society
  http://www.geocities.com/Heartland/6854/noble.html

- North East Ohio-Computer Aided Genealogy—
  NEO-CAG
  http://members.harborcom.net/~kliotj/neocag/

- Ohio Genealogical Society
  http://www.ogs.org/

  - Ashtabula County Genealogical Society, Inc.
    http://www.ashtabulagen.org/

  - Athens County Chapter
    http://www.seorf.ohiou.edu/~xx024/

  - Auglaize County Chapter
    http://www.rootsweb.com/~ohaugogs/index.html

  - Belmont County Chapter
    http://www.rootsweb.com/~ohbelogs/

  - Clinton County Genealogical Society and the
    Clinton County Historical Society
    http://www.postcom.com/ccgshs/
    Wilmington

  - Columbiana County Chapter
    http://www.rootsweb.com/~ohcolumb/

  - Coshocton County Chapter
    http://www.pe.net/~sharyn/cccogs.html

  - The Delaware County Genealogy Society and
    The Delaware County Historical Society
    http://www.midohio.net/dchsdcgs/

  - Fairfield County Genealogical Society
    http://www.fairfieldgenealogy.org/

  - Franklin County Genealogical Society
    http://www.geocities.com/Heartland/Meadows/5179/
    fcgs.html
    Columbus, Ohio

  - The Hamilton County Chapter of the Ohio
    Genealogical Society
    http://members.aol.com/ogshc/index.htm

  - Hancock Chapter
    http://www.bright.net/~hanogs/index.html

  - Hudson Genealogical Study Group
    http://www.rootsweb.com/~ohhudogs/hudson.htm

  - Huron County
    http://www.rootsweb.com/~ohhuron/

  - Jefferson County Chapter
    http://www.rootsweb.com/~ohjefogs/

  - Lake County Genealogical Society
    http://www.morleylibrary.org/genealogy/lcgs.htm

  - Lorain County Chapter
    http://www.centuryinter.net/lorgen/

  - Marion Area Genealogy Society and the Marion
    County Historical Society
    http://www.genealogy.org/~smoore/marion/aboutsoc.htm

  - Montgomery County Chapter
    http://members.aol.com/ogsmont/

  - Morrow County
    http://www.rootsweb.com/~ohmorrow/

  - Preble County
    http://www.pcdl.lib.oh.us/pcgs.htm

  - Richland County Genealogical Society
    http://www.rootsweb.com/~ohrichgs/

  - Union County Genealogical Society
    http://www.geocities.com/Heartland/Prairie/3391/

  - Van Wert Chapter
    http://www.rootsweb.com/~ohvanwer/vwc_ogs.htm

  - Wyandot Tracers—Wyandot County Genealogical
    Society
    http://www.udata.com/users/hsbaker/tracers.htm

- Ohio Historical Society
  http://www.ohiohistory.org/

- Ohio Society Daughters of the American Revolution
  http://members.aol.com/osdar/index.html

- Old Northwest Historical Society
  http://home.fuse.net/rrowan/
  *Dedicated to preserving and perpetuating the history of the
  Old Northwest Territory. The region northwest of the Ohio river
  that became the states of Ohio, Indiana, Illinios, Michigan, and
  Wisconsin.*

- Pemberville-Freedom Area Historical Society
  http://www.wcnet.org/organizations/p/pemhistsoc.html

- Perry County Historical Society
  http://www.netpluscom.com/~pchs/

- Portage County Historical Society
  http://www2.clearlight.com/~pchs/

- Roseville Historical Society
  http://www.netpluscom.com/~pchs/rosevill.htm

- Ross County Historical Society
  http://www.rosscountyhistorical.org/
- Shelby County Historical Society
  http://www.bright.net/~richnsus/
- Slovenian Genealogy Society, Ohio Chapter
  http://feefhs.org/slovenia/frgsgsoh.html
- Southwest Butler County Genealogical Society
  http://www2.eos.net/dajend/swbcgs.html
  Hamilton, Ohio
- Summit County Historical Society
  http://www.neo.lrun.com/Summit_County_Historical_Society/
- Transylvania Saxon Genealogy and Heritage Society, Inc.
  http://feefhs.org/ah/hu/tsghs/frgtsghs.html
- Troy Historical Society
  http://www.virtualcityohio.com/troy/history/troyhistory.html
- The Wayne County Genealogical Society
  http://www.rootsweb.com/~ohwayne/wcgs.htm

- The Wayne County Historical Society Campus
  http://members.aol.com/jnwelty/Hist.html
- Western Reserve Historical Society
  http://www.wrhs.org/
- Willoughby Historical Society
  http://www.wepl.lib.oh.us/wybhisoc.html
- Wooster-Wayne Chapter National Society of the Daughters of the American Revolution
  http://members.aol.com/jnwelty/wwchapter.html

◆ USGenWeb Project

- Ohio Genealogy—USGenWeb Project State Page
  http://www.usgenweb.org/oh
- Ohio—USGenWeb Archives Table of Contents
  http://www.rootsweb.com/~usgenweb/oh/ohfiles.htm
- Ohio—USGenWeb FTP Archives
  ftp://ftp.rootsweb.com/pub/usgenweb/oh/

U.S.—OKLAHOMA—OK
http://www.CyndisList.com/ok.htm

Category Index:

- General Resource Sites
- Government & Cities
- History & Culture
- Libraries, Archives & Museums
- Mailing Lists, Newsgroups & Chat
- Maps, Gazetteers & Geographical Information
- Military
- Newspapers
- People & Families

- Professional Researchers, Volunteers & Other Research Services
- Publications, Software & Supplies
- Queries, Message Boards & Surname Lists
- Records: Census, Cemeteries, Land, Obituaries, Personal, Taxes and Vital
- Religion & Churches
- Societies & Groups
- USGenWeb Project

◆ General Resource Sites

- Everton's Sources of Genealogical Information in Oklahoma
  http://www.everton.com/usa/ok.htm

- Family Tree Maker's Genealogy "How To" Guide—Oklahoma
  http://www.familytreemaker.com/00000211.html

- Genealogy Bulletin Board Systems for Oklahoma
  http://www.genealogy.org/~gbbs/gblok.html

- Genealogy Exchange & Surname Registry—OKGenExchange
  http://www.genexchange.com/ok/index.cfm

- Genealogy Resources on the Internet: Oklahoma
  http://www-personal.umich.edu/~cgaunt/ok.html

- Goodland Presbyterian Children's Home
  http://www2.1starnet.com/goodland/
  With History links for the area.

- LDS Research Outline for Oklahoma
  http://www.everton.com/usa/ok-0837b.txt

- Lineages' Genealogy Site: Oklahoma
  http://www.lineages.com/rooms/usa/state.asp?StateCode=OK

- ROOTS-L United States Resources: Oklahoma
  http://www.rootsweb.com/roots-l/USA/ok.html
  Comprehensive list of research links, including many to history-related sites.

- Texas County, Oklahoma Genealogy and History
  http://www.geocities.com/Heartland/Estates/7166
  This site includes marriage records, newspaper articles, family histories and will include many other things that will relate to area.

◆ Government & Cities

- 50states.com—Oklahoma State Information Resource
  http://www.50states.com/oklahoma.htm
  A list of general information for each state, including a list of colleges, state symbols, links to maps, newspapers, and other miscellaneous state information.

- Excite Travel by City.Net—Oklahoma
  http://www.city.net/countries/united_states/oklahoma/

- Official City Web Sites for the State of Oklahoma
  http://OfficialCitySites.org/Oklahoma.htm

- Oklahoma State Government Information Server
  http://www.oklaosf.state.ok.us/

- Yahoo! Get Local...Oklahoma Cities
  http://dir.yahoo.com/Regional/U_S__States/Oklahoma/Cities/
  Maps, yellow pages, white pages, newspapers and other local information.

- Yahoo! Get Local...Oklahoma Counties and Regions
  http://dir.yahoo.com/Regional/U_S__States/Oklahoma/Counties_and_Regions/
  Maps, yellow pages, white pages, newspapers and other local information.

◆ History & Culture

- OKLAHOMBRES Online!
  http://www.qns.com/~dcordry/hombres.html
  Dedicated to the careful, correct research and preservation of lawman and outlaw history.

- Yahoo!...History...Oklahoma
  http://dir.yahoo.com/Arts/Humanities/History/Browse_By_Region/U_S__States/Oklahoma/

◆ Libraries, Archives & Museums

- Family History Centers—Oklahoma
  http://www.deseretbook.com/famhis/ok.html

- Family History Centers—Oklahoma
  http://www.lib.byu.edu/~uvrfhc/centers/oklahoma.html

- HYTELNET—Library Catalogs: USA: Oklahoma
  http://library.usask.ca/hytelnet/usa/OK.html
  Before you use any of the Telnet links, make note of the user name, password and any other logon information.

- NUCMC Listing of Archives and Manuscript Repositories in Oklahoma
  http://lcweb.loc.gov/coll/nucmc/oksites.html
  Links to information about resources other than those held in the Library of Congress.

- ODL Online: Oklahoma Department of Libraries
  http://www.odl.state.ok.us/
  - Oklahoma Public Libraries on the Web
    http://www.odl.state.ok.us/servlibs/pldirect/pllinks.htm
  - Records Management Division
    http://www.odl.state.ok.us/oar/records.htm
  - State Archives Division
    http://www.odl.state.ok.us/oar/index.htm
    - Genealogical Material
      http://www.odl.state.ok.us/oar/arcgene.htm

- Oklahoma Family History Centers
  http://www.genhomepage.com/FHC/Oklahoma.html
  A list of addresses, phone numbers and hours of operation from the Genealogy Home Page.

- Oklahoma State University Library
  http://www.library.okstate.edu/
  - Special Collections and University Archives
    http://www.library.okstate.edu/dept/scua/scuahp.htm

- Repositories of Primary Sources: Oklahoma
  http://www.uidaho.edu/special-collections/west.html#usok
  A list of links to online resources from the Univ. of Idaho Library, Special Collections and Archives.

- The Tillman County Historical Museum
  http://www.frisco.org/msw/mswtil.htm

- University of Oklahoma Libraries
  http://www-lib.ou.edu/index.htm
  - Western History Collection
    http://www-lib.ou.edu/depts/west/index.htm

- University of Tulsa—McFarlin Library
  http://www.lib.utulsa.edu/
  - Special Collections Department
    http://www.lib.utulsa.edu/speccoll/speccoll.htm

- webCATS: Library Catalogues on the World Wide Web—Oklahoma
  http://library.usask.ca/hywebcat/states/OK.html

◆ Mailing Lists, Newsgroups & Chat

- Genealogy Resources on the Internet—Oklahoma Mailing Lists
  http://members.aol.com/gfsjohnf/gen_mail_states-ok.html
  Each of the mailing list links below points to this site, wonderfully maintained by John Fuller. Visit this site for county-specific mailing lists as well.

- Indian-Territory-Roots Mailing List
  http://members.aol.com/gfsjohnf/gen_mail_states-ok.html#Indian-Territory-Roots
  For anyone with a genealogical interest in Indian Territory—an area that in 1907 became the eastern and south/south-eastern part of Oklahoma.

- ITCREEKN Mailing List
  http://members.aol.com/gfsjohnf/gen_mail_states-ok.html#ITCREEKN
  For anyone with a genealogical interest in the Creek Nation, Indian Territory.

- No_Mans_Land Mailing List
  http://members.aol.com/gfsjohnf/gen_mail_states-ok.html#No_Mans_Land
  For anyone with a genealogical or historical interest in the territory of early Oklahoma history that became what is now known as the Panhandle; touches Kansas, Texas, New Mexico, and Colorado; and is comprised of the Oklahoma counties of Beaver, Texas, and Cimmaron.

- OKROOTS Mailing List
  http://members.aol.com/gfsjohnf/gen_mail_states-ok.html#OKROOTS

- TEXAHOMA-ROOTS-L Mailing List
  http://members.aol.com/gfsjohnf/gen_mail_states-ok.html#TEXAHOMA-ROOTS
  Oklahoma & Texas

◆ Maps, Gazetteers & Geographical Information

- 1872 County Map of East Indian Nations
  http://www.ismi.net/chnegw/1872eindian.htm

- 1872 County Map of West Indian Nations
  http://www.ismi.net/chnegw/1872windian.htm

- 1895 U.S. Atlas—Indian Nations
  http://www.LivGenMI.com/1895inna.htm

- 1895 U.S. Atlas—Oklahoma
  http://www.LivGenMI.com/1895ok.htm

- American Memory Panoramic Maps 1847–1929—Oklahoma
  http://lcweb2.loc.gov/cgi-bin/query/S?ammem/gmd:@filreq(@field(STATE+oklahoma)+@field(COLLID+pmmap))
  From the Geography and Map Division, Library of Congress.

- American Memory Railroad Maps 1828–1900—Oklahoma
  http://memory.loc.gov/cgi-bin/query/S?ammem/gmd:@filreq(@field(STATE+oklahoma)+@field(COLLID+rrmap))
  From the Geography and Map Division, Library of Congress.

Color Landform Atlas: Oklahoma
http://fermi.jhuapl.edu/states/ok_0.html
Including a map of counties and a map for 1895.

Excite Maps: Oklahoma Maps
http://www.city.net/maps/view/?mapurl=/countries/
united_states/oklahoma
Zoom in on these maps all the way to the street level.

HPI County InfoSystem—Counties in Oklahoma
http://www.com/hpi/okcty/index.html

K.B. Slocum Books and Maps—Oklahoma
http://www.treasurenet.com/cgi-bin/treasure/kbslocum/scan/
se=Oklahoma/sf=mapstate

List of Oklahoma Counties
http://www.genealogy.org/~st-clair/counties/state_ok.html

Map of Oklahoma Counties
http://govinfo.kerr.orst.edu/gif/states/ok.gif
*From the Government Information Sharing Project, Information
Services, Oklahoma State University.*

Map of Oklahoma Counties
http://www.lib.utexas.edu/Libs/PCL/Map_collection/states/
Oklahoma.gif
*From the Perry-Castañeda Library at the Univ. of Texas at
Austin.*

U.S. Census Bureau—Oklahoma Profiles
http://www.census.gov/datamap/www/40.html

Yale Peabody Museum: GNIS—Oklahoma
http://www.peabody.yale.edu/other/gnis/OK.html
*Search the USGS Geographic Names Database. You can limit
the search to a specific county in this state and search for any of
the following features: airport arch area arroyo bar basin bay
beach bench bend bridge* **building** *canal cape* **cemetery** *channel*
church *cliff crater crossing dam falls flat forest gap geyser
glacier gut harbor hospital island isthmus lake lava levee locale
mine oilfield other park pillar plain ppl range rapids reserve
reservoir ridge* **school** *sea slope spring stream summit swamp
tower trail tunnel valley well woods.*

◆ Military

The Civil War in Indian Territory
http://www.geocities.com/Heartland/Hills/1263/
itcheyarapindx.html

Korean Conflict State-Level Casualty Lists—
Oklahoma
http://www.nara.gov/nara/electronic/okhrlist.html
*From the National Archives and Records Administration,
Center for Electronic Records.*

Trans-Mississippi Rifles (TMR)
http://members.aol.com/rlhtmr/index.html

Vietnam Conflict State-Level Casualty Lists—
Oklahoma
http://www.nara.gov/nara/electronic/okhrviet.html
*From the National Archives and Records Administration,
Center for Electronic Records.*

The Vietnam Veterans Memorial—Oklahoma
http://grunt.space.swri.edu/statewall/oklahoma/ok.htm

◆ Newspapers

AJR NewsLink—Oklahoma Newspapers
http://www.newslink.org/oknews.html

E&P Media Info Links—Newspaper Sites in
Oklahoma
http://www.mediainfo.com/emedia/browse-results.
htm?region=oklahoma&category=newspaper+++++++++

Ecola Newstand: Oklahoma
http://www.ecola.com/news/press/na/us/ok/

NAA Hotlinks to Newspapers Online—Oklahoma
http://www.naa.org/hotlinks/searchResult.asp?param=
OK-Oklahoma&City=1

N-Net—Oklahoma Newspapers
http://www.n-net.com/ok.htm

Oklahoma Newspaper Project
http://www.keytech.com:80/~frizzell/
A project to preserver newspapers on microfilm.

The Oklahoman Online
http://www.oklahoman.com/

The Ultimate Collection of News Links:
USA—Oklahoma
http://www.pppp.net/links/news/USA-OK.html

Western Oklahoma Newspaper Research
http://members.tripod.com/~smcb/research.html

Yahoo!...Newspapers...Oklahoma
http://dir.yahoo.com/News_and_Media/Newspapers/
Browse_By_Region/U_S__States/Oklahoma/

◆ People & Families

The African—Native Genealogy Homepage
http://members.aol.com/angelaw859/index.html
*Celebrating the Estelusti. The Freedmen Oklahoma's Black
Indians of the Cherokee, Chickasaw, Choctaw, Creek, and
Seminole Nations.*

Boyhood Memories of Col. Ed NIX, U.S. Marshal of
the Oklahoma Territory
http://www.geocities.com/Heartland/Hills/5391/nix.html
By Gene KUYKENDALL.

Links to Plains Indians
http://www.moore-information.com/overland/indians.html

Seminole Nation of Oklahoma—Historic
Preservation Office
http://www.cowboy.net/native/seminole/historic.html

Terri Moore's Native American Home Page
http://cherokee.digigo.com/tmoore/
Arkansas, Oklahoma and Native American Information.

Tribes and Villages of Oklahoma
http://hanksville.phast.umass.edu:8000/cultprop/contacts/
tribal/OK.html

◆ Professional Researchers, Volunteers & Other Research Services

- Board for Certification of Genealogists—Roster of Those Certified—Specializing in Oklahoma
  http://www.genealogy.org/~bcg/rosts_ok.html

- Genealogy Helplist—Oklahoma
  http://posom.com/hl/usa/ok.shtml

- The Official Iowa Counties Professional Genealogist and Researcher's Registry for Oklahoma
  http://www.iowa-counties.com/gene/ok.htm

- Oklahoma and Arkansas Research by Monroe Davis
  http://www.geocities.com/Eureka/Park/5315/research.htm

◆ Publications, Software & Supplies

- AncestorSpy—CDs and Microfiche for Oklahoma
  http://www.ancestorspy.com/ok.htm

- Barbara Green's Used Genealogy Books—Oklahoma
  http://home.earthlink.net/~genbooks/lochist.html#OK

- Barnette's Family Tree Books—Oklahoma
  http://www.barnettesbooks.com/oklahoma.htm

- Books We Own—Oklahoma
  http://www.rootsweb.com/~bwo/oklahoma.html

- Boyd Publishing Company—Oklahoma
  http://www.hom.net/~gac/oklahom.htm

- Frontier Press Bookstore—Oklahoma
  http://www.frontierpress.com/frontier.cgi?category=ok

- The Gregath Publishing Company
  http://www.gregathcompany.com/
  Wyandotte, Oklahoma

- Hearthstone Bookshop—Oklahoma
  http://www.hearthstonebooks.com/cgi-bin/webc.cgi/
  st_main.html?catid=95&sid=2PH5t29sm

- Heritage Books—Oklahoma
  http://www.heritagebooks.com/ok.htm

- Heritage Quest—Microfilm Records for the State of Oklahoma
  http://www.heritagequest.com/genealogy/microfilm/oklahoma/

- Lost in Time Books—Oklahoma
  http://www.lostintime.com/catalog/books/bookst/bo25000.htm

- The Memorabilia Corner
  http://members.aol.com/TMCorner/index.html
  Forms, flags, maps, software, CDs, tapes, microfilm & microfiche, books, periodicals, photographic conservation & archival materials.

- Southern Queries Genealogy Magazine
  http://www.mindspring.com/~freedom1/sq/sq.htm

- Willow Bend Bookstore—Oklahoma
  http://www.willowbend.net/ok.htm

◆ Queries, Message Boards & Surname Lists

- GenConnect Oklahoma Visitor Center
  http://cgi.rootsweb.com/~genbbs/indx/Ok.html
  A system for posting queries, Bibles, biographies, deeds, obituaries, pensions, wills.

- Oklahoma Surnames
  http://www.rootsweb.com/~oknames/

◆ Records: Census, Cemeteries, Land, Obituaries, Personal, Taxes and Vital (Born, Married, Died & Buried)

- The 1790–1890 Federal Population Censuses: Catalog of National Archives Microfilm
  http://www.genealogy.org/census/contents.shtml
  - Census Schedules and Microfilm Roll Numbers for Virginia:
    1890 Special Schedules—Oklahoma and Indian Territories
    http://www.genealogy.org/census/1890-special_schedules/Oklahoma.html

- Cemeteries of the United States—Oklahoma Cemeteries—County Index
  http://www.gac.edu/~kengelha/uscemeteries/oklahoma.html

- Census Online—Links to Census Sites on the Web—Oklahoma
  http://www.census-online.com/links/OK_data.html

- County Courthouse Addresses
  http://www.familytreemaker.com/00000265.html

- Federal Tract Books of Oklahoma Territory
  http://www.sirinet.net/~lgarris/swogs/tract.html

- Find-A-Grave by Location: Oklahoma
  http://www.findagrave.com/grave/lok.html
  Graves of noteworthy people.

- Interment.net: Oklahoma Cemeteries
  http://www.interment.net/us/ok/index.htm
  A list of links to other sites.

- Intruders and Non-Citizens in the Creek Nation 1875–1895
  http://www.rootsweb.com/~itcreek/records2.htm

- Lincoln County, Oklahoma Early Marriages
  http://www.skypoint.com/~jkm/oklincoln/marriage.html

- National Archives—Southwest Region (Fort Worth)
  http://www.nara.gov/regional/ftworth.html

- National Archives—Southwest Region
  http://www.familytreemaker.com/00000105.html
  Records for Arkansas, Louisiana, Oklahoma, Texas, and a portion of New Mexico.
- OKbits—1883–1997 Obits & Tidbits
  http://www.rootsweb.com/~okbits/index.htm
- Oklahoma Vital Records Information
  http://vitalrec.com/ok.html
- Old Obituaries in Stephens County Oklahoma
  http://www.geocities.com/Heartland/Ridge/1308/OBITS.html
- The Political Graveyard—Cemeteries in Oklahoma
  http://politicalgraveyard.com/geo/OK/kmindex.html
- Preplanning Network—Funeral Home and Cemetery Directory—Oklahoma
  http://www.preplannet.com/oklfhcem.htm
- Selected Index of Intruders and Non-Citizens in the Creek Nation (1876–1897)
  http://www.rootsweb.com/~itcreek/records1.htm
- Stephens County Oklahoma Cemeteries
  http://www.geocities.com/Heartland/Ridge/1308/MAPS.html
- USGenWeb Census Project Oklahoma
  http://www.usgenweb.org/census/states/oklahoma.htm
- USGenWeb Tombstone Transcription Project—Oklahoma
  http://www.rootsweb.com/~cemetery/oklahoma.html
- VitalChek Network—Oklahoma
  http://www.vitalchek.com/stateselect.asp?state=OK
- Where to Write for Vital Records—Oklahoma
  http://www.cdc.gov/nchswww/howto/w2w/oklahoma.htm
  From the National Center for Health Statistics (NCHS).

◆ Religion & Churches

- Christianity.Net Church Locator—Oklahoma
  http://www.christianity.net/cgi/location.exe?United_States+Oklahoma
- Church Online!—Oklahoma
  http://www.churchonline.com/usas/ok/ok.html
- Church Profiles—Oklahoma
  http://www.church-profiles.com/ok/ok.html
- Churches dot Net—Global Church Web Pages—Oklahoma
  http://www.churches.net/churches/oklahoma.html
- Churches of the World—Oklahoma
  http://www.churchsurf.com/churches/Oklahoma/index.htm
  From the ChurchSurf Christian Directory.

◆ Societies & Groups

- American Historical Society of Germans from Russia—Central Oklahoma Chapter
  http://www.ahsgr.org/okcentra.html

- Archer's Computer Interest Group List—Oklahoma
  http://www.genealogy.org/~ngs/cigs/ngl1usok.html
- Canadian County Genealogical Society
  http://www.rootsweb.com/~okccgs/
- Choctaw County Genealogical Society
  http://www2.1starnet.com/davelee/History/hsge_01.html
- Cleveland County Genealogical Society
  http://www.telepath.com/ccgs/
- Delaware County Genealogical Society
  http://www.rootsweb.com/~okdelawa/dcgs.htm
- Drummond Historical Society
  http://www.rootsweb.com/~okgarfie/drummond.htm
- Garfield County Genealogists, Inc.
  http://www.harvestcomm.net/org/garfield_genealogy/
- IOOF Lodge Website Directory—Oklahoma
  http://norm28.hsc.usc.edu/IOOF/USA/Oklahoma/Oklahoma.html
  Independent Order of Odd Fellows and Rebekahs.
- Logan County, Oklahoma, Genealogical Society Home Page
  http://www.rootsweb.com/~oklcgs/lcgsmain.htm
- Oklahoma Genealogical Society
  http://www.rootsweb.com/~okgs/
- Oklahoma Historical Society
  http://www.ok-history.mus.ok.us/
- Oklahoma Society Daughters of the American Revolution
  http://connections.oklahoman.net/okdar/
- Payne County Genealogical Society
  http://www.pcgsok.org/
- Pioneer Genealogical Society
  http://www.poncacitynews.com/community/localhistory/genhis/pgs/
  Ponca City, Oklahoma
- Poteau Valley Genealogical Society
  http://www.rootsweb.com/~okleflor/pvgs.htm
- Southwest Oklahoma Genealogical Society
  http://www.sirinet.net/~lgarris/swogs/
- Tulsa Genealogical Society
  http://www.geocities.com/Heartland/Park/8391/Tgspage.htm

◆ USGenWeb Project

- Oklahoma Genealogy—USGenWeb Project State Page
  http://www.usgenweb.org/ok
- Oklahoma—USGenWeb Archives Table of Contents
  http://www.rootsweb.com/~usgenweb/ok/okfiles.htm
- Oklahoma—USGenWeb FTP Archives
  ftp://ftp.rootsweb.com/pub/usgenweb/ok/
- Twin Territories—Oklahoma/Indian Territory Project
  http://www.rootsweb.com/~itgenweb/index.htm

U.S.—OREGON—OR
http://www.CyndisList.com/or.htm

Category Index:

- General Resource Sites
- Government & Cities
- History & Culture
- Libraries, Archives & Museums
- Mailing Lists, Newsgroups & Chat
- Maps, Gazetteers & Geographical Information
- Military
- Newspapers
- People & Families

- Professional Researchers, Volunteers & Other Research Services
- Publications, Software & Supplies
- Queries, Message Boards & Surname Lists
- Records: Census, Cemeteries, Land, Obituaries, Personal, Taxes and Vital
- Religion & Churches
- Societies & Groups
- USGenWeb Project

◆ General Resource Sites

- Everton's Sources of Genealogical Information in Oregon
  http://www.everton.com/usa/or.htm
- Family Tree Maker's Genealogy "How To" Guide—Oregon
  http://www.familytreemaker.com/00000212.html
- Genealogy Bulletin Board Systems for Oregon
  http://www.genealogy.org/~gbbs/gblor.html
- Genealogy Exchange & Surname Registry—ORGenExchange
  http://www.genexchange.com/or/index.cfm
- Genealogy Resources on the Internet: Oregon
  http://www-personal.umich.edu/~cgaunt/oregon.html
- LDS Research Outline for Oregon
  http://www.everton.com/usa/or-0838b.txt
- Lineages' Genealogy Site: Oregon
  http://www.lineages.com/rooms/usa/state.asp?StateCode=OR
- Oregon History & Genealogy Resources
  http://www.rootsweb.com/~genepool/oregon.htm
- ROOTS-L United States Resources: Oregon
  http://www.rootsweb.com/roots-l/USA/or.html
  Comprehensive list of research links, including many to history-related sites.

◆ Government & Cities

- 50states.com—Oregon State Information Resource
  http://www.50states.com/oregon.htm
  A list of general information for each state, including a list of colleges, state symbols, links to maps, newspapers, and other miscellaneous state information.

- Excite Travel by City.Net—Oregon
  http://www.city.net/countries/united_states/oregon/
- City of Coos Bay, Oregon
  http://www.coosbay.org/
- Official City Web Sites for the State of Oregon
  http://OfficialCitySites.org/oregon.htm
- Oregon Online
  http://www.state.or.us/
- Yahoo! Get Local...Oregon Cities
  http://dir.yahoo.com/Regional/U_S__States/Oregon/Cities/
  Maps, yellow pages, white pages, newspapers and other local information.
- Yahoo! Get Local...Oregon Counties and Regions
  http://dir.yahoo.com/Regional/U_S__States/Oregon/Counties_and_Regions/
  Maps, yellow pages, white pages, newspapers and other local information.

◆ History & Culture

- Ghost Towns of Oregon
  http://www.ghosttowns.com/states/or/or.html
- Oregon Trail Pioneers—The Oregon Territory
  http://www.teleport.com/~sflora/ortrail.htm
- Oregon Pioneers—The Wagon Train of 1843
  http://www.peak.org/~mransom/pioneers.html
- Yahoo!...History...Oregon
  http://dir.yahoo.com/Arts/Humanities/History/Browse_By_Region/U_S__States/Oregon/

◆ Libraries, Archives & Museums

- Coos Bay Public Library
  http://www.coos.or.us/~cblib/

- Family History Centers—Oregon
  http://www.deseretbook.com/famhis/or.html

- Family History Centers—Oregon
  http://www.lib.byu.edu/~uvrfhc/centers/oregon.html

- The Hudson's Bay Company Archives
  http://www.gov.mb.ca/chc/archives/hbca/index.html
  From the Provincial Archives of Manitoba, Canada.

- HYTELNET—Library Catalogs: USA: Oregon
  http://library.usask.ca/hytelnet/usa/OR.html
  Before you use any of the Telnet links, make note of the user name, password and any other logon information.

- Multnomah County Library Home Page
  http://www.multnomah.lib.or.us/lib/index.html
  Portland, Oregon

- NUCMC Listing of Archives and Manuscript Repositories in Oregon
  http://lcweb.loc.gov/coll/nucmc/orsites.html
  Links to information about resources other than those held in the Library of Congress.

- Oregon Family History Centers
  http://www.genhomepage.com/FHC/Oregon.html
  A list of addresses, phone numbers and hours of operation from the Genealogy Home Page.

- Oregon Libraries
  http://www.open.org/ola/oregon-libraries.html
  A list from the Oregon Library Association web site.

- Oregon State Archives Public Information Server
  http://arcweb.sos.state.or.us/

  o Oregon Historical County Records Guide
    http://arcweb.sos.state.or.us/county/cphome.html

  o Records of Interest to Genealogists and Students of Family History
    http://arcweb.sos.state.or.us/geneal.html

    • Census records in the Oregon State Archives
      http://arcweb.sos.state.or.us/census.html

    • Guide to Oregon Provisional and Territorial Government Records
      http://arcweb.sos.state.or.us/territ.html

    • Land Records in the Oregon State Archives
      http://arcweb.sos.state.or.us/land.html

    • Military Records in the Oregon State Archives
      http://arcweb.sos.state.or.us/milit.html

    • Naturalization Records in the Oregon State Archives
      http://arcweb.sos.state.or.us/natural.html

    • Probate Records in the Oregon State Archives
      http://arcweb.sos.state.or.us/prob.html

    • Vital Records in the Oregon State Archives
      http://arcweb.sos.state.or.us/vital.html

- Oregon State Library
  http://www.osl.state.or.us/oslhome.html

- Oregon State University Valley Library
  http://www.orst.edu/dept/library/

  o Oregon State University Archives
    http://www.orst.edu/dept/archives/

  o Special Collections
    http://www.orst.edu/dept/Special_Collections/

- Repositories of Primary Sources: Oregon
  http://www.uidaho.edu/special-collections/west.html#usor
  A list of links to online resources from the Univ. of Idaho Library, Special Collections and Archives.

- webCATS: Library Catalogues on the World Wide Web—Oregon
  http://library.usask.ca/hywebcat/states/OR.html

◆ Mailing Lists, Newsgroups & Chat

- Genealogy Resources on the Internet—Oregon Mailing Lists
  http://members.aol.com/gfsjohnf/gen_mail_states-or.html
  Each of the mailing list links below points to this site, wonderfully maintained by John Fuller. Visit this site for county-specific mailing lists as well.

- OREGON Mailing List
  http://members.aol.com/gfsjohnf/gen_mail_states-or.html#OREGON

- OR-ROOTS Mailing List
  http://members.aol.com/gfsjohnf/gen_mail_states-or.html#OR-ROOTS

- OR-WVGS Mailing List
  http://members.aol.com/gfsjohnf/gen_mail_states-or.html#OR-WVGS
  Sponsored by the Williamette Valley Genealogical Society, for anyone with a genealogical interest in the Williamette Valley area of Oregon.

- WESTERN-ROOTS-L Mailing list
  http://members.aol.com/gfsjohnf/gen_mail_states-or.html#WESTERN-ROOTS-L
  Washington, Oregon, Alaska, Idaho, Montana, Wyoming, California, Nevada, Hawaii, Colorado, Utah, Arizona, and New Mexico.

◆ Maps, Gazetteers & Geographical Information

- 1895 U.S. Atlas—Oregon
  http://www.LivGenMI.com/1895or.htm

- American Memory Panoramic Maps 1847–1929—Oregon
  http://lcweb2.loc.gov/cgi-bin/query/S?ammem/gmd:@filreq(@field(STATE+oregon)+@field(COLLID+pmmap))
  From the Geography and Map Division, Library of Congress.

- American Memory Railroad Maps 1828–1900—Oregon
  http://memory.loc.gov/cgi-bin/query/S?ammem/gmd:@filreq(@field(STATE+oregon)+@field(COLLID+rrmap))
  From the Geography and Map Division, Library of Congress.

- Color Landform Atlas: Oregon
  http://fermi.jhuapl.edu/states/or_0.html
  Including a map of counties and a map for 1895.

- County Boundary Changes—County Boundaries in 1843
  http://arcweb.sos.state.or.us/county/cpmapboundary.html
- Excite Maps: Oregon Maps
  http://www.city.net/maps/view/?mapurl=/countries/
  united_states/oregon
  Zoom in on these maps all the way to the street level.
- Historical Maps of Oregon—Oregon Counties and County Seats
  http://arcweb.sos.state.or.us/county/cpmapor.html
- HPI County InfoSystem—Counties in Oregon
  http://www.com/hpi/orcty/index.html
- K.B. Slocum Books and Maps—Oregon
  http://www.treasurenet.com/cgi-bin/treasure/kbslocum/scan/
  se=Oregon/sf=mapstate
- List of Oregon Counties
  http://www.genealogy.org/~st-clair/counties/state_or.html
- Map of Oregon Counties
  http://govinfo.kerr.orst.edu/gif/states/or.gif
  From the Government Information Sharing Project, Information Services, Oregon State University.
- Map of Oregon Counties
  http://www.lib.utexas.edu/Libs/PCL/Map_collection/states/
  Oregon.gif
  From the Perry-Castañeda Library at the Univ. of Texas at Austin.
- U.S. Census Bureau—Oregon Profiles
  http://www.census.gov/datamap/www/41.html
- Yale Peabody Museum: GNIS—Oregon
  http://www.peabody.yale.edu/other/gnis/OR.html
  *Search the USGS Geographic Names Database. You can limit the search to a specific county in this state and search for any of the following features: airport arch area arroyo bar basin bay beach bench bend bridge **building** canal cape **cemetery** channel **church** cliff crater crossing dam falls flat forest gap geyser glacier gut harbor hospital island isthmus lake lava levee locale mine oilfield other park pillar plain ppl range rapids reserve reservoir ridge **school** sea slope spring stream summit swamp tower trail tunnel valley well woods.*

◆ Military

- The Civil War Archive—Union Regiments—Oregon
  http://www.civilwararchive.com/unionor.htm
- Korean Conflict State-Level Casualty Lists—Oregon
  http://www.nara.gov/nara/electronic/orhrlist.html
  From the National Archives and Records Administration, Center for Electronic Records.
- Pacific Northwest Military History and Reenacting Web Site
  http://www.hevanet.com/1860colt/pnwmain.html
- Vietnam Conflict State-Level Casualty Lists—Oregon
  http://www.nara.gov/nara/electronic/orhrviet.html
  From the National Archives and Records Administration, Center for Electronic Records.
- The Vietnam Veterans Memorial—Oregon
  http://grunt.space.swri.edu/statewall/oregon/or.htm

◆ Newspapers

- AJR NewsLink—Oregon Newspapers
  http://www.newslink.org/ornews.html
- E&P Media Info Links—Newspaper Sites in Oregon
  http://www.mediainfo.com/emedia/browse-results.
  htm?region=oregon&category=newspaper+++++++++
- Ecola Newstand: Oregon
  http://www.ecola.com/news/press/na/us/or/
- NAA Hotlinks to Newspapers Online—Oregon
  http://www.naa.org/hotlinks/searchResult.asp?param=
  OR-Oregon&City=1
- N-Net—Oregon Newspapers
  http://www.n-net.com/or.htm
- The Oregon Newspaper Project
  http://libweb.uoregon.edu/preservn/usnp/usnp.html
- The Ultimate Collection of News Links: USA—Oregon
  http://www.pppp.net/links/news/USA-OR.html
- Yahoo!...Newspapers...Oregon
  http://dir.yahoo.com/News_and_Media/Newspapers/
  Browse_By_Region/U_S__States/Oregon/

◆ People & Families

- Affiliated Tribes of Northwest Indians
  http://www.atni.org/~tribes/
  For Alaska, California, Idaho, Montana, Oregon, Washington.
- Tribes and Villages of Oregon
  http://hanksville.phast.umass.edu:8000/cultprop/contacts/
  tribal/OR.html
- WPA Life Histories from Oregon
  http://lcweb2.loc.gov/ammem/wpaintro/orcat.html
  Manuscripts from the Federal Writer's Project, 1936–1940, Library of Congress.

◆ Professional Researchers, Volunteers & Other Research Services

- Ancestors in the Attic
  http://ladyecloud.hypermart.net/Ancestors.htm
- Board for Certification of Genealogists—Roster of Those Certified—Specializing in Oregon
  http://www.genealogy.org/~bcg/rosts_or.html
- Connie LENZEN—Certified Genealogical Research Specialist
  http://www.orednet.org/~clenzen/
  Research in Oregon and southwest Washington.
- Gail GRAHAM, Independent Genealogist & Research Specialist
  http://www.spessart.com/users/ggraham/gailg.htm
  Specializing in Yamhill County, Oregon; and Oregon in General.

- Genealogy Helplist—Oregon
  http://members.aol.com/DFBradshaw/or.html
- The Official Iowa Counties Professional Genealogist and Researcher's Registry for Oregon
  http://www.iowa-counties.com/gene/or.htm
- Past Tracker
  http://www.harborside.com/home/r/rice/index.html
  Coos Bay, Oregon. Native American and New England specialty searches.

◆ Publications, Software & Supplies

- Barbara Green's Used Genealogy Books—Oregon
  http://home.earthlink.net/~genbooks/lochist.html#OR
- Books We Own—Oregon
  http://www.rootsweb.com/~bwo/oregon.html
- Boyd Publishing Company—Oregon
  http://www.hom.net/~gac/oregon.htm
- Frontier Press Bookstore—Oregon
  http://www.frontierpress.com/frontier.cgi?category=or
- Heritage Quest—Microfilm Records for the State of Oregon
  http://www.heritagequest.com/genealogy/microfilm/oregon/
- Powell's Books
  http://www.powells.com/
  Portland. Used, new and out of print books.

◆ Queries, Message Boards & Surname Lists

- CRITESER Crossroad: QUERIES!
  http://ourworld.compuserve.com/homepages/waltcr/queries.htm
  For the CRITESER Surname. Also published on this site are the queries from the Genealogical Society of Douglas County (OR) as published in their quarterly publication the Douglas County Pioneer.
- GenConnect Oregon Visitor Center
  http://cgi.rootsweb.com/~genbbs/indx/Or.html
  A system for posting queries, Bibles, biographies, deeds, obituaries, pensions, wills.

◆ Records: Census, Cemeteries, Land, Obituaries, Personal, Taxes and Vital (Born, Married, Died & Buried)

- The 1790–1890 Federal Population Censuses: Catalog of National Archives Microfilm
  http://www.genealogy.org/census/contents.shtml
  - Census Schedules and Microfilm Roll Numbers for Oregon:
    1850
    http://www.genealogy.org/census/1850_schedules/Oregon.html

1860
http://www.genealogy.org/census/1860_schedules/Oregon.html

1870
http://www.genealogy.org/census/1870_schedules/Oregon.html

1880
http://www.genealogy.org/census/1880_schedules/Oregon.html

1880 soundex
http://www.genealogy.org/census/1880.sdx_schedules/T768.html

1890 Special Schedules
http://www.genealogy.org/census/1890-special_schedules/Oregon.html

- BLM—Oregon's Electronic Reading Room
  http://www.blm.gov/nhp/efoia/or/
  United States Bureau of Land Management.
- Cemeteries of the United States—Oregon Cemeteries—County Index
  http://www.gac.edu/~kengelha/uscemeteries/oregon.html
- Census Online—Links to Census Sites on the Web—Oregon
  http://www.census-online.com/links/OR_data.html
- Census Records in the Oregon State Archives
  http://arcweb.sos.state.or.us/censuslist.html
- County Courthouse Addresses
  http://www.familytreemaker.com/00000266.html
- Find-A-Grave by Location: Oregon
  http://www.findagrave.com/grave/lor.html
  Graves of noteworthy people.
- Interment.net: Oregon Cemeteries
  http://www.interment.net/us/or/index.htm
  A list of links to other sites.
- National Archives—Pacific Alaska Region (Seattle)
  http://www.nara.gov/regional/seattle.html
- National Archives—Pacific Northwest Region
  http://www.familytreemaker.com/00000100.html
  Records for Idaho, Oregon and Washington.
- Oregon Vital Records Information
  http://vitalrec.com/or.html
- The Political Graveyard—Cemeteries in Oregon
  http://politicalgraveyard.com/geo/OR/kmindex.html
- Preplanning Network—Funeral Home and Cemetery Directory—Oregon
  http://www.preplannet.com/orfhcem.htm
- Ricks College—Family History Center Genesis Project
  http://abish.ricks.edu/fhc/gbsearch.asp
  Search engine for marriages in Arizona, Idaho, Nevada, Oregon, Utah 1850–1951.

- SAMPUBCO
  http://www.wasatch.com/~dsam/sampubco/index.htm
  *Will Testators Indexes, Naturalization Records Indexes and
  Census Indexes online. You can order copies of the original
  source documents for a small fee.*

- Umatilla County, Oregon—USGenWeb Archives
  http://www.rootsweb.com/~usgenweb/or/umfiles.htm
  Includes Abstracts of obituaries from Hermiston newspapers.

- USGenWeb Census Project Oregon
  http://www.usgenweb.org/census/states/oregon/oregon.htm

- USGenWeb Tombstone Transcription Project—
  Oregon
  http://www.rootsweb.com/~cemetery/oregon.html

- VitalChek Network—Oregon
  http://www.vitalchek.com/stateselect.asp?state=OR

- Where to Write for Vital Records—Oregon
  http://www.cdc.gov/nchswww/howto/w2w/oregon.htm
  From the National Center for Health Statistics (NCHS).

◆ Religion & Churches

- Christianity.Net Church Locator—Oregon
  http://www.christianity.net/cgi/
  location.exe?United_States+Oregon

- Church Online!—Oregon
  http://www.churchonline.com/usas/or/or.html

- Church Profiles—Oregon
  http://www.church-profiles.com/or/or.html

- Churches dot Net—Global Church Web Pages—
  Oregon
  http://www.churches.net/churches/oregon.html

- Churches of the World—Oregon
  http://www.churchsurf.com/churches/Oregon/index.htm
  From the ChurchSurf Christian Directory.

◆ Societies & Groups

- American Historical Society of Germans from
  Russia—Oregon Chapter
  http://www.ahsgr.org/orportla.html

- Archer's Computer Interest Group List—Oregon
  http://www.genealogy.org/~ngs/cigs/ngl1usor.html

- Beaver Chapter, Oregon State Society Daughters of
  the American Revolution
  http://www.teleport.com/~carolynk/dar.htm

- Benton County Genealogical Society
  http://www.rootsweb.com/~orbentgs/
  Originally the Mid-Valley Genealogical Society.

- Blue Mountain PAF Users Group
  http://www.eoni.com/~paf/
  Eastern Oregon & Southeast Washington.

- Clackamas County Family History Society
  http://www.rootsweb.com/~genepool/ccfhs.htm

- Cottage Grove Genealogical Society
  http://www.rootsweb.com/~genepool/cggs.htm

- Finnish-American Historical Society of the West
  http://www.teleport.com/~finamhsw/
  Portland, Oregon

- Genealogical Forum of Oregon
  http://www.gfo.org/

- IOOF Lodge Website Directory—Oregon
  http://norm28.hsc.usc.edu/IOOF/USA/Oregon/Oregon.html
  Independent Order of Odd Fellows and Rebekahs.

- Lebanon Genealogical Society
  http://www.rootsweb.com/~orlgs/

- Linn Genealogical Society
  http://www.rootsweb.com/~orlinngs/

- Oregon Adoptive Rights Association
  http://www.oara.org/

- Oregon Electric Railway Historical Society
  http://www.reed.edu/~reyn/oerhs.html

- Oregon Genealogical Society
  http://www.rootsweb.com/~genepool/ogs.htm

- Oregon Historical Society
  http://www.ohs.org/

- Oregon State Society Daughters of the
  American Revolution
  http://www.teleport.com/~dareth/DAR/index.htm

- The Pacific Northwest Chapter of the National
  Railway Historical Society
  http://www.easystreet.com/pnwc/
  Portland, Oregon

- Rogue Valley Genealogical Society
  http://www.grrtech.com/rvgs/
  Medford, Oregon

- Southern Oregon Historical Society
  http://www.sohs.org/
  Jackson County

- Southern Oregon PAF Users Group (SO-PAF-UG)
  http://www.webtrail.com/sopafug/

- Willamette Valley Genealogical Society
  http://www.osl.state.or.us/oslhome/wvgs.html
  Salem, Oregon

◆ USGenWeb Project

- Oregon Genealogy—USGenWeb Project State Page
  http://www.usgenweb.org/or

- Oregon—USGenWeb Archives Table of Contents
  http://www.rootsweb.com/~usgenweb/or/orfiles.htm

- Oregon—USGenWeb FTP Archives
  ftp://ftp.rootsweb.com/pub/usgenweb/or/

U.S.—PENNSYLVANIA—PA
http://www.CyndisList.com/pa.htm

Category Index:

- General Resource Sites
- Government & Cities
- History & Culture
- Libraries, Archives & Museums
- Locality Specific
- Mailing Lists, Newsgroups & Chat
- Maps, Gazetteers & Geographical Information
- Military
- Newspapers
- People & Families

- Professional Researchers, Volunteers & Other Research Services
- Publications, Software & Supplies
- Queries, Message Boards & Surname Lists
- Records: Census, Cemeteries, Land, Obituaries, Personal, Taxes and Vital
- Religion & Churches
- Societies & Groups
- USGenWeb Project

◆ General Resource Sites

- Brenda's Guide to Online Pennsylvania Genealogy
  http://www.geocities.com/Heartland/Plains/8021/palinks.htm
  A wonderful collection of resources for PA research!

- Everton's Sources of Genealogical Information in Pennsylvania
  http://www.everton.com/usa/pa.htm

- Family Tree Maker's Genealogy "How To" Guide—Pennsylvania
  http://www.familytreemaker.com/00000213.html

- Genealogy Bulletin Board Systems for Pennsylvania
  http://www.genealogy.org/~gbbs/gblpa.html

- Genealogy Exchange & Surname Registry—PAGenExchange
  http://www.genexchange.com/pa/index.cfm

- Genealogy Resources on the Internet: Pennsylvania
  http://www-personal.umich.edu/~cgaunt/penn.html

- LDS Research Outline for Pennsylvania
  http://www.everton.com/usa/pa-0839b.txt

- Lineages' Genealogy Site: Pennsylvania
  http://www.lineages.com/rooms/usa/state.asp?StateCode=PA

- PA Roots
  http://www.pa-roots.com/
  Dedicated to Pennsylvania Genealogical Research.

- Pennsylvania Genealogy Clues
  http://www.geocities.com/Heartland/6464/

- Pennsylvania Genealogy—Etc.
  http://www.geocities.com/Heartland/6468/

- ROOTS-L United States Resources: Pennsylvania
  http://www.rootsweb.com/roots-l/USA/pa.html
  Comprehensive list of research links, including many to history-related sites.

◆ Government & Cities

- 50states.com—Pennsylvania State Information Resource
  http://www.50states.com/pennsylv.htm
  A list of general information for each state, including a list of colleges, state symbols, links to maps, newspapers, and other miscellaneous state information.

- Excerpts from "History of Bucks County"
  http://www.geocities.com/heartland/6508/BED.HTM
  Bedminster Township

- Excite Travel by City.Net—Pennsylvania
  http://www.city.net/countries/united_states/pennsylvania/

- Commonwealth of Pennsylvania
  http://www.state.pa.us/

- Official City Web Sites for the State of Pennsylvania
  http://OfficialCitySites.org/Pennsylvania.htm

- Township History
  http://www.willistown.pa.us/history.htm
  Willistown Township

- Yahoo! Get Local...Pennsylvania Cities
  http://dir.yahoo.com/Regional/U_S__States/Pennsylvania/Cities/
  Maps, yellow pages, white pages, newspapers and other local information.

- Yahoo! Get Local...Pennsylvania Counties and Regions
  http://dir.yahoo.com/Regional/U_S__States/Pennsylvania/Counties_and_Regions/
  Maps, yellow pages, white pages, newspapers and other local information.

◆ History & Culture

- History of Washington County, Pennsylvania
  http://www.chartiers.com/crumrine/twp-index.html
  Transcription of Boyd Crumrine's 1882 work entitled "History of Washington County, Pennsylvania with Biographical Sketches of Many of Its Pioneers and Prominent Men."

- Pennsylvania State History
  http://www.state.pa.us/PA_Exec/Historical_Museum/pahist.htm

- A Short History of the City of Philadelphia, From Its Foundation to the Present Time (1880)
  http://www.libertynet.org/ardenpop/appshort.html
  Complete text of an 1880 book on the history of Philadelphia.

- Township History
  http://www.willistown.pa.us/history.htm
  Willistown Township

- Yahoo!...History...Pennsylvania
  http://dir.yahoo.com/Arts/Humanities/History/Browse_By_Region/U_S__States/Pennsylvania/

◆ Libraries, Archives & Museums

- Access Pennsylvania
  http://accesspa.brodart.com/
  Searchable database of library catalogs.

- Allentown Public Library
  http://www.allentownpl.org/

- American Swedish Historical Museum
  http://www.libertynet.org/~ashm/
  Philadelphia

- Bloomsburg Public Library
  http://www.BAFN.ORG/library/bloom.htm

- Bryn Mawr College Libraries
  http://www.brynmawr.edu/library/
  See Tripod information below.

  ○ Special Collections
    http://www.brynmawr.edu/library/Docs/speccol.html

- Butler Area Public Library
  http://www.ButlerCounty.com/comminfo/libraries/butapl/library.htm

- Carnegie Library of Pittsburgh
  http://www.clpgh.org/clp/

  ○ Pennsylvania Department
    http://www.clpgh.org/CLP/Pennsylvania/

    • Genealogy
      http://www.clpgh.org/CLP/Pennsylvania/pagen.html

    • Local History
      http://www.clpgh.org/CLP/Pennsylvania/pahistory.html

    • Pa Pitt's Master Index
      http://www.clpgh.org/CLP/Pennsylvania/pahomex2.html

- Chester County Historical Society Library
  http://www.chesco.com/~cchs/library.html

- Delaware County Library System
  http://www.libertynet.org/delcolib/

- Erie County Public Library
  http://www.ecls.lib.pa.us/

- Family History Centers—Pennsylvania
  http://www.deseretbook.com/famhis/pa.html

- Family History Centers—Pennsylvania
  http://www.lib.byu.edu/~uvrfhc/centers/pennsylvania.html

- The Free Library of Philadelphia
  http://www.library.phila.gov/

- Haverford College Libraries
  http://www.haverford.edu/library/web/library.html
  See Tripod information below.

  ○ Special Collections
    http://www.haverford.edu/library/sc/sc.html

    • Quaker Collection
      http://www.haverford.edu/library/sc/qcoll.html

- Historical Society of Pennsylvania—Special Collections Research Library
  http://www.libertynet.org:80/~pahist/library.html

- HYTELNET—Library Catalogs: USA: Pennsylvania
  http://library.usask.ca/hytelnet/usa/PA.html
  Before you use any of the Telnet links, make note of the user name, password and any other logon information.

- James V. Brown Library
  http://www.jvbrown.edu/
  Williamsport

- The Library Company of Philadelphia
  http://www.libertynet.org/gencap/licophil.html

- NUCMC Listing of Archives and Manuscript Repositories in Pennsylvania
  http://lcweb.loc.gov/coll/nucmc/pasites.html
  Links to information about resources other than those held in the Library of Congress.

- PACSCL—Philadelphia Area Consortium of Special Collections Libraries
  http://www.libertynet.org/~pacscl/

- Palatine & Pennsylvania-Dutch Genealogy Guide to the Pennsylvania Archives
  http://www.geocities.com/Heartland/3955/PAarchives.html

- Penn State Libraries
  http://www.libraries.psu.edu/

- Pennsylvania Family History Centers
  http://www.genhomepage.com/FHC/Pennsylvania.html
  A list of addresses, phone numbers and hours of operation from the Genealogy Home Page.
- Philadelphia Archdiocesan Historical Research Center (PAHRC)
  http://www.archdiocese-phl.org/ch/archives.html
- The Philadelphia City Archives
  http://www.phila.gov/phils/carchive.htm
  - Genealogical Resources at the Philadelphia City Archives
    http://www.phila.gov/phils/Docs/Inventor/genealgy.htm
  - Philadelphia City Archives
    http://www.libertynet.org/gencap/philcity.html
    Description from GENCAP.
- Pottsville Free Public Library
  http://www.pottsville.com/library/
- Repositories of Primary Sources: Pennsylvania
  http://www.uidaho.edu/special-collections/east2.html#uspa
  A list of links to online resources from the Univ. of Idaho Library, Special Collections and Archives.
- Somerset Historical Center
  http://www.rootsweb.com/~pasomers/schs/
- The State Archives of Pennsylvania
  http://www.state.pa.us/PA_Exec/Historical_Museum/DAM/psa.htm
  - Genealogical Records at the State Archives
    http://www.state.pa.us/PA_Exec/Historical_Museum/DAM/genie1.htm
- Southern Lehigh Public Library
  http://members.spree.com/sip/slpl/
  Coopersburg, Pennsylvania
- State Library of Pennsylvania
  http://www.cas.psu.edu/docs/pde/libstate.html
  - Collections
    http://www.cas.psu.edu/docs/pde/LIBCOLL.HTML
  - Other Information
    http://www.cas.psu.edu/docs/pde/LIBINFO.HTML
    Includes links for census records, naturalization, genealogy resources and more.
- Swarthmore College Libraries
  http://www.swarthmore.edu/Library/
  See Tripod information below.
  - Friends Historical Library
    http://www.swarthmore.edu/Library/friends/
- Tripod is an online library program shared by three colleges in Pennsylvania with Quaker resources and collections:
  - Quaker Collection—Haverford College Special Collections
    http://www.haverford.edu/library/sc/qcoll.html

- Friends Historical Library at Swarthmore College
  http://www.swarthmore.edu/Library/friends/
- Bryn Mawr
  http://tripod.brynmawr.edu/
- Read A Guide to Searching Tripod
  http://www.brynmawr.edu/Library/Docs/tripod_guide.html
  Then connect to the telnet://tripod.brynmawr.edu Tripod program directly using your telnet software and access capabilities. Must have Telnet software to access. Make note of logon and password when you begin. Read more about Telnet above.
- University of Pennsylvania Library
  http://www.library.upenn.edu/
- webCATS: Library Catalogues on the World Wide Web—Pennsylvania
  http://library.usask.ca/hywebcat/states/PA.html
- Whitehall Township Public Library
  http://whitehall.lib.pa.us/
- York County Library System
  http://www.martinlibrary.org/ycls.html

◆ Locality Specific

- Also see the USGenWeb section for links to county-specific resources.
- Adams Genealogy & Columbia County, Pennsylvania Information and Resources
  http://home.ptd.net/~tombwk/
- The Allegheny River Archives
  http://www.geocities.com/Heartland/Acres/7967
  Genealogical and historical information on Allegheny County residents, past and present, and the areas they live in (local communities). Includes cemetery records and tombstone transcriptions.
- Donna's Berks County Genealogy Page
  http://members.aol.com/Nodoubtay/index.html
- From Cemetery to Tree
  http://home.stny.lrun.com/brown/
  Cemeteries, will docket surnames, births, marriages, soldiers, orphans' schools/homes, etc. for Susquehanna County, Pennsylvania.
- Genealogy/Pa. Northampton/Lehigh Co.
  http://www.geocities.com/Heartland/6508/
  Bits & Pieces of Church & Cemetery Records.
- Pennsylvania Genealogy, Luzerne County
  http://www.geocities.com/Heartland/plains/3558/
- The Philadelphia Story
  http://www.geocities.com/Heartland/Prairie/8088/philly.html
  Information regarding Philadelphia genealogy research.
- Robert Simms' Genealogy Page
  http://www.math.clemson.edu/~rsimms/genealogy.html
  Genealogies from the Chesapeake Bay Area and Western Pennsylvania.

- Schuylkill County Genealogy Ties
  http://www.geocities.com/Heartland/Prairie/4280/
- Tri-County Genealogy Sites of Joyce M. Tice
  http://www.rootsweb.com/~srgp/jmtindex.htm
  Bradford and Tioga Counties in Pennsylvania and Chemung County in New York.

◆ Mailing Lists, Newsgroups & Chat

- Genealogy Resources on the Internet—Pennsylvania Mailing Lists
  http://members.aol.com/gfsjohnf/gen_mail_states-pa.html
  Each of the mailing list links below points to this site, wonderfully maintained by John Fuller. Visit this site for county-specific mailing lists as well.
- BRETHREN Mailing List
  http://members.aol.com/johnf14246/
  gen_mail_general.html#BRETHREN
  Includes such church groups as Tunkers/Dunkers, Church of the Brethren, and German Baptists. Also see the associated web page at http://homepages.rootsweb.com/~padutch/lists.html
- COALMINERS Mailing List
  http://members.aol.com/gfsjohnf/gen_mail_country-unk.
  html#COALMINERS
  For anyone whose ancestors were coalminers in the United Kingdom or the United States.
- NorthFayette Mailing List
  http://members.aol.com/gfsjohnf/gen_mail_states-pa.
  html#NorthFayette
  For anyone with a genealogical interest in North Fayette Township and the surrounding areas including South Fayette, Collier and Moon townships and the towns of Oakdale, Robinson, McDonald and Noblestown. North Fayette township is located in Allegheny County, Pennsylvania.
- OHIO-VALLEY Mailing List
  http://members.aol.com/gfsjohnf/gen_mail_states-pa.
  html#OHIO-VALLEY
  For anyone with a genealogical or historical interest in the Ohio Valley including the states of Ohio, West Virginia, and Pennsylvania.
- PACATHOLICS Mailing List
  http://members.aol.com/gfsjohnf/gen_mail_states-pa.
  html#PACATHOLICS
  For messages, queries, and tips for finding your Catholic ancestors that lived in Pennsylvania.
- PADUTCHgenONLY Mailing List
  http://members.aol.com/gfsjohnf/gen_mail_states-pa.
  html#PADUTCHgenONLY
  For anyone interested in doing Pennsylvania Dutch genealogical research. This list is for genealogical discussions only. Also see the associated web page at http://homepages.rootsweb.com/~padutch/lists.html
- PADUTCH-LIFE Mailing List
  http://members.aol.com/gfsjohnf/gen_mail_states-pa.
  html#PADUTCH-LIFE
  For anyone interested in discussing and sharing information and memories of the Pennsylvania-German people commonly called Pennsylvania Dutch. Topics include customs, everyday lives, recipes and genealogy to give insight as to how our present day lives are a continuation of our Penna-Dutch heritage. Also see the associated web page at http://homepages.rootsweb.com/~padutch/lists.html

- PA-Rooters Mailing List
  http://members.aol.com/gfsjohnf/gen_mail_states-pa.
  html#PA-Rooters
- PA-SUSQUEHANNA Mailing List
  http://members.aol.com/gfsjohnf/gen_mail_states-pa.
  html#PA-SUSQUEHANNA
  For researchers with an interest in the surnames of people who settled on or near the Susquehanna River in Pennsylvania; and in the social history and geography of the River.
- PENNA-DUTCH Mailing List
  http://members.aol.com/gfsjohnf/gen_mail_states-pa.
  html#PENNA-DUTCH
  For anyone who is researching their Pennsylvania Dutch ancestry or has other genealogical or historical interests in the Pennsylvania Dutch. Also see the associated web page at http://homepages.rootsweb.com/~padutch/lists.html
- PENNSYLVANIA-ROOTS-L Mailing List
  http://members.aol.com/gfsjohnf/gen_mail_states-pa.
  html#PENNSYLVANIA-ROOTS
- PHILLY-ROOTS Mailing List
  http://members.aol.com/gfsjohnf/gen_mail_states-pa.
  html#PHILLY-ROOTS
  For the city & county of Philadelphia.
- SOMGEN Mailing List
  http://members.aol.com/gfsjohnf/gen_mail_states-wv.
  html#SOMGEN-L
  For anyone with a genealogical interest in the Pennsylvania counties of Somerset, Bedford, Cambria and Fayette; the Maryland counties of Garrett and Allegany; and the border counties in West Virginia.

◆ Maps, Gazetteers & Geographical Information

- 1895 U.S. Atlas—Pennsylvania
  http://www.LivGenMI.com/1895pa.htm
- American Memory Panoramic Maps 1847–1929—Pennsylvania
  http://lcweb2.loc.gov/cgi-bin/query/S?ammem/gmd:
  @filreq(@field(STATE+pennsylvania)+@field(COLLID+pmmap))
  From the Geography and Map Division, Library of Congress.
- American Memory Railroad Maps 1828–1900—Pennsylvania
  http://memory.loc.gov/cgi-bin/query/S?ammem/gmd:
  @filreq(@field(STATE+pennsylvania)+@field(COLLID+rrmap))
  From the Geography and Map Division, Library of Congress.
- Color Landform Atlas: Pennsylvania
  http://fermi.jhuapl.edu/states/pa_0.html
  Including a map of counties and a map for 1895.
- Excite Maps: Pennsylvania Maps
  http://www.city.net/maps/view/?mapurl=/countries/
  united_states/pennsylvania
  Zoom in on these maps all the way to the street level.
- Gleason's Old Maps Etc.
  http://members.aol.com/oldmapsetc/penn.html
  Photocopies of Old Maps, Prints and Articles of Historical and Genealogical Interest from Pennsylvania.

- HPI County InfoSystem—Counties in Pennsylvania
  http://www.com/hpi/pacty/index.html

- K.B. Slocum Books and Maps—Pennsylvania
  http://www.treasurenet.com/cgi-bin/treasure/kbslocum/scan/
  se=Pennsylvania/sf=mapstate

- List of Pennsylvania Counties
  http://www.genealogy.org/~st-clair/counties/state_pa.html

- Map of Pennsylvania Counties
  http://govinfo.kerr.orst.edu/gif/states/pa.gif
  *From the Government Information Sharing Project, Information
  Services, Oregon State University.*

- Map of Pennsylvania Counties
  http://www.lib.utexas.edu/Libs/PCL/Map_collection/states/
  Pennsylvania.gif
  *From the Perry-Castañeda Library at the Univ. of Texas at
  Austin.*

- Pennsylvania Counties—from GENCAP
  http://www.libertynet.org/gencap/pacounties.html

- Pittsburgh Map Database from Scandal Project
  http://parallel.scandal.cs.cmu.edu/cgi-bin/map

- U.S. Census Bureau—Pennsylvania Profiles
  http://www.census.gov/datamap/www/42.html

- Yale Peabody Museum: GNIS—Pennsylvania
  http://www.peabody.yale.edu/other/gnis/PA.html
  *Search the USGS Geographic Names Database. You can limit
  the search to a specific county in this state and search for any of
  the following features: airport arch area arroyo bar basin bay
  beach bench bend bridge **building** canal cape **cemetery** channel
  church cliff crater crossing dam falls flat forest gap geyser
  glacier gut harbor hospital island isthmus lake lava levee locale
  mine oilfield other park pillar plain ppl range rapids reserve
  reservoir ridge **school** sea slope spring stream summit swamp
  tower trail tunnel valley well woods.*

◆ Military

- 61st PA Volunteers, Regimental History
  http://www.access.digex.net/~bdboyle/61st.txt

- 101st Pennsylvania Volunteer Infantry
  http://members.aol.com/qmsgtboots/101pa.html

- 103d Regiment Pennsylvania Volunteer Infantry
  http://users.aol.com/evanslaug/103rd.html

- 104th Pa. Volunteer Infantry
  http://www.voicenet.com/~104pa/

- 114th Pennsylvania Volunteer Infantry, Co. A—
  "Collis' Zouaves"
  http://www.concentric.net/~sthutch/114th.html

- 125th Pennsylvania Regiment—Memorial
  http://members.aol.com/PA125thReg/home.htm
  *Roster of all companies of the 125th Pennsylvania Regiment
  Volunteers in the Civil War.*

- 187th Regiment Pennsylvania Volunteer Infantry
  http://Bip.concept.se/user/187pvi/

- The Civil War Archive—Union Regiments—
  Pennsylvania
  http://www.civilwararchive.com/unionpa.htm

- Civil War Battle Summaries by State—Pennsylvania
  http://www2.cr.nps.gov/abpp/battles/bystate.htm#pa

- Civil War Diary of Bingham Findley Junkin, 100th
  Pennsylvania Volunteer Infantry ("Roundheads")
  http://www.iwaynet.net/~lsci/junkin/

- The Civil War Pages—78th Pennsylvania
  Volunteer Infantry
  http://members.tripod.com/~ProlificPains/cwpages.htm

- Civil War ... Pennsylvania Regiments
  http://ourworld.compuserve.com/homepages/hmore/

- Civil War Records of Bucks and Northampton
  Counties
  http://www.geocities.com/heartland/6508/DURHAM6.HTM

- Civil War Rolls for Washington County,
  Pennsylvania
  http://www.chartiers.com/crumrine/civil-index.html

- Civil War Soldiers From Jefferson County,
  Pennsylvania
  http://www.geocities.com/Heartland/Plains/8021/civil1.htm

- Conneaut Valley Area Soldiers' Graves
  http://www.granniesworld.com/cvahs/cem/sold/index.html

- The Eighty-Fourth Pennsylvania Volunteer
  http://mason.gmu.edu/~rgainer/

- Gettysburg National Military Park
  http://www.nps.gov/gett/

- Grand Army of the Republic Civil War Museum
  and Library
  http://www.libertynet.org/gencap/gar.html

- Index—Company I, Second Pennsylvania Cavalry
  http://www.granniesworld.com/cvahs/CompanyI/

- Korean Conflict State-Level Casualty Lists—
  Pennsylvania
  http://www.nara.gov/nara/electronic/pahrlist.html
  *From the National Archives and Records Administration,
  Center for Electronic Records.*

- Pennsylvania in the Civil War
  http://www.libertynet.org/gencap/pacw.html

- Pennsylvania Volunteers of the Civil War, 81st
  Regiment Company D
  http://www.geocities.com/Heartland/Hills/3916/cwpa81d.html

- Pennsylvania Volunteers of the Civil War,
  Emergency and State Militia Troops of 1863,
  53rd Regiment Company I
  http://www.geocities.com/Heartland/Hills/3916/cwpa53i.html

- Pennsylvania Volunteers of the Civil War, Ninety-Sixth Regiment, Company F
  http://www.geocities.com/Heartland/Hills/3916/cwpa96f.html

- Pennsylvania Volunteers of the Civil War, Sixteenth Regiment, Company D
  http://www.geocities.com/Heartland/Hills/3916/cwpa16d.html

- Pennsylvania Volunteers of the Civil War, Sixteenth Regiment, Company I
  http://www.geocities.com/Heartland/Hills/3916/cwpa16i.html

- Regimental History 148th Pennsylvania Volunteers
  http://www.gettysburg.edu/~sdreese/148.html

- Revolutionary War Muster Rolls Northampton County, Pennsylvania
  http://www.geocities.com/Heartland/3955/rev.htm
  Names extracted from the Pennsylvania Archives, 2nd Series, Volume XIV.

- Roster Members of 187th Regiment, Pennsylvania Volunteer Infantry
  http://www.clark.net/pub/monte/files/187rost.txt
  Still Living 35 years from the date of discharge, 3 August 1865.

- Roster of the 101st Pennsylvania Volunteer Infantry
  http://members.aol.com/qmsgtboots/101roster.html

- The U.S. Army Military History Institute
  http://carlisle-www.army.mil/usamhi/
  and a description from GENCAP
  http://www.libertynet.org/gencap/usarmymhi.html

- Vietnam Conflict State-Level Casualty Lists— Pennsylvania
  http://www.nara.gov/nara/electronic/pahrviet.html
  From the National Archives and Records Administration, Center for Electronic Records.

- The Vietnam Veterans Memorial—Pennsylvania
  http://grunt.space.swri.edu/statewall/penn/pa.htm

◆ Newspapers

- AJR NewsLink—Pennsylvania Newspapers
  http://www.newslink.org/panews.html

- E&P Media Info Links—Newspaper Sites in Pennsylvania
  http://www.mediainfo.com/emedia/browse-results.htm?region=pennsylvania&category=newspapers++++++++

- Ecola Newstand: Pennsylvania
  http://www.ecola.com/news/press/na/us/pa/

- NAA Hotlinks to Newspapers Online—Pennsylvania
  http://www.naa.org/hotlinks/searchResult.asp?param=PA-Pennsylvania&City=1

- N-Net—Pennsylvania Newspapers
  http://www.n-net.com/pa.htm

- Observer-Reporter Online
  http://www.observer-reporter.com/
  Washington, Pennsylvania

- The Ultimate Collection of News Links: USA— Pennsylvania
  http://www.pppp.net/links/news/USA-PA.html

- Yahoo!...Newspapers...Pennsylvania
  http://dir.yahoo.com/News_and_Media/Newspapers/Browse_By_Region/U_S__States/Pennsylvania/

◆ People & Families

- 18th Century Pennsylvania German Naming Customs
  http://www.kalglo.com/germname.htm

- 18th Century Pennsylvania German Nicknames
  http://www.kalglo.com/nickname.htm

- Beers Biographical Record Online—Washington County, Pennsylvania
  http://www.chartiers.com/beers-project/beers.html
  Biographical Sketches of Prominent and Representative Citizens and of many of the Early Settled Families.

- Directory of Underground Railroad Operators— Pennsylvania
  http://www.ugrr.org//names/map-pa.htm

- Kraig Ruckel's Palatine & Pennsylvania Dutch Genealogy Home Page
  http://www.geocities.com/Heartland/3955/

- Mennonites
  http://www.CyndisList.com/menno.htm
  See this category on Cyndi's List for related links.

- Ohio River Valley Families
  http://orvf.com/
  By Allen David Distler.

- PA Dutch of German Heritage, Not Dutch
  http://www.kalglo.com/padutch.htm

- Palatine Emigrants by Kraig Ruckel
  http://www.geocities.com/Heartland/3955/palatine.htm

- Pennsylvania Dutch Family History
  http://homepages.rootsweb.com/~padutch/

- Quakers
  http://www.CyndisList.com/quaker.htm
  See this category on Cyndi's List for related links.

- Slavery in Dauphin County, Pennsylvania
  http://www.geocities.com/Athens/Parthenon/6329/

- Sullivan-Rutland Genealogy Project
  http://www.rootsweb.com/~srgp/srgpmain.htm
  54,000 Ancestors and Descendants of the early nineteenth century pioneers of Sullivan Township and Rutland Township in Tioga County, Pennsylvania.

- Tim's Tips on Pennsylvania German Research
  http://www.geocities.com/Heartland/Plains/3816/how2.html

- Tribes and Villages of Pennsylvania
  http://hanksville.phast.umass.edu:8000/cultprop/contacts/tribal/PA.html

◆ Professional Researchers, Volunteers & Other Research Services

- Board for Certification of Genealogists—Roster of Those Certified—Specializing in Pennsylvania
  http://www.genealogy.org/~bcg/rosts_pa.html
- Genealogy Helplist—Pennsylvania
  http://www.omeganet.es/~boet/hl/pa.htm
- James F. Justin Family Tree Research Services
  http://members.aol.com/jkjustin/gensrch.html
  Geneology Research Service for New Jersey marriage records, birth records, death certificates, census returns, wills, court records and deeds also Philadelphia National Archives.
- The Official Iowa Counties Professional Genealogist and Researcher's Registry for Pennsylvania
  http://www.iowa-counties.com/gene/pa.htm
- The PA1776 Researchers List
  http://www.pa1776.com/PAGENE/rsr01.htm
- Palatine & Pennsylvania-Dutch Genealogy Personally Owned Genealogy Resources
  http://www.geocities.com/Heartland/3955/resources.htm
- Philadelphia Family Finder
  http://hometown.aol.com/ladybrvhrt/private/index.html
- So Many Branches
  http://www.angelfire.com/biz/SoManyBranches/
  Western New York, Northern Pennsylvania, Michigan and Northern Ohio Genealogical Research.

◆ Publications, Software & Supplies

- AncestorSpy—CDs and Microfiche for Pennsylvania
  http://www.ancestorspy.com/pacat.htm
- Barbara Green's Used Genealogy Books— Pennsylvania
  http://home.earthlink.net/~genbooks/lochist.html#PA
- Barnette's Family Tree Books—Pennsylvania
  http://www.barnettesbooks.com/pennsylv.htm
- Books We Own—Pennsylvania
  http://www.rootsweb.com/~bwo/penn.html
- Boyd Publishing Company—Pennsylvania
  http://www.hom.net/~gac/pennsyl.htm
- Family Line Publications
  http://pages.prodigy.com/Strawn/family.htm
  Books covering Delaware, Maryland, New Jersey, Pennsylvania, Virginia, and Washington DC.
- Frontier Press Bookstore—Pennsylvania
  http://www.frontierpress.com/frontier.cgi?category=pa

- GenealogyBookShop.com—Pennsylvania
  http://www.genealogybookshop.com/genealogybookshop/files/The_United_States,Pennsylvania/index.html
  The online store of Genealogical Publishing Co., Inc. & Clearfield Company.
- The Grannies' Book Emporium
  http://www.granniesworld.com/books/
  Books for Ohio and Pennsylvania.
- Hearthstone Bookshop—Pennsylvania
  http://www.hearthstonebooks.com/cgi-bin/webc.cgi/st_main.html?catid=96&sid=2PH5t29sm
- Heritage Books—Pennsylvania
  http://www.heritagebooks.com/pa.htm
- Heritage Quest—Microfilm Records for the State of Pennsylvania
  http://www.heritagequest.com/genealogy/microfilm/pennsylvania/
- Lost in Time Books—Pennsylvania
  http://www.lostintime.com/catalog/books/bookst/bo26000.htm
- Mechling Associates, Inc. Western Pennsylvania Genealogy & History Books
  http://members.aol.com/armechling/mechweb.html
- The Memorabilia Corner—Books: Pennsylvania
  http://members.aol.com/TMCorner/book_pn.htm
- Picton Press—Pennsylvania
  http://www.midcoast.com/~picton/public_html.BASK/catalog/state_pa.htm
- S-K Publications—Pennsylvania 1800–1850 Census Books
  http://www.skpub.com/genie/census/pa/
- TLC Genealogy Books
  http://www.tlc-gen.com/
  Specializing in Colonial VA, KY, MD, OH, PA, NC, etc.
- Tracing Our Roots
  http://www.harrisburg.com/root.html
  Column by Schuyler Brossman, featured in The Press And Journal Extra, Middletown, Pennsylvania.
- Willow Bend Bookstore—Pennsylvania
  http://www.willowbend.net/pa.htm
- Ye Olde Genealogie Shoppe Books—Pennsylvania
  http://www.yogs.com/maincat.htm#PENNSYLVANIA

◆ Queries, Message Boards & Surname Lists

- Early Pennsylvania Settlers
  http://www.geocities.com/Heartland/3955/early.htm
- GenConnect Pennsylvania Visitor Center
  http://cgi.rootsweb.com/~genbbs/indx/Pa.html
  A system for posting queries, Bibles, biographies, deeds, obituaries, pensions, wills.

- Genealogy Index—10,000 Individuals
  http://www.natins.com/gen/index.html
  Starting in 1750 in Pennsylvania, with the German Immigrants to the present time.

- Palatine & Pennsylvania-Dutch Queries
  http://www.rootsweb.com/~panames/queries.html

- Pennsylvania Dutch (Queries Posted Immediately and Surnames Indexed Every Tuesday)
  http://cgi.rootsweb.com/~genbbs/genbbs.cgi/USA/Pa/Dutch

- Queries—Washington Co., Pennsylvania
  http://www.chartiers.com/pages-new/queries.html

- Surname Registry for Washington Co., Pennsylvania
  http://www.chartiers.com/pages-new/sur.html

◆ Records: Census, Cemeteries, Land, Obituaries, Personal, Taxes and Vital (Born, Married, Died & Buried)

- The 1790–1890 Federal Population Censuses: Catalog of National Archives Microfilm
  http://www.genealogy.org/census/contents.shtml
  - Census Schedules and Microfilm Roll Numbers for Pennsylvania:
    1790
    http://www.genealogy.org/census/1790.html
    1800
    http://www.genealogy.org/census/1800_schedules/Pennsylvania.html
    1810
    http://www.genealogy.org/census/1810_schedules/Pennsylvania.html
    1820
    http://www.genealogy.org/census/1820_schedules/Pennsylvania.html
    1830
    http://www.genealogy.org/census/1830_schedules/Pennsylvania.html
    1840
    http://www.genealogy.org/census/1840_schedules/Pennsylvania.html
    1850
    http://www.genealogy.org/census/1850_schedules/Pennsylvania.html
    1860
    http://www.genealogy.org/census/1860_schedules/Pennsylvania.html
    1870
    http://www.genealogy.org/census/1870_schedules/Pennsylvania.html
    1880
    http://www.genealogy.org/census/1880_schedules/Pennsylvania.html
    1880 Soundex
    http://www.genealogy.org/census/1880.sdx_schedules/T769.html
    1890 Special Schedules
    http://www.genealogy.org/census/1890-special_schedules/Virginia.html

- 1830 Crawford County Census Index
  http://www.granniesworld.com/cvahs/1830/index.html

- 1850 Census Beaver Township, Crawford County, Pennsylvania
  http://www.granniesworld.com/cvahs/bcen/

- 1850 Census Conneautville, Crawford County, Pennsylvania
  http://www.granniesworld.com/cvahs/census/index.html

- 1850 Census Summerhill Township, Crawford County, Pennsylvania
  http://www.granniesworld.com/cvahs/scen/

- Burials of Easton, Plainfield, Mount Bethel, Forks and Dryland
  http://www.geocities.com/Heartland/6508/#Burials of Easton,Plainfield,Mount Bethel,Forks and Dryland

- Cemeteries of the United States—Pennsylvania Cemeteries—County Index
  http://www.gac.edu/~kengelha/uscemeteries/pennsylvania.html

- Cemeteries Online!
  http://martin.simplenet.com/Cemeteries/
  Database of cemeteries in south-eastern and south-central Pennsylvania.

- Cemetery Index for Tioga and Bradford Counties in PA and Chemung County in NY
  http://www.rootsweb.com/~pabradfo/cemindex.htm

- Census Online—Links to Census Sites on the Web—Pennsylvania
  http://www.census-online.com/links/PA_data.html

- Chester Cemeteries Online
  http://www.rootsweb.com/~pacheste/chetgrav.htm

- Congregation Mikveh Israel Cemetery
  http://199.234.236.10/iha/_mikvehc.html
  Philadelphia

- County Courthouse Addresses
  http://www.familytreemaker.com/00000267.html

- Cumberlink Obituaries
  http://www.cumberlink.com/obits/archive.html
  From the Sentinel, Carlisle, Pennsylvania.

- Dauphin County Tax Lists
  http://maley.net/dauphin/tax_lists.htm

- Deed Data Pool
  http://www.ultranet.com/~deeds/pool.htm
  Downloadable deed files for Kentucky, New York, Pennsylvania, Virginia & West Virginia.

- Find-A-Grave by Location: Pennsylvania
  http://www.findagrave.com/grave/lpa.html
  Graves of noteworthy people.

- Forks Church Old Graveyard—Outside Easton, Pa.
  http://www.geocities.com/Heartland/6508/#Forks Church Old Graveyard

- Ground Work Genealogy on the Internet: Pennsylvania
  http://members.aol.com/ssmadonna/pa.htm

- Historic Laurel Hill Cemetery
  http://design.coda.drexel.edu/students/rmiller/assn2b.html
  Philadelphia, Pennsylvania

- Interment.net: Pennsylvania Cemeteries
  http://www.interment.net/us/pa/index.htm
  A list of links to other sites.

- Larry Medaglia: Register of Wills and Clerk of the Orphans' Court, Berks County, PA
  http://www.berksregofwills.com/

- Lehigh County Cemetery Locations
  http://www.geocities.com/Heartland/6508/#Lehigh County

- Lehigh County Historical Society Church Records Collection
  http://www.geocities.com/Heartland/3955/lehchurches.htm
  Pennsylvania

- Lehigh County, Pennsylvania Tax & Census Records
  http://www.geocities.com/Heartland/3955/lehtax.htm

- Marriages and Deaths, A–D
  http://www.geocities.com/Heartland/Plains/3558/admarrig.htm
  1810–1818. Many from Luzerne, Bradford, & Susquehanna Counties.

- Marriages and Deaths, E–G
  http://www.geocities.com/Heartland/Plains/3558/egmarrig.htm
  1810–1818. Many from Luzerne, Bradford, & Susquehanna Counties.

- Montgomery County Cemetery Project
  http://members.aol.com/tmyers8644/mccem.html

- National Archives—Mid Atlantic Region (Philadelphia)
  http://www.nara.gov/regional/philacc.html

- National Archives—Mid-Atlantic Region
  http://www.familytreemaker.com/00000097.html
  Records for Delaware, Maryland, Pennsylvania, Virginia, and West Virginia.

- Naturalizations: Researching Philadelphia Records
  http://www.phila.gov/phils/Docs/Inventor/natz.htm

- Northampton County Cemetery Locations
  http://www.geocities.com/Heartland/6508/#Cemeteries

- Northumberland County Will Index 1772–1859
  ftp://ftp.rootsweb.com/pub/usgenweb/pa/northumberland/wills/willindx.txt

- Obituaries, The Citizens' Voice Newspaper, Wilkes-Barre, PA
  http://citizensvoice.com/obituaries.html

- Observer-Reporter Obituary Archive
  http://www.chartiers.com/worobits/index.html
  Obituaries for Washington and Greene counties from August 1997 through present.

- Old Methodist Church Cemetery, Venus, Pennsylvania
  http://members.aol.com/jadolby/index.htm

- Partial 1680 Pennsylvania Census—Along the Delaware River
  http://www.geocities.com/Heartland/3955/1680census.htm

- Passenger Ship Records—PA Archives
  http://www.rootsweb.com/~usgenweb/pa/1pa/ship.htm

- Pennsylvania Family Bibles
  http://www.geocities.com/Heartland/3955/bibles.htm

- Pennsylvania Counties Addresses for Vital Records
  http://www.geocities.com/Heartland/3955/PAcounties.htm

- Pennsylvania Original Land Records
  http://www.innernet.net/hively/
  Series for York County.

- Pennsylvania Vital Records Information
  http://vitalrec.com/pa.html

- Philadelphia Daily News: Deaths
  http://www.phillynews.com/programs/go-pdn/deaths/

- Philadelphia Inquirer: Obituaries
  http://www.phillynews.com/programs/go-inq/obituaries/

- The Political Graveyard—Cemeteries in Pennsylvania
  http://politicalgraveyard.com/geo/PA/kmindex.html

- Preplanning Network—Funeral Home and Cemetery Directory—Pennsylvania
  http://www.preplannet.com/pennfhcem.htm

- Record of Marriages and Deaths 1826–1836
  http://www.geocities.com/Heartland/Plains/3558/voliv.htm
  Pennsylvania. Found in "Proceedings and Collections of the Wyoming Historical & Geological Society", Vol. IV.

- Records of Egypt Reformed Church Lehigh County, Pennsylvania 1734–1834
  http://www.geocities.com/Heartland/3955/lehegypt.htm
  From Pennsylvania Archives, Sixth Series, Volume 6.

- SAMPUBCO
  http://www.wasatch.com/~dsam/sampubco/index.htm
  Will Testators Indexes, Naturalization Records Indexes and Census Indexes online. You can order copies of the original source documents for a small fee.

- Search the 1860 Franklin County Census
  http://jefferson.village.virginia.edu/vshadow2/govdoc/fr.census1860.html

- Slaveowners and Slaves in and around Dauphin County, Pennsylvania
http://www.geocities.com/Athens/Parthenon/6329/index.html

- Tax Lists: 1734 Philadelphia County Taxables: Berks County Portion
ftp://ftp.rootsweb.com/pub/usgenweb/pa/berks/taxlist/tax1734.txt

- Tax Lists: 1753 Assessment List—Heidelberg Township, Lancaster County
ftp://ftp.rootsweb.com/pub/usgenweb/pa/berks/taxlist/1753heid.txt

- USGenWeb Census Project Pennsylvania
http://www.usgenweb.org/census/states/pennsylv.htm

- USGenWeb Tombstone Transcription Project— Pennsylvania
http://www.rootsweb.com/~cemetery/pennsyl.html

- VitalChek Network—Pennsylvania
http://www.vitalchek.com/stateselect.asp?state=PA

- Werkheiser Cemetery—Forks Township
http://www.geocities.com/Heartland/6508/#Werkheiser Cemetery

- Where to Write for Vital Records—Pennsylvania
http://www.cdc.gov/nchswww/howto/w2w/pennsylv.htm
From the National Center for Health Statistics (NCHS).

◆ Religion & Churches

- The Amish, the Mennonites, and the Plain People of the Pennsylvania Dutch Country
http://www.800padutch.com/amish.html

- Christianity.Net Church Locator—Pennsylvania
http://www.christianity.net/cgi/location.exe?United_States+Pennsylvania

- Church Online!—Pennsylvania
http://www.churchonline.com/usas/pa/pa.html

- Church Profiles—Pennsylvania
http://www.church-profiles.com/pa/pa.html

- Churches dot Net—Global Church Web Pages— Pennsylvania
http://www.churches.net/churches/pennsylv.html

- Churches of the World—Pennsylvania
http://www.churchsurf.com/churches/Pennsylvania/index.htm
From the ChurchSurf Christian Directory.

- Mennonites
http://www.CyndisList.com/menno.htm
See this category on Cyndi's List for related links.

- The Mennonite Historians of Eastern Pennsylvania
http://www.pond.com/~mennhist/

- Pennsylvania Catholic Database
http://WWW.ELINK.NET/bobbi/bo04000.htm

- The Presbyterian Historical Society
http://www.libertynet.org/gencap/presbyhs.html
Philadelphia

- Quakers
http://www.CyndisList.com/quaker.htm
See this category on Cyndi's List for related links.

- The Roman Catholic Archdiocese of Philadelphia
http://www.archdiocese-phl.org/

◆ Societies & Groups

- African-American Genealogy Group (AAGG)
http://www.libertynet.org/gencap/aagg.html
Philadelphia, Pennsylvania

- Allegheny Regional Family History Society
http://www.swcp.com/~dhickman/arfhs.html
Area covers counties in northeast West Virginia, southwest Pennsylvania, western Maryland and northwest Virginia.

- Archer's Computer Interest Group List— Pennsylvania
http://www.genealogy.org/~ngs/cigs/ngl1uspa.html

- The Berks County Genealogical Society
http://www.berksgenes.org/

- Bucks County Genealogical Society
http://www.libertynet.org/gencap/bcgs.html

- The Bucks County Historical Society
http://www.libertynet.org/bchs/index.html

- Butler County Historical Society
http://www.ButlerCounty.com/local/historical/historical.htm

- Centre County Genealogical Society
http://www.ancestry.com/societyhall/pages/sochall-27/main.htm

- The Chadds Ford Historical Society
http://www.de.psu.edu/cfhs/home.html

- The Chester County Historical Society
http://www.chesco.com/~cchs/

- Conemaugh Township Historical Society
http://www.ctcnet.net/ConemaughTwp/history.htm

- Conneaut Valley Area Historical Society
http://www.granniesworld.com/cvahs/

- Cumberland County Historical Society
http://www1.trib.com/CUMBERLINK/cumb/hist.groups.html

- The Delaware County Historical Society
http://www.libertynet.org/gencap/delcopa.html

- The Derry Area Historical Society
http://www.icubed.com/~cheetles/DAHS.html

- GENCAP: Genealogical Computing Association of Pennsylvania
http://www.libertynet.org/gencap/

- Genealogical Research Society of Northeastern Pennsylvania
http://www.clark.net/pub/mjloyd/grsnp/grsnp.html
Counties of: Lackawanna, Luzerne, Wayne, Pike, Monroe and Susquehanna.

- Genealogical Society of Pennsylvania
http://www.libertynet.org/gspa/

- German Society of Pennsylvania
http://www.german-society.org/
and a description from GENCAP
http://www.libertynet.org/gencap/germanpa.html

- Germantown Historical Society
http://www.libertynet.org/gencap/germantown.html

- Greene County Historical Society and Museum
http://www.greenepa.net/~museum/

- Historic Catasauqua Preservation Association
http://www.hcpa.org/

- Historical and Genealogical Society of Somerset County, Inc.
http://www.rootsweb.com/~pasomers/schs/member.htm

- Historical Society of Berks County
http://www.berksweb.com/histsoc.html

- The Historical Society of Frankford
http://www.libertynet.org/gencap/frankford.html

- The Historical Society of Montgomery County
http://www.libertynet.org/gencap/montcopa.html

- Historical Society of Pennsylvania
http://www.libertynet.org/pahist/

- Huntingdon County Historical Society'
http://www.huntingdon.net/hchs/

- IOOF Lodge Website Directory—Pennsylvania
http://norm28.hsc.usc.edu/IOOF/USA/Pennsylvania/Pennsylvania.html
Independent Order of Odd Fellows and Rebekahs.

- Jewish Genealogical Society of Philadelphia
http://www.jewishgen.org/jgsp/

- Lancaster County Historical Society
http://lanclio.org/

- Lancaster Mennonite Historical Society
http://lanclio.org/lmhs.htm

- Lebanon County Historical Society
http://www.leba.net/~history2/

- Lehigh County Historical Society
http://www.geocities.com/Heartland/plains/3955/LCHS.htm

- Lenni Lenape Historical Society
http://www.lenape.org/

- Lycoming County Genealogical Society
http://members.aol.com/LCGSgen/lcgs.htm

- Mahanoy and Mahantongo Historical & Preservation Society
http://www.mahantongo.org/index.htm

- The Maryland and Pennsylvania Railroad Preservation and Historical Society
http://www.arrowweb.com/Ma&Pa/
Spring Grove, Pennsylvania

- The Mennonite Historians of Eastern Pennsylvania
http://www.mhep.org/

- Northeast Pennsylvania Genealogical Society
http://www.rootsweb.com/~panepags/nepa.html

- Pennsylvania American Legion
http://www.pa-legion.com/

- Pennsylvania Daughters of the American Revolution, Bellefonte Chapter
http://www.pa1776.com/DAR/

- Pioneer Historical Society of Bedford County, Inc.
http://bedfordsprings.com/PHS/

- The Presbyterian Historical Society
http://www.libertynet.org/gencap/presbyhs.html
Philadelphia

- Punxsutawney Area Historical and Genealogical Society
http://users.penn.com/~mweimer/historcl.html

- Susquehanna County Historical Society & Free Library Association
http://www.epix.net/~suspulib/

- The Swedish Colonial Society
http://www.libertynet.org/gencap/scs.html
Philadelphia

- Valley Forge Historical Society
http://www.libertynet.org/iha/valleyforge/

- Western Pennsylvania Genealogical Society
http://www.clpgh.org/CLP/Pennsylvania/wpgs.html

◆ USGenWeb Project

- Pennsylvania Genealogy—USGenWeb Project State Page
http://www.usgenweb.org/pa

- PAUSGWARCH Mailing List
http://members.aol.com/gfsjohnf/gen_mail_states-pa.html#PAUSGWARCH
For volunteers assisting in receiving, formatting, and uploading files to the PA archives, part of the USGenWeb Archives Project.

- Pennsylvania—USGenWeb Archives Table of Contents
http://www.rootsweb.com/~usgenweb/pa/pafiles.htm

- Pennsylvania—USGenWeb FTP Archives
ftp://ftp.rootsweb.com/pub/usgenweb/pa/

U.S.—RHODE ISLAND—RI
http://www.CyndisList.com/ri.htm

Category Index:

- General Resource Sites
- Government & Cities
- History & Culture
- Libraries, Archives & Museums
- Mailing Lists, Newsgroups & Chat
- Maps, Gazetteers & Geographical Information
- Military
- Newspapers
- People & Families

- Professional Researchers, Volunteers & Other Research Services
- Publications, Software & Supplies
- Queries, Message Boards & Surname Lists
- Records: Census, Cemeteries, Land, Obituaries, Personal, Taxes and Vital
- Religion & Churches
- Societies & Groups
- USGenWeb Project

◆ General Resource Sites

- Everton's Sources of Genealogical Information in Rhode Island
  http://www.everton.com/usa/ri.htm
- Family Tree Maker's Genealogy "How To" Guide—Rhode Island
  http://www.familytreemaker.com/00000214.html
- Genealogy Exchange & Surname Registry—RIGenExchange
  http://www.genexchange.com/ri/index.cfm
- Genealogy Resources on the Internet: Rhode Island
  http://www-personal.umich.edu/~cgaunt/ri.html
- LDS Research Outline for Rhode Island
  http://www.everton.com/usa/ri-0840b.txt
- Lineages' Genealogy Site: Rhode Island
  http://www.lineages.com/rooms/usa/state.asp?StateCode=RI
- New England Connections
  http://www.geocities.com/Heartland/5274/nec.htm
- Rhode Island Genealogy
  http://users.ids.net/~jcraig/
- ROOTS-L United States Resources: Rhode Island
  http://www.rootsweb.com/roots-l/USA/ri.html
  Comprehensive list of research links, including many to history-related sites.

◆ Government & Cities

- 50states.com—Rhode Island State Information Resource
  http://www.50states.com/rdisland.htm
  A list of general information for each state, including a list of colleges, state symbols, links to maps, newspapers, and other miscellaneous state information.

- Excite Travel by City.Net—Rhode Island
  http://www.city.net/countries/united_states/rhode_island/
- Official City Web Sites for the State of Rhode Island
  http://OfficialCitySites.org/Rhode-Island.htm
- Rhode Island Bestlinx
  http://members.aol.com/squidnunc/bestlinx/index.html
- Rhode Island Online
  http://users.ids.net/ri/
- RI State Government Information Page
  http://www.athena.state.ri.us/info/
- Yahoo! Get Local...Rhode Island Cities
  http://dir.yahoo.com/Regional/U_S__States/Rhode_Island/Cities/
  Maps, yellow pages, white pages, newspapers and other local information.
- Yahoo! Get Local...Rhode Island Counties and Regions
  http://dir.yahoo.com/Regional/U_S__States/Rhode_Island/Counties_and_Regions/
  Maps, yellow pages, white pages, newspapers and other local information.

◆ History & Culture

- Yahoo!...History...Rhode Island
  http://dir.yahoo.com/Arts/Humanities/History/Browse_By_Region/U_S__States/Rhode_Island/

◆ Libraries, Archives & Museums

- Archives in New England on the Internet
  http://www.lib.umb.edu/newengarch/nearch.html
- Barrington Public Library
  http://www.ultranet.com/~bpl/

- East Greenwich Free Library
  http://www.ultranet.com/~egrlib/

- Family History Centers—Rhode Island
  http://www.deseretbook.com/famhis/ri.html

- Family History Centers—Rhode Island
  http://www.lib.byu.edu/~uvrfhc/centers/rhodeisland.html

- HYTELNET—Library Catalogs: USA: Rhode Island
  http://library.usask.ca/hytelnet/usa/RI.html
  Before you use any of the Telnet links, make note of the user name, password and any other logon information.

- NUCMC Listing of Archives and Manuscript Repositories in Rhode Island
  http://lcweb.loc.gov/coll/nucmc/risites.html
  Links to information about resources other than those held in the Library of Congress.

- OLIS: Office of Library & Information Services
  http://www.athena.state.ri.us/olis/

- Repositories of Primary Sources: Rhode Island
  http://www.uidaho.edu/special-collections/east2.html#usri
  A list of links to online resources from the Univ. of Idaho Library, Special Collections and Archives.

- Rhode Island Family History Centers
  http://www.genhomepage.com/FHC/Rhode_Island.html
  A list of addresses, phone numbers and hours of operation from the Genealogy Home Page.

- Rhode Island State Archives
  http://archives.state.ri.us/

- University of Rhode Island Libraries
  http://www.library.uri.edu/
  o Special Collections
    http://www.library.uri.edu/Special_Collections/

- Warwick Public Library
  http://users.ids.net/warwickpl/home.htm

- webCATS: Library Catalogues on the World Wide Web—Rhode Island
  http://library.usask.ca/hywebcat/states/RI.html

◆ Mailing Lists, Newsgroups & Chat

- Genealogy Resources on the Internet—Rhode Island Mailing Lists
  http://members.aol.com/gfsjohnf/gen_mail_states-ri.html
  Each of the mailing list links below points to this site, wonderfully maintained by John Fuller. Visit this site for county-specific mailing lists as well.

- NORTHEAST-ROOTS-L Mailing List
  http://members.aol.com/gfsjohnf/gen_mail_states-ri.html#NORTHEAST-ROOTS
  Connecticut, Maine, Massachusetts, New Hampshire, Rhode Island & Vermont.

- Rhode-Island Mailing List
  http://members.aol.com/gfsjohnf/gen_mail_states-ri.html#Rhode-Island

◆ Maps, Gazetteers & Geographical Information

- 1895 U.S. Atlas—Rhode Island
  http://www.LivGenMI.com/1895ri.htm

- American Memory Panoramic Maps 1847–1929—Rhode Island
  http://lcweb2.loc.gov/cgi-bin/query/S?ammem/gmd:@filreq(@field(STATE+@band(+rhode+island))+@field(COLLID+pmmap))
  From the Geography and Map Division, Library of Congress.

- American Memory Railroad Maps 1828–1900—Rhode Island
  http://memory.loc.gov/cgi-bin/query/S?ammem/gmd:@filreq(@field(STATE+@band(+rhode+island))+@field(COLLID+rrmap))
  From the Geography and Map Division, Library of Congress.

- Color Landform Atlas: Rhode Island
  http://fermi.jhuapl.edu/states/ri_0.html
  Including a map of counties and a map for 1895.

- Excite Maps: Rhode Island Maps
  http://www.city.net/maps/view/?mapurl=/countries/united_states/rhode_island
  Zoom in on these maps all the way to the street level.

- HPI County InfoSystem—Counties in Rhode Island
  http://www.com/hpi/ricty/index.html

- K.B. Slocum Books and Maps—Rhode Island
  http://www.treasurenet.com/cgi-bin/treasure/kbslocum/scan/se=Rhode.20Island/sf=mapstate

- List of Rhode Island Counties
  http://www.genealogy.org/~st-clair/counties/state_ri.html

- Map of Rhode Island Counties
  http://govinfo.kerr.orst.edu/gif/states/ri.gif
  From the Government Information Sharing Project, Information Services, Oregon State University.

- Map of Rhode Island Counties
  http://www.lib.utexas.edu/Libs/PCL/Map_collection/states/Rhode_Island.gif
  From the Perry-Castañeda Library at the Univ. of Texas at Austin.

- Old Maps of New England (Maine, New Hampshire, Vermont, Connecticut, Rhode Island, Massachusetts) and New York
  http://members.aol.com/oldmapsne/index.html

- Reproductions of Old Town Maps in New England
  http://www.biddeford.com/~lkane/

- U.S. Census Bureau—Rhode Island Profiles
  http://www.census.gov/datamap/www/44.html

- Yale Peabody Museum: GNIS—Rhode Island
  http://www.peabody.yale.edu/other/gnis/RI.html
  *Search the USGS Geographic Names Database. You can limit
  the search to a specific county in this state and search for any of
  the following features: airport arch area arroyo bar basin bay
  beach bench bend bridge **building** canal cape **cemetery** channel
  church cliff crater crossing dam falls flat forest gap geyser
  glacier gut harbor hospital island isthmus lake lava levee locale
  mine oilfield other park pillar plain ppl range rapids reserve
  reservoir ridge **school** sea slope spring stream summit swamp
  tower trail tunnel valley well woods.*

◆ Military

- The Civil War Archive—Union Regiments—
  Rhode Island
  http://www.civilwararchive.com/unionri.htm

- Korean Conflict State-Level Casualty Lists—
  Rhode Island
  http://www.nara.gov/nara/electronic/rihrlist.html
  *From the National Archives and Records Administration,
  Center for Electronic Records.*

- Vietnam Conflict State-Level Casualty Lists—
  Rhode Island
  http://www.nara.gov/nara/electronic/rihrviet.html
  *From the National Archives and Records Administration,
  Center for Electronic Records.*

◆ Newspapers

- AJR NewsLink—Rhode Island Newspapers
  http://www.newslink.org/rinews.html

- E&P Media Info Links—Newspaper Sites in
  Rhode Island
  http://www.mediainfo.com/emedia/browse-results.
  htm?region=rhodeisland&category=newspaper+++++++++

- Ecola Newstand: Rhode Island
  http://www.ecola.com/news/press/na/us/ri/

- NAA Hotlinks to Newspapers Online—Rhode Island
  http://www.naa.org/hotlinks/searchResult.asp?param=
  RI-Rhode+Island&City=1

- N-Net—Rhode Island Newspapers
  http://www.n-net.com/ri.htm

- The Providence Journal-Bulletin
  http://www.providencejournal.com/main.htm

- The Ultimate Collection of News Links: USA—
  Rhode Island
  http://www.pppp.net/links/news/USA-RI.html

◆ People & Families

- Directory of Underground Railroad Operators—
  Rhode Island
  http://www.ugrr.org//names/map-ri.htm

- Tribes and Villages of Rhode Island
  http://hanksville.phast.umass.edu:8000/cultprop/contacts/
  tribal/RI.html

- WPA Life Histories from Rhode Island
  http://lcweb2.loc.gov/ammem/wpaintro/ricat.html
  *Manuscripts from the Federal Writer's Project, 1936–1940,
  Library of Congress.*

◆ Professional Researchers, Volunteers & Other Research Services

- Board for Certification of Genealogists—Roster of
  Those Certified—Specializing in Rhode Island
  http://www.genealogy.org/~bcg/rosts_ri.html

- Genealogy Helplist—Rhode Island
  http://www.cyberbeach.net/~mkelly/helplistUSA/ri.htm

- The Official Iowa Counties Professional Genealogist
  and Researcher's Registry for Rhode Island
  http://www.iowa-counties.com/gene/ri.htm

- Rhode Island Families Association—Genealogical
  Publications and Research
  http://www.erols.com/rigr/
  *Research for Rhode Island, New England, Probate, and DAR
  including membership.*

◆ Publications, Software & Supplies

- AncestorSpy—CDs and Microfiche for Rhode Island
  http://www.ancestorspy.com/ri.htm

- Barbara Green's Used Genealogy Books—
  Rhode Island
  http://home.earthlink.net/~genbooks/lochist.html#RI

- Barnette's Family Tree Books—Rhode Island
  http://www.barnettesbooks.com/rhode-is.htm

- Books We Own—Rhode Island
  http://www.rootsweb.com/~bwo/ri.html

- Boyd Publishing Company—New England
  http://www.hom.net/~gac/newengla.htm

- Broad View Books
  http://broadviewbooks.com/
  *Used Genealogy Books, Local History of Massachusetts,
  Connecticut, Rhode Island, Vermont and New England.*

- Essex Books—New England
  http://www.HERTGE.COM/essex/neweng.htm

- Frontier Press Bookstore—Rhode Island
  http://www.frontierpress.com/frontier.cgi?category=ri

- GenealogyBookShop.com—Rhode Island
  http://www.genealogybookshop.com/genealogybookshop/files/
  The_United_States,Rhode_Island/index.html
  *The online store of Genealogical Publishing Co., Inc. &
  Clearfield Company.*

- Hearthstone Bookshop—Rhode Island
  http://www.hearthstonebooks.com/cgi-bin/webc.cgi/st_main.
  html?catid=97&sid=2PH5t29sm

- Heritage Books—Rhode Island
  http://www.heritagebooks.com/ri.htm
- Heritage Quest—Microfilm Records for the State of Rhode Island
  http://www.heritagequest.com/genealogy/microfilm/rhode_island/
- Lost in Time Books—Rhode Island
  http://www.lostintime.com/catalog/books/bookst/bo27000.htm
- The Memorabilia Corner—Books: Rhode Island
  http://members.aol.com/TMCorner/book_ri.htm
- Picton Press—Rhode Island
  http://www.midcoast.com/~picton/public_html.BASK/catalog/state_ri.htm
- Rhode Island Families Association—Genealogical Publications and Research
  http://www.erols.com/rigr/
  Indexed articles from the Rhode Island Genealogical Register, as well as publications from a variety of records: probate, wills, vital, cemeteries, etc.
- Willow Bend Bookstore—Rhode Island
  http://www.willowbend.net/ri.htm

◆ Queries, Message Boards & Surname Lists

- GenConnect Rhode Island Visitor Center
  http://cgi.rootsweb.com/~genbbs/indx/RI.html
  A system for posting queries, Bibles, biographies, deeds, obituaries, pensions, wills.
- New England Connections Query Archive
  http://www.geocities.com/Heartland/5274/nequery.htm

◆ Records: Census, Cemeteries, Land, Obituaries, Personal, Taxes and Vital (Born, Married, Died & Buried)

- The 1790–1890 Federal Population Censuses: Catalog of National Archives Microfilm
  http://www.genealogy.org/census/contents.shtml
  - Census Schedules and Microfilm Roll Numbers for Rhode Island:
    1790
    http://www.genealogy.org/census/1790.html
    1800
    http://www.genealogy.org/census/1800_schedules/Rhode.Island.html
    1810
    http://www.genealogy.org/census/1810_schedules/Rhode.Island.html
    1820
    http://www.genealogy.org/census/1820_schedules/Rhode.Island.html
    1830
    http://www.genealogy.org/census/1830_schedules/Rhode.Island.html
    1840
    http://www.genealogy.org/census/1840_schedules/Rhode.Island.html
    1850
    http://www.genealogy.org/census/1850_schedules/Rhode.Island.html
    1860
    http://www.genealogy.org/census/1860_schedules/Rhode.Island.html
    1870
    http://www.genealogy.org/census/1870_schedules/Rhode.Island.html
    1880
    http://www.genealogy.org/census/1880_schedules/Rhode.Island.html
    1880 Soundex
    http://www.genealogy.org/census/1880.sdx_schedules/T770.html
    1890 Special Schedules
    http://www.genealogy.org/census/1890-special_schedules/Rhode.Island.html
- Cemetery Inscriptions In Little Compton, Newport County, Rhode Island
  ftp://ftp.rootsweb.com/pub/usgenweb/ri/newport/cemetery/cemetery.txt
- County Courthouse Addresses
  http://www.familytreemaker.com/00000268.html
- Find-A-Grave by Location: Rhode Island
  http://www.findagrave.com/grave/lri.html
  Graves of noteworthy people.
- Interment.net: Rhode Island Cemeteries
  http://www.interment.net/us/ri/index.htm
  A list of links to other sites.
- National Archives—Northeast Region (Boston)
  http://www.nara.gov/regional/boston.html
- National Archives—New England Region
  http://www.familytreemaker.com/00000098.html
  Records for Connecticut, Maine, Massachusetts, New Hampshire, Rhode Island, and Vermont.
- The Political Graveyard—Cemeteries in Rhode Island
  http://politicalgraveyard.com/geo/RI/kmindex.html
- Preplanning Network—Funeral Home and Cemetery Directory—Rhode Island
  http://www.preplannet.com/usafh.htm#Rhode Island
- Providence Journal Obituaries
  http://www.projo.com/report/pjb/indexes/ob.htm
- Rhode Island Cemeteries Database Home Page
  http://members.tripod.com/~debyns/cemetery.html

- Rhode Island Vital Records Information
  http://vitalrec.com/ri.html
- Tiverton Grand Deed
  http://www.rootsweb.com/~rinewpor/gnd_deed.html
- USGenWeb Census Project Rhode Island
  http://www.usgenweb.org/census/states/rhodeisl.htm
- USGenWeb Tombstone Transcription Project—
  Rhode Island
  http://www.rootsweb.com/~cemetery/rho-isl.html
- VitalChek Network—Rhode Island
  http://www.vitalchek.com/stateselect.asp?state=RI
- Where to Write for Vital Records—Rhode Island
  http://www.cdc.gov/nchswww/howto/w2w/rdisland.htm
  From the National Center for Health Statistics (NCHS).

◆ Religion & Churches

- Christianity.Net Church Locator—Rhode Island
  http://www.christianity.net/cgi/
  location.exe?United_States+Rhode_Island
- Church Online!—Rhode Island
  http://www.churchonline.com/usas/ri/ri.html
- Church Profiles—Rhode Island
  http://www.church-profiles.com/ri/ri.html
- Churches dot Net—Global Church Web Pages—
  Rhode Island
  http://www.churches.net/churches/risland.html
- Churches of the World—Rhode Island
  http://www.churchsurf.com/churches/Rhode_Island/index.htm
  From the ChurchSurf Christian Directory.

◆ Societies & Groups

- The American-French Genealogical Society
  http://users.ids.net/~afgs/afgshome.html
- Archer's Computer Interest Group List—Rhode
  Island
  http://www.genealogy.org/~ngs/cigs/ngl1usri.html
- Charlestown Historical Society
  http://www.charlestown.com/ri/historicalsociety/index.htm
- The Cranston Historical Society
  http://www.geocities.com/Heartland/4678/sprague.html

- IOOF Lodge Website Directory—Rhode Island
  http://norm28.hsc.usc.edu/IOOF/USA/Rhode_Island/
  Rhode_Island.html
  Independent Order of Odd Fellows and Rebekahs.
- Italian Genealogical Society of America
  http://users.loa.com/~del2jdcd/igsa.html
  Cranston
- Little Compton Historical Society
  http://www.rootsweb.com/~rinewpor/compton.html
- Military Order of the Loyal Legion of the United
  States—Rhode Island Commandery
  http://www.geocities.com/Pentagon/3901/rimollus.html
- Most Worshipful Grand Lodge of the Most Ancient
  and Honorable Society of Free and Accepted Masons
  for the State of Rhode Island and Providence
  Plantations
  http://www.freemason-ri.org/masons/home.htm
- New England Historic Genealogical Society
  http://www.nehgs.org/
- Society Hill: Rhode Island, United States
  http://www.daddezio.com/society/hill/SH-RI-NDX.html
  *A list of addresses for genealogical and historical societies in
  the state.*

◆ USGenWeb Project

- Rhode Island Genealogy—USGenWeb Project State
  Page
  http://www.usgenweb.org/ri
- Rhode Island—USGenWeb Archives Table of
  Contents
  http://www.rootsweb.com/~usgenweb/ri/rifiles.htm
- Rhode Island—USGenWeb FTP Archives
  ftp://ftp.rootsweb.com/pub/usgenweb/ri/
- Rhode Island—Add Query
  http://www.rootsweb.com/~usgenweb/ri/riquery.html
- RIGENWEB Mailing List
  http://members.aol.com/gfsjohnf/gen_mail_states-
  ri.html#RIGENWEB
  Also: RIGenWeb Mailing List
  http://www.rootsweb.com/~rigenweb/mailist.html
  *For discussions with others researching their Rhode Island
  ancestry, or who have other genealogical or historical interests
  in the state of Rhode Island.*

U.S.—SOUTH CAROLINA—SC

http://www.CyndisList.com/sc.htm

Category Index:

- General Resource Sites
- Government & Cities
- History & Culture
- Libraries, Archives & Museums
- Locality Specific
- Mailing Lists, Newsgroups & Chat
- Maps, Gazetteers & Geographical Information
- Military
- Newspapers
- People & Families

- Professional Researchers, Volunteers & Other Research Services
- Publications, Software & Supplies
- Queries, Message Boards & Surname Lists
- Records: Census, Cemeteries, Land, Obituaries, Personal, Taxes and Vital
- Religion & Churches
- Societies & Groups
- USGenWeb Project

◆ General Resource Sites

- Everton's Sources of Genealogical Information in South Carolina
  http://www.everton.com/usa/sc.htm

- Family Tree Maker's Genealogy "How To" Guide—South Carolina
  http://www.familytreemaker.com/00000215.html

- Genealogy Exchange & Surname Registry—SCGenExchange
  http://www.genexchange.com/sc/index.cfm

- Genealogy Resources on the Internet: South Carolina
  http://www-personal.umich.edu/~cgaunt/scarolina.html

- LDS Research Outline for South Carolina
  http://www.everton.com/usa/sc-0841b.txt

- Lineages' Genealogy Site: South Carolina
  http://www.lineages.com/rooms/usa/state.asp?StateCode=SC

- ROOTS-L United States Resources: South Carolina
  http://www.rootsweb.com/roots-l/USA/sc.html
  Comprehensive list of research links, including many to history-related sites.

◆ Government & Cities

- 50states.com—South Carolina State Information Resource
  http://www.50states.com/scarolin.htm
  A list of general information for each state, including a list of colleges, state symbols, links to maps, newspapers, and other miscellaneous state information.

- Excite Travel by City.Net—South Carolina
  http://www.city.net/countries/united_states/south_carolina/

- Official City Web Sites for the State of South Carolina
  http://OfficialCitySites.org/South-Carolina.htm

- South Carolina State Government World Wide Web (WWW) server
  http://www.state.sc.us/

- Yahoo! Get Local...South Carolina Cities
  http://dir.yahoo.com/Regional/U_S__States/South_Carolina/Cities/
  Maps, yellow pages, white pages, newspapers and other local information.

- Yahoo! Get Local...South Carolina Counties and Regions
  http://dir.yahoo.com/Regional/U_S__States/South_Carolina/Counties_and_Regions/
  Maps, yellow pages, white pages, newspapers and other local information.

◆ History & Culture

- Yahoo!...History...South Carolina
  http://dir.yahoo.com/Arts/Humanities/History/Browse_By_Region/U_S__States/South_Carolina

◆ Libraries, Archives & Museums

- Family History Centers—South Carolina
  http://www.deseretbook.com/famhis/sc.html

- Family History Centers—South Carolina
  http://www.lib.byu.edu/~uvrfhc/centers/southcarolina.html

- Greenville (SC) County Library
  http://gcl.greenville.lib.sc.us/

- James A. Rogers Library—Francis Marion
  University
  http://vax.fmarion.edu/
  Florence, South Carolina

- HYTELNET—Library Catalogs: USA:
  South Carolina
  http://library.usask.ca/hytelnet/usa/SC.html
  Before you use any of the Telnet links, make note of the user name, password and any other logon information.

- NUCMC Listing of Archives and Manuscript
  Repositories in South Carolina
  http://lcweb.loc.gov/coll/nucmc/scsites.html
  Links to information about resources other than those held in the Library of Congress.

- Repositories of Primary Sources: South Carolina
  http://www.uidaho.edu/special-collections/east2.html#ussc
  A list of links to online resources from the Univ. of Idaho Library, Special Collections and Archives.

- South Carolina Department of Archives and History
  http://www.state.sc.us/scdah/
  - Research at the Archives
    http://www.state.sc.us/scdah/research.htm
    - Confederate Military Records at the Archives
      http://www.state.sc.us/scdah/confedrc.htm
    - Genealogical Research at the SC Archives
      http://www.state.sc.us/scdah/genealre.htm
    - Researching Family History at the South
      Carolina Archives
      http://www.state.sc.us/scdah/famhstry.htm

- South Carolina State Library
  http://www.state.sc.us/scsl/
  - South Carolina Public Libraries
    http://www.state.sc.us/scsl/colibs1.html
  - South Carolina Reference Room: History and
    Culture
    http://www.state.sc.us/scsl/histcult.html

- University of South Carolina Libraries
  http://www.sc.edu/library/
  - Rare Books and Special Collections
    http://www.sc.edu/library/spcoll/rarebook.html
  - South Caroliniana Library
    http://www.sc.edu/library/socar/index.html
    - Finding Aids
      http://www.sc.edu/library/socar/mnscrpts/findaids.html
  - Special Collections
    http://www.sc.edu/library/spcoll.html

- webCATS: Library Catalogues on the World Wide
  Web—South Carolina
  http://library.usask.ca/hywebcat/states/SC.html

◆ Locality Specific

- Also see the USGenWeb section for links to
  county-specific resources.
- Chesterfield County, SC Genealogical Services
  http://www.charlotte.infi.net/~jpigg/index.htm

◆ Mailing Lists, Newsgroups & Chat

- Genealogy Resources on the Internet—South
  Carolina Mailing Lists
  http://members.aol.com/gfsjohnf/gen_mail_states-sc.html
  Each of the mailing list links below points to this site, wonderfully maintained by John Fuller. Visit this site for county-specific mailing lists as well.

- Appalachianfamily Mailing List
  http://members.aol.com/gfsjohnf/gen_mail_states-va.html#Appalachianfamily
  Appalachian Mountain Families including families from Georgia, North Carolina, South Carolina, Tennessee, Kentucky, Virginia, and West Virginia.

- LONGCANE Mailing List
  http://members.aol.com/gfsjohnf/gen_mail_states-sc.html#LONGCANE
  For anyone with a genealogical or historical interest in the Long Cane Creek area of upstate South Carolina.

- Lowcountry Mailing List
  http://members.aol.com/gfsjohnf/gen_mail_states-sc.html#Lowcountry
  Including Beaufort, Hampton, Jasper, Charleston, and neighboring counties.

- Melungeon Mailing List
  http://members.aol.com/gfsjohnf/gen_mail_states-gen.html#MELUNGEO
  For people conducting Melungeon and/or Appalachian research including Native American, Portuguese, Turkish, Black Dutch, and other unverifiable mixed statements of ancestry or unexplained rumors, with ancestors in TN, KY, VA, NC, SC, GA, AL, WV, and possibly other places.

- NC-SC-ROOTS-L Mailing List
  http://members.aol.com/gfsjohnf/gen_mail_states-sc.html#NC/SC-ROOTS
  North Carolina and South Carolina.

- ORANGEBURGH SC Mailing list
  http://members.aol.com/gfsjohnf/gen_mail_states-sc.html#ORANGEBURGH_SC
  For all serious researchers of the people of Orangeburgh Township, South Carolina.

- SCBATTLES Mailing List
  http://members.aol.com/gfsjohnf/gen_mail_states-sc.html#SCBATTLES
  For anyone having an interest in South Carolina military history including battles, skirmishes, soldiers, units, fortifications, armament, re-enactments or preservation efforts.

- SC-Genealogy Mailing List
  http://members.aol.com/gfsjohnf/gen_mail_states-sc.html#SC-Genealogy

- SCROOTS Mailing List
  http://members.aol.com/gfsjohnf/gen_mail_states-sc.html#SCROOTS

◆ Maps, Gazetteers & Geographical Information

- 1790 South Carolina Census Map
  http://www.historyu.com/Village/SurvHouse/1790pages/90scarolina.html

- 1895 U.S. Atlas—South Carolina
  http://www.LivGenMI.com/1895sc.htm

- American Memory Panoramic Maps 1847–1929—South Carolina
  http://lcweb2.loc.gov/cgi-bin/query/S?ammem/gmd:@filreq(@field(STATE+@band(+south+carolina))+@field(COLLID+pmmap))
  From the Geography and Map Division, Library of Congress.

- American Memory Railroad Maps 1828–1900—South Carolina
  http://memory.loc.gov/cgi-bin/query/S?ammem/gmd:@filreq(@field(STATE+@band(+south+carolina))+@field(COLLID+rrmap))
  From the Geography and Map Division, Library of Congress.

- Color Landform Atlas: South Carolina
  http://fermi.jhuapl.edu/states/sc_0.html
  Including a map of counties and a map for 1895.

- Excite Maps: South Carolina Maps
  http://www.city.net/maps/view/?mapurl=/countries/united_states/south_carolina
  Zoom in on these maps all the way to the street level.

- HPI County InfoSystem—Counties in South Carolina
  http://www.com/hpi/sccty/index.html

- K.B. Slocum Books and Maps—South Carolina
  http://www.treasurenet.com/cgi-bin/treasure/kbslocum/scan/se=South.20Carolina/sf=mapstate

- List of South Carolina Counties
  http://www.genealogy.org/~st-clair/counties/state_sc.html

- Map of South Carolina Counties
  http://govinfo.kerr.orst.edu/gif/states/sc.gif
  From the Government Information Sharing Project, Information Services, Oregon State University.

- Map of South Carolina Counties
  http://www.lib.utexas.edu/Libs/PCL/Map_collection/states/South_Carolina.gif
  From the Perry-Castañeda Library at the Univ. of Texas at Austin.

- U.S. Census Bureau—South Carolina Profiles
  http://www.census.gov/datamap/www/45.html

- Yale Peabody Museum: GNIS—South Carolina
  http://www.peabody.yale.edu/other/gnis/SC.html
  *Search the USGS Geographic Names Database. You can limit the search to a specific county in this state and search for any of the following features: airport arch area arroyo bar basin bay beach bench bend bridge **building** canal cape **cemetery** channel **church** cliff crater crossing dam falls flat forest gap geyser glacier gut harbor hospital island isthmus lake lava levee locale mine oilfield other park pillar plain ppl range rapids reserve reservoir ridge **school** sea slope spring stream summit swamp tower trail tunnel valley well woods.*

◆ Military

- The Civil War Archive—Union Regiments—South Carolina
  http://www.civilwararchive.com/unionsc.htm

- Civil War Battle Summaries by State—South Carolina
  http://www2.cr.nps.gov/abpp/battles/bystate.htm#sc

- Confederate Military Records at the Archives
  http://www.state.sc.us/scdah/confedrc.htm

- Friends of the Florence Stockade
  http://members.aol.com/qmsgtboots/florence.html

- Korean Conflict State-Level Casualty Lists—South Carolina
  http://www.nara.gov/nara/electronic/schrlist.html
  From the National Archives and Records Administration, Center for Electronic Records.

- Vietnam Conflict State-Level Casualty Lists—South Carolina
  http://www.nara.gov/nara/electronic/schrviet.html
  From the National Archives and Records Administration, Center for Electronic Records.

◆ Newspapers

- AJR NewsLink—South Carolina Newspapers
  http://www.newslink.org/scnews.html

- E&P Media Info Links—Newspaper Sites in South Carolina
  http://www.mediainfo.com/emedia/browse-results.htm?region=southcarolina&category=newspaper+++++++++

- Ecola Newstand: South Carolina
  http://www.ecola.com/news/press/na/us/sc/

- ESCN Database Reports
  http://ourworld.compuserve.com/homepages/escn_database_reports/
  Quick Reference Indexes to the Early South Carolina Newspapers.

- NAA Hotlinks to Newspapers Online—South Carolina
  http://www.naa.org/hotlinks/searchResult.asp?param=SC-South+Carolina&City=1

- N-Net—South Carolina Newspapers
  http://www.n-net.com/sc.htm
- The Ultimate Collection of News Links: USA—South Carolina
  http://www.pppp.net/links/news/USA-SC.html
- Yahoo!...Newspapers...South Carolina
  http://dir.yahoo.com/News_and_Media/Newspapers/Browse_By_Region/U_S__States/South_Carolina/

◆ People & Families

- African American History and Genealogy Resources
  http://www.ilinks.net/~mcmaster/
  Includes a partial list of Charleston's antebellum black Catholics, tax records, etc.
- Tribes and Villages of South Carolina
  http://hanksville.phast.umass.edu:8000/cultprop/contacts/tribal/SC.html
- WPA Life Histories from South Carolina
  http://lcweb2.loc.gov/ammem/wpaintro/sccat.html
  Manuscripts from the Federal Writer's Project, 1936–1940, Library of Congress.

◆ Professional Researchers, Volunteers & Other Research Services

- Board for Certification of Genealogists—Roster of Those Certified—Specializing in South Carolina
  http://www.genealogy.org/~bcg/rosts_sc.html
- Genealogy Helplist—South Carolina
  http://posom.com/hl/usa/sc.shtml
- The Official Iowa Counties Professional Genealogist and Researcher's Registry for South Carolina
  http://www.iowa-counties.com/gene/sc.htm

◆ Publications, Software & Supplies

- AncestorSpy—CDs and Microfiche for South Carolina
  http://www.ancestorspy.com/sc.htm
- Barbara Green's Used Genealogy Books—South Carolina
  http://home.earthlink.net/~genbooks/lochist.html#SC
- Barnette's Family Tree Books—South Carolina
  http://www.barnettesbooks.com/south-ca.htm
- Books We Own—South Carolina
  http://www.rootsweb.com/~bwo/scar.html
- Boyd Publishing Company—South Carolina
  http://www.hom.net/~gac/southcar.htm

- Frontier Press Bookstore—South Carolina
  http://www.frontierpress.com/frontier.cgi?category=sc
- GenealogyBookShop.com—South Carolina
  http://www.genealogybookshop.com/genealogybookshop/files/The_United_States,South_Carolina/index.html
  The online store of Genealogical Publishing Co., Inc. & Clearfield Company.
- Hearthstone Bookshop—South Carolina
  http://www.hearthstonebooks.com/cgi-bin/webc.cgi/st_main.html?catid=98&sid=2PH5t29sm
- Heritage Books—South Carolina
  http://www.heritagebooks.com/sc.htm
- Heritage Quest—Microfilm Records for the State of South Carolina
  http://www.heritagequest.com/genealogy/microfilm/south_carolina/
- J & W Enterprises
  http://www.dhc.net/~jw/
  One stop book source on the Internet, specializing in southern states source material.
- Lost in Time Books—South Carolina
  http://www.lostintime.com/catalog/books/bookst/bo28000.htm
- The Memorabilia Corner Books—South Carolina
  http://members.aol.com/TMCorner/book_sc.htm
- The Memorabilia Corner Census View CDs—South Carolina
  http://members.aol.com/TMCorner/cen_sc.htm
- S-K Publications—South Carolina 1850 Census Books
  http://www.skpub.com/genie/census/sc/
- Southern Queries Genealogy Magazine
  http://www.mindspring.com/~freedom1/sq/sq.htm
- Willow Bend Bookstore—South Carolina
  http://www.willowbend.net/sc.htm

◆ Queries, Message Boards & Surname Lists

- GenConnect South Carolina Visitor Center
  http://cgi.rootsweb.com/~genbbs/indx/SC.html
  A system for posting queries, Bibles, biographies, deeds, obituaries, pensions, wills.
- Orangeburgh German-Swiss Genealogical Society Surnames List
  http://www.netside.com/~genealogy/surnames.shtml
  Immigrants and First Families in South Carolina Townships, Amelia, Orangeburgh, Saxe Gotha, Purrysburg, New Windsor, and others.
- South Carolina Historical Society—Surname Guide
  http://www.historic.com/schs/gbrowse/browse.html

◆ Records: Census, Cemeteries, Land, Obituaries, Personal, Taxes and Vital (Born, Married, Died & Buried)

- 1768 Ship Arrivals, Charleston, SC
  ftp://ftp.rootsweb.com/pub/usgenweb/sc/ships/1768ship.txt

- The 1790–1890 Federal Population Censuses: Catalog of National Archives Microfilm
  http://www.genealogy.org/census/contents.shtml

  ○ Census Schedules and Microfilm Roll Numbers for South Carolina:

    1790
    http://www.genealogy.org/census/1790.html

    1800
    http://www.genealogy.org/census/1800_schedules/South.Carolina.html

    1810
    http://www.genealogy.org/census/1810_schedules/South.Carolina.html

    1820
    http://www.genealogy.org/census/1820_schedules/South.Carolina.html

    1830
    http://www.genealogy.org/census/1830_schedules/South.Carolina.html

    1840
    http://www.genealogy.org/census/1840_schedules/South.Carolina.html

    1850
    http://www.genealogy.org/census/1850_schedules/South.Carolina.html

    1860
    http://www.genealogy.org/census/1860_schedules/South.Carolina.html

    1870
    http://www.genealogy.org/census/1870_schedules/South.Carolina.html

    1880
    http://www.genealogy.org/census/1880_schedules/South.Carolina.html

    1880 Soundex
    http://www.genealogy.org/census/1880.sdx_schedules/T771.html

    1890 Special Schedules
    http://www.genealogy.org/census/1890-special_schedules/South.Carolina.html

- The 1800 Horry County South Carolina Census
  http://ourworld.compuserve.com/homepages/jotajota/horry1.htm

- African-American History and Genealogy Resources
  http://www.ilinks.net/~mcmaster/
  Includes a partial list of Charleston's antebellum black Catholics, tax records, etc.

- Allendale / Bamberg / Barnwell County Cemeteries
  http://www.rootsweb.com/~scbarnwe/Cemeteries.htm

- Census Online—Links to Census Sites on the Web—South Carolina
  http://www.census-online.com/links/SC_data.html

- Charleston Race Course Prison Dead, SC
  http://members.aol.com/edboots/charlestondead.html
  Union Civil War Prisoners of War originally buried at the Charleston Race Course Cemetery and later reinterred at the Beaufort National Cemetery.

- County Courthouse Addresses
  http://www.familytreemaker.com/00000269.html

- ESCN (Early South Carolina Newspapers) Database Reports
  http://ourworld.compuserve.com/homepages/escn_database_reports/
  Quick reference indexes to data found in the early South Carolina newspapers.

- Find-A-Grave by Location: South Carolina
  http://www.findagrave.com/grave/lsc.html
  Graves of noteworthy people.

- Ground Work Genealogy on the Internet: South Carolina
  http://members.aol.com/ssmadonna/sc.htm
  Links to sites with a variety of records.

- Index to Probate Court Records in the Union County Courthouse, 1787–1865
  http://members.aol.com/unionscgen/probindx/unscprob.htm

- Interment.net: South Carolina Cemeteries
  http://www.interment.net/us/sc/index.htm
  A list of links to other sites.

- Kershaw County, South Carolina 1800 Federal Census
  http://homepages.rootsweb.com/~marykozy/census/kers1800.txt

- National Archives—Southeast Region (Atlanta)
  http://www.nara.gov/regional/atlanta.html

- National Archives—Southeast Region from Family Tree Maker
  http://www.familytreemaker.com/00000104.html
  Records for Alabama, Florida, Georgia, Kentucky, Mississippi, North Carolina, South Carolina, and Tennessee.

- The Political Graveyard—Cemeteries in South Carolina
  http://politicalgraveyard.com/geo/SC/kmindex.html

- Preplanning Network—Funeral Home and Cemetery Directory—South Carolina
  http://www.preplannet.com/scfhcem.htm

- Slave Entries in Wills, Deeds, Etc.
  http://www.netcom.com/~jog1/slavedocs.html
  Kentucky, South Carolina, Tennessee, Virginia

- South Carolina Vital Records Information
  http://vitalrec.com/sc.html

- USGenWeb Census Project South Carolina
  http://www.usgenweb.org/census/states/southcar/southcar.htm

- USGenWeb Tombstone Transcription Project—South Carolina
  http://www.rootsweb.com/~cemetery/s-car.html

- VitalChek Network—South Carolina
  http://www.vitalchek.com/stateselect.asp?state=SC

- York County, South Carolina, Census Index—Interactive Search
  http://www.rootsweb.com/cgi-bin/scyork/scyork.pl
  1790 to 1850 heads of household.

- Where to Write for Vital Records—South Carolina
  http://www.cdc.gov/nchswww/howto/w2w/scarolin.htm
  From the National Center for Health Statistics (NCHS).

◆ Religion & Churches

- Christianity.Net Church Locator—South Carolina
  http://www.christianity.net/cgi/location.exe?
  United_States+South_Carolina

- Church Online!—South Carolina
  http://www.churchonline.com/usas/sc/sc.html

- Church Profiles—South Carolina
  http://www.church-profiles.com/sc/sc.html

- Churches dot Net—Global Church Web Pages—South Carolina
  http://www.churches.net/churches/scarolin.html

- Churches of the World—South Carolina
  http://www.churchsurf.com/churches/South_Carolina/
  index.htm
  From the ChurchSurf Christian Directory.

◆ Societies & Groups

- Aiken-Barnwell Genealogical Society of South Carolina
  http://www.ifx.net/~lhutto/page2.html

- Archer's Computer Interest Group List—South Carolina
  http://www.genealogy.org/~ngs/cigs/ngl1ussc.html

- Catawba Wateree Genealogical Society
  http://members.aol.com/SCSunset/index.html
  Camden, South Carolina

- Chesterfield District Chapter of the South Carolina Genealogical Society
  http://www.charlotte.infi.net/~jpigg/CDC.htm

- Friends of the Florence Stockade
  http://members.aol.com/qmsgtboots/florence.html
  Florence, South Carolina

- Greenville County Historical Society
  http://www.greenvillehistory.org/

- IOOF Lodge Website Directory—South Carolina
  http://norm28.hsc.usc.edu/IOOF/USA/South_Carolina/
  South_Carolina.html
  Independent Order of Odd Fellows and Rebekahs.

- Jewish Historical Society of South Carolina
  http://www.scsn.net/users/efolley/jhssc/jhssc_home.html

- Kershaw County Historical Society
  http://www.historic.com/kchs/

- Old Darlington District Chapter of the South Carolina Genealogical Society
  http://www.geocities.com/Heartland/Estates/7212/

- Orangeburgh German-Swiss Genealogical Society
  http://www.netside.com/~genealogy/orangeburgh.htm

- Piedmont Historical Society
  http://www.angelfire.com/sc/piedmonths/

- Society Hill: South Carolina, United States
  http://www.daddezio.com/society/hill/SH-SC-NDX.html
  A list of addresses for genealogical and historical societies in the state.

- South Carolina Division, Sons of Confederate Veterans
  http://www.scscv.org

- South Carolina Genealogical Society, Inc.
  http://www.geocities.com/Heartland/Woods/2548/

- South Carolina Historical Society
  http://www.schistory.org

- The Spartanburg Historical Association
  http://www.spartanarts.org/history/index.html

- Three Rivers Historical Society
  http://www.rootsweb.com/~scwillia/htmr.htm

◆ USGenWeb Project

- South Carolina Genealogy—USGenWeb Project State Page
  http://www.usgenweb.org/sc

- South Carolina—USGenWeb Archives Table of Contents
  http://www.rootsweb.com/~usgenweb/sc/scfiles.htm

- South Carolina—USGenWeb FTP Archives
  ftp://ftp.rootsweb.com/pub/usgenweb/sc/

U.S.—SOUTH DAKOTA—SD
http://www.CyndisList.com/sd.htm

Category Index:

- General Resource Sites
- Government & Cities
- History & Culture
- Libraries, Archives & Museums
- Mailing Lists, Newsgroups & Chat
- Maps, Gazetteers & Geographical Information
- Military
- Newspapers
- People & Families

- Professional Researchers, Volunteers & Other Research Services
- Publications, Software & Supplies
- Queries, Message Boards & Surname Lists
- Records: Census, Cemeteries, Land, Obituaries, Personal, Taxes and Vital
- Religion & Churches
- Societies & Groups
- USGenWeb Project

◆ General Resource Sites

- Everton's Sources of Genealogical Information in South Dakota
  http://www.everton.com/usa/sd.htm

- Family Tree Maker's Genealogy "How To" Guide—South Dakota
  http://www.familytreemaker.com/00000216.html

- Genealogy Exchange & Surname Registry—SDGenExchange
  http://www.genexchange.com/sd/index.cfm

- Genealogy Resources on the Internet: South Dakota
  http://www-personal.umich.edu/~cgaunt/sdakota.html

- Hutterite Genealogy HomePage and Cross-Index
  http://feefhs.org/hut/indexhut.html

- LDS Research Outline for South Dakota
  http://www.everton.com/usa/sd-0842b.txt

- Lineages' Genealogy Site: South Dakota
  http://www.lineages.com/rooms/usa/state.asp?StateCode=SD

- ROOTS-L United States Resources: South Dakota
  http://www.rootsweb.com/roots-l/USA/sd.html
  Comprehensive list of research links, including many to history-related sites.

◆ Government & Cities

- 50states.com—South Dakota State Information Resource
  http://www.50states.com/sdakota.htm
  A list of general information for each state, including a list of colleges, state symbols, links to maps, newspapers, and other miscellaneous state information.

- Excite Travel by City.Net—South Dakota
  http://www.city.net/countries/united_states/south_dakota/

- Official City Web Sites for the State of South Dakota
  http://OfficialCitySites.org/South-Dakota.htm

- State of South Dakota
  http://www.state.sd.us/

- Yahoo! Get Local...South Dakota Cities
  http://dir.yahoo.com/Regional/U_S__States/South_Dakota/Cities/
  Maps, yellow pages, white pages, newspapers and other local information.

- Yahoo! Get Local...South Dakota Counties and Regions
  http://dir.yahoo.com/Regional/U_S__States/South_Dakota/Counties_and_Regions/
  Maps, yellow pages, white pages, newspapers and other local information.

◆ History & Culture

- History of South Dakota
  http://www.rapidweb.com/sdhistory/

- Yahoo!...History...South Dakota
  http://dir.yahoo.com/Arts/Humanities/History/Browse_By_Region/U_S__States/South_Dakota

◆ Libraries, Archives & Museums

- Family History Centers—South Dakota
  http://www.deseretbook.com/famhis/sd.html

- Family History Centers—South Dakota
  http://www.lib.byu.edu/~uvrfhc/centers/southdakota.html

- HYTELNET—Library Catalogs: USA: South Dakota
  http://library.usask.ca/hytelnet/usa/SD.html
  Before you use any of the Telnet links, make note of the user name, password and any other logon information.

- NUCMC Listing of Archives and Manuscript
  Repositories in South Dakota
  http://lcweb.loc.gov/coll/nucmc/sdsites.html
  *Links to information about resources other than those held in the
  Library of Congress.*

- Repositories of Primary Sources: South Dakota
  http://www.uidaho.edu/special-collections/west.html#ussd
  *A list of links to online resources from the Univ. of Idaho
  Library, Special Collections and Archives.*

- South Dakota Family History Centers
  http://www.genhomepage.com/FHC/South_Dakota.html
  *A list of addresses, phone numbers and hours of operation from
  the Genealogy Home Page.*

- South Dakota State Archives
  http://www.state.sd.us/state/executive/deca/cultural/
  archives.htm

- South Dakota State Library
  http://www.state.sd.us/state/executive/deca/ST_LIB/st_lib.htm

- State Agricultural Heritage Museum—Genealogy
  Resources
  http://www.sdstate.edu/~wure/http/geneal.htm

- webCATS: Library Catalogues on the World Wide
  Web—South Dakota
  http://library.usask.ca/hywebcat/states/SD.html

◆ Mailing Lists, Newsgroups & Chat

- Genealogy Resources on the Internet—South Dakota
  Mailing Lists
  http://members.aol.com/gfsjohnf/gen_mail_states-sd.html
  *Each of the mailing list links below points to this site, wonder-
  fully maintained by John Fuller. Visit this site for county-specific
  mailing lists as well.*

- NDSDMN-L Mailing List
  http://members.aol.com/gfsjohnf/gen_mail_states-sd.
  html#NDSDMN-L
  North Dakota, South Dakota and Minnesota.

◆ Maps, Gazetteers & Geographical Information

- 1872 County Map of Dakota
  http://www.ismi.net/chnegw/1872dakota.htm

- 1895 U.S. Atlas—South Dakota
  http://www.LivGenMI.com/1895sd.htm

- American Memory Panoramic Maps 1847–1929—
  South Dakota
  http://lcweb2.loc.gov/cgi-bin/query/S?ammem/gmd:@filreq
  (@field(STATE+@band(south+dakota+))+@field(COLLID+pmmap))
  From the Geography and Map Division, Library of Congress.

- American Memory Railroad Maps 1828–1900—
  South Dakota
  http://memory.loc.gov/cgi-bin/query/S?ammem/gmd:@filreq
  (@field(STATE+@band(south+dakota+))+@field(COLLID+rrmap))
  From the Geography and Map Division, Library of Congress.

- Andreas' Historical Atlas of Dakota
  http://www.rootsweb.com/~usgenweb/sd/andreas/
  1884

- Color Landform Atlas: South Dakota
  http://fermi.jhuapl.edu/states/sd_0.html
  Including a map of counties and a map for 1895.

- Excite Maps: South Dakota Maps
  http://www.city.net/maps/view/?mapurl=/countries/
  united_states/south_dakota
  Zoom in on these maps all the way to the street level.

- HPI County InfoSystem—Counties in South Dakota
  http://www.com/hpi/sdcty/index.html

- K.B. Slocum Books and Maps—South Dakota
  http://www.treasurenet.com/cgi-bin/treasure/kbslocum/scan/
  se=South.20Dakota/sf=mapstate

- List of South Dakota Counties
  http://www.genealogy.org/~st-clair/counties/state_sd.html

- Map of South Dakota Counties
  http://govinfo.kerr.orst.edu/gif/states/sd.gif
  *From the Government Information Sharing Project, Information
  Services, Oregon State University.*

- Map of South Dakota Counties
  http://www.lib.utexas.edu/Libs/PCL/Map_collection/states/
  South_Dakota.gif
  *From the Perry-Castañeda Library at the Univ. of Texas at
  Austin.*

- U.S. Census Bureau—South Dakota Profiles
  http://www.census.gov/datamap/www/46.html

- Yale Peabody Museum: GNIS—South Dakota
  http://www.peabody.yale.edu/other/gnis/SD.html
  *Search the USGS Geographic Names Database. You can limit
  the search to a specific county in this state and search for any of
  the following features: airport arch area arroyo bar basin bay
  beach bench bend bridge **building** canal cape **cemetery** channel
  church cliff crater crossing dam falls flat forest gap geyser
  glacier gut harbor hospital island isthmus lake lava levee locale
  mine oilfield other park pillar plain ppl range rapids reserve
  reservoir ridge **school** sea slope spring stream summit swamp
  tower trail tunnel valley well woods.*

◆ Military

- Dakota Territory During the Civil War
  http://www.rootsweb.com/~usgenweb/sd/military/cw.htm
  Includes a roster of all known 1st Dakota Cavalry personnel.

- Korean Conflict State-Level Casualty Lists—
  South Dakota
  http://www.nara.gov/nara/electronic/sdhrlist.html
  *From the National Archives and Records Administration,
  Center for Electronic Records.*

- Vietnam Conflict State-Level Casualty Lists—
  South Dakota
  http://www.nara.gov/nara/electronic/sdhrviet.html
  *From the National Archives and Records Administration,
  Center for Electronic Records.*

◆ Newspapers

- AJR NewsLink—South Dakota Newspapers
  http://www.newslink.org/sdnews.html
- E&P Media Info Links—Newspaper Sites in
  South Dakota
  http://www.mediainfo.com/emedia/browse-results.
  htm?region=southdakota&category=newspaper+++++++++
- Ecola Newstand: South Dakota
  http://www.ecola.com/news/press/na/us/sd/
- NAA Hotlinks to Newspapers Online—
  South Dakota
  http://www.naa.org/hotlinks/searchResult.asp?param=
  SD-South+Dakota&City=1
- N-Net—South Dakota Newspapers
  http://www.n-net.com/sd.htm
- South Dakota Newspaper Project
  http://www.state.sd.us/state/executive/deca/cultural/
  newspap.htm
- The Ultimate Collection of News Links: USA—
  South Dakota
  http://www.pppp.net/links/news/USA-SD.html
- Yahoo!...Newspapers...South Dakota
  http://dir.yahoo.com/News_and_Media/Newspapers/
  Browse_By_Region/U_S__States/South_Dakota/

◆ People & Families

- Biographies from the Memorial and
  Biographical Record
  http://www.rootsweb.com/~usgenweb/sd/biography/
  memor.htm
- The Life and Times of South Dakota Pioneers
  http://members.aol.com/drfransen/letters/home.htm
- SD Biographies
  http://www.rootsweb.com/~usgenweb/sd/biography/bios.htm
- Tribes and Villages of South Dakota
  http://hanksville.phast.umass.edu:8000/cultprop/contacts/
  tribal/SD.html

◆ Professional Researchers, Volunteers & Other Research Services

- Board for Certification of Genealogists—Roster of
  Those Certified—Specializing in South Dakota
  http://www.genealogy.org/~bcg/rosts_sd.html
- Genealogy Helplist—South Dakota
  http://posom.com/hl/usa/sd.shtml
- The Official Iowa Counties Professional Genealogist
  and Researcher's Registry for South Dakota
  http://www.iowa-counties.com/gene/sd.htm

◆ Publications, Software & Supplies

- AncestorSpy—CDs and Microfiche for
  South Dakota
  http://www.ancestorspy.com/sd.htm
- Barbara Green's Used Genealogy Books—
  South Dakota
  http://home.earthlink.net/~genbooks/lochist.html#SD
- Books We Own—South Dakota
  http://www.rootsweb.com/~bwo/sdakota.html
- Boyd Publishing Company—South Dakota
  http://www.hom.net/~gac/southdak.htm
- Brule County, SD, History Index—Interactive
  Search
  http://www.rootsweb.com/cgi-bin/sdbrulehist/sdbrule.pl
  *From the South Dakota Historical Collections, Vol. XXIII,
  pages 1–184 (1947).*
- Frontier Press Bookstore—South Dakota
  http://www.frontierpress.com/frontier.cgi?category=sd
- Heritage Quest—Microfilm Records for the State of
  South Dakota
  http://www.heritagequest.com/genealogy/microfilm/
  south_dakota/
- Park Genealogical Books
  http://www.parkbooks.com/
  *Specialists in genealogy and local history for Minnesota,
  Wisconsin, North and South Dakota and the surrounding area.*

◆ Queries, Message Boards & Surname Lists

- GenConnect South Dakota Visitor Center
  http://cgi.rootsweb.com/~genbbs/indx/SD.html
  *A system for posting queries, Bibles, biographies, deeds,
  obituaries, pensions, wills.*

◆ Records: Census, Cemeteries, Land, Obituaries, Personal, Taxes and Vital (Born, Married, Died & Buried)

- The 1790–1890 Federal Population Censuses:
  Catalog of National Archives Microfilm
  http://www.genealogy.org/census/contents.shtml
  - Census Schedules and Microfilm Roll Numbers
    for South Dakota:
    1860
    http://www.genealogy.org/census/1860_schedules/
    Dakota.html
    1870
    http://www.genealogy.org/census/1870_schedules/
    Dakota.html

1880
http://www.genealogy.org/census/1880_schedules/
Dakota.html

1880 Soundex
http://www.genealogy.org/census/1880.sdx_schedules/
T740.html

1890 Special Schedules
http://www.genealogy.org/census/1890-special_schedules/
South.Dakota.html

- 1885 Dakota Territory Census Database
http://www.lib.ndsu.nodak.edu/database/1885census.html

- Campbell County, South Dakota 1910 Census of German Russians
http://pixel.cs.vt.edu/library/census/link/camp10.txt

- Campbell County, South Dakota, Obitbook— Interactive Search
http://www.rootsweb.com/cgi-bin/sdcampbell/obitbook.pl

- Charles Mix County, South Dakota 1910 Census of German Russians
http://pixel.cs.vt.edu/library/census/link/cmix10.txt

- Chas. Mix County, South Dakota, Atlas Index— Interactive Search
http://www.rootsweb.com/cgi-bin/sdchasmix/1906atlas.pl

- Clark County, South Dakota 1910 Census of German Russians
http://pixel.cs.vt.edu/library/census/link/clark10.txt

- County Courthouse Addresses
http://www.familytreemaker.com/00000270.html

- Dakota Territory 1860 Census—Interactive Search
http://www.rootsweb.com/cgi-bin/sdcensus/sd1860cen.pl

- Edmunds County, South Dakota, Cemetery Census—Interactive Search
http://www.rootsweb.com/cgi-bin/sdedmunds/cemetery.pl

- Find-A-Grave by Location: South Dakota
http://www.findagrave.com/grave/lsd.html
Graves of noteworthy people.

- The Gluecksthal Reformed Church, Odessa Township, McPherson Co, South Dakota
http://pixel.cs.vt.edu/library/churches/link/glueck.txt
Birth records, now in the possession of the Eureka Reformed Church.

- Greenway Cemetery, Greenway, South Dakota
http://pixel.cs.vt.edu/library/cemeteries/sodak/link/grnway.txt

- Homesteading Records—Tracking Your Ancestors in South Dakota
http://members.aol.com/gkrell/homestead/home.html

- Interment.net: South Dakota Cemeteries
http://www.interment.net/us/sd/index.htm
A list of links to other sites.

- Jerauld County Cemetery Index
http://pixel.cs.vt.edu/library/cemeteries/sodak/link/jerauld.txt

- McPherson County, South Dakota 1900 Census of German Russians
http://pixel.cs.vt.edu/library/census/link/mcpher00.txt

- McPherson County, South Dakota 1910 Census of German Russians
http://pixel.cs.vt.edu/library/census/link/mcpher10.txt

- National Archives—Rocky Mountain Region (Denver)
http://www.nara.gov/regional/denver.html

- National Archives—Rocky Mountain Region
http://www.familytreemaker.com/00000103.html
Records for Colorado, Montana, North Dakota, South Dakota, Utah, Wyoming, and a portion of New Mexico.

- The Political Graveyard—Cemeteries in South Dakota
http://politicalgraveyard.com/geo/SD/kmindex.html

- Preplanning Network—Funeral Home and Cemetery Directory—South Dakota
http://www.preplannet.com/usafh.htm#South Dakota

- SDGenWeb County Land Records
http://members.aol.com/drfransen/land/home.htm

- South Dakota Land Records
http://pixel.cs.vt.edu/library/land/sodak/

- South Dakota Vital Records Information
http://vitalrec.com/sd.html

- USGenWeb Census Project South Dakota
http://www.usgenweb.org/census/states/southdak.htm

- USGenWeb Tombstone Transcription Project— South Dakota
http://www.rootsweb.com/~cemetery/sdakota.html

- VitalChek Network—South Dakota
http://www.vitalchek.com/stateselect.asp?state=SD

- Walworth County, South Dakota 1900 Census of German Russians
http://pixel.cs.vt.edu/library/census/link/wal00.txt

- Walworth County, South Dakota 1910 Census of German Russians
http://pixel.cs.vt.edu/library/census/link/wal10.txt

- Where to Write for Vital Records—South Dakota
http://www.cdc.gov/nchswww/howto/w2w/sdakota.htm
From the National Center for Health Statistics (NCHS).

◆ Religion & Churches

- Christianity.Net Church Locator—South Dakota
http://www.christianity.net/cgi/
location.exe?United_States+South_Dakota

- Church Profiles—South Dakota
http://www.church-profiles.com/sd/sd.html

- Churches dot Net—Global Church Web Pages— South Dakota
  http://www.churches.net/churches/sdakota.html
- Churches of the World—South Dakota
  http://www.churchsurf.com/churches/South_Dakota/index.htm
  From the ChurchSurf Christian Directory.

◆ Societies & Groups

- Archer's Computer Interest Group List— South Dakota
  http://www.genealogy.org/~ngs/cigs/ngl1ussd.html
- IOOF Lodge Website Directory—South Dakota
  http://norm28.hsc.usc.edu/IOOF/USA/South_Dakota/South_Dakota.html
  Independent Order of Odd Fellows and Rebekahs.
- SD-GOLD—South Dakota Genealogy of Lyman Descendants
  http://www.geocities.com/Heartland/Ridge/8591/
  Lyman County, South Dakota
- Sioux Valley Genealogical Society
  http://www.rootsweb.com/~sdsvgs
  Minnehaha County, South Dakota
- Society Hill: South Dakota, United States
  http://www.daddezio.com/society/hill/SH-SD-NDX.html
  A list of addresses for genealogical and historical societies in the state.

- South Dakota Genealogical & Historical Societies
  http://www.rootsweb.com/~sdgenweb/gensoc/gensoc.html
- South Dakota Genealogical Society
  http://www.rootsweb.com/~sdgenweb/gensoc/sdgensoc.html
- South Dakota Genealogical Society Quarterly Index—Interactive Search
  http://www.rootsweb.com/cgi-bin/sdgsqart/sdgsqart.pl
- South Dakota State Historical Society / Office of History
  http://www.state.sd.us/state/executive/deca/cultural/sdshs.htm
- Tri-State Genealogical Society
  http://scream.iw.net/~shepherd/
  South Dakota, Wyoming, and Montana.

◆ USGenWeb Project

- South Dakota Genealogy—USGenWeb Project State Page
  http://www.usgenweb.org/sd
- South Dakota—USGenWeb Archives Table of Contents
  http://www.rootsweb.com/~usgenweb/sd/sdfiles.htm
- South Dakota—USGenWeb FTP Archives
  ftp://ftp.rootsweb.com/pub/usgenweb/sd/

U.S.—TENNESSEE—TN
http://www.CyndisList.com/tn.htm

Category Index:

- General Resource Sites
- Government & Cities
- History & Culture
- Libraries, Archives & Museums
- Locality Specific
- Mailing Lists, Newsgroups & Chat
- Maps, Gazetteers & Geographical Information
- Military
- Newspapers
- People & Families

- Professional Researchers, Volunteers & Other Research Services
- Publications, Software & Supplies
- Queries, Message Boards & Surname Lists
- Records: Census, Cemeteries, Land, Obituaries, Personal, Taxes and Vital
- Religion & Churches
- Societies & Groups
- USGenWeb Project

◆ General Resource Sites

- Everton's Sources of Genealogical Information in Tennessee
  http://www.everton.com/usa/tn.htm

- Family Tree Maker's Genealogy "How To" Guide—Tennessee
  http://www.familytreemaker.com/00000217.html

- Genealogy Bulletin Board Systems for Tennessee
  http://www.genealogy.org/~gbbs/gbltn.html

- Genealogy Exchange & Surname Registry—TNGenExchange
  http://www.genexchange.com/tn/index.cfm

- Genealogy Resources on the Internet: Tennessee
  http://www-personal.umich.edu/~cgaunt/tenn.html

- LDS Research Outline for Tennessee
  http://www.everton.com/usa/tn-0843b.txt

- Lineages' Genealogy Site: Tennessee
  http://www.lineages.com/rooms/usa/state.asp?StateCode=TN

- ROOTS-L United States Resources: Tennessee
  http://www.rootsweb.com/roots-l/USA/tn.html
  Comprehensive list of research links, including many to history-related sites.

- Tennessee Genealogy & History
  http://web.utk.edu/~kizzer/genehist/

◆ Government & Cities

- 50states.com—Tennessee State Information Resource
  http://www.50states.com/tennesse.htm
  A list of general information for each state, including a list of colleges, state symbols, links to maps, newspapers, and other miscellaneous state information.

- Excite Travel by City.Net—Tennessee
  http://www.city.net/countries/united_states/tennessee/

- Official City Web Sites for the State of Tennessee
  http://OfficialCitySites.org/Tennessee.htm

- Tennessee: America at Its Best ~ State of Tennessee
  http://www.state.tn.us/

- Yahoo! Get Local...Tennessee Cities
  http://dir.yahoo.com/Regional/U_S__States/Tennessee/Cities/
  Maps, yellow pages, white pages, newspapers and other local information.

- Yahoo! Get Local...Tennessee Counties and Regions
  http://dir.yahoo.com/Regional/U_S__States/Tennessee/Counties_and_Regions/
  Maps, yellow pages, white pages, newspapers and other local information.

◆ History & Culture

- A Little History of Tennessee
  http://www.wizard.com/~bascs/tennhist.htm

- Memphis History and Facts
  http://www.memphislibrary.lib.tn.us/history/memphis2.htm

- Tennessee Chronology
  http://www.wizard.com/~bascs/tnchron.htm

- Tennessee Online
  http://www.vic.com/tnchron/
  Tennessee's only on-line historical magazine.

- Yahoo!...History...Tennessee
  http://dir.yahoo.com/Arts/Humanities/History/
  Browse_By_Region/U_S__States/Tennessee

◆ Libraries, Archives & Museums

- East Tennessee Historical Center
  http://www.korrnet.org/knoxlib/ethc.htm
  In downtown Knoxville, it houses: McClung Historical Collection, Knox County Archives, East Tennessee Historical Society, Museum of East Tennessee History, Tennessee Society, Sons of the Revolution.

- Family History Centers—Tennessee
  http://www.deseretbook.com/famhis/tn.html

- Family History Centers—Tennessee
  http://www.lib.byu.edu/~uvrfhc/centers/tennessee.html

- HYTELNET—Library Catalogs: USA: Tennessee
  http://library.usask.ca/hytelnet/usa/TN.html
  Before you use any of the Telnet links, make note of the user name, password and any other logon information.

- Knox County Public Library System
  http://www.xrnet.org/knoxlib/index.htm
  - Calvin M. McClung Historical Collection
    http://www.korrnet.org/knoxlib/mcclung.htm

- Memphis / Shelby County Public Library & Information Center
  http://www.memphislibrary.lib.tn.us/
  - History and Travel Department
    http://www.memphislibrary.lib.tn.us/history/index.html
    - The Genealogy Collection
      http://www.memphislibrary.lib.tn.us/history/genea1.htm
    - Guide to the Genealogy Collection
      http://www.memphislibrary.lib.tn.us/history/guigen.htm
  - Memphis and Shelby County Archives
    http://www.memphislibrary.lib.tn.us/history/archiv1.htm
  - Memphis and Shelby County Room
    http://www.memphislibrary.lib.tn.us/history/memshe1.htm

- Museum of East Tennessee History
  http://www.korrnet.org/eths/museum.htm

- NUCMC Listing of Archives and Manuscript Repositories in Tennessee
  http://lcweb.loc.gov/coll/nucmc/tnsites.html
  Links to information about resources other than those held in the Library of Congress.

- Repositories of Primary Sources: Tennessee
  http://www.uidaho.edu/special-collections/east2.html#ustn
  A list of links to online resources from the Univ. of Idaho Library, Special Collections and Archives.

- Tennessee Family History Centers
  http://www.genhomepage.com/FHC/Tennessee.html
  A list of addresses, phone numbers and hours of operation from the Genealogy Home Page.

- Tennessee State Library and Archives
  http://www.state.tn.us/sos/statelib/tslahome.htm
  - Genealogical Fact Sheets About Tennessee Counties
    http://www.state.tn.us/sos/statelib/pubsvs/countypg.htm
  - Historical and Genealogical Information
    http://www.state.tn.us/sos/statelib/pubsvs/intro.htm
  - Historical and Genealogical Information—Suggestions for Native American Research (Cherokee)
    http://www.state.tn.us/sos/statelib/pubsvs/cherokee.htm

- UTK LibLink—University of Tennessee, Knoxville, Libraries
  http://www.lib.utk.edu/
  - Library Guides from the UTK Libraries
    http://www.lib.utk.edu/collect/library_guides/
    You will need to have a copy of the free Adobe Acrobat Reader Software program in order to view the following library guides. (File extensions are .pdf).
    http://www.adobe.com/prodindex/acrobat/readstep.html
    - Genealogical Research
      http://www.lib.utk.edu/collect/library_guides/guide_030.pdf
    - Genealogical Research at at the Special Collections Library, The University of Tennessee, Knoxville
      http://www.lib.utk.edu/collect/library_guides/guide_152.pdf
    - How to Use the Online Catalog
      http://www.lib.utk.edu/collect/library_guides/guide_090.pdf
  - Manuscript Collections
    http://toltec.lib.utk.edu/~spec_coll/manuscripts/
    - Herbert E. Copeland Railroadiana Collection
      http://toltec.lib.utk.edu/~spec_coll/manuscripts/a0847
    - Knoxville Railway and Light Company
      http://toltec.lib.utk.edu/~spec_coll/manuscripts/a1502
    - Railroad Records Collection
      http://toltec.lib.utk.edu/~spec_coll/manuscripts/a1108
    - Smoky Mountain Railroad Collection
      http://toltec.lib.utk.edu/~spec_coll/manuscripts/a0424
    - Tennessee Central Railroad Company Collection
      http://toltec.lib.utk.edu/~spec_coll/manuscripts/a1702

- webCATS: Library Catalogues on the World Wide Web—Tennessee
  http://library.usask.ca/hywebcat/states/TN.html

◆ Locality Specific

- Also see the USGenWeb section for links to county-specific resources.

- Cannon County, Tennessee Genealogy Project
  http://www.geocities.com/Heartland/Hills/9624/

- Coffee County, Tennessee Genealogy Project
  http://members.xoom.com/spurlock/

- Fayette County, Tennessee Genealogy
  http://home.mem.net/~rac7253/fayette/

- Genealogy in Sumner County, Tennessee
  http://members.aol.com/cathelk/sumner/keen.htm

- Grainger County, Tennessee Genealogy
  http://web.utk.edu/~kizzer/grainger/

- Hardin County, TN History Pages
  http://www.hardincountytn.com/history/
  Includes links to Civil War information for Hardin County as well.

- The Original Hawkins County, Tennessee Genealogy Website
  http://web.utk.edu/~kizzer/hawkins/

- The Original Jefferson County, Tennessee Genealogy Website
  http://web.utk.edu/~kizzer/jefferson/

- Roots of Roane
  http://www.roanetn.com/

- Smoky Mountain Ancestral Quest
  http://www.SmokyKin.com/

- Tennessee Connections—Middle Tennessee Genealogy
  http://members.xoom.com/TNGenealogy/index.html

- Yesterday, Henderson County, Tennessee History Page
  http://funnelweb.utcc.utk.edu/~ddonahue/he-stuff/yester.htm

◆ Mailing Lists, Newsgroups & Chat

- Genealogy Resources on the Internet—Tennessee Mailing Lists
  http://members.aol.com/gfsjohnf/gen_mail_states-tn.html
  Each of the mailing list links below points to this site, wonderfully maintained by John Fuller. Visit this site for county-specific mailing lists as well.

- Appalachianfamily Mailing List
  http://members.aol.com/gfsjohnf/gen_mail_states-va.html#Appalachianfamily
  Appalachian Mountain Families including families from Georgia, North Carolina, South Carolina, Tennessee, Kentucky, Virginia, and West Virginia.

- DanvilleCrossing Mailing List
  http://members.aol.com/gfsjohnf/gen_mail_states-tn.html#DanvilleCrossing
  For Benton, Henry, Humphreys, Stewart and Houston Counties.

- DumplinTN Mailing List
  http://members.aol.com/gfsjohnf/gen_mail_states-tn.html#DumplinTN
  For anyone with a genealogical or historical interest in Jefferson and Sevier Counties, Tennessee.

- ETN Mailing List
  http://members.aol.com/gfsjohnf/gen_mail_states-tn.html#ETN
  For anyone with a genealogical interest in the eastern 3rd Grand Division of the state of Tennessee as well as the lost State of Franklin.

- ETN-OZ Mailing List
  http://members.aol.com/gfsjohnf/gen_mail_states-tn.html#ETN-OZ
  For anyone interested in families that migrated from East Tennessee to the Ozarks region.

- JACKSON-CLAY-OVERTON-CO-TN Mailing List
  http://members.aol.com/gfsjohnf/gen_mail_states-tn.html#JACKSON/CLAY
  Jackson, Clay and/or Overton Counties, as well as Smith County, Tennessee which was the parent county and bordering Monroe County, Kentucky.

- Melungeon Mailing List
  http://members.aol.com/gfsjohnf/gen_mail_states-gen.html#MELUNGEO
  For people conducting Melungeon and/or Appalachian research including Native American, Portuguese, Turkish, Black Dutch, and other unverifiable mixed statements of ancestry or unexplained rumors, with ancestors in TN, KY, VA, NC, SC, GA, AL, WV, and possibly other places.

- SE-TN Mailing List
  http://members.aol.com/gfsjohnf/gen_mail_states-tn.html#SE-TN
  For anyone with a genealogical interest in Southeast Tennessee consisting of Polk, McMinn, Bradley, Hamilton and Meigs Counties.

- TENNESSEE Mailing List
  http://members.aol.com/gfsjohnf/gen_mail_states-tn.html#TENNESSEE

- TN-Rooters Mailing List
  http://members.aol.com/gfsjohnf/gen_mail_states-tn.html#TN-Rooters

- TNROOTS-L Mailing List
  http://members.aol.com/gfsjohnf/gen_mail_states-tn.html#TNROOTS

◆ Maps, Gazetteers & Geographical Information

- 1895 U.S. Atlas—Tennessee
  http://www.LivGenMI.com/1895tn.htm

- American Memory Panoramic Maps 1847–1929—Tennessee
  http://lcweb2.loc.gov/cgi-bin/query/S?ammem/gmd:@filreq(@field(STATE+@band(+tennessee))+@field(COLLID+pmmap))
  From the Geography and Map Division, Library of Congress.

- American Memory Railroad Maps 1828–1900—Tennessee
  http://memory.loc.gov/cgi-bin/query/S?ammem/gmd:@filreq(@field(STATE+tennessee)+@field(COLLID+rrmap))
  From the Geography and Map Division, Library of Congress.

- Color Landform Atlas: Tennessee
  http://fermi.jhuapl.edu/states/tn_0.html
  Including a map of counties and a map for 1895.

- Excite Maps: Tennessee Maps
  http://www.city.net/maps/view/?mapurl=/countries/
  united_states/tennessee
  Zoom in on these maps all the way to the street level.

- Genealogical Fact Sheets about Tennessee Counties
  http://www.state.tn.us/other/statelib/pubsvs/countypg.htm

- HPI County InfoSystem—Counties in Tennessee
  http://www.com/hpi/tncty/index.html

- Introduction to Tennessee Land History
  http://www.ultranet.com/~deeds/tenn.htm

- K.B. Slocum Books and Maps—Tennessee
  http://www.treasurenet.com/cgi-bin/treasure/kbslocum/scan/
  se=Tennessee/sf=mapstate

- List of Tennessee Counties
  http://www.genealogy.org/~st-clair/counties/state_tn.html

- Map of Tennessee Counties, Map #1
  http://govinfo.kerr.orst.edu/gif/states/tn.gif

  Map #2
  http://govinfo.kerr.orst.edu/gif/states/tn1.gif

  Map #3
  http://govinfo.kerr.orst.edu/gif/states/tn2.gif

  Map #4
  http://govinfo.kerr.orst.edu/gif/states/tnorig.gif
  *From the Government Information Sharing Project, Information
  Services, Oregon State University.*

- Map of Tennessee Counties
  http://www.lib.utexas.edu/Libs/PCL/Map_collection/states/
  Tennessee3.gif
  *From the Perry-Castañeda Library at the Univ. of Texas at
  Austin.*

- The Maps Our Ancestors Followed—A TNGenWeb
  History Project
  http://www.tngenweb.usit.com/maps/

- Tennessee Roads Before 1800
  http://web.utk.edu/~kizzer/genehist/maps/1800road.htm

- U.S. Census Bureau—Tennessee Profiles
  http://www.census.gov/datamap/www/47.html

- Yale Peabody Museum: GNIS—Tennessee
  http://www.peabody.yale.edu/other/gnis/TN.html
  *Search the USGS Geographic Names Database. You can limit
  the search to a specific county in this state and search for any of
  the following features: airport arch area arroyo bar basin bay
  beach bench bend bridge **building** canal cape **cemetery** channel
  church cliff crater crossing dam falls flat forest gap geyser
  glacier gut harbor hospital island isthmus lake lava levee locale
  mine oilfield other park pillar plain ppl range rapids reserve
  reservoir ridge **school** sea slope spring stream summit swamp
  tower trail tunnel valley well woods.*

◆ Military

- 8th Tennessee Cavalry, C.S.A.
  http://www.jagunet.com/~mbar/8tncav.htm

- 20th (Russell's) Tennessee Cavalry, C.S.A.
  http://home.olemiss.edu/~cmprice/cav.html

- 25th. TN. Inf. CSA
  http://userzweb.lightspeed.net/~richardm/zolly.htm

- 44th Tennessee Infantry Regiment, C.S.A.
  http://www.geocities.com/BourbonStreet/4455/

- 47th Tennessee Infantry Regiment, C.S.A.
  http://www.geocities.com/Pentagon/4740/

- The Civil War Archive—Union Regiments—
  Tennessee
  http://www.civilwararchive.com/uniontn.htm

- Civil War Battle Summaries by State—Tennessee
  http://www2.cr.nps.gov/abpp/battles/bystate.htm#tn

- Korean Conflict State-Level Casualty Lists—
  Tennessee
  http://www.nara.gov/nara/electronic/tnhrlist.html
  *From the National Archives and Records Administration,
  Center for Electronic Records.*

- Tennessee Confederate Soldiers' Home Applications
  http://www.state.tn.us/sos/statelib/pubsvs/csh_intr.htm

- Tennessee Military Department
  http://www.state.tn.us/military/
  *Office of the Adjutant General and the War Records Division
  Tennessee World War I Veterans.*
  http://www.state.tn.us/sos/statelib/pubsvs/ww1intro.htm
  *A database for select counties in Tennessee. From the Tennessee
  State Library and Archives.*

- TNGenWeb Civil War Resource Page
  http://www.tngenweb.org/cwsource.htm

- Vietnam Conflict State-Level Casualty Lists—
  Tennessee
  http://www.nara.gov/nara/electronic/tnhrviet.html
  *From the National Archives and Records Administration,
  Center for Electronic Records.*

◆ Newspapers

- AJR NewsLink—Tennessee Newspapers
  http://www.newslink.org/tnnews.html

- E&P Media Info Links—Newspaper Sites in
  Tennessee
  http://www.mediainfo.com/emedia/browse-results.
  htm?region=tennessee&category=newspaper+++++++++

- Ecola Newstand: Tennessee
  http://www.ecola.com/news/press/na/us/tn/

- The Knoxville Gazette
  http://www.ultranet.com/~smack/news.htm
  *Transcribed historical articles related to genealogy, from
  November 5, 1791 thru January 14, 1792. More transcriptions
  to come in this ongoing project.*

- NAA Hotlinks to Newspapers Online—Tennessee
  http://www.naa.org/hotlinks/searchResult.asp?param=
  TN-Tennessee&City=1

- N-Net—Tennessee Newspapers
  http://www.n-net.com/tn.htm

- The Tennessee Newspaper Project
  http://toltec.lib.utk.edu/~spec_coll/newspaper/tnphome.htm
- The Ultimate Collection of News Links: USA—
  Tennessee
  http://www.pppp.net/links/news/USA-TN.html
- Yahoo!...Newspapers...Tennessee
  http://dir.yahoo.com/News_and_Media/Newspapers/
  Browse_By_Region/U_S__States/Tennessee/

◆ People & Families

- The Chickasaw and Their Cessions
  http://www.tngenweb.usit.com/tnfirst/chicksaw/
- First Families of Tennessee
  http://www.korrnet.org/eths/firstfam.htm
- First People of Tennessee
  http://www.tngenweb.usit.com/tnfirst/
- A Melungeon Home Page
  http://www.clinch.edu/appalachia/melungeon/
- Southeastern Kentucky Melungeon Information
  Exchange
  http://www.bright.net/~kat/skmie.htm
  Also Tennessee, North Carolina and Virginia.
- Tribes and Villages of Tennessee
  http://hanksville.phast.umass.edu:8000/cultprop/contacts/
  tribal/TN.html

◆ Professional Researchers, Volunteers & Other Research Services

- AL, GA, TN Genealogy Researcher
  http://members.aol.com/CindyJ4/algatn.htm
- Board for Certification of Genealogists—Roster of
  Those Certified—Specializing in Tennessee
  http://www.genealogy.org/~bcg/rosts_tn.html
- Genealogy Helplist—Tennessee
  http://posom.com/hl/usa/tn.shtml
- The Official Iowa Counties Professional Genealogist
  and Researcher's Registry for Tennessee
  http://www.iowa-counties.com/gene/tn.htm

◆ Publications, Software & Supplies

- AncestorSpy—CDs and Microfiche for Tennessee
  http://www.ancestorspy.com/tn.htm
- Barbara Green's Used Genealogy Books—
  Tennessee
  http://home.earthlink.net/~genbooks/lochist.html#TN
- Barnette's Family Tree Books—Tennessee
  http://www.barnettesbooks.com/tennessee.htm

- Books We Own—Tennessee
  http://www.rootsweb.com/~bwo/tennessee.html
- Boyd Publishing Company—Tennessee
  http://www.hom.net/~gac/tenn.htm
- Byron Sistler and Associates, Inc.
  http://www.mindspring.com/~sistler/
  *Over 900 books covering records from Tennessee, Virginia,
  North Carolina, and Kentucky.*
- Frontier Press Bookstore—Tennessee
  http://www.frontierpress.com/frontier.cgi?category=tn
- GenealogyBookShop.com—Tennessee
  http://www.genealogybookshop.com/genealogybookshop/files/
  The_United_States,Tennessee/index.html
  *The online store of Genealogical Publishing Co., Inc. &
  Clearfield Company.*
- Genealogy and Tennessee—GENEALOGY
  FRIENDS:Partyline News
  http://members.aol.com/genny1/genny1.html
  FREE Queries, mail or e-mail.
- Gorin Genealogical Publishing
  http://members.tripod.com/~GorinS/index.html
  and an alternate address
  http://members.aol.com/kygen/gorin.htm
  *Publications cover mostly Kentucky, also has some for Logan
  County, Illinois and Fentress & Overton Counties, Tennessee.*
- Hearthstone Bookshop—Tennessee
  http://www.hearthstonebooks.com/cgi-bin/webc.cgi/st_main.
  html?catid=99&sid=2PH5t29sm
- Heritage Books—Tennessee
  http://www.heritagebooks.com/tn.htm
- Heritage Quest—Microfilm Records for the State of
  Tennessee
  http://www.heritagequest.com/genealogy/microfilm/tennessee/
- J & W Enterprises
  http://www.dhc.net/~jw/
  *One stop book source on the Internet, specializing in southern
  states source material.*
- Lost in Time Books—Tennessee
  http://www.lostintime.com/catalog/books/bookst/bo29000.htm
- The Memorabilia Corner Books—Tennessee
  http://members.aol.com/TMCorner/book_tn.htm
- The Memorabilia Corner Census View CDs—
  Tennessee
  http://members.aol.com/TMCorner/cen_tenn.htm
- Mountain Press
  http://www.mountainpress.com
  *Books for the south-eastern section of the United States from
  Pennsylvania to Texas, with the emphasis on Tennessee and
  Virginia.*
- S-K Publications—Tennessee 1820–1850 Census
  Books
  http://www.skpub.com/genie/census/tn/

- Southern Queries Genealogy Magazine
  http://www.mindspring.com/~freedom1/sq/sq.htm
- Willow Bend Bookstore—Tennessee
  http://www.willowbend.net/tn.htm
- Ye Olde Genealogie Shoppe Books—Tennessee
  http://www.yogs.com/tennesse.htm

◆ Queries, Message Boards & Surname Lists

- GenConnect Tennessee Visitor Center
  http://cgi.rootsweb.com/~genbbs/indx/Tn.html
  A system for posting queries, Bibles, biographies, deeds, obituaries, pensions, wills.

◆ Records: Census, Cemeteries, Land, Obituaries, Personal, Taxes and Vital (Born, Married, Died & Buried)

- The 1790–1890 Federal Population Censuses: Catalog of National Archives Microfilm
  http://www.genealogy.org/census/contents.shtml
  - Census Schedules and Microfilm Roll Numbers for Tennessee:
    1810
    http://www.genealogy.org/census/1810_schedules/Tennessee.html
    1820
    http://www.genealogy.org/census/1820_schedules/Tennessee.html
    1830
    http://www.genealogy.org/census/1830_schedules/Tennessee.html
    1840
    http://www.genealogy.org/census/1840_schedules/Tennessee.html
    1850
    http://www.genealogy.org/census/1850_schedules/Tennessee.html
    1860
    http://www.genealogy.org/census/1860_schedules/Tennessee.html
    1870
    http://www.genealogy.org/census/1870_schedules/Tennessee.html
    1880
    http://www.genealogy.org/census/1880_schedules/Tennessee.html
    1880 Soundex
    http://www.genealogy.org/census/1880.sdx_schedules/T772.html

- 1890 Special Schedules
  http://www.genealogy.org/census/1890-special_schedules/Tennessee.html
- 1820 United States Census Robertson County Tennessee
  http://home.earthlink.net/~howardorjeff/1820.htm
- 1830 Greene County, Tennessee Census Index
  http://www.geocities.com/Heartland/Hills/8214/indextn.html
- 1830 Sumner County, TN Census Index
  http://www.tngenweb.usit.com/sumner/sumncndx.htm
- 1850 Census, Greene Co., Tennessee
  http://www.census-online.com/transcript/tn/greene/index.html
- 1850 Cocke Co., Tennessee Census
  http://www.liberty.com/home/hannibal/cocke.html
- 1850 Census, Jackson County, Tennessee
  http://www2.aros.net/~cbutler//census/jack50x.htm
- African Americans listed in the 1850 & 1860 Madison County, Tennessee Free Census Schedule
  http://www.ccharity.com/tennessee/freetenn.htm
- Census Online—Links to Census Sites on the Web—Tennessee
  http://www.census-online.com/links/TN_data.html
- Confederate Soldiers Rest, Elmwood Cemetery, Memphis, Tennessee
  http://www.people.memphis.edu/~jcothern/soldrest.htm
- Correlations: Warren County, Tennessee 1850 Census Database Project
  http://members.aol.com/APTurner/wctnhome.htm
  "The goal is to correlate the 1850 census records for Warren County, Tennessee with other types of records which show family connections: marriage, probate, court, land, Bible, Ancestral File, personal GEDCOM files, magazine articles, Internet newsgroup messages, and so forth."
- County Courthouse Addresses
  http://www.familytreemaker.com/00000271.html
- Deaths and Funerals—Chattanooga Free Press
  http://www.chatfreepress.com/obituary/
- Decatur County, Tennessee Cemeteries
  http://funnelweb.utcc.utk.edu/~ddonahue/decatur/decatur.htm
- Find-A-Grave by Location: Tennessee
  http://www.findagrave.com/grave/ltn.html
  Graves of noteworthy people.
- Finding Birth & Death Records in Tennessee
  http://www.state.tn.us/sos/statelib/pubsvs/vital3.htm
  From the Tennessee State Library and Archives.
- Freedman's Bureau, Marriages in Tennessee 1865–1869
  http://ccharity.com/freedmens/tennesseemarriages.htm
- Genealogical Research in Tennessee County Courthouses
  http://www.wizard.com/~bascs/edbyler.htm

- Greene County, Tennessee 1783 Tax List
  http://www.tngenweb.org/greene/tax001.htm

- Greene County, TN, Early Tax Lists
  http://www.tngenweb.org/greene/earlytax.htm

- Ground Work Genealogy on the Internet: Tennessee
  http://members.aol.com/ssmadonna/tn.htm
  Links to sites with a variety of records.

- Henderson County, Tennessee Cemeteries
  http://funnelweb.utcc.utk.edu/~ddonahue/henderson/hender.htm

- Index to the Shelby County Death Records (1848–1885)
  http://www.memphislibrary.lib.tn.us/ShelbyDR18/index.html

- Interment.net: Tennessee Cemeteries
  http://www.interment.net/us/tn/index.htm
  A list of links to other sites.

- An Introduction to the History of Tennessee's Confusing Land Laws
  http://web.utk.edu/~kizzer/genehist/research/landlaws.htm
  By Billie R. McNamara.

- KnoxNews.com—News—Obituaries
  http://www.knoxnews.com/news/obituaries/
  Knoxville News-Sentinel Online.

- Lincoln County, Tennessee, Marriages—Interactive Search
  http://www.rootsweb.com/cgi-bin/tnlincoln/tnlincoln.pl

- Making the Best Use of Tennessee Census Index Books, 1820–1840
  http://www.state.tn.us/sos/statelib/pubsvs/cen1820.htm
  From the Tennessee State Library and Archives, Historical and Genealogical Information.

- Making the Best Use of Tennessee Census Index Books, 1850–1880
  http://www.state.tn.us/sos/statelib/pubsvs/cen1850.htm
  From the Tennessee State Library and Archives, Historical and Genealogical Information.

- Memphis and Shelby County Death Certificates (1902–1939) & Miscellaneous
  http://www.memphislibrary.lib.tn.us/ShelbyDR/index.html

- Memphis and Shelby County Death Certificates (1940–1945)
  http://www.memphislibrary.lib.tn.us/ShelbyDR40/index.html

- National Archives—Southeast Region (Atlanta)
  http://www.nara.gov/regional/atlanta.html

- National Archives—Southeast Region from Family Tree Maker
  http://www.familytreemaker.com/00000104.html
  Records for Tennessee, Florida, Georgia, Kentucky, Mississippi, North Carolina, South Carolina, and Tennessee.

- The Political Graveyard—Cemeteries in Tennessee
  http://politicalgraveyard.com/geo/TN/kmindex.html

- Preplanning Network—Funeral Home and Cemetery Directory—Tennessee
  http://www.preplannet.com/tennfhcem.htm

- Researching in Tennessee Courthouses
  http://www.hardincountytn.com/history/tnch.htm

- SAMPUBCO
  http://www.wasatch.com/~dsam/sampubco/index.htm
  Will Testators Indexes, Naturalization Records Indexes and Census Indexes online. You can order copies of the original source documents for a small fee.

- Slave Entries in Wills, Deeds, Etc.
  http://www.netcom.com/~jog1/slavedocs.html
  Kentucky, South Carolina, Tennessee, Virginia

- Sumner County Tax Records and Other Lists
  http://www.tngenweb.org/sumner/sumnlist.htm

- Sumner County, Tennessee Bible Records
  http://www.tngenweb.org/sumner/sumnbibl.htm

- Tennessee Vital Records Information
  http://vitalrec.com/tn.html

- USGenWeb Census Project Tennessee
  http://www.usgenweb.org/census/states/tennesse.htm

- USGenWeb Tombstone Transcription Project—Tennessee
  http://www.rootsweb.com/~cemetery/tenn.html

- Using Tennessee Census Records, 1880–1920
  http://www.state.tn.us/sos/statelib/pubsvs/cen1880.htm
  From the Tennessee State Library and Archives, Historical and Genealogical Information.

- VitalChek Network—Tennessee
  http://www.vitalchek.com/stateselect.asp?state=TN

- Wayne County Tennessee Bible Records
  http://www.netease.net/wayne/bible.htm

- Where to Write for Vital Records—Tennessee
  http://www.cdc.gov/nchswww/howto/w2w/tennesse.htm
  From the National Center for Health Statistics (NCHS).

◆ Religion & Churches

- Christianity.Net Church Locator—Tennessee
  http://www.christianity.net/cgi/location.exe?United_States+Tennessee

- Church Online!—Tennessee
  http://www.churchonline.com/usas/tn/tn.html

- Church Profiles—Tennessee
  http://www.church-profiles.com/tn/tn.html

- Churches dot Net—Global Church Web Pages—Tennessee
  http://www.churches.net/churches/tennesse.html

- Churches of the World—Tennessee
  http://www.churchsurf.com/churches/Tennessee/index.htm
  From the ChurchSurf Christian Directory.

- The Historical Foundation of the Cumberland Presbyterian Church and the Cumberland Presbyterian Church in America
  http://www.cumberland.org/hfcpc/
  Memphis, Tennessee
- Sumner County Churches
  http://www.tngenweb.org/sumner/sumnchur.htm

◆ Societies & Groups

- Archer's Computer Interest Group List—Tennessee
  http://www.genealogy.org/~ngs/cigs/ngl1ustn.html
- Coffee County Historical Society—Info. & Pubs.
  http://www.cafes.net/jlewis/pubs.htm
- East Tennessee Historical Society
  http://www.korrnet.org/eths/
- First Families of Tennessee
  http://www.korrnet.org/eths/firstfam.htm
  A Heritage Program of the East Tennessee Historical Society.
- Hardin County Historical Society
  http://www.hardincountytn.com/history/history.htm
- IOOF Lodge Website Directory—Tennessee
  http://norm28.hsc.usc.edu/IOOF/USA/Tennessee/Tennessee.html
  Independent Order of Odd Fellows and Rebekahs.
- Middle Tennessee Genealogical Society
  http://www.dogtrot.com/mtgs/
- Roane County Heritage Commission
  http://www.roanetnheritage.com/
- Society Hill: Tennessee, United States
  http://www.daddezio.com/society/hill/SH-TN-NDX.html
  A list of addresses for genealogical and historical societies in the state.

- Smoky Mountain Historical Society
  http://www.SmokyKin.com/smhs
  Eastern Tennessee
- Tennessee Division, Sons of Confederate Veterans
  http://www.tennessee-scv.org/
- Tennessee Genealogical Society
  http://www.rootsweb.com/~tngs/
- Tennessee Historical Commission
  http://www.vic.com/tnchron/resource/thc.htm
- Tennessee Society Daughters of the American Revolution
  http://members.aol.com/chucalissa/tnsdar/tnsdar.htm
- Tennessee Society Sons of the Revolution
  http://members.aol.com/tnsor/
- Upper Cumberland Genealogical Association
  http://www.jagunet.com/~mbar/ucga.htm
  Cookeville, Tennessee
- Wayne County Historical Society
  http://www.netease.net/wayne/wchs.htm

◆ USGenWeb Project

- Tennessee Genealogy—USGenWeb Project State Page
  http://www.usgenweb.org/tn
- Letters from Forgotten Ancestors
  http://www.tngenweb.usit.com/tnletters/
  A Tennessee Genealogy History Project.
- Tennessee—USGenWeb Archives Table of Contents
  http://www.rootsweb.com/~usgenweb/tn/tnfiles.htm
- Tennessee—USGenWeb FTP Archives
  ftp://ftp.rootsweb.com/pub/usgenweb/tn/

U.S.—TEXAS—TX
http://www.CyndisList.com/tx.htm

Category Index:

- Events
- General Resource Sites
- Government & Cities
- History & Culture
- Libraries, Archives & Museums
- Locality Specific
- Mailing Lists, Newsgroups & Chat
- Maps, Gazetteers & Geographical Information
- Military
- Newspapers

- People & Families
- Professional Researchers, Volunteers & Other Research Services
- Publications, Software & Supplies
- Queries, Message Boards & Surname Lists
- Records: Census, Cemeteries, Land, Obituaries, Personal, Taxes and Vital
- Religion & Churches
- Societies & Groups
- USGenWeb Project

◆ Events

- The Family History Show
  http://familyhistory.flash.net/
  A radio talk show on the Texas State Network with Michael Matthews.

- Family Reunion Page for the Central Texas Area
  http://www.aisi.net/GenWeb/mclennanco/mainreun.htm

- Institute of Genealogical Studies
  http://www.cyberramp.net/~igs/

◆ General Resource Sites

- Everton's Sources of Genealogical Information in Texas
  http://www.everton.com/usa/tx.htm

- Family Tree Maker's Genealogy "How To" Guide—Texas
  http://www.familytreemaker.com/00000218.html

- Genealogy Bulletin Board Systems for Texas
  http://www.genealogy.org/~gbbs/gbltx.html

- Genealogy Exchange & Surname Registry—TXGenExchange
  http://www.genexchange.com/tx/index.cfm

- Genealogy Resources on the Internet: Texas
  http://www-personal.umich.edu/~cgaunt/texas.html

- LDS Research Outline for Texas
  http://www.everton.com/usa/tx-0844b.txt

- Lineages' Genealogy Site: Texas
  http://www.lineages.com/rooms/usa/state.asp?StateCode=TX

- ROOTS-L United States Resources: Texas
  http://www.rootsweb.com/roots-l/USA/tx.html
  Comprehensive list of research links, including many to history-related sites.

◆ Government & Cities

- 50states.com—Texas State Information Resource
  http://www.50states.com/texas.htm
  A list of general information for each state, including a list of colleges, state symbols, links to maps, newspapers, and other miscellaneous state information.

- Excite Travel by City.Net—Texas
  http://www.city.net/countries/united_states/texas/

- Official City Web Sites for the State of Texas
  http://OfficialCitySites.org/Texas.htm

- State of Texas Government Information
  http://www.texas.gov/

- Virtual Victoria
  http://www.viptx.net/victoria/index.html

- Yahoo! Get Local...Texas Cities
  http://dir.yahoo.com/Regional/U_S__States/Texas/Cities/
  Maps, yellow pages, white pages, newspapers and other local information.

- Yahoo! Get Local...Texas Counties and Regions
  http://dir.yahoo.com/Regional/U_S__States/Texas/Counties_and_Regions/
  Maps, yellow pages, white pages, newspapers and other local information.

◆ History & Culture

- Brazoria County Historical Museum
  http://www.tgn.net/~bchm/default.html

- Center for Studies in Texas History—Texas State Historical Association
  http://www.dla.utexas.edu/texhist/
- Ghost Towns of Texas
  http://www.ghosttowns.com/states/tx/tx.html
- Lone Star Junction: A Texas Almanac
  http://www.lsjunction.com/
- Virtual Victoria: Cattle Brands
  http://www.viptx.net/victoria/history/brands.html
  Ranchers' names with examples of brands for 1838–1932 from Victoria County, Texas.
- Yahoo!...History...Texas
  http://dir.yahoo.com/Arts/Humanities/History/Browse_By_Region/U_S__States/Texas

◆ Libraries, Archives & Museums

- Austin Public Library
  http://www.library.ci.austin.tx.us/
- Catholic Archives of Texas
  http://www.onr.com/user/cat/
- Corpus Christi Public Library
  http://www.library.ci.corpus-christi.tx.us/
  - Local History Department
    http://www.library.ci.corpus-christi.tx.us/localhis/lh.htm
- Dallas Public Library
  http://www.lib.ci.dallas.tx.us/home.htm
- Daughters of the Republic of Texas Library
  http://hotx.com/drtl/public_html/
  At the Alamo, San Antonio, Texas.
- Family History Centers—Texas
  http://www.deseretbook.com/famhis/tx.html
- Family History Centers—Texas
  http://www.lib.byu.edu/~uvrfhc/centers/texas.html
- Fort Worth Public Library
  http://198.215.16.8:443/fortworth/fwpl/
  - Fort Worth Public Library Genealogy/ Local History
    http://198.215.16.8:443/fortworth/fwpl/genlhst.htm
- Genealogy Friends of Plano Libraries, Inc.
  http://www.geocities.com/Heartland/Estates/4167/
  Collin County, Texas
- Houston Public Library
  http://www.hpl.lib.tx.us/hpl/hplhome.html
  - Clayton Library—Center for Genealogical Research
    http://www.hpl.lib.tx.us/clayton/
  - Texas and Local History Department
    http://www.hpl.lib.tx.us/hpl/txr.html

- HYTELNET—Library Catalogs: USA: Texas
  http://library.usask.ca/hytelnet/usa/TX.html
  Before you use any of the Telnet links, make note of the user name, password and any other logon information.
- NUCMC Listing of Archives and Manuscript Repositories in Texas
  http://lcweb.loc.gov/coll/nucmc/txsites.html
  Links to information about resources other than those held in the Library of Congress.
- Repositories of Primary Sources: Texas
  http://www.uidaho.edu/special-collections/west.html#ustx
  A list of links to online resources from the Univ. of Idaho Library, Special Collections and Archives.
- San Antonio Public Library
  http://www.sat.lib.tx.us/
  - Genealogy
    http://www.sat.lib.tx.us/html/genealog.htm
- Sophienburg Museum & Archives
  http://www.new-braunfels.com/sophienburg/index.html
  "Dedicated to the preservation of the history of German settlement in New Braunfels and German genealogy in Texas and the West."
- Texas Family History Centers
  http://www.genhomepage.com/FHC/Texas.html
  A list of addresses, phone numbers and hours of operation from the Genealogy Home Page.
- Texas State Library & Archives Commission— Archives & Information Services Lobby
  http://www.tsl.state.tx.us/lobby/
  - Archival Services
    http://www.tsl.state.tx.us/lobby/arcfirst.htm
  - Genealogy Collection
    http://www.tsl.state.tx.us/lobby/genfirst.htm
  - Online Catalog
    http://www.tsl.state.tx.us/catalog/index.html
  - Reference / Documents Collection
    http://www.tsl.state.tx.us/lobby/reffirst.htm
  - Sam Houston Center
    http://www.tsl.state.tx.us/lobby/samfirst.htm
- University of Texas Libraries Online
  http://www.lib.utexas.edu/
  - Center for American History
    http://www.lib.utexas.edu/Libs/CAH/
  - Mexican Archives Project Index
    http://www.lib.utexas.edu/Libs/Benson/Mex_Archives/Collection_list.html
  - Perry-Castañeda Library Map Collection
    http://www.lib.utexas.edu/Libs/PCL/Map_collection/Map_collection.html
- webCATS: Library Catalogues on the World Wide Web—Texas
  http://library.usask.ca/hywebcat/states/TX.html

◆ Locality Specific

- Also see the USGenWeb section for links to county-specific resources.
- Franklin County Genealogy Resource Page
  http://www.polatteu.com/franklin/
- Gray, Texas . . . A community, a family, a door to the past . . .
  http://www.ghgcorp.com/rgcoleman/index.htm
- Marilyn Hoye's Home Page
  http://www.geocities.com/Vienna/1516/index.html
  Many Texas resources, especially some for Houston.
- Milam County, Texas Information Compiled by James David Walker
  http://www.geocities.com/Heartland/Hills/7475/
  Cemetery lists, lists of towns, etc. WALKER, ADAMS, MORGAN, MASSENGALE, RICE, HARRELL, ROGERS, JONES, AYCOCK, IVY.
- Piney Woods Rooters of Southeast Texas
  http://members.aol.com/RootsLady/rooters/piney.htm

◆ Mailing Lists, Newsgroups & Chat

- Genealogy Resources on the Internet—Texas Mailing Lists
  http://members.aol.com/gfsjohnf/gen_mail_states-tx.html
  Each of the mailing list links below points to this site, wonderfully maintained by John Fuller. Visit this site for county-specific mailing lists as well.
- EAST-TEXAS-ROOTS Mailing List
  http://members.aol.com/gfsjohnf/gen_mail_states-tx.html#EAST-TEXAS-ROOTS
  A mailing list for anyone who has an interest in genealogy and family history research in Nacogdoches County, Texas and surrounding counties.
- GERMAN-TEXAN Mailing List
  http://members.aol.com/gfsjohnf/gen_mail_states-tx.html#GERMAN-TEXAN
  For anyone with a genealogical interest in German and Central European immigrants to Texas, especially Germans in the 19th century.
- GRAY_TX Mailing List
  http://members.aol.com/gfsjohnf/gen_mail_states-tx.html#GRAY_TX
  For those who are researching family lines in the Gray community of Marion County, Texas.
- PERMIAN_BASIN Mailing List
  http://members.aol.com/gfsjohnf/gen_mail_states-tx.html#PERMIAN_BASIN
  For anyone with a genealogical interest in the Permian Basin area of Texas including Andrews, Ector, Midland, Ward, and Winkler counties.
- TEXAHOMA-ROOTS-L Mailing List
  http://members.aol.com/gfsjohnf/gen_mail_states-tx.html#TEXAHOMA-ROOTS
  Oklahoma & Texas

- TX_HILL_COUNTRY Mailing List
  http://members.aol.com/gfsjohnf/gen_mail_states-tx.html#TX_HILL_COUNTRY
  Dedicated to the discussion and exchange of information regarding the history and genealogy of the 22 counties that make up the region known as the "Texas Hill Country" Also see the associated web page at http://lonestar.texas.net/~dwatson/blanco/txhillco.htm
- TX-Landmark Mailing List
  http://members.aol.com/gfsjohnf/gen_mail_states-tx.html#TX-Landmark
  For anyone with a genealogical or historical interest in Texas landmarks and vanished communities.
- TX-MEX Mailing List
  http://members.aol.com/gfsjohnf/gen_mail_states-tx.html#TX-MEX
  For anyone with ancestors who immigrated to Texas from Mexico.
- TX-Rooters Mailing List
  http://members.aol.com/gfsjohnf/gen_mail_states-tx.html#TX-Rooters
- WESTEX-ROOTS
  http://members.aol.com/gfsjohnf/gen_mail_states-tx.html#WESTEX-ROOTS
  For anyone with a genealogical or historical interest in West Texas.

◆ Maps, Gazetteers & Geographical Information

- 1895 U.S. Atlas—Texas
  http://www.LivGenMI.com/1895tx.htm
- American Memory Panoramic Maps 1847–1929—Texas
  http://lcweb2.loc.gov/cgi-bin/query/S?ammem/gmd:@filreq(@field(STATE+@band(+texas))+@field(COLLID+pmmap))
  From the Geography and Map Division, Library of Congress.
- American Memory Railroad Maps 1828–1900—Texas
  http://memory.loc.gov/cgi-bin/query/S?ammem/gmd:@filreq(@field(STATE+texas)+@field(COLLID+rrmap))
  From the Geography and Map Division, Library of Congress.
- Color Landform Atlas: Texas
  http://fermi.jhuapl.edu/states/tx_0.html
  Including a map of counties and a map for 1895.
- Excite Maps: Texas Maps
  http://www.city.net/maps/view/?mapurl=/countries/united_states/texas
  Zoom in on these maps all the way to the street level.
- HPI County InfoSystem—Counties in Texas
  http://www.com/hpi/txcty/index.html
- K.B. Slocum Books and Maps—Texas
  http://www.treasurenet.com/cgi-bin/treasure/kbslocum/scan/se=Texas/sf=mapstate

- List of Texas Counties
  http://www.genealogy.org/~st-clair/counties/state_tx.html
- Map of Texas Counties, Map #1
  http://govinfo.kerr.orst.edu/gif/states/tx.gif

  Map #2
  http://govinfo.kerr.orst.edu/gif/states/tx1.gif

  Map #3
  http://govinfo.kerr.orst.edu/gif/states/tx2.gif

  Map #4
  http://govinfo.kerr.orst.edu/gif/states/tx3.gif

  Map #5
  http://govinfo.kerr.orst.edu/gif/states/txorig.gif
  From the Government Information Sharing Project, Information Services, Oregon State University.
- Map of Texas Counties
  http://www.lib.utexas.edu/Libs/PCL/Map_collection/states/Texas3.gif
  From the Perry-Castañeda Library at the Univ. of Texas at Austin.
- Texas Department of Transportation County Maps
  http://www.lib.utexas.edu/Libs/PCL/txdot/TXDOTCounty.html
- Texas General Land Office Archives—Map Collection
  http://www.glo.state.tx.us/central/arc/mapscol.html
- Texas Historic Sites Atlas
  http://atlas.thc.state.tx.us/
- Texas Map Collection
  http://www.texas.gov/maps.html
- University of Texas Map Collection
  gopher://rowan.lib.utexas.edu/
- U.S. Census Bureau—Texas Profiles
  http://www.census.gov/datamap/www/48.html
- Yale Peabody Museum: GNIS—Texas
  http://www.peabody.yale.edu/other/gnis/TX.html
  *Search the USGS Geographic Names Database. You can limit the search to a specific county in this state and search for any of the following features: airport arch area arroyo bar basin bay beach bench bend bridge **building** canal cape **cemetery** channel **church** cliff crater crossing dam falls flat forest gap geyser glacier gut harbor hospital island isthmus lake lava levee locale mine oilfield other park pillar plain ppl range rapids reserve reservoir ridge **school** sea slope spring stream summit swamp tower trail tunnel valley well woods.*

◆ Military

- 6th Texas Cavalry Battalion—Gould's Texas Battalion
  http://www.io.com/~dwhite/gould.html
  A history of the battalion and a muster roll for company E.
- 6th Texas Infantry—A Civil War Historical and Genealogical Resource Page
  http://lonestar.texas.net/~thompson/
- 7th Texas Infantry
  http://www.why.net/home/sdavis/7thTexas/index.htm

- The 35th Texas Cavalry
  http://www.io.com/~dwhite/35thTX.html
  A brief history of the 35th Texas Cavalry and extracts from the pension application of Mrs. John Hale.
- Adjutant General Texas Volunteers (Spanish-American War) Records, 1898–1902
  http://link.tsl.state.tx.us/.dir/adj.dir/.files/adjsaw.ans
- The Civil War Archive—Union Regiments—Texas
  http://www.civilwararchive.com/uniontx.htm
- Civil War Battle Summaries by State—Texas
  http://www2.cr.nps.gov/abpp/battles/bystate.htm#tx
- The Civil War Round Table of Dallas
  http://members.tripod.com/~DallasCWRT
- Index to Confederate Pension Applications
  http://www.tsl.state.tx.us/lobby/cpi/introcpi.htm
- Korean Conflict State-Level Casualty Lists—Texas
  http://www.nara.gov/nara/electronic/txhrlist.html
  From the National Archives and Records Administration, Center for Electronic Records.
- Milam County, Texas: List of Honor
  http://www.geocities.com/Athens/Academy/2670/
  Individuals Who Have Given Their Lives in the Defense of Their Country from World War I through Vietnam.
- Muster Roll Captain R. R. Sissell's Company, Hopkins County, Texas
  http://www.geocities.com/Vienna/1516/muster.html
- Official Historic Web site of the 10th Texas Infantry
  http://members.aol.com/SMckay1234/
- Parsons' Texas Cavalry Brigade
  http://www.why.net/home/sdavis/Parsons/index.htm
  Regimental rosters for the 12th, 19th, 21st, 30th and Morgan's Regiment Texas Cavalry.
- Roster of Company I, 28th Texas Cavalry (Dismounted)
  http://www.io.com/~dwhite/col28.html
- Texas Adjutant General Service Records 1836–1935
  http://www.tsl.state.tx.us/lobby/servrecs.htm
- Texas Volunteers, Spanish-American War Military Rolls, 1898–1901
  http://isadore.tsl.state.tx.us/.dir/mil.dir/.files/mrw.txt
- Vietnam Conflict State-Level Casualty Lists—Texas
  http://www.nara.gov/nara/electronic/txhrviet.html
  From the National Archives and Records Administration, Center for Electronic Records.
- Virtual Victoria: Confederate Pension Applicant Index
  http://www.viptx.net/victoria/history/pensions/index.html
  An index to all of the applicants from Victoria County, Texas.
- Virtual Victoria: Confederate Soldiers
  http://www.viptx.net/victoria/history/soldiers.html
  Rosters of soldiers from Victoria County, Texas.

◆ Newspapers

- AJR NewsLink—Texas Newspapers
  http://www.newslink.org/txnews.html

- Austin 360: News: Austin American-Statesman
  http://www.Austin360.com/news/

- The Dallas Morning News
  http://www.dallasnews.com/

- E&P Media Info Links—Newspaper Sites in Texas
  http://www.mediainfo.com/emedia/browse-results.
  htm?region=texas&category=newspaper+++++++++

- Ecola Newstand: Texas
  http://www.ecola.com/news/press/na/us/tx/

- Houston Chronicle Interactive
  http://www.chron.com/

- Lubbock Online
  http://www.lubbockonline.com/

- Montague County Shopper Online
  http://www.morgan.net/shopper/

- NAA Hotlinks to Newspapers Online—Texas
  http://www.naa.org/hotlinks/searchResult.asp?param=
  TX-Texas&City=1

- N-Net—Texas Newspapers
  http://www.n-net.com/tx.htm

- Tracing Our Roots
  http://www.hhcn.com/family/kellow/index.html
  *Column by Brenda Burns Kellow, featured in the Plano Star
  Courier, Plano, Texas.*

- The Ultimate Collection of News Links:
  USA—Texas
  http://www.pppp.net/links/news/USA-TX.html

- Yahoo!...Newspapers...Texas
  http://dir.yahoo.com/News_and_Media/Newspapers/
  Browse_By_Region/U_S__States/Texas/

◆ People & Families

- Dallas Virtual Jewish Community—Jewish
  Genealogy Home Page
  http://www.dvjc.org/history/genealogy.shtml

- Polish Texan Genealogy Page
  http://shell.idt.net/~u1211419/Polish/Polishtx.htm

- Tribes and Villages of Texas
  http://hanksville.phast.umass.edu:8000/cultprop/contacts/
  tribal/TX.html

- Virtual Victoria: The Original Colonists
  http://www.viptx.net/victoria/history/colonists/index.html
  Victoria County, Texas

- WPA Life Histories from Texas
  http://lcweb2.loc.gov/ammem/wpaintro/txcat.html
  *Manuscripts from the Federal Writer's Project, 1936–1940,
  Library of Congress.*

◆ Professional Researchers, Volunteers & Other Research Services

- Board for Certification of Genealogists—Roster of
  Those Certified—Specializing in Texas
  http://www.genealogy.org/~bcg/rosts_tx.html

- Dickenson Research & Photo-Video Evidence
  http://PersonalWebs.myriad.net/jdickenson/
  *Huntsville, Texas. Specializing in Locating Missing Heirs in
  Estate Cases and General Genealogical Research.*

- Genealogy Helplist—Texas
  http://posom.com/hl/usa/tx.shtml

- Genealogy Research by Diane Tofte Kropp
  http://lonestar.simplenet.com/genres.html
  Pearland, Texas

- Higgins Family History and Other Services
  http://www.concentric.net/~Higginsj/
  *Family history typing & publishing, document scanning for
  documentation, research Dallas/Fort Worth available resources
  including government archives.*

- Holly Heinsohn Texas Genealogy
  http://www.hrkropp.com/wizzf.html

- JET Genealogical Research
  http://members.tripod.com/~Janet_E_Tabares/index.html
  Houston, Texas

- Lonestar Genealogy
  http://lonestar.simplenet.com/genealogy.html
  *Jeannette Prouse is a professional researcher living in Texas
  who does research services for the entire United States.*

- The Official Iowa Counties Professional Genealogist
  and Researcher's Registry for Texas
  http://www.iowa-counties.com/gene/tx.htm

◆ Publications, Software & Supplies

- AncestorSpy—CDs and Microfiche for Texas
  http://www.ancestorspy.com/tx.htm

- Barbara Green's Used Genealogy Books—Texas
  http://home.earthlink.net/~genbooks/lochist.html#TX

- Barnette's Family Tree Book Company
  http://www.barnettesbooks.com/

- Books We Own—Texas
  http://www.rootsweb.com/~bwo/texas.html

- Boyd Publishing Company—Texas
  http://www.hom.net/~gac/texas.htm

- Curtis Media, Inc.
  http://members.aol.com/curmedia/curtish.htm
  Bedford, Texas. Publishers of genealogy and history books.

- Design Software
  http://www.dhc.net/~design/
  *Burleson, Texas. A variety of genealogical research software
  products.*

- Ericson Books
  http://www.ericsonbooks.com/
  Nacogdoches, Texas

- Frontier Press Bookstore—Texas
  http://www.frontierpress.com/frontier.cgi?category=tx

- GenealogyBookShop.com—Texas
  http://www.genealogybookshop.com/genealogybookshop/files/
  The_United_States,Texas/index.html
  *The online store of Genealogical Publishing Co., Inc. &
  Clearfield Company.*

- Hearthstone Bookshop—Texas
  http://www.hearthstonebooks.com/cgi-bin/webc.cgi/st_main.
  html?catid=100&sid=2PH5t29sm

- Heritage Books—Texas
  http://www.heritagebooks.com/tx.htm

- Heritage Quest—Microfilm Records for the State
  of Texas
  http://www.heritagequest.com/genealogy/microfilm/texas/

- J & W Enterprises
  http://www.dhc.net/~jw/
  *One stop book source on the Internet, specializing in southern
  states source material.*

- Lost in Time Books—Texas
  http://www.lostintime.com/catalog/books/bookst/bo30000.htm

- The Memorabilia Corner Books—Texas
  http://members.aol.com/TMCorner/book_tx.htm

- Ovilla, Texas History Book
  http://www.flash.net/~cmiracle/

- S-K Publications—Texas 1850 Census Books
  http://www.skpub.com/genie/census/tx/

- Southern Queries Genealogy Magazine
  http://www.mindspring.com/~freedom1/sq/sq.htm

- Texas State Historical Association Publications
  http://www.dla.utexas.edu/texhist/TSHApub.html

- Willow Bend Bookstore—Texas
  http://www.willowbend.net/tx.htm

◆ Queries, Message Boards & Surname Lists

- Dallas County, Texas QueryBase
  http://www.geocities.com/TheTropics/1926/dallasquery.html
  Postings thru present date.

- GenConnect Texas Visitor Center
  http://cgi.rootsweb.com/~genbbs/indx/Tx.html
  *A system for posting queries, Bibles, biographies, deeds,
  obituaries, pensions, wills.*

- Lonestar Genealogy—Texas Surnames
  http://lonestar.simplenet.com/genealogy/txqueries.html

- The Texas Genealogy Register
  http://www.lsjunction.com/gen.htm

- Texas Surnames
  http://www.rootsweb.com/~txrusk/txsurnames.html

◆ Records: Census, Cemeteries, Land, Obituaries, Personal, Taxes and Vital (Born, Married, Died & Buried)

- The 1790–1890 Federal Population Censuses:
  Catalog of National Archives Microfilm
  http://www.genealogy.org/census/contents.shtml
  - Census Schedules and Microfilm Roll Numbers
    for Texas:
    1850
    http://www.genealogy.org/census/1850_schedules/
    Texas.html
    1860
    http://www.genealogy.org/census/1860_schedules/
    Texas.html
    1870
    http://www.genealogy.org/census/1870_schedules/
    Texas.html
    1880
    http://www.genealogy.org/census/1880_schedules/
    Texas.html
    1880 Soundex
    http://www.genealogy.org/census/1880.sdx_schedules/
    T773.html
    1890 Special Schedules
    http://www.genealogy.org/census/1890-special_schedules/
    Texas.html

- 1850 Census for Robertson County, Texas
  http://www.geocities.com/Heartland/Plains/3451/1850.htm

- 1850 Census, Victoria County, Texas
  http://www.viptx.net/victoria/history/1850/

- 1870 Dimmit County, Texas Census
  http://www.rootsweb.com/~txdimmit/DC1870.htm

- 1880 Karnes County Census (Polish Areas)
  http://paris.chem.yale.edu/~zondlo/karnes1880.html

- 1900 Dimmit County Census Index
  http://www.rootsweb.com/~txdimmit/DC1900.htm

- 1910 Dimmit County Census Index
  http://www.rootsweb.com/~txdimmit/dc1910.htm

- Boren-Reagor Springs Cemetery
  http://www.geocities.com/Heartland/Prairie/1746/boren.html
  *The Boren-Reagor Springs Cemetery page has biographical
  information on individuals buried in the cemetery with a
  complete listing of all who are buried there. Links included to
  Civil War History of those buried in the cemetery and of other
  Boren descendants. Also included in the history of the Lee-
  Peacock Feud.*

- Caldwell County, Texas Marriages, 1848–1886
  ftp://ftp.rootsweb.com/pub/usgenweb/tx/caldwell/marriage/
  1848.txt
- Census Online—Links to Census Sites on the Web—
  Texas
  http://www.census-online.com/links/TX_data.html
- County Courthouse Addresses
  http://www.familytreemaker.com/00000272.html
- Eakins Cemetery Records
  http://www.geocities.com/SoHo/Lofts/6448/EakinsCem.html
  Ponder, Denton County
- Find-A-Grave by Location: Texas
  http://www.findagrave.com/grave/ltx.html
  Graves of noteworthy people.
- Fort Worth Star-Telegram Local Death Notices
  http://www.startext.com/today/news/local/fw/
  *Scroll to the bottom of this page and click on the link for "Local
  Death Notices."*
- Fragments of the 1890 Census for Texas
  http://lonestar.simplenet.com/genealogy/genweb/1890tx.html
- Grimes County Texas 1900 Census, Germans
  from Russia
  http://pixel.cs.vt.edu/library/census/link/grimes00.txt
- Grimes County Texas 1910 Census, Germans
  from Russia
  http://pixel.cs.vt.edu/library/census/link/grimes10.txt
- Grimes County Texas 1920 Census, Germans
  from Russia
  http://pixel.cs.vt.edu/library/census/link/grimes20.txt
- Ground Work Genealogy on the Internet: Texas
  http://members.aol.com/ssmadonna/tx.htm
  Links to sites with a variety of records.
- History of the Seminole Indian Scout Cemetery
  http://www.coax.net/people/lwf/his_sisc.htm
  Brackettville, Texas
- Hood County Texas Genealogical Society Index
  of Records
  http://www.genealogy.org/~granbury/index.htm
  Including birth, marriage, tax, & many other online records.
- Houston, Texas Tax List, September, 1839
  http://www.geocities.com/Vienna/1516/taxlist.html
  From the Houston Morning Star Newspaper.
- Index to Confederate Pension Applications
  http://www.tsl.state.tx.us/lobby/cpi/introcpi.htm
- Interment.net: Texas Cemeteries
  http://www.interment.net/us/tx/index.htm
  A list of links to other sites.
- Jefferson County, Texas Cemeteries
  http://www.rootsweb.com/~txjeffer/burials/cemeteri.htm
- Marriages from the Texas Telegraph, 1841–50
  http://www.geocities.com/Vienna/1516/houmart.html
  Houston, Texas

- Mills Cemetery, Garland, Texas
  http://www.geocities.com/TheTropics/1127/mills.html
- Montague County Shopper Online—Obituaries
  http://ww2.morgan.net/Shopper/obits.htm
- National Archives—Southwest Region (Fort Worth)
  http://www.nara.gov/regional/ftworth.html
- National Archives—Southwest Region
  http://www.familytreemaker.com/00000105.html
  *Records for Arkansas, Louisiana, Oklahoma, Texas, and a
  portion of New Mexico.*
- Obituaries from the Houston Morning Star, 1839
  http://www.geocities.com/Vienna/1516/houobi.html
  1840
  http://www.geocities.com/Vienna/1516/houobi40.html
  1841
  http://www.geocities.com/Vienna/1516/houobi41.html
  1842
  http://www.geocities.com/Vienna/1516/houobi42.html
  1843
  http://www.geocities.com/Vienna/1516/houobi43.html
  1844
  http://www.geocities.com/Vienna/1516/houobi44.html
- The Old 300 Genealogical Database
  http://www.tgn.net/~bchm/Genealogy/gene.html
  *"The 'Old 300' database actually includes a core listing of all
  settlers who had received land grants in Austin's Colony by the
  eve of the war for independence from Mexico."*
- Passenger List of Ship Ben Nevis
  http://home.sprynet.com/sprynet/harrisfarm/bennevis.htm
  *Ship Register Wendish Colonists of Texas, 1854, from Liverpool,
  England to Queenstown, Ireland to Galveston, Texas.*
- Pin Oak Cemetery, Milam County, Texas
  http://www.geocities.com/Heartland/Hills/7475/poc.html
- The Political Graveyard—Cemeteries in Texas
  http://politicalgraveyard.com/geo/TX/kmindex.html
- Preplanning Network—Funeral Home and
  Cemetery Directory—Texas
  http://www.preplannet.com/texfhcem.htm
- Shiloh Cemetery, Delta County, Texas
  http://www.geocities.com/Vienna/1516/shiloh.html
- SouthEast Texas Obituaries
  http://members.aol.com/RootsLady/universal/obituari.htm
- Stony Cemetery
  http://www.geocities.com/SoHo/Lofts/6448/StonyCem.html
  Denton County
- Texas County Tax Rolls
  http://isadore.tsl.state.tx.us/g/genealogy/.files/tax
  Information on how to order these records on microfilm.
- Texas General Land Office—Archives and Records
  http://www.glo.state.tx.us/central/arc/index.html
- Texas General Land Office—Map Collection
  http://www.glo.state.tx.us/central/arc/mapscol.html

- Texas General Land Office—Spanish and Mexican Land Titles in Texas
  http://www.glo.state.tx.us/central/arc/spanmex.html
- Texas State Cemetery
  http://www.cemetery.state.tx.us/
- Texas Vital Records Information
  http://vitalrec.com/tx.html
- USGenWeb Census Project Texas
  http://www.usgenweb.org/census/states/texas.htm
- USGenWeb Tombstone Transcription Project— Texas
  http://www.rootsweb.com/~cemetery/Texas/index1.html
- VitalChek Network—Texas
  http://www.vitalchek.com/stateselect.asp?state=TX
- Where to Write for Vital Records—Texas
  http://www.cdc.gov/nchswww/howto/w2w/texas.htm
  From the National Center for Health Statistics (NCHS).

◆ Religion & Churches

- Christianity.Net Church Locator—Texas
  http://www.christianity.net/cgi/location.exe?United_States+Texas
- Church Online!—Texas
  http://www.churchonline.com/usas/tx/tx.html
- Church Profiles—Texas
  http://www.church-profiles.com/tx/tx.html
- Churches dot Net—Global Church Web Pages— Texas
  http://www.churches.net/churches/texas.html
- Churches of the World—Texas
  http://www.churchsurf.com/churches/Texas/index.htm
  From the ChurchSurf Christian Directory.
- First Baptist Church, Ladonia, Texas
  http://www.geocities.com/~fannincounty/GenWeb/fbc-lad.html
  History and information on this church which was established circa 1860.

◆ Societies & Groups

- The American Legion—Department of Texas
  http://www.txlegion.org
- Anderson County Genealogy Society
  http://www.e-tex.com/personal/bonniew/acgs/acgs2.htm
  Palestine, Texas
- Archer's Computer Interest Group List—Texas
  http://www.genealogy.org/~ngs/cigs/ngl1ustx.html
- Ark-La-Tex Genealogical Association
  http://www.softdisk.com/comp/aga/
- Athens Genealogical Organization—Athens, Henderson County, Texas
  http://www.rootsweb.com/~txhender/heago.html

- The Austin Genealogical Society
  http://www.main.org/ags/
- Brazos Genealogical Association, Brazos County, Texas
  http://www2.cy-net.net/~bga/
- Brazosport Genealogy Society
  http://gator1.brazosport.cc.tx.us/~gensoc/
  Lake Jackson, Texas
- Caldwell County Genealogical and Historical Society
  http://www.rootsweb.com/~txcaldwe/socpage.htm
- Central Texas PC Users Group, Austin— Genealogy SIG
  http://www.ctpcug.com./sigs.htm#gen
- Coastal Bend Genealogy Society
  http://www.rootsweb.com/~txcbgs/
  Nueces County, Texas
- Comal County Genealogy Society
  http://www.hal-pc.org/~dcrane/txgenweb/comal/co-ccgs.htm
- Czech Heritage Society of Texas
  http://www.genealogy.org/~czech/
- Dallas Genealogical Society
  http://www.dallasgenealogy.org/
- Dallas Historical Society
  http://www.arlington.net/interact/dhs.htm
- Dallas Jewish Historical Society
  http://www.dvjc.org/history/
- East Texas Genealogical Society
  http://www.rootsweb.com/~txetgs/txetgs/index.html
  Tyler, Texas
- The El Paso Genealogical Society
  http://rgfn.epcc.edu/users/az289/
- Ellis County Genealogical Society
  http://www.rootsweb.com/~txellis/esoc.htm
- Fort Worth Genealogical Society
  http://www.rootsweb.com/~txfwgs/
- German-Texan Heritage Society
  http://www.main.org/germantxn/
- Garland Genealogical Society
  http://www.geocities.com/TheTropics/1926/society.html
- Greater Houston Jewish Genealogical Society
  http://dirac.bcm.tmc.edu/~david/jgs.html
- HAL-PC Genealogy SIG Home Page
  http://www.hal-pc.org/~jeans/gene.shtml
  Houston, Texas
- Hi-Plains Genealogical Society
  http://www.texasonline.net/schools/unger/geneal.htm
  Plainview, Hale County, Texas

- Hispanic Genealogical Society
  http://www.brokersys.com/~joguerra/jose.html
  Houston, Texas

- The Historical Society of Denton County
  http://www.iglobal.net/mayhouse/Historical_Society.html

- Hood County, Texas Genealogical Society
  http://www.genealogy.org/~granbury/welcome.html
  Granbury, Texas

- The Huguenot Society of Texas of the National
  Huguenot Society
  http://www.startext.net/homes/huguenot/

- IOOF Lodge Website Directory—Texas
  http://norm28.hsc.usc.edu/IOOF/USA/Texas/Texas.html
  Independent Order of Odd Fellows and Rebekahs.

- Kingsland Genealogical Society
  http://www.rootsweb.com/~txkinggs/

- Lamar County Genealogical Society Home Page
  http://gen.1starnet.com/lamargen.htm

- Lower Gulf Coast Genealogy Group
  http://www.phoenix.net/~dsk/genealogy.html

- Mesquite Historical & Genealogical Society
  http://members.aol.com/dstuart101/mesquite/page1.htm

- Mid-Cities Genealogical Society
  http://www.geocities.com/Heartland/Ranch/3825/
  Bedford, Texas

- The Milam County Genealogical Society
  http://www.aisi.net/GenWeb/MilamCo/mcgs.htm

- Montgomery County Genealogical &
  Historical Society, Inc.
  http://mcia.com/gsociety.htm

- Nacogdoches Genealogical Society
  http://users.aol.com/pphill235/ngs/ngshome.html

- North Collin County Genealogical Society
  http://www.psyberlink.net/~kcole/nccgs.htm

- North Texas Genealogical Association
  http://www.wf.net/~fmaier/

- Peters Colony Historical Society of Dallas County,
  Texas
  http://www.starbase21.com/PSGenealogy/

- San Angelo Genealogical & Historical Society
  http://www.rootsweb.com/~saghs/index.htm

- Society Hill: Texas, United States
  http://www.daddezio.com/society/hill/SH-TX-NDX.html
  *A list of addresses for genealogical and historical societies in
  the state.*

- Sons of Dewitt Colony Texas
  http://www.tamu.edu/ccbn/dewitt.htm
  *History, politics, life and genealogy of the area covered by the
  colony from 1700–1846: Caldwell, Comal, DeWitt, Fayette,
  Gonzales, Guadalupe, Hays, Jackson, Lavaca, Victoria and
  Wilson Counties.*

- Sons of Norway, NordTex Lodge 1-594,
  Dallas, Texas
  http://web2.airmail.net/gus/nordtex.htm

- SouthEast Texas Genealogical & Historical Society
  http://members.aol.com/RootsLady/setghs/setghs.htm
  Beaumont, Texas

- South Plains Genealogical Society
  http://www.door.net/spgs/
  Lubbock, Texas

- Spanish American Genealogical Association
  (SAGA)
  http://members.aol.com/sagacorpus/saga.htm
  Corpus Christi

- Texas Catholic Historical Society
  http://www.history.swt.edu/Catholic_Southwest.htm

- Texas Division, Sons of Confederate Veterans
  http://www.texas-scv.org/

- The Texas Historical Commission
  http://www.thc.state.tx.us/

- Texas Roots—Limestone County Cemetery Surveys
  http://www.glade.net/~hcox/cemeteries/cemeteryintro.html

- Texas Wendish Heritage Society
  http://home.sprynet.com/sprynet/harrisfarm/wendish.htm

- Texas Society Daughters of the American
  Revolution
  http://www.tsdar.org/

- Texas Society Sons of the American Revolution
  http://www.txssar.org/

- Tyler County Genealogical Society
  http://members.tripod.com/~KCfalcon/TCGS
  Woodville, Texas

- Van Zandt County Genealogical Society
  http://www.rootsweb.com/~txvzcgs/vzgs.htm
  Canton, Texas

- Victoria County Genealogical Society
  http://www.viptx.net/vcgs/vcgs.html

- Walker County Genealogical Society
  http://personalwebs.myriad.net/jdickenson/wcgen.htm
  Huntsville, Texas

- Wood County, Texas Genealogical Society
  http://www.rootsweb.com/~txwood/wcgs.htm

◆ USGenWeb Project

- Texas Genealogy—USGenWeb Project State Page
  http://www.usgenweb.org/tx

- Texas—USGenWeb Archives Table of Contents
  http://www.rootsweb.com/~usgenweb/tx/txfiles.htm

- Texas—USGenWeb FTP Archives
  ftp://ftp.rootsweb.com/pub/usgenweb/tx/

U.S.—UTAH—UT
http://www.CyndisList.com/ut.htm

Category Index:

- General Resource Sites
- Government & Cities
- History & Culture
- History of the LDS Church
- Libraries, Archives & Museums
- Mailing Lists, Newsgroups & Chat
- Maps, Gazetteers & Geographical Information
- Military
- Newspapers
- People & Families

- Professional Researchers, Volunteers & Other Research Services
- Publications, Software & Supplies
- Queries, Message Boards & Surname Lists
- Records: Census, Cemeteries, Land, Obituaries, Personal, Taxes and Vital
- Religion & Churches
- Societies & Groups
- USGenWeb Project

◆ General Resource Sites

- Everton's Sources of Genealogical Information in Utah
  http://www.everton.com/usa/ut.htm

- Family Tree Maker's Genealogy "How To" Guide—Utah
  http://www.familytreemaker.com/00000219.html

- Genealogy Exchange & Surname Registry—UTGenExchange
  http://www.genexchange.com/ut/index.cfm

- Genealogy Resources on the Internet: Utah
  http://www-personal.umich.edu/~cgaunt/utah.html

- LDS Research Outline for Utah
  http://www.everton.com/usa/ut-0845b.txt

- Lineages' Genealogy Site: Utah
  http://www.lineages.com/rooms/usa/state.asp?StateCode=UT

- ROOTS-L United States Resources: Utah
  http://www.rootsweb.com/roots-l/USA/ut.html
  Comprehensive list of research links, including many to history-related sites.

◆ Government & Cities

- 50states.com—Utah State Information Resource
  http://www.50states.com/utah.htm
  A list of general information for each state, including a list of colleges, state symbols, links to maps, newspapers, and other miscellaneous state information.

- Excite Travel by City.Net—Utah
  http://www.city.net/countries/united_states/utah/

- Official City Web Sites for the State of Utah
  http://OfficialCitySites.org/utah.htm

- Official State of Utah Web Site
  http://www.state.ut.us/

- Yahoo! Get Local...Utah Cities
  http://dir.yahoo.com/Regional/U_S__States/Utah/Cities/
  Maps, yellow pages, white pages, newspapers and other local information.

- Yahoo! Get Local...Utah Counties and Regions
  http://dir.yahoo.com/Regional/U_S__States/Utah/Counties_and_Regions/
  Maps, yellow pages, white pages, newspapers and other local information.

◆ History & Culture

- Ghost Towns of Utah
  http://www.ghosttowns.com/states/ut/ut.html

- Mountain Men and the Fur Trade
  http://www.xmission.com/~drudy/amm.html
  Sources of the History of the Fur Trade in the Rocky Mountain West.

- Utah History Home Page
  http://www.ce.ex.state.ut.us/history/

- Weston Memories
  http://www.vii.com/~nelsonb/weston.htm

- Yahoo!...History...Utah
  http://dir.yahoo.com/Arts/Humanities/History/Browse_By_Region/U_S__States/Utah

◆ History of the LDS Church

- Handcart Companies
  http://eddy.media.utah.edu/medsol/UCME/h/HANDCART.html

- **LDS & Family History Centers**
  http://www.CyndisList.com/lds.htm
  See this category on Cyndi's List for related links.

- **Max Bertola's—The Mormon Pioneer Story**
  http://www.uvol.com/pioneer/homepage.html

- **Mormon History Resource Page**
  http://www.indirect.com:80/www/crockett/history.html
  - **Mormon Diaries/Journals and Biographies**
    http://www.indirect.com:80/www/crockett/bios.html
  - **Mormon History Resource Page—Pioneer Period**
    http://www.indirect.com:80/www/crockett/pioneer.html

- **The Mormon Pioneer Trail**
  http://www.americanwest.com/trails/pages/mormtrl.htm
  From the American West Home Page.

- **The Mormon Pioneer Trail**
  http://www.omaha.org/trails/main.htm
  From the Douglas-Sarpy Counties Mormon Trails Association.

- **The Mormon Trail**
  http://www.esu3.k12.ne.us:80/districts/elkhorn/ms/curriculum/Mormon1.html

- **MormonTrail.com—The Pioneer Experience**
  http://www.mormontrail.com/
  The Official Web Site for Stories, Facts, and Ship Logs on the Mormon Trail Pioneers.

- **Tracing Mormon Pioneers**
  http://www.vii.com/~nelsonb/pioneer.htm
  - **Mormon Emigrant Ships (1840–1868)**
    http://www.vii.com/~nelsonb/pioneer.htm#ships

◆ Libraries, Archives & Museums

- **Brigham Young University Libraries**
  http://www.byu.edu/libraries/
  - **Utah Valley Regional Family History Center**
    http://www.lib.byu.edu/dept/uvrfhc/
    On the fourth floor of the Harold B. Lee Library on the campus of Brigham Young University.

- **Family History Centers—Utah**
  http://www.deseretbook.com/famhis/ut.html

- **Family History Centers—Utah**
  http://www.lib.byu.edu/~uvrfhc/centers/utah.html

- **HYTELNET—Library Catalogs: USA: Utah**
  http://library.usask.ca/hytelnet/usa/UT.html
  Before you use any of the Telnet links, make note of the user name, password and any other logon information.

- **J. Willard Marriott Library, University of Utah**
  http://www.lib.utah.edu/index.phtml
  - **Special Collections**
    http://www.lib.utah.edu/spc/spc.html

- **LDS & Family History Centers**
  http://www.CyndisList.com/lds.htm
  See this category on Cyndi's List for related links.

- **Libraries in Utah**
  http://www.state.lib.ut.us/resource/utahlib.htm

- **The Logan Library**
  http://www.logan.lib.ut.us/

- **NUCMC Listing of Archives and Manuscript Repositories in Utah**
  http://lcweb.loc.gov/coll/nucmc/utsites.html
  Links to information about resources other than those held in the Library of Congress.

- **Pioneer Utah's Online Library**
  http://pioneer.lib.ut.us/
  - **Library & Library Catalogs**
    http://pioneer.lib.ut.us/pioneer_dir/libraries2.htm

- **Provo City Library**
  http://www.provo.lib.ut.us/

- **Repositories of Primary Sources: Utah**
  http://www.uidaho.edu/special-collections/west.html#usut
  A list of links to online resources from the Univ. of Idaho Library, Special Collections and Archives.

- **Salt Lake City Public Library**
  http://www.slcpl.lib.ut.us/

- **Southern Utah University—Sherratt Library Web**
  http://www.li.suu.edu/

- **Utah Family History Centers**
  http://www.genhomepage.com/FHC/Utah.html
  A list of addresses, phone numbers and hours of operation from the Genealogy Home Page.

- **Utah State Archives**
  http://www.archives.state.ut.us/
  - **Finding Aids**
    http://www.archives.state.ut.us/referenc/!faids.htm
  - **Frequently Asked Questions**
    http://www.archives.state.ut.us/referenc/faq.htm
  - **Public Services**
    http://www.archives.state.ut.us/referenc/!public.htm

- **Utah State Library Division Home Page**
  http://www.state.lib.ut.us/

- **Utah Valley PAF Users Group—Salt Lake Family History Library**
  http://www.genealogy.org/~uvpafug/fhlslc.html

- **webCATS: Library Catalogues on the World Wide Web—Utah**
  http://library.usask.ca/hywebcat/states/UT.html

◆ Mailing Lists, Newsgroups & Chat

- **Genealogy Resources on the Internet—Utah Mailing Lists**
  http://members.aol.com/gfsjohnf/gen_mail_states-ut.html
  Each of the mailing list links below points to this site, wonderfully maintained by John Fuller. Visit this site for county-specific mailing lists as well.

- **ELIJAH-L Mailing List**
  http://members.aol.com/johnf14246/
  gen_mail_general.html#ELIJAH-L
  For believing members of the Church of Jesus Christ of Latter-day Saints to discuss their ideas and experiences relating with genealogy in the LDS Church.

- **emery-ut-gen Mailing List**
  http://members.aol.com/gfsjohnf/gen_mail_states-ut.html#emery-ut-gen

- **HANDCART Mailing List**
  http://members.aol.com/gfsjohnf/gen_mail_states-ut.html#HANDCART
  For anyone who has an interest in the genealogy, journals, and stories of the Pioneers of the Church of Jesus Christ of Latter-day Saints who settled in the Salt Lake Valley from 1847 to 1860.

- **Utah Mailing List**
  http://members.aol.com/gfsjohnf/gen_mail_states-ut.html#Utah

- **WESTERN-ROOTS-L Mailing list**
  http://members.aol.com/gfsjohnf/gen_mail_states-ut.html#WESTERN-ROOTS-L
  Washington, Oregon, Alaska, Idaho, Montana, Wyoming, California, Nevada, Hawaii, Colorado, Utah, Arizona, and New Mexico.

◆ Maps, Gazetteers & Geographical Information

- **1895 U.S. Atlas—Utah**
  http://www.LivGenMI.com/1895ut.htm

- **American Memory Panoramic Maps 1847–1929—Utah**
  http://lcweb2.loc.gov/cgi-bin/query/S?ammem/gmd:@filreq(@field(STATE+@band(+utah))+@field(COLLID+pmmap))
  From the Geography and Map Division, Library of Congress.

- **American Memory Railroad Maps 1828–1900—Utah**
  http://memory.loc.gov/cgi-bin/query/S?ammem/gmd:@filreq(@field(STATE+utah)+@field(COLLID+rrmap))
  From the Geography and Map Division, Library of Congress.

- **Color Landform Atlas: Utah**
  http://fermi.jhuapl.edu/states/ut_0.html
  Including a map of counties and a map for 1895.

- **Excite Maps: Utah Maps**
  http://www.city.net/maps/view/?mapurl=/countries/united_states/utah
  Zoom in on these maps all the way to the street level.

- **HPI County InfoSystem—Counties in Utah**
  http://www.com/hpi/utcty/index.html

- **K.B. Slocum Books and Maps—Utah**
  http://www.treasurenet.com/cgi-bin/treasure/kbslocum/scan/se=Utah/sf=mapstate

- **List of Utah Counties**
  http://www.genealogy.org/~st-clair/counties/state_ut.html

- **Map of Utah Counties**
  http://govinfo.kerr.orst.edu/gif/states/ut.gif
  From the Government Information Sharing Project, Information Services, Oregon State University.

- **Map of Utah Counties**
  http://www.lib.utexas.edu/Libs/PCL/Map_collection/states/Utah.jpg
  From the Perry-Castañeda Library at the Univ. of Texas at Austin.

- **U.S. Census Bureau—Utah Profiles**
  http://www.census.gov/datamap/www/49.html

- **Yale Peabody Museum: GNIS—Utah**
  http://www.peabody.yale.edu/other/gnis/UT.html
  *Search the USGS Geographic Names Database. You can limit the search to a specific county in this state and search for any of the following features: airport arch area arroyo bar basin bay beach bench bend bridge **building** canal cape **cemetery** channel **church** cliff crater crossing dam falls flat forest gap geyser glacier gut harbor hospital island isthmus lake lava levee locale mine oilfield other park pillar plain ppl range rapids reserve reservoir ridge **school** sea slope spring stream summit swamp tower trail tunnel valley well woods.*

◆ Military

- **Korean Conflict State-Level Casualty Lists—Utah**
  http://www.nara.gov/nara/electronic/uthrlist.html
  From the National Archives and Records Administration, Center for Electronic Records.

- **Vietnam Conflict State-Level Casualty Lists—Utah**
  http://www.nara.gov/nara/electronic/uthrviet.html
  From the National Archives and Records Administration, Center for Electronic Records.

◆ Newspapers

- **AJR NewsLink—Utah Newspapers**
  http://www.newslink.org/utnews.html

- **E&P Media Info Links—Newspaper Sites in Utah**
  http://www.mediainfo.com/emedia/browse-results.htm?region=utah&category=newspaper+++++++++

- **Ecola Newstand: Utah**
  http://www.ecola.com/news/press/na/us/ut/

- **NAA Hotlinks to Newspapers Online—Utah**
  http://www.naa.org/hotlinks/searchResult.asp?param=UT-Utah&City=1

- **N-Net—Utah Newspapers**
  http://www.n-net.com/ut.htm

- **The Salt Lake Tribune**
  http://www.sltrib.com/

- **The Ultimate Collection of News Links: USA—Utah**
  http://www.pppp.net/links/news/USA-UT.html

- **Yahoo!...Newspapers...Utah**
  http://dir.yahoo.com/News_and_Media/Newspapers/Browse_By_Region/U_S__States/Utah/

◆ People & Families

- Tribes and Villages of Utah
  http://hanksville.phast.umass.edu:8000/cultprop/contacts/
  tribal/UT.html

- WPA Life Histories from Utah
  http://lcweb2.loc.gov/ammem/wpaintro/utcat.html
  *Manuscripts from the Federal Writer's Project, 1936–1940,
  Library of Congress.*

◆ Professional Researchers, Volunteers & Other Research Services

- Ancestors Lost and Found
  http://www.ancestorsfound.com/
  Salt Lake City, Utah

- Board for Certification of Genealogists—Roster of
  Those Certified—Specializing in Utah
  http://www.genealogy.org/~bcg/rosts_ut.html

- Genealogy Helplist—Utah
  http://members.aol.com/DFBradshaw/ut.html

- Genie Genealogy Research
  http://genealogy.hypermart.net
  *Genie Genealogy provides professional genealogy research
  services to help you find your ancestors. Whether you're a
  novice or expert, discover your family tree now—quickly and
  affordably. Genie also offers web page design, picture scanning,
  report printing, data entry, and LDS-specific genealogy services.*

- Heirlines Family History and Genealogy Research
  Services
  http://www.heirlines.com

- Heritage Consulting and Services
  http://www.heritageconsulting.com/
  Salt Lake City, Utah

- Kinsearch Genealogical Services
  http://home.utah-inter.net/kinsearch/index.html
  *Provides genealogical research services at the Family History
  Library (FHL) in Salt Lake City.*

- Natalie Cottrill Genealogical Research
  http://www.nataliesnet.com/
  *United States research at the Salt Lake City, Utah Family
  History Library.*

- The Official Iowa Counties Professional Genealogist
  and Researcher's Registry for Utah
  http://www.iowa-counties.com/gene/ut.htm

- Salt Lake Chapter—Association of Professional
  Genealogists
  http://www.lofthouse.com/slcapg/slcapg.htm

- Susan Ybarra, Basque Researcher
  http://www.iosphere.net/~jholwell/fam-find/spa/9701072.html
  *Specializing in Basque records from the province of Vizcaya.
  These records are on microfilm at the Salt Lake Family History
  Library, but do not get circulated.*

◆ Publications, Software & Supplies

- Barbara Green's Used Genealogy Books—Utah
  http://home.earthlink.net/~genbooks/lochist.html#UT

- Books We Own—Utah
  http://www.rootsweb.com/~bwo/utah.html

- Frontier Press Bookstore—Utah
  http://www.frontierpress.com/frontier.cgi?category=ut

- Heritage Quest—Microfilm Records for the State
  of Utah
  http://www.heritagequest.com/genealogy/microfilm/utah/

◆ Queries, Message Boards & Surname Lists

- GenConnect Utah Visitor Center
  http://cgi.rootsweb.com/~genbbs/indx/Ut.html
  *A system for posting queries, Bibles, biographies, deeds,
  obituaries, pensions, wills.*

◆ Records: Census, Cemeteries, Land, Obituaries, Personal, Taxes and Vital (Born, Married, Died & Buried)

- The 1790–1890 Federal Population Censuses:
  Catalog of National Archives Microfilm
  http://www.genealogy.org/census/contents.shtml
  - Census Schedules and Microfilm Roll Numbers
    for Utah:
    1850
    http://www.genealogy.org/census/1850_schedules/Utah.html
    1860
    http://www.genealogy.org/census/1860_schedules/Utah.html
    1870
    http://www.genealogy.org/census/1870_schedules/Utah.html
    1880
    http://www.genealogy.org/census/1880_schedules/Utah.html
    1880 Soundex
    http://www.genealogy.org/census/1880.sdx_schedules/
    T774.html
    1890 Special Schedules
    http://www.genealogy.org/census/1890-special_schedules/
    Utah.html

- BLM—Utah's Electronic Reading Room
  http://www.blm.gov/nhp/efoia/ut/
  United States Bureau of Land Management.

- County Courthouse Addresses
  http://www.familytreemaker.com/00000273.html

- Find-A-Grave by Location: Utah
  http://www.findagrave.com/grave/lut.html
  Graves of noteworthy people.

- Interment.net: Utah Cemeteries
  http://www.interment.net/us/ut/index.htm
  A list of links to other sites.

- National Archives—Rocky Mountain Region
  (Denver)
  http://www.nara.gov/regional/denver.html

- National Archives—Rocky Mountain Region
  http://www.familytreemaker.com/00000103.html
  *Records for Colorado, Montana, North Dakota, South Dakota,
  Utah, Wyoming, and a portion of New Mexico.*

- The Political Graveyard—Cemeteries in Utah
  http://politicalgraveyard.com/geo/UT/kmindex.html

- Preplanning Network—Funeral Home and
  Cemetery Directory—Utah
  http://www.preplannet.com/utahfh.htm

- Ricks College—Family History Center Genesis
  Project
  http://abish.ricks.edu/fhc/gbsearch.asp
  *Search engine for marriages in Arizona, Idaho, Nevada, Oregon,
  Utah 1850–1951.*

- The Salt Lake Tribune—Utah Section
  http://www.sltrib.com/
  *Go to the Utah section and find the links for Utah Births and
  Utah Deaths.*

- USGenWeb Census Project Utah
  http://www.usgenweb.org/census/states/utah.htm

- USGenWeb Tombstone Transcription Project—Utah
  http://www.rootsweb.com/~cemetery/utah.html

- Utah Vital Records Information
  http://vitalrec.com/ut.html

- VitalChek Network—Utah
  http://www.vitalchek.com/stateselect.asp?state=UT

- Vital Records Extracted from "The Life, Travels, and
  Ministry of Milton M. Everly"
  http://www.aloha.net/~jan/milton.txt
  *June 1904–November 1904. Extractions of records for
  marriages, some baptisms, and funerals.*

- Where to Write for Vital Records—Utah
  http://www.cdc.gov/nchswww/howto/w2w/utah.htm
  From the National Center for Health Statistics (NCHS).

◆ Religion & Churches

- Christianity.Net Church Locator—Utah
  http://www.christianity.net/cgi/
  location.exe?United_States+Utah

- Church Profiles—Utah
  http://www.church-profiles.com/ut/ut.html

- Churches dot Net—Global Church Web Pages—
  Utah
  http://www.churches.net/churches/utah.html

- Churches of the World—Utah
  http://www.churchsurf.com/churches/Utah/index.htm
  From the ChurchSurf Christian Directory.

- LDS & Family History Centers
  http://www.CyndisList.com/lds.htm
  See this category on Cyndi's List for related links.

◆ Societies & Groups

- Archer's Computer Interest Group List—Utah
  http://www.genealogy.org/~ngs/cigs/ngl1usut.html

- Genealogical Society of Utah
  http://www.mormons.org/daily/family_history/
  genealogical_society_eom.htm
  Description from All About Mormons.

- Genealogical Society of Utah
  http://www.itd.nps.gov/cwss/gsu.html
  *Description from the National Park Service, Civil War Soldiers
  and Sailors System web site.*

- IOOF Lodge Website Directory—Utah
  http://norm28.hsc.usc.edu/IOOF/USA/Utah/Utah.html
  Independent Order of Odd Fellows and Rebekahs.

- Society Hill: Utah, United States
  http://www.daddezio.com/society/hill/SH-UT-NDX.html
  *A list of addresses for genealogical and historical societies in
  the state.*

- Sons of the American Revolution Utah Society
  http://sar.org/utssar/

- Sons of Utah Pioneers
  http://www.uvol.com/sup/

- The Utah Genealogical Association
  http://www.infouga.org/home.htm

- Utah State Historical Society—Utah History
  Home Page
  http://www.history.state.ut.us/

- Utah State Society Daughters of the American
  Revolution
  http://www.geocities.com/Heartland/Pointe/1077/

- Utah Valley PAF Users Group—Home Page
  http://www.genealogy.org/~uvpafug/

- Washington County Historical Society
  http://www.ci.st-george.ut.us/Tourism/History/historical.html

◆ USGenWeb Project

- Utah Genealogy—USGenWeb Project State Page
  http://www.usgenweb.org/ut

- Utah—USGenWeb Archives Table of Contents
  http://www.rootsweb.com/~usgenweb/ut/utfiles.htm

- Utah—USGenWeb FTP Archives
  ftp://ftp.rootsweb.com/pub/usgenweb/ut/

U.S.—VERMONT—VT
http://www.CyndisList.com/vt.htm

Category Index:

- General Resource Sites
- Government & Cities
- History & Culture
- Libraries, Archives & Museums
- Mailing Lists, Newsgroups & Chat
- Maps, Gazetteers & Geographical Information
- Military
- Newspapers
- People & Families

- Professional Researchers, Volunteers & Other Research Services
- Publications, Software & Supplies
- Queries, Message Boards & Surname Lists
- Records: Census, Cemeteries, Land, Obituaries, Personal, Taxes and Vital
- Religion & Churches
- Societies & Groups
- USGenWeb Project

◆ General Resource Sites

- Everton's Sources of Genealogical Information in Vermont
  http://www.everton.com/usa/vt.htm

- Family Tree Maker's Genealogy "How To" Guide—Vermont
  http://www.familytreemaker.com/00000220.html

- Genealogical Society of Vermont
  http://ourworld.compuserve.com:80/homepages/induni_n_J/

- Genealogy Exchange & Surname Registry—VTGenExchange
  http://www.genexchange.com/vt/index.cfm

- Genealogy Resources on the Internet: Vermont
  http://www-personal.umich.edu/~cgaunt/vermont.html

- LDS Research Outline for Vermont
  http://www.everton.com/usa/vt-0846b.txt

- Lineages' Genealogy Site: Vermont
  http://www.lineages.com/rooms/usa/state.asp?StateCode=VT

- New England Connections
  http://www.geocities.com/Heartland/5274/nec.htm

- ROOTS-L United States Resources: Vermont
  http://www.rootsweb.com/roots-l/USA/vt.html
  Comprehensive list of research links, including many to history-related sites.

- Vermont Genealogy Site
  http://www.web-home.com/vt-genealogy/
  Information on the FARR family, the Town of Cavendish.

◆ Government & Cities

- 50states.com—Vermont State Information Resource
  http://www.50states.com/vermont.htm
  A list of general information for each state, including a list of colleges, state symbols, links to maps, newspapers, and other miscellaneous state information.

- Excite Travel by City.Net—Vermont
  http://www.city.net/countries/united_states/vermont/

- Official City Web Sites for the State of Vermont
  http://OfficialCitySites.org/Vermont.htm

- State of Vermont Home Page
  http://www.state.vt.us/

- Virtual Vermont Internet Magazine—Vermont Town and City Clerks
  http://www.virtualvermont.com/clerks/index.html

- Yahoo! Get Local...Vermont Cities
  http://dir.yahoo.com/Regional/U_S__States/Vermont/Cities/
  Maps, yellow pages, white pages, newspapers and other local information.

- Yahoo! Get Local...Vermont Counties and Regions
  http://dir.yahoo.com/Regional/U_S__States/Vermont/Counties_and_Regions/
  Maps, yellow pages, white pages, newspapers and other local information.

◆ History & Culture

- Vermont Historic Sites Guide
  http://www.state.vt.us/dca/historic/hp_sites.htm

- Vermont, The Green Mountain State—Some Vermont History
  http://mole.uvm.edu/state/vthist.html

- Virtual Vermont Internet Magazine—
Vermont History
http://www.virtualvermont.com/history/index.html
"Native Vermonters and Those Less Fortunate," "A Vermonter Was First" and "It Happened Here."

- Yahoo!...History...Vermont
http://dir.yahoo.com/Arts/Humanities/History/
Browse_By_Region/U_S__States/Vermont/

◆ Libraries, Archives & Museums

- Archives in New England on the Internet
http://www.lib.umb.edu/newengarch/nearch.html

- The Bennington Museum
http://www.bennington.com/museum/gene.html
The Genealogy and History Research Library has family genealogies, town and county histories, census indexes, biographies and local research materials.

- Family History Centers—Vermont
http://www.deseretbook.com/famhis/vt.html

- Family History Centers—Vermont
http://www.lib.byu.edu/~uvrfhc/centers/vermont.html

- HYTELNET—Library Catalogs: USA: Vermont
http://library.usask.ca/hytelnet/usa/VT.html
Before you use any of the Telnet links, make note of the user name, password and any other logon information.

- NUCMC Listing of Archives and Manuscript Repositories in Vermont
http://lcweb.loc.gov/coll/nucmc/vtsites.html
Links to information about resources other than those held in the Library of Congress.

- Repositories of Primary Sources: Vermont
http://www.uidaho.edu/special-collections/east2.html#usvt
A list of links to online resources from the Univ. of Idaho Library, Special Collections and Archives.

- University of Vermont Libraries
http://sageunix.uvm.edu/

  o UVM Special Collections
http://sageunix.uvm.edu/~sc/

- Vermont Department of Libraries
http://dol.state.vt.us/

- Vermont Genealogy—from Middlebury College Library
http://www.middlebury.edu/library/genealogy.html

- The Vermont State Archives
http://www.sec.state.vt.us/archives/archdex.htm

- Vermontiana Collections
http://www.uvm.edu/~histpres/vtiana/vccont.html
A guide to Vermontiana collections at academic, special and selected public libraries.

- Virtual Vermont Internet Magazine—Vermont Library Directory, 1997
http://www.virtualvermont.com/ind/libraries.html

- webCATS: Library Catalogues on the World Wide Web—Vermont
http://library.usask.ca/hywebcat/states/VT.html

◆ Mailing Lists, Newsgroups & Chat

- Genealogy Resources on the Internet—Vermont Mailing Lists
http://members.aol.com/gfsjohnf/gen_mail_states-vt.html
Each of the mailing list links below points to this site, wonderfully maintained by John Fuller. Visit this site for county-specific mailing lists as well.

- NORTHEAST-ROOTS-L Mailing List
http://members.aol.com/gfsjohnf/gen_mail_states-vt.html#NORTHEAST-ROOTS
Connecticut, Maine, Massachusetts, New Hampshire, Rhode Island & Vermont.

- Vermont Mailing List
http://members.aol.com/gfsjohnf/gen_mail_states-vt.html#Vermont

◆ Maps, Gazetteers & Geographical Information

- 1895 U.S. Atlas—Vermont
http://www.LivGenMI.com/1895vt.htm

- American Memory Panoramic Maps 1847–1929—Vermont
http://lcweb2.loc.gov/cgi-bin/query/S?ammem/gmd:@filreq(@field(STATE+@band(+vermont))+@field(COLLID+pmmap))
From the Geography and Map Division, Library of Congress.

- American Memory Railroad Maps 1828–1900—Vermont
http://memory.loc.gov/cgi-bin/query/S?ammem/gmd:@filreq(@field(STATE+vermont)+@field(COLLID+rrmap))
From the Geography and Map Division, Library of Congress.

- Color Landform Atlas: Vermont
http://fermi.jhuapl.edu/states/vt_0.html
Including a map of counties and a map for 1895.

- Excite Maps: Vermont Maps
http://www.city.net/maps/view/?mapurl=/countries/united_states/vermont
Zoom in on these maps all the way to the street level.

- HPI County InfoSystem—Counties in Vermont
http://www.com/hpi/vtcty/index.html

- K.B. Slocum Books and Maps—Vermont
http://www.treasurenet.com/cgi-bin/treasure/kbslocum/scan/se=Vermont/sf=mapstate

- List of Vermont Counties
http://www.genealogy.org/~st-clair/counties/state_vt.html

- Map of Vermont Counties
http://govinfo.kerr.orst.edu/gif/states/vt.gif
From the Government Information Sharing Project, Information Services, Oregon State University.

- Map of Vermont Counties
  http://www.lib.utexas.edu/Libs/PCL/Map_collection/states/
  Vermont.gif
  From the Perry-Castañeda Library at the Univ. of Texas at Austin.

- Old Maps of New England (Maine, New Hampshire, Vermont, Connecticut, Rhode Island, Massachusetts) and New York
  http://members.aol.com/oldmapsne/index.html

- Reproductions of Old Town Maps in New England
  http://www.biddeford.com/~lkane/

- U.S. Census Bureau—Vermont Profiles
  http://www.census.gov/datamap/www/50.html

- Vermont, The Green Mountain State—Some Vermont Geography
  http://mole.uvm.edu/state/vtgeog.html

- Yale Peabody Museum: GNIS—Vermont
  http://www.peabody.yale.edu/other/gnis/VT.html
  *Search the USGS Geographic Names Database. You can limit the search to a specific county in this state and search for any of the following features: airport arch area arroyo bar basin bay beach bench bend bridge **building** canal cape **cemetery** channel **church** cliff crater crossing dam falls flat forest gap geyser glacier gut harbor hospital island isthmus lake lava levee locale mine oilfield other park pillar plain ppl range rapids reserve reservoir ridge **school** sea slope spring stream summit swamp tower trail tunnel valley well woods.*

◆ Military

- The Civil War Archive—Union Regiments—Vermont
  http://www.civilwararchive.com/unionvt.htm

- Korean Conflict State-Level Casualty Lists—Vermont
  http://www.nara.gov/nara/electronic/vthrlist.html
  From the National Archives and Records Administration, Center for Electronic Records.

- Vermont in the Civil War
  http://www.geocities.com/Pentagon/1861/vt-cw.htm

- Vietnam Conflict State-Level Casualty Lists—Vermont
  http://www.nara.gov/nara/electronic/vthrviet.html
  From the National Archives and Records Administration, Center for Electronic Records.

◆ Newspapers

- AJR NewsLink—Vermont Newspapers
  http://www.newslink.org/vtnews.html

- E&P Media Info Links—Newspaper Sites in Vermont
  http://www.mediainfo.com/emedia/browse-results.
  htm?region=vermont&category=newspaper+++++++++

- Ecola Newstand: Vermont
  http://www.ecola.com/news/press/na/us/vt/

- NAA Hotlinks to Newspapers Online—Vermont
  http://www.naa.org/hotlinks/searchResult.asp?param=
  VT-Vermont&City=1

- N-Net—Vermont Newspapers
  http://www.n-net.com/vt.htm

- The Ultimate Collection of News Links: USA—Vermont
  http://www.pppp.net/links/news/USA-VT.html

- Yahoo!...Newspapers...Vermont
  http://dir.yahoo.com/News_and_Media/Newspapers/
  Browse_By_Region/U_S__States/Vermont/Complete_Listing/

◆ People & Families

- Directory of Underground Railroad Operators—Vermont
  http://www.ugrr.org//names/map-vt.htm

- Tribes and Villages of Vermont
  http://hanksville.phast.umass.edu:8000/cultprop/contacts/
  tribal/VT.html

- WPA Life Histories from Vermont
  http://lcweb2.loc.gov/ammem/wpaintro/vtcat.html
  Manuscripts from the Federal Writer's Project, 1936–1940, Library of Congress.

◆ Professional Researchers, Volunteers & Other Research Services

- Board for Certification of Genealogists—Roster of Those Certified—Specializing in Vermont
  http://www.genealogy.org/~bcg/rosts_vt.html

- Eastern Townships of Quebec Genealogy
  http://www.virtuel.qc.ca/simmons/
  Marlene Simmons has indexed 490,000 church, census, newspaper, cemetery, some Vermont vital records, and other miscellaneous records.

- Genealogy Helplist—Vermont
  http://www.cybercomm.net/~freddie/helplist/vt.htm

◆ Publications, Software & Supplies

- AncestorSpy—CDs and Microfiche for Vermont
  http://www.ancestorspy.com/vt.htm

- Barbara Green's Used Genealogy Books—Vermont
  http://home.earthlink.net/~genbooks/lochist.html#VT

- Barnette's Family Tree Books—Vermont
  http://www.barnettesbooks.com/vermont.htm

- Books We Own—Vermont
  http://www.rootsweb.com/~bwo/vermont.html

- Boyd Publishing Company—New England
  http://www.hom.net/~gac/newengla.htm
- Broad View Books
  http://broadviewbooks.com/
  Used Genealogy Books, Local History of Massachusetts, Connecticut, Rhode Island, Vermont and New England.
- Essex Books—New England
  http://www.HERTGE.COM/essex/neweng.htm
- Frontier Press Bookstore—Vermont
  http://www.frontierpress.com/frontier.cgi?category=vt
- GenealogyBookShop.com—Vermont
  http://www.genealogybookshop.com/genealogybookshop/files/The_United_States,Vermont/index.html
  The online store of Genealogical Publishing Co., Inc. & Clearfield Company.
- Genealogy Titles from the Vermont Historical Society Book List
  http://www.state.vt.us/vhs/shop/genebks.htm
- Hearthstone Bookshop—Vermont
  http://www.hearthstonebooks.com/cgi-bin/webc.cgi/st_main.html?catid=101&sid=2PH5t29sm
- Heritage Books—Vermont
  http://www.heritagebooks.com/vt.htm
- Heritage Quest—Microfilm Records for the State of Vermont
  http://www.heritagequest.com/genealogy/microfilm/vermont/
- Lost in Time Books—Vermont
  http://www.lostintime.com/catalog/books/bookst/bo31000.htm
- The Memorabilia Corner Books—Vermont
  http://members.aol.com/TMCorner/book_vt.htm
- Picton Press—Vermont
  http://www.midcoast.com/~picton/public_html.BASK/catalog/state_vt.htm
- Tuttle Antiquarian Books
  http://www.rmharris.com/pub/rmharris/alldlrs/ne/05701tut.html
  Rutland, Vermont
- Willow Bend Bookstore—Vermont
  http://www.willowbend.net/vt.htm

◆ Queries, Message Boards & Surname Lists

- GenConnect Vermont Visitor Center
  http://cgi.rootsweb.com/~genbbs/indx/Vt.html
  A system for posting queries, Bibles, biographies, deeds, obituaries, pensions, wills.
- New England Connections Query Archive
  http://www.geocities.com/Heartland/5274/nequery.htm

◆ Records: Census, Cemeteries, Land, Obituaries, Personal, Taxes and Vital (Born, Married, Died & Buried)

- The 1790–1890 Federal Population Censuses: Catalog of National Archives Microfilm
  http://www.genealogy.org/census/contents.shtml
  - Census Schedules and Microfilm Roll Numbers for Vermont:
    1790
    http://www.genealogy.org/census/1790.html
    1800
    http://www.genealogy.org/census/1800_schedules/Vermont.html
    1810
    http://www.genealogy.org/census/1810_schedules/Vermont.html
    1820
    http://www.genealogy.org/census/1820_schedules/Vermont.html
    1830
    http://www.genealogy.org/census/1830_schedules/Vermont.html
    1840
    http://www.genealogy.org/census/1840_schedules/Vermont.html
    1850
    http://www.genealogy.org/census/1850_schedules/Vermont.html
    1860
    http://www.genealogy.org/census/1860_schedules/Vermont.html
    1870
    http://www.genealogy.org/census/1870_schedules/Vermont.html
    1880
    http://www.genealogy.org/census/1880_schedules/Vermont.html
    1880 Soundex
    http://www.genealogy.org/census/1880.sdx_schedules/T775.html
    1890 Special Schedules
    http://www.genealogy.org/census/1890-special_schedules/Vermont.html
- 1920 Census of Saxtons River, Windham County, Vermont
  http://www.rootsweb.com/rootsweb/searches/vtsaxriv/
- Census Online—Links to Census Sites on the Web—Vermont
  http://www.census-online.com/links/VT_data.html

- County Courthouse Addresses
  http://www.familytreemaker.com/00000274.html

- Find-A-Grave by Location: Vermont
  http://www.findagrave.com/grave/lvt.html
  Graves of noteworthy people.

- Interment.net: Vermont Cemeteries
  http://www.interment.net/us/vt/index.htm
  A list of links to other sites.

- National Archives—Northeast Region (Boston)
  http://www.nara.gov/regional/boston.html

- National Archives—New England Region
  http://www.familytreemaker.com/00000098.html
  Records for Connecticut, Maine, Massachusetts, New Hampshire, Rhode Island, and Vermont.

- The Political Graveyard—Cemeteries in Vermont
  http://politicalgraveyard.com/geo/VT/kmindex.html

- Preplanning Network—Funeral Home and Cemetery Directory—Vermont
  http://www.preplannet.com/verfhcemhtm.htm

- USGenWeb Census Project Vermont
  http://www.usgenweb.org/census/states/vermont.htm

- USGenWeb Tombstone Transcription Project—Vermont
  http://www.rootsweb.com/~cemetery/vermont.html

- Vermont Vital Records Information
  http://vitalrec.com/vt.html

- VitalChek Network—Vermont
  http://www.vitalchek.com/stateselect.asp?state=VT

- Where to Write for Vital Records—Vermont
  http://www.cdc.gov/nchswww/howto/w2w/vermont.htm
  From the National Center for Health Statistics (NCHS).

◆ Religion & Churches

- Christianity.Net Church Locator—Vermont
  http://www.christianity.net/cgi/location.exe?
  United_States+Vermont

- Church Online!—Vermont
  http://www.churchonline.com/usas/vt/vt.html

- Church Profiles—Vermont
  http://www.church-profiles.com/vt/vt.html

- Churches dot Net—Global Church Web Pages—Vermont
  http://www.churches.net/churches/vermont.html

- Churches of the World—Vermont
  http://www.churchsurf.com/churches/Vermont/index.htm
  From the ChurchSurf Christian Directory.

◆ Societies & Groups

- Genealogical Society of Vermont
  http://ourworld.compuserve.com:80/homepages/induni_n_J/

- IOOF Lodge Website Directory—Vermont
  http://norm28.hsc.usc.edu/IOOF/USA/Vermont/Vermont.html
  Independent Order of Odd Fellows and Rebekahs.

- Local Historical Societies—Index from VHS
  http://www.state.vt.us/vhs/lhs/lhsindex.htm

- New England Historic Genealogical Society
  http://www.nehgs.org/

- Society Hill: Vermont, United States
  http://www.daddezio.com/society/hill/SH-VT-NDX.html
  A list of addresses for genealogical and historical societies in the state.

- Swanton Historical Society
  http://www.rootsweb.com/~vtfrankl/shs.htm

- The Vermont French-Canadian Genealogical Society
  http://members.aol.com/vtfcgs/genealogy/index.html
  Burlington, Vermont

- The Vermont Historical Society
  http://www.state.vt.us/vhs/

- The Vermont Old Cemetery Association
  http://homepages.together.net/~btrutor/voca/vocahome.htm

- Virtual Vermont Internet Magazine—Local Historical Societies
  http://www.virtualvermont.com/ind/historicals.html

◆ USGenWeb Project

- Vermont Genealogy—USGenWeb Project State Page
  http://www.usgenweb.org/vt

- Vermont—USGenWeb Archives Table of Contents
  http://www.rootsweb.com/~usgenweb/vt/vtfiles.htm

- Vermont—USGenWeb FTP Archives
  ftp://ftp.rootsweb.com/pub/usgenweb/vt/

U.S.—VIRGINIA—VA

http://www.CyndisList.com/va.htm

Category Index:

- General Resource Sites
- Government & Cities
- History & Culture
- Libraries, Archives & Museums
- Locality Specific
- Mailing Lists, Newsgroups & Chat
- Maps, Gazetteers & Geographical Information
- Military
- Newspapers
- People & Families

- Professional Researchers, Volunteers & Other Research Services
- Publications, Software & Supplies
- Queries, Message Boards & Surname Lists
- Records: Census, Cemeteries, Land, Obituaries, Personal, Taxes and Vital
- Religion & Churches
- Societies & Groups
- USGenWeb Project

◆ General Resource Sites

- Everton's Sources of Genealogical Information in Virginia
  http://www.everton.com/usa/va.htm

- Family Tree Maker's Genealogy "How To" Guide—Virginia
  http://www.familytreemaker.com/00000221.html

- Genealogy Bulletin Board Systems for Virginia
  http://www.genealogy.org/~gbbs/gblva.html

- Genealogy Exchange & Surname Registry—VAGenExchange
  http://www.genexchange.com/va/index.cfm

- Genealogy Resources on the Internet: Virginia
  http://www-personal.umich.edu/~cgaunt/virginia.html

- LDS Research Outline for Virginia
  http://www.everton.com/usa/va-0847b.txt

- Lineages' Genealogy Site: Virginia
  http://www.lineages.com/rooms/usa/state.asp?StateCode=VA

- ROOTS-L United States Resources: Virginia
  http://www.rootsweb.com/roots-l/USA/va.html
  Comprehensive list of research links, including many to history-related sites.

◆ Government & Cities

- 50states.com—Virginia State Information Resource
  http://www.50states.com/virginia.htm
  A list of general information for each state, including a list of colleges, state symbols, links to maps, newspapers, and other miscellaneous state information.

- Excite Travel by City.Net—Virginia
  http://www.city.net/countries/united_states/virginia/

- Official City Web Sites for the State of Virginia
  http://OfficialCitySites.org/Virginia.htm

- Virginia State Page
  http://www.state.va.us/

- Yahoo! Get Local...Virginia Cities
  http://dir.yahoo.com/Regional/U_S__States/Virginia/Cities/
  Maps, yellow pages, white pages, newspapers and other local information.

- Yahoo! Get Local...Virginia Counties and Regions
  http://dir.yahoo.com/Regional/U_S__States/Virginia/Counties_and_Regions/
  Maps, yellow pages, white pages, newspapers and other local information.

◆ History & Culture

- Association for the Preservation of Virginia Antiquities (APVA)
  http://www.apva.org/apva/index.html

  ○ Association for the Preservation of Virginia Antiquities—Jamestown Rediscovery
    http://www.apva.org/

    • A Brief History of Jamestown
      http://www.apva.org/history/index.html

- James River Plantations
  http://www.jamesriverplantations.org/

- Yahoo!...History...Virginia
  http://dir.yahoo.com/Arts/Humanities/History/Browse_By_Region/U_S__States/Virginia

◆ Libraries, Archives & Museums

- Carrier Library, James Madison University
  http://library.jmu.edu/
  - Genealogy Research Bibliography
    http://library.jmu.edu/library/guides/history/genealogy.htm
  - History Research Bibliography Directory
    http://library.jmu.edu/library/guides/historydir.htm
  - Special Collections
    http://library.jmu.edu/libliaison/sc/aboutsc.htm
- Chesapeake, Virginia Family History Center
  http://sites.communitylink.org/cpl/famhistory.html
- Directory of Virginia Libraries
  http://www.vsla.edu:80/directory/
- Directory of Virginia Repositories
  http://www.vsla.edu/reposit/reposit.html
- Family History Centers—Virginia
  http://www.deseretbook.com/famhis/va.html
- Family History Centers—Virginia
  http://www.lib.byu.edu/~uvrfhc/centers/virginia.html
- Hampton Roads Naval Museum
  http://naval-station.norfolk.va.us/navy.html
  Norfolk, Virginia
- HYTELNET—Library Catalogs: USA: Virginia
  http://library.usask.ca/hytelnet/usa/VA.html
  Before you use any of the Telnet links, make note of the user name, password and any other logon information.
- The Library of Virginia
  http://www.vsla.edu/index.html
  - The Library of Virginia—Archival and Information Services
    http://www.vsla.edu/archives/index.html
  - The Library of Virginia Digital Collections
    http://198.17.62.51/
    - LVA Electronically Available Card Indexes
      http://198.17.62.51/collections/
  - The Library of Virginia Genealogy Home Page
    http://www.vsla.edu/archives/genie.html
  - The Library of Virginia—Online Catalogs and Image Databases
    http://www.vsla.edu/lva/col.html
  - Research Guides and Finding Aids at the Library of Virginia
    http://www.vsla.edu/research.html
- The Mariners' Museum—Newport News, Virginia
  http://www.mariner.org/
  Archives, manuscripts, manifests & research services available.
- National Genealogical Society—Library Services
  http://www.genealogy.org/~ngs/library.html
  Arlington, Virginia

- NUCMC Listing of Archives and Manuscript Repositories in Virginia
  http://lcweb.loc.gov/coll/nucmc/vasites.html
  Links to information about resources other than those held in the Library of Congress.
- Old Dominion University Library
  http://www.lib.odu.edu/
  - Special Collections
    http://www.lib.odu.edu/aboutlib/spccol/
    - Manuscript Collections
      http://www.lib.odu.edu/aboutlib/spccol/tidewater/indexmain.shtml
      Civil War Collections
      http://www.lib.odu.edu/aboutlib/spccol/civilwar/index.shtml
      Local History
      http://www.lib.odu.edu/aboutlib/spccol/norfolk.shtml
      Military History
      http://www.lib.odu.edu/aboutlib/spccol/military/military.shtml
      Women's History
      http://www.lib.odu.edu/aboutlib/spccol/women.shtml
- Repositories of Primary Sources: Virginia
  http://www.uidaho.edu/special-collections/east2.html#usva
  A list of links to online resources from the Univ. of Idaho Library, Special Collections and Archives.
- Rockingham Public Library
  http://home.rica.net/rpl/
- Shenandoah County Library System
  http://www.shenandoah.co.lib.va.us/
  - Local History & Genealogy
    http://www.shenandoah.co.lib.va.us/genealogy.htm
- Swem Library—The College of William and Mary
  http://www.swem.wm.edu/
  - Special Collections Division
    http://www.swem.wm.edu/SPCOL/spcolhp.html
- University of Virginia Library
  http://www.lib.virginia.edu/
  - Special Collections Department
    http://www.lib.virginia.edu/speccol/
  - Special Collections Digital Center
    http://www.lib.virginia.edu/speccol/scdc/scdc.html
- Virginia Family History Centers
  http://www.genhomepage.com/FHC/Virginia.html
  A list of addresses, phone numbers and hours of operation from the Genealogy Home Page.
- Virginia Military Institute Archives
  http://www.vmi.edu/~archtml/index.html
- Virginia Tech University Libraries
  http://www.lib.vt.edu/

- ○ Appalachian Studies
  http://www.lib.vt.edu/Subjects/appalachian.html
- ○ History Resources
  http://www.lib.vt.edu/Subjects/history.html
- ○ Special Collections Department
  http://scholar2.lib.vt.edu/spec/spechp.htm
  - • The Manuscript Collections
    http://scholar2.lib.vt.edu/spec/mss/msshp.htm
    Includes Southern Appalachian history and culture, Civil War, Railroad History and much more.

    Manuscript Sources for Civil War Research
    http://scholar2.lib.vt.edu/spec/civwar/guidecw.htm

    Manuscript Sources for Railroad History Research
    http://scholar2.lib.vt.edu/spec/railroad/rrintro.htm
- • Washington & Lee University Libraries
  http://www.wlu.edu/library/
  - ○ History Resources
    http://liberty.uc.wlu.edu/~vstanley/newhist/index.html
  - ○ Resources for Genealogical Research
    http://www.wlu.edu/~vstanley/geneal.txt
- • webCATS: Library Catalogues on the World Wide Web—Virginia
  http://library.usask.ca/hywebcat/states/VA.html
- • Williamsburg Regional Library
  http://www.wrl.org/
  Serving Williamsburg, James City County and York County, Virginia.

◆ Locality Specific

- • Also see the USGenWeb section for links to county-specific resources.
- • GHOTES—The "Genealogy and History of the Eastern Shore" of Virginia
  http://www.esva.net/ghotes/
- • Golden Lyon II Genealogical Research
  http://www.erols.com/rariggin/lyon.html
  Resource for studying related families of the Lower Eastern Shore—Allied Families of the Delmarva Peninsula.
- • Loudoun County, Virginia
  http://www.rootsweb.com/~inclinto/loudoun.html
  Links to Loudoun Co., VA Resources and Sue Beach's Loudoun Co., VA Research Interests.
- • Mt.View Research Page County, Virginia
  http://www.geocities.com/Heartland/Valley/9793/index.html
- • Russell County, 1860–1865
  http://rhobard.com/russell/
  Contains Civil War and census information.
- • Shenandoah Ancestry
  http://home.tampabay.rr.com/shenandoah/

◆ Mailing Lists, Newsgroups & Chat

- • Genealogy Resources on the Internet—Virginia Mailing Lists
  http://members.aol.com/gfsjohnf/gen_mail_states-va.html
  Each of the mailing list links below points to this site, wonderfully maintained by John Fuller. Visit this site for county-specific mailing lists as well.
- • Appalachianfamily Mailing List
  http://members.aol.com/gfsjohnf/gen_mail_states-va.html#Appalachianfamily
  Appalachian Mountain Families including families from Georgia, North Carolina, South Carolina, Tennessee, Kentucky, Virginia, and West Virginia.
- • GERMANNA_COLONIES Mailing List
  http://members.aol.com/gfsjohnf/gen_mail_states-va.html#GERMAN_COLONIES
  For descendants of the Germanna Colonies (i.e., the original German settlements in Virginia under Governor Spotswood; there were three colonies established, the first being in 1714).
- • GHOTES Mailing List
  http://members.aol.com/gfsjohnf/gen_mail_states-va.html#GHOTES
  For anyone who has an active research interest in the Genealogy and History of the Eastern Shore (GHOTES) of Virginia (specifically Accomack and Northampton Counties).
- • HARRISON-MONONGALIA.VA Mailing List
  http://members.aol.com/gfsjohnf/gen_mail_states-va.html#HARRISON-M
  For Harrison and Monongalia counties, now West Virginia.
- • JACKSON-ROANE.VA Mailing List
  http://members.aol.com/gfsjohnf/gen_mail_states-va.html#JACKSON
  For Jackson and Roane Counties, now West Virginia.
- • LOWER-DELMARVA-ROOTS Mailing List
  http://members.aol.com/gfsjohnf/gen_mail_states-va.html#LOWER-DELMARVA-ROOTS
  Sussex and Kent Counties in Delaware; Dorchester, Wicomico, Somerset, and Worcester in Maryland; Northampton and Accomack in Virginia.
- • Melungeon Mailing List
  http://members.aol.com/gfsjohnf/gen_mail_states-gen.html#MELUNGEO
  For people conducting Melungeon and/or Appalachian research including Native American, Portuguese, Turkish, Black Dutch, and other unverifiable mixed statements of ancestry or unexplained rumors, with ancestors in TN, KY, VA, NC, SC, GA, AL, WV, and possibly other places.
- • OLD-FREDERICK-CO-VA Mailing List
  http://members.aol.com/gfsjohnf/gen_mail_states-wv.html#OLD-FREDERICK.CO.VA
  For anyone with a genealogical or historical interest in old Frederick County, Virginia. The boundaries of old Frederick County today encompass 12 counties: Frederick, Clarke, Warren, Shenandoah and Page counties in Virginia; and Jefferson, Berkeley, Morgan, Hampshire, Mineral, Hardy and Grant counties in West Virginia.
- • ROANOKE_CO_VA Mailing List
  http://members.aol.com/gfsjohnf/gen_mail_states-va.html#ROANOKE_CO_VA

- SHENANDOAH Mailing List
  http://members.aol.com/gfsjohnf/gen_mail_states-va.
  html#SHENANDOAH
  For anyone who has an interest in genealogy related to families of the Shenandoah Valley of Virginia.

- SW_VA-L Mailing List
  http://members.aol.com/gfsjohnf/gen_mail_states-va.
  html#SW_VA-L
  For those with genealogical research in southwest Virginia: Lee, Scott, Washington, Russell and Tazewell counties.

- VAFINCAS Mailing List
  http://members.aol.com/gfsjohnf/gen_mail_states-va.
  html#VAFINCAS
  For anyone with an interest in the history of Southwestern Virginia. It includes that region of the the old, former county of Fincastle, Virginia.

- VA-Rooters Mailing List
  http://members.aol.com/gfsjohnf/gen_mail_states-va.
  html#VA-Rooters

- VA-ROOTS Mailing List
  http://members.aol.com/gfsjohnf/gen_mail_states-va.
  html#VA-ROOTS

- VAROOTS Mailing List
  http://members.aol.com/gfsjohnf/gen_mail_states-
  va.html#VAROOTS

- VA-SOUTHSIDE Mailing List
  http://members.aol.com/gfsjohnf/gen_mail_states-va.
  html#VA-SOUTHSIDE
  Amelia, Appomattox, Brunswick, Charlotte, Dinwiddie, Franklin, Greensville, Halifax, Henry, Isle of Wight, Lunenburg, Mecklenburg, Nottway, Patrick, Pittsylvania, Prince Edward, Prince George, Southampton, Surry and Sussex Counties, and cities of Petersburg, Colonial Heights, Hopewell, Danville, Suffolk, Emporia, South Boston, Franklin and Martinsville.

- VATIDEWATER Mailing List
  http://members.aol.com/gfsjohnf/gen_mail_states-va.
  html#VATIDEWATER
  For anyone with a genealogical interest in the Tidewater area of Virginia.

- VAWBTSVETS Mailing List
  http://members.aol.com/gfsjohnf/gen_mail_states-va.
  html#VAWBTSVETS
  For anyone with a genealogical interest in the Virginia veterans of the War Between the States.

- VA-WVA-ROOTS-L Mailing List
  http://members.aol.com/gfsjohnf/gen_mail_states-va.
  html#VA/WVA-ROOTS
  For Virginia and West Virginia.

- WDC-GenWeb Mailing List
  http://members.aol.com/gfsjohnf/gen_mail_states-wv.
  html#WDC-GenWeb
  For those interested in the World Descendant Charts (WDC) Genealogy Web Project. The WDC specializes in Virginia and West Virginia families.
  http://www.primenet.com/~dlytton/wdc

- WVPENDLE Mailing List
  http://members.aol.com/gfsjohnf/gen_mail_states-va.
  html#WVPENDLE
  Pendleton County area of West Virginia which includes the bordering Virginia counties of Highland and Rockingham.

◆ Maps, Gazetteers & Geographical Information

- 1790 Virginia Census Map
  http://www.historyu.com/Village/SurvHouse/1790pages/
  90virginia.html

- 1895 U.S. Atlas—Virginia
  http://www.LivGenMl.com/1895va.htm

- American Memory Panoramic Maps 1847–1929—Virginia
  http://lcweb2.loc.gov/cgi-bin/query/S?ammem/gmd:@filreq
  (@field(STATE+@band(+virginia))+@field(COLLID+pmmap))
  From the Geography and Map Division, Library of Congress.

- American Memory Railroad Maps 1828–1900—Virginia
  http://memory.loc.gov/cgi-bin/query/S?ammem/gmd:@filreq
  (@field(STATE+virginia)+@field(COLLID+rrmap))
  From the Geography and Map Division, Library of Congress.

- Color Landform Atlas: Virginia
  http://fermi.jhuapl.edu/states/va_0.html
  Including a map of counties and a map for 1895.

- Excite Maps: Virginia Maps
  http://www.city.net/maps/view/?mapurl=/countries/
  united_states/virginia
  Zoom in on these maps all the way to the street level.

- HPI County InfoSystem—Counties in Virginia
  http://www.com/hpi/vacty/index.html

- Introduction to Virginia Land History
  http://www.ultranet.com/~deeds/virg.htm

- K.B. Slocum Books and Maps—Virginia
  http://www.treasurenet.com/cgi-bin/treasure/kbslocum/scan/
  se=Virginia/sf=mapstate

- A List of the Parishes in Virginia. June the 30th, 1680
  http://www.lineages.com/archives/VAPSH680.HTM

- List of Virginia Counties
  http://www.genealogy.org/~st-clair/counties/state_va.html

- Map of Virginia Counties, Map #1
  http://govinfo.kerr.orst.edu/gif/states/va.gif
  Map #2
  http://govinfo.kerr.orst.edu/gif/states/va1.gif
  Map #3
  http://govinfo.kerr.orst.edu/gif/states/va2.gif
  From the Government Information Sharing Project, Information Services, Oregon State University.

- Map of Virginia Counties
  http://www.lib.utexas.edu/Libs/PCL/Map_collection/states/
  Virginia3.gif
  From the Perry-Castañeda Library at the Univ. of Texas at Austin.

- Parishes of Virginia 1600–1790
  http://www.wp.com/genealogy/page15.html

- UVa Library Geographic Information Center
  http://viva.lib.virginia.edu/gic/
  - Digital Resources Catalog
    http://viva.lib.virginia.edu/gic/catalog/
  - Maps Collection
    http://viva.lib.virginia.edu/gic/services/services_maps.html
  - Virginia Digital Map Library
    http://viva.lib.virginia.edu/gic/maps/maps_va.html
  - Virginia Locator Service
    http://viva.lib.virginia.edu/gic/va_locator/locator.html
- U.S. Census Bureau—Virginia Profiles
  http://www.census.gov/datamap/www/51.html
- VA Cities, Counties and Towns
  http://www.rootsweb.com/~varockbr/vatown.htm
  A list of towns with their respective counties, zip codes and incorporation dates.
- Virginia County Interactive Mapper
  http://ptolemy.gis.virginia.edu/gicdoc/mapper/tiger.html
- Yale Peabody Museum: GNIS—Virginia
  http://www.peabody.yale.edu/other/gnis/VA.html
  *Search the USGS Geographic Names Database. You can limit the search to a specific county in this state and search for any of the following features: airport arch area arroyo bar basin bay beach bench bend bridge **building** canal cape **cemetery** channel **church** cliff crater crossing dam falls flat forest gap geyser glacier gut harbor hospital island isthmus lake lava levee locale mine oilfield other park pillar plain ppl range rapids reserve reservoir ridge **school** sea slope spring stream summit swamp tower trail tunnel valley well woods.*

◆ Military

- 30th Regiment of Virginia Infantry, Regimental History
  http://www.access.digex.net/~bdboyle/30thva.html
- 51st Virginia Infantry
  http://www.clark.net/pub/mjloyd/home.html
  On Mary Jo Loyd's Home Page.
- The Civil War Archive—Union Regiments— Virginia
  http://www.civilwararchive.com/unionva.htm
- Civil War Battle Summaries by State—Virginia
  http://www2.cr.nps.gov/abpp/battles/bystate.htm#va
- Confederate Soldiers from the Shenandoah Valley
  http://home.tampabay.rr.com/shenandoah/civilwar.html
- Culpeper Minute Battalion
  http://www.meridiantc.com/nwta/index.html
- A Guide to the Civil War Materials of the Earl Gregg Swem Library at the College of William and Mary
  http://www.swem.wm.edu/SPCOL/CivilWar/webcw2.html
- Korean Conflict State-Level Casualty Lists— Virginia
  http://www.nara.gov/nara/electronic/vahrlist.html
  From the National Archives and Records Administration, Center for Electronic Records.

- Russell County, Virginia Civil War Website
  http://rhobard.com/russell/civilwar.html
- Search the Virginia Rosters
  http://jefferson.village.virginia.edu/vshadow/rostersearch.html
- Swann's Battalion Virginia Cavalry
  http://members.aol.com/jweaver302/CW/swann.htm
- Thurmond's Virginia Partisan Rangers
  http://members.aol.com/jweaver302/CW/thurmond.htm
- Vietnam Conflict State-Level Casualty Lists— Virginia
  http://www.nara.gov/nara/electronic/vahrviet.html
  From the National Archives and Records Administration, Center for Electronic Records.
- Virginia Civil War Home Page
  http://members.aol.com/jweaver300/grayson/vacwhp.htm
- Virginia's Confederate Military Hospitals
  http://members.aol.com/jweaver300/grayson/hospital.htm

◆ Newspapers

- AJR NewsLink—Virginia Newspapers
  http://www.newslink.org/vanews.html
- E&P Media Info Links—Newspaper Sites in Virginia
  http://www.mediainfo.com/emedia/browse-results.htm?region=virginia&category=newspaper+++++++++
- Ecola Newstand: Virginia
  http://www.ecola.com/news/press/na/us/va/
- NAA Hotlinks to Newspapers Online—Virginia
  http://www.naa.org/hotlinks/searchResult.asp?param=VA-Virginia&City=1
- N-Net—Virginia Newspapers
  http://www.n-net.com/va.htm
- Pilot Online—The Virginian-Pilot
  http://www.pilotonline.com/
  Hampton Roads
- The Richmond Times-Dispatch
  http://www.gateway-va.com/pages/tdmain.htm
- The Roanoke Times Online
  http://www.roanoke.com/
- Southwest Virginia Enterprise
  http://www.wythenews.com/
  Wytheville, Virginia
- The Ultimate Collection of News Links: USA—Virginia
  http://www.pppp.net/links/news/USA-VA.html
- The Virginia Newspaper Project
  http://vsla.edu/vnp/home.html
- Yahoo!...Newspapers...Virginia
  http://dir.yahoo.com/News_and_Media/Newspapers/Browse_By_Region/U_S__States/Virginia/

◆ People & Families

- Afro-American Sources in Virginia—A Guide to Manuscripts
  http://www.upress.virginia.edu/plunkett/mfp.html

- Chronicles of the Scotch-Irish Settlement in Virginia
  http://www.rootsweb.com/~chalkley/
  Extracted from the Original Court Records of Augusta County 1745–1800 by Lyman Chalkley.

- Directory of Underground Railroad Operators—Virginia
  http://www.ugrr.org//names/map-va.htm

- Early Virginia / WVA Genealogy
  http://www.sonic.net/~melvaw/
  A collection of family trees based on those who were the first settlers (1800s) of Monroe County, West Virginia. These early pioneers came primarily from nearby counties in Virginia, lying in what we currently know as Albemarle, Augusta, Botetourt, Fincastle, Giles, Greenbriar, Montgomery, Orange, Rockingham, and Rockbridge.

- Southeastern Kentucky Melungeon Information Exchange
  http://www.bright.net/~kat/skmie.htm
  Also Tennessee, North Carolina and Virginia.

- Tribes and Villages of Virginia
  http://hanksville.phast.umass.edu:8000/cultprop/contacts/tribal/VA.html

◆ Professional Researchers, Volunteers & Other Research Services

- Board for Certification of Genealogists—Roster of Those Certified—Specializing in Virginia
  http://www.genealogy.org/~bcg/rosts_va.html

- The Cavalier Research Group
  http://www.cavaliergroup.org/

- Genealogy Helplist—Virginia
  http://home.sprynet.com/sprynet/mttaylor/va.htm

- Lassen & Lassen: Certified Genealogical Records Specialists
  E-mail:slassen@infoave.net
  Work in Ashe, Wilkes, Watauga, and Alleghany Cos., NC and in Grayson Co., VA. Additional nearby counties by special arrangement. Specialties are research, reportage, and on-site photography. For details e-mail slassen@infoave.net

- The Official Iowa Counties Professional Genealogist and Researcher's Registry for Virginia
  http://www.iowa-counties.com/gene/va.htm

- Virginia Family Research
  http://www.mindspring.com/~jkward/Index.html
  Virginia genealogy, Virginia Confederate records, Revolutionary records.

- The Virginia Genealogy Store—Research Services
  http://www.wp.com/genealogy/page9.html

◆ Publications, Software & Supplies

- AncestorSpy—CDs and Microfiche for Virginia
  http://www.ancestorspy.com/va.htm

- Barbara Green's Used Genealogy Books—Virginia
  http://home.earthlink.net/~genbooks/lochist.html#VA

- Barnette's Family Tree Books—Virginia
  http://www.barnettesbooks.com/virginia.htm

- BEYOND GERMANNA: A Newsletter of Genealogy and History
  http://www.wp.com/germanna/

- Books We Own—Virginia
  http://www.rootsweb.com/~bwo/virginia.html

- Boyd Publishing Company—Virginia
  http://www.hom.net/~gac/vigin.htm

- Byron Sistler and Associates, Inc.
  http://www.mindspring.com/~sistler/
  Over 900 books covering records from Tennessee, Virginia, North Carolina, and Kentucky.

- Family Line Publications
  http://pages.prodigy.com/Strawn/family.htm
  Books covering Delaware, Maryland, New Jersey, Pennsylvania, Virginia, and Washington DC.

- Frontier Press Bookstore—Virginia
  http://www.frontierpress.com/frontier.cgi?category=va

- GenealogyBookShop.com—Virginia
  http://www.genealogybookshop.com/genealogybookshop/files/The_United_States,Virginia/index.html
  The online store of Genealogical Publishing Co., Inc. & Clearfield Company.

- Hearthstone Bookshop Home Page
  http://www.hearthstonebooks.com/
  Alexandria, Virginia

- Hearthstone Bookshop—Virginia
  http://www.hearthstonebooks.com/cgi-bin/webc.cgi/st_main.html?catid=102&sid=2PH5t29sm

- Heritage Books—Virginia
  http://www.heritagebooks.com/va.htm

- Heritage Quest—Microfilm Records for the State of Virginia
  http://www.heritagequest.com/genealogy/microfilm/virginia/

- Iberian Publishing Company's Online Catalog
  http://www.iberian.com/
  Specializing in reference works for genealogists and historians researching the Virginias and other Southeastern U.S. States circa. 1650–1850.

- J & W Enterprises
  http://www.dhc.net/~jw/
  One stop book source on the Internet, specializing in southern states source material.

- Lost in Time Books—Virginia
  http://www.lostintime.com/catalog/books/bookst/bo32000.htm

- Marriages of Norfolk County, Virginia, 1851–1865
  E-mail:ehanbury@pilot.infi.net
  This book, compiled and published by Elizabeth B. Hanbury, lists the 1300+ marriages and all pertinent information for each given in the county marriage register for that period. Arranged alphabetically by grooms' last names; brides' names are indexed. For details send e-mail to Elizabeth at:ehanbury@pilot.infi.net

- The Memorabilia Corner Books—Virginia
  http://members.aol.com/TMCorner/book_vir.htm

- The Memorabilia Corner Census View CDs—Virginia
  http://members.aol.com/TMCorner/cen_virg.htm

- Mountain Press
  http://www.mountainpress.com
  Books for the south-eastern section of the United States from Pennsylvania to Texas, with the emphasis on Tennessee and Virginia.

- Picton Press—Virginia
  http://www.midcoast.com/~picton/public_html.BASK/catalog/state_va.htm

- S-K Publications—Virginia 1810–1850 Census Books
  http://www.skpub.com/genie/census/va/

- Southern Queries Genealogy Magazine
  http://www.mindspring.com/~freedom1/sq/sq.htm

- Tidewater Virginia Families
  http://www.erols.com/tvf/
  "A Magazine of History and Genealogy." An independent quarterly journal.

- TLC Genealogy Books
  http://www.tlc-gen.com/
  Specializing in Colonial VA, KY, MD, OH, PA, NC, etc.

- The William and Mary Quarterly
  http://www.jstor.org/journals/00435597.html
  A searchable database from the JSTOR Journal Collection online. This covers three series dating from 1892 through 1991.

- Willow Bend Bookstore—Virginia
  http://www.willowbend.net/va.htm

- Ye Olde Genealogie Shoppe Books—Virginia & West Virginia
  http://www.yogs.com/virginia.htm

◆ Queries, Message Boards & Surname Lists

- GenConnect Virginia Visitor Center
  http://cgi.rootsweb.com/~genbbs/indx/Va.html
  A system for posting queries, Bibles, biographies, deeds, obituaries, pensions, wills.

- Virginia Genealogical Society Queries
  http://www.vgs.org/queries.htm

- Virginia Surname HOMEPAGE Register
  http://people.delphi.com/fspradlin/vasurnam.htm

◆ Records: Census, Cemeteries, Land, Obituaries, Personal, Taxes and Vital (Born, Married, Died & Buried)

- 1785 Halifax County VA Heads of Families
  http://www.genealogy.org/~ajmorris/misc/va1785hf.htm

- The 1790–1890 Federal Population Censuses: Catalog of National Archives Microfilm
  http://www.genealogy.org/census/contents.shtml
  - Census Schedules and Microfilm Roll Numbers for Virginia:

    1790
    http://www.genealogy.org/census/1790.html

    1810
    http://www.genealogy.org/census/1810_schedules/Virginia.html

    1820
    http://www.genealogy.org/census/1820_schedules/Virginia.html

    1830
    http://www.genealogy.org/census/1830_schedules/Virginia.html

    1840
    http://www.genealogy.org/census/1840_schedules/Virginia.html

    1850
    http://www.genealogy.org/census/1850_schedules/Virginia.html

    1860
    http://www.genealogy.org/census/1860_schedules/Virginia.html

    1870
    http://www.genealogy.org/census/1870_schedules/Virginia.html

    1880
    http://www.genealogy.org/census/1880_schedules/Virginia.html

    1880 Soundex
    http://www.genealogy.org/census/1880.sdx_schedules/T776.html

    1890 Special Schedules
    http://www.genealogy.org/census/1890-special_schedules/Virginia.html

- 1810 Census Culpeper County, Virginia
  http://www.rootsweb.com/~takelley/culp1810/culp1810.htm

- 1850 Census, Shenandoah Co, VA
  http://www.rootsweb.com/~vashenan/census.html

- 1860 Census Northumberland County, Virginia
  http://www.mosquitonet.com/~luht/CENSUS.HTM

- Aquia Church Page
  http://www.illuminet.net/aquiachurch/cemetary.html
  Cemetery listing of Aquia Episcopal Church, Stafford, Virginia (Stafford County). Includes cemetery locations and map.

- Arlington National Cemetery
  http://www.arlingtoncemetery.com/

- Arlington National Cemetery
  http://www.mdw.army.mil/cemetery.htm
  General information and a map.

- Census Online—Links to Census Sites on the Web—Virginia
  http://www.census-online.com/links/VA_data.html

- County Courthouse Addresses
  http://www.familytreemaker.com/00000275.html

- Deed Data Pool
  http://www.ultranet.com/~deeds/pool.htm
  Downloadable deed files for Kentucky, New York, Pennsylvania, Virginia & West Virginia.

- Find-A-Grave by Location: Virginia
  http://www.findagrave.com/grave/lva.html
  Graves of noteworthy people.

- Freedmen's Bureau Register of Marriages in Gloucester, Virginia 1861–1869
  http://ccharity.com/freedmens/gloucester.htm

- The Genealogy Bookshelf
  http://www.win.net/~camorrison/
  Online Bible records, marriage, church & cemetery, land, order, tax, will & estate, orphan & guardian, death, patent records from several families, cities & counties in Virginia.

- Ground Work Genealogy on the Internet: Virginia
  http://members.aol.com/ssmadonna/va.htm
  Links to sites with a variety of records.

- Interment.net: Virginia Cemeteries
  http://www.interment.net/us/va/index.htm
  A list of links to other sites.

- Land Office Patents and Grants Collection Index
  http://image.vtls.com/collections/LO.html
  Electronic Card Indexes, Digital Collections Home Page, The Library of Virginia.

- List of Ships Conveying Emigrants to Virginia Before 1625–6
  http://www.rootsweb.com/~ote/vaship.htm
  From the Olive Tree.

- A List of Tithables in Fauquier County, Virginia, in the Year 1759
  http://www.tlc-gen.com/fauquier.htm

- Mt. View Research 1860 Federal Census Page Co., Va.
  http://www.geocities.com/Heartland/Valley/9793/census1860a.htm

- Mt. View Research 1870 Federal Census Page Co., Va.
  http://www.geocities.com/Heartland/Valley/9793/census1870a.htm

- Mt. View Research Cemetery Index Page County, Virginia
  http://www.geocities.com/Heartland/Valley/9793/cemeteryindex.htm

- Mt. View Research Page County, Virginia Marriages 1831–1864
  http://www.rootsweb.com/~vapage/marriages.htm

- Mt. View Research Page County, Virginia Marriages 1831–1864 Bride Index
  http://www.rootsweb.com/~vapage/marriagesbride.htm

- Mt. View Research Shenandoah County, Virginia Marriages 1850–1859
  http://www.rootsweb.com/~vapage/shenandoahmarrac.htm

- National Archives—Mid Atlantic Region (Philadelphia)
  http://www.nara.gov/regional/philacc.html

- National Archives—Mid-Atlantic Region
  http://www.familytreemaker.com/00000097.html
  Records for Delaware, Maryland, Pennsylvania, Virginia, and West Virginia.

- New Kent Co. Land Tax—1782
  http://www.geocities.com/Heartland/4945/nktax1782.html

- Old Blandford Church and Cemetery
  http://www.rootsweb.com/~vacpeter/cemetery/blandfd1.htm
  Petersburg, Virginia

- The Political Graveyard—Cemeteries in Virginia
  http://politicalgraveyard.com/geo/VA/kmindex.html

- Preplanning Network—Funeral Home and Cemetery Directory—Virginia
  http://www.preplannet.com/virgfhcem.htm

- Register of Free Blacks Augusta County, Virginia
  http://jefferson.village.virginia.edu/vshadow2/govdoc/fblack.html

- Register of Free Negroes and Mulattoes in the Corporation of Staunton
  http://jefferson.village.virginia.edu/vshadow2/govdoc/fblack2.html

- Roanoke Times Online Obituaries
  http://www.roanoke.com/classifieds/obits.html

- Russell County, Virginia 1860 Census
  http://rhobard.com/census/index.shtml

- Search the 1860 Augusta County Census
  http://jefferson.village.virginia.edu/vshadow2/govdoc/au.census1860.html

- Slave Entries in Wills, Deeds, Etc.
  http://www.netcom.com/~jog1/slavedocs.html
  Kentucky, South Carolina, Tennessee, Virginia

- Slave Information from Various Loudoun Co., VA Documents, 13 Dec 1809 to 30 June 1861
  http://www.rootsweb.com/~valoudou/slaves.html

- Southwest Virginia Enterprise—Obituaries
  http://www.wythenews.com/obit.htm
  Obituaries from the latest edition of this newspaper in Wythe County, Virginia. Also see their archives for past editions from previous dates which also include obituaries.
  http://www.wythenews.com/archive.htm

- Times-Dispatch Obituaries—Richmond, Virginia
  http://www.gateway-va.com/pages/tdstory/obtindex.htm

- USGenWeb Census Project Virginia
  http://www.usgenweb.org/census/states/virginia/virginia.htm

- USGenWeb Tombstone Transcription Project—Virginia
  http://www.rootsweb.com/~cemetery/virginia.html

- Virginia Quit Rent Rolls, 1704
  http://www.lineages.com/vault/rents_1704_results.asp
  Searchable database.

- Virginia 1704 Rent Rolls
  ftp://ftp.rootsweb.com/pub/usgenweb/va/1704va.txt
  Text file.

- Virginia Vital Records Information
  http://vitalrec.com/va.html

- VitalChek Network—Virginia
  http://www.vitalchek.com/stateselect.asp?state=VA

- Where to Write for Vital Records—Virginia
  http://www.cdc.gov/nchswww/howto/w2w/virginia.htm
  From the National Center for Health Statistics (NCHS).

- WPA Reports for Culpeper Co., VA—Bibles
  http://www.rootsweb.com/~takelley/cbibles.htm

◆ Religion & Churches

- Christianity.Net Church Locator—Virginia
  http://www.christianity.net/cgi/location.exe?United_States+Virginia

- Church Online!—Virginia
  http://www.churchonline.com/usas/va/va.html

- Church Profiles—Virginia
  http://www.church-profiles.com/va/va.html

- Churches dot Net—Global Church Web Pages—Virginia
  http://www.churches.net/churches/virginia.html

- Churches of the World—Virginia
  http://www.churchsurf.com/churches/Virginia/index.htm
  From the ChurchSurf Christian Directory.

◆ Societies & Groups

- Albemarle County Historical Society
  http://monticello.avenue.gen.va.us/Community/Agencies/ACHS/

- Allegheny Regional Family History Society
  http://www.swcp.com/~dhickman/arfhs.html
  Area covers counties in northeast West Virginia, southwest Pennsylvania, western Maryland and northwest Virginia.

- American Legion, Dept. of Virginia
  http://members.aol.com/valeg/valegion.htm

- Archer's Computer Interest Group List—Virginia
  http://www.genealogy.org/~ngs/cigs/ngl1usva.html

- Central Virginia Genealogical Association
  http://monticello.avenue.gen.va.us/Community/Agencies/CVGA/home.html

- Fairfax Genealogical Society
  http://www.fxgs.org
  Official site of the Fairfax Genealogical Society of Fairfax County, Virginia, a non-profit organization. Describes the Society and its activities and presents information on research resources in the County and surrounding areas, including links.

- Genealogical Society of Page County, Virginia
  http://www.rootsweb.com/~vagspc/pcgs.htm

- IOOF Lodge Website Directory—Virginia
  http://norm28.hsc.usc.edu/IOOF/USA/Virginia/Virginia.html
  Independent Order of Odd Fellows and Rebekahs.

- Jamestowne Society
  http://www.jamestowne.org/index.html
  For descendants of the Virginia settlers in the first permanent English settlement in America.

- Lower Delmarva Genealogical Society
  http://bay.intercom.net/ldgs/index.html
  Delaware, Maryland and Virginia

- The Memorial Foundation of the Germanna Colonies in Virginia, Inc
  http://www.summit.net/GERMANNA/
  Foundation information and publications for sale also.

- National Genealogical Society
  http://www.ngsgenealogy.org/
  Arlington, Virginia

- Nelson County Historical Society
  http://www.mindspring.com/~wcoffey/nelson/nchs.htm

- Orange County Historical Society, Inc.
  http://www.gemlink.com/~ochistsoc/

- Order of Descendants of Ancient Planters
  http://tyner.simplenet.com/PLANTERS.HTM
  People who arrived in Virginia before 1616, remained for a period of three years, paid their passage, and survived the massacre of 1622.

- Prince William County Genealogical Society
  http://www.rootsweb.com/~vapwcgs/pwcgs.htm
  Manassas

- Roots Users Group of Arlington, Virginia
  http://www.genealogy.org/~rug/

- Society Hill: Virginia, United States
  http://www.daddezio.com/society/hill/SH-VA-NDX.html
  A list of addresses for genealogical and historical societies in the state.

- Sons of Confederate Veterans, Virginia Division
  http://www.cstone.net/~wmm/SCV-VIRGINIA/index.html

- Tazewell County Historical Society
  http://www.cc.utah.edu/~pdp7277/taze-soc.html
- Virginia Beach Genealogical Society
  http://www.tschoice.com/vbgs/
- The Virginia Genealogical Society
  http://www.vgs.org/
- Virginia Historical Society
  http://www.vahistorical.org/

◆ USGenWeb Project

- Virginia Genealogy—USGenWeb Project State Page
  http://www.usgenweb.org/va
- Virginia—USGenWeb Archives Table of Contents
  for the
  http://www.rootsweb.com/~usgenweb/va/vafiles.htm
- Virginia—USGenWeb FTP Archives
  ftp://ftp.rootsweb.com/pub/usgenweb/va/

U.S.—WASHINGTON—WA
http://www.CyndisList.com/wa.htm

Category Index:

- General Resource Sites
- Government & Cities
- History & Culture
- Libraries, Archives & Museums
- Mailing Lists, Newsgroups & Chat
- Maps, Gazetteers & Geographical Information
- Military
- Newspapers
- People & Families

- Professional Researchers, Volunteers & Other Research Services
- Publications, Software & Supplies
- Queries, Message Boards & Surname Lists
- Records: Census, Cemeteries, Land, Obituaries, Personal, Taxes and Vital
- Religion & Churches
- Societies & Groups
- USGenWeb Project

◆ General Resource Sites

- Everton's Sources of Genealogical Information in Washington
  http://www.everton.com/usa/wa.htm

- Family Tree Maker's Genealogy "How To" Guide—Washington
  http://www.familytreemaker.com/00000222.html

- Genealogy Bulletin Board Systems for Washington
  http://www.genealogy.org/~gbbs/gblwa.html

- Genealogy Exchange & Surname Registry—WAGenExchange
  http://www.genexchange.com/wa/index.cfm

- Genealogy Resources on the Internet: Washington
  http://www-personal.umich.edu/~cgaunt/wa.html

- LDS Research Outline for Washington
  http://www.everton.com/usa/wa-0848b.txt

- Lineages' Genealogy Site: Washington
  http://www.lineages.com/rooms/usa/state.asp?StateCode=WA

- ROOTS-L United States Resources: Washington
  http://www.rootsweb.com/roots-l/USA/wa.html
  Comprehensive list of research links, including many to history-related sites.

- UW Certificate Program in Genealogy and Family History
  http://www.edoutreach.washington.edu/extinfo/certprog/gfh/default.htm
  From the University of Washington in Seattle.

- Washington State Genealogical Society—Genealogical Events Calendar
  http://www.rootsweb.com/~wasgs/wsgscal.htm

◆ Government & Cities

- 50states.com—Washington State Information Resource
  http://www.50states.com/washingt.htm
  A list of general information for each state, including a list of colleges, state symbols, links to maps, newspapers, and other miscellaneous state information.

- Excite Travel by City.Net—Washington
  http://www.city.net/countries/united_states/washington/

- Official City Web Sites for the State of Washington
  http://OfficialCitySites.org/Washington.htm

- Home Page Washington State of Washington
  http://www.wa.gov/

- Kent
  http://www.kent.wednet.edu/curriculum/soc_studies/text/grade3/Kent_Hist/Kent_Page.html
  A list of history resources from the Kent School District Social Studies program.

- Yahoo! Get Local...Washington Cities
  http://dir.yahoo.com/Regional/U_S__States/Washington/Cities/
  Maps, yellow pages, white pages, newspapers and other local information.

- Yahoo! Get Local...Washington Counties and Regions
  http://dir.yahoo.com/Regional/U_S__States/Washington/Counties_and_Regions/
  Maps, yellow pages, white pages, newspapers and other local information.

◆ History & Culture

- Ghost Towns of Washington
  http://www.ghosttowns.com/states/wa/wa.html

- History of Bellingham
  http://nwcorner.com/tour/history.html
- Kitsap County History
  http://www.paveweb.com/vr/history/
  - Kitsap County, Washington History Bibliography
    http://www.oz.net/vr/history/bibliography.html
- Klondike Gold Rush National Historical Park Seattle Unit
  http://www.nps.gov/klse/klse_vvc.htm
- Northwest of the West: the Frontier Experience on the Northwest Coast
  http://www.lib.washington.edu/exhibits/FRONTIER/Local/
- The Pacific Northwest Forum
  http://www.narhist.ewu.edu/pnf/pnf.html
  A Journal Devoted to the History, Literature, and Environment of the Northwest.
- Photo Adventures—Museum of History and Industry
  http://www.historymuse-nw.org/photo%20adventures/photo_ad.htm
  A collection of historical photographs from the Pacific Northwest and Alaska.
- San Juan Island National Historic Park
  http://www.nps.gov/sajh/
- Yahoo!...History...Washington
  http://dir.yahoo.com/Arts/Humanities/History/Browse_By_Region/U_S__States/Washington

◆ Libraries, Archives & Museums

- Anacortes Public Library
  http://www.library.anacortes.wa.us/hom.htm
- Bellingham Public Library
  http://www.city-govt.ci.bellingham.wa.us/bplhome.htm
- Collins Memorial Library—University of Puget Sound
  http://www.ups.edu/library/home.htm
- Family History Centers—Washington
  http://www.deseretbook.com/famhis/wa.html
- Family History Centers—Washington
  http://www.lib.byu.edu/~uvrfhc/centers/washington.html
- Heritage Quest Research Library
  http://members.aol.com/hqrl/index.htm
  Orting
- Historical Museums—Washington Online Highways
  http://www.ohwy.com/wa/h/histmuse.htm
  List of historical museums in Washington state, along with addresses, photographs, related links and other details.
- The Hudson's Bay Company Archives
  http://www.gov.mb.ca/chc/archives/hbca/index.html
  From the Provincial Archives of Manitoba, Canada.

- HYTELNET—Library Catalogs: USA: Washington
  http://library.usask.ca/hytelnet/usa/WA.html
  Before you use any of the Telnet links, make note of the user name, password and any other logon information.
- King County Archives & Records Management Section
  http://www.metrokc.gov/recelec/archives/
- King County Library System
  http://www.kcls.org/kcls/kcls.html
- Longview Public Library
  http://ci.longview.wa.us/information/library/index.html
  - The Genealogy Room: Local Records and Research Help
    http://ci.longview.wa.us/information/library/genealogy/index.html
- Museum of History and Industry
  http://www.historymuse-nw.org/index.html
  Seattle
- North Central Regional Library
  http://www.ncrl.org/ncrl/home.html
  For Chelan, Douglas, Ferry, Grant and Okanogan counties.
- NUCMC Listing of Archives and Manuscript Repositories in Washington
  http://lcweb.loc.gov/coll/nucmc/wasites.html
  Links to information about resources other than those held in the Library of Congress.
- Pacific Lutheran University—Robert A. L. Mortvedt Library
  http://www.plu.edu/~libr/
  - Archives and Special Collections
    http://www.plu.edu/~archives/
    - Scandinavian Immigrant Experience Collection
      http://www.plu.edu/~archives/sieindex.html
    - University Archives
      http://www.plu.edu/~archives/uaindex.html
- Pierce County Library System
  http://www.pcl.lib.wa.us/
- Puget Sound Genealogy Resources
  http://www.rootsweb.com/~watpcgs/pugetres.htm
  A list of research libraries and institutions in the greater Puget Sound area.
- Repositories of Primary Sources: Washington
  http://www.uidaho.edu/special-collections/west.html#uswa
  A list of links to online resources from the Univ. of Idaho Library, Special Collections and Archives.
- Seattle Pacific University Library
  http://www.spu.edu:80/depts/library/
- Seattle Public Library
  http://www.spl.org/
  - Seattle Public Library Genealogy Collection
    http://www.spl.org/humanities/genealogy/genealogy.html

- ○ Seattle Public Library Humanities Department
  http://www.spl.org/humanities/humanities.html
- ○ Seattle Public Library—Seattle Room
  http://www.spl.org/humanities/seattleroom.html
- ○ Seattle Public Library's On-Line Catalog, QUEST
  telnet://spl.lib.wa.us
- Seattle Public Schools Archives and Records Management Center
  http://sea-css.ssd.k12.wa.us/archives/welcome.htm
- Seattle University Lemieux Library
  http://www.seattleu.edu/lemlib/llhomepg.htm
- Secretary of State—Division of Archives & Records Management
  http://www.wa.gov/sec/archives.htm
  - ○ Washington State Regional Archives
    http://www.wa.gov/sec/archives/branches.htm
  - ○ Washington State Archives Center in Olympia
    http://www.wa.gov/sec/archives/main.htm
- Spokane Public Library
  http://splnet.spokpl.lib.wa.us/
  - ○ Genealogy Research
    http://splnet.spokpl.lib.wa.us/subject/findingaids/genea.html
  - ○ Northwest Room
    http://splnet.spokpl.lib.wa.us/aboutspl/nwroom.html
- Tacoma Public Library
  http://www.tpl.lib.wa.us/
  - ○ The Genealogy Collection at the Tacoma Public Library
    http://www.tpl.lib.wa.us/nwr/tplgene.htm
    Be sure to see the listing for the Topical Shelf List of the Genealogical Collection at the Tacoma Public Library, which is for sale through the TPCGS web site.
    http://www.rootsweb.com/~watpcgs/pubs.htm
  - ○ Northwest History Databases from the Tacoma Public Library
    http://www.tpl.lib.wa.us/nwr/nwdata.htm
  - ○ Northwest Room & Special Collections at the Tacoma Public Library
    http://www.tpl.lib.wa.us/nwr/nwhome.htm
- University of Washington Libraries Information Gateway
  http://www.lib.washington.edu
  - ○ Special Collections and Preservation Division
    http://www.lib.washington.edu/Specialcoll/
  - ○ Suzzallo and Allen Libraries
    http://www.lib.washington.edu/Suzzallo/
  - ○ University of Washington Library Telnet
    telnet://uwin.u.washington.edu
    Must have Telnet software to access. Make note of logon and password when you begin.

- Washington Family History Centers
  http://www.genhomepage.com/FHC/Washington.html
  A list of addresses, phone numbers and hours of operation from the Genealogy Home Page.
- Washington Public Libraries Online
  http://www.walib.spl.org/home.html
- Washington State Library (WSL)
  http://www.wa.gov/WSL/
- webCATS: Library Catalogues on the World Wide Web—Washington
  http://library.usask.ca/hywebcat/states/WA.html
- Woodinville Library—King County Library System
  http://www.kcls.lib.wa.us/wood/wood.html

◆ Mailing Lists, Newsgroups & Chat

- Genealogy Resources on the Internet—Washington Mailing Lists
  http://members.aol.com/gfsjohnf/gen_mail_states-wa.html
  Each of the mailing list links below points to this site, wonderfully maintained by John Fuller. Visit this site for county-specific mailing lists as well.
- PSROOTS-L Mailing List
  http://www.rootsweb.com/~watpcgs/psroots.htm
  Sponsored by the Tacoma-Pierce County Genealogical Society. The list is available to all genealogical & historical societies and their membership in the greater Puget Sound region. It is also available to anyone who is doing genealogical research in the Puget Sound area of Washington state. We hope this list will become a regularly used forum for the exchange of information regarding anything related to genealogy and our area.
- Washington Mailing List
  http://members.aol.com/gfsjohnf/gen_mail_states-wa.html#Washington
- WASHINGTON Mailing List
  http://members.aol.com/gfsjohnf/gen_mail_states-wa.html#WASHINGTON
- WESTERN-ROOTS-L Mailing List
  http://members.aol.com/gfsjohnf/gen_mail_states-wa.html#WESTERN-ROOTS-L
  Washington, Oregon, Alaska, Idaho, Montana, Wyoming, California, Nevada, Hawaii, Colorado, Utah, Arizona, and New Mexico.

◆ Maps, Gazetteers & Geographical Information

- 1895 U.S. Atlas—Washington
  http://www.LivGenMI.com/1895wa.htm
- American Memory Panoramic Maps 1847–1929—Washington
  http://lcweb2.loc.gov/cgi-bin/query/S?ammem/gmd:@filreq(@field(STATE+@band(+washington))+@field(COLLID+pmmap))
  From the Geography and Map Division, Library of Congress.

- American Memory Railroad Maps 1828–1900—
  Washington
  http://memory.loc.gov/cgi-bin/query/S?ammem/gmd:@filreq
  (@field(STATE+washington)+@field(COLLID+rrmap))
  From the Geography and Map Division, Library of Congress.

- Color Landform Atlas: Washington
  http://fermi.jhuapl.edu/states/wa_0.html
  Including a map of counties and a map for 1895.

- Excite Maps: Washington Maps
  http://www.city.net/maps/view/?mapurl=/countries/
  united_states/washington
  Zoom in on these maps all the way to the street level.

- HPI County InfoSystem—Counties in Washington
  http://www.com/hpi/wacty/index.html

- K.B. Slocum Books and Maps—Washington
  http://www.treasurenet.com/cgi-bin/treasure/kbslocum/scan/
  se=Washington/sf=mapstate

- List of Washington Counties
  http://www.genealogy.org/~st-clair/counties/state_wa.html

- Map of Washington Counties
  http://govinfo.kerr.orst.edu/gif/states/wa.gif
  *From the Government Information Sharing Project, Information
  Services, Oregon State University.*

- Map of Washington Counties
  http://www.lib.utexas.edu/Libs/PCL/Map_collection/states/
  Washington.gif
  *From the Perry-Castañeda Library at the Univ. of Texas at
  Austin.*

- U.S. Census Bureau—Washington Profiles
  http://www.census.gov/datamap/www/53.html

- Washington Place Names Origins
  http://www.tpl.lib.wa.us/nwr/placecgi.htm
  A searchable database from the Tacoma Public Library.

- Yale Peabody Museum: GNIS—Washington
  http://www.peabody.yale.edu/other/gnis/WA.html
  *Search the USGS Geographic Names Database. You can limit
  the search to a specific county in this state and search for any of
  the following features: airport arch area arroyo bar basin bay
  beach bench bend bridge **building** canal cape **cemetery** channel
  church cliff crater crossing dam falls flat forest gap geyser
  glacier gut harbor hospital island isthmus lake lava levee locale
  mine oilfield other park pillar plain ppl range rapids reserve
  reservoir ridge **school** sea slope spring stream summit swamp
  tower trail tunnel valley well woods.*

◆ Military

- The Civil War Archive—Union Regiments—
  Washington
  http://www.civilwararchive.com/unionwa.htm

- Korean Conflict State-Level Casualty Lists—
  Washington
  http://www.nara.gov/nara/electronic/wahrlist.html
  *From the National Archives and Records Administration,
  Center for Electronic Records.*

- Pacific Northwest Military History and
  Reenacting Web Site
  http://www.hevanet.com/1860colt/pnwmain.html

- Vietnam Conflict State-Level Casualty Lists—
  Washington
  http://www.nara.gov/nara/electronic/wahrviet.html
  *From the National Archives and Records Administration,
  Center for Electronic Records.*

◆ Newspapers

- AJR NewsLink—Washington Newspapers
  http://www.newslink.org/wanews.html

- The Daily News Online
  http://www.tdn.com/
  Longview-Kelso

- E&P Media Info Links—Newspaper Sites
  in Washington
  http://www.mediainfo.com/emedia/browse-results.
  htm?region=washington&category=newspaper+++++++++

- Ecola Newstand: Washington
  http://www.ecola.com/news/press/na/us/wa/

- The Issaquah Press
  http://www.blueworld.com/iol/isspress/
  Includes Historic Articles.

- NAA Hotlinks to Newspapers Online—Washington
  http://www.naa.org/hotlinks/searchResult.asp?param=
  WA-Washington&City=1

- N-Net—Washington Newspapers
  http://www.n-net.com/wa.htm

- The Seattle Times
  http://www.seattletimes.com/

- Trib-Net—The News Tribune
  http://www.tribnet.com/
  Tacoma

- Tri-City Herald Online
  http://www.tri-cityherald.com/
  Kennewick, Pasco and Richland, Washington.

- The Ultimate Collection of News Links:
  USA—Washington
  http://www.pppp.net/links/news/USA-WA.html

- UW Suzzallo Library Microform and Newspaper
  Collections
  http://www.lib.washington.edu/libinfo/libunits/suzzallo/
  mcnews/

- Washington Newspaper Publishers Association
  http://www.wnpa.com/editor/

- The Wenatchee World
  http://www.wenworld.com/

- Yahoo!...Newspapers...Washington
  http://dir.yahoo.com/News_and_Media/Newspapers/
  Browse_By_Region/U_S__States/Washington/

◆ People & Families

- Affiliated Tribes of Northwest Indians
  http://www.atni.org/~tribes/
  For Alaska, California, Idaho, Montana, Oregon, Washington.

- Confederated Tribes of the Chehalis
  http://coopext.cahe.wsu.edu/~chehalis/

- Issaquah Historic Families
  http://www.blueworld.com/iol/isspress/histfamilies/toc.html

- Lewis County Biographies
  http://www.halcyon.com/jennyrt/bios/bios.html

- Mercer's Maids—Pioneer Brides of 1864
  http://members.tripod.com/~PeriM/Brides.html

- Stevens County Biographies
  http://www.rootsweb.com/~usgenweb/wa/stevens/bios.htm

- Suquamish Tribe
  http://www.redshift.com/~hdt/suquamish/index.html

- Tribes and Villages of Washington
  http://hanksville.phast.umass.edu:8000/cultprop/contacts/tribal/WA.html

- Washington Indian Reservation Orders
  http://www.rootsweb.com/~usgenweb/wa/indians/resorder.htm

- Washington Indian Treaties
  http://www.rootsweb.com/~usgenweb/wa/indians/treaties.htm

- Washington Tribes
  http://www.travel-in-wa.com/DISTINCTLY/tribes.html
  List of addresses for tribes in the state.

- WPA Life Histories from Washington
  http://lcweb2.loc.gov/ammem/wpaintro/wacat.html
  Manuscripts from the Federal Writer's Project, 1936–1940, Library of Congress.

◆ Professional Researchers, Volunteers & Other Research Services

- Ancestral Investigations
  http://www.ancestralinvestigation.com/
  "Offers a variety of research services at a reasonable rate, including internet research, US Archive research, CD and book searches, and organization of family information."

- Board for Certification of Genealogists—Roster of Those Certified—Specializing in Washington
  http://www.genealogy.org/~bcg/rosts_wa.html

- Connie Lenzen—Certified Genealogical Research Specialist
  http://www.orednet.org/~clenzen/
  Research in Oregon and southwest Washington.

- Tacoma-Pierce County Genealogical Society—Family Line Research
  http://www.rootsweb.com/~watpcgs/famline.htm
  For help in the Tacoma-Pierce County, Washington area.

- Genealogy Helplist—Washington
  http://members.aol.com/DFBradshaw/wa.html

- The Official Iowa Counties Professional Genealogist and Researcher's Registry for Washington
  http://www.iowa-counties.com/gene/wa.htm

◆ Publications, Software & Supplies

- Barbara Green's Used Genealogy Books—Washington
  http://home.earthlink.net/~genbooks/lochist.html#WA

- Books We Own—Washington
  http://www.rootsweb.com/~bwo/washington.html

- family Backtracking—The Newsletter of the Puget Sound Genealogical Society
  http://www.rootsweb.com/~wapsgs/news.htm

- Frontier Press Bookstore—Washington
  http://www.frontierpress.com/frontier.cgi?category=wa

- Heritage Books—Washington
  http://www.heritagebooks.com/wa.htm

- Heritage Quest—Microfilm Records for the State of Washington
  http://www.heritagequest.com/genealogy/microfilm/washington/

- Local History Publications—King County Area
  http://www.bcc.ctc.edu/cpsha/books/books_kc.html

- Lost in Time Books—Washington
  http://www.lostintime.com/catalog/books/bookst/bo33000.htm

- The Memorabilia Corner Books—Washington
  http://members.aol.com/TMCorner/book_wa.htm

- Shorey's Bookstore Inc.
  http://www.serv.net/shorey/
  Seattle. Used & rare books, out-of-print book searches.

- Tacoma-Pierce County Genealogical Society—Publications for Sale
  http://www.rootsweb.com/~watpcgs/pubs.htm

- Tri-City Herald Genealogy Online
  http://www.tri-cityherald.com/genealogy/
  Dozens of helpful columns written by Terry Day and Donna Potter Phillips.

- Willow Bend Bookstore—Washington
  http://www.willowbend.net/wa.htm

◆ Queries, Message Boards & Surname Lists

- GenConnect Washington Visitor Center
  http://cgi.rootsweb.com/~genbbs/indx/Wa.html
  A system for posting queries, Bibles, biographies, deeds, obituaries, pensions, wills.

- Tacoma-Pierce County Genealogical Society—
Ancestor Exchange
http://www.rootsweb.com/~watpcgs/ancexch.htm

- Tacoma-Pierce County Genealogical Society—
Queries
http://www.rootsweb.com/~watpcgs/queries.htm

◆ Records: Census, Cemeteries, Land, Obituaries, Personal, Taxes and Vital (Born, Married, Died & Buried)

- The 1790–1890 Federal Population Censuses: Catalog of National Archives Microfilm
http://www.genealogy.org/census/contents.shtml

  - Census Schedules and Microfilm Roll Numbers for Washington:

    1860
http://www.genealogy.org/census/1860_schedules/Washington.html

    1870
http://www.genealogy.org/census/1870_schedules/Washington.html

    1880
http://www.genealogy.org/census/1880_schedules/Washington.html

    1880 Soundex
http://www.genealogy.org/census/1880.sdx_schedules/T777.html

    1890 Special Schedules
http://www.genealogy.org/census/1890-special_schedules/Washington.html

- 1910 Benton County Census
http://www.owt.com/ebchs/census.htm

- Associated Catholic Cemeteries, Archdiocese of Seattle
http://www.acc-seattle.com/

- Census Online—Links to Census Sites on the Web—Washington
http://www.census-online.com/links/WA_data.html

- County Courthouse Addresses
http://www.familytreemaker.com/00000276.html

- Find-A-Grave by Location: Washington
http://www.findagrave.com/grave/lwa.html
Graves of noteworthy people.

- Grays Harbor County, Washington Cemeteries
http://www.geocities.com/Heartland/Hills/6201/cemeteries.html
A list of cemeteries and their addresses, plus information on a book in the works from the Grays Harbor Genealogical Society.

- Historical Notes—Calvary Cemetery
http://www.acc-seattle.com/cchistry.html
Seattle

- Interment.net: Washington Cemeteries
http://www.interment.net/us/wa/index.htm
A list of links to other sites.

- National Archives Microfilm Collection in Seattle
http://www.rootsweb.com/~watpcgs/narafilm.htm
A list of 549 microfilm publications available at the Pacific Alaska Region branch of NARA.

- National Archives—Pacific Alaska Region (Seattle)
http://www.nara.gov/regional/seattle.html

- National Archives—Pacific Northwest Region
http://www.familytreemaker.com/00000100.html
Records for Idaho, Oregon and Washington.

- The Political Graveyard—Cemeteries in Washington
http://politicalgraveyard.com/geo/WA/kmindex.html

- Preplanning Network—Funeral Home and Cemetery Directory—Washington
http://www.preplannet.com/washfhcem.htm

- Stevens County Death Register, 1891–1907
ftp://ftp.rootsweb.com/pub/usgenweb/wa/stevens/vital/death.txt

- Tacoma Obituary Database
http://www.tpl.lib.wa.us/nwr/obitscgi.htm

- USGenWeb Census Project Washington
http://www.usgenweb.org/census/states/washingt.htm

- USGenWeb Tombstone Transcription Project— Washington
http://www.rootsweb.com/~cemetery/washing.html

- VitalChek Network—Washington
http://www.vitalchek.com/stateselect.asp?state=WA

- Washington Cemetery Project
http://www.rootsweb.com/~usgenweb/wa/wacem.htm
From the US GenWeb Archives.

  - Eden Valley Cemetery
ftp://ftp.rootsweb.com/pub/usgenweb/wa/wahkiakum/cemetery/edenvall.txt
Also known as Buskala Family Cemetery.

  - Elma Catholic Cemetery
ftp://ftp.rootsweb.com/pub/usgenweb/wa/graysharbor/cemetery/elmacath.txt
Also known as St. Joseph's Cemetery.

  - Fern Hill Cemetery, Wahkiakum County
ftp://ftp.rootsweb.com/pub/usgenweb/wa/wahkiakum/cemetery/fernhill.txt

  - Grays River Grange Cemetery, Wahkiakum County
ftp://ftp.rootsweb.com/pub/usgenweb/wa/wahkiakum/cemetery/graysriv.txt

  - Greenwood Cemetery, Cathlamet, Wahkiakum County
ftp://ftp.rootsweb.com/pub/usgenweb/wa/wahkiakum/cemetery/greenwd.txt

- ○ Johns River Cemetery, Markham, Washington
  ftp://ftp.rootsweb.com/pub/usgenweb/wa/graysharbor/cemetery/jriver.txt
- ○ Mt. Adams Cemetery, Glenwood, Klickitat County, Washington
  ftp://ftp.rootsweb.com/pub/usgenweb/wa/klickitat/cemetery/mtadams.txt
- ○ Old Schafer Homestead Cemetery
  ftp://ftp.rootsweb.com/pub/usgenweb/wa/graysharbor/cemetery/schafer.txt
  Also known as Schafer Valley Cemetery and Satsop Valley Cemetery. Some of the graves here were moved to Shafer Cemetery and to Fern Hill Cemetery.
- ○ Pioneer Cemetery in Cathlamet, Wahkiakum County
  ftp://ftp.rootsweb.com/pub/usgenweb/wa/wahkiakum/cemetery/pioneer.txt
- ○ Rosburg Cemetery, Wahkiakum County
  ftp://ftp.rootsweb.com/pub/usgenweb/wa/wahkiakum/cemetery/rosburg.txt
- ○ Seal River Cemetery, Wahkiakum County
  ftp://ftp.rootsweb.com/pub/usgenweb/wa/wahkiakum/cemetery/sealriv.txt
- • Washington Census Project
  http://www.usgenweb.org/census/states/washingt.htm
  From the US GenWeb Archives.
- ○ 1850 Federal Census for Lewis County, Oregon Territory
  ftp://ftp.rootsweb.com/pub/usgenweb/wa/lewis/census/50lc.txt
  Included what is now Lewis, Thurston, and Pierce counties.
- ○ 1858 Chehalis County Territorial Census
  ftp://ftp.rootsweb.com/pub/usgenweb/wa/graysharbor/census/58ccterr.txt
  Now Gray's Harbor County.
- ○ 1860 Thurston County Territorial Census
  ftp://ftp.rootsweb.com/pub/usgenweb/wa/thurston/census/60tcterr.txt
- ○ 1910 Federal Census—Fox Island Precinct, Pierce County, Washington
  ftp://ftp.rootsweb.com/pub/usgenweb/wa/pierce/census/10pcfoxi.txt
- ○ Buckley, Pierce County, Washington 1890 Census
  ftp://ftp.rootsweb.com/pub/usgenweb/wa/pierce/census/90bucktn.txt
- ○ Douglas Co., Washington Territory, 1885 Territorial Census
  ftp://ftp.rootsweb.com/pub/usgenweb/wa/douglas/census/85dcterr.txt
- ○ Index of 1910 Federal Census, Pierce County, Wilkeson, Washington
  ftp://ftp.rootsweb.com/pub/usgenweb/wa/pierce/census/10pcwkin.txt
- ○ School Census of Students, Arline, Washington, 1911
  ftp://ftp.rootsweb.com/pub/usgenweb/wa/pierce/school/11arline.txt
- ○ Territorial and State Census Schedules in Washington
  ftp://ftp.rootsweb.com/pub/usgenweb/wa/census/waterr.txt
- • Washington Vital Records Information
  http://vitalrec.com/wa.html
- • Where to Write for Vital Records—Washington
  http://www.cdc.gov/nchswww/howto/w2w/washnton.htm
  From the National Center for Health Statistics (NCHS).

◆ Religion & Churches

- • Christianity.Net Church Locator—Washington
  http://www.christianity.net/cgi/location.exe?United_States+Washington
- • Church Online!—Washington
  http://www.churchonline.com/usas/wa/wa.html
- • Church Profiles—Washington
  http://www.church-profiles.com/wa/wa.html
- • Churches dot Net—Global Church Web Pages—Washington
  http://www.churches.net/churches/washingt.html
- • Churches of the World—Washington
  http://www.churchsurf.com/churches/Washington/index.htm
  From the ChurchSurf Christian Directory.

◆ Societies & Groups

- • American Historical Society of Germans from Russia—Central Washington Chapter
  http://www.ahsgr.org/wacentra.html
- • American Historical Society of Germans from Russia—Greater Seattle Chapter
  http://www.ahsgr.org/waseattl.html
- • American Historical Society of Germans from Russia—Olympic Peninsula Chapter—Washington
  http://www.ahsgr.org/waolypen.html
- • American Historical Society of Germans from Russia—Washington Rainier Chapter of Tacoma
  http://www.ahsgr.org/warainer.html
- • Archer's Computer Interest Group List—Washington
  http://www.genealogy.org/~ngs/cigs/ngl1uswa.html
- • Blue Mountain PAF Users Group
  http://www.eoni.com/~paf/
  Eastern Oregon & Southeast Washington.
- • Clark County Genealogical Society
  http://www.worldaccessnet.com/NonProfitOrganizations/ccgs/

- Daylight Lodge #232, M.W. Grand Lodge of Free and Accepted Masons of Washington
  http://www.eskimo.com/~daylight/
  Seattle

- East Benton County Historical Society Museum
  http://www.owt.com/ebchs/
  Kennewick, Washington

- Eastern Washington Genealogical Society
  http://www.onlinepub.net/ewgs/
  Spokane

- Eastside Genealogical Society, King County, Washington
  http://www.rootsweb.com/~wakcegs/index.htm

- Fort Vancouver Historical Society of Clark County, Inc.
  http://www.teleport.com/~gcermak/clarkcohistory/

- Genealogical Societies in Washington State
  http://www.rootsweb.com/~wasgs/wsgssocs.htm

- GRHS Puget Sound Chapter
  http://www.grhs.com/pugetsnd.html
  Germans From Russia Heritage Society.

- IOOF Lodge Website Directory—Washington
  http://norm28.hsc.usc.edu/IOOF/USA/Washington/Washington.html
  Independent Order of Odd Fellows and Rebekahs.

- Issaquah Historical Society
  http://www.issaquah.org/comorg/past/mpast.htm

- Jefferson County Genealogical Society
  http://www.rootsweb.com/~wajcgs/
  Port Townsend, Washington

- Kitsap County Historical Society Museum
  http://www.waynes.net/kchsm/

- Lewis County Genealogical Society
  http://www.localaccess.com/lcgs/
  Chehalis, Washington. Also serving South Thurston County.

- Lower Columbia Genealogical Society
  http://ci.longview.wa.us/information/library//genealogy/lcgs.html
  For Cowlitz & Wahkiakum Counties.

- Olympia Genealogical Society
  http://www.rootsweb.com/~waogs/

- Puget Sound Genealogical Society (PSGS)
  http://www.rootsweb.com/~wapsgs/
  Port Orchard, Kitsap County and also a group meeting in Belfair, Mason County.

- Puget Sound Maritime Historical Society
  http://www.psmaritime.org/
  Seattle

- Sacajawea Chapter, Washington State Society, Daughters of the American Revolution
  http://members.home.net/jmccoy1/sacaj.htm

- Seattle, Portland & Spokane (SP&S) Railway Historical Society
  http://www.teleport.com/~amacha/spsrhs.htm
  Vancouver, Washington

- Skagit Valley Genealogical Society
  http://www.ncia.com/~svgs/
  Mount Vernon, Washington

- Society Hill: Washington, United States
  http://www.daddezio.com/society/hill/SH-WA-NDX.html
  A list of addresses for genealogical and historical societies in the state.

- Stillaguamish Valley Genealogical Society
  http://home1.gte.net/bhuson/stilly.html
  Arlington

- Swedish Finn Historical Society
  http://home1.gte.net/SFHS/index.htm
  Seattle, Washington

- Tacoma Historical Society
  http://www.powerscourt.com/ths/

- Tacoma-Pierce County Genealogical Society
  http://www.rootsweb.com/~watpcgs/tpcgs.htm

- The Tri-City Genealogical Society
  http://www.cbvcp.com/tcgs/
  Richland

- Washington Freemasonry—State of Washington, USA
  http://www.telebyte.com/masons/masons.html

- Washington State Genealogical Society
  http://www.rootsweb.com/~wasgs/

- Washington State Historical Society
  http://www.wshs.org/

- The Washington State Railroads Historical Society
  http://home1.gte.net/jimbowe/WSRHS1.htm
  Pasco, Washington

- Washington State Society Daughters of the American Revolution
  http://members.aol.com/darlifer/index.html

- Wenatchee Area Genealogical Society
  http://www.crcwnet.com/~wags/

- Whatcom Genealogical Society
  http://www.rootsweb.com/~wawhatco/wgs/index.htm
  Bellingham

- Whitman County Genealogical Society
  http://www.wsu.edu:8080/~mbsimon/wcgs/index.html

- Whitman County Historical Society
  http://www.wsu.edu:8080/~kemeyer/wchs.html

- Yakima Valley Genealogical Society
  http://www.rootsweb.com/~wayvgs/

◆ USGenWeb Project

- Washington Genealogy—USGenWeb Project State Page
  http://www.usgenweb.org/wa

- USGenWeb Archives—Washington Cemetery Project
  http://www.rootsweb.com/~usgenweb/wa/wacem.htm

- USGenWeb Archives—Washington Census Project
  http://www.rootsweb.com/~usgenweb/wa/wacensus.htm

- Washington—USGenWeb Archives Table of Contents
  http://www.rootsweb.com/~usgenweb/wa/wafiles.htm

- Washington—USGenWeb FTP Archives
  ftp://ftp.rootsweb.com/pub/usgenweb/wa/

U.S.—WEST VIRGINIA—WV

http://www.CyndisList.com/wv.htm

Category Index:

- General Resource Sites
- Government & Cities
- History & Culture
- Libraries, Archives & Museums
- Locality Specific
- Mailing Lists, Newsgroups & Chat
- Maps, Gazetteers & Geographical Information
- Military
- Newspapers

- People & Families
- Professional Researchers, Volunteers & Other Research Services
- Publications, Software & Supplies
- Queries, Message Boards & Surname Lists
- Records: Census, Cemeteries, Land, Obituaries, Personal, Taxes and Vital
- Religion & Churches
- Societies & Groups
- USGenWeb Project

◆ General Resource Sites

- Everton's Sources of Genealogical Information in West Virginia
  http://www.everton.com/usa/wv.htm

- Family Tree Maker's Genealogy "How To" Guide—West Virginia
  http://www.familytreemaker.com/00000224.html

- Genealogy Exchange & Surname Registry—WVGenExchange
  http://www.genexchange.com/wv/index.cfm

- Genealogy in Wyoming Co., West Virginia
  http://members.aol.com/jlcooke/cook.htm

- Genealogy Resources on the Internet: West Virginia
  http://www-personal.umich.edu/~cgaunt/westva.html

- Lineages' Genealogy Site: West Virginia
  http://www.lineages.com/rooms/usa/state.asp?StateCode=WV

- ROOTS-L United States Resources: West Virginia
  http://www.rootsweb.com/roots-l/USA/wv.html
  Comprehensive list of research links, including many to history-related sites.

◆ Government & Cities

- 50states.com—West Virginia State Information Resource
  http://www.50states.com/wvirgini.htm
  A list of general information for each state, including a list of colleges, state symbols, links to maps, newspapers, and other miscellaneous state information.

- Excite Travel by City.Net—West Virginia
  http://www.city.net/countries/united_states/west_virginia/

- Official City Web Sites for the State of West Virginia
  http://OfficialCitySites.org/West-Virginia.htm

- West Virginia Web
  http://www.wvweb.com/

- Yahoo! Get Local...West Virginia Cities
  http://dir.yahoo.com/Regional/U_S__States/West_Virginia/Cities/
  Maps, yellow pages, white pages, newspapers and other local information.

- Yahoo! Get Local...West Virginia Counties and Regions
  http://dir.yahoo.com/Regional/U_S__States/West_Virginia/Counties_and_Regions/
  Maps, yellow pages, white pages, newspapers and other local information.

◆ History & Culture

- West Virginia Histories
  http://www.clearlight.com/~wvhh/

- Yahoo!...History...West Virginia
  http://dir.yahoo.com/Arts/Humanities/History/Browse_By_Region/U_S__States/West_Virginia

◆ Libraries, Archives & Museums

- Family History Centers—West Virginia
  http://www.deseretbook.com/famhis/wv.html

- Family History Centers—West Virginia
  http://www.lib.byu.edu/~uvrfhc/centers/westvirginia.html

- HYTELNET—Library Catalogs: USA: West Virginia
  http://library.usask.ca/hytelnet/usa/WV.html
  Before you use any of the Telnet links, make note of the user name, password and any other logon information.

- Marshall University Libraries
  http://www.marshall.edu/library/
  - James E. Morrow Library Special Collections and University Archives
    http://www.marshall.edu/speccoll/
    - Guide to the Local History and Genealogy Holdings in the Special Collections Department
      http://www.marshall.edu/speccoll/title.html
    - Manuscript Collections
      http://www.marshall.edu/speccoll/mss.html
    - West Virginia: A Historical Resource Guide
      http://www.marshall.edu/speccoll/RG-title.html
    - West Virginia Collection
      http://www.marshall.edu/speccoll/wvcoll.html
- NUCMC Listing of Archives and Manuscript Repositories in West Virginia
  http://lcweb.loc.gov/coll/nucmc/wvsites.html
  Links to information about resources other than those held in the Library of Congress.
- Ohio County Public Library
  http://129.71.122.114/main/index.htm
  - Special and Unique Holdings
    http://129.71.122.114/main/special.htm
    - Wheeling Room
      http://129.71.122.114/main/wheelrm.htm
- Repositories of Primary Sources: West Virginia
  http://www.uidaho.edu/special-collections/east2.html#uswv
  A list of links to online resources from the Univ. of Idaho Library, Special Collections and Archives.
- webCATS: Library Catalogues on the World Wide Web—West Virginia
  http://library.usask.ca/hywebcat/states/WV.html
- West Virginia Library Commission Home Page
  http://www.wvlc.wvnet.edu/
- West Virginia State Archives
  http://www.wvlc.wvnet.edu/history/wvsamenu.html
  - County Court Records at the West Virginia State Archives
    http://www.wvlc.wvnet.edu/history/countrec.html
  - Naturalization Records at the West Virginia State Archives
    http://www.wvlc.wvnet.edu/history/natural.html
  - West Virginia State Archives Genealogy Surname Exchange
    http://www.wvlc.wvnet.edu/history/surintro.html
  - West Virginia State Archives Manuscript Collection
    http://www.wvlc.wvnet.edu/history/mancoll.html
  - West Virginia State Archives Map Collection
    http://www.wvlc.wvnet.edu/history/maps.html

- West Virginia University Libraries
  http://www.wvu.edu/~library/
  - Libraries & Collections
    http://www.wvu.edu/~library/branches.htm
    - Appalachian Collection
      http://www.wvu.edu/~library/appal.htm
    - Map Collection
      http://www.wvu.edu/~library/maplib.htm
    - West Virginia and Regional History Collection
      http://www.wvu.edu/~library/wvarhc.htm

◆ Locality Specific

- Also see the USGenWeb section for links to county-specific resources.
- Lincoln Co., WV Genealogy Chat Room
  http://www.oklahoma.net/~davidm/lincoln/chat.htm
- Michelle's Mineral County, West Virginia Genealogy Page
  http://www.fortunecity.com/millenium/meadowbank/347/index.html
  Births, deaths, marriages, wills, cemeteries and census data for Mineral County, WV.
- North Central West Virginia
  http://al7fl.abts.net/Chenoweth/chenowet.htm
  Randolph, Tucker, Preston, Taylor, Harrison, Upshur and other counties.

◆ Mailing Lists, Newsgroups & Chat

- Genealogy Resources on the Internet—West Virginia Mailing Lists
  http://members.aol.com/gfsjohnf/gen_mail_states-wv.html
  Each of the mailing list links below points to this site, wonderfully maintained by John Fuller. Visit this site for county-specific mailing lists as well.
- Appalachianfamily Mailing List
  http://members.aol.com/gfsjohnf/gen_mail_states-va.html#Appalachianfamily
  Appalachian Mountain Families including families from Georgia, North Carolina, South Carolina, Tennessee, Kentucky, Virginia, and West Virginia.
- COALMINERS Mailing List
  http://members.aol.com/gfsjohnf/gen_mail_country-unk.html#COALMINERS
  For anyone whose ancestors were coalminers in the United Kingdom or the United States.
- HARRISON-MONONGALIA.VA Mailing List
  http://members.aol.com/gfsjohnf/gen_mail_states-wv.html#HARRISON-M
  For Harrison and Monongalia counties of Virginia, now West Virginia.
- JACKSON-ROANE.VA Mailing List
  http://members.aol.com/gfsjohnf/gen_mail_states-wv.html#JACKSON
  For Jackson and Roane Counties of Virginia, now West Virginia.

- Melungeon Mailing List
  http://members.aol.com/gfsjohnf/gen_mail_states-gen.
  html#MELUNGEO
  *For people conducting Melungeon and/or Appalachian research
  including Native American, Portuguese, Turkish, Black Dutch,
  and other unverifiable mixed statements of ancestry or unexplained rumors, with ancestors in TN, KY, VA, NC, SC, GA, AL,
  WV, and possibly other places.*

- OHIO-VALLEY Mailing List
  http://members.aol.com/gfsjohnf/gen_mail_states-wv.
  html#OHIO-VALLEY
  *For anyone with a genealogical or historical interest in the
  Ohio Valley including the states of Ohio, West Virginia, and
  Pennsylvania.*

- OLD-FREDERICK-CO-VA Mailing List
  http://members.aol.com/gfsjohnf/gen_mail_states-wv.
  html#OLD-FREDERICK.CO.VA
  *For anyone with a genealogical or historical interest in old
  Frederick County, Virginia. The boundaries of old Frederick
  County today encompass 12 counties: Frederick, Clarke,
  Warren, Shenandoah and Page counties in Virginia; and
  Jefferson, Berkeley, Morgan, Hampshire, Mineral, Hardy and
  Grant counties in West Virginia.*

- SOMGEN-L Mailing List
  http://members.aol.com/gfsjohnf/gen_mail_states-wv.
  html#SOMGEN-L
  *For anyone with a genealogical interest in the Pennsylvania
  counties of Somerset, Bedford, Cambria and Fayette; the
  Maryland counties of Garrett and Allegany; and the border
  counties in West Virginia.*

- VA-WVA-ROOTS-L Mailing List
  http://members.aol.com/gfsjohnf/gen_mail_states-wv.
  html#VA/WVA-ROOTS
  Virginia and West Virginia.

- WDC-GenWeb Mailing List
  http://members.aol.com/gfsjohnf/gen_mail_states-wv.
  html#WDC-GenWeb
  *For those interested in the World Descendant Charts (WDC)
  Genealogy Web Project. The WDC specializes in Virginia and
  West Virginia families.*
  http://www.primenet.com/~dlytton/wdc

- WVA Mailing List
  http://members.aol.com/gfsjohnf/gen_mail_states-wv.
  html#WVA

- WV-MetroValley Mailing List
  http://members.aol.com/gfsjohnf/gen_mail_states-wv.
  html#WV-MetroValley
  *For the counties of Boone, Cabell, Kanawha, Lincoln, Logan,
  Mason, Mingo, Putnam, and Wayne.*

- WV-SOUTHERN Mailing List
  http://members.aol.com/gfsjohnf/gen_mail_states-wv.
  html#WV-SOUTHERN
  *Primarily the counties of Fayette, Greenbrier, McDowell,
  Mercer, Monroe, Nicholas, Summers, Raleigh, and Wyoming.*

- WVWBTSVETS Mailing List
  http://members.aol.com/gfsjohnf/gen_mail_states-wv.
  html#WVWBTSVETS
  *For anyone researching Civil War Veterans, both Confederate
  and Union, in West Virginia.*

◆ Maps, Gazetteers & Geographical Information

- 1790 West Virginia Census Map
  http://www.historyu.com/Village/SurvHouse/1790pages/
  90wvirginia.html

- 1895 U.S. Atlas—West Virginia
  http://www.LivGenMI.com/1895wv.htm

- American Memory Panoramic Maps 1847–1929—
  West Virginia
  http://lcweb2.loc.gov/cgi-bin/query/S?ammem/gmd:@filreq
  (@field(STATE+@band(+west+virginia))+@field(COLLID+pmmap))
  From the Geography and Map Division, Library of Congress.

- American Memory Railroad Maps 1828–1900—
  West Virginia
  http://memory.loc.gov/cgi-bin/query/S?ammem/gmd:@filreq
  (@field(STATE+@band(+west+virginia))+@field(COLLID+rrmap))
  From the Geography and Map Division, Library of Congress.

- Color Landform Atlas: West Virginia
  http://fermi.jhuapl.edu/states/wv_0.html
  Including a map of counties and a map for 1895.

- Excite Maps: West Virginia Maps
  http://www.city.net/maps/view/?mapurl=/countries/
  united_states/west_virginia
  Zoom in on these maps all the way to the street level.

- HPI County InfoSystem—Counties in West Virginia
  http://www.com/hpi/wvcty/index.html

- K.B. Slocum Books and Maps—West Virginia
  http://www.treasurenet.com/cgi-bin/treasure/kbslocum/scan/
  se=West.20Virginia/sf=mapstate

- List of West Virginia Counties
  http://www.genealogy.org/~st-clair/counties/state_wv.html

- Map of West Virginia Counties
  http://govinfo.kerr.orst.edu/gif/states/wv.gif
  *From the Government Information Sharing Project, Information
  Services, Oregon State University.*

- Map of West Virginia
  http://www.lib.utexas.edu/Libs/PCL/Map_collection/states/
  West_Virginia.gif
  *From the Perry-Castañeda Library at the Univ. of Texas at
  Austin.*

- U.S. Census Bureau—West Virginia Profiles
  http://www.census.gov/datamap/www/54.html

- Yale Peabody Museum: GNIS—West Virginia
  http://www.peabody.yale.edu/other/gnis/WV.html
  *Search the USGS Geographic Names Database. You can limit
  the search to a specific county in this state and search for any of
  the following features: airport arch area arroyo bar basin bay
  beach bench bend bridge **building** canal cape **cemetery** channel
  church cliff crater crossing dam falls flat forest gap geyser
  glacier gut harbor hospital island isthmus lake lava levee locale
  mine oilfield other park pillar plain ppl range rapids reserve
  reservoir ridge **school** sea slope spring stream summit swamp
  tower trail tunnel valley well woods.*

◆ Military

- The 7th West Virginia Infantry Homepage
  http://members.aol.com/dwmellott/7wv.htm
  "The voice of the Bloody Seventh."

- 8th Virginia Cavalry—Wayne County, West Virginia
  http://ourworld.compuserve.com/homepages/GlenGallagher/
  8thva.htm

- 16th Virginia Cavalry—Wayne County, West Virginia
  http://ourworld.compuserve.com/homepages/GlenGallagher/
  16thva.htm

- The Civil War Archive—Union Regiments—West Virginia
  http://www.civilwararchive.com/unionwv.htm

- Civil War Battle Summaries by State—West Virginia
  http://www2.cr.nps.gov/abpp/battles/bystate.htm#wv

- Civil War in West Virginia
  http://www.rootsweb.com/~hcpd/civilwar.htm

- Civil War Roundtable of Southern West Virginia
  http://members.tripod.com/~cwrswv/index.html

- Company D, Tenth WV Volunteers (116 men)
  http://members.tripod.com/~drmalec/cod10.htm

- Korean Conflict State-Level Casualty Lists—West Virginia
  http://www.nara.gov/nara/electronic/wvhrlist.html
  From the National Archives and Records Administration, Center for Electronic Records.

- Muster Roll—West Virginia 15th Vol. Infantry
  http://sunsite.utk.edu/civil-war/wvamuster.html

- The Seventh West Virginia Cavalry
  http://members.aol.com/stevecunni/wv7thcav/index.html
  Formerly the Eighth [West] Virginia Infantry and the Eighth West Virginia Mounted Infantry U.S. Civil War, Union Army, 1861–1865.

- Third West Virginia Infantry
  http://www.rootsweb.com/~hcpd/3rdinf/3rdinf.htm
  aka Sixth West Virginia Vets Volunteer Cavalry.

- USGenWeb Archives: West Virginia: Civil War Files
  http://www.rootsweb.com/usgenweb/wv/civilwar/

- USGenWeb Archives: West Virginia: Early Military Files
  http://www.rootsweb.com/usgenweb/wv/earlymil/

- Vietnam Conflict State-Level Casualty Lists—West Virginia
  http://www.nara.gov/nara/electronic/wvhrviet.html
  From the National Archives and Records Administration, Center for Electronic Records.

- West Virginia in the Civil War
  http://www.wvcivilwar.com/

- West Virginia Military Research
  http://www.rootsweb.com/~wvgenweb/military/index.html

◆ Newspapers

- AJR NewsLink—West Virginia Newspapers
  http://www.newslink.org/wvnews.html

- The Braxton Democrat-Central
  http://access.mountain.net/~braxton/braxton.html
  Serving Braxton County, West Virginia since 1883.

- E&P Media Info Links—Newspaper Sites in West Virginia
  http://www.mediainfo.com/emedia/browse-results.
  htm?region=westvirginia&category=newspaper+++++++++

- Ecola Newstand: West Virginia
  http://www.ecola.com/news/press/na/us/wv/

- NAA Hotlinks to Newspapers Online—West Virginia
  http://www.naa.org/hotlinks/searchResult.asp?param=
  WV-West+Virginia&City=1

- N-Net—West Virginia Newspapers
  http://www.n-net.com/wv.htm

- The Ultimate Collection of News Links: USA—West Virginia
  http://www.pppp.net/links/news/USA-WV.html

- Yahoo!...Newspapers...West Virginia
  http://dir.yahoo.com/News_and_Media/Newspapers/
  Browse_By_Region/U_S__States/West_Virginia/

◆ People & Families

- Don Norman's Family Histories from West Virginia
  http://www.everton.com/norman/norman.don/norman.htm

- Early Virginia / WVA Genealogy
  http://www.sonic.net/~melvaw/
  A collection of family trees based on those who were the first settlers (1800s) of Monroe County, West Virginia. These early pioneers came primarily from nearby counties in Virginia, lying in what we currently know as Albemarle, Augusta, Botetourt, Fincastle, Giles, Greenbriar, Montgomery, Orange, Rockingham, and Rockbridge.

- Tribes and Villages of West Virginia
  http://hanksville.phast.umass.edu:8000/cultprop/contacts/
  tribal/WV.html

◆ Professional Researchers, Volunteers & Other Research Services

- Board for Certification of Genealogists—Roster of Those Certified—Specializing in West Virginia
  http://www.genealogy.org/~bcg/rosts_wv.html

- Genealogy Helplist—West Virginia
  http://www.cybercomm.net/~freddie/helplist/wv.htm

- The Official Iowa Counties Professional Genealogist and Researcher's Registry for West Virginia
  http://www.iowa-counties.com/gene/wv.htm

◆ Publications, Software & Supplies

- Barbara Green's Used Genealogy Books—
  West Virginia
  http://home.earthlink.net/~genbooks/lochist.html#WV

- Barnette's Family Tree Books—West Virginia
  http://www.barnettesbooks.com/west-vir.htm

- Books We Own—West Virginia
  http://www.rootsweb.com/~bwo/wv.html

- Boyd Publishing Company—West Virginia
  http://www.hom.net/~gac/westvin.htm

- Frontier Press Bookstore—West Virginia
  http://www.frontierpress.com/frontier.cgi?category=wv

- GenealogyBookShop.com—West Virginia
  http://www.genealogybookshop.com/genealogybookshop/files/
  The_United_States,West_Virginia/index.html
  *The online store of Genealogical Publishing Co., Inc. &
  Clearfield Company.*

- Hearthstone Bookshop—West Virginia
  http://www.hearthstonebooks.com/cgi-bin/webc.cgi/
  st_main.html?catid=103&sid=2PH5t29sm

- Heritage Books—West Virginia
  http://www.heritagebooks.com/wv.htm

- Heritage Quest—Microfilm Records for the State of
  West Virginia
  http://www.heritagequest.com/genealogy/microfilm/
  west_virginia/

- Iberian Publishing Company's Online Catalog
  http://www.iberian.com/
  *Specializing in reference works for genealogists and historians
  researching the Virginias and other Southeastern U.S. States
  circa. 1650–1850.*

- Lost in Time Books—West Virginia
  http://www.lostintime.com/catalog/books/bookst/bo34000.htm

- The Memorabilia Corner Books—West Virginia
  http://members.aol.com/TMCorner/book_wv.htm

- Picton Press—West Virginia
  http://www.midcoast.com/~picton/public_html.BASK/catalog/
  state_wv.htm

- S-K Publications—West Virginia 1810–1850
  Census Books
  http://www.skpub.com/genie/census/wv/

- Southern Queries Genealogy Magazine
  http://www.mindspring.com/~freedom1/sq/sq.htm

- The Tri-County Researcher
  http://www.ovnet.com/~tcr/
  *A West Virginia Genealogical Publication covering Marshall,
  Tyler, & Wetzel Counties.*

- West Virginia Book Company
  http://www.wvbookco.com/

- West Virginia Histories Homepage
  http://www.clearlight.com/~wvhh/
  *A listing of history books that have been published relating to
  West Virginia.*

- Willow Bend Bookstore—West Virginia
  http://www.willowbend.net/wv.htm

- Ye Olde Genealogie Shoppe Books—Virginia &
  West Virginia
  http://www.yogs.com/virginia.htm

◆ Queries, Message Boards & Surname Lists

- GenConnect West Virginia Visitor Center
  http://cgi.rootsweb.com/~genbbs/indx/WV.html
  *A system for posting queries, Bibles, biographies, deeds,
  obituaries, pensions, wills.*

- West Virginia Surname Researchers
  http://www.rootsweb.com/~wvgenweb/surname/

◆ Records: Census, Cemeteries, Land, Obituaries, Personal, Taxes and Vital (Born, Married, Died & Buried)

- The 1790–1890 Federal Population Censuses:
  Catalog of National Archives Microfilm
  http://www.genealogy.org/census/contents.shtml

  ○ Census Schedules and Microfilm Roll Numbers
    for West Virginia:

    1790
    http://www.genealogy.org/census/1790.html

    1810
    http://www.genealogy.org/census/1810_schedules/
    Virginia.html

    1820
    http://www.genealogy.org/census/1820_schedules/
    Virginia.html

    1830
    http://www.genealogy.org/census/1830_schedules/
    Virginia.html

    1840
    http://www.genealogy.org/census/1840_schedules/
    Virginia.html

    1850
    http://www.genealogy.org/census/1850_schedules/
    Virginia.html

    1860
    http://www.genealogy.org/census/1860_schedules/
    Virginia.html

    1870
    http://www.genealogy.org/census/1870_schedules/
    West.Virginia.html

1880
http://www.genealogy.org/census/1880_schedules/
West.Virginia.html

1880 Soundex
http://www.genealogy.org/census/1880.sdx_schedules/
T778.html

1890 Special Schedules
http://www.genealogy.org/census/1890-special_schedules/
West.Virginia.html

- 1850 Federal Census of Wayne County, Virginia
http://www.rootsweb.com/~wvwayne/wayne50.htm

- Cemeteries
http://www.geocities.com/Heartland/Acres/4348/
cemeteries.html
Two abandoned cemeteries in Cabell County and Wayne County, West Virginia.

- Census Online—Links to Census Sites on the Web—West Virginia
http://www.census-online.com/links/WV_data.html

- County Courthouse Addresses
http://www.familytreemaker.com/00000278.html

- Deed Data Pool
http://www.ultranet.com/~deeds/pool.htm
Downloadable deed files for Kentucky, New York, Pennsylvania, Virginia & West Virginia.

- Early Marriages of Wood County
http://home.sprynet.com/sprynet/bweiford/woodcoma.htm

- Find-A-Grave by Location: West Virginia
http://www.findagrave.com/grave/lwv.html
Graves of noteworthy people.

- Interment.net: West Virginia Cemeteries
http://www.interment.net/us/wv/index.htm
A list of links to other sites.

- Kanawha County Tax Lists
http://www.rootsweb.com/~wvkanawh/Tax/index.html

- National Archives—Mid-Atlantic Region (Philadelphia)
http://www.nara.gov/regional/philacc.html

- National Archives—Mid-Atlantic Region
http://www.familytreemaker.com/00000097.html
Records for Delaware, Maryland, Pennsylvania, Virginia, and West Virginia.

- The Political Graveyard—Cemeteries in West Virginia
http://politicalgraveyard.com/geo/WV/kmindex.html

- Preplanning Network—Funeral Home and Cemetery Directory—West Virginia
http://www.preplannet.com/usafh.htm#West Virgina

- USGenWeb Census Project West Virginia
http://www.usgenweb.org/census/states/westvirg.htm

- USGenWeb Tombstone Transcription Project—West Virginia
http://www.rootsweb.com/~cemetery/westvirg.html

- VitalChek Network—West Virginia
http://www.vitalchek.com/stateselect.asp?state=WV

- Vital Records Extracted From "The Life, Travels, and Ministry of Milton M. Everly"
http://www.aloha.net/~jan/milton.txt
August 1885–September 1897. Extractions of records for marriages, some baptisms, and funerals.

- West Virginia Vital Records Information
http://vitalrec.com/wv.html

- Where to Write for Vital Records—West Virginia
http://www.cdc.gov/nchswww/howto/w2w/westva.htm
From the National Center for Health Statistics (NCHS).

◆ Religion & Churches

- Christianity.Net Church Locator—West Virginia
http://www.christianity.net/cgi/location.exe?
United_States+West_Virginia

- Church Profiles—West Virginia
http://www.church-profiles.com/wv/wv.html

- Churches dot Net—Global Church Web Pages—West Virginia
http://www.churches.net/churches/wvirgini.html

- Churches of the World—West Virginia
http://www.churchsurf.com/churches/West_Virginia/index.htm
From the ChurchSurf Christian Directory.

◆ Societies & Groups

- Allegheny Regional Family History Society
http://www.swcp.com/~dhickman/arfhs.html
Area covers counties in northeast West Virginia, southwest Pennsylvania, western Maryland and northwest Virginia.

- Collis P. Huntington Railroad Historical Society
http://www.serve.com/cphrrhs/

- The Greenbrier Historical Society, Inc.
http://web.mountain.net/~ghs/ghs.html

- Hacker's Creek Pioneer Descendants
http://www.rootsweb.com/~hcpd/

- IOOF Lodge Website Directory—West Virginia
http://norm28.hsc.usc.edu/IOOF/USA/West_Virginia/
West_Virginia.html
Independent Order of Odd Fellows and Rebekahs.

- Kanawha Valley Genealogy Society
http://www.rootsweb.com/~wvkvgs/

- Mining Your History Foundation
http://www.rootsweb.com/~myhf/
A Statewide Genealogy and Local History Society for "Almost Heaven" West Virginia.

- Society Hill: West Virginia, United States
  http://www.daddezio.com/society/hill/SH-WV-NDX.html
  A list of addresses for genealogical and historical societies in the state.

- West Virginia Division, Sons of Confederate Veterans
  http://hometown.aol.com/SteveCSA/SCVWVD.html

- West Virginia State Society National Society Daughters of the American Revolution
  http://www.geocities.com/CapitolHill/9133/

- Wheeling Area Genealogical Society
  http://www.hostville.com/wags/

- Wyoming County Genealogical Society
  http://members.aol.com/jlcooke/gensoc.htm
  Also a list of Genealogical Societies in West Virginia.

◆ USGenWeb Project

- West Virginia Genealogy—USGenWeb Project State Page
  http://www.usgenweb.org/wv

- General West Virginia Queries
  http://www.rootsweb.com/~wvgenweb/query/

- West Virginia—USGenWeb Archives Table of Contents
  http://www.rootsweb.com/~usgenweb/wv/wvfiles.htm

- West Virginia—USGenWeb FTP Archives
  ftp://ftp.rootsweb.com/pub/usgenweb/wv/

- WVGenWeb Community Bulletin Board
  http://www.rootsweb.com/~wvgenweb/announce/index.html

U.S.—WISCONSIN—WI
http://www.CyndisList.com/wi.htm

Category Index:

- General Resource Sites
- Government & Cities
- History & Culture
- Libraries, Archives & Museums
- Mailing Lists, Newsgroups & Chat
- Maps, Gazetteers & Geographical Information
- Military
- Newspapers
- People & Families

- Professional Researchers, Volunteers & Other Research Services
- Publications, Software & Supplies
- Queries, Message Boards & Surname Lists
- Records: Census, Cemeteries, Land, Obituaries, Personal, Taxes and Vital
- Religion & Churches
- Societies & Groups
- USGenWeb Project

◆ General Resource Sites

- Everton's Sources of Genealogical Information in Wisconsin
  http://www.everton.com/usa/wi.htm
- Family Tree Maker's Genealogy "How To" Guide—Wisconsin
  http://www.familytreemaker.com/00000225.html
- Genealogy Classes offered through Madison Area Technical College
  http://www.rootsweb.com/~widane/class.htm
- Genealogy Exchange & Surname Registry—WIGenExchange
  http://www.genexchange.com/wi/index.cfm
- Genealogy Resources on the Internet: Wisconsin
  http://www-personal.umich.edu/~cgaunt/wisconsin.html
- Kent Peterson's Genealogy Trading Post
  http://www.execpc.com/~kap/
- LDS Research Outline for Wisconsin
  http://www.everton.com/usa/wi-0850b.txt
- Lineages' Genealogy Site: Wisconsin
  http://www.lineages.com/rooms/usa/state.asp?StateCode=WI
- ROOTS-L United States Resources: Wisconsin
  http://www.rootsweb.com/roots-l/USA/wi.html
  Comprehensive list of research links, including many to history-related sites.
- Wisconsin Calendar of Lineage Events
  http://www.execpc.com/~drg/drgllcal.html

◆ Government & Cities

- 50states.com—Wisconsin State Information Resource
  http://www.50states.com/wisconsi.htm
  A list of general information for each state, including a list of colleges, state symbols, links to maps, newspapers, and other miscellaneous state information.
- Excite Travel by City.Net—Wisconsin
  http://www.city.net/countries/united_states/wisconsin/
- Official City Web Sites for the State of Wisconsin
  http://OfficialCitySites.org/Wisconsin.htm
- Sauk County, Wisconsin
  http://www.saukcounty.com
- State of Wisconsin Information Server—Badger
  http://badger.state.wi.us/
- Yahoo! Get Local...Wisconsin Cities
  http://dir.yahoo.com/Regional/U_S__States/Wisconsin/Cities/
  Maps, yellow pages, white pages, newspapers and other local information.
- Yahoo! Get Local...Wisconsin Counties and Regions
  http://dir.yahoo.com/Regional/U_S__States/Wisconsin/Counties_and_Regions/
  Maps, yellow pages, white pages, newspapers and other local information.

◆ History & Culture

- The Milton House Museum Historic Site
  http://www.inwave.com/Milton/MiltonHouse/
  Includes information about the Underground Railroad in Wisconsin.
- Yahoo!...History...Wisconsin

http://dir.yahoo.com/Arts/Humanities/History/
Browse_By_Region/U_S__States/Wisconsin

◆ Libraries, Archives & Museums

- Academic Libraries in Wisconsin
  http://facstaff.uww.edu/WAAL/acadlibs.html

- Family History Centers—Wisconsin
  http://www.deseretbook.com/famhis/wi.html

- Family History Centers—Wisconsin
  http://www.lib.byu.edu/~uvrfhc/centers/wisconsin.html

- HYTELNET—Library Catalogs: USA: Wisconsin
  http://library.usask.ca/hytelnet/usa/WI.html
  Before you use any of the Telnet links, make note of the user name, password and any other logon information.

- The Madison, WI Stake Family History Center
  http://www.cae.wisc.edu/~porterb/lds/fam_hist.html

- NUCMC Listing of Archives and Manuscript Repositories in Wisconsin
  http://lcweb.loc.gov/coll/nucmc/wisites.html
  Links to information about resources other than those held in the Library of Congress.

- Repositories of Primary Sources: Wisconsin
  http://www.uidaho.edu/special-collections/east2.html#uswi
  A list of links to online resources from the Univ. of Idaho Library, Special Collections and Archives.

- State Historical Society of Wisconsin, Archives Division
  http://www.wisc.edu/shs-archives/

- State Historical Society of Wisconsin, Library Division
  http://www.wisc.edu/shs-library/

- University of Wisconsin—Madison Electronic Library
  http://www.library.wisc.edu/

- University of Wisconsin—Milwaukee Golda Meir Library
  http://www.uwm.edu:80/Library/
  - Milwaukee Urban Archives
    http://www.uwm.edu:80/Dept/Library/arch/
    - Genealogical Collections
      http://www.uwm.edu:80/Dept/Library/arch/genie.htm
    - Naturalization Records
      http://www.uwm.edu:80/Dept/Library/arch/citizen.htm
    - Pioneers of Southeastern Wisconsin Collections, A–I
      http://www.uwm.edu:80/Dept/Library/arch/pionr1.htm
      J–R
      http://www.uwm.edu:80/Dept/Library/arch/pionr2.htm
      S–Z
      http://www.uwm.edu:80/Dept/Library/arch/pionr3.htm
    - Railroad Collections
      http://www.uwm.edu:80/Dept/Library/arch/rail.htm

  - Special Collections and Rare Books
    http://www.uwm.edu:80/Dept/Library/special/

- Vesterheim Genealogical Center and Naeseth Library
  http://www.vesterheim.org/genealogy/
  Madison, Wisconsin

- webCATS: Library Catalogues on the World Wide Web—Wisconsin
  http://library.usask.ca/hywebcat/states/WI.html

- Wisconsin Family History Centers
  http://www.genhomepage.com/FHC/Wisconsin.html
  A list of addresses, phone numbers and hours of operation from the Genealogy Home Page.

- Wisconsin Library and Library-related Web Sites
  http://www.dpi.state.wi.us/dpi/dlcl/pld/wis_lib.html

- Wisconsin Veterans Museum
  http://badger.state.wi.us/agencies/dva/museum/wvmmain.html

◆ Mailing Lists, Newsgroups & Chat

- Genealogy Resources on the Internet—Wisconsin Mailing Lists
  http://members.aol.com/gfsjohnf/gen_mail_states-wi.html
  Each of the mailing list links below points to this site, wonderfully maintained by John Fuller. Visit this site for county-specific mailing lists as well.

- GenWisconsin Mailing List
  http://members.aol.com/gfsjohnf/gen_mail_states-wi.html#GenWisconsin

- MI-WI-ROOTS-L Mailing List
  http://members.aol.com/gfsjohnf/gen_mail_states-wi.html#MI/WI-ROOTS
  Michigan & Wisconsin

- NISHNAWBE Mailing List
  http://members.aol.com/gfsjohnf/gen_mail_states-wi.html#NISHNAWBE
  For anyone researching Native Americans in Michigan and Wisconsin, and the fur traders connected with them.

- WauShaOcon Mailing List
  http://members.aol.com/gfsjohnf/gen_mail_states-wi.html#WauShaOcon
  For Waupaca, Shawano, and Oconto counties.

- WI-Walworth-Rooters Mailing List
  http://members.aol.com/gfsjohnf/gen_mail_states-wi.html#WI-Walworth-Rooters
  For anyone with a historic or genealogical interest in Walworth County, Wisconsin. This list is associated with the Walworth County Genealogical Society and the WIGenExchange site.

◆ Maps, Gazetteers & Geographical Information

- 1895 U.S. Atlas—Wisconsin
  http://www.LivGenMI.com/1895wi.htm

- American Memory Panoramic Maps 1847–1929—Wisconsin
  http://lcweb2.loc.gov/cgi-bin/query/S?ammem/gmd:@filreq
  (@field(STATE+@band(+wisconsin))+@field(COLLID+pmmap))
  From the Geography and Map Division, Library of Congress.

- American Memory Railroad Maps 1828–1900—Wisconsin
  http://memory.loc.gov/cgi-bin/query/S?ammem/gmd:@filreq
  (@field(STATE+wisconsin)+@field(COLLID+rrmap))
  From the Geography and Map Division, Library of Congress.

- Color Landform Atlas: Wisconsin
  http://fermi.jhuapl.edu/states/wi_0.html
  Including a map of counties and a map for 1895.

- Excite Maps: Wisconsin Maps
  http://www.city.net/maps/view/?mapurl=/countries/
  united_states/wisconsin
  Zoom in on these maps all the way to the street level.

- HPI County InfoSystem—Counties in Wisconsin
  http://www.com/hpi/wicty/index.html

- K.B. Slocum Books and Maps—Wisconsin
  http://www.treasurenet.com/cgi-bin/treasure/kbslocum/scan/
  se=Wisconsin/sf=mapstate

- List of Wisconsin Counties
  http://www.genealogy.org/~st-clair/counties/state_wi.html

- Map of Wisconsin Counties
  http://govinfo.kerr.orst.edu/gif/states/wi.gif
  From the Government Information Sharing Project, Information Services, Oregon State University.

- Map of Wisconsin Counties
  http://www.lib.utexas.edu/Libs/PCL/Map_collection/states/
  Wisconsin.gif
  From the Perry-Castañeda Library at the Univ. of Texas at Austin.

- U.S. Census Bureau—Wisconsin Profiles
  http://www.census.gov/datamap/www/55.html

- Wisconsin County Maps, 1901
  http://www.kinquest.com/1901Atlas/1901atlas.html

- Yale Peabody Museum: GNIS—Wisconsin
  http://www.peabody.yale.edu/other/gnis/WI.html
  *Search the USGS Geographic Names Database. You can limit the search to a specific county in this state and search for any of the following features: airport arch area arroyo bar basin bay beach bench bend bridge **building** canal cape **cemetery** channel **church** cliff crater crossing dam falls flat forest gap geyser glacier gut harbor hospital island isthmus lake lava levee locale mine oilfield other park pillar plain ppl range rapids reserve reservoir ridge **school** sea slope spring stream summit swamp tower trail tunnel valley well woods.*

◆ Military

- 28th Regiment, Wisconsin Volunteer Infantry
  http://www.execpc.com/~kap/wisc28.html

- The Civil War Archive—Union Regiments—Wisconsin
  http://www.civilwararchive.com/unionwi.htm

- Finding Your Civil War Ancestor in Wisconsin
  http://www.execpc.com/~kap/wisc-cw.html

- Korean Conflict State-Level Casualty Lists—Wisconsin
  http://www.nara.gov/nara/electronic/wihrlist.html
  From the National Archives and Records Administration, Center for Electronic Records.

- Vietnam Conflict State-Level Casualty Lists—Wisconsin
  http://www.nara.gov/nara/electronic/wihrviet.html
  From the National Archives and Records Administration, Center for Electronic Records.

- Wisconsin Veterans Museum
  http://badger.state.wi.us/agencies/dva/museum/wvmmain.html

◆ Newspapers

- AJR NewsLink—Wisconsin Newspapers
  http://www.newslink.org/winews.html

- E&P Media Info Links—Newspaper Sites in Wisconsin
  http://www.mediainfo.com/emedia/browse-results.
  htm?region=wisconsin&category=newspaper+++++++++

- Ecola Newstand: Wisconsin
  http://www.ecola.com/news/press/na/us/wi/

- NAA Hotlinks to Newspapers Online—Wisconsin
  http://www.naa.org/hotlinks/searchResult.asp?param=
  WI-Wisconsin&City=1

- N-Net—Wisconsin Newspapers
  http://www.n-net.com/wi.htm

- The Ultimate Collection of News Links: USA—Wisconsin
  http://www.pppp.net/links/news/USA-WI.html

- Yahoo!...Newspapers...Wisconsin
  http://dir.yahoo.com/News_and_Media/Newspapers/
  Browse_By_Region/U_S__States/Wisconsin/

◆ People & Families

- Directory of Underground Railroad Operators—Wisconsin
  http://www.ugrr.org//names/map-wi.htm

- Native American Research in Wisconsin
  http://members.aol.com/RoundSky/Wis-intro.html

- Tribes and Villages of Wisconsin
  http://hanksville.phast.umass.edu:8000/cultprop/contacts/
  tribal/WI.html

- WPA Life Histories from Wisconsin
  http://lcweb2.loc.gov/ammem/wpaintro/wicat.html
  Manuscripts from the Federal Writer's Project, 1936–1940, Library of Congress.

◆ Professional Researchers, Volunteers & Other Research Services

- Board for Certification of Genealogists—Roster of Those Certified—Specializing in Wisconsin
  http://www.genealogy.org/~bcg/rosts_wi.html
- Donna's Genealogy Services
  http://www.globaldialog.com/~kilroyd/genserv.htm
  Watertown, Wisconsin
- Genealogy Helplist—Wisconsin
  http://www.calarts.edu/~karynw/helplist/wi.html
- The Official Iowa Counties Professional Genealogist and Researcher's Registry for Wisconsin
  http://www.iowa-counties.com/gene/wi.htm
- WiSearch
  http://www.msn.fullfeed.com/~wisearch/
  Professional research into your Wisconsin roots, specializing in the 1820–1920 time period. Census, vital records, land records, naturalization and much more. Offering on-site photography too!

◆ Publications, Software & Supplies

- AncestorSpy—CDs and Microfiche for Wisconsin
  http://www.ancestorspy.com/wi.htm
- Barbara Green's Used Genealogy Books— Wisconsin
  http://home.earthlink.net/~genbooks/lochist.html#WI
- Books We Own—Wisconsin
  http://www.rootsweb.com/~bwo/wisconsin.html
- Frontier Press Bookstore—Wisconsin
  http://www.frontierpress.com/frontier.cgi?category=wi
- Hearthstone Bookshop—Wisconsin
  http://www.hearthstonebooks.com/cgi-bin/webc.cgi/st_main.html?catid=104&sid=2PH5t29sm
- Heritage Books—Wisconsin
  http://www.heritagebooks.com/wi.htm
- Heritage Quest—Microfilm Records for the State of Wisconsin
  http://www.heritagequest.com/genealogy/microfilm/wisconsin/
- Kinseeker Publications
  http://www.angelfire.com/biz/Kinseeker/index.html
- Lost in Time Books—Wisconsin
  http://www.lostintime.com/catalog/books/bookst/bo35000.htm
- The Memorabilia Corner Books—Wisconsin
  http://members.aol.com/TMCorner/book_wis.htm
- Origins—A Genealogy Book Store
  http://www.angelfire.com/biz/origins1/

- Park Genealogical Books
  http://www.parkbooks.com/
  Specialists in genealogy and local history for Minnesota, Wisconsin, North and South Dakota and the surrounding area.
- S-K Publications—Wisconsin 1850 Census Books
  http://www.skpub.com/genie/census/wi/
- Willow Bend Bookstore—Wisconsin
  http://www.willowbend.net/wi.htm

◆ Queries, Message Boards & Surname Lists

- GenConnect Wisconsin Visitor Center
  http://cgi.rootsweb.com/~genbbs/indx/Wi.html
  A system for posting queries, Bibles, biographies, deeds, obituaries, pensions, wills.

◆ Records: Census, Cemeteries, Land, Obituaries, Personal, Taxes and Vital (Born, Married, Died & Buried)

- The 1790–1890 Federal Population Censuses: Catalog of National Archives Microfilm
  http://www.genealogy.org/census/contents.shtml
  - Census Schedules and Microfilm Roll Numbers for Wisconsin:
    1840
    http://www.genealogy.org/census/1840_schedules/Wisconsin.html
    1850
    http://www.genealogy.org/census/1850_schedules/Wisconsin.html
    1860
    http://www.genealogy.org/census/1860_schedules/Wisconsin.html
    1870
    http://www.genealogy.org/census/1870_schedules/Wisconsin.html
    1880
    http://www.genealogy.org/census/1880_schedules/Wisconsin.html
    1880 Soundex
    http://www.genealogy.org/census/1880.sdx_schedules/T779.html
    1890 Special Schedules
    http://www.genealogy.org/census/1890-special_schedules/Wisconsin.html
- The Bureau of Land Management—Eastern States, General Land Office
  http://www.glorecords.blm.gov/
  The Official Land Patent Records Site. This site has a searchable database of over two million pre-1908 Federal land title records, including scanned images of those records. The Eastern Public Land States covered in this database are: Alabama, Arkansas, Florida, Illinois, Indiana, Louisiana, Michigan, Minnesota, Mississippi, Missouri, Ohio, Wisconsin.

- Census Online—Links to Census Sites on the Web—Wisconsin
  http://www.census-online.com/links/WI_data.html
- County Courthouse Addresses
  http://www.familytreemaker.com/00000279.html
- Find-A-Grave by Location: Wisconsin
  http://www.findagrave.com/grave/lwi.html
  Graves of noteworthy people.
- Index to 1910 Federal Census for Berlin Township, Marathon County, Wisconsin
  http://www.goodnet.com/~eb43571/berlin.htm
- Interment.net: Wisconsin Cemeteries
  http://www.interment.net/us/wi/index.htm
  A list of links to other sites.
- National Archives—Great Lakes Region (Chicago)
  http://www.nara.gov/regional/chicago.html
- National Archives—Great Lakes Region
  http://www.familytreemaker.com/00000096.html
  Records from Illinois, Indiana, Michigan, Minnesota, Ohio, and Wisconsin.
- The Political Graveyard—Cemeteries in Wisconsin
  http://politicalgraveyard.com/geo/WI/kmindex.html
- Preplanning Network—Funeral Home and Cemetery Directory—Wisconsin
  http://www.preplannet.com/wisfhcem.htm
- USGenWeb Census Project Wisconsin
  http://www.usgenweb.org/census/states/wisconsi.htm
- USGenWeb Tombstone Transcription Project—Wisconsin
  http://www.rootsweb.com/~cemetery/wiscon.html
- VitalChek Network—Wisconsin
  http://www.vitalchek.com/stateselect.asp?state=WI
- Where to Write for Vital Records—Wisconsin
  http://www.cdc.gov/nchswww/howto/w2w/wisconsn.htm
  From the National Center for Health Statistics (NCHS).
- Wisconsin Land Records—Interactive Search
  http://searches.rootsweb.com/cgi-bin/wisconsin/wisconsin.pl
  Pre-1908 Homestead and Cash Entry Patents from the BLM.
- Wisconsin Vital Records Information
  http://vitalrec.com/wi.html

◆ Religion & Churches

- Christianity.Net Church Locator—Wisconsin
  http://www.christianity.net/cgi/location.exe?United_States+Wisconsin
- Church Online!—Wisconsin
  http://www.churchonline.com/usas/wi/wi.html
- Church Profiles—Wisconsin
  http://www.church-profiles.com/wi/wi.html

- Churches dot Net—Global Church Web Pages—Wisconsin
  http://www.churches.net/churches/wisconsi.html
- Churches of the World—Wisconsin
  http://www.churchsurf.com/churches/Wisconsin/index.htm
  From the ChurchSurf Christian Directory.

◆ Societies & Groups

- American Historical Society of Germans from Russia—Southeastern Wisconsin Chapter
  http://www.ahsgr.org/wisouthe.html
- Archer's Computer Interest Group List—Wisconsin
  http://www.genealogy.org/~ngs/cigs/ngl1uswi.html
- Buffalo County Historical Society
  http://www.rootsweb.com/~wibuffal/bchs.htm
- Dodge/Jefferson Counties Genealogical Society
  http://members.tripod.com/~djcgs/
- Fond du Lac County Genealogical Society
  http://www.rootsweb.com/~wifonddu/resources/organizations/fdlgensoc.htm
- Fond du Lac County Historical Society
  http://www.rootsweb.com/~wifonddu/resources/organizations/fdlhistsoc.html
- Grant County Genealogical Society
  http://www.rootsweb.com/~wigrant/gcgensoc.htm
- Grantsburg Area Historical Society
  http://www.mwd.com/tourism/history.html
- Heart O' Wisconsin Genealogical Society
  http://www.rootsweb.com/~wiwood/HeartOWi/h-master.htm
  Wisconsin Rapids
- Huguenot Society of Wisconsin
  http://www.execpc.com/~drg/wihs.html
- IOOF Lodge Website Directory—Wisconsin
  http://norm28.hsc.usc.edu/IOOF/USA/Wisconsin/Wisconsin.html
  Independent Order of Odd Fellows and Rebekahs.
- Iowa County Wisconsin Genealogical Society
  http://www.friendsnfamily.net/wiiowagensoc/index.html
- Irish Genealogical Society of Wisconsin
  http://www.execpc.com/~igsw/
- La Crosse County Historical Society
  http://www.centuryinter.net/lchs/
- Links to Wisconsin Heritage & Lineage Societies
  http://www.execpc.com/~drg/drgll.html
- Marathon County Genealogical Society
  http://members.aol.com/mcgswebs/
- Mazomanie Historical Society
  http://www.mazoarea.com/ypahist.htm

- Military Order of the Loyal Legion of the United States—Wisconsin Commandery
  http://www.execpc.com/~drg/wimol.html

- Milwaukee PAF Users Group Home Page
  http://www.execpc.com/~bheck/mpafug.html

- The Oak Creek Historical Society
  http://members.aol.com/larryr3670/OC_HISTR/Ochsocie.htm

- Sauk County Historical Society
  http://www.saukcounty.com/schs/
  Baraboo, Wisconsin

- The Saukville Area Historical Society
  http://www.execpc.com/~artin/sahs/main.html

- Society Hill: Wisconsin, United States
  http://www.daddezio.com/society/hill/SH-WI-NDX.html
  A list of addresses for genealogical and historical societies in the state.

- Society of the War of 1812 in the State of Wisconsin
  http://www.execpc.com/~drg/wihs.html

- Soo Line Historical and Technical Society
  http://www.rrhistorical.com/sooline/index.html

- State Historical Society of Wisconsin
  http://www.shsw.wisc.edu/

- Walworth County (WI) Genealogical Society
  E-mail: PGleich@aol.com
  Delavan. For details send e-mail to President Peggy Gleich at PGleich@aol.com

- Watertown Historical Society
  http://members.tripod.com/~watertownhs/

- Wauwatosa Historical Society
  http://www.icomplete.com/tosahistoricalsoc/

- Wisconsin Marine Historical Society
  http://www.wisconsinwebdesign.com/wmhs/homeport.htm

- Wisconsin Society Daughters of the American Revolution
  http://www.execpc.com/~ekuchta/wisdar.html

- Wisconsin State Genealogical Society
  http://www.rootsweb.com/~wsgs/

◆ USGenWeb Project

- Wisconsin Genealogy—USGenWeb Project State Page
  http://www.usgenweb.org/wi

- Wisconsin—USGenWeb Archives Table of Contents
  http://www.rootsweb.com/~usgenweb/wi/wifiles.htm

- Wisconsin—USGenWeb FTP Archives
  ftp://ftp.rootsweb.com/pub/usgenweb/wi/

U.S.—WYOMING—WY

http://www.CyndisList.com/wy.htm

Category Index:

- General Resource Sites
- Government & Cities
- History & Culture
- Libraries, Archives & Museums
- Mailing Lists, Newsgroups & Chat
- Maps, Gazetteers & Geographical Information
- Military
- Newspapers
- People & Families

- Professional Researchers, Volunteers & Other Research Services
- Publications, Software & Supplies
- Queries, Message Boards & Surname Lists
- Records: Census, Cemeteries, Land, Obituaries, Personal, Taxes and Vital
- Religion & Churches
- Societies & Groups
- USGenWeb Project

◆ General Resource Sites

- Everton's Sources of Genealogical Information in Wyoming
  http://www.everton.com/usa/wy.htm
- Family Tree Maker's Genealogy "How To" Guide— Wyoming
  http://www.familytreemaker.com/00000226.html
- Genealogy Exchange & Surname Registry— WYGenExchange
  http://www.genexchange.com/wy/index.cfm
- Genealogy Resources on the Internet: Wyoming
  http://www-personal.umich.edu/~cgaunt/wyoming.html
- Lineages' Genealogy Site: Wyoming
  http://www.lineages.com/rooms/usa/state.asp?StateCode=WY
- ROOTS-L United States Resources: Wyoming
  http://www.rootsweb.com/roots-l/USA/wy.html
  Comprehensive list of research links, including many to history-related sites.

◆ Government & Cities

- 50states.com—Wyoming State Information Resource
  http://www.50states.com/wyoming.htm
  A list of general information for each state, including a list of colleges, state symbols, links to maps, newspapers, and other miscellaneous state information.
- Excite Travel by City.Net—Wyoming
  http://www.city.net/countries/united_states/wyoming/
- Official City Web Sites for the State of Wyoming
  http://OfficialCitySites.org/Wyoming.htm

- State of Wyoming
  http://www.state.wy.us/
- Yahoo! Get Local...Wyoming Cities
  http://dir.yahoo.com/Regional/U_S__States/Wyoming/Cities/
  Maps, yellow pages, white pages, newspapers and other local information.
- Yahoo! Get Local...Wyoming Counties and Regions
  http://dir.yahoo.com/Regional/U_S__States/Wyoming/Counties_and_Regions/
  Maps, yellow pages, white pages, newspapers and other local information.

◆ History & Culture

- Ghost Towns of Wyoming
  http://www.ghosttowns.com/states/wy/wy.html
- Mountain Men and the Fur Trade
  http://www.xmission.com/~drudy/amm.html
  Sources of the History of the Fur Trade in the Rocky Mountain West.
- The Wyoming Companion—Heritage and History
  http://www.wyomingcompanion.com/wchh.html
- Wyoming Historical Facts
  http://www.state.wy.us/state/wyoming_news/general/text_history.html
- Wyoming State Parks & Historic Sites
  http://www.trib.com/WYOMING/WYOPARKS/
- Yahoo!...History...Wyoming
  http://dir.yahoo.com/Arts/Humanities/History/Browse_By_Region/U_S__States/Wyoming/
- Yellowstone National Park History Page
  http://www.yellowstone.net/history.htm

◆ Libraries, Archives & Museums

- Buffalo Bill Historical Center
  http://www.truewest.com/BBHC/
- Family History Centers—Wyoming
  http://www.deseretbook.com/famhis/wy.html
- Family History Centers—Wyoming
  http://www.lib.byu.edu/~uvrfhc/centers/wyoming.html
- Genealogical Research At UW Libraries
  http://www.uwyo.edu/lib/gene.htm
  Univ. of Wyoming
- HYTELNET—Library Catalogs: USA: Washington
  http://library.usask.ca/hytelnet/usa/WA.html
  Before you use any of the Telnet links, make note of the user name, password and any other logon information.
- NUCMC Listing of Archives and Manuscript Repositories in Wyoming
  http://lcweb.loc.gov/coll/nucmc/wysites.html
  Links to information about resources other than those held in the Library of Congress.
- Repositories of Primary Sources: Wyoming
  http://www.uidaho.edu/special-collections/west.html#uswy
  A list of links to online resources from the Univ. of Idaho Library, Special Collections and Archives.
- Sweetwater County Historical Museum
  http://www.wwcc.cc.wy.us/community/sweetwater/museum/index.html
- University of Wyoming Libraries
  http://www-lib.uwyo.edu/
  - American Heritage Center (AHC)
    http://www.uwyo.edu/ahc/ahcinfo.htm
- Wyoming Family History Centers
  http://www.genhomepage.com/FHC/Wyoming.html
  A list of addresses, phone numbers and hours of operation from the Genealogy Home Page.
- Wyoming Libraries on the Web
  http://www-wsl.state.wy.us/wyld/libraries/index.html
- Wyoming State Archives
  http://commerce.state.wy.us/cr/Archives/
- Wyoming State Library
  http://www-wsl.state.wy.us/
- Wyoming State Museum
  http://commerce.state.wy.us/cr/WSM/
- Yellowstone National Park Archives Index
  http://www.nps.gov/yell/archives.htm

◆ Mailing Lists, Newsgroups & Chat

- Genealogy Resources on the Internet—Wyoming Mailing Lists
  http://members.aol.com/gfsjohnf/gen_mail_states-wy.html
  Each of the mailing list links below points to this site, wonderfully maintained by John Fuller. Visit this site for county-specific mailing lists as well.

- COALMINERS Mailing List
  http://members.aol.com/gfsjohnf/gen_mail_country-unk.html#COALMINERS
  For anyone whose ancestors were coalminers in the United Kingdom or the United States.
- WESTERN-ROOTS-L Mailing list
  http://members.aol.com/gfsjohnf/gen_mail_states-wy.html#WESTERN-ROOTS-L
  Washington, Oregon, Alaska, Idaho, Montana, Wyoming, California, Nevada, Hawaii, Colorado, Utah, Arizona, and New Mexico.
- WYOMING Mailing List
  http://members.aol.com/gfsjohnf/gen_mail_states-wy.html#WYOMING

◆ Maps, Gazetteers & Geographical Information

- 1872 County Map of Wyoming
  http://www.ismi.net/chnegw/1872wyoming.htm
- 1895 U.S. Atlas—Wyoming
  http://www.LivGenMI.com/1895wy.htm
- American Memory Panoramic Maps 1847–1929—Wyoming
  http://lcweb2.loc.gov/cgi-bin/query/S?ammem/gmd:@filreq(@field(STATE+wyoming)+@field(COLLID+pmmap))
  From the Geography and Map Division, Library of Congress.
- American Memory Railroad Maps 1828–1900—Wyoming
  http://memory.loc.gov/cgi-bin/query/S?ammem/gmd:@filreq(@field(STATE+wyoming)+@field(COLLID+rrmap))
  From the Geography and Map Division, Library of Congress.
- Color Landform Atlas: Wyoming
  http://fermi.jhuapl.edu/states/wy_0.html
  Including a map of counties and a map for 1895.
- Excite Maps: Wyoming Maps
  http://www.city.net/maps/view/?mapurl=/countries/united_states/wyoming
  Zoom in on these maps all the way to the street level.
- HPI County InfoSystem—Counties in Wyoming
  http://www.com/hpi/wycty/index.html
- K.B. Slocum Books and Maps—Wyoming
  http://www.treasurenet.com/cgi-bin/treasure/kbslocum/scan/se=Wyoming/sf=mapstate
- List of Wyoming Counties
  http://www.genealogy.org/~st-clair/counties/state_wy.html
- Map of Wyoming Counties
  http://govinfo.kerr.orst.edu/gif/states/wy.gif
  From the Government Information Sharing Project, Information Services, Oregon State University.
- Map of Wyoming Counties
  http://www.lib.utexas.edu/Libs/PCL/Map_collection/states/Wyoming.gif
  From the Perry-Castañeda Library at the Univ. of Texas at Austin.

- U.S. Census Bureau—Wyoming Profiles
  http://www.census.gov/datamap/www/56.html

- Yale Peabody Museum: GNIS—Wyoming
  http://www.peabody.yale.edu/other/gnis/WY.html
  Search the USGS Geographic Names Database. You can limit the search to a specific county in this state and search for any of the following features: airport arch area arroyo bar basin bay beach bench bend bridge **building** *canal cape* **cemetery** *channel* **church** *cliff crater crossing dam falls flat forest gap geyser glacier gut harbor hospital island isthmus lake lava levee locale mine oilfield other park pillar plain ppl range rapids reserve reservoir ridge* **school** *sea slope spring stream summit swamp tower trail tunnel valley well woods.*

◆ Military

- Korean Conflict State-Level Casualty Lists—Wyoming
  http://www.nara.gov/nara/electronic/wyhrlist.html
  From the National Archives and Records Administration, Center for Electronic Records.

- Vietnam Conflict State-Level Casualty Lists—Wyoming
  http://www.nara.gov/nara/electronic/wyhrviet.html
  From the National Archives and Records Administration, Center for Electronic Records.

◆ Newspapers

- AJR NewsLink—Wyoming Newspapers
  http://www.newslink.org/wynews.html

- E&P Media Info Links—Newspaper Sites in Wyoming
  http://www.mediainfo.com/emedia/browse-results.htm?region=wyoming&category=newspaper+++++++++

- Ecola Newstand: Wyoming
  http://www.ecola.com/news/press/na/us/wy/

- NAA Hotlinks to Newspapers Online—Wyoming
  http://www.naa.org/hotlinks/searchResult.asp?param=WY-Wyoming&City=1

- N-Net—Wyoming Newspapers
  http://www.n-net.com/wy.htm

- The Ultimate Collection of News Links: USA—Wyoming
  http://www.pppp.net/links/news/USA-WY.html

- Yahoo!...Newspapers...Wyoming
  http://dir.yahoo.com/News_and_Media/Newspapers/Browse_By_Region/U_S__States/Wyoming/

◆ People & Families

- Tribes and Villages of Wyoming
  http://hanksville.phast.umass.edu:8000/cultprop/contacts/tribal/WY.html

◆ Professional Researchers, Volunteers & Other Research Services

- Board for Certification of Genealogists—Roster of Those Certified—Specializing in Wyoming
  http://www.genealogy.org/~bcg/rosts_wy.html

- Genealogy Helplist—Wyoming
  http://members.aol.com/DFBradshaw/wy.html

- The Official Iowa Counties Professional Genealogist and Researcher's Registry for Wyoming
  http://www.iowa-counties.com/gene/wy.htm

◆ Publications, Software & Supplies

- AncestorSpy—CDs and Microfiche for Wyoming
  http://www.ancestorspy.com/wy.htm

- Barbara Green's Used Genealogy Books—Wyoming
  http://home.earthlink.net/~genbooks/lochist.html#WY

- Books We Own—Wyoming
  http://www.rootsweb.com/~bwo/wyoming.html

- Frontier Press Bookstore—Wyoming
  http://www.frontierpress.com/frontier.cgi?category=wy

- Heritage Quest—Microfilm Records for the State of Wyoming
  http://www.heritagequest.com/genealogy/microfilm/wyoming/

◆ Queries, Message Boards & Surname Lists

- GenConnect Wyoming Visitor Center
  http://cgi.rootsweb.com/~genbbs/indx/Wy.html
  A system for posting queries, Bibles, biographies, deeds, obituaries, pensions, wills.

◆ Records: Census, Cemeteries, Land, Obituaries, Personal, Taxes and Vital (Born, Married, Died & Buried)

- The 1790–1890 Federal Population Censuses: Catalog of National Archives Microfilm
  http://www.genealogy.org/census/contents.shtml
  - Census Schedules and Microfilm Roll Numbers for Wyoming:
    1870
    http://www.genealogy.org/census/1870_schedules/Wyoming.html
    1880
    http://www.genealogy.org/census/1880_schedules/Wyoming.html
    1880 Soundex
    http://www.genealogy.org/census/1880.sdx_schedules/T780.html

1890 Special Schedules
http://www.genealogy.org/census/1890-special_schedules/
Wyoming.html

- BLM—Wyoming's Electronic Reading Room
http://www.blm.gov/nhp/efoia/wy/
United States Bureau of Land Management.

- Census Online—Links to Census Sites on the Web—
Wyoming
http://www.census-online.com/links/WY_data.html

- County Courthouse Addresses
http://www.familytreemaker.com/00000280.html

- Find-A-Grave by Location: Wyoming
http://www.findagrave.com/grave/lwy.html
Graves of noteworthy people.

- National Archives-Rocky Mountain Region
(Denver)
http://www.nara.gov/regional/denver.html

- National Archives—Rocky Mountain Region
http://www.familytreemaker.com/00000103.html
*Records for Colorado, Montana, North Dakota, South Dakota,
Utah, Wyoming, and a portion of New Mexico.*

- The Political Graveyard—Cemeteries in Wyoming
http://politicalgraveyard.com/geo/WY/kmindex.html

- Preplanning Network—Funeral Home and
Cemetery Directory—Wyoming
http://www.preplannet.com/usafh.htm#Wyoming

- USGenWeb Census Project Wyoming
http://www.usgenweb.org/census/states/wyoming.htm

- USGenWeb Tombstone Transcription Project—
Wyoming
http://www.rootsweb.com/~cemetery/wyoming.html

- VitalChek Network—Wyoming
http://www.vitalchek.com/stateselect.asp?state=WY

- Where to Write for Vital Records—Wyoming
http://www.cdc.gov/nchswww/howto/w2w/wyoming.htm
From the National Center for Health Statistics (NCHS).

- Wyoming Vital Records Information
http://vitalrec.com/wy.html

◆ Religion & Churches

- Christianity.Net Church Locator—Wyoming
http://www.christianity.net/cgi/location.exe?
United_States+Wyoming

- Church Online!—Wyoming
http://www.churchonline.com/usas/wy/wy.html

- Church Profiles—Wyoming
http://www.church-profiles.com/wy/wy.html

- Churches dot Net—Global Church Web Pages—
Wyoming
http://www.churches.net/churches/wyoming.html

- Churches of the World—Wyoming
http://www.churchsurf.com/churches/Wyoming/index.htm
From the ChurchSurf Christian Directory.

◆ Societies & Groups

- Albany County Historical Society
http://www.uwyo.edu/ahc/achs/index.htm

- Archer's Computer Interest Group List—Wyoming
http://www.genealogy.org/~ngs/cigs/ngl1uswy.html

- IOOF Lodge Website Directory—Wyoming
http://norm28.hsc.usc.edu/IOOF/USA/Wyoming/Wyoming.html
Independent Order of Odd Fellows and Rebekahs.

- Sheridan Genealogical Society
http://www.rootsweb.com/~wyshergs/sheridan.htm

- Society Hill: Wyoming, United States
http://www.daddezio.com/society/hill/SH-WY-NDX.html
*A list of addresses for genealogical and historical societies in
the state.*

- Tri-State Genealogical Society
http://scream.iw.net/~shepherd/
South Dakota, Wyoming, and Montana.

- Union Pacific Historical Society
http://www.uphs.org/
Cheyenne, Wyoming

◆ USGenWeb Project

- Wyoming Genealogy—USGenWeb Project
State Page
http://www.usgenweb.org/wy

- Wyoming—USGenWeb Archives Table of Contents
http://www.rootsweb.com/~usgenweb/wy/wyfiles.htm

- Wyoming—USGenWeb FTP Archives
ftp://ftp.rootsweb.com/pub/usgenweb/wy/

USGENWEB & WORLDGENWEB PROJECTS
http://www.CyndisList.com/genweb.htm

Category Index:
- ◆ Canada GenWeb Project
- ◆ Mailing Lists—USGenWeb
- ◆ Mailing Lists—WorldGenWeb

- ◆ Miscellaneous USGenWeb & WorldGenWeb Links
- ◆ The USGenWeb Project
- ◆ WorldGenWeb Project

◆ Canada GenWeb Project

- ● Canada GenWeb Project
  http://www.rootsweb.com/~canwgw/index.html
  - ○ Acadian GenWeb
    http://www.geocities.com/Heartland/Acres/2162/
  - ○ Alberta GenWeb
    http://www.geocities.com/~dhomme/genweb/albertagenweb.html
  - ○ British Columbia GenWeb Project
    http://www.islandnet.com/~jveinot/genweb/bcgenweb.html
  - ○ New Brunswick / Nouveau-Brunswick GenWeb
    http://www.bitheads.ca/nbgenweb/index.htm
  - ○ Newfoundland & Labrador GenWeb Project
    http://www.huronweb.com/genweb/nf.htm
  - ○ Nova Scotia GenWeb Project
    http://www.geocities.com/Heartland/6625/nsgenweb.html
  - ○ Ontario GenWeb
    http://www.geneofun.on.ca/ongenweb/
  - ○ The Island Register—Prince Edward Island GenWeb Project
    http://www.isn.net/~dhunter/pegenweb.html
  - ○ Québec GenWeb Project / GenWeb du Québec
    http://www.cam.org/~beaur/gen/qcgenweb.html
  - ○ Saskatchewan GenWeb
    http://www.rootsweb.com/~cansk/Saskatchewan/

◆ Mailing Lists—USGenWeb

The following mailing lists for each state are for discussing the creation of a single source for all US state genealogy databases. These lists are for use by county coordinators in the USGenWeb project:

- ● AKGEN Mailing List
  http://members.aol.com/gfsjohnf/gen_mail_states-ak.html#AKGEN-L
- ● AZGEN-L Mailing List
  http://members.aol.com/gfsjohnf/gen_mail_states-az.html#AZGEN-L

- ● CAGEN-L Mailing List
  http://members.aol.com/gfsjohnf/gen_mail_states-ca.html#CAGEN-L
- ● COGEN-L Mailing List
  http://members.aol.com/gfsjohnf/gen_mail_states-co.html#COGEN-L
- ● CTGEN Mailing List
  http://members.aol.com/gfsjohnf/gen_mail_states-ct.html#CTGEN
- ● GALINA Mailing List
  http://members.aol.com/gfsjohnf/gen_mail_states-ga.html#GALINA
  Georgia and South Carolina
- ● IAGEN Mailing List
  http://members.aol.com/gfsjohnf/gen_mail_states-ia.html#IAGEN-L
- ● IDGEN-L Mailing List
  http://members.aol.com/gfsjohnf/gen_mail_states-id.html#IDGEN-L
- ● MAGEN Mailing List
  http://members.aol.com/gfsjohnf/gen_mail_states-ma.html#MAGEN-L
- ● MDGEN-L Mailing List
  http://members.aol.com/gfsjohnf/gen_mail_states-md.html#MDGEN-L
- ● MTGEN Mailing List
  http://members.aol.com/gfsjohnf/gen_mail_states-mt.html#MTGEN-L
- ● NDGENWEB Mailing List
  http://members.aol.com/gfsjohnf/gen_mail_states-nd.html#NDGENWEB
- ● NMGEN-L Mailing List
  http://members.aol.com/gfsjohnf/gen_mail_states-nm.html#NMGEN-L
- ● NVGEN Mailing List
  http://members.aol.com/gfsjohnf/gen_mail_states-nv.html#NVGEN-L
- ● NYS Mailing List
  http://members.aol.com/gfsjohnf/gen_mail_states-ny.html#NYS

- OKGEN Mailing List
  http://members.aol.com/gfsjohnf/gen_mail_states-ok.
  html#OKGEN-L
- QEXPRESS Mailing List
  http://members.aol.com/johnf14246/
  gen_mail_general.html#QEXPRESS
  *For people who are using the USGenWeb/WorldGenWeb Query
  Express system.*
- TNGEN-L Mailing List
  http://members.aol.com/gfsjohnf/gen_mail_states-tn.
  html#TNGEN-L
- WAGEN-L Mailing List
  http://members.aol.com/gfsjohnf/gen_mail_states-wa.
  html#WAGEN-L
- WVGEN Mailing List
  http://members.aol.com/gfsjohnf/gen_mail_states-wv.
  html#WVGEN-L
- WYGEN Mailing List
  http://members.aol.com/gfsjohnf/gen_mail_states-wy.
  html#WYGEN-L

◆ Mailing Lists—WorldGenWeb

- IrelandGenWeb Mailing List
  http://members.aol.com/gfsjohnf/gen_mail_country-unk.
  html#IrelandGenWeb
- IsraelGenWeb Mailing List
  http://members.aol.com/gfsjohnf/gen_mail_country-isr.
  html#IsraelGenWeb
- MidEastGenWeb Mailing List
  http://members.aol.com/gfsjohnf/gen_mail_country-gen.
  html#MidEastGenWeb
- NorthernIrelandGenWeb Mailing List
  http://members.aol.com/gfsjohnf/gen_mail_country-ire.
  html#NorthernIrelandGenWeb
- QEXPRESS Mailing List
  http://members.aol.com/johnf14246/
  gen_mail_general.html#QEXPRESS
  *For people who are using the USGenWeb/WorldGenWeb Query
  Express system.*
- SCOTLAND-GENWEB Mailing List
  http://members.aol.com/gfsjohnf/gen_mail_country-unk.
  html#SCOTLAND-GENWEB
- WorldGenWeb Mailing List
  http://members.aol.com/gfsjohnf/gen_mail_country-gen.
  html#WorldGenWeb
- WorldGenWeb-Preussen Mailing List
  http://members.aol.com/gfsjohnf/gen_mail_country-ger.
  html#WorldGenWeb-Preussen

◆ Miscellaneous USGenWeb & WorldGenWeb Links

- County Coordinator's Helper
  http://www.rootsweb.com/~cchelper/

- GenConnect
  http://cgi.rootsweb.com/~genbbs/index.html
  *For queries, biographies and obituaries from the USGenWeb
  and WorldGenWeb projects.*
- Search the USGenWeb Archives Digital Library
  http://www.rootsweb.com/~usgenweb/ussearch.htm
- Surname Helper—Search for a Surname
  http://cgi.rootsweb.com/surhelp/srchall.html
  *A searchable database of queries and surname registrations
  posted on various genealogy sites, including USGenWeb and
  WorldGenWeb.*
- USGenWeb Archives
  http://www.rootsweb.com/~usgenweb/
- USGenWeb Census Project
  http://www.usgenweb.org/census/
- USGenWeb County Help Page
  http://www.rootsweb.com/~mioaklan/help/genweb-county-
  help.html
- USGenWeb Kids' Page
  http://www.rootsweb.com/~usgwkidz/
- USGenWeb Lineage Researcher Pages
  http://www.rootsweb.com/~lineage/
- The USGenWeb Project Official Announcements
  http://www.usgenweb.org/official/official.html
- USGenWeb Tombstone Transcription Project
  http://www.rootsweb.com/~cemetery/
- WorldGenWeb Archives
  http://www.rootsweb.com/~wggenweb/wgfiles.htm

◆ The USGenWeb Project

- The USGenWeb Project
  http://www.usgenweb.org
  - Alabama
    http://www.usgenweb.org/al
  - Alaska
    http://www.usgenweb.org/ak
  - Arizona
    http://www.usgenweb.org/az
  - Arkansas
    http://www.usgenweb.org/ar
  - California
    http://www.usgenweb.org/ca
  - Colorado
    http://www.usgenweb.org/co
  - Connecticut
    http://www.usgenweb.org/ct
  - Delaware
    http://www.usgenweb.org/de
  - District of Columbia
    http://www.usgenweb.org/dc

- o Florida
  http://www.usgenweb.org/fl
- o Georgia
  http://www.usgenweb.org/ga
- o Hawaii
  http://www.usgenweb.org/hi
- o Idaho
  http://www.usgenweb.org/id
- o Illinois
  http://www.usgenweb.org/il
- o Indiana
  http://www.usgenweb.org/in
- o Iowa
  http://www.usgenweb.org/ia
- o Kansas
  http://www.usgenweb.org/ks
- o Kentucky
  http://www.usgenweb.org/ky
- o Louisiana
  http://www.usgenweb.org/la
- o Maine
  http://www.usgenweb.org/me
- o Maryland
  http://www.usgenweb.org/md
- o Massachusetts
  http://www.usgenweb.org/ma
- o Michigan
  http://www.usgenweb.org/mi
- o Minnesota
  http://www.usgenweb.org/mn
- o Mississippi
  http://www.usgenweb.org/ms
- o Missouri
  http://www.usgenweb.org/mo
- o Montana
  http://www.usgenweb.org/mt
- o Nebraska
  http://www.usgenweb.org/ne
- o Nevada
  http://www.usgenweb.org/nv
- o New Hampshire
  http://www.usgenweb.org/nh
- o New Jersey
  http://www.usgenweb.org/nj
- o New Mexico
  http://www.usgenweb.org/nm
- o New York
  http://www.usgenweb.org/ny
- o North Carolina
  http://www.usgenweb.org/nc

- o North Dakota
  http://www.usgenweb.org/nd
- o Ohio
  http://www.usgenweb.org/oh
- o Oklahoma
  http://www.usgenweb.org/ok
- o Oregon
  http://www.usgenweb.org/or
- o Pennsylvania
  http://www.usgenweb.org/pa
- o Rhode Island
  http://www.usgenweb.org/ri
- o South Carolina
  http://www.usgenweb.org/sc
- o South Dakota
  http://www.usgenweb.org/sd
- o Tennessee
  http://www.usgenweb.org/tn
- o Texas
  http://www.usgenweb.org/tx
- o Utah
  http://www.usgenweb.org/ut
- o Vermont
  http://www.usgenweb.org/vt
- o Virginia
  http://www.usgenweb.org/va
- o Washington
  http://www.usgenweb.org/wa
- o West Virginia
  http://www.usgenweb.org/wv
- o Wisconsin
  http://www.usgenweb.org/wi
- o Wyoming
  http://www.usgenweb.org/wy

◆ WorldGenWeb Project

- ● The WorldGenWeb Project
  http://www.worldgenweb.org
  - o AfricaGenWeb
    http://www.rootsweb.com/~africagw/
  - o AsianGenWeb
    http://www.rootsweb.com/~asiagw/
  - o AustraliaGenWeb
    http://www.rootsweb.com/~auswgw/
  - o CanadaGenWeb
    http://www.geocities.com/Heartland/6625/cngenweb.html
    See the CanadaGenWeb Project section above.
  - o CaribbeanGenWeb
    http://www.rootsweb.com/~caribgw/
  - o CentralAmGenWeb
    http://www.rootsweb.com/~centamgw/

○ EuroGenWeb
http://worldgenweb.org/eurogenweb/

- BalticSeaGenWeb
http://www.worldgenweb.org/eurogenweb/bsgw.html
Includes: Antarctica, Finland, Lithuania, Denmark, Greenland, Norway, Estonia, Iceland, Sweden, Faroe Islands, Latvia.

- CenEuroGenWeb
http://www.rootsweb.com/~deusaa/ceneuro.htm
Includes: Belgium, Leichtenstein, The Netherlands, Czech Republic, Luxembourg, Slovak Republic, Germany, Moravia, Switzerland.

- EastEuroGenWeb
http://www.rootsweb.com/~easeurgw/
Includes: Austria, Albania, Belarus, Bosnia-Herzegovina, Bulgaria, Croatia, Hungary, Macedonia, Moldova, Montenegro, Romania, Russia, Serbia, Slovenia, Ukraine.

- MediterraneanGenWeb
http://www.rootsweb.com/~sthamgw/medgw.html
Includes: Andorra, Azores, Cape Verde, Cyprus, France, Greece, Italy, Madria, Malta, Monaco, Portugal, San Marino, Spain, Turkey, Vatican City.

- UKGenWeb
http://www.rootsweb.com/~ukwgw/
Includes: Channel Islands, England, Gilbraltar, Ireland, Northern Ireland, Scotland, St. Helena, Wales.

○ MexicoGenWeb Project
http://www.rootsweb.com/~mexwgw/

○ MidEastGenWeb
http://www.rootsweb.com/~mdeastgw/

○ PacificGenWeb
http://www.rootsweb.com/~pacifgw/

○ SouthAmGenWeb
http://www.rootsweb.com/~sthamgw/

○ USGenWeb Project
http://www.usgenweb.org/
See the USGenWeb project section above.

WESTERN EUROPE
http://www.CyndisList.com/westeuro.htm

Category Index:

- General Resource Sites
- Libraries, Archives & Museums
- Mailing Lists, Newsgroups & Chat
- Maps, Gazetteers & Geographical Information

- Professional Researchers, Volunteers & Other Research Services
- Publications, Software & Supplies
- Societies & Groups

◆ General Resource Sites

- Andorra Genealogy—World GenWeb
  http://www.rootsweb.com/~wgandorr/

- Austria / Österreich
  http://www.CyndisList.com/austria.htm
  See this category on Cyndi's List for related links.

- Belgium / Belgique / België
  http://www.CyndisList.com/belgium.htm
  See this category on Cyndi's List for related links.

- Channel Islands
  http://www.CyndisList.com/channel.htm
  See this category on Cyndi's List for related links.

- Denmark / Danmark
  http://www.CyndisList.com/denmark.htm
  See this category on Cyndi's List for related links.

- England
  http://www.CyndisList.com/england.htm
  See this category on Cyndi's List for related links.

- European Focus
  http://www.eurofocus.com/
  Photographic portfolios of ancestral towns in Europe created for Genealogy enthusiasts in Germany, Italy, Poland, Scandinavia, Great Britain and more.

- Finland / Suomi
  http://www.CyndisList.com/finland.htm
  See this category on Cyndi's List for related links.

- France
  http://www.CyndisList.com/france.htm
  See this category on Cyndi's List for related links.

- Genealogy Benelux Home Page
  http://www.ufsia.ac.be/genealogy/

- Germany / Deutschland
  http://www.CyndisList.com/germany.htm
  See this category on Cyndi's List for related links.

- Ireland & Northern Ireland
  http://www.CyndisList.com/ireland.htm
  See this category on Cyndi's List for related links.

- Italy / Italia
  http://www.CyndisList.com/italy.htm
  See this category on Cyndi's List for related links.

- Iceland / Ísland
  http://www.CyndisList.com/iceland.htm
  See this category on Cyndi's List for related links.

- Isle of Man
  http://www.CyndisList.com/isleman.htm
  See this category on Cyndi's List for related links.

- LUXEMBOURG: Help for Genealogical Research by Therese Becker
  http://www.pi.se/collings-system/a-fam-tb.htm#to

- Luxembourg on My Mind
  http://members.aol.com/VailCorp/lux.html
  Dedicated to the many descendants of emigrants from Luxembourg.

- Maltese Genealogy Corner
  http://www.fred.net/malta/roots.html

- MEDERNACH
  http://gallery.uunet.lu/M.Brouwer/index.html
  The village Medernach or the name Medernach from Luxembourg.

- Netherlands / Nederland
  http://www.CyndisList.com/nether.htm
  See this category on Cyndi's List for related links.

- Norway / Norge
  http://www.CyndisList.com/norway.htm
  See this category on Cyndi's List for related links.

- P & T Luxembourg OnLine!
  http://www.editus.lu/
  Online telephone directory.

- Scotland
  http://www.CyndisList.com/scotland.htm
  See this category on Cyndi's List for related links.

- Spain, Portugal & the Basque Country / España, Portugal, y El País Vasco
  http://www.CyndisList.com/spain.htm
  See this category on Cyndi's List for related links.

- Sweden / Sverige
  http://www.CyndisList.com/sweden.htm
  See this category on Cyndi's List for related links.

- Switzerland / Suisse / Schweiz
  http://www.CyndisList.com/swiss.htm
  See this category on Cyndi's List for related links.

- United Kingdom & Ireland
  http://www.CyndisList.com/uksites.htm
  See this category on Cyndi's List for related links.

- Wales
  http://www.CyndisList.com/wales.htm
  See this category on Cyndi's List for related links.

◆ Libraries, Archives & Museums

- Institut Grand-Ducal—Section de Linguistique, de Folklore et de Toponymie
  http://www.igd-leo.lu/
  Luxembourg

- Public Libraries of Europe
  http://dspace.dial.pipex.com/town/square/ac940/eurolib.html

◆ Mailing Lists, Newsgroups & Chat

- EURO-JEWISH Mailing List
  http://members.aol.com/johnf14246/
  gen_mail_general.html#EURO-JEWISH
  For anyone with a genealogical interest in the Migration, History, Culture, Heritage and Surname search of the Jewish people from Europe to the United States and their descendants in the United States.

- GENBNL-L Mailing List
  http://members.aol.com/gfsjohnf/gen_mail_country-blg.
  html#DUTCH
  For research in the Benelux region (Belgium, the Netherlands, and Luxembourg). Gatewayed with the soc.genealogy.benelux newsgroup.

- med-gene Mailing List
  http://members.aol.com/gfsjohnf/gen_mail_country-gen.
  html#med-gene
  For anyone with a genealogical interest in the Mediterranean area.

- SARDINIA Mailing List
  http://members.aol.com/gfsjohnf/gen_mail_country-sar.
  html#SARDINIA

- TRIER-ROOTS Mailing List
  http://members.aol.com/gfsjohnf/gen_mail_country-lux.
  html#GER-TRIER-ROOTS
  For anyone with a genealogical interest in Luxembourg, the Saarland, the Rheinland, Westfalen (Westphalia), and the Pfalz (used to be between Rheinland and Baden, belonged to Bavaria but is now part of Rheinpfalz).

◆ Maps, Gazetteers & Geographical Information

- From the Perry-Castañeda Library at the Univ. of Texas at Austin:

  - Map of Andorra
    http://www.lib.utexas.edu/Libs/PCL/Map_collection/europe/
    Andorra.jpg

  - Map of Gibraltar
    http://www.lib.utexas.edu/Libs/PCL/Map_collection/europe/
    Gibraltar.jpg

  - Map of Luxembourg
    http://www.lib.utexas.edu/Libs/PCL/Map_collection/europe/
    Luxembourg.jpg

  - Map of Liechtenstein
    http://www.lib.utexas.edu/Libs/PCL/Map_collection/europe/
    Liechtenstein.jpg

  - Map of Malta
    http://www.lib.utexas.edu/Libs/PCL/Map_collection/europe/
    Malta.GIF

  - Map of Monaco
    http://www.lib.utexas.edu/Libs/PCL/Map_collection/europe/
    Monaco.jpg

  - Map of San Marino
    http://www.lib.utexas.edu/Libs/PCL/Map_collection/europe/
    SanMarino.jpg

  - Map of Vatican City
    http://www.lib.utexas.edu/Libs/PCL/Map_collection/europe/
    Vaticancity.jpg

◆ Professional Researchers, Volunteers & Other Research Services

- Board for Certification of Genealogists—Roster of Those Certified—Specializing in Europe/USSR
  http://www.genealogy.org/~bcg/rosts_@e.html

- Genealogy Services, Malta
  http://www.waldonet.net.mt/~sultan/gene.htm

- IHFF Genealogie Gesellschaft mbH
  http://www.netway.at/ihff/index.htm
  Professional Researcher specializing in: Austria, Czech & Slovak Republics, Hungary, Slovenian Republic, Croatia, Galicia, others.

◆ Publications, Software & Supplies

- Books We Own—Luxembourg
  http://www.rootsweb.com/~bwo/lux.html

- Frontier Press Bookstore—European Ancestry
  http://www.frontierpress.com/frontier.cgi?category=europe

◆ Societies & Groups

- Archer's Computer Interest Group List— Luxembourg
  http://www.genealogy.org/~ngs/cigs/ngl3otlu.html

- Cercle de Généalogie et d'Héraldique de l'U.E.
  http://ourworld.compuserve.com/homepages/cghue_eusgh/
  cghue2.htm

WILLS & PROBATE
http://www.CyndisList.com/wills.htm

- Abstracts from the Court of Probate Records for Annapolis County, Nova Scotia
  http://www.widomaker.com/~gwk/abstract.htm
  Canada. We are indebted to Wayne W. Walker for making a copy of his Abstracts from the Court of Probate Records for Annapolis County, Nova Scotia available to us on the Internet. The Abstracts are available for download as a ZIP (compressed) file. The text is in ASCII text format which can be read by all word processors.

- Abstracts of Ellis County Wills
  http://www.rootsweb.com/~txellis/ewill2.htm
  Texas

- Analyzing Wills for Useful Clues
  http://www.genealogy.org/~bcg/skbld955.html
  From the Board for Certification of Genealogists—Skill Building—May 1995.

- Baltimore & Anne Arundel County Last Will and Testaments
  http://www.rootsweb.com/~mdbaltim/wills/xxwills.htm

- Bladen Co, NC Will of Matthew PRIDGEN 1818
  ftp://ftp.rootsweb.com/pub/usgenweb/nc/bladen/wills/pr0008.txt

- Cheshire Wills
  http://www.users.zetnet.co.uk/blangston/chswills/
  England

- Consolidated Index to Lunenburg County Probated Wills 1770–1996
  http://www.geocities.com/Heartland/Ranch/8785/willndx.html
  Nova Scotia, Canada

- Delmarva Genealogy Wills Page
  http://www.shoreweb.com/cindy/wills.htm

- Elizabeth Blackwell's Will (1859 Fauquier County, VA)
  http://ccharity.com/contributors/eblackwellswill.htm

- Family Tree Genealogical and Probate Research Bureau Ltd.
  http://www.familytree.hu/
  Professional research service covering the area of what was formerly the Austro-Hungarian Empire, including: Hungary, Slovakia, Czech Republic, Austria, Italy, Transylvania, Croatia, Slovenia, former Yugoslavia (Banat), and the Ukraine (Sub-Carpathian).

- GenealogyBookShop.com—Wills and Probate Records
  http://www.genealogybookshop.com/genealogybookshop/files/General,Wills_and_Probate_Records/index.html
  The online store of Genealogical Publishing Co., Inc. & Clearfield Company.

- Glossary of Unusual Words Found in Wills, Etc.
  http://ourworld.compuserve.com/homepages/dave_tylcoat/gloss.htm

- Index to PEI Probate Records
  http://www.eskimo.com/~mvreid/peiprbt.html
  Prince Edward Island, Canada

- Irish Ancestors: Wills
  http://www.irish-times.com/ancestor/browse/records/wills/index.htm

- Kentuckiana Genealogy—Wills and Probate in Kentuckiana
  http://www.floyd-pavey.com/kentuckiana/kyiana/prbtewill.html

- Kosciusko County, Indiana—Index to the Early Wills 1844–1920
  http://www.rootsweb.com/~inkosciu/willsndx.htm

- Larry Medaglia: Register of Wills and Clerk of the Orphans' Court, Berks County, PA
  http://www.berksregofwills.com/

- Loudoun Co., Virginia Documents
  http://www.rootsweb.com/~valoudou/document.html
  Includes transcripts of wills for the following surnames: BRADEN, DEMORY, DULIN, ELGIN, FOX, GIDEON, HAGUE, HIXSON, HUMPHREY, MARKS, MOORE, PANCOAST, RAMEY, STEVENS and more.

- Lunenburg, Nova Scotia Will Extracts
  http://www.geocities.com/Heartland/Meadows/5699/willidx.html

- Northumberland County Will Index 1772–1859
  ftp://ftp.rootsweb.com/pub/usgenweb/pa/northumberland/wills/willindx.txt
  Pennsylvania

- Probate Records ~ U.K.
  http://www.pro.gov.uk/leaflets/ri031.htm
  Public Record Office, Records Information Leaflet No. 31.

- Probate Records of David THOMAS
  http://www.rootsweb.com/~inclinto/tomas.html
  Clinton County, Indiana

- RAIFORD, Matthew—1752, Bladen County, North Carolina—Wills
  ftp://ftp.rootsweb.com/pub/usgenweb/nc/bladen/wills/mraiford.txt

- SAMPUBCO—Will Testator Indexes
  http://www.wasatch.com/~dsam/sampubco/index.htm

- SHERMANs of Yaxley
  http://www.geocities.com/Heartland/Ranch/3064/sherman.htm
  This site contains wills transcribed from "Some of the Descendants of Philip Sherman, First Secretary of Rhode Island" by Roy V. Sherman.

- Sussex County Will Abstracts Index
  http://www.gate.net/~pascalfl/wlabsdex.html
  New Jersey

- **Will of Burr BRADEN**
  http://www.rootsweb.com/~valoudou/willburr.html
  Signed Nov. 19, 1861 in Clinton Co., Indiana.

- **Will of John WINGATE**
  http://www.genealogy.org/~ajmorris/misc/will01.htm

- **Wills and Administration Collection Index**
  http://198.17.62.51/collections/WI.html
  Part of the Electronic Card Indexes from the Library of Virginia.

- **Wills—Giles County**
  http://www.rootsweb.com/~tngiles/wills/wills.htm
  Tennessee

- **Wills of Mayflower Passengers**
  http://members.aol.com/mayflo1620/wills.html

- **Wills on the Web**
  http://www.ca-probate.com/wills.htm
  Actual Wills of Celebrities and Ordinary People, 1615–1997.